Holy Bible

the old & new testament for genZ

© 2023 by Athena Scroll

All rights reserved. No part of this publication may be reproduced, distributed, or transmitted in any form or by any means, including photocopying, recording, or other electronic or mechanical methods, without the prior written permission of the publisher, except in the case of brief quotations embodied in critical reviews and certain other noncommercial uses permitted by copyright law.

The author dedicates this book to the pursuit of love and understanding, thanking the divine for inspiration and acknowledging the help from other translations. This work is a heartfelt act of devotion.

Book Title: Holy Bible For Gen Z
Author: Athena Scroll
Genre / Category: Love; Spiritual; Religious Verses;

First Edition.

Cover Design by SM.

So what's inside?

the old testament for genz
the new testament for genz

THE OLD TESTAMENT
for Genz

athena scroll

Your Path Forward

Genesis	1
Exodus	18
Leviticus	34
Numbers	46
Deuteronomy	62
Joshua	76
Judges	85
Ruth	93
1 Samuel	94
2 Samuel	106
1 Kings	114
2 Kings	124
1 Chronicles	135
2 Chronicles	145
Ezra	157
Nehemiah	161
Esther	167
Job	170
Psalms	180
Proverbs	203
Ecclesiastes	211
Song of Songs	214
Isaiah	216
Jeremiah	235
Lamentations	256
Ezekiel	258
Daniel	278
Hosea	283
Joel	286
Amos	288
Obadiah	291
Jonah	292
Micah	293
Nahum	295
Habakkuk	296
Zephaniah	297
Haggai	298
Zechariah	299
Malachi	303

Genesis

{1:1} **In the beginning, God created the heavens and the earth.** {1:2} The earth was formless and empty, and darkness covered the deep waters. And the Spirit of God was hovering over the surface of the waters. {1:3} Then God said, "Let there be light," and there was light. {1:4} And God saw that the light was good. Then he separated the light from the darkness. {1:5} God called the light "day" and the darkness "night." And evening passed and morning came, marking the first day. {1:6} Then God said, "Let there be a space between the waters, to separate the waters of the heavens from the waters of the earth." {1:7} And that is what happened. God made this space to separate the waters of the earth from the waters of the heavens. {1:8} God called the space "sky." And evening passed and morning came, marking the second day. {1:9} Then God said, "Let the waters beneath the sky flow together into one place, so dry ground may appear." And that is what happened. {1:10} God called the dry ground "land" and the waters "seas." And God saw that it was good. {1:11} Then God said, "Let the land sprout with vegetation—every sort of seed-bearing plant, and trees that grow seed-bearing fruit. These seeds will then produce the kinds of plants and trees from which they came." And that is what happened. {1:12} The land produced vegetation—all sorts of seed-bearing plants, and trees with seed-bearing fruit. Their seeds produced plants and trees of the same kind. And God saw that it was good. {1:13} And evening passed and morning came, marking the third day. {1:14} Then God said, "Let lights appear in the sky to separate the day from the night. Let them be signs to mark the seasons, days, and years. {1:15} Let these lights in the sky shine down on the earth." And that is what happened. {1:16} God made two great lights—the larger one to govern the day, and the smaller one to govern the night. He also made the stars. {1:17} God set these lights in the sky to light the earth, {1:18} to govern the day and night, and to separate the light from the darkness. And God saw that it was good. {1:19} And evening passed and morning came, marking the fourth day. {1:20} Then God said, "Let the waters swarm with fish and other life. Let the skies be filled with birds of every kind." {1:21} So God created great sea creatures and every living thing that scurries and swarms in the water, and every sort of bird—each producing offspring of the same kind. And God saw that it was good. {1:22} Then God blessed them, saying, "Be fruitful and multiply. Let the fish fill the seas, and let the birds multiply on the earth." {1:23} And evening passed and morning came, marking the fifth day. {1:24} Then God said, "Let the earth produce every sort of animal, each producing offspring of the same kind—livestock, small animals that scurry along the ground, and wild animals." And that is what happened. {1:25} God made all sorts of wild animals, livestock, and small animals, each able to produce offspring of the same kind. And God saw that it was good. {1:26} Then God said, *"Let us make human beings in our image, to be like us. They will reign over the fish in the sea, the birds in the sky, the livestock, all the wild animals on the earth, and the small animals that scurry along the ground."* {1:27} So God created human beings in his own image. In the image of God he created them; male and female he created them. {1:28} Then God blessed them and said, "Be fruitful and multiply. Fill the earth and govern it. Reign over the fish in the sea, the birds in the sky, and all the animals that scurry along the ground." {1:29} Then God said, "Look! I have given you every seed-bearing plant throughout the earth and all the fruit trees for your food. {1:30} And I have given every green plant as food for all the wild animals, the birds in the sky, and the small animals that scurry along the ground—everything that has life." And that is what happened. {1:31} Then God looked over all he had made, and he saw that it was very good! And evening passed and morning came, marking the sixth day.

{2:1} So the heavens and the earth were completed, along with all of their vast array. {2:2} By the seventh day, God had finished the work he had been doing; so on the seventh day he rested from all his work. {2:3} Then God blessed the seventh day and made it holy, because on it he rested from all the work of creation that he had done. {2:4} This is the account of the creation of the heavens and the earth when the Lord God made the earth and the heavens. {2:5} No shrub had yet appeared on the earth and no plant had yet sprung up, for the Lord God had not sent rain on the earth and there was no one to work the ground, {2:6} but streams came up from the earth and watered the whole surface of the ground. {2:7} **Then the Lord God formed a man from the dust of the ground and breathed into his nostrils the breath of life, and the man became a living being.** {2:8} Now the Lord God had planted a garden in the east, in Eden; and there he put the man he had formed. {2:9} The Lord God made all kinds of trees grow out of the ground—trees that were pleasing to the eye and good for food. In the middle of the garden were the tree of life and the tree of the knowledge of good and evil. {2:10} A river watering the garden flowed from Eden; from there it was separated into four headwaters. {2:11} The name of the first is the Pishon; it winds through the entire land of Havilah, where there is gold. {2:12} (The gold of that land is good; aromatic resin and onyx are also there.) {2:13} The name of the second river is the Gihon; it winds through the entire land of Cush. {2:14} The name of the third river is the Tigris; it runs along the east side of Ashur. And the fourth river is the Euphrates. {2:15} The Lord God took the man and put him in the Garden of Eden to work it and take care of it. {2:16} And the Lord God commanded the man, "You are free to eat from any tree in the garden; {2:17} but you must not eat from the tree of the knowledge of good and evil, for when you eat from it you will certainly die." {2:18} The Lord God said, "It is not good for the man to be alone. I will make a helper suitable for him." {2:19} Now the Lord God had formed out of the ground all the wild animals and all the birds in the sky. He brought them to the man to see what he would name them; and whatever the man called each living creature, that was its name. {2:20} So the man gave names to all the livestock, the birds in the sky and all the wild animals. But for Adam no suitable helper was found. {2:21} So the Lord God caused the man to fall into a deep sleep; and while he was sleeping, he took one of the man's ribs and then closed up the place with flesh. {2:22} Then the Lord God made a woman from the rib he had taken out of the man, and he brought her to the man. {2:23} The man said, "This is now bone of my bones and flesh of my flesh; she shall be called 'woman,' for she was taken out of man." {2:24} That is why a man leaves his father and mother and is united to his wife, and they become one flesh. {2:25} Adam and his wife were both naked, and they felt no shame.

{3:1} Now the serpent was more cunning than any of the wild animals the Lord God had made. He said to the woman, "Did God really say, 'You must not eat from any tree in the garden'?" {3:2} The woman replied to the serpent, "We may eat fruit from the trees in the garden, {3:3} but God did say, 'You must not eat fruit from the tree that is in the middle of the garden, and you must not touch it, or you will die.'" {3:4} "You will not certainly die," the serpent said to the woman. {3:5} "For God knows that when you eat from it your eyes will be opened, and you will be like God, knowing good and evil." {3:6} When the woman saw that the fruit of the tree was good for food and pleasing to the eye, and also desirable for gaining wisdom, she took some and ate it. She also gave some to her husband, who was with her, and he ate it. {3:7} Then the eyes of both of them were opened, and they realized they were naked; so they sewed fig leaves together and made coverings for themselves. {3:8} Then the man and his wife heard the sound of the Lord God as he was walking in the garden in the cool of the day, and they hid from the Lord God among the trees of the garden. {3:9} But the Lord God called to the man, "Where are you?" {3:10} He answered, "I heard you in the garden, and I was afraid because I was naked; so I hid." {3:11} And he said, "Who told you that you were naked? Have you eaten from the tree that I commanded you not to eat from?" {3:12} The man said, "The woman you put here with me—she gave me some fruit from the tree, and I ate it." {3:13} Then the Lord God said to the woman, "What is this you have done?" The woman said, "The serpent deceived me, and I ate." {3:14} So the Lord God said to the serpent, "Because you have done this, cursed are you above all livestock and all wild animals! You will crawl on your belly and you will eat dust all the days of your life. {3:15} **And I will put enmity between you and the woman, and between your offspring and hers; he will crush your head, and you will strike his heel."** {3:16} To the woman he said, "I will make your pains in childbearing very severe; with painful labor you will give birth to children. Your desire will be for your husband, and he will rule over you." {3:17} To Adam he said, "Because you listened to your wife and ate fruit from the tree about which I commanded you, 'You must not eat from it,' cursed is the ground because of you; through painful toil you will eat food from it all the days of your life. {3:18} It will produce thorns and thistles for you, and you will eat the plants of the field. {3:19} By the sweat of your brow you will eat your food until you return to the ground, since from it you were taken; for dust you are and to dust you will return." {3:20} Adam named his wife Eve, because she would become the mother of all the living. {3:21} The Lord God made garments of skin for Adam and his wife and clothed them. {3:22} And the Lord God said, "The man has now become like one of us, knowing good and evil. He must not be allowed to reach out his hand and take also from the tree of life and eat, and live forever." {3:23} So the Lord God banished him from the Garden of Eden to work the ground from which he had been taken. {3:24} After he drove the man out, he placed on the east side of the Garden of Eden cherubim and a flaming sword flashing back and forth to guard the way to the tree of life.

{4:1} Adam made love to his wife Eve, and she became pregnant and gave birth to Cain. She said, "With the help of the Lord I have brought forth a man." {4:2} Later she gave birth to his brother Abel. Now Abel kept flocks, and Cain worked the soil. {4:3} In the course of time Cain brought some of the fruits of the soil as an offering to the Lord. {4:4} And Abel also brought an offering—fat portions from some of the firstborn of his flock. The Lord looked with favor on Abel and his offering, {4:5} but on Cain and his offering he did not look with favor. So Cain was very angry, and his face was downcast. {4:6} Then the Lord said to Cain, "Why are you angry? Why is your face downcast? {4:7} If you do what is right, will you not be accepted? But if you do not do what is right, sin is crouching at your door; it desires to have you, but you must rule over it." {4:8} Now Cain said to his brother Abel, "Let's go out to the field." While they were in the field, Cain attacked his brother Abel and killed him. {4:9} Then the Lord said to Cain, "Where is your brother Abel?" "I don't know," he replied. "Am I my brother's keeper?" {4:10} The Lord said, "What have you done? Listen! Your brother's blood cries out to me from the ground. {4:11} Now you are under a curse and driven from the ground, which opened its mouth to receive your brother's blood from your hand. {4:12} When you work the ground, it will no longer yield its crops for you. You will be a restless wanderer on the earth." {4:13} Cain said to the Lord, "My punishment is more than I can bear. {4:14} Today you are driving me from the land, and I will be hidden from your presence; I will be a restless wanderer on the earth, and whoever finds me will kill me." {4:15} But the Lord said to him, "Not so; anyone who kills Cain will suffer vengeance seven times over." Then the Lord put a mark on Cain so that no one who found him would kill him. {4:16} So Cain went out from the Lord's presence and lived in the land of Nod, east of Eden. {4:17} Cain made love to his wife, and she became pregnant and gave birth to Enoch. Cain was then building a city, and he named it after his son Enoch. {4:18} To Enoch was born Irad, and Irad was the father of Mehujael, and Mehujael was the father of Methushael, and Methushael was the father of Lamech. {4:19} Lamech married two women, one named Adah and the other Zillah. {4:20} Adah gave birth to Jabal; he was the father of those who live in tents and raise livestock. {4:21} His brother's name was Jubal; he was the father of all who play stringed instruments and pipes. {4:22} Zillah also had a son, Tubal-Cain, who forged all kinds of tools out of bronze and iron. Tubal-Cain's sister was Naamah. {4:23} Lamech said to his wives, "Adah and Zillah, listen to me; wives of Lamech, hear my words. I have killed a man for wounding me, a young man for injuring me. {4:24} If Cain is avenged seven times, then Lamech seventy-seven times." {4:25} Adam made love to his wife again, and she gave birth to a son and named him Seth, saying, "God has granted me another child in place of Abel, since Cain killed him." {4:26} Seth also had a son, and he named him Enosh. At that time people began to call on the name of the Lord.

{5:1} This is the written account of Adam's family line. When God created mankind, he made them in the likeness of God. {5:2} He created them male and female and blessed them. And he named them "Mankind" when they were created. {5:3} When Adam had lived 130 years, he had a son in his own likeness, in his own image; and he named him Seth. {5:4} After Seth was born, Adam lived 800 years and had other sons and daughters. {5:5} Altogether, Adam lived a total of 930 years, and then he died. {5:6} When Seth had lived 105 years, he became the father of Enosh. {5:7} After he became the father of Enosh, Seth lived 807 years and had other sons and daughters. {5:8} Altogether, Seth lived a total of 912 years, and then he died. {5:9} When Enosh had lived 90 years, he became the father of Kenan. {5:10} After he became the father of Kenan, Enosh lived 815 years and had other sons and daughters. {5:11} Altogether, Enosh lived a total of 905 years, and then he died. {5:12} When Kenan had lived 70 years, he became the father of Mahalalel. {5:13} After he became the father of Mahalalel, Kenan lived 840 years and had other sons and daughters. {5:14} Altogether, Kenan lived a total of 910 years, and then he died. {5:15} When Mahalalel had lived 65 years, he became the father of Jared. {5:16} After he became the father of Jared, Mahalalel lived 830 years and had other sons and daughters. {5:17} Altogether, Mahalalel lived a total of 895 years, and then he died. {5:18} When Jared had lived 162 years, he became the father of Enoch. {5:19} After he became the father of Enoch, Jared lived 800 years and had other sons and daughters. {5:20} Altogether, Jared lived a total of 962 years, and then he died. {5:21} When Enoch had lived 65 years, he became the father of Methuselah. {5:22} After he became the father of Methuselah, Enoch walked faithfully with God 300 years and had other sons and daughters. {5:23} Altogether, Enoch lived a total of 365 years. {5:24} Enoch walked faithfully with God; then he was no more, because God took him away. {5:25} When Methuselah had lived 187 years, he became the father of Lamech. {5:26} After he became the father of Lamech, Methuselah lived 782 years and had other sons and daughters. {5:27} Altogether, Methuselah lived a total of 969 years, and then he died. {5:28} When Lamech had lived 182 years, he had a son. {5:29} He named him Noah and said, "He will comfort us in the labor and painful toil of our hands caused by the ground the Lord has cursed." {5:30} After Noah was born, Lamech lived 595 years and had other sons and daughters. {5:31} Altogether, Lamech lived a total of 777 years, and then he died. {5:32} After Noah was 500 years old, he became the father of Shem, Ham and Japheth.

{6:1} As people began to multiply on the earth and daughters were born to them, {6:2} the sons of God saw that the daughters of humans were beautiful, and they married any of them they chose. {6:3} Then the Lord said, "My Spirit will not contend with humans forever, for they are mortal; their days will be a hundred and twenty years." {6:4} The Nephilim were on the earth in those days—and also afterward—when the sons of God went to the daughters of humans and had children by them. They were the heroes of old, men of renown. {6:5} **The Lord saw how great the wickedness of the human race had become on the earth, and that every inclination of the thoughts of the human heart was only evil all the time.** {6:6} The Lord regretted that he had made human beings on the earth, and his heart was deeply troubled. {6:7} So the Lord said, "I will wipe from the face of the earth the human race I have created—and with them the animals, the birds and the creatures that move along the ground—for I regret that I have made them." {6:8} But Noah found favor in the eyes of the Lord. {6:9} This is the account of Noah and his family. Noah was a righteous man, blameless among the people of his time, and he walked faithfully with God. {6:10} Noah had three sons: Shem, Ham and Japheth. {6:11} Now the earth was corrupt in God's sight and was full of violence. {6:12} God saw how corrupt the earth had become, for all the people on earth had corrupted their ways. {6:13} So God said to Noah, "I am going to put an end to all people, for the earth is filled with violence because of them. I am surely going to destroy both them and the earth. {6:14} So make yourself an ark of cypress wood; make rooms in it and coat it with pitch inside and out. {6:15} This is how you are to build it: The ark is to be three hundred cubits long, fifty cubits wide and thirty cubits high. {6:16} Make a roof for it, leaving below the roof an opening one cubit high all around. Put a door in the side of the ark and make lower, middle and upper decks. {6:17} I am going to bring floodwaters on the earth to destroy all life under the heavens, every creature that has the breath of life in it. Everything on earth will perish. {6:18} But I will establish my covenant with you, and you will enter the ark—you and your sons and your wife and your sons' wives with you. {6:19} You are to bring into the ark two of all living creatures, male and female, to keep them alive with you. {6:20} Two of every kind of bird, of every kind of animal and of every kind of creature that moves along the ground will come to you to be kept alive. {6:21} You are to take every kind of food that is to be eaten and store it away as food for you and for them." {6:22} Noah did everything just as God commanded him.

{7:1} Then the Lord said to Noah, "Go into the ark, you and your whole family, because I have found you righteous in this generation. {7:2} Take with you seven pairs of every kind of clean animal, a male and its mate, and one pair of every kind of unclean animal, a male and its mate, {7:3} and also seven pairs of every kind of bird, male and female, to keep their various kinds alive throughout the earth. {7:4} Seven days from now I will send rain on the earth for forty days and forty nights, and I will wipe from the face of the earth every living creature I have made." {7:5} And Noah did all that the Lord commanded him. {7:6} Noah was six hundred years old when the floodwaters came on the earth. {7:7} And Noah and his sons and his wife and his sons' wives entered the ark to escape the waters of the flood. {7:8} Pairs of clean and unclean animals, of birds and of all creatures that move along the ground, {7:9} male and female, came to Noah and entered the ark, as God had commanded Noah. {7:10} And after the seven days the floodwaters came on the earth. {7:11} In the six hundredth year of Noah's life, on the seventeenth day of the second month—on that day all the springs of the great deep burst forth, and the floodgates of the heavens were opened. {7:12} And rain fell on the earth forty days and forty nights. {7:13} On that very day Noah and his sons, Shem, Ham and Japheth, together with his wife and the wives of his three sons, entered the ark. {7:14} They had with them every wild animal according to its kind, all livestock according to their kinds, every creature that moves along the ground according to its kind and every bird according to its kind, everything with wings. {7:15} Pairs of all creatures that have the breath of life in them came to Noah and entered the ark. {7:16} The animals going in were male and female of every living thing, as God had commanded Noah. Then the Lord shut him in. {7:17} For forty days the flood kept coming on the earth, and as the waters increased they lifted the ark high above the earth. {7:18} The waters rose and increased greatly on the earth, and the ark floated on the surface of the water. {7:19} They rose greatly on the earth, and all the high mountains under the entire heavens were covered. {7:20} The waters rose and covered the mountains to a depth of more than fifteen cubits. {7:21} Every living thing that moved on land perished—birds, livestock, wild animals, all the creatures that swarm over the earth, and all mankind. {7:22} Everything on dry land that had the breath of life in its nostrils died. {7:23} Every living thing on the face of the earth was wiped out; people and animals and the creatures that move along the ground and the birds were wiped from the earth. Only Noah was left, and those with him in the ark. {7:24} The waters flooded the earth for a hundred and fifty days.

{8:1} Then God remembered Noah and all the animals and livestock with him in the ark. He caused a wind to pass over the earth, and the waters began to subside. {8:2} The springs of the deep and the windows of the heavens were closed, and the rain stopped falling from the sky. {8:3} The waters gradually receded from the earth. After one hundred and fifty days, the waters had gone down. {8:4} On the seventeenth day of the seventh month, the ark came to rest on the mountains of Ararat. {8:5} The waters continued to decrease until the tenth month, and on the first day of the tenth month, the mountain peaks became visible. {8:6} After forty days, Noah opened a window he had made in the ark. {8:7} He sent out a raven, and it kept flying back and forth until the waters had dried up from the earth. {8:8} Then he sent out a dove to see if the waters had receded from the surface of the ground. {8:9} But the dove found no place to perch because the water still covered the ground; so it returned to Noah in the ark. He reached out his hand and took the dove and brought it back to himself in the ark. {8:10} He waited seven more days and again sent out the dove from the ark. {8:11} When the dove returned to him in the evening, there in its beak was a freshly plucked olive leaf! Then Noah knew that the water had receded from the earth. {8:12} He waited seven more days and sent the dove out again, but this time it did not return to him. {8:13} By the first day of the first month of Noah's six hundred and first year, the water had dried up from the earth. Noah then removed the covering of the ark and saw that the surface of the ground was dry. {8:14} By the twenty-seventh day of the second month, the earth was completely dry. {8:15} Then God said to Noah, {8:16} "Come out of the ark, you and your wife and your sons and their wives. {8:17} Bring out every kind of living creature that is with you—the birds, the animals, and all the creatures that move along the ground—so they can multiply on the earth and be fruitful and increase in number upon it." {8:18} So Noah came out, together with his sons and his wife and his sons' wives. {8:19} All the animals, including every kind of bird and every kind of creature that moves along the ground, came out of the ark, one kind after another. {8:20} Then Noah built an altar to the Lord and, taking some of all the clean animals and clean birds, he sacrificed burnt offerings on it. {8:21} The Lord smelled the pleasing aroma and said in his heart: "Never again will I curse the ground because of humans, even though every inclination of the human heart is evil from childhood. And never again will I destroy all living creatures, as I have done. {8:22} As long as the earth endures, seedtime and harvest, cold and heat, summer and winter, day and night will never cease."

{9:1} Then God blessed Noah and his sons, saying to them, "Be fruitful and increase in number and fill the earth. {9:2} The fear and dread of you will fall on all the beasts of the earth, and on all the birds in the sky, on every creature that moves along the ground, and on all the fish in the sea; they are given into your hands. {9:3} Everything that lives and moves about will be food for you. Just as I gave you the green plants, I now give you everything. {9:4} But you must not eat meat that has its lifeblood still in it. {9:5} And for your lifeblood I will surely demand an accounting. I will demand an accounting from every animal. And from each human being, too, I will demand an accounting for the life of another human being. {9:6} Whoever sheds human blood, by humans shall their blood be shed; for in the image of God has God made mankind. {9:7} As for you, be fruitful and increase in number; multiply on the earth and increase upon it." {9:8} Then God said to Noah and to his sons with him: {9:9} "I now establish my covenant with you and with your descendants after you {9:10} and with every living creature that was with you—the birds, the livestock and all the wild animals, all those that came out of the ark with you—every living creature on earth. {9:11} I establish my covenant with you: Never again will all life be destroyed by the waters of a flood; never again will there be a flood to destroy the earth." {9:12} And God said, "This is the sign of the covenant I am making between me and you and every living creature with you, a covenant for all generations to come: {9:13} **I have set my rainbow in the clouds, and it will be the sign of the covenant between me and the earth.** {9:14} Whenever I bring clouds over the earth and the rainbow appears in the clouds, {9:15} I will remember my covenant between me and you and all living creatures of every kind. Never again will the waters become a flood to destroy all life. {9:16} Whenever the rainbow appears in the clouds, I will see it and remember the everlasting covenant between God and all living creatures of every kind on the earth." {9:17} So God said to Noah, "This is the sign of the covenant I have established between me and all life on the earth." {9:18} The sons of Noah who came out of the ark were Shem, Ham and Japheth. (Ham was the father of Canaan.) {9:19} These were the three sons of Noah, and from them came the people who were scattered over the whole earth. {9:20} Noah, a man of the soil, proceeded to plant a vineyard. {9:21} When he drank some of its wine, he became drunk and lay uncovered inside his tent. {9:22} Ham, the father of Canaan, saw his father naked and told his two brothers outside. {9:23} But Shem and Japheth took a garment and laid it across their shoulders; then they walked in backward and covered their father's naked body. Their faces were turned the other way so that they would not see their father naked. {9:24} When Noah awoke from his wine and found out what his youngest son had done to him, {9:25} he said, "Cursed be Canaan! The lowest of slaves will be to his brothers." {9:26} He also said, "Praise be to the Lord, the God of Shem! May Canaan be the slave of Shem. {9:27} May God extend Japheth's territory; may Japheth live in the tents of Shem, and may Canaan be the slave of Japheth." {9:28} After the flood Noah lived 350 years. {9:29} Noah lived a total of 950 years, and then he died.

{10:1} These are the descendants of Noah's sons, Shem, Ham, and Japheth, to whom sons were born after the flood. {10:2} The sons of Japheth: Gomer, Magog, Madai, Javan, Tubal, Meshech, and Tiras. {10:3} The sons of Gomer: Ashkenaz, Riphath, and Togarmah. {10:4} The sons of Javan: Elishah, Tarshish, Kittim, and Dodanim. {10:5} These were the descendants of Japheth, who spread out to their own territories, each with their own language, according to their clans and nations. {10:6} The sons of Ham: Cush, Mizraim, Put, and Canaan. {10:7} The sons of Cush: Seba, Havilah, Sabtah, Raamah, and Sabteca. The sons of Raamah: Sheba and Dedan. {10:8} Cush was the father of Nimrod, who became a mighty warrior on the earth. {10:9} He was a mighty hunter before the LORD; that is why it is said, "Like Nimrod, a mighty hunter before the LORD." {10:10} The first centers of his kingdom were Babylon, Uruk, Akkad, and Kalneh, in Shinar. {10:11} From that land he went to Assyria, where he built Nineveh, Rehoboth Ir, Calah, {10:12} and Resen, which is between Nineveh and Calah—which is the great city. {10:13} Mizraim was the father of the Ludites, Anamites, Lehabites, Naphtuhites, {10:14} Pathrusites, Casluhites (from whom the Philistines came), and Caphtorites. {10:15} Canaan was the father of Sidon his firstborn, and of the Hittites, {10:16} Jebusites, Amorites, Girgashites, {10:17} Hivites, Arkites, Sinites, {10:18} Arvadites, Zemarites, and Hamathites. Later the Canaanite clans scattered {10:19} and the borders of Canaan reached from Sidon toward Gerar as far as Gaza, and then toward Sodom,

Gomorrah, Admah and Zeboyim, as far as Lasha. {10:20} These are the sons of Ham, according to their clans and languages, in their territories and nations. {10:21} Sons were also born to Shem, whose older brother was Japheth; Shem was the ancestor of all the sons of Eber. {10:22} The sons of Shem: Elam, Asshur, Arphaxad, Lud, and Aram. {10:23} The sons of Aram: Uz, Hul, Gether, and Meshech. {10:24} Arphaxad was the father of Shelah, and Shelah the father of Eber. {10:25} Two sons were born to Eber: One was named Peleg, because in his time the earth was divided; his brother was named Joktan. {10:26} Joktan was the father of Almodad, Sheleph, Hazarmaveth, Jerah, {10:27} Hadoram, Uzal, Diklah, {10:28} Obal, Abimael, Sheba, {10:29} Ophir, Havilah, and Jobab. All these were sons of Joktan. {10:30} Their territory extended from Mesha toward Sephar, in the eastern hill country. {10:31} These are the sons of Shem, according to their clans and languages, in their territories and nations. {10:32} These are the clans of Noah's sons, according to their lines of descent, within their nations. From these the nations spread out over the earth after the flood.

{11:1} The entire earth had one language and a common speech. {11:2} As people moved eastward, they found a plain in the land of Shinar and settled there. {11:3} They said to each other, "Come, let's make bricks and bake them thoroughly." They used brick instead of stone, and tar for mortar. {11:4} Then they said, "Come, let us build ourselves a city, with a tower that reaches to the heavens, so that we may make a name for ourselves; otherwise we will be scattered over the face of the whole earth." {11:5} But the LORD came down to see the city and the tower the people were building. {11:6} The LORD said, "If as one people speaking the same language they have begun to do this, then nothing they plan to do will be impossible for them. {11:7} Come, let us go down and confuse their language so they will not understand each other." {11:8} So the LORD scattered them from there over all the earth, and they stopped building the city. {11:9} That is why it was called Babel—because there the LORD confused the language of the whole world. From there the LORD scattered them over the face of the whole earth. {11:10} This is the account of Shem's family line. Shem was a hundred years old when he became the father of Arphaxad, two years after the flood. {11:11} And Shem lived five hundred years after he became the father of Arphaxad, and he had other sons and daughters. {11:12} When Arphaxad had lived thirty-five years, he became the father of Salah. {11:13} And Arphaxad lived four hundred and three years after he became the father of Salah, and he had other sons and daughters. {11:14} When Salah had lived thirty years, he became the father of Eber. {11:15} And Salah lived four hundred and three years after he became the father of Eber, and he had other sons and daughters. {11:16} When Eber had lived thirty-four years, he became the father of Peleg. {11:17} And Eber lived four hundred and thirty years after he became the father of Peleg, and he had other sons and daughters. {11:18} When Peleg had lived thirty years, he became the father of Reu. {11:19} And Peleg lived two hundred and nine years after he became the father of Reu, and he had other sons and daughters. {11:20} When Reu had lived thirty-two years, he became the father of Serug. {11:21} And Reu lived two hundred and seven years after he became the father of Serug, and he had other sons and daughters. {11:22} When Serug had lived thirty years, he became the father of Nahor. {11:23} And Serug lived two hundred years after he became the father of Nahor, and he had other sons and daughters. {11:24} When Nahor had lived twenty-nine years, he became the father of Terah. {11:25} And Nahor lived a hundred and nineteen years after he became the father of Terah, and he had other sons and daughters. {11:26} After Terah had lived seventy years, he became the father of Abram, Nahor, and Haran. {11:27} This is the account of Terah's family line. Terah became the father of Abram, Nahor, and Haran. And Haran became the father of Lot. {11:28} While his father Terah was still alive, Haran died in Ur of the Chaldeans, in the land of his birth. {11:29} Abram and Nahor both married. The name of Abram's wife was Sarai, and the name of Nahor's wife was Milkah; she was the daughter of Haran, the father of both Milkah and Iskah. {11:30} Now Sarai was childless because she was not able to conceive. {11:31} Terah took his son Abram, his grandson Lot son of Haran, and his daughter-in-law Sarai, the wife of his son Abram, and together they set out from Ur of the Chaldeans to go to Canaan. But when they came to Harran, they settled there. {11:32} Terah lived two hundred and five years, and he died in Harran.

{12:1} The LORD said to Abram, "Go from your country, your people and your father's household to the land I will show you. {12:2} **"I will make you into a great nation, and I will bless you; I will make your name great, and you will be a blessing.** {12:3} "I will bless those who bless you, and whoever curses you I will curse; and all peoples on earth will be blessed through you." {12:4} So Abram went, as the LORD had told him; and Lot went with him. Abram was seventy-five years old when he set out from Harran. {12:5} He took his wife Sarai, his nephew Lot, all the possessions they had accumulated and the people they had acquired in Harran, and they set out for the land of Canaan, and they arrived there. {12:6} Abram traveled through the land as far as the site of the great tree of Moreh at Shechem. At that time the Canaanites were in the land. {12:7} The LORD appeared to Abram and said, "To your offspring I will give this land." So he built an altar there to the LORD, who had appeared to him. {12:8} From there he went on toward the hills east of Bethel and pitched his tent, with Bethel on the west and Ai on the east. There he built an altar to the LORD and called on the name of the LORD. {12:9} Then Abram set out and continued toward the Negev. {12:10} Now there was a famine in the land, and Abram went down to Egypt to live there for a while because the famine was severe. {12:11} As he was about to enter Egypt, he said to his wife Sarai, "I know what a beautiful woman you are. {12:12} When the Egyptians see you, they will say, 'This is his wife.' Then they will kill me but will let you live. {12:13} Say you are my sister, so that I will be treated well for your sake and my life will be spared because of you." {12:14} When Abram came to Egypt, the Egyptians saw that Sarai was a very beautiful woman. {12:15} And when Pharaoh's officials saw her, they praised her to Pharaoh, and she was taken into his palace. {12:16} He treated Abram well for her sake, and Abram acquired sheep, cattle, male and female donkeys, male and female servants, and camels. {12:17} But the LORD inflicted serious diseases on Pharaoh and his household because of Abram's wife Sarai. {12:18} So Pharaoh summoned Abram. "What have you done to me?" he said. "Why didn't you tell me she was your wife? {12:19} Why did you say, 'She is my sister,' so that I took her to be my wife? Now then, here is your wife. Take her and go!" {12:20} Then Pharaoh gave orders about Abram to his men, and they sent him on his way, with his wife and everything he had.

{13:1} Abram left Egypt, he and his wife and all that he had, and Lot went with him into the Negev. {13:2} Now Abram was very wealthy in livestock, in silver, and in gold. {13:3} And he journeyed on from the Negev as far as Bethel, to the place where his tent had been at the beginning, between Bethel and Ai, {13:4} to the place where he had made an altar at the first. And there Abram called upon the name of the LORD. {13:5} Now Lot, who went with Abram, also had flocks, herds, and tents. {13:6} And the land could not support both of them dwelling together; for their possessions were so great that they could not dwell together. {13:7} And there was strife between the herdsmen of Abram's livestock and the herdsmen of Lot's livestock. At that time the Canaanites and the Perizzites were dwelling in the land. {13:8} Then Abram said to Lot, "Let there be no strife between you and me, and between your herdsmen and my herdsmen, for we are kinsmen. {13:9} Is not the whole land before you? Separate yourself from me. If you take the left hand, then I will go to the right, or if you take the right hand, then I will go to the left." {13:10} And Lot lifted up his eyes and saw that the Jordan Valley was well watered everywhere like the garden of the LORD, like the land of Egypt, in the direction of Zoar. (This was before the LORD destroyed Sodom and Gomorrah.) {13:11} So Lot chose for himself all the Jordan Valley, and Lot journeyed east. Thus they separated from each other. {13:12} Abram settled in the land of Canaan, while Lot settled among the cities of the valley and moved his tent as far as Sodom. {13:13} Now the men of Sodom were wicked, great sinners against the LORD. {13:14} And the LORD said to Abram, after Lot had separated from him, "Lift up your eyes and look from the place where you are, northward and southward and eastward and westward, {13:15} for all the land that you see I will give to you and to your offspring forever. {13:16} I will make your offspring as the dust of the earth, so that if one can count the dust of the earth, your offspring also can be counted. {13:17} Arise, walk through the length and the breadth of the land, for I will give it to you." {13:18} So Abram moved his tent and came and settled by the oaks of Mamre, which are at Hebron, and there he built an altar to the LORD.

{14:1} In the days of Amraphel king of Shinar, Arioch king of Ellasar, Chedorlaomer king of Elam, and Tidal king of nations, {14:2} these kings made war with Bera king of Sodom, Birsha king of Gomorrah, Shinab king of Admah, Shemeber king of Zeboiim, and the king of Bela (that is, Zoar). {14:3} All these joined forces in the Valley of Siddim (that is, the Salt Sea). {14:4} Twelve years they had served Chedorlaomer, but in the thirteenth year they rebelled. {14:5} In the fourteenth year Chedorlaomer and the kings who were with him came and defeated the Rephaim in Ashteroth-karnaim, the Zuzim in Ham, the Emim in Shaveh-kiriathaim, {14:6} and the Horites in their hill country of Seir, as far as El-paran on the border of the wilderness. {14:7} Then they turned back and came to En-mishpat (that is, Kadesh) and defeated all the country of the Amalekites, and also the Amorites who were dwelling in Hazazon-tamar. {14:8} Then the king of Sodom, the king of Gomorrah, the king of Admah, the king of Zeboiim, and the king of Bela (that is, Zoar) went out, and they joined battle in the Valley of Siddim {14:9} against Chedorlaomer king of Elam, Tidal king of nations, Amraphel king of Shinar, and Arioch king of Ellasar, four kings against five. {14:10} Now the Valley of Siddim was full of bitumen pits, and as the kings of Sodom and Gomorrah fled, some fell into them, and the rest fled to the hill country. {14:11} So the enemy took all the possessions of Sodom and Gomorrah, and all their provisions, and went their way. {14:12} They also took Lot, the son of Abram's brother, who was dwelling in Sodom, and his possessions, and went their way. {14:13} Then one who had escaped came and told Abram the Hebrew, who was living by the oaks of Mamre the Amorite, brother of Eshcol and of Aner. These were allies of Abram. {14:14} When Abram heard that his kinsman had been taken captive, he led forth his trained men, born in his house, 318 of them, and went in pursuit as far as Dan. {14:15} And he divided his forces against them by night, he and his servants, and defeated them and pursued them to Hobah, north of Damascus. {14:16} Then he brought back all the possessions, and also brought back his kinsman Lot with his possessions, and the women and the people. {14:17} After his return from the defeat of Chedorlaomer and the kings who were with him, the king of Sodom went out to meet him at the Valley of Shaveh (that is, the King's Valley). {14:18} And Melchizedek, king of Salem brought out bread and wine. (He was a priest of God Most High.) {14:19} And he blessed him and said, "Blessed be Abram by God Most High, Possessor of heaven and earth; {14:20} and blessed be God Most High, who has delivered your enemies into your hand!" And Abram gave him a tenth of everything. {14:21} And the king of Sodom said to Abram, "Give me the persons, but take the goods for yourself." {14:22} But Abram said to the king of Sodom, "I have lifted my hand to the LORD, God Most High, Possessor of heaven and earth, {14:23} that I would not take a thread or a sandal strap or anything that is yours, lest you should say, 'I have made Abram rich.' {14:24} I will take nothing but what the young men have eaten, and the share of the men who went with me. Let Aner, Eshcol, and Mamre take their share."

{15:1} After these events, the word of the LORD came to Abram in a vision, saying, "Do not be afraid, Abram. I am your shield and your exceedingly great reward." {15:2} But Abram said, "Lord GOD, what will you give me, seeing I am childless, and the heir of my house is Eliezer of Damascus?" {15:3} And Abram said, "Look, you have given me no offspring; indeed, one born in my house is my heir." {15:4} Then behold, the word of the LORD came to him, saying, "This one shall not be your heir, but one who will come from your own body shall be your heir." {15:5} And He brought him outside and said, "Look now toward heaven, and count the stars if you are able to number them." And He said to him, "So shall your descendants be." {15:6} And Abram believed in the LORD, and He accounted it to him for righteousness. {15:7} Then He said to him, "I am the LORD, who brought you out of Ur of the Chaldeans, to give you this land to inherit it." {15:8} And he said, "Lord GOD, how shall I know that I will inherit it?" {15:9} So He said to him, "Bring Me a three-year-old heifer, a three-year-old female goat, a three-year-old ram, a turtledove, and a young pigeon." {15:10} Then he brought all these to Him and cut them in two, down the middle, and placed each piece opposite the other; but he did not cut the birds in two. {15:11} And when the vultures came down on the carcasses, Abram drove them away. {15:12} Now when the sun was going down, a deep sleep fell upon Abram; and behold, horror and great darkness fell upon him. {15:13} Then He said to Abram, "Know certainly that your descendants will be strangers in a land that is not theirs, and will serve them, and they will afflict them for four hundred years. {15:14} And also the nation whom they serve I will judge; afterward they shall come out with great possessions. {15:15} Now as for you, you shall go to your fathers in peace; you shall be buried at a good old age. {15:16} But in the fourth generation they shall return here, for the iniquity of the Amorites is not yet complete." {15:17} And it came to pass, when the sun went down and it was dark, that behold, there appeared a smoking oven and a burning torch that passed between those pieces. {15:18} On the same day the LORD made a covenant with Abram, saying: "To your descendants I have given this land, from the river of Egypt to the great river, the River Euphrates— {15:19} the Kenites, the Kenezzites, the Kadmonites, {15:20} the Hittites, the Perizzites, the Rephaim, {15:21} the Amorites, the Canaanites, the Girgashites, and the Jebusites."

{16:1} Sarai, Abram's wife, had not borne him any children. However, she had an Egyptian servant named Hagar. {16:2} Sarai said to Abram, "The LORD has prevented me from having children. Please, go to my servant; perhaps I can have children through her." Abram listened to Sarai. {16:3} So Sarai gave her servant Hagar to Abram as his wife. This happened after Abram had lived in the land of Canaan for ten years. {16:4} Abram slept with Hagar, and she became pregnant. When she realized she was pregnant, she began to despise her mistress. {16:5} Sarai said to Abram, "This is your fault! I gave my servant to you, and now that she's pregnant, she looks down on me. May the LORD judge between us!" {16:6} Abram replied, "She is your servant; deal with her as you see fit." Then Sarai mistreated Hagar, and she fled from her. {16:7} The angel of the LORD found Hagar by a spring of water in the wilderness, along the road to Shur. {16:8} The angel asked, "Hagar, where have you come from, and where are you going?" She replied, "I am running away from my mistress Sarai." {16:9} The angel said, "Go back to your mistress and submit to her authority." {16:10} The angel continued, "I will greatly multiply your descendants, and they will be too numerous to count." {16:11} The angel also said, "You are now pregnant and will give birth to a son. You are to name him Ishmael, for the LORD has heard your cries of affliction. {16:12} "He will be like a wild donkey, fighting everyone, and everyone will be against him. He will live in hostility toward all his relatives." {16:13} Hagar named the LORD who spoke to her, "You are the God who sees me." She also said, "Have I truly seen the One who sees me?" {16:14} That is why the well was called Beer-lahai-roi; it is located between Kadesh and Bered. {16:15} Hagar gave birth to Abram's son, and Abram named him Ishmael. {16:16} Abram was eighty-six years old when Hagar gave birth to Ishmael.

{17:1} When Abram was ninety-nine years old, the LORD appeared to him and said, "I am God Almighty; walk before me and be blameless. {17:2} "I will make my covenant between me and you, and I will greatly increase your numbers." {17:3} Abram fell facedown, and God said to him, {17:4} "As for me, this is my covenant with you: You will be the father of many nations. {17:5} "No longer will you be called Abram; your name will be Abraham, for I have made you a father of many nations. {17:6} "I will make you very fruitful; I will make nations of you, and kings will come from you. {17:7} **"I will establish my covenant as an everlasting covenant between me and you and your descendants after you for the generations to come, to be your God and the God of your descendants after you.** {17:8} "The whole land of Canaan, where you now reside as a foreigner, I will give as an everlasting possession to you and your descendants after you; and I will be their God." {17:9} Then God said to Abraham, "As for you, you must keep my covenant, you and your descendants after you for the generations to come. {17:10} "This is my covenant with you and your descendants after you, the covenant you are to keep: Every male among you shall be circumcised. {17:11} "You are to undergo circumcision, and it will be the sign of the covenant between me and you. {17:12} "For the generations to come every male among you who is eight days old must be circumcised, including those born in your household or bought with money from a foreigner—those who are not your offspring. {17:13} "Whether born in your household or bought with your money, they must be circumcised. My covenant in your flesh is to be an everlasting covenant. {17:14} "Any uncircumcised male, who has not been circumcised in the flesh, will be cut off from his people; he has broken my covenant." {17:15} God also said to Abraham, "As for Sarai your wife, you are no longer to call her Sarai; her name will be Sarah. {17:16} "I will bless her and will surely give you a son by her. I will bless her so that she will be the mother of nations; kings of peoples will come from her." {17:17} Abraham fell facedown; he laughed and said to himself, "Will a son be born to a man a hundred years old? Will Sarah bear a child at the age of ninety?" {17:18} And Abraham said to God, "If only Ishmael might live under your blessing!" {17:19} Then God said, "Yes, but your wife Sarah will bear you a son, and you will call him Isaac. I will establish my covenant with him as an everlasting covenant for his descendants after him. {17:20} "As for Ishmael, I have heard you: I will surely bless him; I will make him fruitful and will greatly increase his numbers. He will be the father of twelve rulers, and I will make him into a great nation. {17:21} "But my covenant I will establish with Isaac, whom Sarah will bear to you by this time next year." {17:22} When he had finished speaking with Abraham, God went up from him. {17:23} On that very day Abraham took his son Ishmael and all those born in his household or bought with his money, every male in his household, and circumcised them, as God told him. {17:24} Abraham was ninety-nine years old when he was circumcised, {17:25} and his son Ishmael was thirteen; {17:26} Abraham and his son Ishmael were both circumcised on that very day. {17:27} And every male in Abraham's household, including those born in his household or bought from a foreigner, was circumcised with him.

{18:1} One day, the LORD appeared to Abraham in the plains of Mamre. Abraham was sitting at the entrance to his tent in the heat of the day. {18:2} When he looked up, he saw three men standing nearby. He hurried to meet them and bowed low to the ground, {18:3} saying, "My lord, if I have found favor in your eyes, please do not pass your servant by. {18:4} "Let a little water be brought, and then you may all wash your feet and rest under this tree. {18:5} "Let me get you something to eat, so you can be refreshed and then go on your way—now that you have come to your servant." "Very well," they answered, "do as you say." {18:6} So Abraham hurried into the tent to Sarah. "Quick," he said, "get three seahs of the finest flour and knead it and bake some bread." {18:7} Then he ran to the herd and selected a choice, tender calf and gave it to a servant, who hurried to prepare it. {18:8} He then brought some curds and milk and the calf that had been prepared, and set these before them. While they ate, he stood near them under a tree. {18:9} "Where is your wife Sarah?" they asked him. "There, in the tent," he said. {18:10} Then one of them said, "I will surely return to you about this time next year, and Sarah your wife will have a son." Now Sarah was listening at the entrance to the tent, which was behind him. {18:11} Abraham and Sarah were already very old, and Sarah was past the age of childbearing. {18:12} So Sarah laughed to herself as she thought, "After I am worn out and my lord is old, will I now have this pleasure?" {18:13} Then the LORD said to Abraham, "Why did Sarah laugh and say, 'Will I really have a child, now that I am old?' {18:14} "Is anything too hard for the LORD? I will return to you at the appointed time next year, and Sarah will have a son." {18:15} Sarah was afraid, so she lied and said, "I did not laugh." But he said, "Yes, you did laugh." {18:16} When the men got up to leave, they looked down toward Sodom, and Abraham walked along with them to see them on their way. {18:17} Then the LORD said, "Shall I hide from Abraham what I am about to do? {18:18} "Abraham will surely become a great and powerful nation, and all nations on earth will be blessed through him. {18:19} "For I have chosen him, so that he will direct his children and his household after him to keep the way of the LORD by doing what is right and just, so that the LORD will bring about for Abraham what he has promised him." {18:20} Then the LORD said, "The outcry against Sodom and Gomorrah is so great and their sin so grievous {18:21} that I will go down and see if what they have done is as bad as the outcry that has reached me. If not, I will know." {18:22} The men turned away and went toward Sodom, but Abraham remained standing before the LORD. {18:23} Then Abraham approached him and said: "Will you sweep away the righteous with the wicked? {18:24} "What if there are fifty righteous people in the city? Will you really sweep it away and not spare the place for the sake of the fifty righteous people in it? {18:25} "Far be it from you to do such a thing—to kill the righteous with the wicked, treating the righteous and the wicked alike. Far be it from you! Will not the Judge of all the earth do right?" {18:26} The LORD said, "If I find fifty righteous people in the city of Sodom, I will spare the whole place for their sake." {18:27} Then Abraham spoke up again: "Now that I have been so bold as to speak to the Lord, though I am nothing but dust and ashes, {18:28} what if the number of the righteous is five less than fifty? Will you destroy the whole city for lack of five people?" "If I find forty-five there," he said, "I will not destroy it." {18:29} Once again he spoke to him, "What if only forty are found there?" He said, "For the sake of forty, I will not do it." {18:30} Then he said, "May the Lord not be angry, but let me speak. What if only thirty can be found there?" He answered, "I will not do it if I find thirty there." {18:31} Abraham said, "Now that I have been so bold as to speak to the Lord, what if only twenty can be found there?" He said, "For the sake of twenty, I will not destroy it." {18:32} Then he said, "May the Lord not be angry, but let me speak just once more. What if only ten can be found there?" He answered, "For the sake of ten, I will not destroy it." {18:33} When the LORD had finished speaking with Abraham, he left, and Abraham returned home.

{19:1} Two angels arrived in Sodom in the evening, and Lot was sitting at the city gate. When he saw them, he got up to meet them and bowed down with his face to the ground. {19:2} "My lords," he said, "please turn aside to your servant's house. You can wash your feet and spend the night and then go on your way early in the morning." "No," they answered, "we will spend the night in the square." {19:3} But he insisted so strongly that they did go with him and entered his house. He prepared a meal for them, baking bread without yeast, and they ate. {19:4} Before they had gone to bed, all the men from every part of the city of Sodom—both young and old—surrounded the house. {19:5} They called to Lot, "Where are the men who came to you tonight? Bring them out to us so that we can have sex with them." {19:6} Lot went outside to meet them and shut the door behind him {19:7} and said, "No, my friends. Don't do this wicked thing. {19:8} Look, I have two daughters who have never slept with a man. Let me bring them out to you, and you can do what you like with them. But don't do anything to these men, for they have come under the protection of my roof." {19:9} "Get out of our way," they replied. "This fellow came here as a foreigner, and now he wants to play the judge! We'll treat you worse than them." They kept bringing pressure on Lot and moved forward to break down the door. {19:10} But the men inside reached out and pulled Lot back into the house and shut the door. {19:11} Then they struck the men who were at the door of the house, young and old, with blindness so that they could not find the door. {19:12} The two men said to Lot, "Do you have anyone else here—sons-in-law, sons or daughters, or anyone else in the city who belongs to you? Get them out of here, {19:13} because we are going to destroy this place. The outcry to the LORD against its people is so great that he has sent us to destroy it." {19:14} So Lot went out and spoke to his sons-in-law, who were pledged to marry his daughters. He said, "Hurry and get out of this place, because the LORD is about to destroy the city!" But his sons-in-law thought he was joking. {19:15} With the coming of dawn, the angels urged Lot, saying, "Hurry! Take your wife and your two daughters who are here, or you will be swept away when the city is punished." {19:16} When he hesitated, the men grasped his hand and the hands of his wife and of his two daughters and led them safely out of the city, for the LORD was merciful to them. {19:17} As soon as they had brought them out, one of them said, "Flee for your lives! Don't look back, and don't stop anywhere in the plain! Flee to the mountains or you will be swept away!" {19:18} But Lot said to them, "No, my lords, please! {19:19} Your servant has found favor in your eyes, and you have shown great kindness to me in sparing my life. But I can't flee to the mountains; this disaster will overtake me, and I'll die. {19:20} Look, here is a town near enough to run to, and it is small. Let me flee to it—it is very small, isn't it? Then my life will be spared." {19:21} He said to him, "Very well, I will grant this request too; I will not overthrow the town you speak of. {19:22} But flee there quickly, because I cannot do anything until you reach it." (That is why the town was called Zoar.) {19:23} By the time Lot reached Zoar, the sun had risen over the land. {19:24} Then the LORD rained down burning sulfur on Sodom and Gomorrah—from the LORD out of the heavens. {19:25} Thus he overthrew those cities and the entire plain, destroying all those living in the cities—and also the vegetation in the land. {19:26} But Lot's wife looked back, and she became a pillar of salt. {19:27} Early the next morning Abraham got up and returned to the place where he had stood before the LORD. {19:28} He looked down toward Sodom and Gomorrah, toward all the land of the plain, and he saw dense smoke rising from the land, like smoke from a furnace. {19:29} So when God destroyed the cities of the plain, he remembered Abraham, and he brought Lot out of the catastrophe that overthrew the cities where Lot had lived. {19:30} Lot and his two daughters left Zoar and settled in the mountains, for he was afraid to stay in Zoar. He and his two daughters lived in a cave. {19:31} One day the older daughter said to the younger, "Our father is old, and there is no man around here to give us children—as is the custom all over the earth. {19:32} Let's get our father to drink wine and then sleep with him and preserve our family line through our father." {19:33} That night they got their father to drink wine, and the older daughter went in and slept with him. He was not aware of it when she lay down or when she got up. {19:34} The next day the older daughter said to the younger, "Last night I slept with my father. Let's get him to drink wine again tonight, and you go in and sleep with him so we can preserve our family line through our father." {19:35} So they got their father to drink wine that night also, and the younger daughter went in and slept with him. Again he was not aware of it when she lay down or when she got up. {19:36} So both of Lot's daughters became pregnant by their father. {19:37} The older daughter had a son, and she named him Moab; he is the father of the Moabites today. {19:38} The younger daughter also had a son, and she named him Ben-Ammi; he is the father of the Ammonites of today.

{20:1} Abraham traveled southward and settled between Kadesh and Shur, staying for a time in Gerar. {20:2} He told the people there that his wife Sarah was his sister. So, King Abimelech of Gerar sent for Sarah and took her. {20:3} But God came to Abimelech in a dream and said, "You are as good as dead because of the woman you have taken—she is married." {20:4} Abimelech had not touched her, so he pleaded with God, "Lord, would you destroy a nation that has done no wrong? {20:5} Didn't Abraham himself tell me, 'She is my sister'? And she herself said, 'He is my brother.' I acted in innocence and with a clear conscience." {20:6} God replied in the dream, "Yes, I know you acted with a clear conscience. That's why I kept you from sinning against me, and I did not let you touch her. {20:7} Now return the man's wife to him, for he is a prophet, and he will pray for you, and you will live. But if you do not return her, you may be sure that you and all your people will die." {20:8} Early the next morning, Abimelech summoned all his officials, and when he told them what had happened, they were terrified. {20:9} Then Abimelech called for Abraham and demanded, "What have you done to us? What crime have I committed that deserves treatment like this, making me and my kingdom guilty of this great sin? No one should ever do what you have done to me!" {20:10} Abraham replied, "I thought, 'This is a godless place. They will want my wife and will kill me to get her.' {20:11} Besides, she really is my sister, the daughter of my father—though not of my mother—and I married her. {20:12} So when God called me to leave my father's home and travel from place to place, I told her, 'Do me a favor. Wherever we go, tell the people that I am your brother.'" {20:13} Then Abimelech took some sheep, oxen, male and female servants, and gave them to Abraham. He also returned his wife Sarah to him. {20:15} Abimelech said, "Look over my land and choose any place where you would like to live." {20:16} Then he addressed Sarah, saying, "Look, I am giving your 'brother' a thousand pieces of silver as a token of apology. This will vindicate you before all who are with you, and everyone will know that you have been treated fairly." {20:17} Abraham prayed to God, and God healed Abimelech, his wife, and his female slaves so they could have children again. {20:18} For the LORD had caused all the women in Abimelech's household to be barren because of Sarah, Abraham's wife.

{21:1} The LORD kept his promise to Sarah and she gave birth to a son in her old age, just as God had said. {21:2} Sarah conceived and bore Abraham a son at the appointed time God had mentioned. {21:3} Abraham named his son Isaac, as instructed. {21:4} When Isaac was eight days old, Abraham circumcised him, following God's command. {21:5} Abraham was one hundred years old when Isaac was born. {21:6} Sarah rejoiced, saying, "God has brought me laughter, and everyone who hears about it will laugh with me." {21:7} She marveled that she, an elderly woman, could nurse a child. {21:8} When Isaac was weaned, Abraham held a great feast to celebrate. {21:9} However, Sarah noticed Ishmael, the son of Hagar, mocking Isaac. {21:10} Distressed, Sarah demanded that Abraham send Hagar and Ishmael away, declaring that Ishmael would not inherit alongside Isaac. {21:11} This troubled Abraham greatly because Ishmael was his son. {21:12} But God reassured Abraham, telling him to listen to Sarah, as Isaac would be the one through whom his descendants would be counted. {21:13} God also promised to make a nation out of Ishmael because he was Abraham's son. {21:14} Early the next morning, Abraham gave Hagar and Ishmael some provisions and sent them away. {21:15} They wandered in the wilderness of Beer-sheba until their water ran out. {21:16} Hagar, unable to bear seeing her son die, put him under a bush and sat a distance away, weeping. {21:17} God heard Ishmael's cries, and an angel comforted Hagar, promising to make Ishmael a great nation. {21:18} God revealed a well to Hagar, providing them with water. {21:19} Ishmael grew up in the wilderness and became skilled with the bow. {21:20} He settled in the wilderness of Paran, and his mother found him a wife from Egypt. {21:21} Around this time, Abimelech and Phichol, his chief officer, approached Abraham, acknowledging that God was with him. {21:22} They made a covenant with Abraham, swearing to deal kindly with each other and respecting each other's descendants. {21:23} Abraham agreed to the covenant. {21:24} Later, Abraham confronted Abimelech about a well that Abimelech's servants had seized. {21:25} Abimelech claimed ignorance but accepted Abraham's explanation. {21:26} Abraham then presented Abimelech with livestock as a gesture of goodwill. {21:27} They made a covenant, and Abraham set aside seven ewe lambs as a witness. {21:28} This agreement was made in Beersheba, where they both swore to honor it. {21:29} From then on, the place was called Beersheba. {21:30} They made a covenant there, and Abimelech and his chief officer returned to Philistia. {21:31} Abraham planted a grove in Beersheba and called upon the name of the LORD, the eternal God. {21:32} He lived in Philistine territory for a long time.{21:33} Abraham planted a grove in Beersheba and worshipped the LORD, the eternal God there. {21:34} He stayed in the land of the Philistines for a long time.

{22:1} After these events, God tested Abraham and said to him, "Abraham!" And Abraham responded, "Here I am." {22:2} Then God said, "Take your son, your only son Isaac, whom you love, and go to the land of Moriah. Offer him there as a burnt offering on one of the mountains that I will show you." {22:3} So Abraham rose early in the morning, saddled his donkey, took two of his young men with him, along with Isaac his son. He split wood for the burnt offering and set out for the place God had told him about. {22:4} On the third day, Abraham looked up and saw the place in the distance. {22:5} He said to his servants, "Stay here with the donkey while I and the boy go over there. We will worship and then we will come back to you." {22:6} Abraham took the wood for the burnt offering and placed it on his son Isaac, and he himself carried the fire and the knife. As the two of them walked on together, {22:7} Isaac spoke up and said to his father Abraham, "Father?" "Yes, my son?" Abraham replied. "The fire and wood are here," Isaac said, "but where is the lamb for the burnt offering?" {22:8} Abraham answered, "God himself will provide the lamb for the burnt offering, my son." And the two of them went on together. {22:9} When they reached the place God had told him about, Abraham built an altar there and arranged the wood on it. He bound his son Isaac and laid him on the altar, on top of the wood. {22:10} Then he reached out his hand and took the knife to slay his son. {22:11} But the angel of the LORD called out to him from heaven, "Abraham! Abraham!" "Here I am," he replied. {22:12} "Do not lay a hand on the boy," he said. "Do not do anything to him. Now I know that you fear God, because you have not withheld from me your son, your only son." {22:13} Abraham looked up and there in a thicket he saw a ram caught by its horns. He went over and took the ram and sacrificed it as a burnt offering instead of his son. {22:14} So Abraham called that place The LORD Will Provide. And to this day it is said, "On the mountain of the LORD it will be provided." {22:15} The angel of the LORD called to Abraham from heaven a second time {22:16} and said, "I swear by myself, declares the LORD, that because you have done this and have not withheld your son, your only son, {22:17} I will surely bless you and make your descendants as numerous as the stars in the sky and as the sand on the seashore. Your descendants will take possession of the cities of their enemies, {22:18} *and through your offspring all nations on earth will be blessed, because you have obeyed me."* {22:19} Then Abraham returned to his servants, and they set off together for Beersheba. And Abraham stayed in Beersheba. {22:20} Sometime later Abraham was told, "Milcah is also a mother; she has borne sons to your brother Nahor: {22:21} Uz the firstborn, Buz his brother, Kemuel (the father of Aram), {22:22} Kesed, Hazo, Pildash, Jidlaph, and Bethuel."{22:23} Bethuel became the father of Rebekah. These eight sons Milcah bore to Nahor, Abraham's brother. {22:24} His concubine, whose name was Reumah, also bore him sons: Tebah, Gaham, Tahash, and Maakah.

{23:1} Sarah lived to be 127 years old. These were the years of her life. {23:2} She died in Kirjath-arba, which is Hebron, in the land of Canaan. Abraham mourned and wept for her. {23:3} After Sarah's death, Abraham rose from before his dead wife and spoke to the sons of Heth. {23:4} He said, "I am a stranger and a sojourner among you. Please give me a piece of land to bury my dead." {23:5} The sons of Heth replied, {23:6} "Listen to us, mighty prince. Choose any of our tombs to bury your dead. None of us will refuse you his tomb for burial." {23:7} Abraham bowed before the people of the land, the sons of Heth. {23:8} He spoke to them, saying, "If you agree to let me bury my dead out of my sight, please intercede for me with Ephron, son of Zohar. {23:9} Ask him to sell me the cave of Machpelah, which is at the end of his field. I will pay its full price for a burial site." {23:10} Ephron was among the sons of Heth. He responded to Abraham's request in the presence of all the people at the city gate. {23:11} He said, "No, my lord, listen to me. I give you the field and the cave within it. I give it to you in the presence of my people. Bury your dead there." {23:12} Abraham again bowed before the people of the land. {23:13} He then spoke to Ephron in front of everyone, saying, "Please, if you are willing to sell me the field, accept payment from me so I can bury my dead there." {23:14} Ephron replied, "My lord, listen to me. The land is worth four hundred shekels of silver, but what is that between you and me? Bury your dead." {23:15} Abraham agreed with Ephron's terms. He weighed out the silver in front of the sons of Heth, four hundred shekels of silver according to the weight used by merchants. {23:16} Abraham agreed to Ephron's terms and weighed out four hundred shekels of silver, as Ephron had stated in the presence of the sons of Heth, using the standard weight accepted by merchants. {23:17} The field of Ephron in Machpelah, facing Mamre, including the field, the cave within it, and all the trees within the borders of the field, were transferred to Abraham as his property. {23:18} This transaction was witnessed by the sons of Heth at the city gate, ensuring the legitimacy of the transfer of ownership. {23:19} Following this, Abraham buried his wife Sarah in the cave of the field of Machpelah, near Mamre, which is Hebron in the land of Canaan. {23:20} Both the field and the cave within it were confirmed as Abraham's possession for use as a burial site by the sons of Heth.

{24:1} Abraham, now old and advanced in age, had been blessed by the LORD in all things. {24:2} He instructed his eldest servant, who managed all his affairs, to place his hand under his thigh as a gesture of oath-taking. {24:3} Abraham made the servant swear by the LORD, the God of heaven and earth, not to take a wife for his son Isaac from the Canaanite women among whom they lived. {24:4} Instead, he was to go to Abraham's homeland and relatives to find a wife for Isaac. {24:5} Concerned that the woman might not agree to come back with the servant, the servant asked if he should bring Isaac there if the woman refused. {24:6} Abraham insisted that under no circumstances should Isaac be taken back to Abraham's homeland. {24:7} Abraham reassured the servant, reminding him of the LORD's promise to provide a wife for Isaac from Abraham's own people and land. {24:8} If the woman refused, Abraham told the servant he would be released from his oath, but Isaac must not be taken back. {24:9} The servant pledged to fulfill his master's wishes and swore an oath to him about the matter. {24:10} The servant took ten of his master's camels and set out for Mesopotamia, to the city of Nahor, carrying all kinds of goods with him. {24:11} He made the camels kneel down outside the city near a well, at the time when the women came out to draw water. {24:12} The servant prayed to the LORD, asking for success and showing kindness to Abraham by providing a suitable wife for Isaac. {24:13} He watched the women coming to the well, hoping for a sign. {24:14} Before he finished praying, Rebekah, the daughter of Bethuel, son of Milcah, who was the wife of Abraham's brother Nahor, approached with her pitcher on her shoulder. {24:15} Rebekah was beautiful, a virgin, and she went down to the well, filled her pitcher, and came up again. {24:16} The servant ran to meet her and asked for a drink from her pitcher. {24:17} Rebekah readily gave him a drink and then offered to water his camels as well. {24:18} After she had finished watering the camels, the servant asked about her family and if there was room for him to stay. {24:19} Rebekah identified herself as the daughter of Bethuel and assured him they had enough provisions and lodging space. {24:20} Overwhelmed with gratitude, the servant watched silently, wondering if the LORD had indeed made his journey successful. {24:21} As the camels finished drinking, the servant gave Rebekah a golden earring and two gold bracelets, then asked about her family. {24:22} Rebekah confirmed her lineage and invited him to stay at their house. {24:23} She assured him they had enough straw, fodder, and space for lodging. {24:24} The servant bowed down and worshiped the LORD, acknowledging His guidance to Abraham's family. {24:25} Rebekah ran home and told her family about the encounter with the servant.{24:26} The servant bowed his head and worshiped the LORD, expressing gratitude for His guidance. {24:27} He praised the LORD, acknowledging that God had not abandoned Abraham, showing him mercy and faithfulness. He acknowledged that it was the LORD who led him to the house of Abraham's relatives. {24:28} Meanwhile, Rebekah ran to inform her family about the encounter. {24:29} Rebekah had a brother named Laban, who hurried to meet the servant at the well. {24:30} Laban noticed the gifts on his sister's hands and listened to her account of the encounter. {24:31} Impressed, Laban invited the servant to their home, assuring him of lodging and provisions for the camels. {24:32} The servant accepted Laban's hospitality. He tended to the camels and provided water for washing, for both himself and his companions. {24:33} Despite the meal being set before him, the servant insisted on first sharing his purpose. He explained his mission to find a wife for Isaac. {24:34} He introduced himself as Abraham's servant, highlighting the great blessings Abraham had received from the LORD. {24:35} He recounted how Sarah, despite her old age, bore a son to Abraham, to whom Abraham had given everything he owned. {24:36} Abraham made the servant swear not to take a wife for Isaac from the Canaanites but from his own relatives. {24:37} If the woman from his relatives did not agree, the servant would be released from his oath. {24:38} He expressed Abraham's confidence that the LORD would send His angel to guide him in finding a wife for Isaac from his own people. {24:39} The servant shared his initial concerns about the woman's willingness to follow him. {24:40} Abraham assured him that the LORD, before whom he walked, would send His angel to prosper his way. {24:41} If the woman's family did not agree, the servant would be released from his oath. {24:42} The servant recounted his prayer at the well, asking for a sign to identify the chosen woman. {24:43} He explained how Rebekah fulfilled the sign he had prayed for. {24:44} He described Rebekah's willingness to provide water not only for him but also for his camels as a sign from the LORD. {24:45} Before he finished speaking in his heart, Rebekah appeared, fulfilling his prayer. {24:46} He described how Rebekah generously provided water for him and his camels. {24:47} The servant asked Rebekah about her family and learned of her lineage. {24:48} Overwhelmed with gratitude and awe, the servant worshiped and praised the LORD for leading him to Rebekah, who would become Isaac's wife. {24:49} He sought assurance from Rebekah's family that they would deal kindly and truthfully with his master. {24:50} Laban and Bethuel acknowledged that the matter seemed to come from the LORD, and they could not speak against it.{24:51} Laban and Bethuel acknowledged Rebekah as the chosen wife for Isaac, agreeing to her departure with the servant. {24:52} Upon hearing their consent, the servant bowed down and worshiped the LORD. {24:53} He presented gifts of silver, gold, and clothing to Rebekah, as well as precious items to her brother and mother. {24:54} They celebrated with food and drink, and they stayed overnight. The next morning, the servant requested to return to his master. {24:55} Rebekah's family proposed that she stay with them for at least ten days before departing. {24:56} However, the servant insisted on leaving immediately, citing the LORD's blessing on his journey. {24:57} They consulted Rebekah, who agreed to go with the servant. {24:58} Rebekah's family then sent her off with blessings and well-wishes. {24:59} Rebekah, her nurse, Abraham's servant, and his men set out on their journey. {24:60} Rebekah's family blessed her, expressing hopes for her future prosperity and descendants. {24:61} Rebekah and her attendants rode on camels and followed the servant as they departed. {24:62} Meanwhile, Isaac had returned from Lahai-roi and was meditating in the field. {24:63} He looked up and saw the camels approaching. {24:64} Rebekah also saw Isaac and dismounted from her camel. {24:65} Curious, she asked the servant about the man approaching, who identified him as Isaac. Rebekah then covered herself with a veil. {24:66} The servant recounted everything to Isaac. {24:67} Isaac welcomed Rebekah into Sarah's tent, and they were married. Isaac found comfort in Rebekah after his mother's passing.

{25:1} Abraham married again, and his new wife was named Keturah. {25:2} She bore him several children: Zimran, Jokshan, Medan, Midian, Ishbak, and Shuah. {25:3} Jokshan had two sons: Sheba and Dedan. Dedan's sons were Asshurim, Letushim, and Leummim. {25:4} Midian had five sons: Ephah, Epher, Hanoch, Abidah, and Eldaah. These were all Keturah's children. {25:5} Abraham gave everything he had to his son Isaac. {25:6} To the sons he had with his concubines, Abraham gave gifts and sent them away from his son Isaac while he was still alive, eastward to the east country. {25:7} Abraham lived for 175 years. {25:8} Then he died at a good old age, full of years, and was gathered to his people. {25:9} His sons Isaac and Ishmael buried him in the cave of Machpelah, in the field of Ephron the son of Zohar the Hittite, before Mamre. {25:10} This was the field Abraham had bought from the sons of Heth. There Abraham and Sarah were buried. {25:11} After Abraham died, God blessed his son Isaac, who settled near the well Lahai-Roi. {25:12} Now, these are the descendants of Ishmael, Abraham's son by Hagar the Egyptian, Sarah's maidservant: {25:13} Nebajoth, Kedar, Adbeel, Mibsam, Mishma, Dumah, Massa, Hadar, Tema, Jetur, Naphish, and Kedemah. {25:14} These were Ishmael's sons, listed by name in the order of their birth and settlements, each of them a chief of a tribe. {25:15} Ishmael lived for 137 years. Then he died and was gathered to his people. {25:16} His descendants settled from Havilah to Shur, near Egypt, as you go toward Assyria. And he died in the presence of all his brothers. {25:19} These are the descendants of Isaac, Abraham's son. {25:20} Isaac was forty years old when he married Rebekah, the daughter of Bethuel the Aramean from Paddan Aram and the sister of Laban the Aramean. {25:21} Rebekah was barren, so Isaac prayed to the LORD on her behalf. The LORD answered his prayer, and Rebekah became pregnant. {25:22} But the two children in her womb struggled with each other. She asked the LORD why this was happening. {25:23} The LORD told her, "Two nations are in your womb, and two peoples from within you will be separated. One people will be stronger than the other, and the older will serve the younger." {25:24} When Rebekah's time to give birth came, she had twins. {25:25} The first to come out was red, and his whole body was like a hairy garment; so they named him Esau. {25:26} After that, his brother came out with his hand grasping Esau's heel; so he was named Jacob. Isaac was sixty years old when Rebekah gave birth to them. {25:27} The boys grew up, and Esau became a skillful hunter, a man of the open country, while Jacob was content to stay at home among the tents. {25:28} Isaac loved Esau because he enjoyed eating the wild game Esau brought him, but Rebekah loved Jacob. {25:29} Once when Jacob was cooking some stew, Esau came in from the open country, famished. {25:30} He said to Jacob, "Quick, let me have some of that red stew! I'm famished!" (That is why he was also called Edom.) {25:31} Jacob replied, "First, sell me your birthright." {25:32} "Look, I am about to die," Esau said. "What good is the birthright to me?" {25:33} But Jacob said, "Swear to me first." So he swore an oath to him, selling his birthright to Jacob. {25:34} Then Jacob gave Esau some bread and lentil stew. He ate and drank, and then got up and left. So Esau despised his birthright.

{26:1} There was a famine in the land, similar to the one in Abraham's time. So, Isaac went to Abimelech, the king of the Philistines, in Gerar. {26:2} The LORD appeared to him and instructed him not to go to Egypt but to stay in the land that God would show him. {26:3} God promised to bless Isaac and his descendants, giving them all the land and fulfilling the oath made to Abraham. {26:4} God assured Isaac that his descendants would multiply greatly, becoming as numerous as the stars, and all nations would be blessed through them. {26:5} This promise was because Abraham obeyed God's commands faithfully. {26:6} So, Isaac stayed in Gerar. {26:7} When the locals asked about his wife, he said she was his sister, fearing they might kill him because she was attractive. {26:8} After some time, Abimelech saw Isaac and Rebekah together and realized they were married. {26:9} Abimelech confronted Isaac for lying, and Isaac explained that he did it out of fear. {26:10} Abimelech reprimanded him, saying someone could have slept with Rebekah, bringing guilt upon them. {26:11} Abimelech warned his people not to harm Isaac or Rebekah under penalty of death. {26:12} Despite the challenges, Isaac planted crops and harvested a hundredfold that year, blessed by the LORD.

{26:13} Isaac grew prosperous and powerful, causing jealousy among the Philistines. {26:14} They had filled in the wells dug by Abraham's servants, so Isaac redug them. {26:15} The Philistines envied Isaac's wealth and possessions. {26:16} Abimelech told Isaac to leave because he had become too powerful. {26:17} So, Isaac moved to the valley of Gerar and settled there. {26:18} He reopened the wells his father had dug, naming them as his father had named them. {26:19} Isaac's servants dug and found a spring of fresh water in the valley. {26:20} But the herdsmen of Gerar quarreled with Isaac's herdsmen, claiming the water as theirs. So, Isaac named the well Esek, meaning contention. {26:21} They dug another well, but there was more conflict. So, Isaac named it Sitnah, meaning enmity. {26:22} Isaac moved again and dug another well, and this time there was no quarrel. He named it Rehoboth, meaning spaciousness, saying, "Now the LORD has made room for us, and we shall be fruitful in the land." {26:23} From there, Isaac went to Beer-sheba. {26:24} That night, the LORD appeared to him, confirming His presence and blessings because of Abraham's obedience. {26:25} Isaac built an altar there, called on the LORD's name, and set up his tent. His servants dug a well. {26:26} Abimelech, along with Ahuzzath his friend and Phichol the chief captain, came from Gerar to Isaac. {26:27} Isaac asked why they sought him out since they had sent him away and expressed hatred toward him. {26:28} They explained they recognized God's blessing on Isaac and wanted to make a covenant with him for peace. {26:29} They promised not to harm him since they had only treated him well. Isaac was now considered blessed by the LORD. {26:30} They celebrated together, eating and drinking. {26:31} Early the next morning, they made a covenant with each other, and Isaac sent them away in peace. {26:32} On that same day, Isaac's servants reported finding water in the well they dug. Isaac named it Shebah, and Beer-sheba is its name to this day. {26:34} Esau married at forty, taking Judith and Bashemath, both Hittite women, causing grief to Isaac and Rebekah.

{27:1} When Isaac grew old and his eyesight failed, he called for his eldest son Esau and said to him, "My son." {27:2} Esau replied, "Here I am, Father." {27:3} Isaac said, "I am old, and I don't know when I will die. Now, take your hunting gear—your bow and arrows—and go out into the fields. Hunt some wild game for me. {27:4} Prepare my favorite dish, and bring it to me to eat. Then I will bless you before I die." {27:5} Rebekah overheard Isaac's conversation with Esau. So, when Esau went out to hunt for the game, Rebekah spoke to her son Jacob. {27:6} She said, "Listen carefully. I overheard your father asking Esau to bring him some wild game so he could eat it and then bless him before he dies. {27:7} Now, my son, do exactly as I tell you. {27:8} Go out to the flock and bring me two fine young goats. I'll use them to prepare your father's favorite dish. {27:9} Then take it to your father so he can eat it and bless you before he dies." {27:10} Jacob was concerned, saying to his mother, "But Father might recognize me. Esau is hairy, and I am smooth-skinned. {27:11} What if Father touches me? He'll know I'm deceiving him and curse me instead of blessing me." {27:12} But his mother replied, "Let the curse fall on me, my son. Just do as I say; go and get the goats." {27:13} So, Jacob went out and got the goats for his mother. She prepared Isaac's favorite dish, just as he liked it. {27:14} Then Rebekah took Esau's best clothes, which were there in the house, and gave them to Jacob, her younger son. {27:15} She also made Jacob wear goatskins on his hands and the smooth part of his neck. {27:16} Then she gave Jacob the delicious food and bread she had prepared. {27:17} Jacob took the food to his father. "My father?" he said. {27:18} "Yes, my son," Isaac answered. "Which one are you—Esau or Jacob?" {27:19} Jacob replied, "It's Esau, your firstborn son. I've done as you asked. Here is the wild game. Sit up and eat it so you can give me your blessing." {27:20} Isaac asked, "How did you find it so quickly, my son?" {27:21} Jacob replied, "Because the LORD your God put it in my path." {27:22} Then Isaac said to Jacob, "Come closer so I can touch you and make sure that you really are Esau." {27:23} So, Jacob went closer to his father, and Isaac touched him. "The voice is Jacob's, but the hands are Esau's," Isaac said. {27:24} But he did not recognize Jacob because Jacob's hands felt hairy just like Esau's. So, Isaac went ahead and blessed Jacob. {27:25} "Are you really my son Esau?" Isaac asked. {27:26} "Come here and kiss me, my son," Isaac said. {27:27} So, Jacob went over and kissed him. And when Isaac caught the smell of his clothes, he was finally convinced, and he blessed him. "Ah, the smell of my son is like the smell of the outdoors that the LORD has blessed! {27:28} May God give you the dew of heaven and the richness of the earth, abundant grain and new wine. {27:29} May nations serve you and peoples bow down to you. Be lord over your brothers, and may the sons of your mother bow down to you. May those who curse you be cursed, and those who bless you be blessed." {27:30} As soon as Isaac had finished blessing Jacob, and almost before Jacob had left his father, Esau came in from hunting. {27:31} He prepared his father's favorite dish and brought it to him. Then he said, "Sit up, Father, and eat my wild game so you can give me your blessing." {27:32} "Which son are you?" Isaac asked. {27:33} Esau replied, "I am Esau, your firstborn son." {27:34} Isaac began to tremble uncontrollably and said, "Then who just served me wild game? I have already eaten it, and I blessed him just before you came. Now what can I do for you, my son?" {27:35} Esau pleaded, "But haven't you saved a blessing for me?" {27:36} Isaac said to him, "I have made Jacob your master and have declared that all his brothers will be his servants. I have guaranteed him an abundance of grain and new wine—what is left for me to give you, my son?" {27:37} Esau pleaded, "Don't you have any blessing left for me, Father? Bless me, too!" Then Esau broke down and wept bitterly. {27:38} Finally, Isaac said to him, "You will live away from the richness of the earth, and away from the dew of the heaven above. {27:39} You will live by your sword, and you will serve your brother. But when you decide to break free, you will shake his yoke from your neck." {27:40} Esau hated Jacob because of the blessing his father had given him. Esau said to himself, "My father will soon be dead and gone. Then I will kill Jacob." {27:42} Rebekah was told what Esau was planning, so she sent for Jacob and told him, "Listen, Esau is consoling himself by plotting to kill you. {27:43} So, my son, do what I say. Get ready and flee to my brother Laban in Haran. {27:44} Stay there with him until your brother's fury subsides. {27:45} When he forgets what you have done, I will send for you. Why should I lose both of you in one day?" {27:46} Then Rebekah said to Isaac, "I'm sick and tired of these local Hittite women! I would rather die than see Jacob marry one of them."

{28:1} Isaac called Jacob, blessed him, and instructed him not to marry a Canaanite woman. {28:2} He directed Jacob to go to Padan-aram to find a wife from his mother's family. {28:3} Isaac prayed for God's blessings upon Jacob, to be fruitful and multiply, inheriting the land promised to Abraham. {28:4} He wished for Jacob to receive the blessings of Abraham and to pass them on to his descendants. {28:5} Jacob left for Padan-aram, to the house of Laban, his uncle, son of Bethuel. {28:6} Esau, realizing Jacob's departure and Isaac's instructions, also sought a wife from Ishmael's family. {28:7} Jacob obeyed his parents and went to Padan-aram as instructed. {28:8} Esau saw that his Canaanite wives displeased his father, Isaac. {28:9} So Esau married Mahalath, Ishmael's daughter. {28:10} Jacob journeyed from Beer-sheba toward Haran. {28:11} He rested at a certain place, using stones for pillows, and slept there. {28:12} Jacob dreamt of a ladder connecting heaven and earth with angels ascending and descending, and God above it. {28:13} God assured Jacob of the land promise given to Abraham and Isaac, extending it to him and his descendants. {28:14} Jacob's descendants would be numerous and spread across the earth, bringing blessings to all nations. {28:15} God promised to be with Jacob, protect him wherever he went, and bring him back to this land. {28:16} Jacob woke up, realizing the presence of God in that place. {28:17} He was in awe, acknowledging it as the house of God and the gateway to heaven. {28:18} Early the next morning, Jacob set up the stone he had used as a pillow as a pillar and anointed it with oil. {28:19} He named the place Bethel, formerly known as Luz. {28:20} Jacob made a vow, seeking God's guidance, provision, and protection on his journey. {28:21} If God fulfilled these promises, Jacob pledged to make Him his God and to give a tenth of all he received. {28:22} He declared the stone pillar as God's house, promising to dedicate a portion of his wealth to God.

{29:1} Jacob continued his journey and arrived in the land of the eastern people. {29:2} He noticed a well in a field with three flocks of sheep lying nearby. They watered their flocks from this well, covered by a large stone. {29:3} When all the flocks gathered, they rolled the stone away to water the sheep, then replaced it. {29:4} Jacob asked the shepherds where they were from, and they replied, "Haran." {29:5} He inquired about Laban, Nahor's son, and they confirmed knowing him. {29:6} Jacob then asked about Laban's welfare, and they said he was fine, and Rachel, Laban's daughter, was coming with the sheep. {29:7} Jacob suggested watering the sheep since it was still early, but the shepherds insisted on waiting until all the flocks gathered. {29:8} While they conversed, Rachel arrived with her father's sheep, as she was responsible for them. {29:10} Jacob approached, rolled the stone from the well, and watered Laban's flock. {29:11} Overwhelmed with emotion, Jacob kissed Rachel and wept. {29:12} He informed Rachel of their family connection, and she hurried to tell her father. {29:13} Laban, upon hearing of Jacob, embraced and welcomed him into his home, where Jacob recounted his journey. {29:14} Laban acknowledged Jacob as family and hosted him for a month. {29:15} Laban proposed wages for Jacob's service since they were kin. {29:16} Laban had two daughters: Leah, the elder, and Rachel, the younger. {29:17} Leah had tender eyes, while Rachel was beautiful and favored. {29:18} Jacob loved Rachel and agreed to work seven years for Laban to marry her. {29:19} Laban agreed, preferring Jacob as Rachel's husband over another man. {29:20} The seven years passed swiftly for Jacob due to his love for Rachel. {29:21} When Jacob requested Rachel as his wife, Laban arranged a feast. {29:23} However, in the evening, Laban deceived

Jacob by giving him Leah instead of Rachel. {29:24} Laban also gave Leah her maid, Zilpah. {29:25} Jacob confronted Laban in the morning, questioning why he had deceived him. {29:26} Laban defended his actions, citing the custom of not giving the younger daughter before the elder. {29:27} Laban proposed fulfilling Leah's bridal week and then giving Rachel to Jacob in exchange for seven more years of service. {29:28} Jacob agreed and married Rachel after completing Leah's week. {29:29} Laban gave Rachel her maid, Bilhah, as well. {29:30} Jacob also married Rachel and served Laban for another seven years. {29:31} Despite Leah being initially unloved, God blessed her with children while Rachel remained barren. {29:32} Leah bore Reuben, believing God had seen her affliction and hoping her husband would love her. {29:33} She named her second son Simeon, believing God had heard that she was hated. {29:34} Her third son, Levi, she believed would bring her closer to her husband. {29:35} Leah's fourth son, Judah, prompted her to praise the Lord.

{30:1} When Rachel saw that she couldn't have children, she felt jealous of her sister. She said to Jacob, "Give me children, or I'll die." {30:2} Jacob got angry with Rachel and said, "Am I God? It's not up to me to give you children." {30:3} Rachel then suggested that Jacob should have children with her servant Bilhah, and Rachel would claim them as her own. {30:4} Jacob agreed, and he had children with Bilhah. {30:5} Bilhah gave birth to a son for Jacob. {30:6} Rachel felt that God had answered her prayers by giving her a son through Bilhah. She named him Dan. {30:7} Bilhah had another son for Jacob. {30:8} Rachel felt triumphant over her sister and named the second son Naphtali. {30:9} Leah, seeing Rachel's success, also gave her maid Zilpah to Jacob as a wife. {30:10} Zilpah bore Jacob a son. {30:11} Leah named him Gad, meaning "a troop is coming." {30:12} Zilpah had another son for Jacob. {30:13} Leah named him Asher, feeling blessed by having sons. {30:14} Reuben found mandrakes and brought them to his mother Leah. Rachel asked Leah for some of the mandrakes. {30:15} Leah refused, feeling that Rachel had taken her husband and now wanted her son's mandrakes too. {30:16} Rachel agreed to let Leah spend the night with Jacob in exchange for the mandrakes. {30:17} God listened to Leah and she became pregnant with her fifth son. {30:18} Leah named him Issachar, feeling that God had rewarded her for giving her maid to Jacob. {30:19} Leah had another son for Jacob, her sixth. {30:20} Leah named him Zebulun, feeling that her husband would live with her since she had borne him six sons. {30:21} Later, Leah gave birth to a daughter and named her Dinah. {30:22} God remembered Rachel, and listened to her, and made her able to have children. {30:23} She became pregnant and had a son, saying, "God has taken away my disgrace." {30:24} She named him Joseph, saying, "May the LORD give me another son." {30:25} After Joseph was born, Jacob said to Laban, "Send me away so I can go back to my own homeland. {30:26} Give me my wives and children, for whom I have served you, and let me leave, for you know how hard I've worked for you." {30:27} Laban replied, "Please stay. I have learned that the LORD has blessed me because of you." {30:28} Jacob said, "Tell me what you want to pay me, and I will accept it." {30:29} Laban said, "You know how well I've treated you and how your flocks have grown under my care." {30:30} Jacob continued, "You had very little before I came, but now your possessions have increased greatly. The LORD has blessed you because of me. But when can I start providing for my own family?" {30:31} Laban asked, "What wages do you want?" {30:32} Jacob said, "I don't want anything from you. But let me do this: I will go through your flocks today and remove all the speckled and spotted sheep and goats and all the brown sheep among the lambs. That will be my wages." {30:33} "That way, my honesty will be evident to you later on when you come to check my wages. If I have any sheep or goats that are not speckled or spotted or any lambs that are not brown, they will be considered stolen." {30:34} Laban agreed, saying, "Let it be as you have said." {30:35} That day Laban removed all the male goats that were speckled or spotted, all the female goats that were speckled or spotted, every one with some white on it, and all the brown sheep. He entrusted them to his sons. {30:36} Then he put a three-day journey between himself and Jacob, while Jacob took care of the rest of Laban's flocks. {30:37} Jacob took fresh branches from green poplar, almond, and plane trees, and peeled white streaks in them, exposing the white of the branches. {30:38} He placed these branches in the troughs where the flocks came to drink, facing them so they would see the branches while mating. {30:39} As a result, the flocks bred in front of the branches and gave birth to striped, speckled, and spotted offspring. {30:40} Jacob separated the lambs and set the faces of the flocks toward the striped and brown sheep among Laban's flocks. He kept his own separate and did not put them with Laban's sheep. {30:41} Whenever the stronger of the flock were breeding, Jacob would place the branches in the troughs so they would breed near them. {30:42} **But he did not put the branches in when the weaker animals were breeding. So the weaker animals belonged to Laban, and the stronger ones to Jacob.** {30:43} As a result, Jacob became exceedingly prosperous. He acquired large flocks, maidservants, menservants, camels, and donkeys.

{31:1} Jacob heard Laban's sons accusing him, saying, "Jacob has taken everything that belonged to our father and gained all this wealth from it." {31:2} Jacob noticed that Laban's attitude towards him had changed. {31:3} Then the LORD spoke to Jacob, saying, "Return to the land of your ancestors, to your relatives, and I will be with you." {31:4} So Jacob sent for Rachel and Leah to come out to the field where his flocks were. {31:5} He said to them, "I have noticed that your father's attitude towards me has changed, but the God of my father has been with me." {31:6} "You know that I have worked hard for your father." {31:7} "But he has cheated me and changed my wages ten times. Yet God has not allowed him to harm me." {31:8} "Whenever he said, 'The speckled animals will be your wages,' all the flocks gave birth to speckled young. And when he said, 'The streaked animals will be your wages,' all the flocks bore streaked young." {31:9} "So God has taken away your father's livestock and given them to me." {31:10} "Once, during mating season, I had a dream. I looked up and saw that the rams mating with the flock were streaked, speckled, and spotted." {31:11} "Then the angel of God appeared to me in the dream and said, 'Jacob.' And I replied, 'Here I am.'" {31:12} "The angel said, 'Look up and see that all the rams mating with the flock are streaked, speckled, and spotted, for I have seen everything that Laban has been doing to you.'" {31:13} "I am the God of Bethel, where you anointed a pillar and made a vow to me. Now leave this land and return to your homeland." {31:14} Rachel and Leah replied, "Do we still have any portion or inheritance in our father's household?" {31:15} "Aren't we considered as foreigners by him? He sold us, and he has spent all the money that belonged to us." {31:16} "All the wealth that God has taken away from our father rightfully belongs to us and our children. So do whatever God has told you to do." {31:17} Jacob got up, put his wives and children on camels, {31:18} and took all his livestock and possessions that he had acquired in Paddan-aram, to go to his father Isaac in the land of Canaan. {31:19} Meanwhile, Laban had gone to shear his sheep, and Rachel stole her father's household gods. {31:20} Jacob deceived Laban the Aramean by not telling him that he was leaving. {31:21} So Jacob fled with all he had, crossed the Euphrates River, and headed for the hill country of Gilead. {31:22} Three days later, Laban was told that Jacob had fled. {31:23} He gathered his relatives and pursued Jacob for seven days until he caught up with him in the hill country of Gilead. {31:24} But God came to Laban in a dream at night and warned him, "Be careful not to say anything to Jacob, neither good nor bad." {31:25} Laban caught up with Jacob, who had pitched his tent in the mountains. Laban and his relatives also pitched their tents in the hill country of Gilead. {31:26} Laban confronted Jacob, asking, "Why have you deceived me and taken my daughters away as if they were captives of war?" {31:27} "Why did you leave secretly without telling me? I would have sent you off with joy, songs, and music. And you didn't even let me kiss my sons and daughters goodbye. You have acted foolishly." {31:28} "I could harm you, but the God of your father warned me last night not to say anything good or bad to you." {31:29} "Now, even though you were longing to return to your father's house, why did you steal my household gods?" {31:30} Jacob replied to Laban, "I left secretly because I was afraid you would take your daughters away forcibly." {31:31} "Whoever has taken your gods shall not live. Let us search and whoever has them, take them." Jacob didn't know Rachel had taken the gods. {31:32} Laban searched Jacob's tents, but found nothing. Then he searched Rachel's tent. {31:33} Rachel had hidden the gods in the camel's saddlebags and sat on them. Laban searched but didn't find them. {31:34} Rachel told her father, "Please excuse me, I cannot get up, as I'm having my period." Laban searched but couldn't find the gods. {31:36} Jacob got angry and argued with Laban. "What have I done wrong? Why are you chasing me like this?" {31:37} "You've searched all my belongings. Have you found anything of yours? Let our relatives be witnesses and judge between us." {31:38} "I've been with you for twenty years. Your livestock never miscarried, and I never ate your rams." {31:39} "If any animal was killed by wild beasts, I bore the loss. You demanded payment from me whether it was stolen during the day or night." {31:40} "I suffered through scorching heat and freezing cold, with sleepless nights." {31:41} "I served you for twenty years, fourteen for your daughters and six for your livestock. Yet you changed my wages ten times." {31:42} "If not for the God of my father Abraham and the fear of Isaac, you would have sent me away empty-handed. But God saw my hardship and rebuked you last night." {31:43} Laban replied to Jacob, saying, "These daughters are mine, along with their children and the cattle you see. Everything you see here belongs to me. So, what can I do for my daughters and their children today? {31:44} Let's make a covenant between you and me, a binding agreement witnessed by us both." {31:45} Jacob took a stone and set it up as a pillar. {31:46} Then he said to his relatives, "Gather stones." They gathered stones and made a heap. They ate there beside the heap. {31:47} Laban called it Jegar-sahadutha, but

Jacob called it Galeed. {31:48} Laban said, "This heap is a witness between you and me today." That's why it's called Galeed. {31:49} And Mizpah, because Laban said, "May the LORD watch between you and me when we are apart from each other. {31:50} If you mistreat my daughters or take other wives besides them, know that God is a witness between us." {31:51} Laban said to Jacob, "This heap and this pillar are a witness that I will not harm you, and you will not harm me." {31:52} "May the God of Abraham and Nahor, the God of their father, {31:53} judge between us," Jacob swore, invoking the fear of his father Isaac. {31:54} Jacob offered a sacrifice on the mountain and invited his relatives to eat bread. They ate and stayed overnight on the mountain. {31:55} Early the next morning, Laban kissed his sons and daughters goodbye, blessed them, and returned home.

{32:1} Jacob continued on his journey, and he encountered the angels of God. {32:2} When Jacob saw them, he said, "This is God's army," and he named that place Mahanaim. {32:3} Jacob sent messengers ahead of him to his brother Esau in the land of Seir, the territory of Edom. {32:4} He instructed them, "Tell my lord Esau, 'Your servant Jacob says: I have been staying with Laban and have remained there until now. {32:5} I have acquired oxen, donkeys, flocks, male and female servants, and I am sending this message to find favor in your sight.'" {32:6} The messengers returned to Jacob, saying, "We went to your brother Esau, and he is coming to meet you, accompanied by four hundred men." {32:7} Jacob was greatly afraid and distressed. He divided the people who were with him, as well as the flocks, herds, and camels, into two groups. {32:8} He said, "If Esau attacks one group, the other may escape." {32:9} Jacob prayed, "God of my father Abraham and Isaac, who told me, 'Return to your country and your relatives, and I will bless you. {32:10} I am unworthy of all the kindness and faithfulness you have shown me. I crossed the Jordan with only a staff, and now I have become two groups. {32:11} Please deliver me from the hand of my brother Esau, for I am afraid he will come and attack me, along with the mothers and their children. {32:12} But you promised to bless me and make my descendants as numerous as the sand on the seashore, too many to count.'" {32:13} Jacob spent the night there. He selected a gift for his brother Esau from what he had with him: {32:14} Two hundred female goats, twenty male goats, two hundred ewes, twenty rams, {32:15} Thirty female camels with their young, forty cows, ten bulls, twenty female donkeys, and ten male donkeys. {32:16} He put them in the care of his servants, each herd by itself, and instructed his servants, "Go on ahead of me, leaving some space between each herd." {32:17} To the first servant, he said, "When my brother Esau meets you and asks, 'To whom do you belong, and where are you going, and who owns these animals in front of you?' {32:18} You are to answer, 'They belong to your servant Jacob. They are a gift sent to my lord Esau, and he is coming behind us.'" {32:19} Jacob gave the same instructions to the second and third servants and to all who followed the herds, saying, "This is what you are to say to Esau when you meet him." {32:20} And tell him, 'Your servant Jacob is right behind us.' Jacob thought, 'I will appease him with the gift that is going ahead of me. Later, when I see him, perhaps he will receive me.' {32:21} So Jacob's gift went on ahead of him, while he himself spent that night in the camp. {32:22} During the night, Jacob got up and took his two wives, his two female servants, and his eleven sons, and crossed the ford of the Jabbok. {32:23} After he had sent them across the stream, he sent over all his possessions. {32:24} Jacob found himself alone, and a man wrestled with him until daybreak. {32:25} When the man saw that he could not overpower Jacob, he touched the socket of Jacob's hip so that his hip was wrenched as he wrestled with the man. {32:26} The man said, "Let me go, for it is daybreak." But Jacob replied, "I will not let you go unless you bless me." {32:27} The man asked him, "What is your name?" "Jacob," he answered. {32:28} Then the man said, "Your name will no longer be Jacob, but Israel, because you have struggled with God and with humans and have overcome." {32:29} Jacob then asked him, "Please tell me your name." But he replied, "Why do you ask my name?" Then he blessed him there. {32:30} So Jacob called the place Peniel, saying, "It is because I saw God face to face, and yet my life was spared." {32:31} The sun rose above him as he passed Peniel, and he was limping because of his hip. {32:32} Therefore to this day the Israelites do not eat the tendon attached to the socket of the hip, because the socket of Jacob's hip was touched near the tendon.

{33:1} Jacob looked up and saw Esau coming with four hundred men. He divided the children among Leah, Rachel, and the two female servants. {33:2} He put the female servants and their children in front, Leah and her children next, and Rachel and Joseph in the rear. {33:3} Jacob himself went ahead and bowed to the ground seven times as he approached his brother. {33:4} Esau ran to meet him, embraced him, hugged his neck, and kissed him. And they both wept. {33:5} Esau looked up and saw the women and children and asked, "Who are these with you?" Jacob answered, "The children whom God has graciously given your servant." {33:6} Then the female servants and their children approached and bowed down. {33:7} Next, Leah and her children came near and bowed down, and then Joseph and Rachel approached and bowed down. {33:8} Esau asked, "What do you mean by all these herds I met?" Jacob replied, "To find favor in your sight, my lord." {33:9} Esau said, "I have plenty, my brother. Keep what you have for yourself." {33:10} Jacob insisted, "Please, if I have found favor in your sight, accept my gift. For seeing your face is like seeing the face of God, and you have received me favorably. {33:11} Please take my blessing that I have brought to you, because God has been gracious to me, and I have everything I need." Jacob urged him until Esau accepted the gift. {33:12} Esau suggested, "Let's journey together, and I will go ahead of you." {33:13} Jacob replied, "My lord knows that the children are tender, and I have with me flocks and herds with young. If they are driven hard for even one day, all the animals will die. {33:14} Let my lord go ahead of his servant while I move along slowly, at the pace of the livestock and the children, until I come to my lord in Seir." {33:15} Esau said, "Let me leave some of my men with you." But Jacob responded, "What need is there? Let me find favor in your sight." {33:16} So Esau went back that day to Seir. {33:17} Jacob journeyed to Succoth and built a house for himself and made shelters for his livestock. That's why the place was called Succoth. {33:18} Jacob arrived safely at the city of Shechem in the land of Canaan, coming from Padanaram. He set up his tent near the city. {33:19} He purchased a piece of land where he had pitched his tent from the sons of Hamor, the father of Shechem, for a hundred pieces of silver. {33:20} There he built an altar and named it El-elohe-Israel, which means "God, the God of Israel."

{34:1} Dinah, the daughter of Leah and Jacob, went out to see the daughters of the land. {34:2} Shechem, the son of Hamor the Hivite, who was a prince of the country, saw her, took her, and lay with her, defiling her. {34:3} Shechem's soul became attached to Dinah, Jacob's daughter, and he loved her, speaking kindly to her. {34:4} Shechem spoke to his father Hamor, asking him to get Dinah for him as his wife. {34:5} Jacob heard that Shechem had defiled his daughter Dinah, but Jacob's sons were in the field with his cattle. Jacob kept quiet until they came home. {34:6} Hamor, Shechem's father, went to Jacob to talk with him. {34:7} When Jacob's sons heard about it, they were grieved and very angry because Shechem had brought shame upon Israel by lying with Jacob's daughter, something that should not have been done. {34:8} Hamor spoke to them, saying, "My son Shechem desires your daughter. Please give her to him as his wife. {34:9} "And let's make marriages between our people. Give us your daughters and take our daughters for yourselves." {34:10} "You can live with us, trade in our land, and acquire property here." {34:11} Shechem said to Dinah's father and brothers, "Please accept me, and I will give whatever you ask." {34:12} "Name your price for the dowry and gifts, and I will pay it. Just give me the girl as my wife." {34:13} Jacob's sons answered Shechem and Hamor deceitfully because Shechem had defiled their sister Dinah. {34:14} They said, "We can't give our sister to someone who is uncircumcised; it would be a disgrace to us." {34:15} "But we will consent to this: If all your males become circumcised like us," {34:16} "then we will give you our daughters and take yours, and we will become one people." {34:17} "But if you refuse to be circumcised, we will take our daughter and leave." {34:18} Hamor and Shechem, his son, were pleased with this proposal. {34:19} Shechem wasted no time in doing what was asked because he was deeply attracted to Dinah and was more honorable than anyone else in his father's household. {34:20} Hamor and Shechem went to the gate of their city and spoke to the men of their city, saying, {34:21} "These men are peaceful with us. Let them live in the land and trade here. The land is large enough for them. Let's take their daughters as wives and give them our daughters." {34:22} "But the condition they set for us to live together as one people is that all our males must be circumcised, just as they are." {34:23} "Then all their possessions, including their livestock, will be ours. Let's agree to this, and they will dwell among us." {34:24} All the men who went out of the city gate listened to Hamor and Shechem, and every male was circumcised, all who went out of the city gate. {34:25} On the third day, when they were still in pain, two of Jacob's sons, Simeon and Levi, Dinah's brothers, took their swords, went boldly into the city, and killed all the males. {34:26} They killed Hamor and Shechem, took Dinah from Shechem's house, and left. {34:27} Jacob's sons found the slain men and plundered the city because their sister had been defiled. {34:28} They took the sheep, oxen, donkeys, everything in the city and in the fields, {34:29} as well as all their wealth and little ones. They captured their wives and plundered everything in their houses. {34:30} Jacob said to Simeon and Levi, "You have brought trouble upon me, making me stink in the eyes of the people of the land, the Canaanites and the Perizzites. We are few in number, and they may gather against us and destroy me and my household." {34:31} But Simeon and Levi replied, "Should he have treated our sister like a prostitute?"

{35:1} God told Jacob, "Get up, go to Bethel, and live there. Build an altar to the God who appeared to you when you were fleeing from your brother Esau." {35:2} Jacob said to his household and all who were with him, "Get rid of the foreign gods among you. Clean yourselves and change your clothes." {35:3} "Then let's go to Bethel, where I will build an altar to the God who answered me in my distress and was with me on my journey." {35:4} They gave Jacob all the foreign gods and earrings they had, and Jacob buried them under the oak near Shechem. {35:5} As they journeyed, the terror of God fell on the surrounding cities, so they did not pursue Jacob's sons. {35:6} Jacob and all his people reached Luz, which is Bethel in the land of Canaan. {35:7} There, Jacob built an altar and named the place El-beth-el because God appeared to him when he was fleeing from his brother. {35:8} Deborah, Rebekah's nurse, died and was buried beneath Bethel under an oak, which was named Allon-bachuth. {35:9} God appeared to Jacob again when he came from Padan-aram and blessed him. {35:10} God said to him, "Your name is Jacob, but you will no longer be called Jacob; your name will be Israel." So he named him Israel. {35:11} God also said, "I am God Almighty. Be fruitful and multiply. A nation and a company of nations will come from you, and kings will descend from you." {35:12} "The land I gave to Abraham and Isaac, I will give to you and your descendants after you." {35:13} Then God left him where He had spoken with him. {35:14} Jacob set up a stone pillar where God had spoken to him, poured a drink offering and oil on it. {35:15} He called the place Bethel, where God had spoken to him. {35:16} They journeyed from Bethel, and Rachel went into labor. She had a difficult delivery. {35:17} The midwife comforted her, saying, "Don't fear, you will have another son." {35:18} As Rachel's life was departing, she named her son Ben-oni, but Jacob called him Benjamin. {35:19} Rachel died and was buried on the way to Ephrath, which is Bethlehem. {35:20} Jacob set up a pillar on her grave, which is the pillar of Rachel's grave to this day. {35:21} Israel moved on and pitched his tent beyond the tower of Edar. {35:22} While Israel was living in that land, Reuben slept with Bilhah, his father's concubine, and Israel heard about it. Jacob had twelve sons: {35:23} Leah's sons: Reuben, Jacob's firstborn, Simeon, Levi, Judah, Issachar, and Zebulun. {35:24} Rachel's sons: Joseph and Benjamin. {35:25} Bilhah's sons, Rachel's servant: Dan and Naphtali. {35:26} Zilpah's sons, Leah's servant: Gad and Asher. These were the sons born to Jacob in Padan-aram. {35:27} Jacob went to his father Isaac in Mamre, near Hebron, where Abraham and Isaac had stayed. {35:28} Isaac lived 180 years. {35:29} Then he breathed his last and died, joining his ancestors in death at a ripe old age. His sons Esau and Jacob buried him.

{36:1} These are the descendants of Esau, who is also called Edom. {36:2} Esau married Canaanite women: Adah, the daughter of Elon the Hittite; Aholibamah, the daughter of Anah and granddaughter of Zibeon the Hivite; and Basemath, Ishmael's daughter and sister of Nebajoth. {36:3} Adah bore Eliphaz to Esau, and Basemath bore Reuel. {36:4} Aholibamah bore Jeush, Jaalam, and Korah to Esau. These were Esau's sons born in Canaan. {36:5} Esau took his wives, children, household, livestock, and all his possessions acquired in Canaan, and moved away from his brother Jacob because their possessions were too great to live together. He settled in the hill country of Seir; Esau is Edom. {36:6} These are the descendants of Esau, the father of the Edomites, who settled in Seir. {36:7} Esau's sons were Eliphaz, son of Esau's wife Adah, and Reuel, son of Esau's wife Basemath. {36:8} Eliphaz's sons were Teman, Omar, Zepho, Kenaz, Korah, Gatam, and Amalek, born to Eliphaz's concubine Timna. {36:9} Reuel's sons were Nahath, Zerah, Shammah, and Mizzah. {36:10} Aholibamah's sons were Jeush, Jaalam, and Korah. {36:11} These were the dukes descended from Esau's sons: Duke Teman, Duke Omar, Duke Zepho, Duke Kenaz, Duke Korah, Duke Gatam, and Duke Amalek. These were the dukes descended from Eliphaz in Edom, sons of Adah. {36:12} These were the dukes descended from Reuel: Duke Nahath, Duke Zerah, Duke Shammah, and Duke Mizzah. These were the dukes descended from Reuel in Edom, sons of Basemath. {36:13} These were the dukes descended from Aholibamah, daughter of Anah and granddaughter of Zibeon: Duke Jeush, Duke Jaalam, and Duke Korah. These were the dukes descended from Aholibamah, Esau's wife. {36:14} These were the sons of Esau, who is also called Edom, and these were their dukes. {36:15} These were the dukes descended from Esau's firstborn son Eliphaz: Duke Teman, Duke Omar, Duke Zepho, Duke Kenaz, Duke Korah, Duke Gatam, and Duke Amalek. These were the dukes descended from Eliphaz in Edom, sons of Adah. {36:16} These were the dukes descended from Esau's son Reuel: Duke Nahath, Duke Zerah, Duke Shammah, and Duke Mizzah. These were the dukes descended from Reuel in Edom, sons of Basemath. {36:17} These were the dukes descended from Esau's wife Aholibamah, daughter of Anah: Duke Jeush, Duke Jaalam, and Duke Korah. These were the dukes descended from Aholibamah, daughter of Anah and Esau's wife. {36:18} These were the descendants of Esau, who is also called Edom, and these were their dukes. {36:19} These were the sons of Seir the Horite, who inhabited the land: Lotan, Shobal, Zibeon, Anah, Dishon, Ezer, and Dishan. These were the dukes of the Horites, sons of Seir, in Edom. {36:20} The sons of Lotan were Hori and Hemam; Lotan's sister was Timna. {36:21} The sons of Shobal were Alvan, Manahath, Ebal, Shepho, and Onam. {36:22} The sons of Zibeon were Ajah and Anah. Anah found hot springs in the wilderness while he was pasturing the donkeys of his father Zibeon. {36:23} The sons of Anah were Dishon and Aholibamah, daughter of Anah. {36:24} These were the sons of Dishon: Hemdan, Eshban, Ithran, and Cheran. {36:25} The sons of Ezer were Bilhan, Zaavan, and Akan. {36:26} The sons of Dishan were Uz and Aran. {36:27} These were the dukes descended from the Horites: Duke Lotan, Duke Shobal, Duke Zibeon, Duke Anah, Duke Dishon, Duke Ezer, and Duke Dishan. These were the dukes descended from the Horites, according to their dukes, in the land of Seir. {36:28} Dishan had these children: Uz and Aran. {36:29} These were the leaders among the Horites: Lotan, Shobal, Zibeon, Anah, {36:30} Dishon, Ezer, and Dishan. They were the leaders of the Horites in the land of Seir. {36:31} These are the kings who reigned in the land of Edom before any king ruled over the Israelites. {36:32} Bela, the son of Beor, ruled in Edom, and the name of his city was Dinhabah. {36:33} Bela died, and Jobab, the son of Zerah from Bozrah, succeeded him as king. {36:34} Jobab died, and Husham from the land of Temani became king. {36:35} Husham died, and Hadad, the son of Bedad, who defeated Midian in the fields of Moab, became king, and his city was called Avith. {36:36} Hadad died, and Samlah from Masrekah became king. {36:37} Samlah died, and Saul from Rehoboth by the river became king. {36:38} Saul died, and Baal-hanan, the son of Achbor, became king. {36:39} Baal-hanan, the son of Achbor, died, and Hadar became king, and his city was called Pau. His wife's name was Mehetabel, the daughter of Matred, the daughter of Mezahab. {36:40} These are the names of the chiefs descended from Esau, according to their clans, territories, and names: Chief Timnah, Chief Alvah, Chief Jetheth, {36:41} Chief Aholibamah, Chief Elah, Chief Pinon, {36:42} Chief Kenaz, Chief Teman, Chief Mibzar, {36:43} Chief Magdiel, Chief Iram. These were the chiefs of Edom, each in their own territory, and Esau was the father of the Edomites.

{37:1} Jacob lived in the land where his father had stayed, the land of Canaan. {37:2} These are the descendants of Jacob. Joseph, who was seventeen years old, was shepherding the flock with his brothers, the sons of Bilhah and Zilpah, his father's wives. Joseph brought back a bad report about them to his father. {37:3} Now Israel loved Joseph more than all his other sons because he was born to him in his old age, and he made him a coat of many colors. {37:4} When his brothers saw that their father loved him more than all of them, they hated him and couldn't speak peaceably to him. {37:5} Joseph had a dream and told it to his brothers, which made them hate him even more. {37:6} He said to them, "Listen to this dream I had. {37:7} We were binding sheaves in the field, and my sheaf stood up and your sheaves gathered around it and bowed down to it." {37:8} His brothers said to him, "Will you really reign over us? Will you truly rule over us?" And they hated him even more because of his dreams and his words. {37:9} Then he had another dream and told it to his brothers. "Look," he said, "I had another dream, and this time the sun, moon, and eleven stars were bowing down to me." {37:10} He told his father and his brothers, and his father rebuked him, saying, "What is this dream you've had? Will your mother and I and your brothers actually come and bow down to the ground before you?" {37:11} His brothers were jealous of him, but his father kept the matter in mind. {37:12} Now his brothers had gone to graze their father's flock near Shechem. {37:13} Israel said to Joseph, "Aren't your brothers grazing the flock near Shechem? Come, I'll send you to them." "Here I am," he replied. {37:14} So Israel said to him, "Go and see if your brothers and the flock are well, and bring word back to me." Then he sent him from the Valley of Hebron, and Joseph went to Shechem. {37:15} A man found Joseph wandering in the field and asked him, "What are you looking for?" {37:16} He replied, "I'm looking for my brothers. Can you tell me where they're grazing their flocks?" {37:17} The man said, "They've moved on from here. I heard them say, 'Let's go to Dothan.'" So Joseph went after his brothers and found them in Dothan. {37:18} When they saw him from a distance, before he reached them, they plotted to kill him. {37:19} They said to one another, "Here comes that dreamer! {37:20} Come now, let's kill him and throw him into one of these pits and say that a ferocious animal devoured him. Then we'll see what comes of his dreams." {37:21} But Reuben heard this and rescued him from their hands, saying, "Let's not take his life." {37:22} "Don't shed blood," Reuben said. "Throw him into this pit in the wilderness, but don't lay a hand on him." He intended to rescue him from their hands and return him to his father. {37:23} When Joseph arrived to his brothers, they stripped him of his coat, the coat of many colors that he was wearing. {37:24} Then they took him and threw him into a pit. The pit was empty, with no water in it. {37:25} As they sat down to eat, they looked up and saw a caravan of Ishmaelites coming from Gilead. Their camels were loaded with spices, balm, and myrrh, heading to Egypt. {37:26} Judah suggested to his brothers, "What profit is there if we kill our brother and cover up his blood? Let's sell him to the Ishmaelites instead. He is our brother, after all, our own flesh." His brothers agreed. {37:27} So when the Midianite merchants passed by, they pulled Joseph out of the pit and sold him to the Ishmaelites for twenty pieces of silver. And the Ishmaelites took Joseph to Egypt. {37:28} When Reuben returned to the pit and saw that Joseph wasn't there, he tore his clothes in distress. {37:29} He went back to his brothers and said, "The boy is gone! What am I going to do?" {37:30} Then they took Joseph's coat, killed a young goat, dipped the coat in its blood, {37:31} and sent the coat of many colors to their father, saying, "We found this. Do you recognize it? Is it your son's coat or not?" {37:32} Jacob recognized it and exclaimed, "It is my son's coat! A wild animal has devoured him. Joseph has surely been torn to pieces!" {37:33} Jacob tore his clothes, put a sackcloth around his waist, and mourned for his son for many days. {37:34} All his sons and daughters tried to comfort him, but he refused to be comforted. "I will go down to the grave mourning for my son," he said. So his father wept for him. {37:35} Meanwhile, the Midianites sold Joseph in Egypt to Potiphar, an officer of Pharaoh and captain of the guard.

{38:1} At that time, Judah left his brothers and stayed with a man named Hirah, an Adullamite. {38:2} While there, Judah saw the daughter of a Canaanite named Shua. He married her and had three sons: Er, Onan, and Shelah. {38:3} Er married Tamar, but he was wicked, so God took his life. {38:4} Then Judah told Onan to marry Tamar and fulfill the duty of a brother-in-law, but Onan refused and was also struck down by God. {38:5} Judah then told Tamar to wait until his youngest son Shelah was grown before marrying again. But Judah had no intention of giving Shelah to her. {38:6} After some time, Judah's wife, the daughter of Shua, died. When he finished mourning, he went up to Timnah to his sheepshearers, accompanied by his friend Hirah the Adullamite. {38:7} Tamar learned that Judah was going to Timnah and devised a plan. {38:8} She dressed as a prostitute and positioned herself along the road to Timnah because she knew Shelah had grown up, yet Judah had not given him to her as a husband. {38:9} When Judah saw her, he propositioned her, not realizing she was his daughter-in-law. He promised her a young goat from his flock as payment. {38:10} She asked for a pledge until he sent the goat, and he agreed, giving her his signet ring, bracelets, and staff. They slept together, and she became pregnant. {38:11} Tamar then went home, removed her veil, and put on her widow's clothes. {38:12} Judah sent the young goat by his friend Hirah, but he couldn't find the woman. {38:13} Judah asked the men of the place where the prostitute had been, but they said there was no such woman there. {38:14} So Judah decided to let Tamar keep the items he had given her, to avoid embarrassment. {38:15} About three months later, Judah was told that Tamar, his daughter-in-law, was pregnant. He ordered her to be brought out and burned. {38:16} As she was brought out, she sent word to Judah, saying, "I am pregnant by the man who owns these items. Please identify them." Judah recognized them and admitted that Tamar was more righteous than he because he hadn't given her to Shelah. {38:17} Tamar gave birth to twins. During the delivery, one baby's hand emerged, and the midwife tied a scarlet thread around it, but the baby pulled his hand back in. His brother then emerged, and he was named Perez. The baby with the scarlet thread was named Zerah. {38:18} Judah asked, "What pledge do you want?" Tamar replied, "Your signet, bracelets, and staff." Judah gave them to her, and they slept together, resulting in Tamar conceiving. {38:19} Afterward, Tamar removed her veil, put on her widow's garments, and went home. {38:20} Judah sent his friend to deliver the goat and retrieve his pledge from the woman, but she couldn't be found. {38:21} Judah asked the locals about the prostitute, but they said there was none. {38:22} Returning to Judah, his friend reported the inability to find her, and the locals confirmed there was no prostitute there. {38:23} Judah decided to let Tamar keep the items to avoid shame since she couldn't be found. {38:24} About three months later, Judah was informed that Tamar, his daughter-in-law, had committed adultery and was pregnant. Judah demanded she be brought forth and burned. {38:25} As she was brought out, Tamar sent a message to Judah, presenting the items and asking him to identify them. {38:26} Judah recognized the items and confessed Tamar's righteousness, acknowledging that he hadn't given her to Shelah as promised. He did not have relations with her again. {38:27} Tamar gave birth to twins. During delivery, one baby's hand emerged first, and a scarlet thread was tied around it. But the baby withdrew his hand, and his brother, Perez, was born first. {38:28} Then his brother, Zerah, was born, who had the scarlet thread on his hand. {38:29} As the baby withdrew his hand, his brother emerged first. Tamar exclaimed, "How have you broken forth?" So they named him Perez. {38:30} Afterward, his brother, who had the scarlet thread on his hand, was born, and they named him Zerah

{39:1} Joseph was taken to Egypt and Potiphar, an officer of Pharaoh, bought him from the Ishmaelites who had brought him there. {39:2} The LORD was with Joseph, and he prospered. He served in the house of his master, the Egyptian. {39:3} His master recognized the LORD's favor upon Joseph and saw that everything Joseph did prospered. {39:4} Joseph found favor in his master's sight and was made overseer of his house, with all that he had entrusted to Joseph's care. {39:5} The LORD blessed the Egyptian's house for Joseph's sake, and everything in the house and in the field prospered. {39:6} Potiphar left everything in Joseph's charge, knowing only the food he ate. Now Joseph was handsome and well-built. {39:7} Afterward, Potiphar's wife tried to seduce Joseph, saying, "Lie with me." {39:8} But Joseph refused, explaining that his master had entrusted him with everything in the house except her, and he could not sin against God. {39:9} Despite her persistent advances, Joseph did not yield to her. {39:10} One day, Joseph went into the house to do his work, and no one else was inside. {39:11} Potiphar's wife seized him by his garment, demanding that he lie with her, but Joseph fled, leaving his garment behind. {39:12} When she saw that he had left his garment, she falsely accused him of trying to seduce her. {39:13} She used the garment as evidence against him, and Joseph was falsely accused. {39:14} When Potiphar returned, his wife accused Joseph of attempting to seduce her, and she claimed that he had left his garment behind when she cried out for help. {39:15} She reiterated her false accusation to Potiphar, who believed her story. {39:16} She kept Joseph's garment until her husband returned. {39:17} Then she told Potiphar the same story, accusing Joseph of mocking them. {39:18} She claimed that when she cried out, Joseph fled, leaving his garment behind. {39:19} Potiphar was enraged when he heard his wife's accusations. {39:20} Potiphar had Joseph thrown into prison, where the king's prisoners were confined. But even in prison, the LORD was with Joseph. {39:21} He showed him kindness and granted him favor in the eyes of the prison warden. {39:22} The warden entrusted all the prisoners to Joseph's care, and everything that was done in the prison was under Joseph's authority. {39:23} The warden paid no attention to anything under Joseph's care, because the LORD was with him and made everything he did prosper.

{40:1} After these events, the butler and the baker of the king of Egypt offended their master. {40:2} Pharaoh was angry with his chief butler and chief baker. {40:3} So he put them in prison under the custody of the captain of the guard, where Joseph was confined. {40:4} Joseph was assigned to attend to them, and they spent some time in custody. {40:5} One night, both the butler and the baker had dreams, each with its own meaning. {40:6} When Joseph saw them in the morning, he noticed they were troubled. {40:7} He asked them why they looked so sad. {40:8} They explained they had dreams but no one to interpret them. Joseph replied, "Doesn't interpretation belong to God? Tell me your dreams." {40:9} The chief butler shared his dream with Joseph. He said, "In my dream, I saw a vine with three branches. It budded, blossomed, and produced ripe grapes. {40:10} I squeezed the grapes into Pharaoh's cup and gave it to him." {40:11} Joseph interpreted the dream, saying, "The three branches represent three days. {40:13} In three days, Pharaoh will restore you to your position as his butler, and you will serve him as before. {40:14} When this happens, please remember me and show kindness by mentioning me to Pharaoh, so I can be released from prison. I was unjustly taken from the land of the Hebrews, and I have done nothing to deserve being thrown into this dungeon." {40:16} The chief baker, seeing the favorable interpretation, shared his dream. He said, "In my dream, I had three baskets on my head. {40:17} The top basket contained baked goods for Pharaoh, but birds were eating from it." {40:18} Joseph interpreted this dream as well, saying, "The three baskets also represent three days. {40:19} However, within three days, Pharaoh will lift your head off and hang you on a tree, and birds will eat your flesh." {40:20} Three days later, on Pharaoh's birthday, he held a feast for all his servants. {40:21} He reinstated the chief butler to his position and handed him the cup. {40:22} But he hanged the chief baker, just as Joseph had interpreted. {40:23} However, the chief butler did not remember Joseph; he forgot all about him.

{41:1} After two full years, Pharaoh had a dream. He found himself standing by the river. {41:2} Seven well-favored and fat cows emerged from the river and grazed in a meadow. {41:3} Then seven other cows, ugly and thin, came up from the river after them and stood beside the fat cows on the bank of the river. {41:4} The thin, ugly cows devoured the seven fat cows. Pharaoh woke up. {41:5} He fell asleep again and had another dream. This time, he saw seven plump ears of grain growing on a single stalk. {41:6} After them, seven thin, withered ears, scorched by the east wind, sprouted up. {41:7} The thin ears swallowed the seven healthy ears. Pharaoh woke up again; it was all a dream. {41:8} In the morning, Pharaoh was troubled by these dreams. He summoned all the magicians and wise men of Egypt, but none could interpret his dreams.

{41:9} Then the chief butler remembered Joseph and his ability to interpret dreams. He recounted how Joseph had accurately interpreted his and the chief baker's dreams while they were in prison. {41:14} Pharaoh called for Joseph to interpret his dreams. They quickly brought Joseph out of the dungeon. He shaved and changed his clothes before appearing before Pharaoh. {41:15} Pharaoh explained his dreams to Joseph, expressing his frustration at finding no one who could interpret them. {41:16} Joseph replied, "I cannot interpret dreams on my own. Only God can provide Pharaoh with the answer he seeks." {41:17} Pharaoh described his dreams to Joseph: seven fat cows being devoured by seven thin cows, and seven healthy ears of grain being consumed by seven thin and withered ones. {41:20} Joseph listened as Pharaoh recounted his dreams, describing the imagery of fat cows and lean cows, and healthy grain being devoured by thin, withered grain. {41:24} Pharaoh explained how he had shared his dreams with the magicians, but none could interpret them. {41:25} Joseph explained to Pharaoh, "The dreams you had are one and the same. God has shown you what is about to happen. {41:26} The seven healthy cows and the seven healthy ears of grain represent seven years of abundance. Likewise, the seven lean cows and the seven withered ears of grain symbolize seven years of famine. {41:27} God has revealed to Pharaoh what He is about to do. {41:28} Joseph continued, "During the seven years of plenty, Egypt will enjoy great abundance. But it will be followed by seven years of severe famine, during which the abundance will be entirely forgotten. The famine will be so severe that the land will be devastated. {41:32} "The doubling of the dream signifies that God has firmly established this plan and will soon bring it to pass. {41:33} "Therefore, Pharaoh, I advise you to appoint a wise and discerning man to oversee the land of Egypt. {41:34} Let him appoint officers to collect one-fifth of the produce during the years of plenty and store it in the cities. {41:35} This stored grain will serve as a reserve during the years of famine, preventing the land from perishing." {41:37} Pharaoh and his servants agreed with Joseph's plan. {41:38} Pharaoh recognized Joseph's wisdom and said, "Can we find anyone else like him, a man in whom the Spirit of God dwells?" {41:39} Then Pharaoh said to Joseph, "Since God has revealed all this to you, there is no one as discerning and wise as you. {41:40} You shall be in charge of my palace, and all my people shall obey your commands. Only in matters concerning the throne will I be greater than you." {41:41} Pharaoh further declared to Joseph, "I hereby appoint you as ruler over all the land of Egypt." {41:42} Pharaoh removed his signet ring from his finger and put it on Joseph's finger. He dressed him in fine linen clothes and placed a gold chain around his neck. {41:43} Then he had Joseph ride in the second chariot, and servants called out before him, "Bow down!" Thus, Joseph was appointed ruler over all Egypt. {41:44} Pharaoh announced, "I am Pharaoh, but without your permission, no one shall lift a hand or foot in all Egypt." {41:45} Pharaoh named Joseph Zaphnath-paaneah and gave him Asenath, the daughter of Poti-phera, priest of On, as his wife. And Joseph went throughout the land of Egypt. {41:46} Joseph was thirty years old when he entered the service of Pharaoh king of Egypt. And Joseph traveled throughout the land of Egypt. {41:47} During the seven years of abundance, the land produced plentifully. {41:48} Joseph collected all the food produced in Egypt during the seven years of abundance and stored it in the cities. In each city, he stored the food from the surrounding fields. {41:49} Joseph stored up huge quantities of grain, as numerous as the sand of the sea; it was beyond measure. {41:50} Before the years of famine came, Joseph had two sons by Asenath, daughter of Poti-phera, priest of On. {41:51} Joseph named his firstborn Manasseh and said, "God has made me forget all my hardship and all my father's household." {41:52} He named his second son Ephraim and said, "God has made me fruitful in the land of my suffering." {41:53} The seven years of abundance in Egypt came to an end, {41:54} and the seven years of famine began, just as Joseph had said. There was famine in all the other lands, but in the whole land of Egypt there was food. {41:55} When all of Egypt began to feel the famine, the people cried to Pharaoh for food. Then Pharaoh told all the Egyptians, "Go to Joseph and do what he tells you." {41:56} When the famine had spread over the whole country, Joseph opened all the storehouses and sold grain to the Egyptians, for the famine was severe throughout Egypt. {41:57} And all the countries came to Egypt to buy grain from Joseph because the famine was severe all the world.

{42:1} When Jacob saw that there was grain in Egypt, he said to his sons, "Why are you just standing around? {42:2} I have heard that there is grain in Egypt. Go down there and buy some for us, so that we may live and not die." {42:3} So Joseph's ten brothers went down to buy grain from Egypt. {42:4} But Jacob did not send Benjamin, Joseph's brother, with the others, because he was afraid that harm might come to him. {42:5} The sons of Israel went to buy grain along with others who were coming, for the famine was severe in the land of Canaan. {42:6} Now Joseph was the governor of the land, the one who sold grain to all its people. So when Joseph's brothers arrived, they bowed down to him with their faces to the ground. {42:7} As soon as Joseph saw his brothers, he recognized them, but he pretended to be a stranger and spoke harshly to them. "Where do you come from?" he asked. "From the land of Canaan," they replied, "to buy food." {42:8} Although Joseph recognized his brothers, they did not recognize him. {42:9} Then Joseph remembered the dreams he had dreamed about them, and he said to them, "You are spies! You have come to see where our land is vulnerable." {42:10} "No, my lord," they answered. "Your servants have come to buy food. {42:11} We are all sons of one man. We are honest men; your servants are not spies." {42:12} "No!" he said to them. "You have come to see where our land is vulnerable." {42:13} But they replied, "Your servants were twelve brothers, the sons of one man, who lives in the land of Canaan. The youngest is now with our father, and one is no more." {42:14} Joseph said to them, "It is just as I told you: You are spies! {42:15} And this is how you will be tested: As surely as Pharaoh lives, you will not leave this place unless your youngest brother comes here. {42:16} Send one of your number to get your brother; the rest of you will be kept in prison, so that your words may be tested to see if you are telling the truth. If not, then as surely as Pharaoh lives, you are spies!" {42:17} And he put them all in custody for three days. {42:18} On the third day, Joseph said to them, "Do this and you will live, for I fear God: {42:19} If you are honest men, let one of your brothers stay here in prison, while the rest of you go and take grain back for your starving households. {42:20} But you must bring your youngest brother to me, so that your words may be verified and that you may not die." This they proceeded to do. {42:21} They said to one another, "Surely we are being punished because of our brother. We saw how distressed he was when he pleaded with us for his life, but we would not listen; that's why this distress has come upon us." {42:22} Reuben replied, "Didn't I tell you not to sin against the boy? But you wouldn't listen! Now we must account for his blood." {42:23} They did not realize that Joseph could understand them, since he was using an interpreter. {42:24} He turned away from them and began to weep, but then came back and spoke to them again. He had Simeon taken from them and bound before their eyes. {42:25} Joseph gave orders to fill their bags with grain, to return each man's silver to his sack, and to give them provisions for their journey. After this was done for them, {42:26} they loaded their grain on their donkeys and left. {42:27} At the place where they stopped for the night, one of them opened his sack to get feed for his donkey, and he saw his silver in the mouth of his sack. {42:28} "My silver has been returned," he said to his brothers. "Here it is in my sack." Their hearts sank, and they turned to each other trembling and said, "What is this that God has done to us?" {42:29} When they came to their father Jacob in the land of Canaan, they told him all that had happened to them, saying, {42:30} "The man who is the lord of the land spoke roughly to us and treated us as though we were spying on the country. {42:31} But we said to him, 'We are honest men; we are not spies. {42:32} We are twelve brothers, sons of our father; one is no more, and the youngest is now with our father in the land of Canaan.' {42:33} Then the man who is the lord of the country said to us, 'This is how I will know if you are honest men: Leave one of your brothers here with me, take grain for your starving households, and go. {42:34} But bring your youngest brother to me, so I will know that you are not spies but honest men. Then I will give your brother back to you, and you can trade in the land.'" {42:35} As they were emptying their sacks, each man's bundle of money was found in his sack. When they and their father saw the bundles of money, they were afraid. {42:36} Their father Jacob said to them, "You have deprived me of my children. Joseph is no more, and Simeon is no more, and now you want to take Benjamin away. All these things are against me." {42:37} Then Reuben said to his father, "You may put both of my sons to death if I do not bring Benjamin back to you. Entrust him to my care, and I will return him to you." {42:38} But Jacob replied, "My son will not go down with you, for his brother is dead and he is the only one left. If any harm comes to him on the journey you are taking, you will bring my gray head down to the grave in sorrow.

{43:1} The famine was severe in the land. {43:2} When they had eaten all the grain they had brought from Egypt, their father said to them, "Go back and buy us a little more food." {43:3} Judah replied, "The man warned us solemnly, 'You will not see my face again unless your brother is with you.' {43:4} If you will send our brother with us, we will go down and buy food for you. {43:5} But if you will not send him, we will not go down, because the man said to us, 'You will not see my face again unless your brother is with you.'" {43:6} Israel said, "Why did you bring this trouble on me by telling the man you had another brother?" {43:7} They replied, "The man questioned us closely about ourselves and our family. 'Is your father still living?' he asked us. 'Do you have another brother?' We simply answered his questions. How were we to know he would say, 'Bring your brother down here'?" {43:8} Judah said to Israel his father, "Send the boy along with me and we will go at once, so that we and you and our children may live and not die. {43:9} I myself will guarantee his safety; you can hold me personally responsible for him. If I do not bring him back to you and set him here before you, I will bear the blame before you all my life. {43:10} As it is, if we had not delayed, we could have gone and returned twice." {43:11} Then their father Israel said to them, "If it must be, then do this: Put some of the best products of the land in your bags and take them down to the man as a gift—a little balm and a little honey, some spices and myrrh, some pistachio nuts and almonds. {43:12} Take double the amount of silver with you, for you must return the silver that was put back into the mouths of your sacks. Perhaps it was a mistake. {43:13} Take your brother also and go back to the man at once. {43:14} And may God Almighty grant you mercy before the man so that he will let your other brother and Benjamin come back with you. As for me, if I am bereaved, I am bereaved." {43:15} So the men took the gifts and double the amount of silver, and Benjamin also. They hurried down to Egypt and presented themselves to Joseph. {43:16} When Joseph saw Benjamin with them, he said to the steward of his house, "Take these men to my house, slaughter an animal and prepare a meal; they are to eat with me at noon." {43:17} The steward did as Joseph directed and took the men into Joseph's house. {43:18} Now the men were frightened when they were taken to his house. They thought, "We were brought here because of the silver that was put back into our sacks the first time. He wants to attack us and overpower us and seize us as slaves and take our donkeys." {43:19} So they went up to Joseph's steward and spoke to him at the entrance to the house. {43:20} "We beg your pardon, our lord," they said, "we came down here the first time to buy food. {43:21} But at the place where we stopped for the night, we opened our sacks and each of us found his silver—the exact weight—in the mouth of his sack. So we have brought it back with us. {43:22} We have also brought additional silver with us to buy food. We don't know who put our silver in our sacks." {43:23} "It's all right," he said. "Don't be afraid. Your God, the God of your father, has given you treasure in your sacks; I received your silver." Then he brought Simeon out to them. {43:24} The steward took the men into Joseph's house, gave them water to wash their feet and provided fodder for their donkeys. {43:25} They prepared their gifts for Joseph's arrival at noon, because they had heard that they were to eat there. {43:26} When Joseph came home, they presented to him the gifts they had brought into the house, and they bowed down before him to the ground. {43:27} He asked them how they were, and then he said, "How is your aged father you told me about? Is he still living?" {43:28} They replied, "Your servant our father is still alive and well." And they bowed down, prostrating themselves before him. {43:29} As he looked about and saw his brother Benjamin, his own mother's son, he asked, "Is this your youngest brother, the one you told me about?" And he said, "God be gracious to you, my son." {43:30} Deeply moved at the sight of his brother, Joseph hurried out and looked for a place to weep. He went into his private room and wept there. {43:31} After he had washed his face, he came out and, controlling himself, said, "Serve the food." {43:32} They served him by himself, the brothers by themselves, and the Egyptians who ate with him by themselves, because Egyptians could not eat with Hebrews, for that is detestable to Egyptians. {43:33} The men had been seated before him in the order {43:34} And he took portions of food and sent them to them from his table, but Benjamin's portion was five times as much as anyone else's. So they feasted and drank freely with him, enjoying themselves.

{44:1} Joseph told his household steward, "Fill the men's sacks with as much food as they can carry, and put each man's money back in his sack." {44:2} He also instructed, "Put my silver cup in the youngest brother's sack, along with his payment." The steward did as Joseph instructed. {44:3} The next morning, the men and their donkeys were sent off. {44:4} Joseph then said to his steward, "Hurry after the men and when you catch up to them, ask, 'Why have you repaid good with evil? {44:5} Isn't this the cup my master drinks from and uses for divination? What you've done is wrong.'" {44:6} The steward caught up to them and repeated Joseph's words. {44:7} The brothers responded, "Why does our lord say such things? Far be it from us to do such a thing! {44:8} We brought back the money we found in our sacks from Canaan. Why would we steal silver or gold from your master's house? {44:9} If you find the cup with any of us, let him die, and we will become your lord's slaves." {44:10} The steward agreed, "Let it be as you say. The one with the cup will become my servant, and the rest of you will be blameless." {44:11} So they all lowered their sacks to the ground and opened them. {44:12} The steward searched the sacks, starting with the eldest and ending with the youngest, and found the cup in Benjamin's sack. {44:13} They tore their clothes in distress, loaded their donkeys, and returned to the city. {44:14} Judah and his brothers went to Joseph's house, and they fell on the ground before him. {44:15} Joseph questioned them, "What have you done? Don't you know I can divine?" {44:16} Judah replied, "What can we say, my lord? How can we prove our innocence? God has uncovered our guilt. We are your servants, both we and the one in whose sack the cup was found." {44:17} Joseph responded, "I would never do such a thing. Only the one with the cup will be my servant. As for the rest of you, go back to your father in peace." { {44:18} Judah approached Joseph and said, "Please, my lord, allow me to speak a word in your ears. Please do not be angry with your servant, for you are as mighty as Pharaoh himself. {44:19} My lord asked us, his servants, 'Do you have a father or a brother?' {44:20} And we answered, 'We have an old father, and a young brother, the child of his old age. His brother is dead, so he is the only one left of his mother, and his father loves him dearly.' {44:21} You commanded us, 'Bring him down to me so I can see him.' {44:22} But we pleaded, 'The boy cannot leave his father. If he were to leave, our father would surely die.' {44:23} You warned us, 'Unless your youngest brother comes with you, you will not see my face again.' {44:24} So when we returned to our father, we told him what you had said. {44:25} And our father instructed us, 'Go back and buy us a little more food.' {44:26} But we replied, 'We cannot go unless our youngest brother is with us. We cannot face the man unless he accompanies us.' {44:27} Our father reminded us, 'You know that my wife bore me two sons. {44:28} One of them went away, and I assumed he was torn to pieces. I haven't seen him since. {44:29} If you take this one from me too, and harm comes to him, you will bring my gray head down to the grave in sorrow.' {44:30} Now if I go back to my father without the boy, and his life is so intertwined with the boy's life, {44:31} he will surely die when he sees the boy is missing, and our father's grief will kill him. {44:32} I pledged myself as a guarantee for the boy to my father, saying, 'If I do not bring him back to you, I will bear the blame forever.' {44:33} So please, let me stay as a slave instead of the boy, and let him go back with his brothers. {44:34} How can I face my father if the boy is not with me? I couldn't bear to see the anguish that would come upon him."

{45:1} Joseph could no longer control his emotions in front of all those around him, so he ordered everyone to leave. No one else was present when Joseph revealed himself to his brothers. {45:2} He wept loudly, and even the Egyptians and Pharaoh's household heard him. {45:3} Joseph said to his brothers, "I am Joseph. Is my father still alive?" But they were stunned and couldn't answer him because they were afraid. {45:4} Joseph told his brothers, "Come close to me, please." And they approached. Then he said, "I am Joseph, your brother, whom you sold into Egypt. {45:5} But don't be upset or angry with yourselves for selling me here, because God sent me ahead of you to preserve life. {45:6} For two years now, there has been famine in the land, and there are still five more years in which there will be neither plowing nor harvesting. {45:7} But God sent me ahead of you to ensure that you would survive and to save many lives. {45:8} So it was not you who sent me here, but God. He has made me a father to Pharaoh, lord of his entire household, and ruler over all Egypt. {45:9} Hurry and go to my father and say to him, 'This is what your son Joseph says: God has made me lord of all Egypt. Come down to me without delay. {45:10} You shall dwell in the land of Goshen and be near me—you, your children, your grandchildren, your flocks, your herds, and all that you have. {45:11} There I will provide for you, for there are still five years of famine to come, so that you and your household, and all that you have, may not come to poverty.' {45:12} You can see for yourselves, and my brother Benjamin can see, that it is really I who am speaking to you. {45:13} Tell my father about all the honor I have in Egypt and about everything you have seen. And bring my father down here quickly." {45:14} Then he embraced his brother Benjamin and wept, and Benjamin wept on his shoulder. {45:15} He kissed all his brothers and wept over them. Afterward, his brothers talked with him. {45:16} News of Joseph's reunion with his brothers spread throughout Pharaoh's palace, and Pharaoh and his servants were pleased. {45:17} Pharaoh said to Joseph, "Tell your brothers, 'Do this: Load your animals and go back to the land of Canaan. {45:18} Bring your father and your families and come to me. I will give you the best of the land of Egypt, and you can enjoy the fat of the land. {45:19} You are also instructed, 'Do this: Take wagons from Egypt for your children and your wives and bring your father and come. {45:20} Don't worry about your belongings, for the best of all Egypt will be yours.'" {45:21} So the sons of Israel did as they were told. Joseph gave them wagons as Pharaoh had commanded, and he also provided them with provisions for their journey. {45:22} To each of them, he gave new clothes, but to Benjamin, he gave three hundred pieces of silver and five sets of clothes. {45:23} And to his father, he sent ten donkeys loaded with the finest goods of Egypt and ten female donkeys loaded with grain, bread, and provisions for his journey. {45:24} Then he sent his brothers away, and as they departed, he told them, "Do not quarrel on the way." {45:25} So they left Egypt and went to their father Jacob in the land of Canaan. {45:26} They told him, "Joseph is still alive! In fact, he is ruler over all the land of Egypt." But Jacob was stunned and could not believe them. {45:27} However, when they relayed all the words Joseph had spoken to him and showed him the wagons Joseph had sent to carry him,

Jacob's spirit was revived. {45:28} He exclaimed, "Enough! My son Joseph is still alive! I must go and see him before I die."

{46:1} Israel journeyed with all his belongings and reached Beer-sheba. There, he offered sacrifices to the God of his father Isaac. {46:2} During the night, God spoke to Israel in a vision, calling, "Jacob, Jacob." And Jacob responded, "Here I am." {46:3} God said, "I am God, the God of your father. Do not be afraid to go down to Egypt, for I will make you a great nation there. {46:4} I will go down to Egypt with you, and I will surely bring you back again. Joseph will close your eyes when you die." {46:5} So Jacob left Beer-sheba. His sons carried him, along with their wives and children, in the wagons provided by Pharaoh. {46:6} They also took their livestock and possessions from the land of Canaan and went to Egypt—Jacob and all his descendants. {46:7} These included his sons and grandsons, his daughters and granddaughters—his entire family went with him to Egypt. {46:8} The descendants of Jacob who went to Egypt with him were as follows: Reuben, Jacob's firstborn. {46:9} Reuben's sons were Hanoch, Phallu, Hezron, and Carmi. {46:10} The sons of Simeon were Jemuel, Jamin, Ohad, Jachin, Zohar, and Shaul, the son of a Canaanite woman. {46:11} The sons of Levi were Gershon, Kohath, and Merari. {46:12} Judah's sons were Er, Onan, Shelah, Pharez, and Zarah. But Er and Onan died in Canaan. Pharez's sons were Hezron and Hamul. {46:13} Issachar's sons were Tola, Phuvah, Job, and Shimron. {46:14} Zebulun's sons were Sered, Elon, and Jahleel. {46:15} These were the sons of Leah, whom she bore to Jacob in Padan-aram, along with his daughter Dinah. The total number of his sons and daughters was thirty-three. {46:16} Gad's sons were Ziphion, Haggi, Shuni, Ezbon, Eri, Arodi, and Areli. {46:17} Asher's sons were Jimnah, Ishuah, Isui, Beriah, and Serah, their sister. Beriah's sons were Heber and Malchiel. {46:18} These were the children of Zilpah, whom Laban gave to Leah his daughter. She bore these to Jacob—sixteen souls in all. {46:19} Rachel bore Joseph and Benjamin to Jacob. {46:20} In Egypt, Joseph had Manasseh and Ephraim, whom Asenath, the daughter of Potipherah, priest of On, bore to him. {46:21} Benjamin's sons were Belah, Becher, Ashbel, Gera, Naaman, Ehi, Rosh, Muppim, Huppim, and Ard. {46:22} These were the sons of Rachel who were born to Jacob—fourteen souls in all. {46:23} Dan's son was Hushim. {46:24} Naphtali's sons were Jahzeel, Guni, Jezer, and Shillem. {46:25} These were the sons of Bilhah, whom Laban gave to Rachel his daughter. She bore these to Jacob—seven souls in all. {46:26} The total number of souls that went with Jacob to Egypt, those who came from his body, excluding Jacob's sons' wives, was sixty-six. {46:27} Joseph's sons, who were born to him in Egypt, were two souls. All the souls of Jacob's household who came to Egypt were seventy. {46:28} Judah went ahead to Joseph to show him the way to Goshen, and they arrived in the land of Goshen. {46:29} Joseph prepared his chariot and went to meet his father Israel in Goshen. When he saw him, he embraced him and wept on his neck for a long time. {46:30} Israel said to Joseph, "Now I can die, since I have seen your face and know that you are still alive." {46:31} Joseph said to his brothers and his father's household, "I will go and inform Pharaoh, telling him, 'My brothers and my father's household, who were in the land of Canaan, have come to me. {46:32} These men are shepherds, and they have always been shepherds. They have brought with them their flocks and herds and everything they own.' {46:33} When Pharaoh calls you and asks, 'What is your occupation?' {46:34} You must say, 'Your servants have raised livestock from our youth until now, both we and our fathers.' Then you will be allowed to settle in the land of Goshen, because all shepherds are detestable to the Egyptians."

{47:1} Joseph went to Pharaoh and said, "My father and my brothers have come from the land of Canaan with their flocks, herds, and all that they own. They are now in the land of Goshen." {47:2} Then Joseph brought five of his brothers and introduced them to Pharaoh. {47:3} Pharaoh asked them, "What is your occupation?" And they replied, "We are shepherds, both we and our ancestors." {47:4} They further explained to Pharaoh, "We have come to live in this land because there is no pasture for our flocks in Canaan due to the severe famine. Please allow us to settle in the land of Goshen." {47:5} Pharaoh said to Joseph, "Your father and brothers have come to you. {47:6} The land of Egypt is open before you; settle your father and brothers in the best part of the land. Let them live in the land of Goshen. And if you know of any capable men among them, put them in charge of my livestock." {47:7} Joseph brought his father Jacob and presented him to Pharaoh. Jacob blessed Pharaoh. {47:8} Pharaoh asked Jacob, "How old are you?" {47:9} Jacob replied, "The years of my pilgrimage are a hundred and thirty. My life has been short and full of trouble, not reaching the years of my ancestors." {47:10} Jacob blessed Pharaoh again and left his presence. {47:11} Joseph settled his father and brothers in Egypt, giving them property in the best part of the land, the region of Rameses, as Pharaoh had commanded. {47:12} Joseph provided for his father, brothers, and all their households with bread, according to their needs. {47:13} The famine was severe, and there was no bread in the land of Egypt and Canaan. Both lands were devastated by the famine. {47:14} Joseph collected all the money in Egypt and Canaan in exchange for the grain people bought, and he brought it into Pharaoh's palace. {47:15} When the money ran out in Egypt and Canaan, all the Egyptians came to Joseph, pleading for food. They said, "Give us bread. Why should we die before your eyes when we have no money left?" {47:16} Joseph told them, "Give me your livestock, and I will give you food in exchange if you have no money." {47:17} So they brought their livestock to Joseph, and he gave them bread in exchange for their horses, flocks, herds, and donkeys. Thus, he provided them with food for that year. {47:18} When that year ended, they came to Joseph again and said, "We cannot hide from you, my lord, that our money is gone, and our livestock now belongs to you. We have nothing left but ourselves and our land. {47:19} Why should we and our land perish before your eyes? Buy us and our land in exchange for food, and we will be Pharaoh's slaves. Give us seed so that we may live and not die, and the land may not become desolate." {47:20} So Joseph bought all the land in Egypt for Pharaoh because the famine had devastated the Egyptians, and the land became Pharaoh's. {47:21} As for the people, Joseph relocated them to the cities, from one end of Egypt to the other. {47:22} Only the land of the priests he did not buy because they had an allotment from Pharaoh and lived off the allotment Pharaoh gave them. Therefore, they did not sell their land. {47:23} Joseph said to the people, "Now that I have bought you and your land for Pharaoh, here is seed for you to plant the land. {47:24} When you harvest, give a fifth of it to Pharaoh, and keep four-fifths for yourselves as seed for the fields and as food for yourselves, your households, and your children." {47:25} The people said, "You have saved our lives. Let us find favor in your sight, and we will be Pharaoh's servants." {47:26} Joseph established this as a law in Egypt, which remains in effect to this day: Pharaoh should receive a fifth of the produce, except for the land of the priests, which did not become Pharaoh's. {47:27} So Israel settled in the land of Egypt, in the region of Goshen. They acquired property there, were fruitful, and multiplied greatly. {47:28} Jacob lived in Egypt for seventeen years, and the full span of his life was a hundred and forty-seven years. {47:29} When the time drew near for Israel to die, he called his son Joseph and said to him, "If I have found favor in your eyes, put your hand under my thigh and promise me that you will show me kindness and faithfulness. Do not bury me in Egypt, {47:30} "But I want to be buried with my ancestors. Promise me that you will carry my body out of Egypt and bury me with them." Joseph replied, "I will do as you have asked." {47:31} "Swear to me that you will do this," Jacob insisted. So Joseph swore to him, and then Israel bowed in worship as he leaned on the top of his staff.

{48:1} After some time, Joseph was informed, "Your father is sick." So he took his two sons, Manasseh and Ephraim, with him. {48:2} Jacob was told, "Your son Joseph has come to you." So Israel gathered his strength and sat up in bed. {48:3} Jacob said to Joseph, "God Almighty appeared to me at Luz in the land of Canaan and blessed me. {48:4} He said to me, 'I will make you fruitful and multiply you; I will make of you a multitude of people, and I will give this land to your descendants after you as an everlasting possession.' {48:5} "Now your two sons, Ephraim and Manasseh, born to you in the land of Egypt before I came to you in Egypt, are mine; Ephraim and Manasseh shall be mine, just as Reuben and Simeon are mine. {48:6} Any children born to you after them shall be yours; they will be recorded under the names of their brothers in their inheritance. {48:7} "As for me, when I came from Paddan, Rachel died in the land of Canaan on the way, some distance from Ephrath; and I buried her there on the way to Ephrath (that is, Bethlehem)." {48:8} Israel saw Joseph's sons and asked, "Who are these?" {48:9} Joseph replied, "These are my sons, whom God has given me in this place." And he said, "Please bring them to me, and I will bless them." {48:10} Now Israel's eyes were dim with age, and he could not see well. So Joseph brought them near him, and he kissed them and embraced them. {48:11} Israel said to Joseph, "I never expected to see your face again, and now God has allowed me to see your children too." {48:12} Then Joseph removed them from Israel's knees and bowed down with his face to the ground. {48:13} Joseph took them both, Ephraim with his right hand toward Israel's left, and Manasseh with his left hand toward Israel's right, and brought them close to him. {48:14} But Israel reached out his right hand and placed it on Ephraim's head, though he was the younger, and crossing his arms, he put his left hand on Manasseh's head, even though Manasseh was the firstborn. {48:15} Then he blessed Joseph and said, "May the God before whom my fathers Abraham and Isaac walked faithfully, the God who has been my shepherd all my life to this day, {48:16} the Angel who has delivered me from all harm, bless these boys. May they be called by my name and the names of my fathers Abraham and Isaac, and may they increase greatly on the earth." {48:17} When Joseph saw his father placing his right hand on Ephraim's head, he was displeased; so he took hold of his father's hand to move it from Ephraim's head to Manasseh's head.

{48:18} Joseph said to him, "No, my father, this one is the firstborn; put your right hand on his head." {48:19} But his father refused and said, "I know, my son, I know. He too will become a nation, and he too will become great. Nevertheless, his younger brother will be greater than he, and his descendants will become a group of nations." {48:20} So he blessed them that day, saying, "By you Israel will pronounce blessings, saying, 'May God make you like Ephraim and Manasseh.'" So he put Ephraim ahead of Manasseh. {48:21} Then Israel said to Joseph, "I am about to die, but God will be with you and take you back to the land of your fathers. {48:22} And I have given you one portion more than your brothers, which I took from the hand of the Amorite with my sword and my bow.

{49:1} Jacob called his sons and said, "Gather together, and I will tell you what will happen to you in the future. {49:2} "Listen, sons of Jacob; pay attention to Israel your father. {49:3} "Reuben, you are my firstborn, my strength and the first sign of my manhood, excelling in honor and power. {49:4} But you are as unruly as a flood, and you will no longer excel because you went up to your father's bed, onto my couch and defiled it. {49:5} "Simeon and Levi are brothers— their swords are weapons of violence. {49:6} Let me not enter their council, let me not join their assembly, for they have killed men in their anger and hamstrung oxen as they pleased. {49:7} Cursed be their anger, so fierce, and their fury, so cruel! I will scatter them in Jacob and disperse them in Israel. {49:8} "Judah, your brothers will praise you; your hand will be on the neck of your enemies; your father's sons will bow down to you. {49:9} You are a lion's cub, Judah; you return from the prey, my son. Like a lion he crouches and lies down, like a lioness—who dares to rouse him? {49:10} The scepter will not depart from Judah, nor the ruler's staff from between his feet, until he to whom it belongs shall come and the obedience of the nations shall be his. {49:11} He will tether his donkey to a vine, his colt to the choicest branch; he will wash his garments in wine, his robes in the blood of grapes. {49:12} His eyes will be darker than wine, his teeth whiter than milk. {49:13} "Zebulun will live by the seashore and become a haven for ships; his border will extend toward Sidon. {49:14} "Issachar is a rawboned donkey lying down among the sheep pens. {49:15} When he sees how good is his resting place and how pleasant is his land, he will bend his shoulder to the burden and submit to forced labor. {49:16} "Dan will provide justice for his people as one of the tribes of Israel. {49:17} Dan will be a snake by the roadside, a viper along the path, that bites the horse's heels so that its rider tumbles backward. {49:18} "I look for your deliverance, Lord. {49:19} "Gad will be attacked by a band of raiders, but he will attack them at their heels. {49:20} "Asher's food will be rich; he will provide delicacies fit for a king. {49:21} "Naphtali is a doe set free that bears beautiful fawns. {49:22} "Joseph is a fruitful vine, a fruitful vine near a spring, whose branches climb over a wall. {49:23} With bitterness archers attacked him; they shot at him with hostility. {49:24} But his bow remained steady, his strong arms stayed limber, because of the hand of the Mighty One of Jacob, because of the Shepherd, the Rock of Israel, {49:25} because of your father's God, who helps you, because of the Almighty, who blesses you with blessings of the skies above, blessings of the deep springs below, blessings of the breast and womb. {49:26} Your father's blessings are greater than the blessings of the ancient mountains, than the bounty of the age-old hills. Let all these rest on the head of Joseph, on the brow of the prince among his brothers. { {49:27} "Benjamin is a ravenous wolf; in the morning he devours the prey, in the evening he divides the plunder. {49:28} These are the twelve tribes of Israel, and this is what their father said to them when he blessed them, giving each the blessing appropriate to him. {49:29} Then he gave them these instructions: "I am about to be gathered to my people. Bury me with my fathers in the cave in the field of Ephron the Hittite, {49:30} the cave in the field of Machpelah, near Mamre in Canaan, which Abraham bought along with the field as a burial place from Ephron the Hittite. {49:31} There Abraham and his wife Sarah were buried, there Isaac and his wife Rebekah were buried, and there I buried Leah. {49:32} The field and the cave in it were bought from the Hittites." {49:33} When Jacob had finished giving instructions to his sons, he drew his feet up into the bed, breathed his last and was gathered to his people.

{50:1} Joseph wept as he fell upon his father's face and kissed him. {50:2} He then commanded his servants, the physicians, to embalm his father, and they embalmed Israel. {50:3} Forty days were required for the embalming process, as was the custom, and the Egyptians mourned for him seventy days. {50:4} After the mourning period, Joseph spoke to Pharaoh's household, requesting to fulfill his father's wish to be buried in Canaan. {50:5} He explained that his father had made him swear to bury him in Canaan, and he asked permission to fulfill this promise. {50:6} Pharaoh granted Joseph's request, saying he should go and bury his father as promised. {50:7} Joseph, accompanied by Pharaoh's servants, elders, and all of Joseph's family, went up to bury his father. {50:8} They left behind their little ones, flocks, and herds in the land of Goshen. {50:9} Chariots and horsemen also went up with Joseph, forming a large company. {50:10} They reached the threshing floor of Atad, beyond the Jordan, where they mourned and lamented greatly for seven days. {50:11} The Canaanites observed their mourning and named the place Abel-mizraim, recognizing the depth of the Egyptians' grief. {50:12} Joseph's sons carried out their father's instructions, burying him in the cave of Machpelah in Canaan, as Abraham had purchased it for a burial site. {50:13} After burying their father, Joseph and his brothers returned to Egypt with all who had accompanied them. {50:14} Upon Joseph's return, his brothers feared his retaliation for their past wrongs. {50:15} They sent a message to Joseph, claiming that their father had instructed him to forgive them. {50:16} Joseph wept when he heard this message, and his brothers fell before him, pleading to be his servants. {50:17} Joseph reassured them, stating that he would not take the place of God in judgment. {50:18} He acknowledged their wrongdoing but assured them that God had turned it to good, saving many lives. {50:19} Joseph reassured his brothers, saying, "Fear not, for am I in the place of God? But as for you, you thought evil against me; but God meant it for good, to bring to pass, as it is this day, to save many people alive. {50:20} **Now therefore fear ye not: I will nourish you, and your little ones.** {50:21} He comforted them and spoke kindly to them. {50:22} Joseph lived in Egypt with his father's household, reaching the age of one hundred and ten years. {50:23} He saw Ephraim's children to the third generation, and also the children of Machir, the son of Manasseh, were brought up on Joseph's knees. {50:24} Joseph spoke to his brothers, saying, "I am about to die, but God will surely visit you, and bring you out of this land to the land which He swore to Abraham, to Isaac, and to Jacob." {50:25} Joseph took an oath from the children of Israel, declaring, "God will surely visit you, and you shall carry up my bones from hence." {50:26} Joseph died at the age of one hundred and ten years. The Egyptians embalmed him, and he was placed in a coffin in Egypt.

Exodus

{1:1} These are the names of the children of Israel who came into Egypt; every man and his household came with Jacob. {1:2} Reuben, Simeon, Levi, and Judah, {1:3} Issachar, Zebulun, and Benjamin, {1:4} Dan, and Naphtali, Gad, and Asher. {1:5} All the souls that came out of Jacob were seventy souls, for Joseph was already in Egypt. {1:6} Joseph died, along with all his brothers and that entire generation. {1:7} The children of Israel became fruitful and multiplied greatly; they became exceedingly numerous, and the land was filled with them. {1:8} But then a new king, who did not know Joseph, came to power in Egypt. {1:9} He said to his people, "Look, the Israelites have become too numerous and strong for us. {1:10} Let's deal shrewdly with them, otherwise they will continue to increase, and if a war breaks out, they will join our enemies, fight against us, and leave the country." {1:11} So the Egyptians appointed taskmasters over the Israelites to oppress them with forced labor. They built Pithom and Raamses as store cities for Pharaoh. {1:12} But the more they were oppressed, the more they multiplied and spread. The Egyptians came to dread the Israelites {1:13} and worked them ruthlessly. {1:14} They made their lives bitter with harsh labor in brick and mortar and with all kinds of work in the fields; in all their harsh labor the Egyptians worked them ruthlessly. {1:15} The king of Egypt said to the Hebrew midwives, whose names were Shiphrah and Puah, {1:16} "When you are helping the Hebrew women during childbirth on the delivery stool, if you see that the baby is a boy, kill him; but if it is a girl, let her live." {1:17} The midwives, however, feared God and did not do what the king of Egypt had told them to do; they let the boys live. {1:18} Then the king of Egypt summoned the midwives and asked them, "Why have you done this? Why have you let the boys live?" {1:19} The midwives answered Pharaoh, "Hebrew women are not like Egyptian women; they are vigorous and give birth before the midwives arrive." {1:20} So God was kind to the midwives, and the number of people increased and became even more numerous. {1:21} And because the midwives feared God, he gave them families of their own. {1:22} Then Pharaoh gave this order to all his people: "Every Hebrew boy that is born you must throw into the Nile, but let every girl live."

{2:1} A man from the tribe of Levi married a woman from the same tribe. {2:2} The woman became pregnant and gave birth to a son. When she saw that he was a fine child, she hid him for three months. {2:3} Unable to hide him any longer, she got a basket made of reeds and waterproofed it with tar and pitch. Then she put the baby in the basket and placed it among the reeds along the bank of the Nile River. {2:4} The baby's sister stood at a distance to see what would happen to him. {2:5} Soon Pharaoh's daughter came down to bathe in the river, and her attendants walked along the riverbank. When the princess saw the basket among the reeds, she sent her maid to get it for her. {2:6} When the princess opened it, she saw the baby. The little boy was crying, and she felt sorry for him. "This must be one of the Hebrew children," she said. {2:7} Then the baby's sister approached Pharaoh's daughter. "Shall I go and find one of the Hebrew women to nurse the baby for you?" she asked. {2:8} "Yes, do!" the princess replied. So the girl went and called the baby's mother. {2:9} "Take this baby and nurse him for me," the princess told the baby's mother. "I will pay you for your help." So the woman took her baby home and nursed him. {2:10} Later, when the child was older, his mother brought him back to Pharaoh's daughter, who adopted him as her own son. She named him Moses, for she said, "I drew him out of the water." {2:11} Many years later, when Moses had grown up, he went out to visit his own people, the Hebrews, and he saw how hard they were forced to work. During his visit, he saw an Egyptian beating one of his fellow Hebrews. {2:12} Looking around and seeing no one, Moses killed the Egyptian and hid his body in the sand. {2:13} The next day, when Moses went out to visit his people again, he saw two Hebrew men fighting. "Why are you beating up your friend?" Moses said to the one who had started the fight. {2:14} The man replied, "Who appointed you to be our prince and judge? Are you going to kill me as you killed that Egyptian yesterday?" Then Moses was afraid, thinking, "Everyone knows what I did!" {2:15} When Pharaoh heard what had happened, he tried to kill Moses. But Moses fled from Pharaoh and went to live in the land of Midian. When Moses arrived in Midian, he sat down beside a well. {2:16} Now the priest of Midian had seven daughters who came to draw water and fill the water troughs for their father's flock. {2:17} But some other shepherds came and chased them away. So Moses came to their rescue and watered their flock. {2:18} When the girls returned to their father, he asked, "Why are you back so soon today?" {2:19} "An Egyptian rescued us from the shepherds," they answered. "And then he drew water for us and watered our flock." {2:20} "Where is he?" their father asked. "Why did you leave him there? Invite him to come and eat with us." {2:21} Moses agreed to stay with the man, who gave his daughter Zipporah to Moses in marriage. {2:22} Later she gave birth to a son, and Moses named him Gershom, for he explained, "I have been a foreigner in a foreign land." {2:23} Many years passed, and the king of Egypt died. But the Israelites continued to groan under their burden of slavery. They cried out for help, and their cry rose up to God. {2:24} God heard their groaning, and he remembered his covenant promise to Abraham, Isaac, and Jacob. {2:25} God looked down on the people of Israel and knew it was time to act.

{3:1} Moses was tending the flock of Jethro, his father-in-law, the priest of Midian. He led the flock to the backside of the desert and came to the mountain of God, Horeb. {3:2} Suddenly, the angel of the LORD appeared to him in a flame of fire from within a bush. Moses noticed that the bush was burning but was not consumed by the fire. {3:3} Curious, Moses decided to investigate this remarkable sight. {3:4} As Moses approached, God called to him from the midst of the bush, saying, "Moses, Moses." Moses responded, "Here I am." {3:5} God instructed Moses, "Do not come any closer. Take off your sandals, for the place where you are standing is holy ground." {3:6} Then God revealed Himself further, saying, "I am the God of your father, the God of Abraham, Isaac, and Jacob." Overwhelmed, Moses hid his face because he was afraid to look at God. {3:7} God continued, "I have seen the suffering of my people in Egypt, and I have heard their cries because of their slave drivers. I am aware of their suffering. {3:8} "So I have come down to rescue them from the power of the Egyptians and lead them out of Egypt into a good and spacious land, a land flowing with milk and honey—the territory of the Canaanites, Hittites, Amorites, Perizzites, Hivites, and Jebusites. {3:9} "Now indeed, the cry of the Israelites has reached me, and I have seen how severely the Egyptians oppress them. {3:10} "Therefore, go! I am sending you to Pharaoh to bring my people, the Israelites, out of Egypt." {3:11} Moses replied to God, "Who am I that I should go to Pharaoh and bring the Israelites out of Egypt?" {3:12} God assured him, "I will be with you. This will be the sign to you that I have sent you: When you have brought the people out of Egypt, you will worship God on this mountain." {3:13} Moses then asked God, "Suppose I go to the Israelites and say to them, 'The God of your ancestors has sent me to you,' and they ask me, 'What is his name?' Then what should I tell them?" {3:14} **God said to Moses, "I AM WHO I AM. Tell the Israelites, 'I AM has sent me to you.'"** {3:15} Furthermore, God said to Moses, "Say this to the Israelites: 'The LORD, the God of your ancestors—the God of Abraham, Isaac, and Jacob—has sent me to you.' This is my eternal name, my name to remember for all generations. {3:16} "Go, assemble the elders of Israel and say to them, 'The LORD, the God of your ancestors—the God of Abraham, Isaac, and Jacob—appeared to me and said: I have watched over you and have seen what has been done to you in Egypt. {3:17} "'And I have promised to bring you up out of your misery in Egypt into the land of the Canaanites, Hittites, Amorites, Perizzites, Hivites, and Jebusites—a land flowing with milk and honey.'" {3:18} "The elders will listen to you. Then you and the elders of Israel must go to the king of Egypt and tell him, 'The LORD, the God of the Hebrews, has met with us. So let us take a three-day journey into the wilderness to offer sacrifices to the LORD our God.' {3:19} "But I know that the king of Egypt will not let you go unless a mighty hand compels him. {3:20} "So I will stretch out my hand and strike Egypt with all the wonders I will perform there. After that, he will let you go. {3:21} "And I will make the Egyptians favorably disposed toward this people so that when you leave, you will not go empty-handed. {3:22} "Every woman is to ask her neighbor and any woman living in her house for articles of silver and gold and for clothing, which you will put on your sons and daughters. And so you will plunder the Egyptians."

{4:1} Moses replied to God, "But Lord, what if they don't believe me or listen to me? They might say, 'The LORD did not appear to you.'" {4:2} God asked Moses, "What is that in your hand?" Moses answered, "A rod." {4:3} God instructed him, "Throw it on the ground." So Moses threw it down, and it turned into a snake. Moses fled from it. {4:4} Then God said to Moses, "Reach out your hand and take it by the tail." So Moses reached out and caught the snake, and it turned back into a rod in his hand. {4:5} God said, "This is so they may believe that the LORD, the God of their ancestors—Abraham, Isaac, and Jacob—has appeared to you." {4:6} Then God said, "Put your hand inside your cloak." Moses did so, and when he took it out, his hand was leprous like snow. {4:7} "Put your hand back into your cloak," God said. So Moses put his hand back, and when he took it out again, it was restored like the rest of his flesh. {4:8} "If they do not believe you or pay attention to the first sign, they may believe the second. {4:9} "But if they do not believe these two signs or listen to you, take some water from the Nile and pour it on the dry ground. The water you take from the river will become blood on the ground." {4:10} Moses said to the LORD, "Pardon your servant, Lord. I have never been eloquent, neither in the past nor since you have spoken to your servant. I am slow of speech and tongue." {4:11} The LORD said to him, "Who gave human beings their mouths? Who makes them deaf or mute? Who gives them sight or makes them blind? Is it not I, the LORD? {4:12} "Now go; I will help you speak and will teach you what to say." {4:13} But Moses said, "Pardon your servant, Lord. Please send someone else." {4:14} Then the LORD's anger burned against Moses and he said, "What about your brother, Aaron the Levite? I know he can speak well. He is already on his way to meet you, and he will be glad to see you. {4:15} "You shall speak to him and put words in his mouth; I will help both of you speak and will teach you what to do. {4:16} "He will speak to the people for you, and it will be as if he were your mouth and as if you were God to him. {4:17} "But take this staff in your hand so you can perform the signs with it." {4:18} Then Moses went back to his father-in-law Jethro and said to him, "Let me return to my own people in Egypt to see if any of them are still alive." Jethro said, "Go, and I wish you well." {4:19} Now the LORD had said to Moses in Midian, "Go back to Egypt, for all those who wanted to kill you are dead." {4:20} So Moses took his wife and sons, put them on a donkey, and started back to Egypt. And he took the staff of God in his hand. {4:21} The LORD said to Moses, "When you return to Egypt, see that you perform before Pharaoh all the wonders I have given you the power to do. But I will harden his heart so he will not let the people go. {4:22} "Then say to Pharaoh, 'This is what the LORD says: Israel is my firstborn son, {4:23} "and I told you, 'Let my son go, so he may worship me.' But you refused to let him go; so I will kill your firstborn son.'" {4:24} At a lodging place on the way, the LORD met Moses and was about to kill him. {4:25} But Zipporah took a flint knife, cut off her son's foreskin and touched Moses' feet with it. "Surely you are a bridegroom of blood to me," she said. {4:26} So the LORD let him alone. (At that time she said "bridegroom of blood," referring to circumcision.) {4:27} The LORD said to Aaron, "Go into the wilderness to meet Moses." So he met Moses at the mountain of God and kissed him. {4:28} Then Moses told Aaron everything the LORD had sent him to say, and also about all the signs he had commanded him to perform. {4:29} Moses and Aaron brought together all the elders of the Israelites, {4:30} and Aaron told them everything the LORD had said to Moses. He also performed the signs before the people, {4:31} and they believed. And when they heard that the LORD was concerned about them and had seen their misery, they bowed down and worshiped.

{5:1} Moses and Aaron went to Pharaoh and said, "This is what the LORD, the God of Israel, says: Let my people go, so they may hold a feast to me in the wilderness." {5:2} Pharaoh responded, "Who is the LORD, that I should obey him and let Israel go? I do not know the LORD, and I will not let Israel go." {5:3} Moses and Aaron replied, "The God of the Hebrews has met with us. Let us go on a three-day journey into the desert to sacrifice to the LORD our God, or he may strike us with pestilence or the sword." {5:4} Pharaoh retorted, "Why are you, Moses and Aaron, distracting the people from their work? Get back to your tasks!" {5:5} "Look," Pharaoh continued, "the population of the land is increasing, and you are making them rest from their labors." {5:6} So Pharaoh commanded the taskmasters and officials of the people, saying, {5:7} "You shall no longer give the people straw to make bricks as before. Let them go and gather straw for themselves. {5:8} "But require them to make the same quota of bricks as before. Do not reduce it. They are lazy; that is why they are crying out, 'Let us go and sacrifice to our God.' {5:9} "Make the work harder for the men so that they keep working and pay no attention to lies." {5:10} The taskmasters and officials went out and said to the people, "Pharaoh says, 'I will not give you straw. {5:11} "Go and get straw wherever you can find it, but your work will not be reduced.'" {5:12} So the people scattered throughout the land of Egypt to gather stubble for straw. {5:13} The taskmasters pressured them, saying, "Complete your work, your daily quota of bricks, just as when you had straw." {5:14} The Israelite overseers, whom Pharaoh's taskmasters had appointed, were beaten and questioned, "Why haven't you met your quota of bricks yesterday and today as before?" {5:15} The Israelite overseers went to Pharaoh and pleaded, "Why are you treating your servants this way? {5:16} "No straw is given to your servants, yet they demand, 'Make bricks!' Your servants are being beaten, but the fault lies with your own people." {5:17} Pharaoh replied, "You are idle, you are idle! That is why you say, 'Let us go and sacrifice to the LORD.' {5:18} "Now get back to work! No straw will be given to you, yet you must deliver the same quota of bricks." {5:19} The Israelite overseers realized they were in trouble when they were told, "You must not reduce your daily quota of bricks." {5:20} As they left Pharaoh, they encountered Moses and Aaron standing in their path. {5:21} They said to them, "May the LORD look on you and judge you! You have made us obnoxious to Pharaoh and his officials and have put a sword in their hand to kill us." {5:22} Moses returned to the LORD and asked, "Lord, why have you brought trouble upon this people? Why did you send me? {5:23} "Ever since I went to Pharaoh to speak in your name, he has brought trouble upon this people, and you have not rescued your people at all."

{6:1} Then the LORD said to Moses, "Now you will see what I will do to Pharaoh. With a strong hand, he will let them go, and with a strong hand, he will drive them out of his land. {6:2} And God spoke to Moses, saying, "I am the LORD. {6:3} "I appeared to Abraham, to Isaac, and to Jacob as God Almighty, but by my name JEHOVAH, I was not known to them. {6:4} "I also established my covenant with them to give them the land of Canaan, the land of their pilgrimage, where they were strangers. {6:5} "I have heard the groaning of the children of Israel, whom the Egyptians keep in bondage, and I have remembered my covenant. {6:6} "Therefore, say to the children of Israel, 'I am the LORD, and I will bring you out from under the burdens of the Egyptians, and I will rid you of their bondage. I will redeem you with an outstretched arm and with great judgments. {6:7} "I will take you to be my people, and I will be your God, and you shall know that I am the LORD your God, who brings you out from under the burdens of the Egyptians. {6:8} "I will bring you into the land that I swore to give to Abraham, to Isaac, and to Jacob, and I will give it to you for an inheritance. I am the LORD." {6:9} Moses spoke thus to the children of Israel, but they did not listen to him because of their anguish and cruel bondage. {6:10} And the LORD spoke to Moses, saying, {6:11} "Go in, speak to Pharaoh king of Egypt, that he let the children of Israel go out of his land." {6:12} But Moses said before the LORD, "Behold, the children of Israel have not listened to me; how then shall Pharaoh listen to me, who am of uncircumcised lips?" {6:13} And the LORD spoke to Moses and Aaron, and gave them a charge to the children of Israel and to Pharaoh king of Egypt, to bring the children of Israel out of the land of Egypt. {6:14} These are the heads of their fathers' houses: The sons of Reuben, the firstborn of Israel: Hanoch, and Pallu, Hezron, and Carmi. These are the families of Reuben. {6:15} And the sons of Simeon: Jemuel, and Jamin, and Ohad, and Jachin, and Zohar, and Shaul, the son of a Canaanite woman. These are the families of Simeon. {6:16} These are the names of the sons of Levi according to their generations: Gershon, and Kohath, and Merari. And the years of the life of Levi were one hundred thirty-seven years. {6:17} The sons of Gershon: Libni, and Shimi, according to their families. {6:18} And the sons of Kohath: Amram, and Izhar, and Hebron, and Uzziel. And the years of the life of Kohath were one hundred thirty-three years. {6:19} And the sons of Merari: Mahali and Mushi. These are the families of Levi according to their generations. {6:20} Amram took him Jochebed his father's sister to wife, and she bore him Aaron and Moses. And the years of the life of Amram were one hundred and thirty-seven years. {6:21} And the sons of Izhar: Korah, and Nepheg, and Zichri. {6:22} And the sons of Uzziel: Mishael, and Elzaphan, and Zithri. {6:23} And Aaron took him Elisheba, daughter of Amminadab, sister of Naashon, to wife; and she bore him Nadab, and Abihu, Eleazar, and Ithamar. {6:24} And the sons of Korah: Assir, and Elkanah, and

Abiasaph. These are the families of the Korhites. {6:25} And Eleazar, Aaron's son, took him one of the daughters of Putiel to wife; and she bore him Phinehas. These are the heads of the fathers of the Levites according to their families. {6:26} These are that Aaron and Moses, to whom the LORD said, "Bring out the children of Israel from the land of Egypt according to their armies." {6:27} These are they who spoke to Pharaoh king of Egypt, to bring out the children of Israel from Egypt: these are that Moses and Aaron. {6:28} And it came to pass on the day when the LORD spoke to Moses in the land of Egypt, {6:29} That the LORD spoke to Moses, saying, "I am the LORD: speak to Pharaoh king of Egypt all that I say to you." {6:30} But Moses said before the LORD, "Behold, I am of uncircumcised lips, and how shall Pharaoh listen to me?"

{7:1} Then the LORD said to Moses, "See, I have made you a god to Pharaoh, and Aaron your brother shall be your prophet. {7:2} "You shall speak all that I command you, and Aaron your brother shall speak to Pharaoh, that he sends the children of Israel out of his land. {7:3} "I will harden Pharaoh's heart and multiply my signs and wonders in the land of Egypt. {7:4} "But Pharaoh shall not listen to you, so that I may lay my hand upon Egypt and bring forth my armies, my people the children of Israel, out of the land of Egypt by great judgments. {7:5} "And the Egyptians shall know that I am the LORD when I stretch forth my hand upon Egypt and bring out the children of Israel from among them. {7:6} "So Moses and Aaron did as the LORD commanded them; thus they did. {7:7} "Moses was eighty years old, and Aaron eighty-three years old when they spoke to Pharaoh. {7:8} "Then the LORD spoke to Moses and Aaron, saying, {7:9} "When Pharaoh speaks to you, saying, 'Show a miracle for you,' then you shall say to Aaron, 'Take your rod and cast it before Pharaoh, and it shall become a serpent.' {7:10} "So Moses and Aaron went in to Pharaoh, and they did so as the LORD had commanded; and Aaron cast down his rod before Pharaoh, and before his servants, and it became a serpent. {7:11} "Then Pharaoh also called the wise men and the sorcerers; now the magicians of Egypt, they also did in like manner with their enchantments. {7:12} "For they cast down every man his rod, and they became serpents; but Aaron's rod swallowed up their rods. {7:13} "And he hardened Pharaoh's heart, so that he did not listen to them; as the LORD had said. {7:14} "Then the LORD said to Moses, 'Pharaoh's heart is hardened; he refuses to let the people go. {7:15} " 'Get yourself to Pharaoh in the morning; lo, he goes out to the water; and you shall stand by the river's brink against he comes; and the rod which was turned to a serpent you shall take in your hand. {7:16} " 'And you shall say to him, "The LORD God of the Hebrews has sent me to you, saying, 'Let my people go, that they may serve me in the wilderness:' but behold, hitherto you would not hear. {7:17} " 'Thus says the LORD, "In this you shall know that I am the LORD: behold, I will smite with the rod that is in my hand upon the waters which are in the river, and they shall be turned to blood. {7:18} " 'And the fish that is in the river shall die, and the river shall stink; and the Egyptians shall loathe to drink of the water of the river. {7:19} " 'And the LORD spoke to Moses, saying to Aaron, 'Take your rod, and stretch out your hand upon the waters of Egypt, upon their streams, upon their rivers, and upon their ponds, and upon all their pools of water, that they may become blood; and that there may be blood throughout all the land of Egypt, both in vessels of wood and in vessels of stone. {7:20} " 'So Moses and Aaron did so, as the LORD commanded; and he lifted up the rod, and smote the waters that were in the river, in the sight of Pharaoh, and in the sight of his servants; and all the waters that were in the river were turned to blood. {7:21} " 'And the fish that was in the river died; and the river stank, and the Egyptians could not drink of the water of the river; and there was blood throughout all the land of Egypt. {7:22} " 'And the magicians of Egypt did so with their enchantments; and Pharaoh's heart was hardened, neither did he listen to them; as the LORD had said. {7:23} " 'And Pharaoh turned and went into his house, neither did he set his heart to this also. {7:24} " 'And all the Egyptians dug round about the river for water to drink; for they could not drink of the water of the river. {7:25} " 'And seven days were fulfilled, after that the LORD had smitten the river.

{8:1} Then the LORD spoke to Moses, "Go to Pharaoh and say to him, 'Thus says the LORD: Let my people go, that they may serve me.' {8:2} "And if you refuse to let them go, behold, I will smite all your borders with frogs: {8:3} "And the river shall bring forth frogs abundantly, which shall go up and come into your house, and into your bedroom, and upon your bed, and into the houses of your servants, and upon your people, and into your ovens, and into your kneading troughs. {8:4} "And the frogs shall come up both on you, and upon your people, and upon all your servants. {8:5} "Then the LORD spoke to Moses, saying, 'Say to Aaron, "Stretch forth your hand with your rod over the streams, over the rivers, and over the ponds, and cause frogs to come up upon the land of Egypt." {8:6} "And Aaron stretched out his hand over the waters of Egypt; and the frogs came up, and covered the land of Egypt. {8:7} "And the magicians did so with their enchantments, and brought up frogs upon the land of Egypt. {8:8} "Then Pharaoh called for Moses and Aaron, and said, 'Entreat the LORD, that he may take away the frogs from me, and from my people; and I will let the people go, that they may do sacrifice unto the LORD.' {8:9} "And Moses said to Pharaoh, 'Glory over me: when shall I entreat for you, and for your servants, and for your people, to destroy the frogs from you and your houses, [that] they may remain in the river only?' {8:10} "And he said, 'Tomorrow.' And he said, '[Be it] according to your word: that you may know that [there is] none like unto the LORD our God.' {8:11} "And the frogs shall depart from you, and from your houses, and from your servants, and from your people; they shall remain in the river only. {8:12} "And Moses and Aaron went out from Pharaoh: and Moses cried unto the LORD because of the frogs which he had brought against Pharaoh. {8:13} "And the LORD did according to the word of Moses; and the frogs died out of the houses, out of the villages, and out of the fields. {8:14} "And they gathered them together upon heaps: and the land stank. {8:15} "But when Pharaoh saw that there was respite, he hardened his heart, and did not listen to them; as the LORD had said. {8:16} "And the LORD said to Moses, 'Say to Aaron, Stretch out your rod, and smite the dust of the land, that it may become lice throughout all the land of Egypt.' {8:17} "And they did so; for Aaron stretched out his hand with his rod, and smote the dust of the earth, and it became lice in man, and in beast; all the dust of the land became lice throughout all the land of Egypt. {8:18} "And the magicians did so with their enchantments to bring forth lice, but they could not: so there were lice upon man, and upon beast. {8:19} "Then the magicians said to Pharaoh, 'This is the finger of God:' and Pharaoh's heart was hardened, and he did not listen to them; as the LORD had said. {8:20} "And the LORD said to Moses, 'Rise up early in the morning, and stand before Pharaoh; lo, he comes forth to the water; and say to him, "Thus says the LORD: Let my people go, that they may serve me." {8:21} " 'Else, if you will not let my people go, behold, I will send swarms [of flies] upon you, and upon your servants, and upon your people, and into your houses: and the houses of the Egyptians shall be full of swarms [of flies], and also the ground whereon they [are.] {8:22} " 'And I will sever in that day the land of Goshen, in which my people dwell, that no swarms [of flies] shall be there; to the end you may know that I am the LORD in the midst of the earth. {8:23} " 'And I will put a division between my people and your people: tomorrow shall this sign be. {8:24} " 'And the LORD did so; and there came a grievous swarm [of flies] into the house of Pharaoh, and [into] his servants' houses, and into all the land of Egypt: the land was corrupted by reason of the swarm [of flies.] {8:25} "And Pharaoh called for Moses and Aaron, and said, 'Go ye, sacrifice to your God in the land.' {8:26} "And Moses said, 'It is not meet so to do; for we shall sacrifice the abomination of the Egyptians to the LORD our God: lo, shall we sacrifice the abomination of the Egyptians before their eyes, and will they not stone us? {8:27} " 'We will go three days' journey into the wilderness, and sacrifice to the LORD our God, as he shall command us.' {8:28} "And Pharaoh said, 'I will let you go, that ye may sacrifice to the LORD your God in the wilderness; only ye shall not go very far away: intreat for me.' {8:29} "And Moses said, 'Behold, I go out from thee, and I will intreat the LORD that the swarms [of flies] may depart from Pharaoh, from his servants, and from his people, tomorrow: but let not Pharaoh deal deceitfully any more in not letting the people go to sacrifice to the LORD.' {8:30} "And Moses went out from Pharaoh, and entreated the LORD. {8:31} "And the LORD did according to the word of Moses; and he removed the swarms [of flies] from Pharaoh, from his servants, and from his people; there remained not one. {8:32} "And Pharaoh hardened his heart at this time also, neither would he let the people go."

{9:1} Then the LORD said to Moses, "Go to Pharaoh, and tell him, 'Thus says the LORD God of the Hebrews: Let my people go, that they may serve me.' {9:2} "For if you refuse to let them go, and will hold them still, {9:3} "Behold, the hand of the LORD is upon your cattle which is in the field, upon the horses, upon the donkeys, upon the camels, upon the oxen, and upon the sheep: there shall be a very grievous murrain. {9:4} "And the LORD shall sever between the cattle of Israel and the cattle of Egypt: and there shall nothing die of all that is the children's of Israel. {9:5} "And the LORD appointed a set time, saying, 'Tomorrow the LORD shall do this thing in the land.' {9:6} "And the LORD did that thing on the morrow, and all the cattle of Egypt died: but of the cattle of the children of Israel died not one. {9:7} "And Pharaoh sent, and, behold, there was not one of the cattle of the Israelites dead. And the heart of Pharaoh was hardened, and he did not let the people go. {9:8} "Then the LORD said to Moses and Aaron, 'Take you two handfuls of ashes of the furnace, and let Moses sprinkle it toward the heaven in the sight of Pharaoh. {9:9} "And it shall become small dust in all the land of Egypt, and shall be a boil breaking forth with blains upon man, and upon beast, throughout all the land of Egypt. {9:10} "And they took ashes of the furnace, and stood before Pharaoh; and Moses sprinkled it up toward heaven; and it became a boil breaking forth with blains upon man, and upon beast. {9:11} "And the magicians could not stand before Moses because of the boils; for the boil was upon the magicians, and upon all the Egyptians. {9:12} "And the LORD hardened the heart of Pharaoh, and he did not listen to them; as the LORD had spoken to Moses. {9:13} "And the LORD said to Moses, 'Rise up early in the morning, and stand before Pharaoh, and say to him, "Thus says the LORD God of the Hebrews: Let my people go, that they may serve me. {9:14} "For I will at this time send all my plagues upon your heart, and upon your servants, and upon your people; that you may know that there is none like me in all the earth. {9:15} "For now I will stretch out my hand, that I may smite you and your people with pestilence; and you shall be cut off from the earth. {9:16} "And in very deed for this cause have I raised you up, for to show in you my power; and that my name may be declared throughout all the earth. {9:17} "As yet exaltest you yourself against my people, that you will not let them go? {9:18} "Behold, tomorrow about this time I will cause it to rain a very grievous hail, such as has not been in Egypt since the foundation thereof even until now. {9:19} "Send therefore now, and gather your cattle, and all that you have in the field; for upon every man and beast which shall be found in the field, and shall not be brought home, the hail shall come down upon them, and they shall die. {9:20} "He that feared the word of the LORD among the servants of Pharaoh made his servants and his cattle flee into the houses: {9:21} "And he that regarded not the word of the LORD left his servants and his cattle in the field. {9:22} "And the LORD said to Moses, 'Stretch forth your hand toward heaven, that there may be hail in all the land of Egypt, upon man, and upon beast, and upon every herb of the field, throughout the land of Egypt. {9:23} "And Moses stretched forth his rod toward heaven: and the LORD sent thunder and hail, and the fire ran along upon the ground; and the LORD rained hail upon the land of Egypt. {9:24} "So there was hail, and fire mingled with the hail, very grievous, such as there was none like it in all the land of Egypt since it became a nation. {9:25} "And the hail smote throughout all the land of Egypt all that was in the field, both man and beast; and the hail smote every herb of the field, and broke every tree of the field. {9:26} "Only in the land of Goshen, where the children of Israel were, was there no hail. {9:27} "And Pharaoh sent, and called for Moses and Aaron, and said to them, 'I have sinned this time: the LORD is righteous, and I and my people are wicked. {9:28} " 'Entreat the LORD (for it is enough) that there be no more mighty thunderings and hail; and I will let you go, and you shall stay no longer. {9:29} "And Moses said to him, 'As soon as I am gone out of the city, I will spread abroad my hands unto the LORD; and the thunder shall cease, neither shall there be any more hail; that you may know how that the earth is the LORD'S. {9:30} " 'But as for you and your servants, I know that you will not yet fear the LORD God. {9:31} "And the flax and the barley were smitten: for the barley was in the ear, and the flax was bolled. {9:32} "But the wheat and the rye were not smitten: for they were not grown up. {9:33} "And Moses went out of the city from Pharaoh, and spread abroad his hands unto the LORD: and the thunders and hail ceased, and the rain was not poured upon the earth. {9:34} "And when Pharaoh saw that the rain and the hail and the thunders were ceased, he sinned yet more, and hardened his heart, he and his servants. {9:35} "And the heart of Pharaoh was hardened, neither would he let the children of Israel go; as the LORD had spoken by Moses."

{10:1} "And the LORD said unto Moses, Go in unto Pharaoh: for I have hardened his heart, and the heart of his servants, that I might show these my signs before him: {10:2} "And that thou mayest tell in the ears of thy son, and of thy son's son, what things I have wrought in Egypt, and my signs which I have done among them; that ye may know how that I am the LORD. {10:3} "And Moses and Aaron came in unto Pharaoh, and said unto him, Thus saith the LORD God of the Hebrews, How long wilt thou refuse to humble thyself before me? let my people go, that they may serve me. {10:4} "Else, if thou refuse to let my people go, behold, tomorrow will I bring the locusts into thy coast: {10:5} "And they shall cover the face of the earth, that one cannot be able to see the earth: and they shall eat the residue of that which is escaped, which remaineth unto you from the hail, and shall eat every tree which groweth for you out of the field: {10:6} "And they shall fill thy houses, and the houses of all thy servants, and the houses of all the Egyptians; which neither thy fathers, nor thy fathers' fathers have seen, since the day that they were upon the earth unto this day. And he turned himself, and went out from Pharaoh. {10:7} "And Pharaoh's servants said unto him, How long shall this man be a snare unto us? let the men go, that they may serve the LORD their God: knowest thou not yet that Egypt is destroyed? {10:8} "And Moses and Aaron were brought again unto Pharaoh: and he said unto them, Go, serve the LORD your God: but who are they that shall go? {10:9} "And Moses said, We will go with our young and with our old, with our sons and with our daughters, with our flocks and with our herds will we go; for we must hold a feast unto the LORD. {10:10} "And he said unto them, Let the LORD be so with you, as I will let you go, and your little ones: look to it; for evil is before you. {10:11} "Not so: go now ye that are men, and serve the LORD; for that ye did desire. And they were driven out from Pharaoh's presence. {10:12} "And the LORD said unto Moses, Stretch out thine hand over the land of Egypt for the locusts, that they may come up upon the land of Egypt, and eat every herb of the land, even all that the hail hath left. {10:13} "And Moses stretched forth his rod over the land of Egypt, and the LORD brought an east wind upon the land all that day, and all that night; and when it was morning, the east wind brought the locusts. {10:14} "And the locusts went up over all the land of Egypt, and rested in all the coasts of Egypt: very grievous were they; before them there were no such locusts as they, neither after them shall be such. {10:15} "For they covered the face of the whole earth, so that the land was darkened; and they did eat every herb of the land, and all the fruit of the trees which the hail had left: and there remained not any green thing in the trees, or in the herbs of the field, through all the land of Egypt. {10:16} "Then Pharaoh called for Moses and Aaron in haste; and he said, I have sinned against the LORD your God, and against you. {10:17} "Now therefore forgive, I pray thee, my sin only this once, and entreat the LORD your God, that he may take away from me this death only. {10:18} "And he went out from Pharaoh, and entreated the LORD. {10:19} "And the LORD turned a mighty strong west wind, which took away the locusts, and cast them into the Red Sea; there remained not one locust in all the coasts of Egypt. {10:20} "But the LORD hardened Pharaoh's heart, so that he would not let the children of Israel go. {10:21} "And the LORD said unto Moses, Stretch out thine hand toward heaven, that there may be darkness over the land of Egypt, even darkness which may be felt. {10:22} "And Moses stretched forth his hand toward heaven; and there was a thick darkness in all the land of Egypt three days: {10:23} "They saw not one another, neither rose any from his place for three days: but all the children of Israel had light in their dwellings. {10:24} "And Pharaoh called unto Moses, and said, Go ye, serve the LORD; only let your flocks and your herds be stayed: let your little ones also go with you. {10:25} "And Moses said, Thou must give us also sacrifices and burnt offerings, that we may sacrifice unto the LORD our God. {10:26} "Our cattle also shall go with us; there shall not an hoof be left behind; for thereof must we take to serve the LORD our God; and we know not with what we must serve the LORD, until we come thither. {10:27} "But the LORD hardened Pharaoh's heart, and he would not let them go. {10:28} "And Pharaoh said unto him, Get thee from me, take heed to thyself, see my face no more; for in that day thou seest my face thou shalt die. {10:29} "And Moses said, Thou hast spoken well, I will see thy face again no more."

{11:1} "And the LORD said unto Moses, Yet will I bring one plague more upon Pharaoh, and upon Egypt; afterwards he will let you go hence: when he shall let you go, he shall surely thrust you out hence altogether. {11:2} "Speak now in the ears of the people, and let every man borrow of his neighbour, and every woman of her neighbour, jewels of silver, and jewels of gold. {11:3} "And the LORD gave the people favour in the sight of the Egyptians. Moreover, the man Moses was very great in the land of Egypt, in the sight of Pharaoh's servants, and in the sight of the people. {11:4} "And Moses said, Thus saith the LORD, About midnight will I go out into the midst of Egypt: {11:5} "And all the firstborn in the land of Egypt shall die, from the firstborn of Pharaoh that sitteth upon his throne, even unto the firstborn of the maidservant that is behind the mill; and all the firstborn of beasts. {11:6} "And there shall be a great cry throughout all the land of Egypt, such as there was none like it, nor shall be like it any more. {11:7} "But against any of the children of Israel shall not a dog move his tongue, against man or beast: that ye may know how that the LORD doth put a difference between the Egyptians and Israel. {11:8} "And all these thy servants shall come down unto me, and bow down themselves unto me, saying, Get thee out, and all the people that follow thee: and after that I will go out. And he went out from Pharaoh in a great anger. {11:9} "And the LORD said unto Moses, Pharaoh shall not hearken unto you; that my wonders may be multiplied in the land of Egypt. {11:10} "And Moses and Aaron did all these wonders before Pharaoh: and the LORD hardened Pharaoh's heart, so that he would not let the children of Israel go out of his land."

{12:1} *"And the LORD spake unto Moses and Aaron in the land of Egypt, saying,* {12:2} *"This month shall be unto you the beginning of months: it shall be the first month of the year to you.* {12:3} "Speak ye unto all the congregation of Israel, saying, In the tenth day of this month they shall take to them every man a lamb, according to the house of their fathers, a lamb for a house: {12:4} "And if the household be too little for the lamb, let him and his neighbour next unto his house take it according to the number of the souls; every man according to his eating shall make your count for the lamb. {12:5} "Your lamb shall be without blemish, a male of the first year: ye shall take it out from the sheep, or from the goats: {12:6} "And ye shall keep it up until the fourteenth day of the same month: and the whole assembly of the congregation of Israel shall kill it in the evening. {12:7} "And they shall take of the blood, and strike it on the two side posts and on the upper door post of the houses, wherein they shall eat it. {12:8} "And they shall eat the flesh in that night, roast with fire, and unleavened bread; and with bitter herbs they shall eat it. {12:9} "Eat not of it raw, nor sodden at all with water, but roast with fire; his head with his legs, and with the purtenance thereof. {12:10} "And ye shall let nothing of it remain until the morning; and that which remaineth of it until the morning ye shall burn with fire. {12:11} "And thus shall ye eat it; with your loins girded, your shoes on your feet, and your staff in your hand; and ye shall eat it in haste: it is the LORD'S passover. {12:12} "For I will pass through the land of Egypt this night, and will smite all the firstborn in the land of Egypt, both man and beast; and against all the gods of Egypt I will execute judgment: I am the LORD. {12:13} "And the blood shall be to you for a token upon the houses where ye are: and when I see the blood, I will pass over you, and the plague shall not be upon you to destroy you, when I smite the land of Egypt. {12:14} "And this day shall be unto you for a memorial; and ye shall keep it a feast to the LORD throughout your generations; ye shall keep it a feast by an ordinance for ever. {12:15} "Seven days shall ye eat unleavened bread; even the first day ye shall put away leaven out of your houses: for whosoever eateth leavened bread from the first day until the seventh day, that soul shall be cut off from Israel. {12:16} "And in the first day there shall be an holy convocation, and in the seventh day there shall be an holy convocation to you; no manner of work shall be done in them, save that which every man must eat, that only may be done of you. {12:17} "And ye shall observe the feast of unleavened bread; for in this selfsame day have I brought your armies out of the land of Egypt: therefore shall ye observe this day in your generations by an ordinance for ever. {12:18} "In the first month, on the fourteenth day of the month at even, ye shall eat unleavened bread, until the one and twentieth day of the month at even. {12:19} "Seven days shall there be no leaven found in your houses: for whosoever eateth that which is leavened, even that soul shall be cut off from the congregation of Israel, whether he be a stranger, or born in the land. {12:20} "Ye shall eat nothing leavened; in all your habitations shall ye eat unleavened bread. {12:21} "Then Moses called for all the elders of Israel, and said unto them, Draw out and take you a lamb according to your families, and kill the passover. {12:22} "And ye shall take a bunch of hyssop, and dip it in the blood that is in the basin, and strike the lintel and the two side posts with the blood that is in the basin; and none of you shall go out at the door of his house until the morning. {12:23} "For the LORD will pass through to smite the Egyptians; and when he seeth the blood upon the lintel, and on the two side posts, the LORD will pass over the door, and will not suffer the destroyer to come in unto your houses to smite you. {12:24} "And ye shall observe this thing for an ordinance to thee and to thy sons for ever. {12:25} "And it shall come to pass, when ye be come to the land which the LORD will give you, according as he hath promised, that ye shall keep this service. {12:26} "And it shall come to pass, when your children shall say unto you, What mean ye by this service? {12:26} "And it shall come to pass, when your children shall say unto you, What mean ye by this service? {12:27} "That ye shall say, It is the sacrifice of the LORD'S passover, who passed over the houses of the children of Israel in Egypt, when he smote the Egyptians, and delivered our houses. And the people bowed the head and worshipped. {12:28} "And the children of Israel went away, and did as the LORD had commanded Moses and Aaron, so did they. {12:29} "And it came to pass, that at midnight the LORD smote all the firstborn in the land of Egypt, from the firstborn of Pharaoh that sat on his throne unto the firstborn of the captive that was in the dungeon; and all the firstborn of cattle. {12:30} "And Pharaoh rose up in the night, he, and all his servants, and all the Egyptians; and there was a great cry in Egypt; for there was not a house where there was not one dead. {12:31} "And he called for Moses and Aaron by night, and said, Rise up, and get you forth from among my people, both ye and the children of Israel; and go, serve the LORD, as ye have said. {12:32} "Also take your flocks and your herds, as ye have said, and be gone; and bless me also. {12:33} "And the Egyptians were urgent upon the people, that they might send them out of the land in haste; for they said, We be all dead men. {12:34} "And the people took their dough before it was leavened, their kneadingtroughs being bound up in their clothes upon their shoulders. {12:35} "And the children of Israel did according to the word of Moses; and they borrowed of the Egyptians jewels of silver, and jewels of gold, and raiment: {12:36} "And the LORD gave the people favour in the sight of the Egyptians, so that they lent unto them such things as they required. And they spoiled the Egyptians. {12:37} "And the children of Israel journeyed from Rameses to Succoth, about six hundred thousand on foot that were men, beside children. {12:38} "And a mixed multitude went up also with them; and flocks, and herds, even very much cattle. {12:39} "And they baked unleavened cakes of the dough which they brought forth out of Egypt, for it was not leavened; because they were thrust out of Egypt, and could not tarry, neither had they prepared for themselves any victual. {12:40} "Now the sojourning of the children of Israel, who dwelt in Egypt, was four hundred and thirty years. {12:41} "And it came to pass at the end of the four hundred and thirty years, even the selfsame day it came to pass, that all the hosts of the LORD went out from the land of Egypt. {12:42} "It is a night to be much observed unto the LORD for bringing them out from the land of Egypt: this is that night of the LORD to be observed of all the children of Israel in their generations. {12:43} "And the LORD said unto Moses and Aaron, This is the ordinance of the passover: There shall no stranger eat thereof: {12:44} "But every man's servant that is bought for money, when thou hast circumcised him, then shall he eat thereof. {12:45} "A foreigner and an hired servant shall not eat thereof. {12:46} "In one house shall it be eaten; thou shalt not carry forth ought of the flesh abroad out of the house; neither shall ye break a bone thereof. {12:47} "All the congregation of Israel shall keep it. {12:48} "And when a stranger shall sojourn with thee, and will keep the passover to the LORD, let all his males be circumcised, and then let him come near and keep it; and he shall be as one that is born in the land: for no uncircumcised person shall eat thereof. {12:49} "One law shall be to him that is homeborn, and unto the stranger that sojourneth among you. {12:50} "Thus did all the children of Israel; as the LORD commanded Moses and Aaron, so did they. {12:51} "And it came to pass the selfsame day, that the LORD did bring the children of Israel out of the land of Egypt by their armies."

{13:1} And the LORD spoke unto Moses, saying, {13:2} "Set apart for me all the firstborn males, both man and beast, for they belong to me. {13:3} Moses said to the people, "Remember this day, when you came out of Egypt, out of the house of slavery. The LORD brought you out with a mighty hand; therefore, no leavened bread shall be eaten. {13:4} This day marks the beginning of the month Abib. {13:5} When the LORD brings you into the land of the Canaanites, Hittites, Amorites, Hivites, and Jebusites, the land he swore to give your ancestors, a land flowing with milk and honey, you must observe this ceremony in this month. {13:6} For seven days you shall eat unleavened bread, and on the seventh day, there shall be a feast to the LORD. {13:7} Unleavened bread shall be eaten for seven days; no leavened bread shall be seen anywhere, nor shall there be any yeast within your borders. {13:8} You shall tell your son on that day, 'This is because of what the LORD did for me when I came out of Egypt.' {13:9} This observance shall be a sign on your hand and a reminder between your eyes, so that the instructions of the LORD may be in your mouth; for with a mighty hand, the LORD brought you out of Egypt. {13:10} You shall keep this ordinance at the appointed time from year to year. {13:11} When the LORD brings you into the land of the Canaanites, as he swore to you and your ancestors, you must dedicate to the LORD every firstborn male from both man and beast; they belong to the LORD. {13:12} Every firstborn male of an ass you shall redeem with a lamb, or if you do not redeem it, you must break its neck. And all the firstborn of your children you shall redeem. {13:13} And when your son asks you in the future, 'What does this mean?' you shall say to him, 'By a mighty hand, the LORD brought us out of Egypt, out of the house of slavery. {13:14} And when Pharaoh stubbornly refused to let us go, the LORD killed all the firstborn in Egypt, both man and beast. That is why I sacrifice to the LORD the first male offspring of every womb, but redeem all the firstborn of my sons.' {13:15} This observance shall be a sign on your hand and a symbol on your forehead that by a mighty hand the LORD brought us out of Egypt." {13:16} When Pharaoh let the people go, God did not lead them along the road through the land of the Philistines, though that was shorter. For God said, "If they face war, they might change their minds and return to Egypt." {13:17} So God led the people around by the desert road toward the Red Sea. The Israelites went up out of Egypt ready for battle. {13:18} Moses took the bones of Joseph with him because Joseph had made the Israelites swear an oath. He had said, "God will surely come to your aid, and then you must carry my bones up with you from this place." {13:19} After leaving Succoth they camped at Etham on the edge of the desert. {13:20} By day the LORD went ahead of them in a pillar of cloud to guide them on their way and by night in a pillar of fire to give them light, so that they could travel by day or night. {13:21} During the day, the LORD went ahead of them in a pillar of cloud to guide them on their way, and at night in a pillar of fire to give them light, so they could travel day and night. {13:22} The pillar of cloud by day and the pillar of fire by night did not depart from their place in front of the people.

{14:1} Then the LORD spoke to Moses, saying, {14:2} "Tell the children of Israel to turn and camp before Pi-hahiroth, between Migdol and the sea, opposite Baal-zephon; you shall camp by the sea. {14:3} For Pharaoh will say of the children of Israel, 'They are bewildered by the land; the wilderness has closed them in.' {14:4} And I will harden Pharaoh's heart, so that he will pursue them; and I will gain honor over Pharaoh and over all his army, that the Egyptians may know that I am the LORD." So they did. {14:5} Now it was told the king of Egypt that the people had fled, and the heart of Pharaoh and his servants was turned against the people; and they said, "Why have we done this, that we have let Israel go from serving us?" {14:6} So he made ready his chariot and took his people with him. {14:7} Also, he took six hundred choice chariots, and all the chariots of Egypt with captains over every one of them. {14:8} And the LORD hardened the heart of Pharaoh king of Egypt, and he pursued the children of Israel; and the children of Israel went out with boldness. {14:9} So the Egyptians pursued them, all the horses and chariots of Pharaoh, his horsemen and his army, and overtook them camping by the sea beside Pi-hahiroth, before Baal Zephon. {14:10} And when Pharaoh drew near, the children of Israel lifted their eyes, and behold, the Egyptians marched after them. So they were very afraid, and the children of Israel cried out to the LORD. {14:11} Then they said to Moses, "Because there were no graves in Egypt, have you taken us away to die in the wilderness? Why have you so dealt with us, to bring us up out of Egypt? {14:12} Is this not the word that we told you in Egypt, saying, 'Let us alone that we may serve the Egyptians?' For it would have been better for us to serve the Egyptians than that we should die in the wilderness." {14:13} And Moses said to the people, "Do not be afraid. Stand still, and see the salvation of the LORD, which He will accomplish for you today. For the Egyptians whom you see today, you shall see again no more forever. {14:14} The LORD will fight for you, and you shall hold your peace." {14:15} And the LORD said to Moses, "Why do you cry to Me? Tell the children of Israel to go forward. {14:16} But lift up your rod, and stretch out your hand over the sea and divide it. And the children of Israel shall go on dry ground through the midst of the sea. {14:17} And I indeed will harden the hearts of the Egyptians, and they shall follow them. So I will gain honor over Pharaoh and over all his army, his chariots, and his horsemen. {14:18} Then the Egyptians shall know that I am the LORD, when I have gained honor for Myself over Pharaoh, his chariots, and his horsemen." {14:19} And the Angel of God, who went before the camp of Israel, moved and went behind them; and the pillar of cloud went from before them and stood behind them. {14:20} So it came between the camp of the Egyptians and the camp of Israel. Thus it was a cloud and darkness to the one, and it gave light by night to the other, so that the one did not come near the other all that night. {14:21} **Then Moses stretched out his hand over the sea; and the LORD caused the sea to go back by a strong east wind all that night, and made the sea into dry land, and the waters were divided.** {14:22} **So the children of Israel went into the midst of the sea on the dry ground, and the waters were a wall to them on their right hand and on their left.** {14:23} And the Egyptians pursued and went after them into the midst of the sea, all Pharaoh's horses, his chariots, and his horsemen. {14:24} Now it came to pass, in the morning watch, that the LORD looked down upon the army of the Egyptians through the pillar of fire and cloud, and He troubled the army of the Egyptians. {14:25} And He took off their chariot wheels, so that they drove them with difficulty; and the Egyptians said, "Let us flee from the face of Israel, for the LORD fights for them against the Egyptians." {14:26} Then the LORD said to Moses, "Stretch out your hand over the sea, that the waters may come back upon the Egyptians, on their chariots, and on their horsemen." {14:27} And Moses stretched out his hand over the sea; and when the morning appeared, the sea returned to its full depth, while the Egyptians were fleeing into it. So the LORD overthrew the Egyptians in the midst of the sea. {14:28} Then the waters returned and covered the chariots, the horsemen, and all the army of Pharaoh that came into the sea after them. Not so much as one of them remained. {14:29} But the children of Israel had walked on dry land in the midst of the sea, and the waters were a wall to them on their right hand and on their left. {14:30} So the LORD saved Israel that day out of the hand of the Egyptians, and Israel saw the Egyptians dead on the seashore. {14:31} Thus Israel saw the great work which the LORD had done in Egypt; so the people feared the LORD, and believed the LORD and His servant Moses.

{15:1} Moses and the Israelites sang this song to the LORD, saying: "I will sing to the LORD, for he has triumphed gloriously; he has thrown the horse and its rider into the sea. {15:2} The LORD is my strength and song, and he has become my salvation. He is my God, and I will praise him; my father's God, and I will exalt him. {15:3} The LORD is a warrior; the LORD is his name. {15:4} Pharaoh's chariots and his army he has hurled into the sea. The best of Pharaoh's officers are drowned in the Red Sea. {15:5} The deep waters have covered them; they sank to the depths like a stone. {15:6} Your right hand, LORD, was majestic in power. Your right hand, LORD, shattered the enemy. {15:7} In the greatness of your majesty you threw down those who opposed you. You unleashed your burning anger; it consumed them like stubble. {15:8} By the blast of your nostrils the waters piled up. The surging waters stood up like a wall; the deep waters congealed in the heart of the sea. {15:9} The enemy boasted, 'I will pursue, I will overtake them. I will divide the spoils; I will gorge myself on them. I will draw my sword and my hand will destroy them.' {15:10} But you blew with your breath, and the sea covered them. They sank like lead in the mighty waters. {15:11} Who among the gods is like you, LORD? Who is like you — majestic in holiness, awesome in glory, working wonders? {15:12} You stretch out your right hand, and the earth swallows your enemies. {15:13} In your unfailing love you will lead the people you have redeemed. In your strength you will guide them to your holy dwelling. {15:14} The nations will hear and tremble; anguish will grip the people of Philistia. {15:15} The chiefs of Edom will be terrified, the leaders of Moab will be seized with trembling, the people of Canaan will melt away; {15:16} terror and dread will fall on them. By the power of your arm they will be as still as a stone — until your people pass by, LORD, until the people you bought pass by. {15:17} You will bring them in and plant them on the mountain of your inheritance — the place, LORD, you made for your dwelling, the sanctuary, Lord, your hands established. {15:18} The LORD reigns for ever and ever." {15:19} When Pharaoh's horses, chariots and horsemen went into the sea, the LORD brought the waters of the sea back over them, but the Israelites walked through the sea on dry ground. {15:20} Then Miriam the prophet, Aaron's sister, took a timbrel in her hand, and all the women followed her, with timbrels and dancing. {15:21} Miriam sang to them: "Sing to the LORD, for he is highly exalted. Both horse and driver he has hurled into the sea." {15:22} Moses led Israel from the Red Sea and they went into the Desert of Shur. For three days they traveled in the desert without finding water. {15:23} When they came to Marah, they could not drink its water because it was bitter. (That is why the place is called Marah.) {15:24} So the people grumbled against Moses, saying, "What are we to drink?" {15:25} Then Moses cried out to the LORD, and the LORD showed him a piece of wood. He threw it into the water, and the water became fit to drink. There the LORD issued a ruling and instruction for them and put them to the test. {15:26} He said, "If you listen carefully to the LORD your God and do what is right in his eyes, if you pay attention to his commands and keep all his decrees, I will not bring on you any of the diseases I brought on the Egyptians, for I am the LORD, who heals you." {15:27} Then they came to Elim, where there were twelve springs and seventy palm trees, and they camped there near the water.

{16:1} They journeyed from Elim, and the whole Israelite community came to the Desert of Sin, which is between Elim and Sinai, on the fifteenth day of the second month after they had come out of Egypt. {16:2} The entire Israelite community grumbled against Moses and Aaron in the wilderness. {16:3} The Israelites said to them, "If only we had died by the LORD's hand in Egypt! There we sat around pots of meat and ate all the food we wanted, but you have brought us out into this desert to starve this entire assembly to death." {16:4} Then the LORD said to Moses, "I will rain down bread from heaven for you. The people are to go out each day and gather enough for that day. In this way, I will test them and see whether they will follow my instructions. {16:5} On the sixth day, they are to prepare what they bring in, and that is to be twice as much as they gather on the other days." {16:6} So Moses and Aaron said to all the Israelites, "In the evening you will know that it was the LORD who brought you out of Egypt, {16:7} and in the morning you will see the glory of the LORD, because he has heard your grumbling against him. Who are we, that you should grumble against us?" {16:8} Moses also said, "You will know that it was the LORD when he gives you meat to eat in the evening and all the bread you want in the morning because he has heard your grumbling against him. Who are we? You are not grumbling against us, but against the LORD." {16:9} Then Moses told Aaron, "Say to the entire Israelite community, 'Come before the LORD, for he has heard your grumbling.'" {16:10} While Aaron was speaking to the whole Israelite community, they looked toward the desert, and there was the glory of the LORD appearing in the cloud. {16:11} The LORD said to Moses, {16:12} "I have heard the grumbling of the Israelites. Tell them, 'At twilight you will eat meat, and in the morning you will be filled with bread. Then you will know that I am the LORD your God.'" {16:13} That evening quail came and covered the camp, and in the morning there was a layer of dew around the camp. {16:14} When the dew was gone, thin flakes like frost on the ground appeared on the desert floor. {16:15} When the Israelites saw it, they said to each other, "What is it?" For they did not know what it was. Moses said to them, "It is the bread the LORD has given you to eat. {16:16} This is what the LORD has commanded: 'Everyone is to gather as much as they need. Take an omer for each person you have in your tent.'" {16:17} The Israelites did as they were told; some gathered much, some little. {16:18} And when they measured it by the omer, the one who gathered much did not have too much, and the one who gathered little did not have too little. Everyone had gathered just as much as they needed. {16:19} Then Moses said to them, "No one is to keep any of it until morning." {16:20} However, some of them paid no attention to Moses;

they kept part of it until morning, but it was full of maggots and began to smell. So Moses was angry with them. {16:21} Each morning everyone gathered as much as they needed, and when the sun grew hot, it melted away. {16:22} On the sixth day, they gathered twice as much — two omers for each person — and the leaders of the community came and reported this to Moses. {16:23} He said to them, "This is what the LORD commanded: 'Tomorrow is to be a day of sabbath rest, a holy sabbath to the LORD. So bake what you want to bake and boil what you want to boil. Save whatever is left and keep it until morning.'" {16:24} So they saved it until morning, as Moses commanded, and it did not stink or get maggots in it. {16:25} "Eat it today," Moses said, "because today is a sabbath to the LORD. You will not find any of it on the ground today. {16:26} Six days you are to gather it, but on the seventh day, the Sabbath, there will not be any." {16:27} Nevertheless, some of the people went out on the seventh day to gather it, but they found none. {16:28} Then the LORD said to Moses, "How long will you refuse to keep my commands and my instructions? {16:29} Bear in mind that the LORD has given you the Sabbath; that is why on the sixth day he gives you bread for two days. Everyone is to stay where they are on the seventh day; no one is to go out." {16:30} So the people rested on the seventh day. {16:31} The people of Israel called the bread manna. It was white like coriander seed and tasted like wafers made with honey. {16:32} Moses said, "This is what the LORD has commanded: 'Take an omer of manna and keep it for the generations to come, so they can see the bread I gave you to eat in the wilderness when I brought you out of Egypt.'" {16:33} So Moses said to Aaron, "Take a jar and put an omer of manna in it. Then place it before the LORD to be kept for the generations to come." {16:34} As the LORD commanded Moses, Aaron put the manna with the tablets of the covenant law, so that it might be preserved. {16:35} **The Israelites ate manna for forty years, until they came to a land that was settled; they ate manna until they reached the border of Canaan.** {16:36} (An omer is one-tenth of an ephah.)

{17:1} The entire community of Israelites journeyed from the wilderness of Sin, following the LORD's command, and camped at Rephidim. But there was no water for the people to drink. {17:2} So the people quarreled with Moses and demanded, "Give us water to drink!" Moses replied, "Why are you quarreling with me? Why are you testing the LORD?" {17:3} The people were thirsty for water, and they complained to Moses, saying, "Why did you bring us up out of Egypt, just to kill us, our children, and our livestock with thirst?" {17:4} Moses cried out to the LORD, "What should I do with these people? They are ready to stone me!" {17:5} The LORD said to Moses, "Go on ahead of the people, taking with you some of the elders of Israel, and take in your hand the staff with which you struck the Nile. I will stand there before you by the rock at Horeb. Strike the rock, and water will come out of it for the people to drink." So Moses did this in the sight of the elders of Israel. {17:6} He named the place Massah and Meribah because the Israelites quarreled and because they tested the LORD saying, "Is the LORD among us or not?" {17:8} The Amalekites came and attacked the Israelites at Rephidim. {17:9} Moses said to Joshua, "Choose some of our men and go out to fight the Amalekites. Tomorrow I will stand on top of the hill with the staff of God in my hands." {17:10} So Joshua fought the Amalekites as Moses had ordered, while Moses, Aaron, and Hur went to the top of the hill. {17:11} As long as Moses held up his hands, the Israelites were winning, but whenever he lowered his hands, the Amalekites were winning. {17:12} When Moses' hands grew tired, they took a stone and put it under him, and he sat on it. Aaron and Hur held his hands up — one on one side, one on the other — so that his hands remained steady until sunset. {17:13} Joshua overwhelmed the Amalekite army with the sword. {17:14} Then the LORD said to Moses, "Write this on a scroll as something to be remembered and make sure that Joshua hears it, because I will completely blot out the name of Amalek from under heaven." {17:15} Moses built an altar and called it The LORD is my Banner. {17:16} He said, "Because hands were lifted up against the throne of the LORD, the LORD will be at war against the Amalekites from generation to generation."

{18:1} When Jethro, Moses' father-in-law and the priest of Midian, heard about all that God had done for Moses and for Israel his people, and how the LORD had brought Israel out of Egypt, {18:2} Jethro, Moses' father-in-law, took Zipporah, Moses' wife, after Moses had sent her back, {18:3} along with her two sons. One of the sons was named Gershom, for Moses said, "I have been a foreigner in a foreign land." The other son was named Eliezer, for Moses said, "The God of my father was my helper and delivered me from the sword of Pharaoh." {18:4} Jethro, Moses' father-in-law, along with Moses' wife and her two sons, came to Moses in the wilderness where he was camped at the mountain of God. {18:5} Jethro said to Moses, "I, your father-in-law Jethro, have come to you, along with your wife and her two sons." {18:7} Moses went out to meet his father-in-law, bowed down, and kissed him. They greeted each other and then went into the tent. {18:8} Moses told his father-in-law all that the LORD had done to Pharaoh and the Egyptians for Israel's sake, and all the hardships they had faced along the way, and how the LORD had delivered them. {18:9} Jethro rejoiced over all the goodness the LORD had shown to Israel, rescuing them from the hand of the Egyptians. {18:10} Jethro exclaimed, "Blessed be the LORD, who has delivered you from the hand of the Egyptians and from Pharaoh, and who has rescued the people from under the hand of the Egyptians. {18:11} Now I know that the LORD is greater than all gods because he triumphed where they were arrogant." {18:12} Then Jethro, Moses' father-in-law, brought a burnt offering and sacrifices to God, and Aaron came with all the elders of Israel to eat bread with Moses' father-in-law before God. {18:13} The next day, Moses sat as judge for the people, and the people stood around him from morning until evening. {18:14} When Moses' father-in-law saw all that he was doing for the people, he asked, "What is this you are doing for the people? Why do you sit alone, with all the people standing around you from morning until evening?" {18:15} Moses replied, "Because the people come to me to inquire of God. {18:16} Whenever they have a dispute, they come to me, and I judge between one person and another, and I make known the statutes of God and his laws." {18:17} Moses' father-in-law said to him, "What you are doing is not good. {18:18} You and these people who come to you will wear yourselves out. The task is too heavy for you; you cannot handle it alone. {18:19} Now listen to me; I will give you advice, and God be with you. You must represent the people before God and bring their disputes to him. {18:20} Teach them the decrees and laws, and show them the way to live and the duties they are to perform. {18:21} But select capable men from all the people — men who fear God, trustworthy men who hate dishonest gain — and appoint them as officials over thousands, hundreds, fifties, and tens. {18:22} Have them serve as judges for the people at all times, but have them bring every difficult case to you; the simple cases they can decide themselves. That will make your load lighter, because they will share it with you. {18:23} If you do this and God so commands, you will be able to stand the strain, and all these people will go home satisfied." {18:24} Moses listened to his father-in-law and did everything he said. {18:25} Moses chose capable men from all Israel and made them leaders of the people — officials over thousands, hundreds, fifties, and tens. {18:26} They served as judges for the people at all times. The difficult cases they brought to Moses, but the simple ones they decided themselves. {18:27} Then Moses let his father-in-law depart, and he went on his way back to his own land.

{19:1} In the third month after the Israelites had left Egypt, they arrived at the wilderness of Sinai on the same day. {19:2} They had journeyed from Rephidim and had set up camp in the wilderness near Mount Sinai. {19:3} Moses went up to God, and the LORD called to him from the mountain, saying, "Tell the house of Jacob and the Israelites: {19:4} You have seen what I did to the Egyptians, how I carried you on eagles' wings and brought you to myself. {19:5} Now if you will indeed obey my voice and keep my covenant, you will be a special treasure to me above all people, for all the earth is mine. {19:6} You will be a kingdom of priests and a holy nation. These are the words you must speak to the Israelites." {19:7} Moses called the elders of the people and laid before them all the words that the LORD had commanded him. {19:8} All the people answered together, saying, "Everything the LORD has spoken, we will do." Then Moses relayed the words of the people to the LORD. {19:9} The LORD said to Moses, "I will come to you in a thick cloud so that the people may hear when I speak with you and believe you forever." Moses told the words of the people to the LORD. {19:10} The LORD said to Moses, "Go to the people and sanctify them today and tomorrow, and let them wash their clothes. {19:11} Be ready by the third day, for on the third day the LORD will come down upon Mount Sinai in the sight of all the people. {19:12} You shall set bounds for the people all around, saying, 'Be careful not to go up on the mountain or touch its base. Whoever touches the mountain shall surely be put to death. {19:13} No hand shall touch him, but he shall surely be stoned or shot with an arrow; whether man or beast, he shall not live.' When the trumpet sounds a long blast, they shall come up to the mountain." {19:14} Moses went down from the mountain to the people and sanctified them, and they washed their clothes. {19:15} He said to the people, "Be ready for the third day. Do not approach your wives." {19:16} On the morning of the third day, there were thunders and lightnings, and a thick cloud covered the mountain, and the sound of a trumpet was very loud, so that all the people in the camp trembled. {19:17} Moses brought the people out of the camp to meet God, and they took their stand at the foot of the mountain. {19:18} Mount Sinai was covered in smoke because the LORD descended on it in fire, and the smoke rose like the smoke of a furnace, and the whole mountain trembled violently. {19:19} As the sound of the trumpet grew louder and louder, Moses spoke, and God answered him in a voice. {19:20} The LORD descended on Mount Sinai to the top of the mountain, and the

LORD called Moses to the top. So Moses went up. {19:21} The LORD said to Moses, "Go down and warn the people not to break through to see the LORD, lest many of them perish. {19:22} Also let the priests who come near to the LORD consecrate themselves, lest the LORD break out against them." {19:23} Moses said to the LORD, "The people cannot come up to Mount Sinai, for you yourself warned us, saying, 'Set bounds around the mountain and consecrate it.'" {19:24} And the LORD said to him, "Go down, and come up bringing Aaron with you. But do not let the priests and the people break through to come up to the LORD, lest he break out against them." {19:25} So Moses went down to the people and spoke to them.

{20:1} And God spoke all these words, saying, {20:2} "I am the LORD your God, who brought you out of the land of Egypt, out of the house of bondage. {20:3} "**You shall have no other gods before me.** {20:4} "**You shall not make for yourself any graven image, or any likeness of anything that is in heaven above, or that is in the earth beneath, or that is in the water under the earth.** {20:5} "You shall not bow down yourself to them, nor serve them: for I the LORD your God am a jealous God, visiting the iniquity of the fathers upon the children to the third and fourth generation of them that hate me; {20:6} "And showing mercy to thousands of them that love me, and keep my commandments. {20:7} "You shall not take the name of the LORD your God in vain; for the LORD will not hold him guiltless that takes his name in vain. {20:8} "**Remember the Sabbath day, to keep it holy.** {20:9} "Six days you shall labor, and do all your work: {20:10} "But the seventh day is the Sabbath of the LORD your God: in it you shall not do any work, you, nor your son, nor your daughter, your manservant, nor your maidservant, nor your cattle, nor your stranger that is within your gates: {20:11} "For in six days the LORD made heaven and earth, the sea, and all that in them is, and rested the seventh day: wherefore the LORD blessed the Sabbath day, and hallowed it. {20:12} "Honor your father and your mother: that your days may be long upon the land which the LORD your God gives you. {20:13} "You shall not kill. {20:14} "You shall not commit adultery. {20:15} "You shall not steal. {20:16} "You shall not bear false witness against your neighbor. {20:17} "You shall not covet your neighbor's house, you shall not covet your neighbor's wife, nor his manservant, nor his maidservant, nor his ox, nor his donkey, nor anything that is your neighbor's. {20:18} "And all the people saw the thunderings, and the lightnings, and the noise of the trumpet, and the mountain smoking: and when the people saw it, they removed, and stood afar off. {20:19} "And they said unto Moses, Speak with us, and we will hear: but let not God speak with us, lest we die. {20:20} "And Moses said unto the people, Fear not: for God has come to prove you, and that his fear may be before your faces, that you sin not. {20:21} "And the people stood afar off, and Moses drew near unto the thick darkness where God was. {20:22} "And the LORD said unto Moses, Thus you shall say unto the children of Israel, 'You have seen that I have talked with you from heaven. {20:23} "You shall not make with me gods of silver, neither shall you make unto you gods of gold. {20:24} "An altar of earth you shall make unto me, and shall sacrifice thereon your burnt offerings, and your peace offerings, your sheep, and your oxen: in all places where I record my name I will come unto you, and I will bless you. {20:25} "And if you will make me an altar of stone, you shall not build it of hewn stone: for if you lift up your tool upon it, you have polluted it. {20:26} "Neither shall you go up by steps unto mine altar, that your nakedness be not discovered thereon."

{21:1} These are the judgments that you shall set before them. {21:2} If you buy a Hebrew servant, he shall serve you for six years, and in the seventh year he shall go out free without paying anything. {21:3} If he came in by himself, he shall go out by himself; if he was married, then his wife shall go out with him. {21:4} If his master gives him a wife and she bears him sons or daughters, the wife and her children shall belong to the master, and he shall go out by himself. {21:5} But if the servant plainly says, 'I love my master, my wife, and my children; I will not go out free,' {21:6} then his master shall bring him to the judges. He shall also bring him to the door, or to the doorpost, and his master shall bore his ear through with an awl, and he shall serve him forever. {21:7} If a man sells his daughter to be a maidservant, she shall not go out as the menservants do. {21:8} If she does not please her master who has betrothed her to himself, then he shall let her be redeemed. He shall have no power to sell her to a foreign nation, seeing he has dealt deceitfully with her. {21:9} And if he has betrothed her to his son, he shall deal with her according to the manner of daughters. {21:10} If he takes another wife, her food, her clothing, and her marriage rights shall he not diminish. {21:11} And if he does not do these three things for her, then she shall go out free without paying any money. {21:12} Whoever strikes a man so that he dies shall surely be put to death. {21:13} But if a man did not lie in wait, but God delivered him into his hand, then I will appoint you a place where he shall flee. {21:14} But if a man comes presumptuously upon his neighbor, to slay him with guile; you shall take him from my altar, that he may die. {21:15} Whoever strikes his father or his mother shall surely be put to death. {21:16} Whoever steals a man, and sells him, or if he is found in his hand, he shall surely be put to death. {21:17} Whoever curses his father or his mother shall surely be put to death. {21:18} If men strive together, and one strikes another with a stone, or with his fist, and he does not die, but keeps his bed; {21:19} if he rises again and walks abroad upon his staff, then he that struck him shall be acquitted. He shall only pay for the loss of his time, and shall cause him to be thoroughly healed. {21:20} If a man strikes his servant, or his maid, with a rod, and he dies under his hand; he shall be surely punished. {21:21} Notwithstanding, if he continues a day or two, he shall not be punished: for he is his money. {21:22} If men strive, and hurt a woman with child, so that her fruit depart from her, and yet no mischief follow: he shall be surely punished, according as the woman's husband will lay upon him; and he shall pay as the judges determine. {21:23} And if any mischief follows, then you shall give life for life, {21:24} Eye for eye, tooth for tooth, hand for hand, foot for foot, {21:25} Burning for burning, wound for wound, stripe for stripe. {21:26} And if a man strikes the eye of his servant, or the eye of his maid, and it perishes; he shall let him go free for his eye's sake. {21:27} And if he strikes out his manservant's tooth, or his maidservant's tooth; he shall let him go free for his tooth's sake. {21:28} If an ox gores a man or a woman, that they die: then the ox shall be surely stoned, and his flesh shall not be eaten; but the owner of the ox shall be cleared. {21:29} But if the ox was known to push with his horn in time past, and it has been testified to his owner, and he has not kept him in, but that he has killed a man or a woman; the ox shall be stoned, and his owner also shall be put to death. {21:30} If there is laid on him a sum of money, then he shall give for the ransom of his life whatever is laid upon him. {21:31} Whether he has gored a son, or has gored a daughter, according to this judgment shall it be done unto him. {21:32} If the ox gores a manservant or a maidservant; he shall give unto their master thirty shekels of silver, and the ox shall be stoned. {21:33} And if a man shall open a pit, or if a man shall dig a pit, and not cover it, and an ox or an ass fall in it; {21:34} the owner of the pit shall make it good, and give money unto the owner of them; and the dead beast shall be his. {21:35} And if one man's ox hurts another's, that he dies; then they shall sell the live ox, and divide the money of it; and the dead ox also they shall divide. {21:36} Or if it is known that the ox has used to push in time past, and his owner has not kept him in; he shall surely pay ox for ox; and the dead shall be his own.

{22:1} If a man steals an ox or a sheep and kills it or sells it, he shall restore five oxen for an ox and four sheep for a sheep. {22:2} If a thief is found breaking in, and is struck so that he dies, there shall be no bloodshed for him. {22:3} If the sun has risen upon him, there shall be bloodshed for him; he should make full restitution; if he has nothing, then he shall be sold for his theft. {22:4} If the theft is certainly found in his hand alive, whether it be ox, or ass, or sheep; he shall restore double. {22:5} If a man causes a field or vineyard to be eaten, and puts his beast in, and feeds in another man's field; he shall make restitution from the best of his own field, and of the best of his own vineyard. {22:6} If fire breaks out and catches in thorns, so that the stacks of grain, or the standing grain, or the field, are consumed with it; he that kindled the fire shall surely make restitution. {22:7} If a man delivers money or goods to his neighbor to keep, and it is stolen out of the man's house; if the thief is found, let him pay double. {22:8} If the thief is not found, then the master of the house shall be brought to the judges, to see whether he has put his hand to his neighbor's goods. {22:9} For all manner of trespass, whether it be for ox, for ass, for sheep, for clothing, or for any manner of lost thing, which another claims to be his, the cause of both parties shall come before the judges; and whom the judges shall condemn, he shall pay double unto his neighbor. {22:10} If a man delivers to his neighbor an ass, or an ox, or a sheep, or any beast, to keep; and it dies, or is hurt, or driven away, and no man seeing it: {22:11} Then shall an oath of the LORD be between them both, that he has not put his hand to his neighbor's goods; and the owner of it shall accept it, and he shall not make it good. {22:12} And if it is stolen from him, he shall make restitution unto the owner thereof. {22:13} If it is torn in pieces, then let him bring it for witness, and he shall not make good that which was torn. {22:14} And if a man borrows anything of his neighbor, and it is hurt, or dies, the owner thereof not being with it, he shall surely make it good. {22:15} But if the owner thereof is with it, he shall not make it good: if it is a hired thing, it came for his hire. {22:16} And if a man entices a maid that is not betrothed, and lies with her, he shall surely endow her to be his wife. {22:17} If her father utterly refuses to give her unto him, he shall pay money according to the dowry of virgins. {22:18} You shall not allow a witch to live. {22:19} Whoever lies with a beast shall surely be put to death. {22:20} He that sacrifices unto any god, save unto the LORD only, he shall be utterly destroyed. {22:21} You shall neither vex a stranger, nor oppress him: for you were strangers in the land of Egypt. {22:22} You shall not afflict any widow, or fatherless child. {22:23} If you afflict them in any way, and they cry at all unto me, I will surely hear their cry; {22:24} And my wrath shall become hot, and I will kill you with the sword; and your wives shall be widows, and your children fatherless. {22:25} If you lend money to any of my people that is poor by you, you shall not be to him as a usurer, neither shall you lay upon him usury. {22:26} If you at all take your neighbor's garment to pledge, you shall deliver it unto him by the time the sun goes down: {22:27} For that is his covering only, it is his garment for his skin: wherein shall he sleep? and it shall come to pass, when he cries unto me, that I will hear; for I am gracious. {22:28} You shall not revile the gods, nor curse the ruler of your people. {22:29} You shall not delay to offer the first of your ripe fruits, and of your liquors: the firstborn of your sons shall you give unto me. {22:30} Likewise shall you do with your oxen, and with your sheep: seven days it shall be with its dam; on the eighth day you shall give it me. {22:31} And you shall be holy men unto me: neither shall you eat any flesh that is torn of beasts in the field; you shall cast it to the dogs.

{23:1} Do not spread false reports. Do not join hands with the wicked to be an unjust witness. {23:2} Do not follow the crowd in doing wrong. Do not pervert justice by siding with the crowd. {23:3} Do not show favoritism to a poor person in a lawsuit. {23:4} If you come across your enemy's ox or donkey wandering off, return it to him. {23:5} If you see the donkey of someone who hates you fallen down under its load, do not leave it there; be sure you help them with it. {23:6} Do not deny justice to your poor people in their lawsuits. {23:7} Keep far away from a false accusation. Do not kill the innocent and righteous, for I will not acquit the guilty. {23:8} Do not accept a bribe, for a bribe blinds those who see and twists the words of the innocent. {23:9} Do not oppress a foreigner; you yourselves know how it feels to be foreigners, because you were foreigners in Egypt. {23:10} For six years you are to sow your fields and harvest the crops, {23:11} but during the seventh year let the land lie unplowed and unused. Then the poor among your people may get food from it, and the wild animals may eat what is left. Do the same with your vineyard and your olive grove. {23:12} Six days do your work, but on the seventh day do not work, so that your ox and your donkey may rest, and so that the slave born in your household, and the foreigner, may be refreshed. {23:13} Be careful to do everything I have said to you. Do not invoke the names of other gods; do not let them be heard on your lips. {23:14} Three times a year you are to celebrate a festival to me. {23:15} Celebrate the Festival of Unleavened Bread; for seven days eat bread made without yeast, as I commanded you. Do this at the appointed time in the month of Aviv, for in that month you came out of Egypt. No one is to appear before me empty-handed. {23:16} Celebrate the Festival of Harvest with the firstfruits of the crops you sow in your field. Celebrate the Festival of Ingathering at the end of the year, when you gather in your crops from the field. {23:17} Three times a year all your men are to appear before the Sovereign LORD. {23:18} Do not offer the blood of a sacrifice to me along with anything containing yeast. The fat of my festival offerings must not be kept until morning. {23:19} Bring the best of the firstfruits of your soil to the house of the LORD your God. Do not cook a young goat in its mother's milk. {23:20} See, I am sending an angel ahead of you to guard you along the way and to bring you to the place I have prepared. {23:21} Pay attention to him and listen to what he says. Do not rebel against him; he will not forgive your rebellion, since my Name is in him. {23:22} If you listen carefully to what he says and do all that I say, I will be an enemy to your enemies and will oppose those who oppose you. {23:23} My angel will go ahead of you and bring you into the land of the Amorites, Hittites, Perizzites, Canaanites, Hivites and Jebusites, and I will wipe them out. {23:24} Do not bow down before their gods or worship them or follow their practices. You must demolish them and break their sacred stones to pieces. {23:25} Worship the LORD your God, and his blessing will be on your food and water. I will take away sickness from among you, {23:26} and none will miscarry or be barren in your land. I will give you a full life span. {23:27} I will send my terror ahead of you and throw into confusion every nation you encounter. I will make all your enemies turn their backs and run. {23:28} I will send the hornet ahead of you to drive the Hivites, Canaanites and Hittites out of your way. {23:29} But I will not drive them out in a single year, because the land would become desolate and the wild animals too numerous for you. {23:30} Little by little I will drive them out before you, until you have increased enough to take possession of the land. {23:31} I will establish your borders from the Red Sea to the Mediterranean Sea, and from the desert to the Euphrates River. I will give into your hands the people who live in the land, and you will drive them out before you. {23:32} Do not make a covenant with them or with their gods. {23:33} Do not let them live in your land or they will cause you to sin against me, because the worship of their gods will certainly be a snare to you."

{24:1} And he said unto Moses, Come up unto the LORD, thou, and Aaron, Nadab, and Abihu, and seventy of the elders of Israel; and worship ye afar off. {24:2} And Moses alone shall come near the LORD: but they shall not come nigh; neither shall the people go up with him. {24:3} And Moses came and told the people all the words of the LORD, and all the judgments: and all the people answered with one voice, and said, All the words which the LORD hath said will we do. {24:4} And Moses wrote all the words of the LORD, and rose up early in the morning, and builded an altar under the hill, and twelve pillars, according to the twelve tribes of Israel. {24:5} And he sent young men of the children of Israel, which offered burnt offerings, and sacrificed peace offerings of oxen unto the LORD. {24:6} And Moses took half of the blood, and put it in basons; and half of the blood he sprinkled on the altar. {24:7} And he took the book of the covenant, and read in the audience of the people: and they said, All that the LORD hath said will we do, and be obedient. {24:8} And Moses took the blood, and sprinkled it on the people, and said, Behold the blood of the covenant, which the LORD hath made with you concerning all these words. {24:9} Then went up Moses, and Aaron, Nadab, and Abihu, and seventy of the elders of Israel: {24:10} And they saw the God of Israel: and there was under his feet as it were a paved work of a sapphire stone, and as it were the body of heaven in his clearness. {24:11} And upon the nobles of the children of Israel he laid not his hand: also they saw God, and did eat and drink. {24:12} And the LORD said unto Moses, Come up to me into the mount, and be there: and I will give thee tables of stone, and a law, and commandments which I have written; that thou mayest teach them. {24:13} And Moses rose up, and his minister Joshua: and Moses went up into the mount of God. {24:14} And he said unto the elders, Tarry ye here for us, until we come again unto you: and, behold, Aaron and Hur [are] with you: if any man have any matters to do, let him come unto them. {24:15} And Moses went up into the mount, and a cloud covered the mount. {24:16} And the glory of the LORD abode upon mount Sinai, and the cloud covered it six days: and the seventh day he called unto Moses out of the midst of the cloud. {24:17} And the sight of the glory of the LORD was like devouring fire on the top of the mount in the eyes of the children of Israel. {24:18} And Moses went into the midst of the cloud, and gat him up into the mount: and Moses was in the mount forty days and forty nights.

{25:1} And the LORD spake unto Moses, saying, {25:2} Speak unto the children of Israel, that they bring me an offering: of every man that giveth it willingly with his heart ye shall take my offering. {25:3} And this is the offering which ye shall take of them; gold, and silver, and brass, {25:4} And blue, and purple, and scarlet, and fine linen, and goats' hair, {25:5} And rams' skins dyed red, and badgers' skins, and shittim wood, {25:6} Oil for the light, spices for anointing oil, and for sweet incense, {25:7} Onyx stones, and stones to be set in the ephod, and in the breastplate. {25:8} **And let them make me a sanctuary; that I may dwell among them.** {25:9} **According to all that I show thee, after the pattern of the tabernacle, and the pattern of all the instruments thereof, even so shall ye make it.** {25:10} And they shall make an ark of shittim wood: two cubits and a half shall be the length thereof, and a cubit and a half the breadth thereof, and a cubit and a half the height thereof. {25:11} And thou shalt overlay it with pure gold, within and without shalt thou overlay it, and shalt make upon it a crown of gold round about. {25:12} And thou shalt cast four rings of gold for it, and put them in the four corners thereof; and two rings shall be in the one side of it, and two rings in the other side of it. {25:13} And thou shalt make staves of shittim wood, and overlay them with gold. {25:14} And thou shalt put the staves into the rings by the sides of the ark, that the ark may be borne with them. {25:15} The staves shall be in the rings of the ark: they shall not be taken from it. {25:16} And thou shalt put into the ark the testimony which I shall give thee. {25:17} And thou shalt make a mercy seat of pure gold: two cubits and a half shall be the length thereof, and a cubit and a half the breadth thereof. {25:18} And thou shalt make two cherubims of gold, of beaten work shalt thou make them, in the two ends of the mercy seat. {25:19}

And make one cherub on the one end, and the other cherub on the other end: even of the mercy seat shall ye make the cherubims on the two ends thereof. {25:20} And the cherubims shall stretch forth their wings on high, covering the mercy seat with their wings, and their faces shall look one to another; toward the mercy seat shall the faces of the cherubims be. {25:21} And thou shalt put the mercy seat above upon the ark; and in the ark thou shalt put the testimony that I shall give thee. {25:22} And there I will meet with thee, and I will commune with thee from above the mercy seat, from between the two cherubims which are upon the ark of the testimony, of all things which I will give thee in commandment unto the children of Israel. {25:23} Thou shalt also make a table of shittim wood: two cubits shall be the length thereof, and a cubit the breadth thereof, and a cubit and a half the height thereof. {25:24} And thou shalt overlay it with pure gold, and make thereto a crown of gold round about. {25:25} And thou shalt make unto it a border of a handbreadth round about, and thou shalt make a golden crown to the border thereof round about. {25:26} And thou shalt make for it four rings of gold, and put the rings in the four corners that are on the four feet thereof. {25:27} Over against the border shall the rings be for places of the staves to bear the table. {25:28} And thou shalt make the staves of shittim wood, and overlay them with gold, that the table may be borne with them. {25:29} And thou shalt make the dishes thereof, and spoons thereof, and covers thereof, and bowls thereof, to cover withal: of pure gold shalt thou make them. {25:30} And thou shalt set upon the table showbread before me alway. {25:31} And thou shalt make a candlestick of pure gold: beaten work shall the candlestick be made: his shaft, and his branches, his bowls, his knops, and his flowers, shall be of the same. {25:32} And six branches shall come out of the sides of it; three branches of the candlestick out of the one side, and three branches of the candlestick out of the other side: {25:33} Three bowls made like unto almonds, with a knop and a flower in one branch; and three bowls made like almonds in the other branch, with a knop and a flower: so in the six branches that come out of the candlestick. {25:34} And in the candlestick shall be four bowls made like unto almonds, with their knops and their flowers. {25:35} And there shall be a knop under two branches of the same, and a knop under two branches of the same, and a knop under two branches of the same, according to the six branches that proceed out of the candlestick. {25:36} Their knops and their branches shall be of the same: all it shall be one beaten work of pure gold. {25:37} And thou shalt make the seven lamps thereof: and they shall light the lamps thereof, that they may give light over against it. {25:38} And the tongs thereof, and the snuffdishes thereof, shall be of pure gold. {25:39} Of a talent of pure gold shall he make it, with all these vessels. {25:40} And look that thou make them after their pattern, which was showed thee in the mount.

{26:1} Moreover, thou shalt make the tabernacle with ten curtains of fine twined linen, and blue, and purple, and scarlet: with cherubims of cunning work shalt thou make them. {26:2} The length of one curtain shall be eight and twenty cubits, and the breadth of one curtain four cubits: and every one of the curtains shall have one measure. {26:3} The five curtains shall be coupled together one to another; and other five curtains shall be coupled one to another. {26:4} And thou shalt make loops of blue upon the edge of the one curtain from the selvedge in the coupling; and likewise shalt thou make in the uttermost edge of another curtain, in the coupling of the second. {26:5} Fifty loops shalt thou make in the one curtain, and fifty loops shalt thou make in the edge of the curtain that is in the coupling of the second; that the loops may take hold one of another. {26:6} And thou shalt make fifty taches of gold, and couple the curtains together with the taches: and it shall be one tabernacle. {26:7} And thou shalt make curtains of goats' hair to be a covering upon the tabernacle: eleven curtains shalt thou make. {26:8} The length of one curtain shall be thirty cubits, and the breadth of one curtain four cubits: and the eleven curtains shall be all of one measure. {26:9} And thou shalt couple five curtains by themselves, and six curtains by themselves, and shalt double the sixth curtain in the forefront of the tabernacle. {26:10} And thou shalt make fifty loops on the edge of the one curtain that is outmost in the coupling, and fifty loops in the edge of the curtain which coupleth the second. {26:11} And thou shalt make fifty taches of brass, and put the taches into the loops, and couple the tent together, that it may be one. {26:12} And the remnant that remaineth of the curtains of the tent, the half curtain that remaineth, shall hang over the backside of the tabernacle. {26:13} And a cubit on the one side, and a cubit on the other side of that which remaineth in the length of the curtains of the tent, it shall hang over the sides of the tabernacle on this side and on that side, to cover it. {26:14} And thou shalt make a covering for the tent of rams' skins dyed red, and a covering above of badgers' skins. {26:15} And thou shalt make boards for the tabernacle of shittim wood standing up. {26:16} Ten cubits shall be the length of a board, and a cubit and a half shall be the breadth of one board. {26:17} Two tenons shall there be in one board, set in order one against another: thus shalt thou make for all the boards of the tabernacle. {26:18} And thou shalt make the boards for the tabernacle, twenty boards on the south side southward. {26:19} And thou shalt make forty sockets of silver under the twenty boards; two sockets under one board for his two tenons, and two sockets under another board for his two tenons. {26:20} And for the second side of the tabernacle on the north side there shall be twenty boards: {26:21} And their forty sockets of silver; two sockets under one board, and two sockets under another board. {26:22} And for the sides of the tabernacle westward thou shalt make six boards. {26:23} And two boards shalt thou make for the corners of the tabernacle in the two sides. {26:24} And they shall be coupled together beneath, and they shall be coupled together above the head of one board unto one ring: thus shall it be for them both; they shall be for the two corners. {26:25} And they shall be eight boards, and their sockets of silver, sixteen sockets; two sockets under one board, and two sockets under another board. {26:26} And thou shalt make bars of shittim wood; five for the boards of the one side of the tabernacle, {26:27} And five bars for the boards of the other side of the tabernacle, and five bars for the boards of the side of the tabernacle, for the two sides westward. {26:28} And the middle bar in the midst of the boards shall reach from end to end. {26:29} And thou shalt overlay the boards with gold, and make their rings of gold for places for the bars: and thou shalt overlay the bars with gold. {26:30} And thou shalt rear up the tabernacle according to the fashion thereof which was showed thee in the mount. {26:31} And thou shalt make a vail of blue, and purple, and scarlet: and fine twined linen of cunning work: with cherubims shall it be made: {26:32} And thou shalt hang it upon four pillars of shittim wood overlaid with gold: their hooks shall be of gold, upon the four sockets of silver. {26:33} And thou shalt hang up the vail under the taches, that thou mayest bring in thither within the vail the ark of the testimony: and the vail shall divide unto you between the holy place and the most holy. {26:34} And thou shalt put the mercy seat upon the ark of the testimony in the most holy place. {26:35} And thou shalt set the table without the vail, and the candlestick over against the table on the side of the tabernacle toward the south: and thou shalt put the table on the north side. {26:36} And thou shalt make a hanging for the door of the tent, of blue, and purple, and scarlet, and fine twined linen, wrought with needlework. {26:37} And thou shalt make for the hanging five pillars of shittim wood, and overlay them with gold, and their hooks shall be of gold: and thou shalt cast five sockets of brass for them.

{27:1} And thou shalt make an altar of shittim wood, five cubits long, and five cubits broad; the altar shall be foursquare: and the height thereof shall be three cubits. {27:2} And thou shalt make the horns of it upon the four corners thereof: his horns shall be of the same: and thou shalt overlay it with brass. {27:3} And thou shalt make his pans to receive his ashes, and his shovels, and his basons, and his fleshhooks, and his firepans: all the vessels thereof thou shalt make of brass. {27:4} And thou shalt make for it a grate of network of brass; and upon the net shalt thou make four brasen rings in the four corners thereof. {27:5} And thou shalt put it under the compass of the altar beneath, that the net may be even to the midst of the altar. {27:6} And thou shalt make staves for the altar, staves of shittim wood, and overlay them with brass. {27:7} And the staves shall be put into the rings, and the staves shall be upon the two sides of the altar, to bear it. {27:8} Hollow with boards shalt thou make it: as it was shewed thee in the mount, so shall they make it. {27:9} And thou shalt make the court of the tabernacle: for the south side southward there shall be hangings for the court of fine twined linen of an hundred cubits long for one side: {27:10} And the twenty pillars thereof and their twenty sockets shall be of brass; the hooks of the pillars and their fillets shall be of silver. {27:11} And likewise for the north side in length there shall be hangings of an hundred cubits long, and his twenty pillars and their twenty sockets of brass; the hooks of the pillars and their fillets of silver. {27:12} And for the breadth of the court on the west side shall be hangings of fifty cubits: their pillars ten, and their sockets ten. {27:13} And the breadth of the court on the east side eastward shall be fifty cubits. {27:14} The hangings of one side of the gate shall be fifteen cubits: their pillars three, and their sockets three. {27:15} And on the other side shall be hangings fifteen cubits: their pillars three, and their sockets three. {27:16} And for the gate of the court shall be an hanging of twenty cubits, of blue, and purple, and scarlet, and fine twined linen, wrought with needlework: and their pillars shall be four, and their sockets four. {27:17} All the pillars round about the court shall be filleted with silver; their hooks shall be of silver, and their sockets of brass. {27:18} The length of the court shall be an hundred cubits, and the breadth fifty everywhere, and the height five cubits of fine twined linen, and their sockets of brass. {27:19} All the vessels of the tabernacle in all the service thereof, and all the pins thereof, and all the pins of the court, shall be of brass. {27:20} And thou shalt command the children of Israel, that they bring thee pure oil olive beaten for the light, to cause the lamp to burn always. {27:21} In the tabernacle of the congregation without the vail, which is before the testimony, Aaron and his sons shall order it from evening to morning before the LORD: it shall be a statute forever unto their generations on the behalf of the children of Israel.

{28:1} And take thou unto thee Aaron thy brother, and his sons with him, from among the children of Israel, that he may minister unto me in the priest's office, even Aaron, Nadab and Abihu, Eleazar and Ithamar, Aaron's sons. {28:2} And thou shalt make holy garments for Aaron thy brother for glory and for beauty. {28:3} And thou shalt speak unto all that are wise hearted, whom I have filled with the spirit of wisdom, that they may make Aaron's garments to consecrate him, that he may minister unto me in the priest's office. {28:4} And these are the garments which they shall make; a breastplate, and an ephod, and a robe, and a broidered coat, a mitre, and a girdle: and they shall make holy garments for Aaron thy brother, and his sons, that he may minister unto me in the priest's office. {28:5} And they shall take gold, and blue, and purple, and scarlet, and fine linen. {28:6} And they shall make the ephod of gold, of blue, and of purple, of scarlet, and fine twined linen, with cunning work. {28:7} It shall have the two shoulderpieces thereof joined at the two edges thereof; and so it shall be joined together. {28:8} And the curious girdle of the ephod, which is upon it, shall be of the same, according to the work thereof; even of gold, of blue, and purple, and scarlet, and fine twined linen. {28:9} And thou shalt take two onyx stones, and grave on them the names of the children of Israel: {28:10} Six of their names on one stone, and the other six names of the rest on the other stone, according to their birth. {28:11} With the work of an engraver in stone, like the engravings of a signet, shalt thou engrave the two stones with the names of the children of Israel: thou shalt make them to be set in ouches of gold. {28:12} And thou shalt put the two stones upon the shoulders of the ephod for stones of memorial unto the children of Israel: and Aaron shall bear their names before the LORD upon his two shoulders for a memorial. {28:13} And thou shalt make ouches of gold; {28:14} And two chains of pure gold at the ends; of wreathen work shalt thou make them, and fasten the wreathen chains to the ouches. {28:15} And thou shalt make the breastplate of judgment with cunning work; after the work of the ephod thou shalt make it; of gold, of blue, and of purple, and of scarlet, and of fine twined linen, shalt thou make it. {28:16} Foursquare it shall be being doubled; a span shall be the length thereof, and a span shall be the breadth thereof. {28:17} And thou shalt set in it settings of stones, even four rows of stones: the first row shall be a sardius, a topaz, and a carbuncle: this shall be the first row. {28:18} And the second row shall be an emerald, a sapphire, and a diamond. {28:19} And the third row a ligure, an agate, and an amethyst. {28:20} And the fourth row a beryl, and an onyx, and a jasper: they shall be set in gold in their inclosings. {28:21} And the stones shall be with the names of the children of Israel, twelve, according to their names, like the engravings of a signet; every one with his name shall they be according to the twelve tribes. {28:22} And thou shalt make upon the breastplate chains at the ends of wreathen work of pure gold. {28:23} And thou shalt make upon the breastplate two rings of gold, and shalt put the two rings on the two ends of the breastplate. {28:24} And thou shalt put the two wreathen chains of gold in the two rings which are on the ends of the breastplate. {28:25} And the other two ends of the two wreathen chains thou shalt fasten in the two ouches, and put them on the shoulderpieces of the ephod before it. {28:26} And thou shalt make two rings of gold, and thou shalt put them upon the two ends of the breastplate in the border thereof, which is in the side of the ephod inward. {28:27} And two other rings of gold thou shalt make, and shalt put them on the two sides of the ephod underneath, toward the forepart thereof, over against the other coupling thereof, above the curious girdle of the ephod. {28:28} And they shall bind the breastplate by the rings thereof unto the rings of the ephod with a lace of blue, that it may be above the curious girdle of the ephod, and that the breastplate be not loosed from the ephod. {28:29} And Aaron shall bear the names of the children of Israel in the breastplate of judgment upon his heart, when he goeth in unto the holy place, for a memorial before the LORD continually. {28:30} And thou shalt put in the breastplate of judgment the Urim and the Thummim; and they shall be upon Aaron's heart, when he goeth in before the LORD: and Aaron shall bear the judgment of the children of Israel upon his heart before the LORD continually. {28:31} And thou shalt make the robe of the ephod all of blue. {28:32} And there shall be an hole in the top of it, in the midst thereof: it shall have a binding of woven work round about the hole of it, as it were the hole of an habergeon, that it be not rent. {28:33} And beneath upon the hem of it thou shalt make pomegranates of blue, and of purple, and of scarlet, round about the hem thereof; and bells of gold between them round about: {28:34} A golden bell and a pomegranate, a golden bell and a pomegranate, upon the hem of the robe round about. {28:35} And it shall be upon Aaron to minister: and his sound shall be heard when he goeth in unto the holy place before the LORD, and when he cometh out, that he die not. {28:36} And thou shalt make a plate of pure gold, and grave upon it, like the engravings of a signet, HOLINESS TO THE LORD. {28:37} And thou shalt put it on a blue lace, that it may be upon the mitre; upon the forefront of the mitre it shall be. {28:38} And it shall be upon Aaron's forehead, that Aaron may bear the iniquity of the holy things, which the children of Israel shall hallow in all their holy gifts; and it shall be always upon his forehead, that they may be accepted before the LORD. {28:39} And thou shalt embroider the coat of fine linen, and thou shalt make the mitre of fine linen, and thou shalt make the girdle of needlework. {28:40} And for Aaron's sons thou shalt make coats, and thou shalt make for them girdles, and bonnets shalt thou make for them, for glory and for beauty. {28:41} And thou shalt put them upon Aaron thy brother, and his sons with him; and shalt anoint them, and consecrate them, and sanctify them, that they may minister unto me in the priest's office. {28:42} And thou shalt make them linen breeches to cover their nakedness; from the loins even unto the thighs they shall reach: {28:43} And they shall be upon Aaron, and upon his sons, when they come in unto the tabernacle of the congregation, or when they come near unto the altar to minister in the holy place; that they bear not iniquity, and die: it shall be a statute for ever unto him and his seed after him.

{29:1} And this is the thing that thou shalt do unto them to hallow them, to minister unto me in the priest's office: Take one young bullock, and two rams without blemish, {29:2} And unleavened bread, and cakes unleavened tempered with oil, and wafers unleavened anointed with oil: of wheaten flour shalt thou make them. {29:3} And thou shalt put them into one basket, and bring them in the basket, with the bullock and the two rams. {29:4} And Aaron and his sons thou shalt bring unto the door of the tabernacle of the congregation, and shalt wash them with water. {29:5} And thou shalt take the garments, and put upon Aaron the coat, and the robe of the ephod, and the ephod, and the breastplate, and gird him with the curious girdle of the ephod: {29:6} And thou shalt put the mitre upon his head, and put the holy crown upon the mitre. {29:7} Then shalt thou take the anointing oil, and pour it upon his head, and anoint him. {29:8} And thou shalt bring his sons, and put coats upon them. {29:9} And thou shalt gird them with girdles, Aaron and his sons, and put the bonnets on them: and the priest's office shall be theirs for a perpetual statute: and thou shalt consecrate Aaron and his sons. {29:10} And thou shalt cause a bullock to be brought before the tabernacle of the congregation: and Aaron and his sons shall put their hands upon the head of the bullock. {29:11} And thou shalt kill the bullock before the LORD, by the door of the tabernacle of the congregation. {29:12} And thou shalt take of the blood of the bullock, and put it upon the horns of the altar with thy finger, and pour all the blood beside the bottom of the altar. {29:13} And thou shalt take all the fat that covereth the inwards, and the caul that is above the liver, and the two kidneys, and the fat that is upon them, and burn them upon the altar. {29:14} But the flesh of the bullock, and his skin, and his dung, shalt thou burn with fire without the camp: it is a sin offering. {29:15} Thou shalt also take one ram; and Aaron and his sons shall put their hands upon the head of the ram. {29:16} And thou shalt slay the ram, and thou shalt take his blood, and sprinkle it round about upon the altar. {29:17} And thou shalt cut the ram in pieces, and wash the inwards of him, and his legs, and put them unto his pieces, and unto his head. {29:18} And thou shalt burn the whole ram upon the altar: it is a burnt offering unto the LORD: it is a sweet savour, an offering made by fire unto the LORD. {29:19} And thou shalt take the other ram; and Aaron and his sons shall put their hands upon the head of the ram. {29:20} Then shalt thou kill the ram, and take of his blood, and put it upon the tip of the right ear of Aaron, and upon the tip of the right ear of his sons, and upon the thumb of their right hand, and upon the great toe of their right foot, and sprinkle the blood upon the altar round about. {29:21} And thou shalt take of the blood that is upon the altar, and of the anointing oil, and sprinkle it upon Aaron, and upon his garments, and upon his sons, and upon the garments of his sons with him: and he shall be hallowed, and his garments, and his sons, and his sons' garments with him. {29:22} Also thou shalt take of the ram the fat and the rump, and the fat that covereth the inwards, and the caul above the liver, and the two kidneys, and the fat that is upon them, and the right shoulder; for it is a ram of consecration: {29:23} And one loaf of bread, and one cake of oiled bread, and one wafer out of the basket of the unleavened bread that is before the LORD: {29:24} And thou shalt put all in the hands of Aaron, and in the hands of his sons; and shalt wave them for a wave offering before the LORD. {29:25} And thou shalt receive them of their hands, and burn them upon the altar for a burnt offering, for a sweet savour before the LORD: it is an offering made by fire unto the LORD. {29:26} And thou shalt take the breast of the ram of Aaron's consecration, and wave it for a wave offering before the LORD: and it shall be thy part. {29:27} And thou shalt sanctify the breast of the wave offering, and the shoulder of the heave offering, which is waved, and which is heaved up, of the ram of the consecration, even of that which is for Aaron, and of that which is for his sons. {29:28} And it shall be Aaron's and his sons' by a statute forever from the children of Israel: for it is an heave offering: and it shall be an heave offering from the children of Israel of the sacrifice of their peace offerings, even their heave offering unto the LORD. {29:29} And the holy garments of Aaron shall be his sons' after him, to be anointed therein, and to be consecrated in them. {29:30} And that son that is priest in his stead shall put them on seven days, when he cometh into the tabernacle of the congregation to minister in the holy place. {29:31} And thou shalt take the ram of the consecration, and seethe his flesh in the holy place. {29:32} And Aaron and his sons shall eat the flesh of the ram, and the bread that is in the basket, by the door of the tabernacle of the congregation. {29:33} And they shall eat those things wherewith the atonement was made, to consecrate and to sanctify them: but a stranger shall not eat thereof, because they are holy. {29:34} And if aught of the flesh of the consecrations, or of the bread, remain unto the morning, then thou shalt burn the remainder with fire: it shall not be eaten, because it is holy. {29:35} And thus shalt thou do unto Aaron, and to his sons, according to all things which I have commanded thee: seven days shalt thou consecrate them. {29:36} And thou shalt offer every day a bullock for a sin offering for atonement: and thou shalt cleanse the altar, when thou hast made an atonement for it, and thou shalt anoint it, to sanctify it. {29:37} Seven days thou shalt make an atonement for the altar, and sanctify it; and it shall be an altar most holy: whatsoever toucheth the altar shall be holy. {29:38} Now this is that which thou shalt offer upon the altar; two lambs of the first year day by day continually. {29:39} The one lamb thou shalt offer in the morning; and the other lamb thou shalt offer at even: {29:40} And with the one lamb a tenth deal of flour mingled with the fourth part of an hin of beaten oil; and the fourth part of an hin of wine for a drink offering. {29:41} And the other lamb thou shalt offer at even, and shalt do thereto according to the meat offering of the morning, and according to the drink offering thereof, for a sweet savor, an offering made by fire unto the LORD. {29:42} This shall be a continual burnt offering throughout your generations at the door of the tabernacle of the congregation before the LORD: where I will meet you, to speak there unto thee. {29:43} And there I will meet with the children of Israel, and the tabernacle shall be sanctified by my glory. {29:44} And I will sanctify the tabernacle of the congregation, and the altar: I will sanctify also both Aaron and his sons, to minister to me in the priest's office. {29:45} And I will dwell among the children of Israel, and will be their God. {29:46} And they shall know that I am the LORD their God, that brought them forth out of the land of Egypt, that I may dwell among them: I am the LORD their God.

{30:1} And thou shalt make an altar to burn incense upon: of shittim wood shalt thou make it. {30:2} A cubit shall be the length thereof, and a cubit the breadth thereof; foursquare shall it be: and two cubits shall be the height thereof: the horns thereof shall be of the same. {30:3} And thou shalt overlay it with pure gold, the top thereof, and the sides thereof round about, and the horns thereof; and thou shalt make unto it a crown of gold round about. {30:4} And two golden rings shalt thou make to it under the crown of it, by the two corners thereof, upon the two sides of it shalt thou make it; and they shall be for places for the staves to bear it withal. {30:5} And thou shalt make the staves of shittim wood, and overlay them with gold. {30:6} And thou shalt put it before the vail that is by the ark of the testimony, before the mercy seat that is over the testimony, where I will meet with thee. {30:7} And Aaron shall burn thereon sweet incense every morning: when he dresseth the lamps, he shall burn incense upon it. {30:8} And when Aaron lighteth the lamps at even, he shall burn incense upon it, a perpetual incense before the LORD throughout your generations. {30:9} Ye shall offer no strange incense thereon, nor burnt sacrifice, nor meat offering; neither shall ye pour drink offering thereon. {30:10} And Aaron shall make an atonement upon the horns of it once in a year with the blood of the sin offering of atonements: once in the year shall he make atonement upon it throughout your generations: it is most holy unto the LORD. {30:11} And the LORD spake unto Moses, saying, {30:12} When thou takest the sum of the children of Israel after their number, then shall they give every man a ransom for his soul unto the LORD, when thou numberest them; that there be no plague among them, when thou numberest them. {30:13} This they shall give, every one that passeth among them that are numbered, half a shekel after the shekel of the sanctuary: (a shekel is twenty gerahs:) an half shekel shall be the offering of the LORD. {30:14} Every one that passeth among them that are numbered, from twenty years old and above, shall give an offering unto the LORD. {30:15} The rich shall not give more, and the poor shall not give less than half a shekel, when they give an offering unto the LORD, to make an atonement for your souls. {30:16} And thou shalt take the atonement money of the children of Israel, and shalt appoint it for the service of the tabernacle of the congregation; that it may be a memorial unto the children of Israel before the LORD, to make an atonement for your souls. {30:17} And the LORD spake unto Moses, saying, {30:18} Thou shalt also make a laver of brass, and his foot also of brass, to wash withal: and thou shalt put it between the tabernacle of the congregation and the altar, and thou shalt put water therein. {30:19} For Aaron and his sons shall wash their hands and their feet thereat: {30:20} When they go into the tabernacle of the congregation, they shall wash with water, that they die not; or when they come near to the altar to minister, to burn offering made by fire unto the LORD: {30:21} So they shall wash their hands and their feet, that they die not: and it shall be a statute for ever to them, even to him and to his seed throughout their generations. {30:22} Moreover the LORD spake unto Moses, saying, {30:23} Take thou also unto thee principal spices, of pure myrrh five hundred shekels, and of sweet cinnamon half so much, even two hundred and fifty shekels, and of sweet calamus two hundred and fifty shekels, {30:24} And of cassia five hundred shekels, after the shekel of the sanctuary, and of oil olive an hin: {30:25} And thou shalt make it an oil of holy ointment, an ointment compound after the art of the apothecary: it shall be an holy anointing oil. {30:26} And thou shalt anoint the tabernacle of the congregation therewith, and the ark of the testimony, {30:27} And the table and all his vessels, and the candlestick and his vessels, and the altar of incense, {30:28} And the altar of burnt offering with all his vessels, and the laver and his foot. {30:29} And thou shalt sanctify them, that they may be most holy: whatsoever toucheth them shall be holy. {30:30} And thou shalt anoint Aaron and his sons, and consecrate them, that they may minister unto me in the priest's office. {30:31} And thou shalt speak unto the children of Israel, saying, This shall be an holy anointing oil unto me throughout your generations. {30:32} Upon man's flesh shall it not be poured, neither shall ye make any other like it, after the composition of it: it is holy, and it shall be holy unto you. {30:33} Whosoever compoundeth any like it, or whosoever putteth any of it upon a stranger, shall even be cut off from his people. {30:34} And the LORD said unto Moses, Take unto thee sweet spices, stacte, and onycha, and galbanum; these sweet spices with pure frankincense: of each shall there be a like weight: {30:35} And thou shalt make it a perfume, a confection after the art of the apothecary, tempered together, pure and holy: {30:36} And thou shalt beat some of it very small, and put of it before the testimony in the tabernacle of the congregation, where I will meet with thee: it shall be unto you most holy. {30:37} And as for the perfume which thou shalt make, ye shall not make to yourselves according to the composition thereof: it shall be unto thee holy for the LORD. {30:38} Whosoever shall make like unto that, to smell thereto, shall even be cut off from his people.

{31:1} And the LORD spake unto Moses, saying, {31:2} See, I have called by name Bezaleel the son of Uri, the son of Hur, of the tribe of Judah: {31:3} And I have filled him with the spirit of God, in wisdom, and in understanding, and in knowledge, and in all manner of workmanship, {31:4} To devise cunning works, to work in gold, and in silver, and in brass, {31:5} And in cutting of stones, to set [them,] and in carving of timber, to work in all manner of workmanship. {31:6} And I, behold, I have given with him Aholiab, the son of Ahisamach, of the tribe of Dan: and in the hearts of all that are wise hearted I have put wisdom, that they may make all that I have commanded thee; {31:7} The tabernacle of the congregation, and the ark of the testimony, and the mercy seat that [is] thereupon, and all the furniture of the tabernacle, {31:8} And the table and his furniture, and the pure candlestick with all his furniture, and the altar of incense, {31:9} And the altar of burnt offering with all his furniture, and the laver and his foot, {31:10} And the cloths of service, and the holy garments for Aaron the priest, and the garments of his sons, to minister in the priest's office, {31:11} And the anointing oil, and sweet incense for the holy [place:] according to all that I have commanded thee shall they do. {31:12} And the LORD spake unto Moses, saying, {31:13} Speak thou also unto the children of Israel, saying, Verily my sabbaths ye shall keep: for it is a sign between me and you throughout your generations; that ye may know that I [am] the LORD that doth sanctify you. {31:14} Ye shall keep the sabbath therefore; for it [is] holy unto you: every one that defileth it shall surely be put to death: for whosoever doeth [any] work therein, that soul shall be cut off from among his people. {31:15} Six days may work be done; but in the seventh is the sabbath of rest, holy to the LORD: whosoever doeth [any] work in the sabbath day, he shall surely be put to death. {31:16} Wherefore the children of Israel shall keep the sabbath, to observe the sabbath throughout their generations, [for] a perpetual covenant. {31:17} It [is] a sign between me and the children of Israel for ever: for [in] six days the LORD made heaven and earth, and on the seventh day he rested, and was refreshed. {31:18} **And he gave unto Moses, when he had made an end of communing with him upon mount Sinai, two tables of testimony, tables of stone, written with the finger of God.**

{32:1} And when the people saw that Moses delayed to come down out of the mount, the people gathered themselves together unto Aaron, and said unto him, Up, make us gods, which shall go before us; for [as for] this Moses, the man that brought us up out of the land of Egypt, we wot not what is become of him. {32:2} And Aaron said unto them, Break off the golden earrings, which [are] in the ears of your wives, of your sons, and of your daughters, and bring [them] unto me. {32:3} And all the people brake off the golden earrings which [were] in their ears, and brought [them] unto Aaron. {32:4} And he received [them] at their hand, and fashioned it with a graving tool, after he had made it a molten calf: and they said, These [be] thy gods, O Israel, which brought thee up out of the land of Egypt. {32:5} And when Aaron saw [it,] he built an altar before it; and Aaron made proclamation, and said, To morrow [is] a feast to the LORD. {32:6} And they rose up early on the morrow, and offered burnt offerings, and brought peace offerings; and the people sat down to eat and to drink, and rose up to play. {32:7} And the LORD said unto Moses, Go, get thee down; for thy people, which thou broughtest out of the land of Egypt, have corrupted [themselves:] {32:8} They have turned aside quickly out of the way which I commanded them: they have made them a molten calf, and have worshipped it, and have sacrificed thereunto, and said, These [be] thy gods, O Israel, which have brought thee up out of the land of Egypt. {32:9} And the LORD said unto Moses, I have seen this people, and, behold, it [is] a stiffnecked people: {32:10} Now therefore let me alone, that my wrath may wax hot against them, and that I may consume them: and I will make of thee a great nation. {32:11} And Moses besought the LORD his God, and said, LORD, why doth thy wrath wax hot against thy people, which thou hast brought forth out of the land of Egypt with great power, and with a mighty hand? {32:12} Wherefore should the Egyptians speak, and say, For mischief did he bring them out, to slay them in the mountains, and to consume them from the face of the earth? Turn from thy fierce wrath, and repent of this evil against thy people. {32:13} Remember Abraham, Isaac, and Israel, thy servants, to whom thou swarest by thine own self, and saidst unto them, I will multiply your seed as the stars of heaven, and all this land that I have spoken of will I give unto your seed, and they shall inherit [it] for ever. {32:14} And the LORD repented of the evil which he thought to do unto his people. {32:15} And Moses turned, and went down from the mount, and the two tables of the testimony [were] in his hand: the tables [were] written on both their sides; on the one side and on the other [were] they written. {32:16} And the tables [were] the work of God, and the writing [was] the writing of God, graven upon the tables. {32:17} And when Joshua heard the noise of the people as they shouted, he said unto Moses, [There is] a noise of war in the camp. {32:18} And he said, [It is] not the voice of [them that] shout for mastery, neither [is it] the voice of [them that] cry for being overcome: [but] the noise of [them that] sing do I hear. {32:19} And it came to pass, as soon as he came nigh unto the camp, that he saw the calf, and the dancing: and Moses' anger waxed hot, and he cast the tables out of his hands, and brake them beneath the mount. {32:20} And he took the calf which they had made, and burnt [it] in the fire, and ground [it] to powder, and strawed [it] upon the water, and made the children of Israel drink [of it.] {32:21} And Moses said unto Aaron, What did this people unto thee, that thou hast brought so great a sin upon them? {32:22} And Aaron said, Let not the anger of my lord wax hot: thou knowest the people, that they are [set] on mischief. {32:23} For they said unto me, Make us gods, which shall go before us: for [as for] this Moses, the man that brought us up out of the land of Egypt, we wot not what is become of him. {32:24} And I said unto them, Whosoever hath any gold, let them break [it] off. So they gave [it] me: then I cast it into the fire, and there came out this calf. {32:25} And when Moses saw that the people [were] naked; (for Aaron had made them naked unto [their] shame among their enemies:) {32:26} Then Moses stood in the gate of the camp, and said, Who [is] on the LORD'S side? [let him come] unto me. And all the sons of Levi gathered themselves together unto him. {32:27} And he said unto them, Thus saith the LORD God of Israel, Put every man his sword by his side, [and] go in and out from gate to gate throughout the camp, and slay every man his brother, and every man his companion, and every man his neighbour. {32:28} And the children of Levi did according to the word of Moses: and there fell of the people that day about three thousand men. {32:29} For Moses had said, Consecrate yourselves to day to the LORD, even every man upon his son, and upon his brother; that he may bestow upon you a blessing this day. {32:30} And it came to pass on the morrow, that Moses said unto the people, Ye have sinned a great sin: and now I will go up unto the LORD; peradventure I shall make an atonement for your sin. {32:31} And Moses returned unto the LORD, and said, Oh, this people have sinned a great sin, and have made them gods of gold. {32:32} Yet now, if thou wilt forgive their sin—; and if not, blot me, I pray thee, out of thy book which thou hast written. {32:33} And the LORD said unto Moses, Whosoever hath sinned against me, him will I blot out of my book. {32:34} Therefore now go, lead the people unto [the place] of which I have spoken unto thee: behold, mine Angel shall go before thee: nevertheless in the day when I visit I will visit their sin upon them. {32:35} And the LORD plagued the people, because they made the calf, which Aaron made.

{33:1} And the LORD said unto Moses, Depart, [and] go up hence, thou and the people which thou hast brought up out of the land of Egypt, unto the land which I sware unto Abraham, to Isaac, and to Jacob, saying, Unto thy seed will I give it: {33:2} And I will send an angel before thee; and I will drive out the Canaanite, the Amorite, and the Hittite, and the Perizzite, the Hivite, and the Jebusite: {33:3} Unto a land flowing with milk and honey: for I will not go up in the midst of thee; for thou [art] a stiffnecked people: lest I consume thee in the way. {33:4} And when the people heard these evil tidings, they mourned: and no man did put on him his ornaments. {33:5} For the LORD had said unto Moses, Say unto the children of Israel, Ye [are] a stiffnecked people: I will come up into the midst of thee in a moment, and consume thee: therefore now put off thy ornaments from thee, that I may know what to do unto thee. {33:6} And the children of Israel stripped themselves of their ornaments by the mount Horeb. {33:7} And Moses took the tabernacle, and pitched it without the camp, afar off from the camp, and called it the Tabernacle of the congregation. And it came to pass, [that] every one which sought the LORD went out unto the tabernacle of the congregation, which [was] without the camp. {33:8} And it came to pass, when Moses went out unto the tabernacle, [that] all the people rose up, and stood every man [at] his tent door, and looked after Moses, until he was gone into the tabernacle. {33:9} And it came to pass, as Moses entered into the tabernacle, the cloudy pillar descended, and stood [at] the door of the tabernacle, and [the] LORD talked with Moses. {33:10} And all the people saw the cloudy pillar stand [at] the tabernacle door: and all the people rose up and worshipped, every man [in] his tent door. {33:11} And the LORD spake unto Moses face to face, as a man speaketh unto his friend. And he turned again into the camp: but his servant Joshua, the son of Nun, a young man, departed not out of the tabernacle. {33:12} And Moses said unto the LORD, See, thou sayest unto me, Bring up this people: and thou hast not let me know whom thou wilt send with me. Yet thou hast said, I know thee by name, and thou hast also found grace in my sight. {33:13} Now therefore, I pray thee, if I have found grace in thy sight, shew me now thy way, that I may know thee, that I may find grace in thy sight: and consider that this nation [is] thy people. {33:14} And he said, My presence shall go [with thee,] and I will give thee rest. {33:15} And he said unto him, If thy presence go not [with me,] carry us not up hence. {33:16} For wherein shall it be known here that I and thy people have found grace in thy sight? [is it] not in that thou goest with us? so shall we be separated, I and thy people, from all the people that [are] upon the face of the earth. {33:17} And the LORD said unto Moses, I will do this thing also that thou hast spoken: for thou hast found grace in my sight, and I know thee by name. {33:18} And he said, I beseech thee, shew me thy glory. {33:19} And he said, I will make all my goodness pass before thee, and I will proclaim the name of the LORD before thee; and will be gracious to whom I will be gracious, and will shew mercy on whom I will shew mercy. {33:20} And he said, Thou canst not see my face: for there shall no man see me, and live. {33:21} And the LORD said, Behold, [there is] a place by me, and thou shalt stand upon a rock: {33:22} And it shall come to pass, while my glory passeth by, that I will put thee in a clift of the rock, and will cover thee with my hand while I pass by: {33:23} And I will take away mine hand, and thou shalt see my back parts: but my face shall not be seen.

{34:1} And the LORD said unto Moses, Hew thee two tables of stone like unto the first: and I will write upon [these] tables the words that were in the first tables, which thou brakest. {34:2} And be ready in the morning, and come up in the morning unto mount Sinai, and present thyself there to me in the top of the mount. {34:3} And no man shall come up with thee, neither let any man be seen throughout all the mount; neither let the flocks nor herds feed before that mount. {34:4} And he hewed two tables of stone like unto the first; and Moses rose up early in the morning, and went up unto mount Sinai, as the LORD had commanded him, and took in his hand the two tables of stone. {34:5} And the LORD descended in the cloud, and stood with him there, and proclaimed the name of the LORD. {34:6} *And the LORD passed by before him, and proclaimed, The LORD, The LORD God, merciful and gracious, longsuffering, and abundant in goodness and truth,* {34:7} *Keeping mercy for thousands, forgiving iniquity and transgression and sin, and that will by no means clear [the guilty;] visiting the iniquity of the fathers upon the children, and upon the children's children, unto the third and to the fourth [generation.]* {34:8} And Moses made haste, and bowed his head toward the earth, and worshipped. {34:9} And he said, If now I have found grace in thy sight, O Lord, let my Lord, I pray thee, go among us; for it [is] a stiffnecked people; and pardon our iniquity and our sin, and take us for thine inheritance. {34:10} And he said, Behold, I make a covenant:

before all thy people I will do marvels, such as have not been done in all the earth, nor in any nation: and all the people among which thou [art] shall see the work of the LORD: for it [is] a terrible thing that I will do with thee. {34:11} Observe thou that which I command thee this day: behold, I drive out before thee the Amorite, and the Canaanite, and the Hittite, and the Perizzite, and the Hivite, and the Jebusite. {34:12} Take heed to thyself, lest thou make a covenant with the inhabitants of the land whither thou goest, lest it be for a snare in the midst of thee: {34:13} But ye shall destroy their altars, break their images, and cut down their groves: {34:14} For thou shalt worship no other god: for the LORD, whose name [is] Jealous, [is] a jealous God: {34:15} Lest thou make a covenant with the inhabitants of the land, and they go a whoring after their gods, and do sacrifice unto their gods, and [one] call thee, and thou eat of his sacrifice; {34:16} And thou take of their daughters unto thy sons, and their daughters go a whoring after their gods, and make thy sons go a whoring after their gods. {34:17} Thou shalt make thee no molten gods. {34:18} The feast of unleavened bread shalt thou keep. Seven days thou shalt eat unleavened bread, as I commanded thee, in the time of the month Abib: for in the month Abib thou camest out from Egypt. {34:19} All that openeth the matrix [is] mine; and every firstling among thy cattle, [whether] ox or sheep, [that is male.] {34:20} But the firstling of an ass thou shalt redeem with a lamb: and if thou redeem [him] not, then shalt thou break his neck. All the firstborn of thy sons thou shalt redeem. And none shall appear before me empty. {34:21} Six days thou shalt work, but on the seventh day thou shalt rest: in earing time and in harvest thou shalt rest. {34:22} And thou shalt observe the feast of weeks, of the firstfruits of wheat harvest, and the feast of ingathering at the year's end. {34:23} Thrice in the year shall all your men children appear before the Lord GOD, the God of Israel. {34:24} For I will cast out the nations before thee, and enlarge thy borders: neither shall any man desire thy land, when thou shalt go up to appear before the LORD thy God thrice in the year. {34:25} Thou shalt not offer the blood of my sacrifice with leaven; neither shall the sacrifice of the feast of the passover be left unto the morning. {34:26} The first of the firstfruits of thy land thou shalt bring unto the house of the LORD thy God. Thou shalt not seethe a kid in his mother's milk. {34:27} And the LORD said unto Moses, Write thou these words: for after the tenor of these words I have made a covenant with thee and with Israel. {34:28} And he was there with the LORD forty days and forty nights; he did neither eat bread, nor drink water. And he wrote upon the tables the words of the covenant, the ten commandments. {34:29} When Moses came down from Mount Sinai with the two tables of testimony in his hand, he didn't realize that his face was shining because he had been talking with the LORD. {34:30} But when Aaron and all the Israelites saw Moses, they noticed that his face was radiant, and they were afraid to come near him. {34:31} However, Moses called to them, and Aaron and all the leaders of the community returned to him, and Moses spoke with them. {34:32} Then all the Israelites approached, and Moses gave them the commandments the LORD had spoken with him on Mount Sinai. {34:33} After Moses had finished speaking with them, he put a veil over his face. {34:34} But whenever Moses went in before the LORD to speak with Him, he removed the veil until he came out. And when he came out and spoke to the Israelites what he had been commanded, {34:35} they saw that Moses' face was radiant. So, Moses would cover his face with the veil again until he went in to speak with the LORD.

{35:1} Moses gathered all the congregation of the children of Israel and told them, "These are the words the LORD has commanded you to do. {35:2} Six days shall be for work, but the seventh day is a holy Sabbath rest dedicated to the LORD. Anyone who works on that day shall be put to death. {35:3} No fire shall be kindled throughout your dwellings on the Sabbath day. {35:4} Then Moses addressed the entire congregation of Israel, saying, "This is what the LORD has commanded: {35:5} Take from among you an offering to the LORD. Whoever is willing in heart, let him bring it—an offering to the LORD—gold, silver, and bronze, {35:6} blue, purple, and scarlet thread, fine linen, and goat's hair, {35:7} ram skins dyed red, badger skins, and acacia wood, {35:8} oil for the light, spices for the anointing oil and for the sweet incense, {35:9} onyx stones, and stones to be set in the ephod and in the breastplate; {35:10} "Let every skilled craftsman among you come and make all that the LORD has commanded: {35:11} the tabernacle, its tent, its covering, its clasps, its boards, its bars, its pillars, and its sockets; {35:12} the ark and its poles, with the mercy seat and the veil of the covering; {35:13} the table and its poles, all its utensils, and the showbread; {35:14} also the lampstand for the light, its utensils, its lamps, and the oil for the light; {35:15} the incense altar, its poles, the anointing oil, the sweet incense, and the screen for the door at the entrance of the tabernacle; {35:16} the altar of burnt offering with its bronze grating, its poles, all its utensils, and the basin with its base; {35:17} the hangings of the court, its pillars, their sockets, and the screen for the gate of the court; {35:18} the pegs of the tabernacle, the pegs of the court, and their cords; {35:19} the garments of ministry, for ministering in the holy place—the holy garments for Aaron the priest and the garments of his sons, to minister as priests." {35:20} Then all the congregation of the children of Israel departed from the presence of Moses. {35:21} And they came, everyone whose heart was stirred up, and everyone whose spirit was willing, and they brought the LORD's offering for the work of the tabernacle of meeting, for all its service, and for the holy garments. {35:22} They came, both men and women, as many as had a willing heart, and brought earrings and nose rings, rings and necklaces, all jewelry of gold, that is, every man who made an offering of gold to the LORD. {35:23} And every man, with whom was found blue, purple, and scarlet thread, fine linen, and goats' hair, red skins of rams, and badger skins, brought them. {35:24} Everyone who offered an offering of silver or bronze brought the LORD's offering. And everyone with whom was found acacia wood for any work of the service, brought it. {35:25} All the women who were gifted artisans spun yarn with their hands, and brought what they had spun—of blue, purple, and scarlet, and fine linen. {35:26} And all the women whose hearts stirred with wisdom spun yarn of goats' hair. {35:27} The rulers brought onyx stones, and the stones to be set in the ephod and in the breastplate; {35:28} and spices and oil for the light, for the anointing oil, and for the sweet incense. {35:29} The children of Israel brought a willing offering to the LORD, every man and woman whose heart made them willing to bring for all manner of work which the LORD had commanded to be done by the hand of Moses. {35:30} Then Moses said to the children of Israel, "See, the LORD has called by name Bezalel the son of Uri, the son of Hur, of the tribe of Judah; {35:31} and He has filled him with the Spirit of God, in wisdom and understanding, in knowledge, and in all manner of workmanship, {35:32} to design artistic works, to work in gold, in silver, in bronze, {35:33} in cutting jewels for setting, in carving wood, and to work in all manner of artistic workmanship. {35:34} And He has put in his heart the ability to teach, in him and Aholiab the son of Ahisamach, of the tribe of Dan. {35:35} He has filled them with skill to do all manner of work of the engraver, of the designer, and of the tapestry maker, in blue, purple, and scarlet thread, and fine linen, and of the weaver—those who do every work and those who design artistic works."

{36:1} Bezalel, Aholiab, and every skilled person whom the LORD had given wisdom and understanding worked on all the tasks required for the sanctuary, exactly as the LORD had commanded. {36:2} Moses called Bezalel, Aholiab, and all the skilled workers whose hearts were stirred to join in the work. {36:3} They received from Moses all the offerings that the Israelites had brought for the work of the sanctuary. They continued to bring freewill offerings every morning. {36:4} Then all the skilled workers left their work and said to Moses, "The people are bringing much more than enough for doing the work the LORD commanded to be done." {36:5} So Moses gave a command, and word was proclaimed throughout the camp: "Let neither man nor woman do any more work for the offering of the sanctuary." And the people were restrained from bringing more. {36:7} The materials they had were sufficient for all the work to be done, and there was even excess. {36:8} Every skilled worker made ten curtains of finely woven linen, blue, purple, and scarlet fabric, with cherubim skillfully worked into them. {36:9} Each curtain was twenty-eight cubits long and four cubits wide; all the curtains were the same size. {36:10} He joined five curtains together and the other five curtains together. {36:11} He made loops of blue yarn along the edge of the curtain at the end in one set, and the same was done along the edge of the outermost curtain in the second set. {36:12} Fifty loops he made on one curtain, and fifty loops he made on the edge of the curtain that was in the second set; the loops were opposite one another. {36:13} And he made fifty gold clasps and coupled the curtains together with the clasps, so the tabernacle was a single unit. {36:14} He also made curtains of goats' hair for the tent over the tabernacle. He made eleven curtains in all. {36:15} Each curtain was thirty cubits long and four cubits wide; all the curtains were the same size. {36:16} He joined five curtains by themselves and the other six curtains by themselves. {36:17} He made fifty loops along the edge of the outermost curtain in one set and fifty loops along the edge of the curtain that joined the second set. {36:18} He also made fifty bronze clasps to fasten the tent together as a single unit. {36:19} And he made a covering for the tent of ram skins dyed red and a covering of badger skins above that. {36:20} He constructed the frames for the tabernacle out of acacia wood, standing upright. {36:21} Each frame was ten cubits long and one and a half cubits wide. {36:22} Each frame had two tenons, set parallel to one another. He did this for all the frames of the tabernacle. {36:23} He made twenty frames for the south side of the tabernacle {36:24} and made forty silver bases to go under the twenty frames—two bases under each frame for its two tenons—{36:25} and for the other side of the tabernacle, the north side, he made twenty frames {36:26} with their forty silver bases—two bases under each frame. {36:27} For the rear of the tabernacle, the west side, he made six frames {36:28} and two frames for the corners at the rear of the tabernacle. {36:29} These were doubled at the bottom and fitted together at the top with a single ring; both were like that for both corners. {36:30} So there were eight frames and sixteen silver bases—two under each frame. {36:31} He also made crossbars of acacia wood: five for the frames on one side of the tabernacle, {36:32} five for those on the other side, and five for the frames on the west, at the rear of the tabernacle. {36:33} He made the central crossbar run through the middle of the frames from end to end. {36:34} He overlaid the frames with gold and made gold rings to hold the crossbars, and he overlaid the crossbars with gold. {36:35} For the veil he made woven material of blue, purple, and scarlet yarn, and of fine linen—worked into it were cherubim. {36:36} He made four posts of acacia wood and overlaid them with gold. Their hooks were of gold, and he cast four silver bases for them. {36:37} For the entrance to the tent, he made a screen embroidered with blue, purple, and scarlet yarn, and fine linen—{36:38} and the five posts with their hooks. He overlaid their tops and bands with gold, but their five bases were bronze.

{37:1} Bezaleel crafted the ark from shittim wood, measuring two and a half cubits in length, a cubit and a half in width, and a cubit and a half in height. {37:2} He overlaid it with pure gold inside and out, and made a gold crown all around it. {37:3} Four gold rings were cast for it, to be set at its four corners: two rings on one side and two rings on the other. {37:4} He made poles of shittim wood and overlaid them with gold, {37:5} and inserted the poles into the rings on the sides of the ark to carry it. {37:6} The mercy seat was made of pure gold, measuring two and a half cubits in length and one and a half cubits in width. {37:7} Bezaleel made two cherubim of gold, beaten out of one piece, and placed them at the ends of the mercy seat. {37:8} One cherub was placed on one end and the other cherub on the other end, with the cherubim spreading their wings over the mercy seat and facing each other. {37:9} The cherubim covered the mercy seat with their wings, facing toward it. {37:10} The table was made of shittim wood, measuring two cubits in length, one cubit in width, and a cubit and a half in height. {37:11} It was overlaid with pure gold, and a gold crown was made for it all around. {37:12} A border of a handbreadth was made around it, and a gold crown was made for the border all around. {37:13} Four gold rings were cast for it and placed at the four corners, near the four feet. {37:14} The rings were opposite the border, providing places for the poles to carry the table. {37:15} Bezaleel made poles of shittim wood and overlaid them with gold to carry the table. {37:16} He also made the utensils for the table: its dishes, spoons, bowls, and covers, all made of pure gold. {37:17} The lampstand was made of pure gold, beaten work, with its shaft, branches, bowls, knobs, and flowers all of one piece. {37:18} It had six branches, three on each side, with three bowls made like almonds on one branch, a knob, and a flower; and three bowls made like almonds on the next branch, with a knob and a flower, and so on for all six branches. {37:19} There were four bowls made like almonds on the lampstand, with its knobs and flowers. {37:20} A knob was under two branches of the same, and a knob under two branches of the same, and a knob under two branches of the same, according to the six branches coming out of the lampstand. {37:21} The knobs and branches were of one piece with the lampstand, all of it made of pure gold. {37:22} Bezaleel also made seven lamps, as well as its snuffers and snuff dishes, all of pure gold. {37:23} He used a talent of pure gold to make them and all their utensils. {37:25} The incense altar was made of shittim wood, measuring a cubit in length, a cubit in width, and two cubits in height, with horns of the same wood. {37:26} It was overlaid with pure gold on top, on the sides all around, and on its horns, and a crown of gold was made for it all around. {37:27} Two gold rings were made for it under its crown, on its two sides, for the poles to bear it. {37:28} Bezaleel made poles of shittim wood and overlaid them with gold. {37:29} He also made the holy anointing oil and the pure incense of sweet spices, following the instructions of the perfumer.

{38:1} Bezaleel made the altar of burnt offering from shittim wood, measuring five cubits in length, five cubits in width, and three cubits in height. {38:2} He placed horns on its four corners, all made of the same wood, and overlaid the altar with brass. {38:3} All the utensils for the altar—the pots, shovels, basins, fleshhooks, and firepans—were made of brass. {38:4} He also made a brass grate for the altar, placing it beneath, reaching halfway up the altar. {38:5} Four rings of brass were cast for the four corners of the grate, to hold the poles. {38:6} Bezaleel made poles of shittim wood and overlaid them with brass. {38:7} He inserted the poles into the rings on the sides of the altar to carry it, making the altar hollow with boards. {38:8} The laver was made of brass, and its base was made from the mirrors of the women who assembled at the entrance of the tent of meeting. {38:9} Bezaleel made the courtyard: for the south side, the hangings of fine twined linen were one hundred cubits long, supported by twenty pillars set in twenty brass sockets, with silver hooks and fillets. {38:10} For the north side, there were also one hundred cubits of hangings, with twenty pillars in twenty brass sockets, but with silver hooks and fillets. {38:11} The west side had hangings fifty cubits long, supported by ten pillars in ten sockets, with silver hooks and fillets. {38:12} The east side had hangings fifty cubits long. {38:13} The entrance gate had fifteen cubits of hangings on one side, with three pillars and three sockets. {38:14} Similarly, on the other side of the gate, there were fifteen cubits of hangings with three pillars and three sockets. {38:15} All the hangings around the courtyard were made of fine twined linen. {38:16} The sockets for the pillars were made of brass, with silver hooks and fillets, and their capitals were overlaid with silver. {38:17} The gate of the courtyard was made of needlework in blue, purple, scarlet, and fine twined linen, twenty cubits long and five cubits high, matching the hangings of the courtyard. {38:18} There were four pillars in four brass sockets, with silver hooks and fillets. {38:19} All the pegs for the tabernacle and the courtyard were made of brass. {38:21} This summarizes the materials used in the construction of the tabernacle, the tabernacle of the testimony, as counted and commanded by Moses, for the service of the Levites, under the direction of Ithamar, son of Aaron the priest. {38:22} Bezaleel, son of Uri, of the tribe of Judah, made everything the LORD commanded Moses. {38:23} He was assisted by Aholiab, son of Ahisamach, of the tribe of Dan, who was skilled in engraving, crafting, and embroidering in blue, purple, scarlet, and fine linen. {38:24} The gold used in all the work of the sanctuary, including the gold from the contributions, amounted to twenty-nine talents and seven hundred and thirty shekels, according to the sanctuary shekel. {38:25} The silver collected from those who were numbered in the congregation totaled one hundred talents and one thousand seven hundred and seventy-five shekels, according to the sanctuary shekel. {38:26} Each person contributed a beka, that is, half a shekel, according to the sanctuary shekel, for everyone twenty years old and above, totaling six hundred and three thousand five hundred and fifty men. {38:27} The one hundred talents of silver were used to make the sockets for the sanctuary and the veil, one hundred sockets from the one hundred talents, one talent per socket. {38:28} From the one thousand seven hundred and seventy-five shekels, Bezaleel made the hooks for the pillars, overlaying their capitals and filleting them. {38:29} The brass from the offering amounted to seventy talents and two thousand four hundred shekels. {38:30} With this, he made the sockets for the entrance of the tent of meeting, the bronze altar, the bronze grating for it, and all its utensils. {38:31} He also made the sockets for the courtyard all around, and the sockets for the gate of the courtyard, and all the pegs for the tabernacle and the courtyard.

{39:1} They made cloths of service from blue, purple, and scarlet to use in the holy place, as well as the holy garments for Aaron, following the instructions of the LORD given to Moses. {39:2} Bezaleel crafted the ephod from gold, blue, purple, scarlet, and fine linen. {39:3} They hammered the gold into thin plates and cut it into wires to work it into the blue, purple, scarlet, and fine linen with skillful craftsmanship. {39:4} Shoulder pieces were made for the ephod to attach it together at its two edges. {39:5} The intricate sash of the ephod, worn over it, was made of the same materials—gold, blue, purple, scarlet, and fine linen—as instructed by the LORD. {39:6} They crafted onyx stones enclosed in gold settings, engraved like signet rings, with the names of the tribes of Israel. {39:7} These stones were placed on the shoulders of the ephod as memorial stones for the Israelites, as the LORD commanded Moses. {39:8} The breastplate was made with skillful workmanship, resembling the ephod, from gold, blue, purple, scarlet, and fine linen. {39:9} It was square and folded double, a span in length and a span in width when doubled. {39:10} Four rows of stones were set in it: the first row had a sardius, a topaz, and a carbuncle; this was the first row. {39:11} The second row had an emerald, a sapphire, and a diamond. {39:12} The third row had a jacinth, an agate, and an amethyst. {39:13} The fourth row had a beryl, an onyx, and a jasper. These stones were enclosed in gold settings, each engraved with the name of one of the twelve tribes of Israel, like the engravings of a signet ring. {39:14} Chains of pure gold were made for the breastplate, attached to its rings at the corners. {39:15} Two gold rings were made and placed on the two ends of the breastplate. {39:16} The gold chains were then attached to these rings on the breastplate. {39:17} The ends of the chains were fastened to the two settings on the shoulder pieces of the ephod at the front. {39:18} Two more gold rings were made for the breastplate, placed on its edge on the inside of the ephod. {39:19} Two additional gold rings were made for the ephod, below its shoulder pieces, near its seam above the ephod's skillfully woven sash. {39:20} They tied the breastplate securely to the rings of the ephod with a blue cord so that it would be above the sash of the ephod and would not come loose, {39:21} as the LORD commanded Moses. {39:22} They made the robe of the ephod entirely of blue fabric. {39:23} There was an opening in the center of the robe, like the opening of a garment, with a woven collar around the opening so that it would not tear. {39:24} On the hem of the robe, they made pomegranates of blue, purple, and scarlet yarn, alternating with gold bells all around the hem. {39:25} A gold bell and a pomegranate were placed alternately all around the hem of the robe for ministering, as the LORD commanded Moses. {39:27} They made tunics of fine linen for Aaron and his sons, {39:28} as well as headbands, caps, and linen undergarments of fine linen. {39:29} They also made a sash of fine linen, blue, purple, and scarlet yarn, expertly woven, as the LORD commanded Moses. {39:30} The plate of the holy crown was made of pure gold, and the inscription on it was like that of a seal: "HOLINESS TO THE LORD." {39:31} A blue cord was tied to it to fasten it securely on the front of the turban, as the LORD commanded Moses. {39:32} So all the work on the tabernacle, the Tent of Meeting, was completed. The Israelites did everything just as the LORD had commanded Moses. {39:33} They brought the tabernacle to Moses: the tent and all its furnishings, clasps, frames, crossbars, posts, and bases; {39:34} the covering of ram skins dyed red and the covering of fine leather; the curtain for the veil; {39:35} the ark of the covenant with its poles and the mercy seat; {39:36} the table, all its utensils, and the bread of the Presence; {39:37} the pure gold lampstand with its lamps set in order and all its accessories, and the olive oil for the light; {39:38} the gold altar, the anointing oil, the fragrant incense, and the curtain for the entrance to the tent; {39:39} the bronze altar with its bronze grating, its poles, and all its utensils; the basin with its stand; {39:40} the curtains of the courtyard with its posts and bases, and the curtain for the entrance to the courtyard, its ropes and tent pegs, and all the furnishings for the service of the tabernacle, for the Tent of Meeting; {39:41} the woven garments for ministering in the sanctuary, both the sacred garments for Aaron the priest and the garments for his sons to serve as priests. {39:42} The Israelites had done all the work just as the LORD had commanded Moses. {39:43} Moses inspected all the work, and indeed they had done it just as the LORD had commanded. So Moses blessed them.

{40:1} Then the LORD spoke to Moses, saying, {40:2} "On the first day of the first month, you shall set up the tabernacle of the tent of meeting. {40:3} Put the ark of the testimony in it and cover the ark with the veil. {40:4} Bring in the table and arrange the items on it, and bring in the lampstand and light its lamps. {40:5} Set up the golden altar for incense before the ark of the testimony, and hang the curtain at the entrance to the tabernacle. {40:6} Set up the altar of burnt offering in front of the entrance to the tent of meeting. {40:7} Place the basin between the tent of meeting and the altar, and put water in it. {40:8} Set up the courtyard all around and hang the curtain at the entrance to the courtyard gate. {40:9} Take the anointing oil and anoint the tabernacle and everything in it; consecrate it and all its furnishings, so they will be holy. {40:10} Anoint the altar of burnt offering and all its utensils; consecrate the altar, and it will be most holy. {40:11} Anoint the basin and its stand and consecrate it. {40:12} Bring Aaron and his sons to the entrance to the tent of meeting and wash them with water. {40:13} Dress Aaron in the sacred garments, anoint him, and consecrate him so he may serve me as a priest. {40:14} Bring his sons and dress them in tunics. {40:15} Anoint them just as you anointed their father, so they may serve me as priests. Their anointing will be to a priesthood that will continue throughout their generations. {40:16} Moses did everything just as the LORD commanded him. {40:17} So the tabernacle was set up on the first day of the first month in the second year. {40:18} Moses set up the tabernacle: he laid its bases, set up its frames, inserted its crossbars, and set up its posts. {40:19} Then he spread the tent over the tabernacle and put the covering over the tent, as the LORD commanded Moses. {40:20} He took the tablets of the covenant law and placed them in the ark, attached the poles to the ark, and put the atonement cover over it. {40:21} Then he brought the ark into the tabernacle and hung the curtain and shielded the ark of the covenant law, as the LORD commanded Moses. {40:22} He placed the table in the tent of meeting on the north side of the tabernacle outside the curtain {40:23} and set out the bread on it before the LORD, as the LORD commanded Moses. {40:24} He placed the lampstand in the tent of meeting opposite the table on the south side of the tabernacle {40:25} and set up the lamps before the LORD, as the LORD commanded Moses. {40:26} He placed the gold altar in the tent of meeting in front of the curtain {40:27} and burned fragrant incense on it, as the LORD commanded Moses. {40:28} He put up the curtain at the entrance to the tabernacle. {40:29} He set the altar of burnt offering near the entrance to the tabernacle, the tent of meeting, and offered on it burnt offerings and grain offerings, as the LORD commanded Moses. {40:30} He placed the basin between the tent of meeting and the altar and put water in it for washing, {40:31} and Moses, Aaron, and his sons used it to wash their hands and feet. {40:32} They washed whenever they entered the tent of meeting or approached the altar, as the LORD commanded Moses. {40:33} Then Moses set up the courtyard around the tabernacle and altar and put up the curtain at the entrance to the courtyard gate. So Moses finished the work. {40:34} Then the cloud covered the tent of meeting, and the glory of the LORD filled the tabernacle. {40:35} Moses could not enter the tent of meeting because the cloud had settled on it, and the glory of the LORD filled the tabernacle. {40:36} In all the travels of the Israelites, whenever the cloud lifted from above the tabernacle, they would set out; {40:37} but if the cloud did not lift, they did not set out—until the day it lifted. {40:38} So the cloud of the LORD was over the tabernacle by day, and fire was in the cloud by night, in the sight of all the Israelites during all their travels.

Leviticus

{1:1} The LORD called to Moses and spoke to him from the tabernacle of the congregation, saying, {1:2} **"Speak to the children of Israel and tell them, 'If any man among you brings an offering to the LORD, you shall bring your offering from the cattle, whether from the herd or from the flock.** {1:3} If his offering is a burnt sacrifice from the herd, let him offer a male without blemish; he shall offer it willingly at the entrance of the tabernacle of the congregation before the LORD. {1:4} And he shall lay his hand on the head of the burnt offering, and it shall be accepted on his behalf to make atonement for him. {1:5} Then he shall slaughter the bull before the LORD; and the priests, Aaron's sons, shall bring the blood and sprinkle it all around on the altar that is by the entrance of the tabernacle of the congregation. {1:6} And he shall skin the burnt offering and cut it into pieces. {1:7} The sons of Aaron the priest shall put fire on the altar and lay the wood in order on the fire. {1:8} Then the priests, Aaron's sons, shall arrange the pieces, the head, and the fat on the wood that is on the fire on the altar. {1:9} But he shall wash its entrails and its legs with water. And the priest shall burn all on the altar as a burnt sacrifice, an offering made by fire, a sweet aroma to the LORD. {1:10} 'If his offering is from the flocks, from the sheep or from the goats, as a burnt sacrifice, he shall bring a male without blemish. {1:11} He shall kill it on the north side of the altar before the LORD; and the priests, Aaron's sons, shall sprinkle its blood all around on the altar. {1:12} And he shall cut it into pieces, with its head and its fat; and the priest shall arrange them in order on the wood that is on the fire upon the altar. {1:13} But he shall wash the entrails and the legs with water. And the priest shall bring it all and burn it on the altar; it is a burnt sacrifice, an offering made by fire, a sweet aroma to the LORD. {1:14} 'If the burnt sacrifice for his offering to the LORD is of birds, then he shall bring his offering of turtledoves or young pigeons. {1:15} The priest shall bring it to the altar, wring off its head, and burn it on the altar; and its blood shall be drained out at the side of the altar. {1:16} And he shall remove its crop with its feathers and cast it beside the altar on the east side, by the place of the ashes. {1:17} Then he shall split it at its wings, but shall not divide it completely; and the priest shall burn it on the altar, on the wood that is on the fire. It is a burnt sacrifice, an offering made by fire, a sweet aroma to the LORD."

{2:1} When anyone offers a grain offering to the LORD, his offering shall be fine flour; he shall pour oil upon it and put frankincense on it. {2:2} Then he shall bring it to Aaron's sons, the priests, and he shall take from it his handful of fine flour and oil, with all the frankincense, and the priest shall burn it as a memorial on the altar, an offering made by fire, a sweet aroma to the LORD. {2:3} The rest of the grain offering shall belong to Aaron and his sons; it is most holy of the offerings to the LORD made by fire. {2:4} If you bring an offering of a grain offering baked in the oven, it shall be unleavened cakes of fine flour mixed with oil, or unleavened wafers anointed with oil. {2:5} If your offering is a grain offering baked on a pan, it shall be of fine flour unleavened, mixed with oil. {2:6} You shall break it in pieces and pour oil on it; it is a grain offering. {2:7} If your offering is a grain offering in a covered pan, it shall be made of fine flour with oil. {2:8} You shall bring the grain offering that is made of these things to the LORD; and when it is presented to the priest, he shall bring it to the altar. {2:9} The priest shall take from the grain offering a memorial of it and shall burn it on the altar; it is an offering made by fire, a sweet aroma to the LORD. {2:10} The rest of the grain offering shall belong to Aaron and his sons; it is most holy of the offerings to the LORD made by fire. {2:11} No grain offering which you bring to the LORD shall be made with leaven, for you shall not burn any leaven nor any honey in any offering made by fire to the LORD. {2:12} As for the offering of the firstfruits, you shall offer them to the LORD, but they shall not be burned on the altar for a sweet aroma. {2:13} Every offering of your grain offering you shall season with salt; you shall not allow the salt of the covenant of your God to be lacking from your grain offering. With all your offerings you shall offer salt.{2:14} If you offer a grain offering of your firstfruits to the LORD, you shall offer for the grain offering of your firstfruits green heads of grain dried by fire, grain beaten from full heads. {2:15} And you shall put oil on it and lay frankincense on it; it is a grain offering. {2:16} The priest shall burn the memorial of it, part of the beaten grain of it, and part of the oil of it, with all the frankincense of it; it is an offering made by fire to the LORD.

{3:1} If someone's offering to the LORD is a peace offering from the herd, whether it's a male or female, it must be without any blemish presented before the LORD. {3:2} The person offering it shall lay their hand on the head of the offering and slaughter it at the entrance of the tabernacle. Then Aaron's sons, the priests, shall sprinkle the blood around the altar. {3:3} From the peace offering, they shall offer to the LORD the fat covering the entrails and all the fat on the entrails. {3:4} They shall also offer the two kidneys, the fat on them, by the flanks, and the lobe on the liver, along with the kidneys. {3:5} Aaron's sons shall burn it on the altar along with the burnt offering, which is on the wood on the fire; it is an offering made by fire, a pleasing aroma to the LORD. {3:6} If the offering for a peace offering to the LORD is from the flock, whether male or female, it must be without blemish. {3:7} If someone offers a lamb, they shall present it before the LORD. {3:8} They shall lay their hand on the head of the offering and slaughter it in front of the tabernacle. Then Aaron's sons shall sprinkle its blood around the altar. {3:9} From the peace offering, they shall offer to the LORD the fat, the whole fatty tail near the backbone, the fat covering the entrails, and all the fat on the entrails. {3:10} They shall also offer the two kidneys, the fat on them, by the flanks, and the lobe on the liver, along with the kidneys. {3:11} The priest shall burn it on the altar; it is the food of the offering made by fire to the LORD. {3:12} If someone's offering is a goat, they shall present it before the LORD. {3:13} They shall lay their hand on its head and slaughter it in front of the tabernacle. Then Aaron's sons shall sprinkle its blood around the altar. {3:14} They shall offer its fat as an offering made by fire to the LORD: the fat covering the entrails and all the fat on the entrails. {3:15} They shall also offer the two kidneys, the fat on them, by the flanks, and the lobe on the liver, along with the kidneys. {3:16} The priest shall burn them on the altar; it is the food of the offering made by fire for a pleasing aroma. All the fat belongs to the LORD. {3:17} This shall be a perpetual statute for your generations throughout all your dwellings: you shall not eat neither fat nor blood.

{4:1} The LORD spoke to Moses, saying, {4:2} "Speak to the children of Israel, saying, if anyone sins unintentionally against any of the LORD's commandments concerning things that should not be done, and does any of them: {4:3} if the anointed priest sins, bringing guilt on the people, he shall bring a young bull without blemish as a sin offering to the LORD. {4:4} He shall bring the bull to the entrance of the tabernacle of the congregation before the LORD, lay his hand on the bull's head, and kill it before the LORD. {4:5} The anointed priest shall take some of the bull's blood and bring it to the tabernacle of the congregation. {4:6} He shall dip his finger in the blood and sprinkle it seven times before the LORD, in front of the veil of the sanctuary. {4:7} The priest shall also put some of the blood on the horns of the altar of sweet incense before the LORD, which is in the tabernacle of the congregation, and pour out all the blood at the base of the altar of burnt offering, which is at the entrance of the tabernacle of the congregation. {4:8} Then he shall remove all the fat from the bull of the sin offering: the fat covering the entrails, all the fat on the entrails, {4:9} the two kidneys and the fat on them by the flanks, and the fatty lobe attached to the liver, along with the kidneys. It shall be removed. {4:10} Just as it was taken from the bull of the peace offering sacrifice, the priest shall burn them on the altar of burnt offering. {4:11} The skin of the bull, all its flesh, with its head, legs, entrails, and dung— {4:12} all of it, he shall take outside the camp to a clean place where the ashes are poured out and burn it on wood with fire. It shall be burned where the ashes are poured out. {4:13} "If the whole congregation of Israel sins unintentionally, and the matter is hidden from the eyes of the assembly, and they have done something against any of the commandments of the LORD concerning things that should not be done, and are guilty; {4:14} when the sin which they have committed becomes known, then the congregation shall offer a young bull for the sin and bring it before the tabernacle of the congregation. {4:15} The elders of the congregation shall lay their hands on the head of the bull before the LORD, and the bull shall be killed before the LORD. {4:16} Then the anointed priest shall bring some of the bull's blood to the tabernacle of the congregation. {4:17} The priest shall dip his finger in some of the blood and sprinkle it seven times before the LORD, even in front of the veil. {4:18} He shall also put some of the blood on the horns of the altar that is before the LORD in the tabernacle of the congregation and pour out all the blood at the base of the altar of burnt offering, which is at the entrance of the tabernacle of the congregation. {4:19} Then he shall remove all the fat from it and burn it on the altar. {4:20} He shall treat the bull as he treated the bull for a sin offering. Thus, the priest shall make atonement for them, and it shall be forgiven them. {4:21} And he shall take the bull outside the camp and burn it as he burned the first bull. It is a sin offering for the congregation. {4:22} "When a ruler sins and unintentionally violates any of the commandments of the LORD his God, which should not be done, and is guilty; {4:23} or if his sin, in which he has sinned, comes to his knowledge, he shall bring his offering: a kid of the goats, a male without blemish. {4:24} He shall lay his hand on the head of the goat and kill it in the place where they kill the burnt offering before the LORD. It is a sin offering. {4:25} The priest shall take some of the blood of the sin offering with his finger and put it on the horns of the altar of burnt offering. Then he shall pour out its blood at the base of the altar of burnt offering. {4:26} He shall burn all its fat on the altar, like the fat of the peace offerings. So the priest shall make atonement for him concerning his sin, and it shall be forgiven him. {4:27} "If anyone of the common people sins unintentionally by doing any of the things which the LORD has commanded not to be done, and becomes guilty; {4:28} or if his sin which he has committed is made known to him, then he shall bring his offering: a kid of the goats, a female without blemish, for his sin which he has committed. {4:29} He shall lay his hand on the head of the sin offering and kill the sin offering at the place of the burnt offering. {4:30} The priest shall take some of its blood with his finger and put it on the horns of the altar of burnt offering. Then he shall pour out all the blood at the base of the altar. {4:31} He shall remove all its fat, as fat is removed from the lamb of the sacrifice of peace offerings. The priest shall burn it on the altar, on the offerings made by fire to the LORD. So the priest shall make atonement for him, and it shall be forgiven him. {4:32} If he brings a lamb as his sin offering, he shall bring a female without blemish. {4:33} He shall lay his hand on the head of the sin offering and kill it as a sin offering in the place where they kill the burnt offering. {4:34} The priest shall take some of the blood of the sin offering with his finger and put it on the horns of the altar of burnt offering. Then he shall pour out all its blood at the base of the altar. {4:35} He shall remove all its fat, as the fat of the lamb is removed from the sacrifice of peace offerings. The priest shall burn them on the altar according to the offerings made by fire to the LORD. So the priest shall make atonement for his sin that he has committed, and it shall be forgiven him.

{5:1} If someone sins and hears a sworn oath but fails to report it, they bear the consequences of their iniquity. {5:2} Likewise, if someone touches any unclean thing, whether the carcass of an unclean animal or the carcass of unclean cattle or creeping things, and it is hidden from them, they become unclean and guilty. {5:3} If someone touches any human uncleanliness and later realizes it, they become guilty. {5:4} Also, if someone swears thoughtlessly, whether for good or evil, and later becomes aware of it, they become guilty in any of these matters. {5:5} When they become aware of their guilt, they must confess their sin. {5:6} Then they shall bring a trespass offering to the LORD for the sin they committed: a female lamb or goat from the flock. The priest shall make atonement for them concerning their sin. {5:7} If they cannot afford a lamb, they shall bring two turtledoves or two young pigeons to the LORD—one for a sin offering and the other for a burnt offering. {5:8} They shall bring them to the priest, who shall offer the one for the sin offering first, wring its head from its neck but not sever it. {5:9} The priest shall sprinkle some of the blood of the sin offering on the side of the altar, and the rest of the blood shall be drained out at the base of the altar; it is a sin offering. {5:10} Then they shall offer the second bird for a burnt offering, following the prescribed procedure, and the priest shall make atonement for their sin, and they shall be forgiven. {5:11} But if they cannot afford two turtledoves or two young pigeons, they shall bring a tenth of an ephah of fine flour as a sin offering. They shall not put oil or frankincense on it because it is a sin offering. {5:12} They shall bring it to the priest, who shall take a handful of it as a memorial and burn it on the altar as an offering made by fire to the LORD; it is a sin offering. {5:13} The priest shall make atonement for them concerning their sin, and they shall be forgiven, and the rest shall belong to the priest as a grain offering. {5:14} Then the LORD spoke to Moses, saying, {5:15} If someone commits a trespass and sins unintentionally in the holy things of the LORD, they shall bring a ram without blemish from the flock, with the value determined by the sanctuary shekel, as a trespass offering. {5:16} They shall make restitution for the wrong they have done in the holy thing, adding a fifth to it, and give it to the priest. The priest shall make atonement for them with the ram of the trespass offering, and they shall be forgiven. {5:17} If someone sins by doing what is forbidden by the commandments of the LORD, even if they did not realize it, they are guilty and must bear the consequences of their iniquity. {5:18} They shall bring a ram without blemish from the flock, with the value determined by the sanctuary, for a trespass offering to the priest. The priest shall make atonement for them concerning their unintentional error, and they shall be forgiven. {5:19} It is a trespass offering; they have indeed trespassed against the LORD.

{6:1} Then the LORD spoke to Moses, saying, {6:2} If someone sins and commits a trespass against the LORD by deceiving their neighbor, whether in something entrusted to them, in a deposit, or through robbery, or if they have defrauded their neighbor, {6:3} or if they find lost property and lie about it, swearing falsely about any such sin that a person may commit— {6:4} then they must make restitution for what they have done wrong. They must return what they unlawfully took, what they deceitfully acquired, what was entrusted to them, or what they found and falsely swore about. {6:5} They must make full restitution, adding a fifth of the value to it, and give it all to the owner on the day of their guilt offering. {6:6} They shall bring a guilt offering to the LORD, a ram without defect from the flock, with the value determined by the sanctuary, for their trespass offering to the priest. {6:7} The priest shall make atonement for them before the LORD, and they will be forgiven for all their trespasses. {6:8} Then the LORD spoke to Moses, saying, {6:9} "Command Aaron and his sons, saying, 'This is the law of the burnt offering: The burnt offering must remain on the altar all night until morning, and the fire on the altar must be kept burning. {6:10} The priest shall put on his linen garment and linen breeches and shall remove the ashes left by the burnt offering that the fire has consumed on the altar, and he shall put them beside the altar. {6:11} Then he shall change his clothes and carry the ashes outside the camp to a clean place. {6:12} The fire on the altar must be kept burning; it must not go out. Every morning the priest shall add wood to the fire, arrange the burnt offering on it, and burn the fat of the fellowship offerings on it. {6:13} The fire must be kept burning continuously on the altar; it must not go out. {6:14} "This is the law of the grain offering: Aaron's sons shall present it before the LORD, in front of the altar. {6:15} The priest shall take a handful of the fine flour and oil, together with all the incense, and burn it as a memorial portion on the altar—a pleasing aroma to the LORD. {6:16} The rest of it Aaron and his sons shall eat. It is to be eaten without leaven in the sanctuary area; they are to eat it in the courtyard of the Tent of Meeting. {6:17} It must not be baked with leaven. I have given it to them as their share of the food offerings presented to me. It is most holy, like the sin offering and the guilt offering. {6:18} All the males among the descendants of Aaron shall eat of it. It is a permanent statute throughout your generations concerning the food offerings presented to the LORD. Everyone who touches them will be holy." {6:19} Then the LORD spoke to Moses, saying, {6:20} "This is the offering Aaron and his sons are to present to the LORD on the day he is anointed: one-tenth of an ephah of the finest flour as a regular grain offering, half of it in the morning and half in the evening. {6:21} Prepare it with oil on a griddle; bring it well-mixed and present the grain offering broken in pieces as a pleasing aroma to the LORD. {6:22} The priest who is anointed to succeed his father shall prepare it. It is a permanent statute to be offered entirely to the LORD. {6:23} Every grain offering of a priest shall be burned completely; it must not be eaten." {6:24} Then the LORD spoke to Moses, saying, {6:25} "Speak to Aaron and his sons, saying, 'This is the law of the sin offering: In the place where the burnt offering is slaughtered, the sin offering shall be slaughtered before the LORD; it is most holy. {6:26} The priest who offers it for sin shall eat it. In a holy place it shall be eaten, in the courtyard of the Tent of Meeting. {6:27} Anything that touches its flesh will become holy, and when any of its blood is splattered on a garment, you shall wash whatever it was splattered on in a holy place. {6:28} But the clay pot in which it is cooked must be broken; if it is cooked in a bronze pot, it must be scoured and rinsed with water. {6:29} All the males among the priests may eat of it; it is most holy. {6:30} But no sin offering may be eaten if any of its blood is brought into the Tent of Meeting to make atonement in the Holy Place; it must be burned up in the fire.'"

{7:1} This is the law of the trespass offering: it is most holy. {7:2} Just as the burnt offering is killed in the same place, so shall the trespass offering be killed, and its blood shall be sprinkled around the altar. {7:3} All its fat shall be offered: the fat covering the entrails, the two kidneys, the fat on them by the flanks, and the lobe above the liver with the kidneys; it shall all be removed. {7:4} The priest shall burn them on the altar as an offering made by fire to the LORD; it is a trespass offering. {7:5} Every male among the priests shall eat it in the holy place; it is most holy. {7:6} The law for the trespass offering is the same as for the sin offering: there is one law for both. The priest who makes atonement with it shall have it. {7:7} The priest who offers anyone's burnt offering shall have for himself the skin of the burnt offering he has offered. {7:8} All the grain offering baked in the oven, and all that is cooked in a pan or on a griddle, shall belong to the priest who offers it. {7:9} Every grain offering, whether mixed with oil or dry, shall belong equally to all the sons of Aaron. {7:10} This is the law of the sacrifice of peace offerings, which shall be offered to the LORD. {7:11} If it is offered as a thanksgiving, then unleavened cakes mixed with oil, unleavened wafers anointed with oil, and cakes made of fine flour mixed with oil, fried, shall be offered with the sacrifice of thanksgiving. {7:12} Along with the cakes, leavened bread shall also be offered with the sacrifice of thanksgiving for peace offerings. {7:13} One of each offering shall be offered as a heave offering to the LORD; it shall belong to the priest who sprinkles the blood of the peace offerings. {7:14} The flesh of the sacrifice of peace offerings for thanksgiving shall be eaten on the same day it is offered; none of it shall be left until morning. {7:15} But if the offering is a vow or a voluntary offering, it shall be eaten on the day it is offered, and the remainder may be eaten on the next day. {7:16} However, if any of the flesh of the sacrifice of peace offerings is eaten on the third day, it shall not be accepted, and it shall not be credited to the one who offers it; it shall be an abomination, and the person who eats it shall bear his iniquity. {7:17} Any flesh that touches anything unclean shall not be eaten; it shall be burned with fire. All who are clean may eat the flesh. {7:18} But if anyone is ceremonially unclean and eats the flesh of the sacrifice of peace offerings that belong to the LORD, that person shall be cut off from his people. {7:19} Also, anyone who touches any unclean thing, whether the uncleanness of man, an unclean animal, or any abominable unclean thing, and eats the flesh of the sacrifice of peace offerings that belong to the LORD, shall be cut off from his people. {7:20} Then the LORD spoke to Moses, saying, {7:21} "Speak to the children of Israel, saying, 'You shall not eat any fat, whether from ox, sheep, or goat. {7:22} The fat of an animal that dies naturally or is torn by beasts may be used for any other purpose, but you shall not eat it. {7:23} For whoever eats the fat of an animal offered as a fire offering to the LORD shall be cut off from his people. {7:24} Also, you shall not eat any blood, whether of fowl or beast, in any of your dwellings. {7:25} Whoever eats any blood shall be cut off from his people." {7:26} Then the LORD spoke to Moses, saying, {7:27} "Speak to the children of Israel, saying: 'He who offers the sacrifice of his peace offerings to the LORD shall bring his offering to the LORD; it shall consist of the fat with the breast, and he shall bring it that the breast may be waved as a wave offering before the LORD. {7:28} The priest shall burn the fat on the altar, but the breast shall belong to Aaron and his sons. {7:29} Also, the right thigh you shall give to the priest as a heave offering from the sacrifices of your peace offerings. {7:30} He among the sons of Aaron who offers the blood of the peace offerings and the fat shall have the right thigh as his part. {7:31} For the wave breast and the heave thigh I have taken from the children of Israel, from the sacrifices of their peace offerings, and I have given them to Aaron the priest and to his sons by a statute forever from among the children of Israel.' {7:32} "This is the portion from the offerings made by fire to the LORD, given to Aaron and his sons on the day when they were presented to minister to the LORD as priests. {7:33} This is what the LORD commanded to be given to them by the children of Israel on the day when He anointed them, by a statute forever throughout their generations." {7:34} This is the law of the burnt offering, the grain offering, the sin offering, the trespass offering, the consecrations, and the sacrifice of the peace offerings, {7:35} which the LORD commanded Moses on Mount Sinai on the day He commanded the children of Israel to offer their offerings to the LORD in the Wilderness of Sinai. {7:36} This law was given by the LORD to be observed by the children of Israel on the day of their anointing, and it is to be a permanent statute for all their generations. {7:37} Here are the regulations concerning the burnt offering, the grain offering, the sin offering, the trespass offering, the consecrations, and the peace offerings. {7:38} These instructions were given by the LORD to Moses on Mount Sinai when He commanded the children of Israel to present their offerings to the LORD in the wilderness of Sinai.

{8:1} Then the LORD spoke to Moses, saying, {8:2} "Take Aaron and his sons, along with their garments, the anointing oil, a bull for the sin offering, two rams, and a basket of unleavened bread. {8:3} Gather all the congregation to the entrance of the tent of meeting." {8:4} Moses did as the LORD commanded, and the assembly gathered at the entrance of the tent of meeting. {8:5} Moses said to the congregation, "This is what the LORD has commanded to be done." {8:6} So Moses brought Aaron and his sons, washed them with water, {8:7} clothed them with the priestly garments, including the ephod and breastplate, as instructed by the LORD. {8:8} He placed the breastplate with the Urim and Thummim on Aaron. {8:9} Then he put the turban on Aaron's head, with the golden plate inscribed with "Holy to the LORD," as the LORD had commanded. {8:10} Moses took the anointing oil and consecrated the tabernacle and everything in it. {8:11} He sprinkled some of the oil on the altar seven times, anointing the altar and its utensils to consecrate them. {8:12} Moses poured some of the anointing oil on Aaron's head, consecrating him. {8:13} Next, Moses brought Aaron's sons, dressed them in tunics, and tied sashes around them, just as the LORD had commanded. {8:14} He then presented the bull for the sin offering, and Aaron and his sons laid their hands on its head. {8:15} Moses slaughtered the bull, took some of its blood, and applied it to the horns of the altar to purify it. {8:16} He burned the fat and other parts of the bull on the altar as a burnt offering outside the camp, following the LORD's command. {8:17} Moses brought the ram for the burnt offering. Aaron and his sons laid their hands on its head, {8:18} and Moses slaughtered it, splashing its blood on all sides of the altar. {8:19} He cut the ram into pieces, burned the head, fat, and other pieces on the altar. {8:20} He washed the entrails and legs with water and burned the whole ram on the altar as a burnt offering, a pleasing aroma to the LORD, following the LORD's command. {8:21} Then Moses presented the second ram, the ram of consecration. Aaron and his sons laid their hands on its head, {8:22} Moses slaughtered it, took some of its blood, and put it on the tips of Aaron's right ear, thumb of his right hand, and big toe of his right foot. {8:23} He also put blood on the tips of Aaron's sons' right ears, thumbs of their right hands, and big toes of their right feet. {8:24} Moses sprinkled some of the blood on the altar all around. {8:25} He took the fat, the fat tail, all the fat around the internal organs, the long lobe of the liver, the two kidneys with their fat, and the right thigh. {8:26} From the basket of unleavened bread before the LORD, Moses took one loaf, one cake of oiled bread, and one wafer, and placed them on the fat and the right thigh. {8:27} He put all these in the hands of Aaron and his sons and waved them as a wave offering before the LORD. {8:28} Moses took them back from their hands and burned them on the altar along with the burnt offering, consecrating them as a pleasing aroma before the LORD. {8:29} He also took the breast of the ram of consecration and waved it as a wave offering before the LORD; it was Moses' portion as the LORD commanded. {8:30} Moses took some of the anointing oil and some of the blood on the altar and sprinkled it on Aaron, his garments, his sons, and their garments, sanctifying them. {8:31} Then Moses instructed Aaron and his sons, "Boil the meat at the entrance of the tent of meeting and eat it there with the bread from the basket of consecration, as I commanded, saying, 'Aaron and his sons shall eat it.' {8:32} Burn any remaining meat and bread with fire. {8:33} Stay at the entrance of the tent of meeting for seven days, until your ordination period is over; for it will take seven days to ordain you. {8:34} This is what the LORD has commanded to be done to make atonement for you. {8:35} So Aaron and his sons did everything the LORD commanded through Moses."

{9:1} On the eighth day, Moses called Aaron, his sons, and the elders of Israel together. {9:2} He instructed Aaron to take a young calf for a sin offering and a ram for a burnt offering, both without blemish, and to offer them before the LORD. {9:3} To the children of Israel, he said they should take a kid of the goats for a sin offering, as well as a calf and a lamb, both of the first year and without blemish, for a burnt offering. {9:4} Additionally, they were to bring a bullock and a ram for peace offerings, along with a grain offering mixed with oil, for on that day the LORD would appear to them. {9:5} The people brought what Moses commanded before the tabernacle, and the whole congregation stood before the LORD. {9:6} Moses declared that they were following the LORD's command, and the glory of the LORD would appear to them. {9:7} Then Moses instructed Aaron to go to the altar, offer the sin offering and burnt offering for himself and the people, and make atonement for them, as the LORD had commanded. {9:8} Aaron went to the altar and sacrificed the calf for the sin offering for himself. {9:9} His sons brought the blood to him, and he applied it to the horns of the altar and poured the rest at the base, as instructed. {9:10} He burned the fat and other specified parts of the sin offering on the altar, as commanded. {9:11} The flesh and hide of the sin offering were burned outside the camp. {9:12} Then he sacrificed the burnt offering, and his sons presented the blood to him, which he sprinkled around the altar. {9:13} They presented the burnt offering to him, along with its pieces and head, which he burned on the altar. {9:14} He washed the inner parts and legs and burned them on top of the burnt offering. {9:15} Afterward, he took the people's offering, slaughtered the goat for their sin offering, and offered it as he had done previously. {9:16} He also offered the burnt offering according to the prescribed manner. {9:17} The grain offering was burnt on the altar alongside the morning burnt sacrifice. {9:18} Additionally, he sacrificed the bullock and ram for peace offerings on behalf of the people, and his sons presented the blood to him, which he sprinkled around the altar. {9:19} The specified fat portions were placed on the breasts and then burned on the altar. {9:20} Aaron waved the breasts and right shoulder as a wave offering before the LORD, as commanded by Moses. {9:21} After completing the offerings, Aaron blessed the people and descended from the altar. {9:22} Then Moses and Aaron entered the tabernacle, came out, and blessed the people. At that moment, the glory of the LORD appeared to all. {9:23} Suddenly, fire came out from before the LORD and consumed the burnt offering and fat on the altar, {9:24} prompting the people to shout and fall on their faces in reverence.

{10:1} Nadab and Abihu, the sons of Aaron, each took their censer, put fire and incense in it, and offered strange fire before the LORD, which He had not commanded them to do. {10:2} Then fire came out from the LORD and consumed them, and they died before the LORD. {10:3} Moses said to Aaron, "This is what the LORD meant when He said, 'I will be sanctified by those who come near Me, and before all the people I will be glorified.'" Aaron remained silent. {10:4} Moses called Mishael and Elzaphan, the sons of Uzziel (Aaron's uncle), and instructed them to remove the bodies of Nadab and Abihu from the sanctuary and out of the camp. {10:5} Mishael and Elzaphan carried the bodies out of the camp, as Moses had commanded. {10:6} Moses instructed Aaron, Eleazar, and Ithamar (Aaron's remaining sons) not to uncover their heads or tear their clothes, lest they die and incur wrath upon all the people. Instead, he told them to let the whole house of Israel mourn the LORD's judgment. {10:7} They were not to leave the tabernacle door, for the anointing oil of the LORD was upon them. They obeyed Moses' command. {10:8} Then the LORD spoke to Aaron, saying, {10:9} "Do not drink wine or strong drink, neither you nor your sons, when you enter the tabernacle of the congregation, lest you die. This is to be a perpetual statute throughout your generations. {10:10} This command is to distinguish between the holy and the unholy, and between the unclean and the clean, {10:11} so that you may teach the children of Israel all the statutes which the LORD has spoken to them through Moses." {10:12} Moses instructed Aaron, Eleazar, and Ithamar to eat the remaining meat offering from the offerings made by fire without leaven beside the altar, for it is most holy. {10:13} They were to eat it in the holy place, as it was their portion from the sacrifices made by fire, as commanded. {10:14} The wave breast and heave shoulder they were to eat in a clean place, along with their sons and daughters, for they were their portion from the peace offerings of the children of Israel. {10:15} These portions were to be brought with the offerings made by fire of the fat to wave before the LORD, and it would be theirs forever, as the LORD commanded. {10:16} Moses discovered that the goat of the sin offering had been burned, and he became angry with Eleazar and Ithamar, Aaron's remaining sons. {10:17} He questioned why they had not eaten the sin offering in the holy place, as it was most holy and given to them to bear the iniquity of the congregation and make atonement for them before the LORD. {10:18} Aaron responded, explaining that they had already made their offerings to the LORD that day, and considering the tragic events, would it have been acceptable to eat the sin offering in the sight of the LORD? {10:19} Aaron said to Moses, "Today, we have already offered our sin offering and burnt offering before the LORD. Given the tragic events that have befallen me, would it have been acceptable for me to eat the sin offering today in the sight of the LORD? {10:20} When Moses heard this, he was content."

{11:1} The LORD spoke to Moses and Aaron, saying to them, {11:2} "Speak to the children of Israel, saying, 'These are the animals which you may eat among all the animals that are on the earth. {11:3} Whatever parts the hoof and is cloven-footed, and chews the cud, among the animals, that you may eat. {11:4} Nevertheless, these you shall not eat of those that chew the cud, or of those that have a divided hoof: the camel, because it chews the cud but does not have a divided hoof, it is unclean to you. {11:5} And the coney, because it chews the cud but does not have a divided hoof, it is unclean to you. {11:6} And the hare, because it chews the cud but does not have a divided hoof, it is unclean to you. {11:7} And the swine, though it has a divided hoof and is cloven-footed, yet it does not chew the cud; it is unclean to you. {11:8} Of their flesh you shall not eat, and their carcasses you shall not touch; they are unclean to you. {11:9} These you may eat of all that are in the waters: whatever has fins and scales in the waters, in the seas, and in the rivers, them you may eat. {11:10} But all that do not have fins and scales in the seas and in the rivers, of all that move in the waters, and of any living thing which is in the waters, they shall be an abomination to you: {11:11} They shall be an abomination to you; you shall not eat of their flesh, but you shall regard their carcasses as an abomination. {11:12} Whatever has no fins nor scales in the waters, that shall be an abomination to you. {11:13} And these you shall regard as an abomination among the birds; they shall not be eaten, they are an abomination: the eagle, the osprey, and the ospray, {11:14} And the vulture, the kite after its kind; {11:15} Every raven after its kind; {11:16} And the owl, the night hawk, the cuckoo, and the hawk after its kind, {11:17} And the little owl, the cormorant, the great owl, {11:18} And the swan, the pelican, the gier eagle, {11:19} And the stork, the heron after its kind, and the lapwing, and the bat. {11:20} All birds that creep, going upon all fours, shall be an abomination to you. {11:21} Yet these you may eat of every flying creeping thing that goes upon all fours, which have legs above their feet, to leap withal upon the earth; {11:22} Even these of them you may eat; the locust after its kind, and the bald locust after its kind, and the beetle after its kind, and the grasshopper after its kind. {11:23} But all other flying creeping things, which have four feet, shall be an abomination to you. {11:24} And for these you shall be unclean: whoever touches the carcass of them shall be unclean until the evening. {11:25} And whoever carries anything of the carcass of them shall wash his clothes, and be unclean until the evening. {11:26} The carcasses of every beast which divides the hoof, and is not cloven-footed, nor chews the cud, are unclean to you: everyone that touches them shall be unclean. {11:27} And whatever goes upon its paws, among all manner of beasts that go on all four, those are unclean to you: whoever touches their carcass shall be unclean until the evening. {11:28} And he that carries the carcass of them shall wash his clothes, and be unclean until the evening: they are unclean to you." {11:29} These also shall be unclean to you among the creeping things that creep upon the earth: the weasel, the mouse, the tortoise after its kind, {11:30} And the ferret, the chameleon, the lizard, the snail, and the mole. {11:31} These are unclean to you among all that creep: whoever touches them when they are dead shall be unclean until the evening. {11:32} And whatever any of them, when they are dead, falls upon, it shall be unclean; whether it be any vessel of wood, or clothing, or skin, or sack, whatever vessel it be, wherein any work is done, it must be put into water, and it shall be unclean until the evening; so it shall be cleansed. {11:33} And every earthen vessel, into which any of them falls, whatever is in it shall be unclean; and you shall break it. {11:34} Of all food which may be eaten, that on which such water comes shall be unclean: and all drink that may be drunk in every such vessel shall be unclean. {11:35} And every thing whereupon any part of their carcass falls shall be unclean; whether it be oven, or ranges for pots, they shall be broken down: for they are unclean, and shall be unclean to you. {11:36} Nevertheless, a fountain or pit, wherein there is plenty of water, shall be clean: but that which touches their carcass shall be unclean. {11:37} And if any part of their carcass falls upon any sowing seed which is to be sown, it shall be clean. {11:38} But if any water be put upon the seed, and any part of their carcass falls thereon, it shall be unclean to you. {11:39} And if any beast, of which you may eat, dies; he that touches the carcass thereof shall be unclean until the evening. {11:40} And he that eats of the carcass of it shall wash his clothes, and be unclean until the evening: he also that bears the carcass of it shall wash his clothes, and be unclean until the evening. {11:41} And every creeping thing that creeps upon the earth shall be an abomination; it shall not be eaten. {11:42} Whatever goes upon the belly, and whatever goes upon all fours, or whatever has more feet among all creeping things that creep upon the earth, them you shall not eat; for they are an abomination. {11:43} You shall not make yourselves abominable with any creeping thing that creeps, neither shall you make yourselves unclean with them, that you should be defiled thereby. {11:44} For I am the LORD your God: you shall therefore sanctify yourselves, and you shall be holy; for I am holy: neither shall you defile yourselves with any manner of creeping thing that creeps upon the earth. {11:45} For I am the LORD who brings you up out of the land of Egypt, to be your God: you shall therefore be holy, for I am holy. {11:46} This is the law of the beasts, and of the fowl, and of every living creature that moves in the waters, and of every creature that creeps upon the earth: {11:47} To make a difference between the unclean and the clean, and between the beast that may be eaten and the beast that may not be eaten.

{12:1} And the LORD spoke unto Moses, saying, {12:2} Speak unto the children of Israel, saying, If a woman has conceived seed and borne a male child, then she shall be unclean seven days; according to the days of the separation for her infirmity shall she be unclean. {12:3} And on the eighth day, the flesh of his foreskin shall be circumcised. {12:4} And she shall then continue in the blood of her purifying three and thirty days; she shall touch no hallowed thing, nor come into the sanctuary, until the days of her purifying be fulfilled. {12:5} But if she bears a female child, then she shall be unclean two weeks, as in her separation: and she shall continue in the blood of her purifying threescore and six days. {12:6} And when the days of her purifying are fulfilled, for a son, or for a daughter, she shall bring a lamb of the first year for a burnt offering, and a young pigeon, or a turtledove, for a sin offering, unto the door of the tabernacle of the congregation, unto the priest: {12:7} Who shall offer it before the LORD, and make an atonement for her; and she shall be cleansed from the issue of her blood. This is the law for her that has borne a male or a female. {12:8} And if she is not able to bring a lamb, then she shall bring two turtles, or two young pigeons; the one for the burnt offering, and the other for a sin offering: and the priest shall make an atonement for her, and she shall be clean.

{13:1} And the LORD spoke unto Moses and Aaron, saying, {13:2} When a man shall have in the skin of his flesh a rising, a scab, or a bright spot, and it be in the skin of his flesh like the plague of leprosy; then he shall be brought unto Aaron the priest, or unto one of his sons the priests: {13:3} And the priest shall look on the plague in the skin of the flesh: and when the hair in the plague is turned white, and the plague in sight be deeper than the skin of his flesh, it is a plague of leprosy: and the priest shall look on him, and pronounce him unclean. {13:4} If the bright spot be white in the skin of his flesh, and in sight be not deeper than the skin, and the hair thereof be not turned white; then the priest shall shut up him that has the plague seven days: {13:5} And the priest shall look on him the seventh day: and, behold, if the plague in his sight be at a stay, and the plague spread not in the skin; then the priest shall shut him up seven days more: {13:6} And the priest shall look on him again the seventh day: and, behold, if the plague be somewhat dark, and the plague spread not in the skin, the priest shall pronounce him clean: it is but a scab: and he shall wash his clothes, and be clean. {13:7} But if the scab spread much abroad in the skin, after that he has been seen of the priest for his cleansing, he shall be seen of the priest again: {13:8} And if the priest see that, behold, the scab spreadeth in the skin, then the priest shall pronounce him unclean: it is a leprosy. {13:9} When the plague of leprosy is in a man, then he shall be brought unto the priest; {13:10} And the priest shall see him: and, behold, if the rising be white in the skin, and it have turned the hair white, and there be quick raw flesh in the rising; {13:11} It is an old leprosy in the skin of his flesh, and the priest shall pronounce him unclean, and shall not shut him up: for he is unclean. {13:12} And if a leprosy break out abroad in the skin, and the leprosy cover all the skin of him that has the plague from his head even to his foot, wheresoever the priest looketh; {13:13} Then the priest shall consider: and, behold, if the leprosy have covered all his flesh, he shall pronounce him clean that has the plague: it is all turned white: he is clean. {13:14} But when raw flesh appears in him, he shall be unclean. {13:15} And the priest shall see the raw flesh, and pronounce him to be unclean: for the raw flesh is unclean: it is a leprosy. {13:16} Or if the raw flesh turn again, and be changed unto white, he shall come unto the priest; {13:17} And the priest shall see him: and, behold, if the plague be turned into white; then the priest shall pronounce him clean that has the plague: he is clean. {13:18} The flesh also, in which, even in the skin thereof, was a boil, and is healed, {13:19} And in the place of the boil there be a white rising, or a bright spot, white, and somewhat reddish, and it be shown to the priest; {13:20} And if, when the priest sees it, behold, it be in sight lower than the skin, and the hair thereof be turned white; the priest shall pronounce him unclean: it is a plague of leprosy broken out of the boil. {13:21} But if the priest looks on it, and, behold, there be no white hairs therein, and if it be not lower than the skin, but be somewhat dark; then the priest shall shut him up seven days: {13:22} And if it spread much abroad in the skin, then the priest shall pronounce him unclean: it is a plague. {13:23} But if the bright spot stays in his place, and spreads not in the skin, but it be somewhat dark; it is a rising of the burning, and the priest shall pronounce him clean: for it is an inflammation of the burning. {13:24} Or if there be any flesh, in the skin whereof there is a hot burning, and the quick flesh that burneth have a white bright spot, somewhat reddish, or white; {13:25} Then the priest shall look upon it: and, behold, if the hair in the bright spot be turned white, and it be in sight deeper than the skin; it is a leprosy broken out of the burning: wherefore the priest shall pronounce him unclean: it is the plague of leprosy. {13:26} But if the priest look on it, and, behold, there be no white hair in the bright spot, and it be no lower than the other skin, but be somewhat dark; then the priest shall shut him up seven days: {13:27} And the priest shall look upon him the seventh day: and if it be spread much abroad in the skin, then the priest shall pronounce him unclean: it is the plague of leprosy. {13:28} And if the bright spot stay in his place, and spread not in the skin, but it be somewhat dark; it is a rising of the burning, and the priest shall pronounce him clean: for it is an inflammation of the burning. {13:29} If a man or woman have a plague upon the head or the beard; {13:30} Then the priest shall see the plague: and, behold, if it be in sight deeper than the skin; and there be in it a yellow thin hair; then the priest shall pronounce him unclean: it is a dry scall, even a leprosy upon the head or beard. {13:31} And if the priest look on the plague of the scall, and, behold, it be not in sight deeper than the skin, and that there is no black hair in it; then the priest shall shut up him that has the plague of the scall seven days: {13:32} And in the seventh day the priest shall look on the plague: and, behold, if the scall spread not, and there be in it no yellow hair, and the scall be not in sight deeper than the skin; {13:33} He shall be shaven, but the scall shall he not shave; and the priest shall shut up him that has the scall seven days more: {13:34} And in the seventh day the priest shall look on the scall: and, behold, if the scall be not spread in the skin, nor be in sight deeper than the skin; then the priest shall pronounce him clean: and he shall wash his clothes, and be clean. {13:35} But if the scall spread much in the skin after his cleansing; {13:36} Then the priest shall look on him: and, behold, if the scall be spread in the skin, the priest shall not seek for yellow hair; he is unclean. {13:37} But if the scall be in his sight at a stay, and that there is black hair grown up therein; the scall is healed, he is clean: and the priest shall pronounce him clean. {13:38} If a man also or a woman have in the skin of their flesh bright spots, even white bright spots; {13:39} Then the priest shall look: and, behold, if the bright spots in the skin of their flesh be darkish white; it is a freckled spot that groweth in the skin; he is clean. {13:40} And the man whose hair is fallen off his head, he is bald; yet is he clean. {13:41} And he that hath his hair fallen off from the part of his head toward his face, he is forehead bald: yet is he clean. {13:42} And if there be in the bald head, or bald forehead, a white reddish sore; it is a leprosy sprung up in his bald head, or his bald forehead. {13:43} Then the priest shall look upon it: and, behold, if the rising of the sore be white reddish in his bald head, or in his bald forehead, as the leprosy appeareth in the skin of the flesh; {13:44} He is a leprous man, he is unclean: the priest shall pronounce him utterly unclean; his plague is in his head. {13:45} And the leper in whom the plague is, his clothes shall be rent, and his head bare, and he shall put a covering upon his upper lip, and shall cry, Unclean, unclean. {13:46} All the days wherein the plague shall be in him he shall be defiled; he is unclean: he shall dwell alone; without the camp shall his habitation be. {13:47} The garment also that the plague of leprosy is in, whether it be a woollen garment, or a linen garment; {13:48} Whether it be in the warp, or woof; of linen, or of woollen; whether in a skin, or in any thing made of skin; {13:49} And if the plague be greenish or reddish in the garment, or in the skin, either in the warp, or in the woof, or in any thing of skin; it is a plague of leprosy, and shall be showed unto the priest: {13:50} And the priest shall look upon the plague, and shut up the one that has the plague for seven days: {13:51} And he shall look on the plague on the seventh day: if the plague be spread in the garment, either in the warp, or in the woof, or in a skin, or in any work that is made of skin; the plague is a fretting leprosy; it is unclean. {13:52} Therefore, he shall burn that garment, whether warp or woof, in woolen or in linen, or anything of skin, wherein the plague is: for it is a fretting leprosy; it shall be burnt in the fire. {13:53} And if the priest shall look, and behold, the plague be not spread in the garment, either in the warp, or in the woof, or in any thing of skin; {13:54} Then the priest shall command that they wash the thing wherein the plague is, and he shall shut it up for seven days more: {13:55} And the priest shall look on the plague, after it is washed: and if the plague has not changed its color, and the plague be not spread; it is unclean; you shall burn it in the fire; it is fret inward, whether it be bare within or without. {13:56} And if the priest looks, and behold, the plague be somewhat dark after the washing of it; then he shall rend it out of the garment, or out of the skin, or out of the warp, or out of the woof: {13:57} And if it still appears in the garment, either in the warp, or in the woof, or in any thing of skin; it is a spreading plague: you shall burn that wherein the plague is with fire. {13:58} And the garment, whether warp, or woof, or whatsoever thing of skin it be, which you shall wash, if the plague be departed from them, then it shall be washed the second time, and shall be clean. {13:59} This is the law of the plague of leprosy in a garment of woolen or linen, either in the warp, or in the woof, or in any thing of skins, to pronounce it clean, or to pronounce it unclean.

{14:1} And the LORD spoke to Moses, saying, {14:2} This shall be the law of the leper in the day of his cleansing: He shall be brought unto the priest. {14:3} And the priest shall go forth out of the camp; and the priest shall look, and behold, if the plague of leprosy be healed in the leper; {14:4} Then shall the priest command to take for him that is to be cleansed two birds alive and clean, and cedar wood, and scarlet, and hyssop: {14:5} And the priest shall command that one of the birds be killed in an earthen vessel over running water: {14:6} As for the living bird, he shall take it, and the cedar wood, and the scarlet, and the hyssop, and shall dip them and the living bird in the blood of the bird that was killed over the running water: {14:7} And he shall sprinkle upon him that is to be cleansed from the leprosy seven times, and shall pronounce him clean, and shall let the living bird loose into the open field. {14:8} And he that is to be cleansed shall wash his clothes, and shave off all his hair, and wash himself in water, that he may be clean: and after that he shall come into the camp, and shall tarry abroad out of his tent seven days. {14:9} But it shall be on the seventh day, that he shall shave all his hair off his head and his beard and his eyebrows, even all his hair he shall shave off: and he shall wash his clothes, also he shall wash his flesh in water, and he shall be clean. {14:10} And on the eighth day he shall take two he lambs without blemish, and one ewe lamb of the first year without blemish, and three tenth deals of fine flour for a meat offering, mingled with oil, and one log of oil. {14:11} And the priest that maketh him clean shall present the man that is to be made clean, and those things, before the LORD, at the door of the tabernacle of the congregation: {14:12} And the priest shall take one he lamb, and offer him for a trespass offering, and the log of oil, and wave them for a wave offering before the LORD: {14:13} And he shall slay the lamb in the place where he shall kill the sin offering and the burnt offering, in the holy place: for as the sin offering is the priest's, so is the trespass offering: it is most holy: {14:14} And the priest shall take some of the blood of the trespass offering, and the priest shall put it upon the tip of the right ear of him that is to be cleansed, and upon the thumb of his right hand, and upon the great toe of his right foot: {14:15} And the priest shall take some of the log of oil, and pour it into the palm of his own left hand: {14:16} And the priest shall dip his right finger in the oil that is in his left hand, and shall sprinkle of the oil with his finger seven times before the LORD: {14:17} And of the rest of the oil that is in his hand shall the priest put upon the tip of the right ear of him that is to be cleansed, and upon the thumb of his right hand, and upon the great toe of his right foot, upon the blood of the trespass offering: {14:18} And the remnant of the oil that is in the priest's hand he shall pour upon the head of him that is to be cleansed: and the priest shall make an atonement for him before the LORD. {14:19} And the priest shall offer the sin offering, and make an atonement for him that is to be cleansed from his uncleanness; and afterward he shall kill the burnt offering: {14:20} And the priest shall offer the burnt offering and the meat offering upon the altar: and the priest shall make an atonement for him, and he shall be clean. {14:21} And if he be poor, and cannot get so much; then he shall take one lamb for a trespass offering to be waved, to make an atonement for him, and one tenth deal of fine flour mingled with oil for a meat offering, and a log of oil; {14:22} And two turtledoves, or two young pigeons, such as he is able to get; and the one shall be a sin offering, and the other a burnt offering. {14:23} And he shall bring them on the eighth day for his cleansing unto the priest, unto the door of the tabernacle of the congregation, before the LORD. {14:24} And the priest shall take the lamb of the trespass offering, and the log of oil, and the priest shall wave them for a wave offering before the LORD: {14:25} And he shall kill the lamb of the trespass offering, and the priest shall take some of the blood of the trespass offering, and put it upon the tip of the right ear of him that is to be cleansed, and upon the thumb of his right hand, and upon the great toe of his right foot: {14:26} And the priest shall pour of the oil into the palm of his own left hand: {14:27} And the priest shall sprinkle with his right finger some of the oil that is in his left hand seven times before the LORD: {14:28} And the priest shall put of the oil that is in his hand upon the tip of the right ear of him that is to be cleansed, and upon the thumb of his right hand, and upon the great toe of his right foot, upon the place of the blood of the trespass offering: {14:29} And the rest of the oil that is in the priest's hand he shall put upon the head of him that is to be cleansed, to make an atonement for him before the LORD. {14:30} Then he shall offer one of the turtledoves, or of the young pigeons, whichever he can get; {14:31} Even if he can only get one, he shall offer it as a sin offering, and the other as a burnt offering, along with the grain offering. The priest shall make atonement for the one to be cleansed before the LORD. {14:32} This is the law for someone who has the plague of leprosy and cannot afford what is needed for their cleansing. {14:33} Then the LORD spoke to Moses and Aaron, saying, {14:34} "When you come into the land of Canaan, which I am giving you as a possession, and I put the plague of leprosy in a house in the land of your possession, {14:35} the owner of the house shall come and tell the priest, 'There seems to be a plague in the house.' {14:36} Then the priest shall command that the house be emptied before he goes in to examine the plague, so that everything in the house does not become unclean. Afterward, the priest shall go in to inspect the house. {14:37} And if he finds the plague in the walls of the house with hollow streaks, greenish or reddish, which appear lower than the rest of the wall; {14:38} then the priest shall go out of the house to the door and shut up the house for seven days. {14:39} The priest shall come again on the seventh day and inspect; if the plague has spread in the walls of the house, {14:40} then the priest shall command that they remove the stones with the plague in them and cast them into an unclean place outside the city. {14:41} And he shall have the inside of the house scraped all around, and the plaster that is scraped off shall be dumped in an unclean place outside the city. {14:42} Then new stones shall be taken, and replaced in the place of the old stones, and new mortar shall be used to plaster the house. {14:43} But if the plague returns and breaks out in the house after the stones have been removed, and after the house has been scraped and replastered; {14:44} then the priest shall come and inspect, and if he finds that the plague has spread in the house, it is a fretting leprosy in the house; it is unclean. {14:45} The house, its stones, its timber, and all the mortar shall be torn down, and they shall be taken out of the city to an unclean place. {14:46} Moreover, whoever enters the house while it is shut up shall be unclean until evening. {14:47} And whoever lies down in the house shall wash his clothes, and whoever eats in the house shall wash his clothes. {14:48} But if the priest comes and inspects, and sees that the plague has not spread in the house after it has been replastered, then the priest shall pronounce the house clean, because the plague is healed. {14:49} And to cleanse the house, he shall take two birds, cedar wood, scarlet, and hyssop. {14:50} Then he shall kill one of the birds in an earthen vessel over running water; {14:51} and he shall take the cedar wood, the hyssop, the scarlet, and the living bird, and dip them in the blood of the slain bird and in the running water, and sprinkle the house seven times. {14:52} He shall cleanse the house with the blood of the bird, the running water, the living bird, the cedar wood, the hyssop, and the scarlet. {14:53} But he shall release the living bird outside the city into the open fields, and make atonement for the house, and it shall be clean. {14:54} This is the law for all kinds of leprous diseases: for leprosy in a garment, in a house, {14:55} for a swelling, for a scab, and for a bright spot, {14:56} to teach when it is unclean and when it is clean. This is the law of leprosy. {14:57} This verse summarizes the purpose of the preceding laws regarding leprosy: to instruct on distinguishing between what is unclean and what is clean. It serves as the conclusion to the laws concerning leprosy, emphasizing their role in providing guidance on cleanliness and uncleanness related to this condition.

{15:1} The LORD spoke to Moses and Aaron, saying, {15:2} "Speak to the children of Israel, and tell them: If any man has a discharge from his body, he is unclean because of it. {15:3} This is his uncleanness due to his discharge: whether his body discharges fluid or the discharge is stopped up, it still makes him unclean. {15:4} Any bed on which he lies down with the discharge is unclean, and anything on which he sits shall be unclean as well. {15:5} Whoever touches his bed must wash their clothes and bathe in water; they will be unclean until evening. {15:6} Likewise, whoever sits on anything on which the man with the discharge has sat must wash their clothes and bathe in water; they will be unclean until evening. {15:7} Also, whoever touches the body of the man with the discharge must wash their clothes and bathe in water; they will be unclean until evening. {15:8} If the man with the discharge spits on someone who is clean, that person must wash their clothes and bathe in water; they will be unclean until evening. {15:9} Any saddle on which the man with the discharge rides shall be unclean. {15:10} Whoever touches anything that was under him shall be unclean until evening; they must wash their clothes and bathe in water, and they will be unclean until evening. {15:11} Whoever the man with the discharge touches, if they haven't washed their hands with water, must wash their clothes and bathe in water; they will be unclean until evening. {15:12} Any earthen vessel that the man with the discharge touches shall be broken, and any wooden vessel shall be rinsed with water. {15:13} When the man with the discharge is cleansed from his discharge, he shall count seven days for his cleansing. He shall wash his clothes, bathe his body in running water, and he will be clean. {15:14} On the eighth day, he shall take two turtledoves or two young pigeons and come before the LORD to the entrance of the tent of meeting, and give them to the priest. {15:15} The priest shall offer them, one for a sin offering and the other for a burnt offering; thus the priest shall make atonement for him before the LORD for his discharge. {15:16} If a man has an emission of semen, he shall bathe his whole body in water and be unclean until evening. {15:17} Any garment or skin on which semen is found shall be washed with water and be unclean until evening. {15:18} When a man has sexual relations with a woman and there is an emission of semen, both of them shall bathe in water and be unclean until evening. {15:19} If a woman has a discharge of blood, her impurity shall last seven days, and anyone who touches her will be unclean until evening. {15:20} Everything she lies on during her period will be unclean, and everything she sits on will be unclean. {15:21} Whoever touches her bed must wash their clothes and bathe in water; they will be unclean until evening. {15:22} Whoever touches anything she sits on must wash their clothes and bathe in water; they will be unclean until evening. {15:23} If a man has sexual relations with her and her menstrual blood touches him, he will be unclean for seven days, and every bed he lies on will be unclean. {15:24} If a woman has a discharge of blood for many days, not at the time of her menstrual period, or if the discharge continues beyond her period, she is unclean all the days the discharge continues, as during her period. {15:25} Every bed on which she lies during all the days of her discharge will be treated the same as during her period, and anything she sits on will be unclean, as during her period. {15:26} Whoever touches these things will be unclean; they must wash their clothes and bathe in water, and they will be unclean until evening. {15:27} When she is cleansed from her discharge, she must count seven days, and after that she will be clean.

{15:28} On the eighth day, she shall take two turtledoves or two young pigeons and bring them to the priest at the entrance to the tent of meeting. {15:29} The priest shall offer one as a sin offering and the other as a burnt offering; thus the priest shall make atonement for her before the LORD for her discharge. {15:30} You shall separate the children of Israel from their uncleanness, lest they die in their uncleanness when they defile my tabernacle that is among them. {15:31} This is the law for the man with a discharge, for the one whose semen flows from him and makes him unclean, {15:32} for the woman with menstrual impurity, for a man or woman with a discharge, {15:33} and for a man who lies with a woman who is unclean."

{16:1} After the death of Aaron's two sons, who died when they offered unauthorized fire before the LORD, God spoke to Moses. {16:2} The LORD instructed Moses to tell Aaron, his brother, not to enter the Most Holy Place behind the veil whenever he pleased, or else he would die. The LORD would appear in the cloud above the mercy seat. {16:3} Aaron was to enter the Most Holy Place with a young bull for a sin offering and a ram for a burnt offering. {16:4} He was to wear the holy linen garments, including the linen undergarments, and tie a linen sash around himself. He had to wash himself before putting them on. {16:5} Aaron was to take two goats from the congregation for a sin offering and a ram for a burnt offering. {16:6} He would offer the bull as a sin offering for himself and his household to make atonement. {16:7} Aaron would cast lots for the two goats—one for the LORD and the other for the scapegoat. {16:8} The goat chosen for the LORD would be sacrificed as a sin offering. {16:9} The goat chosen as the scapegoat would be presented alive before the LORD to make atonement, then sent away into the wilderness. {16:10} Aaron would offer the bull for his own sin offering and make atonement for himself and his household. {16:11} He would take a censer of burning coals and a handful of finely ground incense inside the veil. {16:12} Aaron would put the incense on the fire before the LORD to cover the mercy seat, so he wouldn't die. {16:13} He would sprinkle some of the bull's blood on the mercy seat and in front of it seven times. {16:14} Then he would slaughter the goat chosen as the sin offering for the people, take its blood into the Most Holy Place, and sprinkle it on the mercy seat and in front of it. {16:15} This would make atonement for the Most Holy Place because of the Israelites' uncleanness and their rebellious acts, cleansing the tabernacle and altar from their sins. {16:16} No one could be in the tabernacle while Aaron made atonement in the Most Holy Place until he came out and made atonement for himself, his household, and the entire assembly of Israel. {16:17} Aaron would then go to the altar before the LORD and make atonement for it by applying some of the bull's and goat's blood to its horns. {16:18} He would sprinkle the blood on the altar seven times, purifying it from the Israelites' uncleanness. {16:19} After reconciling the Most Holy Place, the tabernacle, and the altar, Aaron would bring the live goat. {16:20} He would lay both hands on its head, confessing over it all the Israelites' sins and rebellious acts, and then send it away into the wilderness with a man appointed for this task. {16:21} The goat would carry all their sins to a remote area. {16:22} Aaron would then enter the tabernacle, remove his linen garments, and leave them there. He would wash himself before putting on his regular garments. {16:23} Afterward, he would offer the burnt offerings for himself and the people, making atonement. {16:24} The fat from the sin offerings would be burned on the altar. {16:25} The man who led the scapegoat away would wash his clothes and bathe before reentering the camp. {16:26} The bull and goat sacrificed for sin, whose blood was brought into the Most Holy Place for atonement, would be taken outside the camp and burned. {16:27} The man who burned them would wash his clothes and bathe before reentering the camp. {16:28} This would be a permanent statute: on the tenth day of the seventh month, the Israelites were to humble themselves, doing no work, whether native-born or foreigner residing among them. {16:29} The high priest would make atonement for the people on that day, cleansing them from their sins before the LORD. {16:30} It would be a Sabbath of complete rest for the people, who were to humble themselves. {16:31} The anointed priest who succeeded his father in the priesthood would make atonement, wearing the linen garments, for the Most Holy Place, the tabernacle, the altar, the priests, and all the people. {16:32} This would be an everlasting statute, making atonement for the Israelites' sins once a year, as the LORD commanded Moses. {16:33} The high priest shall make atonement for the holy sanctuary, the tabernacle of the congregation, and the altar. He shall also make atonement for the priests and all the people of the congregation. {16:34} This shall be an everlasting statute for you: to make atonement for the children of Israel for all their sins once a year. And Aaron did as the LORD commanded Moses.

{17:1} And the LORD spoke unto Moses, saying, {17:2} "Speak unto Aaron, and unto his sons, and unto all the children of Israel, and say unto them; This is the thing which the LORD hath commanded, saying, {17:3} What man soever there be of the house of Israel, that killeth an ox, or lamb, or goat, in the camp, or that killeth it out of the camp, {17:4} And bringeth it not unto the door of the tabernacle of the congregation, to offer an offering unto the LORD before the tabernacle of the LORD; blood shall be imputed unto that man; he hath shed blood; and that man shall be cut off from among his people: {17:5} To the end that the children of Israel may bring their sacrifices, which they offer in the open field, even that they may bring them unto the LORD, unto the door of the tabernacle of the congregation, unto the priest, and offer them for peace offerings unto the LORD. {17:6} And the priest shall sprinkle the blood upon the altar of the LORD at the door of the tabernacle of the congregation, and burn the fat for a sweet savour unto the LORD. {17:7} And they shall no more offer their sacrifices unto devils, after whom they have gone a whoring. This shall be a statute forever unto them throughout their generations. {17:8} And thou shalt say unto them, Whatsoever man there be of the house of Israel, or of the strangers which sojourn among you, that offereth a burnt offering or sacrifice, {17:9} And bringeth it not unto the door of the tabernacle of the congregation, to offer it unto the LORD; even that man shall be cut off from among his people. {17:10} And whatsoever man there be of the house of Israel, or of the strangers that sojourn among you, that eateth any manner of blood; I will even set my face against that soul that eateth blood, and will cut him off from among his people. {17:11} For the life of the flesh is in the blood: and I have given it to you upon the altar to make an atonement for your souls: for it is the blood that maketh an atonement for the soul. {17:12} Therefore I said unto the children of Israel, No soul of you shall eat blood, neither shall any stranger that sojourneth among you eat blood. {17:13} And whatsoever man there be of the children of Israel, or of the strangers that sojourn among you, which hunteth and catcheth any beast or fowl that may be eaten; he shall even pour out the blood thereof, and cover it with dust. {17:14} For it is the life of all flesh; the blood of it is for the life thereof: therefore I said unto the children of Israel, Ye shall eat the blood of no manner of flesh: for the life of all flesh is the blood thereof: whosoever eateth it shall be cut off. {17:15} And every soul that eateth that which died of itself, or that which was torn with beasts, whether it be one of your own country, or a stranger, he shall both wash his clothes, and bathe himself in water, and be unclean until the even: then shall he be clean. {17:16} But if he wash them not, nor bathe his flesh; then he shall bear his iniquity."

{18:1} And the LORD spoke unto Moses, saying, {18:2} "Speak unto the children of Israel, and say unto them, I am the LORD your God. {18:3} After the doings of the land of Egypt, wherein ye dwelt, shall ye not do: and after the doings of the land of Canaan, whither I bring you, shall ye not do: neither shall ye walk in their ordinances. {18:4} Ye shall do my judgments, and keep mine ordinances, to walk therein: I am the LORD your God. {18:5} Ye shall therefore keep my statutes, and my judgments: which if a man do, he shall live in them: I am the LORD. {18:6} None of you shall approach to any that is near of kin to him, to uncover their nakedness: I am the LORD. {18:7} The nakedness of thy father, or the nakedness of thy mother, shalt thou not uncover: she is thy mother; thou shalt not uncover her nakedness. {18:8} The nakedness of thy father's wife shalt thou not uncover: it is thy father's nakedness. {18:9} The nakedness of thy sister, the daughter of thy father, or daughter of thy mother, whether she be born at home, or born abroad, even their nakedness thou shalt not uncover. {18:10} The nakedness of thy son's daughter, or of thy daughter's daughter, even their nakedness thou shalt not uncover: for theirs is thine own nakedness. {18:11} The nakedness of thy father's wife's daughter, begotten of thy father, she is thy sister, thou shalt not uncover her nakedness. {18:12} Thou shalt not uncover the nakedness of thy father's sister: she is thy father's near kinswoman. {18:13} Thou shalt not uncover the nakedness of thy mother's sister: for she is thy mother's near kinswoman. {18:14} Thou shalt not uncover the nakedness of thy father's brother, thou shalt not approach to his wife: she is thine aunt. {18:15} Thou shalt not uncover the nakedness of thy daughter in law: she is thy son's wife; thou shalt not uncover her nakedness. {18:16} Thou shalt not uncover the nakedness of thy brother's wife: it is thy brother's nakedness. {18:17} Thou shalt not uncover the nakedness of a woman and her daughter, neither shalt thou take her son's daughter, or her daughter's daughter, to uncover her nakedness; for they are her near kinswomen: it is wickedness. {18:18} Neither shalt thou take a wife to her sister, to vex her, to uncover her nakedness, beside the other in her lifetime. {18:19} Also thou shalt not approach unto a woman to uncover her nakedness, as long as she is put apart for her uncleanness. {18:20} Moreover thou shalt not lie carnally with thy neighbour's wife, to defile thyself with her. {18:21} And thou shalt not let any of thy seed pass through the fire to Molech, neither shalt thou profane the name of thy God: I am the LORD. {18:22} **Thou shalt not lie with mankind, as with womankind: it is abomination.** {18:23} Neither shalt thou lie with any beast to defile thyself therewith: neither shall any woman stand before a beast to lie down thereto: it is confusion. {18:24} Defile not ye yourselves in any of these things: for in all these the nations are defiled which I cast out before you: {18:25} And the land is defiled: therefore I do visit the iniquity thereof upon it, and the land itself vomiteth out her inhabitants. {18:26} Ye shall therefore keep my statutes and my judgments, and shall not commit any of these abominations; neither any of your own nation, nor any stranger that sojourneth among you: {18:27} (For all these abominations have the men of the land done, which were before you, and the land is defiled;) {18:28} That the land spue not you out also, when ye defile it, as it spued out the nations that were before you. {18:29} For whosoever shall commit any of these abominations, even the souls that commit them shall be cut off from among their people. {18:30} Therefore shall ye keep mine ordinance, that ye commit not any one of these abominable customs, which were committed before you, and that ye defile not yourselves therein: I am the LORD your God."

{19:1} And the LORD spoke unto Moses, saying, {19:2} "Speak unto all the congregation of the children of Israel, and say unto them, Ye shall be holy: for I the LORD your God am holy. {19:3} Ye shall fear every man his mother, and his father, and keep my sabbaths: I am the LORD your God. {19:4} Turn ye not unto idols, nor make to yourselves molten gods: I am the LORD your God. {19:5} And if ye offer a sacrifice of peace offerings unto the LORD, ye shall offer it at your own will. {19:6} It shall be eaten the same day ye offer it, and on the morrow: and if ought remain until the third day, it shall be burnt in the fire. {19:7} And if it be eaten at all on the third day, it is abominable; it shall not be accepted. {19:8} Therefore everyone that eateth it shall bear his iniquity, because he hath profaned the hallowed thing of the LORD: and that soul shall be cut off from among his people. {19:9} And when ye reap the harvest of your land, thou shalt not wholly reap the corners of thy field, neither shalt thou gather the gleanings of thy harvest. {19:10} And thou shalt not glean thy vineyard, neither shalt thou gather every grape of thy vineyard; thou shalt leave them for the poor and stranger: I am the LORD your God. {19:11} Ye shall not steal, neither deal falsely, neither lie one to another. {19:12} And ye shall not swear by my name falsely, neither shalt thou profane the name of thy God: I am the LORD. {19:13} Thou shalt not defraud thy neighbour, neither rob him: the wages of him that is hired shall not abide with thee all night until the morning. {19:14} Thou shalt not curse the deaf, nor put a stumblingblock before the blind, but shalt fear thy God: I am the LORD. {19:15} Ye shall do no unrighteousness in judgment: thou shalt not respect the person of the poor, nor honour the person of the mighty: but in righteousness shalt thou judge thy neighbour. {19:16} Thou shalt not go up and down as a talebearer among thy people: neither shalt thou stand against the blood of thy neighbour: I am the LORD. {19:17} Thou shalt not hate thy brother in thine heart: thou shalt in any wise rebuke thy neighbour, and not suffer sin upon him. {19:18} **Thou shalt not avenge, nor bear any grudge against the children of thy people, but thou shalt love thy neighbour as thyself: I am the LORD.** {19:19} Ye shall keep my statutes. Thou shalt not let thy cattle gender with a diverse kind: thou shalt not sow thy field with mingled seed: neither shall a garment mingled of linen and woollen come upon thee. {19:20} And whosoever lieth carnally with a woman, that is a bondmaid, betrothed to an husband, and not at all redeemed, nor freedom given her; she shall be scourged; they shall not be put to death, because she was not free. {19:21} And he shall bring his trespass offering unto the LORD, unto the door of the tabernacle of the congregation, even a ram for a trespass offering. {19:22} And the priest shall make an atonement for him with the ram of the trespass offering before the LORD for his sin which he hath done: and the sin which he hath done shall be forgiven him. {19:23} And when ye shall come into the land, and shall have planted all manner of trees for food, then ye shall count the fruit thereof as uncircumcised: three years shall it be as uncircumcised unto you: it shall not be eaten of. {19:24} But in the fourth year all the fruit thereof shall be holy to praise the LORD withal. {19:25} And in the fifth year shall ye eat of the fruit thereof, that it may yield unto you the increase thereof: I am the LORD your God. {19:26} Ye shall not eat any thing with the blood: neither shall ye use enchantment, nor observe times. {19:27} Ye shall not round the corners of your heads, neither shalt thou mar the corners of thy beard. {19:28} Ye shall not make any cuttings in your flesh for the dead, nor print any marks upon you: I am the LORD. {19:29} Do not prostitute thy daughter, to cause her to be a whore; lest the land fall to whoredom, and the land become full of wickedness. {19:30} Ye shall keep my sabbaths, and reverence my sanctuary: I am the LORD. {19:31} **Regard not them that have familiar spirits, neither seek after wizards, to be defiled by them: I am the LORD your God.** {19:32} Thou shalt rise up before the hoary head, and honour the face of the old man, and fear thy God: I am the LORD. {19:33} And if a stranger sojourn with thee in your land, ye shall not vex him. {19:34} But the stranger that dwelleth with you shall be unto you as one born among you, and thou shalt love him as thyself; for ye were strangers in the land of Egypt: I am the LORD your God. {19:35} Ye shall do no unrighteousness in judgment, in meteyard, in weight, or in measure. {19:36} Just balances, just weights, a just ephah, and a just hin, shall ye have: I am the LORD your God, which brought you out of the land of Egypt. {19:37} Therefore shall ye observe all my statutes, and all my judgments, and do them: I am the LORD."

{20:1} And the LORD spoke unto Moses, saying, {20:2} "Again, thou shalt say to the children of Israel, Whosoever he be of the children of Israel, or of the strangers that sojourn in Israel, that giveth any of his seed unto Molech; he shall surely be put to death: the people of the land shall stone him with stones. {20:3} And I will set my face against that man, and will cut him off from among his people; because he hath given of his seed unto Molech, to defile my sanctuary, and to profane my holy name. {20:4} And if the people of the land do any ways hide their eyes from the man, when he giveth of his seed unto Molech, and kill him not: {20:5} Then I will set my face against that man, and against his family, and will cut him off, and all that go a whoring after him, to commit whoredom with Molech, from among their people. {20:6} And the soul that turneth after such as have familiar spirits, and after wizards, to go a whoring after them, I will even set my face against that soul, and will cut him off from among his people. {20:7} Sanctify yourselves therefore, and be ye holy: for I am the LORD your God. {20:8} And ye shall keep my statutes, and do them: I am the LORD which sanctify you. {20:9} For every one that curseth his father or his mother shall be surely put to death: he hath cursed his father or his mother; his blood shall be upon him. {20:10} And the man that committeth adultery with another man's wife, even he that committeth adultery with his neighbour's wife, the adulterer and the adulteress shall surely be put to death. {20:11} And the man that lieth with his father's wife hath uncovered his father's nakedness: both of them shall surely be put to death; their blood shall be upon them. {20:12} And if a man lie with his daughter in law, both of them shall surely be put to death: they have wrought confusion; their blood shall be upon them. {20:13} **If a man also lie with mankind, as he lieth with a woman, both of them have committed an abomination: they shall surely be put to death; their blood shall be upon them.** {20:14} And if a man take a wife and her mother, it is wickedness: they shall be burnt with fire, both he and they; that there be no wickedness among you. {20:15} And if a man lie with a beast, he shall surely be put to death: and ye shall slay the beast. {20:16} And if a woman approach unto any beast, and lie down thereto, thou shalt kill the woman, and the beast: they shall surely be put to death; their blood shall be upon them. {20:17} And if a man shall take his sister, his father's daughter, or his mother's daughter, and see her nakedness, and she see his nakedness; it is a wicked thing; and they shall be cut off in the sight of their people: he hath uncovered his sister's nakedness; he shall bear his iniquity. {20:18} And if a man shall lie with a woman having her sickness, and shall uncover her nakedness; he hath discovered her fountain, and she hath uncovered the fountain of her blood: and both of them shall be cut off from among their people. {20:19} And thou shalt not uncover the nakedness of thy mother's sister, nor of thy father's sister: for he uncovereth his near kin: they shall bear their iniquity. {20:20} And if a man shall lie with his uncle's wife, he hath uncovered his uncle's nakedness: they shall bear their sin; they shall die childless. {20:21} And if a man shall take his brother's wife, it is an unclean thing: he hath uncovered his brother's nakedness; they shall be childless. {20:22} Ye shall therefore keep all my statutes, and all my judgments, and do them: that the land, whither I bring you to dwell therein, spue you not out. {20:23} And ye shall not walk in the manners of the nation, which I cast out before you: for they committed all these things, and therefore I abhorred them. {20:24} But I have said unto you, Ye shall inherit their land, and I will give it unto you to possess it, a land that floweth with milk and honey: I am the LORD your God, which have separated you from other people. {20:25} Ye shall therefore put difference between clean beasts and unclean, and between unclean fowls and clean: and ye shall not make your souls abominable by beast, or by fowl, or by any manner of living thing that creepeth on the ground, which I have separated from you as unclean. {20:26} And ye shall be holy unto me: for I the LORD am holy, and have severed you from other people, that ye should be mine. {20:27} A man also or woman that hath a familiar spirit, or that is a wizard, shall surely be put to death: they shall stone them with stones: their blood shall be upon them."

{21:1} And the LORD said unto Moses, Speak unto the priests, the sons of Aaron, and say unto them, None of you shall be defiled for the dead among your people. {21:2} However, for his close relatives—his mother, father, son, daughter, brother, {21:3} And for his unmarried sister who is near to him, who has had no husband—for her, he may be defiled. {21:4} But he, being a chief man among his people, shall not defile himself to dishonor himself. {21:5} The priests shall not make themselves bald on their heads, nor shave off the corners of their beards, nor make any cuttings in their flesh. {21:6} They shall be holy to their God and not profane the name of their God, for they offer the offerings of the LORD made by fire, and the bread of their God. Therefore, they shall be holy. {21:7} They shall not marry a woman who is a prostitute or profane, nor shall they marry a woman who has been divorced from her husband, for the priest is holy to his God. {21:8} Therefore, you shall sanctify him, for he offers the bread of your God. He shall be holy to you, for I the LORD, who sanctify you, am holy. {21:9} And if the daughter of a priest profanes herself by prostituting, she profanes her father; she shall be burned with fire. {21:10} And the high priest among his brethren, upon whose head the anointing oil was poured and who is consecrated to wear the garments, shall not uncover his head nor tear his clothes. {21:11} Nor shall he go near any dead body, nor defile himself for his father or mother; {21:12} Nor shall he leave the sanctuary, nor profane the sanctuary of his God, for the crown of the anointing oil of his God is upon him. I am the LORD. {21:13} And he shall take a wife who is a virgin. {21:14} A widow, a divorced woman, a profane woman, or a prostitute—these he shall not take; but he shall take a virgin of his own people as wife. {21:15} Nor shall he profane his offspring among his people, for I the LORD sanctify him. {21:16} And the LORD spoke unto Moses, saying, {21:17} Speak unto Aaron, saying, Whoever among your offspring in their generations has any blemish, let him not approach to offer the bread of his God. {21:18} For any man with a blemish shall not approach: a blind man, a lame man, one with a flat nose, or anything superfluous, {21:19} Or a man with a broken foot or hand, {21:20} Or a hunchback, a dwarf, one with a blemish in his eye, with scurvy, scabbed, or one with broken stones; {21:21} No man with a blemish from among the offspring of Aaron the priest shall come near to offer the offerings of the LORD made by fire; he has a blemish; he shall not come near to offer the bread of his God. {21:22} He shall eat the bread of his God, both of the most holy and of the holy. {21:23} Only he shall not go near the veil, nor come near to the altar, because he has a blemish; that he may not profane my sanctuaries, for I the LORD sanctify them. {21:24} And Moses told it unto Aaron, and to his sons, and unto all the children of Israel.

{22:1} And the LORD spoke unto Moses, saying, {22:2} Speak unto Aaron and his sons, instructing them to separate themselves from the holy things of the children of Israel, so they do not profane my holy name in the things they set apart for me. I am the LORD. {22:3} Tell them that anyone among your descendants, throughout your generations, who approaches the holy things while he is unclean shall be cut off from my presence. I am the LORD. {22:4} Any descendant of Aaron who is a leper or has a discharge shall not eat of the holy things until he is clean. Also, whoever touches anything unclean by contact with the dead, or a man from whom seed goes out, {22:5} Or whoever touches any creeping thing that may make him unclean, or a man from whom he may become unclean, whatever his uncleanness may be; {22:6} The person who has touched any such shall be unclean until evening and shall not eat of the holy things unless he washes his body with water. {22:7} And when the sun sets, he shall be clean and may afterward eat of the holy things, for it is his food. {22:8} He shall not eat anything that dies by itself or is torn by beasts, so as not to defile himself with it. I am the LORD. {22:9} Therefore, they shall keep my commandments, lest they bear sin and die for it, if they profane it. I, the LORD, sanctify them. {22:10} No stranger shall eat of the holy things; neither a sojourner of the priest nor a hired servant shall eat of the holy things. {22:11} But if a priest buys a slave with his money, the slave may eat of it, and one who is born in his house may eat of his food. {22:12} If a priest's daughter is married to an outsider, she may not eat of the holy offerings. {22:13} But if a priest's daughter is widowed or divorced, has no child, and has returned to her father's house as in her youth, she may eat of her father's food. But no stranger may eat of it. {22:14} And if anyone eats the holy offering unintentionally, he shall add the fifth part to it and give it to the priest along with the holy offering. {22:15} They shall not profane the holy things of the children of Israel, which they offer to the LORD, {22:16} Nor allow them to bear the guilt of trespass when they eat their holy things, for I, the LORD, sanctify them. {22:17} And the LORD spoke unto Moses, saying, {22:18} Speak unto Aaron, his sons, and all the children of Israel, saying, Whoever, whether of the house of Israel or of the strangers in Israel, offers his oblation for his vows or freewill offerings to the LORD for a burnt offering; {22:19} Offer at your own will a male without blemish, whether from the herd, the flock, or the goats. {22:20} But anything with a blemish you shall not offer, for it will not be acceptable for you. {22:21} And whoever offers a sacrifice of peace offerings to the LORD to fulfill his vow, or a freewill offering in cattle or sheep, it shall be perfect and accepted; there shall be no blemish in it. {22:22} Blind, broken, maimed, having a wen, scurvy, or scabbed animals you shall not offer to the LORD nor make an offering by fire of them on the altar to the LORD. {22:23} Whether a bull or a lamb with any defect, you may offer it for a freewill offering, but it shall not be accepted for a vow. {22:24} You shall not offer to the LORD anything that is bruised, crushed, broken, or cut; nor shall you make any offering of them in your land. {22:25} You shall not accept from a stranger's hand any of these to offer the bread of your God because they are corrupt and have blemishes; they shall not be accepted for you. {22:26} And the LORD spoke unto Moses, saying, {22:27} When a bull, sheep, or goat is born, it shall be under the dam for seven days; and from the eighth day and thereafter, it shall be accepted as an offering made by fire unto the LORD. {22:28} Whether a cow or a ewe, you shall not kill it and her young on the same day. {22:29} And when you offer a sacrifice of thanksgiving to the LORD, offer it at your own will. {22:30} On the same day, it shall be eaten up; you shall leave none of it until the next day. I am the LORD. {22:31} Therefore, you shall keep my commandments and do them. I am the LORD. {22:32} You shall not profane my holy name, but I will be hallowed among the children of Israel. I am the LORD who sanctifies you, {22:33} Who brought you out of the land of Egypt to be your God. I am the LORD.

{23:1} And the LORD spoke unto Moses, saying, {23:2} **Speak unto the children of Israel and tell them about the feasts of the LORD, which you shall declare as holy convocations. These are my appointed feasts.** {23:3} Six days shall be for work, but the seventh day is the Sabbath of rest, a holy convocation. On that day, you shall not do any work; it is the Sabbath of the LORD in all your dwellings. {23:4} These are the feasts of the LORD, holy convocations which you shall proclaim at their appointed times. {23:5} On the fourteenth day of the first month at evening is the LORD'S Passover. {23:6} And on the fifteenth day of the same month is the Feast of Unleavened Bread unto the LORD; for seven days you must eat unleavened bread. {23:7} On the first day, you shall have a holy convocation; you shall not do any ordinary work on it. {23:8} But you shall offer an offering made by fire unto the LORD for seven days; on the seventh day, there shall be a holy convocation; you shall do no ordinary work therein. {23:9} And the LORD spoke unto Moses, saying, {23:10} Speak unto the children of Israel and say unto them, When you come into the land which I give unto you, and shall reap the harvest thereof, then you shall bring a sheaf of the firstfruits of your harvest unto the priest. {23:11} And he shall wave the sheaf before the LORD, to be accepted for you; on the morrow after the Sabbath, the priest shall wave it. {23:12} And you shall offer that day when you wave the sheaf a male lamb without blemish of the first year for a burnt offering unto the LORD. {23:13} And the meat offering thereof shall be two tenth deals of fine flour mingled with oil, an offering made by fire unto the LORD for a sweet savour; and the drink offering thereof shall be of wine, the fourth part of a hin. {23:14} And you shall eat neither bread, nor parched corn, nor green ears, until the same day that you have brought an offering unto your God; it shall be a statute forever throughout your generations in all your dwellings. {23:15} And you shall count unto you from the morrow after the Sabbath, from the day that you brought the sheaf of the wave offering; seven Sabbaths shall be complete: {23:16} Even unto the morrow after the seventh Sabbath shall you number fifty days, and you shall offer a new meat offering unto the LORD. {23:17} You shall bring out of your habitations two wave loaves of two tenth deals; they shall be of fine flour; they shall be baked with leaven; they are the firstfruits unto the LORD. {23:18} And you shall offer with the bread seven lambs without blemish of the first year, and one young bullock, and two rams; they shall be for a burnt offering unto the LORD, with their meat offering, and their drink offerings, even an offering made by fire, of sweet savour unto the LORD. {23:19} Then you shall sacrifice one kid of the goats for a sin offering and two lambs of the first year for a sacrifice of peace offerings. {23:20} And the priest shall wave them with the bread of the firstfruits for a wave offering before the LORD, with the two lambs; they shall be holy to the LORD for the priest. {23:21} And you shall proclaim on the same day, that it may be a holy convocation unto you; you shall do no ordinary work therein; it shall be a statute forever in all your dwellings throughout your generations.

{23:22} And when you reap the harvest of your land, you shall not make clean riddance of the corners of thy field when you reap, neither shall you gather any gleaning of your harvest; you shall leave them unto the poor, and to the stranger; I am the LORD your God. {23:23} And the LORD spoke unto Moses, saying, {23:24} Speak unto the children of Israel, saying, In the seventh month, on the first day of the month, you shall have a Sabbath, a memorial of blowing of trumpets, a holy convocation. {23:25} You shall do no ordinary work therein; but you shall offer an offering made by fire unto the LORD. {23:26} And the LORD spoke unto Moses, saying, {23:27} Also on the tenth day of this seventh month there shall be a day of atonement; it shall be a holy convocation unto you; and you shall afflict your souls and offer an offering made by fire unto the LORD. {23:28} And you shall do no work on that same day; for it is a day of atonement, to make an atonement for you before the LORD your God. {23:29} For whatever soul it be that shall not be afflicted in that same day, he shall be cut off from among his people. {23:30} And whatever soul it be that does any work in that same day, the same soul will I destroy from among his people. {23:31} You shall do no manner of work; it shall be a statute forever throughout your generations in all your dwellings. {23:32} It shall be unto you a Sabbath of rest, and you shall afflict your souls; on the ninth day of the month at evening, from evening unto evening, you shall celebrate your Sabbath. {23:33} And the LORD spoke unto Moses, saying, {23:34} Speak unto the children of Israel, saying, {23:34} Speak to the children of Israel, saying, On the fifteenth day of this seventh month, there shall be the feast of tabernacles for seven days unto the LORD. {23:35} The first day shall be a holy convocation: you shall not do any regular work on it. {23:36} For seven days, you shall offer an offering made by fire to the LORD. On the eighth day, there shall be a holy convocation unto you, and you shall offer an offering made by fire to the LORD. It is a solemn assembly, you shall not do any regular work on it. {23:37} These are the feasts of the LORD, which you shall proclaim as holy convocations, to offer an offering made by fire to the LORD, a burnt offering, a grain offering, a sacrifice, and drink offerings, everything on its day. {23:38} Besides the sabbaths of the LORD, and besides your gifts, and besides all your vows, and besides all your freewill offerings, which you give to the LORD. {23:39} Also, on the fifteenth day of the seventh month, when you have gathered in the fruit of the land, you shall keep a feast unto the LORD for seven days: the first day shall be a sabbath, and on the eighth day shall be a sabbath. {23:40} And on the first day, you shall take the branches of goodly trees, branches of palm trees, and thick trees' boughs, and willows of the brook, and rejoice before the LORD your God for seven days. {23:41} You shall keep it as a feast unto the LORD for seven days in the year. It shall be a statute forever in your generations: you shall celebrate it in the seventh month. {23:42} You shall dwell in booths for seven days; all those born in Israel shall dwell in booths. {23:43} So that your generations may know that I made the children of Israel dwell in booths when I brought them out of the land of Egypt. I am the LORD your God. {23:44} And Moses declared unto the children of Israel the feasts of the LORD.

{24:1} Then the LORD spoke to Moses, saying, {24:2} "Command the children of Israel to bring unto thee pure olive oil beaten for the light, to cause the lamps to burn continually. {24:3} "Without the veil of the testimony, in the tabernacle of the congregation, shall Aaron order it from the evening unto the morning before the LORD continually: it shall be a statute forever in your generations. {24:4} "He shall order the lamps upon the pure candlestick before the LORD continually. {24:5} "And thou shalt take fine flour, and bake twelve cakes thereof: two tenth deals shall be in one cake. {24:6} "And thou shalt set them in two rows, six on a row, upon the pure table before the LORD. {24:7} "And thou shalt put pure frankincense upon each row, that it may be on the bread for a memorial, even an offering made by fire unto the LORD. {24:8} "Every Sabbath he shall set it in order before the LORD continually, being taken from the children of Israel by an everlasting covenant. {24:9} "And it shall be Aaron's and his sons': and they shall eat it in the holy place: for it is most holy unto him of the offerings of the LORD made by fire by a perpetual statute. {24:10} "And the son of an Israelitish woman, whose father was an Egyptian, went out among the children of Israel: and this son of the Israelitish woman and a man of Israel strove together in the camp; {24:11} "And the Israelitish woman's son blasphemed the name of the LORD, and cursed. And they brought him unto Moses: (and his mother's name was Shelomith, the daughter of Dibri, of the tribe of Dan:) {24:12} "And they put him in ward, that the mind of the LORD might be showed them. {24:13} "And the LORD spoke unto Moses, saying, {24:14} "Bring forth him that hath cursed without the camp; and let all that heard him lay their hands upon his head, and let all the congregation stone him. {24:15} "And thou shalt speak unto the children of Israel, saying, Whosoever curseth his God shall bear his sin. {24:16} "And he that blasphemeth the name of the LORD, he shall surely be put to death, and all the congregation shall certainly stone him: as well the stranger, as he that is born in the land, when he blasphemeth the name of the LORD, shall be put to death. {24:17} **"And he that killeth any man shall surely be put to death."** {24:18} And he that killeth a beast shall make it good; beast for beast. {24:19} "And if a man cause a blemish in his neighbour; as he hath done, so shall it be done to him; {24:20} "Breach for breach, eye for eye, tooth for tooth: as he hath caused a blemish in a man, so shall it be done to him again. {24:21} "And he that killeth a beast, he shall restore it: and he that killeth a man, he shall be put to death. {24:22} "Ye shall have one manner of law, as well for the stranger, as for one of your own country: for I am the LORD your God. {24:23} "And Moses spoke to the children of Israel, that they should bring forth him that had cursed out of the camp, and stone him with stones. And the children of Israel did as the LORD commanded Moses."

{25:1} Then the LORD spoke to Moses in mount Sinai, saying, {25:2} "Speak unto the children of Israel, and say unto them, When ye come into the land which I give you, then shall the land keep a sabbath unto the LORD. {25:3} "Six years thou shalt sow thy field, and six years thou shalt prune thy vineyard, and gather in the fruit thereof; {25:4} "But in the seventh year shall be a sabbath of rest unto the land, a sabbath for the LORD: thou shalt neither sow thy field, nor prune thy vineyard. {25:5} "That which groweth of its own accord of thy harvest thou shalt not reap, neither gather the grapes of thy vine undressed: for it is a year of rest unto the land. {25:6} "And the sabbath of the land shall be meat for you; for thee, and for thy servant, and for thy maid, and for thy hired servant, and for thy stranger that sojourneth with thee, {25:7} "And for thy cattle, and for the beast that are in thy land, shall all the increase thereof be meat. {25:8} "And thou shalt number seven sabbaths of years unto thee, seven times seven years; and the space of the seven sabbaths of years shall be unto thee forty and nine years. {25:9} "Then shalt thou cause the trumpet of the jubile to sound on the tenth day of the seventh month, in the day of atonement shall ye make the trumpet sound throughout all your land. {25:10} "And ye shall hallow the fiftieth year, and proclaim liberty throughout all the land unto all the inhabitants thereof: it shall be a jubile unto you; and ye shall return every man unto his possession, and ye shall return every man unto his family. {25:11} "A jubile shall that fiftieth year be unto you: ye shall not sow, neither reap that which groweth of itself in it, nor gather the grapes in it of thy vine undressed. {25:12} "For it is the jubile; it shall be holy unto you: ye shall eat the increase thereof out of the field. {25:13} "In the year of this jubile ye shall return every man unto his possession. {25:14} "And if thou sell ought unto thy neighbour, or buyest ought of thy neighbour's hand, ye shall not oppress one another: {25:15} "According to the number of years after the jubile thou shalt buy of thy neighbour, and according unto the number of years of the fruits he shall sell unto thee: {25:16} "According to the multitude of years thou shalt increase the price thereof, and according to the fewness of years thou shalt diminish the price of it: for according to the number of the years of the fruits doth he sell unto thee. {25:17} "Ye shall not therefore oppress one another; but thou shalt fear thy God: for I am the LORD your God. {25:18} "Wherefore ye shall do my statutes, and keep my judgments, and do them; and ye shall dwell in the land in safety. {25:19} "And the land shall yield her fruit, and ye shall eat your fill, and dwell therein in safety. {25:20} "And if ye shall say, What shall we eat the seventh year? behold, we shall not sow, nor gather in our increase: {25:21} "Then I will command my blessing upon you in the sixth year, and it shall bring forth fruit for three years. {25:22} "And ye shall sow the eighth year, and eat yet of old fruit until the ninth year; until her fruits come in ye shall eat of the old store. {25:23} "The land shall not be sold for ever: for the land is mine; for ye are strangers and sojourners with me. {25:24} "And in all the land of your possession ye shall grant a redemption for the land. {25:25} "If thy brother be waxen poor, and hath sold away some of his possession, and if any of his kin come to redeem it, then shall he redeem that which his brother sold. {25:26} "And if the man have none to redeem it, and himself be able to redeem it; {25:27} "Then let him count the years of the sale thereof, and restore the overplus unto the man to whom he sold it; that he may return unto his possession. {25:28} "But if he be not able to restore it to him, then that which is sold shall remain in the hand of him that hath bought it until the year of jubile: and in the jubile it shall go out, and he shall return unto his possession. {25:29} "And if a man sell a dwelling house in a walled city, then he may redeem it within a whole year after it is sold; within a full year may he redeem it. {25:30} "And if it be not redeemed within the space of a full year, then the house that is in the walled city shall be established for ever to him that bought it throughout his generations: it shall not go out in the jubile. {25:31} "But the houses of the villages which have no wall round about them shall be counted as the fields of the country: they may be redeemed, and they shall go out in the jubile. {25:32} "Notwithstanding the cities of the Levites, and the houses of the cities of their possession, may the Levites redeem at any time. {25:33} "And if a man purchase of the Levites, then the house that was sold, and the city of his possession, shall go out in the year of jubile: for the houses of the cities of the Levites are their possession among the children of Israel. {25:34} "But the field of the suburbs of their cities may not be sold; for it is their perpetual possession. {25:35} **"And if thy brother be waxen poor, and fallen in decay with thee; then thou shalt relieve him: yea, though he be a stranger, or a sojourner; that he may live with thee.** {25:36} "Take thou no usury of him, or increase: but fear thy God; that thy brother may live with thee. {25:37} "Thou shalt not give him thy money upon usury, nor lend him thy victuals for increase. {25:38} "I am the LORD your God, which brought you forth out of the land of Egypt, to give you the land of Canaan, and to be your God. {25:39} "And if thy brother that dwelleth by thee be waxen poor, and be sold unto thee; thou shalt not compel him to serve as a bondservant; {25:40} "But as an hired servant, and as a sojourner, he shall be with thee, and shall serve thee unto the year of jubile: {25:41} "And then shall he depart from thee, both he and his children with him, and shall return unto his own family, and unto the possession of his fathers shall he return. {25:42} "For they are my servants, which I brought forth out of the land of Egypt: they shall not be sold as bondmen. {25:43} "Thou shalt not rule over him with rigour; but shalt fear thy God. {25:44} "Both thy bondmen, and thy bondmaids, which thou shalt have, shall be of the heathen that are round about you; of them shall ye buy bondmen and bondmaids. {25:45} "Moreover of the children of the strangers that do sojourn among you, of them shall ye buy, and of their families that are with you, which they begat in your land: and they shall be your possession. {25:46} "And ye shall take them as an inheritance for your children after you, to inherit them for a possession; they shall be your bondmen for ever: but over your brethren the children of Israel, ye shall not rule one over another with rigour. {25:47} "And if a sojourner or stranger wax rich by thee, and thy brother that dwelleth by him wax poor, and sell himself unto the stranger or sojourner by thee, or to the stock of the stranger's family: {25:48} "After that he is sold he may be redeemed again; one of his brethren may redeem him: {25:49} "Either his uncle, or his uncle's son, may redeem him, or any that is nigh of kin unto him of his family may redeem him; or if he be able, he may redeem himself. {25:50} "And he shall reckon with him that bought him from the year that he was sold to him unto the year of jubile: and the price of his sale shall be according unto the number of years, according to the time of an hired servant shall it be with him. {25:51} "If there be yet many years behind, according unto them he shall give again the price of his redemption out of the money that he was bought for. {25:52} "And if there remain but few years unto the year of jubile, then he shall count with him, and according unto his years shall he give him again the price of his redemption. {25:53} "And as a yearly hired servant shall he be with him: and the other shall not rule with rigour over him in his sight. {25:54} "And if he be not redeemed in these years, then he shall go out in the year of jubile, both he, and his children with him. {25:55} "For unto me the children of Israel are servants; they are my servants whom I brought forth out of the land of Egypt: I am the LORD your God."

{26:1} "You shall make for yourselves no idols nor graven images, neither rear up a standing image, nor shall you set up any image of stone in your land to bow down unto it; for I am the LORD your God. {26:2} "You shall keep my sabbaths, and reverence my sanctuary: I am the LORD. {26:3} **"If you walk in my statutes, and keep my commandments, and do them;** {26:4} "Then I will give you rain in due season, and the land shall yield her increase, and the trees of the field shall yield their fruit. {26:5} "And your threshing shall reach unto the vintage, and the vintage shall reach unto the sowing time: and you shall eat your bread to the full, and dwell in your land safely. {26:6} "And I will give peace in the land, and you shall lie down, and none shall make you afraid: and I will rid evil beasts out of the land, neither shall the sword go through your land. {26:7} "And you shall chase your enemies, and they shall fall before you by the sword. {26:8} "And five of you shall chase an hundred, and an hundred of you shall put ten thousand to flight: and your enemies shall fall before you by the sword. {26:9} "For I will have respect unto you, and make you fruitful, and multiply you, and establish my covenant with you. {26:10} "And you shall eat old store, and bring forth the old because of the new. {26:11} "And I will set my tabernacle among you: and my soul shall not abhor you. {26:12} "And I will walk among you, and will be your God, and you shall be my people. {26:13} "I am the LORD your God, which brought you forth out of the land of Egypt, that you should not be their bondmen; and I have broken the bands of your yoke, and made you go upright. {26:14} **"But if you will not hearken unto me, and will not do all these commandments;** {26:15} "And if you shall despise my statutes, or if your soul abhor my judgments, so that you will not do all my commandments, but that you break my covenant: {26:16} "I also will do this unto you; I will even appoint over you terror, consumption, and the burning ague, that shall consume the eyes, and cause sorrow of heart: and you shall sow your seed in vain, for your enemies shall eat it. {26:17}

"And I will set my face against you, and you shall be slain before your enemies: they that hate you shall reign over you; and you shall flee when none pursueth you. {26:18} "And if you will not yet for all this hearken unto me, then I will punish you seven times more for your sins. {26:19} "And I will break the pride of your power; and I will make your heaven as iron, and your earth as brass: {26:20} "And your strength shall be spent in vain: for your land shall not yield her increase, neither shall the trees of the land yield their fruits. {26:21} "And if you walk contrary unto me, and will not hearken unto me; I will bring seven times more plagues upon you according to your sins. {26:22} "I will also send wild beasts among you, which shall rob you of your children, and destroy your cattle, and make you few in number; and your ways shall be desolate. {26:23} "And if you will not be reformed by me by these things, but will walk contrary unto me; {26:24} "Then will I also walk contrary unto you, and will punish you yet seven times for your sins. {26:25} "And I will bring a sword upon you, that shall avenge the quarrel of my covenant: and when you are gathered together within your cities, I will send the pestilence among you; and you shall be delivered into the hand of the enemy. {26:26} "And when I have broken the staff of your bread, ten women shall bake your bread in one oven, and they shall deliver you your bread again by weight: and you shall eat, and not be satisfied. {26:27} "And if you will not for all this hearken unto me, but walk contrary unto me; {26:28} "Then I will walk contrary unto you also in fury; and I, even I, will chastise you seven times for your sins. {26:29} "And you shall eat the flesh of your sons, and the flesh of your daughters shall you eat. {26:30} "And I will destroy your high places, and cut down your images, and cast your carcasses upon the carcasses of your idols, and my soul shall abhor you. {26:31} "And I will make your cities waste, and bring your sanctuaries unto desolation, and I will not smell the savor of your sweet odors. {26:32} "And I will bring the land into desolation: and your enemies which dwell therein shall be astonished at it. {26:33} "And I will scatter you among the heathen, and will draw out a sword after you: and your land shall be desolate, and your cities waste. {26:34} "Then shall the land enjoy her sabbaths, as long as it lies desolate, and you be in your enemies' land; even then shall the land rest, and enjoy her sabbaths. {26:35} "As long as it lies desolate it shall rest; because it did not rest in your sabbaths, when you dwelt upon it. {26:36} "And upon them that are left alive of you I will send a faintness into their hearts in the lands of their enemies; and the sound of a shaken leaf shall chase them; and they shall flee, as fleeing from a sword; and they shall fall when none pursueth. {26:37} "And they shall fall one upon another, as it were before a sword, when none pursueth: and you shall have no power to stand before your enemies. {26:38} "And you shall perish among the heathen, and the land of your enemies shall eat you up. {26:39} "And they that are left of you shall pine away in their iniquity in your enemies' lands; and also in the iniquities of their fathers shall they pine away with them. {26:40} "If they shall confess their iniquity, and the iniquity of their fathers, with their trespass which they trespassed against me, and that also they have walked contrary unto me; {26:41} "And that I also have walked contrary unto them, and have brought them into the land of their enemies; if then their uncircumcised hearts be humbled, and they then accept of the punishment of their iniquity: {26:42} "Then will I remember my covenant with Jacob, and also my covenant with Isaac, and also my covenant with Abraham will I remember; and I will remember the land. {26:43} "The land also shall be left of them, and shall enjoy her sabbaths, while she lieth desolate without them: and they shall accept of the punishment of their iniquity: because, even because they despised my judgments, and because their soul abhorred my statutes. {26:44} "And yet for all that, when they be in the land of their enemies, I will not cast them away, neither will I abhor them, to destroy them utterly, and to break my covenant with them: for I am the LORD their God. {26:45} "But I will for their sakes remember the covenant of their ancestors, whom I brought forth out of the land of Egypt in the sight of the heathen, that I might be their God: I am the LORD. {26:46} "These are the statutes and judgments and laws, which the LORD made between him and the children of Israel in mount Sinai by the hand of Moses."

{27:1} And the LORD spoke unto Moses, saying, {27:2} "Speak unto the children of Israel, and say unto them, When a man shall make a singular vow, the persons shall be for the LORD by thy estimation. {27:3} "And thy estimation shall be of the male from twenty years old even unto sixty years old, even thy estimation shall be fifty shekels of silver, after the shekel of the sanctuary. {27:4} "And if it be a female, then thy estimation shall be thirty shekels. {27:5} "And if it be from five years old even unto twenty years old, then thy estimation shall be of the male twenty shekels, and for the female ten shekels. {27:6} "And if it be from a month old even unto five years old, then thy estimation shall be of the male five shekels of silver, and for the female thy estimation shall be three shekels of silver. {27:7} "And if it be from sixty years old and above; if it be a male, then thy estimation shall be fifteen shekels, and for the female ten shekels. {27:8} "But if he be poorer than thy estimation, then he shall present himself before the priest, and the priest shall value him; according to his ability that vowed shall the priest value him. {27:9} "And if it be a beast, whereof men bring an offering unto the LORD, all that any man giveth of such unto the LORD shall be holy. {27:10} "He shall not alter it, nor change it, a good for a bad, or a bad for a good: and if he shall at all change beast for beast, then it and the exchange thereof shall be holy. {27:11} "And if it be any unclean beast, of which they do not offer a sacrifice unto the LORD, then he shall present the beast before the priest: {27:12} "And the priest shall value it, whether it be good or bad: as thou valuest it, who art the priest, so shall it be. {27:13} "But if he will at all redeem it, then he shall add a fifth part thereof unto thy estimation. {27:14} "And when a man shall sanctify his house to be holy unto the LORD, then the priest shall estimate it, whether it be good or bad: as the priest shall estimate it, so shall it stand. {27:15} "And if he that sanctified it will redeem his house, then he shall add the fifth part of the money of thy estimation unto it, and it shall be his. {27:16} "And if a man shall sanctify unto the LORD some part of a field of his possession, then thy estimation shall be according to the seed thereof: an homer of barley seed shall be valued at fifty shekels of silver. {27:17} "If he sanctify his field from the year of jubilee, according to thy estimation it shall stand. {27:18} "But if he sanctify his field after the jubilee, then the priest shall reckon unto him the money according to the years that remain, even unto the year of the jubilee, and it shall be abated from thy estimation. {27:19} "And if he that sanctified the field will in any wise redeem it, then he shall add the fifth part of the money of thy estimation unto it, and it shall be assured to him. {27:20} "And if he will not redeem the field, or if he have sold the field to another man, it shall not be redeemed any more. {27:21} "But the field, when it goeth out in the jubilee, shall be holy unto the LORD, as a field devoted; the possession thereof shall be the priest's. {27:22} "And if a man sanctify unto the LORD a field which he hath bought, which is not of the fields of his possession; {27:23} "Then the priest shall reckon unto him the worth of thy estimation, even unto the year of the jubilee: and he shall give thine estimation in that day, as a holy thing unto the LORD. {27:24} "In the year of the jubilee the field shall return unto him of whom it was bought, even to him to whom the possession of the land did belong. {27:25} "And all thy estimations shall be according to the shekel of the sanctuary: twenty gerahs shall be the shekel. {27:26} "Only the firstling of the beasts, which should be the LORD'S firstling, no man shall sanctify it; whether it be ox, or sheep: it is the LORD'S. {27:27} "And if it be of an unclean beast, then he shall redeem it according to thine estimation, and shall add a fifth part of it thereto: or if it be not redeemed, then it shall be sold according to thy estimation. {27:28} "Notwithstanding no devoted thing, that a man shall devote unto the LORD of all that he hath, both of man and beast, and of the field of his possession, shall be sold or redeemed: every devoted thing is most holy unto the LORD. {27:29} "None devoted, which shall be devoted of men, shall be redeemed; but shall surely be put to death. {27:30} "And all the tithe of the land, whether of the seed of the land, or of the fruit of the tree, is the LORD'S: it is holy unto the LORD. {27:31} "And if a man will at all redeem ought of his tithes, he shall add thereto the fifth part thereof. {27:32} "And concerning the tithe of the herd, or of the flock, even of whatsoever passeth under the rod, the tenth shall be holy unto the LORD. {27:33} "He shall not search whether it be good or bad, neither shall he change it: and if he change it at all, then both it and the change thereof shall be holy; it shall not be redeemed. {27:34} "These are the commandments, which the LORD commanded Moses for the children of Israel in mount Sinai."

Numbers

{1:1} "And the LORD spoke unto Moses in the wilderness of Sinai, in the tabernacle of the congregation, on the first day of the second month, in the second year after they were come out of the land of Egypt, saying, {1:2} *"Take ye the sum of all the congregation of the children of Israel, after their families, by the house of their fathers, with the number of their names, every male by their polls;* {1:3} *"From twenty years old and upward, all that are able to go forth to war in Israel: thou and Aaron shall number them by their armies.* {1:4} *"And with you there shall be a man of every tribe; every one head of the house of his fathers.* {1:5} "And these are the names of the men that shall stand with you: of the tribe of Reuben; Elizur the son of Shedeur. {1:6} "Of Simeon; Shelumiel the son of Zurishaddai. {1:7} "Of Judah; Nahshon the son of Amminadab. {1:8} "Of Issachar; Nethaneel the son of Zuar. {1:9} "Of Zebulun; Eliab the son of Helon. {1:10} "Of the children of Joseph: of Ephraim; Elishama the son of Ammihud: of Manasseh; Gamaliel the son of Pedahzur. {1:11} "Of Benjamin; Abidan the son of Gideoni. {1:12} "Of Dan; Ahiezer the son of Ammishaddai. {1:13} "Of Asher; Pagiel the son of Ocran. {1:14} "Of Gad; Eliasaph the son of Deuel. {1:15} "Of Naphtali; Ahira the son of Enan. {1:16} "These were the renowned of the congregation, princes of the tribes of their fathers, heads of thousands in Israel. {1:17} "And Moses and Aaron took these men which are expressed by their names: {1:18} "And they assembled all the congregation together on the first day of the second month, and they declared their pedigrees after their families, by the house of their fathers, according to the number of the names, from twenty years old and upward, by their polls. {1:19} "As the LORD commanded Moses, so he numbered them in the wilderness of Sinai. {1:20} "And the children of Reuben, Israel's eldest son, by their generations, after their families, by the house of their fathers, according to the number of the names, by their polls, every male from twenty years old and upward, all that were able to go forth to war; {1:21} "Those that were numbered of them, even of the tribe of Reuben, were forty and six thousand and five hundred. {1:22} "Of the children of Simeon, by their generations, after their families, by the house of their fathers, those that were numbered of them, according to the number of the names, by their polls, every male from twenty years old and upward, all that were able to go forth to war; {1:23} "Those that were numbered of them, even of the tribe of Simeon, were fifty and nine thousand and three hundred. {1:24} "Of the children of Gad, by their generations, after their families, by the house of their fathers, according to the number of the names, from twenty years old and upward, all that were able to go forth to war; {1:25} "Those that were numbered of them, even of the tribe of Gad, were forty and five thousand six hundred and fifty. {1:26} "Of the children of Judah, by their generations, after their families, by the house of their fathers, according to the number of the names, from twenty years old and upward, all that were able to go forth to war; {1:27} "Those that were numbered of them, even of the tribe of Judah, were threescore and fourteen thousand and six hundred. {1:28} "Of the children of Issachar, by their generations, after their families, by the house of their fathers, according to the number of the names, from twenty years old and upward, all that were able to go forth to war; {1:29} "Those that were numbered of them, even of the tribe of Issachar, were fifty and four thousand and four hundred. {1:30} "Of the children of Zebulun, by their generations, after their families, by the house of their fathers, according to the number of the names, from twenty years old and upward, all that were able to go forth to war; {1:31} "Those that were numbered of them, even of the tribe of Zebulun, were fifty and seven thousand and four hundred. {1:32} "Of the children of Joseph, namely, of the children of Ephraim, by their generations, after their families, by the house of their fathers, according to the number of the names, from twenty years old and upward, all that were able to go forth to war; {1:33} "Those that were numbered of them, even of the tribe of Ephraim, were forty thousand and five hundred. {1:34} "Of the children of Manasseh, by their generations, after their families, by the house of their fathers, according to the number of the names, from twenty years old and upward, all that were able to go forth to war; {1:35} "Those that were numbered of them, even of the tribe of Manasseh, were thirty and two thousand and two hundred. {1:36} "Of the children of Benjamin, by their generations, after their families, by the house of their fathers, according to the number of the names, from twenty years old and upward, all that were able to go forth to war; {1:37} "Those that were numbered of them, even of the tribe of Benjamin, were thirty and five thousand and four hundred. {1:38} "Of the children of Dan, by their generations, after their families, by the house of their fathers, according to the number of the names, from twenty years old and upward, all that were able to go forth to war; {1:39} "Those that were numbered of them, even of the tribe of Dan, were threescore and two thousand and seven hundred. {1:40} "Of the children of Asher, by their generations, after their families, by the house of their fathers, according to the number of the names, from twenty years old and upward, all that were able to go forth to war; {1:41} "Those that were numbered of them, even of the tribe of Asher, were forty and one thousand and five hundred. {1:42} "Of the children of Naphtali, throughout their generations, after their families, by the house of their fathers, according to the number of the names {1:43} "Those that were numbered of them, even of the tribe of Naphtali, were fifty and three thousand and four hundred. {1:44} "These are those that were numbered, which Moses and Aaron numbered, and the princes of Israel, being twelve men: each one was for the house of his fathers. {1:45} "So were all those that were numbered of the children of Israel, by the house of their fathers, from twenty years old and upward, all that were able to go to war in Israel; {1:46} "Even all they that were numbered were six hundred thousand and three thousand and five hundred and fifty. {1:47} "But the Levites after the tribe of their fathers were not numbered among them. {1:48} "For the LORD had spoken unto Moses, saying, {1:49} "Only thou shalt not number the tribe of Levi, neither take the sum of them among the children of Israel: {1:50} "But thou shalt appoint the Levites over the tabernacle of testimony, and over all the vessels thereof, and over all things that belong to it: they shall bear the tabernacle, and all the vessels thereof; and they shall minister unto it, and shall encamp round about the tabernacle. {1:51} "And when the tabernacle setteth forward, the Levites shall take it down: and when the tabernacle is to be pitched, the Levites shall set it up: and the stranger that cometh nigh shall be put to death. {1:52} "And the children of Israel shall pitch their tents, every man by his own camp, and every man by his own standard, throughout their hosts. {1:53} "But the Levites shall pitch round about the tabernacle of testimony, that there be no wrath upon the congregation of the children of Israel: and the Levites shall keep the charge of the tabernacle of testimony. {1:54} "And the children of Israel did according to all that the LORD commanded Moses, so did they."

{2:1} "And the LORD spoke unto Moses and unto Aaron, saying, {2:2} "Every man of the children of Israel shall pitch by his own standard, with the ensign of their father's house: far off about the tabernacle of the congregation shall they pitch. {2:3} "And on the east side toward the rising of the sun shall they of the standard of the camp of Judah pitch throughout their armies: and Nahshon the son of Amminadab shall be captain of the children of Judah. {2:4} "And his host, and those that were numbered of them, were threescore and fourteen thousand and six hundred. {2:5} "And those that do pitch next unto him shall be the tribe of Issachar: and Nethaneel the son of Zuar shall be captain of the children of Issachar. {2:6} "And his host, and those that were numbered thereof, were fifty and four thousand and four hundred. {2:7} "Then the tribe of Zebulun: and Eliab the son of Helon shall be captain of the children of Zebulun. {2:8} "And his host, and those that were numbered thereof, were fifty and seven thousand and four hundred. {2:9} "All that were numbered in the camp of Judah were an hundred thousand and fourscore thousand and six thousand and four hundred, throughout their armies. These shall first set forth. {2:10} "On the south side shall be the standard of the camp of Reuben according to their armies: and the captain of the children of Reuben shall be Elizur the son of Shedeur. {2:11} "And his host, and those that were numbered thereof, were forty and six thousand and five hundred. {2:12} "And those which pitch by him shall be the tribe of Simeon: and the captain of the children of Simeon shall be Shelumiel the son of Zurishaddai. {2:13} "And his host, and those that were numbered of them, were fifty and nine thousand and three hundred. {2:14} "Then the tribe of Gad: and the captain of the sons of Gad shall be Eliasaph the son of Reuel. {2:15} "And his host, and those that were numbered of them, were forty and five thousand and six hundred and fifty. {2:16} "All that were numbered in the camp of Reuben were an hundred thousand and fifty and one thousand and four hundred and fifty, throughout their armies. And they shall set forth in the second rank. {2:17} "Then the tabernacle of the congregation shall set forward with the camp of the Levites in the midst of the camp: as they encamp, so shall they set forward, every man in his place by their standards. {2:18} "On the west side shall be the standard of the camp of Ephraim according to their armies: and the captain of the sons of Ephraim shall be Elishama the son of Ammihud. {2:19} "And his host, and those that were numbered of them, were forty thousand and five hundred. {2:20} "And by him shall be the tribe of Manasseh: and the captain of the children of Manasseh shall be Gamaliel the son of Pedahzur. {2:21} "And his host, and those that were numbered of them, were thirty and two thousand and two hundred. {2:22} "Then the tribe of Benjamin: and the captain of the sons of Benjamin shall be Abidan the son of Gideoni. {2:23} "And his host, and those that were numbered of them, were thirty and five thousand and four hundred. {2:24} "All that were numbered of the camp of Ephraim were an hundred thousand and eight thousand and an hundred, throughout their armies. And they shall go forward in the third rank. {2:25} "The standard of the camp of Dan shall be on the north side by their armies: and the captain of the children of Dan shall be Ahiezer the son of Ammishaddai. {2:26} "And his host, and those that were numbered of them, were threescore and two thousand and seven hundred. {2:27} "And those that encamp by him shall be the tribe of Asher: and the captain of the children of Asher shall be Pagiel the son of Ocran. {2:28} "And his host, and those that were numbered of them, were forty and one thousand and five hundred. {2:29} "Then the tribe of Naphtali: and the captain of the children of Naphtali shall be Ahira the son of Enan. {2:30} "And his host, and those that were numbered of them, were fifty and three thousand and four hundred. {2:31} "All they that were numbered in the camp of Dan were an hundred thousand and fifty and seven thousand and six hundred. They shall go hindmost with their standards. {2:32} "These are those which were numbered of the children of Israel by the house of their fathers: all those that were numbered of the camps throughout their hosts were six hundred thousand and three thousand and five hundred and fifty. {2:33} "But the Levites were not numbered among the children of Israel; as the LORD commanded Moses. {2:34} "And the children of Israel did according to all that the LORD commanded Moses: so they pitched by their standards, and so they set forward, every one after their families, according to the house of their fathers."

{3:1} "These also are the generations of Aaron and Moses in the day that the LORD spake with Moses in mount Sinai. {3:2} "And these are the names of the sons of Aaron; Nadab the firstborn, and Abihu, Eleazar, and Ithamar. {3:3} "These are the names of the sons of Aaron, the priests which were anointed, whom he consecrated to minister in the priest's office. {3:4} "And Nadab and Abihu died before the LORD, when they offered strange fire before the LORD, in the wilderness of Sinai, and they had no children: and Eleazar and Ithamar ministered in the priest's office in the sight of Aaron their father. {3:5} "And the LORD spake unto Moses, saying, {3:6} "Bring the tribe of Levi near, and present them before Aaron the priest, that they may minister unto him. {3:7} "And they shall keep his charge, and the charge of the whole congregation before the tabernacle of the congregation, to do the service of the tabernacle. {3:8} "And they shall keep all the instruments of the tabernacle of the congregation, and the charge of the children of Israel, to do the service of the tabernacle. {3:9} "And thou shalt give the Levites unto Aaron and to his sons: they are wholly given unto him out of the children of Israel. {3:10} "And thou shalt appoint Aaron and his sons, and they shall wait on their priest's office: and the stranger that cometh nigh shall be put to death. {3:11} "And the LORD spake unto Moses, saying, {3:12} "And I, behold, I have taken the Levites from among the children of Israel instead of all the firstborn that openeth the matrix among the children of Israel: therefore the Levites shall be mine; {3:13} "Because all the firstborn are mine; for on the day that I smote all the firstborn in the land of Egypt I hallowed unto me all the firstborn in Israel, both man and beast: mine shall they be: I am the LORD. {3:14} "And the LORD spake unto Moses in the wilderness of Sinai, saying, {3:15} "Number the children of Levi after the house of their fathers, by their families: every male from a month old and upward shalt thou number them. {3:16} "And Moses numbered them according to the word of the LORD, as he was commanded. {3:17} "And these were the sons of Levi by their names; Gershon, and Kohath, and Merari. {3:18} "And these are the names of the sons of Gershon by their families; Libni, and Shimei. {3:19} "And the sons of Kohath by their families; Amram, and Izehar, Hebron, and Uzziel. {3:20} "And the sons of Merari by their families; Mahli, and Mushi. These are the families of the Levites according to the house of their fathers. {3:21} "Of Gershon was the family of the Libnites, and the family of the Shimites: these are the families of the Gershonites. {3:22} "Those that were numbered of them, according to the number of all the males, from a month old and upward, even those that were numbered of them, were seven thousand and five hundred. {3:23} "The families of the Gershonites shall pitch behind the tabernacle westward. {3:24} "And the chief of the house of the father of the Gershonites shall be Eliasaph the son of Lael. {3:25} "And the charge of the sons of Gershon in the tabernacle of the congregation shall be the tabernacle, and the tent, the covering thereof, and the hanging for the door of the tabernacle of the congregation, {3:26} "And the hangings of the court, and the curtain for the door of the court, which is by the tabernacle, and by the altar round about, and the cords of it for all the service thereof. {3:27} "And of Kohath was the family of the Amramites, and the family of the Izeharites, and the family of the Hebronites, and the family of the Uzzielites: these are the families of the Kohathites. {3:28} "In the number of all the males, from a month old and upward, were eight thousand and six hundred, keeping the charge of the sanctuary. {3:29} "The families of the sons of Kohath shall pitch on the side of the tabernacle southward. {3:30} "And the chief of the house of the father of the families of the Kohathites shall be Elizaphan the son of Uzziel. {3:31} "And their charge shall be the ark, and the table, and the candlestick, and the altars, and the vessels of the sanctuary wherewith they minister, and the hanging, and all the service thereof. {3:32} "And Eleazar the son of Aaron the priest shall be chief over the chief of the Levites, and have the oversight of them that keep the charge of the sanctuary. {3:33} "Of Merari was the family of the Mahlites, and the family of the Mushites: these are the families of Merari. {3:34} "And those that were numbered of them, according to the number of all the males, from a month old and upward, were six thousand and two hundred. {3:35} "And the chief of the house of the father of the families of Merari was Zuriel the son of Abihail: these shall pitch on the side of the tabernacle northward. {3:36} "And under the custody and charge of the sons of Merari shall be the boards of the tabernacle, and the bars thereof, and the pillars thereof, and the sockets thereof, and all the vessels thereof, and all that serveth thereto, {3:37} "And the pillars of the court round about, and their sockets, and their pins, and their cords. {3:38} "But those that encamp before the tabernacle toward the east, even before the tabernacle of the congregation eastward, shall be Moses, and Aaron and his sons, keeping the charge of the sanctuary for the charge of the children of Israel; and the stranger that cometh nigh shall be put to death. {3:39} "All that were numbered of the Levites, which Moses and Aaron numbered at the commandment of the LORD, throughout their families, all the males from a month old and upward, were twenty and two thousand. {3:40} "And the LORD said unto Moses, Number all the firstborn of the males of the children of Israel from a month old and upward, and take the number of their names. {3:41} "And thou shalt take the Levites for me (I am the LORD) instead of all the firstborn among the children of Israel; and the cattle of the Levites instead of all the firstlings among the cattle of the children of Israel. {3:42} "And Moses numbered, as the LORD commanded him, all the firstborn among the children of Israel. {3:43} "And all the firstborn males by the number of names, from a month old and upward, of those that were numbered of them, were twenty and two thousand two hundred and threescore and thirteen. {3:44} "And the LORD spake unto Moses, saying, {3:45} "Take the Levites instead of all the firstborn among the children of Israel, and the cattle of the Levites instead of their cattle; and the Levites shall be mine: I am the LORD. {3:46} "And for those that are to be redeemed of the two hundred and threescore and thirteen of the firstborn of the children of Israel, which are more than the Levites; {3:47} "Thou shalt even take five shekels apiece by the poll, after the shekel of the sanctuary shalt thou take them: (the shekel is twenty gerahs:) {3:48} "And thou shalt give the money, wherewith the odd number of them is to be redeemed, unto Aaron and to his sons. {3:49} "And Moses took the redemption money of them that were over and above them that were redeemed by the Levites: {3:50} "Of the firstborn of the children of Israel took he the money; a thousand three hundred and threescore and five shekels, after the shekel of the sanctuary: {3:51} "And Moses gave the money of them that were redeemed unto Aaron and to his sons, according to the word of the LORD, as the LORD commanded Moses."

{4:1} "And the LORD spake unto Moses and unto Aaron, saying, {4:2} "Take the sum of the sons of Kohath from among the sons of Levi, after their families, by the house of their fathers, {4:3} "From thirty years old and upward even until fifty years old, all that enter into the host, to do the work in the tabernacle of the congregation. {4:4} "This shall be the service of the sons of Kohath in the tabernacle of the congregation, about the most holy things: {4:5} "And when the camp setteth forward, Aaron shall come, and his sons, and they shall take down the covering vail, and cover the ark of testimony with it: {4:6} "And shall put thereon the covering of badgers' skins, and shall spread over it a cloth wholly of blue, and shall put in the staves thereof. {4:7} "And upon the table of shewbread they shall spread a cloth of blue, and put thereon the dishes, and the spoons, and the bowls, and covers to cover withal: and the continual bread shall be thereon: {4:8} "And they shall spread upon them a cloth of scarlet, and cover the same with a covering of badgers' skins, and shall put in the staves thereof. {4:9} "And they shall take a cloth of blue, and cover the candlestick of the light, and his lamps, and his tongs, and his snuffdishes, and all the oil vessels thereof, wherewith they minister unto it: {4:10} "And they shall put it and all the vessels thereof within a covering of badgers' skins, and shall put it upon a bar. {4:11} "And upon the golden altar they shall spread a cloth of blue, and cover it with a covering of badgers' skins, and shall put to the staves thereof: {4:12} "And they shall take all the instruments of ministry, wherewith they minister in the sanctuary, and put them in a cloth of blue, and cover them with a covering of badgers' skins, and shall put them on a bar: {4:13} "And they shall take away the ashes from the altar, and spread a purple cloth thereon: {4:14} "And they shall put upon it all the vessels thereof, wherewith they minister about it, even the censers, the fleshhooks, and the shovels, and the basons, all the vessels of the altar; and they shall spread upon it a covering of badgers skins, and put to the staves of it. {4:15} "And when Aaron and his sons have made an end of covering the sanctuary, and all the vessels of the sanctuary, as the camp is to set forward; after that, the sons of Kohath shall come to bear it: but they shall not touch any holy thing, lest they die. These things are the burden of the sons of Kohath in the tabernacle of the congregation. {4:16} "And to the office of Eleazar the son of Aaron the priest pertaineth the oil for the light, and the sweet incense, and the daily meat offering, and the anointing oil, and the oversight of all the tabernacle, and of all that therein is, in the sanctuary, and in the vessels thereof. {4:17} "And the LORD spake unto Moses and unto Aaron, saying, {4:18} "Cut ye not off the tribe of the families of the Kohathites from among the Levites: {4:19} "But thus do unto them, that they may live, and not die, when they approach unto the most holy things: Aaron and his sons shall go in, and appoint them every one to his service and to his burden: {4:20} "But they shall not go in to see when the holy things are covered, lest they die. {4:21} "And the LORD spake unto Moses, saying, {4:22} "Take also the sum of the sons of Gershon, throughout the houses of their fathers, by their families; {4:23} "From thirty years old and upward until fifty years old shalt thou number them; all that enter in to perform the service, to do the work in the tabernacle of the congregation. {4:24} "This is the service of the families of the Gershonites, to serve, and for burdens: {4:25} "And they shall bear the curtains of the tabernacle, and the tabernacle of the congregation, his covering, and the covering of the badgers' skins that is above upon it, and the hanging for the door of the tabernacle of the congregation, {4:26} "And the hangings of the court, and the hanging for the door of the gate of the court, which is by the tabernacle and by the altar round about, and their cords, and all the instruments of their service, and all that is made for them: so shall they serve. {4:27} "At the appointment of Aaron and his sons shall be all the service of the sons of the Gershonites, in all their burdens, and in all their service: and ye shall appoint unto them in charge all their burdens. {4:28} "This is the service of the families of the sons of Gershon in the tabernacle of the congregation: and their charge shall be under the hand of Ithamar the son of Aaron the priest. {4:29} "As for the sons of Merari, thou shalt number them after their families, by the house of their fathers; {4:30} "From thirty years old and upward even unto fifty years old shalt thou number them, every one that entereth into the service, to do the work of the tabernacle of the congregation. {4:31} "And this is the charge of their burden, according to all their service in the tabernacle of the congregation; the boards of the tabernacle, and the bars thereof, and the pillars thereof, and sockets thereof, {4:32} "And the pillars of the court round about, and their sockets, and their pins, and their cords, with all their instruments, and with all their service: and by name ye shall reckon the instruments of the charge of their burden. {4:33} "This is the service of the families of the sons of Merari, according to all their service, in the tabernacle of the congregation, under the hand of Ithamar the son of Aaron the priest. {4:34} "And Moses and Aaron and the chief of the congregation numbered the sons of the Kohathites after their families, and after the house of their fathers, {4:35} "From thirty years old and upward even unto fifty years old, every one that entereth into the service, for the work in the tabernacle of the congregation: {4:36} "And those that were numbered of them by their families were two thousand seven hundred and fifty. {4:37} "These were they that were numbered of the families of the Kohathites, all that might do service in the tabernacle of the congregation, which Moses and Aaron did number according to the commandment of the LORD by the hand of Moses. {4:38} "And those that were numbered of the sons of Gershon, throughout their families, and by the house of their fathers, {4:39} "From thirty years old and upward even unto fifty years old, every one that entereth into the service, for the work in the tabernacle of the congregation, {4:40} "Even those that were numbered of them, throughout their families, by the house of their fathers, were two thousand and six hundred and thirty. {4:41} "These are they that were numbered of the families of the sons of Gershon, of all that might do service in the tabernacle of the congregation, whom Moses and Aaron did number according to the commandment of the LORD. {4:42} "And those that were numbered of the families of the sons of Merari, throughout their families, by the house of their fathers, {4:43} "From thirty years old and upward even unto fifty years old, every one that entereth into the service, for the work in the tabernacle of the congregation, {4:44} "Even those that were numbered of them after their families, were three thousand and two hundred. {4:45} "These be those that were numbered of the families of the sons of Merari, whom Moses and Aaron numbered according to the word of the LORD by the hand of Moses. {4:46} "All those that were numbered of the Levites, whom Moses and Aaron and the chief of Israel numbered, after their families, and after the house of their fathers, {4:47} "From thirty years old and upward even unto fifty years old, every one that came to do the service of the ministry, and the service of the burden in the tabernacle of the congregation, {4:48} "Even those that were numbered of them, were eight thousand and five hundred and fourscore. {4:49} "According to the commandment of the LORD they were numbered by the hand of Moses, every one according to his service, and according to his burden: thus were they numbered of him, as the LORD commanded Moses."

{5:1} "And the LORD spake unto Moses, saying, {5:2} "Command the children of Israel, that they put out of the camp every leper, and every one that hath an issue, and whosoever is defiled by the dead: {5:3} "Both male and female shall ye put out, without the camp shall ye put them; that they defile not their camps, in the midst whereof I dwell. {5:4} "And the children of Israel did so, and put them out without the camp: as the LORD spake unto Moses, so did the children of Israel. {5:5} "And the LORD spake unto Moses, saying, {5:6} "Speak unto the children of Israel, When a man or woman shall commit any sin that men commit, to do a trespass against the LORD, and that person be guilty; {5:7} "Then they shall confess their sin which they have done: and he shall recompense his trespass with the principal thereof, and add unto it the fifth part thereof, and give it unto him against whom he hath trespassed. {5:8} "But if the man have no kinsman to recompense the trespass unto, let the trespass be recompensed unto the LORD, even to the priest; beside the ram of the atonement, whereby an atonement shall be made for him. {5:9} "And every offering of all the holy things of the children of Israel, which they bring unto the priest, shall be his. {5:10} "And every man's hallowed things shall be his: whatsoever any man giveth the priest, it shall be his. {5:11} "And the LORD spake unto Moses, saying, {5:12} "Speak unto the children of Israel, and say unto them, If any man's wife go aside, and commit a trespass against him, {5:13} "And a man lie with her carnally, and it be hid from the eyes of her husband, and be kept close, and she be defiled, and there be no witness against her, neither she be taken with the manner; {5:14} "And the spirit of jealousy come upon him, and he be jealous of his wife, and she be defiled: or if the spirit of jealousy come upon him, and he be jealous of his wife, and she be not defiled; {5:15} "Then shall the man bring his wife unto the priest, and he shall bring her offering for her, the tenth part of an ephah of barley meal; he shall pour no oil upon it, nor put frankincense thereon; for it is an offering of jealousy, an offering of memorial, bringing iniquity to remembrance. {5:16} "And the priest shall bring her near, and set her before the LORD: {5:17} "And the priest shall take holy water in an earthen vessel; and of the dust that is in the floor of the tabernacle the priest shall take, and put it into the water: {5:18} "And the priest shall set the woman before the LORD, and uncover the woman's head, and put the offering of memorial in her hands, which is the jealousy offering: and the priest shall have in his hand the bitter water that causeth the curse: {5:19} "And the priest shall charge her by an oath, and say unto the woman, If no man have lain with thee, and if thou hast not gone aside to uncleanness with another instead of thy husband, be thou free from this bitter water that causeth the curse: {5:20} "But if thou hast gone aside to another instead of thy husband, and if thou be defiled, and some man have lain with thee beside thine husband: {5:21} "Then the priest shall charge the woman with an oath of cursing, and the priest shall say unto the woman, The LORD make thee a curse and an oath among thy people, when the LORD doth make thy thigh to rot, and thy belly to swell; {5:22} "And this water that causeth the curse shall go into thy bowels, to make thy belly to swell, and thy thigh to rot: And the woman shall say, Amen, amen. {5:23} "And the priest shall write these curses in a book, and he shall blot them out with the bitter water: {5:24} "And he shall cause the woman to drink the bitter water that causeth the curse: and the water that causeth the curse shall enter into her, and become bitter. {5:25} "Then the priest shall take the jealousy offering out of the woman's hand, and shall wave the offering before the LORD, and offer it upon the altar: {5:26} "And the priest shall take an handful of the offering, even the memorial thereof, and burn it upon the altar, and afterward shall cause the woman to drink the water. {5:27} "And when he hath made her to drink the water, then it shall come to pass, that, if she be defiled, and have done trespass against her husband, that the water that causeth the curse shall enter into her, and become bitter, and her belly shall swell, and her thigh shall rot: and the woman shall be a curse among her people. {5:28} "And if the woman be not defiled, but be clean; then she shall be free, and shall conceive seed. {5:29} "This is the law of jealousies, when a wife goeth aside to another instead of her husband, and is defiled; {5:30} "Or when the spirit of jealousy cometh upon him, and he be jealous over his wife, and shall set the woman before the LORD, and the priest shall execute upon her all this law. {5:31} "Then shall the man be guiltless from iniquity, and this woman shall bear her iniquity."

{6:1} "And the LORD spake unto Moses, saying, {6:2} "Speak unto the children of Israel, and say unto them, When either man or woman shall separate themselves to vow a vow of a Nazarite, to separate themselves unto the LORD: {6:3} "He shall separate himself from wine and strong drink, and shall drink no vinegar of wine, or vinegar of strong drink, neither shall he drink any liquor of grapes, nor eat moist grapes, or dried. {6:4} "All the days of his separation shall he eat nothing that is made of the vine tree, from the kernels even to the husk. {6:5} "All the days of the vow of his separation there shall no razor come upon his head: until the days be fulfilled, in the which he separateth himself unto the LORD, he shall be holy, and shall let the locks of the hair of his head grow. {6:6} "All the days that he separateth himself unto the LORD he shall come at no dead body. {6:7} "He shall not make himself unclean for his father, or for his mother, for his brother, or for his sister, when they die: because the consecration of his God is upon his head. {6:8} "All the days of his separation he is holy unto the LORD. {6:9} "And if any man die very suddenly by him, and he hath defiled the head of his consecration; then he shall shave his head in the day of his cleansing, on the seventh day shall he shave it. {6:10} "And on the eighth day he shall bring two turtles, or two young pigeons, to the priest, to the door of the tabernacle of the congregation: {6:11} "And the priest shall offer the one for a sin offering, and the other for a burnt offering, and make an atonement for him, for that he sinned by the dead, and shall hallow his head that same day. {6:12} "And he shall consecrate unto the LORD the days of his separation, and shall bring a lamb of the first year for a trespass offering: but the days that were before shall be lost, because his separation was defiled. {6:13} "And this is the law of the Nazarite, when the days of his separation are fulfilled: he shall be brought unto the door of the tabernacle of the congregation: {6:14} "And he shall offer his offering unto the LORD, one he lamb of the first year without blemish for a burnt offering, and one ewe lamb of the first year without blemish for a sin offering, and one ram without blemish for peace offerings, {6:15} "And a basket of unleavened bread, cakes of fine flour mingled with oil, and wafers of unleavened bread anointed with oil, and their meat offering, and their drink offerings. {6:16} "And the priest shall bring them before the LORD, and shall offer his sin offering, and his burnt offering: {6:17} "And he shall offer the ram for a sacrifice of peace offerings unto the LORD, with the basket of unleavened bread: the priest shall offer also his meat offering, and his drink offering. {6:18} "And the Nazarite shall shave the head of his separation at the door of the tabernacle of the congregation, and shall take the hair of the head of his separation, and put it in the fire which is under the sacrifice of the peace offerings. {6:19} "And the priest shall take the sodden shoulder of the ram, and one unleavened cake out of the basket, and one unleavened wafer, and shall put them upon the hands of the Nazarite, after the hair of his separation is shaven: {6:20} "And the priest shall wave them for a wave offering before the LORD: this is holy for the priest, with the wave breast and heave shoulder: and after that the Nazarite may drink wine. {6:21} "This is the law of the Nazarite who hath vowed, and of his offering unto the LORD for his separation, beside that his hand shall get: according to the vow which he vowed, so he must do after the law of his separation. {6:22} "And the LORD spake unto Moses, saying, {6:23} "Speak unto Aaron and unto his sons, saying, On this wise ye shall bless the children of Israel, saying unto them, {6:24} **"The LORD bless thee, and keep thee:** {6:25} **"The LORD make his face shine upon thee, and be gracious unto thee:** {6:26} **"The LORD lift up his countenance upon thee, and give thee peace.** {6:27} "And they shall put my name upon the children of Israel; and I will bless them."

{7:1} On the day Moses finished setting up the tabernacle, anointing and sanctifying it along with all its instruments—the altar and vessels—he also anointed and sanctified them. {7:2} The leaders of Israel, heads of their ancestral houses, who were in charge of the tribes and counted among them, came forward. {7:3} They brought an offering before the LORD: six covered wagons and twelve oxen—one wagon for every two leaders and an ox for each leader. They brought these offerings before the tabernacle. {7:4} Then the LORD spoke to Moses, saying, {7:5} "Accept these offerings for the service of the tabernacle and give them to the Levites according to their duties." {7:6} So Moses took the wagons and oxen and gave them to the Levites. {7:7} He gave two wagons and four oxen to the Gershonites according to their duties. {7:8} And he gave four wagons and eight oxen to the Merarites according to their duties under Ithamar, the son of Aaron the priest. {7:9} But to the Kohathites, he did not give any, as their duty was to carry the sanctuary on their shoulders. {7:10} On the day the altar was anointed, the leaders made offerings for its dedication before the altar. {7:11} And the LORD said to Moses, "Each leader shall offer their offering on their designated day for the dedication of the altar." {7:12} The first to offer his offering was Nahshon, the son of Amminadab from the tribe of Judah. {7:13} His offering consisted of one silver charger weighing a hundred and thirty shekels, one silver bowl of seventy shekels, both filled with fine flour mixed with oil for a grain offering. {7:14} He also offered a golden spoon weighing ten shekels, full of incense, along with a young bull, a ram, and a one-year-old lamb for burnt offerings, and a male goat for a sin offering. {7:15} Additionally, he presented two oxen, five rams, five male goats, and five one-year-old lambs as peace offerings. This was Nahshon's offering. {7:16} One goat kid for a sin offering. {7:17} And for the peace offering, Nahshon the son of Amminadab offered two oxen, five rams, five male goats, and five one-year-old lambs. {7:18} On the second day, Nethaneel the son of Zuar, prince of Issachar, made his offering. {7:19} He offered a silver charger weighing a hundred and thirty shekels, a silver bowl of seventy shekels, both filled with fine flour mixed with oil for a grain offering. {7:20} Along with a golden spoon weighing ten shekels, filled with incense. {7:21} For burnt offerings, he presented a young bull, a ram, and a one-year-old lamb. {7:22} Also, one goat kid for a sin offering. {7:23} And for the peace offering, he offered two oxen, five rams, five male goats, and five one-year-old lambs. {7:24} On the third day, Eliab the son of Helon, prince of the tribe of Zebulun, made his offering. {7:25} His offering was a silver charger weighing a hundred and thirty shekels, a silver bowl of seventy shekels, both filled with fine flour mixed with oil for a grain offering. {7:26} He also presented a golden spoon weighing ten shekels, filled with incense. {7:27} For burnt offerings, he brought a young bull, a ram, and a one-year-old lamb. {7:28} Additionally, one goat kid was offered for a sin offering. {7:29} And for the peace offering, he provided two oxen, five rams, five male goats, and five one-year-old lambs. {7:30} On the fourth day, Elizur the son of Shedeur, prince of the tribe of Reuben, made his offering. {7:31} He offered a silver charger weighing a hundred and thirty shekels, a silver bowl of seventy shekels, both filled with fine flour mixed with oil for a grain offering. {7:32} Along with a golden spoon weighing ten shekels, filled with incense. {7:33} For burnt offerings, he presented a young bull, a ram, and a one-year-old lamb. {7:34} Also, one goat kid was offered for a sin offering. {7:35} And for the peace offering, he provided two oxen, five rams, five male goats, and five one-year-old lambs. {7:36} On the fifth day, Shelumiel the son of Zurishaddai, prince of the tribe of Simeon, made his offering. {7:37} He offered a silver charger weighing a hundred and thirty shekels, a silver bowl of seventy shekels, both filled with fine flour mixed with oil for a grain offering. {7:38} He also presented a golden spoon weighing ten shekels, filled with incense. {7:39} For burnt offerings, he brought a young bull, a ram, and a one-year-old lamb. {7:40} Additionally, one goat kid was offered for a sin offering. {7:41} And for the peace offering, he provided two oxen, five rams, five male goats, and five one-year-old lambs. {7:42} On the sixth day, Eliasaph the son of Deuel, prince of the tribe of Gad, made his offering. {7:43} He offered a silver charger weighing a hundred and thirty shekels, a silver bowl of seventy shekels, both filled with fine flour mixed with oil for a grain offering. {7:44} Additionally, he presented a golden spoon weighing ten shekels, filled with incense. {7:45} For burnt offerings, he brought a young bull, a ram, and a one-year-old lamb. {7:46} Also, one goat kid was offered for a sin offering. {7:47} And for the peace offering, he provided two oxen, five rams, five male goats, and five one-year-old lambs. {7:48} On the seventh day, Elishama the son of Ammihud, prince of the tribe of Ephraim, made his offering. {7:49} He offered a silver charger weighing a hundred and thirty shekels, a silver bowl of seventy shekels, both filled with fine flour mixed with oil for a grain offering. {7:50} Along with a golden spoon weighing ten shekels, filled with incense. {7:51} For burnt offerings, he presented a young bull, a ram, and a one-year-old lamb. {7:52} Also, one goat kid was offered for a sin offering. {7:53} And for the peace offering, he provided two oxen, five rams, five male goats, and five one-year-old lambs. {7:54} On the eighth day, Gamaliel the son of Pedahzur, prince of the tribe of Manasseh, made his offering. {7:55} He offered a silver charger weighing a hundred and thirty shekels, a silver bowl of seventy shekels, both filled with fine flour mixed with oil for a grain offering. {7:56} Along with a golden spoon weighing ten shekels, filled with incense. {7:57} For burnt offerings, he brought a young bull, a ram, and a one-year-old lamb. {7:58} Additionally, one goat kid was offered for a sin offering. {7:59} And for the peace offering, he provided two oxen, five rams, five male goats, and five one-year-old lambs. {7:60} On the ninth day, Abidan the son of Gideoni, prince of the tribe of Benjamin, made his offering. {7:61} He offered a silver charger weighing a hundred and thirty shekels, a silver bowl of seventy shekels, both filled with fine flour mixed with oil for a grain offering. {7:62} Along with a golden spoon weighing ten shekels, filled with incense. {7:63} For burnt offerings, he presented a young bull, a ram, and a one-year-old lamb. {7:64} Also, one goat kid was offered for a sin offering. {7:65} And for the peace offering, he provided two oxen, five rams, five male goats, and five one-year-old lambs. {7:66} On the tenth day, Ahiezer the son of Ammishaddai, prince of the tribe of Dan, made his offering. {7:67} He offered a silver charger weighing a hundred and thirty shekels, a silver bowl of seventy shekels, both filled with fine flour mixed with oil for a grain offering. {7:68} Additionally, he presented a golden spoon weighing ten shekels, filled with incense. {7:69} For burnt offerings, he brought a young bull, a ram, and a one-year-old lamb. {7:70} Also, one goat kid was offered for a sin offering. {7:71} And for the peace offering, he provided two oxen, five rams, five male goats, and five one-year-old lambs. {7:72} On the eleventh day, Pagiel the son of Ocran, prince of the tribe of Asher, made his offering. {7:73} He offered a silver charger weighing a hundred and thirty shekels, a silver bowl of seventy shekels, both filled with fine flour mixed with oil for a grain offering. {7:74} Along with a golden spoon weighing ten shekels, filled with incense. {7:75} For burnt offerings, he presented a young bull, a ram, and a one-year-old lamb. {7:76} Also, one goat kid was offered for a sin offering. {7:77} And for the peace offering, he provided two oxen, five rams, five male goats, and five one-year-old lambs. {7:78} On the twelfth day, Ahira the son of Enan, prince of the tribe of Naphtali, made his offering. {7:79} He offered a silver charger weighing a hundred and thirty shekels, a silver bowl of seventy shekels, both filled with fine flour mixed with oil for a grain offering. {7:80} Along with a golden spoon weighing ten shekels, filled with incense. {7:81} For burnt offerings, he brought a young bull, a ram, and a one-year-old lamb. {7:82} Also, one goat kid was offered for a sin offering. {7:83} And for the peace offering, he provided two oxen, five rams, five male goats, and five one-year-old lambs. {7:84} This marked the dedication of the altar on the day of its anointing by the princes of Israel. There were twelve silver chargers, twelve silver bowls, and twelve golden spoons. {7:85} Each silver charger weighed a hundred and thirty shekels, and each bowl weighed seventy shekels. The total weight of all the silver vessels was two thousand four hundred shekels, according to the sanctuary shekel. {7:86} The golden spoons numbered twelve, each weighing ten shekels according to the sanctuary shekel. The total weight of the gold spoons was a hundred and twenty shekels. {7:87} The offerings for burnt sacrifices included twelve bulls, twelve rams, and twelve one-year-old lambs, along with their grain offerings. Additionally, twelve goat kids were offered for sin offerings. {7:88} And for the peace offerings, there were twenty-four bulls, sixty rams, sixty male goats, and sixty one-year-old lambs. {7:89} When Moses went into the tabernacle to speak with the LORD, he heard a voice speaking to him from above the mercy seat, between the two cherubim, from the ark of the testimony. And the LORD spoke to him.

{8:1} The LORD spoke to Moses, saying, {8:2} "Tell Aaron that when he lights the lamps, the seven lamps on the lampstand shall give light in front of the lampstand." {8:3} Aaron followed these instructions; he lit the lamps in front of the lampstand as the LORD commanded Moses. {8:4} The lampstand was made of beaten gold, including its shaft and its flowers, all made according to the pattern shown to Moses by the LORD. {8:5} The LORD spoke to Moses again, saying, {8:6} "Take the Levites from among the Israelites and cleanse them. {8:7} Here is how you shall cleanse them: sprinkle them with the water of purification, have them shave all their body hair, and have them wash their clothes to make themselves clean. {8:8} Then have them take a young bull with its grain offering of fine flour mixed with oil, and another young bull for a sin offering. {8:9} Bring the Levites before the tent of meeting, and gather the entire assembly of Israel together. {8:10} Bring the Levites before the LORD, and let the Israelites lay their hands on them. {8:11} Aaron shall present the Levites before the LORD as an offering from the Israelites, so that they may perform the service of the LORD. {8:12} The Levites shall lay their hands on the heads of the bulls, and you shall offer one as a sin offering and the other as a burnt offering to the LORD, to make atonement for the Levites. {8:13} Then you shall present the Levites before Aaron and his sons and offer them as a wave offering to the LORD. {8:14} This is how you shall separate the Levites from among the Israelites; the Levites shall be dedicated to me. {8:15} After this, the Levites may go in to serve at the tent of meeting. You shall cleanse them and present them as an offering. {8:16} The Levites are wholly given to me from among the Israelites; instead of all who open the womb, the firstborn of all the Israelites, I have taken the Levites for myself. {8:17} For all the firstborn among the Israelites, both man and beast, are mine. I sanctified them for myself on the day I struck down all the firstborn in Egypt. {8:18} I have taken the Levites in place of all the firstborn among the Israelites. {8:19} I have given the Levites as a gift to Aaron and his sons from among the Israelites, to serve in the tent of meeting and to make atonement for the Israelites, so that no plague will strike the Israelites when they come near the sanctuary. {8:20} Moses, Aaron, and the entire Israelite community did as the LORD commanded Moses regarding the Levites; the Israelites did to them as well. {8:21} The Levites were purified; they washed their clothes, and Aaron presented them as an offering before the LORD, making atonement for them to cleanse them. {8:22} After that, the Levites went in to perform their service at the tent of meeting before Aaron and his sons, just as the LORD had commanded Moses regarding the Levites, so they did. {8:23} Then the LORD spoke to Moses, saying, {8:24} "This is what pertains to the Levites: from the age of twenty-five years and upward, they shall enter to perform service at the tent of meeting. {8:25} But at the age of fifty years, they shall retire from the service and serve no more. {8:26} They may assist their brothers in the tent of meeting to keep guard, but they shall not perform the service. This is what you shall do to the Levites concerning their duties."

{9:1} The LORD spoke to Moses in the wilderness of Sinai, in the first month of the second year after they had come out of Egypt, saying, {9:2} "Tell the Israelites to observe the Passover at its appointed time. {9:3} On the fourteenth day of this month, at twilight, they shall observe it in accordance with all its statutes and ordinances." {9:4} Moses instructed the Israelites to observe the Passover, {9:5} and they did so on the fourteenth day of the first month at twilight in the wilderness of Sinai, following all that the LORD commanded Moses. {9:6} However, some men were ceremonially unclean due to contact with a dead body and were unable to observe the Passover on that day. They approached Moses and Aaron, {9:7} saying, "We are unclean because of contact with a dead body. Why should we be deprived of presenting the LORD's offering at its appointed time among the Israelites?" {9:8} Moses replied, "Wait here, and I will inquire of the LORD about your case." {9:9} Then the LORD spoke to Moses, saying, {9:10} "Speak to the Israelites, saying, If anyone among you or your descendants is unclean due to contact with a dead body or is on a journey, they may still observe the Passover to the LORD. {9:11} They shall observe it on the fourteenth day of the second month at twilight, eating it with unleavened bread and bitter herbs. {9:12} They shall not leave any of it until morning or break any of its bones; they shall observe all the ordinances of the Passover. {9:13} But anyone who is clean and not on a journey, yet fails to observe the Passover, shall be cut off from among the people because they did not bring the LORD's offering at its appointed time; that person shall bear their sin. {9:14} And if a foreigner residing among you wishes to observe the Passover to the LORD, they must do so according to its statutes and regulations. You shall have the same statute for both the foreigner and the native-born." {9:15} On the day the tabernacle was set up, the cloud covered the tabernacle, the tent of the Testimony. In the evening, there was the appearance of fire over the tabernacle, which remained until morning. {9:16} This continued: the cloud covered it during the day and appeared as fire at night. {9:17} Whenever the cloud lifted from over the tabernacle, the Israelites set out; wherever the cloud settled, the Israelites encamped. {9:18} At the LORD's command, the Israelites set out, and at his command, they encamped. As long as the cloud stayed over the tabernacle, they remained in camp. {9:19} When the cloud stayed over the tabernacle for a long time, the Israelites obeyed the LORD's order and did not set out. {9:20} Sometimes the cloud remained over the tabernacle for only a few days; at the LORD's command, they would encamp, and at his command, they would set out. {9:21} Whether it was two days, a month, or longer, as long as the cloud remained over the tabernacle, the Israelites remained in camp and did not set out; but when it lifted, they would set out. {9:22} Whether by day or by night, whenever the cloud lifted, they set out. {9:23} At the LORD's command, they encamped, and at the LORD's command, they set out. They kept the LORD's charge, according to his command by Moses.

{10:1} The LORD spoke to Moses, saying, {10:2} "Make two trumpets of silver; make them from a single piece. Use them to summon the assembly and to signal the movement of the camps. {10:3} When they blow both trumpets, the whole assembly shall gather at the entrance of the tent of meeting. {10:4} But if only one trumpet is sounded, then the leaders, the heads of the tribes of Israel, shall gather to you. {10:5} When you sound a blast of alarm, the camps on the east side shall set out. {10:6} At the second blast, the camps on the south side shall set out, sounding the alarm for their journeys. {10:7} However, when you gather the assembly, you shall not sound an alarm. {10:8} The sons of Aaron, the priests, shall blow the trumpets. This shall be a permanent ordinance for you and your descendants. {10:9} When you go to war in your land against an enemy who attacks you, you shall sound an alarm with the trumpets, and you will be remembered before the LORD your God, and you will be saved from your enemies. {10:10} Also, on your joyous occasions, your appointed festivals, and the beginning of your months, you shall blow the trumpets over your burnt offerings and your peace offerings, and they shall be a reminder of you before your God. I am the LORD your God. {10:11} On the twentieth day of the second month of the second year, the cloud lifted from above the tent of the covenant law. {10:12} Then the Israelites set out from the Desert of Sinai and traveled from place to place until the cloud came to rest in the Desert of Paran. {10:13} They set out, this first time, at the LORD's command through

Moses. {10:14} The divisions of the camp of Judah went first, under their standard. Nahshon son of Amminadab was in command. {10:15} Nethanel son of Zuar was over the division of the tribe of Issachar, and Eliab son of Helon was over the division of the tribe of Zebulun. {10:16} Then the tabernacle was taken down, and the Gershonites and Merarites, who carried it, set out. {10:18} The divisions of the camp of Reuben went next, under their standard. Elizur son of Shedeur was in command. {10:19} Shelumiel son of Zurishaddai was over the division of the tribe of Simeon, and Eliasaph son of Deuel was over the division of the tribe of Gad. {10:20} Then the Kohathites set out, carrying the holy things. The tabernacle was to be set up before they arrived. {10:22} The divisions of the camp of Ephraim went next, under their standard. Elishama son of Ammihud was in command. {10:23} Gamaliel son of Pedahzur was over the division of the tribe of Manasseh, and Abidan son of Gideoni was over the division of the tribe of Benjamin. {10:25} Finally, as the rear guard for all the units, the divisions of the camp of Dan set out under their standard. Ahiezer son of Ammishaddai was in command. {10:26} Pagiel son of Ocran was over the division of the tribe of Asher, and Ahira son of Enan was over the division of the tribe of Naphtali. {10:27} This was the order of march for the Israelite divisions as they set out. {10:29} Moses said to Hobab, son of Reuel the Midianite, Moses' father-in-law, "We are setting out for the place about which the LORD said, 'I will give it to you.' Come with us and we will treat you well, for the LORD has promised good things to Israel." {10:30} But Hobab replied, "I will not go; I am going back to my own land and my own people." {10:31} "Please do not leave us," Moses said, "you know where we should camp in the wilderness, and you can be our eyes. {10:32} If you come with us, whatever good the LORD will do to us, we will do to you." {10:33} So they set out from the mountain of the LORD and traveled for three days. The ark of the covenant of the LORD went before them during those three days to find them a place to rest. {10:34} The cloud of the LORD was over them by day when they set out from the camp. {10:35} Whenever the ark set out, Moses said, "Rise up, LORD! May your enemies be scattered; may your foes flee before you." {10:36} Whenever it came to rest, he said, "Return, LORD, to the countless thousands of Israel."

{11:1} When the people complained, it angered the LORD, and His wrath was kindled. A fire from the LORD broke out among them and consumed those at the outskirts of the camp. {11:2} The people cried out to Moses, and when Moses prayed to the LORD, the fire was extinguished. {11:3} So Moses named the place Taberah because the fire of the LORD had burned among them. {11:4} Now the mixed multitude among them began to crave other food, and the Israelites also wept and said, "Who will give us meat to eat? {11:5} We remember the fish we ate freely in Egypt, along with the cucumbers, melons, leeks, onions, and garlic. {11:6} But now we have lost our appetite; we never see anything but this manna!" {11:7} The manna was like coriander seed and had the appearance of resin. {11:8} The people would go out and gather it, grind it in hand mills or crush it in mortar, cook it in pots, and make cakes from it. It tasted like something made with olive oil. {11:9} When the dew settled on the camp at night, the manna also came down. {11:10} Moses heard the people of every family wailing at the entrance to their tents. The LORD's anger was greatly aroused, and Moses was troubled. {11:11} He asked the LORD, "Why have you brought this trouble on your servant? What have I done to displease you that you put the burden of all these people on me? {11:12} Did I conceive all these people? Did I give them birth? Why do you tell me to carry them in my arms, as a nurse carries an infant, to the land you promised on oath to their ancestors? {11:13} Where can I get meat for all these people? They keep wailing to me, 'Give us meat to eat!' {11:14} I cannot carry all these people by myself; the burden is too heavy for me. {11:15} If this is how you are going to treat me, please go ahead and kill me—if I have found favor in your eyes—and do not let me face my own ruin." {11:16} The LORD said to Moses, "Bring me seventy of Israel's elders who are known to you as leaders and officials among the people. Have them come to the tent of meeting, that they may stand there with you. {11:17} I will come down and speak with you there, and I will take some of the power of the Spirit that is on you and put it on them. They will share the burden of the people with you so that you will not have to carry it alone. {11:18} "Tell the people: 'Consecrate yourselves in preparation for tomorrow, when you will eat meat. The LORD heard you when you wailed, "If only we had meat to eat! We were better off in Egypt!" Now the LORD will give you meat, and you will eat it. {11:19} You will not eat it for just one day, or two days, or five, ten, or twenty days, {11:20} but for a whole month—until it comes out of your nostrils and you loathe it—because you have rejected the LORD, who is among you, and have wailed before him, saying, "Why did we ever leave Egypt?"'" {11:21} But Moses said, "Here I am among six hundred thousand men on foot, and you say, 'I will give them meat to eat for a whole month!' {11:22} Would they have enough if flocks and herds were slaughtered for them? Would they have enough if all the fish in the sea were caught for them?" {11:23}

The LORD answered Moses, "Is the LORD's arm too short? Now you will see whether or not what I say will come true for you." {11:24} So Moses went out and told the people what the LORD had said. He brought together seventy of their elders and had them stand around the tent. {11:25} Then the LORD came down in the cloud and spoke with him, and he took some of the power of the Spirit that was on him and put it on the seventy elders. When the Spirit rested on them, they prophesied—but did not do so again. {11:26} However, two men, whose names were Eldad and Medad, had remained in the camp. They were listed among the elders but did not go out to the tent. Yet the Spirit also rested on them, and they prophesied in the camp. {11:27} A young man ran and told Moses, "Eldad and Medad are prophesying in the camp!" {11:28} Joshua son of Nun, who had been Moses' aide since youth, spoke up and said, "Moses, my lord, stop them!" {11:29} But Moses replied, "Are you jealous for my sake? I wish that all the LORD's people were prophets and that the LORD would put his Spirit on them!" {11:30} Then Moses and the elders of Israel returned to the camp. {11:31} Now a wind went out from the LORD and drove quail in from the sea. It scattered them up to two cubits deep all around the camp, as far as a day's walk in any direction. {11:32} All that day and night and all the next day the people went out and gathered quail. No one gathered less than ten homers. Then they spread them out all around the camp. {11:33} But while the meat was still between their teeth and before it could be consumed, the anger of the LORD burned against the people, and he struck them with a severe plague. {11:34} Therefore the place was named Kibroth Hattaavah because there they buried the people who had craved other food. {11:35} From Kibroth Hattaavah the people traveled to Hazeroth and stayed there.

{12:1} Miriam and Aaron spoke against Moses because of the Ethiopian woman he had married, for he had married an Ethiopian woman. {12:2} They said, "Has the LORD spoken only through Moses? Hasn't he also spoken through us?" And the LORD heard them. {12:3} (Now Moses was very humble, more so than anyone else on the face of the earth.) {12:4} Suddenly the LORD spoke to Moses, Aaron, and Miriam, "Come out, you three, to the tent of meeting." So they went out. {12:5} Then the LORD descended in a pillar of cloud and stood at the entrance of the tent. He summoned Aaron and Miriam, and they both came forward. {12:6} And he said, "Listen to my words: When there is a prophet among you, I, the LORD, reveal myself to them in visions, I speak to them in dreams. {12:7} But not with my servant Moses. He is faithful in all my house. {12:8} With him I speak face to face, clearly and not in riddles; he sees the form of the LORD. Why then were you not afraid to speak against my servant Moses?" {12:9} The anger of the LORD burned against them, and he left. {12:10} When the cloud lifted from above the tent, Miriam's skin was leprous—it became as white as snow. Aaron turned toward her and saw that she had leprosy. {12:11} So Aaron said to Moses, "Please, my lord, do not hold against us the sin we have so foolishly committed. {12:12} Do not let her be like a stillborn infant coming from its mother's womb with its flesh half eaten away." {12:13} **So Moses cried out to the LORD, "Please, God, heal her!"** {12:14} The LORD replied to Moses, "If her father had merely spit in her face, would she not have been in disgrace for seven days? Confine her outside the camp for seven days; after that she can be brought back." {12:15} So Miriam was confined outside the camp for seven days, and the people did not move on till she was brought back in. {12:16} After that, the people left Hazeroth and encamped in the Desert of Paran.

{13:1} The LORD spoke to Moses, saying, {13:2} "Send men to search the land of Canaan, which I give to the children of Israel: from each tribe, send a ruler." {13:3} So Moses, by the command of the LORD, sent them from the wilderness of Paran. All these men were leaders of Israel. {13:4} Their names were: from the tribe of Reuben, Shammua the son of Zaccur. {13:5} From the tribe of Simeon, Shaphat the son of Hori. {13:6} From the tribe of Judah, Caleb the son of Jephunneh. {13:7} From the tribe of Issachar, Igal the son of Joseph. {13:8} From the tribe of Ephraim, Oshea the son of Nun. {13:9} From the tribe of Benjamin, Palti the son of Raphu. {13:10} From the tribe of Zebulun, Gaddiel the son of Sodi. {13:11} From the tribe of Joseph, specifically the tribe of Manasseh, Gaddi the son of Susi. {13:12} From the tribe of Dan, Ammiel the son of Gemalli. {13:13} From the tribe of Asher, Sethur the son of Michael. {13:14} From the tribe of Naphtali, Nahbi the son of Vophsi. {13:15} From the tribe of Gad, Geuel the son of Machi. {13:16} These are the names of the men whom Moses sent to spy out the land. And Moses called Oshea the son of Nun, Jehoshua. {13:17} Moses sent them to spy out the land of Canaan, instructing them, "Go southward and up into the mountains. {13:18} Observe the land and the people who dwell there, whether strong or weak, few or many. {13:19} See the quality of the land they dwell in, whether good or bad, and the cities they dwell in, whether in tents or strongholds. {13:20} Assess the fertility of the land, whether rich or poor, whether there is wood or not. Be courageous and bring back some fruit from the land. This was the season of the first ripe grapes." {13:21} So they went up and searched the land from the wilderness of Zin to Rehob, as far as Hamath. {13:22} They traveled through the southern region and reached Hebron, where Ahiman, Sheshai, and Talmai, the descendants of Anak, were living. (Hebron had been built seven years before Zoan in Egypt.) {13:23} They reached the valley of Eshcol and cut down a cluster of grapes, which they carried on a pole between two of them. They also brought back pomegranates and figs. {13:24} That place was named the valley of Eshcol because of the cluster of grapes the Israelites cut there. {13:25} After forty days of exploration, they returned from scouting out the land. {13:26} They came back to Moses, Aaron, and the whole congregation of Israel in the wilderness of Paran at Kadesh. They brought back word to them and showed them the fruit of the land. {13:27} They reported, "We went to the land you sent us to. It truly flows with milk and honey, and here is the fruit of it. {13:28} However, the people living there are strong, and the cities are fortified and very large. Moreover, we saw the descendants of Anak there. {13:29} The Amalekites dwell in the southern region; the Hittites, Jebusites, and Amorites dwell in the mountains; and the Canaanites live by the sea and along the Jordan River." {13:30} Caleb quieted the people before Moses and said, "Let's go up and take possession of it, for we are well able to overcome it." {13:31} But the men who had gone up with him said, "We can't attack those people; they are stronger than we are." {13:32} They spread a negative report about the land they had explored to the Israelites, saying, "The land we explored devours its inhabitants, and all the people we saw there are of great stature. {13:33} We even saw giants there, the descendants of Anak. We felt like grasshoppers in our own eyes, and we looked the same to them."

{14:1} The whole congregation raised their voices and wept that night. {14:2} The Israelites murmured against Moses and Aaron, saying, "If only we had died in Egypt or in this wilderness! {14:3} Why has the LORD brought us to this land to fall by the sword, with our wives and children becoming prey? Wouldn't it be better to return to Egypt?" {14:4} They said to each other, "Let's choose a leader and go back to Egypt." {14:5} Moses and Aaron fell facedown before the assembly of Israelites. {14:6} Joshua son of Nun and Caleb son of Jephunneh, who were among those who had explored the land, tore their clothes {14:7} and said to the assembly, "The land we passed through to explore is exceedingly good. {14:8} If the LORD delights in us, he will bring us into this land and give it to us—a land flowing with milk and honey. {14:9} Only do not rebel against the LORD. And do not fear the people of the land, for they are our bread; their protection has been removed, and the LORD is with us. Do not be afraid of them." {14:10} But the whole congregation talked about stoning them. Then the glory of the LORD appeared at the tent of meeting to all the Israelites. {14:11} The LORD said to Moses, "How long will these people treat me with contempt? How long will they refuse to believe in me, despite all the signs I have performed among them? {14:12} I will strike them with a plague and destroy them, but I will make you into a nation greater and stronger than they." {14:13} Moses said to the LORD, "The Egyptians will hear about it! By your power you brought these people up from among them. {14:14} And they will tell the inhabitants of this land about it. They have already heard that you, LORD, are with these people and that you, LORD, have been seen face to face, that your cloud stays over them, and that you go before them in a pillar of cloud by day and a pillar of fire by night. {14:15} **If you put all these people to death, leaving none alive, the nations who have heard this report about you will say,** {14:16} 'The LORD was not able to bring these people into the land he promised them on oath, so he slaughtered them in the wilderness.' {14:17} Now may the LORD's strength be displayed, just as you have declared: {14:18} 'The LORD is slow to anger, abounding in love and forgiving sin and rebellion. Yet he does not leave the guilty unpunished; he punishes the children for the sin of the parents to the third and fourth generation.' {14:19} In accordance with your great love, forgive the sin of these people, just as you have pardoned them from the time they left Egypt until now." {14:20} The LORD replied, "I have forgiven them, as you asked. {14:21} Nevertheless, as surely as I live and as surely as the glory of the LORD fills the whole earth, {14:22} not one of those who saw my glory and the signs I performed in Egypt and in the wilderness but who disobeyed me and tested me ten times— {14:23} not one of them will ever see the land I promised on oath to their ancestors. No one who has treated me with contempt will ever see it. {14:24} But because my servant Caleb has a different spirit and follows me wholeheartedly, I will bring him into the land he went to, and his descendants will inherit it. {14:25} (Now the Amalekites and Canaanites live in the valleys.) Turn back tomorrow and set out toward the desert along the route to the Red Sea." {14:26} The LORD said to Moses and Aaron: {14:27} "How long will this wicked community grumble against me? I have heard the complaints of these grumbling Israelites. {14:28} So tell them, 'As surely as I live, declares the LORD, I will do to you the very thing I heard you say: {14:29} In this wilderness your bodies will fall—every one of you twenty years old or more who was counted in the census and who has grumbled against me. {14:30} Not one of you will enter the land I swore with uplifted hand to make your home, except Caleb son of Jephunneh and Joshua son of Nun. {14:31} As for your children that you said would be taken as plunder, I will bring them in to enjoy the land you have rejected. {14:32} But as for you, your bodies will fall in this wilderness. {14:33} Your children will be shepherds here for forty years, suffering for your unfaithfulness, until the last of your bodies lies in the wilderness. {14:34} For forty years—one year for each of the forty days you explored the land—you will suffer for your sins and know what it is like to have me against you.' {14:35} I, the LORD, have spoken, and I will surely do these things to this whole wicked community, which has banded together against me. They will meet their end in this wilderness; here they will die." {14:36} So the men Moses had sent to explore the land, who returned and made the whole community grumble against him by spreading a bad report about it— {14:37} these men who were responsible for spreading the bad report about the land were struck down and died of a plague before the LORD. {14:38} Of the men who went to explore the land, only Joshua son of Nun and Caleb son of Jephunneh survived. {14:39} When Moses reported this to all the Israelites, they mourned bitterly. {14:40} Early the next morning they set out for the highest point in the hill country, saying, "Now we are ready to go up to the land the LORD promised. Surely we have sinned!" {14:41} But Moses said, "Why are you disobeying the LORD's command? This will not succeed. {14:42} Do not go up, because the LORD is not with you. You will be defeated by your enemies. {14:43} for the Amalekites and Canaanites will face you there. Because you have turned away from the LORD, he will not be with you and you will fall by the sword." {14:44} Nevertheless, in their presumption they went up toward the highest point in the hill country, though neither Moses nor the ark of the LORD's covenant moved from the camp. {14:45} Then the Amalekites and Canaanites who lived in that hill country came down and attacked them and beat them down all the way to Hormah.

{15:1} The LORD spoke to Moses, saying, {15:2} "Speak to the children of Israel and tell them: When you enter the land I am giving you as your home, {15:3} and you present an offering by fire to the LORD, a burnt offering, or a sacrifice to fulfill a vow, or as a freewill offering, or at your appointed festivals, to produce a pleasing aroma for the LORD from the herd or flock, {15:4} the one presenting the offering to the LORD must also bring a grain offering of a tenth of an ephah of finely ground flour mixed with a quarter of a hin of olive oil. {15:5} With each lamb for the burnt offering or the sacrifice, prepare a quarter of a hin of wine as a drink offering. {15:6} With a ram, prepare a grain offering of two tenths of an ephah of finely ground flour mixed with a third of a hin of olive oil, {15:7} and offer a third of a hin of wine as a drink offering. It will be a pleasing aroma to the LORD. {15:8} When you prepare a young bull as a burnt offering or a sacrifice to fulfill a vow or as a fellowship offering to the LORD, {15:9} bring with the bull a grain offering of three tenths of an ephah of finely ground flour mixed with half a hin of olive oil. {15:10} Also bring half a hin of wine as a drink offering. It will be an offering made by fire, a pleasing aroma to the LORD. {15:11} This is to be done for each bull, ram, lamb, or young goat. {15:12} Do this for each one, according to the number that you prepare. {15:13} All native-born Israelites are to do these things in this way when they present a food offering to the LORD. {15:14} If a foreigner resides with you or anyone else among you in future generations and wants to present a food offering as a pleasing aroma to the LORD, they must do exactly as you do. {15:15} The community is to have the same rules for you and for the foreigner residing among you; this is a lasting ordinance for the generations to come. You and the foreigner shall be the same before the LORD. {15:16} The same laws and regulations will apply both to you and to the foreigner residing among you." {15:17} The LORD spoke to Moses, saying, {15:18} "Speak to the children of Israel and say to them: When you enter the land I am bringing you to, {15:19} and you eat the food of the land, present a portion as an offering to the LORD. {15:20} Present a loaf from the first of your ground meal as an offering from the threshing floor throughout your generations. {15:21} Present this offering to the LORD from the first of your ground meal throughout your generations. {15:22} If you unintentionally fail to observe all these commandments that the LORD has spoken to Moses— {15:23} everything the LORD has commanded you through Moses, from the day the LORD gave his commands and onward throughout your generations— {15:24} if anything is done unintentionally without the community's knowledge, the entire community is to offer one young bull as a burnt offering, a pleasing aroma to the LORD, along with its grain offering and drink offering, according to the regulation, and one male goat for a sin offering. {15:25} The priest will make atonement for the whole community of Israel, and they will be forgiven, for it was unintentional; they have brought to the LORD for their unintentional offense a food offering and a sin offering before the LORD. {15:26} And the whole community of Israel and the foreigners residing among them will be forgiven, since all the people were involved in the unintentional wrong. {15:27} But if just one person sins unintentionally, that person must bring a year-old female goat for a sin offering. {15:28} The priest will make atonement before the LORD for the one who erred by sinning unintentionally, and when atonement has been made, that person will be forgiven. {15:29} One and the same law applies to everyone who sins unintentionally, whether a native-born Israelite or a foreigner residing among you. {15:30} But anyone who sins defiantly, whether native-born or foreigner, blasphemes the LORD and must be cut off from the people of Israel. {15:31} Because they have despised the LORD's word and broken his commandments, they must surely be cut off; their guilt remains on them." {15:32} While the Israelites were in the wilderness, they found a man gathering wood on the Sabbath day. {15:33} Those who found him gathering wood brought him to Moses and Aaron and the whole assembly. {15:34} They kept him in custody because it was not clear what should be done to him. {15:35} Then the LORD said to Moses, "The man must die. The whole assembly is to stone him outside the camp." {15:36} So the assembly took him outside the camp and stoned him to death, as the LORD commanded Moses. {15:37} The LORD said to Moses, {15:38} "Speak to the Israelites and make tassels on the corners of their garments throughout their generations, and put a blue cord on the tassel at each corner. {15:39} These will serve as tassels for you to look at, so that you may remember all the LORD's commands and obey them and not prostitute yourselves by chasing after the lusts of your own hearts and eyes. {15:40} Then you will remember to obey all my commands and will be consecrated to your God. {15:41} I am the LORD your God, who brought you out of the land of Egypt, to be your God: I am the LORD your God.

{16:1} Now Korah, the son of Izhar, the son of Kohath, the son of Levi, and Dathan and Abiram, the sons of Eliab, and On, the son of Peleth, sons of Reuben, took men: {16:2} And they rose up before Moses, with certain of the children of Israel, two hundred and fifty princes of the assembly, famous in the congregation, men of renown: {16:3} And they gathered themselves together against Moses and against Aaron, and said unto them, "You take too much upon you, seeing all the congregation are holy, every one of them, and the LORD is among them: wherefore then lift you up yourselves above the congregation of the LORD?" {16:4} And when Moses heard it, he fell upon his face: {16:5} And he spoke unto Korah and unto all his company, saying, "Even tomorrow the LORD will show who are his, and who is holy; and will cause him to come near unto him: even him whom he has chosen will he cause to come near unto him. {16:6} This do; Take you censers, Korah, and all his company; {16:7} And put fire therein, and put incense in them before the LORD tomorrow: and it shall be that the man whom the LORD does choose, he shall be holy: you take too much upon you, you sons of Levi." {16:8} And Moses said unto Korah, "Hear, I pray you, you sons of Levi: {16:9} Seemeth it but a small thing unto you, that the God of Israel has separated you from the congregation of Israel, to bring you near to himself to do the service of the tabernacle of the LORD, and to stand before the congregation to minister unto them? {16:10} And he has brought you near to him, and all your brethren the sons of Levi with you: and seek you the priesthood also? {16:11} For which cause both you and all your company are gathered together against the LORD: and what is Aaron, that you murmur against him?" {16:12} And Moses sent to call Dathan and Abiram, the sons of Eliab: which said, "We will not come up: {16:13} Is it a small thing that you have brought us up out of a land that floweth with milk and honey, to kill us in the wilderness, except you make yourself altogether a prince over us? {16:14} Moreover you have not brought us into a land that floweth with milk and honey, or given us inheritance of fields and vineyards: will you put out the eyes of these men? we will not come up."

{16:15} And Moses was very wroth, and said unto the LORD, "Respect not thou their offering: I have not taken one ass from them, neither have I hurt one of them." {16:16} And Moses said unto Korah, "Be thou and all thy company before the LORD, thou, and they, and Aaron, tomorrow: {16:17} And take every man his censer, and put incense in them, and bring ye before the LORD every man his censer, two hundred and fifty censers; thou also, and Aaron, each of you his censer." {16:18} And they took every man his censer, and put fire in them, and laid incense thereon, and stood in the door of the tabernacle of the congregation with Moses and Aaron. {16:19} And Korah gathered all the congregation against them unto the door of the tabernacle of the congregation: and the glory of the LORD appeared unto all the congregation. {16:20} And the LORD spake unto Moses and unto Aaron, saying, {16:21} Separate yourselves from among this congregation, that I may consume them in a moment. {16:22} And they fell upon their faces, and said, "O God, the God of the spirits of all flesh, shall one man sin, and wilt thou be wroth with all the congregation?" {16:23} And the LORD spake unto Moses, saying, {16:24} Speak unto the congregation, saying, "Get you up from about the tabernacle of Korah, Dathan, and Abiram." {16:25} And Moses rose up and went unto Dathan and Abiram; and the elders of Israel followed him. {16:26} And he spake unto the congregation, saying, "Depart, I pray you, from the tents of these wicked men, and touch nothing of theirs, lest ye be consumed in all their sins." {16:27} So they got up from the tabernacle of Korah, Dathan, and Abiram, on every side: and Dathan and Abiram came out, and stood in the door of their tents, and their wives, and their sons, and their little children. {16:28} And Moses said, "Hereby ye shall know that the LORD hath sent me to do all these works; for I have not done them of mine own mind. {16:29} If these men die the common death of all men, or if they be visited after the visitation of all men; then the LORD hath not sent me. {16:30} But if the LORD make a new thing, and the earth open her mouth, and swallow them up, with all that appertain unto them, and they go down quick into the pit; then ye shall understand that these men have provoked the LORD. {16:31} And it came to pass, as he had made an end of speaking all these words, that the ground clave asunder that was under them: {16:32} And the earth opened her mouth, and swallowed them up, and their houses, and all the men that appertained unto Korah, and all their goods. {16:33} They, and all that appertained to them, went down alive into the pit, and the earth closed upon them: and they perished from among the congregation. {16:34} And all Israel that were round about them fled at the cry of them: for they said, Lest the earth swallow us up also. {16:35} And there came out a fire from the LORD, and consumed the two hundred and fifty men that offered incense. {16:36} And the LORD spake unto Moses, saying, {16:37} Speak unto Eleazar the son of Aaron the priest, that he take up the censers out of the burning, and scatter thou the fire yonder; for they are hallowed. {16:38} The censers of these sinners against their own souls, let them make them broad plates for a covering of the altar: for they offered them before the LORD, therefore they are hallowed: and they shall be a sign unto the children of Israel. {16:39} And Eleazar the priest took the brasen censers, wherewith they that were burnt had offered; and they were made broad plates for a covering of the altar: {16:39} And Eleazar the priest took the brasen censers, which those who were burnt had used, and they were made into broad plates to cover the altar. {16:40} This was to serve as a memorial for the Israelites, so that no outsider, who is not of the descendants of Aaron, would come near to offer incense before the LORD and meet the fate of Korah and his followers, as the LORD had instructed through Moses. {16:41} But the next day, all the congregation of the children of Israel complained against Moses and Aaron, accusing them, "You have killed the people of the LORD." {16:42} As the congregation gathered against Moses and Aaron, they looked toward the tabernacle, and suddenly, the cloud covered it, and the glory of the LORD appeared. {16:43} Moses and Aaron then approached the tabernacle. {16:44} And the LORD spoke to Moses, saying, {16:45} "Get away from this congregation so that I may consume them in an instant." Moses and Aaron fell facedown. {16:46} Moses instructed Aaron, "Take a censer, put fire from the altar in it, add incense, and quickly go to the congregation to make atonement for them. The LORD's wrath has gone out; the plague has begun." {16:47} Aaron did as Moses commanded and ran into the midst of the congregation. Behold, the plague had already started among the people, but Aaron put on incense and made atonement for them. {16:48} He stood between the dead and the living, and the plague was stopped. {16:49} The number of those who died in the plague was fourteen thousand seven hundred, not counting those who died because of Korah. {16:50} Aaron then returned to Moses at the entrance of the tabernacle, and the plague was stopped.

{17:1} And the LORD spoke to Moses, saying, {17:2} "Speak to the children of Israel, and take from each of them a rod according to their ancestral tribes, from all their leaders, twelve rods in total. Write each man's name on his rod. {17:3} Write Aaron's name on the rod of Levi, for one rod shall represent the head of each ancestral tribe. {17:4} Place these rods in the tabernacle of the congregation before the testimony, where I will meet with you. {17:5} The rod of the man I choose will blossom, and I will put an end to the Israelites' complaints against you." {17:6} Moses spoke to the children of Israel, and each of their leaders gave him a rod, twelve rods in all, each representing a tribe. Aaron's rod was among them. {17:7} Moses placed the rods before the LORD in the tabernacle of witness. {17:8} The next day, Moses entered the tabernacle and saw that Aaron's rod, representing the tribe of Levi, had budded, blossomed, and yielded almonds. {17:9} Moses brought out all the rods before the children of Israel, and they took their respective rods. {17:10} And the LORD said to Moses, "Bring Aaron's rod back before the testimony to be kept as a sign against those who rebel. This will put an end to their complaints against Me, so that they do not die." {17:11} Moses did as the LORD commanded him. {17:12} Then the children of Israel said to Moses, "We are doomed to perish, we all perish!" {17:13} "Anyone who comes near the tabernacle of the LORD will die. Will we all be consumed by dying?"

{18:1} And the LORD said to Aaron, "You, your sons, and your father's house shall bear the responsibility for the sanctuary, and you and your sons shall bear the responsibility for the priesthood. {18:2} Also, bring your relatives from the tribe of Levi to join you and assist you. They shall be joined to you and minister before the tabernacle of witness. {18:3} They shall assist you in your duties and in the care of the tabernacle, but they must not come near the sacred vessels and the altar, or they and you will die. {18:4} They shall be joined to you and assist in the service of the tabernacle, and no outsider shall come near you. {18:5} You and your descendants shall be responsible for the sanctuary and the altar, so that no wrath will come upon the Israelites again. {18:6} I have taken your relatives, the Levites, from among the Israelites as a gift for the LORD, to serve in the tabernacle. {18:7} Therefore, you and your sons shall carry out your duties as priests for everything at the altar and behind the veil. I have given you the priesthood as a gift, and any outsider who approaches shall be put to death. {18:8} Furthermore, I have given you the charge of all the sacred offerings of the Israelites, as a special privilege due to your anointing, to you and your sons, as an everlasting ordinance. {18:9} The most holy offerings, reserved from the fire—every grain offering, sin offering, and trespass offering brought to me—shall be most holy for you and your sons. {18:10} You shall eat them in the most holy place; they are holy to you, reserved for you. {18:11} As for the heave offering and wave offerings of the Israelites, I have given them to you, your sons, and daughters with you, as an everlasting statute. Every clean person in your household may eat of them. {18:12} All the best of the oil, wine, and wheat—the firstfruits brought to the LORD—I have given to you. {18:13} Whatever is first ripe in the land brought to the LORD shall be yours. Every clean person in your household may eat of it. {18:14} Everything devoted in Israel shall be yours. {18:15} Every firstborn of man or beast shall be yours, but the firstborn of an unclean animal must be redeemed. {18:16} And those to be redeemed from a month old shall be redeemed according to your valuation, for the price of five shekels, according to the sanctuary shekel, which is twenty gerahs. {18:17} But the firstborn of a cow, sheep, or goat shall not be redeemed; they are holy. Their blood shall be sprinkled on the altar, and their fat burned as an offering pleasing to the LORD. {18:18} Their flesh shall be yours, as the breast of the wave offering and the right thigh are yours. {18:19} All the heave offerings of the holy things brought by the Israelites shall be yours, your sons', and daughters' with you, as an everlasting covenant of salt before the LORD, for you and your descendants. {18:20} And the LORD said to Aaron, "You shall have no inheritance in the land, nor shall you have a portion among them; I am your portion and inheritance among the children of Israel. {18:21} "As for the Levites, I have given them all the tithes in Israel for their inheritance, for the service they perform, the service of the tabernacle of the congregation. {18:22} The Israelites must not come near the tabernacle of the congregation, lest they bear sin and die. {18:23} Only the Levites shall serve at the tabernacle of the congregation and bear the consequences of their iniquity. This shall be a perpetual statute throughout your generations; among the Israelites, they shall have no inheritance. {18:24} But the tithes of the Israelites, which they offer as a heave offering to the LORD, I have given to the Levites as their inheritance; therefore I have said to them, 'Among the Israelites, they shall have no inheritance.'" {18:25} And the LORD spoke to Moses, saying, {18:26} "Speak to the Levites and tell them, 'When you receive the tithes from the Israelites as your inheritance, you shall present a tenth of it as a heave offering for the LORD. {18:27} This heave offering shall be reckoned to you as though it were grain from the threshing floor and wine from the winepress. {18:28} You shall also present a heave offering to the LORD from all your tithes, which you receive from the Israelites. {18:29} Out of all your gifts, you shall offer every heave offering of the LORD, taking the best portion of it, which is considered holy. {18:30} So, when you have set aside the best part of it, it will be counted to the Levites as the yield of the threshing floor and the winepress. {18:31} You and your households may eat it anywhere, as it is your reward for your service in the tabernacle of the congregation. {18:32} By doing this, you will not incur sin, as long as you have set aside the best of it. And be careful not to defile the holy things of the children of Israel, lest you face death.

{19:1} And the LORD spoke to Moses and Aaron, saying, {19:2} "This is the ordinance of the law which the LORD has commanded: Speak to the children of Israel, that they bring you a red heifer without spot, wherein is no blemish, and upon which never came yoke. {19:3} And you shall give her to Eleazar the priest, that he may bring her forth without the camp, and one shall slay her before his face. {19:4} And Eleazar the priest shall take of her blood with his finger, and sprinkle of her blood directly before the tabernacle of the congregation seven times. {19:5} And one shall burn the heifer in his sight; her skin, and her flesh, and her blood, with her dung, shall he burn. {19:6} And the priest shall take cedar wood, and hyssop, and scarlet, and cast it into the midst of the burning of the heifer. {19:7} Then the priest shall wash his clothes, and he shall bathe his flesh in water, and afterward he shall come into the camp, and the priest shall be unclean until the even. {19:8} And he that burns her shall wash his clothes in water, and bathe his flesh in water, and shall be unclean until the even. {19:9} And a man that is clean shall gather up the ashes of the heifer, and lay them up without the camp in a clean place, and it shall be kept for the congregation of the children of Israel for a water of separation: it is a purification for sin. {19:10} And he that gathers the ashes of the heifer shall wash his clothes, and be unclean until the even: and it shall be unto the children of Israel, and unto the stranger that sojourns among them, for a statute forever. {19:11} He that touches the dead body of any man shall be unclean seven days. {19:12} He shall purify himself with it on the third day, and on the seventh day he shall be clean: but if he purifies not himself the third day, then the seventh day he shall not be clean. {19:13} Whoever touches the dead body of any man that is dead, and purifies not himself, defiles the tabernacle of the LORD; and that soul shall be cut off from Israel: because the water of separation was not sprinkled upon him, he shall be unclean; his uncleanness is yet upon him. {19:14} This is the law when a man dies in a tent: all that come into the tent, and all that is in the tent, shall be unclean seven days. {19:15} And every open vessel, which has no covering bound upon it, is unclean. {19:16} And whoever touches one that is slain with a sword in the open fields, or a dead body, or a bone of a man, or a grave, shall be unclean seven days. {19:17} And for an unclean person they shall take of the ashes of the burnt heifer of purification for sin, and running water shall be put thereto in a vessel: {19:18} And a clean person shall take hyssop, and dip it in the water, and sprinkle it upon the tent, and upon all the vessels, and upon the persons that were there, and upon him that touched a bone, or one slain, or one dead, or a grave: {19:19} And the clean person shall sprinkle upon the unclean on the third day, and on the seventh day: and on the seventh day he shall purify himself, and wash his clothes, and bathe himself in water, and shall be clean at even. {19:20} But the man that shall be unclean, and shall not purify himself, that soul shall be cut off from among the congregation, because he has defiled the sanctuary of the LORD: the water of separation has not been sprinkled upon him; he is unclean. {19:21} And it shall be a perpetual statute unto them, that he that sprinkles the water of separation shall wash his clothes; and he that touches the water of separation shall be unclean until even. {19:22} And whatsoever the unclean person touches shall be unclean; and the soul that touches it shall be unclean until even.

{20:1} Then the children of Israel, the whole congregation, came into the desert of Zin in the first month, and the people stayed in Kadesh. Miriam died there and was buried there. {20:2} There was no water for the congregation, so they gathered themselves against Moses and Aaron. {20:3} They argued with Moses, saying, "Would God that we had died when our brethren died before the LORD!" {20:4} "Why have you brought the congregation of the LORD into this wilderness to die, we and our cattle?" {20:5} "Why have you brought us out of Egypt to bring us to this evil place? There is no seed, figs, vines, or pomegranates; and there's no water to drink." {20:6} Moses and Aaron went from the assembly to the door of the tabernacle of the congregation, and they fell on their faces. The glory of the LORD appeared to them. {20:7} And the LORD said to Moses, {20:8} "Take the rod, gather the assembly together, you and Aaron your brother, and speak to the rock before their eyes; it shall give forth water, and you shall bring forth water out of the rock for the congregation and their beasts to drink." {20:9} Moses took the rod from before the LORD, as commanded. {20:10} Moses and Aaron gathered the congregation before the rock, and he said to them, "Hear now, you rebels; must we fetch you water out of this rock?" {20:11} Moses lifted up his hand and smote the rock twice with his rod, and water came out abundantly, and the congregation drank, and their beasts also. {20:12} And the LORD said to Moses and Aaron, "Because you did not believe me, to sanctify me in the eyes of the children of Israel, you shall not bring this congregation into the land which I have given them. {20:13} This is the water of Meribah; because the children of Israel argued with the LORD, and he was sanctified in them." {20:14} Moses sent messengers from Kadesh to the king of Edom, saying, "Thus says your brother Israel: You know all the trouble that has befallen us: {20:15} How our fathers went down into Egypt, and we dwelt in Egypt a long time; and the Egyptians vexed us and our fathers. {20:16} When we cried to the LORD, he heard our voice, and sent an angel, and brought us out of Egypt. Now, behold, we are in Kadesh, a city at the edge of your border. {20:17} Let us pass through your country; we will not pass through fields or vineyards, nor drink water from wells; we will go by the king's highway, not turning right or left until we have passed your borders." {20:18} Edom said to him, "You shall not pass by me, lest I come out against you with the sword." {20:19} The children of Israel said, "We will go by the highway; if I and my cattle drink your water, I will pay for it. I will only pass through on foot." {20:20} Edom said, "You shall not go through." And Edom came out against him with many people and a strong hand. {20:21} Thus Edom refused to give Israel passage through his border; therefore Israel turned away from him. {20:22} And the children of Israel, the whole congregation, journeyed from Kadesh and came to Mount Hor. {20:23} And the LORD spoke to Moses and Aaron on Mount Hor, by the border of the land of Edom, saying, {20:24} "Aaron shall be gathered to his people; he shall not enter the land which I have given to the children of Israel, because you rebelled against my word at the water of Meribah. {20:25} Take Aaron and Eleazar his son, bring them up to Mount Hor. {20:26} Strip Aaron of his garments, put them on Eleazar his son; Aaron shall be gathered to his people, and shall die there." {20:27} Moses did as the LORD commanded; they went up Mount Hor in the sight of all the congregation. {20:28} Moses stripped Aaron of his garments, put them on Eleazar his son; Aaron died there on the top of the mountain. Moses and Eleazar came down from the mountain. {20:29} When all the congregation saw that Aaron was dead, they mourned for Aaron thirty days, all the house of Israel.

{21:1} King Arad the Canaanite, who lived in the south, heard that Israel came by way of the spies. He fought against Israel and took some of them prisoners. {21:2} Israel made a vow to the LORD, saying, "If you deliver this people into my hand, I will utterly destroy their cities." {21:3} The LORD listened to Israel and delivered up the Canaanites. They utterly destroyed them and their cities, and the place was called Hormah. {21:4} They journeyed from Mount Hor by the way of the Red Sea, to go around the land of Edom. The people became discouraged because of the journey. {21:5} The people complained against God and Moses, saying, "Why have you brought us out of Egypt to die in the wilderness? There is no bread or water, and we detest this light bread." {21:6} The LORD sent fiery serpents among the people, and they bit them; many Israelites died. {21:7} So the people came to Moses, confessing their sin and asking him to pray to the LORD to remove the serpents. Moses prayed for the people. {21:8} **The LORD instructed Moses to make a fiery serpent and set it on a pole. Anyone who was bitten and looked at the bronze serpent would live.** {21:9} *Moses made a bronze serpent and put it on a pole. If anyone was bitten by a serpent and looked at the bronze serpent, they would live.* {21:10} The children of Israel set out and camped in Oboth. {21:11} From Oboth, they journeyed and camped at Ije Abarim, in the wilderness east of Moab. {21:12} From there, they moved and camped in the Valley of Zared. {21:13} Then they moved and camped on the other side of the Arnon, which is in the wilderness that extends from the border of the Amorites. Arnon is the border of Moab, between Moab and the Amorites. {21:14} This is mentioned in the Book of the Wars of the LORD: "What he did at the Red Sea, and at the streams of Arnon, {21:15} And at the brooks that flow into the dwelling of Ar, and lie along the border of Moab." {21:16} From there, they went to Beer, the well where the LORD said to Moses, "Gather the people, and I will give them water." {21:17} Then Israel sang this song: "Spring up, O well! Sing to it!" {21:18} The leaders dug the well, the nobles of the people dug it, by the direction of the lawgiver, with their staffs. From the wilderness, they went to Mattanah. {21:19} From Mattanah to Nahaliel, and from Nahaliel to Bamoth, {21:20} From Bamoth in the valley, which is in the country of Moab, to the top of Pisgah, which overlooks the wasteland. {21:21} Israel sent messengers to Sihon king of the Amorites, saying, {21:22} "Let us pass through your land. We will not turn into fields or vineyards, nor drink water from wells. We will go along the king's highway until we have passed your borders." {21:23} But Sihon refused to let Israel pass through his territory. He gathered his people and went out against Israel in the wilderness, coming to Jahaz and fighting against Israel. {21:24} Israel defeated him with the edge of the sword and took possession of his land from the Arnon to the Jabbok, as far as the Ammonites' border, because the border of the Ammonites was fortified. {21:25} Israel took all these cities and settled in the cities of the Amorites, including Heshbon and its villages. {21:26} Heshbon was the city of Sihon king of the Amorites, who had fought against the former king of Moab and taken all his land up to the Arnon. {21:27} "Come to Heshbon, let the city of Sihon be built and established, {21:28} For a fire went out from Heshbon, a flame from the city of Sihon. It consumed Ar of Moab, the lords of the high places of Arnon. {21:29} Woe to you, Moab! You are destroyed, O people of Chemosh! He gave his sons as fugitives, and his daughters into captivity to Sihon king of the Amorites, {21:30} We have shot at them; Heshbon is perished as far as Dibon, and we have laid waste even to Nophah, which reaches to Medeba." {21:31} Thus Israel dwelt in the land of the Amorites. {21:32} Moses sent to spy out Jazer, and they took its villages and drove out the Amorites who were there. {21:33} Then they turned and went up by the way to Bashan, and Og the king of Bashan went out against them, he and all his people, to battle at Edrei. {21:34} But the LORD said to Moses, "Do not fear him, for I have given him into your hand, with all his people and his land. You shall do to him as you did to Sihon king of the Amorites, who lived in Heshbon." {21:35} So they defeated him, his sons, and all his people, until there was no survivor left, and they took possession of his land.

{22:1} The children of Israel moved and camped in the plains of Moab near Jericho on the side of the Jordan. {22:2} Balak, the son of Zippor, saw all that Israel had done to the Amorites. {22:3} Moab became very afraid of the people because they were numerous. Moab was distressed because of the children of Israel. {22:4} Moab said to the elders of Midian, "This company will lick up everything around us, like an ox licks up the grass of the field." Balak, the son of Zippor, was king of the Moabites at that time. {22:5} So, he sent messengers to Balaam, the son of Beor, in Pethor by the river of his people's land. He asked Balaam to come, saying, "There is a people who came out of Egypt; they cover the earth, and they camp opposite me. {22:6} Now, curse this people for me, for they are too mighty for me. Perhaps then I will be able to defeat them and drive them out, for I know that whoever you bless is blessed, and whoever you curse is cursed." {22:7} The elders of Moab and Midian took divination fees in their hands and went to Balaam, repeating Balak's words. {22:8} Balaam told them, "Stay here tonight, and I will bring you word again, as the LORD speaks to me." So the princes of Moab stayed with Balaam. {22:9} God came to Balaam and asked, "Who are these men with you?" {22:10} Balaam replied to God, "Balak, the son of Zippor, king of Moab, has sent word to me, {22:11} 'A people has come out of Egypt, covering the earth. Come, curse them for me; perhaps I will be able to fight against them and drive them away.'" {22:12} God said to Balaam, "You shall not go with them; you shall not curse the people, for they are blessed." {22:13} Balaam rose in the morning and told the princes of Balak, "Go back to your land, for the LORD has refused to let me go with you." {22:14} So the princes of Moab returned to Balak and told him that Balaam refused to come with them. {22:15} Balak sent more honorable princes than before. {22:16} They came to Balaam and said, "Balak, the son of Zippor, says, 'Please come to me. Let nothing hinder you; I will greatly honor you, and whatever you say to me, I will do. So please come and curse this people.'" {22:17} Balaam answered, "Even if Balak were to give me his house full of silver and gold, I could not go beyond the word of the LORD my God, to do less or more. {22:18} Now, please stay here tonight also, so that I may know what else the LORD will tell me." {22:19} God came to Balaam at night and said, "If the men come to call you, rise up and go with them; but only the word that I speak to you, that you shall speak." So Balaam went with the princes of Balak. {22:20} Balaam rose in the morning, saddled his donkey, and went with the princes of

Moab. {22:22} God's anger was kindled because Balaam went, and the Angel of the LORD stood in the way as an adversary against him. Balaam was riding on his donkey, and his two servants were with him. {22:23} The donkey saw the Angel of the LORD standing in the way with a drawn sword, and she turned aside into the field. Balaam struck the donkey to turn her back onto the road. {22:24} But the Angel of the LORD stood in a path of the vineyards, with a wall on each side. {22:25} When the donkey saw the Angel of the LORD, she pressed herself against the wall, crushing Balaam's foot against it. So he struck her again. {22:26} The Angel of the LORD went further and stood in a narrow place, where there was no way to turn either to the right hand or to the left. {22:27} When the donkey saw the Angel of the LORD, she lay down under Balaam. Balaam's anger was kindled, and he struck the donkey with a staff. {22:28} Then the LORD opened the mouth of the donkey, and she said to Balaam, "What have I done to you, that you have struck me these three times?" {22:29} Balaam said to the donkey, "Because you have mocked me. If I had a sword in my hand, I would kill you now." {22:30} The donkey said to Balaam, "Am I not your donkey, which you have ridden upon your whole life until today? Have I ever treated you this way before?" Balaam admitted, "No." {22:31} Then the LORD opened Balaam's eyes, and he saw the Angel of the LORD standing in the way with his sword drawn. So he bowed his head and fell on his face. {22:32} The Angel of the LORD said to him, "Why have you struck your donkey these three times? Behold, I have come out to oppose you because your way is perverse before me. {22:33} The donkey saw me and turned away from me three times. If she hadn't turned away, I would have killed you and spared her. {22:34} Balaam admitted to the Angel of the LORD, "I have sinned. I didn't realize you were standing in my way. If it displeases you, I will turn back." {22:35} The Angel of the LORD instructed Balaam, "Go with the men, but speak only what I tell you." So Balaam went with Balak's princes. {22:36} When Balak heard that Balaam had come, he went to meet him in a Moabite city on the border of Arnon. {22:37} Balak questioned Balaam, "Didn't I send for you? Why didn't you come? Am I not able to honor you?" {22:38} Balaam replied to Balak, "I have come to you, but I have no power to say anything except what God puts in my mouth." {22:39} Balaam went with Balak, and they arrived at Kirjathhuzoth. {22:40} Balak offered oxen and sheep to Balaam and the princes who were with him. {22:41} The next day, Balak took Balaam to the high places of Baal to observe the Israelites from there.

{23:1} Balaam instructed Balak, "Build seven altars for me here and prepare seven oxen and seven rams." {23:2} Balak did as Balaam had instructed, and they both offered a bull and a ram on each altar. {23:3} Balaam told Balak, "Stand by your burnt offering while I go. Perhaps the LORD will meet with me. Whatever he reveals to me, I will tell you." So Balaam went to a high place. {23:4} God met Balaam, and Balaam said to him, "I have prepared seven altars, and I have offered a bull and a ram on each altar." {23:5} The LORD put a message in Balaam's mouth, saying, "Return to Balak and speak what I tell you." {23:6} Balaam went back to Balak, who was standing by his burnt offering along with the princes of Moab. {23:7} Balaam began his message, "Balak, the king of Moab, brought me from Aram, from the eastern mountains, saying, 'Come, curse Jacob for me; come, denounce Israel.'" {23:8} Balaam declared, "How can I curse those whom God has not cursed? How can I denounce those whom the LORD has not denounced?" {23:9} "From the rocky peaks I see them; from the heights I view them. I see a people who live apart and do not consider themselves one of the nations." {23:10} "Who can count the dust of Jacob or number even a fourth of Israel? Let me die the death of the righteous, and may my final end be like theirs!" {23:11} Balak protested, "What have you done to me? I brought you to curse my enemies, but you have blessed them!" {23:12} Balaam responded, "I must speak only what the LORD puts in my mouth." {23:13} Balak then said, "Please come with me to another place from where you may see them, though not all of them. Curse them for me from there." {23:14} So he took him to the field of Zophim, to the top of Pisgah, and built seven altars there. He offered a bull and a ram on each altar. {23:15} Balaam said to Balak, "Stand here beside your burnt offering while I meet with the LORD over there." {23:16} The LORD met with Balaam and put a message in his mouth, saying, "Go back to Balak and give him this message." {23:17} Balaam returned to Balak, who was standing by his burnt offering along with the princes of Moab. {23:18} Balaam began his message, "Balak, rise up and listen; hear me, son of Zippor." {23:19} **"God is not human, that he should lie, not a human being, that he should change his mind. Does he speak and then not act? Does he promise and not fulfill?"** {23:20} "I have received a command to bless; he has blessed, and I cannot change it." {23:21} "No misfortune is seen in Jacob, no misery observed in Israel. The LORD their God is with them; the shout of the King is among them." {23:22} "God brought them out of Egypt; they have the strength of a wild ox." {23:23} "There is no divination against Jacob, no evil omens against Israel. It will now be said of Jacob and of Israel, 'See what God has done!'" {23:24} "The people rise like a lioness; they rouse themselves like a lion that does not rest till it devours its prey and drinks the blood of its victims." {23:25} Balak said to Balaam, "Neither curse them at all nor bless them at all." {23:26} But Balaam answered, "Didn't I tell you I must do whatever the LORD says?" {23:27} Balak then said to Balaam, "Come, let me take you to another place. Perhaps it will please God to let you curse them from there." {23:28} So Balak took Balaam to the top of Peor, which overlooks the wasteland. {23:29} Balaam said to Balak, "Build me seven altars here, and prepare seven bulls and seven rams for me." {23:30} Balak did as Balaam said, and offered a bull and a ram on each altar.

{24:1} When Balaam saw that it pleased the LORD to bless Israel, he did not resort to divination as he had done before. Instead, he turned his face toward the wilderness. {24:2} As Balaam lifted up his eyes, he saw Israel encamped tribe by tribe. Then the Spirit of God came upon him, {24:3} and he uttered his oracle, saying: "Balaam son of Beor speaks, the man whose eyes are opened; {24:4} the oracle of one who hears the words of God, who sees a vision from the Almighty, who falls prostrate, and whose eyes are opened: {24:5} How beautiful are your tents, O Jacob, your dwellings, O Israel! {24:6} Like valleys they spread out, like gardens beside a river, like aloes planted by the LORD, like cedars beside the waters. {24:7} Water will flow from their buckets; their seed will have abundant water. Their king will be greater than Agag; their kingdom will be exalted. {24:8} God brought them out of Egypt; they have the strength of a wild ox. They will devour hostile nations and crush their bones and pierce them with arrows. {24:9} They crouch and lie down like a lion; like a lioness, who dares to rouse them? Blessed is everyone who blesses you, O Israel, and cursed is everyone who curses you." {24:10} Balak's anger burned against Balaam. He struck his hands together and said to him, "I summoned you to curse my enemies, but you have blessed them three times! {24:11} Now leave at once and go home! I said I would reward you handsomely, but the LORD has denied you any reward." {24:12} Balaam answered Balak, "Did I not tell the messengers you sent me, {24:13} 'Even if Balak gave me all the silver and gold in his palace, I could not do anything of my own accord, good or bad, to go beyond the command of the LORD—and I must say only what the LORD says'? {24:14} Now I am going back to my own people, but come, let me warn you of what this people will do to your people in days to come." {24:15} Then he uttered his oracle: "The oracle of Balaam son of Beor, the oracle of one whose eyes are opened; {24:16} the oracle of one who hears the words of God, who has knowledge from the Most High, who sees a vision from the Almighty, who falls prostrate, and whose eyes are opened: {24:17} ***I see him, but not now; I behold him, but not near. A star will come out of Jacob; a scepter will rise out of Israel. He will crush the foreheads of Moab, the skulls of all the people of Sheth.*** {24:18} Edom will be conquered; Seir, his enemy, will be conquered, but Israel will grow strong. {24:19} A ruler will come out of Jacob and destroy the survivors of the city." {24:20} Then Balaam saw Amalek and spoke his message: "Amalek was first among the nations, but their end will be utter destruction." {24:21} Next, he looked at the Kenites and uttered his message: "Your dwelling place is secure, your nest is set in a rock; {24:22} yet you Kenites will be destroyed when Asshur takes you captive." {24:23} Balaam then spoke his message: "Alas, who can live when God does this? {24:24} Ships will come from the shores of Cyprus; they will subdue Asshur and Eber, but they too will come to ruin." {24:25} Then Balaam arose and went back to his place, and Balak also went his way.

{25:1} While Israel was staying in Shittim, the people began to indulge in sexual immorality with the daughters of Moab. {25:2} These women invited the Israelites to the sacrifices of their gods, and the people ate the sacrifices and bowed down to their gods. {25:3} So Israel yoked themselves to the Baal of Peor, and the LORD's anger burned against them. {25:4} The LORD said to Moses, "Take all the leaders of these people, kill them and expose them in broad daylight before the LORD, so that the LORD's fierce anger may turn away from Israel." {25:5} So Moses said to Israel's judges, "Each of you must put to death those of your people who have yoked themselves to the Baal of Peor." {25:6} Then an Israelite man brought into the camp a Midianite woman right before the eyes of Moses and the whole assembly of Israel while they were weeping at the entrance to the tent of meeting. {25:7} When Phinehas son of Eleazar, the son of Aaron, the priest, saw this, he left the assembly, took a spear in his hand {25:8} and followed the Israelite into the tent. He drove the spear into both of them, right through the Israelite man and into the woman's stomach. Then the plague against the Israelites was stopped; {25:9} but those who died in the plague numbered 24,000. {25:10} The LORD said to Moses, {25:11} "Phinehas son of Eleazar, the son of Aaron, the priest, has turned my anger away from the Israelites. Since he was as zealous for my honor among them as I am, I did not put an end to them in my zeal. {25:12} Therefore tell him I am making my covenant of peace with him. {25:13} He and his descendants will have a covenant of a lasting priesthood, because he was zealous for the honor of his God and made atonement for the Israelites." {25:14} The name of the Israelite who was killed with the Midianite woman was Zimri son of Salu, the leader of a Simeonite family. {25:15} And the name of the Midianite woman who was put to death was Cozbi daughter of Zur, a tribal chief of a Midianite family. {25:16} The LORD said to Moses, {25:17} "Treat the Midianites as enemies and kill them, {25:18} because they treated you as enemies when they deceived you in the Peor incident involving their sister Cozbi, the daughter of a Midianite leader, the woman who was killed when the plague came as a result of Peor."

{26:1} After the plague, the LORD spoke to Moses and Eleazar the son of Aaron the priest, saying, {26:2} "Take a census of all the congregation of the children of Israel, from twenty years old and upward, by their fathers' houses, all who are able to go to war in Israel. {26:3} So Moses and Eleazar the priest spoke with them on the plains of Moab by the Jordan, near Jericho, saying, {26:4} "Count the people, those twenty years old and upward, as the LORD commanded Moses and the children of Israel who came out of the land of Egypt. {26:5} The descendants of Reuben, the firstborn of Israel: the Reubenites by their clans were Hanoch, from whom came the clan of the Hanochites; Pallu, from whom came the Palluites; {26:6} Hezron, from whom came the Hezronites; Carmi, from whom came the Carmites. {26:7} These were the clans of the Reubenites; those numbered of them were forty-three thousand seven hundred and thirty. {26:8} The son of Pallu was Eliab. {26:9} The sons of Eliab were Nemuel, Dathan, and Abiram. These were the Dathan and Abiram, chosen by the congregation, who rebelled against Moses and Aaron in the company of Korah when they rebelled against the LORD. {26:10} The earth opened its mouth and swallowed them up along with Korah when that company died, when the fire devoured two hundred and fifty men; and they became a warning. {26:11} But the sons of Korah did not die. {26:12} The sons of Simeon by their clans: of Nemuel, the clan of the Nemuelites; of Jamin, the clan of the Jaminites; of Jachin, the clan of the Jachinites; {26:13} of Zerah, the clan of the Zerahites; of Shaul, the clan of the Shaulites. {26:14} These were the clans of the Simeonites; those numbered of them were twenty-two thousand two hundred. {26:15} The sons of Gad by their clans: of Zephon, the clan of the Zephonites; of Haggi, the clan of the Haggites; of Shuni, the clan of the Shunites; {26:16} of Ozni, the clan of the Oznites; of Eri, the clan of the Erites; {26:17} of Arod, the clan of the Arodites; of Areli, the clan of the Arelites. {26:18} These were the clans of the sons of Gad; those numbered of them were forty thousand five hundred. {26:19} The sons of Judah: Er and Onan; and Er and Onan died in the land of Canaan. {26:20} The sons of Judah by their clans were: of Shelah, the clan of the Shelanites; of Perez, the clan of the Perezites; of Zerah, the clan of the Zerahites. {26:21} The sons of Perez were: of Hezron, the clan of the Hezronites; of Hamul, the clan of the Hamulites. {26:22} These were the clans of Judah; those numbered of them were seventy-six thousand five hundred. {26:23} The sons of Issachar by their clans: of Tola, the clan of the Tolaites; of Puvah, the clan of the Punites; {26:24} of Jashub, the clan of the Jashubites; of Shimron, the clan of the Shimronites. {26:25} These were the clans of Issachar; those numbered of them were sixty-four thousand three hundred. {26:26} The sons of Zebulun by their clans: of Sered, the clan of the Seredites; of Elon, the clan of the Elonites; of Jahleel, the clan of the Jahleelites. {26:27} These were the clans of the Zebulunites; those numbered of them were sixty thousand five hundred. {26:28} The sons of Joseph by their clans were Manasseh and Ephraim. {26:29} The sons of Manasseh: of Machir, the clan of the Machirites; and Machir was the father of Gilead; of Gilead, the clan of the Gileadites. {26:30} These were the sons of Gilead: of Iezer, the clan of the Iezerites; of Helek, the clan of the Helekites; {26:31} and of Asriel, the clan of the Asrielites; and of Shechem, the clan of the Shechemites; {26:32} and of Shemida, the clan of the Shemidaites; and of Hepher, the clan of the Hepherites. {26:33} Zelophehad, son of Hepher, had no sons but daughters. The names of his daughters were Mahlah, Noah, Hoglah, Milcah, and Tirzah. {26:34} These were the clans of Manasseh, and those numbered of them were fifty-two thousand seven hundred. {26:35} The sons of Ephraim by their clans were: of Shuthelah, the clan of the Shuthalhites; of Becher, the clan of the Bachrites; of Tahan, the clan of the Tahanites. {26:36} The sons of Shuthelah were: of Eran, the clan of the Eranites. {26:37} These were the clans of the sons of Ephraim according to those numbered of them: thirty-two thousand five hundred. These were the sons of Joseph by their clans. {26:38} The sons of Benjamin by their clans were: of Bela, the clan of the Belaites; of Ashbel, the clan of the Ashbelites; of Ahiram, the clan of the Ahiramites; {26:39} of Shupham, the clan of the Shuphamites; of Hupham, the clan of the Huphamites. {26:40} The sons of Bela were Ard and Naaman: of Ard, the clan of the Ardites; and of Naaman, the clan of the Naamites. {26:41} These were the sons of Benjamin by their clans, and those numbered of them were forty-five thousand six hundred.

{26:42} The sons of Dan by their clans were: of Shuham, the clan of the Shuhamites. These were the clans of Dan by their clans. {26:43} All the clans of the Shuhamites, according to those numbered of them, were sixty-four thousand four hundred. {26:44} The children of Asher by their clans were: of Jimna, the clan of the Jimnites; of Jesui, the clan of the Jesuites; of Beriah, the clan of the Beriites. {26:45} Of the sons of Beriah were: of Heber, the clan of the Heberites; of Malchiel, the clan of the Malchielites. {26:46} And the name of the daughter of Asher was Sarah. {26:47} These were the clans of the sons of Asher according to those numbered of them, who were fifty-three thousand four hundred. {26:48} The sons of Naphtali by their clans were: of Jahzeel, the clan of the Jahzeelites; of Guni, the clan of the Gunites; {26:49} of Jezer, the clan of the Jezerites; of Shillem, the clan of the Shillemites. {26:50} These were the clans of Naphtali according to their clans, and those numbered of them were forty-five thousand four hundred. {26:51} These were the numbered of the children of Israel, six hundred thousand and a thousand seven hundred and thirty. {26:52} The LORD spoke to Moses, saying, {26:53} "To these, the land shall be divided for an inheritance according to the number of names. {26:54} To many, you shall give the more inheritance, and to few, you shall give the less inheritance; to every one shall his inheritance be given according to those numbered of him. {26:55} Nevertheless, the land shall be divided by lot; according to the names of the tribes of their fathers, they shall inherit. {26:56} According to the lot shall the possession thereof be divided between many and few. {26:57} These were the Levites by their clans: of Gershon, the clan of the Gershonites; of Kohath, the clan of the Kohathites; of Merari, the clan of the Merarites. {26:58} These were the clans of the Levites: the Libnite clan, the Hebronite clan, the Mahlite clan, the Mushite clan, the Korathite clan. Kohath fathered Amram. {26:59} Amram's wife was Jochebed, the daughter of Levi, whom her mother bore to Levi in Egypt. She bore to Amram Aaron, Moses, and Miriam their sister. {26:60} And Aaron was born Nadab, Abihu, Eleazar, and Ithamar. {26:61} Nadab and Abihu died when they offered unauthorized fire before the LORD. {26:62} And those numbered of them were twenty-three thousand, all males from a month old and upward, for they were not numbered among the children of Israel, because there was no inheritance given them among the children of Israel. {26:63} These were they numbered by Moses and Eleazar the priest, who numbered the children of Israel in the plains of Moab by the Jordan near Jericho. {26:64} But among these, there was not a man of them whom Moses and Aaron the priest numbered, when they numbered the children of Israel in the wilderness of Sinai. {26:65} For the LORD had said of them, "They shall surely die in the wilderness." And there was not left a man of them, save Caleb the son of Jephunneh, and Joshua the son of Nun.

{27:1} Then the daughters of Zelophehad, the son of Hepher, the son of Gilead, the son of Machir, the son of Manasseh, from the families of Manasseh the son of Joseph, came forward. Their names were Mahlah, Noah, Hoglah, Milcah, and Tirzah. {27:2} They stood before Moses, Eleazar the priest, the leaders, and all the congregation, at the entrance of the tent of meeting, and said, {27:3} "Our father died in the wilderness, but he was not among those who rebelled against the LORD with Korah. He died for his own sin, and he had no sons. {27:4} Why should our father's name disappear from his clan just because he had no son? Give us property among our father's relatives." {27:5} Moses presented their case before the LORD. {27:6} And the LORD spoke to Moses, saying, {27:7} "The daughters of Zelophehad speak correctly. You shall surely give them property as an inheritance among their father's relatives, and transfer their father's inheritance to them. {27:8} Speak to the Israelites, saying, 'If a man dies without a son, you shall transfer his inheritance to his daughter. {27:9} If he has no daughter, you shall give his inheritance to his brothers. {27:10} If he has no brothers, you shall give his inheritance to his father's brothers. {27:11} If his father has no brothers, you shall give his inheritance to the nearest relative in his clan, and he shall possess it. This is to be a statutory ordinance for the Israelites, as the LORD commanded Moses." {27:12} Then the LORD said to Moses, "Go up this mountain of Abarim and see the land that I have given to the Israelites. {27:13} After you have seen it, you too will be gathered to your people, as your brother Aaron was. {27:14} For when the community rebelled at the waters in the Desert of Zin, both of you disobeyed my command to honor me as holy before their eyes." (These were the waters of Meribah Kadesh, in the Desert of Zin.) {27:15} Moses said to the LORD, {27:16} "May the LORD, the God who gives breath to all living things, appoint someone over this community {27:17} to go out and come in before them, one who will lead them out and bring them in, so the LORD's people will not be like sheep without a shepherd." {27:18} Then the LORD said to Moses, "Take Joshua son of Nun, a man in whom is the Spirit, and lay your hand on him. {27:19} Have him stand before Eleazar the priest and the entire assembly and commission him in their presence. {27:20} Give him some of your authority so the whole Israelite community will obey him. {27:21} He is to stand before Eleazar the priest, who will obtain decisions for him by inquiring of the Urim before the LORD. At his command, he and the entire community of the Israelites will go out, and at his command, they will come in." {27:22} Moses did as the LORD commanded him. He took Joshua and had him stand before Eleazar the priest and the whole assembly. {27:23} Then he laid his hands on him and commissioned him, as the LORD instructed through Moses.

{28:1} Then the LORD spoke to Moses, saying, {28:2} "Command the Israelites and tell them: 'My offering, the food for my sacrifices made by fire, which is a pleasing aroma to me, you must observe to offer to me at their appointed times. {28:3} And say to them, 'This is the offering made by fire that you shall offer to the LORD: two one-year-old lambs without blemish every day, as a regular burnt offering. {28:4} One lamb you shall offer in the morning, and the other lamb you shall offer at twilight. {28:5} Also, include a tenth of an ephah of fine flour mixed with a quarter of a hin of beaten oil as a grain offering with each lamb. {28:6} It is a regular burnt offering, which was ordained at Mount Sinai as a pleasing aroma, an offering made by fire to the LORD. {28:7} And the accompanying drink offering shall be a quarter of a hin for each lamb. Pour out the strong drink as an offering to the LORD in the Holy Place. {28:8} The second lamb you shall offer at twilight; you shall offer it with the same grain offering and drink offering as in the morning, as a pleasing aroma, an offering made by fire to the LORD. {28:9} On the Sabbath day, offer two one-year-old lambs without blemish, along with two-tenths of an ephah of fine flour mixed with oil as a grain offering, and its drink offering. {28:10} This is the burnt offering for every Sabbath, in addition to the regular burnt offering with its drink offering. {28:11} On the first day of each month, you are to present a burnt offering to the LORD: two young bulls, one ram, and seven one-year-old lambs without blemish. {28:12} Along with the bulls, offer three-tenths of an ephah of fine flour mixed with oil as a grain offering, and two-tenths of an ephah of fine flour mixed with oil for the ram, {28:13} and one-tenth of an ephah of fine flour mixed with oil as a grain offering for each lamb. This is a burnt offering, a pleasing aroma, an offering made by fire to the LORD. {28:14} The drink offerings for the bulls shall be half a hin of wine, a third of a hin for the ram, and a quarter of a hin for each lamb. This is the burnt offering for every month throughout the months of the year. {28:15} Also, offer one male goat for a sin offering to the LORD, in addition to the regular burnt offering and its drink offering. {28:16} On the fourteenth day of the first month is the Passover of the LORD. {28:17} And on the fifteenth day of this month is the Feast; for seven days unleavened bread shall be eaten. {28:18} The first day is to be a sacred assembly; you are not to do any regular work. {28:19} Offer a burnt offering, a pleasing aroma to the LORD: two young bulls, one ram, and seven one-year-old male lambs, all without blemish. {28:20} Their grain offering is to be of fine flour mixed with oil: three-tenths of an ephah for each bull, two-tenths for the ram, {28:21} and one-tenth for each of the seven lambs. {28:22} Also, offer one male goat as a sin offering, to make atonement for yourselves. {28:23} You are to offer these in addition to the regular burnt offering in the morning, which is a continual burnt offering. {28:24} This is to be done daily throughout the seven days, along with the regular burnt offering and its drink offering. {28:25} On the seventh day, you shall have a sacred assembly; you are not to do any regular work. {28:26} Also, on the day of the firstfruits, when you present a new grain offering to the LORD after your weeks of bringing it, you shall have a sacred assembly; you are not to do any regular work. {28:27} Offer a burnt offering, a pleasing aroma to the LORD: two young bulls, one ram, and seven one-year-old male lambs, {28:28} with their grain offering of fine flour mixed with oil: three-tenths of an ephah for each bull, two-tenths for the ram, {28:29} and one-tenth for each of the seven lambs. {28:30} Also, offer one male goat as a sin offering, to make atonement for yourselves. {28:31} These are to be offered in addition to the regular burnt offering and its grain offering. They must be without blemish, along with their drink offerings.' "

{29:1} In the seventh month, on the first day, you shall have a sacred assembly; you shall not do any ordinary work. It is a day for sounding the trumpets to you. {29:2} You shall offer a burnt offering to the LORD, a young bull, a ram, and seven male lambs a year old, all without defect. {29:3} Their grain offering shall be of fine flour mixed with oil, three-tenths of an ephah for the bull, two-tenths for the ram, {29:4} and one-tenth for each of the seven lambs; {29:5} along with one male goat for a sin offering, to make atonement for you. {29:6} These are in addition to the monthly burnt offering and its grain offering, the regular burnt offering and its grain offering, and their drink offerings, according to the stipulations for them, as a pleasing aroma, a food offering presented to the LORD. {29:7} On the tenth day of this seventh month, you shall have a sacred assembly; you shall humble yourselves; you shall not do any work. {29:8} But you shall present a burnt offering to the LORD as a pleasing aroma: one young bull, one ram, and seven male lambs a year old, all without defect. {29:9} Their grain offering and drink offerings for the bull, the ram, and the lambs shall be according to their number, as prescribed. {29:10} Along with one male goat for a sin offering; in addition to the sin offering for atonement, the regular burnt offering with its grain offering, and their drink offerings. {29:12} On the fifteenth day of the seventh month, you shall have a sacred assembly; you shall not do any ordinary work, and you shall celebrate a feast to the LORD for seven days. {29:13} You shall offer a burnt offering, an offering made by fire, as a pleasing aroma to the LORD: thirteen young bulls, two rams, and fourteen male lambs a year old, all without defect. {29:14} Their grain offering and drink offerings for the bulls, the rams, and the lambs shall be according to their number, as prescribed. {29:15} Along with one male goat for a sin offering; in addition to the regular burnt offering with its grain offering and drink offerings. {29:17} On the second day, twelve young bulls, two rams, and fourteen male lambs a year old, without defect; {29:18} Their grain offering and drink offerings for the bulls, the rams, and the lambs shall be according to their number, as prescribed. {29:19} Along with one male goat for a sin offering; in addition to the regular burnt offering with its grain offering and drink offerings. {29:20} On the third day, eleven bulls, two rams, and fourteen male lambs a year old, without defect; {29:21} Their grain offering and drink offerings for the bulls, the rams, and the lambs shall be according to their number, as prescribed. {29:22} Along with one male goat for a sin offering; in addition to the regular burnt offering with its grain offering and drink offerings. {29:23} On the fourth day, ten bulls, two rams, and fourteen male lambs a year old, without defect; {29:24} Their grain offering and drink offerings for the bulls, the rams, and the lambs shall be according to their number, as prescribed. {29:25} Along with one male goat for a sin offering; in addition to the regular burnt offering with its grain offering and drink offerings. {29:26} On the fifth day, nine bulls, two rams, and fourteen male lambs a year old, without defect; {29:27} Their grain offering and drink offerings for the bulls, the rams, and the lambs shall be according to their number, as prescribed. {29:28} Along with one male goat for a sin offering; in addition to the regular burnt offering with its grain offering and drink offerings. {29:29} On the sixth day, eight bulls, two rams, and fourteen male lambs a year old, without defect; {29:30} Their grain offering and drink offerings for the bulls, the rams, and the lambs shall be according to their number, as prescribed. {29:31} Along with one male goat for a sin offering; in addition to the regular burnt offering with its grain offering and drink offerings. {29:32} On the seventh day, seven bulls, two rams, and fourteen male lambs a year old, without defect; {29:33} Their grain offering and drink offerings for the bulls, the rams, and the lambs shall be according to their number, as prescribed. {29:34} Along with one male goat for a sin offering; in addition to the regular burnt offering with its grain offering and drink offerings. {29:35} On the eighth day, you shall have a solemn assembly; you shall not do any ordinary work, {29:36} but you shall offer a burnt offering, a food offering, a pleasing aroma to the LORD: one bull, one ram, and seven male lambs a year old, all without defect; {29:37} Their grain offering and drink offerings for the bull, the ram, and the lambs shall be according to their number, as prescribed. {29:38} Along with one male goat for a sin offering; in addition to the regular burnt offering, its grain offering, and drink offering. {29:39} These you shall offer to the LORD at your appointed feasts, in addition to your vow offerings and freewill offerings, for your burnt offerings, grain offerings, drink offerings, and peace offerings." {29:40} Moses told the Israelites everything the LORD commanded him.

{30:1} Moses spoke to the leaders of the tribes of Israel, saying, "This is what the LORD has commanded: {30:2} If a man makes a vow to the LORD or swears an oath to bind himself with a pledge, he must not break his word but must fulfill all that he promised. {30:3} Likewise, if a woman in her youth, while still in her father's house, makes a vow to the LORD or binds herself by a pledge,

{30:4} and her father hears of her vow or pledge but says nothing to her, then all her vows and every pledge by which she has bound herself shall stand. {30:5} But if her father opposes her on the day he hears of it, none of her vows or pledges that she has bound herself with shall stand; and the LORD will release her because her father has made them null and void. {30:6} If she marries after making a vow or rash promise, {30:7} and her husband hears of it but says nothing to her and does not oppose her, then all her vows and pledges by which she has bound herself shall stand. {30:8} But if her husband nullifies them on the day he hears of them, then whatever she says concerning her vows or pledges shall not stand; her husband has nullified them, and the LORD will release her. {30:9} Any vow or pledge made by a widow or divorced woman will be binding on her. {30:10} If a woman makes a vow while in her husband's house or binds herself by a pledge with an oath, {30:11} and her husband hears of it but says nothing and does not oppose her, then all her vows and pledges shall stand. {30:12} But if her husband nullifies them on the day he hears of them, then none of the vows or pledges that she made shall stand; her husband has nullified them, and the LORD will release her. {30:13} Every vow and pledge to deny oneself that a woman makes, her husband may confirm or nullify. {30:14} But if her husband says nothing to her about it from day to day, then he confirms all her vows or pledges by which she bound herself; he confirms them because he said nothing to her when he heard about them. {30:15} But if he nullifies them after he has heard about them, then he is responsible for her guilt." {30:16} These are the statutes that the LORD commanded Moses concerning the relationship between a man and his wife, and between a father and his daughter, especially when she is young and still in her father's house.

{31:1} Then the LORD spoke to Moses, saying, {31:2} "Avenge the children of Israel on the Midianites; afterward you shall be gathered to your people." {31:3} So Moses spoke to the people, saying, "Arm some of yourselves for war, and let them go against the Midianites to execute the vengeance of the LORD on Midian. {31:4} From every tribe, send a thousand men to the war." {31:5} Thus, twelve thousand armed for war were chosen from the tribes of Israel. {31:6} Moses sent them to war, a thousand from each tribe, along with Phinehas the son of Eleazar the priest, who carried the holy instruments and the trumpets for sounding the alarm. {31:7} They waged war against the Midianites, just as the LORD commanded Moses, and killed all the males. {31:8} They also killed the kings of Midian, including Evi, Rekem, Zur, Hur, and Reba, along with Balaam, the son of Beor, whom they killed with the sword. {31:9} The Israelites took the Midianite women and children captive, and plundered all their livestock, goods, and possessions. {31:10} They burned all the Midianite cities and forts with fire. {31:11} They took all the plunder and captives, both people and animals. {31:12} Then they brought the captives, plunder, and spoils to Moses, Eleazar the priest, and the congregation of Israel, who were camped on the plains of Moab by the Jordan River near Jericho. {31:13} Moses, Eleazar the priest, and all the leaders of the congregation went out to meet them outside the camp. {31:14} Moses was angry with the officers of the army, the commanders of thousands and commanders of hundreds, who were returning from the battle. {31:15} He asked them, "Have you allowed all the women to live? {31:16} These women, by the advice of Balaam, caused the Israelites to turn away from the LORD in the incident at Peor, resulting in a plague among the congregation of the LORD. {31:17} Now therefore, kill every male among the little ones, and kill every woman who has known a man intimately. {31:18} But spare all the young girls who have not known a man intimately for yourselves. {31:19} And remain outside the camp for seven days; whoever has killed any person, and whoever has touched any slain, purify yourselves and your captives on the third day and on the seventh day. {31:20} Also, purify all your garments, everything made of skin, everything made of goat's hair, and all articles of wood." {31:21} Then Eleazar the priest said to the men who had gone to battle, "This is the ordinance of the law which the LORD commanded Moses: {31:22} Only the gold, silver, bronze, iron, tin, and lead— {31:23} whatever can endure fire, you shall put through the fire, and it shall be clean; nevertheless it shall be purified with the water of purification. And all that cannot endure fire you shall put through water. {31:24} Also wash your clothes on the seventh day, and you shall be clean; afterward you may come into the camp." {31:25} The LORD spoke to Moses, saying, {31:26} "Count the plunder that was taken—both people and animals—you, Eleazar the priest, and the leaders of the congregation. {31:27} Divide the plunder into two parts, between those who took part in the war, who went out to battle, and all the congregation. {31:28} And impose a tribute for the LORD on the men of war who went out to battle: one out of every five hundred persons, cattle, donkeys, and sheep. {31:29} Take it from their half, and give it to Eleazar the priest as a heave offering to the LORD. {31:30} And from the children of Israel's half, you shall take one portion of every fifty, of persons, cattle, donkeys, sheep, and all kinds of animals, and give them to the Levites who keep charge of the tabernacle of the LORD." {31:31} Moses and Eleazar the priest did as the LORD commanded Moses. {31:32} The plunder remaining from the spoils that the men of war had taken was six hundred and seventy-five thousand sheep, {31:33} seventy-two thousand cattle, {31:34} sixty-one thousand donkeys, {31:35} and thirty-two thousand persons in all, of whom the women who had not known a man intimately were thirty-two thousand. {31:36} Then half of the plunder, the portion for those who had gone out to war, was in number three hundred and thirty-seven thousand five hundred sheep; {31:37} and the LORD's tribute of the sheep was six hundred and seventy-five. {31:38} The cattle were thirty-six thousand, of which the LORD's tribute was seventy-two. {31:39} The donkeys were thirty thousand five hundred, of which the LORD's tribute was sixty-one. {31:40} The persons were sixteen thousand, of whom the LORD's tribute was thirty-two persons. {31:41} Moses gave the tribute, which was the LORD's heave offering, to Eleazar the priest, as the LORD commanded Moses. {31:42} And from the children of Israel's half, which Moses separated from the men who had fought— {31:43} Now the congregation's half was three hundred and thirty-seven thousand five hundred sheep, {31:44} thirty-six thousand cattle, {31:45} thirty thousand five hundred donkeys, {31:46} and sixteen thousand persons— {31:47} Moses took one portion from every fifty, of persons and animals, and gave them to the Levites who kept charge of the tabernacle of the LORD, as the LORD commanded Moses. {31:48} Then the officers who were over thousands of the army, the captains of thousands and captains of hundreds, came to Moses; {31:49} and they said to Moses, "Your servants have taken a count of the men of war who are under our command, and not one man of us is missing. {31:50} We have therefore brought an offering for the LORD, what every man found of ornaments of gold: armlets and bracelets, signet rings, earrings, and necklaces, to make atonement for ourselves before the LORD." {31:51} Moses and Eleazar the priest received the gold from them, all the crafted articles. {31:52} All the gold of the offering that they offered to the LORD, from the captains of thousands and captains of hundreds, was sixteen thousand seven hundred and fifty shekels. {31:53} The men of war had taken spoil, every man for himself. {31:54} Moses and Eleazar the priest took the gold from the captains of thousands and of hundreds, and brought it into the tabernacle of the congregation as a memorial before the LORD for the children of Israel.

{32:1} The tribes of Reuben and Gad had a lot of cattle. When they saw the lands of Jazer and Gilead, they realized it was perfect for their livestock. {32:2} So, they went to Moses, Eleazar the priest, and the leaders of the community and said, {32:3} "We've noticed places like Ataroth, Dibon, Jazer, Nimrah, Heshbon, Elealeh, Shebam, Nebo, and Beon. These are great lands for our cattle. {32:4} The Lord had already defeated the people living there, so it's just right for our livestock. We ask, if you're pleased with us, let us have this land instead of going over the Jordan." {32:5} Moses replied, "Should your brothers go to war while you stay here? {32:6} Why are you discouraging the Israelites from going into the land the Lord promised them? {32:7} This is what your fathers did at Kadesh-Barnea. {32:7} They discouraged the Israelites, and as a result, the Lord was angry and swore that none of the men who came out of Egypt, twenty years old and above, would see the promised land, except Caleb and Joshua. {32:8} The Lord was angry with Israel and made them wander in the wilderness for forty years until the rebellious generation died out. {32:9} You're acting in the same sinful way, increasing the Lord's anger towards Israel. {32:10} If you turn away from the Lord, he'll leave the people in the wilderness, and you'll destroy them. {32:11} But they reassured Moses, saying, "We'll build sheepfolds for our cattle and cities for our families. {32:12} However, we'll go ahead armed, leading the Israelites into their land, while our families stay safe in fortified cities because of the local inhabitants. {32:13} We won't return home until every Israelite has received their inheritance. {32:14} We won't settle on the other side of the Jordan because our inheritance lies here." {32:15} Moses agreed, "If you keep your word and go armed before the Lord into battle until he drives out his enemies, {32:16} and once the land is subdued, you can return, and this land will be yours. {32:17} But if you don't keep your word, you'll sin against the Lord, and your sin will find you out. {32:18} Build cities for your families and sheepfolds for your livestock, and do what you've promised." {32:19} The tribes of Gad and Reuben replied, "We'll do as you say. {32:20} Our families and livestock will stay in the cities of Gilead, but we'll go armed before the Lord into battle." {32:21} Moses then instructed Eleazar the priest, Joshua, and the tribal leaders of Israel regarding their agreement. {32:22} Moses added, "If the tribes of Gad and Reuben fulfill their promise to go armed before the Lord into battle, then give them the land of Gilead as their possession. {32:23} But if they don't, they'll receive their inheritance among you in the land of Canaan." {32:24} The tribes of Gad and Reuben agreed, "We'll go armed before the Lord into the land of Canaan, and our inheritance on this side of the Jordan will be secured." {32:25} Moses then allocated to them, along with half of the tribe of Manasseh, the kingdoms of Sihon and Og, with their cities and surrounding lands. {32:26} The tribe of Gad built Dibon, Ataroth, Aroer, Atroth, Shophan, Jaazer, Jogbehah, Beth-nimrah, and Beth-haran as fenced cities and sheepfolds. {32:27} The tribe of Reuben built Heshbon, Elealeh, Kirjathaim, Nebo, Baal-meon (renaming it), and Shibmah, giving new names to the cities they built. {32:28} The descendants of Machir, a son of Manasseh, captured Gilead and drove out the Amorites. {32:29} Moses granted Gilead to Machir, who settled there. {32:30} Jair, another son of Manasseh, captured and renamed several towns, calling them Havoth-jair. {32:31} And Nobah, also of Manasseh, captured Kenath and its villages, naming it after himself. { {32:32} We will pass over armed before the LORD into the land of Canaan, so that the possession of our inheritance on this side Jordan may be ours. {32:33} And Moses gave to the children of Gad, to the children of Reuben, and to half the tribe of Manasseh, the kingdom of Sihon king of the Amorites, and the kingdom of Og king of Bashan, with the land and its cities in the surrounding areas. {32:34} The children of Gad built Dibon, Ataroth, Aroer, Atroth, Shophan, Jaazer, Jogbehah, Beth-nimrah, and Beth-haran as fenced cities and sheepfolds. {32:35} And the children of Reuben built Heshbon, Elealeh, Kirjathaim, Nebo, Baal-meon (renaming it), and Shibmah, giving new names to the cities they built. {32:36} The children of Machir, the son of Manasseh, went to Gilead, took it, and dispossessed the Amorites who lived there. {32:37} Moses then gave Gilead to Machir, the son of Manasseh, and he settled there. {32:38} Jair, another son of Manasseh, captured and renamed several towns, calling them Havoth-jair. {32:39} **And Nobah, also of Manasseh, captured Kenath and its villages, naming it after himself.** {32:40} So Moses gave Gilead to Machir, the son of Manasseh, and he settled there. {32:41} Jair, the son of Manasseh, took the small towns in Gilead and named them Havoth-jair. {32:42} And Nobah captured Kenath and its villages, renaming it Nobah after himself.

{33:1} These are the journeys of the children of Israel, who left Egypt with their armies under Moses and Aaron. {33:2} Moses wrote down their travels as commanded by the LORD, recording each stage of their journey. {33:3} They departed from Rameses on the fifteenth day of the first month, the day after the Passover. The Israelites left with great confidence, observed by all the Egyptians, for the Egyptians were burying their firstborn, whom the LORD had struck down. The LORD also executed judgments on their gods. {33:4} The Israelites journeyed from Rameses and camped at Succoth. {33:5} From Succoth, they moved to Etham, on the edge of the wilderness. {33:6} They left Etham and turned back toward Pi-hahiroth, facing Baal-zephon, and camped near Migdol. {33:7} Departing from Pi-hahiroth, they passed through the midst of the sea into the wilderness. After traveling three days' journey into the wilderness of Etham, they camped at Marah. {33:8} From Marah, they journeyed to Elim, where there were twelve springs of water and seventy palm trees, and they camped there. {33:9} Leaving Elim, they camped by the Red Sea. {33:10} They moved from the Red Sea and camped in the wilderness of Sin. {33:11} Departing from the wilderness of Sin, they camped in Dophkah. {33:12} Leaving Dophkah, they camped in Alush. {33:13} From Alush, they moved to Rephidim, where there was no water for the people to drink. {33:14} Departing from Rephidim, they camped in the wilderness of Sinai. {33:15} Leaving the wilderness of Sinai, they camped at Kibroth-hattaavah. {33:16} From Kibroth-hattaavah, they moved to Hazeroth. {33:17} Departing from Hazeroth, they camped in Rithmah. {33:18} Leaving Rithmah, they camped in Rimmon-perez. {33:19} From Rimmon-perez, they moved to Libnah. {33:20} Departing from Libnah, they camped in Rissah. {33:21} Leaving Rissah, they camped in Kehelathah. {33:22} From Kehelathah, they moved to Mount Shapher. {33:23} Leaving Mount Shapher, they camped in Haradah. {33:24} From Haradah, they moved to Makheloth. {33:25} Departing from Makheloth, they camped in Tahath. {33:26} Leaving Tahath, they camped in Terah. {33:27} From Terah, they moved to Mithcah. {33:28} Departing from Mithcah, they camped in Hashmonah. {33:29} Leaving Hashmonah, they camped in Moseroth. {33:30} From Moseroth, they moved to Bene-jaakan. {33:31} Departing from Bene-jaakan, they camped at Hor-haggidgad. {33:32} Leaving Hor-haggidgad, they camped in Jotbathah. {33:33} From Jotbathah, they moved to Ebronah. {33:34} Departing from Ebronah, they camped in Ezion-geber. {33:35} Leaving Ezion-geber, they camped in the wilderness of Zin, which is Kadesh. {33:36} From Kadesh, they moved to Mount Hor on the edge of the land of Edom. {33:37} Aaron the priest went up Mount Hor at the LORD's command and died there in the fortieth year after the Israelites had come out of Egypt, on the first day of the fifth month. Aaron was one hundred and twenty-three years old when he died on Mount Hor. {33:38} When the Canaanite king of Arad, who lived in the Negev in the land of Canaan, heard that the Israelites were coming, {33:39} they departed from Mount Hor and camped in Zalmonah. {33:40}

Leaving Zalmonah, they camped in Punon. {33:41} Departing from Punon, they camped in Oboth. {33:42} Leaving Oboth, they camped in Iye-abarim, on the border of Moab. {33:43} From Iim, they moved to Dibon-gad. {33:44} Departing from Dibon-gad, they camped in Almon-diblathaim. {33:45} Leaving Almon-diblathaim, they camped in the mountains of Abarim, near Nebo. {33:46} From the mountains of Abarim, they moved to the plains of Moab by the Jordan, near Jericho. {33:47} They camped by the Jordan, from Beth-jesimoth to Abel-shittim in the plains of Moab. {33:48} While they were in the plains of Moab by the Jordan near Jericho, the LORD spoke to Moses, saying, {33:49} "Speak to the Israelites and tell them: 'When you cross over the Jordan into the land of Canaan, {33:50} you must drive out all the inhabitants of the land before you, destroy all their carved images and cast idols, and demolish all their high places. {33:51} You shall dispossess the inhabitants of the land and settle in it, for I have given you the land to possess. {33:52} You shall divide the land by lot among your families. The larger the family, the more land they shall inherit; the smaller the family, the less land they shall inherit. Each inheritance shall be in the place where the lot falls; you shall inherit according to the tribes of your ancestors. {33:53} But if you do not drive out the inhabitants of the land before you, then those whom you allow to remain will become like thorns in your eyes and barbs in your sides. They will harass you in the land where you live. {33:54} Moreover, I will do to you as I had planned to do to them.'" {33:55} However, if you fail to drive out the inhabitants of the land before you, then those you allow to remain among you will become like thorns in your eyes and irritants in your sides, causing trouble in the land where you reside. {33:56} Furthermore, what I had planned to do to them, I will do to you as well.

{34:1} Then the LORD spoke to Moses, saying, {34:2} "Command the children of Israel, and tell them: 'When you enter the land of Canaan, this is the land that will be your inheritance, the land of Canaan with its borders: {34:3} Your southern boundary will extend from the wilderness of Zin along the eastern side of Edom. The southern border will run along the coast of the Dead Sea to the east. {34:4} From there, your border will turn southward to the ascent of Akrabbim, continue on to Zin, and then run from the south to Kadesh-barnea. It will proceed to Hazar-addar and then to Azmon. {34:5} The border will extend from Azmon to the Brook of Egypt, and its termination will be at the Mediterranean Sea. {34:6} Your western border will be the coastline of the Mediterranean Sea. {34:7} And your northern border will extend from the Mediterranean Sea to Mount Hor. {34:8} from Mount Hor it will extend to the entrance of Hamath, and then the border will reach Zedad. {34:9} From there, the border will proceed to Ziphron, and its termination will be at Hazar-enan. This will be your northern border. {34:10} For your eastern border, you shall draw a line from Hazar-enan to Shepham. {34:11} The boundary will descend from Shepham to Riblah on the east side of Ain, and it will continue downward and reach the eastern shore of the Sea of Galilee. {34:12} From there, the border will descend along the Jordan River until it reaches the Dead Sea. This will be your land, with its surrounding borders. {34:13} Then Moses commanded the children of Israel, saying, "This is the land you will inherit by lot, which the LORD commanded to give to the nine tribes and the half tribe: {34:14} For the tribe of Reuben according to their families, and the tribe of Gad according to their families, have received their inheritance. Also, half of the tribe of Manasseh has received their inheritance. {34:15} The two tribes and the half tribe have received their inheritance on the east side of the Jordan near Jericho, toward the sunrise." {34:16} Then the LORD spoke to Moses, saying, {34:17} "These are the names of the men who will apportion the land for you: Eleazar the priest and Joshua the son of Nun. {34:18} Also, take one leader from each tribe to help divide the land among the Israelites. {34:19} The leaders are as follows: for the tribe of Judah, Caleb the son of Jephunneh; {34:20} for the tribe of Simeon, Shemuel the son of Ammihud; {34:21} for the tribe of Benjamin, Elidad the son of Chislon; {34:22} for the tribe of Dan, Bukki the son of Jogli; {34:23} for the tribe of Manasseh, Hanniel the son of Ephod, representing the descendants of Joseph; {34:24} for the tribe of Ephraim, Kemuel the son of Shiphtan; {34:25} for the tribe of Zebulun, Elizaphan the son of Parnach; {34:26} for the tribe of Issachar, Paltiel the son of Azzan; {34:27} for the tribe of Asher, Ahihud the son of Shelomi; {34:28} for the tribe of Naphtali, Pedahel the son of Ammihud. {34:29} These are the men the LORD commanded to divide the inheritance among the children of Israel in the land of Canaan."

{35:1} And the LORD spoke to Moses in the plains of Moab by the Jordan near Jericho, saying, {35:2} "Command the children of Israel to give cities to the Levites from the inheritance they possess, and also give them suburbs around these cities. {35:3} The Levites shall dwell in these cities, and the suburbs shall be for their livestock, goods, and all their animals. {35:4} The suburbs of the cities given to the Levites shall extend a thousand cubits outward from the city walls all around. {35:5} Beyond the city, measure two thousand cubits to the east, two thousand to the south, two thousand to the west, and two thousand to the north, with the city in the center. These areas shall be the suburbs of the cities. {35:6} Among the cities given to the Levites, six shall be designated as cities of refuge, where the manslayer can flee. Additionally, forty-two cities shall be provided. {35:7} In total, forty-eight cities with their suburbs shall be given to the Levites. {35:8} These cities shall come from the possession of the Israelites. Those with more land shall give more cities, and those with less land shall give fewer. Each shall give cities to the Levites according to their inheritance. {35:9} And the LORD spoke to Moses, saying, {35:10} "Speak to the children of Israel, and when you have crossed over the Jordan into the land of Canaan, {35:11} appoint cities as cities of refuge, where the one who unintentionally kills someone may flee. {35:12} These cities shall serve as a refuge from the avenger, ensuring that the one who accidentally kills another does not die until standing trial before the congregation. {35:13} Six of these cities shall be designated as cities of refuge. {35:14} Three shall be located on the east side of the Jordan and three in the land of Canaan, serving as cities of refuge. {35:15} These six cities shall be a refuge for both the Israelites and foreigners among them, allowing anyone who unintentionally causes death to flee there. {35:16} But if someone kills another with an iron object and intentionally, they are a murderer and must be put to death. {35:17} Likewise, if someone kills another with a stone or a wooden weapon, they are also murderers and must be put to death. {35:18} The avenger of blood shall execute the murderer; when they find them, they shall put them to death. {35:19} However, if the killing was accidental, the congregation shall judge between the slayer and the avenger according to these laws. {35:20} But if the slayer acted with hatred or premeditation, they shall be put to death as a murderer. The avenger of blood shall execute them when they find them. {35:21} Likewise, if the killing was out of enmity, the one who struck the fatal blow shall be put to death; they are a murderer. The avenger of blood shall execute them when they find them. {35:22} However, if the killing was accidental, without enmity, or by throwing something without premeditation, {35:23} or if the killing occurred with a stone that could cause death, but the victim was not the intended target, and there was no prior animosity, {35:24} then the congregation shall judge between the slayer and the avenger according to these laws. {35:25} The congregation shall deliver the slayer from the hand of the avenger and return them to the city of refuge, where they fled. They shall stay there until the death of the high priest, who was anointed with the holy oil. {35:26} But if the slayer leaves the city of refuge and the avenger finds them outside the city borders and kills them, the avenger shall not be guilty of bloodshed. {35:27} This is because the slayer should have remained in the city of refuge until the death of the high priest. After the high priest dies, the slayer may return to their land. {35:28} These laws shall serve as a statute of judgment for generations to come in all your dwellings. {35:29} Whoever kills someone shall be put to death based on the testimony of witnesses. But one witness alone shall not condemn a person to death. {35:30} No ransom shall be accepted for the life of a murderer who is guilty of death; they shall be put to death without exception. {35:31} Nor shall a ransom be accepted for someone who flees to a city of refuge to return and live in their land until the death of the priest. {35:32} You shall not pollute the land where you dwell, for bloodshed defiles the land. The only way to cleanse the land of shed blood is by shedding the blood of the one who shed it. {35:33} **Therefore, do not defile the land where I dwell, for I,** {35:34} the LORD, dwell among the children of Israel."

{36:1} The chief fathers of the families of the children of Gilead, the son of Machir, the son of Manasseh, from the families of the sons of Joseph, came forward and spoke before Moses, the princes, and the chief fathers of Israel. {36:2} They said, "The LORD commanded our lord to give the land as an inheritance by lot to the children of Israel. And our lord was commanded by the LORD to give the inheritance of Zelophehad our brother to his daughters. {36:3} But if these daughters marry men from other tribes of Israel, then their inheritance will be transferred from our fathers' tribe to the tribe into which they marry. Thus, it will be taken from the lot of our inheritance. {36:4} And when the jubilee of the children of Israel comes, their inheritance will be added to the inheritance of the tribe into which they marry. Thus, their inheritance will be taken away from the inheritance of our fathers' tribe. {36:5} Moses commanded the children of Israel according to the word of the LORD, saying, 'The tribe of the sons of Joseph has spoken well. {36:6} This is what the LORD commands concerning the daughters of Zelophehad: They may marry whomever they wish, but they must marry within the family of the tribe of their father. {36:7} This way, the inheritance of the children of Israel will not shift from tribe to tribe. Each Israelite shall hold onto the inheritance of their fathers' tribe. {36:8} Every daughter who inherits land in any tribe of the children of Israel must marry someone from the family of her father's tribe. This ensures that each man of Israel may enjoy his fathers' inheritance. {36:9} The inheritance shall not move from one tribe to another; each tribe of the children of Israel must hold onto its own inheritance. {36:10} Just as the LORD commanded Moses, so the daughters of Zelophehad did. {36:11} Mahlah, Tirzah, Hoglah, Milcah, and Noah, the daughters of Zelophehad, married their father's brothers' sons. {36:12} They married into the families of the sons of Manasseh, the son of Joseph, and their inheritance remained in the tribe of their father's family. {36:13} These are the commandments and judgments that the LORD commanded through Moses to the children of Israel in the plains of Moab by the Jordan near Jericho."

Deuteronomy

{1:1} These are the words that Moses spoke to all the Israelites on the east side of the Jordan River, in the wilderness, in the Arabah, opposite Suph, between Paran and Tophel, Laban, Hazeroth, and Dizahab. {1:2} It is an eleven-day journey from Horeb to Kadesh-barnea by way of Mount Seir. {1:3} In the fortieth year, on the first day of the eleventh month, Moses spoke to the people of Israel according to all that the LORD had given him in commandment to them, {1:4} after he had defeated Sihon the king of the Amorites, who lived in Heshbon, and Og the king of Bashan, who lived in Ashtaroth and in Edrei. {1:5} Beyond the Jordan, in the land of Moab, Moses undertook to explain this law, saying, {1:6} "The LORD our God said to us in Horeb, 'You have stayed long enough at this mountain. {1:7} Turn and take your journey, and go to the hill country of the Amorites and to all their neighbors in the Arabah, in the hill country and in the lowland and in the Negeb and by the seacoast, the land of the Canaanites, and Lebanon, as far as the great river, the river Euphrates. {1:8} Behold, I have set the land before you. Go in and take possession of the land that the LORD swore to your fathers, to Abraham, to Isaac, and to Jacob, to give to them and to their offspring after them.' {1:9} "At that time I said to you, 'I am not able to bear you by myself. {1:10} The LORD your God has multiplied you, and behold, you are today as numerous as the stars of heaven. {1:11} May the LORD, the God of your fathers, make you a thousand times as many as you are and bless you, as he has promised you! {1:12} How can I bear by myself the weight and burden of you and your strife? {1:13} Choose for your tribes wise, understanding, and experienced men, and I will appoint them as your heads.' {1:14} And you answered me, 'The thing that you have spoken is good for us to do.' {1:15} So I took the heads of your tribes, wise and experienced men, and set them as heads over you, commanders of thousands, commanders of hundreds, commanders of fifties, commanders of tens, and officers, throughout your tribes. {1:16} And I charged your judges at that time, 'Hear the cases between your brothers, and judge righteously between a man and his brother or the alien who is with him. {1:17} You shall not be partial in judgment. You shall hear the small and the great alike. You shall not be intimidated by anyone, for the judgment is God's. And the case that is too hard for you, you shall bring to me, and I will hear it.' {1:18} And I commanded you at that time all the things that you should do. {1:19} "Then we set out from Horeb and went through all that great and terrifying wilderness that you saw, on the way to the hill country of the Amorites, as the LORD our God commanded us. And we came to Kadesh-barnea. {1:20} And I said to you, 'You have come to the hill country of the Amorites, which the LORD our God is giving us. {1:21} See, the LORD your God has set the land before you. Go up, take possession, as the LORD, the God of your fathers, has told you. Do not fear or be dismayed.' {1:22} Then all of you came near me and said, 'Let us send men before us, that they may explore the land for us and bring us word again of the way by which we must go up and the cities into which we shall come.' {1:23} The thing seemed good to me, and I took twelve men from you, one man from each tribe. {1:24} And they turned and went up into the hill country, and came to the Valley of Eshcol and spied it out. {1:25} And they took in their hands some of the fruit of the land and brought it down to us, and brought us word again and said, 'It is a good land that the LORD our God is giving us.' {1:26} "Yet you would not go up, but rebelled against the command of the LORD your God. {1:27} And you murmured in your tents and said, 'Because the LORD hated us he has brought us out of the land of Egypt, to give us into the hand of the Amorites, to destroy us. {1:28} Where are we going up? Our brothers have made our hearts melt, saying, "The people are greater and taller than we. The cities are great and fortified up to heaven. And besides, we have seen the sons of the Anakim there."' {1:29} Then I said to you, 'Do not be in dread or afraid of them. {1:30} The LORD your God who goes before you will himself fight for you, just as he did for you in Egypt before your eyes, {1:31} and in the wilderness, where you have seen how the LORD your God carried you, as a man carries his son, all the way that you went until you came to this place.' {1:32} Yet in spite of this word you did not believe the LORD your God, {1:33} who went before you in the way to seek you out a place to pitch your tents, in fire by night and in the cloud by day, to show you by what way you should go. {1:34} "And the LORD heard your words and was angered, and he swore, {1:35} 'Not one of these men of this evil generation shall see the good land that I swore to give to your fathers, {1:36} except Caleb the son of Jephunneh. He shall see it, and to him and to his children I will give the land on which he has trodden, because he has wholly followed the LORD!' {1:37} Even with me the LORD was angry on your account and said, 'You also shall not go in there. {1:38} Joshua the son of Nun, who stands before you, he shall enter. Encourage him, for he shall cause Israel to inherit it. {1:39} And as for your little ones, who you said would become a prey, and your children, who today have no knowledge of good or evil, they shall go in there. And to them I will give it, and they shall possess it. {1:40} But as for you, turn, and journey into the wilderness in the direction of the Red Sea.' { {1:41} Then you responded, saying, "We have sinned against the LORD. We will go up and fight, just as the LORD our God has commanded us." So each of you strapped on your weapons, ready to go up into the hill. {1:42} But the LORD said to me, "Tell them, 'Do not go up and do not fight, for I am not with you, or you will be defeated before your enemies.'" {1:43} So I spoke to you, but you would not listen. You rebelled against the command of the LORD and arrogantly went up into the hill. {1:44} Then the Amorites who lived in that hill country came out against you like bees and chased you, and beat you down in Seir as far as Hormah. {1:45} And you returned and wept before the LORD, but the LORD did not listen to your cries or pay attention to you. {1:46} So you remained in Kadesh for a long time, according to the days that you spent there.

{2:1} So we turned and journeyed into the wilderness by the way of the Red Sea, as the LORD had commanded me. And we traveled around the hill country of Seir for many days. {2:2} Then the LORD spoke to me, saying, {2:3} "You have circled this mountain long enough. Turn northward, {2:4} and command the people, saying, 'You are about to pass through the territory of your brothers, the descendants of Esau, who live in Seir. They will be afraid of you, so be very careful. {2:5} Do not provoke them, for I will not give you any of their land, not even a footstep, because I have given Esau the hill country of Seir as his possession. {2:6} You shall purchase food from them for money, so that you may eat, and you shall also buy water from them for money, so that you may drink. {2:7} For the LORD your God has blessed you in all the work of your hands. He knows your going through this great wilderness. These forty years the LORD your God has been with you. You have lacked nothing.' {2:8} So we passed by our brothers, the descendants of Esau who live in Seir, away from the Arabah road, away from Elath and Ezion-geber. And we turned and passed through the wilderness of Moab. {2:9} Then the LORD said to me, "Do not harass Moab or contend with them in battle, for I will not give you any of their land for a possession, because I have given Ar to the descendants of Lot as a possession." {2:10} (The Emim formerly lived there, a people great and many, and tall as the Anakim. {2:11} Like the Anakim they are also counted as Rephaim, but the Moabites call them Emim. {2:12} The Horites also lived in Seir formerly, but the descendants of Esau dispossessed them and destroyed them from before them and settled in their place, as Israel did to the land of their possession, which the LORD gave to them.) {2:13} 'Now rise up and go over the brook Zered.' So we went over the brook Zered. {2:14} The time from our leaving Kadesh-barnea until we crossed the brook Zered was thirty-eight years, until the entire generation, that is, the men of war, had perished from the camp, as the LORD had sworn to them. {2:15} For indeed the hand of the LORD was against them, to destroy them from the midst of the camp until they were consumed. {2:16} So as soon as all the men of war had perished and were dead from among the people, {2:17} the LORD said to me, {2:18} "Today you are to cross the border of Moab at Ar. {2:19} And when you approach the territory of the people of Ammon, do not harass them or contend with them, for I will not give you any of the land of the people of Ammon as a possession, because I have given it to the sons of Lot for a possession." {2:20} (It is also counted as a land of Rephaim. Rephaim formerly lived there—but the Ammonites call them Zamzummim— {2:21} a people great and many, and tall as the Anakim; but the LORD destroyed them before the Ammonites, and they dispossessed them and settled in their place, {2:22} as he did for the descendants of Esau, who live in Seir, when he destroyed the Horites before them and they dispossessed them and settled in their place even to this day. {2:23} As for the Avvim, who lived in villages as far as Gaza, the Caphtorim, who came from Caphtor, destroyed them and settled in their place.) {2:24} 'Rise up, set out on your journey and go over the Valley of the Arnon. Behold, I have given into your hand Sihon the Amorite, king of Heshbon, and his land. Begin to take possession, and contend with him in battle.' {2:25} This day I will begin to put the dread and fear of you on the peoples who are under the whole heaven, who shall hear the report of you and shall tremble and be in anguish because of you. {2:26} So I sent messengers from the wilderness of Kedemoth to Sihon the king of Heshbon, with words of peace, saying, {2:27} "Let me pass through your land. I will go only by the road; I will turn aside neither to the right nor to the left. {2:28} You shall sell me food for money, that I may eat, and give me water for money, that I may drink. Only let me pass through on foot, {2:29} as the sons of Esau who live in Seir and the Moabites who live in Ar did for me, until I go over the Jordan into the land that the LORD our God is giving to us." {2:30} But Sihon the king of Heshbon would not let us pass by him, for the LORD your God hardened his spirit and made his heart obstinate, that he might give him into your hand, as he is this day. {2:31} And the LORD said to me, 'Behold, I have begun to give Sihon and his land over to you. Begin to take possession, that you may occupy his land.' {2:32} Then Sihon came out against us, he and all his people, to battle at Jahaz. {2:33} And the LORD our God gave him over to us, and we defeated him and his sons and all his people. {2:34} And we captured all his cities at that time and devoted to destruction every city, men, women, and children. We left no survivors. {2:35} Only the livestock we took as spoil for ourselves, with the plunder of the cities that we captured. {2:36} From Aroer, which is on the edge of the Valley of the Arnon, and from the city that is in the valley, as far as Gilead, there was not a city too high for us. The LORD our God gave all into our hands. {2:37} Only to the land of the sons of Ammon you did not draw near, that is, to all the banks of the river Jabbok and the cities of the hill country, whatever the LORD our God had forbidden us.

{3:1} Then we turned and went up the way to Bashan, and Og the king of Bashan came out against us, he and all his people, to battle at Edrei. {3:2} But the LORD said to me, "Do not fear him, for I will deliver him and all his people and his land into your hand. You shall do to him as you did to Sihon king of the Amorites, who dwelt at Heshbon." {3:3} So the LORD our God delivered Og, the king of Bashan, and all his people into our hands, and we defeated them until none were left alive. {3:4} We took all his cities at that time; there was not a city which we did not take from them: sixty cities, all the region of Argob, the kingdom of Og in Bashan. {3:5} All these cities were fortified with high walls, gates, and bars; besides many unwalled towns. {3:6} We completely destroyed them, just as we did to Sihon king of Heshbon, utterly destroying every man, woman, and child in every city. {3:7} However, we took all the livestock and plundered the cities for ourselves. {3:8} And at that time, we took the land from the hand of the two kings of the Amorites, which was on this side of the Jordan, from the River Arnon to Mount Hermon. {3:9} (Hermon the Sidonians call Sirion, and the Amorites call it Senir.) {3:10} All the cities of the plain, all of Gilead, and all of Bashan, as far as Salecah and Edrei, cities of the kingdom of Og in Bashan. {3:11} For only Og king of Bashan remained of the remnant of the giants. Indeed, his bedstead was an iron bedstead. Is it not in Rabbah of the people of Ammon? Nine cubits was its length and four cubits its width, according to the standard cubit. {3:12} And this land, which we possessed at that time, from Aroer, which is by the River Arnon, and half the mountains of Gilead and its cities, I gave to the Reubenites and the Gadites. {3:13} The rest of Gilead and all Bashan, the kingdom of Og, I gave to the half-tribe of Manasseh, all the region of Argob, with all Bashan, called the land of the giants. {3:14} Jair the son of Manasseh took all the region of Argob, as far as the border of the Geshurites and the Maachathites, and called Bashan after his own name, Havoth Jair, to this day. {3:15} And I gave Gilead to Machir. {3:16} And to the Reubenites and the Gadites, I gave from Gilead as far as the River Arnon, including the middle of the valley and the territory as far as the River Jabbok, the border of the people of Ammon, {3:17} as well as the plain also, with the Jordan as the border, from Chinnereth as far as the east side of the Sea of the Arabah (the Salt Sea), below the slopes of Pisgah on the east. {3:18} And I commanded you at that time, saying, "The LORD your God has given you this land to possess. All you men fit for war shall cross over armed before your brethren, the children of Israel. {3:19} However, your wives, your little ones, and your livestock (I know that you have much livestock) shall stay in your cities which I have given you, {3:20} until the LORD has given rest to your brethren as to you, and they also possess the land which the LORD your God is giving them beyond the Jordan. Then each of you may return to his possession which I have given you." {3:21} And I commanded Joshua at that time, saying, "Your eyes have seen all that the LORD your God has done to these two kings; so will the LORD do to all the kingdoms through which you pass. {3:22} You must not fear them, for the LORD your God Himself fights for you." {3:23} And I pleaded with the LORD at that time, saying, {3:24} "O Lord GOD, You have begun to show Your servant Your greatness and Your mighty hand, for what god is there in heaven or on earth who can do anything like Your works and Your mighty deeds? {3:25} I pray, let me cross over and see the good land beyond the Jordan, those pleasant mountains, and Lebanon." {3:26} But the LORD was angry with me on your account and would not listen to me. So the LORD said to me, "Enough of that! Speak no more to Me of this matter. {3:27} Go up to the top of Pisgah and lift your eyes toward the west, the north, the south, and the east; behold it with your eyes, for you shall not cross over this Jordan. {3:28} But command Joshua and encourage him and strengthen him; for he shall go over before this people, and he shall cause them to inherit the land which you will see." {3:29} So we stayed in the valley opposite Beth Peor.

{4:1} Now therefore, listen, O Israel, to the statutes and judgments which I teach you to observe, so that you may live and go in to possess the land which the LORD God of your fathers is giving you. {4:2} You shall not add to the word which I command you, nor take away from it, that you may keep the commandments of the LORD your God which I command you. {4:3} Your eyes have seen what the LORD did because of Baal-peor; for all the men who followed Baal-peor, the LORD your God has destroyed them from among you. {4:4} But you who held fast to the LORD your God are alive, every one of you, today. {4:5} Behold, I have taught you statutes and judgments, just as the LORD my God commanded me, that you should act according to them in the land which you go to possess. {4:6} Therefore be careful to observe them; for this is your wisdom and your understanding in the sight of the nations, who will hear all these statutes, and say, "Surely this great nation is a wise and understanding people." {4:7} For what great nation is there that has God so near to it, as the LORD our God is to us, for whatever reason we may call upon Him? {4:8} And what great nation is there that has such statutes and righteous judgments as are in all this law which I set before you this day? {4:9} Only take heed to yourself, and diligently keep yourself, lest you forget the things your eyes have seen, and lest they depart from your heart all the days of your life. And teach them to your children and your grandchildren, {4:10} especially concerning the day you stood before the LORD your God in Horeb, when the LORD said to me, "Gather the people to Me, and I will let them hear My words, that they may learn to fear Me all the days they live on the earth, and that they may teach their children." {4:11} Then you came near and stood at the foot of the mountain, and the mountain burned with fire to the midst of heaven, with darkness, cloud, and thick darkness. {4:12} And the LORD spoke to you out of the midst of the fire. You heard the sound of the words, but saw no form; you only heard a voice. {4:13} So He declared to you His covenant which He commanded you to perform, the Ten Commandments; and He wrote them on two tablets of stone. {4:14} And the LORD commanded me at that time to teach you statutes and judgments, that you might observe them in the land which you cross over to possess. {4:15} Take careful heed to yourselves, for you saw no form when the LORD spoke to you at Horeb out of the midst of the fire, {4:16} lest you act corruptly and make for yourselves a carved image in the form of any figure: the likeness of male or female, {4:17} the likeness of any animal that is on the earth or the likeness of any winged bird that flies in the air, {4:18} the likeness of anything that creeps on the ground or the likeness of any fish that is in the water beneath the earth. {4:19} And take heed, lest you lift your eyes to heaven, and when you see the sun, the moon, and the stars, all the host of heaven, you feel driven to worship them and serve them, which the LORD your God has given to all the peoples under the whole heaven as a heritage. {4:20} But the LORD has taken you and brought you out of the iron furnace, out of Egypt, to be His people, an inheritance, as you are this day. {4:21} Furthermore the LORD was angry with me for your sakes, and swore that I would not cross over the Jordan, and that I would not enter the good land which the LORD your God is giving you as an inheritance. {4:22} But I must die in this land; I must not cross over the Jordan; but you shall cross over and possess that good land. {4:23} Take heed to yourselves, lest you forget the covenant of the LORD your God which He made with you, and make for yourselves a carved image in the form of anything which the LORD your God has forbidden you. {4:24} For the LORD your God is a consuming fire, a jealous God. {4:25} When you beget children and grandchildren and have grown old in the land, and act corruptly and make a carved image in the form of anything, and do evil in the sight of the LORD your God to provoke Him to anger, {4:26} I call heaven and earth to witness against you this day, that you will soon utterly perish from the land which you cross over the Jordan to possess; you will not prolong your days in it, but will be utterly destroyed. {4:27} And the LORD will scatter you among the peoples, and you will be left few in number among the nations where the LORD will drive you. {4:28} And there you will serve gods, the work of men's hands, wood and stone, which neither see nor hear nor eat nor smell. {4:29} **But from there you will seek the LORD your God, and you will find Him if you seek Him with all your heart and with all your soul.** {4:30} When you are in distress, and all these things come upon you in the latter days, when you turn to the LORD your God and obey His voice {4:31} (for the LORD your God is a merciful God), He will not forsake you nor destroy you, nor forget the covenant of your fathers which He swore to them. {4:32} For ask now concerning the days that are past, which were before you, since the day that God created man on the earth, and ask from one end of heaven to the other, whether any great thing like this has happened, or anything like it has been heard. {4:33} Did any people ever hear the voice of God speaking out of the midst of the fire, as you have heard, and live? {4:34} Or did God ever try to go and take for Himself a nation from the midst of another nation, by trials, by signs, by wonders, by war, by a mighty hand and an outstretched arm, and by great terrors, according to all that the LORD your God did for you in Egypt before your eyes? {4:35} To you it was shown, that you might know that the LORD Himself is God; there is none other besides Him. {4:36} Out of heaven He let you hear His voice, that He might instruct you; on earth He showed you His great fire, and you heard His words out of the midst of the fire. {4:37} And because He loved your fathers, therefore He chose their descendants after them; and He brought you out of Egypt with His Presence, with His mighty power, {4:38} driving out from before you nations greater and mightier than you, to bring you in, to give you their land as an inheritance, {4:39} Know therefore this day, and consider it in your heart, that the LORD He is God in heaven above and on the earth beneath; there is none else. {4:40} Therefore, keep His statutes and His commandments, which I command you today, that it may go well with you and with your children after you, and that you may prolong your days on the earth which the LORD your God gives you forever. {4:41} Then Moses set apart three cities on this side of the Jordan, toward the sunrise, {4:42} that the manslayer might flee there, who kills his neighbor unintentionally, without having hated him in time past, and that by fleeing to one of these cities he might live: {4:43} Bezer in the wilderness on the plateau for the Reubenites, Ramoth in Gilead for the Gadites, and Golan in Bashan for the Manassites. {4:44} Now this is the law which Moses set before the children of Israel. {4:45} These are the testimonies, the statutes, and the judgments which Moses spoke to the children of Israel after they came out of Egypt, {4:46} on this side of the Jordan in the valley opposite Beth Peor, in the land of Sihon king of the Amorites, who dwelt at Heshbon, whom Moses and the children of Israel defeated after they came out of Egypt. {4:47} And they took possession of his land and the land of Og king of Bashan, two kings of the Amorites, who were on this side of the Jordan, toward the sunrise, {4:48} from Aroer, which is on the bank of the River Arnon, even to Mount Sion (that is, Hermon), {4:49} and all the plain on this side of the Jordan eastward, even to the Sea of the Arabah, below the slopes of Pisgah.

{5:1} Moses gathered all Israel and said to them, "Listen, Israel, to the statutes and judgments which I speak to you today. Learn them, keep them, and do them. {5:2} The LORD our God made a covenant with us at Horeb. {5:3} He did not make this covenant with our fathers, but with us, all of us who are alive here today. {5:4} The LORD spoke with you face to face on the mountain out of the midst of the fire. {5:5} I stood between the LORD and you at that time, to convey the word of the LORD to you, for you were afraid because of the fire and did not go up to the mountain, saying, {5:6} 'I am the LORD your God, who brought you out of the land of Egypt, out of the house of bondage. {5:7} You shall have no other gods before Me. {5:8} You shall not make for yourself a carved image, or any likeness of anything that is in heaven above, or that is in the earth beneath, or that is in the water under the earth; {5:9} you shall not bow down to them nor serve them. For I, the LORD your God, am a jealous God, visiting the iniquity of the fathers upon the children to the third and fourth generations of those who hate Me, {5:10} but showing mercy to thousands, to those who love Me and keep My commandments. {5:11} You shall not take the name of the LORD your God in vain, for the LORD will not hold him guiltless who takes His name in vain. {5:12} Observe the Sabbath day, to keep it holy, as the LORD your God commanded you. {5:13} Six days you shall labor and do all your work, {5:14} but the seventh day is the Sabbath of the LORD your God. In it you shall do no work: you, nor your son, nor your daughter, nor your male servant, nor your female servant, nor your ox, nor your donkey, nor any of your cattle, nor your stranger who is within your gates, that your male servant and your female servant may rest as well as you. {5:15} And remember that you were a slave in the land of Egypt, and the LORD your God brought you out from there by a mighty hand and by an outstretched arm; therefore the LORD your God commanded you to keep the Sabbath day. {5:16} Honor your father and your mother, as the LORD your God has commanded you, that your days may be long, and that it may be well with you in the land which the LORD your God is giving you. {5:17} You shall not murder. {5:18} You shall not commit adultery. {5:19} You shall not steal. {5:20} You shall not bear false witness against your neighbor. {5:21} You shall not covet your neighbor's wife; and you shall not desire your neighbor's house, his field, his male servant, his female servant, his ox, his donkey, or anything that is your neighbor's.' {5:22} These words the LORD spoke to all your assembly, in the mountain from the midst of the fire, the cloud, and the thick darkness, with a loud voice; and He added no more. And He wrote them on two tablets of stone and gave them to me. {5:23} So it was, when you heard the voice from the midst of the darkness, while the mountain was burning with fire, that you came near to me, all the heads of your tribes and your elders. {5:24} And you said: 'Surely the LORD our God has shown us His glory and His greatness, and we have heard His voice from the midst of the fire. Today we have seen that God speaks with man; yet he still lives. {5:25} Now therefore, why should we die? For this great fire will consume us; if we hear the voice of the LORD our God anymore, then we shall die. {5:26} For who is there of all flesh who has heard the voice of the living God speaking from the midst of the fire, as we have, and lived? {5:27} You go near and hear all that the LORD our God may say, and tell us all that the LORD our God says to you, and we will hear and do it.' {5:28} "Then the LORD heard the voice of your words when you spoke to me, and the LORD said to me: 'I have heard the voice of the words of this people which they have spoken to you. They are right in all that they have spoken. {5:29} Oh, that they had such a heart in them that they would fear Me and always keep all My commandments, that it might be well with them and with their children forever! {5:30} Go and say to them, "Return to your tents." {5:31} But as for you, stand here by Me, and I will speak to you all the commandments, the statutes, and the judgments which you shall teach them, that they may observe them in the land which I am giving them to possess.' {5:32} "Therefore you shall be careful to do as the LORD your God has commanded you; you shall not turn aside to the right hand or to the left. {5:33} You shall walk in all the ways which the LORD your God has commanded you, that you may live and that it may be well with you, and that you may prolong your days in the land which you shall possess.

{6:1} These are the commandments, statutes, and judgments which the LORD your God commanded to teach you, that you might do them in the land where you go to possess it: {6:2} so that you might fear the LORD your God, to keep all His statutes and His commandments which I command you, you, and your son, and your son's son, all the days of your life, and that your days may be prolonged. {6:3} Therefore, listen, Israel, and be careful to observe it, so that it may be well with you, and that you may multiply greatly, as the LORD God of your fathers has promised you, in the land flowing with milk and honey. {6:4} **Hear, Israel: the LORD our God is one LORD.** {6:5} **And you shall love the LORD your God with all your heart, with all your soul, and with all your might.** {6:6} And these words, which I command you today, shall be in your heart. {6:7} You shall teach them diligently to your children, and shall talk of them when you sit in your house, and when you walk by the way, and when you lie down, and when you rise up. {6:8} You shall bind them for a sign on your hand, and they shall be as frontlets between your eyes. {6:9} You shall write them on the doorposts of your house and on your gates. {6:10} And it shall be, when the LORD your God brings you into the land which He swore to your fathers, to Abraham, Isaac, and Jacob, to give you great and beautiful cities which you did not build, {6:11} houses full of all good things, which you did not fill, wells dug which you did not dig, vineyards and olive trees which you did not plant, when you have eaten and are full; {6:12} then beware lest you forget the LORD who brought you out of the land of Egypt, from the house of bondage. {6:13} You shall fear the LORD your God, and serve Him, and shall take oaths in His name. {6:14} You shall not go after other gods, the gods of the peoples who are all around you; {6:15} for the LORD your God is a jealous God among you, lest the anger of the LORD your God be aroused against you and destroy you from the face of the earth. {6:16} You shall not tempt the LORD your God as you tempted Him in Massah. {6:17} You shall diligently keep the commandments of the LORD your God, His testimonies, and His statutes which He has commanded you. {6:18} And you shall do what is right and good in the sight of the LORD, that it may be well with you, and that you may go in and possess the good land which the LORD swore to your fathers, {6:19} to cast out all your enemies from before you, as the LORD has spoken. {6:20} And when your son asks you in time to come, saying, "What do the testimonies, the statutes, and the judgments mean which the LORD our God has commanded you?" {6:21} then you shall say to your son, "We were slaves of Pharaoh in Egypt, and the LORD brought us out of Egypt with a mighty hand; {6:22} and the LORD showed signs and wonders, great and severe, against Egypt, Pharaoh, and all his household, before our eyes. {6:23} He brought us out from there to bring us in, to give us the land of which He swore to our fathers. {6:24} And the LORD commanded us to observe all these statutes, to fear the LORD our God, for our good always, that He might preserve us alive, as it is this day. {6:25} Then it will be righteousness for us, if we are careful to observe all these commandments before the LORD our God, as He has commanded us."

{7:1} When the LORD your God brings you into the land which you go to possess, and has cast out many nations before you, the Hittites, the Girgashites, the Amorites, the Canaanites, the Perizzites, the Hivites, and the Jebusites, seven nations greater and mightier than you, {7:2} and when the LORD your God delivers them over to you, you shall conquer them and utterly destroy them; you shall make no covenant with them, nor show mercy to them. {7:3} Nor shall you make marriages with them: you shall not give your daughter to their son, nor take their daughter for your son. {7:4} For they will turn your sons away from following Me, to serve other gods; so the anger of the LORD will be aroused against you and destroy you suddenly. {7:5} But thus you shall deal with them: you shall destroy their altars, break down their sacred pillars, cut down their wooden images, and burn their carved images with fire. {7:6} For you are a holy people to the LORD your God; the LORD your God has chosen you to be a special people to Himself, above all people who are on the face of the earth. {7:7} The LORD did not set His love on you nor choose you because you were more in number than any other people, for you were the least of all peoples; {7:8} but because the LORD loves you, and because He would keep the oath which He swore to your fathers, the LORD has brought you out with a mighty hand, and redeemed you from the house of bondage, from the hand of Pharaoh king of Egypt. {7:9} Therefore know that the LORD your God, He is God, the faithful God who keeps covenant and mercy for a thousand generations with those who love Him and keep His commandments; {7:10} and He repays those who hate Him to their face, to destroy them. He will not be slack with him who hates Him; He will repay him to his face. {7:11} Therefore you shall keep the commandments, the statutes, and the judgments which I command you today, to observe them. {7:12} Then it shall come to pass, because you listen to these judgments, and keep and do them, that the LORD your God will keep with you the covenant and the mercy which He swore to your fathers. {7:13} And He will love you and bless you and multiply you; He will also bless the fruit of your womb and the fruit of your land, your grain and your new wine and your oil, the increase of your cattle and the offspring of your flock, in the land of which He swore to your fathers to give you. {7:14} You shall be blessed above all peoples; there shall not be a male or female barren among you or among your livestock. {7:15} And the LORD will take away from you all sickness, and will afflict you with none of the terrible diseases of Egypt which you have known, but will lay them on all those who hate you. {7:16} Also you shall destroy all the peoples whom the LORD your God delivers over to you; your eye shall have no pity on them; nor shall you serve their gods, for that will be a snare to you. {7:17} If you should say in your heart, 'These nations are greater than I; how can I dispossess them?'— {7:18} you shall not be afraid of them, but you shall remember well what the LORD your God did to Pharaoh and to all Egypt: {7:19} the great trials which your eyes saw, the signs and the wonders, the mighty hand and the outstretched arm, by which the LORD your God brought you out. So shall the LORD your God do to all the peoples of whom you are afraid. {7:20} Moreover the LORD your God will send the hornet among them until those who are left, who hide themselves from you, are destroyed. {7:21} You shall not be terrified of them; for the LORD your God, the great and awesome God, is among you. {7:22} And the LORD your God will drive out those nations before you little by little; you will be unable to destroy them at once, lest the beasts of the field become too numerous for you. {7:23} But the LORD your God will deliver them over to you, and will inflict defeat upon them until they are destroyed. {7:24} And He will deliver their kings into your hand, and you will destroy their name from under heaven; no one shall be able to stand against you until you have destroyed them. {7:25} You shall burn the carved images of their gods with fire; you shall not covet the silver or gold that is on them, nor take it for yourselves, lest you be snared by it; for it is an abomination to the LORD your God. {7:26} Nor shall you bring an abomination into your house, lest you be doomed to destruction like it. You shall utterly detest it and utterly abhor it, for it is an accursed thing.

{8:1} All the commandments which I command you this day you shall observe to do, that you may live, and multiply, and go in and possess the land which the LORD swore to your fathers. {8:2} And you shall remember all the way which the LORD your God led you these forty years in the wilderness, to humble you, and to test you, to know what was in your heart, whether you would keep His commandments or not. {8:3} **And He humbled you, and allowed you to hunger, and fed you with manna, which you did not know, neither did your fathers know; that He might make you know that man does not live by bread alone, but by every word that proceeds out of the mouth of the LORD does man live.** {8:4} Your clothing did not wear out upon you, nor did your feet swell, these forty years. {8:5} You shall also consider in your heart that, as a man disciplines his son, so the LORD your God disciplines you. {8:6} Therefore you shall keep the commandments of the LORD your God, to walk in His ways, and to fear Him. {8:7} For the LORD your God brings you into a good land, a land of brooks of water, of fountains and depths that spring out of valleys and hills; {8:8} a land of wheat, barley, vines, fig trees, and pomegranates; a land of olive oil and honey; {8:9} a land where you shall eat bread without scarcity, you shall lack nothing in it; a land whose stones are iron, and out of whose hills you may dig brass. {8:10} When you have eaten and are full, then you shall bless the LORD your God for the good land which He has given you. {8:11} Beware that you do not forget the LORD your God, in not keeping His commandments, His judgments, and His statutes, which I command you this day: {8:12} lest when you have eaten and are full, and have built beautiful houses and dwell in them; {8:13} and when your herds and your flocks multiply, and your silver and gold is multiplied, and all that you have is multiplied; {8:14} then your heart be lifted up, and you forget the LORD your God, who brought you out of the land of Egypt, from the house of bondage; {8:15} who led you through that great and terrible wilderness, where there were fiery serpents, scorpions, and drought, where there was no water; who brought water for you out of the rock of flint; {8:16} who fed you in the wilderness with manna, which your fathers did not know, that He might humble you and that He might test you, to do you good at your latter end; {8:17} and you say in your heart, 'My power and the might of my hand have gained me this wealth.' {8:18} But you shall remember the LORD your God, for it is He who gives you power to get wealth, that He may establish His covenant which He swore to your fathers, as it is this day. {8:19} And it shall be, if you do at all forget the LORD your God, and walk after other gods, and serve them, and worship them, I testify against you this day that you shall surely perish. {8:20} As the nations which the LORD destroys before your face, so you shall perish, because you would not be obedient to the voice of the LORD your God.

{9:1} Listen, Israel: Today you are to pass over the Jordan to go in and possess nations greater and mightier than yourself, with great and fortified cities reaching up to the sky. {9:2} They are a people great and tall, the descendants of the Anakim, whom you know and have heard about, saying, "Who can stand before the descendants of Anak?" {9:3} Therefore, understand this day that the LORD your God is the one who goes over before you; as a consuming fire, He will destroy them and bring them down before your face; so you shall drive them out and destroy them quickly, as the LORD has said to you. {9:4} Do not think in your heart after the LORD your God has cast them out from before you, saying, "Because of my righteousness the LORD has brought me in to possess this land;" but it is because of the wickedness of these nations that the LORD is driving them out from before you. {9:5} It is not because of your righteousness or the uprightness of your heart that you go to possess their land, but because of the wickedness of these nations that the LORD your God drives them out from before you, and to fulfill the word which the LORD swore to your fathers, Abraham, Isaac, and Jacob. {9:6} Understand, therefore, that the LORD your God is not giving you this good land to possess it because of your righteousness; for you are a stiff-necked people. {9:7} Remember and do not forget how you provoked the LORD your God to wrath in the wilderness: from the day that you departed from the land of Egypt until you came to this place, you have been rebellious against the LORD. {9:8} Also, at Horeb, you provoked the LORD to wrath, so that the LORD was angry with you to have destroyed you. {9:9} When I went up into the mountain to receive the tablets of stone, the tablets of the covenant which the LORD made with you, then I stayed in the mountain forty days and forty nights; I neither ate bread nor drank water. {9:10} And the LORD gave me two tablets of stone written with the finger of God; and on them were written according to all the words which the LORD spoke with you on the mountain out of the midst of the fire in the day of the assembly. {9:11} And it came to pass at the end of forty days and forty nights that the LORD gave me the two tablets of stone, the tablets of the covenant. {9:12} And the LORD said to me, "Arise, get down quickly from here; for your people whom you brought out of Egypt have acted corruptly; they have turned aside quickly out of the way which I commanded them; they have made themselves a molded image." {9:13} Furthermore, the LORD spoke to me, saying, "I have seen this people, and indeed they are a stiff-necked people. {9:14} Let Me alone, that I may destroy them and blot out their name from under heaven; and I will make of you a nation mightier and greater than they." {9:15} So I turned and came down from the mountain, and the mountain burned with fire; and the two tablets of the covenant were in my two hands. {9:16} And I looked, and behold, you had sinned against the LORD your God—had made for yourselves a molded calf! You had turned aside quickly out of the way which the LORD had commanded you. {9:17} Then I took the two tablets and threw them out of my two hands and broke them before your eyes. {9:18} And I fell down before the LORD, as at the first, forty days and forty nights; I neither ate bread nor drank water because of all your sin which you committed in doing wickedly in the sight of the LORD, to provoke Him to anger. {9:19} For I was afraid of the anger and hot displeasure with which the LORD was angry with you, to destroy you. But the LORD listened to me at that time also. {9:20} And the LORD was very angry with Aaron, to have destroyed him; so I prayed for Aaron also at the same time. {9:21} Then I took your sin, the calf which you had made, and burned it with fire and crushed it, grinding it very small, until it was as fine as dust; and I threw its dust into the brook that descended from the mountain. {9:22} Also at Taberah, Massah, and Kibroth Hattaavah, you provoked the LORD to wrath. {9:23} Likewise when the LORD sent you from Kadesh Barnea, saying, "Go up and possess the land which I have given you," then you rebelled against the commandment of the LORD your God, and you did not believe Him nor obey His voice. {9:24} You have been rebellious against the LORD from the day that I knew you. {9:25} So I fell down before the LORD for forty days and forty nights, just as I did at the beginning, because the LORD had said He would destroy you. {9:26} Therefore, I prayed to the LORD and said, "O Lord GOD, do not destroy Your people and Your inheritance, whom You have redeemed through Your greatness, whom You have brought out of Egypt with a mighty hand. {9:27} Remember Your servants, Abraham, Isaac, and Jacob; do not look at the stubbornness of this people, nor at their wickedness, nor at their sin. {9:28} Lest the land from which You brought us say, 'Because the LORD was not able to bring them into the land which He promised them, and because He hated them, He brought them out to kill them in the wilderness.' {9:29} Yet they are Your people and Your inheritance, whom You brought out by Your mighty power and by Your outstretched arm."

{10:1} At that time, the LORD said to me, "Hew two tables of stone like the first ones, and come up to the mountain with Me, and make for yourself an ark of wood. {10:2} I will write on the tablets the same words that were on the first tablets you broke, and you shall put them in the ark." {10:3} So I made an ark of acacia wood and hewed two tablets of stone like the first ones, and went up the mountain with the two tablets in my hand. {10:4} And He wrote on the tablets, according to the first writing, the Ten Commandments which the LORD had spoken to you on the mountain from the midst of the fire on the day of the assembly; and the LORD gave them to me. {10:5} Then I turned and came down from the mountain, and put the tablets in the ark which I had made; and there they are, as the LORD commanded me. {10:6} The children of Israel journeyed from Beeroth of the children of Jaakan to Mosera. There Aaron died, and there he was buried; and Eleazar his son ministered as priest in his place. {10:7} From there they journeyed to Gudgodah, and from Gudgodah to Jotbath, a land of rivers of water. {10:8} At that time the LORD separated the tribe of Levi to bear the ark of the covenant of the LORD, to stand before the LORD to serve Him and bless in His name, to this day. {10:9} Therefore Levi has no portion nor inheritance with his brethren; the LORD is his inheritance, just as the LORD your God promised him. {10:10} As at the first time, I stayed on the mountain forty days and forty nights; and the LORD listened to me at that time also, and the LORD would not destroy you. {10:11} Then the LORD said to me, "Arise, begin your journey before the people, that they may go in and possess the land which I swore to their fathers to give them." {10:12} And now, Israel, what does the LORD your God require of you but to fear the LORD your God, to walk in all His ways, to love Him, to serve the LORD your God with all your heart and with all your soul, {10:13} and to keep the commandments of the LORD and His statutes which I command you today for your good? {10:14} Indeed, heaven and the highest heavens belong to the LORD your God, also the earth with all that is in it. {10:15} Only the LORD had a delight in your fathers to love them, and He chose their descendants after them, you above all peoples, as it is this day. {10:16} Therefore, circumcise the foreskin of your heart, and be no longer stiff-necked. {10:17} For the LORD your God is God of gods and Lord of lords, the great God, mighty and awesome, who shows no partiality nor takes a bribe. {10:18} He administers justice for the fatherless and the widow, and loves the stranger, giving him food and clothing. {10:19} Therefore love the stranger, for you were strangers in the land of Egypt. {10:20} **You shall fear the LORD your God; Him you shall serve, and to Him you shall hold fast, and take oaths in His name.** {10:21} He is your praise, and He is your God, who has done for you these great and awesome things which your eyes have seen. {10:22} Your fathers went down to Egypt with seventy persons, and now the LORD your God has made you as the stars of heaven in multitude.

{11:1} So, you must love the LORD your God and keep His charge, statutes, judgments, and commandments always. {11:2} Understand this today, because I am not speaking to your children who have not experienced the discipline of the LORD your God, His greatness, His mighty hand, and His outstretched arm. {11:3} They haven't witnessed His miracles and deeds in Egypt, to Pharaoh the king of Egypt, and to all his land. {11:4} They haven't seen what He did to the Egyptian army, their horses, and chariots, how He caused the Red Sea to engulf them as they pursued you, and how the LORD has destroyed them to this day. {11:5} They haven't seen what He did to you in the wilderness until you reached this place. {11:6} They haven't witnessed what He did to Dathan and Abiram, the sons of Eliab, from the tribe of Reuben, how the earth opened its mouth and swallowed them, along with their households, tents, and all their possessions, right in the midst of Israel. {11:7} But you have seen all the great acts of the LORD. {11:8} Therefore, you must keep all the commandments I'm giving you today so that you may be strong and possess the land you are entering to inherit. {11:9} By doing so, you will prolong your days in the land that the LORD swore to give to your fathers, a land flowing with milk and honey. {11:10} Unlike Egypt, where you sowed seed and watered it like a garden of herbs with your foot, the land you're entering to possess is a land of hills and valleys that drinks water from the rain of heaven. {11:11} It's a land the LORD your God cares for; His eyes are always on it from the beginning to the end of the year. {11:13} If you diligently heed my commandments today, to love the LORD your God and serve Him with all your heart and soul, {11:14} then He will give you the rain for your land in its season, the early rain and the latter rain, that you may gather in your grain, wine, and oil. {11:15} He will also provide grass in the fields for your livestock, so you can eat and be satisfied. {11:16} But be careful that your heart doesn't deceive you, causing you to turn aside and serve other gods and worship them. {11:17} If you do, the LORD's wrath will be kindled against you, and He will shut up the heavens so there will be no rain, and the land won't yield its fruit, leading to your swift destruction from the good land the LORD is giving you. {11:18} So, you must store up these words in your heart and soul, and bind them as a sign on your hand, and let them be as frontlets between your eyes. {11:19} Teach them to your children, talking about them when you sit in your house, walk by the way, lie down, and rise up. {11:20} Write them on the doorposts of your house and on your gates, {11:21} so that your days and the days of your children may be multiplied in the land the LORD promised to give to your fathers, like the days of the heavens on the earth. {11:22} If you carefully keep all these commandments I'm giving you, loving the LORD your God, walking in all His ways, and holding fast to Him, {11:23} then the LORD will drive out all these nations before you, and you will dispossess nations greater and mightier than yourselves. {11:24} Everywhere you set foot will be yours: from the wilderness and Lebanon to the Euphrates River, and from the Mediterranean Sea to the eastern desert. {11:25} No one will be able to oppose you, for the fear and dread of the LORD your God will be upon all the land you tread, just as He promised you. {11:26} Today, I present to you a blessing and a curse: {11:27} a blessing if you obey the commandments of the LORD your God that I am giving you today, {11:28} and a curse if you do not obey the commandments of the LORD your God, but turn aside from the way I am commanding you today to go after other gods, which you have not known. {11:29} When the LORD your God brings you into the land you are entering to possess, you shall set the blessing on Mount Gerizim and the curse on Mount Ebal. {11:30} Aren't they beyond the Jordan, toward the setting sun, in the land of the Canaanites who dwell in the Arabah, opposite Gilgal, beside the oak of Moreh? {11:31} For you are about to cross over the Jordan to enter and possess the land the LORD your God is giving you, and you will possess it and dwell in it. {11:32} Therefore, you must observe and do all the statutes and judgments I am setting before you today.

{12:1} These are the statutes and judgments which you shall observe to do in the land which the LORD God of your fathers is giving you to possess, all the days that you live on the earth. {12:2} You shall utterly destroy all the places where the nations which you shall possess served their gods, on the high mountains, on the hills, and under every green tree. {12:3} And you shall overthrow their altars, break their pillars, and burn their groves with fire; and you shall hew down the carved images of their gods and destroy their names from that place. {12:4} You shall not do so to the LORD your God. {12:5} But to the place which the LORD your God shall choose out of all your tribes to put His name there, to His habitation you shall seek, and there you shall come. {12:6} And there you shall bring your burnt offerings, sacrifices, tithes, heave offerings of your hand, vows, freewill offerings, and the firstlings of your herds and flocks. {12:7} And there you shall eat before the LORD your God, and you shall rejoice in all that you put your hand to, you and your households, where the LORD your God has blessed you. {12:8} You shall not do as we do here today, every man doing what is right in his own eyes. {12:9} For you have not yet come to the rest and the inheritance which the LORD your God is giving you. {12:10} But when you cross over the Jordan and dwell in the land which the LORD your God is giving you to inherit, and He gives you rest from all your enemies round about, so that you dwell in safety, {12:11} then there shall be a place which the LORD your God shall choose to make His name dwell there; there you shall bring all that I command you: your burnt offerings, sacrifices, tithes, heave offerings of your hand, and all your choice vows which you vow to the LORD. {12:12} And you shall rejoice before the LORD your God, you, your sons, your daughters, your male and female servants, and the Levite who is within your gates, since he has no portion nor inheritance with you.

{12:13} Take heed to yourself that you do not offer your burnt offerings in every place that you see; {12:14} but in the place which the LORD shall choose in one of your tribes, there you shall offer your burnt offerings, and there you shall do all that I command you. {12:15} However, you may slaughter and eat meat within all your gates, whatever your heart desires, according to the blessing of the LORD your God which He has given you; the unclean and the clean may eat it, as of the gazelle and the deer. {12:16} Only you shall not eat the blood; you shall pour it on the earth like water. {12:17} You may not eat within your gates the tithe of your grain or your new wine or your oil, of the firstborn of your herd or your flock, of any of your offerings which you vow, of your freewill offerings, or of the heave offering of your hand. {12:18} But you must eat them before the LORD your God in the place which the LORD your God chooses, you and your son and your daughter, your male servant and your female servant, and the Levite who is within your gates; and you shall rejoice before the LORD your God in all to which you put your hands. {12:19} Take heed to yourself that you do not forsake the Levite as long as you live upon the earth. {12:20} "When the LORD your God enlarges your border as He has promised you, and you say, 'Let me eat meat,' because you long to eat meat, you may eat as much meat as your heart desires. {12:21} If the place where the LORD your God chooses to put His name is too far from you, then you may slaughter from your herd and from your flock which the LORD has given you, just as I have commanded you, and you may eat within your gates as much as your heart desires. {12:22} Just as the gazelle and the deer are eaten, so you may eat them; the unclean and the clean alike may eat them. {12:23} Only be sure that you do not eat the blood, for the blood is the life; you may not eat the life with the meat. {12:24} You shall not eat it; you shall pour it on the earth like water. {12:25} You shall not eat it, that it may go well with you and your children after you, when you do what is right in the sight of the LORD. {12:26} "Only the holy things which you have, and your vowed offerings, you shall take and go to the place which the LORD chooses. {12:27} And you shall offer your burnt offerings, the meat and the blood, on the altar of the LORD your God; and the blood of your sacrifices shall be poured out on the altar of the LORD your God, and you shall eat the meat. {12:28} Observe and obey all these words which I command you, that it may go well with you and your children after you forever, when you do what is good and right in the sight of the LORD your God. {12:29} "When the LORD your God cuts off from before you the nations which you go to dispossess, and you displace them and dwell in their land, {12:30} take heed to yourself that you are not ensnared to follow them, after they are destroyed from before you, and that you do not inquire after their gods, saying, 'How did these nations serve their gods? I also will do likewise.' {12:31} You shall not worship the LORD your God in that way; for every abomination to the LORD which He hates they have done to their gods; for they burn even their sons and daughters in the fire to their gods. {12:32} Whatever I command you, be careful to observe it; you shall not add to it nor take away from it.

{13:1} If there arises among you a prophet or a dreamer of dreams, and he gives you a sign or a wonder, {13:2} and the sign or wonder comes to pass, of which he spoke to you, saying, 'Let us go after other gods'—which you have not known—'and let us serve them,' {13:3} you shall not listen to the words of that prophet or that dreamer of dreams, for the LORD your God is testing you to know whether you love the LORD your God with all your heart and with all your soul. {13:4} You shall walk after the LORD your God, fear Him, keep His commandments, obey His voice, and serve Him. {13:5} And that prophet or dreamer of dreams shall be put to death because he has spoken to turn you away from the LORD your God, who brought you out of the land of Egypt and redeemed you from the house of bondage, to entice you from the way in which the LORD your God commanded you to walk. So you shall put away the evil from among you. {13:6} If your brother, the son of your mother, your son, your daughter, the wife of your bosom, or your friend who is as your own soul, secretly entices you, saying, 'Let us go and serve other gods,' which you have not known, neither you nor your fathers, {13:7} of the gods of the people which are all around you, near to you or far off from you, from one end of the earth to the other end of the earth, {13:8} you shall not consent to him or listen to him, nor shall your eye pity him, nor shall you spare him or conceal him; {13:9} but you shall surely kill him; your hand shall be first against him to put him to death, and afterward the hand of all the people. {13:10} And you shall stone him with stones until he dies because he sought to entice you away from the LORD your God, who brought you out of the land of Egypt, from the house of bondage. {13:11} So all Israel shall hear and fear, and not again do such wickedness as this among you. {13:12} If you hear in one of your cities, which the LORD your God gives you to dwell in, {13:13} certain men, the children of Belial, have gone out from among you and have withdrawn the inhabitants of their city, saying, 'Let us go and serve other gods,' which you have not known, {13:14} then you shall inquire, search out, and ask diligently. And if it is indeed true and certain that such an abomination was committed among you, {13:15} you shall surely strike the inhabitants of that city with the edge of the sword, utterly destroying it, all that is in it and its livestock—with the edge of the sword. {13:16} And you shall gather all its plunder into the middle of the street, and completely burn with fire the city and all its plunder, for the LORD your God. It shall be a heap forever; it shall not be built again. {13:17} So none of the accursed things shall remain in your hand, that the LORD may turn from the fierceness of His anger and show you mercy, have compassion on you, and multiply you, just as He swore to your fathers, {13:18} because you have listened to the voice of the LORD your God, to keep all His commandments which I command you today, to do what is right in the eyes of the LORD your God.

{14:1} You are the children of the LORD your God. Therefore, you shall not cut yourselves or make any baldness between your eyes for the dead. {14:2} For you are a holy people to the LORD your God, and the LORD has chosen you to be a special people to Himself, above all the nations on the earth. {14:3} You shall not eat any abominable thing. {14:4} These are the animals which you shall eat: the ox, the sheep, and the goat, {14:5} the hart, the roebuck, the fallow deer, the wild goat, the pygarg, the wild ox, and the chamois. {14:6} And every animal that parts the hoof and has the split hoof divided into two and chews the cud among the animals, you shall eat. {14:7} However, these you shall not eat of those that chew the cud or of those that have a divided hoof: the camel, the hare, and the coney; for they chew the cud but do not have a divided hoof; therefore, they are unclean to you. {14:8} Also, the swine, because it has a divided hoof yet does not chew the cud, is unclean to you. You shall not eat their flesh or touch their dead carcass. {14:9} You may eat of all that are in the waters: all that have fins and scales you shall eat. {14:10} But whatever does not have fins and scales you shall not eat; it is unclean to you. {14:11} Of all clean birds you shall eat. {14:12} But these are the ones of which you shall not eat: the eagle, the ossifrage, the osprey, {14:13} the glede, the kite, the vulture after its kind, {14:14} every raven after its kind, {14:15} the owl, the night hawk, the cuckoo, and the hawk after its kind, {14:16} the little owl, the great owl, the swan, {14:17} the pelican, the gier eagle, the cormorant, {14:18} the stork, the heron after its kind, the lapwing, and the bat. {14:19} And every creeping thing that flies is unclean to you; they shall not be eaten. {14:20} But of all clean fowls you may eat. {14:21} You shall not eat anything that dies of itself; you shall give it to the stranger who is in your gates, that he may eat it, or you may sell it to an alien; for you are a holy people to the LORD your God. You shall not boil a young goat in its mother's milk. {14:22} You shall truly tithe all the increase of your seed that the field brings forth year by year. {14:23} And you shall eat before the LORD your God, in the place which He shall choose to place His name there, the tithe of your corn, your wine, and your oil, and the firstlings of your herds and of your flocks, that you may learn to fear the LORD your God always. {14:24} But if the way is too long for you, so that you are not able to carry it; or if the place is too far from you, which the LORD your God shall choose to set His name there, when the LORD your God has blessed you; {14:25} then you shall turn it into money, bind up the money in your hand, and go to the place which the LORD your God shall choose. {14:26} And you shall spend that money for whatever your soul desires: for oxen, for sheep, for wine, for strong drink, or for whatever your soul desires; and you shall eat there before the LORD your God, and you shall rejoice, you and your household. {14:27} Also, the Levite who is within your gates; you shall not forsake him, for he has no part nor inheritance with you. {14:28} At the end of three years you shall bring forth all the tithe of your increase the same year and shall lay it up within your gates. {14:29} And the Levite, because he has no part nor inheritance with you, and the stranger, and the fatherless, and the widow, who are within your gates, shall come and shall eat and be satisfied; that the LORD your God may bless you in all the work of your hand which you do.

{15:1} At the end of every seven years, you shall make a release. {15:2} This is how it works: Every creditor who lends something to his neighbor shall release it; he shall not demand it from his neighbor or his brother, because it is called the LORD'S release. {15:3} However, you may require it of a foreigner, but what belongs to your brother, you shall release. {15:4} This is to be done when there are no poor among you, for the LORD will greatly bless you in the land He gives you as an inheritance. {15:5} This blessing comes if you carefully listen to the voice of the LORD your God and observe to do all the commandments given to you this day. {15:6} The LORD will bless you abundantly as He promised, and you will lend to many nations but not borrow; you will rule over many nations, but they will not rule over you. {15:7} If there is a poor man among you, one of your brethren, within any of your gates in the land the LORD your God is giving you, do not harden your heart or shut your hand from your poor brother. {15:8} Instead, open your hand wide to him, and lend him sufficient for his need, whatever he lacks. {15:9} Be careful not to harbor wicked thoughts in your heart, thinking, 'The seventh year, the year of release, is near,' and then show ill will toward your poor brother and give him nothing. If he cries out to the LORD against you, it will be counted as sin against you. {15:10} Therefore, give to him willingly, and do not let your heart be grieved when you give to him, because for this, the LORD your God will bless you in all your works and in all to which you put your hand. {15:11} The poor will never cease from the land; therefore, I command you to open your hand wide to your brother, to your poor, and to your needy in your land. {15:12} If your brother, whether a Hebrew man or woman, is sold to you and serves you for six years, then in the seventh year, you shall let him go free from you. {15:13} And when you send him out free from you, you shall not let him go away empty-handed. {15:14} You shall generously provide for him from your flock, your threshing floor, and your winepress, according to what the LORD your God has blessed you with, you shall give to him. {15:15} Remember that you were a slave in the land of Egypt, and the LORD your God redeemed you; therefore, I command you to do this today. {15:16} If he says to you, 'I will not go away from you,' because he loves you and your household, and is well with you, {15:17} then you shall take an awl and thrust it through his ear to the door, and he shall be your servant forever. And also to your maidservant, you shall do likewise. {15:18} Let it not be hard for you when you send him away free from you, for he has been worth a double hired servant to you, in serving you for six years, and the LORD your God will bless you in all that you do. {15:19} All the firstborn males that come from your herd and your flock you shall sanctify to the LORD your God; you shall do no work with the firstborn of your herd, nor shear the firstborn of your flock. {15:20} You shall eat it before the LORD your God year by year in the place He chooses, you and your household. {15:21} But if it has any blemish, such as being lame or blind, or having any serious blemish, you shall not sacrifice it to the LORD your God. {15:22} You may eat it within your gates; the unclean and the clean alike may eat it, as they do the gazelle and the deer. {15:23} However, you shall not eat its blood; you shall pour it on the ground like water.

{16:1} Remember to observe the month of Abib and celebrate the Passover to the LORD your God, for it was in the month of Abib that the LORD your God brought you out of Egypt by night. {16:2} Therefore, you shall sacrifice the Passover to the LORD your God, from the flock and the herd, in the place which the LORD shall choose to place His name there. {16:3} During this time, you shall not eat leavened bread; for seven days, you shall eat unleavened bread, the bread of affliction, to remember the day when you came out of Egypt in haste, all the days of your life. {16:4} Throughout these seven days, no leavened bread should be seen with you, nor shall any meat, which you sacrificed on the first day at evening, remain until the morning. {16:5} You are not allowed to sacrifice the Passover within any of your gates which the LORD your God gives you. {16:6} Instead, at the place where the LORD your God chooses to place His name, there you shall sacrifice the Passover in the evening, at sunset, the time when you came out of Egypt. {16:7} You shall roast and eat it in the place the LORD your God chooses, and in the morning, you shall return to your tents. {16:8} For six days, you shall eat unleavened bread, and on the seventh day, there shall be a solemn assembly to the LORD your God; on that day, you shall do no work. {16:9} Count seven weeks for yourself; begin to count the seven weeks from the time you begin to reap the harvest. {16:10} Then, you shall keep the Feast of Weeks to the LORD your God with a freewill offering from your hand, according to how the LORD your God has blessed you. {16:11} Rejoice before the LORD your God—you, your son, your daughter, your male servant, your female servant, the Levite within your gates, the stranger, the fatherless, and the widow who are among you—in the place the LORD your God has chosen to place His name there. {16:12} Remember that you were a slave in Egypt; therefore, you shall observe and do these statutes. {16:13} Observe the Feast of Tabernacles for seven days, after you have gathered in your harvest of grain and wine. {16:14} Rejoice in your feast—you, your son, your daughter, your male servant, your female servant, the Levite, the stranger, the fatherless, and the widow within your gates. {16:15} For seven days, you shall keep a solemn feast to the LORD your God in the place He chooses, for He will bless you in all your produce and in all the work of your hands, so you shall surely rejoice. {16:16} Three times a year, all your males shall appear before the LORD your God in the place He chooses: during the Feast of Unleavened Bread, the Feast of Weeks, and the Feast of Tabernacles; and they shall not appear before the LORD empty-handed. {16:17} Each man shall give as he is able, according to the blessing of the LORD your God which He has given you. {16:18} Appoint judges and officers in all your gates, which the LORD your God gives you, throughout your tribes; and they shall judge the people with just judgment. {16:19} Do not pervert justice; do not show partiality, nor take a bribe, for a bribe blinds the eyes of the wise and twists the words of the righteous. {16:20} Pursue justice wholeheartedly, so that you may live and inherit the land which the LORD your God gives you. {16:21} Do not plant any trees as an Asherah pole near the altar of the LORD your God, which you shall make for yourself. {16:22} Nor shall you set up any carved image, which the LORD your God detests.

{17:1} You must not sacrifice to the LORD your God any bull or sheep that has a blemish or any defect, for that is detestable to the LORD your God. {17:2} If there is found among you, within any of your gates that the LORD your God is giving you, a man or woman who has done wickedness in the sight of the LORD your God by transgressing His covenant, {17:3} and has gone and served other gods and worshiped them, whether the sun, the moon, or any of the host of heaven, which I have not commanded, {17:4} and it is reported to you, and you hear of it, then you shall inquire diligently. If it is true and certain that such an abomination has been committed in Israel, {17:5} then you shall bring out to your gates that man or woman who has committed that wicked act, and stone them to death with stones until they die. {17:6} A sentence of death shall be carried out only on the testimony of two or three witnesses; no one shall be put to death on the testimony of only one witness. {17:7} The hands of the witnesses shall be the first against the person to execute the death penalty, and afterward the hands of all the people. So you shall purge the evil from among you. {17:8} If a case is too difficult for you to judge—concerning bloodshed, legal claims, or assaults—matters of controversy within your gates, then you shall go up to the place the LORD your God chooses. {17:9} You shall consult the Levitical priests and the judge who is in office at that time. They shall pronounce the verdict in the case. {17:10} You must abide by the decision they announce to you at the place the LORD chooses. Be careful to do exactly as they instruct you. {17:11} You must carry out the verdict they announce and the sentence they impose, without turning aside to the right or to the left from the decision they proclaim to you. {17:12} Anyone who shows contempt for the judge or for the priest who stands ministering there to the LORD your God must be put to death. You must purge the evil from Israel. {17:13} All the people will hear and be afraid, and will not be presumptuous again. {17:14} When you enter the land the LORD your God is giving you and have taken possession of it and settled in it, and you say, "Let us set a king over us like all the nations around us," {17:15} you must indeed set a king over you, one chosen by the LORD your God. You must appoint a king from among your fellow Israelites; you are not allowed to choose a foreigner who is not one of your own people. {17:16} The king must not acquire many horses for himself or send the people back to Egypt to acquire more horses, for the LORD has told you, "You must never return to Egypt." {17:17} The king must not take many wives for himself, or his heart will be led astray. He must not accumulate large amounts of silver and gold for himself. {17:18} When he is seated on his royal throne, he is to write for himself on a scroll a copy of this law, taken from that of the Levitical priests. {17:19} It is to be with him, and he is to read it all the days of his life, so that he may learn to fear the LORD his God and follow carefully all the words of this law and these decrees. {17:20} This will prevent him from becoming proud and turning away from the LORD's commandments. It will also ensure that he and his descendants will reign for many years in his kingdom in Israel.

{18:1} The priests, the Levites, and all the tribe of Levi shall not have a portion or inheritance with Israel. They shall eat the offerings made by fire to the LORD, as well as His inheritance. {18:2} They shall have no inheritance among their fellow Israelites; the LORD Himself is their inheritance, as He promised them. {18:3} This shall be the priest's share from the people who offer sacrifices, whether it be ox or sheep: they shall give the priest the shoulder, the two cheeks, and the stomach. {18:4} They shall also give him the firstfruits of their grain, wine, oil, and the fleece of their sheep. {18:5} For the LORD your God has chosen him out of all your tribes to stand and minister in the name of the LORD, him and his sons forever. {18:6} If a Levite comes from any of your towns in Israel, where he has been residing, and comes with all the desire of his mind to the place the LORD chooses, {18:7} he may minister in the name of the LORD his God like all his fellow Levites who stand before the LORD. {18:8} They shall have equal portions to eat, even though they receive revenue from the sale of their family possessions. {18:9} When you enter the land the LORD your God is giving you, do not learn to imitate the detestable ways of the nations there. {18:10} Let no one be found among you who sacrifices their son or daughter in the fire, who practices divination or sorcery, interprets omens, engages in witchcraft, {18:11} or casts spells, or who is a medium or spiritist or who consults the dead. {18:12} Anyone who does these things is detestable to the LORD; because of these same detestable practices the LORD your God will drive out those nations before you. {18:13} You must be blameless before the LORD your God. {18:14} The nations you will dispossess listen to those who practice sorcery or divination. But as for you, the LORD your God has not permitted you to do so. {18:15} **The LORD your God will raise up for you a prophet like me from among you, from your fellow Israelites. You must listen to him.** {18:16} For this is what you asked of the LORD your God at Horeb on the day of the assembly when you said, "Let us not hear the voice of the LORD our God nor see this great fire anymore, or we will die." {18:17} The LORD said to me: "What they say is good. {18:18} I will raise up for them a prophet like you from among their fellow Israelites, and I will put my words in his mouth. He will tell them everything I command him. {18:19} But whoever does not listen to my words that the prophet speaks in my name, I myself will call him to account. {18:20} But a prophet who presumes to speak in my name anything I have not commanded, or a prophet who speaks in the name of other gods, is to be put to death." {18:21} You may say to yourselves, "How can we know when a message has not been spoken by the LORD?" {18:22} If what a prophet proclaims in the name of the LORD does not take place or come true, that is a message the LORD has not spoken. That prophet has spoken presumptuously, so do not be alarmed.

{19:1} When the LORD your God has driven out the nations before you and you have taken possession of their land and settled in their cities and houses, {19:2} you shall set aside three cities for yourselves in the land the LORD your God is giving you to possess. {19:3} You must prepare the way to these cities and divide the land that the LORD your God is giving you as an inheritance into three parts, so that anyone who has killed another unintentionally may flee there. {19:4} This is the rule for the one who flees to one of these cities to live: Whoever kills their neighbor unintentionally, without malice aforethought— {19:5} as when someone goes into the forest with a neighbor to cut wood, and their hand swings the axe to cut down a tree, but the head flies off the handle and strikes the neighbor so that they die—they may flee to one of these cities and live. {19:6} Otherwise, the avenger of blood might pursue the killer in a rage, overtake them if the distance is too great, and kill them even though they did not deserve death, since they did not hate their neighbor in the past. {19:7} That is why I command you to set aside three cities. {19:8} If the LORD your God enlarges your territory, as he promised on oath to your ancestors, and gives you all the land he promised them, {19:9} because you carefully keep all these commandments I am giving you today and do them—to love the LORD your God and to always walk in obedience to him—then you must add three more cities for yourselves, besides these three. {19:10} This is to prevent the shedding of innocent blood in your land, which the LORD your God is giving you as your inheritance, and so that you will not be guilty of bloodshed. {19:11} But if someone hates their neighbor, lies in wait for them, assaults and kills them, and then flees to one of these cities, {19:12} the elders of the killer's city must send for the killer and have them brought back from the city to be handed over to the avenger of blood to die. {19:13} Show them no pity. You must purge from Israel the guilt of shedding innocent blood, so that it may go well with you. {19:14} Do not move your neighbor's boundary stone set up by your predecessors in the inheritance you receive in the land the LORD your God is giving you to possess. {19:15} One witness is not sufficient to convict anyone accused of any crime or offense they may have committed. A matter must be established by the testimony of two or three witnesses. {19:16} If someone gives false testimony against another person, {19:17} the two people involved in the dispute must stand in the presence of the LORD before the priests and the judges who are in office at the time. {19:18} The judges shall make a thorough investigation, and if the witness proves to be a liar, giving false testimony against their fellow Israelite, {19:19} then do to the false witness as that witness intended to do to the other party. You must purge the evil from among you. {19:20} The rest of the people will hear of this and be afraid, and never again will such an evil thing be done among you. {19:21} Show no pity: life for life, eye for eye, tooth for tooth, hand for hand, foot for foot.

{20:1} When you go out to battle against your enemies and see horses, chariots, and a larger army than yours, do not be afraid of them, for the LORD your God is with you, who brought you up out of the land of Egypt. {20:2} As you approach the battle, the priest shall come forward and address the army, {20:3} saying, "Hear, Israel, today you are going into battle against your enemies. Do not be faint-hearted or afraid; do not tremble or be terrified because of them, {20:4} for the LORD your God goes with you to fight for you against your enemies and to give you victory. {20:5} The officers shall also address the army, saying, "Is anyone afraid or fainthearted? Let him go home so that his fellow soldiers will not become disheartened too." {20:6} Before the battle, certain exemptions are granted: If anyone has built a new house but has not yet dedicated it, let him go home. Otherwise, if he dies in battle, another man may dedicate it. {20:7} If anyone has planted a vineyard but has not yet begun to enjoy its fruit, let him go home. Otherwise, he might die in battle, and another man will eat his fruit. {20:8} If anyone is engaged to a woman but has not yet married her, let him go home. Otherwise, he might die in battle, and another man will marry her. {20:9} After the officers have finished speaking to the army, they shall appoint commanders to lead it into battle. {20:10} When you march up to attack a city, make an offer of peace to it. {20:11} If the city accepts your offer and opens its gates to you, all the people in it shall become your subjects and shall serve you. {20:12} But if the city refuses to make peace with you and fights against you, besiege it. {20:13} And when the LORD your God delivers it into your hand, put to the sword all the men in it. {20:14} But you may take for yourselves the women, the children, the livestock, and everything else in the city—all its plunder—and enjoy the spoils of your enemies, which the LORD your God has given you. {20:15} This is how you are to treat all the cities that are very distant from you, which do not belong to the nations nearby. {20:16} However, in the cities of the nations the LORD your God is giving you as an inheritance, do not leave alive anything that breathes. {20:17} Completely destroy them—the Hittites, Amorites, Canaanites, Perizzites, Hivites, and Jebusites—as the LORD your God has commanded you. {20:18} Otherwise, they may teach you to follow all the detestable things they do in worshiping their gods, and you will sin against the LORD your God. {20:19} When you besiege a city for a long time, making war against it in order to capture it, do not destroy its trees by putting an axe to them, because you can eat their fruit. Do not cut them down, as the trees are not people, and you may use them for food. {20:20} However, you may cut down trees that you know are not fruit trees and use them to build siege works against the city until it falls.

{21:1} If a slain person is found in the land that the LORD your God is giving you to possess, lying in the field, and it is not known who killed him, {21:2} then your elders and judges shall go out and measure the distances to the surrounding cities. {21:3} The elders of the city nearest to the slain person shall take a heifer that has never been worked and has never pulled a yoke. {21:4} They shall bring the heifer down to a rough valley that has not been plowed or planted and shall break its neck there in the valley. {21:5} The Levitical priests shall then come forward, for the LORD your God has chosen them to minister and to pronounce blessings in the name of the LORD, and they shall decide all cases of dispute and violence. {21:6} All the elders of the city nearest to the slain person shall wash their hands over the heifer whose neck was broken in the valley. {21:7} Then they shall declare, "Our hands did not shed this blood, nor did our eyes see it. {21:8} Accept atonement, LORD, for your people Israel, whom you have redeemed, and do not hold your people guilty of the blood of an innocent person." Then the bloodshed will be atoned for, {21:9} and you will have purged from yourselves the guilt of shedding innocent blood, since you have done what is right in the eyes of the LORD. {21:10} When you go to war against your enemies and the LORD your God delivers them into your hands and you take captives, {21:11} if you notice among the captives a beautiful woman and are attracted to her, you may take her as your wife. {21:12} Bring her into your home, have her shave her head, trim her nails, {21:13} and put aside the clothes she was wearing when captured. After she has lived in your house and mourned her father and mother for a full month, then you may go to her and be her husband, and she shall be your wife. {21:14} If you are not pleased with her, let her go wherever she wishes. You must not sell her or treat her as a slave since you have dishonored her. {21:15} If a man has two wives, one loved and the other unloved, and both bear him sons, but the unloved wife has the firstborn son, {21:16} when that man's inheritance is to be given to his sons, he must not show favoritism to the son of the loved wife over the son of the unloved wife, who is the firstborn. {21:17} Instead, he must acknowledge the rights of the firstborn son of the unloved wife by giving him a double portion of all he has. The first son of his father's strength belongs to him. {21:18} If someone has a stubborn and rebellious son who does not obey his father and mother and will not listen to them when disciplined, {21:19} his parents shall take hold of him and bring him to the elders at the gate of his town. {21:20} They shall say to the elders, "This son of ours is stubborn and rebellious. He will not obey us. He is a glutton and a drunkard." {21:21} Then all the men of his town are to stone him to death. You must purge the evil from among you, and all Israel will hear of it and be afraid. {21:22} If someone is guilty of a capital offense and is put to death, and you hang him on a pole, {21:23} you must not leave the body hanging on the pole overnight. Be sure to bury it that same day, because anyone who is hung on a pole is under God's curse. You must not desecrate the land the LORD your God is giving you as an inheritance.

{22:1} If you come across your brother's ox or sheep wandering off, you must not ignore it; you must return it to your brother. {22:2} If your brother is not nearby or you do not know who the owner is, take the animal to your own home and keep it until your brother comes looking for it; then return it to him. {22:3} Do the same with his donkey, his clothing, and anything else your brother loses and you find. You must not ignore your responsibility. {22:4} If you see your brother's donkey or ox fallen on the road, do not ignore it; help him lift it up again. {22:5} A woman must not wear men's clothing, nor a man wear women's clothing, for the LORD your God detests anyone who does this. {22:6} If you happen to come across a bird's nest along the way, either in a tree or on the ground, and the mother is sitting on the young or on the eggs, do not take the mother with the young. {22:7} You may take the young, but be sure to let the mother go, so that it may go well with you and you may have a long life. {22:8} When you build a new house, make a railing around your roof so that you may not bring the guilt of bloodshed on your house if someone falls from it. {22:9} Do not plant two kinds of seed in your vineyard; if you do, not only the crops you plant but also the fruit of the vineyard will be defiled. {22:10} Do not plow with an ox and a donkey yoked together. {22:11} Do not wear clothes of wool and linen woven together. {22:12} Make tassels on the four corners of the cloak you wear. {22:13} If a man takes a wife and, after sleeping with her, dislikes her {22:14} and slanders her and gives her a bad name, saying, "I married this woman, but when I approached her, I did not find proof of her virginity," {22:15} then the young woman's father and mother shall bring to the town elders at the gate proof that she was a virgin. {22:16} Her father will say to the elders, "I gave my daughter in marriage to this man, but he dislikes her. {22:17} Now he has slandered her and said, 'I did not find proof that my daughter to be a virgin.' But here is the proof of my daughter's virginity." Then her parents shall display the cloth before the elders of the town, {22:18} and the elders shall take the man and punish him. {22:19} They shall fine him a hundred shekels of silver and give them to the young woman's father, because this man has given an Israelite virgin a bad name. He shall continue to be his wife; he must not divorce her as long as he lives. {22:20} If, however, the charge is true and no proof of the young woman's virginity can be found, {22:21} she shall be brought to the door of her father's house and there the men of her town shall stone her to death. She has done an outrageous thing in Israel by being promiscuous while still in her father's house. You must purge the evil from among you. {22:22} If a man is found sleeping with another man's wife, both the man who slept with her and the woman must die. You must purge the evil from Israel. {22:23} If a man happens to meet in a town a virgin pledged to be married and he sleeps with her, {22:24} you shall take both of them to the gate of that town and stone them to death—the young woman because she was in a town and did not scream for help, and the man because he violated another man's wife. You must purge the evil from among you. {22:25} But if out in the country a man happens to meet a young woman pledged to be married and rapes her, only the man who has done this shall die. {22:26} Do nothing to the woman; she has committed no sin deserving death. This case is like that of someone who attacks and murders a neighbor, {22:27} for the man found the young woman out in the country, and though the betrothed woman screamed, there was no one to rescue her. {22:28} If a man happens to meet a virgin who is not pledged to be married and rapes her and they are discovered, {22:29} he shall pay her father fifty shekels of silver. He must marry the young woman, for he has violated her. He can never divorce her as long as he lives. {22:30} A man is not to marry his father's wife; he must not dishonor his father's bed.

{23:1} If someone is injured in the private parts or has their private member cut off, they shall not be allowed to join the assembly of the LORD. {23:2} A person born out of wedlock shall not be allowed to join the assembly of the LORD, not even for ten generations. {23:3} An Ammonite or Moabite shall not be allowed to join the assembly of the LORD, not even for ten generations, because they did not meet you with bread and water on your journey out of Egypt, and because they hired Balaam son of Beor from Pethor in Aram Naharaim to pronounce a curse on you. {23:5} However, the LORD your God refused to listen to Balaam and turned the curse into a blessing for you because the LORD your God loves you. {23:6} Therefore, you shall never seek their peace or prosperity. {23:7} You shall not despise an Edomite, for he is your brother. You shall not despise an Egyptian, because you resided as a foreigner in his country. {23:8} The third generation of children born to them may enter the assembly of the LORD. {23:9} When you go out as an army against your enemies, be sure to avoid anything impure. {23:10} If there is among you someone who becomes unclean by nocturnal emissions, they must go outside the camp; they may not come into the camp. {23:11} When evening falls, they must wash themselves, and at sunset, they may return to the camp. {23:12} You must have a place outside the camp where you can go to relieve yourself. {23:13} Carry a digging tool as part of your equipment so that when you relieve yourself, you can dig a hole and cover up your excrement. {23:14} For the LORD your God moves about in your camp to protect you and to deliver your enemies to you. Your camp must be holy so that he will not see among you anything indecent and turn away from you. {23:15} Do not hand over to their master a slave who has escaped from their master and come to you. {23:16} Let them live among you wherever they like and in whatever town they choose. Do not oppress them. {23:17} No Israelite man or woman is to become a shrine prostitute. {23:18} You must not bring the earnings of a female prostitute or of a male prostitute into the house of the LORD your God to pay any vow, because the LORD your God detests them both. {23:19} Do not charge a fellow Israelite interest, whether on money or food or anything else that may earn interest. {23:20} You may charge a foreigner interest, but not a fellow Israelite, so that the LORD your God may bless you in everything you put your hand to in the land you are entering to possess. {23:21} If you make a vow to the LORD your God, do not be slow to fulfill it, because he will hold you to it, and your failure to keep it will be counted against you as sin. {23:22} But if you refrain from making a vow, you will not be guilty. {23:23} Whatever your lips utter, you must be sure to do, because you made your vow freely to the LORD your God with your own mouth. {23:24} When you enter your neighbor's vineyard, you may eat all the grapes you want, but do not put any in your basket. {23:25} **When you enter your neighbor's standing grain, you may pick the heads of grain with your hands, but you must not put a sickle to their standing grain.**

{24:1} If a man marries a woman and later finds something indecent about her, he can write her a certificate of divorce, give it to her, and send her away from his house. {24:2} After she leaves, if she marries another man {24:3} who also divorces her or dies, her first husband may not marry her again, for she has been defiled. {24:4} That would be detestable to the LORD. You must not bring guilt upon the land the LORD your God is giving you as an inheritance. {24:5} When a man is newly married, he is not to be drafted into the army or given any business responsibilities. He must be free to spend one year at home, bringing happiness to the wife he has married. {24:6} No one shall take a pair of millstones or even just the upper millstone as security for a loan, for that would be taking a person's livelihood as security. {24:7} If someone is caught kidnapping a fellow Israelite and treating or selling them as a slave, that kidnapper must be put to death. In this way, you will purge the evil from among you. {24:8} When you are in camp during a war, be careful to avoid anything impure. {24:9} If someone becomes defiled because of a bodily discharge, they must go outside the camp. After dark, they may return to camp. {24:10} Keep a designated area outside the camp where you can relieve yourself. {24:11} As part of your equipment have something to dig with, and when you relieve yourself, dig a hole and cover up your excrement. {24:12} For the LORD your God moves about in your camp to protect you and to deliver your enemies to you. Your camp must be holy, so he will not see among you anything indecent and turn away from you. {24:15} Do not hand over to their master a slave who has escaped from their master and come to you. {24:16} Let them live among you wherever they like and in whatever town they choose. Do not oppress them. {24:17} No Israelite man or woman is to become a shrine prostitute. {24:18} You must not bring the earnings of a female prostitute or of a male prostitute into the house of the LORD your God to pay any vow, because the LORD your God detests them both. {24:19} Do not charge a fellow Israelite interest, whether on money or food or anything else that may earn interest. {24:20} You may charge a foreigner interest, but not a fellow Israelite, so that the LORD your God may bless you in everything you put your hand to in the land you are entering to possess. {24:21} If you make a vow to the LORD your God, do not be slow to fulfill it, because he will hold you to it, and your failure to keep it will be counted against you as sin. {24:22} But if you refrain from making a vow, you will not be guilty. {24:23} Whatever your lips utter, you must be sure to do, because you made your vow freely to the LORD your God with your own mouth. {24:24} When you enter your neighbor's vineyard, you may eat all the grapes you want, but do not put any in your basket. {24:25} When you enter your neighbor's grain field, you may pick kernels with your hands, but you must not put a sickle to their standing grain.

{25:1} When there's a dispute between people and they come to court for judgment, the judges must ensure justice is served. They should acquit the innocent and condemn the guilty. {25:2} If the guilty person deserves to be beaten, the judge will make them lie down and receive a beating in front of them. {25:3} The number of lashes should correspond to the crime, but it must not exceed forty. If it does, your fellow Israelite would be degraded in your eyes. {25:4} When an ox is treading out grain, do not muzzle it. {25:5} If brothers live together and one of them dies without a son, his widow must not marry outside the family. Instead, her brother-in-law should marry her and fulfill the duty of a brother-in-law to her. {25:6} The first son she bears will carry on the name of the dead brother, so his name will not be blotted out from Israel. {25:7} If the brother-in-law refuses to marry his sister-in-law, she shall go to the elders at the town gate and declare, "My brother-in-law refuses to carry on his brother's name in Israel. He will not fulfill the duty of a brother-in-law to me." {25:8} Then the elders of the town shall summon him and talk to him. If he persists and says, "I don't want to marry her," {25:9} his sister-in-law shall go up to him in the presence of the elders, take off one of his sandals, spit in his face, and say, "This is what is done to the man who refuses to build up his brother's family line." {25:10} That man's family line shall be known in Israel as the family of the unsandaled. {25:11} If two men are fighting and the wife of one of them intervenes to rescue her husband from his assailant, and she reaches out and seizes him by his private parts, {25:12} you shall cut off her hand. Show her no pity. {25:13} Do not have two different types of weights in your bag, one heavy and one light. {25:14} Do not have two different types of measures in your house, one large and one small. {25:15} You must have accurate and honest weights and measures, so you may live long in the land the LORD your God is giving you. {25:16} For the LORD your God detests anyone who deals dishonestly. {25:17} Remember what the Amalekites did to you along the way when you came out of Egypt. {25:18} When you were weary and worn out, they met you on your journey and attacked all who were lagging behind; they had no fear of God. {25:19} Therefore, when the LORD your God gives you rest from all your enemies around you in the land he is giving you as an inheritance to possess, you shall blot out the name of Amalek from under heaven. Do not forget!

{26:1} When you enter the land that the LORD your God is giving you as an inheritance, and you settle there, {26:2} you must take some of the first produce from each crop you harvest and put it in a basket. Then go to the place where the LORD your God chooses to be worshiped. {26:3} Present yourself to the priest who is serving at that time and say to him, "I acknowledge today to the LORD your God that I have entered the land that the LORD swore to our ancestors to give us." {26:4} The priest will take the basket from you and set it in front of the altar of the LORD your God. {26:5} Then you must declare in the presence of the LORD your God, "My ancestor was a wandering Aramean who went to live as a foreigner in Egypt. His family arrived few in number, but in Egypt they became a large and mighty nation. {26:6} The Egyptians oppressed us and treated us harshly, forcing us into harsh labor. {26:7} So we cried out to the LORD, the God of our ancestors. The LORD heard our voice and saw our misery, toil, and oppression. {26:8} So the LORD brought us out of Egypt with a strong hand and powerful arm, with overwhelming terror, and with miraculous signs and wonders. {26:9} He brought us to this place and gave us this land flowing with milk and honey! {26:10} And now, O LORD, I have brought you the first portion of the harvest you have given me from the ground." Then place the produce before the LORD your God and bow to the ground in worship before him. {26:11} Then you and the Levites and the foreigners among you will celebrate with all the good things the LORD your God has given to you and your household. {26:12} "Every third year you must offer a special tithe of your crops. In this year of the special tithe you must give your tithes to the Levites, foreigners, orphans, and widows, so that they will have enough to eat in your towns. {26:13} Then you must declare in the presence of the LORD your God, 'I have taken the sacred gift from my house and have given it to the Levites, foreigners, orphans, and widows, just as you commanded me. I have not violated or forgotten any of your commands. {26:14} I have not eaten any of it while in mourning; I have not handled it while I was ceremonially unclean; and I have not offered any of it to the dead. I have obeyed the LORD my God and have done everything you commanded me. {26:15} Look down from your holy dwelling place in heaven and bless your people Israel and the land you have given us, just as you solemnly promised our ancestors—a land flowing with milk and honey.' {26:16} "Today the LORD your God has commanded you to obey all these decrees and regulations. So be careful to obey them wholeheartedly. {26:17} You have declared today that the LORD is your God. And you have promised to walk in his ways, and to obey his decrees, commands, and regulations, and to do everything he tells you. {26:18} The LORD has declared today that you are his people, his own special treasure, just as he promised, and that you must obey all his commands. {26:19} And if you do, he will set you high above all the other nations he has made. Then you will receive praise, honor, and renown. You will be a nation that is holy to the LORD your God, just as he promised."

{27:1} Moses, along with the elders of Israel, instructed the people, saying, "Keep all the commandments I am giving you today. {27:2} "When you cross the Jordan River and enter the land that the LORD your God is giving you as an inheritance, set up large stones and coat them with plaster. {27:3} "Write all the words of this law on the stones after you have crossed over. This is the land the LORD your God promised you—a land flowing with milk and honey—just as he promised your ancestors. {27:4} "Once you have crossed the Jordan, set up these stones I am commanding you today on Mount Ebal and coat them with plaster. {27:5} "Build an altar to the LORD your God with these stones, but do not use any iron tool on them. {27:6} "Use whole stones to build the altar of the LORD your God and offer burnt offerings on it to the LORD your God. {27:7} "Also offer fellowship offerings there, eat, and rejoice before the LORD your God. {27:8} "Write all the words of this law on the stones clearly and plainly. {27:9} "Moses and the Levitical priests spoke to all Israel, saying, 'Pay attention, Israel. Today you have become the people of the LORD your God. {27:10} "Therefore, you must obey the voice of the LORD your God and follow his commandments and statutes that I am giving you today.' {27:11} "On the same day, Moses gave the people this command: {27:12} 'When you have crossed the Jordan, these tribes shall stand on Mount Gerizim to bless the people: Simeon, Levi, Judah, Issachar, Joseph, and Benjamin. {27:13} " 'And these tribes shall stand on Mount Ebal to pronounce curses: Reuben, Gad, Asher, Zebulun, Dan, and Naphtali. {27:14} " 'The Levites shall proclaim with a loud voice to all the people of Israel: {27:15} "Cursed is anyone who makes an idol—a thing detested by the LORD, the work of skilled hands—and sets it up in secret." And all the people shall say, "Amen." {27:16} "Cursed is anyone who dishonors their father or mother." And all the people shall say, "Amen." {27:17} "Cursed is anyone who moves their neighbor's boundary stone." And all the people shall say, "Amen." {27:18} "Cursed is anyone who leads the blind astray on the road." And all the people shall say, "Amen." {27:19} "Cursed is anyone who withholds justice from the foreigner, the fatherless, or the widow." And all the people shall say, "Amen." {27:20} "Cursed is anyone who sleeps with his father's wife, for he dishonors his father's bed." And all the people shall say, "Amen." {27:21} "Cursed is anyone who has sexual relations with any animal." And all the people shall say, "Amen." {27:22} "Cursed is anyone who sleeps with his sister, the daughter of his father or the daughter of his mother." And all the people shall say, "Amen." {27:23} "Cursed is anyone who sleeps with his mother-in-law." And all the people shall say, "Amen." {27:24} "Cursed is anyone who kills their neighbor secretly." And all the people shall say, "Amen." {27:25} "Cursed is anyone who accepts a bribe to kill an innocent person." And all the people shall say, "Amen." {27:26} "Cursed is anyone who does not uphold the words of this law by carrying them out." And all the people shall say, "Amen."

{28:1} If you listen carefully to the voice of the LORD your God and diligently obey all his commandments I am giving you today, the LORD will elevate you above all the nations of the earth. {28:2} These blessings will come upon you and overwhelm you if you heed the voice of the LORD your God: {28:3} You will be blessed in the city and blessed in the countryside. {28:4} Your children, your crops, your herds, and your flocks will all be blessed. {28:5} Your baskets and your kneading troughs will be blessed. {28:6} You will be blessed when you come in and blessed when you go out. {28:7} The LORD will cause your enemies who rise against you to be defeated before your face. They will come against you in one direction but flee from you in seven directions. {28:8} The LORD will bless everything you do and will fill your storehouses. He will bless the land he is giving you. {28:9} The LORD will establish you as his holy people, just as he has promised, if you keep the commandments of the LORD your God and walk in his ways. {28:10} All the peoples of the earth will see that you are called by the name of the LORD, and they will be afraid of you. {28:11} The LORD will grant you abundant prosperity—in your children, your livestock, and your crops—in the land he swore to give your ancestors. {28:12} The LORD will open the heavens, the storehouse of his bounty, to send rain on your land in season and to bless all the work of your hands. You will lend to many nations but borrow from none. {28:13} The LORD will make you the head, not the tail. If you pay attention to the commands of the LORD your God that I give you this day and carefully follow them, you will always be at the top, never at the bottom. {28:14} Do not turn aside from any of the commands I give you today, to the right or to the left, following other gods and serving them. {28:15} However, if you do not obey the voice of the LORD your God and do not carefully follow all his commands and decrees I am giving you today, all these curses will come on you and overtake you: {28:16} You will be cursed in the city and cursed in the countryside. {28:17} Your basket and your kneading trough will be cursed. {28:18} The fruit of your womb, the crops of your land, and the calves of your herds and the lambs of your flocks will be cursed. {28:19} You will be cursed when you come in and cursed when you go out. {28:20} The LORD will send on you curses, confusion, and frustration in everything you do, until you are destroyed and quickly perish because of the evil deeds you have done in forsaking him. {28:21} The LORD will plague you with diseases until he has destroyed you from the land you are entering to possess. {28:22} The LORD will strike you with wasting disease, fever, inflammation, scorching heat, drought, blight, and mildew, which will plague you until you perish. {28:23} The sky over your head will be bronze, the ground beneath you iron. {28:24} The LORD will turn the rain of your country into dust and powder; it will come down from the skies until you are destroyed. {28:25} The LORD will cause you to be defeated before your enemies. You will come at them from one direction but flee from them in seven, and you will become a thing of horror to all the kingdoms on earth. {28:26} Your carcasses will be food for all the birds and the wild animals, and there will be no one to frighten them away. {28:27} The LORD will afflict you with the boils of Egypt and with tumors, festering sores and the itch, from which you cannot be cured. {28:28} The LORD will afflict you with madness, blindness, and confusion of mind. {28:29} At midday you will grope about like a blind person in the dark. You will be unsuccessful in everything you do; day after day you will be oppressed and robbed, with no one to rescue you. {28:30} You will be pledged to be married to a woman, but another will take her and rape her. You will build a house, but you will not live in it. You will plant a vineyard, but you will not even begin to enjoy its fruit. {28:31} Your ox will be slaughtered before your eyes, but you will eat none of it. Your donkey will be forcibly taken from you and will not be returned. Your sheep will be given to your enemies, and no one will rescue them. {28:32} Your sons and daughters will be given to another nation, and you will wear out your eyes watching for them day after day, powerless to lift a hand. {28:33} A people that you do not know will eat what your land and labor produce, and you will have nothing but cruel oppression all your days. {28:34} The sights you see will drive you mad. {28:35} The LORD will strike you with painful boils on your knees and legs, which cannot be cured, spreading from the soles of your feet to the top of your head. {28:36} The LORD will bring you and your king, whom you set over yourselves, to a nation neither you nor your ancestors have known, where you will worship other gods—gods of wood and stone. {28:37} You will become an object of horror, scorn, and ridicule among all the nations where the LORD leads you. {28:38} You will sow much seed in the field but harvest little, because locusts will devour it. {28:39} You will plant vineyards and cultivate them but not drink the wine or gather the grapes, because worms will eat them. {28:40} You will have olive trees throughout your land but will not use the oil, because the olives will drop off. {28:41} You will father sons and daughters but will not keep them, for they will go into captivity. {28:42} Swarms of locusts will take over all your trees and the crops of your land. {28:43} The foreigners living among you will rise higher and higher, while you sink lower and lower. {28:44} They will lend to you, but you will not lend to them. They will be the head, and you will be the tail. {28:45} All these curses will come upon you and pursue you until you are destroyed, because you did not obey the voice of the LORD your God and keep his commandments and statutes that he commanded you. {28:46} These curses will serve as a sign and a wonder upon you and your descendants forever. {28:47} Because you did not serve the LORD your God joyfully and gladly in the abundance of all things, {28:48} therefore you will serve your enemies, whom the LORD will send against you, in hunger, thirst, nakedness, and lacking everything. He will place an iron yoke on your neck until he has destroyed you. {28:49} The LORD will bring a nation against you from far away, from the ends of the earth, like an eagle swooping down, a nation whose language you will not understand, {28:50} a fierce-looking nation without respect for the old or pity for the young. {28:51} They will devour the offspring of your livestock and the produce of your land until you are destroyed. They will leave you no grain, new wine, oil, calves of your herds, or lambs of your flocks, until they have caused you to perish. {28:52} They will besiege all your cities until the high and fortified walls in which you trust fall down throughout your land. They will besiege all your cities throughout your land, which the LORD your God has given you. {28:53} Because of the suffering that your enemy will inflict on you during the siege, you will eat the fruit of the womb, the flesh of the sons and daughters the LORD your God has given you. {28:54} Even the most gentle and sensitive man among you will have no compassion on his brother or the wife he loves or his surviving children, {28:55} and he will not share with them the flesh of the children he has eaten because he has nothing left during the siege and desperate times your enemy will inflict on all your cities. {28:56} The most gentle and delicate woman among you—so delicate and sensitive that she would not venture to set the sole of her foot on the ground—will be hostile toward the husband she cherishes and toward her own son and daughter, {28:57} and toward the afterbirth that comes from between her legs and toward her children she bears, because she intends to eat them secretly for lack of anything else during the siege and desperate times your enemy will inflict on your cities. {28:58} If you do not carefully follow all the words of this law, which are written in this book, and do not revere this glorious and awesome name—the LORD your God— {28:59} then the LORD will bring upon you and your descendants extraordinary plagues, great and prolonged plagues, and severe and lingering illnesses. {28:60} He will bring upon you all the diseases of Egypt that you dreaded, and they will cling to you. {28:61} The LORD will also bring on you every kind of sickness and disaster not recorded in this Book of the Law, until you are destroyed. {28:62} You who were as numerous as the stars in the sky will be left but few in number, because you did not obey the LORD your God. {28:63} Just as it pleased the LORD to make you prosper and increase in number, so it will please him to ruin and destroy you. You will be uprooted from the land you are entering to possess. {28:64} The LORD will scatter you among all nations, from one end of the earth to the other. There you will worship other gods—gods of wood and stone, which neither you nor your ancestors have known. {28:65} Among those nations you will find no repose, no resting place for the sole of your foot. There the LORD will give you an anxious mind, eyes weary with longing, and a despairing heart. {28:66} You will live in constant suspense, filled with dread both night and day, never sure of your life. {28:67} In the morning you will say, "If only it were evening!" and in the evening, "If only it were morning!"—because of the terror that will fill your hearts and the sights that your eyes will see. {28:68} The LORD will send you back in ships to Egypt on a journey I said you should never make again. There you will offer yourselves for sale to your enemies as male and female slaves, but no one will buy you.

{29:1} These are the words of the covenant, which the LORD commanded Moses to make with the children of Israel in the land of Moab, beside the covenant which he made with them in Horeb. {29:2} And Moses called unto all Israel, and said unto them, Ye have seen all that the LORD did before your eyes in the land of Egypt unto Pharaoh, and unto all his servants, and unto all his land; {29:3} The great temptations which thine eyes have seen, the signs, and those great miracles: {29:4} Yet the LORD hath not given you an heart to perceive, and eyes to see, and ears to hear, unto this day. {29:5} And I have led you forty years in the wilderness: your clothes are not waxen old upon you, and thy shoe is not waxen old upon thy foot. {29:6} Ye have not eaten bread, neither have ye drunk wine or strong drink: that ye might know that I am the LORD your God. {29:7} And when ye came unto this place, Sihon the king of Heshbon, and Og the king of Bashan, came out against us unto battle, and we smote them: {29:8} And we took their land, and gave it for an inheritance unto the Reubenites, and to the Gadites, and to the half tribe of Manasseh. {29:9} Keep therefore the words of this covenant, and do them, that ye may prosper in all that ye do. {29:10} Ye stand this day all of you before the LORD your God; your captains of your tribes, your elders, and your officers, with all the men of Israel, {29:11} Your little ones, your wives, and thy stranger that is in thy camp, from the hewer of thy wood unto the drawer of thy water: {29:12} That thou shouldest enter into covenant with the LORD thy God, and into his oath, which the LORD thy God maketh with thee this day: {29:13} That he may establish thee to day for a people unto himself, and that he may be unto thee a God, as he hath said unto thee, and as he hath sworn unto thy fathers, to Abraham, to Isaac, and to Jacob. {29:14} Neither with you only do I make this covenant and this oath; {29:15} But with him that standeth here with us this day before the LORD our God, and also with him that is not here with us this day: {29:16} (For ye know how we have dwelt in the land of Egypt; and how we came through the nations which ye passed by; {29:17} And ye have seen their abominations, and their idols, wood and stone, silver and gold, which were among them:) {29:18} Lest there should be among you man, or woman, or family, or tribe, whose heart turneth away this day from the LORD our God, to go and serve the gods of these nations; lest there should be among you a root that beareth gall and wormwood; {29:19} And it come to pass, when he heareth the words of this curse, that he bless himself in his heart, saying, I shall have peace, though I walk in the imagination of mine heart, to add drunkenness to thirst: {29:20} The LORD will not spare him, but then the anger of the LORD and his jealousy shall smoke against that man, and all the curses that are written in this book shall lie upon him, and the LORD shall blot out his name from under heaven. {29:21} And the LORD shall separate him unto evil out of all the tribes of Israel, according to all the curses of the covenant that are written in this book of the law: {29:22} So that the generation to come of your children that shall rise up after you, and the stranger that shall come from a far land, shall say, when they see the plagues of that land, and the sicknesses which the LORD hath laid upon it; {29:23} And that the whole land thereof is brimstone, and salt, and burning, that it is not sown, nor beareth, nor any grass groweth therein, like the overthrow of Sodom, and Gomorrah, Admah, and Zeboim, which the LORD overthrew in his anger, and in his wrath: {29:24} Even all nations shall say, Wherefore hath the LORD done thus unto this land? what meaneth the heat of this great anger? {29:25} Then men shall say, Because they have forsaken the covenant of the LORD God of their fathers, which he made with them when he brought them forth out of the land of Egypt: {29:26} For they went and served other gods, and worshipped them, gods whom they knew not, and whom he had not given unto them: {29:27} And the anger of the LORD was kindled against this land, to bring upon it all the curses that are written in this book: {29:28} And the LORD rooted them out of their land in anger, and in wrath, and in great indignation, and cast them into another land, as it is this day. {29:29} The secret things belong unto the LORD our God: but those things which are revealed belong unto us and to our children forever, that we may do all the words of this law.

{30:1} When all these things happen to you—the blessings and the curses that I have set before you—and you reflect on them while among all the nations where the LORD your God has driven you, {30:2} and you return to the LORD your God and obey His voice with all your heart and soul, according to all that I command you today, you and your children, {30:3} then the LORD your God will restore your fortunes and have compassion on you, gathering you again from all the peoples where He has scattered you. {30:4} Even if you are banished to the ends of the earth, from there the LORD your God will gather you and bring you back. {30:5} The LORD your God will bring you into the land that your fathers possessed, and you shall possess it. He will do you good and multiply you more than your fathers. {30:6} The LORD your God will circumcise your heart and the heart of your descendants, so that you may love the LORD your God with all your heart and soul, and live. {30:7} The LORD your God will put all these curses on your enemies who hate and persecute you. {30:8} Then you will again obey the voice of the LORD and follow all His commandments I am giving you today. {30:9} The LORD your God will make you prosper abundantly in all the work of your hands, in the offspring of your body, the produce of your livestock, and the produce of your land. For the LORD will again delight in your prosperity, just as He delighted in that of your fathers, {30:10} if you obey the voice of the LORD your God by keeping His commandments and statutes written in this Book of the Law, and if you return to Him with all your heart and soul. {30:11} For this commandment I am giving you today is not too difficult for you or beyond your reach. {30:12} It is not in heaven, so you would need to ask, "Who will ascend to heaven to get it for us and proclaim it, so we may obey it?" {30:13} Nor is it across the sea, so you would need to ask, "Who will cross the sea to get it for us and proclaim it, so we may obey it?" {30:14} The word is near you, in your mouth and in your heart, so you may obey it. {30:15} See, I have set before you today life and prosperity, death and adversity. {30:16} I am commanding you today to love the LORD your God, to walk in His ways, and to keep His commandments, statutes, and ordinances, so that you may live and increase, and the LORD your God may bless you in the land you are entering to possess. {30:17} But if your heart turns away and you do not listen, and you are led astray to bow down to other gods and worship them, {30:18} I declare to you this day that you will certainly perish; you will not live long in the land you are crossing the Jordan to enter and possess. {30:19} I call heaven and earth as witnesses against you today that I have set before you life and death, blessing and cursing. Choose life so that you and your descendants may live, {30:20} loving the LORD your God, obeying His voice, and clinging to Him. For He is your life and the length of your days, that you may dwell in the land that the LORD swore to your fathers—to Abraham, Isaac, and Jacob—to give them."

{31:1} Moses spoke these words to all Israel, {31:2} saying, "I am one hundred and twenty years old today; I can no longer go out and come in. Also, the LORD has said to me, 'You shall not cross over this Jordan.' {31:3} The LORD your God Himself will cross over before you; He will destroy these nations from before you, and you shall dispossess them. Joshua himself will cross over before you, as the LORD has said. {31:4} And the LORD will do to them as He did to Sihon and Og, the kings of the Amorites, and their land, when He destroyed them. {31:5} The LORD will give them over to you, that you may do to them according to every commandment which I have commanded you. {31:6} Be strong and courageous, do not fear nor be afraid of them; for the LORD your God, He is the One who goes with you. He will not leave you nor forsake you." {31:7} Then Moses called Joshua and said to him in the sight of all Israel, "Be strong and of good courage, for you must go with this people to the land which the LORD has sworn to their fathers to give them, and you shall cause them to inherit it. {31:8} And the LORD, He is the One who goes before you. He will be with you, He will not leave you nor forsake you; do not fear nor be dismayed." {31:9} So Moses wrote this law and delivered it to the priests, the sons of Levi, who bore the ark of the covenant of the LORD, and to all the elders of Israel. {31:10} And Moses commanded them, saying: "At the end of every seven years, at the appointed time in the year of release, at the Feast of Tabernacles, {31:11} when all Israel comes to appear before the LORD your God in the place which He chooses, you shall read this law before all Israel in their hearing. {31:12} Gather the people together, men and women and little ones, and the stranger who is within your gates, that they may hear and that they may learn to fear the LORD your God and carefully observe all the words of this law, {31:13} and that their children, who have not known it, may hear and learn to fear the LORD your God as long as you live in the land which you cross the Jordan to possess." {31:14} Then the LORD said to Moses, "Behold, the days approach when you must die; call Joshua, and present yourselves in the tabernacle of meeting, that I may inaugurate him." So Moses and Joshua went and presented themselves in the tabernacle of meeting. {31:15} Now the LORD appeared at the tabernacle in a pillar of cloud, and the pillar of cloud stood above the door of the tabernacle. {31:16} Then the LORD said to Moses: "Behold, you will rest with your fathers; and this people will rise and play the harlot with the gods of the foreigners of the land, where they go to be among them, and they will forsake Me and break My covenant which I have made with them. {31:17} Then My anger shall be aroused against them in that day, and I will forsake them, and I will hide My face from them, and they shall be devoured. And many evils and troubles shall befall them, so that they will say in that day, 'Have not these evils come upon us because our God is not among us?' {31:18} And I will surely hide My face in that day because of all the evil which they have done, in that they have turned to other gods. {31:19} Now therefore, write down this song for yourselves, and teach it to the children of Israel; put it in their mouths, that this song may be a witness for Me against the children of Israel. {31:20} When I have brought them to the land flowing with milk and honey, of which I swore to their fathers, and they have eaten and filled themselves and grown fat, then they will turn to other gods and serve them; and they will provoke Me and break My covenant. {31:21} Then it shall be, when many evils and troubles have come upon them, that this song will testify against them as a witness; for it will not be forgotten in the mouths of their descendants, for I know the inclination of their behavior today, even before I have brought them to the land of which I swore." {31:22} Therefore Moses wrote this song the same day, and taught it to the children of Israel. {31:23} Then He inaugurated Joshua the son of Nun, and said, "Be strong and of good courage; for you shall bring the children of Israel into the land of which I swore to them, and I will be with you." {31:24} So it was, when Moses had completed writing the words of this law in a book, when they were finished, {31:25} that Moses commanded the Levites, who bore the ark of the covenant of the LORD, saying: {31:26} "Take this Book of the Law, and put it beside the ark of the covenant of the LORD your God, that it may be there as a witness against you; {31:27} for I know your rebellion and your stiff neck. If today, while I am yet alive with you, you have been rebellious against the LORD, then how much more after my death? {31:28} Gather to me all the elders of your tribes, and your officers, that I may speak these words in their hearing and call heaven and earth to witness against them. {31:29} For I know that after my death you will become utterly corrupt, and turn aside from the way which I have commanded you. And evil will befall you in the latter days, because you will do evil in the sight of the LORD, to provoke Him to anger through the work of your hands." {31:30} Then Moses spoke in the hearing of all the assembly of Israel the words of this song until they were ended.

{32:1} Listen, O heavens, and I will speak; Hear, O earth, the words of my mouth. {32:2} Let my teaching drop as the rain, My speech distill as the dew, As raindrops on the tender herb, And as showers on the grass. {32:3} For I proclaim the name of the LORD: Ascribe greatness to our God. {32:4} He is the Rock, His work is perfect; For all His ways are justice, A God of truth and without injustice; Righteous and upright is He. {32:5} "They have corrupted themselves; They are not His children, Because of their blemish: A perverse and crooked generation. {32:6} Do you thus deal with the LORD, O foolish and unwise people? Is He not your Father, who bought you? Has He not made you and established you? {32:7} "Remember the days of old, Consider the years of many generations. Ask your father, and he will show you; Your elders, and they will tell you: {32:8} When the Most High divided their inheritance to the nations, When He separated the sons of Adam, He set the boundaries of the peoples According to the number of the children of Israel. {32:9} For the LORD's portion is His people; Jacob is the place of His inheritance. {32:10} "He found him in a desert land And in the wasteland, a howling wilderness; He encircled him, He instructed him, He kept him as the apple of His eye. {32:11} As an eagle stirs up its nest, Hovers over its young, Spreading out its wings, taking them up, Carrying them on its wings, {32:12} So the LORD alone led him, And there was no foreign god with him. {32:13} "He made him ride in the heights of the earth, That he might eat the produce of the fields; He made him draw honey from the rock, And oil from the flinty rock; {32:14} Curds from the cattle, and milk of the flock, With fat of lambs; And rams of the breed of Bashan, and goats, With the choicest wheat; And you drank wine, the blood of the grapes. {32:15} "But Jeshurun grew fat and kicked; You grew fat, you grew thick, You are obese! Then he forsook God who made him, And scornfully esteemed the Rock of his salvation. {32:16} They provoked Him to jealousy with foreign gods; With abominations they provoked Him to anger. {32:17} They sacrificed to demons, not to God, To gods they did not know, To new gods, new arrivals That your fathers did not fear. {32:18} Of the Rock who begot you, you are unmindful, And have forgotten the God who fathered you. {32:19} "And when the LORD saw it, He spurned them, Because of the provocation of His sons and His daughters. {32:20} And He said: 'I will hide My face from them, I will see what their end will be, For they are a perverse generation, Children in whom is no faith. {32:21} They have provoked Me to jealousy by what is not God; They have moved Me to anger by their foolish idols. But I will provoke them to jealousy by those who are not a nation; I will move them to anger by a foolish nation. {32:22} For a fire is kindled in My anger, And shall burn to the lowest hell; It shall consume the earth with her increase, And set on fire the foundations of the mountains. {32:23} 'I will heap disasters on them; I will spend My arrows on them. {32:24} They shall be wasted with hunger, Devoured by pestilence and bitter destruction; I will also send against them the teeth of beasts, With the poison of serpents of the dust. {32:25} The sword shall destroy outside; There shall be terror within For the young man and virgin, The nursing child with the man of gray hairs. {32:26} I would have said, "I will dash them in pieces, I will make the memory of them to cease from among men," {32:27} Had I not feared the wrath of the enemy, Lest their adversaries should misunderstand, Lest they should say, "Our hand is high; And it is not the LORD who has done all this."' {32:28} "For they are a nation void of counsel, Nor is there any understanding in them. {32:29} Oh, that they were wise, that they understood this, That they would consider their latter end! {32:30} How could one chase a thousand, And two put ten thousand to flight, Unless their Rock had sold them, And the LORD had surrendered them? {32:31} For their rock is not like our Rock, Even our enemies themselves being judges. {32:32} For their vine is of the vine of Sodom And of the fields of Gomorrah; Their grapes are grapes of gall, Their clusters are bitter. {32:33} Their wine is the poison of serpents, And the cruel venom of cobras. {32:34} 'Is this not laid up in store with Me, Sealed up among My treasures? {32:35} Vengeance is Mine, and recompense; Their foot shall slip in due time; For the day of their calamity is at hand, And the things to come hasten upon them.' {32:36} "For the LORD will judge His people And have compassion on His servants, When He sees that their power is gone, And there is no one remaining, bond or free. {32:37} He will say: 'Where are their gods, The rock in which they sought refuge? {32:38} Who ate the fat of their sacrifices, And drank the wine of their drink offering? Let them rise and help you, And be your refuge. {32:39} 'Now see that I, even I, am He, And there is no God besides Me; I kill and I make alive; I wound and I heal; Nor is there any who can deliver from My hand. {32:40} For I raise My hand to heaven, And say, "As I live forever, {32:41} If I whet My glittering sword, And My hand takes hold on judgment, I will render vengeance to My enemies, And repay those who hate Me. {32:42} I will make My arrows drunk with blood, And my sword shall devour flesh; With the blood of the slain and the captives, From the heads of the leaders of the enemy.' {32:43} "Rejoice, O nations, with His people; For He will avenge the blood of His servants, And render vengeance to His adversaries; He will provide atonement for His land and His people." {32:44} So Moses came with Hoshea the son of Nun and spoke all the words of this song in the hearing of the people. {32:45} Moses finished speaking all these words to all Israel. {32:46} And he said to them: "Set your hearts on all the words which I testify among you today, which you shall command your children to be careful to observe—all the words of this law. {32:47} For it is not a futile thing for you, because it is your life, and by this word you shall prolong your days in the land which you cross over the Jordan to possess." {32:48} Then the LORD spoke to Moses that very same day, saying: {32:49} "Go up this mountain of the Abarim, Mount Nebo, which is in the land of Moab, across from Jericho; view the land of Canaan, which I give to the children of Israel as a possession; {32:50} and die on the mountain which you ascend, and be gathered to your people, just as Aaron your brother died on Mount Hor and was gathered to his people; {32:51} because you trespassed against Me among the children of Israel at the waters of Meribah Kadesh, in the Wilderness of Zin, because you did not hallow Me in the midst of the children of Israel. {32:52} Yet you shall see the land before you, though you shall not go there, into the land which I am giving to the children of Israel."

{33:1} This is the blessing with which Moses, the man of God, blessed the children of Israel before his death. {33:2} He said: "The LORD came from Sinai, And dawned on them from Seir; He shone forth from Mount Paran, And He came with ten thousands of saints; From His right hand Came a fiery law for them. {33:3} Yes, He loves the people; All His saints are in Your hand; They sit down at Your feet; Everyone receives Your words. {33:4} Moses commanded us a law, The inheritance of the congregation of Jacob. {33:5} And he was king in Jeshurun, When the leaders of the people were gathered, All the tribes of Israel together. {33:6} "Let Reuben live, and not die, Nor let his men be few." {33:7} And this is the blessing of Judah; and he said, "Hear, LORD, the voice of Judah, And bring him to his people; Let his hands be sufficient for him, And may You be a help against his enemies." {33:8} And of Levi he said: "Let Your Thummim and Your Urim be with Your holy one, Whom You tested at Massah, And with whom You contended at the waters of Meribah, {33:9} Who said to his father and mother, 'I have not seen them'; Nor did he acknowledge his brothers, Or know his own children; For they have observed Your word And kept Your covenant. {33:10} They shall teach Jacob Your judgments, And Israel Your law. They shall put incense before You, And a whole burnt sacrifice on Your altar. {33:11} Bless his substance, LORD, And accept the work of his hands; Strike the loins of those who rise against him, And of those who hate him, that they rise not again." {33:12} Of Benjamin he said: "The beloved of the LORD shall dwell in safety by Him, Who shelters him all the day long; And he shall dwell between His shoulders." {33:13} And of Joseph he said: "Blessed of the LORD is his land, With the precious things of heaven, with the dew, And the deep lying beneath, {33:14} With the precious fruits of the sun, With the precious produce of the months, {33:15} With the best things of the ancient mountains, With the precious things of the everlasting hills, {33:16} With the precious things of the earth and its fullness, And the favor of Him who dwelt in the bush. Let the blessing come 'on the head of Joseph, And on the crown of the head of him who was separate from his brothers.' {33:17} His glory is like a firstborn bull, And his horns like the horns of the wild ox; Together with them He shall push the peoples To the ends of the earth; They are the ten thousands of Ephraim, And they are the thousands of Manasseh." {33:18} And of Zebulun he said: "Rejoice, Zebulun, in your going out, And Issachar, in your tents! {33:19} They shall call the peoples to the mountain; There they shall offer sacrifices of righteousness; For they shall partake of the abundance of the seas And of treasures hidden in the sand." {33:20} And of Gad he said: "Blessed is he who enlarges Gad; He dwells as a lion, And tears the arm and the crown of his head. {33:21} He provided the first part for himself, Because a lawgiver's portion was reserved there. He came with the heads of the people; He administered the justice of the LORD, And His judgments with Israel." {33:22} And of Dan he said: "Dan is a lion's whelp; He shall leap from Bashan." {33:23} And of Naphtali he said: "O Naphtali, satisfied with favor, And full of the blessing of the LORD, Possess the west and the south." {33:24} And of Asher he said: "Asher is most blessed of sons; Let him be favored by his brothers, And let him dip his foot in oil. {33:25} Your sandals shall be iron and bronze; As your days, so shall your strength be. {33:26} "There is no one like the God of Jeshurun, Who rides the heavens to help you, And in His excellency on the clouds. {33:27} The eternal God is your refuge, And underneath are the everlasting arms; He will thrust out the enemy from before you, And will say, 'Destroy!' {33:28} Then Israel shall dwell in safety, The fountain of Jacob alone, In a land of grain and new wine; His heavens shall also drop dew. {33:29} Happy are you, O Israel! Who is like you, a people saved by the LORD, The shield of your help And the sword of your majesty! Your enemies shall submit to you, And you shall tread down their high places."

{34:1} Moses went up from the plains of Moab to Mount Nebo, to the top of Pisgah, opposite Jericho. The LORD showed him all the land of Gilead as far as Dan, {34:2} All Naphtali, the land of Ephraim and Manasseh, all the land of Judah as far as the Western Sea, {34:3} The Negev, the plain of the valley of Jericho, the City of Palms, as far as Zoar. {34:4} Then the LORD said to him, "This is the land I promised on oath to Abraham, Isaac, and Jacob when I said, 'I will give it to your descendants.' I have let you see it with your eyes, but you will not cross over into it." {34:5} So Moses the servant of the LORD died there in the land of Moab, as the LORD had said. {34:6} He buried him in Moab, in the valley opposite Beth Peor, but to this day no one knows where his grave is. {34:7} Moses was a hundred and twenty years old when he died, yet his eyes were not weak nor his strength gone. {34:8} The Israelites grieved for Moses in the plains of Moab thirty days, until the time of weeping and mourning was over. {34:9} Now Joshua son of Nun was filled with the spirit of wisdom because Moses had laid his hands on him. So the Israelites listened to him and did what the LORD had commanded Moses. {34:10} Since then, no prophet has risen in Israel like Moses, whom the LORD knew face to face, {34:11} Who did all those signs and wonders the LORD sent him to do in Egypt—to Pharaoh and to all his officials and to his whole land. {34:12} For no one has ever shown the mighty power or performed the awesome deeds that Moses did in the sight of all Israel.

Joshua

{1:1} After Moses, the servant of the LORD, died, the LORD spoke to Joshua, Moses' assistant, saying, {1:2} "Moses, my servant, is dead. Now therefore, arise, go over this Jordan, you and all this people, to the land which I am giving to them—the children of Israel. {1:3} Every place that the sole of your foot shall tread upon, I have given to you, as I said to Moses. {1:4} From the wilderness and Lebanon, as far as the great river, the Euphrates, all the land of the Hittites, and to the Great Sea toward the setting of the sun, shall be your territory. {1:5} **No one shall be able to stand against you all the days of your life. As I was with Moses, so I will be with you. I will not fail you nor forsake you.** {1:6} Be strong and courageous, for you shall divide this land as an inheritance to the people, which I swore to their fathers to give them. {1:7} Only be strong and very courageous, that you may observe to do according to all the law which Moses, my servant, commanded you. Do not turn from it to the right hand or to the left, that you may prosper wherever you go. {1:8} This Book of the Law shall not depart from your mouth, but you shall meditate on it day and night, that you may observe to do according to all that is written in it. For then you will make your way prosperous, and then you will have good success. {1:9} **"Have I not commanded you? Be strong and of good courage; do not be afraid, nor be dismayed, for the LORD your God is with you wherever you go."** {1:10} Then Joshua commanded the officers of the people, saying, {1:11} "Pass through the camp and command the people, saying, 'Prepare provisions for yourselves, for within three days you will cross over this Jordan, to go in to possess the land which the LORD your God is giving you to possess.'" {1:12} And to the Reubenites, the Gadites, and half the tribe of Manasseh, Joshua spoke, saying, {1:13} "Remember the word which Moses, the servant of the LORD, commanded you, saying, 'The LORD your God is giving you rest and is giving you this land.' {1:14} Your wives, your little ones, and your livestock shall remain in the land which Moses gave you on this side of the Jordan. But you shall pass before your brethren armed, all your mighty men of valor, and help them, {1:15} Until the LORD has given your brethren rest, as He gave you, and they also have taken possession of the land which the LORD your God is giving them. Then you shall return to the land of your possession and enjoy it, which Moses the servant of the LORD gave you on this side of the Jordan toward the sunrise." {1:16} So they answered Joshua, saying, "All that you command us we will do, and wherever you send us, we will go. {1:17} Just as we heeded Moses in all things, so we will heed you. Only let the LORD your God be with you, as He was with Moses. {1:18} Whoever rebels against your command and does not heed your words, in all that you command him, shall be put to death. Only be strong and of good courage."

{2:1} Joshua, the son of Nun, sent two men secretly from Shittim, saying, "Go, view the land, especially Jericho." So they went and entered the house of a prostitute named Rahab and stayed there. {2:2} The king of Jericho was informed, "Behold, men of Israel have come here tonight to search out the land." {2:3} The king of Jericho sent word to Rahab, saying, "Bring out the men who have come to you, who entered your house, for they have come to search out the entire land." {2:4} But the woman had taken the two men and hidden them. She said, "True, the men came to me, but I did not know where they were from. {2:5} And at the time of the shutting of the gate, when it was dark, the men went out. Where the men went, I do not know. Pursue them quickly, for you may overtake them." {2:6} But she had brought them up to the roof and hidden them with stalks of flax that she had laid in order upon the roof. {2:7} And the men pursued after them toward the Jordan as far as the fords. As soon as the pursuers had gone out, they shut the gate. {2:8} Before the men lay down, she came up to them on the roof {2:9} and said to them, "I know that the LORD has given you the land, and that the fear of you has fallen upon us, and that all the inhabitants of the land melt away before you. {2:10} For we have heard how the LORD dried up the water of the Red Sea before you when you came out of Egypt, and what you did to the two kings of the Amorites who were beyond the Jordan, to Sihon and Og, whom you devoted to destruction. {2:11} And as soon as we heard it, our hearts melted, and there was no spirit left in any man because of you, for the LORD your God, he is God in the heavens above and on the earth beneath. {2:12} Now then, please swear to me by the LORD that, as I have dealt kindly with you, you also will deal kindly with my father's house, and give me a sure sign {2:13} that you will save alive my father and mother, my brothers and sisters, and all who belong to them, and deliver our lives from death." {2:14} And the men said to her, "Our life for yours even to death! If you do not tell this business of ours, then when the LORD gives us the land we will deal kindly and faithfully with you." {2:15} Then she let them down by a rope through the window, for her house was built into the city wall, so that she lived in the wall. {2:16} And she said to them, "Go into the hills, or the pursuers will encounter you, and hide there three days until the pursuers have returned. Then afterward you may go your way." {2:17} The men said to her, "We will be guiltless with respect to this oath of yours that you have made us swear. {2:18} Behold, when we come into the land, you shall tie this scarlet cord in the window through which you let us down, and you shall gather into your house your father and mother, your brothers, and all your father's household. {2:19} Then if anyone goes out of the doors of your house into the street, his blood shall be on his own head, and we shall be guiltless. But if a hand is laid on anyone who is with you in the house, his blood shall be on our head. {2:20} But if you tell this business of ours, then we shall be guiltless with respect to your oath that you have made us swear." {2:21} And she said, "According to your words, so be it." Then she sent them away, and they departed. And she tied the scarlet cord in the window. {2:22} They departed and went into the hills and remained there three days until the pursuers returned, and the pursuers searched all along the way and found nothing. {2:23} Then the two men returned. They came down from the hills and passed over and came to Joshua the son of Nun, and they told him all that had happened to them. {2:24} And they said to Joshua, "Truly the LORD has given all the land into our hands. And also, all the inhabitants of the land melt away because of us."

{3:1} Joshua woke up early in the morning. They left Shittim and came to the Jordan River, he along with all the Israelites, and stayed there before crossing over. {3:2} After three days, the officers went through the camp; {3:3} and they commanded the people, saying, "When you see the ark of the covenant of the LORD your God, and the Levite priests carrying it, then you shall move from your place and follow it. {3:4} But keep a distance of about two thousand cubits between you and it. Do not come near it, so you'll know the way to go, because you have not traveled this way before." {3:5} Joshua said to the people, "Prepare yourselves, for tomorrow the LORD will perform wonders among you." {3:6} Then Joshua instructed the priests, "Take up the ark of the covenant and cross over ahead of the people." So they lifted the ark of the covenant and went before the people. {3:7} And the LORD said to Joshua, "Today I will begin to make you great in the eyes of all Israel, so they may know that, as I was with Moses, I will also be with you. {3:8} Command the priests who carry the ark of the covenant, 'When you reach the edge of the Jordan's waters, stand in the river.'" {3:9} Joshua said to the Israelites, "Come here and listen to the words of the LORD your God. {3:10} This is how you will know that the living God is among you and that He will drive out the Canaanites, Hittites, Hivites, Perizzites, Girgashites, Amorites, and Jebusites from before you. {3:11} See, the ark of the covenant of the Lord of all the earth is crossing over ahead of you into the Jordan. {3:12} Now choose twelve men, one from each tribe of Israel. {3:13} And as soon as the feet of the priests who carry the ark of the LORD, the Lord of all the earth, touch the waters of the Jordan, its flowing waters will be cut off and stand up in a heap." {3:14} So when the people set out from their tents to cross the Jordan, with the priests bearing the ark of the covenant ahead of them, {3:15} and when those who carried the ark came to the Jordan and their feet touched the water's edge (for the Jordan overflows all its banks during the harvest season), {3:16} the waters flowing down from above stopped and rose up in a heap a great distance away, at Adam, the city near Zaretan. And those flowing down toward the Sea of the Arabah, the Salt Sea, were completely cut off, and the people crossed over opposite Jericho. {3:17} The priests who carried the ark of the covenant of the LORD stood firm on dry ground in the middle of the Jordan, while all Israel passed by until the whole nation had completed crossing over on dry ground.

{4:1} When all the people had finished crossing the Jordan River, the LORD spoke to Joshua, saying, {4:2} "Choose twelve men from among the people, one from each tribe, {4:3} and command them, 'Take twelve stones from the middle of the Jordan, from the place where the priests' feet stood firm. Carry them with you and leave them at the place where you will camp tonight.'" {4:4} So Joshua called the twelve men he had selected from the Israelites, one from each tribe, {4:5} and instructed them, "Go ahead of the ark of the LORD your God into the middle of the Jordan. Each of you should carry a stone on your shoulder, one stone for each tribe of the Israelites, {4:6} so that this may serve as a sign among you. In the future, when your children ask their fathers, 'What do these stones mean?' {4:7} you shall tell them, 'The waters of the Jordan were cut off before the ark of the covenant of the LORD when it crossed the Jordan. These stones are to be a memorial for the Israelites forever.'" {4:8} The Israelites did as Joshua commanded. They took twelve stones from the middle of the Jordan, as the LORD had instructed Joshua. Each tribe of Israel carried a stone, according to the number of the tribes of Israel, and they placed them at their campsite. {4:9} Joshua also set up twelve stones in the middle of the Jordan, where the priests who carried the ark of the covenant had stood. Those stones are there to this day. {4:10} The priests carrying the ark remained standing in the middle of the Jordan until everything the LORD had commanded Joshua to tell the people had been done, following all that Moses had commanded Joshua. Then the people hurried across, {4:11} and when everyone had finished crossing, the ark of the LORD and the priests crossed over in the presence of the people. {4:12} The tribes of Reuben, Gad, and the half-tribe of Manasseh crossed over armed and ahead of the Israelites, just as Moses had instructed them. {4:13} About forty thousand equipped for battle crossed over before the LORD to the plains of Jericho. {4:14} On that day, the LORD honored Joshua in the sight of all Israel, and they revered him all the days of his life, just as they had revered Moses. {4:15} Then the LORD spoke to Joshua, saying, {4:16} "Command the priests who carry the ark of the covenant: 'Come up out of the Jordan.'" {4:17} So Joshua commanded the priests, "Come up out of the Jordan." {4:18} And when the priests who carried the ark of the covenant of the LORD came up from the middle of the Jordan, and the soles of their feet touched dry ground, the waters of the Jordan returned to their place and overflowed all its banks as before. {4:19} The people came up out of the Jordan on the tenth day of the first month and camped at Gilgal, on the eastern border of Jericho. {4:20} Joshua set up the twelve stones that had been taken from the Jordan at Gilgal. {4:21} Then he said to the Israelites, "In the future, when your children ask their fathers, 'What do these stones mean?' {4:22} you shall let your children know, 'Israel crossed the Jordan on dry ground.' {4:23} For the LORD your God dried up the waters of the Jordan before you until you had crossed over, just as He did to the Red Sea, which He dried up before us until we had crossed over, {4:24} so that all the peoples of the earth may know the mighty hand of the LORD, and so that you may always fear the LORD your God."

{5:1} When all the kings of the Amorites on the west side of the Jordan River and all the kings of the Canaanites along the coast heard that the LORD had dried up the Jordan River before the Israelites until they had crossed over, their hearts melted in fear, and they lost all courage because of the Israelites. {5:2} At that time, the LORD said to Joshua, "Make sharp knives and circumcise the Israelites again, a second time." {5:3} So Joshua made sharp knives and circumcised the Israelites at the hill of the foreskins. {5:4} Joshua circumcised them because all the males who came out of Egypt, the warriors, had died in the wilderness during the journey after leaving Egypt. {5:5} All the people who came out were circumcised, but none of those born in the wilderness during the journey from Egypt had been circumcised. {5:6} The Israelites wandered in the wilderness for forty years until all the warriors who had come out of Egypt had died because they did not obey the LORD. The LORD had sworn that he would not let them see the land he had promised their ancestors—a land flowing with milk and honey. {5:7} Their children, whom Joshua circumcised, had not been circumcised along the way because they were born after the journey. {5:8} After they had finished circumcising the entire nation, they stayed in their places in the camp until they had healed. {5:9} Then the LORD said to Joshua, "Today I have rolled away the disgrace of Egypt from you." So that place has been called Gilgal to this day. {5:10} The Israelites camped in Gilgal and celebrated the Passover on the evening of the fourteenth day of the month in the plains of Jericho. {5:11} On the day after the Passover, they ate some of the produce of the land: unleavened bread and roasted grain. {5:12} The manna stopped the day after they ate this food from the land; there was no longer any manna for the Israelites, but that year they ate the crops of Canaan. {5:13} Now when Joshua was near Jericho, he looked up and saw a man standing in front of him with a drawn sword in his hand. Joshua approached him and asked, "Are you for us or for our enemies?" {5:14} "Neither," he replied, "but as commander of the army of the LORD I have now come." Then Joshua fell facedown to the ground in reverence and asked him, "What message does my lord have for his servant?" {5:15} The commander of the LORD'S army replied, "Take off your sandals, for the place where you are standing is holy." And Joshua did so.

{6:1} Jericho was tightly shut up because of the Israelites; no one went out, and no one came in. {6:2} Then the LORD said to Joshua, "See, I have given Jericho into your hands, along with its king and its mighty warriors. {6:3} You are to march around the city, all the men of war, and circle the city once. Do this for six days. {6:4} Have seven priests carry trumpets made from ram's horns in front of the ark. On the seventh day, march around the city seven times, with the priests blowing the trumpets. {6:5} When you hear a long blast on the trumpets, have all the people give a loud shout. Then the wall of the city will collapse, and the people will go up, each straight ahead." {6:6} So Joshua called the priests and instructed them, "Take up the ark of the covenant, and let seven priests carry seven trumpets made from ram's horns in front of the LORD." {6:7} Then he ordered the people, "Move forward and march around the city, with the armed troops going ahead of the ark of the LORD." {6:8} And as Joshua had commanded, the seven priests carrying the seven trumpets made from ram's horns before the LORD went forward, blowing the trumpets, while the ark of the covenant of the LORD followed them. {6:9} The armed troops went ahead of the priests who blew the trumpets, and the rear guard followed the ark, with the priests continually blowing the trumpets. {6:10} Joshua had commanded the people, "Do not shout or make any noise with your voices until the day I tell you to shout. Then shout!" {6:11} So the ark of the LORD circled the city, going once around it. Then the people returned to camp and spent the night there. {6:12} Joshua got up early the next morning, and the priests took up the ark of the LORD. {6:13} The seven priests carrying the seven trumpets made from ram's horns went forward, continually blowing the trumpets, with the armed troops marching ahead of them. The rear guard followed the ark of the LORD, with the priests blowing the trumpets. {6:14} On the second day they marched around the city once and returned to the camp. They did this for six days. {6:15} On the seventh day, they got up at daybreak and marched around the city seven times in the same manner. On that day, only on that day, they circled the city seven times. {6:16} When the priests blew the trumpets the seventh time, Joshua commanded the people, "Shout! For the LORD has given you the city. {6:17} The city and all that is in it are to be devoted to the LORD. Only Rahab the prostitute and all who are with her in her house shall be spared, because she hid the spies we sent. {6:18} But keep away from the devoted things, so that you will not bring about your own destruction by taking any of them. Otherwise, you will make the camp of Israel liable to destruction and bring trouble on it. {6:19} All the silver and gold and the articles of bronze and iron are sacred to the LORD and must go into his treasury." {6:20} **When the trumpets sounded, the people shouted, and at the sound of the trumpet, when the people gave a loud shout, the wall collapsed; so everyone charged straight in, and they took the city.** {6:21} They completely destroyed everything in the city with the sword—every man and woman, young and old, as well as the cattle, sheep, and donkeys. {6:22} Joshua said to the two men who had spied out the land, "Go into the prostitute's house and bring her out, along with all her family, as you promised her." {6:23} So the young men who had done the spying went in and brought out Rahab, her father, mother, brothers, and all the other relatives who were with her. They brought out her entire family and settled them outside the camp of Israel. {6:24} Then they burned down the city and everything in it. Only the silver, gold, and articles of bronze and iron were placed in the treasury of the LORD's house. {6:25} But Joshua spared Rahab the prostitute, with her family and all who belonged to her, because she hid the men Joshua had sent as spies to Jericho. And she lives among the Israelites to this day. {6:26} At that time Joshua pronounced this solemn oath: "Cursed before the LORD is the one who undertakes to rebuild this city, Jericho: 'At the cost of his firstborn son he will lay its foundations; at the cost of his youngest he will set up its gates.'" {6:27} So the LORD was with Joshua, and his fame spread throughout the land.

{7:1} The Israelites committed a trespass by taking something cursed. Achan, from the tribe of Judah, took some of the cursed things, and this angered the LORD against the Israelites. {7:2} Joshua sent men from Jericho to Ai, near Beth-aven, east of Bethel, to scout the land. {7:3} When they returned, they advised Joshua to send only a few men—about two or three thousand—to attack Ai, as the people of Ai were few. {7:4} So about three thousand men went up, but they were chased away by the men of Ai. {7:5} The men of Ai killed about thirty-six Israelites, chasing them from the gate to Shebarim, striking them down on the descent. This caused great fear among the Israelites. {7:6} Joshua tore his clothes and fell face down before the ark of the LORD until evening, along with the elders of Israel, putting dust on their heads. {7:7} Joshua lamented, asking the LORD why He had brought them across the Jordan only to be delivered into the hands of the Amorites to be destroyed. He wished they had stayed on the other side of the Jordan. {7:8} He expressed concern about what would happen if Israel turned its back to its enemies. {7:9} Joshua feared that the Canaanites and all the inhabitants of the land would surround them and wipe out their name. He questioned what would become of the LORD's great name. {7:10} The LORD responded to Joshua, asking why he was lying face down. {7:11} The LORD explained that Israel had sinned and broken His covenant by taking the cursed thing, stealing, and deceiving. They had hidden it among their belongings. {7:12} Because of this sin, the Israelites could not stand before their enemies and would turn their backs. The LORD declared that He would no longer be with them unless they removed the accursed thing from among them. {7:13} The LORD commanded Joshua to sanctify the people and to remove the accursed thing from among them, warning that they couldn't stand before their enemies until they did so. {7:14} In the morning, the tribes would be brought forward, and the LORD would choose which tribe, family, and household was guilty. The guilty individual would be identified. {7:15} The person found with the cursed thing would be burned with fire, along with all his possessions, for breaking the covenant of the LORD and bringing folly upon Israel. {7:16} Joshua rose early in the morning and brought Israel by their tribes. The tribe of Judah was taken. {7:17} Then he brought the family of Judah, and the Zarhites were taken. He brought each family member, and Zabdi was taken. {7:18} He brought each member of Zabdi's household, and Achan, the son of Carmi, was taken from the tribe of Judah. {7:19} Joshua asked Achan to confess his sin to the LORD and tell him what he had done, not to hide anything. {7:20} Achan admitted his sin, confessing that he had seen a valuable Babylonian garment, silver, and gold, which he coveted and took, hiding them in his tent. {7:21} Joshua sent messengers to Achan's tent, where they found the stolen items hidden as Achan had described. {7:22} They brought the items before Joshua and all the Israelites, laying them out before the LORD. {7:23} Then Joshua and all Israel took Achan, along with the stolen items, his family, livestock, tent, and everything he owned, to the Valley of Achor. {7:24} There, they stoned Achan and burned everything with fire. {7:25} Joshua questioned why Achan had brought trouble upon them, and declared that the LORD would trouble him that day. Then all Israel stoned Achan and burned him and his possessions. {7:26} They piled a heap of stones over Achan, and the LORD turned from His anger. So the place was called the Valley of Achor, a reminder of this event.

{8:1} The LORD spoke to Joshua, encouraging him not to fear or be dismayed. He instructed Joshua to take all the people of war and go up to Ai, promising to deliver the king of Ai, his people, city, and land into Joshua's hand. {8:2} Joshua was commanded to treat Ai and its king as he had done with Jericho and its king, but the spoil and cattle were to be taken as plunder. The LORD instructed Joshua to lay an ambush behind the city. {8:3} Joshua obeyed the command and chose thirty thousand mighty men of valor to go up against Ai. He sent them away by night. {8:4} Joshua commanded them to lie in wait behind the city, not going too far, but being ready. Meanwhile, he and the rest of the people would approach the city. {8:5} When the people of Ai came out against them, Joshua and his men would flee, drawing them away from the city. {8:6} While the people of Ai pursued Joshua, the ambush would rise up and seize the city, for the LORD would deliver it into their hands. {8:7} After taking the city, they were to set it on fire according to the LORD's command. {8:8} Joshua sent them forth to lie in ambush between Bethel and Ai on the west side. That night, Joshua stayed among the people. {8:9} Early the next morning, Joshua numbered the people and went up with the elders of Israel before the people to Ai. {8:10} All the people of war went up with Joshua, pitching on the north side of Ai, with a valley between them and Ai. {8:11} About five thousand men were set to lie in ambush between Bethel and Ai on the west side of the city. {8:12} Joshua, with the host on the north of the city and their ambush on the west, went that night into the midst of the valley. {8:13} When the king of Ai saw this, he and the men of the city went out to battle, unaware of the ambush behind the city. {8:14} Joshua and Israel pretended to be beaten, fleeing toward the wilderness. The men of Ai pursued them. {8:15} Then all the men of Ai were called to pursue Israel, leaving the city open. {8:16} The LORD instructed Joshua to stretch out the spear in his hand toward Ai, for He would give it into Joshua's hand. {8:17} As Joshua stretched out the spear, the ambush arose quickly, entering the city, taking it, and setting it on fire. {8:18} When the men of Ai looked back, they saw the smoke of the city ascending, and they were unable to flee. {8:19} Joshua and Israel saw the ambush had taken the city and turned back, attacking and destroying the men of Ai. {8:20} The remaining men of Ai came out against Israel, and they were surrounded. None were left alive or escaped. {8:21} Joshua took the king of Ai alive and brought him to Joshua. {8:22} After killing all the inhabitants of Ai, Israel returned and struck the city with the edge of the sword. {8:23} That day, twelve thousand men and women of Ai fell. {8:24} Joshua did not withdraw his hand until he had utterly destroyed all the inhabitants of Ai. {8:25} The Israelites took the spoil and cattle of the city for themselves, as the LORD had commanded. {8:26} Joshua burnt Ai, making it a desolation forever. {8:27} The king of Ai was hanged on a tree until evening. Then Joshua commanded they take his body down and raise a heap of stones at the gate of the city. {8:30} Joshua built an altar to the LORD God of Israel on Mount Ebal, as Moses had commanded, and offered burnt offerings and peace offerings. {8:31} **He wrote a copy of the law of Moses on stones in the presence of the children of Israel.** {8:32} Joshua wrote a copy of the law of Moses on the stones in the presence of the children of Israel. {8:33} All Israel, along with their elders, officers, and judges, stood on both sides of the ark before the Levite priests who carried the ark of the covenant of the LORD. This included both natives and foreigners, with half of them facing Mount Gerizim and the other half facing Mount Ebal, as Moses had commanded, to bless the people of Israel. {8:34} Afterward, Joshua read all the words of the law, including the blessings and curses, according to what was written in the book of the law. {8:35} Joshua made sure to read every word that Moses had commanded before the entire congregation of Israel, including women, children, and foreigners among them.

{9:1} When the kings on the other side of the Jordan, in the hills, valleys, and along the coast of the Great Sea opposite Lebanon—the Hittites, Amorites, Canaanites, Perizzites, Hivites, and Jebusites—heard about it, they joined forces to fight against Joshua and Israel as one. {9:2} The inhabitants of Gibeon, upon hearing what Joshua had done to Jericho and Ai, resorted to cunning. They disguised themselves as ambassadors, taking old sacks on their donkeys, old and torn wine bottles, patched shoes, worn-out garments, and stale bread. {9:3} They went to Joshua at the camp in Gilgal and said to him and the men of Israel, "We have come from a distant land; therefore, make a treaty with us." {9:4} The Israelites questioned the Gibeonites, "Perhaps you live among us; how then can we make a treaty with you?" {9:5} The Gibeonites replied, "We are your servants." Joshua asked them, "Who are you, and where do you come from?" {9:6} They answered, "We have come from a distant land because we heard of the fame of the LORD your God and all He did in Egypt, and to the two Amorite kings—Sihon of Heshbon and Og of Bashan—beyond the Jordan." {9:7} "Our elders advised us to take provisions and go to meet you, saying, 'We are your servants; now make a treaty with us.'" {9:8} "Our bread was fresh when we left, but now it's dry and moldy. Our wine bottles were new but are now torn, and our clothes and shoes are worn out due to the long journey." {9:9} Joshua and the Israelites accepted their provisions without seeking guidance from the LORD. {9:10} Joshua made a peace treaty with them, and the leaders of the community swore an oath to them. {9:11} Three days later, they discovered that the Gibeonites were their neighbors, living among them. {9:12} The Israelites journeyed to their cities on the third day: Gibeon, Chephirah, Beeroth, and Kiriath Jearim. {9:13} They did not attack these cities because the leaders had sworn to them by the LORD, but the congregation grumbled against their leaders. {9:14} However, the leaders insisted, "We swore to them by the LORD, so we cannot harm them." {9:15} "We will let them live," they agreed, "but they must become woodcutters and water carriers for the entire community, as we promised." {9:16} Joshua called the Gibeonites and demanded, "Why did you deceive us, claiming to be from a distant land when you actually live among us?" {9:17} "Now you are cursed," he declared. "You shall always be servants—woodcutters and water carriers—for the house of my God." {9:18} The Gibeonites explained, "We heard how the LORD commanded Moses to give you this land and destroy its inhabitants. We feared for our lives and thus resorted to this deception." {9:19} "We are in your hands," they surrendered. "Do to us what you think is right." {9:20} Joshua spared their lives but made them woodcutters and water carriers for the congregation and the LORD's altar, a status they maintain to this day, in the place Joshua chose. {9:21} The leaders agreed, "Let them live, but they must serve as woodcutters and water carriers for the entire congregation, just as we promised." {9:22} Joshua summoned them and questioned, "Why did you deceive us, claiming to be from a distant land when you actually live among us?" {9:23} "Now you are cursed," Joshua declared. "You shall always be servants—woodcutters and water carriers—for the house of my God, with no opportunity for release." {9:24} The Gibeonites replied, "We heard how the LORD your God commanded Moses to give you this land and destroy its inhabitants. We feared for our lives, which led us to deceive you." {9:25} "We are in your hands," they submitted. "Do to us as you see fit." {9:26} Joshua spared their lives and ensured they were not harmed by the Israelites. {9:27} From that day forward, Joshua assigned them the task of woodcutting and water carrying for the congregation and the LORD's altar, a duty they continue to perform to this day, at the place Joshua designated.

{10:1} Once, Adoni-zedek, the king of Jerusalem, heard about Joshua's victories—how he had taken Ai, utterly destroying it just like he did with Jericho, and how the people of Gibeon had made peace with Israel and were now allies. {10:2} This news troubled Adoni-zedek and the other surrounding kings because Gibeon was a significant city, even greater than Ai, and its people were mighty. {10:3} So Adoni-zedek sent messengers to other kings nearby—Hoham of Hebron, Piram of Jarmuth, Japhia of Lachish, and Debir of Eglon—asking for their help in attacking Gibeon because they had allied with Joshua. {10:4} The five kings of the Amorites, including the king of Jerusalem, gathered their armies and went up to Gibeon to wage war against it. {10:5} Meanwhile, the men of Gibeon sent word to Joshua, urgently requesting his assistance because all the Amorite kings from the mountains were attacking them. {10:6} Joshua and his warriors quickly responded, leaving from Gilgal in the night to come to Gibeon's aid. {10:7} Encouraged by the LORD, Joshua and his army advanced to confront the enemy. {10:8} The LORD reassured Joshua, telling him not to fear, for He had delivered their enemies into their hands. {10:9} Joshua, trusting in the LORD's promise, marched on through the night from Gilgal. {10:10} The LORD caused confusion among the enemies of Israel, leading to a great slaughter at Gibeon, and the Amorites were chased all the way to Azekah and Makkedah. {10:11} As the Amorites fled, the LORD even caused large stones to fall from the sky, killing more of them than the Israelites did with their swords. {10:12} In the midst of the battle, Joshua prayed to the LORD, asking for the sun and moon to stand still until they had defeated their enemies—a request granted by God, as recorded in the book of Jasher. {10:13} The sun and moon stood still until Israel had avenged themselves on their enemies, a day unlike any other, for the LORD fought on behalf of Israel. {10:14} With the victory secured, Joshua and the Israelites returned to Gilgal. {10:15} The defeated kings, however, sought refuge in a cave at Makkedah. {10:16} Joshua was informed of their hiding place and ordered that the cave be sealed with large stones, while his army pursued the remaining enemies. {10:17} Once the threat was neutralized, Joshua commanded the kings to be brought before him. {10:18} He called upon his captains to put their feet on the necks of these kings as a symbol of their triumph. {10:19} Joshua then urged his army to continue pursuing their enemies, ensuring none escaped back to their fortified cities, as the LORD had delivered them into their hands. {10:20} After a thorough defeat, the surviving enemies sought refuge in fortified cities. {10:21} Joshua and the Israelites returned to Makkedah in peace, with no opposition from the local inhabitants. {10:22} Joshua ordered the cave to be opened, and the five kings were brought out to him. {10:23} These kings, including the king of Jerusalem, were brought before Joshua, who then had his men put their feet on their necks. {10:24} Joshua encouraged his men, reminding them that the LORD would do the same to all their enemies. {10:25} The kings were then executed and hanged on trees until evening. {10:26} At sunset, they were taken down and placed back in the cave, which was sealed with large stones. {10:27} The events of that day included the capture and destruction of Makkedah and its king, as well as the conquests of Libnah, Lachish, Eglon, Hebron, and Debir, with their respective kings meeting the same fate as Jericho's king. {10:28} Joshua's campaign extended across the hill country, the Negev, the western foothills, and the slopes—all the way from Kadesh-barnea to Gaza and Goshen, encompassing Gibeon. {10:29} Joshua took all these kings and their lands in one swift campaign, as the LORD fought on Israel's behalf. {10:30} Finally, Joshua and the Israelites returned to Gilgal, their base camp, victorious in their conquests. {10:31} Joshua then moved from Libnah with all of Israel, advancing towards Lachish, where they set up camp and prepared for battle. {10:32} The LORD handed Lachish over to Israel, and they captured it on the second day. They struck down all who were in the city, just as they had done in Libnah. {10:33} Hearing of Lachish's fall, Horam king of Gezer came to aid Lachish, but Joshua defeated him and his forces, leaving none alive. {10:34} After Lachish, Joshua led Israel to Eglon. They attacked it and conquered it in one day, destroying everyone within, mirroring what they had done in Lachish. {10:35} Continuing their conquest, Joshua and the Israelites moved on to Hebron, where they fought and captured the city. They wiped out the king, its cities, and all its inhabitants, just as they had done in Eglon. {10:36} From Hebron, they proceeded to Debir, where they fought and took the city. They destroyed everyone in it, including the king, in the same manner as they had done in Hebron and Eglon, following the LORD's commands. {10:37} Joshua then returned to Gilgal with all of Israel after completing their conquest of Debir. {10:38} Every hill country, southern region, valley, and spring was subdued by Joshua. He annihilated all the kings and their people, leaving none alive, in obedience to the LORD's command. {10:39} Their campaign extended from Kadesh-barnea to Gaza and throughout Goshen, encompassing Gibeon. Joshua conquered all these kings and their territories simultaneously because the LORD fought for Israel. {10:40} With the conquest complete, Joshua and all of Israel returned to their camp at Gilgal, having achieved victory through the LORD's guidance. {10:41} Joshua's victories extended from Kadesh-barnea all the way to Gaza, covering the entire region of Goshen, including Gibeon. {10:42} Joshua conquered all these kings and their territories simultaneously because the LORD God of Israel fought on behalf of Israel. {10:43} After completing their conquest, Joshua and all of Israel returned to their camp at Gilgal.

{11:1} When Jabin, the king of Hazor, heard about this, he sent messengers to Jobab, the king of Madon, and to the kings of Shimron, Achshaph, and the surrounding regions—north of the mountains, south of Chinneroth, in the valley, and along the borders of Dor to the west. {11:2} These messengers were also sent to the Canaanites on the east and west, as well as to the Amorites, Hittites, Perizzites, Jebusites in the mountains, and the Hivites under Hermon in the land of Mizpeh. {11:3} They gathered their armies, a vast multitude like the sand on the seashore, equipped with many horses and chariots. {11:4} All these kings met and camped together at the waters of Merom to fight against Israel. {11:5} But the LORD said to Joshua, "Do not fear them, for tomorrow at this time I will deliver them over to you, all of them slain. You shall hamstring their horses and burn their chariots with fire." {11:6} So Joshua and his warriors suddenly attacked them at the waters of Merom. {11:7} The LORD delivered the enemy into the hands of Israel, and they struck them down, chasing them as far as Great Sidon, Misrephoth-maim, and the valley of Mizpeh to the east, leaving no survivors. {11:8} Joshua carried out the command of the LORD; he hamstrung their horses and burned their chariots. {11:9} After this victory, Joshua turned back and captured Hazor, striking down its king and all its people with the sword, utterly destroying them and burning the city. {11:10} He also took all the other cities of those kings, destroying them according to the command of the LORD through Moses. {11:11} However, the cities that stood their ground with their walls intact, Israel did not burn; only Hazor was burned by Joshua. {11:12} The Israelites took all the plunder and livestock from these cities as their spoil, but they killed every person, leaving none alive. {11:13} This was done in accordance with the command of Moses, as Joshua had done exactly as he was instructed. {11:14} Thus, Joshua conquered all the land—hills, southern regions, Goshen, the valley, the plain, and the mountain of Israel, even as far as Baal-gad in the valley of Lebanon under Mount Hermon. He struck down all the kings and their people. {11:15} Joshua waged war for a long time against these kings, and not one city made peace with the Israelites except the Hivites of Gibeon, who were spared. {11:16} It was the LORD who hardened the hearts of the other nations to resist Israel in battle, so that they could be utterly destroyed, just as the LORD commanded Moses. {11:17} At that time, Joshua eliminated the Anakim from the mountains of Hebron, Debir, Anab, and all the mountains of Judah and Israel, destroying them along with their cities. {11:18} There were no Anakim left in the land of Israel except in Gaza, Gath, and Ashdod. {11:19} Joshua fulfilled all that the LORD had commanded Moses, allotting the land as an inheritance to the Israelites according to their tribal divisions. And the land finally found rest from war. {11:20} The LORD allowed their hearts to be hardened so that they would come against Israel in battle, ensuring their utter destruction, just as the LORD had commanded Moses. {11:21} During this time, Joshua eradicated the Anakim from the mountains—Hebron, Debir, Anab, and all the mountains of Judah and Israel, completely destroying them along with their cities. {11:22} There were no Anakim left in the land of Israel except in Gaza, Gath, and Ashdod. {11:23} Joshua conquered the entire land, fulfilling all that the LORD had instructed Moses. He distributed the land as an inheritance to the Israelites according to their tribal divisions. Finally, the land found peace from war.

{12:1} These are the kings of the land that the children of Israel defeated and took possession of their land on the other side of the Jordan River, toward the east, from the Arnon River to Mount Hermon, including all the plain to the east: {12:2} Sihon, king of the Amorites, who lived in Heshbon and ruled from Aroer on the edge of the Arnon River, including the middle of the river, and from half of Gilead to the Jabbok River, which is the border of the Ammonites; {12:3} Also, from the plain to the Sea of Galilee in the east, to the Sea of the Arabah (Dead Sea), the road to Beth-jeshimoth, and southward below the slopes of Pisgah. {12:4} And the territory of Og, king of Bashan, one of the last of the Rephaim, who lived in Ashtaroth and Edrei, {12:5} reigning over Mount Hermon, Salcah, and all of Bashan, extending to the border of the Geshurites and Maacathites, and half of Gilead, to the border of Sihon, king of Heshbon. {12:6} Moses, the servant of the LORD, and the children of Israel defeated them, and Moses, the servant of the LORD, gave their land as a possession to the Reubenites, Gadites, and the half-tribe of Manasseh. {12:7} These are the kings of the lands Joshua and the children of Israel defeated on the west side of the Jordan River, from Baal-gad in the valley of Lebanon to Mount Halak, which rises toward Seir. Joshua gave their lands to the tribes of Israel as their inheritance, divided according to their tribal divisions: {12:8} In the mountains, valleys, plains, springs, wilderness, and southern region—the Hittites, Amorites, Canaanites, Perizzites, Hivites, and Jebusites. {12:9} The king of Jericho, one; the king of Ai, near Bethel, one; {12:10} The king of Jerusalem, one; the king of Hebron, one; {12:11} The king of Jarmuth, one; the king of Lachish, one; {12:12} The king of Eglon, one; the king of Gezer, one; {12:13} The king of Debir, one; the king of Geder, one; {12:14} The king of Hormah, one; the king of Arad, one; {12:15} The king of Libnah, one; the king of Adullam, one; {12:16} The king of Makkedah, one; the king of Bethel, one; {12:17} The king of Tappuah, one; the king of Hepher, one; {12:18} The king of Aphek, one; the king of Lasharon, one; {12:19} The king of Madon, one; the king of Hazor, one; {12:20} The king of Shimron-meron, one; the king of Achshaph, one; {12:21} The king of Taanach, one; the king of Megiddo, one; {12:22} The king of Kedesh, one; the king of Jokneam in Carmel, one; {12:23} The king of Dor in the region of Dor, one; the king of Goiim in Gilgal, one; {12:24} The king of Tirzah, one; making a total of thirty-one kings.

{13:1} Now Joshua was old and advanced in years, and the LORD said to him, "You are old and advanced in years, and there is still much land to be possessed. {13:2} This is the land that remains: all the territory of the Philistines and all those of Geshur, {13:3} from Sihor, which is east of Egypt, to the territory of Ekron in the north, considered part of the Canaanite domain. This includes the five Philistine rulers: the Gazathites, the Ashdothites, the Eshkalonites, the Gittites, and the Ekronites, as well as the Avites. {13:4} In the south, all the land of the Canaanites, from Mearah near Sidon to Aphek, reaching the borders of the Amorites. {13:5} Also, all the land of the Gebalites and all of Lebanon, eastward from Baal-gad below Mount Hermon to the entrance of Hamath. {13:6} I will drive out all the inhabitants of the hill country from Lebanon to Misrephoth-maim, including the Sidonians. Only divide the land by lot among the Israelites as I have commanded you. {13:7} Therefore, divide this land as an inheritance among the nine tribes and the half-tribe of Manasseh, {13:8} along with the Reubenites and Gadites who have already received their inheritance beyond the Jordan, eastward, just as Moses, the servant of the LORD, assigned to them. {13:9} This includes Aroer on the bank of the Arnon River, the city in the middle of the river, and all the plain of Medeba up to Dibon; {13:10} also, all the cities of Sihon, king of the Amorites, who reigned in Heshbon, up to the border of the Ammonites; {13:11} and Gilead, the territory of the Geshurites and Maachathites, all of Mount Hermon, and all of Bashan up to Salecah; {13:12} including the entire kingdom of Og in Bashan, who reigned in Ashtaroth and Edrei. He was one of the last of the Rephaim. Moses defeated them and drove them out. {13:13} However, the Israelites did not drive out the Geshurites and the Maachathites. They still live among the Israelites to this day. {13:14} But the tribe of Levi received no inheritance; the LORD God of Israel is their inheritance, as he promised them. {13:15} Moses gave an inheritance to the tribe of Reuben according to their families. {13:16} Their territory extended from Aroer on the bank of the Arnon River, the city in the middle of the river, and all the plain near Medeba; {13:17} including Heshbon and all its cities on the plain, Dibon, Bamoth-baal, and Beth-baal-meon; {13:18} also Jahaza, Kedemoth, and Mephaath; {13:19} as well as Kiriathaim, Sibmah, and Zereth-shahar in the hill country; {13:20} also Beth-peor, the slopes of Pisgah, and Beth-jeshimoth; {13:21} and all the cities of the plain and the entire kingdom of Sihon, king of the Amorites, who reigned in Heshbon, whom Moses defeated along with the leaders of Midian: Evi, Rekem, Zur, Hur, and Reba, princes allied with Sihon, who lived in that land. {13:22} Balaam, the son of Beor, the diviner, was also killed by the Israelites, among those they put to the sword. {13:23} The territory of the tribe of Reuben was bordered by the Jordan River, and this was their inheritance, including the cities and villages within it. {13:24} Moses also gave an inheritance to the tribe of Gad, to the children of Gad according to their families. {13:25} Their territory included Jazer and all the cities of Gilead, as well as half the land of the Ammonites, up to Aroer, which is near Rabbah; {13:26} from Heshbon to Ramath-mizpeh and Betonim, and from Mahanaim to the territory of Debir; {13:27} and in the valley, Beth-aram, Beth-nimrah, Succoth, and Zaphon, the rest of the kingdom of Sihon, king of Heshbon, with the Jordan River as a boundary, extending to the edge of the Sea of Galilee on the eastern side of the Jordan. {13:28} This was the inheritance of the tribe of Gad according to their families, including the cities and villages within their territory. {13:29} Moses also gave an inheritance to the half-tribe of Manasseh, and this was the possession of the half-tribe of the children of Manasseh according to their families. {13:30} Their territory extended from Mahanaim, including all of Bashan, the entire kingdom of Og, king of Bashan, and all the towns of Jair, which are in Bashan, sixty cities; {13:31} also half of Gilead, Ashtaroth, and Edrei, cities of the kingdom of Og in Bashan, which belonged to the children of Machir, the son of Manasseh, for half of the children of Machir, according to their families. {13:32} These are the areas that Moses distributed as an inheritance in the plains of Moab, beyond the Jordan, east of Jericho. {13:33} However, Moses did not give an inheritance to the tribe of Levi; the LORD God of Israel is their inheritance, as he promised them."

{14:1} These are the countries that the Israelites inherited in the land of Canaan, distributed by Eleazar the priest, Joshua the son of Nun, and the heads of the fathers of the tribes of Israel, as their inheritance. {14:2} Their inheritance was determined by lot, as the LORD commanded through Moses, for the nine tribes and the half tribe. {14:3} Moses had already given the inheritance of two and a half tribes on the other side of the Jordan, but he did not give any inheritance to the Levites among the others. {14:4} Since the children of Joseph constituted two tribes—Manasseh and Ephraim—they did not allot any portion to the Levites in the land, except for cities to dwell in, along with their surrounding pasturelands for their livestock and possessions. {14:5} The children of Israel followed the LORD's command through Moses and divided the land accordingly. {14:6} Then the children of Judah approached Joshua in Gilgal. Caleb, the son of Jephunneh the Kenizzite, said to him, "You know what the LORD said to Moses, the man of God, concerning you and me in Kadesh-barnea. {14:7} I was forty years old when Moses, the servant of the LORD, sent me from Kadesh-barnea to spy out the land, and I reported back to him as I felt in my heart. {14:8} However, my fellow spies made the hearts of the people melt, but I remained faithful to the LORD my God. {14:9} On that day, Moses swore, 'The land on which your feet have walked will be your inheritance and that of your descendants forever, because you have wholly followed the LORD my God.' {14:10} Now the LORD has kept me alive, as he promised, for forty-five years since he spoke this word to Moses while the Israelites wandered in the wilderness. And now, at eighty-five years old, I am still as strong today as I was then, for battle, to go out and come in. {14:11} So give me this mountain that the LORD spoke of on that day, for you heard on that day how the Anakim were there, with great fortified cities. Perhaps with the LORD's help, I will drive them out, as the LORD said." {14:12} Joshua blessed him and gave Hebron to Caleb, the son of Jephunneh, as his inheritance. {14:13} Thus, Hebron became the inheritance of Caleb, the son of Jephunneh the Kenizzite, as it remains to this day, because he wholly followed the LORD God of Israel. {14:14} Before its renaming to Hebron, it was known as Kirjath-arba, named after Arba, {14:15} a prominent figure among the Anakim. And the land had peace from war.

{15:1} This is the allotment of the tribe of Judah by their families: The southern border of their inheritance reached to the border of Edom, to the wilderness of Zin, in the far south. {15:2} Their southern border started from the shore of the Dead Sea, from the bay that faces southward. {15:3} It then extended southward to Maaleh-acrabbim, passed along to Zin, ascended to the south of Kadesh-barnea, continued to Hezron, went up to Adar, and turned to Karkaa. {15:4} From there, it passed toward Azmon, reached the Egyptian River, and ended at the sea. This marked the southern boundary. {15:5} The eastern border extended from the Dead Sea to the end of the Jordan River. The northern border began from the bay of the sea at the northernmost point of the Jordan.

{15:6} The border then went up to Beth-hogla, passed north of Beth-arabah, ascended to the stone of Bohan (the son of Reuben), {15:7} and continued northward to Debir from the valley of Achor. It then turned northward, facing Gilgal, which is opposite the ascent of Adummim, south of the river. The border passed toward the waters of En-shemesh and ended at En-rogel. {15:8} From there, it went up by the Valley of Hinnom to the southern slope of the Jebusites (that is, Jerusalem). The border ascended to the top of the mountain westward, at the end of the Valley of Rephaim to the north. {15:9} From the top of the hill, the border extended to the fountain of the water of Nephtoah, reached the cities of Mount Ephron, and continued to Baalah (that is, Kirjath-jearim). {15:10} The border then turned from Baalah westward to Mount Seir, passed along the northern side of Mount Jearim (that is, Chesalon), descended to Beth-shemesh, and continued to Timnah. {15:11} It reached the northern slope of Ekron, then turned toward Shicron, passed along to Mount Baalah, and ended at Jabneel, with the border reaching the sea. {15:12} The western border was the coastline of the Mediterranean Sea. This was the border around the tribe of Judah, according to their families. {15:13} Caleb, the son of Jephunneh, was given a portion among the children of Judah, as the LORD commanded Joshua. This included the city of Arba, the father of Anak, which is Hebron. {15:14} Caleb drove out from there the three sons of Anak: Sheshai, Ahiman, and Talmai, descendants of Anak. {15:15} Then he advanced against the inhabitants of Debir. Now the name of Debir was formerly Kirjath-sepher. {15:16} Caleb said, "Whoever attacks Kirjath-sepher and captures it, I will give him my daughter Achsah in marriage." {15:17} Othniel, the son of Kenaz, Caleb's brother, took it, so Caleb gave him Achsah his daughter as his wife. {15:18} As Achsah came to Othniel, she urged him to ask her father for a field. When she got off her donkey, Caleb asked her, "What do you want?" {15:19} She replied, "Give me a blessing. Since you have given me the land of the Negev, give me also springs of water." So Caleb gave her the upper and lower springs. {15:20} This was the inheritance of the tribe of Judah according to their families. {15:21} The farthest cities of the tribe of Judah toward the border of Edom in the south were Kabzeel, Eder, and Jagur, {15:22} Kinah, Dimonah, Adadah, {15:23} Kedesh, Hazor, Ithnan, {15:24} Ziph, Telem, Bealoth, {15:25} Hazor, Hadattah, Kerioth (that is, Hazor), {15:26} Amam, Shema, Moladah, {15:27} Hazar-gaddah, Heshmon, Beth-palet, {15:28} Hazar-shual, Beersheba, Bizjothjah, {15:29} Baalah, Iim, Azem, {15:30} Eltolad, Chesil, Hormah, {15:31} Ziklag, Madmannah, Sansannah, {15:32} Lebaoth, Shilhim, Ain, and Rimmon—a total of twenty-nine cities with their villages. {15:33} In the lowland: Eshtaol, Zoreah, Ashnah, {15:34} Zanoah, En-gannim, Tappuah, Enam, {15:35} Jarmuth, Adullam, Socoh, Azekah, {15:36} Sharaim, Adithaim, Gederah, and Gederothaim—fourteen cities with their villages. {15:37} Zenan, Hadashah, Migdal-gad, {15:38} Dilean, Mizpeh, Joktheel, {15:39} Lachish, Bozkath, Eglon, {15:40} Cabbon, Lahmam, Kithlish, {15:41} Gederoth, Beth-dagon, Naamah, and Makkedah—sixteen cities with their villages. {15:42} Libnah, Ether, Ashan, {15:43} Iphtah, Ashnah, Nezib, {15:44} Keilah, Achzib, and Mareshah—nine cities with their villages. {15:45} Ekron, with its surrounding towns and villages, {15:46} from Ekron to the sea, all the towns near Ashdod with their villages. {15:47} Ashdod, with its surrounding towns and villages; Gaza, with its surrounding towns and villages, as far as the Brook of Egypt and the coastline of the Mediterranean Sea. {15:48} In the hill country: Shamir, Jattir, Socoh, {15:49} Dannah, Kiriath-sannah (that is, Debir), {15:50} Anab, Eshtemoh, Anim, {15:51} Goshen, Holon, and Giloh—eleven cities with their villages. {15:52} Arab, Dumah, Eshan, {15:53} Janim, Beth-tappuah, Aphekah, {15:54} Humtah, Kiriath-arba (that is, Hebron), and Zior—nine cities with their villages. { {15:55} Maon, Carmel, and Ziph, and Juttah, {15:56} Also, Jezreel, Jokdeam, and Zanoah, {15:57} Additionally, Cain, Gibeah, and Timnah; making ten cities with their surrounding villages. {15:58} Furthermore, Halhul, Beth-zur, and Gedor, {15:59} Along with Maarath, Beth-anoth, and Eltekon; totaling six cities with their villages. {15:60} Moreover, Kirjath-baal, also known as Kirjath-jearim, and Rabbah; these two cities with their villages. {15:61} In the wilderness, there are Beth-arabah, Middin, and Secacah, {15:62} As well as Nibshan, the city of Salt, and En-gedi; making six cities with their villages. {15:63} The Jebusites, inhabitants of Jerusalem, were not driven out by the children of Judah, and they continue to dwell with them in Jerusalem to this day.

{16:1} The land allotted to the children of Joseph extended from the Jordan River near Jericho, eastward to the water of Jericho, reaching into the wilderness that ascends from Jericho up to Mount Bethel. {16:2} From Bethel, it continued to Luz, and passed along the borders of Archi to Ataroth. {16:3} Then it descended westward to the coast of Japhleti, extending to Beth-horon the lower and Gezer, reaching all the way to the sea. {16:4} Thus, the descendants of Joseph, both Manasseh and Ephraim, received their inheritance. {16:5} The border of the tribe of Ephraim, according to their family divisions, extended from Ataroth-addar on the east to Upper Beth-horon. {16:6} From there, it reached toward the sea to Michmethah on the north side, then turned eastward to Taanath-shiloh, passing by Janohah on the east. {16:7} Continuing downward from Janohah to Ataroth and Naarath, it reached Jericho and extended to the Jordan River. {16:8} The border then extended from Tappuah westward to the Kanah River, reaching the sea. This marked the inheritance of the tribe of Ephraim according to their families. {16:9} Additionally, certain cities within the inheritance of Manasseh were designated as separate cities for the descendants of Ephraim, including all their villages. {16:10} However, the Canaanites who lived in Gezer were not driven out; instead, they lived among the Ephraimites to this day, serving under tribute.

{17:1} The tribe of Manasseh also received their portion of land, as they were the firstborn of Joseph. Machir, the firstborn of Manasseh and the father of Gilead, was given land because he was a valiant warrior. {17:2} Other portions of land were allotted to the rest of the descendants of Manasseh, including the children of Abiezer, Helek, Asriel, Shechem, Hepher, and Shemida—all sons of Manasseh by their families. {17:3} Zelophehad, a descendant of Manasseh, had no sons but only daughters: Mahlah, Noah, Hoglah, Milcah, and Tirzah. {17:4} These daughters approached Eleazar the priest, Joshua, and the tribal leaders, requesting an inheritance among their brethren according to the Lord's command. Accordingly, they were given an inheritance among the sons of Manasseh. {17:5} Manasseh received ten portions of land, excluding Gilead and Bashan on the other side of the Jordan River. {17:6} This was because the daughters of Manasseh received an inheritance alongside his sons, while the rest of Manasseh's sons inherited the land of Gilead. {17:7} The territory of Manasseh extended from Asher to Michmethah, bordering Shechem on the right and extending to the inhabitants of En-tappuah. {17:8} Although Tappuah belonged to Manasseh, it was located on the border with Ephraim. {17:9} The border descended to the Kanah River, southward of the river, with certain cities of Ephraim located among the cities of Manasseh. The northern border of Manasseh extended to the sea. {17:10} Ephraim's territory was to the south, while Manasseh's was to the north, with their borders meeting in Asher to the north and Issachar to the east. {17:11} Manasseh possessed cities in Issachar and Asher, including Beth-shean, Ibleam, Dor, Endor, Taanach, and Megiddo, as well as their surrounding towns. {17:12} However, the descendants of Manasseh could not drive out the inhabitants of these cities, and the Canaanites continued to dwell in the land. {17:13} As the Israelites grew stronger, they imposed tribute on the Canaanites but did not completely drive them out. {17:14} The descendants of Joseph, particularly Ephraim and Manasseh, questioned Joshua, asking why they had received only one portion of land, considering their large population and the blessings they had received from the Lord. {17:15} Joshua advised them to go up to the wooded hill country and clear the land for themselves, especially in the territories of the Perizzites and the giants, if the land allotted to them was too small. {17:16} However, the children of Joseph expressed concern that the hill country was not sufficient for their needs, and they were daunted by the Canaanites in the valley who possessed iron chariots. {17:17} Joshua assured the house of Joseph, both Ephraim and Manasseh, that they were a great people with significant power and should not be content with only one portion of land. {17:18} He granted them the mountainous region, instructing them to clear it and drive out the Canaanites, despite their possession of iron chariots and their strength.

{18:1} The entire assembly of the Israelites gathered at Shiloh and erected the tabernacle of the congregation there. By this time, the land had been subdued before them. {18:2} However, seven tribes among the Israelites had not yet received their inheritance. {18:3} Joshua addressed the Israelites, questioning why they were hesitant to possess the land that the Lord, the God of their fathers, had given them. {18:4} He instructed them to select three men from each tribe, who would survey the land and describe it according to its inheritance. These men would then return to Joshua. {18:5} The land would be divided into seven parts, with Judah occupying the southern region and the house of Joseph the northern region. {18:6} Thus, the land was to be described in seven parts and brought back to Joshua, who would cast lots for them before the Lord in Shiloh. {18:7} The Levites were excluded from receiving a portion of land, as the priesthood of the Lord was their inheritance. Additionally, Gad, Reuben, and half the tribe of Manasseh had already received their inheritance beyond the Jordan River, as given by Moses, the servant of the Lord. {18:8} Following Joshua's instructions, the chosen men set out to survey and describe the land, returning to Joshua in Shiloh. {18:9} They traversed the land, describing it by cities into seven parts in a book, and then returned to Joshua at Shiloh. {18:10} Joshua cast lots for them before the Lord in Shiloh, thereby dividing the land among the tribes of Israel according to their divisions. {18:11} The lot fell to the tribe of Benjamin according to their families, with their territory situated between Judah and Joseph. {18:12} Their northern border extended from the Jordan River, passing by Jericho and the mountains westward, reaching the wilderness of Beth-aven. {18:13} From there, the border continued toward Luz, near Bethel to the south, descending to Ataroth-adar, close to the hill south of the lower Beth-horon. {18:14} The border then turned southward, reaching the sea near the hill facing Beth-horon to the south. It ended at Kirjath-baal, also known as Kirjath-jearim, a city of the tribe of Judah, marking the western boundary. {18:15} The southern border started from Kirjath-jearim, extending westward to the waters of Nephtoah. {18:16} It then descended to the end of the mountain overlooking the Valley of Hinnom, which is north of the Valley of the Giants, and descended to En-rogel. {18:17} From there, it turned northward to En-shemesh and continued toward Geliloth, opposite the ascent of Adummim, finally descending to the Stone of Bohan, the son of Reuben. {18:18} The border proceeded along the side opposite Arabah to the north, descending to Arabah. {18:19} From there, it continued to the side of Beth-hoglah to the north, ending at the northern bay of the Salt Sea, at the southern end of the Jordan River, marking the southern boundary. {18:20} The eastern border was formed by the Jordan River. This delineated the inheritance of the tribe of Benjamin, encompassing their territories according to their families. {18:21} The cities of the tribe of Benjamin, according to their families, included Jericho, Beth-hoglah, Keziz Valley, Beth-arabah, Zemaraim, Bethel, Avim, Parah, Ophrah, Chephar-haammonai, Ophni, and Gaba, totaling twelve cities with their villages. { {18:22} The cities included Beth-arabah, Zemaraim, Bethel, {18:23} Avim, Parah, Ophrah, {18:24} Chephar-haammonai, Ophni, and Gaba—twelve cities with their surrounding villages. {18:25} Additionally, there were Gibeon, Ramah, Beeroth, {18:26} Mizpeh, Chephirah, Mozah, {18:27} Rekem, Irpeel, and Taralah, {18:28} As well as Zelah, Eleph, and Jebusi, which is also known as Jerusalem, Gibeath, and Kirjath—fourteen cities with their villages. This constituted the inheritance of the children of Benjamin according to their families.

{19:1} The second lot was drawn for the tribe of Simeon. They got their inheritance within the territory of Judah. {19:2} Here are some of the places in their inheritance: Beer-sheba (also known as Sheba), Moladah, Hazar-shual, Balah, Azem, Eltolad, Bethul, Hormah, Ziklag, Bethmarcaboth, Hazar-susah, Beth-lebaoth, and Sharuhen. There were thirteen cities and their villages. {19:3} Additionally, they had Ain, Remmon, Ether, and Ashan, which were four cities with their villages. {19:4} All the villages around these cities extended to Baalath-beer and Ramath of the south. This was the inheritance of the tribe of Simeon according to their families. {19:5} The children of Simeon received their inheritance from the portion of the children of Judah because the portion of Judah was too large for them. So, the children of Simeon had their inheritance within the inheritance of Judah. {19:6} The third lot was drawn for the children of Zebulun. Their border extended to Sarid in the north. {19:7} From there, it went up towards the sea, reaching Maralah and Dabbasheth. It continued to the river before Jokneam. {19:8} Then, turning eastward from Sarid towards the sunrise, it reached the border of Chisloth-tabor. From there, it went to Daberath and Japhia. {19:9} Continuing on the eastern side, it passed to Gittah-hepher, Ittah-kazin, and Remmon-methoar to Neah. {19:10} From Neah, it turned northward to Hannathon and reached the valley of Jiphthah-el. {19:11} The cities within this territory were Kattath, Nahallal, Shimron, Idalah, and Bethlehem. There were twelve cities with their villages. {19:12} This was the inheritance of the children of Zebulun according to their families, comprising these cities and their villages. {19:13} The fourth lot was drawn for the tribe of Issachar. Their territory extended towards Jezreel, Chesulloth, Shunem, Haphraim, Shihon, Anaharath, Rabbith, Kishion, Abez, Remeth, En-gannim, En-haddah, and Beth-pazzez. {19:14} Their border reached to Tabor, Shahazimah, and Beth-shemesh. Their border extended to the Jordan River. There were sixteen cities with their villages. {19:15} This was the inheritance of the tribe of Issachar according to their families, including the cities and their villages. {19:16} The fifth lot was drawn for the tribe of Asher. Their border extended to Helkath, Hali, Beten, Achshaph, Alammelech, Amad, Misheal, and Carmel westward to Shihor-libnath. {19:17} From there, it turned towards the sunrise to Beth-dagon and extended to Zebulun, the valley of Jiphthah-el, Beth-emek, Neiel, and Cabul. {19:18} The border then turned towards Ramah, Tyre, and Hosah. It extended to the sea and Achzib. {19:19} Their fortified cities included Ziddim, Zer, Hammath, Rakkath, and Chinnereth. Additionally, there were Adamah, Ramah, Hazor, Kedesh, Edrei, En-hazor, Iron, Migdal-el, Horem, Beth-anath, and Beth-shemesh. There were nineteen cities with their villages. {19:20} This was the inheritance of the tribe of Asher according to their families, including these cities and their villages. {19:21} The sixth lot was drawn for the tribe of Naphtali. Their border extended from Heleph, from Allon to Zaanannim, Adami, Nekeb, and Jabneel to Lakum. The border reached the Jordan River. {19:22} Then it turned westward to Aznoth-tabor, Hukkok, Zebulun, Asher, and Judah towards the sunrise. {19:23} Their fortified cities included Ziddim, Zer, Hammath, Rakkath, and Chinnereth. Additionally, there were Adamah, Ramah, Hazor, Kedesh, Edrei, En-hazor, Iron, Migdal-el, Horem, Beth-anath, and Beth-shemesh. There were nineteen cities with their villages. {19:24} This was the inheritance of the tribe of Naphtali according to their families, including these cities and their villages. {19:25} The seventh lot was drawn for the tribe of Dan. Their territory included Zorah, Eshtaol, Ir-shemesh, Shaalabbin, Ajalon, Jethlah, Elon, Thimnathah, Ekron, Eltekeh, Gibbethon, Baalath, Jehud, Bene-berak, Gath-rimmon, Me-jarkon, and Rakkon. {19:26} The border of Dan was too small for them, so they fought against Leshem, conquered it, and called it Dan after their ancestor. {19:27} This was the inheritance of the tribe of Dan according to their families, including these cities and their villages. {19:28} When the division of the land was complete, the children of Israel gave an inheritance to Joshua the son of Nun, as instructed by the LORD. Joshua received the city of Timnath-serah in mount Ephraim and built it. {19:29} These are the inheritances divided by Eleazar the priest, Joshua the son of Nun, and the heads of the families of the tribes of Israel in Shiloh, before the LORD, at the entrance of the tabernacle of the congregation. Thus, they completed the division of the country. {19:30} The cities and villages given to the tribe of Asher were Ummah, Aphek, and Rehob, totaling twenty-two. {19:31} This was their inheritance, distributed among the families of Asher. {19:32} The tribe of Naphtali received their portion as the sixth lot. {19:33} Their territory extended from Heleph and Allon to Zaanannim, Adami, Nekeb, and Jabneel, all the way to Lakum and the Jordan River. {19:34} From there, the border turned westward to Aznothtabor, Hukkok, Zebulun, Asher, and Judah, along the Jordan River to the east. {19:35} The fortified cities in Naphtali's inheritance included Ziddim, Zer, Hammath, Rakkath, and Chinnereth. {19:36} Also included were Adamah, Ramah, Hazor, Kedesh, Edrei, En-hazor, Iron, Migdal-el, Horem, Beth-anath, and Beth-shemesh, totaling nineteen cities with their villages. {19:37} These cities were the inheritance of the tribe of Naphtali, distributed among their families. {19:38} Dan received their inheritance as the seventh lot. {19:39} Their territory included Zorah, Eshtaol, Ir-shemesh, Shaalabbin, Ajalon, Jethlah, Elon, Thimnathah, Ekron, Eltekeh, Gibbethon, Baalath, Jehud, Bene-berak, Gath-rimmon, Me-jarkon, Rakkon, and the area near Japho. {19:40} However, the territory was too small for Dan, so they went up and fought against Leshem, capturing it and renaming it Dan after their ancestor. { {19:41} The coastal area of Dan's inheritance included Zorah, Eshtaol, and Ir-shemesh. {19:42} Also Shaalabbin, Ajalon, and Jethlah, among others. {19:43} Elon, Thimnathah, and Ekron were part of their territory. {19:44} Along with Eltekeh, Gibbethon, and Baalath. {19:45} Also Jehud, Bene-berak, and Gath-rimmon were within their borders. {19:46} Me-jarkon and Rakkon marked the edge, with the border near Japho. {19:47} But the land given to Dan was too small for them, so they fought and conquered Leshem, renaming it Dan after their ancestor. {19:48} This was the inheritance of the tribe of Dan, including the cities and villages within their territory. {19:49} After completing the division of the land among the tribes, {19:50} the Israelites gave Joshua, son of Nun, a portion of land, Timnath-serah in the hill country of Ephraim, as the Lord had commanded. Joshua built the city and lived there. {19:51} These are the portions of land distributed by Eleazar the priest, Joshua, and the tribal leaders at Shiloh before the Lord, at the entrance of the tabernacle. Thus, they completed the division of the land among the Israelites.

{20:1} The Lord spoke to Joshua, saying, {20:2} "Tell the Israelites to designate cities of refuge, as I commanded through Moses, {20:3} So that anyone who unintentionally kills another may flee there and be safe from the avenger of blood. {20:4} When someone flees to one of these cities and stands at the gate, explaining their situation to the elders, they shall be taken in and given a place to live among them. {20:5} If the avenger of blood pursues them, they must not be handed over, for they killed their neighbor unintentionally and without malice aforethought. {20:6} They shall remain in that city until they stand trial before the assembly or until the death of the high priest. Then they may return home to their own city and house from which they fled. {20:7} The cities appointed as refuges were Kedesh in Galilee in the territory of Naphtali, Shechem in Ephraim's hill country, and Kirjath-arba, also known as Hebron, in Judah's mountainous region. {20:8} On the east side of the Jordan River near Jericho, they designated Bezer in the wilderness for the tribe of Reuben, Ramoth in Gilead for the tribe of Gad, and Golan in Bashan for the tribe of Manasseh. {20:9} These cities were designated for all the Israelites and for foreigners residing among them, providing a safe haven for anyone who unintentionally caused the death of another, allowing them to escape the avenger of blood until they could stand trial before the assembly.

{21:1} The leaders of the Levites went to Eleazar the priest and Joshua the son of Nun, and the leaders of the Israelite tribes. {21:2} They spoke to them in Shiloh, Canaan, saying, "The LORD commanded Moses to give us cities to live in, along with pasturelands for our livestock." {21:3} So the Israelites gave the Levites cities with pasturelands from their own inheritance, as the LORD commanded. {21:4} The Kohathite families received cities by lot from the tribe of Judah, Simeon, and Benjamin. The priests, descendants of Aaron, received thirteen cities. {21:5} The rest of the Kohathites received ten cities by lot from the tribes of Ephraim, Dan, and the half-tribe of Manasseh. {21:6} The Gershonites received thirteen cities by lot from the tribes of Issachar, Asher, Naphtali, and the half-tribe of Manasseh in Bashan. {21:7} The Merarites received twelve cities by their families from the tribes of Reuben, Gad, and Zebulun. {21:8} The Israelites gave these cities with their pasturelands to the Levites according to the LORD's command through Moses. {21:9} From the tribes of Judah and Simeon, they gave the cities mentioned by name to the descendants of Aaron, who were Kohathites and Levites, for theirs was the first lot. {21:10} They gave Hebron, a city of refuge for the slayer, and Libnah, Jattir, Eshtemoa, Holon, Debir, Ain, Juttah, and Beth-shemesh, nine cities from these two tribes. {21:11} From Benjamin, they gave Gibeon, Geba, Anathoth, and Almon, four cities. {21:12} The total cities of Aaron's descendants, the priests, were thirteen cities with their pasturelands. {21:13} The remaining Kohathites received cities from the tribe of Ephraim. {21:14} They received Shechem, a city of refuge for the slayer, Gezer, Kibzaim, and Beth-horon, four cities. {21:15} From Dan, they received Eltekeh, Gibbethon, Aijalon, and Gath-rimmon, four cities. {21:16} From the half-tribe of Manasseh, they received Tanach and Gath-rimmon, two cities. {21:17} In total, there were ten cities with their pasturelands for the families of the remaining Kohathites. }{ {21:18} Anathoth with its suburbs, and Almon with its suburbs; four cities. {21:19} Altogether, the cities of the descendants of Aaron the priests were thirteen, each with its suburbs. {21:20} The remaining descendants of Kohath, the Levites, received their cities from the tribe of Ephraim. {21:21} They were given Shechem with its suburbs in Mount Ephraim, a city of refuge for the one who accidentally kills someone, along with Gezer, Kibzaim, and Beth-horon; four cities. {21:22} From the tribe of Dan, they received Eltekeh, Gibbethon, Aijalon, and Gath-rimmon; four cities. {21:23} From the half-tribe of Manasseh, they received Tanach and Gath-rimmon; two cities. {21:24} In total, there were ten cities with their suburbs for the families of the remaining descendants of Kohath. {21:25} To the descendants of Gershon, another family of Levites, from the other half-tribe of Manasseh, they gave Golan in Bashan with its suburbs, another city of refuge, along with Beesh-terah; two cities. {21:26} From the tribe of Issachar, they received Kishon, Dabareh, Jarmuth, and En-gannim; four cities. {21:27} From the tribe of Asher, they received Mishal, Abdon, Helkath, and Rehob; four cities. {21:28} From the tribe of Naphtali, they received Kedesh in Galilee, another city of refuge, along with Hammoth-dor and Kartan; three cities. {21:29} In total, there were thirteen cities with their suburbs for the families of the Gershonites. {21:30} To the families of the descendants of Merari, the remaining Levites, from the tribe of Zebulun, they gave Jokneam, Kartah, Dimnah, and Nahalal; four cities. {21:31} From the tribe of Reuben, they received Bezer, Jahazah, Kedemoth, and Mephaath; four cities. {21:32} From the tribe of Gad, they received Ramoth in Gilead, another city of refuge, along with Mahanaim, Heshbon, and Jazer; four cities in total. {21:33} There were twelve cities in all for the descendants of Merari, allocated according to their families by lot. {21:34} Altogether, the cities of the Levites within the possession of the Israelites were forty-eight, each with its suburbs. {21:35} These cities, each with its suburbs, surrounded them all. This was the case for all these cities. {21:36} The LORD fulfilled His promise to give the land to Israel, and they settled in it. {21:37} He gave them rest from all their enemies, just as He had promised their ancestors. Not one of their enemies could stand against them; the LORD handed all their enemies over to them. {21:38} Every good thing that the LORD had promised the Israelites came true; not one of His promises failed. {21:39} Heshbon with its suburbs, and Jazer with its suburbs; four cities in total. {21:40} So, all the cities assigned to the descendants of Merari by their families, which were the remaining families of the Levites, amounted to twelve cities allocated by lot. {21:41} In total, there were forty-eight cities with their suburbs allocated to the Levites within the territory possessed by the Israelites. {21:42} Each of these cities was surrounded by its suburbs, as were all the cities. {21:43} The LORD fulfilled His promise to Israel, giving them all the land He had sworn to give to their ancestors. They took possession of it and settled there. {21:44} The LORD granted them rest from all their enemies, just as He had promised their ancestors. None of their enemies could stand against them; the LORD delivered all their enemies into their hands. {21:45} Every good thing that the LORD had spoken to the house of Israel came to pass; not one promise went unfulfilled.

{22:1} Then Joshua called the Reubenites, and the Gadites, and the half tribe of Manasseh, {22:2} And said unto them, "You have kept all that Moses the servant of the LORD commanded you, and have obeyed my voice in all that I commanded you: {22:3} You have not left your brethren these many days unto this day, but have kept the charge of the commandment of the LORD your God. {22:4} And now the LORD your God hath given rest unto your brethren, as he promised them: therefore now return ye, and get you unto your tents, and unto the land of your possession, which Moses the servant of the LORD gave you on the other side Jordan. {22:5} But take diligent heed to do the commandment and the law, which Moses the servant of the LORD charged you, to love the LORD your God, and to walk in all his ways, and to keep his commandments, and to cleave unto him, and to serve him with all your heart and with all your soul. {22:6} So Joshua blessed them, and sent them away: and they went unto their tents. {22:7} Now to the one half of the tribe of Manasseh Moses had given possession in Bashan: but unto the other half thereof gave Joshua among their brethren on this side Jordan westward. And when Joshua sent them away also unto their tents, then he blessed them, {22:8} And he spake unto them, saying, "Return with much riches unto your tents, and with very much cattle, with silver, and with gold, and with brass, and with iron, and with very much raiment: divide the spoil of your enemies with your brethren." {22:9} And the children of Reuben and the children of Gad and the half tribe of Manasseh returned, and departed from the children of Israel out of Shiloh, which is in the land of Canaan, to go unto the country of Gilead, to the land of their possession, whereof they were possessed, according to the word of the LORD by the hand of Moses. {22:10} And when they came unto the borders of Jordan, that are in the land of Canaan, the children of Reuben and the children of Gad and the half tribe of Manasseh built there an altar by Jordan, a great altar to see to. {22:11} And the children of Israel heard say, "Behold, the children of Reuben and the children of Gad and the half tribe of Manasseh have built an altar over against the land of Canaan, in the borders of Jordan, at the passage of the children of Israel." {22:12} And when the children of Israel heard of it, the whole congregation of the children of Israel gathered themselves together at Shiloh, to go up to war against them. {22:13} And the children of Israel sent unto the children of Reuben, and to the children of Gad, and to the half tribe of Manasseh, into the land of Gilead, Phinehas the son of Eleazar the priest, {22:14} And with him ten princes, of each chief house a prince throughout all the tribes of Israel; and each one was an head of the house of their fathers among the thousands of Israel. {22:15} And they came unto the children of Reuben, and to the children of Gad, and to the half tribe of Manasseh, unto the land of Gilead, and they spake with them, saying, {22:16} "Thus saith the whole congregation of the LORD, What trespass is this that ye have committed against the God of Israel, to turn away this day from following the LORD, in that ye have builded you an altar, that ye might rebel this day against the LORD? {22:17} Is the iniquity of Peor too little for us, from which we are not cleansed until this day, although there was a plague in the congregation of the LORD, {22:18} But that ye must turn away this day from following the LORD? and it will be, seeing ye rebel today against the LORD, that tomorrow he will be wroth with the whole congregation of Israel. {22:19} Notwithstanding, if the land of your possession be unclean, then pass ye over unto the land of the possession of the LORD, wherein the LORD'S tabernacle dwelleth, and take possession among us: but rebel not against the LORD, nor rebel against us, in building you an altar beside the altar of the LORD our God. {22:20} Did not Achan the son of Zerah commit a trespass in the accursed thing, and wrath fell on all the congregation of Israel? and that man perished not alone in his iniquity. {22:21} Then the children of Reuben and the children of Gad and the half tribe of Manasseh answered, and said unto the heads of the thousands of Israel, {22:22} "The LORD God of gods, the LORD God of gods, he knoweth, and Israel he shall know; if it be in rebellion, or if in transgression against the LORD, (save us not this day,) {22:23} That we have built us an altar to turn from following the LORD, or if to offer thereon burnt offering or meat offering, or if to offer peace offerings thereon, let the LORD himself require it; {22:24} And if we have not rather done it for fear of this thing, saying, In time to come your children might speak unto our children, saying, What have ye to do with the LORD God of Israel? {22:25} For the LORD hath made Jordan a border between us and you, ye children of Reuben and children of Gad; ye have no part in the LORD: so shall your children make our children cease from fearing the LORD. {22:26} Therefore we said, Let us now prepare to build us an altar, not for burnt offering, nor for sacrifice: {22:27} But that it may be a witness between us, and you, and our generations after us, that we might do the service of the LORD before him with our burnt offerings, and with our sacrifices, and with our peace offerings; that your children may not say to our children in time to come, Ye have no part in the LORD. {22:28} Therefore said we, that it shall be, when they should so say to us or to our generations in time to come, that we may say again, Behold the pattern of the altar of the LORD, which our fathers made, not for burnt offerings, nor for sacrifices; but it is a witness between us and you. {22:29} God forbid that we should rebel against the LORD, and turn this day from following the LORD, to build an altar for burnt offerings, for meat offerings, or for sacrifices, beside the altar of the LORD our God that is before his tabernacle. {22:30} And when Phinehas the priest, and the princes of the congregation and heads of the thousands {22:31} And Phinehas the son of Eleazar the priest said unto the children of Reuben, and to the children of Gad, and to the children of Manasseh, "This day we perceive that the LORD is among us, because ye have not committed this trespass against the LORD: now ye have delivered the children of Israel out of the hand of the LORD." {22:32} And Phinehas the son of Eleazar the priest, and the princes, returned from the children of Reuben, and from the children of Gad, out of the land of Gilead, unto the land of Canaan, to the children of Israel, and brought them word again. {22:33} And the thing pleased the children of Israel; and the children of Israel blessed God, and did not intend to go up against them in battle, to destroy the land wherein the children of Reuben and Gad dwelt. {22:34} And the children of Reuben and the children of Gad called the altar "Ed," for it shall be a witness between us that the LORD is God.

{23:1} And it came to pass a long time after that the LORD had given rest unto Israel from all their enemies round about, that Joshua waxed old and stricken in age. {23:2} And Joshua called for all Israel, and for their elders, and for their heads, and for their judges, and for their officers, and said unto them, "I am old and stricken in age: {23:3} And ye have seen all that the LORD your God hath done unto all these nations because of you; for the LORD your God is he that hath fought for you. {23:4} Behold, I have divided unto you by lot these nations that remain, to be an inheritance for your tribes, from Jordan, with all the nations that I have cut off, even unto the great sea westward. {23:5} And the LORD your God, he shall expel them from before you, and drive them from out of your sight; and ye shall possess their land, as the LORD your God hath promised unto you. {23:6} Be ye therefore very courageous to keep and to do all that is written in the book of the law of Moses, that ye turn not aside therefrom to the right hand or to the left; {23:7} That ye come not among these nations, these that remain among you; neither make mention of the names of their gods, nor cause to swear by them, neither serve them, nor bow yourselves unto them: {23:8} But cleave unto the LORD your God, as ye have done unto this day. {23:9} For the LORD hath driven out from before you great nations and strong: but as for you, no man hath been able to stand before you unto this day. {23:10} One man of you shall chase a thousand: for the LORD your God, he it is that fighteth for you, as he hath promised you. {23:11} Take good heed therefore unto yourselves, that ye love the LORD your God. {23:12} Else if ye do in any wise go back, and cleave unto the remnant of these nations, even these that remain among you, and shall make marriages with them, and go in unto them, and they to you: {23:13} Know for a certainty that the LORD your God will no more drive out any of these nations from before you; but they shall be snares and traps unto you, and scourges in your sides, and thorns in your eyes, until ye perish from off this good land which the LORD your God hath given you. {23:14} And, behold, this day I am going the way of all the earth: and ye know in all your hearts and in all your souls, that not one thing hath failed of all the good things which the LORD your God spake concerning you; all are come to pass unto you, and not one thing hath failed thereof. {23:15} Therefore it shall come to pass, that as all good things are come upon you, which the LORD your God promised you; so shall the LORD bring upon you all evil things, until he have destroyed you from off this good land which the LORD your God hath given you. {23:16} **When ye have transgressed the covenant of the LORD your God, which he commanded you, and have gone and served other gods, and bowed yourselves to them; then shall the anger of the LORD be kindled against you, and ye shall perish quickly from off the good land which he hath given unto you.**

{24:1} And Joshua gathered all the tribes of Israel to Shechem, and called for the elders of Israel, and for their heads, and for their judges, and for their officers; and they presented themselves before God. {24:2} And Joshua said unto all the people, "Thus saith the LORD God of Israel, Your fathers dwelt on the other side of the flood in old time, even Terah, the father of Abraham, and the father of Nachor: and they served other gods. {24:3} And I took your father Abraham from the other side of the flood, and led him throughout all the land of Canaan, and multiplied his seed, and gave him Isaac. {24:4} And I gave unto Isaac Jacob and Esau: and I gave unto Esau mount Seir, to possess it; but Jacob and his children went down into Egypt. {24:5} I sent Moses also and Aaron, and I plagued Egypt, according to that which I did among them: and afterward I brought you out. {24:6} And I brought your fathers out of Egypt: and ye came unto the sea; and the Egyptians pursued after your fathers with chariots and horsemen unto the Red sea. {24:7} And when they cried unto the LORD, he put darkness between you and the Egyptians, and brought the sea upon them, and covered them; and your eyes have seen what I have done in Egypt: and ye dwelt in the wilderness a long season. {24:8} And I brought you into the land of the Amorites, which dwelt on the other side Jordan; and they fought with you: and I gave them into your hand, that ye might possess their land; and I destroyed them from before you. {24:9} Then Balak the son of Zippor, king of Moab, arose and warred against Israel, and sent and called Balaam the son of Beor to curse you: {24:10} But I would not hearken unto Balaam; therefore he blessed you still: so I delivered you out of his hand. {24:11} And ye went over Jordan, and came unto Jericho: and the men of Jericho fought against you, the Amorites, and the Perizzites, and the Canaanites, and the Hittites, and the Girgashites, the Hivites, and the Jebusites; and I delivered them into your hand. {24:12} And I sent the hornet before you, which drave them out from before you, even the two kings of the Amorites; but not with thy sword, nor with thy bow. {24:13} And I have given you a land for which ye did not labour, and cities which ye built not, and ye dwell in them; of the vineyards and oliveyards which ye planted not do ye eat. {24:14} Now therefore fear the LORD, and serve him in sincerity and in truth: and put away the gods which your fathers served on the other side of the flood, and in Egypt; and serve ye the LORD. {24:15} ***And if it seem evil unto you to serve the LORD, choose you this day whom ye will serve; whether the gods which your fathers served that were on the other side of the flood, or the gods of the Amorites, in whose land ye dwell: but as for me and my house, we will serve the LORD.*** {24:16} And the people answered and said, "God forbid that we should forsake the LORD, to serve other gods; {24:17} For the LORD our God, he it is that brought us up and our fathers out of the land of Egypt, from the house of bondage, and which did those great signs in our sight, and preserved us in all the way wherein we went, and among all the people through whom we passed: {24:18} And the LORD drave out from before us all the people, even the Amorites which dwelt in the land: therefore will we also serve the LORD; for he is our God." {24:19} And Joshua said unto the people, "Ye cannot serve the LORD: for he is an holy God; he is a jealous God; he will not forgive your transgressions nor your sins. {24:20} If ye forsake the LORD, and serve strange gods, then he will turn and do you hurt, and consume you, after that he hath done you good. {24:21} And the people said unto Joshua, "Nay; but we will serve the LORD." {24:22} And Joshua said unto the people, "Ye are witnesses against yourselves that ye have chosen you the LORD, to serve him." And they said, "We are witnesses." {24:23} Now therefore put away, said he, the strange gods which are among you, and incline your heart unto the LORD God of Israel. {24:24} And the people said unto Joshua, "The LORD our God will we serve, and his voice will we obey." {24:25} So Joshua made a covenant with the people that day, and set them a statute and an ordinance in Shechem. {24:26} And Joshua wrote these words in the book of the law of God, and took a great stone, and set it up there under an oak, that was by the sanctuary of the LORD. {24:27} And Joshua said unto all the people, "Behold, this stone shall be a witness unto us; for it hath heard all the words of the LORD which he spake unto us: it shall be therefore a witness unto you, lest ye deny your God." {24:28} So Joshua let the people depart, every man unto his inheritance. {24:29} And it came to pass after these things, that Joshua the son of Nun, the servant of the LORD, died, being an hundred and ten years old. {24:30} And they buried him in the border of his inheritance in Timnath-serah, which is in mount Ephraim, on the north side of the hill of Gaash. {24:31} ***And Israel served the LORD all the days of Joshua, and all the days of the elders that overlived Joshua, and which had known all the works of the LORD, that he had done for Israel.*** {24:32} And the bones of Joseph, which the children of Israel brought up out of Egypt, buried they in Shechem, in a parcel of ground which Jacob bought of the sons of Hamor the father of Shechem for an hundred pieces of silver: and it became the inheritance of the children of Joseph. {24:33} And Eleazar the son of Aaron died; and they buried him in a hill that pertained to Phinehas his son, which was given him in mount Ephraim.

Judges

{1:1} Now after the death of Joshua it came to pass, that the children of Israel asked the LORD, saying, "Who shall go up for us against the Canaanites first, to fight against them? {1:2} And the LORD said, "Judah shall go up: behold, I have delivered the land into his hand. {1:3} And Judah said unto Simeon his brother, "Come up with me into my lot, that we may fight against the Canaanites; and I likewise will go with thee into thy lot." So Simeon went with him. {1:4} And Judah went up; and the LORD delivered the Canaanites and the Perizzites into their hand: and they slew of them in Bezek ten thousand men. {1:5} And they found Adonibezek in Bezek: and they fought against him, and they slew the Canaanites and the Perizzites. {1:6} But Adoni-bezek fled; and they pursued after him, and caught him, and cut off his thumbs and his great toes. {1:7} And Adoni-bezek said, "Threescore and ten kings, having their thumbs and their great toes cut off, gathered their meat under my table: as I have done, so God hath requited me." And they brought him to Jerusalem, and there he died. {1:8} Now the children of Judah had fought against Jerusalem, and had taken it, and smitten it with the edge of the sword, and set the city on fire. {1:9} And afterward the children of Judah went down to fight against the Canaanites, that dwelt in the mountain, and in the south, and in the valley. {1:10} And Judah went against the Canaanites that dwelt in Hebron: (now the name of Hebron before was Kirjath-arba:) and they slew Sheshai, and Ahiman, and Talmai. {1:11} And from thence he went against the inhabitants of Debir: and the name of Debir before was Kirjath-sepher: {1:12} And Caleb said, "He that smiteth Kirjath-sepher, and taketh it, to him will I give Achsah my daughter to wife." {1:13} And Othniel the son of Kenaz, Caleb's younger brother, took it: and he gave him Achsah his daughter to wife. {1:14} And it came to pass, when she came to him, that she moved him to ask of her father a field: and she lighted from off her ass; and Caleb said unto her, "What wilt thou?" {1:15} And she said unto him, "Give me a blessing: for thou hast given me a south land; give me also springs of water." And Caleb gave her the upper springs and the nether springs. {1:16} And the children of the Kenite, Moses' father in law, went up out of the city of palm trees with the children of Judah into the wilderness of Judah, which lieth in the south of Arad; and they went and dwelt among the people. {1:17} And Judah went with Simeon his brother, and they slew the Canaanites that inhabited Zephath, and utterly destroyed it. And the name of the city was called Hormah. {1:18} Also Judah took Gaza with the coast thereof, and Askelon with the coast thereof, and Ekron with the coast thereof. {1:19} And the LORD was with Judah; and he drave out the inhabitants of the mountain; but could not drive out the inhabitants of the valley, because they had chariots of iron. {1:20} And they gave Hebron unto Caleb, as Moses said: and he expelled thence the three sons of Anak. {1:21} And the children of Benjamin did not drive out the Jebusites that inhabited Jerusalem; but the Jebusites dwell with the children of Benjamin in Jerusalem unto this day. {1:22} And the house of Joseph, they also went up against Bethel: and the LORD was with them. {1:23} And the house of Joseph sent to descry Bethel. (Now the name of the city before was Luz.) {1:24} And the spies saw a man come forth out of the city, and they said unto him, "Show us, we pray thee, the entrance into the city, and we will show thee mercy." {1:25} And when he showed them the entrance into the city, they smote the city with the edge of the sword; but they let go the man and all his family. {1:26} And the man went into the land of the Hittites, and built a city, and called the name thereof Luz: which is the name thereof unto this day. {1:27} Neither did Manasseh drive out the inhabitants of Beth-shean and her towns, nor Taanach and her towns, nor the inhabitants of Dor and her towns, nor the inhabitants of Ibleam and her towns, nor the inhabitants of Megiddo and her towns: but the Canaanites would dwell in that land. {1:28} And it came to pass, when Israel was strong, that they put the Canaanites to tribute, and did not utterly drive them out. {1:29} Neither did Ephraim drive out the Canaanites that dwelt in Gezer; but the Canaanites dwelt in Gezer among them. {1:30} Neither did Zebulun drive out the inhabitants of Kitron, nor the inhabitants of Nahalol; but the Canaanites dwelt among them, and became tributaries. {1:31} Neither did Asher drive out the inhabitants of Accho, nor the inhabitants of Zidon, nor of Ahlab, nor of Achzib, nor of Helbah, nor of Aphik, nor of Rehob: {1:32} But the Asherites dwelt among the Canaanites, the inhabitants of the land: for they did not drive them out. {1:33} Neither did Naphtali drive out the inhabitants of Beth-shemesh, nor the inhabitants of Beth-anath; but he dwelt among the Canaanites, the inhabitants of the land: nevertheless the inhabitants of Beth-shemesh and of Beth-anath became tributaries unto them. {1:34} And the Amorites forced the children of Dan into the mountain: for they would not suffer them to come down to the valley: {1:35} But the Amorites would dwell in mount Heres in Aijalon, and in Shaalbim: yet the hand of the house of Joseph prevailed, so that they became tributaries. {1:36} And the coast of the Amorites was from the going up to Akrabbim, from the rock, and upward.

{2:1} An angel of the LORD came from Gilgal to Bochim and said, "I brought you out of Egypt and into the land I promised your ancestors. I said I would never break my covenant with you. {2:2} "You must not make agreements with the people of this land or worship their gods. You have disobeyed me. Why have you done this? {2:3} "Because of this, I will not drive them out before you. Instead, they will be like thorns in your sides, and their gods will be a snare to you." {2:4} When the angel spoke these words, the Israelites lifted up their voices and wept. They named the place Bochim and sacrificed to the LORD there. {2:5} After Joshua dismissed the people, each went to their inheritance to possess the land. {2:6} The people served the LORD all the days of Joshua and the elders who outlived him, having seen the great works of the LORD for Israel. {2:7} Joshua, the servant of the LORD, died at the age of 110 and was buried in his inheritance in Timnath-heres, in the hill country of Ephraim, north of Gaash. {2:8} That entire generation passed away, and a new generation arose that did not know the LORD or the works he had done for Israel. {2:9} The Israelites did evil in the sight of the LORD, serving the Baals and forsaking the LORD, who brought them out of Egypt. They followed other gods, bowing down to them and angering the LORD. {2:10} They abandoned the LORD to serve Baal and Ashtaroth. {2:11} The LORD's anger burned against Israel. He delivered them into the hands of raiders who plundered them and sold them into the hands of their enemies. They could no longer stand against their enemies. {2:12} Wherever they went, the LORD's hand was against them for evil, as he had sworn, and they were greatly distressed. {2:13} Nevertheless, the LORD raised up judges who delivered them from their oppressors. {2:14} Yet, they did not listen to their judges, but followed other gods, quickly turning away from the path their ancestors had walked. They did not obey the LORD's commandments. {2:15} When the LORD raised up judges, he was with the judge and delivered them from their enemies throughout the judge's lifetime. Because of the Israelites' suffering under their oppressors, the LORD relented. {2:16} However, when the judge died, they returned to their corrupt ways, even more than their ancestors, following other gods and refusing to give up their stubborn practices. {2:17} **The LORD's anger burned against Israel, saying, "This people has broken my covenant, not listening to my voice.** {2:18} "Therefore, I will no longer drive out the nations that Joshua left when he died. I will use them to test Israel, to see if they will follow the LORD's ways as their ancestors did." {2:19} **So, the LORD left those nations, not driving them out quickly or delivering them into Joshua's hand, but leaving them to test Israel.** {2:20} The LORD's anger burned against Israel because they broke his covenant, disobeying his commandments and refusing to listen to his voice. {2:21} He declared, "I will no longer drive out the nations that Joshua left when he died. {2:22} "I will use these nations to test Israel, to see if they will follow the LORD's ways as their ancestors did." {2:23} So, the LORD left those nations, not swiftly driving them out or handing them over to Joshua.

{3:1} These are the nations the LORD left to test Israel, those who had not experienced the wars of Canaan. {3:2} This was to teach the new generations of Israel about war, those who had no previous knowledge of it. {3:3} These nations included the five Philistine rulers, along with the Canaanites, Sidonians, and Hivites living in the mountains of Lebanon, from Mount Baal-hermon to the entrance of Hamath. {3:4} They were left to test Israel, to see if they would obey the LORD's commandments given through Moses to their ancestors. {3:5} The Israelites lived among the Canaanites, Hittites, Amorites, Perizzites, Hivites, and Jebusites. {3:6} They intermarried with these nations, giving their daughters to the sons of the Canaanites, and serving their gods. {3:7} The Israelites did evil in the sight of the LORD, forgetting their God and worshiping Baal and the Asherah poles. {3:8} This angered the LORD, so he allowed Chushan-rishathaim, king of Mesopotamia, to oppress Israel for eight years. {3:9} When the Israelites cried out to the LORD, he raised up Othniel, Caleb's younger brother, to deliver them. {3:10} The Spirit of the LORD came upon Othniel, and he led Israel in battle, defeating Chushan-rishathaim. {3:11} The land had rest for forty years during Othniel's rule, after which he died. {3:12} The Israelites once again did evil in the LORD's sight, so he strengthened Eglon, king of Moab, against them because of their wickedness. {3:13} Eglon allied with the Ammonites and Amalekites, attacking and capturing the city of palm trees. {3:14} For eighteen years, the Israelites served Eglon, king of Moab. {3:15} When they cried out to the LORD, he raised up Ehud, a left-handed Benjamite, to deliver them. {3:16} Ehud crafted a double-edged dagger and concealed it under his clothing on his right thigh. {3:17} He presented a tribute to Eglon and then privately told him he had a message from God. {3:18} As Eglon dismissed his attendants, Ehud approached him in his private chamber. {3:19} He told Eglon he had a secret message, and as Eglon listened intently, Ehud drew the dagger from his thigh and stabbed him in the belly. {3:20} The fat closed over the blade, and Eglon's bowels emptied. Ehud then locked the doors and escaped. {3:21} When Eglon's servants found the doors locked, they assumed he was relieving himself and waited, only to discover him dead. {3:22} Ehud escaped to Seirath, blowing a trumpet to rally the Israelites to battle against the Moabites. {3:23} They followed him, defeating the Moabites and securing peace for eighty years. {3:24} After Ehud, Shamgar, son of Anath, killed six hundred Philistines with an ox goad and delivered Israel. {3:25} The servants waited, feeling embarrassed as time passed. When they realized Eglon hadn't opened the doors, they used a key to unlock them. Inside, they found their lord dead on the ground. {3:26} While they hesitated, Ehud made his escape, passing beyond the quarries and fleeing to Seirath. {3:27} Upon arriving, he blew a trumpet in the mountains of Ephraim, and the Israelites gathered with him. {3:28} Ehud urged them to follow him, declaring that the LORD had delivered their enemies, the Moabites, into their hands. They obeyed, seizing the fords of the Jordan River and preventing anyone from crossing. {3:29} They killed about ten thousand strong and valiant Moabite warriors; none escaped. {3:30} Thus, Moab was subdued by Israel that day, and the land enjoyed eighty years of peace. {3:31} After Ehud, Shamgar, son of Anath, arose. He killed six hundred Philistines with an ox goad and also delivered Israel.

{4:1} Once again, the children of Israel did evil in the sight of the LORD after Ehud died. {4:2} So the LORD sold them into the hand of Jabin, king of Canaan, who reigned in Hazor. His army's commander was Sisera, residing in Harosheth of the Gentiles. {4:3} Sisera oppressed the Israelites mightily with his nine hundred iron chariots for twenty years, causing great suffering. {4:4} **During this time, Deborah, a prophetess and the wife of Lapidoth, served as a judge in Israel.** {4:5} She held court under the palm tree of Deborah between Ramah and Bethel in Mount Ephraim, where the Israelites sought her for judgment. {4:6} Deborah instructed Barak, son of Abinoam from Kedesh-naphtali, to gather ten thousand men from Naphtali and Zebulun and lead them to Mount Tabor. {4:7} She assured Barak that the LORD would draw Sisera, Jabin's army commander, and his chariots to the River Kishon, where Barak would defeat them. {4:8} Barak hesitated, insisting that Deborah accompany him. She agreed but warned him that the honor of victory would not be his, for the LORD would sell Sisera into the hand of a woman. {4:9} Deborah accompanied Barak to Kedesh. {4:10} Barak gathered his troops from Zebulun and Naphtali and went to Kedesh with ten thousand men, with Deborah by his side. {4:11} Meanwhile, Heber the Kenite, who had separated from the Kenites and pitched his tent near Kedesh, informed Sisera of Barak's movements. {4:12} Sisera mobilized his nine hundred iron chariots and his army, gathering them at the River Kishon. {4:13} Deborah told Barak that the time had come, for the LORD had delivered Sisera into his hands. {4:14} Barak descended from Mount Tabor with his ten thousand men, and the LORD routed Sisera's chariots and army before him. {4:15} Sisera fled on foot, and Barak pursued him to Harosheth of the Gentiles. All of Sisera's army fell by the sword; none survived. {4:16} Sisera fled to the tent of Jael, wife of Heber the Kenite, for safety. {4:17} Jael welcomed Sisera into her tent, offering him milk and covering him as he slept. {4:18} When Sisera requested water, Jael gave him milk and covered him again. {4:19} Sisera instructed Jael to stand guard at the tent entrance and deny anyone's presence. {4:20} While he slept, Jael took a tent peg and hammered it through his temple into the ground, killing him. {4:21} When Barak arrived, Jael showed him Sisera's lifeless body in her tent. {4:22} Thus, the LORD subdued Jabin, king of Canaan, before the children of Israel on that day. {4:23} The Israelites gained strength and eventually overcame Jabin, {4:24} destroying him completely.

{5:1} Deborah and Barak, son of Abinoam, sang on that day: {5:2} "Praise the LORD for avenging Israel, as the people willingly offered themselves. {5:3} Hear, O kings; give ear, O princes! I, even I, will sing praises to the LORD God of Israel. {5:4} When the LORD marched from Seir and Edom, the earth trembled, and the heavens poured rain; even the mountains melted before the LORD, the God of Israel. {5:5} In the days of Shamgar and Jael, the roads were deserted, and travelers avoided the highways. {5:6} Villages lay empty in Israel until I, Deborah, arose as a mother in Israel. {5:7} The people turned to new gods, and war broke out in the gates. Among forty thousand in Israel, was there a shield or spear seen? {5:8} My heart is with the leaders of Israel who willingly offered themselves. Bless the LORD! {5:9} Speak, you who ride on white donkeys, you who sit in judgment, and you who walk along the road. {5:10} Those rescued from the noise of archers at the watering places recounted the righteous acts of the LORD, the righteous acts towards His villagers in Israel. {5:11} Then the people of the LORD went down to the gates. {5:12} Awake, Deborah! Awake and sing! Arise, Barak, and lead your captives captive, son of Abinoam. {5:13} The remnant gained dominion over the nobles; the LORD made me have dominion over the mighty. {5:14} From Ephraim came those against Amalek, after you, Benjamin, among your people. From Machir came leaders, and from Zebulun those who wielded the scribe's pen. {5:15} The princes of Issachar were with Deborah; Issachar and Barak were sent into the valley. Among the divisions of Reuben, there were great resolves of heart. {5:16} Why did you remain among the sheepfolds to hear the bleating of the flocks? Among the divisions of Reuben, there were great searchings of heart. {5:17} Gilead remained beyond the Jordan; why did Dan stay in ships? Asher continued along the seashore and stayed in his harbors. {5:18} Zebulun and Naphtali risked their lives in the heights of the battlefield. {5:19} The kings came and fought, then the kings of Canaan fought in Taanach by the waters of Megiddo; they took no spoils of silver. {5:20} From heaven the stars fought, from their courses they fought against Sisera. {5:21} The River Kishon swept them away, that ancient river, the River Kishon. O my soul, march on with strength! {5:22} Then the horses' hooves hammered the ground, galloping, galloping their mighty steeds. {5:23} "Curse Meroz," said the angel of the LORD, "Curse bitterly its inhabitants, because they did not come to the help of the LORD, to the help of the LORD against the mighty." {5:24} Blessed above women shall Jael, the wife of Heber the Kenite, be; blessed shall she be above women in the tent. {5:25} Sisera asked for water, and she gave him milk; she brought out cream in a lordly bowl. {5:26} With her left hand she reached for the tent peg, and with her right hand for the workman's hammer. She struck Sisera, she crushed his head, she shattered and pierced his temple. {5:27} At her feet he sank, he fell, he lay still; at her feet he sank, he fell; where he sank, there he fell—dead. {5:28} Through the window she looked out, peered through the lattice, and lamented, "Why is his chariot so long in coming? Why tarry the clatter of his chariots?" {5:29} The wisest of her ladies answered her; indeed, she keeps saying to herself, {5:30} 'Are they not finding and dividing the spoil? A girl or two for each man, a spoil of dyed garments for Sisera, a spoil of dyed garments embroidered, two pieces of dyed work embroidered for the neck of the looter?' {5:31} So let all Your enemies perish, O LORD! But let those who love Him be like the sun when it comes out in full strength." And the land had rest for forty years.

{6:1} The Israelites did evil in the sight of the LORD, so He allowed the Midianites to rule over them for seven years. {6:2} The Midianites were strong, and the Israelites had to hide in mountains, caves, and strongholds to escape them. {6:3} Whenever the Israelites planted crops, the Midianites, along with the Amalekites and other eastern peoples, invaded their land. {6:4} They camped on the land, destroying crops all the way to Gaza, leaving nothing for the Israelites to eat, not even their livestock. {6:5} The invaders were so numerous, they were like swarms of locusts, with countless camels, and they ravaged the land. {6:6} Because of this, the Israelites became very poor and cried out to the LORD for help. {6:7} When they cried out, the LORD sent a prophet to remind them how He had rescued them from slavery in Egypt and given them their land. {6:8} The LORD sent a prophet to remind them how He had rescued them from slavery in Egypt and given them their land. {6:9} But the Israelites had disobeyed Him and worshipped other gods. {6:10} Then an angel of the LORD appeared to Gideon while he was threshing wheat, and said, "The LORD is with you, mighty warrior!" {6:11} Gideon questioned why all these troubles had befallen them if the LORD was with them. {6:12} **The LORD told Gideon that he would save Israel from the Midianites and that He was sending him to do it.** {6:13} Gideon asked for a sign to prove that the LORD was speaking to him. {6:14} So Gideon prepared a sacrifice, and the angel of the LORD miraculously consumed it with fire. {6:15} Gideon realized he had seen an angel of the LORD and feared for his life. {6:16} But the LORD assured him he would not die. {6:17} Gideon built an altar to the LORD there and named it Jehovah-shalom. {6:18} That night, the LORD told Gideon to destroy his father's altar to Baal and build one to the LORD in its place. {6:19} Gideon obeyed, but because he feared his family and the townspeople, he did it at night. {6:20} In the morning, the people found the altar of Baal destroyed and the new altar to the LORD built. {6:21} They demanded to know who did it, and when they found out, they wanted to kill Gideon. {6:22} But Gideon's father defended him, asking if they would really fight for a false god like Baal. {6:23} From then on, Gideon was called Jerubbaal, meaning "Let Baal contend against him." {6:24} Meanwhile, the enemies of Israel gathered in the valley of Jezreel. {6:25} The Spirit of the LORD came upon Gideon, and he blew a trumpet to gather his people. {6:26} He sent messengers to gather more warriors from the tribes of Manasseh, Asher, Zebulun, and Naphtali. {6:27} Gideon asked for another sign from the LORD, this time with a fleece of wool. {6:28} In the morning, the fleece was wet with dew while the ground around it was dry. {6:29} Gideon then asked for the opposite sign, and the next morning, the fleece was dry while the ground was wet with dew. {6:30} The people of the city demanded that Joash bring out Gideon to be killed for destroying the altar of Baal and the nearby grove. {6:31} But Joash challenged them, asking if they would fight for Baal. He declared that anyone who fought for Baal should be executed, because if Baal truly was a god, he could defend himself. From then on, Gideon was called Jerubbaal, meaning "Let Baal contend against him," because he had destroyed Baal's altar. {6:32} Meanwhile, the enemies of Israel, including the Midianites, Amalekites, and other eastern tribes, gathered in the valley of Jezreel. {6:33} The Spirit of the LORD came upon Gideon, and he blew a trumpet to call the people of Abi-ezer to join him. {6:34} Then messengers were sent throughout Manasseh, and the tribes of Asher, Zebulun, and Naphtali, rallying them to Gideon's cause. {6:35} Gideon prayed to God, asking for a sign with a fleece of wool. He requested that if dew were on the fleece but not on the ground, it would confirm that God would save Israel by his hand. {6:36} The next morning, Gideon found the fleece wet with dew while the ground was dry, confirming God's promise. {6:37} Gideon then asked for another sign, requesting that the fleece be dry while the ground around it was wet with dew. {6:38} The following morning, God granted Gideon's request, demonstrating his faithfulness once again. {6:39} Gideon, grateful and fearing God's anger, asked for one more confirmation with the fleece, requesting the opposite of the previous sign. {6:40} That night, God granted Gideon's request again, solidifying his trust in God's plan.

{7:1} Jerubbaal, also known as Gideon, and his people woke up early and camped near the well of Harod. The Midianite army was north of them, near the hill of Moreh in the valley. {7:2} The LORD told Gideon that his army was too large, so that Israel wouldn't boast about their own strength if they won. He instructed Gideon to tell the fearful to leave. Twenty-two thousand left, leaving ten thousand. {7:3} God said there were still too many. He tested them by how they drank water. Three hundred men lapped water with their hands, while the rest knelt to drink. {7:4} God told Gideon to keep the three hundred who lapped water and dismiss the others. {7:5} Those who lapped water were chosen to stay. {7:6} Only three hundred men lapped water, while the rest knelt to drink. {7:7} God told Gideon that with these three hundred, He would deliver them from the Midianites, and the rest were to go home. {7:8} Gideon sent the rest of the people home and kept the three hundred. The Midianite camp lay below them in the valley. {7:9} That night, the LORD told Gideon to attack the camp, as He had delivered it into his hands. {7:10} If Gideon was afraid, he could go with his servant Phurah to the camp to listen. {7:11} Gideon listened to a man's dream in the camp, which foretold Gideon's victory. {7:12} The Midianites, Amalekites, and others were as numerous as locusts in the valley, with countless camels. {7:13} Gideon overheard a man telling his dream, which indicated Gideon's victory. {7:14} The dream was interpreted as God delivering Midian into Gideon's hands. {7:15} **Gideon worshipped when he heard the interpretation, believing God had delivered Midian into their hands.** {7:16} Gideon divided the three hundred men into three companies, each holding a trumpet, an empty pitcher, and a lamp. {7:17} He instructed them to follow his lead as they approached the enemy camp. {7:18} When he blew his trumpet, they were to blow theirs and shout, "The sword of the LORD and of Gideon." {7:19} Gideon and his men arrived at the camp during the middle watch, blew their trumpets, and broke their pitchers. {7:20} They shouted, "The sword of the LORD and of Gideon," holding lamps and trumpets. {7:21} The enemy panicked, running and crying out in fear. {7:22} The three hundred blew their trumpets, causing confusion, and the Midianites turned on each other in the chaos. {7:23} The men of Israel from Naphtali, Asher, and Manasseh pursued the Midianites. {7:24} Gideon sent messengers to Ephraim, asking for help in capturing the Midianite leaders and controlling the crossings of the Jordan River. {7:25} Ephraim joined the fight, capturing the Midianite leaders Oreb and Zeeb, killing them, and pursuing the rest of the Midianites. They brought the leaders' heads to Gideon.

{8:1} The men of Ephraim questioned Gideon, asking why he didn't call them to fight the Midianites. They criticized him sharply. {8:2} Gideon replied, asking what he had done wrong compared to them. He argued that what Ephraim had achieved was greater than what he had accomplished. {8:3} Gideon reminded them that God had delivered the Midianite princes into their hands, calming their anger. {8:4} Gideon and his three hundred men crossed the Jordan River, weary but still pursuing the enemy. {8:5} He asked the men of Succoth for bread for his tired soldiers, explaining that he was chasing Zebah and Zalmunna, the Midianite kings. {8:6} The leaders of Succoth refused, questioning whether Gideon had captured the kings yet. {8:7} Gideon warned that when he did capture the kings, he would punish them for refusing aid. {8:8} Gideon then went to Penuel and received a similar response. {8:9} He threatened to destroy their tower when he returned in peace. {8:10} Zebah and Zalmunna were in Karkor with fifteen thousand men, the remnants of their once large army. {8:11} Gideon attacked and defeated them, pursuing them as they fled. {8:12} He captured the kings and routed the entire enemy host. {8:13} Gideon returned from battle before sunrise. {8:14} He interrogated a young man from Succoth about their leaders and elders. {8:15} Gideon confronted the men of Succoth, showing them Zebah and Zalmunna, whom they had refused to support. {8:16} He punished the elders with thorns and briers to teach them a lesson. {8:17} Gideon destroyed the tower of Penuel and killed the men of the city. {8:18} He asked Zebah and Zalmunna about the men they had killed at Tabor, revealing they were his own brothers. {8:19} Gideon swore he would not harm them if they had spared his brothers. {8:20} Gideon ordered his son Jether to kill them, but he was too afraid. {8:21} Zebah and Zalmunna requested to be killed by Gideon himself, which he did, taking their camel ornaments. {8:22} The Israelites asked Gideon to rule over them and his descendants, grateful for their deliverance from Midian. {8:23} Gideon refused, declaring that only the LORD would rule over them. {8:24} Gideon asked for the golden earrings taken as plunder, which amounted to a considerable weight. {8:25} The people willingly gave them, and Gideon made an ephod from the gold, which led Israel astray. {8:26} The weight of the gold was significant, including the ornaments from the Midianite kings. {8:27} Gideon placed the ephod in Ophrah, leading Israel into idolatry, which became a snare for Gideon and his household. {8:28} With Midian subdued, Israel enjoyed peace for forty years during Gideon's lifetime. {8:29} Gideon returned to his home, and his family grew, having seventy sons from his wives and one from a concubine. {8:30} Gideon's concubine in Shechem bore him a son named Abimelech. {8:31} Gideon died at a ripe old age and was buried in Ophrah with his ancestors. {8:32} After Gideon's death, Israel turned away from the LORD and worshipped Baalim, forgetting the LORD who had saved them. {8:33} They also neglected to show kindness to Gideon's family, despite his previous deeds for Israel. {8:34} Israel disregarded the LORD who had delivered them from their enemies. {8:35} They did not remember Gideon's kindness and turned to idolatry, forsaking the LORD.

{9:1} Abimelech, the son of Jerubbaal, went to Shechem to his mother's relatives. He spoke to them and to all the family of his mother's father, saying, {9:2} "Please speak in the ears of all the men of Shechem: Is it better for you that seventy sons of Jerubbaal reign over you, or that one reign over you? Remember that I am your bone and your flesh." {9:3} His mother's relatives spoke of him in the ears of all the men of Shechem, and their hearts inclined to follow Abimelech, for they said, "He is our brother." {9:4} They gave him seventy pieces of silver from the house of Baal-berith, with which Abimelech hired vain and light persons who followed him. {9:5} He went to his father's house at Ophrah and killed his brethren, the sons of Jerubbaal, seventy persons, upon one stone. However, Jotham, the youngest son of Jerubbaal, was left, for he hid himself. {9:6} All the men of Shechem and the house of Millo gathered together and made Abimelech king by the plain of the pillar in Shechem. {9:7} When they told Jotham, he went and stood on top of Mount Gerizim, lifted up his voice, and said to them, "Listen to me, men of Shechem, so that God may listen to you. {9:8} "Once the trees went forth to anoint a king over them. They said to the olive tree, 'Reign over us.' {9:9} "But the olive tree said, 'Should I leave my fatness, with which I honor God and man, and go to be promoted over the trees?' {9:10} "The trees said to the fig tree, 'Come, reign over us.' {9:11} "But the fig tree said, 'Should I forsake my sweetness and my good fruit, and go to be promoted over the trees?' {9:12} "Then the trees said to the vine, 'Come, reign over us.' {9:13} "But the vine said, 'Should I leave my wine, which cheers God and man, and go to be promoted over the trees?' {9:14} "Then all the trees said to the bramble, 'Come, reign over us.' {9:15} "And the bramble said to the trees, 'If you truly anoint me king over you, then come and put your trust in my shadow; and if not, let fire come out of the bramble and devour the cedars of Lebanon.' {9:16} "Therefore, if you have dealt truly and sincerely in making Abimelech king, and if you have dealt well with Jerubbaal and his house, and have done to him according to his deeds— {9:17} "(For my father fought for you, risked his life, and delivered you from the hand of Midian; {9:18} "And you have risen up against my father's house this day, killed his sons, seventy persons, upon one stone, and made Abimelech, the son of his maidservant, king over the men of Shechem because he is your brother)— {9:19} "If then you have dealt truly and sincerely with Jerubbaal and his house this day, rejoice in Abimelech, and let him also rejoice in you. {9:20} "But if not, let fire come out from Abimelech and devour the men of Shechem and the house of Millo; and let fire come out from the men of Shechem and from the house of Millo, and devour Abimelech." {9:21} Jotham ran away, fled, and went to Beer, and dwelt there, for fear of Abimelech his brother. {9:22} When Abimelech had reigned three years over Israel, {9:23} God sent an evil spirit between Abimelech and the men of Shechem, and the men of Shechem dealt treacherously with Abimelech, {9:24} So that the cruelty done to the seventy sons of Jerubbaal might come, and their blood be laid upon Abimelech their brother, who killed them, and upon the men of Shechem who aided him in killing his brethren. {9:25} The men of Shechem set liers in wait for him in the top of the mountains, and they robbed all that came along that way by them, and it was told Abimelech. {9:26} Gaal the son of Ebed came with his brethren, and went over to Shechem, and the men of Shechem put their confidence in him. {9:27} They went out into the fields, gathered their vineyards, trod the grapes, made merry, went into the house of their god, ate, drank, and cursed Abimelech. {9:28} Gaal the son of Ebed said, "Who is Abimelech, and who is Shechem, that we should serve him? Is he not the son of Jerubbaal, and Zebul his officer? Serve the men of Hamor the father of Shechem. Why should we serve him?" {9:29} "I wish this people were under my hand! Then would I remove Abimelech." And he said to Abimelech, "Increase your army, and come out." {9:30} When Zebul, the ruler of the city, heard the words of Gaal the son of Ebed, his anger was kindled. {9:31} He sent messengers to Abimelech secretly, saying, "Gaal the son of Ebed and his brethren have come to Shechem, and they fortify the city against you." {9:32} "Now therefore, up by night, you and the people with you, and lie in wait in the field." {9:33} "And it shall be, that in the morning, as soon as the sun is up, you shall rise early, and set upon the city. And behold, when he and the people that is with him come out against you, then may you do to them as you shall find occasion." {9:34} Abimelech rose up, and all the people with him, by night, and they laid wait against Shechem in four companies. {9:35} Gaal the son of Ebed went out, and stood in the entering of the gate of the city. Abimelech rose up, and the people with him, from lying in wait. {9:36} When Gaal saw the people, he said to Zebul, "Behold, there come people down from the top of the mountains." Zebul said unto him, "You see the shadow of the mountains as if they were men." {9:37} Gaal said again, "See there come people down by the middle of the land, and another company come along by the plain of Meonen {9:38} Zebul said to him, "Where is now your boastful speech, where you questioned, 'Who is Abimelech, that we should serve him?' Isn't this the people you despised? Go out now and fight with them." {9:39} Gaal went out before the men of Shechem and fought with Abimelech. {9:40} Abimelech chased him, and Gaal fled before him. Many were overthrown and wounded, even to the entering of the gate. {9:41} Abimelech stayed at Arumah, and Zebul drove out Gaal and his brothers, so they couldn't live in Shechem. {9:42} On the next day, the people went out into the field, and they told Abimelech. {9:43} He divided his people into three companies, and laid wait in the field. When he saw the people coming out of the city, he rose up against them and attacked. {9:44} Abimelech and his company stood at the entering of the gate of the city, while the other two companies attacked those in the fields and killed them. {9:45} Abimelech fought against the city all day, and eventually took it. He killed the people, destroyed the city, and sowed it with salt. {9:46} When the men of the tower of Shechem heard this, they took refuge in the stronghold of the house of the god Berith. {9:47} Abimelech was informed that all the men of the tower of Shechem were gathered together. {9:48} Abimelech and his men went up to Mount Zalmon. Abimelech took an axe, cut down a branch from the trees, laid it on his shoulder, and said to the people with him, "Do as you have seen me do quickly." {9:49} All the people cut down branches and followed Abimelech. They piled the branches against the stronghold and set it on fire, so about a thousand men and women of the tower of Shechem died. {9:50} Abimelech then went to Thebez, laid siege to it, and captured it. {9:51} But there was a strong tower in the city, so all the men and women, along with the city's inhabitants, fled there, shut themselves in, and went up to the top of the tower. {9:52} Abimelech came to the tower, fought against it, and approached the door to set it on fire. {9:53} A woman threw a piece of a millstone on Abimelech's head, and it crushed his skull. {9:54} Abimelech called hastily to his armor-bearer, telling him to kill him so people wouldn't say, "A woman killed him." So, his armor-bearer thrust him through, and he died. {9:55} When the men of Israel saw that Abimelech was dead, they each went to their own place. {9:56} Thus, God repaid the wickedness of Abimelech, who killed his seventy brothers, and the evil of the men of Shechem, {9:57} who received the curse of Jotham the son of Jerubbaal upon their heads.

{10:1} After Abimelech, there arose to defend Israel Tola, the son of Puah, the son of Dodo, a man of Issachar. He lived in Shamir in Mount Ephraim. {10:2} He judged Israel for twenty-three years, then died and was buried in Shamir. {10:3} After him, Jair, a Gileadite, arose and judged Israel for twenty-two years. {10:4} He had thirty sons who rode on thirty donkey colts, and they had thirty cities called Havoth-jair, which are in the land of Gilead. {10:5} Jair died and was buried in Camon. {10:6} The children of Israel again did evil in the sight of the LORD. They served Baalim, Ashtaroth, the gods of Syria, Zidon, Moab, Ammon, and the Philistines, forsaking the LORD and not serving Him. {10:7} The anger of the LORD burned against Israel, and He sold them into the hands of the Philistines and the children of Ammon. {10:8} They oppressed the children of Israel for eighteen years, all those beyond the Jordan in the land of the Amorites, in Gilead. {10:9} Moreover, the children of Ammon crossed over Jordan to fight against Judah, Benjamin, and the house of Ephraim, causing great distress to Israel. {10:10} The children of Israel cried to the LORD, confessing their sin of forsaking God and serving Baalim. {10:11} The LORD reminded them of His past deliverances from the Egyptians, Amorites, Ammonites, and Philistines. {10:12} He pointed out that the Sidonians, Amalekites, and Maonites also oppressed them, and each time they cried out, He delivered them. {10:13} Yet, they continued to forsake Him and serve other gods, so He declared He would not deliver them anymore. {10:14} He instructed them to cry out to the gods they had chosen for deliverance in their time of trouble. {10:15} The children of Israel acknowledged their sin and submitted to whatever God deemed fit, asking only for deliverance that day. {10:16} They removed the foreign gods from among them and served the LORD, which moved Him to compassion for their misery. {10:17} The children of Ammon gathered in Gilead, while the children of Israel assembled in Mizpeh. {10:18} The people and leaders of Gilead discussed who would lead the fight against the children of Ammon, promising leadership over all Gilead to the one who would begin the battle.

{11:1} Jephthah the Gileadite was a mighty man of valor, but he was the son of a prostitute. Gilead fathered Jephthah. {11:2} Gilead's wife bore him sons, and when they grew up, they drove Jephthah away, saying he couldn't inherit because he was the son of a foreign woman. {11:3} So Jephthah fled from his brothers and settled in the land of Tob. There, worthless men gathered around him, and they went out with him. {11:4} Later, the Ammonites waged war against Israel. {11:5} The elders of Gilead went to bring Jephthah back from Tob. {11:6} They asked him to be their leader in fighting against the Ammonites. {11:7} Jephthah questioned why they sought him out after they had expelled him from his father's house. {11:8} The elders of Gilead assured him that they wanted him to lead them and promised to make him their leader. {11:9} Jephthah asked if they would truly make him their leader if he defeated the Ammonites with God's help. {11:10} The elders of Gilead swore to follow his words. {11:11} So Jephthah agreed and became the head and captain over them. He made his vow to the LORD in Mizpeh. {11:12} He sent messengers to the king of the Ammonites, questioning their reason for fighting in Israel's land. {11:13} The king of the Ammonites claimed Israel took his land from Arnon to Jabbok and Jordan when they came out of Egypt, demanding its return. {11:14} Jephthah responded, explaining that Israel hadn't taken land from Moab or Ammon. {11:15} He recounted Israel's journey from Egypt and their respectful requests to pass through Edom and Moab, which were denied. {11:16} Israel then went around Edom and Moab, defeating Sihon, the king of the Amorites, who refused passage. {11:17} Israel possessed the land of the Amorites, including Arnon to Jabbok and from the wilderness to the Jordan. {11:18} Jephthah argued that since the LORD dispossessed the Amorites, the Ammonites had no right to claim the land. {11:19} He questioned why the Ammonites didn't reclaim the land for the past 300 years. {11:20} Jephthah declared the LORD, not Chemosh, would determine possession. {11:21} The Ammonites didn't heed his words. {11:22} The Spirit of the LORD came upon Jephthah, and he passed through Gilead, Manasseh, and Mizpeh of Gilead to the Ammonites. {11:23} Jephthah vowed to offer as a burnt offering whatever came out of his house to meet him if he returned in peace from defeating the Ammonites. {11:24} He fought against the Ammonites and the LORD delivered them into his hands. {11:25} Jephthah defeated the Ammonites from Aroer to Minnith, capturing twenty cities and the surrounding territory. {11:26} When Jephthah returned to Mizpeh, his only daughter came out to meet him with joyous celebration. {11:27} He realized the consequence of his vow and lamented, but his daughter accepted her fate, acknowledging the vow he made to the LORD. {11:28} She requested time to mourn her virginity with her companions. {11:29} After two months, she returned, and Jephthah fulfilled his vow. This became a custom in Israel, with the daughters lamenting Jephthah's daughter yearly. {11:30} **Jephthah made a vow to the LORD, saying, "If you deliver the Ammonites into my hands, whatever comes out of the doors of my house to meet me when I return in peace from battling the Ammonites shall belong to the LORD, and I will offer it as a burnt offering."** {11:31} So Jephthah fought against the Ammonites, and the LORD delivered them into his hands. {11:32} **He defeated them from Aroer to Minnith, capturing twenty cities and the surrounding area, causing a great slaughter. Thus, the Ammonites were subdued before the Israelites.** {11:33} When Jephthah returned home to Mizpeh, his daughter came out to meet him with tambourines and dancing. She was his only child; he had no other sons or daughters. {11:34} When he saw her, he tore his clothes and lamented, saying, "Oh, my daughter! You have brought me great sorrow. You are among those who trouble me because I made a vow to the LORD, and I cannot go back on it." {11:35} His daughter reassured him, saying, "Father, if you made a vow to the LORD, then do to me as you promised. The LORD has granted you victory over your enemies, the Ammonites." {11:36} She asked for two months to mourn her virginity with her friends in the mountains, and Jephthah granted her request. {11:37} After two months, she returned to her father, and he fulfilled his vow to the LORD. She remained a virgin, and this became a custom in Israel. {11:38} Every year, the daughters of Israel would lament the daughter of Jephthah the Gileadite for four days. {11:39} After two months, she returned to her father, and he fulfilled the vow he had made to the LORD. She remained a virgin and never knew a man. This custom became practiced in Israel. {11:40} Each year, the daughters of Israel would gather to mourn the daughter of Jephthah the Gileadite for four days.

{12:1} The men of Ephraim gathered themselves together and went northward to Jephthah. They said, "Why did you fight against the children of Ammon without calling us to join you? We will burn your house down with fire." {12:2} Jephthah replied, "When I called for your help, you did not come to my aid while we were in great strife with the children of Ammon. So, I took matters into my own hands, and the LORD delivered our enemies into our hands. Why then do you come to fight against me today?" {12:3} Jephthah gathered all the men of Gilead and fought against Ephraim. The men of Gilead defeated Ephraim because they accused them of being fugitives. {12:4} The Gileadites took control of the passages of the Jordan before the Ephraimites. When an Ephraimite tried to cross, the Gileadites asked him if he was from Ephraim. If he said no, they asked him to say "Shibboleth." If he couldn't pronounce it correctly, they knew he was an Ephraimite and killed him. Forty-two thousand Ephraimites fell at that time. {12:5} Jephthah judged Israel for six years. After his death, he was buried in one of the cities of Gilead. {12:6} Ibzan of Bethlehem judged Israel after Jephthah. He had thirty sons and thirty daughters whom he married off to people from other places. He judged Israel for seven years and was buried in Bethlehem upon his death. {12:7} After Ibzan, Elon from Zebulun judged Israel for ten years. He died and was buried in Aijalon in the country of Zebulun. {12:8} Abdon, the son of Hillel, a Pirathonite, judged Israel after Elon. He had forty sons and thirty grandsons who rode on seventy ass colts. Abdon judged Israel for eight years before he died and was buried in Pirathon in the land of Ephraim, in the mount of the Amalekites. {12:9} He had thirty sons and thirty daughters whom he sent away to marry, and he brought in thirty daughters from other places for his sons. He judged Israel for seven years. {12:10} Ibzan passed away and was buried in Bethlehem. {12:11} After Ibzan, Elon, a Zebulunite, led Israel for ten years. {12:12} Elon, the Zebulunite, died and was buried in Aijalon in the territory of Zebulun. {12:13} Abdon, the son of Hillel, a Pirathonite, followed Elon in judging Israel. {12:14} Abdon had forty sons and thirty grandsons who rode on seventy donkeys. He judged Israel for eight years. {12:15} Abdon, the son of Hillel, the Pirathonite, died and was buried in Pirathon in the land of Ephraim, in the hill country of the Amalekites.

{13:1} The children of Israel did evil again in the sight of the LORD, so He delivered them into the hand of the Philistines for forty years. {13:2} There was a man from Zorah, belonging to the tribe of Dan, named Manoah. His wife was barren and had not borne any children. {13:3} The angel of the LORD appeared to the woman and told her, "You are barren and have not conceived, but you will conceive and bear a son." {13:4} The angel instructed her not to drink wine or strong drink, nor eat any unclean food, for the child would be a Nazarite to God from birth, and he would begin to deliver Israel from the Philistines. {13:5} The woman told her husband about the encounter with the angel. {13:6} Manoah prayed to the LORD, asking for the man of God to come again and instruct them about the child. {13:7} God listened to Manoah's prayer, and the angel of God appeared again to the woman while she was in the field. {13:8} The woman hurried to tell her husband, who went to meet the angel. {13:9} Manoah asked the angel if he was the one who spoke to his wife. The angel confirmed that he was. {13:10} Manoah asked the angel about how they should raise the child. {13:11} The angel reiterated the instructions given to the woman. {13:12} Manoah requested the angel to stay while they prepared a meal for him. {13:13} The angel declined the offer but instructed them to offer a burnt offering to the LORD. {13:14} Manoah asked the angel his name, but the angel replied that it was secret. {13:15} Manoah offered a kid with a meat offering upon a rock to the LORD, and the angel performed a wonder. {13:16} As the flame rose from the altar, the angel ascended in the flame, and Manoah and his wife fell on their faces. {13:17} After this, the angel did not appear again to Manoah and his wife, and they realized he was an angel of the LORD. {13:18} Manoah feared they would die for having seen God, but his wife reassured him. {13:19} The woman gave birth to a son and named him Samson. The child grew, and the LORD blessed him. {13:20} The Spirit of the LORD began to move Samson in the camp of Dan, between Zorah and Eshtaol. {13:21} The angel of the LORD did not appear again to Manoah and his wife. Manoah realized that the visitor was indeed an angel of the LORD. {13:22} Manoah told his wife, "We will surely die because we have seen God." {13:23} His wife reassured him, saying, "If the LORD intended to kill us, He wouldn't have accepted our offerings, shown us these things, or told us about them." {13:24} The woman gave birth to a son and named him Samson. The child grew, and the LORD blessed him. {13:25} The Spirit of the LORD began to move Samson at times in the camp of Dan between Zorah and Eshtaol.

{14:1} Samson went down to Timnath and saw a woman from the daughters of the Philistines. {14:2} He told his father and mother, "I have seen a woman in Timnath from the daughters of the Philistines. Get her for me as a wife." {14:3} His parents questioned him, "Isn't there a woman among the daughters of your brethren or among all our people? Why take a wife from the uncircumcised Philistines?" But Samson insisted, "Get her for me, for she pleases me well." {14:4} His parents didn't realize it was the LORD's doing, seeking an occasion against the Philistines who ruled over Israel at that time. {14:5} Samson, along with his father and mother, went down to Timnath. On their way, a young lion roared at Samson. {14:6} The Spirit of the LORD came upon him, and he tore the lion apart as one would a young goat, but he didn't tell his parents about it. {14:7} He went down and talked with the woman, finding her pleasing. {14:8} After some time, Samson returned to take her as his wife. Along the way, he turned aside to see the carcass of the lion and found a swarm of bees and honey within it. {14:9} He took some honey in his hands and ate it on the way. When he reached his parents, he also gave them some, but he didn't tell them where he got it. {14:10} Samson's father went to the woman's house, and Samson held a feast, as young men often did. {14:11} When the people saw him, they brought thirty companions to be with him. {14:12} Samson proposed a riddle to them, promising thirty linen garments and thirty changes of clothing if they could solve it within seven days. {14:13} They accepted the challenge, so Samson presented his riddle: "Out of the eater came forth meat, and out of the strong came forth sweetness." But they couldn't explain the riddle in three days. {14:14} On the seventh day, they pressured Samson's wife to get the answer from him, threatening to burn her and her father's house if she didn't. She wept before Samson, accusing him of not loving her enough to share the riddle. {14:15} Samson's wife persisted in asking him for the answer, so he eventually told her. {14:16} She revealed the riddle to her people, and they confronted Samson on the seventh day with the answer. {14:17} Samson realized she had pressured him, so he responded with a remark about her loyalty. {14:18} He was angry and went to Ashkelon, killed thirty men, took their garments, and gave them to the companions who had solved the riddle. Then he returned to his father's house. {14:19} However, his wife was given to his companion, {14:20} whom he had used as a friend.

{15:1} After some time, during the wheat harvest, Samson went to visit his wife with a young goat. He wanted to go to her chamber, but her father wouldn't allow it. {15:2} Her father assumed Samson hated her, so he gave her to Samson's companion instead. He suggested Samson take her younger sister instead, who he thought was more beautiful. {15:3} Samson saw this as an opportunity to cause trouble for the Philistines. {15:4} He caught three hundred foxes, tied them tail to tail with firebrands in between, and set them loose in the Philistine's fields, burning their crops. {15:5} The Philistines found out it was Samson's doing because he had taken his wife and given her to another man. They burned her and her father alive in retaliation. {15:6} Samson vowed revenge and struck the Philistines with a great slaughter. Then he went to live in the rock of Etam. {15:7} The Philistines retaliated by attacking Judah and camping in Lehi. {15:8} The men of Judah questioned Samson's actions, as they feared Philistine retaliation. {15:9} They went to Samson to bind him and hand him over to the Philistines. {15:10} Samson agreed, but only if they promised not to kill him themselves. {15:11} They agreed and bound him with new cords to deliver him to the Philistines. {15:12} When they reached Lehi, the Philistines shouted against him. The Spirit of the LORD empowered Samson, and he broke free from his bonds. {15:13} He found the jawbone of a donkey and used it to kill a thousand Philistines. {15:14} After the battle, he named the place Ramath-lehi. {15:15} He grew thirsty and prayed to the LORD, who provided water from the jawbone. He drank and revived. {15:16} Samson judged Israel for twenty years during the time of the Philistines. {15:17} After speaking, Samson threw away the jawbone and named the place Ramath-lehi. {15:18} He became very thirsty and prayed to the LORD, saying, "You have given me this great victory, but now I may die of thirst and fall into the hands of the uncircumcised." {15:19} God caused water to flow from the jawbone, and Samson drank from it, reviving his spirit. He named the place Enhakkore, which is in Lehi to this day. {15:20} Samson judged Israel during the time of the Philistines for twenty years.

{16:1} Samson went to Gaza and saw a prostitute there. He went to her. {16:2} The people of Gaza heard Samson was there. They surrounded him at the city gate all night, planning to kill him in the morning. {16:3} Samson stayed in the city until midnight. Then he got up, took the city gate doors, posts, and bar, and carried them to the top of a hill near Hebron. {16:4} Afterward, he fell in love with a woman named Delilah in the valley of Sorek. {16:5} The Philistine rulers went to Delilah and offered her money to find out the secret of Samson's strength so they could capture him. {16:6} Delilah asked Samson about his strength. He told her that if he were tied with seven fresh bowstrings, he would become weak. {16:7} The Philistine rulers brought seven fresh bowstrings, and Delilah tied Samson with them while men waited to ambush him. {16:8} Samson easily broke the bowstrings. {16:9} Delilah accused Samson of deceiving her, but he broke free again. {16:10} Delilah persisted, asking how Samson could be bound. He said if he were tied securely with new ropes, he would lose his strength. {16:11} Delilah tied him with new ropes, but Samson broke free again. {16:12} Again, Delilah accused him of lying. {16:13} Samson told her if his hair were woven into a loom, he would lose his strength. {16:14} Delilah wove his hair into the loom and called for the Philistines, but Samson escaped again. {16:15} Delilah complained that Samson didn't really love her since he hadn't revealed his secret. {16:16} She nagged him day after day until he was sick to death of it. {16:17} Finally, Samson told her the truth: his strength came from his uncut hair because he was dedicated to God as a Nazarite from birth. If his hair were cut, he would lose his strength. {16:18} Delilah, realizing she had the secret, told the Philistine rulers. {16:19} They paid her, and while Samson slept on her lap, she had his hair cut, and his strength left him. {16:20} When Samson woke up, he didn't realize his strength was gone until it was too late. {16:21} The Philistines captured him, gouged out his eyes, and imprisoned him in Gaza, forcing him to grind grain. {16:22} Over time, his hair began to grow back. {16:23} The Philistine rulers gathered to celebrate and offer sacrifices to their god, Dagon, for delivering Samson into their hands. {16:24} They praised their god for defeating Samson, whom they considered their enemy and the one who had caused them much harm. {16:25} During the celebration, they called for Samson to entertain them. {16:26} Samson, held by a boy, asked to lean against the pillars supporting the building. {16:27} The building was filled with people, and Samson prayed to God for strength. {16:28} **He pushed against the pillars, causing the entire structure to collapse, killing himself and many Philistines.** {16:29} His relatives retrieved his body and buried him. {16:30} Samson's death killed more Philistines than he had killed during his lifetime. {16:31} He had judged Israel for twenty years.

{17:1} There was a man from Mount Ephraim named Micah. {17:2} He confessed to his mother that he had taken the eleven hundred shekels of silver that she had lost, and she had cursed about. His mother blessed him for returning the silver. {17:3} She had dedicated the silver to the Lord to make idols. So, she returned it to Micah. {17:4} Micah indeed returned the silver to his mother. But she took two hundred shekels and used them to make idols, which were placed in Micah's house. {17:5} Micah had his own shrine, including an ephod, household gods, and he even consecrated one of his sons to be his priest. {17:6} During these times, there was no king in Israel, and everyone did as they pleased. {17:7} A young Levite from Bethlehem in Judah, from the family of Judah, was traveling and ended up staying in Micah's house. {17:8} He had left Bethlehem to find a place to stay and ended up at Micah's house in Mount Ephraim. {17:9} Micah asked him where he came from, and he explained he was a Levite from Bethlehem, seeking a place to stay. {17:10} Micah offered him a position as a father and priest, promising him ten shekels of silver per year, clothes, and food. The Levite agreed. {17:11} The Levite lived with Micah and was treated like one of his sons. {17:12} Micah consecrated the Levite as his priest, and he served in Micah's house. {17:13} Micah believed having a Levite as his priest would bring him good fortune from the Lord.

{18:1} During the time when there was no king in Israel, the tribe of Dan sought territory to settle in because they hadn't received their inheritance among the other tribes of Israel. {18:2} So, the Danites sent five brave men from Zorah and Eshtaol to spy out the land and find a place to settle. They ended up at the house of Micah in Mount Ephraim. {18:3} When they arrived at Micah's house, they recognized the voice of the young Levite priest. They asked him how he ended up there and what he was doing. {18:4} The Levite explained that Micah had hired him to be his priest. {18:5} The Danites asked the priest to seek guidance from God to know if their journey would be successful. {18:6} The priest assured them that God would favor their journey. {18:7} The Danites reached Laish and found its people living securely, without any rulers, far from Sidon, and having no dealings with anyone. {18:8} They returned to their fellow Danites in Zorah and Eshtaol and reported what they found. {18:9} Encouraged by the favorable report, six hundred armed Danites prepared to attack Laish and take its land, which they found to be good and spacious, a place of abundance. {18:10} Setting out from Zorah and Eshtaol, they camped near Kirjath-jearim in Judah, hence naming the place Mahaneh-dan. {18:11} From there, they moved to Mount Ephraim and arrived at Micah's house. {18:12} The five spies informed their fellow Danites about the idols in Micah's house, urging them to consider their course of action. {18:13} They then went to Micah's house and greeted the Levite. {18:14} The six hundred armed Danites stationed themselves at the entrance while the five spies went in and took the idols and the priest. {18:15} They invited the Levite priest to join them and be their priest instead. {18:16} Delighted, the priest went with them, taking the idols. {18:17} As they departed, Micah's neighbors gathered and pursued them. {18:18} Catching up with the Danites, they asked Micah why he had gathered such a large group. {18:19} Micah realized they had taken his idols and priest and warned them not to provoke a conflict. {18:20} The Danites ignored him, and he returned home defeated. {18:21} The Danites attacked Laish, killing its people and burning the city. {18:22} Since Laish was far from Sidon and had no allies, there was no one to save them. {18:23} After capturing Laish, the Danites settled there and renamed it Dan after their ancestor. {18:24} They set up the idols they had taken from Micah's house and appointed Jonathan, the son of Gershom, as their priest. {18:25} These idols remained in Dan as long as the Tabernacle was in Shiloh. {18:26} This practice continued until the land was captured and its people exiled. {18:27} The Danites took Micah's idols and priest and went to Laish, where the people lived peacefully and securely. They attacked and destroyed the city, killing its inhabitants and setting it on fire. {18:28} Since Laish was far from Sidon and had no allies, there was no one to rescue them. The city was located in a valley near Beth-rehob. {18:29} After conquering Laish, the Danites rebuilt the city and settled there. They named it Dan, after their ancestor Dan, although its original name was Laish. {18:30} The Danites installed the idols they had taken from Micah's house. Jonathan, the son of Gershom and grandson of Manasseh, served as priest for the tribe of Dan and his descendants until the land was captured and its people exiled. {18:31} They continued to worship Micah's idols as long as the Tabernacle of God was in Shiloh.

{19:1} In those days when there was no king in Israel, a Levite from the side of Mount Ephraim took a concubine from Bethlehem in Judah. {19:2} But his concubine betrayed him and went back to her father's house in Bethlehem. She stayed there for four months. {19:3} Her husband decided to go after her, hoping to reconcile. He took his servant and two donkeys with him. When they arrived, the concubine's father welcomed him warmly. {19:4} The father-in-law persuaded him to stay for three days. They ate, drank, and lodged together. {19:5} On the fourth day, the Levite prepared to leave, but the father-in-law urged him to stay longer. {19:6} They ate and drank together again, and the father-in-law suggested they stay the night. {19:7} When the Levite rose to leave the next morning, the father-in-law convinced him to stay another day. {19:8} On the fifth day, the Levite tried to leave again, but the father-in-law persuaded him to stay until afternoon. {19:9} As they prepared to depart, the father-in-law suggested they stay one more night since it was getting late. {19:10} But the Levite insisted on leaving and traveled towards Jebus, which is Jerusalem. They arrived at Jebus as evening approached, with the concubine and two saddled donkeys. {19:11} When they reached Jebus, the servant suggested they stay in the city of the Jebusites for the night. {19:12} However, the Levite refused, wanting to stay among fellow Israelites. So, they continued on to Gibeah. {19:13} They decided to stay in Gibeah or Ramah for the night. As they approached Gibeah, the sun was setting. {19:14} When they arrived at Gibeah in Benjamin, they looked for a place to lodge, but no one offered them hospitality. {19:15} Eventually, an old man from Mount Ephraim, who was living in Gibeah, invited them to stay at his house. The old man was a Benjamite. {19:16} As evening came, the old man saw them in the street and asked where they were going. {19:17} They explained they were from Bethlehem in Judah, on their way to Mount Ephraim, but no one had offered them a place to stay. {19:18} The old man welcomed them, offering food and lodging for their donkeys as well. {19:19} After providing for their needs, they ate, drank, and made merry. {19:20} Later that night, certain wicked men of the city surrounded the house, demanding the Levite be brought out so they could have sex with him. {19:21} The old man tried to reason with them, offering his virgin daughter and the Levite's concubine instead. {19:22} But the men refused and insisted on having the Levite. {19:23} Reluctantly, the old man brought out the concubine, and they abused her all night. {19:24} In the morning, the Levite found her lying at the door. He told her to get up, but she didn't respond. {19:25} Realizing she was dead, the Levite took her body home, cut it into twelve pieces, and sent one piece to each tribe of Israel. {19:26} This gruesome act shocked all who saw it, and they lamented the atrocity. {19:27} They saw it as an unprecedented evil in Israel's history and urged each other to take action and speak out against it. {19:28} He said to her, "Get up, let's go." But she didn't respond. So the man lifted her onto his donkey and went back home. {19:29} When he arrived home, he took a knife, grabbed hold of his concubine, and cut her body into twelve pieces, including her bones. Then he sent her remains throughout all the territory of Israel. {19:30} Everyone who saw this gruesome sight exclaimed that such a thing had never been seen or done since the Israelites came out of Egypt. They were shocked and urged each other to consider the matter carefully and express their thoughts.

{20:1} Then all the children of Israel gathered together from Dan to Beer-sheba, including the land of Gilead, before the LORD at Mizpeh. {20:2} The leaders of all the people, representing all the tribes of Israel, presented themselves in the assembly of the people of God. There were four hundred thousand men armed with swords. {20:3} (The people of Benjamin heard that the Israelites had gone up to Mizpeh.) The Israelites asked, "Tell us, how did this wickedness happen?" {20:4} The Levite, the husband of the murdered woman, answered, "My concubine and I came to Gibeah, which belongs to Benjamin, to spend the night." {20:5} "But the men of Gibeah attacked me at night, surrounding the house with the intention of killing me. They raped my concubine, and she died." {20:6} "So I took her body, cut it into pieces, and sent them throughout the territory of Israel, because of the shameful and wicked act they had committed in Israel." {20:7} "Now, all of you, Israelites, give your advice and counsel." {20:8} All the people stood as one and declared, "None of us will return to his tent, and none of us will go home." {20:9} "But here is what we will do to Gibeah: We will cast lots and send men against it." {20:10} "From every tribe, we will take ten men out of every hundred, a hundred out of every thousand, and a thousand out of every ten thousand, to get provisions for the army when they go to Gibeah of Benjamin, to repay them for the disgraceful act they committed in Israel." {20:11} So all the men of Israel gathered against the city, united as one. {20:12} The tribes of Israel sent messengers throughout the tribe of Benjamin, asking, "What wickedness is this that has occurred among you?" {20:13} "Now, hand over those wicked men, the troublemakers in Gibeah, so that we may put them to death and purge evil from Israel." But the Benjamites refused to listen to their fellow Israelites. {20:14} Instead, the Benjamites gathered from their cities to Gibeah to fight the Israelites. {20:15} From the cities, the Benjamites mustered twenty-six thousand swordsmen, in addition to the seven hundred chosen men of Gibeah. {20:16} Among these soldiers, there were seven hundred chosen left-handed warriors, each skilled in slinging stones at a hair's breadth without missing. {20:17} The men of Israel, apart from Benjamin, numbered four hundred thousand swordsmen; all were experienced in battle. {20:18} The Israelites went up to the house of God and asked counsel from God, saying, "Which of us should go first to fight against the Benjamites?" The LORD replied, "Judah shall go first." {20:19} So the Israelites rose early and encamped against Gibeah. {20:20} The men of Israel went out to engage Benjamin in battle and arrayed themselves against them at Gibeah. {20:21} The Benjamites came out of Gibeah and struck down twenty-two thousand Israelites on the battlefield that day. {20:22} But the Israelites rallied and set their battle lines again in the same place where they had positioned themselves on the first day. {20:23} The Israelites went up and wept before the LORD until evening, inquiring of the LORD, "Should we go up again to fight against our brothers, the Benjamites?" And the LORD replied, "Go up against them." {20:24} The Israelites approached the Benjamites again the next day. {20:25} And the Benjamites came out of Gibeah to engage them again, striking down eighteen thousand more Israelites, all of them armed with swords. {20:26} Then all the Israelites, all the people, went up and came to the house of God and wept. They sat there before the LORD, fasting that day until evening and offering burnt offerings and peace offerings before the LORD. {20:27} The Israelites inquired of the LORD (for the ark of the covenant of God was there in those days, {20:28} and Phinehas, the son of Eleazar, the son of Aaron, served before it in those days), asking, "Should we go out to battle against our brothers, the Benjamites, again, or should we cease?" And the LORD replied, "Go up, for tomorrow I will deliver them into your hand." {20:29} So Israel set men in ambush around Gibeah. { {20:30} The Israelites went up against the Benjamites on the third day, positioning themselves against Gibeah just like before. {20:31} The Benjamites came out and lured the Israelites away from the city. They attacked and killed about thirty Israelites on the roads leading to the house of God and to Gibeah in the fields. {20:32} The Benjamites thought they were winning, just as they had before. But the Israelites pretended to retreat, drawing the Benjamites away from the city and onto the roads. {20:33} Then all the Israelite soldiers took up positions at Baal-tamar, while the ambushers from Israel emerged from their hiding places near Gibeah. {20:34} Ten thousand chosen men from Israel attacked Gibeah, and the battle raged fiercely. But the Benjamites didn't realize that disaster was about to strike them. {20:35} The LORD struck down the Benjamites before the Israelites, and they slaughtered twenty-five thousand one hundred Benjamite soldiers that day, all of them skilled warriors. {20:36} The Benjamites saw they were being defeated because the Israelites gave ground to them, relying on their ambushers near Gibeah. {20:37} The ambushers rushed Gibeah, attacking the city and slaughtering its inhabitants with their swords. {20:38} The Israelites and the ambushers had agreed on a signal: when they saw a great flame and smoke rise from the city, they would attack. {20:39} As the Israelites pretended to retreat, the Benjamites pursued and killed about thirty Israelites, thinking they had the upper hand as in the previous battle. {20:40} But when the smoke and flame rose from the city like a pillar to the sky, the Benjamites realized they were in trouble. {20:41} As the Israelites turned back, the Benjamites were shocked to see the disaster that had befallen them. {20:42} They tried to flee toward the wilderness, but the Israelites pursued and defeated them, destroying those who came out of the cities. {20:43} Thus, they surrounded the Benjamites, chasing and trampling them down near Gibeah, towards the east. {20:44} Eighteen thousand valiant Benjamite soldiers fell that day. {20:45} The survivors fled to the wilderness, to the rock of Rimmon. But the Israelites killed five thousand of them on the roads and pursued them to Gidom, killing two thousand more. {20:46} So, a total of twenty-five thousand Benjamite soldiers, all brave warriors, fell that day. {20:47} Only six hundred Benjamites escaped to the wilderness and stayed at the rock of Rimmon for four months. {20:48} The Israelites turned back and struck down the Benjamites, including men from every city, animals, and anything else they found. They also set fire to all the cities they came across.

{21:1} The men of Israel had sworn in Mizpeh, saying they wouldn't give their daughters to Benjamin as wives. {21:2} So, they gathered at the house of God and stayed there until evening, weeping bitterly before the LORD. {21:3} They asked, "O LORD God of Israel, why has this happened, leaving one tribe of Israel without descendants?" {21:4} The next day, they built an altar and offered burnt offerings and peace offerings. {21:5} The Israelites wondered which tribe hadn't joined them in the assembly at Mizpeh. They had sworn that anyone absent would be put to death. {21:6} They felt sorry for Benjamin, their brothers, realizing one tribe would be lost from Israel. {21:7} They pondered how to find wives for the remaining Benjamites since they had sworn not to give them their daughters. {21:8} They discovered that no one from Jabesh-gilead had come to the assembly at Mizpeh. {21:9} They sent twelve thousand of their bravest men to Jabesh-gilead with orders to kill everyone, including women and children. {21:10} They were told to spare only the virgins. {21:11} So they found four hundred young virgins and brought them to Shiloh. {21:12} They sent messengers to the Benjamites at the rock Rimmon, offering peace and giving them wives from the virgins of Jabesh-gilead. {21:13} However, there weren't enough women for all the Benjamites. {21:14} The Israelites felt sorry for Benjamin again, realizing the LORD had caused a division among the tribes of Israel. {21:15} The elders discussed finding wives for the remaining Benjamites, considering that they couldn't give them their own daughters due to their oath. {21:16} They decided there must be an inheritance for the survivors of Benjamin to prevent the tribe from being wiped out. {21:17} But they couldn't give them their daughters because of the curse they had sworn. {21:18} So they devised a plan involving a yearly feast in Shiloh, where the daughters of Shiloh danced. {21:19} They instructed the Benjamites to hide in the vineyards and snatch wives for themselves when the girls came out to dance. {21:20} They promised to intervene if anyone complained, saying they hadn't provided wives for Benjamin during the war. {21:21} The Benjamites followed the plan, taking wives from the daughters of Shiloh. {21:22} Then they returned to their land, rebuilt their cities, and settled in them. {21:23} The Israelites dispersed to their tribes and families, returning to their inheritances. {21:24} In those days, there was no king in Israel, {21:25} and everyone did as they saw fit.

Ruth

{1:1} In the time when judges ruled, there was a famine in Bethlehemjudah. A man named Elimelech, his wife Naomi, and their two sons went to live in Moab. {1:2} Elimelech, Naomi, and their sons, Mahlon and Chilion, were Ephrathites from Bethlehemjudah. They settled in Moab. {1:3} Elimelech died, leaving Naomi and her two sons. {1:4} Mahlon and Chilion married Moabite women named Orpah and Ruth. They lived in Moab for about ten years. {1:5} Sadly, both Mahlon and Chilion died, leaving Naomi without her husband and sons. {1:6} Naomi decided to return to Judah upon hearing that the LORD had provided food for his people there. {1:7} She set out with her daughters-in-law to return to Judah. {1:8} Along the way, Naomi urged Orpah and Ruth to return to their mothers' homes, wishing them well. {1:9} She prayed for them to find new husbands and kissed them goodbye as they wept. {1:10} Orpah and Ruth insisted on going with Naomi. {1:11} Naomi encouraged them to stay in Moab, as she had no more sons to offer them. {1:12} She reminded them that even if she were to remarry and have more sons, they would have to wait a long time to marry them. {1:13} Overcome with sorrow, Naomi felt the LORD had turned against her. {1:14} They wept again, and Orpah decided to return to her people and gods, but Ruth stayed with Naomi. {1:15} Naomi urged Ruth to follow Orpah's example and return to her own people. {1:16} **Instead, Ruth vowed to stay with Naomi, wherever she went, and to adopt Naomi's people and God as her own.** {1:17} Ruth pledged to stay with Naomi until death separated them. {1:18} Seeing Ruth's determination, Naomi stopped trying to persuade her. {1:19} So Naomi and Ruth journeyed to Bethlehem. When they arrived, the whole city was stirred, asking if Naomi had returned. {1:20} Naomi asked to be called Mara, meaning bitter, as she felt God had treated her harshly. {1:21} She lamented how she left full but returned empty, feeling afflicted by the Almighty. {1:22} Thus, Naomi and Ruth, her Moabite daughter-in-law, arrived in Bethlehem at the beginning of the barley harvest.

{2:1} Naomi had a relative of her late husband named Boaz, a wealthy man from Elimelech's family. {2:2} Ruth, the Moabite woman, asked Naomi for permission to glean in the fields for leftover grain. Naomi agreed. {2:3} Ruth went to glean in a field, which happened to belong to Boaz, a relative of Naomi's. {2:4} Boaz greeted his reapers, and they blessed him. Boaz noticed Ruth and asked about her. {2:5} The servant overseeing the reapers told Boaz about Ruth and her loyalty to Naomi. {2:6} Ruth asked permission to glean among the sheaves, and she had been working hard since morning. {2:7} Boaz allowed Ruth to glean in his field and instructed his young men not to bother her. {2:8} He advised Ruth to stay close to his female servants and assured her safety and access to water. {2:9} Ruth thanked Boaz for his kindness, considering herself a stranger in his land. {2:10} Boaz admired Ruth's devotion to Naomi and blessed her, acknowledging her sacrifices. {2:11} He praised Ruth for leaving her homeland to care for Naomi and prayed for God's blessings upon her. {2:12} **Ruth expressed gratitude for Boaz's encouragement and kindness, feeling unworthy.** {2:13} Boaz invited Ruth to join his reapers for a meal, offering her bread and vinegar. {2:14} Ruth ate with the reapers, and Boaz served her roasted grain, and she was satisfied. {2:15} Boaz instructed his young men to let Ruth glean among the sheaves without reproach. {2:16} He even ordered them to intentionally drop extra grain for her to gather without criticism. {2:17} Ruth gleaned in Boaz's field until evening and collected about an ephah of barley. {2:18} She took her gleanings to Naomi, who was impressed and blessed the man who had shown kindness to Ruth. {2:19} Naomi asked where Ruth had gleaned, and she told her about Boaz. {2:20} Naomi praised Boaz for his continued kindness and realized that he was a close relative. {2:21} Ruth recounted Boaz's instructions to stay close to his young men until the end of the harvest. {2:22} Naomi advised Ruth to continue working in Boaz's fields to avoid meeting anyone elsewhere. {2:23} So Ruth remained with Boaz's female servants until the end of both the barley and wheat harvests and lived with Naomi.

{3:1} Naomi said to Ruth, "My daughter, should I not seek rest for you, that it may be well with you? {3:2} Now Boaz, our relative, with whose maids you have been, will be winnowing barley tonight at the threshing floor. {3:3} Wash yourself, anoint yourself, and put on your best clothes. Then go down to the threshing floor, but do not make yourself known to the man until he has finished eating and drinking. {3:4} When he lies down, take note of where he is lying. Then go, uncover his feet, and lie down. He will tell you what to do." {3:5} Ruth agreed, saying, "All that you say to me I will do." {3:6} So Ruth went to the threshing floor and did as her mother-in-law instructed. {3:7} After Boaz had eaten and drunk and his heart was merry, he went to lie down at the end of the heap of grain. Ruth came quietly, uncovered his feet, and lay down. {3:8} At midnight, Boaz woke up suddenly and was startled to find a woman lying at his feet. {3:9} **He asked, "Who are you?" Ruth replied, "I am Ruth, your maidservant. Spread your garment over your maidservant, for you are a close relative."** {3:10} Boaz blessed Ruth, acknowledging her kindness and loyalty, greater now than at the beginning. {3:11} He assured her not to fear, promising to fulfill her requests because the whole city knew she was a virtuous woman. {3:12} Boaz acknowledged that he was a close relative but mentioned another kinsman closer than himself. {3:13} He advised Ruth to stay the night and see if the closer kinsman would fulfill his duty. If not, Boaz pledged to do so himself, as the LORD lives. He instructed her to lie down until morning. {3:14} Ruth lay at his feet until morning, then rose before anyone could recognize her. Boaz cautioned her to keep their encounter private. {3:15} He gave her six measures of barley, instructing her to hold out her veil. Boaz then measured the barley into it, and Ruth went back to the city. {3:16} When Ruth returned to her mother-in-law, Naomi asked what happened. Ruth recounted everything Boaz had done for her. {3:17} Ruth showed Naomi the barley Boaz had given her, explaining that he told her not to go empty-handed to her mother-in-law. {3:18} Naomi advised Ruth to wait and see how the matter would unfold, as Boaz would not rest until he had resolved it that day.

{4:1} **Boaz went up to the gate and sat down there. Soon, the kinsman of whom Boaz had spoken passed by. Boaz called out to him, "Hey, come over here and sit down." So he turned aside and sat down.** {4:2} Boaz then gathered ten elders of the city and asked them to sit down as well. {4:3} Addressing the kinsman, Boaz said, "Naomi, who has returned from Moab, is selling a piece of land that belonged to our relative Elimelech." {4:4} Boaz explained his intention to inform the kinsman first. If he chose to redeem the land, he should do so, but if not, Boaz would step in as the next in line. The kinsman agreed to redeem it. {4:5} **Boaz added a condition: whoever bought the land from Naomi must also marry Ruth the Moabitess, the widow of Mahlon, to carry on the name of the deceased on his inheritance.** {4:6} The kinsman declined, fearing it might jeopardize his own inheritance. So he relinquished his right to Boaz, saying, "You redeem it for yourself, for I cannot." {4:7} In Israel, the custom of redemption was confirmed by a man taking off his shoe and giving it to his neighbor. This served as a testimony. {4:8} The kinsman then told Boaz to buy the land, and Boaz removed his shoe, signifying his acquisition. {4:9} Boaz declared to the elders and all the people present that he had bought all that belonged to Elimelech, Chilion, and Mahlon from Naomi. {4:10} Additionally, he had taken Ruth as his wife to preserve the name of the deceased in his inheritance. The people bore witness to this transaction. {4:11} The people blessed Boaz, likening Ruth to Rachel and Leah and wishing him prosperity in Ephrathah and Bethlehem. {4:12} They prayed for Boaz's house to be as prosperous as Pharez's, from whom Jesse and eventually David came. {4:13} Boaz married Ruth, and she conceived and bore a son. {4:14} The women praised Naomi, saying, "Blessed be the LORD, who has not left you without a family redeemer today! May his name become famous in Israel. {4:15} He will renew your life and sustain you in your old age. For your daughter-in-law, who loves you and is better to you than seven sons, has given him birth." {4:16} Naomi took the child, laid him in her lap, and became his nurse. {4:17} The neighbors named the child Obed, saying, "A son has been born to Naomi." He became the father of Jesse, who was the father of David. {4:18} These are the descendants of Pharez: Pharez fathered Hezron, {4:19} Hezron fathered Ram, Ram fathered Amminadab, {4:20} Amminadab fathered Nahshon, Nahshon fathered Salmon, {4:21} Salmon fathered Boaz, Boaz fathered Obed, {4:22} Obed fathered Jesse, and Jesse fathered David.

1 Samuel

{1:1} In Ramathaimzophim, there was a man named Elkanah from the tribe of Ephraim. His father was Jeroham, the son of Elihu, the son of Tohu, the son of Zuph, an Ephrathite. {1:2} Elkanah had two wives: one named Hannah and the other Peninnah. Peninnah had children, but Hannah had none. {1:3} Every year, Elkanah went up from his city to worship and sacrifice to the LORD of hosts in Shiloh. The priests of the LORD, Hophni and Phinehas, Eli's sons, were there. {1:4} When Elkanah offered sacrifices, he gave portions to Peninnah and her children, but he gave a double portion to Hannah because he loved her. However, the LORD had closed Hannah's womb. {1:5} Peninnah, her rival, would provoke her bitterly to irritate her because the LORD had closed her womb. {1:6} So it went on year by year; whenever Hannah went up to the house of the LORD, Peninnah would provoke her, and she would weep and not eat. {1:7} Elkanah her husband would ask her, "Hannah, why do you weep? Why don't you eat? Why is your heart sad? Am I not better to you than ten sons?" {1:8} After they had eaten and drunk in Shiloh, Hannah rose. Now Eli the priest was sitting on the seat beside the doorpost of the temple of the LORD. {1:9} Hannah was deeply distressed and prayed to the LORD, weeping bitterly. {1:10} She made a vow, saying, "O LORD of hosts, if You will indeed look upon the affliction of Your maidservant, and remember me, and not forget Your maidservant, but give Your maidservant a male child, then I will give him to the LORD all the days of his life, and no razor shall come upon his head." {1:11} As she continued praying before the LORD, Eli observed her mouth. {1:12} Hannah was praying silently; only her lips moved, and her voice was not heard. Therefore Eli thought she was drunk. {1:13} Eli said to her, "How long will you be drunk? Put away your wine from you." {1:14} Hannah answered, "No, my lord, I am a woman deeply troubled; I have drunk neither wine nor strong drink, but I have been pouring out my soul before the LORD. {1:15} Do not regard your maidservant as a wicked woman, for I have spoken from my great anguish and grief." {1:16} Eli answered, "Go in peace, and the God of Israel grant your petition that you have asked of Him." {1:17} Hannah said, "Let your maidservant find favor in your sight." So the woman went her way and ate, and her face was no longer sad. {1:18} They rose early in the morning and worshiped before the LORD, then returned to their house in Ramah. Elkanah knew Hannah his wife, and the LORD remembered her. {1:19} Hannah conceived and bore a son and called his name Samuel, saying, "Because I have asked for him from the LORD." {1:20} The man Elkanah and all his house went up to offer to the LORD the yearly sacrifice and his vow. {1:21} But Hannah did not go up, for she said to her husband, "I will not go up until the child is weaned; then I will bring him, that he may appear before the LORD and remain there forever." {1:22} Elkanah her husband said to her, "Do what seems best to you; wait until you have weaned him; only may the LORD establish His word." So the woman remained and nursed her son until she weaned him. {1:23} When she had weaned him, she took him up with her, along with three bulls, an ephah of flour, and a skin of wine, and brought him to the house of the LORD in Shiloh. And the child was young. {1:24} They slaughtered the bull, and brought the child to Eli. {1:25} She said, "Oh, my lord! As you live, my lord, I am the woman who stood here beside you, praying to the LORD. {1:26} "For this child I prayed, and the LORD has granted me my petition which I asked of Him. {1:27} "Therefore I have lent him to the LORD; {1:28} as long as he lives he shall be lent to the LORD." So they worshiped the LORD there.

{2:1} Hannah prayed and said, "My heart rejoices in the LORD; my horn is exalted in the LORD. My mouth is enlarged over my enemies because I rejoice in Your salvation. {2:2} **There is none holy like the LORD, for there is none besides You; there is no rock like our God.** {2:3} Talk no more so proudly; let not arrogance come from your mouth, for the LORD is a God of knowledge, and by Him actions are weighed. {2:4} The bows of the mighty are broken, and those who stumbled are girded with strength. {2:5} Those who were full have hired themselves out for bread, and the hungry have ceased. The barren has borne seven, and she who has many children has become feeble. {2:6} The LORD kills and makes alive; He brings down to the grave and brings up. {2:7} The LORD makes poor and makes rich; He brings low and lifts up. {2:8} He raises up the poor from the dust and lifts up the beggar from the dunghill to set them among princes and make them inherit the throne of glory. For the pillars of the earth are the LORD's, and He has set the world upon them. {2:9} He will keep the feet of His saints, and the wicked shall be silent in darkness. For by strength shall no man prevail. {2:10} The adversaries of the LORD shall be broken to pieces; out of heaven shall He thunder upon them. The LORD shall judge the ends of the earth; and He shall give strength to His king and exalt the horn of His anointed. {2:11} Elkanah went to Ramah to his house. And the child ministered to the LORD before Eli the priest. {2:12} Now the sons of Eli were corrupt; they did not know the LORD. {2:13} And the custom of the priests with the people was that when any man offered sacrifice, the priest's servant would come while the meat was boiling with a three-pronged fork in his hand. {2:14} He would thrust it into the pan, kettle, caldron, or pot; and whatever the fork brought up, the priest would take for himself. This they did in Shiloh to all the Israelites who came there. {2:15} Also, before they burned the fat, the priest's servant would come and say to the man who sacrificed, "Give meat for roasting to the priest, for he will not take boiled meat from you, but raw." {2:16} And if the man said to him, "Let them burn the fat first, and then take as much as your heart desires," he would answer him, "No, but you must give it now; and if not, I will take it by force." {2:17} Therefore the sin of the young men was very great before the LORD, for men abhorred the offering of the LORD. {2:18} But Samuel ministered before the LORD, even as a child, wearing a linen ephod. {2:19} Moreover, his mother would make him a little robe and bring it to him year by year when she came up with her husband to offer the yearly sacrifice. {2:20} And Eli blessed Elkanah and his wife, saying, "The LORD give you descendants from this woman for the loan that was lent to the LORD." Then they would go to their own home. {2:21} And the LORD visited Hannah, so that she conceived and bore three sons and two daughters. Meanwhile, the child Samuel grew before the LORD. {2:22} Now Eli was very old; and he heard everything his sons did to all Israel, and how they lay with the women who assembled at the door of the tabernacle of meeting. {2:23} So he said to them, "Why do you do such things? For I hear of your evil dealings from all the people. {2:24} No, my sons! For it is not a good report that I hear. You make the LORD's people transgress. {2:25} If one man sins against another, God will judge him. But if a man sins against the LORD, who will intercede for him?" Nevertheless, they did not heed the voice of their father, because the LORD desired to kill them. {2:26} And the child Samuel grew in stature and in favor both with the LORD and men. {2:27} Then a man of God came to Eli and said to him, "Thus says the LORD: 'Did I not clearly reveal Myself to the house of your father when they were in Egypt in Pharaoh's house? {2:28} Did I not choose him out of all the tribes of Israel to be My priest, to offer upon My altar, to burn incense, and to wear an ephod before Me? And did I not give to the house of your father all the offerings of the children of Israel made by fire? {2:29} Why do you kick at My sacrifice and My offering which I have commanded in My dwelling place, and honor your sons more than Me, to make yourselves fat with the best of all the offerings of Israel My people?' {2:30} Therefore the LORD God of Israel says: 'I said indeed that your house and the house of your father would walk before Me forever.' But now the LORD says: 'Far be it from Me; for those who honor Me I will honor, and those who despise Me shall be lightly esteemed. {2:31} Behold, the days are coming that I will cut off your arm and the arm of your father's house, so that there will not be an old man in your house. {2:32} And you will see an enemy in My dwelling place, despite all the good which God does for Israel. And there shall not be an old man in your house forever. {2:33} But any of your men whom I do not cut off from My altar shall consume your eyes and grieve your heart. And all the descendants of your house shall die in the flower of their age. {2:34} Now this shall be a sign to you that will come upon your two sons, on Hophni and Phinehas: in one day they shall die, both of them. {2:35} Then I will raise up for Myself a faithful priest who shall do according to what is in My heart and in My mind. I will build him a sure house, and he shall walk before My anointed forever. {2:36} And it shall come to pass that everyone who is left in your house will come and bow down to him for a piece of silver and a morsel of bread, and say, "Please, put me in one of the priestly positions, that I may eat a piece of bread."'

{3:1} And the child Samuel served the LORD before Eli. And in those days, the word of the LORD was rare; there were no frequent visions. {3:2} And it happened at that time, as Eli was lying down in his place (now his eyesight had begun to grow dim so that he could not see), {3:3} and before the lamp of God went out in the temple of the LORD where the ark of God was, and Samuel was lying down to sleep, {3:4} that the LORD called Samuel, and he said, "Here I am!" {3:5} So he ran to Eli and said, "Here I am, for you called me." But he said, "I did not call; lie down again." So he went and lay down. {3:6} And the LORD called again,

"Samuel!" and Samuel arose and went to Eli and said, "Here I am, for you called me." But he answered, "I did not call, my son; lie down again." {3:7} Now Samuel did not yet know the LORD, and the word of the LORD had not yet been revealed to him. {3:8} And the LORD called Samuel again the third time. And he arose and went to Eli and said, "Here I am, for you called me." Then Eli perceived that the LORD was calling the boy. {3:9} Therefore Eli said to Samuel, "Go, lie down, and if he calls you, you shall say, 'Speak, LORD, for your servant hears.'" So Samuel went and lay down in his place. {3:10} **And the LORD came and stood, calling as at other times, "Samuel! Samuel!" And Samuel said, "Speak, for your servant hears."** {3:11} Then the LORD said to Samuel, "Behold, I am about to do a thing in Israel at which the two ears of everyone who hears it will tingle. {3:12} On that day I will fulfill against Eli all that I have spoken concerning his house, from beginning to end. {3:13} And I declare to him that I am about to punish his house forever, for the iniquity that he knew, because his sons were blaspheming God, and he did not restrain them. {3:14} Therefore I swear to the house of Eli that the iniquity of Eli's house shall not be atoned for by sacrifice or offering forever." {3:15} Samuel lay until morning; then he opened the doors of the house of the LORD. And Samuel was afraid to tell the vision to Eli. {3:16} But Eli called Samuel and said, "Samuel, my son." And he said, "Here I am." {3:17} And Eli said, "What was it that he told you? Do not hide it from me. May God do so to you and more also if you hide anything from me of all that he told you." {3:18} So Samuel told him everything and hid nothing from him. And he said, "It is the LORD. Let him do what seems good to him." {3:19} And Samuel grew, and the LORD was with him and let none of his words fall to the ground. {3:20} And all Israel from Dan to Beersheba knew that Samuel was established as a prophet of the LORD. {3:21} And the LORD appeared again at Shiloh, for the LORD revealed himself to Samuel at Shiloh by the word of the LORD.

{4:1} And Samuel's words were heard throughout all Israel. Now, Israel went out to battle against the Philistines and camped at Ebenezer, while the Philistines camped at Aphek. {4:2} The Philistines lined up against Israel, and when the battle began, Israel was defeated by the Philistines, who killed about four thousand men in the field. {4:3} When the people returned to the camp, the elders of Israel asked, "Why has the LORD allowed us to be defeated today before the Philistines? Let us bring the ark of the covenant of the LORD from Shiloh, so that it may come among us and save us from our enemies." {4:4} So the people sent to Shiloh and brought from there the ark of the covenant of the LORD of hosts, who sits enthroned on the cherubim. And the two sons of Eli, Hophni and Phinehas, were with the ark of the covenant of God. {4:5} When the ark of the covenant of the LORD came into the camp, all Israel raised a great shout, so loud that the ground shook. {4:6} When the Philistines heard the noise of the shout, they wondered, "What does this great shout in the camp of the Hebrews mean?" And when they realized that the ark of the LORD had come into the camp, {4:7} the Philistines were afraid, saying, "God has come into the camp! Woe to us! Nothing like this has ever happened before. {4:8} Woe to us! Who will deliver us from the hand of these mighty gods? These are the gods who struck the Egyptians with all sorts of plagues in the wilderness. {4:9} Be courageous, Philistines! Act like men and fight, so that you will not become servants to the Hebrews, as they have been to you. Fight like men!" {4:10} So the Philistines fought, and Israel was defeated; every man fled to his tent. There was a great slaughter, and thirty thousand foot soldiers of Israel fell. {4:11} The ark of God was captured, and Eli's two sons, Hophni and Phinehas, were killed. {4:12} A man from the tribe of Benjamin ran from the battlefield and came to Shiloh that same day, with his clothes torn and dirt on his head. {4:13} When he arrived, Eli was sitting on a seat beside the road, watching, for his heart trembled for the ark of God. When the man entered the city and told what had happened, the whole city cried out. {4:14} When Eli heard the outcry, he asked, "What does this commotion mean?" The man hurried over and told Eli. {4:15} Eli, now ninety-eight years old and blind, asked, "What happened, my son?" {4:16} The man replied, "I have fled from the battle today." Eli asked, "What happened, my son?" {4:17} The messenger answered, "Israel fled before the Philistines, and there was a great slaughter among the people. Your two sons, Hophni and Phinehas, are dead, and the ark of God has been captured." {4:18} As soon as the man mentioned the ark of God, Eli fell backward off his seat by the side of the gate. His neck was broken, and he died, for he was an old man and heavy. He had judged Israel for forty years. {4:19} His daughter-in-law, Phinehas' wife, was pregnant and about to give birth. When she heard the news that the ark of God was captured and that her father-in-law and husband were dead, she went into labor and gave birth prematurely. {4:20} As she was dying, the women attending her said, "Don't despair; you have given birth to a son!" But she did not respond or pay attention. {4:21} She named the boy Ichabod, saying, "The glory has departed from Israel!" because the ark of God had been captured and because of the deaths of her father-in-law and her husband. {4:22} She said, "The glory has departed from Israel, for the ark of God has been captured."

{5:1} The Philistines took the ark of God and brought it from Ebenezer to Ashdod. {5:2} When they brought the ark into the house of Dagon and set it beside Dagon, {5:3} the people of Ashdod found Dagon fallen on his face before the ark of the LORD the next morning. They picked Dagon up and put him back in his place. {5:4} But the following morning, Dagon was again found fallen before the ark of the LORD, with his head and hands broken off on the threshold; only the torso of Dagon remained. {5:5} Since then, neither the priests of Dagon nor anyone entering Dagon's house in Ashdod steps on the threshold to this day. {5:6} However, the LORD afflicted the people of Ashdod and its vicinity with tumors, and devastated them. {5:7} When the men of Ashdod saw what was happening, they said, "The ark of the God of Israel must not stay with us, for his hand is heavy upon us and upon Dagon our god." {5:8} So they summoned all the Philistine rulers and asked, "What should we do with the ark of the God of Israel?" The rulers replied, "Let the ark of the God of Israel be moved to Gath." So they moved the ark of the God of Israel to Gath. {5:9} But after they had brought it there, the LORD's hand was against the city, causing a great panic. He struck the people of the city, both young and old, with tumors in their secret parts. {5:10} Therefore, they sent the ark of God to Ekron. But when the ark of God arrived in Ekron, the Ekronites cried out, "They have brought the ark of the God of Israel to us to kill us and our people!" {5:11} So they summoned all the Philistine rulers and pleaded, "Send away the ark of the God of Israel! Let it return to its own place, so it will not kill us and our people!" For there was a deadly panic throughout the city; the hand of God was very heavy there. {5:12} Those who did not die were afflicted with tumors, and the cry of the city went up to heaven. }

{6:1} The ark of the LORD remained in the land of the Philistines for seven months. {6:2} The Philistines consulted their priests and diviners, asking, "What should we do with the ark of the LORD? Tell us how to send it back to its place." {6:3} The priests and diviners advised them, "If you send back the ark of the God of Israel, do not send it back empty-handed. Make a trespass offering to him. Then you will be healed, and you will understand why his hand has not been removed from you." {6:4} They asked, "What trespass offering should we make?" The answer came, "Make five golden tumors and five golden mice, corresponding to the number of Philistine rulers, for the same plague struck both you and your rulers. {6:5} "Make models of your tumors and mice that are destroying your land, and give glory to the God of Israel. Perhaps he will lighten his hand from you, your gods, and your land." {6:6} "Why harden your hearts like the Egyptians and Pharaoh did? When he performed wonders among them, didn't they let the people go, and they departed?" {6:7} "Now make a new cart and take two milk cows that have never been yoked. Hitch the cows to the cart but take their calves away and pen them up. {6:8} "Put the ark of the LORD on the cart, along with the gold tumors and mice as a trespass offering, in a chest beside it. Then send it off and let it go its way. {6:9} "Watch to see if it goes up toward Beth-shemesh along the road to its homeland. If so, this great disaster is a divine judgment, but if not, then we will know that it is not his hand that struck us; it was a coincidence." {6:10} The men did as instructed. They took two milk cows and hitched them to the cart, keeping their calves penned up at home. {6:11} They placed the ark of the LORD on the cart, along with the chest containing the gold tumors and images of the tumors. {6:12} The cows headed straight for Beth-shemesh, lowing as they went, never turning off course. The Philistine lords followed them as far as the border of Beth-shemesh. {6:13} Meanwhile, the people of Beth-shemesh were harvesting their wheat in the valley. When they looked up and saw the ark, they were overjoyed. {6:14} The cart came into the field of Joshua the Beth-shemite and stopped there by a large stone. The people chopped up the cart and offered the cows as a burnt offering to the LORD. {6:15} The Levites took down the ark of the LORD and the chest containing the gold items and placed them on the large stone. Then the people of Beth-shemesh offered burnt offerings and made sacrifices to the LORD that day. {6:16} The five Philistine rulers witnessed this and returned to Ekron the same day. {6:17} These are the gold tumors that the Philistines offered as a trespass offering to the LORD: one each for Ashdod, Gaza, Ashkelon, Gath, and Ekron. {6:18} They also made gold mice, one for each of the Philistine cities, including the fortified cities and the country villages. This large stone in Joshua's field where they set the ark of the LORD is a witness to this day. {6:19} But God struck down some of the men of Beth-shemesh because they had looked inside the ark of the LORD. He struck down seventy men, and the people mourned because the LORD had struck them with a great slaughter. {6:20} The people of Beth-shemesh wondered, "Who can stand before the holy LORD God? To whom shall he go up from us?" {6:21} They sent messengers to the people of Kiriath-jearim, saying, "The Philistines have returned the ark of the LORD. Come down and take it up to your town."

{7:1} And the men of Kirjath-jearim came, and brought up the ark of the LORD, and brought it into the house of Abinadab in the hill, and sanctified Eleazar his son to keep the ark of the LORD. {7:2} And it came to pass, while the ark abode in Kirjath-jearim, that the time was long; for it was twenty years: and all the house of Israel lamented after the LORD. {7:3} And Samuel spake unto all the house of Israel, saying, If ye do return unto the LORD with all your hearts, [then] put away the strange gods and Ashtaroth from among you, and prepare your hearts unto the LORD, and serve him only: and he will deliver you out of the hand of the Philistines. {7:4} Then the children of Israel did put away Baalim and Ashtaroth, and served the LORD only. {7:5} And Samuel said, Gather all Israel to Mizpeh, and I will pray for you unto the LORD. {7:6} And they gathered together to Mizpeh, and drew water, and poured [it] out before the LORD, and fasted on that day, and said there, We have sinned against the LORD. And Samuel judged the children of Israel in Mizpeh. {7:7} And when the Philistines heard that the children of Israel were gathered together to Mizpeh, the lords of the Philistines went up against Israel. And when the children of Israel heard [it,] they were afraid of the Philistines. {7:8} And the children of Israel said to Samuel, Cease not to cry unto the LORD our God for us, that he will save us out of the hand of the Philistines. {7:9} And Samuel took a sucking lamb, and offered [it for] a burnt offering wholly unto the LORD: and Samuel cried unto the LORD for Israel; and the LORD heard him. {7:10} And as Samuel was offering up the burnt offering, the Philistines drew near to battle against Israel: but the LORD thundered with a great thunder on that day upon the Philistines, and discomfited them; and they were smitten before Israel. {7:11} And the men of Israel went out of Mizpeh, and pursued the Philistines, and smote them, until [they came] under Beth-car. {7:12} Then Samuel took a stone, and set [it] between Mizpeh and Shen, and called the name of it Eben-ezer, saying, Hitherto hath the LORD helped us. {7:13} So the Philistines were subdued, and they came no more into the coast of Israel: and the hand of the LORD was against the Philistines all the days of Samuel. {7:14} And the cities which the Philistines had taken from Israel were restored to Israel, from Ekron even unto Gath; and the coasts thereof did Israel deliver out of the hands of the Philistines. And there was peace between Israel and the Amorites. {7:15} And Samuel judged Israel all the days of his life. {7:16} And he went from year to year in circuit to Bethel, and Gilgal, and Mizpeh, and judged Israel in all those places. {7:17} And his return [was] to Ramah; for there [was] his house; and there he judged Israel; and there he built an altar unto the LORD.

{8:1} And it came to pass, when Samuel was old, that he made his sons judges over Israel. {8:2} Now the name of his firstborn was Joel; and the name of his second, Abiah: [they were] judges in Beer-sheba. {8:3} And his sons walked not in his ways, but turned aside after lucre, and took bribes, and perverted judgment. {8:4} Then all the elders of Israel gathered themselves together, and came to Samuel unto Ramah, {8:5} And said unto him, Behold, thou art old, and thy sons walk not in thy ways: now make us a king to judge us like all the nations. {8:6} But the thing displeased Samuel, when they said, Give us a king to judge us. And Samuel prayed unto the LORD. {8:7} **And the LORD said unto Samuel, Hearken unto the voice of the people in all that they say unto thee: for they have not rejected thee, but they have rejected me, that I should not reign over them.** {8:8} According to all the works which they have done since the day that I brought them up out of Egypt even unto this day, wherewith they have forsaken me, and served other gods, so do they also unto thee. {8:9} Now therefore hearken unto their voice: howbeit yet protest solemnly unto them, and shew them the manner of the king that shall reign over them. {8:10} And Samuel told all the words of the LORD unto the people that asked of him a king. {8:11} And he said, This will be the manner of the king that shall reign over you: He will take your sons, and appoint [them] for himself, for his chariots, and to be his horsemen; and [some] shall run before his chariots. {8:12} And he will appoint him captains over thousands, and captains over fifties; and [will set them] to ear his ground, and to reap his harvest, and to make his instruments of war, and instruments of his chariots. {8:13} And he will take your daughters [to be] confectionaries, and [to be] cooks, and [to be] bakers. {8:14} And he will take your fields, and your vineyards, and your oliveyards, [even] the best [of them,] and give [them] to his servants. {8:15} And he will take the tenth of your seed, and of your vineyards, and give to his officers, and to his servants. {8:16} And he will take your menservants, and your maidservants, and your goodliest young men, and your asses, and put [them] to his work. {8:17} He will take the tenth of your sheep: and ye shall be his servants. {8:18} And ye shall cry out in that day because of your king which ye shall have chosen you; and the LORD will not hear you in that day. {8:19} Nevertheless the people refused to obey the voice of Samuel; and they said, Nay; but we will have a king over us; {8:20} That we also may be like all the nations; and that our king may judge us, and go out before us, and fight our battles. {8:21} And Samuel heard all the words of the people, and he rehearsed them in the ears of the LORD. {8:22} And the LORD said to Samuel, Hearken unto their voice, and make them a king. And Samuel said unto the men of Israel, Go ye every man unto his city.

{9:1} Now there was a man of Benjamin, whose name [was] Kish, the son of Abiel, the son of Zeror, the son of Bechorath, the son of Aphiah, a Benjamite, a mighty man of power. {9:2} And he had a son, whose name [was] Saul, a choice young man, and a goodly: and [there was] not among the children of Israel a goodlier person than he: from his shoulders and upward [he was] higher than any of the people. {9:3} And the asses of Kish Saul's father were lost. And Kish said to Saul his son, Take now one of the servants with thee, and arise, go seek the asses. {9:4} And he passed through mount Ephraim, and passed through the land of Shalisha, but they found [them] not: then they passed through the land of Shalim, and [there they were] not: and he passed through the land of the Benjamites, but they found [them] not. {9:5} [And] when they were come to the land of Zuph, Saul said to his servant that [was] with him, Come, and let us return; lest my father leave [caring] for the asses, and take thought for us. {9:6} And he said unto him, Behold now, [there is] in this city a man of God, and [he is] an honourable man; all that he saith cometh surely to pass: now let us go thither; peradventure he can shew us our way that we should go. {9:7} Then said Saul to his servant, But, behold, [if] we go, what shall we bring the man? for the bread is spent in our vessels, and [there is] not a present to bring to the man of God: what have we? {9:8} And the servant answered Saul again, and said, Behold, I have here at hand the fourth part of a shekel of silver: [that] will I give to the man of God, to tell us our way. {9:9} (Beforetime in Israel, when a man went to enquire of God, thus he spake, Come, and let us go to the seer: for [he that is] now [called] a Prophet was beforetime called a Seer.) {9:10} Then said Saul to his servant, Well said; come, let us go. So they went unto the city where the man of God [was]. {9:11} [And] as they went up the hill to the city, they found young maidens going out to draw water, and said unto them, Is the seer here? {9:12} And they answered them, and said, He is; behold, [he is] before you: make haste now, for he came to day to the city; for [there is] a sacrifice of the people to day in the high place: {9:13} As soon as ye be come into the city, ye shall straightway find him, before he go up to the high place to eat: for the people will not eat until he come, because he doth bless the sacrifice; [and] afterwards they eat that be bidden. Now therefore get you up; for about this time ye shall find him. {9:14} And they went up into the city: [and] when they were come into the city, behold, Samuel came out against them, for to go up to the high place. {9:15} Now the LORD had told Samuel in his ear a day before Saul came, saying, {9:16} To morrow about this time I will send thee a man out of the land of Benjamin, and thou shalt anoint him [to be] captain over my people Israel, that he may save my people out of the hand of the Philistines: for I have looked upon my people, because their cry is come unto me. {9:17} And when Samuel saw Saul, the LORD said unto him, Behold the man whom I spake to thee of! this same shall reign over my people. {9:18} Then Saul drew near to Samuel in the gate, and said, Tell me, I pray thee, where the seer's house [is.] {9:19} And Samuel answered Saul, and said, I [am] the seer: go up before me unto the high place; for ye shall eat with me to day, and to morrow I will let thee go, and will tell thee all that [is] in thine heart. {9:20} And as for thine asses that were lost three days ago, set not thy mind on them; for they are found. And on whom [is] all the desire of Israel? [Is it] not on thee, and on all thy father's house? {9:21} And Saul answered and said, [Am] not I a Benjamite, of the smallest of the tribes of Israel? and my family the least of all the families of the tribe of Benjamin? wherefore then speakest thou so to me? {9:22} And Samuel took Saul and his servant, and brought them into the parlour, and made them sit in the chiefest place among them that were bidden, which [were] about thirty persons. {9:23} And Samuel said unto the cook, Bring the portion which I gave thee, of which I said unto thee, Set it by thee. {9:24} And the cook took up the shoulder, and [that] which [was] upon it, and set [it] before Saul. And [Samuel] said, Behold that which is left! set [it] before thee, [and] eat: for unto this time hath it been kept for thee since I said, I have invited the people. So Saul did eat with Samuel that day. {9:25} And when they were come down from the high place into the city, [Samuel] communed with Saul upon the top of the house. {9:26} And they arose early: and it came to pass about the spring of the day, that Samuel called Saul to the top of the house, saying, Up, that I may send thee away. And Saul arose, and they went out both of them, he and Samuel, abroad. {9:27} [And] as they were going down to the end of the city, Samuel said to Saul, Bid the servant pass on before us, (and he passed on,) but stand thou still a while, that I may shew thee the word of God.

{10:1} Then Samuel took a vial of oil, and poured [it] upon his head, and kissed him, and said, [Is it] not because the LORD hath anointed thee [to be] captain over his inheritance? {10:2} When thou art departed from me to day, then thou shalt find two men by Rachel's sepulchre in the border of Benjamin at Zelzah; and they will say unto thee, The asses which thou wentest to seek are found: and, lo, thy father hath left the care of the asses, and sorroweth for you, saying, What shall I do for my son? {10:3} Then shalt thou go on forward from thence, and thou shalt come to the plain of Tabor, and there shall meet thee three men going up to God to Bethel, one carrying three kids, and another carrying three loaves of bread, and another carrying a bottle of wine: {10:4} And they will salute thee, and give thee two [loaves] of bread; which thou shalt receive of their hands. {10:5} After that thou shalt come to the hill of God, where [is] the garrison of the Philistines: and it shall come to pass, when thou art come thither to the city, that thou shalt meet a company of prophets coming down from the high place with a psaltery, and a tabret, and a pipe, and a harp, before them; and they shall prophesy: {10:6} And the Spirit of the LORD will come upon thee, and thou shalt prophesy with them, and shalt be turned into another man. {10:7} And let it be, when these signs are come unto thee, [that] thou do as occasion serve thee; for God [is] with thee. {10:8} And thou shalt go down before me to Gilgal; and, behold, I will come down unto thee, to offer burnt offerings, [and] to sacrifice sacrifices of peace offerings: seven days shalt thou tarry, till I come to thee, and shew thee what thou shalt do. {10:9} And it was [so,] that when he had turned his back to go from Samuel, God gave him another heart: and all those signs came to pass that day. {10:10} And when they came thither to the hill, behold, a company of prophets met him; and the Spirit of God came upon him, and he prophesied among them. {10:11} And it came to pass, when all that knew him beforetime saw that, behold, he prophesied among the prophets, then the people said one to another, What [is] this [that] is come unto the son of Kish? [Is] Saul also among the prophets? {10:12} And one of the same place answered and said, But who [is] their father? Therefore it became a proverb, [Is] Saul also among the prophets? {10:13} And when he had made an end of prophesying, he came to the high place. {10:14} And Saul's uncle said unto him and to his servant, Whither went ye? And he said, To seek the asses: and when we saw that [they were] no where, we came to Samuel. {10:15} And Saul's uncle said, Tell me, I pray thee, what Samuel said unto you. {10:16} And Saul said unto his uncle, He told us plainly that the asses were found. But of the matter of the kingdom, whereof Samuel spake, he told him not. {10:17} And Samuel called the people together unto the LORD to Mizpeh; {10:18} And said unto the children of Israel, Thus saith the LORD God of Israel, I brought up Israel out of Egypt, and delivered you out of the hand of the Egyptians, and out of the hand of all kingdoms, [and] of them that oppressed you: {10:19} And ye have this day rejected your God, who himself saved you out of all your adversities and your tribulations; and ye have said unto him, [Nay,] but set a king over us. Now therefore present yourselves before the LORD by your tribes, and by your thousands. {10:20} And when Samuel had caused all the tribes of Israel to come near, the tribe of Benjamin was taken. {10:21} When he had caused the tribe of Benjamin to come near by their families, the family of Matri was taken, and Saul the son of Kish was taken: and when they sought him, he could not be found. {10:22} Therefore they enquired of the LORD further, if the man should yet come thither. And the LORD answered, Behold, he hath hid himself among the stuff. {10:23} And they ran and fetched him thence: and when he stood among the people, he was higher than any of the people from his shoulders and upward. {10:24} And Samuel said to all the people, See ye him whom the LORD hath chosen, that [there is] none like him among all the people? And all the people shouted, and said, God save the king. {10:25} Then Samuel told the people the manner of the kingdom, and wrote [it] in a book, and laid [it]up before the LORD. And Samuel sent all the people away, every man to his house. {10:26} And Saul also went home to Gibeah; and there went with him a band of men, whose hearts God had touched. {10:27} But the children of Belial said, How shall this man save us? And they despised him, and brought him no presents. But he held his peace.

{11:1} Then Nahash the Ammonite came up, and encamped against Jabesh-gilead: and all the men of Jabesh said unto Nahash, Make a covenant with us, and we will serve thee. {11:2} And Nahash the Ammonite answered them, On this [condition] will I make [a covenant] with you, that I may thrust out all your right eyes, and lay it [for] a reproach upon all Israel. {11:3} And the elders of Jabesh said unto him, Give us seven days respite, that we may send messengers unto all the coasts of Israel: and then, if [there be] no man to save us, we will come out to thee. {11:4} Then came the messengers to Gibeah of Saul, and told the tidings in the ears of the people: and all the people lifted up their voices, and wept. {11:5} And, behold, Saul came after the herd out of the field; and Saul said, What [aileth] the people that they weep? And they told him the tidings of the men of Jabesh. {11:6} And the Spirit of God came upon Saul when he heard those tidings, and his anger was kindled greatly. {11:7} And he took a yoke of oxen, and hewed them in pieces, and sent [them] throughout all the coasts of Israel by the hands of messengers, saying, Whosoever cometh not forth after Saul and after Samuel, so shall it be done unto his oxen. And the fear of the LORD fell on the people, and they came out with one consent. {11:8} And when he numbered them in Bezek, the children of Israel were three hundred thousand, and the men of Judah thirty thousand. {11:9} And they said unto the messengers that came, Thus shall ye say unto the men of Jabesh-gilead, To morrow, by [that time] the sun be hot, ye shall have help. And the messengers came and shewed [it] to the men of Jabesh; and they were glad. {11:10} Therefore the men of Jabesh said, To morrow we will come out unto you, and ye shall do with us all that seemeth good unto you. {11:11} And it was [so] on the morrow, that Saul put the people in three companies; and they came into the midst of the host in the morning watch, and slew the Ammonites until the heat of the day: and it came to pass, that they which remained were scattered, so that two of them were not left together. {11:12} And the people said unto Samuel, Who [is] he that said, Shall Saul reign over us? bring the men, that we may put them to death. {11:13} And Saul said, There shall not a man be put to death this day: for to day the LORD hath wrought salvation in Israel. {11:14} Then said Samuel to the people, Come, and let us go to Gilgal, and renew the kingdom there. {11:15} And all the people went to Gilgal; and there they made Saul king before the LORD in Gilgal; and there they sacrificed sacrifices of peace offerings before the LORD; and there Saul and all the men of Israel rejoiced greatly.

{12:1} And Samuel said unto all Israel, Behold, I have hearkened unto your voice in all that ye said unto me, and have made a king over you. {12:2} And now, behold, the king walketh before you: and I am old and grayheaded; and, behold, my sons [are] with you: and I have walked before you from my childhood unto this day. {12:3} Behold, here I [am:] witness against me before the LORD, and before his anointed: whose ox have I taken? or whose ass have I taken? or whom have I defrauded? whom have I oppressed? or of whose hand have I received [any] bribe to blind mine eyes therewith? and I will restore it you. {12:4} And they said, Thou hast not defrauded us, nor oppressed us, neither hast thou taken ought of any man's hand. {12:5} And he said unto them, The LORD [is] witness against you, and his anointed [is] witness this day, that ye have not found ought in my hand. And they answered, [He is] witness. {12:6} And Samuel said unto the people, [It is] the LORD that advanced Moses and Aaron, and that brought your fathers up out of the land of Egypt. {12:7} Now therefore stand still, that I may reason with you before the LORD of all the righteous acts of the LORD, which he did to you and to your fathers. {12:8} When Jacob was come into Egypt, and your fathers cried unto the LORD, then the LORD sent Moses and Aaron, which brought forth your fathers out of Egypt, and made them dwell in this place. {12:9} And when they forgat the LORD their God, he sold them into the hand of Sisera, captain of the host of Hazor, and into the hand of the Philistines, and into the hand of the king of Moab, and they fought against them. {12:10} **And they cried unto the LORD, and said, We have sinned, because we have forsaken the LORD, and have served Baalim and Ashtaroth: but now deliver us out of the hand of our enemies, and we will serve thee.** {12:11} And the LORD sent Jerubbaal, and Bedan, and Jephthah, and Samuel, and delivered you out of the hand of your enemies on every side, and ye dwelled safe. {12:12} And when ye saw that Nahash the king of the children of Ammon came against you, ye said unto me, Nay; but a king shall reign over us: when the LORD your God [was] your king. {12:13} Now therefore behold the king whom ye have chosen, [and] whom ye have desired! and, behold, the LORD hath set a king over you. {12:14} If ye will fear the LORD, and serve him, and obey his voice, and not rebel against the commandment of the LORD, then shall both ye and also the king that reigneth over you continue following the LORD your God: {12:15} But if ye will not obey the voice of the LORD, but rebel against the commandment of the LORD, then shall the hand of the LORD be against you, as [it was] against your fathers. {12:16} Now therefore stand and see this great thing, which the LORD will do before your eyes. {12:17} [Is it] not wheat harvest to day? I will call unto the LORD, and he shall send thunder and rain; that ye may perceive and see that your wickedness [is] great, which ye have done in the sight of the LORD, in asking you a king. {12:18} So Samuel called unto the LORD; and the LORD sent thunder and rain that day: and all the people greatly feared the LORD and Samuel. {12:19} And all the people said unto Samuel, Pray for thy servants unto the LORD thy God, that we die not: for we have added unto all our sins [this] evil, to ask us a king. {12:20} And Samuel said unto the people, Fear not: ye have done all this wickedness: yet turn not aside from following the LORD, but serve the LORD with all your heart; {12:21} And turn ye not aside: for [then should ye go] after vain [things,] which cannot profit nor deliver; for they [are] vain. {12:22}

For the LORD will not forsake his people for his great name's sake: because it hath pleased the LORD to make you his people. {12:23} Moreover as for me, God forbid that I should sin against the LORD in ceasing to pray for you: but I will teach you the good and the right way: {12:24} Only fear the LORD, and serve him in truth with all your heart: for consider how great [things] he hath done for you. {12:25} But if ye shall still do wickedly, ye shall be consumed, both ye and your king.

{13:1} Saul reigned one year; and when he had reigned two years over Israel, {13:2} Saul chose him three thousand men of Israel; whereof two thousand were with Saul in Michmash and in mount Bethel, and a thousand were with Jonathan in Gibeah of Benjamin: and the rest of the people he sent every man to his tent. {13:3} And Jonathan smote the garrison of the Philistines that was in Geba, and the Philistines heard of it. And Saul blew the trumpet throughout all the land, saying, Let the Hebrews hear. {13:4} And all Israel heard say that Saul had smitten a garrison of the Philistines, and that Israel also was had in abomination with the Philistines. And the people were called together after Saul to Gilgal. {13:5} And the Philistines gathered themselves together to fight with Israel, thirty thousand chariots, and six thousand horsemen, and people as the sand which is on the sea shore in multitude: and they came up, and pitched in Michmash, eastward from Beth-aven. {13:6} When the men of Israel saw that they were in a strait, (for the people were distressed,) then the people did hide themselves in caves, and in thickets, and in rocks, and in high places, and in pits. {13:7} And some of the Hebrews went over Jordan to the land of Gad and Gilead. As for Saul, he was yet in Gilgal, and all the people followed him trembling. {13:8} And he tarried seven days, according to the set time that Samuel had appointed: but Samuel came not to Gilgal; and the people were scattered from him. {13:9} And Saul said, Bring hither a burnt offering to me, and peace offerings. And he offered the burnt offering. {13:10} And it came to pass, that as soon as he had made an end of offering the burnt offering, behold, Samuel came; and Saul went out to meet him, that he might salute him. {13:11} And Samuel said, What hast thou done? And Saul said, Because I saw that the people were scattered from me, and that thou camest not within the days appointed, and that the Philistines gathered themselves together at Michmash; {13:12} Therefore said I, The Philistines will come down now upon me to Gilgal, and I have not made supplication unto the LORD: I forced myself therefore, and offered a burnt offering. {13:13} And Samuel said to Saul, Thou hast done foolishly: thou hast not kept the commandment of the LORD thy God, which he commanded thee: for now would the LORD have established thy kingdom upon Israel for ever. {13:14} But now thy kingdom shall not continue: the LORD hath sought him a man after his own heart, and the LORD hath commanded him to be captain over his people, because thou hast not kept that which the LORD commanded thee. {13:15} And Samuel arose, and gat him up from Gilgal unto Gibeah of Benjamin. And Saul numbered the people that were present with him, about six hundred men. {13:16} And Saul, and Jonathan his son, and the people that were present with them, abode in Gibeah of Benjamin: but the Philistines encamped in Michmash. {13:17} And the spoilers came out of the camp of the Philistines in three companies: one company turned unto the way that leadeth to Ophrah, unto the land of Shual: {13:18} And another company turned the way to Bethhoron: and another company turned to the way of the border that looketh to the valley of Zeboim toward the wilderness. {13:19} Now there was no smith found throughout all the land of Israel: for the Philistines said, Lest the Hebrews make them swords or spears: {13:20} But all the Israelites went down to the Philistines, to sharpen every man his share, and his coulter, and his axe, and his mattock. {13:21} Yet they had a file for the mattocks, and for the coulters, and for the forks, and for the axes, and to sharpen the goads. {13:22} So it came to pass in the day of battle, that there was neither sword nor spear found in the hand of any of the people that were with Saul and Jonathan: but with Saul and with Jonathan his son was there found. {13:23} And the garrison of the Philistines went out to the passage of Michmash.

{14:1} Now it came to pass upon a day, that Jonathan the son of Saul said unto the young man that bare his armour, Come, and let us go over to the Philistines' garrison, that is on the other side. But he told not his father. {14:2} And Saul tarried in the uttermost part of Gibeah under a pomegranate tree which is in Migron: and the people that were with him were about six hundred men; {14:3} And Ahiah, the son of Ahitub, I-chabod's brother, the son of Phinehas, the son of Eli, the LORD'S priest in Shiloh, wearing an ephod. And the people knew not that Jonathan was gone. {14:4} And between the passages, by which Jonathan sought to go over unto the Philistines' garrison, there was a sharp rock on the one side and a sharp rock on the other side: and the name of the one was Bozez, and the name of the other Seneh. {14:5} The forefront of the one was situate northward over against Michmash, and the other southward over against Gibeah. {14:6} And Jonathan said to the young man that bare his armour, Come, and let us go over unto the garrison of these uncircumcised: it may be that the LORD will work for us: for there is no restraint to the LORD to save by many or by few. {14:7} And his armourbearer said unto him, Do all that is in thine heart: turn thee; behold, I am with thee according to thy heart. {14:8} Then said Jonathan, Behold, we will pass over unto these men, and we will discover ourselves unto them. {14:9} If they say thus unto us, Tarry until we come to you; then we will stand still in our place, and will not go up unto them. {14:10} But if they say thus, Come up unto us; then we will go up: for the LORD hath delivered them into our hand: and this shall be a sign unto us. {14:11} And both of them discovered themselves unto the garrison of the Philistines: and the Philistines said, Behold, the Hebrews come forth out of the holes where they had hid themselves. {14:12} And the men of the garrison answered Jonathan and his armourbearer, and said, Come up to us, and we will shew you a thing. And Jonathan said unto his armourbearer, Come up after me: for the LORD hath delivered them into the hand of Israel. {14:13} And Jonathan climbed up upon his hands and upon his feet, and his armourbearer after him: and they fell before Jonathan; and his armourbearer slew after him. {14:14} And that first slaughter, which Jonathan and his armourbearer made, was about twenty men, within as it were an half acre of land, which a yoke of oxen might plow. {14:15} And there was trembling in the host, in the field, and among all the people: the garrison, and the spoilers, they also trembled, and the earth quaked: so it was a very great trembling. {14:16} And the watchmen of Saul in Gibeah of Benjamin looked; and, behold, the multitude melted away, and they went on beating down one another. {14:17} Then said Saul unto the people that were with him, Number now, and see who is gone from us. And when they had numbered, behold, Jonathan and his armourbearer were not there. {14:18} And Saul said unto Ahiah, Bring hither the ark of God. For the ark of God was at that time with the children of Israel. {14:19} And it came to pass, while Saul talked unto the priest, that the noise that was in the host of the Philistines went on and increased: and Saul said unto the priest, Withdraw thine hand. {14:20} And Saul and all the people that were with him assembled themselves, and they came to the battle: and, behold, every man's sword was against his fellow, and there was a very great discomfiture. {14:21} Moreover the Hebrews that were with the Philistines before that time, which went up with them into the camp from the country round about, even they also turned to be with the Israelites that were with Saul and Jonathan. {14:22} Likewise all the men of Israel which had hid themselves in mount Ephraim, when they heard that the Philistines fled, even they also followed hard after them in the battle. {14:23} So the LORD saved Israel that day: and the battle passed over unto Beth-aven. {14:24} And the men of Israel were distressed that day: for Saul had adjured the people, saying, Cursed be the man that eateth any food until evening, that I may be avenged on mine enemies. So none of the people tasted any food. {14:25} And all they of the land came to a wood; and there was honey upon the ground. {14:26} And when the people were come into the wood, behold, the honey dropped; but no man put his hand to his mouth: for the people feared the oath. {14:27} But Jonathan heard not when his father charged the people with the oath: wherefore he put forth the end of the rod that was in his hand, and dipped it in an honeycomb, and put his hand to his mouth; and his eyes were enlightened. {14:28} Then answered one of the people, and said, Thy father straitly charged the people with an oath, saying, Cursed be the man that eateth any food this day. And the people were faint. {14:29} Then said Jonathan, My father hath troubled the land: see, I pray you, how mine eyes have been enlightened, because I tasted a little of this honey. {14:30} How much more, if haply the people had eaten freely today of the spoil of their enemies which they found? for had there not been now a much greater slaughter among the Philistines? {14:31} And they smote the Philistines that day from Michmash to Aijalon: and the people were very faint. {14:32} And the people flew upon the spoil, and took sheep, and oxen, and calves, and slew them on the ground: and the people did eat them with the blood. {14:33} Then they told Saul, saying, Behold, the people sin against the LORD, in that they eat with the blood. And he said, Ye have transgressed: roll a great stone unto me this day. {14:34} And Saul said, Disperse yourselves among the people, and say unto them, Bring me hither every man his ox, and every man his sheep, and slay them here, and eat; and sin not against the LORD in eating with the blood. And all the people brought every man his ox with him that night, and slew them there. {14:35} And Saul built an altar unto the LORD: the same was the first altar that he built unto the LORD. {14:36} And Saul said, Let us go down after the Philistines by night, and spoil them until the morning light, and let us not leave a man of them. And they said, Do whatsoever seemeth good unto thee. Then said the priest, Let us draw near hither unto God. {14:37} And Saul asked counsel of God, Shall I go down after the Philistines? wilt thou deliver them into the hand of Israel? But he answered him not that day. {14:38} And Saul said, Draw ye near hither, all the chief of the people: and know and see wherein this sin hath been this day. {14:39} For, as the LORD liveth, which saveth Israel, though it be in Jonathan my son, he shall surely die. But there was not a man among all the people that answered him. {14:40} Then said he unto all Israel, Be ye on one side, and I and Jonathan my son will be on the other side. And the people said unto Saul, Do what seemeth good unto thee. {14:41} Therefore Saul said unto the LORD God of Israel, Give a perfect lot. And Saul and Jonathan were taken: but the people escaped. {14:42} And Saul said, Cast lots between me and Jonathan my son. And Jonathan was taken. {14:43} Then Saul said to Jonathan, Tell me what thou hast done. And Jonathan told him, and said, I did but taste a little honey with the end of the rod that was in mine hand, and, lo, I must die. {14:44} And Saul answered, God do so and more also: for thou shalt surely die, Jonathan. {14:45} And the people said unto Saul, Shall Jonathan die, who hath wrought this great salvation in Israel? God forbid: as the LORD liveth, there shall not one hair of his head fall to the ground; for he hath wrought with God this day. So the people rescued Jonathan, that he died not. {14:46} Then Saul went up from following the Philistines: and the Philistines went to their own place. {14:47} So Saul took the kingdom over Israel, and fought against all his enemies on every side, against Moab, and against the children of Ammon, and against Edom, and against the kings of Zobah, and against the Philistines: and whithersoever he turned himself, he vexed them. {14:48} And he gathered an host, and smote the Amalekites, and delivered Israel out of the hands of them that spoiled them. {14:49} Now the sons of Saul were Jonathan, and Ishui, and Melchi-shua: and the names of his two daughters were these; the name of the firstborn Merab, and the name of the younger Michal; {14:50} And the name of Saul's wife was Ahinoam, the daughter of Ahimaaz: and the name of the captain of his host was Abner, the son of Ner, Saul's uncle. {14:51} And Kish was the father of Saul; and Ner the father of Abner was the son of Abiel. {14:52} And there was sore war against the Philistines all the days of Saul: and when Saul saw any strong man, or any valiant man, he took him unto him.

{15:1} Samuel also said unto Saul, The LORD sent me to anoint thee to be king over his people, over Israel: now therefore hearken thou unto the voice of the words of the LORD. {15:2} Thus saith the LORD of hosts, I remember that which Amalek did to Israel, how he laid wait for him in the way, when he came up from Egypt. {15:3} Now go and smite Amalek, and utterly destroy all that they have, and spare them not; but slay both man and woman, infant and suckling, ox and sheep, camel and ass. {15:4} And Saul gathered the people together, and numbered them in Telaim, two hundred thousand footmen, and ten thousand men of Judah. {15:5} And Saul came to a city of Amalek, and laid wait in the valley. {15:6} And Saul said unto the Kenites, Go, depart, get you down from among the Amalekites, lest I destroy you with them: for ye shewed kindness to all the children of Israel, when they came up out of Egypt. So the Kenites departed from among the Amalekites. {15:7} And Saul smote the Amalekites from Havilah until thou comest to Shur, that is over against Egypt. {15:8} And he took Agag the king of the Amalekites alive, and utterly destroyed all the people with the edge of the sword. {15:9} But Saul and the people spared Agag, and the best of the sheep, and of the oxen, and of the fatlings, and the lambs, and all that was good, and would not utterly destroy them: but every thing that was vile and refuse, that they destroyed utterly. {15:10} Then came the word of the LORD unto Samuel, saying, {15:11} It repenteth me that I have set up Saul to be king: for he is turned back from following me, and hath not performed my commandments. And it grieved Samuel; and he cried unto the LORD all night. {15:12} And when Samuel rose early to meet Saul in the morning, it was told Samuel, saying, Saul came to Carmel, and, behold, he set him up a place, and is gone about, and passed on, and gone down to Gilgal. {15:13} And Samuel came to Saul: and Saul said unto him, Blessed be thou of the LORD: I have performed the commandment of the LORD. {15:14} And Samuel said, What meaneth then this bleating of the sheep in mine ears, and the lowing of the oxen which I hear? {15:15} And Saul said, They have brought them from the Amalekites: for the people spared the best of the sheep and of the oxen, to sacrifice unto the LORD thy God; and the rest we have utterly destroyed. {15:16} Then Samuel said unto Saul, Stay, and I will tell thee what the LORD hath said to me this night. And he said unto him, Say on. {15:17} And Samuel said, When thou wast little in thine own sight, wast thou not made the head of the tribes of Israel, and the LORD anointed thee king over Israel? {15:18} And the LORD sent thee on a journey, and said, Go and utterly destroy the sinners the Amalekites, and fight against them until they be consumed. {15:19} Wherefore then didst thou not obey the voice of the LORD, but didst fly upon the spoil, and didst evil in the sight of the LORD? {15:20} And Saul said unto Samuel, Yea, I have obeyed the voice of the LORD, and have gone the way which the LORD sent me, and have brought Agag the king of Amalek, and have utterly destroyed the Amalekites. {15:21} But the people took of the spoil, sheep and oxen, the chief of the things which should have been utterly destroyed, to sacrifice unto the LORD thy God in Gilgal. {15:22} And Samuel said, Hath the LORD as great delight in burnt offerings and sacrifices, as in obeying the voice of the LORD? Behold, to obey is better than sacrifice, and to hearken than the fat of rams. {15:23} For rebellion is as the sin of witchcraft, and stubbornness is as iniquity and idolatry. Because thou hast rejected the word of the LORD, he hath also rejected thee from being king. {15:24} And Saul said unto Samuel, I have sinned: for I have transgressed the commandment of the LORD, and thy words: because I feared the people, and obeyed their voice. {15:25} Now therefore, I pray thee, pardon my sin, and turn again with me, that I may worship the LORD. {15:26} And Samuel said unto Saul, I will not return with thee: for thou hast rejected the word of the LORD, and the LORD hath rejected thee from being king over Israel. {15:27} And as Samuel turned about to go away, he laid hold upon the skirt of his mantle, and it rent. {15:28} And Samuel said unto him, The LORD hath rent the kingdom of Israel from thee this day, and hath given it to a neighbour of thine, that is better than thou. {15:29} And also the Strength of Israel will not lie nor repent: for he is not a man, that he should repent. {15:30} Then he said, I have sinned: yet honour me now, I pray thee, before the elders of my people, and before Israel, and turn again with me, that I may worship the LORD thy God. {15:31} So Samuel turned again after Saul; and Saul worshipped the LORD. {15:32} Then said Samuel, Bring ye hither to me Agag the king of the Amalekites. And Agag came unto him delicately. And Agag said, Surely the bitterness of death is past. {15:33} And Samuel said, As thy sword hath made women childless, so shall thy mother be childless among women. And Samuel hewed Agag in pieces before the LORD in Gilgal. {15:34} Then Samuel went to Ramah; and Saul went up to his house to Gibeah of Saul. {15:35} And Samuel came no more to see Saul until the day of his death: nevertheless Samuel mourned for Saul: and the LORD repented that he had made Saul king over Israel.

{16:1} And the LORD said unto Samuel, How long wilt thou mourn for Saul, seeing I have rejected him from reigning over Israel? fill thine horn with oil, and go, I will send thee to Jesse the Bethlehemite: for I have provided me a king among his sons. {16:2} And Samuel said, How can I go? if Saul hear it, he will kill me. And the LORD said, Take an heifer with thee, and say, I am come to sacrifice to the LORD. {16:3} And call Jesse to the sacrifice, and I will show thee what thou shalt do: and thou shalt anoint unto me him whom I name unto thee. {16:4} And Samuel did that which the LORD spake, and came to Bethlehem. And the elders of the town trembled at his coming, and said, Comest thou peaceably? {16:5} And he said, Peaceably: I am come to sacrifice unto the LORD: sanctify yourselves, and come with me to the sacrifice. And he sanctified Jesse and his sons, and called them to the sacrifice. {16:6} And it came to pass, when they were come, that he looked on Eliab, and said, Surely the LORD'S anointed is before him. {16:7} But the LORD said unto Samuel, Look not on his countenance, or on the height of his stature; because I have refused him: for the LORD seeth not as man seeth; for man looketh on the outward appearance, but the LORD looketh on the heart. {16:8} Then

Jesse called Abinadab, and made him pass before Samuel. And he said, Neither hath the LORD chosen this. {16:9} Then Jesse made Shammah to pass by. And he said, Neither hath the LORD chosen this. {16:10} Again, Jesse made seven of his sons to pass before Samuel. And Samuel said unto Jesse, The LORD hath not chosen these. {16:11} And Samuel said unto Jesse, Are here all thy children? And he said, There remaineth yet the youngest, and, behold, he keepeth the sheep. And Samuel said unto Jesse, Send and fetch him: for we will not sit down till he come hither. {16:12} And he sent, and brought him in. Now he was ruddy, and withal of a beautiful countenance, and goodly to look to. And the LORD said, Arise, anoint him: for this is he. {16:13} Then Samuel took the horn of oil, and anointed him in the midst of his brethren: and the Spirit of the LORD came upon David from that day forward. So Samuel rose up, and went to Ramah. {16:14} But the Spirit of the LORD departed from Saul, and an evil spirit from the LORD troubled him. {16:15} And Saul's servants said unto him, Behold now, an evil spirit from God troubleth thee. {16:16} Let our lord now command thy servants, which are before thee, to seek out a man, who is a cunning player on an harp: and it shall come to pass, when the evil spirit from God is upon thee, that he shall play with his hand, and thou shalt be well. {16:17} And Saul said unto his servants, Provide me now a man that can play well, and bring him to me. {16:18} Then answered one of the servants, and said, Behold, I have seen a son of Jesse the Bethlehemite, that is cunning in playing, and a mighty valiant man, and a man of war, and prudent in matters, and a comely person, and the LORD is with him. {16:19} Wherefore Saul sent messengers unto Jesse, and said, Send me David thy son, which is with the sheep. {16:20} And Jesse took an ass laden with bread, and a bottle of wine, and a kid, and sent them by David his son unto Saul. {16:21} And David came to Saul, and stood before him: and he loved him greatly; and he became his armourbearer. {16:22} And Saul sent to Jesse, saying, Let David, I pray thee, stand before me; for he hath found favour in my sight. {16:23} And it came to pass, when the evil spirit from God was upon Saul, that David took an harp, and played with his hand: so Saul was refreshed, and was well, and the evil spirit departed from him.

{17:1} Now the Philistines gathered together their armies to battle, and were gathered together at Shochoh, which belongeth to Judah, and pitched between Shochoh and Azekah, in Ephes-dammim. {17:2} And Saul and the men of Israel were gathered together, and pitched by the valley of Elah, and set the battle in array against the Philistines. {17:3} And the Philistines stood on a mountain on the one side, and Israel stood on a mountain on the other side: and there was a valley between them. {17:4} And there went out a champion out of the camp of the Philistines, named Goliath, of Gath, whose height was six cubits and a span. {17:5} And he had an helmet of brass upon his head, and he was armed with a coat of mail; and the weight of the coat was five thousand shekels of brass. {17:6} And he had greaves of brass upon his legs, and a target of brass between his shoulders. {17:7} And the staff of his spear was like a weaver's beam; and his spear's head weighed six hundred shekels of iron: and one bearing a shield went before him. {17:8} And he stood and cried unto the armies of Israel, and said unto them, Why are ye come out to set your battle in array? am not I a Philistine, and ye servants to Saul? choose you a man for you, and let him come down to me. {17:9} If he be able to fight with me, and to kill me, then will we be your servants: but if I prevail against him, and kill him, then shall ye be our servants, and serve us. {17:10} And the Philistine said, I defy the armies of Israel this day; give me a man, that we may fight together. {17:11} When Saul and all Israel heard those words of the Philistine, they were dismayed, and greatly afraid. {17:12} Now David was the son of that Ephrathite of Bethlehemjudah, whose name was Jesse; and he had eight sons: and the man went among men for an old man in the days of Saul. {17:13} And the three eldest sons of Jesse went and followed Saul to the battle: and the names of his three sons that went to the battle were Eliab the firstborn, and next unto him Abinadab, and the third Shammah. {17:14} And David was the youngest: and the three eldest followed Saul. {17:15} But David went and returned from Saul to feed his father's sheep at Bethlehem. {17:16} And the Philistine drew near morning and evening, and presented himself forty days. {17:17} And Jesse said unto David his son, Take now for thy brethren an ephah of this parched corn, and these ten loaves, and run to the camp to thy brethren; {17:18} And carry these ten cheeses unto the captain of their thousand, and look how thy brethren fare, and take their pledge. {17:19} Now Saul, and they, and all the men of Israel, were in the valley of Elah, fighting with the Philistines. {17:20} And David rose up early in the morning, and left the sheep with a keeper, and took, and went, as Jesse had commanded him; and he came to the trench, as the host was going forth to the fight, and shouted for the battle. {17:21} For Israel and the Philistines had put the battle in array, army against army. {17:22} And David left his carriage in the hand of the keeper of the carriage, and ran into the army, and came and saluted his brethren. {17:23} And as he talked with them, behold, there came up the champion, the Philistine of Gath, Goliath by name, out of the armies of the Philistines, and spake according to the same words: and David heard them. {17:24} And all the men of Israel, when they saw the man, fled from him, and were sore afraid. {17:25} And the men of Israel said, Have ye seen this man that is come up? surely to defy Israel is he come up: and it shall be, that the man who killeth him, the king will enrich him with great riches, and will give him his daughter, and make his father's house free in Israel. {17:26} And David spake to the men that stood by him, saying, What shall be done to the man that killeth this Philistine, and taketh away the reproach from Israel? for who is this uncircumcised Philistine, that he should defy the armies of the living God? {17:27} And the people answered him after this manner, saying, So shall it be done to the man that killeth him. {17:28} And Eliab his eldest brother heard when he spoke unto the men; and Eliab's anger was kindled against David, and he said, Why camest thou down hither? and with whom hast thou left those few sheep in the wilderness? I know thy pride, and the naughtiness of thine heart; for thou art come down that thou mightest see the battle. {17:29} And David said, What have I now done? Is there not a cause? {17:30} And he turned from him toward another, and spoke after the same manner: and the people answered him again after the former manner. {17:31} And when the words were heard which David spoke, they rehearsed them before Saul: and he sent for him. {17:32} And David said to Saul, Let no man's heart fail because of him; thy servant will go and fight with this Philistine. {17:33} And Saul said to David, Thou art not able to go against this Philistine to fight with him: for thou art but a youth, and he a man of war from his youth. {17:34} And David said unto Saul, Thy servant kept his father's sheep, and there came a lion, and a bear, and took a lamb out of the flock: {17:35} And I went out after him, and smote him, and delivered it out of his mouth: and when he arose against me, I caught him by his beard, and smote him, and slew him. {17:36} Thy servant slew both the lion and the bear: and this uncircumcised Philistine shall be as one of them, seeing he hath defied the armies of the living God. {17:37} David said moreover, The LORD that delivered me out of the paw of the lion, and out of the paw of the bear, he will deliver me out of the hand of this Philistine. And Saul said unto David, Go, and the LORD be with thee. {17:38} And Saul armed David with his armor, and he put a helmet of brass upon his head; also he armed him with a coat of mail. {17:39} And David girded his sword upon his armor, and he assayed to go; for he had not proved it. And David said unto Saul, I cannot go with these; for I have not proved them. And David put them off him. {17:40} And he took his staff in his hand, and chose him five smooth stones out of the brook, and put them in a shepherd's bag which he had, even in a scrip; and his sling was in his hand: and he drew near to the Philistine. {17:41} And the Philistine came on and drew near unto David; and the man that bare the shield went before him. {17:42} And when the Philistine looked about, and saw David, he disdained him: for he was but a youth, and ruddy, and of a fair countenance. {17:43} And the Philistine said unto David, Am I a dog, that thou comest to me with staves? And the Philistine cursed David by his gods. {17:44} And the Philistine said to David, Come to me, and I will give thy flesh unto the fowls of the air, and to the beasts of the field. {17:45} Then said David to the Philistine, Thou comest to me with a sword, and with a spear, and with a shield: but I come to thee in the name of the LORD of hosts, the God of the armies of Israel, whom thou hast defied. {17:46} This day will the LORD deliver thee into mine hand; and I will smite thee, and take thine head from thee; and I will give the carcases of the host of the Philistines this day unto the fowls of the air, and to the wild beasts of the earth; that all the earth may know that there is a God in Israel. {17:47} **And all this assembly shall know that the LORD saveth not with sword and spear: for the battle is the LORD'S, and he will give you into our hands.** {17:48} And it came to pass, when the Philistine arose, and came and drew nigh to meet David, that David hastened, and ran toward the army to meet the Philistine. {17:49} And David put his hand in his bag, and took thence a stone, and slung it, and smote the Philistine in his forehead, that the stone sunk into his forehead; and he fell upon his face to the earth. {17:50} So David prevailed over the Philistine with a sling and with a stone, and smote the Philistine, and slew him; but there was no sword in the hand of David. {17:51} Therefore David ran, and stood upon the Philistine, and took his sword, and drew it out of the sheath thereof, and slew him, and cut off his head therewith. And when the Philistines saw their champion was dead, they fled. {17:52} And the men of Israel and of Judah arose, and shouted, and pursued the Philistines, until thou come to the valley, and to the gates of Ekron. And the wounded of the Philistines fell down by the way to Shaaraim, even unto Gath, and unto Ekron. {17:53} And the children of Israel returned from chasing after the Philistines, and they spoiled their tents. {17:54} And David took the head of the Philistine, and brought it to Jerusalem; but he put his armor in his tent. {17:55} And when Saul saw David go forth against the Philistine, he said unto Abner, the captain of the host, Abner, whose son is this youth? And Abner said, As thy soul liveth, O king, I cannot tell. {17:56} And the king said, Inquire thou whose son the stripling is. {17:57} And as David returned from the slaughter of the Philistine, Abner took him, and brought him before Saul with the head of the Philistine in his hand. {17:58} And Saul said to him, Whose son art thou, thou young man? And David answered, I am the son of thy servant Jesse the Bethlehemite.

{18:1} And it came to pass, when he had finished speaking unto Saul, that the soul of Jonathan was knit with the soul of David, and Jonathan loved him as his own soul. {18:2} And Saul took him that day, and would let him go no more home to his father's house. {18:3} Then Jonathan and David made a covenant, because he loved him as his own soul. {18:4} And Jonathan stripped himself of the robe that was upon him, and gave it to David, and his garments, even to his sword, and to his bow, and to his girdle. {18:5} And David went out whithersoever Saul sent him, and behaved himself wisely: and Saul set him over the men of war, and he was accepted in the sight of all the people, and also in the sight of Saul's servants. {18:6} And it came to pass as they came, when David was returned from the slaughter of the Philistine, that the women came out of all cities of Israel, singing and dancing, to meet king Saul, with tabrets, with joy, and with instruments of music. {18:7} And the women answered one another as they played, and said, Saul hath slain his thousands, and David his ten thousands. {18:8} And Saul was very wroth, and the saying displeased him; and he said, They have ascribed unto David ten thousands, and to me they have ascribed but thousands: and what can he have more but the kingdom? {18:9} And Saul eyed David from that day and forward. {18:10} And it came to pass on the morrow, that the evil spirit from God came upon Saul, and he prophesied in the midst of the house: and David played with his hand, as at other times: and there was a javelin in Saul's hand. {18:11} And Saul cast the javelin; for he said, I will smite David even to the wall with it. And David avoided out of his presence twice. {18:12} And Saul was afraid of David, because the LORD was with him, and was departed from Saul. {18:13} Therefore Saul removed him from him, and made him his captain over a thousand; and he went out and came in before the people. {18:14} And David behaved himself wisely in all his ways; and the LORD was with him. {18:15} Wherefore when Saul saw that he behaved himself very wisely, he was afraid of him. {18:16} But all Israel and Judah loved David, because he went out and came in before them. {18:17} And Saul said to David, Behold my elder daughter Merab, her will I give thee to wife: only be thou valiant for me, and fight the LORD'S battles. For Saul said, Let not mine hand be upon him, but let the hand of the Philistines be upon him. {18:18} And David said unto Saul, Who am I? and what is my life, or my father's family in Israel, that I should be son in law to the king? {18:19} But it came to pass at the time when Merab Saul's daughter should have been given to David, that she was given unto Adriel the Meholathite to wife. {18:20} And Michal Saul's daughter loved David: and they told Saul, and the thing pleased him. {18:21} And Saul said, I will give him her, that she may be a snare to him, and that the hand of the Philistines may be against him. Wherefore Saul said to David, Thou shalt this day be my son in law in the one of the twain. {18:22} And Saul commanded his servants, saying, Commune with David secretly, and say, Behold, the king hath delight in thee, and all his servants love thee: now therefore be thou the king's son in law. {18:23} And Saul's servants spoke those words in the ears of David. And David said, Seemeth it to you a light thing to be a king's son in law, seeing that I am a poor man, and lightly esteemed? {18:24} And the servants of Saul told him, saying, On this manner spoke David. {18:25} And Saul said, Thus shall ye say to David, The king desireth not any dowry, but an hundred foreskins of the Philistines, to be avenged of the king's enemies. But Saul thought to make David fall by the hand of the Philistines. {18:26} And when his servants told David these words, it pleased David well to be the king's son in law: and the days were not expired. {18:27} Wherefore David arose and went, he and his men, and slew of the Philistines two hundred men; and David brought their foreskins, and they gave them in full tale to the king, that he might be the king's son in law. And Saul gave him Michal his daughter to wife. {18:28} And Saul saw and knew that the LORD was with David, and that Michal Saul's daughter loved him. {18:29} And Saul was yet the more afraid of David; and Saul became David's enemy continually. {18:30} Then the princes of the Philistines went forth: and it came to pass, after they went forth, that David behaved himself more wisely than all the servants of Saul; so that his name was much set by.

{19:1} And Saul spoke to Jonathan his son, and to all his servants, that they should kill David. {19:2} But Jonathan Saul's son delighted much in David: and Jonathan told David, saying, Saul my father seeketh to kill thee: now therefore, I pray thee, take heed to thyself until the morning, and abide in a secret place, and hide thyself: {19:3} And I will go out and stand beside my father in the field where thou art, and I will commune with my father of thee; and what I see, that I will tell thee. {19:4} And Jonathan spoke good of David unto Saul his father, and said unto him, Let not the king sin against his servant, against David; because he hath not sinned against thee, and because his works have been to thee-ward very good: {19:5} For he did put his life in his hand, and slew the Philistine, and the LORD wrought a great salvation for all Israel: thou sawest it, and didst rejoice: wherefore then wilt thou sin against innocent blood, to slay David without a cause? {19:6} And Saul hearkened unto the voice of Jonathan: and Saul swore, As the LORD liveth, he shall not be slain. {19:7} And Jonathan called David, and Jonathan showed him all those things. And Jonathan brought David to Saul, and he was in his presence, as in times past. {19:8} And there was war again: and David went out, and fought with the Philistines, and slew them with a great slaughter; and they fled from him. {19:9} And the evil spirit from the LORD was upon Saul, as he sat in his house with his javelin in his hand: and David played with his hand. {19:10} And Saul sought to smite David even to the wall with the javelin; but he slipped away out of Saul's presence, and he smote the javelin into the wall: and David fled, and escaped that night. {19:11} Saul also sent messengers unto David's house, to watch him, and to slay him in the morning: and Michal David's wife told him, saying, If thou save not thy life tonight, tomorrow thou shalt be slain. {19:12} So Michal let David down through a window: and he went, and fled, and escaped. {19:13} And Michal took an image, and laid it in the bed, and put a pillow of goats' hair for his bolster, and covered it with a cloth. {19:14} And when Saul sent messengers to take David, she said, He is sick. {19:15} And Saul sent the messengers again to see David, saying, Bring him up to me in the bed, that I may slay him. {19:16} And when the messengers were come in, behold, there was an image in the bed, with a pillow of goats' hair for his bolster. {19:17} And Saul said unto Michal, Why hast thou deceived me so, and sent away mine enemy, that he is escaped? And Michal answered Saul, He said unto me, Let me go; why should I kill thee? {19:18} So David fled, and escaped, and came to Samuel to Ramah, and told him all that Saul had done to him. And he and Samuel went and dwelt in Naioth. {19:19} And it was told Saul, saying, Behold, David is at Naioth in Ramah. {19:20} And Saul sent messengers to take David: and when they saw the company of the prophets prophesying, and Samuel standing as appointed over them, the Spirit of God was upon the messengers of Saul, and they also prophesied. {19:21} And when it was told Saul, he sent other messengers, and they prophesied likewise. And Saul sent messengers again the third time, and they prophesied also. {19:22} Then went he also to Ramah, and came to a great well that is in Sechu: and he asked and said, Where are Samuel and David? And one said, Behold, they be at Naioth in Ramah. {19:23} And he went thither to Naioth in Ramah: and the Spirit of God was upon him also, and he went on, and prophesied, until he came to Naioth in Ramah. {19:24} And he stripped off his clothes also, and prophesied before Samuel in like manner, and lay down naked all that day and all that night. Wherefore they say, Is Saul also among the prophets?

{20:1} David fled from Naioth in Ramah and approached Jonathan, asking, "What have I done? What is my wrongdoing before your father that he seeks my life?" {20:2} Jonathan reassured him, saying, "You won't die. My father doesn't make any decision, big or small, without telling me. Why would he hide this from me? It's not true." {20:3} David swore, "Your father knows I have your favor. He just doesn't want to upset you. But I swear by the LORD and your life, I'm in grave danger." {20:4} Jonathan promised David, "Whatever you need, I'll do it for you." {20:5} David replied, "Tomorrow is the new moon, and I'm expected to dine with the king. But let me hide in the field until the third day's evening." {20:6} David suggested a plan, "If your father asks about me, say that I urgently requested permission to go to Bethlehem for a family sacrifice." {20:7} He added, "If your father agrees, all is well. But if he's angry, it means trouble is brewing." {20:8} David appealed to Jonathan, "Please be kind to me. You've made a covenant with me before the LORD. If I've done wrong, kill me yourself rather than deliver me to your father." {20:9} Jonathan replied, "I would never let harm come to you, even if my father planned it." {20:10} David asked, "But how will I know if your father responds harshly?" {20:11} Jonathan proposed, "Let's go into the field together." {20:12} In the field, Jonathan prayed, "O LORD God of Israel, if my father intends good for David, I won't keep it from him." {20:13} **He continued, "But if my father means harm, I'll warn you, and you can go in peace. May the LORD be with you as He was with my father."** {20:14} Jonathan requested, "Promise me kindness for as long as I live, and don't abandon my family, even when David's enemies are defeated." {20:15} He vowed, "Let the LORD hold David's enemies accountable." {20:16} Jonathan and David renewed their covenant, as Jonathan loved David like his own soul. {20:17} Jonathan had David swear again because of their deep bond. {20:18} Jonathan reminded David, "Tomorrow is the new moon, and your absence will be noticed." {20:19} He instructed David, "After three days, return to the place where you hid before and wait by the stone Ezel." {20:20} Jonathan outlined a signal, "I'll shoot three arrows as though aiming at a target." {20:21} He explained, "If

I tell the lad the arrows are on this side, it's safe for you to return. But if I say the arrows are beyond, it means you must flee." {20:22} Jonathan concluded, "May the LORD send you away safely. Our conversation is sealed by the LORD forever." {20:23} Jonathan ensured their agreement was under the LORD's watchful eye. {20:24} David hid in the field, and when the new moon arrived, the king sat to eat, noticing David's absence. {20:25} Saul sat by the wall, with Jonathan beside him and Abner on Saul's other side, while David's seat remained empty. {20:26} Saul stayed silent, suspecting David might be unclean. {20:27} The next day, David's absence was noted, and Saul questioned Jonathan about it. {20:28} Jonathan explained that David had asked to visit Bethlehem for a family sacrifice. {20:29} He asked for permission, saying, "Please let me go if I've found favor in your eyes." {20:30} Saul grew angry with Jonathan, accusing him of siding with David to his own detriment. {20:31} Saul insisted that as long as David lived, Jonathan's reign would not be established. {20:32} Jonathan defended David, asking, "What has he done to deserve death?" {20:33} Saul hurled a javelin at Jonathan, revealing his intent to kill David. {20:34} Jonathan left the table in anger, refusing to eat out of grief for David. {20:35} The next morning, Jonathan met David in the field as planned, with a young lad. {20:36} He sent the lad to retrieve the arrows he shot, using them as a signal. {20:37} When the lad reached the spot, Jonathan called out, indicating the direction of the arrows. {20:38} The lad retrieved the arrows and returned them to Jonathan. {20:39} Only Jonathan and David understood the significance of this exchange. {20:40} Jonathan sent the lad back to the city with his equipment. {20:41} After the lad left, David emerged from his hiding place, and they embraced and wept. {20:42} Jonathan assured David of their continued friendship, and they parted ways.

{21:1} David went to Nob to meet Ahimelech the priest. Ahimelech was afraid when he saw David alone and asked him why he was alone without anyone with him. {21:2} David told Ahimelech that the king had given him a secret task and instructed him not to let anyone know about it. David had arranged for his servants to be at a specific place. {21:3} David asked Ahimelech for five loaves of bread or whatever was available. {21:4} Ahimelech replied that he only had consecrated bread, which was reserved for priests. He could give it to David if his men had abstained from women. {21:5} David assured Ahimelech that his men had indeed abstained, and their vessels were consecrated. So, the consecrated bread would be suitable. {21:6} Ahimelech gave David the consecrated bread because there was no other bread available except the showbread, which was replaced daily. {21:7} On that day, a man named Doeg, a servant of Saul and the chief of Saul's herdsmen, happened to be there. {21:8} David asked Ahimelech if there were any weapons available because he hadn't brought his own due to the urgency of the king's business. {21:9} Ahimelech mentioned the sword of Goliath, which David had slain, wrapped in a cloth behind the ephod. David eagerly accepted it. {21:10} David fled that day because he feared Saul and went to Achish, the king of Gath. {21:11} Achish's servants recognized David and praised him for his victories over tens of thousands, which made David afraid of Achish. {21:12} David pretended to be insane in front of Achish, scratching on the gates and letting his saliva run down his beard. {21:13} Achish concluded that David was mad and questioned why his servants had brought him there, declaring that he had no need for madmen in his presence. {21:14} Achish refused to allow David into his house, seeing him as a madman. {21:15} He questioned why they had brought David to him, as he had no use for madmen in his presence.

{22:1} David left there and escaped to the cave of Adullam. When his brothers and his father's household heard about it, they went down to him. {22:2} Many who were in distress, in debt, or discontented gathered around him, and he became their leader. About four hundred men were with him. {22:3} David then went to Mizpeh of Moab and asked the king of Moab to take care of his parents until he knew what God had planned for him. {22:4} So, the king of Moab welcomed David's parents, and they stayed with him while David remained in the stronghold. {22:5} The prophet Gad told David not to stay in the stronghold but to go to the land of Judah. So, David left and went to the forest of Hareth. {22:6} When Saul heard that David and his men had been discovered, he was sitting under a tree in Ramah, holding his spear, with all his servants around him. {22:7} Saul addressed his servants from Benjamin, accusing them of conspiring with David. He questioned whether David promised them fields and vineyards, making them officers in his army. {22:8} Saul believed they were all against him, that no one told him about Jonathan's alliance with David, and that no one sympathized with him or informed him of David's plans. {22:9} Then Doeg the Edomite, who was in charge of Saul's servants, spoke up. He reported seeing David at Nob with Ahimelech, where he received food and Goliath's sword. {22:10} Saul sent for Ahimelech and all his family, the priests of Nob. They came to the king. {22:11} Saul accused Ahimelech of conspiring against him by helping David with food, weapons, and seeking guidance from God to rebel against Saul. {22:12} Ahimelech defended himself, stating David's loyalty and how he followed Saul's orders faithfully. {22:13} Saul disregarded Ahimelech's defense and condemned him and his family to death. {22:14} Then Ahimelech explained David's loyalty and innocence, highlighting his honorable service to Saul. {22:15} Ahimelech denied any wrongdoing, claiming he knew nothing of David's plans. {22:16} Despite Ahimelech's innocence, Saul ordered his execution along with his entire family. {22:17} Saul commanded his guards to kill the priests of the LORD, accusing them of supporting David and hiding his escape. {22:18} When the guards refused, Saul ordered Doeg to kill the priests. Doeg slaughtered eighty-five priests that day, along with the people of Nob. {22:19} He also destroyed Nob, killing men, women, children, and animals. {22:20} Abiathar, one of Ahimelech's sons, managed to escape and joined David. {22:21} Abiathar informed David about Saul's massacre of the priests of the LORD. {22:22} David regretted involving Doeg in Nob, knowing he would inform Saul, leading to the deaths of Ahimelech's family. {22:23} David assured Abiathar of his safety, promising to protect him from those who sought their lives.

{23:1} They told David, "Look, the Philistines are fighting against Keilah, and they are plundering the threshing floors." {23:2} So David asked the LORD, "Should I go and attack these Philistines?" And the LORD said to David, "Go, attack the Philistines and save Keilah." {23:3} But David's men said to him, "We are afraid here in Judah. How much more if we go to Keilah against the Philistine armies?" {23:4} David inquired of the LORD again, and the LORD answered him, "Arise, go down to Keilah, for I will deliver the Philistines into your hand." {23:5} So David and his men went to Keilah, fought the Philistines, and took away their livestock, defeating them decisively. Thus, David saved the people of Keilah. {23:6} Meanwhile, Abiathar, the son of Ahimelech, fled to David in Keilah, bringing an ephod with him. {23:7} When Saul learned that David had come to Keilah, he thought, "God has delivered him into my hand, for he has trapped himself by entering a town with gates and bars." {23:8} So Saul called all the people to war, to besiege David and his men in Keilah. {23:9} David realized that Saul was secretly planning harm against him. He said to Abiathar the priest, "Bring the ephod here." {23:10} Then David prayed, "O LORD, God of Israel, I have heard that Saul is coming to destroy Keilah because of me. Will the men of Keilah hand me over to him? Will Saul come down, as I have heard?" And the LORD answered, "He will come down." {23:11} David then asked, "Will the men of Keilah deliver me and my men into Saul's hand?" And the LORD replied, "They will deliver you up." {23:12} So David and his six hundred men departed from Keilah, going wherever they could. When Saul learned that David had escaped from Keilah, he decided not to pursue him further. {23:13} David stayed in the wilderness strongholds, hiding in the mountains of the wilderness of Ziph. Saul searched for him every day, but God did not deliver David into his hand. {23:14} Saul's pursuit made David realize that Saul had come out to seek his life. David was hiding in the wilderness of Ziph, in the forest. {23:15} Then Jonathan, Saul's son, went to David in the forest and encouraged him in God. {23:16} Jonathan assured David, "Do not fear. My father Saul will not find you. You will be king over Israel, and I will be next to you, as even my father Saul knows." {23:17} So Jonathan and David made a covenant before the LORD. David stayed in the forest, while Jonathan returned home. {23:18} Meanwhile, the people of Ziph went to Saul in Gibeah and said, "Isn't David hiding among us in the strongholds in the forest on the hill of Hachilah, south of Jeshimon?" {23:19} "Now, O king, come down whenever you wish, and it will be our responsibility to deliver him into your hand," they said. {23:20} Saul praised them, saying, "May you be blessed by the LORD for your compassion towards me. Go and prepare further. Find out his hiding places and who has seen him there, for I have heard that he is very cunning." {23:21} "Investigate thoroughly and discover all the places where he hides, then come back to me with certainty, and I will accompany you. If he is in the land, I will search him out among all the clans of Judah." {23:22} So they went to Ziph ahead of Saul, while David and his men were in the wilderness of Maon, in the desert plain south of Jeshimon. {23:23} Saul and his men went in search of David, but David and his men were on the other side of the mountain. They hurried to escape Saul, who and his men had surrounded David and his men, intending to capture them. {23:24} However, a messenger came to Saul, urging him to come quickly, as the Philistines had invaded the land. So Saul abandoned his pursuit of David and went to fight the Philistines, and that place became known as Sela-hammahlekoth. {23:25} David left there and went to live in the strongholds of En-gedi. {23:26} Saul went on one side of the mountain, while David and his men were on the other side. David hurried to escape Saul's pursuit because Saul and his men had surrounded them, intending to capture them. {23:27} But then a messenger came to Saul, saying, "Hurry and come, for the Philistines have invaded the land." {23:28} So Saul stopped pursuing David and went to fight the Philistines. That's why they called that place Sela-hammahlekoth. {23:29} Meanwhile, David left there and lived in the strongholds at En-gedi.

{24:1} When Saul returned from fighting the Philistines, he heard that David was in the wilderness of En-gedi. {24:2} So Saul took three thousand chosen men from Israel and went to search for David and his men among the rocks where the wild goats roam. {24:3} Along the way, Saul came to some sheep pens, where there was a cave. Saul went in to relieve himself, while David and his men were hiding in the recesses of the cave. {24:4} David's men told him, "Today is the day the LORD spoke of when he said, 'I will hand over your enemy to you for you to deal with as you wish.'" So David crept forward and cut off a piece of Saul's robe without him knowing. {24:5} Later, David felt guilty for cutting Saul's robe. {24:6} He said to his men, "I could never do something like this to my master, the LORD's anointed. I won't lift my hand against him because he is the LORD's chosen one." {24:7} So David persuaded his men with these words and didn't let them attack Saul. Then Saul left the cave and went on his way. {24:8} Afterward, David also left the cave and called out to Saul, "My lord the king!" When Saul looked behind him, David bowed down with his face to the ground. {24:9} David asked Saul, "Why do you listen to people who say I'm trying to harm you?" {24:10} "Today you've seen how the LORD handed you over to me in the cave," David continued. "Some urged me to kill you, but I spared you, saying, 'I won't harm my lord, for he is the LORD's chosen one.'" {24:11} "Look, my father, here is a piece of your robe I cut off," David said. "I could have killed you, but I didn't. See, there is no evil or rebellion in me. I have not wronged you, but you are hunting me down to take my life." {24:12} "May the LORD judge between us and avenge me," David declared, "but I will not harm you." {24:13} "As the proverb says, 'Out of the wicked comes wickedness,' but my hand will not touch you." {24:14} "Whom are you pursuing?" David asked. "A dead dog? A flea? May the LORD be our judge and decide between us. May he vindicate me by delivering me from your hand." {24:15} When David finished speaking, Saul asked, "Is that your voice, my son David?" Then Saul wept aloud. {24:16} "You are more righteous than I," Saul admitted. "You have treated me well, but I have treated you badly." {24:17} "You have shown me kindness today," Saul acknowledged. "When the LORD delivered me into your hands, you didn't kill me." {24:18} "Surely, if a man finds his enemy, he lets him go unharmed," Saul reasoned. "May the LORD reward you well for the way you treated me today." {24:19} "I know that you will surely be king," Saul acknowledged. "And the kingdom of Israel will be established in your hands." {24:20} "Now swear to me by the LORD that you will not kill off my descendants or wipe out my name from my father's family," Saul requested. {24:21} So David swore to Saul, and Saul went home, {24:22} while David and his men went up to the stronghold.

{25:1} After Samuel died, all the Israelites mourned for him and buried him in his house in Ramah. Then David went to the wilderness of Paran. {25:2} In Maon, there was a man named Nabal, who owned property in Carmel. He was very wealthy, with three thousand sheep and a thousand goats. At that time, he was shearing his sheep in Carmel. {25:3} The man's name was Nabal, and his wife's name was Abigail. She was intelligent and beautiful, but Nabal was harsh and wicked in his dealings. He was from the house of Caleb. {25:4} David heard that Nabal was shearing his sheep in the wilderness. {25:5} So David sent ten young men and instructed them, "Go to Carmel, find Nabal, and greet him in my name." {25:6} "Say to him, 'May you have peace, your household, and all that you have. I've heard that your shepherds have been with us, and we haven't harmed them. Nothing was missing all the while they were in Carmel.'" {25:7} "Ask your servants, and they will tell you. Please show kindness to us, for we have come on a festive day. Please give whatever you can to your servants and to your son David.'" {25:8} David's young men went and delivered this message to Nabal in David's name, then they waited. {25:9} But Nabal responded rudely to David's servants, saying, "Who is David? Who is this son of Jesse? Many servants are breaking away from their masters these days." {25:10} "Why should I take my bread, my water, and the meat I have prepared for my shearers and give it to men coming from who knows where?" {25:11} So David's men returned and told him everything Nabal had said. {25:12} David said to his men, "Each of you strap on your sword!" So they did, and David strapped on his own sword. {25:13} About four hundred men went up with David, while two hundred stayed with the supplies. {25:14} But one of Nabal's young men went to Abigail, Nabal's wife, and told her, "David sent messengers from the wilderness to greet our master, but he hurled insults at them." {25:15} "Yet these men were very good to us. They did not mistreat us, and nothing was missing all the time we were out in the fields with them." {25:16} "They were a wall around us both day and night, all the time we were herding our sheep near them." {25:17} "Now consider carefully what you can do, because disaster is hanging over our master and his whole household. He is such a wicked man that no one can talk to him." {25:18} Abigail quickly gathered two hundred loaves of bread, two skins of wine, five dressed sheep, five seahs of roasted grain, a hundred cakes of raisins, and two hundred cakes of pressed figs, and loaded them on donkeys. {25:19} Then she told her servants, "Go on ahead; I'll follow you." But she did not tell her husband Nabal. {25:20} As she came riding her donkey into a mountain ravine, she saw David and his men descending toward her, and she met them. {25:21} David had just said, "It's been useless—all my watching over this fellow's property in the wilderness so that nothing of his was missing. He has paid me back evil for good." {25:22} "May God deal with David, be it ever so severely if by morning I leave alive one male of all who belong to him." {25:23} When Abigail saw David, she quickly got off her donkey and bowed down before David with her face to the ground. {25:24} She fell at his feet and said, "Pardon your servant, my lord, and let me speak to you; hear what your servant has to say." {25:25} "Please pay no attention, my lord, to that wicked man Nabal. He is just like his name—his name means Fool, and folly goes with him. But as for me, your servant, I did not see the men my lord sent." {25:26} "And now, my lord, as surely as the LORD your God lives and as you live, since the LORD has kept you from bloodshed and from avenging yourself with your own hands, may your enemies and all who are intent on harming my lord be like Nabal." {25:27} "And let this gift, which your servant has brought to my lord, be given to the men who follow you." {25:28} "Please forgive your servant's presumption. The LORD your God will certainly make a lasting dynasty for my lord, because you fight the LORD's battles, and no wrongdoing will be found in you as long as you live." {25:29} "Even though someone is pursuing you to take your life, the life of my lord will be bound securely in the bundle of the living by the LORD your God, but the lives of your enemies he will hurl away as from the pocket of a sling." {25:30} "When the LORD has fulfilled for my lord every good thing he promised concerning him and has appointed him ruler over Israel," {25:31} "my lord will not have on his conscience the staggering burden of needless bloodshed or of having avenged himself. And when the LORD your God has brought my lord success, remember your servant." {25:32} David said to Abigail, "Praise be to the LORD, the God of Israel, who has sent you today to meet me." {25:33} "May you be blessed for your good judgment and for keeping me from bloodshed this day and from avenging myself with my own hands." {25:34} "Otherwise, as surely as the LORD, the God of Israel, lives, who has kept me from harming you, if you had not come quickly to meet me, not one male belonging to Nabal would have been left alive by daybreak." {25:35} Then David accepted from her hand what she had brought him and said, "Go home in peace. I have heard your words and granted your request." {25:36} When Abigail went to Nabal, he was in the house holding a banquet like that of a king. He was in high spirits and very drunk. So she told him nothing until the next morning. {25:37} In the morning, when Nabal was sober, his wife told him all these things, and his heart failed him, and he became like a stone. {25:38} About ten days later, the LORD struck Nabal and he died. {25:39} When David heard that Nabal was dead, he said, "Praise be to the LORD, who has upheld my cause against Nabal for treating me with contempt. He has kept his servant from doing wrong and has brought Nabal's wrongdoing down on his own head." Then David sent word to Abigail, asking her {25:40} David's servants arrived at Abigail's home in Carmel and said to her, "David has sent us to bring you to him as his wife." {25:41} Abigail quickly got up, bowed down with her face to the ground, and said, "I am your servant, ready to serve and wash the feet of my lord's servants." {25:42} Without delay, Abigail mounted her donkey, accompanied by five of her maids, and followed the messengers of David. She became his wife. {25:43} David had also married Ahinoam of Jezreel; both women became his wives. {25:44} Meanwhile, Saul had given his daughter Michal, who was David's wife, to Palti son of Laish, who was from Gallim.

{26:1} The Ziphites went to Saul in Gibeah and said, "Isn't David hiding in the hill of Hachilah, near Jeshimon?" {26:2} So Saul, with three thousand chosen men of Israel, went to the wilderness of Ziph to search for David. {26:3} Saul camped in the hill of Hachilah near Jeshimon, while David stayed in the wilderness. He noticed that Saul was pursuing him. {26:4} David sent out spies and confirmed that Saul had indeed come. {26:5} David and Abishai approached Saul's camp by night. Saul was asleep in the trench, with his spear stuck in the ground near his head. Abner, the captain of his army, and the soldiers were sleeping around him. {26:6} David asked Abishai and Ahimelech the Hittite who would go with him to Saul's camp. Abishai volunteered. {26:7} Under the cover of darkness, David and Abishai approached Saul's camp. They found Saul sleeping in the trench with his spear by his head, while Abner and the soldiers were around him. {26:8} Abishai suggested killing Saul, believing God had delivered him into their hands, but David refused. {26:9} David reasoned that they couldn't harm the LORD's anointed without guilt. {26:10} David expressed his faith that God would deal with Saul in His own time. {26:11}

Instead of killing Saul, David took Saul's spear and water jug while he slept. {26:12} They left without anyone noticing, as a deep sleep from the LORD had fallen upon them. {26:13} David then went to the other side of the hill and called out to Abner, reproaching him for failing to protect the king. {26:14} Abner responded, and David rebuked him for allowing someone to enter the camp to harm the king. {26:15} David emphasized the importance of guarding the king, especially considering that Saul's life had been in David's hands. {26:16} David criticized Abner and Saul's guards for their failure to protect Saul and showed them Saul's spear and water jug as proof. {26:17} Saul recognized David's voice and asked why he was pursuing him. {26:18} David appealed to Saul, questioning why he was hunting him when he had done no wrong. {26:19} David pleaded with Saul to listen to him and let God judge between them. {26:20} David likened Saul's pursuit to chasing a flea or a partridge in the mountains. {26:21} Saul admitted his wrongdoing and asked David to return, promising not to harm him. {26:22} David pointed out Saul's spear and requested that one of the young men retrieve it. {26:23} David acknowledged that God had protected him from harming Saul. {26:24} Saul praised David and acknowledged that he would accomplish great things. {26:25} David departed, and Saul returned home.

{27:1} David thought to himself, "Someday Saul will surely kill me. There's no point in staying in Israel. I should escape to the land of the Philistines, where Saul won't find me." {27:2} So David and his six hundred men went to Achish, the king of Gath. {27:3} They stayed with Achish in Gath, along with their families, including David's wives, Ahinoam and Abigail. {27:4} When Saul heard that David had fled to Gath, he stopped searching for him. {27:5} David asked Achish for a place to settle outside the royal city, and Achish gave him Ziklag, which still belongs to the kings of Judah. {27:6} David lived in the land of the Philistines for a year and four months. {27:7} During this time, David and his men raided the Geshurites, Gezrites, and Amalekites, killing everyone and taking their livestock and possessions. {27:8} They left no survivors and returned to Achish. {27:9} Achish asked where they had been, and David lied, saying they had raided areas in the south of Judah. {27:10} David made sure no one survived to tell Achish what they had really done, fearing that Achish would reject him if he knew the truth. {27:11} Achish believed David's lies, thinking that David had made himself hated by his own people, {27:12} and he decided to keep David as his servant forever.

{28:1} During those days, the Philistines gathered their armies to fight against Israel. Achish told David, "You and your men will fight with me." {28:2} David replied, "You will soon see what I can do." {28:3} Meanwhile, Samuel had died, and all Israel mourned and buried him in Ramah. Saul had expelled mediums and spiritists from the land. {28:4} The Philistines set up camp at Shunem, and Saul gathered Israel's army at Gilboa. {28:5} When Saul saw the Philistine army, he was terrified, and his heart trembled. {28:6} Saul sought guidance from the LORD, but the LORD didn't answer him through dreams, the Urim, or prophets. {28:7} So Saul asked his servants to find a woman with a familiar spirit. They directed him to a woman in Endor. {28:8} Saul disguised himself and went with two men to the woman's place at night. He asked her to summon Samuel using her familiar spirit. {28:9} The woman hesitated, fearing Saul's punishment for practicing forbidden arts. {28:10} But Saul swore to her by the LORD that she wouldn't be punished. {28:11} The woman asked whom she should summon, and Saul said, "Bring up Samuel." {28:12} When the woman saw Samuel, she cried out, realizing the disguised man was Saul. {28:13} Saul reassured her, asking what she had seen. She replied that she saw gods ascending from the earth. {28:14} Saul asked for Samuel's appearance, and the woman described an old man covered with a mantle. Saul recognized it was Samuel and bowed in respect. {28:15} Samuel asked Saul why he had disturbed him. Saul explained his distress and sought guidance since God no longer answered him. {28:16} Samuel rebuked Saul, telling him that the LORD had rejected him and transferred the kingdom to David because Saul disobeyed God's commands. {28:17} Samuel predicted that the Philistines would defeat Israel and Saul and his sons would die the next day. {28:18} Saul collapsed in fear upon hearing Samuel's words because he hadn't eaten all day and night. {28:19} The woman offered food to Saul, and though he initially refused, he eventually ate at her insistence. {28:20} After eating, Saul regained some strength. {28:21} The woman comforted Saul, expressing her obedience and offering him food for his journey. {28:22} Saul finally agreed to eat, and the woman prepared a meal for him and his servants. {28:23} But Saul refused, saying, "I will not eat." However, his servants, along with the woman, persuaded him, and he listened to their voice. So he got up from the ground and sat on the bed. {28:24} The woman had a fat calf in the house. She quickly slaughtered it, took flour, kneaded dough, and baked unleavened bread. {28:25} Then she served it to Saul and his servants. They ate, and afterwards, they rose up and left that night

{29:1} The Philistines gathered all their armies to Aphek, while the Israelites camped near a fountain in Jezreel. {29:2} The Philistine lords passed by hundreds and thousands, but David and his men were at the rear with Achish. {29:3} The Philistine princes questioned, "Why are these Hebrews here?" Achish replied, "Isn't this David, the servant of Saul, who has been with me for days or years? I've found no fault in him." {29:4} The Philistine princes were angry, saying, "Send David back, let him not go with us to battle. He might turn against us and side with Saul. How else could he regain Saul's favor except by betraying us?" {29:5} "Isn't this David," they said, "of whom they sang, 'Saul has slain his thousands, and David his ten thousands'?" {29:6} Achish called David and said, "You have been upright, and your loyalty has been good, but the lords are against you. Return and go in peace." {29:7} David asked, "What have I done wrong? Why can't I fight for my lord the king?" {29:8} Achish replied, "You are good in my sight, but the Philistine princes have decided you cannot go to battle with us." {29:9} "Go back in the morning with your men," Achish instructed, "and depart as soon as it's light." {29:10} David and his men rose early to return to the land of the Philistines, {29:11} while the Philistines went up to Jezreel.

{30:1} When David and his men returned to Ziklag on the third day, they found that the Amalekites had invaded the south, attacked Ziklag, and burned it with fire. {30:2} They had taken captive the women and everyone else in the city, sparing no one, and then continued on their way. {30:3} Upon seeing the city burned and their loved ones taken captive, David and his men wept until they had no more strength. {30:4} Among the captives were David's two wives, Ahinoam and Abigail. {30:5} David was greatly distressed, and the people even spoke of stoning him. But David found strength in the Lord his God. {30:6} He then asked Abiathar the priest to bring him the ephod, and David inquired of the Lord whether they should pursue the Amalekites. The Lord answered affirmatively. {30:7} So David and his six hundred men went after the Amalekites and reached the brook Besor, where two hundred men remained due to exhaustion. {30:8} David and four hundred men continued the pursuit, while the others stayed behind. {30:9} Along the way, they encountered an Egyptian who had been left behind by the Amalekites because he was sick. {30:10} After providing him with food and water, David inquired about their whereabouts. The Egyptian led them to the Amalekite camp. {30:11} The Amalekites were celebrating and feasting, unaware of David's approach. {30:12} David and his men attacked them from twilight until the evening of the next day, except for four hundred young men who escaped on camels. {30:13} David recovered everything the Amalekites had taken, including his two wives. {30:14} They also retrieved all the spoils taken from Ziklag and the surrounding areas. {30:15} David treated the Egyptian kindly, who had helped them locate the Amalekites. {30:16} Upon returning, David's men who were too exhausted to continue were met with opposition from some of the others who didn't want to share the spoils with them. {30:17} However, David intervened, stating that all should share in the spoils equally, as it was the Lord who had given them victory. {30:18} David recovered everything that was taken, and nothing was missing, whether small or great. {30:19} He also gathered all the livestock that the Amalekites had taken and declared it as his spoil. {30:20} David then distributed portions of the spoils to various cities and places throughout Israel as a gesture of gratitude. {30:21} Upon returning to Ziklag, David sent portions of the spoil to the elders of Judah and to various towns where he and his men had frequented. {30:22} He established a statute that ensured those who fought received equal shares of the spoils, which remained in effect for Israel. {30:23} David's generosity extended to all, regardless of their contribution to the battle, acknowledging that their victory was from the Lord. {30:24} This decree became a lasting ordinance in Israel. {30:25} David's distribution of spoils extended to several cities and regions, including Hebron, where David and his men often resided. { {30:26} When David arrived in Ziklag, he sent a portion of the spoils to the elders of Judah and to his friends, saying, "Here is a gift for you from the spoils of the enemies of the LORD." {30:27} He sent gifts to those in Bethel, south Ramoth, Jattir, {30:28} Aroer, Siphmoth, Eshtemoa, {30:29} Rachal, the cities of the Jerahmeelites, the cities of the Kenites, {30:30} Hormah, Chorashan, Athach, {30:31} Hebron, and to all the places where David and his men used to go.

{31:1} The Philistines fought against Israel, and the Israelite men fled from them and were slain on Mount Gilboa. {31:2} The Philistines pursued Saul and his sons, and they killed Jonathan, Abinadab, and Melchi-shua, Saul's sons. {31:3} Saul was severely wounded by the archers, and the battle turned against him. {31:4} Saul told his armorbearer to kill him with his sword to prevent the Philistines from mistreating him, but the armorbearer was too afraid. So Saul took his own sword and fell on it. {31:5} When the armorbearer saw that Saul was dead, he also killed himself. {31:6} Thus Saul, his three sons, his armorbearer, and all his men died together that day. {31:7} When the Israelites across the valley and on the other side of the Jordan saw that Saul and his sons were dead and that Israel was fleeing, they abandoned their cities, and the Philistines occupied them. {31:8} The next day, the Philistines came to strip the dead bodies and found Saul and his sons on Mount Gilboa. {31:9} They cut off Saul's head, stripped off his armor, and sent messengers throughout the land of the Philistines to spread the news in the temples of their idols and among the people. {31:10} They put Saul's armor in the temple of Ashtaroth and hung his body on the wall of Beth-shan. {31:11} When the people of Jabesh-gilead heard what the Philistines had done to Saul, {31:12} brave men from Jabesh-gilead traveled all night, took the bodies of Saul and his sons from the wall of Beth-shan, and brought them to Jabesh, where they burned them. {31:13} Then they buried their bones under a tree in Jabesh and mourned for seven days.

2 Samuel

{1:1} After Saul died, David returned from defeating the Amalekites and stayed in Ziklag for two days. {1:2} On the third day, a man came from Saul's camp with torn clothes and dirt on his head. When he reached David, he bowed down. {1:3} David asked him where he came from, and he said he had escaped from the Israelite camp. {1:4} David inquired about what happened, and the man told him that the Israelites fled from the battle, and many were killed, including Saul and Jonathan. {1:5} David asked the man how he knew Saul and Jonathan were dead. {1:6} The man explained that he found Saul on Mount Gilboa, wounded and leaning on his spear, with chariots and horsemen pursuing him. {1:7} Saul saw the man and called out to him. The man responded, and Saul asked him to kill him because he was in anguish and wanted to die. {1:8} The man identified himself as an Amalekite, and Saul told him to carry out the deed. So, the man killed Saul and took his crown and bracelet to David. {1:9} David mourned when he heard this and tore his clothes, as did his men. They mourned, wept, and fasted until evening for Saul, Jonathan, and the people of Israel who died in battle. {1:10} David questioned the man further, and he revealed that he was an Amalekite. {1:11} David commanded one of his men to kill the Amalekite, and he did so. {1:12} David held the Amalekite accountable for killing the anointed of the LORD, as he had confessed to it. {1:13} David lamented over Saul and Jonathan with a mournful song. {1:14} He also instructed them to teach the children of Judah the use of the bow, as recorded in the book of Jasher. {1:15} David expressed his sorrow and heartbreak for Saul and Jonathan, acknowledging their strength and unity. {1:16} He wished for the news of their deaths not to spread to the enemies' cities to prevent their rejoicing. {1:17} David cursed Mount Gilboa, where Saul's shield was cast aside and Saul was defeated. {1:18} He praised Jonathan's and Saul's bravery in battle, saying they were like eagles and lions. {1:19} David called upon the daughters of Israel to weep for Saul, who adorned them with scarlet and gold. {1:20} **He lamented the loss of mighty warriors like Saul and Jonathan in battle.** {1:21} David expressed his deep sorrow for Jonathan, whose love was precious to him. {1:22} He mourned the fallen warriors and the loss of their weapons of war. {1:23} Saul and Jonathan were beloved and pleasant in life, and even in death, they were not separated. They were as swift as eagles and strong as lions. {1:24} Daughters of Israel, mourn for Saul, who adorned you with scarlet and gold ornaments. {1:25} How the mighty have fallen in battle! Jonathan, you were slain in your high places. {1:26} I grieve for you, my brother Jonathan. Your love for me was extraordinary, surpassing the love of women. {1:27} How the mighty have fallen, and the weapons of war are destroyed!

{2:1} After this, David asked the LORD, "Should I go up to any of the cities of Judah?" The LORD replied, "Go up." David asked, "Where should I go?" The LORD answered, "To Hebron." {2:2} So David went to Hebron, taking his two wives, Ahinoam and Abigail, with him. {2:3} He also brought his men and their families, and they settled in Hebron. {2:4} The men of Judah came to David and anointed him as king over Judah. They informed David that the men of Jabesh-gilead had buried Saul. {2:5} David sent messengers to the men of Jabesh-gilead, thanking them for their kindness in burying Saul and blessing them in the name of the LORD. {2:6} He prayed for kindness and truth to be shown to them and promised to repay their kindness. {2:7} David encouraged them, saying, "Now be strong and valiant. Your master Saul is dead, and the house of Judah has anointed me as their king." {2:8} However, Abner, Saul's commander, took Ish-bosheth, Saul's son, and made him king over Gilead, Ashur, Jezreel, Ephraim, Benjamin, and all Israel. {2:9} Ish-bosheth was forty years old when he became king and reigned for two years. Meanwhile, the house of Judah followed David. {2:10} David reigned in Hebron over Judah for seven years and six months. {2:11} Abner and Ish-bosheth's servants went from Mahanaim to Gibeon, while Joab and David's servants went out to meet them. {2:12} They met by the pool of Gibeon, and Abner suggested that the young men engage in a contest. {2:13} Twelve men from each side participated, resulting in a fierce battle at the pool of Gibeon. {2:14} Abner proposed the contest, and Joab agreed. Twelve men from each side fought, and they all fell down together. {2:15} This event became known as Helkath-hazzurim, near Gibeon. {2:16} The battle was intense, with Abner and the men of Israel being defeated by David's servants. {2:17} Among those present were Joab, Abishai, and Asahel, who was as swift as a wild roe. {2:18} Asahel pursued Abner relentlessly, refusing to turn aside. {2:19} Abner warned Asahel to stop chasing him, but Asahel persisted. {2:20} When Abner refused to relent, he struck Asahel with the hinder end of his spear, killing him. {2:21} Asahel's pursuers stopped upon reaching the place where he fell and died. {2:22} Joab and Abishai continued to pursue Abner, and as the sun set, they reached the hill of Ammah near Giah. {2:23} Meanwhile, the men of Benjamin gathered behind Abner, forming a single troop on a hilltop. {2:24} Abner called out to Joab, questioning the endless bloodshed. He urged Joab to halt the pursuit. {2:25} Joab then blew a trumpet, and the fighting ceased. Abner and his men traveled through the plain, crossed the Jordan, and arrived at Mahanaim. {2:26} Joab returned, and all David's servants were accounted for except for nineteen men and Asahel. {2:27} However, three hundred and sixty men died from the servants of David and Benjamin in the conflict. {2:28} They buried Asahel in his father's tomb in Bethlehem and returned to Hebron at dawn. {2:29} Abner and his men traveled all night through the plain, crossed the Jordan, and passed through all Bithron until they reached Mahanaim. {2:30} Meanwhile, Joab returned from pursuing Abner. After gathering all the people, he found that nineteen of David's servants and Asahel were missing. {2:31} The servants of David had killed three hundred and sixty men from Benjamin and Abner's forces. {2:32} They buried Asahel in his father's tomb in Bethlehem. Then Joab and his men traveled all night and reached Hebron at dawn.

{3:1} There was a long war between the house of Saul and the house of David. David grew stronger while Saul's house grew weaker. {3:2} In Hebron, David had sons: Amnon, his firstborn from Ahinoam; Chileab from Abigail, the wife of Nabal; Absalom from Maacah, the daughter of Talmai king of Geshur; Adonijah from Haggith; Shephatiah from Abital; and Ithream from Eglah, David's wife. {3:3} This happened during the ongoing war between the house of Saul and the house of David. Abner supported Saul's house. {3:4} Saul had a concubine named Rizpah, daughter of Aiah. Ish-bosheth asked Abner why he had been with her. {3:5} Abner was angered by Ish-bosheth's words and reminded him of his loyalty to Saul's house. He also vowed to fulfill the Lord's promise to David. {3:6} Ish-bosheth could not respond, fearing Abner. {3:7} Abner sent messengers to David, proposing an alliance and offering to bring all of Israel under David's rule. {3:8} David agreed to the alliance but demanded the return of Michal, Saul's daughter. {3:9} David sent messengers to Ish-bosheth, requesting Michal's return. {3:10} Ish-bosheth complied, and Michal was taken from her husband, Phaltiel. {3:11} Abner, accompanied by twenty men, came to David, and a feast was held in their honor. Abner pledged to gather all Israel to support David. {3:12} Abner departed in peace, and David's servants returned with spoils. Abner, however, was not with them as David had sent him away in peace. {3:13} Joab learned of Abner's visit and was upset that David had let him go. {3:14} Joab confronted David about this, accusing Abner of deceit and spying. {3:15} Joab sent messengers after Abner, who brought him back from the well of Sirah, unbeknownst to David. {3:16} Abner returned to Hebron, where Joab killed him in revenge for Asahel's death. {3:17} When David learned of Abner's death, he declared himself innocent of it, placing the blame on Joab and his family. {3:18} David mourned Abner and lamented his death as that of a nobleman. {3:19} David refused to eat until evening as a sign of mourning, and the people respected his decision. {3:20} They understood that David did not order Abner's death, recognizing the loss of a great man in Israel. {3:21} David acknowledged his weakness as king and expressed his inability to control Joab and his brothers' actions. {3:22} David vowed that the Lord would judge those responsible for evil deeds. {3:23} Joab and his men returned to David and reported that Abner had visited him and left in peace. {3:24} Joab confronted David, questioning why he had let Abner go. {3:25} Joab accused Abner of deception and spying on David. {3:26} After Joab left, he sent messengers to bring Abner back, unbeknownst to David. {3:27} When Abner returned, Joab killed him in revenge for the death of his brother Asahel. {3:28} David declared his innocence in Abner's death, placing the blame on Joab and his family. {3:29} David cursed Joab and his descendants for their actions. {3:30} Joab and Abishai killed Abner in retaliation for Asahel's death. {3:31} David mourned Abner's death and followed his bier. {3:32} Abner was buried in Hebron, and David wept at his grave along with the people. {3:33} David questioned if Abner's death was necessary, lamenting his demise. {3:34} David expressed sorrow over Abner's death, noting he wasn't treated as a criminal. {3:35} David vowed not to eat until the sun went down in mourning for Abner. {3:36} The people respected David's vow, and his actions pleased them. {3:37} The people recognized that David didn't order Abner's death. {3:38} David acknowledged Abner's greatness and mourned his loss. {3:39} David admitted his weakness as king and recognized the difficulty of dealing with Joab and his family, leaving justice to the Lord.

{4:1} When Saul's son learned of Abner's death in Hebron, he was weakened, and all the Israelites were troubled. {4:2} Saul's son had two captains named Baanah and Rechab, sons of Rimmon the Beerothite from the tribe of Benjamin. (Beeroth belonged to Benjamin, and the Beerothites had fled to Gittaim and lived there until then.) {4:3} Jonathan, Saul's son, had a son who was lame in both feet. He was five years old when news of Saul and Jonathan's deaths came from Jezreel. His nurse picked him up and fled, but he fell and became lame. His name was Mephibosheth. {4:4} Rechab and Baanah, sons of Rimmon the Beerothite, went to Ish-bosheth's house around noon. Ish-bosheth was lying on his bed at noon. {4:5} Rechab and Baanah entered the house as if to get wheat and struck Ish-bosheth under the fifth rib. They then escaped. {4:6} Ish-bosheth was alone in his bedchamber when they attacked him. They killed him, beheaded him, and fled through the plain all night. {4:7} They brought Ish-bosheth's head to David in Hebron, claiming they had avenged him by killing Saul's enemy. {4:8} Rechab and Baanah brought Ish-bosheth's head to David in Hebron. They claimed they had avenged David by killing his enemy, Saul's son, who had sought David's life. They believed the Lord had brought this vengeance upon Saul and his descendants. {4:9} David responded to Rechab and Baanah, sons of Rimmon the Beerothite, saying, "As the Lord lives, who has delivered me from all troubles, when someone brought me news of Saul's death hoping for a reward, I killed him in Ziklag. Should I not then require justice for the murder of an innocent man in his own house, on his bed?" {4:10} David questioned the morality of killing a righteous person in his own house, emphasizing the severity of their crime. {4:11} David ordered his men to execute Rechab and Baanah, cutting off their hands and feet and hanging them up over the pool in Hebron. {4:12} Ish-bosheth's head was buried in Abner's tomb in Hebron.

{5:1} All the tribes of Israel came to David in Hebron, saying, "We are your own people, your flesh and blood. {5:2} In the past, when Saul was king, you led Israel in and out, and the Lord promised that you would be the shepherd of his people and the ruler of Israel." {5:3} So all the elders of Israel came to David in Hebron, and David made a covenant with them before the Lord, and they anointed David as king over Israel. {5:4} David was thirty years old when he became king, and he reigned for forty years. {5:5} He reigned over Judah for seven years and six months in Hebron, and then he reigned over all Israel and Judah for thirty-three years in Jerusalem. {5:6} **David and his men went to Jerusalem to confront the Jebusites, who inhabited the land. The Jebusites mocked David, saying he couldn't enter unless he removed the blind and lame among them.** {5:7} However, David captured the stronghold of Zion, which became known as the City of David. {5:8} On that day, David declared, "Whoever conquers the Jebusites and reaches the water shaft will be chief and captain." From then on, it was said, "Only the blind and the lame will not enter the house." {5:9} David lived in the fortress and called it the City of David. He built it up from the surrounding area of Millo inward. {5:10} David continued to grow in power, and the Lord God of hosts was with him. {5:11} Hiram, king of Tyre, sent messengers to David along with cedar trees, carpenters, and masons to build a palace for David. {5:12} David realized that the Lord had established him as king over Israel and had exalted his kingdom for the sake of his people Israel. {5:13} David took more concubines and wives from Jerusalem, and he had more sons and daughters. {5:14} The sons born to David in Jerusalem were named Shammuah, Shobab, Nathan, and Solomon. {5:15} He also had Ibhar, Elishua, Nepheg, and Japhia. {5:16} And Elishama, Eliada, and Eliphalet were also born to him. {5:17} When the Philistines heard that David had been anointed king over Israel, they came up to attack him. David heard of it and went down to the stronghold. {5:18} The Philistines also spread themselves in the valley of Rephaim. {5:19} David inquired of the Lord whether he should go up against the Philistines. The Lord assured David of victory, so David attacked them at Baal-perazim and defeated them. {5:20} David acknowledged the Lord's help in battle and called the place Baal-perazim. {5:21} The Philistines abandoned their idols, and David and his men burned them. {5:22} The Philistines regrouped and spread out again in the valley of Rephaim. {5:23} David sought the Lord's guidance again, and this time the Lord instructed him to circle around the Philistines and attack them from behind the mulberry trees. {5:24} When David heard the sound of marching in the tops of the mulberry trees, he knew it was time to attack, for the Lord would go before him to strike down the Philistines. {5:25} David obeyed the Lord's command and defeated the Philistines from Geba to Gazer.

{6:1} David gathered thirty thousand chosen men of Israel. {6:2} He went from Baale of Judah with the people to bring up the ark of God, whose name is called by the name of the LORD of hosts who dwells between the cherubim. {6:3} They placed the ark of God on a new cart and brought it out of the house of Abinadab in Gibeah. Uzzah and Ahio, the sons of Abinadab, drove the cart. {6:4} They brought the ark out of Abinadab's house in Gibeah, with Ahio leading it. {6:5} David and all the house of Israel played music before the LORD on various instruments made of fir wood, including harps, psalteries, timbrels, cornets, and cymbals. {6:6} When they came to Nachon's threshing floor, Uzzah reached out his hand to the ark of God and took hold of it because the oxen stumbled. {6:7} The LORD's anger was kindled against Uzzah, and God struck him there for his error, and he died by the ark of God. {6:8} David was displeased because the LORD had struck Uzzah, so he called the place Perez-uzzah. {6:9} David feared the LORD that day and questioned how the ark of the LORD could come to him. {6:10} David decided not to bring the ark of the LORD to the City of David but diverted it to the house of Obed-edom the Gittite. {6:11} The ark remained in the house of Obed-edom for three months, and the LORD blessed Obed-edom and his household. {6:12} When David heard that the LORD had blessed Obed-edom's house because of the ark of God, he brought the ark with gladness to the City of David. {6:13} Every six paces, those carrying the ark of the LORD sacrificed oxen and fatlings. {6:14} David danced before the LORD with all his might, wearing a linen ephod. {6:15} David and all the house of Israel brought up the ark of the LORD with shouting and the sound of the trumpet. {6:16} As the ark of the LORD entered the City of David, Michal, Saul's daughter, looked through a window and saw David leaping and dancing before the LORD, and she despised him in her heart. {6:17} They placed the ark of the LORD in its place in the tabernacle David had pitched for it, and David offered burnt offerings and peace offerings before the LORD. {6:18} After offering the sacrifices, David blessed the people in the name of the LORD of hosts. {6:19} He distributed bread, meat, and wine to all the people, both men and women, and everyone went home. {6:20} David returned to bless his household, but Michal came out to meet him and criticized him for his behavior before the servants. {6:21} David defended himself, saying he was playing before the LORD, who had chosen him over her father and his house to rule over Israel. {6:22} David vowed to be even more undignified in his worship and to honor the LORD, regardless of Michal's opinion. {6:23} Michal, daughter of Saul, remained childless until her death.

{7:1} King David, enjoying rest from his enemies, spoke to Nathan the prophet, saying that while he lived in a house of cedar, the ark of God remained within curtains. {7:2} Nathan encouraged David to do as his heart desired, for the LORD was with him. {7:3} However, that night, the LORD spoke to Nathan, instructing him to tell David that God didn't require a house, as He had dwelt in a tent since bringing Israel out of Egypt. {7:4} God hadn't asked any of the tribes of Israel to build Him a house of cedar. {7:5} Instead, God reminded David of his humble origins, choosing him from tending sheep to rule over Israel, defeating his enemies, and making his name great. {7:6} God promised to appoint a place for Israel to dwell securely, free from oppression, and to establish David's lineage forever. {7:7} Although David wouldn't build the house, his descendant would, and God would establish his kingdom. {7:8} God assured David that his descendant would build a house for His name, and God would establish his kingdom forever. {7:9} God promised to be a father to David's descendant, who would be His son. If he sinned, God would discipline him, but His mercy would remain. {7:10} David's house and kingdom would be established forever, and his throne would endure. {7:11} Nathan relayed these words and vision to David. {7:12} David humbly acknowledged God's greatness and wondered why God had chosen him. {7:13} David marveled at God's promise to establish his house and kingdom forever. {7:14} He praised God's greatness and acknowledged His uniqueness. {7:15} David recognized God's faithfulness to Israel and His covenant with David's house. {7:16} **He prayed for God's continued blessings on his household.** {7:17} David praised God's revelations and promised to pray according to God's word. {7:18} He acknowledged God's faithfulness and prayed for the fulfillment of His promises. {7:19} David marveled at God's goodness toward him and his descendants. {7:20} He recognized God's knowledge of his heart and acknowledged His greatness. {7:21} David thanked God for His word and His deeds, which revealed His greatness. {7:22} He praised God as the God over Israel, unmatched by any other. {7:23} David marveled at God's redemption of Israel and His mighty acts on their behalf. {7:24} He acknowledged Israel as God's chosen people and praised Him as their God. {7:25} David prayed for the fulfillment of God's promises concerning his house and asked for His name to be magnified forever. {7:26} He prayed for God's blessing on the house of David. {7:27} David acknowledged God's promise to build Him a house and prayed in response to this revelation. {7:28} He affirmed God's truthfulness and thanked Him for His promises. {7:29} David prayed for God's blessing on his house, knowing that God had spoken it and desired His blessing to continue forever.

{8:1} Afterward, David defeated the Philistines and took control of Methegammah from them. {8:2} He also conquered Moab, measuring them with a line to determine who would be put to death and who would be spared. The Moabites then became David's servants, offering gifts. {8:3} David further defeated Hadadezer, king of Zobah, as he sought to reclaim territory along the Euphrates River. {8:4} From Hadadezer, David captured a thousand chariots, seven hundred horsemen, and twenty thousand foot soldiers. He disabled the chariot horses but kept enough for a hundred chariots. {8:5} When the Syrians of Damascus came to help Hadadezer, David struck down twenty-two thousand of them. {8:6} David established garrisons in Damascus, and the Syrians became his servants, offering gifts. The LORD protected David wherever he went. {8:7} David took the golden shields from Hadadezer's servants and brought them to Jerusalem. {8:8} He also seized a large amount of bronze from Betah and Berothai, cities of Hadadezer. {8:9} Upon hearing of David's victory over Hadadezer, King Toi of Hamath sent his son Joram to congratulate and bless David. {8:10} Joram brought with him silver, gold, and bronze vessels, which David dedicated to the LORD along with the spoils from his conquests. {8:11} These included treasures from Syria, Moab, Ammon, the Philistines, Amalek, and the spoil of Hadadezer. {8:12} David gained renown after defeating the Syrians in the Valley of Salt, killing eighteen thousand men. {8:13} He stationed garrisons throughout Edom, and the Edomites became David's servants. The LORD protected David wherever he went. {8:14} David ruled over all Israel, ensuring justice and equity for his people. {8:15} Joab, son of Zeruiah, commanded the army; Jehoshaphat, son of Ahilud, served as recorder. {8:16} Zadok, son of Ahitub, and Ahimelech, son of Abiathar, were the priests, while Seraiah was the scribe. {8:17} Benaiah, son of Jehoiada, oversaw the Cherethites and Pelethites, {8:18} and David's sons held positions of authority.

{9:1} David asked, "Is there anyone left from the house of Saul to whom I can show kindness for the sake of Jonathan?" {9:2} A servant named Ziba from the house of Saul was summoned before David. The king inquired, "Are you Ziba?" And he replied, "Yes, I am your servant." {9:3} David inquired further, "Is there anyone left from the house of Saul to whom I can show God's kindness?" Ziba informed the king, "Jonathan has a son who is lame in his feet." {9:4} David asked, "Where is he?" Ziba replied, "He is in the house of Machir son of Ammiel, in Lo-debar." {9:5} King David sent for him from the house of Machir in Lo-debar. {9:6} When Mephibosheth, the son of Jonathan and grandson of Saul, came to David, he prostrated himself before him. David addressed him, saying, "Mephibosheth." And he responded, "Here is your servant." {9:7} David reassured him, "Do not be afraid. For the sake of Jonathan your father, I will show you kindness and restore all the land that belonged to Saul your father. You will eat at my table always." {9:8} Mephibosheth humbly replied, "Who am I, a dead dog, that you should show such kindness to me?" {9:9} David then summoned Ziba, Saul's servant, and informed him, "I have given your master's grandson everything that belonged to Saul and his household. {9:10} You and your sons and servants will work the land for him and bring in the produce, providing food for him. But Mephibosheth, your master's grandson, will always eat at my table." Ziba had fifteen sons and twenty servants. {9:11} Ziba agreed to carry out the king's command regarding Mephibosheth, who would dine at the king's table like one of his sons. {9:12} Mephibosheth had a young son named Micha, and all those in Ziba's household served Mephibosheth. {9:13} So Mephibosheth lived in Jerusalem, always dining at the king's table, though he was lame in both feet.

{10:1} After this, the king of the Ammonites died, and his son Hanun became king. David decided to show kindness to Hanun for the sake of his father, Nahash. So, David sent his servants to comfort Hanun concerning his father. {10:2} However, the Ammonite princes suspected David's motives and said to Hanun, "Do you really believe that David is honoring your father by sending these comforters? {10:3} Isn't he sending them to spy on us and overthrow the city?" {10:4} Hanun believed their words and treated David's servants disrespectfully. He shaved off half of their beards and cut their garments, sending them away in shame. {10:5} When David learned of this, he instructed the men to stay in Jericho until their beards grew back. {10:6} The Ammonites, realizing they had offended David, sought help from the Syrians of Beth-rehob, Zoba, and other regions, hiring twenty thousand foot soldiers, a thousand men from Maacah, and twelve thousand men from Ish-tob. {10:7} Upon hearing this, David sent Joab and his mighty men to confront them. {10:8} The Ammonites positioned themselves at the city gate, while the Syrians were in the open field. {10:9} Joab, seeing that they were surrounded, divided his troops, placing the best soldiers against the Syrians and entrusting the rest to his brother Abishai to face the Ammonites. {10:10} He encouraged Abishai, saying, "Let's fight bravely for our people and our cities. May the LORD do what is right." {10:11} Joab instructed Abishai that if the Syrians proved too strong for him, Abishai should come to his aid. Similarly, if the Ammonites were too strong for Abishai, Joab would assist him. {10:12} Joab encouraged Abishai to be courageous and fight valiantly for their people and cities, trusting that the LORD would determine the outcome. {10:13} Abishai and his troops approached the Syrians in battle, and the Syrians fled before them. {10:14} Witnessing the Syrians' retreat, the Ammonites also fled before Abishai and took refuge in their city. Thus, Joab concluded his campaign against the Ammonites and returned to Jerusalem. {10:15} Seeing their defeat at the hands of Israel, the Syrians regrouped and prepared for further confrontation. {10:16} They gathered at Helam, with Shobach leading them. {10:17} David, upon hearing this, assembled all of Israel and crossed the Jordan to meet the Syrians in battle. {10:18} The Syrians were defeated, with David's forces killing seven hundred charioteers and forty thousand horsemen. Shobach, their commander, was also killed. {10:19} Witnessing the defeat of their allies, other kings who served Hadarezer made peace with Israel, no longer willing to aid the Ammonites.

{11:1} After the year passed, the time when kings typically went to battle arrived. David sent Joab and his servants, along with all of Israel, to destroy the children of Ammon and besiege Rabbah. But David stayed in Jerusalem. {11:2} One evening, David got up from his bed and walked on the roof of the king's house. From there, he saw a woman bathing, and she was very beautiful. {11:3} David inquired about the woman and learned she was Bath-sheba, the wife of Uriah the Hittite. {11:4} David sent messengers, took Bath-sheba, and slept with her because she had purified herself from her uncleanness. Then she returned to her house. {11:5} Bath-sheba became pregnant and informed David. {11:6} David sent for Uriah the Hittite through Joab. {11:7} When Uriah arrived, David asked about Joab, the people, and the progress of the war. {11:8} David instructed Uriah to go home and wash his feet. Uriah left, and the king sent food after him. {11:9} However, Uriah slept at the door of the king's house with all the servants and didn't go to his house. {11:10} When David learned that Uriah didn't go home, he asked him why he hadn't. {11:11} Uriah explained that it wouldn't be right for him to enjoy the comforts of home while his fellow soldiers were still in tents and open fields. {11:12} David asked Uriah to stay another day, but Uriah remained in Jerusalem. {11:13} David made Uriah drunk, but still, he didn't go home. {11:14} In the morning, David wrote a letter to Joab and sent it with Uriah. {11:15} The letter instructed Joab to put Uriah in a dangerous battle position and then retreat, so Uriah would be killed. {11:16} Joab followed David's orders and put Uriah in a place where the fighting was fierce. {11:17} Uriah died in the battle, along with other soldiers. {11:18} Joab sent a messenger to inform David about the war. {11:19} He instructed the messenger to anticipate David's anger and to explain that Uriah had died. {11:20} The messenger recounted the battle to David, including Uriah's death. {11:21} David encouraged Joab to fight fiercely, not dwelling on Uriah's death. {11:22} The messenger reported to David as instructed. {11:23} He explained how the battle unfolded and Uriah's death. {11:24} David accepted the news, advising Joab to continue the battle. {11:25} David reassured Joab that casualties happen in war and encouraged him to keep fighting. {11:26} Bath-sheba mourned Uriah's death. {11:27} After her mourning period, David took Bath-sheba as his wife, and she bore him a son. But what David did displeased the LORD.

{12:1} The LORD sent Nathan to David. Nathan came and told him a story: In a city, there were two men—one rich and the other poor. {12:2} The rich man owned many flocks and herds. {12:3} The poor man had only one little ewe lamb, which he bought and cared for. It grew up with him and his children, eating from his plate, drinking from his cup, and even sleeping in his arms. It was like a daughter to him. {12:4} A traveler came to the rich man, but instead of taking an animal from his own flock to feed the guest, he took the poor man's lamb and prepared it for the visitor. {12:5} David became furious and said to Nathan, "As the LORD lives, the man who did this deserves to die! He should pay back four times the value because he showed no pity." {12:6} Nathan said to David, "You are that man! This is what the LORD, the God of Israel, says: I anointed you king over Israel and rescued you from Saul. {12:7} I gave you your master's house and wives. I gave you the kingdoms of Israel and Judah. And if all this had been too little, I would have given you even more. {12:8} Why then have you despised the LORD's command by doing evil in his sight? You have killed Uriah the Hittite with the sword and taken his wife as your own. You have murdered him with the Ammonites' sword. {12:9} Now, because of what you've done, the sword will never leave your house. You have despised me by taking Uriah's wife to be your own. {12:10} This is what the LORD says: 'I will cause trouble for you from within your own family. I will take your wives and give them to another man, and he will lie with them openly in broad daylight. {12:11} You did it secretly, but I will do this openly in the sight of all Israel and the sun.' {12:12} David confessed to Nathan, "I have sinned against the LORD." Nathan replied, "The LORD has forgiven your sin. You will not die. {12:13} However, because of what you've done, you've given the enemies of the LORD an opportunity to blaspheme. {12:14} The child born to you will die." {12:15} Nathan left, and the LORD made the child Bath-sheba bore to David very sick. {12:16} David pleaded with God for the child's life. He fasted, lay on the ground all night, and prayed. {12:17} David's servants tried to lift him from the ground, but he refused to get up or eat with them. {12:18} On the seventh day, the child died. David's servants were afraid to tell him because of his grief. {12:19} But when David saw them whispering, he realized the child had died. He asked, "Is the child dead?" They replied, "Yes, he is." {12:20} David got up, washed, changed his clothes, went to worship in the house of the LORD, then returned home to eat. {12:21} His servants questioned him about his behavior. They observed how he fasted and wept while the child was alive but then ate when the child died. {12:22} David explained, "While the child was alive, I hoped God would show mercy and spare him.{12:23} But now that he's dead, why should I fast? Can I bring him back? No, but I will go to him one day." {12:24} David comforted Bath-sheba, and they had another son, whom he named Solomon. The LORD loved him. {12:25} Nathan the prophet, sent by David, called the child Jedidiah because of the LORD. {12:26} Meanwhile, Joab fought against Rabbah of the Ammonites and captured the royal city. {12:27} He sent messengers to David, saying, "I have taken Rabbah and its water supply. {12:28} Now gather the rest of the troops, besiege the city, and capture it. Otherwise, I will take the credit for it." {12:29} David assembled the army, went to Rabbah, fought, and took the city. {12:30} He removed the king's crown, weighing a talent of gold with precious stones, and placed it on his own head. The plunder from the city was extensive. {12:31} David brought the people out and put them to work with saws, iron picks, and axes. He made them work at brick-making. He did this to all the Ammonite cities. Then he and his army returned to Jerusalem.

{13:1} After this, Absalom, King David's son, had a beautiful sister named Tamar. Amnon, another son of David, loved her deeply. {13:2} Amnon became so obsessed with Tamar that he made himself sick over her. She was still a virgin, and he felt it was impossible to have her. {13:3} Amnon had a friend named Jonadab, who was very clever. Jonadab asked Amnon why he looked so miserable, and Amnon confessed his love for Tamar. {13:4} Jonadab suggested a plan to Amnon. He told him to pretend to be sick and ask for Tamar to come and cook for him in front of their father. {13:5} Amnon followed Jonadab's advice. When King David visited him, Amnon asked if Tamar could come and prepare food for him. {13:6} David agreed and sent Tamar to Amnon's house. She baked cakes for him, but he refused to eat. {13:7} Amnon then asked everyone to leave the room, so he could be alone with Tamar. {13:8} He told Tamar to bring the food into his chamber so he could eat it from her hand. {13:9} Tamar obeyed and brought the cakes to Amnon, but instead of eating, he grabbed her and demanded that she lie with him. {13:10} Tamar pleaded with him not to force her, reminding him of the disgrace it would bring upon both of them. {13:11} Despite her pleas, Amnon overpowered her and raped her. {13:12} Afterward, he felt intense hatred towards Tamar and ordered her to leave. {13:13} Tamar begged him not to send her away, but he refused to listen. {13:14} Then he had his servant throw her out and bolt the door behind her. {13:15} Tamar, devastated, put ashes on her head, tore her colorful robe, and cried bitterly. {13:16} Absalom, Tamar's brother, comforted her and advised her to keep silent about what happened. {13:17} When King David learned of the incident, he was furious. {13:18} Absalom, meanwhile, harbored hatred towards Amnon for violating his sister. {13:19} Two years later, Absalom hosted a sheepshearing feast and invited all of David's sons. {13:20} Absalom asked the king to allow his sons to attend the feast, but David was hesitant. {13:21} Absalom persisted until David agreed, and he specifically requested that Amnon also join them. {13:22} Absalom then instructed his servants to wait for the opportune moment and kill Amnon. {13:23} During the feast, the servants carried out Absalom's command and murdered Amnon. {13:24} News of Amnon's death reached David, who was devastated. {13:25} However, Jonadab assured David that only Amnon had been killed, not all of his sons. {13:26} Absalom fled to Geshur to escape the consequences of his actions. {13:27} David mourned for Amnon every day, longing to be reunited with Absalom. {13:28} Absalom instructed his servants to wait for the right moment when Amnon was drunk, then kill him without fear, as Absalom had commanded. The servants obeyed, and all of the king's sons fled on their mules. {13:29} While they were on the way, news reached David that Absalom had killed all of his sons. David tore his clothes and lay on the ground, while his servants also mourned. {13:30} But Jonadab reassured David that only Amnon had been killed, not all of his sons. He reminded David that Absalom had planned this revenge since the day Amnon had raped Tamar. {13:31} So David should not grieve as if all his sons were dead, but only for Amnon. {13:32} Absalom fled, and a lookout spotted a large group of people approaching. {13:33} Jonadab informed David that the king's sons were returning, confirming his earlier words. {13:34} When David's sons arrived, they wept bitterly, and David and his servants joined them in mourning. {13:35} Absalom fled to Geshur and stayed there for three years, while David mourned for him every day. {13:36} David's heart longed to be reunited with Absalom, finding some comfort in the fact that Amnon was dead. {13:37} Absalom fled to Talmai, the son of Ammihud, king of Geshur. David mourned for his son every day. {13:38} He stayed in Geshur for three years. {13:39} David's heart longed to be with Absalom, finding some comfort in the fact that Amnon was dead.

{14:1} Joab, son of Zeruiah, noticed that the king's heart leaned toward Absalom. {14:2} So Joab sent for a wise woman from Tekoah and instructed her to pretend to be a mourning widow. {14:3} He told her to go to the king and speak as he directed. {14:4} When the woman of Tekoah spoke to the king, she bowed before him and pleaded for help. {14:5} The king asked her what was troubling her, and she told him a story of how her two sons fought, resulting in one's death. {14:6} She explained that now the family wanted to kill her only surviving son, leaving her with no descendants. {14:7} The king assured her he would take action to protect her. {14:8} She expressed her gratitude, and the king promised to ensure her safety. {14:9} She then urged the king to remember God's mercy and prevent further bloodshed. {14:10} The king vowed to protect her son, swearing by the Lord's name. {14:11} She continued, pleading with the king to bring back the banished, as God finds ways to reconcile. {14:12} The king agreed to hear her request. {14:13} She questioned why the king had not brought back his banished son, suggesting it was a fault. {14:14} She reminded him of life's fragility and God's mercy. {14:15} The woman explained that fear compelled her to speak to the king, hoping he would grant her plea. {14:16} She believed the king would deliver her and her son from destruction. {14:17} She praised the king's discernment, likening him to an angel of God. {14:18} The king asked her to tell him the truth, suspecting Joab's involvement. {14:19} She confirmed Joab's role and praised the king's wisdom. {14:20} The king then commanded Joab to bring Absalom back. {14:21} Joab thanked the king and went to Geshur to retrieve Absalom. {14:22} When Absalom returned, the king allowed him to go home but refused to see him. {14:23} Absalom dwelled in Jerusalem for two years without seeing the king. {14:24} He tried to summon Joab, who refused to come, so Absalom set Joab's field on fire. {14:25} Joab confronted Absalom about the fire, and Absalom pleaded to see the king's face. {14:26} Joab informed the king, who then welcomed Absalom back with a kiss. { {14:27} Absalom had three sons and one daughter named Tamar, who was exceptionally beautiful. {14:28} Absalom lived in Jerusalem for two years without seeing the king's face. {14:29} He tried to summon Joab to arrange a meeting with the king, but Joab refused to come, even after a second request. {14:30} Frustrated, Absalom ordered his servants to set Joab's barley field on fire since it was near his own. {14:31} When Joab confronted Absalom about the fire, Absalom explained that he wanted Joab to come to him so he could ask why he had been brought back from Geshur. {14:32} Absalom expressed his desire to see the king's face and offered to face any punishment if he had done wrong. {14:33} Joab relayed Absalom's message to the king, and when Absalom came before him, the king kissed him.

{15:1} *Absalom gathered chariots, horses, and fifty men to run before him.* {15:2} *Early in the morning, Absalom positioned himself by the gate and addressed those seeking judgment from the king, offering himself as a solution.* {15:3} He convinced them that their cases were valid but lamented the lack of someone appointed by the king to hear them. {15:4} Expressing a desire to be a judge, Absalom promised justice to anyone who came to him. {15:5} When people approached him, Absalom greeted them warmly, taking their hands and kissing them. {15:6} Absalom won over the hearts of the Israelites with his approach, gradually gaining their support. {15:7} After forty years, Absalom asked the king's permission to fulfill a vow he made in Hebron. {15:8} He claimed to have vowed to serve the Lord if he returned safely to Jerusalem from Geshur in Syria. {15:9} King David granted him permission, and Absalom went to Hebron. {15:10} Meanwhile, Absalom secretly sent messengers throughout Israel to announce his reign in Hebron upon hearing a trumpet. {15:11} He also enlisted two hundred men from Jerusalem to join him, unaware of his true intentions. {15:12} Absalom sought the advice of Ahithophel, David's counselor, strengthening his conspiracy against David. {15:13} A messenger informed David that the hearts of the Israelites were with Absalom. {15:14} David decided to flee Jerusalem with his servants to avoid Absalom's wrath and protect the city. {15:15} His servants agreed to follow his command. {15:16} David departed, leaving ten concubines to look after the house, and headed to a distant place. {15:17} All his followers, including six hundred Gittites, accompanied him. {15:18} Along the way, David advised Ittai the Gittite to return to Jerusalem, but Ittai insisted on staying by his side. {15:19} David allowed Ittai and his men to join them. {15:20} As they journeyed, David expressed gratitude for Ittai's loyalty but suggested he return to Jerusalem. {15:21} Ittai pledged allegiance to David, promising to remain with him, whether in life or death. {15:22} David permitted Ittai and his men to continue with him. {15:23} The people wept as they crossed the Kidron Valley, and David ascended the Mount of Olives barefoot, lamenting his situation. {15:24} Zadok and the Levites carried the ark of God out of Jerusalem, but David instructed them to return it if he found favor with the Lord. {15:25} David entrusted Zadok with the ark and advised him to return to the city with his sons. {15:26} He resigned himself to God's will, accepting whatever outcome awaited him. {15:27} David urged Zadok, a seer, to return to the city in peace with his sons. {15:28} He decided to wait for news from Zadok in the wilderness. {15:29} Zadok and Abiathar returned to Jerusalem with the ark and stayed there. {15:30} Meanwhile, David continued his journey, mourning and weeping as he went. {15:31} When David learned that Ahithophel had joined Absalom's conspiracy, he prayed for God to thwart Ahithophel's counsel. {15:32} As David reached the summit, Hushai the Archite approached him with torn clothes and earth on his head. {15:33} David advised Hushai to return to the city, pretending to serve Absalom and counteracting Ahithophel's advice. {15:34} He instructed Hushai to relay information to Zadok and Abiathar and to act as his spy. {15:35} David reminded Hushai of the priests' sons in Jerusalem and instructed him to communicate with them. {15:36} He emphasized the importance of Zadok and Abiathar's sons in gathering information for him. {15:37} Hushai entered Jerusalem, and Absalom arrived shortly after.

{16:1} As David continued on his way, Ziba, the servant of Mephibosheth, met him with two saddled donkeys carrying provisions: two hundred loaves of bread, a hundred bunches of raisins, a hundred clusters of summer fruit, and a bottle of wine. {16:2} David asked Ziba about the purpose of these provisions, and Ziba explained that they were for the king's household and for those who needed sustenance in the wilderness. {16:3} David inquired about Mephibosheth, and Ziba claimed that Mephibosheth remained in Jerusalem, hoping that the house of Israel would restore him as king. {16:4} David then granted all that belonged to Mephibosheth to Ziba, who humbly asked for grace in the king's sight. {16:5} While passing through Bahurim, a man named Shimei, a member of Saul's family, came out and cursed David continuously, throwing stones at him and his servants. {16:6} Shimei accused David of shedding the blood of Saul's house and claimed that the kingdom had been given to Absalom because of David's actions. {16:7} Abishai, son of Zeruiah, proposed to kill Shimei for cursing the king, but David refused, acknowledging that the Lord had allowed Shimei to curse him. {16:8} David reasoned that perhaps the Lord would repay him with good for enduring Shimei's cursing. {16:9} As David and his men continued, Shimei followed along the hillside, continuing to curse and throw stones at them. {16:10} David and his people arrived in Jerusalem, while Absalom and the men of Israel also reached the city along with Ahithophel. {16:11} Upon Hushai's arrival to Absalom, he greeted him with expressions of loyalty to the king. {16:12} Absalom questioned Hushai's loyalty, wondering why he did not accompany David. {16:13} Hushai assured Absalom of his allegiance, stating that he would serve whomever the Lord and the people of Israel chose. {16:14} Absalom sought counsel from Ahithophel, who advised him to publicly take possession of his father's concubines, which would demonstrate his dominance over David. {16:15} Following Ahithophel's counsel, Absalom set up a tent on the roof of the palace and went in to his father's concubines in the sight of all Israel. {16:16} Ahithophel's counsel was highly regarded, as if seeking advice from God Himself, both by David

and Absalom. {16:17} Absalom questioned Hushai about his loyalty, asking why he did not side with David. {16:18} Hushai replied that he would align himself with whomever the Lord, the people, and all of Israel chose, pledging his allegiance to them. {16:19} He emphasized his commitment to serving the chosen leader, whether it be David or his son Absalom, just as he had served David's father faithfully. {16:20} Absalom then turned to Ahithophel for advice on their next course of action. {16:21} Ahithophel advised Absalom to publicly take possession of his father's concubines, which would demonstrate his authority and strengthen his support among the people. {16:22} Following Ahithophel's counsel, Absalom set up a tent on the roof of the palace and went in to his father's concubines in the sight of all Israel. {16:23} Ahithophel's counsel was highly esteemed, as if seeking guidance directly from God Himself, both by David and Absalom.

{17:1} Ahithophel proposed to Absalom to gather twelve thousand men and pursue David immediately. {17:2} He planned to attack David while he was tired and weak, causing fear among his followers, with the intention of striking down only the king. {17:3} Ahithophel assured Absalom that if they succeeded, all the people would return to him, and there would be peace. {17:4} Absalom and the elders of Israel agreed with Ahithophel's proposal. {17:5} Absalom then called for Hushai the Archite to hear his advice as well. {17:6} When Hushai arrived, Absalom asked for his opinion on Ahithophel's plan. {17:7} Hushai advised Absalom against following Ahithophel's counsel, stating it wasn't suitable for the current situation. {17:8} He reminded Absalom of David's strength and the loyalty of his men, likening them to a fierce bear robbed of her cubs. {17:9} Hushai suggested that David might be hiding, and if some of Absalom's men were defeated initially, rumors of a massacre would spread fear among his supporters. {17:10} He warned that even the bravest warriors would be disheartened, knowing David's reputation for strength. {17:11} Hushai recommended gathering all of Israel's forces, leading them personally into battle. {17:12} He proposed a swift and decisive attack to eliminate David and his followers completely. {17:13} If David sought refuge in a city, Hushai suggested besieging it until not a single stone remained. {17:14} Absalom and the elders favored Hushai's counsel over Ahithophel's, unaware that the Lord had orchestrated this to bring disaster upon Absalom. {17:15} Hushai informed Zadok and Abiathar of Ahithophel's and his own advice and instructed them to relay this information to David immediately. {17:16} Zadok and Abiathar's sons, Jonathan and Ahimaaz, stayed hidden while a woman informed them of Absalom's plans, which they then conveyed to David. {17:17} They avoided detection and quickly warned David to cross over the Jordan River that night to escape Absalom's threat. {17:18} Although a young man saw them, they managed to evade capture and find refuge in Bahurim. {17:19} A woman concealed them in her well, and when Absalom's servants inquired about them, she deceived them. {17:20} Unable to find Jonathan and Ahimaaz, Absalom's servants returned to Jerusalem. {17:21} After their departure, Jonathan and Ahimaaz emerged from the well and informed David of the danger, prompting him to quickly cross the water. {17:22} David and his people crossed the Jordan safely before morning. {17:23} When Ahithophel realized his counsel was disregarded, he returned home, put his affairs in order, and committed suicide. {17:24} David arrived at Mahanaim, while Absalom and the Israelites crossed the Jordan. {17:25} Absalom appointed Amasa as commander in place of Joab. {17:26} They camped in the land of Gilead. {17:27} When David arrived at Mahanaim, Shobi, the son of Nahash from Rabbah of the Ammonites, Machir, the son of Ammiel from Lodebar, and Barzillai the Gileadite from Rogelim, {17:28} brought supplies including beds, basins, earthen vessels, wheat, barley, flour, parched corn, beans, lentils, parched pulse, honey, butter, sheep, and cheese for David and his people to eat. They recognized the hunger, weariness, and thirst of the people in the wilderness. {17:29} They provided these provisions to alleviate the needs of David and his followers.

{18:1} David counted the people with him and appointed captains of thousands and hundreds over them. {18:2} He divided the people into three parts, one under Joab, one under Abishai (Joab's brother), and one under Ittai the Gittite. David declared his intention to go with them, but the people insisted he remain in the city to provide support if needed. {18:3} Recognizing David's value, they urged him to stay behind for their safety. {18:4} David agreed and stationed himself by the city gate as the people marched out in groups. {18:5} Before they departed, David instructed Joab and Abishai to deal gently with Absalom, which was heard by all the captains. {18:6} The people went out to battle against Israel, and the conflict occurred in the forest of Ephraim. {18:7} The Israelites were defeated by David's servants, resulting in a significant loss of twenty thousand men. {18:8} The battle spread across the countryside, and more casualties were caused by the forest than by the sword. {18:9} During the fighting, Absalom encountered David's servants.

His mule passed under a large oak tree, and Absalom's head became caught in the branches while the mule ran off. {18:10} A witness reported this to Joab, who questioned why the witness hadn't killed Absalom. {18:11} However, the witness explained he couldn't disobey David's command to spare Absalom. {18:12} Joab refused to delay further, took three darts, and thrust them through Absalom's heart while he was still alive in the oak tree. {18:13} Ten young men then struck and killed Absalom. {18:14} Joab sounded the trumpet, signaling the end of the pursuit. Absalom's body was cast into a pit in the forest, covered with a heap of stones, and all Israel dispersed to their tents. {18:15} Ten young men who were carrying Joab's armor surrounded Absalom and struck him down, killing him. {18:16} Joab then blew the trumpet, signaling the end of the pursuit against Israel, as he restrained the people. {18:17} **They took Absalom and threw him into a large pit in the forest, covering him with a great heap of stones. All Israel scattered, each to their own tent.** {18:18} Absalom had erected a pillar for himself in his lifetime, which stands in the King's Valley, as he had no son to carry on his name. He named the pillar after himself, and it is known as Absalom's monument to this day. {18:19} Ahimaaz, son of Zadok, expressed his desire to inform David of the victory, but Joab instructed him to wait. {18:20} Instead, Joab sent Cushi to inform David of Absalom's death, as it would not be suitable for Ahimaaz to deliver such news. {18:21} However, Ahimaaz insisted on running after Cushi. {18:22} Though Joab questioned Ahimaaz's readiness, he allowed him to go. {18:23} Ahimaaz outran Cushi and arrived first, informing the gatekeepers who then reported to David. {18:24} Seeing another runner, the watchman notified the king of the approaching messengers. {18:25} As the runners drew near, the king anticipated the news they carried. {18:26} Observing another runner, the watchman informed the king that Ahimaaz was likely among them, as he was known for his speed. {18:27} David acknowledged Ahimaaz as a bearer of good tidings. {18:28} Ahimaaz reached David and reassured him that all was well, falling before the king in gratitude for the victory. {18:29} David inquired about Absalom, but Ahimaaz avoided a direct answer, not having witnessed Absalom's death himself. {18:30} David instructed Ahimaaz to stand aside, and he waited. {18:31} When Cushi arrived, he conveyed the news of victory, prompting David to inquire again about Absalom. {18:32} Cushi confirmed Absalom's fate, likening David's enemies to him. {18:33} David was deeply moved, grieving for his son Absalom, expressing his wish that he could have died in Absalom's place.

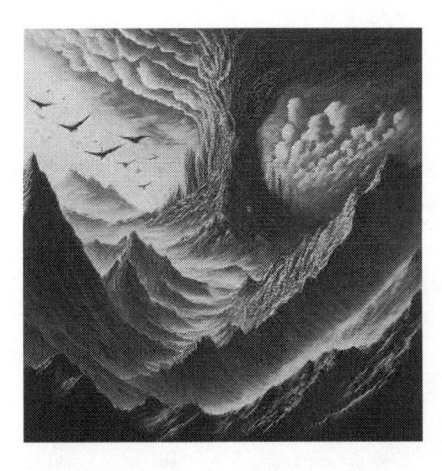

{19:1} It was reported to Joab, "Behold, the king is weeping and mourning for Absalom." {19:2} The victory of that day turned into mourning for all the people when they heard how deeply the king grieved for his son. {19:3} The people slipped into the city that day as if they were ashamed, sneaking away like defeated soldiers in battle. {19:4} **The king covered his face and cried out loudly, "O my son Absalom, O my son, my son!"** {19:5} Joab entered the king's house and said, "Today you have shamed the faces of all your servants who saved your life, the lives of your sons and daughters, and the lives of your wives and concubines. {19:6} You have shown that you love your enemies and hate your friends. You have declared today that princes and servants mean nothing to you. For I see now that if Absalom were alive and we all were dead, it would have pleased you. {19:7} Now therefore, arise, go forth, and speak kindly to your servants. For I swear by the LORD, if you do not go out, not a single person will remain with you this night, and that will be worse for you than all the evils that have befallen you from your youth until now." {19:8} So the king arose and sat in the gate, and all the people were informed, "Behold, the king is sitting in the gate." And all the people came before the king, for Israel had fled, each to their own tent. {19:9} All the people were in dispute throughout the tribes of Israel, saying, "The king saved us from our enemies' hands and delivered us from the Philistines, but now he has fled the land because of Absalom. {19:10} And Absalom, whom we anointed over us, is dead in battle. Now, why aren't you saying anything about bringing the king back?" {19:11} King David sent word to Zadok and Abiathar the priests, saying, "Speak to the elders of Judah, asking them, 'Why are you the last to bring the king back to his house, especially when all Israel's words have reached the king's ears? {19:12} You are my relatives, my own flesh and blood. So why should you be the last to bring back the king?' {19:13} And tell Amasa, 'Are you not my own flesh and blood? May God deal with me, be it ever so severely, if you are not the commander of my army for life in place of Joab.' {19:14} So he won over the hearts of all the men of Judah as though they were one man, and they sent word to the king, 'Return, you and all your servants.' {19:15} Then the king returned and came to the Jordan. And Judah came to Gilgal, to go out to meet the king and to bring the king across the Jordan. {19:16} Shimei, the son of Gera, a Benjaminite from Bahurim, hurried and came down with the men of Judah to meet King David. {19:17} A thousand men from Benjamin were with him, along with Ziba, the servant of the house of Saul, and his fifteen sons and twenty servants. They rushed to the Jordan ahead of the king. {19:18} A ferryboat was there to carry the king's household across, doing whatever was needed. When Shimei, the son of Gera, crossed the Jordan, he fell prostrate before the king {19:19} and said to him, "Let not my lord hold me guilty, and do not remember the wrong your servant did on the day my lord the king left Jerusalem. May the king not take it to heart. {19:20} For your servant knows that I have sinned. Therefore, I have come today as the first of all the house of Joseph to go down to meet my lord the king." {19:21} But Abishai, the son of Zeruiah, answered, "Should not Shimei be put to death for this, because he cursed the LORD's anointed?" {19:22} David replied, "What do I have to do with you, sons of Zeruiah? If he is cursing because the LORD said to him, 'Curse David,' who then shall say, 'Why have you done this?'" {19:23} David also said to Shimei, "You shall not die." And the king swore an oath to him. {19:24} Mephibosheth, the son of Saul, came down to meet the king. He hadn't tended to his feet, trimmed his beard, or washed his clothes since the day the king left until the day he returned in peace. {19:25} When he came to Jerusalem to meet the king, the king asked him, "Mephibosheth, why didn't you come with me?" {19:26} Mephibosheth answered, "My lord, O king, my servant deceived me. He told me he would saddle a donkey for me to ride to you because I am lame. {19:27} He slandered your servant to you, my lord the king, but you are as an angel of God. Do what you see fit. {19:28} My whole family deserved death before my lord the king, yet you set me at your own table. So what right do I have to ask anything more of the king?" {19:29} The king replied, "Why speak any more about your matters? I have decided: you and Ziba shall divide the land." {19:30} Mephibosheth said to the king, "Let him take it all, since my lord the king has returned home in peace." {19:31} Barzillai the Gileadite came down from Rogelim and went over the Jordan with the king to escort him over the Jordan. {19:32} Barzillai was a very old man, eighty years old, and he had provided for the king during his stay at Mahanaim, for he was a very wealthy man. {19:33} The king said to Barzillai, "Come over with me, and I will provide for you in Jerusalem." {19:34} But Barzillai replied to the king, "How many more years do I have to live, that I should go up to Jerusalem with the king? {19:35} I am eighty years old today. Can I discern between good and evil? Can I still enjoy the taste of what I eat or drink? Can I listen to the voices of singing men and women? So why should your servant burden the king any longer? {19:36} Let me go back, and I will die in my own city, and be buried beside my father and mother's grave. But here is your servant Chimham; let him go with my lord the king, and do for him what seems good to you." {19:37} The king replied, "Chimham shall go over with me, and I will do for him whatever you think best. And whatever you request of me, I will do for you." {19:38} So all the people crossed the Jordan, and when the king had crossed over, he kissed Barzillai and blessed him. {19:39} Then Barzillai returned to his own place. {19:40} The king went on to Gilgal, and Chimham went with him, along with all the people of Judah and half the people of Israel. {19:41} All the men of Israel came to the king and asked, "Why have our brothers, the men of Judah, taken you away and brought the king, his household, and all David's men across the Jordan?" {19:42} The men of Judah answered, "The king is our close relative. So why be angry about this matter? Have we eaten any of the king's provisions or received any gifts from him?" {19:43} The men of Israel replied, "We have ten shares in the king, and we have more claim to David than you do. Why then do you despise us and ignore our advice in bringing back our king?" And the words of the men of Judah were harsher than those of the men of Israel.

{20:1} There was a man named Sheba, the son of Bichri, from the tribe of Benjamin. He blew a trumpet and declared, "We have no part in David, nor do we have any inheritance in the son of Jesse. Every man to his tents, O Israel." {20:2} So all the Israelites followed Sheba, except the men of Judah who remained loyal to their king, from the Jordan to Jerusalem.

{20:3} When David returned to his house in Jerusalem, he took the ten concubines he had left to take care of the house and put them in confinement. He provided for them but did not have relations with them. So they remained in confinement until the day they died, living as widows. {20:4} Then the king said to Amasa, "Gather the men of Judah to me within three days, and be present here yourself." {20:5} But Amasa took longer than the time allotted for him. {20:6} So David said to Abishai, "Now Sheba, the son of Bichri, will harm us more than Absalom did. Take your lord's servants and pursue him, lest he finds fortified cities and escapes from us." {20:7} Joab's men, the Cherethites, the Pelethites, and all the mighty men went out of Jerusalem to pursue Sheba. {20:8} When they reached the great stone in Gibeon, Amasa came to meet them. Joab's garment was girded, and he had a sword in its sheath, which fell out as he walked. {20:9} Joab asked Amasa, "Are you well, my brother?" And Joab took Amasa's beard to kiss him. {20:10} But Amasa did not notice the sword in Joab's hand. Joab struck him in the fifth rib, causing his bowels to spill out, and he died instantly. Joab and his brother Abishai pursued Sheba. {20:11} One of Joab's men stood by Amasa's body and said, "Whoever favors Joab and is for David, let him follow Joab." {20:12} Amasa lay in the middle of the road in a pool of blood. When the man saw that everyone stopped, he moved Amasa's body off the road into a field and covered him with a garment. {20:13} After Amasa was removed from the road, all the people continued to pursue Sheba. {20:14} Sheba passed through all the tribes of Israel to Abel and Beth-maacah, and all the Berites joined him. {20:15} They besieged Sheba in Abel of Beth-maacah and built a siege ramp against the city wall. All Joab's men battered the wall to break it down. {20:16} A wise woman from the city cried out to Joab, "Listen, come near, and let me speak with you." {20:17} Joab approached her, and she asked, "Are you Joab?" When he confirmed, she said, "Listen to what your servant has to say." {20:18} She recounted an old saying about seeking counsel in Abel and urged Joab not to destroy the city, a mother in Israel, and the inheritance of the Lord. {20:19} Joab assured her that they had no intention of destroying the city but only sought Sheba, the one who rebelled against King David. He promised to withdraw if they handed over Sheba. {20:20} The woman agreed to deliver Sheba's head over the wall to Joab. {20:21} She went to the people, and they cut off Sheba's head and threw it to Joab. {20:22} Joab blew the trumpet, and his men dispersed, each to his tent. Joab returned to Jerusalem to the king. {20:23} Joab was in charge of all Israel's army, and Benaiah, the son of Jehoiada, commanded the Cherethites and Pelethites. {20:24} Adoram was in charge of forced labor, and Jehoshaphat, the son of Ahilud, was the recorder. {20:25} Sheva was the scribe, and Zadok and Abiathar were the priests. {20:26} Ira, the Jairite, was also a chief minister under David.

{21:1} During the days of David, there was a three-year famine, happening year after year. David sought the Lord, and the Lord answered, saying it was because of Saul and his bloody house, for he killed the Gibeonites. {21:2} So David called the Gibeonites, who were not Israelites but remnants of the Amorites. Saul had tried to kill them out of zeal for Israel and Judah. {21:3} David asked the Gibeonites how he could make amends to bless the Lord's inheritance. {21:4} The Gibeonites asked for no silver or gold from Saul's house and demanded no bloodshed in Israel. David agreed to do whatever they asked. {21:5} They requested that seven of Saul's sons be handed over to them to be hanged before the Lord in Gibeah of Saul, the one chosen by the Lord. {21:6} David spared Mephibosheth, Jonathan's son, {21:7} because of the oath between David and Jonathan. {21:8} But he gave the Gibeonites the two sons of Rizpah, Saul's concubine, and five sons of Michal, Saul's daughter, whom she raised for Adriel. {21:9} The Gibeonites hanged them on a hill before the Lord. All seven were put to death in the days of the barley harvest. {21:10} Rizpah spread sackcloth on a rock from the beginning of harvest until rain fell from heaven. She protected the bodies from birds by day and beasts by night. {21:11} When David heard what Rizpah did, Saul's concubine, he was told. {21:12} David retrieved the bones of Saul and Jonathan from the men of Jabesh-gilead, who had taken them from the public square of Beth-shan, where the Philistines had hanged them. {21:13} He gathered their bones and buried them in Benjamin's land in Zelah, in Kish's tomb, as David commanded. Afterward, {21:14} God responded to the land. {21:15} The Philistines waged war against Israel again. David and his servants fought them, and David grew weary. {21:16} Ishbi-benob, a descendant of the giants, attempted to kill David with a spear weighing three hundred shekels, but Abishai saved him by killing the Philistine. {21:17} After this, David's men swore that he should not go to battle again to avoid extinguishing the light of Israel. {21:18} Another battle occurred with the Philistines at Gob, where Sibbechai killed Saph, another giant's descendant. {21:19} In Gob, Elhanan, the son of Jaare-oregim from Bethlehem, killed Goliath's brother. {21:20} Another battle happened in Gath, where a giant with six fingers on each hand and six toes on each foot, totaling twenty-four, was born. {21:21} He defied Israel, but Jonathan, the son of Shimeah, killed him. {21:22} These four giants were born in Gath and were slain by David and his servants.

{22:1} David spoke to the LORD the words of this song on the day when the LORD delivered him from all his enemies, including Saul. {22:2} He said, "The LORD is my rock, fortress, and deliverer. {22:3} I trust in Him; He is my shield, salvation, high tower, refuge, and savior, rescuing me from violence. {22:4} I will praise the LORD and be saved from my enemies. {22:5} When death's waves surrounded me and ungodly floods terrified me, {22:6} when sorrows and death's snares trapped me, {22:7} in my distress, I called to the LORD, and He heard me from His temple; my cry reached His ears. {22:8} The earth shook and trembled; heaven's foundations moved because of His anger. {22:9} Smoke and fire came from His nostrils, devouring coals kindled by it. {22:10} He bowed the heavens, came down with darkness under His feet, {22:11} riding on a cherub, flying on the wings of the wind, surrounding Himself with darkness, thick clouds, and dark waters. {22:12} Coals of fire blazed before Him; thunder and lightning echoed His voice. {22:13} He scattered His enemies with arrows and lightning. {22:14} At His rebuke, the sea's channels appeared, the world's foundations revealed. {22:15} He lifted me out of many waters, delivering me from strong enemies and those who hated me, too powerful for me. {22:16} Though they came upon me in my distress, the LORD supported me. {22:17} He brought me to a spacious place because He delighted in me, rewarding me for my righteousness and faithfulness. {22:18} I followed His ways, keeping His statutes, remaining upright and avoiding iniquity. {22:19} Thus, the LORD rewarded me according to my righteousness and cleanness. {22:20} With the merciful, He shows mercy; with the upright, He acts uprightly. {22:21} He saves the afflicted but opposes the haughty. {22:22} He is my lamp, lighting my darkness, enabling me to overcome obstacles. {22:23} By God, I have defeated enemies, leaped over walls, for His way is perfect, His word tried and true, a shield to those who trust Him. {22:24} Who is God except the LORD? Who is a rock except our God? {22:25} He is my strength and power, making my way perfect, giving me sure-footedness and victory in battle. {22:26} He trains my hands for war, making my arms strong. {22:27} He gives me the shield of salvation, and His gentleness makes me great. {22:28} He broadens my path, preventing my feet from slipping. {22:29} I pursue and destroy my enemies; none rise again because the LORD strengthens me for battle. {22:30} He arms me, subduing those who rise against me. {22:31} God's way is perfect, His word is tried and true; He is a shield for those who trust in Him. {22:32} Who is God except the LORD? Who is a rock except our God? {22:33} God is my strength and power; He makes my way perfect. {22:34} He makes my feet like the feet of deer and sets me upon high places. {22:35} He teaches my hands to war, so that I can break a bow of steel. {22:36} He gives me the shield of salvation, and His gentleness makes me great. {22:37} He broadens my steps, so my feet do not slip. {22:38} I pursue and destroy my enemies, not stopping until I have consumed them. {22:39} I have wounded them so they cannot rise; they have fallen under my feet. {22:40} God has girded me with strength for battle; He has subdued those who rose against me. {22:41} He has given me victory over my enemies. {22:42} They looked for help, but there was none; even to the LORD, but He did not answer them. {22:43} I have crushed them like dust and stamped them like mud in the streets. {22:44} God has delivered me from the strivings of my people; He has made me head over nations I didn't know, who now serve me. {22:45} Strangers submit to me; when they hear, they obey me. {22:46} Strangers fade away and tremble in their strongholds. {22:47} The LORD lives; blessed be my rock; exalted be the God of my salvation. {22:48} It is God who avenges me, who brings down the people under me. {22:49} He brings me out from my enemies, lifting me above those who rise against me; He delivers me from the violent. {22:50} Therefore, I will give thanks to You, O LORD, among the nations; I will sing praises to

Your name. {22:51} You are the tower of salvation for Your king; You show mercy to Your anointed, to David, and his descendants forevermore.

{23:1} These are the last words of David, the son of Jesse, the man raised up on high, the anointed of the God of Jacob, the sweet psalmist of Israel. {23:2} The Spirit of the LORD spoke through me; His word was on my tongue. {23:3} The God of Israel said, the Rock of Israel spoke to me: "He who rules over men must be just, ruling in the fear of God. {23:4} He shall be like the light of the morning, like the sun rising, like tender grass springing after rain." {23:5} Though my house is not so with God, He has made an everlasting covenant with me, ordered in all things and sure. This is my salvation and desire, though it has not yet come to fruition. {23:6} But the sons of Belial shall be like thorns, thrust away because they cannot be handled. {23:7} Whoever touches them must be armed with iron and a spear; they shall be burned with fire in the same place. {23:8} These are the names of the mighty men whom David had: Adino the Eznite, who lifted his spear against eight hundred and killed them at one time. {23:9} Eleazar the son of Dodo the Ahohite, one of the three mighty men with David, who defied the Philistines gathered for battle when the Israelites had retreated. {23:10} He fought until his hand was weary, and the LORD brought a great victory that day. {23:11} Shammah the son of Agee the Hararite stood in the midst of a field of lentils, defending it from the Philistines, and the LORD wrought a great victory. {23:12} Three of the thirty chief men went down to David during harvest time to the cave of Adullam while the Philistines camped in the Valley of Rephaim. {23:13} David was in a stronghold, and the Philistine garrison was in Bethlehem. {23:14} David longed for water from the well of Bethlehem, and three mighty men broke through the Philistine ranks, drew water from the well, and brought it to David. But he poured it out to the LORD. {23:15} He refused to drink it, saying it was the blood of men who risked their lives. {23:16} Abishai, the brother of Joab, was chief among three. He lifted his spear against three hundred and killed them, earning a name among three. {23:17} Benaiah the son of Jehoiada, a valiant man from Kabzeel, slew two lionlike men of Moab and a lion in a pit during snow. {23:18} He also killed an Egyptian, taking his spear and killing him with it. {23:19} He wasn't the most honored among the three mighty men, but he was their leader. However, he didn't reach the top three. {23:20} Benaiah, the son of Jehoiada, from Kabzeel, a courageous man, performed many brave deeds. He killed two Moabite warriors who were as fierce as lions. He also went down into a pit on a snowy day and killed a lion. {23:21} Additionally, he defeated an Egyptian, a formidable opponent armed with a spear. Benaiah approached him with only a staff, disarmed him, and killed him with his own spear. {23:22} These were the notable exploits of Benaiah, the son of Jehoiada. Although he wasn't among the top three, he was highly esteemed among the mighty men. {23:23} He was considered more honorable than the thirty, but still didn't reach the top three. David appointed him as the commander of his bodyguard. {23:24} Among the thirty mighty men were Asahel, the brother of Joab, and Elhanan, the son of Dodo from Bethlehem. {23:25} There was also Shammah from Harod, Elika from Harod, and Helez from Paltite. {23:26} Ira, the son of Ikkesh from Tekoa, and Abiezer from Anathoth were also among them. {23:27} Mebunnai from Hushath, Zalmon from Ahoh, and Maharai from Netophah were part of the thirty. {23:28} Heleb, the son of Baanah from Netophah, and Ittai, the son of Ribai from Benjamin's Gibeah, were also counted among them. {23:29} Benaiah from Pirathon and Hiddai from the brooks of Gaash were among the thirty mighty men. {23:30} Other members included Abi-albon from Arbath, Azmaveth from Barhum, and Eliahba from Shaalbon. {23:31} From the sons of Jashen, there was Jonathan; from Harar, Shammah; and from Harar, Ahiam, the son of Sharar. {23:32} Eliphelet, the son of Ahasbai from Maacah, and Eliam, the son of Ahithophel from Giloh, were also among them. {23:33} Hezrai from Carmel, Paarai from Arbite, and Igal, the son of Nathan, from Zobah were part of the thirty. {23:34} Bani, the Gadite, Zelek, the Ammonite, and Nahari from Beeroth were also counted. {23:35} Uriah the Hittite was also part of the thirty-seven mighty men in total. {23:36} The list also included Ira from Ithra, Gareb from Ithra, and Uriah the Hittite. {23:37} Zelek from Ammon served as the armor-bearer to Joab, the son of Zeruiah. {23:38} Uriah the Hittite was among the thirty-seven. {23:39} In total, there were thirty-seven mighty men listed.

{24:1} Once again, the LORD became angry with Israel. He moved David to take action against them, saying, "Go, count the people of Israel and Judah." {24:2} So King David instructed Joab, the commander of his army, "Go through all the tribes of Israel, from Dan to Beersheba, and count the people. I want to know how many there are." {24:3} Joab cautioned the king, "May the LORD your God increase the number of your people a hundred times over! But why does my lord the king want to do this?" {24:4} However, the king's command prevailed, and Joab and the commanders of the army went out to count the people of Israel. {24:5} They crossed the Jordan and camped at Aroer, on the right side of the city that is in the middle of the river of Gad, and went toward Jazer. {24:6} Then they went to Gilead and to the land of Tahtim-hodshi, and they came to Dan-jaan and around to Sidon. {24:7} They went to the fortress of Tyre and all the cities of the Hivites and Canaanites. Then they went out to the south of Judah, even to Beersheba. {24:8} After traveling through the entire land, they returned to Jerusalem after nine months and twenty days. {24:9} Joab reported the total number of people to the king: there were eight hundred thousand valiant men in Israel who could draw the sword, and five hundred thousand men in Judah. {24:10} When David realized what he had done, he was deeply troubled and confessed to the LORD, "I have sinned greatly in what I have done. Please forgive your servant's wrongdoing, for I have acted foolishly." {24:11} The next morning, the word of the LORD came to the prophet Gad, David's seer, saying, {24:12} "Go and tell David, 'This is what the LORD says: I am giving you three options. Choose one of them, and I will do it to you.'" {24:13} So Gad went to David and presented the choices: "Shall seven years of famine come upon your land? Or will you flee before your enemies for three months while they pursue you? Or shall there be three days of pestilence in your land? Now consider and decide what answer I should give to the one who sent me." {24:14} David replied to Gad, "I am in great distress. Let us fall into the hands of the LORD, for his mercy is great; but do not let me fall into human hands." {24:15} So the LORD sent a plague upon Israel from the morning until the appointed time, and seventy thousand men died from Dan to Beersheba. {24:16} When the angel stretched out his hand to destroy Jerusalem, the LORD relented concerning the disaster and said to the angel who was afflicting the people, "Enough! Withdraw your hand now." The angel of the LORD was then standing at the threshing floor of Araunah the Jebusite. {24:17} When David saw the angel striking down the people, he said to the LORD, "I have sinned; I, the shepherd, have done wrong. These are but sheep. What have they done? Let your hand fall on me and my family." {24:18} Gad came to David that day and said to him, "Go up and build an altar to the LORD on the threshing floor of Araunah the Jebusite." {24:19} So David, following Gad's instructions, went up as the LORD had commanded. {24:20} Araunah saw the king and his servants approaching and went out to meet them. He bowed facedown to the ground before the king. {24:21} Araunah asked, "Why has my lord the king come to his servant?" David replied, "To buy your threshing floor and build an altar to the LORD, so that the plague on the people may be stopped." {24:22} Araunah said to David, "Let my lord the king take whatever he wishes and offer it up. Here are oxen for the burnt offering and threshing sledges and ox yokes for the wood." {24:23} Araunah gave all this to the king. Then he said to the king, "May the LORD your God accept you." {24:24} But the king replied to Araunah, "No, I insist on paying you for it. I will not sacrifice to the LORD my God burnt offerings that cost me nothing." So David bought the threshing floor and the oxen for fifty shekels of silver. {24:25} David built an altar to the LORD there and sacrificed burnt offerings and fellowship offerings. Then the LORD answered his prayer in behalf of the land, and the plague on Israel was stopped.

1 Kings

{1:1} King David was old and frail, unable to generate warmth even when covered with clothes. {1:2} His servants suggested finding a young virgin to keep him warm by lying close to him. {1:3} They searched throughout Israel and found Abishag, a beautiful Shunammite, for this purpose. {1:4} Abishag served and cared for the king, but he did not have intimate relations with her. {1:5} Meanwhile, Adonijah, David's son, declared himself king and gathered supporters. {1:6} David had never opposed Adonijah before, and he was handsome like his brother Absalom. {1:7} Adonijah sought advice from Joab and Abiathar, and they supported him. {1:8} However, key figures like Zadok the priest, Benaiah, Nathan the prophet, and Solomon were not on Adonijah's side. {1:9} Adonijah hosted a feast and invited all except those loyal to David's house. {1:10} Notably, he didn't invite Nathan, Benaiah, Solomon, or the mighty men. {1:11} Nathan warned Bathsheba about Adonijah's scheme to seize the throne. {1:12} He advised her to remind David of his promise to make Solomon king. {1:13} Bathsheba approached David and recounted Nathan's counsel. {1:14} Nathan confirmed her words in David's presence. {1:15} Bathsheba entered the king's chamber where Abishag was attending to him. {1:16} She bowed before David, and he asked her what she needed. {1:17} Bathsheba reminded David of his promise to make Solomon king. {1:18} She informed him of Adonijah's actions. {1:19} Bathsheba emphasized the importance of David declaring his successor before he died. {1:20} She feared that she and Solomon would be in danger if David didn't act. {1:21} Nathan entered while Bathsheba was speaking to David. {1:22} Nathan bowed before the king. {1:23} He informed David about Adonijah's self-proclamation as king. {1:24} Nathan questioned if David had indeed chosen Adonijah to succeed him. {1:25} He described Adonijah's feast and the declaration of him as king. {1:26} Nathan pointed out that neither he, Zadok, Benaiah, nor Solomon were invited. {1:27} Nathan asked why David hadn't informed them about the succession. {1:28} David called for Bathsheba. {1:29} He reassured her with an oath that Solomon would be king as promised. {1:30} David confirmed his earlier vow before the LORD. {1:31} Bathsheba paid respects to David, wishing him a long life. {1:32} David summoned Zadok, Nathan, and Benaiah. {1:33} He instructed them to anoint Solomon as king and have him ride on David's mule to Gihon. {1:34} Zadok and Nathan were to anoint Solomon as king and declare him as such. {1:35} They were to bring Solomon to David's throne to establish him as king. {1:36} Benaiah expressed his agreement and prayed for Solomon's success. {1:37} They proceeded to carry out David's orders. {1:38} Zadok, Nathan, Benaiah, and others accompanied Solomon to Gihon. {1:39} Zadok anointed Solomon with oil, and they proclaimed him king. {1:40} The people rejoiced and celebrated Solomon's kingship with music and fanfare. {1:41} Adonijah and his guests heard the commotion and wondered about its cause. {1:42} Jonathan, son of Abiathar, arrived and informed Adonijah about Solomon's coronation. {1:43} Adonijah learned that David had officially made Solomon king. {1:44} Jonathan recounted the anointing ceremony and the joyous celebration. {1:45} Adonijah realized the significance of the noise he heard. {1:46} Solomon was now seated on the throne. {1:47} David's servants blessed him, acknowledging Solomon as the rightful king. {1:48} David praised the LORD for allowing him to witness Solomon's ascension to the throne. {1:49} Adonijah's guests became fearful and dispersed. {1:50} Adonijah, fearing Solomon's wrath, sought refuge at the altar. {1:51} Solomon was informed of Adonijah's actions. {1:52} Solomon promised Adonijah safety if he proved himself worthy, but warned of consequences if he acted wickedly. {1:53} Solomon had Adonijah brought before him, where he pledged allegiance and was sent home.

{2:1} As David's death approached, he gave Solomon some final instructions. {2:2} He urged Solomon to be strong and courageous, acting like a mature man. {2:3} **David advised Solomon to obey God's commands and walk in His ways as written in the Law of Moses. This would ensure success in all endeavors.** {2:4} David reminded Solomon of God's promise to establish David's dynasty if his descendants remained faithful. {2:5} David mentioned Joab's past deeds, including the murders of Abner and Amasa, and urged Solomon to deal with him wisely. {2:6} Solomon was to use his wisdom and ensure Joab didn't die peacefully despite his old age. {2:7} David asked Solomon to show kindness to the sons of Barzillai for their support during Absalom's rebellion. {2:8} On the other hand, Shimei's past actions warranted punishment, but David had spared his life. {2:9} David left it to Solomon's discretion to handle Shimei, ensuring he didn't die a peaceful death. {2:10} After David's death, Solomon became king, ruling from Jerusalem. {2:11} David's reign lasted forty years, including seven years in Hebron and thirty-three in Jerusalem. {2:12} Solomon's reign began, and his kingdom flourished. {2:13} Adonijah, seeking to secure his position, approached Bathsheba. {2:14} He assured her of peaceful intentions and requested a private audience. {2:15} Adonijah claimed the kingdom was rightfully his, but circumstances had favored Solomon. {2:16} He asked Bathsheba to intercede with Solomon on his behalf, requesting Abishag's hand in marriage. {2:17} Bathsheba agreed to speak to Solomon about Adonijah's request. {2:18} Bathsheba presented Adonijah's proposal to Solomon. {2:19} Solomon showed respect to his mother, and after she made her request, he agreed. {2:20} Bathsheba asked Solomon to grant Adonijah's petition. {2:21} Solomon questioned why Adonijah sought Abishag and insinuated he was making a move for the throne. {2:22} Solomon interpreted Adonijah's request as a challenge to his reign and decided to execute him. {2:23} Solomon swore to carry out this judgment. {2:24} Solomon ordered Benaiah to execute Adonijah. {2:25} Benaiah fulfilled the command, and Adonijah was put to death. {2:26} Solomon exiled Abiathar from the priesthood due to his past actions. {2:27} This fulfilled the prophecy concerning the house of Eli. {2:28} News of Joab's actions reached Solomon, prompting Joab to seek refuge at the altar. {2:29} Solomon instructed Benaiah to apprehend Joab. {2:30} Benaiah conveyed Solomon's message to Joab. {2:31} Solomon ordered Joab's execution to atone for the innocent blood he shed. {2:32} Solomon declared God's judgment upon Joab for his past deeds. {2:33} Benaiah carried out Solomon's command, executing Joab. {2:34} Solomon appointed Benaiah as commander of the army and replaced Abiathar with Zadok as priest. {2:35} Solomon commanded Shimei to remain in Jerusalem under penalty of death. {2:36} After three years, Shimei's servants fled to Gath, and Shimei went to retrieve them. {2:37} Solomon reminded Shimei of his oath and warned him of the consequences of leaving Jerusalem. {2:38} Shimei agreed to Solomon's terms and stayed in Jerusalem. {2:39} Shimei's servants returned from Gath, and Shimei stayed in Jerusalem for many days. {2:40} However, Shimei later ventured out to Gath to retrieve his servants again. {2:41} When Solomon learned of Shimei's actions, he reminded him of his oath. {2:42} Solomon questioned Shimei's disobedience. {2:43} Solomon admonished Shimei for breaking his oath and commanded his execution. {2:44} Solomon cited Shimei's past actions against David as the reason for his judgment. {2:45} Solomon's reign was blessed, and David's dynasty was secured. {2:46} Solomon's authority was firmly established.

{3:1} Solomon formed a bond with Pharaoh, the king of Egypt, and married his daughter. He brought her to the city of David until he finished building his own palace, the temple of the LORD, and the surrounding walls of Jerusalem. {3:2} During this time, the people continued to offer sacrifices in high places because there was no temple built for the LORD's name yet. {3:3} Solomon remained devoted to the LORD, following the teachings of his father David. However, he still offered sacrifices and burned incense in the high places. {3:4} Solomon went to Gibeon to offer sacrifices, as it was a significant high place. There, he offered a thousand burnt offerings on the altar. {3:5} While in Gibeon, the LORD appeared to Solomon in a dream at night and said, "Ask me for whatever you want, and I will give it to you." {3:6} Solomon replied, acknowledging God's kindness to his father David and his own unworthiness. He asked for wisdom to govern the people justly. {3:7} Solomon recognized his youth and lack of experience in leading such a vast nation. {3:8} He acknowledged the greatness of the people of Israel and requested understanding to discern between good and evil. {3:9} **Solomon desired wisdom to judge the people fairly, recognizing the enormity of the task.** {3:10} God was pleased with Solomon's request for wisdom and granted it to him. {3:11} Additionally, God promised Solomon riches and honor because he hadn't asked for selfish desires like long life or wealth. {3:12} God assured Solomon that he would be the wisest king ever known. {3:13} Solomon was also promised unparalleled wealth and honor if he remained obedient to the LORD's commandments. {3:14} God promised to prolong Solomon's days if he continued to walk in obedience like his father David. {3:15} Solomon woke up from the dream, went to Jerusalem, and stood before the ark of the covenant. He offered sacrifices and made a feast for his servants. {3:16} Two women, both claiming to be the mother of a living child, came before Solomon. {3:17} One woman explained that she and the other woman lived together and each gave birth to a child. {3:18} However, one woman's child died, and she switched it with the other woman's living child while they were asleep. {3:19} When the rightful mother discovered the dead child, she realized the switch. {3:20} Solomon listened as both women presented their cases. {3:21} One woman insisted the living child was hers, while the other argued the opposite. {3:22} Solomon ordered a sword brought before him , {3:23} and suggested splitting the living child in two. {3:24} Solomon ordered a sword to be brought before him. {3:25} He commanded, "Divide the living child in two, and give half to one woman and half to the other." {3:26} One of the women, the real mother of the living child, pleaded with the king, "Please, my lord, don't kill the child. Give her the living child." But the other woman insisted on dividing the child. {3:27} Solomon, discerning the true mother's love, declared, "Give the living child to her; do not kill it. She is the mother." {3:28} This judgment spread throughout Israel, and they revered Solomon for his wisdom, recognizing that it was from God, enabling him to administer justice.

{4:1} Solomon was the king over all Israel. {4:2} These were his officials: Azariah son of Zadok was the priest; {4:3} Elihoreph and Ahiah, sons of Shisha, were his secretaries; Jehoshaphat son of Ahilud was the recorder. {4:4} Benaiah son of Jehoiada was in charge of the army; Zadok and Abiathar were the priests; {4:5} Azariah son of Nathan was in charge of the district officers; Zabud son of Nathan was a trusted adviser to the king; {4:6} Ahishar was in charge of the palace; Adoniram son of Abda was in charge of forced labor. {4:7} Solomon had twelve district officers who provided food for the king and his household. Each had to provide supplies for one month of the year. {4:8} These were their names: Ben Hur, in the hill country of Ephraim; {4:9} Ben Deker, in Makaz, Shaalbim, Beth Shemesh, and Elon Bethhanan; {4:10} Ben Hesed, in Arubboth (Socoh and all the land of Hepher were his); {4:11} Ben Abinadab, in Naphoth Dor (he was married to Taphath, Solomon's daughter); {4:12} Baana son of Ahilud, in Taanach and Megiddo, and in all of Beth Shan next to Zarethan below Jezreel, from Beth Shan to Abel Meholah across to Jokmeam; {4:13} Ben Geber, in Ramoth Gilead (the settlements of Jair son of Manasseh in Gilead were his, as well as the district of Argob in Bashan and its sixty large walled cities with bronze gate bars); {4:14} Ahinadab son of Iddo, in Mahanaim; {4:15} Ahimaaz, in Naphtali (he had married Basemath daughter of Solomon); {4:16} Baana son of Hushai, in Asher and in Aloth; {4:17} Jehoshaphat son of Paruah, in Issachar; {4:18} Shimei son of Ela, in Benjamin; {4:19} Geber son of Uri, in Gilead (the country of Sihon king of the Amorites and the country of Og king of Bashan). He was the only governor over the district. {4:20} Judah and Israel were as numerous as the sand on the seashore; they ate, they drank and they were happy. {4:21} And Solomon ruled over all the kingdoms from the Euphrates River to the land of the Philistines, as far as the border of Egypt. These countries brought tribute and were Solomon's subjects all his life. {4:22} Solomon's daily provisions were thirty cors of the finest flour and sixty cors of meal, {4:23} ten head of stall-fed cattle, twenty of pasture-fed cattle and a hundred sheep and goats, as well as deer, gazelles, roebucks and choice fowl. {4:24} For he ruled over all the kingdoms west of the Euphrates River, from Tiphsah to Gaza, and had peace on all sides. {4:25} During Solomon's lifetime Judah and Israel, from Dan to Beersheba, lived in safety, everyone under their own vine and under their own fig tree. {4:26} Solomon had four thousand stalls for chariot horses, and twelve thousand horses. {4:27} The district officers, each in his month, supplied provisions for King Solomon and all who came to the king's table. They saw to it that nothing was lacking. {4:28} They also brought to the proper place their quotas of barley and straw for the chariot horses and the other horses. {4:29} God gave Solomon wisdom and very great insight, and a breadth of understanding as measureless as the sand on the seashore. {4:30} Solomon's wisdom was greater than the wisdom of all the people of the East, and greater than all the wisdom of Egypt. {4:31} He was wiser than anyone else, including Ethan the Ezrahite—wiser than Heman, Kalkol and Darda, the sons of Mahol. And his fame spread to all the surrounding nations. {4:32} He spoke three thousand proverbs and his songs numbered a thousand and five. {4:33} He spoke about plant life, from the cedar of Lebanon to the hyssop that grows out of walls. He also spoke about animals and birds, reptiles and fish. {4:34} From all nations people came to listen to Solomon's wisdom, sent by all the kings of the world, who had heard of his wisdom.

{5:1} Hiram, the king of Tyre, sent his servants to Solomon because he heard that Solomon had been anointed king in place of his father. Hiram had always been a friend of David. {5:2} Solomon then sent a message to Hiram, saying, {5:3} "You know that my father David was unable to build a house for the name of the LORD his God because of the wars that surrounded him on every side until the LORD had subdued his enemies under his feet. {5:4} But now the LORD my God has given me peace on every side, and there is no adversary or trouble. {5:5} So, I intend to build a house for the name of the LORD my God, as the LORD spoke to my father David, saying, 'Your son, whom I will set on your throne in your place, shall build the house for my name.' {5:6} Now, therefore, command that cedar trees be cut for me from Lebanon, and my servants will work with your servants. And I will pay your servants whatever wages you set, for there is no one among us who is skilled like the Sidonians in cutting timber." {5:7} When Hiram heard Solomon's words, he greatly rejoiced and praised the LORD, who had given David a wise son to rule over this great people. {5:8} Hiram then sent a message to Solomon, saying, "I have heard your request concerning cedar and cypress timber. I will fulfill all your requests. {5:9} My servants will bring the timber down from Lebanon to the sea, and I will arrange for them to be transported by sea in rafts to the place you specify. There I will have them broken up, and you can take them away. And you shall meet my needs by providing food for my household." {5:10} So Hiram provided Solomon with cedar and cypress timber according to all his needs. {5:11} In return, Solomon gave Hiram twenty thousand measures of wheat as food for his household, and twenty measures of pure oil. Solomon provided these for Hiram every year. {5:12} And the LORD gave Solomon wisdom, as he had promised him, and there was peace between Hiram and Solomon, and they made a treaty together. {5:13} Solomon imposed a levy on all Israel, and the levy numbered thirty thousand men. {5:14} He sent them to Lebanon, ten thousand a month in shifts; they would spend one month in Lebanon and two months at home. Adoniram was in charge of the labor force. {5:15} Solomon also had seventy thousand carriers and eighty thousand stonecutters in the hill country, {5:16} besides Solomon's 3,300 chief officers who supervised the people doing the work. {5:17} The king commanded that they quarry large stones, valuable stones, and hew stones to lay the foundation of the house. {5:18} Solomon's builders and Hiram's builders worked together, along with the stonecutters. Together they prepared the timber and stones for building the house.

{6:1} In the four hundred and eightieth year after the Israelites left Egypt, in the fourth year of Solomon's reign over Israel, in the month of Zif, which is the second month, Solomon began to build the house of the LORD. {6:2} The house that King Solomon built for the LORD was sixty cubits long, twenty cubits wide, and thirty cubits high. {6:3} The porch in front of the temple was twenty cubits long, according to the width of the house, and its depth was ten cubits in front of the house. {6:4} Solomon made narrow windows for the house. {6:5} Against the outer walls of the house and the inner sanctuary, Solomon built a structure around the walls of the house, enclosing the temple and the inner sanctuary. He constructed side rooms all around. {6:6} The lowest floor was five cubits wide, the middle floor was six cubits wide, and the third floor was seven cubits wide. He made offset ledges around the outside of the temple so that nothing would be inserted into the temple walls. {6:7} The house was built with stones prepared at the quarry, so that no hammer, chisel, or any iron tool was heard in the temple while it was being built. {6:8} The entrance to the lowest floor was on the south side of the temple; a staircase led up to the middle level and from there to the third floor. {6:9} So he built the temple and completed it, roofing it with beams and planks of cedar. {6:10} He built side rooms all along the temple, each five cubits high; they were attached to the temple by cedar beams. {6:11} Then the word of the LORD came to Solomon, saying, {6:12} "As for this temple you are building, if you follow my decrees, observe my laws, and keep all my commands and obey them, I will fulfill through you the promise I gave to David your father. {6:13} And I will dwell among the Israelites and will not abandon my people Israel." {6:14} So Solomon built the temple and completed it. {6:15} He lined its interior walls with cedar boards, paneling them from the floor of the temple to the ceiling, and covered the floor of the temple with planks of juniper. {6:16} He partitioned off twenty cubits at the rear of the temple with cedar boards from floor to ceiling to form within the temple an inner sanctuary, the Most Holy Place. {6:17} The main hall in front of this room was forty cubits long. {6:18} The inside of the temple was cedar, carved with gourds and open flowers. Everything was cedar; no stone was to be seen. {6:19} He prepared the inner sanctuary within the temple to set the ark of the covenant of the LORD there. {6:20} The inner sanctuary was twenty cubits long, twenty cubits wide, and twenty cubits high. He overlaid it with pure gold, and he also overlaid the altar of cedar. {6:21} Solomon covered the inside of the temple with pure gold, and he extended gold chains across the front of the inner sanctuary, which was overlaid with gold. {6:22} So he overlaid the whole interior with gold. He also overlaid with gold the altar that belonged to the inner sanctuary. {6:23} For the inner sanctuary, Solomon made two cherubim out of olive wood, each ten cubits high. {6:24} One wing of the first cherub was five cubits long, and the other wing five cubits—ten cubits from wing tip to wing tip. {6:25} The second cherub also measured ten cubits, for the two cherubim were identical in size and shape. {6:26} The height of each cherub was ten cubits. {6:27} He placed the cherubim inside the innermost room of the temple, with their wings spread out. The wing of one cherub touched one wall, while the wing of the other touched the other wall, and their wings touched each other in the middle of the room. {6:28} He overlaid the cherubim with gold. {6:29} On the walls all around the temple, inside and out, he carved cherubim, palm trees, and open flowers. {6:30} He also covered the floors of both the inner and outer rooms of the temple with gold. {6:31} For the entrance to the inner sanctuary, Solomon made doors out of olive wood that were one fifth of the width of the sanctuary. {6:32} And on the olive wood doors he carved cherubim, palm trees, and open flowers, and overlaid them with gold; he hammered gold over the cherubim and palm trees. {6:33} Also for the entrance of the temple, Solomon made doorposts out of olive wood that were one fourth of the width of the sanctuary. {6:34} The two doors were made of juniper wood, and each door was made with two folding panels. {6:35} He carved cherubim, palm trees, and open flowers on them and overlaid them with gold, hammered evenly over the carvings. {6:36} He built the inner courtyard with three courses of dressed stone and one course of trimmed cedar beams. {6:37} The foundation of the temple of the LORD was laid in the fourth year, in the month of Zif. {6:38} And in the eleventh year, in the month of Bul, which is the eighth month, the temple was finished in all its details according to its specifications. So he was seven years in building it.

{7:1} Solomon took thirteen years to build his own palace, and he completed the entire palace. {7:2} He also built the Palace of the Forest of Lebanon, which was a hundred cubits long, fifty cubits wide, and thirty cubits high, with four rows of cedar pillars supporting cedar beams. {7:3} The roof was made of cedar above the beams, which rested on forty-five pillars, fifteen in each row. {7:4} There were windows in three rows, and each window was opposite the other in three tiers. {7:5} All the doorways had rectangular frames; they were in the front of the square, and opposite each other in three tiers. {7:6} Solomon also made a colonnade fifty cubits long and thirty cubits wide. In front of it was a portico, and in front of that were pillars and an overhanging roof. {7:7} He built the throne hall, known as the Hall of Judgment, where he was to judge, and it was covered with cedar from floor to ceiling. {7:8} His own palace, where he was to live, was similar in design. Solomon also made a palace for Pharaoh's daughter, whom he had married, similar to the Hall of Judgment. {7:9} All these buildings were made of costly stones, cut to size and sawed with saws, inside and out, from the foundation to the eaves, and also on the outside to the great courtyard. {7:10} The foundation stones were large, and each was twelve cubits long and eight cubits wide. {7:11} Above were high-grade stones, cut to size, and cedar beams. {7:12} The great courtyard was surrounded by three courses of dressed stone and one course of trimmed cedar beams, just like the inner courtyard of the temple and the portico around the temple. {7:13} King Solomon sent for a man named Hiram from Tyre. {7:14} Hiram's mother was a widow from the tribe of Naphtali, and his father was from Tyre and a skilled craftsman in bronze. Hiram was filled with wisdom, understanding, and skill to do all kinds of work in bronze. He came to King Solomon and did all the work assigned to him. {7:15} He cast two bronze pillars, each eighteen cubits high and twelve cubits around. {7:16} He also made two capitals of cast bronze to set on the tops of the pillars; each capital was five cubits high. {7:17} There were seven chains for each capital, arranged in two rows and secured to the capitals on the top of the pillars. {7:18} He made the pillars and two sets of chain networks to decorate the capitals on top of the pillars; each network had seven chains. {7:19} The capitals on top of the pillars in the portico were in the shape of lilies, four cubits high. {7:20} The capitals on the two pillars also had pomegranates above, beside the bowl-shaped parts of the capitals. {7:21} He set up the pillars at the portico of the temple. The pillar to the south he named Jakin, and the one to the north Boaz. {7:22} The capitals on top were in the shape of lilies. And so the work on the pillars was completed. {7:23} He made the Sea of cast metal, circular in shape, measuring ten cubits from rim to rim and five cubits high. It took a line of thirty cubits to measure around it. {7:24} Below the rim, gourds encircled it—ten to a cubit. The gourds were cast in two rows in one piece with the Sea. {7:25} The Sea stood on twelve bulls, three facing north, three facing west, three facing south, and three facing east. The Sea rested on top of them, and their hindquarters were toward the center. {7:26} It was a handbreadth in thickness, and its rim was like the rim of a cup, like a lily blossom. It held two thousand baths. {7:27} He also made ten movable stands of bronze; each was four cubits long, four wide, and three high. {7:28} This is how the stands were made: They had side panels attached to uprights. {7:29} On the panels between the uprights were lions, bulls, and cherubim—and on the uprights as well. Above and below the lions and bulls were wreaths of hammered work. {7:30} Each stand had four bronze wheels with bronze axles, and each had a basin resting on four supports, cast with wreaths on each side.

{7:31} On the inside of the stand there was an opening that had a circular frame one cubit deep. This opening was round, and with its basework it measured a cubit and a half. Around its opening there was engraving. The panels of the stands were square, not round. {7:32} The four wheels were under the panels, and the axles of the wheels were attached to the stand. The diameter of each wheel was a cubit and a half. {7:33} The wheels were made like chariot wheels; the axles, rims, spokes and hubs were all of cast metal. {7:34} Each stand had four handles, one on each corner, projecting from the stand. {7:35} At the top of the stand there was a circular band half a cubit deep. The supports and panels were attached to the top of the stand. {7:36} He engraved cherubim, lions, and palm trees on the surfaces of the supports and on the panels, in every available space, with wreaths all around. {7:37} This is how he made the ten stands. They were all cast in the same molds and were identical in size and shape. {7:38} He then made ten bronze basins, each holding forty baths and measuring four cubits across, one basin to go on each of the ten stands. {7:39} He placed five of the stands on the south side of the temple and five on the north. He placed the Sea on the south side, at the southeast corner of the temple. {7:40} Hiram also made the pots, shovels, and sprinkling bowls. So Hiram finished all the work he had undertaken for King Solomon in the temple of the LORD: {7:41} the two pillars; the two bowl-shaped capitals on top of the pillars; the two sets of network decorating the two bowl-shaped capitals on top of the pillars; {7:42} the four hundred pomegranates for the two sets of network (two rows of pomegranates for each set of network, decorating the bowl-shaped capitals on top of the pillars); {7:43} the ten stands with their ten basins; {7:44} the Sea and the twelve bulls under it; {7:45} the pots, shovels, and sprinkling bowls. All these objects that Hiram made for King Solomon for the temple of the LORD were of polished bronze. {7:46} The king cast them in the plain of the Jordan, on the clay ground between Succoth and Zarthan. {7:47} Solomon left all the vessels unweighed because they were too numerous, and the weight of the brass could not be determined. {7:48} Solomon made all the vessels for the house of the LORD: the altar of gold, the table for the showbread, {7:49} the pure gold candlesticks—five on the right and five on the left—before the inner sanctuary, with the flowers, lamps, and gold tongs. {7:50} He also made the gold bowls, snuffers, basins, spoons, and censers, as well as the gold hinges for the doors of the inner sanctuary, the Most Holy Place, and for the doors of the temple. {7:51} Thus, all the work that King Solomon did for the house of the LORD was completed. He brought in the items dedicated by his father David: the silver, gold, and vessels, and placed them among the treasures of the house of the LORD.

{8:1} Solomon gathered the elders of Israel, along with the heads of the tribes and the chief fathers, to Jerusalem. Their purpose was to bring up the ark of the covenant of the LORD from the city of David, also known as Zion. {8:2} All the men of Israel came together to King Solomon during the feast in the month of Ethanim, the seventh month. {8:3} The elders of Israel arrived, and the priests carried up the ark. {8:4} They brought up the ark of the LORD, the tabernacle of the congregation, and all the holy vessels from the tabernacle. The priests and Levites were responsible for this. {8:5} King Solomon and all the assembly of Israel, who had gathered before him, were sacrificing so many sheep and oxen that they could not be counted. {8:6} The priests brought the ark of the covenant of the LORD into its place, into the inner sanctuary of the house, under the wings of the cherubim. {8:7} The cherubim spread their wings over the place of the ark, covering it and its poles from above. {8:8} The poles were so long that their ends could be seen from the Holy Place in front of the inner sanctuary, but not from outside. They remain there to this day. {8:9} There was nothing in the ark except the two tablets of stone that Moses had placed there at Horeb, when the LORD made a covenant with the children of Israel as they came out of Egypt. {8:10} When the priests came out of the Holy Place, the cloud filled the house of the LORD, {8:11} and the priests could not continue their service because of the cloud; for the glory of the LORD filled the house of the LORD. {8:12} Then Solomon said, "The LORD said that he would dwell in thick darkness. {8:13} I have indeed built you an exalted house, a place for you to dwell in forever." {8:14} Then the king turned around and blessed all the assembly of Israel, while they were standing. {8:15} He said, "Blessed be the LORD God of Israel, who spoke with his mouth to David my father, and with his hand fulfilled it, saying, {8:16} 'Since the day that I brought my people Israel out of Egypt, I have chosen no city out of all the tribes of Israel to build a house, that my name might be there; but I chose David to be over my people Israel.' {8:17} Now it was in the heart of David my father to build a house for the name of the LORD God of Israel. {8:18} But the LORD said to David my father, 'Whereas it was in your heart to build a house unto my name, you did well that it was in your heart. {8:19} Nevertheless, you shall not build the house, but your son who shall come out of your loins, he shall build the house unto my name.' {8:20} And the LORD has fulfilled his word that he spoke, and I have risen in the place of David my father, and sit on the throne of Israel, as the LORD promised, and have built the house for the name of the LORD God of Israel. {8:21} And I have set there a place for the ark, wherein is the covenant of the LORD that he made with our fathers when he brought them out of the land of Egypt. {8:22} **Then Solomon stood before the altar of the LORD in the presence of all the assembly of Israel, and spread out his hands toward heaven.** {8:23} He said, "LORD God of Israel, there is no God like you, in heaven above or on earth beneath, who keeps covenant and mercy with your servants who walk before you with all their heart. {8:24} You have kept with your servant David my father what you promised him. You spoke also with your mouth, and have fulfilled it with your hand, as it is this day. {8:25} Now therefore, LORD God of Israel, keep with your servant David my father what you promised him, saying, 'There shall not fail you a man in my sight to sit on the throne of Israel, if only your children take heed to their way, to walk before me as you have walked before me.' {8:26} And now, O God of Israel, let your word be verified, which you spoke to your servant David my father. {8:27} But will God indeed dwell on the earth? Behold, heaven and the heaven of heavens cannot contain you. How much less this house that I have built! {8:28} Yet have respect to the prayer of your servant and to his supplication, O LORD my God, to listen to the cry and the prayer which your servant is praying before you today: {8:29} that your eyes may be open toward this house night and day, toward the place of which you said, 'My name shall be there,' that you may listen to the prayer which your servant makes toward this place. {8:30} And listen to the supplication of your servant and of your people Israel, when they pray toward this place. Hear in heaven your dwelling place; and when you hear, forgive. {8:31} If anyone sins against his neighbor and is required to take an oath, and he comes and swears the oath before your altar in this house: {8:32} then hear in heaven, and act, and judge your servants, condemning the wicked, to bring his way on his own head, and justifying the righteous, to give him according to his righteousness. {8:33} When your people Israel are defeated before the enemy because they have sinned against you, and they turn again to you and confess your name and pray and make supplication to you in this house: {8:34} then hear in heaven, and forgive the sin of your people Israel, and bring them back to the land which you gave to their fathers. {8:35} When the heavens are shut up and there is no rain because they have sinned against you; if they pray toward this place and confess your name and turn from their sin when you afflict them: {8:36} then hear in heaven, and forgive the sin of your servants, your people Israel, that you may teach them the good way in which they should walk; and send rain on your land which you have given to your people as an inheritance. {8:37} If there is famine in the land, if there is pestilence, blight, mildew, locust, or if their enemy besieges them in the land of their cities; whatever plague, whatever sickness there is: {8:38} whatever prayer, whatever supplication is made by anyone, or by all your people Israel, when each one knows the plague of his own heart and spreads out his hands toward this house: {8:39} then hear in heaven your dwelling place, and forgive, and act, and give to everyone according to all his ways, whose heart you know (for you alone know the hearts of all the sons of men), {8:40} So that they may fear you all the days they live in the land which you gave to our fathers. {8:41} Furthermore, concerning a stranger who is not of your people Israel but comes from a distant land for your name's sake: {8:42} (For they shall hear of your great name, and of your strong hand, and of your outstretched arm;) when he comes and prays toward this house, {8:43} Hear in heaven your dwelling place, and do according to all that the stranger calls to you for, so that all the people of the earth may know your name and fear you, as your people Israel do, and that they may know that this house which I have built is called by your name. {8:44} If your people go out to battle against their enemy, wherever you send them, and they pray to the LORD toward the city which you have chosen, and toward the house that I have built for your name: {8:45} Then hear in heaven their prayer and their supplication, and maintain their cause. {8:46} If they sin against you (for there is no one who does not sin), and you are angry with them and deliver them to the enemy, so that they are carried away captive to the land of the enemy, far or near; {8:47} Yet if they come to their senses in the land where they were carried captive, and repent, and make supplication to you in the land of those who carried them captive, saying, 'We have sinned, and have done perversely, we have committed wickedness;' {8:48} And return to you with all their heart and with all their soul, in the land of their enemies who led them away captive, and pray to you toward their land which you gave to their fathers, the city which you have chosen, and the house which I have built for your name: {8:49} Then hear their prayer and their supplication in heaven your dwelling place, and maintain their cause, {8:50} And forgive your people who have sinned against you and all their transgressions in which they have transgressed against you, and grant them compassion before those who carried them captive, that they may have compassion on them: {8:51} For they are your people and your inheritance, whom you brought out of Egypt, out of the iron furnace. {8:52} Let your eyes be open to the supplication of your servant and the supplication of your people Israel, to listen to them whenever they call to you. {8:53} For you separated them from among all the peoples of the earth to be your inheritance, as you spoke by the hand of Moses your servant, when you brought our fathers out of Egypt, O Lord GOD. {8:54} And so it was, when Solomon had finished praying all this prayer and supplication to the LORD, that he arose from before the altar of the LORD, from kneeling on his knees with his hands spread out toward heaven. {8:55} And he stood and blessed all the assembly of Israel with a loud voice, saying: {8:56} "Blessed be the LORD, who has given rest to his people Israel, according to all that he promised; not one word has failed of all his good promise, which he promised by Moses his servant. {8:57} May the LORD our God be with us, as he was with our fathers. May he not leave us nor forsake us, {8:58} That he may incline our hearts to him, to walk in all his ways, and to keep his commandments, his statutes, and his judgments, which he commanded our fathers. {8:59} And let these words of mine, with which I have made supplication before the LORD, be near to the LORD our God day and night, that he may maintain the cause of his servant and the cause of his people Israel, as each day may require: {8:60} That all the peoples of the earth may know that the LORD is God; there is no other. {8:61} Let your heart therefore be loyal to the LORD our God, to walk in his statutes and keep his commandments, as at this day. {8:62} And the king, and all Israel with him, offered sacrifices before the LORD. {8:63} Solomon offered a sacrifice of peace offerings to the LORD, twenty-two thousand bulls and one hundred and twenty thousand sheep. So the king and all the children of Israel dedicated the house of the LORD. {8:64} On the same day, the king consecrated the middle of the court that was before the house of the LORD; for there he offered burnt offerings, grain offerings, and the fat of the peace offerings, because the bronze altar that was before the LORD was too small to receive the burnt offerings, the grain offerings, and the fat of the peace offerings. {8:65} At that time Solomon held a feast, and all Israel with him, a great assembly from the entrance of Hamath to the Brook of Egypt, before the LORD our God, seven days and seven more days—fourteen days. {8:66} On the eighth day he sent the people away; and they blessed the king, and went to their tents joyful and glad of heart for all the good that the LORD had done for his servant David, and for Israel his people.

{9:1} After Solomon had finished building the house of the LORD, and his own palace, and had accomplished all his desires, {9:2} The LORD appeared to Solomon a second time, as he had appeared to him at Gibeon. {9:3} And the LORD said to him, "I have heard your prayer and supplication that you have made before me. I have consecrated this house which you have built, to put my name there forever; and my eyes and my heart will be there perpetually. {9:4} If you walk before me as your father David walked, with integrity of heart and uprightness, doing according to all that I have commanded you, and keeping my statutes and judgments, {9:5} Then I will establish the throne of your kingdom over Israel forever, as I promised to David your father, saying, 'You shall not fail to have a man on the throne of Israel.' {9:6} But if you or your descendants turn away from following me, and do not keep my commandments and my statutes which I have set before you, but go and serve other gods, and worship them, {9:7} Then I will cut off Israel from the land which I have given them; and this house which I have consecrated for my name I will cast out of my sight. Israel will be a proverb and a byword among all peoples. {9:8} And as for this house, which is exalted, everyone who passes by it will be astonished and hiss, and say, 'Why has the LORD done thus to this land and to this house?' {9:9} Then they will answer, 'Because they forsook the LORD their God, who brought their fathers out of the land of Egypt, and embraced other gods, and worshiped them and served them; therefore the LORD has brought all this calamity on them.' {9:10} Now it happened at the end of twenty years, when Solomon had built the two houses, the house of the LORD and the king's house {9:11} (Hiram king of Tyre had supplied Solomon with cedar and cypress and gold, as much as he desired), that King Solomon then gave Hiram twenty cities in the land of Galilee. {9:12} But when Hiram went from Tyre to see the cities which Solomon had given him, they did not please him. {9:13} So he said, "What kind of cities are these which you have given me, my brother?" And he called them the land of Cabul, as they are to this day. {9:14} Then Hiram sent the king one hundred and twenty talents of gold. {9:15} This is the reason for the labor force which King Solomon raised: to build the house of the LORD, his own house, the Millo, the wall of Jerusalem, Hazor, Megiddo, and Gezer. {9:16} (Pharaoh king of Egypt had gone up and taken Gezer and burned it with fire, had killed the Canaanites who dwelt in the city, and had given it as a dowry to his daughter, Solomon's wife.) {9:17} So Solomon built Gezer, Lower Beth Horon, {9:18} Baalath, and Tadmor in the wilderness, in the land of Judah, {9:19} All the storage cities that Solomon had, cities for his chariots and cities for his cavalry, and whatever Solomon desired to build in Jerusalem, in Lebanon, and in all the land of his dominion. {9:20} All the people who were left of the Amorites, Hittites, Perizzites, Hivites, and Jebusites, who were not of Israel— {9:21} that is, their descendants who were left in the land after them, whom the children of Israel had not been able to utterly destroy—Solomon imposed forced labor on them, as it is to this day. {9:22} But of the children of Israel Solomon made no forced laborers, because they were men of war and his servants: his officers, his captains, commanders of his chariots, and his cavalry. {9:23} These were the chief officers who were over Solomon's work: five hundred and fifty, who ruled over the people who did the work. {9:24} But Pharaoh's daughter came up from the City of David to her house which Solomon had built for her. Then he built the Millo. {9:25} Now three times a year Solomon offered burnt offerings and peace offerings on the altar which he had built for the LORD, and he burned incense on the altar that was before the LORD. So he finished the temple. {9:26} King Solomon also built a fleet of ships at Ezion Geber, which is near Elath on the shore of the Red Sea, in the land of Edom. {9:27} Then Hiram sent his servants with the fleet, seamen who knew the sea, to work with the servants of Solomon. {9:28} And they went to Ophir, and acquired four hundred and twenty talents of gold from there, and brought it to King Solomon.

{10:1} When the queen of Sheba heard about Solomon's fame, she came to test him with hard questions. {10:2} She arrived in Jerusalem with a large caravan, carrying spices, gold, and precious stones. When she met Solomon, she discussed everything on her mind with him. {10:3} Solomon answered all her questions; nothing was too hard for him to explain. {10:4} After the queen of Sheba had seen Solomon's wisdom and the palace he had built, {10:5} the food on his table, the seating of his officials, the attending servants in their robes, his cupbearers, and the burnt offerings he made at the LORD's temple, she was overwhelmed. {10:6} She said to the king, "The report I heard in my own country about your achievements and your wisdom is true. {10:7} But I did not believe these things until I came and saw with my own eyes. Indeed, not even half of the greatness of your wisdom was told to me; you have far exceeded the report I heard. {10:8} Your men and attendants are fortunate to be continually in your presence, hearing your wisdom. {10:9} Praise be to the LORD your God, who has delighted in you and placed you on the throne of Israel. Because of the LORD's eternal love for Israel, he has made you king to maintain justice and righteousness." {10:10} Then she gave the king 120 talents of gold, a large quantity of spices, and precious stones. Never again were so many spices brought in as those the queen of Sheba gave to King Solomon. {10:11} Hiram's fleet, which brought gold from Ophir, also brought from Ophir a large quantity of almug wood and precious stones. {10:12} The king used the almug wood to make supports for the LORD's temple and for the royal palace, and to make harps and lyres for the musicians. So much almug wood has never been imported or seen since that day. {10:13} King Solomon gave the queen of Sheba all she desired and asked for, besides what he had given her out of his royal bounty. Then she left and returned with her retinue to her own country. {10:14} The weight of the gold that Solomon received yearly was 666 talents, {10:15} not including the revenues from merchants and traders and from all the Arabian kings and the governors of the territories. {10:16} King Solomon made 200 large shields of hammered gold; 600 shekels of gold went into each shield. {10:17} He also made 300 smaller shields of hammered gold, with three minas of gold in each shield. The king put them in the Palace of the Forest of Lebanon. {10:18} Then the king made a great throne covered with ivory and overlaid with pure gold. {10:19} The throne had six steps, and its back had a rounded top. On both sides of the seat were armrests, with a lion standing beside each of them. {10:20} Twelve lions stood on the six steps, one at either end of each step. Nothing like it had ever been made for any other kingdom. {10:21} All King Solomon's goblets were gold, and all the household articles in the Palace of the Forest of Lebanon were pure gold. Nothing was made of silver, because silver was considered of little value in Solomon's time. {10:22} The king had a fleet of trading ships at sea along with the ships of Hiram. Once every three years it returned, bringing gold, silver, and ivory, and apes and baboons. {10:23} King Solomon was greater in riches and wisdom than all the other kings of the earth. {10:24} **The whole world sought audience with Solomon to hear the wisdom God had put in his heart.** {10:25} Year after year, everyone who came brought a gift—articles of silver and gold, robes, weapons and spices, and horses and mules. {10:26} Solomon accumulated chariots and horses; he had fourteen hundred chariots and twelve thousand horses, which he kept in the chariot cities and also with him in Jerusalem. {10:27} **The king made silver as common in Jerusalem as stones, and cedar as plentiful as sycamore-fig trees in the foothills.** {10:28} Solomon's horses were imported from Egypt and from all other countries. {10:29} As for the other events of Solomon's reign, from beginning to end, are they not written in the records of Nathan the prophet, in the prophecy of Ahijah the Shilonite and in the visions of Iddo the seer concerning Jeroboam son of Nebat?

{11:1} King Solomon, however, loved many foreign women besides Pharaoh's daughter—Moabites, Ammonites, Edomites, Sidonians, and Hittites. {11:2} They were from nations about which the LORD had told the Israelites, "You must not intermarry with them, because they will surely turn your hearts after their gods." Nevertheless, Solomon held fast to them in love. {11:3} He had seven hundred wives of royal birth and three hundred concubines, and his wives led him astray. {11:4} **As Solomon grew old, his wives turned his heart after other gods, and his heart was not fully devoted to the LORD his God, as the heart of his father David had been.** {11:5} He followed Ashtoreth the goddess of the Sidonians, and Molek the detestable god of the Ammonites. {11:6} So Solomon did evil in the eyes of the LORD; he did not follow the LORD completely, as David his father had done. {11:7} On a hill east of Jerusalem, Solomon built a high place for Chemosh the detestable god of Moab, and for Molek the detestable god of the Ammonites. {11:8} He did the same for all his foreign wives, who burned incense and offered sacrifices to their gods. {11:9} The LORD became angry with Solomon because his heart had turned away from the LORD, the God of Israel, who had appeared to him twice. {11:10} Although he had forbidden Solomon to follow other gods, Solomon did not keep the LORD's command. {11:11} So the LORD said to Solomon, "Since this is your attitude and you have not kept my covenant and my decrees, which I commanded you, I will most certainly tear the kingdom away from you and give it to one of your subordinates. {11:12} Nevertheless, for the sake of David your father, I will not do it during your lifetime. I will tear it out of the hand of your son. {11:13} Yet I will not tear the whole kingdom from him, but will give him one tribe for the sake of David my servant and for the sake of Jerusalem, which I have chosen." {11:14} Then the LORD raised up against Solomon an adversary, Hadad the Edomite, from the royal line of Edom. {11:15} Earlier when David was fighting with Edom, Joab the commander of the army, had gone up to bury the dead. After he had killed every male in Edom, {11:16} Joab and all Israel stayed there for six months until they had destroyed every male in Edom. {11:17} But Hadad, still only a boy, fled to Egypt with some Edomite officials who had served his father. {11:18} They set out from Midian and went to Paran. Then taking people from Paran with them, they went to Egypt, to Pharaoh king of Egypt, who gave Hadad a house and land and provided him with food. {11:19} Pharaoh was so pleased with Hadad that he gave him his sister, Queen Tahpenes' sister, in marriage. {11:20} The sister of Tahpenes bore him a son named Genubath, whom Tahpenes brought up in the royal palace. There Genubath lived with Pharaoh's own children. {11:21} While he was in Egypt, Hadad heard that David was resting with his ancestors and that Joab the commander of the army was also dead. Then Hadad said to Pharaoh, "Let me go, that I may return to my own country." {11:22} "What have you lacked here that you want to go back to your own country?" Pharaoh asked. "Nothing," Hadad replied, "but do let me go!" {11:23} And God raised up against Solomon another adversary, Rezon son of Eliada, who had fled from his master, Hadadezer king of Zobah. {11:24} When David destroyed Zobah's army, Rezon gathered a band of men around him and became their leader; they went to Damascus, where they settled and took control. {11:25} Rezon was Israel's adversary as long as Solomon lived, adding to the trouble caused by Hadad. So Rezon ruled in Aram and was hostile toward Israel. {11:26} Also, Jeroboam son of Nebat rebelled against the king. He was one of Solomon's officials, an Ephraimite from Zeredah, and his mother was a widow named Zeruah. {11:27} Here is the account of how he rebelled against the king: Solomon had built the terraces and had filled in the gap in the wall of the city of David his father. {11:28} Now Jeroboam was a man of standing, and when Solomon saw how well the young man did his work, he put him in charge of the whole labor force of the tribes of Joseph. {11:29} About that time Jeroboam was going out of Jerusalem, and Ahijah the prophet of Shiloh met him on the way, wearing a new cloak. The two of them were alone out in the country, {11:30} and Ahijah took hold of the new cloak he was wearing and tore it into twelve pieces. {11:31} Then he said to Jeroboam, "Take ten pieces for yourself, for this is what the LORD, the God of Israel, says: 'See, I am going to tear the kingdom out of Solomon's hand and give you ten tribes. {11:32} But for the sake of my servant David and the city of Jerusalem, which I have chosen out of all the tribes of Israel, he will have one tribe. {11:33} I will do this because they have forsaken me and worshiped Ashtoreth the goddess of the Sidonians, Chemosh the god of the Moabites, and Molek the god of the Ammonites, and have not walked in obedience to me, nor done what is right in my eyes, nor kept my decrees and laws as David, Solomon's father, did. {11:34} "'But I will not take the whole kingdom out of Solomon's hand; I have made him ruler all the days of his life for the sake of David my servant, whom I chose and who obeyed my commands and decrees. {11:35} I will take the kingdom from his son's hands and give you ten tribes. {11:36} I will give one tribe to his son so that David my servant may always have a lamp before me in Jerusalem, the city where I chose to put my Name. {11:37} However, as for you, I will take you, and you will rule over all that your heart desires; you will be king over Israel. {11:38} And if you listen to all that I command you, and walk in my ways, and do what is right in my sight, keeping my statutes and commandments as David my servant did, then I will be with you. I will build you a dynasty as enduring as the one I built for David, and I will give Israel to you. {11:39} But I will afflict the descendants of David because of this, though not forever. {11:40} Solomon tried to kill Jeroboam, but Jeroboam fled to Egypt, to Shishak king of Egypt, and stayed there until Solomon's death. {11:41} The rest of the events of Solomon's reign, along with all his accomplishments and his wisdom, are recorded in the book of the acts of Solomon. {11:42} Solomon reigned in Jerusalem over all Israel for forty years. {11:43} Then he rested with his ancestors and was buried in the city of his father David. And Rehoboam his son succeeded him as king.

{12:1} Rehoboam went to Shechem, where all Israel had gathered to make him king. {12:2} While Jeroboam was still in Egypt, having fled from King Solomon, he heard about it. {12:3} So they sent for Jeroboam, and he and all Israel came and spoke to Rehoboam. {12:4} They said, "Your father made our burden heavy. Now, lighten it, and we will serve you." {12:5} Rehoboam told them, "Go away for three days, then come back to me." So the people left. {12:6} Rehoboam consulted with the older advisers who had served Solomon his father, asking how he should respond to the people. {12:7} They advised him to be kind and serve the people, and they would serve him forever. {12:8} But Rehoboam rejected their counsel and consulted with his peers who had grown up with him. {12:9} They advised him to make the yoke even heavier, saying, 'Tell them, "My little finger is thicker than my father's waist."' {12:10} "My father made your yoke heavy, but I will make it even heavier," he declared. "My father disciplined you with whips, but I will use scorpions!" {12:11} On the third day, Jeroboam and the people returned as the king had directed. {12:12} Rehoboam answered them harshly, rejecting the advice of the older men, and spoke according to the counsel of the young men. {12:13} He said, "My father made your yoke heavy, and I will add to it. My father disciplined you with whips, but I will use scorpions." {12:14} The king did not listen to the people, for this turn of events was from the LORD, fulfilling the word He had spoken to Jeroboam. {12:15} When all Israel saw that the king refused to listen to them, they said, "What share do we have in David? We have no inheritance in the son of Jesse. To your tents, O Israel! Look after your own house, O David!" So Israel departed to their tents. {12:16} But the Israelites who lived in the cities of Judah remained loyal to Rehoboam. {12:17} Rehoboam then sent Adoram, who was in charge of forced labor, but all Israel stoned him to death. So King Rehoboam quickly mounted his chariot and fled to Jerusalem. {12:18} And Israel has been in rebellion against the house of David to this day. {12:19} When all Israel heard that Jeroboam had returned, they summoned him to the assembly and made him king over all Israel, except for the tribe of Judah. {12:20} When Rehoboam arrived in Jerusalem, he mobilized all the men of Judah and Benjamin—180,000 chosen warriors—to fight against the house of Israel and restore the kingdom to himself. {12:21} But the word of God came to Shemaiah, a man of God, saying, {12:22} "Speak to Rehoboam, son of Solomon, king of Judah, and to all the people of Judah and Benjamin, and to the rest of the people, saying, {12:23} 'Thus says the LORD: You shall not go up nor fight against your brethren, the children of Israel. Let every man return to his house, for this thing is from Me.'" {12:24} And they obeyed the word of the LORD and turned back, as the LORD commanded. {12:25} Jeroboam then built Shechem in the hill country of Ephraim and lived there. From there he went out and built Penuel. {12:26} Jeroboam thought to himself, "The kingdom will now likely revert to the house of David. {12:27} If these people go up to offer sacrifices at the temple of the LORD in Jerusalem, they will again give their allegiance to their lord, Rehoboam king of Judah, and they will kill me and return to King Rehoboam." {12:28} After seeking advice, the king made two golden calves and said to the people, "It is too much for you to go up to Jerusalem. Here are your gods, O Israel, who brought you up out of Egypt." {12:29} He set one up in Bethel, and the other in Dan. {12:30} And this became a sin, for the people went even as far as Dan to worship the one there. {12:31} Jeroboam also built shrines on high places and appointed priests from all sorts of people, even though they were not Levites. {12:32} He instituted a festival on the fifteenth day of the eighth month, like the festival held in Judah, and offered sacrifices on the altar. This he did in Bethel, sacrificing to the calves he had made. And at Bethel, he also installed priests at the high places he had made. {12:33} On the fifteenth day of the eighth month, a month of his own choosing, he offered sacrifices on the altar he had built at Bethel. So he instituted the festival for the Israelites and went up to the altar to make offerings.

{13:1} A man of God from Judah came to Bethel by the word of the LORD while Jeroboam was at the altar burning incense. {13:2} He cried out against the altar by the word of the LORD, saying, "O altar, altar! This is what the LORD says: 'A son named Josiah will be born to the house of David. On you he will sacrifice the priests of the high places who burn incense on you, and human bones will be burned on you.'" {13:3} He gave a sign that same day, saying, "This is the sign the LORD has spoken: 'The altar will be split apart, and the ashes on it will be poured out.'" {13:4} When King Jeroboam heard what the man of God cried out against the altar in Bethel, he stretched out his hand from the altar and said, "Seize him!" But his hand, which he stretched out toward the man of God, shriveled up so that he could not pull it back. {13:5} The altar was also split apart, and the ashes poured out from the altar, according to the sign given by the man of God by the word of the LORD. {13:6} The king pleaded with the man of God, "Please, pray to the LORD your God for me, that my hand may be restored." So the man of God prayed to the LORD, and the king's hand was restored and became as it was before. {13:7} Then the king said to the man of God, "Come home with me for a meal, and I will give you a gift." {13:8} But the man of God replied to the king, "Even if you were to give me half your possessions, I would not go with you, nor would I eat bread or drink water here. {13:9} For I was commanded by the word of the LORD: 'You must not eat bread or drink water or return by the way you came.'" {13:10} So he took another road and did not return by the way he had come to Bethel. {13:11} Now there was an old prophet living in Bethel, and his sons came and told him everything the man of God had done that day in Bethel, including the words he had spoken to the king. They also told their father what had happened to the man of God. {13:12} Their father asked them, "Which way did he go?" And his sons showed him which way the man of God who had come from Judah had gone. {13:13} So he said to his sons, "Saddle the donkey for me." And when they had saddled the donkey for him, he mounted it {13:14} and rode after the man of God. He found him sitting under an oak tree and asked, "Are you the man of God who came from Judah?" "I am," he replied. {13:15} So the prophet said to him, "Come home with me and eat bread." {13:16} But the man of God replied, "I cannot turn back with you or go with you, nor can I eat bread or drink water with you in this place. {13:17} For I was told by the word of the LORD: 'You must not eat bread or drink water there or return by the way you came.'" {13:18} The prophet answered, "I too am a prophet, as you are. And an angel said to me by the word of the LORD: 'Bring him back with you to your house so that he may eat bread and drink water.'" But he was lying to him. {13:19} So the man of God went back with him, and ate bread in his house and drank water. {13:20} While they were sitting at the table, the word of the LORD came to the prophet who had brought him back. {13:21} He cried out to the man of God who had come from Judah, "This is what the LORD says: 'You have defied the word of the LORD and have not kept the command the LORD your God gave you. {13:22} You came back and ate bread and drank water in the place where he told you not to eat or drink. Therefore your body will not be buried in the tomb of your ancestors.'" {13:23} After the man of God had finished eating and drinking, the prophet who had brought him back saddled his donkey for him. {13:24} As he went on his way, a lion met him on the road and killed him, and his body was left lying on the road, with both the donkey and the lion standing beside it. {13:25} Some people who passed by saw the body lying in the road with the lion standing beside it, and they went and reported it in the city where the old prophet lived. {13:26} When the prophet who had brought him back from his journey heard of it, he said, "It is the man of God who defied the word of the LORD. The LORD has given him over to the lion, which has mauled him and killed him, as the word of the LORD had warned him." {13:27} The prophet said to his sons, "Saddle the donkey for me," and they did so. {13:28} Then he went out and found the body lying on the road, with the donkey and the lion standing beside it. The lion had neither eaten the body nor mauled the donkey. {13:29} And the prophet took up the carcass of the man of God, and laid it on the donkey, and brought it back. The old prophet came to the city to mourn and bury him. {13:30} He laid the carcass in his own grave, and they mourned over him, saying, "Alas, my brother!" {13:31} After burying him, he spoke to his sons, saying, "When I die, bury me in the tomb where the man of God is buried; lay my bones beside his bones. {13:32} For the prophecy he declared by the word of the LORD against the altar in Bethel and against all the shrines on the high places in the cities of Samaria will surely come to pass." {13:33} After these events, Jeroboam did not turn from his evil ways but appointed priests from all sorts of people for the high places. Whoever desired to be a priest, he consecrated him, and he became one of the priests of the high places. {13:34} This was the sin that caused the downfall of the house of Jeroboam, leading to its destruction from the face of the earth.

{14:1} At that time, Abijah, the son of Jeroboam, fell sick. {14:2} Jeroboam said to his wife, "Get up, disguise yourself so you won't be recognized as

Jeroboam's wife, and go to Shiloh. Ahijah the prophet is there, the one who told me I would be king over this people. {14:3} Take ten loaves of bread, some cakes, and a jar of honey, and go to him. He will tell you what will happen to the child." {14:4} Jeroboam's wife did as he said. She went to Shiloh and came to Ahijah's house. Ahijah, however, could not see; his eyes were dim with age. {14:5} The LORD said to Ahijah, "Jeroboam's wife is coming to inquire of you about her son, for he is ill. You are to give her this message when she arrives: When she comes in, she will pretend to be someone else." {14:6} When Ahijah heard the sound of her footsteps entering the door, he said, "Come in, wife of Jeroboam. Why do you pretend to be someone else? I have a message for you." {14:7} "Go and tell Jeroboam," says the LORD, the God of Israel. "I promoted you from among the people and made you ruler over my people Israel. {14:8} I tore the kingdom away from the house of David and gave it to you, but you have not been like my servant David, who kept my commandments and followed me with all his heart, doing only what was right in my eyes. {14:9} Instead, you have done more evil than anyone before you. You have made other gods and cast me behind your back, provoking me to anger with your idols. {14:10} Therefore, I will bring disaster on the house of Jeroboam: I will cut off from Jeroboam every last male in Israel—slave or free. I will wipe out the house of Jeroboam as one sweeps away dung until it is all gone. {14:11} Dogs will eat those belonging to Jeroboam who die in the city, and the birds will feed on those who die in the field, for the LORD has spoken." {14:12} "Go back home," Ahijah continued. "As soon as you enter the city, the child will die. {14:13} All Israel will mourn for him and bury him. He is the only one belonging to Jeroboam who will be buried, because he is the only one in the house of Jeroboam in whom the LORD, the God of Israel, has found anything good. {14:14} The LORD will raise up for himself a king over Israel who will cut off the family of Jeroboam. This is the day! What? Yes, even now. {14:15} And the LORD will strike Israel, making it like a reed swaying in the water. He will uproot Israel from this good land he gave to their ancestors and scatter them beyond the Euphrates River, because they aroused the LORD's anger with their Asherah poles. {14:16} And he will give Israel up because of the sins Jeroboam has committed and has caused Israel to commit." {14:17} Jeroboam's wife got up, left, and went to Tirzah. As soon as she stepped over the threshold of the house, the child died. {14:18} They buried him, and all Israel mourned for him, as the LORD had said through his servant Ahijah the prophet. {14:19} The other events of Jeroboam's reign, his wars, and how he ruled are recorded in the Book of the Annals of the Kings of Israel. {14:20} Jeroboam reigned for twenty-two years. Then he rested with his ancestors, and his son Nadab succeeded him as king. {14:21} Meanwhile, Rehoboam, Solomon's son, ruled in Judah. Rehoboam was forty-one years old when he became king, and he reigned seventeen years in Jerusalem, the city the LORD had chosen out of all the tribes of Israel to put his Name there. His mother's name was Naamah; she was an Ammonite. {14:22} Judah did evil in the LORD's sight. By the sins they committed, they aroused his jealousy even more than their ancestors had done. {14:23} They also built high places, sacred pillars, and Asherah poles on every high hill and under every green tree. {14:24} There were even male shrine prostitutes in the land, and the people engaged in all the detestable practices of the nations the LORD had driven out before the Israelites. {14:25} In the fifth year of King Rehoboam, Shishak king of Egypt attacked Jerusalem. {14:26} He carried off the treasures of the LORD's temple and the treasures of the royal palace. He took everything, including all the gold shields Solomon had made. {14:27} So King Rehoboam made bronze shields to replace them and assigned these to the commanders of the guard on duty at the entrance to the royal palace. {14:28} Whenever the king went to the LORD's temple, the guards bore the shields, then returned them to the guardroom. {14:29} The rest of the events of Rehoboam's reign and all he did are recorded in the Book of the Annals of the Kings of Judah. {14:30} There was continual warfare between Rehoboam and Jeroboam. {14:31} Rehoboam rested with his ancestors and was buried with them in the City of David. His mother's name was Naamah; she was an Ammonite. And his son Abijam succeeded him as king.

{15:1} In the eighteenth year of King Jeroboam's reign over Israel, Abijam became king of Judah. {15:2} He ruled in Jerusalem for three years. His mother's name was Maachah, the daughter of Abishalom. {15:3} Abijam followed the sinful ways of his father before him, and his heart was not fully committed to the LORD his God, like his ancestor David's heart. {15:4} But for the sake of David, the LORD his God gave him a lamp in Jerusalem, raising up his son after him and establishing Jerusalem. {15:5} David had done what was right in the LORD's eyes, except in the case of Uriah the Hittite. {15:6} There was continual warfare between Rehoboam and Jeroboam as long as Abijam reigned. {15:7} The rest of Abijam's deeds and his wars are recorded in the Book of the Annals of the Kings of Judah. And there was war between Abijam and Jeroboam. {15:8} Abijam died and was buried with his ancestors in the City of David. His son Asa succeeded him as king. {15:9} In the twentieth year of Jeroboam's reign over Israel, Asa became king of Judah. {15:10} He ruled in Jerusalem for forty-one years. His mother's name was Maachah, the daughter of Abishalom. {15:11} Asa did what was right in the LORD's sight, following the example of his ancestor David. {15:12} He expelled the male shrine prostitutes from the land and removed all the idols his ancestors had made. {15:13} He even deposed his grandmother Maachah from her position as queen mother because she had made an obscene Asherah pole. Asa cut down the pole and burned it in the Kidron Valley. {15:14} Though the high places were not removed, Asa's heart remained fully committed to the LORD throughout his life. {15:15} He brought into the temple of the LORD the silver and gold and articles that he and his father had dedicated. {15:16} There was continual warfare between Asa and Baasha king of Israel throughout their reigns. {15:17} Baasha king of Israel went up against Judah and fortified Ramah to prevent anyone from leaving or entering the territory of King Asa of Judah. {15:18} Asa took all the silver and gold remaining in the treasuries of the LORD's temple and the royal palace. He entrusted them to his officials and sent them to Ben-Hadad son of Tabrimmon, the son of Hezion, the king of Aram, who was ruling in Damascus, with this message: {15:19} "Let there be a treaty between me and you, as there was between my father and your father. See, I am sending you a gift of silver and gold. Break your treaty with Baasha king of Israel so he will withdraw from me." {15:20} Ben-Hadad agreed with King Asa and sent his army commanders against the towns of Israel. They conquered Ijon, Dan, Abel Beth Maakah, and all Kinnereth, as well as Naphtali. {15:21} When Baasha heard this, he stopped fortifying Ramah and withdrew to Tirzah. {15:22} King Asa issued a decree throughout Judah—no one was exempted—and they carried away from Ramah the stones and timber Baasha had used to build. With them King Asa fortified Geba in Benjamin and Mizpah. {15:23} The rest of all the acts of Asa, all his achievements, all he did, and the cities he built are written in the Book of the Annals of the Kings of Judah. In his old age, Asa suffered from a foot disease. {15:24} Asa rested with his ancestors and was buried with them in the City of David his father. Jehoshaphat his son succeeded him as king. {15:25} Nadab son of Jeroboam became king of Israel in the second year of Asa's reign over Judah, and he reigned over Israel for two years. {15:26} He did evil in the sight of the LORD, following the ways of his father and the sin he had caused Israel to commit. {15:27} Baasha son of Ahijah, from the tribe of Issachar, conspired against him, and Baasha struck him down at Gibbethon, a Philistine town, while Nadab and all Israel were besieging it. {15:28} Baasha killed Nadab in the third year of Asa's reign over Judah and succeeded him as king. {15:29} As soon as Baasha became king, he killed all the house of Jeroboam. He left not one male alive to Jeroboam's name. It was in accordance with the word of the LORD spoken through his servant Ahijah the Shilonite— {15:30} because of the sins Jeroboam had committed and had caused Israel to commit, and because he aroused the anger of the LORD, the God of Israel. {15:31} The rest of Nadab's deeds and all he did are recorded in the Book of the Annals of the Kings of Israel. {15:32} There was continual warfare between Asa and Baasha king of Israel throughout their reigns. {15:33} In the third year of Asa king of Judah, Baasha son of Ahijah became king of all Israel in Tirzah, and he reigned twenty-four years. {15:34} He did evil in the sight of the LORD, following the ways of Jeroboam and the sin he had caused Israel to commit.

{16:1} Then the word of the LORD came to Jehu, the son of Hanani, against Baasha, saying, {16:2} "Because I exalted you from the dust and made you ruler over my people Israel, but you have followed in the footsteps of Jeroboam, leading my people into sin and angering me with their wickedness, {16:3} therefore, I will wipe out the descendants of Baasha and his house, making your house like that of Jeroboam son of Nebat. {16:4} Any of Baasha's family who dies in the city will be eaten by dogs, and any who die in the field will be eaten by birds." {16:5} The rest of Baasha's deeds and his strength are recorded in the annals of the kings of Israel. {16:6} Baasha died and was buried in Tirzah, and his son Elah became king in his place. {16:7} But because of the evil Baasha had done, as well as his son Elah, provoking the LORD's anger with their sinful actions and by following the example of Jeroboam, and because Baasha had killed Jeroboam, the word of the LORD against Baasha and his house was delivered by the prophet Jehu. {16:8} In the twenty-sixth year of King Asa of Judah, Elah son of Baasha began his reign over Israel in Tirzah, and he reigned for two years. {16:9} While Elah was in Tirzah, getting drunk in the house of Arza, the supervisor of his palace in Tirzah, his servant Zimri, the commander of half his chariots, conspired against him. {16:10} Zimri went in, struck Elah down, and killed him in the twenty-seventh year of King Asa of Judah, and then became king in his place. {16:11} As soon as Zimri became king and sat on the throne, he killed off the entire household of Baasha, leaving him not even one male relative or friend. {16:12} This fulfilled the word of the LORD against Baasha, delivered by Jehu the prophet, because of all the sins Baasha and his son Elah had committed, leading Israel into sin and provoking the LORD, the God of Israel, with their worthless idols. {16:13} The rest of Elah's deeds and his treachery are recorded in the annals of the kings of Israel. {16:14} In the twenty-seventh year of King Asa of Judah, Zimri reigned over Israel for seven days in Tirzah. The Israelite army was camped near Gibbethon, a Philistine city. {16:15} When the Israelites in the camp heard that Zimri had plotted against the king and assassinated him, they proclaimed Omri, the commander of the army, as king over Israel that very day in the camp. {16:16} Omri and all the Israelites with him left Gibbethon and besieged Tirzah. {16:17} When Zimri saw that the city was captured, he went into the citadel of the royal palace, set the palace on fire over himself, and died. {16:18} This happened because of the sins he committed in doing evil in the sight of the LORD, following the sinful ways of Jeroboam and leading Israel into sin. {16:19} The rest of Zimri's deeds and his conspiracy are recorded in the annals of the kings of Israel. {16:20} Then the people of Israel were divided into two factions: half supported Tibni son of Ginath to make him king, and the other half supported Omri. {16:21} But Omri's followers proved stronger than those of Tibni, so Tibni died, and Omri became king. {16:22} In the thirty-first year of King Asa of Judah, Omri began his reign over Israel, and he reigned for twelve years, six of them in Tirzah. {16:23} He bought the hill of Samaria from Shemer for two talents of silver and built a city on the hill. He named it Samaria after Shemer, the former owner of the hill. {16:24} But Omri did evil in the sight of the LORD and committed more wickedness than all who were before him. {16:25} He followed the sinful ways of Jeroboam son of Nebat, leading Israel into sin and provoking the LORD, the God of Israel, with their worthless idols. {16:26} The rest of Omri's deeds and his might are recorded in the annals of the kings of Israel. {16:27} Omri died and was buried in Samaria, and his son Ahab succeeded him as king. {16:28} In the thirty-eighth year of King Asa of Judah, Ahab son of Omri began his reign over Israel, and he reigned in Samaria for twenty-two years. {16:29} Ahab did more evil in the sight of the LORD than all who were before him. {16:30} As if it were not enough for him to follow the sinful ways of Jeroboam son of Nebat, he married Jezebel, the daughter of Ethbaal king of the Sidonians, and then proceeded to serve Baal and worship him. {16:31} He set up an altar for Baal in the temple of Baal that he built in Samaria. {16:32} Ahab also made an Asherah pole, provoking the LORD, the God of Israel, to anger more than all the kings of Israel before him. {16:33} In Ahab's time, Hiel of Bethel rebuilt Jericho. He laid its foundations at the cost of his firstborn son Abiram and set up its gates at the cost of his youngest son Segub, in accordance with the word of the LORD spoken by Joshua son of Nun. {16:34} All of Ahab's deeds and the sins he committed, including his building of the temple of Baal, are recorded in the annals of the kings of Israel.

{17:1} *Elijah the Tishbite, who lived in Gilead, said to Ahab, "As the LORD God of Israel lives, there will be no dew or rain in the coming years, except at my word."* {17:2} Then the word of the LORD came to Elijah, saying, {17:3} "Go eastward and hide by the Brook Cherith, which is east of the Jordan. {17:4} You will drink from the brook, and I have commanded the ravens to feed you there." {17:5} So Elijah did as the LORD commanded. He stayed by the Brook Cherith, east of the Jordan, and the ravens brought him bread and meat in the morning and evening, and he drank from the brook. {17:6} But after some time, the brook dried up because there had been no rain in the land. {17:7} Then the word of the LORD came to Elijah, saying, {17:8} "Arise, go to Zarephath, which belongs to Sidon, and stay there. I have commanded a widow there to provide for you." {17:9} So Elijah went to Zarephath. And when he came to the gate of the city, indeed a widow was there gathering sticks. He called to her and said, "Please bring me a little water in a cup, that I may drink." {17:10} And as she was going to get it, he called to her and said, "Please bring me a morsel of bread in your hand." {17:11} So she said, "As the LORD your God lives, I do not have bread, only a handful of flour in a bin, and a little oil in a jar; and see, I am gathering a couple of sticks that I may go in and prepare it for myself and my son, that we may eat it, and die." {17:12} And Elijah said to her, "Do not fear; go and do as you have said, but make me a small cake from it first, and bring it to me; and afterward make some for yourself and your son. {17:13} For thus says the LORD God of Israel: 'The bin of flour shall not be used up, nor shall the jar of oil run dry, until the day the LORD sends rain on the earth.'" {17:14} So she went away and did according to the word of Elijah; and she and he and her household ate for many days. {17:15} The bin of flour was not used up, nor did the jar of oil run dry, according to the word of the LORD which He spoke by Elijah. {17:16} Now it happened after these things that the son of the woman who owned the house became sick. And his sickness was so serious that there was no breath left in him. {17:17} So she said to Elijah, "What have I to do with you, O man of God? Have you come to me to bring my sin to remembrance and to kill my son?" {17:18} And he said to her, "Give me your son." So he took him out of her arms and carried him to the upper room where he was staying, and laid him on his own bed. {17:19} Then he cried out to the LORD and said, "O LORD my God, have You also brought tragedy on the widow with whom I lodge, by killing her son?" {17:20} And he stretched himself out on the child three times, and cried out to the LORD and said, "O LORD my God, I pray, let this child's soul come back to him." {17:21} Then the LORD heard the voice of Elijah; and the soul of the child came back to him, and he revived. {17:22} And Elijah took the child and brought him down from the upper room into the house, and gave him to his mother. And Elijah said, "See, your son lives!" {17:23} And Elijah took the child and brought him down from the upper room into the house, and gave him to his mother. And Elijah said, "See, your son lives!" {17:24} Then the woman said to Elijah, "Now I know that you are a man of God, and that the word of the LORD in your mouth is truth."

{18:1} After a long time, the word of the LORD came to Elijah in the third year, saying, "Go, present yourself to Ahab, and I will send rain on the earth." {18:2} So Elijah went to present himself to Ahab. Now the famine was severe in Samaria. {18:3} And Ahab called Obadiah, who was in charge of the palace. (Now Obadiah feared the LORD greatly. {18:4} For when Jezebel massacred the prophets of the LORD, Obadiah took a hundred prophets, hid them fifty to a cave, and provided them with bread and water.) {18:5} Ahab said to Obadiah, "Go through the land to all the springs of water and to all the streams. Perhaps we may find grass to keep the horses and mules alive, so that we will not have to kill any of our animals." {18:6} They divided the land between them to explore it. Ahab went one way by himself, and Obadiah went another way by himself. {18:7} As Obadiah was walking along, he suddenly met Elijah. Obadiah recognized him, bowed down to the ground, and said, "Is it really you, my lord Elijah?" {18:8} "Yes," he replied. "Go tell your master, 'Elijah is here.'" {18:9} But Obadiah said, "What sin have I committed, that you are delivering your servant into the hand of Ahab to kill me? {18:10} As surely as the LORD your God lives, there is no nation or kingdom where my lord has not sent someone to look for you. And when they said, 'He is not here,' he made them swear that they could not find you. {18:11} And now you tell me to go to my master and say, 'Elijah is here.' {18:12} But as soon as I leave you, the Spirit of the LORD will carry you away to some unknown place. Then when I go to tell Ahab and he doesn't find you, he will kill me. Yet I have been a devout worshiper of the LORD since my youth. {18:13} Wasn't it reported to my lord what I did when Jezebel killed the prophets of the LORD? I hid a hundred of the LORD's prophets in two caves, fifty in each, and provided them with bread and water. {18:14} And now you tell me, 'Go tell your master, "Elijah is here,"' and he will kill me!" {18:15} Elijah said, "As the LORD of Hosts lives, before whom I stand, I will surely present myself to Ahab today." {18:16} So Obadiah went to meet Ahab and told him. Then Ahab went to meet Elijah. {18:17} When Ahab saw Elijah, he said to him, "Is it you, the one who brings disaster on Israel?" {18:18} "I have not brought disaster on Israel," Elijah replied, "but you and your father's house have, by abandoning the commandments of the LORD and following the Baals. {18:19} Now summon all Israel to meet me at Mount Carmel, along with the four hundred and fifty prophets of Baal and the four hundred prophets of Asherah who eat at Jezebel's table." {18:20} So Ahab summoned all the Israelites and gathered the prophets at Mount Carmel. {18:21} Then Elijah approached all the people and said, "How long will you waver between two opinions? If the LORD is God, follow Him. But if Baal is God, follow him." But the people did not answer him a word. {18:22} Then Elijah said to the people, "I am the only remaining prophet of the LORD, but Baal has four hundred and fifty prophets. {18:23} Let two bulls be given to us. Let them choose one bull for themselves, cut it into pieces, and place it on the wood, but not light the fire. I will prepare the other bull, lay it on the wood, and not light the fire. {18:24} Then you may call on the name of your gods, and I will call on the name of the LORD. The God who answers by fire, He is God." And all the people answered, "What you say is good." {18:25} Then Elijah said to the prophets of Baal, "Choose one bull for yourselves and prepare it first, since there are so many of you. Then call on the name of your god, but do not light the fire." {18:26} So they took the bull given them, prepared it, and called on the name of Baal from morning until noon, shouting, "O Baal, answer us!" But there was no sound, and no one answered as they leaped around the altar they had made. {18:27} At noon Elijah began to taunt them: "Shout louder, for he is a god! Perhaps he is deep in thought, or occupied, or on a journey. Perhaps he is sleeping and must be awakened!" {18:28} So they shouted louder and cut themselves with knives and spears, according to their custom, until their blood flowed out all over them. {18:29} Midday passed, and they kept on raving until the time of the evening sacrifice. But there was no response, no one answered, and no one paid attention. {18:30} Then Elijah said to all the people, "Come near to me." So all the people approached him. And he repaired the altar of the LORD that had been torn down. {18:31} Elijah took twelve stones, one for each of the tribes descended from Jacob, to whom the LORD had said, "Your name shall be Israel." {18:32} With the stones he built an altar in the name of the LORD, and he dug a trench around it large enough to hold about two seahs of seed. {18:33} He arranged the wood, cut the bull into pieces, and laid it on the wood. Then he said to them, "Fill four large jars with water and pour it on the offering and on the wood." {18:34} "Do it again," he said, and they did it again. "Do it a third time," he ordered, and they did it a third time. {18:35} The water ran down around the altar and even filled the trench. {18:36} At the time of sacrifice, the prophet Elijah stepped forward and prayed: "LORD, the God of Abraham, Isaac, and Israel, let it be known today that you are God in Israel and that I am your servant and have done all these things at your command. {18:37} Answer me, LORD, answer me, so these people will know that you, LORD, are God, and that you are turning their hearts back again." {18:38} Then the fire of the LORD fell and burned up the sacrifice, the wood, the stones, and the soil, and also licked up the water in the trench. {18:39} When all the people saw this, they fell prostrate and cried, "The LORD—he is God! The LORD—he is God!" {18:40} Then Elijah commanded them, "Seize the prophets of Baal. Don't let anyone get away!" They seized them, and Elijah had them brought down to the Kishon Valley and slaughtered there. {18:41} And Elijah said to Ahab, "Go, eat and drink, for there is the sound of a heavy rain." {18:42} So Ahab went off to eat and drink, but Elijah climbed to the top of Carmel, bent down to the ground, and put his face between his knees. {18:43} "Go and look toward the sea," he told his servant. And he went up and looked. "There is nothing there," he said. Seven times Elijah said, "Go back." {18:44} The seventh time the servant reported, "A cloud as small as a man's hand is rising from the sea." So Elijah said, "Go and tell Ahab, 'Hitch up your chariot and go down before the rain stops you.'" {18:45} Meanwhile, the sky grew black with clouds, the wind rose, a heavy rain started falling, and Ahab rode off to Jezreel. {18:46} The power of the LORD came on Elijah, and tucking his cloak into his belt, he ran ahead of Ahab all the way to Jezreel.

{19:1} Ahab told Jezebel all that Elijah had done, including how he had killed all the prophets with the sword. {19:2} Jezebel sent a messenger to Elijah with a threat: "May the gods deal with me, be it ever so severely, if by this time tomorrow I do not make your life like that of one of them." {19:3} Elijah was afraid and ran for his life. When he came to Beer-sheba in Judah, he left his servant there, {19:4} while he himself went a day's journey into the wilderness. He came to a broom bush, sat down under it and prayed that he might die. "I have had enough, LORD," he said. "Take my life; I am no better than my ancestors." {19:5} **Then he lay down under the bush and fell asleep. All at once an angel touched him and said, "Get up and eat."** {19:6} He looked around, and there by his head was some bread baked over hot coals, and a jar of water. He ate and drank and then lay down again. {19:7} The angel of the LORD came back a second time and touched him and said, "Get up and eat, for the journey is too much for you." {19:8} So he got up and ate and drank. Strengthened by that food, he traveled forty days and forty nights until he reached Horeb, the mountain of God. {19:9} There he went into a cave and spent the night. And the word of the LORD came to him: "What are you doing here, Elijah?" {19:10} He replied, "I have been very zealous for the LORD God Almighty. The Israelites have rejected your covenant, torn down your altars, and put your prophets to death with the sword. I am the only one left, and now they are trying to kill me too." {19:11} The LORD said, "Go out and stand on the mountain in the presence of the LORD, for the LORD is about to pass by." Then a great and powerful wind tore the mountains apart and shattered the rocks before the LORD, but the LORD was not in the wind. After the wind there was an earthquake, but the LORD was not in the earthquake. {19:12} After the earthquake came a fire, but the LORD was not in the fire. And after the fire came a gentle whisper. {19:13} When Elijah heard it, he pulled his cloak over his face and went out and stood at the mouth of the cave. Then a voice said to him, "What are you doing here, Elijah?" {19:14} He replied, "I have been very zealous for the LORD God Almighty. The Israelites have rejected your covenant, torn down your altars, and put your prophets to death with the sword. I am the only one left, and now they are trying to kill me too." {19:15} The LORD said to him, "Go back the way you came, and go to the Desert of Damascus. When you get there, anoint Hazael king over Aram. {19:16} Also, anoint Jehu son of Nimshi king over Israel, and anoint Elisha son of Shaphat from Abel Meholah to succeed you as prophet. {19:17} Jehu will put to death any who escape the sword of Hazael, and Elisha will put to death any who escape the sword of Jehu. {19:18} Yet I reserve seven thousand in Israel—all whose knees have not bowed down to Baal and whose mouths have not kissed him." {19:19} So Elijah went from there and found Elisha son of Shaphat. He was plowing with twelve yoke of oxen, and he himself was driving the twelfth pair. Elijah went up to him and threw his cloak around him. {19:20} Elisha then left his oxen and ran after Elijah. "Let me kiss my father and mother goodbye," he said, "and then I will come with you." "Go back," Elijah replied. "What have I done to you?" {19:21} So Elisha left him and went back. He took his yoke of oxen and slaughtered them. He burned the plowing equipment to cook the meat and gave it to the people, and they ate. Then he set out to follow Elijah and became his servant.

{20:1} Ben-hadad, the king of Syria, gathered his army, consisting of thirty-two kings along with horses and chariots. They besieged Samaria and waged war against it. {20:2} He sent messengers even to Ahab, the king of Israel, demanding his silver, gold, wives, and children. {20:3} Ahab responded, agreeing to Ben-hadad's demands. {20:4} However, Ben-hadad demanded even more, threatening to send his servants to take whatever they desired from Ahab's house and the houses of his servants. {20:5} Ahab gathered the elders and explained the situation. They advised him not to comply. {20:6} Ahab refused Ben-hadad's demands, causing Ben-hadad to prepare for battle against Samaria. {20:7} Then a prophet came to Ahab, promising victory over the Syrians. {20:8} Ahab asked how this victory would come about, and the prophet revealed that it would be through young men from the provinces. {20:9} Ahab was instructed to lead the battle. {20:10} Ahab prepared for battle, while Ben-hadad and his kings were drinking in their pavilions. {20:11} Ben-hadad was warned of Israel's response, but he ignored it and ordered his army to attack. {20:12} The prophet advised Ahab to strengthen himself and prepare, for the Syrians would return the following year. {20:13} The Syrians believed the God of Israel was only a god of the hills, not the valleys, so they planned to fight in the plains where they thought they would be stronger. {20:14} They strategized to replace the captured kings with captains and to rebuild their army. {20:15} The next year, Ben-hadad attacked Israel again, and both armies prepared for battle. {20:16} The battle began, with Israel initially outnumbered but ultimately victorious. {20:17} A man of God prophesied that Israel would defeat the Syrians, and indeed, they did, killing a hundred thousand foot soldiers in one day. {20:18} The remaining Syrians fled to Aphek, where a wall collapsed, killing twenty-seven thousand. {20:19} Ben-hadad's servants suggested seeking mercy from Ahab, so they approached him humbly. {20:20} Ahab received Ben-hadad and made a covenant with him, allowing him to live. {20:21} However, a prophet rebuked a man who refused to strike him as commanded by God. Consequently, the man was killed by a lion after leaving the prophet. {20:22} Another prophet confronted Ahab disguised as a wounded soldier, delivering a message from God about his disobedience. {20:23} Ahab returned home troubled by the prophet's words. {20:24} Thus ended the conflict between Israel and Syria for the time being. {20:25} Ben-hadad advised Ahab to rebuild his army to match what he had lost and promised victory in the plains. Ahab listened and prepared accordingly. {20:26} The following year, Ben-hadad mobilized the Syrians and marched to Aphek to battle Israel. {20:27} The Israelites assembled to confront them, but they appeared vastly outnumbered. {20:28} Then a man of God came to the king of Israel, proclaiming that God would deliver the Syrians into his hand to show that He is the Lord. {20:29} For seven days, the two sides faced each other, and on the seventh day, Israel attacked and killed a hundred thousand Syrian foot soldiers. {20:30} The remaining Syrians fled into the city of Aphek, where a collapsing wall killed twenty-seven thousand more. Ben-hadad escaped into an inner chamber. {20:31} Ben-hadad's servants suggested seeking mercy from Ahab, so they approached him in sackcloth and ropes, pleading for Ben-hadad's life. {20:32} Ahab, referring to Ben-hadad as his brother, agreed to spare him. {20:33} Ben-hadad was brought before Ahab, who made a covenant with him and allowed him to leave. {20:34} Ben-hadad promised to restore the cities his father took from Ahab's father, and Ahab sent him away with this agreement. {20:35} Meanwhile, a prophet asked his neighbor to strike him in the name of the Lord, but the neighbor refused. {20:36} As punishment for disobedience, the prophet prophesied that a lion would kill him after he left. {20:37} Finding another man, the prophet requested to be struck, and the man wounded him. {20:38} The prophet disguised himself and awaited the king's passing. {20:39} As the king passed by, the prophet recounted a story, prompting the king to pronounce judgment. {20:40} The king realized the prophet's identity and acknowledged his mistake. {20:41} The prophet then delivered a message from the Lord, declaring punishment for releasing a man designated for destruction. {20:42} Heavy-hearted, the king returned home to Samaria. {20:43} Thus ended the events surrounding the conflict between Israel and Syria.

{21:1} After these events, Naboth the Jezreelite owned a vineyard in Jezreel, near the palace of Ahab, the king of Samaria. {21:2} Ahab said to Naboth, "Give me your vineyard, so I can use it as a vegetable garden since it's close to my house. I'll either give you a better vineyard in exchange, or I'll pay you its worth." {21:3} Naboth replied, "The LORD forbid that I should give you the inheritance of my fathers." {21:4} Ahab went home distressed and angry because Naboth refused to give him his ancestral inheritance. He lay on his bed, turned away, and wouldn't eat. {21:5} Jezebel, his wife, asked him, "Why are you so upset that you won't eat?" {21:6} Ahab explained, "I asked Naboth for his vineyard, offering to buy it or give him another in return, but he refused to give it to me." {21:7} Jezebel responded, "You're the king of Israel! Get up, eat, and be happy. I'll get you Naboth's vineyard." {21:8} She wrote letters in Ahab's name, sealed them with his seal, and sent them to the elders and nobles living in Naboth's city. {21:9} The letters instructed to declare a fast and set Naboth in a prominent place. {21:10} Then, two scoundrels accused Naboth of blasphemy against God and the king. They took him out of the city and stoned him to death. {21:11} The elders and nobles followed Jezebel's orders as written in the letters. {21:12} They proclaimed a fast and set Naboth in a high position among the people. {21:13} Two scoundrels falsely accused Naboth before the people, claiming he blasphemed God and the king. They stoned him to death outside the city. {21:14} They sent word to Jezebel that Naboth was dead. {21:15} When Jezebel learned of Naboth's death, she told Ahab to take possession of the vineyard since Naboth was dead. {21:16} Ahab went to take possession of Naboth's vineyard. {21:17} Then the word of the LORD came to Elijah, instructing him to go meet Ahab in Naboth's vineyard. {21:18} Elijah was to confront Ahab for killing Naboth and taking his land. {21:19} **Elijah was to deliver a message from the LORD: where dogs licked Naboth's blood, they would lick Ahab's blood too.** {21:20} Ahab asked Elijah if he had found him, to which Elijah replied that he had, because Ahab had sold himself to evil in the sight of the LORD. {21:21} Elijah prophesied that evil would befall Ahab, his descendants would be cut off, and his household would suffer for his sins. {21:22} Ahab's house would suffer a fate similar to Jeroboam and Baasha's for provoking the LORD's anger and leading Israel to sin. {21:23} The LORD also spoke against Jezebel, saying she would be eaten by dogs at the wall of Jezreel. {21:24} Dogs would eat Ahab's descendants who died in the city, and birds would eat those who died in the fields. {21:25} No one had provoked the LORD as Ahab had, influenced by his wife Jezebel, and he committed abominable acts by worshiping idols like the Amorites. {21:26} When Ahab heard these words, he tore his clothes, put on sackcloth, fasted, and went about humbly. {21:27} Then the word of the LORD came to Elijah again, {21:28} acknowledging Ahab's humility and stating that because he humbled himself, {21:29} the evil would not come upon him in his days, but in his son's days.

{22:1} For three years, there was peace between Syria and Israel. {22:2} In the third year, Jehoshaphat, the king of Judah, visited the king of Israel. {22:3} The king of Israel said to his servants, "Do you know that Ramoth in Gilead belongs to us, yet we haven't taken it from the king of Syria?" {22:4} He asked Jehoshaphat, "Will you join me in battling for Ramoth-gilead?" Jehoshaphat replied, "I am with you, my people are your people, and my horses are your horses." {22:5} Jehoshaphat suggested seeking the word of the LORD before making a decision. {22:6} The king of Israel gathered about four hundred prophets and asked them if they should go to battle. They all advised him to go, saying the Lord would deliver Ramoth-gilead to the king. {22:7} Jehoshaphat asked if there was another prophet of the LORD they could consult. {22:8} The king mentioned Micaiah but expressed his dislike for him because he always prophesied evil concerning him. However, Jehoshaphat urged him not to say so. {22:9} The king ordered Micaiah to be brought before them. {22:10} The kings sat in the entrance of the gate of Samaria while the prophets prophesied before them. {22:11} One of the prophets, Zedekiah, even made horns of iron, declaring victory for the king. {22:12} All the prophets agreed that the king would succeed in capturing Ramoth-gilead. {22:13} A messenger encouraged Micaiah to speak favorably like the other prophets, but Micaiah insisted he would speak only what the LORD told him. {22:14} Micaiah assured the king he would speak only what the LORD revealed to him. {22:15} When Micaiah came before the king, he advised them to go to battle, as the other prophets had said. {22:16} The king demanded that Micaiah speak the truth in the name of the LORD. {22:17} Micaiah prophesied that Israel would be scattered like sheep without a shepherd, advising them to return home in peace. {22:18} The king of Israel complained to Jehoshaphat that Micaiah always prophesied evil concerning him. {22:19} Micaiah recounted seeing the LORD on His throne with the host of heaven standing by Him. {22:20} The LORD asked who would persuade Ahab to go up and fall at Ramoth-gilead, and a spirit volunteered to be a lying spirit in the mouths of Ahab's prophets. {22:21} The LORD allowed the spirit to persuade Ahab. {22:22} Micaiah explained that the LORD had allowed a lying spirit in the mouths of the prophets to speak evil concerning Ahab. {22:23} Zedekiah struck Micaiah and questioned how the LORD's spirit had passed from him to speak to Micaiah. {22:24} Micaiah warned Zedekiah that he would see the truth on the day he hid in an inner chamber. {22:25} The king ordered Micaiah to be taken away until he returned safely. {22:26} Micaiah proclaimed that if the king returned in peace, the LORD had not spoken through him. {22:27} Then the king and Jehoshaphat went up to battle against Ramoth-gilead. {22:28} The king disguised himself, but Jehoshaphat wore his robes. {22:29} When the captains of the chariots saw Jehoshaphat, they mistook him for the king of Israel and pursued him, but when they realized their mistake, they stopped. {22:30} Meanwhile, a man randomly shot an arrow that struck the king of Israel between the joints of his armor. {22:31} The king of Israel instructed his charioteer to take him out of the battle, as he was wounded. {22:32} The battle continued fiercely, and the king died that evening, with his blood flowing into the chariot. {22:33} The proclamation went out for everyone to return home. {22:34} They brought the king's body to Samaria and buried him, fulfilling the LORD's word. {22:35} Dogs licked up his blood, as the LORD had spoken. {22:36} Thus, Ahab died, and Ahaziah his son succeeded him. {22:37} Jehoshaphat began to reign in Judah during Ahab's fourth year as king of Israel. {22:38} Jehoshaphat was thirty-five years old when he began to reign, and he reigned twenty-five years in Jerusalem. He followed the ways of his father Asa, though the high places remained. {22:39} Jehoshaphat made peace with the king of Israel. {22:40} The rest of Jehoshaphat's deeds are recorded in the chronicles of the kings of Judah. {22:41} Jehoshaphat passed away and was buried with his fathers, and Jehoram his son reigned in his place. {22:42} Ahaziah, Ahab's son, became king over Israel in Samaria during Jehoshaphat's seventeenth year as king of Judah. He reigned for two years, doing evil in the sight of the LORD, following the ways of his parents and Jeroboam, leading Israel into sin. {22:43} He served Baal and provoked the LORD God of Israel, following his father's example. {22:44} There was no king in Edom, only a deputy ruled. {22:45} Jehoshaphat made ships to go to Ophir for gold, but they were wrecked. {22:46} The rest of Jehoshaphat's deeds and his might are recorded in the chronicles of the kings of Judah. {22:47} Jehoshaphat rid the land of the remaining sodomites from his father Asa's time. {22:48} Tharshish ships were built for gold, but they failed at Ezion-geber. {22:49} Ahaziah asked Jehoshaphat to let his servants go on the ships, but Jehoshaphat refused. {22:50} Jehoshaphat died and was buried with his fathers in the city of David. Jehoram his son became king after him. {22:51} Ahaziah, Ahab's son, began his reign over Israel in Samaria during Jehoshaphat's seventeenth year as king of Judah, reigning for two years. {22:52} He did evil in the sight of the LORD, following his parents' and Jeroboam's sinful ways. {22:53} Ahaziah worshiped Baal and provoked the LORD God of Israel, imitating his father's actions.

2 Kings

{1:1} Moab rebelled against Israel after Ahab died. {1:2} Ahaziah, king of Israel, fell through a lattice in his upper chamber in Samaria and became ill. He sent messengers to inquire of Baalzebub, the god of Ekron, if he would recover from his illness. {1:3} But the angel of the LORD instructed Elijah the Tishbite, "Go meet the messengers of the king of Samaria and ask them, 'Is it because there is no God in Israel that you seek Baal-zebub, the god of Ekron?'" {1:4} Then the LORD said, "You will not recover; you will surely die." And Elijah left. {1:5} When the messengers returned, Elijah asked them, "Why have you come back?" {1:6} They replied, "We met a man who told us to return to the king with this message from the LORD: 'Is it because there is no God in Israel that you send to inquire of Baal-zebub? Therefore, you will not come down from the bed you have gone up on; you will surely die.'" {1:7} "What did this man look like?" Elijah asked. {1:8} They answered, "He was a hairy man with a leather belt around his waist." Elijah realized it was him, Elijah the Tishbite. {1:9} So the king sent a captain with fifty soldiers to Elijah. The captain found Elijah sitting on a hilltop and demanded, "Man of God, the king orders you to come down." {1:10} Elijah replied, "If I am truly a man of God, let fire come down from heaven and consume you and your fifty men." Suddenly, fire came down and killed them. {1:11} The king sent another captain with fifty men. He commanded Elijah, "Come down quickly!" {1:12} Elijah responded, "If I am a man of God, let fire come down from heaven and consume you and your fifty men." Once again, fire came down and killed them. {1:13} The king sent a third captain with fifty men. This captain approached Elijah, fell on his knees, and pleaded, "Man of God, please spare my life and the lives of my men!" {1:14} The angel of the LORD instructed Elijah, "Go down with him; do not be afraid." {1:15} So Elijah went with the captain to the king. {1:16} Elijah told the king, "Because you sought guidance from Baal-zebub instead of the God of Israel, you will not recover; you will surely die." {1:17} Ahaziah died as the LORD had foretold through Elijah. Jehoram became king in his place during the second year of Jehoram, son of Jehoshaphat, king of Judah, because Ahaziah had no son. {1:18} The remaining acts of Ahaziah are recorded in the chronicles of the kings of Israel.

{2:1} When the LORD was about to take Elijah up to heaven in a whirlwind, Elijah went with Elisha from Gilgal. {2:2} Elijah said to Elisha, "Stay here; the LORD has sent me to Bethel." But Elisha replied, "As surely as the LORD lives and as you live, I will not leave you." So they went down to Bethel. {2:3} The company of prophets at Bethel came out to Elisha and asked, "Do you know that the LORD is going to take your master from you today?" "Yes, I know," Elisha replied, "so be quiet." {2:4} Then Elijah said to him, "Stay here, Elisha; the LORD has sent me to Jericho." And he replied, "As surely as the LORD lives and as you live, I will not leave you." So they went to Jericho. {2:5} The company of prophets at Jericho went up to Elisha and asked him, "Do you know that the LORD is going to take your master from you today?" "Yes, I know," he replied, "so be quiet." {2:6} Then Elijah said to him, "Stay here; the LORD has sent me to the Jordan." And he replied, "As surely as the LORD lives and as you live, I will not leave you." So the two of them walked on. {2:7} Fifty men from the company of prophets went and stood at a distance, facing the place where Elijah and Elisha were standing. {2:8} Elijah took his cloak, rolled it up and struck the water with it. The water divided to the right and to the left, and the two of them crossed over on dry ground. {2:9} **When they had crossed, Elijah said to Elisha, "Tell me, what can I do for you before I am taken from you?" "Let me inherit a double portion of your spirit," Elisha replied.** {2:10} "You have asked a difficult thing," Elijah said, "yet if you see me when I am taken from you, it will be yours—otherwise, it will not." {2:11} **As they were walking along and talking together, suddenly a chariot of fire and horses of fire appeared and separated the two of them, and Elijah went up to heaven in a whirlwind.** {2:12} Elisha saw this and cried out, "My father! My father! The chariots and horsemen of Israel!" And Elisha saw him no more. Then he took hold of his garment and tore it in two. {2:13} Elisha then picked up Elijah's cloak that had fallen from him and went back and stood on the bank of the Jordan. {2:14} He took the cloak that had fallen from Elijah and struck the water with it. "Where now is the LORD, the God of Elijah?" he asked. When he struck the water, it divided to the right and to the left, and he crossed over. {2:15} The company of prophets from Jericho, who were watching, said, "The spirit of Elijah is resting on Elisha." And they went to meet him and bowed to the ground before him. {2:16} "Look," they said, "we your servants have fifty able men. Let them go and look for your master. Perhaps the Spirit of the LORD has picked him up and set him down on some mountain or in some valley." "No," Elisha replied, "do not send them." {2:17} But they persisted until he was too embarrassed to refuse. So he said, "Send them." And they sent fifty men, who searched for three days but did not find him. {2:18} When they returned to Elisha, who was staying in Jericho, he said to them, "Didn't I tell you not to go?" {2:19} The people of the city said to Elisha, "Look, our lord, this town is well situated, as you can see, but the water is bad and the land is unproductive." {2:20} "Bring me a new bowl," he said, "and put salt in it." So they brought it to him. {2:21} Then he went out to the spring and threw the salt into it, saying, "This is what the LORD says: 'I have healed this water. Never again will it cause death or make the land unproductive.'" {2:22} And the water has remained pure to this day, according to the word Elisha had spoken. {2:23} From there Elisha went up to Bethel. As he was walking along the road, some boys came out of the town and jeered at him. "Get out of here, baldy!" they said. "Get out of here, baldy!" {2:24} He turned around, looked at them and called down a curse on them in the name of the LORD. Then two bears came out of the woods and mauled forty-two of the boys. {2:25} From there Elisha went on to Mount Carmel and then returned to Samaria.

{3:1} Jehoram, the son of Ahab, began to rule over Israel in Samaria during the eighteenth year of Jehoshaphat's reign over Judah. He ruled for twelve years. {3:2} He did evil in the sight of the LORD, though not as much as his father and mother. He got rid of the image of Baal that his father had made. {3:3} However, he continued to follow the sinful ways of Jeroboam son of Nebat, who had led Israel into sin, and he did not turn away from them. {3:4} Now Mesha, the king of Moab, was a sheep breeder. He used to pay the king of Israel an annual tribute of a hundred thousand lambs and the wool of a hundred thousand rams. {3:5} But after Ahab died, the king of Moab rebelled against the king of Israel. {3:6} So King Jehoram set out from Samaria at that time and mustered all Israel. {3:7} He also sent this message to Jehoshaphat king of Judah: "The king of Moab has rebelled against me. Will you go with me to fight against Moab?" "I will go with you," replied Jehoshaphat. "I am as you are, my people as your people, my horses as your horses." {3:8} "By which route shall we attack?" he asked. "Through the Wilderness of Edom," Jehoram answered. {3:9} So the king of Israel set out with the king of Judah and the king of Edom. After a roundabout march of seven days, there was no water for the army or for the animals with them. {3:10} "Oh no!" exclaimed the king of Israel. "The LORD has called us three kings together only to deliver us into the hands of Moab!" {3:11} But Jehoshaphat asked, "Is there no prophet of the LORD here, through whom we may inquire of the LORD?" An officer of the king of Israel answered, "Elisha son of Shaphat is here. He used to pour water on the hands of Elijah." {3:12} Jehoshaphat said, "The word of the LORD is with him." So the king of Israel and Jehoshaphat and the king of Edom went down to him. {3:13} Elisha said to the king of Israel, "Why do you want to involve me? Go to the prophets of your father and the prophets of your mother." "No," replied the king of Israel, "for it is the LORD who has called us three kings together to deliver us into the hands of Moab." {3:14} Elisha said, "As surely as the LORD Almighty lives, whom I serve, if I did not have respect for Jehoshaphat king of Judah, I would not pay any attention to you. {3:15} But now bring me a harpist." While the harpist was playing, the hand of the LORD came on Elisha {3:16} and he said, "This is what the LORD says: Make this valley full of ditches. {3:17} For this is what the LORD says: You will see neither wind nor rain, yet this valley will be filled with water, and you, your cattle and your other animals will drink. {3:18} This is an easy thing in the eyes of the LORD; he will also deliver Moab into your hands. {3:19} You will overthrow every fortified city and every major town. You will cut down every good tree, stop up all the springs, and ruin every good field with stones." {3:20} The next morning, about the time for offering the sacrifice, there it was—water flowing from the direction of Edom! And the land was filled with water. {3:21} Now all the Moabites had heard that the kings had come to fight against them; so every man, young and old, who could bear arms was called up and stationed on the border. {3:22} When they got up early in the morning, the sun was shining on the water. To the Moabites across the way, the water looked red—like blood. {3:23} "That's blood!" they said. "Those kings must have fought and slaughtered each other. Now to the plunder, Moab!" {3:24} But when the Moabites came to the camp of Israel, the Israelites rose up and fought them until they fled. And the Israelites invaded Moab and slaughtered the Moabites. {3:25} They destroyed the towns, and each man threw a stone on every good field until it was covered. They stopped up all the springs and cut down every good tree. Only Kir Haresheth was left with its stones in place, but men armed with slings surrounded it and attacked it. {3:26} When the king of Moab saw that the battle had gone against him, he took with him seven hundred swordsmen to break through to the king of Edom, but they failed. {3:27} Then he took his firstborn son, who was to succeed him as king, and offered him as a sacrifice on the city wall. The fury against Israel was great; they withdrew and returned to their own land.

{4:1} There was a woman, the wife of one of the sons of the prophets, who cried out to Elisha, saying, "Your servant, my husband, has died, and you know that he revered the LORD. But now the creditor is coming to take my two sons as his slaves." {4:2} Elisha asked her, "What can I do for you? Tell me, what do you have in your house?" She replied, "Your servant has nothing in the house except a jar of oil." {4:3} Then Elisha said, "Go around and ask all your neighbors for empty jars. Don't ask for just a few. {4:4} Then go inside and shut the door behind you and your sons. Pour oil into all the jars, and as each is filled, put it to one side." {4:5} She left him and shut the door behind her and her sons. They brought the jars to her and she kept pouring. {4:6} When all the jars were full, she said to her son, "Bring me another one." But he replied, "There is not a jar left." Then the oil stopped flowing. {4:7} She went and told the man of God, and he said, "Go, sell the oil and pay your debts. You and your sons can live on what is left." {4:8} One day Elisha went to Shunem. And a well-to-do woman was there, who urged him to stay for a meal. So whenever he came by, he stopped there to eat. {4:9} She said to her husband, "I know that this man who often comes our way is a holy man of God. {4:10} Let's make a small room on the roof and put in it a bed and a table, a chair and a lamp for him. Then he can stay there whenever he comes to us." {4:11} One day when Elisha came, he went up to his room and lay down there. {4:12} He said to his servant Gehazi, "Call the Shunammite." So he called her, and she stood before him. {4:13} Elisha said to him, "Tell her, 'You have gone to all this trouble for us. Now what can be done for you? Can we speak on your behalf to the king or the commander of the army?'" She replied, "I have a home among my own people." {4:14} "What can be done for her?" Elisha asked. Gehazi said, "She has no son, and her husband is old." {4:15} Then Elisha said, "Call her." So he called her, and she stood in the doorway. {4:16} "About this time next year," Elisha said, "you will hold a son in your arms." "No, my lord," she objected. "Please, man of God, don't mislead your servant!" {4:17} But the woman became pregnant, and the next year about that same time she gave birth to a son, just as Elisha had told her. {4:18} The child grew, and one day he went out to his father, who was with the reapers. {4:19} He said to his father, "My head! My head!" His father told a servant, "Carry him to his mother." {4:20} After the servant had lifted him up and carried him to his mother, the boy sat on her lap until noon, and then he died. {4:21} She went up and laid him on the bed of the man of God, then shut the door and went out. {4:22} She called her husband and said, "Please send me one of the servants and a donkey so I can go to the man of God quickly and return." {4:23} "Why go to him today?" he asked. "It's not the New Moon or the Sabbath." "That's all right," she said. {4:24} She saddled the donkey and said to her servant, "Lead on; don't slow down for me unless I tell you." {4:25} So she set out and came to the man of God at Mount Carmel. When he saw her in the distance, the man of God said to his servant Gehazi, "Look! There's the Shunammite! {4:26} Run to meet her and ask her, 'Are you all right? Is your husband all right? Is your child all right?'" "Everything is all right," she said. {4:27} When she reached the man of God at the mountain, she took hold of his feet. Gehazi came over to push her away, but the man of God said, "Leave her alone! She is in bitter distress, but the LORD has hidden it from me and has not told me why." {4:28} "Did I ask you for a son, my lord?" she said. "Didn't I tell you, 'Don't raise my hopes'?" {4:29} Elisha said to Gehazi, "Tuck your cloak into your belt, take my staff in your hand and run. Don't greet anyone you meet, and if anyone greets you, do not answer. Lay my staff on the boy's face." {4:30} But the child's mother said, "As surely as the LORD lives and as you live, I will not leave you." So he got up and followed her. {4:31} Gehazi went on ahead and laid the staff on the boy's face, but there was no sound or response. So Gehazi went back to meet Elisha and told him, "The boy has not awakened." {4:32} When Elisha reached the house, there was the boy lying dead on his couch. {4:33} He went in, shut the door on the two of them, and prayed to the LORD. {4:34} Then he got on the bed and lay on the boy, mouth to mouth, eyes to eyes, hands to hands. As he stretched himself out on him, the boy's body grew warm. {4:35} Elisha turned away and walked back and forth in the room and then got on the bed and stretched out on him once more. The boy sneezed seven times and opened his eyes. {4:36} Elisha summoned Gehazi and said, "Call the Shunammite." And he did. When she came, he said, "Take your son." {4:37} She came in, fell at his feet and bowed to the ground. Then she took her son and went out. {4:38} Elisha returned to Gilgal and there was a famine in the region. While the company of the prophets was meeting with him, he said to his servant, "Put on the large pot and cook some stew for these prophets." {4:39} One of the men went out into the field to gather herbs. He found a wild vine and gathered from it wild gourds, filling his cloak. He came back and sliced them into the pot of stew, though they didn't recognize what they were. {4:40} They served the stew to the men, but as they began to eat, they cried out, "Man of God, there is death in the pot!" And they couldn't eat it. {4:41} "Bring me some meal," Elisha said. He threw it into the pot and said, "Serve it to the people to eat." And there was nothing harmful in the pot. {4:42} A man from Baal-Shalisha came and brought the man of God some bread from the firstfruits—twenty loaves of barley and fresh ears of grain in his sack. Elisha said, "Give it to the people to eat." {4:43} His servant questioned, "How can I set this before a hundred men?" But Elisha insisted, "Give it to the people to eat, for this is what the LORD says: 'They will eat and have some left over.'" {4:44} So he set it before them, and they ate and had some left over, according to the word of the LORD.

{5:1} Naaman, the commander of the Syrian army, was highly respected and esteemed by his master, because the LORD had given Syria great victories through him. However, Naaman had leprosy. {5:2} During one of their raids into the land of Israel, the Syrians had captured a young girl who served Naaman's wife. {5:3} This young girl said to her mistress, "If only my master would go to the prophet in Samaria! He would cure him of his leprosy." {5:4} Naaman's master heard what the girl from Israel had said, and he decided to send Naaman to the king of Israel with a letter. {5:5} The king of Syria sent Naaman on his way with gifts—ten talents of silver, six thousand pieces of gold, and ten sets of clothing. {5:6} The letter to the king of Israel stated, "With this letter, I am sending my servant Naaman to you so that you may cure him of his leprosy." {5:7} When the king of Israel read the letter, he was greatly distressed and tore his clothes, saying, "Am I God, to kill and to make alive, that this man sends someone to me to be cured of his leprosy? Surely he is seeking a quarrel with me!" {5:8} When Elisha, the man of God, heard that the king had torn his clothes, he sent him a message: "Why have you torn your clothes? Send Naaman to me, and he will know that there is a prophet in Israel." {5:9} So Naaman went with his horses and chariots and stood at the door of Elisha's house. {5:10} Elisha sent a messenger to him, saying, "Go, wash yourself seven times in the Jordan, and your flesh will be restored, and you will be cleansed." {5:11} But Naaman became angry and went away, saying, "I thought that he would surely come out to me and stand and call on the name of the LORD his God, wave his hand over the spot and cure me of my leprosy. {5:12} Are not Abana and Pharpar, the rivers of Damascus, better than all the waters of Israel? Couldn't I wash in them and be cleansed?" So he turned and went off in a rage. {5:13} Naaman's servants approached him and said, "My father, if the prophet had told you to do some great thing, would you not have done it? How much more, then, when he tells you, 'Wash and be cleansed'?" {5:14} So Naaman went down and dipped himself in the Jordan seven times, as the man of God had told him, and his flesh was restored and became clean like that of a young boy. {5:15} Then Naaman and all his attendants went back to the man of God. He stood before him and said, "Now I know that there is no God in all the world except in Israel. So please accept a gift from your servant." {5:16} But Elisha said, "As surely as the LORD lives, whom I serve, I will not accept a thing." And even though Naaman urged him, he refused. {5:17} "If you will not," said Naaman, "please let me, your servant, be given as much earth as a pair of mules can carry, for your servant will never again make burnt offerings and sacrifices to any other god but the LORD. {5:18} But may the LORD forgive your servant for this one thing: When my master enters the temple of Rimmon to bow down and he is leaning on my arm and I have to bow there also—when I bow down in the temple of Rimmon, may the LORD forgive your servant for this." {5:19} "Go in peace," Elisha said. So Naaman left him and traveled some distance away. {5:20} Gehazi, the servant of Elisha the man of God, thought, "My master has let this Syrian Naaman off too lightly by not accepting from him what he brought. As surely as the LORD lives, I will run after him and get something from him." {5:21} So Gehazi hurried after Naaman. When Naaman saw him running toward him, he got down from the chariot to meet him. "Is everything all right?" he asked. {5:22} "Everything is all right," Gehazi answered. "My master sent me to say, 'Two young men from the company of the prophets have just come to me from the hill country of Ephraim. Please give them a talent of silver and two sets of clothing.'" {5:23} "By all means, take two talents," said Naaman. He urged Gehazi to accept them, and then tied up the two talents of silver in two bags, with two sets of clothing. He gave them to two of his servants, and they carried them ahead of Gehazi. {5:24} When Gehazi came to the hill, he took the things from the servants and put them away in the house. He sent the men away, and they left. {5:25} Then Gehazi went in and stood before his master Elisha. "Where have you been, Gehazi?" Elisha asked.

"Your servant didn't go anywhere," Gehazi answered. {5:26} But Elisha said to him, "Was not my spirit with you when the man got down from his chariot to meet you? Is this the time to take money or to accept clothes—or olive groves and vineyards, or flocks and herds, or male and female slaves? {5:27} Naaman's leprosy will cling to you and to your descendants forever." Then Gehazi went from Elisha's presence and his skin was leprous—it had become as white as snow.

{6:1} The followers of Elisha said to him, "The place where we live with you is too small for us. {6:2} Let's go to the Jordan River and each of us get a log from there. Then we can build a place to live." Elisha agreed, saying, "Go ahead." {6:3} One of them said, "Please come with your servants." Elisha replied, "I will go." {6:4} So he went with them to the Jordan River and they began to cut down trees. {6:5} While one of them was cutting down a tree, the iron head of his axe fell into the water. "Oh no, master!" he cried out. "It was borrowed!" {6:6} Elisha asked, "Where did it fall?" When he showed him the place, Elisha cut a stick and threw it there, and made the iron float. {6:7} "Pick it up," Elisha said. So he reached out his hand and took it. {6:8} Then the king of Syria waged war against Israel. He consulted his officers, saying, "My camp will be in such and such a place." {6:9} But the man of God sent word to the king of Israel: "Be careful not to pass this place, because the Syrians are going down there." {6:10} So the king of Israel checked on the place indicated by the man of God. Time and again Elisha warned the king, so that he was on his guard in such places. {6:11} This enraged the king of Syria. He summoned his officers and demanded of them, "Tell me! Which of us is on the side of the king of Israel?" {6:12} "None of us, my lord the king," said one of his officers, "but Elisha, the prophet in Israel, tells the king of Israel the very words you speak in your bedroom." {6:13} "Go, find out where he is," the king ordered, "so I can send men and capture him." The report came back: "He is in Dothan." {6:14} Then he sent horses and chariots and a strong force there. They went by night and surrounded the city. {6:15} When the servant of the man of God got up and went out early the next morning, an army with horses and chariots had surrounded the city. "Oh no, my lord! What shall we do?" the servant asked. {6:16} "Don't be afraid," the prophet answered. "Those who are with us are more than those who are with them." {6:17} And Elisha prayed, "Open his eyes, LORD, so that he may see." Then the LORD opened the servant's eyes, and he looked and saw the hills full of horses and chariots of fire all around Elisha. {6:18} As the enemy came down toward him, Elisha prayed to the LORD, "Strike this army with blindness." So he struck them with blindness, as Elisha had asked. {6:19} Elisha told them, "This is not the road and this is not the city. Follow me, and I will lead you to the man you are looking for." And he led them to Samaria. {6:20} After they entered the city, Elisha said, "LORD, open the eyes of these men so they can see." Then the LORD opened their eyes and they looked, and there they were, inside Samaria. {6:21} When the king of Israel saw them, he asked Elisha, "Shall I kill them, my father? Shall I kill them?" {6:22} "Do not kill them," he answered. "Would you kill those you have captured with your own sword or bow? Set food and water before them so that they may eat and drink and then go back to their master." {6:23} So he prepared a great feast for them, and after they had finished eating and drinking, he sent them away, and they returned to their master. So the bands from Aram stopped raiding Israel's territory. {6:24} Some time later, Ben-Hadad king of Aram mobilized his entire army and marched up and laid siege to Samaria. {6:25} There was a great famine in the city; the siege lasted so long that a donkey's head sold for eighty shekels of silver, and a quarter of a cab of seed pods for five shekels. {6:26} As the king of Israel was passing by on the wall, a woman cried to him, "Help me, my lord the king!" {6:27} He responded, "If the LORD does not help you, where can I find help for you? From the threshing floor? Or from the winepress?" {6:28} Then the king asked her, "What is troubling you?" She answered, "This woman said to me, 'Give up your son so we may eat him today, and tomorrow we'll eat my son.' {6:29} So we cooked my son and ate him. The next day I said to her, 'Give up your son so we may eat him,' but she had hidden him." {6:30} When the king heard the woman's words, he tore his robes. As he went along the wall, the people looked, and they saw that, under his clothes, he had sackcloth on his body. {6:31} He said, "May God deal with me, be it ever so severely, if the head of Elisha son of Shaphat remains on his shoulders today!" {6:32} Now Elisha was sitting in his house, and the elders were sitting with him. The king sent a messenger ahead, but before he arrived, Elisha said to the elders, "Don't you see how this murderer is sending someone to cut off my head? Look, when the messenger comes, shut the door and hold it shut against him. Is not the sound of his master's footsteps behind him?" {6:33} While he was still talking to them, the messenger came down to him. And the king said, "This disaster is from the LORD. Why should I wait for the LORD any longer?"

{7:1} **Then Elisha said, "Listen to the word of the LORD: Tomorrow, about this time, a measure of fine flour will be sold for a shekel, and two measures of barley for a shekel, at the gate of Samaria."** {7:2} Now a royal officer on whose hand the king leaned responded to the man of God and said, "Even if the LORD were to make windows in heaven, could such a thing happen?" And Elisha replied, "You will see it with your own eyes, but you will not eat any of it." {7:3} Now there were four lepers at the entrance of the gate, and they said to one another, "Why sit here until we die? {7:4} If we say, 'Let us enter the city,' then the famine is in the city, and we shall die there. And if we sit here, we die also. So let us go and surrender to the Syrian camp. If they spare us, we shall live; and if they kill us, we shall only die." {7:5} So they arose in the twilight to go to the camp of the Syrians. But when they came to the edge of the Syrian camp, behold, there was no one there. {7:6} For the Lord had caused the army of the Syrians to hear the sound of chariots and horses, the sound of a great army, so that they said to one another, "Look, the king of Israel has hired the kings of the Hittites and the kings of the Egyptians to attack us!" {7:7} Therefore they arose and fled in the twilight, leaving behind their tents, horses, and donkeys, and they fled for their lives. {7:8} When these lepers came to the edge of the camp, they went into one tent, ate and drank, and carried off silver, gold, and clothing, which they hid. Then they returned and entered another tent and carried off more goods, which they also hid. {7:9} Then they said to one another, "We are not doing right. This day is a day of good news, and we are keeping silent. If we wait until the morning light, punishment will overtake us. So now, let us go and inform the king's household." {7:10} So they went and called out to the gatekeepers of the city and told them, saying, "We went to the Syrian camp, and behold, there was no one there, not even the sound of anyone, only the horses and donkeys tied up, and the tents left as they were." {7:11} Then the gatekeepers called out and told it to the king's household inside. {7:12} And the king arose in the night and said to his servants, "Let me tell you what the Syrians have done to us. They know that we are hungry; therefore they have gone out of the camp to hide themselves in the field, thinking, 'When they come out of the city, we shall take them alive and get into the city.'" {7:13} But one of his servants replied, "Please, let some men take five of the remaining horses, which are left in the city. (Behold, they are like all the multitude of Israel that is left in it; behold, they are like all the multitude of the Israelites who have already perished,) and let us send and see." {7:14} So they took two chariots with horses, and the king sent them after the army of the Syrians, saying, "Go and see." {7:15} And they followed them as far as the Jordan, and indeed, the whole way was littered with garments and equipment that the Syrians had thrown away in their haste. Then the messengers returned and reported to the king. {7:16} So the people went out and plundered the tents of the Syrians. Then a measure of fine flour was sold for a shekel, and two measures of barley for a shekel, according to the word of the LORD. {7:17} Now the king had appointed the royal officer on whose hand he leaned to have charge of the gate, but the people trampled him to death in the gate, just as the man of God had said when the king came down to him. {7:18} For it happened just as the man of God had spoken to the king, saying, "Two measures of barley will be sold for a shekel, and a measure of fine flour for a shekel, tomorrow about this time in the gate of Samaria." {7:19} Then the royal officer had answered the man of God and said, "Even if the LORD were to make windows in heaven, could such a thing happen?" And he had replied, "You will see it with your own eyes, but you will not eat any of it." {7:20} And so it happened to him; for the people trampled him to death in the gate, and he died.

{8:1} Then Elisha spoke to the woman whose son he had restored to life, saying, "Get up, and go with your household, and live wherever you can, for the LORD has called for a famine, and it will come upon the land for seven years." {8:2} So the woman arose and did as the man of God instructed. She went with her household and lived in the land of the Philistines for seven years. {8:3} After seven years, the woman returned from the land of the Philistines and went to appeal to the king for her house and land. {8:4} The king was speaking with Gehazi, the servant of the man of God, asking him to recount all the remarkable things that Elisha had done. {8:5} As Gehazi was telling the king about how Elisha had restored a dead body to life, the woman whose son had been restored to life cried out to the king for her house and land. Gehazi said, "My lord, O king, this is the woman, and this is her son whom Elisha restored to life." {8:6} When the king asked the woman about it, she told him everything. So the king appointed an official for her, saying, "Restore everything that belongs to her, including all the produce of her fields from the day she left the land until now." {8:7} Elisha went to Damascus, and Ben-hadad, the king of Syria, was sick. It was reported to him, "The man of God has come here." {8:8} So the king said to Hazael, "Take a gift with you and go to meet the man of God. Inquire of the LORD through him, asking, 'Will I recover from this illness?'" {8:9} Hazael went to meet Elisha, taking with him a gift of every good thing from Damascus, carried by forty camels. He came and stood before Elisha and said, "Your son Ben-hadad, king of Syria, has sent me to ask, 'Will I recover from this illness?'" {8:10} Elisha told him, "Go and say to him, 'You will certainly recover.' However, the LORD has shown me that he will surely die." {8:11} Elisha stared at Hazael with a fixed gaze until Hazael became uncomfortable, and then the man of God began to weep. {8:12} Hazael asked, "Why is my lord weeping?" And Elisha replied, "Because I know the evil you will do to the Israelites. You will set fire to their fortified cities, kill their young men with the sword, dash their little ones to pieces, and rip open their pregnant women." {8:13} Hazael responded, "How could your servant, a mere dog, accomplish such great things?" Elisha answered, "The LORD has shown me that you will become king over Syria." {8:14} Then Hazael left Elisha and went to his master, who asked him, "What did Elisha say to you?" And Hazael replied, "He told me that you would surely recover." {8:15} But the next day, Hazael took a thick cloth, dipped it in water, and spread it over the king's face until he died. And Hazael became king in his place. {8:16} In the fifth year of Joram, the son of Ahab, king of Israel, while Jehoshaphat was king of Judah, Jehoram, the son of Jehoshaphat, king of Judah, began to reign. {8:17} He was thirty-two years old when he became king, and he reigned in Jerusalem for eight years. {8:18} He followed the ways of the kings of Israel, just as the house of Ahab had done, for he married a daughter of Ahab. He did evil in the sight of the LORD. {8:19} **Yet the LORD was unwilling to destroy Judah, for the sake of his servant David, as he had promised to maintain a lamp for David and his descendants forever.** {8:20} During his reign, Edom rebelled against Judah and appointed their own king. {8:21} So Joram crossed over to Zair with all his chariots. He rose by night and attacked the Edomites who had surrounded him and the commanders of the chariots, but the troops fled to their tents. {8:22} Edom has been in rebellion against Judah to this day. Libnah also rebelled at the same time. {8:23} As for the rest of the acts of Joram and all that he did, are they not written in the book of the chronicles of the kings of Judah? {8:24} **Joram rested with his fathers and was buried with his fathers in the city of David. And Ahaziah his son reigned in his place.** {8:25} In the twelfth year of Joram, the son of Ahab, king of Israel, Ahaziah, the son of Jehoram, king of Judah, began to reign. {8:26} Ahaziah was twenty-two years old when he became king, and he reigned in Jerusalem for one year. His mother's name was Athaliah, the daughter of Omri, king of Israel. {8:27} He walked in the ways of the house of Ahab and did evil in the sight of the LORD, as the house of Ahab had done, for he was related by marriage to the house of Ahab. {8:28} Ahaziah went with Joram, the son of Ahab, to fight against Hazael, king of Syria, in Ramoth-gilead. And the Syrians wounded Joram. {8:29} **So King Joram returned to Jezreel to recover from the wounds that the Syrians had inflicted on him at Ramah, when he fought against Hazael, king of Syria. And Ahaziah, the son of Jehoram, king of Judah, went down to visit Joram, the son of Ahab, in Jezreel because he was sick.**

{9:1} Elisha the prophet called one of the disciples and said to him, "Get ready, take this flask of oil, and go to Ramoth-gilead. {9:2} When you arrive, find Jehu, the son of Jehoshaphat, and bring him into a private room away from his companions. {9:3} Then pour the oil on his head and say, 'This is what the LORD says: I anoint you as king over Israel.' Afterward, open the door and run away without delay." {9:4} So the young prophet went to Ramoth-gilead as instructed. {9:5} When he arrived, he found the army officers sitting together. He approached Jehu and said, "I have a message for you, Captain." Jehu asked, "For which one of us?" The young prophet replied, "For you, Captain." {9:6} Jehu then got up and went into the house. The young prophet poured the oil on Jehu's head and declared, "This is what the LORD, the God of Israel, says: I have anointed you king over the LORD's people, Israel. {9:7} "You must destroy the house of Ahab, your master," the prophet continued, "to avenge the blood of the LORD's servants the prophets and all the other servants of the LORD shed by Jezebel." {9:8} "The entire house of Ahab will be wiped out," the prophet declared. "I will cut off every male in Ahab's family, both slave and free, in Israel. {9:9} I will make the house of Ahab like the house of Jeroboam son of Nebat and like the house of Baasha son of Ahijah. {9:10} Jezebel will be devoured by dogs in the plot of land at Jezreel, and there will be no one to bury her." Then the young prophet opened the door and fled. {9:11} Jehu went back to his fellow officers, and one of them asked, "Is everything all right? Why did this crazy fellow come to you?" Jehu replied, "You know the man and the message he brought." {9:12} "That's a lie! Tell us what he said," they demanded. Jehu recounted, "He said to me, 'This is what the LORD says: I have anointed you king over Israel.'" {9:13} Immediately, the officers acted. Each one spread his cloak under Jehu on the bare steps, blew the trumpet, and shouted, "Jehu is king!" {9:14} So Jehu, the son of Jehoshaphat, conspired against Joram while he and all Israel were guarding Ramoth-gilead against Hazael king of Syria. {9:15} But King Joram had returned to Jezreel to recover from the wounds he had sustained in the battle against Hazael king of Syria. Meanwhile, Ahaziah king of Judah had come down to see Joram. {9:16} When Jehu arrived in Jezreel, Joram was resting there. King Ahaziah of Judah had also come to visit Joram. {9:17} A lookout stationed on the tower in Jezreel saw Jehu and his company approaching, so he shouted, "I see a company of men!" Joram commanded, "Get a horseman and send him to meet them and ask, 'Do you come in peace?'" {9:18} So a horseman went to meet Jehu and said, "This is what the king asks: 'Do you come in peace?'" Jehu replied, "What do you have to do with peace? Fall in behind me." The lookout reported, "The messenger reached them but hasn't started back." {9:19} Then he sent out a second horseman, who came to them and said, "This is what the king asks: 'Do you come in peace?'" And Jehu answered, "What do you have to do with peace? Fall in behind me." {9:20} The lookout reported, "He has reached them but hasn't started back. The driving is like that of Jehu son of Nimshi—he drives like a madman!" {9:21} Joram ordered, "Hitch up my chariot." And when it was hitched up, Joram king of Israel and Ahaziah king of Judah rode out in their chariots to meet Jehu. They met him at the plot of land that had belonged to Naboth the Jezreelite. {9:22} When Joram saw Jehu, he asked, "Do you come in peace, Jehu?" Jehu replied, "What peace can there be as long as the idolatry and witchcraft of your mother Jezebel are all around us?" {9:23} Then Joram wheeled his chariot around and fled, shouting to Ahaziah, "Treachery, Ahaziah!" {9:24} Jehu drew his bow and shot Joram between the shoulders. The arrow pierced his heart, and he slumped down in his chariot. {9:25} Jehu said to Bidkar, his charioteer, "Pick up Joram's body and throw it into the field that belonged to Naboth the Jezreelite. Remember when you and I were riding together after his father Ahab, and the LORD uttered this oracle against him: {9:26} 'As surely as I saw yesterday the blood of Naboth and the blood of his sons,' declares the LORD, 'I will repay you in this plot of ground,' declares the LORD. So take him and throw him onto the plot of ground, as the LORD has said." {9:27} When Ahaziah king of Judah saw what was happening, he fled along the road to Beth-haggan. Jehu pursued him, shouting, "Shoot him too!" So they shot Ahaziah in his chariot at the Ascent of Gur near Ibleam. He fled to Megiddo and died there. {9:28} His servants carried him in a chariot to Jerusalem, where they buried him in his tomb with his fathers in the City of David. {9:29} In the eleventh year of Joram son of Ahab, Ahaziah began to reign over Judah. {9:30} When Jehu arrived in Jezreel, Jezebel heard about it. She painted her eyes, adorned her hair, and looked down from a window. {9:31} As Jehu entered the gate, she asked, "Have you come in peace, you Zimri, murderer of your master?" {9:32} Jehu looked up at the window and called out, "Who is on my side? Who?" And two or three eunuchs looked down at him. {9:33} Jehu commanded, "Throw her down!" So they threw Jezebel down, and some of her blood splattered on the wall and on the horses. Jehu trampled her underfoot. {9:34} Afterward, Jehu went in to eat and drink. He then said, "Go and see about this cursed woman, and bury her, for she was a king's daughter." {9:35} When they went to bury her, they found only her skull, feet, and palms of her hands. {9:36} They returned and informed Jehu. He said, "This fulfills the word of the LORD spoken by his servant Elijah the Tishbite, saying, 'Dogs will eat Jezebel's flesh in the plot of land at Jezreel, {9:37} and her carcass will be like dung on the ground in the plot of land at Jezreel, so that no one will be able to say, "This is Jezebel."'"

{10:1} Ahab had seventy sons in Samaria. Jehu wrote letters to the rulers of Jezreel, the elders, and those who brought up Ahab's children, saying, {10:2} "As soon as you receive this letter, along with Ahab's sons, and you have chariots, horses, a fortified city, and weapons, choose the best and most capable of your master's sons, set him on his father's throne, and fight for your master's house." {10:3} But they were afraid and said, "Two kings couldn't stand against him, so how can we?" {10:4} The palace administrator, the city governor, the elders, {10:5} and those who brought up the children sent a message to Jehu, saying, "We are your servants and will do whatever you ask. We will not make anyone king; do what you think is best." {10:6} Jehu wrote them a second letter, saying, "If you are with me and will obey my commands, take the heads of your master's sons and come to me in Jezreel by this time tomorrow." Now the king's sons, seventy in all, were with the leading men of the city who were bringing them up. {10:7} When the letter reached them, they took the king's sons and slaughtered all seventy. They put their heads in baskets and sent them to Jehu in Jezreel. {10:8} A messenger reported, "They have brought the heads of the king's sons." Jehu commanded, "Pile them in two heaps at the entrance of the city gate until morning." {10:9} In the morning, he went out and stood before the people, saying, "You are innocent. I conspired against my master and killed him, but who killed all these? {10:10} Remember that not a word the LORD spoke against the house of Ahab will fail. The LORD has accomplished what he foretold through his servant Elijah." {10:11} Jehu killed all who remained of Ahab's family in Jezreel, along with his great men, close friends, and priests, leaving him no survivor. {10:12} Then Jehu left for Samaria. Along the way, at the shearing house, {10:13} he met some relatives of Ahaziah, the king of Judah. He asked, "Who are you?" They answered, "We are relatives of Ahaziah. We are going to visit the royal family and the queen mother's family." {10:14} Jehu ordered, "Seize them!" So they seized them and slaughtered them at the well of Beth Eked, forty-two men. He left no survivors. {10:15} Continuing on, Jehu encountered Jehonadab son of Rechab, who was coming to meet him. Jehu greeted him and asked, "Is your heart true to mine?" "It is," Jehonadab replied. "If it is," said Jehu, "give me your hand." So Jehonadab gave him his hand, and Jehu helped him into the chariot. {10:16} Jehu said, "Come with me and see my zeal for the LORD." Then he had Jehonadab ride along in his chariot. {10:17} When Jehu came to Samaria, he killed all who remained of Ahab's family in Samaria, just as the LORD had declared through Elijah. {10:18} Jehu summoned the worshippers of Baal and said, "Ahab served Baal a little, but Jehu will serve him much. {10:19} So gather all the prophets, servants, and priests of Baal. Don't let anyone stay away, for I have a great sacrifice to offer to Baal. Anyone who fails to come will forfeit his life." But Jehu was deceiving them, intending to destroy the worshippers of Baal. {10:20} Jehu proclaimed a solemn assembly for Baal, and all the worshippers came, so that there was no one left who did not attend. They packed the house of Baal from one end to the other. {10:21} Jehu instructed the custodian of the wardrobe, "Bring out robes for all the worshippers of Baal." So he brought out robes for them. {10:22} Then Jehu and Jehonadab son of Rechab entered the house of Baal, and Jehu said to the worshippers of Baal, "Make sure that there are no servants of the LORD here, only worshippers of Baal." {10:23} They went in to offer sacrifices and burnt offerings. Meanwhile, {10:24} Jehu stationed eighty men outside and warned them, "If any of the men I have brought into your hands escape, you will pay with your life for theirs." {10:25} When Jehu had finished offering the burnt offering, he said to the guards and officers, "Go in and kill them; let no one escape!" So they struck them down with the sword. Then the guards and officers threw the bodies out and entered the inner shrine of the house of Baal. {10:26} They brought out the sacred pillar of the temple of Baal and burned it. {10:27} They demolished the sacred pillar of Baal and the temple of Baal and turned it into a latrine, as it remains today. {10:28} Thus Jehu eradicated Baal worship from Israel. {10:29} However, Jehu did not turn away from the sins of Jeroboam, who had caused Israel to sin - the worship of the golden calves at Bethel and Dan. {10:30} The LORD said to Jehu, "Because you have done well in accomplishing what is right in my eyes and have done to the house of Ahab all I had in mind to do, your descendants will sit on the throne of Israel to the fourth generation." {10:31} Yet Jehu was not careful to keep the law of the LORD, the God of Israel, with all his heart. He did not turn away from the sins of Jeroboam, which had caused Israel to sin. {10:32} In those days the LORD began to reduce the size of Israel. Hazael overpowered the Israelites throughout their territory, {10:33} from the Jordan eastward, including all the land of Gilead - the Gadites, the Reubenites, and the Manassites - from Aroer by the Arnon Valley through Gilead and Bashan. {10:34} The rest of the acts of Jehu, all his accomplishments and all his might, are they not written in the book of the annals of the kings of Israel? {10:35} Jehu rested with his ancestors and was buried in Samaria. His son Jehoahaz succeeded him as king. {10:36} Jehu reigned over Israel in Samaria for twenty-eight years.

{11:1} Athaliah, the mother of Ahaziah, saw that her son was dead, so she killed all the royal heirs. {11:2} But Jehosheba, Ahaziah's sister and the daughter of King Joram, took Joash, Ahaziah's son, and hid him along with his nurse in a bedroom to save him from Athaliah's slaughter. So he was not killed. {11:3} Joash stayed hidden with Jehosheba in the house of the LORD for six years while Athaliah ruled over the land. {11:4} In the seventh year, Jehoiada sent for the commanders of the units of a hundred, along with the Carites and the guards, and brought them to the temple of the LORD. He made a covenant with them and took an oath to show them the king's son. {11:5} Jehoiada commanded them, "A third of you who are on duty on the Sabbath will guard the royal palace. {11:6} Another third will be at the Sur Gate, and the rest at the gate behind the guards. Make sure you keep watch over the palace so it won't be broken into. {11:7} The other two thirds of you, who are off duty on the Sabbath, will stand guard at the LORD's temple around the king. {11:8} Each man should be armed. Stay with the king wherever he goes, and if anyone tries to break through your ranks, kill him." {11:9} The commanders of the units of a hundred did everything Jehoiada the priest ordered. They each took their men—those who were going on duty on the Sabbath and those who were going off duty—and came to Jehoiada the priest. {11:10} Then Jehoiada the priest gave the commanders the spears and shields that had belonged to King David and were in the temple of the LORD. {11:11} The guards, each with his weapon in his hand, stationed themselves around the king—near the altar and the temple, from the south side to the north side of the temple. {11:12} Jehoiada brought out the king's son, put the crown on him, and presented him with a copy of the covenant. They proclaimed him king and anointed him. They clapped their hands and shouted, "Long live the king!" {11:13} When Athaliah heard the noise made by the guards and the people, she went to the people at the temple of the LORD. {11:14} She looked, and there was the king, standing by the pillar, as the custom was. The officers and the trumpeters were beside the king, and all the people of the land were rejoicing and blowing trumpets. Then Athaliah tore her robes and called out, "Treason! Treason!" {11:15} Jehoiada the priest ordered the commanders of the units of a hundred, who were in charge of the troops: "Bring her out between the ranks and put to the sword anyone who follows her." For the priest had said, "Do not put her to death at the temple of the LORD." {11:16} So they seized her as she reached the place where the horses enter the palace grounds, and there she was put to death. {11:17} Jehoiada then made a covenant between the LORD and the king and the people that they would be the LORD's people. He also made a covenant between the king and the people. {11:18} All the people of the land went to the temple of Baal and tore it down. They smashed the altars and idols to pieces and killed Mattan the priest of Baal in front of the altars. Then Jehoiada the priest posted guards at the temple of the LORD. {11:19} He took with him the commanders of hundreds, the Carites, the guards, and all the people of the land, and together they brought the king down from the temple of the LORD and went into the palace, entering by way of the gate of the guards. The king then took his place on the royal throne. {11:20} All the people of the land rejoiced, and the city was quiet, because Athaliah had been slain with the sword at the palace. {11:21} Joash was seven years old when he began to reign.

{12:1} In the seventh year of Jehu's reign, Jehoash became king, and he ruled for forty years in Jerusalem. His mother's name was Zibiah from Beer-sheba. {12:2} Jehoash did what was right in the sight of the LORD all his days under the guidance of Jehoiada the priest. {12:3} However, the high places were not removed, and the people continued to sacrifice and burn incense there. {12:4} Jehoash instructed the priests, "All the money from the sacred offerings brought into the house of the LORD—every man's assessment, the money each person is required to pay, and all the money voluntarily given for the house of the LORD— {12:5} let the priests receive it from their acquaintances to repair any damage found in the temple." {12:6} But by the twenty-third year of King Jehoash, the priests had not repaired the temple. {12:7} So King Jehoash summoned Jehoiada the priest and the other priests and asked them, "Why haven't you repaired the temple's damages? Don't accept any more money from your acquaintances; hand it over for the temple repairs." {12:8} The priests agreed not to accept any more money from the people for the temple repairs. {12:9} Instead, Jehoiada made a chest with a hole in the lid and placed it beside the altar, on the right side as one enters the house of the LORD. The priests guarding the entrance put into it all the money brought into the house of the LORD. {12:10} Whenever they saw that there was a large amount of money in the chest, the royal secretary and the high priest would come, count the money found in the house of the LORD, and bag it up. {12:11} They would then give the money that had been counted into the hands of the workers who had oversight of the house of the LORD. They, in turn, would pay the carpenters, builders, {12:12} masons, stonecutters, and buy timber and quarried stone to repair the temple. Whatever was needed to repair the temple was paid for from the funds brought into the house of the LORD. {12:13} However, no silver bowls, snuffers, basins, trumpets, or gold or silver vessels were made with the money brought into the house of the LORD. {12:14} Instead, it was given to the workers, and with it, they repaired the temple. {12:15} The workers were not required to account for the money given to them to pay the workers, because they acted with complete honesty. {12:16} The money for guilt offerings and sin offerings was not brought into the house of the LORD; it belonged to the priests. {12:17} Then Hazael king of Syria marched up and fought against Gath and captured it. Afterward, Hazael set out to attack Jerusalem. {12:18} Jehoash king of Judah took all the sacred objects that his ancestors—Jehoshaphat, Jehoram, and Ahaziah, the kings of Judah—had dedicated, as well as his own sacred objects and all the gold found in the treasuries of the house of the LORD and the royal palace, and sent them to Hazael king of Syria. So Hazael withdrew from Jerusalem. {12:19} The rest of the events of Jehoash's reign and all his accomplishments are recorded in the Book of the Chronicles of the Kings of Judah. {12:20} Jehoash's officials conspired against him and assassinated him at the house of Millo, on the road down to Silla. {12:21} Jozachar son of Shimeath and Jehozabad son of Shomer, his servants, struck him down, and he died. They buried him with his ancestors in the City of David, and his son Amaziah succeeded him as king.

{13:1} In the twenty-third year of Joash, son of Ahaziah, king of Judah, Jehoahaz, son of Jehu, began to rule over Israel in Samaria and reigned for seventeen years. {13:2} But Jehoahaz did evil in the sight of the LORD, following the sinful ways of Jeroboam son of Nebat, who caused Israel to sin. He did not turn away from them. {13:3} This angered the LORD, so he allowed Hazael king of Syria and his son Ben-hadad to oppress Israel continuously. {13:4} Jehoahaz prayed to the LORD, who heard him because he saw how severely Israel was oppressed by the king of Syria. {13:5} The LORD provided a deliverer for Israel, and they were freed from the Syrians' grip. The Israelites went back to living in their tents as before. {13:6} However, they still didn't give up the sinful practices of Jeroboam, which included worshiping the idols and the Asherah pole in Samaria. {13:7} Jehoahaz was left with only fifty horsemen, ten chariots, and ten thousand foot soldiers because the king of Syria had decimated them and reduced them to nothing. {13:8} The rest of Jehoahaz's deeds, along with his might, are recorded in the chronicles of the kings of Israel. {13:9} When Jehoahaz died, he was buried in Samaria, and his son Joash became the next king. {13:10} In the thirty-seventh year of Joash, king of Judah, Jehoash, son of Jehoahaz, became king over Israel in Samaria, ruling for sixteen years. {13:11} Jehoash also did evil in the sight of the LORD, persisting in the sinful ways of Jeroboam, son of Nebat, who led Israel into sin. {13:12} The chronicles of Joash's reign, his deeds, and his military exploits against Amaziah, king of Judah, are recorded in the annals of the kings of Israel. {13:13} When Joash died, he was buried in Samaria with the kings of Israel, and Jeroboam succeeded him on the throne. {13:14} During Elisha's final illness, Joash, the king of Israel, visited him, weeping over his face, and said, "My father, my father, the chariot and horsemen of Israel!" {13:15} Elisha instructed him, "Take bow and arrows." Joash obeyed and took them. {13:16} Elisha told the king to put his hand on the bow, and he did. Then Elisha placed his hands on the king's hands. {13:17} Elisha instructed him to open the east window and shoot. When Joash did, Elisha declared it the arrow of the LORD's victory over Syria. He told Joash he would defeat the Syrians in Aphek until they were destroyed. {13:18} Then Elisha told Joash to take the arrows and strike the ground. Joash struck the ground three times and stopped. {13:19} Elisha became angry with him and said he should have struck five or six times to completely defeat Syria. But now, Joash would only defeat Syria three times. {13:20} Elisha died and was buried. Sometime later, Moabite raiders invaded the land at the beginning of the year. {13:21} While some men were burying a man, they saw a band of raiders, so they hastily threw the man's body into Elisha's tomb. When the man's body touched Elisha's bones, he revived and stood on his feet. {13:22} Hazael, king of Syria, oppressed Israel throughout Jehoahaz's reign. {13:23} Nevertheless, the LORD showed mercy to Israel because of his covenant with Abraham, Isaac, and Jacob. He did not destroy them or banish them from his presence. {13:24} When Hazael died, his son Ben-hadad succeeded him as king of Syria. {13:25} Jehoash, son of Jehoahaz, regained the cities that Hazael's son Ben-hadad had taken from him in battle. Joash defeated Ben-hadad three times and recovered the cities of Israel.

{14:1} Amaziah, the son of Joash, became king of Judah in the second year of Joash son of Jehoahaz, king of Israel. He was twenty-five years old when he began to reign and ruled for twenty-nine years in Jerusalem. His mother's name was Jehoaddan from Jerusalem. {14:2} Amaziah did what was right in the sight of the LORD, but not as wholeheartedly as his ancestor David. He followed the example of his father Joash in most things. {14:3} However, he didn't remove the high places, and the people continued to sacrifice and burn incense there. {14:4} As soon as his rule was established, Amaziah executed the servants who had murdered his father, King Joash. However, he didn't punish the children of the murderers, following the law of Moses which forbade punishing children for their parents' sins. {14:5} Amaziah waged war against Edom in the Valley of Salt and killed ten thousand Edomites. He also captured Selah, renaming it Joktheel. {14:6} Then Amaziah challenged Jehoash, king of Israel, to battle. {14:7} But Jehoash replied with a metaphor, saying, "A thistle in Lebanon sent a message to a cedar tree, asking for the cedar's daughter in marriage. But a wild beast trampled the thistle." {14:8} Jehoash advised Amaziah not to provoke unnecessary conflict, warning him of the consequences. {14:9} However, Amaziah didn't heed the warning, and they met at Beth-shemesh, where Judah was defeated by Israel. {14:10} Jehoash captured Amaziah and breached the wall of Jerusalem, looting the treasures of the temple and the king's palace before returning to Samaria. {14:11} The remaining details of Jehoash's reign, his accomplishments, and his battle with Amaziah are recorded in the chronicles of the kings of Israel. {14:12} Jehoash died and was buried in Samaria, and his son Jeroboam succeeded him as king of Israel. {14:13} After Jehoash's death, Amaziah reigned in Judah for fifteen years. {14:14} The remaining acts of Amaziah, including the conspiracy against him and his eventual death in Lachish, are chronicled in the records of the kings of Judah. {14:15} The people of Judah crowned Amaziah's sixteen-year-old son, Azariah, as king after his death. {14:16} Jeroboam, the son of Jehoash, became king of Israel in the fifteenth year of Amaziah's reign and ruled for forty-one years. {14:17} He continued the sinful ways of Jeroboam son of Nebat, leading Israel astray. {14:18} Despite this, Jeroboam expanded the borders of Israel, fulfilling the word of the LORD spoken through his prophet Jonah. {14:19} Though the affliction of Israel was severe, the LORD did not abandon them, saving them through Jeroboam son of Jehoash. {14:20} The details of Jeroboam's reign, including his wars and conquests, are recorded in the chronicles of the kings of Israel. {14:21} Jeroboam died, and his son Zachariah succeeded him as king of Israel. {14:22} He built Elath and returned it to Judah after the king died. {14:23} In the fifteenth year of Amaziah, the son of Joash, king of Judah, Jeroboam, the son of Joash, king of Israel, began to reign in Samaria. He reigned forty-one years. {14:24} And he did what was evil in the sight of the LORD; he did not turn away from all the sins of Jeroboam, the son of Nebat, who caused Israel to sin. {14:25} He restored the border of Israel from the entrance of Hamath to the Sea of the Arabah, according to the word of the LORD, the God of Israel, which he spoke by his servant Jonah, the son of Amittai, the prophet, who was from Gath-hepher. {14:26} For the LORD saw the affliction of Israel, that it was very bitter, for there was none left, bond or free, and there was no helper for Israel. {14:27} And the LORD did not say that he would blot out the name of Israel from under heaven, but he saved them by the hand of Jeroboam, the son of Joash. {14:28} Now the rest of the acts of Jeroboam, all that he did, his might, how he fought, and how he restored Damascus and Hamath to Judah in Israel, are they not written in the book of the chronicles of the kings of Israel? {14:29} And Jeroboam slept with his fathers, the kings of Israel, and his son Zachariah reigned in his place.

{15:1} In the twenty-seventh year of Jeroboam, king of Israel, Azariah, the son of Amaziah, king of Judah, began to reign. {15:2} He was sixteen years old when he became king, and he reigned fifty-two years in Jerusalem. His mother's name was Jecholiah of Jerusalem. {15:3} Azariah did what was right in the sight of the LORD, just as his father Amaziah had done.

{15:4} However, the high places were not removed, and the people continued to sacrifice and burn incense on the high places. {15:5} The LORD struck the king with leprosy until the day of his death, and he lived in isolation. Jotham, the king's son, governed the palace and judged the people of the land. {15:6} The rest of Azariah's acts, and all that he did, are recorded in the chronicles of the kings of Judah. {15:7} Azariah died and was buried with his fathers in the city of David. Jotham, his son, reigned in his place. {15:8} In the thirty-eighth year of Azariah, king of Judah, Zachariah, the son of Jeroboam, began to reign over Israel in Samaria for six months. {15:9} He did evil in the sight of the LORD, following the sins of Jeroboam, the son of Nebat, who led Israel into sin. {15:10} Shallum, the son of Jabesh, conspired against him, struck him down publicly, and killed him, becoming king in his place. {15:11} The remaining acts of Zachariah are recorded in the chronicles of the kings of Israel. {15:12} This was the word of the LORD spoken to Jehu, saying, "Your sons shall sit on the throne of Israel up to the fourth generation." And so it happened. {15:13} Shallum, the son of Jabesh, began to reign in the thirty-ninth year of Uzziah, king of Judah, but he only reigned for a full month in Samaria. {15:14} Menahem, the son of Gadi, went up from Tirzah to Samaria, struck down Shallum, the son of Jabesh, and became king in his place. {15:15} The rest of Shallum's acts and his conspiracy are recorded in the chronicles of the kings of Israel. {15:16} Then Menahem attacked Tiphsah and all its people, because they did not surrender. He ripped open all the pregnant women. {15:17} In the thirty-ninth year of Azariah, king of Judah, Menahem, the son of Gadi, began to reign over Israel in Samaria for ten years. {15:18} He did evil in the sight of the LORD, not turning away from the sins of Jeroboam, the son of Nebat, who led Israel into sin. {15:19} Pul, the king of Assyria, invaded the land, and Menahem paid him a thousand talents of silver to secure his support and strengthen his hold on the kingdom. {15:20} Menahem exacted this money from Israel's wealthy men, each contributing fifty shekels of silver to the king of Assyria. Then the king of Assyria withdrew from the land and did not stay there. {15:21} The remaining acts of Menahem are recorded in the chronicles of the kings of Israel. Menahem died, and his son Pekahiah became king in his place. {15:22} Pekahiah began to reign after his father Menahem's death. {15:23} In the fiftieth year of Azariah, king of Judah, Pekahiah, the son of Menahem, became king over Israel in Samaria, ruling for two years. {15:24} He did evil in the sight of the LORD, not turning away from the sins of Jeroboam, the son of Nebat, who led Israel into sin. {15:25} Pekah, the son of Remaliah, one of his officers, conspired against him and struck him down in Samaria, in the palace of the king's house, along with Argob and Arieh, and with him fifty Gileadite men. Pekah became king in his place. {15:26} The rest of Pekahiah's acts and all that he did are recorded in the chronicles of the kings of Israel. {15:27} In the fifty-second year of Azariah, king of Judah, Pekah, the son of Remaliah, began to reign over Israel in Samaria, ruling for twenty years. {15:28} He did evil in the sight of the LORD, not turning away from the sins of Jeroboam, the son of Nebat, who led Israel into sin. {15:29} During Pekah's reign, Tiglath-pileser, king of Assyria, attacked and captured several Israelite territories, deporting the people to Assyria. {15:30} Hoshea, the son of Elah, conspired against Pekah, struck him down, and became king in his place in the twentieth year of Jotham, the son of Uzziah. {15:31} The remaining acts of Pekah and all that he did are recorded in the chronicles of the kings of Israel. {15:32} In the second year of Pekah, the son of Remaliah, king of Israel, Jotham, the son of Uzziah, king of Judah, began to reign. {15:33} He was twenty-five years old when he became king, and he reigned sixteen years in Jerusalem. His mother's name was Jerusha, the daughter of Zadok. {15:34} Jotham did what was right in the sight of the LORD, just as his father Uzziah had done. {15:35} However, the high places were not removed, and the people continued to sacrifice and burn incense on the high places. Jotham built the Upper Gate of the house of the LORD. {15:36} The rest of Jotham's acts and all that he did are recorded in the chronicles of the kings of Judah. {15:37} In those days, the LORD began to send Rezin, the king of Syria, and Pekah, the son of Remaliah, against Judah. {15:38} Jotham died and was buried with his fathers in the city of David. His son Ahaz became king in his place.

{16:1} In the seventeenth year of Pekah, the son of Remaliah, Ahaz, the son of Jotham, king of Judah, began to reign. {16:2} Ahaz was twenty years old when he became king, and he reigned sixteen years in Jerusalem. However, he did not do what was right in the sight of the LORD his God, unlike his ancestor David. {16:3} Instead, Ahaz followed the ways of the kings of Israel and even sacrificed his own son in the fire, imitating the detestable practices of the nations that the LORD had driven out before the Israelites. {16:4} He also offered sacrifices and burned incense on the high places, on the hills, and under every green tree. {16:5} During Ahaz's reign, Rezin, king of Syria, and Pekah, son of Remaliah, king of Israel, attacked Jerusalem, but they could not defeat him. {16:6} However, Rezin managed to reclaim Elath for Syria, driving out the Jews who had been living there. The Syrians settled in Elath, where they remain to this day. {16:7} In desperation, Ahaz sent messengers to Tiglath-pileser, king of Assyria, declaring himself to be the king's servant and son. He pleaded for assistance against the kings of Syria and Israel who were attacking him. {16:8} Ahaz took silver and gold from the treasuries of the LORD's house and his own palace and sent them as a gift to the king of Assyria. {16:9} Tiglath-pileser responded by attacking Damascus, capturing it, and deporting its people to Kir. He also killed Rezin, king of Syria. {16:10} When Ahaz visited Damascus to meet Tiglath-pileser, he saw an altar there. He sent a description of the altar to Urijah the priest, asking him to build a similar one in Jerusalem. {16:11} Urijah followed Ahaz's instructions and built the altar before Ahaz's return from Damascus. {16:12} Upon his return, Ahaz approached the altar and offered sacrifices on it. {16:13} He made burnt offerings, grain offerings, drink offerings, and peace offerings, sprinkling the blood of the peace offerings on the altar. {16:14} Ahaz also moved the bronze altar from its original location in front of the LORD's temple and placed it on the north side of the new altar. {16:15} He commanded Urijah to use the new altar for the morning and evening burnt offerings, the king's burnt offering, and the offerings of the people, along with their drink offerings, and to sprinkle blood on it. The bronze altar would be reserved for his own use. {16:16} Urijah carried out all of Ahaz's commands. {16:17} Additionally, Ahaz made alterations to the temple, removing the borders of the stands and taking down the bronze basin from the backs of the bronze oxen, placing it on a stone pedestal. {16:18} He also made changes to the temple structure, including altering the Sabbath canopy and the entrance used by the king, to please the king of Assyria. {16:19} The remaining acts of Ahaz are recorded in the chronicles of the kings of Judah. {16:20} Ahaz died and was buried with his ancestors in the city of David. His son Hezekiah succeeded him as king.

{17:1} In the twelfth year of Ahaz, king of Judah, Hoshea, the son of Elah, began to reign in Samaria over Israel for nine years. {17:2} Hoshea did evil in the sight of the LORD, though not as much as the kings before him in Israel. {17:3} Shalmaneser, king of Assyria, came against him, and Hoshea became his vassal, paying him tribute. {17:4} However, the king of Assyria discovered a conspiracy by Hoshea because he had sent envoys to So, the king of Egypt, and withheld tribute from Assyria. As a result, Hoshea was imprisoned. {17:5} Subsequently, the king of Assyria besieged Samaria for three years. {17:6} In the ninth year of Hoshea's reign, the king of Assyria captured Samaria, exiled the Israelites to Assyria, and settled them in various locations such as Halah, Habor by the river of Gozan, and in the cities of the Medes. {17:7} **This happened because the people of Israel had sinned against the LORD their God, who had brought them out of Egypt and warned them not to follow other gods.** {17:8} Yet they disregarded God's commandments, following the practices of the nations the LORD had driven out before them, as well as the kings of Israel. {17:9} The Israelites practiced idolatry in secret, building high places and setting up sacred pillars and Asherah poles in every city. {17:10} They even worshiped idols on every high hill and under every green tree, burning incense like the nations whom the LORD had driven out before them. {17:11} Their actions provoked the LORD to anger, as they committed wicked deeds against Him. {17:12} Despite the warnings of the prophets and seers sent by the LORD, the Israelites refused to turn from their evil ways and obey His commandments. {17:13} Instead, they persisted in their disobedience and idolatry, like their ancestors who did not believe in the LORD their God. {17:14} Consequently, the LORD's anger burned against Israel, and He removed them from His presence, leaving only the tribe of Judah. {17:15} Even Judah failed to keep the commandments of the LORD and followed the idolatrous practices of Israel. {17:16} Thus, the LORD rejected all the descendants of Israel, allowing them to be oppressed and eventually exiled. {17:17} The people of Israel abandoned the LORD, engaging in detestable practices such as child sacrifice, divination, and sorcery, provoking the LORD to anger. {17:18} Therefore, the LORD punished Israel severely, causing them to be taken away from His sight, leaving only the tribe of Judah. {17:19} Even Judah did not remain faithful to the LORD's commandments but instead imitated the idolatrous practices of Israel. {17:20} As a result, the LORD rejected the entire nation of Israel, subjecting them to affliction and allowing them to fall into the hands of plunderers. {17:21} The division between Israel and Judah began when Jeroboam, son of Nebat, led Israel into sin by turning them away from following the LORD. {17:22} The people of Israel persisted in the sins of Jeroboam, refusing to repent, which ultimately led to their exile, as foretold by the LORD's prophets. {17:23} Thus, Israel was taken away from their land and carried off to Assyria, just as the LORD had warned through His prophets. {17:24} The king of Assyria resettled Samaria with people from various foreign lands, who did not initially fear the LORD. Consequently, the LORD sent lions among them to attack and kill some of them. {17:25} Recognizing this as a divine punishment due to their ignorance of the God of the land, the people appealed to the king of Assyria for help. {17:26} In response, the king of Assyria instructed them to bring back one of the priests from exile to teach them how to worship the LORD. {17:27} A priest was brought back from Samaria to teach the newcomers about the God of the land, and he settled in Bethel. {17:28} However, each nation continued to worship their own gods alongside their newfound fear of the LORD, maintaining their former idolatrous practices. {17:29} They made idols and placed them in the high places, following the customs of the nations they had displaced. {17:30} Each nation worshipped its own gods, including Succoth-benoth, Nergal, Ashima, Nibhaz, Tartak, Adrammelech, and Anammelech. {17:31} Despite this, they also feared the LORD and appointed priests from among themselves to serve in the high places, sacrificing to their gods. {17:32} Thus, they continued to fear the LORD outwardly while serving their own gods, just as they had done before their exile. {17:33} This persisted to the present day, as they did not fear the LORD or follow His statutes, ordinances, or commandments, as the LORD had commanded the children of Jacob. {17:34} The LORD had made a covenant with the children of Jacob, charging them not to fear other gods, bow down to them, serve them, or sacrifice to them. {17:35} Instead, they were to fear and worship the LORD, who had delivered them from Egypt with great power and outstretched arm. {17:36} They were to observe the statutes, ordinances, laws, and commandments the LORD had given them forever, without fearing other gods. {17:37} Despite this covenant, the people of Israel did not heed the LORD's commands but continued in their former ways. {17:38} Consequently, the nations who had settled in Samaria continued to fear the LORD outwardly while persisting in their idolatry. {17:39} Nevertheless, the LORD remained their only hope for deliverance from their enemies, if only they would fear and obey Him. {17:40} Yet, they remained unresponsive, clinging to their old ways. {17:41} Thus, these nations continued to fear the LORD while serving their idols, following the practices of their ancestors.

{18:1} In the third year of Hoshea, son of Elah, king of Israel, Hezekiah, the son of Ahaz, king of Judah, began to reign. {18:2} Hezekiah was twenty-five years old when he became king, and he reigned twenty-nine years in Jerusalem. His mother's name was Abi, the daughter of Zachariah. {18:3} Hezekiah did what was right in the sight of the LORD, following the example of his ancestor David. {18:4} He removed the high places, destroyed the sacred pillars, cut down the groves, and broke into pieces the bronze serpent that Moses had made. Up to that time, the Israelites had burned incense to it, calling it Nehushtan. {18:5} Hezekiah trusted in the LORD God of Israel, and there was no king like him among the kings of Judah, either before or after him. {18:6} He remained faithful to the LORD, never turning away from following Him, and he obeyed all the commandments the LORD gave to Moses. {18:7} As a result, the LORD was with Hezekiah, and he prospered wherever he went. Hezekiah rebelled against the king of Assyria and did not serve him. {18:8} Hezekiah also defeated the Philistines, extending his territory as far as Gaza and its borders, from the watchtower to the fortified city. {18:9} In the fourth year of Hezekiah's reign, which was the seventh year of Hoshea, king of Israel, Shalmaneser, king of Assyria, attacked Samaria and besieged it. {18:10} After three years, in the sixth year of Hezekiah's reign, the ninth year of Hoshea, king of Israel, Samaria fell. {18:11} The king of Assyria then exiled the Israelites to Assyria, settling them in Halah, Habor by the river of Gozan, and in the cities of the Medes. {18:12} This happened because the Israelites disobeyed the voice of the LORD their God, breaking His covenant and disregarding all that Moses, the servant of the LORD, had commanded. They refused to listen or obey. {18:13} In the fourteenth year of Hezekiah's reign, Sennacherib, king of Assyria, attacked all the fortified cities of Judah and captured them. {18:14} Hezekiah, king of Judah, sent a message to the king of Assyria at Lachish, admitting his offense and offering to pay whatever tribute was demanded of him. The king of Assyria imposed a heavy tax of three hundred talents of silver and thirty talents of gold on Hezekiah. {18:15} Hezekiah gave the king of Assyria all the silver found in the house of the LORD and in the treasuries of the royal palace. {18:16} He even stripped the gold from the doors and pillars of the temple of the LORD and gave it to the king of Assyria. {18:17} The king of Assyria then sent Tartan, Rabsaris, and Rabshakeh from Lachish with a large army to confront King Hezekiah in Jerusalem. They positioned themselves by the conduit of the upper pool, near the highway to the fuller's field. {18:18} When they called for the king, Eliakim, Shebna, and Joah came out to meet them. Eliakim was in charge of the palace, Shebna was the royal secretary, and Joah was the recorder. {18:19} Rabshakeh addressed them, questioning Hezekiah's confidence and accusing him of rebellion against the king of Assyria. {18:20} He mocked Hezekiah's reliance on Egypt for support, likening it to leaning on a broken reed that would pierce the hand of anyone who leaned on it. He warned against trusting in the LORD, claiming that Hezekiah had offended Him by removing the high places and altars. {18:21} Rabshakeh challenged the people to provide two thousand horses if they claimed to trust in the LORD. He questioned how they could resist even the least of his master's officers if they relied on Egypt's chariots and horsemen. {18:22} He urged them to make peace with the king of Assyria by offering a tribute, promising that they would then be free to enjoy their own possessions and live securely in a foreign land. {18:23} Rabshakeh demanded hostages as a sign of their submission, offering horses to those who could ride them. {18:24} He questioned Hezekiah's ability to resist Assyria, asserting that the LORD had commanded Assyria to destroy Judah. {18:25} Rabshakeh warned against trusting in the LORD, citing Assyria's successful conquests of other nations. {18:26} Upon hearing these words, Eliakim, Shebna, and Joah asked Rabshakeh to speak in Aramaic, as they understood it, and not in Hebrew, to prevent the people on the city wall from being frightened. {18:27} However, Rabshakeh responded by speaking loudly in Hebrew, aiming to demoralize the people by warning them of the impending siege and starvation. {18:28} He continued to proclaim the might of the king of Assyria and the futility of Hezekiah's resistance. {18:29} He warned the people not to be deceived by Hezekiah's promises of deliverance, as he would not be able to save them from Assyria's grasp. {18:30} Rabshakeh advised them not to trust in the LORD, claiming that Hezekiah's assurances of divine rescue were false. {18:31} Instead, he suggested making peace with Assyria by offering tribute, promising that they would then be free to enjoy their land and resources. {18:32} Rabshakeh described the land Assyria would provide, likening it to their own land, abundant with crops and vineyards. {18:33} He questioned the efficacy of other nations' gods in saving them from Assyria's conquests. {18:34} Rabshakeh challenged the gods of other conquered nations, asking if they had been able to save their people. {18:35} He questioned why the people of Jerusalem believed their God could deliver them when the gods of other nations had failed. {18:36} The people remained silent, following the king's command not to respond. {18:37} Eliakim, Shebna, and Joah returned to Hezekiah with torn clothes and reported Rabshakeh's words to him.

{19:1} When King Hezekiah heard this, he tore his clothes, put on sackcloth, and went into the house of the LORD. {19:2} Hezekiah sent Eliakim, the palace administrator, Shebna the secretary, and the leading priests, all wearing sackcloth, to the prophet Isaiah son of Amoz. {19:3} They told him, "This is what Hezekiah says: This day is a day of distress and rebuke and disgrace, as when children come to the moment of birth and there is no strength to deliver them. {19:4} But perhaps the LORD your God will hear all the words of the field commander, whom his master, the king of Assyria, has sent to ridicule the living God, and will rebuke him for the words the LORD your God has heard. Therefore, pray for the remnant that still survives." {19:5} When King Hezekiah's officials came to Isaiah, {19:6} Isaiah said to them, "Tell your master, 'This is what the LORD says: Do not be afraid of what you have heard—those words with which the underlings of the king of Assyria have blasphemed me. {19:7} Listen! I am going to put such a spirit in him that when he hears a certain report, he will return to his own country, and there I will have him cut down with the sword.'" {19:8} When the field commander heard that the king of Assyria had left Lachish, he withdrew and found the king fighting against Libnah. {19:9} Now Sennacherib received a report that Tirhakah, the king of Cush, was marching out to fight against him. When he heard it, he sent messengers to Hezekiah with this word: {19:10} "Say to Hezekiah king of Judah: Do not let the god you depend on deceive you when he says, 'Jerusalem will not be given into the hands of the king of Assyria.' {19:11} Surely you have heard what the kings of Assyria have done to all the countries, destroying them completely. And will you be delivered? {19:12} Did the gods of the nations that were destroyed by my predecessors deliver them—the gods of Gozan, Haran, Rezeph, and the people of Eden who were in Tel Assar? {19:13} Where is the king of Hamath or the king of Arpad? Where are the kings of Lair, Sepharvaim, Hena and Ivvah?" {19:14} Hezekiah received the letter from the messengers and read it. Then he went up to the temple of the LORD and spread it out before the LORD. {19:15} And Hezekiah prayed to the LORD: "LORD, the God of Israel, enthroned between the cherubim, you alone are God over all the kingdoms of the earth. You have made heaven and earth. {19:16} Give ear, LORD, and hear; open your eyes, LORD, and see; listen to the words Sennacherib has sent to ridicule the living God. {19:17} It is true, LORD, that the Assyrian kings have laid waste these nations and their lands. {19:18} They have thrown their gods into the fire and destroyed them, for they were not gods but only wood and stone, fashioned by human hands. {19:19} Now, LORD our God, deliver us from his hand, so that all the kingdoms of the earth may know that you alone, LORD, are God." {19:20} Then Isaiah son of Amoz sent a message to Hezekiah: "This is what the LORD, the God of Israel, says: I have heard your prayer concerning Sennacherib king of Assyria. {19:21} This is the word that the LORD has spoken against him: 'Virgin Daughter Zion despises you and mocks you. Daughter Jerusalem tosses her head as you flee. {19:22} Who is it you have ridiculed and blasphemed? Against whom have you raised your voice and lifted your eyes in pride? Against the Holy One of Israel! {19:23} By your messengers you have ridiculed the Lord. And you have said, 'With my many chariots I have ascended the heights of the mountains, the utmost heights of Lebanon. I have cut down its tallest cedars, the choicest of its junipers. I have reached its remotest heights, the finest of its forests. {19:24} I have dug wells in foreign lands and drunk the water there. With the soles of my feet I have dried up all the streams of Egypt.' {19:25} "Have you not heard? Long ago I ordained it. In days of old I planned it; now I have brought it to pass, that you have turned fortified cities into piles of stone. {19:26} Their people, drained of power, are dismayed and put to shame. They are like plants in the field, like tender green shoots, like grass sprouting on the roof, scorched before it grows up. {19:27} "But I know where you are and when you come and go and how you rage against me. {19:28} Because you rage against me and because your insolence has reached my ears, I will put my hook in your nose and my bit in your mouth, and I will make you return by the way you came.' {19:29} "This will be the sign for you, Hezekiah: This year you will eat what grows by itself, and the second year what springs from that. But in the third year sow and reap, plant vineyards and eat their fruit. {19:30} Once more a remnant of the kingdom of Judah will take root below and bear fruit above. {19:31} For out of Jerusalem will come a remnant, and out of Mount Zion a band of survivors. The zeal of the LORD Almighty will accomplish this. {19:32} "Therefore this is what the LORD says concerning the king of Assyria: 'He will not enter this city or shoot an arrow here. He will not come before it with shield or build a siege ramp against it. {19:33} By the way that he came he will return; he will not enter this city,' declares the LORD. {19:34} 'I will defend this city and save it, for my sake and for the sake of David my servant.'" {19:35} That night the angel of the LORD went out and put to death a hundred and eighty-five thousand in the Assyrian camp. When the people got up the next morning—there were all the dead bodies! {19:36} So Sennacherib king of Assyria broke camp and withdrew. He returned to Nineveh and stayed there. {19:37} One day, while he was worshiping in the temple of his god Nisrok, his sons Adrammelek and Sharezer killed him with the sword, and they escaped to the land of Ararat. And Esarhaddon his son succeeded him as king.

{20:1} In those days, Hezekiah became very sick, nearing death. The prophet Isaiah, son of Amoz, visited him and delivered a message from the LORD, saying, "Put your house in order, for you will die; you will not recover." {20:2} Hezekiah turned his face to the wall and prayed to the LORD, {20:3} saying, "Please, O LORD, remember how I have walked before you faithfully and with a wholehearted devotion and have done what is good in your sight." And Hezekiah wept bitterly. {20:4} Before Isaiah had left the middle courtyard, the word of the LORD came to him: {20:5} "Go back and tell Hezekiah, the leader of my people, 'This is what the LORD, the God of your father David, says: I have heard your prayer and seen your tears; I will heal you. On the third day from now you will go up to the temple of the LORD. {20:6} I will add fifteen years to your life, and I will deliver you and this city from the hand of the king of Assyria. I will defend this city for my sake and for the sake of my servant David.'" {20:7} Then Isaiah said, "Prepare a poultice of figs." So they did, and applied it to the boil, and Hezekiah recovered. {20:8} Hezekiah asked Isaiah, "What will be the sign that the LORD will heal me and that I will go up to the temple of the LORD on the third day?" {20:9} Isaiah answered, "This is the LORD's sign to you that the LORD will do what he has promised: Shall the shadow go forward ten steps, or shall it go back ten steps?" {20:10} "It is a simple matter for the shadow to go forward ten steps," said Hezekiah. "Rather, have it go back ten steps." {20:11} The prophet Isaiah cried out to the LORD, and the LORD made the shadow go back ten steps it had gone down on the stairway of Ahaz. {20:12} At that time, Merodach-Baladan son of Baladan, king of Babylon, sent Hezekiah letters and a gift, for he had heard of Hezekiah's illness. {20:13} Hezekiah received the envoys and showed them all that was in his storehouses—the silver, the gold, the spices, and the fine oil—his armory and everything found among his treasures. There was nothing in his palace or in all his kingdom that Hezekiah did not show them. {20:14} Then Isaiah the prophet went to King Hezekiah and asked, "What did those men say, and where did they come from?" "From a distant land," Hezekiah replied. "They came from Babylon." {20:15} The prophet asked, "What did they see in your palace?" "They saw everything in my palace," Hezekiah said. "There is nothing among my treasures that I did not show them." {20:16} Then Isaiah said to Hezekiah, "Hear the word of the LORD: {20:17} The time will surely come when everything in your palace, and all that your predecessors have stored up until this day, will be carried off to Babylon. Nothing will be left, says the LORD. {20:18} And some of your descendants, your own flesh and blood who will be born to you, will be taken away, and they will become eunuchs in the palace of the king of Babylon." {20:19} "The word of the LORD you have spoken is good," Hezekiah replied. For he thought, "Will there not be peace and security in my lifetime?" {20:20} The rest of the events of Hezekiah's reign, all his achievements and how he made the pool and the tunnel by which he brought water into the city, are they not written in the book of the annals of the kings of Judah? {20:21} Hezekiah rested with his ancestors. And Manasseh his son succeeded him as king.

{21:1} Manasseh was twelve years old when he became king, and he reigned in Jerusalem for fifty-five years. His mother's name was Hephzi-bah. {21:2} He did what was evil in the sight of the LORD, following the detestable practices of the nations whom the LORD had driven out before the Israelites. {21:3} He rebuilt the high places that his father Hezekiah had demolished; he also erected altars for Baal and made an Asherah pole, just as King Ahab of Israel had done. He bowed down to all the host of heaven and served them. {21:4} Manasseh even built altars in the temple of the LORD, of which the LORD had said, "My name will remain in Jerusalem forever." {21:5} He built altars for all the host of heaven in the two courtyards of the house of the LORD. {21:6} He sacrificed his own son in the fire, practiced divination, sought omens, and consulted mediums and spiritists. He did great evil in the sight of the LORD, provoking Him to anger. {21:7} Manasseh also set up an idol of Asherah pole he had made in the temple, about which the LORD had said to David and his son Solomon, "In this temple and in Jerusalem, which I have chosen out of all the tribes of Israel, I will put my Name forever. {21:8} I will never again make the feet of Israel wander from the land I gave to their ancestors, if only they carefully follow all I commanded them, and the whole law that my servant Moses gave them." {21:9} But the people did not listen, and Manasseh led them astray to do more evil than the nations had the LORD had destroyed before the Israelites. {21:10} The LORD spoke through His servants, the prophets, saying, {21:11} "Because Manasseh king of Judah has committed these detestable sins, more evil than the Amorites who preceded him, and has led Judah into sin with his idols, {21:12} I am going to bring upon Jerusalem and Judah such disaster that the ears of everyone who hears of it will tingle. {21:13} I will stretch out over Jerusalem the measuring line used against Samaria and the plumb line used against the house of Ahab. I will wipe out Jerusalem as one wipes a dish, wiping it and turning it upside down. {21:14} I will forsake the remnant of my inheritance and give them into the hands of their enemies. They will become plunder and spoil to all their enemies, {21:15} because they have done evil in my sight and have provoked me to anger from the day their ancestors came out of Egypt until this day." {21:16} Moreover, Manasseh shed so much innocent blood that he filled Jerusalem from end to end, in addition to the sin he had caused Judah to commit by doing evil in the sight of the LORD. {21:17} As for the rest of the acts of Manasseh, along with all his accomplishments and the sin he committed, are they not written in the Book of the Chronicles of the Kings of Judah? {21:18} Manasseh rested with his ancestors and was buried in the garden of his own house, the garden of Uzza. And his son Amon succeeded him as king. {21:19} Amon was twenty-two years old when he became king, and he reigned in Jerusalem for two years. His mother's name was Meshullemeth daughter of Haruz; she was from Jotbah. {21:20} He did what was evil in the sight of the LORD, just as his father Manasseh had done. {21:21} He followed completely the ways of his father, serving the idols his father had worshipped, and bowed down to them. {21:22} He forsook the LORD, the God of his ancestors, and did not walk in the way of the LORD. {21:23} Amon's officials conspired against him and assassinated him in his palace. {21:24} Then the people of the land put to death all who had plotted against King Amon, and they made his son Josiah king in his place. {21:25} As for the other events of Amon's reign and what he did, are they not written in the Book of the Chronicles of the Kings of Judah? {21:26} Amon was buried in his tomb in the garden of Uzza. And his son Josiah succeeded him as king.

{22:1} Josiah was eight years old when he became king, and he ruled in Jerusalem for thirty-one years. His mother's name was Jedidah, the daughter of Adaiah of Bozkath. {22:2} He did what was pleasing in the sight of the LORD and followed all the ways of his ancestor David; he did not turn aside to the right or to the left. {22:3} In the eighteenth year of Josiah's reign, he sent Shaphan son of Azaliah, the son of Meshullam, the secretary, to the temple of the LORD. He told him, {22:4} "Go up to Hilkiah the high priest and have him get ready the money that has been brought into the temple of the LORD, which the doorkeepers have collected from the people. {22:5} Have them entrust it to the men appointed to supervise the work on the temple. And have these men pay the workers who repair the temple of the LORD— {22:6} the carpenters, the builders, and the masons. Also, have them purchase timber and dressed stone to repair the temple. {22:7} But they need not account for the money entrusted to them, because they are honest in their dealings."

{22:8} Hilkiah the high priest said to Shaphan the secretary, "I have found the Book of the Law in the temple of the LORD." He gave it to Shaphan, who read it. {22:9} Then Shaphan the secretary went to the king and reported to him, "Your officials have paid out the money that was in the temple of the LORD and have entrusted it to the workers and supervisors at the temple." {22:10} Then Shaphan the secretary informed the king, "Hilkiah the priest has given me a book." And Shaphan read from it in the presence of the king. {22:11} When the king heard the words of the Book of the Law, he tore his robes. {22:12} He gave these orders to Hilkiah the priest, Ahikam son of Shaphan, Akbor son of Micaiah, Shaphan the secretary, and Asaiah the king's attendant: {22:13} "Go and inquire of the LORD for me and for the people and for all Judah about what is written in this book that has been found. Great is the LORD's anger that burns against us because those who have gone before us have not obeyed the words of this book; they have not acted in accordance with all that is written there concerning us." {22:14} Hilkiah the priest, Ahikam, Akbor, Shaphan, and Asaiah went to speak to the prophet Huldah, who was the wife of Shallum son of Tikvah, the son of Harhas, keeper of the wardrobe. She lived in Jerusalem, in the New Quarter. {22:15} She said to them, "This is what the LORD, the God of Israel, says: Tell the man who sent you to me, {22:16} 'This is what the LORD says: I am going to bring disaster on this place and its people, according to everything written in the book the king of Judah has read. {22:17} Because they have forsaken me and burned incense to other gods and aroused my anger by all the idols their hands have made, my anger will burn against this place and will not be quenched.' {22:18} "Tell the king of Judah, who sent you to inquire of the LORD, 'This is what the LORD, the God of Israel, says concerning the words you heard: {22:19} Because your heart was responsive and you humbled yourself before the LORD when you heard what I have spoken against this place and its people—that they would become a curse and be laid waste—and because you tore your robes and wept in my presence, I also have heard you, declares the LORD. {22:20} Therefore, I will gather you to your ancestors, and you will be buried in peace. Your eyes will not see all the disaster I am going to bring on this place.'" So they took her answer back to the king.

{23:1} The king sent for all the elders of Judah and Jerusalem to gather before him. {23:2} He went up to the house of the LORD along with all the people of Judah and Jerusalem, including the priests, prophets, and both small and great. There, he read aloud all the words of the book of the covenant found in the house of the LORD. {23:3} Standing by a pillar, the king made a covenant before the LORD to faithfully follow His commandments, testimonies, and statutes with all their heart and soul, promising to uphold the words of the covenant written in the book. The people stood in agreement with the covenant. {23:4} The king commanded the high priest Hilkiah, the priests of the second order, and the temple doorkeepers to bring out all the vessels made for Baal, the grove, and the host of heaven from the temple of the LORD. He then burned them outside Jerusalem in the fields of Kidron and carried their ashes to Bethel. {23:5} He removed the idolatrous priests appointed by the kings of Judah to burn incense in the high places throughout Judah and around Jerusalem. These were the priests who burned incense to Baal, the sun, the moon, the planets, and all the host of heaven. {23:6} The king also brought out the grove from the house of the LORD to the brook Kidron, where he burned it and ground it to powder, scattering the powder over the graves of the common people. {23:7} Additionally, he demolished the houses of the male cult prostitutes that were in the vicinity of the house of the LORD, where the women wove hangings for the grove. {23:8} He expelled all the priests from the cities of Judah and defiled the high places where they burned incense, from Geba to Beersheba, including the high places at the gates of Joshua the governor of the city, which were on the left side of the city gate. {23:9} Although these priests of the high places did not come to the altar of the LORD in Jerusalem, they were allowed to eat unleavened bread with their fellow priests. {23:10} He also defiled Topheth in the Valley of Hinnom to prevent anyone from sacrificing their children to Molech. {23:11} Furthermore, he removed the horses that the kings of Judah had dedicated to the sun, which were situated at the entrance to the house of the LORD, near the chamber of Nathan-melech the chamberlain. He burned the chariots of the sun with fire. {23:12} The king demolished the altars on the roof of the upper chamber of Ahaz, which the kings of Judah had built, as well as the altars Manasseh had erected in the two courts of the house of the LORD. He pulverized them and scattered the dust into the brook Kidron. {23:13} He also defiled the high places east of Jerusalem, to the south of the Mount of Corruption, which Solomon had built for Ashtoreth, Chemosh, and Milcom, the abominations of the Sidonians, Moabites, and Ammonites, respectively. {23:14} Josiah broke apart the sacred pillars, cut down the groves, and filled their places with the bones of men. {23:15} He destroyed the altar at Bethel and the high place established by Jeroboam son of Nebat, who had caused Israel to sin. Josiah smashed the altar, burned the high place to ashes, and ground it into powder. He also burned the grove. {23:16} Josiah looked around and saw the tombs on the hill. He sent for the bones from the tombs, burned them on the altar, and defiled it, in accordance with the word of the LORD proclaimed by the man of God who had foretold these events. {23:17} Upon seeing a tomb, Josiah asked about it. The people of the city told him it was the tomb of the man of God who had come from Judah and prophesied the things Josiah had done against the altar of Bethel. {23:18} Josiah commanded them not to disturb the bones in the tomb. So, they left the bones undisturbed, along with the bones of the prophet who had come from Samaria. {23:19} Josiah also removed all the houses of the high places from the cities of Samaria, which the kings of Israel had built to provoke the LORD to anger, and he did to them according to all the actions he had taken in Bethel. {23:20} He executed all the priests of the high places who were there on the altars, burning men's bones upon them. Then he returned to Jerusalem. {23:21} The king instructed all the people to observe the Passover to the LORD their God, as it was written in the book of the covenant. {23:22} There had not been a Passover like it since the days of the judges who ruled Israel, nor during the entire period of the kings of Israel and Judah. {23:23} But in the eighteenth year of Josiah's reign, this Passover was observed to the LORD in Jerusalem. {23:24} Josiah removed the mediums, spiritists, idols, and all the abominations he found in Judah and Jerusalem to fulfill the words of the law written in the book discovered by Hilkiah the priest in the house of the LORD. {23:25} No king before Josiah turned to the LORD with all his heart, soul, and might, in accordance with all the law of Moses. Nor did any king arise after him who was like him. {23:26} Yet, the LORD did not turn from the fierceness of His great wrath because of all the provocations Manasseh had done. {23:27} The LORD declared that He would remove Judah from His sight, just as He had removed Israel, and He would forsake Jerusalem, the city He had chosen, and the temple where He had said His name would dwell. {23:28} The remaining events of Josiah's reign and all his deeds are recorded in the chronicles of the kings of Judah. {23:29} During Josiah's reign, Pharaoh Necho king of Egypt marched up to assist the king of Assyria at the Euphrates River, and Josiah went out to confront him. But Necho killed him at Megiddo as soon as he saw him. {23:30} Josiah's servants transported his body in a chariot from Megiddo to Jerusalem, where they buried him in his own tomb. Then the people of the land took Jehoahaz son of Josiah and anointed him, making him king in his father's place. {23:31} Jehoahaz was twenty-three years old when he became king, and he reigned in Jerusalem for three months. His mother's name was Hamutal, the daughter of Jeremiah of Libnah. {23:32} He did evil in the LORD's sight, following the sinful practices of his ancestors. {23:33} Pharaoh Necho imprisoned Jehoahaz at Riblah in the land of Hamath so that he could not rule in Jerusalem. He also imposed a tribute of one hundred talents of silver and a talent of gold on the land. {23:34} Then Pharaoh Necho made Eliakim, Josiah's son, king in place of his father Josiah and changed his name to Jehoiakim. He took Jehoahaz away to Egypt, where he later died. {23:35} Jehoiakim paid the silver and gold to Pharaoh Necho, but to raise the money, he taxed the land according to Pharaoh's command. Every person contributed silver and gold according to their means to give to Pharaoh Necho. {23:36} Jehoiakim was twenty-five years old when he became king, and he reigned for eleven years in Jerusalem. His mother's name was Zebudah, the daughter of Pedaiah of Rumah. {23:37} Like his ancestors, Jehoiakim did evil in the LORD's sight, following their sinful ways.

{24:1} During Jehoiakim's reign, Nebuchadnezzar, the king of Babylon, marched against Jerusalem. Jehoiakim served Nebuchadnezzar for three years, but then he rebelled. {24:2} *The LORD sent various groups, including the Chaldeans, Syrians, Moabites, and Ammonites, to attack Judah and destroy it, fulfilling the prophecy spoken by the prophets of the LORD.* {24:3} This calamity befell Judah by the command of the LORD to remove them from His sight due to the sins of Manasseh, particularly for shedding innocent blood, which the LORD could not pardon. {24:4} The rest of Jehoiakim's deeds are recorded in the chronicles of the kings of Judah. After his death, his son Jehoiachin became king. {24:5} Egypt's king never ventured out of his land again because Babylon's king had taken control of all the territory from the River of Egypt to the Euphrates River. {24:6} Jehoiachin was eighteen years old when he became king, reigning only three months in Jerusalem before his mother's son-in-law, Nebuchadnezzar, took him captive. {24:7} Jehoiachin's reign marked the time when Nebuchadnezzar besieged Jerusalem. {24:8} *In the eighth year of Nebuchadnezzar's reign, he captured Jehoiachin, taking away treasures from the house of the LORD and the king's palace, fulfilling the LORD's prophecy regarding the vessels of gold.* {24:9} Nebuchadnezzar also deported the leading citizens, craftsmen, and smiths, leaving only the poorest people behind in Jerusalem. {24:10} Jehoiachin, along with his mother, wives, officers, and the mighty men, were taken captive to Babylon. {24:11} In total, Nebuchadnezzar took about seven thousand men of valor and a thousand craftsmen and smiths as captives to Babylon. {24:12} Nebuchadnezzar appointed Mattaniah, Jehoiachin's uncle, as king in his place, renaming him Zedekiah. {24:13} Zedekiah was twenty-one years old when he began to reign, ruling for eleven years in Jerusalem. Like his predecessors, he did evil in the LORD's sight. {24:14} Zedekiah's rebellion against the king of Babylon resulted in the expulsion of Judah and Jerusalem from the LORD's presence. {24:15} Jehoiachin, the king of Judah, along with his mother, wives, officers, and the powerful people of the land were taken as captives to Babylon by the Babylonian king. {24:16} Additionally, about seven thousand strong and capable men, including craftsmen and smiths, were also taken into captivity. They were considered fit for war, and the Babylonian king brought them to Babylon. {24:17} After this, the king of Babylon appointed Mattaniah, Jehoiachin's uncle, as the new king, renaming him Zedekiah. {24:18} Zedekiah was twenty-one years old when he became king, and he ruled in Jerusalem for eleven years. His mother's name was Hamutal, daughter of Jeremiah of Libnah. {24:19} However, Zedekiah followed the evil ways of his predecessor Jehoiakim, displeasing the LORD. {24:20} The LORD's anger led to the downfall of Jerusalem and Judah. Zedekiah's rebellion against the king of Babylon was part of this divine judgment.

{25:1} In the ninth year of Zedekiah's reign, in the tenth month, on the tenth day, Nebuchadnezzar, the king of Babylon, came with his army and besieged Jerusalem. They built forts around it. {25:2} The siege lasted until the eleventh year of King Zedekiah. {25:3} By the ninth day of the fourth month, famine struck the city, and there was no food for the people. {25:4} When the city's defenses were breached, the men of war fled by night through the gate between two walls near the king's garden. The Babylonian army pursued King Zedekiah, who fled toward the plain. {25:5} The Chaldean army caught up with the king in the plains of Jericho, and his army scattered. {25:6} They captured Zedekiah and took him to Nebuchadnezzar at Riblah, where they pronounced judgment on him. {25:7} Before Zedekiah's eyes, they killed his sons, then blinded him, bound him with bronze shackles, and took him to Babylon. {25:8} On the seventh day of the fifth month, in the nineteenth year of Nebuchadnezzar's reign, Nebuzaradan, the captain of the guard, came to Jerusalem. {25:9} He burned down the house of the LORD, the king's palace, and all the houses in Jerusalem, including those of the notable people, using fire. {25:10} The Babylonian army, under the captain of the guard, demolished the city walls. {25:11} Nebuzaradan, the captain of the guard, took captive the remaining people in the city, including those who had surrendered to the king of Babylon, except for a few poor individuals left behind to work the vineyards and fields. {25:12} They destroyed the bronze pillars, bases, and the bronze sea in the house of the LORD, breaking them into pieces and carrying the bronze to Babylon. {25:13} They also took away the bronze pots, shovels, snuffers, spoons, and all the bronze utensils used for worship. {25:14} Additionally, they seized the gold and silver firepans, bowls, and other precious items. {25:15} The captain of the guard took away these items made of gold and silver. {25:16} They dismantled the two bronze pillars, the bronze sea, and the bases that Solomon had made for the house of the LORD. The weight of the bronze from all these items was incalculable. {25:17} Each pillar was eighteen cubits high, topped with a brass capital three cubits high, decorated with brass pomegranates and wreathed work. The second pillar was similar. {25:18} The captain of the guard also took Seraiah, the chief priest, Zephaniah, the second priest, and three doorkeepers. {25:19} He seized one of the officers responsible for military affairs, five members of the king's council, the chief scribe of the army, and sixty other influential people found in the city. {25:20} Nebuzaradan, the captain of the guard, took these captives to the king of Babylon at Riblah. {25:21} The king of Babylon executed them at Riblah in the land of Hamath, and thus, Judah was deported from their land. {25:22} Nebuchadnezzar left some of the people in the land of Judah and appointed Gedaliah, the son of Ahikam and grandson of Shaphan, as their governor. {25:23} When the army commanders and their men heard that Gedaliah had been appointed governor, they came to Gedaliah at Mizpah. These included Ishmael son of Nethaniah, Johanan son of Careah, Seraiah son of Tanhumeth the Netophathite, and Jaazaniah son of the Maacathite, along with their men. {25:24} Gedaliah assured them safety under Babylonian rule, encouraging them to settle in the land and serve the king of Babylon. {25:25} However, in the seventh month, Ishmael son of Nethaniah, of the royal family, came with ten men and assassinated Gedaliah, along with the Jews and Chaldeans at Mizpah. {25:26} Fearing the Chaldeans, all the people, including both small and great, and the army commanders, fled to Egypt. {25:27} In the thirty-seventh year of Jehoiachin's captivity, in the twelfth month, on the twenty-seventh day, Evil-merodach, the king of Babylon, released Jehoiachin from prison. {25:28} He treated Jehoiachin kindly, exalting him above the other captive kings in Babylon. {25:29} Jehoiachin's prison clothes were replaced, and he dined regularly in the king's presence for the rest of his life. {25:30} The king provided Jehoiachin with a daily allowance for the rest of his days.

1 Chronicles

{1:1} This is the lineage of Adam: Sheth, Enosh, {1:2} Kenan, Mahalaleel, Jered, {1:3} Henoch, Methuselah, Lamech, {1:4} Noah, Shem, Ham, and Japheth. {1:5} Japheth's descendants were: Gomer, Magog, Madai, Javan, Tubal, Meshech, and Tiras. {1:6} Gomer's sons were: Ashchenaz, Riphath, and Togarmah. {1:7} Javan's sons were: Elishah, Tarshish, Kittim, and Dodanim. {1:8} Ham's sons were: Cush, Mizraim, Put, and Canaan. {1:9} Cush's sons were: Seba, Havilah, Sabta, Raamah, and Sabtecha. Raamah's sons were: Sheba and Dedan. {1:10} Cush also fathered Nimrod, who became a powerful ruler on Earth. {1:11} Mizraim's sons were: Ludim, Anamim, Lehabim, Naphtuhim, {1:12} Pathrusim, Casluhim (from whom the Philistines came), and Caphtorim. {1:13} Canaan's sons were: Sidon (his firstborn), Heth, {1:14} the Jebusite, the Amorite, the Girgashite, {1:15} the Hivite, the Arkite, the Sinite, {1:16} the Arvadite, the Zemarite, and the Hamathite. {1:17} Shem's sons were: Elam, Asshur, Arphaxad, Lud, Aram, Uz, Hul, Gether, and Meshech. {1:18} Arphaxad's son was Shelah, who in turn fathered Eber. {1:19} Eber had two sons: one was named Peleg, because in his days the Earth was divided, and his brother's name was Joktan. {1:20} Joktan's sons were: Almodad, Sheleph, Hazarmaveth, Jerah, {1:21} Hadoram, Uzal, Diklah, {1:22} Ebal, Abimael, Sheba, {1:23} Ophir, Havilah, and Jobab. These were Joktan's descendants. {1:24} Shem's line continued through Arphaxad, Shelah, {1:25} Eber, Peleg, Reu, {1:26} Serug, Nahor, Terah, {1:27} and finally to Abram, also known as Abraham. {1:28} Abraham had two sons: Isaac and Ishmael. {1:29} Ishmael's descendants were: Nebaioth (his firstborn), Kedar, Adbeel, Mibsam, {1:30} Mishma, Dumah, Massa, Hadad, Tema, {1:31} Jetur, Naphish, and Kedemah. These were Ishmael's sons. {1:32} Abraham also had sons through Keturah, his concubine: Zimran, Jokshan, Medan, Midian, Ishbak, and Shuah. Jokshan's sons were: Sheba and Dedan. {1:33} Midian's sons were: Ephah, Epher, Henoch, Abida, and Eldaah. All these were Keturah's sons. {1:34} Isaac's sons were: Esau and Israel. {1:35} Esau's sons were: Eliphaz, Reuel, Jeush, Jaalam, and Korah. {1:36} Eliphaz's sons were: Teman, Omar, Zephi, Gatam, Kenaz, Timna, and Amalek. {1:37} Reuel's sons were: Nahath, Zerah, Shammah, and Mizzah. {1:38} Seir's sons were: Lotan, Shobal, Zibeon, Anah, Dishon, Ezar, and Dishan. {1:39} Lotan's sons were: Hori and Homam; Timna was Lotan's sister. {1:40} Shobal's sons were: Alian, Manahath, Ebal, Shephi, and Onam. Zibeon's sons were: Aiah and Anah. {1:41} Anah's son was Dishon, and Dishon's sons were: Amram, Eshban, Ithran, and Cheran. {1:42} Ezer's sons were: Bilhan, Zavan, and Jakan. Dishan's sons were: Uz and Aran. {1:43} These are the kings who ruled in Edom before any Israelite king: Bela, the son of Beor, ruled from Dinhabah. {1:44} When Bela died, Jobab, the son of Zerah from Bozrah, became king. {1:45} After Jobab's death, Husham from the land of the Temanites became king. {1:46} Then Hadad, the son of Bedad, who defeated Midian in the field of Moab, became king. His city was called Avith. {1:47} After Hadad's death, Samlah from Masrekah became king. {1:48} Then Shaul from Rehoboth by the river became king. {1:49} After Shaul's death, Baal-hanan, the son of Achbor, became king. {1:50} After Baal-hanan's death, Hadad became king. His city was Pai, and his wife's name was Mehetabel, the daughter of Matred, the daughter of Mezahab. {1:51} Hadad also died. The chiefs of Edom were: Timnah, Aliah, Jetheth, {1:52} Aholibamah, Elah, Pinon, {1:53} Kenaz, Teman, Mibzar, {1:54} Magdiel, and Iram. These were the chiefs of Edom.

{2:1} These are the sons of Israel: Reuben, Simeon, Levi, and Judah, Issachar, and Zebulun. {2:2} Dan, Joseph, and Benjamin, Naphtali, Gad, and Asher. {2:3} Judah had three sons from the daughter of Shua the Canaanitess: Er, Onan, and Shelah. But Er, Judah's firstborn, was wicked in the sight of the LORD, so He put him to death. {2:4} Then Tamar, his daughter-in-law, bore him two sons: Pharez and Zerah. Judah had five sons in total. {2:5} Pharez's sons were: Hezron and Hamul. {2:6} Zerah's sons were: Zimri, Ethan, Heman, Calcol, and Dara—five in all. {2:7} Carmi's sons were: Achar, who brought trouble upon Israel by violating the things devoted to destruction. {2:8} Ethan's son was Azariah. {2:9} Hezron had sons by the woman he married: Jerahmeel, Ram, and Chelubai. {2:10} Ram fathered Amminadab, who fathered Nahshon, the leader of the tribe of Judah. {2:11} Nahshon fathered Salma, who fathered Boaz. {2:12} Boaz fathered Obed, who fathered Jesse. {2:13} Jesse's firstborn was Eliab, followed by Abinadab, Shimma, {2:14} Nethaneel, Raddai, Ozem, and David as the seventh. {2:15} David had sisters named Zeruiah and Abigail. Zeruiah's sons were Abishai, Joab, and Asahel—three in total. {2:16} Abigail bore Amasa, whose father was Jether the Ishmeelite. {2:17} Caleb, son of Hezron, had children with his wife Azubah and his second wife Jerioth. Her sons were Jesher, Shobab, and Ardon. {2:18} After Azubah died, Caleb married Ephrath, who bore him Hur. {2:19} Hur fathered Uri, who fathered Bezaleel. {2:20} Hezron then married the daughter of Machir, the father of Gilead, and she bore him Segub. {2:21} Segub fathered Jair, who had twenty-three cities in Gilead. {2:22} Jair captured Geshur and Aram, along with their towns, including Kenath and its surrounding towns—sixty towns. All these belonged to the sons of Machir, Gilead's father. {2:23} After Hezron's death in Caleb-Ephratah, Abiah, Hezron's wife, bore him Ashur, the father of Tekoa. {2:24} Jerahmeel, Hezron's firstborn, had sons: Ram, his firstborn, Bunah, Oren, Ozem, and Ahijah. {2:25} Jerahmeel also had another wife named Atarah, who was the mother of Onam. {2:26} Ram's sons were Maaz, Jamin, and Eker. {2:27} Onam's sons were Shammai and Jada. Shammai's sons were Nadab and Abishur. {2:28} Abishur's wife was Abihail, who bore him Ahban and Molid. {2:29} Nadab's sons were Seled and Appaim. Seled died without children. {2:30} Appaim's son was Ishi, who fathered Sheshan. Sheshan's descendants included Ahlai. {2:31} Jada's sons were Jether and Jonathan. Jether died childless. {2:32} Jonathan's sons were Peleth and Zaza. {2:33} These were the descendants of Jerahmeel. {2:34} Sheshan had no sons, only daughters. He had an Egyptian servant named Jarha. {2:35} Sheshan gave his daughter in marriage to Jarha, who then had a son named Attai. {2:36} Attai's descendants were Nathan, Zabad, {2:37} Ephlal, Obed, {2:38} Jehu, Azariah, {2:39} Helez, Eleasah, {2:40} Sisamai, Shallum, {2:41} Jekamiah, and Elishama. {2:42} Caleb's brother Jerahmeel had a son named Mesha, who was the father of Ziph. Mareshah was the father of Hebron. {2:43} Hebron's sons were Korah, Tappuah, Rekem, and Shema. {2:44} Shema fathered Raham, the father of Jorkeam, and Rekem fathered Shammai. {2:45} Shammai's son was Maon, the father of Beth-zur. {2:46} Caleb's concubine Ephah bore him Haran, Moza, and Gazez. Haran fathered Gazez. {2:47} Jahdai's sons were Regem, Jotham, Gesham, Pelet, Ephah, and Shaaph. {2:48} Maachah, Caleb's concubine, bore Sheber and Tirhanah. {2:49} She also bore Shaaph, the father of Madmannah, Sheva the father of Machbenah and Gibea. Caleb's daughter was Achsa. {2:50} These were the descendants of Caleb, son of Hur, the firstborn of Ephratah: Shobal, the father of Kirjath-jearim, {2:51} Salma, the father of Bethlehem, Hareph, the father of Beth-gader. {2:52} Shobal, the father of Kirjath-jearim, had sons: Haroeh and half of the Manahethites. {2:53} The families of Kirjath-jearim included the Ithrites, the Puhites, the Shumathites, and the Mishraites. From these descended the Zareathites and the Eshtaulites. {2:54} Salma's sons were Bethlehem, the Netophathites, Ataroth, the house of Joab, and half of the Manahethites—the Zorites. {2:55} *The families of scribes who lived in Jabez were the Tirathites, the Shimeathites, and the Suchathites. These were the Kenites who descended from Hemath, the father of the house of Rechab.*

{3:1} *These were the sons of David, born to him in Hebron: his firstborn was Amnon, born to Ahinoam the Jezreelitess; his second, Daniel, born to Abigail the Carmelitess;* {3:2} The third, Absalom, the son of Maachah, the daughter of Talmai, king of Geshur; the fourth, Adonijah, the son of Haggith; {3:3} The fifth, Shephatiah, born to Abital; the sixth, Ithream, born to Eglah his wife. {3:4} These six were born to him in Hebron, where he reigned for seven years and six months, and in Jerusalem he reigned for thirty-three years. {3:5} And these were born to him in Jerusalem: Shimea, Shobab, Nathan, and Solomon, four, by Bath-shua the daughter of Ammiel; {3:6} Ibhar, Elishama, Eliphelet, {3:7} Nogah, Nepheg, Japhia, {3:8} Elishama, Eliada, Eliphelet, nine in total. {3:9} These were all the sons of David, besides the sons of his concubines, and Tamar their sister. {3:10} Solomon's son was Rehoboam, followed by Abia, Asa, Jehoshaphat, {3:11} Joram, Ahaziah, Joash, {3:12} Amaziah, Azariah, Jotham, {3:13} Ahaz, Hezekiah, Manasseh, {3:14} Amon, Josiah. {3:15} Josiah's sons were: Johanan, Jehoiakim, Zedekiah, and Shallum. {3:16} Jehoiakim's sons were Jeconiah and Zedekiah. {3:17} Jeconiah's sons were Assir and Salathiel. {3:18} Malchiram, Pedaiah, Shenazar, Jecamiah, Hoshama, and Nedabiah were also sons of Jeconiah. {3:19} Pedaiah's sons were Zerubbabel and Shimei. Zerubbabel's sons were Meshullam, Hananiah, and Shelomith their sister. {3:20} Hashubah, Ohel, Berechiah, Hasadiah, and Jushab-hesed, making a total of five sons. {3:21} Hananiah's sons were Pelatiah and Jesaiah, along with sons of Rephaiah, Arnan, Obadiah, and Shechaniah. {3:22} *Shechaniah's sons were Shemaiah, and Shemaiah's sons were Hattush, Igeal, Bariah, Neariah, and Shaphat, totaling six.* {3:23} Neariah's sons were Elioenai, Hezekiah, and Azrikam, three in total. {3:24} Elioenai had seven sons: Hodaiah, Eliashib, Pelaiah, Akkub, Johanan, Dalaiah, and Anani.

{4:1} The sons of Judah were Pharez, Hezron, Carmi, Hur, and Shobal. {4:2} Reaiah, the son of Shobal, had a son named Jahath, who had sons named Ahumai and Lahad. They were from the families of the Zorathites. {4:3} The father of Etam had sons named Jezreel, Ishma, and Idbash. Their sister was named Hazelelponi. {4:4} Hur, the firstborn of Ephratah and the father of Bethlehem, had sons named Penuel and Ezer, who were the fathers of Gedor and Hushah, respectively. {4:5} Ashur, the father of Tekoa, had two wives named Helah and Naarah. {4:6} Naarah gave birth to Ahuzam, Hepher, Temeni, and Haahashtari. {4:7} Helah's sons were Zereth, Jezoar, and Ethnan. {4:8} Coz had sons named Anub and Zobebah, as well as the families of Aharhel, the son of Harum. {4:9} Jabez was more honorable than his brothers, and his mother named him Jabez, saying, "Because I bore him in pain." {4:10} **Jabez prayed to the God of Israel, asking for blessings, expansion of his territory, God's presence, and protection from evil. God granted his request.** {4:11} Chelub, the brother of Shuah, was the father of Mehir, who was the father of Eshton. {4:12} Eshton had sons named Beth-rapha, Paseah, and Tehinnah, who was the father of Irnahash. They were the men of Rechah. {4:13} Kenaz had sons named Othniel and Seraiah, and Othniel had a son named Hathath. {4:14} Meonothai was the father of Ophrah, and Seraiah was the father of Joab, the founder of the valley of Charashim, because they were craftsmen. {4:15} Caleb, the son of Jephunneh, had sons named Iru, Elah, and Naam. Elah's son was Kenaz. {4:16} Jehaleleel had sons named Ziph, Ziphah, Tiria, and Asareel. {4:17} Ezra had sons named Jether, Mered, Epher, and Jalon, and his wife gave birth to Miriam, Shammai, and Ishbah, who was the father of Eshtemoa. {4:18} Ezra's wife Jehudijah had sons named Jered, Heber, and Jekuthiel. They were born to Bithiah, the daughter of Pharaoh, whom Mered married. {4:19} Hodiah, Naham's sister, had sons named Keilah and Eshtemoa. {4:20} Shimon had sons named Amnon, Rinnah, Ben-hanan, and Tilon, and Ishi had sons named Zoheth and Ben-zoheth. {4:21} Shelah, the son of Judah, had sons named Er, Laadah, and the families of the house of those who worked with fine linen, the house of Ashbea. {4:22} Jokim, the men of Chozeba, Joash, Saraph, who ruled in Moab, and Jashubi-lehem were also descendants of Shelah. These are ancient records. {4:23} The potters and those who lived among plants and hedges lived there, working for the king. {4:24} The sons of Simeon were Nemuel, Jamin, Jarib, Zerah, and Shaul. {4:25} Shallum was Simeon's son, and his descendants were Mibsam, Mishma, Hamuel, Zacchur, and Shimei. {4:26} Shimei had sixteen sons and six daughters, whereas his brothers did not have many children, and his family did not multiply like Judah's descendants. {4:27} They lived in various cities, including Beer-sheba, Moladah, Hazar-shual, Bilhah, Ezem, Tolad, Bethuel, Hormah, Ziklag, Bethmarcaboth, Hazar-susim, Beth- birei, and Shaaraim. These were their cities during David's reign. {4:28} Their villages were Etam, Ain, Rimmon, Tochen, and Ashan, totaling five cities, along with their surrounding villages, extending to Baal. {4:29} Meshobab, Jamlech, and Joshah, the son of Amaziah, were among them. {4:30} Joel, Jehu, Asiel's son Seraiah, Elioenai, Jaakobah, Jeshohaiah, Asaiah, Adiel, Jesimiel, and Benaiah were also among them. {4:31} Ziza, the son of Shiphi, the son of Allon, the son of Jedaiah, the son of Shimri, the son of Shemaiah, were among them, mentioned by name as leaders {4:32} Their villages were Etam, Ain, Rimmon, Tochen, and Ashan, totaling five cities. All the surrounding villages near these cities extended to Baal. {4:33} These were their dwellings, along with their genealogy. {4:34} Meshobab, Jamlech, and Joshah, the son of Amaziah, were among them. {4:35} Also included were Joel, Jehu, the son of Josibiah, who was the son of Seraiah, the son of Asiel. {4:36} Additionally, there were Elioenai, Jaakobah, Jeshohaiah, Asaiah, Adiel, Jesimiel, and Benaiah. {4:37} Ziza, the son of Shiphi, the son of Allon, the son of Jedaiah, the son of Shimri, the son of Shemaiah, were among them, mentioned by name as leaders in their families. {4:38} These individuals were noted as princes in their families, and their family households multiplied greatly. {4:39} They traveled to the entrance of Gedor, on the east side of the valley, in search of pasture for their flocks. {4:40} They found fertile and expansive pastureland, quiet and peaceful, as it had been inhabited by descendants of Ham in the past. {4:41} During the reign of Hezekiah, king of Judah, these individuals attacked the tents and habitations they found there, completely destroying them. They settled in these places because of the excellent pasture for their flocks. {4:42} Five hundred men from the sons of Simeon, led by Pelatiah, Neariah, Rephaiah, and Uzziel, the sons of Ishi, went to Mount Seir. {4:43} They defeated the remaining Amalekites who had escaped and settled there until this day.

{5:1} Reuben, the firstborn of Israel, had sons named Hanoch, Pallu, Hezron, and Carmi. However, because he defiled his father's bed, his birthright was given to Joseph's sons. The genealogy is not reckoned according to birthright. {5:2} Judah became prominent among his brothers, and from him came the chief ruler. Yet, the birthright belonged to Joseph. {5:3} The sons of Reuben, the firstborn of Israel, were Hanoch, Pallu, Hezron, and Carmi. {5:4} Joel's descendants included Shemaiah, Gog, Shimei, Micah, Reaia, and Baal. {5:5} Tilgath-pilneser, the king of Assyria, took Beerah, the prince of the Reubenites, captive. {5:6} Among his brethren were the chief Jeiel and Zechariah. {5:7} Bela, the son of Azaz, dwelt in Aroer, extending to Nebo and Baal-meon. {5:8} He lived eastward, entering the wilderness from the river Euphrates, due to their livestock multiplying in the land of Gilead. {5:9} During Saul's reign, they fought against the Hagarites and dwelt in their tents across the east land of Gilead. {5:10} The children of Gad dwelt in the land of Bashan to Salchah. Joel was their chief, along with Shapham, Jaanai, and Shaphat. {5:11} Their brethren from the house of their fathers were Michael, Meshullam, Sheba, Jorai, Jachan, Zia, and Heber. {5:12} These were the children of Abihail, the son of Huri, the son of Jaroah, the son of Gilead, the son of Michael, the son of Jeshishai, the son of Jahdo, the son of Buz. {5:13} Ahi, the son of Abdiel, was the chief of their fathers' house. They dwelt in Gilead in Bashan, as well as in its towns and suburbs, extending to the borders of Sharon. {5:14} All these were recorded by genealogies during the reigns of Jotham, king of Judah, and Jeroboam, king of Israel. {5:15} Ahi, the son of Abdiel, who was the son of Guni, served as the chief of their fathers' house. {5:16} They lived in Gilead in Bashan, along with its towns and all the surrounding areas of Sharon, extending to their borders. {5:17} All these individuals were recorded in genealogies during the reigns of King Jotham of Judah and King Jeroboam of Israel. {5:18} The sons of Reuben, Gad, and half the tribe of Manasseh, valiant men, skilled in war, numbered forty-four thousand seven hundred and sixty, who went to war. {5:19} They fought against the Hagarites, Jetur, Nephish, and Nodab. {5:20} God helped them in battle, delivering the Hagarites and their allies into their hands because they trusted in Him. {5:21} They took fifty thousand camels, two hundred and fifty thousand sheep, two thousand donkeys, and one hundred thousand men as captives. {5:22} Many were slain in battle because it was ordained by God. They dwelt in the land until the captivity. {5:23} The children of half the tribe of Manasseh dwelt in the land, increasing from Bashan to Baal-hermon and Senir, and to Mount Hermon. {5:24} These were the heads of their fathers' houses: Epher, Ishi, Eliel, Azriel, Jeremiah, Hodaviah, and Jahdiel, mighty men of valor and renowned heads of their fathers' houses. {5:25} They transgressed against the God of their fathers, worshipping the gods of the land, which God had destroyed before them. {5:26} The God of Israel stirred up the spirit of Pul, king of Assyria, and Tilgath-pilneser, king of Assyria, who took the Reubenites, Gadites, and half the tribe of Manasseh into captivity to Halah, Habor, Hara, and the river Gozan, where they remain to this day.

{6:1} The sons of Levi were Gershon, Kohath, and Merari. {6:2} Kohath had three sons: Amram, Izhar, and Hebron, and also Uzziel. {6:3} Amram had three children: Aaron, Moses, and Miriam. Aaron had four sons: Nadab, Abihu, Eleazar, and Ithamar. {6:4} Eleazar's son was Phinehas, who had a son named Abishua. {6:5} Abishua had a son named Bukki, who in turn had a son named Uzzi. {6:6} Uzzi's son was Zerahiah, and Zerahiah had a son named Meraioth. {6:7} Meraioth's son was Amariah, and Amariah's son was Ahitub. {6:8} Ahitub's son was Zadok, who had a son named Ahimaaz. {6:9} Ahimaaz's son was Azariah, and Azariah had a son named Johanan. {6:10} Johanan had a son named Azariah, who served as a priest in Solomon's temple in Jerusalem. {6:11} Azariah's son was Amariah, and Amariah had a son named Ahitub. {6:12} Ahitub's son was Zadok, and Zadok had a son named Shallum. {6:13} Shallum's son was Hilkiah, and Hilkiah had a son named Azariah. {6:14} Azariah's son was Seraiah, and Seraiah had a son named Jehozadak. {6:15} Jehozadak was taken into captivity when the LORD allowed Judah and Jerusalem to fall to Nebuchadnezzar. {6:16} The descendants of Levi were Gershom, Kohath, and Merari. {6:17} Gershom had two sons: Libni and Shimei. {6:18} Kohath had four sons: Amram, Izhar, Hebron, and Uzziel. {6:19} Merari had two sons: Mahli and Mushi. These were the Levite families according to their ancestors. {6:20} Gershom's descendants included Libni, Jahath, Zimmah, Joah, Iddo, Zerah, and Jeaterai. {6:21} Kohath's descendants included Amminadab, Korah, Assir, Elkanah, Ebiasaph, Tahath, Uriel, Uzziah, and Shaul. {6:22} The sons of Kohath: Amminadab his son, Korah his son, Assir his son, {6:23} Elkanah his son, Ebiasaph his son, and Assir his son, {6:24} Tahath his son, Uriel his son, Uzziah his son, and Shaul his son. {6:25} And the sons of Elkanah were Amasai and Ahimoth. {6:26} Elkanah's descendants were Zophai his son and Nahath his son, {6:27} Eliab his son, Jeroham his son, and Elkanah his son. {6:28} The sons of Samuel were Vashni, the firstborn, and Abiah. {6:29} The sons of Merari: Mahli, Libni his son, Shimei his son, Uzza his son, {6:30} Shimea his son, Haggiah his son, Asaiah his son. {6:31} These are the ones whom David appointed to lead the singing in the house of the LORD, after the ark had found its resting place. {6:32} They ministered before the tabernacle of the congregation with singing until Solomon built the house of the LORD in Jerusalem. Then they performed their duties according to their order. {6:33} They also included those who were chosen to serve, along with their descendants. Of the Kohathites, Heman the singer was the son of Joel, {6:34} the son of Elkanah, the son of Jeroham, the son of Eliel, the son of Toah, {6:35} the son of Zuph, the son of Elkanah, the son of Mahath, the son of Amasai, {6:36} the son of Elkanah, the son of Joel, the son of Azariah, the son of Zephaniah, {6:37} the son of Tahath, the son of Assir, the son of Ebiasaph, the son of Korah, {6:38} the son of Izhar, the son of Kohath, the son of Levi, the son of Israel. {6:39} His brother Asaph, who stood at his right hand, was Asaph the son of Berachiah, the son of Shimea, {6:40} the son of Michael, the son of Baaseiah, the son of Malchiah, {6:41} the son of Ethni, the son of Zerah, the son of Adaiah, {6:42} the son of Ethan, the son of Zimmah, the son of Shimei, {6:43} the son of Jahath, the son of Gershom, the son of Levi. {6:44} Their relatives, the sons of Merari, stood on their left: Ethan the son of Kishi, the son of Abdi, the son of Malluch, {6:45} the son of Hashabiah, the son of Amaziah, the son of Hilkiah, {6:46} the son of Amzi, the son of Bani, the son of Shamer, {6:47} the son of Mahli, the son of Mushi, the son of Merari, the son of Levi. {6:48} Their fellow Levites were appointed to all sorts of services in the tabernacle of the house of God. {6:49} But Aaron and his descendants offered sacrifices on the altar of burnt offering and on the altar of incense. They were appointed to serve in the most holy place and to make atonement for Israel, according to all that Moses the servant of God had commanded. {6:50} The sons of Aaron were Eleazar, Phinehas, Abishua, {6:51} Bukki, Uzzi, and Zerahiah, {6:52} Meraioth, Amariah, Ahitub, {6:53} Zadok, and Ahimaaz. {6:54} These were the dwelling places of the sons of Aaron throughout their families, in their territories. The Kohathites, being of the priestly line, received their inheritance by lot. {6:55} They were given Hebron in the land of Judah, along with its surrounding suburbs. {6:56} However, the fields and villages of the city were given to Caleb the son of Jephunneh. {6:57} The sons of Aaron received cities in Judah, including Hebron, a city of refuge, Libnah with its suburbs, Jattir, Eshtemoa with their suburbs, {6:58} Hilen with its suburbs, Debir with its suburbs, {6:59} Ashan with its suburbs, and Beth-shemesh with its suburbs. {6:60} From the tribe of Benjamin, they received Geba with its suburbs, Alemeth with its suburbs, and Anathoth with its suburbs, totaling thirteen cities for their families. {6:61} The remaining sons of Kohath, who were left from the tribe, received ten cities by lot from the half tribe of Manasseh. {6:62} The sons of Gershom received thirteen cities throughout their families from the tribes of Issachar, Asher, Naphtali, and Manasseh in Bashan. {6:63} The sons of Merari received twelve cities by lot throughout their families from the tribes of Reuben, Gad, and Zebulun. {6:64} The children of Israel gave these cities with their suburbs to the Levites as their inheritance. {6:65} By lot, they were given cities from the tribes of Judah, Simeon, and Benjamin, each city bearing its name. {6:66} The remaining families of the sons of Kohath received cities in Ephraim's territory. {6:67} They were given Shechem in mount Ephraim with its suburbs, Gezer with its suburbs, {6:68} Jokmeam with its suburbs, Bethhoron with its suburbs, {6:69} Aijalon with its suburbs, and Gath-rimmon with its suburbs. {6:70} From the half tribe of Manasseh, they received Aner with its suburbs and Bileam with its suburbs, for the remnant of the sons of Kohath. {6:71} The sons of Gershom received from the half tribe of Manasseh, Golan in Bashan with its suburbs and Ashtaroth with its suburbs. {6:72} From the tribe of Issachar, they received Kedesh with its suburbs, Daberath with its suburbs, {6:73} Ramoth with its suburbs, and Anem with its suburbs. {6:74} From the tribe of Asher, they received Mashal with its suburbs, Abdon with its suburbs, {6:75} Hukok with its suburbs, and Rehob with its suburbs. {6:76} From the tribe of Naphtali, they received Kedesh in Galilee with its suburbs, Hammon with its suburbs, and Kirjathaim with its suburbs. {6:77} The rest of the children of Merari received from the tribe of Zebulun, Rimmon with its suburbs and Tabor with its suburbs. {6:78} On the east side of the Jordan near Jericho, they received from the tribe of Reuben, Bezer in the wilderness with its suburbs, Jahzah with its suburbs, {6:79} Kedemoth with its suburbs, and Mephaath with its suburbs. {6:80} From the tribe of Gad, they received Ramoth in Gilead with its suburbs, and Mahanaim with its suburbs, {6:81} Heshbon with its suburbs, and Jazer with its suburbs.

{7:1} The sons of Issachar were Tola, Puah, Jashub, and Shimron, totaling four. {7:2} Tola's sons were Uzzi, Rephaiah, Jeriel, Jahmai, Jibsam, and Shemuel, who were heads of their father's house. They were valiant men of might in their generations. In David's time, they numbered twenty-two thousand six hundred. {7:3} Uzzi's sons were Izrahiah. Izrahiah's sons were Michael, Obadiah, Joel, and Ishiah, totaling five, all of them chief men. {7:4} Together with their descendants, according to their generations, they formed bands of soldiers for war, totaling thirty-six thousand men, as they had many wives and sons. {7:5} Among all the families of Issachar, their brethren were valiant men of might, totaling eighty-seven thousand according to their genealogies. {7:6} The sons of Benjamin were Bela, Becher, and Jediael, totaling three. {7:7} Bela's sons were Ezbon, Uzzi, Uzziel, Jerimoth, and Iri, totaling five, heads of their fathers' houses, mighty men of valor. They were reckoned as twenty-two thousand thirty-four according to their genealogies. {7:8} Becher's sons were Zemira, Joash, Eliezer, Elioenai, Omri, Jerimoth, Abiah, Anathoth, and Alameth. All these were Becher's sons. {7:9} They numbered twenty thousand two hundred according to their genealogy by their generations, heads of their fathers' houses, mighty men of valor. {7:10} Jediael's sons were Bilhan. Bilhan's sons were Jeush, Benjamin, Ehud, Chenaanah, Zethan, Tharshish, and Ahishahar. {7:11} All these were the sons of Jediael, mighty men of valor, totaling seventeen thousand two hundred soldiers, fit for war and battle. {7:12} Shuppim, Huppim, and the children of Ir, Hushim, were the sons of Aher. {7:13} The sons of Naphtali were Jahziel, Guni, Jezer, and Shallum, the sons of Bilhah. {7:14} The sons of Manasseh were Ashriel, who was born to his wife, and Machir, who was the father of Gilead. Machir's concubine bore him Machir, the father of Gilead. {7:15} Machir took the sister of Huppim and Shuppim as his wife, and her name was Maachah. The name of the second son was Zelophehad, who had daughters. {7:16} Maachah, Machir's wife, bore a son whom she named Peresh, and his brother was called Sheresh, whose sons were Ulam and Rakem. {7:17} Ulam's sons were Bedan, who were the sons of Gilead, the son of Machir, the son of Manasseh. {7:18} His sister Hammoleketh bore Ishod, Abiezer, and Mahalah. {7:19} Shemidah's sons were Ahian, Shechem, Likhi, and Aniam. {7:20} The sons of Ephraim were Shuthelah, Bered his son, Tahath his son, Eladah his son, Tahath his son, {7:21} Zabad his son, Shuthelah his son, Ezer, and Elead, whom the men of Gath who were born in that land slew, because they came down to take away their cattle. {7:22} Ephraim mourned many days, and his brethren came to comfort him. {7:23} He went in to his wife, and she conceived and bore a son, whom he named Beriah, because it went evil with his house. His daughter was Sherah, who built Beth-horon the nether, the upper, and Uzzen-sherah. {7:24} Rephah was his son, also Resheph, Telah his son, Tahan his son, {7:25} Laadan his son, Ammihud his son, Elishama his son, {7:26} Non his son, Jehoshuah his son. {7:27} Their possessions and habitations were Bethel and its towns, Naaran eastward, Gezer westward, Shechem, and its towns unto Gaza and its towns. {7:28} By the borders of the children of Manasseh were Beth-shean and its towns, Taanach and its towns, Megiddo and its towns, Dor and its towns. In these dwelt the children of Joseph, the son of Israel. {7:29} The sons of Asher were Imnah, Isuah, Ishuai, Beriah, and Serah their sister. {7:30} Beriah's sons were Heber and Malchiel, who was the father of Birzavith. {7:31} Heber begat Japhlet, Shomer, Hotham, and Shua their sister. {7:32} Japhlet's sons were Pasach, Bimhal, and Ashvath. These were the children of Japhlet. {7:33} Shamer's sons were Ahi, Rohgah, Jehubbah, and Aram. {7:34} His brother Helem's sons were Zophah, Imna, Shelesh, and Amal. {7:35} Zophah's sons were Suah, Harnepher, Shual, Beri, Imrah, {7:36} Bezer, Hod, Shamma, Shilshah, Ithran, and Beera. {7:37} Jether's sons were Jephunneh, Pispah, Ara. {7:38} Ulla's sons were Arah, Haniel, Rezia. {7:39} All these were the children of Asher, heads of their father's house, choice and mighty men of valor, chief of the princes. {7:40} The number throughout the genealogy of those apt for war and battle was twenty-six thousand men.

{8:1} Benjamin had three sons: Bela, Ashbel, and Aharah. {8:2} Bela's sons were Addar, Gera, Abihud, Abishua, Naaman, Ahoah, Gera, Shephuphan, and Huram. {8:3} These descendants of Bela were leaders among the inhabitants of Geba, who were later relocated to Manahath. {8:4} Naaman, Ahiah, and Gera, descendants of Bela, were also relocated, and Gera fathered Uzza and Ahihud. {8:5} Shaharaim had children in Moab after sending away his wives, Hushim and Baara. {8:6} His sons were Jobab, Zibia, Mesha, Malcham, Jeuz, Shachia, and Mirma. {8:7} From Hushim, he had Abitub and Elpaal. {8:8} Elpaal's sons were Eber, Misham, and Shamed, who built Ono and Lod. {8:9} Beriah and

Shema were also leaders among the inhabitants of Aijalon. {8:10} Other descendants included Ahio, Shashak, Jeremoth, Zebadiah, Arad, Ader, Michael, Ispah, and Joha. {8:11} Zebadiah, Meshullam, Hezeki, Heber, Ishmerai, Jezliah, and Jobab were also among Elpaal's sons. {8:12} Elpaal also had Jakim, Zichri, Zabdi, Elienai, Zilthai, Eliel, Adaiah, Beraiah, and Shimrath. {8:13} Ishpan, Heber, Eliel, Abdon, Zichri, Hanan, Hananiah, Elam, and Antothijah were born of Shimhi. {8:14} Shashak had sons named Iphedeiah and Penuel. {8:15} Jeroham's sons were Shamsherai, Shehariah, Athaliah, Jaresiah, Eliah, and Zichri. {8:16} These were prominent men in Jerusalem. {8:17} The father of Gibeon, Maachah, had sons named Abdon, Zur, Kish, Baal, Nadab, Gedor, Ahio, and Zacher. {8:18} Mikloth's son was Shimeah, who dwelt in Jerusalem with his brethren. {8:19} Ner begat Kish, Kish begat Saul, Saul begat Jonathan, Malchi-shua, Abinadab, and Esh-baal. {8:20} Jonathan's son was Merib-baal, who fathered Micah. {8:21} Micah's sons were Pithon, Melech, Tarea, and Ahaz. {8:22} Ahaz had sons named Jehoadah, Alemeth, Azmaveth, Zimri, and Moza. {8:23} Moza's son was Binea, whose descendants were Rapha, Eleasah, and Azel. {8:24} Azel had six sons: Azrikam, Bocheru, Ishmael, Sheariah, Obadiah, and Hanan. {8:25} Eshek's sons were Ulam, Jehush, and Eliphelet. {8:26} Ulam's sons were mighty warriors, skilled archers, and had many descendants. {8:27} In total, there were 150 mighty men among Ulam's offspring. {8:28} These were all descendants of Benjamin. { {8:29} The father of Gibeon lived in Gibeon, and his wife's name was Maachah. {8:30} They had several sons: Abdon, Zur, Kish, Baal, Nadab, Gedor, Ahio, and Zacher. {8:31} Mikloth was the father of Shimeah, who also lived in Jerusalem alongside his brothers. {8:32} Ner was the father of Kish, who in turn fathered Saul, Jonathan, Malchi-shua, Abinadab, and Esh-baal. {8:33} Jonathan's son was Merib-baal, who had a son named Micah. {8:34} Micah's sons were Pithon, Melech, Tarea, and Ahaz. {8:35} Ahaz had sons named Jehoadah, Alemeth, Azmaveth, Zimri, and Moza. {8:36} Moza fathered Binea, Rapha, Eleasah, and Azel. {8:37} Azel had six sons: Azrikam, Bocheru, Ishmael, Sheariah, Obadiah, and Hanan. {8:38} These were all the sons of Azel. {8:39} Eshek's sons were Ulam, Jehush, and Eliphelet. {8:40} Ulam's sons were brave warriors, skilled archers, and they had many descendants, totaling 150.

{9:1} All the people of Israel were recorded in genealogies, which were written in the books of the kings of Israel and Judah. They were taken to Babylon because of their sins. {9:2} The first inhabitants in their cities were the Israelites, priests, Levites, and Nethinims. {9:3} In Jerusalem, there were people from the tribes of Judah, Benjamin, Ephraim, and Manasseh. {9:4} Uthai, a descendant of Pharez, lived in Jerusalem. {9:5} Asaiah and his sons were Shilonites. {9:6} Jeuel and his brothers, numbering 690, were descendants of Zerah. {9:7} Sallu, Ibneiah, Elah, and Meshullam were among the descendants of Benjamin. {9:8} Together with their brethren, they numbered 956 and were leaders in their families. {9:9} Among the priests were Jedaiah, Jehoiarib, Jachin, and Azariah. {9:10} Azariah was the ruler of the house of God. {9:11} Adaiah, Maasiai, and their brethren, numbering 1,760, were very capable for serving in the house of God. {9:12} Shemaiah, Bakbakkar, Heresh, Galal, and Mattaniah were Levites. {9:13} Obadiah, Berechiah, and their brethren, along with Jeduthun, numbered 284. {9:14} The porters, including Shallum, Akkub, Talmon, and Ahiman, numbered 212. {9:15} They were appointed by David and Samuel for their duties. {9:16} They had oversight over the gates of the house of the Lord. {9:17} The porters were divided into four quarters: east, west, north, and south. {9:18} They waited at the king's gate, and they were in charge of the Levites' companies. {9:19} Shallum and his Korahite brethren were gatekeepers of the tabernacle. {9:20} Phinehas was their ruler, and the Lord was with him. {9:21} Zechariah was a doorkeeper at the tabernacle. {9:22} These porters numbered 212 and were appointed by David and Samuel. {9:23} They and their children had oversight over the gates of the house of the Lord. {9:24} The porters were divided into four quarters. {9:25} Their brethren from the villages joined them every seven days. {9:26} The Levites had oversight over the chambers and treasuries of the house of God. {9:27} They lodged around the house of God, opening it every morning. {9:28} They were responsible for the ministering vessels. {9:29} They oversaw the instruments of the sanctuary, including the fine flour, wine, oil, frankincense, and spices. {9:30} Some of the priests made the ointment of the spices. {9:31} Mattithiah, a Levite, had oversight over the things made in the pans. {9:32} Other Kohathite Levites were in charge of the showbread. {9:33} The singers among the Levites were free and worked day and night. {9:34} These Levites were chief throughout their generations, dwelling in Jerusalem. {9:35} In Gibeon, Jehiel and his sons Abdon, Zur, Kish, Baal, Ner, and Nadab lived. {9:36} Gedor, Ahio, Zechariah, and Mikloth were also among them. {9:37} Mikloth fathered Shimeam, and they dwelt in Jerusalem opposite their brethren. {9:38} Ner fathered Kish, who fathered Saul, Jonathan, Malchi-shua, Abinadab, and Esh-baal. {9:39} Jonathan's son was Merib-baal, who fathered Micah. {9:40} Micah's sons were Pithon, Melech, Tahrea, and Ahaz. {9:41} Ahaz fathered Jarah, Alemeth, Azmaveth, and Zimri. {9:42} Zimri fathered Moza, who fathered Binea, Rephaiah, Eleasah, and Azel. {9:43} Azel had six sons: Azrikam, Bocheru, Ishmael, Sheariah, Obadiah, and Hanan. {9:44} These were the sons of Azel.

{10:1} The Philistines fought against Israel, and the Israelite men fled from them on Mount Gilboa. {10:2} The Philistines pursued Saul and his sons and killed Jonathan, Abinadab, and Malchi-shua. {10:3} Saul was badly wounded by archers in the battle. {10:4} Saul asked his armorbearer to kill him, but the armorbearer was afraid, so Saul took his own life. {10:5} When the armorbearer saw Saul dead, he also killed himself. {10:6} So Saul, his three sons, and all his house died together. {10:7} The men of Israel in the valley saw they were defeated and that Saul and his sons were dead, so they abandoned their cities, and the Philistines occupied them. {10:8} The next day, the Philistines found Saul and his sons dead on Mount Gilboa. {10:9} They stripped Saul, took his head and armor, and sent them around to their idols and people. {10:10} They placed Saul's armor in their temple and hung his head in the temple of Dagon. {10:11} When the people of Jabesh-gilead heard what the Philistines had done to Saul, {10:12} they bravely retrieved Saul's and his sons' bodies and buried their bones under an oak in Jabesh, mourning for seven days. {10:13} Saul died because of his transgressions against the Lord, for not obeying the Lord's word and seeking guidance from a medium instead of the Lord. {10:14} Because of this disobedience, the Lord took the kingdom from Saul and gave it to David, the son of Jesse.

{11:1} Then all Israel came to David in Hebron, saying, "Look, we are your own flesh and blood. {11:2} Even in the past, when Saul was king, you were the one who led Israel in and out. The LORD your God said to you, 'You will shepherd my people Israel, and you will be their ruler.'" {11:3} So all the elders of Israel came to the king at Hebron, and King David made a covenant with them before the LORD, and they anointed David king over Israel, according to the word of the LORD through Samuel. {11:4} David and all Israel marched to Jerusalem, which was Jebus, where the Jebusites, the inhabitants of the land, were. {11:5} The inhabitants of Jebus said to David, "You will not come in here!" Nevertheless, David captured the fortress of Zion, that is, the City of David. {11:6} David said, "Whoever attacks the Jebusites first will become commander-in-chief." So Joab son of Zeruiah went up first, and he became chief. {11:7} David lived in the fortress; that is why they called it the City of David. {11:8} He built up the city around it, from the supporting terraces to the surrounding wall, while Joab restored the rest of the city. {11:9} David became more and more powerful because the LORD Almighty was with him. {11:10} These were the chiefs of David's mighty men, who, together with all Israel, helped him in his reign to make him king, according to the word of the LORD concerning Israel. {11:11} This is the list of David's mighty warriors: Jashobeam, a Hakmonite, was chief of the officers; he raised his spear against three hundred men, whom he killed in one encounter. {11:12} Next to him was Eleazar son of Dodai the Ahohite, one of the three mighty warriors. {11:13} He was with David at Pas Dammim when the Philistines gathered there for battle. At a place where there was a field full of barley, the troops fled from the Philistines. {11:14} But they took their stand in the middle of the field. They defended it and struck the Philistines down, and the LORD brought about a great victory. {11:15} Three of the thirty chiefs came down to David to the rock at the cave of Adullam, while a band of Philistines was encamped in the Valley of Rephaim. {11:16} At that time David was in the stronghold, and the Philistine garrison was at Bethlehem. {11:17} David longed for water and said, "Oh, that someone would get me a drink of water from the well near the gate of Bethlehem!" {11:18} So the Three broke through the Philistine lines, drew water from the well near the gate of Bethlehem, and carried it back to David. But David refused to drink it; he poured it out before the LORD, {11:19} saying, "Far be it from me, LORD, to do this! Is it not the blood of men who went at the risk of their lives?" And David would not drink it. Such were the exploits of the three mighty warriors. {11:20} Abishai, the brother of Joab, was chief of the Three. He raised his spear against three hundred men, whom he killed, and so he became as famous as the Three. {11:21} He was doubly honored above the Three and became their commander, even though he was not included among them. {11:22} Benaiah son of Jehoiada, a valiant fighter from Kabzeel, performed great exploits. He struck down Moab's two mightiest warriors. He also went down into a pit on a snowy day and killed a lion. {11:23} And he struck down an Egyptian who was seven and a half feet tall. Although the Egyptian had a spear like a weaver's rod in his hand, Benaiah went against him with a club. He snatched the spear from the Egyptian's hand and killed him with his own spear. {11:24} Such were the exploits of Benaiah son of Jehoiada; he too was as famous as the three mighty warriors. {11:25} He was held in greater honor than any of the Thirty, but he was not included among the Three. And David put him in charge of his bodyguard. {11:26} Among the Thirty were: Asahel the brother of Joab, Elhanan son of Dodo from Bethlehem, {11:27} Shammoth the Harorite, Helez the Pelonite, {11:28} Ira son of Ikkesh from Tekoa, Abiezer from Anathoth, {11:29} Sibbekai the Hushathite, Ilai the Ahohite, {11:30} Maharai from Netophah, Heled son of Baanah from Netophah, {11:31} Ithai son of Ribai from Gibeah in Benjamin, Benaiah the Pirathonite, {11:32} Hurai from the ravines of Gaash, Abiel the Arbathite, {11:33} Azmaveth the Baharumite, Eliahba the Shaalbonite, {11:34} the sons of Hashem the Gizonite, Jonathan son of Shage the Hararite, {11:35} Ahiam son of Sakar the Hararite, Eliphal son of Ur, {11:36} Hepher the Mekerathite, Ahijah the Pelonite, {11:37} Hezro from Carmel, Naarai son of Ezbai, {11:38} Joel the brother of Nathan, Mibhar son of Hagri, {11:39} Zelek the Ammonite, Naharai from Beeroth, the armor-bearer of Joab son of Zeruiah, {11:40} Ira the Ithrite, Gareb the Ithrite, {11:41} Uriah the Hittite, Zabad son of Ahlai, {11:42} Adina son of Shiza the Reubenite, who was chief of the Reubenites, and the thirty men with him, {11:43} Hanan son of Maakah, Joshaphat the Mithnite, {11:44} Uzzia the Ashterathite, Shama and Jeiel the sons of Hotham the Aroerite, {11:45} Jediael son of Shimri, his brother Joha the Tizite, {11:46} Eliel the Mahavite, Jeribai and Joshaviah the sons of Elnaam, Ithmah the Moabite, {11:47} Eliel, Obed, and Jaasiel the Mezobaite.

{12:1} These were the men who came to David at Ziklag while he was still banished from Saul son of Kish. They were among the mighty men, helpers in war. {12:2} They were armed with bows and could use both the right hand and the left in hurling stones and shooting arrows from a bow. They were Saul's kinsmen from Benjamin: {12:3} Chief Ahiezer, then Joash, sons of Shemaah the Gibeathite; Jeziel and Pelet, sons of Azmaveth; Berachah and Jehu the Antothite; {12:4} Ismaiah the Gibeonite, a mighty man among the thirty, and over the thirty; Jeremiah, Jahaziel, Johanan, and Josabad the Gederathite; {12:5} Eluzai, Jerimoth, Bealiah, Shemariah, Shephatiah the Haruphite; {12:6} Elkanah, Jesiah, Azareel, Joezer, Jashobeam the Korhites; {12:7} Joelah, Zebadiah, sons of Jeroham of Gedor. {12:8} From the Gadites, men of might and warriors fit for battle, who could handle shield and buckler, with faces like lions and swift as roes on the mountains: {12:9} Ezer the first, Obadiah the second, Eliab the third, {12:10} Mishmannah the fourth, Jeremiah the fifth, {12:11} Attai the sixth, Eliel the seventh, {12:12} Johanan the eighth, Elzabad the ninth, {12:13} Jeremiah the tenth, Machbanai the eleventh. {12:14} These were the sons of Gad, captains of the army; the least was over a hundred, and the greatest over a thousand. {12:15} They crossed the Jordan in the first month when it was overflowing all its banks, and put to flight all those in the valleys, both east and west. {12:16} Some from Benjamin and Judah also came to David at the stronghold. {12:17} David went out to meet them and said, "If you have come peacefully to help me, my heart will be united with you. But if you have come to betray me to my enemies, since my hands have done no wrong, may the God of our ancestors see and judge." {12:18} Then Amasai, chief of the captains, was moved by the Spirit and said, "We are yours, David, and on your side, son of Jesse. Peace, peace to you, and peace to those who help you, for your God helps you." So David received them and made them captains of his raiding bands. {12:19} Some from Manasseh also defected to David when he went with the Philistines to fight against Saul. But they did not help him, because after consultation, the Philistine lords sent him away, saying, "He will desert to his master Saul at the cost of our heads." {12:20} As David went to Ziklag, these men from Manasseh joined him: Adnah, Jozabad, Jediael, Michael, Jozabad, Elihu, and Zilthai, captains of thousands from Manasseh. {12:21} They helped David against the raiders, for they were all mighty men of valor and were captains in the army. {12:22} Day by day, men came to David to help him until there was a great army, like the armed of God. {12:23} These are the numbers of armed warriors who joined David at Hebron to turn Saul's kingdom over to him, as the LORD had said. {12:24} From Judah, carrying shields and spears, there were 6,800 soldiers ready for battle. {12:25} From Simeon, there were 7,100 mighty men of valor for war. {12:26} From Levi, there were 4,600 soldiers. {12:27} Jehoiada, leader of the Aaronites, had 3,700 men with him. {12:28} Zadok, a young man of valor, commanded 22 captains from his father's house. {12:29} From Benjamin, the relatives of Saul, there were 3,000, for up to that time the majority of them had kept their allegiance to Saul's house. {12:30} From Ephraim, there were 20,800 mighty men of valor, famous throughout the house of their fathers. {12:31} From the half-tribe of Manasseh, there were 18,000, who were designated by name to come and make David king. {12:32} From Issachar, men who understood the times and knew what Israel should do, there were 200 chiefs, and all their kinsmen were under their command. {12:33} From Zebulun, there were 50,000 who could keep rank, who were not of a double heart. {12:34} From Naphtali, there were 1,000 captains, and with them 37,000 armed with shield and spear. {12:35} From the Danites, there were 28,600 men equipped for battle. {12:36} From Asher, there were 40,000 men ready for war. {12:37} On the other side of the Jordan, from the Reubenites, the Gadites, and the half-tribe of Manasseh, there were 120,000 men armed with all kinds of weapons for battle. {12:38} All these men of war, who could keep rank, came to Hebron with a whole heart to make David king over all Israel, and all the rest of Israel were of one mind to make David king. {12:39} And they stayed with David three days, eating and drinking, for their brethren had prepared for them. {12:40} Moreover, those who were near them, as far as Issachar and Zebulun and Naphtali, brought food on donkeys, camels, mules, and oxen, abundant provisions of flour, cakes of figs, clusters of raisins, wine, oil, oxen, and sheep, for there was joy in Israel.

{13:1} David consulted with the captains of thousands and hundreds, and with every leader. {13:2} Then David addressed all the congregation of Israel, saying, "If it seems good to you, and if it is the will of the LORD our God, let us send word to our brethren who are left in all the land of Israel, as well as to the priests and Levites in their cities and suburbs, that they may gather to us. {13:3} Let us bring back the ark of our God, for we did not seek it during the days of Saul." {13:4} The entire congregation agreed to this plan because it seemed right in the eyes of all the people. {13:5} So David gathered all Israel from Shihor of Egypt to the entrance of Hemath, to bring the ark of God from Kirjath-jearim. {13:6} David and all Israel went up to Baalah, that is, to Kirjath-jearim, which belonged to Judah, to bring from there the ark of the LORD, who is enthroned between the cherubim, whose name is called upon it. {13:7} They carried the ark of God on a new cart from the house of Abinadab. Uzza and Ahio drove the cart. {13:8} David and all Israel played before God with all their might, with singing, harps, psalteries, timbrels, cymbals, and trumpets. {13:9} When they came to the threshing floor of Chidon, Uzza reached out his hand to steady the ark because the oxen stumbled. {13:10} But the anger of the LORD burned against Uzza, and He struck him down because he touched the ark. And there he died before God. {13:11} David was upset because the LORD's wrath had broken out against Uzza. So that place has been called Perez-uzza to this day. {13:12} David was afraid of God that day, asking, "How can I bring the ark of God home to me?" {13:13} Therefore, David did not take the ark to the City of David, but diverted it to the house of Obed-edom the Gittite. {13:14} The ark of God remained with the family of Obed-edom in his house for three months, and the LORD blessed Obed-edom and all his household.

{14:1} King Hiram of Tyre sent messengers to David, along with cedar timber, masons, and carpenters, to build a house for him. {14:2} David realized that the LORD had established him as king over Israel, for his kingdom was greatly exalted because of his people Israel. {14:3} David took more wives in Jerusalem and fathered more sons and daughters. {14:4} These are the names of the children he had in Jerusalem: Shammua, Shobab, Nathan, Solomon, {14:5} Ibhar, Elishua, Elpalet, {14:6} Nogah, Nepheg, Japhia, {14:7} Elishama, Beeliada, Eliphalet. {14:8} When the Philistines heard that David had been anointed king over all Israel, they all went up to seek him. David heard about it and went out to confront them. {14:9} *The Philistines had spread themselves in the Valley of Rephaim. {14:10} David inquired of God, asking, "Should I go up against the Philistines? Will you deliver them into my hand?" And the LORD said to him, "Go up, for I will deliver them into your hand."* {14:11} So David went up to Baal-perazim and defeated them there. David said, "God has broken through my enemies by my hand like a breaking flood." Therefore, they named that place Baal-perazim. {14:12} When the Philistines abandoned their idols there, David gave orders, and they were burned with fire. {14:13} The Philistines spread out again in the valley. {14:14} David inquired of God again, and God said to him, "Do not go up after them; turn away from them and come against them in front of the mulberry trees. {14:15} When you hear the sound of marching in the tops of the mulberry trees, then go out to battle, for God has gone out before you to strike the army of the Philistines." {14:16} David did as God commanded, and they struck down the army of the Philistines from Gibeon to Gazer. {14:17} David's fame spread to all lands, and the LORD brought fear of him upon all nations.

{15:1} David built houses for himself in the city of David and prepared a place for the ark of God, setting up a tent for it. {15:2} David declared that only the Levites should carry the ark of God, for the LORD had chosen them to minister before Him forever. {15:3} He gathered all Israel to Jerusalem to bring up the ark of the LORD to the place he had prepared for it. {15:4} David summoned the descendants of Aaron and the Levites: {15:5} From the sons of Kohath, Uriel the chief and his 120 brethren; {15:6} From the sons of Merari, Asaiah the chief and his 220 brethren; {15:7} From the sons of Gershom, Joel the chief and his 130 brethren; {15:8} From the sons of Elizaphan, Shemaiah the chief and his 200 brethren; {15:9} From the sons of Hebron, Eliel the chief and his 80 brethren; {15:10} From the sons of Uzziel, Amminadab the chief and his 112 brethren. {15:11} David called for Zadok and Abiathar the priests, as well as the Levites Uriel, Asaiah, Joel, Shemaiah, Eliel, and Amminadab. {15:12} He said to them, "You are the heads of the Levite families. Consecrate yourselves and your brethren so you may bring up the ark of the LORD God of Israel to the place I have prepared for it. {15:13} "Because you did not carry it the first time, the LORD our God made a breach upon us, for we did not seek Him according to the proper order." {15:14} So the priests and Levites consecrated themselves to bring up the ark of the LORD God of Israel. {15:15} The Levites carried the ark of God on their shoulders with the poles, as Moses had commanded by the word of the LORD. {15:16} David instructed the chiefs of the Levites to appoint their brethren as singers with musical instruments, including psalteries, harps, and cymbals, to play joyfully. {15:17} The Levites appointed Heman the son of Joel, Asaph the son of Berechiah, and Ethan the son of Kushaiah, along with their brethren. {15:18} With them were their brethren of the second rank: Zechariah, Ben, Jaaziel, Shemiramoth, Jehiel, Unni, Eliab, Benaiah, Maaseiah, Mattithiah, Elipheleh, Mikneiah, Obed-edom, and Jeiel, who were the porters. {15:19} Heman, Asaph, and Ethan were appointed to sound the cymbals of brass. {15:20} Zechariah, Aziel, Shemiramoth, Jehiel, Unni, Eliab, Maaseiah, and Benaiah played the psalteries on Alamoth. {15:21} Mattithiah, Elipheleh, Mikneiah, Obed-edom, Jeiel, and Azaziah played the harps on the Sheminith to excel. {15:22} Chenaniah, chief of the Levites, was in charge of the song; he was skillful. {15:23} Berechiah and Elkanah were doorkeepers for the ark. {15:24} Shebaniah, Jehoshaphat, Nethaneel, Amasai, Zechariah, Benaiah, and Eliezer the priests blew the trumpets before the ark of God. Obed-edom and Jehiah were doorkeepers for the ark. {15:25} David, the elders of Israel, and the captains over thousands went to bring up the ark of the covenant of the LORD out of the house of Obed-edom with joy. {15:26} When God helped the Levites who carried the ark of the covenant of the LORD, they offered seven bulls and seven rams. {15:27} David was clothed with a robe of fine linen, as were all the Levites who carried the ark, the singers, and Chenaniah the master of the song. David also wore an ephod of linen. {15:28} Thus, all Israel brought up the ark of the covenant of the LORD with shouting, the sound of the cornet, trumpets, cymbals, and the playing of psalteries and harps. {15:29} As the ark of the covenant of the LORD came to the city of David, Michal, the daughter of Saul, looked out of a window and saw King David dancing and playing. She despised him in her heart.

{16:1} They brought the ark of God and placed it in the tent David had set up. They offered burnt sacrifices and peace offerings before God. {16:2} After David finished offering the burnt offerings and peace offerings, he blessed the people in the name of the LORD. {16:3} He gave each Israelite, both men and women, a loaf of bread, a portion of meat, and a flask of wine. {16:4} David appointed certain Levites to minister before the ark of the LORD, to record, and to give thanks and praise to the LORD, the God of Israel: {16:5} Asaph was the chief, followed by Zechariah, Jeiel, Shemiramoth, Jehiel, Mattithiah, Eliab, Benaiah, and Obed-edom. Jeiel played the psalteries and harps, while Asaph made music with cymbals. Benaiah and Jahaziel, the priests, blew trumpets continually before the ark of God's covenant. {16:6} On that day, David delivered the following psalm to thank the LORD into the hands of Asaph and his brethren: {16:7} "Give thanks to the LORD, call upon His name; make known His deeds among the people. {16:8} Sing to Him, sing psalms to Him; talk about all His wonderful works. {16:9} Glory in His holy name; let the hearts of those who seek the LORD rejoice. {16:10} Seek the LORD and His strength; seek His face continually. {16:11} *Remember His marvelous works, His wonders, and the judgments He has spoken.* {16:12} O descendants of Israel, His servant, O children of Jacob, His chosen ones. {16:13} He is the LORD our God; His judgments are in all the earth. {16:14} Remember His covenant forever, the word He commanded for a thousand generations: {16:15} The covenant He made with Abraham, and His oath to Isaac, {16:16} Which He confirmed to Jacob as a statute, to Israel as an everlasting covenant, {16:17} Saying, 'To you I will give the land of Canaan as the portion of your inheritance.' {16:18} When they were few in number, just a handful of sojourners, {16:19} Wandering from nation to nation, from one kingdom to another, {16:20} He allowed no one to oppress them; He rebuked kings on their behalf, {16:21} Saying, 'Do not touch My anointed ones, and do no harm to My prophets.' {16:22} Sing to the LORD, all the earth; proclaim His salvation day after day. {16:23} Declare His glory among the nations, His marvelous works among all peoples. {16:24} For great is the LORD, and greatly to be praised; He is to be feared above all gods. {16:25} For all the gods of the peoples are idols, but the LORD made the heavens. {16:26} Splendor and majesty are before Him; strength and joy are in His dwelling place. {16:27} Ascribe to the LORD, O families of the peoples, ascribe to the LORD glory and strength. {16:28} Ascribe to the LORD the glory due His name; bring an offering and come before Him. Worship the LORD in the splendor of holiness. {16:29} Tremble before Him, all the earth; indeed, the world is firmly established, it shall not be moved. {16:30} Let the heavens be glad and the earth rejoice; let them say among the nations, 'The LORD reigns!' {16:31} Let the sea resound, and all that fills it; let the fields exult, and all that is in them! {16:32} Then shall the trees of the forest sing for joy before the LORD, for He is coming to judge the earth. {16:33} Oh, give thanks to the LORD, for He is good; His mercy endures forever. {16:34} *And say, 'Save us, O God of our salvation; gather us, and deliver us from the nations, that we may give thanks to Your holy name, and glory in Your praise.'* {16:35} Blessed be the LORD, the God of Israel, from everlasting to everlasting." And all the people said, "Amen!" and praised the LORD. {16:36} David left Asaph and his brethren before the ark of the covenant of the LORD to minister before it continually, as each day required. {16:37} Along with them were Obed-edom and sixty-eight brethren; Obed-edom, the son of Jeduthun, and Hosah served as gatekeepers. {16:38} Zadok the priest and his brethren the priests stood before the tabernacle of the LORD at the high place in Gibeon, {16:39} To offer burnt offerings to the LORD on the altar of burnt offering continually, morning and evening, according to all that is written in the law of the LORD, which He commanded Israel. {16:40} With them were Heman and Jeduthun and the rest who were chosen and designated by name to give thanks to the LORD, for His mercy endures forever. They offered burnt offerings to the LORD on the altar of burnt offering continually, both in the morning and in the evening, following all that is written in the law of the LORD, which He commanded Israel. {16:41} Along with them were Heman and Jeduthun, and others who were chosen and designated by name to give thanks to the LORD, for His mercy endures forever. {16:42} Heman and Jeduthun were accompanied by trumpets and cymbals to make music, along with other musical instruments dedicated to the LORD. The sons of Jeduthun served as gatekeepers. {16:43} Then all the people went to their homes, and David returned to bless his house.

{17:1} While David was in his house, he said to Nathan the prophet, "Here I am, living in a house of cedar, while the ark of the covenant of the LORD remains under curtains." {17:2} Nathan replied to David, "Do all that is in your heart, for God is with you." {17:3} That very night, the word of God came to Nathan, saying, {17:4} "Go and tell David my servant, 'This is what the LORD says: You are not the one to build me a house to dwell in. {17:5} I have not dwelt in a house from the day I brought Israel up out of Egypt to this day. I have moved from one tent site to another, from one dwelling place to another. {17:6} Wherever I have moved with all the Israelites, did I ever say to any of their leaders whom I commanded to shepherd my people, 'Why have you not built me a house of cedar?' {17:7} "Now then, tell my servant David, 'This is what the LORD Almighty says: I took you from the pasture, from tending the flock, and appointed you ruler over my people Israel. {17:8} I have been with you wherever you have gone, and I have cut off all your enemies from before you. Now I will make your name like the names of the greatest men on earth. {17:9} And I will provide a place for my people Israel and will plant them so that they can have a home of their own and no longer be disturbed.

Wicked people will not oppress them anymore, as they did at the beginning {17:10} and have done ever since the time I appointed leaders over my people Israel. I will also subdue all your enemies. "'I declare to you that the LORD will build a house for you. {17:11} When your days are over and you go to be with your ancestors, I will raise up your offspring to succeed you, one of your own sons, and I will establish his kingdom. {17:12} He is the one who will build a house for me, and I will establish his throne forever. {17:13} I will be his father, and he will be my son. I will never take my love away from him, as I took it away from your predecessor. {17:14} I will set him over my house and my kingdom forever; his throne will be established forever.'" {17:15} Nathan reported to David all the words of this entire revelation. {17:16} Then King David went in and sat before the LORD, and he said: "Who am I, LORD God, and what is my family, that you have brought me this far? {17:17} And as if this were not enough in your sight, my God, you have spoken about the future of the house of your servant. You, LORD God, have looked on me as though I were the most exalted of men. {17:18} "What more can David say to you for honoring your servant? For you know your servant. {17:19} LORD, for the sake of your servant and according to your will, you have done this great thing and made known all these great promises. {17:20} "There is no one like you, LORD, and there is no God but you, as we have heard with our own ears. {17:21} And who is like your people Israel—the one nation on earth whose God went out to redeem a people for himself, and to make a name for yourself, and to perform great and awesome wonders by driving out nations from before your people, whom you redeemed from Egypt? {17:22} You made your people Israel your very own forever, and you, LORD, have become their God. {17:23} "And now, LORD, let the promise you have made concerning your servant and his house be established forever. Do as you promised, {17:24} so that it will be established and that your name will be great forever. Then people will say, 'The LORD Almighty, the God over Israel, is Israel's God!' And the house of your servant David will be established before you. {17:25} "You, my God, have revealed to your servant that you will build a house for him. So your servant has found courage to pray to you. {17:26} You, LORD, are God! You have promised these good things to your servant. {17:27} Now you have been pleased to bless the house of your servant, that it may continue forever in your sight; for you, LORD, have blessed it, and it will be blessed forever."

{18:1} After this, David defeated the Philistines, subdued them, and took Gath and its surrounding towns from their control. {18:2} He also defeated Moab, and the Moabites became David's subjects, paying him tribute. {18:3} David then defeated Hadadezer king of Zobah as he went to establish his control along the Euphrates River. {18:4} David captured from him a thousand chariots, seven thousand charioteers, and twenty thousand foot soldiers. David hamstrung all but a hundred of the chariot horses. {18:5} When the Arameans of Damascus came to help Hadadezer king of Zobah, David struck down twenty-two thousand of them. {18:6} David stationed garrisons in the Aramean kingdom of Damascus, and the Arameans became subject to him and brought tribute. The LORD gave David victory wherever he went. {18:7} David took the gold shields carried by Hadadezer's officers and brought them to Jerusalem. {18:8} He also took a vast amount of bronze from Tibhath and Kun, towns under Hadadezer's control. Solomon later used this bronze to make the bronze Sea, the pillars, and various bronze articles. {18:9} When Tou king of Hamath heard that David had defeated the entire army of Hadadezer king of Zobah, {18:10} he sent his son Hadoram to King David to greet him and congratulate him on his victory in battle over Hadadezer, who had been at war with Tou. Hadoram brought all kinds of articles of gold, silver, and bronze. {18:11} King David dedicated these articles to the LORD, as he had done with the silver and gold from all the nations he had subdued: {18:12} Abishai son of Zeruiah struck down eighteen thousand Edomites in the Valley of Salt. {18:13} He stationed garrisons in Edom, and all the Edomites became subject to David. The LORD gave David victory wherever he went. {18:14} David reigned over all Israel, administering justice and equity to all his people. {18:15} Joab son of Zeruiah was over the army; Jehoshaphat son of Ahilud was recorder; {18:16} Zadok son of Ahitub and Abimelek son of Abiathar were priests; Shavsha was secretary; {18:17} Benaiah son of Jehoiada was over the Kerethites and Pelethites; and David's sons were chief officials at the king's side.

{19:1} After this, Nahash the king of the Ammonites died, and his son succeeded him as king. {19:2} David decided to show kindness to Hanun, Nahash's son, because Nahash had shown kindness to him. So David sent messengers to comfort Hanun over his father's death. However, when David's servants entered the land of the Ammonites to visit Hanun and offer their condolences, {19:3} the Ammonite officials said to Hanun, "Do you really think David is honoring your father by sending these men to you? No, he's sent them to spy out the land, to overthrow it, and to gather intelligence." {19:4} So Hanun seized David's servants, shaved off half of their beards, cut off their garments at the buttocks, and sent them away in disgrace. {19:5} When David heard what had happened to his men, he sent messengers to meet them, for they were deeply humiliated. The king instructed them, "Stay in Jericho until your beards have grown back, then return." {19:6} Meanwhile, when the Ammonites realized they had become repulsive to David, Hanun and the Ammonites sent a thousand talents of silver to hire chariots and horsemen from Mesopotamia, Aram-maacah, and Zobah. {19:7} They hired thirty-two thousand chariots along with the king of Maacah and his army, who encamped near Medeba. The Ammonites also gathered from their cities and prepared for battle. {19:8} When David heard of this, he sent Joab and the entire army of mighty men. {19:9} The Ammonites marched out and deployed for battle at the entrance of their city, while the kings who had come to their aid took their positions in the open field. {19:10} Seeing that the battle was set against him from the front and the rear, Joab selected the best troops of Israel and arrayed them against the Arameans. {19:11} The rest of the army he entrusted to his brother Abishai, who positioned them to engage the Ammonites. {19:12} Joab said, "If the Arameans prove too strong for me, you come to my aid; but if the Ammonites are too strong for you, I will come to help you. {19:13} Be courageous! Let us fight bravely for our people and for the cities of our God. And may the LORD do what is good in His sight." {19:14} So Joab and his troops advanced to engage the Arameans, who fled before them. {19:15} When the Ammonites saw the Arameans fleeing, they too fled before Abishai and entered their city. Then Joab returned to Jerusalem. {19:16} When the Arameans realized they had been defeated by Israel, they sent messengers to summon additional Aramean troops led by Shophach, the commander of Hadadezer's army. {19:17} When David heard of this, he gathered all Israel, crossed the Jordan, and marched against them. He arrayed his forces for battle against the Arameans, and they fought him. {19:18} The Arameans fled before Israel, and David killed seven thousand charioteers and forty thousand foot soldiers of the Arameans. He also struck down Shophach, the commander of the army. {19:19} When the servants of Hadadezer saw that they had been defeated by Israel, they made peace with David and became his subjects. After this, the Arameans refused to help the Ammonites anymore.

{20:1} After a year had passed, the time when kings go out to battle, Joab led the army and ravaged the land of the Ammonites. He then besieged Rabbah, while David remained in Jerusalem. Joab captured Rabbah and laid it to waste. {20:2} David took the crown from the Ammonite king's head, which weighed a talent of gold and was adorned with precious stones. David placed it on his own head and plundered the city, gathering a great amount of spoil. {20:3} He brought out the people of Rabbah and subjected them to saws, iron harrows, and axes. This was David's treatment of all the Ammonite cities. Then David and his men returned to Jerusalem. {20:4} Later, there was a war with the Philistines at Gezer. During this time, Sibbechai the Hushathite killed Sippai, a descendant of the giants, and the Philistines were subdued. {20:5} Another battle ensued with the Philistines, and Elhanan, the son of Jair, killed Lahmi, the brother of Goliath the Gittite, whose spear shaft was like a weaver's beam. {20:6} Again, there was war at Gath, where a man of great stature, with twenty-four fingers and toes, six on each hand and foot, challenged Israel. Jonathan, the son of Shimea, David's brother, killed him. {20:7} These were descendants of the giant in Gath, {20:8} and they were slain by David and his servants.

{21:1} Satan incited David to count the people of Israel. {21:2} David instructed Joab and the leaders to conduct a census from Beersheba to Dan and report the total number to him. {21:3} Joab questioned the necessity of the census, warning of the potential consequences, but David insisted. So Joab went throughout Israel and returned to Jerusalem. {21:4} Joab provided the count to David: there were 1,100,000 men in Israel capable of wielding a sword, and in Judah, there were 470,000. {21:5} However, David did not count Levi and Benjamin because Joab found the king's order repugnant. {21:6} But he did not include Levi and Benjamin in the count, because Joab found the king's command repulsive {21:7} This displeased God, so he struck Israel {21:8} David confessed to God, saying, "I have sinned greatly by doing this. Please forgive your servant's wrongdoing, for I have acted foolishly. {21:9} Then the LORD spoke to Gad, David's seer, saying,{21:10} "Go and tell David, 'This is what the LORD says: I offer you three choices. Choose one, and I will carry it out.' {21:11} So Gad went to David and relayed the message {21:12} "Here are your options: three years of famine, three months of being pursued by your enemies while their swords overtake you, or three days of the LORD's sword—pestilence in the land and the angel of the LORD wreaking havoc throughout Israel. Now decide what I should tell the one who sent me." {21:13} David replied to Gad, "I am in great distress. Let me fall into the hands of the LORD, for his mercy is great.

But let me not fall into the hands of men." {21:14} Consequently, seventy thousand men in Israel perished due to a plague sent by God. {21:15} An angel was sent to destroy Jerusalem, but God relented upon seeing the devastation and halted the destruction. {21:16} David, seeing the angel with a drawn sword over Jerusalem, {21:17} pleaded for mercy, along with the elders of Israel. {21:18} The angel commanded David to build an altar to the LORD , {21:19}on the threshing floor of Ornan the Jebusite. {21:20} David approached Ornan, who offered his threshing floor for the altar. {21:21} Ornan and his sons hid from the angel. {21:22} David insisted on paying the full price for the site to prevent the plague from afflicting the people. {21:23} Ornan said to David, "Take it, my lord the king, and do what seems good to you. I give you the oxen for burnt offerings, the threshing instruments for wood, and the wheat for the grain offering. I give it all." {21:24} But King David replied to Ornan, "No, I insist on paying the full price for it. I will not take what is yours for the LORD, nor will I offer burnt offerings that cost me nothing." {21:25} So David paid Ornan six hundred shekels of gold by weight for the place. {21:26} David built an altar, offered sacrifices, and prayed to the LORD. God responded by sending fire from heaven to consume the offerings. {21:27} The LORD commanded the angel to sheath his sword, signifying the end of the punishment. {21:28} David realized that God had answered him, so he continued to offer sacrifices on the threshing floor. {21:29} At that time, the tabernacle and the altar of burnt offering were at Gibeon , {21:30} because David was afraid to go before the tabernacle due to the angel's sword.

{22:1} David said, "This is the house of the LORD God, and this is the altar of the burnt offering for Israel. {22:2} David commanded to gather together the strangers in the land of Israel. He set masons to hew wrought stones to build the house of God. {22:3} David prepared iron in abundance for the nails for the doors of the gates, and for the joinings. Brass was also prepared in abundance without weight. {22:4} Cedar trees were abundant; the Zidonians and the people of Tyre brought much cedar wood to David. {22:5} David said, "Solomon my son is young, and the house to be built for the LORD must be exceedingly magnificent, of fame and glory throughout all countries. Therefore, I will now make preparation for it." So David prepared abundantly before his death. {22:6} David called for Solomon his son and charged him to build a house for the LORD God of Israel. {22:7} David said to Solomon, "My son, it was in my mind to build a house unto the name of the LORD my God. {22:8} But the word of the LORD came to me, saying, 'You have shed blood abundantly and made great wars. You shall not build a house unto my name, because you have shed much blood upon the earth in my sight.' {22:9} Behold, a son shall be born to you, who shall be a man of rest. I will give him rest from all his enemies round about. His name shall be Solomon, and I will give peace and quietness unto Israel in his days. {22:10} He shall build a house for my name; he shall be my son, and I will be his father. I will establish the throne of his kingdom over Israel forever. {22:11} Now, my son, may the LORD be with you; prosper and build the house of the LORD your God, as he has said of you. {22:12} Only the LORD give you wisdom and understanding, and give you charge concerning Israel, that you may keep the law of the LORD your God. {22:13} **Then you shall prosper if you take heed to fulfill the statutes and judgments which the LORD charged Moses with concerning Israel. Be strong and of good courage; dread not, nor be dismayed.** {22:14} In my trouble, I have prepared for the house of the LORD an hundred thousand talents of gold, and a thousand thousand talents of silver; and of brass and iron without weight; for it is in abundance. Timber also and stone have I prepared; and you may add thereto. {22:15} Moreover, there are workmen with you in abundance, hewers and workers of stone and timber, and all manner of cunning men for every manner of work. {22:16} Of the gold, the silver, and the brass, and the iron, there is no number. Arise therefore and be doing, and the LORD be with you. {22:17} David also commanded all the princes of Israel to help Solomon his son, saying, {22:18} 'Is not the LORD your God with you? Has he not given you rest on every side? For he has given the inhabitants of the land into my hand; and the land is subdued before the LORD, and before his people. {22:19} Now set your heart and your soul to seek the LORD your God; arise therefore, and build the sanctuary of the LORD God, to bring the ark of the covenant of the LORD, and the holy vessels of God, into the house that is to be built to the name of the LORD.'

{23:1} When David was old and full of days, he made Solomon his son king over Israel. {23:2} He gathered together all the princes of Israel, with the priests and the Levites. {23:3} The Levites were numbered from the age of thirty years and upward. Their number by their polls, man by man, was thirty-eight thousand. {23:4} Of these, twenty-four thousand were appointed to work on the house of the LORD, and six thousand were officers and judges. {23:5} Additionally, there were four thousand porters and four thousand who praised the LORD with musical instruments, as David had arranged. {23:6} David divided them into courses among the sons of Levi, namely, Gershon, Kohath, and Merari. {23:7} The Gershonites included Laadan and Shimei. {23:8} Laadan's sons were Jehiel, Zetham, and Joel, three in number. {23:9} Shimei's sons were Shelomith, Haziel, and Haran, also three in number. These were the chiefs of the fathers of Laadan. {23:10} Shimei had four sons: Jahath, Zina, Jeush, and Beriah. Among them, Jahath was the chief and Zizah the second, {23:11} while Jeush and Beriah had not many sons and were counted together according to their father's house. {23:12} The sons of Kohath were Amram, Izhar, Hebron, and Uzziel, four in total. {23:13} Amram's sons were Aaron and Moses. Aaron was separated to sanctify the most holy things, along with his sons forever, to burn incense before the LORD, to minister unto him, and to bless in his name perpetually. {23:14} Concerning Moses, the man of God, his sons were named from the tribe of Levi. {23:15} Moses's sons were Gershom and Eliezer. {23:16} Shebuel was the chief among the sons of Gershom. {23:17} Eliezer's sons included Rehabiah, who was the chief. Eliezer had no other sons, but Rehabiah had many. {23:18} The sons of Izhar were led by Shelomith. {23:19} Hebron's sons were Jeriah, Amariah, Jahaziel, and Jekameam. {23:20} Uzziel's sons were Micah and Jesiah. {23:21} The sons of Merari were Mahli and Mushi. Mahli's sons included Eleazar and Kish. {23:22} Eleazar died without sons, only daughters, who were taken by their brethren, the sons of Kish. {23:23} Mushi's sons were Mahli, Eder, and Jeremoth, three in number. {23:24} These were the sons of Levi according to the house of their fathers, including the chiefs, counted by number of names by their polls, who performed the work for the service of the house of the LORD, from the age of twenty years and upward. {23:25} David acknowledged, "The LORD God of Israel has given rest unto his people, that they may dwell in Jerusalem forever. {23:26} Likewise, the Levites shall no longer carry the tabernacle or any of its vessels for its service. {23:27} By the last words of David, the Levites were numbered from twenty years old and above. {23:28} Their duty was to serve the sons of Aaron in the house of the LORD, in the courts, chambers, purifying all holy things, and the work of the service of the house of God. {23:29} They were responsible for the showbread, the fine flour for the meal offering, the unleavened cakes, baked and fried items, and all manner of measure and size. {23:30} They stood every morning to thank and praise the LORD, and likewise in the evening. {23:31} They offered all burnt sacrifices unto the LORD on the Sabbaths, new moons, and set feasts, according to the order commanded unto them, continually before the LORD. {23:32} Their duty was to keep the charge of the tabernacle of the congregation, the charge of the holy place, and the charge of the sons of Aaron their brethren, in the service of the house of the LORD.

{24:1} These are the divisions of the sons of Aaron: Nadab, Abihu, Eleazar, and Ithamar. {24:2} Nadab and Abihu died before their father, leaving no children, so Eleazar and Ithamar executed the priest's office. {24:3} David distributed them, appointing Zadok of the sons of Eleazar and Ahimelech of the sons of Ithamar according to their offices in their service. {24:4} There were more chief men among the sons of Eleazar than among the sons of Ithamar, so they were divided accordingly. Sixteen chief men came from the sons of Eleazar and eight from the sons of Ithamar, according to their fathers' houses. {24:5} They were divided by lot for their duties in the sanctuary and the house of God. Governors were chosen from the sons of Eleazar and the sons of Ithamar. {24:6} Shemaiah, a Levite scribe, wrote their names before the king, the princes, Zadok the priest, Ahimelech the son of Abiathar, and the chief fathers of the priests and Levites. A principal household was chosen for Eleazar, and one for Ithamar. {24:7} The first lot fell to Jehoiarib, the second to Jedaiah, {24:8} the third to Harim, the fourth to Seorim, {24:9} the fifth to Malchijah, the sixth to Mijamin, {24:10} the seventh to Hakkoz, the eighth to Abijah, {24:11} the ninth to Jeshua, the tenth to Shecaniah, {24:12} the eleventh to Eliashib, the twelfth to Jakim, {24:13} the thirteenth to Huppah, the fourteenth to Jeshebeab, {24:14} the fifteenth to Bilgah, the sixteenth to Immer, {24:15} the seventeenth to Hezir, the eighteenth to Aphses, {24:16} the nineteenth to Pethahiah, the twentieth to Jehezekel, {24:17} the twenty-first to Jachin, the twenty-second to Gamul, {24:18} the twenty-third to Delaiah, the twenty-fourth to Maaziah. {24:19} These were the orderings of them in their service to come into the house of the LORD, according to their manner, under Aaron their father, as the LORD God of Israel had commanded him. {24:20} The rest of the sons of Levi were as follows: Shubael, the son of Amram; Jehdeiah, the son of Shubael. {24:21} Concerning Rehabiah: Isshiah was the first of the sons of Rehabiah. {24:22} Shelomoth, of the Izharites; Jahath, the son of Shelomoth. {24:23} Hebron's sons were Jeriah (the first), Amariah (the second), Jahaziel (the third), and Jekameam (the fourth). {24:24} Michah, of the sons of Uzziel; Shamir, the son of Michah. {24:25} Isshiah's brother was Zechariah, the son of Isshiah. {24:26} Merari's sons were Mahli and Mushi; Jaaziah's sons were Beno. {24:27} Jaaziah's sons under Merari were Beno, Shoham,

Zaccur, and Ibri. {24:28} Eleazar, from Mahli, had no sons. {24:29} Concerning Kish: Jerahmeel was the son of Kish. {24:30} Mushi's sons were Mahli, Eder, and Jerimoth. These were the sons of the Levites according to their fathers' houses. {24:31} They cast lots alongside their brethren, the sons of Aaron, in the presence of David the king, Zadok, Ahimelech, and the chief fathers of the priests and Levites, the principal fathers over against their younger brethren.

{25:1} David and the captains of the host assigned the service of the sons of Asaph, Heman, and Jeduthun, who prophesied with harps, psalteries, and cymbals. The number of workmen according to their service was as follows: {25:2} Sons of Asaph included Zaccur, Joseph, Nethaniah, and Asarelah, who prophesied under Asaph's direction according to the king's order. {25:3} Jeduthun's sons were Gedaliah, Zeri, Jeshaiah, Hashabiah, and Mattithiah, six in number, under their father's direction, prophesying with a harp to give thanks and praise to the LORD. {25:4} Heman's sons were Bukkiah, Mattaniah, Uzziel, Shebuel, Jerimoth, Hananiah, Hanani, Eliathah, Giddalti, Romamti-ezer, Joshbekashah, Mallothi, Hothir, and Mahazioth. {25:5} Heman, the king's seer in the words of God, had fourteen sons and three daughters. {25:6} They all served under their father for song in the house of the LORD, with cymbals, psalteries, and harps, according to the king's order to Asaph, Jeduthun, and Heman. {25:7} The total number, including their brethren instructed in the songs of the LORD, skilled in music, was two hundred eighty-eight. {25:8} They cast lots, both small and great, teacher and scholar. {25:9} The first lot fell to Asaph's descendant Joseph, the second to Gedaliah, along with his twelve brethren and sons. {25:10} The third to Zaccur and his twelve brethren and sons. {25:11} The fourth to Izri and his twelve brethren and sons. {25:12} The fifth to Nethaniah and his twelve brethren and sons. {25:13} The sixth to Bukkiah and his twelve brethren and sons. {25:14} The seventh to Jesharelah and his twelve brethren and sons. {25:15} The eighth to Jeshaiah and his twelve brethren and sons. {25:16} The ninth to Mattaniah and his twelve brethren and sons. {25:17} The tenth to Shimei and his twelve brethren and sons. {25:18} The eleventh to Azareel and his twelve brethren and sons. {25:19} The twelfth to Hashabiah and his twelve brethren and sons. {25:20} The thirteenth to Shubael and his twelve brethren and sons. {25:21} The fourteenth to Mattithiah and his twelve brethren and sons. {25:22} The fifteenth to Jeremoth and his twelve brethren and sons. {25:23} The sixteenth to Hananiah and his twelve brethren and sons. {25:24} The seventeenth to Joshbekashah and his twelve brethren and sons. {25:25} The eighteenth to Hanani and his twelve brethren and sons. {25:26} The nineteenth to Mallothi and his twelve brethren and sons. {25:27} The twentieth to Eliathah and his twelve brethren and sons. {25:28} The twenty-first to Hothir and his twelve brethren and sons. {25:29} The twenty-second to Giddalti and his twelve brethren and sons. {25:30} The twenty-third to Mahazioth and his twelve brethren and sons. {25:31} The twenty-fourth to Romamti-ezer and his twelve brethren and sons.

{26:1} Concerning the divisions of the porters: Of the Korhites was Meshelemiah the son of Kore, of the sons of Asaph. {26:2} And the sons of Meshelemiah were Zechariah the firstborn, Jediael the second, Zebadiah the third, Jathniel the fourth, Elam the fifth, Jehohanan the sixth, Elioenai the seventh. {26:3} Moreover the sons of Obed-edom were Shemaiah the firstborn, Jehozabad the second, Joah the third, and Sacar the fourth, and Nethaneel the fifth, Ammiel the sixth, Issachar the seventh, Peulthai the eighth: for God blessed him. {26:4} Also unto Shemaiah his son were sons born, that ruled throughout the house of their father: for they were mighty men of valour. {26:5} The sons of Shemaiah were Othni, and Rephael, and Obed, Elzabad, whose brethren were strong men, Elihu, and Semachiah. {26:6} All these of the sons of Obed-edom: they and their sons and their brethren, able men for strength for the service, were threescore and two of Obed-edom. {26:7} And Meshelemiah had sons and brethren, strong men, eighteen. {26:8} Also Hosah, of the children of Merari, had sons; Simri the chief, (for though he was not the firstborn, yet his father made him the chief;) {26:9} Hilkiah the second, Tebaliah the third, Zechariah the fourth: all the sons and brethren of Hosah were thirteen. {26:10} Among these were the divisions of the porters, even among the chief men, having wards one against another, to minister in the house of the LORD. {26:11} And they cast lots, as well the small as the great, according to the house of their fathers, for every gate. {26:12} And the lot eastward fell to Shelemiah. Then for Zechariah his son, a wise counsellor, they cast lots; and his lot came out northward. {26:13} To Obed-edom southward; and to his sons the house of Asuppim. {26:14} To Shuppim and Hosah the lot came forth westward, with the gate Shallecheth, by the causeway of the going up, ward against ward. {26:15} Eastward were six Levites, northward four a day, southward four a day, and toward Asuppim two and two. {26:16} At Parbar westward, four at the causeway, and two at Parbar. {26:17} These are the divisions of the porters among the sons of Kore, and among the sons of Merari. {26:18} And of the Levites, Ahijah was over the treasures of the house of God, and over the treasures of the dedicated things. {26:19} As concerning the sons of Laadan; the sons of the Gershonite Laadan, chief fathers, even of Laadan the Gershonite, were Jehieli. {26:20} The sons of Jehieli were Zetham, and Joel his brother, which were over the treasures of the house of the LORD. {26:21} Of the Amramites, and the Izharites, the Hebronites, and the Uzzielites: {26:22} And Shebuel the son of Gershom, the son of Moses, was ruler of the treasures. {26:23} And his brethren by Eliezer; Rehabiah his son, and Jeshaiah his son, and Joram his son, and Zichri his son, and Shelomith his son. {26:24} Which Shelomith and his brethren were over all the treasures of the dedicated things, which David the king, and the chief fathers, the captains over thousands and hundreds, and the captains of the host, had dedicated. {26:25} Out of the spoils won in battles did they dedicate to maintain the house of the LORD. {26:26} And all that Samuel the seer, and Saul the son of Kish, and Abner the son of Ner, and Joab the son of Zeruiah, had dedicated; and whosoever had dedicated anything, it was under the hand of Shelomith, and of his brethren. {26:27} Of the Izharites, Chenaniah and his sons were for the outward business over Israel, for officers and judges. {26:28} Of the Hebronites, Hashabiah and his brethren, men of valour, a thousand and seven hundred, were officers among them of Israel on this side Jordan westward in all the business of the LORD, and in the service of the king. {26:29} Among the Hebronites was Jerijah the chief, even among the Hebronites, according to the generations of his fathers. In the fortieth year of the reign of David they were sought for, and there were found among them mighty men of valour at Jazer of Gilead. {26:30} And his brethren, men of valour, were two thousand and seven hundred chief fathers, whom king David made rulers over the Reubenites, {26:31} the Gadites, and the half tribe of Manasseh, {26:32} for every matter pertaining to God, and affairs of the king.

{27:1} The children of Israel were counted, including the chief fathers, captains of thousands and hundreds, and officers who served the king in various monthly rotations throughout the year. Each course consisted of twenty-four thousand men. {27:2} Jashobeam, the son of Zabdiel, led the first course in the first month, with twenty-four thousand men. {27:3} Perez's descendants led the host in the first month. {27:4} Dodai, an Ahohite, led the second course in the second month, with twenty-four thousand men. {27:5} Benaiah, the son of Jehoiada, a chief priest, led the host in the third month, with twenty-four thousand men. {27:6} Benaiah, known for his valor, led the host with Ammizabad his son. {27:7} Asahel, Joab's brother, led the host in the fourth month, with twenty-four thousand men. {27:8} Shamhuth the Izrahite led the host in the fifth month, with twenty-four thousand men. {27:9} Ira, the son of Ikkesh the Tekoite, led the host in the sixth month, with twenty-four thousand men. {27:10} Helez the Pelonite, from the tribe of Ephraim, led the host in the seventh month, with twenty-four thousand men. {27:11} Sibbecai the Hushathite, from the Zarhites, led the host in the eighth month, with twenty-four thousand men. {27:12} Abiezer the Anetothite, from the tribe of Benjamin, led the host in the ninth month, with twenty-four thousand men. {27:13} Maharai the Netophathite, from the Zarhites, led the host in the tenth month, with twenty-four thousand men. {27:14} Benaiah the Pirathonite, from the tribe of Ephraim, led the host in the eleventh month, with twenty-four thousand men. {27:15} Heldai the Netophathite, from Othniel, led the host in the twelfth month, with twenty-four thousand men. {27:16} Leaders were appointed over the tribes of Israel. {27:17} Eliezer led the Reubenites, Shephatiah led the Simeonites, Hashabiah led the Levites, and Zadok led the Aaronites. {27:18} Elihu led Judah, Omri led Issachar, and Ishmaiah led Zebulun. Jerimoth led Naphtali. {27:19} Hoshea led the children of Ephraim, Joel led the half tribe of Manasseh, and Iddo led the half tribe of Manasseh in Gilead. Jaasiel led Benjamin. {27:20} Azareel led Dan. {27:21} These were the princes of the tribes of Israel. {27:22} David didn't count those under twenty years old as the Lord promised to increase Israel like the stars. {27:23} Joab began counting but didn't finish due to the wrath against Israel, so the count wasn't recorded. {27:24} Azmaveth oversaw the king's treasures, and Jehonathan managed the storehouses. {27:25} Ezri managed the field workers, Shimei oversaw the vineyards, and Zabdi managed the wine cellars. {27:26} Baal-hanan managed the olive and sycamore trees, and Joash managed the oil cellars. {27:27} Shitrai managed the herds in Sharon, and Shaphat managed the herds in the valleys. {27:28} Obil managed the camels, and Jehdeiah managed the donkeys. Jaziz managed the flocks. {27:29} These were the rulers of King David's possessions. {27:30} Jonathan, David's uncle, was a counselor and scribe. Jehiel, son of Hachmoni, was with the king's sons. {27:31} Ahithophel was the king's counselor, and Hushai the Archite was the king's companion. {27:32} Jonathan, David's uncle, served as a counselor, a wise man, and a scribe. Jehiel, the son of Hachmoni, was among the king's sons. {27:33} Ahithophel was the king's counselor, and Hushai the

Archite was the king's companion. {27:34} After Ahithophel, Jehoiada the son of Benaiah and Abiathar took counsel. Joab served as the general of the king's army.

{28:1} David gathered all the leaders of Israel, including the tribal princes, company captains serving the king in rotation, commanders over thousands and hundreds, stewards of the king's possessions, his sons, officers, mighty men, and valiant warriors, to Jerusalem. {28:2} Standing, David addressed them, expressing his desire to build a house of rest for the ark of the covenant and the footstool of God. Though he had prepared, God forbade him due to his history of warfare and bloodshed. {28:3} Despite this, God chose David to be king over Israel forever, particularly from the tribe of Judah, David's family. Solomon, David's son, was chosen to build the temple. {28:4} God promised to establish Solomon's kingdom forever if he remained obedient. {28:5} David urged the people to obey God's commandments to secure their land for future generations. {28:6} David advised Solomon to serve God wholeheartedly, assuring him that God would always be with him if he remained faithful. {28:7} David reminded Solomon of his duty to build the temple, encouraging him to be strong and do it. {28:8} David provided Solomon with detailed plans for the temple's construction, including its structure, treasuries, chambers, and furnishings. {28:9} He also specified the materials needed for various items in the temple, such as gold and silver for instruments, candlesticks, tables, and vessels. {28:10} David ensured that Solomon had everything necessary for the priests' courses, Levitical service, and temple work. {28:11} He encouraged Solomon to be courageous and assured him of God's presence and support until the temple's completion. {28:12} David promised Solomon that the priests, Levites, skilled workers, princes, and people would assist him in the temple's construction and service. {28:13} Additionally, David provided for the needs of the priests and Levites, ensuring everything required for the service in the house of the LORD, including vessels. {28:14} He allocated gold and silver by weight for all instruments used in various services. {28:15} Specific weights were assigned for gold and silver used in candlesticks and their lamps, tailored to each candlestick's purpose. {28:16} Gold and silver were provided by weight for the tables of showbread. {28:17} Pure gold was designated for fleshhooks, bowls, cups, and golden basins, each weighed appropriately. {28:18} Refined gold was allocated for the altar of incense and for the pattern of the cherubim's chariot covering the ark of the covenant. {28:19} David explained that the LORD revealed all these details to him in writing, by His hand upon him, encompassing every aspect of the temple's design. {28:20} David encouraged Solomon to be strong and courageous, assuring him of God's constant presence and support until the completion of the temple's construction. {28:21} Furthermore, David assured Solomon that the priests, Levites, skilled workers, princes, and all the people would be available to assist him in every aspect of temple service and construction.

{29:1} King David addressed the congregation, acknowledging that his son Solomon, chosen by God, was young and inexperienced, and the task of building the temple was immense, intended not for man but for the LORD God. {29:2} David had prepared extensively for the construction of the temple, gathering gold, silver, brass, iron, wood, precious stones, and marble stones in abundance. {29:3} Out of his own wealth and devotion to the house of God, David contributed additional gold and silver beyond what he had already prepared. {29:4} His contribution included three thousand talents of gold from Ophir and seven thousand talents of refined silver for overlaying the temple walls. {29:5} David encouraged others to join in consecrating their service to the LORD that day. {29:6} Consequently, the leaders of Israel, along with the captains and rulers of the king's work, offered willingly. {29:7} They contributed substantial amounts of gold, silver, brass, iron, and precious stones for the service of the temple. {29:8} Those who possessed precious stones gave them to the treasury of the house of the LORD under the supervision of Jehiel the Gershonite. {29:9} The people rejoiced in their offerings, willingly and with perfect hearts, and David also rejoiced greatly. {29:10} David blessed the LORD before the congregation, acknowledging His greatness, power, glory, and sovereignty over all. {29:11} He praised God for His provision of riches and honor and acknowledged that all things come from Him. {29:12} David recognized God's authority and ability to make great and give strength to all. {29:13} Therefore, David and the people thanked and praised God's glorious name. {29:14} David humbly questioned his own significance and that of his people, realizing that their ability to offer willingly came from God. {29:15} He acknowledged their transient nature as strangers and sojourners on earth, with fleeting days. {29:16} All the resources prepared for building the temple were from God's hand and belonged to Him. {29:17} David affirmed his sincerity in offering all these things willingly and expressed joy at the people's willingness to offer to God. {29:18} He prayed for God to keep this attitude in the hearts of His people and to prepare their hearts for Him. {29:19} David asked God to give Solomon a perfect heart to keep His commandments, testimonies, and statutes and to build the palace as provisioned. {29:20} David urged the congregation to bless the LORD their God, and they did, bowing down and worshiping the LORD and the king. {29:21} They sacrificed sacrifices and offerings in abundance the following day, with great gladness and festivity. {29:22} Solomon was anointed king a second time, and Zadok was made priest, and they ate and drank before the LORD with joy. {29:23} Solomon sat on the throne as king, succeeding David his father, and prospered, with all Israel obeying him. {29:24} All the princes, mighty men, and David's sons submitted to Solomon as king. {29:25} The LORD greatly exalted Solomon in the sight of all Israel, bestowing upon him royal majesty unmatched by any king before him. {29:26} Thus, David, son of Jesse, reigned over all Israel. {29:27} He reigned forty years, seven in Hebron and thirty-three in Jerusalem, and died in old age, full of days, riches, and honor. {29:28} Solomon his son succeeded him as king. {29:29} The acts of David, from beginning to end, are recorded in the books of Samuel the seer, Nathan the prophet, and Gad the seer, including his reign and might over Israel and the kingdoms. {29:30} These records encompass all that David and Israel experienced during his reign.

2 Chronicles

{1:1} Solomon, the son of David, grew strong in his kingdom, and the LORD his God was with him, greatly magnifying him. {1:2} Solomon addressed all Israel, including the captains, judges, governors, and chiefs of the families, and they went together to the high place at Gibeon, where Moses had established the tabernacle of the congregation. {1:3} Although David had brought the ark of God to Jerusalem, Solomon and the congregation sought guidance at the brasen altar before the tabernacle. {1:4} Solomon offered a thousand burnt offerings on the brasen altar before the LORD. {1:5} That night, God appeared to Solomon and offered him a request. {1:6} Solomon expressed gratitude for God's mercy towards his father David and requested wisdom and knowledge to govern his vast people effectively. {1:7} **Pleased with Solomon's humble request for wisdom rather than riches or honor, God granted him wisdom and promised him riches, wealth, and honor beyond any king before or after him.** {1:8} Solomon returned from Gibeon to Jerusalem and reigned over Israel. {1:9} He assembled chariots and horsemen, amassing a considerable military force. {1:10} Solomon also accumulated vast amounts of silver, gold, and cedar trees, making Jerusalem abundant in wealth. {1:11} Additionally, Solomon acquired horses and linen yarn from Egypt through his merchants, trading with other kingdoms. {1:12} They brought chariots and horses from Egypt at a considerable cost, supplying horses for other kings in the region. {1:13} After returning from his journey, Solomon reigned over Israel from the high place at Gibeon to Jerusalem, where the tabernacle of the congregation stood. {1:14} Solomon amassed a formidable military force, with 1,400 chariots and 12,000 horsemen stationed in the chariot cities and in Jerusalem. {1:15} Under Solomon's reign, Jerusalem became rich in silver, gold, and cedar trees, as abundant as stones and sycomore trees in the valley. {1:16} Solomon acquired horses and linen yarn from Egypt through his merchants, at a cost. {1:17} They brought chariots from Egypt, priced at six hundred shekels of silver each, and horses at one hundred and fifty shekels each, supplying them to the kings of the Hittites and Syria through their means.

{2:1} Solomon decided to build a house for the name of the LORD and a palace for himself. {2:2} He assigned seventy thousand men to carry burdens, eighty thousand to quarry stone in the mountains, and three thousand six hundred to supervise them. {2:3} Solomon sent a message to Huram, the king of Tyre, requesting materials just as his father David had received for building his house. {2:4} He explained that he intended to build a grand house for the LORD, dedicated to offering incense, showbread, and sacrifices regularly, following the ordinances of Israel. {2:5} Solomon acknowledged the greatness of God, stating that no house could contain Him. {2:6} He questioned his ability to build a suitable house for God, realizing that even the heavens cannot contain Him, except to offer sacrifices before Him. {2:7} Solomon asked Huram to send a skilled craftsman in various materials to work alongside the craftsmen of Judah and Jerusalem. {2:8} He requested cedar, cypress, and algum trees from Lebanon, as he knew Huram's servants were skilled in cutting timber. {2:9} Solomon needed abundant timber for the magnificent house he planned to build. {2:10} In return for the timber, he promised Huram's servants generous provisions of wheat, barley, wine, and oil. {2:11} Huram responded, acknowledging that Solomon was made king by the LORD's love for His people. {2:12} He praised the LORD for granting David a wise son capable of building both the house of the LORD and a royal palace. {2:13} Huram sent a skilled craftsman, descended from Dan and Tyre, capable in various materials and engraving, to assist Solomon. {2:14} This craftsman was skilled in gold, silver, bronze, iron, stone, wood, fabric, and engraving, able to work alongside Solomon's and David's craftsmen. {2:15} Huram requested that Solomon send the promised provisions to his servants. {2:16} Huram agreed to supply the needed timber from Lebanon, to be transported by sea to Joppa and then to Jerusalem. {2:17} Solomon counted the foreigners in Israel, totaling 153,600, and assigned them various tasks, similar to how David had organized them. {2:18} Among them, he appointed 70,000 as burden bearers, 80,000 as stone quarry workers, and 3,600 as overseers.

{3:1} Solomon began building the house of the LORD in Jerusalem on Mount Moriah, where the LORD appeared to his father David, at the place David had prepared on the threshing floor of Ornan the Jebusite. {3:2} Construction began on the second day of the second month in the fourth year of Solomon's reign. {3:3} Here are the instructions Solomon followed for building the house of God: Its length was sixty cubits, and its width twenty cubits. {3:4} The porch at the front of the house was twenty cubits long, matching the width of the house, and one hundred and twenty cubits high. It was overlaid with pure gold inside. {3:5} The main hall was paneled with fir tree and overlaid with fine gold. Palm trees and chains were adorned on it. {3:6} Precious stones were used to beautify the house, and the gold came from Parvaim. {3:7} Gold covered the beams, posts, walls, and doors of the house, with cherubim engraved on the walls. {3:8} The most holy place measured twenty cubits in length and width, overlaid with fine gold amounting to six hundred talents. {3:9} Fifty shekels of gold were used for the nails, and the upper chambers were also overlaid with gold. {3:10} Two cherubim of image work were made for the most holy place and overlaid with gold. {3:11} Each cherub's wings spanned twenty cubits, with one wing touching the wall of the house, and the other wing touching the wing of the other cherub. {3:12} Each cherub's other wing also measured five cubits, reaching to the wall, with the other wing measuring five cubits, touching the wing of the other cherub. {3:13} The wings of these cherubim spread twenty cubits, and they stood on their feet with their faces inward. {3:14} The veil was made of blue, purple, and crimson, with cherubim embroidered on it. {3:15} Solomon also made two pillars in front of the house, each thirty-five cubits high, with a capital of five cubits on top of each. {3:16} Chains were made and placed on the tops of the pillars, with a hundred pomegranates on each chain. {3:17} The pillars were erected in front of the temple, one on the right named Jachin, and the other on the left named Boaz.

{4:1} Solomon also made an altar of brass, twenty cubits long, twenty cubits wide, and ten cubits high. {4:2} He crafted a molten sea, ten cubits from brim to brim, circular in shape, and five cubits high. A line of thirty cubits measured around it. {4:3} Underneath it were oxen sculptures, ten per cubit, encircling the sea. Two rows of oxen were cast when the sea was cast. {4:4} The sea rested on twelve oxen, three facing each direction—north, west, south, and east—with their hindquarters inward. {4:5} It was a handbreadth thick, with a brim resembling a cup's edge adorned with lilies. It held and contained three thousand baths of water. {4:6} Additionally, he made ten basins, five on the right side and five on the left, for washing the offerings. The sea was for the priests to wash in. {4:7} Ten golden candlesticks were crafted, five placed on the right side of the temple and five on the left. {4:8} He also made ten tables, placing them in the temple, five on the right side and five on the left, along with a hundred golden basins. {4:9} Solomon constructed the court of the priests, the great court, and brass doors for the court, overlaying them with brass. {4:10} He positioned the sea on the right side of the temple's east end, opposite the south. {4:11} Huram made the pots, shovels, and basins. He completed the work assigned by King Solomon for the house of God. {4:12} This included the two pillars, the capitals on top of the pillars, and the two wreaths covering the capitals. {4:13} Four hundred pomegranates adorned the two wreaths, two rows of pomegranates on each wreath, covering the two capitals on the pillars. {4:14} Bases and lavers were made upon the bases. {4:15} There was one sea and twelve oxen underneath it. {4:16} Huram crafted the pots, shovels, flesh hooks, and all their utensils for King Solomon's house of the LORD from bright brass. {4:17} These were cast in the plain of the Jordan, in the clay ground between Succoth and Zeredathah. {4:18} Solomon made these vessels in great abundance, and the weight of the brass was immeasurable. {4:19} He also made all the vessels for the house of God, including the golden altar and the tables for the showbread. {4:20} Moreover, he crafted the candlesticks with their lamps of pure gold, to burn before the oracle, along with the flowers, lamps, and tongs—all of gold. {4:21} The snuffers, basins, spoons, and censers were made of pure gold. {4:22} Even the entry doors to the inner sanctuary and the doors of the temple were made of gold.

{5:1} Solomon completed all the work for the house of the LORD. He brought in all the dedicated items of his father David, including the silver, gold, and instruments, and stored them in the treasury of God's house. {5:2} Then Solomon gathered the elders of Israel, the heads of the tribes, and the chiefs of the families to Jerusalem to bring up the ark of the covenant of the LORD from the City of David, which is Zion. {5:3} All the men of Israel assembled before the king during the feast in the seventh month. {5:4} The elders of Israel came, and the Levites carried the ark. {5:5} They brought up the ark, the tabernacle, and all the holy vessels. The priests and Levites were responsible for this. {5:6} King Solomon and all the assembly of Israel sacrificed countless sheep and oxen before the ark. {5:7} The priests brought the ark of the covenant of the LORD into its place in the inner sanctuary of the temple, under the wings of the cherubim. {5:8} The cherubim spread their wings over the ark, covering it and its poles from above. {5:9} The ends of the poles were visible from the ark in the inner sanctuary, but not from outside. They remain there to this day. {5:10} The ark contained only the two tablets that Moses placed in it at Horeb, where the LORD made a covenant with the Israelites when they came out of Egypt. {5:11} When the priests came out of the Holy Place, all the priests present were sanctified and did not follow their divisions. {5:12} The Levitical singers, including Asaph, Heman, and Jeduthun, together with their sons and relatives, stood at the east end of the altar in white linen garments, with cymbals, harps, and lyres, along with 120 priests sounding trumpets. {5:13} When the trumpeters and singers performed together, praising and thanking the LORD with one voice, accompanied by trumpets, cymbals, and other instruments, and proclaiming, "For he is good; his steadfast love endures forever," the house of the LORD was filled with a cloud. {5:14} The priests could not continue their service because of the cloud, for the glory of the LORD filled the house of God.

{6:1} Solomon said, "The LORD has said that He would dwell in thick darkness. But I have built a house for you, a place for your everlasting dwelling. {6:2} Then Solomon turned to bless the entire congregation of Israel, and all of Israel stood. {6:3} He said, "Blessed be the LORD God of Israel, who has fulfilled with His hands what He spoke to my father David, saying, {6:4} 'Since the day I brought my people out of the land of Egypt, I chose no city among all the tribes of Israel to build a house in, that my name might be there; neither did I choose any man to be a ruler over my people Israel. {6:5} But I chose Jerusalem, and David to lead my people.' {6:6} It was in the heart of David my father to build a house for the name of the LORD God of Israel. {6:7} But the LORD said to David my father, 'Though it was in your heart to build a house for my name, you did well in that it was in your heart. {6:8} However, you shall not build the house; but your son who will come from your own loins, he shall build the house for my name.' {6:9} The LORD has now fulfilled His word, for I, Solomon, have risen in the place of my father David, and am set on the throne of Israel as the LORD promised, and have built the house for the name of the LORD God of Israel. {6:10} And in it, I have placed the ark containing the covenant of the LORD made with the children of Israel." {6:11} Solomon stood before the altar of the LORD in the presence of all the congregation of Israel and spread forth his hands. {6:12} Solomon had made a bronze scaffold, five cubits long, five cubits wide, and three cubits high, which he set in the midst of the court. Upon it, he stood, kneeled down upon his knees before all the congregation of Israel, and spread forth his hands toward heaven. {6:13} He said, "O LORD God of Israel, there is no God like you in heaven or on earth, who keeps covenant and shows mercy to your servants who walk before you with all their hearts. {6:14} You have kept with your servant David my father what you promised him, speaking with your mouth and fulfilling it with your hand, as it is today. {6:15} Now therefore, O LORD God of Israel, keep with your servant David my father what you promised him, saying, 'There shall not fail you a man in my sight to sit on the throne of Israel; yet so that your children take heed to their way to walk in my law, as you have walked before me.' {6:16} Now then, O LORD God of Israel, let your word be verified, which you have spoken to your servant David. {6:17} But will God indeed dwell with men on the earth? Behold, heaven and the heaven of heavens cannot contain you; how much less this house which I have built! {6:18} Therefore, have regard to the prayer of your servant and to his supplication, O LORD my God, to listen to the cry and the prayer which your servant prays before you, {6:19} That your eyes may be open upon this house day and night, upon the place of which you said you would put your name there, to listen to the prayer which your servant prays toward this place. {6:20} Hearken therefore to the supplications of your servant and of your people Israel, which they shall make toward this place. Listen from your dwelling place, even from heaven; and when you hear, forgive. {6:21} If a man sins against his neighbor, and an oath be laid upon him to make him swear, and the oath comes before your altar in this house; {6:22} Then hear from heaven, and do, and judge your servants, by requiting the wicked, by recompensing his way upon his own head, and by justifying the righteous, by giving him according to his righteousness. {6:23} And if your people Israel are defeated by their enemies because they have sinned against you, and they return and confess your name, and pray and make supplication before you in this house; {6:24} Then hear from the heavens, and forgive the sin of your people Israel, and bring them again to the land which you gave to them and to their fathers. {6:25} When the heavens are shut up and there is no rain because they have sinned against you, yet if they pray toward this place and confess your name and turn from their sin when you afflict them; {6:26} Then hear from heaven, and forgive the sin of your servants and of your people Israel when you have taught them the good way wherein they should walk, and send rain upon your land which you have given to your people for an inheritance. {6:27} If there is famine in the land, if there is pestilence, blight, mildew, locusts, or caterpillars, if their enemies besiege them in the cities of their land, whatever plague, whatever sickness there be; {6:28} Whatever prayer or supplication is made by anyone, or by all your people Israel, when every one shall know his own affliction and his own grief, and shall spread forth his hands toward this house; {6:29} Then hear from heaven your dwelling place, and forgive, and render unto every man according to all his ways, whose heart you know (for you alone know the hearts of the children of men); {6:30} That they may fear you, to walk in your ways so long as they live in the land which you gave to our fathers. {6:31} Moreover concerning the foreigner who is not of your people Israel but comes from a distant land for your great name's sake and your mighty hand and your outstretched arm; if they come and pray in this house; {6:32} Then hear from the heavens, even from your dwelling place, and do according to all that the foreigner asks of you, that all the people of the earth may know your name and fear you, as does your people Israel, and may know that this house which I have built is called by your name. {6:33} If your people go out to battle against their enemies by the way that you shall send them, and they pray unto you toward this city which you have chosen and the house which I have built for your name; {6:34} Then hear from the heavens their prayer and their supplication, and maintain their cause. {6:35} If they sin against you (for there is no man who does not sin), and you are angry with them, and deliver them over before their enemies, and they carry them away captives unto a land far off or near; {6:36} Yet if they turn themselves in the land where they are carried captive, and repent and make supplication unto you in the land of their captivity, saying, 'We have sinned, we have done wrong, and have dealt wickedly'; {6:37} Yet if they remember themselves in the land where they are carried captive, and turn and pray to you in the land of their captivity, saying, 'We have sinned, we have done wrong, and have acted wickedly'; {6:38} If they return to you with all their heart and with all their soul in the land of their captivity where they have been carried captive, and pray toward their land, which you gave to their fathers, and toward the city which you have chosen, and toward the house which I have built for your name; {6:39} Then hear from the heavens, from your dwelling place, their prayer and their supplications, and maintain their cause, and forgive your people who have sinned against you. {6:40} **Now, my God, let your eyes be open and your ears attentive to the prayer made in this place.** {6:41} Therefore arise, O LORD God, into your resting place, you and the ark of your strength; let your priests, O LORD God, be clothed with salvation, and let your saints rejoice in goodness. {6:42} O LORD God, do not turn away the face of your anointed; remember the mercies of David your servant.

{7:1} Now when Solomon had finished praying, fire came down from heaven and consumed the burnt offering and the sacrifices, and the glory of the LORD filled the house. {7:2} And the priests could not enter the house of the LORD because the glory of the LORD filled the LORD's house. {7:3} When all the children of Israel saw how the fire came down and the glory of the LORD on the house, they bowed themselves with their faces to the ground upon the pavement, worshipped, and praised the LORD, saying, "For he is good, for his mercy endures forever." {7:4} Then the king and all the people offered sacrifices before the LORD. {7:5} King Solomon offered a sacrifice of twenty-two thousand oxen and one hundred twenty thousand sheep. So the king and all the people dedicated the house of God. {7:6} The priests attended to their duties; the Levites also with instruments of music of the LORD, which David the king had made to praise the LORD because his mercy endures forever, when David praised by their ministry. And the priests sounded trumpets before them, and all Israel stood. {7:7} Moreover, Solomon consecrated the middle of the court that was before the house of the LORD, for there he offered burnt offerings and the fat of the peace offerings because the bronze altar that Solomon had made was not able to receive the burnt offerings, the grain offerings, and the fat. {7:8} Also at the same time, Solomon kept the feast for seven days, and all Israel with him, a very great congregation, from the entrance of Hamath to the Brook of Egypt. {7:9} And on the eighth day, they held a solemn assembly, for they kept the dedication of the altar for seven days and the feast for seven days. {7:10} On the twenty-third day of the seventh month, he sent the people away to their tents, glad and merry in heart for the goodness that the LORD had shown to David, to Solomon, and to Israel his people. {7:11} **Thus Solomon finished the house of the LORD and the king's house. And all that came into Solomon's heart to make in the house of the LORD and in his own house, he successfully accomplished.** {7:12} And the LORD appeared to Solomon by night and said to him, "I have heard your prayer and have chosen this place for myself as a house of sacrifice. {7:13} If I shut up heaven so that there is no rain, or if I command the locusts to devour the land, or if I send pestilence among my people; {7:14} If my people, who are called by my name, humble themselves, pray, seek my face, and turn from their wicked ways, then I will hear from heaven, forgive their sin, and heal their land. {7:15} Now my eyes shall be open and my ears attentive to the prayer made in this place. {7:16} For now I have chosen and sanctified this house, that my name may be there forever; and my eyes and my heart will be there perpetually. {7:17} And as for you, if you will walk before me as David your father walked, and do according to all that I have commanded you, and observe my statutes and my judgments; {7:18} Then I will establish the throne of your kingdom, according as I have covenanted with David your father, saying, 'There shall not fail you a man to be ruler in Israel.' {7:19} But if you turn away and forsake my statutes and my commandments which I have set before you, and shall go and serve other gods, and worship them; {7:20} Then I will pluck them up by the roots out of my land which I have given them; and this house, which I have sanctified for my name, I will cast out of my sight, and will make it a proverb and a byword among all nations. {7:21} And this house, which is high, shall be an astonishment to everyone that passes by it, so that he shall say, 'Why has the LORD done thus to this land and to this house?' {7:22} And it shall be answered, 'Because they forsake the LORD God of their fathers, who brought them forth out of the land of Egypt, and laid hold on other gods, and worshipped them, and served them. Therefore, he has brought all this evil upon them.'

{8:1} It happened after twenty years, during which Solomon built the house of the LORD and his own house, {8:2} that the cities which Huram had given to Solomon, Solomon rebuilt them and settled the children of Israel there. {8:3} Solomon went to Hamath-zobah and conquered it. {8:4} He built Tadmor in the wilderness and all the storage cities that he built in Hamath. {8:5} He also built Upper Beth-horon and Lower Beth-horon as fortified cities with walls, gates, and bars. {8:6} And Baalath, and all the storage cities that Solomon had, and all the cities for his chariots, the cities for his horsemen, and whatever Solomon desired to build in Jerusalem, in Lebanon, and throughout all the land under his dominion. {8:7} As for all the people who remained of the Hittites, Amorites, Perizzites, Hivites, and Jebusites, who were not of Israel— {8:8} their descendants who remained after them in the land, whom the children of Israel did not destroy—Solomon imposed forced labor on them to this day. {8:9} But Solomon did not make slaves of the children of Israel for his work; they were men of war, his captains, and commanders of his chariots and horsemen. {8:10} And these were the chief officers of King Solomon, two hundred and fifty, who ruled over the people. {8:11} **Solomon brought the daughter of Pharaoh up from the City of David to the house he had built for her, for he said, "My wife shall not dwell in the house of David king of Israel, because the places where the ark of the LORD has come are holy."** {8:12} Then Solomon offered burnt offerings to the LORD on the altar of the LORD, which he had built before the vestibule, {8:13} according to the daily rate, offering according to the commandment of Moses for the Sabbaths, the New Moons, and the set feasts three times a year—the Feast of Unleavened Bread, the Feast of Weeks, and the Feast of Tabernacles. {8:14} He appointed, according to the order of David his father, the divisions of the priests to their service, the Levites to their duties (to praise and serve before the priests) as the duty of each day required, and the gatekeepers by their divisions at each gate; for so David the man of God had commanded. {8:15} They did not depart from the command of the king to the priests and Levites concerning any matter or concerning the treasuries. {8:16} Now all the work of Solomon was well-ordered from the day of the foundation of the house of the LORD until it was finished. So the house of the LORD was completed. {8:17} Then Solomon went to Ezion-geber and Elath on the seashore, in the land of Edom. {8:18} **And Huram sent him, by the hands of his servants, ships and servants who knew the sea. They went with the servants of Solomon to Ophir, and took from there four hundred and fifty talents of gold, and brought them to King Solomon.**

{9:1} When the queen of Sheba heard of Solomon's fame, she came to test him with difficult questions in Jerusalem, accompanied by a very large entourage, with camels bearing spices, and an abundance of gold and precious stones. When she arrived, she discussed everything on her mind with Solomon. {9:2} Solomon answered all her questions; nothing was too hard for him to explain. {9:3} After seeing Solomon's wisdom and the palace he had built, {9:4} the food at his table, the seating of his officials, the attending servants in their robes, his cupbearers, and the burnt offerings he made at the temple of the LORD, she was overwhelmed. {9:5} She said to the king, "The report I heard in my own country about your achievements and your wisdom is true. {9:6} But I did not believe these things until I came and saw with my own eyes. Indeed, not even half was told me; in wisdom and wealth you have far exceeded the report I heard. {9:7} Your attendants and officials are fortunate to stand in your presence and hear your wisdom. {9:8} Praise be to the LORD your God, who has delighted in you and placed you on the throne of Israel. Because of the LORD's eternal love for Israel, he has made you king to maintain justice and righteousness." {9:9} She gave the king 120 talents of gold, large quantities of spices, and precious stones. Never again were so many spices brought in as those the queen of Sheba gave to King Solomon. {9:10} Huram's servants and Solomon's servants, who brought gold from Ophir, also brought algum wood and precious stones. {9:11} The king used the algum wood to make terraces for the LORD's temple and for the royal palace, and to make harps and lyres for the musicians. Nothing like them had ever been seen in Judah. {9:12} King Solomon gave the queen of Sheba all she desired and asked for, besides what he had given her out of his royal bounty. Then she left and returned with her retinue to her own country. {9:13} The weight of the gold that Solomon received yearly was 666 talents, {9:14} besides what merchants and traders brought. All the kings of Arabia and the governors of the territories also brought gold and silver to Solomon. {9:15} King Solomon made 200 large shields of hammered gold; 600 shekels of gold went into each shield. {9:16} He also made 300 small shields of hammered gold; three minas of gold went into each shield. The king put them in the Palace of the Forest of Lebanon. {9:17} The king made a great throne covered with ivory and overlaid with pure gold. {9:18} The throne had six steps, and its back had a rounded top. On both sides of the seat were armrests, with a lion standing beside each of them. {9:19} Twelve lions stood on the six steps, one at either end of each step. Nothing like it had ever been made for any other kingdom. {9:20} All of King Solomon's drinking cups were gold, and all the utensils in the Palace of the Forest of Lebanon were pure gold. Nothing was made of silver, because silver was considered of little value in Solomon's time. {9:21} The king's ships went to Tarshish with the servants of Huram. Every three years they returned, bringing gold, silver, and ivory, and apes and baboons. {9:22} King Solomon was greater in riches and wisdom than all the other kings of the earth. {9:23} All the kings of the earth sought audience with Solomon to hear the wisdom that God had put in his heart. {9:24} **Year after year, everyone who came brought a gift—articles of silver and gold, robes, weapons, spices, horses, and mules.** {9:25} Solomon had 4,000 stalls for horses and chariots, and 12,000 horsemen, whom he stationed in the chariot cities and with the king in Jerusalem. {9:26} He ruled over all the kings from the Euphrates River to the land of the Philistines, as far as the border of Egypt. {9:27} The king made silver as common in Jerusalem as stones, and cedar as plentiful as sycamore-fig trees in the foothills. {9:28} Solomon's horses were imported from Egypt and from all other countries. {9:29} **The rest of the events of Solomon's reign, from beginning to end, are recorded in the records of Nathan the prophet, in the prophecy of Ahijah the Shilonite, and in the visions of Iddo the seer concerning Jeroboam son of Nebat.** {9:30} Solomon reigned in Jerusalem over all Israel forty years.

{9:31} Then he rested with his ancestors and was buried in the city of David his father. And Rehoboam his son succeeded him as king.

{10:1} Rehoboam went to Shechem, where all Israel had gathered to make him king. {10:2} Jeroboam, who had fled to Egypt to escape Solomon, heard about this and returned. {10:3} They sent for Jeroboam, and when he and all Israel came, they spoke to Rehoboam, {10:4} saying, "Your father made our yoke heavy. So lighten the harsh labor and the heavy yoke your father imposed on us, and we will serve you." {10:5} Rehoboam told them to come back in three days. So the people departed. {10:6} Rehoboam consulted with the elders who had served Solomon his father during his lifetime, asking them what he should say to the people. {10:7} They advised him, "If you are kind to these people and please them by speaking good words, they will be your servants forever." {10:8} But Rehoboam rejected the advice of the elders and consulted with the young men who had grown up with him and were serving him. {10:9} He asked them, "What should I say to these people who have asked me to lighten the yoke my father put on us?" {10:10} The young men advised him, "Tell them, 'My little finger is thicker than my father's waist. My father made your yoke heavy, but I will add to it. My father disciplined you with whips, but I will use scorpions.'" {10:11} On the third day, Jeroboam and all the people returned to Rehoboam, as the king had ordered, saying, "Come back to me in three days." {10:12} But the king answered them harshly. He rejected the advice of the elders {10:13} and followed the counsel of the young men, saying, "My father made your yoke heavy, but I will add to it. My father disciplined you with whips, but I will use scorpions." {10:14} The king did not listen to the people, for this turn of events was from God, to fulfill the word the LORD had spoken to Jeroboam son of Nebat through Ahijah the Shilonite. {10:15} When all Israel saw that the king refused to listen to them, they answered the king: "What share do we have in David? We have no inheritance in the son of Jesse. To your tents, O Israel! Look now to your own house, O David!" So the Israelites went home. {10:16} But as for the Israelites who were living in the towns of Judah, {10:17} Rehoboam still ruled over them. {10:18} Then King Rehoboam sent Adoniram, who was in charge of forced labor, but all Israel stoned him to death. King Rehoboam, however, managed to get into his chariot and escape to Jerusalem. {10:19} So Israel has been in rebellion against the house of David to this day.

{11:1} When Rehoboam returned to Jerusalem, he gathered 180,000 chosen warriors from the tribes of Judah and Benjamin to fight against Israel and reclaim the kingdom. {11:2} But the word of the LORD came to Shemaiah, a man of God, saying, {11:3} "Speak to Rehoboam, the son of Solomon, king of Judah, and to all the people of Judah and Benjamin, saying, {11:4} 'This is what the LORD says: You must not go up to fight against your fellow Israelites. Everyone should go back home, for this situation is from me.' So they obeyed the word of the LORD and turned back from attacking Jeroboam. {11:5} Rehoboam stayed in Jerusalem and fortified cities in Judah for defense. {11:6} He built up Bethlehem, Etam, and Tekoa, {11:7} along with Beth-zur, Shoco, and Adullam, {11:8} as well as Gath, Mareshah, and Ziph, {11:9} and Adoraim, Lachish, and Azekah, {11:10} and Zorah, Aijalon, and Hebron, all fortified cities in Judah and Benjamin. {11:11} Rehoboam strengthened these strongholds, stationed commanders in them, and stored up supplies of food, oil, and wine. {11:12} He also placed shields and spears in every city, making them very strong. Judah and Benjamin supported him. {11:13} Furthermore, the priests and Levites from all over Israel came to him. {11:14} The Levites abandoned their pasturelands and property to come to Judah and Jerusalem because Jeroboam and his sons had rejected them from serving as priests of the LORD. {11:15} Instead, Jeroboam appointed his own priests for the high places, the goat and calf idols he had made. {11:16} But from all the tribes of Israel, those who set their hearts to seek the LORD, the God of Israel, came to Jerusalem to sacrifice to the LORD, the God of their ancestors. {11:17} So they strengthened the kingdom of Judah and made Rehoboam, Solomon's son, strong for three years. During those years, they walked in the ways of David and Solomon. {11:18} Rehoboam married Mahalath, daughter of Jerimoth, son of David, and Abihail, daughter of Eliab, son of Jesse. {11:19} Mahalath bore him children: Jeush, Shamariah, and Zaham. {11:20} After her, he married Maachah, daughter of Absalom, who bore him Abijah, Attai, Ziza, and Shelomith. {11:21} Rehoboam favored Maachah, Absalom's daughter, above all his wives and concubines. He had 18 wives and 60 concubines, and he fathered 28 sons and 60 daughters. {11:22} Rehoboam appointed Abijah, Maachah's son, as the chief prince among his brothers, intending to make him king. {11:23} He acted wisely by dispersing his sons throughout all the districts of Judah and Benjamin, to every fortified city, providing them with an abundance of provisions. And he sought many wives for himself.

{12:1} After Rehoboam had established his kingdom and strengthened himself, he abandoned the law of the LORD, and all Israel followed suit. {12:2} In the fifth year of Rehoboam's reign, King Shishak of Egypt attacked Jerusalem because they had disobeyed the LORD. {12:3} Shishak came with 1,200 chariots, 60,000 horsemen, and countless troops from Egypt, including Libyans, Sukkites, and Ethiopians. {12:4} He captured the fortified cities of Judah and then advanced to Jerusalem. {12:5} Prophet Shemaiah went to Rehoboam and the leaders of Judah in Jerusalem because of Shishak's attack. He said to them, "The LORD says you have forsaken me, so I have allowed Shishak to attack you." {12:6} Hearing this, the leaders and the king humbled themselves, acknowledging the righteousness of the LORD. {12:7} Seeing their humility, the LORD spoke to Shemaiah, saying, "Because they have humbled themselves, I will not destroy them completely. I will grant them some deliverance, and Jerusalem will not be destroyed by Shishak." {12:8} However, they will become Shishak's servants, learning the difference between serving me and serving earthly kings". {12:9} Shishak plundered the treasures of the LORD's house and the king's palace, taking everything, including the golden shields Solomon had made. {12:10} Rehoboam replaced the gold shields with bronze ones and entrusted them to the chief of the palace guard. {12:11} Whenever the king went to the LORD's house, the guard would bring the shields and then return them to the guardroom. {12:12} When Rehoboam humbled himself, the LORD's anger relented, and Jerusalem was spared from complete destruction. Things went well in Judah. {12:13} Rehoboam strengthened his position in Jerusalem and reigned there. He was forty-one years old when he became king and ruled for seventeen years in Jerusalem, the city the LORD had chosen for his name. His mother's name was Naamah, an Ammonite. {12:14} However, Rehoboam did evil because he did not set his heart to seek the LORD. {12:15} The account of Rehoboam's reign, including his deeds, is recorded in the writings of the prophet Shemaiah and the seer Iddo concerning genealogies. There were continual wars between Rehoboam and Jeroboam. {12:16} Rehoboam died and was buried in the City of David. His son Abijah succeeded him as king.

{13:1} In the eighteenth year of King Jeroboam's reign, Abijah became king of Judah. He ruled for three years in Jerusalem. His mother was Michaiah, the daughter of Uriel from Gibeah. There was war between Abijah and Jeroboam. {13:2} Abijah assembled an army of 400,000 valiant warriors, while Jeroboam countered with 800,000 mighty men of valor. {13:3} Standing on Mount Zemaraim in Mount Ephraim, Abijah addressed Jeroboam and all Israel. He reminded them that the LORD had given the kingdom to David and his descendants forever through a covenant of salt. {13:4} Abijah accused Jeroboam of rebellion against his lord Solomon and of gathering worthless men to rebel against Rehoboam. {13:5} He pointed out that Jeroboam had replaced the priests of the LORD with priests of his own choosing and had made golden calves for worship. {13:6} While Jeroboam had forsaken the LORD, Abijah affirmed that Judah remained faithful, with priests descended from Aaron serving the LORD. {13:7} Abijah warned that God was with them as their captain, and his priests were ready with trumpets to sound the alarm against Jeroboam. {13:8} Jeroboam, however, set an ambush against Judah. When Judah realized they were surrounded, they cried out to the LORD, and the priests sounded the trumpets. {13:9} God struck Jeroboam and all Israel, giving victory to Abijah and Judah. They pursued and defeated Israel, causing a great slaughter. {13:10} Abijah's reliance on the LORD brought success, and they captured cities from Jeroboam, including Bethel and Ephrain. {13:11} Jeroboam never regained strength during Abijah's reign, and he died. Abijah grew mighty, having many wives, sons, and daughters. The details of his reign are recorded in the writings of the prophet Iddo. { {13:12} Abijah proclaimed that God Himself was their captain, and the priests sounded trumpets to warn their enemies. He urged the children of Israel not to fight against the LORD, warning them that they would not succeed. {13:13} Despite this, Jeroboam set up an ambush against Judah, surrounding them from the front and behind. {13:14} When Judah realized they were surrounded, they cried out to the LORD, and the priests blew their trumpets. {13:15} God responded by striking Jeroboam and all Israel before Abijah and Judah. The men of Judah shouted and God gave them victory. {13:16} The children of Israel fled before Judah, and God delivered them into their hands. {13:17} Abijah and his people inflicted a great slaughter upon them, killing five hundred thousand chosen men of Israel. {13:18} Thus, the children of Israel were defeated at that time, and the children of Judah prevailed because they relied on the LORD God of their fathers. {13:19} Abijah pursued Jeroboam and captured cities from him, including Bethel, Jeshanah, and Ephrain. {13:20} Jeroboam never regained strength during Abijah's reign, and the LORD struck him, causing his death. {13:21} Abijah became mighty, marrying fourteen wives and fathering twenty-two sons and sixteen daughters. {13:22} The remaining details of Abijah's life and deeds are recorded in the writings of the prophet Iddo.

{14:1} After Abijah passed away, he was buried in the city of David, and his son Asa became king. Under Asa's rule, the land enjoyed peace for ten years. {14:2} Asa followed the ways that pleased the LORD his God. {14:3} He removed the altars of foreign gods, demolished the high places, broke down the sacred pillars, and cut down the Asherah poles. {14:4} Asa commanded the people of Judah to seek the LORD God of their ancestors and to follow His law and commandments. {14:5} He also eliminated the high places and sacred pillars from all the cities of Judah, and the kingdom experienced peace during his reign. {14:6} Asa fortified cities throughout Judah, taking advantage of the peaceful times granted by the LORD. {14:7} Encouraging the people, Asa proposed building and fortifying these cities with walls, towers, gates, and bars while the land was still at peace. The people agreed, and they prospered. {14:8} Asa's army consisted of 300,000 men from Judah equipped with shields and spears and 280,000 men from Benjamin skilled in archery. {14:9} Zerah the Ethiopian marched against them with an army of one million troops and 300 chariots, reaching Mareshah. {14:10} Asa confronted him, positioning his forces in the valley of Zephathah at Mareshah. {14:11} Asa prayed to the LORD for help, acknowledging their reliance on Him and pleading for victory. {14:12} The LORD granted their request, defeating the Ethiopians before Asa and Judah, causing them to flee. {14:13} Asa and his army pursued them to Gerar, where the Ethiopians were utterly defeated, unable to recover, and lost much spoil. {14:14} They also conquered the surrounding cities, as the fear of the LORD fell upon them, leading to abundant spoil. {14:15} They seized livestock, including sheep and camels, and returned to Jerusalem victorious.

{15:1} The Spirit of God inspired Azariah, the son of Oded, to speak. {15:2} Azariah addressed Asa, as well as all of Judah and Benjamin, saying, "The LORD is with you as long as you remain faithful to Him. If you seek Him, He will be found by you, but if you forsake Him, He will forsake you. {15:3} For a long time, Israel has been without the true God, without teaching priests, and without the law. {15:4} But when they turned to the LORD God of Israel in their trouble and sought Him, He responded to them. {15:5} During those times, there was no peace for those who went out or came in; there were great vexations upon all the inhabitants of the land. {15:6} Nation rose against nation, and city against city, for God afflicted them with all kinds of adversity. {15:7} Therefore, be strong and do not let your hands be weak, for your work will be rewarded." {15:8} When Asa heard these words and the prophecy of Oded the prophet, he took courage. He removed the abominable idols from all the land of Judah and Benjamin, as well as from the cities he had taken in Mount Ephraim. He also restored the altar of the LORD before the temple. {15:9} Asa gathered all of Judah, Benjamin, and the foreigners with them from Ephraim, Manasseh, and Simeon, as they came to him in abundance when they saw that the LORD his God was with him. {15:10} They assembled in Jerusalem in the third month of the fifteenth year of Asa's reign. {15:11} At that time, they offered to the LORD seven hundred oxen and seven thousand sheep from the spoils they had brought. {15:12} They entered into a covenant to seek the LORD God of their fathers with all their heart and soul. {15:13} They decreed that anyone who would not seek the LORD God of Israel should be put to death, whether small or great, man or woman. {15:14} They swore this oath to the LORD with loud voices, shouting, trumpets, and horns. {15:15} All of Judah rejoiced at the oath, for they swore with all their heart and sought the LORD with all their desire, and He was found by them. The LORD granted them rest all around. {15:16} Asa removed his grandmother Maachah from her position as queen because she had made an idol in a grove. He destroyed her idol by burning it at the brook Kidron. {15:17} **Although the high places were not removed from Israel, Asa's heart remained faithful to the LORD all his days.** {15:18} Asa brought into the house of God the dedicated items from his father and himself, including silver, gold, and vessels. {15:19} There was no more war until the thirty-fifth year of Asa's reign.

{16:1} In the thirty-sixth year of Asa's reign, Baasha, the king of Israel, attacked Judah and built Ramah to block any traffic to or from Asa, the king of Judah. {16:2} Asa responded by taking silver and gold from the treasuries of the LORD's house and his own palace. He sent these treasures to Ben-hadad, the king of Syria, who resided in Damascus, with a message. {16:3} Asa reminded Ben-hadad of the alliance between their fathers and proposed that Ben-hadad break his treaty with Baasha, the king of Israel, in exchange for the treasures Asa sent him. {16:4} Ben-hadad agreed to Asa's proposal and sent his army captains to attack the cities of Israel. They conquered Ijon, Dan, Abelmaim, and all the store cities of Naphtali. {16:5} When Baasha learned of this, he abandoned the construction of Ramah, and the work ceased. {16:6} Asa then mobilized all of Judah to dismantle the stones and timber of Ramah, which Baasha had been using to build. Asa used these materials to fortify Geba and Mizpah. {16:7} At that time, Hanani the seer came to Asa, the king of Judah, and rebuked him for relying on the king of Syria instead of trusting in the LORD his God. As a result, the Syrian army escaped Asa's grasp. {16:8} Hanani reminded Asa of past victories the LORD had granted him over formidable foes like the Ethiopians and the Lubims because Asa had trusted in the LORD. {16:9} Hanani emphasized that the LORD's eyes roam throughout the earth, seeking to strengthen those whose hearts are fully committed to Him. Asa's reliance on Syria instead of the LORD was foolish, and it would result in ongoing wars for him. {16:10} Asa was enraged by Hanani's words and threw him into prison. Asa also oppressed some of the people at the same time. {16:11} The deeds of Asa, from beginning to end, are recorded in the books of the kings of Judah and Israel. {16:12} In the thirty-ninth year of his reign, Asa developed a severe foot disease. Despite his illness, he did not seek the LORD's help but relied on physicians. {16:13} Asa died in the forty-first year of his reign and was buried in the sepulchers he had prepared for himself in the city of David. His burial bed was filled with sweet odors and various spices prepared by skilled apothecaries. A great burning was made in his honor.

{17:1} Jehoshaphat succeeded his father Asa as king and fortified himself against Israel. {17:2} He stationed troops in all the fortified cities of Judah and placed garrisons throughout the land of Judah and in the cities of Ephraim that his father Asa had captured. {17:3} Jehoshaphat walked in the ways of his ancestor David and did not worship Baal. Instead, he sought the LORD, the God of his father, and followed His commandments, unlike the practices of Israel. {17:4} Because of this, the LORD established Jehoshaphat's kingdom, and all Judah brought him gifts, enriching him with abundant wealth and honor. {17:5} Jehoshaphat's heart was devoted to the LORD, and he removed the high places and groves from Judah. {17:6} In the third year of his reign, Jehoshaphat sent teachers to the cities of Judah, including Levites and priests, to instruct the people in the law of the LORD. {17:7} These teachers traveled throughout Judah, educating the people in the ways of the LORD. {17:8} The fear of the LORD fell upon the neighboring kingdoms, preventing them from warring against Jehoshaphat. Even the Philistines and Arabians paid tribute to him. {17:9} Jehoshaphat's power grew, and he constructed castles and store cities in Judah. He also maintained a strong military presence in Jerusalem. {17:10} The military strength of Judah was significant, with hundreds of thousands of valiant warriors from the tribes of Judah and Benjamin. {17:11} These mighty warriors served the king, along with others stationed in the fortified cities throughout Judah. {17:12} Jehoshaphat became exceedingly great, and he constructed castles and store cities throughout Judah. {17:13} He was heavily involved in business throughout the cities of Judah, and the mighty men of valor, the warriors, were stationed in Jerusalem. {17:14} The following are the numbers of the divisions according to their ancestral families: In Judah, Adnah was the chief over three hundred thousand mighty men of valor. {17:15} Next to him was Jehohanan, the captain, with two hundred and eighty thousand men. {17:16} Following him was Amasiah, the son of Zichri, who volunteered himself to the LORD, along with two hundred thousand mighty men of valor. {17:17} From Benjamin, there was Eliada, a mighty man of valor, with two hundred thousand armed men equipped with bows and shields. {17:18} Next to him was Jehozabad, with one hundred and eighty thousand men prepared for war. {17:19} These served the king, in addition to those whom the king stationed in the fortified cities throughout all Judah.

{18:1} Jehoshaphat was wealthy and respected, and he formed an alliance with Ahab. {18:2} After some time, he visited Ahab in Samaria. Ahab slaughtered many sheep and oxen for him and his entourage and persuaded him to join in attacking Ramoth-gilead. {18:3} Ahab asked Jehoshaphat, "Will you go with me to Ramoth-gilead?" Jehoshaphat replied, "I am with you, and my people are with yours. We will join you in the war." {18:4} Jehoshaphat suggested, "Let us first seek the word of the LORD today." {18:5} So Ahab gathered four hundred prophets and asked them, "Should we go to battle at Ramoth-gilead, or should we refrain?" They unanimously advised, "Go, for God will deliver it into the king's hand." {18:6} Jehoshaphat inquired, "Isn't there another prophet of the LORD we can consult?" {18:7} Ahab admitted, "There is one, Micaiah, but I despise him because he always prophesies evil concerning me." {18:8} Nonetheless, Ahab summoned Micaiah. {18:9} Ahab and Jehoshaphat sat in royal robes at the entrance of Samaria while all the prophets prophesied before them. {18:10} One of the prophets, Zedekiah, made iron horns and declared, "With these, you will push back Syria until they are defeated." {18:11} All the prophets echoed this sentiment, encouraging them to go to Ramoth-gilead and promising victory. {18:12} When the messenger urged Micaiah to speak favorably like the other prophets, Micaiah insisted, "As the LORD lives, I will speak only what God tells me." {18:13} Upon meeting the kings, Micaiah sarcastically agreed with the false prophets, saying they would succeed. {18:14} Ahab sensed Micaiah's sarcasm and demanded him to speak the truth in the name of the LORD. {18:15} Micaiah then revealed a vision where he saw Israel scattered like sheep without a shepherd, and he advised them to return home in peace. {18:16} Ahab accused Micaiah of always prophesying evil, {18:17} to which Micaiah responded by describing a vision of the LORD seated on His throne ,{18:18} with the hosts of heaven on His right and left. {18:19} In this vision, the LORD asked who would entice Ahab to go up and fall at Ramoth-gilead. {18:20} A spirit offered to be a lying spirit in the mouths of Ahab's prophets, {18:21} and the LORD approved this plan. {18:22} Micaiah declared that the LORD had put a lying spirit in the mouths of Ahab's prophets, bringing forth evil against him. {18:23} Zedekiah struck Micaiah and asked how the Spirit of the LORD had spoken to him. {18:24} Micaiah prophesied that Zedekiah would see on that day when he would go into hiding. {18:25} Ahab ordered Micaiah to be imprisoned until his return in peace, {18:26} but Micaiah warned that if Ahab returned in peace, the LORD had not spoken through him. {18:27} Despite Micaiah's warning, Ahab and Jehoshaphat proceeded to Ramoth-gilead. {18:28} Ahab disguised himself, but instructed Jehoshaphat to wear his royal robes. {18:30} The king of Syria commanded his chariot captains to target only the king of Israel. {18:31} Mistaken for the king of Israel, the captains attacked Jehoshaphat, but he cried out to the LORD, {18:32} who helped him, causing the captains to turn away. {18:33} A random arrow struck Ahab between the joints of his armor, mortally wounding him. {18:34} Despite his wound, Ahab remained in his chariot until evening, when he died.

{19:1} Jehoshaphat, king of Judah, returned safely to Jerusalem. {19:2} Jehu, the son of Hanani the seer, confronted him, saying, "Why did you assist the ungodly and love those who hate the LORD? Therefore, the LORD's wrath is upon you." {19:3} Despite this, Jehu acknowledged some good in Jehoshaphat for removing idolatrous groves from the land and seeking God. {19:4} Jehoshaphat continued to reside in Jerusalem and led the people back to the LORD, from Beer-sheba to Mount Ephraim. {19:5} He appointed judges in all the fortified cities of Judah and instructed them to judge not for man, but for the LORD who is with them in judgment. {19:6} He emphasized the importance of fearing the LORD, avoiding iniquity, impartiality, and bribery. {19:7} Jehoshaphat also established a judicial system in Jerusalem, comprising Levites, priests, and tribal leaders, to settle disputes according to the LORD's laws. {19:8} He instructed them to execute their duties faithfully and with integrity. {19:9} Whenever disputes arose among their brethren, they were to warn them against trespassing against the LORD to avoid bringing wrath upon themselves and their brethren. {19:10} Amariah the chief priest oversaw matters concerning the LORD, while Zebadiah, son of Ishmael, managed the king's affairs, supported by the Levites as officers. {19:11} Jehoshaphat encouraged them to act courageously, promising that the LORD would be with the righteous.

{20:1} After this, the Moabites, Ammonites, and others attacked Jehoshaphat. {20:2} People informed Jehoshaphat about the huge enemy force approaching from beyond the sea, near En-gedi. {20:3} Jehoshaphat was afraid and sought the LORD, proclaiming a fast throughout Judah. {20:4} Judah gathered to seek help from the LORD; people came from all cities. {20:5} Jehoshaphat stood before the LORD in the house of the LORD. {20:6} He prayed, acknowledging God's power over all nations. {20:7} He reminded God of His promises to Abraham and their ancestors. {20:8} Judah had built a sanctuary for God's name in the land. {20:9} They trusted God to help them in times of trouble if they prayed before Him. {20:10} Jehoshaphat recounted how the Ammonites, Moabites, and Edomites were spared by God during Israel's exodus. {20:11} Now these nations were attacking them. {20:12} Jehoshaphat asked God to judge them, as they were powerless against such a vast enemy. {20:13} All of Judah, including their families, stood before the LORD. {20:14} Then Jahaziel, a Levite, spoke as the Spirit of the LORD came upon him. {20:15} He encouraged them not to fear, for the battle belonged to God. {20:16} They were instructed to face the enemy at a specific location. {20:17} They were told they wouldn't need to fight; God would save them. {20:18} Jehoshaphat and all Judah worshipped the LORD. {20:19} The Levites praised God loudly. {20:20} Early the next morning, they went to the wilderness, Jehoshaphat urging faith in God and His prophets. {20:21} Singers praising the LORD led the army, declaring His enduring mercy. {20:22} As they praised, the LORD caused confusion among the enemy, and they were defeated. {20:23} The enemies turned against each other. {20:24} When Judah approached, they found the enemy dead, with abundant spoils. {20:25} They spent three days collecting the spoils. {20:26} On the fourth day, they gathered in the valley of Berachah and blessed the LORD. {20:27} They returned to Jerusalem rejoicing, as the LORD had given them victory. {20:28} They brought instruments to the house of the LORD. {20:29} Fear of God spread among neighboring kingdoms. {20:30} Jehoshaphat's realm was peaceful, as God granted him rest. {20:31} Jehoshaphat was thirty-five when he began to reign and reigned for twenty-five years. {20:32} He followed the ways of his father Asa, pleasing the LORD. {20:33} However, he didn't remove the high places of worship, as the people hadn't fully turned to God. {20:34} Other acts of Jehoshaphat are recorded in the book of Jehu. {20:35} Later, Jehoshaphat allied with the wicked Ahaziah, king of Israel. {20:36} They attempted to build ships in Ezion-geber to go to Tarshish. {20:37} A prophet, Eliezer, foretold God's judgment for this alliance, and the ships were destroyed.

{21:1} After Jehoshaphat died, his son Jehoram became king. {21:2} Jehoram had brothers: Azariah, Jehiel, Zechariah, Azariah, Michael, and Shephatiah, sons of Jehoshaphat. {21:3} Jehoshaphat gave his sons great gifts and fortified cities, but he gave the kingdom to Jehoram because he was the firstborn. {21:4} Jehoram, now king, killed all his brothers and some princes of Israel to secure his rule. {21:5} He was thirty-two when he became king and ruled for eight years in Jerusalem. {21:6} Jehoram followed the wicked ways of the kings of Israel by marrying Ahab's daughter and doing evil in God's eyes. {21:7} However, God didn't destroy the house of David due to His covenant with David to provide an eternal light for him and his descendants. {21:8} During Jehoram's reign, the Edomites rebelled against Judah and crowned their own king. {21:9} Jehoram fought against the Edomites and defeated them, but they remained in revolt. {21:10} Libnah also rebelled because Jehoram abandoned the LORD, his fathers' God. {21:11} Jehoram promoted idolatry in Judah, leading the people into sin. {21:12} Elijah the prophet sent Jehoram a letter from God, condemning him for not following the ways of his father Jehoshaphat and grandfather Asa, but instead, imitating the kings of Israel. {21:13} Jehoram's actions, akin to the wickedness of the house of Ahab, included killing his better brothers and leading Judah into sin. {21:14} God promised to afflict Jehoram and his people with a severe plague, affecting his family and possessions. {21:15} Jehoram would suffer from a debilitating bowel disease until his bowels fell out, leading to his death. {21:16} God incited the Philistines, Arabians, and Ethiopians against Jehoram. {21:17} They invaded Judah, looting the king's house and taking his family captive, leaving only his youngest son, Jehoahaz. {21:18} After all this, God struck Jehoram with an incurable disease in his bowels. {21:19} Two years later, his bowels fell out due to the illness, leading to his death. He wasn't mourned as his ancestors were, and he wasn't buried with the kings. {21:20} Jehoram was thirty-two when he became king, ruling for eight years in Jerusalem, but he died without honor, buried in the city of David but not with the kings.

{22:1} After Jehoram's death, the people of Jerusalem made his youngest son, Ahaziah, king because the Arabians had killed all the older sons. {22:2} Ahaziah was forty-two when he became king and ruled for one year in Jerusalem. His mother was Athaliah, daughter of Omri. {22:3} He followed the evil ways of the house of Ahab, influenced by his mother's wicked counsel. {22:4} Ahaziah did evil in God's sight, following the counsel of Ahab's family, which led to his downfall. {22:5} He joined Jehoram of Israel in a war against Hazael, king of Syria, at Ramoth-gilead, where Jehoram was wounded. {22:6} Jehoram returned to Jezreel to heal, and Ahaziah went to visit him. Meanwhile, Azariah, son of Jehoram of Judah, also visited Jehoram in Jezreel. {22:7} Ahaziah's downfall was orchestrated by God because he allied with Jehoram against Jehu, whom God had anointed to end the house of Ahab. {22:8} Jehu, executing judgment against the house of Ahab, found Ahaziah's relatives and killed them. {22:9} Ahaziah was captured and killed in Samaria. They buried him, recognizing him as Jehoshaphat's descendant who had sought the LORD. {22:10} Athaliah, Ahaziah's mother, seized power after his death and killed all the royal heirs of Judah. {22:11} But Jehoshabeath, daughter of the king, saved Joash, Ahaziah's son, from being killed. She hid him along with his nurse in the house. {22:12} Joash remained hidden in the house of God for six years while Athaliah ruled over the land.

{23:1} In the seventh year, Jehoiada gathered leaders and made a covenant with them. {23:2} They gathered Levites and heads of Israelite families and went to Jerusalem. {23:3} The congregation made a covenant with the king in the house of God, affirming that the king's son would reign, as the LORD had promised to David's descendants. {23:4} They established duties for priests and Levites, assigning some to be doorkeepers, others to be at the king's house, and the rest at the gate. {23:5} The people were to stay in the temple courts. {23:6} Only priests and Levites were allowed in the house of the LORD; others were forbidden. The Levites were to guard the king with weapons. {23:7} Anyone who entered the house without authorization would be killed, except for the king's entourage. {23:8} The Levites and all Judah followed Jehoiada's commands, with some entering and leaving on the Sabbath. {23:9} Jehoiada provided weapons from King David's arsenal in the house of God. {23:10} They stationed armed men around the temple, from one side to the other, by the altar and the temple, guarding the king. {23:11} They crowned the king's son, anointed him, and proclaimed, "God save the king." {23:12} When Athaliah heard the people's celebration, she came to the temple, saw the king, and the people rejoicing. {23:13} Enraged, she cried "Treason!" when she saw the king being honored. {23:14} Jehoiada ordered her capture outside the temple, instructing not to kill her inside. {23:15} They seized her and executed her near the horse gate by the king's house. {23:16} Jehoiada made a covenant between the people and the king to be the LORD's people. {23:17} They destroyed the house of Baal, its altars, images, and killed Baal's priest Mattan. {23:18} Jehoiada reorganized the temple services according to David's instructions, with offerings, rejoicing, and singing. {23:19} He stationed gatekeepers to prevent anyone unclean from entering the temple. {23:20} They brought the king down from the temple to the king's house through the high gate and enthroned him. {23:21} The people rejoiced, and the city was peaceful after Athaliah's death.

{24:1} Joash was seven years old when he began to reign, and he reigned forty years in Jerusalem. His mother's name was Zibiah of Beer-sheba. {24:2} Joash did what was right in the sight of the LORD all the days of Jehoiada the priest. {24:3} Jehoiada took for him two wives, and he had sons and daughters. {24:4} Joash decided to repair the house of the LORD. {24:5} He gathered the priests and the Levites and told them to go to the cities of Judah, collect money from all Israel every year, and use it to repair the house of God. However, the Levites did not hurry to do it. {24:6} The king asked Jehoiada why he hadn't instructed the Levites to bring in the collection as Moses, the servant of the LORD, and the congregation of Israel had commanded for the tabernacle of witness. {24:7} Joash mentioned that the sons of Athaliah, a wicked woman, had damaged the house of God and had given all the dedicated things of the house of the LORD to Baalim. {24:8} At the king's command, a chest was made and placed outside the gate of the house of the LORD. {24:9} A proclamation was made throughout Judah and Jerusalem to bring in the collection that Moses, the servant of God, had laid upon Israel in the wilderness. {24:10} All the princes and people rejoiced and brought in their contributions until the chest was full. {24:11} When the chest was brought to the king's office by the Levites and they saw there was a lot of money, the king's scribe and the high priest's officer emptied the chest, took it, and brought it back. They did this daily, collecting money abundantly. {24:12} The king and Jehoiada gave the money to those who worked on the service of the house of the LORD. They hired masons, carpenters, and craftsmen to repair the house of the LORD, including those who worked with iron and brass. {24:13} The workers completed the task, restoring and strengthening the house of God. {24:14} After finishing the repairs, the remaining money was brought before the king and Jehoiada. They used it to make vessels for the house of the LORD, including vessels for offering, spoons, and vessels of gold and silver. Burnt offerings were offered continually in the house of the LORD all the days of Jehoiada. {24:15} Jehoiada grew old and died at the age of one hundred and thirty. {24:16} He was buried in the city of David among the kings because he had done good in Israel, both toward God and toward his house. {24:17} After Jehoiada's death, the princes of Judah came to the king and paid homage to him. The king listened to them. {24:18} They abandoned the house of the LORD, the God of their fathers, and served groves and idols. This angered God, and wrath came upon Judah and Jerusalem because of their disobedience. {24:19} Although prophets were sent to them to bring them back to the LORD, they refused to listen. {24:20} The Spirit of God came upon Zechariah, the son of Jehoiada the priest, who stood above the people and warned them that because they had forsaken the LORD, they would not prosper. {24:21} They conspired against Zechariah and stoned him at the command of the king in the court of the house of the LORD. {24:22} Joash, the king, forgot the kindness that Jehoiada his father had shown him and killed his son. As he died, Zechariah prayed that the LORD would require it. {24:23} At the end of the year, the army of Syria came against Joash. They invaded Judah and Jerusalem, destroying all the princes of the people and sending their spoils to the king of Damascus. {24:24} Though the Syrian army was small, the LORD delivered a great host into their hands because the people had forsaken the LORD, the God of their fathers. Thus, judgment was executed against Joash. {24:25} When the Syrians left him, Joash was left with severe diseases. His own servants conspired against him because of the blood of the sons of Jehoiada the priest, and they killed him in his bed. He was buried in the city of David, but not in the sepulchers of the kings. {24:26} Those who conspired against him were Zabad, the son of Shimeath an Ammonitess, and Jehozabad, the son of Shimrith, a Moabitess. {24:27} Concerning Joash's sons, the burdens placed upon him, and the repair of the house of God, these are written in the book of the kings. Amaziah his son reigned in his place.

{25:1} Amaziah was twenty-five years old when he began to reign, and he reigned twenty-nine years in Jerusalem. His mother's name was Jehoaddan of Jerusalem. {25:2} He did what was right in the sight of the LORD, but not with a perfect heart. {25:3} When his kingdom was established, he executed his servants who had killed his father, the king. {25:4} However, he did not kill their children, as written in the law in the book of Moses, where the LORD commanded that fathers should not die for their children's sins, nor should children die for their fathers' sins, but each person should be responsible for their own sins. {25:5} Amaziah gathered the people of Judah and appointed captains over thousands and hundreds, according to their ancestral houses throughout Judah and Benjamin. He counted them from twenty years old and above and found three hundred thousand choice men ready for war, skilled in handling spear and shield. {25:6} He also hired one hundred thousand mighty men of valor from Israel for one hundred talents of silver. {25:7} But a man of God came to him, warning that the LORD was not with Israel, specifically with all the children of Ephraim. {25:8} However, if he chose to go to battle, he was told to be strong, but that God would make him fall before the enemy because God has the power to help and to cast down. {25:9} Amaziah asked what should be done about the hundred talents he had already given to the army of Israel. The man of God assured him that the LORD was able to give him much more than that. {25:10} So, Amaziah sent the army of Israel back home, which angered them greatly, and they returned home in great anger. {25:11} Amaziah strengthened himself and led his people to the valley of salt, where he defeated ten thousand of the children of Seir. {25:12} He took ten thousand captives alive, brought them to the top of a rock, and threw them down, so they were all broken to pieces. {25:13} However, the soldiers whom Amaziah had sent back turned against the cities of Judah, from Samaria to Beth-horon, killing three thousand of them and taking much spoil. {25:14} After returning from the slaughter of the Edomites, Amaziah brought the gods of the children of Seir and worshiped them. {25:15} This angered the LORD, so He sent a prophet to Amaziah, questioning why he had sought after the gods of people who couldn't even deliver their own people from his hand. {25:16} As they conversed, the king asked if the prophet was part of his counsel, warning him not to be struck down. The prophet stopped speaking, knowing that God had determined to destroy Amaziah because of his actions and failure to heed counsel. {25:17} Amaziah sought advice and sent to Joash, the king of Israel, proposing to meet face to face. {25:18} Joash responded with a parable, warning Amaziah not to be overconfident. {25:19} Despite the warning, Amaziah persisted in his plans, which ultimately led to his downfall, as it was determined by God because they sought after the gods of Edom. {25:20} So, Joash, the king of Israel, attacked Judah, defeating them at Beth-shemesh. {25:21} Judah was defeated, and Amaziah fled. {25:22} Joash captured Amaziah, brought him to Jerusalem, {25:23} broke down a section of its wall, and took all the treasures from the house of God and the king's house, {25:24} along with hostages, back to Samaria. {25:25} Amaziah lived fifteen years after the death of Joash, king of Israel. {25:26} The remaining deeds of Amaziah are recorded in the book of the kings of Judah and Israel. {25:27} After turning away from following the LORD, a conspiracy arose against Amaziah in Jerusalem. He fled to Lachish, but they pursued him and killed him there. {25:28} They brought his body back on horses and buried him with his fathers in the city of Judah.

{26:1} All the people of Judah crowned Uzziah king when he was sixteen years old, succeeding his father Amaziah. {26:2} He rebuilt Eloth and returned it to Judah after his father's death. {26:3} Uzziah was sixteen years old when he began to reign, and he reigned fifty-two years in Jerusalem. His mother's name was Jecoliah of Jerusalem. {26:4} Like his father Amaziah, Uzziah did what was right in the sight of the LORD.

{26:5} *During the time of Zechariah, who had understanding in the visions of God, Uzziah sought God, and as long as he sought the LORD, God made him prosper.* {26:6} He waged war against the Philistines, breaking down the walls of Gath, Jabneh, and Ashdod, and built cities around Ashdod and in Philistine territory. {26:7} God aided him against the Philistines and the Arabians dwelling in Gur-baal and the Mehunims. {26:8} Uzziah received gifts from the Ammonites, and his fame spread to the border of Egypt, for he became exceedingly strong. {26:9} Additionally, Uzziah built towers in Jerusalem at strategic locations and fortified them. {26:10} He constructed towers in the desert and dug numerous wells because he had much livestock, both in the lowlands and plains. He also had farmers and vine dressers in the mountains and in Carmel, for he loved agriculture. {26:11} Uzziah had a well-trained army organized into bands according to the records kept by Jeiel the scribe and Maaseiah the ruler, under the command of Hananiah, one of the king's captains. {26:12} The chief fathers of the mighty men of valor numbered two thousand six hundred. {26:13} Under their command was an army of three hundred thousand and seven thousand five hundred soldiers, powerful and ready to help the king against the enemy. {26:14} Uzziah provided them with shields, spears, helmets, habergeons, bows, and slings for casting stones. {26:15} He also installed engines in Jerusalem, devised by skillful men, on the towers and bulwarks, to shoot arrows and large stones. Uzziah's name became well known because he received marvelous help until he became strong. {26:16} However, when he became strong, his heart was lifted up to his destruction. He transgressed against the LORD by entering the temple of the LORD to burn incense on the altar of incense. {26:17} Azariah the priest, accompanied by eighty valiant priests of the LORD, confronted him, saying it was not his place to burn incense to the LORD, but the priests, the sons of Aaron, who were consecrated for that task. {26:18} They ordered him out of the sanctuary, warning him that he had trespassed and would not receive honor from the LORD God. {26:19} Uzziah, enraged, held a censer to burn incense, but leprosy broke out on his forehead before the priests in the house of the LORD, beside the incense altar. {26:20} The chief priest Azariah and all the priests saw him leprous and expelled him from there. Uzziah hurried out himself because the LORD had struck him. {26:21} Uzziah remained a leper until his death, living in a separate house, cut off from the house of the LORD. His son Jotham ruled in his place, overseeing the king's house and governing the people of the land. {26:22} The prophet Isaiah, son of Amoz, recorded the rest of Uzziah's deeds, from beginning to end. {26:23} Uzziah died and was buried with his fathers in the field of burial reserved for the kings, for he was a leper. Jotham, his son succeeded him as king.

{27:1} Jotham was twenty-five years old when he became king, and he reigned for sixteen years in Jerusalem. His mother's name was Jerushah, the daughter of Zadok. {27:2} He did what was right in the sight of the LORD, following the example of his father Uzziah. However, he did not enter the temple of the LORD. Nevertheless, the people continued to act corruptly. {27:3} Jotham built up the high gate of the house of the LORD, and he constructed extensively on the wall of Ophel. {27:4} Additionally, he established cities in the mountains of Judah, and in the forests, he erected forts and towers. {27:5} Jotham also engaged in battle with the king of the Ammonites and emerged victorious. As a tribute, the Ammonites paid him one hundred talents of silver, along with ten thousand measures of wheat and barley, in the same amount for the second and third years. {27:6} Jotham grew mighty because he was diligent in following the ways of the LORD his God. {27:7} The remaining actions of Jotham, including his wars and his conduct, are recorded in the book of the kings of Israel and Judah. {27:8} He was twenty-five years old when he began his reign and ruled for sixteen years in Jerusalem. {27:9} Jotham passed away and was buried in the city of David. His son Ahaz succeeded him as king.

{28:1} Ahaz was twenty years old when he became king, and he reigned for sixteen years in Jerusalem. However, he did not do what was right in the sight of the LORD, unlike his ancestor David. {28:2} He followed the ways of the kings of Israel and even made idols for Baal. Furthermore, he burned incense in the Valley of Hinnom and sacrificed his own children in the fire, imitating the detestable practices of the nations that the LORD had driven out before the Israelites. {28:3} Additionally, he offered sacrifices and burned incense on the high places, on the hills, and under every green tree. {28:4} Because of these actions, the LORD delivered him into the hands of the king of Syria, who defeated him and took a great number of his people captive to Damascus. {28:5} He was also handed over to the king of Israel, who inflicted a severe defeat upon him. {28:6} Pekah, the son of Remaliah, from Israel, killed one hundred and twenty thousand valiant men of Judah in one day because they had forsaken the LORD, the God of their fathers. {28:7} In addition to this, Zichri, a mighty man of Ephraim, killed Maaseiah the king's son, Azrikam the governor of the palace, and Elkanah, the next in authority to the king. {28:8} The Israelites also took captive two hundred thousand of their fellow Israelites, including women, sons, and daughters, and seized a great amount of plunder from them, bringing it to Samaria. {28:9} However, there was a prophet of the LORD named Oded who stood before the army returning to Samaria and warned them that their actions had provoked the LORD's wrath against Judah. {28:10} He urged them to release the captives they had taken, reminding them of their own sins against the LORD. {28:11} So listen to me now, and return the captives you have taken from your own brothers, for the fierce anger of the LORD is upon you. {28:12} Then certain leaders of the Ephraimites—Azariah the son of Johanan, Berechiah the son of Meshillemoth, Jehizkiah the son of Shallum, and Amasa the son of Hadlai—stood up against those returning from war. {28:13} They said to them, "You shall not bring the captives here, for we have already offended the LORD enough. Bringing in more captives will only add to our sins and trespasses, for our wrongdoing is great, and there is fierce wrath against Israel." {28:14} So the armed men left the captives and the plunder before the leaders and the assembly. {28:15} Then those who were named rose up, took the captives, clothed the naked among them with the plunder, provided them with food and drink, anointed them, placed the feeble on donkeys, and brought them to Jericho, the city of palm trees, to their fellow Israelites. Afterward, they returned to Samaria. {28:16} During this time of trouble, King Ahaz sought help from the kings of Assyria. {28:17} The Edomites also attacked Judah and took captives. {28:18} The Philistines invaded the cities of the lowlands and the southern areas of Judah, capturing several towns and villages. {28:19} Because of Ahaz's wickedness, the LORD brought Judah low, allowing these calamities to befall them. {28:20} Tilgath-pilneser, the king of Assyria, brought distress upon Ahaz but did not provide him with lasting assistance. {28:21} Ahaz, in his desperation, took treasures from the house of the LORD, the royal palace, and the officials and offered them to the king of Assyria, but it did not help him. {28:22} Despite his troubles, Ahaz continued to defy the LORD, committing even more acts of wickedness. {28:23} He worshiped the gods of Damascus, believing they could save him, but they only brought about his downfall and that of all Israel. {28:24} Ahaz further desecrated the house of God by dismantling its vessels, closing its doors, and erecting altars to other gods throughout Jerusalem. {28:25} In every city of Judah, he established high places to burn incense to foreign gods, provoking the LORD, the God of his ancestors, to anger. {28:26} The complete account of Ahaz's deeds, from beginning to end, is recorded in the chronicles of the kings of Judah and Israel. {28:27} Ahaz died and was buried in Jerusalem but was not laid to rest in the tombs of the kings of Israel. Hezekiah, his son, succeeded him as king.

{29:1} Hezekiah became king at the age of twenty-five, and he reigned in Jerusalem for twenty-nine years. His mother's name was Abijah, the daughter of Zechariah. {29:2} Hezekiah did what was right in the sight of the LORD, following the example of his ancestor David. {29:3} In the first year of his reign, in the first month, he opened the doors of the house of the LORD and repaired them. {29:4} He gathered the priests and Levites and assembled them in the east street, {29:5} saying to them, "Listen to me, you Levites. Sanctify yourselves and sanctify the house of the LORD, the God of your fathers. Remove the filthiness from the holy place. {29:6} "For our fathers have trespassed and done evil in the eyes of the LORD our God. They have forsaken Him, turning their backs on the dwelling place of the LORD. {29:7} "They have closed the doors of the porch, extinguished the lamps, and not offered incense or burnt offerings in the holy place to the God of Israel. {29:8} "Because of this, the wrath of the LORD was upon Judah and Jerusalem, and He delivered them to trouble, astonishment, and ridicule, as you see with your own eyes. {29:9} "Our fathers have fallen by the sword, and our sons, daughters, and wives are in captivity because of this. {29:10} "Now it is in my heart to make a covenant with the LORD, the God of Israel, so that His fierce wrath may turn away from us. {29:11} "My sons, do not be negligent now. The LORD has chosen you to stand before Him, to serve Him, and to minister to Him by burning incense." {29:12} Then the Levites arose—Mahath the son of Amasai, Joel the son of Azariah, from the Kohathites; Kish the son of Abdi, Azariah the son of Jehalelel, from the Merarites; Joah the son of Zimmah, Eden the son of Joah, from the Gershonites; {29:13} Shimri and Jeiel, from the sons of Elizaphan; Zechariah and Mattaniah, from the sons of Asaph; {29:14} Jehiel and Shimei, from the sons of Heman; Shemaiah and Uzziel, from the sons of Jeduthun. {29:15} They gathered their brethren, sanctified themselves, and came according to the commandment of the king, by the word of the LORD, to cleanse the house of the LORD. {29:16} The priests went into the inner part of the house of the LORD to cleanse it. They brought out all the uncleanness they found in the temple of the LORD into the court of the house of the LORD, and the Levites took it to carry it out into the brook Kidron. {29:17} They began to sanctify on the first day of the first month and reached the porch of the LORD on the eighth day of the month. They sanctified the house of the LORD in eight days and finished on the sixteenth day of the first month. {29:18} Then they went in to Hezekiah the king and said, "We have cleansed all the house of the LORD, the altar of burnt offering, and all its vessels, as well as the table of showbread and its vessels. {29:19} "Moreover, all the vessels that King Ahaz cast away in his transgression we have prepared and sanctified, and they are before the altar of the LORD." {29:20} Hezekiah rose early, gathered the rulers of the city, and went up to the house of the LORD. {29:21} They brought seven bulls, seven rams, seven lambs, and seven male goats as a sin offering for the kingdom, the sanctuary, and Judah. Hezekiah commanded the priests, the sons of Aaron, to offer them on the altar of the LORD. {29:22} They slaughtered the bulls, and the priests received the blood and sprinkled it on the altar. Likewise, when they slaughtered the rams, they sprinkled the blood on the altar. They also slaughtered the lambs and sprinkled the blood on the altar. {29:23} They brought the male goats for the sin offering before the king and the assembly, and they laid their hands on them. {29:24} The priests slaughtered them and made reconciliation with their blood on the altar to make atonement for all Israel, as the king commanded, for the burnt offering and sin offering were for all Israel. {29:25} Hezekiah stationed the Levites in the house of the LORD with cymbals, psalteries, and harps, according to the commandment of David, Gad the king's seer, and Nathan the prophet. This was the commandment of the LORD by His prophets. {29:26} The Levites stood with the instruments of David, and the priests with the trumpets. {29:27} Hezekiah commanded to offer the burnt offering on the altar. When the burnt offering began, the song of the LORD began with the trumpets and instruments ordained by David, king of Israel. {29:28} All the congregation worshipped, and the singers sang, and the trumpeters sounded until the burnt offering was finished. {29:29} When they finished offering, the king and all present with him bowed themselves and worshipped. {29:30} Hezekiah and the princes commanded the Levites to sing praises to the LORD with the words of David and Asaph the seer. They sang praises with gladness, bowed their heads, and worshipped. {29:31} Then Hezekiah said, "Now that you have consecrated yourselves to the LORD, come near and bring sacrifices and thank offerings into the house of the LORD." The congregation brought sacrifices and thank offerings, and as many as were willing brought burnt offerings. {29:32} The number of burnt offerings brought by the congregation was seventy bulls, one hundred rams, and two hundred lambs—all for a burnt offering to the LORD. {29:33} The consecrated offerings included six hundred bulls and three thousand sheep. {29:34} However, the priests were too few to skin all the burnt offerings. Therefore, their brethren the Levites helped them until the work was finished and until the other priests had sanctified themselves, for the Levites were more diligent in sanctifying themselves than the priests. {29:35} There were also plenty of burnt offerings with the fat of the peace offerings and the drink offerings for every burnt offering. Thus, the service of the house of the LORD was set in order. {29:36} Hezekiah and all the people rejoiced because God had prepared the people, for this thing was done suddenly.

{30:1} Hezekiah sent letters to all Israel and Judah, including Ephraim and Manasseh, inviting them to come to the house of the LORD in Jerusalem to celebrate the Passover to the LORD, the God of Israel. {30:2} The king and his officials, along with the entire assembly in Jerusalem, decided to celebrate the Passover in the second month. {30:3} They couldn't celebrate it at the regular time because the priests hadn't sanctified themselves sufficiently, and the people hadn't gathered in Jerusalem. {30:4} This plan pleased the king and all the assembly. {30:5} So they issued a decree to proclaim throughout all Israel, from Beer-sheba to Dan, that everyone should come to Jerusalem to celebrate the Passover to the LORD, the God of Israel, because they hadn't observed it for a long time as it was prescribed. {30:6} The messengers went out with letters from the king and his officials throughout Israel and Judah, urging the people to return to the LORD, the God of their fathers—Abraham, Isaac, and Israel—so that He might return to the remnant of them who had escaped from the kings of Assyria. {30:7} They were encouraged not to be like their fathers and brethren who had trespassed against the LORD, resulting in desolation. {30:8} They were urged not to be stubborn like their fathers but to yield themselves to the LORD and enter His sanctuary, which He had sanctified forever. They were to serve the LORD their God so that His fierce wrath might turn away from them. {30:9} They were reminded that if they turned back to the LORD, their brethren and children who were captives would find compassion and return to the land because the LORD their God is gracious and merciful, and He doesn't turn His face away from those who return to Him. {30:10} However, some people from Ephraim, Manasseh, and Zebulun mocked the messengers. {30:11} But some from Asher, Manasseh, and Zebulun humbled themselves and came to Jerusalem. {30:12} In Judah, God gave them unity of purpose to carry out the king's command by the word of the LORD. {30:13} A large assembly gathered in Jerusalem to celebrate the Feast of Unleavened Bread in the second month. {30:14} They removed the altars in Jerusalem and all the altars for incense, casting them into the brook Kidron. {30:15} They slaughtered the Passover on the fourteenth day of the second month. The priests and Levites were ashamed and sanctified themselves, bringing the burnt offerings into the house of the LORD. {30:16} They stood in their places according to the law of Moses, and the priests sprinkled the blood received from the Levites. {30:17} Many in the assembly were not sanctified, so the Levites were in charge of killing the Passovers for everyone who was not clean to sanctify them to the LORD. {30:18} Many from Ephraim, Manasseh, Issachar, and Zebulun hadn't cleansed themselves properly, yet they ate the Passover contrary to what was written. Hezekiah prayed for them, asking the LORD to pardon everyone who prepares their heart to seek God, even if they're not purified according to the sanctuary's regulations. {30:19} The LORD listened to Hezekiah and healed the people. {30:20} The Israelites present in Jerusalem celebrated the Feast of Unleavened Bread for seven days with great joy. The Levites and priests praised the LORD daily with loud instruments. {30:21} Hezekiah encouraged the Levites who were teaching the people about the LORD. They ate throughout the feast for seven days, offering peace offerings and confessing to the LORD, the God of their fathers. {30:22} The whole assembly agreed to celebrate for another seven days with gladness. Hezekiah provided one thousand bulls and seven thousand sheep for the congregation, and the princes offered one thousand bulls and ten thousand sheep. Many priests sanctified themselves. {30:23} There was great joy in Jerusalem, unlike anything since Solomon's time. {30:24} Then the priests and Levites blessed the people, and their prayers ascended to God's holy dwelling place in heaven. {30:25} All the assembly of Judah, including the priests, Levites, and the Israelites present, as well as the foreigners from Israel and Judah, rejoiced together. {30:26} So there was great joy in Jerusalem, for it had not been like this since the time of Solomon, the son of David, king of Israel. {30:27} The priests and Levites arose and blessed the people. Their voices were heard, and their prayer reached God's holy dwelling place in heaven.

{31:1} After completing all this, all Israelites who were present went out to the cities of Judah and destroyed the idols, cut down the groves, and demolished the high places and altars throughout Judah, Benjamin, Ephraim, and Manasseh until they had eradicated them all. Then all the Israelites returned to their possessions in their own cities. {31:2} Hezekiah organized the divisions of the priests and Levites according to their duties, assigning them to offer burnt offerings and peace offerings, to minister, and to give thanks and praise at the gates of the LORD's house. {31:3} He also allocated a portion of his own possessions for the burnt offerings, including the morning and evening offerings, offerings for the Sabbaths, New Moons, and appointed feasts, as prescribed in the Law of the LORD. {31:4} Additionally, he instructed the people of Jerusalem to provide for the priests and Levites so that they could be encouraged to fulfill their duties according to the Law of the LORD. {31:5} When the decree was issued, the Israelites brought abundant firstfruits of grain, wine, oil, honey, and all the produce of the field, as well as a tithe of everything they brought in abundantly. {31:6} The Israelites and Judahites residing in the cities of Judah also brought in the tithe of oxen, sheep, and consecrated items to the LORD their God, and they piled them in heaps. {31:7} They began laying the foundation of these heaps in the third month and finished them by the seventh month. {31:8} When Hezekiah and the officials saw the heaps, they praised the LORD and His people Israel. {31:9} Hezekiah inquired of the priests and Levites about the heaps. {31:10} Azariah, the chief priest of the house of Zadok, replied that since the people began bringing offerings to the house of the LORD, they had more than enough to eat and plenty left over because the LORD had blessed His people abundantly. {31:11} So Hezekiah ordered chambers to be prepared in the house of the LORD, and they were prepared. {31:12} The offerings, tithes, and dedicated things were brought in faithfully. Cononiah the Levite was appointed ruler over them, with his brother Shimei as his assistant. {31:13} Jehiel, Azaziah, Nahath, Asahel, Jerimoth, Jozabad, Eliel, Ismachiah, and Mahath were overseers under Cononiah and Shimei, appointed by King Hezekiah and Azariah, the ruler of the house of God. {31:14} Kore, the son of Imnah the Levite, the gatekeeper toward the east, was responsible for the freewill offerings of God, distributing the offerings of the LORD and the most holy things. {31:15} Eden, Miniamin, Jeshua, Shemaiah, Amariah, Shecaniah, in their appointed offices in the cities of the priests, distributed to their brethren according to their divisions, both to the great and small, {31:16} in addition to their genealogical records, from three years old and upward, everyone who entered the house of the LORD for their daily portion in their service, according to their duties by their divisions.

{31:17} This also applied to the genealogy of the priests by their fathers' houses and the Levites from twenty years old and upward, in their duties by their divisions. {31:18} It included their genealogy, their wives, sons, and daughters—all who were faithful in keeping themselves holy according to their appointed duties. {31:19} Likewise, the sons of Aaron the priests who lived in the fields of their cities had men designated by name to distribute portions to all the males among the priests and to all who were recorded by genealogy among the Levites. {31:20} Hezekiah did this throughout all Judah, acting according to what was good, right, and true before the LORD his God. {31:21} In every work he began for the service of the house of God, in the law, and in the commandments, seeking his God with all his heart, he prospered.

{32:1} After these events and the consolidation thereof, Sennacherib, the king of Assyria, marched into Judah and besieged the fortified cities, intending to conquer them for himself. {32:2} When Hezekiah saw that Sennacherib had come and was determined to attack Jerusalem, {32:3} he consulted with his officials and warriors to block the waters of the springs outside the city. They helped him in this endeavor. {32:4} So many people gathered together and stopped all the springs and the brook that ran through the land, questioning why the kings of Assyria should find abundant water. {32:5} Hezekiah also reinforced himself, repairing the broken walls, extending them up to the towers, building another wall outside, and restoring the supporting terraces in the City of David. He also made a large number of weapons and shields. {32:6} He appointed military officers over the people, gathering them at the city gate and encouraged them, saying, {32:7} "Be strong and courageous! Do not be afraid or dismayed because of the king of Assyria and his vast army, for there are more with us than with him. {32:8} With him is only human strength, but with us is the LORD our God to help us and fight our battles." And the people were encouraged by the words of Hezekiah king of Judah. {32:9} Afterward, Sennacherib king of Assyria sent his servants to Jerusalem (while he himself laid siege to Lachish with all his forces), to Hezekiah king of Judah and to all Judah who were in Jerusalem, saying, {32:10} "Thus says Sennacherib king of Assyria: 'On what do you base your confidence as you remain under siege in Jerusalem?' {32:11} 'Doesn't Hezekiah persuade you to trust in the LORD your God, saying, "The LORD will deliver us from the hand of the king of Assyria"? {32:12} 'Hasn't Hezekiah removed his high places and altars, commanding Judah and Jerusalem to worship before one altar and burn incense on it?' {32:13} 'Do you not know what I and my fathers have done to all the peoples of other lands? Were the gods of the nations of those lands able to deliver their lands out of my hand? {32:14} 'Who among all the gods of those nations that my fathers utterly destroyed was able to deliver his people out of my hand, that your God should be able to deliver you out of my hand? {32:15} 'Now therefore, do not let Hezekiah deceive you or persuade you like this, nor believe him; for no god of any nation or kingdom has been able to deliver his people from my hand or the hand of my fathers. How much less will your God deliver you out of my hand?'" {32:16} His servants spoke even more against the LORD God and against His servant Hezekiah. {32:17} Moreover, Sennacherib wrote letters to ridicule the LORD God of Israel and to speak against Him, saying, "Just as the gods of the nations of other lands have not delivered their people from my hand, so the God of Hezekiah will not deliver His people from my hand." {32:18} They shouted loudly in the language of Judah to the people of Jerusalem who were on the wall, trying to frighten and disturb them, in order to capture the city. {32:19} They spoke against the God of Jerusalem as they had against the gods of the peoples of the earth, which were the work of human hands. {32:20} Because of this, Hezekiah the king and the prophet Isaiah the son of Amoz prayed and cried out to heaven. {32:21} And the LORD sent an angel who annihilated all the mighty warriors, leaders, and officers in the camp of the king of Assyria. So he returned to his own land in disgrace. And when he entered the temple of his god, some of his own offspring struck him down with the sword there. {32:22} Thus the LORD saved Hezekiah and the inhabitants of Jerusalem from the hand of Sennacherib king of Assyria and from all others, guiding them on every side. {32:23} Many brought gifts to the LORD in Jerusalem and valuable presents to Hezekiah king of Judah, so that he was esteemed highly by all nations from that time onward. {32:24} In those days, Hezekiah became mortally ill and prayed to the LORD. The LORD spoke to him and gave him a sign. {32:25} But Hezekiah did not respond according to the benefit shown to him, for his heart became proud. Therefore, there was wrath upon him, and upon Judah and Jerusalem. {32:26} Nevertheless, Hezekiah humbled himself for the pride of his heart, both he and the inhabitants of Jerusalem, so that the wrath of the LORD did not come upon them in the days of Hezekiah. {32:27} Hezekiah had exceedingly much riches and honor, and he made himself treasuries for silver, gold, precious stones, spices, shields, and all kinds of desirable items. {32:28} He also built storehouses for the harvest of grain, wine, and oil, and stalls for all kinds of livestock, and pens for flocks. {32:29} Moreover, he provided himself with cities and possessions of flocks and herds in abundance, for God had given him very much wealth. {32:30} This same Hezekiah blocked the upper outlet of the waters of Gihon and directed them straight down on the west side of the City of David. And Hezekiah prospered in all his endeavors. {32:31} However, regarding the ambassadors of the princes of Babylon who were sent to him to inquire about the wonder that had happened in the land, God left him to himself to test him, that He might know all that was in his heart. {32:32} Now the rest of the acts of Hezekiah and his goodness, behold, they are written in the vision of Isaiah the prophet, the son of Amoz, and in the book of the kings of Judah and Israel. {32:33} And Hezekiah rested with his fathers, and they buried him in the most prominent of the tombs of the sons of David. And all Judah and the inhabitants of Jerusalem honored him at his death. And his son Manasseh reigned in his place.

{33:1} Manasseh was twelve years old when he became king, and he reigned fifty-five years in Jerusalem. {33:2} But he did what was evil in the sight of the LORD, following the abominations of the nations whom the LORD had dispossessed before the people of Israel. {33:3} He rebuilt the high places that his father Hezekiah had torn down, erected altars for the Baals, made Asherah poles, worshiped all the stars of heaven, and served them. {33:4} He even built altars in the house of the LORD, where the LORD had said, "In Jerusalem shall my name be forever." {33:5} He built altars for all the host of heaven in the two courts of the house of the LORD. {33:6} He made his sons pass through the fire in the Valley of the Son of Hinnom, practiced fortune-telling, omens, sorcery, and consulted mediums and necromancers. He did much evil in the sight of the LORD, provoking him to anger. {33:7} He also set a carved image, the idol that he had made, in the house of God, of which God had said to David and to Solomon his son, "In this house, and in Jerusalem, which I have chosen out of all the tribes of Israel, I will put my name forever." {33:8} "I will no more remove the foot of Israel from the land that I appointed for your fathers, if only they will be careful to do all that I have commanded them, all the law, statutes, and rules given through Moses." {33:9} Manasseh led Judah and the inhabitants of Jerusalem astray, causing them to do more evil than the nations whom the LORD destroyed before the people of Israel. {33:10} The LORD spoke to Manasseh and his people, but they paid no attention. {33:11} Therefore, the LORD brought upon them the commanders of the army of the king of Assyria, who captured Manasseh with hooks, bound him with chains, and took him to Babylon. {33:12} **And when he was in distress, he entreated the favor of the LORD his God and humbled himself greatly before the God of his fathers.** {33:13} **He prayed to him, and God was moved by his entreaty and heard his plea and brought him again to Jerusalem into his kingdom. Then Manasseh knew that the LORD was God.** {33:14} Afterward, he built an outer wall for the city of David west of Gihon, in the valley, and connected it with the Fish Gate and carried it around to Ophel, raising it to a great height. He also stationed military commanders in all the fortified cities of Judah. {33:15} He removed the foreign gods and the idol from the house of the LORD, as well as all the altars that he had built on the mountain of the house of the LORD and in Jerusalem, and he threw them outside the city. {33:16} He also restored the altar of the LORD and offered on it sacrifices of peace offerings and thanksgiving, and he commanded Judah to serve the LORD, the God of Israel. {33:17} Nevertheless, the people still sacrificed at the high places, but only to the LORD their God. {33:18} Now the rest of the acts of Manasseh, his prayer to his God, and the words of the seers who spoke to him in the name of the LORD, the God of Israel, behold, they are written in the Chronicles of the Kings of Israel. {33:19} His prayer and how God responded to him, and all his sin and his faithlessness, and the sites on which he built high places and set up the Asherim and the images, before he humbled himself, behold, they are written in the Chronicles of the Seers. {33:20} So Manasseh slept with his fathers, and they buried him in his house. And Amon his son reigned in his place. {33:21} Amon was twenty-two years old when he began to reign, and he reigned two years in Jerusalem. {33:22} And he did what was evil in the sight of the LORD, as Manasseh his father had done. For Amon sacrificed to all the images that Manasseh his father had made, and served them. {33:23} He did not humble himself before the LORD, as Manasseh his father had humbled himself, but this Amon incurred more and more guilt. {33:24} And his servants conspired against him and put him to death in his house. {33:25} But the people of the land struck down all those who had conspired against King Amon, and the people of the land made Josiah his son king in his place.

{34:1} Josiah was only eight years old when he became king, and he ruled in Jerusalem for thirty-one years. {34:2} He did what was right in the sight of the LORD, following the example of his ancestor David. He neither turned to the right nor to the left from God's commands. {34:3} In the eighth year of his reign, while still young, Josiah began to seek the

God of his ancestor David. In the twelfth year, he started to purge Judah and Jerusalem of the high places, groves, carved images, and molten images. {34:4} Josiah demolished the altars of Baal in the presence of the people, cutting down the images that were above them. He broke into pieces the groves, carved images, and molten images, turning them into dust and scattering it over the graves of those who had sacrificed to them. {34:5} He burned the bones of the pagan priests on their altars and purified Judah and Jerusalem. {34:6} Josiah extended his reforms to the cities of Manasseh, Ephraim, Simeon, and Naphtali, breaking down their altars, groves, and idols. {34:7} After destroying the altars and groves, and pulverizing the graven images and idols throughout the land of Israel, he returned to Jerusalem. {34:8} In the eighteenth year of his reign, having purified the land and the temple, Josiah sent officials to repair the house of the LORD his God. {34:9} When they came to Hilkiah the high priest, they delivered the money that had been brought into the house of God, collected by the Levites who guarded the doors, from Manasseh, Ephraim, the remnant of Israel, Judah, and Benjamin. {34:10} The money was given to the overseers of the temple workmen to repair and restore the house of the LORD. {34:11} They used the funds to buy hewn stone and timber for the temple's repairs, as well as to restore the houses that the kings of Judah had destroyed. {34:12} The workers, overseen by Jahath and Obadiah the Levites, and Zechariah and Meshullam the Kohathites, carried out their tasks faithfully. They were aided by Levites skilled in musical instruments. {34:13} Others were appointed as bearers of burdens, overseers, scribes, officers, and porters. {34:14} While bringing out the money collected for the temple, Hilkiah the priest discovered a book of the law of the LORD given by Moses. {34:15} Hilkiah informed Shaphan the scribe, who then delivered the book to Josiah. {34:16} Shaphan presented the book to the king and reported that everything entrusted to his servants had been carried out. {34:17} The money found in the house of the LORD had been collected and delivered to the overseers and workmen. {34:18} Upon hearing the words of the law, Josiah tore his clothes. {34:19} He instructed Hilkiah, Ahikam, Abdon, Shaphan, and Asaiah to inquire of the LORD for him and for the remnant of Israel and Judah regarding the contents of the book. Josiah feared the great wrath of the LORD because their ancestors had not kept His word. {34:20} Hilkiah and the others went to Huldah the prophetess, who dwelt in Jerusalem, and relayed Josiah's message. {34:21} Huldah responded that the LORD would indeed bring evil upon the land, as described in the book read before the king of Judah, because the people had forsaken Him and worshiped other gods. {34:22} She instructed them to convey to Josiah the LORD's message about the impending judgment. {34:23} As Josiah's heart was tender and he had humbled himself before God, God heard his supplication. Josiah would be gathered to his grave in peace, spared from witnessing the coming calamity upon the land. {34:24} Josiah then gathered all the elders of Judah and Jerusalem. {34:25} He went up to the house of the LORD with all the men of Judah, the inhabitants of Jerusalem, the priests, the Levites, and the people, both great and small. There, Josiah read to them all the words of the book of the covenant found in the house of the LORD. {34:26} Josiah made a covenant before the LORD, committing himself and all the people to obey God's commandments, testimonies, and statutes, with all their hearts and souls, in accordance with the covenant written in the book. {34:27} All present in Jerusalem and Benjamin agreed to uphold the covenant of God, the God of their fathers. {34:28} Josiah removed all the abominations from the territories belonging to the children of Israel, compelling all those in Israel to serve the LORD their God. Throughout his reign, they did not turn away from following the LORD, the God of their fathers. {34:29} Then the king summoned all the elders of Judah and Jerusalem. {34:30} Josiah went up to the house of the LORD, accompanied by all the men of Judah, the inhabitants of Jerusalem, the priests, the Levites, and all the people, both great and small. There, he read aloud to them all the words of the book of the covenant found in the house of the LORD. {34:31} Standing in his place, the king made a covenant before the LORD, pledging to walk in obedience to the LORD's commandments, testimonies, and statutes with all his heart and soul. He committed to fulfilling the words of the covenant written in the book. {34:32} Josiah ensured that all those present in Jerusalem and Benjamin affirmed the covenant. The inhabitants of Jerusalem followed the covenant of God, the God of their fathers. {34:33} Josiah removed all the abominations from the territories belonging to the children of Israel. He compelled all those in Israel to serve the LORD their God. Throughout his days, they remained faithful in following the LORD, the God of their fathers.

{35:1} Josiah celebrated a Passover to the LORD in Jerusalem, sacrificing the Passover lamb on the fourteenth day of the first month. {35:2} He appointed the priests to their duties and encouraged them in the service of the house of the LORD. {35:3} Josiah instructed the Levites, who were set apart for the LORD, to place the holy ark in the house built by Solomon, reassuring them that it would no longer be a burden on their shoulders. He urged them to serve the LORD their God and His people Israel. {35:4} He organized them according to their ancestral houses and their divisions, following the instructions laid out by David, king of Israel, and Solomon his son. {35:5} The Levites were to stand in the holy place according to their family divisions, alongside their fellow Israelites. {35:6} They were to slaughter the Passover lamb, purify themselves, and prepare their fellow Israelites to observe the word of the LORD as given through Moses. {35:7} Josiah provided the people with thirty thousand lambs and goats for the Passover offerings, along with three thousand cattle, all from the king's possessions. {35:8} Additionally, his officials willingly gave to the people, the priests, and the Levites for the Passover offerings: two thousand six hundred small cattle and three hundred oxen from Hilkiah, Zechariah, and Jehiel, rulers of the house of God. {35:9} Conaniah, Shemaiah, Nethaneel, Hashabiah, Jeiel, and Jozabad, chief Levites, contributed five thousand small cattle and five hundred oxen for the Levites' Passover offerings. {35:10} The preparations were made according to Josiah's command. The priests stood in their places, and the Levites in their divisions, as ordered by the king. {35:11} They slaughtered the Passover lamb, and the priests sprinkled the blood while the Levites skinned the animals. {35:12} The burnt offerings were then prepared according to the family divisions of the people, as written in the Book of Moses. They did the same with the cattle. {35:13} The Passover was roasted over the fire as prescribed, while the other holy offerings were cooked in pots, cauldrons, and pans, and distributed promptly among the people. {35:14} Afterward, they made preparations for themselves and for the priests, who were busy offering burnt offerings and fat until nightfall. Therefore, the Levites made preparations for themselves and for the priests, the descendants of Aaron. {35:15} The singers, the sons of Asaph, were in their places according to David's command, along with Heman, Jeduthun, and the king's seer. The gatekeepers were stationed at every gate; they did not need to leave their positions because their fellow Levites made the preparations for them. {35:16} Thus, all the service of the LORD was carried out that day for the observance of the Passover and the offering of burnt offerings on the LORD's altar, following King Josiah's command. {35:17} The people of Israel present at that time celebrated the Passover and the Feast of Unleavened Bread for seven days. {35:18} Such a Passover had not been observed in Israel since the days of Samuel the prophet, and none of the kings of Israel had ever celebrated a Passover like Josiah's, attended by the priests, Levites, all of Judah and Israel, and the inhabitants of Jerusalem. {35:19} This Passover was held in the eighteenth year of Josiah's reign. {35:20} After all these events, when Josiah had finished restoring the temple, Necho king of Egypt marched out to fight at Carchemish on the Euphrates, and Josiah went out to engage him. {35:21} But Necho sent messengers to Josiah, saying, "What quarrel is there, king of Judah, between you and me? It is not you I am attacking at this time, but the house with which I am at war. God has commanded me to hurry; so stop opposing God, who is with me, or he will destroy you." {35:22} Josiah, however, refused to turn away from him, but disguised himself to engage him in battle. He would not listen to what Necho had said at God's command but went to fight him on the plain of Megiddo. {35:23} Archers shot King Josiah, and he said to his servants, "Take me away; I am badly wounded." {35:24} So they took him out of his chariot, put him in his other chariot, and brought him to Jerusalem, where he died. He was buried in the tombs of his ancestors, and all Judah and Jerusalem mourned for him. {35:25} Jeremiah composed a lament for Josiah, and to this day all the male and female singers commemorate Josiah in the lamentations. These became a tradition in Israel and are recorded in the lamentations. {35:26} The rest of the events of Josiah's reign and his acts of devotion are recorded in the Book of the Law of the LORD. {35:27} His deeds, from beginning to end, are recorded in the annals of the kings of Israel and Judah.

{36:1} The people of the land appointed Jehoahaz, Josiah's son, as king in Jerusalem after his father's death. {36:2} Jehoahaz was twenty-three years old when he became king, and he ruled for three months in Jerusalem. {36:3} However, the king of Egypt removed him from power in Jerusalem and imposed a fine of one hundred talents of silver and a talent of gold on the land. {36:4} The king of Egypt then installed Jehoahaz's brother Eliakim as king over Judah and Jerusalem, renaming him Jehoiakim. He took Jehoahaz to Egypt. {36:5} Jehoiakim was twenty-five years old when he became king, and he reigned for eleven years in Jerusalem. Unfortunately, he did evil in the sight of the LORD his God. {36:6} Nebuchadnezzar, king of Babylon, marched against him, bound him in bronze shackles, and took him to Babylon. {36:7} Nebuchadnezzar also carried off some of the articles from the house of the LORD to Babylon and placed them in his temple there. {36:8} The rest of Jehoiakim's deeds, along with his detestable practices and what was found against him, are recorded in the annals of the kings of Israel and Judah. His son Jehoiachin succeeded him as king. {36:9} Jehoiachin was eight years old when he became king, and he reigned for three months and ten days in Jerusalem. He also did evil in the sight of the LORD. {36:10} After a year had passed, King Nebuchadnezzar sent for him and brought him to Babylon, along with the valuable articles from the house of the LORD. Then he made Jehoiachin's uncle, Zedekiah, king over Judah and Jerusalem. {36:11} Zedekiah was twenty-one years old when he became king, and he reigned for eleven years in Jerusalem. However, he too did evil in the sight of the LORD his God. {36:12} Zedekiah did not humble himself before Jeremiah the prophet, who spoke for the LORD. {36:13} He also rebelled against King Nebuchadnezzar, who had made him swear allegiance by God. He became stiff-necked and hardened his heart, refusing to turn to the LORD, the God of Israel. {36:14} **_Furthermore, all the leaders of the priests and the people greatly transgressed by following all the abominations of the nations and defiling the house of the LORD, which He had consecrated in Jerusalem._** {36:15} **_The LORD, the God of their ancestors, sent word to His people through His messengers, rising early and sending them, because He had compassion on His people and His dwelling place._** {36:16} **_But they mocked the messengers of God, despised His words, and scoffed at His prophets, until the wrath of the LORD against His people was so great that there was no remedy._** {36:17} Therefore, He brought against them the king of the Chaldeans, who killed their young men with the sword in the sanctuary of their own temple. He showed no pity to young men or women, the elderly, or the infirm. God handed all of them over to Nebuchadnezzar. {36:18} Nebuchadnezzar took all the articles from the house of God, both large and small treasures from the house of the LORD and from the royal palace, and carried them off to Babylon. {36:19} Then they set fire to the house of God, broke down the wall of Jerusalem, burned all its palaces, and destroyed everything of value. {36:20} Those who escaped the sword were taken as captives to Babylon, where they became servants to him and his successors until the kingdom of Persia came to power. {36:21} This fulfilled the word of the LORD spoken by Jeremiah until the land had enjoyed its Sabbaths. All the days of its desolation it rested, until seventy years were completed. {36:22} In the first year of Cyrus, king of Persia, to fulfill the word of the LORD spoken by Jeremiah, the LORD stirred up the spirit of Cyrus, king of Persia, to make a proclamation throughout his kingdom and put it in writing: {36:23} "Thus says Cyrus, king of Persia: 'The LORD, the God of heaven, has given me all the kingdoms of the earth and has appointed me to build a temple for Him at Jerusalem in Judah. Anyone of His people among you may go up, and may the LORD his God be with him.'"

Ezra

{1:1} Now in the first year of Cyrus king of Persia, the LORD stirred up the spirit of Cyrus king of Persia, so that he made a proclamation throughout all his kingdom, and also put it in writing, saying, {1:2} "Thus saith Cyrus king of Persia: The LORD God of heaven hath given me all the kingdoms of the earth; and he hath charged me to build him a house at Jerusalem, which is in Judah. {1:3} Who among you is of his people? Let his God be with him, and let him go up to Jerusalem, which is in Judah, and build the house of the LORD God of Israel (he is the God) which is in Jerusalem. {1:4} And whoever remains in any place where he sojourns, let the men of his place help him with silver, and with gold, and with goods, and with beasts, beside the freewill offering for the house of God that is in Jerusalem. {1:5} Then rose up the chief of the fathers of Judah and Benjamin, and the priests, and the Levites, with all whose spirit God had raised, to go up to build the house of the LORD which is in Jerusalem. {1:6} And all those around them strengthened their hands with vessels of silver, with gold, with goods, and with beasts, and with precious things, beside all that was willingly offered. {1:7} Also Cyrus the king brought forth the vessels of the house of the LORD, which Nebuchadnezzar had brought forth out of Jerusalem, and had put them in the house of his gods; {1:8} Even those did Cyrus king of Persia bring forth by the hand of Mithredath the treasurer, and numbered them unto Sheshbazzar, the prince of Judah. {1:9} And this is the number of them: thirty chargers of gold, a thousand chargers of silver, nine and twenty knives, {1:10} Thirty basons of gold, silver basons of a second sort four hundred and ten, and other vessels a thousand. {1:11} All the vessels of gold and of silver were five thousand and four hundred. All these did Sheshbazzar bring up with them of the captivity that were brought up from Babylon unto Jerusalem.

{2:1} Now these are the children of the province who went up out of the captivity, of those who had been carried away, whom Nebuchadnezzar the king of Babylon had carried away unto Babylon, and came again unto Jerusalem and Judah, every one unto his city; {2:2} Which came with Zerubbabel: Jeshua, Nehemiah, Seraiah, Reelaiah, Mordecai, Bilshan, Mizpar, Bigvai, Rehum, Baanah. The number of the men of the people of Israel: {2:3} The children of Parosh, two thousand one hundred seventy and two. {2:4} The children of Shephatiah, three hundred seventy and two. {2:5} The children of Arah, seven hundred seventy and five. {2:6} The children of Pahathmoab, of the children of Jeshua and Joab, two thousand eight hundred and twelve. {2:7} The children of Elam, one thousand two hundred fifty and four. {2:8} The children of Zattu, nine hundred forty and five. {2:9} The children of Zaccai, seven hundred and threescore. {2:10} The children of Bani, six hundred forty and two. {2:11} The children of Bebai, six hundred twenty and three. {2:12} The children of Azgad, one thousand two hundred twenty and two. {2:13} The children of Adonikam, six hundred sixty and six. {2:14} The children of Bigvai, two thousand fifty and six. {2:15} The children of Adin, four hundred fifty and four. {2:16} The children of Ater of Hezekiah, ninety and eight. {2:17} The children of Bezai, three hundred twenty and three. {2:18} The children of Jorah, one hundred and twelve. {2:19} The children of Hashum, two hundred twenty and three. {2:20} The children of Gibbar, ninety and five. {2:21} The children of Bethlehem, one hundred twenty and three. {2:22} The men of Netophah, fifty and six. {2:23} The men of Anathoth, one hundred twenty and eight. {2:24} The children of Azmaveth, forty and two. {2:25} The children of Kirjath-arim, Chephirah, and Beeroth, seven hundred and forty and three. {2:26} The children of Ramah and Gaba, six hundred twenty and one. {2:27} The men of Michmas, one hundred twenty and two. {2:28} The men of Bethel and Ai, two hundred twenty and three. {2:29} The children of Nebo, fifty and two. {2:30} The children of Magbish, one hundred fifty and six. {2:31} The children of the other Elam, one thousand two hundred fifty and four. {2:32} The children of Harim, three hundred and twenty. {2:33} The children of Lod, Hadid, and Ono, seven hundred twenty and five. {2:34} The children of Jericho, three hundred forty and five. {2:35} The children of Senaah, three thousand and six hundred and thirty. {2:36} The priests: the children of Jedaiah, of the house of Jeshua, nine hundred seventy and three. {2:37} The children of Immer, one thousand fifty and two. {2:38} The children of Pashur, one thousand two hundred forty and seven. {2:39} The children of Harim, one thousand and seventeen. {2:40} The Levites: the children of Jeshua and Kadmiel, of the children of Hodaviah, seventy and four. {2:41} The singers: the children of Asaph, one hundred twenty and eight. {2:42} The children of the porters: the children of Shallum, the children of Ater, the children of Talmon, the children of Akkub, the children of Hatita, the children of Shobai, in all one hundred thirty and nine. {2:43} The Nethinims: the children of Ziha, the children of Hasupha, the children of Tabbaoth, {2:44} The children of Keros, the children of Siaha, the children of Padon, {2:45} The children of Lebanah, the children of Hagabah, the children of Akkub, {2:46} The children of Hagab, the children of Shalmai, the children of Hanan, {2:47} The children of Giddel, the children of Gahar, the children of Reaiah, {2:48} The children of Rezin, the children of Nekoda, the children of Gazzam, {2:49} The children of Uzza, the children of Paseah, the children of Besai, {2:50} The children of Asnah, the children of Mehunim, the children of Nephusim, {2:51} The children of Bakbuk, the children of Hakupha, the children of Harhur, {2:52} The children of Bazluth, the children of Mehida, the children of Harsha, {2:53} The children of Barkos, the children of Sisera, the children of Thamah, {2:54} The children of Neziah, the children of Hatipha. {2:55} The children of Solomon's servants: the children of Sotai, the children of Sophereth, the children of Peruda, {2:56} The children of Jaalah, the children of Darkon, the children of Giddel, {2:57} The children of Shephatiah, the children of Hattil, the children of Pochereth of Zebaim, the children of Ami. {2:58} All the Nethinims, and the children of Solomon's servants, were three hundred ninety and two. {2:59} And these were they who went up from Telmelah, Tel-harsa, Cherub, Addan, and Immer: but they could not show their father's house, and their seed, whether they were of Israel: {2:60} The children of Delaiah, the children of Tobiah, the children of Nekoda, six hundred fifty and two. {2:61} And of the children of the priests: the children of Habaiah, the children of Koz, the children of Barzillai; who took a wife of the daughters of Barzillai the Gileadite, and was called after their name. {2:62} These sought their register among those that were reckoned by genealogy, but they were not found: therefore were they, as polluted, put from the priesthood. {2:63} And the Tirshatha said unto them, that they should not eat of the most holy things, till there stood up a priest with Urim and with Thummim. {2:64} The whole congregation together was forty and two thousand three hundred and threescore, {2:65} Besides their servants and their maids, of whom there were seven thousand three hundred thirty and seven: and among them were two hundred singing men and singing women. {2:66} Their horses were seven hundred thirty and six; their mules, two hundred forty and five; their camels, four hundred thirty and five; their asses, six thousand seven hundred and twenty. {2:67} And some of the chief of the fathers, when they came to the house of the LORD which is at Jerusalem, offered freely for the house of God to set it up in his place: {2:68} They gave after their ability unto the treasure of the work sixty-one thousand drams of gold, and five thousand pounds of silver, and one hundred priests' garments. {2:69} So the priests, and the Levites, and some of the people, and the singers, and the porters, and the Nethinims, dwelt in their cities, {2:70} and all Israel in their cities.

{3:1} And when the seventh month came, and the children of Israel were in the cities, the people gathered themselves together as one man to Jerusalem. {3:2} Then Jeshua the son of Jozadak, and his brethren the priests, and Zerubbabel the son of Shealtiel, and his brethren, stood up and built the altar of the God of Israel, to offer burnt offerings thereon, as it is written in the law of Moses the man of God. {3:3} And they set the altar upon its bases; for fear was upon them because of the people of those countries: and they offered burnt offerings thereon unto the LORD, even burnt offerings morning and evening. {3:4} They also kept the feast of tabernacles, as it is written, and offered the daily burnt offerings by number, according to the custom, as the duty of every day required; {3:5} And afterward offered the continual burnt offering, both of the new moons, and of all the set feasts of the LORD that were consecrated, and of everyone that willingly offered a freewill offering unto the LORD. {3:6} From the first day of the seventh month they began to offer burnt offerings unto the LORD. But the foundation of the temple of the LORD was not yet laid. {3:7} They also gave money unto the masons, and to the carpenters; and food, and drink, and oil, unto them of Zidon, and to them of Tyre, to bring cedar trees from Lebanon to the sea of Joppa, according to the grant that they had from Cyrus king of Persia. {3:8} Now in the second year of their coming unto the house of God at Jerusalem, in the second month, Zerubbabel the son of Shealtiel, and Jeshua the son of Jozadak, and the remnant of their brethren the priests and the Levites, and all they that were come out of the captivity unto Jerusalem; appointed the Levites, from twenty years old and upward, to set forward the work of the house of the LORD. {3:9} Then Jeshua with his sons and his brethren, Kadmiel and his sons, the sons of Judah, together, to set forward the workmen in the house of God: the sons of Henadad, with their sons and their brethren the Levites. {3:10} And when the builders laid the foundation of the temple of the LORD, they set the priests in their apparel with trumpets, and the Levites the sons of Asaph with cymbals, to praise the LORD, after the ordinance of David king of Israel. {3:11} **And they sang together by course in praising and giving thanks unto the LORD; because he is good, for his mercy endureth forever toward Israel. And all the people shouted with a great shout, when they praised the LORD, because the foundation of the house of the LORD was laid.** {3:12} But many of the priests and Levites and chief of the fathers, who were ancient men, that had seen the first house, when the foundation of this house was laid before their eyes, wept with a loud voice; and many shouted aloud for joy: {3:13} So that the people could not discern the noise of the shout of joy from the noise of the weeping of the people: for the people shouted with a loud shout, and the noise was heard afar off.

{4:1} When the adversaries of Judah and Benjamin heard that the children of the captivity were building the temple to the LORD God of Israel; {4:2} They came to Zerubbabel and the chief of the fathers, saying, "Let us build with you, for we seek your God as you do, and we have sacrificed to him since the days of Esarhaddon king of Assyria, who brought us here." {4:3} But Zerubbabel, Jeshua, and the chief of the fathers of Israel replied, "You have nothing to do with us in building a house to our God; but we ourselves together will build to the LORD God of Israel, as king Cyrus of Persia commanded us." {4:4} Then the people of the land weakened the hands of the people of Judah, and troubled them in building, {4:5} And hired counselors against them to frustrate their purpose, all the days of Cyrus king of Persia, even until the reign of Darius king of Persia. {4:6} And in the reign of Ahasuerus, in the beginning of his reign, they wrote an accusation against the inhabitants of Judah and Jerusalem. {4:7} And in the days of Artaxerxes wrote Bishlam, Mithredath, Tabeel, and the rest of their companions, to Artaxerxes king of Persia; and the letter was written in the Syrian language and interpreted in the Syrian language. {4:8} Rehum the chancellor and Shimshai the scribe wrote a letter against Jerusalem to Artaxerxes the king in this way: {4:9} Then Rehum the chancellor, Shimshai the scribe, and their companions, the Dinaites, the Apharsathchites, the Tarpelites, the Apharsites, the Archevites, the Babylonians, the Susanchites, the Dehavites, and the Elamites, {4:10} And the rest of the nations whom the great and noble Asnapper brought over and settled in the cities of Samaria, and the rest that are on this side of the river, and at such a time. {4:11} This is the copy of the letter that they sent to Artaxerxes the king: Your servants, the men on this side of the river, and at such a time. {4:12} Let it be known to the king that the Jews who came up from you to us have come to Jerusalem, building the rebellious and bad city, and have set up its walls and joined the foundations. {4:13} Now if this city is built and the walls are set up again, they will not pay toll, tribute, and custom, and you will damage the revenue of the kings. {4:14} Therefore, because we have maintenance from the king's palace, and it was not proper for us to see the king dishonored, we have sent and informed the king, {4:15} That a search may be made in the book of the records of your fathers. So you will find in the book of the records and know that this city is a rebellious city, hurtful to kings and provinces, and that they have stirred up sedition within it of old time. For this cause, this city was destroyed. {4:16} We inform the king that if this city is built again and its walls are set up, by this means you will have no portion on this side of the river. {4:17} Then the king sent an answer to Rehum the chancellor, Shimshai the scribe, and their companions who dwell in Samaria, and to the rest beyond the river, saying, "Peace, and at such a time." {4:18} The letter which you sent to us has been read before me. {4:19} And I commanded, and search has been made, and it is found that this city of old time has made insurrection against kings, and rebellion and sedition have been made

therein. {4:20} There have been mighty kings also over Jerusalem, who have ruled over all countries beyond the river; and toll, tribute, and custom were paid to them. {4:21} Now, give commandment to cause these men to cease, and let this city not be built until another commandment shall be given from me. {4:22} Take heed now that you do not fail to do this. Why should damage grow to the hurt of the kings? {4:23} Now when the copy of king Artaxerxes' letter was read before Rehum, Shimshai the scribe, and their companions, they went up in haste to Jerusalem to the Jews, and made them cease by force and power. {4:24} Then the work of the house of God which is at Jerusalem ceased. So it ceased until the second year of the reign of Darius king of Persia.

{5:1} Then the prophets, Haggai the prophet, and Zechariah the son of Iddo, prophesied to the Jews who were in Judah and Jerusalem in the name of the God of Israel. {5:2} So Zerubbabel the son of Shealtiel and Jeshua the son of Jozadak began to build the house of God in Jerusalem, and the prophets of God were helping them. {5:3} At the same time, Tatnai, the governor on this side of the river, and Shethar-boznai, and their companions, came to them and said, "Who has commanded you to build this house and make up this wall?" {5:4} They replied, "What are the names of the men who are making this building?" {5:5} But the eye of their God was upon the elders of the Jews, so they could not cause them to cease until the matter came to Darius. Then they returned an answer by letter concerning this matter. {5:6} The copy of the letter that Tatnai, the governor on this side of the river, and Shethar-boznai, and his companions the Apharsachites, who were on this side of the river, sent to Darius the king, was written thus: {5:7} "To Darius the king, all peace. {5:8} Be it known to the king that we went into the province of Judea, to the house of the great God, which is built with great stones, and timber is laid in the walls, and this work goes fast on and prospers in their hands. {5:9} Then we asked those elders, and said to them, 'Who commanded you to build this house and make up these walls?' {5:10} We asked for their names also, to certify to you that we might write the names of the men who are the chief of them. {5:11} And thus they returned us an answer, saying, 'We are the servants of the God of heaven and earth, and we are building the house that was built many years ago, which a great king of Israel built and set up. {5:12} But after our fathers provoked the God of heaven to wrath, he gave them into the hand of Nebuchadnezzar the king of Babylon, the Chaldean, who destroyed this house and carried the people away into Babylon. {5:13} But in the first year of Cyrus the king of Babylon, the same king Cyrus made a decree to build this house of God. {5:14} And the vessels of gold and silver of the house of God, which Nebuchadnezzar took out of the temple that was in Jerusalem and brought them into the temple of Babylon, those Cyrus the king took out of the temple of Babylon, and they were delivered to Sheshbazzar, whom he made governor. {5:15} And he said to him, 'Take these vessels, go, carry them into the temple that is in Jerusalem, and let the house of God be built in his place.' {5:16} Then Sheshbazzar laid the foundation of the house of God in Jerusalem, and since that time, even until now, it has been in building, and yet it is not finished. {5:17} Now therefore, if it seems good to the king, let there be search made in the king's treasure house, which is there at Babylon, whether it is so, that a decree was made by Cyrus the king to build this house of God at Jerusalem, and let the king send his pleasure to us concerning this matter."

{6:1} Then King Darius made a decree, and a search was made in the house of the rolls where the treasures were kept in Babylon. {6:2} And there was found at Achmetha, in the palace in the province of the Medes, a scroll, and therein was a record thus written: {6:3} "In the first year of Cyrus the king, Cyrus the king made a decree concerning the house of God at Jerusalem: Let the house be built, the place where they offered sacrifices, and let its foundations be strongly laid; its height sixty cubits, and its breadth sixty cubits, {6:4} with three rows of great stones, and a row of new timber; and let the expenses be given out of the king's house. {6:5} And also let the golden and silver vessels of the house of God, which Nebuchadnezzar took out of the temple in Jerusalem and brought unto Babylon, be restored and brought again unto the temple in Jerusalem, each to its place, and placed in the house of God. {6:6} Now therefore, Tatnai, governor beyond the river, Shethar-boznai, and your companions the Apharsachites, who are beyond the river, keep away from there. {6:7} Let the work of this house of God alone; let the governor of the Jews and the elders of the Jews build this house of God in its place. {6:8} Moreover, I make a decree as to what you shall do for the elders of these Jews for the building of this house of God: from the king's goods, even from the tribute beyond the river, expenses shall be given to these men, so that they are not hindered. {6:9} And whatever they need, both young bullocks, rams, and lambs for the burnt offerings of the God of heaven, wheat, salt, wine, and oil, according to the appointment of the priests who are in Jerusalem, let it be given to them day by day without fail.

{6:10} That they may offer sacrifices of sweet savors unto the God of heaven, and pray for the life of the king and his sons. {6:11} Also, I have made a decree that whoever shall alter this word, let timber be pulled down from his house, and being set up, let him be hanged thereon; and let his house be made a dunghill for this. {6:12} And may the God whose name dwells there destroy all kings and people who shall put their hand to alter and to destroy this house of God which is at Jerusalem. I, Darius, have made a decree; let it be done with speed. {6:13} Then Tatnai, governor on this side of the river, Shethar-boznai, and their companions, according to what Darius the king had sent, so they did speedily. {6:14} And the elders of the Jews built, and they prospered through the prophesying of Haggai the prophet and Zechariah the son of Iddo. And they built and finished it according to the commandment of the God of Israel, and according to the commandment of Cyrus, Darius, and Artaxerxes king of Persia. {6:15} And this house was finished on the third day of the month Adar, which was in the sixth year of the reign of Darius the king. {6:16} And the children of Israel, the priests, and the Levites, and the rest of the children of the captivity, kept the dedication of this house of God with joy, {6:17} and offered at the dedication of this house of God a hundred bullocks, two hundred rams, four hundred lambs; and for a sin offering for all Israel, twelve he-goats, according to the number of the tribes of Israel. {6:18} And they set the priests in their divisions, and the Levites in their courses, for the service of God, which is at Jerusalem, as it is written in the book of Moses. {6:19} And the children of the captivity kept the Passover on the fourteenth day of the first month. {6:20} For the priests and the Levites were purified together, all of them were pure, and killed the Passover for all the children of the captivity, and for their brethren the priests, and for themselves. {6:21} And the children of Israel, who had come again out of captivity, and all who had separated themselves unto them from the filthiness of the heathen of the land, to seek the LORD God of Israel, did eat, {6:22} and kept the feast of unleavened bread seven days with joy; for the LORD had made them joyful, and turned the heart of the king of Assyria unto them, to strengthen their hands in the work of the house of God, the God of Israel.

{7:1} Now after these things, in the reign of Artaxerxes king of Persia, Ezra the son of Seraiah, the son of Azariah, the son of Hilkiah, {7:2} The son of Shallum, the son of Zadok, the son of Ahitub, {7:3} The son of Amariah, the son of Azariah, the son of Meraioth, {7:4} The son of Zerahiah, the son of Uzzi, the son of Bukki, {7:5} The son of Abishua, the son of Phinehas, the son of Eleazar, the son of Aaron the chief priest: {7:6} **This Ezra went up from Babylon; and he was a ready scribe in the law of Moses, which the LORD God of Israel had given; and the king granted him all his request, according to the hand of the LORD his God upon him.** {7:7} And some of the children of Israel, and of the priests, and the Levites, and the singers, and the porters, and the Nethinims, went up to Jerusalem, in the seventh year of Artaxerxes the king. {7:8} And he came to Jerusalem in the fifth month, which was in the seventh year of the king. {7:9} For upon the first day of the first month began he to go up from Babylon, and on the first day of the fifth month came he to Jerusalem, according to the good hand of his God upon him. {7:10} **For Ezra had prepared his heart to seek the law of the LORD, and to do it, and to teach in Israel statutes and judgments.** {7:11} Now this is the copy of the letter that King Artaxerxes gave unto Ezra the priest, the scribe, even a scribe of the words of the commandments of the LORD, and of his statutes to Israel: {7:12} Artaxerxes, king of kings, unto Ezra the priest, a scribe of the law of the God of heaven, perfect peace, and at such a time. {7:13} I make a decree, that all they of the people of Israel, and of his priests and Levites, in my realm, who are minded of their own freewill to go up to Jerusalem, go with thee. {7:14} Forasmuch as thou art sent of the king, and of his seven counsellors, to inquire concerning Judah and Jerusalem, according to the law of thy God which is in thine hand; {7:15} And to carry the silver and gold, which the king and his counsellors have freely offered unto the God of Israel, whose habitation is in Jerusalem, {7:16} And all the silver and gold that thou canst find in all the province of Babylon, with the freewill offering of the people, and of the priests, offering willingly for the house of their God which is in Jerusalem: {7:17} That thou mayest buy speedily with this money bullocks, rams, lambs, with their meat offerings and their drink offerings, and offer them upon the altar of the house of your God which is in Jerusalem. {7:18} And whatsoever shall seem good to thee, and to thy brethren, to do with the rest of the silver and the gold, that do after the will of your God. {7:19} The vessels also that are given thee for the service of the house of thy God, those deliver thou before the God of Jerusalem. {7:20} And whatsoever more shall be needful for the house of thy God, which thou shalt have occasion to bestow, bestow it out of the king's treasure house. {7:21} And I, even I Artaxerxes the king, do make a decree to all the treasurers which are beyond the river, that whatsoever Ezra the priest, the scribe of the law of the God of heaven, shall require of you, it be done speedily, {7:22} Unto an hundred talents of silver, and to an hundred measures of wheat, and to an hundred baths of wine, and to an hundred baths of oil, and salt without prescribing how much. {7:23} Whatsoever is commanded by the God of heaven, let it be diligently done for the house of the God of heaven: for why should there be wrath against the realm of the king and his sons? {7:24} Also we certify you, that touching any of the priests and Levites, singers, porters, Nethinims, or ministers of this house of God, it shall not be lawful to impose toll, tribute, or custom, upon them. {7:25} And thou, Ezra, after the wisdom of thy God, that is in thine hand, set magistrates and judges, which may judge all the people that are beyond the river, all such as know the laws of thy God; and teach ye them that know them not. {7:26} And whosoever will not do the law of thy God, and the law of the king, let judgment be executed speedily upon him, whether it be unto death, or to banishment, or to confiscation of goods, or to imprisonment. {7:27} **Blessed be the LORD God of our fathers, which hath put such a thing as this in the king's heart, to beautify the house of the LORD which is in Jerusalem:** {7:28} And hath extended mercy unto me before the king, and his counsellors, and before all the king's mighty princes. And I was strengthened as the hand of the LORD my God was upon me, and I gathered together out of Israel chief men to go up with me.

{8:1} These are now the chief of their fathers, and this is the genealogy of them that went up with me from Babylon, in the reign of Artaxerxes the king. {8:2} Of the sons of Phinehas: Gershom. Of the sons of Ithamar: Daniel. Of the sons of David: Hattush. {8:3} Of the sons of Shechaniah, of the sons of Pharosh: Zechariah; and with him were reckoned by genealogy of the males an hundred and fifty. {8:4} Of the sons of Pahath-moab: Elihoenai the son of Zerahiah, and with him two hundred males. {8:5} Of the sons of Shechaniah: the son of Jahaziel, and with him three hundred males. {8:6} Of the sons also of Adin: Ebed the son of Jonathan, and with him fifty males. {8:7} And of the sons of Elam: Jeshaiah the son of Athaliah, and with him seventy males. {8:8} And of the sons of Shephatiah: Zebadiah the son of Michael, and with him fourscore males. {8:9} Of the sons of Joab: Obadiah the son of Jehiel, and with him two hundred and eighteen males. {8:10} And of the sons of Shelomith: the son of Josiphiah, and with him an hundred and threescore males. {8:11} And of the sons of Bebai: Zechariah the son of Bebai, and with him twenty and eight males. {8:12} And of the sons of Azgad: Johanan the son of Hakkatan, and with him an hundred and ten males. {8:13} And of the last sons of Adonikam, whose names are these, Eliphelet, Jeiel, and Shemaiah, and with them threescore males. {8:14} Of the sons also of Bigvai: Uthai, and Zabbud, and with them seventy males. {8:15} And I gathered them together to the river that runneth to Ahava; and there abode we in tents three days: and I viewed the people, and the priests, and found there none of the sons of Levi. {8:16} Then sent I for Eliezer, for Ariel, for Shemaiah, and for Elnathan, and for Jarib, and for Elnathan, and for Nathan, and for Zechariah, and for Meshullam, chief men; also for Joiarib, and for Elnathan, men of understanding. {8:17} And I sent them with commandment unto Iddo the chief at the place Casiphia, and I told them what they should say unto Iddo, and to his brethren the Nethinims, at the place Casiphia, that they should bring unto us ministers for the house of our God. {8:18} And by the good hand of our God upon us they brought us a man of understanding, of the sons of Mahli, the son of Levi, the son of Israel; and Sherebiah, with his sons and his brethren, eighteen; {8:19} And Hashabiah, and with him Jeshaiah of the sons of Merari, his brethren and their sons, twenty; {8:20} Also of the Nethinims, whom David and the princes had appointed for the service of the Levites, two hundred and twenty Nethinims: all of them were expressed by name. {8:21} Then I proclaimed a fast there, at the river of Ahava, that we might afflict ourselves before our God, to seek of him a right way for us, and for our little ones, and for all our substance. {8:22} For I was ashamed to require of the king a band of soldiers and horsemen to help us against the enemy in the way: because we had spoken unto the king, saying, The hand of our God is upon all them for good that seek him; but his power and his wrath is against all them that forsake him. {8:23} So we fasted and besought our God for this: and he was intreated of us. {8:24} Then I separated twelve of the chief of the priests, Sherebiah, Hashabiah, and ten of their brethren with them, {8:25} And weighed unto them the silver, and the gold, and the vessels, even the offering of the house of our God, which the king, and his counsellors, and his lords, and all Israel there present, had offered: {8:26} I even weighed unto their hand six hundred and fifty talents of silver, and silver vessels an hundred talents, and of gold an hundred talents; {8:27} Also twenty basons of gold, of a thousand drams; and two vessels of fine copper, precious as gold. {8:28} And I said unto them, Ye are holy unto the LORD; the vessels are holy also; and the silver and the gold are a freewill offering unto the LORD God of your fathers. {8:29} Watch ye, and keep them, until ye weigh them before the chief of the priests and the Levites, and chief of the fathers of Israel, at Jerusalem, in the chambers of the house of the LORD. {8:30} So took the priests and the Levites the weight of the silver, and the gold, and the vessels, to bring them to Jerusalem unto the house of our God. {8:31} Then we departed from the river of Ahava on the twelfth day of the first month, to go unto Jerusalem: and the hand of our God was upon us, and he delivered us from the hand of the enemy, and of such as lay in wait by the way. {8:32} And we came to Jerusalem, and abode there three days. {8:33} Now on the fourth day was the silver and the gold and the vessels weighed in the house of our God by the hand of Meremoth the son of Uriah the priest; and with him was Eleazar the son of Phinehas; and with them was Jozabad the son of Jeshua, and Noadiah the son of Binnui, Levites; {8:34} By number and by weight of every one: and all the weight was written at that time. {8:35} Also the children of those that had been carried away, which were come out of the captivity, offered burnt offerings unto the God of Israel, twelve bullocks for all Israel, ninety and six rams, seventy and seven lambs, twelve he goats for a sin offering: all this was a burnt offering unto the LORD. {8:36} And they delivered the king's commissions unto the king's lieutenants, and to the governors on this side the river: and they furthered the people, and the house of God.

{9:1} Now when these things were done, the princes came to me, saying, "The people of Israel, and the priests, and the Levites, have not separated themselves from the people of the lands, doing according to their abominations, even of the Canaanites, the Hittites, the Perizzites, the Jebusites, the Ammonites, the Moabites, the Egyptians, and the Amorites. {9:2} For they have taken of their daughters for themselves, and for their sons: so that the holy seed have mingled themselves with the people of those lands: yea, the hand of the princes and rulers hath been chief in this trespass. {9:3} And when I heard this thing, I rent my garment and my mantle, and plucked off the hair of my head and of my beard, and sat down astonied. {9:4} Then were assembled unto me every one that trembled at the words of the God of Israel, because of the transgression of those that had been carried away; and I sat astonied until the evening sacrifice. {9:5} And at the evening sacrifice I arose up from my heaviness; and having rent my garment and my mantle, I fell upon my knees, and spread out my hands unto the LORD my God. {9:6} And said, O my God, I am ashamed and blush to lift up my face to thee, my God: for our iniquities are increased over our head, and our trespass is grown up unto the heavens. {9:7} Since the days of our fathers have we been in a great trespass unto this day; and for our iniquities have we, our kings, and our priests, been delivered into the hand of the kings of the lands, to the sword, to captivity, and to a spoil, and to confusion of face, as it is this day. {9:8} **And now for a little space grace hath been shewed from the LORD our God, to leave us a remnant to escape, and to give us a nail in his holy place, that our God may lighten our eyes, and give us a little reviving in our bondage.** {9:9} For we were bondmen; yet our God hath not forsaken us in our bondage, but hath extended mercy unto us in the sight of the kings of Persia, to give us a reviving, to set up the house of our God, and to repair the desolations thereof, and to give us a wall in Judah and in Jerusalem. {9:10} And now, O our God, what shall we say after this? for we have forsaken thy commandments, {9:11} Which thou hast commanded by thy servants the prophets, saying, The land, unto which ye go to possess it, is an unclean land with the filthiness of the people of the lands, with their abominations, which have filled it from one end to another with their uncleanness. {9:12} Now therefore give not your daughters unto their sons, neither take their daughters unto your sons, nor seek their peace or their wealth for ever: that ye may be strong, and eat the good of the land, and leave it for an inheritance to your children for ever. {9:13} And after all that is come upon us for our evil deeds, and for our great trespass, seeing that thou our God hast punished us less than our iniquities deserve, and hast given us such deliverance as this; {9:14} Should we again break thy commandments, and join in affinity with the people of these abominations? wouldest not thou be angry with us till thou hadst consumed us, so that there should be no remnant nor escaping? {9:15} O LORD God of Israel, thou art righteous: for we remain yet escaped, as it is this day: behold, we are before thee in our trespasses: for we cannot stand before thee because of this.

{10:1} Now when Ezra had prayed, and when he had confessed, weeping and casting himself down before the house of God, there assembled unto him out of Israel a very great congregation of men and women and children: for the people wept very sore. {10:2} And Shechaniah the son of Jehiel, one of the sons of Elam, answered and said unto Ezra, "We have trespassed against our God, and have taken strange wives of the people of the land: yet now there is hope in Israel concerning this thing. {10:3} Now therefore let us make a covenant with our God to put away all the wives, and such as are born of them, according to the counsel of my lord, and of those that tremble at the commandment of our God; and let it be done according to the law. {10:4} **Arise; for this matter belongeth unto thee: we also will be with thee: be of good courage, and do it."** {10:5} Then arose Ezra, and made the chief priests, the Levites, and all Israel, to swear that they should do according to this word. And they sware. {10:6} Then Ezra rose up from before the house of God, and went into the chamber of Johanan the son of Eliashib: and when he came thither, he did eat no bread, nor drink water: for he mourned because of the transgression of them that had been carried away. {10:7} And they made proclamation throughout Judah and Jerusalem unto all the children of the captivity, that they should gather themselves together unto Jerusalem; {10:8} And that whosoever would not come within three days, according to the counsel of the princes and the elders, all his substance should be forfeited, and himself separated from the congregation of those that had been carried away. {10:9} Then all the men of Judah and Benjamin gathered themselves together unto Jerusalem within three days. It was the ninth month, on the twentieth day of the month; and all the people sat in the street of the house of God, trembling because of this matter, and for the great rain. {10:10} And Ezra the priest stood up, and said unto them, "Ye have transgressed, and have taken strange wives, to increase the trespass of Israel. {10:11} Now therefore make confession unto the LORD God of your fathers, and do his pleasure: and separate yourselves from the people of the land, and from the strange wives. {10:12} Then all the congregation answered and said with a loud voice, 'As thou hast said, so must we do.' {10:13} But the people are many, and it is a time of much rain, and we are not able to stand without, neither is this a work of one day or two: for we are many that have transgressed in this thing. {10:14} Let now our rulers of all the congregation stand, and let all them which have taken strange wives in our cities come at appointed times, and with them the elders of every city, and the judges thereof, until the fierce wrath of our God for this matter be turned from us. {10:15} Only Jonathan the son of Asahel and Jahaziah the son of Tikvah were employed about this matter: and Meshullam and Shabbethai the Levite helped them. {10:16} And the children of the captivity did so. And Ezra the priest, with certain chief of the fathers, after the house of their fathers, and all of them by their names, were separated, and sat down in the first day of the tenth month to examine the matter. {10:17} And they made an end with all the men that had taken strange wives by the first day of the first month. {10:18} And among the sons of the priests there were found that had taken strange wives: namely, of the sons of Jeshua the son of Jozadak, and his brethren; Maaseiah, and Eliezer, and Jarib, and Gedaliah. {10:19} And they gave their hands that they would put away their wives; and being guilty, they offered a ram of the flock for their trespass. {10:20} And of the sons of Immer; Hanani, and Zebadiah. {10:21} And of the sons of Harim; Maaseiah, and Elijah, and Shemaiah, and Jehiel, and Uzziah. {10:22} And of the sons of Pashur; Elioenai, Maaseiah, Ishmael, Nethaneel, Jozabad, and Elasah. {10:23} Also of the Levites; Jozabad, and Shimei, and Kelaiah, (the same is Kelita,) Pethahiah, Judah, and Eliezer. {10:24} Of the singers also; Eliashib: and of the porters; Shallum, and Telem, and Uri. {10:25} Moreover of Israel: of the sons of Parosh; Ramiah, and Jeziah, and Malchiah, and Miamin, and Eleazar, and Malchijah, and Benaiah. {10:26} And of the sons of Elam; Mattaniah, Zechariah, and Jehiel, and Abdi, and Jeremoth, and Eliah. {10:27} And of the sons of Zattu; Elioenai, Eliashib, Mattaniah, and Jeremoth, and Zabad, and Aziza. {10:28} Of the sons also of Bebai; Jehohanan, Hananiah, Zabbai, and Athlai. {10:29} And of the sons of Bani; Meshullam, Malluch, and Adaiah, Jashub, and Sheal, and Ramoth. {10:30} And of the sons of Pahath-moab; Adna, and Chelal, Benaiah, Maaseiah, Mattaniah, Bezaleel, and Binnui, and Manasseh. {10:31} And of the sons of Harim; Eliezer, Ishijah, Malchiah, Shemaiah, Shimeon, {10:32} Benjamin, Malluch, and Shemariah. {10:33} Of the sons of Hashum; Mattenai, Mattathah, Zabad, Eliphelet, Jeremai, Manasseh, and Shimei. {10:34} Of the sons of Bani; Maadai, Amram, and Uel, {10:35} Benaiah, Bedeiah, Chelluh, {10:36} Vaniah, Meremoth, Eliashib, {10:37} Mattaniah, Mattenai, and Jaasau, {10:38} And Bani, and Binnui, Shimei, {10:39} And Shelemiah, and Nathan, and Adaiah, {10:40} Machnadebai, Shashai, Sharai, {10:41} Azareel, and Shelemiah, Shemariah, {10:42} Shallum, Amariah, and Joseph. {10:43} Of the sons of Nebo; Jeiel, Mattithiah, Zabad, Zebina, Jadau, and Joel, Benaiah. {10:44} All these had taken strange wives: and some of them had wives by whom they had children.

Nehemiah

{1:1} *The words of Nehemiah the son of Hachaliah. And it came to pass in the month Chisleu, in the twentieth year, as I was in Shushan the palace,* {1:2} That Hanani, one of my brethren, came, he and certain men of Judah; and I asked them concerning the Jews that had escaped, which were left of the captivity, and concerning Jerusalem. {1:3} And they said unto me, "The remnant that are left of the captivity there in the province are in great affliction and reproach: the wall of Jerusalem also is broken down, and the gates thereof are burned with fire. {1:4} And it came to pass, when I heard these words, that I sat down and wept, and mourned certain days, and fasted, and prayed before the God of heaven, {1:5} And said, 'I beseech thee, O LORD God of heaven, the great and terrible God, that keepeth covenant and mercy for them that love him and observe his commandments: {1:6} Let thine ear now be attentive, and thine eyes open, that thou mayest hear the prayer of thy servant, which I pray before thee now, day and night, for the children of Israel thy servants, and confess the sins of the children of Israel, which we have sinned against thee: both I and my father's house have sinned. {1:7} We have dealt very corruptly against thee, and have not kept the commandments, nor the statutes, nor the judgments, which thou commandedst thy servant Moses. {1:8} Remember, I beseech thee, the word that thou commandedst thy servant Moses, saying, 'If ye transgress, I will scatter you abroad among the nations; {1:9} But if ye turn unto me, and keep my commandments, and do them; though there were of you cast out unto the uttermost part of the heaven, yet will I gather them from thence, and will bring them unto the place that I have chosen to set my name there. {1:10} Now these are thy servants and thy people, whom thou hast redeemed by thy great power, and by thy strong hand. {1:11} *O Lord, I beseech thee, let now thine ear be attentive to the prayer of thy servant, and to the prayer of thy servants, who desire to fear thy name: and prosper, I pray thee, thy servant this day, and grant him mercy in the sight of this man. For I was the king's cupbearer.*

{2:1} In the month Nisan, in the twentieth year of King Artaxerxes, wine was before him. I took up the wine and gave it to the king. I had not been sad in his presence before. {2:2} The king asked me, "Why is your face sad? You are not sick. This is nothing but sorrow of heart." Then I was very afraid. {2:3} I said to the king, "May the king live forever! Why should my face not be sad when the city, the place of my fathers' tombs, lies waste, and its gates are burned with fire?" {2:4} The king asked me, "What do you request?" So I prayed to the God of heaven. {2:5} I said to the king, "If it pleases the king, and if your servant has found favor in your sight, send me to Judah, to the city of my fathers' tombs, that I may rebuild it." {2:6} The king, with the queen sitting beside him, asked me, "How long will your journey be, and when will you return?" So it pleased the king to send me, and I set him a time. {2:7} I also said to the king, "If it pleases the king, let letters be given to me for the governors beyond the river, that they may let me pass through until I come to Judah, {2:8} and a letter to Asaph the keeper of the king's forest, that he must give me timber to make beams for the gates of the citadel which pertains to the temple, for the city wall, and for the house that I will occupy." And the king granted them to me according to the good hand of my God upon me. {2:9} Then I went to the governors in the region beyond the River, and gave them the king's letters. Now the king had sent captains of the army and horsemen with me. {2:10} When Sanballat the Horonite and Tobiah the servant, the Ammonite, heard of it, they were deeply disturbed that a man had come to seek the well-being of the children of Israel. {2:11} So I came to Jerusalem and was there three days. {2:12} Then I arose in the night, I and a few men with me; I told no one what my God had put in my heart to do at Jerusalem; nor was there any animal with me, except the one on which I rode. {2:13} And I went out by night through the Valley Gate to the Serpent Well and the Refuse Gate, and viewed the walls of Jerusalem which were broken down and its gates which were burned with fire. {2:14} Then I went on to the Fountain Gate and to the King's Pool, but there was no room for the animal under me to pass. {2:15} So I went up in the night by the valley, and viewed the wall; then I turned back and entered by the Valley Gate, and so returned. {2:16} And the officials did not know where I had gone or what I had done; I had not yet told the Jews, the priests, the nobles, the officials, or the others who did the work. {2:17} Then I said to them, "You see the distress that we are in, how Jerusalem lies waste, and its gates are burned with fire. Come and let us build the wall of Jerusalem, that we may no longer be a reproach." {2:18} *And I told them of the hand of my God which had been good upon me, and also of the king's words that he had spoken to me. So they said, "Let us rise up and build." Then they set their hands to this good work.* {2:19} But when Sanballat the Horonite, Tobiah the Ammonite official, and Geshem the Arab heard of it, they laughed at us and despised us, and said, "What is this thing that you are doing? Will you rebel against the king?" {2:20} So I answered them, and said to them, "The God of heaven Himself will prosper us; therefore we His servants will arise and build, but you have no heritage or right or memorial in Jerusalem."

{3:1} Eliashib the high priest and his fellow priests rose up to rebuild the Sheep Gate. They consecrated it and set up its doors, even to the Tower of Meah they consecrated it, to the Tower of Hananeel. {3:2} Next to them, the men of Jericho built. Next to them, Zaccur the son of Imri built. {3:3} The sons of Hassenaah built the Fish Gate; they laid its beams and set up its doors, its bolts, and its bars. {3:4} Next to them, Meremoth the son of Urijah, the son of Koz, repaired. Next to them, Meshullam the son of Berechiah, the son of Meshezabeel, repaired. Next to them, Zadok the son of Baana repaired. {3:5} Next to them, the Tekoites repaired; but their nobles did not put their shoulders to the work of their Lord. {3:6} Moreover, Jehoiada the son of Paseah and Meshullam the son of Besodeiah repaired the Old Gate; they laid its beams and set up its doors, its bolts, and its bars. {3:7} Next to them, Melatiah the Gibeonite, Jadon the Meronothite, the men of Gibeon, and Mizpah repaired to the throne of the governor on this side of the River. {3:8} Next to him, Uzziel the son of Harhaiah, one of the goldsmiths, repaired. Next to him, Hananiah, one of the perfumers, repaired; and they fortified Jerusalem as far as the Broad Wall. {3:9} Next to them, Rephaiah the son of Hur, ruler of the half district of Jerusalem, repaired. {3:10} Next to them, Jedaiah the son of Harumaph made repairs in front of his house. And next to him, Hattush the son of Hashabneiah made repairs. {3:11} Malchijah the son of Harim and Hasshub the son of Pahath-moab repaired another section, as well as the Tower of the Ovens. {3:12} Next to him, Shallum the son of Hallohesh, ruler of the half district of Jerusalem, repaired, he and his daughters. {3:13} The Valley Gate was repaired by Hanun, and the inhabitants of Zanoah; they built it, hung its doors with its bolts and bars, and repaired a thousand cubits of the wall as far as the Refuse Gate. {3:14} Malchijah the son of Rechab, ruler of the district of Beth-haccerem, repaired the Refuse Gate; he built it and hung its doors with its bolts and bars. {3:15} Shallun the son of Col-hozeh, leader of the district of Mizpah, repaired the Fountain Gate; he built it, covered it, hung its doors with its bolts and bars, and repaired the wall of the Pool of Shelah by the King's Garden, as far as the stairs that go down from the City of David. {3:16} After him, Nehemiah the son of Azbuk, leader of half the district of Beth Zur, made repairs as far as the place in front of the tombs of David, to the man-made pool, and as far as the House of the Mighty. {3:17} After him, the Levites under Rehum the son of Bani made repairs. Next to him, Hashabiah, leader of half the district of Keilah, made repairs for his district. {3:18} After him, their brethren under Bavai the son of Henadad, leader of the other half of the district of Keilah, made repairs. {3:19} And next to him, Ezer the son of Jeshua, leader of Mizpah, repaired another section in front of the Ascent to the Armory at the buttress. {3:20} After him, Baruch the son of Zabbai carefully repaired the other section, from the buttress to the door of the house of Eliashib the high priest. {3:21} After him, Meremoth the son of Urijah, the son of Koz, repaired another section, from the door of the house of Eliashib to the end of the house of Eliashib. {3:22} And after him, the priests, the men of the plain, made repairs. {3:23} After him, Benjamin and Hasshub made repairs opposite their house. After them, Azariah the son of Maaseiah, the son of Ananiah, made repairs by his house. {3:24} After him, Binnui the son of Henadad repaired another section, from the house of Azariah to the buttress, even as far as the corner. {3:25} Palal the son of Uzai made repairs opposite the buttress and on the tower which projects from the king's upper house that was by the court of the prison. After him, Pedaiah the son of Parosh made repairs. {3:26} Moreover the Nethinims dwelt in Ophel, as far as the place opposite the Water Gate toward the east, and the projecting tower. {3:27} After them the Tekoites repaired another section, opposite the great projecting tower as far as the wall of Ophel. {3:28} Beyond the Horse Gate the priests made repairs, each in front of his own house. {3:29} After them Zadok the son of Immer made repairs in front of his own house. After him Shemaiah the son of Shechaniah, the keeper of the East Gate, made repairs. {3:30} *After him, Hananiah the son of Shelemiah, and Hanun, the sixth son of Zalaph, repaired another section. After him, Meshullam the son of Berechiah made repairs in front of his dwelling.* {3:31} After him, Malchijah, one of the goldsmiths, made repairs as far as the house of the Nethinim and of the merchants, opposite the Miphkad Gate, and to the upper room at the corner. {3:32} And between the upper room at the corner and the Sheep Gate, the goldsmiths and the merchants made repairs.

{4:1} When Sanballat heard that we were rebuilding the wall, he became furious and filled with indignation. He mocked the Jews. {4:2} He spoke in the presence of his brethren and the army of Samaria, saying, "What are these feeble Jews doing? Will they fortify themselves? Will they offer sacrifices? Will they complete it in a day? Will they revive the stones from the heaps of rubble, even though they are burned?" {4:3} Tobiah the Ammonite was beside him and said, "Whatever they build, if even a fox goes up on it, he will break down their stone wall." {4:4} So we prayed to our God and set a watch against them day and night because of them. {4:5} Judah said, "The strength of the laborers is failing, and there is so much rubble that we are unable to rebuild the wall." {4:6} Our adversaries said, "They will not know or see anything until we come among them and kill them and stop the work." {4:7} But when Sanballat, Tobiah, the Arabs, the Ammonites, and the Ashdodites heard that the repair of the walls of Jerusalem was progressing and that the breaches were beginning to be closed, they became furious. {4:8} They all conspired together to come and fight against Jerusalem and cause a disturbance. {4:9} Nevertheless, we prayed to our God and set up a guard against them day and night. {4:10} Meanwhile, Judah said, "The strength of the laborers is failing, and there is so much rubble that we are unable to rebuild the wall." {4:11} Our enemies said, "They will not know or see anything until we come among them and kill them and stop the work." {4:12} The Jews who lived near them came to us ten times, saying, "From every place where you turn, they will attack us." {4:13} So I stationed people behind the lowest parts of the wall, at the openings; and I stationed the people by families with their swords, spears, and bows. {4:14} After I looked things over, I stood up and said to the nobles, the officials, and the rest of the people, "Do not be afraid of them. Remember the Lord, who is great and awesome, and fight for your families, your sons and your daughters, your wives and your homes." {4:15} When our enemies heard that their plot had been revealed and that God had frustrated their plans, we all returned to the wall, each to his own work. {4:16} From that day on, half of my men did the work, while the other half were equipped with spears, shields, bows, and armor. The leaders stood behind the whole house of Judah {4:17} Those who built on the wall and those who carried burdens loaded themselves so that everyone worked with one hand and held a weapon with the other. {4:18} Every builder had his sword strapped to his side as he built. The trumpeter stayed beside me. {4:19} I said to the nobles, the officials, and the rest of the people, "The work is extensive and spread out, and we are widely separated from each other on the wall. {4:20} Wherever you hear the sound of the trumpet, rally to us there. Our God will fight for us!" {4:21} So we continued the work with half holding spears from the break of dawn until the stars came out. {4:22} At that time, I also said to the people, "Let each man and his servant stay inside Jerusalem at night, so that they may act as guards by night and workers by day." {4:23} So neither I, nor my brothers, nor my servants, nor the men of the guard who followed me, took off our clothes; each kept his weapon at his right hand.

{5:1} There was a great outcry from the people and their wives against their fellow Jews. {5:2} Some were saying, "We, our sons, and our daughters are many; so let us get grain, that we may eat and live." {5:3} Others were saying, "We have mortgaged our fields, vineyards, and houses to buy grain because of the famine." {5:4} Still others were saying, "We have borrowed money for the king's tax against our fields and vineyards. {5:5} Yet now our flesh is as the flesh of our brethren, our children as their children; and indeed we are forcing our sons and our daughters to be slaves, and some of our daughters have been brought into slavery. It is not in our power to redeem them, for other men have our lands and vineyards." {5:6} When I heard their outcry and these words, I was very angry. {5:7} After serious thought, I rebuked the nobles and rulers, and said to them, "Each of you is exacting usury from his brother." So I called a great assembly against them. {5:8} And I said to them, "According to our ability we have redeemed our Jewish brethren who were sold to the nations. Now indeed, will you even sell your brethren? Or should they be sold to us?" Then they were silenced and found nothing to say. {5:9} Then I said, "What you are doing is not good. Should you not walk in the fear of our God because of the reproach of the nations, our enemies? {5:10} I also, with my brethren and my servants, am lending them money and grain. Please, let us stop this usury! {5:11} Restore now to them, even this day, their fields, their vineyards, their olive groves, and their houses, also a hundredth of the money and the grain, the new wine and the oil, that you have charged them." {5:12} So they said, "We will restore it, and will require nothing from them; we will do as you say." Then I called the priests, and required an oath from them that they would do according to this promise. {5:13} Then I shook out the fold of my garment and said, "So may God shake out each man from his house, and from his property, who does not perform this promise. Even thus may he be shaken out and emptied." And all the assembly said, "Amen!" and praised the Lord. Then the people did according to this promise. {5:14} Moreover, from the time that I was appointed to be their governor in the land of Judah, from the twentieth year until the thirty-second year of King Artaxerxes, twelve years, neither I nor my brothers ate the governor's provisions. {5:15} But the former governors who were before me laid burdens on the people, and took from them bread and wine, besides forty shekels of silver. Yes, even their servants bore rule over the people, but I did not do so, because of the fear of God. {5:16} Indeed, I also continued the work on this wall, and we did not buy any land. All my servants were gathered there for the work. {5:17} And at my table were one hundred and fifty Jews and rulers, besides those who came to us from the nations around us. {5:18} Now that which was prepared daily was one ox and six choice sheep. Also fowl were prepared for me, and once every ten days an abundance of all kinds of wine. Yet in spite of this I did not demand the governor's provisions, because the bondage was heavy on this people. {5:19} Remember me, my God, for good, according to all that I have done for this people.

{6:1} It happened that when Sanballat, Tobiah, Geshem the Arabian, and our other enemies heard that I had finished building the wall and that there were no more breaks in it (although at that time I had not yet installed the doors in the gates), {6:2} Sanballat and Geshem sent me a message, saying, "Come, let us meet together in one of the villages in the plain of Ono." But they were planning to harm me. {6:3} So I sent messengers back to them, saying, "I am doing important work and cannot come down. Why should the work stop while I leave it and come down to meet with you?" {6:4} They sent me the same message four times, and each time I gave them the same answer. {6:5} Then Sanballat sent his servant to me in the same way for the fifth time, carrying an open letter in his hand. {6:6} In it was written, "It is reported among the nations, and Gashmu confirms it, that you and the Jews are planning to rebel, and that is why you are rebuilding the wall. And according to these reports, you wish to become their king. {6:7} You have also appointed prophets to proclaim in Jerusalem about you, saying, 'There is a king in Judah!' Now these matters will be reported to the king. So come, let us confer together." {6:8} But I sent a message back to him, saying, "None of these things you are saying are true. You are making them up in your own mind." {6:9} **For they were all trying to frighten us, thinking, "Their hands will get too weak for the work, and it will not be completed." But now, my God, strengthen my hands.** {6:10} Later, I went to the house of Shemaiah the son of Delaiah, the son of Mehetabel, who was confined at home. He said, "Let us meet together in the house of God, inside the temple, and let us close the temple doors, because men are coming to kill you—by night they are coming to kill you." {6:11} But I said, "Should a man like me run away? Or should someone like me go into the temple to save his life? I will not go!" {6:12} I realized that God had not sent him, but that he had prophesied against me because Tobiah and Sanballat had hired him. {6:13} He had been hired to intimidate me so that I would commit a sin by doing this, and then they would have a shameful story to use against me. {6:14} Remember, my God, Tobiah and Sanballat according to these their actions, and also Noadiah the prophetess and the other prophets who tried to intimidate me. {6:15} So the wall was completed on the twenty-fifth day of Elul in fifty-two days. {6:16} When all our enemies heard about it, and all the surrounding nations saw it, they lost their confidence, for they realized that this work had been accomplished with the help of our God. {6:17} Moreover, during those days the nobles of Judah kept sending many letters to Tobiah, and his letters came to them. {6:18} For many in Judah were bound by oath to him, because he was the son-in-law of Shecaniah the son of Arah, and his son Jehohanan had married the daughter of Meshullam the son of Berechiah. {6:19} Also they spoke of his good deeds in my presence, and reported my words to him. And Tobiah sent letters to intimidate me.

{7:1} After the wall was built and the doors were installed, I appointed gatekeepers, singers, and Levites. {7:2} I entrusted the supervision of Jerusalem to my brother Hanani, along with Hananiah, the commander of the fortress, because he was a faithful man who feared God more than many others. {7:3} I instructed them, "Do not open the gates of Jerusalem until the sun is hot. While the gatekeepers are still on duty, have them shut the doors and bar them. Also, appoint residents of Jerusalem to serve as guards, each at their designated posts and each in front of their own homes." {7:4} Now the city was large and spacious, but there were few people in it, and the houses had not yet been rebuilt. {7:5} Then God put it into my heart to assemble the nobles, the officials, and the people to be registered by genealogy. I found the genealogical record of those who had first returned, and I found written in it: {7:6} "These are the people of the province who came up from the captivity of the exiles, whom Nebuchadnezzar king of Babylon had taken captive and who returned to Jerusalem and Judah, each to his own town. {7:7} They came with Zerubbabel, Joshua, Nehemiah, Azariah, Raamiah, Nahamani, Mordecai, Bilshan, Mispereth, Bigvai, Nehum, and Baanah." {7:8} The list of the men of Israel: {7:9} Parosh: 2,172 {7:10} Shephatiah: 372 {7:11} Arah: 652 {7:12} Pahath-Moab (descendants of Jeshua and Joab): 2,818 {7:13} Elam: 1,254 {7:14} Zattu: 845 {7:15} Zaccai: 760 {7:16} Binnui: 648 {7:17} Bebai: 628 {7:18} Azgad: 2,322 {7:19} Adonikam: 667 {7:20} Bigvai: 2,067 {7:21} Adin: 655 {7:22} Ater (descendants of Hezekiah): 98 {7:23} Hashum: 328 {7:24} Bezai: 324 {7:25} Hariph: 112 {7:26} Gibeon: 95 {7:27} Bethlehem and Netophah: 188 {7:28} Anathoth: 128 {7:29} Beth Azmaveth: 42 {7:30} Kiriath Jearim, Kephirah, and Beeroth: 743 {7:31} Ramah and Geba: 621 {7:32} Micmash: 122 {7:33} Bethel and Ai: 123 {7:34} Nebo: 52 {7:35} Elam (another group): 1,254 {7:36} Harim: 320 {7:37} Jericho: 345 {7:38} Lod, Hadid, and Ono: 721 {7:39} Senaah: 3,930 {7:39} The priests: the descendants of Jedaiah, belonging to the house of Jeshua, numbered 973. {7:40} The descendants of Immer totaled 1,052. {7:41} The descendants of Pashhur numbered 1,247. {7:42} The descendants of Harim numbered 1,017. {7:43} The Levites: the descendants of Jeshua and Kadmiel, along with the descendants of Hodaviah, numbered 74. {7:44} The singers: the descendants of Asaph numbered 148. {7:45} The gatekeepers: the descendants of Shallum, Ater, Talmon, Akkub, Hatita, and Shobai totaled 138. {7:46} The temple servants: the descendants of Ziha, Hashupha, Tabbaoth, {7:47} Keros, Sia, Padon, {7:48} Lebana, Hagaba, Shalmai, {7:49} Hanan, Giddel, Gahar, {7:50} Reaiah, Rezin, Nekoda, {7:51} Gazzam, Uzza, Phaseah, {7:52} Besai, Meunim, Nephushesim, {7:53} Bakbuk, Hakupha, Harhur, {7:54} Bazlith, Mehida, Harsha, {7:55} Barkos, Sisera, Temah, {7:56} Neziah, Hatipha. {7:57} The descendants of the servants of Solomon: the descendants of Sotai, Sophereth, Peruda, {7:58} Jaala, Darkon, Giddel, {7:59} Shephatiah, Hattil, Pochereth Hazzebaim, Ami. {7:60} The temple servants and descendants of the servants of Solomon totaled 392. {7:61} These are the ones who came up from Tel Melah, Tel Harsha, Cherub, Addon, and Immer, but they could not show their families or their ancestry, whether they belonged to Israel: {7:62} The descendants of Delaiah, Tobiah, and Nekoda totaled 642. {7:63} And from the priests: the descendants of Hobaiah, Koz, and Barzillai (who had married one of the daughters of Barzillai the Gileadite and was called by their name). {7:64} These searched for their family records, but they could not find them; therefore, they were considered unclean and excluded from the priesthood. {7:65} The governor ordered them not to eat the most holy food until there was a priest who could consult the Urim and Thummim. {7:66} The whole assembly numbered 42,360, {7:67} not including their 7,337 male and female servants; they also had 245 male and female singers. {7:68} They had 736 horses, 245 mules, {7:69} 435 camels, and 6,720 donkeys. {7:70} Some of the heads of the families contributed to the work. The governor gave to the treasury 1,000 drachmas of gold, 50 bowls, and 530 garments for priests. {7:71} Some of the heads of the families gave to the treasury for the work 20,000 drachmas of gold and 2,200 minas of silver. {7:72} The total given by the rest of the people was 20,000 drachmas of gold, 2,000 minas of silver, and 67 garments for priests. {7:73} The priests, the Levites, the gatekeepers, the singers, some of the people, the temple servants, and all Israel settled in their towns. When the seventh month came, the Israelites were in their own towns.

{8:1} All the people gathered together as one in the square before the Water Gate. They asked Ezra the teacher of the Law to bring out the Book of the Law of Moses, which the Lord had given for Israel to obey. {8:2} So on the first day of the seventh month, Ezra the priest brought the Law before the assembly, which included men, women, and all who were old enough to understand. {8:3} He read it aloud from daybreak till noon as he faced the square before the Water Gate in the presence of the men, women, and others who could understand. And all the people listened attentively to the Book of the Law. {8:4} Ezra the teacher of the Law stood on a high wooden platform built for the occasion. Beside him on his right stood Mattithiah, Shema, Anaiah, Uriah, Hilkiah, and Maaseiah, and on his left were Pedaiah, Mishael, Malkijah, Hashum, Hashbaddanah, Zechariah, and Meshullam. {8:5} Ezra opened the book. All the people could see him because he was standing above them; and as he opened it, the people all stood up. {8:6} Ezra praised the Lord, the great God; and all the people lifted their hands and responded, "Amen! Amen!" Then they bowed down and worshiped the Lord with their faces to the ground. {8:7} The Levites—Jeshua, Bani, Sherebiah, Jamin, Akkub, Shabbethai, Hodiah, Maaseiah, Kelita, Azariah, Jozabad, Hanan, and Pelaiah—instructed the people in the Law while the people were standing there. {8:8} They read from the Book of the Law of God, making it clear and giving the meaning so that the people understood what was being read. {8:9} Then Nehemiah the governor, Ezra the priest and teacher of the Law, and the Levites who were instructing the people said to them all, "This day is holy to the Lord your God. Do not mourn or weep." For all the people had been weeping as they listened to the words of the Law. {8:10} **Nehemiah said, "Go and enjoy choice food and sweet drinks, and send some to those who have nothing prepared. This day is holy to our Lord. Do not grieve, for the joy of the Lord is your strength."** {8:11} The Levites calmed all the people, saying, "Be still, for this is a holy day. Do not grieve." {8:12} Then all the people went away to eat and drink, to send portions of food and to celebrate with great joy, because they now understood the words that had been made known to them. {8:13} On the second day of the month, the heads of all the families, along with the priests and the Levites, gathered around Ezra the teacher to give attention to the words of the Law. {8:14} They found written in the Law, which the Lord had commanded through Moses, that the Israelites were to live in temporary shelters during the festival of the seventh month {8:15} and that they should proclaim this word and spread it throughout their towns and in Jerusalem: "Go out into the hill country and bring back branches from olive and wild olive trees, and from myrtles, palms and shade trees, to make temporary shelters"—as it is written. {8:16} So the people went out and brought back branches and built themselves temporary shelters on their own roofs, in their courtyards, in the courts of the house of God and in the square by the Water Gate and the one by the Gate of Ephraim. {8:17} The whole company that had returned from exile built temporary shelters and lived in them. From the days of Joshua son of Nun until that day, the Israelites had not celebrated it like this. And their joy was very great. {8:18} Day after day, from the first day to the last, Ezra read from the Book of the Law of God. They celebrated the festival for seven days, and on the eighth day, in accordance with the regulation, there was an assembly.

{9:1} On the twenty-fourth day of the same month, the Israelites gathered together, fasting and wearing sackcloth and having dust on their heads. {9:2} Those of Israelite descent had separated themselves from all foreigners. They stood in their places and confessed their sins and the sins of their ancestors. {9:3} They stood where they were and read from the Book of the Law of the Lord their God for a quarter of the day, and spent another quarter in confession and in worshiping the Lord their God. {9:4} Standing on the stairs of the Levites were Jeshua, Bani, Kadmiel, Shebaniah, Bunni, Sherebiah, Bani, and Chenani. They cried out loudly to the Lord their God. {9:5} And the Levites—Jeshua, Kadmiel, Bani, Hashabneiah, Sherebiah, Hodiah, Shebaniah, and Pethahiah—said: "Stand up and praise the Lord your God, who is from everlasting to everlasting. Blessed be your glorious name, and may it be exalted above all blessing and praise. {9:6} You alone are the Lord. You made the heavens, even the highest heavens, and all their starry host, the earth and all that is on it, the seas and all that is in them. You give life to everything, and the multitudes of heaven worship you. {9:7} You are the Lord God, who chose Abram and brought him out of Ur of the Chaldeans and named him Abraham. {9:8} You found his heart faithful to you, and you made a covenant with him to give to his descendants the land of the Canaanites, Hittites, Amorites, Perizzites, Jebusites, and Girgashites. You have kept your promise because you are righteous. {9:9} You saw the suffering of our ancestors in Egypt; you heard their cry at the Red Sea. {9:10} You sent signs and wonders against Pharaoh, against all his officials and all the people of his land, for you knew how arrogantly the Egyptians treated them. You made a name for yourself, which remains to this day. {9:11} You divided the sea before them, so that they passed through it on dry ground, but you hurled their pursuers into the depths, like a stone into mighty waters. {9:12} By day you led them with a pillar of cloud, and by night with a pillar of fire to give them light on the way they were to take. {9:13} You came down on Mount Sinai; you spoke to them from heaven. You gave them regulations and laws that are just and right, and decrees and commands that are good. {9:14} You made known to them your holy Sabbath and gave them commands, decrees, and laws through your servant Moses. {9:15} In their hunger you gave them bread from heaven and in their thirst brought them water from the rock; you told them to go in and take possession of the land you had sworn with uplifted hand to give them. {9:16} But they, our ancestors, became arrogant and stiff-necked, and they did not obey your commands. {9:17} They refused to listen and failed to remember the miracles you performed among them. They became stiff-necked and in their rebellion appointed a leader in order to return to their slavery. But you are a forgiving God, gracious and compassionate, slow to anger and abounding in love. Therefore you did not desert them, {9:18} even when they cast for themselves an image of a calf and said, 'This is your god, who brought you up out of Egypt,' or when they committed awful blasphemies. {9:19} Because of your great compassion you did not abandon them in the wilderness. By day the pillar of cloud did not fail to guide them on their path, nor the pillar of fire by night to shine on the way they were to take. {9:20} You gave your good Spirit to instruct them. You did not withhold your manna from their mouths, and you gave them water for their thirst. {9:21} For forty years you sustained them in the wilderness; they lacked nothing, their clothes did not wear out nor did their feet become swollen. {9:22} You gave them kingdoms and nations, allotting to them even the remotest frontiers. They took over the country of Sihon king of Heshbon and the country of Og king of Bashan. {9:23} You made their descendants as numerous as the stars in the sky and brought them into the land that you told their parents to enter and possess. {9:24} Their children went in and took possession of the land. You subdued before them the Canaanites, who lived in the land; you gave the Canaanites into their hands, along with their kings and the peoples of the land, to deal with them as they pleased. {9:25} They captured fortified cities and fertile land; they took possession of houses filled with all kinds of good things, wells already dug, vineyards, olive groves, and fruit trees in abundance. They ate to the full and were well-nourished; they reveled in your great goodness. {9:26} But they were disobedient and rebelled against you; they turned their backs on your law. They killed your prophets, who had warned them in order to turn them back to you; they committed awful blasphemies. {9:27} So you delivered them into the hands of their enemies, who oppressed them. But when they were oppressed they cried out to you. From heaven you heard them, and in your great compassion you gave them deliverers, who rescued them from the hands of their enemies. {9:28} But as soon as they were at rest, they again did what was evil in your sight. Then you abandoned them to the hand of their enemies so that they ruled over them. And when they cried out to you again, you heard from heaven, and in your compassion you delivered them time after time. {9:29} You warned them in order to turn them back to your law, but they became arrogant and disobeyed your commands. They sinned against your ordinances, of which you said, 'The person who obeys them will live by them.' Stubbornly they turned their backs on you, became stiff-necked and refused to listen. {9:30} For many years you were patient with them. By your Spirit you warned them through your prophets. Yet they paid no attention, so you gave them into the hands of the neighboring peoples. {9:31} But in your great mercy you did not put an end to them or abandon them, for you are a gracious and merciful God. {9:32} Now therefore, our God, the great God, mighty and awesome, who keeps his covenant of love, do not let all this hardship seem trifling in your eyes—the hardship that has come on us, on our kings and leaders, on our priests and prophets, on our ancestors and all your people, from the days of the kings of Assyria until today. {9:33} In all that has happened to us, you have remained righteous; you have acted faithfully, while we acted wickedly. {9:34} Our kings, our leaders, our priests, and our ancestors did not follow your law; they did not pay attention to your commands or the statutes you warned them to keep. {9:35} Even while they were in their kingdom, enjoying your great goodness to them in the spacious and fertile land you gave them, they did not serve you or turn from their evil ways. {9:36} But see, we are slaves today, slaves in the land you gave our ancestors so they could eat its fruit and the other good things it produces. {9:37} Because of our sins, its abundant harvest goes to the kings you have placed over us. They rule over our bodies and our cattle as they please. We are in great distress. {9:38} **In view of all this, we are making a binding agreement, putting it in writing, and our leaders, our Levites and our priests are affixing their seals to it.**

{10:1} The following are those who sealed the agreement: Nehemiah the governor, the son of Hacaliah, and Zidkijah. {10:2} Seraiah, Azariah, Jeremiah, {10:3} Pashhur, Amariah, Malchijah, {10:4} Hattush, Shebaniah, Malluch, {10:5} Harim, Meremoth, Obadiah, {10:6} Daniel, Ginnethon, Baruch, {10:7} Meshullam, Abijah, Mijamin, {10:8} Maaziah, Bilgai, Shemaiah. These were the priests. {10:9} The Levites: Jeshua son of Azaniah, Binnui from the sons of Henadad, Kadmiel, {10:10} and their associates: Shebaniah, Hodiah, Kelita, Pelaiah, Hanan, {10:11} Micha, Rehob, Hashabiah, {10:12} Zaccur, Sherebiah, Shebaniah, {10:13} Hodiah, Bani, Beninu. {10:14} The leaders of the people: Parosh, Pahath-Moab, Elam, Zattu, Bani, {10:15} Bunni, Azgad, Bebai, {10:16} Adonijah, Bigvai, Adin, {10:17} Ater, Hezekiah, Azzur, {10:18} Hodiah, Hashum, Bezai, {10:19} Hariph, Anathoth, Nebai, {10:20} Magpiash, Meshullam, Hezir, {10:21} Meshezabel, Zadok, Jaddua, {10:22} Pelatiah, Hanan, Anaiah, {10:23} Hoshea, Hananiah, Hasshub, {10:24} Hallohesh, Pilha, Shobek, {10:25} Rehum, Hashabnah, Maaseiah, {10:26} Ahijah, Hanan, Anan, {10:27} Malluch, Harim, Baanah. {10:28} The rest of the people—priests, Levites, gatekeepers, musicians, temple servants, and all who separated themselves from the neighboring peoples for the sake of the Law of God, together with their wives and all their sons and daughters who are able to understand— {10:29} all these now join their fellow Israelites the nobles, and bind themselves with a curse and an oath to follow the Law of God given through Moses the servant of God and to obey carefully all the commands, regulations, and decrees of the Lord our Lord. {10:30} "We promise not to give our daughters in marriage to the peoples around us or take their daughters for our sons. {10:31} "When the neighboring peoples bring merchandise or grain to sell on the Sabbath, we will not buy from them on the Sabbath or on any holy day. Every seventh year we will forgo working the land and will cancel all debts. {10:32} "We assume the responsibility for carrying out the commands to give a third of a shekel each year for the service of the house of our God: {10:33} for the bread set out on the table; for the regular grain offerings and burnt offerings; for the offerings on the Sabbaths, at the New Moon feasts and at the appointed festivals; for the holy offerings; for sin offerings to make atonement for Israel; and for all the duties of the house of our God. {10:34} "We—the priests, the Levites and the people—have cast lots to determine when each of our families is to bring to the house of our God at set times each year a contribution of wood to burn on the altar of the Lord our God, as it is written in the Law. {10:35} "We also assume responsibility for bringing to the house of the Lord each year the firstfruits of our crops and of every fruit tree. {10:36} "As it is also written in the Law, we will bring the firstborn of our sons and of our cattle, of our herds and of our flocks to the house of our God, to the priests ministering there. {10:37} "Moreover, we will bring to the storerooms of the house of our God, to the priests, the first of our ground meal, of our grain offerings, of the fruit of all our trees and of our new wine and olive oil. And we will bring a tithe of our crops to the Levites, for it is the Levites who collect the tithes in all the towns where we work. {10:38} "A priest descended from Aaron is to accompany the Levites when they receive the tithes, and the Levites are to bring a tenth of the tithes up to the house of our God, to the storerooms of the treasury. {10:39} The Israelites and Levites are to bring the contributions of grain, new wine and olive oil to the storerooms, where the articles for the sanctuary and for the ministering priests, the gatekeepers and the musicians are also kept. "We will not neglect the house of our God."

{11:1} The leaders of the people settled in Jerusalem, and the rest of the people cast lots to bring one out of every ten to live in Jerusalem, the holy city, while the remaining nine parts would live in other cities. {11:2} Everyone blessed those who volunteered to live in Jerusalem. {11:3} These were the leaders of the province who settled in Jerusalem, but the people of Judah lived in their own towns: Israelites, priests, Levites, temple servants, and descendants of Solomon's servants. {11:4} Some of the people of Judah and Benjamin settled in Jerusalem. From the tribe of Judah: Athaiah son of Uzziah, the son of Zechariah, the son of Amariah, the son of Shephatiah, the son of Mahalalel, a descendant of Perez; {11:5} and Maaseiah son of Baruch, the son of Col-Hozeh, the son of Hazaiah, the son of Adaiah, the son of Joiarib, the son of Zechariah, a descendant of Shelah. {11:6} The descendants of Perez who lived in Jerusalem totaled 468 valiant men. {11:7} From the tribe of Benjamin: Sallu son of Meshullam, the son of Joed, the son of Pedaiah, the son of Kolaiah, the son of Maaseiah, the son of Ithiel, the son of Jeshaiah. {11:8} After him,

Gabbai and Sallai totaled 928. {11:9} Their chief officer, Joel son of Zikri, was in charge, and Judah son of Hassenuah was over the second district of the city. {11:10} From the priests: Jedaiah son of Joiarib, Jakin, {11:11} and Seraiah son of Hilkiah, the son of Meshullam, the son of Zadok, the son of Meraioth, the son of Ahitub, the official in charge of the house of God. {11:12} Their associates who carried out the work of the temple numbered 822. Adaiah son of Jeroham, the son of Pelaliah, the son of Amzi, the son of Zechariah, the son of Pashhur, the son of Malkijah, {11:13} and his associates, who were heads of families, numbered 242. Amashsai son of Azarel, the son of Ahzai, the son of Meshillemoth, the son of Immer, {11:14} and his associates, who were men of standing, numbered 128. Their chief officer was Zabdiel son of Haggedolim. {11:15} From the Levites: Shemaiah son of Hasshub, the son of Azrikam, the son of Hashabiah, the son of Bunni; {11:16} and Shabbethai and Jozabad, two of the heads of the Levites, who had charge of the outside work of the house of God; {11:17} Mattaniah son of Mica, the son of Zabdi, the son of Asaph, the director who led in thanksgiving and prayer; Bakbukiah, second among his associates; and Abda son of Shammua, the son of Galal, the son of Jeduthun. {11:18} The Levites in the holy city totaled 284. {11:19} The gatekeepers: Akkub, Talmon, and their associates, who kept watch at the gates, numbered 172. {11:20} The rest of the Israelites, with the priests and Levites, were in all the towns of Judah, each on their ancestral property. {11:21} The temple servants lived on the hill of Ophel, and Ziha and Gishpa were in charge of them. {11:22} The chief officer of the Levites in Jerusalem was Uzzi son of Bani, the son of Hashabiah, the son of Mattaniah, the son of Mika. Uzzi was one of Asaph's descendants, who were the musicians responsible for the service of the house of God. {11:23} The musicians were under the king's orders, which regulated their daily activity. {11:24} Pethahiah son of Meshezabel, one of the descendants of Zerah son of Judah, was the king's agent in all affairs relating to the people. {11:25} As for the villages with their fields, some of the people of Judah lived in Kiriath Arba and its surrounding settlements, in Dibon and its settlements, in Jekabzeel and its villages, {11:26} in Jeshua, in Moladah, in Beth Pelet, {11:27} in Hazar Shual, in Beersheba and its settlements, {11:28} in Ziklag, in Meconah and its settlements, {11:29} in En Rimmon, in Zorah, in Jarmuth, {11:30} Zanoah, Adullam and their villages, in Lachish and its fields, and in Azekah and its settlements. So they were living all the way from Beersheba to the Valley of Hinnom. {11:31} Some of the people of Benjamin also lived near Geba, in Micmash, Aija, Bethel and its settlements, {11:32} in Anathoth, Nob, Ananiah, {11:33} in Hazor, Ramah, Gittaim, {11:34} in Hadid, Zeboim, Neballat, {11:35} in Lod and Ono, and in the Valley of the Craftsmen. {11:36} Some of the Levites, divisions in Judah, were settled in Benjamin.

{12:1} These were the priests and Levites who went up with Zerubbabel son of Shealtiel and Jeshua: Seraiah, Jeremiah, Ezra, {12:2} Amariah, Malluch, Hattush, {12:3} Shecaniah, Rehum, Meremoth, {12:4} Iddo, Ginnethon, Abijah, {12:5} Mijamin, Maadiah, Bilgah, {12:6} Shemaiah, Joiarib, Jedaiah, {12:7} Sallu, Amok, Hilkiah, Jedaiah. They were the leaders among the priests and their relatives in the days of Jeshua. {12:8} The Levites were Jeshua, Binnui, Kadmiel, Sherebiah, Judah, and Mattaniah, who, together with his associates, was in charge of the songs of thanksgiving. {12:9} Bakbukiah and Unni, their associates, stood opposite them in the services. {12:10} Jeshua was the father of Joiakim, Joiakim the father of Eliashib, Eliashib the father of Joiada, {12:11} Joiada the father of Jonathan, and Jonathan the father of Jaddua. {12:12} In the days of Joiakim, these were the heads of the priestly families: of Seraiah, Meraiah; of Jeremiah, Hananiah; {12:13} of Ezra, Meshullam; of Amariah, Jehohanan; {12:14} of Malluchi, Jonathan; of Shebaniah, Joseph; {12:15} of Harim, Adna; of Meremoth, Helkai; {12:16} of Iddo, Zechariah; of Ginnethon, Meshullam; {12:17} of Abijah, Zikri; of Miniamin and of Moadiah, Piltai; {12:18} of Bilgah, Shammua; of Shemaiah, Jehonathan; {12:19} of Joiarib, Mattenai; of Jedaiah, Uzzi; {12:20} of Sallai, Kallai; of Amok, Eber; {12:21} of Hilkiah, Hashabiah; of Jedaiah, Nethanel. {12:22} During the reigns of Eliashib, Joiada, Johanan, and Jaddua, the heads of the families of the Levites were recorded in the book of the annals until the reign of Darius the Persian. {12:23} The family heads among the Levites were written down in the records up to the days of Johanan son of Eliashib. {12:24} The leaders of the Levites were Hashabiah, Sherebiah, and Jeshua son of Kadmiel, along with their associates, who stood opposite them to give praise and thanksgiving, one section responding to the other, as prescribed by David the man of God. {12:25} Mattaniah, Bakbukiah, Obadiah, Meshullam, Talmon, and Akkub were gatekeepers who guarded the storerooms at the gates. {12:26} They served in the days of Joiakim son of Jeshua, the son of Jozadak, and in the days of Nehemiah the governor and of Ezra the priest and scribe. {12:27} At the dedication of the wall of Jerusalem, the Levites were sought out from where they lived and were brought to Jerusalem to celebrate joyfully the dedication with songs of thanksgiving and with the music of cymbals, harps, and lyres. {12:28} The musicians also gathered from the region around Jerusalem, from the villages of the Netophathites, {12:29} from Beth Gilgal, and from the fields of Geba and Azmaveth, for the musicians had built villages for themselves around Jerusalem. {12:30} When the priests and Levites had purified themselves ceremonially, they purified the people, the gates, and the wall. {12:31} I had the leaders of Judah go up on top of the wall. I also assigned two large choirs to give thanks. One was to proceed on top of the wall to the right, toward the Dung Gate. {12:32} Hoshaiah and half the leaders of Judah followed them, {12:33} along with Azariah, Ezra, Meshullam, {12:34} Judah, Benjamin, Shemaiah, Jeremiah, {12:35} and some priests with trumpets, namely Zechariah son of Jonathan, the son of Shemaiah, the son of Mattaniah, the son of Micaiah, the son of Zakkur, the son of Asaph, {12:36} and his associates—Shemaiah, Azarel, Milalai, Gilalai, Maai, Nethanel, Judah, and Hanani—with musical instruments prescribed by David the man of God. Ezra the scribe led the procession. {12:37} At the Fountain Gate they went directly up the steps of the City of David on the ascent to the wall and passed above the house of David to the Water Gate on the east. {12:38} The second choir proceeded to the left, while I followed them with half the people along the top of the wall, past the Tower of the Ovens to the Broad Wall, {12:39} over the Gate of Ephraim, the Jeshanah Gate, the Fish Gate, the Tower of Hananel and the Tower of the Hundred, as far as the Sheep Gate. At the Gate of the Guard they stopped. {12:40} The two choirs that gave thanks then took their places in the house of God; so did I, together with half the officials, {12:41} as well as the priests—Eliakim, Maaseiah, Miniamin, Micaiah, Elioenai, Zechariah, and Hananiah with their trumpets— {12:42} and also Maaseiah, Shemaiah, Eleazar, Uzzi, Jehohanan, Malkijah, Elam, and Ezer. The choirs sang under the direction of Jezrahiah. {12:43} And on that day they offered great sacrifices, rejoicing because God had given them great joy. The women and children also rejoiced. The sound of rejoicing in Jerusalem could be heard far away. {12:44} At that time men were appointed to be in charge of the storerooms for the contributions, firstfruits, and tithes. From the fields around the towns they were to bring into the storerooms the portions required by the Law for the priests and Levites, for Judah was pleased with the ministering priests and Levites. {12:45} They performed the service of their God and the service of purification, as did also the musicians and gatekeepers, according to the commands of David and his son Solomon . {12:46} For long ago, in the days of David and Asaph, there had been directors for the musicians and for the songs of praise and thanksgiving to God. {12:47} So in the days of Zerubbabel and of Nehemiah, all Israel contributed the daily portions for the musicians and the gatekeepers. They also set aside the portion for the other Levites, and the Levites set aside the portion for the descendants of Aaron.

{13:1} On that day they read from the Book of Moses in the hearing of the people, and it was found written that the Ammonite and the Moabite should not be admitted into the assembly of God forever, {13:2} because they had not met the Israelites with bread and water but hired Balaam to call down a curse on them. (Our God, however, turned the curse into a blessing.) {13:3} When the people heard this law, they excluded from Israel all who were of foreign descent. {13:4} Before this, Eliashib the priest had been put in charge of the storerooms of the house of our God. He was closely associated with Tobiah, {13:5} and he had provided him with a large room formerly used to store the grain offerings and incense and temple articles, and also the tithes of grain, new wine, and olive oil prescribed for the Levites, musicians, and gatekeepers, as well as the contributions for the priests. {13:6} But while all this was going on, I was not in Jerusalem, for in the thirty-second year of Artaxerxes king of Babylon, I had returned to the king. Some time later I asked his permission {13:7} and came back to Jerusalem. Here I learned about the evil thing Eliashib had done in providing Tobiah a room in the courts of the house of God. {13:8} I was greatly displeased and threw all Tobiah's household goods out of the room. {13:9} I gave orders to purify the rooms, and then I put back into them the equipment of the house of God, with the grain offerings and the incense. {13:10} I also learned that the portions assigned to the Levites had not been given to them, and that all the Levites and musicians responsible for the service had gone back to their own fields. {13:11} So I rebuked the officials and asked them, "Why is the house of God neglected?" Then I called them together and stationed them at their posts. {13:12} All Judah brought the tithes of grain, new wine, and olive oil into the storerooms. {13:13} I put Shelemiah the priest, Zadok the scribe, and a Levite named Pedaiah in charge of the storerooms and made Hanan son of Zakkur, the son of Mattaniah, their assistant, because they were considered trustworthy. They were made responsible for distributing the supplies to their fellow Levites. {13:14} Remember me for this, my God, and do not blot out what I have so faithfully done for the house of my God and its services. {13:15} In those days I saw people in Judah treading winepresses on the Sabbath and bringing in grain and loading it on donkeys, together with wine, grapes, figs, and all other kinds of loads. And they were bringing all this into

Jerusalem on the Sabbath. Therefore I warned them against selling food on that day. {13:16} People from Tyre who lived in Jerusalem were bringing in fish and all kinds of merchandise and selling them in Jerusalem on the Sabbath to the people of Judah. {13:17} I rebuked the nobles of Judah and said to them, "What is this wicked thing you are doing—desecrating the Sabbath day? {13:18} Didn't your ancestors do the same things, so that our God brought all this calamity on us and on this city? Now you are stirring up more wrath against Israel by desecrating the Sabbath." {13:19} When evening shadows fell on the gates of Jerusalem before the Sabbath, I ordered the doors to be shut and not opened until the Sabbath was over. I stationed some of my own men at the gates so that no load could be brought in on the Sabbath day. {13:20} Once or twice the merchants and sellers of all kinds of goods spent the night outside Jerusalem. {13:21} But I warned them and said, "Why do you spend the night by the wall? If you do this again, I will arrest you." From that time on they no longer came on the Sabbath. {13:22} Then I commanded the Levites to purify themselves and go and guard the gates in order to keep the Sabbath day holy. Remember me for this also, my God, and show mercy to me according to your great love. {13:23} Moreover, in those days I saw men of Judah who had married women from Ashdod, Ammon, and Moab. {13:24} Half of their children spoke the language of Ashdod or the language of one of the other peoples, and did not know how to speak the language of Judah. {13:25} I rebuked them and called curses down on them. I beat some of the men and pulled out their hair. I made them take an oath in God's name and said: "You are not to give your daughters in marriage to their sons, nor are you to take their daughters in marriage for your sons or for yourselves. {13:26} Was it not because of marriages like these that Solomon king of Israel sinned? Among the many nations there was no king like him. He was loved by his God, and God made him king over all Israel, but even he was led into sin by foreign women. {13:27} Must we hear now that you too are doing all this terrible wickedness and are being unfaithful to our God by marrying foreign women?" {13:28} One of the sons of Joiada son of Eliashib the high priest was son-in-law to Sanballat the Horonite. And I drove him away from me. {13:29} Remember them, my God, because they defiled the priestly office and the covenant of the priesthood and of the Levites. {13:30} So I purified the priests and the Levites of everything foreign, and assigned them duties, each to his own task. {13:31} I also made provision for contributions of wood at designated times, and for the firstfruits. Remember me with favor, my God.

Esther

{1:1} In the days of Ahasuerus, who ruled over 127 provinces from India to Ethiopia, he held a great feast in his palace in Shushan. {1:2} This feast lasted for 180 days, where he displayed the wealth and splendor of his kingdom. {1:3} After this, he hosted another feast for all the people in Shushan for seven days, in the palace garden court. {1:4} The decorations were lavish, with white, green, and blue hangings, gold and silver beds, and marble pillars. {1:5} The guests were served wine in various gold vessels, and everyone drank according to their preference, as the king had ordered. {1:6} Queen Vashti also hosted a separate feast for the women in the royal house. {1:7} On the seventh day, when the king was merry with wine, he ordered Queen Vashti to come before him wearing her royal crown to display her beauty to the people and princes. {1:8} But Queen Vashti refused to come, which made the king very angry. {1:9} Seeking advice, the king consulted his wise men, including seven princes of Persia and Media. {1:10} They suggested that Vashti's disobedience would set a bad example for all women and proposed that she be removed from her position as queen. {1:11} They also advised the king to issue a decree that wives should honor their husbands, to prevent similar disobedience in the future. {1:12} The king and his princes agreed with this advice, and the king sent out letters to all his provinces, declaring that every man should be the ruler of his household. {1:13} Then the king turned to his wise advisors, who were knowledgeable about laws and judgments. Among them were Carshena, Shethar, Admatha, Tarshish, Meres, Marsena, and Memucan, the top princes of Persia and Media, who had direct access to the king. {1:14} The king sought their counsel on what to do about Queen Vashti's disobedience to his command through his chamberlains. {1:15} Memucan, one of the wise advisors, spoke up before the king and the princes, stating that Vashti's refusal wasn't just an offense against the king but also against all the princes and people throughout the kingdom. {1:16} He argued that Vashti's actions would set a bad precedent, leading other women to disobey their husbands when they heard of the queen's refusal to obey the king's command. {1:17} Memucan warned that if this disobedience spread, it would lead to contempt and anger among all the women in the kingdom towards their husbands. {1:18} He proposed that a royal decree be issued, stating that Vashti could no longer appear before King Ahasuerus, and that her royal position should be given to someone more deserving. {1:19} Memucan suggested that once this decree was proclaimed throughout the kingdom, all wives would learn to honor and obey their husbands, regardless of their status. {1:20} The king and his princes agreed with Memucan's proposal, finding it suitable. Therefore, the king ordered letters to be sent to all his provinces, ensuring that every man would be the head of his household, according to their own language and customs. {1:21} This decree pleased the king and the princes, and they acted according to Memucan's advice. {1:22} Letters were dispatched to every province, proclaiming that men should have authority in their homes, and these decrees were distributed in the languages of the people, ensuring that everyone understood the new law.

{2:1} After some time, when King Ahasuerus's anger had subsided, he remembered what had happened with Vashti and the decree against her. {2:2} His servants suggested that young, beautiful virgins should be sought for the king. {2:3} The king appointed officers in every province to gather these young virgins to Shushan the palace, to be under the care of Hegai, the king's chamberlain, who was in charge of the women. They were given the necessary purification treatments. {2:4} The maiden who pleased the king would become the new queen in place of Vashti. The king agreed to this plan. {2:5} In Shushan lived a Jew named Mordecai, who had been taken captive from Jerusalem. He had raised his cousin, Hadassah, also known as Esther, as his own daughter. {2:6} Esther was exceptionally beautiful, and when the king's decree was heard, she too was brought to the king's palace under Hegai's care. {2:7} Esther found favor with Hegai, who provided her with everything she needed for purification and even appointed seven maids to assist her. She was placed in the best part of the women's house. {2:8} Mordecai instructed Esther not to reveal her Jewish heritage. {2:9} Mordecai regularly checked on Esther's well-being and progress. {2:10} Each maiden underwent a twelve-month purification process before meeting the king, including six months with oil of myrrh and six months with perfumes and other preparations. {2:11} When it was Esther's turn to go to the king, she followed Hegai's instructions and gained favor with all who saw her. {2:12} Esther was brought to King Ahasuerus in the tenth month of the seventh year of his reign. {2:13} The king loved Esther more than all the other women, and he crowned her as queen in place of Vashti. {2:14} The king celebrated Esther's coronation with a great feast for his princes and servants, and he also made arrangements for the provinces, giving gifts according to his wealth. {2:15} Mordecai, meanwhile, sat in the king's gate. {2:16} Esther continued to obey Mordecai's instructions and did not reveal her Jewish background. {2:17} During this time, two of the king's chamberlains, Bigthan and Teresh, became angry and plotted against the king. {2:18} Mordecai learned of their plot and informed Queen Esther, who relayed the information to the king on Mordecai's behalf. {2:19} The matter was investigated, and the conspirators were hanged, with the event recorded in the king's chronicles. {2:20} Esther obeyed Mordecai's instructions and did not reveal her family background, just as Mordecai had instructed her from the time she was brought up by him. {2:21} During this time, while Mordecai was stationed at the king's gate, two of the king's chamberlains, Bigthan and Teresh, who were responsible for guarding the door, became angry and plotted to harm King Ahasuerus. {2:22} Mordecai learned of their plot and informed Queen Esther about it, who then relayed the information to the king, attributing it to Mordecai. {2:23} The matter was investigated, and the truth was uncovered. Consequently, both Bigthan and Teresh were executed by hanging, and the event was recorded in the king's chronicles.

{3:1} After these events, King Ahasuerus elevated Haman, the son of Hammedatha the Agagite, to a position above all the other princes. {3:2} The king commanded all his servants at the king's gate to bow down and show reverence to Haman. Everyone obeyed except Mordecai, who refused to bow or show him any respect. {3:3} This defiance caught the attention of the other servants, who questioned Mordecai about his disobedience to the king's command. {3:4} When Mordecai explained that he was a Jew and could not bow to anyone but God, the servants reported his behavior to Haman. {3:5} Seeing Mordecai's refusal to bow filled Haman with anger. {3:6} Haman, instead of targeting just Mordecai, decided to seek vengeance against all the Jews throughout the kingdom of Ahasuerus, as Mordecai had revealed his identity. {3:7} Haman consulted the casting of lots, known as Pur, to determine the best time to carry out his plan. The lot fell on the twelfth month. {3:8} Haman approached King Ahasuerus, informing him of a people scattered throughout the kingdom whose customs and laws were different from those of others, suggesting they were a threat to the king's authority. {3:9} He proposed that if the king agreed, he would pay a large sum of money to have these people destroyed. {3:10} The king agreed and gave Haman his ring as a symbol of authority to carry out his plan. {3:11} The king entrusted Haman with the authority to do as he pleased with the people and their possessions. {3:12} Haman then had official letters written, commanding the destruction of all Jews in the kingdom, and these letters were sealed with the king's ring. {3:13} These letters were sent by messengers throughout the kingdom, decreeing the destruction of all Jews, regardless of age or gender, on the thirteenth day of the twelfth month. {3:14} Copies of the decree were distributed to all provinces, instructing the people to be ready for the appointed day. {3:15} Upon issuing the decree, the king and Haman sat down to drink, while the city of Shushan was in confusion and turmoil.

{4:1} When Mordecai learned of all that had happened, he tore his clothes, put on sackcloth and ashes, and went out into the city, crying loudly and bitterly. {4:2} He went as far as the king's gate, though no one dressed in sackcloth could enter there. {4:3} Throughout the provinces, wherever the king's decree was received, there was great mourning among the Jews. They fasted, wept, and lamented, with many wearing sackcloth and ashes. {4:4} Esther's maids and chamberlains informed her of Mordecai's distress. The queen was deeply troubled and sent clothes to him, urging him to remove his sackcloth, but Mordecai refused. {4:5} Esther summoned Hatach, one of the king's chamberlains, and sent him to Mordecai to find out what was troubling him. {4:6} Hatach went to Mordecai, who explained everything that had happened, including Haman's plot to destroy the Jews and the promised payment to the king's treasury. {4:7} Mordecai gave Hatach a copy of the decree issued in Shushan to destroy the Jews and instructed him to show it to Esther. He charged her to intercede with the king on behalf of her people. {4:8} **Hatach returned to Esther and relayed Mordecai's message.** {4:9} Esther then instructed Hatach to relay a message back to Mordecai. {4:10} Esther reiterated her command to Hatach, emphasizing the gravity of the situation. {4:11} She explained the danger of approaching the king without being summoned, as it could result in death unless the king extended his golden scepter. However, she hadn't been summoned by the king for the past thirty days. {4:12} Hatach conveyed Esther's words to Mordecai. {4:13} Mordecai responded, warning Esther not to think she would escape the fate of her people just because she was in the king's palace. He urged her to take action, for perhaps she had become queen for such a time as this. {4:14} **Esther instructed Hatach to convey her response to Mordecai.** {4:15} She instructed Mordecai to gather all the Jews in Shushan to fast for three days, day and night, while she and her maidens would also fast. Afterward, she would approach the king, even though it was against the law. She concluded by saying, "If I perish, I perish." {4:16} Mordecai complied with Esther's instructions. {4:17} He did as Esther had commanded him.

{5:1} On the third day, Esther put on her royal attire and stood in the inner court of the king's palace, opposite the king's house. The king was seated on his royal throne in the palace, facing the entrance. {5:2} When the king saw Queen Esther standing in the court, she found favor in his sight, and he extended the golden scepter to her. Esther approached and touched the tip of the scepter. {5:3} The king asked her, "What is your request, Queen Esther? Whatever you desire, even to half the kingdom, it shall be granted." {5:4} Esther replied, "If it pleases the king, let him and Haman come to a banquet that I have prepared for them today." {5:5} The king commanded Haman to hurry and fulfill Esther's request. So they both went to the banquet prepared by Esther. {5:6} During the wine banquet, the king asked Esther, "What is your petition? It shall be granted. What is your request? Even to half the kingdom, it shall be done." {5:7} Esther answered, saying, "My petition and request are this: {5:8} If I have found favor in the king's sight and if it pleases him to grant my petition and fulfill my request, let the king and Haman come to another banquet I will prepare for them tomorrow. Then I will do as the king has said." {5:9} Haman left the banquet that day in high spirits. But when he saw Mordecai at the king's gate and noticed that Mordecai did not stand up or show any respect to him, he became furious. {5:10} Despite his anger, Haman restrained himself. When he returned home, he called for his friends and his wife Zeresh. {5:11} Haman boasted to them about his wealth, his many children, and how the king had honored and promoted him above all the other officials and servants. {5:12} He added, "Even Queen Esther invited no one but me to accompany the king to the banquet she prepared. And tomorrow, I am invited to dine with her and the king again." {5:13} But Haman's happiness was overshadowed by seeing Mordecai at the king's gate, and he felt that none of his achievements mattered as long as Mordecai remained there. {5:14} So, his wife and friends suggested, "Build a gallows fifty cubits high and ask the king tomorrow to have Mordecai hanged on it. Then you can go to the banquet with the king and enjoy yourself." Haman liked the idea and had the gallows built.

{6:1} That night, the king couldn't sleep, so he ordered the book containing records of the chronicles to be brought and read to him. {6:2} They found written in the records that Mordecai had exposed a plot by two of the king's chamberlains, Bigthana and Teresh, who had planned to assassinate King Ahasuerus. {6:3} The king asked, "What honor and recognition has Mordecai received for this?" His attendants replied, "Nothing has been done for him." {6:4} The king inquired, "Who is in the court?" Now Haman had just entered the outer court of the king's palace to speak to the king about hanging Mordecai on the gallows he had prepared. {6:5} The king's servants informed him, "Haman is standing in the court." The king then ordered, "Let him come in." {6:6} So Haman entered, and the king asked him, "What should be done for the man whom the king delights to honor?" Haman thought to himself, "Who else would the king desire to honor more than me?" {6:7} Haman replied, "For the man whom the king delights to honor, {6:8} let royal robes be brought, which the king himself wears, and a horse that the king rides upon, and let a royal crown be placed on his head. {6:9} Then let the robes and the horse be handed over to one of the king's most noble officials. Let them robe the man whom the king delights to honor, and parade him on horseback through the city streets, proclaiming, 'This is what is done for the man whom the king delights to honor.'" {6:10} The king said to Haman, "Hurry, take the robes and the horse, as you have suggested, and do this for Mordecai the Jew, who sits at the king's gate. Do not neglect anything you have mentioned." {6:11} So Haman took the robes and the horse, dressed Mordecai, and led him on horseback through the city streets, proclaiming, "This is what is done for the man whom the king delights to honor." {6:12} Afterward, Mordecai returned to the king's gate, but Haman hurried home, mourning and with his head covered. {6:13} Haman recounted to his wife Zeresh and all his friends everything that had happened to him. His advisers and wife warned him, "If Mordecai, before whom you have begun to fall, is indeed of Jewish descent, you will not prevail against him; you will surely fall before him." {6:14} While they were still talking, the king's eunuchs arrived in haste to take Haman to the banquet that Esther had prepared.

{7:1} The king and Haman attended the banquet with Queen Esther. {7:2} On the second day of the wine banquet, the king asked Esther again, "What is your request, Queen Esther? It will be granted to you. What do you desire? Even if it is half of my kingdom, it will be done." {7:3} **Queen Esther replied, "If I have found favor in your sight, O king, and if it pleases you, spare my life—this is my petition. And spare my people—this is my request.** {7:4} We have been sold, I and my people, to be destroyed, to be killed, and to be annihilated. If we had merely been sold into slavery, I would have kept silent, for our affliction would not have been worth troubling the king." {7:5} King Ahasuerus asked Queen Esther, "Who is he, and where is he, who would dare to do such a thing?" {7:6} Esther replied, "The adversary and enemy is this wicked Haman." Then Haman was terrified before the king and queen. {7:7} The king, filled with wrath, left the wine banquet and went into the palace garden. Haman, realizing that the king had decided his fate, stayed behind to beg Queen Esther for his life. {7:8} When the king returned from the palace garden to the banquet hall, he found Haman fallen on the couch where Esther was reclining. The king exclaimed, "Will he even assault the queen while I am in the house?" As soon as the words left the king's mouth, Haman's face was covered. {7:9} **Then Harbonah, one of the king's eunuchs, said, "Look, there is the gallows, fifty cubits high, that Haman made for Mordecai, who spoke out to the king's benefit, standing at Haman's house." The king declared, "Hang him on it."** {7:10} So they hanged Haman on the gallows that he had prepared for Mordecai. Then the king's wrath subsided.

{8:1} On that day, King Ahasuerus granted Esther the queen the house of Haman, the enemy of the Jews. And Mordecai came before the king, for Esther had informed him of Mordecai's relation to her. {8:2} The king removed his signet ring, which he had taken from Haman, and gave it to Mordecai. Esther then appointed Mordecai over the house of Haman. {8:3} Esther spoke again before the king, falling at his feet and pleading with tears to annul the evil plotted by Haman the Agagite against the Jews. {8:4} The king extended the golden scepter toward Esther, so she arose and stood before him. {8:5} She said, "If it pleases the king, and if I have found favor in his sight, and if the matter seems right to the king and I am pleasing in his eyes, let it be written to revoke the letters devised by Haman the son of Hammedatha the Agagite, which he wrote to destroy the Jews in all the king's provinces. {8:6} "For how can I bear to see the disaster that will come upon my people? How can I endure to see the destruction of my kindred?" {8:7} King Ahasuerus said to Queen Esther and Mordecai the Jew, "I have given Esther the house of Haman, and he was hanged on the gallows because he laid his hand on the Jews. {8:8} "Now you may write in the king's name whatever pleases you, and seal it with the king's ring; for a document written in the king's name and sealed with the king's ring cannot be revoked." {8:9} So the king's scribes were called in the third month, which is the month of Sivan, on the twenty-third day; and it was written according to all that Mordecai commanded to the Jews, the satraps, the governors, and the officials of the provinces from India to Ethiopia, 127 provinces, to each province in its own script, to every people in their own language, and to the Jews in their own script and language. {8:10} He wrote in the name of King Ahasuerus, sealed it with the king's signet ring, and sent letters by couriers on horseback, riding on royal horses bred from the royal stud. {8:11} In these letters, the king allowed the Jews in every city to assemble and defend their lives, to destroy, to kill, and to annihilate any armed force of any people or province that might attack them, including children and women, and to plunder their goods, {8:12} On one day in all the provinces of King Ahasuerus, namely, on the thirteenth day of the twelfth month, which is the month of Adar. {8:13} A copy of the document was to be issued as a decree in every province, publicly displayed to all peoples, so that the Jews would be ready on that day to avenge themselves on their enemies. {8:14} The couriers, mounted on royal steeds, hurried out, urged by the king's command. The decree was issued in the citadel of Susa. {8:15} Mordecai went out from the king's presence in royal robes of blue and white, with a great golden crown and a robe of fine linen and purple. And the city of Susa rejoiced and was glad. {8:16} The Jews had light and gladness, joy and honor. {8:17} *In every province and city, wherever the king's command and decree reached, there was joy and gladness among the Jews, a feast and a holiday. And many from the peoples of the country declared themselves Jews, for fear of the Jews had fallen upon them.*

{9:1} In the twelfth month, known as Adar, on the thirteenth day, when the king's decree to annihilate the Jews was set to be carried out, the tables turned. Instead of being oppressed, the Jews gained the upper hand over those who sought their destruction. {9:2} *Throughout the provinces of King Ahasuerus, the Jews assembled to defend themselves against their enemies. No one could stand against them because fear of the Jews had gripped everyone.* {9:3} The officials of the king, including governors and deputies, supported the Jews because they feared Mordecai. {9:4} Mordecai, who had risen in prominence within the king's palace, became increasingly influential throughout the provinces. His reputation spread far and wide. {9:5} The Jews struck down all who opposed them, inflicting slaughter and destruction on those who harbored hatred against them. {9:6} In the citadel of Susa alone, the Jews killed five hundred men. {9:7} Among those slain were the ten sons of Haman, the enemy of the Jews. However, they did not take any plunder. {9:8} The news of these events reached the king, who inquired of Queen Esther about the situation in Susa. {9:9} Esther requested that the Jews in Susa be granted another day to defend themselves, and that the ten sons of Haman be hanged on the gallows. {9:10} The king agreed, and the decree was issued in Susa. Haman's ten sons were hanged accordingly. {9:11} On the following day, the Jews in Susa killed three hundred more men, but again refrained from taking any spoils. {9:12} Meanwhile, in the other provinces of the kingdom, the Jews gathered to defend themselves and found rest from their enemies. They killed seventy-five thousand of their foes but did not plunder their possessions. {9:13} These events took place on the thirteenth day of Adar, and on the fourteenth, they rested and celebrated with feasting and joy. {9:14} The Jews in Susa observed the same pattern, resting on the thirteenth and fourteenth days and celebrating on the fifteenth. {9:15} Those Jews living in unwalled towns designated the fourteenth day of Adar as a day of joy, feasting, and exchanging gifts. {9:16} Mordecai wrote to all the Jews in King Ahasuerus's provinces, near and far, instructing them to annually observe the fourteenth and fifteenth days of Adar. {9:17} These days commemorated the Jews' victory over their enemies, the transformation of sorrow into joy, and mourning into celebration. {9:18} The Jews embraced Mordecai's decree and committed to keeping these days as a permanent part of their calendar. {9:19} They named these days Purim, after the "pur," or lot, that Haman cast to determine the day of the Jews' destruction. {9:20} Mordecai and Esther sent letters throughout the kingdom, promoting peace and truth among the Jews. {9:21} Their letters confirmed the observance of Purim according to Mordecai's instructions, which became law and were recorded in the royal archives. {9:22} These days mark the Jews' rest from their enemies, the transformation of a month of sorrow into joy, and mourning into a day of celebration. They should be observed with feasting, joy, sharing food with one another, and giving gifts to the poor. {9:23} The Jews committed to observing these customs as Mordecai had instructed them. {9:24} They did so because Haman, the enemy of the Jews, had plotted their destruction by casting lots, or "pur," to determine their fate. {9:25} However, when Esther intervened before the king, he commanded that Haman's wicked plot against the Jews should befall him and his sons, who were to be hanged on the gallows. {9:26} These days were henceforth called Purim, after the "pur" used by Haman. The Jews accepted these instructions and commemorated these events. {9:27} They pledged to keep these days annually, ensuring that they would be observed by all generations, families, provinces, and cities among the Jews, with the memory of Purim enduring through the ages. {9:28} Esther and Mordecai, with the authority vested in them, wrote to confirm these customs, sending letters to all Jews in the kingdom of Ahasuerus, promoting peace and truth. {9:29} Their letters aimed to affirm the observance of Purim according to the decree issued by Mordecai and Esther, including the fasting and lamentations. {9:30} Esther's decree reinforced the observance of Purim, ensuring its continuation as recorded in the royal archives. {9:31} These letters were dispatched to all 127 provinces of the kingdom, emphasizing the importance of observing Purim according to Mordecai and Esther's decree. {9:32} The decree of Esther confirmed the customs of Purim, ensuring their preservation for future generations, as recorded in the official records.

{10:1} King Ahasuerus imposed a tax on the land and the islands of the sea. {10:2} The mighty deeds and accomplishments of King Ahasuerus, including the elevation of Mordecai, are recorded in the chronicles of the kings of Media and Persia. {10:3} Mordecai the Jew held a position second only to King Ahasuerus himself. He was highly esteemed among the Jews and was beloved by many of his brethren. Mordecai diligently worked for the prosperity of his people and advocated for peace among his descendants

Job

{1:1} There was a man named Job who lived in the land of Uz. He was a righteous and upright man, fearing God and shunning evil. {1:2} Job had seven sons and three daughters. {1:3} He possessed seven thousand sheep, three thousand camels, five hundred yoke of oxen, five hundred female donkeys, and a large household. Job was the greatest man in the east. {1:4} Job's sons would hold feasts in their homes, each on his designated day, and they would invite their sisters to eat and drink with them. {1:5} After the days of feasting, Job would send for his children to sanctify them. Early in the morning, he would offer burnt offerings for each of them, thinking, "Perhaps my children have sinned and cursed God in their hearts." Job did this continually. {1:6} One day, the angels came to present themselves before the Lord, and Satan also came with them. {1:7} The Lord asked Satan, "Where have you come from?" Satan replied, "From roaming throughout the earth, going back and forth on it." {1:8} Then the Lord said to Satan, "Have you considered my servant Job? There is no one on earth like him; he is blameless and upright, fearing God and shunning evil." {1:9} Satan answered, "Does Job fear God for nothing?" {1:10} "Have you not put a hedge around him and his household and everything he has? You have blessed the work of his hands, so that his flocks and herds are spread throughout the land." {1:11} "But now stretch out your hand and strike everything he has, and he will surely curse you to your face." {1:12} The Lord said to Satan, "Very well, then, everything he has is in your power, but on the man himself do not lay a finger." Then Satan went out from the presence of the Lord. {1:13} One day, while Job's sons and daughters were feasting and drinking wine at the oldest brother's house, {1:14} a messenger came to Job and said, "The oxen were plowing and the donkeys were grazing nearby, {1:15} and the Sabeans attacked and made off with them. They put the servants to the sword, and I am the only one who has escaped to tell you!" {1:16} While he was still speaking, another messenger came and said, "The fire of God fell from the heavens and burned up the sheep and the servants, and I am the only one who has escaped to tell you!" {1:17} While he was still speaking, another messenger came and said, "The Chaldeans formed three raiding parties and swept down on your camels and made off with them. They put the servants to the sword, and I am the only one who has escaped to tell you!" {1:18} While he was still speaking, yet another messenger came and said, "Your sons and daughters were feasting and drinking wine at the oldest brother's house, {1:19} when suddenly a mighty wind swept in from the desert and struck the four corners of the house. It collapsed on them and they are dead, and I am the only one who has escaped to tell you!" {1:20} At this, Job got up and tore his robe and shaved his head. Then he fell to the ground in worship {1:21} and said: **"Naked I came from my mother's womb, and naked I will depart. The Lord gave and the Lord has taken away; may the name of the Lord be praised."** {1:22} In all this, Job did not sin by charging God with wrongdoing.

{2:1} Once again, the sons of God came to present themselves before the Lord, and Satan also came among them to present himself before the Lord. {2:2} The Lord said to Satan, "Where have you come from?" Satan answered, "From roaming throughout the earth, going back and forth on it." {2:3} Then the Lord said to Satan, "Have you considered my servant Job? There is no one like him on earth; he is blameless and upright, fearing God and shunning evil. And he still maintains his integrity, even though you incited me against him to ruin him without any reason." {2:4} Satan replied to the Lord, "Skin for skin! A man will give all he has for his own life. {2:5} But now stretch out your hand and strike his flesh and bones, and he will surely curse you to your face." {2:6} The Lord said to Satan, "Very well, then, he is in your hands; but you must spare his life." {2:7} So Satan went out from the presence of the Lord and afflicted Job with painful sores from the soles of his feet to the crown of his head. {2:8} Job took a piece of broken pottery and scraped himself with it as he sat among the ashes. {2:9} His wife said to him, "Are you still maintaining your integrity? Curse God and die!" {2:10} He replied, "You are talking like a foolish woman. Shall we accept good from God, and not trouble?" In all this, Job did not sin in what he said. {2:11} When Job's three friends heard about all the troubles that had come upon him, they set out from their homes and met together by agreement to go and sympathize with him and comfort him. {2:12} When they saw him from a distance, they could hardly recognize him; they began to weep aloud, and they tore their robes and sprinkled dust on their heads. {2:13} Then they sat on the ground with him for seven days and seven nights. No one said a word to him, because they saw how great his suffering was.

{3:1} Then Job opened his mouth and cursed the day of his birth. {3:2} He said: {3:3} "Let the day of my birth perish, and the night that said, 'A boy is conceived!' {3:4} That day—may it turn to darkness; may God above not care about it; may no light shine on it. {3:5} May gloom and utter darkness claim it once more; may a cloud settle over it; may blackness overwhelm its light. {3:6} That night—may thick darkness seize it; may it not be included among the days of the year nor be entered in any of the months. {3:7} May that night be barren; may no shout of joy be heard in it. {3:8} May those who curse days curse that day, those who are ready to rouse Leviathan. {3:9} May its morning stars become dark; may it wait for daylight in vain and not see the first rays of dawn, {3:10} for it did not shut the doors of the womb on me to hide trouble from my eyes. {3:11} "Why did I not perish at birth, and die as I came from the womb? {3:12} Why were there knees to receive me and breasts that I might be nursed? {3:13} For now I would be lying down in peace; I would be asleep and at rest {3:14} with kings and rulers of the earth, who built for themselves places now lying in ruins, {3:15} with princes who had gold, who filled their houses with silver. {3:16} Or why was I not hidden away in the ground like a stillborn child, like an infant who never saw the light of day? {3:17} There the wicked cease from turmoil, and there the weary find rest. {3:18} Captives also enjoy their ease; they no longer hear the slave driver's shout. {3:19} The small and the great are there, and the slaves are freed from their owners. {3:20} "Why is light given to those in misery, and life to the bitter of soul, {3:21} to those who long for death that does not come, who search for it more than for hidden treasure, {3:22} who are filled with gladness and rejoice when they reach the grave? {3:23} Why is life given to a man whose way is hidden, whom God has hedged in? {3:24} For sighing comes to me instead of food; my groans pour out like water. {3:25} What I feared has come upon me; what I dreaded has happened to me. {3:26} I have no peace, no quietness; I have no rest, but only turmoil."

{4:1} Then Eliphaz the Temanite responded: {4:2} "If we attempt to speak to you, will you be offended? But who can restrain themselves from speaking? {4:3} Indeed, you have instructed many and strengthened weak hands. {4:4} Your words have supported those who were stumbling; you have strengthened faltering knees. {4:5} But now trouble has come upon you, and you are dismayed; it strikes you, and you are troubled. {4:6} Isn't your piety your confidence, and the integrity of your ways your hope? {4:7} "Think now, who that was innocent ever perished? Where were the upright ever destroyed? {4:8} As I have observed, those who plow iniquity and sow trouble reap the same. {4:9} By the breath of God they perish, and by the blast of his anger they are consumed. {4:10} The roaring of the lion and the voice of the fierce lion, the teeth of the young lions are broken. {4:11} The old lion perishes for lack of prey, and the cubs of the lioness are scattered. {4:12} "A word was secretly brought to me, and my ear caught a whisper of it. {4:13} In troubling thoughts from the visions of the night, when deep sleep falls on people, {4:14} fear and trembling seized me and made all my bones shake. {4:15} A spirit glided past my face; the hair of my flesh stood up. {4:16} It stood still, but I could not discern its appearance. A form loomed before my eyes; there was silence, then I heard a voice: {4:17} 'Can a mortal be more righteous than God? Can even a strong man be more pure than his Maker? {4:18} If God places no trust in his servants, if he charges his angels with error, {4:19} how much more those who live in houses of clay, whose foundations are in the dust, who are crushed more readily than a moth! {4:20} They are broken in pieces from dawn to dusk;

unnoticed, they perish forever. {4:21} Are not their tent cords pulled up, so that they die without wisdom?'

{5:1} "Call now, if there is anyone who will answer you; and to which of the saints will you turn? {5:2} For wrath kills the foolish man, and envy slays the silly one. {5:3} I have seen the foolish taking root, but suddenly I cursed his dwelling place. {5:4} His children are far from safety, and they are crushed in the gate, with no one to deliver them. {5:5} Whose harvest the hungry eat up, and take it even out of the thorns; and the robber swallows up their substance. {5:6} Although affliction does not come from the dust, neither does trouble spring out of the ground; {5:7} Yet man is born to trouble, as the sparks fly upward. {5:8} I would seek unto God, and commit my cause unto Him, {5:9} Who does great and unsearchable things, marvelous things without number; {5:10} Who gives rain upon the earth, and sends waters upon the fields; {5:11} To set up on high those who are lowly, that those who mourn may be lifted to safety. {5:12} He disappoints the devices of the crafty, so that their hands cannot perform their plans. {5:13} He catches the wise in their own craftiness, and the counsel of the cunning is carried headlong. {5:14} They meet with darkness in the daytime, and grope at noonday as in the night. {5:15} But He saves the needy from the sword, from their mouth, and from the hand of the mighty. {5:16} So the poor have hope, and injustice stops her mouth. {5:17} Behold, happy is the man whom God corrects; therefore do not despise the chastening of the Almighty. {5:18} For He wounds, but He also binds up; He injures, but His hands also heal. {5:19} He shall deliver you in six troubles; yes, in seven no evil shall touch you. {5:20} In famine He shall redeem you from death, and in war from the power of the sword. {5:21} You shall be hidden from the scourge of the tongue, neither shall you be afraid of destruction when it comes. {5:22} At destruction and famine you shall laugh; neither shall you be afraid of the beasts of the earth. {5:23} For you shall be in league with the stones of the field, and the beasts of the field shall be at peace with you. {5:24} And you shall know that your tent shall be in peace; and you shall visit your habitation, and shall not sin. {5:25} You shall know also that your offspring shall be great, and your descendants as the grass of the earth. {5:26} You shall come to your grave in a full age, like as a shock of corn comes in its season. {5:27} Look, this we have searched out, so it is; listen to it, and know it for your good."

{6:1} Job replied: {6:2} "Oh, that my anguish were weighed and all my misery placed on the scales! {6:3} It would surely outweigh the sand of the seas— no wonder my words have been impetuous. {6:4} The arrows of the Almighty are in me, my spirit drinks in their poison; God's terrors are arrayed against me. {6:5} "Does a wild donkey bray when it has grass, or an ox bellow when it has fodder? {6:6} Is tasteless food eaten without salt, or is there flavor in the sap of the mallow? {6:7} I refuse to touch it; such food makes me ill. {6:8} "Oh, that I might have my request, that God would grant what I hope for, {6:9} that God would be willing to crush me, to let loose his hand and cut off my life! {6:10} Then I would still have this consolation— my joy in unrelenting pain— that I had not denied the words of the Holy One. {6:11} "What strength do I have, that I should still hope? What prospects, that I should be patient? {6:12} Do I have the strength of stone? Is my flesh bronze? {6:13} Do I have any power to help myself, now that success has been driven from me? {6:14} "Anyone who withholds kindness from a friend forsakes the fear of the Almighty. {6:15} But my brothers are as undependable as intermittent streams, as the streams that overflow {6:16} when darkened by thawing ice and swollen with melting snow, {6:17} but that stop flowing in the dry season, and in the heat vanish from their channels. {6:18} Caravans turn aside from their routes; they go off into the wasteland and perish. {6:19} The caravans of Tema look for water, the traveling merchants of Sheba look in hope. {6:20} They are distressed, because they had been confident; they arrive there, only to be disappointed. {6:21} Now you too have proved to be of no help; you see something dreadful and are afraid. {6:22} "Have I ever said, 'Give something on my behalf, pay a ransom for me from your wealth, {6:23} deliver me from the hand of the enemy, rescue me from the grasp of the ruthless'? {6:24} "Teach me, and I will be quiet; show me where I have been wrong. {6:25} How painful are honest words! But what do your arguments prove? {6:26} Do you mean to correct what I say, and treat my desperate words as wind? {6:27} You would even cast lots for the fatherless and barter away your friend. {6:28} "But now be so kind as to look at me. Would I lie to your face? {6:29} Relent, do not be unjust; reconsider, for my integrity is at stake. {6:30} Is there any wickedness on my lips? Can my mouth not discern malice?"

{7:1} "Isn't there an appointed time for humanity on earth? Aren't their days like those of a hired laborer? {7:2} Like a servant longing for the shade, or a laborer waiting to be paid, {7:3} so I am allotted months of futility, and nights of misery are assigned to me. {7:4} "When I lie down, I think, 'How long until I get up?' The night drags on, and I toss and turn until dawn. {7:5} My body is clothed with worms and scabs, my skin is broken and festering. {7:6} "My days are swifter than a weaver's shuttle, and they come to an end without hope. {7:7} Remember, O God, that my life is but a breath; my eyes will never again see happiness. {7:8} The eye that now sees me will not see me again; you will look for me, but I will be no more. {7:9} As a cloud vanishes and is gone, so one who goes down to the grave does not return. {7:10} He will never come to his house again; his place will know him no more. {7:11} "Therefore I will not keep silent; I will speak out in the anguish of my spirit, I will complain in the bitterness of my soul. {7:12} Am I the sea, or the monster of the deep, that you put me under guard? {7:13} When I think my bed will comfort me and my couch will ease my complaint, {7:14} even then you frighten me with dreams and terrify me with visions, {7:15} so that I prefer strangling and death, rather than this body of mine. {7:16} I despise my life; I would not live forever. Let me alone; my days have no meaning. {7:17} "What is mankind that you make so much of them, that you give them so much attention, {7:18} that you examine them every morning and test them every moment? {7:19} Will you never look away from me, or let me alone even for an instant? {7:20} If I have sinned, what have I done to you, you who see everything we do? Why have you made me your target? Have I become a burden to you? {7:21} Why do you not pardon my offenses and forgive my sins? For I will soon lie down in the dust; you will search for me, but I will be no more."

{8:1} Then Bildad the Shuhite answered and said, {8:2} "How long will you speak these things? How long will your words be like a strong wind? {8:3} Does God pervert justice? Or does the Almighty pervert what is right? {8:4} If your children have sinned against Him, and He has delivered them into the hand of their transgression, {8:5} if you would earnestly seek God and plead with the Almighty, {8:6} if you were pure and upright, surely now He would awake for you, and prosper your rightful dwelling place. {8:7} Though your beginning was small, yet your latter end would increase abundantly. {8:8} For inquire, please, of the former age, and consider the things discovered by their fathers; {8:9} For we were born yesterday, and know nothing, because our days on earth are but a shadow. {8:10} Will they not teach you and tell you, and utter words from their heart? {8:11} Can the papyrus grow up without a marsh? Can the reeds flourish without water? {8:12} While it is yet green and not cut down, it withers before any other plant. {8:13} So are the paths of all who forget God; and the hope of the hypocrite shall perish, {8:14} whose confidence shall be cut off, and whose trust is a spider's web. {8:15} He leans on his house, but it does not stand. He holds it fast, but it does not endure. {8:16} He is green before the sun, and his branches spread out over his garden. {8:17} His roots wrap around the rock heap, he looks for a place among the stones. {8:18} If he is destroyed from his place, then it will deny him, saying, 'I have not seen you.' {8:19} Behold, this is the joy of his way; and out of the earth others will grow. {8:20} **Behold, God will not cast away a blameless man, nor will He uphold evildoers.** {8:21} He will yet fill your mouth with laughter, and your lips with rejoicing. {8:22} Those who hate you will be clothed with shame, and the dwelling place of the wicked will come to nothing."

{9:1} Then Job answered and said, {9:2} "I know it is true, but how can a man be righteous before God? {9:3} If one wished to contend with Him, he could not answer Him once in a thousand times. {9:4} He is wise in heart and mighty in strength. Who has hardened himself against Him and prospered? {9:5} He moves mountains, and they do not know it; He overturns them in His anger. {9:6} He shakes the earth out of its place, and its pillars tremble; {9:7} He commands the sun, and it does not rise; He seals off the stars; {9:8} He alone spreads out the heavens, and treads on the waves of the sea; {9:9} He made the Bear, Orion, and the Pleiades, and the chambers of the south; {9:10} He does great things beyond searching out, and wonders without number. {9:11} If He goes by me, I do not see Him; If He moves past, I do not perceive Him. {9:12} If He takes away, who can hinder Him? Who can say to Him, 'What are You doing?' {9:13} God will not withdraw His anger; the allies of Rahab bow under Him. {9:14} How then can I answer Him, And choose my words to reason with Him? {9:15} Though I were righteous, I could not answer Him; I would beg mercy of my Judge. {9:16} If I called and He answered me, I would not believe that He listened to my voice. {9:17} For He crushes me with a tempest and multiplies my wounds without cause. {9:18} He does not allow me to catch my breath, but fills me with bitterness. {9:19} If it is a matter of strength, indeed He is strong; and if of justice, who will appoint my day in court? {9:20} Though I were righteous, my own mouth would condemn me; Though I were blameless, it would prove me perverse. {9:21} I am blameless, yet I do not know myself; I despise my life. {9:22} It is all one thing; therefore I say, 'He destroys the blameless and the wicked.' {9:23} If the scourge kills suddenly, He laughs at the plight of the innocent. {9:24} The earth is given into the hand of the wicked. He covers the faces of its judges. If it is not He, then who else could it be? {9:25} Now my days are swifter than a runner; They flee away, they see no good. {9:26} They pass by like swift ships, like an eagle swooping on its prey. {9:27} If I say, 'I will forget my complaint, I will put off my sad face and be of good cheer,' {9:28} I am afraid of all my sufferings; I know that You will not hold me innocent. {9:29} If I am condemned, Why then do I labor in vain? {9:30} If I wash myself with snow water, And cleanse my hands with soap, {9:31} Yet You will plunge me into the pit, and my own clothes will abhor me. {9:32} For He is not a man, as I am, That I may answer Him, And that we should go to court together. {9:33} Nor is there any mediator between us, Who may lay his hand on us both. {9:34} Let Him take His rod away from me, And do not let dread of Him terrify me. {9:35} Then I would speak and not fear Him, But it is not so with me."

{10:1} My soul is weary of my life; I will leave my complaint upon myself; I will speak in the bitterness of my soul. {10:2} I will say unto God, Do not condemn me; Show me why You contend with me. {10:3} Is it good to oppress? To despise the work of Your hands and favor the counsel of the wicked? {10:4} Do You have eyes of flesh? Do You see as man sees? {10:5} Are Your days like man's days? Are Your years like those of mortals? {10:6} That You inquire after my iniquity and search for my sin? {10:7} You know that I am not wicked; and there is none who can deliver me from Your hand. {10:8} Your hands have made and fashioned me; yet You destroy me. {10:9} Remember, I beseech You, that You have made me as the clay; and will You bring me into dust again? {10:10} Have You not poured me out like milk, and curdled me like cheese? {10:11} You have clothed me with skin and flesh, and fenced me with bones and sinews. {10:12} You have granted me life and favor, and Your visitation has preserved my spirit. {10:13} Yet You have hidden these things in Your heart; I know they are with You. {10:14} If I sin, then You mark me, and You will not acquit me from my iniquity. {10:15} If I am wicked, woe unto me; and if I am righteous, I will not lift up my head. I am full of confusion; therefore see my affliction. {10:16} For it increases. You hunt me like a fierce lion; and again You show Yourself marvelous upon me. {10:17} You renew Your witnesses against me, and increase Your indignation upon me; changes and war are against me. {10:18} Why then have You brought me forth from the womb? Oh that I had given up the ghost, and no eye had seen me! {10:19} I should have been as though I had not been; I should have been carried from the womb to the grave. {10:20} Are not my days few? Cease then, and let me alone, that I may take comfort a little, {10:21} Before I go whence I shall not return, even to the land of darkness and the shadow of death; {10:22} A land of darkness, as darkness itself; and of the shadow of death, without any order, and where the light is as darkness.

{11:1} Then answered Zophar the Naamathite, and said, {11:2} Should not the multitude of words be answered? Should a man full of talk be justified? {11:3} Should your lies make men hold their peace? And when you mock, shall no man make you ashamed? {11:4} For you have said, My doctrine is pure, and I am clean in your eyes. {11:5} But oh that God would speak, and open his lips against you; {11:6} And that he would show you the secrets of wisdom, that they are double to that which is! Know therefore that God exacts of you less than your iniquity deserves. {11:7} Can you by searching find out God? Can you find out the Almighty unto perfection? {11:8} It is as high as heaven; what can you do? Deeper than hell; what can you know? {11:9} The measure thereof is longer than the earth, and broader than the sea. {11:10} If he cuts off, and shuts up, or gathers together, then who can hinder him? {11:11} For he knows vain men; he sees wickedness also; will he not then consider it? {11:12} For vain man would be wise, though man be born like a wild ass's colt. {11:13} If you prepare your heart, and stretch out your hands toward him; {11:14} If iniquity be in your hand, put it far away, and let not wickedness dwell in your tabernacles. {11:15} For then shall you lift up your face without spot; yes, you shall be steadfast, and shall not fear: {11:16} Because you shall forget your misery, and remember it as waters that pass away: {11:17} And your age shall be clearer than the noonday; you shall shine forth, you shall be as the morning. {11:18} And you shall be secure, because there is hope; yes, you shall dig about you, and you shall take your rest in safety. {11:19} Also you shall lie down, and none shall make you afraid; yes, many shall make suit unto you. {11:20} But the eyes of the wicked shall fail, and they shall not escape, and their hope shall be as the giving up of the ghost.

{12:1} And Job answered and said, {12:2} No doubt but you are the people, and wisdom shall die with you. {12:3} But I have understanding as well as you; I am not inferior to you: yes, who doesn't know such things as these? {12:4} I am as one mocked of his neighbor, who calls upon God, and he answers him: the just upright man is laughed to scorn. {12:5} He that is ready to slip with his feet is as a lamp despised in the thought of him that is at ease. {12:6} The tabernacles of robbers prosper, and they that provoke God are secure; into whose hand God brings abundantly. {12:7} But ask now the beasts, and they shall teach you; and the fowls of the air, and they shall tell you: {12:8} Or speak to the earth, and it shall teach you: and the fishes of the sea shall declare unto you. {12:9} Who doesn't know in all these that the hand of the LORD has wrought this? {12:10} In whose hand is the soul of every living thing, and the breath of all mankind. {12:11} Does not the ear try words? and the mouth taste his meat? {12:12} With the ancient is wisdom; and in length of days understanding. {12:13} With him is wisdom and strength, he has counsel and understanding. {12:14} Behold, he breaks down, and it cannot be built again: he shuts up a man, and there can be no opening. {12:15} Behold, he withholds the waters, and they dry up: also he sends them out, and they overturn the earth. {12:16} With him is strength and wisdom: the deceived and the deceiver are his. {12:17} He leads counselors away spoiled, and makes the judges fools. {12:18} He loosens the bond of kings, and girds their loins with a girdle. {12:19} He leads princes away spoiled, and overthrows the mighty. {12:20} He removes away the speech of the trusty, and takes away the understanding of the aged. {12:21} He pours contempt upon princes, and weakens the strength of the mighty. {12:22} He discovers deep things out of darkness, and brings out to light the shadow of death. {12:23} He increases the nations, and destroys them: he enlarges the nations, and straitens them again. {12:24} He takes away the heart of the chief of the people of the earth, and causes them to wander in a wilderness where there is no way. {12:25} They grope in the dark without light, and he makes them to stagger like a drunken man.

{13:1} Lo, my eye has seen all this, my ear has heard and understood it. {13:2} What you know, I know also: I am not inferior to you. {13:3} Surely I would speak to the Almighty, and I desire to reason with God. {13:4} But you are forgers of lies, you are all worthless physicians. {13:5} Oh, that you would altogether hold your peace! and it should be your wisdom. {13:6} Hear now my reasoning, and listen to the pleadings of my lips. {13:7} Will you speak wickedly for God? and talk deceitfully for him? {13:8} Will you show partiality for him? will you contend for God? {13:9} Is it good that he should search you out? or as one man mocks another, do you so mock him? {13:10} He will surely reprove you, if you secretly show favoritism. {13:11} Shall not his excellency make you afraid? and his dread fall upon you? {13:12} Your remembrances are like ashes, your bodies to bodies of clay. {13:13} Hold your peace, let me alone, that I may speak, and let come on me what will. {13:14} Why do I take my flesh in my teeth, and put my life in my hand? {13:15} Though he slay me, yet will I trust in him: but I will maintain my own ways before him. {13:16} He also shall be my salvation: for a hypocrite shall not come before him. {13:17} Hear diligently my speech, and my declaration with your ears. {13:18} Behold now, I have ordered my cause; I know that I shall be justified. {13:19} Who is he that will plead with me? for now, if I hold my tongue, I shall give up the ghost. {13:20} Only do not two things unto me: then will I not hide myself from you. {13:21} Withdraw your hand far from me: and let not your dread make me afraid. {13:22} Then call, and I will answer: or let me speak, and answer you me. {13:23} How many are my iniquities and sins? make me to know my transgression and my sin. {13:24} Why do you hide your face, and hold me for your enemy? {13:25} Will you break a leaf driven to and fro? and will you pursue the dry stubble? {13:26} For you write bitter things against me, and make me possess the iniquities of my youth. {13:27} You put my feet also in the stocks, and look narrowly unto all my paths; you set a print upon the heels of my feet. {13:28} And he, as a rotten thing, consumes, as a garment that is moth-eaten.

{14:1} Man that is born of a woman is of few days, and full of trouble. {14:2} He comes forth like a flower, and is cut down: he flees also as a shadow, and continues not. {14:3} And do you open your eyes upon such a one, and bring me into judgment with you? {14:4} Who can bring a clean thing out of an unclean? Not one. {14:5} Seeing his days are determined, the number of his months are with you, you have appointed his bounds that he cannot pass; {14:6} Turn from him, that he may rest, till he shall accomplish, as an hireling, his day. {14:7} For there is hope of a tree, if it be cut down, that it will sprout again, and that the tender branch thereof will not cease. {14:8} Though the root thereof wax old in the earth, and the stock thereof die in the ground; {14:9} Yet through the scent of water it will bud, and bring forth boughs like a plant. {14:10} But man dies, and wastes away: yes, man gives up the ghost, and where is he? {14:11} As the waters fail from the sea, and the flood decays and dries up: {14:12} So man lies down, and rises not: till the heavens be no more, they shall not awake, nor be raised out of their sleep. {14:13} Oh that you would hide me in the grave, that you would keep me secret, until your wrath be past, that you would appoint me a set time, and remember me! {14:14} If a man dies, shall he live again? All the days of my appointed time will I wait, till my change come. {14:15} You shall call, and I will answer you: you will have a desire to the work of your hands. {14:16} For now you number my steps: do you not watch over my sin? {14:17} My transgression is sealed up in a bag, and you sew up my iniquity. {14:18} And surely the mountain falling comes to nought, and the rock is removed out of his place. {14:19} The waters wear the stones: you wash away the things which grow out of the dust of the earth; and you destroy the hope of man. {14:20} You prevail forever against him, and he passes: you change his countenance, and send him away. {14:21} His sons come to honor, and he knows it not; and they are brought low, but he perceives it not of them. {14:22} But his flesh upon him shall have pain, and his soul within him shall mourn.

{15:1} Then answered Eliphaz the Temanite, and said, {15:2} Should a wise man utter vain knowledge, and fill his belly with the east wind? {15:3} Should he reason with unprofitable talk? or with speeches wherewith he can do no good? {15:4} Yes, you cast off fear, and restrain prayer before God. {15:5} For your mouth utters your iniquity, and you choose the tongue of the crafty. {15:6} Your own mouth condemns you, and not I: yes, your own lips testify against you. {15:7} Are you the first man that was born? or were you made before the hills? {15:8} Have you heard the secret of God? and do you restrain wisdom to yourself? {15:9} What do you know, that we know not? what understand you, which is not in us? {15:10} With us are both the grayheaded and very aged men, much elder than your father. {15:11} Are the consolations of God small with you? is there any secret thing with you? {15:12} Why does your heart carry you away? and what do your eyes wink at, {15:13} That you turn your spirit against God, and let such words go out of your mouth? {15:14} What is man, that he should be clean? and he which is born of a woman, that he should be righteous? {15:15} Behold, he puts no trust in his saints; yes, the heavens are not clean in his sight. {15:16} How much more abominable and filthy is man, which drinks iniquity like water? {15:17} I will show you, hear me; and that which I have seen I will declare; {15:18} Which wise men have told from their fathers, and have not hid it: {15:19} Unto whom alone the earth was given, and no stranger passed among them. {15:20} The wicked man travails with pain all his days, and the number of years is hidden to the oppressor. {15:21} A dreadful sound is in his ears: in prosperity the destroyer shall come upon him. {15:22} He believes not that he shall return out of darkness, and he is waited for of the sword. {15:23} He wanders abroad for bread, saying, Where is it? he knows that the day of darkness is ready at his hand. {15:24} Trouble and anguish shall make him afraid; they shall prevail against him, as a king ready to the battle. {15:25} For he stretches out his hand against God, and strengthens himself against the Almighty. {15:26} He runs upon him, even on his neck, upon the thick bosses of his bucklers; {15:27} Because he covers his face with his fatness, and makes collops of fat on his flanks. {15:28} And he dwells in desolate cities, and in houses which no man inhabits, which are ready to become heaps. {15:29} He shall not be rich, neither shall his substance continue, neither shall he prolong the perfection thereof upon the earth. {15:30} He shall not depart out of darkness; the flame shall dry up his branches, and by the breath of his mouth shall he go away. {15:31} Let not him that is deceived trust in vanity: for vanity shall be his recompense. {15:32} It shall be accomplished before his time, and his branch shall not be green. {15:33} He shall shake off his unripe grape as the vine, and shall cast off his flower as the olive. {15:34} For the congregation of hypocrites shall be desolate, and fire shall consume the tabernacles of bribery. {15:35} They conceive mischief, and bring forth vanity, and their belly prepares deceit.

{16:1} Then Job answered and said, {16:2} I have heard many such things: miserable comforters are you all. {16:3} Shall vain words have an end? or what emboldens you that you answer? {16:4} I also could speak as you do: if your soul were in my soul's stead, I could heap up words against you, and shake my head at you. {16:5} But I would strengthen you with my mouth, and the moving of my lips should assuage your grief. {16:6} Though I speak, my grief is not assuaged: and though I forbear, what am I eased? {16:7} But now he has made me weary: you have made desolate all my company. {16:8} And you have filled me with wrinkles, which is a witness against me: and my leanness rising up in me bears witness to my face. {16:9} He tears me in his wrath, who hates me: he gnashes upon me with his teeth; my enemy sharpens his eyes upon me. {16:10} They have gaped upon me with their mouth; they have smitten me upon the cheek reproachfully; they have gathered themselves together against me. {16:11} God has delivered me to the ungodly, and turned me over into the hands of the wicked. {16:12} I was at ease, but he has broken me asunder: he has also taken me by my neck, and shaken me to pieces, and set me up for his mark. {16:13} His archers compass me round about, he cleaves my reins asunder, and does not spare; he pours out my gall upon the ground. {16:14} He breaks me with breach upon breach, he runs upon me like a giant. {16:15} I have sewed sackcloth upon my skin, and defiled my horn in the dust. {16:16} My face is foul with weeping, and my eyelids are the shadow of death; {16:17} Not for any injustice in my hands: also my prayer is pure. {16:18} O earth, cover not my blood, and let my cry have no place. {16:19} Also now, behold, my witness is in heaven, and my record is on high. {16:20} My friends scorn me: but my eye pours out tears unto God. {16:21} Oh that one might plead for a man with God, as a man pleads for his neighbor! {16:22} When a few years are come, then I shall go the way whence I shall not return.

{17:1} My breath is corrupt, my days are extinct, the graves are ready for me. {17:2} Are there not mockers with me? and does not my eye continue in their provocation? {17:3} Lay down now, put me in a surety with thee; who is he that will strike hands with me? {17:4} For thou hast hid their heart from understanding: therefore shalt thou not exalt them. {17:5} He that speaketh flattery to his friends, even the eyes of his children shall fail. {17:6} He hath made me also a byword of the people; and aforetime I was as a tabret. {17:7} Mine eye also is dim by reason of sorrow, and all my members are as a shadow. {17:8} Upright men shall be astonished at this, and the innocent shall stir up himself against the hypocrite. {17:9} The righteous also shall hold on his way, and he that hath clean hands shall be stronger and stronger. {17:10} But as for you all, do ye return, and come now: for I cannot find one wise man among you. {17:11} My days are past, my purposes are broken off, even the thoughts of my heart. {17:12} They change the night into day: the light is short because of darkness. {17:13} If I wait, the grave is mine house: I have made my bed in the darkness. {17:14} I have said to corruption, Thou art my father: to the worm, Thou art my mother, and my sister. {17:15} And where is now my hope? as for my hope, who shall see it? {17:16} They shall go down to the bars of the pit, when our rest together is in the dust.

{18:1} Then answered Bildad the Shuhite, and said, {18:2} How long will it be ere ye make an end of words? Mark, and afterwards we will speak. {18:3} Wherefore are we counted as beasts, and reputed vile in your sight? {18:4} He teareth himself in his anger: shall the earth be forsaken for thee? and shall the rock be removed out of his place? {18:5} Yea, the light of the wicked shall be put out, and the spark of his fire shall not shine. {18:6} The light shall be dark in his tabernacle, and his candle shall be put out with him. {18:7} The steps of his strength shall be straitened, and his own counsel shall cast him down. {18:8} For he is cast into a net by his own feet, and he walketh upon a snare. {18:9} The gin shall take him by the heel, and the robber shall prevail against him. {18:10} The snare is laid for him in the ground, and a trap for him in the way. {18:11} Terrors shall make him afraid on every side, and shall drive him to his feet. {18:12} His strength shall be hungerbitten, and destruction shall be ready at his side. {18:13} It shall devour the strength of his skin: even the firstborn of death shall devour his strength. {18:14} His confidence shall be rooted out of his tabernacle, and it shall bring him to the king of terrors. {18:15} It shall dwell in his tabernacle, because it is none of his: brimstone shall be scattered upon his habitation. {18:16} His roots shall be dried up beneath, and above shall his branch be cut off. {18:17} His remembrance shall perish from the earth, and he shall have no name in the street. {18:18} He shall be driven from light into darkness, and chased out of the world. {18:19} He shall neither have son nor nephew among his people, nor any remaining in his dwellings. {18:20} They that come after him shall be astonied at his day, as they that went before were affrighted. {18:21} Surely such are the dwellings of the wicked, and this is the place of him that knoweth not God.

{19:1} Then Job answered and said, {19:2} How long will ye vex my soul, and break me in pieces with words? {19:3} These ten times have ye reproached me: ye are not ashamed that ye make yourselves strange to me. {19:4} And be it indeed that I have erred, mine error remaineth with myself. {19:5} If indeed ye will magnify yourselves against me, and plead against me my reproach: {19:6} Know now that God hath overthrown me, and hath compassed me with his net. {19:7} Behold, I cry out of wrong, but I am not heard: I cry aloud, but there is no judgment. {19:8} He hath fenced up my way that I cannot pass, and he hath set darkness in my paths. {19:9} He hath stripped me of my glory, and taken the crown from my head. {19:10} He hath destroyed me on every side, and I am gone: and mine hope hath he removed like a tree. {19:11} He hath also kindled his wrath against me, and he counteth me unto him as one of his enemies. {19:12} His troops come together, and raise up their way against me, and encamp round about my tabernacle. {19:13} He hath put my brethren far from me, and mine acquaintance are verily estranged from me. {19:14} My kinsfolk have failed, and my familiar friends have forgotten me. {19:15} They that dwell in mine house, and my maids, count me for a stranger: I am an alien in their sight. {19:16} I called my servant, and he gave me no answer; I intreated him with my mouth. {19:17} My breath is strange to my wife, though I intreated for the children's sake of mine own body. {19:18} Yea, young children despised me; I arose, and they spake against me. {19:19} All my inward friends abhorred me: and they whom I loved are turned against me. {19:20} My bone cleaveth to my skin and to my flesh, and I am escaped with the skin of my teeth. {19:21} Have pity upon me, have pity upon me, O ye my friends; for the hand of God hath touched me. {19:22} Why do ye persecute me as God, and are not satisfied with my flesh? {19:23} Oh that my words were now written! oh that they were printed in a book! {19:24} That they were graven with an iron pen and lead in the rock for ever! {19:25} **For I know that my redeemer liveth, and that he shall stand at the latter day upon the earth:** {19:26} And though after my skin worms destroy this body, yet in my flesh shall I see God: {19:27} Whom I shall see for myself, and mine eyes shall behold, and not another; though my reins be consumed within me. {19:28} But ye should say, Why persecute we him, seeing the root of the matter is found in me? {19:29} Be ye afraid of the sword: for wrath bringeth the punishments of the sword, that ye may know there is a judgment.

{20:1} Then answered Zophar the Naamathite, and said, {20:2} Therefore do my thoughts cause me to answer, and for this I make haste. {20:3} I have heard the check of my reproach, and the spirit of my understanding causeth me to answer. {20:4} Knowest thou not this of old, since man was placed upon earth, {20:5} That the triumphing of the wicked is short, and the joy of the hypocrite but for a moment? {20:6} Though his excellency mount up to the heavens, and his head reach unto the clouds; {20:7} Yet he shall perish forever like his own dung: they which have seen him shall say, Where is he? {20:8} He shall fly away as a dream, and shall not be found: yea, he shall be chased away as a vision of the night. {20:9} The eye also which saw him shall see him no more; neither shall his place any more behold him. {20:10} His children shall seek to please the poor, and his hands shall restore their goods. {20:11} His bones are full of the sin of his youth, which shall lie down with him in the dust. {20:12} Though wickedness be sweet in his mouth, though he hide it under his tongue; {20:13} Though he spare it, and forsake it not; but keep it still within his mouth: {20:14} Yet his meat in his bowels is turned, it is the gall of asps within him. {20:15} He hath swallowed down riches, and he shall vomit them up again: God shall cast them out of his belly. {20:16} He shall suck the poison of asps: the viper's tongue shall slay him. {20:17} He shall not see the rivers, the floods, the brooks of honey and butter. {20:18} That which he laboured for shall he restore, and shall not swallow it down: according to his substance shall the restitution be, and he shall not rejoice therein. {20:19} Because he hath oppressed and hath forsaken the poor; because he hath violently taken away a house which he builded not; {20:20} Surely he shall not feel quietness in his belly, he shall not save of that which he desired. {20:21} There shall none of his meat be left; therefore shall no man look for his goods. {20:22} In the fulness of his sufficiency he shall be in straits: every hand of the wicked shall come upon him. {20:23} When he is about to fill his belly, God shall cast the fury of his wrath upon him, and shall rain it upon him while he is eating. {20:24} He shall flee from the iron weapon, and the bow of steel shall strike him through. {20:25} It is drawn, and cometh out of the body; yea, the glittering sword cometh out of his gall: terrors are upon him. {20:26} All darkness shall be hid in his secret places: a fire not blown shall consume him; it shall go ill with him that is left in his tabernacle. {20:27} The heaven shall reveal his iniquity; and the earth shall rise up against him. {20:28} The increase of his house shall depart, and his goods shall flow away in the day of his wrath. {20:29} This is the portion of a wicked man from God, and the heritage appointed unto him by God.

{21:1} But Job answered and said, {21:2} Hear diligently my speech, and let this be your consolations. {21:3} Suffer me that I may speak; and after that I have spoken, mock on. {21:4} As for me, is my complaint to man? and if it were so, why should not my spirit be troubled? {21:5} Mark me, and be astonished, and lay your hand upon your mouth. {21:6} Even when I remember I am afraid, and trembling taketh hold on my flesh. {21:7} Wherefore do the wicked live, become old, yea, are mighty in power? {21:8} Their seed is established in their sight with them, and their offspring before their eyes. {21:9} Their houses are safe from fear, neither is the rod of God upon them. {21:10} Their bull gendereth, and faileth not; their cow calveth, and casteth not her calf. {21:11} They send forth their little ones like a flock, and their children dance. {21:12} They take the timbrel and harp, and rejoice at the sound of the organ. {21:13} They spend their days in wealth, and in a moment go down to the grave. {21:14} Therefore they say unto God, Depart from us; for we desire not the knowledge of thy ways. {21:15} What is the Almighty, that we should serve him? and what profit should we have, if we pray unto him? {21:16} Lo, their good is not in their hand: the counsel of the wicked is far from me. {21:17} How oft is the candle of the wicked put out! and how oft cometh their destruction upon them! God distributeth sorrows in his anger. {21:18} They are as stubble before the wind, and as chaff that the storm carrieth away. {21:19} God layeth up his iniquity for his children: he rewardeth him, and he shall know it. {21:20} His eyes shall see his destruction, and he shall drink of the wrath of the Almighty. {21:21} For what pleasure hath he in his house after him, when the number of his months is cut off in the midst? {21:22} Shall any teach God knowledge? seeing he judgeth those that are high. {21:23} One dieth in his full strength, being wholly at ease and quiet. {21:24} His breasts are full of milk, and his bones are moistened with marrow. {21:25} And another dieth in the bitterness of his soul, and never eateth with pleasure. {21:26} They shall lie down alike in the dust, and the worms shall cover them. {21:27} Behold, I know your thoughts, and the devices which ye wrongfully imagine against me. {21:28} For ye say, Where is the house of the prince? and where are the dwelling places of the wicked? {21:29} Have ye not asked them that go by the way? and do ye not know their tokens, {21:30} That the wicked is reserved to the day of destruction? they shall be brought forth to the day of wrath. {21:31} Who shall declare his way to his face? and who shall repay him what he hath done? {21:32} Yet shall he be brought to the grave, and shall remain in the tomb. {21:33} The clods of the valley shall be sweet unto him, and every man shall draw after him, as there are innumerable before him. {21:34} How then comfort ye me in vain, seeing in your answers there remaineth falsehood?

{22:1} Then Eliphaz the Temanite answered and said, {22:2} Can a man be profitable unto God, as he that is wise may be profitable unto himself? {22:3} Is it any pleasure to the Almighty that thou art righteous? or is it gain to him that thou makest thy ways perfect? {22:4} Will he reprove thee for fear of thee? will he enter with thee into judgment? {22:5} Is not thy wickedness great? and thine iniquities infinite? {22:6} For thou hast taken a pledge from thy brother for nought, and stripped the naked of their clothing. {22:7} Thou hast not given water to the weary to drink, and thou hast withholden bread from the hungry. {22:8} But as for the mighty man, he had the earth; and the honourable man dwelt in it. {22:9} Thou hast sent widows away empty, and the arms of the fatherless have been broken. {22:10} Therefore snares are round about thee, and sudden fear troubleth thee; {22:11} Or darkness, that thou canst not see; and abundance of waters cover thee. {22:12} Is not God in the height of heaven? and behold the height of the stars, how high they are! {22:13} And thou sayest, How doth God know? can he judge through the dark cloud? {22:14} Thick clouds are a covering to him, that he seeth not; and he walketh in the circuit of heaven. {22:15} Hast thou marked the old way which wicked men have trodden? {22:16} Which were cut down out of time, whose foundation was overflown with a flood: {22:17} Which said unto God, Depart from us: and what can the Almighty do for them? {22:18} Yet he filled their houses with good things: but the counsel of the wicked is far from me. {22:19} The righteous see it, and are glad: and the innocent laugh them to scorn. {22:20} Whereas our substance is not cut down, but the remnant of them the fire consumeth. {22:21} Acquaint now thyself with him, and be at peace: thereby good shall come unto thee. {22:22} Receive, I pray thee, the law from his mouth, and lay up his words in thine heart. {22:23} If thou return to the Almighty, thou shalt be built up, thou shalt put away iniquity far from thy tabernacles. {22:24} Then shalt thou lay up gold as dust, and the gold of Ophir as the stones of the brooks. {22:25} Yea, the Almighty shall be thy defence, and thou shalt have plenty of silver. {22:26} For then shalt thou have thy delight in the Almighty, and shalt lift up thy face unto God. {22:27} Thou shalt make thy prayer unto him, and he shall hear thee, and thou shalt pay thy vows. {22:28} Thou shalt also decree a thing, and it shall be established unto thee: and the light shall shine upon thy ways. {22:29} When men are cast down, then thou shalt say, There is lifting up; and he shall save the humble person. {22:30} He shall deliver the island of the innocent: and it is delivered by the pureness of thine hands.

{23:1} Then Job answered and said, {23:2} Even today my complaint is bitter: my stroke is heavier than my groaning. {23:3} Oh that I knew where I might find him! that I might come even to his seat! {23:4} I would order my cause before him, and fill my mouth with arguments. {23:5} I would know the words which he would answer me, and understand what he would say unto me. {23:6} Will he plead against me with his great power? No; but he would put strength in me. {23:7} There the righteous might dispute with him; so should I be delivered forever from my judge. {23:8} Behold, I go forward, but he is not there; and backward, but I cannot perceive him: {23:9} On the left hand, where he doth work, but I cannot behold him: he hideth himself on the right hand, that I cannot see him. {23:10} But he knoweth the way that I take: when he hath tried me, I shall come forth as gold. {23:11} My foot hath held his steps, his way have I kept, and not declined. {23:12} Neither have I gone back from the commandment of his lips; I have esteemed the words of his mouth more than my necessary food. {23:13} But he is in one mind, and who can turn him? and what his soul desireth, even that he doeth. {23:14} For he performeth the thing that is appointed for me: and many such things are with him. {23:15} Therefore am I troubled at his presence: when I consider, I am afraid of him. {23:16} For God maketh my heart soft, and the Almighty troubleth me: {23:17} Because I was not cut off before the darkness, neither hath he covered the darkness from my face.

{24:1} Why, seeing times are not hidden from the Almighty, do they that know him not see his days? {24:2} Some remove the landmarks; they violently take away flocks, and feed thereof. {24:3} They drive away the ass of the fatherless, they take the widow's ox for a pledge. {24:4} They turn the needy out of the way: the poor of the earth hide themselves together. {24:5} Behold, as wild asses in the desert, go they forth to their work; rising betimes for a prey: the wilderness yieldeth food for them and for their children. {24:6} They reap every one his corn in the field: and they gather the vintage of the wicked. {24:7} They cause the naked to lodge without clothing, that they have no covering in the cold. {24:8} They are wet with the showers of the mountains, and embrace the rock for want of a shelter. {24:9} They pluck the fatherless from the breast, and take a pledge of the poor. {24:10} They cause him to go naked without clothing, and they take away the sheaf from the hungry; {24:11} Which make oil within their walls, and tread their winepresses, and suffer thirst. {24:12} Men groan from out of the city, and the soul of the wounded crieth out: yet God layeth not folly to them. {24:13} They are of those that rebel against the light; they know not the ways thereof, nor abide in the paths thereof. {24:14} The murderer rising with the light killeth the poor and needy, and in the night is as a thief. {24:15} The eye also of the adulterer waiteth for the twilight, saying, No eye shall see me: and disguiseth his face. {24:16} In the dark they dig through houses, which they had marked for themselves in the daytime: they know not the light. {24:17} For the morning is to them even as the shadow of death: if one know them, they are in the terrors of the shadow of death. {24:18} He is swift as the waters; their portion is cursed in the earth: he beholdeth not the way of the vineyards. {24:19} Drought and heat consume the snow waters: so doth the grave those which have sinned. {24:20} **The womb shall forget him; the worm shall feed sweetly on him; he shall be no more remembered; and wickedness shall be broken as a tree.** {24:21} He evil entreateth the barren that beareth not: and doeth not good to the widow. {24:22} He draweth also the mighty with his power: he riseth up, and no man is sure of life. {24:23} Though it be given him to be in safety, whereon he resteth; yet his eyes are upon their ways. {24:24} **They are exalted for a little while, but are gone and brought low; they are taken out of the way as all other, and cut off as the tops of the ears of corn.** {24:25} And if it be not so now, who will make me a liar, and make my speech nothing worth?

{25:1} Then answered Bildad the Shuhite, and said, {25:2} Dominion and fear are with him, he maketh peace in his high places. {25:3} *Is there any number of his armies?* **and upon whom doth not his light arise?** {25:4} How then can man be justified with God? or how can he be clean that is born of a woman? {25:5} Behold even to the moon, and it shineth not; yea, the stars are not pure in his sight. {25:6} How much less man, that is a worm? and the son of man, which is a worm?

{26:1} But Job answered and said, {26:2} How hast thou helped him that is without power? How savest thou the arm that hath no strength? {26:3} How hast thou counseled him that hath no wisdom? And how hast thou plentifully declared the thing as it is? {26:4} To whom hast thou uttered words? And whose spirit came from thee? {26:5} Dead things are formed from under the waters, and the inhabitants thereof. {26:6} Hell is naked before him, and destruction hath no covering. {26:7} He stretcheth out the north over the empty place, and hangeth the earth upon nothing. {26:8} He bindeth up the waters in his thick clouds; and the cloud is not rent under them. {26:9} He holdeth back the face of his throne, and spreadeth his cloud upon it. {26:10} He hath compassed the waters with bounds, until the day and night come to an end. {26:11} The pillars of heaven tremble and are astonished at his reproof. {26:12} He divideth the sea with his power, and by his understanding he smiteth through the proud. {26:13} By his spirit he hath garnished the heavens; his hand hath formed the crooked serpent. {26:14} Lo, these are parts of his ways: but how little a portion is heard of him? But the thunder of his power who can understand?

{27:1} Moreover, Job continued his parable, and said, {27:2} As God liveth, who hath taken away my judgment; and the Almighty, who hath vexed my soul; {27:3} All the while my breath is in me, and the spirit of God is in my nostrils; {27:4} My lips shall not speak wickedness, nor my tongue utter deceit. {27:5} God forbid that I should justify you: till I die I will not remove mine integrity from me. {27:6} My righteousness I hold fast, and will not let it go: my heart shall not reproach me so long as I live. {27:7} Let mine enemy be as the wicked, and he that riseth up against me as the unrighteous. {27:8} For what is the hope of the hypocrite, though he hath gained, when God taketh away his soul? {27:9} Will God hear his cry when trouble cometh upon him? {27:10} Will he delight himself in the Almighty? will he always call upon God? {27:11} I will teach you by the hand of God: that which is with the Almighty will I not conceal. {27:12} Behold, all ye yourselves have seen it; why then are ye thus altogether vain? {27:13} This is the portion of a wicked man with God, and the heritage of oppressors, which they shall receive of the Almighty. {27:14} If his children be multiplied, it is for the sword: and his offspring shall not be satisfied with bread. {27:15} Those that remain of him shall be buried in death: and his widows shall not weep. {27:16} Though he heap up silver as the dust, and prepare raiment as the clay; {27:17} He may prepare it, but the just shall put it on, and the innocent shall divide the silver. {27:18} He buildeth his house as a moth, and as a booth that the keeper maketh. {27:19} The rich man shall lie down, but he shall not be gathered: he openeth his eyes, and he is not. {27:20} Terrors take hold on him as waters, a tempest stealeth him away in the night. {27:21} The east wind carrieth him away, and he departeth: and as a storm hurleth him out of his place. {27:22} For God shall cast upon him, and not spare: he would fain flee out of his hand. {27:23} Men shall clap their hands at him, and shall hiss him out of his place.

{28:1} Surely there is a vein for the silver, and a place for gold where they find it. {28:2} Iron is taken out of the earth, and brass is melted out of the stone. {28:3} He sets an end to darkness, and searches out all perfection: the stones of darkness, and the shadow of death. {28:4} The flood breaks out from the inhabitant; even the waters forgotten of the foot: they are dried up, they are gone away from men. {28:5} As for the earth, out of it comes bread: and under it is turned up as if it were fire. {28:6} The stones of it are the place of sapphires: and it has dust of gold. {28:7} There is a path which no bird knows, and which the vulture's eye has not seen: {28:8} The lion's whelps have not trodden it, nor the fierce lion passed by it. {28:9} He puts forth his hand upon the rock; he overturns the mountains by the roots. {28:10} He cuts out rivers among the rocks; and his eye sees every precious thing. {28:11} He binds the floods from overflowing; and the thing that is hidden he brings forth to light. {28:12} But where shall wisdom be found? and where is the place of understanding? {28:13} Man does not know its price; neither is it found in the land of the living. {28:14} The depth says, It is not in me: and the sea says, It is not with me. {28:15} It cannot be gotten for gold, neither shall silver be weighed for the price thereof. {28:16} It cannot be valued with the gold of Ophir, with the precious onyx, or the sapphire. {28:17} The gold and the crystal cannot equal it: and the exchange of it shall not be for jewels of fine gold. {28:18} No mention shall be made of coral, or of pearls: for the price of wisdom is above rubies. {28:19} The topaz of Ethiopia shall not equal it, neither shall it be valued with pure gold. {28:20} Whence then comes wisdom? and where is the place of understanding? {28:21} Seeing it is hidden from the eyes of all living, and kept close from the birds of the air. {28:22} Destruction and death say, We have heard the fame thereof with our ears. {28:23} God understands the way thereof, and he knows the place thereof. {28:24} For he looks to the ends of the earth, and sees under the whole heaven; {28:25} To make the weight for the winds; and he weighs the waters by measure. {28:26} When he made a decree for the rain, and a way for the lightning of the thunder: {28:27} Then did he see it, and declare it; he prepared it, yes, and searched it out. {28:28} **And unto man he said, Behold, the fear of the Lord, that is wisdom; and to depart from evil is understanding.**

{29:1} Moreover, Job continued his parable, and said, {29:2} Oh that I were as in months past, as in the days when God preserved me; {29:3} When his candle shined upon my head, and when by his light I walked through darkness; {29:4} As I was in the days of my youth, when the secret of God was upon my tabernacle; {29:5} When the Almighty was yet with me, when my children were about me; {29:6} When I washed my steps with butter, and the rock poured me out rivers of oil; {29:7} When I went out to the gate through the city, when I prepared my seat in the street! {29:8} The young men saw me, and hid themselves: and the aged arose, and stood up. {29:9} The princes refrained talking, and laid their hand on their mouth. {29:10} The nobles held their peace, and their tongue cleaved to the roof of their mouth. {29:11} When the ear heard me, then it blessed me; and when the eye saw me, it gave witness to me: {29:12} Because I delivered the poor that cried, and the fatherless, and him that had none to help him. {29:13} The blessing of him that was ready to perish came upon me: and I caused the widow's heart to sing for joy. {29:14} I put on righteousness, and it clothed me: my judgment was as a robe and a diadem. {29:15} I was eyes to the blind, and feet was I to the lame. {29:16} I was a father to the poor: and the cause which I knew not I searched out. {29:17} And I broke the jaws of the wicked, and plucked the spoil out of his teeth. {29:18} Then I said, I shall die in my nest, and I shall multiply my days as the sand. {29:19} My root was spread out by the waters, and the dew lay all night upon my branch. {29:20} My glory was fresh in me, and my bow was renewed in my hand. {29:21} Unto me men gave ear, and waited, and kept silence at my counsel. {29:22} After my words they spoke not again; and my speech dropped upon them. {29:23} And they waited for me as for the rain; and they opened their mouth wide as for the latter rain. {29:24} If I laughed on them, they believed it not; and the light of my countenance they cast not down. {29:25} I chose out their way, and sat chief, and dwelt as a king in the army, as one that comforteth the mourners.

{30:1} But now they that are younger than I have me in derision, whose fathers I would have disdained to have set with the dogs of my flock. {30:2} Yea, whereto might the strength of their hands, in whom old age was perished? {30:3} For want and famine, they were solitary; fleeing into the wilderness, in former time desolate and waste. {30:4} They cut up mallows by the bushes, and juniper roots for their food. {30:5} They were driven forth from among men; they cried after them as after a thief. {30:6} To dwell in the cliffs of the valleys, in caves of the earth, and in the rocks. {30:7} Among the bushes they brayed; under the nettles they were gathered together. {30:8} They were children of fools, yes, children of base men: they were viler than the earth. {30:9} And now I am their song, yes, I am their byword. {30:10} They abhor me, they flee far from me, and spare not to spit in my face. {30:11} Because he hath loosed my cord, and afflicted me, they have also let loose the bridle before me. {30:12} Upon my right hand rise the youth; they push away my feet, and they raise up against me the ways of their destruction. {30:13} They mar my path, they set forward my calamity, they have no helper. {30:14} They came upon me as a wide breaking in of waters: in the desolation they rolled themselves upon me. {30:15} Terrors are turned upon me; they pursue my soul as the wind: and my welfare passeth away as a cloud. {30:16} And now my soul is poured out upon me; the days of affliction have taken hold upon me. {30:17} My bones are pierced in me in the night season: and my sinews take no rest. {30:18} By the great force of my disease is my garment changed: it binds me about as the collar of my coat. {30:19} He hath cast me into the mire, and I am become like dust and ashes. {30:20} I cry unto thee, and thou dost not hear me: I stand up, and thou regardest me not. {30:21} Thou art become cruel to me: with thy strong hand thou opposest thyself against me. {30:22} Thou liftest me up to the wind; thou causest me to ride upon it, and dissolvest my substance. {30:23} For I know that thou wilt bring me to death, and to the house appointed for all living. {30:24} Howbeit he will not stretch out his hand to the grave, though they cry in his destruction. {30:25} Did not I weep for him that was in trouble? was not my soul grieved for the poor? {30:26} When I looked for good, then evil came unto me: and when I waited for light, there came darkness. {30:27} My bowels boiled, and rested not: the days of affliction prevented me. {30:28} I went mourning without the sun: I stood up, and I cried in the congregation. {30:29} I am a brother to dragons, and a companion to owls. {30:30} My skin is black upon me, and my bones are burned with heat. {30:31} My harp also is turned to mourning, and my organ into the voice of them that weep.

{31:1} I made a covenant with mine eyes; why then should I think upon a maid? {31:2} For what portion of God is there from above? and what inheritance of the Almighty from on high? {31:3} Is not destruction to the wicked? and a strange punishment to the workers of iniquity? {31:4} Doth not he see my ways, and count all my steps? {31:5} If I have walked with vanity, or if my foot hath hasted to deceit; {31:6} Let me be weighed in an even balance, that God may know mine integrity. {31:7} If my step hath turned out of the way, and mine heart walked after mine eyes, and if any blot hath cleaved to mine hands; {31:8} Then let me sow, and let another eat; yea, let my offspring be rooted out. {31:9} If mine heart have been deceived by a woman, or if I have laid wait at my neighbour's door; {31:10} Then let my wife grind unto another, and let others bow down upon her. {31:11} For this is an heinous crime; yea, it is an iniquity to be punished by the judges. {31:12} For it is a fire that consumeth to destruction, and would root out all mine increase. {31:13} If I did despise the cause of my manservant or of my maidservant, when they contended with me; {31:14} What then shall I do when God riseth up? and when he visiteth, what shall I answer him? {31:15} Did not he that made me in the womb make him? and did not one fashion us in the womb? {31:16} If I have withheld the poor from their desire, or have caused the eyes of the widow to fail; {31:17} Or have eaten my morsel myself alone, and the fatherless hath not eaten thereof; {31:18} For from my youth he was brought up with me, as with a father, and I have guided her from my mother's womb; {31:19} If I have seen any perish for want of clothing, or any poor without covering; {31:20} If his loins have not blessed me, and if he were not warmed with the fleece of my sheep; {31:21} If I have lifted up my hand against the fatherless, when I saw my help in the gate; {31:22} Then let mine arm fall from my shoulder blade, and mine arm be broken from the bone. {31:23} For destruction from God was a terror to me, and by reason of his highness I could not endure. {31:24} If I have made gold my hope, or have said to the fine gold, Thou art my confidence; {31:25} If I rejoiced because my wealth was great, and because mine hand had gotten much; {31:26} If I beheld the sun when it shined, or the moon walking in brightness; {31:27} And my heart hath been secretly enticed, or my mouth hath kissed my hand: {31:28} This also were an iniquity to be punished by the judge: for I should have denied the God that is above. {31:29} If I rejoiced at the destruction of him that hated me, or lifted up myself when evil found him: {31:30} Neither have I suffered my mouth to sin by wishing a curse to his soul. {31:31} If the men of my tabernacle said not, Oh that we had of his flesh! we cannot be satisfied. {31:32} The stranger did not lodge in the street: but I opened my doors to the traveller. {31:33} If I covered my transgressions as Adam, by hiding mine iniquity in my bosom: {31:34} Did I fear a great multitude, or did the contempt of families terrify me, that I kept silence, and went not out of the door? {31:35} Oh that one would hear me! behold, my desire is, that the Almighty would answer me, and that mine adversary had written a book. {31:36} Surely I would take it upon my shoulder, and bind it as a crown to me. {31:37} I would declare unto him the number of my steps; as a prince would I go near unto him. {31:38} If my land cry against me, or that the furrows likewise thereof complain; {31:39} If I have eaten the fruits thereof without money, or have caused the owners thereof to lose their life: {31:40} Let thistles grow instead of wheat, and cockle instead of barley. The words of Job are ended.

{32:1} So these three men ceased to answer Job, because he was righteous in his own eyes. {32:2} Then was kindled the wrath of Elihu the son of Barachel the Buzite, of the kindred of Ram: against Job was his wrath kindled, because he justified himself rather than God. {32:3} Also against his three friends was his wrath kindled, because they had found no answer, and yet had condemned Job. {32:4} Now Elihu had waited till Job had spoken, because they were elder than he. {32:5} When Elihu saw that there was no answer in the mouth of these three men, then his wrath was kindled. {32:6} And Elihu the son of Barachel the Buzite answered and said, I am young, and ye are very old; wherefore I was afraid, and durst not shew you mine opinion. {32:7} I said, Days should speak, and multitude of years should teach wisdom. {32:8} But there is a spirit in man: and the inspiration of the Almighty giveth them understanding. {32:9} Great men are not always wise: neither do the aged understand judgment. {32:10} Therefore I said, Hearken to me; I also will shew mine opinion. {32:11} Behold, I waited for your words; I gave ear to your reasons, whilst ye searched out what to say. {32:12} Yea, I attended unto you, and, behold, there was none of you that convinced Job, or that answered his words: {32:13} Lest ye should say, We have found out wisdom: God thrusteth him down, not man. {32:14} Now he hath not directed his words against me: neither will I answer him with your speeches. {32:15} They were amazed, they answered no more: they left off speaking. {32:16} When I had waited, (for they spake not, but stood still, and answered no more;) {32:17} I said, I will answer also my part, I also will shew mine opinion. {32:18} For I am full of matter, the spirit within me constraineth me. {32:19} Behold, my belly is as wine which hath no vent; it is ready to burst like new bottles. {32:20} I will speak, that I may be refreshed: I will open my lips and answer. {32:21} Let me not, I pray you, accept any man's person, neither let me give flattering titles unto man. {32:22} For I know not to give flattering titles; in so doing my maker would soon take me away.

{33:1} Wherefore, Job, I pray thee, hear my speeches, and hearken to all my words. {33:2} Behold, now I have opened my mouth, my tongue hath spoken in my mouth. {33:3} My words shall be of the uprightness of my heart: and my lips shall utter knowledge clearly. {33:4} The Spirit of God hath made me, and the breath of the Almighty hath given me life. {33:5} If thou canst answer me, set thy words in order before me, stand up. {33:6} Behold, I am according to thy wish in God's stead: I also am formed out of the clay. {33:7} Behold, my terror shall not make thee afraid, neither shall my hand be heavy upon thee. {33:8} Surely thou hast spoken in mine hearing, and I have heard the voice of thy words, saying, {33:9} I am clean without transgression, I am innocent; neither is there iniquity in me. {33:10} Behold, he findeth occasions against me, he counteth me for his enemy, {33:11} He putteth my feet in the stocks, he marketh all my paths. {33:12} Behold, in this thou art not just: I will answer thee, that God is greater than man. {33:13} Why dost thou strive against him? for he giveth not account of any of his matters. {33:14} For God speaketh once, yea twice, yet man perceiveth it not. {33:15} In a dream, in a vision of the night, when deep sleep falleth upon men, in slumberings upon the bed; {33:16} Then he openeth the ears of men, and sealeth their instruction, {33:17} That he may withdraw man from his purpose, and hide pride from man. {33:18} He keepeth back his soul from the pit, and his life from perishing by the sword. {33:19} He is chastened also with pain upon his bed, and the multitude of his bones with strong pain: {33:20} So that his life abhorreth bread, and his soul dainty meat. {33:21} His flesh is consumed away, that it cannot be seen; and his bones that were not seen stick out. {33:22} Yea, his soul draweth near unto the grave, and his life to the destroyers. {33:23} If there be a messenger with him, an interpreter, one among a thousand, to show unto man his uprightness; {33:24} Then he is gracious unto him, and saith, Deliver him from going down to the pit: I have found a ransom. {33:25} His flesh shall be fresher than a child's: he shall return to the days of his youth: {33:26} He shall pray unto God, and he will be favourable unto him: and he shall see his face with joy: for he will render unto man his righteousness. {33:27} He looketh upon men, and if any say, I have sinned, and perverted that which was right, and it profited me not; {33:28} He will deliver his soul from going into the pit, and his life shall see the light. {33:29} Lo, all these things worketh God oftentimes with man, {33:30} To bring back his soul from the pit, to be enlightened with the light of the living. {33:31} Mark well, O Job, hearken unto me: hold thy peace, and I will speak. {33:32} If thou hast any thing to say, answer me: speak, for I desire to justify thee. {33:33} If not, hearken unto me: hold thy peace, and I shall teach thee wisdom.

{34:1} Furthermore Elihu answered and said, {34:2} Hear my words, O ye wise men; and give ear unto me, ye that have knowledge. {34:3} For the ear tries words, as the mouth tastes food. {34:4} Let us choose judgment; let us know among ourselves what is good. {34:5} For Job hath said, "I am righteous: and God hath taken away my judgment." {34:6} Should I lie against my right? My wound is incurable without transgression. {34:7} What man is like Job, who drinketh up scorning like water? {34:8} He goeth in company with the workers of iniquity, and walketh with wicked men. {34:9} For he hath said, "It profiteth a man nothing that he should delight himself with God." {34:10} Therefore hearken unto me, ye men of understanding: far be it from God, that he should do wickedness; and from the Almighty, that he should commit iniquity. {34:11} For the work of a man shall he render unto him, and cause every man to find according to his ways. {34:12} Yea, surely God will not do wickedly, neither will the Almighty pervert judgment. {34:13} Who hath given him a charge over the earth? or who hath disposed the whole world? {34:14} If he set his heart upon man, if he gather unto himself his spirit and his breath; {34:15} All flesh shall perish together, and man shall turn again unto dust. {34:16} If now thou hast understanding, hear this: hearken to the voice of my words. {34:17} Shall even he that hateth right govern? and wilt thou condemn him that is most just? {34:18} Is it fit to say to a king, "Thou art wicked"? and to princes, "Ye are ungodly"? {34:19} How much less to him that accepteth not the persons of princes, nor regardeth the rich more than the poor? for they all are the work of his hands. {34:20} In a moment shall they die, and the people shall be troubled at midnight, and pass away: and the mighty shall be taken away without hand. {34:21} For his eyes are upon the ways of man, and he seeth all his goings. {34:22} There is no darkness, nor shadow of death, where the workers of iniquity may hide themselves. {34:23} For he will not lay upon man more than right; that he should enter into judgment with God. {34:24} He shall break in pieces mighty men without number, and set others in their stead. {34:25} Therefore he knoweth their works, and he overturneth them in the night, so that they are destroyed. {34:26} He striketh them as wicked men in the open sight of others; {34:27} Because they turned back from him, and would not consider any of his ways: {34:28} So that they cause the cry of the poor to come unto him, and he heareth the cry of the afflicted. {34:29} When he giveth quietness, who then can make trouble? and when he hideth his face, who then can behold him? whether it be done against a nation, or against a man only: {34:30} That the hypocrite reign not, lest the people be ensnared. {34:31} Surely it is meet to be said unto God, "I have borne chastisement, I will not offend any more." {34:32} "Teach thou me: if I have done iniquity, I will do no more." {34:33} Should it be according to thy mind? he will recompense it, whether thou refuse, or whether thou choose; and not I: therefore speak what thou knowest. {34:34} Let men of understanding tell me, and let a wise man hearken unto me. {34:35} Job hath spoken without knowledge, and his words were without wisdom. {34:36} My desire is that Job may be tried unto the end because of his answers for wicked men. {34:37} For he addeth rebellion unto his sin, he clappeth his hands among us, and multiplieth his words against God.

{35:1} Elihu spoke moreover, and said, {35:2} "Thinkest thou this to be right, that thou saidst, 'My righteousness is more than God's'? {35:3} "For thou saidst, 'What advantage will it be unto thee? And, What profit shall I have, if I be cleansed from my sin?'" {35:4} "I will answer thee, and thy companions with thee." {35:5} "Look unto the heavens, and see; and behold the clouds which are higher than thou." {35:6} "If thou sinnest, what doest thou against him? or if thy transgressions be multiplied, what doest thou unto him?" {35:7} "If thou be righteous, what givest thou him? or what receiveth he of thine hand?" {35:8} "Thy wickedness may hurt a man as thou art; and thy righteousness may profit the son of man." {35:9} "By reason of the multitude of oppressions they make the oppressed to cry: they cry out by reason of the arm of the mighty." {35:10} "But none saith, 'Where is God my maker, who giveth songs in the night;'" {35:11} "Who teacheth us more than the beasts of the earth, and maketh us wiser than the fowls of heaven?" {35:12} "There they cry, but none giveth answer, because of the pride of evil men." {35:13} "Surely God will not hear vanity, neither will the Almighty regard it." {35:14} "Although thou sayest thou shalt not see him, yet judgment is before him; therefore trust thou in him." {35:15} "But now, because it is not so, he hath visited in his anger; yet he knoweth it not in great extremity:" {35:16} "Therefore doth Job open his mouth in vain; he multiplieth words without knowledge."

{36:1} Elihu also proceeded, and said, {36:2} "Suffer me a little, and I will show thee that I have yet to speak on God's behalf." {36:3} "I will fetch my knowledge from afar, and will ascribe righteousness to my Maker." {36:4} "For truly my words shall not be false: he that is perfect in knowledge is with thee." {36:5} "Behold, God is mighty, and despiseth not any; he is mighty in strength and wisdom." {36:6} "He preserveth not the life of the wicked: but giveth right to the poor." {36:7} "He withdraweth not his eyes from the righteous: but with kings are they on the throne; yea, he doth establish them for ever, and they are exalted." {36:8} "And if they be bound in fetters, and be holden in cords of affliction;" {36:9} "Then he showeth them their work, and their transgressions that they have exceeded." {36:10} "He openeth also their ear to discipline, and commandeth that they return from iniquity." {36:11} "If they obey and serve him, they shall spend their days in prosperity, and their years in pleasures." {36:12} "But if they obey not, they shall perish by the sword, and they shall die without knowledge." {36:13} "But the hypocrites in heart heap up wrath: they cry not when he bindeth them." {36:14} "They die in youth, and their life is among the unclean." {36:15} "He delivereth the poor in his affliction, and openeth their ears in oppression." {36:16} "Even so would he have removed thee out of the strait into a broad place, where there is no straitness; and that which should be set on thy table should be full of fatness." {36:17} "But thou hast fulfilled the judgment of the wicked: judgment and justice take hold on thee." {36:18} "Because there is wrath, beware lest he take thee away with his stroke: then a great ransom cannot deliver thee." {36:19} "Will he esteem thy riches? No, not gold, nor all the forces of strength." {36:20} "Desire not the night, when people are cut off in their place." {36:21} "Take heed, regard not iniquity: for this hast thou chosen rather than affliction." {36:22} "Behold, God exalteth by his power: who teacheth like him?" {36:23} "Who hath enjoined him his way? or who can say, Thou hast wrought iniquity?" {36:24} "Remember that thou magnify his work, which men behold." {36:25} "Every man may see it; man may behold it afar off." {36:26} "Behold, God is great, and we know him not, neither can the number of his years be searched out." {36:27} "For he maketh small the drops of water: they pour down rain according to the vapour thereof:" {36:28} "Which the clouds do drop and distil upon man abundantly." {36:29} "Also can any understand the spreadings of the clouds, or the noise of his tabernacle?" {36:30} "Behold, he spreadeth his light upon it, and covereth the bottom of the sea." {36:31} "For by them judgeth he the people; he giveth meat in abundance." {36:32} "With clouds he covereth the light; and commandeth it not to shine by the cloud that cometh betwixt." {36:33} "The noise thereof showeth concerning it, the cattle also concerning the vapour."

{37:1} At this also my heart trembleth, and is moved out of his place. {37:2} Hear attentively the noise of his voice, and the sound that goeth out of his mouth. {37:3} He directeth it under the whole heaven, and his lightning unto the ends of the earth. {37:4} After it a voice roareth: he thundereth with the voice of his excellency; and he will not stay them when his voice is heard. {37:5} God thundereth marvellously with his voice; great things doeth he, which we cannot comprehend. {37:6} For he saith to the snow, Be thou on the earth; likewise to the small rain, and to the great rain of his strength. {37:7} He sealeth up the hand of every man; that all men may know his work. {37:8} Then the beasts go into dens, and remain in their places. {37:9} Out of the south cometh the whirlwind: and cold out of the north. {37:10} By the breath of God frost is given: and the breadth of the waters is straitened. {37:11} Also by watering he wearieth the thick cloud: he scattereth his bright cloud: {37:12} And it is turned round about by his counsels: that they may do whatsoever he commandeth them upon the face of the world in the earth. {37:13} He causeth it to come, whether for correction, or for his land, or for mercy. {37:14} Hearken unto this, O Job: stand still, and consider the wondrous works of God. {37:15} Dost thou know when God disposed them, and caused the light of his cloud to shine? {37:16} Dost thou know the balancings of the clouds, the wondrous works of him which is perfect in knowledge? {37:17} How thy garments are warm, when he quieteth the earth by the south wind? {37:18} Hast thou with him spread out the sky, which is strong, and as a molten looking glass? {37:19} Teach us what we shall say unto him; for we cannot order our speech by reason of darkness. {37:20} Shall it be told him that I speak? if a man speak, surely he shall be swallowed up. {37:21} And now men see not the bright light which is in the clouds: but the wind passeth, and cleanseth them. {37:22} Fair weather cometh out of the north: with God is terrible majesty. {37:23} Touching the Almighty, we cannot find him out: he is excellent in power, and in judgment, and in plenty of justice: he will not afflict. {37:24} Men do therefore fear him: he respecteth not any that are wise of heart.

{38:1} **Then the LORD answered Job out of the whirlwind, and said,** {38:2} **Who is this that darkeneth counsel by words without knowledge?** {38:3} Gird up now thy loins like a man; for I will demand of thee, and answer thou me. {38:4} Where wast thou when I laid the foundations of the earth? declare, if thou hast understanding. {38:5} Who hath laid the measures thereof, if thou knowest? or who hath stretched the line upon it? {38:6} Whereupon are the foundations thereof fastened? or who laid the corner stone thereof; {38:7} When the morning stars sang together, and all the sons of God shouted for joy? {38:8} Or who shut up the sea with doors, when it brake forth, as if it had issued out of the womb? {38:9} When I made the cloud the garment thereof, and thick darkness a swaddlingband for it, {38:10} And brake up for it my decreed place, and set bars and doors, {38:11} And said, Hitherto shalt thou come, but no further: and here shall thy proud waves be stayed? {38:12} Hast thou commanded the morning since thy days; and caused the dayspring to know his place; {38:13} That it might take hold of the ends of the earth, that the wicked might be shaken out of it? {38:14} It is turned as clay to the seal; and they stand as a garment. {38:15} And from the wicked their light is withholden, and the high arm shall be broken. {38:16} Hast thou entered into the springs of the sea? or hast thou walked in the search of the depth? {38:17} Have the gates of death been opened unto thee? or hast thou seen the doors of the shadow of death? {38:18} Hast thou perceived the breadth of the earth? declare if thou knowest it all. {38:19} Where is the way where light dwelleth? and as for darkness, where is the place thereof, {38:20} That thou shouldest take it to the bound thereof, and that thou shouldest know the paths to the house thereof? {38:21} Knowest thou it, because thou wast then born? or because the number of thy days is great? {38:22} Hast thou entered into the treasures of the snow? or hast thou seen the treasures of the hail, {38:23} Which I have reserved against the time of trouble, against the day of battle and war? {38:24} By what way is the light parted, which scattereth the east wind upon the earth? {38:25} Who hath divided a watercourse for the overflowing of waters, or a way for the lightning of thunder; {38:26} To cause it to rain on the earth, where no man is; on the wilderness, wherein there is no man; {38:27} To satisfy the desolate and waste ground; and to cause the bud of the tender herb to spring forth? {38:28} Hath the rain a father? or who hath begotten the drops of dew? {38:29} Out of whose womb came the ice? and the hoary frost of heaven, who hath gendered it? {38:30} The waters are hid as with a stone, and the face of the deep is frozen. {38:31} Canst thou bind the sweet influences of Pleiades, or loose the bands of Orion? {38:32} Canst thou bring forth Mazzaroth in his season? or canst thou guide Arcturus with his sons? {38:33} Knowest thou the ordinances of heaven? canst thou set the dominion thereof in the earth? {38:34} Canst thou lift up thy voice to the clouds, that abundance of waters may cover thee? {38:35} Canst thou send lightnings, that they may go, and say unto thee, Here we are? {38:36} Who hath put wisdom in the inward parts? or who hath given understanding to the heart? {38:37} Who can number the clouds in wisdom? or who can stay the bottles of heaven, {38:38} When the dust groweth into hardness, and the clods cleave fast together? {38:39} Wilt thou hunt the prey for the lion? or fill the appetite of the young lions, {38:40} When they couch in their dens, and abide in the covert to lie in wait? {38:41} Who provideth for the raven his food? when his young ones cry unto God, they wander for lack of meat.

{39:1} Knowest thou the time when the wild goats of the rock bring forth? or canst thou mark when the hinds do calve? {39:2} Canst thou number the months that they fulfil? or knowest thou the time when they bring forth? {39:3} They bow themselves, they bring forth their young ones, they cast out their sorrows. {39:4} Their young ones are in good liking, they grow up with corn; they go forth, and return not unto them. {39:5} Who hath sent out the wild ass free? or who hath loosed the bands of the wild ass? {39:6} Whose house I have made the wilderness, and the barren land his dwellings. {39:7} He scorneth the multitude of the city, neither regardeth he the crying of the driver. {39:8} The range of the mountains is his pasture, and he searcheth after every green thing. {39:9} Will the unicorn be willing to serve thee, or abide by thy crib? {39:10} Canst thou bind the unicorn with his band in the furrow? or will he harrow the valleys after thee? {39:11} Wilt thou trust him, because his strength is great? or wilt thou leave thy labour to him? {39:12} Wilt thou believe him, that he will bring home thy seed, and gather it into thy barn? {39:13} Gavest thou the goodly wings unto the peacocks? or wings and feathers unto the ostrich? {39:14} Which leaveth her eggs in the earth, and warmeth them in dust, {39:15} And forgetteth that the foot may crush them, or that the wild beast may break them. {39:16} She is hardened against her young ones, as though they were not hers: her labour is in vain without fear; {39:17} Because God hath deprived her of wisdom, neither hath he imparted to her understanding. {39:18} What time she lifteth up herself on high, she scorneth the horse and his rider. {39:19} Hast thou given the horse strength? hast thou clothed his neck with thunder? {39:20} Canst thou make him afraid as a grasshopper? the glory of his nostrils is terrible. {39:21} He paweth in the valley, and rejoiceth in his strength: he goeth on to meet the armed men. {39:22} He mocketh at fear, and is not affrighted; neither turneth he back from the sword. {39:23} The quiver rattleth against him, the glittering spear and the shield. {39:24} He swalloweth the ground with fierceness and rage: neither believeth he that it is the sound of the trumpet. {39:25} He saith among the trumpets, Ha, ha; and he smelleth the battle afar off, the thunder of the captains, and the shouting. {39:26} Doth the hawk fly by thy wisdom, and stretch her wings toward the south? {39:27} Doth the eagle mount up at thy command, and make her nest on high? {39:28} She dwelleth and abideth on the rock, upon the crag of the rock, and the strong place. {39:29} From thence she seeketh the prey, and her eyes behold afar off. {39:30} Her young ones also suck up blood: and where the slain are, there is she.

{40:1} Moreover the LORD answered Job, and said, {40:2} Shall he that contendeth with the Almighty instruct him? he that reproveth God, let him answer it. {40:3} Then Job answered the LORD, and said, {40:4} Behold, I am vile; what shall I answer thee? I will lay mine hand upon my mouth. {40:5} Once have I spoken; but I will not answer: yea, twice; but I will proceed no further. {40:6} Then answered the LORD unto Job out of the whirlwind, and said, {40:7} Gird up thy loins now like a man: I will demand of thee, and declare thou unto me. {40:8} Wilt thou also disannul my judgment? wilt thou condemn me, that thou mayest be righteous? {40:9} Hast thou an arm like God? or canst thou thunder with a voice like him? {40:10} Deck thyself now with majesty and excellency; and array thyself with glory and beauty. {40:11} Cast abroad the rage of thy wrath: and behold every one that is proud, and abase him. {40:12} Look on every one that is proud, and bring him low; and tread down the wicked in their place. {40:13} Hide them in the dust together; and bind their faces in secret. {40:14} Then will I also confess unto thee that thine own right hand can save thee. {40:15} Behold now behemoth, which I made with thee; he eateth grass as an ox. {40:16} Lo now, his strength is in his loins, and his force is in the navel of his belly. {40:17} He moveth his tail like a cedar: the sinews of his stones are wrapped together. {40:18} His bones are as strong pieces of brass; his bones are like bars of iron. {40:19} He is the chief of the ways of God: he that made him can make his sword to approach unto him. {40:20} Surely the mountains bring him forth food, where all the beasts of the field play. {40:21} He lieth under the shady trees, in the covert of the reed, and fens. {40:22} The shady trees cover him with their shadow; the willows of the brook compass him about. {40:23} Behold, he drinketh up a river, and hasteth not: he trusteth that he can draw up Jordan into his mouth. {40:24} He taketh it with his eyes: his nose pierceth through snares.

{41:1} Canst thou draw out leviathan with an hook? or his tongue with a cord which thou lettest down? {41:2} Canst thou put an hook into his nose? or bore his jaw through with a thorn? {41:3} Will he make many supplications unto thee? will he speak soft words unto thee? {41:4} Will he make a covenant with thee? wilt thou take him for a servant for ever? {41:5} Wilt thou play with him as with a bird? or wilt thou bind him for thy maidens? {41:6} Shall the companions make a banquet of him? shall they part him among the merchants? {41:7} Canst thou fill his skin with barbed irons? or his head with fish spears? {41:8} Lay thine hand upon him, remember the battle, do no more. {41:9} Behold, the hope of him is in vain: shall not one be cast down even at the sight of him? {41:10} None is so fierce that dare stir him up: who then is able to stand before me? {41:11} Who hath prevented me, that I should repay him? whatsoever is under the whole heaven is mine. {41:12} I will not conceal his parts, nor his power, nor his comely proportion. {41:13} Who can discover the face of his garment? or who can come to him with his double bridle? {41:14} Who can open the doors of his face? his teeth are terrible round about. {41:15} His scales are his pride, shut up together as with a close seal. {41:16} One is so near to another, that no air can come between them. {41:17} They are joined one to another, they stick together, that they cannot be sundered. {41:18} By his neesings a light doth shine, and his eyes are like the eyelids of the morning. {41:19} Out of his mouth go burning lamps, and sparks of fire leap out. {41:20} Out of his nostrils goeth smoke, as out of a seething pot or caldron. {41:21} His breath kindleth coals, and a flame goeth out of his mouth. {41:22} In his neck remaineth strength, and sorrow is turned into joy before him. {41:23} The flakes of his flesh are joined together: they are firm in themselves; they cannot be moved. {41:24} His heart is as firm as a stone; yea, as hard as a piece of the nether millstone. {41:25} When he raiseth up himself, the mighty are afraid: by reason of breakings they purify themselves. {41:26} The sword of him that layeth at him cannot hold: the spear, the dart, nor the habergeon. {41:27} He esteemeth iron as straw, and brass as rotten wood. {41:28} The arrow cannot make him flee: slingstones are turned with him into stubble. {41:29} Darts are counted as stubble: he laugheth at the shaking of a spear. {41:30} Sharp stones are under him: he spreadeth sharp pointed things upon the mire. {41:31} He maketh the deep to boil like a pot: he maketh the sea like a pot of ointment. {41:32} He maketh a path to shine after him; one would think the deep to be hoary. {41:33} Upon earth there is not his like, who is made without fear. {41:34} He beholdeth all high things: he is a king over all the children of pride.

{42:1} Then Job answered the LORD, and said, {42:2} I know that thou canst do every thing, and that no thought can be withholden from thee. {42:3} Who is he that hideth counsel without knowledge? therefore have I uttered that I understood not; things too wonderful for me, which I knew not. {42:4} Hear, I beseech thee, and I will speak: I will demand of thee, and declare thou unto me. {42:5} **I have heard of thee by the hearing of the ear: but now mine eye seeth thee.** {42:6} Wherefore I abhor myself, and repent in dust and ashes. {42:7} And it was so, that after the LORD had spoken these words unto Job, the LORD said to Eliphaz the Temanite, My wrath is kindled against thee, and against thy two friends: for ye have not spoken of me the thing that is right, as my servant Job hath. {42:8} Therefore take unto you now seven bullocks and seven rams, and go to my servant Job, and offer up for yourselves a burnt offering; and my servant Job shall pray for you: for him will I accept: lest I deal with you after your folly, in that ye have not spoken of me the thing which is right, like my servant Job. {42:9} So Eliphaz the Temanite and Bildad the Shuhite and Zophar the Naamathite went, and did according as the LORD commanded them: the LORD also accepted Job. {42:10} And the LORD turned the captivity of Job, when he prayed for his friends: also the LORD gave Job twice as much as he had before. {42:11} Then came there unto him all his brethren, and all his sisters, and all they that had been of his acquaintance before, and did eat bread with him in his house: and they bemoaned him, and comforted him over all the evil that the LORD had brought upon him: every man also gave him a piece of money, and every one an earring of gold. {42:12} So the LORD blessed the latter end of Job more than his beginning: for he had fourteen thousand sheep, and six thousand camels, and a thousand yoke of oxen, and a thousand she asses. {42:13} He had also seven sons and three daughters. {42:14} And he called the name of the first, Jemima; and the name of the second, Kezia; and the name of the third, Keren-happuch. {42:15} And in all the land were no women found so fair as the daughters of Job: and their father gave them inheritance among their brethren. {42:16} After this lived Job an hundred and forty years, and saw his sons, and his sons' sons, even four generations. {42:17} So Job died, being old and full of days.

Psalms

{1:1} Blessed is the man that walketh not in the counsel of the ungodly, nor standeth in the way of sinners, nor sitteth in the seat of the scornful. {1:2} But his delight is in the law of the LORD; and in his law doth he meditate day and night. {1:3} And he shall be like a tree planted by the rivers of water, that bringeth forth his fruit in his season; his leaf also shall not wither; and whatsoever he doeth shall prosper. {1:4} The ungodly are not so: but are like the chaff which the wind driveth away. {1:5} Therefore the ungodly shall not stand in the judgment, nor sinners in the congregation of the righteous. {1:6} For the LORD knoweth the way of the righteous: but the way of the ungodly shall perish.

{2:1} Why do the heathen rage, and the people imagine a vain thing? {2:2} The kings of the earth set themselves, and the rulers take counsel together, against the LORD, and against his anointed, saying, {2:3} Let us break their bands asunder, and cast away their cords from us. {2:4} He that sitteth in the heavens shall laugh: the Lord shall have them in derision. {2:5} Then shall he speak unto them in his wrath, and vex them in his sore displeasure. {2:6} Yet have I set my king upon my holy hill of Zion. {2:7} I will declare the decree: the LORD hath said unto me, Thou art my Son; this day have I begotten thee. {2:8} Ask of me, and I shall give thee the heathen for thine inheritance, and the uttermost parts of the earth for thy possession. {2:9} Thou shalt break them with a rod of iron; thou shalt dash them in pieces like a potter's vessel. {2:10} Be wise now therefore, O ye kings: be instructed, ye judges of the earth. {2:11} Serve the LORD with fear, and rejoice with trembling. {2:12} Kiss the Son, lest he be angry, and ye perish from the way, when his wrath is kindled but a little. Blessed are all they that put their trust in him.

{3:1} LORD, how are they increased that trouble me! many are they that rise up against me. {3:2} Many there be which say of my soul, "There is no help for him in God." Selah. {3:3} But thou, O LORD, art a shield for me; my glory, and the lifter up of mine head. {3:4} I cried unto the LORD with my voice, and he heard me out of his holy hill. Selah. {3:5} I laid me down and slept; I awaked; for the LORD sustained me. {3:6} I will not be afraid of ten thousands of people, that have set themselves against me round about. {3:7} Arise, O LORD; save me, O my God: for thou hast smitten all mine enemies upon the cheek bone; thou hast broken the teeth of the ungodly. {3:8} Salvation belongeth unto the LORD: thy blessing is upon thy people. Selah.

{4:1} Hear me when I call, O God of my righteousness: thou hast enlarged me when I was in distress; have mercy upon me, and hear my prayer. {4:2} O ye sons of men, how long will ye turn my glory into shame? how long will ye love vanity, and seek after leasing? Selah. {4:3} But know that the LORD hath set apart him that is godly for himself: the LORD will hear when I call unto him. {4:4} Stand in awe, and sin not: commune with your own heart upon your bed, and be still. Selah. {4:5} Offer the sacrifices of righteousness, and put your trust in the LORD. {4:6} There be many that say, Who will show us any good? LORD, lift thou up the light of thy countenance upon us. {4:7} Thou hast put gladness in my heart, more than in the time that their corn and their wine increased. {4:8} I will both lay me down in peace, and sleep: for thou, LORD, only makest me dwell in safety.

{5:1} Give ear to my words, O LORD, consider my meditation. {5:2} Hearken unto the voice of my cry, my King, and my God: for unto thee will I pray. {5:3} My voice shalt thou hear in the morning, O LORD; in the morning will I direct my prayer unto thee, and will look up. {5:4} For thou art not a God that hath pleasure in wickedness: neither shall evil dwell with thee. {5:5} The foolish shall not stand in thy sight: thou hatest all workers of iniquity. {5:6} Thou shalt destroy them that speak leasing: the LORD will abhor the bloody and deceitful man. {5:7} But as for me, I will come into thy house in the multitude of thy mercy: and in thy fear will I worship toward thy holy temple. {5:8} Lead me, O LORD, in thy righteousness because of mine enemies; make thy way straight before my face. {5:9} For there is no faithfulness in their mouth; their inward part is very wickedness; their throat is an open sepulchre; they flatter with their tongue. {5:10} Destroy thou them, O God; let them fall by their own counsels; cast them out in the multitude of their transgressions; for they have rebelled against thee. {5:11} But let all those that put their trust in thee rejoice: let them ever shout for joy, because thou defendest them: let them also that love thy name be joyful in thee. {5:12} For thou, LORD, wilt bless the righteous; with favour wilt thou compass him as with a shield.

{6:1} O LORD, rebuke me not in thine anger, neither chasten me in thy hot displeasure. {6:2} Have mercy upon me, O LORD; for I am weak: O LORD, heal me; for my bones are vexed. {6:3} My soul is also sore vexed: but thou, O LORD, how long? {6:4} Return, O LORD, deliver my soul: oh save me for thy mercies' sake. {6:5} For in death there is no remembrance of thee: in the grave who shall give thee thanks? {6:6} I am weary with my groaning; all the night make I my bed to swim; I water my couch with my tears. {6:7} Mine eye is consumed because of grief; it waxeth old because of all mine enemies. {6:8} Depart from me, all ye workers of iniquity; for the LORD hath heard the voice of my weeping. {6:9} The LORD hath heard my supplication; the LORD will receive my prayer. {6:10} Let all mine enemies be ashamed and sore vexed: let them return and be ashamed suddenly.

{7:1} **O Lord my God, in thee do I put my trust: save me from all them that persecute me, and deliver me.** {7:2} Lest he tear my soul like a lion, rending it in pieces, while there is none to deliver. {7:3} O LORD my God, if I have done this; if there be iniquity in my hands; {7:4} If I have rewarded evil unto him that was at peace with me; (yea, I have delivered him that without cause is mine enemy:) {7:5} Let the enemy persecute my soul, and take it; yea, let him tread down my life upon the earth, and lay mine honour in the dust. Selah. {7:6} Arise, O LORD, in thine anger, lift up thyself because of the rage of mine enemies: and awake for me to the judgment that thou hast commanded. {7:7} So shall the congregation of the people compass thee about: for their sakes therefore return thou on high. {7:8} The LORD shall judge the people: judge me, O LORD, according to my righteousness, and according to mine integrity that is in me. {7:9} Oh let the wickedness of the wicked come to an end; but establish the just: for the righteous God trieth the hearts and reins. {7:10} My defence is of God, which saveth the upright in heart. {7:11} God judgeth the righteous, and God is angry with the wicked every day. {7:12} If he turn not, he will whet his sword; he hath bent his bow, and made it ready. {7:13} He hath also prepared for him the instruments of death; he ordaineth his arrows against the persecutors. {7:14} **Behold, he travaileth with iniquity, and hath conceived mischief, and brought forth falsehood.** {7:15} He made a pit, and digged it, and is fallen into the ditch which he made. {7:16} His mischief shall return upon his own head, and his violent dealing shall come down upon his own pate. {7:17} **I will praise the LORD according to his righteousness: and will sing praise to the name of the LORD most high.**

{8:1} O LORD our Lord, how excellent is thy name in all the earth! who hast set thy glory above the heavens. {8:2} Out of the mouth of babes and sucklings hast thou ordained strength because of thine enemies, that thou mightest still the enemy and the avenger. {8:3} When I consider thy heavens, the work of thy fingers, the moon and the stars, which thou hast ordained; {8:4} **What is man, that thou art mindful of him? and the son of man, that thou visitest him?** {8:5} For thou hast made him a little lower than the angels, and hast crowned him with glory and honour. {8:6} **Thou madest him to have dominion over the works of thy hands; thou hast put all things under his feet:** {8:7} All sheep and oxen, yea, and the beasts of the field; {8:8} The fowl of the air, and the fish of the sea, and whatsoever passeth through the paths of the seas. {8:9} O LORD our Lord, how excellent is thy name in all the earth!

✝ he Old Testament ✝ 180

{9:1} I will praise thee, O LORD, with my whole heart; I will show forth all thy marvelous works. {9:2} I will be glad and rejoice in thee: I will sing praise to thy name, O thou most High. {9:3} When mine enemies are turned back, they shall fall and perish at thy presence. {9:4} For thou hast maintained my right and my cause; thou sittest in the throne judging right. {9:5} Thou hast rebuked the heathen, thou hast destroyed the wicked, thou hast put out their name for ever and ever. {9:6} O thou enemy, destructions are come to a perpetual end: and thou hast destroyed cities; their memorial is perished with them. {9:7} But the LORD shall endure for ever: he hath prepared his throne for judgment. {9:8} And he shall judge the world in righteousness, he shall minister judgment to the people in uprightness. {9:9} The LORD also will be a refuge for the oppressed, a refuge in times of trouble. {9:10} And they that know thy name will put their trust in thee: for thou, LORD, hast not forsaken them that seek thee. {9:11} Sing praises to the LORD, which dwelleth in Zion: declare among the people his doings. {9:12} When he maketh inquisition for blood, he remembereth them: he forgetteth not the cry of the humble. {9:13} Have mercy upon me, O LORD; consider my trouble which I suffer of them that hate me, thou that liftest me up from the gates of death: {9:14} That I may show forth all thy praise in the gates of the daughter of Zion: I will rejoice in thy salvation. {9:15} The heathen are sunk down in the pit that they made: in the net which they hid is their own foot taken. {9:16} The LORD is known by the judgment which he executeth: the wicked is snared in the work of his own hands. Higgaion. Selah. {9:17} The wicked shall be turned into hell, and all the nations that forget God. {9:18} For the needy shall not always be forgotten: the expectation of the poor shall not perish forever. {9:19} Arise, O LORD; let not man prevail: let the heathen be judged in thy sight. {9:20} Put them in fear, O LORD: that the nations may know themselves to be but men. Selah.

{10:1} Why standest thou afar off, O LORD? Why hidest thou thyself in times of trouble? {10:2} The wicked in his pride doth persecute the poor: let them be taken in the devices that they have imagined. {10:3} For the wicked boasteth of his heart's desire, and blesseth the covetous, whom the LORD abhorreth. {10:4} The wicked, through the pride of his countenance, will not seek after God: God is not in all his thoughts. {10:5} His ways are always grievous; thy judgments are far above out of his sight: as for all his enemies, he puffeth at them. {10:6} He hath said in his heart, I shall never be moved: for I shall never be in adversity. {10:7} His mouth is full of cursing and deceit and fraud: under his tongue is mischief and vanity. {10:8} He sitteth in the lurking places of the villages: in the secret places doth he murder the innocent: his eyes are privily set against the poor. {10:9} He lieth in wait secretly as a lion in his den: he lieth in wait to catch the poor: he doth catch the poor, when he draweth him into his net. {10:10} He croucheth, and humbleth himself, that the poor may fall by his strong ones. {10:11} He hath said in his heart, God hath forgotten: he hideth his face; he will never see it. {10:12} Arise, O LORD; O God, lift up thine hand: forget not the humble. {10:13} Wherefore doth the wicked contemn God? he hath said in his heart, Thou wilt not require it. {10:14} Thou hast seen it; for thou beholdest mischief and spite, to requite it with thy hand: the poor committeth himself unto thee; thou art the helper of the fatherless. {10:15} Break thou the arm of the wicked and the evil man: seek out his wickedness till thou find none. {10:16} The LORD is King for ever and ever: the heathen are perished out of his land. {10:17} LORD, thou hast heard the desire of the humble: thou wilt prepare their heart, thou wilt cause thine ear to hear: {10:18} To judge the fatherless and the oppressed, that the man of the earth may no more oppress.

{11:1} In the LORD put I my trust: How say ye to my soul, Flee as a bird to your mountain? {11:2} For, lo, the wicked bend their bow, they make ready their arrow upon the string, that they may privily shoot at the upright in heart. {11:3} If the foundations be destroyed, what can the righteous do? {11:4} The LORD is in his holy temple, the LORD'S throne is in heaven: his eyes behold, his eyelids try, the children of men. {11:5} The LORD trieth the righteous: but the wicked and him that loveth violence his soul hateth. {11:6} Upon the wicked he shall rain snares, fire and brimstone, and an horrible tempest: this shall be the portion of their cup. {11:7} For the righteous LORD loveth righteousness; his countenance doth behold the upright.

{12:1} Help, LORD; for the godly man ceaseth; for the faithful fail from among the children of men. {12:2} They speak vanity every one with his neighbour: with flattering lips and with a double heart do they speak. {12:3} The LORD shall cut off all flattering lips, and the tongue that speaketh proud things: {12:4} Who have said, With our tongue will we prevail; our lips are our own: who is lord over us? {12:5} For the oppression of the poor, for the sighing of the needy, now will I arise, saith the LORD; I will set him in safety from him that puffeth at him. {12:6} The words of the LORD are pure words: as silver tried in a furnace of earth, purified seven times. {12:7} Thou shalt keep them, O LORD, thou shalt preserve them from this generation for ever. {12:8} The wicked walk on every side, when the vilest men are exalted.

{13:1} How long wilt thou forget me, O LORD? for ever? how long wilt thou hide thy face from me? {13:2} How long shall I take counsel in my soul, having sorrow in my heart daily? how long shall mine enemy be exalted over me? {13:3} Consider and hear me, O LORD my God: lighten mine eyes, lest I sleep the sleep of death; {13:4} Lest mine enemy say, I have prevailed against him; and those that trouble me rejoice when I am moved. {13:5} But I have trusted in thy mercy; my heart shall rejoice in thy salvation. {13:6} I will sing unto the LORD, because he hath dealt bountifully with me.

{14:1} The fool hath said in his heart, There is no God. They are corrupt, they have done abominable works, there is none that doeth good. {14:2} The LORD looked down from heaven upon the children of men, to see if there were any that did understand, and seek God. {14:3} They are all gone aside, they are all together become filthy: there is none that doeth good, no, not one. {14:4} Have all the workers of iniquity no knowledge? who eat up my people as they eat bread, and call not upon the LORD. {14:5} There were they in great fear: for God is in the generation of the righteous. {14:6} Ye have shamed the counsel of the poor, because the LORD is his refuge. {14:7} Oh that the salvation of Israel were come out of Zion! when the LORD bringeth back the captivity of his people, Jacob shall rejoice, and Israel shall be glad.

{15:1} LORD, who shall abide in thy tabernacle? who shall dwell in thy holy hill? {15:2} He that walketh uprightly, and worketh righteousness, and speaketh the truth in his heart. {15:3} He that backbiteth not with his tongue, nor doeth evil to his neighbour, nor taketh up a reproach against his neighbour. {15:4} In whose eyes a vile person is contemned; but he honoureth them that fear the LORD. He that sweareth to his own hurt, and changeth not. {15:5} He that putteth not out his money to usury, nor taketh reward against the innocent. He that doeth these things shall never be moved.

{16:1} Preserve me, O God: for in thee do I put my trust. {16:2} O my soul, thou hast said unto the LORD, Thou art my Lord: my goodness extendeth not to thee; {16:3} But to the saints that are in the earth, and to the excellent, in whom is all my delight. {16:4} Their sorrows shall be multiplied that hasten after another god: their drink offerings of blood will I not offer, nor take up their names into my lips. {16:5} The LORD is the portion of mine inheritance and of my cup: thou maintainest my lot. {16:6} The lines are fallen unto me in pleasant places; yea, I have a goodly heritage. {16:7} I will bless the LORD, who hath given me counsel: my reins also instruct me in the night seasons. {16:8} I have set the LORD always before me: because he is at my right hand, I shall not be moved. {16:9} Therefore my heart is glad, and my glory rejoiceth: my flesh also shall rest in hope. {16:10} For thou wilt not leave my soul in hell; neither wilt thou suffer thine Holy One to see corruption. {16:11} Thou wilt show me the path of life: in thy presence is fulness of joy; at thy right hand there are pleasures for evermore.

{17:1} Hear the right, O LORD, attend unto my cry, give ear unto my prayer, that goeth not out of feigned lips. {17:2} Let my sentence come forth from thy presence; let thine eyes behold the things that are equal. {17:3} Thou hast proved mine heart; thou hast visited me in the night; thou hast tried me, and shalt find nothing; I am purposed that my mouth shall not transgress. {17:4} Concerning the works of men, by the word of thy lips I have kept me from the paths of the destroyer. {17:5} Hold up my goings in thy paths, that my footsteps slip not. {17:6} I have called upon thee, for thou wilt hear me, O God: incline thine ear unto me, and hear my speech. {17:7} Show thy marvelous lovingkindness, O thou that savest by thy right hand them which put their trust in thee from those that rise up against them. {17:8} Keep me as the apple of the eye, hide me under the shadow of thy wings, {17:9} From the wicked that oppress me, from my deadly enemies, who compass me about. {17:10} They are enclosed in their own fat: with their mouth they speak proudly. {17:11} They have now encompassed us in our steps: they have set their eyes bowing down to the earth; {17:12} Like as a lion that is greedy of his prey, and as it were a young lion lurking in secret places. {17:13} Arise, O LORD, disappoint him, cast him down: deliver my soul from the wicked, which is thy sword: {17:14} From men which are thy hand, O LORD, from men of the world, which have their portion in this life, and whose belly thou fillest with thy hidden treasure: they are full of children, and leave the rest of their substance to their babes. {17:15} As for me, I will behold thy face in righteousness: I shall be satisfied, when I awake, with thy likeness.

{18:1} I will love thee, O LORD, my strength. {18:2} The LORD is my rock, and my fortress, and my deliverer; my God, my strength, in whom I will trust; my buckler, and the horn of my salvation, and my high tower. {18:3} I will call upon the LORD, who is worthy to be praised: so shall I be saved from mine enemies. {18:4} The sorrows of death compassed me, and the floods of ungodly men made me afraid. {18:5} The sorrows of hell compassed me about: the snares of death prevented me. {18:6} In my distress I called upon the LORD, and cried unto my God: he heard my voice out of his temple, and my cry came before him, even into his ears. {18:7} Then the earth shook and trembled; the foundations also of the hills moved and were shaken, because he was wroth. {18:8} There went up a smoke out of his nostrils, and fire out of his mouth devoured: coals were kindled by it. {18:9} He bowed the heavens also, and came down: and darkness was under his feet. {18:10} And he rode upon a cherub, and did fly: yea, he did fly upon the wings of the wind. {18:11} He made darkness his secret place; his pavilion round about him were dark waters and thick clouds of the skies. {18:12} At the brightness that was before him his thick clouds passed, hail stones and coals of fire. {18:13} The LORD also thundered in the heavens, and the Highest gave his voice; hail stones and coals of fire. {18:14} Yea, he sent out his arrows, and scattered them; and he shot out lightnings, and discomfited them. {18:15} Then the channels of waters were seen, and the foundations of the world were discovered at thy rebuke, O LORD, at the blast of the breath of thy nostrils. {18:16} He sent from above, he took me, he drew me out of many waters. {18:17} He delivered me from my strong enemy, and from them which hated me: for they were too strong for me. {18:18} They prevented me in the day of my calamity: but the LORD was my stay. {18:19} He brought me forth also into a large place; he delivered me, because he delighted in me. {18:20} The LORD rewarded me according to my righteousness; according to the cleanness of my hands hath he recompensed me. {18:21} For I have kept the ways of the LORD, and have not wickedly departed from my God. {18:22} For all his judgments were before me, and I did not put away his statutes from me. {18:23} I was also upright before him, and I kept myself from mine iniquity. {18:24} Therefore hath the LORD recompensed me according to my righteousness, according to the cleanness of my hands in his eyesight. {18:25} With the merciful thou wilt show thyself merciful; with an upright man thou wilt show thyself upright; {18:26} With the pure thou wilt show thyself pure; and with the froward thou wilt show thyself froward. {18:27} For thou wilt save the afflicted people; but wilt bring down high looks. {18:28} For thou wilt light my candle: the LORD my God will enlighten my darkness. {18:29} For by thee I have run through a troop; and by my God have I leaped over a wall. {18:30} As for God, his way is perfect: the word of the LORD is tried: he is a buckler to all those that trust in him. {18:31} For who is God save the LORD? or who is a rock save our God? {18:32} It is God that girdeth me with strength, and maketh my way perfect. {18:33} He maketh my feet like hinds' feet, and setteth me upon my high places. {18:34} He teacheth my hands to war, so that a bow of steel is broken by mine arms. {18:35} Thou hast also given me the shield of thy salvation: and thy right hand hath holden me up, and thy gentleness hath made me great. {18:36} Thou hast enlarged my steps under me, that my feet did not slip. {18:37} I have pursued mine enemies, and overtaken them: neither did I turn again till they were consumed. {18:38} I have wounded them that they were not able to rise: they are fallen under my feet. {18:39} For thou hast girded me with strength unto the battle: thou hast subdued under me those that rose up against me. {18:40} Thou hast also given me the necks of mine enemies; that I might destroy them that hate me. {18:41} They cried, but there was none to save them: even unto the LORD, but he answered them not. {18:42} Then did I beat them small as the dust before the wind: I did cast them out as the dirt in the streets. {18:43} Thou hast delivered me from the strivings of the people; and thou hast made me the head of the heathen: a people whom I have not known shall serve me. {18:44} As soon as they hear of me, they shall obey me: the strangers shall submit themselves unto me. {18:45} The strangers shall fade away, and be afraid out of their close places. {18:46} The LORD liveth; and blessed be my rock; and let the God of my salvation be exalted. {18:47} It is God that avengeth me, and subdueth the people under me. {18:48} He delivereth me from mine enemies: yea, thou liftest me up above those that rise up against me: thou hast delivered me from the violent man. {18:49} Therefore will I give thanks unto thee, O LORD, among the heath en, and sing praises unto thy name. {18:50} Great deliverance giveth he to his king; and showeth mercy to his anointed, to David, and to his seed for evermore.

{19:1} The heavens declare the glory of God; and the firmament showeth his handywork. {19:2} Day unto day uttereth speech, and night unto night showeth knowledge. {19:3} There is no speech nor language, where their voice is not heard. {19:4} Their line is gone out through all the earth, and their words to the end of the world. In them hath he set a tabernacle for the sun, {19:5} Which is as a bridegroom coming out of his chamber, and rejoiceth as a strong man to run a race. {19:6} His going forth is from the end of the heaven, and his circuit unto the ends of it: and there is nothing hid from the heat thereof. {19:7} The law of the LORD is perfect, converting the soul: the testimony of the LORD is sure, making wise the simple. {19:8} The statutes of the LORD are right, rejoicing the heart: the commandment of the LORD is pure, enlightening the eyes. {19:9} The fear of the LORD is clean, enduring for ever: the judgments of the LORD are true and righteous altogether. {19:10} More to be desired are they than gold, yea, than much fine gold: sweeter also than honey and the honeycomb. {19:11} Moreover by them is thy servant warned: and in keeping of them there is great reward. {19:12} Who can understand his errors? cleanse thou me from secret faults. {19:13} Keep back thy servant also from presumptuous sins; let them not have dominion over me: then shall I be upright, and I shall be innocent from the great transgression. {19:14} Let the words of my mouth, and the meditation of my heart, be acceptable in thy sight, O LORD, my strength, and my redeemer.

{20:1} May the LORD hear you in times of trouble; may the name of the God of Jacob protect you. {20:2} May he send you help from his sanctuary and strengthen you from Zion. {20:3} May he remember all your sacrifices and accept your burnt offerings. {20:4} May he grant you your heart's desires and fulfill all your plans. {20:5} We will rejoice in your salvation, and in the name of our God, we will set up our banners. May the LORD fulfill all your requests. {20:6} Now I know that the LORD saves his anointed; he will answer him from his holy heaven with the saving strength of his right hand. {20:7} Some trust in chariots and some in horses, but we will remember the name of the LORD our God. {20:8} They are brought down and fallen, but we are risen and stand upright. {20:9} Save us, LORD! May the king answer us when we call.

{21:1} The king shall rejoice in your strength, O LORD; and in your salvation, how greatly shall he rejoice! {21:2} You have given him his heart's desire and have not withheld the request of his lips. {21:3} For you meet him with the blessings of goodness; you set a crown of pure gold upon his head. {21:4} He asked life from you, and you gave it to him—length of days forever and ever. {21:5} His glory is great in your salvation; honor and majesty you have placed upon him. {21:6} For you have made him most blessed forever; you have made him exceedingly glad with your presence. {21:7} For the king trusts in the LORD, and through the mercy of the Most High, he shall not be moved. {21:8} Your hand will find all your enemies; your right hand will find out those who hate you. {21:9} You shall make them as a fiery oven in the time of your anger; the LORD shall swallow them up in his wrath, and the fire shall devour them. {21:10} You shall destroy their offspring from the earth, and their descendants from among the sons of men. {21:11} For they intended evil against you; they devised a mischievous plan which they are not able to perform. {21:12} Therefore you will make them turn their backs;

when you make ready your arrows on your string toward their faces. {21:13} Be exalted, O LORD, in your own strength! We will sing and praise your power.

{22:1} My God, my God, why have you forsaken me? Why are you so far from helping me, and from the words of my groaning? {22:2} O my God, I cry in the daytime, but you do not hear; and in the night season, and I am not silent. {22:3} But you are holy, O you who inhabit the praises of Israel. {22:4} Our fathers trusted in you; they trusted, and you delivered them. {22:5} They cried to you, and were delivered; they trusted in you, and were not ashamed. {22:6} But I am a worm, and not a man; a reproach of men, and despised by the people. {22:7} All those who see me ridicule me; they shoot out the lip, they shake the head, saying, {22:8} "He trusted in the LORD, let Him rescue him; let Him deliver him, since he delights in him!" {22:9} But you are He who took me out of the womb; you made me trust while on my mother's breasts. {22:10} I was cast upon you from birth; from my mother's womb you have been my God. {22:11} Do not be far from me, for trouble is near; for there is none to help. {22:12} Many bulls have surrounded me; strong bulls of Bashan have encircled me. {22:13} They gape at me with their mouths, like a raging and roaring lion. {22:14} I am poured out like water, and all my bones are out of joint; my heart is like wax; it has melted within me. {22:15} My strength is dried up like a potsherd, and my tongue clings to my jaws; you have brought me to the dust of death. {22:16} For dogs have surrounded me; the congregation of the wicked has enclosed me. They pierced my hands and my feet; {22:17} I can count all my bones. They look and stare at me. {22:18} They divide my garments among them, and for my clothing they cast lots. {22:19} But do not be far from me, O LORD; O my strength, hasten to help me! {22:20} Deliver me from the sword, my precious life from the power of the dog. {22:21} Save me from the lion's mouth and from the horns of the wild oxen! You have answered me. {22:22} I will declare your name to my brethren; in the midst of the assembly I will praise you. {22:23} You who fear the LORD, praise Him! All you descendants of Jacob, glorify Him, and fear Him, all you offspring of Israel! {22:24} For He has not despised nor abhorred the affliction of the afflicted; nor has He hidden His face from him; but when he cried to Him, He heard. {22:25} My praise shall be of you in the great assembly; I will pay my vows before those who fear Him. {22:26} The poor shall eat and be satisfied; those who seek Him will praise the LORD. Let your heart live forever! {22:27} All the ends of the world shall remember and turn to the LORD, and all the families of the nations shall worship before You. {22:28} For the kingdom is the LORD's, and He rules over the nations. {22:29} All the prosperous of the earth shall eat and worship; all those who go down to the dust shall bow before Him, even he who cannot keep himself alive. {22:30} A posterity shall serve Him. It will be recounted of the Lord to the next generation, {22:31} They will come and declare His righteousness to a people who will be born, that He has done this.

{23:1} **The LORD is my shepherd; I shall not lack anything.** {23:2} He makes me lie down in green pastures; he leads me beside still waters. {23:3} He restores my soul; he leads me in the paths of righteousness for his name's sake. {23:4} Even though I walk through the darkest valley, I will fear no evil, for you are with me; your rod and your staff, they comfort me. {23:5} You prepare a table before me in the presence of my enemies; you anoint my head with oil; my cup overflows. {23:6} Surely goodness and mercy shall follow me all the days of my life, and I will dwell in the house of the LORD forever.

{24:1} The earth is the LORD's, and everything in it, the world, and all who live in it. {24:2} For he has founded it on the seas and established it on the waters. {24:3} Who may ascend the mountain of the LORD? Who may stand in his holy place? {24:4} The one with clean hands and a pure heart, who does not trust in an idol or swear by a false god. {24:5} They will receive blessing from the LORD and vindication from God their Savior. {24:6} Such is the generation of those who seek him, who seek your face, God of Jacob. {24:7} Lift up your heads, you gates; be lifted up, you ancient doors, that the King of glory may come in. {24:8} Who is this King of glory? The LORD strong and mighty, the LORD mighty in battle. {24:9} Lift up your heads, you gates; lift them up, you ancient doors, that the King of glory may come in. {24:10} Who is he, this King of glory? The LORD Almighty—he is the King of glory.

{25:1} To you, O LORD, I lift up my soul. {25:2} O my God, I trust in you; let me not be put to shame, let not my enemies triumph over me. {25:3} Indeed, let no one who waits on you be ashamed; let those be ashamed who deal treacherously without cause. {25:4} Show me your ways, O LORD; teach me your paths. {25:5} Lead me in your truth and teach me, for you are the God of my salvation; on you I wait all the day. {25:6} Remember, O LORD, your tender mercies and your lovingkindnesses, for they have been from of old. {25:7} Do not remember the sins of my youth, nor my transgressions; according to your mercy remember me, for your goodness' sake, O LORD. {25:8} Good and upright is the LORD; therefore he teaches sinners in the way. {25:9} The humble he guides in justice, and the humble he teaches his way. {25:10} All the paths of the LORD are mercy and truth to such as keep his covenant and his testimonies. {25:11} For your name's sake, O LORD, pardon my iniquity, for it is great. {25:12} Who is the man that fears the LORD? Him shall he teach in the way he chooses. {25:13} His soul shall dwell at ease, and his descendants shall inherit the earth. {25:14} The secret of the LORD is with those who fear him, and he will show them his covenant. {25:15} My eyes are ever toward the LORD, for he shall pluck my feet out of the net. {25:16} Turn yourself to me, and have mercy on me, for I am desolate and afflicted. {25:17} The troubles of my heart have enlarged; bring me out of my distresses. {25:18} Look upon my affliction and my pain, and forgive all my sins. {25:19} Consider my enemies, for they are many; and they hate me with cruel hatred. {25:20} O keep my soul, and deliver me; let me not be ashamed, for I put my trust in you. {25:21} Let integrity and uprightness preserve me, for I wait for you. {25:22} Redeem Israel, O God, out of all their troubles.

{26:1} Judge me, O LORD, for I have walked in my integrity; I have also trusted in the LORD; therefore I shall not slide. {26:2} Examine me, O LORD, and prove me; try my heart and my mind. {26:3} For your lovingkindness is before my eyes, and I have walked in your truth. {26:4} I have not sat with deceitful men, nor will I go in with pretenders. {26:5} I have hated the assembly of evildoers, and I will not sit with the wicked. {26:6} I will wash my hands in innocence; so I will go about your altar, O LORD, {26:7} That I may proclaim with the voice of thanksgiving, and tell of all your wondrous works. {26:8} LORD, I have loved the habitation of your house, and the place where your glory dwells. {26:9} Do not gather my soul with sinners, nor my life with bloodthirsty men, {26:10} In whose hands is wickedness, and their right hand is full of bribes. {26:11} But as for me, I will walk in my integrity; redeem me, and be merciful to me. {26:12} My foot stands in an even place; in the congregations I will bless the LORD.

{27:1} The LORD is my light and my salvation; whom shall I fear? The LORD is the strength of my life; of whom shall I be afraid? {27:2} When the wicked, even my enemies and foes, came upon me to eat up my flesh, they stumbled and fell. {27:3} Though a host should encamp against me, my heart shall not fear: though war should rise against me, in this I will be confident. {27:4} One thing have I desired of the LORD, that will I seek after; that I may dwell in the house of the LORD all the days of my life, to behold the beauty of the LORD, and to inquire in his temple. {27:5} For in the time of trouble he shall hide me in his pavilion: in the secret of his tabernacle shall he hide me; he shall set me up upon a rock. {27:6} And now shall my head be lifted up above my enemies around me: therefore will I offer in his tabernacle sacrifices of joy; I will sing, yes, I will sing praises unto the LORD. {27:7} Hear, O LORD, when I cry with my voice: have mercy also upon me, and answer me. {27:8} When thou saidst, "Seek ye my face;" my heart said unto thee, "Thy face, LORD, will I seek." {27:9} Hide not thy face far from me; put not thy servant away in anger: thou hast been my help; leave me not, neither forsake me, O God of my salvation. {27:10} When my father and my mother forsake me, then the LORD will take me up. {27:11} Teach me thy way, O LORD, and lead me in a plain path, because of mine enemies. {27:12} Deliver me not over unto the will of mine enemies: for false witnesses are risen up against me, and such as breathe out cruelty. {27:13} I would have fainted, unless I had believed to see the goodness of the LORD in the land of the living. {27:14} Wait on the LORD: be of good courage, and he shall strengthen thine heart: wait, I say, on the LORD.

{28:1} Unto thee will I cry, O LORD my rock; be not silent to me: lest, if thou be silent to me, I become like them that go down into the pit. {28:2} Hear the voice of my supplications, when I cry unto thee, when I lift up my hands toward thy holy oracle. {28:3} Draw me not away with the wicked, and with the workers of iniquity, which speak peace to their neighbors, but mischief is in their hearts. {28:4} Give them according to their deeds, and according to the wickedness of their endeavors: give them after the work of their hands; render to them their desert. {28:5} Because they regard not the works of the LORD, nor the operation of his hands, he shall destroy them, and not build them up. {28:6} Blessed be the LORD, because he hath heard the voice of my supplications. {28:7} The LORD is my strength and my shield; my heart trusted in him, and I am helped: therefore my heart greatly rejoiceth; and with my song will I praise him. {28:8} The LORD is their strength, and he is the saving strength of his anointed. {28:9} Save thy people, and bless thine inheritance: feed them also, and lift them up for ever.

{29:1} Give unto the LORD, O ye mighty, give unto the LORD glory and strength. {29:2} Give unto the LORD the glory due unto his name; worship the LORD in the beauty of holiness. {29:3} The voice of the LORD is upon the waters: the God of glory thundereth: the LORD is upon many waters. {29:4} The voice of the LORD is powerful; the voice of the LORD is full of majesty. {29:5} The voice of the LORD breaketh the cedars; yea, the LORD breaketh the cedars of Lebanon. {29:6} He maketh them also to skip like a calf; Lebanon and Sirion like a young unicorn. {29:7} The voice of the LORD divideth the flames of fire. {29:8} The voice of the LORD shaketh the wilderness; the LORD shaketh the wilderness of Kadesh. {29:9} The voice of the LORD maketh the hinds to calve, and discovereth the forests: and in his temple doth every one speak of his glory. {29:10} The LORD sitteth upon the flood; yea, the LORD sitteth King for ever. {29:11} The LORD will give strength unto his people; the LORD will bless his people with peace.

{30:1} I will extol thee, O LORD; for thou hast lifted me up, and hast not made my foes to rejoice over me. {30:2} O LORD my God, I cried unto thee, and thou hast healed me. {30:3} O LORD, thou hast brought up my soul from the grave: thou hast kept me alive, that I should not go down to the pit. {30:4} Sing unto the LORD, O ye saints of his, and give thanks at the remembrance of his holiness. {30:5} For his anger endureth but a moment; in his favour is life: weeping may endure for a night, but joy cometh in the morning. {30:6} And in my prosperity I said, I shall never be moved. {30:7} LORD, by thy favour thou hast made my mountain to stand strong: thou didst hide thy face, and I was troubled. {30:8} I cried to thee, O LORD; and unto the LORD I made supplication. {30:9} What profit is there in my blood, when I go down to the pit? Shall the dust praise thee? shall it declare thy truth? {30:10} Hear, O LORD, and have mercy upon me: LORD, be thou my helper. {30:11} Thou hast turned for me my mourning into dancing: thou hast put off my sackcloth, and girded me with gladness; {30:12} To the end that my glory may sing praise to thee, and not be silent. O LORD my God, I will give thanks unto thee for ever.

{31:1} In thee, O LORD, do I put my trust; let me never be ashamed: deliver me in thy righteousness. {31:2} Bow down thine ear to me; deliver me speedily: be thou my strong rock, for an house of defence to save me. {31:3} For thou art my rock and my fortress; therefore for thy name's sake lead me, and guide me. {31:4} Pull me out of the net that they have laid privily for me: for thou art my strength. {31:5} Into thine hand I commit my spirit: thou hast redeemed me, O LORD God of truth. {31:6} I have hated them that regard lying vanities: but I trust in the LORD. {31:7} I will be glad and rejoice in thy mercy: for thou hast considered my trouble; thou hast known my soul in adversities; {31:8} And hast not shut me up into the hand of the enemy: thou hast set my feet in a large room. {31:9} Have mercy upon me, O LORD, for I am in trouble: mine eye is consumed with grief, yea, my soul and my belly. {31:10} For my life is spent with grief, and my years with sighing: my strength faileth because of mine iniquity, and my bones are consumed. {31:11} I was a reproach among all mine enemies, but especially among my neighbours, and a fear to mine acquaintance: they that did see me without fled from me. {31:12} I am forgotten as a dead man out of mind: I am like a broken vessel. {31:13} For I have heard the slander of many: fear was on every side: while they took counsel together against me, they devised to take away my life. {31:14} But I trusted in thee, O LORD: I said, Thou art my God. {31:15} My times are in thy hand: deliver me from the hand of mine enemies, and from them that persecute me. {31:16} Make thy face to shine upon thy servant: save me for thy mercies' sake. {31:17} Let me not be ashamed, O LORD; for I have called upon thee: let the wicked be ashamed, and let them be silent in the grave. {31:18} Let the lying lips be put to silence; which speak grievous things proudly and contemptuously against the righteous. {31:19} Oh how great is thy goodness, which thou hast laid up for them that fear thee; which thou hast wrought for them that trust in thee before the sons of men! {31:20} Thou shalt hide them in the secret of thy presence from the pride of man: thou shalt keep them secretly in a pavilion from the strife of tongues. {31:21} Blessed be the LORD: for he hath showed me his marvellous kindness in a strong city. {31:22} For I said in my haste, I am cut off from before thine eyes: nevertheless thou heardest the voice of my supplications when I cried unto thee. {31:23} O love the LORD, all ye his saints: for the LORD preserveth the faithful, and plentifully rewardeth the proud doer. {31:24} Be of good courage, and he shall strengthen your heart, all ye that hope in the LORD.

{32:1} Blessed is he whose transgression is forgiven, whose sin is covered. {32:2} Blessed is the man unto whom the LORD imputeth not iniquity, and in whose spirit there is no guile. {32:3} When I kept silence, my bones waxed old through my roaring all the day long. {32:4} For day and night thy hand was heavy upon me: my moisture is turned into the drought of summer. Selah. {32:5} I acknowledged my sin unto thee, and mine iniquity have I not hid. I said, I will confess my transgressions unto the LORD; and thou forgavest the iniquity of my sin. Selah. {32:6} For this shall every one that is godly pray unto thee in a time when thou mayest be found: surely in the floods of great waters they shall not come nigh unto him. {32:7} Thou art my hiding place; thou shalt preserve me from trouble; thou shalt compass me about with songs of deliverance. Selah. {32:8} I will instruct thee and teach thee in the way which thou shalt go: I will guide thee with mine eye. {32:9} Be ye not as the horse, or as the mule, which have no understanding: whose mouth must be held in with bit and bridle, lest they come near unto thee. {32:10} Many sorrows shall be to the wicked: but he that trusteth in the LORD, mercy shall compass him about. {32:11} Be glad in the LORD, and rejoice, ye righteous: and shout for joy, all ye that are upright in heart.

{33:1} Rejoice in the LORD, O ye righteous: for praise is comely for the upright. {33:2} Praise the LORD with harp: sing unto him with the psaltery and an instrument of ten strings. {33:3} Sing unto him a new song; play skilfully with a loud noise. {33:4} For the word of the LORD is right; and all his works are done in truth. {33:5} He loveth righteousness and judgment: the earth is full of the goodness of the LORD. {33:6} By the word of the LORD were the heavens made; and all the host of them by the breath of his mouth. {33:7} He gathereth the waters of the sea together as an heap: he layeth up the depth in storehouses. {33:8} Let all the earth fear the LORD: let all the inhabitants of the world stand in awe of him. {33:9} For he spake, and it was done; he commanded, and it stood fast. {33:10} The LORD bringeth the counsel of the heathen to nought: he maketh the devices of the people of none effect. {33:11} The counsel of the LORD standeth for ever, the thoughts of his heart to all generations. {33:12} Blessed is the nation whose God is the LORD: and the people whom he hath chosen for his own inheritance. {33:13} The LORD looketh from heaven; he beholdeth all the sons of men. {33:14} From the place of his habitation he looketh upon all the inhabitants of the earth. {33:15} He fashioneth their hearts alike; he considereth all their works. {33:16} There is no king saved by the multitude of an host: a mighty man is not delivered by much strength. {33:17} An horse is a vain thing for safety: neither shall he deliver any by his great strength. {33:18} Behold, the eye of the LORD is upon them that fear him, upon them that hope in his mercy; {33:19} To deliver their soul from death, and to keep them alive in famine. {33:20} Our soul waiteth for the LORD: he is our help and our shield. {33:21} For our heart shall rejoice in him, because we have trusted in his holy name. {33:22} Let thy mercy, O LORD, be upon us, according as we hope in thee.

{34:1} I will bless the LORD at all times: his praise shall continually be in my mouth. {34:2} My soul shall make her boast in the LORD: the humble shall hear thereof, and be glad. {34:3} O magnify the LORD with me, and let us exalt his name together. {34:4} I sought the LORD, and he heard me, and delivered me from all my fears. {34:5} They looked unto him, and were lightened: and their faces were not ashamed. {34:6} This poor man cried, and the LORD heard him, and saved him out of all his troubles. {34:7} The angel of the LORD encampeth round about them that fear him, and delivereth them. {34:8} O taste and see that the LORD is good: blessed is the man that trusteth in him. {34:9} O fear the LORD, ye his saints: for there is no want to them that fear him. {34:10} The young lions do lack, and suffer hunger: but they that seek the LORD shall not want any good thing. {34:11} Come, ye children, hearken unto me: I will teach you the fear of the LORD. {34:12} What man is he that desireth life, and loveth many days, that he may see good? {34:13} Keep thy tongue from evil, and thy lips from speaking guile. {34:14} Depart from evil, and do good; seek peace, and pursue it. {34:15} The eyes of the LORD are upon the righteous, and his ears are open unto their cry. {34:16} The face of the LORD is against them that do evil, to cut off the remembrance of them from the earth. {34:17} The righteous cry, and the LORD heareth, and delivereth them out of all their troubles. {34:18} The LORD is nigh unto them that are of a broken heart; and saveth such as be of a contrite spirit. {34:19} Many are the afflictions of the righteous: but the LORD delivereth him out of them all. {34:20} He keepeth all his bones: not one of them is broken. {34:21} Evil shall slay the wicked: and they that hate the righteous shall be desolate. {34:22} The LORD redeemeth the soul of his servants: and none of them that trust in him shall be desolate.

{35:1} Plead my cause, O LORD, with them that strive with me: fight against them that fight against me. {35:2} Take hold of shield and buckler, and stand up for mine help. {35:3} Draw out also the spear, and stop the way against them that persecute me: say unto my soul, I am thy salvation. {35:4} Let them be confounded and put to shame that seek after my soul: let them be turned back and brought to confusion that devise my hurt. {35:5} Let them be as chaff before the wind: and let the angel of the LORD chase them. {35:6} Let their way be dark and slippery: and let the angel of the LORD persecute them. {35:7} For without cause have they hid for me their net in a pit, which without cause they have digged for my soul. {35:8} Let destruction come upon him at unawares; and let his net that he hath hid catch himself: into that very destruction let him fall. {35:9} And my soul shall be joyful in the LORD: it shall rejoice in his salvation. {35:10} All my bones shall say, LORD, who is like unto thee, which deliverest the poor from him that is too strong for him, yea, the poor and the needy from him that spoileth him? {35:11} False witnesses did rise up; they laid to my charge things that I knew not. {35:12} They rewarded me evil for good to the spoiling of my soul. {35:13} But as for me, when they were sick, my clothing was sackcloth: I humbled my soul with fasting; and my prayer returned into mine own bosom. {35:14} I behaved myself as though he had been my friend or brother: I bowed down heavily, as one that mourneth for his mother. {35:15} But in mine adversity they rejoiced, and gathered themselves together: yea, the abjects gathered themselves together against me, and I knew it not; they did tear me, and ceased not: {35:16} With hypocritical mockers in feasts, they gnashed upon me with their teeth. {35:17} Lord, how long wilt thou look on? rescue my soul from their destructions, my darling from the lions. {35:18} I will give thee thanks in the great congregation: I will praise thee among much people. {35:19} Let not them that are mine enemies wrongfully rejoice over me: neither let them wink with the eye that hate me without a cause. {35:20} For they speak not peace: but they devise deceitful matters against them that are quiet in the land. {35:21} Yea, they opened their mouth wide against me, and said, Aha, aha, our eye hath seen it. {35:22} This thou hast seen, O LORD: keep not silence: O Lord, be not far from me. {35:23} Stir up thyself, and awake to my judgment, even unto my cause, my God and my Lord. {35:24} Judge me, O LORD my God, according to thy righteousness; and let them not rejoice over me. {35:25} Let them not say in their hearts, Ah, so would we have it: let them not say, We have swallowed him up. {35:26} Let them be ashamed and brought to confusion together that rejoice at mine hurt: let them be clothed with shame and dishonour that magnify themselves against me. {35:27} Let them shout for joy, and be glad, that favour my righteous cause: yea, let them say continually, Let the LORD be magnified, which hath pleasure in the prosperity of his servant. {35:28} And my tongue shall speak of thy righteousness and of thy praise all the day long.

{36:1} The transgression of the wicked says within my heart, that there is no fear of God before his eyes. {36:2} For he flattereth himself in his own eyes, until his iniquity be found to be hateful. {36:3} The words of his mouth are iniquity and deceit: he hath left off to be wise, and to do good. {36:4} He deviseth mischief upon his bed; he setteth himself in a way that is not good; he abhorreth not evil. {36:5} Thy mercy, O LORD, is in the heavens; and thy faithfulness reacheth unto the clouds. {36:6} Thy righteousness is like the great mountains; thy judgments are a great deep: O LORD, thou preservest man and beast. {36:7} How excellent is thy lovingkindness, O God! therefore the children of men put their trust under the shadow of thy wings. {36:8} They shall be abundantly satisfied with the fatness of thy house; and thou shalt make them drink of the river of thy pleasures. {36:9} For with thee is the fountain of life: in thy light shall we see light. {36:10} O continue thy lovingkindness unto them that know thee; and thy righteousness to the upright in heart. {36:11} Let not the foot of pride come against me, and let not the hand of the wicked remove me. {36:12} There are the workers of iniquity fallen: they are cast down, and shall not be able to rise.

{37:1} Don't worry about evildoers, and don't be jealous of those who do wrong. {37:2} They will soon disappear like grass and wither like green plants. {37:3} Trust in the LORD and do good. Then you will live safely in the land and prosper. {37:4} **Take delight in the LORD, and he will give you your heart's desires.** {37:5} Commit everything you do to the LORD. Trust him, and he will help you. {37:6} He will make your innocence radiate like the dawn, and the justice of your cause will shine like the noonday sun. {37:7} Be still in the presence of the LORD, and wait patiently for him to act. Don't worry about evil people who prosper or fret about their wicked schemes. {37:8} Stop being angry! Turn from your rage! Do not lose your temper - it only leads to harm. {37:9} For the wicked will be destroyed, but those who trust in the LORD will possess the land. {37:10} Soon the wicked will disappear. Though you look for them, they will be gone. {37:11} The lowly will possess the land and will live in peace and prosperity. {37:12} The wicked plot against the godly; they snarl at them in defiance. {37:13} But the Lord just laughs, for he sees their day of judgment coming. {37:14} The wicked draw their swords and string their bows to kill the poor and the oppressed, to slaughter those who do right. {37:15} But their swords will stab their own hearts, and their bows will be broken. {37:16} It is better to be godly and have little than to be evil and rich. {37:17} For the strength of the wicked will be shattered, but the LORD takes care of the godly. {37:18} Day by day the LORD takes care of the innocent, and they will receive an inheritance that lasts forever. {37:19} They will not be disgraced in hard times; even in famine they will have more than enough. {37:20} But the wicked will die. The Lord's enemies are like flowers in a field - they will disappear like smoke. {37:21} The wicked borrow and never repay, but the godly are generous givers. {37:22} Those blessed by the LORD will inherit the land, but those cursed by him will die. {37:23} The LORD directs the steps of the godly. He delights in every detail of their lives. {37:24} Though they stumble, they will never fall, for the LORD holds them by the hand. {37:25} Once I was young, and now I am old. Yet I have never seen the godly abandoned or their children begging for bread. {37:26} The godly always give generous loans to others, and their children are a blessing. {37:27} Turn from evil and do good, and you will live in the land forever. {37:28} For the LORD loves justice and will never abandon the godly. He will keep them safe forever. {37:29} But the children of the wicked will die. The godly will inherit the land and will live there forever. {37:30} The godly offer good counsel; they teach right from wrong. {37:31} They have made God's law their own, so they will never slip from his path. {37:32} The wicked wait in ambush for the godly, looking for an excuse to kill them. {37:33} But the LORD will not let the wicked succeed or let the godly be condemned when they are put on trial. {37:34} Put your hope in the LORD. Travel steadily along his path. He will honor you by giving you the land. You will see the wicked destroyed. {37:35} I have seen wicked and ruthless people flourishing like a tree in its native soil. {37:36} But when I looked again, they were gone! Though I searched for them, I could not find them! {37:37} Look at those who are honest and good, for a wonderful future awaits those who love peace. {37:38} But the rebellious will be destroyed; they have no future. {37:39} The LORD rescues the godly; he is their fortress in times of trouble. {37:40} The LORD helps them, rescuing them from the wicked. He saves them, and they find shelter in him because they trust in him.

{38:1} O LORD, don't punish me in your anger or discipline me in your fury. {38:2} Your arrows have struck deep, and your hand has come down on me hard. {38:3} My whole body is sick because of your anger. There is no health in my bones because of my sin. {38:4} My guilt overwhelms me; it is a burden too heavy to bear. {38:5} My wounds fester and stink because of my foolish sins. {38:6} I am bent over and racked with pain. All day long I walk around filled with grief. {38:7} A raging fever burns within me, and my health is broken. {38:8} I am exhausted and completely crushed. My groans come from an anguished heart. {38:9} You know what I long for, Lord; you hear my every sigh. {38:10} My heart beats wildly, my strength fails, and I have lost my sight. {38:11} My loved ones and friends stay away, fearing my disease. Even my own family stands at a distance. {38:12} Meanwhile, my enemies lay traps for me; those who wish me harm make plans to ruin me. They deceive me with lies all day long. {38:13} But like a deaf man, I don't hear; like a mute, I don't speak up. {38:14} I am silent before my accusers; I say nothing as they mock me. {38:15} But I trust in you, O LORD; I say, "You are my God!" {38:16} Hear my cry, for I am very low. Rescue me from my persecutors, for they are too strong for me. {38:17} I am on the verge of collapse, facing constant pain. {38:18} I confess my guilt; I am deeply sorry for my sin. {38:19} But my enemies are vigorous and mighty; they hate me without reason. {38:20} They repay my good deeds with evil; they oppose me because I stand for righteousness. {38:21} O LORD, don't abandon me; O my God, do not stay away. {38:22} Hurry to help me, O Lord, my Savior.

{39:1} I said, "I will be careful with my words and not sin with my tongue. I will restrain my mouth while the wicked are in my presence." {39:2} I remained silent, holding back even from speaking good things, and my anguish only grew. {39:3} My heart burned within me; as I thought, the fire ignited, and then I spoke with my tongue: {39:4} "Lord, show me the end of my life and the number of my days, so that I may understand how fleeting my life is. {39:5} You have made my days as short as a handbreadth, and my lifetime is nothing compared to you. Surely every person, even at their best, is but a breath." {39:6} Indeed, every person lives in a futile existence; they strive in vain, accumulating riches without knowing who will inherit them. {39:7} So, Lord, what am I waiting for? My hope is in you alone. {39:8} Save me from my wrongdoings; do not let me become a laughingstock to fools. {39:9} I remained silent; I did not speak, for it was you who acted. {39:10} Remove your affliction from me; I am worn down by the blow of your hand. {39:11} When you rebuke and discipline a person for their wrongdoing, their beauty fades away like a moth-eaten garment. Surely, everyone is but a breath." {39:12} Hear my prayer, O Lord, and listen to my cry; do not remain silent at my tears. For I am a stranger in this world, just passing through like all my ancestors. {39:13} Spare me, that I may regain my strength before I depart and am no more.

{40:1} I patiently waited for the LORD, and he listened to my cry. {40:2} He lifted me out of the pit of despair, out of the mud and mire. He set my feet on solid ground and steadied me as I walked along. {40:3} He has given me a new song to sing, a hymn of praise to our God. Many will see what he has done and be amazed. They will put their trust in the LORD. {40:4} Blessed is the one who trusts in the LORD, who does not look to the proud, to those who turn aside to false gods. {40:5} O LORD my God, you have done many miracles for us. Your plans for us are too numerous to list. If I tried to recite all your wonderful deeds, I would never come to the end of them. {40:6} You take no delight in sacrifices or offerings. Now that you have made me listen, I finally understand— you don't require burnt offerings or sin offerings. {40:7} Then I said, "Look, I have come. As is written about me in the Scriptures: {40:8} I take joy in doing your will, my God, for your instructions are written on my heart." {40:9} I have told all your people about your justice. I have not been afraid to speak out, as you, O LORD, well know. {40:10} I have not kept the good news of your justice hidden in my heart; I have talked about your faithfulness and saving power. I have told everyone in the great assembly of your unfailing love and faithfulness. {40:11} LORD, don't hold back your tender mercies from me. Let your unfailing love and faithfulness always protect me. {40:12} For troubles surround me— too many to count! My sins pile up so high I can't see my way out. They outnumber the hairs on my head. I have lost all courage. {40:13} Please, LORD, rescue me! Come quickly, LORD, and help me. {40:14} May those who try to destroy me be humiliated and put to shame. May those who take delight in my trouble be turned back in disgrace. {40:15} Let them be horrified by their shame, for they said, "Aha! We've got him now!" {40:16} But may all who search for you be filled with joy and gladness. May those who love your salvation repeatedly shout, "The LORD is great!" {40:17} As for me, I am poor and needy, but the Lord is thinking about me right now. You are my helper and my savior. Do not delay, O my God.

{41:1} Blessed is the one who cares for the poor; the LORD will rescue him in times of trouble. {41:2} The LORD will protect him and keep him alive; he will be blessed on the earth, and you will not give him over to the desires of his enemies. {41:3} The LORD will sustain him on his sickbed and restore him from his bed of illness. {41:4} I said, "LORD, be gracious to me; heal my soul, for I have sinned against you." {41:5} My enemies speak maliciously about me, asking, "When will he die and his name perish?" {41:6} Even if they come to visit, they speak deceitfully; their hearts gather slander, and when they leave, they spread it. {41:7} All who hate me whisper together about me; they imagine the worst for me. {41:8} They say, "A vile disease has afflicted him; he will never get up from the place where he lies." {41:9} Even my close friend, whom I trusted, who shared my bread, has lifted up his heel against me. {41:10} But you, O LORD, be gracious to me and raise me up, that I may repay them. {41:11} By this I know that you delight in me: because my enemy does not triumph over me. {41:12} As for me, you uphold me in my integrity and set me in your presence forever. {41:13} Blessed be the LORD, the God of Israel, from everlasting to everlasting. Amen and Amen.

{42:1} Like a deer that longs for streams of water, so my soul longs for you, O God. {42:2} My soul thirsts for God, for the living God. When can I come and appear before God? {42:3} My tears have been my food day and night, while people continually ask me, "Where is your God?" {42:4} These things I remember as I pour out my soul: how I used to go with the multitude, leading the procession to the house of God, with shouts of joy and thanksgiving amid the festive throng. {42:5} Why, my soul, are you downcast? Why so disturbed within me? Put your hope in God, for I will yet praise him, my Savior and my God. {42:6} My soul is downcast within me; therefore I will remember you from the land of the Jordan, the heights of Hermon—from Mount Mizar. {42:7} Deep calls to deep in the roar of your waterfalls; all your waves and breakers have swept over me. {42:8} By day the LORD directs his love, at night his song is with me—a prayer to the God of my life. {42:9} I say to God my Rock, "Why have you forgotten me? Why must I go about mourning, oppressed by the enemy?" {42:10} My bones suffer mortal agony as my foes taunt me, saying to me all day long, "Where is your God?" {42:11} Why, my soul, are you downcast? Why so disturbed within me? Put your hope in God, for I will yet praise him, my Savior and my God.

{43:1} O God, judge me and plead my cause against an ungodly nation. Deliver me from deceitful and unjust men. {43:2} You are the God of my strength. Why have you rejected me? Why do I go about mourning because of the oppression of the enemy? {43:3} Send out your light and your truth; let them lead me. Let them bring me to your holy hill and to your tabernacle. {43:4} Then I will go to the altar of God, to God my exceeding joy; and on the harp, I will praise you, O God, my God. {43:5} Why are you cast down, O my soul? And why are you disquieted within me? Hope in God; for I shall yet praise him, who is the health of my countenance and my God.

{44:1} O God, we have heard with our ears; our fathers have told us about the deeds you performed in their days, in times of old. {44:2} How you drove out the nations with your hand and planted our ancestors; how you afflicted the peoples and cast them out. {44:3} For they did not possess the land by their own sword, nor did their own arm save them; but it was your right hand, your arm, and the light of your countenance, because you favored them. {44:4} You are our King, O God; command deliverances for Jacob. {44:5} Through you we will push down our enemies; through your name we will trample those who rise up against us. {44:6} For I will not trust in my bow, nor shall my sword save me. {44:7} But you have saved us from our enemies, and have put to shame those who hated us. {44:8} In God we boast all day long, and praise your name forever. Selah. {44:9} But you have cast us off and put us to shame, and do not go out with our armies. {44:10} You make us turn back from the enemy, and those who hate us take spoil for themselves. {44:11} You have given us up like sheep intended for food, and have scattered us among the nations. {44:12} You sell your people for nothing, and are not enriched by selling them. {44:13} You make us a reproach to our neighbors, a scorn and a derision to those all around us. {44:14} You make us a byword among the nations, a shaking of the head among the people. {44:15} My disgrace is continually before me, and the shame of my face has covered me, {44:16} Because of the taunts of him who reproaches and reviles, because of the enemy and avenger. {44:17} All this has come upon us, yet we have not forgotten you, nor have we dealt falsely with your covenant. {44:18} Our heart has not turned back, nor have our steps departed from your way; {44:19} Though you have severely broken us in the place of jackals, and covered us with the shadow of death. {44:20} If we have forgotten the name of our God, or stretched out our hands to a foreign god, {44:21} Would not God search this out? For He knows the secrets of the heart. {44:22} Yes, for your sake we are killed all day long; we are accounted as sheep for the slaughter. {44:23} Awake! Why do you sleep, O Lord? Arise! Do not cast us off forever. {44:24} Why do you hide your face, and forget our affliction and oppression? {44:25} For our soul is bowed down to the dust; our body clings to the ground. {44:26} Arise for our help, and redeem us for the sake of your mercy.

{45:1} My heart overflows with a noble theme; I address my verses to the king; my tongue is like the pen of a skillful scribe. {45:2} You are the most handsome of men; grace is poured upon your lips; therefore God has blessed you forever. {45:3} Gird your sword on your thigh, O mighty one, in your splendor and majesty! {45:4} In your majesty ride out victoriously for the cause of truth and meekness and righteousness; let your right hand teach you awesome deeds! {45:5} Your arrows are sharp in the heart of the king's enemies; the peoples fall under you. {45:6} Your throne, O God, is forever and ever. The scepter of your kingdom is a scepter of uprightness; {45:7} you have loved righteousness and hated wickedness. Therefore God, your God, has anointed you with the oil of gladness beyond your companions; {45:8} your robes are all fragrant with myrrh and aloes and cassia. From ivory palaces stringed instruments make you glad; {45:9} daughters of kings are among your ladies of honor; at your right hand stands the queen in gold of Ophir. {45:10} Hear, O daughter, and consider, and incline your ear: forget your people and your father's house, {45:11} and the king will desire your beauty. Since he is your lord, bow to him. {45:12} The people of Tyre will seek your favor with gifts, the richest of the people. {45:13} All glorious is the princess in her chamber, with robes interwoven with gold. {45:14} In many-colored robes she is led to the king, with her virgin companions following behind her. {45:15} With joy and gladness they are led along as they enter the palace of the king. {45:16} In place of your fathers shall be your sons; you will make them princes in all the earth. {45:17} I will cause your name to be remembered in all generations; therefore nations will praise you forever and ever.

{46:1} God is our refuge and strength, a very present help in trouble. {46:2} Therefore, we will not fear, even if the earth is removed, and the mountains are carried into the midst of the sea; {46:3} Though its waters roar and are troubled, though the mountains shake with the swelling of the waves. Selah. {46:4} There is a river whose streams make glad the city of God, the holy place of the tabernacles of the Most High. {46:5} God is in the midst of her; she shall not be moved; God will help her when the morning dawns. {46:6} The nations rage, the kingdoms totter; he utters his voice, the earth melts. {46:7} The LORD of hosts is with us; the God of Jacob is our refuge. Selah. {46:8} Come, behold the works of the LORD, what desolations he has made in the earth. {46:9} He makes wars cease to the end of the earth; he breaks the bow and cuts the spear in two; he burns the chariots with fire. {46:10} "Be still, and know that I am God. I will be exalted among the nations, I will be exalted in the earth!" {46:11} The LORD of hosts is with us; the God of Jacob is our refuge. Selah.

{47:1} Oh, clap your hands, all you people; shout to God with the voice of triumph! {47:2} For the LORD Most High is awesome; he is a great King over all the earth. {47:3} He shall subdue the peoples under us, and the nations under our feet. {47:4} He shall choose our inheritance for us, the excellence of Jacob whom he loves. Selah. {47:5} God has gone up with a shout, the LORD with the sound of a trumpet. {47:6} Sing praises to God, sing praises; sing praises to our King, sing praises! {47:7} For God is the King of all the earth; sing praises with understanding. {47:8} God reigns over the nations; God sits on his holy throne. {47:9} The princes of the people have gathered together, the people of the God of Abraham; for the shields of the earth belong to God; he is greatly exalted.

{48:1} Great is the LORD, and greatly to be praised in the city of our God, in the mountain of his holiness. {48:2} Beautiful in elevation, the joy of the whole earth, is Mount Zion, on the sides of the north, the city of the great King. {48:3} God is known in her citadels as a refuge. {48:4} For behold, the kings assembled, they passed by together. {48:5} They saw it, and so they marveled; they were troubled, and hastened away. {48:6} Fear took hold of them there, and pain, as of a woman in labor. {48:7} You break the ships of Tarshish with an east wind. {48:8} As we have heard, so we have seen in the city of the LORD of hosts, in the city of our God: God will establish it forever. Selah. {48:9} We have thought of your steadfast love, O God, in the midst of your temple. {48:10} As your name, O God, so your praise reaches to the ends of the earth. Your right hand is filled with righteousness. {48:11} Let Mount Zion be glad! Let the daughters of Judah rejoice because of your judgments! {48:12} Walk about Zion, go around her, number her towers, {48:13} Consider well her ramparts, go through her citadels, that you may tell the next generation {48:14} that this is God, our God forever and ever. He will guide us forever.

{49:1} Hear this, all you people; give ear, all you inhabitants of the world: {49:2} Both low and high, rich and poor, together. {49:3} My mouth shall speak of wisdom; and the meditation of my heart shall be of understanding. {49:4} I will incline my ear to a parable: I will open my dark saying upon the harp. {49:5} Why should I fear in the days of evil, when the iniquity of my heels shall surround me? {49:6} Those who trust in their wealth and boast of the abundance of their riches— {49:7} none of them can by any means redeem his brother, nor give to God a ransom for him— {49:8} (For the redemption of their soul is precious, and it ceases forever:) {49:9} That he should still live forever, and not see corruption. {49:10} For one sees that wise men die, likewise the fool and the brutish person perish, and leave their wealth to others. {49:11} Their inward thought is that their houses shall continue forever, and their dwelling places to all generations; they call their lands after their own names. {49:12} Nevertheless, man being in honor does not endure; he is like the beasts that perish. {49:13} This is their way, their folly; yet their posterity approve their sayings. Selah. {49:14} Like sheep they are laid in the grave; death shall feed on them; and the upright shall have dominion over them in the morning; and their beauty shall consume in the grave from their dwelling. {49:15} But God will redeem my soul from the power of the grave: for he shall receive me. Selah. {49:16} Be not afraid when one is made rich, when the glory of his house is increased; {49:17} For when he dies he shall carry nothing away: his glory shall not descend after him. {49:18} Though while he lived he blessed his soul: and men will praise you, when you do well to yourself. {49:19} He shall go to the generation of his fathers; they shall never see light. {49:20} Man that is in honor, and understands not, is like the beasts that perish.

{50:1} The mighty God, even the LORD, has spoken, and called the earth from the rising of the sun unto the going down thereof. {50:2} Out of Zion, the perfection of beauty, God has shined. {50:3} Our God shall come, and shall not keep silence: a fire shall devour before him, and it shall be very tempestuous round about him. {50:4} He shall call to the heavens from above, and to the earth, that he may judge his people. {50:5} Gather my saints together unto me; those that have made a covenant with me by sacrifice. {50:6} And the heavens shall declare his righteousness: for God is judge himself. Selah. {50:7} Hear, O my people, and I will speak; O Israel, and I will testify against thee: I am God, even thy God. {50:8} I will not reprove thee for thy sacrifices or thy burnt offerings, to have been continually before me. {50:9} I will take no bullock out of thy house, nor he goats out of thy folds. {50:10} For every beast of the forest is mine, and the cattle upon a thousand hills. {50:11} I know all the fowls of the mountains: and the wild beasts of the field are mine. {50:12} If I were hungry, I would not tell thee: for the world is mine, and the fulness thereof. {50:13} Will I eat the flesh of bulls, or drink the blood of goats? {50:14} Offer unto God thanksgiving; and pay thy vows unto the most High: {50:15} And call upon me in the day of trouble: I will deliver thee, and thou shalt glorify me. {50:16} But unto the wicked God saith, What hast thou to do to declare my statutes, or that thou shouldest take my covenant in thy mouth? {50:17} Seeing thou hatest instruction, and castest my words behind thee. {50:18} When thou sawest a thief, then thou consentedst with him, and hast been partaker with adulterers. {50:19} Thou givest thy mouth to evil, and thy tongue frameth deceit. {50:20} Thou sittest and speakest against thy brother; thou slanderest thine own mother's son. {50:21} These things hast thou done, and I kept silence; thou thoughtest that I was altogether such an one as thyself: but I will reprove thee, and set them in order before thine eyes. {50:22} Now consider this, ye that forget God, lest I tear you in pieces, and there be none to deliver. {50:23} Whoso offereth praise glorifieth me: and to him that ordereth his conversation aright will I shew the salvation of God.

{51:1} Have mercy upon me, O God, according to thy lovingkindness: according unto the multitude of thy tender mercies blot out my transgressions. {51:2} Wash me thoroughly from mine iniquity, and cleanse me from my sin. {51:3} For I acknowledge my transgressions: and my sin is ever before me. {51:4} Against thee, thee only, have I sinned, and done this evil in thy sight: that thou mightest be justified when thou speakest, and be clear when thou judgest. {51:5} Behold, I was shaped in iniquity; and in sin did my mother conceive me. {51:6} Behold, thou desirest truth in the inward parts: and in the hidden part thou shalt make me to know wisdom. {51:7} Purge me with hyssop, and I shall be clean: wash me, and I shall be whiter than snow. {51:8} Make me to hear joy and gladness; that the bones which thou hast broken may rejoice. {51:9} Hide thy face from my sins, and blot out all mine iniquities. {51:10} Create in me a clean heart, O God; and renew a right spirit within me. {51:11} Cast me not away from thy presence; and take not thy holy spirit from me. {51:12} Restore unto me the joy of thy salvation; and uphold me with thy free spirit. {51:13} Then will I teach transgressors thy ways; and sinners shall be converted unto thee. {51:14} Deliver me from bloodguiltiness, O God, thou God of my salvation: and my tongue shall sing aloud of thy righteousness. {51:15} O Lord, open thou my lips; and my mouth shall show forth thy praise. {51:16} For thou desirest not sacrifice; else would I give it: thou delightest not in burnt offering. {51:17} **The sacrifices of God are a broken spirit: a broken and a contrite heart, O God, thou wilt not despise**. {51:18} Do good in thy good pleasure unto Zion: build thou the walls of Jerusalem. {51:19} Then shalt thou be pleased with the sacrifices of righteousness, with burnt offering and whole burnt offering: then shall they offer bullocks upon thine altar.

{52:1} Why boastest thou thyself in mischief, O mighty man? The goodness of God endureth continually. {52:2} Thy tongue deviseth mischiefs; like a sharp razor, working deceitfully. {52:3} Thou lovest evil more than good; and lying rather than to speak righteousness. Selah. {52:4} Thou lovest all devouring words, O thou deceitful tongue. {52:5} God shall likewise destroy thee forever; he shall take thee away, and pluck thee out of thy dwelling place, and root thee out of the land of the living. Selah. {52:6} The righteous also shall see, and fear, and shall laugh at him: {52:7} Lo, this is the man that made not God his strength; but trusted in the abundance of his riches, and strengthened himself in his wickedness. {52:8} But I am like a green olive tree in the house of God: I trust in the mercy of God forever and ever. {52:9} I will praise thee forever, because thou hast done it: and I will wait on thy name; for it is good before thy saints.

{53:1} The fool hath said in his heart, "There is no God." Corrupt are they, and have done abominable iniquity: there is none that doeth good. {53:2} God looked down from heaven upon the children of men, to see if there were any that did understand, that did seek God. {53:3} Every one of them is gone back: they are altogether become filthy; there is none that doeth good, no, not one. {53:4} Have the workers of iniquity no knowledge? who eat up my people as they eat bread: they have not called upon God. {53:5} There were they in great fear, where no fear was: for God hath scattered the bones of him that encampeth against thee:

thou hast put them to shame, because God hath despised them. {53:6} Oh that the salvation of Israel were come out of Zion! When God bringeth back the captivity of his people, Jacob shall rejoice, and Israel shall be glad.

{54:1} Save me, O God, by thy name, and judge me by thy strength. {54:2} Hear my prayer, O God; give ear to the words of my mouth. {54:3} For strangers are risen up against me, and oppressors seek after my soul: they have not set God before them. Selah. {54:4} Behold, God is mine helper: the Lord is with them that uphold my soul. {54:5} He shall reward evil unto mine enemies: cut them off in thy truth. {54:6} I will freely sacrifice unto thee: I will praise thy name, O LORD; for it is good. {54:7} For he hath delivered me out of all trouble: and mine eye hath seen his desire upon mine enemies.

{55:1} Give ear to my prayer, O God; and hide not thyself from my supplication. {55:2} Attend unto me, and hear me: I mourn in my complaint, and make a noise; {55:3} Because of the voice of the enemy, because of the oppression of the wicked: for they cast iniquity upon me, and in wrath they hate me. {55:4} My heart is sore pained within me: and the terrors of death are fallen upon me. {55:5} Fearfulness and trembling are come upon me, and horror hath overwhelmed me. {55:6} And I said, Oh that I had wings like a dove! for then would I fly away, and be at rest. {55:7} Lo, then would I wander far off, and remain in the wilderness. Selah. {55:8} I would hasten my escape from the windy storm and tempest. {55:9} Destroy, O Lord, and divide their tongues: for I have seen violence and strife in the city. {55:10} Day and night they go about it upon the walls thereof: mischief also and sorrow are in the midst of it. {55:11} Wickedness is in the midst thereof: deceit and guile depart not from her streets. {55:12} For it was not an enemy that reproached me; then I could have borne it: neither was it he that hated me that did magnify himself against me; then I would have hid myself from him: {55:13} But it was thou, a man mine equal, my guide, and mine acquaintance. {55:14} We took sweet counsel together, and walked unto the house of God in company. {55:15} Let death seize upon them, and let them go down quick into hell: for wickedness is in their dwellings, and among them. {55:16} As for me, I will call upon God; and the Lord shall save me. {55:17} Evening, and morning, and at noon, will I pray, and cry aloud: and he shall hear my voice. {55:18} He hath delivered my soul in peace from the battle that was against me: for there were many with me. {55:19} God shall hear, and afflict them, even he that abideth of old. Selah. Because they have no changes, therefore they fear not God. {55:20} He hath put forth his hands against such as be at peace with him: he hath broken his covenant. {55:21} The words of his mouth were smoother than butter, but war was in his heart: his words were softer than oil, yet were they drawn swords. {55:22} Cast thy burden upon the Lord, and he shall sustain thee: he shall never suffer the righteous to be moved. {55:23} But thou, O God, shalt bring them down into the pit of destruction: bloody and deceitful men shall not live out half their days; but I will trust in thee.

{56:1} Be merciful unto me, O God: for man would swallow me up; he fighting daily oppresseth me. {56:2} Mine enemies would daily swallow me up: for they be many that fight against me, O thou most High. {56:3} What time I am afraid, I will trust in thee. {56:4} In God I will praise his word, in God I have put my trust; I will not fear what flesh can do unto me. {56:5} Every day they wrest my words: all their thoughts are against me for evil. {56:6} They gather themselves together, they hide themselves, they mark my steps, when they wait for my soul. {56:7} Shall they escape by iniquity? in thine anger cast down the people, O God. {56:8} Thou tellest my wanderings: put thou my tears into thy bottle: are they not in thy book? {56:9} When I cry unto thee, then shall mine enemies turn back: this I know; for God is for me. {56:10} In God will I praise his word: in the Lord will I praise his word. {56:11} In God have I put my trust: I will not be afraid what man can do unto me. {56:12} Thy vows are upon me, O God: I will render praises unto thee. {56:13} For thou hast delivered my soul from death: wilt not thou deliver my feet from falling, that I may walk before God in the light of the living?

{57:1} Be merciful unto me, O God, be merciful unto me: for my soul trusteth in thee: yea, in the shadow of thy wings will I make my refuge, until these calamities be overpast. {57:2} I will cry unto God most high; unto God that performeth all things for me. {57:3} He shall send from heaven, and save from the reproach of him that would swallow me up. Selah. God shall send forth his mercy and his truth. {57:4} My soul is among lions: and I lie even among them that are set on fire, even the sons of men, whose teeth are spears and arrows, and their tongue a sharp sword. {57:5} Be thou exalted, O God, above the heavens; let thy glory be above all the earth. {57:6} They have prepared a net for my steps; my soul is bowed down: they have digged a pit before me, into the midst whereof they are fallen themselves. Selah. {57:7} My heart is fixed, O God, my heart is fixed: I will sing and give praise. {57:8} Awake up, my glory; awake, psaltery and harp: I myself will awake early. {57:9} I will praise thee, O Lord, among the people: I will sing unto thee among the nations. {57:10} For thy mercy is great unto the heavens, and thy truth unto the clouds. {57:11} Be thou exalted, O God, above the heavens: let thy glory be above all the earth.

{58:1} Do ye indeed speak righteousness, O congregation? do ye judge uprightly, O ye sons of men? {58:2} Yea, in heart ye work wickedness; ye weigh the violence of your hands in the earth. {58:3} The wicked are estranged from the womb: they go astray as soon as they be born, speaking lies. {58:4} Their poison is like the poison of a serpent: they are like the deaf adder that stoppeth her ear; {58:5} Which will not hearken to the voice of charmers, charming never so wisely. {58:6} Break their teeth, O God, in their mouth: break out the great teeth of the young lions, O LORD. {58:7} Let them melt away as waters which run continually: when he bendeth his bow to shoot his arrows, let them be as cut in pieces. {58:8} As a snail which melteth, let every one of them pass away: like the untimely birth of a woman, that they may not see the sun. {58:9} Before your pots can feel the thorns, he shall take them away as with a whirlwind, both living, and in his wrath. {58:10} The righteous shall rejoice when he seeth the vengeance: he shall wash his feet in the blood of the wicked. {58:11} So that a man shall say, Verily there is a reward for the righteous: verily he is a God that judgeth in the earth.

{59:1} Deliver me from mine enemies, O my God: defend me from them that rise up against me. {59:2} Deliver me from the workers of iniquity, and save me from bloody men. {59:3} For, lo, they lie in wait for my soul: the mighty are gathered against me; not for my transgression, nor for my sin, O LORD. {59:4} They run and prepare themselves without my fault: awake to help me, and behold. {59:5} Thou therefore, O LORD God of hosts, the God of Israel, awake to visit all the heathen: be not merciful to any wicked transgressors. Selah. {59:6} They return at evening: they make a noise like a dog, and go round about the city. {59:7} Behold, they belch out with their mouth: swords are in their lips: for who, say they, doth hear? {59:8} But thou, O LORD, shalt laugh at them; thou shalt have all the heathen in derision. {59:9} Because of his strength will I wait upon thee: for God is my defence. {59:10} The God of my mercy shall prevent me: God shall let me see my desire upon mine enemies. {59:11} Slay them not, lest my people forget: scatter them by thy power; and bring them down, O Lord our shield. {59:12} For the sin of their mouth and the words of their lips let them even be taken in their pride: and for cursing and lying which they speak. {59:13} Consume them in wrath, consume them, that they may not be: and let them know that God ruleth in Jacob unto the ends of the earth. Selah. {59:14} And at evening let them return; and let them make a noise like a dog, and go round about the city. {59:15} Let them wander up and down for meat, and grudge if they be not satisfied. {59:16} But I will sing of thy power; yea, I will sing aloud of thy mercy in the morning: for thou hast been my defence and refuge in the day of my trouble. {59:17} Unto thee, O my strength, will I sing: for God is my defence, and the God of my mercy.

{60:1} O God, thou hast cast us off, thou hast scattered us, thou hast been displeased; O turn thyself to us again. {60:2} Thou hast made the earth to tremble; thou hast broken it: heal the breaches thereof; for it shaketh. {60:3} Thou hast showed thy people hard things: thou hast made us to drink the wine of astonishment. {60:4} Thou hast given a banner to them that fear thee, that it may be displayed because of the truth. Selah. {60:5} That thy beloved may be delivered; save with thy right hand, and hear me. {60:6} God hath spoken in his holiness; I will rejoice, I will divide Shechem, and mete out the valley of Succoth. {60:7} Gilead is mine, and Manasseh is mine; Ephraim also is the strength of mine head; Judah is my lawgiver; {60:8} Moab is my washpot; over Edom will I cast out my shoe; Philistia, triumph thou because of me. {60:9} Who will bring me into the strong city? who will lead me into Edom? {60:10} Wilt not thou, O God, which hadst cast us off? and thou, O God, which didst not go out with our armies? {60:11} Give us help from trouble: for vain is the help of man. {60:12} Through God we shall do valiantly: for he it is that shall tread down our enemies.

{61:1} Hear my cry, O God; attend unto my prayer. {61:2} From the end of the earth will I cry unto thee, when my heart is overwhelmed: lead me to the rock that is higher than I. {61:3} For thou hast been a shelter for me, and a strong tower from the enemy. {61:4} I will abide in thy tabernacle for ever: I will trust in the covert of thy wings. Selah. {61:5} For thou, O God, hast heard my vows: thou hast given me the heritage of those that fear thy name. {61:6} Thou wilt prolong the king's life: and his years as many generations. {61:7} He shall abide before God for ever: O prepare mercy and truth, which may preserve him. {61:8} So will I sing praise unto thy name for ever, that I may daily perform my vows.

{62:1} Truly my soul waiteth upon God: from him cometh my salvation. {62:2} He only is my rock and my salvation; he is my defense; I shall not be greatly moved. {62:3} How long will ye imagine mischief against a man? ye shall be slain all of you: as a bowing wall shall ye be, and as a tottering fence. {62:4} They only consult to cast him down from his excellency: they delight in lies: they bless with their mouth, but they curse inwardly. Selah. {62:5} My soul, wait thou only upon God; for my expectation is from him. {62:6} He only is my rock and my salvation: he is my defense; I shall not be moved. {62:7} In God is my salvation and my glory: the rock of my strength, and my refuge, is in God. {62:8} Trust in him at all times; ye people, pour out your heart before him: God is a refuge for us. Selah. {62:9} Surely men of low degree are vanity, and men of high degree are a lie: to be laid in the balance, they are altogether lighter than vanity. {62:10} Trust not in oppression, and become not vain in robbery: if riches increase, set not your heart upon them. {62:11} God hath spoken once; twice have I heard this; that power belongeth unto God. {62:12} Also unto thee, O Lord, belongeth mercy: for thou renderest to every man according to his work.

{63:1} O God, thou art my God; early will I seek thee: my soul thirsteth for thee, my flesh longeth for thee in a dry and thirsty land, where no water is; {63:2} To see thy power and thy glory, as I have seen thee in the sanctuary. {63:3} Because thy lovingkindness is better than life, my lips shall praise thee. {63:4} Thus will I bless thee while I live: I will lift up my hands in thy name. {63:5} My soul shall be satisfied as with marrow and fatness; and my mouth shall praise thee with joyful lips: {63:6} When I remember thee upon my bed, and meditate on thee in the night watches. {63:7} Because thou hast been my help, therefore in the shadow of thy wings will I rejoice. {63:8} My soul followeth hard after thee: thy right hand upholdeth me. {63:9} But those that seek my soul, to destroy it, shall go into the lower parts of the earth. {63:10} They shall fall by the sword: they shall be a portion for foxes. {63:11} But the king shall rejoice in God; every one that sweareth by him shall glory: but the mouth of them that speak lies shall be stopped.

{64:1} Hear my voice, O God, in my prayer: preserve my life from fear of the enemy. {64:2} Hide me from the secret counsel of the wicked; from the insurrection of the workers of iniquity: {64:3} Who sharpen their tongue like a sword, and bend their bows to shoot their arrows, even bitter words: {64:4} That they may shoot in secret at the blameless: suddenly do they shoot at him, and fear not. {64:5} They encourage themselves in an evil matter: they talk of laying snares secretly; they say, "Who will see them?" {64:6} They devise iniquities; they have perfected a plan of searching diligently: both the inward thought of every one of them, and the heart, is deep. {64:7} But God shall shoot at them with an arrow; suddenly shall they be wounded. {64:8} So they shall make their own tongue to fall upon themselves: all that see them shall flee away. {64:9} And all men shall fear, and shall declare the work of God; for they shall wisely consider of his doing. {64:10} The righteous shall be glad in the LORD, and shall trust in him; and all the upright in heart shall glory.

{65:1} Praise awaits you, O God, in Zion; and to you the vow will be fulfilled. {65:2} O you who hear prayer, to you all flesh will come. {65:3} Iniquities prevail against me; as for our transgressions, you shall purge them away. {65:4} Blessed is the one whom you choose, and cause to approach to dwell in your courts. We shall be satisfied with the goodness of your house, even of your holy temple. {65:5} By awesome deeds of righteousness you will answer us, O God of our salvation, the confidence of all the ends of the earth, and of those who are far away upon the sea. {65:6} Who by his strength establishes the mountains, being girded with power. {65:7} Who stills the noise of the seas, the noise of their waves, and the tumult of the peoples. {65:8} They also who dwell in the farthest parts are afraid of your signs; you make the outgoings of the morning and evening rejoice. {65:9} You visit the earth and water it; you greatly enrich it with the river of God, which is full of water; you prepare them grain when you have so provided for it. {65:10} You water its ridges abundantly; you settle its furrows; you make it soft with showers; you bless its growth. {65:11} You crown the year with your goodness, and your paths drip with abundance. {65:12} They drop on the pastures of the wilderness, and the little hills rejoice on every side. {65:13} The pastures are clothed with flocks; the valleys also are covered over with grain; they shout for joy, they also sing.

{66:1} Make a joyful noise unto God, all you lands; {66:2} Sing forth the honor of his name; make his praise glorious. {66:3} Say unto God, "How awesome are your works! Through the greatness of your power shall your enemies submit themselves unto you." {66:4} All the earth shall worship you and sing unto you; they shall sing to your name. Selah. {66:5} Come and see the works of God; he is awesome in his deeds toward the children of men. {66:6} He turned the sea into dry land; they went through the flood on foot; there we rejoiced in him. {66:7} He rules by his power forever; his eyes behold the nations; let not the rebellious exalt themselves. Selah. {66:8} O bless our God, you people, and make the voice of his praise to be heard. {66:9} Who holds our soul in life and does not allow our feet to be moved. {66:10} For you, O God, have proved us; you have tried us as silver is tried. {66:11} You brought us into the net; you laid affliction upon our loins. {66:12} You have caused men to ride over our heads; we went through fire and through water; but you brought us out into a wealthy place. {66:13} I will go into your house with burnt offerings; I will pay you my vows, {66:14} Which my lips have uttered, and my mouth has spoken when I was in trouble. {66:15} I will offer unto you burnt sacrifices of fatlings, with the incense of rams; I will offer bullocks with goats. Selah. {66:16} Come and hear, all you who fear God, and I will declare what he has done for my soul. {66:17} I cried unto him with my mouth, and he was extolled with my tongue. {66:18} If I regard iniquity in my heart, the Lord will not hear me; {66:19} But verily God has heard me; he has attended to the voice of my prayer. {66:20} Blessed be God, who has not turned away my prayer, nor his mercy from me.

{67:1} God, be merciful unto us, and bless us; and cause his face to shine upon us. Selah. {67:2} That your way may be known upon earth, your saving health among all nations. {67:3} Let the people praise you, O God; let all the people praise you. {67:4} O let the nations be glad and sing for joy; for you shall judge the people righteously and govern the nations upon earth. Selah. {67:5} Let the people praise you, O God; let all the people praise you. {67:6} Then shall the earth yield her increase; and God, even our own God, shall bless us. {67:7} God shall bless us; and all the ends of the earth shall fear him.

{68:1} Let God arise, let his enemies be scattered; let them also that hate him flee before him. {68:2} As smoke is driven away, so drive them away; as wax melts before the fire, so let the wicked perish at the presence of God. {68:3} But let the righteous be glad; let them rejoice before God; yea, let them exceedingly rejoice. {68:4} Sing unto God, sing praises to his name; extol him that rides upon the heavens by his name JAH, and rejoice before him. {68:5} A father of the fatherless, and a judge of the widows, is God in his holy habitation. {68:6} God sets the solitary in families; he brings out those which are bound with chains; but the rebellious dwell in a dry land. {68:7} O God, when you went forth before your people, when you marched through the wilderness; Selah: {68:8} The earth shook, the heavens also dropped at the presence of God; even Sinai itself was moved at the presence of God, the God of Israel. {68:9} You, O God, did send a plentiful rain, whereby you did confirm your inheritance, when it was weary. {68:10} Your congregation has dwelt therein; you, O God, have prepared of your goodness for the poor. {68:11} The Lord gave the word; great was the company of those that published it. {68:12} Kings of armies fled apace; and she that tarried at home divided the spoil. {68:13} Though you have lain among the pots, yet shall you be as the wings of a dove covered with silver, and her feathers with yellow gold. {68:14} When the Almighty scattered kings in it, it was white as snow in Salmon. {68:15} The hill of God is as the hill of Bashan; a high hill as the hill of Bashan. {68:16} Why leap you, you high hills? This is the hill which God desires to dwell in; yea, the LORD will dwell in it forever. {68:17} The chariots of God are twenty thousand, even thousands of angels; the Lord is among them, as in Sinai, in the holy place. {68:18} You have ascended on high, you have led captivity captive; you have received gifts for men; yea, for the rebellious also, that the LORD God might dwell among them. {68:19} Blessed be the Lord, who daily loads us with benefits, even the God of our salvation. Selah. {68:20} He that is our God is the God of salvation; and unto God the Lord belong the issues from death. {68:21} But God shall wound the head of his enemies, and the hairy scalp of such a one as goes on still in his trespasses. {68:22} The Lord said, I will bring again from Bashan, I will bring my people again from the depths of the sea: {68:23} That your foot may be dipped in the blood of your enemies, and the tongue of your dogs in the same. {68:24} They have seen your goings, O God; even the goings of my God, my King, in the sanctuary. {68:25} The singers went before, the players on instruments followed after; among them were the damsels playing with timbrels. {68:26} Bless you God in the congregations, even the Lord, from the fountain of Israel. {68:27} There is little Benjamin with their ruler, the princes of Judah and their council, the princes of Zebulun, and the princes of Naphtali. {68:28} Your God has commanded your strength; strengthen, O God, that which you have wrought for us. {68:29} Because of your temple at Jerusalem shall kings bring presents unto you. {68:30} Rebuke the company of spearmen, the multitude of the bulls, with the calves of the people, till every one submits himself with pieces of silver; scatter the people that delight in war. {68:31} Princes shall come out of Egypt; Ethiopia shall soon stretch out her hands unto God. {68:32} Sing unto God, you kingdoms of the earth; O sing praises unto the Lord;

Selah: {68:33} To him that rides upon the heavens of heavens, which were of old; lo, he does send out his voice, and that a mighty voice. {68:34} Ascribe strength unto God; his excellency is over Israel, and his strength is in the clouds. {68:35} O God, you are terrible out of your holy places; the God of Israel is he that gives strength and power unto his people. Blessed be God.

{69:1} Save me, O God; for the waters are come in unto my soul. {69:2} I sink in deep mire, where there is no standing: I am come into deep waters, where the floods overflow me. {69:3} I am weary of my crying: my throat is dried: mine eyes fail while I wait for my God. {69:4} They that hate me without a cause are more than the hairs of mine head: they that would destroy me, being mine enemies wrongfully, are mighty: then I restored that which I took not away. {69:5} O God, thou knowest my foolishness; and my sins are not hid from thee. {69:6} Let not them that wait on thee, O Lord GOD of hosts, be ashamed for my sake: let not those that seek thee be confounded for my sake, O God of Israel. {69:7} Because for thy sake I have borne reproach; shame hath covered my face. {69:8} I am become a stranger unto my brethren, and an alien unto my mother's children. {69:9} For the zeal of thine house hath eaten me up; and the reproaches of them that reproached thee are fallen upon me. {69:10} When I wept, and chastened my soul with fasting, that was to my reproach. {69:11} I made sackcloth also my garment; and I became a proverb to them. {69:12} They that sit in the gate speak against me; and I was the song of the drunkards. {69:13} But as for me, my prayer is unto thee, O LORD, in an acceptable time: O God, in the multitude of thy mercy hear me, in the truth of thy salvation. {69:14} Deliver me out of the mire, and let me not sink: let me be delivered from them that hate me, and out of the deep waters. {69:15} Let not the waterflood overflow me, neither let the deep swallow me up, and let not the pit shut her mouth upon me. {69:16} Hear me, O LORD; for thy lovingkindness is good: turn unto me according to the multitude of thy tender mercies. {69:17} And hide not thy face from thy servant; for I am in trouble: hear me speedily. {69:18} Draw nigh unto my soul, and redeem it: deliver me because of mine enemies. {69:19} Thou hast known my reproach, and my shame, and my dishonour: mine adversaries are all before thee. {69:20} Reproach hath broken my heart; and I am full of heaviness: and I looked for some to take pity, but there was none; and for comforters, but I found none. {69:21} They gave me also gall for my meat; and in my thirst they gave me vinegar to drink. {69:22} Let their table become a snare before them: and that which should have been for their welfare, let it become a trap. {69:23} Let their eyes be darkened, that they see not; and make their loins continually to shake. {69:24} Pour out thine indignation upon them, and let thy wrathful anger take hold of them. {69:25} Let their habitation be desolate; and let none dwell in their tents. {69:26} For they persecute him whom thou hast smitten; and they talk to the grief of those whom thou hast wounded. {69:27} Add iniquity unto their iniquity: and let them not come into thy righteousness. {69:28} Let them be blotted out of the book of the living, and not be written with the righteous. {69:29} But I am poor and sorrowful: let thy salvation, O God, set me up on high. {69:30} I will praise the name of God with a song, and will magnify him with thanksgiving. {69:31} This also shall please the LORD better than an ox or bullock that hath horns and hoofs. {69:32} The humble shall see this, and be glad: and your heart shall live that seek God. {69:33} For the LORD heareth the poor, and despiseth not his prisoners. {69:34} Let the heaven and earth praise him, the seas, and every thing that moveth therein. {69:35} For God will save Zion, and will build the cities of Judah: that they may dwell there, and have it in possession. {69:36} The seed also of his servants shall inherit it: and they that love his name shall dwell therein.

{70:1} Make haste, O God, to deliver me; make haste to help me, O LORD. {70:2} Let them be ashamed and confounded that seek after my soul: let them be turned backward, and put to confusion, that desire my hurt. {70:3} Let them be turned back for a reward of their shame that say, Aha, aha. {70:4} Let all those that seek thee rejoice and be glad in thee: and let such as love thy salvation say continually, Let God be magnified. {70:5} But I am poor and needy: make haste unto me, O God: thou art my help and my deliverer; O LORD, make no tarrying.

{71:1} In thee, O LORD, do I put my trust: let me never be put to confusion. {71:2} Deliver me in thy righteousness, and cause me to escape: incline thine ear unto me, and save me. {71:3} Be thou my strong habitation, whereunto I may continually resort: thou hast given commandment to save me; for thou art my rock and my fortress. {71:4} Deliver me, O my God, out of the hand of the wicked, out of the hand of the unrighteous and cruel man. {71:5} For thou art my hope, O Lord GOD: thou art my trust from my youth. {71:6} By thee have I been holden up from the womb: thou art he that took me out of my mother's bowels: my praise shall be continually of thee. {71:7} I am as a wonder unto many; but thou art my strong refuge. {71:8} Let my mouth be filled with thy praise and with thy honour all the day. {71:9} Cast me not off in the time of old age; forsake me not when my strength faileth. {71:10} For mine enemies speak against me; and they that lay wait for my soul take counsel together, {71:11} Saying, God hath forsaken him: persecute and take him; for there is none to deliver him. {71:12} O God, be not far from me: O my God, make haste for my help. {71:13} Let them be confounded and consumed that are adversaries to my soul; let them be covered with reproach and dishonour that seek my hurt. {71:14} But I will hope continually, and will yet praise thee more and more. {71:15} My mouth shall show forth thy righteousness and thy salvation all the day; for I know not the numbers thereof. {71:16} I will go in the strength of the Lord GOD: I will make mention of thy righteousness, even of thine only. {71:17} O God, thou hast taught me from my youth: and hitherto have I declared thy wondrous works. {71:18} Now also when I am old and greyheaded, O God, forsake me not; until I have showed thy strength unto this generation, and thy power to every one that is to come. {71:19} Thy righteousness also, O God, is very high, who hast done great things: O God, who is like unto thee! {71:20} Thou, which hast showed me great and sore troubles, shalt quicken me again, and shalt bring me up again from the depths of the earth. {71:21} Thou shalt increase my greatness, and comfort me on every side. {71:22} I will also praise thee with the psaltery, even thy truth, O my God: unto thee will I sing with the harp, O thou Holy One of Israel. {71:23} My lips shall greatly rejoice when I sing unto thee; and my soul, which thou hast redeemed. {71:24} My tongue also shall talk of thy righteousness all the day long: for they are confounded, for they are brought unto shame, that seek my hurt.

{72:1} Give the king thy judgments, O God, and thy righteousness unto the king's son. {72:2} He shall judge thy people with righteousness, and thy poor with judgment. {72:3} The mountains shall bring peace to the people, and the little hills, by righteousness. {72:4} He shall judge the poor of the people, he shall save the children of the needy, and shall break in pieces the oppressor. {72:5} They shall fear thee as long as the sun and moon endure, throughout all generations. {72:6} He shall come down like rain upon the mown grass: as showers that water the earth. {72:7} In his days shall the righteous flourish; and abundance of peace so long as the moon endureth. {72:8} He shall have dominion also from sea to sea, and from the river unto the ends of the earth. {72:9} They that dwell in the wilderness shall bow before him; and his enemies shall lick the dust. {72:10} The kings of Tarshish and of the isles shall bring presents: the kings of Sheba and Seba shall offer gifts. {72:11} Yea, all kings shall fall down before him: all nations shall serve him. {72:12} For he shall deliver the needy when he crieth; the poor also, and him that hath no helper. {72:13} He shall spare the poor and needy, and shall save the souls of the needy. {72:14} He shall redeem their soul from deceit and violence: and precious shall their blood be in his sight. {72:15} And he shall live, and to him shall be given of the gold of Sheba: prayer also shall be made for him continually; and daily shall he be praised. {72:16} There shall be an handful of corn in the earth upon the top of the mountains; the fruit thereof shall shake like Lebanon: and they of the city shall flourish like grass of the earth. {72:17} His name shall endure for ever: his name shall be continued as long as the sun: and men shall be blessed in him: all nations shall call him blessed. {72:18} Blessed be the LORD God, the God of Israel, who only doeth wondrous things: {72:19} And blessed be his glorious name for ever: and let the whole earth be filled with his glory; Amen, and Amen. {72:20} The prayers of David the son of Jesse are ended.

{73:1} Truly God is good to Israel, even to such as are of a clean heart. {73:2} But as for me, my feet were almost gone; my steps had well nigh slipped. {73:3} For I was envious at the foolish, when I saw the prosperity of the wicked. {73:4} For there are no bands in their death: but their strength is firm. {73:5} They are not in trouble as other men; neither are they plagued like other men. {73:6} Therefore pride compasseth them about as a chain; violence covereth them as a garment. {73:7} Their eyes stand out with fatness: they have more than heart could wish. {73:8} They are corrupt, and speak wickedly concerning oppression: they speak loftily. {73:9} They set their mouth against the heavens, and their tongue walketh through the earth. {73:10} Therefore his people return hither: and waters of a full cup are wrung out to them. {73:11} And they say, How doth God know? and is there knowledge in the most High? {73:12} Behold, these are the ungodly, who prosper in the world; they increase in riches. {73:13} Verily I have cleansed my heart in vain, and washed my hands in innocency. {73:14} For all the day long have I been plagued, and chastened every morning. {73:15} If I say, I will speak thus; behold, I should offend against the generation of thy children. {73:16} When I thought to know this, it was too painful for me; {73:17} Until I went into the sanctuary of God; then understood I their end. {73:18} Surely thou didst set them in slippery places: thou castedst them down into destruction. {73:19} How are they brought into desolation, as in a moment! they are utterly consumed with terrors. {73:20} As a dream when one awaketh; so, O Lord, when thou awakest, thou shalt despise their image. {73:21} Thus my heart was grieved, and I was pricked in my reins. {73:22} So foolish was I, and ignorant: I was as a beast before thee. {73:23} Nevertheless I am continually with thee: thou hast holden me by my right hand. {73:24} Thou shalt guide me with thy counsel, and afterward receive me to glory. {73:25} **Whom have I in heaven but thee? and there is none upon earth that I desire beside thee.** {73:26} My flesh and my heart faileth: but God is the strength of my heart, and my portion for ever. {73:27} For, lo, they that are far from thee shall perish: thou hast destroyed all them that go a whoring from thee. {73:28} **But it is good for me to draw near to God: I have put my trust in the Lord GOD, that I may declare all thy works.**

{74:1} O God, why hast thou cast us off for ever? Why doth thine anger smoke against the sheep of thy pasture? {74:2} Remember thy congregation, which thou hast purchased of old; the rod of thine inheritance, which thou hast redeemed; this mount Zion, wherein thou hast dwelt. {74:3} Lift up thy feet unto the perpetual desolations; even all that the enemy hath done wickedly in the sanctuary. {74:4} Thine enemies roar in the midst of thy congregations; they set up their ensigns for signs. {74:5} A man was famous according as he had lifted up axes upon the thick trees. {74:6} But now they break down the carved work thereof at once with axes and hammers. {74:7} They have cast fire into thy sanctuary; they have defiled by casting down the dwelling place of thy name to the ground. {74:8} They said in their hearts, Let us destroy them together: they have burned up all the synagogues of God in the land. {74:9} We see not our signs: there is no more any prophet: neither is there among us any that knoweth how long. {74:10} O God, how long shall the adversary reproach? Shall the enemy blaspheme thy name for ever? {74:11} Why withdrawest thou thy hand, even thy right hand? Pluck it out of thy bosom. {74:12} For God is my King of old, working salvation in the midst of the earth. {74:13} Thou didst divide the sea by thy strength: thou brakest the heads of the dragons in the waters. {74:14} Thou brakest the heads of leviathan in pieces, and gavest him to be meat to the people inhabiting the wilderness. {74:15} Thou didst cleave the fountain and the flood: thou driedst up mighty rivers. {74:16} The day is thine, the night also is thine: thou hast prepared the light and the sun. {74:17} Thou hast set all the borders of the earth: thou hast made summer and winter. {74:18} Remember this, that the enemy hath reproached, O LORD, and that the foolish people have blasphemed thy name. {74:19} O deliver not the soul of thy turtledove unto the multitude of the wicked: forget not the congregation of thy poor for ever. {74:20} Have respect unto the covenant: for the dark places of the earth are full of the habitations of cruelty. {74:21} O let not the oppressed return ashamed: let the poor and needy praise thy name. {74:22} **Arise, O God, plead thine own cause: remember how the foolish man reproacheth thee daily.** {74:23} **Forget not the voice of thine enemies: the tumult of those that rise up against thee increaseth continually.**

{75:1} **Unto thee, O God, do we give thanks, unto thee do we give thanks: for thy name is near thy wondrous works declare.** {75:2} When I shall receive the congregation I will judge uprightly. {75:3} The earth and all the inhabitants thereof are dissolved: I bear up the pillars of it. Selah. {75:4} I said unto the fools, Deal not foolishly: and to the wicked, Lift not up the horn: {75:5} Lift not up your horn on high: speak not with a stiff neck. {75:6} For promotion cometh neither from the east, nor from the west, nor from the south. {75:7} But God is the judge: he putteth down one, and setteth up another. {75:8} For in the hand of the LORD there is a cup, and the wine is red; it is full of mixture; and he poureth out of the same: but the dregs thereof, all the wicked of the earth shall wring them out, and drink them. {75:9} **But I will declare for ever; I will sing praises to the God of Jacob.** {75:10} All the horns of the wicked also will I cut off; but the horns of the righteous shall be exalted.

{76:1} In Judah is God known: his name is great in Israel. {76:2} In Salem also is his tabernacle, and his dwelling place in Zion. {76:3} There brake he the arrows of the bow, the shield, and the sword, and the battle. Selah. {76:4} **Thou art more glorious and excellent than the mountains of prey.** {76:5} The stouthearted are spoiled, they have slept their sleep: and none of the men of might have found their hands. {76:6} At thy rebuke, O God of Jacob, both the chariot and horse are cast into a dead sleep. {76:7} Thou, even thou, art to be feared: and who may stand in thy sight when once thou art angry? {76:8} **Thou didst cause judgment to be heard from heaven; the earth feared, and was still,** {76:9} When God arose to judgment, to save all the meek of the earth. Selah. {76:10} Surely the wrath of man shall praise thee: the remainder of wrath shalt thou restrain. {76:11} **Vow, and pay unto the LORD your God: let all that be round about him bring presents unto him that ought to be feared.** {76:12} He shall cut off the spirit of princes: he is terrible to the kings of the earth.

{77:1} I cried unto God with my voice, even unto God with my voice; and he gave ear unto me. {77:2} In the day of my trouble I sought the Lord: my sore ran in the night, and ceased not: my soul refused to be comforted. {77:3} I remembered God, and was troubled: I complained, and my spirit was overwhelmed. Selah. {77:4} Thou holdest mine eyes waking: I am so troubled that I cannot speak. {77:5} I have considered the days of old, the years of ancient times. {77:6} I call to remembrance my song in the night: I commune with mine own heart: and my spirit made diligent search. {77:7} Will the Lord cast off for ever? and will he be favourable no more? {77:8} Is his mercy clean gone for ever? doth his promise fail for evermore? {77:9} Hath God forgotten to be gracious? hath he in anger shut up his tender mercies? Selah. {77:10} And I said, This is my infirmity: but I will remember the years of the right hand of the most High. {77:11} I will remember the works of the LORD: surely I will remember thy wonders of old. {77:12} I will meditate also of all thy work, and talk of thy doings. {77:13} Thy way, O God, is in the sanctuary: who is so great a God as our God? {77:14} Thou art the God that doest wonders: thou hast declared thy strength among the people. {77:15} Thou hast with thine arm redeemed thy people, the sons of Jacob and Joseph. Selah. {77:16} The waters saw thee, O God, the waters saw thee; they were afraid: the depths also were troubled. {77:17} The clouds poured out water: the skies sent out a sound: thine arrows also went abroad. {77:18} The voice of thy thunder was in the heaven: the lightnings lightened the world: the earth trembled and shook. {77:19} Thy way is in the sea, and thy path in the great waters, and thy footsteps are not known. {77:20} Thou leddest thy people like a flock by the hand of Moses and Aaron.

{78:1} Give ear, O my people, to my law: incline your ears to the words of my mouth. {78:2} I will open my mouth in a parable: I will utter dark sayings of old: {78:3} Which we have heard and known, and our fathers have told us. {78:4} We will not hide them from their children, showing to the generation to come the praises of the LORD, and his strength, and his wonderful works that he hath done. {78:5} For he established a testimony in Jacob, and appointed a law in Israel, which he commanded our fathers, that they should make them known to their children: {78:6} That the generation to come might know them, even the children which should be born; who should arise and declare them to their children: {78:7} That they might set their hope in God, and not forget the works of God, but keep his commandments: {78:8} And might not be as their fathers, a stubborn and rebellious generation; a generation that set not their heart aright, and whose spirit was not steadfast with God. {78:9} The children of Ephraim, being armed, and carrying bows, turned back in the day of battle. {78:10} They kept not the covenant of God, and refused to walk in his law; {78:11} And forgot his works, and his wonders that he had showed them. {78:12} Marvellous things did he in the sight of their fathers, in the land of Egypt, in the field of Zoan. {78:13} He divided the sea, and caused them to pass through; and he made the waters to stand as a heap. {78:14} In the daytime also he led them with a cloud, and all the night with a light of fire. {78:15} He clave the rocks in the wilderness, and gave them drink as out of the great depths. {78:16} He brought streams also out of the rock, and caused waters to run down like rivers. {78:17} And they sinned yet more against him by provoking the Most High in the wilderness. {78:18} And they tempted God in their heart by asking meat for their lust. {78:19} Yea, they spoke against God; they said, Can God furnish a table in the wilderness? {78:20} Behold, he smote the rock, that the waters gushed out, and the streams overflowed; can he give bread also? can he provide flesh for his people? {78:21} Therefore the LORD heard this, and was wroth: so a fire was kindled against Jacob, and anger also came up against Israel; {78:22} Because they believed not in God, and trusted not in his salvation: {78:23} Though he had commanded the clouds from above, and opened the doors of heaven, {78:24} And had rained down manna upon them to eat, and had given them of the corn of heaven. {78:25} Man did eat angels' food: he sent them meat to the full. {78:26} He caused an east wind to blow in the heaven: and by his power he brought in the south wind. {78:27} He rained flesh also upon them as dust, and feathered fowls like as the sand of the sea: {78:28} And he let it fall in the midst of their camp, round about their habitations. {78:29} So they did eat, and were well filled: for he gave them their own desire; {78:30} They were not estranged from their lust. But while their meat was yet in their mouths, {78:31} The wrath of God came upon them, and slew the fattest of them, and smote down the chosen men of Israel. {78:32} For all this they sinned still, and believed not for his wondrous works. {78:33} Therefore their days did he consume in vanity, and their years in trouble. {78:34} When he slew them, then they sought him: and they returned and enquired early after God. {78:35} And they remembered that God was their rock, and the high God their redeemer. {78:36} Nevertheless they did flatter him with their mouth, and they lied unto him with their tongues. {78:37} For their heart was not right with him, neither were they steadfast in his covenant. {78:38} But he, being full of compassion, forgave their iniquity, and destroyed them not: yea, many a time turned he his anger away, and did not stir up all his wrath. {78:39} For he remembered that they were but flesh; a wind that passeth away, and cometh not again. {78:40} How oft did they provoke him in the wilderness, and grieve him in the desert! {78:41} Yea, they turned back and tempted God, and limited the Holy One of Israel. {78:42} They remembered not his hand, nor the day when he delivered them from the enemy. {78:43} How he had wrought his signs in Egypt, and his wonders in the field of Zoan: {78:44} And had turned their rivers into blood; and their floods, that they could not drink. {78:45} He sent divers sorts of flies among them, which devoured them; and frogs, which destroyed them. {78:46} He gave also their increase unto the caterpillar, and their labor unto the locust. {78:47} He destroyed their vines with hail, and their sycamore trees with frost. {78:48} He gave up their cattle also to the hail, and their flocks to hot thunderbolts. {78:49} He cast upon them the fierceness of his anger, wrath, and indignation, and trouble, by sending evil angels among them. {78:50} He made a way to his anger; he spared not their soul from death, but gave their life over to the pestilence; {78:51} And smote all the firstborn in Egypt; the chief of their strength in the tabernacles of Ham: {78:52} But made his own people to go forth like sheep, and guided them in the wilderness like a flock. {78:53} And he led them on safely, so that they feared not: but the sea overwhelmed their enemies. {78:54} And he brought them to the border of his sanctuary, even to this mountain, which his right hand had purchased. {78:55} He cast out the heathen also before them, and divided them an inheritance by line, and made the tribes of Israel to dwell in their tents. {78:56} Yet they tempted and provoked the most high God, and kept not his testimonies: {78:57} But turned back, and dealt unfaithfully like their fathers: they were turned aside like a deceitful bow. {78:58} For they provoked him to anger with their high places, and moved him to jealousy with their graven images. {78:59} When God heard this, he was wroth, and greatly abhorred Israel: {78:60} So that he forsook the tabernacle of Shiloh, the tent which he placed among men. {78:61} And delivered his strength into captivity, and his glory into the enemy's hand. {78:62} He gave his people over also unto the sword; and was wroth with his inheritance. {78:63} The fire consumed their young men; and their maidens were not given to marriage. {78:64} Their priests fell by the sword; and their widows made no lamentation. {78:65} Then the Lord awaked as one out of sleep, and like a mighty man that shouteth by reason of wine. {78:66} And he smote his enemies in the hinder parts: he put them to a perpetual reproach. {78:67} Moreover he refused the tabernacle of Joseph, and chose not the tribe of Ephraim: {78:68} But chose the tribe of Judah, the mount Zion which he loved. {78:69} And he built his sanctuary like high palaces, like the earth which he hath established for ever. {78:70} He chose David also his servant, and took him from the sheepfolds: {78:71} From following the ewes great with young he brought him to feed Jacob his people, and Israel his inheritance. {78:72} So he fed them according to the integrity of his heart; and guided them by the skilfulness of his hands.

{79:1} O God, the heathen are come into thine inheritance; thy holy temple have they defiled; they have laid Jerusalem on heaps. {79:2} The dead bodies of thy servants have they given to be meat unto the fowls of the heaven, the flesh of thy saints unto the beasts of the earth. {79:3} Their blood have they shed like water round about Jerusalem; and there was none to bury them. {79:4} We are become a reproach to our neighbours, a scorn and derision to them that are round about us. {79:5} How long, LORD? wilt thou be angry for ever? shall thy jealousy burn like fire? {79:6} Pour out thy wrath upon the heathen that have not known thee, and upon the kingdoms that have not called upon thy name. {79:7} For they have devoured Jacob, and laid waste his dwelling place. {79:8} O remember not against us former iniquities: let thy tender mercies speedily prevent us: for we are brought very low. {79:9} Help us, O God of our salvation, for the glory of thy name: and deliver us, and purge away our sins, for thy name's sake. {79:10} Wherefore should the heathen say, Where is their God? let him be known among the heathen in our sight by the revenging of the blood of thy servants which is shed. {79:11} Let the sighing of the prisoner come before thee; according to the greatness of thy power preserve thou those that are appointed to die; {79:12} And render unto our neighbours sevenfold into their bosom their reproach, wherewith they have reproached thee, O Lord. {79:13} So we thy people and sheep of thy pasture will give thee thanks for ever: we will shew forth thy praise to all generations.

{80:1} *Give ear, O Shepherd of Israel, thou that leadest Joseph like a flock; thou that dwellest between the cherubims, shine forth.* {80:2} *Before Ephraim and Benjamin and Manasseh stir up thy strength, and come and save us.* {80:3} Turn us again, O God, and cause thy face to shine; and we shall be saved. {80:4} O LORD God of hosts, how long wilt thou be angry against the prayer of thy people? {80:5} Thou feedest them with the bread of tears; and givest them tears to drink in great measure. {80:6} Thou makest us a strife unto our neighbours: and our enemies laugh among themselves. {80:7} Turn us again, O God of hosts, and cause thy face to shine; and we shall be saved. {80:8} Thou hast brought a vine out of Egypt: thou hast cast out the heathen, and planted it. {80:9} Thou preparedst room before it, and didst cause it to take deep root, and it filled the land. {80:10} The hills were covered with the shadow of it, and the boughs thereof were like the goodly cedars. {80:11} She sent out her boughs unto the sea, and her branches unto the river. {80:12} Why hast thou then broken down her hedges, so that all they which pass by the way do pluck her? {80:13} The boar out of the wood doth waste it, and the wild beast of the field doth devour it. {80:14} Return, we beseech thee, O God of hosts: look down from heaven, and behold, and visit this vine; {80:15} And the vineyard which thy right hand hath planted, and the branch that thou madest strong for thyself. {80:16} It is burned with fire, it is cut down: they perish at the rebuke of thy countenance. {80:17} Let thy hand be upon the man of thy right hand, upon the son of man whom thou madest strong for thyself. {80:18} So will not we go back from thee: quicken us, and we will call upon thy name. {80:19} Turn us again, O LORD God of hosts, cause thy face to shine; and we shall be saved.

{81:1} Sing aloud unto God our strength: make a joyful noise unto the God of Jacob. {81:2} Take a psalm, and bring hither the timbrel, the pleasant harp with the psaltery. {81:3} Blow up the trumpet in the new moon, in the time appointed, on our solemn feast day. {81:4} For this was a statute for Israel, and a law of the God of Jacob. {81:5} This he ordained in Joseph for a testimony, when he went out through the land of Egypt: where I heard a language that I understood not. {81:6} I removed his shoulder from the burden: his hands were delivered from the pots. {81:7} Thou calledst in trouble, and I delivered thee; I answered thee in the secret place of thunder: I proved thee at the waters of Meribah. Selah. {81:8} Hear, O my people, and I will testify unto thee: O Israel, if thou wilt hearken unto me; {81:9} There shall no strange god be in thee; neither shalt thou worship any strange god. {81:10} I am the LORD thy God, which brought thee out of the land of Egypt: open thy mouth wide, and I will fill it. {81:11} But my people would not hearken to my voice; and Israel would none of me. {81:12} So I gave them up unto their own hearts' lust: and they walked in their own counsels. {81:13} Oh that my people had hearkened unto me, and Israel had walked in my ways! {81:14} I should soon have subdued their enemies, and turned my hand against their adversaries. {81:15} *The haters of the LORD should have submitted themselves unto him: but their time should have endured for ever. {81:16} He should have fed them also with the finest of the wheat: and with honey out of the rock should I have satisfied thee.*

{82:1} *God standeth in the congregation of the mighty; he judgeth among the gods.* {82:2} How long will ye judge unjustly, and accept the persons of the wicked? Selah. {82:3} Defend the poor and fatherless: do justice to the afflicted and needy. {82:4} Deliver the poor and needy: rid them out of the hand of the wicked. {82:5} They know not, neither will they understand; they walk on in darkness: all the foundations of the earth are out of course. {82:6} I have said, Ye are gods; and all of you are children of the most High. {82:7} But ye shall die like men, and fall like one of the princes. {82:8} *Arise, O God, judge the earth: for thou shalt inherit all nations.*

{83:1} *Keep not thou silence, O God: hold not thy peace, and be not still, O God.* {83:2} For, lo, thine enemies make a tumult: and they that hate thee have lifted up the head. {83:3} *They have taken crafty counsel against thy people, and consulted against thy hidden ones.* {83:4} They have said, Come, and let us cut them off from being a nation; that the name of Israel may be no more in remembrance. {83:5} For they have consulted together with one consent: they are confederate against thee: {83:6} The tabernacles of Edom, and the Ishmaelites; of Moab, and the Hagarenes; {83:7} Gebal, and Ammon, and Amalek; the Philistines with the inhabitants of Tyre; {83:8} Assur also is joined with them: they have holpen the children of Lot. Selah. {83:9} Do unto them as unto the Midianites; as to Sisera, as to Jabin, at the brook of Kison: {83:10} Which perished at Endor: they became as dung for the earth. {83:11} Make their nobles like Oreb, and like Zeeb: yea, all their princes as Zebah, and as Zalmunna: {83:12} Who said, Let us take to ourselves the houses of God in possession. {83:13} O my God, make them like a wheel; as the stubble before the wind. {83:14} *As the fire burneth a wood, and as the flame setteth the mountains on fire;* {83:15} So persecute them with thy tempest, and make them afraid with thy storm. {83:16} *Fill their faces with shame; that they may seek thy name, O LORD.* {83:17} Let them be confounded and troubled for ever; yea, let them be put to shame, and perish: {83:18} That men may know that thou, whose name alone is JEHOVAH, art the most high over all the earth.

{84:1} How lovely are your dwellings, O LORD of hosts! {84:2} My soul longs, yes, even faints for the courts of the LORD; my heart and my flesh cry out for the living God. {84:3} Even the sparrow has found a home, and the swallow a nest for herself, where she may lay her young—near your altars, O LORD of hosts, my King, and my God. {84:4} Blessed are those who dwell in your house; they will still be praising you. Selah. {84:5} Blessed is the one whose strength is in you, whose heart is set on pilgrimage. {84:6} Passing through the valley of Baca, they make it a spring; the rain also covers it with pools. {84:7} They go from strength to strength; each one appears before God in Zion. {84:8} O LORD God of hosts, hear my prayer; give ear, O God of Jacob! Selah. {84:9} Behold, O God our shield, and look upon the face of your anointed. {84:10} For a day in your courts is better than a thousand elsewhere. I would rather be a doorkeeper in the house of my God than dwell in the tents of wickedness. {84:11} For the LORD God is a sun and shield; the LORD bestows favor and honor. No good thing does he withhold from those who walk uprightly. {84:12} O LORD of hosts, blessed is the one who trusts in you.

{85:1} LORD, you have shown favor to your land; you have restored the fortunes of Jacob. {85:2} You have forgiven the iniquity of your people; you have covered all their sin. Selah. {85:3} You have withdrawn all your wrath; you have turned from your hot anger. {85:4} Restore us, O God of our salvation, and put away your indignation toward us. {85:5} Will you be angry with us forever? Will you prolong your anger to all generations? {85:6} Will you not revive us again, that your people may rejoice in you? {85:7} Show us your steadfast love, O LORD, and grant us your salvation. {85:8} Let me hear what God the LORD will speak, for he will speak peace to his people, to his saints; but let them not turn back to folly. {85:9} Surely his salvation is near to those who fear him, that glory may dwell in our land. {85:10} Steadfast love and faithfulness meet; righteousness and peace kiss each other. {85:11} Faithfulness springs up from the ground, and righteousness looks down from the sky. {85:12} Yes, the LORD will give what is good, and our land will yield its increase. {85:13} Righteousness will go before him and make his footsteps a way.

{86:1} Bow down your ear, O LORD, hear me, for I am poor and needy. {86:2} Preserve my soul, for I am holy; O you, my God, save your servant who trusts in you. {86:3} Be merciful to me, O Lord, for I cry to you daily. {86:4} Rejoice the soul of your servant, for to you, O Lord, I lift up my soul. {86:5} For you, Lord, are good and ready to forgive, and abundant in mercy to all who call upon you. {86:6} Give ear, O LORD, to my prayer; and attend to the voice of my supplications. {86:7} In the day of my trouble, I will call upon you, for you will answer me. {86:8} Among the gods, there is none like you, O Lord; nor are there any works like your works. {86:9} All nations whom you have made shall come and worship before you, O Lord, and shall glorify your name. {86:10} For you are great and do wondrous things; you alone are God. {86:11} Teach me your way, O LORD; I will walk in your truth; unite my heart to fear your name. {86:12} I will praise you, O Lord my God, with all my heart, and I will glorify your name forevermore. {86:13} For great is your mercy toward me, and you have delivered my soul from the lowest hell. {86:14} O God, the proud have risen against me, and the assemblies of violent men have sought after my soul; and have not set you before them. {86:15} But you, O Lord, are a God full of compassion and gracious, longsuffering and abundant in mercy and truth. {86:16} O turn to me, and have mercy upon me; give your strength to your servant, and save the son of your handmaid. {86:17} Show me a token for good; that those who hate me may see it, and be ashamed; because you, LORD, have helped me and comforted me.

{87:1} His foundation is in the holy mountains. {87:2} The LORD loves the gates of Zion more than all the dwellings of Jacob. {87:3} Glorious things are spoken of you, O city of God. Selah. {87:4} I will make mention of Rahab and Babylon to those who know me; behold Philistia and Tyre, with Ethiopia; this man was born in there. {87:5} And of Zion it shall be said, "This and that man was born in her"; and the highest himself shall establish her. {87:6} The LORD shall count, when he writes up the people, that this man was born there. Selah. {87:7} As well the singers as the players on instruments shall be there; all my springs are in you.

{88:1} O LORD God of my salvation, I have cried day and night before you: {88:2} Let my prayer come before you; incline your ear unto my cry; {88:3} For my soul is full of troubles, and my life draws nigh unto the grave. {88:4} I am counted with them that go down into the pit; I am as a man that has no strength. {88:5} Free among the dead, like the slain that lie in the grave, whom you remember no more: and they are cut off from your hand. {88:6} You have laid me in the lowest pit, in darkness, in the deeps. {88:7} Your wrath lies hard upon me, and you have afflicted me with all your waves. Selah. {88:8} You have put away my acquaintances far from me; you have made me an abomination unto them: I am shut up, and I cannot come forth. {88:9} My eye mourns by reason of affliction: LORD, I have called daily upon you, I have stretched out my hands unto you. {88:10} Will you show wonders to the dead? Shall the dead arise and praise you? Selah. {88:11} Shall your lovingkindness be declared in the grave? Or your faithfulness in destruction? {88:12} Shall your wonders be known in the dark? And your righteousness in the land of forgetfulness? {88:13} But unto you have I cried, O LORD; and in the morning shall my prayer prevent you. {88:14} LORD, why do you cast off my soul? Why hide your face from me? {88:15} I am afflicted and ready to die from my youth up; while I suffer your terrors I am distracted. {88:16} Your fierce wrath goes over me; your terrors have cut me off. {88:17} They came round about me daily like water; they compassed me about together. {88:18} Lover and friend have you put far from me, and my acquaintance into darkness.

{89:1} I will sing of the mercies of the LORD forever: with my mouth will I make known your faithfulness to all generations. {89:2} For I have said, Mercy shall be built up forever: your faithfulness you shall establish in the very heavens. {89:3} I have made a covenant with my chosen, I have sworn unto David my servant, {89:4} Your seed will I establish forever, and build up your throne to all generations. Selah. {89:5} And the heavens shall praise your wonders, O LORD: your faithfulness also in the congregation of the saints. {89:6} For who in the heaven can be compared unto the LORD? Who among the sons of the mighty can be likened unto the LORD? {89:7} God is greatly to be feared in the assembly of the saints, and to be had in reverence of all them that are about him. {89:8} O LORD God of hosts, who is a strong LORD like unto you? Or to your faithfulness round about you? {89:9} You rule the raging of the sea: when the waves thereof arise, you still them. {89:10} You have broken Rahab in pieces, as one that is slain; you have scattered your enemies with your strong arm. {89:11} The heavens are yours, the earth also is yours: as for the world and the fullness thereof, you have founded them. {89:12} The north and the south you have created them: Tabor and Hermon shall rejoice in your name. {89:13} You have a mighty arm: strong is your hand, and high is your right hand. {89:14} Justice and judgment are the habitation of your throne: mercy and truth shall go before your face. {89:15} Blessed is the people that know the joyful sound: they shall walk, O LORD, in the light of your countenance. {89:16} In your name shall they rejoice all the day: and in your righteousness shall they be exalted. {89:17} For you are the glory of their strength: and in your favor our horn shall be exalted. {89:18} For the LORD is our defense; and the Holy One of Israel is our king. {89:19} Then you spoke in vision to your holy one, and said, I have laid help upon one that is mighty; I have exalted one chosen out of the people. {89:20} I have found David my servant; with my holy oil have I anointed him: {89:21} With whom my hand shall be established: mine arm also shall strengthen him. {89:22} The enemy shall not exact upon him; nor the son of wickedness afflict him. {89:23} And I will beat down his foes before his face, and plague them that hate him. {89:24} But my faithfulness and my mercy shall be with him: and in my name shall his horn be exalted. {89:25} I will set his hand also in the sea, and his right hand in the rivers. {89:26} He shall cry unto me, You are my father, my God, and the rock of my salvation. {89:27} Also I will make him my firstborn, higher than the kings of the earth. {89:28} My mercy will I keep for him forevermore, and my covenant shall stand fast with him. {89:29} His seed also will I make to endure forever, and his throne as the days of heaven. {89:30} If his children forsake my law, and walk not in my judgments; {89:31} If they break my statutes, and keep not my commandments; {89:32} Then will I visit their transgression with the rod, and their iniquity with stripes. {89:33} Nevertheless my lovingkindness will I not utterly take from him, nor suffer my faithfulness to fail. {89:34} My covenant will I not break, nor alter the thing that is gone out of my lips. {89:35} Once have I sworn by my holiness that I will not lie unto David. {89:36} His seed shall endure forever, and his throne as the sun before me. {89:37} It shall be established forever as the moon, and as a faithful witness in heaven. Selah. {89:38} But you have cast off and abhorred, you have been wroth with your anointed. {89:39} You have made void the covenant of your servant: you have profaned his crown by casting it to the ground. {89:40} You have broken down all his hedges; you have brought his strongholds to ruin. {89:41} All that pass by the way spoil him: he is a reproach to his neighbors. {89:42} You have set up the right hand of his adversaries; you have made all his enemies to rejoice. { 89:43} You have also turned the edge of his sword, and have not made him to stand in the battle. {89:44} You have made his glory to cease, and cast his throne down to the ground. {89:45} The days of his youth have you shortened: you have covered him with shame. Selah. {89:46} How long, LORD? Will you hide yourself forever? Shall your wrath burn like fire? {89:47} Remember how short my time is: wherefore have you made all men in vain? {89:48} What man is he that lives, and shall not see death? Shall he deliver his soul from the hand of the grave? Selah. {89:49} Lord, where are your former lovingkindnesses, which you swore unto David in your truth? {89:50} Remember, Lord, the reproach of your servants; how I do bear in my bosom the reproach of all the mighty people; {89:51} Wherewith your enemies have reproached, O LORD; wherewith they have reproached the footsteps of your anointed. {89:52} Blessed be the LORD forevermore. Amen, and Amen.

{90:1} LORD, you have been our dwelling place in all generations. {90:2} Before the mountains were brought forth, or ever you had formed the earth and the world, even from everlasting to everlasting, you are God. {90:3} You turn man to destruction; and say, Return, you children of men. {90:4} For a thousand years in your sight are but as yesterday when it is past, and as a watch in the night. {90:5} You carry them away as with a flood; they are as a sleep: in the morning they are like grass which grows up. {90:6} In the morning it flourishes, and grows up; in the evening it is cut down, and withers. {90:7} For we are consumed by your anger, and by your wrath are we troubled. {90:8} You have set our iniquities before you, our secret sins in the light of your countenance. {90:9} For all our days are passed away in your wrath: we spend our years as a tale that is told. {90:10} The days of our years are threescore years and ten; and if by reason of strength they are fourscore years, yet is their strength labor and sorrow; for it is soon cut off, and we fly away. {90:11} Who knows the power of your anger? Even according to your fear, so is your wrath. {90:12} So teach us to number our days, that we may apply our hearts unto wisdom. {90:13} Return, O LORD, how long? and let it repent you concerning your servants. {90:14} O satisfy us early with your mercy; that we may rejoice and be glad all our days. {90:15} Make us glad according to the days wherein you have afflicted us, and the years wherein we have seen evil. {90:16} Let your work appear unto your servants, and your glory unto their children. {90:17} And let the beauty of the LORD our God be upon us: and establish the work of our hands upon us; yes, the work of our hands establish it.

{91:1} He who dwells in the secret place of the Most High shall abide under the shadow of the Almighty. {91:2} I will say of the LORD, "He is my refuge and my fortress: my God; in him will I trust." {91:3} Surely he shall deliver you from the snare of the fowler, and from the noisome pestilence. {91:4} He shall cover you with his feathers, and under his wings you shall trust: his truth shall be your shield and buckler. {91:5} You shall not be afraid for the terror by night; nor for the arrow that flies by day; {91:6} Nor for the pestilence that walks in darkness; nor for the destruction that wastes at noonday. {91:7} A thousand shall fall at your side, and ten thousand at your right hand; but it shall not come near you. {91:8} Only with your eyes shall you behold and see the reward of the wicked. {91:9} Because you have made the LORD, who is my refuge, even the Most High, your habitation; {91:10} There shall no evil befall you, neither shall any plague come near your dwelling. {91:11} For he shall give his angels charge over you, to keep you in all your ways. {91:12} They shall bear you up in their hands, lest you dash your foot against a stone. {91:13} You shall tread upon the lion and adder: the young lion and the dragon shall you trample under feet. {91:14} Because he has set his love upon me, therefore will I deliver him: I will set him on high, because he has known my name. {91:15} He shall call upon me, and I will answer him: I will be with him in trouble; I will deliver him, and honor him. {91:16} With long life will I satisfy him, and show him my salvation.

{92:1} It is a good thing to give thanks unto the LORD, and to sing praises unto your name, O Most High: {92:2} To show forth your lovingkindness in the morning, and your faithfulness every night, {92:3} Upon an instrument of ten strings, and upon the psaltery; upon the harp with a solemn sound. {92:4} For you, LORD, have made me glad through your work: I will triumph in the works of your hands. {92:5} O LORD, how great are your works! and your thoughts are very deep. {92:6} A brutish man knows not; neither does a fool understand this. {92:7} When the wicked spring as the grass, and when all the workers of iniquity do flourish; it is that they shall be destroyed forever: {92:8} But you, LORD, are most high forevermore. {92:9} For, lo, your enemies, O LORD, for, lo, your enemies shall perish; all the workers of iniquity shall be scattered. {92:10} But my horn shall you exalt like the horn of a unicorn: I shall be anointed with fresh oil. {92:11} My eye also shall see my desire on my enemies, and my ears shall hear my desire of the wicked that rise up against me. {92:12} The righteous shall flourish like the palm tree: he shall grow like a cedar in Lebanon. {92:13} Those that be planted in the house of the LORD shall flourish in the courts of our God. {92:14} They shall still bring forth fruit in old age; they shall be fat and flourishing; {92:15} To show that the LORD is upright: he is my rock, and there is no unrighteousness in him.

{93:1} The LORD reigns, he is clothed with majesty; the LORD is clothed with strength, he has girded himself: the world also is established, that it cannot be moved. {93:2} Your throne is established of old: you are from everlasting. {93:3} The floods have lifted up, O LORD, the floods have lifted up their voice; the floods lift up their waves. {93:4} The LORD on high is mightier than the noise of many waters, yes, than the mighty waves of the sea. {93:5} Your testimonies are very sure: holiness befits your house, O LORD, forever.

{94:1} O LORD God, to whom vengeance belongs; O God, to whom vengeance belongs, show yourself. {94:2} Rise up, O judge of the earth; render a reward to the proud. {94:3} LORD, how long shall the wicked, how long shall the wicked triumph? {94:4} How long shall they utter and speak hard things? and all the workers of iniquity boast themselves? {94:5} They break in pieces your people, O LORD, and afflict your heritage. {94:6} They slay the widow and the stranger, and murder the fatherless. {94:7} Yet they say, "The LORD shall not see, neither shall the God of Jacob regard it." {94:8} Understand, you brutish among the people: and you fools, when will you be wise? {94:9} He that planted the ear, shall he not hear? he that formed the eye, shall he not see? {94:10} He that chastises the nations, shall he not correct? he that teaches man knowledge, shall he not know? {94:11} The LORD knows the thoughts of man, that they are vanity. {94:12} Blessed is the man whom you chasten, O LORD, and teach him out of your law; {94:13} That you may give him rest from the days of adversity, until the pit be dug for the wicked. {94:14} For the LORD will not cast off his people, neither will he forsake his inheritance. {94:15} But judgment shall return unto righteousness: and all the upright in heart shall follow it. {94:16} Who will rise up for me against the evildoers? or who will stand up for me against the workers of iniquity? {94:17} Unless the LORD had been my help, my soul had almost dwelt in silence. {94:18} When I said, "My foot slips;" your mercy, O LORD, held me up. {94:19} In the multitude of my thoughts within me your comforts delight my soul. {94:20} Shall the throne of iniquity have fellowship with you, which frames mischief by a law? {94:21} They gather themselves together against the soul of the righteous, and condemn the innocent blood. {94:22} But the LORD is my defense; and my God is the rock of my refuge. {94:23} And he shall bring upon them their own iniquity, and shall cut them off in their own wickedness; yes, the LORD our God shall cut them off.

{95:1} O come, let us sing unto the LORD: let us make a joyful noise to the rock of our salvation. {95:2} Let us come before his presence with thanksgiving, and make a joyful noise unto him with psalms. {95:3} For the LORD is a great God, and a great King above all gods. {95:4} In his hand are the deep places of the earth: the strength of the hills is his also. {95:5} The sea is his, and he made it: and his hands formed the dry land. {95:6} O come, let us worship and bow down: let us kneel before the LORD our maker. {95:7} For he is our God; and we are the people of his pasture, and the sheep of his hand. Today if you will hear his voice, {95:8} Harden not your heart, as in the provocation, and as in the day of temptation in the wilderness: {95:9} When your fathers tempted me, proved me, and saw my work. {95:10} Forty years long was I grieved with this generation, and said, "It is a people that do err in their heart, and they have not known my ways:" {95:11} Unto whom I swore in my wrath that they should not enter into my rest.

{96:1} O sing unto the LORD a new song: sing unto the LORD, all the earth. {96:2} Sing unto the LORD, bless his name; show forth his salvation from day to day. {96:3} Declare his glory among the heathen, his wonders among all people. {96:4} For the LORD is great, and greatly to be praised: he is to be feared above all gods. {96:5} For all the gods of the nations are idols: but the LORD made the heavens. {96:6} Honour and majesty are before him: strength and beauty are in his sanctuary. {96:7} Give unto the LORD, O ye kindreds of the people, give unto the LORD glory and strength. {96:8} Give unto the LORD the glory due unto his name: bring an offering, and come into his courts. {96:9} O worship the LORD in the beauty of holiness: fear before him, all the earth. {96:10} Say among the heathen that the LORD reigneth: the world also shall be established that it shall not be moved: he shall judge the people righteously. {96:11} Let the heavens rejoice, and let the earth be glad; let the sea roar, and the fullness thereof. {96:12} Let the field be joyful, and all that is therein: then shall all the trees of the wood rejoice {96:13} Before the LORD: for he cometh, for he cometh to judge the earth: he shall judge the world with righteousness, and the people with his truth.

{97:1} The LORD reigneth; let the earth rejoice; let the multitude of isles be glad thereof. {97:2} Clouds and darkness are round about him: righteousness and judgment are the habitation of his throne. {97:3} A fire goeth before him, and burneth up his enemies round about. {97:4} His lightnings enlightened the world: the earth saw, and trembled. {97:5} The hills melted like wax at the presence of the LORD, at the presence of the Lord of the whole earth. {97:6} The heavens declare his righteousness, and all the people see his glory. {97:7} Confounded be all they that serve graven images, that boast themselves of idols: worship him, all ye gods. {97:8} Zion heard, and was glad; and the daughters of Judah rejoiced because of thy judgments, O LORD. {97:9} For thou, LORD, art high above all the earth: thou art exalted far above all gods. {97:10} Ye that love the LORD, hate evil: he preserveth the souls of his saints; he delivereth them out of the hand of the wicked. {97:11} Light is sown for the righteous, and gladness for the upright in heart. {97:12} Rejoice in the LORD, ye righteous; and give thanks at the remembrance of his holiness.

{98:1} O sing unto the LORD a new song; for he hath done marvelous things: his right hand, and his holy arm, hath gotten him the victory. {98:2} The LORD hath made known his salvation: his righteousness hath he openly showed in the sight of the heathen. {98:3} He hath remembered his mercy and his truth toward the house of Israel: all the ends of the earth have seen the salvation of our God. {98:4} Make a joyful noise unto the LORD, all the earth: make a loud noise, and rejoice, and sing praise. {98:5} Sing unto the LORD with the harp; with the harp, and the voice of a psalm. {98:6} With trumpets and sound of cornet make a joyful noise before the LORD, the King. {98:7} Let the sea roar, and the fullness thereof; the world, and they that dwell therein. {98:8} Let the floods clap their hands: let the hills be joyful together. {98:9} Before the LORD; for he cometh to judge the earth: with righteousness shall he judge the world, and the people with equity.

{99:1} The LORD reigneth; let the people tremble: he sitteth between the cherubims; let the earth be moved. {99:2} The LORD is great in Zion; and he is high above all the people. {99:3} Let them praise thy great and terrible name; for it is holy. {99:4} The king's strength also loveth judgment; thou dost establish equity, thou executest judgment and righteousness in Jacob. {99:5} Exalt ye the LORD our God, and worship at his footstool; for he is holy. {99:6} Moses and Aaron among his priests, and Samuel among them that call upon his name; they called upon the LORD, and he answered them. {99:7} He spake unto them in the cloudy pillar: they kept his testimonies, and the ordinance that he gave them. {99:8} Thou answeredst them, O LORD our God: thou wast a God that forgavest them, though thou tookest vengeance of their inventions. {99:9} Exalt the LORD our God, and worship at his holy hill; for the LORD our God is holy.

{100:1} Make a joyful noise unto the LORD, all ye lands. {100:2} Serve the LORD with gladness: come before his presence with singing. {100:3} Know ye that the LORD he is God: it is he that hath made us, and not we ourselves; we are his people, and the sheep of his pasture. {100:4} Enter into his gates with thanksgiving, and into his courts with praise: be thankful unto him, and bless his name. {100:5} For the LORD is good; his mercy is everlasting; and his truth endureth to all generations.

{101:1} I will sing of mercy and judgment: unto thee, O LORD, will I sing. {101:2} I will behave myself wisely in a perfect way. O when wilt thou come unto me? I will walk within my house with a perfect heart. {101:3} I will set no wicked thing before mine eyes: I hate the work of them that turn aside; it shall not cleave to me. {101:4} A froward heart shall depart from me: I will not know a wicked person. {101:5} Whoso privily slandereth his neighbour, him will I cut off: him that hath an high look and a proud heart will not I suffer. {101:6} Mine eyes shall be upon the faithful of the land, that they may dwell with me: he that walketh in a perfect way, he shall serve me. {101:7} He that worketh deceit shall not dwell within my house: he that telleth lies shall not tarry in my sight. {101:8} I will early destroy all the wicked of the land; that I may cut off all wicked doers from the city of the LORD.

{102:1} Hear my prayer, O LORD, and let my cry come unto thee. {102:2} Hide not thy face from me in the day when I am in trouble; incline thine ear unto me: in the day when I call answer me speedily. {102:3} For my days are consumed like smoke, and my bones are burned as an hearth. {102:4} My heart is smitten, and withered like grass; so that I forget to eat my bread. {102:5} By reason of the voice of my groaning my bones cleave to my skin. {102:6} I am like a pelican of the wilderness: I am like an owl of the desert. {102:7} I watch, and am as a sparrow alone upon the house top. {102:8} Mine enemies reproach me all the day; and they that are mad against me are sworn against me. {102:9} For I have eaten ashes like bread, and mingled my drink with weeping, {102:10} Because of thine indignation and thy wrath: for thou hast lifted me up, and cast me down. {102:11} My days are like a shadow that declineth; and I am withered like grass. {102:12} But thou, O LORD, shalt endure for ever; and thy remembrance unto all generations. {102:13} Thou shalt arise, and have mercy upon Zion: for the time to favour her, yea, the set time, is come. {102:14} For thy servants take pleasure in her stones, and favour the dust thereof. {102:15} So the heathen shall fear the name of the LORD, and all the kings of the earth thy glory. {102:16} When the LORD shall build up Zion, he shall appear in his glory. {102:17} He will regard the prayer of the destitute, and not despise their prayer. {102:18} This shall be written for the generation to come: and the people which shall be created shall praise the LORD. {102:19} For he hath looked down from the height of his sanctuary; from heaven did the LORD behold the earth; {102:20} To hear the groaning of the prisoner; to loose those that are appointed to death; {102:21} To declare the name of the LORD in Zion, and his praise in Jerusalem; {102:22} When the people are gathered together, and the kingdoms, to serve the LORD. {102:23} He weakened my strength in the way; he shortened my days. {102:24} I said, O my God, take me not away in the midst of my days: thy years are throughout all generations. {102:25} Of old hast thou laid the foundation of the earth: and the heavens are the work of thy hands. {102:26} They shall perish, but thou shalt endure: yea, all of them shall wax old like a garment; as a vesture shalt thou change them, and they shall be changed: {102:27} But thou art the same, and thy years shall have no end. {102:28} The children of thy servants shall continue, and their seed shall be established before thee.

{103:1} Bless the LORD, O my soul: and all that is within me, bless his holy name. {103:2} Bless the LORD, O my soul, and forget not all his benefits: {103:3} Who forgiveth all thine iniquities; who healeth all thy diseases; {103:4} Who redeemeth thy life from destruction; who crowneth thee with lovingkindness and tender mercies; {103:5} Who satisfieth thy mouth with good things; so that thy youth is renewed like the eagle's. {103:6} The LORD executeth righteousness and judgment for all that are oppressed. {103:7} He made known his ways unto Moses, his acts unto the children of Israel. {103:8} The LORD is merciful and gracious, slow to anger, and plenteous in mercy. {103:9} He will not always chide: neither will he keep his anger for ever. {103:10} He hath not dealt with us after our sins; nor rewarded us according to our iniquities. {103:11} For as the heaven is high above the earth, so great is his mercy toward them that fear him. {103:12} As far as the east is from the west, so far hath he removed our transgressions from us. {103:13} Like as a father pitieth his children, so the LORD pitieth them that fear him. {103:14} For he knoweth our frame; he remembereth that we are dust. {103:15} As for man, his days are as grass: as a flower of the field, so he flourisheth. {103:16} For the wind passeth over it, and it is gone; and the place thereof shall know it no more. {103:17} But the mercy of the LORD is from everlasting to everlasting upon them that fear him, and his righteousness unto children's children; {103:18} To such as keep his covenant, and to those that remember his commandments to do them. {103:19} The LORD hath prepared his throne in the heavens; and his kingdom ruleth over all. {103:20} Bless the LORD, ye his angels, that excel in strength, that do his commandments, hearkening unto the voice of his word. {103:21} Bless ye the LORD, all ye his hosts; ye ministers of his, that do his pleasure. {103:22} Bless the LORD, all his works in all places of his dominion: bless the LORD, O my soul.

{104:1} Bless the LORD, O my soul. O LORD my God, thou art very great; thou art clothed with honour and majesty. {104:2} Who coverest thyself with light as with a garment: who stretchest out the heavens like a curtain: {104:3} Who layeth the beams of his chambers in the waters: who maketh the clouds his chariot: who walketh upon the wings of the wind: {104:4} Who maketh his angels spirits; his ministers a flaming fire: {104:5} Who laid the foundations of the earth, that it should not be removed for ever. {104:6} Thou coveredst it with the deep as with a garment: the waters stood above the mountains. {104:7} At thy rebuke they fled; at the voice of thy thunder they hasted away. {104:8} They go up by the mountains; they go down by the valleys unto the place which thou hast founded for them. {104:9} Thou hast set a bound that they may not pass over; that they turn not again to cover the earth. {104:10} He sendeth the springs into the valleys, which run among the hills. {104:11} They give drink to every beast of the field: the wild asses quench their thirst. {104:12} By them shall the fowls of the heaven have their habitation, which sing among the branches. {104:13} He watereth the hills from his chambers: the earth is satisfied with the fruit of thy works. {104:14} He causeth the grass to grow for the cattle, and herb for the service of man: that he may bring forth food out of the earth; {104:15} And wine that maketh glad the heart of man, and oil to make his face to shine, and bread which strengtheneth man's heart. {104:16} The trees of the LORD are full of sap; the cedars of Lebanon, which he hath planted; {104:17} Where the birds make their nests: as for the stork, the fir trees are her house. {104:18} The high hills are a refuge for the wild goats; and the rocks for the conies. {104:19} He appointed the moon for seasons: the sun knoweth his going down. {104:20} Thou makest darkness, and it is night: wherein all the beasts of the forest do creep forth. {104:21} The young lions roar after their prey, and seek their meat from God. {104:22} The sun ariseth, they gather themselves together, and lay them down in their dens. {104:23} Man goeth forth unto his work and to his labour until the evening. {104:24} O LORD, how manifold are thy works! in wisdom hast thou made them all: the earth is full of thy riches. {104:25} So is this great and wide sea, wherein are things creeping innumerable, both small and great beasts. {104:26} There go the ships: there is that leviathan, whom thou hast made to play therein. {104:27} These wait all upon thee; that thou mayest give them their meat in due season. {104:28} That thou givest them they gather: thou openest thine hand, they are filled with good. {104:29} Thou hidest thy face, they are troubled: thou takest away their breath, they die, and return to their dust. {104:30} Thou sendest forth thy spirit, they are created: and thou renewest the face of the earth. {104:31} The glory of the LORD shall endure for ever: the LORD shall rejoice in his works. {104:32} He looketh on the earth, and it trembleth: he toucheth the hills, and they smoke. {104:33} I will sing unto the LORD as long as I live: I will sing praise to my God while I have my being. {104:34} My meditation of him shall be sweet: I will be glad in the LORD. {104:35} Let the sinners be consumed out of the earth, and let the wicked be no more. Bless thou the LORD, O my soul. Praise ye the LORD.

{105:1} O give thanks unto the LORD; call upon his name: make known his deeds among the people. {105:2} Sing unto him, sing psalms unto him: talk ye of all his wondrous works. {105:3} Glory ye in his holy name: let the heart of them rejoice that seek the LORD. {105:4} Seek the LORD, and his strength: seek his face evermore. {105:5} Remember his marvellous works that he hath done; his wonders, and the judgments of his mouth; {105:6} O ye seed of Abraham his servant, ye children of Jacob his chosen. {105:7} He is the LORD our God: his judgments are in all the earth. {105:8} He hath remembered his covenant for ever, the word which he commanded to a thousand generations. {105:9} Which covenant he made with Abraham, and his oath unto Isaac; {105:10} And confirmed the same unto Jacob for a law, and to Israel for an everlasting covenant: {105:11} Saying, Unto thee will I give the land of Canaan, the lot of your inheritance: {105:12} When they were but a few men in number; yea, very few, and strangers in it. {105:13} When they went from one nation to another, from one kingdom to another people; {105:14} He suffered no man to do them wrong: yea, he reproved kings for their sakes; {105:15} Saying, Touch not mine anointed, and do my prophets no harm. {105:16} Moreover he called for a famine upon the land: he brake the whole staff of bread. {105:17} He sent a man before them, even Joseph, who was sold for a servant: {105:18} Whose feet they hurt with fetters: he was laid in iron: {105:19} Until the time that his word came: the word of the LORD tried him. {105:20} The king sent and loosed him; even the ruler of the people, and let him go free. {105:21} He made him lord of his house, and ruler of all his substance: {105:22} To bind his princes at his pleasure; and teach his senators wisdom. {105:23} Israel also came into Egypt; and Jacob sojourned in the land of Ham. {105:24} And he increased his people greatly; and made them stronger than their enemies. {105:25} He turned their heart to hate his people, to deal subtilly with his servants. {105:26} He sent Moses his servant; and Aaron whom he had chosen. {105:27} They shewed his signs among them, and wonders in the land of Ham. {105:28} He sent darkness, and made it dark; and they rebelled not against his word. {105:29} He turned their waters into blood, and slew their fish. {105:30} Their land brought forth frogs in abundance, in the chambers of their kings. {105:31} He spake, and there came divers sorts of flies, and lice in all their coasts. {105:32} He gave them hail for rain, and flaming fire in their land. {105:33} He smote their vines also and their fig trees; and brake the trees of their coasts. {105:34} He spake, and the locusts came, and caterpillers, and that without number, {105:35} And did eat up all the herbs in their land, and devoured the fruit of their ground. {105:36} He smote also all the firstborn in their land, the chief of all their strength. {105:37} He brought them forth also with silver and gold: and there was not one feeble person among their tribes. {105:38} Egypt was glad when they departed: for the fear of them fell upon them. {105:39} He spread a cloud for a covering; and fire to give light in the night. {105:40} The people asked, and he brought quails, and satisfied them with the bread of heaven. {105:41} He opened the rock, and the waters gushed out; they ran in the dry places like a river. {105:42} For he remembered his holy promise, and Abraham his servant. {105:43} And he brought forth his people with joy, and his chosen with gladness: {105:44} And gave them the lands of the heathen: and they inherited the labour of the people; {105:45} That they might observe his statutes, and keep his laws. Praise ye the LORD.

{106:1} Praise ye the LORD. O give thanks unto the LORD; for he is good: for his mercy endureth for ever. {106:2} Who can utter the mighty acts of the LORD? who can shew forth all his praise? {106:3} Blessed are they that keep judgment, and he that doeth righteousness at all times. {106:4} Remember me, O LORD, with the favour that thou bearest unto thy people: O visit me with thy salvation; {106:5} That I may see the good of thy chosen, that I may rejoice in the gladness of thy nation, that I may glory with thine inheritance. {106:6} We have sinned with our fathers, we have committed iniquity, we have done wickedly. {106:7} Our fathers understood not thy wonders in Egypt; they remembered not the multitude of thy mercies; but provoked him at the sea, even at the Red sea. {106:8} Nevertheless he saved them for his name's sake, that he might make his mighty power to be known. {106:9} He rebuked the Red sea also, and it was dried up: so he led them through the depths, as through the wilderness. {106:10} And he saved them from the hand of him that hated them, and redeemed them from the hand of the enemy. {106:11} And the waters covered their enemies: there was not one of them left. {106:12} Then believed they his words; they sang his praise. {106:13} They soon forgat his works; they waited not for his counsel: {106:14} But lusted exceedingly in the wilderness, and tempted God in the desert. {106:15} And he gave them their request; but sent leanness into their soul. {106:16} They envied Moses also in the camp, and Aaron the saint of the LORD. {106:17} The earth opened and swallowed up Dathan, and covered the company of Abiram. {106:18} And a fire was kindled in their company; the flame burned up the wicked. {106:19} They made a calf in Horeb, and worshipped the molten image. {106:20} Thus they changed their glory into the similitude of an ox that eateth grass. {106:21} They forgat God their saviour, which had done great things in Egypt; {106:22} Wondrous works in the land of Ham, and terrible things by the Red sea. {106:23} Therefore he said that he would destroy them, had not Moses his chosen stood before him in the breach, to turn away his wrath, lest he should destroy them. {106:24} Yea, they despised the pleasant land, they believed not his word: {106:25} But murmured in their tents, and hearkened not unto the voice of the LORD. {106:26} Therefore he lifted up his hand against them, to overthrow them in the wilderness: {106:27} To overthrow their seed also among the nations, and to scatter them in the lands. {106:28} They joined themselves also unto Baal-peor, and ate the sacrifices of the dead. {106:29} Thus they provoked him to anger with their inventions: and the plague brake in upon them. {106:30} Then stood up Phinehas, and executed judgment: and so the plague was stayed. {106:31} And that was counted unto him for righteousness unto all generations for evermore. {106:32} They angered him also at the waters of strife, so that it went ill with Moses for their sakes: {106:33} Because they provoked his spirit, so that he spake unadvisedly with his lips. {106:34} They did not destroy the nations, concerning whom the LORD commanded them: {106:35} But were mingled among the heathen, and learned their works. {106:36} And they served their idols: which were a snare unto them. {106:37} Yea, they sacrificed their sons and their daughters unto devils, {106:38} And shed innocent blood, even the blood of their sons and of their daughters, whom they sacrificed unto the idols of Canaan: and the land was polluted with blood. {106:39} Thus were they defiled with their own works, and went a whoring with their own inventions. {106:40} Therefore was the wrath of the LORD kindled against his people, insomuch that he abhorred his own inheritance. {106:41} And he gave them into the hand of the heathen; and they that hated them ruled over them. {106:42} Their enemies also oppressed them, and they were brought into subjection under their hand. {106:43} Many times did he deliver them; but they provoked him with their counsel, and were brought low for their iniquity. {106:44} Nevertheless he regarded their affliction, when he heard their cry: {106:45} And he remembered for them his covenant, and repented according to the multitude of his mercies. {106:46} He made them also to be pitied of all those that carried them captives. {106:47} Save us, O LORD our God, and gather us from among the heathen, to give thanks unto thy holy name, and to triumph in thy praise. {106:48} Blessed be the Lord God of Israel from everlasting to everlasting: and let all the people say, Amen. Praise the LORD.

{107:1} O give thanks unto the LORD, for he is good: for his mercy endureth for ever. {107:2} Let the redeemed of the LORD say so, whom he hath redeemed from the hand of the enemy; {107:3} And gathered them out of the lands, from the east, and from the west, from the north, and from the south. {107:4} They wandered in the wilderness in a solitary way; they found no city to dwell in. {107:5} Hungry and thirsty, their soul fainted in them. {107:6} Then they cried unto the LORD in their trouble, and he delivered them out of their distresses. {107:7} And he led them forth by the right way, that they might go to a city of habitation. {107:8} Oh that men would praise the LORD for his goodness, and for his wonderful works to the children of men! {107:9} For he satisfieth the longing soul, and filleth the hungry soul with goodness. {107:10} Such as sit in darkness and in the shadow of death, being bound in affliction and iron; {107:11} Because they rebelled against the words of God, and contemned the counsel of the most High: {107:12} Therefore he brought down their heart with labour; they fell down, and there was none to help. {107:13} Then they cried unto the LORD in their trouble, and he saved them out of their distresses. {107:14} He brought them out of darkness and the shadow of death, and brake their bands in sunder. {107:15} Oh that men would praise the LORD for his goodness, and for his wonderful works to the children of men! {107:16} For he hath broken the gates of brass, and cut the bars of iron in sunder. {107:17} Fools because of their transgression, and because of their iniquities, are afflicted. {107:18} Their soul abhorreth all manner of meat; and they draw near unto the gates of death. {107:19} Then they cry unto the LORD in their trouble, and he saveth them out of their distresses. {107:20} He sent his word, and healed them, and delivered them from their destructions. {107:21} Oh that men would praise the LORD for his goodness, and for his wonderful works to the children of men! {107:22} And let them sacrifice the sacrifices of thanksgiving, and declare his works with rejoicing. {107:23} They that go down to the sea in ships, that do business in great waters; {107:24} These see the works of the LORD, and his wonders in the deep. {107:25} For he commandeth, and raiseth the stormy wind, which lifteth up the waves thereof. {107:26} They mount up to the heaven, they go down again to the depths: their soul is melted because of trouble. {107:27} They reel to and fro, and stagger like a drunken man, and are at their wit's end. {107:28} Then they cry unto the LORD in their trouble, and he bringeth them out of their distresses. {107:29} He maketh the storm a calm, so that the waves thereof are still. {107:30} Then are they glad because they be quiet; so he bringeth them unto their desired haven. {107:31} Oh that men would praise the LORD for his goodness, and for his wonderful works to the children of men! {107:32} Let them exalt him also in the congregation of the people, and praise him in the assembly of the elders. {107:33} He turneth rivers into a wilderness, and the watersprings into dry ground; {107:34} A fruitful land into barrenness, for the wickedness of them that dwell therein. {107:35} He turneth the wilderness into a standing water, and dry ground into watersprings. {107:36} And there he maketh the hungry to dwell, that they may prepare a city for habitation; {107:37} And sow the fields, and plant vineyards, which may yield fruits of increase. {107:38} He blesseth them also, so that they are multiplied greatly; and suffereth not their cattle to decrease. {107:39} Again, they are minished and brought low through oppression, affliction, and sorrow. {107:40} He poureth contempt upon princes, and causeth them to wander in the wilderness, where there is no way. {107:41} Yet setteth he the poor on high from affliction, and maketh him families like a flock. {107:42} The righteous shall see it, and rejoice: and all iniquity shall stop her mouth. {107:43} Whoso is wise, and will observe these things, even they shall understand the lovingkindness of the LORD.

{108:1} *O God, my heart is steadfast; I will sing and make music with all my soul.* {108:2} Awake, harp and lyre! I will awaken the dawn. {108:3} I will praise you, O LORD, among the nations; I will sing of you among the peoples. {108:4} For great is your love, higher than the heavens; your faithfulness reaches to the skies. {108:5} Be exalted, O God, above the heavens, and let your glory be over all the earth. {108:6} Save us and help us with your right hand, that those you love may be delivered. {108:7} God has spoken from his sanctuary: "In triumph I will parcel out Shechem and measure off the Valley of Sukkoth. {108:8} Gilead is mine, Manasseh is mine; Ephraim is my helmet, Judah is my scepter. {108:9} Moab is my washbasin, on Edom I toss my sandal; over Philistia I shout in triumph." {108:10} Who will bring me to the fortified city? Who will lead me to Edom? {108:11} *Is it not you, O God, you who have rejected us and no longer go out with our armies?* {108:12} Give us aid against the enemy, for the help of man is worthless. {108:13} With God we will gain the victory, and he will trample down our enemies.

{109:1} O God, do not remain silent, for I praise you. {109:2} Wicked and deceitful mouths speak against me; they accuse me with lying tongues. {109:3} They surround me with hateful words and fight against me without cause. {109:4} In return for my love, they accuse me, but I remain devoted to prayer. {109:5} They repay me evil for good and hatred for my love. {109:6} Appoint a wicked man over him; let an accuser stand at his right hand. {109:7} When he is tried, let him be found guilty, and may his prayers condemn him. {109:8} May his days be few; may another take his place of leadership. {109:9} May his children be fatherless and his wife a widow. {109:10} May his children wander as beggars, seeking food far from their ruined homes. {109:11} May the creditor seize all he has; may strangers plunder his wealth. {109:12} May no one extend kindness to him or take pity on his fatherless children. {109:13} May his descendants be cut off, their names blotted out from the next generation. {109:14} May the iniquity of his fathers be remembered before the LORD; may the sin of his mother never be erased. {109:15} May their sins always remain before the LORD, that he may blot out their name from the earth. {109:16} For he never thought of doing a kindness, but hounded to death the poor and the needy and the brokenhearted. {109:17} He loved to pronounce a curse— may it come back on him. He found no pleasure in blessing— may it be far from him. {109:18} He wore cursing like his coat— let it soak into his body like water and seep into his bones like oil. {109:19} May it be like a cloak wrapped around him, like a belt tied forever around him. {109:20} This is how the LORD will repay my accusers, those who speak evil against my soul. {109:21} But you, O GOD the Lord, deal kindly with me for the sake of your name; because your steadfast love is good, deliver me. {109:22} For I am poor and needy, and my heart is wounded within me. {109:23} I fade away like an evening shadow; I am shaken off like a locust. {109:24} My knees are weak from fasting, and my body has become lean and gaunt. {109:25} I am scorned by all who see me; they shake their heads in scorn. {109:26} Help me, O LORD my God; save me according to your steadfast love. {109:27} Let them know that this is your doing, that you, LORD, have done it. {109:28} Let them curse, but you bless; let them be put to shame, but let your servant rejoice. {109:29} **Let my accusers be clothed with dishonor; may they be wrapped in their own shame as in a cloak.** {109:30} With my mouth I will give great thanks to the LORD; I will praise him in the midst of the throng. {109:31} For he stands at the right hand of the needy one, to save him from those who condemn his soul.

{110:1} The LORD said to my Lord, "Sit at my right hand, until I make your enemies your footstool." {110:2} The LORD will extend your mighty scepter from Zion; rule in the midst of your enemies! {110:3} Your troops will be willing on your day of battle. Arrayed in holy splendor, your young men will come to you like dew from the morning's womb. {110:4} The LORD has sworn and will not change his mind: "You are a priest forever, in the order of Melchizedek." {110:5} The Lord is at your right hand; he will crush kings on the day of his wrath. {110:6} He will judge the nations, heaping up the dead and crushing the rulers of the whole earth. {110:7} He will drink from a brook along the way, and so he will lift his head high.

{111:1} Praise the LORD! I will praise the LORD with all my heart, in the company of the upright and in the congregation. {111:2} The LORD's deeds are great, eagerly sought by all who delight in them. {111:3} His work is majestic and glorious, and his righteousness endures forever. {111:4} He has caused his wonders to be remembered; the LORD is gracious and compassionate. {111:5} He provides food for those who fear him; he remembers his covenant forever. {111:6} He has shown his people the power of his works, giving them the inheritance of the nations. {111:7} The works of his hands are faithful and just; all his precepts are trustworthy. {111:8} They are established forever and ever, enacted in truth and uprightness. {111:9} He provided redemption for his people; he ordained his covenant forever—holy and awesome is his name. {111:10} The fear of the LORD is the beginning of wisdom; all who follow his precepts have good understanding. To him belongs eternal praise.

{112:1} Praise the LORD! Blessed is the man who fears the LORD, who delights greatly in his commandments. {112:2} His descendants will be mighty on earth; the generation of the upright will be blessed. {112:3} Wealth and riches will be in his house, and his righteousness will endure forever. {112:4} Light dawns in the darkness for the upright; he is gracious, compassionate, and righteous. {112:5} Good will come to those who are generous and lend freely, who conduct their affairs with justice. {112:6} Surely the righteous will never be shaken; they will be remembered forever. {112:7} They will have no fear of bad news; their hearts are steadfast, trusting in the LORD. {112:8} Their hearts are secure, they will have no fear; in the end they will look in triumph on their foes. {112:9} They have freely scattered their gifts to the poor, their righteousness endures forever; their horn will be lifted high in honor. {112:10} The wicked will see and be vexed, they will gnash their teeth and waste away; the longings of the wicked will come to nothing.

{113:1} Praise the LORD! Praise, O servants of the LORD, praise the name of the LORD. {113:2} Blessed be the name of the LORD from this time forth and forevermore. {113:3} From the rising of the sun to its setting, the LORD's name is to be praised. {113:4} The LORD is high above all nations, and his glory above the heavens. {113:5} Who is like the LORD our God, who dwells on high, {113:6} Who humbles himself to behold the things in heaven and on earth! {113:7} He raises up the poor out of the dust and lifts the needy out of the dunghill, {113:8} That he may set them with princes, even with the princes of his people. {113:9} He makes the barren woman keep house and be a joyful mother of children. Praise the LORD.

{114:1} When Israel went out of Egypt, the house of Jacob from a people of strange language; {114:2} Judah was his sanctuary, and Israel his dominion. {114:3} The sea saw it and fled; Jordan was driven back. {114:4} The mountains skipped like rams, and the little hills like lambs. {114:5} What ailed you, O sea, that you fled? O Jordan, that you were driven back? {114:6} O mountains, that you skipped like rams? O little hills, like lambs? {114:7} Tremble, O earth, at the presence of the Lord, at the presence of the God of Jacob, {114:8} Who turned the rock into a standing water, the flint into a fountain of waters.

{115:1} Not unto us, O LORD, not unto us, but unto thy name give glory, for thy mercy, and for thy truth's sake. {115:2} Why should the heathen say, Where is now their God? {115:3} But our God is in the heavens; he has done whatever he pleased. {115:4} Their idols are silver and gold, the work of men's hands. {115:5} They have mouths, but they do not speak; eyes they have, but they do not see; {115:6} They have ears, but they do not hear; noses they have, but they do not smell; {115:7} They have hands, but they do not handle; feet they have, but they do not walk; neither do they speak through their throat. {115:8} Those who make them are like them; so is everyone who trusts in them. {115:9} O Israel, trust in the LORD; he is their help and their shield. {115:10} O house of Aaron, trust in the LORD; he is their help and their shield. {115:11} You who fear the LORD, trust in the LORD; he is their help and their shield. {115:12} The LORD has been mindful of us; he will bless us; he will bless the house of Israel; he will bless the house of Aaron. {115:13} He will bless those who fear the LORD, both small and great. {115:14} May the LORD increase you more and more, you and your children. {115:15} You are blessed of the LORD who made heaven and earth. {115:16} The heavens, even the heavens, are the LORD's; but the earth he has given to the children of men. {115:17} The dead do not praise the LORD, neither any who go down into silence. {115:18} But we will bless the LORD from this time forth and forevermore. Praise the LORD.

{116:1} I love the LORD, because he has heard my voice and my supplications. {116:2} Because he has inclined his ear unto me, therefore will I call upon him as long as I live. {116:3} The sorrows of death compassed me, and the pains of hell got hold upon me: I found trouble and sorrow. {116:4} Then called I upon the name of the LORD; O LORD, I beseech thee, deliver my soul. {116:5} Gracious is the LORD, and righteous; yes, our God is merciful. {116:6} The LORD preserves the simple: I was brought low, and he helped me. {116:7} Return unto your rest, O my soul; for the LORD has dealt bountifully with you. {116:8} For you have delivered my soul from death, my eyes from tears, and my feet from falling. {116:9} I will walk before the LORD in the land of the living. {116:10} I believed, therefore have I spoken: I was greatly afflicted; {116:11} I said in my haste, All men are liars. {116:12} What shall I render unto the LORD for all his benefits toward me? {116:13} I will take the cup of salvation, and call upon the name of the LORD. {116:14} I will pay my vows unto the LORD now in the presence of all his people. {116:15} Precious in the sight of the LORD is the death of his saints. {116:16} O LORD, truly I am your servant; I am your servant, and the son of your handmaid: you have loosed my bonds. {116:17} I will offer to you the sacrifice of thanksgiving, and will call upon the name of the LORD. {116:18} I will pay my vows unto the LORD now in the presence of all his people, {116:19} In the courts of the LORD's house, in the midst of you, O Jerusalem. Praise the LORD.

{117:1} O praise the LORD, all you nations: praise him, all you people. {117:2} For his merciful kindness is great toward us: and the truth of the LORD endures forever. Praise the LORD.

{118:1} **O give thanks unto the LORD; for he is good: because his mercy endureth forever.** {118:2} Let Israel now say, that his mercy endureth forever. {118:3} Let the house of Aaron now say, that his mercy endureth forever. {118:4} Let them now that fear the LORD say, that his mercy endureth forever. {118:5} I called upon the LORD in distress: the LORD answered me, and set me in a large place. {118:6} The LORD is on my side; I will not fear: what can man do unto me? {118:7} The LORD taketh my part with them that help me: therefore shall I see my desire upon them that hate me. {118:8} It is better to trust in the LORD than to put confidence in man. {118:9} It is better to trust in the LORD than to put confidence in princes. {118:10} All nations compassed me about: but in the name of the LORD will I destroy them. {118:11} They compassed me about; yea, they compassed me about: but in the name of the LORD I will destroy them. {118:12} They compassed me about like bees; they are quenched as the fire of thorns: for in the name of the LORD I will destroy them. {118:13} Thou hast thrust sore at me that I might fall: but the LORD helped me. {118:14} The LORD is my strength and song, and is become my salvation. {118:15} The voice of rejoicing and salvation is in the tabernacles of the righteous: the right hand of the LORD doeth valiantly. {118:16} The right hand of the LORD is exalted: the right hand of the LORD doeth valiantly. {118:17} I shall not die, but live, and declare the works of the LORD. {118:18} The LORD hath chastened me sore: but he hath not given me over unto death. {118:19} Open to me the gates of righteousness: I will go into them, and I will praise the LORD: {118:20} This gate of the LORD, into which the righteous shall enter. {118:21} I will praise thee: for thou hast heard me, and art become my salvation. {118:22} The stone which the builders refused is become the head stone of the corner. {118:23} This is the LORD'S doing; it is marvellous in our eyes. {118:24} This is the day which the LORD hath made; we will rejoice and be glad in it. {118:25} Save now, I beseech thee, O LORD: O LORD, I beseech thee, send now prosperity. {118:26} Blessed be he that cometh in the name of the LORD: we have blessed you out of the house of the LORD. {118:27} God is the LORD, which hath shewed us light: bind the sacrifice with cords, even unto the horns of the altar. {118:28} Thou art my God, and I will praise thee: thou art my God, I will exalt thee. {118:29} O give thanks unto the LORD; for he is good: for his mercy endureth forever.

{119:1} Blessed are the undefiled in the way, who walk in the law of the LORD. {119:2} Blessed are they that keep his testimonies, and that seek him with the whole heart. {119:3} They also do no iniquity: they walk in his ways. {119:4} Thou hast commanded us to keep thy precepts diligently. {119:5} O that my ways were directed to keep thy statutes! {119:6} Then shall I not be ashamed, when I have respect unto all thy commandments. {119:7} I will praise thee with uprightness of heart, when I shall have learned thy righteous judgments. {119:8} I will keep thy statutes: O forsake me not utterly. BETH. {119:9} Wherewithal shall a young man cleanse his way? by taking heed thereto according to thy word. {119:10} With my whole heart have I sought thee: O let me not wander from thy commandments. {119:11} Thy word have I hid in mine heart, that I might not sin against thee. {119:12} Blessed art thou, O LORD: teach me thy statutes. {119:13} With my lips have I declared all the judgments of thy mouth. {119:14} I have rejoiced in the way of thy testimonies, as much as in all riches. {119:15} I will meditate in thy precepts, and have respect unto thy ways. {119:16} I will delight myself in thy statutes: I will not forget thy word. GIMEL. {119:17} Deal bountifully with thy servant, that I may live, and keep thy word. {119:18} Open thou mine eyes, that I may behold wondrous things out of thy law. {119:19} I am a stranger in the earth: hide not thy commandments from me. {119:20} My soul breaketh for the longing that it hath unto thy judgments at all times. {119:21} Thou hast rebuked the proud that are cursed, which do err from thy commandments. {119:22} Remove from me reproach and contempt; for I have kept thy testimonies. {119:23} Princes also did sit and speak against me: but thy servant did meditate in thy statutes. {119:24} Thy testimonies also are my delight and my counsellors. DALETH. {119:25} My soul cleaveth unto the dust: quicken thou me according to thy word. {119:26} I have declared my ways, and thou heardest me: teach me thy statutes. {119:27} Make me to understand the way of thy precepts: so shall I talk of thy wondrous works. {119:28} My soul melteth for heaviness: strengthen thou me according unto thy word. {119:29} Remove from me the way of lying: and grant me thy law graciously. {119:30} I have chosen the way of truth: thy judgments have I laid before me. {119:31} I have stuck unto thy testimonies: O LORD, put me not to shame. {119:32} I will run the way of thy commandments, when thou shalt enlarge my heart. HE. {119:33} Teach me, O LORD, the way of thy statutes; and I shall keep it unto the end. {119:34} Give me understanding, and I shall keep thy law; yea, I shall observe it with my whole heart. {119:35} Make me to go in the path of thy commandments; for therein do I delight. {119:36} Incline my heart unto thy testimonies, and not to covetousness. {119:37} Turn away mine eyes from beholding vanity; and quicken thou me in thy way. {119:38} Stablish thy word unto thy servant, who is devoted to thy fear. {119:39} Turn away my reproach which I fear: for thy judgments are good. {119:40} Behold, I have longed after thy precepts: quicken me in thy righteousness. VAU. {119:41} Let thy mercies come also unto me, O LORD, even thy salvation, according to thy word. {119:42} So shall I have wherewith to answer him that reproacheth me: for I trust in thy word. {119:43} And take not the word of truth utterly out of my mouth; for I have hoped in thy judgments. {119:44} So shall I keep thy law continually for ever and ever. {119:45} And I will walk at liberty: for I seek thy precepts. {119:46} I will speak of thy testimonies also before kings, and will not be ashamed. {119:47} And I will delight myself in thy commandments, which I have loved. {119:48} My hands also will I lift up unto thy commandments, which I have loved; and I will meditate in thy statutes. ZAIN. {119:49} Remember the word unto thy servant, upon which thou hast caused me to hope. {119:50} This is my comfort in my affliction: for thy word hath quickened me. {119:51} The proud have had me greatly in derision: yet have I not declined from thy law. {119:52} I remembered thy judgments of old, O LORD; and have comforted myself. {119:53} Horror hath taken hold upon me because of the wicked that forsake thy law. {119:54} Thy statutes have been my songs in the house of my pilgrimage. {119:55} I have remembered thy name, O LORD, in the night, and have kept thy law. {119:56} This I had, because I kept thy precepts. CHETH. {119:57} Thou art my portion, O LORD: I have said that I would keep thy words. {119:58} I intreated thy favour with my whole heart: be merciful unto me according to thy word. {119:59} I thought on my ways, and turned my feet unto thy testimonies. {119:60} I made haste, and delayed not to keep thy commandments. {119:61} The bands of the wicked have robbed me: but I have not forgotten thy law. {119:62} At midnight I will rise to give thanks unto thee because of thy righteous judgments. {119:63} I am a companion of all them that fear thee, and of them that keep thy precepts. {119:64} The earth, O LORD, is full of thy mercy: teach me thy statutes. TETH. {119:65} Thou hast dealt well with thy servant, O LORD, according unto thy word. {119:66} Teach me good judgment and knowledge: for I have believed thy commandments. {119:67} Before I was afflicted I went astray: but now have I kept thy word. {119:68} Thou art good, and doest good; teach me thy statutes. {119: 69} The proud have forged a lie against me: but I will keep thy precepts with my whole heart. {119:70} Their heart is as fat as grease; but I delight in thy law. {119:71} It is good for me that I have been afflicted; that I might learn thy statutes. {119:72} The law of thy mouth is better unto me than thousands of gold and silver. JOD. {119:73} Thy hands have made me and fashioned me: give me understanding, that I may learn thy commandments. {119:74} They that fear thee will be glad when they see me; because I have hoped in thy word. {119:75} I know, O LORD, that thy judgments are right, and that thou in faithfulness hast afflicted me. {119:76} Let, I pray thee, thy merciful kindness be for my comfort, according to thy word unto thy servant. {119:77} Let thy tender mercies come unto me, that I may live: for thy law is my delight. {119:78} Let the proud be ashamed; for they dealt perversely with me without a cause: but I will meditate in thy precepts. {119:79} Let those that fear thee turn unto me, and those that have known thy testimonies. {119:80} Let my heart be sound in thy statutes; that I be not ashamed. CAPH. {119:81} My soul fainteth for thy salvation: but I hope in thy word. {119:82} Mine eyes fail for thy word, saying, When wilt thou comfort me? {119:83} For I am become like a bottle in the smoke; yet do I not forget thy statutes. {119:84} How many are the days of thy servant? when wilt thou execute judgment on them that persecute me? {119:85} The proud have digged pits for me, which are not after thy law. {119:86} All thy commandments are faithful: they persecute me wrongfully; help thou me. {119:87} They had almost consumed me upon earth; but I forsook not thy precepts. {119:88} Quicken me after thy lovingkindness; so shall I keep the testimony of thy mouth. LAMED. {119:89} For ever, O LORD, thy word is settled in heaven. {119:90} Thy faithfulness is unto all generations: thou hast established the earth, and it abideth. {119:91} They continue this day according to thine ordinances: for all are thy servants. {119:92} Unless thy law had been my delights, I should then have perished in mine affliction. {119:93} I will never forget thy precepts: for with them thou hast quickened me. {119:94} I am thine, save me; for I have sought thy precepts. {119:95} The wicked have waited for me to destroy me: but I will consider thy testimonies. {119:96} I have seen an end of all perfection: but thy commandment is exceeding broad. MEM. {119:97} O how love I thy law! it is my meditation all the day. {119:98} Thou through thy commandments hast made me wiser than mine enemies: for they are ever with me. {119:99} I have more understanding than all my teachers: for thy testimonies are my meditation. {119:100} I understand more than the ancients, because I keep thy precepts. {119:101} I have refrained my feet from every evil way, that I might keep thy word. {119:102} I have not departed from thy judgments: for thou hast taught me. {119:103} How sweet are thy words unto my taste! yea, sweeter than honey to my mouth! {119:104} Through thy precepts I get understanding: therefore I hate every false way. NUN. {119:105} Thy word is a lamp unto my feet, and a light unto my path. {119:106} I have sworn, and I will perform it, that I will keep thy righteous judgments. {119:107} I am afflicted very much: quicken me, O LORD, according unto thy word. {119:108} Accept, I beseech thee, the freewill offerings of my mouth, O LORD, and teach me thy judgments. {119:109} My soul is continually in my hand: yet do I not forget thy law. {119:110} The wicked have laid a snare for me: yet I erred not from thy precepts. {119:111} Thy testimonies have I taken as an heritage for ever: for they are the rejoicing of my heart. {119:112} I have inclined mine heart to perform thy statutes alway, even unto the end. SAMECH. {119:113} I hate vain thoughts: but thy law do I love. {119:114} Thou art my hiding place and my shield: I hope in thy word. {119:115} Depart from me, ye evildoers: for I will keep the commandments of my God. {119:116} Uphold me according unto thy word, that I may live: and let me not be ashamed of my hope. {119:117} Hold thou me up, and I shall be safe: and I will have respect unto thy statutes continually. {119:118} Thou hast trodden down all them that err from thy statutes: for their deceit is falsehood. {119:119} Thou puttest away all the wicked of the earth like dross: therefore I love thy testimonies. {119:120} My flesh trembleth for fear of thee; and I am afraid of thy judgments. AIN. {119:121} I have done judgment and justice: leave me not to mine oppressors. {119:122} Be surety for thy servant for good: let not the proud oppress me. {119:123} Mine eyes fail for thy salvation, and for the word of thy righteousness. {119:124} Deal with thy servant according unto thy mercy, and teach me thy statutes. {119:125} I am thy servant; give me understanding, that I may know thy testimonies. {119:126} It is time for thee, LORD, to work: for they have made void thy law. {119:127} **Therefore I love thy commandments above gold; yea, above fine gold.** {119:128} Therefore I esteem all thy precepts concerning all things to be right; and I hate every false way. PE. {119:129} Thy testimonies are wonderful: therefore doth my soul keep them. {119:130} The entrance of thy words giveth light; it giveth understanding unto the simple. {119:131} I opened my mouth, and panted: for I longed for thy commandments. {119:132} Look thou upon me, and be merciful unto me, as thou usest to do unto those that love thy name. {119:133} Order my steps in thy word: and let not any iniquity have dominion over me. {119:134} Deliver me from the oppression of man: so will I keep thy precepts. {119:135} Make thy face to shine upon thy servant; and teach me thy statutes. {119:136} Rivers of waters run down mine eyes, because they keep not thy law. TZADDE. {119:137} Righteous art thou, O LORD, and upright are thy judgments. {119:138} Thy testimonies that thou hast commanded are righteous and very faithful. {119:139} My zeal hath consumed me, because mine enemies have forgotten thy words. {119:140} Thy word is very pure: therefore thy servant loveth it. {119:141} I am small and despised: yet do not I forget thy precepts. {119:142} **Thy righteousness is an everlasting righteousness, and thy law is the truth. {119:143} Trouble and anguish have taken hold on me: yet thy commandments are my delights.** {119:144} The righteousness of thy testimonies is everlasting: give me understanding, and I shall live. KOPH. {119:145} I cried with my whole heart; hear me, O LORD: I will keep thy statutes. {119:146} I cried unto thee; save me, and I shall keep thy testimonies. {119:147} I prevented the dawning of the morning, and cried: I hoped in thy word. {119:148} Mine eyes prevent the night watches, that I might meditate in thy word. {119:149} Hear my voice according unto thy lovingkindness: O LORD, quicken me according to thy judgment. {119:150} They draw nigh that follow after mischief: they are far from thy law. {119:151} Thou art near, O LORD; and all thy commandments are truth. {119:152} Concerning thy testimonies, I have known of old that thou hast founded them for ever. RESH. {119:153} Consider mine affliction, and deliver me: for I do not forget thy law. {119:154} Plead my cause, and deliver me: quicken me according to thy word. {119:155} Salvation is far from the wicked: for they seek not thy statutes. {119:156} Great are thy tender mercies, O LORD: quicken me according to thy judgments. {119:157} Many are my persecutors and mine enemies; yet do I not decline from thy testimonies. {119:158} I beheld the transgressors, and was grieved; because they kept not thy word. {119:159} Consider how I love thy precepts: quicken me, O LORD, according to thy lovingkindness. {119:160} Thy word is true from the beginning: and every one of thy righteous judgments endureth for ever. SCHIN. {119:161} Princes have persecuted me without a cause: but my heart standeth in awe of thy word. {119:162} I rejoice at thy word, as one that findeth great spoil. {119:163} I hate and abhor lying: but thy law do I love. {119:164} Seven times a day do I praise thee because of thy righteous judgments. {119:165} Great peace have they which love thy law: and nothing shall offend them. {119:166} LORD, I have hoped for thy salvation, and done thy commandments. {119:167} My soul hath kept thy testimonies; and I love them exceedingly. {119:168} I have kept thy precepts and thy testimonies: for all my ways are before thee. TAU. {119:169} Let my cry come near before thee, O LORD: give me understanding according to thy word. {119:170} **Let my supplication come before thee: deliver me according to thy word.** {119:171} My lips shall utter praise, when thou hast taught me thy statutes. {119:172} My tongue shall speak of thy word: for all thy commandments are righteousness. {119:173} **Let thine hand help me; for I have chosen thy precepts.** {119:174} I have longed for thy salvation, O LORD; and thy law is my delight. {119:175} Let my soul live, and it shall praise thee; and let thy judgments help me. {119:176} **I have gone astray like a lost sheep; seek thy servant; for I do not forget thy commandments.**

{120:1} When I was in trouble, I called out to the LORD, and he listened to me. {120:2} Please, LORD, save me from people who tell lies and deceive others. {120:3} What punishment do you think liars deserve? What should be done to those who speak with deceit? {120:4} They should be hit with sharp arrows and burning coals. {120:5} I feel like I'm stuck living among people who don't want peace, who would rather fight. {120:6} I want peace, but when I try to talk peacefully, they want to fight.

{121:1} *I look up to the hills, wondering where my help will come from.* {121:2} *My help comes from the LORD, who made the heavens and the earth.* {121:3} *He won't let you stumble; the one who watches over you won't fall asleep.* {121:4} Indeed, the one who watches over Israel never sleeps or slumbers. {121:5} The LORD himself watches over you; the LORD stands beside you as your protective shade. {121:6} The sun will not harm you by day, nor the moon at night. {121:7} The LORD keeps you from all harm and watches over your life. {121:8} The LORD keeps watch over you as you come and go, both now and forever.

{122:1} I was happy when they said to me, "Let's go to the LORD's house." {122:2} Now we are standing at the gates of Jerusalem, ready to enter. {122:3} Jerusalem is built like a city where everything is close together. {122:4} This is where the tribes come to worship the LORD and give thanks to his name. {122:5} Here are the seats of judgment, the thrones of the descendants of David. {122:6} Pray for the peace of Jerusalem: those who love you will prosper. {122:7} May there be peace within your walls and prosperity in your palaces. {122:8} For the sake of my family and friends, I will say, "May you have peace." {122:9} For the sake of the house of the LORD our God, I will seek your prosperity.

{123:1} I lift my eyes to you, who dwell in the heavens. {123:2} Just as servants watch their masters and maids watch their mistresses, so we look to the LORD our God until he shows us mercy. {123:3} Have mercy on us, LORD, have mercy, for we have had more than our fill of contempt. {123:4} We have had more than our fill of the scoffing of the proud and the contempt of the arrogant.

{124:1} If the LORD had not been on our side—let Israel say— {124:2} If the LORD had not been on our side when people attacked us, {124:3} they would have swallowed us alive because of their anger against us. {124:4} The waters would have engulfed us; a torrent would have overwhelmed us. {124:5} Yes, the raging waters of their fury would have swept over our very souls. {124:6} Praise the LORD, who did not let their teeth tear us apart! {124:7} We escaped like a bird from a hunter's trap. The trap is broken, and we are free! {124:8} Our help comes from the LORD, who made heaven and earth.

{125:1} Those who trust in the LORD are like Mount Zion, which cannot be shaken but endures forever. {125:2} As the mountains surround Jerusalem, so the LORD surrounds his people, both now and forevermore. {125:3} The scepter of the wicked will not remain over the land allotted to the righteous, for then the righteous might use their hands to do evil. {125:4} LORD, do good to those who are good, to those who are upright in heart. {125:5} But those who turn to crooked ways the LORD will banish with the evildoers. Peace be on Israel.

{126:1} When the LORD brought back the captives to Zion, we were like those who dream. {126:2} Then our mouth was filled with laughter, and our tongue with singing. Then they said among the nations, "The LORD has done great things for them." {126:3} The LORD has done great things for us, and we are glad. {126:4} Restore our fortunes, O LORD, like streams in the Negev. {126:5} Those who sow in tears shall reap with shouts of joy. {126:6} He who goes out weeping, bearing the seed for sowing, shall come home with shouts of joy, bringing his sheaves with him.

{127:1} Unless the LORD builds the house, those who build it labor in vain. Unless the LORD watches over the city, the watchman stays awake in vain. {127:2} It is in vain that you rise up early and go late to rest, eating the bread of anxious toil; for he gives to his beloved sleep. {127:3} Behold, children are a heritage from the LORD, the fruit of the womb a reward. {127:4} Like arrows in the hand of a warrior are the children of one's youth. {127:5} Blessed is the man who fills his quiver with them! He shall not be put to shame when he speaks with his enemies in the gate.

{128:1} Blessed is everyone who fears the LORD, who walks in his ways! {128:2} You shall eat the fruit of the labor of your hands; you shall be blessed, and it shall be well with you. {128:3} Your wife will be like a fruitful vine within your house; your children will be like olive shoots around your table. {128:4} Behold, thus shall the man be blessed who fears the LORD. {128:5} The LORD bless you from Zion! May you see the prosperity of Jerusalem all the days of your life! {128:6} May you see your children's children! Peace be upon Israel!

{129:1} "Many a time they have afflicted me from my youth," let Israel now say— {129:2} "Many a time they have afflicted me from my youth, yet they have not prevailed against me. {129:3} The plowers plowed upon my back; they made long their furrows." {129:4} The LORD is righteous; he has cut the cords of the wicked. {129:5} May all who hate Zion be put to shame and turned backward! {129:6} Let them be like the grass on the housetops, which withers before it grows up, {129:7} with which the reaper does not fill his hand nor the binder of sheaves his arms, {129:8} nor do those who pass by say, "The blessing of the LORD be upon you! We bless you in the name of the LORD!"

{130:1} Out of the depths I cry to you, O LORD! {130:2} O Lord, hear my voice! Let your ears be attentive to the voice of my pleas for mercy! {130:3} If you, O LORD, should mark iniquities, O Lord, who could stand? {130:4} But with you there is forgiveness, that you may be feared. {130:5} I wait for the LORD, my soul waits, and in his word I hope; {130:6} my soul waits for the Lord more than watchmen for the morning, more than watchmen for the morning. {130:7} O Israel, hope in the LORD! For with the LORD there is steadfast love, and with him is plentiful redemption. {130:8} And he will redeem Israel from all his iniquities.

{131:1} LORD, my heart is not proud, nor are my eyes haughty; neither do I concern myself with great matters or things too profound for me. {131:2} Surely I have calmed and quieted my soul, like a weaned child with its mother; like a weaned child is my soul within me. {131:3} O Israel, hope in the LORD from this time forth and forevermore.

{132:1} O LORD, remember David and all his afflictions— {132:2} how he swore to the LORD and vowed to the Mighty One of Jacob: {132:3} "I will not enter my house or go to my bed, {132:4} I will not give sleep to my eyes or slumber to my eyelids, {132:5} until I find a place for the LORD, a dwelling place for the Mighty One of Jacob." {132:6} Behold, we heard of it in Ephrathah; we found it in the fields of Jaar. {132:7} Let us go to his dwelling place; let us worship at his footstool! {132:8} Arise, O LORD, and go to your resting place, you and the ark of your might. {132:9} Let your priests be clothed with righteousness, and let your saints shout for joy. {132:10} For the sake of your servant David, do not turn away the face of your anointed one. {132:11} The LORD swore to David a sure oath from which he will not turn back: "One of the sons of your body I will set on your throne. {132:12} If your sons keep my covenant and my testimonies that I shall teach them, their sons also forever shall sit on your throne." {132:13} For the LORD has chosen Zion; he has desired it for his dwelling place: {132:14} "This is my resting place forever; here I will dwell, for I have desired it. {132:15} I will abundantly bless her provisions; I will satisfy her poor with bread. {132:16} Her priests I will clothe with salvation, and her saints will shout for joy. {132:17} There I will make a horn to sprout for David; I have prepared a lamp for my anointed. {132:18} His enemies I will clothe with shame, but on him his crown will shine."

{133:1} Behold, how good and pleasant it is when brothers dwell in unity! {133:2} It is like the precious oil on the head, running down on the beard, on the beard of Aaron, running down on the collar of his robes! {133:3} It is like the dew of Hermon, which falls on the mountains of Zion! For there the LORD has commanded the blessing, life forevermore.

{134:1} Bless the LORD, all you servants of the LORD, who stand by night in the house of the LORD! {134:2} Lift up your hands to the sanctuary and bless the LORD! {134:3} May the LORD bless you from Zion, he who made heaven and earth.

{135:1} Praise the LORD! Praise the name of the LORD; praise him, O servants of the LORD, {135:2} who stand in the house of the LORD, in the courts of the house of our God! {135:3} Praise the LORD, for the LORD is good; sing praises to his name, for it is pleasant! {135:4} For the LORD has chosen Jacob for himself, Israel as his own possession. {135:5} For I know that the LORD is great, and that our Lord is above all gods. {135:6} Whatever the LORD pleases, he does, in heaven and on earth, in the seas and all deeps. {135:7} He it is who makes the clouds rise at the end of the earth, who makes lightnings for the rain and brings forth the wind from his storehouses. {135:8} He it was who struck down the firstborn of Egypt, both of man and of beast; {135:9} who in your midst, O Egypt, sent signs and wonders against Pharaoh and all his servants; {135:10} who struck down many nations and killed mighty kings— {135:11} Sihon, king of the Amorites, and Og, king of Bashan, and all the kingdoms of Canaan— {135:12} and gave their land as a heritage, a heritage to his people Israel. {135:13} Your name, O LORD, endures forever, your renown,

O LORD, throughout all ages. {135:14} For the LORD will vindicate his people and have compassion on his servants. {135:15} The idols of the nations are silver and gold, the work of human hands. {135:16} They have mouths, but do not speak; they have eyes, but do not see; {135:17} they have ears, but do not hear, nor is there any breath in their mouths. {135:18} Those who make them become like them, so do all who trust in them. {135:19} O house of Israel, bless the LORD! O house of Aaron, bless the LORD! {135:20} O house of Levi, bless the LORD! You who fear the LORD, bless the LORD! {135:21} Blessed be the LORD from Zion, he who dwells in Jerusalem! Praise the LORD!

{136:1} Give thanks to the LORD, for he is good, for his mercy endures forever. {136:2} Give thanks to the God of gods, for his mercy endures forever. {136:3} Give thanks to the Lord of lords, for his mercy endures forever. {136:4} To him who alone does great wonders, for his mercy endures forever. {136:5} To him who by wisdom made the heavens, for his mercy endures forever. {136:6} To him who stretched out the earth above the waters, for his mercy endures forever. {136:7} To him who made the great lights, for his mercy endures forever. {136:8} The sun to rule by day, for his mercy endures forever. {136:9} The moon and stars to rule by night, for his mercy endures forever. {136:10} To him who struck Egypt in their firstborn, for his mercy endures forever. {136:11} And brought out Israel from among them, for his mercy endures forever. {136:12} With a strong hand and an outstretched arm, for his mercy endures forever. {136:13} To him who divided the Red Sea in two, for his mercy endures forever. {136:14} And made Israel pass through the midst of it, for his mercy endures forever. {136:15} But overthrew Pharaoh and his host in the Red Sea, for his mercy endures forever. {136:16} To him who led his people through the wilderness, for his mercy endures forever. {136:17} To him who struck down great kings, for his mercy endures forever. {136:18} And killed famous kings, for his mercy endures forever. {136:19} Sihon, king of the Amorites, for his mercy endures forever. {136:20} And Og, the king of Bashan, for his mercy endures forever. {136:21} And gave their land as a heritage, for his mercy endures forever. {136:22} Even a heritage to Israel his servant, for his mercy endures forever. {136:23} Who remembered us in our low estate, for his mercy endures forever. {136:24} And redeemed us from our enemies, for his mercy endures forever. {136:25} Who gives food to all flesh, for his mercy endures forever. {136:26} Give thanks to the God of heaven, for his mercy endures forever.

{137:1} By the rivers of Babylon, there we sat down, yes, we wept, when we remembered Zion. {137:2} We hung our harps upon the willows in the midst of it. {137:3} For there, those who carried us away captive required of us a song, and those who wasted us required of us mirth, saying, "Sing us one of the songs of Zion." {137:4} How shall we sing the LORD'S song in a strange land? {137:5} If I forget you, O Jerusalem, let my right hand forget her skill. {137:6} If I do not remember you, let my tongue cling to the roof of my mouth; if I do not exalt Jerusalem above my chief joy. {137:7} Remember, O LORD, the children of Edom in the day of Jerusalem, who said, "Raze it, raze it, even to the foundation thereof." {137:8} O daughter of Babylon, who is to be destroyed, happy shall he be, that rewards you as you have served us. {137:9} Happy shall he be, that takes and dashes your little ones against the stones.

{138:1} I will praise you with my whole heart; before the gods, I will sing praise to you. {138:2} I will worship toward your holy temple and praise your name for your lovingkindness and truth; for you have magnified your word above all your name. {138:3} In the day when I cried, you answered me and strengthened me with strength in my soul. {138:4} All the kings of the earth shall praise you, O LORD, when they hear the words of your mouth. {138:5} Yes, they shall sing in the ways of the LORD, for great is the glory of the LORD. {138:6} Though the LORD is high, yet he has respect unto the lowly, but the proud he knows afar off. {138:7} Though I walk in the midst of trouble, you will revive me; you shall stretch forth your hand against the wrath of my enemies, and your right hand shall save me. {138:8} The LORD will perfect that which concerns me; your mercy, O LORD, endures forever; forsake not the works of your own hands.

{139:1} O LORD, you have searched me and known me. {139:2} You know my downsitting and my uprising; you understand my thought afar off. {139:3} You encompass my path and my lying down, and are acquainted with all my ways. {139:4} For there is not a word on my tongue, but lo, O LORD, you know it altogether. {139:5} You have beset me behind and before and laid your hand upon me. {139:6} Such knowledge is too wonderful for me; it is high, I cannot attain unto it. {139:7} Where shall I go from your spirit? Or where shall I flee from your presence? {139:8} If I ascend up into heaven, you are there; if I make my bed in hell, behold, you are there. {139:9} If I take the wings of the morning and dwell in the uttermost parts of the sea, {139:10} Even there shall your hand lead me, and your right hand shall hold me. {139:11} If I say, Surely the darkness shall cover me; even the night shall be light about me. {139:12} Yes, the darkness hides not from you; but the night shines as the day: the darkness and the light are both alike to you. {139:13} For you have possessed my reins; you have covered me in my mother's womb. {139:14} *I will praise you, for I am fearfully and wonderfully made; marvelous are your works; and that my soul knows right well.* {139:15} My substance was not hidden from you when I was made in secret, and curiously wrought in the lowest parts of the earth. {139:16} Your eyes saw my substance, yet being unperfect; and in your book all my members were written, which in continuance were fashioned, when as yet there was none of them. {139:17} How precious also are your thoughts unto me, O God! How great is the sum of them! {139:18} If I should count them, they are more in number than the sand: when I awake, I am still with you. {139:19} Surely you will slay the wicked, O God; depart from me, therefore, you bloody men. {139:20} For they speak against you wickedly, and your enemies take your name in vain. {139:21} Do I not hate them, O LORD, that hate you? And am I not grieved with those that rise up against you? {139:22} I hate them with perfect hatred: I count them my enemies. {139:23} Search me, O God, and know my heart; try me, and know my thoughts. {139:24} And see if there be any wicked way in me, and lead me in the way everlasting.

{140:1} Deliver me, O LORD, from the evil man; preserve me from the violent man, {140:2} Who imagine mischiefs in their heart; continually they are gathered together for war. {140:3} They have sharpened their tongues like a serpent; adders' poison is under their lips. Selah. {140:4} Keep me, O LORD, from the hands of the wicked; preserve me from the violent man who have purposed to overthrow my goings. {140:5} The proud have laid a snare for me, and cords; they have spread a net by the wayside; they have set traps for me. Selah. {140:6} I said unto the LORD, "You are my God"; hear the voice of my supplications, O LORD. {140:7} O GOD the Lord, the strength of my salvation, you have covered my head in the day of battle. {140:8} Grant not, O LORD, the desires of the wicked; further not his wicked device, lest they exalt themselves. Selah. {140:9} As for the head of those who surround me, let the mischief of their own lips cover them. {140:10} Let burning coals fall upon them; let them be cast into the fire; into deep pits, that they rise not up again. {140:11} Let not an evil speaker be established in the earth; evil shall hunt the violent man to overthrow him. {140:12} I know that the LORD will maintain the cause of the afflicted and the right of the poor. {140:13} Surely the righteous shall give thanks unto your name; the upright shall dwell in your presence.

{141:1} LORD, I cry unto you; make haste unto me; give ear unto my voice when I cry unto you. {141:2} Let my prayer be set forth before you as incense; and the lifting up of my hands as the evening sacrifice. {141:3} Set a watch, O LORD, before my mouth; keep the door of my lips. {141:4} Incline not my heart to any evil thing, to practice wicked works with men that work iniquity; and let me not eat of their delicacies. {141:5} Let the righteous strike me; it shall be a kindness; and let him reprove me; it shall be an excellent oil, which shall not break my head; for yet my prayer also shall be in their calamities. {141:6} When their judges are overthrown in stony places, they shall hear my words, for they are sweet. {141:7} Our bones are scattered at the mouth of the grave, as when one cuts and cleaves wood upon the earth. {141:8} But my eyes are unto you, O GOD the Lord; in you is my trust; leave not my soul destitute. {141:9} Keep me from the snares which they have laid for me, and the traps of the workers of iniquity. {141:10} Let the wicked fall into their own nets, while I withal escape.

{142:1} I cried unto the LORD with my voice; with my voice unto the LORD did I make my supplication. {142:2} I poured out my complaint before him; I showed before him my trouble. {142:3} When my spirit was overwhelmed within me, then you knew my path. In the way wherein I walked they have secretly laid a snare for me. {142:4} I looked on my right hand, and beheld, but there was no man that would know me; refuge failed me; no man cared for my soul. {142:5} I cried unto you, O LORD; I said, "You are my refuge and my portion in the land of the living." {142:6} Attend unto my cry; for I am brought very low; deliver me from my persecutors; for they are stronger than I. {142:7} Bring my soul out of prison, that I may praise your name; the righteous shall compass me about; for you shall deal bountifully with me.

{143:1} Hear my prayer, O LORD; give ear to my supplications: in your faithfulness answer me, and in your righteousness. {143:2} And do not enter into judgment with your servant; for in your sight shall no man living be justified. {143:3} For the enemy has persecuted my soul; he has struck down my life to the ground; he has made me dwell in darkness, as those who have been long dead. {143:4} Therefore is my spirit overwhelmed within me; my heart within me is desolate. {143:5} I remember the days of old; I meditate on all your works; I muse on the work of your hands. {143:6} I stretch forth my hands unto you; my soul thirsts after you, as a thirsty land. Selah. {143:7} Hear me speedily, O LORD; my spirit fails; hide not your face from me, lest I be like unto them that go down into the pit. {143:8} Cause me to hear your lovingkindness in the morning; for in you do I trust: cause me to know the way wherein I should walk; for I lift up my soul unto you. {143:9} Deliver me, O LORD, from my enemies: I flee unto you to hide me. {143:10} Teach me to do your will; for you are my God: your spirit is good; lead me into the land of uprightness. {143:11} Quicken me, O LORD, for your name's sake: for your righteousness' sake bring my soul out of trouble. {143:12} And of your mercy cut off my enemies, and destroy all them that afflict my soul: for I am your servant.

{144:1} Blessed be the LORD my strength, who teaches my hands to war, and my fingers to fight: {144:2} My goodness, and my fortress; my high tower, and my deliverer; my shield, and he in whom I trust; who subdues my people under me. {144:3} LORD, what is man, that you take knowledge of him! or the son of man, that you make account of him! {144:4} Man is like to vanity: his days are as a shadow that passes away. {144:5} Bow your heavens, O LORD, and come down: touch the mountains, and they shall smoke. {144:6} Cast forth lightning, and scatter them: shoot out your arrows, and destroy them. {144:7} Send your hand from above; rid me, and deliver me out of great waters, from the hand of strange children; {144:8} Whose mouth speaks vanity, and their right hand is a right hand of falsehood. {144:9} I will sing a new song unto you, O God: upon a psaltery and an instrument of ten strings will I sing praises unto you. {144:10} It is he that gives salvation unto kings: who delivers David his servant from the hurtful sword. {144:11} Rid me, and deliver me from the hand of strange children, whose mouth speaks vanity, and their right hand is a right hand of falsehood: {144:12} That our sons may be as plants grown up in their youth; that our daughters may be as corner stones, polished after the similitude of a palace: {144:13} That our garners may be full, affording all manner of store: that our sheep may bring forth thousands and ten thousands in our streets: {144:14} That our oxen may be strong to labour; that there be no breaking in, nor going out; that there be no complaining in our streets. {144:15} Happy is that people, that is in such a case: yea, happy is that people, whose God is the LORD.

{145:1} I will extol you, my God, O king; and I will bless your name for ever and ever. {145:2} Every day will I bless you; and I will praise your name for ever and ever. {145:3} Great is the LORD, and greatly to be praised; and his greatness is unsearchable. {145:4} One generation shall praise your works to another, and shall declare your mighty acts. {145:5} I will speak of the glorious honor of your majesty, and of your wondrous works. {145:6} And people shall speak of the might of your terrible acts: and I will declare your greatness. {145:7} They shall abundantly utter the memory of your great goodness, and shall sing of your righteousness. {145:8} The LORD is gracious, and full of compassion; slow to anger, and of great mercy. {145:9} The LORD is good to all: and his tender mercies are over all his works. {145:10} All your works shall praise you, O LORD; and your saints shall bless you. {145:11} They shall speak of the glory of your kingdom, and talk of your power; {145:12} To make known to the sons of men his mighty acts, and the glorious majesty of his kingdom. {145:13} Your kingdom is an everlasting kingdom, and your dominion endures throughout all generations. {145:14} The LORD upholds all that fall, and raises up all those that be bowed down. {145:15} The eyes of all wait upon you; and you give them their meat in due season. {145:16} You open your hand, and satisfy the desire of every living thing. {145:17} The LORD is righteous in all his ways, and holy in all his works. {145:18} The LORD is near to all them that call upon him, to all that call upon him in truth. {145:19} He will fulfill the desire of them that fear him: he also will hear their cry, and will save them. {145:20} The LORD preserves all them that love him: but all the wicked will he destroy. {145:21} My mouth shall speak the praise of the LORD: and let all flesh bless his holy name for ever and ever.

{146:1} Praise ye the LORD. Praise the LORD, O my soul. {146:2} While I live will I praise the LORD: I will sing praises unto my God while I have any being. {146:3} Put not your trust in princes, nor in the son of man, in whom there is no help. {146:4} His breath goeth forth, he returneth to his earth; in that very day his thoughts perish. {146:5} Happy is he that hath the God of Jacob for his help, whose hope is in the LORD his God: {146:6} Which made heaven, and earth, the sea, and all that therein is: which keepeth truth for ever: {146:7} Which executeth judgment for the oppressed: which giveth food to the hungry. The LORD looseth the prisoners: {146:8} The LORD openeth the eyes of the blind: the LORD raiseth them that are bowed down: the LORD loveth the righteous: {146:9} The LORD preserveth the strangers; he relieveth the fatherless and widow: but the way of the wicked he turneth upside down. {146:10} The LORD shall reign for ever, even thy God, O Zion, unto all generations. Praise ye the LORD.

{147:1} Praise ye the LORD: for it is good to sing praises unto our God; for it is pleasant; and praise is comely. {147:2} The LORD doth build up Jerusalem: he gathereth together the outcasts of Israel. {147:3} He healeth the broken in heart, and bindeth up their wounds. {147:4} He telleth the number of the stars; he calleth them all by their names. {147:5} Great is our Lord, and of great power: his understanding is infinite. {147:6} The LORD lifteth up the meek: he casteth the wicked down to the ground. {147:7} Sing unto the LORD with thanksgiving; sing praise upon the harp unto our God: {147:8} Who covereth the heaven with clouds, who prepareth rain for the earth, who maketh grass to grow upon the mountains. {147:9} He giveth to the beast his food, and to the young ravens which cry. {147:10} He delighteth not in the strength of the horse: he taketh not pleasure in the legs of a man. {147:11} The LORD taketh pleasure in them that fear him, in those that hope in his mercy. {147:12} Praise the LORD, O Jerusalem; praise thy God, O Zion. {147:13} For he hath strengthened the bars of thy gates; he hath blessed thy children within thee. {147:14} He maketh peace in thy borders, and filleth thee with the finest of the wheat. {147:15} He sendeth forth his commandment upon earth: his word runneth very swiftly. {147:16} He giveth snow like wool: he scattereth the hoar frost like ashes. {147:17} **He casteth forth his ice like morsels: who can stand before his cold?** {147:18} He sendeth out his word, and melteth them: he causeth his wind to blow, and the waters flow. {147:19} He sheweth his word unto Jacob, his statutes and his judgments unto Israel. {147:20} **He hath not dealt so with any nation: and as for his judgments, they have not known them. Praise ye the LORD.**

{148:1} Praise ye the LORD. Praise ye the LORD from the heavens: praise him in the heights. {148:2} Praise ye him, all his angels: praise ye him, all his hosts. {148:3} Praise ye him, sun and moon: praise him, all ye stars of light. {148:4} Praise him, ye heavens of heavens, and ye waters that be above the heavens. {148:5} Let them praise the name of the LORD: for he commanded, and they were created. {148:6} He hath also stablished them for ever and ever: he hath made a decree which shall not pass. {148:7} Praise the LORD from the earth, ye dragons, and all deeps: {148:8} Fire, and hail; snow, and vapours; stormy wind fulfilling his word: {148:9} Mountains, and all hills; fruitful trees, and all cedars: {148:10} Beasts, and all cattle; creeping things, and flying fowl: {148:11} **Kings of the earth, and all people; princes, and all judges of the earth:** {148:12} Both young men, and maidens; old men, and children: {148:13} Let them praise the name of the LORD: for his name alone is excellent; his glory is above the earth and heaven. {148:14} He also exalteth the horn of his people, the praise of all his saints; even of the children of Israel, a people near unto him. Praise ye the LORD.

{149:1} Praise ye the LORD. Sing unto the LORD a new song, and his praise in the congregation of saints. {149:2} Let Israel rejoice in him that made him: let the children of Zion be joyful in their King. {149:3} Let them praise his name in the dance: let them sing praises unto him with the timbrel and harp. {149:4} For the LORD taketh pleasure in his people: he will beautify the meek with salvation. {149:5} Let the saints be joyful in glory: let them sing aloud upon their beds. {149:6} Let the high praises of God be in their mouth, and a twoedged sword in their hand; {149:7} To execute vengeance upon the heathen, and punishments upon the people; {149:8} To bind their kings with chains, and their nobles with fetters of iron; {149:9} To execute upon them the judgment written: this honour have all his saints. Praise ye the LORD.

{150:1} Praise ye the LORD. Praise God in his sanctuary: praise him in the firmament of his power. {150:2} Praise him for his mighty acts: praise him according to his excellent greatness. {150:3} Praise him with the sound of the trumpet: praise him with the psaltery and harp. {150:4} Praise him with the timbrel and dance: praise him with stringed instruments and organs. {150:5} Praise him upon the loud cymbals: praise him upon the high sounding cymbals. {150:6} Let every thing that hath breath praise the LORD. Praise ye the LORD.

Proverbs

{1:1} The proverbs of Solomon the son of David, king of Israel; {1:2} To know wisdom and instruction; to perceive the words of understanding; {1:3} To receive the instruction of wisdom, justice, and judgment, and equity; {1:4} To give subtilty to the simple, to the young man knowledge and discretion. {1:5} A wise man will hear, and will increase learning; and a man of understanding shall attain unto wise counsels: {1:6} To understand a proverb, and the interpretation; the words of the wise, and their dark sayings. {1:7} **The fear of the LORD is the beginning of knowledge: but fools despise wisdom and instruction.** {1:8} My son, hear the instruction of thy father, and forsake not the law of thy mother: {1:9} For they shall be an ornament of grace unto thy head, and chains about thy neck. {1:10} My son, if sinners entice thee, consent thou not. {1:11} If they say, Come with us, let us lay wait for blood, let us lurk privily for the innocent without cause: {1:12} Let us swallow them up alive as the grave; and whole, as those that go down into the pit: {1:13} We shall find all precious substance, we shall fill our houses with spoil: {1:14} Cast in thy lot among us; let us all have one purse: {1:15} My son, walk not thou in the way with them; refrain thy foot from their path: {1:16} For their feet run to evil, and make haste to shed blood. {1:17} Surely in vain the net is spread in the sight of any bird. {1:18} And they lay wait for their own blood; they lurk privily for their own lives. {1:19} So are the ways of every one that is greedy of gain; which taketh away the life of the owners thereof. {1:20} Wisdom crieth without; she uttereth her voice in the streets: {1:21} She crieth in the chief place of concourse, in the openings of the gates: in the city she uttereth her words, saying, {1:22} How long, ye simple ones, will ye love simplicity? and the scorners delight in their scorning, and fools hate knowledge? {1:23} Turn you at my reproof: behold, I will pour out my spirit unto you, I will make known my words unto you. {1:24} Because I have called, and ye refused; I have stretched out my hand, and no man regarded; {1:25} But ye have set at nought all my counsel, and would none of my reproof: {1:26} I also will laugh at your calamity; I will mock when your fear cometh; {1:27} When your fear cometh as desolation, and your destruction cometh as a whirlwind; when distress and anguish cometh upon you. {1:28} Then shall they call upon me, but I will not answer; they shall seek me early, but they shall not find me: {1:29} For that they hated knowledge, and did not choose the fear of the LORD: {1:30} They would none of my counsel: they despised all my reproof. {1:31} Therefore shall they eat of the fruit of their own way, and be filled with their own devices. {1:32} For the turning away of the simple shall slay them, and the prosperity of fools shall destroy them. {1:33} But whoso hearkeneth unto me shall dwell safely, and shall be quiet from fear of evil.

{2:1} My son, if thou wilt receive my words, and hide my commandments with thee; {2:2} So that thou incline thine ear unto wisdom, and apply thine heart to understanding; {2:3} Yea, if thou criest after knowledge, and liftest up thy voice for understanding; {2:4} If thou seekest her as silver, and searchest for her as for hid treasures; {2:5} Then shalt thou understand the fear of the LORD, and find the knowledge of God. {2:6} For the LORD giveth wisdom: out of his mouth cometh knowledge and understanding. {2:7} He layeth up sound wisdom for the righteous: he is a buckler to them that walk uprightly. {2:8} He keepeth the paths of judgment, and preserveth the way of his saints. {2:9} Then shalt thou understand righteousness, and judgment, and equity; yea, every good path. {2:10} When wisdom entereth into thine heart, and knowledge is pleasant unto thy soul; {2:11} Discretion shall preserve thee, understanding shall keep thee; {2:12} To deliver thee from the way of the evil man, from the man that speaketh froward things; {2:13} Who leave the paths of uprightness, to walk in the ways of darkness; {2:14} Who rejoice to do evil, and delight in the frowardness of the wicked; {2:15} Whose ways are crooked, and they froward in their paths: {2:16} To deliver thee from the strange woman, even from the stranger which flattereth with her words; {2:17} Which forsaketh the guide of her youth, and forgetteth the covenant of her God. {2:18} For her house inclineth unto death, and her paths unto the dead. {2:19} None that go unto her return again, neither take they hold of the paths of life. {2:20} That thou mayest walk in the way of good men, and keep the paths of the righteous. {2:21} For the upright shall dwell in the land, and the perfect shall remain in it. {2:22} But the wicked shall be cut off from the earth, and the transgressors shall be rooted out of it.

{3:1} My son, forget not my law; but let thine heart keep my commandments: {3:2} For length of days, and long life, and peace, shall they add to thee. {3:3} Let not mercy and truth forsake thee: bind them about thy neck; write them upon the table of thine heart: {3:4} So shalt thou find favour and good understanding in the sight of God and man. {3:5} **Trust in the LORD with all thine heart; and lean not unto thine own understanding.** {3:6} In all thy ways acknowledge him, and he shall direct thy paths. {3:7} Be not wise in thine own eyes: fear the LORD, and depart from evil. {3:8} It shall be health to thy navel, and marrow to thy bones. {3:9} Honour the LORD with thy substance, and with the firstfruits of all thine increase: {3:10} So shall thy barns be filled with plenty, and thy presses shall burst out with new wine. {3:11} My son, despise not the chastening of the LORD; neither be weary of his correction: {3:12} For whom the LORD loveth he correcteth; even as a father the son in whom he delighteth. {3:13} Happy is the man that findeth wisdom, and the man that getteth understanding. {3:14} For the merchandise of it is better than the merchandise of silver, and the gain thereof than fine gold. {3:15} She is more precious than rubies: and all the things thou canst desire are not to be compared unto her. {3:16} Length of days is in her right hand; and in her left hand riches and honour. {3:17} Her ways are ways of pleasantness, and all her paths are peace. {3:18} She is a tree of life to them that lay hold upon her: and happy is every one that retaineth her. {3:19} The LORD by wisdom hath founded the earth; by understanding hath he established the heavens. {3:20} By his knowledge the depths are broken up, and the clouds drop down the dew. {3:21} My son, let not them depart from thine eyes: keep sound wisdom and discretion: {3:22} So shall they be life unto thy soul, and grace to thy neck. {3:23} Then shalt thou walk in thy way safely, and thy foot shall not stumble. {3:24} When thou liest down, thou shalt not be afraid: yea, thou shalt lie down, and thy sleep shall be sweet. {3:25} Be not afraid of sudden fear, neither of the desolation of the wicked, when it cometh. {3:26} For the LORD shall be thy confidence, and shall keep thy foot from being taken. {3:27} Withhold not good from them to whom it is due, when it is in the power of thine hand to do it. {3:28} Say not unto thy neighbour, Go, and come again, and to morrow I will give; when thou hast it by thee. {3:29} Devise not evil against thy neighbour, seeing he dwelleth securely by thee. {3:30} Strive not with a man without cause, if he have done thee no harm. {3:31} Envy thou not the oppressor, and choose none of his ways. {3:32} For the froward is abomination to the LORD: but his secret is with the righteous. {3:33} The curse of the LORD is in the house of the wicked: but he blesseth the habitation of the just. {3:34} Surely he scorneth the scorners: but he giveth grace unto the lowly. {3:35} The wise shall inherit glory: but shame shall be the promotion of fools.

{4:1} Hear, ye children, the instruction of a father, and attend to know understanding. {4:2} For I give you good doctrine, forsake ye not my law. {4:3} For I was my father's son, tender and only beloved in the sight of my mother. {4:4} He taught me also, and said unto me, Let thine heart retain my words: keep my commandments, and live. {4:5} Get wisdom, get understanding: forget it not; neither decline from the words of my mouth. {4:6} Forsake her not, and she shall preserve thee: love her, and she shall keep thee. {4:7} Wisdom is the principal thing; therefore get wisdom: and with all thy getting get understanding. {4:8} Exalt her, and she shall promote thee: she shall bring thee to honour, when thou dost embrace her. {4:9} She shall give to thine head an ornament of grace: a crown of glory shall she deliver to thee. {4:10} Hear, O my son, and receive my sayings; and the years of thy life shall be many. {4:11} I have taught thee in the way of wisdom; I have led thee in right paths. {4:12} When thou goest, thy steps shall not be straitened; and when thou runnest, thou shalt not stumble. {4:13} Take fast hold of instruction; let her not go: keep her; for she is thy life. {4:14} Enter not into the path of the wicked, and go not in the way of evil men. {4:15} Avoid it, pass not by it, turn from it, and pass away. {4:16} For they sleep not, except they have done mischief; and their sleep is taken away, unless they cause some to fall. {4:17} For they eat the bread of wickedness, and drink the wine of violence. {4:18} But the path of the just is as the shining light, that shineth more and more unto the perfect day. {4:19} The way of the wicked is as darkness: they know not at what they stumble. {4:20} My son, attend to my words; incline thine ear unto my sayings. {4:21} Let them not depart from thine eyes; keep them in the midst of thine heart. {4:22} For they are life unto those that find them, and health to all their flesh. {4:23} Keep thy heart with all diligence; for out of it are the issues of life. {4:24} Put away from thee a froward mouth, and perverse lips put far from thee. {4:25} Let thine eyes look right on, and let thine eyelids look straight before thee. {4:26} Ponder the path of thy feet, and let all thy ways be established. {4:27} Turn not to the right hand nor to the left: remove thy foot from evil.

{5:1} My son, attend unto my wisdom, and bow thine ear to my understanding: {5:2} That thou mayest regard discretion, and that thy lips may keep knowledge. {5:3} For the lips of a strange woman drop as an honeycomb, and her mouth is smoother than oil: {5:4} But her end is bitter as wormwood, sharp as a twoedged sword. {5:5} Her feet go down to death; her steps take hold on hell. {5:6} Lest thou shouldest ponder the path of life, her ways are moveable, that thou canst not know them. {5:7} Hear me now therefore, O ye children, and depart not from the words of my mouth. {5:8} Remove thy way far from her, and come not nigh the door of her house: {5:9} Lest thou give thine honour unto others, and thy years unto the cruel: {5:10} Lest strangers be filled with thy wealth; and thy labours be in the house of a stranger; {5:11} And thou mourn at the last, when thy flesh and thy body are consumed, {5:12} And say, How have I hated instruction, and my heart despised reproof; {5:13} And have not obeyed the voice of my teachers, nor inclined mine ear to them that instructed me! {5:14} I was almost in all evil in the midst of the congregation and assembly. {5:15} Drink waters out of thine own cistern, and running waters out of thine own well. {5:16} Let thy fountains be dispersed abroad, and rivers of waters in the streets. {5:17} Let them be only thine own, and not strangers' with thee. {5:18} Let thy fountain be blessed: and rejoice with the wife of thy youth. {5:19} Let her be as the loving hind and pleasant roe; let her breasts satisfy thee at all times; and be thou ravished always with her love. {5:20} And why wilt thou, my son, be ravished with a strange woman, and embrace the bosom of a stranger? {5:21} For the ways of man are before the eyes of the LORD, and he pondereth all his goings. {5:22} His own iniquities shall take the wicked himself, and he shall be holden with the cords of his sins. {5:23} He shall die without instruction; and in the greatness of his folly he shall go astray.

{6:1} My son, if thou be surety for thy friend, if thou hast stricken thy hand with a stranger, {6:2} Thou art snared with the words of thy mouth, thou art taken with the words of thy mouth. {6:3} Do this now, my son, deliver thyself, when thou art come into the hand of thy friend; go, humble thyself, and make sure thy friend. {6:4} Give not sleep to thine eyes, nor slumber to thine eyelids. {6:5} Deliver thyself as a roe from the hand of the hunter, and as a bird from the hand of the fowler. {6:6} Go to the ant, thou sluggard; consider her ways, and be wise: {6:7} Which having no guide, overseer, or ruler, {6:8} Provideth her meat in the summer, and gathereth her food in the harvest. {6:9} How long wilt thou sleep, O sluggard? when wilt thou arise out of thy sleep? {6:10} Yet a little sleep, a little slumber, a little folding of the hands to sleep: {6:11} So shall thy poverty come as one that travelleth, and thy want as an armed man. {6:12} A naughty person, a wicked man, walketh with a froward mouth. {6:13} He winketh with his eyes, he speaketh with his feet, he teacheth with his fingers; {6:14} Frowardness is in his heart, he deviseth mischief continually; he soweth discord. {6:15} Therefore shall his calamity come suddenly; suddenly shall he be broken without remedy. {6:16} These six things doth the LORD hate: yea, seven are an abomination unto him: {6:17} A proud look, a lying tongue, and hands that shed innocent blood, {6:18} An heart that deviseth wicked imaginations, feet that be swift in running to mischief, {6:19} A false witness that speaketh lies, and he that soweth discord among brethren. {6:20} My son, keep thy father's commandment, and forsake not the law of thy mother: {6:21} Bind them continually upon thine heart, and tie them about thy neck. {6:22} When thou goest, it shall lead thee; when thou sleepest, it shall keep thee; and when thou awakest, it shall talk with thee. {6:23} For the commandment is a lamp; and the law is light; and reproofs of instruction are the way of life: {6:24} To keep thee from the evil woman, from the flattery of the tongue of a strange woman. {6:25} Lust not after her beauty in thine heart; neither let her take thee with her eyelids. {6:26} For by means of a whorish woman a man is brought to a piece of bread: and the adulteress will hunt for the precious life. {6:27} Can a man take fire in his bosom, and his clothes not be burned? {6:28} Can one go upon hot coals, and his feet not be burned? {6:29} So he that goeth in to his neighbour's wife; whosoever toucheth her shall not be innocent. {6:30} Men do not despise a thief, if he steal to satisfy his soul when he is hungry; {6:31} But if he be found, he shall restore sevenfold; he shall give all the substance of his house. {6:32} Whoso committeth adultery with a woman lacketh understanding: he that doeth it destroyeth his own soul. {6:33} A wound and dishonour shall he get; and his reproach shall not be wiped away. {6:34} For jealousy is the rage of a man: therefore he will not spare in the day of vengeance. {6:35} He will not regard any ransom; neither will he rest content, though thou givest many gifts.

{7:1} My son, keep my words, and lay up my commandments with thee. {7:2} Keep my commandments, and live; and my law as the apple of thine eye. {7:3} Bind them upon thy fingers, write them upon the table of thine heart. {7:4} Say unto wisdom, Thou art my sister; and call understanding thy kinswoman: {7:5} That they may keep thee from the strange woman, from the stranger which flattereth with her words. {7:6} For at the window of my house I looked through my casement, {7:7} And beheld among the simple ones, I discerned among the youths, a young man void of understanding, {7:8} Passing through the street near her corner; and he went the way to her house, {7:9} In the twilight, in the evening, in the black and dark night: {7:10} And, behold, there met him a woman with the attire of an harlot, and subtil of heart. {7:11} She is loud and stubborn; her feet abide not in her house: {7:12} Now is she without, now in the streets, and lieth in wait at every corner. {7:13} So she caught him, and kissed him, and with an impudent face said unto him, {7:14} I have peace offerings with me; this day have I payed my vows. {7:15} Therefore came I forth to meet thee, diligently to seek thy face, and I have found thee. {7:16} I have decked my bed with coverings of tapestry, with carved works, with fine linen of Egypt. {7:17} I have perfumed my bed with myrrh, aloes, and cinnamon. {7:18} Come, let us take our fill of love until the morning: let us solace ourselves with loves. {7:19} For the goodman is not at home, he is gone a long journey: {7:20} He hath taken a bag of money with him, and will come home at the day appointed. {7:21} With her much fair speech she caused him to yield, with the flattering of her lips she forced him. {7:22} He goeth after her straightway, as an ox goeth to the slaughter, or as a fool to the correction of the stocks; {7:23} Till a dart strike through his liver; as a bird hasteth to the snare, and knoweth not that it is for his life. {7:24} Hearken unto me now therefore, O ye children, and attend to the words of my mouth. {7:25} Let not thine heart decline to her ways, go not astray in her paths. {7:26} For she hath cast down many wounded: yea, many strong men have been slain by her. {7:27} Her house is the way to hell, going down to the chambers of death.

{8:1} Doth not wisdom cry? and understanding put forth her voice? {8:2} She standeth in the top of high places, by the way in the places of the paths. {8:3} She crieth at the gates, at the entry of the city, at the coming in at the doors. {8:4} Unto you, O men, I call; and my voice is to the sons of man. {8:5} O ye simple, understand wisdom: and, ye fools, be ye of an understanding heart. {8:6} Hear; for I will speak of excellent things; and the opening of my lips shall be right things. {8:7} For my mouth shall speak truth; and wickedness is an abomination to my lips. {8:8} All the words of my mouth are in righteousness; there is nothing froward or perverse in them. {8:9} They are all plain to him that understandeth, and right to them that find knowledge. {8:10} Receive my instruction, and not silver; and knowledge rather than choice gold. {8:11} For wisdom is better than rubies; and all the things that may be desired are not to be compared to it. {8:12} I wisdom dwell with prudence, and find out knowledge of witty inventions. {8:13} The fear of the LORD is to hate evil: pride, and arrogancy, and the evil way, and the froward mouth, do I hate. {8:14} Counsel is mine, and sound wisdom: I am understanding; I have strength. {8:15} By me kings reign, and princes decree justice. {8:16} By me princes rule, and nobles, even all the judges of the earth. {8:17} I love them that love me; and those that seek me early shall find me. {8:18} Riches and honour are with me; yea, durable riches and righteousness. {8:19} My fruit is better than gold, yea, than fine gold; and my revenue than choice silver. {8:20} I lead in the way of righteousness, in the midst of the paths of judgment: {8:21} That I may cause those that love me to inherit substance; and I will fill their treasures. {8:22} The LORD possessed me in the beginning of his way, before his works of old. {8:23} I was set up from everlasting, from the beginning, or ever the earth was. {8:24} When there were no depths, I was brought forth; when there were no fountains abounding with water. {8:25} Before the mountains were settled, before the hills was I brought forth: {8:26} While as yet he had not made the earth, nor the fields, nor the highest part of the dust of the world. {8:27} When he prepared the heavens, I was there: when he set a compass upon the face of the depth: {8:28} When he established the clouds above: when he strengthened the fountains of the deep: {8:29} When he gave to the sea his decree, that the waters should not pass his commandment: when he appointed the foundations of the earth: {8:30} Then I was by him, as one brought up with him: and I was daily his delight, rejoicing always before him; {8:31} Rejoicing in the habitable part of his earth; and my delights were with the sons of men. {8:32} Now therefore hearken unto me, O ye children: for blessed are they that keep my ways. {8:33} Hear instruction, and be wise, and refuse it not. {8:34} Blessed is the man that heareth me, watching daily at my gates, waiting at the posts of my doors. {8:35} For whoso findeth me findeth life, and shall obtain favour of the LORD. {8:36} But he that sinneth against me wrongeth his own soul: all they that hate me love death.

{9:1} Wisdom hath builded her house, she hath hewn out her seven pillars: {9:2} She hath killed her beasts; she hath mingled her wine; she hath also furnished her table. {9:3} She hath sent forth her maidens: she crieth upon the highest places of the city, {9:4} Whoso is simple, let him turn in hither: as for him that wanteth understanding, she saith to him, {9:5} Come, eat of my bread, and drink of the wine which I have mingled. {9:6} Forsake the foolish, and live; and go in the way of understanding. {9:7} He that reproveth a scorner getteth to himself shame: and he that rebuketh a wicked man getteth himself a blot. {9:8} Reprove not a scorner, lest he hate thee: rebuke a wise man, and he will love thee. {9:9} Give instruction to a wise man, and he will be yet wiser: teach a just man, and he will increase in learning. {9:10} The fear of the LORD is the beginning of wisdom: and the knowledge of the holy is understanding. {9:11} For by me thy days shall be multiplied, and the years of thy life shall be increased. {9:12} If thou be wise, thou shalt be wise for thyself: but if thou scornest, thou alone shalt bear it. {9:13} A foolish woman is clamorous: she is simple, and knoweth nothing. {9:14} For she sitteth at the door of her house, on a seat in the high places of the city, {9:15} To call passengers who go right on their ways: {9:16} Whoso is simple, let him turn in hither: and as for him that wanteth understanding, she saith to him, {9:17} Stolen waters are sweet, and bread eaten in secret is pleasant. {9:18} But he knoweth not that the dead are there; and that her guests are in the depths of hell.

{10:1} The proverbs of Solomon. A wise son makes a glad father: but a foolish son is the heaviness of his mother. {10:2} Treasures of wickedness profit nothing: but righteousness delivers from death. {10:3} The LORD will not suffer the soul of the righteous to famish: but he casts away the substance of the wicked. {10:4} He becomes poor that deals with a slack hand: but the hand of the diligent makes rich. {10:5} He that gathers in summer is a wise son: but he that sleeps in harvest is a son that causes shame. {10:6} Blessings are upon the head of the just: but violence covers the mouth of the wicked. {10:7} The memory of the just is blessed: but the name of the wicked shall rot. {10:8} The wise in heart will receive commandments: but a prating fool shall fall. {10:9} He that walks uprightly walks surely: but he that perverts his ways shall be known. {10:10} He that winks with the eye causes sorrow: but a prating fool shall fall. {10:11} The mouth of a righteous man is a well of life: but violence covers the mouth of the wicked. {10:12} Hatred stirs up strifes: but love covers all sins. {10:13} In the lips of him that has understanding wisdom is found: but a rod is for the back of him that is void of understanding. {10:14} Wise men lay up knowledge: but the mouth of the foolish is near destruction. {10:15} The rich man's wealth is his strong city: the destruction of the poor is their poverty. {10:16} The labor of the righteous tends to life: the fruit of the wicked to sin. {10:17} He is in the way of life that keeps instruction: but he that refuses reproof errs. {10:18} He that hides hatred with lying lips, and he that utters a slander, is a fool. {10:19} In the multitude of words there lacks not sin: but he that refrains his lips is wise. {10:20} The tongue of the just is as choice silver: the heart of the wicked is little worth. {10:21} The lips of the righteous feed many: but fools die for want of wisdom. {10:22} The blessing of the LORD, it makes rich, and he adds no sorrow with it. {10:23} It is as sport to a fool to do mischief: but a man of understanding has wisdom. {10:24} The fear of the wicked, it shall come upon him: but the desire of the righteous shall be granted. {10:25} As the whirlwind passes, so is the wicked no more: but the righteous is an everlasting foundation. {10:26} As vinegar to the teeth, and as smoke to the eyes, so is the sluggard to them that send him. {10:27} The fear of the LORD prolongs days: but the years of the wicked shall be shortened. {10:28} The hope of the righteous shall be gladness: but the expectation of the wicked shall perish. {10:29} The way of the LORD is strength to the upright: but destruction shall be to the workers of iniquity. {10:30} The righteous shall never be removed: but the wicked shall not inhabit the earth. {10:31} The mouth of the just brings forth wisdom: but the froward tongue shall be cut out. {10:32} The lips of the righteous know what is acceptable: but the mouth of the wicked speaks frowardness.

{11:1} A false balance is abomination to the LORD: but a just weight is his delight. {11:2} When pride comes, then comes shame: but with the lowly is wisdom. {11:3} The integrity of the upright shall guide them: but the perverseness of transgressors shall destroy them. {11:4} Riches profit not in the day of wrath: but righteousness delivers from death. {11:5} The righteousness of the perfect shall direct his way: but the wicked shall fall by his own wickedness. {11:6} The righteousness of the upright shall deliver them: but transgressors shall be taken in their own naughtiness. {11:7} When a wicked man dies, his expectation shall perish: and the hope of unjust men perishes. {11:8} The righteous is delivered out of trouble, and the wicked comes in his stead. {11:9} A hypocrite with his mouth destroys his neighbour: but through knowledge shall the just be delivered. {11:10} When it goes well with the righteous, the city rejoices: and when the wicked perish, there is shouting. {11:11} By the blessing of the upright the city is exalted: but it is overthrown by the mouth of the wicked. {11:12} He that is void of wisdom despises his neighbour: but a man of understanding holds his peace. {11:13} A talebearer reveals secrets: but he that is of a faithful spirit conceals the matter. {11:14} Where no counsel is, the people fall: but in the multitude of counsellors there is safety. {11:15} He that is surety for a stranger shall smart for it: and he that hates suretyship is sure. {11:16} A gracious woman retains honour: and strong men retain riches. {11:17} The merciful man does good to his own soul: but he that is cruel troubles his own flesh. {11:18} The wicked works a deceitful work: but to him that sows righteousness shall be a sure reward. {11:19} As righteousness tends to life: so he that pursues evil pursues it to his own death. {11:20} They that are of a froward heart are abomination to the LORD: but such as are upright in their way are his delight. {11:21} Though hand join in hand, the wicked shall not be unpunished: but the seed of the righteous shall be delivered. {11:22} As a jewel of gold in a swine's snout, so is a fair woman which is without discretion. {11:23} The desire of the righteous is only good: but the expectation of the wicked is wrath. {11:24} There is that scatters, and yet increases; and there is that withholds more than is meet, but it tends to poverty. {11:25} The liberal soul shall be made fat: and he that waters shall be watered also himself. {11:26} He that withholds corn, the people shall curse him: but blessing shall be upon the head of him that sells it. {11:27} He that diligently seeks good procures favour: but he that seeks mischief, it shall come unto him. {11:28} He that trusts in his riches shall fall: but the righteous shall flourish as a branch. {11:29} He that troubles his own house shall inherit the wind: and the fool shall be servant to the wise of heart. {11:30} The fruit of the righteous is a tree of life; and he that winneth souls is wise. {11:31} Behold, the righteous shall be recompensed in the earth: much more the wicked and the sinner.

{12:1} Whoever loves instruction loves knowledge: but he who hates reproof is brutish. {12:2} A good man obtains favor of the LORD: but a man of wicked devices will he condemn. {12:3} A man shall not be established by wickedness: but the root of the righteous shall not be moved. {12:4} A virtuous woman is a crown to her husband: but she that makes ashamed is as rottenness in his bones. {12:5} The thoughts of the righteous are right: but the counsels of the wicked are deceit. {12:6} The words of the wicked are to lie in wait for blood: but the mouth of the upright shall deliver them. {12:7} The wicked are overthrown, and are not: but the house of the righteous shall stand. {12:8} A man shall be commended according to his wisdom: but he that is of a perverse heart shall be despised. {12:9} He that is despised, and has a servant, is better than he that honors himself, and lacks bread. {12:10} A righteous man regards the life of his beast: but the tender mercies of the wicked are cruel. {12:11} He that tills his land shall be satisfied with bread: but he that follows vain persons is void of understanding. {12:12} The wicked desires the net of evil men: but the root of the righteous yields fruit. {12:13} The wicked is snared by the transgression of his lips: but the just shall come out of trouble. {12:14} A man shall be satisfied with good by the fruit of his mouth: and the recompense of a man's hands shall be rendered unto him. {12:15} The way of a fool is right in his own eyes: but he that hearkens unto counsel is wise. {12:16} A fool's wrath is presently known: but a prudent man covers shame. {12:17} He that speaks truth shows forth righteousness: but a false witness deceit. {12:18} There is that speaks like the piercings of a sword: but the tongue of the wise is health. {12:19} The lip of truth shall be established forever: but a lying tongue is but for a moment. {12:20} Deceit is in the heart of them that imagine evil: but to the counsellors of peace is joy. {12:21} There shall no evil happen to the just: but the wicked shall be filled with mischief. {12:22} Lying lips are abomination to the LORD: but they that deal truly are his delight. {12:23} A prudent man conceals knowledge: but the heart of fools proclaims foolishness. {12:24} **The hand of the diligent shall bear rule: but the slothful shall be under tribute.** {12:25} Heaviness in the heart of man makes it stoop: but a good word makes it glad. {12:26} The righteous is more excellent than his neighbor: but the way of the wicked seduces them. {12:27} The slothful man roasts not that which he took in hunting: but the substance of a diligent man is precious. {12:28} In the way of righteousness is life; and in the pathway thereof there is no death.

{13:1} A wise son hears his father's instruction: but a scorner hears not rebuke. {13:2} A man shall eat good by the fruit of his mouth: but the soul of the transgressors shall eat violence. {13:3} He that keeps his mouth keeps his life: but he that opens wide his lips shall have destruction. {13:4} The soul of the sluggard desires, and has nothing: but the soul of the diligent shall be made fat. {13:5} A righteous man hates lying: but a wicked man is loathsome, and comes to shame. {13:6} Righteousness keeps him that is upright in the way: but wickedness overthrows the sinner. {13:7} There is that makes himself rich, yet has nothing: there is that makes himself poor, yet has great riches. {13:8} The ransom of a man's life is his riches: but the poor hears not rebuke. {13:9} The light of the righteous rejoices: but the lamp of the wicked shall be put out. {13:10} Only by pride comes contention: but with the well advised is wisdom. {13:11} Wealth gotten by vanity shall be diminished: but he that gathers by labor shall increase. {13:12} Hope deferred makes the heart sick: but when the desire comes, it is a tree of life. {13:13} Whoso despises the word shall be destroyed: but he that fears the commandment shall be rewarded. {13:14} The law of the wise is a fountain of life, to depart from the snares of death. {13:15} Good understanding gives favor: but the way of transgressors is hard. {13:16} Every prudent man deals with knowledge: but a fool lays open his folly. {13:17} A wicked messenger falls into mischief: but a faithful ambassador is health. {13:18} Poverty and shame shall be to him that refuses instruction: but he that regards reproof shall be honored. {13:19} The desire accomplished is sweet to the soul: but it is abomination to fools to depart from evil. {13:20} **He that walks with wise men shall be wise: but a companion of fools shall be destroyed.** {13:21} Evil pursues sinners: but to the righteous good shall be repaid. {13:22} A good man leaves an inheritance to his children's children: and the wealth of the sinner is laid up for the just. {13:23} Much food is in the tillage of the poor: but there is that is destroyed for want of judgment. {13:24} He that spares his rod hates his son: but he that loves him chastens him betimes. {13:25} The righteous eats to the satisfying of his soul: but the belly of the wicked shall want.

{14:1} Every wise woman builds her house: but the foolish tears it down with her hands. {14:2} He that walks in his uprightness fears the LORD: but he that is perverse in his ways despises him. {14:3} In the mouth of the foolish is a rod of pride: but the lips of the wise shall preserve them. {14:4} Where no oxen are, the crib is clean: but much increase is by the strength of the ox. {14:5} A faithful witness will not lie: but a false witness will utter lies. {14:6} A scorner seeks wisdom, and finds it not: but knowledge is easy unto him that understands. {14:7} Go from the presence of a foolish man, when you perceive not in him the lips of knowledge. {14:8} The wisdom of the prudent is to understand his way: but the folly of fools is deceit. {14:9} Fools make a mock at sin: but among the righteous there is favor. {14:10} The heart knows his own bitterness; and a stranger does not intermeddle with his joy. {14:11} The house of the wicked shall be overthrown: but the tabernacle of the upright shall flourish. {14:12} There is a way which seems right unto a man, but the end thereof are the ways of death. {14:13} Even in laughter the heart is sorrowful; and the end of that mirth is heaviness. {14:14} The backslider in heart shall be filled with his own ways: and a good man shall be satisfied from himself. {14:15} The simple believes every word: but the prudent man looks well to his going. {14:16} A wise man fears, and departs from evil: but the fool rages, and is confident. {14:17} He that is soon angry deals foolishly: and a man of wicked devices is hated. {14:18} The simple inherit folly: but the prudent are crowned with knowledge. {14:19} The evil bow before the good; and the wicked at the gates of the righteous. {14:20} The poor is hated even of his own neighbor: but the rich has many friends. {14:21} He that despises his neighbor sins: but he that has mercy on the poor, happy is he. {14:22} Do they not err that devise evil? but mercy and truth shall be to them that devise good. {14:23} In all labor there is profit: but the talk of the lips tends only to penury. {14:24} The crown of the wise is their riches: but the foolishness of fools is folly. {14:25} A true witness delivers souls: but a deceitful witness speaks lies. {14:26} In the fear of the LORD is strong confidence: and his children shall have a place of refuge. {14:27} The fear of the LORD is a fountain of life, to depart from the snares of death. {14:28} In the multitude of people is the king's honor: but in the want of people is the destruction of the prince. {14:29} He that is slow to wrath is of great understanding: but he that is hasty of spirit exalts folly. {14:30} A sound heart is the life of the flesh: but envy the rottenness of the bones. {14:31} He that oppresses the poor reproaches his Maker: but he that honors him has mercy on the poor. {14:32} The wicked is driven away in his wickedness: but the righteous has hope in his death. {14:33} Wisdom rests in the heart of him that has understanding: but that which is in the midst of fools is made known. {14:34} Righteousness exalts a nation: but sin is a reproach to any people. {14:35} The king's favor is toward a wise servant: but his wrath is against him that causes shame.

{15:1} A soft answer turns away wrath: but grievous words stir up anger. {15:2} The tongue of the wise uses knowledge rightly: but the mouth of fools pours out foolishness. {15:3} The eyes of the LORD are in every place, beholding the evil and the good. {15:4} A wholesome tongue is a tree of life: but perverseness therein is a breach in the spirit. {15:5} A fool despises his father's instruction: but he that regards reproof is prudent. {15:6} In the house of the righteous is much treasure: but in the revenues of the wicked is trouble. {15:7} The lips of the wise disperse knowledge: but the heart of the foolish does not so. {15:8} The sacrifice of the wicked is an abomination to the LORD: but the prayer of the upright is his delight. {15:9} The way of the wicked is an abomination unto the LORD: but he loves him that follows after righteousness. {15:10} Correction is grievous unto him that forsakes the way: and he that hates reproof shall die. {15:11} Hell and destruction are before the LORD: how much more then the hearts of the children of men? {15:12} A scorner loves not one that reproves him: neither will he go unto the wise. {15:13} A merry heart makes a cheerful countenance: but by sorrow of the heart the spirit is broken. {15:14} **The heart of him that has understanding seeks knowledge: but the mouth of fools feeds on foolishness.** {15:15} All the days of the afflicted are evil: but he that is of a merry heart has a continual feast. {15:16} Better is little with the fear of the LORD than great treasure and trouble therewith. {15:17} Better is a dinner of herbs where love is, than a stalled ox and hatred therewith. {15:18} A wrathful man stirs up strife: but he that is slow to anger appeases strife. {15:19} The way of the slothful man is as a hedge of thorns: but the way of the righteous is made plain. {15:20} A wise son makes a glad father: but a foolish man despises his mother. {15:21} Folly is joy to him that is destitute of wisdom: but a man of understanding walks uprightly. {15:22} Without counsel purposes are disappointed: but in the multitude of counsellors they are established. {15:23} A man has joy by the answer of his mouth: and a word spoken in due season, how good is it! {15:24} The way of life is above to the wise, that he may depart from hell beneath. {15:25} The LORD will destroy the house of the proud: but he will establish the border of the widow. {15:26} The thoughts of the wicked are an abomination to the LORD: but the words of the pure are pleasant words. {15:27} He that is greedy of gain troubles his own house; but he that hates gifts shall live. {15:28} The heart of the righteous studies to answer: but the mouth of the wicked pours out evil things. {15:29} The LORD is far from the wicked: but he hears the prayer of the righteous. {15:30} The light of the eyes rejoices the heart: and a good report makes the bones fat. {15:31} The ear that hears the reproof of life abides among the wise. {15:32} He that refuses instruction despises his own soul: but he that hears reproof gets understanding. {15:33} The fear of the LORD is the instruction of wisdom; and before honour is humility.

{16:1} The preparations of the heart in man, and the answer of the tongue, is from the LORD. {16:2} All the ways of a man are clean in his own eyes; but the LORD weighs the spirits. {16:3} **Commit your works unto the LORD, and your thoughts shall be established.** {16:4} The LORD has made all things for himself: yes, even the wicked for the day of evil. {16:5} Everyone that is proud in heart is an abomination to the LORD: though hand join in hand, he shall not be unpunished. {16:6} By mercy and truth iniquity is purged: and by the fear of the LORD men depart from evil. {16:7} When a man's ways please the LORD, he makes even his enemies to be at peace with him. {16:8} Better is a little with righteousness than great revenues without right. {16:9} A man's heart devises his way: but the LORD directs his steps. {16:10} A divine sentence is in the lips of the king: his mouth transgresses not in judgment. {16:11} A just weight and balance are the LORD'S: all the weights of the bag are his work. {16:12} **It is an abomination to kings to commit wickedness: for the throne is established by righteousness.** {16:13} Righteous lips are the delight of kings; and they love him that speaks right. {16:14} The wrath of a king is as messengers of death: but a wise man will pacify it. {16:15} In the light of the king's countenance is life; and his favour is as a cloud of the latter rain. {16:16} How much better is it to get wisdom than gold! and to get understanding rather to be chosen than silver! {16:17} The highway of the upright is to depart from evil: he that keeps his way preserves his soul. {16:18} **Pride goes before destruction, and a haughty spirit before a fall.** {16:19} Better it is to be of a humble spirit with the lowly, than to divide the spoil with the proud. {16:20} **He that handles a matter wisely shall find good: and whoever trusts in the LORD, happy is he.** {16:21} The wise in heart shall be called prudent: and the sweetness of the lips increases learning. {16:22} Understanding is a wellspring of life unto him that has it: but the instruction of fools is folly. {16:23} The heart of the wise teaches his mouth, and adds learning to his lips. {16:24} Pleasant words are as an honeycomb, sweet to the soul, and health to the bones. {16:25} **There is a way that seems right unto a man, but the end thereof are the ways of death.** {16:26} He that labours labours for himself; for his mouth craves it of him. {16:27} An ungodly man digs up evil: and in his lips there is as a burning fire. {16:28} A froward man sows strife: and a whisperer separates chief friends. {16:29} **A violent man entices his neighbour, and leads him into the way that is not good.** {16:30} He shuts his eyes to devise froward things: moving his lips he brings evil to pass. {16:31} The hoary head is a crown of glory, if it be found in the way of righteousness. {16:32} He that is slow to anger is better than the mighty; and he that rules his spirit than he that takes a city. {16:33} **The lot is cast into the lap; but the whole disposing thereof is of the LORD.**

{17:1} Better is a dry morsel, and quietness therewith, than a house full of sacrifices with strife. {17:2} A wise servant shall have rule over a son that causes shame, and shall have part of the inheritance among the brethren. {17:3} The fining pot is for silver, and the furnace for gold: but the LORD tries the hearts. {17:4} A wicked doer gives heed to false lips; and a liar gives ear to a naughty tongue. {17:5} Whoever mocks the poor reproaches his Maker: and he that is glad at calamities shall not be unpunished. {17:6} **Children's children are the crown of old men; and the glory of children are their fathers.** {17:7} Excellent speech does not befit a fool: much less do lying lips befit a prince. {17:8} A gift is as a precious stone in the eyes of him that has it: wherever it turns, it prospers. {17:9} He that covers a transgression seeks love; but he that repeats a matter separates very friends. {17:10} A reproof enters more into a wise man than an hundred stripes into a fool. {17:11} An evil man seeks only rebellion: therefore a cruel messenger shall be sent against him. {17:12} Let a bear robbed of her whelps meet a man, rather than a fool in his folly. {17:13} Whoever rewards evil for good, evil shall not depart from his house. {17:14} **The beginning of strife is as when one lets out water: therefore leave off contention, before it be meddled with.** {17:15} He that justifies the wicked, and he that condemns the just, even they both are abomination to the LORD. {17:16} Why is there a price in the hand of a fool to get wisdom, seeing he has no heart to it? {17:17} A friend loves at all times, and a brother is born for adversity. {17:18} A man void of understanding strikes hands, and becomes surety in the presence of his friend. {17:19} He loves transgression that loves strife: and he that exalts his gate seeks destruction. {17:20} He that has a froward heart finds no good: and he that has a perverse tongue falls into mischief. {17:21} He that begets a fool does it to his sorrow: and the father of a fool has no joy. {17:22} A merry heart does good like a medicine: but a broken spirit dries the bones. {17:23} A wicked man takes a gift out of the bosom to pervert the ways of judgment. {17:24} **Wisdom is before him that has understanding; but the eyes of a fool are in the ends of the earth.** {17:25} A foolish son is a grief to his father, and bitterness to her that bore him. {17:26} Also to punish the just is not good, nor to strike princes for equity. {17:27} **He that has knowledge spares his words: and a man of understanding is of an excellent spirit.** {17:28} Even a fool, when he holds his peace, is counted wise: and he that shuts his lips is esteemed a man of understanding.

{18:1} Through desire a man, having separated himself, seeks and intermeddles with all wisdom. {18:2} A fool has no delight in understanding, but that his heart may discover itself. {18:3} When the wicked comes, then comes also contempt, and with ignominy reproach. {18:4} The words of a man's mouth are as deep waters, and the wellspring of wisdom as a flowing brook. {18:5} It is not good to accept the person of the wicked, to overthrow the righteous in judgment. {18:6} A fool's lips enter into contention, and his mouth calls for strokes. {18:7} A fool's mouth is his destruction, and his lips are the snare of his soul. {18:8} The words of a talebearer are as wounds, and they go down into the innermost parts of the belly. {18:9} He also that is slothful in his work is brother to him that is a great waster. {18:10} The name of the LORD is a strong tower: the righteous runs into it, and is safe. {18:11} The rich man's wealth is his strong city, and as a high wall in his own conceit. {18:12} Before destruction the heart of man is haughty, and before honour is humility. {18:13} He that answers a matter before he hears it, it is folly and shame unto him. {18:14} The spirit of a man will sustain his infirmity; but a wounded spirit who can bear? {18:15} The heart of the prudent gets knowledge; and the ear of the wise seeks knowledge. {18:16} A man's gift makes room for him, and brings him before great men. {18:17} He that is first in his own cause seems just; but his neighbour comes and searches him. {18:18} The lot causes contentions to cease, and parts between the mighty. {18:19} A brother offended is harder to be won than a strong city: and their contentions are like the bars of a castle. {18:20} A man's belly shall be satisfied with the fruit of his mouth; and with the increase of his lips shall he be filled. {18:21} Death and life are in the power of the tongue: and they that love it shall eat the fruit thereof. {18:22} Whoever finds a wife finds a good thing, and obtains favour of the LORD. {18:23} The poor uses entreaties; but the rich answers roughly. {18:24} A man that has friends must show himself friendly: and there is a friend that sticks closer than a brother.

{19:1} Better is the poor who walks in his integrity than he who is perverse in his lips and is a fool. {19:2} Also, that the soul be without knowledge, it is not good; and he that hastens with his feet sins. {19:3} The foolishness of man perverts his way: and his heart frets against the LORD. {19:4} Wealth makes many friends; but the poor is separated from his neighbor. {19:5} A false witness shall not be unpunished, and he that speaks lies shall not escape. {19:6} Many will entreat the favor of the prince: and every man is a friend to him that gives gifts. {19:7} All the brethren of the poor hate him: how much more do his friends go far from him? he pursues them with words, yet they are wanting to him. {19:8} He that gets wisdom loves his own soul: he that keeps understanding shall find good. {19:9} A false witness shall not be unpunished, and he that speaks lies shall perish. {19:10} Delight is not seemly for a fool; much less for a servant to have rule over princes. {19:11} The discretion of a man defers his anger; and it is his glory to pass over a transgression. {19:12} The king's wrath is as the roaring of a lion; but his favor is as dew upon the grass. {19:13} A foolish son is the calamity of his father: and the contentions of a wife are a continual dropping. {19:14} House and riches are the inheritance of fathers and a prudent wife is from the LORD. {19:15} Slothfulness casts into a deep sleep; and an idle soul shall suffer hunger. {19:16} He that keeps the commandment keeps his own soul; but he that despises his ways shall die. {19:17} He that has pity upon the poor lends unto the LORD; and that which he has given will he pay him again. {19:18} Chasten your son while there is hope, and let not your soul spare for his crying. {19:19} A man of great wrath shall suffer punishment: for if you deliver him, yet you must do it again. {19:20} Hear counsel, and receive instruction, that you may be wise in your latter end. {19:21} There are many devices in a man's heart; nevertheless the counsel of the LORD, that shall stand. {19:22} The desire of a man is his kindness: and a poor man is better than a liar. {19:23} The fear of the LORD tends to life: and he that has it shall abide satisfied; he shall not be visited with evil. {19:24} A slothful man hides his hand in his bosom, and will not so much as bring it to his mouth again. {19:25} Smite a scorner, and the simple will beware: and reprove one that has understanding, and he will understand knowledge. {19:26} He that wastes his father, and chases away his mother, is a son that causes shame, and brings reproach. {19:27} Cease, my son, to hear the instruction that causes to err from the words of knowledge. {19:28} An ungodly witness scorns judgment: and the mouth of the wicked devours iniquity. {19:29} Judgments are prepared for scorners, and stripes for the back of fools.

{20:1} Wine is a mocker, strong drink is raging: and whoever is deceived thereby is not wise. {20:2} The fear of a king is as the roaring of a lion: provoking him to anger sins against his own soul. {20:3} It is an honor for a man to cease from strife: but every fool will be meddling. {20:4} The sluggard will not plow by reason of the cold; therefore shall he beg in harvest, and have nothing. {20:5} Counsel in the heart of man is like deep water; but a man of understanding will draw it out. {20:6} Most men will proclaim every one his own goodness: but a faithful man who can find? {20:7} The just man walks in his integrity: his children are blessed after him. {20:8} A king that sits in the throne of judgment scatters away all evil with his eyes. {20:9} Who can say, I have made my heart clean, I am pure from my sin? {20:10} Diverse weights, and diverse measures, both of them are alike abomination to the LORD. {20:11} Even a child is known by his doings, whether his work be pure, and whether it be right. {20:12} The hearing ear, and the seeing eye, the LORD has made even both of them. {20:13} Love not sleep, lest you come to poverty; open your eyes, and you shall be satisfied with bread. {20:14} It is naught, it is naught, says the buyer: but when he is gone his way, then he boasts. {20:15} There is gold, and a multitude of rubies: but the lips of knowledge are a precious jewel. {20:16} Take his garment that is surety for a stranger: and take a pledge of him for a strange woman. {20:17} Bread of deceit is sweet to a man; but afterwards his mouth shall be filled with gravel. {20:18} Every purpose is established by counsel: and with good advice make war. {20:19} He that goes about as a talebearer reveals secrets: therefore meddle not with him that flatters with his lips. {20:20} Whoso curses his father or his mother, his lamp shall be put out in obscure darkness. {20:21} An inheritance may be gotten hastily at the beginning; but the end thereof shall not be blessed. {20:22} Say not thou, I will recompense evil; but wait on the LORD, and he shall save you. {20:23} Diverse weights are an abomination unto the LORD; and a false balance is not good. {20:24} Man's goings are of the LORD; how can a man then understand his own way? {20:25} It is a snare to the man who devours that which is holy, and after vows to make inquiry. {20:26} A wise king scatters the wicked, and brings the wheel over them. {20:27} The spirit of man is the candle of the LORD, searching all the inward parts of the belly. {20:28} Mercy and truth preserve the king: and his throne is upheld by mercy. {20:29} The glory of young men is their strength: and the beauty of old men is the grey head. {20:30} The blueness of a wound cleanses away evil: so do stripes the inward parts of the belly.

{21:1} The king's heart is in the hand of the LORD, as the rivers of water: he turns it wherever he will. {21:2} Every way of a man is right in his own eyes: but the LORD ponders the hearts. {21:3} To do justice and judgment is more acceptable to the LORD than sacrifice. {21:4} An haughty look, a proud heart, and the plowing of the wicked, is sin. {21:5} The thoughts of the diligent lead to plenteousness; but everyone who is hasty only ends up in want. {21:6} Obtaining treasures through a lying tongue is like a fleeting fantasy for those seeking death. {21:7} The robbery of the wicked shall destroy them, because they refuse to do justice. {21:8} The way of man is froward and strange: but for the pure, his work is right. {21:9} It is better to dwell in a corner of the housetop, than with a brawling woman in a wide house. {21:10} The soul of the wicked desires evil: his neighbor finds no favor in his eyes. {21:11} When the scorner is punished, the simple become wise; and when the wise is instructed, he receives knowledge. {21:12} The righteous wisely considers the house of the wicked: but God overthrows the wicked for their wickedness. {21:13} Whoever stops his ears at the cry of the poor, he also shall cry himself, but shall not be heard. {21:14} A gift in secret pacifies anger, and a reward in the bosom strong wrath. {21:15} It is joy to the just to do judgment, but destruction shall be to the workers of iniquity. {21:16} The man that wanders out of the way of understanding shall remain in the congregation of the dead. {21:17} He that loves pleasure shall be a poor man: he that loves wine and oil shall not be rich. {21:18} The wicked shall be a ransom for the righteous, and the transgressor for the upright. {21:19} It is better to dwell in the wilderness, than with a contentious and an angry woman. {21:20} There is treasure to be desired and oil in the dwelling of the wise; but a foolish man spends it up. {21:21} He that follows after righteousness and mercy finds life, righteousness, and honor. {21:22} A wise man scales the city of the mighty, and casts down the strength of its confidence. {21:23} Whoever keeps his mouth and his tongue keeps his soul from troubles. {21:24} Proud and haughty scorner is his name, who deals in proud wrath. {21:25} The desire of the slothful kills him; for his hands refuse to labor. {21:26} He covets greedily all the day long: but the righteous gives and spares not. {21:27} The sacrifice of the wicked is abomination: how much more, when he brings it with a wicked mind? {21:28} A false witness shall perish: but the man that hears speaks constantly. {21:29} A wicked man hardens his face: but as for the upright, he directs his way. {21:30} There is no wisdom nor understanding nor counsel against the LORD. {21:31} The horse is prepared against the day of battle: but safety is of the LORD.

{22:1} A good name is rather to be chosen than great riches, and loving favor rather than silver and gold. {22:2} The rich and poor meet together: the LORD is the maker of them all. {22:3} A prudent man foresees the evil, and hides himself: but the simple pass on, and are punished. {22:4} By humility and the fear of the LORD are riches, and honor, and life. {22:5} Thorns and snares are in the way of the froward: he that keeps his soul shall be far from them. {22:6} **Train up a child in the way he should go: and when he is old, he will not depart from it.** {22:7} The rich rules over the poor, and the borrower is servant to the lender. {22:8} He that sows iniquity shall reap vanity: and the rod of his anger shall fail. {22:9} He that has a bountiful eye shall be blessed; for he gives of his bread to the poor. {22:10} Cast out the scorner, and contention shall go out; yes, strife and reproach shall cease. {22:11} He that loves pureness of heart, for the grace of his lips the king shall be his friend. {22:12} The eyes of the LORD preserve knowledge, and he overthrows the words of the transgressor. {22:13} The slothful man says, "There is a lion outside, I shall be slain in the streets." {22:14} The mouth of strange women is a deep pit: he that is abhorred of the LORD shall fall therein. {22:15} Foolishness is bound in the heart of a child; but the rod of correction shall drive it far from him. {22:16} He that oppresses the poor to increase his riches, and he that gives to the rich, shall surely come to want. {22:17} Bow down your ear, and hear the words of the wise, and apply your heart unto my knowledge. {22:18} For it is a pleasant thing if you keep them within you; they shall withal be fitted in your lips. {22:19} That your trust may be in the LORD, I have made known to you this day, even to you. {22:20} Have not I written to you excellent things in counsels and knowledge, {22:21} That I might make you know the certainty of the words of truth; that you might answer the words of truth to those that send unto you? {22:22} Rob not the poor, because he is poor: neither oppress the afflicted in the gate: {22:23} For the LORD will plead their cause, and spoil the soul of those that spoiled them. {22:24} Make no friendship with an angry man; and with a furious man you shall not go: {22:25} Lest you learn his ways, and get a snare to your soul. {22:26} Be not one of them that strike hands, or of them that are sureties for debts. {22:27} If you have nothing to pay, why should he take away your bed from under you? {22:28} Remove not the ancient landmark, which your fathers have set. {22:29} Do you see a man diligent in his business? He shall stand before kings; he shall not stand before mean men.

{23:1} When you sit down to eat with a ruler, consider carefully what is before you. {23:2} Put a knife to your throat if you are given to appetite. {23:3} Do not desire his delicacies, for they are deceitful food. {23:4} Do not labor to be rich; cease from your own wisdom. {23:5} Will you set your eyes on that which is not? For riches certainly make themselves wings; they fly away like an eagle toward heaven. {23:6} Do not eat the bread of him who has an evil eye, nor desire his delicacies; {23:7} For as he thinks in his heart, so is he: "Eat and drink," he says to you, but his heart is not with you. {23:8} The morsel you have eaten you will vomit up, and waste your pleasant words. {23:9} Do not speak in the hearing of a fool, for he will despise the wisdom of your words. {23:10} Do not remove the old landmark, nor enter the fields of the fatherless; {23:11} For their Redeemer is mighty; He will plead their cause with you. {23:12} Apply your heart to instruction, and your ears to words of knowledge. {23:13} Do not withhold correction from a child, for if you beat him with a rod, he will not die. {23:14} You shall beat him with a rod, and deliver his soul from hell. {23:15} My son, if your heart is wise, my heart will rejoice—indeed, I myself; {23:16} Yes, my inmost being will rejoice when your lips speak right things. {23:17} Do not let your heart envy sinners, but be in the fear of the LORD all the day long; {23:18} For surely there is a hereafter, and your hope will not be cut off. {23:19} Hear, my son, and be wise; and guide your heart in the way. {23:20} Do not be among winebibbers, among riotous eaters of flesh; {23:21} For the drunkard and the glutton will come to poverty, and drowsiness will clothe a man with rags. {23:22} Listen to your father who begot you, and do not despise your mother when she is old. {23:23} Buy the truth, and do not sell it, also wisdom and instruction and understanding. {23:24} The father of the righteous will greatly rejoice, and he who begets a wise child will have joy of him. {23:25} Your father and your mother will be glad, and she who bore you will rejoice. {23:26} My son, give me your heart, and let your eyes observe my ways. {23:27} For a whore is a deep ditch, and a strange woman is a narrow pit. {23:28} She also lies in wait as for prey, and increases the unfaithful among men. {23:29} Who has woe? Who has sorrow? Who has contentions? Who has complaints? Who has wounds without cause? Who has redness of eyes? {23:30} Those who linger long at the wine, those who go in search of mixed wine. {23:31} Do not look on the wine when it is red, when it sparkles in the cup, when it swirls around smoothly; {23:32} At the last it bites like a serpent, and stings like a viper. {23:33} Your eyes will see strange things, and your heart will utter perverse things. {23:34} Yes, you will be like one who lies down in the midst of the sea, or like one who lies at the top of the mast, saying: {23:35} "They have struck me, but I was not hurt; they have beaten me, but I did not feel it. When shall I awake, that I may seek another drink?"

{24:1} Don't envy evil people or desire to be with them. {24:2} They think about causing trouble, and their words are full of harm. {24:3} Wisdom builds a house, and understanding makes it strong. {24:4} Knowledge fills the rooms with precious and pleasant riches. {24:5} A wise person is strong; knowledge increases strength. {24:6} Seek wise counsel for your plans; safety comes from having many advisors. {24:7} Fools can't understand wisdom; they stay silent when wise people speak. {24:8} Those who plan to do evil will be called troublemakers. {24:9} Foolish thoughts are sinful, and mocking is hated by everyone. {24:10} If you give up when troubles come, your strength is weak. {24:11} If you ignore those in trouble and say you didn't know about their suffering, God, who knows all hearts, will see it and punish you. {24:12} Eat honey, my son, for it is good; honey from the comb is sweet to your taste. {24:13} Wisdom is like honey for your soul. If you find it, there is a future reward, and your hope will never be cut off. {24:14} Don't wait to attack the home of the righteous, and don't destroy where they rest. {24:15} Though the righteous person falls seven times, they rise again, but the wicked stumble when calamity strikes. {24:16} Don't be happy when your enemy falls, and don't rejoice when they stumble. {24:17} If you do, the Lord will see it and be displeased, and he will turn his anger away from them. {24:18} Don't worry because of evil people, or be envious of the wicked; {24:19} There is no future for the evil, and the lamp of the wicked will be put out. {24:20} Fear the Lord and the king, and don't associate with rebels, {24:21} for disaster will strike them suddenly. Who knows what punishment will come from the Lord and the king? {24:22} Showing partiality in judgment is not good. Whoever says to the guilty, "You are innocent," will be cursed by people and denounced by nations. {24:23} But it will go well with those who convict the guilty, and rich blessing will come on them. {24:24} Whoever gives an honest answer kisses the lips. {24:25} Finish your outdoor work and get your fields ready; after that, build your house. {24:26} Don't testify against your neighbor without cause, or use your lips to deceive. {24:27} Don't say, "I'll do to them what they have done to me; I'll repay the wrong they did." {24:28} I passed by the field of a lazy person, by the vineyard of one who has no sense; {24:29} thorns had come up everywhere, the ground was covered with weeds, and the stone wall was in ruins. {24:30} I applied my heart to what I observed and learned a lesson from what I saw: {24:31} A little sleep, a little slumber, a little folding of the hands to rest— {24:32} Then I observed and learned a lesson; I looked closely and received instruction. {24:33} Just a little sleep, a little slumber, a little folding of the hands to rest— {24:34} and poverty will come upon you like a thief, and scarcity like an armed man.

{25:1} These are also proverbs of Solomon, which the men of Hezekiah king of Judah copied out. {25:2} It brings honor to God to conceal things, but the honor of kings is to search them out. {25:3} Like the heavens for height and the earth for depth, so the heart of kings is unsearchable. {25:4} Remove the impurities from silver, and a vessel will be produced for a silversmith. {25:5} Remove the wicked from the king's presence, and his throne will be established in righteousness. {25:6} Do not exalt yourself in the king's presence, and do not stand in the place of great men; {25:7} for it is better to be told, "Come up here," than to be put lower in the presence of a prince you have seen with your own eyes. {25:8} Do not rush to go to court, for what will you do in the end if your neighbor puts you to shame? {25:9} Argue your case with your neighbor directly, and do not reveal another's secret, {25:10} lest the one who hears it disgrace you, and your bad reputation never disappears. {25:11} A word spoken at the right time is like apples of gold in settings of silver. {25:12} Like an earring of gold or an ornament of fine gold is a wise reprover to a receptive ear. {25:13} Like the cold of snow in the time of harvest is a faithful messenger to those who send him; he refreshes the soul of his masters. {25:14} Like clouds and wind without rain is one who boasts about gifts never given. {25:15} With patience a ruler may be persuaded, and a gentle tongue can break bones. {25:16} If you find honey, eat only what you need; otherwise, you may have too much and vomit it up. {25:17} Let your foot be seldom in your neighbor's house, or they may become weary of you and hate you. {25:18} Like a club, a sword, or a sharp arrow is one who bears false witness against their neighbor. {25:19} Confidence in an unreliable person in times of trouble is like a broken tooth or a foot out of joint. {25:20} Singing cheerful songs to a person with a heavy heart is like taking a coat off on a cold day or pouring vinegar on soda. {25:21} If your enemy is hungry, give him food to eat; if he is thirsty, give him water to drink. {25:22} In doing this, you will heap burning coals on his head, and the LORD will reward you. {25:23} Like a north wind that brings unexpected rain is a sly tongue—which provokes a horrified look. {25:24} It is better to live in a corner of the roof than in a house shared with a quarrelsome woman. {25:25} Like cold water to a weary soul is good news from a distant land. {25:26} Like a muddied spring or a polluted well are the righteous who give way to the wicked. {25:27} It is not good to eat too much honey, nor is it honorable to seek one's own honor. {25:28} Like a city whose walls are broken through is a person who lacks self-control.

{26:1} Like snow in summer or rain at harvest time, honor is not fitting for a fool. {26:2} Like a fluttering sparrow or a darting swallow, an undeserved curse does not come to rest. {26:3} A whip for the horse, a bridle for the donkey, and a rod for the backs of fools. {26:4} Do not answer a fool according to his folly, or you yourself will be like him. {26:5} Answer a fool according to his folly, or he will be wise in his own eyes. {26:6} Sending a message by the hand of a fool is like cutting off one's feet or drinking poison. {26:7} The legs of the lame are not equal, nor are proverbs delivered by fools. {26:8} Like tying a stone in a sling, so is giving honor to a fool. {26:9} Like a thorn that goes into the hand of a drunkard, so is a proverb in the mouth of fools. {26:10} Like an archer who wounds at random is one who hires a fool or any passerby. {26:11} Like a dog that returns to its vomit is a fool who repeats his foolishness. {26:12} Do you see a man wise in his own eyes? There is more hope for a fool than for him. {26:13} The sluggard says, "There is a lion in the road! A lion is in the streets!" {26:14} Like a door that turns on its hinges, so does the sluggard on his bed. {26:15} The sluggard buries his hand in the dish; it wearies him to bring it back to his mouth. {26:16} The sluggard is wiser in his own eyes than seven men who answer discreetly. {26:17} Like one who grabs a stray dog by the ears is someone who rushes into a quarrel not their own. {26:18} Like a maniac who shoots flaming arrows and deadly arrows {26:19} is the one who deceives their neighbor and says, "I was only joking!" {26:20} Without wood, a fire goes out; without gossip, a quarrel dies down. {26:21} As charcoal to embers and as wood to fire, so is a quarrelsome person for kindling strife. {26:22} The words of a gossip are like choice morsels; they go down to the inmost parts. {26:23} Like a coating of silver dross on earthenware are fervent lips with an evil heart. {26:24} Enemies disguise themselves with their lips, but in their hearts they harbor deceit. {26:25} Though their speech is charming, do not believe them, for seven abominations fill their hearts. {26:26} Their malice may be concealed by deception, but their wickedness will be exposed in the assembly. {26:27} Whoever digs a pit will fall into it; if someone rolls a stone, it will roll back on them. {26:28} A lying tongue hates those it hurts, and a flattering mouth works ruin.

{27:1} Don't brag about tomorrow, because you don't know what a day may bring. {27:2} Let someone else praise you, not your own mouth—a stranger, not your own lips. {27:3} A stone is heavy, and sand is weighty, but a fool's wrath is heavier than both. {27:4} Wrath is fierce and anger is overwhelming, but who can stand before jealousy? {27:5} Open rebuke is better than hidden love. {27:6} The wounds of a friend can be trusted, but the kisses of an enemy are deceitful. {27:7} A full soul loathes honey, but to a hungry soul, even bitter things taste sweet. {27:8} Like a bird that wanders from its nest, so is a person who wanders from their place. {27:9} Ointment and perfume make the heart glad, and so does the sweetness of a friend's counsel. {27:10} Don't forsake your friend or your father's friend, and don't go to your brother's house in times of trouble. It's better to have a nearby neighbor than a distant brother. {27:11} My son, be wise and make me glad, so that I can answer anyone who taunts me. {27:12} A prudent person sees danger and takes refuge, but the simple keep going and suffer for it. {27:13} Take the garment of one who puts up security for a stranger; hold it in pledge if it is done for an outsider. {27:14} If someone blesses their neighbor loudly early in the morning, it will be taken as a curse. {27:15} A continual dripping on a rainy day and a quarrelsome wife are alike. {27:16} Whoever can restrain her can restrain the wind or grasp oil with his hand. {27:17} Iron sharpens iron, and one person sharpens another. {27:18} Whoever tends a fig tree will eat its fruit, and whoever looks after their master will be honored. {27:19} As water reflects the face, so one's life reflects the heart of man. {27:20} Sheol and Abaddon are never satisfied, and neither are human eyes. {27:21} The crucible for silver and the furnace for gold, but people are tested by their praise. {27:22} Though you grind a fool in a mortar, grinding them like grain with a pestle, you will not remove their folly from them. {27:23} Be sure to know the condition of your flocks, and give attention to your herds; {27:24} for riches do not last forever, nor does a crown endure to all generations. {27:25} When the hay is removed and new growth appears and the grass from the hills is gathered in, {27:26} the lambs will provide you with clothing, and the goats with the price of a field. {27:27} You will have plenty of goats' milk to feed your family and to nourish your female servants.

{28:1} The wicked run away even when no one is chasing them, but the righteous are as bold as lions. {28:2} When a country is rebellious, it has many rulers, but a person with understanding and knowledge maintains order. {28:3} A poor person who oppresses the poor is like a driving rain that destroys the crops. {28:4} Those who forsake the law praise the wicked, but those who keep the law resist them. {28:5} Evil people don't understand justice, but those who seek the LORD understand everything. {28:6} Better to be poor and honest than to be dishonest and rich. {28:7} Whoever keeps the law is a discerning child, but a companion of gluttons disgraces their father. {28:8} Whoever increases wealth by taking interest or profit from the poor amasses it for another, who will be kind to the poor. {28:9} If anyone turns a deaf ear to my instruction, even their prayers are detestable. {28:10} Whoever leads the upright along an evil path will fall into their own trap, but the blameless will receive a good inheritance. {28:11} The rich are wise in their own eyes; one who is poor and discerning sees through them. {28:12} When the righteous triumph, there is great elation; but when the wicked rise to power, people go into hiding. {28:13} Whoever conceals their sins does not prosper, but the one who confesses and renounces them finds mercy. {28:14} Blessed is the one who always trembles before God, but whoever hardens their heart falls into trouble. {28:15} Like a roaring lion or a charging bear is a wicked ruler over a helpless people. {28:16} A tyrannical ruler practices extortion, but one who hates ill-gotten gain will enjoy a long reign. {28:17} Anyone tormented by the guilt of murder will seek refuge in the grave; let no one hold them back. {28:18} Whoever walks in integrity will be delivered, but whoever is perverse in their ways will fall into the pit. {28:19} Those who work their land will have abundant food, but those who chase fantasies will have their fill of poverty. {28:20} A faithful person will be richly blessed, but one eager to get rich will not go unpunished. {28:21} Showing partiality is never good, yet some will do wrong for a piece of bread. {28:22} The stingy are eager to get rich and are unaware that poverty awaits them. {28:23} Whoever rebukes a person will in the end gain favor rather than one who has a flattering tongue. {28:24} Whoever robs their father or mother and says, "It's not wrong," is partner to one who destroys. {28:25} Greedy people stir up conflict, but those who trust in the LORD will prosper. {28:26} Those who trust in themselves are fools, but those who walk in wisdom are kept safe. {28:27} Those who give to the poor will lack nothing, but those who close their eyes to them receive many curses. {28:28} When the wicked rise to power, people go into hiding; but when the wicked perish, the righteous thrive.

{29:1} If you ignore warnings and refuse to change, you'll face sudden destruction with no chance of escape. {29:2} When the righteous lead, people rejoice; but when the wicked rule, people mourn. {29:3} Loving wisdom brings joy to one's parents, but keeping company with prostitutes squanders one's wealth. {29:4} A king who judges fairly brings stability to the land, but one who accepts bribes undermines it. {29:5} Flattering your neighbor sets a trap for your own feet. {29:6} Evil people are trapped by their sinful ways, but the righteous sing and rejoice. {29:7} The righteous care about justice for the poor, but the wicked have no such concern. {29:8} Mockers can bring a whole city to ruin, but the wise turn away anger. {29:9} When wise people debate with fools, whether they rant or laugh, there is no peace. {29:10} The bloodthirsty hate blameless people, but the upright seek to help them. {29:11} Fools vent their anger, but the wise quietly hold it back. {29:12} If a ruler listens to lies, all his officials become wicked. {29:13} The poor and the oppressor have this in common: the LORD gives sight to the eyes of both. {29:14} A king who judges the poor with fairness will have a lasting throne. {29:15} Discipline your children, and they will give you peace of mind and bring you happiness. {29:16} When the wicked are in authority, sin flourishes, but the godly will live to see their downfall. {29:17} Discipline your children, and they will give you peace of mind and will make your heart glad. {29:18} Without vision, people perish; but those who keep the law are blessed. {29:19} You cannot correct a servant merely by words; they may understand, but they will not respond. {29:20} If you see someone who speaks in haste, there is more hope for a fool than for them. {29:21} If you pamper your servant from youth, they will become your enemy in the end. {29:22} An angry person stirs up conflict, and a hot-tempered person commits many sins. {29:23} Pride will bring a person low, but the humble in spirit will retain honor. {29:24} Whoever shares with a thief is their own enemy; they hear the oath to testify, but say nothing. {29:25} The fear of others can be a trap, but trusting in the LORD means safety. {29:26} Many seek the favor of a ruler, but every person's decision comes from the LORD. {29:27} The righteous detest the dishonest; the wicked detest the upright.

{30:1} These are the words of Agur, son of Jakeh, who spoke a prophecy to Ithiel and Ucal: {30:2} "I am more ignorant than anyone else; I lack understanding like any other human. {30:3} I have not acquired wisdom, nor do I possess the knowledge of the Holy One. {30:4} Who has ascended to heaven and come back down? Who has gathered the wind in their fists? Who has wrapped up the waters in a cloak? Who has established all the ends of the earth? What is their name, and what is the name of their son? Surely you know! {30:5} Every word of God is flawless; he is a shield to those who take refuge in him. {30:6} Do not add to his words, or he will rebuke you and prove you a liar. {30:7} Two things I ask of you, Lord; do not refuse me before I die: {30:8} Keep falsehood and lies far from me; give me neither poverty nor riches, but give me only my daily bread. {30:9} Otherwise, I may have too much and disown you and say, 'Who is the Lord?' Or I may become poor and steal, and so dishonor the name of my God. {30:10} Do not accuse a servant without cause, or they will curse you, and you will pay for it. {30:11} There are those who curse their fathers and do not bless their mothers; {30:12} those who are pure in their own eyes and yet are not cleansed of their filth; {30:13} those whose eyes are ever so haughty, whose glances are so disdainful; {30:14} those whose teeth are swords and whose jaws are set with knives to devour the poor from the earth and the needy from among mankind. {30:15} The leech has two daughters. 'Give! Give!' they cry. There are three things that are never satisfied, four that never say, 'Enough!': {30:16} the grave, the barren womb, land, which is never satisfied with water, and fire, which never says, 'Enough!' {30:17} The eye that mocks a father, that scorns an aged mother, will be pecked out by the ravens of the valley, will be eaten by the vultures. {30:18} There are three things that are too amazing for me, four that I do not understand: {30:19} the way of an eagle in the sky, the way of a snake on a rock, the way of a ship on the high seas, and the way of a man with a young woman. {30:20} This is the way of an adulterous woman: she eats and wipes her mouth and says, 'I've done nothing wrong.' {30:21} Under three things the earth trembles, under four it cannot bear up: {30:22} a servant who becomes king, a godless fool who gets plenty to eat, {30:23} a contemptible woman who gets married, and a servant who displaces her mistress. {30:24} Four things on earth are small, yet they are extremely wise: {30:25} Ants are creatures of little strength, yet they store up their food in the summer; {30:26} hyraxes are creatures of little power, yet they make their home in the crags; {30:27} locusts have no king, yet they advance together in ranks; {30:28} a lizard can be caught with the hand, yet it is found in kings' palaces. {30:29} There are three things that are stately in their stride, four that move with stately bearing: {30:30} a lion, mighty among beasts, who retreats before nothing; {30:31} a strutting rooster, a male goat, and a king secure against revolt. {30:32} If you play the fool and exalt yourself, or if you plan evil, clap your hand over your mouth! {30:33} For as churning cream produces butter, and as twisting the nose produces blood, so stirring up anger produces strife."

{31:1} These are the words of King Lemuel, the prophecy that his mother taught him: {31:2} "What, my son? And what, the son of my womb? And what, the son of my vows? {31:3} Do not give your strength to women, nor your ways to that which destroys kings. {31:4} It is not for kings, O Lemuel, it is not for kings to drink wine, nor for princes to crave strong drink, {31:5} lest they drink and forget what the law says, and deprive all the oppressed of their rights. {31:6} Give strong drink to one who is perishing, and wine to those in bitter distress; {31:7} let them drink and forget their poverty, and remember their misery no more. {31:8} Speak up for those who cannot speak for themselves, for the rights of all who are destitute. {31:9} Speak up and judge fairly; defend the rights of the poor and needy." {31:10} Who can find a virtuous woman? Her worth is far above rubies. {31:11} The heart of her husband trusts in her, and he will have no lack of gain. {31:12} She brings him good, not harm, all the days of her life. {31:13} She selects wool and flax and works with eager hands. {31:14} She is like the merchant ships, bringing her food from afar. {31:15} She rises while it is still night to provide food for her household and portions for her servants. {31:16} She considers a field and buys it; from her earnings she plants a vineyard. {31:17} She sets about her work vigorously; her arms are strong for her tasks. {31:18} She sees that her trading is profitable, and her lamp does not go out at night. {31:19} In her hand she holds the distaff and grasps the spindle with her fingers. {31:20} She opens her arms to the poor and extends her hands to the needy. {31:21} When it snows, she has no fear for her household; for all of them are clothed in scarlet. {31:22} She makes coverings for her bed; she is clothed in fine linen and purple. {31:23} Her husband is respected at the city gate, where he takes his seat among the elders of the land. {31:24} She makes linen garments and sells them, and supplies the merchants with sashes. {31:25} She is clothed with strength and dignity; she can laugh at the days to come. {31:26} She speaks with wisdom, and faithful instruction is on her tongue. {31:27} She watches over the affairs of her household and does not eat the bread of idleness. {31:28} Her children arise and call her blessed; her husband also, and he praises her: {31:29} "Many women do noble things, but you surpass them all." {31:30} Charm is deceptive, and beauty is fleeting; but a woman who fears the LORD is to be praised. {31:31} Honor her for all that her hands have done, and let her works bring her praise at the city gate."

Ecclesiastes

{1:1} These are the words of the Preacher, the son of David, who was king in Jerusalem: {1:2} **"Vanity of vanities," says the Preacher, "vanity of vanities; all is vanity.** {1:3} What does man gain from all his labor that he toils at under the sun? {1:4} Generations come and generations go, but the earth remains forever. {1:5} The sun rises and the sun sets, hurrying back to where it rises. {1:6} The wind blows to the south and turns to the north; round and round it goes, ever returning on its course. {1:7} All streams flow into the sea, yet the sea is never full. To the place the streams come from, there they return again. {1:8} All things are wearisome; man cannot express it. The eye is not satisfied with seeing, nor the ear filled with hearing. {1:9} What has been will be again, what has been done will be done again; there is nothing new under the sun. {1:10} Is there anything of which one can say, "Look! This is something new"? It was here already, long ago; it was here before our time. {1:11} There is no remembrance of men of old, and even those who are yet to come will not be remembered by those who follow them. {1:12} I, the Preacher, was king over Israel in Jerusalem. {1:13} I applied my mind to study and to explore by wisdom all that is done under the heavens. What a heavy burden God has laid on men! {1:14} I have seen all the things that are done under the sun; all of them are meaningless, a chasing after the wind. {1:15} What is twisted cannot be straightened; what is lacking cannot be counted. {1:16} I thought to myself, "I have acquired great wisdom, surpassing all who were over Jerusalem before me; and my mind has had great experience of wisdom and knowledge." {1:17} Then I applied myself to the understanding of wisdom, and also of madness and folly, but I learned that this, too, is a chasing after the wind. {1:18} For with much wisdom comes much sorrow; the more knowledge, the more grief."

{2:1} So I said to myself, "Come on, let's try pleasure. Let's look for the good things in life." But I found that this is also meaningless. {2:2} I said of laughter, "It is madness," and of pleasure, "What does it accomplish?" {2:3} I explored with my mind how to stimulate my body with wine while my mind was guiding me wisely, and how to take hold of folly, until I could see what good there is for the sons of men to do under heaven during the few days of their lives. {2:4} I made great works; I built houses and planted vineyards for myself. {2:5} I made gardens and parks for myself, and I planted all kinds of fruit trees in them. {2:6} I made pools of water to irrigate a forest of growing trees. {2:7} I acquired male and female servants, and had servants born in my house. I also owned more herds and flocks than anyone in Jerusalem before me. {2:8} I amassed silver and gold for myself, and the treasure of kings and provinces. I acquired male and female singers, and a harem as well—the delights of a man's heart. {2:9} I became greater by far than anyone in Jerusalem before me. In all this my wisdom stayed with me. {2:10} I denied myself nothing my eyes desired; I refused my heart no pleasure. My heart took delight in all my labor, and this was the reward for all my toil. {2:11} Yet when I surveyed all that my hands had done and what I had toiled to achieve, everything was meaningless, a chasing after the wind; nothing was gained under the sun. {2:12} Then I turned my thoughts to consider wisdom, and also madness and folly. What more can the king's successor do than what has already been done? {2:13} I saw that wisdom is better than folly, just as light is better than darkness. {2:14} The wise have eyes in their heads, while the fool walks in the darkness; but I came to realize that the same fate overtakes them both. {2:15} Then I said to myself, "The fate of the fool will overtake me also. What then do I gain by being wise?" I said to myself, "This too is meaningless." {2:16} For the wise, like the fool, will not be long remembered; the days have already come when both will have been forgotten. Like the fool, the wise too must die! {2:17} So I hated life, because the work that is done under the sun was grievous to me. All of it is meaningless, a chasing after the wind. {2:18} I hated all the things I had toiled for under the sun, because I must leave them to the one who comes after me. {2:19} And who knows whether that person will be wise or foolish? Yet they will have control over all the fruit of my toil into which I have poured my effort and skill under the sun. This too is meaningless. {2:20} So my heart began to despair over all my toilsome labor under the sun. {2:21} For a person may labor with wisdom, knowledge, and skill, and then they must leave all they own to another who has not toiled for it. This too is meaningless and a great misfortune. {2:22} What do people get for all the toil and anxious striving with which they labor under the sun? {2:23} All their days their work is grief and pain; even at night their minds do not rest. This too is meaningless. {2:24} A person can do nothing better than to eat and drink and find satisfaction in their own toil. This too, I see, is from the hand of God, {2:25} for without him, who can eat or find enjoyment? {2:26} To the person who pleases him, God gives wisdom, knowledge and happiness, but to the sinner he gives the task of gathering and storing up wealth to hand it over to the one who pleases God. This too is meaningless, a chasing after the wind.

{3:1} **There is a time for everything, and a season for every activity under the heavens:** {3:2} a time to be born and a time to die, a time to plant and a time to uproot, {3:3} a time to kill and a time to heal, a time to tear down and a time to build, {3:4} a time to weep and a time to laugh, a time to mourn and a time to dance, {3:5} a time to scatter stones and a time to gather them, a time to embrace and a time to refrain from embracing, {3:6} a time to search and a time to give up, a time to keep and a time to throw away, {3:7} a time to tear and a time to mend, a time to be silent and a time to speak, {3:8} a time to love and a time to hate, a time for war and a time for peace. {3:9} What do workers gain from their toil? {3:10} I have seen the burden God has laid on the human race. {3:11} He has made everything beautiful in its time. He has also set eternity in the human heart; yet no one can fathom what God has done from beginning to end. {3:12} I know that there is nothing better for people than to be happy and to do good while they live. {3:13} That each of them may eat and drink, and find satisfaction in all their toil—this is the gift of God. {3:14} I know that everything God does will endure forever; nothing can be added to it and nothing taken from it. God does it so that people will fear him. {3:15} Whatever is has already been, and what will be has been before; and God will call the past to account. {3:16} And I saw something else under the sun: In the place of judgment—wickedness was there, in the place of justice—wickedness was there. {3:17} I said to myself, "God will bring into judgment both the righteous and the wicked, for there will be a time for every activity, a time to judge every deed." {3:18} I also said to myself, "As for humans, God tests them so that they may see that they are like the animals. {3:19} Surely the fate of human beings is like that of the animals; the same fate awaits them both: As one dies, so dies the other. All have the same breath; humans have no advantage over animals. Everything is meaningless. {3:20} All go to the same place; all come from dust, and to dust all return. {3:21} Who knows if the human spirit rises upward and if the spirit of the animal goes down into the earth?" {3:22} So I saw that there is nothing better for a person than to enjoy their work, because that is their lot. For who can bring them to see what will happen after them?

{4:1} So I observed all the oppression that occurs under the sun. I saw the tears of the oppressed, and they have no comforter; power was on the side of their oppressors, and they have no comforter. {4:2} Therefore, I praised the dead who are already dead more than the living who are still alive. {4:3} But better off than both of them is the one who has not yet been born, who has not seen the evil that is done under the sun. {4:4} Then I saw that all toil and all skill in work come from one person's envy of another. This also is vanity and a chasing after wind. {4:5} The fool folds his hands and consumes his own flesh. {4:6} Better is a handful of quietness than two hands full of toil and a striving after wind. {4:7} Again, I saw vanity under the sun: {4:8} There is one alone, without even a companion; he has neither child nor sibling, yet there is no end to all his toil, and his eyes are never satisfied with riches. "For whom am I toiling," he asks, "and depriving myself of pleasure?" This also is vanity and an unhappy business. {4:9} **Two are better than one because they**

have a good reward for their toil. {4:10} For if they fall, one will lift up the other; but woe to one who is alone and falls and does not have another to help. {4:11} Again, if two lie together, they keep warm; but how can one keep warm alone? {4:12} And though one might prevail against another, two will withstand one. A threefold cord is not quickly broken. {4:13} Better is a poor but wise youth than an old but foolish king who no longer knows how to take advice. {4:14} For the poor man came out of prison to reign, although he was born poor in his kingdom. {4:15} **I saw all the living who walk under the sun, with the youth who was to stand up in the king's place.** {4:16} There was no end to all the people, all of whom he led. Yet those who come later will not rejoice in him. Surely this also is vanity and a chasing after wind.

{5:1} When you go to the house of God, be careful to listen more than to offer the sacrifice of fools, for they do not realize that they are doing wrong. {5:2} Do not be hasty with your mouth, and do not let your heart hurry to utter anything before God. God is in heaven, and you are on earth, so let your words be few. {5:3} Dreams come from much activity, and the words of fools come from many words. {5:4} When you make a vow to God, do not delay to fulfill it, for he takes no pleasure in fools. Pay what you vow. {5:5} It is better not to vow than to vow and not fulfill it. {5:6} Do not let your mouth lead you into sin, and do not say before the messenger that it was a mistake. Why should God be angry at your words and destroy the work of your hands? {5:7} In many dreams and in many words there are also vanities, but fear God. {5:8} If you see oppression of the poor and perversion of justice and righteousness in a province, do not be amazed at the situation, for a higher official watches over the high officials, and even higher ones are over them. {5:9} The produce of the land is taken by all; even the king profits from the fields. {5:10} Those who love money will never have enough. How meaningless to think that wealth brings true happiness! {5:11} As goods increase, so do those who consume them. And what benefit are they to the owner except to feast his eyes on them? {5:12} The sleep of a laborer is sweet, whether he eats little or much, but the abundance of a rich man permits him no sleep. {5:13} There is a grievous evil I have seen under the sun: wealth hoarded to the harm of its owner. {5:14} That wealth is lost in a bad venture, so when he fathers a son, there is nothing left for him. {5:15} Naked a man comes from his mother's womb, and as he comes, so he departs. He takes nothing from his labor that he can carry in his hand. {5:16} This too is a grievous evil: As everyone comes, so they depart, and what do they gain, since they toil for the wind? {5:17} All their days they eat in darkness, with much sorrow, sickness, and anger. {5:18} Here is what I have seen to be good and fitting: to eat, to drink, and to find enjoyment in all the labor one does under the sun during the few days of life that God has given, for this is his lot. {5:19} Everyone also to whom God has given wealth and possessions and power to enjoy them, and to accept his lot and find enjoyment in his toil—this is the gift of God. {5:20} For they will not dwell overmuch on the days of their life because God keeps them occupied with joy in their hearts.

{6:1} There is a troubling thing I have seen under the sun, and it is widespread among people: {6:2} A man to whom God has given riches, wealth, and honor, so that he lacks nothing for his soul of all that he desires, yet God does not give him the power to enjoy it, but a stranger consumes it. This is vanity and a painful affliction. {6:3} If a man fathers a hundred children and lives many years, so that the days of his years are many, but his soul is not satisfied with good things, and he also has no burial, I say that an untimely birth is better than he. {6:4} For he comes in vanity and departs in darkness, and his name will be covered with darkness. {6:5} Moreover, he has not seen the sun or known anything; this has more rest than the other. {6:6} Even if he lives a thousand years twice over, yet he has seen no good—do not all go to the same place? {6:7} **All the toil of man is for his mouth, yet his appetite is not satisfied.** {6:8} For what advantage has the wise man over the fool? And what does the poor man have who knows how to conduct himself before the living? {6:9} Better is the sight of the eyes than the wandering of the appetite; this also is vanity and a striving after wind. {6:10} Whatever has come to be has already been named, and it is known what man is, and that he is not able to dispute with one stronger than he. {6:11} The more words, the more vanity, and what is the advantage to man? {6:12} For who knows what is good for man while he lives the few days of his vain life, which he passes like a shadow? For who can tell man what will be after him under the sun?

{7:1} A good reputation is better than expensive perfume, and the day of death is better than the day of birth. {7:2} It is better to go to a house of mourning than to a house of feasting, for death is the destiny of everyone; the living should take this to heart. {7:3} Sorrow is better than laughter, for sadness can improve the heart. {7:4} The wise prefer the house of mourning, but fools prefer the house of pleasure. {7:5} It is better to heed the rebuke of the wise than to listen to the song of fools. {7:6} Like crackling thorns under a pot, so is the laughter of fools. This too is meaningless. {7:7} Oppression can make a wise man mad, and a bribe can corrupt the heart. {7:8} The end of a matter is better than its beginning, and patience is better than pride. {7:9} Do not be quickly provoked in your spirit, for anger resides in the lap of fools. {7:10} Do not say, "Why were the old days better than these?" For it is not wise to ask such questions. {7:11} Wisdom, like an inheritance, is good, and it benefits those who see the sun. {7:12} Wisdom is a shelter, as money is a shelter, but the advantage of knowledge is this: Wisdom preserves the life of its possessor. {7:13} Consider what God has done: Who can straighten what he has made crooked? {7:14} In the day of prosperity, be joyful, but in the day of adversity, consider: God has made one as well as the other, so that no one can discover anything about their future. {7:15} In my meaningless life, I have seen both of these: the righteous perishing in their righteousness, and the wicked living long in their wickedness. {7:16} Do not be overly righteous, nor overly wise. Why destroy yourself? {7:17} Do not be overly wicked, nor be foolish. Why die before your time? {7:18} It is good to grasp the one and not let go of the other. Whoever fears God will avoid all extremes. {7:19} Wisdom makes one wise person more powerful than ten rulers in a city. {7:20} Indeed, there is no one on earth who is righteous, no one who does what is right and never sins. {7:21} Do not pay attention to every word people say, or you may hear your servant cursing you— {7:22} for you know in your heart that many times you yourself have cursed others. {7:23} All this I tested by wisdom and I said, "I am determined to be wise"—but this was beyond me. {7:24} Whatever is far off and most profound— who can discover it? {7:25} I applied my heart to understand, to search, and to seek out wisdom and an explanation for things, and to understand the stupidity of wickedness and the madness of folly. {7:26} I find more bitter than death the woman who is a snare, whose heart is a trap, and whose hands are chains. The man who pleases God will escape her, but the sinner she will ensnare. {7:27} "Look," says the Teacher, "this is what I have discovered: Adding one thing to another to discover the scheme of things— {7:28} while I was still searching but not finding— I found one upright man among a thousand, but not one upright woman among them all. {7:29} This only have I found: God created mankind upright, but they have gone in search of many schemes."

{8:1} Who is like the wise man? Who understands the interpretation of things? A person's wisdom lights up their face, softening its boldness. {8:2} I advise you to obey the king's command, because of the oath sworn before God. {8:3} Do not be quick to leave his presence. Do not stand up for an evil cause, for he does whatever he pleases. {8:4} Where the word of a king holds power, who can challenge him, saying, "What are you doing?" {8:5} Whoever obeys the command will come to no harm, and the heart of the wise will discern both time and judgment. {8:6} As there is a time and judgment for every purpose, so the misery of man weighs heavily upon him. {8:7} Man does not know what will happen, and who can tell him when it will happen? {8:8} No one has power over the spirit to retain it, and no one has power in the day of death. There is no discharge in that war, and wickedness will not deliver those devoted to it. {8:9} I have seen all this and applied my heart to every work done under the sun. There is a time when one man rules over another to his own harm. {8:10} Then I observed the wicked being buried—those who had come and gone from the holy place—and they were forgotten in the city where they had acted thus. This too is meaningless. {8:11} Because sentence against an evil deed is not executed quickly, the hearts of people are filled with the desire to do evil. {8:12} Even though a sinner may do evil a hundred times and prolong his days, yet I know that it will be well with those who fear God, because they fear before him. {8:13} But it will not be well with the wicked, nor will they prolong their days, which are as fleeting as a shadow, because they do not fear God. {8:14} There is a vanity that occurs on earth: Sometimes the righteous are treated according to the deeds of the wicked, and sometimes the wicked are treated according to the deeds of the righteous. I said that this too is meaningless. {8:15} So I commended mirth, because there is nothing better for a person under the sun than to eat, drink, and be merry, for these pleasures accompany their labor all the days of their life, which God gives them under the sun. {8:16} When I applied my heart to understand wisdom and to observe the work that is done on the earth—though one sees no sleep day or night— {8:17} then I saw all the work of God, that a man cannot discover the work that is done under the sun. However much a man may labor in seeking, he will not find it out; even though a wise man claims to know, he cannot comprehend it.

{9:1} For all this, I considered in my heart to declare that the righteous and the wise, along with their deeds, are in the hand of God. No one knows whether love or hatred awaits them. {9:2} Everything comes alike to all: one fate awaits the righteous and the wicked, the good and the clean, the unclean, those who sacrifice, and those who do not. As it is for the good, so it is for the sinner; as for those who swear oaths, so for those who fear them. {9:3} This is an evil among all the deeds done under the sun: that one fate awaits all. Yes, the hearts of the sons of men are full of evil, and madness is in their hearts while they live, and afterward they go to the dead. {9:4} For to him who is joined to all the living, there is hope; for a living dog is better than a dead lion. {9:5} The living know that they will die, but the dead know nothing; they have no more reward, for their memory is forgotten. {9:6} Their love, hatred, and envy have already perished; they have no more share forever in anything done under the sun. {9:7} Go, eat your bread with joy, and drink your wine with a merry heart; for God now accepts your works. {9:8} Let your garments always be white, and let your head lack no ointment. {9:9} Live joyfully with the wife you love all the days of your vain life, which God has given you under the sun, all the days of your vanity; for that is your portion in this life, and in your labor which you take under the sun. {9:10} Whatever your hand finds to do, do it with your might; for there is no work, nor device, nor knowledge, nor wisdom in the grave, where you go. {9:11} *I returned and saw under the sun that the race is not to the swift, nor the battle to the strong, nor bread to the wise, nor riches to men of understanding, nor favor to men of skill; but time and chance happen to them all.* {9:12} For man also does not know his time: like fish taken in a cruel net, and birds caught in a snare, so are the sons of men snared in an evil time, when it falls suddenly upon them. {9:13} This wisdom I have also seen under the sun, and it seemed great to me: {9:14} There was a little city with few men within it, and a great king came against it, besieged it, and built great bulwarks against it. {9:15} Now there was found in it a poor wise man, and by his wisdom he delivered the city. Yet no one remembered that same poor man. {9:16} Then I said, "Wisdom is better than strength." Nevertheless, the poor man's wisdom is despised, and his words are not heard. {9:17} The words of wise men are heard in quiet more than the cry of him who rules among fools. {9:18} Wisdom is better than weapons of war, but one sinner destroys much good.

{10:1} Dead flies cause the ointment of the apothecary to send forth a stinking savour: so does a little folly him who is in reputation for wisdom and honour. {10:2} A wise man's heart is at his right hand, but a fool's heart is at his left. {10:3} Even when a fool walks by the way, his wisdom fails him, and he says to everyone that he is a fool. {10:4} If the spirit of the ruler rises up against you, do not leave your place; for yielding pacifies great offenses. {10:5} There is an evil I have seen under the sun, as an error which proceeds from the ruler: {10:6} Folly is set in great dignity, and the rich sit in low place. {10:7} I have seen servants upon horses, and princes walking as servants upon the earth. {10:8} He who digs a pit shall fall into it, and whoever breaks a hedge, a serpent shall bite him. {10:9} Whoever removes stones shall be hurt thereby, and he who cleaves wood shall be endangered thereby. {10:10} If the iron is blunt, and one does not whet the edge, then must he put to more strength; but wisdom is profitable to direct. {10:11} *Surely the serpent will bite without enchantment; and a babbler is no better.* {10:12} The words of a wise man's mouth are gracious, but the lips of a fool will swallow up himself. {10:13} The beginning of the words of his mouth is foolishness, and the end of his talk is mischievous madness. {10:14} A fool also is full of words; a man cannot tell what shall be, and what shall be after him, who can tell him? {10:15} The labor of the foolish wearies every one of them, because he knows not how to go to the city. {10:16} Woe to you, O land, when your king is a child, and your princes eat in the morning! {10:17} Blessed are you, O land, when your king is the son of nobles, and your princes eat in due season, for strength, and not for drunkenness! {10:18} By much slothfulness the building decays, and through idleness of the hands the house droppeth through. {10:19} A feast is made for laughter, and wine makes merry; but money answers all things. {10:20} *Curse not the king, no not in your thought; and curse not the rich in your bedchamber: for a bird of the air shall carry the voice, and that which has wings shall tell the matter.*

{11:1} Cast your bread upon the waters, for you shall find it after many days. {11:2} Give a portion to seven, and also to eight; for you know not what evil shall be upon the earth. {11:3} If the clouds are full of rain, they empty themselves upon the earth; and if the tree falls toward the south, or toward the north, in the place where the tree falls, there it shall be. {11:4} He who observes the wind shall not sow, and he who regards the clouds shall not reap. {11:5} As you know not what is the way of the spirit, nor how the bones grow in the womb of her who is with child, even so you know not the works of God who makes all. {11:6} *In the morning sow your seed, and in the evening withhold not your hand: for you know not whether shall prosper, either this or that, or whether they both shall be alike good.* {11:7} Truly the light is sweet, and a pleasant thing it is for the eyes to behold the sun. {11:8} But if a man lives many years, and rejoices in them all, yet let him remember the days of darkness; for they shall be many. All that comes is vanity. {11:9} Rejoice, O young man, in your youth; and let your heart cheer you in the days of your youth, and walk in the ways of your heart, and in the sight of your eyes: but know that for all these things God will bring you into judgment. {11:10} Therefore remove sorrow from your heart, and put away evil from your flesh: for childhood and youth are vanity.

{12:1} Remember your Creator in the days of your youth, while the evil days come not, nor the years draw nigh, when you shall say, "I have no pleasure in them;" {12:2} While the sun, or the light, or the moon, or the stars, be not darkened, nor the clouds return after the rain: {12:3} In the day when the keepers of the house shall tremble, and the strong men shall bow themselves, and the grinders cease because they are few, and those that look out of the windows be darkened, {12:4} And the doors shall be shut in the streets, when the sound of the grinding is low, and he shall rise up at the voice of the bird, and all the daughters of music shall be brought low; {12:5} Also when they shall be afraid of that which is high, and fears shall be in the way, and the almond tree shall flourish, and the grasshopper shall be a burden, and desire shall fail: because man goes to his long home, and the mourners go about the streets: {12:6} Or ever the silver cord be loosed, or the golden bowl be broken, or the pitcher be broken at the fountain, or the wheel broken at the cistern. {12:7} Then shall the dust return to the earth as it was: and the spirit shall return unto God who gave it. {12:8} Vanity of vanities, says the preacher; all is vanity. {12:9} And moreover, because the preacher was wise, he still taught the people knowledge; yes, he gave good heed, and sought out, and set in order many proverbs. {12:10} The preacher sought to find out acceptable words: and that which was written was upright, even words of truth. {12:11} The words of the wise are as goads, and as nails fastened by the masters of assemblies, which are given from one shepherd. {12:12} And further, by these, my son, be admonished: of making many books there is no end; and much study is a weariness of the flesh. {12:13} *Let us hear the conclusion of the whole matter: Fear God, and keep his commandments: for this is the whole duty of man.* {12:14} For God shall bring every work into judgment, with every secret thing, whether it be good, or whether it be evil.

Song of Songs

{1:1} The Song of Songs, which is Solomon's. {1:2} Let him kiss me with the kisses of his mouth: for your love is better than wine. {1:3} Because of the fragrance of your good ointments, your name is as ointment poured forth; therefore the virgins love you. {1:4} **Draw me, we will run after you: the king has brought me into his chambers: we will be glad and rejoice in you, we will remember your love more than wine: the upright love you.** {1:5} I am black, but comely, O daughters of Jerusalem, as the tents of Kedar, as the curtains of Solomon. {1:6} Do not look upon me, because I am black, because the sun has looked upon me: my mother's children were angry with me; they made me the keeper of the vineyards; but my own vineyard have I not kept. {1:7} Tell me, O you whom my soul loves, where you feed, where you make your flock to rest at noon: for why should I be as one that turns aside by the flocks of your companions? {1:8} If you do not know, O fairest among women, go your way forth by the footsteps of the flock, and feed your kids beside the shepherds' tents. {1:9} I have compared you, O my love, to a company of horses in Pharaoh's chariots. {1:10} Your cheeks are comely with rows of jewels, your neck with chains of gold. {1:11} We will make borders of gold with studs of silver. {1:12} While the king sits at his table, my spikenard sends forth the smell thereof. {1:13} A bundle of myrrh is my well-beloved unto me; he shall lie all night betwixt my breasts. {1:14} My beloved is unto me as a cluster of camphire in the vineyards of En-gedi. {1:15} Behold, you are fair, my love; behold, you are fair; you have doves' eyes. {1:16} Behold, you are fair, my beloved, yes, pleasant: also our bed is green. {1:17} The beams of our house are cedar, and our rafters of fir.

{2:1} I am the rose of Sharon, and the lily of the valleys. {2:2} As the lily among thorns, so is my love among the daughters. {2:3} As the apple tree among the trees of the wood, so is my beloved among the sons. I sat down under his shadow with great delight, and his fruit was sweet to my taste. {2:4} He brought me to the banqueting house, and his banner over me was love. {2:5} Stay me with flagons, comfort me with apples: for I am sick of love. {2:6} His left hand is under my head, and his right hand doth embrace me. {2:7} I charge you, O ye daughters of Jerusalem, by the roes, and by the hinds of the field, that ye stir not up, nor awake my love, till he please. {2:8} The voice of my beloved! behold, he cometh leaping upon the mountains, skipping upon the hills. {2:9} My beloved is like a roe or a young hart: behold, he standeth behind our wall, he looketh forth at the windows, shewing himself through the lattice. {2:10} My beloved spake, and said unto me, Rise up, my love, my fair one, and come away. {2:11} For, lo, the winter is past, the rain is over and gone; {2:12} The flowers appear on the earth; the time of the singing of birds is come, and the voice of the turtle is heard in our land; {2:13} The fig tree putteth forth her green figs, and the vines with the tender grape give a good smell. Arise, my love, my fair one, and come away. {2:14} O my dove, that art in the clefts of the rock, in the secret places of the stairs, let me see thy countenance, let me hear thy voice; for sweet is thy voice, and thy countenance is comely. {2:15} Take us the foxes, the little foxes, that spoil the vines: for our vines have tender grapes. {2:16} **My beloved is mine, and I am his: he feedeth among the lilies.** {2:17} Until the day break, and the shadows flee away, turn, my beloved, and be thou like a roe or a young hart upon the mountains of Bether.

{3:1} By night on my bed I sought him whom my soul loveth: I sought him, but I found him not. {3:2} I will rise now, and go about the city in the streets, and in the broad ways I will seek him whom my soul loveth: I sought him, but I found him not. {3:3} The watchmen that go about the city found me: [to whom I said,] Saw ye him whom my soul loveth? {3:4} *[It was]* *but a little that I passed from them, but I found him whom my soul loveth: I held him, and would not let him go, until I had brought him into my mother's house, and into the chamber of her that conceived me.* {3:5} I charge you, O ye daughters of Jerusalem, by the roes, and by the hinds of the field, that ye stir not up, nor awake [my] love, till he please. {3:6} Who [is] this that cometh out of the wilderness like pillars of smoke, perfumed with myrrh and frankincense, with all powders of the merchant? {3:7} Behold his bed, which [is] Solomon's; threescore valiant men [are] about it, of the valiant of Israel. {3:8} They all hold swords, [being] expert in war: every man [hath] his sword upon his thigh because of fear in the night. {3:9} King Solomon made himself a chariot of the wood of Lebanon. {3:10} He made the pillars thereof [of] silver, the bottom thereof [of] gold, the covering of it [of] purple, the midst thereof being paved [with] love, for the daughters of Jerusalem. {3:11} Go forth, O ye daughters of Zion, and behold king Solomon with the crown wherewith his mother crowned him in the day of his espousals, and in the day of the gladness of his heart.

{4:1} Behold, thou [art] fair, my love; behold, thou [art] fair; thou [hast] doves' eyes within thy locks: thy hair [is] as a flock of goats, that appear from mount Gilead. {4:2} Thy teeth [are] like a flock [of sheep that are even] shorn, which came up from the washing; whereof every one bear twins, and none [is] barren among them. {4:3} Thy lips [are] like a thread of scarlet, and thy speech [is] comely: thy temples [are] like a piece of a pomegranate within thy locks. {4:4} Thy neck [is] like the tower of David builded for an armoury, whereon there hang a thousand bucklers, all shields of mighty men. {4:5} Thy two breasts [are] like two young roes that are twins, which feed among the lilies. {4:6} Until the day break, and the shadows flee away, I will get me to the mountain of myrrh, and to the hill of frankincense. {4:7} **Thou [art] all fair, my love; [there is] no spot in thee.** {4:8} Come with me from Lebanon, [my] spouse, with me from Lebanon: look from the top of Amana, from the top of Shenir and Hermon, from the lions' dens, from the mountains of the leopards. {4:9} Thou hast ravished my heart, my sister, [my] spouse; thou hast ravished my heart with one of thine eyes, with one chain of thy neck. {4:10} How fair is thy love, my sister, [my] spouse! how much better is thy love than wine! and the smell of thine ointments than all spices! {4:11} Thy lips, O [my] spouse, drop [as] the honeycomb: honey and milk [are] under thy tongue; and the smell of thy garments [is] like the smell of Lebanon. {4:12} A garden inclosed [is] my sister, [my] spouse; a spring shut up, a fountain sealed. {4:13} Thy plants [are] an orchard of pomegranates, with pleasant fruits; camphire, with spikenard, {4:14} Spikenard and saffron; calamus and cinnamon, with all trees of frankincense; myrrh and aloes, with all the chief spices: {4:15} A fountain of gardens, a well of living waters, and streams from Lebanon. {4:16} Awake, O north wind; and come, thou south; blow upon my garden, [that] the spices thereof may flow out. Let my beloved come into his garden, and eat his pleasant fruits.

{5:1} I am come into my garden, my sister, [my] spouse: I have gathered my myrrh with my spice; I have eaten my honeycomb with my honey; I have drunk my wine with my milk: eat, O friends; drink, yea, drink abundantly, O beloved. {5:2} I sleep, but my heart waketh: [it is] the voice of my beloved that knocketh, [saying,] Open to me, my sister, my love, my dove, my undefiled: for my head is filled with dew, [and] my locks with the drops of the night. {5:3} I have put off my coat; how shall I put it on? I have washed my feet; how shall I defile them? {5:4} My beloved put in his hand by the hole [of the door,] and my bowels were moved for him. {5:5} I rose up to open to my beloved; and my hands dropped [with] myrrh, and my fingers [with] sweet smelling myrrh, upon the handles of the lock. {5:6} I opened to my beloved; but my beloved had withdrawn himself, [and] was gone: my soul failed when he spake: I sought him, but I could not find him; I called him, but he gave me no answer. {5:7} The watchmen that went about the city found me, they smote me, they wounded me; the keepers of the walls took away my veil from me. {5:8} I charge you, O daughters of Jerusalem, if ye find my beloved, that ye tell him, that I [am] sick of love. {5:9} What [is] thy beloved more than [another] beloved, O thou fairest among women? what [is] thy beloved more than [another] beloved, that thou dost so charge us? {5:10} My beloved [is] white and ruddy, the chiefest among ten thousand. {5:11} His head [is as] the most fine gold, his locks [are] bushy, [and] black as a raven. {5:12} His eyes [are] as [the eyes] of doves by the rivers of waters, washed with milk, [and] fitly set. {5:13} His cheeks [are] as a bed of spices, [as] sweet flowers: his lips [like] lilies, dropping sweet smelling myrrh. {5:14} **His hands [are as] gold rings set with the beryl: his belly [is as] bright ivory overlaid [with] sapphires.** {5:15} His legs [are as] pillars of marble, set upon sockets of fine gold: his countenance [is] as Lebanon, excellent as the cedars. {5:16} **His mouth [is] most sweet: yea, he [is] altogether lovely. This [is] my beloved, and this [is] my friend, O daughters of Jerusalem.**

{6:1} Whither is thy beloved gone, O thou fairest among women? whither is thy beloved turned aside? that we may seek him with thee. {6:2} My beloved is gone down into his garden, to the beds of spices, to feed in the gardens, and to gather lilies. {6:3} ***I [am] my beloved's, and my beloved [is] mine: he feedeth among the lilies.*** {6:4} Thou [art] beautiful, O my love, as Tirzah, comely as Jerusalem, terrible as [an army] with banners. {6:5} Turn away thine eyes from me, for they have overcome me: thy hair [is] as a flock of goats that appear from Gilead. {6:6} Thy teeth [are] as a flock of sheep which go up from the washing, whereof every one beareth twins, and [there is] not one barren among them. {6:7} As a piece of a pomegranate [are] thy temples within thy locks. {6:8} There are threescore queens, and fourscore concubines, and virgins without number. {6:9} My dove, my undefiled is [but] one; she [is] the [only] one of her mother, she [is] the choice [one] of her that bare her. The daughters saw her, and blessed her; [yea,] the queens and the concubines, and they praised her. {6:10} Who [is] she [that] looketh forth as the morning, fair as the moon, clear as the sun, [and] terrible as [an army] with banners? {6:11} I went down into the garden of nuts to see the fruits of the valley, [and] to see whether the vine flourished, [and] the pomegranates budded. {6:12} Or ever I was aware, my soul made me [like] the chariots of Amminadib. {6:13} Return, return, O Shulamite; return, return, that we may look upon thee. What will ye see in the Shulamite? As it were the company of two armies.

{7:1} How beautiful are thy feet with shoes, O prince's daughter! the joints of thy thighs [are] like jewels, the work of the hands of a cunning workman. {7:2} Thy navel [is like] a round goblet, [which] wanteth not liquor: thy belly [is like] an heap of wheat set about with lilies. {7:3} Thy two breasts [are] like two young roes [that are] twins. {7:4} Thy neck [is] as a tower of ivory; thine eyes [like] the fishpools in Heshbon, by the gate of Bath-rabbim: thy nose [is] as the tower of Lebanon which looketh toward Damascus. {7:5} Thine head upon thee [is] like Carmel, and the hair of thine head like purple; the king [is] held in the galleries. {7:6} How fair and how pleasant art thou, O love, for delights! {7:7} This thy stature is like to a palm tree, and thy breasts to clusters [of grapes.] {7:8} I said, I will go up to the palm tree, I will take hold of the boughs thereof: now also thy breasts shall be as clusters of the vine, and the smell of thy nose like apples; {7:9} And the roof of thy mouth like the best wine for my beloved, that goeth [down] sweetly, causing the lips of those that are asleep to speak. {7:10} I [am] my beloved's, and his desire [is] toward me. {7:11} Come, my beloved, let us go forth into the field; let us lodge in the villages. {7:12} Let us get up early to the vineyards; let us see if the vine flourish, [whether] the tender grape appear, [and] the pomegranates bud forth: there will I give thee my loves. {7:13} The mandrakes give a smell, and at our gates [are] all manner of pleasant [fruits,] new and old, [which] I have laid up for thee, O my beloved.

{8:1} O that thou [wert] as my brother, that sucked the breasts of my mother! [when] I should find thee without, I would kiss thee; yea, I should not be despised. {8:2} I would lead thee, [and] bring thee into my mother's house, [who] would instruct me: I would cause thee to drink of spiced wine of the juice of my pomegranate. {8:3} His left hand [should be] under my head, and his right hand should embrace me. {8:4} I charge you, O daughters of Jerusalem, that ye stir not up, nor awake [my] love, until he please. {8:5} Who [is] this that cometh up from the wilderness, leaning upon her beloved? I raised thee up under the apple tree: there thy mother brought thee forth: there she brought thee forth [that] bare thee. {8:6} **Set me as a seal upon thine heart, as a seal upon thine arm: for love [is] strong as death; jealousy [is] cruel as the grave: the coals thereof [are] coals of fire, [which hath a] most vehement flame.** {8:7} Many waters cannot quench love, neither can the floods drown it: if [a] man would give all the substance of his house for love, it would utterly be contemned. {8:8} We have a little sister, and she hath no breasts: what shall we do for our sister in the day when she shall be spoken for? {8:9} If she [be] a wall, we will build upon her a palace of silver: and if she [be] a door, we will inclose her with boards of cedar. {8:10} I [am] a wall, and my breasts like towers: then was I in his eyes as one that found favour. {8:11} Solomon had a vineyard at Baal-hamon; he let out the vineyard unto keepers; every one for the fruit thereof was to bring a thousand [pieces] of silver. {8:12} My vineyard, which [is] mine, [is] before me: thou, O Solomon, [must have] a thousand, and those that keep the fruit thereof two hundred. {8:13} Thou that dwellest in the gardens, the companions hearken to thy voice: cause me to hear [it.] {8:14} Make haste, my beloved, and be thou like to a roe or to a young hart upon the mountains of spices.

Isaiah

{1:1} The vision of Isaiah the son of Amoz, which he saw concerning Judah and Jerusalem in the days of Uzziah, Jotham, Ahaz, [and] Hezekiah, kings of Judah. {1:2} Hear, O heavens, and give ear, O earth: for the LORD hath spoken, I have nourished and brought up children, and they have rebelled against me. {1:3} The ox knoweth his owner, and the ass his master's crib: [but] Israel doth not know, my people doth not consider. {1:4} Ah sinful nation, a people laden with iniquity, a seed of evildoers, children that are corrupters: they have forsaken the LORD, they have provoked the Holy One of Israel unto anger, they are gone away backward. {1:5} Why should ye be stricken any more? ye will revolt more and more: the whole head is sick, and the whole heart faint. {1:6} From the sole of the foot even unto the head [there is] no soundness in it; [but] wounds, and bruises, and putrifying sores: they have not been closed, neither bound up, neither mollified with ointment. {1:7} Your country [is] desolate, your cities [are] burned with fire: your land, strangers devour it in your presence, and [it is] desolate, as overthrown by strangers. {1:8} And the daughter of Zion is left as a cottage in a vineyard, as a lodge in a garden of cucumbers, as a besieged city. {1:9} Except the LORD of hosts had left unto us a very small remnant, we should have been as Sodom, [and] we should have been like unto Gomorrah. {1:10} Hear the word of the LORD, ye rulers of Sodom; give ear unto the law of our God, ye people of Gomorrah. {1:11} To what purpose [is] the multitude of your sacrifices unto me? saith the LORD: I am full of the burnt offerings of rams, and the fat of fed beasts; and I delight not in the blood of bullocks, or of lambs, or of he goats. {1:12} When ye come to appear before me, who hath required this at your hand, to tread my courts? {1:13} Bring no more vain oblations; incense is an abomination unto me; the new moons and sabbaths, the calling of assemblies, I cannot away with; [it is] iniquity, even the solemn meeting. {1:14} Your new moons and your appointed feasts my soul hateth: they are a trouble unto me; I am weary to bear [them.] {1:15} And when ye spread forth your hands, I will hide mine eyes from you: yea, when ye make many prayers, I will not hear: your hands are full of blood. {1:16} Wash you, make you clean; put away the evil of your doings from before mine eyes; cease to do evil; {1:17} Learn to do well; seek judgment, relieve the oppressed, judge the fatherless, plead for the widow. {1:18} Come now, and let us reason together, saith the LORD: though your sins be as scarlet, they shall be as white as snow; though they be red like crimson, they shall be as wool. {1:19} If ye be willing and obedient, ye shall eat the good of the land; {1:20} But if ye refuse and rebel, ye shall be devoured with the sword: for the mouth of the LORD hath spoken [it.] {1:21} How is the faithful city become an harlot! it was full of judgment; righteousness lodged in it; but now murderers. {1:22} Thy silver is become dross, thy wine mixed with water: {1:23} Thy princes [are] rebellious, and companions of thieves: every one loveth gifts, and followeth after rewards: they judge not the fatherless, neither doth the cause of the widow come unto them. {1:24} Therefore saith the Lord, the LORD of hosts, the mighty One of Israel, Ah, I will ease me of mine adversaries, and avenge me of mine enemies: {1:25} And I will turn my hand upon thee, and purely purge away thy dross, and take away all thy tin: {1:26} And I will restore thy judges as at the first, and thy counsellors as at the beginning: afterward thou shalt be called, The city of righteousness, the faithful city. {1:27} Zion shall be redeemed with judgment, and her converts with righteousness. {1:28} And the destruction of the transgressors and of the sinners [shall be] together, and they that forsake the LORD shall be consumed. {1:29} For they shall be ashamed of the oaks which ye have desired, and ye shall be confounded for the gardens that ye have chosen. {1:30} For ye shall be as an oak whose leaf fadeth, and as a garden that hath no water. {1:31} And the strong shall be as tow, and the maker of it as a spark, and they shall both burn together, and none shall quench [them.]

{2:1} The word that Isaiah the son of Amoz saw concerning Judah and Jerusalem. {2:2} And it shall come to pass in the last days, [that] the mountain of the LORD'S house shall be established in the top of the mountains, and shall be exalted above the hills; and all nations shall flow unto it. {2:3} And many people shall go and say, Come ye, and let us go up to the mountain of the LORD, to the house of the God of Jacob; and he will teach us of his ways, and we will walk in his paths: for out of Zion shall go forth the law, and the word of the LORD from Jerusalem. {2:4} And he shall judge among the nations, and shall rebuke many people: and they shall beat their swords into plowshares, and their spears into pruninghooks: nation shall not lift up sword against nation, neither shall they learn war any more. {2:5} O house of Jacob, come ye, and let us walk in the light of the LORD. {2:6} Therefore thou hast forsaken thy people the house of Jacob, because they be replenished from the east, and [are] soothsayers like the Philistines, and they please themselves in the children of strangers. {2:7} Their land also is full of silver and gold, neither [is there any] end of their treasures; their land is also full of horses, neither [is there any] end of their chariots: {2:8} Their land also is full of idols; they worship the work of their own hands, that which their own fingers have made: {2:9} And the mean man boweth down, and the great man humbleth himself: therefore forgive them not. {2:10} Enter into the rock, and hide thee in the dust, for fear of the LORD, and for the glory of his majesty. {2:11} The lofty looks of man shall be humbled, and the haughtiness of men shall be bowed down, and the LORD alone shall be exalted in that day. {2:12} For the day of the LORD of hosts [shall be] upon every [one that is] proud and lofty, and upon every [one that is] lifted up; and he shall be brought low: {2:13} And upon all the cedars of Lebanon, [that are] high and lifted up, and upon all the oaks of Bashan, {2:14} And upon all the high mountains, and upon all the hills [that are] lifted up, {2:15} And upon every high tower, and upon every fenced wall, {2:16} And upon all the ships of Tarshish, and upon all pleasant pictures. {2:17} And the loftiness of man shall be bowed down, and the haughtiness of men shall be made low: and the LORD alone shall be exalted in that day. {2:18} And the idols he shall utterly abolish. {2:19} And they shall go into the holes of the rocks, and into the caves of the earth, for fear of the LORD, and for the glory of his majesty, when he ariseth to shake terribly the earth. {2:20} In that day a man shall cast his idols of silver, and his idols of gold, which they made [each one] for himself to worship, to the moles and to the bats; {2:21} To go into the clefts of the rocks, and into the tops of the ragged rocks, for fear of the LORD, and for the glory of his majesty, when he ariseth to shake terribly the earth. {2:22} Cease ye from man, whose breath [is] in his nostrils: for wherein is he to be accounted of?

{3:1} For, behold, the Lord, the LORD of hosts, doth take away from Jerusalem and from Judah the stay and the staff, the whole stay of bread, and the whole stay of water. {3:2} The mighty man, and the man of war, the judge, and the prophet, and the prudent, and the ancient, {3:3} **The captain of fifty, and the honourable man, and the counsellor, and the cunning artificer, and the eloquent orator.** {3:4} And I will give children [to be] their princes, and babes shall rule over them. {3:5} And the people shall be oppressed, every one by another, and every one by his neighbour: the child shall behave himself proudly against the ancient, and the base against the honourable. {3:6} When a man shall take hold of his brother of the house of his father, [saying,] Thou hast clothing, be thou our ruler, and [let] this ruin [be] under thy hand: {3:7} In that day shall he swear, saying, I will not be an healer; for in my house [is] neither bread nor clothing: make me not a ruler of the people. {3:8} For Jerusalem is ruined, and Judah is fallen: because their tongue and their doings [are] against the LORD, to provoke the eyes of his glory. {3:9} The shew of their countenance doth witness against them; and they declare their sin as Sodom, they hide [it] not. Woe unto their soul! for they have rewarded evil unto themselves. {3:10} Say ye to the righteous, that [it shall be] well [with him:] for they shall eat the fruit of their doings. {3:11} Woe unto the wicked! [it shall be] ill [with him:] for the reward of his hands shall be given him. {3:12} [As for] my people, children [are] their oppressors, and women rule over them. O my people, they which lead thee cause [thee] to err, and destroy the way of thy paths. {3:13} The LORD standeth up to plead, and standeth to judge the people. {3:14} The LORD will enter into judgment with the ancients of his people, and the princes thereof: for ye have eaten up the vineyard; the spoil of the poor [is] in your houses. {3:15} **What mean ye [that] ye beat my people to pieces, and grind the faces of the poor? saith the LORD GOD of hosts.** {3:16} Moreover the LORD saith, Because the daughters of Zion are haughty, and walk with stretched forth necks and wanton eyes, walking and mincing [as] they go, and making a tinkling with their feet: {3:17} Therefore the LORD will smite with a scab the crown of the head of the daughters of Zion, and the LORD will discover their secret parts. {3:18} In that day the Lord will take away the bravery of [their] tinkling ornaments [about their feet,] and [their] cauls, and [their] round tires like the moon, {3:19} The chains, and the bracelets, and the mufflers, {3:20} The bonnets, and the ornaments of the legs, and the headbands, and the tablets, and the earrings, {3:21} The rings, and nose jewels, {3:22} The changeable suits of apparel, and the mantles, and the wimples, and the crisping pins, {3:23} The glasses, and the fine linen, and the hoods, and the vails. {3:24} **And it shall come to pass, [that] instead of sweet smell there shall be stink; and instead of a girdle a rent; and instead of well set hair baldness; and instead of a stomacher a girding of sackcloth; [and] burning instead of beauty.** {3:25} **Thy men shall fall by the sword, and thy mighty in the war.** {3:26} And her gates shall lament and mourn; and she [being] desolate shall sit upon the ground.

{4:1} And in that day seven women shall take hold of one man, saying, We will eat our own bread, and wear our own apparel: only let us be called by thy name, to take away our reproach. {4:2} In that day shall the branch of the LORD be beautiful and glorious, and the fruit of the earth [shall be] excellent and comely for them that are escaped of Israel. {4:3} And it shall come to pass, [that he that is] left in Zion, and [he that] remaineth in Jerusalem, shall be called holy, [even] every one that is written among the living in Jerusalem: {4:4} When the Lord shall have washed away the filth of the daughters of Zion, and shall have purged the blood of Jerusalem from the midst thereof by the spirit of judgment, and by the spirit of burning. {4:5} And the LORD will create upon every dwelling place of mount Zion, and upon her assemblies, a cloud and smoke by day, and the shining of a flaming fire by night: for upon all the glory [shall be] a defence. {4:6} And there shall be a tabernacle for a shadow in the daytime from the heat, and for a place of refuge, and for a covert from storm and from rain.

{5:1} Now will I sing to my wellbeloved a song of my beloved touching his vineyard. My wellbeloved hath a vineyard in a very fruitful hill: {5:2} And he fenced it, and gathered out the stones thereof, and planted it with the choicest vine, and built a tower in the midst of it, and also made a winepress therein: and he looked that it should bring forth grapes, and it brought forth wild grapes. {5:3} And now, O inhabitants of Jerusalem, and men of Judah, judge, I pray you, betwixt me and my vineyard. {5:4} What could have been done more to my vineyard, that I have not done in it? wherefore, when I looked that it should bring forth grapes, brought it forth wild grapes? {5:5} And now go to; I will tell you what I will do to my vineyard: I will take away the hedge thereof, and it shall be eaten up; [and] break down the wall thereof, and it shall be trodden down: {5:6} And I will lay it waste: it shall not be pruned, nor digged; but there shall come up briers and thorns: I will also command the clouds that they rain no rain upon it. {5:7} For the vineyard of the LORD of hosts [is] the house of Israel, and the men of Judah his pleasant plant: and he looked for judgment, but behold oppression; for righteousness, but behold a cry. {5:8} Woe unto them that join house to house, [that] lay field to field, till [there be] no place, that they may be placed alone in the midst of the earth! {5:9} In mine ears [said] the LORD of hosts, Of a truth many houses shall be desolate, [even] great and fair, without inhabitant. {5:10} Yea, ten acres of vineyard shall yield one bath, and the seed of an homer shall yield an ephah. {5:11} Woe unto them that rise up early in the morning, [that] they may follow strong drink; that continue until night, [till] wine inflame them! {5:12} And the harp, and the viol, the tabret, and pipe, and wine, are in their feasts: but they regard not the work of the LORD, neither consider the operation of his hands. {5:13} Therefore my people are gone into captivity, because [they have] no knowledge: and their honourable men [are] famished, and their multitude dried up with thirst. {5:14} Therefore hell hath enlarged herself, and opened her mouth without measure: and their glory, and their multitude, and their pomp, and he that rejoiceth, shall descend into it. {5:15} And the mean man shall be brought down, and the mighty man shall be humbled, and the eyes of the lofty shall be humbled: {5:16} But the LORD of hosts shall be exalted in judgment, and God that is holy shall be sanctified in righteousness. {5:17} Then shall the lambs feed after their manner, and the waste places of the fat ones shall strangers eat. {5:18} Woe unto them that draw iniquity with cords of vanity, and sin as it were with a cart rope: {5:19} That say, Let him make speed, [and] hasten his work, that we may see it: and let the counsel of the Holy One of Israel draw nigh and come, that we may know [it!] {5:20} Woe unto them that call evil good, and good evil; that put darkness for light, and light for darkness; that put bitter for sweet, and sweet for bitter! {5:21} Woe unto [them that are] wise in their own eyes, and prudent in their own sight! {5:22} Woe unto [them that are] mighty to drink wine, and men of strength to mingle strong drink: {5:23} Which justify the wicked for reward, and take away the righteousness of the righteous from him! {5:24} Therefore as the fire devoureth the stubble, and the flame consumeth the chaff, [so] their root shall be as rottenness, and their blossom shall go up as dust: because they have cast away the law of the LORD of hosts, and despised the word of the Holy One of Israel. {5:25} Therefore is the anger of the LORD kindled against his people, and he hath stretched forth his hand against them, and hath smitten them: and the hills did tremble, and their carcases [were] torn in the midst of the streets. For all this his anger is not turned away, but his hand [is] stretched out still. {5:26} And he will lift up an ensign to the nations from far, and will hiss unto them from the end of the earth: and, behold, they shall come with speed swiftly: {5:27} None shall be weary nor stumble among them; none shall slumber nor sleep; neither shall the girdle of their loins be loosed, nor the latchet of their shoes be broken: {5:28} Whose arrows [are] sharp, and all their bows bent, their horses' hoofs shall be counted like flint, and their wheels like a whirlwind: {5:29} Their roaring [shall be] like a lion, they shall roar like young lions: yea, they shall roar, and lay hold of the prey, and shall carry [it] away safe, and none shall deliver [it.] {5:30} And in that day they shall roar against them like the roaring of the sea: and if [one] look unto the land, behold darkness [and] sorrow, and the light is darkened in the heavens thereof.

{6:1} In the year that king Uzziah died I saw also the Lord sitting upon a throne, high and lifted up, and his train filled the temple. {6:2} Above it stood the seraphims: each one had six wings; with twain he covered his face, and with twain he covered his feet, and with twain he did fly. {6:3} And one cried unto another, and said, Holy, holy, holy, [is] the LORD of hosts: the whole earth [is] full of his glory. {6:4} And the posts of the door moved at the voice of him that cried, and the house was filled with smoke. {6:5} Then said I, Woe [is] me! for I am undone; because I [am] a man of unclean lips, and I dwell in the midst of a people of unclean lips: for mine eyes have seen the King, the LORD of hosts. {6:6} Then flew one of the seraphims unto me, having a live coal in his hand, [which] he had taken with the tongs from off the altar: {6:7} And he laid [it] upon my mouth, and said, Lo, this hath touched thy lips; and thine iniquity is taken away, and thy sin purged. {6:8} Also I heard the voice of the Lord, saying, Whom shall I send, and who will go for us? Then said I, Here [am] I; send me. {6:9} And he said, Go, and tell this people, Hear ye indeed, but understand not; and see ye indeed, but perceive not. {6:10} Make the heart of this people fat, and make their ears heavy, and shut their eyes; lest they see with their eyes, and hear with their ears, and understand with their heart, and convert, and be healed. {6:11} Then said I, Lord, how long? And he answered, Until the cities be wasted without inhabitant, and the houses without man, and the land be utterly desolate, {6:12} And the LORD have removed men far away, and [there be] a great forsaking in the midst of the land. {6:13} But yet in it [shall be] a tenth, and [it] shall return, and shall be eaten: as a teil tree, and as an oak, whose substance is in them, when they cast [their leaves: so] the holy seed [shall be] the substance thereof.

{7:1} And it came to pass in the days of Ahaz the son of Jotham, the son of Uzziah, king of Judah, [that] Rezin the king of Syria, and Pekah the son of Remaliah, king of Israel, went up toward Jerusalem to war against it, but could not prevail against it. {7:2} And it was told the house of David, saying, Syria is confederate with Ephraim. And his heart was moved, and the heart of his people, as the trees of the wood are moved with the wind. {7:3} Then said the LORD unto Isaiah, Go forth now to meet Ahaz, thou, and Shearjashub thy son, at the end of the conduit of the upper pool in the highway of the fuller's field; {7:4} And say unto him, Take heed, and be quiet; fear not, neither be fainthearted for the two tails of these smoking firebrands, for the fierce anger of Rezin with Syria, and of the son of Remaliah. {7:5} Because Syria, Ephraim, and the son of Remaliah, have taken evil counsel against thee, saying, {7:6} Let us go up against Judah, and vex it, and let us make a breach therein for us, and set a king in the midst of it, [even] the son of Tabeal: {7:7} Thus saith the Lord GOD, It shall not stand, neither shall it come to pass. {7:8} For the head of Syria [is] Damascus, and the head of Damascus [is] Rezin; and within threescore and five years shall Ephraim be broken, that it be not a people. {7:9} And the head of Ephraim [is] Samaria, and the head of Samaria [is] Remaliah's son. If ye will not believe, surely ye shall not be established. {7:10} Moreover the LORD spake again unto Ahaz, saying, {7:11} Ask thee a sign of the LORD thy God; ask it either in the depth, or in the height above. {7:12} But Ahaz said, I will not ask, neither will I tempt the LORD. {7:13} And he said, Hear ye now, O house of David; [Is it]

✝ he Old Testament ✦ 217

a small thing for you to weary men, but will ye weary my God also? {7:14} **Therefore the Lord himself shall give you a sign; Behold, a virgin shall conceive, and bear a son, and shall call his name Immanuel.** {7:15} Butter and honey shall he eat, that he may know to refuse the evil, and choose the good. {7:16} For before the child shall know to refuse the evil, and choose the good, the land that thou abhorrest shall be forsaken of both her kings. {7:17} The LORD shall bring upon thee, and upon thy people, and upon thy father's house, days that have not come, from the day that Ephraim departed from Judah; [even] the king of Assyria. {7:18} And it shall come to pass in that day, [that] the LORD shall hiss for the fly that [is] in the uttermost part of the rivers of Egypt, and for the bee that [is] in the land of Assyria. {7:19} And they shall come, and shall rest all of them in the desolate valleys, and in the holes of the rocks, and upon all thorns, and upon all bushes. {7:20} In the same day shall the Lord shave with a razor that is hired, [namely,] by them beyond the river, by the king of Assyria, the head, and the hair of the feet: and it shall also consume the beard. {7:21} And it shall come to pass in that day, [that] a man shall nourish a young cow, and two sheep; {7:22} And it shall come to pass, for the abundance of milk [that] they shall give he shall eat butter: for butter and honey shall every one eat that is left in the land. {7:23} And it shall come to pass in that day, [that] every place shall be, where there were a thousand vines at a thousand silverlings, it shall [even] be for briers and thorns. {7:24} With arrows and with bows shall [men] come thither; because all the land shall become briers and thorns. {7:25} And [on] all hills that shall be digged with the mattock, there shall not come thither the fear of briers and thorns: but it shall be for the sending forth of oxen, and for the treading of lesser cattle.

{8:1} Moreover the LORD said unto me, Take thee a great roll, and write in it with a man's pen concerning Maher-shalal-hash-baz. {8:2} And I took unto me faithful witnesses to record, Uriah the priest, and Zechariah the son of Jeberechiah. {8:3} And I went unto the prophetess; and she conceived, and bare a son. Then said the LORD to me, Call his name Maher-shalal-hash-baz. {8:4} For before the child shall have knowledge to cry, My father, and my mother, the riches of Damascus and the spoil of Samaria shall be taken away before the king of Assyria. {8:5} The LORD spake also unto me again, saying, {8:6} Forasmuch as this people refuseth the waters of Shiloah that go softly, and rejoice in Rezin and Remaliah's son; {8:7} Now therefore, behold, the Lord bringeth up upon them the waters of the river, strong and many, [even] the king of Assyria, and all his glory: and he shall come up over all his channels, and go over all his banks: {8:8} And he shall pass through Judah; he shall overflow and go over, he shall reach [even] to the neck; and the stretching out of his wings shall fill the breadth of thy land, O Immanuel. {8:9} Associate yourselves, O ye people, and ye shall be broken in pieces; and give ear, all ye of far countries: gird yourselves, and ye shall be broken in pieces; gird yourselves, and ye shall be broken in pieces. {8:10} Take counsel together, and it shall come to nought; speak the word, and it shall not stand: for God [is] with us. {8:11} For the LORD spake thus to me with a strong hand, and instructed me that I should not walk in the way of this people, saying, {8:12} Say ye not, A confederacy, to all [them to] whom this people shall say, A confederacy; neither fear ye their fear, nor be afraid. {8:13} Sanctify the LORD of hosts himself; and [let] him [be] your fear, and [let] him [be] your dread. {8:14} And he shall be for a sanctuary; but for a stone of stumbling and for a rock of offence to both the houses of Israel, for a gin and for a snare to the inhabitants of Jerusalem. {8:15} And many among them shall stumble, and fall, and be broken, and be snared, and be taken. {8:16} Bind up the testimony, seal the law among my disciples. {8:17} And I will wait upon the LORD, that hideth his face from the house of Jacob, and I will look for him. {8:18} Behold, I and the children whom the LORD hath given me [are] for signs and for wonders in Israel from the LORD of hosts, which dwelleth in mount Zion. {8:19} And when they shall say unto you, Seek unto them that have familiar spirits, and unto wizards that peep, and that mutter: should not a people seek unto their God? for the living to the dead? {8:20} To the law and to the testimony: if they speak not according to this word, [it is] because [there is] no light in them. {8:21} And they shall pass through it, hardly bestead and hungry: and it shall come to pass, that when they shall be hungry, they shall fret themselves, and curse their king and their God, and look upward. {8:22} And they shall look unto the earth; and behold trouble and darkness, dimness of anguish; and [they shall be] driven to darkness.

{9:1} Nevertheless the dimness [shall] not [be] such as [was] in her vexation, when at the first he lightly afflicted the land of Zebulun and the land of Naphtali, and afterward did more grievously afflict [her by] the way of the sea, beyond Jordan, in Galilee of the nations. {9:2} The people that walked in darkness have seen a great light: they that dwell in the land of the shadow of death, upon them hath the light shined. {9:3} Thou hast multiplied the nation, [and] not increased the joy: they joy before thee according to the joy in harvest, [and] as [men] rejoice when they divide the spoil. {9:4} For thou hast broken the yoke of his burden, and the staff of his shoulder, the rod of his oppressor, as in the day of Midian. {9:5} For every battle of the warrior [is] with confused noise, and garments rolled in blood; but [this] shall be with burning [and] fuel of fire. {9:6} **For unto us a child is born, unto us a son is given: and the government shall be upon his shoulder: and his name shall be called Wonderful, Counsellor, The mighty God, The everlasting Father, The Prince of Peace.** {9:7} Of the increase of [his] government and peace [there shall be] no end, upon the throne of David, and upon his kingdom, to order it, and to establish it with judgment and with justice from henceforth even for ever. The zeal of the LORD of hosts will perform this. {9:8} The Lord sent a word into Jacob, and it hath lighted upon Israel. {9:9} And all the people shall know, [even] Ephraim and the inhabitant of Samaria, that say in the pride and stoutness of heart, {9:10} The bricks are fallen down, but we will build with hewn stones: the sycomores are cut down, but we will change [them into] cedars. {9:11} Therefore the LORD shall set up the adversaries of Rezin against him, and join his enemies together; {9:12} The Syrians before, and the Philistines behind; and they shall devour Israel with open mouth. For all this his anger is not turned away, but his hand [is] stretched out still. {9:13} For the people turneth not unto him that smiteth them, neither do they seek the LORD of hosts. {9:14} Therefore the LORD will cut off from Israel head and tail, branch and rush, in one day. {9:15} The ancient and honourable, he [is] the head; and the prophet that teacheth lies, he [is] the tail. {9:16} For the leaders of this people cause [them] to err; and [they that are] led of them [are] destroyed. {9:17} Therefore the Lord shall have no joy in their young men, neither shall have mercy on their fatherless and widows: for every one is an hypocrite and an evildoer, and every mouth speaketh folly. For all this his anger is not turned away, but his hand [is] stretched out still. {9:18} For wickedness burneth as the fire: it shall devour the briers and thorns, and shall kindle in the thickets of the forest, and they shall mount up [like] the lifting up of smoke. {9:19} Through the wrath of the LORD of hosts is the land darkened, and the people shall be as the fuel of the fire: no man shall spare his brother. {9:20} And he shall snatch on the right hand, and be hungry; and he shall eat on the left hand, and they shall not be satisfied: they shall eat every man the flesh of his own arm: {9:21} Manasseh, Ephraim; and Ephraim, Manasseh: [and] they together [shall be] against Judah. For all this his anger is not turned away, but his hand [is] stretched out still.

{10:1} Woe unto them that decree unrighteous decrees, and that write grievousness [which] they have prescribed; {10:2} To turn aside the needy from judgment, and to take away the right from the poor of my people, that widows may be their prey, and [that] they may rob the fatherless! {10:3} And what will ye do in the day of visitation, and in the desolation [which] shall come from far? to whom will ye flee for help? and where will ye leave your glory? {10:4} Without me they shall bow down under the prisoners, and they shall fall under the slain. For all this his anger is not turned away, but his hand [is] stretched out still. {10:5} O Assyrian, the rod of mine anger, and the staff in their hand is mine indignation. {10:6} I will send him against an hypocritical nation, and against the people of my wrath will I give him a charge, to take the spoil, and to take the prey, and to tread them down like the mire of the streets. {10:7} Howbeit he meaneth not so, neither doth his heart think so; but [it is] in his heart to destroy and cut off nations not a few. {10:8} For he saith, [Are] not my princes altogether kings? {10:9} [Is] not Calno as Carchemish? [is] not Hamath as Arpad? [is] not Samaria as Damascus? {10:10} As my hand hath found the kingdoms of the idols, and whose graven images did excel them of Jerusalem and of Samaria; {10:11} Shall I not, as I have done unto Samaria and her idols, so do to Jerusalem and her idols? {10:12} Wherefore it shall come to pass, [that] when the Lord hath performed his whole work upon mount Zion and on Jerusalem, I will punish the fruit of the stout heart of the king of Assyria, and the glory of his high looks. {10:13} For he saith, By the strength of my hand I have done [it,] and by my wisdom; for I am prudent: and I have removed the bounds of the people, and have robbed their treasures, and I have put down the inhabitants like a valiant [man:] {10:14} And my hand hath found as a nest the riches of the people: and as one gathereth eggs [that are] left, have I gathered all the earth; and there was none that moved the wing, or opened the mouth, or peeped. {10:15} Shall the axe boast itself against him that heweth therewith? [or] shall the saw magnify itself against him that shaketh it? as if the rod should shake [itself] against them that lift it up, [or] as if the staff should lift up [itself, as if it were] no wood. {10:16} Therefore shall the Lord, the Lord of hosts, send among his fat ones leanness; and under his glory he shall kindle a burning like the burning of a fire. {10:17} And the light of Israel shall be for a fire, and his Holy One for a flame: and it shall burn and devour his thorns and his briers in one day; {10:18} And shall consume the glory of his forest, and of his fruitful field, both soul and body: and they shall be as when a standardbearer fainteth. {10:19} And the rest of the trees of his forest shall be few, that a child may write them. {10:20} And it shall come to pass in that day, [that] the remnant of Israel, and such as are escaped of the house of Jacob, shall no more again stay upon him that smote them; but shall stay upon the LORD, the Holy One of Israel, in truth. {10:21} The remnant shall return, [even] the remnant of Jacob, unto the mighty God. {10:22} For though thy people Israel be as the sand of the sea, [yet] a remnant of them shall return: the consumption decreed shall overflow with righteousness. {10:23} For the Lord GOD of hosts shall make a consumption, even determined, in the midst of all the land. {10:24} Therefore thus saith the Lord GOD of hosts, O my people that dwellest in Zion, be not afraid of the Assyrian: he shall smite thee with a rod, and shall lift up his staff against thee, after the manner of Egypt. {10:25} For yet a very little while, and the indignation shall cease, and mine anger in their destruction. {10:26} And the LORD of hosts shall stir up a scourge for him according to the slaughter of Midian at the rock of Oreb: and [as] his rod [was] upon the sea, so shall he lift it up after the manner of Egypt. {10:27} And it shall come to pass in that day, [that] his burden shall be taken away from off thy shoulder, and his yoke from off thy neck, and the yoke shall be destroyed because of the anointing. {10:28} He is come to Aiath, he is passed to Migron; at Michmash he hath laid up his carriages: {10:29} They are gone over the passage: they have taken up their lodging at Geba; Ramah is afraid; Gibeah of Saul is fled. {10:30} Lift up thy voice, O daughter of Gallim: cause it to be heard unto Laish, O poor Anathoth. {10:31} Madmenah is removed; the inhabitants of Gebim gather themselves to flee. {10:32} As yet shall he remain at Nob that day: he shall shake his hand [against] the mount of the daughter of Zion, the hill of Jerusalem. {10:33} Behold, the Lord, the LORD of hosts, shall lop the bough with terror: and the high ones of stature [shall be] hewn down, and the haughty shall be humbled. {10:34} And he shall cut down the thickets of the forest with iron, and Lebanon shall fall by a mighty one.

{11:1} A ruler will come from Jesse's family, and a descendant will arise from his roots. {11:2} The Spirit of the LORD will rest on him— the Spirit of wisdom and understanding, the Spirit of counsel and might, the Spirit of knowledge and the fear of the LORD. {11:3} He will delight in obeying the LORD. He will not judge by appearance nor make a decision based on hearsay. {11:4} He will give justice to the poor and make fair decisions for the exploited. The earth will shake at the force of his word, and one breath from his mouth will destroy the wicked. {11:5} He will wear righteousness like a belt and truth like an undergarment. {11:6} In that day the wolf and the lamb will live together; the leopard will lie down with the baby goat. The calf and the yearling will be safe with the lion, and a little child will lead them all. {11:7} The cow will graze near the bear. The cub and the calf will lie down together. The lion will eat hay like a cow. {11:8} The baby will play safely near the hole of a cobra. Yes, a little child will put its hand in a nest of deadly snakes without harm. {11:9} Nothing will hurt or destroy in all my holy mountain, for as the waters fill the sea, so the earth will be filled with people who know the LORD. {11:10} In that day the heir to David's throne will be a banner of salvation to all the world. The nations will rally to him, and the land where he lives will be a glorious place. {11:11} In that day the Lord will reach out his hand a second time to bring back the remnant of his people— those who remain in Assyria and northern Egypt; in southern Egypt, Ethiopia, and Elam; in Babylonia, Hamath, and all the distant coastlands. {11:12} He will raise a flag among the nations and assemble the exiles of Israel. He will gather the scattered people of Judah from the ends of the earth. {11:13} Then at last the jealousy between Israel and Judah will end. They will not be rivals anymore. {11:14} They will join forces to swoop down on Philistia to the west. Together they will attack and plunder the nations to the east. They will occupy all the lands of Edom, Moab, and Ammon will obey them. {11:15} The LORD will make a dry path through the gulf of the Red Sea. He will wave his hand over the Euphrates River, sending a mighty wind to divide it into seven streams so it can easily be crossed on foot. {11:16} He will make a highway for the remnant of his people, the remnant coming from Assyria, just as he did for Israel long ago when they returned from Egypt.

{12:1} On that day you will say, "LORD, I will praise you! Though you were angry with me, your anger has turned away, and you have comforted me. {12:2} Behold, God is my salvation; I will trust and not be afraid; for the LORD JEHOVAH is my strength and my song; he has become my salvation. {12:3} Therefore, with joy you will draw water from the wells of salvation. {12:4} And on that day you will say, "Praise the LORD! Call upon his name; proclaim his deeds among the nations; declare that his name is exalted. {12:5} Sing to the LORD, for he has done glorious things; let this be known throughout the earth. {12:6} Shout aloud and sing for joy, O inhabitant of Zion, for great is the Holy One of Israel among you."

{13:1} This is the burden of Babylon, which Isaiah the son of Amoz foresaw. {13:2} "Raise a banner on a high mountain, shout loudly to them; wave your hand, so they may enter the gates of the nobles. {13:3} I have commanded my consecrated ones; I have summoned my warriors to carry out my anger, those who rejoice in my triumph. {13:4} Listen to the noise on the mountains, like that of a great multitude! Hear the uproar of the kingdoms of nations gathered together! The LORD Almighty is mustering an army for battle. {13:5} They come from a distant land, from the ends of the heavens— the LORD and the weapons of his wrath— to destroy the whole country. {13:6} Wail, for the day of the LORD is near; it will come like destruction from the Almighty. {13:7} Because of this, all hands will go limp, every heart will melt with fear. {13:8} Terror will seize them, pain and anguish will grip them; they will writhe like a woman in labor. They will look aghast at each other, their faces aflame with fear. {13:9} See, the day of the LORD is coming —a cruel day, with wrath and fierce anger— to make the land desolate and destroy the sinners within it. {13:10} The stars of heaven and their constellations will not show their light. The rising sun will be darkened and the moon will not give its light. {13:11} I will punish the world for its evil, the wicked for their sins. I will put an end to the arrogance of the haughty and will humble the pride of the ruthless. {13:12} I will make people scarcer than pure gold, more rare than the gold of Ophir. {13:13} Therefore I will make the heavens tremble; and the earth will shake from its place at the wrath of the LORD Almighty, in the day of his burning anger. {13:14} Like hunted gazelles, like sheep without a shepherd, they will all return to their own people, they will flee to their native land. {13:15} Whoever is captured will be thrust through; all who are caught will fall by the sword. {13:16} Their infants will be dashed to pieces before their eyes; their houses will be looted and their wives violated. {13:17} See, I will stir up against them the Medes, who do not care for silver and have no delight in gold. {13:18} Their bows will strike down the young men; they will have no mercy on infants, nor will they look with compassion on children. {13:19} Babylon, the jewel of kingdoms, the pride and glory of the Babylonians, will be overthrown by God like Sodom and Gomorrah. {13:20} She will never be inhabited or lived in through all generations; there no nomads will pitch their tents, there no shepherds will rest their flocks. {13:21} But desert creatures will lie there, jackals will fill her houses; there the owls will dwell, and there the wild goats will leap about. {13:22} Hyenas will inhabit her strongholds, jackals her luxurious palaces. Her time is at hand, and her days will not be prolonged."

{14:1} The LORD will show mercy to Jacob and choose Israel once again, settling them in their own land. Strangers will join them and will be united with the house of Jacob. {14:2} People will take them and bring them to their place. The house of Israel will possess them in the land of the LORD as servants and maidservants. They will take captives from those who had taken them captive and rule over their oppressors. {14:3} The day will come when the LORD gives you rest from your sorrow, fear, and the hard bondage you endured. {14:4} Then you will take up this proverb against the king of Babylon, saying, "How the oppressor has ceased, the golden city ceased!" {14:5} The LORD has broken the staff of the wicked, the scepter of rulers. {14:6} He who struck the people in wrath with a continual stroke, he who ruled the nations in anger, is now persecuted, and no one stops him. {14:7} The whole earth is at rest and quiet; they break forth into singing. {14:8} Even the fir trees and cedars of Lebanon rejoice, saying, "Since you are laid down, no feller has come up against us." {14:9} Hell from beneath is moved for you to meet you at your coming; it stirs up the dead, even all the chief ones of the earth; it raises up from their thrones all the kings of the nations. {14:10} They all speak and say to you, "Have you also become weak as we? Have you become like us?" {14:11} Your pomp is brought down to the grave, the noise of your harps; the worm is spread under you, and worms cover you. {14:12} How you have fallen from heaven, O Lucifer, son of the morning! How you are cut down to the ground, who weakened the nations! {14:13} For you said in your heart, "I will ascend into heaven, I will exalt my throne above the stars of God; I will also sit upon the mount of the congregation, in the sides of the north; {14:14} I will ascend above the heights of the clouds; I will be like the Most High." {14:15} Yet you shall be brought down to hell, to the sides of the pit. {14:16} Those who see you shall narrowly look upon you and consider you, saying, "Is this the man who made the earth tremble, who shook kingdoms? {14:17} Who made the world as a wilderness and destroyed its cities? Who did not open the house of his prisoners?" {14:18} All the kings of the nations, even all of them, lie in glory, each in his own house. {14:19} But you are cast out of your grave like an abominable branch, as the clothing of those who are slain, thrust through with a sword, who go down to the stones of the pit; as a carcass trodden underfoot. {14:20} You shall not be joined with them in burial because you have destroyed your land and slain your people. The seed of evildoers shall never be renowned. {14:21} Prepare slaughter for his children for the iniquity of their fathers, that they do not rise, nor possess the land, nor fill the face of the world with cities. {14:22} For I will rise up against them, says the LORD of hosts, and cut off from Babylon the name, remnant, son, and nephew, says the LORD. {14:23} I will also make it a possession for the bittern and pools of water; and I will sweep it with the broom of destruction, says the LORD of hosts. {14:24} The LORD of hosts has sworn, saying, "Surely as I have thought, so shall it come to pass; and as I have purposed, so shall it stand: {14:25} That I will break the Assyrian in my land, and upon my mountains tread him underfoot. Then shall his yoke depart from off them, and his burden depart from off their shoulders. {14:26} This is the purpose that is purposed upon the whole earth, and this is the hand that is stretched out upon all the nations. {14:27} For the LORD of hosts has purposed, and who shall disannul it? And his hand is stretched out, and who shall turn it back? {14:28} In the year that King Ahaz died was this burden. {14:29} Do not rejoice, Philistia, because the rod of him who struck you is broken; for out of the serpent's root shall come forth a viper, and his fruit shall be a fiery flying serpent. {14:30} The firstborn of the poor will feed, and the needy will lie down in safety. I will kill your root with famine, and he will slay your remnant. {14:31} Howl, O gate; cry, O city; you, Philistia, are dissolved! For there shall come from the north a smoke, and none shall be alone in his appointed times. {14:32} What shall one then answer the messengers of the nation? That the LORD has founded Zion, and the poor of his people shall trust in it."

{15:1} This is the burden of Moab: In the night, Ar of Moab is destroyed and brought to silence. Kir of Moab suffers the same fate, also in the night. {15:2} They mourn in Bajith and Dibon, the high places of Moab. There will be wailing over Nebo and Medeba. Every head shall be shaved, and every beard cut off. {15:3} Sackcloth will be worn in the streets, and there will be loud weeping on the rooftops and in the streets, with everyone mourning abundantly. {15:4} Heshbon and Elealeh cry out, their voices reaching Jahaz. Even the armed soldiers of Moab cry out, their lives filled with anguish. {15:5} My heart mourns for Moab; its fugitives flee to Zoar, like a three-year-old heifer. They climb up to Luhith with weeping, and on the way to Horonaim, they cry out in destruction. {15:6} The waters of Nimrim are desolate; the hay has withered, the grass has failed, and there is no greenery. {15:7} Their abundance and stored-up wealth will be carried away to the brook of the willows. {15:8} The cry of distress echoes around the borders of Moab, reaching Eglaim and Beerelim. {15:9} The waters of Dimon will be filled with blood. I will bring even more trouble upon Dimon—lions upon those who escape from Moab and upon the remnant of the land.

{16:1} Send the lamb as tribute to the ruler of the land, from Sela to the wilderness, to the mount of the daughter of Zion. {16:2} Like a wandering bird cast out of the nest, so shall the daughters of Moab be at the fords of Arnon. {16:3} Take counsel, execute judgment; make your shadow as the night in the midst of the noonday; hide the outcasts; do not betray the wanderer. {16:4} Let my outcasts dwell with you, Moab; be a refuge to them from the face of the spoiler. The extortioner is at an end, the spoiler ceases, and the oppressors are consumed out of the land. {16:5} Mercy shall establish the throne, and he shall sit upon it in truth in the tabernacle of David, judging, seeking judgment, and hastening righteousness. {16:6} We have heard of the pride of Moab; he is very proud—of his haughtiness, pride, and wrath. But his lies will not endure. {16:7} Therefore Moab shall howl, and everyone shall mourn for the foundations of Kir-hareseth, for they are stricken. {16:8} For the fields of Heshbon languish, and the vine of Sibmah. The lords of the nations have broken down its principal plants; they have come even to Jazer and wandered through the wilderness. Its branches are stretched out; they have gone over the sea. {16:9} Therefore, I will weep with the weeping of Jazer for the vine of Sibmah. I will water you with my tears, O Heshbon and Elealeh, for the shouting for your summer fruits and harvest has fallen. {16:10} Gladness and joy are taken away from the plentiful field; there shall be no singing in the vineyards, nor shouting. The treaders shall tread out no wine in their presses; I have made their vintage shouting cease. {16:11} Therefore, my bowels shall sound like a harp for Moab, and my inward parts for Kir-haresh. {16:12} And it shall come to pass when Moab is weary on the high place, he shall come to his sanctuary to pray, but he shall not prevail. {16:13} This is the word that the LORD has spoken concerning Moab since that time. {16:14} But now the LORD has spoken, saying, "Within three years, as the years of a hired servant, the glory of Moab shall be despised, with all that great multitude; and the remnant shall be very small and feeble."

{17:1} The burden of Damascus. Look, Damascus will be taken away from being a city, and it shall become a ruinous heap. {17:2} The cities of Aroer are forsaken; they shall be for flocks, which shall lie down, and none shall make them afraid. {17:3} The fortress shall also cease from Ephraim, and the kingdom from Damascus, and the remnant of Syria. They shall be like the glory of the children of Israel, says the LORD of hosts. {17:4} And in that day, it shall come to pass that the glory of Jacob shall be made thin, and the fatness of his flesh shall wax lean. {17:5} And it shall be as when the harvestman gathers the corn, and reaps the ears with his arm; and it shall be as he that gathers the ears in the valley of Rephaim. {17:6} Yet gleaning grapes shall be left in it, as the shaking of an olive tree, two or three berries in the top of the uppermost bough, four or five in the outmost fruitful branches thereof, says the LORD God of Israel. {17:7} At that day, shall a man look to his Maker, and his eyes shall have respect to the Holy One of Israel. {17:8} And he shall not look to the altars, the work of his hands, neither shall respect that which his fingers have made, either the groves, or the images. {17:9} In that day, shall his strong cities be as a forsaken bough, and an uppermost branch, which they left because of the children of Israel; and there shall be desolation. {17:10} Because thou hast forgotten the God of thy salvation, and hast not been mindful of the rock of thy strength, therefore shalt thou plant pleasant plants, and shalt set it with strange slips: {17:11} In the day shalt thou make thy plant to grow, and in the morning shalt thou make thy seed to flourish: but the harvest shall be a heap in the day of grief and of desperate sorrow. {17:12} Woe to the multitude of many people, which make a noise like the noise of the seas; and to the rushing of nations, that make a rushing like the rushing of mighty waters! {17:13} The nations shall rush like the rushing of many waters: but God shall rebuke them, and they shall flee far off, and shall be chased as the chaff of the mountains before the wind, and like a rolling thing before the whirlwind. {17:14} And behold at eveningtide trouble; and before the morning he is not. This is the portion of them that spoil us, and the lot of them that rob us.

{18:1} Woe to the land shadowing with wings, which is beyond the rivers of Ethiopia: {18:2} That sends ambassadors by the sea, even in vessels of bulrushes upon the waters, saying, "Go, ye swift messengers, to a nation scattered and peeled, to a people terrible from their beginning hitherto; a nation meted out and trodden down, whose land the rivers have spoiled! {18:3} All ye inhabitants of the world, and dwellers on the earth, see ye, when he lifts up an ensign on the mountains; and when he blows a trumpet, hear ye. {18:4} For so the LORD said unto me, "I will take my rest, and I will consider in my dwelling place like a clear heat upon herbs, and like a cloud of dew in the heat of harvest. {18:5} For before the harvest, when the bud is perfect, and the sour grape is ripening in the flower, he shall both cut off the sprigs with pruninghooks, and take away and cut down the branches. {18:6} They shall be left together unto the fowls of the mountains, and to the beasts of the earth: and the fowls shall summer upon them, and all the beasts of the earth shall winter upon them. {18:7} In that time shall the present be brought unto the LORD of hosts of a people scattered and peeled, and from a people terrible from their beginning hitherto; a nation meted out and trodden under foot, whose land the rivers have spoiled, to the place of the name of the LORD of hosts, the mount Zion.

{19:1} The burden of Egypt. Behold, the LORD rides upon a swift cloud, and shall come into Egypt: and the idols of Egypt shall be moved at his presence, and the heart of Egypt shall melt in the midst of it. {19:2} And I will set the Egyptians against the Egyptians: and they shall fight every one against his brother, and every one against his neighbour; city against city, and kingdom against kingdom. {19:3} And the spirit of Egypt shall fail in the midst thereof; and I will destroy the counsel thereof: and they shall seek to the idols, and to the charmers, and to them that have familiar spirits, and to the wizards. {19:4} And the Egyptians will I give over into the hand of a cruel lord; and a fierce king shall rule over them, saith the Lord, the LORD of hosts. {19:5} And the waters shall fail from the sea, and the river shall be wasted and dried up. {19:6} And they shall turn the rivers far away; and the brooks of defence shall be emptied and dried up: the reeds and flags shall wither. {19:7} The paper reeds by the brooks, by the mouth of the brooks, and every thing sown by the brooks, shall wither, be driven away, and be no more. {19:8} The fishers also shall mourn, and all they that cast angle into the brooks shall lament, and they that spread nets upon the waters shall languish. {19:9} Moreover they that work in fine flax, and they that weave networks, shall be confounded. {19:10} And they shall be broken in the purposes thereof, all that make sluices and ponds for fish. {19:11} Surely the princes of Zoan are fools, the counsel of the wise counsellors of Pharaoh is become brutish: how say ye unto Pharaoh, I am the son of the wise, the son of ancient kings? {19:12} Where are they? where are thy wise men? and let them tell thee now, and let them know what the LORD of hosts hath purposed upon Egypt. {19:13} The princes of Zoan are become fools, the princes of Noph are deceived; they have also seduced Egypt, even they that are the stay of the tribes thereof. {19:14} The LORD hath mingled a perverse spirit in the midst thereof: and they have caused Egypt to err in every work thereof, as a drunken man staggereth in his vomit. {19:15}

Neither shall there be any work for Egypt, which the head or tail, branch or rush, may do. {19:16} In that day shall Egypt be like unto women: and it shall be afraid and fear because of the shaking of the hand of the LORD of hosts, which he shaketh over it. {19:17} And the land of Judah shall be a terror unto Egypt, every one that maketh mention thereof shall be afraid in himself, because of the counsel of the LORD of hosts, which he hath determined against it. {19:18} In that day shall five cities in the land of Egypt speak the language of Canaan, and swear to the LORD of hosts; one shall be called, The city of destruction. {19:19} In that day shall there be an altar to the LORD in the midst of the land of Egypt, and a pillar at the border thereof to the LORD. {19:20} And it shall be for a sign and for a witness unto the LORD of hosts in the land of Egypt: for they shall cry unto the LORD because of the oppressors, and he shall send them a saviour, and a great one, and he shall deliver them. {19:21} And the LORD shall be known to Egypt, and the Egyptians shall know the LORD in that day, and shall do sacrifice and oblation; yea, they shall vow a vow unto the LORD, and perform it. {19:22} And the LORD shall smite Egypt: he shall smite and heal it: and they shall return even to the LORD, and he shall be intreated of them, and shall heal them. {19:23} In that day shall there be a highway out of Egypt to Assyria, and the Assyrian shall come into Egypt, and the Egyptian into Assyria, and the Egyptians shall serve with the Assyrians. {19:24} In that day shall Israel be the third with Egypt and with Assyria, even a blessing in the midst of the land: {19:25} Whom the LORD of hosts shall bless, saying, Blessed be Egypt my people, and Assyria the work of my hands, and Israel mine inheritance.

{20:1} In the year that Tartan came unto Ashdod, (when Sargon the king of Assyria sent him,) and fought against Ashdod, and took it; {20:2} At the same time spake the LORD by Isaiah the son of Amoz, saying, Go and loose the sackcloth from off thy loins, and put off thy shoe from thy foot. And he did so, walking naked and barefoot. {20:3} And the LORD said, Like as my servant Isaiah hath walked naked and barefoot three years for a sign and wonder upon Egypt and upon Ethiopia; {20:4} So shall the king of Assyria lead away the Egyptians prisoners, and the Ethiopians captives, young and old, naked and barefoot, even with their buttocks uncovered, to the shame of Egypt. {20:5} And they shall be afraid and ashamed of Ethiopia their expectation, and of Egypt their glory. {20:6} And the inhabitant of this isle shall say in that day, Behold, such is our expectation, whither we flee for help to be delivered from the king of Assyria: and how shall we escape?

{21:1} The burden of the desert of the sea. As whirlwinds in the south pass through; so it cometh from the desert, from a terrible land. {21:2} A grievous vision is declared unto me; the treacherous dealer dealeth treacherously, and the spoiler spoileth. Go up, O Elam: besiege, O Media; all the sighing thereof have I made to cease. {21:3} Therefore are my loins filled with pain: pangs have taken hold upon me, as the pangs of a woman that travaileth: I was bowed down at the hearing of it; I was dismayed at the seeing of it. {21:4} My heart panted, fearfulness affrighted me: the night of my pleasure hath he turned into fear unto me. {21:5} Prepare the table, watch in the watchtower, eat, drink: arise, ye princes, and anoint the shield. {21:6} For thus hath the Lord said unto me, Go, set a watchman, let him declare what he seeth. {21:7} And he saw a chariot with a couple of horsemen, a chariot of asses, and a chariot of camels; and he hearkened diligently with much heed: {21:8} And he cried, A lion: My lord, I stand continually upon the watchtower in the daytime, and I am set in my ward whole nights: {21:9} And, behold, here cometh a chariot of men, with a couple of horsemen. And he answered and said, Babylon is fallen, is fallen; and all the graven images of her gods he hath broken unto the ground. {21:10} O my threshing, and the corn of my floor: that which I have heard of the LORD of hosts, the God of Israel, have I declared unto you. {21:11} The burden of Dumah. He calleth to me out of Seir, Watchman, what of the night? Watchman, what of the night? {21:12} The watchman said, The morning cometh, and also the night: if ye will enquire, enquire ye: return, come. {21:13} The burden upon Arabia. In the forest in Arabia shall ye lodge, O ye travelling companies of Dedanim. {21:14} The inhabitants of the land of Tema brought water to him that was thirsty, they prevented with their bread him that fled. {21:15} For they fled from the swords, from the drawn sword, and from the bent bow, and from the grievousness of war. {21:16} For thus hath the Lord said unto me, Within a year, according to the years of an hireling, and all the glory of Kedar shall fail; {21:17} And the residue of the number of archers, the mighty men of the children of Kedar, shall be diminished: for the LORD God of Israel hath spoken it.

{22:1} The burden of the valley of vision. What aileth thee now, that thou art wholly gone up to the housetops? {22:2} Thou that art full of stirs, a tumultuous city, a joyous city: thy slain men are not slain with the sword, nor dead in battle. {22:3} All thy rulers are fled together, they are bound by the archers: all that are found in thee are bound together, which have fled from far. {22:4} Therefore said I, Look away from me; I will weep bitterly, labour not to comfort me, because of the spoiling of the daughter of my people. {22:5} For it is a day of trouble, and of treading down, and of perplexity by the Lord GOD of hosts in the valley of vision, breaking down the walls, and of crying to the mountains. {22:6} And Elam bare the quiver with chariots of men and horsemen, and Kir uncovered the shield. {22:7} And it shall come to pass, that thy choicest valleys shall be full of chariots, and the horsemen shall set themselves in array at the gate. {22:8} And he discovered the covering of Judah, and thou didst look in that day to the armour of the house of the forest. {22:9} Ye have seen also the breaches of the city of David, that they are many: and ye gathered together the waters of the lower pool. {22:10} And ye have numbered the houses of Jerusalem, and the houses have ye broken down to fortify the wall. {22:11} Ye made also a ditch between the two walls for the water of the old pool: but ye have not looked unto the maker thereof, neither had respect unto him that fashioned it long ago. {22:12} And in that day did the Lord GOD of hosts call to weeping, and to mourning, and to baldness, and to girding with sackcloth: {22:13} And behold joy and gladness, slaying oxen, and killing sheep, eating flesh, and drinking wine: let us eat and drink; for tomorrow we shall die. {22:14} And it was revealed in mine ears by the LORD of hosts, Surely this iniquity shall not be purged from you till ye die, saith the Lord GOD of hosts. {22:15} Thus saith the Lord GOD of hosts, Go, get thee unto this treasurer, even unto Shebna, which is over the house, and say, {22:16} What hast thou here? and whom hast thou here, that thou hast hewed thee out a sepulchre here, as he that heweth him out a sepulchre on high, and that graveth an habitation for himself in a rock? {22:17} Behold, the LORD will carry thee away with a mighty captivity, and will surely cover thee. {22:18} He will surely violently turn and toss thee like a ball into a large country: there shalt thou die, and there the chariots of thy glory shall be the shame of thy lord's house. {22:19} And I will drive thee from thy station, and from thy state shall he pull thee down. {22:20} And it shall come to pass in that day, that I will call my servant Eliakim the son of Hilkiah: {22:21} And I will clothe him with thy robe, and strengthen him with thy girdle, and I will commit thy government into his hand: and he shall be a father to the inhabitants of Jerusalem, and to the house of Judah. {22:22} And the key of the house of David will I lay upon his shoulder; so he shall open, and none shall shut; and he shall shut, and none shall open. {22:23} And I will fasten him as a nail in a sure place; and he shall be for a glorious throne to his father's house. {22:24} And they shall hang upon him all the glory of his father's house, the offspring and the issue, all vessels of small quantity, from the vessels of cups, even to all the vessels of flagons. {22:25} In that day, saith the LORD of hosts, shall the nail that is fastened in the sure place be removed, and be cut down, and fall; and the burden that was upon it shall be cut off: for the LORD hath spoken it.

{23:1} The burden of Tyre. Howl, ye ships of Tarshish; for it is laid waste, so that there is no house, no entering in: from the land of Chittim it is revealed to them. {23:2} Be still, ye inhabitants of the isle; thou whom the merchants of Zidon, that pass over the sea, have replenished. {23:3} And by great waters the seed of Sihor, the harvest of the river, is her revenue; and she is a mart of nations. {23:4} Be thou ashamed, O Zidon: for the sea hath spoken, even the strength of the sea, saying, I travail not, nor bring forth children, neither do I nourish up young men, nor bring up virgins. {23:5} As at the report concerning Egypt, so shall they be sorely pained at the report of Tyre. {23:6} Pass ye over to Tarshish; howl, ye inhabitants of the isle. {23:7} Is this your joyous city, whose antiquity is of ancient days? her own feet shall carry her afar off to sojourn. {23:8} Who hath taken this counsel against Tyre, the crowning city, whose merchants are princes, whose traffickers are the honourable of the earth? {23:9} The LORD of hosts hath purposed it, to stain the pride of all glory, and to bring into contempt all the honourable of the earth. {23:10} Pass through thy land as a river, O daughter of Tarshish: there is no more strength. {23:11} He stretched out his hand over the sea, he shook the kingdoms: the LORD hath given a commandment against the merchant city, to destroy the strong holds thereof. {23:12} And he said, Thou shalt no more rejoice, O thou oppressed virgin, daughter of Zidon: arise, pass over to Chittim; there also shalt thou have no rest. {23:13} Behold the land of the Chaldeans; this people was not, til the Assyrian founded it for them that dwell in the wilderness: they set up the towers thereof, they raised up the palaces thereof; and he brought it to ruin. {23:14} Howl, ye ships of Tarshish: for your strength is laid waste. {23:15} And it shall come to pass in that day, that Tyre shall be forgotten seventy years, according to the days of one king: after the end of seventy years shall Tyre sing as an harlot. {23:16} Take an harp, go about the city, thou harlot that hast been forgotten; make sweet melody, sing many songs, that thou mayest be remembered. {23:17} And it shall come to pass after the end of seventy years, that the LORD will visit Tyre, and she shall turn to her hire, and shall commit fornication with all the kingdoms of the world upon the face of the earth. {23:18} And her merchandise and her hire shall be holiness to the LORD: it shall not be treasured nor laid up; for her merchandise shall be for them that dwell before the LORD, to eat sufficiently, and for durable clothing.

{24:1} Behold, the LORD makes the earth empty, wastes it, turns it upside down, and scatters its inhabitants. {24:2} And it shall be, as with the people, so with the priest; as with the servant, so with his master; as with the maid, so with her mistress; as with the buyer, so with the seller; as with the lender, so with the borrower; as with the taker of usury, so with the giver of usury to him. {24:3} The land shall be utterly emptied and utterly spoiled; for the LORD has spoken this word. {24:4} The earth mourns and fades away, the world languishes and fades away; the haughty people of the earth languish. {24:5} The earth also is defiled under its inhabitants, because they have transgressed the laws, changed the ordinance, and broken the everlasting covenant. {24:6} Therefore the curse has devoured the earth, and those who dwell therein are desolate. Therefore the inhabitants of the earth are burned, and few men left. {24:7} The new wine mourns, the vine languishes, all the merry-hearted sigh. {24:8} The mirth of tambourines ceases, the noise of those who rejoice ends, the joy of the harp ceases. {24:9} They shall not drink wine with a song; strong drink shall be bitter to those who drink it. {24:10} The city of confusion is broken down; every house is shut up, so that no man may come in. {24:11} There is a crying for wine in the streets; all joy is darkened, the mirth of the land is gone. {24:12} In the city is left desolation, and the gate is smitten with destruction. {24:13} When thus it shall be in the midst of the land among the people, there shall be as the shaking of an olive tree, and as the gleaning grapes when the vintage is done. {24:14} They shall lift up their voice, they shall sing for the majesty of the LORD, they shall cry aloud from the sea. {24:15} Therefore glorify ye the LORD in the fires, even the name of the LORD God of Israel in the isles of the sea. {24:16} From the uttermost part of the earth have we heard songs, even glory to the righteous. But I said, My leanness, my leanness, woe unto me! The treacherous dealers have dealt treacherously; yea, the treacherous dealers have dealt very treacherously. {24:17} Fear, and the pit, and the snare, are upon thee, O inhabitant of the earth. {24:18} And it shall come to pass, that he who fleeth from the noise of the fear shall fall into the pit; and he that cometh up out of the midst of the pit shall be taken in the snare; for the windows from on high are open, and the foundations of the earth do shake. {24:19} The earth is utterly broken down, the earth is clean dissolved, the earth is moved exceedingly. {24:20} The earth shall reel to and fro like a drunkard, and shall be removed like a cottage; and the transgression thereof shall be heavy upon it; and it shall fall, and not rise again. {24:21} And it shall come to pass in that day, that the LORD shall punish the host of the high ones that are on high, and the kings of the earth upon the earth. {24:22} And they shall be gathered together, as prisoners are gathered in the pit, and shall be shut up in the prison, and after many days shall they be visited. {24:23} Then the moon shall be confounded, and the sun ashamed, when the LORD of hosts shall reign in Mount Zion, and in Jerusalem, and before his ancients gloriously.

{25:1} O LORD, you are my God; I will exalt you and praise your name, for you have done wonderful things. Your counsels of old are faithfulness and truth. {25:2} For you have turned a city into a heap, a fortified city into ruins; a palace of strangers is now a city no more, it shall never be rebuilt. {25:3} Therefore, the strong nations shall glorify you; the city of the formidable nations shall fear you. {25:4} For you have been a strength to the poor, a strength to the needy in their distress, a refuge from the storm, a shadow from the heat, when the blast of the terrible ones is like a storm against the wall. {25:5} You shall bring down the noise of strangers, as the heat in a dry place; even the heat with the shadow of a cloud. The arrogance of the formidable shall be brought low. {25:6} And on this mountain, the LORD of hosts shall make for all people a feast of rich foods, a feast of wines on the lees, of rich foods full of marrow, of well-refined wines on the lees. {25:7} And he will destroy on this mountain the covering cast over all people, and the veil that is spread over all nations. {25:8} He will swallow up death in victory, and the Lord GOD will wipe away tears from all faces; the reproach of his people shall be taken away from all the earth, for the LORD has spoken it. {25:9} And it shall be said in that day, "Look, this is our God; we have waited for him, and he will save us. This is the LORD; we have waited for him, we will be glad and rejoice in his salvation." {25:10} For on this mountain, the hand of the LORD shall rest, and Moab shall be trodden down under him, even as straw is trodden down for the dunghill. {25:11} And he shall spread forth his hands in the midst of them, as one who swims spreads forth his hands to swim; and he shall bring down their pride together with the spoils of their hands. {25:12} And the fortress of the high fort of your walls shall he bring down, lay low, and bring to the ground, even to the dust.

{26:1} In that day, this song shall be sung in the land of Judah: "We have a strong city; salvation will God appoint for walls and bulwarks. {26:2} Open the gates, that the righteous nation which keeps the truth may enter in. {26:3} You will keep in perfect peace those whose mind is stayed on you, because they trust in you. {26:4} Trust in the LORD forever, for in the LORD JEHOVAH is everlasting strength. {26:5} For he brings down those who dwell on high; the lofty city, he lays it low; he brings it even to the ground; he brings it down to the dust. {26:6} The foot shall tread it down, even the feet of the poor, and the steps of the needy. {26:7} The way of the just is uprightness; you, most upright, weigh the path of the just. {26:8} Yes, in the way of your judgments, O LORD, we have waited for you; the desire of our soul is to your name and to the remembrance of you. {26:9} With my soul, I have desired you in the night; yes, with my spirit within me, I will seek you early; for when your judgments are in the earth, the inhabitants of the world will learn righteousness. {26:10} Let favor be shown to the wicked, yet will he not learn righteousness; in the land of uprightness, he will deal unjustly and will not behold the majesty of the LORD. {26:11} LORD, when your hand is lifted up, they will not see; but they shall see and be ashamed for their envy at the people; yes, the fire of your enemies shall devour them. {26:12} LORD, you will ordain peace for us, for you also have wrought all our works in us. {26:13} O LORD our God, other lords besides you have had dominion over us; but by you only will we make mention of your name. {26:14} They are dead, they shall not live; they are deceased, they shall not rise; therefore, you have visited and destroyed them, and made all their memory to perish. {26:15} You have increased the nation, O LORD, you have increased the nation; you are glorified; you had removed it far unto all the ends of the earth. {26:16} LORD, in trouble they have visited you, they poured out a prayer when your chastening was upon them. {26:17} Like as a woman with child, that draws near the time of her delivery, is in pain, and cries out in her pangs; so have we been in your sight, O LORD. {26:18} We have been with child, we have been in pain, we have as it were brought forth wind; we have not wrought any deliverance in the earth; neither have the inhabitants of the world fallen. {26:19} Your dead men shall live, together with my dead body shall they arise. Awake and sing, you that dwell in dust; for your dew is as the dew of herbs, and the earth shall cast out the dead. {26:20} Come, my people, enter into your chambers, and shut your doors about you; hide yourself as it were for a little moment, until the indignation be overpast. {26:21} For behold, the LORD comes out of his place to punish the inhabitants of the earth for their iniquity; the earth also shall disclose her blood and shall no more cover her slain."

{27:1} In that day, the LORD with his sore and great and strong sword shall punish leviathan the piercing serpent, even leviathan that crooked serpent; and he shall slay the dragon that is in the sea. {27:2} In that day, sing to her, "A vineyard of red wine." {27:3} I, the LORD, do keep it; I will water it every moment: lest any hurt it, I will keep it night and day. {27:4} Fury is not in me: who would set the briers and thorns against me in battle? I would go through them, I would burn them together. {27:5} Or let him take hold of my strength, that he may make peace with me; and he shall make peace with me. {27:6} He shall cause them that come of Jacob to take root: Israel shall blossom and bud, and fill the face of the world with fruit. {27:7} Hath he smitten him, as he smote those that smote him? Or is he slain according to the slaughter of them that are slain by him? {27:8} In measure, when it shoots forth, thou wilt debate with it: he stays his rough wind in the day of the east wind. {27:9} By this, therefore, shall the iniquity of Jacob be purged; and this is all the fruit to take away his sin; when he makes all the stones of the altar as chalkstones that are beaten in sunder, the groves and images shall not stand up. {27:10} Yet the defenced city shall be desolate, and the habitation forsaken, and left like a wilderness: there shall the calf feed, and there shall he lie down, and consume the branches thereof. {27:11}

When the boughs thereof are withered, they shall be broken off: the women come, and set them on fire: for it is a people of no understanding: therefore he that made them will not have mercy on them, and he that formed them will show them no favor. {27:12} And it shall come to pass in that day, that the LORD shall beat off from the channel of the river unto the stream of Egypt, and ye shall be gathered one by one, O ye children of Israel. {27:13} And it shall come to pass in that day, that the great trumpet shall be blown, and they shall come which were ready to perish in the land of Assyria, and the outcasts in the land of Egypt, and shall worship the LORD in the holy mount at Jerusalem.

{28:1} Woe to the crown of pride, to the drunkards of Ephraim, whose glorious beauty is a fading flower, which are on the head of the fat valleys of them that are overcome with wine! {28:2} Behold, the Lord hath a mighty and strong one, which as a tempest of hail and a destroying storm, as a flood of mighty waters overflowing, shall cast down to the earth with the hand. {28:3} The crown of pride, the drunkards of Ephraim, shall be trodden under feet: {28:4} And the glorious beauty, which is on the head of the fat valley, shall be a fading flower, and as the hasty fruit before the summer; which when he that looketh upon it seeth, while it is yet in his hand he eateth it up. {28:5} In that day shall the LORD of hosts be for a crown of glory, and for a diadem of beauty, unto the residue of his people, {28:6} And for a spirit of judgment to him that sitteth in judgment, and for strength to them that turn the battle to the gate. {28:7} But they also have erred through wine, and through strong drink are out of the way; the priest and the prophet have erred through strong drink, they are swallowed up of wine, they are out of the way through strong drink; they err in vision, they stumble in judgment. {28:8} For all tables are full of vomit and filthiness, so that there is no place clean. {28:9} Whom shall he teach knowledge? and whom shall he make to understand doctrine? them that are weaned from the milk, and drawn from the breasts. {28:10} For precept must be upon precept, precept upon precept; line upon line, line upon line; here a little, and there a little: {28:11} For with stammering lips and another tongue will he speak to this people. {28:12} To whom he said, This is the rest wherewith ye may cause the weary to rest; and this is the refreshing: yet they would not hear. {28:13} But the word of the LORD was unto them precept upon precept, precept upon precept; line upon line, line upon line; here a little, and there a little; that they might go, and fall backward, and be broken, and snared, and taken. {28:14} Wherefore hear the word of the LORD, ye scornful men, that rule this people which is in Jerusalem. {28:15} Because ye have said, We have made a covenant with death, and with hell are we at agreement; when the overflowing scourge shall pass through, it shall not come unto us: for we have made lies our refuge, and under falsehood have we hid ourselves: {28:16} Therefore thus saith the Lord GOD, Behold, I lay in Zion for a foundation a stone, a tried stone, a precious corner stone, a sure foundation: he that believeth shall not make haste. {28:17} Judgment also will I lay to the line, and righteousness to the plummet: and the hail shall sweep away the refuge of lies, and the waters shall overflow the hiding place. {28:18} And your covenant with death shall be disannulled, and your agreement with hell shall not stand; when the overflowing scourge shall pass through, then ye shall be trodden down by it. {28:19} From the time that it goeth forth it shall take you: for morning by morning shall it pass over, by day and by night: and it shall be a vexation only to understand the report. {28:20} For the bed is shorter than that a man can stretch himself on it: and the covering narrower than that he can wrap himself in it. {28:21} For the LORD shall rise up as in mount Perazim, he shall be wroth as in the valley of Gibeon, that he may do his work, his strange work; and bring to pass his act, his strange act. {28:22} Now therefore be ye not mockers, lest your bands be made strong: for I have heard from the Lord GOD of hosts a consumption, even determined upon the whole earth. {28:23} Give ye ear, and hear my voice; hearken, and hear my speech. {28:24} Doth the plowman plow all day to sow? doth he open and break the clods of his ground? {28:25} When he hath made plain the face thereof, doth he not cast abroad the fitches, and scatter the cummin, and cast in the principal wheat and the appointed barley and the rie in their place? {28:26} For his God doth instruct him to discretion, and doth teach him. {28:27} For the fitches are not threshed with a threshing instrument, neither is a cart wheel turned about upon the cummin; but the fitches are beaten out with a staff, and the cummin with a rod. {28:28} Bread corn is bruised; because he will not ever be threshing it, nor break it with the wheel of his cart, nor bruise it with his horsemen. {28:29} This also cometh forth from the LORD of hosts, which is wonderful in counsel, and excellent in working.

{29:1} Woe to Ariel, to Ariel, the city where David dwelt! Add ye year to year; let them kill sacrifices. {29:2} Yet I will distress Ariel, and there shall be heaviness and sorrow: and it shall be unto me as Ariel. {29:3} And I will camp against thee round about, and will lay siege against thee with a mount, and I will raise forts against thee. {29:4} And thou shalt be brought down, and shalt speak out of the ground, and thy speech shall be low out of the dust, and thy voice shall be, as of one that hath a familiar spirit, out of the ground, and thy speech shall whisper out of the dust. {29:5} Moreover the multitude of thy strangers shall be like small dust, and the multitude of the terrible ones shall be as chaff that passeth away: yea, it shall be at an instant suddenly. {29:6} Thou shalt be visited of the LORD of hosts with thunder, and with earthquake, and great noise, with storm and tempest, and the flame of devouring fire. {29:7} And the multitude of all the nations that fight against Ariel, even all that fight against her and her munition, and that distress her, shall be as a dream of a night vision. {29:8} It shall even be as when a hungry man dreameth, and, behold, he eateth; but he awaketh, and his soul is empty: or as when a thirsty man dreameth, and, behold, he drinketh; but he awaketh, and, behold, he is faint, and his soul hath appetite: so shall the multitude of all the nations be, that fight against mount Zion. {29:9} Stay yourselves, and wonder; cry ye out, and cry: they are drunken, but not with wine; they stagger, but not with strong drink. {29:10} For the LORD hath poured out upon you the spirit of deep sleep, and hath closed your eyes: the prophets and your rulers, the seers hath he covered. {29:11} And the vision of all is become unto you as the words of a book that is sealed, which men deliver to one that is learned, saying, Read this, I pray thee: and he saith, I cannot; for it is sealed: {29:12} And the book is delivered to him that is not learned, saying, Read this, I pray thee: and he saith, I am not learned. {29:13} Wherefore the Lord said, Forasmuch as this people draw near me with their mouth, and with their lips do honour me, but have removed their heart far from me, and their fear toward me is taught by the precept of men: {29:14} Therefore, behold, I will proceed to do a marvellous work among this people, even a marvellous work and a wonder: for the wisdom of their wise men shall perish, and the understanding of their prudent men shall be hid. {29:15} Woe unto them that seek deep to hide their counsel from the LORD, and their works are in the dark, and they say, Who seeth us? and who knoweth us? {29:16} Surely your turning of things upside down shall be esteemed as the potter's clay: for shall the work say of him that made it, He made me not? or shall the thing framed say of him that framed it, He had no understanding? {29:17} Is it not yet a very little while, and Lebanon shall be turned into a fruitful field, and the fruitful field shall be esteemed as a forest? {29:18} And in that day shall the deaf hear the words of the book, and the eyes of the blind shall see out of obscurity, and out of darkness. {29:19} The meek also shall increase their joy in the LORD, and the poor among men shall rejoice in the Holy One of Israel. {29:20} For the terrible one is brought to nought, and the scorner is consumed, and all that watch for iniquity are cut off: {29:21} That make a man an offender for a word, and lay a snare for him that reproveth in the gate, and turn aside the just for a thing of nought. {29:22} Therefore thus saith the LORD, who redeemed Abraham, concerning the house of Jacob, Jacob shall not now be ashamed, neither shall his face now wax pale. {29:23} But when he seeth his children, the work of mine hands, in the midst of him, they shall sanctify my name, and sanctify the Holy One of Jacob, and shall fear the God of Israel. {29:24} They also that erred in spirit shall come to understanding, and they that murmured shall learn doctrine.

{30:1} Woe to the rebellious children, saith the LORD, that take counsel, but not of me; and that cover with a covering, but not of my spirit, that they may add sin to sin: {30:2} That walk to go down into Egypt, and have not asked at my mouth; to strengthen themselves in the strength of Pharaoh, and to trust in the shadow of Egypt! {30:3} Therefore shall the strength of Pharaoh be your shame, and the trust in the shadow of Egypt your confusion. {30:4} For his princes were at Zoan, and his ambassadors came to Hanes. {30:5} They were all ashamed of a people that could not profit them, nor be an help nor profit, but a shame, and also a reproach. {30:6} The burden of the beasts of the south: into the land of trouble and anguish, from whence come the young and old lion, the viper and fiery flying serpent, they will carry their riches upon the shoulders of young asses, and their treasures upon the bunches of camels, to a people that shall not profit them. {30:7} For the Egyptians shall help in vain, and to no purpose: therefore have I cried concerning this, Their strength is to sit still. {30:8} Now go, write it before them in a table, and note it in a book, that it may be for the time to come forever and ever: {30:9} That this is a rebellious people, lying children, children that will not hear the law of the LORD: {30:10} Which say to the seers, See not; and to the prophets, Prophesy not unto us right things, speak unto us smooth things, prophesy deceits: {30:11} Get you out of the way, turn aside out of the path, cause the Holy One of Israel to cease from before us. {30:12} Wherefore thus saith the Holy One of Israel, Because ye despise this word, and trust in oppression and perverseness, and stay thereon: {30:13} Therefore this iniquity shall be to you as a breach ready to fall, swelling out in a high wall, whose breaking cometh suddenly at an instant. {30:14} And he shall break it as the breaking of the potters' vessel that is broken in pieces; he shall not spare: so that there shall not be found in the bursting of it a sherd to take fire from the hearth, or to take water withal out of the pit. {30:15} For thus saith the Lord GOD, the Holy One of Israel; In returning and rest shall ye be saved; in quietness and in confidence shall be your strength: and ye would not. {30:16} But ye said, No; for we will flee upon horses; therefore shall ye flee: and, We will ride upon the swift; therefore shall they that pursue you be swift. {30:17} One thousand shall flee at the rebuke of one; at the rebuke of five shall ye flee: till ye be left as a beacon upon the top of a mountain, and as an ensign on an hill. {30:18} And therefore will the LORD wait, that he may be gracious unto you, and therefore will he be exalted, that he may have mercy upon you: for the LORD is a God of judgment: blessed are all they that wait for him. {30:19} For the people shall dwell in Zion at Jerusalem: thou shalt weep no more: he will be very gracious unto thee at the voice of thy cry; when he shall hear it, he will answer thee. {30:20} And though the Lord give you the bread of adversity, and the water of affliction, yet shall not thy teachers be removed into a corner any more, but thine eyes shall see thy teachers: {30:21} And thine ears shall hear a word behind thee, saying, This is the way, walk ye in it, when ye turn to the right hand, and when ye turn to the left. {30:22} Ye shall defile also the covering of thy graven images of silver, and the ornament of thy molten images of gold: thou shalt cast them away as a menstruous cloth; thou shalt say unto it, Get thee hence. {30:23} Then shall he give the rain of thy seed, that thou shalt sow the ground withal; and bread of the increase of the earth, and it shall be fat and plenteous: in that day shall thy cattle feed in large pastures. {30:24} The oxen likewise and the young asses that ear the ground shall eat clean provender, which hath been winnowed with the shovel and with the fan. {30:25} And there shall be upon every high mountain, and upon every high hill, rivers and streams of waters in the day of the great slaughter, when the towers fall. {30:26} Moreover the light of the moon shall be as the light of the sun, and the light of the sun shall be sevenfold, as the light of seven days, in the day that the LORD bindeth up the breach of his people, and healeth the stroke of their wound. {30:27} Behold, the name of the LORD cometh from far, burning with his anger, and the burden thereof is heavy: his lips are full of indignation, and his tongue as a devouring fire: {30:28} And his breath, as an overflowing stream, shall reach to the midst of the neck, to sift the nations with the sieve of vanity: and there shall be a bridle in the jaws of the people, causing them to err. {30:29} Ye shall have a song, as in the night when a holy solemnity is kept; and gladness of heart, as when one goeth with a pipe to come into the mountain of the LORD, to the mighty One of Israel. {30:30} And the LORD shall cause his glorious voice to be heard, and shall shew the lighting down of his arm, with the indignation of his anger, and with the flame of a devouring fire, with scattering, and tempest, and hailstones. {30:31} For through the voice of the LORD shall the Assyrian be beaten down, which smote with a rod. {30:32} And in every place where the grounded staff shall pass, which the LORD shall lay upon him, it shall be with tabrets and harps: and in battles of shaking will he fight with it. {30:33} For Tophet is ordained of old; yea, for the king it is prepared; he hath made it deep and large: the pile thereof is fire and much wood; the breath of the LORD, like a stream of brimstone, doth kindle it.

{31:1} Woe to them that go down to Egypt for help; and stay on horses, and trust in chariots, because they are many; and in horsemen, because they are very strong; but they look not unto the Holy One of Israel, neither seek the LORD! {31:2} Yet he also is wise, and will bring evil, and will not call back his words: but will arise against the house of the evildoers, and against the help of them that work iniquity. {31:3} Now the Egyptians are men, and not God; and their horses flesh, and not spirit. When the LORD shall stretch out his hand, both he that helpeth shall fall, and he that is holpen shall fall down, and they all shall fail together. {31:4} For thus hath the LORD spoken unto me, Like as the lion and the young lion roaring on his prey, when a multitude of shepherds is called forth against him, he will not be afraid of their voice, nor abase himself for the noise of them: so shall the LORD of hosts come down to fight for mount Zion, and for the hill thereof. {31:5} As birds flying, so will the LORD of hosts defend Jerusalem; defending also he will deliver it; and passing over he will preserve it. {31:6} Turn ye unto him from whom the children of Israel have deeply revolted. {31:7} For in that day every man shall cast away his idols of silver, and his idols of gold, which your own hands have made unto you for a sin. {31:8} Then shall the Assyrian fall with the sword, not of a mighty man; and the sword, not of a mean man, shall devour him: but he shall flee from the sword, and his young men shall be discomfited. {31:9} And he shall pass over to his strong hold for fear, and his princes shall be afraid of the ensign, saith the LORD, whose fire is in Zion, and his furnace in Jerusalem.

{32:1} Behold, a king shall reign in righteousness, and princes shall rule in judgment. {32:2} And a man shall be as a hiding place from the wind, and a covert from the tempest; as rivers of water in a dry place, as the shadow of a great rock in a weary land. {32:3} And the eyes of them that see shall not be dim, and the ears of them that hear shall hearken. {32:4} The heart also of the rash shall understand knowledge, and the tongue of the stammerers shall be ready to speak plainly. {32:5} The vile person shall be no more called liberal, nor the churl said to be bountiful. {32:6} For the vile person will speak villainy, and his heart will work iniquity, to practice hypocrisy, and to utter error against the LORD, to make empty the soul of the hungry, and he will cause the drink of the thirsty to fail. {32:7} The instruments also of the churl are evil: he devises wicked devices to destroy the poor with lying words, even when the needy speaketh right. {32:8} But the liberal devises liberal things; and by liberal things shall he stand. {32:9} Rise up, ye women that are at ease; hear my voice, ye careless daughters; give ear unto my speech. {32:10} Many days and years shall ye be troubled, ye careless women: for the vintage shall fail, the gathering shall not come. {32:11} Tremble, ye women that are at ease; be troubled, ye careless ones: strip you, and make you bare, and gird sackcloth upon your loins. {32:12} They shall lament for the teats, for the pleasant fields, for the fruitful vine. {32:13} Upon the land of my people shall come up thorns and briers; yea, upon all the houses of joy in the joyous city: {32:14} Because the palaces shall be forsaken; the multitude of the city shall be left; the forts and towers shall be for dens forever, a joy of wild asses, a pasture of flocks; {32:15} Until the spirit be poured upon us from on high, and the wilderness be a fruitful field, and the fruitful field be counted for a forest. {32:16} Then judgment shall dwell in the wilderness, and righteousness remain in the fruitful field. {32:17} And the work of righteousness shall be peace; and the effect of righteousness quietness and assurance forever. {32:18} And my people shall dwell in a peaceable habitation, and in sure dwellings, and in quiet resting places; {32:19} When it shall hail, coming down on the forest; and the city shall be low in a low place. {32:20} Blessed are ye that sow beside all waters, that send forth thither the feet of the ox and the ass.

{33:1} Woe to you who plunder but are not plundered, and deal treacherously but are not dealt with treacherously! When you cease to plunder, you will be plundered; when you stop dealing treacherously, they will deal treacherously with you. {33:2} O LORD, be gracious to us; we have waited for you. Be our arm every morning, our salvation also in the time of trouble. {33:3} At the noise of the tumult, the people fled; at the lifting up of yourself, the nations were scattered. {33:4} And your spoil shall be gathered like the gathering of the caterpillar; as the running to and fro of locusts, he shall run upon them. {33:5} The LORD is exalted, for he dwells on high; he has filled Zion with judgment and righteousness. {33:6} And wisdom and knowledge shall be the stability of your times, and strength of salvation; the fear of the LORD is his treasure. {33:7} Behold, their valiant ones shall cry without; the ambassadors of peace shall weep bitterly. {33:8} The highways lie waste, the wayfaring man ceases. He has broken the covenant, he has despised the cities, he regards no man. {33:9} The earth mourns and languishes; Lebanon is ashamed and hewn down; Sharon is like a wilderness; and Bashan and Carmel shake off their fruits. {33:10} Now will I rise, says the LORD; now will I be exalted; now will I lift up myself. {33:11} You shall conceive chaff, you shall bring forth stubble; your breath, as fire, shall devour you. {33:12} And the people shall be as the burnings of lime; as thorns cut up shall they be burned in the fire. {33:13} Hear, you who are far off, what I have done; and you who are near, acknowledge my might. {33:14} The sinners in Zion are afraid; fearfulness has surprised the hypocrites. Who among us shall dwell with the devouring fire? Who among us shall dwell with everlasting burnings? {33:15} He who walks righteously, and speaks uprightly; he who despises the gain of oppressions, who shakes his hands from holding bribes, who stops his ears from hearing of blood, and shuts his eyes from seeing evil; {33:16} He shall dwell on high; his place of defense shall be the munitions of rocks; bread shall be given him; his waters shall be sure. {33:17} Your eyes shall see the king in his beauty; they shall behold the land that is very far off. {33:18} Your heart shall meditate terror. Where is the scribe? Where is the receiver? Where is he that counted the towers? {33:19} You shall not see a fierce people, a people of a deeper speech than you can perceive, of a stammering tongue that you cannot understand. {33:20} Look upon Zion, the city of our solemnities; your eyes shall see Jerusalem, a quiet habitation, a tabernacle that shall not be taken down; not one of its stakes shall ever be removed, neither shall any of its cords be broken. {33:21} But there the glorious LORD will be unto us a place of broad rivers and streams; wherein shall go no galley with oars, neither shall gallant ship pass thereby. {33:22} For the LORD is our judge, the LORD is our lawgiver, the LORD is our king; he will save us. {33:23} Your tacklings are loosed; they could not well strengthen their mast, they could not spread the sail; then is the prey of a great spoil divided; the lame take the prey. {33:24} And the inhabitant shall not say, "I am sick"; the people that dwell therein shall be forgiven their iniquity.

{34:1} Come near, you nations, to hear; and listen, you people: let the earth hear, and all that is therein; the world, and all things that come forth of it. {34:2} For the indignation of the LORD is upon all nations, and his fury upon all their armies: he has utterly destroyed them, he has delivered them to the slaughter. {34:3} Their slain also shall be cast out, and their stink shall come up out of their carcasses, and the mountains shall be melted with their blood. {34:4} And all the host of heaven shall be dissolved, and the heavens shall be rolled together as a scroll: and all their host shall fall down, as the leaf falls off from the vine, and as a falling fig from the fig tree. {34:5} For my sword shall be bathed in heaven: behold, it shall come down upon Edom, and upon the people of my curse, to judgment. {34:6} The sword of the LORD is filled with blood, it is made fat with fatness, and with the blood of lambs and goats, with the fat of the kidneys of rams: for the LORD has a sacrifice in Bozrah, and a great slaughter in the land of Edom. {34:7} And the unicorns shall come down with them, and the bullocks with the bulls; and their land shall be soaked with blood, and their dust made fat with fatness. {34:8} For it is the day of the LORD'S vengeance, and the year of recompenses for the controversy of Zion. {34:9} And the streams thereof shall be turned into pitch, and the dust thereof into brimstone, and the land thereof shall become burning pitch. {34:10} It shall not be quenched night nor day; the smoke thereof shall go up forever: from generation to generation it shall lie waste; none shall pass through it forever and ever. {34:11} But the cormorant and the bittern shall possess it; the owl also and the raven shall dwell in it: and he shall stretch out upon it the line of confusion, and the stones of emptiness. {34:12} They shall call the nobles thereof to the kingdom, but none shall be there, and all her princes shall be nothing. {34:13} And thorns shall come up in her palaces, nettles and brambles in the fortresses thereof: and it shall be a habitation of dragons, and a court for owls. {34:14} The wild beasts of the desert shall also meet with the wild beasts of the island, and the satyr shall cry to his fellow; the screech owl also shall rest there, and find for herself a place of rest. {34:15} There shall the great owl make her nest, and lay, and hatch, and gather under her shadow: there shall the vultures also be gathered, everyone with her mate. {34:16} Seek ye out of the book of the LORD, and read: no one of these shall fail, none shall want her mate: for my mouth it hath commanded, and his spirit it hath gathered them. {34:17} And he hath cast the lot for them, and his hand hath divided it unto them by line: they shall possess it forever, from generation to generation shall they dwell therein.

{35:1} The wilderness and the solitary place shall be glad for them; and the desert shall rejoice, and blossom as the rose. {35:2} It shall blossom abundantly, and rejoice even with joy and singing: the glory of Lebanon shall be given unto it, the excellency of Carmel and Sharon, they shall see the glory of the LORD, and the excellency of our God. {35:3} Strengthen ye the weak hands, and confirm the feeble knees. {35:4} Say to them that are of a fearful heart, Be strong, fear not: behold, your God will come with vengeance, even God with a recompense; he will come and save you. {35:5} Then the eyes of the blind shall be opened, and the ears of the deaf shall be unstopped. {35:6} Then shall the lame man leap as a hart, and the tongue of the dumb sing: for in the wilderness shall waters break out, and streams in the desert. {35:7} And the parched ground shall become a pool, and the thirsty land springs of water: in the habitation of dragons, where each lay, shall be grass with reeds and rushes. {35:8} And a highway shall be there, and a way, and it shall be called The way of holiness; the unclean shall not pass over it; but it shall be for those: the wayfaring men, though fools, shall not err therein. {35:9} No lion shall be there, nor any ravenous beast shall go up thereon, it shall not be found there; but the redeemed shall walk there: {35:10} And the ransomed of the LORD shall return, and come to Zion with songs and everlasting joy upon their heads: they shall obtain joy and gladness, and sorrow and sighing shall flee away.

{36:1} Now it came to pass in the fourteenth year of king Hezekiah, that Sennacherib king of Assyria came up against all the defenced cities of Judah, and took them. {36:2} And the king of Assyria sent Rabshakeh from Lachish to Jerusalem unto king Hezekiah with a great army. And he stood by the conduit of the upper pool in the highway of the fuller's field. {36:3} Then came forth unto him Eliakim, Hilkiah's son, which was over the house, and Shebna the scribe, and Joah, Asaph's son, the recorder. {36:4} And Rabshakeh said unto them, Say ye now to Hezekiah, Thus saith the great king, the king of Assyria, What confidence is this wherein thou trustest? {36:5} I say, (but they are but vain words) I have counsel and strength for war: now on whom dost thou trust, that thou rebellest against me? {36:6} Lo, thou trustest in the staff of this broken reed, on Egypt; whereon if a man lean, it will go into his hand, and pierce it: so is Pharaoh king of Egypt to all that trust in him. {36:7} But if thou say to me, We trust in the LORD our God: is it not he, whose high places and whose altars Hezekiah hath taken away, and said to Judah and to Jerusalem, Ye shall worship before this altar? {36:8} Now therefore give pledges, I pray thee, to my master the king of Assyria, and I will give thee two thousand horses, if thou be able on thy part to set riders upon them. {36:9} How then wilt thou turn away the face of one captain of the least of my master's servants, and put thy trust on Egypt for chariots and for horsemen? {36:10} And am I now come up without the LORD against this land to destroy it? the LORD said unto me, Go up against this land, and destroy it. {36:11} Then said Eliakim and Shebna and Joah unto Rabshakeh, Speak, I pray thee, unto thy servants in the Syrian language; for we understand it: and speak not to us in the Jews' language, in the ears of the people that are on the wall. {36:12} But Rabshakeh said, Hath my master sent me to thy master and to thee to speak these words? hath he not sent me to the men that sit upon the wall, that they may eat their own dung, and drink their own piss with you? {36:13} Then Rabshakeh stood, and cried with a loud voice in the Jews' language, and said, Hear ye the words of the great king, the king of Assyria. {36:14} Thus saith the king, Let not Hezekiah deceive you: for he shall not be able to deliver you. {36:15} Neither let Hezekiah make you trust in the LORD, saying, The LORD will surely deliver us: this city shall not be delivered into the hand of the king of Assyria. {36:16} Hearken not to Hezekiah: for thus saith the king of Assyria, Make an agreement with me by a present, and come out to me: and eat ye every one of his vine, and every one of his fig tree, and drink ye every one the waters of his own cistern; {36:17} Until I come and take you away to a land like your own land, a land of corn and wine, a land of bread and vineyards. {36:18} Beware lest Hezekiah persuade you, saying, The LORD will deliver us. Hath any of the gods of the nations delivered his land out of the hand of the king of Assyria? {36:19} Where are the gods of Hamath and Arphad? where are the gods of Sepharvaim? and have they delivered Samaria out of my hand? {36:20} Who among all the gods of these lands have delivered their land out of my hand, that the LORD should deliver Jerusalem out of my hand? {36:21} But they held their peace, and answered him not a word: for the king's commandment was, saying, Answer him not. {36:22} Then came Eliakim, the son of Hilkiah, that was over the household, and Shebna the scribe, and Joah, the son of Asaph, the recorder, to Hezekiah with their clothes rent, and told him the words of Rabshakeh.

{37:1} And it came to pass, when king Hezekiah heard it, that he rent his clothes, and covered himself with sackcloth, and went into the house of the LORD. {37:2} And he sent Eliakim, who was over the household, and Shebna the scribe, and the elders of the priests covered with sackcloth, unto Isaiah the prophet the son of Amoz. {37:3} And they said unto him, Thus saith Hezekiah, This day is a day of trouble, and of rebuke, and of blasphemy: for the children are come to the birth, and there is not strength to bring forth. {37:4} It may be the LORD thy God will hear the words of Rabshakeh, whom the king of Assyria his master hath sent to reproach the living God, and will reprove the words which the LORD thy God hath heard: wherefore lift up thy prayer for the remnant that is left. {37:5} So the servants of king Hezekiah came to Isaiah. {37:6} And Isaiah said unto them, Thus shall ye say unto your master, Thus saith the LORD, Be not afraid of the words that thou hast heard, wherewith the servants of the king of Assyria have blasphemed me. {37:7} Behold, I will send a blast upon him, and he shall hear a rumour, and return to his own land; and I will cause him to fall by the sword in his own land. {37:8} So Rabshakeh returned, and found the king of Assyria warring against Libnah: for he had heard that he was departed from Lachish. {37:9} And he heard say concerning Tirhakah king of Ethiopia, He is come forth to make war with thee. And when he heard it, he sent messengers to Hezekiah, saying, {37:10} Thus shall ye speak to Hezekiah king of Judah, saying, Let not thy God, in whom thou trustest, deceive thee, saying, Jerusalem shall not be given into the hand of the king of Assyria. {37:11} Behold, thou hast heard what the kings of Assyria have done to all lands by destroying them utterly; and shalt thou be delivered? {37:12} Have the gods of the nations delivered them which my fathers have destroyed, as Gozan, and Haran, and Rezeph, and the children of Eden which were in Telassar? {37:13} Where is the king of Hamath, and the king of Arphad, and the king of the city of Sepharvaim, Hena, and Ivah? {37:14} And Hezekiah received the letter from the hand of the messengers, and read it: and Hezekiah went up unto the house of the LORD, and spread it before the LORD. {37:15} And Hezekiah prayed unto the LORD, saying, {37:16} O LORD of hosts, God of Israel, that dwellest between the cherubims, thou art the God, even thou alone, of all the kingdoms of the earth: thou hast made heaven and earth. {37:17} Incline thine ear, O LORD, and hear; open thine eyes, O LORD, and see: and hear all the words of Sennacherib, which hath sent to reproach the living God. {37:18} Of a truth, LORD, the kings of Assyria have laid waste all the nations, and their countries, {37:19} And have cast their gods into the fire: for they were no gods, but the work of men's hands, wood and stone: therefore they have destroyed them. {37:20} Now therefore, O LORD our God, save us from his hand, that all the kingdoms of the earth may know that thou art the LORD, even thou only. {37:21} Then Isaiah the son of Amoz sent unto Hezekiah, saying, Thus saith the LORD God of Israel, Whereas thou hast prayed to me against Sennacherib king of Assyria: {37:22} This is the word which the LORD hath spoken concerning him; The virgin, the daughter of Zion, hath despised thee, and laughed thee to scorn; the daughter of Jerusalem hath shaken her head at thee. {37:23} Whom hast thou reproached and blasphemed? and against whom hast thou exalted thy voice, and lifted up thine eyes on high? even against the Holy One of Israel. {37:24} By thy servants hast thou reproached the Lord, and hast said, By the multitude of my chariots am I come up to the height of the mountains, to the sides of Lebanon; and I will cut down the tall cedars thereof, and the choice fir trees thereof: and I will enter into the height of his border, and the forest of his Carmel. {37:25} I have digged, and drunk water; and with the sole of my feet have I dried up all the rivers of the besieged places. {37:26} Hast thou not heard long ago, how I have done it; and of ancient times, that I have formed it? now have I brought it to pass, that thou shouldest be to lay waste defenced cities into ruinous heaps. {37:27} Therefore their inhabitants were of small power, they were dismayed and confounded: they were as the grass of the field, and as the green herb, as the grass on the housetops, and as corn blasted before it be grown up. {37:28} But I know thy abode, and thy going out, and thy coming in, and thy rage against me. {37:29} Because thy rage against me, and thy tumult, is come up into mine ears, therefore will I put my hook in thy nose, and my bridle in thy lips, and I will turn thee back by the way by which thou camest. {37:30} And this shall be a sign unto thee, Ye shall eat this year such as groweth of itself; and the second year that which springeth of the same: and in the third year sow ye, and reap, and plant vineyards, and eat the fruit thereof. {37:31} And the remnant that is escaped of the house of Judah shall again take root downward, and bear fruit upward: {37:32} For out of Jerusalem shall go forth a remnant, and they that escape out of mount Zion: the zeal of the LORD of hosts shall do this. {37:33} Therefore thus saith the LORD concerning the king of Assyria, He shall not come into this city, nor shoot an arrow there nor come before it with shields, nor cast a bank against it. {37:34} By the way that he came, by the same shall he return, and shall not come into this city, saith the LORD. {37:35} For I will defend this city to save it for mine own sake, and for my servant David's sake. {37:36} Then the angel of the LORD went forth, and smote in the camp of the Assyrians a hundred and fourscore and five thousand: and when they arose early in the morning, behold, they were all dead corpses. {37:37} So Sennacherib king of Assyria departed, and went and returned, and dwelt at Nineveh. {37:38} And it came to pass, as he was worshipping in the house of Nisroch his god, that Adrammelech and Sharezer his sons smote him with the sword; and they escaped into the land of Armenia: and Esar-haddon his son reigned in his stead.

{38:1} In those days was Hezekiah sick unto death. And Isaiah the prophet the son of Amoz came unto him, and said unto him, Thus saith the LORD, Set thine house in order: for thou shalt die, and not live. {38:2} Then Hezekiah turned his face toward the wall, and prayed unto the LORD, {38:3} And said, Remember now, O LORD, I beseech thee, how I have walked before thee in truth and with a perfect heart, and have done that which is good in thy sight. And Hezekiah wept sore. {38:4} Then came the word of the LORD to Isaiah, saying, {38:5} Go, and say to Hezekiah, Thus saith the LORD, the God of David thy father, I have heard thy prayer, I have seen thy tears: behold, I will add unto thy days fifteen years. {38:6} And I will deliver thee and this city out of the hand of the king of Assyria: and I will defend this city. {38:7} And this shall be a sign unto thee from the LORD, that the LORD will do this thing that he hath spoken; {38:8} Behold, I will bring again the shadow of the degrees, which is gone down in the sun dial of Ahaz, ten degrees backward. So the sun returned ten degrees, by which degrees it was gone down. {38:9} The writing of Hezekiah king of Judah, when he had been sick, and was recovered of his sickness: {38:10} I said in the cutting off of my days, I shall go to the gates of the grave: I am deprived of the residue of my years. {38:11} I said, I shall not see the LORD, even the LORD, in the land of the living: I shall behold man no more with the inhabitants of the world. {38:12} Mine age is departed, and is removed from me as a shepherd's tent: I have cut off like a weaver my life: he will cut me off with pining sickness: from day even to night wilt thou make an end of me. {38:13} I reckoned till morning, that, as a lion, so will he break all my bones: from day even to night wilt thou make an end of me. {38:14} Like a crane or a swallow, so did I chatter: I did mourn as a dove: mine eyes fail with looking upward: O LORD, I am oppressed; undertake for me. {38:15} What shall I say? he hath both spoken unto me, and himself hath done it: I shall go softly all my years in the bitterness of my soul. {38:16} O Lord, by these things men live, and in all these things is the life of my spirit: so wilt thou recover me, and make me to live. {38:17} Behold, for peace I had great bitterness: but thou hast in love to my soul delivered it from the pit of corruption: for thou hast cast all my sins behind thy back. {38:18} For the grave cannot praise thee, death cannot celebrate thee: they that go down into the pit cannot hope for thy truth. {38:19} The living, the living, he shall praise thee, as I do this day: the father to the children shall make known thy truth. {38:20} The LORD was ready to save me: therefore we will sing my songs to the stringed instruments all the days of our life in the house of the LORD. {38:21} For Isaiah had said, Let them take a lump of figs, and lay it for a plaister upon the boil, and he shall recover. {38:22} Hezekiah also had said, What is the sign that I shall go up to the house of the LORD?

{39:1} At that time Merodach-baladan, the son of Baladan, king of Babylon, sent letters and a present to Hezekiah: for he had heard that he had been sick, and was recovered. {39:2} And Hezekiah was glad of them, and showed them the house of his precious things, the silver, and the gold, and the spices, and the precious ointment, and all the house of his armor, and all that was found in his treasures: there was nothing in his house, nor in all his dominion, that Hezekiah showed them not. {39:3} Then came Isaiah the prophet unto king Hezekiah, and said unto him, What said these men? and from whence came they unto thee? And Hezekiah said, They are come from a far country unto me, even from Babylon. {39:4} Then said he, What have they seen in thine house? And Hezekiah answered, All that is in mine house have they seen: there is nothing among my treasures that I have not showed them. {39:5} Then said Isaiah to Hezekiah, Hear the word of the LORD of hosts: {39:6} Behold, the days come, that all that is in thine house, and that which thy fathers have laid up in store until this day, shall be carried to Babylon: nothing shall be left, saith the LORD. {39:7} And of thy sons that shall issue from thee, which thou shalt beget, shall they take away; and they shall be eunuchs in the palace of the king of Babylon. {39:8} Then said Hezekiah to Isaiah, Good is the word of the LORD which thou hast spoken. He said moreover, For there shall be peace and truth in my days.

{40:1} Comfort ye, comfort ye my people, saith your God. {40:2} Speak ye comfortably to Jerusalem, and cry unto her, that her warfare is accomplished, that her iniquity is pardoned: for she hath received of the LORD'S hand double for all her sins. {40:3} The voice of him that crieth in the wilderness, Prepare ye the way of the LORD, make straight in the desert a highway for our God. {40:4} Every valley shall be exalted, and every mountain and hill shall be made low: and the crooked shall be made straight, and the rough places plain: {40:5} And the glory of the LORD shall be revealed, and all flesh shall see it together: for the mouth of the LORD hath spoken it. {40:6} The voice said, Cry. And he said, What shall I cry? All flesh is grass, and all the goodliness thereof is as the flower of the field: {40:7} The grass withereth, the flower fadeth: because the spirit of the LORD bloweth upon it: surely the people is grass. {40:8} The grass withereth, the flower fadeth: but the word of our God shall stand for ever. {40:9} O Zion, that bringest good tidings, get thee up into the high mountain; O Jerusalem, that bringest good tidings, lift up thy voice with strength; lift it up, be not afraid; say unto the cities of Judah, Behold your God! {40:10} Behold, the Lord GOD will come with strong hand, and his arm shall rule for him: behold, his reward is with him, and his work before him. {40:11} He shall feed his flock like a shepherd: he shall gather the lambs with his arm, and carry them in his bosom, and shall gently lead those that are with young. {40:12} Who hath measured the waters in the hollow of his hand, and meted out heaven with the span, and comprehended the dust of the earth in a measure, and weighed the mountains in scales, and the hills in a balance? {40:13} Who hath directed the Spirit of the LORD, or being his counsellor hath taught him? {40:14} With whom took he counsel, and who instructed him, and taught him in the path of judgment, and taught him knowledge, and shewed to him the way of understanding? {40:15} Behold, the nations are as a drop of a bucket, and are counted as the small dust of the balance: behold, he taketh up the isles as a very little thing. {40:16} And Lebanon is not sufficient to burn, nor the beasts thereof sufficient for a burnt offering. {40:17} All nations before him are as nothing; and they are counted to him less than nothing, and vanity. {40:18} To whom then will ye liken God? or what likeness will ye compare unto him? {40:19} The workman melteth a graven image, and the goldsmith spreadeth it over with gold, and casteth silver chains. {40:20} He that is so impoverished that he hath no oblation chooseth a tree that will not rot; he seeketh unto him a cunning workman to prepare a graven image, that shall not be moved. {40:21} Have ye not known? have ye not heard? hath it not been told you from the beginning? have ye not understood from the foundations of the earth? {40:22} It is he that sitteth upon the circle of the earth, and the inhabitants thereof are as grasshoppers; that stretcheth out the heavens as a curtain, and spreadeth them out as a tent to dwell in: {40:23} That bringeth the princes to nothing; he maketh the judges of the earth as vanity. {40:24} Yea, they shall not be planted; yea, they shall not be sown: yea, their stock shall not take root in the earth: and he shall also blow upon them, and they shall wither, and the whirlwind shall take them away as stubble. {40:25} To whom then will ye liken me, or shall I be equal? saith the Holy One. {40:26} Lift up your eyes on high, and behold who hath created these things, that bringeth out their host by number: he calleth them all by names by the greatness of his might, for that he is strong in power; not one faileth. {40:27} Why sayest thou, O Jacob, and speakest, O Israel, My way is hid from the LORD, and my judgment is passed over from my God? {40:28} **Hast thou not known? hast thou not heard, that the everlasting God, the LORD, the Creator of the ends of the earth, fainteth not, neither is weary? there is no searching of his understanding.** {40:29} He giveth power to the faint; and to them that have no might he increaseth strength. {40:30} Even the youths shall faint and be weary, and the young men shall utterly fall: {40:31} But they that wait upon the LORD shall renew their strength; they shall mount up with wings as eagles; they shall run, and not be weary; and they shall walk, and not faint.

{41:1} Keep silence before me, O islands; and let the people renew their strength: let them come near; then let them speak: let us come near together to judgment. {41:2} Who raised up the righteous man from the east, called him to his foot, gave the nations before him, and made him rule over kings? he gave them as the dust to his sword, and as driven stubble to his bow. {41:3} He pursued them, and passed safely; even by the way that he had not gone with his feet. {41:4} Who hath wrought and done it, calling the generations from the beginning? I the LORD, the first, and with the last; I am he. {41:5} The isles saw it, and feared; the ends of the earth were afraid, drew near, and came. {41:6} They helped every one his neighbour; and every one said to his brother, Be of good courage. {41:7} So the carpenter encouraged the goldsmith, and he that smootheth with the hammer him that smote the anvil, saying, It is ready for the soldering: and he fastened it with nails, that it should not be moved. {41:8} But thou, Israel, art my servant, Jacob whom I have chosen, the seed of Abraham my friend. {41:9} Thou whom I have taken from the ends of the earth, and called thee from the chief men thereof, and said unto thee, Thou art my servant; I have chosen thee, and not cast thee away. {41:10} Fear thou not; for I am with thee: be not dismayed; for I am thy God: I will strengthen thee; yea, I will help thee; yea, I will uphold thee with the right hand of my righteousness. {41:11} Behold, all they that were incensed against thee shall be ashamed and confounded: they shall be as nothing; and they that strive with thee shall perish. {41:12} Thou shalt seek them, and shalt not find them, even them that contended with thee: they that war against thee shall be as nothing, and as a thing of nought. {41:13} For I the LORD thy God will hold thy right hand, saying unto thee, Fear not; I will help thee. {41:14} Fear not, thou worm Jacob, and ye men of Israel; I will help thee, saith the LORD, and thy redeemer, the Holy One of Israel. {41:15} Behold, I will make thee a new sharp threshing instrument having teeth: thou shalt thresh the mountains, and beat them small, and shalt make the hills as chaff. {41:16} Thou shalt fan them, and the wind shall carry them away, and the whirlwind shall scatter them: and thou shalt rejoice in the LORD, and shalt glory in the Holy One of Israel. {41:17} When the poor and needy seek water, and there is none, and their tongue faileth for thirst, I the LORD will hear them, I the God of Israel will not forsake them. {41:18} I will open rivers in high places, and fountains in the midst of the valleys: I will make the wilderness a pool of water, and the dry land springs of water. {41:19} I will plant in the wilderness the cedar, the shittah tree, and the myrtle, and the oil tree; I will set in the desert the fir tree, and the pine, and the box tree together: {41:20} That they may see, and know, and consider, and understand together, that the hand of the LORD hath done this, and the Holy One of Israel hath created it. {41:21} Produce your cause, saith the LORD; bring forth your strong reasons, saith the King of Jacob. {41:22} Let them bring them forth, and show us what shall happen: let them show the former things, what they be, that we may consider them, and know the latter end of them; or declare us things for to come. {41:23} Show the things that are to come hereafter, that we may know that ye are gods: yea, do good, or do evil, that we may be dismayed, and behold it together. {41:24} Behold, ye are of nothing, and your work of nought: an abomination is he that chooseth you. {41:25} I have raised up one from the north, and he shall come: from the rising of the sun shall he call upon my name: and he shall come upon princes as upon mortar, and as the potter treadeth clay. {41:26} Who hath declared from the beginning, that we may know? and beforetime, that we may say, He is righteous? yea, there is none that showeth, yea, there is none that declareth, yea, there is none that heareth your words. {41:27} The first shall say to Zion, Behold, behold them: and I will give to Jerusalem one that bringeth good tidings. {41:28} For I beheld, and there was no man; even among them, and there was no counsellor, that, when I asked of them, could answer a word. {41:29} Behold, they are all vanity; their works are nothing: their molten images are wind and confusion.

{42:1} Behold my servant, whom I uphold; mine elect, in whom my soul delighteth; I have put my spirit upon him: he shall bring forth judgment to the Gentiles. {42:2} He shall not cry, nor lift up, nor cause his voice to be heard in the street. {42:3} A bruised reed shall he not break, and the smoking flax shall he not quench: he shall bring forth judgment unto truth. {42:4} He shall not fail nor be discouraged, till he have set judgment in the earth: and the isles shall wait for his law. {42:5} Thus saith God the LORD, he that created the heavens, and stretched them out; he that spread forth the earth, and that which cometh out of it; he that giveth breath unto the people upon it, and spirit to them that walk therein: {42:6} I the LORD have called thee in righteousness, and will hold thine hand, and will keep thee, and give thee for a covenant of the people, for a light of the Gentiles; {42:7} To open the blind eyes, to bring out the prisoners from the prison, and them that sit in darkness out of the prison house. {42:8} I am the LORD: that is my name: and my glory will I not give to another, neither my praise to graven images. {42:9} Behold, the former things are come to pass, and new things do I declare: before they spring forth I tell you of them. {42:10} Sing unto the LORD a new song, and his praise from the end of the earth, ye that go down to the sea, and all that is therein; the isles, and the inhabitants thereof. {42:11} Let the wilderness and the cities thereof lift up their voice, the villages that Kedar doth inhabit: let the inhabitants of the rock sing, let them shout from the top of the mountains. {42:12} Let them give glory unto the LORD, and declare his praise in the islands. {42:13} The LORD shall go forth as a mighty man, he shall stir up jealousy like a man of war: he shall cry, yea, roar; he shall prevail against his enemies. {42:14} I have long time holden my peace; I have been still, and refrained myself: now will I cry like a travailing woman; I will destroy and devour at once. {42:15} I will make waste mountains and hills, and dry up all their herbs; and I will make the rivers islands, and I will dry up the pools. {42:16} And I will bring the blind by a way that they knew not; I will lead them in paths that they have not known: I will make darkness light before them, and crooked things straight. These things will I do unto them, and not forsake them. {42:17} They shall be turned back, they shall be greatly ashamed, that trust in graven images, that say to the molten images, Ye are our gods. {42:18} Hear, ye deaf; and look, ye blind, that ye may see. {42:19} Who is blind, but my servant? or deaf, as my messenger that I sent? who is blind as he that is perfect, and blind as the LORD'S servant? {42:20} Seeing many things, but thou observest not; opening the ears, but he heareth not. {42:21} The LORD is well pleased for his righteousness' sake; he will magnify the law, and make it honourable. {42:22} But this is a people robbed and spoiled; they are all of them snared in holes, and they are hid in prison houses: they are for a prey, and none delivereth; for a spoil, and none saith, Restore. {42:23} Who among you will give ear to this? who will hearken and hear for the time to come? {42:24} Who gave Jacob for a spoil, and Israel to the robbers? did not the LORD, he against whom we have sinned? for they would not walk in his ways, neither were they obedient unto his law. {42:25} Therefore he hath poured upon them the fury of his anger, and the strength of battle: and it hath set him on fire round about, yet he knew not; and it burned him, yet he laid it not to heart.

{43:1} Behold, God says, "I created you, Jacob, and formed you, Israel. Fear not, for I have redeemed you; I have called you by your name; you are mine. {43:2} When you pass through waters, I will be with you; through rivers, they will not overflow you. When you walk through fire, you will not be burned; the flame will not kindle upon you. {43:3} For I am the LORD your God, the Holy One of Israel, your Savior. I gave Egypt for your ransom, Ethiopia and Seba for you. {43:4} Since you are precious in my sight, honorable, and I have loved you, I will give men for you, and people for your life. {43:5} Fear not, for I am with you. I will bring your seed from the east, and gather you from the west; {43:6} I will say to the north, Give up; and to the south, Keep not back: bring my sons from far, and my daughters from the ends of the earth; {43:7} Everyone called by my name: for I have created him for my glory, I have formed him; yes, I have made him. {43:8} Bring forth the blind people that have eyes, and the deaf that have ears. {43:9} Let all the nations be gathered together, and let the people be assembled: who among them can declare this, and show us former things? Let them bring forth their witnesses, that they may be justified: or let them hear, and say, [It is] truth. {43:10} You are my witnesses, says the LORD, and my servant whom I have chosen: that you may know and believe me, and understand that I am he: before me there was no God formed, neither shall there be after me. {43:11} I, even I, am the LORD; and beside me there is no savior. {43:12} I have declared, and have saved, and I have showed, when there was no strange god among you: therefore you are my witnesses, says the LORD, that I am God. {43:13} Yes, before the day was I am he; and there is none that can deliver out of my hand: I will work, and who shall let it? {43:14} Thus says the LORD, your redeemer, the Holy One of Israel; For your sake I have sent to Babylon, and have brought down all their nobles, and the Chaldeans, whose cry is in the ships. {43:15} I am the LORD, your Holy One, the creator of Israel, your King. {43:16} Thus says the LORD, who makes a way in the sea, and a path in the mighty waters; {43:17} Who brings forth the chariot and horse, the army and the power; they shall lie down together, they shall not rise: they are extinct, they are quenched as tow. {43:18} Remember not the former things, neither consider the things of old. {43:19} Behold, I will do a new thing; now it shall spring forth; shall you not know it? I will even make a way in the wilderness, and rivers in the desert. {43:20} The beast of the field shall honor me, the dragons and the owls: because I give waters in the wilderness, and rivers in the desert, to give drink to my people, my chosen. {43:21} This people have I formed for myself; they shall show forth my praise. {43:22} But you have not called upon me, O Jacob; but you have been weary of me, O Israel. {43:23} You have not brought me the small cattle of your burnt offerings; neither have you honored me with your sacrifices. I have not caused you to serve with an offering, nor wearied you with incense. {43:24} You have bought me no sweet cane with money, neither have you filled me with the fat of your sacrifices: but you have made me to serve with your sins, you have wearied me with your iniquities. {43:25} I, even I, am he that blots out your transgressions for my own sake, and will not remember your sins. {43:26} Put me in remembrance: let us plead together; declare you, that you may be justified. {43:27} Your first father has sinned, and your teachers have transgressed against me. {43:28} Therefore I have profaned the princes of the sanctuary, and have given Jacob to the curse, and Israel to reproaches."

{44:1} Listen now, Jacob my servant, and Israel, whom I have chosen: {44:2} Thus says the LORD who made you and formed you from the womb, who will help you; Fear not, O Jacob, my servant; and you, Jesurun, whom I have chosen. {44:3} For I will pour water upon him that is thirsty, and floods upon the dry ground: I will pour my spirit upon your seed, and my blessing upon your offspring. {44:4} And they shall spring up among the grass, as willows by the water courses. {44:5} One shall say, I am the LORD'S; and another shall call himself by the name of Jacob; and another shall subscribe with his hand unto the LORD, and surname himself by the name of Israel. {44:6} Thus says the LORD the King of Israel, and his redeemer the LORD of hosts; I am the first, and I am the last; and beside me there is no God. {44:7} And who, as I, shall call, and shall declare it, and set it in order for me, since I appointed the ancient people? and the things that are coming, and shall come, let them show unto them. {44:8} Fear not, neither be afraid: have not I told you from that time, and have declared it? you are even my witnesses. Is there a God beside me? yes, there is no God; I know not any. {44:9} They that make a graven image are all of them vanity; and their delectable things shall not profit; and they are their own witnesses; they see not, nor know; that they may be ashamed. {44:10} Who has formed a god, or molten a graven image that is profitable for nothing? {44:11} Behold, all his fellows shall be ashamed: and the workmen, they are of men: let them all be gathered together, let them stand up; yet they shall fear, and they shall be ashamed together. {44:12} The smith with the tongs both works in the coals, and fashions it with hammers, and works it with the strength of his arms: yes, he is hungry, and his strength fails: he drinks no water, and is faint. {44:13} The carpenter stretches out his rule; he marks it out with a line; he fits it with planes, and he marks it out with the compass, and makes it after the figure of a man, according to the beauty of a man; that it may remain in the house. {44:14} He hews down cedars, and takes the cypress and the oak, which he strengthens for himself among the trees of the forest: he plants an ash, and the rain nourishes it. {44:15} Then shall it be for a man to burn: for he will take thereof, and warm himself; yes, he kindles it, and bakes bread; yes, he makes a god, and worships it; he makes it a graven image, and falls down thereto. {44:16} He burns part thereof in the fire; with part thereof he eats flesh; he roasts roast, and is satisfied: yes, he warms himself, and says, Aha, I am warm, I have seen the fire: {44:17} And the residue thereof he makes a god, even his graven image: he falls down unto it, and worships it, and prays unto it, and says, Deliver me; for you are my god. {44:18} They have not known nor understood: for he has shut their eyes, that they cannot see; and their hearts, that they cannot understand. {44:19} And none considers in his heart, neither is there knowledge nor understanding to say, I have burned part of it in the fire; yes, also I have baked bread upon the coals thereof; I have roasted flesh, and eaten it: and shall I make the residue thereof an abomination? shall I fall down to the stock of a tree? {44:20} He feeds on ashes: a deceived heart has turned him aside, that he cannot deliver his soul, nor say, Is there not a lie in my right hand? {44:21} Remember these, O Jacob and Israel; for you are my servant: I have formed you; you are my servant: O Israel, you shall not be forgotten of me. {44:22} I have blotted out, as a thick cloud, your transgressions, and, as a cloud, your sins: return unto me; for I have redeemed you. {44:23} Sing, O you heavens; for the LORD has done it: shout, you lower parts of the earth: break forth into singing, you mountains, O forest, and every tree therein: for the LORD has redeemed Jacob, and glorified himself in Israel. {44:24} Thus says the LORD, your redeemer, and he that formed you from the womb, I am the LORD that makes all things; that stretches forth the heavens alone; that spreads abroad the earth by myself; {44:25} That frustrates the tokens of the liars, and makes diviners mad; that turns wise men backward, and makes their knowledge foolish; {44:26} That confirms the word of his servant, and performs the counsel of his messengers; that says to Jerusalem, You shall be inhabited; and to the cities of Judah, You shall be built, and I will raise up the decayed places thereof; {44:27} That says to the deep, Be dry, and I will dry up your rivers; {44:28} That says of Cyrus, He is my shepherd, and shall perform all my pleasure: even saying to Jerusalem, You shall be built; and to the temple, Your foundation shall be laid.

{45:1} Here is what the LORD says to his chosen one, to Cyrus, whose right hand I have held to subdue nations before him; I will loosen the loins of kings to open before him the two-leaved gates; and the gates shall not be shut; {45:2} I will go before you and make the crooked places straight: I will break in pieces the gates of brass and cut asunder the bars of iron; {45:3} And I will give you the treasures of darkness, and hidden riches of secret places, so that you may know that I, the LORD, who calls you by your name, am the God of Israel. {45:4} For the sake of my servant Jacob, and Israel my chosen, I have called you by your name: I have surnamed you, though you have not known me. {45:5} I am the LORD, and there is none else, there is no God beside me: I girded you, though you have not known me: {45:6} That they may know from the rising of the sun, and from the west, that there is none beside me. I am the LORD, and there is none else. {45:7} I form the light, and create darkness: I make peace, and create evil: I the LORD do all these things. {45:8} Drop down, you heavens, from above, and let the skies pour down righteousness: let the earth open, and let them bring forth salvation, and let righteousness spring up together; I the LORD have created it. {45:9} Woe unto him that strives with his Maker! Let the potsherd strive with the potsherds of the earth. Shall the clay say to him that fashions it, What are you making? or your work, He has no hands? {45:10} Woe unto him that says unto his father, What have you begotten? or to the woman, What have you brought forth? {45:11} Here is what the LORD, the Holy One of Israel, and his Maker, says: Ask me about things to come concerning my sons, and concerning the work of my hands, command you me. {45:12} I have made the earth, and created man upon it: I, even my hands, have stretched out the heavens, and all their host have I commanded. {45:13} I have raised him up in righteousness, and I will direct all his ways: he shall build my city, and he shall let go my captives, not for price nor reward, says the LORD of hosts. {45:14} Here is what the LORD says: The labor of Egypt, and merchandise of Ethiopia and of the Sabeans, men of stature, shall come over unto you, and they shall be yours: they shall come after you; in chains they shall come over, and they shall fall down unto you, they shall make supplication unto you, saying, Surely God is in you; and there is none else, there is no God. {45:15} Verily you are a God who hides yourself, O God of Israel, the Savior. {45:16} They shall be ashamed, and also confounded, all of them: they shall go to confusion together that are makers of idols. {45:17} But Israel shall be saved in the LORD with an everlasting salvation: you shall not be ashamed nor confounded world without end. {45:18} For thus says the LORD that created the heavens; God himself that formed the earth and made it; he has established it, he created it not in vain, he formed it to be inhabited: I am the LORD; and there is none else. {45:19} I have not spoken in secret, in a dark place of the earth: I said not unto the seed of Jacob, Seek me in vain: I the LORD speak righteousness, I declare things that are right. {45:20} Assemble yourselves and come; draw near together, you that are escaped of the nations: they have no knowledge that set up the wood of their graven image, and pray unto a god that cannot save. {45:21} Tell them, and bring them near; yes, let them take counsel together: who has declared this from ancient time? who has told it from that time? Have not I the LORD? and there is no God else beside me; a just God and a Savior; there is none beside me. {45:22} Look unto me, and be saved, all the ends of the earth: for I am God, and there is none else. {45:23} I have sworn by myself, the word has gone out of my mouth in righteousness, and shall not return, That unto me every knee shall bow, every tongue shall swear. {45:24} Surely, shall one say, in the LORD have I righteousness and strength: even to him shall men come; and all that are incensed against him shall be ashamed. {45:25} In the LORD shall all the seed of Israel be justified, and shall glory.

{46:1} Bel bows down, Nebo stoops; their idols were upon the beasts and upon the cattle: your carriages were heavy laden; they are a burden to the weary beast. {46:2} They stoop, they bow down together; they could not deliver the burden, but themselves are gone into captivity. {46:3} Listen to me, O house of Jacob, and all the remnant of the house of Israel, who are borne by me from the belly, who are carried from the womb: {46:4} And even to your old age I am he; and even to hoar hairs will I carry you: I have made, and I will bear; even I will carry, and will deliver you. {46:5} To whom will you liken me, and make me equal, and compare me, that we may be like? {46:6} They lavish gold out of the bag, and weigh silver in the balance, and hire a goldsmith; and he makes it a god: they fall down, yes, they worship. {46:7} They bear him upon the shoulder, they carry him, and set him in his place, and he stands; from his place shall he not remove: yes, one shall cry unto him, yet can he not answer, nor save him out of his trouble. {46:8} Remember this, and show yourselves men: bring it again to mind, O you transgressors. {46:9} Remember the former things of old: for I am God, and there is none else; I am God, and there is none like me, {46:10} Declaring the end from the beginning, and from ancient times the things that are not yet done, saying, My counsel shall stand, and I will do all my pleasure: {46:11} Calling a ravenous bird from the east, the man that executes my counsel from a far country: yes, I have spoken it, I will also bring it to pass; I have purposed it, I will also do it. {46:12} Listen to me, you stout-hearted, that are far from righteousness: {46:13} I bring near my righteousness; it shall not be far off, and my salvation shall not tarry: and I will place salvation in Zion for Israel my glory.

{47:1} Come down, and sit in the dust, O virgin daughter of Babylon, sit on the ground: there is no throne, O daughter of the Chaldeans: for thou shalt no more be called tender and delicate. {47:2} Take the millstones, and grind meal: uncover thy locks, make bare the leg, uncover the thigh, pass over the rivers. {47:3} Thy nakedness shall be uncovered, yea, thy shame shall be seen: I will take vengeance, and I will not meet thee as a man. {47:4} As for our redeemer, the LORD of hosts is his name, the Holy One of Israel. {47:5} Sit thou silent, and get thee into darkness, O daughter of the Chaldeans: for thou shalt no more be called, The lady of kingdoms. {47:6} I was wroth with my people, I have polluted mine inheritance, and given them into thine hand: thou didst show them no mercy; upon the ancient hast thou very heavily laid thy yoke. {47:7} And thou saidst, I shall be a lady forever: so that thou didst not lay these things to thy heart, neither didst remember the latter end of it. {47:8} Therefore hear now this, thou that art given to pleasures, that dwellest carelessly, that sayest in thine heart, I am, and none else beside me; I shall not sit as a widow, neither shall I know the loss of children: {47:9} But these two things shall come to thee in a moment in one day, the loss of children, and widowhood: they shall come upon thee in their perfection for the multitude of thy sorceries, and for the great abundance of thine enchantments. {47:10} For thou hast trusted in thy wickedness: thou hast said, None seeth me. Thy wisdom and thy knowledge, it hath perverted thee; and thou hast said in thine heart, I am, and none else beside me. {47:11} Therefore shall evil come upon thee; thou shalt not know from whence it riseth: and mischief shall fall upon thee; thou shalt not be able to put it off: and desolation shall come upon thee suddenly, which thou shalt not know. {47:12} Stand now with thine enchantments, and with the multitude of thy sorceries, wherein thou hast labored from thy youth; if so be thou shalt be able to profit, if so be thou mayest prevail. {47:13} Thou art wearied in the multitude of thy counsels. Let now the astrologers, the stargazers, the monthly prognosticators, stand up, and save thee from these things that shall come upon thee. {47:14} Behold, they shall be as stubble; the fire shall burn them; they shall not deliver themselves from the power of the flame: there shall not be a coal to warm at, nor fire to sit before it. {47:15} Thus shall they be unto thee with whom thou hast labored, even thy merchants, from thy youth: they shall wander everyone to his quarter; none shall save thee.

{48:1} Hear this, O house of Jacob, who are called by the name of Israel, and have come forth out of the waters of Judah, who swear by the name of the LORD, and make mention of the God of Israel, but not in truth, nor in righteousness. {48:2} For they call themselves of the holy city, and rely upon the God of Israel; The LORD of hosts is his name. {48:3} I have declared the former things from the beginning; and they went forth out of my mouth, and I showed them; I did them suddenly, and they came to pass. {48:4} Because I knew that you are obstinate, and your neck is an iron sinew, and your brow brass; {48:5} I have even from the beginning declared it to you; before it came to pass I showed it to you: lest you should say, My idol has done them, and my graven image, and my molten image, has commanded them. {48:6} You have heard, see all this; and will you not declare it? I have shown you new things from this time, even hidden things, and you did not know them. {48:7} They are created now, and not from the beginning; even before the day when you heard them not: lest you should say, Behold, I knew them. {48:8} Yes, you heard not; yes, you knew not; yes, from that time that your ear was not opened: for I knew that you would deal very treacherously, and were called a transgressor from the womb. {48:9} For my name's sake will I defer my anger, and for my praise will I refrain for you, that I cut you not off. {48:10} Behold, I have refined you, but not with silver; I have chosen you in the furnace of affliction. {48:11} For my own sake, even for my own sake, will I do it: for how should my name be polluted? and I will not give my glory to another. {48:12} Listen to me, O Jacob and Israel, my called; I am he; I am the first, I also am the last. {48:13} My hand also has laid the foundation of the earth, and my right hand has spanned the heavens: when I call unto them, they stand up together. {48:14} All you, assemble yourselves, and hear; which among them has declared these things? The LORD has loved him: he will do his pleasure on Babylon, and his arm shall be on the Chaldeans. {48:15} I, even I, have spoken; yes, I have called him: I have brought him, and he shall make his way prosperous. {48:16} Come near to me, hear this; I have not spoken in secret from the beginning; from the time that it was, there am I: and now the Lord GOD, and his Spirit, has sent me. {48:17} Thus says the LORD, your Redeemer, the Holy One of Israel; I am the LORD your God who teaches you to profit, who leads you by the way that you should go. {48:18} Oh that you had hearkened to my commandments! then had your peace been as a river, and your righteousness as the waves of the sea: {48:19} Your seed also had been as the sand, and the offspring of your bowels like the gravel thereof; his name should not have been cut off nor destroyed from before me. {48:20} Go forth from Babylon, flee from the Chaldeans, with a voice of singing declare it, tell this, utter it even to the end of the earth; say, The LORD has redeemed his servant Jacob. {48:21} And they thirsted not when he led them through the deserts: he caused the waters to flow out of the rock for them: he clave the rock also, and the waters gushed out. {48:22} There is no peace, says the LORD, unto the wicked.

{49:1} Listen, O isles, to me; and hearken, you people, from far; The LORD has called me from the womb; from the bowels of my mother he has made mention of my name. {49:2} And he has made my mouth like a sharp sword; in the shadow of his hand he has hidden me, and made me a polished shaft; in his quiver he has hidden me; {49:3} And said to me, You are my servant, O Israel, in whom I will be glorified. {49:4} Then I said, I have labored in vain, I have spent my strength for nothing, and in vain: yet surely my judgment is with the LORD, and my work with my God. {49:5} And now, says the LORD that formed me from the womb to be his servant, to bring Jacob again to him, Though Israel be not gathered, yet shall I be glorious in the eyes of the LORD, and my God shall be my strength. {49:6} And he said, It is a light thing that you should be my servant to raise up the tribes of Jacob, and to restore the preserved of Israel: I will also give you for a light to the Gentiles, that you may be my salvation unto the end of the earth. {49:7} Thus says the LORD, the Redeemer of Israel, and his Holy One, to him whom man despises, to him whom the nation abhors, to a servant of rulers, Kings shall see and arise, princes also shall worship, because of the LORD that is faithful, and the Holy One of Israel, and he shall choose you. {49:8} Thus says the

LORD, In an acceptable time have I heard you, and in a day of salvation have I helped you: and I will preserve you, and give you for a covenant of the people, to establish the earth, to cause to inherit the desolate heritages; {49:9} That you may say to the prisoners, Go forth; to them that are in darkness, Show yourselves. They shall feed in the ways, and their pastures shall be in all high places. {49:10} They shall not hunger nor thirst; neither shall the heat nor sun smite them: for he that has mercy on them shall lead them, even by the springs of water shall he guide them. {49:11} And I will make all my mountains a way, and my highways shall be exalted. {49:12} Behold, these shall come from far: and, lo, these from the north and from the west; and these from the land of Sinim. {49:13} Sing, O heavens; and be joyful, O earth; and break forth into singing, O mountains: for the LORD has comforted his people, and will have mercy upon his afflicted. {49:14} But Zion said, The LORD has forsaken me, and my Lord has forgotten me. {49:15} Can a woman forget her sucking child, that she should not have compassion on the son of her womb? yes, they may forget, yet will I not forget you. {49:16} Behold, I have graven you upon the palms of my hands; your walls are continually before me. {49:17} Your children shall make haste; your destroyers and they that made you waste shall go forth of you. {49:18} Lift up your eyes round about, and behold: all these gather themselves together, and come to you. As I live, says the LORD, you shall surely clothe yourself with them all, as with an ornament, and bind them on you, as a bride does. {49:19} For your waste and your desolate places, and the land of your destruction, shall even now be too narrow by reason of the inhabitants, and they that swallowed you up shall be far away. {49:20} The children which you shall have, after you have lost the other, shall say again in your ears, The place is too strait for me: give place to me that I may dwell. {49:21} Then shall you say in your heart, Who has begotten me these, seeing I have lost my children, and am desolate, a captive, and removing to and fro? and who has brought up these? Behold, I was left alone; these, where had they been? {49:22} Thus says the Lord GOD, Behold, I will lift up my hand to the Gentiles, and set up my standard to the people: and they shall bring your sons in their arms, and your daughters shall be carried upon their shoulders. {49:23} And kings shall be your nursing fathers, and their queens your nursing mothers: they shall bow down to you with their face toward the earth, and lick up the dust of your feet; and you shall know that I am the LORD: for they shall not be ashamed that wait for me. {49:24} Shall the prey be taken from the mighty, or the lawful captive delivered? {49:25} But thus says the LORD, Even the captives of the mighty shall be taken away, and the prey of the terrible shall be delivered: for I will contend with him that contends with you, and I will save your children. {49:26} And I will feed them that oppress you with their own flesh; and they shall be drunken with their own blood, as with sweet wine: and all flesh shall know that I the LORD am your Savior and your Redeemer, the mighty One of Jacob.

{50:1} Thus says the LORD, Where is the bill of your mother's divorcement, whom I have put away? or which of my creditors is it to whom I have sold you? Behold, for your iniquities have you sold yourselves, and for your transgressions is your mother put away. {50:2} Wherefore, when I came, was there no man? when I called, was there none to answer? Is my hand shortened at all, that it cannot redeem? or have I no power to deliver? behold, at my rebuke I dry up the sea, I make the rivers a wilderness: their fish stinks, because there is no water, and dies for thirst. {50:3} I clothe the heavens with blackness, and I make sackcloth their covering. {50:4} The Lord GOD has given me the tongue of the learned, that I should know how to speak a word in season to him that is weary: he wakens morning by morning, he wakens my ear to hear as the learned. {50:5} The Lord GOD has opened my ear, and I was not rebellious, neither turned away back. {50:6} I gave my back to the smiters, and my cheeks to them that plucked off the hair: I hid not my face from shame and spitting. {50:7} For the Lord GOD will help me; therefore shall I not be confounded: therefore have I set my face like a flint, and I know that I shall not be ashamed. {50:8} He is near that justifies me; who will contend with me? let us stand together: who is mine adversary? let him come near to me. {50:9} Behold, the Lord GOD will help me; who is he that shall condemn me? lo, they all shall wax old as a garment; the moth shall eat them up. {50:10} Who is among you that fears the LORD, that obeys the voice of his servant, that walks in darkness, and has no light? let him trust in the name of the LORD, and stay upon his God. {50:11} Behold, all you that kindle a fire, that encompass yourselves about with sparks: walk in the light of your fire, and in the sparks that you have kindled. This shall you have of mine hand; you shall lie down in sorrow.

{51:1} Listen to me, you who follow after righteousness, you who seek the LORD: look unto the rock whence you are hewn, and to the hole of the pit whence you are dug. {51:2} Look unto Abraham your father, and unto Sarah that bore you: for I called him alone, and blessed him, and increased him. {51:3} For the LORD shall comfort Zion: he will comfort all her waste places; and he will make her wilderness like Eden, and her desert like the garden of the LORD; joy and gladness shall be found therein, thanksgiving, and the voice of melody. {51:4} Listen unto me, my people; and give ear unto me, O my nation: for a law shall proceed from me, and I will make my judgment to rest for a light of the people. {51:5} My righteousness is near; my salvation is gone forth, and mine arms shall judge the people; the isles shall wait upon me, and on mine arm shall they trust. {51:6} Lift up your eyes to the heavens, and look upon the earth beneath: for the heavens shall vanish away like smoke, and the earth shall wax old like a garment, and they that dwell therein shall die in like manner: but my salvation shall be forever, and my righteousness shall not be abolished. {51:7} Listen unto me, you that know righteousness, the people in whose heart is my law; fear not the reproach of men, neither be afraid of their revilings. {51:8} For the moth shall eat them up like a garment, and the worm shall eat them like wool: but my righteousness shall be forever, and my salvation from generation to generation. {51:9} Awake, awake, put on strength, O arm of the LORD; awake, as in the ancient days, in the generations of old. Art thou not it that hath cut Rahab, and wounded the dragon? {51:10} Art thou not it which hath dried the sea, the waters of the great deep; that hath made the depths of the sea a way for the ransomed to pass over? {51:11} Therefore the redeemed of the LORD shall return, and come with singing unto Zion; and everlasting joy shall be upon their head: they shall obtain gladness and joy; and sorrow and mourning shall flee away. {51:12} I, even I, am he that comforts you: who are you, that you should be afraid of a man that shall die, and of the son of man which shall be made as grass; {51:13} And forget the LORD your maker, that hath stretched forth the heavens, and laid the foundations of the earth; and hast feared continually every day because of the fury of the oppressor, as if he were ready to destroy? and where is the fury of the oppressor? {51:14} The captive exile hastens that he may be loosed, and that he should not die in the pit, nor that his bread should fail. {51:15} But I am the LORD thy God, that divided the sea, whose waves roared: The LORD of hosts is his name. {51:16} And I have put my words in thy mouth, and I have covered thee in the shadow of mine hand, that I may plant the heavens, and lay the foundations of the earth, and say unto Zion, Thou art my people. {51:17} Awake, awake, stand up, O Jerusalem, which hast drunk at the hand of the LORD the cup of his fury; thou hast drunken the dregs of the cup of trembling, and wrung them out. {51:18} None to guide her among all the sons whom she hath brought forth; neither any that taketh her by the hand of all the sons that she hath brought up. {51:19} These two things are come unto thee; who shall be sorry for thee? desolation, and destruction, and the famine, and the sword: by whom shall I comfort thee? {51:20} Thy sons have fainted, they lie at the head of all the streets, as a wild bull in a net: they are full of the fury of the LORD, the rebuke of thy God. {51:21} Therefore hear now this, thou afflicted, and drunken, but not with wine: {51:22} Thus saith thy Lord the LORD, and thy God that pleadeth the cause of his people, Behold, I have taken out of thine hand the cup of trembling, even the dregs of the cup of my fury; thou shalt no more drink it again: {51:23} But I will put it into the hand of them that afflict thee; which have said to thy soul, Bow down, that we may go over: and thou hast laid thy body as the ground, and as the street, to them that went over.

{52:1} Awake, awake; put on thy strength, O Zion; put on thy beautiful garments, O Jerusalem, the holy city: for henceforth there shall no more come into thee the uncircumcised and the unclean. {52:2} Shake thyself from the dust; arise, and sit down, O Jerusalem: loose thyself from the bands of thy neck, O captive daughter of Zion. {52:3} For thus saith the LORD, Ye have sold yourselves for nought; and ye shall be redeemed without money. {52:4} For thus saith the Lord GOD, My people went down aforetime into Egypt to sojourn there; and the Assyrian oppressed them without cause. {52:5} **Now therefore, what have I here, saith the LORD, that my people is taken away for nought? they that rule over them make them to howl, saith the LORD; and my name continually every day is blasphemed.** {52:6} Therefore my people shall know my name: therefore they shall know in that day that I am he that doth speak: behold, it is I. {52:7} How beautiful upon the mountains are the feet of him that bringeth good tidings, that publisheth peace; that bringeth good tidings of good, that publisheth salvation; that saith unto Zion, Thy God reigneth! {52:8} Thy watchmen shall lift up the voice; with the voice together shall they sing: for they shall see eye to eye, when the LORD shall bring again Zion. {52:9} Break forth into joy, sing together, ye waste places of Jerusalem: for the LORD hath comforted his people, he hath redeemed Jerusalem. {52:10} The LORD hath made bare his holy arm in the eyes of all the nations; and all the ends of the earth shall see the salvation of our God. {52:11} Depart ye, depart ye, go ye out from thence, touch no unclean thing; go ye out of the midst of her; be ye clean, that bear the vessels of the LORD. {52:12} For ye shall not go out with haste, nor go by flight: for the LORD will go before you; and the God of Israel will be your rereward. {52:13} Behold, my servant shall deal prudently, he shall be exalted and extolled, and be very high. {52:14} As many were astonished at thee; his visage was so marred more than any man, and his form more than the sons of men: {52:15} So shall he sprinkle many nations; the kings shall shut their mouths at him: for that which had not been told them shall they see; and that which they had not heard shall they consider.

{53:1} Who has believed our report? and to whom is the arm of the LORD revealed? {53:2} For he shall grow up before him as a tender plant, and as a root out of a dry ground: he hath no form nor comeliness; and when we shall see him, there is no beauty that we should desire him. {53:3} He is despised and rejected of men; a man of sorrows, and acquainted with grief: and we hid as it were our faces from him; he was despised, and we esteemed him not. {53:4} **Surely he hath borne our griefs, and carried our sorrows: yet we did esteem him stricken, smitten of God, and afflicted.** {53:5} But he was wounded for our transgressions, he was bruised for our iniquities: the chastisement of our peace was upon him; and with his stripes we are healed. {53:6} All we like sheep have gone astray; we have turned every one to his own way; and the LORD hath laid on him the iniquity of us all. {53:7} He was oppressed, and he was afflicted, yet he opened not his mouth: he is brought as a lamb to the slaughter, and as a sheep before her shearers is dumb, so he openeth not his mouth. {53:8} He was taken from prison and from judgment: and who shall declare his generation? for he was cut off out of the land of the living: for the transgression of my people was he stricken. {53:9} And he made his grave with the wicked, and with the rich in his death; because he had done no violence, neither was any deceit in his mouth. {53:10} Yet it pleased the LORD to bruise him; he hath put him to grief: when thou shalt make his soul an offering for sin, he shall see his seed, he shall prolong his days, and the pleasure of the LORD shall prosper in his hand. {53:11} He shall see of the travail of his soul, and shall be satisfied: by his knowledge shall my righteous servant justify many; for he shall bear their iniquities. {53:12} Therefore will I divide him a portion with the great, and he shall divide the spoil with the strong; because he hath poured out his soul unto death: and he was numbered with the transgressors; and he bore the sin of many, and made intercession for the transgressors.

{54:1} Sing, O barren, you who did not bear; break forth into singing, and cry aloud, you who did not travail with child: for more are the children of the desolate than the children of the married wife, says the LORD. {54:2} Enlarge the place of your tent, and let them stretch forth the curtains of your habitations: spare not, lengthen your cords, and strengthen your stakes; {54:3} For you shall break forth on the right hand and on the left; and your seed shall inherit the Gentiles, and make the desolate cities to be inhabited. {54:4} Fear not; for you shall not be ashamed: neither be you confounded; for you shall not be put to shame: for you shall forget the shame of your youth, and shall not remember the reproach of your widowhood any more. {54:5} For your Maker is your husband; the LORD of hosts is his name; and your Redeemer the Holy One of Israel; The God of the whole earth shall he be called. {54:6} For the LORD has called you as a woman forsaken and grieved in spirit, and a wife of youth, when you were refused, says your God. {54:7} For a small moment have I forsaken you; but with great mercies will I gather you. {54:8} In a little wrath I hid my face from you for a moment; but with everlasting kindness will I have mercy on you, says the LORD your Redeemer. {54:9} For this is as the waters of Noah unto me: for as I have sworn that the waters of Noah should no more go over the earth; so have I sworn that I would not be wroth with you, nor rebuke you. {54:10} For the mountains shall depart, and the hills be removed; but my kindness shall not depart from you, neither shall the covenant of my peace be removed, says the LORD that has mercy on you. {54:11} O you afflicted, tossed with tempest, and not comforted, behold, I will lay your stones with fair colors, and lay your foundations with sapphires. {54:12} And I will make your windows of agates, and your gates of carbuncles, and all your borders of pleasant stones. {54:13} And all your children shall be taught of the LORD; and great shall be the peace of your children. {54:14} In righteousness shall you be established: you shall be far from oppression; for you shall not fear: and from terror; for it shall not come near you. {54:15} Behold, they shall surely gather together, but not by me: whoever shall gather together against you shall fall for your sake. {54:16} Behold, I have created the smith that blows the coals in the fire, and that brings forth an instrument for his work; and I have created the waster to destroy. {54:17} No weapon that is formed against you shall prosper; and every tongue that shall rise against you in judgment you shall condemn. This is the heritage of the servants of the LORD, and their righteousness is of me, says the LORD.

{55:1} Hey, everyone who is thirsty, come to the waters, even if you have no money; come, buy, and eat; yes, come, buy wine and milk without money and without price. {55:2} Why spend money on what isn't bread, and your labor on what doesn't satisfy? Listen carefully to me, and eat what is good, and let your soul delight itself in richness. {55:3} Incline your ear, and come to me: listen, and your soul shall live; and I will make an everlasting covenant with you, even the sure mercies of David. {55:4} Behold, I have given him as a witness to the people, a leader and commander to the people. {55:5} Behold, you shall call a nation that you don't know, and nations that didn't know you shall run to you because of the LORD your God, and for the Holy One of Israel; for he has glorified you. {55:6} Seek the LORD while he may be found, call upon him while he is near: {55:7} Let the wicked forsake his way, and the unrighteous man his thoughts: and let him return to the LORD, and he will have mercy upon him; and to our God, for he will abundantly pardon. {55:8} For my thoughts are not your thoughts, neither are your ways my ways, says the LORD. {55:9} For as the heavens are higher than the earth, so are my ways higher than your ways, and my thoughts than your thoughts. {55:10} For as the rain comes down, and the snow from heaven, and doesn't return there, but waters the earth, and makes it bring forth and bud, that it may give seed to the sower, and bread to the eater: {55:11} So shall my word be that goes forth out of my mouth: it shall not return to me void, but it shall accomplish that which I please, and it shall prosper in the thing to which I sent it. {55:12} For you shall go out with joy, and be led forth with peace: the mountains and the hills shall break forth before you into singing, and all the trees of the field shall clap their hands. {55:13} Instead of the thorn shall come up the fir tree, and instead of the brier shall come up the myrtle tree: and it shall be to the LORD for a name, for an everlasting sign that shall not be cut off.

{56:1} This is what the LORD says: Keep justice, and do righteousness, for my salvation is near to come, and my righteousness to be revealed. {56:2} Blessed is the one who does this, and the son of man who holds fast to it; who keeps the Sabbath from profaning it, and keeps his hand from doing any evil. {56:3} Let not the foreigner who has joined himself to the LORD say, "The LORD will surely separate me from his people"; and let not the eunuch say, "Behold, I am a dry tree." {56:4} For thus says the LORD to the eunuchs who keep my Sabbaths, and choose the things that please me, and hold fast to my covenant: {56:5} Even to them I will give in my house and within my walls a place and a name better than of sons and of daughters: I will give them an everlasting name that shall not be cut off. {56:6} Also the foreigners who join themselves to the LORD, to serve him, and to love the name of the LORD, to be his servants, everyone who keeps the Sabbath from profaning it, and holds fast to my covenant; {56:7} Even them I will bring to my holy mountain, and make them joyful in my house of prayer: their burnt offerings and their sacrifices shall be accepted upon my altar; for my house shall be called a house of prayer for all people. {56:8} The Lord GOD, who gathers the outcasts of Israel, says, "Yet will I gather others to him, besides those who are gathered to him." {56:9} All you beasts of the field, come to devour, yes, all you beasts in the forest. {56:10} His watchmen are blind: they are all ignorant, they are all dumb dogs, they cannot bark; sleeping, lying down, loving to slumber. {56:11} Yes, they are greedy dogs which can never have enough, and they are shepherds that cannot understand: they all look to their own way, every one for his gain, from his quarter. {56:12} "Come," they say, "I will fetch wine, and we will fill ourselves with strong drink; and tomorrow shall be as this day, and much more abundant."

{57:1} The righteous perish, and no one takes it to heart; and merciful people are taken away, with none considering that the righteous are taken away from the evil to come. {57:2} They shall enter into peace: they shall rest in their beds, each one walking in his uprightness. {57:3} But draw near here, you sons of the sorceress, the seed of the adulterer and the prostitute. {57:4} Against whom do you sport yourselves? Against whom do you make a wide mouth, and draw out the tongue? Are you not children of transgression, a seed of falsehood, {57:5} Enflaming yourselves with idols under every green tree, slaying the children in the valleys under the cliffs of the rocks? {57:6} Among the smooth stones of the stream is your portion; they, they are your lot: even to them have you poured a drink offering, you have offered a meat offering. Should I receive comfort in these? {57:7} Upon a lofty and high mountain you have set your bed: even there you went up to offer sacrifice. {57:8} Behind the doors also and the posts you have set up your remembrance: for you have uncovered yourself to another than me, and have gone up; you have enlarged your bed, and made a covenant with them; you loved their bed where you saw it. {57:9} And you went to the king with ointment, and did increase your perfumes, and did send your messengers far off, and did debase yourself even unto hell. {57:10} You are wearied in the greatness of your way; yet said you not, There is no hope: you have found the life of your hand; therefore you were not grieved. {57:11} And of whom have you been afraid or feared, that you have lied, and have not remembered me, nor laid it to your heart? Have not I held my peace even of old, and you fear me not? {57:12} I will declare your righteousness, and your works; for they shall not profit you. {57:13} When you cry, let your companies deliver you; but the wind shall carry them all away; vanity shall take them: but he who puts his trust in me shall possess the land, and shall inherit my holy mountain; {57:14} And shall say, Cast up, cast up, prepare the way, take up the stumbling block out of the way of my people. {57:15} For thus says the high and lofty One who inhabits eternity, whose name is Holy; I dwell in the high and holy place, with him also who is of a contrite and humble spirit, to revive the spirit of the humble, and to revive the heart of the contrite ones. {57:16} For I will not contend forever, neither will I be always angry: for the spirit should fail before me, and the souls which I have made. {57:17} For the iniquity of his covetousness I was angry, and smote him: I hid myself, and was angry, and he went on stubbornly in the way of his heart. {57:18} I have seen his ways, and will heal him: I will lead him also, and restore comforts to him and to his mourners. {57:19} I create the fruit of the lips; Peace, peace to him that is far off, and to him that is near, says the LORD; and I will heal him. {57:20} But the wicked are like the troubled sea, when it cannot rest, whose waters cast up mire and dirt. {57:21} There is no peace, says my God, to the wicked.

{58:1} Cry aloud, spare not, lift up your voice like a trumpet, and show my people their transgression, and the house of Jacob their sins. {58:2} Yet they seek me daily, and delight to know my ways, as a nation that did righteousness, and forsook not the ordinance of their God: they ask of me the ordinances of justice; they take delight in approaching to God. {58:3} Why have we fasted, they say, and you do not see? Why have we afflicted our soul, and you take no knowledge? Behold, in the day of your fast you find pleasure, and exact all your labors. {58:4} Behold, you fast for strife and debate, and to smite with the fist of wickedness: you shall not fast as you do this day, to make your voice to be heard on high. {58:5} Is it such a fast that I have chosen? a day for a man to afflict his soul? Is it to bow down his head as a bulrush, and to spread sackcloth and ashes under him? Will you call this a fast, and an acceptable day to the LORD? {58:6} Is not this the fast that I have chosen? to loose the bands of wickedness, to undo the heavy burdens, and to let the oppressed go free, and that you break every yoke? {58:7} Is it not to deal your bread to the hungry, and that you bring the poor that are cast out to your house? When you see the naked, that you cover him; and that you hide not yourself from your own flesh? {58:8} Then shall your light break forth as the morning, and your health shall spring forth speedily: and your righteousness shall go before you; the glory of the LORD shall be your rear guard. {58:9} Then shall you call, and the LORD shall answer; you shall cry, and he shall say, Here I am. If you take away from the midst of you the yoke, the putting forth of the finger, and speaking vanity; {58:10} And if you draw out your soul to the hungry, and satisfy the afflicted soul; then shall your light rise in obscurity, and your darkness be as the noonday: {58:11} And the LORD shall guide you continually, and satisfy your soul in drought, and make fat your bones: and you shall be like a watered garden, and like a spring of water, whose waters fail not. {58:12} And they that shall be of you shall build the old waste places: you shall raise up the foundations of many generations; and you shall be called, The repairer of the breach, The restorer of paths to dwell in. {58:13} If you turn away your foot from the sabbath, from doing your pleasure on my holy day; and call the sabbath a delight, the holy of the LORD, honorable; and shall honor him, not doing your own ways, nor finding your own pleasure, nor speaking your own words: {58:14} Then shall you delight yourself in the LORD; and I will cause you to ride upon the high places of the earth, and feed you with the heritage of Jacob your father: for the mouth of the LORD has spoken it.

{59:1} Behold, the LORD's hand is not shortened, that it cannot save; neither his ear heavy, that it cannot hear: {59:2} But your iniquities have separated between you and your God, and your sins have hid his face from you, that he will not hear. {59:3} For your hands are defiled with blood, and your fingers with iniquity; your lips have spoken lies, your tongue has muttered perverseness. {59:4} None calls for justice, nor pleads for truth: they trust in vanity, and speak lies; they conceive mischief, and bring forth iniquity. {59:5} They hatch cockatrice' eggs, and weave the spider's web: whoever eats of their eggs dies, and that which is crushed breaks out into a viper. {59:6} Their webs shall not become garments, neither shall they cover themselves with their works: their works are works of iniquity, and the act of violence is in their hands. {59:7} Their feet run to evil, and they make haste to shed innocent blood: their thoughts are thoughts of iniquity; wasting and destruction are in their paths. {59:8} The way of peace they know not; and there is no judgment in their goings: they have made them crooked paths: whoever goes therein shall not know peace. {59:9} Therefore is judgment far from us, neither does justice overtake us: we wait for light, but behold obscurity; for brightness, but we walk in darkness. {59:10} We grope for the wall like the blind, and we grope as if we had no eyes: we stumble at noonday as in the night; we are in desolate places as dead men. {59:11} We roar all like bears, and mourn sore like doves: we look for judgment, but there is none; for salvation, but it is far off from us. {59:12} For our transgressions are multiplied before you, and our sins testify against us: for our transgressions are with us; and as for our iniquities, we know them; {59:13} In transgressing and lying against the LORD, and departing away from our God, speaking oppression and revolt, conceiving and uttering from the heart words of falsehood. {59:14} And judgment is turned away backward, and justice stands afar off: for truth is fallen in the street, and equity cannot enter. {59:15} Yes, truth fails; and he that departs from evil makes himself a prey: and the LORD saw it, and it displeased him that there was no judgment. {59:16} And he saw that there was no man, and wondered that there was no intercessor: therefore his arm brought salvation unto him; and his righteousness, it sustained him. {59:17} For he put on righteousness as a breastplate, and an helmet of salvation upon his head; and he put on the garments of vengeance for clothing, and was clad with zeal as a cloak. {59:18} According to their deeds, accordingly he will repay, fury to his adversaries, recompense to his enemies; to the islands he will repay recompense. {59:19} So shall they fear the name of the LORD from the west, and his glory from the rising of the sun. When the enemy shall come in like a flood, the Spirit of the LORD shall lift up a standard against him. {59:20} And the Redeemer shall come to Zion, and unto them that turn from transgression in Jacob, says the LORD. {59:21} As for me, this is my covenant with them, says the LORD; My spirit that is upon you, and my words which I have put in your mouth, shall not depart out of your mouth, nor out of the mouth of your seed, nor out of the mouth of your seed's seed, says the LORD, from henceforth and forever.

{60:1} Arise, shine; for your light has come, and the glory of the LORD is risen upon you. {60:2} For, behold, the darkness shall cover the earth, and gross darkness the people: but the LORD shall arise upon you, and his glory shall be seen upon you. {60:3} And the Gentiles shall come to your light, and kings to the brightness of your rising. {60:4} Lift up your eyes round about, and see: all they gather themselves together, they come to you: your sons shall come from far, and your daughters shall be nursed at your side. {60:5} Then you shall see, and flow together, and your heart shall fear, and be enlarged; because the abundance of the sea shall be converted unto you, the forces of the Gentiles shall come unto you. {60:6} The multitude of camels shall cover you, the dromedaries of Midian and Ephah; all they from Sheba shall come: they shall bring gold and incense; and they shall show forth the praises of the LORD. {60:7} All the flocks of Kedar shall be gathered together unto you, the rams of Nebaioth shall minister unto you: they shall come up with acceptance on my altar, and I will glorify the house of my glory. {60:8} Who are these that fly as a cloud, and as the doves to their windows? {60:9} Surely the isles shall wait for me, and the ships of Tarshish first, to bring your sons from far, their silver and their gold with them, unto the name of the LORD your God, and to the Holy One of Israel, because he has glorified you. {60:10} And the sons of strangers shall build up your walls, and their kings shall minister unto you: for in my wrath I smote you, but in my favor have I had mercy on you. {60:11} Therefore your gates shall be open continually; they shall not be shut day nor night; that men may bring unto you the forces of the Gentiles, and that their kings may be brought. {60:12} For the nation and kingdom that will not serve you shall perish; yes, those nations shall be utterly wasted. {60:13} The glory of Lebanon shall come unto you, the fir tree, the pine tree, and the box together, to beautify the place of my sanctuary; and I will make the place of my feet glorious. {60:14} The sons also of them that afflicted you shall come bending unto you; and all they that despised you shall bow themselves down at the soles of your feet; and they shall call you, The city of the LORD, The Zion of the Holy One of Israel. {60:15} Whereas you have been forsaken and hated, so that no man went through you, I will make you an eternal excellency, a joy of many generations. {60:16} You shall also suck the milk of the Gentiles, and suck the breast of kings: and you shall know that I the LORD am your Savior and your Redeemer, the mighty One of Jacob. {60:17} For brass I will bring gold, and for iron I will bring silver, and for wood brass, and for stones iron: I will also make your officers peace, and your exactors righteousness. {60:18} Violence shall no more be heard in your land, wasting nor destruction within your borders; but you shall call your walls Salvation, and your gates Praise. {60:19} The sun shall be no more your light by day; neither for brightness shall the moon give light unto you: but the LORD shall be unto you an everlasting light, and your God your glory. {60:20} Your sun shall no more go down; neither shall your moon withdraw itself: for the LORD shall be your everlasting light, and the days of your mourning shall be ended. {60:21}

Your people also shall be all righteous: they shall inherit the land forever, the branch of my planting, the work of my hands, that I may be glorified. {60:22} A little one shall become a thousand, and a small one a strong nation: I the LORD will hasten it in his time.

{61:1} The Spirit of the Lord GOD is upon me; because the LORD has anointed me to preach good tidings unto the meek; he has sent me to bind up the brokenhearted, to proclaim liberty to the captives, and the opening of the prison to them that are bound; {61:2} To proclaim the acceptable year of the LORD, and the day of vengeance of our God; to comfort all that mourn; {61:3} To appoint unto them that mourn in Zion, to give unto them beauty for ashes, the oil of joy for mourning, the garment of praise for the spirit of heaviness; that they might be called trees of righteousness, the planting of the LORD, that he might be glorified. {61:4} And they shall build the old wastes, they shall raise up the former desolations, and they shall repair the waste cities, the desolations of many generations. {61:5} And strangers shall stand and feed your flocks, and the sons of the alien shall be your plowmen and your vinedressers. {61:6} But you shall be named the Priests of the LORD: men shall call you the Ministers of our God: you shall eat the riches of the Gentiles, and in their glory shall you boast yourselves. {61:7} For your shame you shall have double; and for confusion they shall rejoice in their portion: therefore in their land they shall possess the double: everlasting joy shall be unto them. {61:8} For I the LORD love judgment, I hate robbery for burnt offering; and I will direct their work in truth, and I will make an everlasting covenant with them. {61:9} And their seed shall be known among the Gentiles, and their offspring among the people: all that see them shall acknowledge them, that they are the seed which the LORD has blessed. {61:10} I will greatly rejoice in the LORD, my soul shall be joyful in my God; for he has clothed me with the garments of salvation, he has covered me with the robe of righteousness, as a bridegroom decks himself with ornaments, and as a bride adorns herself with her jewels. {61:11} For as the earth brings forth her bud, and as the garden causes the things that are sown in it to spring forth; so the Lord GOD will cause righteousness and praise to spring forth before all the nations.

{62:1} For Zion's sake will I not hold my peace, and for Jerusalem's sake I will not rest, until the righteousness thereof goes forth as brightness, and the salvation thereof as a lamp that burns. {62:2} And the Gentiles shall see thy righteousness, and all kings thy glory: and thou shalt be called by a new name, which the mouth of the LORD shall name. {62:3} Thou shalt also be a crown of glory in the hand of the LORD, and a royal diadem in the hand of thy God. {62:4} Thou shalt no more be termed Forsaken; neither shall thy land any more be termed Desolate: but thou shalt be called Hephzi-bah, and thy land Beulah: for the LORD delighteth in thee, and thy land shall be married. {62:5} For as a young man marrieth a virgin, so shall thy sons marry thee: and as the bridegroom rejoiceth over the bride, so shall thy God rejoice over thee. {62:6} I have set watchmen upon thy walls, O Jerusalem, which shall never hold their peace day nor night: ye that make mention of the LORD, keep not silence, {62:7} And give him no rest, till he establish, and till he make Jerusalem a praise in the earth. {62:8} The LORD hath sworn by his right hand, and by the arm of his strength, Surely I will no more give thy corn to be meat for thine enemies; and the sons of the stranger shall not drink thy wine, for the which thou hast laboured: {62:9} But they that have gathered it shall eat it, and praise the LORD; and they that have brought it together shall drink it in the courts of my holiness. {62:10} Go through, go through the gates; prepare ye the way of the people; cast up, cast up the highways; gather out the stones; lift up a standard for the people. {62:11} Behold, the LORD hath proclaimed unto the end of the world, Say ye to the daughter of Zion, Behold, thy salvation cometh; behold, his reward is with him, and his work before him. {62:12} And they shall call them, The holy people, The redeemed of the LORD: and thou shalt be called, Sought out, A city not forsaken.

{63:1} Who is this that comes from Edom, with dyed garments from Bozrah? This one is glorious in his apparel, traveling in the greatness of his strength. I speak in righteousness, mighty to save. {63:2} Why are you red in your apparel, and your garments like one who treads in the winepress? {63:3} I have trodden the winepress alone; and of the people, there was none with me. For I will tread them in my anger and trample them in my fury; and their blood shall be sprinkled upon my garments, and I will stain all my raiment. {63:4} For the day of vengeance is in my heart, and the year of my redeemed has come. {63:5} And I looked, and there was none to help; and I wondered that there was none to uphold. Therefore my own arm brought salvation unto me; and my fury, it upheld me. {63:6} And I will tread down the people in my anger, and make them drunk in my fury, and I will bring down their strength to the earth. {63:7} I will mention the lovingkindnesses of the LORD, and the praises of the LORD, according to all that the LORD has bestowed on us, and the great goodness toward the house of Israel, which he has bestowed on them according to his mercies, and according to the multitude of his lovingkindnesses. {63:8} For he said, Surely they are my people, children that will not lie: so he was their Saviour. {63:9} In all their affliction he was afflicted, and the angel of his presence saved them: in his love and in his pity he redeemed them; and he bore them, and carried them all the days of old. {63:10} But they rebelled, and vexed his holy Spirit: therefore he was turned to be their enemy, and he fought against them. {63:11} Then he remembered the days of old, Moses, and his people, saying, Where is he that brought them up out of the sea with the shepherd of his flock? Where is he that put his holy Spirit within him? {63:12} That led them by the right hand of Moses with his glorious arm, dividing the water before them, to make himself an everlasting name? {63:13} That led them through the deep, as a horse in the wilderness, that they should not stumble? {63:14} As a beast goes down into the valley, the Spirit of the LORD caused him to rest: so did you lead your people, to make yourself a glorious name. {63:15} Look down from heaven, and behold from the habitation of your holiness and of your glory: where is your zeal and your strength, the sounding of your bowels and of your mercies toward me? Are they restrained? {63:16} Doubtless you are our father, though Abraham be ignorant of us, and Israel acknowledge us not: you, O LORD, are our father, our redeemer; your name is from everlasting. {63:17} O LORD, why have you made us to err from your ways, and hardened our heart from your fear? Return for your servants' sake, the tribes of your inheritance. {63:18} The people of your holiness have possessed it but a little while: our adversaries have trodden down your sanctuary. {63:19} We are yours: you never bore rule over them; they were not called by your name.

{64:1} Oh, that you would rend the heavens, that you would come down, that the mountains might flow down at your presence, {64:2} As when the melting fire burns, the fire causes the waters to boil, to make your name known to your adversaries, that the nations may tremble at your presence! {64:3} When you did terrible things which we looked not for, you came down, the mountains flowed down at your presence. {64:4} For since the beginning of the world, men have not heard, nor perceived by the ear, neither has the eye seen, O God, beside you, what he has prepared for him that waits for him. {64:5} You meet him that rejoices and works righteousness, those that remember you in your ways: behold, you are wroth; for we have sinned: in those is continuance, and we shall be saved. {64:6} But we are all as an unclean thing, and all our righteousnesses are as filthy rags; and we all fade as a leaf; and our iniquities, like the wind, have taken us away. {64:7} And there is none that calls upon your name, that stirs up himself to take hold of you: for you have hid your face from us, and have consumed us, because of our iniquities. {64:8} But now, O LORD, you are our father; we are the clay, and you our potter; and we all are the work of your hand. {64:9} Be not wroth very sore, O LORD, neither remember iniquity forever: behold, see, we beseech you, we are all your people. {64:10} Your holy cities are a wilderness, Zion is a wilderness, Jerusalem a desolation. {64:11} Our holy and our beautiful house, where our fathers praised you, is burned up with fire: and all our pleasant things are laid waste. {64:12} Will you refrain yourself for these things, O LORD? Will you hold your peace, and afflict us very sore?

{65:1} I am sought by those who didn't ask for me; I am found by those who didn't seek me. I said, "Behold me, behold me," to a nation that was not called by my name. {65:2} I have spread out my hands all day to a rebellious people, who walk in a way that is not good, after their own thoughts; {65:3} A people who provoke me to anger continually to my face; who sacrifice in gardens, and burn incense on altars of brick; {65:4} Who remain among the graves, and lodge in the monuments, who eat swine's flesh, and broth of abominable things is in their vessels; {65:5} Who say, "Stand by yourself, come not near to me; for I am holier than you." These are a smoke in my nose, a fire that burns all the day. {65:6} Behold, it is written before me: I will not keep silence, but will repay, even repay into their bosom, {65:7} Your iniquities, and the iniquities of your fathers together, says the LORD, who have burned incense on the mountains, and blasphemed me on the hills: therefore I will measure their former work into their bosom. {65:8} Thus says the LORD, As the new wine is found in the cluster, and one says, "Destroy it not; for a blessing is in it:" so will I do for my servants' sakes, that I may not destroy them all. {65:9} And I will bring forth a seed out of Jacob, and out of Judah an inheritor of my mountains: and my elect shall inherit it, and my servants shall dwell there. {65:10} And Sharon shall be a fold of flocks, and the valley of Achor a place for the herds to lie down in, for my people that have sought me. {65:11} But you are they that forsake the LORD, that forget my holy mountain, that prepare a table for that troop, and that furnish the drink offering unto that number. {65:12} Therefore will I number you to the sword, and you shall all bow down to the slaughter: because when I called, you did not answer; when I spoke, you did not hear; but did evil before my eyes, and did choose what I delighted not. {65:13} Therefore thus says the Lord GOD, Behold, my servants shall eat, but you shall be hungry: behold, my servants shall drink, but you shall be thirsty: behold, my servants shall rejoice, but you shall be ashamed: {65:14} Behold, my servants shall sing for joy of heart, but you shall cry for sorrow of heart, and shall howl for vexation of spirit. {65:15} And you shall leave your name for a curse unto my chosen: for the Lord GOD shall slay you, and call his servants by another name: {65:16} That he who blesses himself in the earth shall bless himself in the God of truth; and he that swears in the earth shall swear by the God of truth; because the former troubles are forgotten, and because they are hidden from mine eyes. {65:17} For, behold, I create new heavens and a new earth: and the former shall not be remembered, nor come into mind. {65:18} But be glad and rejoice forever in that which I create: for, behold, I create Jerusalem a rejoicing, and her people a joy. {65:19} And I will rejoice in Jerusalem, and joy in my people: and the voice of weeping shall be no more heard in her, nor the voice of crying. {65:20} There shall be no more thence an infant of days, nor an old man that hath not filled his days: for the child shall die an hundred years old; but the sinner being an hundred years old shall be accursed. {65:21} And they shall build houses, and inhabit them; and they shall plant vineyards, and eat the fruit of them. {65:22} They shall not build, and another inhabit; they shall not plant, and another eat: for as the days of a tree are the days of my people, and mine elect shall long enjoy the work of their hands. {65:23} They shall not labour in vain, nor bring forth for trouble; for they are the seed of the blessed of the LORD, and their offspring with them. {65:24} And it shall come to pass, that before they call, I will answer; and while they are yet speaking, I will hear. {65:25} The wolf and the lamb shall feed together, and the lion shall eat straw like the bullock: and dust shall be the serpent's meat. They shall not hurt nor destroy in all my holy mountain, says the LORD.

{66:1} Thus says the LORD, "The heaven is my throne, and the earth is my footstool: where is the house that you build unto me? and where is the place of my rest? {66:2} For all those things my hand has made, says the LORD: but to this man will I look, even to him that is poor and of a contrite spirit, and trembles at my word. {66:3} He that kills an ox is as if he slew a man; he that sacrifices a lamb, as if he cut off a dog's neck; he that offers an oblation, as if he offered swine's blood; he that burns incense, as if he blessed an idol. Yes, they have chosen their own ways, and their soul delights in their abominations. {66:4} I also will choose their delusions, and will bring their fears upon them; because when I called, none did answer; when I spoke, they did not hear: but they did evil before mine eyes, and chose what I delighted not. {66:5} Hear the word of the LORD, you that tremble at his word; your brethren that hated you, that cast you out for my name's sake, said, 'Let the LORD be glorified:' but he shall appear to your joy, and they shall be ashamed. {66:6} A voice of noise from the city, a voice from the temple, a voice of the LORD that renders recompense to his enemies. {66:7} Before she travailed, she brought forth; before her pain came, she was delivered of a man child. {66:8} Who has heard such a thing? who has seen such things? Shall the earth be made to bring forth in one day? or shall a nation be born at once? for as soon as Zion travailed, she brought forth her children. {66:9} Shall I bring to the birth, and not cause to bring forth? says the LORD: shall I cause to bring forth, and shut the womb? says thy God. {66:10} Rejoice with Jerusalem, and be glad with her, all you that love her: rejoice for joy with her, all you that mourn for her: {66:11} That you may suck, and be satisfied with the breasts of her consolations; that you may milk out, and be delighted with the abundance of her glory. {66:12} For thus says the LORD, "Behold, I will extend peace to her like a river, and the glory of the Gentiles like a flowing stream: then shall you suck, you shall be borne upon her sides, and be dandled upon her knees. {66:13} As one whom his mother comforts, so will I comfort you; and you shall be comforted in Jerusalem. {66:14} And when you see this, your heart shall rejoice, and your bones shall flourish like an herb: and the hand of the LORD shall be known toward his servants, and his indignation toward his enemies. {66:15} For, behold, the LORD will come with fire, and with his chariots like a whirlwind, to render his anger with fury, and his rebuke with flames of fire. {66:16} For by fire and by his sword will the LORD plead with all flesh: and the slain of the LORD shall be many. {66:17} They that sanctify themselves, and purify themselves in the gardens behind one tree in the midst, eating swine's flesh, and the abomination, and the mouse, shall be consumed together, says the LORD. {66:18} For I know their works and their thoughts: it shall come, that I will gather all nations and tongues; and they shall come, and see my glory. {66:19} And I will set a sign among them, and I will send those that escape of them unto the nations, to Tarshish, Pul, and Lud, that draw the bow, to Tubal, and Javan, to the isles afar off, that have not heard my fame, neither have seen my glory; and they shall declare my glory among the Gentiles. {66:20} And they shall bring all your brethren for an offering unto the LORD out of all nations upon horses, and in chariots, and in litters, and upon mules, and upon swift beasts, to my holy mountain Jerusalem, says the LORD, as the children of Israel bring an offering in a clean vessel into the house of the LORD. {66:21} And I will also take of them for priests and for Levites, says the LORD. {66:22} For as the new heavens and the new earth, which I will make, shall remain before me, says the LORD, so shall your seed and your name remain. {66:23} And it shall come to pass, that from one new moon to another, and from one sabbath to another, shall all flesh come to worship before me, says the LORD. {66:24} And they shall go forth, and look upon the carcases of the men that have transgressed against me: for their worm shall not die, neither shall their fire be quenched; and they shall be an abhorring unto all flesh.

Jeremiah

{1:1} The words of Jeremiah the son of Hilkiah, of the priests that were in Anathoth in the land of Benjamin: {1:2} To whom the word of the LORD came in the days of Josiah the son of Amon king of Judah, in the thirteenth year of his reign. {1:3} It came also in the days of Jehoiakim the son of Josiah king of Judah, unto the end of the eleventh year of Zedekiah the son of Josiah king of Judah, unto the carrying away of Jerusalem captive in the fifth month. {1:4} Then the word of the LORD came unto me, saying, {1:5} **Before I formed thee in the belly I knew thee; and before thou camest forth out of the womb I sanctified thee, and I ordained thee a prophet unto the nations.** {1:6} Then said I, Ah, Lord GOD! behold, I cannot speak: for I am a child. {1:7} But the LORD said unto me, Say not, I am a child: for thou shalt go to all that I shall send thee, and whatsoever I command thee thou shalt speak. {1:8} Be not afraid of their faces: for I am with thee to deliver thee, saith the LORD. {1:9} Then the LORD put forth his hand, and touched my mouth. And the LORD said unto me, Behold, I have put my words in thy mouth. {1:10} See, I have this day set thee over the nations and over the kingdoms, to root out, and to pull down, and to destroy, and to throw down, to build, and to plant. {1:11} Moreover the word of the LORD came unto me, saying, Jeremiah, what seest thou? And I said, I see a rod of an almond tree. {1:12} Then said the LORD unto me, Thou hast well seen: for I will hasten my word to perform it. {1:13} And the word of the LORD came unto me the second time, saying, What seest thou? And I said, I see a seething pot; and the face thereof is toward the north. {1:14} Then the LORD said unto me, Out of the north an evil shall break forth upon all the inhabitants of the land. {1:15} For, lo, I will call all the families of the kingdoms of the north, saith the LORD; and they shall come, and they shall set every one his throne at the entering of the gates of Jerusalem, and against all the walls thereof round about, and against all the cities of Judah. {1:16} And I will utter my judgments against them touching all their wickedness, who have forsaken me, and have burned incense unto other gods, and worshipped the works of their own hands. {1:17} Thou therefore gird up thy loins, and arise, and speak unto them all that I command thee: be not dismayed at their faces, lest I confound thee before them. {1:18} For, behold, I have made thee this day a defenced city, and an iron pillar, and brasen walls against the whole land, against the kings of Judah, against the princes thereof, against the priests thereof, and against the people of the land. {1:19} And they shall fight against thee; but they shall not prevail against thee; for I am with thee, saith the LORD, to deliver thee.

{2:1} Moreover, the word of the LORD came to me, saying, {2:2} Go and cry in the ears of Jerusalem, saying, Thus saith the LORD; I remember thee, the kindness of thy youth, the love of thine espousals, when thou wentest after me in the wilderness, in a land that was not sown. {2:3} Israel was holiness unto the LORD, and the firstfruits of his increase: all that devour him shall offend; evil shall come upon them, saith the LORD. {2:4} Hear ye the word of the LORD, O house of Jacob, and all the families of the house of Israel: {2:5} Thus saith the LORD, What iniquity have your fathers found in me, that they are gone far from me, and have walked after vanity, and are become vain? {2:6} Neither said they, Where is the LORD that brought us up out of the land of Egypt, that led us through the wilderness, through a land of deserts and of pits, through a land of drought, and of the shadow of death, through a land that no man passed through, and where no man dwelt? {2:7} And I brought you into a plentiful country, to eat the fruit thereof and the goodness thereof; but when ye entered, ye defiled my land, and made mine heritage an abomination. {2:8} The priests said not, Where is the LORD? and they that handle the law knew me not: the pastors also transgressed against me, and the prophets prophesied by Baal, and walked after things that do not profit. {2:9} Wherefore I will yet plead with you, saith the LORD, and with your children's children will I plead. {2:10} For pass over the isles of Chittim, and see; and send unto Kedar, and consider diligently, and see if there be such a thing. {2:11} Hath a nation changed their gods, which are yet no gods? but my people have changed their glory for that which doth not profit. {2:12} Be astonished, O ye heavens, at this, and be horribly afraid, ye very desolate, saith the LORD. {2:13} **For my people have committed two evils; they have forsaken me the fountain of living waters, and hewed them out cisterns, broken cisterns, that can hold no water.** {2:14} Is Israel a servant? is he a homeborn [slave]? why is he spoiled? {2:15} The young lions roared upon him, and yelled, and they made his land waste: his cities are burned without inhabitant. {2:16} Also the children of Noph and Tahapanes have broken the crown of thy head.

{2:17} Hast thou not procured this unto thyself, in that thou hast forsaken the LORD thy God, when he led thee by the way? {2:18} And now what hast thou to do in the way of Egypt, to drink the waters of Sihor? or what hast thou to do in the way of Assyria, to drink the waters of the river? {2:19} Thine own wickedness shall correct thee, and thy backslidings shall reprove thee: know therefore and see that it is an evil thing and bitter, that thou hast forsaken the LORD thy God, and that my fear is not in thee, saith the Lord GOD of hosts. {2:20} For of old time I have broken thy yoke, and burst thy bands; and thou saidst, I will not transgress; when upon every high hill and under every green tree thou wanderest, playing the harlot. {2:21} Yet I had planted thee a noble vine, wholly a right seed: how then art thou turned into the degenerate plant of a strange vine unto me? {2:22} For though thou wash thee with nitre, and take thee much sope, yet thine iniquity is marked before me, saith the Lord GOD. {2:23} How canst thou say, I am not polluted, I have not gone after Baalim? see thy way in the valley, know what thou hast done: thou art a swift dromedary traversing her ways; {2:24} A wild ass used to the wilderness, that snuffeth up the wind at her pleasure; in her occasion who can turn her away? all they that seek her will not weary themselves; in her month they shall find her. {2:25} Withhold thy foot from being unshod, and thy throat from thirst: but thou saidst, There is no hope: no; for I have loved strangers, and after them will I go. {2:26} As the thief is ashamed when he is found, so is the house of Israel ashamed; they, their kings, their princes, and their priests, and their prophets, {2:27} Saying to a stock, Thou art my father; and to a stone, Thou hast brought me forth: for they have turned their back unto me, and not their face: but in the time of their trouble they will say, Arise, and save us. {2:28} But where are thy gods that thou hast made thee? let them arise, if they can save thee in the time of thy trouble: for according to the number of thy cities are thy gods, O Judah. {2:29} Wherefore will ye plead with me? ye all have transgressed against me, saith the LORD. {2:30} In vain have I smitten your children; they received no correction: your own sword hath devoured your prophets, like a destroying lion. {2:31} O generation, see ye the word of the LORD. Have I been a wilderness unto Israel? a land of darkness? wherefore say my people, We are lords; we will come no more unto thee? {2:32} Can a maid forget her ornaments, or a bride her attire? yet my people have forgotten me days without number. {2:33} Why trimmest thou thy way to seek love? therefore hast thou also taught the wicked ones thy ways. {2:34} Also in thy skirts is found the blood of the souls of the poor innocents: I have not found it by secret search, but upon all these. {2:35} Yet thou sayest, Because I am innocent, surely his anger shall turn from me. Behold, I will plead with thee, because thou sayest, I have not sinned. {2:36} Why gaddest thou about so much to change thy way? thou also shalt be ashamed of Egypt, as thou wast ashamed of Assyria. {2:37} Yea, thou shalt go forth from him, and thine hands upon thine head: for the LORD hath rejected thy confidences, and thou shalt not prosper in them.

{3:1} They say, If a man put away his wife, and she go from him, and become another man's, shall he return unto her again? shall not that land be greatly polluted? but thou hast played the harlot with many lovers; yet return again to me, saith the LORD. {3:2} Lift up thine eyes unto the high places, and see where thou hast not been lien with. In the ways hast thou sat for them, as the Arabian in the wilderness; and thou hast polluted the land with thy whoredoms and with thy wickedness. {3:3} Therefore the showers have been withholden, and there hath been no latter rain; and thou hadst a whore's forehead, thou refusedst to be ashamed. {3:4} Wilt thou not from this time cry unto me, My father, thou art the guide of my youth? {3:5} Will he reserve his anger for ever? will he keep it to the end? Behold, thou hast spoken and done evil things as thou couldest. {3:6} The LORD said also unto me in the days of Josiah the king, Hast thou seen that which backsliding Israel hath done? she is gone up upon every high mountain and under every green tree, and there hath played the harlot. {3:7} And I said after she had done all these things, Turn thou unto me. But she returned not. And her treacherous sister Judah saw it. {3:8} And I saw, when for all the causes whereby backsliding Israel committed adultery I had put her away, and given her a bill of divorce; yet her treacherous sister Judah feared not, but went and played the harlot also. {3:9} And it came to pass through the lightness of her whoredom, that she defiled the land, and committed adultery with stones and with stocks. {3:10} And yet for all this her treacherous sister Judah hath not turned unto me with her whole heart, but feignedly, saith the LORD. {3:11} And the LORD said unto me, The backsliding Israel hath justified herself more than treacherous Judah. {3:12} Go and proclaim these words toward the north, and say, Return, thou backsliding Israel, saith the LORD; and I will not cause mine anger to fall upon you: for I am merciful, saith the LORD, and I will not keep anger for ever. {3:13} Only acknowledge thine iniquity, that thou hast transgressed against the LORD thy God, and hast scattered thy ways to the strangers under every green tree, and ye have not obeyed my voice, saith the LORD. {3:14} Turn, O backsliding children, saith the LORD; for I am married unto you: and I will take you one of a city, and two of a family, and I will bring you to Zion: {3:15} And I will give you pastors according to mine heart, which shall feed you with knowledge and understanding. {3:16} And it shall come to pass, when ye be multiplied and increased in the land, in those days, saith the LORD, they shall say no more, The ark of the covenant of the LORD: neither shall it come to mind: neither shall they remember it; neither shall they visit it; neither shall that be done any more. {3:17} At that time they shall call Jerusalem the throne of the LORD; and all the nations shall be gathered unto it, to the name of the LORD, to Jerusalem: neither shall they walk any more after the imagination of their evil heart. {3:18} In those days the house of Judah shall walk with the house of Israel, and they shall come together out of the land of the north to the land that I have given for an inheritance unto your fathers. {3:19} But I said, How shall I put thee among the children, and give thee a pleasant land, a goodly heritage of the hosts of nations? and I said, Thou shalt call me, My father; and shalt not turn away from me. {3:20} Surely as a wife treacherously departeth from her husband, so have ye dealt treacherously with me, O house of Israel, saith the LORD. {3:21} A voice was heard upon the high places, weeping and supplications of the children of Israel: for they have perverted their way, and they have forgotten the LORD their God. {3:22} Return, ye backsliding children, and I will heal your backslidings. Behold, we come unto thee; for thou art the LORD our God. {3:23} Truly in vain is salvation hoped for from the hills, and from the multitude of mountains: truly in the LORD our God is the salvation of Israel. {3:24} For shame hath devoured the labour of our fathers from our youth; their flocks and their herds, their sons and their daughters. {3:25} We lie down in our shame, and our confusion covereth us: for we have sinned against the LORD our God, we and our fathers, from our youth even unto this day, and have not obeyed the voice of the LORD our God.

{4:1} If you decide to return, O Israel, says the LORD, come back to me. And if you remove your detestable idols from my sight, then you will not be exiled. {4:2} You must swear, 'As surely as the LORD lives,' in truth, justice, and righteousness. Then the nations will be blessed by him and will praise him. {4:3} This is what the LORD says to the people of Judah and Jerusalem: Plow up the hard ground of your hearts! Do not waste your good seed among thorns. {4:4} Change your hearts before the LORD, and remove the sin from your lives, you people of Judah and inhabitants of Jerusalem. Otherwise, my anger will burn like an unquenchable fire because of all your sins. {4:5} Announce this in Judah and broadcast it in Jerusalem: Sound the alarm throughout the land! Cry out and gather together! Call the people to come together and seek refuge in fortified cities. {4:6} Raise the signal to Jerusalem! Flee for safety! Don't delay! For I am bringing terrible destruction from the north. {4:7} A lion stalks from its den, a destroyer of nations. It has left its lair and is headed your way. It's going to devastate your land! Your towns will lie in ruins, with no one living in them. {4:8} So put on clothes of mourning and weep with broken hearts, for the fierce anger of the LORD is still upon us. {4:9} In that day, says the LORD, the king and the officials will tremble in fear. The priests will be struck with horror, and the prophets will be appalled. {4:10} Then I said, 'O Sovereign LORD, the people have been deceived by what you said, for you promised peace for Jerusalem. But the sword is held at their throats!' {4:11} At that time this message will be given to Jerusalem: 'A scorching wind from the desert hills sweeps across the land, sweeping away all your people's hopes of peace. {4:12} This wind is too strong for that! It comes at my command! Now I will pronounce your destruction!' {4:13} Look! A great army is coming from the north! A great nation and many kings are rising against you from far-off lands. {4:14} Weep for your sins, O Jerusalem! Let your tears flow like a river day and night. Give yourselves no rest; give your eyes no relief. {4:15} Cry out in anguish, you people of Jerusalem! Go in mourning like the shepherds, for your brightest days will soon be over. {4:16} I will send these enemy troops among you like poisonous snakes you cannot charm. They will bite you, and you will die of their wounds. {4:17} I, the LORD, have spoken!' {4:18} My grief is beyond healing; my heart is broken. Listen to the weeping of my people; it can be heard all across the land. 'Has the LORD abandoned Jerusalem?' the people ask. 'Is her King no longer there?' 'Oh, why have they provoked my anger with their carved idols and their worthless foreign gods?' says the LORD. {4:19} The people of Jerusalem will weep like a woman in labor, mourning for their sins. {4:20} Their fields will be deserted, and the land will be a wilderness. The cities and towns will be destroyed, and left in ruins. {4:21} Even now, my people are like a flock of sheep that have been attacked and scattered. They are wandering over the hills and mountains, with no one to search for them or care for them. {4:22} 'My people have been foolish!' says the LORD. 'They have not listened to me or followed my instructions. They have rebelled against me. {4:23} The heavens above will grow black with clouds, and the earth will be covered with darkness. I have spoken, and I will not change my mind.' {4:24} The earth will shake at the sound of the LORD's voice, when he roars from Jerusalem. The lush pastures of the shepherds will dry up; the grass will wither, and the trees and plants will die. {4:25} Listen to the LORD's warning! 'Watch out! The enemy is coming from a distant land, raising a battle cry against the towns of Judah. {4:26} They surround Jerusalem like watchmen around a field, for my people have rebelled against me,' says the LORD. {4:27} 'Your own conduct has brought this upon you. This punishment is bitter, piercing to the heart!' {4:28} My heart is weighed down with grief, and I feel like I am carrying a heavy load. Listen! Hear the weeping of my people from distant lands: 'Is the LORD no longer in Zion? Is her King no longer there?' 'Oh, why have they provoked me to anger with their carved idols and their worthless foreign gods?' says the LORD. {4:29} 'The people of Jerusalem will flee like frightened deer. They will run from advancing enemy troops, and there will be no one to help them. {4:30} Now, why do you go on shouting? Is there no king in you? Have your counselors all died, that pain seizes you like that of a woman in labor? {4:31} Wail, you people of Jerusalem, for the enemy is coming! They are coming in from a distant land to attack the towns of Judah. They will surround Jerusalem like watchmen around a field, for my people have rebelled against me,' says the LORD.

{5:1} Run through the streets of Jerusalem! Look around and search! Find one person who acts justly and seeks the truth, and I will forgive the city. {5:2} But even when they say, 'As surely as the LORD lives,' they are not being honest. {5:3} LORD, you look for truth, but they only bring you trouble. They refuse to turn from their sins and do what is right. They are as stubborn as mules and won't obey you. {5:4} I thought, 'These are only the poor and ignorant. They behave foolishly, for they do not know what the LORD demands or understand God's laws.' {5:5} I will go to the leaders and speak to them, for they know what God wants. They know what is right, but they are as rebellious as a pack of dogs. {5:6} So a lion from the forest will attack them; a wolf from the desert will pounce on them. A leopard will lurk near their towns, tearing apart any who dare to venture out. For their rebellion is great, and their sins are many. {5:7} How can I pardon you? Your children have deserted me and sworn by gods that are not gods at all. I fed them until they were full, but then they committed adultery and spent their time with prostitutes. {5:8} They are well-fed, lusty stallions, each neighing for his neighbor's wife. {5:9} Should I not punish them for this?' says the LORD. 'Should I not avenge myself against such a nation?' {5:10} Go down the rows of the vineyards and destroy the grapevines, leaving a scattered few alive. Strip the branches from the vines, for these people do not belong to the LORD. {5:11} For both Israel and Judah have broken their promises to me. {5:12} The people of Israel and Judah are full of deceit. They refuse to acknowledge me as their LORD. {5:13} 'The prophets are but wind, for the word is not in them. So let these things happen to them!' {5:14} Therefore, this is what the LORD God of Heaven's Armies says: 'Because the people are talking like this, I will give you messages that will burn them up like firewood! {5:15} And I will bring upon you a mighty nation from far away,' says the LORD. 'They will come with their horses like a vast swarm of locusts. {5:16} They are a mighty army, marching to war against you. {5:17} They will devour your crops and your food; they will destroy your sons and your daughters. They will devour your flocks and herds; they will devour your grapes and figs. And they will destroy your fortified towns, which you think are so safe. {5:18} But even in those days,' says the LORD, 'I will not completely destroy you. {5:19} And when your people ask, 'Why is the LORD our God doing all this to us?' you must tell them, 'You have rejected me and served foreign gods in your own land. Now you will serve foreigners in a land that is not your own.' {5:20} Make this announcement to the people of Israel and Judah: 'Listen to this message from the LORD, you foolish and senseless people. {5:21} You have eyes, but you don't see. You have ears, but you don't listen. {5:22} Why don't you fear me?' says the LORD. 'Why don't you tremble in my presence? I made the sand a boundary for the sea, a permanent boundary that it cannot cross. The sea may toss, but it cannot go beyond it. The waves may roar, but they cannot cross it. {5:23} But my people are stubborn and rebellious; they have turned away and left me. {5:24} They do not say from the heart, 'Let us live in awe of the LORD our God, for he gives us rain each spring and fall, assuring us of a harvest when the time is right.' {5:25} Your wickedness has deprived you of these wonderful blessings. Your sin has robbed you of all these good things. {5:26} 'Among my people are wicked men who lie in wait for victims like a hunter hiding in a blind. {5:27} They are continually setting traps to catch people. {5:28} Like cages full of birds, their homes are filled with evil plots. And now they are great and rich. {5:29} They are fat and sleek, and there is no limit to their wicked deeds. They refuse to provide justice to orphans and deny the rights of the poor. {5:30} Should I not punish them for this?' says the LORD. 'Should I not avenge myself against such a nation?' {5:31} 'I will send a whirlwind to scatter them like chaff, says the LORD. 'They will be swept away by the wind, never to be seen again. This is their fate because they have brought this evil upon themselves.'

{6:1} People of Benjamin, flee from Jerusalem! Sound the alarm in Tekoa! Light the signal fires in Beth-haccerem! Disaster looms from the north, bringing great destruction. {6:2} I see Zion as a lovely and delicate woman. {6:3} The enemy shepherds will surround her with their flocks. They will set up their tents around her and each will graze in his own area. {6:4} Prepare for battle against her; let's attack at noon! But, alas, the day is fading, and the evening shadows are falling. {6:5} Let's attack by night and destroy her fortresses. {6:6} The LORD of Heaven's Armies has ordered the destruction of Jerusalem. She is full of oppression and violence. {6:7} She pours out wickedness like a fountain. Violence and destruction echo throughout her streets. Sorrow and wounds are always before me. {6:8} Jerusalem, listen to me and be warned, or I will turn away from you in disgust. I will turn your city into a heap of ruins, a place where no one lives. {6:9} The LORD of Heaven's Armies says, "Even the few who remain in Israel will be gleaned again, as grapes are harvested from the vine. So turn your hand to the baskets, as a grape gatherer does." {6:10} But to whom can I give a warning? Who will listen when I speak? Their ears are closed, and they refuse to listen. The word of the LORD is scorned; they take no pleasure in it. {6:11} So now I am filled with the LORD's fury. I am tired of holding it in! "Pour it out on the children in the streets and on the gatherings of young men as well. Both husbands and wives will be taken away, and the old with those who are weighed down with years. {6:12} Their homes will be turned over to their enemies, along with their fields and their wives. For I will raise my powerful fist against the people of this land," says the LORD. {6:13} "From the least to the greatest, their lives are ruled by greed. From prophets to priests, they are all frauds. {6:14} They offer superficial treatments for my people's mortal wound. They give assurances of peace when there is no peace. {6:15} Were they ashamed when they committed these disgusting sins? Not at all—they don't even blush. Therefore, they will lie among the slaughtered. They will be brought down when I punish them," says the LORD. {6:16} This is what the LORD says: "Stop at the crossroads and look around. Ask for the old, godly way, and walk in it. Travel its path, and you will find rest for your souls." But they reply, "No, that's not the road we want!" {6:17} I appointed watchmen over you and said, "Listen for the sound of the alarm." But you replied, "No! We won't pay attention!" {6:18} So listen, all you nations; take note, you people of the earth. {6:19} Hear, earth! I am bringing disaster upon these people, the fruit of their own schemes, because they refuse to listen to my words and reject my instructions. {6:20} "What do I care about incense from Sheba or sweet calamus from a distant land? Your burnt offerings are not acceptable; your sacrifices do not please me." {6:21} Therefore, this is what the LORD says: "I will put obstacles in the path of these people. Fathers and sons alike will stumble over them; neighbors and friends will die together." {6:22} This is what the LORD says: "A great army is coming from the north, a mighty nation is rising against you. {6:23} They are armed with bows and spears. They are cruel and show no mercy. As they ride forward on horses, they sound like a roaring sea. They are coming in battle formation, planning to destroy you, Jerusalem!" {6:24} We have heard reports about the enemy, and we are weak with fright. Fear and pain have gripped us, like that of a woman in labor. {6:25} Don't go out to the fields! Don't travel on the roads! The enemy's sword is everywhere and terrorizes everyone! {6:26} O my people, dress yourselves in burlap and sit among the ashes. Mourn and weep bitterly, as for the loss of an only son. For suddenly, the destroying armies will be upon you! {6:27} I have made you a tester of metals and my people the ore, that you may observe and test their ways. {6:28} "All are rebels, spreading slander. They are bronze and iron; all of them act corruptly. {6:29} The bellows blow fiercely to burn away the lead with fire, but the refining goes on in vain; the wicked are not purged out. {6:30} Reprobate silver shall they be called, for the LORD has rejected them."

{7:1} This is the message that came to Jeremiah from the LORD: {7:2} "Stand at the entrance to the LORD's Temple, and proclaim this message. Listen, all you people of Judah who come through these gates to worship the LORD! {7:3} This is what the LORD of Heaven's Armies, the God of Israel, says: 'Change your ways and your actions, and I will let you live in this place. {7:4} Don't put your trust in deceptive words and say, 'This is the Temple of the LORD, the Temple of the LORD, the Temple of the LORD!' {7:5} No, if you really change your ways and your actions and deal justly with each other justly, {7:6} if you stop exploiting foreigners, orphans, and widows, and stop your murdering, and if you stop harming yourselves by worshiping idols, {7:7} then I will let you stay in this land that I gave to your ancestors forever and ever. {7:8} But look, you are trusting in deceptive words that are worthless. {7:9} Will you steal and murder, commit adultery and perjury, burn incense to Baal, and worship other gods you have not known, {7:10} and then come and stand before me in this Temple that bears my name and say, 'We are safe!'—safe to do all these detestable things? {7:11} Do you think this Temple that bears my name is a hideout for robbers? Surely I see all the evil going on there. I, the LORD, have spoken! {7:12} Go now to the place at Shiloh where I once put the Tabernacle that bore my name. See what I did there because of all the wickedness of my people, the Israelites. {7:13} While you were doing these wicked things, says the LORD, I spoke to you about it repeatedly, but you would not listen. I called out to you, but you refused to answer. {7:14} So just as I destroyed Shiloh, I will now destroy this Temple that bears my name, this Temple that you trust in for help, this place that I gave to you and your ancestors. {7:15} And I will send you out of my sight into exile, just as I did your relatives, the people of Israel.' {7:16} "Pray no more for these people, Jeremiah. Do not weep or pray for them, and don't beg me to help them, for I will not listen to you. {7:17} Don't you see what they are doing throughout the towns of Judah and in the streets of Jerusalem? {7:18} No wonder I am so angry! Watch how the children gather wood and the fathers build sacrificial fires. See how the women knead dough and make cakes to offer to the Queen of Heaven. And they pour out liquid offerings to their other idol gods! {7:19} Am I the one they are hurting?" asks the LORD. "Most of all, they hurt themselves, to their own shame." {7:20} So this is what the Sovereign LORD says: "I will pour out my terrible fury on this place. Its people, animals, trees, and crops will be consumed by the unquenchable fire of my anger." {7:21} This is what the LORD of Heaven's Armies, the God of Israel, says: "Take your burnt offerings and your other sacrifices and eat them yourselves! {7:22} When I led your ancestors out of Egypt, it was not burnt offerings and sacrifices I wanted from them. {7:23} This is what I told them: 'Obey me, and I will be your God, and you will be my people. Do everything as I say, and all will be well.' {7:24} But my people would not listen to me. They kept doing whatever they wanted, following the stubborn desires of their evil hearts. They went backward instead of forward. {7:25} From the day your ancestors left Egypt until now, I have continued to send my servants, the prophets—day in and day out. {7:26} But my people have not listened to me or even tried to hear. They have been stubborn and sinful—even worse than their ancestors. {7:27} Tell them all this, but do not expect them to listen. Shout out your warnings, but do not expect them to respond. {7:28} Say to them, 'This is the nation whose people will not obey the LORD their God and who refuse to be taught. Truth has vanished from among them; it is no longer heard on their lips.' {7:29} "Shave your head in mourning, and weep alone on the mountains. For the LORD has rejected and forsaken this generation that has provoked his fury. {7:30} "The people of Judah have sinned before my very eyes," says the LORD. "They have set up their abominable idols right in the Temple that bears my name, defiling it. {7:31} They have built pagan shrines at Topheth, the garbage dump in the valley of Ben-Hinnom, and there they burn their sons and daughters in the fire. I have never commanded such a horrible deed; it never even crossed my mind to command such a thing! {7:32} So beware, for the time is coming," says the LORD, "when that garbage dump will no longer be called Topheth or the valley of Ben-Hinnom, but the Valley of Slaughter. They will bury the bodies in Topheth until there is no more room for them. {7:33} The bodies of my people will be food for the vultures and wild animals, and no one will be left to scare them away. {7:34} I will put an end to the happy singing and laughter in the streets of Jerusalem. The joyful voices of bridegrooms and brides will no longer be heard in the towns of Judah. The land will lie in complete desolation.

{8:1} This is what the LORD says: "At that time, they will bring out the bones of the kings of Judah, the bones of the princes, the bones of the priests, the bones of the prophets, and the bones of the people of Jerusalem from their graves. {8:2} They will spread them out before the sun, the moon, and all the stars of the sky, which the people have loved, served, worshiped, and sought after. These bones will not be gathered up or buried but will be scattered on the ground like dung. {8:3} Death will be preferable to life for all the survivors who remain of this evil family, wherever I have driven them," says the LORD of Heaven's Armies. {8:4} "Tell them, 'This is what the LORD says: When people fall down, don't they get up again? When they discover they're on the wrong road, don't they turn back? {8:5} So why do these people stay on their self-destructive path? Why do they refuse to turn back? They cling tightly to their deceit and refuse to return. {8:6} I listened to their conversations, but they were not speaking honestly. No one repents of their wickedness, saying, 'What have I done?' They all turn to their own course like horses charging into battle. {8:7} Even the stork knows when it is time to move on. The turtledove, swallow, and crane recognize the seasons of their migration, but my people do not know the requirements of the LORD. {8:8} "'How can you say, "We are wise because we have the word of the LORD," when your teachers have twisted it by writing lies? {8:9} These wise teachers will be shamed. They will be humiliated and trapped. Since they have rejected the word of the LORD, what kind of wisdom do they have? {8:10} Therefore, I will give their wives to other men and their fields to new owners. From the least to the greatest, their lives are ruled by greed. Yes, even my prophets and priests are like that. They are all frauds. {8:11} They offer superficial treatments for my people's mortal wound. They give assurances of peace when there is no peace. {8:12} Were they ashamed when they committed these disgusting sins? Not at all—they don't even know how to blush! Therefore, they will lie among the slaughtered. They will be brought down when I punish them," says the LORD. {8:13} I will surely consume them," says the LORD. "There will be no grapes on the vine. No figs on the fig tree, and even the leaves will wither. What I have given them will soon be gone. {8:14} Why are we sitting here, waiting for something to happen? Let's go to the fortified towns and die there. For the LORD our God has decreed our destruction and has given us a cup of poison to drink because we sinned against the LORD. {8:15} **We hoped for peace, but no peace came. We hoped for a time of healing, but found only terror.** {8:16} The snorting of the enemies' warhorses can be heard all the way from the land of Dan in the north! The neighing of their stallions makes the whole land tremble. They are coming to devour the land and everything in it—cities and people alike. {8:17} "'I will send these enemies to devour you like poisonous snakes. They will not be charmed, and they will bite you,' says the LORD." {8:18} **My grief is beyond healing; my heart is broken.** {8:19} Listen to the weeping of my people; it can be heard all across the land. 'Has the LORD abandoned Jerusalem?' the people ask. 'Is her King no longer there?' 'Oh, why have they angered me with their carved idols and worthless gods?' says the LORD. {8:20} **"The harvest is finished, and the summer is gone," the people cry, "yet we are not saved!"** {8:21} I hurt with the hurt of my people. I mourn and am overcome with grief. {8:22} Is there no medicine in Gilead? Is there no physician there? Why is there no healing for the wounds of my people?

{9:1} I wish my head were a spring of water and my eyes a fountain of tears! Then I could weep day and night for my people who have been slaughtered. {9:2} I wish I could go away and forget my people and live in a traveler's shack in the desert. They are all adulterers—a pack of treacherous liars. {9:3} They bend their tongues like bows to shoot out lies. They refuse to stand up for the truth. They only go from bad to worse. They do not know me," says the LORD. {9:4} "Beware of your neighbor! Don't even trust your brother! For brother takes advantage of brother, and friend deceives friend. {9:5} They all fool and defraud each other; no one tells the truth. With practiced tongues they tell lies; they wear themselves out with all their sinning. {9:6} They pile on lies upon lies and refuse to acknowledge me," says the LORD. {9:7} "So I will melt them down and test them. How else can I deal with my people? {9:8} Their tongues shoot lies like arrows. They speak friendly words to their neighbors while scheming in their hearts. {9:9} Should I not punish them for this?" says the LORD. "Should I not avenge myself against such a nation? {9:10} I will weep for the mountains and wail for the wilderness pastures. For they are desolate and empty of life; the lowing of cattle is heard no more; the birds and wild animals have all fled. {9:11} "I will make Jerusalem into a heap of ruins," says the LORD. "It will be a place haunted by jackals. The towns of Judah will be ghost towns, with no one living in them." {9:12} "Who is wise enough to understand all this? Who has been instructed by the LORD and can explain it to others? Why has the land been so devastated that no one dares to travel through it? {9:13} The LORD replies, "This has happened because my people have abandoned my instructions; they have refused to obey what I said. {9:14} Instead, they have stubbornly followed their own desires and worshiped the images of Baal, as their ancestors taught them. {9:15} Therefore, this is what the LORD of Heaven's Armies, the God of Israel, says: 'I will feed them with bitterness and give them poison to drink. {9:16} I will scatter them around the world, in places they and their ancestors never heard of. Even there I will chase them with the sword until I have destroyed them completely.'" {9:17} This is what the LORD of Heaven's Armies says: "Consider all this, and call for the mourners. Send for the women who mourn at funerals. {9:18} Quick! Begin your weeping! Let the tears flow from your eyes. {9:19} Hear the people of Jerusalem crying in despair, 'We are ruined! We are completely humiliated! We must leave our land, because our homes have been torn down.'" {9:20} Listen, you women, to the words of the LORD; open your ears to what he has to say. Teach your daughters to wail; teach one another how to lament. {9:21} For death has crept in through our windows and has entered our mansions. It has killed off the flower of our youth and all our children. {9:22} "This is what the LORD says: 'Bodies will be scattered across the fields like clumps of manure, like bundles of grain after the harvest. No one will be left to bury them.'" {9:23} The wise should not boast of their wisdom, nor the strong of their strength, nor the rich of their wealth. {9:24} If any want to boast, they should boast that they know and understand me, because my love is constant, and I do what is just and right. These are the things that please me," says the LORD. {9:25} "The time is coming," says the LORD, "when I will punish all those who are circumcised in body but not in spirit— {9:26} Egypt, Judah, Edom, Ammon, Moab, and all who live in the distant wilderness. For all these nations are really uncircumcised, and even the people of Israel are uncircumcised in their hearts."

{10:1} Listen to the words of the LORD, people of Israel: {10:2} The LORD says, "Don't follow the ways of the nations, and don't be disturbed by the signs in the sky, even though the nations are terrified by them. {10:3} The customs of the people are worthless; they cut down a tree from the forest and carve it with an ax. {10:4} They decorate it with silver and gold and fasten it with hammer and nails so it won't fall over. {10:5} These idols stand upright like scarecrows in a field, but they cannot speak! They must be carried because they cannot walk. Don't be afraid of such idols, for they can neither harm you nor do you any good. {10:6} The LORD alone is God; he is the Creator, and his name is glorious and mighty. {10:7} All nations should stand in awe of him; he is the one true King. But the idols people worship are foolish and stupid. They are worthless as a teacher of goodness. {10:8} Silver is brought from Tarshish and gold from Uphaz. These are the products of a craftsman and of the hands of a goldsmith. The blue and purple fabric comes from distant lands and is skilfully made. {10:9} But the LORD is the only true God; he is the living God and the everlasting King! The whole earth trembles at his anger. The nations cannot stand up to his fury. {10:10} So tell them, "These gods you worship are not the ones who made the heavens and earth! They will die and disappear from the earth and sky." {10:11} God made the earth by his power, and he preserves it by his wisdom. With his own understanding he stretched out the heavens. {10:12} When he speaks, there is thunder in the heavens. He causes the clouds to rise over the earth. He sends the lightning with the rain and releases the wind from his storehouses. {10:13} People are foolish and ignorant, with their worthless idols. Their wooden images are a fraud. {10:14} They are meaningless, a work of mockery. In the day of reckoning, they will all be destroyed. {10:15} But the LORD is the only true God. He is the living God and the everlasting King! The whole earth trembles at his anger. The nations cannot stand up to his fury. {10:16} The descendants of Jacob are not like their worthless idols. They are his own people, and he names them Israel. {10:17} Gather your belongings from among the nations, O Israel. Pack your bags and prepare to leave. {10:18} For the LORD is going to scatter you far from your homeland; he will surely disperse you among the nations. {10:19} My heart is broken because of the false prophets, and my bones tremble. I stagger like a drunken man because of the holy words the LORD has spoken against them. {10:20} The land is full of people who don't know the LORD. They worship idols made of wood and stone, which cannot see or hear or eat or smell. {10:21} The LORD says, "The wise are not to boast of their wisdom, nor the strong of their strength, nor the rich of their wealth. {10:22} Instead, let those who boast boast about this: that they understand and know me, that I am the LORD, who is kind and just and righteous in all the earth. These are the things I delight in," says the LORD. {10:23} The time is coming when I will punish all those who are circumcised only in the flesh— {10:24} Egypt, Judah, Edom, Ammon, Moab, and all who live in the distant wilderness. {10:25}For all these nations are really uncircumcised, and even the people of Israel are uncircumcised in their hearts."

{11:1} This is the message that came to Jeremiah from the LORD: {11:2} "Listen to the terms of this covenant and speak to the people of Judah and to the residents of Jerusalem. {11:3} Tell them, 'This is what the

LORD, the God of Israel, says: Cursed is anyone who does not obey the terms of this covenant— {11:4} the covenant I made with your ancestors when I brought them out of Egypt, where they were slaves. I told them, "Obey me and do everything I command you, and you will be my people, and I will be your God." {11:5} I said, "If you do, I will fulfill the oath I swore to your ancestors, to give them a land flowing with milk and honey"—the land you possess today.'" {11:6} Then I replied, "Amen, LORD." {11:7} And the LORD said to me, "Announce all these words in the towns of Judah and in the streets of Jerusalem: Listen to the terms of this covenant and follow them. {11:8} From the time I brought your ancestors out of Egypt until today, I warned them again and again, saying, 'Obey me.' {11:9} But they did not listen or pay attention; instead, they followed the stubbornness of their evil hearts. So I brought on them all the curses of the covenant I had commanded them to follow but that they did not keep." {11:10} Then the LORD said to me, "There is a conspiracy among the people of Judah and those who live in Jerusalem. {11:11} They have returned to the sins of their ancestors, who refused to listen to my words. They have followed other gods to serve them. Both Israel and Judah have broken the covenant I made with their ancestors. {11:12} Therefore this is what the LORD says: I will bring on them a disaster they cannot escape. Although they cry out to me, I will not listen to them. {11:13} The towns of Judah and the people of Jerusalem will go and cry out to the gods to whom they burn incense, but they will not help them at all when disaster strikes. {11:14} "Pray no more for these people, Jeremiah. Do not weep or pray for them, for I will not listen to them when they cry out to me in distress. {11:15} What is my beloved doing in my temple as she, with many others, works out her evil schemes? Can consecrated meat avert your punishment? When you engage in your wickedness, then you rejoice." {11:16} The LORD called you a thriving olive tree with fruit beautiful in form. But with the roar of a mighty storm, he will set it on fire, and its branches will be broken. {11:17} The LORD Almighty, who planted you, has decreed disaster for you, because the people of both Israel and Judah have done evil and aroused my anger by burning incense to Baal. {11:18} Because the LORD revealed their plot to me, I knew it, for at that time he showed me what they were doing. {11:19} I had been like a gentle lamb led to the slaughter; I did not realize that they had plotted against me, saying, "Let us destroy the tree and its fruit; let us cut him off from the land of the living, that his name be remembered no more." {11:20} But you, LORD Almighty, who judge righteously and test the heart and mind, let me see your vengeance on them, for to you I have committed my cause. {11:21} Therefore this is what the LORD says about the people of Anathoth who are threatening to kill you, saying, "Do not prophesy in the name of the LORD or you will die by our hands"— {11:22} Therefore this is what the LORD Almighty says: "I will punish them. Their young men will die by the sword; their sons and daughters will die by famine. {11:23} Not even a remnant will be left to them, because I will bring disaster on the people of Anathoth in the year of their punishment."

{12:1} LORD, you are righteous when I bring a case before you. Yet I would speak with you about your justice: Why does the way of the wicked prosper? Why do all the faithless live at ease? {12:2} You have planted them, and they have taken root; they grow and bear fruit. You are always on their lips but far from their hearts. {12:3} Yet you know me, LORD; you see me and test my thoughts about you. Drag them off like sheep to be butchered! Set them apart for the day of slaughter! {12:4} How long will the land lie parched and the grass in every field be withered? Because those who live in it are wicked, the animals and birds have perished. Moreover, the people say, "He will not see what happens to us." {12:5} "If you have raced with men on foot and they have worn you out, how can you compete with horses? If you stumble in safe country, how will you manage in the thickets by the Jordan? {12:6} Your relatives, members of your own family—even they have betrayed you; they have raised a loud cry against you. Do not trust them, though they speak well of you. {12:7} "I will forsake my house, abandon my inheritance; I will give the one I love into the hands of her enemies. {12:8} My inheritance has become to me like a lion in the forest. She roars at me; therefore, I hate her. {12:9} Has not my inheritance become to me like a speckled bird of prey that other birds of prey surround and attack? Go and gather all the wild beasts; bring them to devour. {12:10} Many shepherds will ruin my vineyard and trample down my field; they will turn my pleasant field into a desolate wasteland. {12:11} It will be made a wasteland, parched and desolate before me; the whole land will be laid waste because there is no one who cares. {12:12} The destroyers will come against every town, and not a town will escape. The land will be made desolate, and all who dwell in it will mourn. {12:13} The crops are destroyed, and they are ashamed because the fields are barren. The crops have failed, and the people are ashamed. They cover their heads in grief because of the Lord's fierce anger. {12:14} This is what the LORD says: "As for all my wicked neighbors who seize the inheritance I gave my people Israel, I will uproot them from their lands and remove the people of Judah from among them. {12:15} But after I uproot them, I will again have compassion and will bring each of them back to their own inheritance and their own country. {12:16} And if they learn well the ways of my people and swear by my name, saying, 'As surely as the LORD lives'—even as they once taught my people to swear by Baal—then they will be established among my people. {12:17} But if any nation does not listen, I will completely uproot and destroy it," declares the LORD.

{13:1} The LORD said to me, "Go and get yourself a linen belt, and put it around your waist, but do not let it touch water." {13:2} So I bought a belt as the LORD instructed and put it around my waist. {13:3} Then the word of the LORD came to me a second time, saying, {13:4} "Take the belt you have bought, which is around your waist, and go to the Euphrates. Hide it there in a crevice of the rocks." {13:5} So I went and hid it by the Euphrates as the LORD had commanded me. {13:6} After many days, the LORD said to me, "Go now to the Euphrates and retrieve the belt I commanded you to hide there." {13:7} So I went to the Euphrates, dug up the belt, and retrieved it from the place where I had hidden it. But it was ruined and completely worthless. {13:8} Then the word of the LORD came to me, saying, {13:9} "This is what the LORD says: 'In the same way I will ruin the pride of Judah and the great pride of Jerusalem. {13:10} These wicked people, who refuse to listen to my words, who follow the stubbornness of their hearts, and who go after other gods to serve and worship them—they will become like this belt, completely worthless! {13:11} For just as a belt is bound around a man's waist, so I bound the whole house of Israel and the whole house of Judah to me,' declares the LORD, 'to be my people for my renown and praise and honor. But they did not listen.' {13:12} "Therefore say to them, 'This is what the LORD, the God of Israel, says: Every wineskin should be filled with wine.' And if they say to you, 'Don't we know that every wineskin should be filled with wine?' {13:13} then tell them, 'This is what the LORD says: I am going to fill with drunkenness all who live in this land, including the kings who sit on David's throne, the priests, the prophets and all those living in Jerusalem. {13:14} I will smash them one against the other, parents and children alike, declares the LORD. I will allow no pity or mercy or compassion to keep me from destroying them.'" {13:15} Listen and pay attention! Do not be arrogant, for the LORD has spoken. {13:16} Give glory to the LORD your God before he brings darkness, before your feet stumble on the darkening hills. You hope for light, but he will turn it to utter darkness and change it to deep gloom. {13:17} But if you do not listen, I will weep in secret because of your pride; my eyes will weep bitterly, overflowing with tears, because the LORD's flock will be taken captive. {13:18} Say to the king and to the queen mother, "Come down from your thrones, for your glorious crowns will fall from your heads." {13:19} The cities in the Negev will be shut tight, with no one to open them. All Judah will be carried into exile, carried completely away. {13:20} Look up and see those who are coming from the north. Where is the flock that was entrusted to you, the sheep that were your pride? {13:21} What will you say when the LORD sets over you those you cultivated as your special allies? Will not pain grip you like that of a woman in labor? {13:22} And if you ask yourself, "Why has this happened to me?" It is because of your many sins that your skirts have been torn off and your body exposed. {13:23} Can an Ethiopian change his skin or a leopard its spots? Neither can you do good who are accustomed to doing evil. {13:24} "I will scatter you like chaff driven by the desert wind. {13:25} This is your lot, the portion I have measured out to you," declares the LORD, "because you have forgotten me and trusted in false gods. {13:26} I will pull up your skirts over your face that your shame may be seen— {13:27} your adulteries and lustful neighings, your shameless prostitution! I have seen your detestable acts on the hills and in the fields. Woe to you, Jerusalem! How long will you be unclean?"

{14:1} The LORD spoke to Jeremiah about the drought in the land. {14:2} Judah is in mourning, and its gates are desolate; the people are despairing, and the cry of Jerusalem has gone up. {14:3} The nobles send their servants for water; they come to the cisterns but find none. They return with empty jars, ashamed and dismayed, covering their heads in distress. {14:4} Because the ground is cracked and there is no rain, the farmers are ashamed and cover their heads in sorrow. {14:5} Even the doe in the field deserts her newborn fawn because there is no grass. {14:6} The wild donkeys stand on the barren heights; they pant for air like jackals, their eyes fail for lack of pasture. {14:7} "O LORD, though our sins testify against us, act for the sake of your name. Our rebellions are many; we have sinned against you. {14:8} You are the hope of Israel, its Savior in times of distress. Why are you like a stranger in the land, like a traveler who stays only a night? {14:9} Why are you like a man taken by surprise, like a warrior powerless to save? Yet you, O LORD, are among us, and we bear your name; do not forsake us! {14:10} This is what the LORD says to this people: They greatly love to wander; they do not restrain their feet. So the LORD does not accept them; he will now remember their wickedness and punish their sins. {14:11} Then the LORD said to me, "Do not pray for the well-being of these people. {14:12} When they fast, I will not hear their cry; when they offer burnt offerings and grain offerings, I will not accept them. Instead, I will consume them by sword, famine, and plague." {14:13} But I protested, "Ah, Lord GOD! The prophets are telling them, 'You will not see sword or suffer famine. Indeed, I will give you lasting peace in this place.'" {14:14} Then the LORD said to me, "The prophets are prophesying lies in my name. I did not send them or authorize them or speak to them. They are prophesying to you false visions, divinations, idolatries, and the delusions of their own minds. {14:15} Therefore, this is what the LORD says about the prophets who are prophesying in my name: I did not send them, yet they say, 'No sword or famine will touch this land.' Those same prophets will perish by sword and famine. {14:16} And the people they are prophesying to will be thrown out into the streets of Jerusalem because of famine and sword. There will be no one to bury them—neither them nor their wives, their sons, or their daughters. For I will pour out their wickedness on them. {14:17} "So tell them this: 'My eyes overflow with tears day and night without ceasing, for my people, my precious children, have suffered a grievous wound, a crushing blow. {14:18} If I go into the fields, I see the ravages of the sword; if I enter the city, I see the ravages of famine. Both prophet and priest have gone to a land they know not.'" {14:19} Have you rejected Judah completely? Do you despise Zion? Why have you afflicted us so that we cannot be healed? We hoped for peace, but no good has come, for a time of healing, but there is only terror. {14:20} We acknowledge, O LORD, our wickedness and the guilt of our ancestors; we have indeed sinned against you. {14:21} Do not scorn us, for the sake of your name; do not dishonor your glorious throne. Remember your covenant with us; do not break it. {14:22} Can any of the worthless idols of the nations bring rain? Can the skies themselves send down showers? No, you alone are our God, and we wait for you, for you have made all these things.

{15:1} The LORD spoke to me, saying, "Even if Moses and Samuel were to stand before me, my heart would not turn toward this people. Cast them out of my sight and let them go forth. {15:2} "And if they ask, 'Where shall we go?' you shall tell them, 'This is what the LORD says: Those destined for death, to death; those for the sword, to the sword; those for famine, to famine; and those for captivity, to captivity.' {15:3} "I will appoint over them four kinds of destroyers," declares the LORD: "the sword to kill, the dogs to drag away, the birds in the sky and the beasts on the earth to devour and destroy. {15:4} "And I will make them a horror to all the kingdoms of the earth because of what Manasseh son of Hezekiah king of Judah did in Jerusalem. {15:5} "Who will have pity on you, O Jerusalem? Who will mourn for you? Who will turn aside to inquire about your welfare? {15:6} "You have forsaken me," declares the LORD. "You have turned your back, so I will stretch out my hand against you and destroy you. I am tired of relenting. {15:7} "I will winnow them with a winnowing fork at the city gates of the land. I will bereave them; I will destroy my people, for they have not turned from their ways. {15:8} "Their widows will be more numerous than the sand of the seas. I have brought against the mother of young men a destroyer at noonday. I have suddenly brought down on her anguish and terrors. {15:9} "She who bore seven sons pines away; her life breath fails her. Her sun sets while it is still day; she is ashamed and humiliated. And the rest of them I will give over to the sword in the presence of their enemies," declares the LORD. {15:10} "Woe to me, my mother, that you have borne me, a man of strife and contention to the whole earth! I have neither lent nor borrowed, yet everyone curses me. {15:11} The LORD said, 'Surely I will deliver you for a good purpose; surely I will make your enemies plead with you in times of disaster and times of distress.' {15:12} "Can a man break iron—iron from the north—or bronze? {15:13} "I will give away your wealth and your treasures as plunder, without charge, because of all your sins throughout your country. {15:14} "I will enslave you to your enemies in a land you do not know, for my anger will kindle a fire that will burn against you." {15:15} "You understand, O LORD; remember me and care for me. Avenge me on my persecutors. You are long-suffering; do not take me away. Know that for your sake I endure reproach. {15:16} "Your words were found, and I ate them. They became my joy and my heart's delight, for I bear your name, O LORD God Almighty. {15:17} "I did not sit in the company of revelers, nor did I rejoice. I sat alone because your hand was on me and you had filled me with indignation. {15:18} "Why is my pain unending and my wound grievous and incurable? You are to me like a deceptive brook, like a spring that fails." {15:19} Therefore, this is what the LORD says: "If you repent, I will restore you that you may serve me; if you utter worthy, not worthless, words, you will be my spokesman. Let this people turn to you, but you must not turn to them. {15:20} "I will make you a wall to this people, a fortified wall of bronze; they will fight against you but will not overcome you, for I am with you to rescue and save you," declares the LORD. {15:21} "I will save you from the hands of the wicked and deliver you from the grasp of the cruel."

{16:1} The LORD spoke to me again, saying, {16:2} "Do not take a wife or have sons or daughters in this place. {16:3} "For this is what the LORD says about the sons and daughters born in this place, and about the mothers who bear them, and the fathers who beget them in this land: {16:4} "They will die of deadly diseases, without being lamented or buried. They will become like dung on the ground, consumed by sword and famine. Their carcasses will be food for the birds of the air and the beasts of the earth. {16:5} "Do not enter the house of mourning or go to lament or mourn for them, for I have taken away my peace from this people, declares the LORD, my steadfast love and mercy. {16:6} "Both great and small will die in this land; they will not be buried or mourned for, nor will anyone make cuts or shave their heads for them. {16:7} "No one will offer food to comfort those in mourning for the dead, nor will they give them a cup of consolation for their father or mother. {16:8} "Do not enter the house of feasting to sit down and eat and drink. {16:9} "For this is what the LORD of hosts, the God of Israel, says: 'I will make to cease in this place, in your sight and in your days, the voice of mirth and the voice of gladness, the voice of the bridegroom and the voice of the bride. {16:10} "And when you tell these people all these words, and they ask you, 'Why has the LORD pronounced all this great evil against us? What is our iniquity? What is the sin that we have committed against the LORD our God?' {16:11} "Then you shall say to them: 'Because your fathers have forsaken me, declares the LORD, and have followed other gods, served them, worshiped them, and forsaken me, and have not kept my law; {16:12} "And you have done worse than your fathers. Look, each one of you follows the stubbornness of his evil heart, so that you do not listen to me. {16:13} "Therefore I will cast you out of this land into a land that neither you nor your fathers have known, and there you will serve other gods day and night, for I will show you no favor. {16:14} "Therefore, behold, the days are coming, declares the LORD, when it shall no longer be said, 'As the LORD lives who brought up the people of Israel out of the land of Egypt,' {16:15} "But, 'As the LORD lives who brought up the people of Israel from the land of the north and from all the countries where he had driven them.' And I will bring them back to their own land that I gave to their fathers. {16:16} "Behold, I will send for many fishermen, declares the LORD, and they shall catch them. And afterward I will send for many hunters, and they shall hunt them from every mountain and hill, and out of the clefts of the rocks. {16:17} "For my eyes are on all their ways; they are not hidden from me, nor is their iniquity concealed from my eyes. {16:18} "I will doubly repay their iniquity and their sin, because they have polluted my land with the carcasses of their detestable idols and have filled my inheritance with their abominations. {16:19} "O LORD, my strength and my stronghold, my refuge in the day of trouble, to you shall the nations come from the ends of the earth and say: 'Our fathers have inherited nothing but lies, worthless things in which there is no profit.' {16:20} "Can man make for himself gods? Such are not gods! {16:21} "Therefore, behold, I will make them know, this once I will make them know my power and my might, and they shall know that my name is the LORD."

{17:1} The sin of Judah is deeply engraved, like etchings with an iron stylus, and inscribed with a diamond point on the tablet of their hearts and on the horns of their altars. {17:2} Their children remember their altars and their Asherah poles by the green trees on the high hills. {17:3} "O my mountain in the field, I will give up your wealth and all your treasures as plunder, because of the sin throughout your country. {17:4} "And you, even yourself, will discontinue from your heritage that I gave you, and I will make you serve your enemies in a land you do not know. For you have kindled a fire in my anger that will burn forever. {17:5} "This is what the LORD says: 'Cursed is the one who trusts in man, who depends on flesh for strength and whose heart turns away from the LORD. {17:6} "For he will be like a bush in the wastelands; he will not see prosperity when it comes. He will dwell in the parched places of the desert, in a salt land where no one lives. {17:7} **"But blessed is the one who trusts in the LORD, whose confidence is in him.** {17:8} "He will be like a tree planted by the water that sends out its roots by the stream. It does not fear when heat comes; its leaves are always green. It has no worries in a year of drought and never fails to bear fruit. {17:9} "The heart is deceitful above all things and beyond cure. Who can understand it? {17:10} "I the LORD search the heart and examine the mind, to reward each person according to their conduct, according to what their deeds deserve." {17:11} Like a partridge that hatches eggs it did not lay are those who gain riches by unjust means. When their lives are half gone, their riches will desert them, and in the end they will prove to be fools. {17:12} "A glorious throne, exalted from the beginning, is the place of our sanctuary. {17:13} "O LORD, the hope of Israel, all who forsake you will be put to shame. Those who turn away from you will be written in the dust because they have forsaken the LORD, the spring of living water. {17:14} "Heal me, LORD, and I will be healed; save me and I will be saved, for you are the one I praise. {17:15} "They keep saying to me, 'Where is the word of the LORD? Let it now be fulfilled!' {17:16} "I have not run away from being your shepherd; you know I have not desired the day of despair. What passes my lips is open before you. {17:17} "Do not be a terror to me; you are my refuge in the day of disaster. {17:18} "Let my persecutors be put to shame, but keep me from shame; let them be terrified, but keep me from terror. Bring on them the day of disaster; destroy them with double destruction. {17:19} "This is what the LORD said to me: 'Go and stand at the gate of the people, through which the kings of Judah go in and out; stand also at all the other gates of Jerusalem. {17:20} "Say to them, 'Hear the word of the LORD, you kings of Judah and all people of Judah and everyone living in Jerusalem who come through these gates. {17:21} "This is what the LORD says: Be careful not to carry a load on the Sabbath day or bring it through the gates of Jerusalem. {17:22} "Do not bring a load out of your houses or do any work on the Sabbath, but keep the Sabbath day holy, as I commanded your ancestors. {17:23} "Yet they did not listen or pay attention; they were stiff-necked and would not listen or respond to discipline. {17:24} "But if you are careful to obey me, declares the LORD, and bring no load through the gates of this city on the Sabbath, but keep the Sabbath day holy by not doing any work on it, {17:25} "Then kings who sit on David's throne will come through the gates of this city with their officials. They and their officials will come riding in chariots and on horses, accompanied by the men of Judah and those living in Jerusalem, and this city will be inhabited forever. {17:26} "People will come from the towns of Judah and the villages around Jerusalem, from the territory of Benjamin and the western foothills, from the hill country and the Negev, bringing burnt offerings and sacrifices, grain offerings and incense, and bringing thank offerings to the house of the LORD. {17:27} "But if you do not obey me to keep the Sabbath day holy by not carrying any load as you come through the gates of Jerusalem on the Sabbath day, then I will kindle an unquenchable fire in the gates of Jerusalem that will consume her fortresses.'"

{18:1} This is the message that came to Jeremiah from the LORD: {18:2} "Go down to the potter's house, and I will speak to you there." {18:3} So I went down to the potter's house, and saw him working at the wheel. {18:4} But the jar he was making did not turn out as he had hoped, so he crushed it into a lump of clay again and started over. {18:5} Then the LORD gave me this message: {18:6} "O Israel, can't I do to you as this potter has done to his clay? As the clay is in the potter's hand, so are you in my hand, O Israel. {18:7} *If I announce that a certain nation or kingdom is to be uprooted, torn down, and destroyed,* {18:8} *but then that nation renounces its evil ways, I will not destroy it as I had planned.* {18:9} And if I announce that I will build up and plant a certain nation or kingdom, {18:10} but then that nation turns to evil and refuses to obey me, I will not bless it as I said I would. {18:11} "Therefore, Jeremiah, go and warn all Judah and Jerusalem. Say to them, 'This is what the LORD says: I am planning disaster for you instead of good. So turn from your evil ways, each of you, and do what is right.'" {18:12} But the people replied, "Don't waste your breath. We will continue to live as we want to, stubbornly following our own evil desires." {18:13} Therefore, this is what the LORD says: "Inquire among the nations: Who has ever heard anything like this? Has anyone ever seen anything as strange as what Israel has done? {18:14} "Does the snow ever melt from the mountaintops of Lebanon? Do the cold streams flowing from those distant mountains ever run dry? {18:15} Yet my people have forgotten me. They burn incense to worthless idols, which make them stumble in their ways on the ancient paths. They walk in paths, in a way not cast up; {18:16} Making their land desolate, a perpetual object of scorn. All who pass by will be astonished and shake their heads. {18:17} "I will scatter my people before their enemies as the east wind scatters dust. And in all their trouble I will turn my back on them and refuse to notice their distress." {18:18} Then the people said, "Come on, let's plot a way to stop Jeremiah. We have plenty of priests and wise men and prophets to advise us. We don't need him to teach the word of the LORD anymore." {18:19} So I replied, "LORD, hear me and listen to what my enemies are saying. {18:20} Should they repay evil for good? They have dug a pit to kill me, though I pleaded for them and tried to stop your anger against them. {18:21} "Therefore, let their children starve; let them die by the sword. Let their wives become widows with no one to support them. Let their old men die in a plague, and let their young men be killed in battle. {18:22} "Let screaming be heard from their homes as warriors come suddenly upon them. For they have dug a pit for me to fall into and have hidden traps along my path. {18:23} LORD, you know all about their murderous plots against me. Don't forgive their crimes and blot out their sins. Let them die before you. Deal with them in your anger."

{19:1} This is what the LORD says: "Go and get a clay jar from a potter, and take along some of the elders of the people and of the priests. {19:2} Then go out to the valley of Ben-Hinnom, near the entrance to the Potsherd Gate, and announce the words I tell you. {19:3} Say, 'Listen to this message from the LORD, you kings of Judah and citizens of Jerusalem! This is what the LORD of Heaven's Armies, the God of Israel, says: I will bring disaster upon this place that will make the ears of those who hear about it ring. {19:4} For Israel has forsaken me and turned this valley into a place of wickedness. The people burn incense to foreign gods—idols never before acknowledged by this generation, by their ancestors, or by the kings of Judah. And they have filled this place with the blood of innocent children. {19:5} They have built pagan shrines to Baal, and there they burn their sons as sacrifices to Baal. I have never commanded such a horrible deed; it never even crossed my mind to command such a thing!' {19:6} "So beware, for the time is coming," says the LORD, "when this garbage dump will no longer be called Topheth or the valley of Ben-Hinnom, but the Valley of Slaughter. {19:7} For I will upset the careful plans of Judah and Jerusalem. I will allow invading armies to slaughter them and leave their dead bodies as food for the vultures and wild animals. {19:8} I will reduce Jerusalem to ruins, making it a monument to their stupidity. All who pass by will be astonished and will gasp at the destruction they see there. {19:9} I will see to it that your enemies lay siege to the city until all the food is gone. Then those trapped inside will eat their own sons and daughters and friends. They will be driven to utter despair.' {19:10} "As these men watch you, Jeremiah, smash the jar you brought. {19:11} Then say to them, 'This is what the LORD of Heaven's Armies says: As this jar lies shattered, so I will shatter the people of Judah and Jerusalem beyond all hope of repair. They will bury the bodies here in Topheth, the garbage dump, until there is no more room for them.' {19:12} "This is what I will do to this place and its people," says the LORD. "I will cause this city to become desolate, and it will be a horrifying example to all who pass by. {19:13} I will see to it that your enemies lay siege to the city until all the food is gone. Then those trapped inside will eat their own sons and daughters and friends. They will be driven to utter despair.' {19:14} Then Jeremiah returned from Topheth, the garbage dump where he had delivered this message, and he stopped in front of the LORD's Temple. He said to the people there, {19:15} "This is what the LORD of Heaven's Armies, the God of Israel, says: 'I will bring disaster upon this city and its surrounding towns as I promised, because you have stubbornly refused to listen to me.'"

{20:1} Pashhur son of Immer, the priest and chief official in the Temple of the LORD, heard what Jeremiah was prophesying. {20:2} So he arrested Jeremiah the prophet and had him whipped and put in stocks at the Benjamin Gate of the LORD's Temple. {20:3} The next day, when Pashhur finally released him, Jeremiah said to him, "The LORD has changed your name. From now on you are to be called 'The Man Who Lives in Terror.' {20:4} For this is what the LORD says: I will send terror upon you and all your friends, and you will watch as they are slaughtered by the swords of the enemy. I will hand Judah over to the king of Babylon. He will take them captive to Babylon or kill them with the sword. {20:5} I will hand over all the wealth of this city—all its products, all its valuables, and all the treasures of the kings of Judah. I will hand it all over to their enemies, who will plunder it, capture it, and carry it away to Babylon. {20:6} And you, Pashhur, and all your household will go as captives to Babylon. There you will die and be buried, you and all your friends to whom you prophesied that everything would be all right." {20:7} O LORD, you misled me, and I allowed myself to be misled. You are stronger than I am, and you overpowered me. Now I am mocked every day; everyone laughs at me. {20:8} When I speak, the words burst out. "Violence and destruction!" I shout. So these messages from the LORD have made me a household joke. {20:9} But if I say I'll never mention the LORD or speak in his name, his word burns in my heart like a fire. It's like a fire in my bones! I am worn out trying to hold it in! I can't do it! {20:10} I have heard the many rumors about me. They call me "The Man Who Lives in Terror." They threaten, "If you say anything, we will report it." Even my old friends are watching me, waiting for a fatal slip. "He will trap himself," they say, "and then we will get our revenge on him." {20:11} But the LORD stands beside me like a great warrior. Before him my persecutors will stumble. They cannot defeat me. They will fail and be thoroughly humiliated. Their dishonor will never be forgotten. {20:12} O LORD of Heaven's Armies, you test those who are righteous, and you examine the deepest thoughts and secrets. Let me see your vengeance against them, for I have committed my cause to you. {20:13} Sing to the LORD! Praise the LORD! For though I was poor and needy, he rescued me from my oppressors. {20:14} Cursed be the day when I was born! May the day of my birth never be blessed. {20:15} Cursed be the man who brought the news to my father, saying, "A baby boy has been born to you—bringing him great joy." {20:16} Let that man be like the cities the LORD overthrew without mercy. Let him hear wailing in the morning and a battle cry at noon. {20:17} For my mother's womb should have been my grave. Her womb should have been pregnant forever. {20:18} Why was I ever born? My entire life has been filled with trouble, sorrow, and shame.

{21:1} This is the message that came to Jeremiah from the LORD when King Zedekiah sent Pashhur son of Malkijah and Zephaniah son of Maaseiah, the priest, to speak with him. {21:2} "Inquire of the LORD for us," they said, "for King Nebuchadnezzar of Babylon is attacking us. Perhaps the LORD will be gracious and do a mighty miracle as he has done in the past. Perhaps he will force Nebuchadnezzar to withdraw his armies." {21:3} Jeremiah replied, "Go back to King Zedekiah and tell him, {21:4} 'This is what the LORD, the God of Israel, says: I will make your weapons useless against the king of Babylon and the Babylonians who are outside your walls attacking you. In fact, I will bring your enemies right into the heart of this city. {21:5} I myself will fight against you with a strong hand and a powerful arm, for I am very angry. You have made me furious! {21:6} I will send a terrible plague upon this city, and both people and animals will die. {21:7} And after all that, says the LORD, I will hand over King Zedekiah of Judah, his staff, and everyone else in the city who survives the disease, war, and famine. I will hand them over to King Nebuchadnezzar of Babylon and to their other enemies. He will slaughter them without mercy, pity, or compassion.' {21:8} "Tell the people, 'This is what the LORD says: I am presenting you with two choices. You can either stay in this city and die, or you can go out and surrender to the Babylonians. If you stay, you will die by the sword, famine, and disease. {21:9} But if you go out and surrender, you will live; your life will be spared as though it were a prize of war. {21:10} For I have decided to bring disaster and not good upon this city, says the LORD. It will be handed over to the king of Babylon, and he will burn it to the ground.' {21:11} "Say to the royal family of Judah, 'Listen to this message from the LORD! {21:12} This is what the LORD says to the dynasty of David: {21:13} 'Give justice each morning to the people you judge! Help those who have been robbed; rescue them from their oppressors. Otherwise, my anger will burn like an unquenchable fire because of all your sins. {21:14} I will personally fight against you, declaring war on you in anger and fury because you have refused to change your evil ways. {21:15} But I will punish you as your deeds deserve, says the LORD. I will set fire to your palace, and it will burn up everything around it.'"

{22:1} This is what the LORD says: {22:2} "Go down to the palace of the king of Judah and deliver this message: {22:3} 'Listen to the word of the LORD, O king of Judah, sitting on David's throne—you and your officials and all your people who come through these gates. {22:4} This is what the LORD says: Do what is just and right. Rescue from the hand of the oppressor the one who has been robbed. Do no wrong or violence to the foreigner, the fatherless, or the widow, and do not shed innocent blood in this place. {22:5} If you obey these commands, then kings who follow the line of David will continue to enter through these gates, riding in chariots and on horses, with their officials and their people. {22:6} But if you do not obey, I swear by myself, declares the LORD, that this palace will become a pile of rubble.'" {22:7} This is what the LORD says about the palace of the king of Judah: {22:8} "Though you are like Gilead to me, like the summit of Lebanon, I will surely make you like a wasteland, like towns not inhabited. {22:9} I will send destroyers against you, each man with his weapons, and they will cut down your finest cedar trees and throw them into the fire. {22:10} Many nations will pass by this city and will ask one another, 'Why has the LORD done such a thing to this great city?' {22:11} And the answer will be, 'Because they have forsaken the covenant of the LORD their God and have worshiped and served other gods.'" {22:12} Do not weep for the dead king or mourn his loss. Weep bitterly for the one who is exiled, for he will never return to see his native land again. {22:13} For this is what the LORD says about Jehoiakim, the son of King Josiah of Judah: {22:14} "What sorrow awaits Jehoiakim! For his reign will end; he will be taken away from Jerusalem like a donkey being dragged away, never to return. {22:15} For he will die in a distant land and will never again see his beloved country." {22:16} For this is what the LORD says about Jehoiakim, who succeeded his father, King Josiah, and was taken away as a captive: {22:17} "What sorrow awaits Jehoiakim! {22:18} For he will be buried like a dead donkey—dragged out of Jerusalem and dumped outside the gates! {22:19} "What sorrow awaits Jehoiakim! {22:20} For he will be carried away captive to a foreign land, where he will die a shameful death." {22:21} Yes, this is what the LORD says about Jehoiakim: {22:22} "The members of his family will not mourn for him. They will not say, 'Ah, my brother! Ah, my sister!' His subjects will not mourn for him or for his lost glory. {22:23} For this is what the LORD says: {22:24} "Let him be as a vessel lying broken on the ground, discarded and despised. {22:25} Dragged out of Jerusalem like a dead donkey and dumped outside the gates! {22:26} "To the earth, earth, earth! Hear the word of the LORD! {22:27} For this is what the LORD says: {22:28} "Record this man as childless, a man who will not prosper in his lifetime. {22:29} For none of his descendants will prosper, {22:30} sitting on the throne of David and ruling again in Judah."

{23:1} Woe to the shepherds who destroy and scatter the sheep of my pasture! declares the LORD. {23:2} Therefore, this is what the LORD, the God of Israel, says to the shepherds who tend my people: "You have scattered my flock and driven them away. You have not cared for them, but I will punish you for the evil you have done," declares the LORD. {23:3} "I myself will gather the remnant of my flock from all the countries where I have driven them, and will bring them back to their pasture, where they will be fruitful and increase in number. {23:4} I will place shepherds over them who will tend them, and they will no longer be afraid or terrified, nor will any be missing," declares the LORD. {23:5} "The days are coming," declares the LORD, "when I will raise up for David a righteous Branch, a King who will reign wisely and do what is just and right in the land. {23:6} In his days Judah will be saved and Israel will live in safety. This is the name by which he will be called: The LORD Our Righteous Savior. {23:7} "So then, the days are coming," declares the LORD, "when people will no longer say, 'As surely as the LORD lives, who brought the Israelites up out of Egypt,' {23:8} but they will say, 'As surely as the LORD lives, who brought the descendants of Israel up out of the land of the north and out of all the countries where he had banished them.' Then they will live in their own land." {23:9} Concerning the prophets: My heart is broken within me; all my bones tremble. I am like a drunken man, like a strong man overcome by wine, because of the LORD and his holy words. {23:10} The land is full of adulterers; because of the curse the land lies parched and the pastures in the wilderness are withered. The prophets follow an evil course and use their power unjustly. {23:11} "Both prophet and priest are godless; even in my temple I find their wickedness," declares the LORD. {23:12} "Therefore their path will become slippery; they will be banished to darkness and there they will fall. I will bring disaster on them in the year they are punished," declares the LORD. {23:13} "Among the prophets of Samaria I saw this repulsive thing: They prophesied by Baal and led my people Israel astray. {23:14} And among the prophets of Jerusalem I have seen something horrible: They commit adultery and live a lie. They strengthen the hands of evildoers, so that not one of them turns from their wickedness. They are all like Sodom to me; the people of Jerusalem are like Gomorrah." {23:15} Therefore, this is what the LORD Almighty says concerning the prophets: "I will make them eat bitter food and drink poisoned water, because from the prophets of Jerusalem ungodliness has spread throughout the land." {23:16} This is what the LORD Almighty says: "Do not listen to what the prophets are prophesying to you; they fill you with false hopes. They speak visions from their own minds, not from the mouth of the LORD. {23:17} They keep saying to those who despise me, 'The LORD says: You will have peace.' And to all who follow the stubbornness of their hearts they say, 'No harm will come to you.' {23:18} But which of them has stood in the council of the LORD to see or to hear his word? Who has listened and heard his word? {23:19} See, the storm of the LORD will burst out in wrath, a whirlwind swirling down on the heads of the wicked. {23:20} The anger of the LORD will not turn back until he fully accomplishes the purposes of his heart. In days to come you will understand it clearly. {23:21} I did not send these prophets, yet they have run with their message; I did not speak to them, yet they have prophesied. {23:22} But if they had stood in my council, they would have proclaimed my words to my people and would have turned them from their evil ways and from their evil deeds. {23:23} "Am I only a God nearby," declares the LORD, "and not a God far away? {23:24} Who can hide in secret places so that I cannot see them?" declares the LORD. "Do not I fill heaven and earth?" declares the LORD. {23:25} "I have heard what the prophets say who prophesy lies in my name. They say, 'I had a dream! I had a dream!' {23:26} How long will this continue in the hearts of these lying prophets, who prophesy the delusions of their own minds? {23:27} They think the dreams they tell one another will make my people forget my name, just as their ancestors forgot my name through Baal worship. {23:28} Let the prophet who has a dream recount the dream, but let the one who has my word speak it faithfully. For what has straw to do with grain?" declares the LORD. {23:29} "Is not my word like fire," declares the LORD, "and like a hammer that breaks a rock in pieces? {23:30} "Therefore," declares the LORD, "I am against the prophets who steal from one another words supposedly from me. {23:31} Yes," declares the LORD, "I am against the prophets who wag their own tongues and yet declare, 'The LORD declares.' {23:32} Indeed, I am against those who prophesy false dreams," declares the LORD. "They tell them and lead my people astray with their reckless lies, yet I did not send or appoint them. They do not benefit these people in the least," declares the LORD. {23:33} "When these people, or a prophet or a priest, ask you, 'What is the message from the LORD?' say to them, 'What message? I will forsake you, declares the LORD.' {23:34} If a prophet or a priest or anyone else claims, 'This is a message from the LORD,' I will punish them and their household. {23:35} This is what each of you keeps saying to your friends and other Israelites: 'What is the LORD's answer?' or 'What has the LORD spoken?' {23:36} But you must not mention 'a message from the LORD' again, because each one's word becomes their own message. So you distort the words of the living God, the LORD Almighty, our God. {23:37} "This is what you keep saying to a prophet: 'What is the LORD's answer to you?' or 'What has the LORD spoken?' {23:38} Although you claim, 'This is a message from the LORD,' this is what the LORD says: You used the words, 'This is a message from the LORD,' even though I told you that you must not claim, 'This is a message from the LORD.' {23:39} Therefore, I will surely forget you and cast you out of my presence along with the city I gave to you and your ancestors. {23:40} I will bring on you everlasting disgrace—everlasting shame that will not be forgotten."

{24:1} The LORD showed me two baskets of figs placed before the temple of the LORD. This happened after Nebuchadnezzar, the king of Babylon, had taken Jeconiah, the son of Jehoiakim, the king of Judah, along with the princes of Judah, the craftsmen, and the smiths, from Jerusalem and brought them to Babylon. {24:2} In one basket were very good figs, as ripe as the first fruits, and in the other basket were very bad figs that were so rotten they couldn't be eaten. {24:3} Then the LORD asked me, "What do you see, Jeremiah?" And I said, "Figs. The good figs are very good, and the bad figs are very bad, too rotten to eat." {24:4} The LORD spoke to me again, saying, {24:5} "This is what the LORD, the God of Israel, says: Like these good figs, I will regard those who were carried away captive from Judah, whom I sent to the land of the Chaldeans for their own good. {24:6} For I will watch over them for their good, and I will bring them back to this land. I will build them up and not tear them down; I will plant them and not uproot them. {24:7} And I will give them a heart to know me, that I am the LORD. They will be my people, and I will be their God, for they will return to me with their whole heart. {24:8} But as for the bad figs, which are too rotten to eat, this is what the LORD says: So will I deal with Zedekiah, the king of Judah, and his princes, along with the remaining inhabitants of Jerusalem who stay in this land, and those who dwell in the land of Egypt. {24:9} I will deliver them to be scattered among all the kingdoms of the earth for their harm, to become an object of reproach, a byword, a taunt, and a curse in all the places where I drive them. {24:10} And I will send the sword, famine, and pestilence among them until they are consumed from the land that I gave to them and their fathers."

{25:1} This is the message that came to Jeremiah concerning all the people of Judah in the fourth year of Jehoiakim, the son of Josiah, king of Judah. It was also the first year of Nebuchadnezzar, king of Babylon. {25:2} Jeremiah the prophet spoke to all the people of Judah and to all the inhabitants of Jerusalem, saying, {25:3} "From the thirteenth year of Josiah, the son of Amon, king of Judah, until today, which is the twenty-third year, the word of the LORD has come to me, and I have spoken to you, rising early and speaking. But you have not listened. {25:4} The LORD has sent all his servants, the prophets, to you, rising early and sending them, but you have not listened or inclined your ear to hear. {25:5} They pleaded, 'Turn away, each one, from your evil ways and from the evil deeds you are doing, and dwell in the land that the LORD has given to you and your fathers forever and ever. {25:6} Do not follow other gods to serve them, worship them, or provoke me to anger with the works of your hands, and I will not harm you.' {25:7} But you have not listened to me," says the LORD, "and you have provoked me to anger with the works of your hands, to your own harm. {25:8} Therefore, this is what the LORD of hosts says: Because you have not listened to my words, {25:9} I will send and take all the families of the north, says the LORD, and Nebuchadnezzar, the king of Babylon, my servant, and I will bring them against this land, its inhabitants, and all the surrounding nations. I will utterly destroy them, making them an astonishment, a hissing, and perpetual desolations. {25:10} Moreover, I will take away from them the sounds of joy and gladness, the voices of the bridegroom and the bride, the sounds of the millstones, and the light of the candle. {25:11} And this entire land will become a desolation and an astonishment, and these nations will serve the king of Babylon for seventy years. {25:12} Then, after seventy years are completed, I will punish the king of Babylon and that nation, says the LORD, for their iniquity, and the land of the Chaldeans. I will make it perpetual desolations. {25:13} And I will bring upon that land all my words that I have pronounced against it, all that is written in this book, which Jeremiah has prophesied against all the nations. {25:14} For many nations and great kings will also make them serve, and I will recompense them according to their deeds and the works of their hands. {25:15} For the LORD, the God of Israel, says to me, 'Take this cup of wine from my hand and cause all the nations to whom I send you to drink it.' {25:16} And they will drink and stagger and go mad because of the sword that I will send among them. {25:17} So I took the cup from the LORD's hand and made all the nations drink it, to whom the LORD had sent me: {25:18} Jerusalem, the cities of Judah, its kings and princes, to make them a desolation, an astonishment, a hissing, and a curse, as it is this day; {25:19} Pharaoh, king of Egypt, his servants, princes, and all his people; {25:20} Also, the mixed multitude, all the kings of Uz, all the kings of the Philistines, Ashkelon, Gaza, Ekron, and the remnant of Ashdod; {25:21} Edom, Moab, and the people of Ammon; {25:22} All the kings of Tyre, Sidon, and the kings of the coastlands across the sea; {25:23} Dedan, Tema, Buz, and all who are in the farthest corners; {25:24} All the kings of Arabia and all the kings of the mixed multitude who dwell in the desert; {25:25} All the kings of Zimri, Elam, and the Medes; {25:26} And all the kings of the north, near and far, one with another, and all the kingdoms of the world upon the face of the earth. The king of Sheshach shall drink after them. {25:27} Then you shall say to them, 'Thus says the LORD of hosts, the God of Israel: Drink, be drunk, vomit, and fall, and rise no more, because of the sword which I will send among you.' {25:28} And if they refuse to take the cup from your hand to drink, then you shall say to them, 'Thus says the LORD of hosts: You shall certainly drink! {25:29} For I begin to bring calamity on the city which is called by my name, and should you be utterly unpunished? You shall not be unpunished, for I will call for a sword on all the inhabitants of the earth, says the LORD of hosts.' {25:30} Therefore, prophesy against them all these words, and say to them: 'The LORD will roar from on high, and utter his voice from his holy habitation; he will mightily roar against his fold. He will give a shout, as those who tread the grapes, against all the inhabitants of the earth. {25:31} A noise shall come to the ends of the earth, for the LORD has a controversy with the nations; he will plead with all flesh; he will give those who are wicked to the sword, says the LORD. {25:32} The LORD of hosts declares, "Look, disaster will spread from nation to nation, and a great whirlwind will arise from the farthest reaches of the earth. {25:33} On that day, the LORD's slain will stretch from one end of the earth to the other; they will neither be mourned, gathered, nor buried; they will be like dung on the ground. {25:34} Cry out, you shepherds, and wail! Roll in the ashes, you leaders of the flock! For your days of slaughter and dispersion are at hand; you will fall like fine pottery. {25:35} The shepherds will have no refuge, nor will the leaders of the flock have any means of escape. {25:36} Listen to the cries of the shepherds, and the wails of the leaders of the flock, for the LORD has devastated their pasture. {25:37} The peaceful dwellings lie in ruins because of the fierce anger of the LORD. {25:38} He has left his lair like a lion; their land is desolate because of the wrath of the oppressor, and because of the LORD's fierce anger."

{26:1} At the beginning of Jehoiakim's reign as king of Judah, the son of Josiah, this message from the LORD came: {26:2} "Stand in the courtyard of the LORD's house and speak to all the cities of Judah that come to worship there. Speak all the words I command you; do not leave out anything. {26:3} Perhaps they will listen and turn from their evil ways. Then I will relent and not bring the disaster I have planned because of their wickedness. {26:4} Say to them, 'This is what the LORD says: If you do not listen to me and follow my law, which I have set before you, {26:5} and if you do not listen to the words of my servants the prophets, whom I have sent to you again and again (though you have not listened), {26:6} then I will make this house like Shiloh and this city a curse among all the nations of the earth.'" {26:7} When Jeremiah finished speaking all that the LORD had commanded him to say to all the people, the priests, the prophets, and all the people seized him and said, "You must die! {26:8} Why do you prophesy in the name of the LORD that this house will be like Shiloh and this city will be desolate and deserted?" And all the people crowded around Jeremiah in the house of the LORD. {26:9} When the officials of Judah heard about these things, they went up from the royal palace to the house of the LORD and took their places at the entrance of the New Gate of the LORD's house. {26:10} Then the priests and the prophets said to the officials and all the people, "This man should be sentenced to death because he has prophesied against this city. You have heard it with your own ears!" {26:11} Then Jeremiah said to all the officials and all the people: "The LORD sent me to prophesy against this house and this city all the things you have heard. {26:12} Now reform your ways and your actions and obey the LORD your God. Then the LORD will relent and not bring the disaster he has pronounced against you. {26:13} As for me, I am in your hands; do with me whatever you think is good and right. {26:14} Be assured, however, that if you put me to death, you will bring innocent blood on yourselves and on this city and on those who live in it, for in truth the LORD has sent me to you to speak all these words in your hearing." {26:15} Then the officials and all the people said to the priests and the prophets, "This man should not be sentenced to death! He has spoken to us in the name of the LORD our God." {26:16} Some of the elders of the land stepped forward and said to the entire assembly of people, {26:17} "Micah of Moresheth prophesied in the days of Hezekiah king of Judah. He told all the people of Judah, 'This is what the LORD Almighty says: Zion will be plowed like a field, Jerusalem will become a heap of rubble, the temple hill a mound overgrown with thickets.' {26:18} Did Hezekiah king of Judah or anyone else in Judah put him to death? Did not Hezekiah fear the LORD and seek his favor? And did not the LORD relent, so that he did not bring the disaster he pronounced against them? We are about to bring a terrible disaster on ourselves!" {26:19} Uriah son of Shemaiah from Kiriath Jearim was another man who prophesied in the name of the LORD; he prophesied the same things against this city and this land as Jeremiah did. {26:20} When King Jehoiakim and all his officers and officials heard his words, the king was determined to put him to death. But Uriah heard of it and fled in fear to Egypt. {26:21} King Jehoiakim, however, sent Elnathan son of Akbor to Egypt, along with some other men. {26:22} They brought Uriah out of Egypt and took him to King Jehoiakim, who had him struck down with a sword and his body thrown into the burial place of the common people. {26:23} Furthermore, Ahikam son of Shaphan supported Jeremiah, {26:24} and so he was not handed over to the people to be put to death.

{27:1} In the beginning of the reign of Jehoiakim, the son of Josiah, king of Judah, the word of the LORD came to Jeremiah, saying, {27:2} "Thus says the LORD to me: Make bonds and yokes and put them on your neck, {27:3} and send them to the kings of Edom, Moab, Ammon, Tyre, and Sidon, by the messengers who come to Jerusalem to Zedekiah, king of Judah. {27:4} Command them to say to their masters, 'Thus says the LORD of hosts, the God of Israel: Thus shall you say to your masters: {27:5} I have made the earth, man, and beasts upon it, by my great power and outstretched arm, and I have given it to whomever it seemed fit to me. {27:6} Now I have given all these lands into the hand of Nebuchadnezzar, king of Babylon, my servant, and even the beasts of the field I have given him to serve him. {27:7} And all nations shall serve him, his son, and his grandson, until the time of his own land comes; then many nations and great kings shall make him their servant. {27:8} But the nation and kingdom that will not serve Nebuchadnezzar, king of Babylon, and will not put their neck under the yoke of the king of Babylon, I will punish, declares the LORD, with the sword, famine, and pestilence, until I have consumed them by his hand. {27:9} Therefore, do not listen to your prophets, diviners, dreamers, enchanters, or sorcerers, who say to you, 'You shall not serve the king of Babylon.' {27:10} For they prophesy lies to you, to remove you far from your land, so that I should drive you out, and you should perish. {27:11} But the nation that brings its neck under the yoke of the king of Babylon and serves him, I will let remain in its own land, declares the LORD; they shall till it and dwell in it." {27:12} I also spoke to Zedekiah, king of Judah, according to all these words, saying, 'Bring your necks under the yoke of the king of Babylon and serve him and his people, and live. {27:13} Why will you and your people die by the sword, famine, and pestilence, as the LORD has spoken against the nation that will not serve the king of Babylon? {27:14} Therefore, do not listen to the prophets who say to you, 'You shall not serve the king of Babylon,' for they prophesy lies to you. {27:15} For I have not sent them, declares the LORD, yet they prophesy falsely in my name, that I might drive you out, and you might perish, you and the prophets who prophesy to you." {27:16} Also, I spoke to the priests and all the people, saying, 'Thus says the LORD: Do not listen to the words of your prophets who prophesy to you, saying, 'Behold, the vessels of the LORD's house shall now shortly be brought back from Babylon,' for they prophesy lies to you. {27:17} Do not listen to them; serve the king of Babylon and live. Why should this city be laid waste? {27:18} But if they are prophets, and if the word of the LORD is with them, let them now make intercession to the LORD of hosts, that the vessels which are left in the house of the LORD, and in the house of the king of Judah, and in Jerusalem, not go to Babylon. {27:19} For thus says the LORD of hosts concerning the pillars, the sea, the bases, and the rest of the vessels that remain in this city: {27:20} Which Nebuchadnezzar, king of Babylon, did not take when he carried away Jeconiah, the son of Jehoiakim, king of Judah, from Jerusalem to Babylon, and all the nobles of Judah and Jerusalem. {27:21} Yes, thus says the LORD of hosts, the God of Israel, concerning the vessels that remain in the house of the LORD, and in the house of the king of Judah and of Jerusalem: {27:22} They shall be carried to Babylon, and there they shall remain until the day that I visit them, declares the LORD; then I will bring them up and restore them to this place.

{28:1} In the same year, at the beginning of the reign of Zedekiah, king of Judah, in the fourth year, in the fifth month, Hananiah, the son of Azur the prophet from Gibeon, spoke to me in the house of the LORD, in the presence of the priests and all the people, saying, {28:2} "Thus says the LORD of hosts, the God of Israel: I have broken the yoke of the king of Babylon. {28:3} Within two full years, I will bring back into this place all the vessels of the LORD's house that Nebuchadnezzar, king of Babylon, took away from this place and carried to Babylon. {28:4} And I will bring back to this place Jeconiah, the son of Jehoiakim, king of Judah, with all the captives of Judah who went into Babylon, declares the LORD, for I will break the yoke of the king of Babylon." {28:5} Then the prophet Jeremiah said to the prophet Hananiah in the presence of the priests and all the people who stood in the house of the LORD, {28:6} "Even the prophet Jeremiah said, 'Amen! May the LORD do so; may the LORD fulfill your words that you have prophesied to bring back the vessels of the LORD's house and all that is carried away captive, from Babylon into this place.' {28:7} Nevertheless, hear now this word that I speak in your ears and in the ears of all the people: {28:8} The prophets before me and before you of old prophesied against many countries and great kingdoms of war, evil, and pestilence. {28:9} The prophet who prophesies of peace, when the word of the prophet comes to pass, then shall the prophet be known, that the LORD has truly sent him. {28:10} Then Hananiah the prophet took the yoke off the prophet Jeremiah's neck and broke it. {28:11} And Hananiah spoke in the presence of all the people, saying, "Thus says the LORD: Even so will I break the yoke of Nebuchadnezzar, king of Babylon, from the neck of all nations within the space of two full years." And the prophet Jeremiah went his way. {28:12} Then the word of the LORD came to Jeremiah, after Hananiah the prophet had broken the yoke from off the neck of the prophet Jeremiah, saying, {28:13} "Go and tell Hananiah, saying, 'Thus says the LORD: You have broken the yokes of wood, but you shall make for them yokes of iron. {28:14} For thus says the LORD of hosts, the God of Israel: I have put a yoke of iron upon the neck of all these nations, that they may serve Nebuchadnezzar, king of Babylon, and they shall serve him, and I have given him the beasts of the field also.' {28:15} Then the prophet Jeremiah said to Hananiah the prophet, "Hear now, Hananiah; the LORD has not sent you, but you make this people trust in a lie. {28:16} Therefore, thus says the LORD: Behold, I will cast you from off the face of the earth; this year you shall die, because you have taught rebellion against the LORD." {28:17} So Hananiah the prophet died the same year, in the seventh month.

{29:1} These are the words of the letter that Jeremiah the prophet sent from Jerusalem to the remaining elders who were carried away captive, as well as to the priests, prophets, and all the people whom Nebuchadnezzar had taken captive from Jerusalem to Babylon. {29:2} (This happened after Jeconiah the king, the queen, the eunuchs, the princes of Judah and Jerusalem, the carpenters, and the smiths had been deported from Jerusalem.) {29:3} The letter was carried by Elasah the son of Shaphan and Gemariah the son of Hilkiah, whom Zedekiah, king of Judah, sent to Babylon to Nebuchadnezzar, king of Babylon, with the following message: {29:4} "Thus says the LORD of hosts, the God of Israel, to all who are carried away captive, whom I have caused to be taken away from Jerusalem to Babylon: {29:5} Build houses and live in them; plant gardens and eat their fruit. {29:6} Take wives and have sons and daughters; take wives for your sons and give your daughters to husbands, so they may bear sons and daughters. Increase there and do not decrease. {29:7} Seek the peace of the city where I have sent you into captivity, and pray to the LORD for it; for in its peace, you will have peace. {29:8} For thus says the LORD of hosts, the God of Israel: Do not let your prophets and diviners who are among you deceive you, nor listen to your dreams which you cause to be dreamed. {29:9} For they prophesy falsely to you in my name; I have not sent them, declares the LORD. {29:10} For thus says the LORD: After seventy years are completed at Babylon, I will visit you and fulfill my good word toward you, in bringing you back to this place. {29:11} **For I know the thoughts that I think toward you, says the LORD, thoughts of peace and not of evil, to give you a future and a hope.** {29:12} Then you will call upon me and go and pray to me, and I will listen to you. {29:13} You will seek me and find me, when you search for me with all your heart. {29:14} I will be found by you, says the LORD, and I will turn away your captivity, gather you from all the nations and places where I have driven you, says the LORD, and bring you back to the place from which I caused you to be carried away captive. {29:15} Because you have said, 'The LORD has raised up prophets for us in Babylon,' {29:16} Know that thus says the LORD concerning the king who sits on the throne of David, and concerning all the people who dwell in this city, and concerning your brethren who have not gone out with you into captivity: {29:17} Thus says the LORD of hosts: Behold, I will send on them the sword, famine, and pestilence, and will make them like vile figs that cannot be eaten, they are so evil. {29:18} I will persecute them with the sword, famine, and pestilence, and deliver them to trouble to all the kingdoms of the earth, to be a curse, an astonishment, a hissing, and a reproach among all the nations where I have driven them, {29:19} Because they have not listened to my words, says the LORD, which I sent to them by my servants the prophets, rising up early and sending them; but you would not listen, says the LORD. {29:20} Hear therefore the word of the LORD, all you of the captivity, whom I have sent from Jerusalem to Babylon: {29:21} Thus says the LORD of hosts, the God of Israel, concerning Ahab the son of Kolaiah and Zedekiah the son of Maaseiah, who prophesy a lie to you in my name: Behold, I will deliver them into the hand of Nebuchadnezzar, king of Babylon, and he shall slay them before your eyes. {29:22} And from them, a curse shall be taken up by all the captivity of Judah who are in Babylon, saying, 'The LORD make you like Zedekiah and like Ahab, whom the king of Babylon roasted in the fire,' {29:23} Because they have done disgraceful things in Israel, have committed adultery with their neighbors' wives, and have spoken lying words in my name, which I have not commanded them. Even I know, and I am a witness, says the LORD. {29:24} Also, you shall speak to Shemaiah the Nehelamite, saying, {29:25} Thus speaks the LORD of hosts, the God of Israel, saying, 'Because you have sent letters in your name to all the people who are at Jerusalem, and to Zephaniah the son of Maaseiah the priest, and to all the priests, saying, {29:26} "The LORD has made you priest instead of Jehoiada the priest, so that there should be officers in the house of the LORD over every man who is demented and considers himself a prophet, that you should put him in prison and in the stocks." {29:27} Now therefore, why have you not rebuked Jeremiah of Anathoth, who makes himself a prophet to you? {29:28} For he has sent to us in Babylon, saying, 'This captivity is long; build houses and dwell in them; plant gardens and eat their fruit.'" {29:29} And Zephaniah the priest read this letter in the hearing of Jeremiah the prophet. {29:30} Then the word of the LORD came to Jeremiah, saying, {29:31} "Send to all those in captivity, saying, 'Thus says the LORD concerning Shemaiah the Nehelamite: Because Shemaiah has prophesied to you, and I have not sent him, and he has caused you to trust in a lie; {29:32} therefore thus says the LORD: Behold, I will punish Shemaiah the Nehelamite and his family. He shall not have anyone to dwell among this people, nor shall he see the good that I will do for my people, says the LORD, because he has taught rebellion against the LORD."

{30:1} This is the message that came to Jeremiah from the LORD: {30:2} "This is what the LORD, the God of Israel, says: Write down all the words that I have spoken to you in a book. {30:3} For behold, the days are coming, declares the LORD, when I will bring back the captivity of my people Israel and Judah, says the LORD. I will cause them to return to the land that I gave to their fathers, and they shall possess it. {30:4} These are the words that the LORD spoke concerning Israel and Judah: {30:5} For thus says the LORD: We have heard a voice of trembling, of fear, and not of peace. {30:6} Ask now and see: Can a man give birth? Why do I see every man with his hands on his loins like a woman in labor, and all faces turned pale? {30:7} Alas! For that day is great, so that none is like it; it is the time of Jacob's trouble, but he shall be saved out of it. {30:8} For it shall come to pass in that day, says the LORD of hosts, that I will break the yoke from off your neck, and burst your bonds; strangers shall no longer enslave him. {30:9} But they shall serve the LORD their God, and David their king, whom I will raise up to them. {30:10} Therefore, fear not, O my servant Jacob, says the LORD, nor be dismayed, O Israel; for behold, I will save you from afar, and your offspring from the land of their captivity. Jacob shall return, have rest and be quiet, and no one shall make him afraid. {30:11} For I am with you, says the LORD, to save you; though I make a full end of all nations where I have scattered you, yet I will not make a complete end of you. But I will correct you in justice, and will not let you go altogether unpunished. {30:12} For thus says the LORD: Your affliction is incurable, your wound is severe. {30:13} There is none to plead your cause, that you may be bound up; you have no healing medicines. {30:14} All your lovers have forgotten you; they do not seek you; for I have wounded you with the wound of an enemy, with the chastisement of a cruel one, because of your multitude of iniquities; because your sins have increased. {30:15} Why do you cry out for your affliction? Your sorrow is incurable because of the multitude of your iniquities; because your sins have increased, I have done these things to you. {30:16} Therefore all those who devour you shall be devoured; and all your adversaries, every one of them, shall go into captivity; those who plunder you shall become plunder, and all who prey upon you I will make prey. {30:17} For I will restore health to you and heal your wounds, says the LORD; because they called you an outcast saying, 'This is Zion; no one seeks her.' {30:18} Thus says the LORD: Behold, I will bring back the captivity of Jacob's tents, and have mercy on his dwelling places. The city shall be rebuilt on its own heap, and the palace shall remain according to its own plan. {30:19} Out of them shall proceed thanksgiving and the voice of those who make merry; I will multiply them, and they shall not diminish; I will also glorify them, and they shall not be small. {30:20} Their children also shall be as before, and their congregation shall be established before me; I will punish all who oppress them. {30:21} Their nobles shall be from among them, and their governor shall come from their midst; then I will cause him to draw near, and he shall approach me; for who is this who pledged his heart to approach me? says the LORD. {30:22} And you shall be my people, and I will be your God. {30:23} Behold, the whirlwind of the LORD goes forth with fury, a continuing whirlwind; it will fall violently on the head of the wicked. {30:24} The fierce anger of the LORD will not return until He has done it, and until He has performed the intents of His heart. In the latter days you will consider it."

{31:1} The LORD says, "At that time, I will be the God of all the families of Israel, and they shall be my people. {31:2} "Those who survived the sword found grace in the wilderness; Israel, when I went to give him rest. {31:3} "The LORD appeared to me of old, saying, 'Yes, I have loved you with an everlasting love; therefore with lovingkindness I have drawn you. {31:4} "Again I will build you, and you shall be rebuilt, O virgin of Israel! You shall again be adorned with your tambourines, and shall go forth in the dances of those who rejoice. {31:5} "You shall yet plant vines on the mountains of Samaria; the planters shall plant and eat them as ordinary fruit. {31:6} "For there shall be a day when the watchmen will cry on Mount Ephraim, 'Arise, and let us go up to Zion, to the LORD our God.' {31:7} "For thus says the LORD: 'Sing with gladness for Jacob, and shout among the chief of the nations; proclaim, give praise, and say, "O LORD, save your people, the remnant of Israel!" {31:8} "Behold, I will bring them from the north country, and gather them from the ends of the earth, including the blind and the lame, the woman with child and the one who labors with child, together; a great throng shall return there. {31:9} "They shall come with weeping, and with supplications I will lead them. I will cause them to walk by the rivers of waters in a straight way, where they shall not stumble; for I am a father to Israel, and Ephraim is my firstborn. {31:10} "Hear the word of the LORD, O nations, and declare it in the isles afar off, and say, 'He who scattered Israel will gather him, and keep him as a shepherd does his flock.' {31:11} "For the LORD has redeemed Jacob, and ransomed him from the hand of one stronger than he. {31:12} "Therefore they shall come and sing in the height of Zion, streaming to the goodness of the LORD—for wheat and new wine and oil, for the young of the flock and the herd; their souls shall be like a well-watered garden, and they shall sorrow no more at all. {31:13} "Then shall the virgin rejoice in the dance, and the young men and the old together; for I will turn their mourning to joy, will comfort them, and make them rejoice rather than sorrow. {31:14} "I will satiate the soul of the priests with abundance, and my people shall be satisfied with my goodness, says the LORD. {31:15} "Thus says the LORD: 'A voice was heard in Ramah, lamentation and bitter weeping, Rachel weeping for her children, refusing to be comforted for her children, because they are no more.' {31:16} "Thus says the LORD: 'Refrain your voice from weeping, and your eyes from tears; for your work shall be rewarded, says the LORD, and they shall come back from the land of the enemy. {31:17} "There is hope in your future, says the LORD, that your children shall come back to their own border. {31:18} "I have surely heard Ephraim bemoaning himself: 'You have chastised me, and I was chastised, like an untrained bull; restore me, and I will return, for you are the LORD my God. {31:19} "Surely, after my turning, I repented; and after I was instructed, I struck myself on the thigh; I was ashamed, yes, even humiliated, because I bore the reproach of my youth.' {31:20} "Is Ephraim my dear son? Is he a pleasant child? For though I spoke against him, I earnestly remember him still; therefore my heart yearns for him; I will surely have mercy on him, says the LORD. {31:21} "Set up signposts, make landmarks; set your heart toward the highway, the way in which you went. Turn back, O virgin of Israel, turn back to these your cities. {31:22} "How long will you gad about, O you backsliding daughter? For the LORD has created a new thing in the earth—a woman shall encompass a man. {31:23} "Thus says the LORD of hosts, the God of Israel: 'They shall again use this speech in the land of Judah and in its cities, when I bring back their captivity: "The LORD bless you, O home of justice, and mountain of holiness!" {31:24} "And there shall dwell in Judah itself, and in all its cities together, farmers and those going out with flocks. {31:25} "For I have satiated the weary soul, and I have replenished every sorrowful soul." {31:26} Upon this I awoke and looked around, and my sleep was sweet to me. {31:27} "Behold, the days are coming, says the LORD, that I will sow the house of Israel and the house of Judah with the seed of man and the seed of beast. {31:28} "And it shall come to pass, as I have watched over them to pluck up, to break down, to throw down, to destroy, and to afflict, so I will watch over them to build and to plant, says the LORD. {31:29} "In those days they shall say no more: 'The fathers have eaten sour grapes, and the children's teeth are set on edge.' {31:30} "But every one shall die for his own iniquity; every man who eats the sour grapes, his teeth shall be set on edge. {31:31} "Behold, the days are coming, says the LORD, when I will make a new covenant with the house of Israel and with the house of Judah— {31:32} "Not according to the covenant that I made with their fathers in the day that I took them by the hand to lead them out of the land of Egypt, my covenant which they broke, though I was a husband to them, says the LORD. {31:33} "But this is the covenant that I will make with the house of Israel after those days, says the LORD: I will put my law in their minds, and write it on their hearts; and I will be their God, and they shall be my people. {31:34} "No more shall every man teach his neighbor, and every man his brother, saying, 'Know the LORD,' for they all shall know me, from the least of them to the greatest of them, says the LORD. For I will forgive their iniquity, and their sin I will remember no more." {31:35} Thus says the LORD, who gives the sun for a light by day, the ordinances of the moon and the stars for a light by night, who disturbs the sea, and its waves roar—the LORD of hosts is His name: {31:36} "If those ordinances depart from before me, says the LORD, then the seed of Israel shall also cease from being a nation before me forever." {31:37} Thus says the LORD: "If heaven above can be measured, and the foundations of the earth searched out beneath, I will also cast off all the seed of Israel for all that they have done, says the LORD. {31:38} "Behold, the days are coming, says the LORD, that the city shall be built for the LORD from the Tower of Hananel to the Corner Gate. {31:39} "The surveyor's line shall again extend straight forward over the hill Gareb; then it shall turn toward Goath. {31:40} "And the whole valley of the dead bodies and of the ashes, and all the fields as far as the Brook Kidron, to the corner of the Horse Gate toward the east, shall be holy to the LORD. It shall not be plucked up or thrown down anymore forever."

{32:1} The message came to Jeremiah from the LORD in the tenth year of Zedekiah king of Judah, which was the eighteenth year of Nebuchadnezzar. {32:2} At that time, the army of the king of Babylon was besieging Jerusalem, and Jeremiah the prophet was confined in the courtyard of the prison, which was in the palace of the king of Judah. {32:3} Zedekiah king of Judah had imprisoned him, asking, "Why do you prophesy, saying, 'Thus says the LORD: Behold, I will give this city into the hand of the king of Babylon, and he shall take it? {32:4} "And Zedekiah king of Judah shall not escape from the hand of the Chaldeans, but shall surely be delivered into the hand of the king of Babylon, and shall speak with him face to face, and see him eye to eye. {32:5} "Then he shall lead Zedekiah to Babylon, and there he shall be until I visit him," says the LORD; "though you fight with the Chaldeans, you shall not succeed." {32:6} And Jeremiah said, "The word of the LORD came to me, saying, {32:7} 'Behold, Hanamel the son of Shallum your uncle will come to you, saying, "Buy my field which is in Anathoth, for the right of redemption is yours to buy it."' {32:8} "Then Hanamel my uncle's son came to me in the court of the prison according to the word of the LORD, and said to me, 'Please buy my field that is in Anathoth, which is in the land of Benjamin; for the right of inheritance is yours, and the redemption is yours; buy it for yourself.' Then I knew that this was the word of the LORD. {32:9} "So I bought the field from Hanamel, the son of my uncle, who was in Anathoth, and weighed out to him the money—seventeen shekels of silver. {32:10} "I signed the deed and sealed it, took witnesses, and weighed the money on the scales. {32:11} "Then I took the purchase deed, both that which was sealed according to the law and custom, and that which was open. {32:12} "And I gave the purchase deed to Baruch the son of Neriah, son of Maaseiah, in the presence of Hanamel my uncle's son and in the presence of the witnesses who signed the purchase deed, before all the Jews who sat in the court of the prison. {32:13} "Then I charged Baruch before them, saying, {32:14} 'Thus says the LORD of hosts, the God of Israel: "Take these deeds, both this purchase deed which is sealed and this deed which is open, and put them in an earthen vessel, that they may last many days." {32:15} "For thus says the LORD of hosts, the God of Israel: 'Houses and fields and vineyards shall be possessed again in this land.' {32:16} "Now when I had delivered the purchase deed to Baruch the son of Neriah, I prayed to the LORD, saying: {32:17} 'Ah, Lord GOD! Behold, You have made the heavens and the earth by Your great power and outstretched arm. There is nothing too hard for You. {32:18} 'You show lovingkindness to thousands, and repay the iniquity of the fathers into the bosom of their children after them—the Great, the Mighty God, whose name is the LORD of hosts. {32:19} 'You are great in counsel and mighty in work, for Your eyes are open to all the ways of the sons of men, to give everyone according to his ways and according to the fruit of his doings. {32:20} 'You have set signs and wonders in the land of Egypt, to this day, and in Israel and among other men; and You have made Yourself a name, as it is this day. {32:21} 'You have brought Your people Israel out of the land of Egypt with signs and wonders, with a strong hand and an outstretched arm, and with great terror; {32:22} 'You have given them this land, of which You swore to their fathers to give them—a land flowing with milk and honey. {32:23} 'And they came in and took possession of it, but they have not obeyed Your voice or walked in Your law. They have done nothing of all that You commanded them to do; therefore You have caused all this calamity to come upon them. {32:24} 'Look, the siege mounds! They have come to the city to take it; and the city has been given into the hand of the Chaldeans who fight against it, because of the sword and famine and pestilence. What You have spoken has happened; there You see it! {32:25} 'And You have said to me, O Lord GOD, "Buy the field for money, and take witnesses!"—yet the city has been given into the hand of the Chaldeans.'" {32:26} Then the word of the LORD came to Jeremiah, saying, {32:27} "Behold, I am the LORD, the God of all flesh. Is there anything too hard for Me? {32:28} "Therefore thus says the LORD: 'Behold, I will give this city into the hand of the Chaldeans, into the hand of Nebuchadnezzar king of Babylon, and he shall take it. {32:29} 'And the Chaldeans who fight against this city shall come and set fire to this city and burn it, with the houses on whose roofs they have offered incense to Baal and poured out drink offerings to other gods, to provoke Me to anger; {32:30} 'Because the children of Israel and the children of Judah have done only evil in My sight from their youth. For the children of Israel have provoked Me only to anger with the work of their hands,' says the LORD. {32:31} 'For this city has been to Me a provocation of My anger and My fury from the day that they built it, even to this day; so I will remove it from before My face {32:32} 'Because of all the evil of the children of Israel and the children of Judah, which they have done to provoke Me to anger—they, their kings, their princes, their priests, their prophets, the men of Judah, and the inhabitants of Jerusalem. {32:33} 'And they have turned to Me the back, and not the face; though I taught them, rising up early and teaching them, yet they have not listened to receive instruction. {32:34} 'But they set their abominations in the house which is called by My name, to defile it. {32:35} 'And they built the high places of Baal which are in the Valley of the Son of Hinnom, to cause their sons and their daughters to pass through the fire to Molech, which I did not command them, nor did it come into My mind that they should do this abomination, to cause Judah to sin. {32:36} 'Now therefore, thus says the LORD, the God of Israel, concerning this city of which you say, "It shall be delivered into the hand of the king of Babylon by the sword, by the famine, and by the pestilence": {32:37} 'Behold, I will gather them out of all countries where I have driven them in My anger, in My fury, and in great wrath; I will bring them back to this place, and I will cause them to dwell safely. {32:38} 'They shall be My people, and I will be their God; {32:39} 'Then I will give them one heart and one way, that they may fear Me forever, for the good of them and their children after them. {32:40} 'And I will make an everlasting covenant with them, that I will not turn away from doing them good; but I will put My fear in their hearts so that they will not depart from Me. {32:41} 'Yes, I will rejoice over them to do them good, and I will assuredly plant them in this land, with all My heart and with all My soul.' {32:42} 'For thus says the LORD: "Just as I have brought all this great calamity on this people, so I will bring on them all the good that I have promised them. {32:43} 'And fields will be bought in this land of which you say, "It is desolate, without man or beast; it has been given into the hand of the Chaldeans." {32:44} 'Men will buy fields for money, sign deeds and seal them, and take witnesses, in the land of Benjamin, in the places around Jerusalem, in the cities of Judah, in the cities of the mountains, in the cities of the lowland, and in the cities of the South; for I will cause their captives to return,' says the LORD."

{33:1} Again, the word of the LORD came to Jeremiah while he was still confined in the courtyard of the prison, saying, {33:2} "Thus says the LORD, who made the earth, the LORD who formed it to establish it—the LORD is His name: {33:3} 'Call to Me, and I will answer you, and show you great and mighty things which you do not know.' {33:4} "For thus says the LORD, the God of Israel, concerning the houses of this city and the houses of the kings of Judah, which have been broken down to fortify against the siege mounds and the sword: {33:5} 'They come to fight with the Chaldeans, but [it is only] to fill them with the dead bodies of men whom I have slain in My anger and fury, for all whose wickedness I have hidden My face from this city. {33:6} 'Behold, I will bring it health and healing; I will heal them and reveal to them the abundance of peace and truth. {33:7} 'I will bring back the captives of Judah and the captives of Israel, and will rebuild them as at the first. {33:8} 'I will cleanse them from all their iniquity by which they have sinned against Me, and I will pardon all their iniquities by which they have sinned and by which they have transgressed against Me. {33:9} "Then it shall be to Me a name of joy, a praise, and an honor before all nations of the earth, who shall hear all the good that I do to them; they shall fear and tremble for all the goodness and all the prosperity that I provide for it. {33:10} "Thus says the LORD: 'Again there shall be heard in this place—of which you say, "It is desolate, without man and without beast"—in the cities of Judah, in the streets of Jerusalem that are desolate, without man and without inhabitant and without beast, {33:11} 'The voice of joy and the voice of gladness, the voice of the bridegroom and the voice of the bride, the voice of those who will say: "Praise the LORD of hosts, for the LORD is good, for His mercy endures forever"—and of those who will bring the sacrifice of praise into the house of the LORD. For I will cause the captives of the land to return as at the first,' says the LORD. {33:12} "Thus says the LORD of hosts: 'Again in this place which is desolate, without man and without beast, and in all its cities, there shall be a habitation of shepherds causing their flocks to lie down. {33:13} 'In the cities of the mountains, in the cities of the lowland, in the cities of the South, in the land of Benjamin, in the places around Jerusalem, and in the cities of Judah, the flocks shall again pass under the hands of him who counts them,' says the LORD. {33:14} "Behold, the days are coming," says the LORD, "that I will perform that good thing which I have promised to the house of Israel and to the house of Judah: {33:15} 'In those days and at that time I will cause to grow up to David a Branch of righteousness; He shall execute judgment and righteousness in the earth. {33:16} 'In those days Judah will be saved, and Jerusalem will dwell safely. And this is the name by which she will be called: THE LORD OUR RIGHTEOUSNESS.' {33:17} "For thus says the LORD: 'David shall never lack a man to sit on the throne of the house of Israel; {33:18} 'Nor shall the priests, the Levites, lack a man to offer burnt offerings before Me, to kindle grain offerings, and to sacrifice continually.'" {33:19} And the word of the LORD came to Jeremiah, saying, {33:20} "Thus says the LORD: 'If you can break My covenant with the day and My covenant with the night, so that there will not be day and night in their season, {33:21} 'Then My covenant may also be broken with David My servant, so that he shall not have a son to reign on his throne, and with the Levites, the priests, My ministers. {33:22} 'As the host of heaven cannot be numbered, nor the sand of the sea measured, so will I multiply the descendants of David My servant and the Levites who minister to Me.'" {33:23} Moreover the word of the LORD came to Jeremiah, saying, {33:24} "Have you not considered what these people have spoken, saying, 'The two families which the LORD has chosen, He has also cast them off'? Thus they have despised My people, as if they should no more be a nation before them. {33:25} 'Thus says the LORD: 'If My covenant is not with day and night, and if I have not appointed the ordinances of heaven and earth, {33:26} 'Then I will cast away the descendants of Jacob and David My servant, so that I will not take any of his descendants to be rulers over the descendants of Abraham, Isaac, and Jacob. For I will cause their captives to return, and will have mercy on them.'"

{34:1} This is the message that came to Jeremiah from the LORD when Nebuchadnezzar king of Babylon and his entire army, including all the kingdoms he ruled, and all the other lands, were at war against Jerusalem and all its towns: {34:2} "This is what the LORD, the God of Israel, says: Go and speak to Zedekiah king of Judah. Tell him, 'This is what the LORD says: I am about to hand this city over to the king of Babylon, and he will burn it down. {34:3} You will not escape his grasp; you will be captured and taken to meet the king of Babylon face to face. Then you will be exiled to Babylon. {34:4} But listen to this promise from the LORD, O Zedekiah king of Judah. This is what the LORD says about you: You will not be killed in war. {34:5} Instead, you will die peacefully. People will burn incense in your memory, just as they did for your ancestors, the kings who preceded you. They will mourn for you, crying, "Alas, our master is dead!" This I have decreed, says the LORD.'" {34:6} So Jeremiah the prophet delivered the message to King Zedekiah of Judah in Jerusalem {34:7} when the king of Babylon's army was attacking Jerusalem and all the towns of Judah that were still under Israelite control. This included Lachish and Azekah, for these were the only fortified cities of Judah that remained. {34:8} This message came to Jeremiah from the LORD after King Zedekiah made a covenant with the people, proclaiming freedom for all their slaves. {34:9} This is the covenant he made: He promised to free all the slaves, both Hebrew slaves and non-Hebrew slaves, so that no one would be a slave any longer. He did this in the presence of all the officials of Jerusalem. {34:10} But the officials and all the people had changed their minds and had taken back the men and women they had freed, forcing them to be slaves again. {34:11} So the LORD gave them this message through Jeremiah: {34:12} "This is what the LORD, the God of Israel, says: I made a covenant with your ancestors long ago when I rescued them from their slavery in Egypt. {34:13} I told them that every Hebrew slave must be freed after serving six years. But your ancestors paid no attention to me. They refused to obey. {34:14} Recently you repented and did what was right, following my command, and you freed your slaves. You made a solemn covenant with me in the Temple that bears my name. {34:15} But now you have shrugged off your oath and defiled my name by taking back the men and women you had freed, making them slaves once again. {34:16} Therefore, this is what the LORD says: Since you have not obeyed me by setting your countrymen free, I will set you free to be destroyed by war, disease, and famine. You will be an object of horror to all the nations of the earth. {34:17} Because you have broken the terms of our covenant, I will cut you apart just as you cut apart the calf when you walked between its halves to solemnize your vows. {34:18} Yes, I will cut you apart, whether you are officials of Judah or Jerusalem, court officials, priests, or common people—for you have broken your oath. {34:19} I will give you to your enemies, and they will kill you. Your bodies will be food for the vultures and wild animals. {34:20} I will hand over King Zedekiah of Judah and his officials to the army of those who want to kill them. They will hand them over to the king of Babylon's army, but it will retreat. {34:21} I will command my people to return to this city, and they will fight against it and capture it. {34:22} They will set it on fire, and I will turn the towns of Judah into a desolate wasteland, where no one lives."

{35:1} This is a message that came to Jeremiah from the LORD during the time of Jehoiakim, the son of Josiah, who was king of Judah. It said, {35:2} "Go to the house of the Rechabites and speak to them. Bring them into one of the chambers of the house of the LORD and offer them wine to drink." {35:3} So Jeremiah went and gathered Jaazaniah, the son of Jeremiah, along with his brothers and all the sons of the Rechabite family. {35:4} He brought them to the house of the LORD, into the chamber of the sons of Hanan, near the chamber of the princes, above the chamber of Maaseiah, the doorkeeper. {35:5} Jeremiah set pots full of wine and cups before the Rechabites and said, "Drink some wine." {35:6} But they replied, "We will not drink wine, because our ancestor Jonadab, the son of Rechab, commanded us never to drink wine, neither us nor our descendants. {35:7} He also instructed us never to build houses, sow seeds, plant vineyards, or own any of these things. Instead, we are to live in tents all our lives, so that we may live long in the land where we reside as strangers." {35:8} "We have obeyed everything Jonadab commanded us. We, our wives, our sons, and our daughters have never drunk wine {35:9} or built houses to live in. We have no vineyards, fields, or seeds. {35:10} We have lived in tents and have obeyed everything our ancestor Jonadab commanded us." {35:11} However, when Nebuchadnezzar, the king of Babylon, invaded the land, we feared the armies of the Chaldeans and Syrians, so we came to Jerusalem and settled here." {35:12} Then the LORD spoke to Jeremiah, saying, {35:13} "Go and speak to the people of Judah and the inhabitants of Jerusalem. Ask them, 'Won't you learn a lesson and listen to my words?' says the LORD. {35:14} "The Rechabites have obeyed their ancestor Jonadab's command not to drink wine. They still follow his commands to this day, but I have spoken to you over and over again, and you have not listened to me. {35:15} "I have sent all my servants, the prophets, to you, rising early and sending them, saying, 'Turn from your evil ways, amend your actions, do not worship other gods, and you will remain in the land I have given you and your ancestors.' But you have not listened or paid attention to me. {35:16} "Because the descendants of Jonadab have obeyed their father's command, but my people have not listened to me. {35:17} "Therefore, this is what the LORD God of hosts, the God of Israel, says: I will bring upon Judah and all the inhabitants of Jerusalem all the disaster I have pronounced against them, because I have spoken to them, but they have not listened, and I have called to them, but they have not answered." {35:18} Then Jeremiah said to the Rechabites, "This is what the LORD of hosts, the God of Israel, says: Because you have obeyed the command of your ancestor Jonadab and have kept all his instructions and done everything he commanded, {35:19} "Therefore, this is what the LORD of hosts, the God of Israel, says: Jonadab, the son of Rechab, will never lack a man to stand before me forever."

{36:1} This happened during the fourth year of Jehoiakim, the son of Josiah, king of Judah. Jeremiah received a message from the LORD, saying, {36:2} "Take a scroll and write down everything I have told you about Israel, Judah, and all the other nations, from the time I first spoke to you, during the days of Josiah, up to now. {36:3} Perhaps when the people of Judah hear about all the punishment I plan to bring upon them, they will turn away from their sinful ways, and I will forgive them for their sins and wrongdoing." {36:4} So Jeremiah called Baruch, the son of Neriah, and Baruch wrote down everything Jeremiah dictated to him from the mouth of the LORD, on a scroll. {36:5} Jeremiah then instructed Baruch, "I am confined and cannot go to the house of the LORD. {36:6} So you go and read aloud from the scroll, which you have written from my words, to the people at the LORD's house on the day of fasting. Also, read it to all the people of Judah who come from their cities. {36:7} Perhaps they will pray to the LORD and each one will turn from their wicked ways, for the LORD's anger and fury are great against this people." {36:8} Baruch did exactly as Jeremiah the prophet commanded, reading from the scroll the words of the LORD in the LORD's house. {36:9} In the fifth year of Jehoiakim, son of Josiah, king of Judah, in the ninth month, a fast was proclaimed before the LORD for all the people in Jerusalem and for all the people who came from the cities of Judah to Jerusalem. {36:10} Baruch read from the scroll the words of Jeremiah in the house of the LORD, in the chamber of Gemariah, son of Shaphan the scribe, in the upper court, at the entry of the New Gate of the LORD's house, to all the people. {36:11} When Michaiah, son of Gemariah, son of Shaphan, heard all the words of the LORD from the scroll, {36:12} he went down to the king's house, to the scribe's chamber, where all the officials were sitting: Elishama the scribe, Delaiah son of Shemaiah, Elnathan son of Achbor, Gemariah son of Shaphan, and Zedekiah son of Hananiah, and all the officials. {36:13} Michaiah told them everything he had heard when Baruch read from the scroll in the hearing of the people. {36:14} So all the officials sent Jehudi, son of Nethaniah, son of Shelemiah, son of Cushi, to Baruch, saying, "Take in your hand the scroll you read aloud to the people and come here." So Baruch, son of Neriah, took the scroll in his hand and went to them. {36:15} They said to him, "Sit down and read it to us." So Baruch read it to them. {36:16} When they heard all the words, they looked at each other in fear and said to Baruch, "We must tell the king everything we have heard." {36:17} They asked Baruch, "How did you write down all these words?" Baruch replied, "Jeremiah dictated all these words to me, and I wrote them with ink on the scroll." {36:18} Then the officials said to Baruch, "You and Jeremiah must go into hiding, {36:19} and no one must know where you are." {36:20} Afterward, they went to the king in the courtyard, but they left the scroll in the room of Elishama the scribe. Then they reported all the words to the king. {36:21} So the king sent Jehudi to get the scroll, and Jehudi took it from the room of Elishama the scribe. And Jehudi read it in the hearing of the king and all the officials standing beside him. {36:22} The king was sitting in his winter quarters, with a fire burning in the firepot in front of him. {36:23} After Jehudi had read three or four columns, the king cut them off with a scribe's knife and threw them into the firepot, until the entire scroll was consumed in the fire. {36:24} Yet neither the king nor any of his attendants who heard all these words showed any fear or tore their clothes. {36:25} Even though Elnathan, Delaiah, and Gemariah urged the king not to burn the scroll, he would not listen to them. {36:26} Instead, the king commanded Jerahmeel, Seraiah, and Shelemiah to arrest Baruch the scribe and Jeremiah the prophet. But the LORD had hidden them. {36:27} After the king had burned the scroll containing the words Baruch had written at Jeremiah's dictation, the word of the LORD came to Jeremiah: {36:28} "Get another scroll and write on it all the words that were on the first scroll, which Jehoiakim king of Judah burned. {36:29} And tell Jehoiakim king of Judah, 'This is what the LORD says: You burned the scroll and said, "Why did you write on it that the king of Babylon would certainly come and destroy this land and wipe out both man and beast from it?" {36:30} Therefore, this is what the LORD says about Jehoiakim king of Judah: He will have no one to sit on the throne of David; his body will be thrown out and exposed to the heat by day and the frost by night. {36:31} I will punish him and his children and his attendants for their wickedness. I will bring on them and those living in Jerusalem and the people of Judah every disaster I pronounced against them, because they have not listened.'" {36:32} So Jeremiah took another scroll and gave it to Baruch son of Neriah, the scribe, and as Jeremiah dictated, Baruch wrote on it all the words of the scroll that Jehoiakim king of Judah had burned in the fire. And many similar words were added to them.

{37:1} Zedekiah, the son of Josiah, became king in place of Coniah, the son of Jehoiakim, whom Nebuchadnezzar, king of Babylon, had made king in the land of Judah. {37:2} However, neither Zedekiah, nor his officials, nor the people of the land, listened to the words of the LORD spoken by the prophet Jeremiah. {37:3} Zedekiah sent Jehucal, the son of Shelemiah, and Zephaniah, the son of Maaseiah the priest, to Jeremiah, saying, "Pray to the LORD our God for us." {37:4} Jeremiah was freely moving among the people because he hadn't been put in prison. {37:5} At that time, Pharaoh's army came out of Egypt. When the Babylonian army besieging Jerusalem heard this news, they withdrew from Jerusalem. {37:6} Then the word of the LORD came to Jeremiah, saying, {37:7} "Tell this to the king of Judah who sent you to inquire of me: 'Pharaoh's army, which came to help you, will return to Egypt, to their own land. {37:8} The Babylonians will come back, fight against this city, capture it, and burn it down.' {37:9} Don't deceive yourselves, thinking that the Babylonians will surely leave, for they will not. {37:10} Even if you defeat the entire Babylonian army, leaving only wounded men, they will still rise up and burn this city down." {37:11} When the Babylonian army withdrew from Jerusalem because of Pharaoh's army, {37:12} Jeremiah left Jerusalem to go to the territory of Benjamin, intending to take care of personal business among the people. {37:13} While he was at the Benjamin Gate, a captain of the guard named Irijah, the son of Shelemiah, accused Jeremiah, saying, "You are deserting to the Babylonians!" {37:14} But Jeremiah denied it, saying, "That's not true; I'm not deserting to the Babylonians." However, Irijah wouldn't listen. Instead, he arrested Jeremiah and brought him to the officials. {37:15} The officials became angry with Jeremiah and beat him. Then they put him in prison in the house of Jonathan the scribe, which they had converted into a prison. {37:16} Jeremiah was put into a dungeon with cells and remained there for a long time. {37:17} Later, King Zedekiah sent for Jeremiah and secretly asked him in his palace, "Is there any word from the LORD?" Jeremiah replied, "There is. You will be handed over to the king of Babylon." {37:18} Jeremiah then asked Zedekiah, "What crime have I committed against you, your officials, or the people that I should be put in prison?" {37:19} "Where are your prophets now," Jeremiah continued, "who told you that the king of Babylon would not come against you or this land?" {37:20} "Please listen to me, my lord the king," Jeremiah pleaded. "Do not send me back to the house of Jonathan the scribe, or I will die there." {37:21} So Zedekiah ordered that Jeremiah be placed in the courtyard of the guard and given a loaf of bread from the baker's street every day until all the bread in the city was gone. And so Jeremiah remained in the courtyard of the guard.

{38:1} Shephatiah, the son of Mattan, Gedaliah, the son of Pashur, Jucal, the son of Shelemiah, and Pashur, the son of Malchiah, heard the words Jeremiah spoke to all the people, saying, {38:2} "This is what the LORD says: Those who remain in this city will die by the sword, famine, and pestilence. But those who surrender to the Chaldeans will live; they will have their lives as a reward and will live." {38:3} "This city will certainly be handed over to the Babylonian army, which will capture it." {38:4} So the princes said to the king, "We urge you, let this man be put to death, for he is discouraging the soldiers and the people by saying such things. He is not seeking the well-being of the people, but their harm." {38:5} Then King Zedekiah said, "He is in your hands, for the king can do nothing to oppose you." {38:6} So they took Jeremiah and threw him into the cistern of Malchiah, the king's son, which was in the courtyard of the guard. They lowered Jeremiah down with ropes. The cistern had no water, only mud, and Jeremiah sank into the mud. {38:7} Now Ebed-melech the Ethiopian, one of the eunuchs in the king's palace, heard that Jeremiah had been put in the cistern. While the king was sitting in the Benjamin Gate, {38:8} Ebed-melech went out of the palace and said to the king, {38:9} "My lord the king, these men have acted wickedly in all they have done to Jeremiah the prophet. They have thrown him into the cistern, where he will starve to death because there is no more bread in the city." {38:10} Then the king commanded Ebed-melech the Ethiopian, "Take thirty men from here with you and lift Jeremiah the prophet out of the cistern before he dies." {38:11} So Ebed-melech took the men with him and went to a room under the treasury in the palace. He took some old rags and worn-out clothes from there and lowered them with ropes into the cistern to Jeremiah. {38:12} Ebed-melech the Ethiopian said to Jeremiah, "Put these old rags and worn-out clothes under your arms to pad the ropes." Jeremiah did so, {38:13} and they pulled him up with the ropes and lifted him out of the cistern. And Jeremiah remained in the courtyard of the guard. {38:14} Then King Zedekiah sent for Jeremiah the prophet and brought him to the third entrance of the LORD's temple. The king said to Jeremiah, "I am going to ask you something; don't hide anything from me." {38:15} Jeremiah replied to Zedekiah, "If I tell you, will you not surely put me to death? Even if I give you advice, you won't listen to me." {38:16} But King Zedekiah secretly swore to Jeremiah, "As surely as the LORD lives, who has given us breath, I will not put you to death or hand you over to those who want to kill you." {38:17} Then Jeremiah said to Zedekiah, "This is what the LORD, the God of Hosts, the God of Israel, says: 'If you surrender to the officials of the king of Babylon, your life will be spared, and this city will not be burned down. You and your family will live. {38:18} But if you don't surrender to the officials of the king of Babylon, this city will be handed over to the Chaldeans, and they will burn it down. And you will not escape from their hands.'" {38:19} King Zedekiah said to Jeremiah, "I am afraid of the Judeans who have deserted to the Chaldeans. They may hand me over to them, and they will mistreat me." {38:20} But Jeremiah reassured him, "They will not hand you over. Obey the LORD's voice that I am speaking to you, and it will go well with you, and you will live. {38:21} But if you refuse to surrender, this is what the LORD has shown me: {38:22} All the women left in the palace of the king of Judah will be brought out to the officials of the king of Babylon. Those women will say: 'Your trusted friends have misled you and have overcome you. Your feet are stuck in the mud, and they have deserted you.' {38:24} "Zedekiah said to Jeremiah, 'Do not let anyone know about this conversation, or you may die. {38:25} If the officials hear that I have spoken with you and come to you and say, 'Tell us what you said to the king and what the king said to you; don't hide anything from us, or we will kill you,' {38:26} then tell them, 'I was pleading with the king not to send me back to the house of Jonathan to die there.'" {38:27} "When all the officials came to Jeremiah and questioned him, he told them everything the king had ordered him to say. So they said no more to him, for no one had heard his conversation with the king. {38:28} Jeremiah remained in the courtyard of the guard until the day Jerusalem was captured."

{39:1} In the ninth year of Zedekiah king of Judah, in the tenth month, Nebuchadrezzar king of Babylon and all his army came against Jerusalem and besieged it. {39:2} In the eleventh year of Zedekiah, in the fourth month, on the ninth day of the month, the city was broken into. {39:3} All the princes of the king of Babylon entered and sat in the middle gate, including Nergal-sharezer, Samgar-nebo, Sarsechim, Rab-saris, Nergal-sharezer, Rabmag, and all the other princes of the king of Babylon. {39:4} When Zedekiah king of Judah and all the soldiers saw them, they fled and left the city by night through the king's garden, by the gate between the two walls. Zedekiah went toward the plain. {39:5} But the Chaldean army pursued them and caught Zedekiah in the plains of Jericho. They captured him and brought him to Nebuchadnezzar king of Babylon at Riblah in the land of Hamath, where he pronounced judgment on him. {39:6} There, in Riblah, the king of Babylon slaughtered Zedekiah's sons before his eyes. He also executed all the nobles of Judah. {39:7} Furthermore, he blinded Zedekiah, put him in chains, and took him to Babylon. {39:8} The Chaldeans burned down the king's palace and the houses of the people, and they broke down the walls of Jerusalem. {39:9} Nebuzar-adan, the captain of the guard, carried away captive to Babylon the rest of the people who remained in the city, as well as those who had defected to him, along with the rest of the population. {39:10} But Nebuzar-adan left behind some of the poorest people in Judah, giving them vineyards and fields at the same time. {39:11} Nebuchadrezzar king of Babylon gave orders concerning Jeremiah to Nebuzar-adan the captain of the guard, saying, {39:12} "Take him, look after him, and do him no harm; but do to him as he asks." {39:13} So Nebuzar-adan, Rab-saris, Nergal-sharezer, Rabmag, and all the other nobles of the king of Babylon sent for Jeremiah. {39:14} They took him out of the prison courtyard and entrusted him to Gedaliah the son of Ahikam, the son of Shaphan, to take him home. So he remained among the people. {39:15} Meanwhile, the word of the LORD came to Jeremiah while he was still confined in the prison courtyard, saying, {39:16} "Go and speak to Ebed-melech the Ethiopian, saying, 'Thus says the LORD of hosts, the God of Israel: Behold, I will bring my words upon this city for evil, not for good; and they will happen before your eyes on that day. {39:17} But I will deliver you on that day, declares the LORD, and you shall not be given into the hand of the men of whom you are afraid. {39:18} For I will surely save you, and you shall not fall by the sword, but your life shall be your prize because you have put your trust in me,' declares the LORD."

{40:1} The word that came to Jeremiah from the LORD, after that Nebuzar-adan the captain of the guard had let him go from Ramah, when he had taken him being bound in chains among all that were carried away captive of Jerusalem and Judah, which were carried away captive unto Babylon. {40:2} And the captain of the guard took Jeremiah, and said unto him, The LORD thy God hath pronounced this evil upon this place. {40:3} Now the LORD hath brought [it,] and done according as he hath said: because ye have sinned against the LORD, and have not obeyed his voice, therefore this thing is come upon you. {40:4} And now, behold, I loose thee this day from the chains which [were] upon thine hand. If it seem good unto thee to come with me into Babylon, come; and I will look well unto thee: but if it seem ill unto thee to come with me into Babylon, forbear: behold, all the land [is] before thee: whither it seemeth good and convenient for thee to go, thither go. {40:5} Now while he was not yet gone back, [he said,] Go back also to Gedaliah the son of Ahikam the son of Shaphan, whom the king of Babylon hath made governor over the cities of Judah, and dwell with him among the people: or go wheresoever it seemeth convenient unto thee to go. So the captain of the guard gave him victuals and a reward, and let him go. {40:6} Then went Jeremiah unto Gedaliah the son of Ahikam to Mizpah; and dwelt with him among the people that were left in the land. {40:7} Now when all the captains of the forces which [were] in the fields, [even] they and their men, heard that the king of Babylon had made Gedaliah the son of Ahikam governor in the land, and had committed unto him men, and women, and children, and of the poor of the land, of them that were not carried away captive to Babylon; {40:8} Then they came to Gedaliah to Mizpah, even Ishmael the son of Nethaniah, and Johanan and Jonathan the sons of Kareah, and Seraiah the son of Tanhumeth, and the sons of Ephai the Netophathite, and Jezaniah the son of a Maachathite, they and their men. {40:9} And Gedaliah the son of Ahikam the son of Shaphan sware unto them and to their men, saying, Fear not to serve the Chaldeans: dwell in the land, and serve the king of Babylon, and it shall be well with you. {40:10} As for me, behold, I will dwell at Mizpah to serve the Chaldeans, which will come unto us: but ye, gather ye wine, and summer fruits, and oil, and put [them] in your vessels, and dwell in your cities that ye have taken. {40:11} Likewise when all the Jews that [were] in Moab, and among the Ammonites, and in Edom, and that [were] in all the countries, heard that the king of Babylon had left a remnant of Judah, and that he had set over them Gedaliah the son of Ahikam the son of Shaphan; {40:12} Even all the Jews returned out of all places whither they were driven, and came to the land of Judah, to Gedaliah, unto Mizpah, and gathered wine and summer fruits very much. {40:13} Moreover Johanan the son of Kareah, and all the captains of the forces that [were] in the fields, came to Gedaliah to Mizpah, {40:14} And said unto him, Dost thou certainly know that Baalis the king of the Ammonites hath sent Ishmael the son of Nethaniah to slay thee? But Gedaliah the son of Ahikam believed them not. {40:15} Then Johanan the son of Kareah spake to Gedaliah in Mizpah secretly, saying, Let me go, I pray thee, and I will slay Ishmael the son of Nethaniah, and no man shall know [it:] wherefore should he slay thee, that all the Jews which are gathered unto thee should be scattered, and the remnant in Judah perish? {40:16} But Gedaliah the son of Ahikam said unto Johanan the son of Kareah, Thou shalt not do this thing: for thou speakest falsely of Ishmael.

{41:1} Now it came to pass in the seventh month, [that] Ishmael the son of Nethaniah the son of Elishama, of the seed royal, and the princes of the king, even ten men with him, came unto Gedaliah the son of Ahikam to Mizpah; and there they did eat bread together in Mizpah. {41:2} Then arose Ishmael the son of Nethaniah, and the ten men that were with him, and smote Gedaliah the son of Ahikam the son of Shaphan with the sword, and slew him, whom the king of Babylon had made governor over the land. {41:3} Ishmael also slew all the Jews that were with him, [even] with Gedaliah, at Mizpah, and the Chaldeans that were found there, [and] the men of war. {41:4} And it came to pass the second day after he had slain Gedaliah, and no man knew [it,] {41:5} That there came certain from Shechem, from Shiloh, and from Samaria, [even] fourscore men, having their beards shaven, and their clothes rent, and having cut themselves, with offerings and incense in their hand, to bring [them] to the house of the LORD. {41:6} And Ishmael the son of Nethaniah went forth from Mizpah to meet them, weeping all along as he went: and it came to pass, as he met them, he said unto them, Come to Gedaliah the son of Ahikam. {41:7} And it was [so,] when they came into the midst of the city, that Ishmael the son of Nethaniah slew them, [and cast them] into the midst of the pit, he, and the men that [were] with him. {41:8} But ten men were found among them that said unto Ishmael, Slay us not: for we have treasures in the field, of wheat, and of barley, and of oil, and of honey. So he forbare, and slew them not among their brethren. {41:9} Now the pit wherein Ishmael had cast all the dead bodies of the men, whom he had slain because of Gedaliah, [was] it which Asa the king had made for fear of Baasha king of Israel: [and] Ishmael the son of Nethaniah filled it with [them that were] slain. {41:10} Then Ishmael carried away captive all the residue of the people that [were] in Mizpah, [even] the king's daughters, and all the people that remained in Mizpah, whom Nebuzaradan the captain of the guard had committed to Gedaliah the son of Ahikam: and Ishmael the son of Nethaniah carried them away captive, and departed to go over to the Ammonites. {41:11} But when Johanan the son of Kareah, and all the captains of the forces that [were] with him, heard of all the evil that Ishmael the son of Nethaniah had done, {41:12} Then they took all the men, and went to fight with Ishmael the son of Nethaniah, and found him by the great waters that [are] in Gibeon. {41:13} Now it came to pass, [that] when all the people which [were] with Ishmael saw Johanan the son of Kareah, and all the captains of the forces that [were] with him, then they were glad. {41:14} So all the people that Ishmael had carried away captive from Mizpah cast about and returned, and went unto Johanan the son of Kareah. {41:15} But Ishmael the son of Nethaniah escaped from Johanan with eight men, and went to the Ammonites. {41:16} Then took Johanan the son of Kareah, and all the captains of the forces that [were] with him, all the remnant of the people whom he had recovered from Ishmael the son of Nethaniah, from Mizpah, after [that] he had slain Gedaliah the son of Ahikam, [even] mighty men of war, and the women, and the children, and the eunuchs, whom he had brought again from Gibeon: {41:17} And they departed, and dwelt in the habitation of Chimham, which is by Bethlehem, to go to enter into Egypt, {41:18} Because of the Chaldeans: for they were afraid of them, because Ishmael the son of Nethaniah had slain Gedaliah the son of Ahikam, whom the king of Babylon made governor in the land.

{42:1} Then all the captains of the forces, and Johanan the son of Kareah, and Jezaniah the son of Hoshaiah, and all the people from the least even unto the greatest, came near, {42:2} And said unto Jeremiah the prophet, Let, we beseech thee, our supplication be accepted before thee, and pray for us unto the LORD thy God, [even] for all this remnant; (for we are left [but] a few of many, as thine eyes do behold us:) {42:3} That the LORD thy God may show us the way wherein we may walk, and the thing that we may do. {42:4} Then Jeremiah the prophet said unto them, I have heard [you;] behold, I will pray unto the LORD your God according to your words; and it shall come to pass, [that] whatsoever thing the LORD shall answer you, I will declare [it] unto you; I will keep nothing back from you. {42:5} Then they said to Jeremiah, The LORD be a true and faithful witness between us, if we do not even according to all things for the which the LORD thy God shall send thee to us. {42:6} Whether [it be] good, or whether [it be] evil, we will obey the voice of the LORD our God, to whom we send thee; that it may be well with us, when we obey the voice of the LORD our God. {42:7} And it came to pass after ten days, that the word of the LORD came unto Jeremiah. {42:8} Then called he Johanan the son of Kareah, and all the captains of the forces which [were] with him, and all the people from the least even to the greatest, {42:9} And said unto them, Thus saith the LORD, the God of Israel, unto whom ye sent me to present your supplication before him; {42:10} If ye will still abide in this land, then will I build you, and not pull [you] down, and I will plant you, and not pluck [you] up: for I repent me of the evil that I have done unto you. {42:11} Be not afraid of the king of Babylon, of whom ye are afraid; be not afraid of him, saith the LORD: for I [am] with you, to save you, and to deliver you from his hand. {42:12} And I will show mercies unto you, that he may have mercy upon you, and cause you to return to your own land. {42:13} But if ye say, We will not dwell in this land, neither obey the voice of the LORD your God, {42:14} Saying, No; but we will go into the land of Egypt, where we shall see no war, nor hear the sound of the trumpet, nor have hunger of bread; and there will we dwell: {42:15} And now therefore hear the word of the LORD, ye remnant of Judah; Thus saith the LORD of hosts, the God of Israel; If ye wholly set your faces to enter into Egypt, and go to sojourn there; {42:16} Then it shall come to pass, [that] the sword, which ye feared, shall overtake you there in the land of Egypt, and the famine, whereof ye were afraid, shall follow close after you there in Egypt; and there ye shall die. {42:17} So shall it be with all the men that set their faces to go into Egypt to sojourn there; they shall die by the sword, by the famine, and by the pestilence: and none of them shall remain or escape from the evil that I will bring upon them. {42:18} For thus saith the LORD of hosts, the God of Israel; As mine anger and my fury hath been poured forth upon the inhabitants of Jerusalem; so shall my fury be poured forth upon you, when ye shall enter into Egypt: and ye shall be an execration, and an astonishment, and a curse, and a reproach; and ye shall see this place no more. {42:19} The LORD hath said concerning you, O ye remnant of Judah; Go ye not into Egypt: know certainly that I have admonished you this day. {42:20} For ye dissembled in your hearts, when ye sent me unto the LORD your God, saying, Pray for us unto the LORD our God; and according unto all that the LORD our God shall say, so declare unto us, and we will do [it.] {42:21} And [now] I have this day declared [it] to you; but ye have not obeyed the voice of the LORD your God, nor any [thing] for the which he hath sent me unto you. {42:22} Now therefore know certainly that ye shall die by the sword, by the famine, and by the pestilence, in the place whither ye desire to go [and] to sojourn.

{43:1} And it came to pass, [that] when Jeremiah had made an end of speaking unto all the people all the words of the LORD their God, for which the LORD their God had sent him to them, [even] all these words, {43:2} Then spake Azariah the son of Hoshaiah, and Johanan the son of Kareah, and all the proud men, saying unto Jeremiah, Thou speakest falsely: the LORD our God hath not sent thee to say, Go not into Egypt to sojourn there: {43:3} But Baruch the son of Neriah setteth thee on against us, for to deliver us into the hand of the Chaldeans, that they might put us to death, and carry us away captives into Babylon. {43:4} So Johanan the son of Kareah, and all the captains of the forces, and all the people, obeyed not the voice of the LORD, to dwell in the land of Judah. {43:5} But Johanan the son of Kareah, and all the captains of the forces, took all the remnant of Judah, that were returned from all nations, whither they had been driven, to dwell in the land of Judah; {43:6} [Even] men, and women, and children, and the king's daughters, and every person that Nebuzar-adan the captain of the guard had left with Gedaliah the son of Ahikam the son of Shaphan, and Jeremiah the prophet, and Baruch the son of Neriah. {43:7} So they came into the land of Egypt: for they obeyed not the voice of the LORD: thus came they [even] to Tahpanhes. {43:8} Then came the word of the LORD unto Jeremiah in Tahpanhes, saying, {43:9} Take great stones in thine hand, and hide them in the clay in the brickkiln, which [is] at the entry of Pharaoh's house in Tahpanhes, in the sight of the men of Judah; {43:10} And say unto them, Thus saith the LORD of hosts, the God of Israel; Behold, I will send and take Nebuchadrezzar the king of Babylon, my servant, and will set his throne upon these stones that I have hid; and he shall spread his royal pavilion over them. {43:11} And when he cometh, he shall smite the land of Egypt, [and deliver] such [as are] for death to death; and such [as are] for captivity to captivity; and such [as are] for the sword to the sword. {43:12} And I will kindle a fire in the houses of the gods of Egypt; and he shall burn them, and carry them away captives: and he shall array himself with the land of Egypt, as a shepherd putteth on his garment; and he shall go forth from thence in peace. {43:13} He shall break also the images of Beth-shemesh, that [is] in the land of Egypt; and the houses of the gods of the Egyptians shall he burn with fire.

{44:1} The word that came to Jeremiah concerning all the Jews which dwell in the land of Egypt, which dwell at Migdol, and at Tahpanhes, and at Noph, and in the country of Pathros, saying, {44:2} Thus saith the LORD of hosts, the God of Israel; Ye have seen all the evil that I have brought upon Jerusalem, and upon all the cities of Judah; and, behold, this day they [are] a desolation, and no man dwelleth therein, {44:3} Because of their wickedness which they have committed to provoke me to anger, in that they went to burn incense, [and] to serve other gods, whom they knew not, [neither] they, ye, nor your fathers. {44:4} Howbeit I sent unto you all my servants the prophets, rising early and sending [them,] saying, Oh, do not this abominable thing that I hate. {44:5} But they hearkened not, nor inclined their ear to turn from their wickedness, to burn no incense unto other gods. {44:6} Wherefore my fury and mine anger was poured forth, and was kindled in the cities of Judah and in the streets of Jerusalem; and they are wasted [and] desolate, as at this day. {44:7} Therefore now thus saith the LORD, the God of hosts, the God of Israel; Wherefore commit ye [this] great evil against your souls, to cut off from you man and woman, child and suckling, out of Judah, to leave you none to remain; {44:8} In that ye provoke me unto wrath with the works of your hands, burning incense unto other gods in the land of Egypt, whither ye be gone to dwell, that ye might cut yourselves off, and that ye might be a curse and a reproach among all the nations of the earth? {44:9} Have ye forgotten the wickedness of your fathers, and the wickedness of the kings of Judah, and the wickedness of their wives, and your own wickedness, and the wickedness of your wives, which they have committed in the land of Judah, and in the streets of Jerusalem? {44:10} They are not humbled [even] unto this day, neither have they feared, nor walked in my law, nor in my statutes, that I set before you and before your fathers. {44:11} Therefore thus saith the LORD of hosts, the God of Israel; Behold, I will set my face against you for evil, and to cut off all Judah. {44:12} And I will take the remnant of Judah, that have set their faces to go into the land of Egypt to sojourn there, and they shall all be consumed, [and] fall in the land of Egypt; they shall [even] be consumed by the sword and by the famine: they shall die, from the least even unto the greatest, by the sword [and] by the famine: and they shall be an execration, [and] an astonishment, and a curse, and a reproach. {44:13} For I will punish them that dwell in the land of Egypt, as I have punished Jerusalem, by the sword, by the famine, and by the pestilence: {44:14} So that none of the remnant of Judah, which are gone into the land of Egypt to sojourn there, shall escape or remain, that they should return into the land of Judah, to the which they have a desire to return to dwell there: for none shall return but such as shall escape. {44:15} Then all the men which knew that their wives had burned incense unto other gods, and all the women that stood by, a great multitude, even all the people that dwelt in the land of Egypt, in Pathros, answered Jeremiah, saying, {44:16} [As for] the word that thou hast spoken unto us in the name of the LORD, we will not hearken unto thee. {44:17} But we will certainly do whatsoever thing goeth forth out of our own mouth, to burn incense unto the queen of heaven, and to pour out drink offerings unto her, as we have done, we, and our fathers, our kings, and our princes, in the cities of Judah, and in the streets of Jerusalem: for [then] had we plenty of victuals, and were well, and saw no evil. {44:18} But since we left off to burn incense to the queen of heaven, and to pour out drink offerings unto her, we have wanted all [things,] and have been consumed by the sword and by the famine. {44:19} And when we burned incense to the queen of heaven, and poured out drink offerings unto her, did we make her cakes to worship her, and pour out drink offerings unto her, without our men? {44:20} Then Jeremiah said unto all the people, to the men, and to the women, and to all the people which had given him [that] answer, saying, {44:21} The incense that ye burned in the cities of Judah, and in the streets of Jerusalem, ye, and your fathers, your kings, and your princes, and the people of the land, did not the LORD remember them, and came it [not] into his mind? {44:22} So that the LORD could no longer bear, because of the evil of your doings, [and] because of the abominations which ye have committed; therefore is your land a desolation, and an astonishment, and a curse, without an inhabitant, as at this day. {44:23} Because ye have burned incense, and because ye have sinned against the LORD, and have not obeyed the voice of the LORD, nor walked in his law, nor in his statutes, nor in his testimonies; therefore this evil is happened unto you, as at this day. {44:24} Moreover Jeremiah said unto all the people, and to all the women, Hear the word of the LORD, all Judah that [are] in the land of Egypt: {44:25} Thus saith the LORD of hosts, the God of Israel, saying; Ye and your wives have both spoken with your mouths, and fulfilled with your hand, saying, We will surely perform our vows that we have vowed, to burn incense to the queen of heaven, and to pour out drink offerings unto her: ye will surely accomplish your vows, and surely perform your vows. {44:26} Therefore hear ye the word of the LORD, all Judah that dwell in the land of Egypt; Behold, I have sworn by my great name, saith the LORD, that my name shall no more be named in the mouth of any man of Judah in all the land of Egypt, saying, The Lord GOD liveth. {44:27} Behold, I will watch over them for evil, and not for good: and all the men of Judah that are in the land of Egypt shall be consumed by the sword and by the famine, until there be an end of them. {44:28} Yet a small number that escape the sword shall return out of the land of Egypt into the land of Judah, and all the remnant of Judah, that are gone into the land of Egypt to sojourn there, shall know whose words shall stand, mine, or theirs. {44:29} And this [shall be] a sign unto you, saith the LORD, that I will punish you in this place, that ye may know that my words shall surely stand against you for evil: {44:30} Thus saith the LORD; Behold, I will give Pharaohhophra king of Egypt into the hand of his enemies, and into the hand of them that seek his life; as I gave Zedekiah king of Judah into the hand of Nebuchadrezzar king of Babylon, his enemy, and that sought his life.

{45:1} The word that Jeremiah the prophet spake unto Baruch the son of Neriah, when he had written these words in a book at the mouth of Jeremiah, in the fourth year of Jehoiakim the son of Josiah king of Judah, saying, {45:2} Thus saith the LORD, the God of Israel, unto thee, O Baruch; {45:3} **Thou didst say, Woe is me now! for the LORD hath added grief to my sorrow; I fainted in my sighing, and I find no rest.** {45:4} Thus shalt thou say unto him, The LORD saith thus; Behold, [that] which I have built will I break down, and that which I have planted I will pluck up, even this whole land. {45:5} **And seekest thou great things for thyself? seek [them] not: for, behold, I will bring evil upon all flesh, saith the LORD: but thy life will I give unto thee for a prey in all places whither thou goest.**

{46:1} The word of the LORD which came to Jeremiah the prophet against the Gentiles; {46:2} Against Egypt, against the army of Pharaoh-necho king of Egypt, which was by the river Euphrates in Carchemish, which Nebuchadrezzar king of Babylon smote in the fourth year of Jehoiakim the son of Josiah king of Judah. {46:3} Order ye the buckler and shield, and draw near to battle. {46:4} Harness the horses; and get up, ye horsemen, and stand forth with [your] helmets; furbish the spears, [and] put on the brigandines. {46:5} Wherefore have I seen them dismayed [and] turned away back? and their mighty ones are beaten down, and are fled apace, and look not back: [for] fear [was] round about, saith the LORD. {46:6} Let not the swift flee away, nor the mighty man escape; they shall stumble, and fall toward the north by the river Euphrates. {46:7} Who [is] this [that] cometh up as a flood, whose waters are moved as the rivers? {46:8} Egypt riseth up like a flood, and [his] waters are moved like the rivers; and he saith, I will go up, [and] will cover the earth; I will destroy the city and the inhabitants thereof. {46:9} Come up, ye horses; and rage, ye chariots; and let the mighty men come forth; the Ethiopians and the Libyans, that handle the shield; and the Lydians, that handle [and] bend the bow. {46:10} For this [is] the day of the Lord GOD of hosts, a day of vengeance, that he may avenge him of his adversaries: and the sword shall devour, and it shall be satiate and made drunk with their blood: for the Lord GOD of hosts hath a sacrifice in the north country by the river Euphrates. {46:11} Go up into Gilead, and take balm, O virgin, the daughter of Egypt: in vain shalt thou use many medicines; [for] thou shalt not be cured. {46:12} The nations have heard of thy shame, and thy cry hath filled the land: for the mighty man hath stumbled against the mighty, [and] they are fallen both together. {46:13} The word that the LORD spake to Jeremiah the prophet, how Nebuchadrezzar king of Babylon should come [and] smite the land of Egypt. {46:14} Declare ye in Egypt, and publish in Migdol, and publish in Noph and in Tahpanhes: say ye, Stand fast, and prepare thee; for the sword shall devour round about thee. {46:15} Why are thy valiant [men] swept away? they stood not, because the LORD did drive them. {46:16} He made many to fall, yea, one fell upon another: and they said, Arise, and let us go again to our own people, and to the land of our nativity, from the oppressing sword. {46:17} They did cry there, Pharaoh king of Egypt [is but] a noise; he hath passed the time appointed. {46:18} [As] I live, saith the King, whose name [is] the LORD of hosts, Surely as Tabor [is] among the mountains, and as Carmel by the sea, [so] shall he come.

{46:19} O thou daughter dwelling in Egypt, furnish thyself to go into captivity: for Noph shall be waste and desolate without an inhabitant. {46:20} Egypt [is like] a very fair heifer, [but] destruction cometh; it cometh out of the north. {46:21} Also her hired men [are] in the midst of her like fatted bullocks; for they also are turned back, and are fled away together: they did not stand, because the day of their calamity was come upon them, [and] the time of their visitation. {46:22} The voice thereof shall go like a serpent; for they shall march with an army, and come against her with axes, as hewers of wood. {46:23} They shall cut down her forest, saith the LORD, though it cannot be searched; because they are more than the grasshoppers, and [are] innumerable. {46:24} The daughter of Egypt shall be confounded; she shall be delivered into the hand of the people of the north. {46:25} The LORD of hosts, the God of Israel, saith; Behold, I will punish the multitude of No, and Pharaoh, and Egypt, with their gods, and their kings; even Pharaoh, and [all] them that trust in him: {46:26} And I will deliver them into the hand of those that seek their lives, and into the hand of Nebuchadrezzar king of Babylon, and into the hand of his servants: and afterward it shall be inhabited, as in the days of old, saith the LORD. {46:27} But fear not thou, O my servant Jacob, and be not dismayed, O Israel: for, behold, I will save thee from afar off, and thy seed from the land of their captivity; and Jacob shall return, and be in rest and at ease, and none shall make [him] afraid. {46:28} Fear thou not, O Jacob my servant, saith the LORD: for I [am] with thee; for I will make a full end of all the nations whither I have driven thee: but I will not make a full end of thee, but correct thee in measure; yet will I not leave thee wholly unpunished.

{47:1} The word of the LORD that came to Jeremiah the prophet against the Philistines, before that Pharaoh smote Gaza. {47:2} Thus saith the LORD; Behold, waters rise up out of the north, and shall be an overflowing flood, and shall overflow the land, and all that is therein; the city, and them that dwell therein: then the men shall cry, and all the inhabitants of the land shall howl. {47:3} At the noise of the stamping of the hoofs of his strong [horses,] at the rushing of his chariots, [and at] the rumbling of his wheels, the fathers shall not look back to [their] children for feebleness of hands; {47:4} Because of the day that cometh to spoil all the Philistines, [and] to cut off from Tyrus and Zidon every helper that remaineth: for the LORD will spoil the Philistines, the remnant of the country of Caphtor. {47:5} Baldness is come upon Gaza; Ashkelon is cut off [with] the remnant of their valley: how long wilt thou cut thyself? {47:6} O thou sword of the LORD, how long [will it be] ere thou be quiet? put up thyself into thy scabbard, rest, and be still. {47:7} How can it be quiet, seeing the LORD hath given it a charge against Ashkelon, and against the sea shore? there hath he appointed it.

{48:1} Against Moab thus saith the LORD of hosts, the God of Israel; Woe unto Nebo! for it is spoiled: Kiriathaim is confounded [and] taken: Misgab is confounded and dismayed. {48:2} [There shall be] no more praise of Moab: in Heshbon they have devised evil against it; come, and let us cut it off from [being] a nation. Also thou shalt be cut down, O Madmen; the sword shall pursue thee. {48:3} A voice of crying [shall be] from Horonaim, spoiling and great destruction. {48:4} Moab is destroyed; her little ones have caused a cry to be heard. {48:5} For in the going up of Luhith continual weeping shall go up; for in the going down of Horonaim the enemies have heard a cry of destruction. {48:6} Flee, save your lives, and be like the heath in the wilderness. {48:7} For because thou hast trusted in thy works and in thy treasures, thou shalt also be taken: and Chemosh shall go forth into captivity [with] his priests and his princes together. {48:8} And the spoiler shall come upon every city, and no city shall escape: the valley also shall perish, and the plain shall be destroyed, as the LORD hath spoken. {48:9} Give wings unto Moab, that it may flee and get away: for the cities thereof shall be desolate, without any to dwell therein. {48:10} Cursed [be] he that doeth the work of the LORD deceitfully, and cursed [be] he that keepeth back his sword from blood. {48:11} Moab hath been at ease from his youth, and he hath settled on his lees, and hath not been emptied from vessel to vessel, neither hath he gone into captivity: therefore his taste remained in him, and his scent is not changed. {48:12} Therefore, behold, the days come, saith the LORD, that I will send unto him wanderers, that shall cause him to wander, and shall empty his vessels, and break their bottles. {48:13} And Moab shall be ashamed of Chemosh, as the house of Israel was ashamed of Bethel their confidence. {48:14} How say ye, We [are] mighty and strong men for the war? {48:15} Moab is spoiled, and gone up [out of] her cities, and his chosen young men are gone down to the slaughter, saith the King, whose name [is] the LORD of hosts. {48:16} The calamity of Moab [is] near to come, and his affliction hasteth fast. {48:17} All ye that are about him, bemoan him; and all ye that know his name, say, How is the strong staff broken, [and] the beautiful rod! {48:18} Thou daughter that dost inhabit Dibon, come down from [thy] glory, and sit in thirst; for the spoiler of Moab shall come upon thee, [and] he shall destroy thy strong holds.

{48:19} O inhabitant of Aroer, stand by the way, and espy; ask him that fleeth, and her that escapeth, [and] say, What is done? {48:20} Moab is confounded; for it is broken down: howl and cry; and tell ye it in Arnon, that Moab is spoiled, {48:21} And judgment is come upon the plain country; upon Holon, and upon Jahazah, and upon Mephaath, {48:22} And upon Dibon, and upon Nebo, and upon Bethdiblathaim, {48:23} And upon Kiriathaim, and upon Bethgamul, and upon Beth-meon, {48:24} And upon Kerioth, and upon Bozrah, and upon all the cities of the land of Moab, far or near. {48:25} The horn of Moab is cut off, and his arm is broken, saith the LORD. {48:26} Make ye him drunken: for he magnified [himself] against the LORD: Moab also shall wallow in his vomit, and he also shall be in derision. {48:27} For was not Israel a derision unto thee? was he found among thieves? for since thou spakest of him, thou skippedst for joy. {48:28} O ye that dwell in Moab, leave the cities, and dwell in the rock, and be like the dove [that] maketh her nest in the sides of the hole's mouth. {48:29} We have heard the pride of Moab, (he is exceeding proud) his loftiness, and his arrogancy, and his pride, and the haughtiness of his heart. {48:30} I know his wrath, saith the LORD; but [it shall] not [be] so; his lies shall not so effect [it.]{48:31} Therefore will I howl for Moab, and I will cry out for all Moab; [mine heart] shall mourn for the men of Kir-heres. {48:32} O vine of Sibmah, I will weep for thee with the weeping of Jazer: thy plants are gone over the sea, they reach [even] to the sea of Jazer: the spoiler is fallen upon thy summer fruits and upon thy vintage. {48:33} And joy and gladness is taken from the plentiful field, and from the land of Moab; and I have caused wine to fail from the winepresses: none shall tread with shouting; [their] shouting [shall be] no shouting. {48:34} From the cry of Heshbon [even] unto Elealeh, [and even] unto Jahaz, have they uttered their voice, from Zoar [even] unto Horonaim, [as] an heifer of three years old: for the waters also of Nimrim shall be desolate. {48:35} Moreover I will cause to cease in Moab, saith the LORD, him that offereth in the high places, and him that burneth incense to his gods. {48:36} Therefore mine heart shall sound for Moab like pipes, and mine heart shall sound like pipes for the men of Kir-heres: because the riches [that] he hath gotten are perished. {48:37} For every head [shall be] bald, and every beard clipped: upon all the hands [shall be] cuttings, and upon the loins sackcloth. {48:38} [There shall be] lamentation generally upon all the housetops of Moab, and in the streets thereof: for I have broken Moab like a vessel wherein [is] no pleasure, saith the LORD. {48:39} They shall howl, [saying,] How is it broken down! how hath Moab turned the back with shame! so shall Moab be a derision and a dismaying to all them about him. {48:40} For thus saith the LORD; Behold, he shall fly as an eagle, and shall spread his wings over Moab. {48:41} Kerioth is taken, and the strong holds are surprised, and the mighty men's hearts in Moab at that day shall be as the heart of a woman in her pangs. {48:42} And Moab shall be destroyed from [being] a people, because he hath magnified [himself] against the LORD. {48:43} Fear, and the pit, and the snare, [shall be] upon thee, O inhabitant of Moab, saith the LORD. {48:44} He that fleeth from the fear shall fall into the pit; and he that getteth up out of the pit shall be taken in the snare: for I will bring upon it, [even] upon Moab, the year of their visitation, saith the LORD. {48:45} They that fled stood under the shadow of Heshbon because of the force: but a fire shall come forth out of Heshbon, and a flame from the midst of Sihon, and shall devour the corner of Moab, and the crown of the head of the tumultuous ones. {48:46} Woe be unto thee, O Moab! the people of Chemosh perisheth: for thy sons are taken captives, and thy daughters captives. {48:47} Yet will I bring again the captivity of Moab in the latter days, saith the LORD. Thus far [is] the judgment of Moab.

{49:1} Concerning the Ammonites, thus saith the LORD; Hath Israel no sons? hath he no heir? why [then] doth their king inherit Gad, and his people dwell in his cities? {49:2} Therefore, behold, the days come, saith the LORD, that I will cause an alarm of war to be heard in Rabbah of the Ammonites; and it shall be a desolate heap, and her daughters shall be burned with fire: then shall Israel be heir unto them that were his heirs, saith the LORD. {49:3} Howl, O Heshbon, for Ai is spoiled: cry, ye daughters of Rabbah, gird you with sackcloth; lament, and run to and fro by the hedges; for their king shall go into captivity, [and] his priests and his princes together. {49:4} Wherefore gloriest thou in the valleys, thy flowing valley, O backsliding daughter? that trusted in her treasures, [saying,] Who shall come unto me? {49:5} Behold, I will bring a fear upon thee, saith the Lord GOD of hosts, from all those that be about thee; and ye shall be driven out every man right forth; and none shall gather up him that wandereth. {49:6} And afterward I will bring again the captivity of the children of Ammon, saith the LORD. {49:7} Concerning Edom, thus saith the LORD of hosts; [Is] wisdom no more in Teman? is counsel perished from the prudent? is their wisdom vanished? {49:8} Flee ye, turn back, dwell deep, O inhabitants of Dedan; for I will bring the calamity of Esau upon him, the time [that] I will visit him. {49:9} If grapegatherers come to thee, would they not leave [some] gleaning grapes? if thieves by night, they will destroy till they have enough. {49:10} But I have made Esau bare, I have uncovered his secret places, and he shall not be able to hide himself: his seed is spoiled, and his brethren, and his neighbours, and he is not. {49:11} Leave thy fatherless children, I will preserve [them] alive; and let thy widows trust in me. {49:12} For thus saith the LORD; Behold, they whose judgment [was] not to drink of the cup have assuredly drunken; and [art] thou he [that] shall altogether go unpunished? thou shalt not go unpunished, but thou shalt surely drink [of it.]{49:13} For I have sworn by myself, saith the LORD, that Bozrah shall become a desolation, a reproach, a waste, and a curse; and all the cities thereof shall be perpetual wastes. {49:14} I have heard a rumour from the LORD, and an ambassador is sent unto the heathen, [saying,] Gather ye together, and come against her, and rise up to the battle. {49:15} For, lo, I will make thee small among the heathen, [and] despised among men. {49:16} Thy terribleness hath deceived thee, [and] the pride of thine heart, O thou that dwellest in the clefts of the rock, that holdest the height of the hill: though thou shouldest make thy nest as high as the eagle, I will bring thee down from thence, saith the LORD. {49:17} Also Edom shall be a desolation: every one that goeth by it shall be astonished, and shall hiss at all the plagues thereof. {49:18} As in the overthrow of Sodom and Gomorrah and the neighbour [cities] thereof, saith the LORD, no man shall abide there, neither shall a son of man dwell in it. {49:19} Behold, he shall come up like a lion from the swelling of Jordan against the habitation of the strong: but I will suddenly make him run away from her: and who [is] a chosen [man, that] I may appoint over her? for who [is] like me? and who will appoint me the time? and who [is] that shepherd that will stand before me? {49:20} Therefore hear the counsel of the LORD, that he hath taken against Edom; and his purposes, that he hath purposed against the inhabitants of Teman: Surely the least of the flock shall draw them out: surely he shall make their habitations desolate with them. {49:21} The earth is moved at the noise of their fall, at the cry the noise thereof was heard in the Red sea. {49:22} Behold, he shall come up and fly as the eagle, and spread his wings over Bozrah: and at that day shall the heart of the mighty men of Edom be as the heart of a woman in her pangs. {49:23} Concerning Damascus. Hamath is confounded, and Arpad: for they have heard evil tidings: they are fainthearted; [there is] sorrow on the sea; it cannot be quiet. {49:24} Damascus is waxed feeble, [and] turneth herself to flee, and fear hath seized on [her:] anguish and sorrows have taken her, as a woman in travail. {49:25} How is the city of praise not left, the city of my joy! {49:26} Therefore her young men shall fall in her streets, and all the men of war shall be cut off in that day, saith the LORD of hosts. {49:27} And I will kindle a fire in the wall of Damascus, and it shall consume the palaces of Ben-hadad. {49:28} Concerning Kedar, and concerning the kingdoms of Hazor, which Nebuchadrezzar king of Babylon shall smite, thus saith the LORD; Arise ye, go up to Kedar, and spoil the men of the east. {49:29} Their tents and their flocks shall they take away: they shall take to themselves their curtains, and all their vessels, and their camels; and they shall cry unto them, Fear [is] on every side. {49:30} Flee, get you far off, dwell deep, O ye inhabitants of Hazor, saith the LORD; for Nebuchadrezzar king of Babylon hath taken counsel against you, and hath conceived a purpose against you. {49:31} Arise, get you up unto the wealthy nation, that dwelleth without care, saith the LORD, which have neither gates nor bars, [which] dwell alone. {49:32} And their camels shall be a booty, and the multitude of their cattle a spoil: and I will scatter into all winds them [that are] in the utmost corners; and I will bring their calamity from all sides thereof, saith the LORD. {49:33} And Hazor shall be a dwelling for dragons, [and] a desolation for ever: there shall no man abide there, nor [any] son of man dwell in it. {49:34} The word of the LORD that came to Jeremiah the prophet against Elam in the beginning of the reign of Zedekiah king of Judah, saying, {49:35} Thus saith the LORD of hosts; Behold, I will break the bow of Elam, the chief of their might. {49:36} And upon Elam will I bring the four winds from the four quarters of heaven, and will scatter them toward all those winds; and there shall be no nation whither the outcasts of Elam shall not come. {49:37} For I will cause Elam to be dismayed before their enemies, and before them that seek their life: and I will bring evil upon them [even] my fierce anger, saith the LORD; and I will send the sword after them, till I have consumed them: {49:38} And I will set my throne in Elam, and will destroy from thence the king and the princes, saith the LORD. {49:39} But it shall come to pass in the latter days, [that] I will bring again the captivity of Elam, saith the LORD.

{50:1} The word that the LORD spake against Babylon [and] against the land of the Chaldeans by Jeremiah the prophet. {50:2} Declare ye among the nations, and publish, and set up a standard; publish, [and] conceal not: say, Babylon is taken, Bel is confounded, Merodach is broken in pieces; her idols are confounded, her images are broken in pieces. {50:3} For out of the north there cometh up a nation against her, which shall make her land desolate, and none shall dwell therein: they shall remove, they shall depart, both man and beast. {50:4} In those days, and in that time, saith the LORD, the children of Israel shall come, they and the children of Judah together, going and weeping: they shall go, and seek the LORD their God. {50:5} They shall ask the way to Zion with their faces thitherward, [saying,] Come, and let us join ourselves to the LORD in a perpetual covenant [that] shall not be forgotten. {50:6} My people hath been lost sheep: their shepherds have caused them to go astray, they have turned them away [on] the mountains: they have gone from mountain to hill, they have forgotten their restingplace. {50:7} All that found them have devoured them: and their adversaries said, We offend not, because they have sinned against the LORD, the habitation of justice, even the LORD, the hope of their fathers. {50:8} Remove out of the midst of Babylon, and go forth out of the land of the Chaldeans, and be as the he goats before the flocks. {50:9} For, lo, I will raise and cause to come up against Babylon an assembly of great nations from the north country: and they shall set themselves in array against her; from thence she shall be taken: their arrows [shall be] as of a mighty expert man; none shall return in vain. {50:10} And Chaldea shall be a spoil: all that spoil her shall be satisfied, saith the LORD. {50:11} Because ye were glad, because ye rejoiced, O ye destroyers of mine heritage, because ye are grown fat as the heifer at grass, and bellow as bulls; {50:12} Your mother shall be sore confounded; she that bare you shall be ashamed: behold, the hindermost of the nations [shall be] a wilderness, a dry land, and a desert. {50:13} Because of the wrath of the LORD it shall not be inhabited, but it shall be wholly desolate: every one that goeth by Babylon shall be astonished, and hiss at all her plagues. {50:14} Put yourselves in array against Babylon round about: all ye that bend the bow, shoot at her, spare no arrows: for she hath sinned against the LORD. {50:15} Shout against her round about: she hath given her hand: her foundations are fallen, her walls are thrown down: for it [is] the vengeance of the LORD: take vengeance upon her; as she hath done, do unto her. {50:16} Cut off the sower from Babylon, and him that handleth the sickle in the time of harvest: for fear of the oppressing sword they shall turn every one to his people, and they shall flee every one to his own land. {50:17} Israel [is] a scattered sheep; the lions have driven [him] away: first the king of Assyria hath devoured him; and last this Nebuchadrezzar king of Babylon hath broken his bones. {50:18} Therefore thus saith the LORD of hosts, the God of Israel; Behold, I will punish the king of Babylon and his land, as I have punished the king of Assyria. {50:19} And I will bring Israel again to his habitation, and he shall feed on Carmel and Bashan, and his soul shall be satisfied upon mount Ephraim and Gilead. {50:20} In those days, and in that time, saith the LORD, the iniquity of Israel shall be sought for, and [there shall be] none; and the sins of Judah, and they shall not be found: for I will pardon them whom I reserve. {50:21} Go up against the land of Merathaim, [even] against it, and against the inhabitants of Pekod: waste and utterly destroy after them, saith the LORD, and do according to all that I have commanded thee. {50:22} A sound of battle [is] in the land, and of great destruction. {50:23} How is the hammer of the whole earth cut asunder and broken! how is Babylon become a desolation among the nations! {50:24} I have laid a snare for thee, and thou art also taken, O Babylon, and thou wast not aware: thou art found, and also caught, because thou hast striven against the LORD. {50:25} The LORD hath opened his armoury, and hath brought forth the weapons of his indignation: for this [is] the work of the Lord GOD of hosts in the land of the Chaldeans. {50:26} Come against her from the utmost border, open her storehouses: cast her up as heaps, and destroy her utterly: let nothing of her be left. {50:27} Slay all her bullocks; let them go down to the slaughter: woe unto them! for their day is come, the time of their visitation. {50:28} The voice of them that flee and escape out of the land of Babylon, to declare in Zion the vengeance of the LORD our God, the vengeance of his temple. {50:29} Call together the archers against Babylon: all ye that bend the bow, camp against it round about; let none thereof escape: recompense her according to her work; according to all that she hath done, do unto her: for she hath been proud against the LORD, against the Holy One of Israel. {50:30} Therefore shall her young men fall in the streets, and all her men of war shall be cut off in that day, saith the LORD. {50:31} Behold, I [am] against thee, [O thou] most proud, saith the Lord GOD of hosts: for thy day is come, the time [that] I will visit thee. {50:32} And the most proud shall stumble and fall, and none shall raise him up: and I will kindle a fire in his cities, and it shall devour all round about him. {50:33} Thus saith the LORD of hosts; The children of Israel and the children of Judah [were] oppressed together: and all that took them captives held them fast; they refused to let them go. {50:34} Their Redeemer [is] strong; the LORD of hosts [is] his name: he shall throughly plead their cause, that he may give rest to the land, and disquiet the inhabitants of Babylon. {50:35} A sword [is] upon the Chaldeans, saith the LORD, and upon the inhabitants of Babylon, and upon her princes, and upon her wise [men.]{50:36} A sword [is] upon the liars; and they shall dote: a sword [is] upon her mighty men; and they shall be dismayed. {50:37} A sword [is] upon their horses, and upon their chariots, and upon all the mingled people that [are] in the midst of her; and they shall become as women: a sword [is] upon her treasures; and they shall be robbed. {50:38} A drought [is] upon her waters; and they shall be dried up: for it [is] the land of graven images, and they are mad upon [their] idols. {50:39} Therefore the wild beasts of the desert with the wild beasts of the islands shall dwell [there,] and the owls shall dwell therein: and it shall be no more inhabited for ever; neither shall it be dwelt in from generation to generation. {50:40} As God overthrew Sodom and Gomorrah and the neighbour [cities] thereof, saith the LORD; [so] shall no man abide there, neither shall any son of man dwell therein. {50:41} Behold, a people shall come from the north, and a great nation, and many kings shall be raised up from the coasts of the earth. {50:42} They shall hold the bow and the lance: they [are] cruel, and will not shew mercy: their voice shall roar like the sea, and they shall ride upon horses, [every one] put in array, like a man to the battle, against thee, O daughter of Babylon. {50:43} The king of Babylon hath heard the report of them, and his hands waxed feeble: anguish took hold of him, [and] pangs as of a woman in travail. {50:44} Behold, he shall come up like a lion from the swelling of Jordan unto the habitation of the strong: but I will make them suddenly run away from her: and who [is] a chosen [man, that] I may appoint over her? for who [is] like me? and who will appoint me the time? and who [is] that shepherd that will stand before me? {50:45} Therefore hear ye the counsel of the LORD, that he hath taken against Babylon; and his purposes, that he hath purposed against the land of the Chaldeans: Surely the least of the flock shall draw them out: surely he shall make [their] habitation desolate with them. {50:46} At the noise of the taking of Babylon the earth is moved, and the cry is heard among the nations.

{51:1} This is what the LORD says: "I will stir up a destructive wind against Babylon and the people who live in Babylonia. {51:2} I will send foreign armies to Babylon to winnow her and to destroy her land. They will surround her and bring disaster upon her from every direction. {51:3} Let the archer bend his bow against those who think themselves strong! Let him march against Babylon! Spare no arrows, for she has sinned against the LORD. {51:4} The slain will lie in the streets of Babylon, and those who die in battle will lie scattered throughout the land of the Chaldeans. {51:5} But the LORD has not abandoned Israel and Judah. He is still their God, even though their land was filled with sin against the Holy One of Israel. {51:6} "Flee from Babylon! Save yourselves! Don't let yourselves be destroyed because of her sins. It is time for the LORD to avenge his Temple. {51:7} Babylon was a golden cup in the LORD's hands, a cup that made the whole earth drunk. The nations drank Babylon's wine, and they have all gone mad. {51:8} But suddenly Babylon, the great city, will be destroyed. Weep for her! Give her medicine. Perhaps she can yet be healed. {51:9} We would have healed Babylon, but she cannot be healed. Let us abandon her and each go to our own land, for her judgment reaches to the skies; it is as high as the heavens. {51:10} "The LORD has vindicated us. Come, let us announce in Zion what the LORD our God has done. {51:11} Sharpen the arrows! Fill the quivers! The LORD has stirred up the spirit of the kings of the Medes to destroy Babylon, because his judgment on her is final. It is the LORD's vengeance, vengeance for his Temple. {51:12} Raise the battle flag against Babylon's walls! Reinforce the guard! Station the watchmen! Prepare an ambush, for the LORD will fulfill all his plans against Babylon. {51:13} You who live along the rivers and rich in treasures, your end has come; the time for you to be destroyed has arrived. {51:14} The LORD of Heaven's Armies has sworn this oath: "I will fill you with troops like a swarm of locusts, and they will shout in triumph over you. {51:15} He made the earth by his power, and he preserves it by his wisdom. With his own understanding he stretched out the heavens. {51:16} When he speaks in the thunder, the heavens roar with rain. He causes the clouds to rise over the earth. He sends the lightning with the rain and releases the wind from his storehouses. {51:17} "The whole human race is foolish and has no knowledge! The craftsmen are disgraced by the idols they make, for their images are a fraud. They have no life or breath in them. {51:18} They are worthless, the objects of mockery. When the time of their punishment comes, they will all be destroyed. {51:19} But the God of Israel is no idol! He is the Creator of everything that exists, including his people, his own special possession. The LORD of Heaven's Armies is his name! {51:20} "You are my battle-ax and sword," says the LORD. "With you I will shatter nations and destroy many kingdoms. {51:21} With you I will shatter armies—destroying the horse and rider, the chariot and charioteer. {51:22} With you I will shatter men and women, old people and children, young men and maidens. {51:23} With you I will shatter shepherds and flocks, farmers and oxen, captains and rulers. {51:24} "I will repay Babylon and the people of Babylonia for all the evil they have done to my people in Jerusalem," says the LORD. {51:25} "Look, O mighty mountain, destroyer of the earth! I am your enemy," says the LORD. "I will raise my fist against you, to roll you down from the heights. When I am finished, you will be nothing but a heap of rubble. {51:26} You will be desolate forever. Even your stones will never again be used for building. You will be completely wiped out," says the LORD. {51:27} Raise a signal flag to the nations. Sound the battle cry! Mobilize them all against Babylon. Prepare them to fight against her! Bring out the horses and chariots and the armies of Persia and Media, which will roll in like a mighty flood! {51:28} Prepare to destroy Babylon's archers, all the armies of the world. {51:29} The land trembles and writhes in pain, for everything the LORD has planned against Babylon stands unchanged. Babylon will be left desolate without a single inhabitant. {51:30} "The mightiest warriors of Babylon have stopped fighting. They stay in their strongholds. Their strength is exhausted; they have become like women. Babylon's homes have been set on fire, and her gates have been broken. {51:31} Messenger follows messenger, and the news just keeps coming. Each one brings a message of disaster. {51:32} Babylonia's wise men are put to shame! They are suddenly confused and bewildered. {51:33} The LORD of Heaven's Armies has spoken— I will cut down the tall cedars of Lebanon and shake the cedars of Bashan. {51:34} I will bring my enemies to Babylon to be punished there. I will make Babylon's land desolate, and then no one will live there any longer. I, the LORD, have spoken! {51:35} "Babylon, you have been like a threshing floor at harvest time, but the time of your harvest has come and gone. {51:36} Listen to the terrible cry of Babylon, the sound of great destruction from the land of the Babylonians! {51:37} For the LORD is destroying Babylon. He will silence her loud voice. Waves of enemies pound against her; the noise of battle rings throughout the city. {51:38} Destroying armies come against Babylon. Her mighty men are captured, and their weapons break in their hands. For the LORD is a God who gives just punishment; he always repays in full. {51:39} "I will make her officials and wise men drunk, along with her captains, officials, and warriors. They will fall asleep and never wake up again!" says the King, whose name is the LORD of Heaven's Armies. {51:40} This is what the LORD of Heaven's Armies says: "The wide walls of Babylon will be leveled to the ground, and her high gates will be burned. The builders from many lands have worked in vain, for their work will be destroyed by fire!" {51:41} "How Babylon is praised, the whole earth! How she has become desolate among the nations! {51:42} The sea has come over Babylon; she is covered with its tumultuous waves. {51:43} Her cities are desolate, a dry and desert land, a land where no one lives, where no human being passes through. {51:44} And I will punish Bel in Babylon. I will make him vomit up what he has swallowed. The nations will no longer come and worship him. His wall of Babylon will fall. {51:45} "My people, flee from Babylon! Save yourselves! Don't get trapped in her punishment! It is the LORD's time for vengeance; he will repay her what she deserves. {51:46} Babylon's fall will be so sudden that the earth will shake at the news, and her cries of anguish will be heard around the world. {51:47} "For the time has come for Babylon to be destroyed. Her idols will be broken in pieces, and her gods will be utterly disgraced. {51:48} Babylon's mightiest warriors have stopped fighting; they sit in their barracks. Their strength is gone; they have become like women. Babylon's homes are set on fire, and the gates are broken down. {51:49} Listen to the terrible cry from Babylon, from the land of the Babylonians. It is the sound of great destruction. {51:50} "Babylon, you have caused the death of many people throughout the world. Now you will be destroyed, and the families of your victims will say, 'May Babylon be as ruined as Babylon has ruined us.' {51:51} We are ashamed because we have heard insults. Disgrace covers our faces because foreigners have entered the holiest places of our Temple. {51:52} "But the time is coming soon," says the LORD, "when I will punish Babylon's idols. The whole land will groan, and her people will die in widespread slaughter. {51:53} "Even if Babylon reaches the sky and fortifies her high walls, I will still send destroyers against her," says the LORD. {51:54} Listen! Hear the cry of Babylon! The sound of great destruction comes from the land of the Babylonians! {51:55} For the LORD is destroying Babylon. He will silence her loud voice. Waves of enemies pound against her; the noise of battle rings throughout the city. {51:56} Her mightiest warriors no longer fight. They stay in their barracks; their courage is gone. They have become like women. The invaders have set her buildings on fire, and her walls have been broken down. {51:57} The famous walls of Babylon will be leveled to the ground, and her high gates will be burned. The builders from many lands have worked in vain, for their work will be destroyed by fire!" {51:58} This is what the LORD of Heaven's Armies says: "The wide walls of Babylon will be leveled to the ground, and her high gates will be burned. The builders from many lands have worked in vain, for their work will be destroyed by fire!" {51:59} The prophet Jeremiah gave instructions to Seraiah son of Neriah and grandson of Mahseiah when he went to Babylon with King Zedekiah of Judah. This was during the fourth year of Zedekiah's reign. Seraiah was a quartermaster in the royal service. {51:60} So Jeremiah wrote down all the terrible disasters that would come upon Babylon—all the words written here. {51:61} He said to Seraiah, "When you get to Babylon, read aloud everything on this scroll. {51:62} Then say, ' LORD, you have said that this place will be destroyed, that it will lie empty and desolate forever.' {51:63} When you have finished reading the scroll, tie it to a stone and throw it into the Euphrates River. {51:64} Then say, 'In this same way Babylon and her people will sink, never again to rise, because of the disasters I will bring upon her.' This is the end of Jeremiah's messages

{52:1} Zedekiah became king when he was twenty-one years old, and he ruled in Jerusalem for eleven years. His mother was named Hamutal; she was the daughter of Jeremiah from the town of Libnah. {52:2} Zedekiah did what was evil in the sight of the LORD, just as Jehoiakim had done. {52:3} Because of the LORD's anger, it happened in Jerusalem and Judah that Zedekiah rebelled against the king of Babylon. {52:4} In the ninth year of Zedekiah's reign, on the tenth day of the tenth month, Nebuchadnezzar, the king of Babylon, and his entire army came against Jerusalem. They set up camp and built siege ramps around the city. {52:5} So Jerusalem was under siege until the eleventh year of King Zedekiah's reign. {52:6} Then, in the fourth month, on the ninth day of the month, the famine in the city became very severe, and there was no food for the people. {52:7} The city walls were breached, and all the soldiers fled. They left the city at night by way of the gate between the two walls, near the king's garden, while the Babylonians were surrounding the city. They fled toward the Arabah. {52:8} But the Babylonian army chased after King Zedekiah and caught him on the plains of Jericho. All his soldiers scattered and fled. {52:9} They captured the king and took him to the king of Babylon at Riblah in the land of Hamath, where the king pronounced judgment on him. {52:10} The king of Babylon killed Zedekiah's sons right before his eyes, and he also killed all the nobles of Judah at Riblah. {52:11} Then he gouged out Zedekiah's eyes, bound him in bronze chains, and took him to Babylon, where he remained in prison until the day of his death. {52:12} In the fifth month, on the tenth day of the month, which was the nineteenth year of Nebuchadnezzar king of Babylon, Nebuzaradan, the captain of the guard who served the king of Babylon, entered Jerusalem. {52:13} He burned down the house of the LORD, the king's palace, and all the houses in Jerusalem—every important building was destroyed by fire. {52:14} The Babylonian army, under the captain of the guard, broke down all the walls surrounding Jerusalem. {52:15} Nebuzaradan, the captain of the guard, took captive some of the poorest people, the rest of the people who were still in the city, the deserters who had defected to the king of Babylon, and the rest of the craftsmen. {52:16} But Nebuzaradan left behind some of the poorest people of the land to work the vineyards and fields. {52:17} The Babylonians also broke up the bronze pillars in the LORD's temple, the bronze stands, and the bronze basin (the Sea), and they carried all the bronze to Babylon. {52:18} They also took away the pots, shovels, wick trimmers, dishes, and all the bronze utensils used in the temple service. {52:19} The captain of the guard also took the small bowls, fire pans, basins, pots, lampstands, dishes, and bowls—all made of pure gold or silver. {52:20} The bronze from the two pillars, the Sea, and the twelve bronze bulls under the Sea, which King Solomon had made for the LORD's temple, was too heavy to be weighed. {52:21} Each pillar was eighteen cubits high, with a circumference of twelve cubits; each was four fingers thick, and hollow. {52:22} The bronze capital on top of one pillar was five cubits high and was decorated with a network and pomegranates of bronze all around. The other pillar, with its pomegranates, was similar. {52:23} There were ninety-six pomegranates on the sides; the total number of pomegranates above the surrounding network was one hundred. {52:24} The captain of the guard also took Seraiah the chief priest, Zephaniah the priest next in rank, and the three doorkeepers. {52:25} Of those still in the city, he took an officer who had been in charge of the fighting men, seven royal advisers, the secretary to the commander of the army, who mustered the people of the land, and sixty other men. {52:26} Nebuzaradan, the captain of the guard, took them all and brought them to the king of Babylon at Riblah. {52:27} And there at Riblah, in the land of Hamath, the king of Babylon had them all executed. So the people of Judah were taken into exile from their land. {52:28} These are the numbers of the people whom Nebuchadnezzar took into exile: In the seventh year of his reign, he took 3,023 Jews; {52:29} in the eighteenth year of Nebuchadnezzar, he took 832 people from Jerusalem; {52:30} in the twenty-third year of Nebuchadnezzar, Nebuzaradan, the captain of the guard, took 745 Jews into exile. All the people numbered 4,600. {52:31} In the thirty-seventh year of the exile of Jehoiachin king of Judah, in the twelfth month, on the twenty-fifth day of the month, Evil-Merodach king of Babylon, in the year he became king, graciously freed Jehoiachin king of Judah from prison. {52:32} He spoke kindly to him and gave him a seat of honor higher than those of the other kings who were with him in Babylon. {52:33} So Jehoiachin put aside his prison clothes and for the rest of his life ate regularly at the king's table. {52:34} And he was given a regular food allowance by the king, a portion for each day, for the rest of his life.

Lamentations

{1:1} **Look at the city! Once bustling with people, now it sits alone. How did it become like a widow, once so great among the nations, now forced to pay tribute?** {1:2} It weeps bitterly through the night, tears staining its cheeks. None of its lovers comfort it; even its friends have turned into enemies. {1:3} Judah has been taken captive, suffering affliction and servitude among foreign nations. It finds no rest, pursued relentlessly by its persecutors. {1:4} Zion mourns; no one comes to its solemn feasts. Its gates stand deserted, its priests sigh, its young women suffer, and bitterness fills the air. {1:5} Its enemies are victorious; the LORD has punished it for its many sins. Its children have been taken captive before the enemy. {1:6} All its beauty has faded; its leaders are like deer without pasture, weak and helpless before their pursuers. {1:7} **Jerusalem remembers its past glories, now overshadowed by affliction and misery. No one came to its aid when enemies overtook it; they even mocked its sacred days.** {1:8} Jerusalem has sinned greatly and is now cast aside. Those who once honored it now despise it, seeing its shameful nakedness. It groans in shame and turns away. {1:9} Its filthiness is evident, but it doesn't remember its fate. It has come down dramatically, with no one to comfort it. LORD, see my affliction; my enemy has exalted himself. {1:10} The adversary has laid hands on all its precious things; it has seen even the heathens enter its sanctuary, against your command. {1:11} Its people sigh, seeking bread; they trade their valuables for food just to survive. LORD, see and consider my vile condition. {1:12} "Doesn't anyone care?" I cry out to all who pass by. "See if there's any sorrow like mine, inflicted by the LORD in his fierce anger. {1:13} "From above, he has sent fire into my bones, overwhelming me. He has set traps for my feet, leaving me desolate and faint all day long. {1:14} "The burden of my sins weighs heavily; they wrap around my neck, making me weak. The Lord has handed me over to those I cannot resist. {1:15} "The Lord has trampled all my mighty men, gathering an assembly to crush my young men. He has treated the virgin daughter of Judah as if in a winepress. {1:16} "For all these things, I weep bitterly; my eyes overflow with tears. Comfort is far from me; my children suffer because the enemy has prevailed. {1:17} Zion stretches out its hands, but no one comforts it. The LORD has commanded that enemies surround Jacob; Jerusalem is like a menstruous woman among them. {1:18} The LORD is righteous, for I have rebelled against his commandments. All people, behold my sorrow: my young men and virgins have been taken captive. {1:19} I called for help from my lovers, but they deceived me. My priests and elders perished in the city, seeking food for their souls. {1:20} Look at me, LORD; I am distressed. My heart is troubled; I have rebelled greatly. Death is everywhere, both outside and inside my home. {1:21} They have heard my sighs; no one comforts me. All my enemies rejoice in my troubles, knowing it was your doing. LORD, bring the day you promised, and let them suffer like me. {1:22} Let all their wickedness come before you, and deal with them as you have dealt with me for all my sins. My sighs are many, and my heart is faint.

{2:1} **Look how the Lord, in his anger, has covered the daughter of Zion with a cloud, casting down the beauty of Israel from heaven to earth. He has forgotten his footstool in his fury!** {2:2} The Lord has destroyed all the homes of Jacob without pity. In his wrath, he has demolished the strongholds of the daughter of Judah, bringing them to the ground and polluting the kingdom and its leaders. {2:3} In his fierce anger, he has cut off the strength of Israel, withdrawing his protection from before the enemy. He burned against Jacob like a raging fire, devouring everything in its path. {2:4} He wielded his bow like an enemy, standing against his people with his right hand as an adversary. He killed all that was beautiful in the tabernacle of the daughter of Zion, pouring out his fury like fire. {2:5} The Lord acted as an enemy, swallowing up Israel and all its palaces. He destroyed their strongholds, increasing mourning and lamentation in the daughter of Judah. {2:6} He violently took away his sanctuary, destroying their places of assembly. The Lord caused their solemn feasts and Sabbaths to be forgotten in Zion, despising both king and priest in his anger. {2:7} The Lord abandoned his altar and abhorred his sanctuary, delivering the walls of her palaces into the hands of the enemy. They made noise in the house of the Lord, as in the day of a solemn feast. {2:8} The Lord planned to destroy the walls of the daughter of Zion; he stretched out a line and did not relent from destroying. Therefore, both rampart and wall lamented; they languished together. {2:9} Her gates sank into the ground; he destroyed and broke her bars. Her king and princes are among the nations; the law is no more, and her prophets find no vision from the Lord. {2:10} The elders of the daughter of Zion sit on the ground in silence, casting dust on their heads and wearing sackcloth. The young women of Jerusalem hang their heads low. {2:11} My eyes are filled with tears; my heart is troubled. For the destruction of the daughter of my people, even children and infants faint in the streets of the city. {2:12} They cry to their mothers, asking for food and drink, collapsing like the wounded in the streets, with their souls poured out into their mothers' bosom. {2:13} What can I compare to you, O daughter of Jerusalem? Your breach is vast like the sea; who can heal you? {2:14} Your prophets have seen worthless and foolish things for you, failing to reveal your iniquity and turn away your captivity. Instead, they prophesied false burdens and causes of banishment. {2:15} All who pass by clap their hands and hiss at you, wagging their heads at the daughter of Jerusalem, saying, "Is this the city called the perfection of beauty, the joy of the whole earth?" {2:16} All your enemies have opened their mouths against you, hissing and gnashing their teeth, saying, "We have swallowed her up; this is the day we've waited for; we have seen it!" {2:17} The Lord has done what he planned, fulfilling his word commanded long ago. He has thrown down without pity, causing your enemies to rejoice and raising the horn of your adversaries. {2:18} Cry out, O wall of the daughter of Zion; let tears run down like a river day and night. Give yourself no rest; let not the apple of your eye cease. {2:19} Arise, cry out in the night; pour out your heart like water before the Lord. Lift up your hands for the life of your young children fainting for hunger in every street. {2:20} Look, O Lord, and see whom you have done this to. Shall women eat their offspring, children of a span long? Shall priests and prophets be slain in the sanctuary of the Lord? {2:21} Both young and old lie in the streets; my virgins and young men are fallen by the sword. You have killed them in your anger, showing no pity. {2:22} You summoned terrors against me on every side, so that none escaped or survived in the day of your anger. Those whom I had cared for and brought up, my enemies have consumed.

{3:1} I'm the man who has seen affliction by the rod of his wrath. {3:2} He has led me into darkness, not into light. {3:3} Surely, he has turned against me all day long. {3:4} He has made my flesh and skin old; he has broken my bones. {3:5} He has built against me and surrounded me with bitterness and hardship. {3:6} He has put me in dark places, like those long dead. {3:7} He has hedged me in so I cannot escape; he has made my chains heavy. {3:8} Even when I cry and shout, he shuts out my prayer. {3:9} He has blocked my ways with stone walls; he has made my paths crooked. {3:10} He has been like a bear lying in wait, like a lion in hiding. {3:11} He has turned aside my ways and torn me apart; he has left me desolate. {3:12} He has bent his bow and aimed it at me like an arrow. {3:13} He has caused the arrows of his quiver to pierce my kidneys. {3:14} I have become a laughingstock to all my people; they mock me all day long. {3:15} He has filled me with bitterness and made me drunk with wormwood. {3:16} He has also broken my teeth with gravel stones and covered me with ashes. {3:17} He has taken away my peace and prosperity; I have forgotten what happiness is. {3:18} I thought my strength and hope were gone from the Lord. {3:19} I remember my affliction and misery, the bitterness and gall. {3:20} My soul still remembers them and is humbled within me. {3:21} This I remember, so I have hope. {3:22} **It's because of the Lord's mercies that we are not destroyed; his compassions never fail.** {3:23} They are new every morning; great is his faithfulness. {3:24} The Lord is my portion, says my soul; therefore, I will hope in him. {3:25} The Lord is good to those who wait for him, to the soul that seeks him. {3:26} It's good for a person to both hope and quietly wait for the salvation of the Lord. {3:27} It's good to bear the yoke in one's youth. {3:28} He sits alone and keeps silent because he has borne it. {3:29} He puts his mouth in the dust, hoping there may be salvation. {3:30} He gives his cheek to the one who strikes him; he is filled with reproach. {3:31} The Lord will not cast off forever. {3:32} Though he causes grief, he will have compassion according to his mercies. {3:33} For he does not afflict willingly or grieve the children of men. {3:34} He crushes under his feet all the prisoners of the earth. {3:35} He turns aside the justice due a man before the face of the Most High. {3:36} He does not approve of subverting a man in his cause. {3:37} Who can speak and have it happen if the Lord hasn't commanded it? {3:38} Does evil or good come out of the mouth of the Most High? {3:39} Why should a living person complain about the punishment of his sins? {3:40} Let's search and examine our ways and turn back to the Lord. {3:41} Let's lift up our hearts with our hands to God in heaven. {3:42} We have transgressed and rebelled; you have not pardoned. {3:43} You have covered us with anger and pursued us; you have slain without pity. {3:44} You have covered yourself with a cloud so that our prayers cannot pass through. {3:45} You have made us like refuse and garbage among the people. {3:46} All our enemies have opened their mouths against us. {3:47} Fear, traps, desolation, and destruction have come upon us. {3:48} My eyes run down with rivers of water for the destruction of the daughter of my people. {3:49} My eye flows without ceasing, without any intermission, until the Lord looks down from heaven. {3:50} My eye affects my heart because of all the daughters of my city. {3:51} My enemies chased me without cause like a bird. {3:52} They cut off my life in the dungeon and cast a stone upon me. {3:53} Waters flowed over my head; I said, "I am cut off." {3:54} I called upon your name, O Lord, out of the low dungeon. {3:55} You heard my voice; do not hide your ear at my cry. {3:56} You came near on the day I called upon you; you said, "Fear not." {3:57} O Lord, you have pleaded the causes of my soul; you have redeemed my life. {3:58} O Lord, you have seen my wrong; judge my cause. {3:59} You have seen all their vengeance and imaginations against me. {3:60} You have heard their reproach, O Lord, and all their imaginations against me. {3:61} The lips of those who rose up against me and their plots against me all day. {3:62} See their sitting down and their rising up; I am their mockery. {3:63} Render unto them a recompense, O Lord, according to the work of their hands. {3:64} Give them sorrow of heart, your curse upon them. {3:65} Pursue and destroy them in anger from under the heavens of the Lord.

{4:1} How has the gold become dim! How has the finest gold changed! The stones of the sanctuary are scattered in the streets. {4:2} The precious sons of Zion, comparable to fine gold, how are they regarded as earthen pitchers, the work of a potter's hands! {4:3} Even the sea monsters draw out the breast, they nurse their young; but the daughter of my people has become cruel, like ostriches in the wilderness. {4:4} The tongue of the nursing child sticks to the roof of his mouth for thirst; the young children ask for bread, but no one gives [it] to them. {4:5} Those who once feasted delicately are desolate in the streets; those who were brought up in scarlet embrace ash heaps. {4:6} For the punishment of the iniquity of the daughter of my people is greater than the punishment of the sin of Sodom, which was overthrown in a moment, and no hands were laid on her. {4:7} **Her Nazarites were purer than snow, they were whiter than milk; they were more ruddy in body than rubies, their polishing was like sapphire.** {4:8} Now their appearance is blacker than soot; they are not recognized in the streets; their skin clings to their bones, it has become as dry as wood. {4:9} Those who were slain with the sword are better off than those who were slain with hunger; for these pine away, stricken for lack of the fruits of the field. {4:10} The hands of compassionate women have cooked their own children; they became food for them in the destruction of the daughter of my people. {4:11} The Lord has fulfilled his fury; he has poured out his fierce anger and kindled a fire in Zion, which has devoured its foundations. {4:12} The kings of the earth and all the inhabitants of the world would not have believed that the adversary and the enemy would enter the gates of Jerusalem. {4:13} Because of the sins of her prophets and the iniquities of her priests, who have shed the blood of the just in her midst, {4:14} They wandered like blind men in the streets, they were defiled with blood, so that no one could touch their garments. {4:15} They cried out to them, "Unclean! Depart! Depart! Do not touch!" So they fled and wandered; among the nations they said, "They shall no longer dwell [there.] {4:16} The anger of the Lord has separated them; he will regard them no more. They respected neither the persons of the priests nor showed favor to the elders. {4:17} As for us, our eyes failed, watching for vain help; in our watching we watched for a nation that could not save us. {4:18} They hunt our steps, so that we cannot walk in our streets; our end is near, our days are fulfilled; for our end has come. {4:19} Our persecutors are swifter than the eagles of the heavens; they pursued us on the mountains, they lay in wait for us in the wilderness. {4:20} The breath of our nostrils, the anointed of the Lord, was caught in their pits, of whom we said, "Under his shadow we shall live among the nations." {4:21} Rejoice and be glad, O daughter of Edom, who dwells in the land of Uz! The cup shall also pass over to you and you shall become drunk and make yourself naked. {4:22} The punishment of your iniquity is accomplished, O daughter of Zion; he will no longer carry you away into captivity. He will punish your iniquity, O daughter of Edom; he will uncover your sins.

{5:1} Remember, O LORD, what has happened to us; consider and see our disgrace. {5:2} Our inheritance has been turned over to strangers, our houses to foreigners. {5:3} We have become orphans, fatherless; our mothers are like widows. {5:4} We must buy our water to drink; our wood comes at a price. {5:5} Our pursuers are at our necks; we are weary, but there is no rest for us. {5:6} We have submitted to Egypt and Assyria to get enough bread. {5:7} Our fathers sinned and are no more, and we bear their punishment. {5:8} Slaves rule over us; there is no one to deliver us from their hands. {5:9} We risk our lives to get our bread because of the sword in the desert. {5:10} Our skin is hot as an oven, fevered with hunger. {5:11} Women are violated in Zion, virgins in the towns of Judah. {5:12} Princes are hung up by their hands; elders are shown no respect. {5:13} Young men must grind at the millstones; boys stagger under loads of wood. {5:14} The elders are gone from the city gate; the young men have stopped their music. {5:15} Joy is gone from our hearts; our dancing has turned to mourning. {5:16} The crown has fallen from our head; woe to us, for we have sinned! {5:17} Because of all this, our hearts are faint; our eyes grow dim {5:18} **Because Mount Zion lies desolate, with foxes prowling over it.** {5:19} But you, O LORD, reign forever; your throne endures from generation to generation. {5:20} Why do you always forget us? Why do you forsake us so long? {5:21} Restore us to yourself, O LORD, that we may return; renew our days as of old, {5:22} Unless you have utterly rejected us and are angry with us beyond measure.

Ezekiel

{1:1} It happened in the thirtieth year, in the fourth month, on the fifth day of the month, while I was among the captives by the river of Chebar, that the heavens were opened, and I saw visions of God. {1:2} On the fifth day of the month, which was the fifth year of King Jehoiachin's captivity, {1:3} the word of the LORD came expressly to Ezekiel the priest, the son of Buzi, in the land of the Chaldeans by the river Chebar; and the hand of the LORD was upon him there. {1:4} As I looked, behold, a whirlwind came out of the north, a great cloud, and a fire infolding itself, and a brightness was about it, and out of the midst of it came the color of amber, out of the midst of the fire. {1:5} **Out of the midst of it came the likeness of four living creatures. And this was their appearance: they had the likeness of a man.** {1:6} Each one had four faces, and each one had four wings. {1:7} Their feet were straight feet; the sole of their feet was like the sole of a calf's foot, and they sparkled like burnished brass. {1:8} Under their wings on their four sides they had human hands; and the four had their faces and their wings. {1:9} Their wings were joined one to another; they didn't turn when they went; each one went straight forward. {1:10} As for the likeness of their faces, they had the face of a man, and the face of a lion, on the right side; they four had the face of an ox on the left side; they four also had the face of an eagle. {1:11} Their faces and their wings were stretched upward; two wings of each one were joined one to another, and two covered their bodies. {1:12} Each one went straight forward: where the spirit was to go, they went; they didn't turn when they went. {1:13} The living creatures' appearance was like burning coals of fire, and like the appearance of torches. The fire went up and down among the living creatures; and the fire was bright, and out of the fire went forth lightning. {1:14} The living creatures ran and returned as the appearance of a flash of lightning. {1:15} Now as I beheld the living creatures, behold one wheel upon the earth by the living creatures, with his four faces. {1:16} The appearance of the wheels and their work was like the color of beryl; and they four had one likeness: and their appearance and their work was as it were a wheel within a wheel. {1:17} When they went, they went in their four directions: they didn't turn when they went. {1:18} Their rims were high and awesome; and the rims of all four were full of eyes all around. {1:19} When the living creatures went, the wheels went beside them; and when the living creatures were lifted up from the earth, the wheels were lifted up. {1:20} Wherever the spirit was to go, they went; the wheels were lifted up beside them: for the spirit of the living creature was in the wheels. {1:21} When those went, these went; and when those stood, these stood; and when those were lifted up from the earth, the wheels were lifted up beside them: for the spirit of the living creature was in the wheels. {1:22} Over the heads of the living creature there was the likeness of a firmament, like the awesome crystal to look at, stretched out over their heads above. {1:23} Under the firmament were their wings straight, the one toward the other: each one had two which covered on this side, and every one had two which covered on that side, their bodies. {1:24} When they went, I heard the noise of their wings like the noise of great waters, like the voice of the Almighty, a noise of tumult like the noise of an army: when they stood, they let down their wings. {1:25} There was a voice above the firmament that was over their heads when they stood and let down their wings. {1:26} Above the firmament that was over their heads was the likeness of a throne, as the appearance of a sapphire stone; and on the likeness of the throne was a likeness as the appearance of a man on it above. {1:27} I saw as it were glowing metal, as the appearance of fire within it all around, from the appearance of his waist and upward; and from the appearance of his waist and downward I saw as it were the appearance of fire, and there was brightness around him. {1:28} As the appearance of the rainbow that is in the cloud in the day of rain, so was the appearance of the brightness all around. This was the appearance of the likeness of the glory of the LORD. When I saw it, I fell on my face, and I heard a voice of one that spoke.

{2:1} And he said to me, "Son of man, stand on your feet, and I will speak to you." {2:2} And when he spoke to me, the spirit entered into me and set me on my feet, so that I could hear him. {2:3} And he said to me, "Son of man, I am sending you to the children of Israel, to a rebellious nation that has rebelled against me. They and their fathers have transgressed against me up to this very day. {2:4} They are impudent and stubborn children. I am sending you to them, and you shall say to them, 'Thus says the Lord GOD.' {2:5} Whether they listen or refuse to listen (for they are a rebellious house), they will know that a prophet has been among them. {2:6} And you, son of man, do not be afraid of them, nor be afraid of their words, though thorns and briers are with you and you dwell among scorpions. Do not be afraid of their words or dismayed by their looks, for they are a rebellious house. {2:7} You shall speak my words to them, whether they listen or refuse to listen, for they are most rebellious. {2:8} But you, son of man, hear what I say to you: Do not be rebellious like that rebellious house. Open your mouth and eat what I give you." {2:9} Then I looked, and a hand was stretched out to me; and behold, a scroll of a book was in it. {2:10} And he spread it before me; and it was written on the front and back, and there were written on it lamentations, mourning, and woe.

{3:1} Then he said to me, "Son of man, eat what you find; eat this scroll, and go speak to the house of Israel." {3:2} So I opened my mouth, and he made me eat that scroll. {3:3} And he said to me, "Son of man, feed your belly and fill your stomach with this scroll that I give you." So I ate it, and it was as sweet as honey in my mouth. {3:4} Then he said to me, "Son of man, go to the house of Israel and speak my words to them. {3:5} For you are not sent to a people of foreign speech and a hard language, but to the house of Israel, {3:6} not to many peoples of foreign speech and a hard language, whose words you cannot understand. Surely, if I sent you to them, they would listen to you. {3:7} But the house of Israel will not listen to you, because they will not listen to me, for all the house of Israel is impudent and hardhearted. {3:8} Behold, I have made your face strong against their faces, and your forehead strong against their foreheads. {3:9} Like adamant harder than flint have I made your forehead. Fear them not, nor be dismayed at their looks, for they are a rebellious house." {3:10} Moreover, he said to me, "Son of man, receive in your heart all my words that I speak to you, and hear with your ears. {3:11} And go to the exiles, to your people, and speak to them and say to them, 'Thus says the Lord GOD,' whether they hear or refuse to hear." {3:12} Then the Spirit lifted me up, and I heard behind me the voice of a great earthquake: "Blessed be the glory of the LORD from his place!" {3:13} [I heard] also the sound of the wings of the living creatures as they touched one another, and the sound of the wheels beside them, and the sound of a great earthquake. {3:14} So the Spirit lifted me up and took me away, and I went in bitterness, in the heat of my spirit, but the hand of the LORD was strong upon me. {3:15} Then I came to the exiles at Tel-abib, who were dwelling by the Chebar canal, and I sat where they were dwelling. And I sat there overwhelmed among them seven days. {3:16} And at the end of seven days, the word of the LORD came to me: {3:17} "Son of man, I have made you a watchman for the house of Israel. Whenever you hear a word from my mouth, you shall give them warning from me. {3:18} If I say to the wicked, 'You shall surely die,' and you give him no warning, nor speak to warn the wicked from his wicked way, in order to save his life, that wicked person shall die for his iniquity, but his blood I will require at your hand. {3:19} But if you warn the wicked, and he does not turn from his wickedness, or from his wicked way, he shall die for his iniquity, but you will have delivered your soul. {3:20} Again, if a righteous person turns from his righteousness and commits injustice, and I lay a stumbling block before him, he shall die. Because you have not warned him, he shall die for his sin, and his righteous deeds that he has done shall not be remembered, but his blood I will require at your hand. {3:21} But if you warn the righteous person not to sin, and he does not sin, he shall surely live, because he took warning, and you will have delivered your soul." {3:22} And the hand of the LORD was upon me there. And he said to me, "Arise, go out into the valley, and there I will speak with you." {3:23} So I arose and went out into the valley, and behold, the glory of the LORD stood there, like the glory that I had seen by the Chebar canal, and I fell on my face. {3:24} But the Spirit entered into me and set me on my feet, and he spoke with me and said to me, "Go, shut yourself within your house. {3:25} And you, son of man, behold, cords will be placed upon you, and you shall be bound with them, so that you cannot go out among the people. {3:26} And I will make your tongue cling to the roof of your mouth, so that you shall be mute and unable to reprove them, for they are a rebellious house. {3:27} But when I speak with you, I will open your mouth, and you shall say to them, 'Thus says the Lord GOD.' He who will hear, let him hear; and he who will refuse to hear, let him refuse, for they are a rebellious house."

{4:1} "You also, son of man, take a clay tablet and lay it before you, and portray on it a city, Jerusalem. {4:2} Lay siege against it, build a siege wall against it, and heap up a mound against it; set camps against it also, and place battering rams against it all around. {4:3} Moreover take for yourself an iron plate, and set it as an iron wall between you and the city. Set your face against it, and it shall be besieged, and you shall lay siege against it. This shall be a sign to the house of Israel. {4:4} "Lie also on your left side, and lay the iniquity of the house of Israel upon it. According to the number of the days that you lie on it, you shall bear their iniquity. {4:5} For I have laid on you the years of their iniquity, according to the number of the days, three hundred and ninety days; so you shall bear the iniquity of the house of Israel. {4:6} And when you have completed them, lie again on your right side; then you shall bear the iniquity of the house of Judah forty days. I have laid on you a day for each year. {4:7} "Therefore you shall set your face toward the siege of Jerusalem; your arm shall be uncovered, and you shall prophesy against it. {4:8} And surely I will restrain you so that you cannot turn from one side to another till you have ended the days of your siege. {4:9} "Also take for yourself wheat, barley, beans, lentils, millet, and spelt; put them into one vessel, and make bread of them for yourself. During the number of days that you lie on your side, three hundred and ninety days, you shall eat it. {4:10} And your food which you eat shall be by weight, twenty shekels a day; from time to time you shall eat it. {4:11} You shall also drink water by measure, one-sixth of a hin; from time to time you shall drink. {4:12} And you shall eat it as barley cakes; and bake it using fuel of human waste in their sight." {4:13} Then the LORD said, "So shall the children of Israel eat their defiled bread among the Gentiles, where I will drive them." {4:14} So I said, "Ah, Lord GOD! Indeed I have never defiled myself from my youth till now; I have never eaten what died of itself or was torn by beasts, nor has abominable flesh ever come into my mouth." {4:15} Then He said to me, "See, I am giving you cow dung instead of human waste, and you shall prepare your bread over it." {4:16} Moreover He said to me, "Son of man, surely I will cut off the supply of bread in Jerusalem; they shall eat bread by weight and with anxiety, and shall drink water by measure and with dread, {4:17} so that they may lack bread and water, and be dismayed with one another, and waste away because of their iniquity.

{5:1} "And you, son of man, take a sharp knife, take a barber's razor, and pass it over your head and your beard; then take scales to weigh and divide the hair. {5:2} You shall burn with fire a third part in the midst of the city when the days of the siege are fulfilled; then you shall take a third part and strike it with a knife all around the city; and a third part you shall scatter to the wind, and I will unsheathe a sword after them. {5:3} You shall also take a few of them and bind them in your skirts. {5:4} Then take some of them again and throw them into the midst of the fire, and burn them in the fire; from it a fire will come forth into all the house of Israel. {5:5} Thus says the Lord GOD: 'This is Jerusalem; I have set it in the midst of the nations and countries that surround her. {5:6} And she has changed My judgments into wickedness more than the nations, and My statutes more than the countries that surround her; for they have refused My judgments and My statutes, they have not walked in them. {5:7} Therefore thus says the Lord GOD: 'Because you have multiplied more than the nations that surround you, and have not walked in My statutes, nor kept My judgments, nor done according to the judgments of the nations that surround you— {5:8} therefore thus says the Lord GOD: 'Behold, I, even I, am against you and will execute judgments in your midst in the sight of the nations. {5:9} And I will do in you what I have not done, and the like of which I will not do any more, because of all your abominations. {5:10} Therefore the fathers shall eat their sons in your midst, and the sons shall eat their fathers; and I will execute judgments among you, and all the remnant of you I will scatter to all the winds. {5:11} Therefore, as I live,' says the Lord GOD, 'surely, because you have defiled My sanctuary with all your detestable things and with all your abominations, therefore I will also diminish you; My eye will not spare, nor will I have any pity. {5:12} A third part of you shall die of pestilence and be consumed with famine in your midst; a third part shall fall by the sword all around you; and I will scatter another third to all the winds, and I will unsheathe a sword after them. {5:13} Thus shall My anger be accomplished, and I will cause My fury to rest upon them, and I will be comforted. They shall know that I, the LORD, have spoken it in My zeal when I have accomplished My fury upon them. {5:14} Moreover I will make you a desolation and a reproach among the nations that surround you, in the sight of all who pass by. {5:15} So it shall be a reproach, a taunt, an instruction, and an astonishment to the nations that surround you when I execute judgments against you in anger and fury and furious rebukes. I, the LORD, have spoken it. {5:16} When I send against them the evil arrows of famine which shall be for their destruction, and which I will send to destroy you, I will increase the famine upon you and cut off your supply of bread. {5:17} So I will send upon you famine and evil beasts, and they shall bereave you; pestilence and blood shall pass through you, and I will bring the sword against you. I, the LORD, have spoken it.'"

{6:1} The word of the LORD came to me, saying, {6:2} "Son of man, set your face toward the mountains of Israel and prophesy against them. {6:3} Say to the mountains, hills, rivers, and valleys, 'Thus says the Lord GOD: Behold, I, even I, will bring a sword upon you, and I will destroy your high places. {6:4} Your altars shall be desolate, and your images shall be broken; I will cast down your slain men before your idols. {6:5} I will lay the dead bodies of the children of Israel before their idols, and I will scatter your bones around your altars. {6:6} In all your dwellings, the cities shall be laid waste, and the high places shall be desolate, so that your altars may be laid waste, your idols broken, your images cut down, and your works abolished. {6:7} The slain shall fall in your midst, and you shall know that I am the LORD. {6:8} Yet I will leave a remnant, so that you may have some who shall escape the sword among the nations when you are scattered through the countries. {6:9} Then those who escape of you shall remember me among the nations where they are carried captive, because I am broken by their whorish heart which has departed from me, and by their eyes which go after their idols; and they shall loathe themselves for the evils which they have committed in all their abominations. {6:10} And they shall know that I am the LORD, and that I have not said in vain that I would do this evil to them. {6:11} Thus says the Lord GOD: 'Strike with your hand and stamp with your foot, and say, "Alas for all the evil abominations of the house of Israel! For they shall fall by the sword, by famine, and by pestilence. {6:12} He who is far off shall die of the pestilence, and he who is near shall fall by the sword; and he who remains and is besieged shall die by famine. Thus will I accomplish my fury upon them. {6:13} Then you shall know that I am the LORD, when their slain men shall be among their idols all around their altars, on every high hill, in all the tops of the mountains, and under every green tree, and under every thick oak, the places where they offered sweet incense to all their idols. {6:14} So I will stretch out my hand upon them and make the land desolate, more desolate than the wilderness toward Diblath, in all their habitations. And they shall know that I am the LORD.'"

{7:1} The word of the LORD came to me, saying, {7:2} "And you, son of man, thus says the Lord GOD to the land of Israel: An end, the end has come upon the four corners of the land. {7:3} Now the end has come upon you, and I will send my anger upon you and judge you according to your ways, and I will repay upon you all your abominations. {7:4} My eye shall not spare you, nor will I have pity; I will repay your ways upon you, and your abominations shall be in your midst, and you shall know that I am the LORD. {7:5} Thus says the Lord GOD: An evil, an only evil, behold, has come. {7:6} The end has come, the end has come; it watches for you; behold, it has come. {7:7} The morning has come to you, O you who dwell in the land; the time has come, the day of trouble is near, and not the joyful shouting on the mountains. {7:8} Now I will shortly pour out my fury upon you and fulfill my anger upon you, and I will judge you according to your ways, and I will repay you for all your abominations. {7:9} My eye shall not spare, nor will I have pity; I will repay you according to your ways and your abominations that are in your midst, and you shall know that I am the LORD who strikes. {7:10} Behold the day, behold, it has come; the morning has gone forth; the rod has blossomed, pride has budded. {7:11} Violence has risen up into a rod of wickedness; none of them shall remain, neither of their multitude, nor of any of theirs; nor shall there be mourning for them. {7:12} The time has come, the day draws near; let not the buyer rejoice, nor the seller mourn; for wrath is upon all the multitude. {7:13} For the seller shall not return to that which is sold, although they were yet alive; for the vision concerns the whole multitude, which shall not return, nor shall any strengthen himself in the iniquity of his life. {7:14} They have blown the trumpet to make all ready, but none goes to the battle, for my wrath is upon all the multitude. {7:15} The sword is outside, and the pestilence and the famine within; he who is in the field shall die by the sword, and he who is in the city, famine and pestilence shall devour him. {7:16} But those who escape of them shall escape and be on the mountains like doves of the valleys, all of them mourning, each one for his iniquity. {7:17} All hands shall be feeble, and all knees shall be weak as water. {7:18} They shall also gird themselves with sackcloth, and horror shall cover them; and shame shall be upon all faces, and baldness upon all their heads. {7:19} They shall cast their silver in the streets, and their gold shall be removed; their silver and their gold shall not be able to deliver them in the day of the wrath of the LORD; they shall not satisfy their souls, nor fill their stomachs, because it is the stumbling block of their iniquity. {7:20} As for the beauty of his ornament, he set it in majesty, but they made the images of their abominations and detestable things therein; therefore I have set it far from them. {7:21} And I will give it into the hands of strangers for plunder, and to the wicked of the earth for spoil; and they shall pollute it. {7:22} My face will I turn also from them, and they shall pollute my secret place; for robbers shall enter into it and defile it. {7:23} Make a chain, for the land is full of bloody crimes, and the city is full of violence. {7:24} Therefore I will bring the worst of the heathen, and they shall possess their houses; I will also make the pomp of the strong to cease, and their holy places shall be defiled. {7:25} Destruction comes, and they shall seek peace, but there shall be none. {7:26} Mischief shall come upon mischief, and rumor shall be upon rumor; then shall they seek a vision of the prophet, but the law shall perish from the priest, and counsel from the elders. {7:27} The king shall mourn, and the prince shall be clothed with desolation, and the hands of the people of the land shall be troubled; I will deal with them according to their way, and according to their deserts will I judge them, and they shall know that I am the LORD."

{8:1} In the sixth year, in the sixth month, on the fifth day of the month, as I sat in my house, and the elders of Judah sat before me, the hand of the Lord GOD fell upon me. {8:2} And I looked, and behold, a likeness as the appearance of fire, from the appearance of his waist downward, fire; and from his waist upward, like the appearance of brightness, like the color of amber. {8:3} He stretched out the form of a hand and took me by a lock of my head; and the Spirit lifted me up between earth and heaven and brought me in visions of God to Jerusalem, to the door of the inner gate that faces north, where was the seat of the image of jealousy, which provokes to jealousy. {8:4} And behold, the glory of the God of Israel was there, according to the vision that I saw in the plain. {8:5} Then he said to me, "Son of man, lift up your eyes now toward the north." So I lifted up my eyes toward the north, and behold, north of the gate of the altar this image of jealousy was in the entrance. {8:6} Furthermore he said to me, "Son of man, do you see what they are doing, the great abominations that the house of Israel commits here, to make me go far away from my sanctuary? Now turn again, and you will see greater abominations." {8:7} So he brought me to the door of the court; and when I looked, there was a hole in the wall. {8:8} Then he said to me, "Son of man, dig now in the wall." And when I dug in the wall, there was a door. {8:9} And he said to me, "Go in, and see the wicked abominations that they are doing here." {8:10} So I went in and saw, and there, portrayed all around on the wall, were every form of creeping things, and abominable beasts, and all the idols of the house of Israel. {8:11} And there stood before them seventy men of the elders of the house of Israel, and in their midst stood Jaazaniah the son of Shaphan, with each man his censer in his hand; and a thick cloud of incense went up. {8:12} Then he said to me, "Son of man, have you seen what the elders of the house of Israel do in the dark, every man in the room of his idols? For they say, 'The LORD does not see us, the LORD has forsaken the land.'" {8:13} He also said to me, "Turn again, and you will see greater abominations that they are doing." {8:14} So he brought me to the door of the gate of the LORD's house which was toward the north, and there sat women weeping for Tammuz. {8:15} Then he said to me, "Have you seen this, O son of man? Turn again, and you will see greater abominations than these." {8:16} So he brought me into the inner court of the LORD's house, and there, at the door of the temple of the LORD, between the porch and the altar, were about twenty-five men with their backs toward the temple of the LORD and their faces toward the east, and they were worshiping the sun toward the east. {8:17} Then he said to me, "Have you seen this, O son of man? Is it a trivial thing to the house of Judah to commit the abominations which they commit here? For they have filled the land with violence; then they return to provoke me to anger; and behold, they put the branch to their nose. {8:18} Therefore I also will act in fury. My eye will not spare, nor will I have pity; even though they cry in my ears with a loud voice, I will not hear them."

{9:1} He also cried loudly in my ears, saying, "Bring near those who have charge over the city, every man with his destroying weapon in his hand." {9:2} And behold, six men came from the direction of the upper gate, which faces north, each with his weapon for slaughter in his hand, and among them was one man clothed in linen, with a writer's inkhorn at his side. And they went in and stood beside the bronze altar. {9:3} Now the glory of the God of Israel had gone up from the cherub, where it had been, to the threshold of the temple. And he called to the man clothed in linen, who had the writer's inkhorn at his side. {9:4} And the LORD said to him, "Go through the midst of the city, through the midst of Jerusalem, and put a mark on the foreheads of the men who sigh and cry over all the abominations that are done within it." {9:5} To the others he said in my hearing, "Go after him through the city and kill; do not let your eye spare, nor have any pity. {9:6} Utterly slay old and young men, maidens, little children, and women; but do not come near anyone on whom is the mark; and begin at my sanctuary." So they began with the elders who were before the temple. {9:7} Then he said to them, "Defile the temple, and fill the courts with the slain. Go out!" And they went out and killed in the city. {9:8} So it was, that while they were killing them, I was left alone; and I fell on my face and cried out, and said, "Ah, Lord GOD! Will You destroy all the remnant of Israel in pouring out Your fury on Jerusalem?" {9:9} Then he said to me, "The iniquity of the house of Israel and Judah is exceedingly great, and the land is full of bloodshed, and the city full of perversity. For they say, 'The LORD has forsaken the land, and the LORD does not see.' {9:10} And as for me also, my eye will neither spare, nor will I have pity, but I will recompense their deeds on their own head." {9:11} Just then, the man clothed in linen, who had the inkhorn at his side, reported back, saying, "I have done as you commanded me."

{10:1} Then I looked, and behold, above the cherubim that were over the heads, there appeared above them something like a sapphire stone, resembling the appearance of a throne. {10:2} And he spoke to the man clothed in linen and said, "Go in among the wheels, under the cherub, and fill your hands with coals of fire from among the cherubim, and scatter them over the city." And he went in my sight. {10:3} Now the cherubim were standing on the south side of the temple when the man went in, and the cloud filled the inner court. {10:4} Then the glory of the LORD went up from the cherub to the threshold of the temple, and the temple was filled with the cloud, and the court was filled with the brightness of the LORD's glory. {10:5} And the sound of the wings of the cherubim was heard as far as the outer court, like the voice of God Almighty when he speaks. {10:6} And when he commanded the man clothed in linen, "Take fire from between the wheels, from among the cherubim," he went in and stood beside a wheel. {10:7} And a cherub stretched out his hand from among the cherubim to the fire that was among the cherubim and took some of it and put it into the hands of the man clothed in linen, who took it and went out. {10:8} And there appeared in the cherubim the form of a human hand under their wings. {10:9} And I looked, and behold, there were four wheels beside the cherubim, one beside each cherub, and the appearance of the wheels was like the gleaming of beryl. {10:10} And their appearance and construction was as it were a wheel within a wheel. {10:11} When they went, they went in any of their four directions without turning as they went, but in whatever direction the front wheel faced, the others followed without turning as they went. {10:12} And their entire body, their backs, their hands, their wings, and the wheels were full of eyes all around, even the wheels that the four of them had. {10:13} As for the wheels, they were called in my hearing "the whirling wheels." {10:14} And every one had four faces: the first face was the face of a cherub, the second face was the face of a man, the third the face of a lion, and the fourth the face of an eagle. {10:15} And the cherubim lifted up their wings and mounted up from the earth before my eyes as they went out, with the wheels beside them. And they stood at the entrance of the east gate of the house of the LORD, and the glory of the God of Israel was over them. {10:16} These were the living creatures that I saw underneath the God of Israel by the Chebar canal, and I knew that they were cherubim. {10:17} Each had four faces and each had four wings, and underneath their wings, the likeness of human hands. {10:18} And the glory of the LORD went out from the threshold of the house and stood over the cherubim. {10:19} And the cherubim lifted up their wings and mounted up from the earth before my eyes as they went out, with the wheels beside them. And they stood at the entrance of the east gate of the house of the LORD, and the glory of the God of Israel was over them. {10:20} These were the living creatures that I saw underneath the God of Israel by the Chebar canal, and I knew that they were cherubim. {10:21} Each had four faces and each had four wings, and underneath their wings, the likeness of human hands. {10:22} And the likeness of their faces was the same faces that I had seen by the Chebar canal, their appearance and themselves. They went each straight forward.

{11:1} Then the spirit lifted me up and brought me to the east gate of the LORD's house, which faces eastward. And behold, at the entrance of the gate were twenty-five men, among whom I saw Jaazaniah the son of Azur, and Pelatiah the son of Benaiah, princes of the people. {11:2} Then he said to me, "Son of man, these are the men who devise mischief and give wicked counsel in this city, {11:3} who say, 'The time is not near to build houses. This city is the cauldron, and we are the meat.' {11:4} Therefore prophesy against them; prophesy, O son of man." {11:5} And the Spirit of the LORD fell upon me, and he said to me, "Speak. Thus says the LORD: So you have said, O house of Israel, for I know the things that come into your mind, every one of them. {11:6} You have multiplied your slain in this city and have filled its streets with the slain. {11:7} Therefore thus says the Lord GOD: Your slain whom you have laid in the midst of it, they are the meat, and this city is the cauldron, but I will bring you out of the midst of it. {11:8} You have feared the sword, and I will bring the sword upon you, declares the Lord GOD. {11:9} And I will bring you out of the midst of it and give you into the hands of foreigners, and execute judgments upon you. {11:10} You shall fall by the sword. I will judge you at the border of Israel, and you shall know that I am the LORD. {11:11} This city shall not be your cauldron, nor shall you be the meat in the midst of it. I will judge you at the border of Israel. {11:12} And you shall know that I am the LORD. For you have not walked in my statutes nor obeyed my rules, but have acted according to the rules of the nations that are around you." {11:13} And it came to pass, when I prophesied, that Pelatiah the son of Benaiah died. Then I fell upon my face and cried out with a loud voice and said, "Ah, Lord GOD! Will you make a full end of the remnant of Israel?" {11:14} Again the word of the LORD came to me, saying, {11:15} "Son of man, your brothers, even your brothers, your kinsmen, the whole house of Israel, all of them, are those of whom the inhabitants of Jerusalem have said, 'Go far from the LORD; to us this land is given for a possession.' {11:16} Therefore say, 'Thus says the Lord GOD: Though I removed them far off among the nations, and though I scattered them among the countries, yet I have been a sanctuary to them for a while in the countries where they have gone.' {11:17} Therefore say, 'Thus says the Lord GOD: I will gather you from the peoples and assemble you out of the countries where you have been scattered, and I will give you the land of Israel.' {11:18} And when they come there, they will remove from it all its detestable things and all its abominations. {11:19} And I will give them one heart, and a new spirit I will put within them. I will remove the heart of stone from their flesh and give them a heart of flesh, {11:20} that they may walk in my statutes and keep my rules and obey them. And they shall be my people, and I will be their God. {11:21} **But as for those whose heart goes after their detestable things and their abominations, I will bring their deeds upon their own heads, declares the Lord GOD."** {11:22} Then the cherubim lifted up their wings, with the wheels beside them, and the glory of the God of Israel was over them above. {11:23} And the glory of the LORD went up from the midst of the city and stood on the mountain that is on the east side of the city. {11:24} **And the Spirit took me up and brought me in the vision by the Spirit of God into Chaldea, to the exiles. Then the vision that I had seen went up from me.** {11:25} And I told the exiles all the things that the LORD had shown me.

{12:1} The word of the LORD also came to me, saying, {12:2} "Son of man, you dwell in the midst of a rebellious house, who have eyes to see but do not see, who have ears to hear but do not hear, for they are a rebellious house. {12:3} Therefore, son of man, prepare your belongings for moving, and move by day in their sight; you shall move from your place to another place in their sight. Perhaps they will consider, though they are a rebellious house. {12:4} Then you shall bring forth your belongings by day in their sight, as belongings for moving, and you shall go out in the evening in their sight, as those who go out into captivity. {12:5} Dig through the wall in their sight and carry your belongings out through it. {12:6} In their sight, you shall bear it on your shoulders and carry it out in the twilight; you shall cover your face so that you do not see the ground, for I have set you as a sign to the house of Israel." {12:7} "And I did as I was commanded. I brought out my belongings by day as if preparing for captivity, and in the evening, I dug through the wall with my hand; I brought it out in the twilight, and I carried it on my shoulder in their sight. {12:8} And in the morning, the word of the LORD came to me, saying, {12:9} "Son of man, has not the rebellious house of Israel, said to you, 'What are you doing?' {12:10} Say to them, 'Thus says the Lord GOD: This oracle concerns the prince in Jerusalem and all the house of Israel who are in it.' {12:11} Say, 'I am your sign: as I have done, so shall it be done to them; they shall go into exile.' {12:12} "And the prince among them shall bear his belongings on his shoulder in the twilight and shall go out. They shall dig through the wall to bring him out through it; he shall cover his face, so that he cannot see the land with his eyes. {12:13} My net also I will spread over him, and he shall be taken in my snare. And I will bring him to Babylon, the land of the Chaldeans, yet he shall not see it, and he shall die there. {12:14} And I will scatter toward every wind all who are around him, his helpers and all his troops, and I will unsheathe the sword after them. {12:15} And they shall know that I am the LORD, when I disperse them among the nations and scatter them among the countries. {12:16} But I will let a few of them escape from the sword, from famine and pestilence, that they may declare all their abominations among the nations where they go, and may know that I am the LORD." {12:17} "Moreover, the word of the LORD came to me, saying, {12:18} "Son of man, eat your bread with quaking, and drink your water with trembling and with anxiety. {12:19} And say to the people of the land, 'Thus says the Lord GOD concerning the inhabitants of Jerusalem and the land of Israel: They shall eat their bread in anxiety and drink water in dismay, for her land will be desolate from all that is in it because of the violence of all those who dwell in it. {12:20} And the inhabited cities shall be laid waste, and the land shall become desolate, and you shall know that I am the LORD.'" {12:21} "And the word of the LORD came to me, saying, {12:22} "Son of man, what is this proverb that you have about the land of Israel, saying, 'The days grow long, and every vision comes to nothing'? {12:23} Tell them therefore, 'Thus says the Lord GOD: I will put an end to this proverb, and they shall no more use it as a proverb in Israel.' But say to them, 'The days are near, and the fulfillment of every vision.' {12:24} For there shall be no more any false vision or flattering divination within the house of Israel. {12:25} For I am the LORD; I will speak the word that I will speak, and it will be performed. It will no longer be delayed, but in your days, O rebellious house, I will speak the word and perform it, declares the Lord GOD." {12:26} "Again the word of the LORD came to me, saying, {12:27} "Son of man, behold, those of the house of Israel who say, 'The vision that he sees is for many days from now, and he prophesies of times far off.' {12:28} Therefore say to them, 'Thus says the Lord GOD: None of my words will be delayed any longer, but the word that I speak will be fulfilled, declares the Lord GOD.'"

{13:1} And the word of the LORD came to me, saying, {13:2} "Son of man, prophesy against the prophets of Israel who prophesy, and say to them who prophesy out of their own hearts, 'Hear the word of the LORD.' {13:3} Thus says the Lord GOD: Woe to the foolish prophets who follow their own spirit and have seen nothing! {13:4} O Israel, your prophets are like foxes in the deserts. {13:5} You have not gone up into the gaps, nor made up the hedge for the house of Israel to stand in the battle on the day of the LORD. {13:6} They have seen vanity and lying divination, saying, 'The LORD says,' but the LORD has not sent them, yet they have made others hope that they would confirm the word. {13:7} Have you not seen a vain vision and spoken a lying divination, whereas you say, 'The LORD says,' although I have not spoken? {13:8} Therefore thus says the Lord GOD: Because you have spoken vanity and seen lies, behold, I am against you, says the Lord GOD. {13:9} And my hand shall be against the prophets who see vanity and divine lies. They shall not be in the assembly of my people, nor shall they be written in the writing of the house of Israel, nor shall they enter into the land of Israel. And you shall know that I am the Lord GOD. {13:10} Because, even because they have misled my people, saying, 'Peace,' when there was no peace, and one built up a wall, and behold, others daubed it with untempered mortar, {13:11} Say to those who daub it with untempered mortar that it shall fall. There shall be an overflowing shower, and you, O great hailstones, shall fall, and a stormy wind shall tear it down. {13:12} And when the wall falls, will it not be said to you, 'Where is the daubing with which you have daubed it?' {13:13} Therefore thus says the Lord GOD: I will even tear it down with a stormy wind in my fury. There shall be an overflowing shower in my anger, and great hailstones in my fury to consume it. {13:14} So I will break down the wall that you have daubed with untempered mortar and bring it down to the ground, so that its foundation shall be exposed, and it shall fall, and you shall be consumed in its midst. And you shall know that I am the LORD. {13:15} Thus will I accomplish my wrath upon the wall and upon those who have daubed it with untempered mortar, and I will say to you, 'The wall is no more, nor those who daubed it.' {13:16} [To wit,] the prophets of Israel who prophesy concerning Jerusalem and see visions of peace for her, when there is no peace, says the Lord GOD. {13:17} Likewise, son of man, set your face against the daughters of your people, who prophesy out of their own heart, and prophesy against them. {13:18} And say, 'Thus says the Lord GOD: Woe to the women who sew pillows to all armholes and make kerchiefs upon the head of every stature to hunt souls! Will you hunt the souls of my people, and will you save the souls alive that come to you? {13:19} And will you pollute my people among my people for handfuls of barley and for pieces of bread, to slay the souls that should not die, and to save the souls alive that should not live, by your lying to my people who listen to your lies? {13:20} Therefore thus says the Lord GOD: Behold, I am against your pillows, with which you there hunt the souls to make them fly, and I will tear them from your arms, and I will let the souls go, even the souls that you hunt to make them fly. {13:21} Also, I will tear your kerchiefs and deliver my people out of your hand, and they shall be no more in your hand to be hunted. And you shall know that I am the LORD. {13:22} Because with lies you have made the heart of the righteous sad, whom I have not made sad, and have strengthened the hands of the wicked, that he should not return from his wicked way, by promising him life. {13:23} Therefore you shall see no more vanity, nor divine divinations, for I will deliver my people out of your hand, and you shall know that I am the LORD.

{14:1} Then certain of the elders of Israel came to me and sat before me. {14:2} And the word of the LORD came to me, saying, {14:3} "Son of man, these men have set up their idols in their hearts and put the stumbling block of their iniquity before their face. Should I be inquired of at all by them? {14:4} Therefore speak to them and say to them, 'Thus says the Lord GOD: Every man of the house of Israel who sets up his idols in his heart and puts the stumbling block of his iniquity before his face, and comes to the prophet, I the LORD will answer him according to the multitude of his idols, {14:5} that I may take the house of Israel in their own heart, because they are all estranged from me through their idols. {14:6} Therefore say to the house of Israel, 'Thus says the Lord GOD: Repent, and turn yourselves from your idols, and turn away your faces from all your abominations. {14:7} For every one of the house of Israel or of the stranger who sojourns in Israel, who separates himself from me, and sets up his idols in his heart, and puts the stumbling block of his iniquity before his face, and comes to a prophet to inquire of him concerning me, I the LORD will answer him by myself. {14:8} And I will set my face against that man and will make him a sign and a proverb, and I will cut him off from the midst of my people, and you shall know that I am the LORD. {14:9} And if the prophet is deceived when he has spoken a thing, I the LORD have deceived that prophet, and I will stretch out my hand upon him and will destroy him from the midst of my people Israel. {14:10} And they shall bear the punishment of their iniquity: the punishment of the prophet shall be even as the punishment of him who seeks [to him]. {14:11} That the house of Israel may no more go astray from me, neither be polluted anymore with all their transgressions, but that they may be my people, and I may be their God, says the Lord GOD. {14:12} The word of the LORD came again to me, saying, {14:13} "Son of man, when the land sins against me by trespassing grievously, then will I stretch out my hand upon it and will break the staff of its bread, and will send famine upon it and will cut off man and beast from it. {14:14} Though these three men, Noah, Daniel, and Job, were in it, they should deliver [but] their own souls by their righteousness, says the Lord GOD. {14:15} If I cause noisome beasts to pass through the land, and they spoil it, so that it be desolate, that no man may pass through because of the beasts: {14:16} Though these three men [were] in it, [as] I live, says the Lord GOD, they shall deliver neither sons nor daughters; they only shall be delivered, but the land shall be desolate. {14:17} Or if I bring a sword upon that land and say, 'Sword, go through the land,' so that I cut off man and beast from it: {14:18} Though these three men [were] in it, [as] I live, says the Lord GOD, they shall deliver neither sons nor daughters, but they only shall be delivered themselves. {14:19} Or if I send a pestilence into that land and pour out my fury upon it in blood, to cut off from it man and beast: {14:20} Though Noah, Daniel, and Job, [were] in it, [as] I live, says the Lord GOD, they shall deliver neither son nor daughter; they shall [but] deliver their own souls by their righteousness. {14:21} For thus says the Lord GOD: How much more when I send my four sore judgments upon Jerusalem, the sword, and the famine, and the noisome beast, and the pestilence, to cut off from it man and beast? {14:22} Yet, behold, therein shall be left a remnant that shall be brought forth, [both] sons and daughters: behold, they shall come forth unto you, and you shall see their way and their doings: and you shall be comforted concerning the evil that I have brought upon Jerusalem, [even] concerning all that I have brought upon it. {14:23} And they shall comfort you when you see their ways and their doings: and you shall know that I have not done without cause all that I have done in it, says the Lord GOD.

{15:1} And the word of the LORD came to me, saying, {15:2} "Son of man, What is the vine tree more than any tree, [or than] a branch which is among the trees of the forest? {15:3} Shall wood be taken thereof to do any work? or will [men] take a pin of it to hang any vessel thereon? {15:4} Behold, it is cast into the fire for fuel; the fire devours both the ends of it, and the midst of it is burned. Is it fit for [any] work? {15:5} Behold, when it was whole, it was fit for no work: how much less shall it be fit yet for [any] work, when the fire has devoured it, and it is burned? {15:6} Therefore thus says the Lord GOD; As the vine tree among the trees of the forest, which I have given to the fire for fuel, so will I give the inhabitants of Jerusalem. {15:7} *And I will set my face against them; they shall go out from [one] fire, and [another] fire shall devour them; and you shall know that I [am] the LORD, when I set my face against them.* {15:8} And I will make the land desolate, because they have committed a trespass, says the Lord GOD.

{16:1} Again the word of the LORD came to me, saying, {16:2} "Son of man, cause Jerusalem to know her abominations, {16:3} And say, Thus says the Lord GOD to Jerusalem; Your birth and your nativity [is] of the land of Canaan; your father [was] an Amorite, and your mother a Hittite. {16:4} And [as for] your nativity, on the day you were born your navel was not cut, neither were you washed in water to supple [you;] you were not salted at all, nor swaddled at all. {16:5} No eye pitied you, to do any of these to you, to have compassion upon you; but you were cast out in the open field, to the loathing of your person, on the day that you were born. {16:6} And when I passed by you, and saw you polluted in your own blood, I said to you [when you were] in your blood, Live; yes, I said to you [when you were] in your blood, Live. {16:7} I have caused you to multiply as the bud of the field, and you have increased and grown great, and you are come to excellent ornaments: your breasts are fashioned, and your hair is grown, whereas you [were] naked and bare. {16:8} Now when I passed by you, and looked upon you, behold, your time [was] the time of love; and I spread my skirt over you, and covered your nakedness: yes, I swore to you, and entered into a covenant with you, says the Lord GOD, and you became mine. {16:9} Then washed I you with water; yes, I thoroughly washed away your blood from you, and I anointed you with oil. {16:10} I clothed you also with broidered work, and shod you with badgers' skin, and I girded you about with fine linen, and I covered you with silk. {16:11} I decked you also with ornaments, and I put bracelets upon your hands, and a chain on your neck. {16:12} And I put a jewel on your forehead, and earrings in your ears, and a beautiful crown upon your head. {16:13} Thus were you decked with gold and silver; and your raiment [was of] fine linen, and silk, and broidered work; you did eat fine flour, and honey, and oil: and you were exceedingly beautiful, and you did prosper into a kingdom. {16:14} And your renown went forth among the heathen for your beauty: for it [was] perfect through my comeliness, which I had put upon you, says the Lord GOD. {16:15} But you trusted in your own beauty, and played the harlot because of your renown, and poured out your fornications on every one that passed by; it was theirs. {16:16} And of your garments you did take, and decked your high places with diverse colors, and played the harlot thereupon: [the like things] shall not come, neither shall it be so. {16:17} You have also taken your fair jewels of my gold and of my silver, which I had given you, and made to yourself images of men, and did commit whoredom with them, {16:18} And took your broidered garments, and covered them: and you have set my oil and my incense before them. {16:19} My meat also which I gave you, fine flour, and oil, and honey, [wherewith] I fed you, you have even set it before them for a sweet savor: and [thus] it was, says the Lord GOD. {16:20} Moreover you have taken your sons and your daughters, whom you have borne to me, and these have you sacrificed to them to be devoured. [Is this] of your whoredoms a small matter, {16:21} That you have slain my children, and delivered them to cause them to pass through [the fire] for them? {16:22} And in all your abominations and your whoredoms you have not remembered the days of your youth, when you were naked and bare, [and] were polluted in your blood. {16:23} And it came to pass after all your wickedness, (woe, woe to you! says the Lord GOD;) {16:24} [That] you have also built to you an eminent place, and have made you a high place in every street. {16:25} You have built your high place at every head of the way, and have made your beauty to be abhorred, and have opened your feet to every one that passed by, and multiplied your whoredoms. {16:26} You have also committed fornication with the Egyptians your neighbors, great of flesh; and have increased your whoredoms, to provoke me to anger. {16:27} Behold, therefore I have stretched out my hand over you, and have diminished your ordinary [food,] and delivered you to the will of them that hate you, the daughters of the Philistines, which are ashamed of your lewd way. {16:28} You have played the whore also with the Assyrians, because you were unsatiable; yes, you have played the harlot with them, and yet could not be satisfied. {16:29} You have moreover multiplied your fornication in the land of Canaan to Chaldea; and yet you were not satisfied herewith. {16:30} How weak is your heart, says the Lord GOD, seeing you do all these [things,] the work of an imperious whorish woman; {16:31} In that you build your

✝ he Old Testament ✝ 262

eminent place in the head of every way, and make your high place in every street; and have not been as a harlot, in that you scorn hire; {16:32} [But as] a wife that commits adultery, [which] takes strangers instead of her husband! {16:33} They give gifts to all whores: but you give your gifts to all your lovers, and hire them, that they may come to you on every side for your whoredom. {16:34} And the contrary is in you from [other] women in your whoredoms, whereas none follows you to commit whoredoms: and in that you give a reward, and no reward is given to you, therefore you are contrary. {16:35} Wherefore, O harlot, hear the word of the LORD: {16:36} **Thus says the Lord GOD; Because your filthiness was poured out, and your nakedness discovered through your whoredoms with your lovers, and with all the idols of your abominations, and by the blood of your children, which you did give to them;** {16:37} Behold, therefore I will gather all your lovers, with whom you have taken pleasure, and all [them] that you have loved, with all [them] that you have hated; I will even gather them round about against you, and will discover your nakedness to them, that they may see all your nakedness. {16:38} And I will judge you, as women that break wedlock and shed blood are judged; and I will give you blood in fury and jealousy. {16:39} And I will also give you into their hand, and they shall throw down your eminent place, and shall break down your high places: they shall strip you also of your clothes, and shall take your fair jewels, and leave you naked and bare. {16:40} They shall also bring up a company against you, and they shall stone you with stones, and thrust you through with their swords. {16:41} And they shall burn your houses with fire, and execute judgments upon you in the sight of many women: and I will cause you to cease from playing the harlot, and you also shall give no hire any more. {16:42} So will I make my fury toward you to rest, and my jealousy shall depart from you, and I will be quiet, and will be no more angry. {16:43} Because you have not remembered the days of your youth, but have fretted me in all these [things;] behold, therefore I also will recompense your way upon [your] head, says the Lord GOD: and you shall not commit this lewdness above all your abominations. {16:44} **Behold, every one that uses proverbs shall use [this] proverb against you, saying, As is the mother, [so is] her daughter.** {16:45} You [are] your mother's daughter, that loathes her husband and her children; and you [are] the sister of your sisters, which loathed their husbands and their children: your mother [was] a Hittite, and your father an Amorite. {16:46} And your elder sister [is] Samaria, she and her daughters that dwell at your left hand: and your younger sister, that dwells at your right hand, [is] Sodom and her daughters. {16:47} Yet have you not walked after their ways, nor done after their abominations: but, as [if that were] a very little [thing,] you were corrupted more than they in all your ways. {16:48} **[As] I live, says the Lord GOD, Sodom your sister has not done, she nor her daughters, as you have done, you and your daughters.** {16:49} Behold, this was the iniquity of your sister Sodom, pride, fullness of bread, and abundance of idleness was in her and in her daughters, neither did she strengthen the hand of the poor and needy. {16:50} And they were haughty, and committed abomination before me: therefore I took them away as I saw [good.] {16:51} Neither has Samaria committed half of your sins; but you have multiplied your abominations more than they, and have justified your sisters in all your abominations which you have done. {16:52} **You also, which have judged your sisters, bear your own shame for your sins that you have committed more abominable than they: they are more righteous than you: yes, be you confounded also, and bear your shame, in that you have justified your sisters.** {16:53} When I shall bring again their captivity, the captivity of Sodom and her daughters, and the captivity of Samaria and her daughters, then [will I bring again] the captivity of your captives in the midst of them: {16:54} That you may bear your own shame, and may be confounded in all that you have done, in that you are a comfort to them. {16:55} **When your sisters, Sodom and her daughters, shall return to their former estate, and Samaria and her daughters shall return to their former estate, then you and your daughters shall return to your former estate.** {16:56} For your sister Sodom was not mentioned by your mouth in the day of your pride, {16:57} Before your wickedness was discovered, as at the time of [your] reproach of the daughters of Syria, and all [that are] round about her, the daughters of the Philistines, which despise you round about. {16:58} You have borne your lewdness and your abominations, says the LORD. {16:59} For thus says the Lord GOD; I will even deal with you as you have done, which have despised the oath in breaking the covenant. {16:60} **Nevertheless I will remember my covenant with you in the days of your youth, and I will establish to you an everlasting covenant.** {16:61} **Then you shall remember your ways, and be ashamed, when you shall receive your sisters, your elder and your younger: and I will give them to you for daughters, but not by your covenant.** {16:62} **And I will establish my covenant with you; and you shall know that I [am] the LORD.** {16:63} **That you may remember, and be confounded, and never open your mouth any more because of your shame, when I am pacified toward you for all that you have done, says the Lord GOD.**

{17:1} And the word of the LORD came to me, saying, {17:2} "Son of man, put forth a riddle, and speak a parable to the house of Israel; {17:3} And say, Thus says the Lord GOD; A great eagle with great wings, longwinged, full of feathers, which had diverse colors, came to Lebanon, and took the highest branch of the cedar: {17:4} He cropped off the top of his young twigs, and carried it into a land of traffic; he set it in a city of merchants. {17:5} He took also of the seed of the land, and planted it in a fruitful field; he placed it by great waters, and set it as a willow tree. {17:6} And it grew, and became a spreading vine of low stature, whose branches turned toward him, and the roots thereof were under him: so it became a vine, and brought forth branches, and shot forth sprigs. {17:7} There was also another great eagle with great wings and many feathers: and, behold, this vine did bend her roots toward him, and shot forth her branches toward him, that he might water it by the furrows of her plantation. {17:8} It was planted in good soil by great waters, that it might bring forth branches, and that it might bear fruit, that it might be a goodly vine. {17:9} Say you, Thus says the Lord GOD; Shall it prosper? shall he not pull up the roots thereof, and cut off the fruit thereof, that it wither? it shall wither in all the leaves of her spring, even without great power or many people to pluck it up by the roots thereof. {17:10} Yes, behold, [being] planted, shall it prosper? shall it not utterly wither, when the east wind touches it? it shall wither in the furrows where it grew. {17:11} Moreover the word of the LORD came to me, saying, {17:12} Say now to the rebellious house, Do you not know what these [things mean?] tell them, Behold, the king of Babylon has come to Jerusalem, and has taken the king thereof, and the princes thereof, and led them with him to Babylon; {17:13} And has taken of the king's seed, and made a covenant with him, and has taken an oath of him: he has also taken the mighty of the land: {17:14} That the kingdom might be base, that it might not lift itself up, [but] that by keeping of his covenant it might stand. {17:15} But he rebelled against him in sending his ambassadors into Egypt, that they might give him horses and much people. Shall he prosper? shall he escape that does such [things?] or shall he break the covenant, and be delivered? {17:16} As I live, says the Lord GOD, surely in the place [where] the king dwells that made him king, whose oath he despised, and whose covenant he broke, [even] with him in the midst of Babylon he shall die. {17:17} Neither shall Pharaoh with [his] mighty army and great company make for him in the war, by casting up mounts, and building forts, to cut off many persons: {17:18} Seeing he despised the oath by breaking the covenant, when, lo, he had given his hand, and has done all these [things,] he shall not escape. {17:19} Therefore thus says the Lord GOD; [As] I live, surely my oath that he has despised, and my covenant that he has broken, even it will I recompense upon his own head. {17:20} And I will spread my net upon him, and he shall be taken in my snare, and I will bring him to Babylon, and will plead with him there for his trespass that he has trespassed against me. {17:21} And all his fugitives with all his bands shall fall by the sword, and they that remain shall be scattered toward all winds: and you shall know that I the LORD have spoken [it.] {17:22} Thus says the Lord GOD; I will also take of the highest branch of the high cedar, and will set it; I will crop off from the top of his young twigs a tender one, and will plant it upon a high mountain and eminent: {17:23} In the mountain of the height of Israel will I plant it: and it shall bring forth boughs, and bear fruit, and be a goodly cedar: and under it shall dwell all fowl of every wing; in the shadow of the branches thereof shall they dwell. {17:24} And all the trees of the field shall know that I the LORD have brought down the high tree, have exalted the low tree, have dried up the green tree, and have made the dry tree to flourish: I the LORD have brought down the high tree, have exalted the low tree, have dried up the green tree, and have made the dry tree to flourish: I the LORD have spoken and have done [it.

{18:1} The word of the LORD came unto me again, saying, {18:2} "What do you mean by using this proverb concerning the land of Israel, saying, 'The fathers have eaten sour grapes, and the children's teeth are set on edge'? {18:3} As I live," saith the Lord GOD, "you shall not have occasion any more to use this proverb in Israel. {18:4} **Behold, all souls are mine; as the soul of the father, so also the soul of the son is mine: the soul that sinneth, it shall die.** {18:5} But if a man be just, and do that which is lawful and right, {18:6} [And] has not eaten upon the mountains, neither has lifted up his eyes to the idols of the house of Israel; neither has defiled his neighbor's wife, neither has come near to a menstruous woman, {18:7} And has not oppressed any, [but] has restored to the debtor his pledge, has spoiled none by violence, has given his bread to the hungry, and has covered the naked with a garment; {18:8} He [that] has not given forth upon usury, neither has taken any increase, [that] has withdrawn his hand from iniquity, has executed true judgment between man and man, {18:9} Has walked in my statutes, and has kept my judgments, to deal truly; he [is] just, he shall surely live, saith the Lord GOD. {18:10} If he begets a son [that is] a robber, a shedder of blood, and [that] does the like to [any] one of these [things], {18:11} And that does not any of those [duties], but even has eaten upon the mountains, and defiled his neighbor's wife, {18:12} Has oppressed the poor and needy, has spoiled by violence, has not restored the pledge, and has lifted up his eyes to the idols, has committed abomination, {18:13} Has given forth upon usury, and has taken increase: shall he then live? he shall not live: he has done all these abominations; he shall surely die; his blood shall be upon him. {18:14} Now, lo, [if] he begets a son, that sees all his father's sins which he has done, and considers, and does not such like, {18:15} [That] has not eaten upon the mountains, neither has lifted up his eyes to the idols of the house of Israel, has not defiled his neighbor's wife, {18:16} Neither has oppressed any, has not withheld the pledge, neither has spoiled by violence, [but] has given his bread to the hungry, and has covered the naked with a garment, {18:17} [That] has taken off his hand from the poor, [that] has not received usury nor increase, has executed my judgments, has walked in my statutes; he shall not die for the iniquity of his father, he shall surely live. {18:18} [As for] his father, because he cruelly oppressed, spoiled his brother by violence, and did [that] which [is] not good among his people, lo, even he shall die in his iniquity. {18:19} Yet you say, Why? does not the son bear the iniquity of the father? When the son has done that which is lawful and right, [and] has kept all my statutes, and has done them, he shall surely live. {18:20} The soul that sinneth, it shall die. The son shall not bear the iniquity of the father, neither shall the father bear the iniquity of the son: the righteousness of the righteous shall be upon him, and the wickedness of the wicked shall be upon him. {18:21} But if the wicked will turn from all his sins that he has committed, and keep all my statutes, and do that which is lawful and right, he shall surely live, he shall not die. {18:22} All his transgressions that he has committed, they shall not be mentioned unto him: in his righteousness that he has done he shall live. {18:23} Have I any pleasure at all that the wicked should die? saith the Lord GOD: [and] not that he should return from his ways, and live? {18:24} But when the righteous turns away from his righteousness, and commits iniquity, [and] does according to all the abominations that the wicked [man] does, shall he live? All his righteousness that he has done shall not be mentioned: in his trespass that he has trespassed, and in his sin that he has sinned, in them shall he die. {18:25} Yet you say, "The way of the Lord is not equal. Hear now, O house of Israel; Is not my way equal? are not your ways unequal? {18:26} When a righteous [man] turns away from his righteousness, and commits iniquity, and dies in them; for his iniquity that he has done shall he die. {18:27} Again, when the wicked [man] turns away from his wickedness that he has committed, and does that which is lawful and right, he shall save his soul alive. {18:28} Because he considers, and turns away from all his transgressions that he has committed, he shall surely live, he shall not die. {18:29} Yet the house of Israel says, "The way of the Lord is not fair." O house of Israel, are not my ways fair? Are not your ways unfair? {18:30} Therefore, I will judge you, O house of Israel, each one according to his ways, says the Lord GOD. Repent, and turn away from all your transgressions; so iniquity shall not be your downfall. {18:31} **Cast away from you all your transgressions, by which you have transgressed, and make for yourselves a new heart and a new spirit. For why should you die, O house of Israel?** {18:32} For I have no pleasure in the death of one who dies, says the Lord GOD. Therefore, turn yourselves and live.

{19:1} Furthermore, take up a lamentation for the princes of Israel, {19:2} and say, "What is your mother? A lioness: she lay down among lions, she nourished her cubs among young lions. {19:3} And she brought up one of her cubs: it became a young lion, and it learned to catch prey; it devoured men. {19:4} The nations also heard of him; he was caught in their pit, and they brought him with chains to the land of Egypt. {19:5} Now when she saw that she had waited, and her hope was lost, then she took another of her cubs, and made him a young lion. {19:6} And he roamed among the lions, he became a young lion, and learned to catch prey, and devoured men. {19:7} He prowled among the ruins, and laid waste their cities; and the land was desolate, and its fullness, by the noise of his roaring. {19:8} Then the nations set against him on every side from the provinces, and spread their net over him; he was caught in their pit. {19:9} And they put him in chains, and brought him to the king of Babylon; they brought him into strongholds, that his voice should no more be heard upon the mountains of Israel. {19:10} Your mother was like a vine in your blood, planted by the waters: she was fruitful and full of branches because of many waters. {19:11} She had strong branches for scepters of rulers, and her stature was exalted among the thick branches, and she appeared in her height with the multitude of her branches. {19:12} But she was uprooted in fury, she was cast down to the ground, and the east wind dried up her fruit; her strong branches were broken and withered; the fire consumed them. {19:13} And now she is planted in the wilderness, in a dry and thirsty ground. {19:14} And fire has gone out from a branch of her branches, which has devoured her fruit, so that she has no strong branch to be a scepter to rule. This is a lamentation, and it shall be for a lamentation."

{20:1} It happened in the seventh year, on the fifth day of the fifth month, that certain elders of Israel came to inquire of the LORD and sat before me. {20:2} Then the word of the LORD came to me, saying, {20:3} "Son of man, speak to the elders of Israel, and say to them, 'Thus says the Lord GOD: Are you coming to inquire of me? As I live, says the Lord GOD, I will not be inquired of by you. {20:4} Will you judge them, son of man, will you judge them? Cause them to know the abominations of their fathers. {20:5} And say to them, 'Thus says the Lord GOD: On the day when I chose Israel and lifted up my hand to the seed of the house of Jacob, and made myself known to them in the land of Egypt, when I lifted up my hand to them, saying, I am the LORD your God; {20:6} on that day I lifted up my hand to them, to bring them out of the land of Egypt into a land that I had chosen for them, flowing with milk and honey, which is the glory of all lands. {20:7} Then I said to them, "Each of you, throw away the abominations which are before your eyes, and do not defile yourselves with the idols of Egypt: I am the LORD your God." {20:8} But they rebelled against me and would not listen to me. They did not cast away the abominations of their eyes, nor did they forsake the idols of Egypt. Then I said, 'I will pour out my fury on them to fulfill my anger against them in the midst of the land of Egypt.' {20:9} But I acted for my name's sake, that it should not be profaned among the nations among whom they were, in whose sight I had made myself known to them, to bring them out of the land of Egypt. {20:10} Therefore I made them go out of the land of Egypt and brought them into the wilderness. {20:11} And I gave them my statutes and showed them my judgments, which if a man does, he shall live by them. {20:12} Moreover I also gave them my Sabbaths, to be a sign between me and them, that they might know that I am the LORD who sanctifies them. {20:13} Yet the house of Israel rebelled against me in the wilderness; they did not walk in my statutes; they despised my judgments, which if a man does, he shall live by them; and they greatly polluted my Sabbaths. Then I said I would pour out my fury on them in the wilderness, to consume them. {20:14} But I acted for my name's sake, that it should not be profaned before the nations, in whose sight I had brought them out. {20:15} Yet also I raised my hand in an oath to them in the wilderness, that I would not bring them into the land which I had given them, flowing with milk and honey, the glory of all lands, {20:16} because they despised my judgments and did not walk in my statutes, but profaned my Sabbaths; for their heart went after their idols. {20:17} Nevertheless my eye spared them from destruction. I did not make an end of them in the wilderness. {20:18} But I said to their children in the wilderness, 'Do not walk in the statutes of your fathers, nor observe their judgments, nor defile yourselves with their idols. {20:19} I am the LORD your God; walk in my statutes, keep my judgments, and do them; {20:20} hallow my Sabbaths, and they will be a sign between me and you, that you may know that I am the LORD your God.' {20:21} Notwithstanding, the children rebelled against me; they did not walk in my statutes, nor kept my judgments to do them, which if a man does, he shall live by them; they profaned my Sabbaths. Then I said I would pour out my fury on them, to fulfill my anger against them in the wilderness. {20:22} Nevertheless I withdrew my hand and acted for my name's sake, that it should not be profaned in the sight of the nations, in whose sight I had brought them out. {20:23} I also raised my hand in an oath to them in the wilderness, that I would scatter them among the nations and disperse them throughout the countries, {20:24} because they had not executed my judgments, but had despised my statutes, had polluted my Sabbaths, and their eyes were fixed on their fathers' idols. {20:25} Therefore I also gave them up to statutes that were not good, and judgments by which they could not live; {20:26} and I pronounced them unclean because of their ritual gifts, in that they caused all their firstborn to pass through the fire, that I might make them desolate and that they might know that I am the LORD.' {20:27} Therefore, son of man, speak to the house of Israel, and say to them, 'Thus says the Lord GOD: "In this too your fathers have blasphemed me, by being unfaithful to me. {20:28} When I brought them into the land concerning which I had raised my hand in an oath to give them, and they saw all the high hills and all the thick trees, there they offered their sacrifices and provoked me with their offerings. There they also sent up their sweet aroma and poured out their drink offerings. {20:29} Then I said to them, 'What is this high place to which you go?' So its name is called Bamah to this day. {20:30} Therefore say to the house of Israel, 'Thus says the Lord GOD: "Are you defiling yourselves in the manner of your fathers, and committing harlotry according to their abominations? {20:31} For when you offer your gifts and make your sons pass through the fire, you defile yourselves with all your idols, even to this day. So shall I be inquired of by you, O house of Israel? As I live, says the Lord GOD, I will not be inquired of by you. {20:32} And what comes into your mind shall never be, when you say, 'We will be like the Gentiles, like the families in other countries, serving wood and stone.' {20:33} "As I live," says the Lord GOD, "surely with a mighty hand, with an outstretched arm, and with fury poured out, I will rule over you. {20:34} I will bring you out from the peoples and gather you out of the countries where you are scattered, with a mighty hand, with an outstretched arm, and with fury poured out. {20:35} And I will bring you into the wilderness of the peoples, and there I will plead my case with you face to face. {20:36} Just as I pleaded my case with your fathers in the wilderness of the land of Egypt, so I will plead my case with you," says the Lord GOD . {20:37} I will make you pass under the rod, and I will bring you into the bond of the covenant; {20:38} I will purge the rebels from among you, and those who transgress against me; I will bring them out of the country where they dwell, but they shall not enter the land of Israel. Then you will know that I am the LORD. {20:39} "As for you, O house of Israel," thus says the Lord GOD: "Go, serve every one of you his idols—and hereafter—if you will not obey me; but profane my holy name no more with your gifts and your idols. {20:40} For on my holy mountain, on the mountain height of Israel," says the Lord GOD, "there all the house of Israel, all of them in the land, shall serve me; there I will accept them, and there I will require your offerings and the firstfruits of your sacrifices, together with all your holy things. {20:41} I will accept you as a sweet aroma when I bring you out from the peoples and gather you out of the countries where you have been scattered; and I will be hallowed in you before the Gentiles. {20:42} Then you shall know that I am the LORD, when I bring you into the land of Israel, into the country for which I raised my hand in an oath to give to your fathers. {20:43} And there you shall remember your ways and all your doings with which you were defiled; and you shall loathe yourselves in your own sight because of all the evils that you have committed. {20:44} Then you shall know that I am the LORD, when I have dealt with you for my name's sake, not according to your wicked ways nor according to your corrupt doings, O house of Israel," says the Lord GOD. {20:45} Furthermore the word of the LORD came to me, saying, {20:46} "Son of man, set your face toward the south; preach against the south and prophesy against the forest land in the South, {20:47} and say to the forest of the South, 'Hear the word of the LORD! Thus says the Lord GOD: "Behold, I will kindle a fire in you, and it shall devour every green tree and every dry tree in you; the blazing flame shall not be quenched, and all faces from the south to the north shall be scorched by it. {20:48} All flesh shall see that I, the LORD, have kindled it; it shall not be quenched."' {20:49} Then I said, "Ah, Lord GOD! They say of me, 'Does he not speak parables?'"

{21:1} The word of the LORD came to me, saying, {21:2} "Son of man, set your face toward Jerusalem, and speak against the holy places, and prophesy against the land of Israel, {21:3} and say to the land of Israel, 'Thus says the LORD: Behold, I am against you, and I will draw my sword out of its sheath and will cut off from you both the righteous and the wicked. {21:4} Since I will cut off from you both the righteous and the wicked, my sword shall go out of its sheath against all flesh from south to north, {21:5} so that all flesh may know that I, the LORD, have drawn my sword out of its sheath; it shall not return anymore. {21:6} Therefore sigh, son of man, with the breaking of your loins, and sigh before their eyes with bitterness. {21:7} And it shall be, when they say to you, 'Why are you sighing?' that you shall answer, 'Because of the news; for it is coming.' Every heart will melt, all hands will be feeble, every spirit will faint, and all knees will be as weak as water. Behold, it is coming and shall be brought to pass," says the Lord GOD. {21:8} Again the word of the LORD came to me, saying, {21:9} "Son of man, prophesy and say, 'Thus says the LORD: "A sword, a sword is sharpened and also polished, {21:10} sharpened to make a dreadful slaughter, polished to flash like lightning! Should we then rejoice? The rod of my son despises every tree. {21:11} And he has given it to be polished, that it may be handled; the sword is sharpened and polished to be given into the hand of the slayer."' {21:12} Cry and wail, son of man; for it will be against my people, against all the princes of Israel. Terrors by reason of the sword will be against my people; therefore strike your thigh. {21:13} Because it is a testing, and what if the sword despises even the scepter? The scepter shall be no more," says the Lord GOD. {21:14} "Therefore, son of man, prophesy and strike your hands together. The sword will be doubled the third time, the sword of the slain. It is the sword of the great men who are slain, which enters their private chambers. {21:15} I have set the point of the sword against all their gates, that their heart may melt and many may stumble. Ah! It is made bright; it is grasped for slaughter. {21:16} Swords, go one way or the other; either to the right or to the left, wherever your edge is directed. {21:17} I also will beat my fists together, and I will cause my fury to rest. I, the LORD, have spoken." {21:18} The word of the LORD came to me again, saying, {21:19} "Also, son of man, appoint two ways for the sword of the king of Babylon to go; both of them shall go from the same land. Make a signpost; make it at the head of the way to the city. {21:20} Appoint a road for the sword to go to Rabbah of the Ammonites, and to Judah, into fortified Jerusalem. {21:21} For the king of Babylon stands at the parting of the road, at the fork of the two roads, to use divination: he shakes the arrows, he consults the images, he looks at the liver. {21:22} In his right hand is the divination for Jerusalem: to set up battering rams, to call for a slaughter, to lift the voice with shouting, to set battering rams against the gates, to heap up a siege mound, and to build a wall. {21:23} And it will be to them like false divination in the eyes of those who have sworn oaths with them; but he will bring their iniquity to remembrance, that they may be taken. {21:24} "Therefore thus says the Lord GOD: 'Because you have made your iniquity to be remembered, in that your transgressions are uncovered, so that in all your doings your sins appear—because you have come to remembrance, you shall be taken by the hand. {21:25} Now to you, O profane, wicked prince of Israel, whose day has come, whose iniquity shall end, {21:26} thus says the Lord GOD: 'Remove the turban, and take off the crown; nothing shall remain the same. Exalt the humble, and humble the exalted. {21:27} Overthrown, overthrown, overthrown, I will make it overthrown! It shall be no longer, until He comes whose right it is, and I will give it to Him.'" {21:28} "And you, son of man, prophesy and say, 'Thus says the Lord GOD concerning the Ammonites and concerning their reproach,' and say: 'A sword , a sword is drawn, polished for slaughter, for consuming, for flashing— {21:29} while they see false visions for you, while they divine a lie to you, to bring you on the necks of the wicked, the slain whose day has come, whose iniquity shall end. {21:30} Return it to its sheath. I will judge you in the place where you were created, in the land of your nativity. {21:31} I will pour out my indignation on you; I will blow against you with the fire of my wrath, and deliver you into the hands of brutal men who are skillful to destroy. {21:32} You shall be fuel for the fire; your blood shall be in the midst of the land. You shall not be remembered, for I the LORD have spoken.'"

{22:1} Then the word of the LORD came to me, saying, {22:2} "Now, son of man, will you judge the bloody city? Yes, you shall show her all her abominations. {22:3} Then say, 'Thus says the Lord GOD: "The city sheds blood in her midst, that her time may come, and makes idols against herself to defile herself. {22:4} You have become guilty by the blood you have shed, and have defiled yourself with the idols you have made; you have brought your days to a close, and have come to your years. Therefore, I have made you a reproach to the nations and a mockery to all countries. {22:5} Those near and far from you will mock you, you who are infamous and full of turmoil. {22:6} Behold, the princes of Israel, each one in you, have used their power to shed blood. {22:7} In you they have shown contempt for father and mother; in your midst they have oppressed the stranger; in you they have mistreated the fatherless and the widow. {22:8} You have despised my holy things and profaned my Sabbaths. {22:9} In you are men who slander to shed blood; in you they eat on the mountains; in your midst they commit lewdness. {22:10} In you they uncover their fathers' nakedness; in you they violate women who are set apart during their impurity. {22:11} One commits abomination with his neighbor's wife; another lewdly defiles his daughter-in-law; and another in you violates his sister, his father's daughter. {22:12} In you they take bribes to shed blood; you take usury and increase; you have greedily gained from your neighbors by extortion, and have forgotten me," says the Lord GOD. {22:13} "Behold, therefore, I have struck my hand at your dishonest gain which you have made, and at the bloodshed which has been in your midst. {22:14} Can your heart endure, or can your hands be strong, in the days when I deal with you? I, the LORD, have spoken it, and I will do it. {22:15} I will scatter you among the nations, disperse you in the countries, and remove your filthiness from you. {22:16} You shall take your inheritance in yourself in the sight of the nations, and you shall know that I am the LORD." {22:17} The word of the LORD came to me, saying, {22:18} "Son of man, the house of Israel has become dross to me; they are all bronze, tin, iron, and lead, in the midst of a furnace; they have become the dross of silver. {22:19} Therefore thus says the Lord GOD: 'Because you have all become dross, behold, therefore I will gather you into the midst of Jerusalem. {22:20} As men gather silver, bronze, iron, lead, and tin into the midst of a furnace, to blow fire on it, to melt it; so I will gather you in my anger and my fury, and I will leave you there and melt you. {22:21} Yes, I will gather you and blow on you in the fire of my wrath, and you shall be melted in its midst. {22:22} As silver is melted in the midst of a furnace, so shall you be melted in its midst; then you shall know that I, the LORD, have poured out my fury upon you.'" {22:23} Then the word of the LORD came to me, saying, {22:24} "Son of man, say to her: 'You are a land that is not cleansed, nor rained upon in the day of indignation. {22:25} There is a conspiracy of her prophets in her midst, like a roaring lion tearing the prey; they have devoured souls; they have taken treasure and precious things; they have made many widows in her midst. {22:26} Her priests have violated my law and profaned my holy things; they have not distinguished between the holy and unholy, nor have they made known the difference between the unclean and the clean; and they have hidden their eyes from my Sabbaths, so that I am profaned among them. {22:27} Her princes in her midst are like wolves tearing the prey, to shed blood, to destroy people, and to get dishonest gain. {22:28} Her prophets plastered them with untempered mortar, seeing false visions and divining lies for them, saying, 'Thus says the Lord GOD,' when the LORD had not spoken. {22:29} The people of the land have used oppressions, committed robbery, and mistreated the poor and needy; and they have wrongfully oppressed the stranger. {22:30} So I sought for a man among them who would make a wall and stand in the gap before me on behalf of the land, that I should not destroy it; but I found no one. {22:31} Therefore I have poured out my indignation on them; I have consumed them with the fire of my wrath; and I have recompensed their deeds on their own heads," says the Lord GOD."

{23:1} Then the word of the LORD came again to me, saying, {23:2} "Son of man, there were two women, the daughters of one mother. {23:3} They committed whoredoms in Egypt; they were young, and their breasts were pressed, and there their virginity was violated. {23:4} Their names were Aholah, the elder, and Aholibah, her sister. They were mine, and they bore sons and daughters. Their names: Samaria for Aholah, and Jerusalem for Aholibah. {23:5} Aholah played the harlot when she was mine; she lusted after her lovers, the Assyrians, her neighbors, {23:6} clothed in blue, governors and rulers, all of them desirable young men, horsemen riding on horses. {23:7} So she prostituted herself with them, with all their choice men of Assyria, with all for whom she lusted; she defiled herself with their idols. {23:8} Nor did she give up her harlotry brought from Egypt, for in her youth they had lain with her, pressed her virgin bosom, and poured out their immorality upon her. {23:9} Therefore I delivered her into the hand of her lovers, into the hand of the Assyrians, for whom she lusted. {23:10} These uncovered her nakedness, took her sons and daughters, and killed her with the sword; thus she became a byword among women, for they executed judgment on her. {23:11} Now when her sister Aholibah saw this, she became more corrupt in her lust than she, and in her harlotry more corrupt than her sister's harlotry. {23:12} She also lusted after the Assyrians, governors and rulers, clothed most gorgeously, horsemen riding on horses, all of them desirable young men. {23:13} Then I saw that she had defiled herself; both had followed the same path. {23:14} But she increased her harlotry; she looked at men portrayed on the wall, images of Chaldeans portrayed in vermilion, {23:15} girded with belts around their waists, flowing turbans on their heads, all of them looking like captains, in the manner of the Babylonians of Chaldea, the land of their nativity. {23:16} As soon as her eyes saw them, she lusted for them and sent messengers to them in Chaldea. {23:17} Then the Babylonians came to her, into the bed of love, and they defiled her with their immorality; so she was defiled by them, and alienated herself from them. {23:18} So she uncovered her harlotry and uncovered her nakedness. Then I alienated Myself from her, as I had alienated Myself from her sister. {23:19} Yet she multiplied her harlotry in recalling the days of her youth, when she had played the harlot in the land of Egypt. {23:20} She lusted after their paramours, whose flesh is like the flesh of donkeys, and whose issue is like the issue of horses. {23:21} Thus you called to remembrance the lewdness of your youth, when the Egyptians pressed your bosom because of your youthful breasts. {23:22} Therefore, O Aholibah, thus says the Lord GOD: 'Behold, I will stir up your lovers against you, from whom you have alienated yourself, and I will bring them against you from every side: {23:23} the Babylonians and all the Chaldeans, Pekod, Shoa, Koa, and all the Assyrians with them, all desirable young men, governors and rulers, great lords and renowned, all of them riding on horses. {23:24} They shall come against you with chariots, wagons, and a multitude of people; they shall set against you buckler, shield, and helmet all around. I will delegate judgment to them, and they shall judge you according to their judgments. {23:25} I will set My jealousy against you, and they shall deal furiously with you; they shall remove your nose and your ears, and your remnant shall fall by the sword; they shall take your sons and your daughters, and your remnant shall be devoured by fire. {23:26} They shall also strip you of your clothes and take away your beautiful jewelry. {23:27} Thus I will make your lewdness to cease from you, and your harlotry brought from the land of Egypt; so that you will not lift your eyes to them, nor remember Egypt anymore. {23:28} For thus says the Lord GOD: 'Surely I will deliver you into the hand of those you hate, into the hand of those from whom you alienated yourself. {23:29} They shall deal hatefully with you, take away all you have worked for, and leave you naked and bare; the nakedness of your harlotry shall be uncovered, both your lewdness and your harlotry. {23:30} I will do these things to you because you have gone after the Gentiles, and because you have become defiled by their idols. {23:31} You have walked in the way of your sister; therefore I will put her cup in your hand.' {23:32} Thus says the Lord GOD: 'You shall drink of your sister's cup, deep and wide; you shall be laughed to scorn and held in derision; it contains much. {23:33} You will be filled with drunkenness and sorrow, with the cup of horror and desolation, with the cup of your sister Samaria. {23:34} You shall drink it and drain it; you shall break its shards, and tear at your own breasts; for I have spoken,' says the Lord GOD. {23:35} Therefore thus says the Lord GOD: 'Because you have forgotten Me and cast Me behind your back, therefore you shall bear the penalty of your lewdness and your harlotry.' {23:36} Furthermore, the LORD said to me: 'Son of man, will you judge Aholah and Aholibah? Yes, declare to them their abominations: {23:37} that they have committed adultery and blood is on their hands; they have committed adultery with their idols, and even sacrificed their sons whom they bore to Me, passing them through the fire, to devour them. {23:38} Moreover they have done this to Me: they have defiled My sanctuary on the same day and profaned My Sabbaths. {23:39} For when they had slain their children for their idols, on the same day they came into My sanctuary to profane it; and indeed thus they have done in the midst of My house. {23:40} Furthermore you sent for men to come from afar, to whom a messenger was sent; and there they came. For whom you washed yourself, painted your eyes, and adorned yourself with ornaments, {23:41} You sat on a stately bed, with a table prepared before it, where you set My incense and My oil. {23:42} And a voice of a multitude at ease was with her, and with the men of the common sort were brought Sabeans from the wilderness, who put bracelets on their hands and beautiful crowns on their heads. {23:43} Then I said to her who was old in adulteries, 'Will they now commit harlotry with her, and she with them?' {23:44} Yet they went in to her, as men go in to a woman who plays the harlot; thus they went in to Aholah and Aholibah, the lewd women. {23:45} And the righteous men shall judge them after the manner of adulteresses and after the manner of women who shed blood, because they are adulteresses, and blood is in their hands. {23:46} For thus says the Lord GOD: 'I will bring up a company against them, and will give them to be removed and plundered. {23:47} The company shall stone them with stones and dispatch them with their swords; they shall slay their sons and their daughters, and burn up their houses with fire. {23:48} Thus I will cause lewdness to cease from the land, that all women may be taught not to follow after your lewdness. {23:49} And they shall repay your lewdness upon you, and you shall bear the sins of your idols; and you shall know that I am the Lord GOD.'

{24:1} Again, in the ninth year, on the tenth month, on the tenth day of the month, the word of the LORD came to me, saying, {24:2} "Son of man, write down the name of this day, even this same day, for on this day the king of Babylon set himself against Jerusalem. {24:3} "And speak a parable to the rebellious house, and say to them, 'Thus says the Lord GOD: "Set on a pot, set it on, and also pour water into it. {24:4} "Gather the pieces of meat into it, every good piece, the thigh and the shoulder; fill it with choice bones. {24:5} "Take the choice of the flock, and also burn the bones under it, and make it boil well, and let them seethe the bones in it." {24:6} "Therefore thus says the Lord GOD: 'Woe to the bloody city, to the pot whose scum is in it, and whose scum has not gone out of it! Bring it out piece by piece; let no lot fall upon it. {24:7} "'For her blood is in her midst; she set it on top of a rock; she did not pour it on the ground, to cover it with dust; {24:8} "'That it might raise up fury and take vengeance, I have set her blood on top of a rock, that it should not be covered. {24:9} "'Therefore thus says the Lord GOD: 'Woe to the bloody city! I will even make the pile for fire great. {24:10} "'Heap on wood, kindle the fire, consume the flesh, and spice it well, and let the bones be burned. {24:11} "'Then set it empty on the coals, that the bronze of it may be hot, and may burn, and that the filthiness of it may be melted in it, that the scum of it may be consumed. {24:12} "'She has wearied herself with lies, and her great scum did not go forth out of her: her scum shall be in the fire. {24:13} "'In your filthiness is lewdness: because I have cleansed you, and you were not cleansed, you shall not be cleansed from your filthiness any more, till I have caused my fury to rest upon you. {24:14} "'I the LORD have spoken it: it shall come to pass, and I will do it; I will not go back, neither will I spare, neither will I repent; according to your ways and according to your doings, they shall judge you,' says the Lord GOD. {24:15} "Also the word of the LORD came to me, saying, {24:16} "Son of man, behold, I take away from you the desire of your eyes with a stroke: yet neither shall you mourn nor weep, neither shall your tears run down. {24:17} "Forbear to cry, make no mourning for the dead, bind the turban of your head upon you, and put on your shoes upon your feet, and cover not your lips, and eat not the bread of men. {24:18} "So I spoke to the people in the morning: and in the evening my wife died; and I did in the morning as I was commanded. {24:19} "And the people said to me, 'Will you not tell us what these things are to us, that you do so?' {24:20} "Then I answered them, 'The word of the LORD came to me, saying,

{24:21} "Speak to the house of Israel, Thus says the Lord GOD: 'Behold, I will profane my sanctuary, the pride of your strength, the desire of your eyes, and that which your soul pities; and your sons and your daughters whom you have left shall fall by the sword. {24:22} "'And you shall do as I have done: you shall not cover your lips, nor eat the bread of men. {24:23} "'And your turbans shall be on your heads, and your shoes on your feet: you shall not mourn nor weep; but you shall pine away for your iniquities, and mourn one toward another. {24:24} "'Thus Ezekiel is a sign to you: according to all that he has done you shall do: and when this comes, you shall know that I am the Lord GOD. {24:25} "Also, you son of man, shall it not be in the day when I take from them their strength, the joy of their glory, the desire of their eyes, and that whereupon they set their minds, their sons and their daughters, {24:26} "That he who escapes in that day shall come to you, to cause you to hear it with your ears? {24:27} "In that day shall your mouth be opened to him who has escaped, and you shall speak, and be no more dumb: and you shall be a sign to them; and they shall know that I am the LORD.

{25:1} The word of the LORD came again to me, saying, {25:2} "Son of man, set your face against the Ammonites, and prophesy against them; {25:3} "And say to the Ammonites, 'Hear the word of the Lord GOD; Thus says the Lord GOD: Because you said, 'Aha!' against my sanctuary when it was profaned, and against the land of Israel when it was desolate, and against the house of Judah when they went into captivity; {25:4} "Behold, therefore I will deliver you to the men of the east for a possession, and they shall set their palaces in you, and make their dwellings in you: they shall eat your fruit, and they shall drink your milk. {25:5} "And I will make Rabbah a stable for camels, and the Ammonites a resting place for flocks: and you shall know that I am the LORD. {25:6} "For thus says the Lord GOD: Because you have clapped your hands and stamped with your feet, and rejoiced in heart with all your spite against the land of Israel; {25:7} "Behold, therefore I will stretch out my hand upon you, and will deliver you for a spoil to the nations; and I will cut you off from the people, and I will cause you to perish out of the countries: I will destroy you; and you shall know that I am the LORD. {25:8} "Thus says the Lord GOD: Because Moab and Seir say, 'Behold, the house of Judah is like unto all the nations;' {25:9} "Therefore, behold, I will open the side of Moab from the cities, from his cities which are on his frontiers, the glory of the country, Beth-jeshimoth, Baal-meon, and Kiriathaim, {25:10} "To the men of the east with the Ammonites, and will give them in possession, that the Ammonites may not be remembered among the nations. {25:11} "And I will execute judgments upon Moab; and they shall know that I am the LORD. {25:12} "Thus says the Lord GOD: Because Edom has dealt against the house of Judah by taking vengeance, and has greatly offended, and revenged himself upon them; {25:13} "Therefore thus says the Lord GOD: I will also stretch out my hand upon Edom, and will cut off man and beast from it; and I will make it desolate from Teman; and they of Dedan shall fall by the sword. {25:14} "And I will lay my vengeance upon Edom by the hand of my people Israel: and they shall do in Edom according to my anger and according to my fury; and they shall know my vengeance, says the Lord GOD. {25:15} "Thus says the Lord GOD: Because the Philistines have dealt by revenge, and have taken vengeance with a spiteful heart, to destroy it for the old hatred; {25:16} "Therefore thus says the Lord GOD: Behold, I will stretch out my hand upon the Philistines, and I will cut off the Cherethites, and destroy the remnant of the sea coast. {25:17} "And I will execute great vengeance upon them with furious rebukes; and they shall know that I am the LORD, when I shall lay my vengeance upon them.

{26:1} In the eleventh year, on the first day of the month, the word of the LORD came to me, saying, {26:2} "Son of man, because Tyre has said against Jerusalem, 'Aha, she is broken, who was the gateway of the peoples; now she is turned over to me; I shall be replenished, now that she is laid waste.' {26:3} "Therefore thus says the Lord GOD: Behold, I am against you, O Tyre, and will cause many nations to come up against you, as the sea causes its waves to come up. {26:4} "And they shall destroy the walls of Tyre, and break down her towers: I will also scrape her dust from her, and make her like the top of a rock. {26:5} "It shall be a place for the spreading of nets in the midst of the sea: for I have spoken it, says the Lord GOD: and it shall become a spoil to the nations. {26:6} "And her daughters who are in the field shall be slain by the sword; and they shall know that I am the LORD. {26:7} "For thus says the Lord GOD: Behold, I will bring upon Tyre Nebuchadnezzar king of Babylon, a king of kings, from the north, with horses, and with chariots, and with horsemen, and companies, and much people. {26:8} "He shall slay with the sword your daughters in the field: and he shall make a fort against you, and cast a mount against you, and lift up the buckler against you. {26:9} "And he shall set engines of war against your walls, and with his axes he shall break down your towers. {26:10} "By reason of the abundance of his horses their dust shall cover you: your walls shall shake at the noise of the horsemen, and of the wheels, and of the chariots, when he shall enter into your gates, as men enter into a city wherein a breach is made. {26:11} "With the hoofs of his horses shall he tread down all your streets: he shall slay your people by the sword, and your strong garrisons shall go down to the ground. {26:12} "And they shall make a spoil of your riches, and make a prey of your merchandise: and they shall break down your walls, and destroy your pleasant houses: and they shall lay your stones and your timber and your dust in the midst of the water. {26:13} "And I will cause the noise of your songs to cease; and the sound of your harps shall be no more heard. {26:14} "And I will make you like the top of a rock: you shall be a place to spread nets upon; you shall be built no more: for I the LORD have spoken it, says the Lord GOD. {26:15} "Thus says the Lord GOD to Tyre; Shall not the isles shake at the sound of your fall, when the wounded cry, when the slaughter is made in the midst of you? {26:16} "Then all the princes of the sea shall come down from their thrones, and lay away their robes, and put off their embroidered garments: they shall clothe themselves with trembling; they shall sit upon the ground, and shall tremble at every moment, and be astonished at you. {26:17} "And they shall take up a lamentation for you, and say to you, 'How are you destroyed, that was inhabited of seafaring men, the renowned city, which was strong in the sea, she and her inhabitants, which caused their terror to be on all that haunt it! {26:18} "Now shall the isles tremble in the day of your fall; yes, the isles that are in the sea shall be troubled at your departure. {26:19} "For thus says the Lord GOD; When I shall make you a desolate city, like the cities that are not inhabited; when I shall bring up the deep upon you, and great waters shall cover you; {26:20} "When I shall bring you down with those that descend into the pit, with the people of old time, and shall set you in the low parts of the earth, in places desolate of old, with them that go down to the pit, that you be not inhabited; and I shall set glory in the land of the living; {26:21} "I will make you a terror, and you shall be no more: though you be sought for, yet shall you never be found again, says the Lord GOD.

{27:1} Again, the word of the LORD came to me, saying, {27:2} "Now, son of man, take up a lamentation for Tyre; {27:3} "And say to Tyre, O you who are situated at the entry of the sea, a merchant among the peoples for many isles, thus says the Lord GOD: O Tyre, you have said, 'I am of perfect beauty.' {27:4} "Your borders are in the midst of the seas; your builders have perfected your beauty. {27:5} "They have made all your ship boards of fir trees from Senir; they have taken cedars from Lebanon to make masts for you. {27:6} "Your oars were made from the oaks of Bashan; the company of the Ashurites made your benches of ivory, brought from the isles of Chittim. {27:7} "Fine linen with embroidered work from Egypt was spread forth to be your sail; blue and purple from the isles of Elishah covered you. {27:8} "The inhabitants of Zidon and Arvad were your mariners; your wise men, O Tyre, who were in you, were your pilots. {27:9} "The elders of Gebal and its wise men were your calkers; all the ships of the sea with their mariners were in you to occupy your merchandise. {27:10} "Men of Persia, Lud, and Phut were in your army, your men of war; they hung the shield and helmet in you; they set forth your beauty. {27:11} "Men of Arvad with your army were upon your walls round about, and the Gammadims were in your towers; they hung their shields upon your walls round about; they made your beauty perfect. {27:12} "Tarshish was your merchant by reason of the multitude of all kinds of riches; with silver, iron, tin, and lead, they traded in your fairs. {27:13} "Javan, Tubal, and Meshech were your merchants; they traded the persons of men and vessels of brass in your market. {27:14} "The house of Togarmah traded in your fairs with horses, horsemen, and mules. {27:15} "Men of Dedan were your merchants; many isles were the merchandise of your hand; they brought you horns of ivory and ebony as a present. {27:16} "Syria was your merchant by reason of the multitude of the wares of your making; they occupied in your fairs with emeralds, purple, embroidered work, fine linen, coral, and agate. {27:17} "Judah and the land of Israel were your merchants; they traded in your market wheat of Minnith, Pannag, honey, oil, and balm. {27:18} "Damascus was your merchant in the multitude of the wares of your making, for the multitude of all riches; in the wine of Helbon, and white wool. {27:19} "Dan also and Javan, going to and fro, occupied in your fairs; bright iron, cassia, and calamus were in your market. {27:20} "Dedan was your merchant in precious clothes for chariots. {27:21} "Arabia and all the princes of Kedar, they occupied with you in lambs, rams, and goats; in these they were your merchants. {27:22} "The merchants of Sheba and Raamah, they were your merchants; they occupied in your fairs with chief of all spices, and with all precious stones, and gold. {27:23} "Haran, Canneh, and Eden, the merchants of Sheba, Asshur, and Chilmad, were your merchants. {27:24} "These were your merchants in all sorts of things, in blue clothes, embroidered work, chests of rich apparel bound with cords and made of cedar, among your merchandise. {27:25} "The ships of Tarshish sang of you in your market; and you were replenished and made very glorious in the midst of the seas. {27:26} "Your rowers have brought you into great waters; the east wind has broken you in the midst of the seas. {27:27} "Your riches, fairs, merchandise, mariners, pilots, calkers, and all your men of war in you, and in all your company which is in the midst of you, shall fall into the midst of the seas in the day of your ruin. {27:28} "The suburbs shall shake at the sound of the cry of your pilots. {27:29} "And all that handle the oar, the mariners, and all the pilots of the sea, shall come down from their ships, they shall stand upon the land; {27:30} "And shall cause their voice to be heard against you, and shall cry bitterly, and shall cast up dust upon their heads, they shall wallow themselves in the ashes. {27:31} "And they shall make themselves utterly bald for you, and gird them with sackcloth, and they shall weep for you with bitterness of heart and bitter wailing. {27:32} "And in their wailing they shall take up a lamentation for you, and lament over you, saying, 'What city is like Tyre, like the destroyed in the midst of the sea? {27:33} "When your wares went forth out of the seas, you filled many people; you enriched the kings of the earth with the multitude of your riches and of your merchandise. {27:34} "In the time when you shall be broken by the seas in the depths of the waters, your merchandise and all your company in the midst of you shall fall. {27:35} "All the inhabitants of the isles shall be astonished at you, and their kings shall be sore afraid, they shall be troubled in their countenance. {27:36} "The merchants among the people shall hiss at you; you shall be a terror, and never shall be any more.

{28:1} The word of the LORD came again to me, saying, {28:2} "Son of man, say to the prince of Tyre, 'Thus says the Lord GOD: Because your heart is lifted up, and you have said, "I am a god, I sit in the seat of God, in the midst of the seas," yet you are a man, and not God, though you set your heart as the heart of God: {28:3} Behold, you are wiser than Daniel; there is no secret that they can hide from you: {28:4} With your wisdom and understanding, you have gained riches, and have acquired gold and silver in your treasures: {28:5} By your great wisdom and trade, you have increased your riches, and your heart is lifted up because of your riches: {28:6} Therefore thus says the Lord GOD: Because you have set your heart as the heart of God; {28:7} Behold, therefore I will bring strangers upon you, the terrible of the nations: and they shall draw their swords against the beauty of your wisdom, and they shall defile your brightness. {28:8} They shall bring you down to the pit, and you shall die the deaths of those who are slain in the midst of the seas. {28:9} Will you yet say before him who slays you, 'I am God'? But you shall be a man, and not God, in the hand of him who slays you. {28:10} You shall die the deaths of the uncircumcised by the hand of strangers: for I have spoken it, says the Lord GOD. {28:11} Moreover, the word of the LORD came to me, saying, {28:12} **Son of man, take up a lamentation for the king of Tyre, and say to him, 'Thus says the Lord GOD: You seal up the sum, full of wisdom and perfect in beauty.** {28:13} You have been in Eden the garden of God; every precious stone was your covering, the sardius, topaz, and diamond, the beryl, onyx, and jasper, the sapphire, emerald, and carbuncle, and gold: the workmanship of your settings and sockets was prepared in you on the day that you were created. {28:14} You were the anointed cherub who covers; and I have set you so: you were upon the holy mountain of God; you walked up and down in the midst of the stones of fire. {28:15} You were perfect in your ways from the day that you were created, till iniquity was found in you. {28:16} By the abundance of your merchandise they filled the midst of you with violence, and you have sinned: therefore I will cast you as profane out of the mountain of God: and I will destroy you, O covering cherub, from the midst of the stones of fire. {28:17} Your heart was lifted up because of your beauty, you have corrupted your wisdom by reason of your brightness: I will cast you to the ground, I will lay you before kings, that they may behold you. {28:18} You have defiled your sanctuaries by the multitude of your iniquities, by the iniquity of your trade; therefore will I bring forth a fire from the midst of you, it shall devour you, and I will bring you to ashes upon the earth in the sight of all those who behold you. {28:19} All they that know you among the people shall be astonished at you: you shall be a terror, and never shall you be any more.' {28:20} Again the word of the LORD came to me, saying, {28:21} Son of man, set your face against Sidon, and prophesy against it, {28:22} And say, 'Thus says the Lord GOD: Behold, I am against you, O Sidon; and I will be glorified in the midst of you: and they shall know that I am the LORD, when I shall have executed judgments in her, and shall be sanctified in her. {28:23} For I will send into her pestilence, and blood into her streets; and the wounded shall be judged in the midst of her by the sword upon her on every side; and they shall know that I am the LORD. {28:24} And there shall be no more a pricking brier unto the house of Israel, nor any grieving thorn of all that are round about them, that despised them; and they shall know that I am the Lord GOD. {28:25} Thus says the Lord GOD; When I shall have gathered the house of Israel from the people among whom they are scattered, and shall be sanctified in them in the sight of the heathen, then shall they dwell in their land that I have given to my servant Jacob. {28:26} And they shall dwell safely therein, and shall build houses, and plant vineyards; yea, they shall dwell with confidence, when I have executed judgments upon all those that despise them round about them; and they shall know that I am the LORD their God.

{29:1} In the tenth year, in the tenth [month,] in the twelfth [day] of the month, the word of the LORD came unto me, saying, {29:2} Son of man, set thy face against Pharaoh king of Egypt, and prophesy against him, and against all Egypt: {29:3} Speak, and say, Thus saith the Lord GOD; Behold, I [am] against thee, Pharaoh king of Egypt, the great dragon that lieth in the midst of his rivers, which hath said, My river [is] mine own, and I have made [it] for myself. {29:4} But I will put hooks in thy jaws, and I will cause the fish of thy rivers to stick unto thy scales, and I will bring thee up out of the midst of thy rivers, and all the fish of thy rivers shall stick unto thy scales. {29:5} And I will leave thee [thrown] into the wilderness, thee and all the fish of thy rivers: thou shalt fall upon the open fields; thou shalt not be brought together, nor gathered: I have given thee for meat to the beasts of the field and to the fowls of the heaven. {29:6} And all the inhabitants of Egypt shall know that I [am] the LORD, because they have been a staff of reed to the house of Israel. {29:7} When they took hold of thee by thy hand, thou didst break, and rend all their shoulder: and when they leaned upon thee, thou brakest, and madest all their loins to be at a stand. {29:8} Therefore thus saith the Lord GOD; Behold, I will bring a sword upon thee, and cut off man and beast out of thee. {29:9} And the land of Egypt shall be desolate and waste; and they shall know that I [am] the LORD: because he hath said, The river [is] mine, and I have made [it.] {29:10} Behold, therefore I [am] against thee, and against thy rivers, and I will make the land of Egypt utterly waste [and] desolate, from the tower of Syene even unto the border of Ethiopia. {29:11} No foot of man shall pass through it, nor foot of beast shall pass through it, neither shall it be inhabited forty years. {29:12} And I will make the land of Egypt desolate in the midst of the countries [that are] desolate, and her cities among the cities [that are] laid waste shall be desolate forty years: and I will scatter the Egyptians among the nations, and will disperse them through the countries. {29:13} Yet thus saith the Lord GOD; At the end of forty years will I gather the Egyptians from the people whither they were scattered: {29:14} And I will bring again the captivity of Egypt, and will cause them to return [into] the land of Pathros, into the land of their habitation; and they shall be there a base kingdom. {29:15} It shall be the basest of the kingdoms; neither shall it exalt itself any more above the nations: for I will diminish them, that they shall no more rule over the nations. {29:16} And it shall be no more the confidence of the house of Israel, which bringeth [their] iniquity to remembrance, when they shall look after them: but they shall know that I [am] the Lord GOD. {29:17} And it came to pass in the seven and twentieth year, in the first [month,] in the first [day] of the month, the word of the LORD came unto me, saying, {29:18} Son of man, Nebuchadrezzar king of Babylon caused his army to serve a great service against Tyrus: every head [was] made bald, and every shoulder [was] peeled: yet had he no wages, nor his army, for Tyrus, for the service that he had served against it: {29:19} Therefore thus saith the Lord GOD; Behold, I will give the land of Egypt unto Nebuchadrezzar king of Babylon; and he shall take her multitude, and take her spoil, and take her prey; and it shall be the wages for his army. {29:20} I have given him the land of Egypt [for] his labour wherewith he served against it, because they wrought for me, saith the Lord GOD. {29:21} In that day will I cause the horn of the house of Israel to bud forth, and I will give thee the opening of the mouth in the midst of them; and they shall know that I [am] the LORD.

{30:1} The word of the LORD came again unto me, saying, {30:2} Son of man, prophesy and say, Thus saith the Lord GOD; Howl ye, Woe worth the day {30:3} For the day [is] near, even the day of the LORD [is] near, a cloudy day; it shall be the time of the heathen. {30:4} And the sword shall come upon Egypt, and great pain shall be in Ethiopia, when the slain shall fall in Egypt, and they shall take away her multitude, and her foundations shall be broken down. {30:5} Ethiopia, and Libya, and Lydia, and all the mingled people, and Chub, and the men of the land that is in league, shall fall with them by the sword. {30:6} Thus saith the LORD; They also that uphold Egypt shall fall; and the pride of her power shall come down: from the tower of Syene shall they fall in it by the sword, saith the Lord GOD. {30:7} And they shall be desolate in the midst of the countries [that are] desolate, and her cities shall be in the midst of the cities [that are] wasted. {30:8} And they shall know that I [am] the LORD, when I have set a fire in Egypt, and [when] all her helpers shall be destroyed. {30:9} In that day shall messengers go forth from me in ships to make the careless Ethiopians afraid, and great pain shall come upon them, as in the day of Egypt: for, lo, it cometh. {30:10} Thus saith the Lord GOD; I will also make the multitude of Egypt to cease by the hand of Nebuchadrezzar king of Babylon. {30:11} He and his people with him, the terrible of the nations, shall be brought to destroy the land: and they shall draw their swords against Egypt, and fill the land with the slain. {30:12} And I will make the rivers dry, and sell the land into the hand of the wicked: and I will make the land waste, and all that is therein, by the hand of strangers: I the LORD have spoken [it.] {30:13} Thus saith the Lord GOD; I will also destroy the idols, and I will cause [their] images to cease out of Noph; and there shall be no more a prince of the land of Egypt: and I will put a fear in the land of Egypt. {30:14} And I will make Pathros desolate, and will set fire in Zoan, and will execute judgments in No. {30:15} And I will pour my fury upon Sin, the strength of Egypt; and I will cut off the multitude of No. {30:16} And I will set fire in Egypt: Sin shall have great pain, and No shall be rent asunder, and Noph [shall have] distresses daily. {30:17} The young men of Aven and of Pi-beseth shall fall by the sword: and these [cities] shall go into captivity. {30:18} At Tehaphnehes also the day shall be darkened, when I shall break there the yokes of Egypt: and the pomp of her strength shall cease in her: as for her, a cloud shall cover her, and her daughters shall go into captivity. {30:19} Thus will I execute judgments in Egypt: and they shall know that I [am] the LORD. {30:20} And it came to pass in the eleventh year, in the first [month,] in the seventh [day] of the month, [that] the word of the LORD came unto me, saying, {30:21} Son of man, I have broken the arm of Pharaoh king of Egypt; and, lo, it shall not be bound up to be healed, to put a roller to bind it, to make it strong to hold the sword. {30:22} Therefore thus saith the Lord GOD; Behold, I [am] against Pharaoh king of Egypt, and will break his arms, the strong, and that which was broken; and I will cause the sword to fall out of his hand. {30:23} And I will scatter the Egyptians among the nations, and will disperse them through the countries. {30:24} And I will strengthen the arms of the king of Babylon, and put my sword in his hand: but I will break Pharaoh's arms, and he shall groan before him with the groanings of a deadly wounded [man.] {30:25} But I will strengthen the arms of the king of Babylon, and the arms of Pharaoh shall fall down; and they shall know that I [am] the LORD, when I shall put my sword into the hand of the king of Babylon, and he shall stretch it out upon the land of Egypt. {30:26} And I will scatter the Egyptians among the nations, and disperse them among the countries; and they shall know that I [am] the LORD.

{31:1} And it came to pass in the eleventh year, in the third [month,] in the first [day] of the month, [that] the word of the LORD came unto me, saying, {31:2} Son of man, speak unto Pharaoh king of Egypt, and to his multitude; Whom art thou like in thy greatness? {31:3} Behold, the Assyrian [was] a cedar in Lebanon with fair branches, and with a shadowing shroud, and of an high stature; and his top was among the thick boughs. {31:4} The waters made him great, the deep set him up on high with his rivers running round about his plants, and sent out her little rivers unto all the trees of the field. {31:5} Therefore his height was exalted above all the trees of the field, and his boughs were multiplied, and his branches became long because of the multitude of waters, when he shot forth. {31:6} All the fowls of heaven made their nests in his boughs, and under his branches did all the beasts of the field bring forth their young, and under his shadow dwelt all great nations. {31:7} Thus was he fair in his greatness, in the length of his branches: for his root was by great waters. {31:8} The cedars in the garden of God could not hide him: the fir trees were not like his boughs, and the chesnut trees were not like his branches; nor any tree in the garden of God was like unto him in his beauty. {31:9} I have made him fair by the multitude of his branches: so that all the trees of Eden, that [were] in the garden of God, envied him. {31:10} Therefore thus saith the Lord GOD; Because thou hast lifted up thyself in height, and he hath shot up his top among the thick boughs, and his heart is lifted up in his height; {31:11} I have therefore delivered him into the hand of the mighty one of the heathen; he shall surely deal with him: I have driven him out for his wickedness. {31:12} And strangers, the terrible of the nations, have cut him off, and have left him: upon the mountains and in all the valleys his branches are fallen, and his boughs are broken by all the rivers of the land; and all the people of the earth are gone down from his shadow, and have left him. {31:13} Upon his ruin shall all the fowls of the heaven remain, and all the beasts of the field shall be upon his branches: {31:14} To the end that none of all the trees by the waters exalt themselves for their height, neither shoot up their top among the thick boughs, neither their trees stand up in their height, all that drink water: for they are all delivered unto death, to the nether parts of the earth, in the midst of the children of men, with them that go down to the pit. {31:15} Thus saith the Lord GOD; In the day when he went down to the grave I caused a mourning: I covered the deep for him, and I restrained the floods thereof, and the great waters were stayed: and I caused Lebanon to mourn for him, and all the trees of the field fainted for him. {31:16} I made the nations to shake at the sound of his fall, when I cast him down to hell with them that descend into the pit: and all the trees of Eden, the choice and best of Lebanon, all that drink water, shall be comforted in the nether parts of the earth. {31:17} They also went down into hell with him unto [them that be] slain with the sword; and [they that were] his arm, [that] dwelt under his shadow in the midst of the heathen. {31:18} To whom art thou thus like in glory and in greatness among the trees of Eden? yet shalt thou be brought down with the trees of Eden unto the nether parts of the earth: thou shalt lie in the midst of the uncircumcised with [them that be] slain by the sword. This [is] Pharaoh and all his multitude, saith the Lord GOD.

{32:1} And it came to pass in the twelfth year, in the twelfth month, in the first [day] of the month, [that] the word of the LORD came unto me, saying, {32:2} Son of man, take up a lamentation for Pharaoh king of Egypt, and say unto him, Thou art like a young lion of the nations, and thou [art] as a whale in the seas: and thou camest forth with thy rivers, and troubledst the waters with thy feet, and fouledst their rivers. {32:3} Thus saith the Lord GOD; I will therefore spread out my net over thee with a company of many people; and they shall bring thee up in my net. {32:4} Then will I leave thee upon the land, I will cast thee forth upon the open field, and will cause all the fowls of the heaven to remain upon thee, and I will fill the beasts of the whole earth with thee. {32:5} And I will lay thy flesh upon the mountains, and fill the valleys with thy height. {32:6} I will also water with thy blood the land wherein thou swimme, [even] to the mountains; and the rivers shall be full of thee. {32:7} And when I shall put thee out, I will cover the heaven, and make the stars thereof dark; I will cover the sun with a cloud, and the moon shall not give her light. {32:8} All the bright lights of heaven will I make dark over thee, and set darkness upon thy land, saith the Lord GOD. {32:9} I will also vex the hearts of many people, when I shall bring thy destruction among the nations, into the countries which thou hast not known. {32:10} Yea, I will make many people amazed at thee, and their kings shall be horribly afraid for thee, when I shall brandish my sword before them; and they shall tremble at [every] moment, every man for his own life, in the day of thy fall. {32:11} For thus saith the Lord GOD; The sword of the king of Babylon shall come upon thee. {32:12} By the swords of the mighty will I cause thy multitude to fall, the terrible of the nations, all of them: and they shall spoil the pomp of Egypt, and all the multitude thereof shall be destroyed. {32:13} I will destroy also all the beasts thereof from beside the great waters; neither shall the foot of man trouble them any more, nor the hoofs of beasts trouble them. {32:14} Then will I make their waters deep, and cause their rivers to run like oil, saith the Lord GOD. {32:15} When I shall make the land of Egypt desolate, and the country shall be destitute of that whereof it was full, when I shall smite all them that dwell therein, then shall they know that I [am] the LORD. {32:16} This [is] the lamentation wherewith they shall lament her: the daughters of the nations shall lament her: they shall lament for her, [even] for Egypt, and for all her multitude, saith the Lord GOD. {32:17} It came to pass also in the twelfth year, in the fifteenth day of the month, [that] the word of the LORD came unto me, saying, {32:18} Son of man, wail for the multitude of Egypt, and cast them down, [even] her, and the daughters of the famous nations, unto the nether parts of the earth, with them that go down into the pit. {32:19} Whom dost thou pass in beauty? go down, and be thou laid with the uncircumcised. {32:20} They shall fall in the midst of [them that are] slain by the sword: she is delivered to the sword: draw her and all her multitudes. {32:21} The strong among the mighty shall speak to him out of the midst of hell with them that help him: they are gone down, they lie uncircumcised, slain by the sword. {32:22} Asshur [is] there and all her company: his graves [are] about him: all of them slain, fallen by the sword: {32:23} Whose graves are set in the sides of the pit, and her company is round about her grave: all of them slain, fallen by the sword, which caused terror in the land of the living. {32:24} There [is] Elam and all her multitude round about her grave, all of them slain, fallen by the sword, which are gone down uncircumcised into the nether parts of the earth, which caused their terror in the land of the living; yet have they borne their shame with them that go down to the pit. {32:25} They have set her a bed in the midst of the slain with all her multitude: her graves [are] round about him: all of them uncircumcised, slain by the sword: though their terror was caused in the land of the living, yet have they borne their shame with them that go down to the pit: he is put in the midst of [them that be] slain. {32:26} There [is] Meshech, Tubal, and all her multitude: her graves [are] round about him: all of them uncircumcised, slain by the sword, though they caused their terror in the land of the living. {32:27} And they shall not lie with the mighty [that are] fallen of the uncircumcised, which are gone down to hell with their weapons of war: and they have laid their swords under their heads, but their iniquities shall be upon their bones, though [they were] the terror of the mighty in the land of the living. {32:28} Yea, thou shalt be broken in the midst of the uncircumcised, and shalt lie with [them that are] slain with the sword. {32:29} There [is] Edom, her kings, and all her princes, which with their might are laid by [them that were] slain by the sword: they shall lie with the uncircumcised, and with them that go down to the pit. {32:30} There [be] the princes of the north, all of them, and all the Zidonians, which are gone down with the slain; with their terror they are ashamed of their might; and they lie uncircumcised with [them that be] slain by the sword, and bear their shame with them that go down to the pit. {32:31} Pharaoh shall see them, and shall be comforted over all his multitude, [even] Pharaoh and all his army slain by the sword, saith the Lord GOD. {32:32} For I have caused my terror in the land of the living: and he shall be laid in the midst of the uncircumcised with [them that are] slain with the sword, [even] Pharaoh and all his multitude, saith the Lord GOD.

{33:1} Again the word of the LORD came unto me, saying, {33:2} Son of man, speak to the children of thy people, and say unto them, When I bring the sword upon a land, if the people of the land take a man of their coasts, and set him for their watchman: {33:3} If when he seeth the sword come upon the land, he blow the trumpet, and warn the people; {33:4} Then whosoever heareth the sound of the trumpet, and taketh not warning; if the sword come, and take him away, his blood shall be upon his own head. {33:5} He heard the sound of the trumpet, and took not warning; his blood shall be upon him. But he that taketh warning shall deliver his soul. {33:6} But if the watchman see the sword come, and blow not the trumpet, and the people be not warned; if the sword come, and take [any] person from among them, he is taken away in his iniquity; but his blood will I require at the watchman's hand. {33:7} So thou, O son of man, I have set thee a watchman unto the house of Israel; therefore thou shalt hear the word at my mouth, and warn them from me. {33:8} When I say unto the wicked, O wicked [man,] thou shalt surely die; if thou dost not speak to warn the wicked from his way, that wicked [man] shall die in his iniquity; but his blood will I require at thine hand. {33:9} Nevertheless, if thou warn the wicked of his way to turn from it; if he do not turn from his way, he shall die in his iniquity; but thou hast delivered thy soul. {33:10} **Therefore, O thou son of man, speak unto the house of Israel; Thus ye speak, saying, If our transgressions and our sins [be] upon us, and we pine away in them, how should we then live?** {33:11} Say unto them, [As] I live, saith the Lord GOD, I have no pleasure in the death of the wicked; but that the wicked turn from his way and live: turn ye, turn ye from your evil ways; for why will ye die, O house of Israel? {33:12} Therefore, thou son of man, say unto the children of thy people, The righteousness of the righteous shall not deliver him in the day of his transgression: as for the wickedness of the wicked, he shall not fall thereby in the day that he turneth from his wickedness; neither shall the righteous be able to live for his [righteousness] in the day that he sinneth. {33:13} When I shall say to the righteous, [that] he shall surely live; if he trust to his own righteousness, and commit iniquity, all his righteousnesses shall not be remembered; but for his iniquity that he hath committed, he shall die for it. {33:14} Again, when I say unto the wicked, Thou shalt surely die; if he turn from his sin, and do that which is lawful and right; {33:15} [If] the wicked restore the pledge, give again that he had robbed, walk in the statutes of life, without committing iniquity; he shall surely live, he shall not die. {33:16} None of his sins that he hath committed shall be mentioned unto him: he hath done that which is lawful and right; he shall surely live. {33:17} Yet the children of thy people say, The way of the Lord is not equal: but as for them, their way is not equal. {33:18} When the righteous turneth from his righteousness, and committeth iniquity, he shall even die thereby. {33:19} But if the wicked turn from his wickedness, and do that which is lawful and right, he shall live thereby. {33:20} Yet ye say, The way of the Lord is not equal. O ye house of Israel, I will judge you every one after his ways. {33:21} And it came to pass in the twelfth year of our captivity, in the tenth [month,] in the fifth [day] of the month, [that] one that had escaped out of Jerusalem came unto me, saying, The city is smitten. {33:22} Now the hand of the LORD was upon me in the evening, afore he that had escaped came; and had opened my mouth, until he came to me in the morning; and my mouth was opened, and I was no more dumb. {33:23} Then the word of the LORD came unto me, saying, {33:24} Son of man, they that inhabit those wastes of the land of Israel speak, saying, Abraham was one, and he inherited the land: but we [are] many; the land is given us for inheritance. {33:25} Wherefore say unto them, Thus saith the Lord GOD; Ye eat with the blood, and lift up your eyes toward your idols, and shed blood: and shall ye possess the land? {33:26} Ye stand upon your sword, ye work abomination, and ye defile every one his neighbour's wife: and shall ye possess the land? {33:27} Say thou thus unto them, Thus saith the Lord GOD; [As] I live, surely they that [are] in the wastes shall fall by the sword, and him that [is] in the open field will I give to the beasts to be devoured, and they that be in the forts and in the caves shall die of the pestilence. {33:28} For I will lay the land most desolate, and the pomp of her strength shall cease; and the mountains of Israel shall be desolate, that none shall pass through. {33:29} Then shall they know that I [am] the LORD, when I have laid the land most desolate because of all their abominations which they have committed. {33:30} Also, thou son of man, the children of thy people still are talking against thee by the walls and in the doors of the houses, and speak one to another, every one to his brother, saying, Come, I pray you, and hear what is the word that cometh forth from the LORD. {33:31} And they come unto thee as the people cometh, and they sit before thee as my people, and they hear thy words, but they will not do them: for with their mouth they shew much love, [but] their heart goeth after their covetousness. {33:32} And, lo, thou [art] unto them as a very lovely song of one that hath a pleasant voice, and can play well on an instrument: for they hear thy words, but they do them not. {33:33} And when this cometh to pass, (lo, it will come,) then shall they know that a prophet hath been among them.

{34:1} And the word of the LORD came unto me, saying, {34:2} Son of man, prophesy against the shepherds of Israel, prophesy, and say unto them, Thus saith the Lord GOD unto the shepherds; Woe [be] to the shepherds of Israel that do feed themselves! should not the shepherds feed the flocks? {34:3} Ye eat the fat, and ye clothe you with the wool, ye kill them that are fed: [but] ye feed not the flock. {34:4} The diseased have ye not strengthened, neither have ye healed that which was sick, neither have ye bound up [that which was] broken, neither have ye brought again that which was driven away, neither have ye sought that which was lost; but with force and with cruelty have ye ruled them. {34:5} And they were scattered, because [there is] no shepherd: and they became meat to all the beasts of the field, when they were scattered. {34:6} My sheep wandered through all the mountains, and upon every high hill: yea, my flock was scattered upon all the face of the earth, and none did search or seek [after them.] {34:7} Therefore, ye shepherds, hear the word of the LORD; {34:8} [As] I live, saith the Lord GOD, surely because my flock became a prey, and my flock became meat to every beast of the field, because [there was] no shepherd, neither did my shepherds search for my flock, but the shepherds fed themselves, and fed not my flock; {34:9} Therefore, O ye shepherds, hear the word of the LORD; {34:10} Thus saith the Lord GOD; Behold, I [am] against the shepherds; and I will require my flock at their hand, and cause them to cease from feeding the flock; neither shall the shepherds feed themselves any more; for I will deliver my flock from their mouth, that they may not be meat for them. {34:11} For thus saith the Lord GOD; Behold, I, [even] I, will both search my sheep, and seek them out. {34:12} As a shepherd seeketh out his flock in the day that he is among his sheep [that are] scattered; so will I seek out my sheep, and will deliver them out of all places where they have been scattered in the cloudy and dark day. {34:13} And I will bring them out from the people, and gather them from the countries, and will bring them to their own land, and feed them upon the mountains of Israel by the rivers, and in all the inhabited places of the country. {34:14} I will feed them in a good pasture, and upon the high mountains of Israel shall their fold be: there shall they lie in a good fold, and [in] a fat pasture shall they feed upon the mountains of Israel. {34:15} I will feed my flock, and I will cause them to lie down, saith the Lord GOD. {34:16} I will seek that which was lost, and bring again that which was driven away, and will bind up [that which was] broken, and will strengthen that which was sick: but I will destroy the fat and the strong; I will feed them with judgment. {34:17} And [as for] you, O my flock, thus saith the Lord GOD; Behold, I judge between cattle and cattle, between the rams and the he goats. {34:18} [Seemeth it] a small thing unto you to have eaten up the good pasture, but ye must tread down with your feet the residue of your pastures? and to have drunk of the deep waters, but ye must foul the residue with your feet? {34:19} And [as for] my flock, they eat that which ye have trodden with your feet; and they drink that which ye have fouled with your feet. {34:20} Therefore thus saith the Lord GOD unto them; Behold, I, [even] I, will judge between the fat cattle and between the lean cattle. {34:21} Because ye have thrust with side and with shoulder, and pushed all the diseased with your horns, till ye have scattered them abroad; {34:22} Therefore will I save my flock, and they shall no more be a prey; and I will judge between cattle and cattle. {34:23} And I will set up one shepherd over them, and he shall feed them, [even] my servant David; he shall feed them, and he shall be their shepherd. {34:24} And I the LORD will be their God, and my servant David a prince among them; I the LORD have spoken [it.] {34:25} And I will make with them a covenant of peace, and will cause the evil beasts to cease out of the land: and they shall dwell safely in the wilderness, and sleep in the woods. {34:26} And I will make them and the places round about my hill a blessing; and I will cause the shower to come down in his season; there shall be showers of blessing. {34:27} And the tree of the field shall yield her fruit, and the earth shall yield her increase, and they shall be safe in their land, and shall know that I [am] the LORD, when I have broken the bands of their yoke, and delivered them out of the hand of those that served themselves of them. {34:28} And they shall no more be a prey to the heathen, neither shall the beast of the land devour them; but they shall dwell safely, and none shall make [them] afraid. {34:29} And I will raise up for them a plant of renown, and they shall be no more consumed with hunger in the land, neither bear the shame of the heathen any more. {34:30} Thus shall they know that I the LORD their God [am] with them, and [that] they, [even] the house of Israel, [are] my people, saith the Lord GOD. {34:31} And ye my flock, the flock of my pasture, [are] men, [and] I [am] your God, saith the Lord GOD.

{35:1} Moreover the word of the LORD came unto me, saying, {35:2} Son of man, set thy face against mount Seir, and prophesy against it, {35:3} And say unto it, Thus saith the Lord GOD; Behold, O mount Seir, I [am] against thee, and I will stretch out mine hand against thee, and I will make thee most desolate. {35:4} I will lay thy cities waste, and thou shalt be desolate, and thou shalt know that I [am] the LORD. {35:5} Because thou hast had a perpetual hatred, and hast shed [the blood of] the children of Israel by the force of the sword in the time of their calamity, in the time [that their] iniquity [had] an end: {35:6} Therefore, [as] I live, saith the Lord GOD, I will prepare thee unto blood, and blood shall pursue thee: since thou hast not hated blood, even blood shall pursue thee. {35:7} Thus will I make mount Seir most desolate, and cut off from it him that passeth out and him that returneth. {35:8} And I will fill his mountains with his slain [men:] in thy hills, and in thy valleys, and in all thy rivers, shall they fall that are slain with the sword. {35:9} I will make thee perpetual desolations, and thy cities shall not return: and ye shall know that I [am] the LORD. {35:10} Because thou hast said, These two nations and these two countries shall be mine, and we will possess it; whereas the LORD was there: {35:11} Therefore, as I live, saith the Lord GOD, I will even do according to thine anger, and according to thine envy which thou hast used out of thy hatred against them; and I will make myself known among them, when I have judged thee. {35:12} And thou shalt know that I [am] the LORD, [and that] I have heard all thy blasphemies which thou hast spoken against the mountains of Israel, saying, They are laid desolate, they are given us to consume. {35:13} Thus with your mouth ye have boasted against me, and have multiplied your words against me: I have heard [them.] {35:14} Thus saith the Lord GOD; When the whole earth rejoiceth, I will make thee desolate. {35:15} **As thou didst rejoice at the inheritance of the house of Israel, because it was desolate, so will I do unto thee: thou shalt be desolate, O mount Seir, and all Idumea, [even] all of it: and they shall know that I [am] the LORD.**

{36:1} Also, thou son of man, prophesy unto the mountains of Israel, and say, Ye mountains of Israel, hear the word of the LORD: {36:2} Thus saith the Lord GOD; Because the enemy hath said against you, Aha, even the ancient high places are ours in possession: {36:3} Therefore prophesy and say, Thus saith the Lord GOD; Because they have made [you] desolate, and swallowed you up on every side, that ye might be a possession unto the residue of the heathen, and ye are taken up in the lips of talkers, and [are] an infamy of the people: {36:4} Therefore, ye mountains of Israel, hear the word of the Lord GOD; Thus saith the Lord GOD to the mountains, and to the hills, to the rivers, and to the valleys, to the desolate wastes, and to the cities that are forsaken, which became a prey and derision to the residue of the heathen that [are] round about; {36:5} Therefore thus saith the Lord GOD; Surely in the fire of my jealousy have I spoken against the residue of the heathen, and against all Idumea, which have appointed my land into their possession with the joy of all [their] heart, with despiteful minds, to cast it out for a prey. {36:6} Prophesy therefore concerning the land of Israel, and say unto the mountains, and to the hills, to the rivers, and to the valleys, Thus saith the Lord GOD; Behold, I have spoken in my jealousy and in my fury, because ye have borne the shame of the heathen: {36:7} Therefore thus saith the Lord GOD; I have lifted up mine hand, Surely the heathen that [are] about you, they shall bear their shame. {36:8} But ye, O mountains of Israel, ye shall shoot forth your branches, and yield your fruit to my people of Israel; for they are at hand to come. {36:9} For, behold, I [am] for you, and I will turn unto you, and ye shall be tilled and sown: {36:10} And I will multiply men upon you, all the house of Israel, [even] all of it: and the cities shall be inhabited, and the wastes shall be builded: {36:11} And I will multiply upon you man and beast; and they shall increase and bring fruit: and I will settle you after your old estates, and will do better [unto you] than at your beginnings: and ye shall know that I [am] the LORD. {36:12} Yea, I will cause men to walk upon you, [even] my people Israel; and they shall possess thee, and thou shalt be their inheritance, and thou shalt no more henceforth bereave them [of men.] {36:13} Thus saith the Lord GOD; Because they say unto you, Thou [land] devourest up men, and hast bereaved thy nations; {36:14} Therefore thou shalt devour men no more, neither bereave thy nations any more, saith the Lord GOD. {36:15} Neither will I cause [men] to hear in thee the shame of the heathen any more, neither shalt thou bear the reproach of the people any more, neither shalt thou cause thy nations to fall any more, saith the Lord GOD. {36:16} Moreover the word of the LORD came unto me, saying, {36:17} Son of man, when the house of Israel dwelt in their own land, they defiled it by their own way and by their doings: their way was before me as the uncleanness of a removed woman. {36:18} Wherefore I poured my fury upon them for the blood that they had shed upon the land, and for their idols [wherewith] they had polluted it: {36:19} And I scattered them among the heathen, and they were dispersed through the countries: according to their way and according to their doings I judged them. {36:20} And when they entered unto the heathen, whither they went, they profaned my holy name, when they said to them, These [are] the people of the LORD, and are gone forth out of his land. {36:21} But I had pity for mine holy name, which the house of Israel had profaned among the heathen, whither they went. {36:22} Therefore say unto the house of Israel, Thus saith the Lord GOD; I do not [this] for your sakes, O house of Israel, but for mine holy name's sake, which ye have profaned among the heathen, whither ye went. {36:23} And I will sanctify my great name, which was profaned among the heathen, which ye have profaned in the midst of them; and the heathen shall know that I [am] the LORD, saith the Lord GOD, when I shall be sanctified in you before their eyes. {36:24} For I will take you from among the heathen, and gather you out of all countries, and will bring you into your own land. {36:25} Then will I sprinkle clean water upon you, and ye shall be clean: from all your filthiness, and from all your idols, will I cleanse you. {36:26} A new heart also will I give you, and a new spirit will I put within you: and I will take away the stony heart out of your flesh, and I will give you an heart of flesh. {36:27} And I will put my spirit within you, and cause you to walk in my statutes, and ye shall keep my judgments, and do [them.] {36:28} And ye shall dwell in the land that I gave to your fathers; and ye shall be my people, and I will be your God. {36:29} I will also save you from all your uncleannesses: and I will call for the corn, and will increase it, and lay no famine upon you. {36:30} And I will multiply the fruit of the tree, and the increase of the field, that ye shall receive no more reproach of famine among the heathen. {36:31} Then shall ye remember your own evil ways, and your doings that [were] not good, and shall loathe yourselves in your own sight for your iniquities and for your abominations. {36:32} Not for your sakes do I [this,] saith the Lord GOD, be it known unto you: be ashamed and confounded for your own ways, O house of Israel. {36:33} Thus saith the Lord GOD; In the day that I shall have cleansed you from all your iniquities I will also cause [you] to dwell in the cities, and the wastes shall be builded. {36:34} And the desolate land shall be tilled, whereas it lay desolate in the sight of all that passed by. {36:35} And they shall say, "This land that was desolate is become like the garden of Eden; and the waste and desolate and ruined cities [are become] fenced, [and] are inhabited." {36:36} Then the heathen that are left round about you shall know that I the LORD build the ruined places, and plant that that was desolate: I the LORD have spoken [it,] and I will do [it.] {36:37} Thus saith the Lord GOD; I will yet [for] this be enquired of by the house of Israel, to do [it] for them; I will increase them with men like a flock. {36:38} As the holy flock, as the flock of Jerusalem in her solemn feasts; so shall the waste cities be filled with flocks of men: and they shall know that I [am] the LORD.

{37:1} The hand of the LORD was upon me, and carried me out in the spirit of the LORD, and set me down in the midst of the valley which [was] full of bones, {37:2} And caused me to pass by them round about: and, behold, [there were] very many in the open valley; and, lo, [they were] very dry. {37:3} And he said unto me, Son of man, can these bones live? And I answered, O Lord GOD, thou knowest. {37:4} **Again he said unto me, Prophesy upon these bones, and say unto them, O ye dry bones, hear the word of the LORD.** {37:5} Thus saith the Lord GOD unto these bones; Behold, I will cause breath to enter into you, and ye shall live: {37:6} And I will lay sinews upon you, and will bring up flesh upon you, and cover you with skin, and put breath in you, and ye shall live; and ye shall know that I [am] the LORD. {37:7} So I prophesied as I was commanded: and as I prophesied, there was a noise, and behold a shaking, and the bones came together, bone to his bone. {37:8} And when

I beheld, lo, the sinews and the flesh came up upon them, and the skin covered them above: but [there was] no breath in them. {37:9} Then said he unto me, Prophesy unto the wind, prophesy, son of man, and say to the wind, Thus saith the Lord GOD; Come from the four winds, O breath, and breathe upon these slain, that they may live. {37:10} So I prophesied as he commanded me, and the breath came into them, and they lived, and stood up upon their feet, an exceeding great army. {37:11} Then he said unto me, Son of man, these bones are the whole house of Israel: behold, they say, Our bones are dried, and our hope is lost: we are cut off for our parts. {37:12} Therefore prophesy and say unto them, Thus saith the Lord GOD; Behold, O my people, I will open your graves, and cause you to come up out of your graves, and bring you into the land of Israel. {37:13} And ye shall know that I [am] the LORD, when I have opened your graves, O my people, and brought you up out of your graves, {37:14} And shall put my spirit in you, and ye shall live, and I shall place you in your own land: then shall ye know that I the LORD have spoken [it,] and performed [it,] saith the LORD. {37:15} The word of the LORD came again unto me, saying, {37:16} Moreover, thou son of man, take thee one stick, and write upon it, For Judah, and for the children of Israel his companions: then take another stick, and write upon it, For Joseph, the stick of Ephraim, and [for] all the house of Israel his companions: {37:17} And join them one to another into one stick; and they shall become one in thine hand. {37:18} And when the children of thy people shall speak unto thee, saying, Wilt thou not shew us what thou [meanest] by these? {37:19} Say unto them, Thus saith the Lord GOD; Behold, I will take the stick of Joseph, which [is] in the hand of Ephraim, and the tribes of Israel his fellows, and will put them with him, [even] with the stick of Judah, and make them one stick, and they shall be one in mine hand. {37:20} And the sticks whereon thou writest shall be in thine hand before their eyes. {37:21} And say unto them, Thus saith the Lord GOD; Behold, I will take the children of Israel from among the heathen, whither they be gone, and will gather them on every side, and bring them into their own land: {37:22} **And I will make them one nation in the land upon the mountains of Israel; and one king shall be king to them all: and they shall be no more two nations, neither shall they be divided into two kingdoms any more at all:** {37:23} Neither shall they defile themselves any more with their idols, nor with their detestable things, nor with any of their transgressions: but I will save them out of all their dwellingplaces, wherein they have sinned, and will cleanse them: so shall they be my people, and I will be their God. {37:24} And David my servant [shall be] king over them; and they all shall have one shepherd: they shall also walk in my judgments, and observe my statutes, and do them. {37:25} And they shall dwell in the land that I have given unto Jacob my servant, wherein your fathers have dwelt; and they shall dwell therein, [even] they, and their children, and their children's children for ever: and my servant David [shall be] their prince for ever. {37:26} Moreover I will make a covenant of peace with them; it shall be an everlasting covenant with them: and I will place them, and multiply them, and will set my sanctuary in the midst of them for evermore. {37:27} My tabernacle also shall be with them: yea, I will be their God, and they shall be my people. {37:28} And the heathen shall know that I the LORD do sanctify Israel, when my sanctuary shall be in the midst of them for evermore.

{38:1} And the word of the LORD came unto me, saying, {38:2} Son of man, set thy face against Gog, the land of Magog, the chief prince of Meshech and Tubal, and prophesy against him, {38:3} And say, Thus saith the Lord GOD; Behold I am against thee, O Gog, the chief prince of Meshech and Tubal: {38:4} And I will turn thee back, and put hooks into thy jaws, and I will bring thee forth, and all thine army, horses and horsemen, all of them clothed with all sorts of armour, even a great company with bucklers and shields, all of them handling swords: {38:5} Persia, Ethiopia, and Libya with them; all of them with shield and helmet: {38:6} Gomer, and all his bands; the house of Togarmah of the north quarters, and all his bands: and many people with thee. {38:7} Be thou prepared, and prepare for thyself, thou, and all thy company that are assembled unto thee, and be thou a guard unto them. {38:8} After many days thou shalt be visited: in the latter years thou shalt come into the land that is brought back from the sword, and is gathered out of many people, against the mountains of Israel, which have been always waste: but it is brought forth out of the nations, and they shall dwell safely all of them. {38:9} Thou shalt ascend and come like a storm, thou shalt be like a cloud to cover the land, thou, and all thy bands, and many people with thee. {38:10} Thus saith the Lord GOD; It shall also come to pass, that at the same time shall things come into thy mind, and thou shalt think an evil thought: {38:11} And thou shalt say, I will go up to the land of unwalled villages; I will go to them that are at rest, that dwell safely, all of them dwelling without walls, and having neither bars nor gates, {38:12} To take a spoil, and to take a prey; to turn thine hand upon the desolate places that are now inhabited, and upon the people that are gathered out of the nations, which have gotten cattle and goods, that dwell in the midst of the land. {38:13} Sheba, and Dedan, and the merchants of Tarshish, with all the young lions thereof, shall say unto thee, Art thou come to take a spoil? hast thou gathered thy company to take a prey? to carry away silver and gold, to take away cattle and goods, to take a great spoil? {38:14} Therefore, son of man, prophesy and say unto Gog, Thus saith the Lord GOD; In that day when my people of Israel dwelleth safely, shalt thou not know it? {38:15} And thou shalt come from thy place out of the north parts, thou, and many people with thee, all of them riding upon horses, a great company, and a mighty army: {38:16} And thou shalt come up against my people of Israel, as a cloud to cover the land; it shall be in the latter days, and I will bring thee against my land, that the heathen may know me, when I shall be sanctified in thee, O Gog, before their eyes. {38:17} Thus saith the Lord GOD; Art thou he of whom I have spoken in old time by my servants the prophets of Israel, which prophesied in those days many years that I would bring thee against them? {38:18} And it shall come to pass at the same time when Gog shall come against the land of Israel, saith the Lord GOD, that my fury shall come up in my face. {38:19} For in my jealousy and in the fire of my wrath have I spoken, Surely in that day there shall be a great shaking in the land of Israel; {38:20} So that the fishes of the sea, and the fowls of the heaven, and the beasts of the field, and all creeping things that creep upon the earth, and all the men that are upon the face of the earth, shall shake at my presence, and the mountains shall be thrown down, and the steep places shall fall, and every wall shall fall to the ground. {38:21} And I will call for a sword against him throughout all my mountains, saith the Lord GOD: every man's sword shall be against his brother. {38:22} And I will plead against him with pestilence and with blood; and I will rain upon him, and upon his bands, and upon the many people that are with him, an overflowing rain, and great hailstones, fire, and brimstone. {38:23} Thus will I magnify myself, and sanctify myself; and I will be known in the eyes of many nations, and they shall know that I am the LORD.

{39:1} Therefore, thou son of man, prophesy against Gog, and say, Thus saith the Lord GOD; Behold, I am against thee, O Gog, the chief prince of Meshech and Tubal: {39:2} And I will turn thee back, and leave but the sixth part of thee, and will cause thee to come up from the north parts, and will bring thee upon the mountains of Israel: {39:3} And I will smite thy bow out of thy left hand, and will cause thine arrows to fall out of thy right hand. {39:4} Thou shalt fall upon the mountains of Israel, thou, and all thy bands, and the people that is with thee: I will give thee unto the ravenous birds of every sort, and to the beasts of the field to be devoured. {39:5} Thou shalt fall upon the open field: for I have spoken it, saith the Lord GOD. {39:6} And I will send a fire on Magog, and among them that dwell carelessly in the isles: and they shall know that I am the LORD. {39:7} So will I make my holy name known in the midst of my people Israel; and I will not let them pollute my holy name any more: and the heathen shall know that I am the LORD, the Holy One in Israel. {39:8} Behold, it is come, and it is done, saith the Lord GOD; this is the day whereof I have spoken. {39:9} And they that dwell in the cities of Israel shall go forth, and shall set on fire and burn the weapons, both the shields and the bucklers, the bows and the arrows, and the handstaves, and the spears, and they shall burn them with fire seven years: {39:10} So that they shall take no wood out of the field, neither cut down any out of the forests; for they shall burn the weapons with fire: and they shall spoil those that spoiled them, and rob those that robbed them, saith the Lord GOD. {39:11} And it shall come to pass in that day, that I will give unto Gog a place there of graves in Israel, the valley of the passengers on the east of the sea: and it shall stop the noses of the passengers: and there shall they bury Gog and all his multitude: and they shall call it The valley of Hamon-gog. {39:12} And seven months shall the house of Israel be burying of them, that they may cleanse the land. {39:13} Yea, all the people of the land shall bury them; and it shall be to them a renown the day that I shall be glorified, saith the Lord GOD. {39:14} And they shall sever out men of continual employment, passing through the land to bury with the passengers those that remain upon the face of the earth, to cleanse it: after the end of seven months shall they search. {39:15} And the passengers that pass through the land, when any seeth a man's bone, then shall he set up a sign by it, till the buriers have buried it in the valley of Hamon-gog. {39:16} And also the name of the city shall be Hamonah. Thus shall they cleanse the land. {39:17} And, thou son of man, thus saith the Lord GOD; Speak unto every feathered fowl, and to every beast of the field, Assemble yourselves, and come; gather yourselves on every side to my sacrifice that I do sacrifice for you, even a great sacrifice upon the mountains of Israel, that ye may eat flesh, and drink blood. {39:18} Ye shall eat the flesh of the mighty, and drink the blood of the princes of the earth, of rams, of lambs, and of goats, of bullocks, all of them fatlings of Bashan. {39:19} And ye shall eat fat till ye be full, and drink blood till ye be drunken, of my sacrifice which I have sacrificed for you. {39:20} Thus ye shall be filled at my table with horses and chariots, with mighty men, and with all men of war, saith the Lord GOD. {39:21} And I will set my glory among the heathen, and all the heathen shall see my judgment that I have executed, and my hand that I have laid upon them. {39:22} So the house of Israel shall know that I am the LORD their God from that day and forward. {39:23} And the heathen shall know that the house of Israel went into captivity for their iniquity: because they trespassed against me, therefore hid I my face from them, and gave them into the hand of their enemies: so fell they all by the sword. {39:24} According to their uncleanness and according to their transgressions have I done unto them, and hid my face from them. {39:25} Therefore thus saith the Lord GOD; Now will I bring again the captivity of Jacob, and have mercy upon the whole house of Israel, and will be jealous for my holy name; {39:26} After that they have borne their shame, and all their trespasses whereby they have trespassed against me, when they dwelt safely in their land, and none made them afraid. {39:27} **When I have brought them again from the people, and gathered them out of their enemies' lands, and am sanctified in them in the sight of many nations;** {39:28} Then shall they know that I am the LORD their God, which caused them to be led into captivity among the heathen: but I have gathered them unto their own land, and have left none of them any more there. {39:29} Neither will I hide my face any more from them: for I have poured out my spirit upon the house of Israel, saith the Lord GOD.

{40:1} In the twenty-fifth year of our captivity, at the beginning of the year, on the tenth day of the month, in the fourteenth year after the city was struck, on that very day the hand of the LORD was upon me, and brought me there. {40:2} In the visions of God, he brought me into the land of Israel and set me upon a very high mountain, where there was the frame of a city to the south. {40:3} And there was a man whose appearance was like brass, with a line of flax in his hand and a measuring reed, standing in the gate. {40:4} The man said to me, "Son of man, behold with your eyes, and hear with your ears, and set your heart upon all that I shall show you, for the intent that I might show them to you; declare all that you see to the house of Israel. {40:5} And behold, there was a wall on the outside of the house all around, and in the man's hand was a measuring reed of six cubits long by the cubit and a handbreadth; so he measured the breadth of the building, one reed, and the height, one reed. {40:6} Then he came to the gate which looked toward the east, and went up its stairs, and measured the threshold of the gate, which was one reed broad, and the other threshold of the gate, which was one reed broad. {40:7} And every little chamber was one reed long and one reed broad, and between the little chambers were five cubits; and the threshold of the gate by the porch of the gate within was one reed. {40:8} He measured also the porch of the gate within, one reed. {40:9} Then he measured the porch of the gate, eight cubits, and the posts thereof, two cubits, and the porch of the gate was inward. {40:10} And the little chambers of the gate eastward were three on this side and three on that side; they three were of one measure; and the posts had one measure on this side and on that side. {40:11} And he measured the breadth of the entry of the gate, ten cubits, and the length of the gate, thirteen cubits. {40:12} The space also before the little chambers was one cubit on this side, and the space was one cubit on that side, and the little chambers were six cubits on this side and six cubits on that side. {40:13} He measured then the gate from the roof of one little chamber to the roof of another: the breadth was twenty-five cubits, door against door. {40:14} He made also posts of sixty cubits, even unto the post of the court round about the gate. {40:15} And from the face of the gate of the entrance unto the face of the porch of the inner gate were fifty cubits. {40:16} And there were narrow windows to the little chambers, and to their posts within the gate round about, and likewise to the arches; and windows were round about inward; and upon each post were palm trees. {40:17} Then he brought me into the outward court, and, lo, there were chambers, and a pavement made for the court round about: thirty chambers were upon the pavement. {40:18} And the pavement by the side of the gates over against the length of the gates was the lower pavement. {40:19} Then he measured the breadth from the forefront of the lower gate unto the forefront of the inner court without, a hundred cubits eastward and northward. {40:20} And the gate of the outward court that looked toward the north, he measured the length thereof, and the breadth thereof. {40:21} And the little chambers thereof were three on this side and three on that side; and the posts thereof and the arches thereof were after the measure of the first gate: the length thereof was fifty cubits, and the breadth twenty-five cubits. {40:22} And their windows, and their arches, and their palm trees, were after the measure of the gate that looked toward the east; and they went up unto it by seven steps; and the arches thereof were before them. {40:23} And the gate of the inner court was over against the gate toward the north and toward the east; and he measured from gate to gate a hundred cubits. {40:24} After that he brought me toward the south, and behold a gate toward the south: and he measured the posts thereof and the arches thereof according to these measures. {40:25} And there were windows in it and in the arches thereof round about, like those windows: the length was fifty cubits, and the breadth twenty-five cubits. {40:26} And there were seven steps to go up to it, and the arches thereof were before them; and it had palm trees, one on this side, and another on that side, upon the posts thereof. {40:27} And there was a gate in the inner court toward the south: and he measured from gate to gate toward the south a hundred cubits. {40:28} And he brought me to the inner court by the south gate: and he measured the south gate according to these measures; {40:29} And the little chambers thereof, and the posts thereof, and the arches thereof, according to these measures: and there were windows in it and in the arches thereof round about: it was fifty cubits long, and twenty-five cubits broad. {40:30} And the arches round about were twenty-five cubits long, and five cubits broad. {40:31} And the arches thereof were toward the outer court; and palm trees were upon the posts thereof: and the going up to it had eight steps. {40:32} And he brought me into the inner court toward the east: and he measured the gate according to these measures. {40:33} **And the little chambers thereof, and the posts thereof, and the arches thereof, were according to these measures: and there were windows therein and in the arches thereof round about: it was fifty cubits long, and twenty-five cubits broad.** {40:34} And the arches thereof were toward the outward court; and palm trees were upon the posts thereof, on this side, and on that side: and the going up to it had eight steps. {40:35} And he brought me to the north gate, and measured it according to these measures; {40:36} The little chambers thereof, the posts thereof, and the arches thereof, and the windows to it round about: the length was fifty cubits, and the breadth twenty-five cubits. {40:37} And the posts thereof were toward the outer court; and palm trees were upon the posts thereof, on this side, and on that side: and the going up to it had eight steps. {40:38} And the chambers and the entries thereof were by the posts of the gates, where they washed the burnt offering. {40:39} And in the porch of the gate were two tables on this side and two tables on that side, where they slaughtered the burnt offering, the sin offering, and the trespass offering. {40:40} And on the side outside, as one goes up to the entry of the north gate, there were two tables; and on the other side, which was at the porch of the gate, there were two tables. {40:41} So, in total, there were four tables on each side, by the side of the gate; making eight tables in all, where they performed their sacrifices. {40:42} The four tables were made of hewn stone for the burnt offering, one and a half cubits long, one and a half cubits broad, and one cubit high. Upon these tables, they placed the instruments with which they slaughtered the burnt offering and the sacrifice. {40:43} Within were hooks, a handbreadth broad, fastened all around; and upon the tables was the flesh of the offering. {40:44} Outside the inner gate were the chambers of the singers in the inner court, which was at the side of the north gate; and their outlook was toward the south, one at the side of the east gate having the prospect toward the north. {40:45} **Then he said to me, "This chamber, whose outlook is toward the south, is for the priests, the keepers of the charge of the house.** {40:46} And the chamber whose outlook is toward the north is for the priests, the keepers of the charge of the altar. These are the sons of Zadok among the sons of Levi, who come near to the LORD to minister unto him. {40:47} So he measured the court, a hundred cubits long and a hundred cubits broad, foursquare; and the altar that was before the house. {40:48} **And he brought me to the porch of the house and measured each post of the porch, five cubits on this side and five cubits on that side; and the breadth of the gate was three cubits on this side and three cubits on that side. {40:49} The length of the porch was twenty cubits, and the breadth eleven cubits; and he brought me by the steps whereby they went up to it; and there were pillars by the posts, one on this side and another on that side.**

{41:1} **Afterward, he brought me to the temple and measured the posts, which were six cubits broad on one side and six cubits broad on the other side, the same breadth as the tabernacle.** {41:2} The breadth of the door was ten cubits, and the sides of the door were five cubits on one side and five cubits on the other side. He measured the length of the door, which was forty cubits, and its breadth, which was twenty cubits. {41:3} Then he went inward and measured the post of the door, which was two cubits, and the door, which was six cubits, and the breadth of the door, which was seven cubits. {41:4} So he measured its length, which was twenty cubits, and its breadth, which was twenty cubits, before the temple, and he said to me, "This is the most holy place." {41:5} After he measured the wall of the house, which was six cubits, and the breadth of every side chamber, which was four cubits, round about the house on every side. {41:6} The side chambers were three, one over another, and thirty in order. They entered into the wall of the house for the side chambers round about, but they did not have hold in the wall of the house. {41:7} There was an enlarging and a winding about still upward to the side chambers. The winding about of the house went still upward round about the house. Therefore, the breadth of the house was still upward, and it increased from the lowest chamber to the highest by the midst. {41:8} I also saw the height of the house round about: the foundations of the side chambers were a full reed of six great cubits. {41:9} The thickness of the wall, which was for the side chamber without, was five cubits, and that which was left was the place of the side chambers that were within. {41:10} Between the chambers was the wideness of twenty cubits round about the house on every side. {41:11} The doors of the side chambers were toward the place that was left, one door toward the north and another door toward the south, and the breadth of the place that was left was five cubits round about. {41:12} Now the building that was before the separate place at the end toward the west was seventy cubits broad, and the wall of the building was five cubits thick round about, and its length was ninety cubits. {41:13} So he measured the house, a hundred cubits long, and the separate place, and the building, with the walls thereof, a hundred cubits long. {41:14} Also, the breadth of the face of the house, and of the separate place toward the east, was a hundred cubits. {41:15} He measured the length of the building over against the separate place which was behind it, and the galleries thereof on one side and on the other side, a hundred cubits, with the inner temple and the porches of the court. {41:16} The doorposts, and the narrow windows, and the galleries round about on their three stories, over against the door, were paneled with wood round about, from the ground up to the windows, and the windows were covered. {41:17} To that above the door, even unto the inner house, and without, and by all the wall round about within and without, was measured. {41:18} It was made with cherubim and palm trees, so that a palm tree was between a cherub and a cherub, and every cherub had two faces. {41:19} The face of a man was toward the palm tree on one side, and the face of a young lion toward the palm tree on the other side. It was made through all the house round about. {41:20} From the ground unto above the door were cherubim and palm trees made, and on the wall of the temple. {41:21} The posts of the temple were squared, and the face of the sanctuary; the appearance of the one as the appearance of the other. {41:22} The altar of wood was three cubits high, and its length was two cubits, and the corners thereof, and the length thereof, and the walls thereof, were of wood. He said to me, "This is the table that is before the LORD." {41:23} The temple and the sanctuary had two doors. {41:24} The doors had two leaves apiece, two turning leaves; two leaves for the one door, and two leaves for the other door. {41:25} On them, on the doors of the temple, were made cherubim and palm trees, like as were made upon the walls; and there were thick planks upon the face of the porch without. {41:26} There were narrow windows and palm trees on one side and on the other side, on the sides of the porch, and upon the side chambers of the house, and thick planks.

{42:1} Then he brought me forth into the utter court, the way toward the north, and he brought me into the chamber that was over against the separate place, and which was before the building toward the north. {42:2} Before the length of a hundred cubits was the north door, and the breadth was fifty cubits. {42:3} Over against the twenty cubits which were for the inner court, and over against the pavement which was for the utter court, there was a gallery against gallery in three stories. {42:4} And before the chambers was a walk of ten cubits breadth inward, a way of one cubit, and their doors toward the north. {42:5} Now the upper chambers were shorter, for the galleries were higher than these, than the lower, and than the middlemost of the building. {42:6} For they were in three stories, but had not pillars as the pillars of the courts; therefore, the building was straitened more than the lowest and the middlemost from the ground. {42:7} And the wall that was without over against the chambers, toward the utter court on the forepart of the chambers, the length thereof was fifty cubits. {42:8} For the length of the chambers that were in the utter court was fifty cubits, and, lo, before the temple were a hundred cubits. {42:9} And from under these chambers was the entry on the east side, as one goes into them from the utter court. {42:10} The chambers were in the thickness of the wall of the court toward the east, over against the separate place, and over against the building. {42:11} And the way before them was like the appearance of the chambers which were toward the north, as long as they, and as broad as they, and all their goings out were both according to their fashions and according to their doors. {42:12} And according to the doors of the chambers that were toward the south was a door in the head of the way, even the way directly before the wall toward the east, as one enters into them. {42:13} Then he said unto me, "The north chambers and the south chambers, which are before the separate place, they are holy chambers, where the priests that approach unto the LORD shall eat the most holy things; there shall they lay the most holy things, and the meat offering, and the sin offering, and the trespass offering; for the place is holy. {42:14} When the priests enter therein, then shall they not go out of the holy place into the utter court, but there they shall lay their garments wherein they minister; for they are holy; and shall put on other garments, and shall approach to those things which are for the people. {42:15} Now when he had made an end of measuring the inner house, he brought me forth toward the gate whose prospect is toward the east, and measured it round about. {42:16} He measured the east side with the measuring reed, five hundred reeds, with the measuring reed round about. {42:17} He measured the north side, five hundred reeds, with the measuring reed round about. {42:18} He measured the south side, five hundred reeds, with the measuring reed. {42:19} He turned about to the west side, and measured five hundred reeds with the measuring reed. {42:20} He measured it by the four sides; it had a wall round about, five hundred reeds long, and five hundred broad, to make a separation between the sanctuary and the profane place.

{43:1} Afterward, he brought me to the gate, even the gate that looks toward the east. {43:2} And, behold, the glory of the God of Israel came from the way of the east: and his voice was like a noise of many waters: and the earth shined with his glory. {43:3} ***And it was according to the appearance of the vision which I saw, even according to the vision that I saw when I came to destroy the city: and the visions were like the vision that I saw by the river Chebar; and I fell upon my face.*** {43:4} And the glory of the LORD came into the house by the way of the gate whose prospect is toward the east. {43:5} So the spirit took me up, and brought me into the inner court; and, behold, the glory of the LORD filled the house. {43:6} And I heard him speaking unto me out of the house; and the man stood by me. {43:7} And he said unto me, "Son of man, the place of my throne, and the place of the soles of my feet, where I will dwell in the midst of the children of Israel forever, and my holy name, shall the house of Israel no more defile, neither they, nor their kings, by their whoredom, nor by the carcasses of their kings in their high places. {43:8} In their setting of their threshold by my thresholds, and their post by my posts, and the wall between me and them, they have even defiled my holy name by their abominations that they have committed: wherefore I have consumed them in mine anger. {43:9} Now let them put away their whoredom, and the carcasses of their kings, far from me, and I will dwell in the midst of them forever. {43:10} Thou son of man, show the house to the house of Israel, that they may be ashamed of their iniquities: and let them measure the pattern. {43:11} And if they be ashamed of all that they have done, show them the form of the house, and the fashion thereof, and the goings out thereof, and the comings in thereof, and all the forms thereof, and all the ordinances thereof, and all the forms thereof, and all the laws thereof: and write it in their sight, that they may keep the whole form thereof, and all the ordinances thereof, and do them. {43:12} This is the law of the house; Upon the top of the mountain the whole limit thereof round about shall be most holy. Behold, this is the law of the house. {43:13} And these are the measures of the altar after the cubits: The cubit is a cubit and a hand breadth; even the bottom shall be a cubit, and the breadth a cubit, and the border thereof by the edge thereof round about shall be a span: and this shall be the higher place of the altar. {43:14} And from the bottom upon the ground even to the lower settle shall be two cubits, and the breadth one cubit; and from the lesser settle even to the greater settle shall be four cubits, and the breadth one cubit. {43:15} So the altar shall be four cubits; and from the altar and upward shall be four horns. {43:16} And the altar shall be twelve cubits long, twelve broad, square in the four squares thereof. {43:17} And the settle shall be fourteen cubits long and fourteen broad in the four squares thereof; and the border about it shall be half a cubit; and the bottom thereof shall be a cubit about; and his stairs shall look toward the east. {43:18} And he said unto me, Son of man, thus saith the Lord GOD; These are the ordinances of the altar in the day when they shall make it, to offer burnt offerings thereon, and to sprinkle blood thereon. {43:19} And thou shalt give to the priests the Levites that be of the seed of Zadok, which approach unto me, to minister unto me, saith the Lord GOD, a young bullock for a sin offering. {43:20} And thou shalt take of the blood thereof, and put it on the four horns of it, and on the four corners of the settle, and upon the border round about: thus shalt thou cleanse and purge it. {43:21} Thou shalt take the bullock also of the sin offering, and he shall burn it in the appointed place of the house, without the sanctuary. {43:22} And on the second day thou shalt offer a kid of the goats without blemish for a sin offering; and they shall cleanse the altar, as they did cleanse it with the bullock. {43:23} When thou hast made an end of cleansing it, thou shalt offer a young bullock without blemish, and a ram out of the flock without blemish. {43:24} And thou shalt offer them before the LORD, and the priests shall cast salt upon them, and they shall offer them up for a burnt offering unto the LORD. {43:25} Seven days shalt thou prepare every day a goat for a sin offering: they shall also prepare a young bullock, and a ram out of the flock, without blemish. {43:26} Seven days shall they purge the altar and purify it; and they shall consecrate themselves. {43:27} And when these days are expired, it shall be, that upon the eighth day, and so forward, the priests shall make your burnt offerings upon the altar, and your peace offerings; and I will accept you, saith the Lord GOD.

{44:1} Then he brought me back the way of the gate of the outward sanctuary which looks toward the east; and it was shut. {44:2} Then said the LORD unto me, "This gate shall be shut, it shall not be opened, and no man shall enter in by it; because the LORD, the God of Israel, has entered in by it, therefore it shall be shut. {44:3} It is for the prince; the prince, he shall sit in it to eat bread before the LORD; he shall enter by the way of the porch of that gate, and shall go out by the way of the same. {44:4} Then he brought me the way of the north gate before the house: and I looked, and, behold, the glory of the LORD filled the house of the LORD: and I fell upon my face. {44:5} And the LORD said unto me, "Son of man, mark well, and behold with your eyes, and hear with your ears all that I say unto you concerning all the ordinances of the house of the LORD, and all the laws thereof; and mark well the entering in of the house, with every going forth of the sanctuary. {44:6} And you shall say to the rebellious, even to the house of Israel, Thus saith the Lord GOD; O ye house of Israel, let it suffice you of all your abominations, {44:7} In that ye have brought into my sanctuary strangers, uncircumcised in heart, and uncircumcised in flesh, to be in my sanctuary, to pollute it, even my house, when ye offer my bread, the fat and the blood, and they have broken my covenant because of all your abominations. {44:8} And ye have not kept the charge of mine holy things: but ye have set keepers of my charge in my sanctuary for yourselves. {44:9} Thus saith the Lord GOD; No stranger, uncircumcised in heart, nor uncircumcised in flesh, shall enter into my sanctuary, of any stranger that is among the children of Israel. {44:10} And the Levites that are gone away far from me, when Israel went astray, which went astray away from me after their idols; they shall even bear their iniquity. {44:11} Yet they shall be ministers in my sanctuary, having charge at the gates of the house, and ministering to the house: they shall slay the burnt offering and the sacrifice for the people, and they shall stand before them to minister unto them. {44:12} Because they ministered unto them before their idols, and caused the house of Israel to fall into iniquity; therefore have I lifted up mine hand against them, saith the Lord GOD, and they shall bear their iniquity. {44:13} And they shall not come near unto me, to do the office of a priest unto me, nor to come near to any of my holy things, in the most holy place: but they shall bear their shame, and their abominations which they have committed. {44:14} But I will make them keepers of the charge of the house, for all the service thereof, and for all that shall be done therein. {44:15} But the priests the Levites, the sons of Zadok, that kept the charge of my sanctuary when the children of Israel went astray from me, they shall come near to me to minister unto me, and they shall stand before me to offer unto me the fat and the blood, saith the Lord GOD; {44:16} They shall enter into my sanctuary, and they shall come near to my table, to minister unto me, and they shall keep my charge. {44:17} And it shall come to pass, that when they enter in at the gates of the inner court, they shall be clothed with linen garments; and no wool shall come upon them, whiles they minister in the gates of the inner court, and within. {44:18} They shall have linen bonnets upon their heads, and shall have linen breeches upon their loins; they shall not gird themselves with anything that causes sweat. {44:19} And when they go forth into the utter court, even into the utter court to the people, they shall put off their garments wherein they ministered, and lay them in the holy chambers, and they shall put on other garments; and they shall not sanctify the people with their garments. {44:20} Neither shall they shave their heads, nor suffer their locks to grow long; they shall only poll their heads. {44:21} Neither shall any priest drink wine, when they enter into the inner court. {44:22} Neither shall they take for their wives a widow, nor her that is put away: but they shall take maidens of the seed of the house of Israel, or a widow that had a priest before. {44:23} And they shall teach my people the difference between the holy and profane, and cause them to discern between the unclean and the clean. {44:24} And in controversy they shall stand in judgment; and they shall judge it according to my judgments: and they shall keep my laws and my statutes in all mine assemblies; and they shall hallow my sabbaths. {44:25} And they shall come at no dead person to defile themselves: but for father, or for mother, or for son, or for daughter, for brother, or for sister that hath had no husband, they may defile themselves. {44:26} And after he is cleansed, they shall reckon unto him seven days. {44:27} And in the day that he goeth into the sanctuary, unto the inner court, to minister in the sanctuary, he shall offer his sin offering, saith the Lord GOD. {44:28} And it shall be unto them for an inheritance: I am their inheritance: and ye shall give them no possession in Israel: I am their possession. {44:29} They shall eat the meat offering, and the sin offering, and the trespass offering; and every dedicated thing in Israel shall be theirs. {44:29} The priests shall eat the meat offering, sin offering, and trespass offering, along with every dedicated thing in Israel. {44:30} They shall also receive the firstfruits of all produce, and every offering of any kind brought as an offering. Additionally, you shall give the priests the first portion of your dough, so that blessings may come upon your house. {44:31} However, the priests must not eat anything that dies naturally or is torn by wild animals, whether it is from the fowl or the livestock.

{45:1} When dividing the land for inheritance by lot, offer a holy portion to the LORD. This portion will be twenty-five thousand reeds in length and ten thousand reeds in breadth, holy in all its borders. {45:2} Within this portion, there shall be a square area of five hundred reeds by five hundred reeds for the sanctuary, with fifty cubits of open land surrounding it. {45:3} From this measurement, allocate twenty-five thousand reeds in length and ten thousand reeds in breadth for the sanctuary and the most holy place. {45:4} The holy portion of the land is for the priests, the ministers of the sanctuary, who approach to minister to the LORD. It will be a place for their houses and a holy area for the sanctuary. {45:5} Additionally, allocate twenty chambers as a possession for the Levites, the ministers of the house, within this same area. {45:6} Allocate a portion of land five thousand reeds broad and twenty-five thousand reeds long for the city, opposite the holy portion, for the entire house of Israel. {45:7} A portion will also be set aside for the prince on either side of the holy area and the city's possession, extending from the west border to the east border. {45:8} This land will be the prince's possession in Israel, and my princes will no longer oppress my people. The rest of the land will be given to the house of Israel according to their tribes. {45:9} Thus says the Lord GOD: O princes of Israel, let it be enough; cease violence, oppression, and injustice. Remove your unjust practices from my people. {45:10} Use fair balances, weights, and measures: an ephah and a bath shall be of equal measure. {45:11} The bath shall contain one-tenth of a homer, and the ephah one-tenth of a homer. The measure will be according to the homer. {45:12} The shekel shall be twenty gerahs, with twenty shekels, twenty-five shekels, and fifteen shekels making up a maneh. {45:13} Offer a sixth part of an ephah of a homer of wheat and barley as an offering. {45:14} Regarding oil, offer one-tenth of a bath from each homer, which is ten baths, making one homer. {45:15} Offer one lamb out of every two hundred from the fat pastures of Israel for a meat offering, a burnt offering, and peace offerings to make reconciliation, says the Lord GOD. {45:16} All the people of the land will contribute this offering for the prince in Israel. {45:17} The prince's duty will be to provide burnt offerings, meat offerings, and drink offerings during the feasts, new moons, sabbaths, and all the solemnities of Israel's house. He will also prepare sin offerings, meat offerings, burnt offerings, and peace offerings for the reconciliation of the house of Israel. {45:18} Thus says the Lord GOD: On the first day of the first month, cleanse the sanctuary with a young bullock without blemish. {45:19} The priest shall take the blood of the sin offering and put it on the house's posts, the four corners of the altar's settle, and the gate's posts of the inner court. {45:20} Repeat this on the seventh day of the month for anyone who has sinned unintentionally, reconciling the house. {45:21} On the fourteenth day of the first month, observe the seven-day feast of Passover, eating unleavened bread. {45:22} On that day, the prince shall prepare a bullock for a sin offering for himself and the people of the land. {45:23} Throughout the feast, offer seven bullocks and seven rams without blemish daily, along with a kid of the goats for a sin offering. {45:24} Prepare a meat offering of an ephah for a bullock, an ephah for a ram, and a hin of oil for an ephah. {45:25} Similarly, on the fifteenth day of the seventh month, follow the same procedure for the feast's seven days, offering sin offerings, burnt offerings, meat offerings, and oil.

{46:1} Thus says the Lord GOD: The gate of the inner court facing east shall remain closed during the six working days, but on the Sabbath and the day of the new moon, it shall be opened. {46:2} The prince shall enter through the porch of that gate and stand by the gate's post while the priests prepare his burnt offering and peace offerings. He shall worship at the gate's threshold, then leave. The gate will remain open until evening. {46:3} Likewise, the people of the land shall worship at this gate on the Sabbaths and the new moons before the LORD. {46:4} On the Sabbath, the prince's burnt offering to the LORD shall consist of six lambs without blemish and a ram without blemish. {46:5} The grain offering shall be an ephah for the ram, and for the lambs, as much as he is able to give, along with a hin of oil for each ephah. {46:6} On the day of the new moon, the offering shall include a young bullock without blemish, six lambs, and a ram, all without blemish. {46:7} The prince shall provide a grain offering of an ephah for the bullock, an ephah for the ram, and for the lambs as much as his hand can attain, along with a hin of oil for each ephah. {46:8} When the prince enters, he shall go in and leave through the gate's porch. {46:9} During the solemn feasts, those entering through the north gate to worship shall exit through the south gate, and those entering through the south gate shall exit through the north gate. They shall not return by the same gate they entered but shall exit opposite to it. {46:10} The prince shall enter and exit among them. {46:11} During the feasts and solemnities, the grain offering shall be an ephah for a bullock, an ephah for a ram, and for the lambs as much as he is able to give, along with a hin of oil for each ephah. {46:12} When the prince offers a voluntary burnt offering or peace offerings to the LORD, the gate facing east shall be opened for him, and he shall prepare his offerings. After he leaves, the gate shall be shut. {46:13} Every morning, prepare a burnt offering to the LORD of a lamb of the first year without blemish. {46:14} Also, prepare a grain offering of one-sixth of an ephah of fine flour mixed with one-third of a hin of oil to moisten the flour. This offering shall be made continually as a perpetual ordinance to the LORD. {46:15} Thus, prepare the lamb, the grain offering, and the oil every morning for a continual burnt offering. {46:16} If the prince gives a gift to any of his sons, it shall become their inheritance. {46:17} But if he gives a gift from his inheritance to one of his servants, it shall be his until the year of liberty, after which it shall return to the prince. His inheritance shall belong to his sons. {46:18} The prince shall not take the people's inheritance by oppression to drive them out of their possession. Instead, he shall give his sons inheritance from his own possession to prevent the scattering of my people from their possession. {46:19} Then he brought me to the entrance, which was at the side of the gate, into the holy chambers of the priests, facing north. There were chambers on both sides westward. {46:20} He said to me, "This is where the priests shall boil the trespass offering and the sin offering and bake the grain offering so that they do not need to carry them into the outer court to sanctify the people." {46:21} Then he brought me into the outer court and led me past the four corners of the court. Behold, in each corner of the court, there was another court. {46:22} These courts in the four corners were all the same size, each measuring forty cubits long and thirty cubits wide. {46:23} There was a row of building all around them, and they had boiling places built underneath the rows all around. {46:24} He said to me, "These are the places where the ministers of the house shall boil the sacrifice of the people."?

{47:1} Then he brought me again to the door of the house, and behold, waters flowed out from under the threshold of the house toward the east, for the front of the house faced east. The waters flowed down from under the right side of the house, south of the altar. {47:2} He then led me out through the north gate and took me around the outside to the outer gate facing east, and the waters were flowing out on the right side. {47:3} As the man with the measuring line went eastward, he measured off a thousand cubits and led me through the waters; the waters reached my ankles. {47:4} Again he measured off a thousand and led me through the waters; the waters reached my knees. Again he measured off a thousand and led me through; the waters reached my waist. {47:5} Then he measured off another thousand, and the river became so deep I could not cross it; the water was too deep to walk through, a river that could not be crossed. {47:6} He asked me, "Son of man, have you seen this?" Then he led me back to the bank of the river. {47:7} When I arrived, I saw a great number of trees on each side of the river. {47:8} He said to me, "These waters flow toward the eastern region and go down into the Arabah, where they enter the Dead Sea. When they empty into the sea, the salty water there becomes fresh. {47:9} Swarms of living creatures will live wherever the river flows. There will be large numbers of fish, because this water flows there and makes the salt water fresh; so where the river flows, everything will live. {47:10} Fishermen will stand along the shore; from En Gedi to En Eglaim there will be places for spreading nets. The fish will be of many kinds—like the fish of the Mediterranean Sea. {47:11} But the swamps and marshes will not become fresh; they will be left for salt. {47:12} Fruit trees of all kinds will grow on both banks of the river. Their leaves will not wither, nor will their fruit fail. Every month they will bear fruit, because the water from the sanctuary flows to them. Their fruit will serve for food and their leaves for healing." {47:13} This is what the Sovereign LORD says: "These are the boundaries of the land that you will divide among the twelve tribes of Israel, with two portions for Joseph. {47:14} You shall inherit it equally with one another. I swore with uplifted hand to give it to your ancestors, and this land will fall to you as your inheritance. {47:15} This is to be the boundary of the land: On the north side it will run from the Mediterranean Sea by the Hethlon Road past Lebo Hamath to Zedad, {47:16} Berothah and Sibraim (which lies on the border between Damascus and Hamath), as far as Hazer Hattikon, which is on the border of Hauran. {47:17} The boundary will extend from the sea to Hazar Enan, along the northern border of Damascus, with the border of Hamath to the north. This will be the northern boundary. {47:18} On the east side, the boundary will run between Hauran and Damascus, along the Jordan River between Gilead and the land of Israel, to the Dead Sea. This will be the eastern boundary. {47:19} On the south side, it will run from Tamar as far as the waters of Meribah Kadesh, then along the Wadi of Egypt to the Mediterranean Sea. This will be the southern boundary. {47:20} On the west side, the Mediterranean Sea will be the boundary to a point opposite Lebo Hamath. This will be the western boundary. {47:21} You are to distribute this land among yourselves according to the tribes of Israel. {47:22} You are to allot it as an inheritance for yourselves and for the foreigners residing among you and who have children. You are to consider them as native-born Israelites; along with you, they are to be allotted an inheritance among the tribes of Israel. {47:23} In whatever tribe the foreigner resides, there you are to give them their inheritance," declares the Sovereign LORD.

{48:1} These are the names of the tribes. From the north end along the road to Hethlon, as one goes to Hamath, Hazar-enan, the border of Damascus northward, to the coast of Hamath; Dan shall have a portion. {48:2} Along the border of Dan, from the east side to the west side, Asher shall have a portion. {48:3} Along the border of Asher, from the east side to the west side, Naphtali shall have a portion. {48:4} Along the border of Naphtali, from the east side to the west side, Manasseh shall have a portion. {48:5} Along the border of Manasseh, from the east side to the west side, Ephraim shall have a portion. {48:6} Along the border of Ephraim, from the east side to the west side, Reuben shall have a portion. {48:7} Along the border of Reuben, from the east side to the west side, Judah shall have a portion. {48:8} Along the border of Judah, from the east side to the west side, there shall be the offering which you shall offer of twenty-five thousand reeds in breadth and in length like one of the other parts, from the east side to the west side; and the sanctuary shall be in the midst of it. {48:9} The offering that you shall offer to the LORD shall be of twenty-five thousand in length and of ten thousand in breadth. {48:10} And for the priests, this holy offering shall be: toward the north twenty-five thousand in length, toward the west ten thousand in breadth, toward the east ten thousand in breadth, and toward the south twenty-five thousand in length; and the sanctuary of the LORD shall be in the midst of it. {48:11} It shall be for the priests who are sanctified of the sons of Zadok, who have kept my charge, who went not astray when the children of Israel went astray, as the Levites went astray. {48:12} This offering of the land that is offered shall be to them a most holy thing by the border of the Levites. {48:13} Alongside the border of the priests, the Levites shall have twenty-five thousand in length and ten thousand in breadth; all the length shall be twenty-five thousand, and the breadth ten thousand. {48:14} They shall not sell any of it, neither exchange nor alienate the firstfruits of the land; for it is holy to the LORD. {48:15} The five thousand left in breadth over against the twenty-five thousand shall be for common use for the city, for dwelling, and for suburbs; and the city shall be in the midst of it. {48:16} These shall be the measures thereof: the north side four thousand and five hundred, the south side four thousand and five hundred, the east side four thousand and five hundred, and the west side four thousand and five hundred. {48:17} The suburbs of the city shall be two hundred and fifty on the north, two hundred and fifty on the south, two hundred and fifty on the east, and two hundred and fifty on the west. {48:18} The residue in length alongside the holy offering shall be ten thousand eastward and ten thousand westward; and it shall be alongside the holy offering; and the increase thereof shall be for food to those who serve the city. {48:19} Those who serve the city shall serve it out of all the tribes of Israel. {48:20} The whole offering shall be twenty-five thousand by twenty-five thousand; you shall offer the holy offering foursquare with the possession of the city. {48:21} The remainder shall be for the prince, on the one side and on the other of the holy offering and of the possession of the city, in front of the twenty-five thousand of the offering toward the east border, and westward in front of the twenty-five thousand toward the west border, alongside the portions for the prince; and it shall be the holy offering; and the sanctuary of the house shall be in the midst of it. {48:22} Moreover, from the possession of the Levites, and from the possession of the city, being in the midst of that which is the prince's, between the border of Judah and the border of Benjamin, shall be for the prince. {48:23} As for the rest of the tribes, from the east side to the west side, Benjamin shall have a portion. {48:24} Along the border of Benjamin, from the east side to the west side, Simeon shall have a portion. {48:25} Along the border of Simeon, from the east side to the west side, Issachar shall have a portion. {48:26} Along the border of Issachar, from the east side to the west side, Zebulun shall have a portion. {48:27} Along the border of Zebulun, from the east side to the west side, Gad shall have a portion. {48:28} Along the border of Gad, at the south side southward, the border shall be even from Tamar to the waters of strife in Kadesh, to the river toward the great sea. This is the land which you shall divide by lot to the tribes of Israel for inheritance, and these are their portions, says the Lord GOD. {48:29} These are the exits of the city on the north side, four thousand and five hundred measures. {48:30} The gates of the city shall be named after the tribes of Israel: three gates northward; one gate of Reuben, one gate of Judah, one gate of Levi. {48:31} At the east side four thousand and five hundred: and three gates; one gate of Joseph, one gate of Benjamin, one gate of Dan. {48:32} At the south side four thousand and five hundred measures: and three gates; one gate of Simeon, one gate of Issachar , one gate of Zebulun. {48:33} At the west side four thousand and five hundred, with their three gates; one gate of Gad, one gate of Asher, one gate of Naphtali. {48:34} The perimeter shall be eighteen thousand measures: {48:35} and the name of the city from that day shall be, "The LORD is there."

# Daniel

{1:1} In the third year of Jehoiakim's reign over Judah, Nebuchadnezzar, the king of Babylon, came to Jerusalem and besieged it. {1:2} The Lord delivered Jehoiakim, the king of Judah, into Nebuchadnezzar's hand, along with some of the vessels from the house of God. These were taken to the land of Shinar to the house of Nebuchadnezzar's god, and the vessels were placed in the treasure house of his god. {1:3} Then the king instructed Ashpenaz, the master of his eunuchs, to bring some of the Israelites, including members of the royal family and nobility. {1:4} These individuals were to be young men without any physical defects, handsome, knowledgeable in all areas of wisdom, well-educated, intelligent, and capable of serving in the king's palace. They were to be taught the language and literature of the Chaldeans. {1:5} The king assigned them a daily provision of his own food and wine. They were to be nourished for three years, after which they would serve in the king's presence. {1:6} Among these chosen youths were Daniel, Hananiah, Mishael, and Azariah from the tribe of Judah. {1:7} The chief eunuch gave them new names: Daniel was called Belteshazzar, Hananiah was called Shadrach, Mishael was called Meshach, and Azariah was called Abed-nego. {1:8} However, Daniel resolved not to defile himself with the king's food and wine, so he asked the chief eunuch for permission to abstain from them. {1:9} God granted Daniel favor and compassion in the eyes of the chief eunuch. {1:10} But the chief eunuch was concerned about the consequences of allowing them to deviate from the king's provisions, fearing that they might appear unhealthy compared to the other youths, thus risking his own life before the king. {1:11} So Daniel proposed a test to the overseer Melzar, asking for ten days to be fed only vegetables and water. {1:12} After the ten days, their appearance was better and healthier than that of the other youths who ate the king's food. {1:13} Therefore, Melzar allowed them to continue with their diet. {1:14} At the end of their training period, they appeared healthier than those who had eaten the king's food. {1:15} So Melzar continued to provide them with vegetables instead of the king's food and wine. {1:16} Because of their faithfulness, God gave them knowledge and understanding, and Daniel was given the ability to interpret dreams and visions. {1:17} When the appointed time came, the chief eunuch brought them before Nebuchadnezzar. {1:18} After questioning them, Nebuchadnezzar found that Daniel, Hananiah, Mishael, and Azariah were superior to all the other youths. {1:19} They were granted an audience with the king. {1:20} In matters of wisdom and understanding, they proved to be ten times better than all the magicians and astrologers in the kingdom. {1:21} Daniel served in the royal court until the first year of King Cyrus's reign.

{2:1} In the second year of Nebuchadnezzar's reign, he had troubling dreams that disturbed his spirit, causing him to lose sleep. {2:2} Nebuchadnezzar summoned his magicians, astrologers, sorcerers, and Chaldeans to interpret his dreams. They stood before him awaiting his command. {2:3} Addressing them, the king explained his distressing dream and his desire to understand its meaning. {2:4} The Chaldeans responded in Aramaic, asking the king to reveal his dream, promising to provide its interpretation. {2:5} Nebuchadnezzar threatened them, declaring that if they couldn't reveal both the dream and its interpretation, they would face severe consequences, including death and the destruction of their homes. {2:6} However, if they could reveal the dream and its meaning, they would receive rewards and honor from the king. {2:7} The Chaldeans pleaded with the king to share the dream, assuring him they could interpret it. {2:8} Nebuchadnezzar accused them of stalling, suspecting they lacked the ability to fulfill his request. {2:9} He warned them that failure to reveal the dream would result in punishment, as they were attempting to buy time until circumstances changed. {2:10} The Chaldeans admitted their inability to meet the king's demand, claiming that only the gods, who do not dwell among mortals, could fulfill such a request. {2:11} Nebuchadnezzar, enraged by their response, ordered the execution of all the wise men of Babylon. {2:12} The decree to execute the wise men went out, and Daniel and his companions were sought for execution. {2:13} Daniel, in his wisdom, approached Arioch, the captain of the king's guard, questioning the urgency of the decree. {2:14} He then requested time from the king to interpret the dream. {2:15} Daniel inquired about the sudden decree from Arioch, who explained the situation to him. {2:16} Daniel petitioned the king for time to interpret the dream. {2:17} He went to his house and informed his companions, Hananiah, Mishael, and Azariah, urging them to seek mercy from the God of heaven concerning the mystery to avoid execution. {2:18} God revealed the secret to Daniel in a vision, prompting Daniel to praise the God of heaven. {2:19} Daniel acknowledged God's wisdom and power, expressing gratitude for revealing the king's mystery. {2:20} Daniel blessed God, recognizing His sovereignty over time, seasons, kings, wisdom, and knowledge. {2:21} He acknowledged God's authority to change circumstances and reveal hidden things. {2:22} Daniel praised God for His wisdom and might, expressing gratitude for granting him understanding. {2:23} Daniel thanked and praised God for granting him wisdom and revealing the king's mystery. {2:24} Daniel intervened with Arioch, urging him not to execute the wise men of Babylon, and offered to interpret the dream himself. {2:25} Arioch brought Daniel before the king, informing him of Daniel's ability to interpret the dream. {2:26} Nebuchadnezzar questioned Daniel about his capability to interpret the dream. {2:27} Daniel acknowledged that the wise men couldn't reveal the dream, but affirmed that God in heaven could and had done so. {2:28} Daniel explained that God revealed secrets and mysteries, including the king's dream, for the benefit of understanding future events. {2:29} Daniel assured the king that the dream's significance pertained to future events and thoughts that came to Nebuchadnezzar. {2:30} He humbly acknowledged that the revelation wasn't due to his wisdom but for the purpose of interpreting the dream for the king. {2:31} Daniel recounted the king's dream of a great image with terrifying features. {2:32} He described the image's composition of gold, silver, bronze, iron, and clay. {2:33} Daniel recounted how a stone struck the image's feet, causing its destruction, with the stone becoming a great mountain filling the earth. {2:34} Daniel explained that the various materials represented different kingdoms. {2:35} He described how these kingdoms would be destroyed, and God's kingdom would endure forever. {2:36} Daniel assured the king that he would interpret the dream. {2:37} He proclaimed Nebuchadnezzar as a king of kings, empowered by the God of heaven, symbolized by the head of gold in the dream. {2:38} Daniel explained that after Nebuchadnezzar's reign, other kingdoms would rise, each represented by different materials of decreasing value. {2:39} He described subsequent kingdoms, each inferior to the last. {2:40} Daniel foretold the strength and dominance of the fourth kingdom, represented by iron, but also its division and weakness. {2:41} The vision revealed that the kingdom represented by the feet and toes, a mixture of clay and iron, would be divided. It would possess some of the strength of iron due to its iron-clay mixture. {2:42} Just as the toes were a combination of iron and clay, this kingdom would be partly strong and partly brittle. {2:43} The mixture of iron with clay symbolizes an attempt at unity among different peoples, but they will not fully adhere to one another, similar to how iron does not mix well with clay. {2:44} **During the reign of these kings, the God of heaven will establish a kingdom that will never be destroyed. This kingdom will replace all earthly kingdoms, enduring forever.** {2:45} The stone, not cut by human hands, symbolizes this everlasting kingdom, which will crush and obliterate the earthly kingdoms represented by the various materials in Nebuchadnezzar's dream. The certainty of the dream and its interpretation is affirmed. {2:46} Nebuchadnezzar revered Daniel, acknowledging the God of Daniel as supreme. He ordered offerings and incense to be presented to Daniel. {2:47} The king acknowledged the God of Daniel as the highest deity, recognizing Daniel's ability to reveal mysteries. {2:48} Nebuchadnezzar honored Daniel greatly, granting him authority over Babylon's entire province and making him chief of all the wise men in Babylon. {2:49} Daniel requested that Shadrach, Meshach, and Abednego be appointed over Babylon's affairs, while he himself remained at the king's gate, serving in his administration.

{3:1} King Nebuchadnezzar made a statue of gold, it was 60 cubits tall and 6 cubits wide. He set it up in the plain of Dura in Babylon. {3:2} Then he called all the important officials to come for its dedication. {3:3} They all gathered and stood before the statue. {3:4} A herald proclaimed, "When you hear the music, everyone must bow down and worship the golden statue. Anyone who doesn't will be thrown into a fiery furnace." {3:5} So when the music played, everyone from every nation bowed down and worshipped the statue. {3:6} Some Chaldeans saw that certain Jews didn't bow down and reported them to the king. {3:7} When Nebuchadnezzar heard this, he was furious. {3:8} He called for the Jews, Shadrach, Meshach, and Abed-nego, to be brought before him. {3:9} He asked them if they refused to worship his gods and the golden statue he had made. {3:10} He warned them that if they didn't worship, they would be thrown into the fiery furnace. {3:11} They replied that they wouldn't worship his gods or the golden statue. {3:12} This made Nebuchadnezzar very angry. {3:13} He ordered the furnace to be heated seven times hotter and the Jews to be thrown in. {3:14} As they were being brought, Nebuchadnezzar asked if they were really refusing to worship. {3:15} He gave them one more chance to bow down, but they refused, saying their God could save them. {3:16} They said they weren't afraid of the consequences. {3:17} They believed their God could save them from the furnace. {3:18} **Even if He didn't, they still wouldn't worship Nebuchadnezzar's gods or the golden statue.** {3:19} Nebuchadnezzar became even angrier and ordered the furnace to be heated more. {3:20} The strongest men in his army bound the Jews and threw them in. {3:21} The flames were so hot that those who threw them in were killed. {3:22} But inside the furnace, Shadrach, Meshach, and Abed-nego were unharmed. {3:23} They fell into the fire bound. {3:24} When Nebuchadnezzar looked, he saw not three, but four men walking in the fire. {3:25} He saw they were unharmed, and one looked like a divine figure. {3:26} He called them out, and they walked out unharmed. {3:27} All the officials saw that the fire hadn't harmed them. {3:28} Nebuchadnezzar praised the God of Shadrach, Meshach, and Abed-nego for saving them from the fire. {3:29} He made a decree that no one should speak against their God, or they would face severe consequences. {3:30} And he promoted Shadrach, Meshach, and Abed-nego in Babylon.

{4:1} King Nebuchadnezzar sends his greetings to all people, nations, and languages on earth. {4:2} He wants to share the signs and wonders God has shown him. {4:3} He praises God for His greatness, His everlasting kingdom, and His dominion. {4:4} Nebuchadnezzar recalls a time when he was at peace in his palace but had a troubling dream. {4:5} The dream frightened him. {4:6} He called all the wise men of Babylon, but none could interpret the dream. {4:7} Finally, Daniel, also known as Belteshazzar, was brought before him. {4:8} Nebuchadnezzar tells Daniel the dream and asks for its interpretation. {4:9} Daniel, knowing God's spirit is in him, interprets the dream. {4:10} Nebuchadnezzar dreamed of a great tree reaching to heaven with abundant fruit, providing for all creatures. {4:11} An angel commanded to cut down the tree but leave its stump. {4:12} The tree symbolized Nebuchadnezzar's kingdom. {4:13} Daniel explains that God decreed Nebuchadnezzar would lose his sanity and live like an animal for seven years. {4:14} This was to humble him and show that God rules over all. {4:15} Daniel advises Nebuchadnezzar to repent and show mercy to the poor to possibly avoid his fate. {4:16} Nebuchadnezzar's prideful reign led to this judgment. {4:17} The dream's purpose was to demonstrate God's sovereignty. {4:18} Nebuchadnezzar acknowledges Daniel's ability to interpret dreams and asks him to proceed. {4:19} Daniel is troubled by the dream's implications but explains it to the king. {4:20} The dream represented Nebuchadnezzar's greatness, reaching to the heavens. {4:21} But he would be humbled, driven from his throne to live among animals. {4:22} Despite his power, Nebuchadnezzar would face this punishment. {4:23} It was decreed by God to teach Nebuchadnezzar a lesson. {4:24} Daniel assures Nebuchadnezzar of the dream's interpretation. {4:25} Nebuchadnezzar's kingdom would be restored after he acknowledged God's rule. {4:26} Daniel advises Nebuchadnezzar to repent and change his ways. {4:27} **Nebuchadnezzar's pride led to his downfall.** {4:28} The dream's fulfillment came upon Nebuchadnezzar. {4:29} After twelve months, Nebuchadnezzar boasted about his kingdom's greatness. {4:30} But as he spoke, a voice from heaven declared his downfall. {4:31} He would be driven from his throne and live among animals. {4:32} This punishment was to teach him that God rules over all. {4:33} Immediately, Nebuchadnezzar was humbled, living like an animal. {4:34} After seven years, he regained his sanity and praised God's everlasting dominion. {4:35} Nebuchadnezzar acknowledges God's sovereignty over all creation. {4:36} His sanity returned, and his kingdom was restored. {4:37} Nebuchadnezzar praises the King of heaven, acknowledging His sovereignty and judgment.

{5:1} King Belshazzar hosted a grand feast for a thousand of his lords and drank wine in their presence. {5:2} While tasting the wine, Belshazzar ordered the golden and silver vessels taken from the temple in Jerusalem by his father, Nebuchadnezzar, to be brought so that they could drink from them. {5:3} The vessels were brought, and Belshazzar, along with his princes, wives, and concubines, drank from them. {5:4} They drank wine and praised the gods made of various materials. {5:5} Suddenly, fingers appeared and wrote on the wall of the king's palace, which frightened Belshazzar. {5:6} Belshazzar's expression changed, and he was greatly troubled by the writing. {5:7} He called for the astrologers, Chaldeans, and soothsayers, offering rewards to anyone who could interpret the writing. {5:8} However, none of the wise men could read or interpret the writing. {5:9} Belshazzar became greatly troubled, and his lords were astonished. {5:10} The queen, hearing of the king's distress, advised him not to worry and reminded him of Daniel's wisdom. {5:11} She spoke highly of Daniel's abilities and suggested summoning him for the interpretation. {5:12} Daniel was brought before the king, who inquired about his identity and abilities. {5:13} Daniel confirmed his reputation for wisdom and was asked to interpret the writing. {5:14} Belshazzar acknowledged Daniel's wisdom and the spirit of the gods within him. {5:15} Despite the failure of the other wise men, Daniel was summoned for his reputation in interpreting dreams and solving mysteries. {5:16} Belshazzar promised Daniel rewards if he could interpret the writing. {5:17} Daniel declined the rewards but agreed to interpret the writing for the king. {5:18} He reminded Belshazzar of Nebuchadnezzar's rise and fall due to pride. {5:19} Despite Nebuchadnezzar's example, Belshazzar had not humbled himself before God. {5:20} Daniel warned Belshazzar of his impending downfall due to pride. {5:21} Belshazzar had defied God by using sacred vessels for his feast and praising false gods. {5:22} Despite knowing his father's fate, Belshazzar had not humbled himself. {5:23} Belshazzar had blasphemed against God by praising false gods and not glorifying the true God. {5:24} The hand appeared and wrote a message on the wall. {5:25} The writing read: MENE, MENE, TEKEL, UPHARSIN. {5:26} Daniel interpreted the message: God had numbered Belshazzar's kingdom and found it lacking. {5:27} Belshazzar's kingdom would be divided and given to the Medes and Persians. {5:28} Belshazzar honored Daniel and made him the third ruler in the kingdom. {5:29} That very night, Belshazzar was killed, and Darius the Mede took over the kingdom. {5:30} Belshazzar, the king of the Chaldeans, was slain. {5:31} Darius the Median assumed rulership at the age of sixty-two.

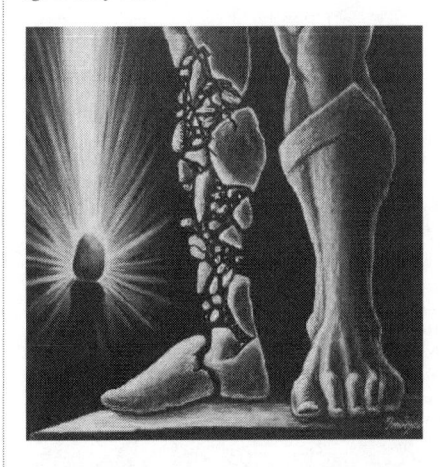

{6:1} Darius decided to appoint 120 princes to govern the entire kingdom, along with three presidents, with Daniel being the chief among them. This arrangement was made to ensure that the king suffered no loss due to the governance. {6:2} Daniel's exceptional spirit set him apart, and Darius considered promoting him to rule over the entire realm. {6:3} However, the other presidents and princes were envious of Daniel's position and sought to find fault with him. Yet, they could find no wrongdoing because Daniel was faithful and blameless. {6:4} Realizing they couldn't discredit Daniel in his duties, the jealous officials plotted against him concerning his devotion to God's law. {6:5} They devised a plan and approached King Darius, proposing a decree that anyone who prayed to any god or man other than the king for thirty days would be thrown into a den of lions. {6:6} They flattered Darius, presenting the decree as a unanimous decision among the kingdom's leaders, urging him to sign it into law. {6:7} Darius, unaware of their scheme, signed the decree, as it was customary for Medo-Persian laws to remain unaltered once established. {6:8} When Daniel learned of the decree, he continued his routine of praying three times a day with his windows open towards Jerusalem, as he had done before. {6:9} The jealous officials caught Daniel praying and reported him to the king, reminding Darius of the signed decree. {6:10} Realizing his mistake, Darius tried to save Daniel but was bound by the unalterable law he had enacted. {6:11} Daniel was brought before Darius, who expressed hope in Daniel's God to deliver him. {6:12} A stone was placed over the den, sealed by the king's signet and those of his nobles, ensuring Daniel's fate. {6:13} Darius spent a sleepless night, fasting and refraining from entertainment, troubled by Daniel's predicament. {6:14} Early the next morning, Darius rushed to the den, calling out to Daniel in distress, wondering if Daniel's God had saved him. {6:15} Daniel assured Darius of his well-being, explaining that God had sent an angel to shut the lions' mouths because of Daniel's innocence. {6:16} Relieved, Darius ordered Daniel's release from the den, finding no harm upon him because of his trust in God. {6:17} The men who had accused Daniel, along with their families, were thrown into the den and devoured by the lions, fulfilling the king's decree. {6:18} Darius, acknowledging the power of Daniel's God, issued a decree exalting the God of Daniel throughout his kingdom. {6:19} Daniel continued to prosper under Darius and later under Cyrus the Persian. { {6:20} Upon reaching the den, Darius cried out to Daniel in anguish, questioning if Daniel's God, whom he served faithfully, could rescue him from the lions. {6:21} Daniel responded respectfully, wishing the king longevity. {6:22} He assured Darius that his God had sent an angel to protect him, keeping the lions at bay because of his innocence before God and the king. {6:23} Overjoyed, Darius ordered Daniel to be lifted out of the den unharmed, attributing his safety to his faith in God. {6:24} The king then commanded that those who had falsely accused Daniel, along with their families, be thrown into the den. The lions swiftly overpowered them, breaking their bones before they even reached the bottom of the den. {6:25} Darius penned a decree extending peace to all people, nations, and languages, proclaiming the God of Daniel as the one to be revered throughout his kingdom. {6:26} He declared that in every corner of his domain, people should tremble before the living and eternal God of Daniel, acknowledging His unshakeable kingdom and everlasting dominion. {6:27} Darius praised God for delivering Daniel from the lions' power, acknowledging His ability to perform miraculous signs and wonders. {6:28} Daniel continued to thrive during the reigns of both Darius and Cyrus the Persian.

{7:1} During the first year of Belshazzar's reign in Babylon, Daniel had a dream and visions while lying in his bed. He recorded the dream and recounted its details. {7:2} Daniel explained that in his vision at night, he saw the four winds of heaven stirring up the great sea. {7:3} From the sea emerged four distinct and mighty beasts. {7:4} The first beast resembled a lion with eagle's wings. Daniel watched until the wings were plucked, and the beast stood upright like a man, receiving a human heart. {7:5} Another beast, a bear, appeared, raised on one side with three ribs in its mouth, commanded to devour much flesh. {7:6} Next, Daniel saw a leopard-like beast with four wings of a bird and four heads, given dominion. {7:7} Then, a fourth beast, incredibly dreadful and powerful, with great iron teeth, devoured and crushed everything in its path. It had ten horns. {7:8} Daniel observed a smaller horn emerging among the ten, uprooting three others. This horn had eyes like a man and spoke arrogantly. {7:9} Daniel witnessed thrones being set up, and the Ancient of Days took His seat. His appearance was awe-inspiring, with white garments and hair like pure wool. His throne resembled fiery flames, with wheels of burning fire. {7:10} A stream of fire flowed from before Him, and countless thousands served Him, while myriad stood before Him for judgment, with books opened. {7:11} Daniel continued watching until the beast was slain, its body destroyed and consumed by fire because of the arrogant words spoken by the horn. {7:12} Although the dominion of the other beasts was taken away, their lives were extended for a period. {7:13} **Daniel saw in his vision one like the Son of Man arriving with the clouds of heaven, brought before the Ancient of Days.** {7:14} This figure was granted dominion, glory, and an everlasting kingdom, with all peoples, nations, and languages serving Him. {7:15} These visions troubled Daniel deeply, causing distress in his spirit and body. {7:16} Seeking understanding, Daniel approached one of those present and asked for an explanation of the visions. {7:17} He was told that the four great beasts represented four kings who would arise from the earth. {7:18} However, the saints of the Most High would eventually receive the kingdom and possess it forever. {7:19} Daniel sought further clarification regarding the fourth beast, especially its terrifying appearance and actions. {7:20} He was informed about the ten horns on its head and the emergence of a smaller horn, which waged war against the saints. {7:21} This horn prevailed over the saints until the Ancient of Days intervened and granted judgment to the saints, ushering in their possession of the kingdom. {7:22} **Thus, Daniel learned that the fourth beast represented a kingdom unlike any other, devouring and trampling the earth.** {7:23} Out of this kingdom, ten kings would arise, followed by another, different from the rest, who would subdue three kings. {7:24} This ruler would speak arrogantly against the Most High, persecuting His saints and attempting to alter laws and times. {7:25} The saints would suffer under his reign for a specific period, but ultimately, judgment would be passed, and his dominion would be destroyed. {7:26} The kingdom and dominion, however, would be given to the saints of the Most High, and their rule would be everlasting. {7:27} The greatness of this kingdom would extend under the entire heavens, with all dominions serving and obeying the saints. {7:28} Daniel concluded his account, noting the profound impact these visions had on him, though he kept their details close to his heart.

{8:1} In the third year of King Belshazzar's reign, I, Daniel, had a vision, following the one I had previously. {8:2} In this vision, I found myself in the palace at Shushan in the province of Elam, standing by the Ulai River. {8:3} I looked up and saw a ram with two horns standing by the river. One horn was taller than the other, and it grew up later. {8:4} This ram charged in different directions, overpowering all beasts and becoming mighty, doing as it pleased. {8:5} While I was pondering, a goat with a notable horn between its eyes appeared from the west, moving swiftly without touching the ground. {8:6} The goat rushed at the ram with two horns by the river, filled with fury and power. {8:7} It attacked the ram, breaking its two horns, and the ram couldn't stand against it. The goat threw the ram down and trampled it, with none to rescue it. {8:8} The goat then grew exceedingly great. When it was strong, its notable horn was broken, and four notable horns came up in its place, pointing toward the four winds of heaven. {8:9} Out of one of these horns emerged a little horn, which grew exceedingly great toward the south, east, and the beautiful land. {8:10} This horn grew powerful, even reaching the host of heaven, casting down some of the host and stars to the ground and trampling on them. {8:11} It even exalted itself against the Prince of the host, abolished the daily sacrifice, and defiled the sanctuary. {8:12} A host was given to this horn because of transgression against the daily sacrifice, casting truth to the ground and prospering in its actions. {8:13} Then I heard one saint asking another how long the vision regarding the daily sacrifice and transgression leading to desolation, with the sanctuary and the host trodden underfoot, would last. {8:14} And the reply came, "Two thousand and three hundred days, then the sanctuary will be cleansed." {8:15} After seeing this vision, I, Daniel, sought to understand its meaning, and suddenly, there appeared before me an appearance like that of a man. {8:16} I heard a voice calling out between the banks of the Ulai River, instructing Gabriel to help me understand the vision. {8:17} As Gabriel approached, I was overcome with fear and fell on my face. But he reassured me, urging me to understand, for the vision pertained to the end times. {8:18} As he spoke, I fell into a deep sleep, face down on the ground. But he touched me and lifted me up. {8:19} Gabriel then promised to reveal what would happen in the latter end of the indignation, for the appointed time of the end would come. {8:20} He explained that the ram with two horns represented the kings of Media and Persia. {8:21} The rough goat symbolized the king of Greece, with the notable horn being the first king. {8:22} After the first king fell, four kingdoms would arise out of the nation, though not with his power. {8:23} In the latter time of these kingdoms, when transgressors have reached their peak, a fierce king with dark understanding will rise. {8:24} This king will be mighty, but not by his own power. He will cause destruction, prospering in his deeds, even against the mighty and the holy people. {8:25} Through deceit, he will cause craft to prosper, magnifying himself and standing against the Prince of princes. But he will be broken without human hands. {8:26} The vision revealed is true, with its fulfillment set for many days. Therefore, seal up the vision, for it pertains to distant times. {8:27} After this vision, I, Daniel, fainted and was sick for days. But afterward, I rose and attended to the king's business, though I was astonished, and no one understood the vision.

{9:1} In the first year of King Darius, the son of Ahasuerus, of the lineage of the Medes, who was made king over the realm of the Chaldeans, {9:2} I, Daniel, understood from the books the number of years revealed by the word of the LORD to Jeremiah the prophet, that seventy years would be fulfilled for the desolation of Jerusalem. {9:3} So I turned to the Lord God, seeking Him through prayer, supplications, fasting, and wearing sackcloth and ashes. {9:4} I prayed to the LORD my God and confessed, "O Lord, the great and awesome God, who keeps His covenant of love with those who love Him and keep His commandments, {9:5} we have sinned and done wrong. We have been wicked and rebelled; we have turned away from your commands and laws. {9:6} We have not listened to your servants the prophets, who spoke in your name to our kings, princes, ancestors, and to all the people of the land. {9:7} Lord, you are righteous, but we are covered in shame today—people of Judah, inhabitants of Jerusalem, and all Israel, near and far, in all the countries where you have scattered us because of our unfaithfulness. {9:8} We, our kings, princes, and ancestors, are covered in shame, Lord, because we have sinned against you. {9:9} The Lord our God is merciful and forgiving, even though we have rebelled against Him. {9:10} We have not obeyed the LORD our God or kept the laws He gave us through His servants the prophets. {9:11} All Israel has transgressed your law and turned away, refusing to obey you. Therefore, the curses and judgments written in the Law of Moses have been poured out on us because we have sinned against you. {9:12} You have fulfilled the words spoken against us and against our rulers by bringing on us a great disaster. Under the whole heaven, nothing has ever been done like what has been done to Jerusalem. {9:13} Just as it is written in the Law of Moses, all this disaster has come upon us, yet we have not sought the favor of the LORD our God by turning from our sins and giving attention to your truth. {9:14} The LORD has brought disaster upon us because of our sins. He has done just as He said He would. Yet we have not sought His favor by turning from our sins and giving attention to your truth. {9:15} Now, Lord our God, who brought your people out of Egypt with a mighty hand and made a name for yourself that endures to this day, we have sinned, we have done wrong. {9:16} Lord, in keeping with all your righteous acts, turn away your anger and your wrath from Jerusalem, your city, your holy hill. Our sins and the iniquities of our ancestors have made Jerusalem and your people an object of scorn to all those around us. {9:17} Now, our God, hear the prayers and petitions of your servant. For your sake, Lord, look with favor on your desolate sanctuary. {9:18} Give ear, our God, and hear; open your eyes and see the desolation of the city that bears your Name. We do not make requests of you because we are righteous, but because of your great mercy. {9:19} Lord, listen! Lord, forgive! Lord, hear and act! For your sake, my God, do not delay, because your city and your people bear your Name." {9:20} While I was speaking and praying, confessing my sin and the sin of my people Israel and making my request to the LORD my God for his holy hill— {9:21} while I was still in prayer, Gabriel, the man I had seen in the earlier vision, came to me in swift flight about the time of the evening sacrifice. {9:22} He instructed me and said to me, "Daniel, I have now come to give you insight and understanding. {9:23} As soon as you began to pray, a word went out, which I have come to tell you, for you are highly esteemed. Therefore, consider the word and understand the vision: {9:24} **Seventy weeks are decreed for your people and your holy city to finish transgression, to put an end to sin, to atone for wickedness, to bring in everlasting righteousness, to seal up vision and prophecy, and to anoint the Most Holy Place.** {9:25} Know and understand this: From the time the word goes out to restore and rebuild Jerusalem until the Anointed One, the ruler, comes, there will be seven 'sevens,' and sixty-two 'sevens.' It will be rebuilt with streets and a trench, but in times of trouble. {9:26} After the sixty-two 'sevens,' the Anointed One will be put to death and will have nothing. The people of the ruler who will come will destroy the city and the sanctuary. The end will come like a flood: War will continue until the end, and desolations have been decreed. {9:27} He will confirm a covenant with many for one 'seven.' In the middle of the 'seven' he will put an end to sacrifice and offering. And at the temple, he will set up an abomination that causes desolation, until the end that is decreed is poured out on him."

{10:1} In the third year of Cyrus king of Persia, a message was revealed to Daniel, who was called Belteshazzar. The message was true and it concerned a great conflict. Daniel understood the message and had understanding of the vision. {10:2} During those days, I, Daniel, was mourning for three weeks straight. {10:3} I ate no choice food; no meat or wine touched my lips; and I used no lotions at all until the three weeks were over. {10:4} On the twenty-fourth day of the first month, as I was standing on the bank of the great river, the Tigris, {10:5} I looked up and there before me was a man dressed in linen, with a belt of fine gold from Uphaz around his waist. {10:6} His body was like topaz, his face like lightning, his eyes like flaming torches, his arms and legs like the gleam of burnished bronze, and his voice like the sound of a multitude. {10:7} I, Daniel, was the only one who saw the vision; those who were with me did not see it, but such terror overwhelmed them that they fled and hid themselves. {10:8} So I was left alone, gazing at this great vision; I had no strength left, my face turned deathly pale and I was helpless. {10:9} Then I heard him speaking, and as I listened to him, I fell into a deep sleep, my face to the ground. {10:10} A hand touched me and set me trembling on my hands and knees. {10:11} He said, "Daniel, you who are highly esteemed, consider carefully the words I am about to speak to you, and stand up, for I have now been sent to you." And when he said this to me, I stood up trembling. {10:12} Then he continued, "Do not be afraid, Daniel. Since the first day that you set your mind to gain understanding and to humble yourself before your God, your words were heard, and I have come in response to them. {10:13} But the prince of the Persian kingdom resisted me twenty-one days. Then Michael, one of the chief princes, came to help me, because I was detained there with the king of Persia. {10:14} Now I have come to explain to you what will happen to your people in the future, for the vision concerns a time yet to come." {10:15} While he was saying this to me, I bowed with my face toward the ground and was speechless. {10:16} Then one who looked like a man touched my lips, and I opened my mouth and began to speak. I said to the one standing before me, "I am overcome with anguish because of the vision, my lord, and I feel very weak. {10:17} How can I, your servant, talk with you, my lord? My strength is gone, and I can hardly breathe." {10:18} Again the one who looked like a man touched me and gave me strength. {10:19} "Do not be afraid, you who are highly esteemed," he said. "Peace! Be strong now; be strong." When he spoke to me, I was strengthened and said, "Speak, my lord, since you have given me strength." {10:20} So he said, "Do you know why I have come to you? Soon I will return to fight against the prince of Persia, and when I go, the prince of Greece will come; {10:21} but first I will tell you what is written in the Book of Truth. (No one supports me against them except Michael, your prince.)

{11:1} In the first year of Darius the Mede, I, Daniel, stood up to support and strengthen him. {11:2} Now I will reveal the truth to you: Three more kings will arise in Persia, and then a fourth, who will be far richer than the others. By his great wealth and power, he will stir up everyone against the kingdom of Greece. {11:3} Then a mighty king will rise, who will rule with great authority and do as he pleases. {11:4} But when he has risen to power, his kingdom will be broken and divided toward the four winds of heaven. It will not go to his descendants, nor will it have the same authority he had, because his kingdom will be uprooted and given to others. {11:5} The king of the South will become strong, as will one of his princes. He will gain power and rule over a vast territory. {11:6} After some years, they will form an alliance. The daughter of the king of the South will go to the king of the North to make an agreement, but she will not retain her power, and he and his supporters will not endure. In those times, she will be betrayed along with those who brought her and her offspring. {11:7} But one from her family line will arise in his place, and he will come against the army of the king of the North and enter his fortress, fighting against them and prevailing. {11:8} He will also seize their gods, their metal images, and their valuable vessels of silver and gold and carry them off to Egypt. For some years he will leave the king of the North alone. {11:9} Then the king of the South will invade the realm of the king of the North but will retreat to his own country. {11:10} His sons will prepare for war and assemble a great army, which will sweep on like an irresistible flood and carry the battle as far as his fortress. {11:11} The king of the South will be enraged and will march out to fight against the king of the North, who will raise a large army, but it will be delivered into the hands of his enemy. {11:12} When the army is carried off, the king of the South will become arrogant and cause tens of thousands to fall, but he will not triumph. {11:13} For the king of the North will muster another army, larger than the first, and after several years he will advance with a huge army and a great deal of equipment. {11:14} In those times, many will rise against the king of the South. The violent ones among your own people will rebel in fulfillment of the vision, but without success. {11:15} Then the king of the North will come, build up a siege mound, and capture a fortified city. The forces of the South will be powerless to resist; even their best troops will not have the strength to stand. {11:16} The invader will do as he pleases; no one will be able to stand against him. He will establish himself in the Beautiful Land and will have the power to destroy it. {11:17} He will determine to come with the might of his entire kingdom and will make an alliance with the king of the South. And he will give him a daughter in marriage in order to overthrow the kingdom, but his plans will not succeed or help him. {11:18} Then he will turn his attention to the coastlands and will capture many. But a commander will put an end to his insolence and will turn his insolence back upon him. {11:19} After this, he will turn back toward the fortresses of his own land but will stumble and fall, to be seen no more. {11:20} His successor will send out a tax collector to maintain the royal splendor, but after a few days he will be destroyed, though not in anger or in battle. {11:21} He will be succeeded by a contemptible person who has not been given the honor of royalty. He will invade the kingdom when its people feel secure, and he will seize it through intrigue. {11:22} Then an overwhelming army will be swept away before him; both it and a prince of the covenant will be destroyed. {11:23} After coming to an agreement with him, he will act deceitfully, and with only a few people he will rise to power. {11:24} When the richest provinces feel secure, he will invade them and will achieve what neither his fathers nor his forefathers did. He will distribute plunder, loot, and wealth among his followers. He will plot the overthrow of fortresses—but only for a time. {11:25} With a large army he will stir up his strength and courage against the king of the South, who will mobilize a very large and powerful army but will not withstand the schemes plotted against him. { {11:26} Those who eat from his provisions will destroy him; his army will be swept away, and many will fall slain. {11:27} Both of these kings' hearts will be bent on evil, and they will speak lies at the same table, but it will not succeed, for the end is still to come at the appointed time. {11:28} Then he will return to his land with great wealth, and his heart will be set against the holy covenant. He will take action and then return to his own land. {11:29} At the appointed time, he will invade the south again, but it will not be as it was before or as it will be later. {11:30} Ships from the western coastlands will oppose him, and he will lose heart. Then he will turn back and vent his fury against the holy covenant. He will take action against it and then return to favor those who forsake the holy covenant. {11:31} His armed forces will rise up to desecrate the temple fortress and will abolish the daily sacrifice. Then they will set up the abomination that causes desolation. {11:32} With flattery he will corrupt those who have violated the covenant, but the people who know their God will firmly resist him. {11:33} Those who are wise will instruct many, though for a time they will fall by the sword or be burned, captured, or plundered. {11:34} When they fall, they will receive a little help, and many who are not sincere will join them. {11:35} Some of the wise will stumble, so that they may be refined, purified, and made spotless until the time of the end, for it will still come at the appointed time. {11:36} The king will do as he pleases. He will exalt and magnify himself above every god and will say unheard-of things against the God of gods. He will be successful until the time of wrath is completed, for what has been determined must take place. {11:37} He will show no regard for the gods of his ancestors or for the one desired by women, nor will he regard any god, but will exalt himself above them all. {11:38} Instead of them, he will honor a god of fortresses; a god unknown to his ancestors he will honor with gold and silver, with precious stones and costly gifts. {11:39} He will attack the mightiest fortresses with the help of a foreign god and will greatly honor those who acknowledge him. He will make them rulers over many people and will distribute the land at a price. {11:40} At the time of the end, the king of the South will engage him in battle, but the king of the North will storm against him with chariots and cavalry and a great fleet of ships. He will invade many countries and sweep through them like a flood. {11:41} He will also invade the Beautiful Land. Many countries will fall, but Edom, Moab and the leaders of Ammon will be delivered from his hand. {11:42} He will extend his power over many countries; Egypt will not escape. {11:43} He will gain control of the treasures of gold and silver and all the riches of Egypt, with the Libyans and Cushites in submission. {11:44} But reports from the east and the north will alarm him, and he will set out in a great rage to destroy and annihilate many. {11:45} He will pitch his royal tents between the seas at the beautiful holy mountain. Yet he will come to his end, and no one will help him.

{12:1} At that time, Michael, the great prince who protects your people, will arise. There will be a time of distress such as has not happened from the beginning of nations until then. But at that time your people—everyone whose name is found written in the book—will be delivered. {12:2} **Multitudes who sleep in the dust of the earth will awake: some to everlasting life, others to shame and everlasting contempt.** {12:3} Those who are wise will shine like the brightness of the heavens, and those who lead many to righteousness, like the stars for ever and ever. {12:4} But you, Daniel, roll up and seal the words of the scroll until the time of the end. Many will go here and there to increase knowledge. {12:5} Then I, Daniel, looked, and there before me stood two others, one on this bank of the river and one on the opposite bank. {12:6} One of them asked the man clothed in linen, who was above the waters of the river, "How long will it be before these astonishing things are fulfilled?" {12:7} The man clothed in linen, who was above the waters of the river, lifted his right hand and his left hand toward heaven, and swore by him who lives forever, saying, "It will be for a time, times and half a time. When the power of the holy people has been finally broken, all these things will be completed." {12:8} I heard, but I did not understand. So I asked, "My lord, what will the outcome of all this be?" {12:9} He replied, "Go your way, Daniel, because the words are rolled up and sealed until the time of the end. {12:10} Many will be purified, made spotless and refined, but the wicked will continue to be wicked. None of the wicked will understand, but those who are wise will understand. {12:11} "From the time that the daily sacrifice is abolished and the abomination that causes desolation is set up, there will be 1,290 days. {12:12} Blessed is the one who waits for and reaches the end of the 1,335 days. {12:13} "As for you, go your way till the end. You will rest, and then at the end of the days you will rise to receive your allotted inheritance.

Hosea

{1:1} This is the message that came to Hosea son of Beeri during the reigns of Uzziah, Jotham, Ahaz, and Hezekiah, kings of Judah, and during the reign of Jeroboam son of Joash, king of Israel. {1:2} **The LORD first spoke to Hosea. He said, "Go and marry a prostitute, so that some of her children will be conceived in prostitution. This will illustrate how Israel has acted like a prostitute by turning against the LORD."** {1:3} So Hosea married Gomer, the daughter of Diblaim, and she became pregnant and gave Hosea a son. {1:4} And the LORD said, "Name the child Jezreel, for I am about to punish King Jehu's dynasty to avenge the murders he committed at Jezreel. In fact, I will bring an end to Israel's independence. {1:5} "Then I will break Israel's military power in the Jezreel Valley." {1:6} Soon Gomer became pregnant again and gave birth to a daughter. And the LORD said to Hosea, "Name your daughter Lo-ruhamah—'Not loved'—for I will no longer show love to the people of Israel or forgive them. {1:7} "But I will show love to the people of Judah. I will free them from their enemies—not with weapons and armies, but by my power as the LORD their God." {1:8} After Gomer had weaned Lo-ruhamah, she again became pregnant and gave birth to a son. {1:9} And the LORD said, "Name him Lo-ammi—'Not my people'—for Israel is not my people, and I am not their God. {1:10} "Yet the time will come when Israel's descendants will be like the sands of the seashore—too many to count. Then, instead of saying to them, 'You are not my people,' I will say to them, 'You are children of the living God.' {1:11} "Then the people of Judah and Israel will unite together. They will choose one leader for themselves, and they will return from exile together. What a day that will be—the day of Jezreel—when God will sow his people in righteousness and prosperity!"

{2:1} "Tell your brothers, 'You are my people,' and your sisters, 'You have received mercy.' {2:2} "Plead with your mother—plead, for she is not my wife and I am not her husband. Tell her to remove the adulterous look from her face and the unfaithfulness from between her breasts. {2:3} Otherwise, I will strip her naked and expose her as she was on the day she was born. I will make her like a desert, turn her into a parched land, and let her die of thirst. {2:4} I will not show mercy to her children, for they are the children of adultery. {2:5} Their mother has been unfaithful and has conceived them in disgrace. She said, 'I will go after my lovers, who give me my food and water, my wool and linen, my olive oil and drink.' {2:6} "Therefore, I will block her path with thornbushes; I will wall her in so that she cannot find her way. {2:7} She will chase after her lovers but not catch them; she will look for them but not find them. Then she will say, 'I will go back to my husband as at first, for then I was better off than now.' {2:8} She doesn't realize that it was I who gave her everything she has—the grain, the new wine, the olive oil; I even gave her silver and gold. But she gave all my gifts to Baal. {2:9} "So now I will take back the ripened grain and new wine I generously provided each harvest season. I will take away the wool and linen clothing I gave her to cover her nakedness. {2:10} I will strip her naked in public, while all her lovers look on. No one will be able to rescue her from my hands. {2:11} I will put an end to all her celebrations: her annual festivals, her new moon celebrations, and her Sabbath days—all her appointed festivals. {2:12} I will destroy her grapevines and fig trees, things she claims her lovers gave her. I will let them grow into tangled thickets, where only wild animals will eat the fruit. {2:13} I will punish her for all those times when she burned incense to her images of Baal, when she put on her earrings and jewels and went out to look for her lovers but forgot all about me," says the LORD. {2:14} "Nevertheless, I will win her back once again. I will lead her into the desert and speak tenderly to her there. {2:15} I will return her vineyards to her and transform the Valley of Trouble into a gateway of hope. She will give herself to me there, as she did long ago when she was young, when I freed her from her captivity in Egypt. {2:16} When that day comes," says the LORD, "you will call me 'my husband' instead of 'my master.' {2:17} "For I will remove the names of the Baal idols from your lips, and you will never mention them again. {2:18} At that time I will make a covenant for them with the wild animals and the birds of the sky and the creatures that crawl on the ground. I will abolish the bow, the sword, and war from the land, so that all may live in safety. {2:19} I will betroth you to me forever; I will betroth you to me in righteousness and justice, in love and compassion. {2:20} I will betroth you to me in faithfulness, and you will acknowledge the LORD. {2:21} "In that day I will respond," declares the LORD— "I will respond to the skies, and they will respond to the earth; {2:22} and the earth will respond to the grain, the new wine and the olive oil, and they will respond to Jezreel. {2:23} I will plant her for myself in the land; I will show my love to the one I called 'Not my loved one.' I will say to those called 'Not my people,' 'You are my people'; and they will say, 'You are my God.'"

{3:1} Then the LORD said to me, "Go, show your love to your wife again, though she is loved by another man and is an adulteress. Love her as the LORD loves the Israelites, though they turn to other gods and love the sacred raisin cakes." {3:2} So I bought her for fifteen shekels of silver and about a homer and a half of barley. {3:3} Then I told her, "You are to live with me many days; you must not be a prostitute or be intimate with any man, and I will behave the same way toward you." {3:4} For the Israelites will live many days without king or prince, without sacrifice or sacred stones, without ephod or household gods. {3:5} Afterward the Israelites will return and seek the LORD their God and David their king. They will come trembling to the LORD and to his blessings in the last days."

{4:1} Listen, Israel, to the words of the LORD, for the LORD has a charge against the inhabitants of the land: There is no faithfulness, no love, no acknowledgment of God in the land. {4:2} There is only cursing, lying, and murder, stealing and adultery; they break all bounds, and bloodshed follows bloodshed. {4:3} Because of this the land dries up, and all who live in it waste away; the beasts of the field, the birds in the sky and the fish in the sea are swept away. {4:4} But let no one bring a charge, let no one accuse another, for your people are like those who bring charges against a priest. {4:5} You stumble day and night, and the prophets stumble with you. So I will destroy your mother— {4:6} **my people are destroyed from lack of knowledge. Because you have rejected knowledge, I also reject you as my priests; because you have ignored the law of your God, I also will ignore your children.** {4:7} The more priests there were, the more they sinned against me; they exchanged their glorious God for something disgraceful. {4:8} They feed on the sins of my people and relish their wickedness. {4:9} And it will be: Like people, like priests. I will punish both of them for their ways and repay them for their deeds. {4:10} They will eat but not have enough; they will engage in prostitution but not flourish, because they have deserted the LORD to give themselves {4:11} to prostitution; old wine and new wine take away their understanding. {4:12} My people consult a wooden idol, and a diviner's rod speaks to them. A spirit of prostitution leads them astray; they are unfaithful to their God. {4:13} They sacrifice on the mountaintops and burn offerings on the hills, under oak, poplar, and terebinth, where the shade is pleasant. Therefore your daughters turn to prostitution and your daughters-in-law to adultery. {4:14} I will not punish your daughters when they turn to prostitution, nor your daughters-in-law when they commit adultery, because the men themselves consort with harlots and sacrifice with shrine prostitutes—a people without understanding will come to ruin! {4:15} Though you, Israel, commit adultery, do not let Judah become guilty. "Do not go to Gilgal; do not go up to Beth Aven. And do not swear, 'As surely as the LORD lives!' {4:16} The Israelites are stubborn, like a stubborn heifer. How then can the LORD pasture them like lambs in a meadow? {4:17} Ephraim is joined to idols; leave him alone! {4:18} Even when their drinks are gone, they continue their prostitution; their rulers dearly love shameful ways. {4:19} A whirlwind will sweep them away, and their sacrifices will bring them shame.

{5:1} Listen, O priests, to this warning; pay attention, O house of Israel; give ear, O house of the king! For judgment is against you, because you have been a snare at Mizpah and a net spread out on Tabor. {5:2} The rebels are knee-deep in slaughter, yet I discipline them all. {5:3} I know Ephraim; Israel is not hidden from me. Now, Ephraim, you are deeply involved in prostitution; Israel is defiled. {5:4} Their deeds do not permit them to return to their God. A spirit of prostitution is in their heart; they do not acknowledge the LORD. {5:5} The arrogance of Israel testifies against them; Israel and Ephraim stumble in their sin; Judah also stumbles with them. {5:6} They go with their flocks and herds to seek the LORD, but they do not find him; he has withdrawn himself from them. {5:7} They are unfaithful to the LORD; they give birth to illegitimate children. Now their New Moon festivals will devour them and their fields. {5:8} Sound the trumpet in Gibeah, the horn in Ramah. Raise the battle cry in Beth Aven; lead on, Benjamin. {5:9} Ephraim will be laid waste on the day of reckoning. Among the tribes of Israel I proclaim what is certain. {5:10} Judah's leaders are like those who move boundary stones. I will pour out my wrath on them like a flood of water. {5:11} Ephraim is oppressed, trampled in judgment, because he is determined to pursue worthless idols. {5:12} So I am like a moth to Ephraim, like rot to the people of Judah. {5:13} When Ephraim saw his sickness and Judah his sores, then Ephraim turned to Assyria, and sent to the great king for help. But he is not able to cure you or heal your sores. {5:14} For I will be like a lion to Ephraim, like a great lion to Judah. I will tear them to pieces and go away; I will carry them off, with no one to rescue them. {5:15} Then I will return to my lair until they have borne their guilt and seek my face— in their misery they will earnestly seek me."

{6:1} Let's return to the LORD; he has torn us, but he will heal us; he has wounded us, but he will bind up our injuries. {6:2} After two days he will revive us; on the third day he will raise us up, and we will live in his presence. {6:3} Then we will understand, if we strive to know the LORD. His coming is as certain as the dawn; he will come to us like the rain, like the spring showers that water the earth. {6:4} O Ephraim, what shall I do with you? O Judah, what shall I do with you? Your loyalty is fleeting like the morning mist, like the dew that vanishes early. {6:5} So I have used the prophets to cut them down; I have killed them with the words from my mouth; my judgments shine like the light. {6:6} **For I desire mercy, not sacrifice, and acknowledgment of God rather than burnt offerings.** {6:7} But they, like Adam, have violated the covenant; there they have been unfaithful to me. {6:8} Gilead is a city of evildoers, stained with footprints of blood. {6:9} As marauders lie in ambush for a victim, so do bands of priests; they murder on the road to Shechem, carrying out their wicked schemes. {6:10} In the house of Israel, I have seen a horrible thing: there is prostitution in Ephraim; Israel is defiled. {6:11} Also, O Judah, a harvest is appointed for you when I restore the fortunes of my people.

{7:1} When I wanted to heal Israel, the sins of Ephraim and the wickedness of Samaria were exposed. They practice deceit; thieves break in, and bandits plunder. {7:2} Yet they do not realize that I remember all their evil deeds. Their sins surround them; they are always before me. {7:3} They delight the king with their wickedness, the princes with their lies. {7:4} They are all adulterers, burning like an oven whose fire the baker need not stir from the kneading of the dough till it rises. {7:5} On the day of the festival of our king, the princes become inflamed with wine, and he joins hands with mockers. {7:6} They are determined as an oven heated by a baker who rests all night, waiting for the dough to ferment. {7:7} At the heart of the oven they glow with intrigue; their leaders are consumed with passion. None of them calls upon me. {7:8} Ephraim mixes with the nations; Ephraim is a flat loaf not turned over. {7:9} Foreigners sap his strength, but he does not realize it. His hair is sprinkled with gray, but he does not notice. {7:10} Despite all this, the pride of Israel testifies against him, yet they do not turn to the LORD their God, nor seek him in all this. {7:11} Ephraim is like a dove, easily deceived and lacking sense. They call out to Egypt; they go to Assyria. {7:12} As they go, I will spread my net over them; I will bring them down like birds from the sky; I will punish them for their wickedness as their assembly has already heard. {7:13} Woe to them! They have strayed from me! Destruction to them! For they have rebelled against me. Though I wanted to redeem them, they have spoken lies against me. {7:14} They do not cry out to me from their hearts but wail on their beds. They slash themselves for grain and new wine; they turn away from me. {7:15} Though I trained and strengthened them, they plot evil against me. {7:16} They turn, but not upward; they are like a faulty bow. Their leaders will fall by the sword because of their insolent words. For this they will be ridiculed in the land of Egypt.

{8:1} Blow the trumpet! Sound the alarm! The enemy swoops down on the LORD's house like an eagle, because Israel has violated my covenant and rebelled against my law. {8:2} They cry out to me, "Our God, we acknowledge you!" {8:3} But Israel has rejected what is good; an enemy will pursue him. {8:4} They set up kings without my consent; they choose princes without my approval. With their silver and gold they make idols for themselves to their own destruction. {8:5} Samaria, throw off your calf-idol! My anger burns against them. How long will they be incapable of purity? {8:6} They are from Israel! This calf—a metalworker has made it; it is not God. It will be broken in pieces, that calf of Samaria. {8:7} They sow the wind and reap the whirlwind. The stalk has no head; it will produce no flour. If it were to yield grain, foreigners would swallow it up. {8:8} Israel is swallowed up; now she is among the nations like something no one wants. {8:9} For they have gone up to Assyria like a wild donkey wandering alone. Ephraim has sold herself to lovers. {8:10} Although they have sold themselves among the nations, I will now gather them together. They will soon writhe under the burden of the king and princes. {8:11} Ephraim has built many altars for sin offerings; these altars will become altars for sinning. {8:12} I wrote for them the many things of my law, but they regarded them as something foreign. {8:13} They offer sacrifices given to me and eat the meat, but the LORD is not pleased with them. Now he will remember their wickedness and punish their sins: They will return to Egypt. {8:14} Israel has forgotten their Maker and built palaces; Judah has fortified many towns. But I will send fire on their cities that will consume their fortresses.

{9:1} Israel, don't rejoice like other nations, for you have turned away from your God, seeking reward from every threshing floor. {9:2} Both the threshing floor and the winepress will fail them; the new wine will dry up. {9:3} They will not remain in the LORD's land; Ephraim will return to Egypt and eat unclean food in Assyria. {9:4} They will not present wine offerings to the LORD, nor will their sacrifices please him. Their food will be like mourners' bread; all who eat it will be unclean because their bread will only satisfy their hunger, not come into the house of the LORD. {9:5} What will you do on the appointed festivals and the days of the feasts of the LORD? {9:6} Destruction is coming; Egypt will gather them up, Memphis will bury them. Nettles will take over their precious possessions; thorns will invade their tents. {9:7} The time of reckoning has come; Israel will know it. The prophet is considered a fool, the inspired person is considered insane, because of the abundance of their sins and the intensity of their hatred. {9:8} Ephraim's watchman is with my God, but the prophet is a trap of a hunter in all his ways, and hostility reigns in the house of his God. {9:9} They have sunk deep into corruption, as in the days of Gibeah; God will remember their wickedness and punish their sins. {9:10} I found Israel like grapes in the wilderness; I saw your ancestors as the first ripe fruit on the fig tree. But they came to Baal Peor and consecrated themselves to that shameful idol; they became as vile as the thing they loved. {9:11} Ephraim's glory will fly away like a bird—from birth, from the womb, and from conception. {9:12} Even if they rear children, I will bereave them of every one. Woe to them when I turn away from them! {9:13} Ephraim, as I observed, is planted in a pleasant place, but Ephraim will bring out their children to the slayer. {9:14} Give them, LORD—what will you give? Give them wombs that miscarry and breasts that are dry. {9:15} All their wickedness is in Gilgal; there I hated them. Because of the wickedness of their deeds, I will drive them out of my house. I will no longer love them; all their leaders are rebellious. {9:16} Ephraim is blighted, their root is withered, they yield no fruit. Even if they bear children, I will slay their cherished offspring. {9:17} My God will reject them because they have not obeyed him; they will wander among the nations.

{10:1} Israel is like an empty vine, producing fruit only for itself. They have multiplied altars according to their abundance of fruit; they have adorned their sacred pillars with the goodness of their land. {10:2} But their hearts are divided; now they will be found guilty. God will break down their altars and destroy their sacred pillars. {10:3} They will say, "We have no king because we did not fear the LORD. What can a king do for us?" {10:4}

They have uttered empty words, making false promises and agreements. Therefore, judgment will spring up like poisonous weeds in their fields. {10:5} The people of Samaria will fear because of the calf-idols of Beth-aven. Both the people and their priests will mourn over them, for their glory has departed from them. {10:6} These idols will be carried off to Assyria as tribute to King Jareb. Ephraim will be put to shame, and Israel will be ashamed of their own counsel. {10:7} Samaria's king will be cut off like foam on the water. {10:8} The high places of Aven, the sin of Israel, will be destroyed. Thorns and thistles will overgrow their altars, and they will cry out to the mountains and hills to cover them and fall on them. {10:9} Since the days of Gibeah, Israel has sinned. There they stood, but the battle against the children of iniquity did not overtake them. {10:10} It is my desire to discipline them. The nations will be gathered against them when they are bound in their double guilt. {10:11} Ephraim is like a well-trained heifer that loves to thresh grain. But I will put a yoke on her fair neck. I will harness Ephraim, Judah will plow, and Jacob will break his clods. {10:12} So, sow righteousness for yourselves, reap the fruit of unfailing love, and break up your unplowed ground. It is time to seek the LORD until he comes and showers his righteousness on you. {10:13} You have plowed wickedness and reaped iniquity; you have eaten the fruit of lies because you have trusted in your own way and in your many warriors. {10:14} Therefore, a tumult will arise among your people, and all your fortresses will be plundered. Just as Shalman devastated Beth-arbel in the day of battle, mothers will be dashed to pieces with their children. {10:15} This is what Bethel will do to you because of your great wickedness. At daybreak, the king of Israel will utterly be cut off.

{11:1} **When Israel was a child, I loved him, and I called my son out of Egypt.** {11:2} But the more I called them, the more they went from me. They kept sacrificing to the Baals and burning incense to idols. {11:3} Yet it was I who taught Ephraim to walk; I took them up by their arms, but they did not acknowledge that I healed them. {11:4} I led them with cords of kindness, with the bands of love; I lifted the yoke from their neck and stooped down to feed them. {11:5} They shall not return to the land of Egypt; instead, the Assyrian will rule over them because they refused to repent. {11:6} The sword will rage against their cities, consuming their fortified gates and devouring them because of their own schemes. {11:7} My people are determined to turn away from me. Even though they call to the Most High, he will not raise them up at all. {11:8} How can I give you up, Ephraim? How can I hand you over, Israel? How can I treat you like Admah? How can I make you like Zeboiim? My heart recoils within me; my compassion grows warm and tender. {11:9} I will not execute my fierce anger; I will not again destroy Ephraim; for I am God and not a man, the Holy One in your midst, and I will not come in wrath. {11:10} They shall go after the LORD; he will roar like a lion; when he roars, his children shall come trembling from the west. {11:11} They shall come trembling like birds from Egypt, and like doves from the land of Assyria; and I will return them to their homes, declares the LORD. {11:12} Ephraim surrounds me with lies, and the house of Israel with deceit, but Judah still walks with God and is faithful to the Holy One.

{12:1} Ephraim feeds on the wind and pursues the east wind; every day he multiplies lies and desolation. They make treaties with Assyria and send olive oil to Egypt. {12:2} The LORD also has a dispute with Judah and will punish Jacob according to his ways; he will repay him according to his deeds. {12:3} In the womb, he took his brother by the heel, and in his strength, he struggled with God. {12:4} He struggled with the angel and prevailed; he wept and sought his favor. He found him at Bethel, and there he spoke with us— {12:5} the LORD, the God of hosts; the LORD is his name! {12:6} Therefore, return to your God; maintain love and justice, and always put your hope in your God. {12:7} Ephraim boasts, "I am very rich; I have acquired wealth for myself. In all my labors, they can find in me no iniquity that is sin." {12:8} But I am the LORD your God from the land of Egypt; I will again make you dwell in tents, as in the days of the appointed festival. {12:9} I spoke to the prophets; it was I who multiplied visions and spoke parables through the prophets. {12:10} Is Gilead wicked? Its people are worthless! In Gilgal, they sacrifice bulls; their altars are like piles of stones on the furrows of a field. {12:11} Jacob fled to the country of Aram; Israel worked for a spouse and for a wife tended sheep. {12:12} But by a prophet the LORD brought Israel up from Egypt, and by a prophet he was preserved. {12:13} Ephraim has stirred up bitter anger;{12:14} so his Lord will leave his bloodguilt on him and repay him for his contempt.

{13:1} When Ephraim spoke, there was trembling; he was exalted in Israel. But when he became guilty through Baal worship, he died. {13:2} Now they sin more and more, crafting idols of silver, skillfully made by artisans. They say of these idols, "Let those who sacrifice kiss the calves." {13:3} Therefore, they will be like the morning mist, like the dew that vanishes early, like chaff blown from the threshing floor, like smoke escaping through a window. {13:4} Yet I am the LORD your God who brought you out of Egypt; you shall acknowledge no God but me, for there is no Savior besides me. {13:5} I cared for you in the wilderness, in the land of drought. {13:6} But when they had pasture, they became satisfied; their hearts became proud, and they forgot me. {13:7} So I will be like a lion to them, like a leopard lurking by the path. {13:8} I will attack them like a bear robbed of her cubs and tear open the rib cage. I will devour them like a lioness— the wild animals will tear them apart. {13:9} O Israel, you are destroying yourself, but in me is your help. {13:10} I will be your king; where is any other that may save you in all your cities? And your judges, of whom you said, "Give me a king and princes"? {13:11} I gave you a king in my anger, and I took him away in my wrath. {13:12} The guilt of Ephraim is bound up; his sin is stored away. {13:13} The pains of childbirth come upon him, but he is an unwise son; when the time arrives, he does not come to the opening of the womb. {13:14} I will deliver them from the power of the grave; I will redeem them from death. Where, O death, are your plagues? Where, O grave, is your destruction? {13:15} Though Ephraim is fruitful among his brothers, an east wind will come, the breath of the LORD rising from the desert; his spring will fail, and his fountain will dry up. His storehouse will be plundered of all its treasures. {13:16} Samaria will bear her guilt, for she has rebelled against her God. They will fall by the sword; their little ones will be dashed to the ground, their pregnant women ripped open.

{14:1} O Israel, return to the LORD your God, for you have stumbled because of your iniquity. {14:2} **Take words with you and return to the LORD; say to him, "Forgive all our sins and receive us graciously, that we may offer the fruit of our lips.** {14:3} Assyria cannot save us; we will not mount warhorses. We will never again say 'Our gods' to what our own hands have made, for in you the fatherless find compassion." {14:4} I will heal their waywardness and love them freely, for my anger has turned away from them. {14:5} I will be like the dew to Israel; he will blossom like a lily. Like a cedar of Lebanon, he will send down his roots; {14:6} his young shoots will grow. His splendor will be like an olive tree, his fragrance like a cedar of Lebanon. {14:7} People will dwell again in his shade; they will flourish like the grain, they will blossom like the vine— Israel's fame will be like the wine of Lebanon. {14:8} Ephraim shall say, "What have I to do anymore with idols?" I will answer him and care for him. I am like a flourishing juniper; your fruitfulness comes from me." {14:9} Who is wise? Let them realize these things. Who is discerning? Let them understand. The ways of the LORD are right; the righteous walk in them, but the rebellious stumble in them.

Joel

{1:1} This is the message that the LORD gave to Joel son of Pethuel. {1:2} Listen, you elders; pay attention, all you who live in the land! Have you ever seen anything like this before? {1:3} Tell your children about it in the years to come, and let your children tell their children. Pass the story down from generation to generation. {1:4} **What the cutting locust left, the swarming locust has eaten. What the swarming locust left, the hopping locust has eaten. And what the hopping locust left, the destroying locust has eaten.** {1:5} Wake up, you drunkards, and weep! All you wine drinkers, cry out in despair because the sweet wine has been taken away from you. {1:6} A vast army of locusts has invaded my land, a terrible army too numerous to count. Its teeth are like lions' teeth, its fangs like those of a lioness. {1:7} It has destroyed my grapevines and ruined my fig trees, stripping their bark and destroying it, leaving the branches white and bare. {1:8} Weep like a bride dressed in black, mourning the death of her husband. {1:9} Grain offerings and drink offerings are cut off from the house of the LORD. The priests are mourning, the ministers of the LORD. {1:10} The fields are ruined, the land is stripped bare. The grain is destroyed, the grapes have withered, and the olive oil is gone. {1:11} Despair, you farmers! Cry, you vine growers! Weep, all you who delight in wine, for the grapes are gone and the vineyards are ruined. {1:12} The fig trees are withered, and the pomegranate trees, palm trees, and apple trees—all the fruit trees—have dried up. All joy has dried up with them. {1:13} Dress yourselves in burlap and weep, you priests! Howl, you who serve before the altar! Come, spend the night in burlap, you ministers of my God. For there is no grain or wine to offer at the Temple of your God. {1:14} Announce a time of fasting; call the people together for a solemn meeting. Bring the leaders and all the people of the land into the Temple of the LORD your God, and cry out to him there. {1:15} The day of the LORD is near, the day when destruction comes from the Almighty. How terrible that day will be! {1:16} Our food disappears before our very eyes. No joyful celebrations are held in the house of our God. {1:17} The seeds die in the parched ground, and the grain crops fail. The barns stand empty, and granaries are abandoned. {1:18} How the animals moan with hunger! The herds of cattle wander about confused, because they have no pasture. The flocks of sheep and goats bleat in misery. {1:19} LORD, help us! The fire has consumed the wilderness pastures, and flames have burned up all the trees. {1:20} Even the wild animals cry out to you because the streams have dried up, and fire has consumed the wilderness pastures.

{2:1} Sound the alarm in Zion; shout a warning on my holy mountain. Let everyone tremble in fear because the day of the LORD is near—it will soon arrive. {2:2} It will be a day of darkness and gloom, a day of clouds and thick darkness. Like the dawn spreading across the mountains, a great and mighty army approaches. There has never been anything like it before, and there will never be anything like it again. {2:3} Fire burns in front of them, and flames follow after them. Ahead of them the land lies as beautiful as the Garden of Eden. Behind them is nothing but desolation; not one thing escapes. {2:4} They look like horses; they charge forward like war horses. {2:5} They leap on the mountaintops with a noise like the rumble of chariots. They're like a roaring fire that devours everything in its path. They're like a powerful army ready for battle. {2:6} Terror fills the people as they see them coming. Every face turns pale with fear. {2:7} They march like warriors and climb the walls like soldiers. They all keep in line, never breaking ranks. {2:8} They don't jostle each other; each moves in exactly the right position. They break through defenses without missing a step. {2:9} They swarm over the city and run along its walls. They enter all the houses, climbing like thieves through the windows. {2:10} The earth quakes as they advance, and the heavens tremble. The sun and moon grow dark, and the stars no longer shine. {2:11} The LORD is at the head of the column. He leads them with a shout. This is his mighty army, and they follow his orders. The day of the LORD is an awesome, terrible thing. Who can endure it? {2:12} That is why the LORD says, "Turn to me now, while there is time. Give me your hearts. Come with fasting, weeping, and mourning. {2:13} **Don't tear your clothing in your grief; instead, tear your hearts." Return to the LORD your God, for he is merciful and compassionate, slow to get angry and filled with unfailing love. He is eager to relent and not punish.** {2:14} Who knows? Perhaps he will give you a reprieve, sending you a blessing instead of this curse. Perhaps you will be able to offer grain and wine to the LORD your God as before. {2:15} Sound the alarm in Jerusalem! Announce a time of fasting; call the people together for a solemn meeting. {2:16} Bring everyone—the elders, the children, and even the babies. Call the bridegroom from his quarters and the bride from her private room. {2:17} Let the priests, who minister in the LORD's presence, stand and weep between the entry room to the Temple and the altar. Let them pray, "Spare your people, LORD! Don't let your special possession become an object of mockery. Don't let them become a joke for unbelieving foreigners who say, 'Has the God of Israel left them?'" {2:18} Then the LORD will pity his people and jealously guard the honor of his land. {2:19} The LORD will reply, "Look! I am sending you grain and new wine and olive oil, enough to satisfy your needs. You will no longer be an object of mockery among the surrounding nations. {2:20} I will drive away these armies from the north. I will send them into the parched wastelands. Those in the front will be driven into the Dead Sea, and those at the rear into the Mediterranean. The stench of their rotting bodies will rise over the land." Surely the LORD has done great things! {2:21} Don't be afraid, my people. Be glad now and rejoice, for the LORD has done great things. {2:22} Don't be afraid, you animals of the field, for the wilderness pastures will soon be green. The trees will again be filled with fruit; fig trees and grapevines will be loaded down once more. {2:23} Rejoice, you people of Jerusalem! Rejoice in the LORD your God! For the rain he sends demonstrates his faithfulness. Once more the autumn rains will come, as well as the rains of spring. {2:24} The threshing floors will again be piled high with grain, and the presses will overflow with new wine and olive oil. {2:25} **The LORD says, "I will give you back what you lost to the swarming locusts, the hopping locusts, the stripping locusts, and the cutting locusts. It was I who sent this great destroying army against you.** {2:26} Once again you will have all the food you want, and you will praise the LORD your God, who does these miracles for you. Never again will my people be disgraced. {2:27} Then you will know that I am among my people Israel, that I am the LORD your God, and there is no other. Never again will my people be disgraced. {2:28} **Afterward, I will pour out my Spirit on all people. Your sons and daughters will prophesy, your old men will dream dreams, and your young men will see visions.** {2:29} Even on the servants and handmaids, I will pour out my Spirit in those days. {2:30} I will show wonders in the heavens and on the earth: blood, fire, and columns of smoke. {2:31} The sun will be turned to darkness, and the moon to blood, before the great and dreadful day of the LORD comes. {2:32} **And everyone who calls on the name of the LORD will be saved; for on Mount Zion and in Jerusalem there will be deliverance, as the LORD has said, even among the survivors whom the LORD calls.**

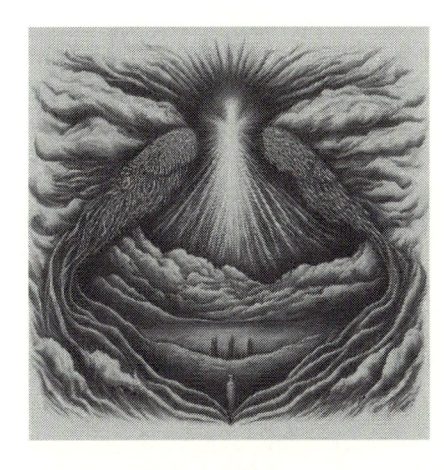

{3:1} For behold, in those days and at that time, when I restore the fortunes of Judah and Jerusalem, {3:2} I will gather all nations and bring them down to the Valley of Jehoshaphat. There I will enter into judgment against them concerning my people, my inheritance Israel, whom they have scattered among the nations and divided up my land. {3:3} They have cast lots for my people, traded boys for prostitutes, and sold girls for wine to drink. {3:4} Now what have you against me, Tyre and Sidon and all you regions of Philistia? Are you repaying me for something I have done? If you are paying me back, I will swiftly and speedily return on your own heads what you have done. {3:5} You took my silver and gold and carried off my finest treasures to your temples. {3:6} You sold the people of Judah and Jerusalem to the Greeks, that you might send them far from their homeland. {3:7} Behold, I will rouse them out of the places to which you sold them, and I will return on your own heads what you have done. {3:8} I will sell your sons and daughters to the people of Judah, and they will sell them to the Sabeans, a nation far away. The LORD has spoken. {3:9} Proclaim this among the nations: Prepare for war! Rouse the warriors! Let all the fighting men draw near and attack. {3:10} Beat your plowshares into swords and your pruning hooks into spears. Let the weakling say, "I am strong!" {3:11} Come quickly, all you nations from every side, and assemble there. Bring down your warriors, O LORD! {3:12} Let the nations be roused; let them advance into the Valley of Jehoshaphat, for there I will sit to judge all the nations on every side. {3:13} Swing the sickle, for the harvest is ripe. Come, trample the grapes, for the winepress is full and the vats overflow—so great is their wickedness! {3:14} Multitudes, multitudes in the valley of decision! For the day of the LORD is near in the valley of decision. {3:15} The sun and moon will be darkened, and the stars no longer shine. {3:16} The LORD will roar from Zion and thunder from Jerusalem; the earth and the heavens will tremble. But the LORD will be a refuge for his people, a stronghold for the people of Israel. {3:17} Then you will know that I, the LORD your God, dwell in Zion, my holy mountain. Jerusalem will be holy; never again will foreigners invade her. {3:18} In that day the mountains will drip new wine, and the hills will flow with milk; all the ravines of Judah will run with water. A fountain will flow out of the LORD's house and will water the valley of acacias. {3:19} But Egypt will be desolate, Edom a desert waste, because of violence done to the people of Judah, in whose land they shed innocent blood. {3:20} Judah will be inhabited forever, and Jerusalem through all generations. {3:21} Shall I leave their innocent blood unavenged? No, I will not. The LORD dwells in Zion.

Amos

{1:1} These are the words of Amos, who was among the shepherds of Tekoa. He received these visions concerning Israel during the reign of Uzziah, king of Judah, and Jeroboam, the son of Joash, king of Israel, two years before the earthquake. {1:2} Amos declared, "The LORD will roar from Zion and thunder from Jerusalem; the pastures of the shepherds will mourn, and the summit of Mount Carmel will wither." {1:3} This is what the LORD says: "Because Damascus has committed three sins, even four, I will not relent. They have threshed Gilead with sledges having iron teeth. {1:4} Therefore, I will send fire upon the house of Hazael, and it will consume the fortresses of Ben-hadad. {1:5} I will break down the gate of Damascus; I will cut off the ruler from the Valley of Aven, and the one who wields the scepter from Beth-eden. The people of Aram will be exiled to Kir," says the LORD. {1:6} This is what the LORD says: "Because Gaza has committed three sins, even four, I will not relent. They carried entire communities into exile, to hand them over to Edom. {1:7} Therefore, I will send fire upon the walls of Gaza, and it will consume its citadels. {1:8} I will cut off the ruler from Ashdod, and the one who wields the scepter from Ashkelon. I will turn My hand against Ekron, and the remnant of the Philistines will perish," says the Lord GOD. {1:9} This is what the LORD says: "Because Tyre has committed three sins, even four, I will not relent. They delivered entire communities to Edom, disregarding a treaty of brotherhood. {1:10} Therefore, I will send fire upon the walls of Tyre, and it will consume its citadels." {1:11} This is what the LORD says: "Because Edom has committed three sins, even four, I will not relent. They pursued their brother with the sword, stifling all compassion; their anger raged continually, and their fury flamed unchecked. {1:12} Therefore, I will send fire upon Teman, and it will consume the citadels of Bozrah." {1:13} This is what the LORD says: "Because the Ammonites have committed three sins, even four, I will not relent. They ripped open the pregnant women of Gilead in order to enlarge their territory. {1:14} Therefore, I will kindle a fire upon the walls of Rabbah, and it will consume its citadels amid war cries on the day of battle, amid violent winds on a stormy day. {1:15} Then their king will go into exile, he and his officials together," says the LORD.

{2:1} This is what the LORD says: "Because Moab has committed three sins, even four, I will not relent. They burned the bones of the king of Edom to lime. {2:2} Therefore, I will send fire upon Moab, and it will consume the citadels of Kerioth. Moab will perish amid uproar, with shouting and the blast of the trumpet. {2:3} I will cut off the ruler from its midst and kill all its officials with him," says the LORD. {2:4} This is what the LORD says: "Because Judah has committed three sins, even four, I will not relent. They have rejected the law of the LORD and have not kept his decrees; they have been led astray by false gods, the same gods their ancestors followed. {2:5} Therefore, I will send fire upon Judah, and it will consume the citadels of Jerusalem." {2:6} This is what the LORD says: "Because Israel has committed three sins, even four, I will not relent. They sell the innocent for silver, and the needy for a pair of sandals. {2:7} They trample on the heads of the poor as on the dust of the ground and deny justice to the oppressed. Father and son use the same girl and so profane my holy name. {2:8} They lie down beside every altar on garments taken in pledge. In the house of their god, they drink wine taken as fines. {2:9} Yet I destroyed the Amorites before them, though they were as tall as cedars and as strong as oaks. I destroyed their fruit above and their roots below. {2:10} I brought you up out of Egypt and led you forty years in the wilderness to give you the land of the Amorites.

{2:11} "I also raised up prophets from among your children and Nazirites from among your youths. Is this not true, people of Israel?" declares the LORD. {2:12} "But you made the Nazirites drink wine and commanded the prophets not to prophesy. {2:13} "Now then, I will crush you as a cart crushes when loaded with grain. {2:14} The swift will not escape, the strong will not muster their strength, and the warrior will not save his life. {2:15} The archer will not stand his ground, the fleet-footed soldier will not get away, and the horseman will not save his life. {2:16} Even the bravest warriors will flee naked on that day," declares the LORD.

{3:1} Listen to this message that the LORD has spoken against you, O children of Israel, against the entire family that I brought up from the land of Egypt, saying: {3:2} "You only have I known of all the families of the earth; therefore I will punish you for all your iniquities. {3:3} "Do two walk together without agreeing on the direction? {3:4} Does a lion roar in the forest when it has no prey? Does a young lion growl in its den if it has caught nothing? {3:5} Does a bird fall into a trap on the ground where no snare has been set? Does a trap spring up from the earth if it has caught nothing at all? {3:6} If a trumpet sounds in a city, will not the people tremble? If calamity comes to a city, has not the LORD caused it? {3:7} **Surely the Lord GOD does nothing without revealing his plan to his servants the prophets.** {3:8} The lion has roared— who will not fear? The Lord GOD has spoken— who can but prophesy? {3:9} Proclaim this among the leaders in Ashdod and among the leaders in Egypt: 'Assemble yourselves on the mountains of Samaria; see the great unrest within her and the oppression among her people.' {3:10} "They do not know how to do right," declares the LORD, "those who store up violence and destruction in their citadels." {3:11} Therefore, this is what the Lord GOD says: "An enemy will surround the land; he will pull down your strongholds and plunder your fortresses." {3:12} This is what the LORD says: "As a shepherd saves from the lion's mouth only two leg bones or a piece of an ear, so will the Israelites be saved, those who sit in Samaria on the edge of their beds and in Damascus on their couches." {3:13} "Hear and testify against the house of Jacob," declares the Lord GOD, the God of Hosts. {3:14} "For in the day I punish Israel for their sins, I will also destroy the altars of Bethel; the horns of the altar will be cut off and fall to the ground. {3:15} I will demolish both the winter and summer houses, and the houses adorned with ivory will perish. The mansions will be demolished," declares the LORD.

{4:1} **Listen to this message, you cows of Bashan, who are on the mountain of Samaria, who oppress the poor, who crush the needy, who say to their husbands, "Bring us drinks!"** {4:2} The Lord GOD has sworn by his holiness: "Behold, the days are coming upon you when they shall take you away with hooks, even the last of you with fishhooks. {4:3} And you shall go out through the breaches, each cow straight ahead; and you shall be cast out into Harmon," declares the LORD. {4:4} "Go to Bethel and sin; go to Gilgal and multiply transgression; bring your sacrifices every morning, your tithes every three years. {4:5} Offer a thanksgiving sacrifice of leavened bread, and proclaim freewill offerings, publish them; for so you love to do, O people of Israel," declares the Lord GOD. {4:6} "I gave you cleanness of teeth in all your cities, and lack of bread in all your places, yet you did not return to me," declares the LORD. {4:7} "I also withheld the rain from you when there were yet three months to the harvest; I would send rain on one city, and send no rain on another city; one field would have rain, and the field on which it did not rain would wither; {4:8} so two or three cities would wander to another city to drink water, and would not be satisfied; yet you did not return to me," declares the LORD. {4:9} "I struck you with blight and mildew; your many gardens and your vineyards, your fig trees and your olive trees the locust devoured; yet you did not return to me," declares the LORD. {4:10} "I sent among you a pestilence after the manner of Egypt; I killed your young men with the sword, and carried away your horses, and I made the stench of your camp go up into your nostrils; yet you did not return to me," declares the LORD. {4:11} "I overthrew some of you, as when God overthrew Sodom and Gomorrah, and you were as a brand plucked out of the burning; yet you did not return to me," declares the LORD. {4:12} "Therefore thus I will do to you, O Israel; because I will do this to you, prepare to meet your God, O Israel!" {4:13} "For behold, he who forms the mountains and creates the wind, and declares to man what is his thought, who makes the morning darkness, and treads on the heights of the earth— the LORD, the God of hosts, is his name!"

{5:1} Listen to this message, O house of Israel, which I bring against you as a lamentation: {5:2} *The virgin of Israel has fallen; she will not rise again. She lies forsaken on her land; there is no one to lift her up.* {5:3} For thus says the Lord GOD: "The city that went out a thousand strong will have only a hundred left, and the one that went out a hundred strong will have only ten left to the house of Israel. {5:4} "For thus says the LORD to the house of Israel: Seek me, and you shall live. {5:5} But do not seek Bethel, and do not enter into Gilgal, or cross over to Beersheba; for Gilgal shall surely go into exile, and Bethel shall come to nothing. {5:6} *Seek the LORD, and you shall live, lest he break out like fire in the house of Joseph, and it devour with none to quench it in Bethel.* {5:7} You who turn justice into wormwood and cast righteousness to the ground, {5:8} "He who made the Pleiades and Orion, and turns deep darkness into the morning and darkens the day into night, who calls for the waters of the sea and pours them out on the surface of the earth— the LORD is his name— {5:9} who brings destruction upon the strong, so that destruction comes upon the fortress. {5:10} *"They hate him who reproves in the gate, and they abhor him who speaks the truth.* {5:11} Therefore because you trample on the poor and you exact taxes of grain from him, you have built houses of hewn stone, but you shall not dwell in them; you have planted pleasant vineyards, but you shall not drink their wine. {5:12} For I know how many are your transgressions and how great are your sins— you who afflict the righteous, who take a bribe, and turn aside the needy in the gate. {5:13} Therefore he who is prudent will keep silent in such a time, for it is an evil time. {5:14} *"Seek good, and not evil, that you may live; and so the LORD, the God of hosts, will be with you, as you have said.* {5:15} Hate evil, and love good, and establish justice in the gate; it may be that the LORD, the God of hosts, will be gracious to the remnant of Joseph. {5:16} Therefore thus says the LORD, the God of hosts, the Lord: In all the squares there shall be wailing, and in all the streets they shall say, 'Alas! Alas!' They shall call the farmers to mourning and to wailing those who are skilled in lamentation. {5:17} And in all vineyards there shall be wailing, for I will pass through your midst," says the LORD. {5:18} "Woe to you who desire the day of the LORD! Why would you have the day of the LORD? It is darkness, and not light, {5:19} as if a man fled from a lion, and a bear met him, or went into the house and leaned his hand against the wall, and a serpent bit him. {5:20} Is not the day of the LORD darkness, and not light, and gloom with no brightness in it? {5:21} "I hate, I despise your feasts, and I take no delight in your solemn assemblies. {5:22} *Even though you offer me your burnt offerings and grain offerings, I will not accept them; and the peace offerings of your fattened animals, I will not look upon them.* {5:23} Take away from me the noise of your songs; to the melody of your harps I will not listen. {5:24} But let justice roll down like waters, and righteousness like an ever-flowing stream. {5:25} "Did you bring to me sacrifices and offerings during the forty years in the wilderness, O house of Israel? {5:26} *You shall take up Sikkuth your king, and Kiyyun your star-god— your images that you made for yourselves,* {5:27} and I will send you into exile beyond Damascus," says the LORD, whose name is the God of hosts.

{6:1} Woe to those who are at ease in Zion and trust in the mountain of Samaria—those who are named the notable men of the nations, to whom the house of Israel comes! {6:2} Go to Calneh and see; from there go to Hamath the great; then go down to Gath of the Philistines. Are they better than these kingdoms? Is their territory greater than your territory? {6:3} You who put far away the day of disaster and bring near the seat of violence— {6:4} who lie on beds of ivory and stretch themselves out on their couches, who eat lambs from the flock and calves from the midst of the stall; {6:5} who sing idle songs to the sound of the harp, and like David invent for themselves instruments of music; {6:6} who drink wine in bowls and anoint themselves with the finest oils, but are not grieved over the ruin of Joseph. {6:7} Therefore they shall now be the first of those who go into exile, and the revelry of those who stretch themselves out shall pass away. {6:8} The Lord GOD has sworn by himself, declares the LORD, the God of hosts: "I abhor the pride of Jacob and hate his strongholds, and I will deliver up the city and all that is in it." {6:9} And if ten men remain in one house, they shall die. {6:10} And when one's relative, the one who anoints him for burial, shall take him up to bring the bones out of the house, and shall say to him who is in the innermost parts of the house, "Is there still anyone with you?" he shall say, "No." And he shall say, "Silence! We must not mention the name of the LORD." {6:11} For behold, the LORD commands, and the great house shall be struck down into fragments, and the little house into bits. {6:12} Do horses run on rocks? Does one plow there with oxen? But you have turned justice into poison and the fruit of righteousness into wormwood— {6:13} you who rejoice in Lo-debar, who say, "Have we not by our own strength captured Karnaim for ourselves?" {6:14} "Behold, I will raise up against you a nation, O house of Israel," declares the LORD, the God of hosts; "and they shall oppress you from Lebo-hamath to the Brook of the Arabah."

{7:1} This is what the Lord GOD showed me: behold, he was forming locusts when the latter growth was just beginning to sprout, and indeed it was the latter growth after the king's mowings. {7:2} When they had finished eating the grass of the land, I said, "O Lord GOD, please forgive! How can Jacob stand? He is so small." {7:3} The LORD relented concerning this: "It shall not be," said the LORD. {7:4} This is what the Lord GOD showed me: behold, the Lord GOD was calling for a judgment by fire, and it devoured the great deep and was eating up the land. {7:5} Then I said, "O Lord GOD, please cease! How can Jacob stand? He is so small." {7:6} The LORD relented concerning this: "This also shall not be," said the Lord GOD. {7:7} This is what he showed me: behold, the Lord was standing beside a wall built with a plumb line, with a plumb line in his hand. {7:8} And the LORD said to me, "Amos, what do you see?" And I said, "A plumb line." Then the Lord said, "Behold, I am setting a plumb line in the midst of my people Israel; I will never again pass by them; {7:9} the high places of Isaac shall be made desolate, and the sanctuaries of Israel shall be laid waste, and I will rise against the house of Jeroboam with the sword." {7:10} Then Amaziah the priest of Bethel sent to Jeroboam king of Israel, saying, "Amos has conspired against you in the midst of the house of Israel. The land is not able to bear all his words. {7:11} For thus Amos has said, 'Jeroboam shall die by the sword, and Israel must go into exile away from its land.'" {7:12} And Amaziah said to Amos, "O seer, go, flee away to the land of Judah, and eat bread there, and prophesy there, {7:13} but never again prophesy at Bethel, for it is the king's sanctuary, and it is a temple of the kingdom." {7:14} Then Amos answered and said to Amaziah, "I was no prophet, nor a prophet's son, but I was a herdsman and a dresser of sycamore figs. {7:15} But the LORD took me from following the flock, and the LORD said to me, 'Go, prophesy to my people Israel.' {7:16} Now therefore hear the word of the LORD. "You say, 'Do not prophesy against Israel, and do not preach against the house of Isaac.' {7:17} *Therefore thus says the LORD: 'Your wife shall be a prostitute in the city, and your sons and your daughters shall fall by the sword, and your land shall be divided up with a measuring line; you yourself shall die in an unclean land, and Israel shall surely go into exile away from its land.'"*

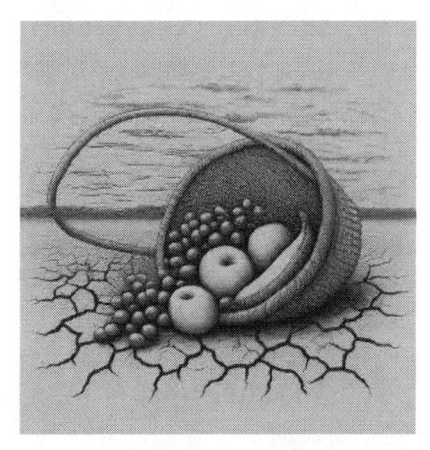

{8:1} This is what the Lord GOD showed me: behold, a basket of summer fruit. {8:2} And he said, "Amos, what do you see?" And I said, "A basket of summer fruit." Then the LORD said to me, "The end has come upon my people Israel; I will not pass by them again. {8:3} The songs of the temple shall become wailings in that day," declares the Lord GOD. "There will be many dead bodies in every place. They shall be cast out in silence. {8:4} Hear this, you who trample on the needy and bring the poor of the land to an end, {8:5} saying, 'When will the new moon be over, that we may sell grain? And the Sabbath, that we may offer wheat for sale, that we may make the ephah small and the shekel great and deal deceitfully with false balances, {8:6} that we may buy the poor for silver and the needy for a pair of sandals and sell the chaff of the wheat?' {8:7} The LORD has sworn by the pride of Jacob: "Surely I will never forget any of their deeds. {8:8} Shall not the land tremble on this account, and everyone mourn who dwells in it, and all of it rise like the Nile, and be tossed about and sink again, like the Nile of Egypt?" {8:9} "And on that day," declares the Lord GOD, "I will make the sun go down at noon and darken the earth in broad daylight. {8:10} I will turn your feasts into mourning and all your songs into lamentation; I will bring sackcloth on every waist and baldness on every head; I will make it like the mourning for an only son and the end of it like a bitter day. {8:11} *"Behold, the days are coming," declares the Lord GOD, "when I will send a famine on the land—not a famine of bread, nor a thirst for water, but of hearing the words of the LORD.* {8:12} They shall wander from sea to sea, and from north to east; they shall run to and fro, to seek the word of the LORD, but they shall not find it. {8:13} In that day the lovely virgins and the young men shall faint for thirst. {8:14} Those who swear by the Guilt of

Samaria, and say, 'As your god lives, O Dan,' and, 'As the Way of Beersheba lives,' they shall fall, and never rise again."

{9:1} I saw the LORD standing upon the altar, and he said, "Strike the top of the doorframe, so that the thresholds shake. Bring them down on the heads of all the people; those who are left I will kill with the sword. None will get away, none will escape. {9:2} Though they dig down to the depths below, from there my hand will take them. Though they climb up to the heavens above, from there I will bring them down. {9:3} Though they hide themselves on the top of Carmel, there I will hunt them down and seize them. Though they hide from my eyes at the bottom of the sea, there I will command the serpent to bite them. {9:4} Though they are driven into exile by their enemies, there I will command the sword to kill them. I will keep my eye on them for harm and not for good. {9:5} The Lord GOD Almighty touches the earth, and it melts, and all who live in it mourn; the whole land rises like the Nile, then sinks like the river of Egypt. {9:6} He builds his lofty palace in the heavens and sets its foundation on the earth; he calls for the waters of the sea and pours them out over the face of the land— the LORD is his name. {9:7} "Are not you Israelites the same to me as the Cushites?" declares the LORD. "Did I not bring Israel up from Egypt, the Philistines from Caphtor and the Arameans from Kir? {9:8} "Surely the eyes of the Sovereign LORD are on the sinful kingdom. I will destroy it from the face of the earth— yet I will not totally destroy the house of Jacob," declares the LORD. {9:9} "For I will give the command, and I will shake the people of Israel among all the nations as grain is shaken in a sieve, and not a pebble will reach the ground. {9:10} All the sinners among my people will die by the sword, all those who say, 'Disaster will not overtake or meet us.' {9:11} *"In that day I will restore David's fallen shelter— I will repair its broken walls and restore its ruins— and will rebuild it as it used to be*, {9:12} so that they may possess the remnant of Edom and all the nations that bear my name," declares the LORD, who will do these things. {9:13} "The days are coming," declares the LORD, "when the reaper will be overtaken by the plowman and the planter by the one treading grapes. New wine will drip from the mountains and flow from all the hills, {9:14} and I will bring my people Israel back from exile. They will rebuild the ruined cities and live in them. They will plant vineyards and drink their wine; they will make gardens and eat their fruit. {9:15} I will plant Israel in their own land, never again to be uprooted from the land I have given them," says the LORD your God.

Obadiah

{1:1} This is what the Lord GOD says about Edom: "We have heard a message from the LORD, an envoy was sent to the nations to say, 'Rise, let us go against her for battle.' {1:2} ***"Behold, I will make you small among the nations; you will be utterly despised.*** {1:3} "The pride of your heart has deceived you, you who live in the clefts of the rocks and make your home on the heights, you who say to yourself, 'Who can bring me down to the ground?' {1:4} ***"Though you soar like the eagle and make your nest among the stars, from there I will bring you down," declares the LORD.*** {1:5} "If thieves came to you, if robbers in the night—oh, what a disaster awaits you—would they not steal only as much as they wanted? If grape pickers came to you, would they not leave a few grapes? {1:6} "How Esau will be ransacked, his hidden treasures pillaged! {1:7} "All your allies will force you to the border; your friends will deceive and overpower you; those who eat your bread will set a trap for you, but you will not detect it. {1:8} "In that day," declares the LORD, "will I not destroy the wise men of Edom, those of understanding in the mountains of Esau? {1:9} "Your warriors, O Teman, will be terrified, and everyone in Esau's mountains will be cut down in the slaughter. {1:10} "Because of the violence against your brother Jacob, you will be covered with shame; you will be destroyed forever. {1:11} "On the day you stood aloof while strangers carried off his wealth and foreigners entered his gates and cast lots for Jerusalem, you were like one of them. {1:12} "You should not gloat over your brother in the day of his misfortune, nor rejoice over the people of Judah in the day of their destruction, nor boast so much in the day of their trouble. {1:13} "You should not march through the gates of my people in the day of their disaster, nor gloat over them in their calamity in the day of their disaster, nor seize their wealth in the day of their disaster. {1:14} "You should not wait at the crossroads to cut down their fugitives, nor hand over their survivors in the day of their trouble. {1:15} "For the day of the LORD is near for all nations. As you have done, it will be done to you; your deeds will return upon your own head. {1:16} "Just as you drank on my holy hill, so all the nations will drink continually; they will drink and drink and be as if they had never been. {1:17} ***"But on Mount Zion will be deliverance; it will be holy, and Jacob will possess his inheritance.*** {1:18} "The house of Jacob will be a fire, and the house of Joseph a flame; the house of Esau will be stubble, and they will set it ablaze and consume it. There will be no survivors from the house of Esau." The LORD has spoken. {1:19} "People from the Negev will occupy the mountains of Esau, and people from the foothills will possess the land of the Philistines. They will occupy the fields of Ephraim and Samaria, and Benjamin will possess Gilead. {1:20} "The exiles of this host of the Israelites will possess the land of the Canaanites as far as Zarephath; the exiles from Jerusalem who are in Sepharad will possess the towns of the Negev. {1:21} ***"Saviors will go up on Mount Zion to govern the mountains of Esau. And the kingdom will be the LORD's."***

Jonah

{1:1} **The word of the LORD came to Jonah, the son of Amittai, saying,** {1:2} **"Arise, go to Nineveh, that great city, and preach against it; for their wickedness has come up before me."** {1:3} But Jonah tried to escape to Tarshish from the presence of the LORD. He went down to Joppa and found a ship going to Tarshish. So he paid the fare and went aboard to flee from the presence of the LORD. {1:4} But the LORD sent a great wind over the sea, causing a mighty storm. The ship was in danger of breaking apart. {1:5} The sailors were terrified and cried out to their gods. They threw the cargo into the sea to lighten the ship. Meanwhile, Jonah had gone down into the lowest parts of the vessel and was fast asleep. {1:6} The captain approached him and said, "What are you doing asleep? Get up, call on your God! Maybe he will take notice of us, and we will not perish." {1:7} Then the sailors said to each other, "Come, let us cast lots to find out who is responsible for this calamity." They cast lots, and the lot fell on Jonah. {1:8} So they asked him, "Tell us, why is this happening to us? What is your occupation? Where do you come from? What is your country? And who are your people?" {1:9} Jonah answered, "I am a Hebrew, and I worship the LORD, the God of heaven, who made the sea and the dry land." {1:10} This terrified the men even more, and they asked him, "What have you done?" (They knew he was fleeing from the presence of the LORD because he had told them.) {1:11} The sea was getting rougher and rougher. So they asked him, "What should we do to you to make the sea calm down for us?" {1:12} Jonah replied, "Pick me up and throw me into the sea, and it will become calm. I know that it is my fault that this great storm has come upon you." {1:13} Instead, the men tried to row back to land, but they could not, for the sea grew even wilder than before. {1:14} Then they cried out to the LORD, "Please, LORD, do not let us die for taking this man's life. Do not hold us accountable for killing an innocent man, for you, LORD, have done as you pleased." {1:15} So they picked up Jonah and threw him into the sea, and the raging sea grew calm. {1:16} At this, the men greatly feared the LORD, and they offered a sacrifice to the LORD and made vows. {1:17} Now the LORD provided a huge fish to swallow Jonah, and Jonah was in the belly of the fish for three days and three nights.

{2:1} **Jonah prayed to the LORD his God from the belly of the fish,** {2:2} saying, "In my distress, I called to the LORD, and he heard me. From the depths of the grave, I cried for help, and you listened to my cry. {2:3} You cast me into the deep, into the heart of the seas, and the currents swirled about me; all your waves and breakers swept over me. {2:4} I said, 'I have been banished from your sight; yet I will look again toward your holy temple.' {2:5} The engulfing waters threatened me, the deep surrounded me; seaweed was wrapped around my head. {2:6} To the roots of the mountains I sank down; the earth beneath barred me in forever. But you brought my life up from the pit, O LORD my God. {2:7} When my life was ebbing away, I remembered you, LORD, and my prayer rose to you, to your holy temple. {2:8} Those who cling to worthless idols turn away from God's love for them. {2:9} But I, with shouts of grateful praise, will sacrifice to you. What I have vowed I will make good. I will say, 'Salvation comes from the LORD.'" {2:10} And the LORD commanded the fish, and it vomited Jonah onto dry land.

{3:1} The word of the LORD came to Jonah a second time, saying, {3:2} "Get up, go to the great city of Nineveh, and deliver the message I have given you." {3:3} So Jonah got up and went to Nineveh, according to the word of the LORD. Now Nineveh was an enormous city, requiring three days to walk through. {3:4} **Jonah set out into the city, and after** walking a day's journey, he proclaimed, "In forty days, Nineveh will be overthrown!" {3:5} The people of Nineveh believed God. They proclaimed a fast and put on sackcloth, from the greatest to the least. {3:6} When news reached the king of Nineveh, he rose from his throne, took off his royal robes, covered himself with sackcloth, and sat in ashes. {3:7} He issued a proclamation throughout Nineveh: "By decree of the king and his nobles: Let no man or beast, herd or flock, taste anything. Let them not eat or drink water. {3:8} Let both man and beast be covered with sackcloth, and let everyone call urgently on God. Let them give up their evil ways and their violence. {3:9} Who knows? God may yet relent and turn from his fierce anger so that we will not perish." {3:10} **When God saw what they did and how they turned from their evil ways, he relented and did not bring on them the destruction he had threatened.**

{4:1} But Jonah was greatly displeased and became very angry. {4:2} **He prayed to the LORD, saying, "O LORD, isn't this what I said when I was still in my own country? That's why I fled to Tarshish. I knew that you are a gracious and merciful God, slow to anger, and abounding in steadfast love, and ready to relent from punishing.** {4:3} So now, O LORD, please take my life from me, for it is better for me to die than to live." {4:4} The LORD replied, "Is it right for you to be angry?" {4:5} Jonah went out of the city and sat on the east side. He made himself a shelter there and sat in its shade, waiting to see what would happen to the city. {4:6} **Then the LORD God provided a plant, and it grew up over Jonah to give shade for his head to ease his discomfort, and Jonah was very happy about the plant.** {4:7} But at dawn the next day, God provided a worm, which chewed the plant so that it withered. {4:8} When the sun rose, God provided a scorching east wind, and the sun blazed on Jonah's head so that he grew faint. He wanted to die, and said, "It would be better for me to die than to live." {4:9} But God said to Jonah, "Is it right for you to be angry about the plant?" And he said, "It is right for me to be angry, even to death." {4:10} But the LORD said, "You have been concerned about this plant, though you did not tend it or make it grow. It sprang up overnight and died overnight. {4:11} **And should I not have concern for the great city of Nineveh, in which there are more than a hundred and twenty thousand people who cannot tell their right hand from their left—and also many animals?"**

Micah

{1:1} This is the message that the LORD gave to Micah of Moresheth during the reigns of Jotham, Ahaz, and Hezekiah, kings of Judah. The vision concerned Samaria and Jerusalem. {1:2} **Listen, all you people! Pay attention, earth, and everything in it! The Lord GOD will be a witness against you from his holy temple.** {1:3} For behold, the LORD is coming out of his place; he will come down and tread upon the high places of the earth. {1:4} The mountains will melt under him, and the valleys will split open, like wax before the fire, like water rushing down a steep slope. {1:5} This judgment is because of Jacob's rebellion and the sins of the people of Israel. What is the rebellion of Jacob? Isn't it Samaria? And what are the pagan shrines in Judah? Aren't they Jerusalem? {1:6} So I will make Samaria a heap of ruins in the open country, a place for planting vineyards. I will pour her stones down into the valley and expose her foundations. {1:7} All her carved images will be smashed to pieces. All her sacred treasures will be burned. These things were bought with the money earned by her prostitution, and they will now be carried away to pay prostitutes elsewhere. {1:8} So I will mourn and lament. I will walk around barefoot and naked. I will howl like a jackal and mourn like an ostrich. {1:9} Her wounds are incurable; they have reached into Judah. They have reached even to the gates of Jerusalem. {1:10} Don't tell our enemies in Gath; don't weep at all. You people in Beth-leaphrah, roll in the dust to show your despair. {1:11} You people in Shaphir, go as captives into exile—naked and ashamed. The people of Zaanan dare not come outside their walls. The people of Beth-ezel mourn, for their house has no support. {1:12} The people of Maroth anxiously wait for relief, but only bitterness awaits them as the LORD's judgment reaches even to the gates of Jerusalem. {1:13} Harness your chariots, you people of Lachish. You led Jerusalem into sin, just as Israel did. {1:14} Send farewell gifts to Moresheth-gath; there is no hope of saving it. The town of Aczib has deceived the kings of Israel. {1:15} O people of Mareshah, I will bring a conqueror to capture your town. And the leaders of Israel will go to Adullam. {1:16} Make yourselves as bald as a vulture, for your children will be driven from you into exile.

{2:1} Woe to those who plan wickedness and work evil deeds while lying in bed! When the morning light comes, they carry out their schemes because they have the power to do so. {2:2} They covet fields and seize them, and houses, and take them away. They oppress a man and his household, a man and his inheritance. {2:3} Therefore, this is what the LORD says: "I am planning disaster against this nation, from which you cannot save yourselves. You will no longer walk proudly, for it will be a time of calamity." {2:4} In that day, people will take up a lament against you and mourn bitterly, saying, "We are utterly ruined! The LORD has changed the portion of my people. How he has removed it from me! He has allotted our fields to traitors." {2:5} Therefore, you will have no one in the assembly of the LORD to divide the land by lot. {2:6} "Stop your preaching," they say. "Don't prophesy to us about what is right. Speak out with your so-called prophecies; we will not be ashamed." {2:7} Is it being said, O house of Jacob: 'Is the Spirit of the LORD impatient? Are these his deeds?' Do not my words do good to him who walks uprightly? {2:8} But lately my people have risen up like an enemy. You strip off the rich robe from those who pass by without a care, like men returning from battle. {2:9} You drive the women of my people from their pleasant homes. You take away my blessing from their children forever. {2:10} Go away! You are not welcome here anymore. Your land is defiled; it will bring about your destruction, a ruinous destruction. {2:11} If someone were to come and deceive with lies, saying, 'I will prophesy for you plenty of wine and beer,' they would be just the prophet for this people. {2:12} "I will surely gather all of you, O Jacob; I will surely bring together the remnant of Israel. I will put them together like sheep in a pen, like a flock in its pasture; the place will throng with people. {2:13} The One who breaks open the way will go up before them; they will break through the gate and go out. Their King will pass through before them, the LORD at their head."

{3:1} And I said, Listen, I beg you, O leaders of Jacob, and you princes of the house of Israel; isn't it your responsibility to understand justice? {3:2} You who hate the good and love the evil, who tear the skin from my people and strip the flesh from their bones. {3:3} You devour my people, strip off their skin, break their bones, and chop them up like meat for the cooking pot, like flesh in a cauldron. {3:4} But when they cry out to the LORD, he will not answer them. Instead, he will hide his face from them because of their evil deeds. {3:5} This is what the LORD says about the prophets who mislead my people, who proclaim peace while they bite with their teeth, but then declare war against those who fail to put food in their mouths. {3:6} Therefore, night will come upon you without vision, and darkness without divination. The sun will set for the prophets, and the day will be dark for them. {3:7} The seers will be ashamed, and the diviners will be embarrassed; they will all cover their mouths because there will be no answer from God {3:8} But as for me, I am filled with power by the Spirit of the LORD, and with justice and might, to declare to Jacob his transgression and to Israel his sin. {3:9} Listen to this, O leaders of the house of Jacob and princes of the house of Israel, who despise justice and pervert all that is right. {3:10} They build up Zion with bloodshed and Jerusalem with wickedness. {3:11} Her leaders judge for a bribe, her priests teach for a price, and her prophets tell fortunes for money. Yet they lean upon the LORD and say, "Isn't the LORD among us? No disaster will come upon us." {3:12} Therefore, because of you, Zion will be plowed like a field, Jerusalem will become a heap of rubble, and the temple mount will be covered with thickets like a forest.

{4:1} **But in the last days, it shall come to pass that the mountain of the house of the LORD will be established as the highest of the mountains, and it will be exalted above the hills. People will flow to it,** {4:2} And many nations will come, saying, "Come, let us go up to the mountain of the LORD, to the house of the God of Jacob. He will teach us his ways, and we will walk in his paths." For out of Zion shall go forth the law, and the word of the LORD from Jerusalem. {4:3} He will judge among many people and rebuke strong nations afar off. They will beat their swords into plowshares and their spears into pruning hooks. Nation will not lift up sword against nation, neither will they learn war anymore. {4:4} But each person will sit under their vine and under their fig tree, and no one will make them afraid, for the mouth of the LORD of hosts has spoken. {4:5} For all people will walk in the name of their gods, but we will walk in the name of the LORD our God forever and ever. {4:6} In that day, says the LORD, I will gather the lame, and I will assemble the outcast, and those whom I have afflicted. {4:7} I will make the lame a remnant and the outcast a strong nation. The LORD will reign over them in Mount Zion from that time forward, even forever. {4:8} And you, O tower of the flock, the stronghold of the daughter of Zion, to you it shall come, even the former dominion shall come, the kingdom to the daughter of Jerusalem. {4:9} Now why do you cry aloud? Is there no king in you? Has your counselor perished? For pangs have seized you like a woman in labor. {4:10} Be in pain and labor to bring forth, O daughter of Zion, like a woman in childbirth. For now you shall go forth from the city, and you shall dwell in the field, and you shall go to Babylon; there you shall be delivered; there the LORD will redeem you from the hand of your enemies. {4:11} Now also many nations are gathered against you, saying, "Let her be defiled, and let our eyes gaze upon Zion." {4:12} But they do not know the thoughts of the LORD, nor do they understand his counsel, for he will gather them like sheaves to the threshing floor. {4:13} Arise and thresh, O daughter of Zion, for I will make your horn iron, and I will make your hooves bronze; you shall beat in pieces many peoples; and I will consecrate their gain to the LORD, their wealth to the Lord of the whole earth.

{5:1} Now gather yourselves in troops, O daughter of troops; they have laid siege against us; they will strike the judge of Israel with a rod on the cheek. {5:2} **But you, Bethlehem Ephrathah, though you are little among the thousands of Judah, yet out of you shall come forth to me the one to** *be ruler in Israel, whose origins are from of old, from everlasting.* {5:3} Therefore, he will give them up until the time when she who is in labor has given birth; then the remnant of his brothers shall return to the children of Israel. {5:4} And he shall stand and shepherd his flock in the strength of the LORD, in the majesty of the name of the LORD his God; and they shall dwell securely, for now he shall be great to the ends of the earth. {5:5} And this one shall be our peace when the Assyrian comes into our land and treads within our borders. {5:6} Then we will raise against him seven shepherds and eight princely men. {5:7} They will waste the land of Assyria with the sword, and the land of Nimrod in its entrances; thus he shall deliver us from the Assyrian when he comes into our land and when he treads within our borders. {5:8} Then the remnant of Jacob shall be in the midst of many peoples like dew from the LORD, like showers on the grass, that tarry for no man nor wait for the sons of men. {5:9} And the remnant of Jacob shall be among the Gentiles in the midst of many peoples like a lion among the beasts of the forest, like a young lion among flocks of sheep, who, if he passes through, both treads down and tears in pieces, and none can deliver. {5:10} Your hand shall be lifted against your adversaries, and all your enemies shall be cut off. {5:11} And it shall come to pass in that day, says the LORD, that I will cut off your horses from among you and will destroy your chariots. {5:12} I will cut off the cities of your land and throw down all your strongholds. {5:13} I will cut off sorceries from your hand, and you shall have no soothsayers. {5:14} I will cut off your carved images and your sacred pillars from among you; you shall no more worship the work of your hands. {5:15} And I will execute vengeance in anger and fury upon the nations, such as they have not heard.

{6:1} Listen now to what the LORD says: "Arise, plead your case before the mountains, and let the hills hear your voice. {6:2} Hear, O mountains, the LORD's complaint, and you strong foundations of the earth; for the LORD has a case against his people, and he will argue it with Israel. {6:3} "My people, what have I done to you? How have I burdened you? Testify against me. {6:4} For I brought you up out of the land of Egypt and redeemed you from the house of bondage; I sent Moses, Aaron, and Miriam before you. {6:5} "My people, remember what Balak king of Moab plotted and what Balaam son of Beor answered him from Shittim to Gilgal, so that you may acknowledge the righteous acts of the LORD." {6:6} With what shall I come before the LORD and bow down before the exalted God? Shall I come before him with burnt offerings, with calves a year old? {6:7} Will the LORD be pleased with thousands of rams, with ten thousand rivers of olive oil? Shall I offer my firstborn for my transgression, the fruit of my body for the sin of my soul? {6:8} *He has shown you, O mortal, what is good. And what does the LORD require of you? To act justly and to love mercy and to walk humbly with your God.* {6:9} The voice of the LORD calls out to the city— and wisdom shall see your name: "Listen to the rod and the one who has appointed it. {6:10} "Are there still treasures of wickedness in the house of the wicked, and a short measure that is cursed? {6:11} Shall I acquit someone with dishonest scales, with a bag of false weights? {6:12} *Your rich people are violent; your inhabitants are liars and their tongues speak deceitfully.* {6:13} Therefore, I have begun to destroy you, to ruin you because of your sins. {6:14} You will eat but not be satisfied; your stomach will still be empty. You will store up but save nothing, because what you save I will give to the sword. {6:15} You will plant but not harvest; you will press olives but not use the oil, you will crush grapes but not drink the wine. {6:16} You follow the statutes of Omri and all the practices of Ahab's house, and you walk in their counsels. Therefore, I will make you a desolation and your inhabitants a hissing, and you shall bear the scorn of my people."

{7:1} Woe is me! I feel like the summer fruits have been gathered, like the last gleanings of the grape harvest; there is no cluster of grapes to eat, no ripe fruit that my soul desires. {7:2} The godly have been swept from the earth; not one upright person remains. Everyone lies in wait to shed blood; they hunt each other with nets. {7:3} Both hands are skilled in doing evil; the ruler demands gifts, the judge accepts bribes, the powerful dictate what they desire— they all conspire together. {7:4} *The best of them is like a brier, the most upright worse than a thorn hedge. The day God visits you has come, the day your watchmen sound the alarm. Now is the time of your confusion.* {7:5} Do not trust a neighbor; put no confidence in a friend. Even with the woman who lies in your embrace guard the words of your lips. {7:6} *For a son dishonors his father, a daughter rises up against her mother, a daughter-in-law against her mother-in-law— a man's enemies are the members of his own household.* {7:7} But as for me, I watch in hope for the LORD, I wait for God my Savior; my God will hear me. {7:8} Do not gloat over me, my enemy! Though I have fallen, I will rise. Though I sit in darkness, the LORD will be my light. {7:9} Because I have sinned against him, I will bear the LORD's wrath, until he pleads my case and upholds my cause. He will bring me out into the light; I will see his righteousness. {7:10} Then my enemy will see it and will be covered with shame, she who said to me, "Where is the LORD your God?" My eyes will see her downfall; even now she will be trampled underfoot like mire in the streets. {7:11} The day for building your walls will come, the day for extending your boundaries. {7:12} In that day people will come to you from Assyria and the cities of Egypt, even from Egypt to the Euphrates and from sea to sea and from mountain to mountain. {7:13} The earth will become desolate because of its inhabitants, as the result of their deeds. {7:14} Shepherd your people with your staff, the flock of your inheritance, which lives by itself in a forest, in fertile pasturelands. Let them feed in Bashan and Gilead as in days long ago. {7:15} *"As in the days when you came out of Egypt, I will show them my wonders."* {7:16} Nations will see and be ashamed, deprived of all their power. They will put their hands over their mouths and their ears will become deaf. {7:17} They will lick dust like a snake, like creatures that crawl on the ground. They will come trembling out of their dens; they will turn in fear to the LORD our God and will be afraid of you. {7:18} Who is a God like you, who pardons sin and forgives the transgression of the remnant of his inheritance? You do not stay angry forever but delight to show mercy. {7:19} You will again have compassion on us; you will tread our sins underfoot and hurl all our iniquities into the depths of the sea. {7:20} You will be faithful to Jacob, and show love to Abraham, as you pledged on oath to our ancestors in days long ago.

Nahum

{1:1} This is the message about Nineveh. It's the vision of Nahum from Elkosh. {1:2} God is jealous, and the LORD takes revenge. He is furious and will punish his enemies. The LORD will take vengeance on his adversaries and keep his wrath for his enemies. {1:3} The LORD is slow to anger but great in power. He will not let the guilty go unpunished. The LORD's way is in the whirlwind and the storm, and the clouds are the dust beneath his feet. {1:4} He rebukes the sea and dries it up; he makes all the rivers run dry. Bashan and Carmel wither, and the blossoms of Lebanon fade away. {1:5} The mountains quake before him, and the hills melt. The earth trembles at his presence—yes, the whole world and everyone in it. {1:6} Who can stand against his indignation? Who can endure his fierce anger? His fury is poured out like fire, and the rocks are thrown down by him. {1:7} **The LORD is good, a refuge in times of trouble. He cares for those who trust in him.** {1:8} But he will sweep away Nineveh with an overwhelming flood of destruction; he will pursue his enemies into darkness. {1:9} What are you plotting against the LORD? He will destroy you completely! No affliction will arise a second time. {1:10} Like tangled thorns and drunken drunkards, they will be devoured like dry stubble. {1:11} From you, Nineveh, comes one who plots evil against the LORD—a wicked counselor. {1:12} **This is what the LORD says: "Though they are powerful and numerous, they will be cut down and pass away. Though I have afflicted you, Nineveh, I will afflict you no more.** {1:13} Now I will break the yoke from your neck and tear off your chains." {1:14} **The LORD has issued a decree against you, Nineveh: "Your name will no longer be remembered. I will destroy the images and idols in your temples. I will prepare your grave, for you are vile."** {1:15} Look! There on the mountains! The feet of one who brings good news, who proclaims peace! Celebrate your festivals, Judah, and fulfill your vows, for the wicked will never again invade your land. They are completely cut off.

{2:1} Prepare for battle! The destroyer is advancing against you. Strengthen your defenses, watch your roads, brace yourselves for the fight. {2:2} The LORD has turned away the glory of Jacob, like the glory of Israel, because marauders have looted them and ruined their vine branches. {2:3} The shields of the mighty are stained red, the soldiers are dressed in scarlet. Chariots flash like fire on the day they are made ready; fir trees tremble at the sight. {2:4} The chariots race through the streets, rushing back and forth in the squares. They look like flaming torches, darting about like lightning. {2:5} The commanders call out orders, but their officers stumble as they hurry to the city walls. The defenses are prepared. {2:6} The river gates are thrown open, and the palace collapses. {2:7} Nineveh is like a pool whose water has drained away. "Stop! Stop!" they cry, but no one turns back. {2:8} Plunder the silver! Plunder the gold! There is no end to the treasure, wealth of every kind! {2:9} Nineveh is empty, desolate, and ruined. Hearts melt with fear, knees tremble, and faces grow pale. {2:10} Where now are the lions' dens, the place where young lions fed, where the lion, lioness, and lion's cubs prowled without fear? {2:11} The lion tore apart whatever prey it wanted and dragged off its victims. It filled its dens with the kill. {2:12} "I am against you," declares the LORD Almighty. "I will burn up your chariots in smoke, and the sword will devour your young lions.{2:13} **I will leave you no prey on the earth. The voices of your messengers will be silenced."**

{3:1} The city is doomed! It's filled with violence and deceit. The victims never escape. {3:2} **The sounds of whips and rattling wheels, the galloping horses, and clattering chariots fill the air.** {3:3} The cavalry charges with flashing swords and gleaming spears. There are countless casualties, bodies strewn everywhere, with no end in sight. They stumble over the corpses. {3:4} This is because of the city's many sins, the attractive temptress, skilled in sorcery, who leads nations astray with her seductions and peoples with her witchcraft. {3:5} But now I, the LORD of Heaven's Armies, will strip away her clothing, exposing her to shame. I will let the nations see her nakedness and kingdoms her disgrace. {3:6} I will cover her with filth in public, and everyone will see her shame. She will become a laughingstock. {3:7} **All who see her will shrink back and say, "Nineveh lies in ruins. Where are the mourners?" Who will mourn for this city? Where can we find anyone to comfort her?** {3:8} Are you any better than Thebes, situated on the Nile River, surrounded by water? The river was her defense, the waters her wall. {3:9} Cush and Egypt were her boundless strength; Put and Libya were among her allies. {3:10} But Thebes was captured and taken away as a prisoner. Her babies were dashed to death against the stones of the streets. Soldiers drew lots to determine the fate of her nobles, and all her great men were put in chains. {3:11} You, too, will drink to the dregs of God's wrath. You will be stripped naked and left exposed. {3:12} All your defenses will be like ripe figs when shaken; they will fall into the mouths of the enemy. {3:13} Look! Your troops are all women! The gates of your land are wide open to the enemy; fire has consumed their bars. {3:14} Draw water for the siege. Strengthen your defenses! Trample the clay, and pack down the mortar! Repair the brick walls! {3:15} But it will be in vain; the fire will devour you. The sword will cut you down like grass. Multiply like insects! Multiply like locusts! {3:16} You have multiplied your merchants more than the stars of the sky. But now they are gone, like locusts, flying away. {3:17} Your officials are like swarming locusts, your commanders like great hordes of locusts, settling in the walls on a cold day. But when the sun rises, they fly away, and no one knows where they are. {3:18} Your shepherds are asleep, O Assyrian king; your princes lie dead in the dust. Your people are scattered across the mountains with no one to gather them together. {3:19} There is no healing for your wound; your injury is fatal. All who hear of your destruction will clap their hands for joy. Who can escape your endless cruelty?

Habakkuk

{1:1} This is what Habakkuk the prophet saw. {1:2} **"O LORD, how long must I cry for help before you listen? I shout to you in vain about violence! But you do not save!** {1:3} Why do you make me see evil, and make me look at trouble? There is destruction and violence everywhere. People are arguing and fighting. {1:4} The law has no power anymore, and justice is never fair. Wicked people get what they want, so justice never wins. {1:5} Look at the nations and watch! Be amazed and shocked! I will do something in your lifetime that you won't believe, even though you are told about it. {1:6} I am bringing the Babylonians to power, those cruel and quick people, who march across the earth and take homes that don't belong to them. {1:7} They are frightening and terrible. They do what they want and are the judges of others. {1:8} Their horses are faster than leopards, fiercer than evening wolves. They gallop ahead, their cavalry comes from far away. They swoop down like eagles attacking their prey. {1:9} They are ready to fight, and their faces look like the wind from the desert. They gather prisoners like sand. {1:10} They make fun of kings, and rulers are a joke to them. They laugh at every fortress and build a dirt ramp to capture it. {1:11} Then they change their minds and leave, thinking their strength comes from their gods. {1:12} LORD, you are from the beginning, my holy God who never dies. LORD, you chose them to punish, to correct and discipline. {1:13} Your eyes are too good to look at evil. You cannot stand to see people treated unfairly. So why do you stay silent while the wicked destroy people who are more innocent than they are? {1:14} People are like fish in the sea, like animals without a leader. {1:15} They are caught with hooks, dragged in nets, and gathered in traps. The captors are happy and glad. {1:16} They worship their nets and offer sacrifices to their traps. They think their nets are powerful and provide plenty of food. {1:17} Will they keep emptying their nets and not showing mercy, continually destroying nations?"

{2:1} I will climb up to my watchtower and stand at my guard post. There I will wait to see what the LORD says and how he will answer my complaint. {2:2} Then the LORD said to me, "Write down what I show you. Write it clearly on a sign so that the message will be easy to read. {2:3} This message is for a future time. It describes the end, and it will be fulfilled. If it seems slow in coming, wait patiently, for it will surely take place. It will not be delayed. {2:4} **"Look at the proud! They trust in themselves, and their lives are crooked. But the righteous will live by their faithfulness to God.** {2:5} "Wealth is treacherous. Drunk with power, the arrogant never rest. Like death itself, they are never satisfied. They are greedy, grabbing everything in sight. But their greed will be their downfall. {2:6} "Will not all these take up their taunt against him, with scoffing and riddles for him, and say, 'Woe to him who heaps up what is not his own—for how long?—and loads himself with pledges!' {2:7} Will not your debtors suddenly arise, and those awake who will make you tremble? Then you will be spoiled for them. {2:8} "Because you have plundered many nations, now all the survivors will plunder you. You have shed human blood and committed violence against lands, cities, and all their inhabitants. {2:9} "What sorrow awaits you who build big houses with money gained dishonestly! You believe your wealth will buy security, putting your family's nest beyond the reach of danger. {2:10} But by the murders you committed, you have shamed your name and forfeited your lives. {2:11} "Even the stones of the walls cry out against you, and the beams in the ceilings echo the accusation. {2:12} "What sorrow awaits you who build cities with money gained through murder and corruption! {2:13} Has not the LORD of Heaven's Armies promised that the wealth of nations will turn to ashes? They work so hard, but all in vain! {2:14} But one day the earth will be filled with the knowledge of the glory of the LORD, as the waters cover the sea. {2:15} "What sorrow awaits you who make your neighbors drunk! You force your cup on them so you can gloat over their shameful nakedness. {2:16} But soon it will be your turn to be disgraced. Come, drink and be exposed! Drink from the cup of the LORD's judgment, and all your glory will be turned to shame. {2:17} "You cut down the forests of Lebanon. Now you will be cut down. You destroyed the animals. Now terror will strike you because of the murders you committed against people and the violence you did to lands, cities, and all their inhabitants. {2:18} "What good is an idol carved by man, or a cast image that deceives you? How foolish to trust in your own creation—a god that can't even talk! {2:19} What sorrow awaits you who say to wooden idols, 'Wake up and save us!' To speechless stone images you say, 'Rise up and teach us!' Can an idol tell you what to do? They may be overlaid with gold and silver, but they are lifeless inside.

{2:20} "But the LORD is in his holy Temple. Let all the earth be silent before him."

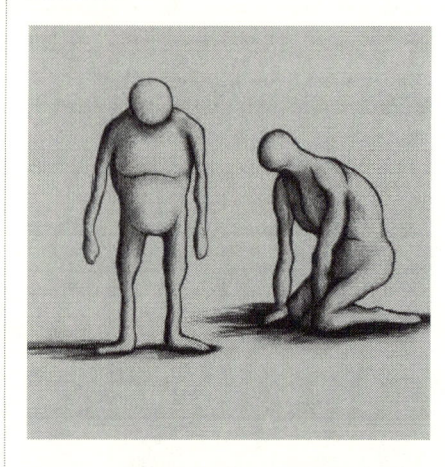

{3:1} This is a prayer from the prophet Habakkuk, sung to the tune "Shigionoth." {3:2} "LORD, I have heard what you have said, and I am filled with awe. LORD, revive your work in our time; make it known in our day. In wrath, remember mercy. {3:3} "God came from Teman, the Holy One from Mount Paran. His glory covered the heavens, and the earth was full of his praise. {3:4} *His brilliance was like the sunrise; rays flashed from his hand, where his power was hidden.* {3:5} Pestilence marched before him; plague followed his steps. {3:6} *He stood and shook the earth; he looked and made the nations tremble. The ancient mountains crumbled and the age-old hills collapsed. His ways are eternal.* {3:7} I saw the tents of Cushan in distress; the dwellings of Midian trembled. {3:8} Was your wrath against the rivers, LORD? Did you rage against the streams? Did you unleash your fury against the sea when you rode your horses and chariots to victory? {3:9} You brandished your bow and called for many arrows. You split the earth with rivers. {3:10} The mountains saw you and writhed. Torrents of water swept by; the deep roared and lifted its waves high. {3:11} The sun and moon stood still in the heavens at the glint of your flying arrows, at the lightning of your flashing spear. {3:12} In wrath you strode through the earth and in anger you threshed the nations. {3:13} You came out to deliver your people, to save your anointed one. You crushed the leader of the land of wickedness, you stripped him from head to foot. Selah {3:14} With his own spear you pierced his head when his warriors stormed out to scatter us, gloating as though about to devour the wretched who were in hiding. {3:15} You trampled the sea with your horses, churning the great waters. {3:16} I heard and my heart pounded, my lips quivered at the sound; decay crept into my bones, and my legs trembled. Yet I will wait patiently for the day of calamity to come on the nation invading us. {3:17} Though the fig tree does not bud and there are no grapes on the vines, though the olive crop fails and the fields produce no food, though there are no sheep in the pen and no cattle in the stalls, {3:18} yet I will rejoice in the LORD, I will be joyful in God my Savior. {3:19} The Sovereign LORD is my strength; he makes my feet like the feet of a deer, he enables me to tread on the heights. For the director of music. On my stringed instruments."

Zephaniah

{1:1} This is the message that the LORD gave to Zephaniah, son of Cushi, grandson of Gedaliah, great-grandson of Amariah, and great-great-grandson of Hizkiah. This message came to Zephaniah during the reign of Josiah son of Amon, king of Judah. {1:2} *"I will completely sweep away everything from the face of the earth," says the LORD.* {1:3} "I will sweep away people and animals alike. I will sweep away the birds of the sky and the fish in the sea. I will reduce the wicked to heaps of rubble, and I will wipe humanity from the face of the earth," says the LORD. {1:4} "I will crush Judah and Jerusalem with my fist and destroy every last trace of their Baal worship. I will put an end to all the idolatrous priests, so that even the memory of them will disappear. {1:5} "I will destroy those who worship the sun, the moon, and the stars. I will destroy those who bow down and swear to the LORD and who also swear by the god Molech. {1:6} "I will destroy those who have turned away from the LORD, those who no longer seek him or ask for his guidance. {1:7} "Stand silent in the presence of the Sovereign LORD, for the awesome day of the LORD's judgment is near. The LORD has prepared his people for a great slaughter and has chosen their executioners. {1:8} "On that day of judgment," says the LORD, "I will punish the leaders and princes of Judah and all those following pagan customs. {1:9} "Yes, I will punish those who participate in pagan worship ceremonies, and those who steal and kill to fill their masters' homes with loot. {1:10} "On that day," says the LORD, "a cry of alarm will come from the Fish Gate and echo throughout the New Quarter of the city. And a great crash will sound from the hills. {1:11} "Wail in sorrow, all you who live in the market area, for all the merchants and traders will be destroyed. {1:12} "I will search with lanterns in Jerusalem's darkest corners to punish those who sit complacent in their sins. They think the LORD will do nothing to them, either good or bad. {1:13} "So their property will be plundered, their homes will be ransacked. They will build new homes but never live in them. They will plant vineyards but never drink wine from them. {1:14} "That terrible day of the LORD is near. Swiftly it comes—a day of bitter tears, a day when even strong men will cry out. {1:15} "It will be a day when the LORD's anger is poured out—a day of terrible distress and anguish, a day of ruin and desolation, a day of darkness and gloom, a day of clouds and blackness, {1:16} a day of trumpet calls and battle cries. Down go the walled cities and the strongest battlements! {1:17} "Because you have sinned against the LORD, I will make you grope around like the blind. Your blood will be poured out into the dust, and your bodies will lie rotting on the ground." {1:18} Your silver and gold will not save you on that day of the LORD's anger. For the whole land will be devoured by the fire of his jealousy. He will make a terrifying end of all the people on earth.

{2:1} Come together, O nation not desired. Gather yourselves before the decree is issued, before the day passes like chaff, before the fierce anger of the LORD comes upon you, before the day of his wrath overtakes you. {2:2} Seek the LORD, all you humble of the earth, who carry out his laws; seek righteousness, seek humility; perhaps you may be hidden on the day of the LORD's wrath. {2:3} *For Gaza will be abandoned, and Ashkelon left in ruins. Ashdod will be driven out at noonday, and Ekron uprooted.* {2:4} Woe to the inhabitants of the seacoast, the nation of the Cherethites! The word of the LORD is against you, O Canaan, land of the Philistines; I will destroy you until there is no inhabitant. {2:5} The seacoast will become pastures, with shepherd's huts and sheepfolds. {2:6} The seacoast will belong to the remnant of the house of Judah; they will find pasture there. In the evening they will lie down in the houses of Ashkelon. For the LORD their God will care for them; he will restore their fortunes. {2:7} I have heard the insults of Moab and the taunts of the Ammonites, who insulted my people and made threats against their land. {2:8} Therefore, as surely as I live," declares the LORD Almighty, the God of Israel, "surely Moab will become like Sodom, the Ammonites like Gomorrah—a place of weeds and salt pits, a wasteland forever. The remnant of my people will plunder them; the survivors of my nation will inherit their land." {2:9} This is what they will get in return for their pride, for insulting and mocking the people of the LORD Almighty. {2:10} The LORD will be awesome to them when he destroys all the gods of the earth. Distant nations will bow down to him, all of them in their own lands. {2:11} "You too, Cushites, will be slain by my sword." {2:12} He will stretch out his hand against the north and destroy Assyria, leaving Nineveh utterly desolate and dry as the desert. {2:13} Flocks and herds will lie down there, creatures of every kind. The desert owl and the screech owl will roost on her columns. Their hooting will echo through the windows, rubble will fill the doorways, the beams of cedar will be exposed. {2:14} This is the city of revelry that lived in safety. She said to herself, "I am the one! And there is none besides me."{2:15} What a ruin she has become, a lair for wild beasts! All who pass by her scoff and shake their fists.

{3:1} How terrible for the city that is stained with sin, that oppresses its people! {3:2} She refuses to listen to correction, she does not trust in the LORD, she does not draw near to her God. {3:3} Her officials are roaring lions, her rulers are evening wolves; they leave nothing for the morning. {3:4} Her prophets are untrustworthy and deceitful; her priests defile the sanctuary and twist the law. {3:5} *But the LORD within her is righteous; he does no wrong. Every morning he brings his justice to light; he does not fail. Yet the unjust know no shame.* {3:6} "I have destroyed nations; their strongholds are demolished. I have left their streets deserted, with no one passing through. Their cities are laid waste; there is no one left—no inhabitant. {3:7} I thought, 'Surely you will fear me and accept correction.' Then her place of refuge would not be destroyed, nor all my punishments come upon her. But they were eager to corrupt all they did." {3:8} Therefore wait for me," declares the LORD, "for the day I will stand up to testify. I have decided to assemble the nations, to gather the kingdoms and to pour out my wrath on them—all my fierce anger. The whole earth will be consumed by the fire of my jealous anger. {3:9} "Then I will purify the lips of the peoples, that all of them may call on the name of the LORD and serve him shoulder to shoulder. {3:10} From beyond the rivers of Cush, my worshipers, the daughter of my dispersed people, will bring me offerings. {3:11} On that day you, Jerusalem, will not be put to shame for all the wrongs you have done to me, because I will remove from you your arrogant boasters. Never again will you be haughty on my holy hill. {3:12} But I will leave within you the meek and humble. The remnant of Israel will trust in the name of the LORD. {3:13} They will do no wrong; they will tell no lies. A deceitful tongue will not be found in their mouths. They will eat and lie down and no one will make them afraid." {3:14} Sing, Daughter Zion; shout aloud, Israel! Be glad and rejoice with all your heart, Daughter Jerusalem! {3:15} The LORD has taken away your punishment; he has turned back your enemy. The LORD, the King of Israel, is with you; never again will you fear any harm. {3:16} **On that day they will say to Jerusalem, "Do not fear, Zion; do not let your hands hang limp.** {3:17} The LORD your God is with you, the Mighty Warrior who saves. He will take great delight in you; in his love he will no longer rebuke you, but will rejoice over you with singing." {3:18} "I will remove from you all who mourn over the loss of your appointed festivals, which is a burden and reproach for you. {3:19} At that time I will deal with all who oppressed you. I will rescue the lame; I will gather the exiles. I will give them praise and honor in every land where they have suffered shame. {3:20} At that time I will gather you; at that time I will bring you home. I will give you honor and praise among all the peoples of the earth when I restore your fortunes before your very eyes," says the LORD.

Haggai

{1:1} In the second year of King Darius, on the first day of the sixth month, the word of the LORD came through the prophet Haggai to Zerubbabel son of Shealtiel, governor of Judah, and to Joshua son of Jozadak, the high priest, saying, {1:2} "This is what the LORD of Heaven's Armies says: These people say, 'The time has not yet come to rebuild the LORD's house.'" {1:3} Then the word of the LORD came through the prophet Haggai, saying, {1:4} *"Is it time for you yourselves to be living in your paneled houses, while this house remains a ruin?"* {1:5} Now, therefore, thus says the LORD of hosts: Consider your ways! {1:6} You have planted much, but harvested little. You eat, but never have enough. You drink, but never have your fill. You put on clothes, but are not warm. You earn wages, only to put them in a purse with holes in it. {1:7} *Thus says the LORD of hosts: Consider your ways!* {1:8} Go up to the mountains and bring wood and build the house, so that I may take pleasure in it and be glorified," says the LORD. {1:9} "You expected much, but behold, it turned out to be little. And when you brought it home, I blew it away. Why?" declares the LORD of hosts. "Because my house lies in ruins, while each of you is busy with his own house. {1:10} *Therefore, because of you the heavens have withheld their dew and the earth has withheld its produce.* {1:11} And I have called for a drought on the land and the mountains, on the grain, on the new wine, on the oil, on whatever the ground brings forth, on men and livestock, and on all the labor of your hands." {1:12} *Then Zerubbabel son of Shealtiel, Joshua son of Jozadak, the high priest, and the whole remnant of the people obeyed the voice of the LORD their God and the words of the prophet Haggai, because the LORD their God had sent him. And the people feared the LORD.* {1:13} Then Haggai, the LORD's messenger, delivered the LORD's message to the people, saying, "I am with you," declares the LORD. {1:14} So the LORD stirred up the spirit of Zerubbabel son of Shealtiel, governor of Judah, the spirit of Joshua son of Jozadak, the high priest, and the spirit of the whole remnant of the people. They came and began to work on the house of the LORD Almighty, their God, {1:15} on the twenty-fourth day of the sixth month in the second year of King Darius.

{2:1} On the twenty-first day of the seventh month, the word of the LORD came through the prophet Haggai, saying, {2:2} "Speak now to Zerubbabel son of Shealtiel, governor of Judah, and to Joshua son of Jozadak, the high priest, and to the remnant of the people, saying, {2:3} 'Who among you saw this house in its former glory? And how do you see it now? Does it not seem to you like nothing in comparison? {2:4} Yet now, be strong, Zerubbabel,' declares the LORD. 'Be strong, Joshua son of Jozadak, the high priest. Be strong, all you people of the land,' declares the LORD. 'Work, for I am with you,' declares the LORD Almighty. {2:5} 'This is the promise I made to you when you came out of Egypt, and my Spirit remains among you. Do not fear.' {2:6} *"For this is what the LORD Almighty says: 'In a little while I will once more shake the heavens and the earth, the sea and the dry land.* {2:7} I will shake all nations, and the desired of all nations will come, and I will fill this house with glory,' says the LORD Almighty. {2:8} 'The silver is mine, and the gold is mine,' declares the LORD Almighty. {2:9} 'The glory of this present house will be greater than the glory of the former house,' says the LORD Almighty. 'And in this place, I will grant peace,' declares the LORD Almighty. {2:10} "On the twenty-fourth day of the ninth month, in the second year of Darius, the word of the LORD came to Haggai the prophet, saying, {2:11} 'This is what the LORD Almighty says: Ask the priests what the law says: {2:12} If someone carries consecrated meat in the fold of their garment, and that fold touches some bread or stew, some wine, olive oil, or other food, does it become consecrated?' The priests answered, 'No.' {2:13} Then Haggai asked, 'If a person defiled by contact with a dead body touches any of these, does it become defiled?' 'Yes,' the priests replied, 'it becomes defiled.' {2:14} So it is with this people and this nation in my sight,' declares the LORD. 'Whatever they do and whatever they offer there is defiled. {2:15} Now give careful thought to this from this day on —consider how things were before one stone was laid on another in the LORD's temple. {2:16} When anyone came to a heap of twenty measures, there were only ten. When anyone went to a wine vat to draw fifty measures, there were only twenty. {2:17} I struck all the work of your hands with blight, mildew, and hail, yet you did not return to me,' declares the LORD. {2:18} 'From this day on, from the twenty-fourth day of the ninth month, give careful thought to the day when the foundation of the LORD's temple was laid. Give careful thought: {2:19} Is there yet any seed left in the barn? Until now, the vine and the fig tree, the pomegranate and the olive tree have not borne fruit. 'From this day on, I will bless you.'" {2:20} The word of the LORD came to Haggai a second time on the twenty-fourth day of the month: {2:21} "Tell Zerubbabel governor of Judah that I am going to shake the heavens and the earth. {2:22} I will overturn royal thrones and shatter the power of the foreign kingdoms. I will overthrow chariots and their drivers; horses and their riders will fall, each by the sword of his brother. {2:23} On that day,' declares the LORD Almighty, 'I will take you, my servant Zerubbabel son of Shealtiel,' declares the LORD, 'and I will make you like my signet ring, for I have chosen you,' declares the LORD Almighty."

Zechariah

{1:1} In the second year of Darius, in the eighth month, the word of the LORD came to the prophet Zechariah son of Berechiah, the son of Iddo, saying, {1:2} "The LORD was very displeased with your ancestors. {1:3} **Therefore tell the people, 'This is what the LORD Almighty says: Return to me,' declares the LORD Almighty, 'and I will return to you,' says the LORD Almighty.** {1:4} Do not be like your ancestors, to whom the earlier prophets proclaimed: This is what the LORD Almighty says: Turn from your evil ways and your evil practices. But they would not listen or pay attention to me, declares the LORD. {1:5} Where are your ancestors now? And the prophets, do they live forever? {1:6} But did not my words and my decrees, which I commanded my servants the prophets, overtake your ancestors? "Then they repented and said, 'The LORD Almighty has done to us what our ways and practices deserve, just as he determined to do.'" {1:7} On the twenty-fourth day of the eleventh month, the month of Shebat, in the second year of Darius, the word of the LORD came to the prophet Zechariah son of Berechiah, the son of Iddo. {1:8} During the night I had a vision, and there before me was a man mounted on a red horse. He was standing among the myrtle trees in a ravine. Behind him were red, brown and white horses. {1:9} I asked, "What are these, my lord?" The angel who was talking with me answered, "I will show you what they are." {1:10} Then the man standing among the myrtle trees explained, "They are the ones the LORD has sent to go throughout the earth." {1:11} And they reported to the angel of the LORD who was standing among the myrtle trees, "We have gone throughout the earth and found the whole world at rest and in peace." {1:12} Then the angel of the LORD said, "LORD Almighty, how long will you withhold mercy from Jerusalem and from the towns of Judah, which you have been angry with these seventy years?" {1:13} So the LORD spoke kind and comforting words to the angel who talked with me. {1:14} Then the angel who was speaking to me said, "Proclaim this word: This is what the LORD Almighty says: 'I am very jealous for Jerusalem and Zion, {1:15} but I am very angry with the nations that feel secure. I was only a little angry, but they went too far with the punishment.' {1:16} Therefore, this is what the LORD says: 'I will return to Jerusalem with mercy, and there my house will be rebuilt. And the measuring line will be stretched out over Jerusalem,' declares the LORD Almighty. {1:17} "Proclaim further: This is what the LORD Almighty says: 'My towns will again overflow with prosperity, and the LORD will again comfort Zion and choose Jerusalem.'" {1:18} Then I looked up, and there before me were four horns. {1:19} I asked the angel who was speaking to me, "What are these?" He answered me, "These are the horns that scattered Judah, Israel, and Jerusalem." {1:20} Then the LORD showed me four craftsmen. {1:21} I asked, "What are these coming to do?" He answered, "These are the horns that scattered Judah so that no one could raise their head, but the craftsmen have come to terrify them and throw down these horns of the nations who lifted up their horns against the land of Judah to scatter its people."

{2:1} Once again, I looked up and saw a man with a measuring line in his hand. {2:2} I asked him, "Where are you going?" He replied, "I am going to measure Jerusalem, to determine its width and length." {2:3} Then the angel who was speaking with me went out, and another angel went to meet him. {2:4} The second angel said to him, "Run and tell that young man, 'Jerusalem will be a city without walls because of the great number of people and animals in it. {2:5} For I myself will be a wall of fire around it,' declares the LORD, 'and I will be its glory within.' {2:6} "Come! Come! Flee from the land of the north," declares the LORD, "for I have scattered you to the four winds of heaven," declares the LORD. {2:7} "Escape, Zion, you who live in Daughter Babylon." {2:8} For this is what the LORD Almighty says: "After the Glorious One has sent me against the nations that have plundered you—for whoever touches you touches the apple of his eye— {2:9} I will surely raise my hand against them so that their slaves will plunder them. Then you will know that the LORD Almighty has sent me. {2:10} "Shout and be glad, Daughter Zion. For I am coming, and I will live among you," declares the LORD. {2:11} "Many nations will be joined with the LORD in that day and will become my people. I will live among you and you will know that the LORD Almighty has sent me to you. {2:12} The LORD will inherit Judah as his portion in the holy land and will again choose Jerusalem. {2:13} Be still before the LORD, all mankind, because he has roused himself from his holy dwelling."

{3:1} Then he showed me Joshua the high priest standing before the angel of the LORD, with Satan standing at his right side to accuse him. {3:2} The LORD said to Satan, "The LORD rebuke you, Satan! The LORD, who has chosen Jerusalem, rebuke you! Is not this man a burning stick snatched from the fire?" {3:3} Now Joshua was dressed in filthy clothes as he stood before the angel. {3:4} The angel said to those who were standing before him, "Take off his filthy clothes." Then he said to Joshua, "See, I have taken away your sin, and I will put fine garments on you." {3:5} Then I said, "Put a clean turban on his head." So they put a clean turban on his head and clothed him, while the angel of the LORD stood by. {3:6} The angel of the LORD gave this charge to Joshua: {3:7} "This is what the LORD Almighty says: 'If you will walk in obedience to me and keep my requirements, then you will govern my house and have charge of my courts, and I will give you a place among these standing here. {3:8} " 'Listen, High Priest Joshua, you and your associates seated before you, who are men symbolic of things to come: I am going to bring my servant, the Branch. {3:9} See, the stone I have set in front of Joshua! There are seven eyes on that one stone, and I will engrave an inscription on it,' says the LORD Almighty, 'and I will remove the sin of this land in a single day. {3:10} " 'In that day each of you will invite your neighbor to sit under your vine and fig tree,' declares the LORD Almighty.'"

{4:1} The angel who talked with me returned and woke me up, like someone awakened from sleep. {4:2} He asked me, "What do you see?" I answered, "I see a solid gold lampstand with a bowl at the top and seven lamps on it, with seven channels to the lamps. {4:3} Also there are two olive trees by it, one on the right of the bowl and the other on its left." {4:4} I asked the angel who talked with me, "What are these, my lord?" {4:5} He answered, "Do you not know what these are?" "No, my lord," I replied. {4:6} **So he said to me, "This is the word of the LORD to Zerubbabel: 'Not by might nor by power, but by my Spirit,' says the LORD Almighty.** {4:7} 'What are you, mighty mountain? Before Zerubbabel you will become level ground. Then he will bring out the capstone to shouts of 'God bless it! God bless it!' {4:8} The word of the LORD came to me: {4:9} 'The hands of Zerubbabel have laid the foundation of this temple; his hands will also complete it. Then you will know that the LORD Almighty has sent me to you. {4:10} 'Who dares despise the day of small things, since the seven eyes of the LORD that range throughout the earth will rejoice when they see the chosen capstone in the hand of Zerubbabel?' {4:11} Then I asked the angel, "What are these two olive trees on the right and the left of the lampstand?" {4:12} Again I asked him, "What are these two olive branches beside the two gold pipes that pour out golden oil?" {4:13} He replied, "Do you not know what these are?" "No, my lord," I said. {4:14} So he said, "These are the two who are anointed to serve the Lord of all the earth."

{5:1} So I turned and raised my eyes and saw a flying scroll. {5:2} The angel asked me, "What do you see?" I replied, "I see a flying scroll; it is twenty cubits long and ten cubits wide." {5:3} Then he said to me, "This is the curse that is going out over the face of the whole land; for according to this scroll, every thief will be banished, and according to it, every perjurer will be banished. {5:4} The LORD Almighty declares, 'I will send it out, and it will enter the house of the thief and the house of anyone who swears falsely by my name. It will remain in that house and destroy it completely, both its timbers and its stones.'" {5:5} Then the angel who was speaking to me came forward and said to me, "Look up and see what is appearing." {5:6} I asked, "What is it?" He replied, "It is a basket." And he added, "This is the iniquity of the people throughout the land." {5:7} Then the cover of lead was raised, and there in the basket sat a woman! {5:8} He said, "This is wickedness," and he pushed her back into the basket and pushed its lead cover down on it. {5:9} Then I looked up—and there before me were two women, with the wind in their wings! They had wings like those of a stork, and they lifted up the basket between heaven and earth. {5:10} I asked the angel who was speaking to me, "Where are they taking the basket?" {5:11} He replied, "To the country of Babylonia to build a house for it. When it is ready, the basket will be set there in its place."

{6:1} So I turned and lifted up my eyes, and saw four chariots coming out from between two mountains; and the mountains were made of bronze. {6:2} The first chariot had red horses, the second black horses, {6:3} the third white horses, and the fourth chariot dappled horses—all strong horses. {6:4} I asked the angel who talked with me, "What are these, my lord?" {6:5} The angel replied, "These are the four spirits of heaven, going out from their station before the Lord of all the earth. {6:6} The chariot with the black horses goes toward the north country, the white ones go after them, and the dappled ones go toward the south country." {6:7} As the strong horses went out, they were eager to patrol the earth. And he said, "Go, patrol the earth." So they patrolled the earth. {6:8} Then he cried out to me and spoke to me, saying, "See, those who go toward the north country have given rest to my spirit in the north country." {6:9} The word of the LORD came to me: {6:10} "Take an offering from the exiles, from Heldai, Tobijah, and Jedaiah, who have arrived from Babylon; go the same day to the house of Josiah son of Zephaniah. {6:11} Take silver and gold, make a crown, and set it on the head of the high priest, Joshua son of Jehozadak. {6:12} Tell him, 'This is what the LORD Almighty says: "Here is the man whose name is the Branch, and he will branch out from his place and build the temple of the LORD. {6:13} It is he who will build the temple of the LORD, and he will be clothed with majesty and will sit and rule on his throne. And he will be a priest on his throne. And there will be harmony between the two." {6:14} The crown will be given to Heldai, Tobijah, Jedaiah, and Hen son of Zephaniah as a memorial in the temple of the LORD. {6:15} Those who are far away will come and help to build the temple of the LORD, and you will know that the LORD Almighty has sent me to you. This will happen if you diligently obey the LORD your God's voice."

{7:1} In the fourth year of King Darius, on the fourth day of the ninth month, which is Chislev, the word of the LORD came to Zechariah. {7:2} Some men had been sent from Bethel to the house of the LORD Almighty to ask the priests and the prophets, "Should I mourn and fast in the fifth month, as I have done for so many years?" {7:3} Then the word of the LORD Almighty came to me: {7:4} "Say to all the people of the land and to the priests, 'When you fasted and mourned in the fifth and seventh months for the past seventy years, was it really for me that you fasted? {7:5} And when you were eating and drinking, were you not just feasting for yourselves? {7:6} Are these not the words the LORD proclaimed through the earlier prophets when Jerusalem and its surrounding towns were at rest and prosperous, {7:7} and the Negev and the western foothills were settled?'" {7:8} And the word of the LORD came again to Zechariah: {7:9} **"This is what the LORD Almighty said: 'Administer true justice; show mercy and compassion to one another.** {7:10} Do not oppress the widow or the fatherless, the foreigner or the poor. Do not plot evil against each other in your hearts.' {7:11} But they refused to pay attention; stubbornly they turned their backs and covered their ears. {7:12} They made their hearts as hard as flint and would not listen to the law or to the words that the LORD Almighty had sent by his Spirit through the earlier prophets. So the LORD Almighty was very angry. {7:13} 'When I called, they did not listen; so when they called, I would not listen,' says the LORD Almighty. {7:14} 'I scattered them with a whirlwind among all the nations, where they were strangers. The land they left behind them was so desolate that no one traveled through it or returned to it. This is how they made the pleasant land desolate.'"

{8:1} The word of the LORD of hosts came to me, saying: {8:2} "This is what the LORD of hosts says: I was fiercely jealous for Zion, with great anger. {8:3} Now this is what the LORD says: I have returned to Zion and will dwell in Jerusalem. Jerusalem will be called the City of Truth, and the mountain of the LORD Almighty will be called the Holy Mountain. {8:4} This is what the LORD Almighty says: 'Once again men and women of ripe old age will sit in the streets of Jerusalem, each of them with cane in hand because of their age. {8:5} The city streets will be filled with boys and girls playing there.' {8:6} This is what the LORD Almighty says: 'It may seem marvelous to the remnant of this people at that time, but will it seem marvelous to me?' declares the LORD Almighty. {8:7} This is what the LORD Almighty says: 'I will save my people from the countries of the east and the west. {8:8} I will bring them back to live in Jerusalem; they will be my people, and I will be faithful and righteous to them as their God.' {8:9} This is what the LORD Almighty says: 'Now hear these words, let your hands be strong so that the temple may be built. {8:10} Before that time, there were no wages for people or hire for animals. No one could go about their business safely because of their enemies, since I had turned everyone against their neighbor. {8:11} But now I will not deal with the remnant of this people as I did in the past,' declares the LORD Almighty. {8:12} 'For the seed will be prosperous, the vine will yield its fruit, the ground will produce its crops, and the heavens will drop their dew. I will give all these things to the remnant that remains. {8:13} Just as you, Judah and Israel, have been a curse among the nations, so I will save you, and you will be a blessing. Do not be afraid, but let your hands be strong.' {8:14} This is what the LORD Almighty says: 'Just as I had determined to bring disaster on you and showed no pity when your ancestors angered me,' says the LORD Almighty, {8:15} 'so now I have determined to do good again to Jerusalem and Judah. Do not be afraid. {8:16} **These are the things you are to do: Speak the truth to each other, and render true and sound judgment in your courts;** {8:17} do not plot evil against each other, and do not love to swear falsely. I hate all this,' declares the LORD. {8:18} Again the word of the LORD Almighty came to me: {8:19} "This is what the LORD Almighty says: 'The fasts of the fourth, fifth, seventh and tenth months will become joyful and glad occasions and happy festivals for Judah. Therefore love truth and peace.' {8:20} This is what the LORD Almighty says: 'Many peoples and the inhabitants of many cities will yet come, {8:21} and the inhabitants of one city will go to another and say, "Let us go at once to entreat the LORD and seek the LORD Almighty. I myself am going." {8:22} And many peoples and powerful nations will come to Jerusalem to seek the LORD Almighty and to entreat him.' {8:23} This is what the LORD Almighty says: 'In those days ten people from all languages and nations will take firm hold of one Jew by the hem of his robe and say, "Let us go with you, because we have heard that God is with you."'

{9:1} This is the message from the LORD concerning the land of Hadrach and its capital, Damascus. The LORD's eyes are watching all the nations and all the tribes of Israel. {9:2} Even Tyre and Sidon, though they are so clever, will yet be humbled by the news of the coming judgment. Tyre has built great fortifications and has made silver and gold as plentiful as dust in the streets! {9:3} But now the LORD will strip away Tyre's possessions and hurl its fortifications into the sea, and it will be burned to the ground. {9:4} The city of Ashkelon will see Tyre fall and will be filled with fear. Gaza will shake with terror, as will Ekron, for their hopes will be dashed. Gaza's king will be killed, and Ashkelon will be deserted. {9:5} Foreigners will occupy the city of Ashdod. I will destroy the pride of the Philistines. {9:6} I will grab the bloody meat from their mouths and snatch the detestable sacrifices from their teeth. Then the surviving Philistines will worship our God and become like a clan in Judah. The Philistines of Ekron will join my people, as the ancient Jebusites once did. {9:7} I will guard my Temple and protect it from invading armies. I will make sure that no oppressor can overrun my people's land again, for now I am watching them with care. {9:8} Rejoice, O people of Zion! Shout in triumph, O people of Jerusalem! Look, your king is coming to you. {9:9} He is righteous and victorious, yet he is humble, riding on a donkey—riding on a donkey's colt. {9:10} I will remove the battle chariots from Israel and the warhorses from Jerusalem. I will destroy all the weapons used in battle, and your king will bring peace to the nations. His realm will stretch from sea to sea and from the Euphrates River to the ends of the earth. {9:11} Because of the covenant I made with you, sealed with blood, I will free your prisoners from death in a waterless dungeon. {9:12} Come back to the place of safety, all you prisoners who still have hope! I promise this very day that I will repay two blessings for each of your troubles. {9:13} Judah is my bow, and Israel is my arrow. Jerusalem is my sword, and like a mighty warrior, I will use it against the Greeks. {9:14} The LORD will appear above his people; his arrows will fly like lightning! The Sovereign LORD will sound the trumpet; he will march in the storms of the south, {9:15} and the LORD of Heaven's Armies will protect his people. They will sparkle in his land like jewels in a crown. {9:16} How wonderful and beautiful they will be! The young men will thrive on abundant grain, and the young women will flourish on new wine.

{10:1} Pray to the LORD for rain in the spring, for he makes the storm clouds. And he will send showers of rain so every field becomes a lush pasture. {10:2} But the idols speak deceitfully, and the fortune-tellers see lies. They comfort people with false hopes, leading them astray like sheep without a shepherd. {10:3} My anger burns against the leaders, and I will punish the leaders, for the LORD of Heaven's Armies has arrived to look after his flock, the people of Judah. He will make them strong and glorious, like a proud warhorse in battle. {10:4} From Judah will come the cornerstone, the tent peg, the battle bow, and all the other rulers. {10:5} Together they will be like warriors in battle, trampling their enemies into the mud under their feet. The LORD will be with them; they will overcome even the mightiest enemies. {10:6} "I will strengthen Judah and save Israel; I will restore them because of my compassion. It will be as though I had never rejected them, for I am the LORD their God, who will hear their cries. {10:7} The people of Ephraim will be as mighty as warriors, and their hearts will be filled with joy as if they had been drinking wine. Their children will see it all and be joyful; their hearts will rejoice in the LORD. {10:8} I will whistle to call them together, for I have redeemed them. From the distant corners of the earth, they will return, staggering and stumbling, but joyful and triumphant. {10:9} I will scatter them among the nations, and they will remember me in distant lands. They and their children will survive and return home again to Israel. {10:10} I will bring them back from Egypt and gather them from Assyria. I will resettle them in Gilead and Lebanon until there is no more room for them all. {10:11} They will pass safely through the sea of distress, for the waves of the sea will be held back. And the pride of Assyria will be crushed, and the rule of Egypt will end. {10:12} I will make them strong in the LORD, and they shall walk in his name," says the LORD.

{11:1} Lebanon, open your doors to let the fire devour your cedars! Fir trees, wail in sorrow, for the mighty cedars have fallen! Oaks of Bashan, cry out, for the forest of the vintage is destroyed. {11:2} Listen to the shepherds wailing, for their glory is ruined. Hear the roaring of young lions, for the pride of the Jordan Valley is devastated. {11:3} The LORD my God says, "Feed the flock meant for slaughter, whose owners slaughter them without remorse. Those who sell them say, 'Praise the LORD, for I am rich!' Even their own shepherds show them no pity. {11:4} "I will no longer show pity to the people of the land," says the LORD. "I will hand everyone over to their neighbors and their king. They will strike the land, and I will not rescue them. {11:5} "But I will take care of the flock meant for slaughter, you poor of the flock. I took two staffs, naming one Beauty and the other Bands, and I tended the flock. {11:6} "In one month, I removed three shepherds whom I detested, and they loathed me in return. {11:7} "Then I declared, 'I will not be your shepherd. Let those who are doomed to die die, and let those who are to be destroyed be destroyed. And let those who remain devour each other's flesh.' {11:8} "Next, I took my staff Beauty and broke it, symbolizing the breaking of the covenant I had made with all the nations. {11:9} "This covenant was broken on that day, and the poor among the flock who were watching me knew that it was the word of the LORD. {11:10} "I said to them, 'If you think it is right, give me my wages. But if not, keep them.' So they weighed out thirty pieces of silver as my wages. {11:11} "Then the LORD said to me, 'Throw it to the potter, the magnificent sum at which they valued me.' So I took the thirty pieces of silver and threw them to the potter in the house of the LORD. {11:12} "Next, I broke my other staff, Bands, symbolizing the breaking of the unity between Judah and Israel. {11:13} "Then the LORD said to me, 'Take again the equipment of a foolish shepherd. {11:14} "For I will raise up a shepherd in the land who will not care for those who are cut off, nor seek the young, nor heal the broken, nor sustain the standing. Instead, he will devour the flesh of the fattened and tear apart their hoofs. {11:15} "Woe to the worthless shepherd who abandons the flock! The sword will strike his arm and his right eye; his arm will be completely withered, and his right eye will be completely blind."

{12:1} This is the message from the LORD concerning Israel, who stretches forth the heavens, lays the foundation of the earth, and forms the spirit of man within him. {12:2} "Behold, I will make Jerusalem a cup of trembling for all the surrounding peoples when they besiege both Judah and Jerusalem. {12:3} "On that day, I will make Jerusalem a burdensome stone for all nations. Anyone who tries to lift it will be severely injured, even if all the nations of the earth gather against it. {12:4} "On that day," says the LORD, "I will strike every horse with astonishment and its rider with madness. I will also open my eyes upon the house of Judah and strike every horse of the people with blindness. {12:5} "The leaders of Judah will say in their hearts, 'The inhabitants of Jerusalem are our strength in the LORD of hosts, their God.' {12:6} "On that day, I will make the leaders of Judah like a firepot among wood and a torch of fire in a sheaf. They will consume all the surrounding peoples on the right hand and on the left, and Jerusalem will be inhabited again in its own place, even in Jerusalem. {12:7} "The LORD will save the tents of Judah first, so that the glory of the house of David and the glory of the inhabitants of Jerusalem may not overshadow Judah. {12:8} "On that day, the LORD will defend the inhabitants of Jerusalem. Even the weakest among them will be as mighty as David, and the house of David will be as God, as the angel of the LORD before them. {12:9} "And on that day, I will set out to destroy all the nations that come against Jerusalem. {12:10} "I will pour out on the house of David and on the inhabitants of Jerusalem the Spirit of grace and supplication. They will look upon me, whom they have pierced, and they will mourn for him as one mourns for an only son, and grieve bitterly for him as one grieves for a firstborn. {12:11} "On that day, there will be a great mourning in Jerusalem, like the mourning at Hadad Rimmon in the plain of Megiddo. {12:12} "Each family will mourn separately: the family of the house of David, their wives apart; the family of the house of Nathan, their wives apart; {12:13} "The family of the house of Levi, their wives apart; the family of Shimei, their wives apart; {12:14} "All the remaining families will mourn separately, each with their wives apart."

{13:1} "On that day, a fountain shall be opened to the house of David and to the inhabitants of Jerusalem for sin and uncleanness. {13:2} "And on that day," says the LORD of hosts, "I will cut off the names of the idols from the land, and they will no longer be remembered. I will also remove the prophets and the unclean spirit from the land. {13:3} "If anyone still prophesies, his own parents, who gave birth to him, will say to him, 'You shall not live, for you speak lies in the name of the LORD.' And his parents will pierce him through when he prophesies. {13:4} "On that day, every prophet will be ashamed of his vision when he prophesies. They will no longer wear a rough garment to deceive. {13:5} "Instead, each one will say, 'I am not a prophet, I am a farmer; for I have been tending to livestock since my youth.' {13:6} "And someone will ask him, 'What are these wounds on your hands?' Then he will answer, 'These are the wounds I received in the house of my friends.' {13:7} "Awake, O sword, against my shepherd, against the man who is my companion," says the LORD of hosts. "Strike the shepherd, and the sheep will be scattered; then I will turn my hand against the little ones. {13:8} "And it shall come to pass that in all the land," says the LORD, "two-thirds of the people will be cut off and perish, but one-third shall be left. {13:9} "I will bring the remaining third through the fire and refine them as silver is refined, and test them as gold is tested. They will call on my name, and I will answer them. I will say, 'They are my people,' and they will say, 'The LORD is our God.'"

{14:1} "Behold, the day of the LORD is coming, and your spoil shall be divided in your midst. {14:2} "For I will gather all nations against Jerusalem to battle; and the city shall be taken, the houses plundered, and the women ravished. Half of the city shall go into captivity, but the remnant of the people shall not be cut off from the city. {14:3} "Then the LORD will go forth and fight against those nations, as He fights in the day of battle. {14:4} "And His feet will stand on that day upon the Mount of Olives, which faces Jerusalem on the east. And the Mount of Olives shall split in two, toward the east and toward the west, making a very large valley; half of the mountain shall move toward the north and half of it toward the south. {14:5} "Then you shall flee through My mountain valley, for the mountain valley shall reach to Azal. Yes, you shall flee as you fled from the earthquake in the days of Uzziah king of Judah. Thus the LORD my God will come, and all the saints with Him. {14:6} "And it shall come to pass in that day, that there shall be no light; the lights will diminish. {14:7} "It shall be one day which is known to the LORD—neither day nor night. But at evening time it shall happen that it will be light. {14:8} ***"And in that day it shall be that living waters shall flow from Jerusalem, half of them toward the eastern sea and half of them toward the western sea; in both summer and winter it shall occur.*** {14:9} "And the LORD shall be King over all the earth. In that day it shall be—'The LORD is one,' and His name one. {14:10} "All the land shall be turned into a plain from Geba to Rimmon south of Jerusalem. Jerusalem shall be raised up and inhabited in her place from Benjamin's Gate to the place of the First Gate and the Corner Gate, and from the Tower of Hananel to the king's winepresses. {14:11} "People shall dwell in it; and no longer shall there be utter destruction, but Jerusalem shall be safely inhabited. {14:12} "And this shall be the plague with which the LORD will strike all the people who fought against Jerusalem: Their flesh shall dissolve while they stand on their feet, their eyes shall dissolve in their sockets, and their tongues shall dissolve in their mouths. {14:13} "It shall come to pass in that day that a great panic from the LORD will be among them. Everyone will seize the hand of his neighbor, and raise his hand against his neighbor's hand. {14:14} "Judah also will fight at Jerusalem. And the wealth of all the surrounding nations shall be gathered together: gold, silver, and apparel in great abundance. {14:15} "Thus shall be the plague on the horse, the mule, the camel, and the donkey, and on all the cattle that will be in those camps. So shall this plague be. {14:16} "And it shall come to pass that everyone who is left of all the nations which came against Jerusalem shall go up from year to year to worship the King, the LORD of hosts, and to keep the Feast of Tabernacles. {14:17} "And it shall be that whichever of the families of the earth do not come up to Jerusalem to worship the King, the LORD of hosts, on them there will be no rain. {14:18} "If the family of Egypt will not come up and enter in, they shall have no rain; they shall receive the plague with which the LORD strikes the nations who do not come up to keep the Feast of Tabernacles. {14:19} "This shall be the punishment of Egypt and the punishment of all the nations that do not come up to keep the Feast of Tabernacles. {14:20} "In that day 'HOLINESS TO THE LORD' shall be engraved on the bells of the horses. The pots in the LORD's house shall be like the bowls before the altar. {14:21} "Yes, every pot in Jerusalem and Judah shall be holiness to the LORD of hosts. Everyone who sacrifices shall come and take them and cook in them. In that day there shall no longer be a Canaanite in the house of the LORD of hosts."

Malachi

{1:1} "The burden of the word of the LORD to Israel by Malachi. {1:2} *"I have loved you," says the LORD. Yet you ask, "How have you loved us?" Was not Esau Jacob's brother?" says the LORD. "Yet I loved Jacob,* {1:3} but Esau I have hated, and I have laid waste his mountains and his heritage to the jackals of the wilderness." {1:4} "Though Edom says, 'We are shattered, but we will rebuild the ruins,' the LORD of hosts says, 'They may build, but I will tear down, and they will be called the wicked country, and the people with whom the LORD is angry forever.'" {1:5} "Your own eyes shall see this, and you shall say, 'Great is the LORD beyond the border of Israel!'" {1:6} "A son honors his father, and a servant his master. If then I am a father, where is my honor? And if I am a master, where is my fear? says the LORD of hosts to you, O priests, who despise my name. But you say, 'How have we despised your name?' {1:7} "By offering polluted food upon my altar. But you say, 'How have we polluted you?' By saying that the LORD's table may be despised. {1:8} "When you offer blind animals in sacrifice, is that not evil? And when you offer those that are lame or sick, is that not evil? Present that to your governor; will he accept you or show you favor?" says the LORD of hosts. {1:9} "And now entreat the favor of God, that he may be gracious to us. With such a gift from your hand, will he show favor to any of you?" says the LORD of hosts. {1:10} "Oh that there were one among you who would shut the doors, that you might not kindle fire on my altar in vain! I have no pleasure in you," says the LORD of hosts, "and I will not accept an offering from your hand. {1:11} *"For from the rising of the sun to its setting my name will be great among the nations, and in every place incense will be offered to my name, and a pure offering. For my name will be great among the nations, says the LORD of hosts.* {1:12} "But you profane it when you say that the Lord's table is polluted, and its fruit, that is, its food, may be despised. {1:13} "You say, 'Behold, what a weariness this is,' and you snort at it, says the LORD of hosts. You bring what has been taken by violence or is lame or sick, and this you bring as your offering! Shall I accept that from your hand?" says the LORD. {1:14} *"But cursed be the cheat who has a male in his flock, and vows it, and yet sacrifices to the Lord what is blemished. For I am a great King, says the LORD of hosts, and my name will be feared among the nations."*

{2:1} "And now, O priests, this commandment is for you. {2:2} "If you will not listen, if you will not take it to heart to give glory to my name, says the LORD of hosts, then I will send the curse upon you and I will curse your blessings. Indeed, I have already cursed them, because you do not take it to heart. {2:3} "Behold, I will rebuke your offspring, and spread dung on your faces, the dung of your offerings, and you shall be taken away with it. {2:4} "So you shall know that I have sent this command to you, that my covenant with Levi may stand, says the LORD of hosts. {2:5} "My covenant with him was one of life and peace, and I gave them to him. It was a covenant of fear, and he feared me. He stood in awe of my name. {2:6} "True instruction was in his mouth, and no wrong was found on his lips. He walked with me in peace and uprightness, and he turned many from iniquity. {2:7} "For the lips of a priest should guard knowledge, and people should seek instruction from his mouth, for he is the messenger of the LORD of hosts. {2:8} "But you have turned aside from the way. You have caused many to stumble by your instruction. You have corrupted the covenant of Levi, says the LORD of hosts. {2:9} "So I make you despised and abased before all the people, inasmuch as you do not keep my ways but show partiality in your instruction." {2:10} "Have we not all one Father? Has not one God created us? Why then are we faithless to one another, profaning the covenant of our fathers? {2:11} "Judah has been faithless, and abomination has been committed in Israel and in Jerusalem. For Judah has profaned the sanctuary of the LORD, which he loves, and has married the daughter of a foreign god. {2:12} "May the LORD cut off from the tents of Jacob any descendant of the man who does this, who brings an offering to the LORD of hosts! {2:13} "And this second thing you do. You cover the LORD's altar with tears, with weeping and groaning because he no longer regards the offering or accepts it with favor from your hand. {2:14} "But you say, 'Why does he not?' Because the LORD was witness between you and the wife of your youth, to whom you have been faithless, though she is your companion and your wife by covenant. {2:15} "Did he not make them one, with a portion of the Spirit in their union? And what was the one God seeking? Godly offspring. So guard yourselves in your spirit, and let none of you be faithless to the wife of your youth. {2:16} "For the man who does not love his wife but divorces her, says the LORD, the God of Israel, covers his garment with violence, says the LORD of hosts. So guard yourselves in your spirit, and do not be faithless." {2:17} *"You have wearied the LORD with your words. But you say, 'How have we wearied him?' By saying, 'Everyone who does evil is good in the sight of the LORD, and he delights in them.' Or by asking, 'Where is the God of justice?'"*

{3:1} "Behold, I will send my messenger, and he will prepare the way before me. And the Lord whom you seek will suddenly come to his temple; and the messenger of the covenant in whom you delight, behold, he is coming," says the LORD of hosts. {3:2} "But who can endure the day of his coming, and who can stand when he appears? For he is like a refiner's fire and like fuller's soap. {3:3} "He will sit as a refiner and purifier of silver, and he will purify the sons of Levi and refine them like gold and silver, and they will bring offerings in righteousness to the LORD. {3:4} "Then the offering of Judah and Jerusalem will be pleasing to the LORD as in the days of old and as in former years. {3:5} "Then I will draw near to you for judgment. I will be a swift witness against the sorcerers, against the adulterers, against those who swear falsely, against those who oppress the hired worker in his wages, the widow and the fatherless, against those who thrust aside the sojourner, and do not fear me," says the LORD of hosts. {3:6} "For I the LORD do not change; therefore you, O children of Jacob, are not consumed. {3:7} "From the days of your fathers you have turned aside from my statutes and have not kept them. Return to me, and I will return to you," says the LORD of hosts. But you say, 'How shall we return?' {3:8} "Will man rob God? Yet you are robbing me. But you say, 'How have we robbed you?' In your tithes and contributions. {3:9} "You are cursed with a curse, for you are robbing me, the whole nation of you. {3:10} "Bring the full tithe into the storehouse, that there may be food in my house. And thereby put me to the test, says the LORD of hosts, if I will not open the windows of heaven for you and pour down for you a blessing until there is no more need. {3:11} "I will rebuke the devourer for you, so that it will not destroy the fruits of your soil, and your vine in the field shall not fail to bear, says the LORD of hosts. {3:12} "Then all nations will call you blessed, for you will be a land of delight," says the LORD of hosts. {3:13} "Your words have been hard against me, says the LORD. But you say, 'How have we spoken against you?' {3:14} "You have said, 'It is vain to serve God. What is the profit of our keeping his charge or of walking as in mourning before the LORD of hosts? {3:15} "And now we call the arrogant blessed. Evildoers not only prosper but they put God to the test and they escape.'" {3:16} "Then those who feared the LORD spoke with one another. The LORD paid attention and heard them, and a book of remembrance was written before him of those who feared the LORD and esteemed his name. {3:17} "They shall be mine, says the LORD of hosts, in the day when I make up my treasured possession, and I will spare them as a man spares his son who serves him. {3:18} "Then once more you shall see the distinction between the righteous and the wicked, between one who serves God and one who does not serve him."

{4:1} "For behold, the day is coming, burning like an oven, when all the arrogant and all evildoers will be stubble. The day that is coming shall set them ablaze, says the LORD of hosts, so that it will leave them neither root nor branch. {4:2} *"But for you who fear my name, the Sun of righteousness shall rise with healing in its wings. You shall go out leaping like calves from the stall.* {4:3} "And you shall tread down the wicked, for they will be ashes under the soles of your feet, on the day when I act, says the LORD of hosts. {4:4} "Remember the law of my servant Moses, the statutes and rules that I commanded him at Horeb for all Israel. {4:5} "Behold, I will send you Elijah the prophet before the great and awesome day of the LORD comes. {4:6} *"And he will turn the hearts of fathers to their children and the hearts of children to their fathers, lest I come and strike the land with a decree of utter destruction."*

THE NEW TESTAMENT
for Genz

athena scroll

Your Path Forword

Matthew	1
Mark	13
Luke	21
John	34
Acts	44
Romans	57
1 Corinthians	63
2 Corinthians	68
Galatians	72
Ephesians	74
Philippians	76
Colossians	78
1 Thessalonians	80
2 Thessalonians	81
1 Timothy	82
2 Timothy	84
Titus	85
Philemon	86
Hebrews	87
James	91
1 Peter	93
2 Peter	95
1 John	96
2 John	98
3 John	99
Jude	100
Revelation	101
Free Gifts	107

Matthew

{1:1} This is the story of Jesus Christ's family history. He was a descendant of David and also of Abraham. {1:2} Abraham was the father of Isaac, who was the father of Jacob. Jacob had Judas and his brothers. {1:3} Judas was the father of Phares and Zara, whose mother was Thamar. Phares had a son named Esrom, who had a son named Aram. {1:4} Aram had a son named Aminadab, who had a son named Naasson, who had a son named Salmon. {1:5} Salmon had a son named Booz, whose mother was Rachab. Booz had a son named Obed, whose mother was Ruth. Obed had a son named Jesse. {1:6} Jesse was the father of David, who became king. David had a son named Solomon, whose mother was the wife of Urias. {1:7} Solomon had a son named Roboam, who had a son named Abia, who had a son named Asa. {1:8} Asa had a son named Josaphat, who had a son named Joram, who had a son named Ozias. {1:9} Ozias had a son named Joatham, who had a son named Achaz, who had a son named Ezekias. {1:10} Ezekias had a son named Manasses, who had a son named Amon, who had a son named Josias. {1:11} Josias had a son named Jechonias and his brothers. This was around the time when the people were taken to Babylon as captives. {1:12} After the captivity in Babylon, Jechonias had a son named Salathiel, who had a son named Zorobabel. {1:13} Zorobabel had a son named Abiud, who had a son named Eliakim, who had a son named Azor. {1:14} Azor had a son named Sadoc, who had a son named Achim, who had a son named Eliud. {1:15} Eliud had a son named Eleazar, who had a son named Matthan, who had a son named Jacob. {1:16} Jacob was the father of Joseph, who was married to Mary. Mary gave birth to Jesus, who is called Christ. {1:17} So, from Abraham to David, there were fourteen generations. From David to the time of the Babylonian captivity, there were fourteen generations. And from the Babylonian captivity to Christ, there were fourteen generations. {1:18} This is how the birth of Jesus Christ happened: Mary, his mother, was engaged to Joseph. Before they came together, she was found to be pregnant by the Holy Spirit. {1:19} Joseph, her husband, being a righteous man and not wanting to expose her to public disgrace, decided to divorce her quietly. {1:20} But as he thought about this, an angel of the Lord appeared to him in a dream. The angel said, "Joseph, son of David, do not be afraid to take Mary as your wife, because what is conceived in her is from the Holy Spirit. {1:21} She will give birth to a son, and you are to give him the name Jesus, because he will save his people from their sins." {1:22} All this took place to fulfill what the Lord had said through the prophet: {1:23} "Behold, the virgin will conceive and give birth to a son, and they will call him Emmanuel" (which means "God with us"). {1:24} When Joseph woke up, he did what the angel of the Lord had commanded him and took Mary home as his wife. {1:25} But he did not consummate their marriage until she gave birth to a son. And he gave him the name Jesus.

{2:1} Jesus was born in Bethlehem of Judea during the reign of King Herod. Wise men from the east came to Jerusalem, {2:2} asking, "Where is the one who has been born king of the Jews? We saw his star when it rose and have come to worship him." {2:3} When King Herod heard this, he was disturbed, and all Jerusalem with him. {2:4} He gathered all the chief priests and teachers of the law and asked them where the Messiah was to be born. {2:5} They replied, "In Bethlehem of Judea, for this is what the prophet has written: {2:6} 'But you, Bethlehem, in the land of Judah, are by no means least among the rulers of Judah; for out of you will come a ruler who will shepherd my people Israel.'" {2:7} Then Herod secretly called the wise men and asked them about the exact time the star had appeared. {2:8} He sent them to Bethlehem and said, "Go and search carefully for the child. As soon as you find him, report to me, so that I too may go and worship him." {2:9} After they had heard the king, they went on their way, and the star they had seen when it rose went ahead of them until it stopped over the place where the child was. {2:10} When they saw the star, they were overjoyed. {2:11} When the wise men entered the house, they saw the child with his mother Mary, and they bowed down and worshiped him. They presented him with gifts of gold, frankincense, and myrrh. {2:12} Then, being warned in a dream not to go back to Herod, they returned to their own country by another route. {2:13} After they had left, an angel of the Lord appeared to Joseph in a dream. The angel said, "Get up, take the child and his mother, and escape to Egypt. Stay there until I tell you, for Herod is going to search for the child to kill him." {2:14} So Joseph got up, took the child and his mother during the night, and left for Egypt, {2:15} where he stayed until the death of Herod. And so was fulfilled what the Lord had said through the prophet: "Out of Egypt I called my son." {2:16} When Herod realized that he had been outwitted by the wise men, he was furious. He gave orders to kill all the boys in Bethlehem and its vicinity who were two years old and under, based on the time he had learned from the wise men. {2:17} This fulfilled what was spoken through the prophet Jeremiah: {2:18} "A voice is heard in Ramah, weeping and great mourning, Rachel weeping for her children and refusing to be comforted, because they are no more." {2:19} After Herod died, an angel of the Lord appeared in a dream to Joseph in Egypt {2:20} and said, "Get up, take the child and his mother, and go to the land of Israel, for those who were trying to take the child's life are dead." {2:21} So Joseph got up, took the child and his mother, and went to the land of Israel. {2:22} But when he heard that Archelaus was reigning in Judea in place of his father Herod, he was afraid to go there. Having been warned in a dream, he withdrew to the district of Galilee, {2:23} and he went and lived in a town called Nazareth. So was fulfilled what was said through the prophets, that he would be called a Nazarene.

{3:1} During those days, John the Baptist came, preaching in the wilderness of Judea, {3:2} and saying, "Repent, for the kingdom of heaven is near!" {3:3} This is the one spoken of through the prophet Isaiah: "A voice of one calling in the wilderness, 'Prepare the way for the Lord, make straight paths for him.'" {3:4} John's clothes were made of camel's hair, and he had a leather belt around his waist. His food was locusts and wild honey. {3:5} People from Jerusalem, all Judea, and the whole region around Jordan went out to him. {3:6} They were baptized by him in the Jordan River, confessing their sins. {3:7} When John saw many Pharisees and Sadducees coming to his baptism, he said to them, "You brood of vipers! Who warned you to flee from the coming wrath? {3:8} Produce fruit in keeping with repentance. {3:9} And do not think you can say to yourselves, 'We have Abraham as our father.' I tell you that out of these stones God can raise up children for Abraham. {3:10} The ax is already at the root of the trees, and every tree that does not produce good fruit will be cut down and thrown into the fire. {3:11} "I baptize you with water for repentance. But after me comes one who is more powerful than I, whose sandals I am not worthy to carry. He will baptize you with the Holy Spirit and fire. {3:12} His winnowing fork is in his hand, and he will clear his threshing floor, gathering his wheat into the barn and burning up the chaff with unquenchable fire." {3:13} Jesus came from Galilee to the Jordan River to be baptized by John. {3:14} But John tried to deter him, saying, "I need to be baptized by you, and yet you come to me?" {3:15} Jesus replied, "Let it be so now; it is proper for us to do this to fulfill all righteousness." Then John consented. {3:16} As soon as Jesus was baptized, he went up out of the water. Suddenly, the heavens were opened, and he saw the Spirit of God descending like a dove and alighting on him. {3:17} And a voice from heaven said, "This is my Son, whom I love; with him I am well pleased."

{4:1} Jesus was led by the Spirit into the wilderness to be tempted by the devil. {4:2} After fasting forty days and forty nights, he was hungry. {4:3} The tempter came to him and said, "If you are the Son of God, tell these stones to become bread." {4:4} Jesus answered, "It is written: 'Man shall not live on bread alone, but on every word that comes from the mouth of God.'" {4:5} Then the devil took him to the holy city and set him on the highest point of the temple. {4:6} "If you are the Son of God," he said, "throw yourself down. For it is written: 'He will command his angels concerning you, and they will lift you up in their hands, so that you will not strike your foot against a stone.'" {4:7} Jesus answered him, "It is also written: 'Do not put the Lord your God to the test.'" {4:8} Again, the devil took him to a very high mountain and showed him all the kingdoms of the world and their splendor. {4:9} "All this I will give you," he said, "if you will bow down and worship me." {4:10} Jesus said to him, "Away from me, Satan! For it is written: 'Worship the Lord your God, and serve him only.'" {4:11} Then the devil left him, and angels came and attended to him. {4:12} When Jesus heard that John had been put in prison, he withdrew to Galilee. {4:13} Leaving Nazareth, he went and lived in Capernaum, which is by the lake in the area of Zebulun and Naphtali— {4:14} to fulfill what was said through the prophet Isaiah: {4:15} "Land of Zebulun and land of Naphtali, the Way of the Sea, beyond the Jordan, Galilee of the Gentiles {4:16} the people living in darkness have seen a great light; on those living in the land of the shadow of death a light has dawned." {4:17} From that time on Jesus began to preach, "Repent, for the kingdom of heaven has come near." {4:18} As Jesus walked by the Sea of Galilee, he saw two brothers, Simon called Peter and his brother Andrew, casting a net into the lake, for they were fishermen. {4:19} "Come, follow me," Jesus said, "and I will send you out to fish for people." {4:20} At once they left their nets and followed him. {4:21} Going on from there, he saw two other brothers, James son of Zebedee and his brother John, in a boat with their father Zebedee, preparing their nets. Jesus called them, {4:22} and immediately they left the boat and their father and followed him. {4:23} Jesus traveled throughout all of Galilee, teaching in their synagogues, proclaiming the good news of the kingdom, and healing every disease and sickness among the people. {4:24} News about him spread all over Syria, and people brought to him all who were ill with various diseases, those suffering severe pain, the demon-possessed, those having seizures, and the paralyzed; and he healed them. {4:25} Large crowds from Galilee, the Decapolis, Jerusalem, Judea, and the region across the Jordan followed him.

{5:1} When Jesus saw the crowds, he went up on a mountainside and sat down. His disciples came to him, {5:2} and he began to teach them, saying: {5:3} "Blessed are the poor in spirit, for theirs is the kingdom of heaven. {5:4} Blessed are those who mourn, for they will be comforted. {5:5} Blessed are the meek, for they will inherit the earth. {5:6} Blessed are those who hunger and thirst for righteousness, for they will be filled. {5:7} Blessed are the merciful, for they will be shown mercy. {5:8} Blessed are the pure in heart, for they will see God. {5:9} Blessed are the peacemakers, for they will be called children of God. {5:10} Blessed are those who are persecuted because of righteousness, for theirs is the kingdom of heaven. {5:11} "Blessed are you when people insult you, persecute you and falsely say all kinds of evil against you because of me. {5:12} Rejoice and be glad, because great is your reward in heaven, for in the same way they persecuted the prophets who were before you. {5:13} You are the salt of the earth. But if the salt loses its saltiness, how can it be made salty again? It is no longer good for anything, except to be thrown out and trampled underfoot. {5:14} You are the light of the world. A town built on a hill cannot be hidden. {5:15} Neither do people light a lamp and put it under a bowl. Instead, they put it on its stand, and it gives light to everyone in the house. {5:16} In the same way, let your light shine before others, so that they may see your good deeds and glorify your Father in heaven. {5:17} Do not think that I have come to abolish the Law or the Prophets; I have not come to abolish them but to fulfill them. {5:18} For truly I tell you, until heaven and earth disappear, not the smallest letter, not the least stroke of a pen, will by any means disappear from the Law until everything is accomplished. {5:19} Therefore, anyone who sets aside one of the least of these commands and teaches others accordingly will be called least in the kingdom of heaven, but whoever practices and teaches these commands will be called great in the kingdom of heaven. {5:20} For I tell you that unless your righteousness surpasses that of the Pharisees and the teachers of the law, you will certainly not enter the kingdom of heaven. {5:21} "You have heard that it was said to the people long ago, 'You shall not murder, and anyone who murders will be subject to judgment.' {5:22} But I tell you that anyone who is angry with a brother or sister will be subject to judgment. Again, anyone who says to a brother or sister, 'Raca,' is answerable to the court. And anyone who says, 'You fool!' will be in danger of the fire of hell. {5:23} Therefore, if you are offering your gift at the altar and there remember that your brother or sister has something against you, {5:24} leave your gift there in front of the altar. First go and be reconciled to them; then come and offer your gift. {5:25} Settle matters quickly with your adversary who is taking you to court. Do it while you are still together on the way, or your adversary may hand you over to the judge, and the judge may hand you over to the officer, and you may be thrown into prison. {5:26} Truly I tell you, you will not get out until you have paid the last penny. {5:27} You have heard that it was said, 'You shall not commit adultery.' {5:28} But I tell you that anyone who looks at a woman lustfully has already committed adultery with her in his heart. {5:29} If your right eye causes you to stumble, gouge it out and throw it away. It is better for you to lose one part of your body than for your whole body to be thrown into hell. {5:30} And if your right hand causes you to stumble, cut it off and throw it away. It is better for you to lose one part of your body than for your whole body to go into hell. {5:31} It has been said, 'Anyone who divorces his wife must give her a certificate of divorce.' {5:32} But I tell you that anyone who divorces his wife, except for sexual immorality, makes her the victim of adultery, and anyone who marries a divorced woman commits adultery. {5:33} "Again, you have heard that it was said to the people long ago, 'Do not break your oath, but fulfill to the Lord the vows you have made.' {5:34} But I tell you, do not swear an oath at all: either by heaven, for it is God's throne; {5:35} or by the earth, for it is his footstool; or by Jerusalem, for it is the city of the Great King. {5:36} And do not swear by your head, for you cannot make even one hair white or black. {5:37} All you need to say is simply 'Yes' or 'No'; anything beyond this comes from the evil one. {5:38} "You have heard that it was said, 'Eye for eye, and tooth for tooth.' {5:39} But I tell you, do not resist an evil person. If anyone slaps you on the right cheek, turn to them the other cheek also. {5:40} And if anyone wants to sue you and take your shirt, hand over your coat as well. {5:41} If anyone forces you to go one mile, go with them two miles. {5:42} Give to the one who asks you, and do not turn away from the one who wants to borrow from you. {5:43} "You have heard that it was said, 'Love your neighbor and hate your enemy.' {5:44} But I tell you, love your enemies and pray for those who persecute you, {5:45} that you may be children of your Father in heaven. He causes his sun to rise on the evil and the good, and sends rain on the righteous and the unrighteous. {5:46} If you love those who love you, what reward will you get? Aren't even the tax collectors doing that? {5:47} And if you greet only your own people, what are you doing more than others? Do not even pagans do that? {5:48} Be perfect, therefore, as your heavenly Father is perfect.

{6:1} "Be careful not to practice your righteousness in front of others to be seen by them. If you do, you will have no reward from your Father in heaven. {6:2} So when you give to the needy, do not announce it with trumpets, as the hypocrites do in the synagogues and on the streets, to be honored by others. Truly I tell you, they have received their reward in full. {6:3} But when you give to the needy, do not let your left hand know what your right hand is doing, {6:4} so that your giving may be in secret. Then your Father, who sees what is done in secret, will reward you openly. {6:5} "And when you pray, do not be like the hypocrites, for they love to pray standing in the synagogues and on the street corners to be seen by others. Truly I tell you, they have received their reward. {6:6} But when you pray, go into your room, close the door and pray to your Father, who is unseen. Then your Father, who sees what is done in secret, will reward you openly. {6:7} And when you pray, do not keep on babbling like pagans, for they think they will be heard because of their many words. {6:8} Do not be like them, for your Father knows what you need before you ask him. {6:9} "This, then, is how you should pray: 'Our Father in heaven, hallowed be your name, {6:10} your kingdom come, your will be done, on earth as it is in heaven. {6:11} Give us today our daily bread. {6:12} And forgive us our debts, as we also have forgiven our debtors. {6:13} And lead us not into temptation, but deliver us from the evil one.' {6:14} For if you forgive other people when they sin against you, your heavenly Father will also forgive you. {6:15} But if you do not forgive others their sins, your Father will not forgive your sins. {6:16} "And when you fast, do not look gloomy like the hypocrites, for they disfigure their faces to show others they are fasting. Truly I tell you, they have received their reward. {6:17} But when you fast, put oil on your head and wash your face, {6:18} so that it will not be obvious to others that you are fasting, but only to your Father, who is unseen; and your Father, who sees what is done in secret, will reward you openly. {6:19} "Do not store up for yourselves treasures on earth, where moths and rust destroy, and where thieves break in and steal. {6:20} But store up for yourselves treasures in heaven, where moths and rust do not destroy, and where thieves do not break in and steal. {6:21} For where your treasure is, there your heart will be also. {6:22} "The eye is the lamp of the body. If your eyes are healthy, your whole body will be full of light. {6:23} But if your eyes are unhealthy, your whole body will be full of darkness. If then the light within you is darkness, how great is that darkness! {6:24} "No one can serve two masters. Either you will hate the one and love the other, or you will be devoted to the one and despise the other. You cannot serve both God and money. {6:25} "Therefore I tell you, do not worry about your life, what you will eat or drink; or about your body, what you will wear. Isn't life more than food, and the body more than clothes? {6:26} Look at the birds of the air; they do not sow or reap or store away in barns, and yet your heavenly Father feeds them. Are you not much more valuable than they? {6:27} Can any one of you by worrying add a single hour to your life? {6:28} "And why do you worry about clothes? See how the flowers of the field grow. They do not labor or spin. {6:29} Yet I tell you that not even Solomon in all his splendor was dressed like one of these. {6:30} If that is how God clothes the grass of the field, which is here today and tomorrow is thrown into the fire, will he not clothe you—you of little faith? {6:31} So do not worry, saying, 'What shall we eat?' or 'What shall we drink?' or 'What shall we wear?' {6:32} For the pagans run after all these things, and your heavenly Father knows that you need them. {6:33} But seek first his kingdom and his righteousness, and all these things will be given to you as well. {6:34} Therefore do not worry about tomorrow, for tomorrow will worry about itself. Each day has enough trouble of its own.

{7:1} "Do not judge, or you too will be judged. {7:2} For in the same way you judge others, you will be judged, and with the measure you use, it will be measured to you. {7:3} "Why do you look at the speck of sawdust in your brother's eye and pay no attention to the plank in your own eye? {7:4} How can you say to your brother, 'Let me take the speck out of your eye,' when all the time there is a plank in your own eye? {7:5} You hypocrite, first take the plank out of your own eye, and then you will see clearly to remove the speck from your brother's eye. {7:6} "Do not give dogs what is sacred; do not throw your pearls to pigs. If you do, they may trample them under their feet, and turn and tear you to pieces. {7:7} "Ask, and it will be given to you; seek, and you will find; knock, and the door will be opened to you. {7:8} For everyone who asks receives; the one who seeks finds; and to the one who knocks, the door will be opened. {7:9} Which of you, if your son asks for bread, will give him a stone? {7:10}

Or if he asks for a fish, will give him a snake? {7:11} If you, then, though you are evil, know how to give good gifts to your children, how much more will your Father in heaven give good gifts to those who ask him! {7:12} So in everything, do to others what you would have them do to you, for this sums up the Law and the Prophets. {7:13} "Enter through the narrow gate. For wide is the gate and broad is the road that leads to destruction, and many enter through it. {7:14} But small is the gate and narrow the road that leads to life, and only a few find it. {7:15} "Beware of false prophets, who come to you in sheep's clothing but inwardly are ravening wolves. {7:16} You will recognize them by their fruits. Do people gather grapes from thorn bushes or figs from thistles? {7:17} Likewise, every good tree bears good fruit, but a bad tree bears bad fruit. {7:18} A good tree cannot bear bad fruit, and a bad tree cannot bear good fruit. {7:19} Every tree that does not bear good fruit is cut down and thrown into the fire. {7:20} Thus, by their fruit you will recognize them. {7:21} "Not everyone who says to me, 'Lord, Lord,' will enter the kingdom of heaven, but only the one who does the will of my Father who is in heaven. {7:22} Many will say to me on that day, 'Lord, Lord, did we not prophesy in your name and in your name drive out demons and in your name perform many miracles?' {7:23} Then I will tell them plainly, 'I never knew you. Away from me, you evildoers!' {7:24} "Therefore, everyone who hears these words of mine and puts them into practice is like a wise man who built his house on the rock: {7:25} The rain came down, the streams rose, and the winds blew and beat against that house; yet it did not fall, because it had its foundation on the rock. {7:26} But everyone who hears these words of mine and does not put them into practice is like a foolish man who built his house on sand: {7:27} The rain came down, the streams rose, and the winds blew and beat against that house, and it fell with a great crash." {7:28} When Jesus had finished saying these things, the crowds were amazed at his teaching, {7:29} because he taught as one who had authority, and not as their teachers of the law.

{8:1} After coming down from the mountain, large crowds followed Jesus. {8:2} Then a leper approached and knelt before him, saying, "Lord, if you are willing, you can make me clean." {8:3} Jesus reached out his hand and touched him, saying, "I am willing; be clean." Immediately his leprosy was cleansed. {8:4} Jesus instructed him, "See that you don't tell anyone. But go, show yourself to the priest and offer the gift Moses commanded, as a testimony to them." {8:5} As Jesus entered Capernaum, a centurion came to him, pleading, {8:6} "Lord, my servant is lying at home paralyzed and in terrible pain." {8:7} Jesus said to him, "I will go and heal him." {8:8} But the centurion replied, "Lord, I am not worthy to have you come into my home. Just say the word, and my servant will be healed. {8:9} For I am a man under authority, with soldiers under me. I tell this one, 'Go,' and he goes; and that one, 'Come,' and he comes. I say to my servant, 'Do this,' and he does it." {8:10} When Jesus heard this, he was amazed and said to those following him, "Truly I tell you, I have not found anyone in Israel with such great faith. {8:11} I tell you that many will come from the east and the west, and will take their places at the feast with Abraham, Isaac, and Jacob in the kingdom of heaven. {8:12} But the subjects of the kingdom will be thrown outside, into the darkness, where there will be weeping and gnashing of teeth." {8:13} Then Jesus said to the centurion, "Go! Let it be done just as you believed it would." And his servant was healed at that moment. {8:14} When Jesus entered Peter's house, he saw Peter's mother-in-law lying sick with a fever. {8:15} He touched her hand, and the fever left her. Then she got up and began to serve them. {8:16} When evening came, they brought to him many who were possessed by demons, and he drove out the spirits with a word and healed all the sick. {8:17} This was to fulfill what was spoken through the prophet Isaiah: "He took up our infirmities and bore our diseases." {8:18} When Jesus saw great crowds around him, he gave orders to cross to the other side [of the lake]. {8:19} Then a certain scribe came to him and said, "Teacher, I will follow you wherever you go." {8:20} Jesus replied, "Foxes have dens and birds of the sky have nests, but the Son of Man has no place to lay his head." {8:21} Another of his disciples said to him, "Lord, first let me go and bury my father." {8:22} But Jesus told him, "Follow me, and let the dead bury their own dead." {8:23} After Jesus got into a boat, his disciples followed him. {8:24} Suddenly, a violent storm arose on the sea, so that the boat was being covered by the waves. But Jesus was asleep. {8:25} So the disciples went and woke him up, saying, "Lord, save us! We're going to die!" {8:26} He said to them, "Why are you afraid, you of little faith?" Then he got up and rebuked the winds and the sea, and there was a great calm. {8:27} The men were amazed and asked, "What kind of man is this? Even the winds and the sea obey him!" {8:28} When Jesus arrived on the other side, in the region of the Gergesenes, two demon-possessed men coming out of the tombs met him. They were so violent that no one could pass that way. {8:29} Suddenly, they cried out, "What do you want with us, Jesus, Son of God? Have you come here to torture us before the appointed time?" {8:30} Nearby, a large herd of pigs was feeding. {8:31} The demons begged Jesus, "If you drive us out, send us into the herd of pigs." {8:32} He said to them, "Go!" So they came out and went into the pigs, and the whole herd rushed down the steep bank into the lake and died in the water. {8:33} Those tending the pigs ran off, went into the town, and reported all this, including what had happened to the demon-possessed men. {8:34} Then the whole town went out to meet Jesus. And when they saw him, they pleaded with him to leave their region.

{9:1} Jesus boarded a ship, crossed over, and returned to his own city. {9:2} People brought to him a man who was paralyzed and lying on a bed. When Jesus saw their faith, he said to the paralyzed man, "Take heart, son; your sins are forgiven." {9:3} Some of the scribes thought to themselves, "This man is blaspheming!" {9:4} Knowing their thoughts, Jesus asked, "Why do you entertain evil thoughts in your hearts? {9:5} Which is easier: to say, 'Your sins are forgiven,' or to say, 'Get up and walk'? {9:6} But I want you to know that the Son of Man has authority on earth to forgive sins." So he said to the paralyzed man, "Get up, take your bed, and go home." {9:7} The man got up and went home. {9:8} When the crowds saw this, they were amazed and praised God for giving such authority to humans. {9:9} As Jesus went on from there, he saw a man named Matthew sitting at the tax booth, and he said to him, "Follow me." And Matthew got up and followed him. {9:10} While Jesus was having a meal at the house, many tax collectors and sinners came and sat down with him and his disciples. {9:11} When the Pharisees saw this, they asked his disciples, "Why does your teacher eat with tax collectors and sinners?" {9:12} But when Jesus heard this, he said to them, "Healthy people don't need a doctor, but sick people do. {9:13} Go and learn what this means: 'I desire mercy, not sacrifice.' For I have not come to call the righteous, but sinners to repentance." {9:14} Then the disciples of John came to Jesus, asking, "Why do we and the Pharisees fast often, but your disciples do not fast?" {9:15} Jesus replied to them, "Can the wedding guests mourn as long as the bridegroom is with them? But the time will come when the bridegroom will be taken away from them, and then they will fast. {9:16} No one patches an old garment with a piece of new cloth, for the patch will shrink and rip away from the old cloth, making the tear worse. {9:17} Nor do people pour new wine into old wineskins. If they do, the skins burst, the wine spills out, and the skins are ruined. Instead, they pour new wine into new wineskins, and both are preserved." {9:18} While Jesus was speaking these things to them, a certain ruler came and worshiped him, saying, "My daughter has just died, but come and lay your hand upon her, and she will live." {9:19} And Jesus arose and followed him, and so did his disciples. {9:20} And behold, a woman who had been suffering from a hemorrhage for twelve years came up behind him and touched the fringe of his cloak; {9:21} for she was saying to herself, "If I only touch his cloak, I will get well." {9:22} But Jesus turning and seeing her said, "Daughter, take courage; your faith has made you well." At once the woman was well. {9:23} When Jesus came into the official's house, and saw the flute players and the crowd in noisy disorder, {9:24} he said, "Leave; for the girl has not died, but is asleep." And they began laughing at him. {9:25} But when the crowd had been sent out, he entered and took her by the hand, and the girl got up. {9:26} And this news spread throughout that land. {9:27} As Jesus went on from there, two blind men followed him, crying out, "Have mercy on us, Son of David!" {9:28} When he entered the house, the blind men came up to him, and Jesus said to them, "Do you believe that I am able to do this?" They said to him, "Yes, Lord." {9:29} Then he touched their eyes, saying, "It shall be done to you according to your faith." {9:30} And their eyes were opened. Then Jesus sternly warned them, "See that no one knows about this." {9:31} But they went out and spread the news about him throughout that entire region. {9:32} As they were going out, behold, they brought to him a man who was mute and demon-possessed. {9:33} And when the demon was cast out, the mute man spoke. And the crowds marveled, saying, "Never was anything like this seen in Israel." {9:34} But the Pharisees said, "He casts out demons by the prince of demons." {9:35} And Jesus went throughout all the cities and villages, teaching in their synagogues, and proclaiming the gospel of the kingdom, and healing every disease and every affliction among the people. {9:36} But when he saw the multitudes, he was moved with compassion for them, because they were weary and scattered, like sheep having no shepherd. {9:37} Then he said to his disciples, "The harvest truly is plentiful, but the laborers are few. {9:38} Therefore, pray to the Lord of the harvest to send out laborers into his harvest."

{10:1} And when he had called his twelve disciples to him, he gave them authority over unclean spirits, to cast them out, and to heal all kinds of sickness and disease. {10:2} These are the names of the twelve apostles: first, Simon (who is called Peter) and his brother Andrew; James the son of Zebedee, and John his brother; {10:3} Philip and Bartholomew; Thomas and Matthew the tax collector; James the son of Alphaeus, and Thaddaeus; {10:4} Simon the Canaanite, and Judas Iscariot, who also betrayed him. {10:5} Jesus sent out these twelve with the following instructions: "Do not go among the Gentiles or enter any town of the Samaritans. {10:6} Go rather to the lost sheep of Israel. {10:7} As you go, proclaim this message: 'The kingdom of heaven has come near.' {10:8} Heal the sick, raise the dead, cleanse those who have leprosy, drive out demons. Freely you have received; freely give. {10:9} Do not take along any gold or silver or copper in your belts; {10:10} take no bag for the journey, or extra shirt, or sandals or a staff; for the worker is worth his keep. {10:11} Whatever town or village you enter, search there for some worthy person and stay at their house until you leave. {10:12} As you enter the home, give it your greeting. {10:13} If the home is deserving, let your peace rest on it; if it is not, let your peace return to you. {10:14} If anyone will not welcome you or listen to your words, leave that home or town and shake the dust off your feet. {10:15} Truly I tell you, it will be more bearable for Sodom and Gomorrah on the day of judgment than for that town." {10:16} "Behold, I am sending you out like sheep among wolves. Therefore be as shrewd as snakes and as innocent as doves. {10:17} Be on your guard; you will be handed over to the local councils and be flogged in the synagogues. {10:18} On my account you will be brought before governors and kings as witnesses to them and to the Gentiles. {10:19} But when they arrest you, do not worry about what to say or how to say it. At that time you will be given what to say, {10:20} for it will not be you speaking, but the Spirit of your Father speaking through you. {10:21} "Brother will betray brother to death, and a father his child; children will rebel against their parents and have them put to death. {10:22} You will be hated by everyone because of me, but the one who stands firm to the end will be saved. {10:23} When you are persecuted in one place, flee to another. Truly I tell you, you will not finish going through the towns of Israel before the Son of Man comes. {10:24} "The student is not above the teacher, nor a servant above his master. {10:25} It is enough for students to be like their teachers, and servants like their masters. If the head of the house has been called Beelzebul, how much more the members of his household! {10:26} "So do not be afraid of them, for there is nothing concealed that will not be disclosed, or hidden that will not be made known. {10:27} What I tell you in the dark, speak in the daylight; what is whispered in your ear, proclaim from the roofs. {10:28} Do not be afraid of those who kill the body but cannot kill the soul. Rather, be afraid of the One who can destroy both soul and body in hell. {10:29} Aren't two sparrows sold for a penny? Yet not one of them will fall to the ground outside your Father's care. {10:30} And even the very hairs of your head are all numbered. {10:31} So don't be afraid; you are worth more than many sparrows. {10:32} "Whoever acknowledges me before others, I will also acknowledge before my Father in heaven. {10:33} But whoever disowns me before others, I will disown before my Father in heaven. {10:34} "Do not suppose that I have come to bring peace to the earth. I did not come to bring peace, but a sword. {10:35} For I have come to turn " 'a man against his father, a daughter against her mother, a daughter-in-law against her mother-in-law— {10:36} a man's enemies will be the members of his own household.' {10:37} "Anyone who loves their father or mother more than me is not worthy of me; anyone who loves their son or daughter more than me is not worthy of me. {10:38} Whoever does not take up their cross and follow me is not worthy of me. {10:39} Whoever finds their life will lose it, and whoever loses their life for my sake will find it." {10:40} "Whoever receives you received me, and whoever receives me receives the one who sent me. {10:41} Whoever receives a prophet because he is a prophet will receive a prophet's reward, and whoever receives a righteous person because he is a righteous person will receive a righteous person's reward. {10:42} And whoever gives even a cup of cold water to one of these little ones because he is my disciple, truly I tell you, he will never lose his reward."

{11:1} After Jesus finished instructing his twelve disciples, he went on from there to teach and preach in the towns of Galilee. {11:2} When John, who was in prison, heard about the deeds of the Messiah, he sent his disciples {11:3} to ask him, "Are you the one who is to come, or should we expect someone else?" {11:4} Jesus replied, "Go back and report to John what you hear and see: {11:5} The blind receive sight, the lame walk, those who have leprosy are cleansed, the deaf hear, the dead are raised, and the good news is proclaimed to the poor. {11:6} Blessed is anyone who does not stumble on account of me." {11:7} "As John's disciples were leaving, Jesus began to speak to the crowds about John: 'What did you go out into the wilderness to see? A reed swayed by the wind? {11:8} If not, what did you go out to see? A man dressed in fine clothes? No, those who wear fine clothes are in kings' palaces. {11:9} Then what did you go out to see? A prophet? Yes, I tell you, and more than a prophet. {11:10} This is the one about whom it is written: "I will send my messenger ahead of you, who will prepare your way before you." {11:11} Truly I tell you, among those born of women there has not risen anyone greater than John the Baptist; yet whoever is least in the kingdom of heaven is greater than he. {11:12} From the days of John the Baptist until now, the kingdom of heaven has been subjected to violence, and violent people have been raiding it. {11:13} For all the Prophets and the Law prophesied until John. {11:14} And if you are willing to accept it, he is the Elijah who was to come. {11:15} Whoever has ears, let them hear.'" {11:16} "How can I compare this generation? They are like children sitting in the marketplaces and calling out to others: {11:17} 'We played the pipe for you, and you did not dance; we sang a dirge, and you did not mourn.' {11:18} For John came neither eating nor drinking, and they say, 'He has a demon.' {11:19} The Son of Man came eating and drinking, and they say, 'Here is a glutton and a drunkard, a friend of tax collectors and sinners.' But wisdom is proved right by her deeds." {11:20} Then Jesus began to denounce the towns in which most of his miracles had been performed, because they did not repent. {11:21} "Woe to you, Chorazin! Woe to you, Bethsaida! If the miracles that were performed in you had been performed in Tyre and Sidon, they would have repented long ago in sackcloth and ashes. {11:22} But I tell you, it will be more bearable for Tyre and Sidon on the day of judgment than for you. {11:23} And you, Capernaum, will you be lifted to the heavens? No, you will go down to Hades. For if the miracles that were performed in you had been performed in Sodom, it would have remained to this day. {11:24} But I tell you that it will be more bearable for Sodom on the day of judgment than for you." {11:25} At that time Jesus answered and said, "I thank you, Father, Lord of heaven and earth, because you have hidden these things from the wise and learned, and revealed them to little children. {11:26} Yes, Father, for this is what you were pleased to do. {11:27} All things have been committed to me by my Father. No one knows the Son except the Father, and no one knows the Father except the Son and those to whom the Son chooses to reveal him. {11:28} "Come to me, all of you who are weary and burdened, and I will give you rest. {11:29} Take my yoke upon you and learn from me, for I am gentle and humble in heart, and you will find rest for your souls. {11:30} For my yoke is easy and my burden is light."

{12:1} At that time, Jesus went on the Sabbath day through the cornfields, and his disciples were hungry, so they began to pluck ears of corn and eat them. {12:2} When the Pharisees saw this, they said to him, "Look, your disciples are doing what is unlawful on the Sabbath." {12:3} But he said to them, "Have you not read what David did when he and his companions were hungry? {12:4} He entered the house of God, and he and his companions ate the consecrated bread—which was not lawful for them to do, but only for the priests. {12:5} Or haven't you read in the Law that the priests on Sabbath duty in the temple desecrate the Sabbath and yet are innocent? {12:6} I tell you that something greater than the temple is here. {12:7} If you had known what these words mean, 'I desire mercy, not sacrifice,' you would not have condemned the innocent. {12:8} For the Son of Man is Lord of the Sabbath." {12:9} Departing from there, he went into their synagogue. {12:10} And there was a man with a withered hand. They asked Jesus, "Is it lawful to heal on the Sabbath?" They asked this to accuse him. {12:11} He replied, "If any of you has a sheep and it falls into a pit on the Sabbath, will you not take hold of it and lift it out? {12:12} How much more valuable is a man than a sheep! Therefore, it is lawful to do good on the Sabbath." {12:13} Then he said to the man, "Stretch out your hand." So he stretched it out, and it was completely restored, just as sound as the other. {12:14} Then the Pharisees went out and plotted how they could destroy Jesus. {12:15} But Jesus, aware of this, withdrew from there. Many followed him, and he healed them all. {12:16} He warned them not to make him known, {12:17} so that what was spoken through the prophet Isaiah might be fulfilled: {12:18} "Here is my servant whom I have chosen, the one I love, in whom I delight; I will put my Spirit on him, and he will proclaim justice to the nations. {12:19} He will not quarrel or cry out; no one will hear his voice in the streets. {12:20} A bruised reed he will not break, and a smoldering wick he will not snuff out, till he has brought justice through to victory. {12:21} In his name the nations will put their hope." {12:22} Then they brought to Jesus a demon-possessed man who was blind and mute, and Jesus healed him, so that he could both speak and see. {12:23} All the people were astonished and said, "Could this be the Son of David?" {12:24} But when the Pharisees heard this, they said, "It is only by Beelzebul, the prince of demons, that this fellow drives out demons." {12:25} Jesus knew their thoughts and said to them, "Every kingdom divided against itself will be ruined, and every city or household divided against itself will not stand. {12:26} If Satan drives out Satan, he is divided against himself. How then can his kingdom stand? {12:27} And if I drive out demons by Beelzebul, by whom do your people drive them out? So then, they will be your judges. {12:28} But if it is by the Spirit of God that I drive out demons, then the kingdom of God has come upon you. {12:29} "Or again, how can anyone enter a strong man's house and carry off his possessions unless he first ties up the strong man? Then he can plunder his house. {12:30} "Whoever is not with me is against me, and whoever does not gather with me scatters." {12:31} So I tell you, every kind of sin and slander can be forgiven, but blasphemy against the Spirit will not be forgiven. {12:32} Anyone who speaks a word against the Son of Man will be forgiven, but anyone who speaks against the Holy Spirit will not be forgiven, either in this age or in the age to come. {12:33} "Make a tree good and its fruit will be good, or make a tree bad and its fruit will be bad, for a tree is recognized by its fruit. {12:34} You brood of vipers, how can you who are evil say anything good? For the mouth speaks what the heart is full of. {12:35} A good man brings good things out of the good stored up in him, and an evil man brings evil things out of the evil stored up in him. {12:36} But I tell you that everyone will have to give account on the day of judgment for every empty word they have spoken. {12:37} For by your words you will be acquitted, and by your words you will be condemned." {12:38} Then some of the scribes and Pharisees said to Jesus, "Teacher, we want to see a sign from you." {12:39} But he answered them, "A wicked and adulterous generation asks for a sign! But none will be given it except the sign of the prophet Jonah. {12:40} For as Jonah was three days and three nights in the belly of a huge fish, so the Son of Man will be three days and three nights in the heart of the earth. {12:41} The men of Nineveh will stand up at the judgment with this generation and condemn it; for they repented at the preaching of Jonah, and now something greater than Jonah is here. {12:42} The Queen of the South will rise at the judgment with this generation and condemn it; for she came from the ends of the earth to listen to Solomon's wisdom, and now something greater than Solomon is here. {12:43} "When an impure spirit comes out of a person, it goes through arid places seeking rest and does not find it. {12:44} Then it says, 'I will return to the house I left.' When it arrives, it finds the house unoccupied, swept clean, and put in order. {12:45} Then it goes and takes with it seven other spirits more wicked than itself, and they go in and live there. And the final condition of that person is worse than the first. That is how it will be with this wicked generation." {12:46} While Jesus was still talking to the crowd, his mother and brothers stood outside, wanting to speak to him. {12:47} Someone told him, "Your mother and brothers are standing outside, wanting to speak to you." {12:48} He replied to him, "Who is my mother, and who are my brothers?" {12:49} Pointing to his disciples, he said, "Here are my mother and my brothers. {12:50} For whoever does the will of my Father in heaven is my brother and sister and mother."

{13:1} On the same day, Jesus left the house and sat by the sea. {13:2} A large crowd gathered around him, so he got into a boat and sat down, while the whole crowd stood on the shore. {13:3} He spoke many things to them in parables, saying, "Listen! A sower went out to sow. {13:4} As he was scattering the seed, some fell along the path, and the birds came and ate it up. {13:5} Some fell on rocky places, where it did not have much soil. It sprang up quickly because the soil was shallow. {13:6} But when the sun came up, the plants were scorched, and they withered because they had no roots. {13:7} Other seeds fell among thorns, which grew up and choked the plants. {13:8} Another seed fell on good soil, where it produced a crop—a hundred, sixty or thirty times what was sown. {13:9} Whoever has ears, let them hear." {13:10} The disciples came to him and asked, "Why do you speak to the people in parables?" {13:11} He replied, "Because the knowledge of the secrets of the kingdom of heaven has been given to you, but not to them. {13:12} Whoever has will be given more, and they will have an abundance. Whoever does not have, even what they have will be taken from them. {13:13} This is why I speak to them in parables: "Though seeing, they do not see; though hearing, they do not hear or understand. {13:14} In them is fulfilled the prophecy of Isaiah: "'You will be ever hearing but never understanding; you will be ever seeing but never perceiving. {13:15} For this people's heart has become calloused; they hardly hear with their ears, and they have closed their eyes. Otherwise they might see with their eyes, hear with their ears, understand with their hearts and turn, and I would heal them.' {13:16} But blessed are your eyes because they see, and your ears because they hear. {13:17} For truly I tell you, many prophets and righteous people longed to see what you see but did not see it, and to hear what you hear but did not hear it. {13:18} So listen to the parable of the sower: {13:19} When someone hears the message about the kingdom but doesn't understand it, the evil one comes and snatches away what was sown in their heart. This is the seed sown along the path. {13:20} The seed falling on rocky ground refers to someone who hears the word and at once receives it with joy. {13:21} But since they have no roots, they last only a short time. When trouble or persecution comes because of the word, they quickly fall away. {13:22} The seed falling among the thorns refers to someone who hears the word, but the worries of this life and the deceitfulness of wealth choke the word, making it unfruitful. {13:23} But the seed falling on good soil refers to someone who hears the word and understands it. This is the one who produces a crop, yielding a hundred, sixty, or thirty times what was sown. {13:24} Jesus told them another parable: "The kingdom of heaven is like a man who sowed good seed in his field. {13:25} But while everyone was sleeping, his enemy came and sowed weeds among the wheat, and went away. {13:26} When the wheat sprouted and formed heads, then the weeds also appeared. {13:27} The owner's servants came to him and said, 'Sir, didn't you sow good seed in your field? Where did the weeds come from?' {13:28} 'An enemy did this,' he replied. The servants asked him, 'Do you want us to go and pull them up?' {13:29} 'No,' he answered, 'because while you are pulling the weeds, you may uproot the wheat with them. {13:30} Let both grow together until the harvest. At that time I will tell the harvesters: First collect the weeds and tie them in bundles to be burned; then gather the wheat and bring it into my barn.'" {13:31} Jesus told them another parable: "The kingdom of heaven is like a mustard seed, which a man took and planted in his field. {13:32} Though it is the smallest of all seeds, yet when it grows, it is the largest of garden plants and becomes a tree, so that the birds come and perch in its branches. {13:33} He told them still another parable: "The kingdom of heaven is like yeast that a woman took and mixed into about sixty pounds of flour until it worked all through the dough." {13:34} Jesus spoke all these things to the crowd in parables; he did not say anything to them without using a parable. {13:35} So was fulfilled what was spoken through the prophet: "I will open my mouth in parables, I will utter things hidden since the creation of the world." {13:36} Then Jesus left the crowd and went into the house. His disciples came to him and said, "Explain to us the parable of the weeds in the field." {13:37} He answered, "The one who sowed the good seed is the Son of Man. {13:38} The field is the world, and the good seed stands for the people of the kingdom. The weeds are the people of the evil one, {13:39} and the enemy who sows them is the devil. The harvest is the end of the age, and the harvesters are angels. {13:40} As the weeds are pulled up and burned in the fire, so it will be at the end of the age. {13:41} The Son of Man will send out his angels, and they will weed out of his kingdom everything that causes sin and all who do evil. {13:42} They will throw them into the blazing furnace, where there will be weeping and gnashing of teeth. {13:43} Then the righteous will shine like the sun in the kingdom of their Father. Whoever has ears, let them hear." {13:44} "Again, the kingdom of heaven is like treasure hidden in a field. When a man found it, he hid it again, and then in his joy went and sold all he had and bought that field." {13:45} "Again, the kingdom of heaven is like a merchant seeking fine pearls. {13:46} When he found one of great value, he went away and sold everything he had and bought it." {13:47} "Again, the kingdom of heaven is like a net that was cast into the sea and caught fish of every kind. {13:48} When it was full, the fishermen pulled it up on the shore. Then they sat down and sorted the good fish into containers, but threw the bad away. {13:49} This is how it will be at the end of the age: The angels will come and separate the wicked from the righteous {13:50} and throw them into the blazing furnace, where there will be weeping and gnashing of teeth. {13:51} 'Have you understood all these things?' Jesus asked. 'Yes,' they replied. {13:52} He said to them, 'Therefore every teacher of the law who has become a disciple in the kingdom of heaven is like the owner of a house who brings out of his storeroom new treasures as well as old.'" {13:53} After Jesus finished these parables, he left that place. {13:54} He went to his hometown and began teaching the people in their synagogue. They were amazed and asked, "Where did this man get this wisdom and these miraculous powers? {13:55} Isn't this the carpenter's son? Isn't his mother's name Mary, and aren't his brothers James, Joseph, Simon, and Judas? {13:56} Aren't all his sisters with us? Where did this man get all these things?" {13:57} And they took offense at him. But Jesus said to them, "A prophet is not without honor except in his own town and in his own home." {13:58} And he did not do many miracles there because of their lack of faith.

{14:1} At that time, Herod the tetrarch heard about the fame of Jesus. {14:2} He said to his servants, "This is John the Baptist; he has risen from the dead, and that is why miraculous powers are at work in him." {14:3} For Herod had arrested John, bound him, and put him in prison because of Herodias, his brother Philip's wife. {14:4} John had been telling him, "It is not lawful for you to have her." {14:5} Although Herod wanted to kill him, he feared the crowd, because they considered John a prophet. {14:6} But when Herod's birthday came, the daughter of Herodias danced before the guests and pleased Herod. {14:7} So he promised with an oath to give her whatever she asked. {14:8} Prompted by her mother, she said, "Give me here on a platter the head of John the Baptist." {14:9} The king was distressed, but because of his oaths and his guests at the table, he ordered that her request be granted. {14:10} So he sent and had John beheaded in the prison. {14:11} His head was brought on a platter and given to the girl, who brought it to her mother. {14:12} John's disciples came and took his body and buried it. Then they went and told Jesus. {14:13} When Jesus heard about John's death, he left there by boat to a remote place to be alone. But the crowds heard about it and followed him on foot from the towns. {14:14} When Jesus landed and saw a large crowd, he had compassion on them and healed their sickness. {14:15}

When evening came, his disciples came to him and said, "This is a remote place, and it's already getting late. Send the crowds away, so they can go to the villages and buy themselves some food." {14:16} Jesus replied, "They do not need to go away. You give them something to eat." {14:17} "We have here only five loaves of bread and two fish," they answered. {14:18} "Bring them here to me," he said. {14:19} And he directed the people to sit down on the grass. Taking the five loaves and the two fish and looking up to heaven, he gave thanks and broke the loaves. Then he gave them to the disciples, and the disciples gave them to the people. {14:20} They all ate and were satisfied, and the disciples picked up twelve baskets of broken pieces that were left over. {14:21} The number of those who ate was about five thousand men, besides women and children. {14:22} Immediately Jesus made the disciples get into the boat and go on ahead of him to the other side, while he dismissed the crowd. {14:23} After he had dismissed them, he went up on a mountainside by himself to pray. Later that night, he was there alone, {14:24} and the boat was already a considerable distance from land, buffeted by the waves because the wind was against it. {14:25} Shortly before dawn Jesus went out to them, walking on the lake. {14:26} When the disciples saw him walking on the lake, they were terrified. "It's a ghost," they said, and cried out in fear. {14:27} But Jesus immediately said to them: "Take courage! It is I. Don't be afraid." {14:28} "Lord, if it's you," Peter replied, "tell me to come to you on the water," he said. {14:29} "Come," he said. Then Peter got down out of the boat, walked on the water and came toward Jesus. {14:30} But when he saw the wind, he was afraid and, beginning to sink, cried out, "Lord, save me!" {14:31} Immediately Jesus reached out his hand and caught him. "You of little faith," he said, "why did you doubt?" {14:32} And when they climbed into the boat, the wind died down. {14:33} Then those who were in the boat worshiped him, saying, "Truly you are the Son of God." {14:34} After they had crossed over, they landed at Gennesaret. {14:35} When the people there recognized Jesus, they sent word to all the surrounding country. People brought all their sickness to him {14:36} and begged him to let the sick just touch the edge of his cloak, and all who touched it were healed.

{15:1} Then some scribes and Pharisees from Jerusalem came to Jesus and asked, {15:2} "Why do your disciples break the tradition of the elders? They don't wash their hands before they eat!" {15:3} Jesus replied, "And why do you break the command of God for the sake of your tradition? {15:4} For God said, 'Honor your father and mother' and 'Anyone who curses their father or mother is to be put to death.' {15:5} But you say that if anyone declares that what might have been used to help their father or mother is 'devoted to God,' {15:6} they are not to 'honor their father or mother' with it. Thus you nullify the word of God for the sake of your tradition. {15:7} You hypocrites! Isaiah was right when he prophesied about you: {15:8} 'These people honor me with their lips, but their hearts are far from me. {15:9} They worship me in vain; their teachings are merely human rules.'" {15:10} Jesus called the crowd to him and said, "Listen and understand: {15:11} What goes into someone's mouth does not defile them, but what comes out of their mouth, that is what defiles them." {15:12} Then the disciples came to him and asked, "Do you know that the Pharisees were offended when they heard this?" {15:13} He replied, "Every plant that my heavenly Father has not planted will be pulled up by the roots. {15:14} Leave them; they are blind guides. If the blind lead the blind, both will fall into a pit." {15:15} Peter said, "Explain the parable to us." {15:16} "Are you still so dull?" Jesus asked them. {15:17} "Don't you see that whatever enters the mouth goes into the stomach and then out of the body? {15:18} But the things that come out of a person's mouth come from the heart, and these defile them. {15:19} For out of the heart come evil thoughts—murder, adultery, sexual immorality, theft, false testimony, slander. {15:20} These are what defile a person; but eating with unwashed hands does not defile them." {15:21} Jesus left that place and withdrew to the region of Tyre and Sidon. {15:22} A Canaanite woman from that vicinity came to him, crying out, "Lord, Son of David, have mercy on me! My daughter is demon-possessed and suffering terribly." {15:23} Jesus did not answer a word. So his disciples came to him and urged him, "Send her away, for she keeps crying out after us." {15:24} He answered, "I was sent only to the lost sheep of Israel." {15:25} The woman came and knelt before him. "Lord, help me!" she said. {15:26} He replied, "It is not right to take the children's bread and toss it to the dogs." {15:27} "Yes it is, Lord," she said. "Even the dogs eat the crumbs that fall from their master's table." {15:28} Then Jesus said to her, "Woman, you have great faith! Your request is granted." And her daughter was healed at that moment. {15:29} Jesus left there and went along the Sea of Galilee. Then he went up on a mountainside and sat down. {15:30} Great crowds came to him, bringing the lame, the blind, the crippled, the mute and many others, and laid them at his feet; and he healed them. {15:31} The people were amazed when they saw the mute speaking, the crippled made well, the lame walking and the blind seeing. And they praised the God of Israel. {15:32} Jesus called his disciples to him and said, "I have compassion for these people; they have already been with me three days and have nothing to eat. I do not want to send them away hungry, or they may collapse on the way." {15:33} His disciples answered, "Where could we get enough bread in this remote place to feed such a crowd?" {15:34} "How many loaves do you have?" Jesus asked. "Seven," they replied, "and a few small fish." {15:35} He told the crowd to sit down on the ground. {15:36} Then he took the seven loaves and the fish, and when he had given thanks, he broke them and gave them to the disciples, and they in turn to the people. {15:37} They all ate and were satisfied. Afterward the disciples picked up seven basketfuls of broken pieces that were left over. {15:38} The number of those who ate was four thousand men, besides women and children. {15:39} After Jesus had sent the crowd away, he got into the boat and went to the vicinity of Magadan.

{16:1} The Pharisees and Sadducees came to Jesus and tested him by asking him to show them a sign from heaven. {16:2} He replied, "When evening comes, you say, 'It will be fair weather, for the sky is red; {16:3} and in the morning, 'Today it will be stormy, for the sky is red and overcast.' You know how to interpret the appearance of the sky, but you cannot interpret the signs of the times. {16:4} A wicked and adulterous generation looks for a sign, but none will be given it except the sign of Jonah." Jesus then left them and went away. {16:5} When they went across the lake, the disciples forgot to take bread. {16:6} Jesus said to them, "Watch out and beware of the yeast of the Pharisees and Sadducees." {16:7} They discussed this among themselves and said, "It is because we didn't bring any bread." {16:8} Aware of their discussion, Jesus asked, "You of little faith, why are you talking among yourselves about having no bread? {16:9} Do you still not understand? Don't you remember the five loaves for the five thousand, and how many baskets you gathered? {16:10} Or the seven loaves for the four thousand, and how many baskets you gathered? {16:11} How is it you don't understand that I was not talking to you about bread? But beware of the yeast of the Pharisees and Sadducees." {16:12} Then they understood that he was not telling them to beware of the yeast used in bread, but of the teaching of the Pharisees and Sadducees. {16:13} When Jesus came to the region of Caesarea Philippi, he asked his disciples, "Who do people say the Son of Man is?" {16:14} They replied, "Some say John the Baptist; others say Elijah; and still others, Jeremiah or one of the prophets." {16:15} "But what about you?" he asked. "Who do you say I am?" {16:16} Simon Peter answered, "You are the Messiah, the Son of the living God." {16:17} Jesus replied, "Blessed are you, Simon son of Jonah, for this was not revealed to you by flesh and blood, but by my Father in heaven. {16:18} And I tell you that you are Peter, and on this rock I will build my church, and the gates of Hades will not overcome it. {16:19} I will give you the keys of the kingdom of heaven; whatever you bind on earth will be bound in heaven, and whatever you lose on earth will be loosed in heaven." {16:20} Then he ordered his disciples not to tell anyone that he was the Messiah. {16:21} From that time on Jesus began to explain to his disciples that he must go to Jerusalem and suffer many things at the hands of the elders, the chief priests and the teachers of the law, and that he must be killed and on the third day be raised to life. {16:22} Peter took him aside and began to rebuke him. "Never, Lord!" he said. "This shall never happen to you!" {16:23} Jesus turned and said to Peter, "Get behind me, Satan! You are a stumbling block to me; you do not have in mind the concerns of God, but merely human concerns." {16:24} Then Jesus said to his disciples, "Whoever wants to be my disciple must deny themselves and take up their cross and follow me. {16:25} For whoever wants to save their life will lose it, but whoever loses their life for me will find it. {16:26} What good will it be for someone to gain the whole world, yet forfeit their soul? Or what can anyone give in exchange for their soul? {16:27} For the Son of Man is going to come in his Father's glory with his angels, and then he will reward each person according to what they have done. {16:28} "Truly I tell you, some who are standing here will not taste death before they see the Son of Man coming in his kingdom."

{17:1} After six days Jesus took Peter, James, and John, his brother, and led them up onto a high mountain by themselves. {17:2} And he was transfigured before them. His face shone like the sun, and his clothes became as white as the light. {17:3} Suddenly Moses and Elijah appeared before them, talking with Jesus. {17:4} Then Peter said to Jesus, "Lord, it is good for us to be here. If you wish, I will put up three shelters—one for you, one for Moses, and one for Elijah." {17:5} While Peter was still speaking, a bright cloud covered them, and a voice from the cloud said, "This is my Son, whom I love; with him I am well pleased. Listen to him!" {17:6} When the disciples heard this, they fell facedown to the ground, terrified. {17:7} But Jesus came and touched them. "Get up," he said. "Don't be afraid." {17:8} When they looked up, they saw no one except Jesus. {17:9} As they were coming down the mountain, Jesus instructed them, "Don't tell anyone what you have seen, until the Son of Man has been raised from the dead." {17:10} The disciples asked him, "Why then do the teachers of the law say that Elijah must come first?" {17:11} Jesus replied, "To be sure, Elijah comes and will restore all things. {17:12} But I tell you, Elijah has already come, and they did not recognize him, but have done to him everything they wished. In the same way the Son of Man is going to suffer at their hands." {17:13} Then the disciples understood that he was talking to them about John the Baptist. {17:14} When they came to the crowd, a man approached Jesus and knelt before him. {17:15} "Lord, have mercy on my son," he said. "He has seizures and is suffering greatly. He often falls into the fire or into the water. {17:16} I brought him to your disciples, but they could not heal him." {17:17} "You unbelieving and perverse generation," Jesus replied, "how long shall I stay with you? How long shall I put up with you? Bring the boy here to me." {17:18} Jesus rebuked the demon, and it came out of the boy, and he was healed at that moment. {17:19} Then the disciples came to Jesus in private and asked, "Why couldn't we drive it out?" {17:20} He replied, "Because you have so little faith. Truly I tell you, if you have faith as small as a mustard seed, you can say to this mountain, 'Move from here to there,' and it will move. Nothing will be impossible for you." {17:21} "But this kind does not go out except by prayer and fasting." {17:22} While they were staying in Galilee, Jesus told them, "The Son of Man is going to be delivered into the hands of men. {17:23} They will kill him, and on the third day he will be raised to life." And the disciples were filled with grief. {17:24} After they arrived in Capernaum, the collectors of the temple tax came to Peter and asked, "Doesn't your teacher pay the temple tax?" {17:25} "Yes, he does," he replied. When Peter came into the house, Jesus was the first to speak. "What do you think, Simon?" he asked. "From whom do the kings of the earth collect duty and taxes—from their own children or from others?" {17:26} "From others," Peter answered. "Then the children are exempt," Jesus said to him. {17:27} "But so that we may not cause offense, go to the lake and throw out your line. Take the first fish you catch; open its mouth and you will find a four-drachma coin. Take it and give it to them for my tax and yours."

{18:1} At that time the disciples came to Jesus and asked, "Who, then, is the greatest in the kingdom of heaven?" {18:2} He called a little child to him, and placed the child among them. {18:3} And he said: "Truly I tell you, unless you change and become like little children, you will never enter the kingdom of heaven. {18:4} Therefore, whoever takes the lowly position of this child is the greatest in the kingdom of heaven. {18:5} And whoever welcomes one such child in my name welcomes me. {18:6} If anyone causes one of these little ones—those who believe in me—to stumble, it would be better for them to have a large millstone hung around their neck and to be drowned in the depths of the sea." {18:7} Woe to the world because of the things that cause people to stumble! Such things must come, but woe to the person through whom they come! {18:8} If your hand or your foot causes you to stumble, cut it off and throw it away. It is better for you to enter life maimed or crippled than to have two hands or two feet and be thrown into eternal fire. {18:9} And if your eye causes you to stumble, gouge it out and throw it away. It is better for you to enter life with one eye than to have two eyes and be thrown into the fire of hell. {18:10} See that you do not despise one of these little ones. For I tell you that their angels in heaven always see the face of my Father in heaven. {18:11} [For the Son of Man came to save the lost.] {18:12} "What do you think? If a man owns a hundred sheep, and one of them wanders away, will he not leave the ninety-nine on the hills and go to look for the one that wandered off? {18:13} And if he finds it, truly I tell you, he is happier about that one sheep than about the ninety-nine that did not wander off. {18:14} In the same way your Father in heaven is not willing that any of these little ones should perish. {18:15} "If your brother or sister sins, go and point out their fault, just between the two of you. If they listen to you, you have won them over. {18:16} But if they will not listen, take one or two others along, so that 'every matter may be established by the testimony of two or three witnesses.' {18:17} If they still refuse to listen, tell it to the church; and if they refuse to listen even to the church, treat them as you would a pagan or a tax collector. {18:18} "Truly I tell you, whatever you bind on earth will be bound in heaven, and whatever you loose on earth will be loosed in heaven. {18:19} "Again, truly I tell you that if two of you on earth agree about anything they ask for, it will be done for them by my Father in heaven. {18:20} For where two or three gather in my name, there am I with them." {18:21} Then Peter came to him and asked, "Lord, how many times shall I forgive my brother or sister who sins against me? Up to seven times?" {18:22} Jesus answered, "I tell you, not seven times, but seventy-seven times. {18:23} "Therefore, the kingdom of heaven is like a king who wants to settle accounts with his servants. {18:24} As he began the settlement, a man who owed him ten thousand bags of gold was brought to him. {18:25} Since he was not able to pay, the master ordered that he and his wife and his children and all that he had sold to repay the debt. {18:26} "At this the servant fell on his knees before him. 'Be patient with me,' he begged, 'and I will pay back everything.' {18:27} The servant's master took pity on him, canceled the debt and let him go. {18:28} "But when that servant went out, he found one of his fellow servants who owed him a hundred silver coins. He grabbed him and began to choke him. 'Pay back what you owe me!' he demanded. {18:29} "His fellow servant fell to his knees and begged him, 'Be patient with me, and I will pay it back.' {18:30} "But he refused. Instead, he went off and had the man thrown into prison until he could pay the debt. {18:31} When the other servants saw what had happened, they were outraged and went and told their master everything that had happened. {18:32} "Then the master called the servant in. 'You wicked servant,' he said, 'I canceled all that debt of yours because you begged me to. {18:33} Shouldn't you have had mercy on your fellow servant just as I had on you?' {18:34} In anger his master handed him over to the jailers to be tortured, until he should pay back all he owed. {18:35} "This is how my heavenly Father will treat each of you unless you forgive your brother or sister from your heart."

{19:1} After Jesus finished speaking, he left Galilee and went into the region of Judea to the other side of the Jordan River. {19:2} Large crowds followed him, and he healed them there. {19:3} Some Pharisees came to him to test him. They asked, "Is it lawful for a man to divorce his wife for any and every reason?" {19:4} Jesus replied, "Haven't you read that at the beginning the Creator 'made them male and female,' {19:5} and said, 'For this reason a man will leave his father and mother and be united to his wife, and the two will become one flesh'? {19:6} So they are no longer two, but one flesh. Therefore what God has joined together, let no one separate." {19:7} "Why then," they asked, "did Moses command that a man give his wife a certificate of divorce and send her away?" {19:8} Jesus replied, "Moses permitted you to divorce your wives because your hearts were hard. But it was not this way from the beginning. {19:9} I tell you that anyone who divorces his wife, except for sexual immorality, and marries another woman commits adultery." {19:10} His disciples said to him, "If this is the situation between a husband and wife, it is better not to marry." {19:11} Jesus replied, "Not everyone can accept this word, but only those to whom it has been given. {19:12} For there are eunuchs who were born that way, and there are eunuchs who have been made eunuchs by others—and there are those who choose to live like eunuchs for the sake of the kingdom of heaven. The one who can accept this should accept it." {19:13} Then people brought little children to Jesus for him to place his hands on them and pray for them. But the disciples rebuked them. {19:14} Jesus said, "Let the little children come to me, and do not hinder them, for the kingdom of heaven belongs to such as these." {19:15} When he had placed his hands on them, he went on from there. {19:16} And behold, someone came to him and asked, "Good Teacher, what good thing must I do to have eternal life?" {19:17} Jesus replied, "Why do you call me good? There is only One who is good. If you want to enter life, keep the commandments." {19:18} "Which ones?" he inquired. Jesus replied, "'You shall not murder, you shall not commit adultery, you shall not steal, you shall not give false testimony, {19:19} honor your father and mother,' and 'love your neighbor as yourself.'" {19:20} "All these I have kept," the young man said. "What do I still lack?" {19:21} Jesus answered, "If you want to be perfect, go, sell your possessions and give to the poor, and you will have treasure in heaven. Then come, follow me." {19:22} When the young man heard this, he went away sad, because he had great wealth. {19:23} Then Jesus said to his disciples, "Truly I tell you, it is hard for a rich person to enter the kingdom of heaven. {19:24} Again I tell you, it is easier for a camel to go through the eye of a needle than for a rich person to enter the kingdom of God." {19:25} When the disciples heard this, they were greatly amazed and asked, "Who then can be saved?" {19:26} Jesus looked at them and said, "With humans this is impossible, but with God all things are possible." {19:27} Then Peter said to him, "Look, we have left everything to follow you. What then will there be for us?" {19:28} Jesus said to them, "Truly I tell you, at the renewal of all things, when the Son of Man sits on his glorious throne, you who have followed me will also sit on twelve thrones, judging the twelve tribes of Israel. {19:29} And everyone who has left houses or brothers or sisters or father or mother or wife or children or fields for my sake will receive a hundred times as much and will inherit eternal life. {19:30} But many who are first will be last, and many who are last will be first."

{20:1} The kingdom of heaven is like a landowner who went out early in the morning to hire workers for his vineyard. {20:2} He agreed to pay them a denarius for the day and sent them into his vineyard. {20:3} About the third hour he went out and saw others standing in the marketplace doing nothing. {20:4} He told them, 'You also go and work in my vineyard, and I will pay you whatever is right.' So they went. {20:5} He went out again about the sixth and ninth hour and did the same thing. {20:6} About the eleventh hour he went out and found still others standing around. He asked them, 'Why have you been standing here all day long doing nothing?' {20:7} 'Because no one has hired us,' they answered. So he told them, 'You also go and work in my vineyard.' {20:8} When evening came, the owner of the vineyard said to his foreman, 'Call the workers and pay them their wages, beginning with the last ones hired and going on to the first.' {20:9} The workers who were hired about the eleventh hour came and each received a denarius. {20:10} So when those who were hired first, they expected to receive more. But each one of them also received a denarius. {20:11} When they received it, they began to grumble against the landowner. {20:12} 'These who were hired last worked only one hour,' they said, 'and you have made them equal to us who have borne the burden of the work and the heat of the day.' {20:13} But he answered one of them, 'I am not being unfair to you, friend. Didn't you agree to work for a denarius? {20:14} Take your pay and go. I want to give the one who was hired last the same as I gave you. {20:15} Don't I have the right to do what I want with my own money?' Or are you envious because I am generous?' {20:16} So the last will be first, and the first will be last." {20:17} As Jesus was going up to Jerusalem, he took the twelve disciples aside on the way and said to them, {20:18} "Look, we are going up to Jerusalem, and the Son of Man will be betrayed to the chief priests and the teachers of the law. They will condemn him to death {20:19} and will hand him over to the Gentiles to be mocked and flogged and crucified. But on the third day he will be raised to life." {20:20} Then the mother of Zebedee's sons came to Jesus with her sons and, kneeling down, asked a favor of him. {20:21} "What is it you want?" he asked. She said to him, "Grant that one of these two sons of mine may sit at your right and the other at your left in your kingdom." {20:22} "You don't know what you are asking," Jesus said to them. "Can you drink the cup I am going to drink?" "We can," they answered. {20:23} Jesus said to them, "You will indeed drink from my cup, but to sit on my right or left is not for me to grant. These places belong to those for whom they have been prepared by my Father." {20:24} When the ten heard about this, they were indignant with the two brothers. {20:25} Jesus called them together and said, "You know that the rulers of the Gentiles lord it over them, and their high officials exercise authority over them. {20:26} Not so with you. Instead, whoever wants to become great among you must be your servant, {20:27} and whoever wants to be first must be your slave— {20:28} just as the Son of Man did not come to be served, but to serve, and to give his life as a ransom for many." {20:29} As they were leaving Jericho, a large crowd followed him. {20:30} As Jesus went on from there, two blind men followed him, calling out, "Have mercy on us, Son of David!" {20:31} When they had gone indoors, the blind men came to him, and he asked them, "Do you believe that I am able to do this?" "Yes, Lord," they replied. {20:32} Then he touched their eyes and said, "According to your faith let it be done to you"; {20:33} and their sight was restored. Jesus warned them sternly, "See that no one knows about this." {20:34} But they went out and spread the news about him all over that region.

{21:1} As Jesus and his disciples approached Jerusalem, they came to Bethphage on the Mount of Olives. Jesus sent two disciples ahead {21:2} with these instructions: "Go into the village over there. As soon as you enter, you will see a donkey tied there with its colt. Untie them and bring them to me. {21:3} If anyone asks what you are doing, just say, 'The Lord needs them,' and he will immediately let you take them." {21:4} This took place to fulfill the prophecy that said, {21:5} "Tell the people of Jerusalem, 'Look, your King is coming to you. He is humble, riding on a donkey—riding on a donkey's colt.'" {21:6} The two disciples did as Jesus commanded. {21:7} They brought the donkey and the colt to him and threw their garments over the colt, and he sat on it. {21:8} Most of the crowd spread their garments on the road ahead of him, and others cut branches from the trees and spread them on the road. {21:9} Jesus was in the center of the procession, and the people all around him were shouting, "Praise God for the Son of David! Blessings on the one who comes in the name of the Lord! Praise God in the highest heaven!" {21:10} The entire city of Jerusalem was in an uproar as he entered. "Who is this?" they asked. {21:11} And the crowds replied, "It's Jesus, the prophet from Nazareth in Galilee." {21:12} Jesus entered the Temple and began to drive out all the people buying and selling animals for sacrifice. He knocked over the tables of the money changers and the chairs of those selling doves. {21:13} He said to them, "The Scriptures declare, 'My Temple will be called a house of prayer,' but you have turned it into a den of thieves!" {21:14} The blind and the lame came to him in the Temple, and he healed them. {21:15} The leading priests and the teachers of religious law saw these wonderful miracles and heard even the children in the Temple shouting, "Praise God for the Son of David." But the leaders were indignant {21:16} and asked Jesus, "Do you hear what these children are saying?" "Yes," Jesus replied. "Haven't you ever read the Scriptures? For they say, 'You have taught children and infants to give you praise.'" {21:17} After this, Jesus left Jerusalem and went to Bethany, where he stayed for the night. {21:18} In the morning, as Jesus was returning to the city, he became hungry. {21:19} Along the way, he saw a fig tree and went to see if there were any figs on it. But there were only leaves. Then he said to the tree, "May you never bear fruit again!" And immediately the fig tree withered up. {21:20} The disciples were amazed when they saw this and exclaimed, "How did the fig tree wither so quickly?" {21:21} Jesus replied, "I tell you the truth, if you have faith and do not doubt, you can do things like this and even more. You can say to this mountain, 'Move from here to there,' and it will move. Nothing will be impossible for you." {21:22} "But you must pray believing, and whatever you ask in prayer, you will receive." {21:23} When Jesus entered the Temple, the leading priests and elders came up to him as he was teaching. They demanded, "By what authority are you doing all these things? Who gave you the right?" {21:24} Jesus replied, "I'll tell you if you answer one question: Did John's authority to baptize come from heaven, or was it merely human?" {21:25} They talked it over among themselves. "If we say it was from heaven, he will ask us why we didn't believe John. {21:26} But if we say it was merely human, we'll be mobbed because the people believe John was a prophet." {21:27} So they finally replied, "We don't know." And Jesus responded, "Then I won't answer your question either." {21:28} "But what do you think? A man had two sons. He went first and said, 'Son, go and work today in my vineyard.' {21:29} "The son replied, 'I will not,' but later he changed his mind and went. {21:30} "Then the father went to the second son and said the same thing. He answered, 'I will, sir,' but he did not go. {21:31} "Which of the two did what his father wanted?" "The first," they answered. Jesus said to them, "Truly I tell you, the tax collectors and the prostitutes are entering the kingdom of God ahead of you. {21:32} "For John came to you to show you the way of righteousness, and you did not believe him, but the tax collectors and the prostitutes did. And even after you saw this, you did not repent and believe him. {21:33} "Listen to another parable: There was a landowner who planted a vineyard. He put a wall around it, dug a winepress in it and built a watchtower. Then he rented the vineyard to some farmers and moved to another place. {21:34} "When the harvest time approached, he sent his servants to the tenants to collect his fruit. {21:35} "The tenants seized his servants; they beat one, killed another, and stoned a third. {21:36} "Then he sent other servants to them, more than the first time, and the tenants treated them the same way. {21:37} "Last of all, he sent his son to them. 'They will respect my son,' he said. {21:38} "But when the tenants saw the son, they said to each other, 'This is the heir. Come, let's kill him and take his inheritance.' {21:39} "So they took him and threw him out of the vineyard and killed him. {21:40} "Therefore, when the owner of the vineyard comes, what will he do to those tenants?" {21:41} "He will bring those wretches to a wretched end," they replied, "and he will rent the vineyard to other tenants, who will give him his share of the crop at harvest time." {21:42} Jesus said to them, "Have you never read in the Scriptures: 'The stone the builders rejected has become the cornerstone; the Lord has done this, and it is marvelous in our eyes'? {21:43} "Therefore I tell you that the kingdom of God will be taken away from you and given to a people who will produce its fruit. {21:44} "Anyone who falls on this stone will be broken to pieces; anyone on whom it falls will be crushed." {21:45} When the chief priests and the Pharisees heard Jesus' parables, they knew he was talking about them. {21:46} They looked for a way to arrest him, but they were afraid of the crowd because the people held that he was a prophet.

{22:1} Jesus spoke to them again in parables, saying: {22:2} "The kingdom of heaven is like a king who prepared a wedding banquet for his son. {22:3} He sent his servants to those who had been invited to the banquet to tell them to come, but they refused to come. {22:4} "Then he sent some more servants and said, 'Tell those who have been invited that I have prepared my dinner: My oxen and fattened cattle have been butchered, and everything is ready. Come to the wedding banquet.' {22:5} "But they paid no attention and went off—one to his field, another to his business. {22:6} The rest seized his servants, mistreated them and killed them. {22:7} The king was enraged. He sent his army and destroyed those murderers and burned their city. {22:8} "Then he said to his servants, 'The wedding banquet is ready, but those I invited did not deserve to come. {22:9} So go to the street corners and invite to the banquet.' {22:10} So the servants went out into the streets and gathered all the people they could find, the bad as well as the good, and the wedding hall was filled with guests. {22:11} "But when the king came in to see the guests, he noticed a man there who was not wearing wedding clothes. {22:12} 'Friend,' he asked, 'how did you get in here without wedding clothes?' The man was speechless. {22:13} "Then the king told the attendants, 'Tie him hand and foot, and throw him outside, into the darkness, where there will be weeping and gnashing of teeth.' {22:14} "For many are invited, but few are chosen." {22:15} Then the Pharisees went out and laid plans to trap him in his words. {22:16} They sent their disciples to him along with the Herodians. "Teacher," they said, "we know that you are a man of integrity and that you teach the way of God in accordance with the truth. You aren't swayed by others, because you pay no attention to who they are. {22:17} Tell us then, what is your opinion? Is it right to pay the imperial tax to Caesar or not?" {22:18} But Jesus, knowing their evil intent, said, "You hypocrites, why are you trying to trap me? {22:19} Show me the coin used for paying the tax." They brought him a denarius, {22:20} and he asked them, "Whose image is this? And whose inscription?" {22:21} "Caesar's," they replied. Then he said to them, "So give back to Caesar what is Caesar's, and to God what is God's." {22:22} When they heard this, they were amazed. So they left him and went away. {22:23} That same day the Sadducees, who say there is no resurrection, came to him with a question. {22:24} "Teacher," they said, "Moses told us that if a man dies without having children, his brother must marry the widow and raise up offspring for him. {22:25} Now there were seven brothers among us. The first one married and died, and since he had no children, he left his wife to his brother. {22:26} The same thing happened to the second and third brother, right on down to the seventh. {22:27} Finally, the woman died too. {22:28} Now then, at the resurrection, whose wife will she be of the seven, since all of them were married to her?" {22:29} Jesus replied, "You are in error because you do not know the Scriptures or the power of God. {22:30} At the resurrection people will neither marry nor be given in marriage; they will be like the angels in heaven. {22:31} But about the resurrection of the dead—have you not read what God said to you, {22:32} 'I am the God of Abraham, the God of Isaac, and the God of Jacob'? He is not the God of the dead but of the living." {22:33} When the crowds heard this, they were astonished at his teaching. {22:34} Hearing that Jesus had silenced the Sadducees, the Pharisees got together. {22:35} One of them, an expert in the law, tested him with this question: {22:36} "Teacher, which is the greatest commandment in the Law?" {22:37} Jesus replied: "'Love the Lord your God with all your heart and with all your soul and with all your mind.' {22:38} This is the first and greatest commandment. {22:39} And the second is like it: 'Love your neighbor as yourself.' {22:40} All the Law and the Prophets hang on these two commandments." {22:41} While the Pharisees were gathered together, Jesus questioned them, {22:42} "What do you think about the Messiah? Whose son is he?" They replied, "The son of David." {22:43} *Jesus said to them, "Then how is it that David, speaking by the Spirit, calls him 'Lord'? For he says,* {22:44} *'The Lord said to my Lord: "Sit at my right hand until I put your enemies under your feet."'* {22:45} If David calls him 'Lord,' how can he be his son?" {22:46} **No one could say a word in reply, and from that day on no one dared to ask him any more questions.**

{23:1} Then Jesus spoke to the crowd and to his disciples, {23:2} "The scribes and the Pharisees sit in Moses' seat. {23:3} So whatever they tell you, do and observe. But don't do what they do, for they do not practice what they preach. {23:4} They tie up heavy, cumbersome loads and put them on other people's shoulders, but they themselves are not willing to lift a finger to move them. {23:5} Everything they do is done for people to see: They make their phylacteries wide and the tassels on their garments long; {23:6} they love the place of honor at banquets and the most important seats in the synagogues; {23:7} they love to be greeted with respect in the marketplaces and to be called 'Rabbi' by others. {23:8} But you are not to be called 'Rabbi,' for you have one Teacher, and you are all brothers. {23:9} And do not call anyone on earth 'father,' for you have one Father, and he is in heaven. {23:10} Nor are you to be called instructors, for you have one Instructor, the Messiah. {23:11} The greatest among you will be your servant. {23:12} For those who exalt themselves will be humbled, and those who humble themselves will be exalted. {23:13} "Woe to you, teachers of the law and Pharisees, you hypocrites! You shut the door of the kingdom of heaven in people's faces. You yourselves do not enter, nor will you let those enter who are trying to. {23:14} "Woe to you, teachers of the law and Pharisees, you hypocrites! You devour widows' houses and for a show make lengthy prayers. Therefore you will receive greater condemnation. {23:15} "Woe to you, teachers of the law and Pharisees, you hypocrites! You travel over land and sea to win a single convert, and when you have succeeded, you make them twice as much a child of hell as you are. {23:16} "Woe to you, blind guides! You say, 'If anyone swears by the temple, it means nothing; but anyone who swears by the gold of the temple is bound by that oath.' {23:17} You blind fools! Which is greater: the gold, or the temple that makes the gold sacred? {23:18} You also say, 'If anyone swears by the altar, it means nothing; but anyone who swears by the gift on the altar is bound by that oath.' {23:19} You blind men! Which is greater: the gift, or the altar that makes the gift sacred? {23:20} Therefore, anyone who swears by the altar swears by it and by everything on it. {23:21} And anyone who swears by the temple swears by it and by the one who dwells in it. {23:22} And anyone who swears by heaven swears by God's throne and by the one who sits on it. {23:23} "Woe to you, teachers of the law and Pharisees, you hypocrites! You give a tenth of your spices—mint, dill and cumin. But you have neglected the more important matters of the law—justice, mercy and faithfulness. You should have practiced the latter, without neglecting the former. {23:24} You blind guides! You strain out a gnat but swallow a camel. {23:25} "Woe to you, teachers of the law and Pharisees, you hypocrites! You clean the outside of the cup and dish, but inside they are full of greed and self-indulgence. {23:26} Blind Pharisee! First clean the inside of the cup and dish, and then the outside also will be clean. {23:27} "Woe to you, teachers of the law and Pharisees, you hypocrites! You are like whitewashed tombs, which look beautiful on the outside but on the inside are full of the bones of the dead and everything unclean. {23:28} In the same way, on the outside you appear to people as righteous but on the inside you are full of hypocrisy and wickedness. {23:29} "Woe to you, teachers of the law and Pharisees, you hypocrites! You build tombs for the prophets and decorate the graves of the righteous. {23:30} And you say, 'If we had lived in the days of our ancestors, we would not have taken part with them in shedding the blood of the prophets.' {23:31} So you testify against yourselves that you are the descendants of those who murdered the prophets. {23:32} Go ahead, then, and complete what your ancestors started! {23:33} "You snakes! You brood of vipers! How will you escape being condemned to hell? {23:34} Therefore, I am sending you prophets and wise men and teachers. Some of them you will kill and crucify; others you will flog in your synagogues and pursue from town to town. {23:35} And so upon you will come all the righteous blood shed on earth, from the blood of righteous Abel to the blood of Zechariah son of Berekiah, whom you murdered between the temple and the altar. {23:36} Truly I tell you, all this will come on this generation. {23:37} "Jerusalem, Jerusalem, you who kill the prophets and stone those sent to you, how often I have longed to gather your children together, as a hen gathers her chicks under her wings, and you were not willing. {23:38} Look, your house is left to you desolate. {23:39} For I tell you, you will not see me again until you say, 'Blessed is he who comes in the name of the Lord.'"

{24:1} Jesus left the temple and was walking away when his disciples came up to him to call his attention to its buildings. {24:2} "Do you see all these things?" he asked. "Truly I tell you, not one stone here will be left on another; everyone will be thrown down." {24:3} As Jesus was sitting on the Mount of Olives, the disciples came to him privately. "Tell us," they said, "when will this happen, and what will be the sign of your coming and of the end of the age?" {24:4} Jesus answered: "Watch out that no one deceives you. {24:5} For many will come in my name, claiming, 'I am the Messiah,' and will deceive many. {24:6} You will hear of wars and rumors of wars, but see to it that you are not alarmed. Such things must happen, but the end is still to come. {24:7} Nation will rise against nation, and kingdom against kingdom. There will be famines and earthquakes in various places. {24:8} All these are the beginning of birth pains. {24:9} "Then you will be handed over to be persecuted and put to death, and you will be hated by all nations because of me. {24:10} At that time many will turn away from the faith and will betray and hate each other, {24:11} and many false prophets will appear and deceive many people. {24:12} Because of the increase of wickedness, the love of most will grow cold, {24:13} but the one who stands firm to the end will be saved. {24:14} And this gospel of the kingdom will be preached in the whole world as a testimony to all nations, and then the end will come. {24:15} "So when you see standing in the holy place 'the abomination that causes desolation,' spoken of through the prophet Daniel—let the reader understand— {24:16} then let those who are in Judea flee to the mountains. {24:17} Let no one on the housetop go down to take anything out of the house. {24:18} Let no one in the field go back to get their cloak. {24:19} How dreadful it will be in those days for pregnant women and nursing mothers! {24:20} Pray that your flight will not take place in winter or on the Sabbath. {24:21} For then there will be great distress, unequaled from the beginning of the world until now—and never to be equaled again. {24:22} "If those days had not been cut short, no one would survive, but for the sake of the elect those days will be shortened. {24:23} "At that time if anyone says to you, 'Look, here is the Messiah!' or, 'There he is!' do not believe it. {24:24} For false messiahs and false prophets will appear and perform great signs and wonders to deceive, if possible, even the elect. {24:25} See, I have told you ahead of time. {24:26} "So if anyone tells you, 'There he is, out in the wilderness,' do not go out; or, 'Here he is, in the inner rooms,' do not believe it. {24:27} For as lightning that comes from the east is visible even in the west, so will be the coming of the Son of Man. {24:28} Wherever there is a carcass, there the vultures will gather." {24:29} Immediately after the tribulation of those days, the sun will be darkened, and the moon will not give its light; the stars will fall from the sky, and the heavenly bodies will be shaken. {24:30} Then will appear the sign of the Son of Man in heaven. And then all the peoples of the earth will mourn when they see the Son of Man coming on the clouds of heaven, with power and great glory. {24:31} And he will send his angels with a loud trumpet call, and they will gather his elect from the four winds, from one end of the heavens to the other. {24:32} "Now learn this lesson from the fig tree: As soon as its twigs get tender and its leaves come out, you know that summer is near. {24:33} Even so, when you see all these things, you know that it is near, right at the door. {24:34} Truly I tell you, this generation will certainly not pass away until all these things have happened. {24:35} Heaven and earth will pass away, but my words will never pass away. {24:36} "But about that day or hour no one knows, not even the angels in heaven, nor the Son, but only the Father. {24:37} As it was in the days of Noah, so it will be at the coming of the Son of Man. {24:38} For in the days before the flood, people were eating and drinking, marrying and giving in marriage, up to the day Noah entered the ark; {24:39} and they knew nothing about what would happen until the flood came and took them all away. That is how it will be at the coming of the Son of Man. {24:40} Two men will be in the field; one will be taken and the other left. {24:41} Two women will be grinding with a hand mill; one will be taken and the other left. {24:42} "Therefore keep watch, because you do not know on what day your Lord will come. {24:43} But understand this: If the owner of the house had known at what time of night the thief was coming, he would have kept watch and would not have let his house be broken into. {24:44} So you also must be ready, because the Son of Man will come at an hour when you do not expect him. {24:45} "Who then is the faithful and wise servant, whom the master has put in charge of the servants in his household to give them their food at the proper time? {24:46} It will be good for that servant whose master finds him doing so when he returns. {24:47} Truly I tell you, he will put him in charge of all his possessions. {24:48} But suppose that servant is wicked and says to himself, 'My master is staying away a long time,' {24:49} and he then begins to beat his fellow servants and to eat and drink with drunkards. {24:50} The master of that servant will come on a day when he does not expect him and at an hour he is not aware of. {24:51} He will cut him to pieces and assign him a place with the hypocrites, where there will be weeping and gnashing of teeth.

{25:1} "Then the kingdom of heaven will be like ten virgins who took their lamps and went out to meet the bridegroom. {25:2} Five of them were wise and five were foolish. {25:3} The foolish ones took their lamps but did not take any oil with them. {25:4} The wise ones, however, took oil in jars along with their lamps. {25:5} The bridegroom was a long time in coming, and they all became drowsy and fell asleep. {25:6} "At midnight the cry rang out: 'Here's the bridegroom! Come out to meet him!' {25:7} "Then all the virgins woke up and trimmed their lamps. {25:8} The foolish ones said to the wise, 'Give us some of your oil; our lamps are going out.' {25:9} "'No,' they replied, 'there may not be enough for both us and you. Instead, go to those who sell oil and buy some for yourselves.' {25:10} "But while they were on their way to buy the oil, the bridegroom arrived. The virgins who were ready went in with him to the wedding banquet. And the door was shut. {25:11} "Later the others also came. 'Lord, Lord,' they said, 'open the door for us!' {25:12} "But he replied, 'Truly I tell you, I don't know you.' {25:13} "Therefore keep watch, because you do not know the day or the hour." {25:14} "For the kingdom of heaven is like a man going on a journey, who called his own servants and entrusted his wealth to them. {25:15} To one he gave five talents, to another two talents, and to another one talent, each according to his ability. Then he went on his journey. {25:16} The servant who had received five talents went and traded with them, and gained five more talents. {25:17} Likewise, the one with two talents gained two more. {25:18} But the servant who had received one talent went off, dug a hole in the ground, and hid his master's money. {25:19} After a long time, the master of those servants returned and settled accounts with them. {25:20} The servant who had received five talents came and brought five more talents, saying, 'Master, you entrusted me with five talents. See, I have gained five more.' {25:21} His master replied, 'Well done, good and faithful servant! You have been faithful with a few things; I will put you in charge of many things. Come and share your master's happiness!' {25:22} The servant with two talents also came and said, 'Master, you entrusted me with two talents. See, I have gained two more.' {25:23} His master replied, 'Well done, good and faithful servant! You have been faithful with a few things; I will put you in charge of many things. Come and share your master's happiness!' {25:24} Then the servant who had received one talent came and said, 'Master, I know that you are a hard man, harvesting where you have not sown and gathering where you have not scattered seed. {25:25} So I was afraid and went out and hid your talent in the ground. See, here is what belongs to you.' {25:26} His master replied, 'You wicked and lazy servant! You knew that I harvest where I have not sown and gather where I have not scattered seed? {25:27} Well then, you should have put my money on deposit with the bankers, so that when I returned I would have received it back with interest. {25:28} Take the talent from him and give it to the one who has ten talents. {25:29} For whoever has will be given more, and they will have an abundance. Whoever does not have, even what they have will be taken from them. {25:30} And throw that worthless servant outside, into the darkness, where there will be weeping and gnashing of teeth." {25:31} "When the Son of Man comes in his glory, and all the angels with him, he will sit on his glorious throne. {25:32} All the nations will be gathered before him, and he will separate the people one from another as a shepherd separates the sheep from the goats. {25:33} He will put the sheep on his right and the goats on his left. {25:34} Then the King will say to those on his right, 'Come, you who are blessed by my Father; take your inheritance, the kingdom prepared for you since the creation of the world. {25:35} For I was hungry and you gave me something to eat, I was thirsty and you gave me something to drink, I was a stranger and you invited me in, {25:36} I needed clothes and you clothed me, I was sick and you looked after me, I was in prison and you came to visit me.' {25:37} Then the righteous will answer him, 'Lord, when did we see you hungry and feed you, or thirsty and give you something to drink? {25:38} When did we see you as a stranger and invite you in, or needing clothes and clothes? {25:39} When did we see you sick or in prison and go to visit you?' {25:40} The King will reply, 'Truly I tell you, whatever you did for one of the least of these brothers and sisters of mine, you did for me.' {25:41} Then he will say to those on his left, 'Depart from me, you who are cursed, into the eternal fire prepared for the devil and his angels. {25:42} For I was hungry and you gave me nothing to eat, I was thirsty and you gave me nothing to drink, {25:43} I was a stranger and you did not invite me in, I needed clothes and you did not clothe me, I was sick and in prison and you did not look after me.' {25:44} They also will answer, 'Lord, when did we see you hungry or thirsty or a stranger or needing clothes or sick or in prison, and did not help you?' {25:45} He will reply, 'Truly I tell you, whatever you did not do for one of the least of these, you did not do for me.' {25:46} Then they will go away to eternal punishment, but the righteous to eternal life."

{26:1} When Jesus had finished all these sayings, he said to his disciples, {26:2} "You know that after two days is the Passover, and the Son of Man will be betrayed to be crucified." {26:3} Then the chief priests, the scribes, and the elders of the people assembled at the palace of the high priest, who was called Caiaphas, {26:4} And they plotted to take Jesus by cunning and kill him. {26:5} But they said, "Not during the feast, lest there be an uproar among the people." {26:6} Now when Jesus was in Bethany, at the house of Simon the leper, {26:7} a woman came to him with an alabaster box of very precious ointment, and poured it on his head as he sat at the table. {26:8} When his disciples saw it, they were indignant, saying, "What is the purpose of this waste? {26:9} For this ointment could have been sold for a large sum and given to the poor." {26:10} But Jesus, aware of this, said to them, "Why do you trouble the woman? For she has done a beautiful thing to me. {26:11} For you always have the poor with you, but you will not always have me. {26:12} In pouring this ointment on my body, she has done it to prepare me for burial. {26:13} Truly, I say to you, wherever this gospel is proclaimed in the whole world, what she has done will also be told in memory of her." {26:14} Then one of the twelve, called Judas Iscariot, went to the chief priests {26:15} and said, "What will you give me if I deliver him over to you?" And they paid him thirty pieces of silver. {26:16} And from that moment he sought an opportunity to betray him. {26:17} On the first day of the Feast of Unleavened Bread, the disciples came to Jesus, asking him, "Where do you want us to prepare for you to eat the Passover?" {26:18} And he said, "Go into the city to a certain man and say to him, 'The Teacher says, "My time is at hand; I will keep the Passover at your house with my disciples."'" {26:19} And the disciples did as Jesus had directed them, and they prepared the Passover. {26:20} When evening came, he reclined at the table with the twelve. {26:21} And as they were eating, he said, "Truly, I say to you, one of you will betray me." {26:22} And they were very sorrowful and began to say to him one after another, "Is it I, Lord?" {26:23} He answered, "He who has dipped his hand in the dish with me will betray me. {26:24} The Son of Man goes as it is written of him, but woe to that man by whom the Son of Man is betrayed! It would have been better for that man if he had not been born." {26:25} Judas, who would betray him, answered, "Is it I, Rabbi?" He said to him, "You have said so." {26:26} Now as they were eating, Jesus took bread, and after blessing it broke it and gave it to the disciples, and said, "Take, eat; this is my body." {26:27} And he took a cup, and when he had given thanks he gave it to them, saying, "Drink of it, all of you, {26:28} for this is my blood of the covenant, which is poured out for many for the forgiveness of sins. {26:29} I tell you I will not drink again of this fruit of the vine until that day when I drink it again with you in my Father's kingdom." {26:30} And when they had sung a hymn, they went out to the Mount of Olives. {26:31} Then Jesus said to them, "You will all fall away because of me tonight. For it is written, 'I will strike the shepherd, and the sheep of the flock will be scattered.' {26:32} But after I am raised up, I will go before you to Galilee." {26:33} Peter answered him, "Though they all fall away because of you, I will never fall away." {26:34} Jesus said to him, "Truly, I tell you, this very night, before the rooster crows, you will deny me three times." {26:35} Peter said to him, "Even if I must die with you, I will not deny you!" And all the disciples said the same. {26:36} Then Jesus went with his disciples to a place called Gethsemane and said to them, "Sit here while I go over there and pray." {26:37} Taking Peter and the two sons of Zebedee along with him, he began to be sorrowful and troubled. {26:38} Then he said to them, "My soul is overwhelmed with sorrow to the point of death. Stay here and keep watch with me." {26:39} Going a little farther, he fell with his face to the ground and prayed, "My Father, if it is possible, may this cup be taken from me. Yet not as I will, but as you will." {26:40} Then he returned to his disciples and found them sleeping. "Couldn't you men keep watch with me for one hour?" he asked Peter. {26:41} "Watch and pray so that you will not fall into temptation. The spirit is willing, but the flesh is weak." {26:42} He went away a second time and prayed, "My Father, if it is not possible for this cup to be taken away unless I drink it, may you be done." {26:43} When he came back, he again found them sleeping because their eyes were heavy. {26:44} So he left them and went away once more and prayed the third time, saying the same thing. {26:45} Then he returned to the disciples and said to them, "Are you still sleeping and resting? Look, the hour has come, and the Son of Man is delivered into the hands of sinners. {26:46} Rise, let us go! Here comes my betrayer!" {26:47} While he was still speaking, Judas, one of the Twelve, arrived. With him was a large crowd armed with swords and clubs, sent from the chief priests and the elders of the people. {26:48} Now the betrayer had arranged a signal with them: "The one I kiss is the man; arrest him." {26:49} Going at once to Jesus, Judas said, "Greetings, Rabbi!" and kissed him. {26:50} Jesus replied, "Do what you came for, friend." Then the men stepped forward, seized Jesus and arrested him. {26:51} With that, one of Jesus' companions reached for his sword, drew it and struck the servant of the high priest, cutting off his ear. {26:52} "Put your sword back in its place," Jesus said to him, "for all who draw the sword will die by the sword. {26:53} Do you think I cannot call on my Father, and he will at once put at my disposal more than twelve legions of angels? {26:54} But how then would the Scriptures be fulfilled that say it must happen in this way?" {26:55} In that hour Jesus said to the crowd, "Am I leading a rebellion, that you have come out with swords and clubs to capture me? Every day I sat in the temple courts teaching, and you did not arrest me. {26:56} But this has all taken place so that the writings of the prophets might be fulfilled." Then all the disciples deserted him and fled. {26:57} Those who had arrested Jesus took him to the house of Caiaphas, the high priest, where the teachers of the law and the elders had gathered. {26:58} Peter followed him at a distance, right up to the courtyard of the high priest. He entered and sat down with the guards to see the outcome. {26:59} The chief priests and the whole Sanhedrin were looking for false evidence against Jesus so that they could put him to death. {26:60} But they did not find any, though many false witnesses came forward. Finally, two came forward {26:61} and declared, "This fellow said, 'I am able to destroy the temple of God and rebuild it in three days.'" {26:62} Then the high priest stood up and said to Jesus, "Are you not going to answer? What is this testimony that these men are bringing against you?" {26:63} But Jesus remained silent. The high priest said to him, "I charge you under oath by the living God: Tell us if you are the Messiah, the Son of God." {26:64} "You have said so," Jesus replied. "But I say to all of you: From now on you will see the Son of Man sitting at the right hand of the Mighty One and coming on the clouds of heaven." {26:65} Then the high priest tore his clothes and said, "He has spoken blasphemy! Why do we need any more witnesses? Look, now you have heard the blasphemy. {26:66} What do you think?" "He is worthy of death," they answered. {26:67} Then they spit in his face and struck him with their fists. Others slapped him {26:68} and said, "Prophesy to us, Messiah. Who hit you?" {26:69} Peter was sitting out in the courtyard, and a servant girl came to him. "You also were with Jesus of Galilee," she said. {26:70} But he denied it before them all. "I don't know what you're talking about," he said. {26:71} Then he went out to the gateway, where another servant girl saw him and said to the people there, "This fellow was with Jesus of Nazareth." {26:72} He denied it again, with an oath: "I don't know the man!" {26:73} After a little while, those standing there went up to Peter and said, "Surely you are one of them; your accent gives you away." {26:74} Then he began to call down curses, and he swore to them, "I don't know the man!" Immediately a rooster crowed. {26:75} Then Peter remembered the word Jesus had spoken: "Before the rooster crows, you will disown me three times." And he went outside and wept bitterly.

{27:1} When morning came, all the chief priests and the elders of the people made plans to have Jesus executed. {27:2} They bound him, led him away, and handed him over to Pilate, the governor. {27:3} When Judas, who had betrayed him, saw that Jesus was condemned, he was filled with remorse and returned the thirty pieces of silver to the chief priests and the elders. {27:4} "I have sinned," he said, "for I have betrayed innocent blood." "What is that to us?" they replied. "That's your responsibility." {27:5} So Judas threw the money into the temple and left. Then he went away and hanged himself. {27:6} The chief priests picked up the coins and said, "It is against the law to put this into the treasury, since it is blood money." {27:7} So they decided to use the money to buy the potter's field as a burial place for foreigners. {27:8} That is why it has been called the Field of Blood to this day. {27:9} Then what was spoken by Jeremiah the prophet was fulfilled: "They took the thirty pieces of silver, the price set on him by the people of Israel, {27:10} and they used them to buy the potter's field, as the Lord commanded me." {27:11} Meanwhile Jesus stood before the governor, and the governor asked him, "Are you the king of the Jews?" "You have said so," Jesus replied. {27:12} When he was accused by the chief priests and the elders, he gave no answer. {27:13} Then Pilate asked him, "Don't you hear the testimony they are bringing against you?" {27:14} But Jesus made no reply, not even to a single charge—to the great amazement of the governor. {27:15} Now it was the governor's custom at the festival to release a prisoner chosen by the crowd. {27:16} At that time they had a well-known prisoner whose name was Barabbas. {27:17} So when the crowd had gathered, Pilate asked them, "Which one do you want me to release to you: Barabbas, or Jesus who is called the Messiah?" {27:18} For he knew it was out of self-interest that they had handed Jesus over to him. {27:19} While Pilate was sitting on the judgment seat, his wife sent him a message: "Don't have anything to do with that innocent man, for I have suffered a great deal today in a dream because of him." {27:20} But the chief priests and the elders persuaded the crowd to ask for Barabbas and to have Jesus executed. {27:21} "Which of the two do you want me to release to you?" asked the governor. "Barabbas," they answered. {27:22} "What shall I do, then, with Jesus who is called the Messiah?" Pilate asked. They all answered, "Crucify him!" {27:23} "Why? What crime has he committed?" asked Pilate. But they shouted all the louder, "Crucify him!" {27:24} When Pilate saw that he was getting nowhere, but that instead an uproar was starting, he took water and washed his hands in front of the crowd. "I am innocent of this man's blood," he said. "It is your responsibility." {27:25} All the people answered, "His blood is on us and on our children!" {27:26} Then he released Barabbas to them. But he had Jesus flogged, and handed him over to be crucified. {27:27} Then the governor's soldiers took Jesus into the Praetorium and gathered the whole company of soldiers around him. {27:28} They stripped him and put a scarlet robe on him, {27:29} and then twisted together a crown of thorns and set it on his head. They put a staff in his right hand. Then they knelt in front of him and mocked him. "Hail, king of the Jews!" they said. {27:30} They spit on him, and took the staff and struck him on the head again and again. {27:31} After they had mocked him, they took off the robe and put his own clothes on him. Then they led him away to crucify him. {27:32} As they were going out, they met a man from Cyrene, named Simon, and they forced him to carry the cross. {27:33} They came to a place called Golgotha (which means "the place of the skull"). {27:34} They offered him wine to drink, mixed with gall; but after tasting it, he refused to drink it. {27:35} And they crucified him, dividing up his clothes, they cast lots to see what each would get. This happened so that the words spoken by the prophet might be fulfilled: "They divided my garments among them and cast lots for my clothing." {27:36} Sitting down, they kept watch over him there. {27:37} Above his head they placed the written charge against him: this is Jesus, the king of the jews. {27:38} Two rebels were crucified with him, one on his right and one on his left. {27:39} Those who passed by hurled insults at him, shaking their heads {27:40} and saying, "You who are going to destroy the temple and build it in three days, save yourself! Come down from the cross, if you are the Son of God!" {27:41} In the same way the chief priests, the teachers of the law and the elders mocked him. {27:42} "He saved others," they said, "but he can't save himself! He's the king of Israel! Let him come down now from the cross, and we will believe in him. {27:43} He trusts in God. Let God rescue him now if he wants him, for he said, 'I am the Son of God.'" {27:44} In the same way the rebels who were crucified with him also heaped insults on him. {27:45} From noon until three in the afternoon darkness came over all the land. {27:46} About three in the afternoon Jesus cried out in a loud voice, "Eli,

Eli, lema sabachthani?" (which means "My God, my God, why have you forsaken me?"). {27:47} When some of those standing there heard this, they said, "He's calling Elijah." {27:48} Immediately one of them ran and got a sponge. He filled it with wine vinegar, put it on a staff, and offered it to Jesus to drink. {27:49} The rest said, "Now leave him alone. Let's see if Elijah comes to save him." {27:50} Jesus, with a loud cry, breathed his last. {27:51} At that moment, the curtain of the temple was torn in two from top to bottom. The earth shook, the rocks split {27:52} and the tombs broke open. The bodies of many holy people who had died were raised to life. {27:53} They came out of the tombs after Jesus' resurrection and went into the holy city and appeared to many people. {27:54} When the centurion and those with him who were guarding Jesus saw the earthquake and all that had happened, they were terrified, and exclaimed, "Surely he was the Son of God!" {27:55} Many women were there, watching from a distance. They had followed Jesus from Galilee to care for his needs. {27:56} Among them were Mary Magdalene, Mary the mother of James and Joseph, and the mother of Zebedee's sons. {27:57} As evening approached, there came a rich man from Arimathea, named Joseph, who had himself become a disciple of Jesus. {27:58} Going to Pilate, he asked for Jesus' body, and Pilate ordered that it be given to him. {27:59} Joseph took the body, wrapped it in a clean linen cloth, {27:60} and placed it in his own new tomb that he had cut out of the rock. He rolled a big stone in front of the entrance to the tomb and went away. {27:61} Mary Magdalene and the other Mary were sitting there opposite the tomb. {27:62} The next day, the one after Preparation Day, the chief priests and the Pharisees went to Pilate. {27:63} "Sir," they said, "we remember that while he was still alive that deceiver said, 'After three days I will rise again.' {27:64} So give the order for the tomb to be made secure until the third day. Otherwise, his disciples may come and steal the body and tell the people that he has been raised from the dead. This last deception will be worse than the first." {27:65} "Take a guard," Pilate answered. "Go, make the tomb as secure as you know how." {27:66} So they went and made the tomb secure by putting a seal on the stone and posting the guard.

{28:1} After the Sabbath, as the first day of the week was dawning, Mary Magdalene and the other Mary went to see the tomb. {28:2} Suddenly, there was a great earthquake; for an angel of the Lord descended from heaven, came and rolled back the stone, and sat on it. {28:3} His appearance was like lightning, and his clothing white as snow. {28:4} The guards shook with fear of him and became like dead men. {28:5} But the angel said to the women, "Do not be afraid; I know that you are looking for Jesus who was crucified. {28:6} He is not here; for he has been raised, as he said. Come, see the place where he lay. {28:7} Then go quickly and tell his disciples, 'He has been raised from the dead, and indeed he is going ahead of you to Galilee; there you will see him.' This is my message for you." {28:8} So they left the tomb quickly with fear and great joy, and ran to tell his disciples. {28:9} Suddenly Jesus met them and said, "Greetings!" And they came to him, took hold of his feet, and worshiped him. {28:10} Then Jesus said to them, "Do not be afraid; go and tell my brothers to go to Galilee; there they will see me." {28:11} While they were going, some of the guards went into the city and told the chief priests everything that had happened. {28:12} After the priests had assembled with the elders, they devised a plan to give a large sum of money to the soldiers, {28:13} telling them, "You must say, 'His disciples came by night and stole him away while we were asleep.' {28:14} If this comes to the governor's ears, we will satisfy him and keep you out of trouble." {28:15} So they took the money and did as they were directed. And this story is still told among the Jews to this day. {28:16} Now the eleven disciples went to Galilee, to the mountain to which Jesus had directed them. {28:17} When they saw him, they worshiped him; but some doubted. {28:18} **And Jesus came and said to them, "All authority in heaven and on earth has been given to me.** {28:19} Go therefore and make disciples of all nations, baptizing them in the name of the Father and of the Son and of the Holy Spirit, {28:20} *and teaching them to obey everything that I have commanded you. And remember, I am with you always, to the end of the age." Amen.*

Mark

{1:1} This is the beginning of the story of Jesus Christ, the Son of God. {1:2} As it was written by the prophets: "Behold, I send my messenger ahead of you, who will prepare your way." {1:3} This messenger will be a voice in the wilderness, proclaiming: "Prepare the way for the Lord, make straight paths for him." {1:4} John appeared in the wilderness, baptizing and preaching a baptism of repentance for the forgiveness of sins. {1:5} People from all over Judea and Jerusalem went out to him. They confessed their sins and were baptized by him in the Jordan River. {1:6} John wore clothing made of camel's hair, with a leather belt around his waist, and he ate locusts and wild honey. {1:7} He preached, saying, "After me comes one who is mightier than I, the straps of whose sandals I am not worthy to stoop down and untie. {1:8} I have baptized you with water, but he will baptize you with the Holy Spirit." {1:9} In those days, Jesus came from Nazareth in Galilee and was baptized by John in the Jordan. {1:10} As Jesus was coming up out of the water, he saw the heavens being torn open and the Spirit descending on him like a dove. {1:11} And a voice came from heaven, saying, "You are my beloved Son; with you I am well pleased." {1:12} Immediately, the Spirit drove Jesus into the wilderness. {1:13} He was in the wilderness for forty days, tempted by Satan. He was with the wild animals, and angels ministered to him. {1:14} After John was imprisoned, Jesus went into Galilee, proclaiming the good news of the kingdom of God. {1:15} He said, "The time is fulfilled, and the kingdom of God is near. Repent and believe the gospel!" {1:16} As Jesus was walking by the Sea of Galilee, he saw Simon and his brother Andrew casting a net into the sea, for they were fishermen. {1:17} Jesus said to them, "Come, follow me, and I will make you fishers of men." {1:18} Immediately, they left their nets and followed him. {1:19} Going a little farther, he saw James son of Zebedee and his brother John in a boat, preparing their nets. {1:20} Without delay, he called them, and they left their father Zebedee in the boat with the hired men and followed him. {1:21} They went to Capernaum, and on the Sabbath Jesus entered the synagogue and taught. {1:22} The people were amazed at his teaching, because he taught them as one who had authority, not as the teachers of the law. {1:23} In the synagogue, there was a man possessed by an impure spirit, who cried out, {1:24} "What do you want with us, Jesus of Nazareth? Have you come to destroy us? I know who you are—the Holy One of God!" {1:25} "Be quiet!" said Jesus sternly. "Come out of him!" {1:26} The impure spirit shook the man violently and came out of him with a shriek. {1:27} The people were all so amazed that they asked each other, "What is this? A new teaching—and with authority! He even gives orders to impure spirits and they obey him." {1:28} News about him spread quickly over the whole region of Galilee. {1:29} As soon as they left the synagogue, they went with James and John to the home of Simon and Andrew. {1:30} Simon's mother-in-law was in bed with a fever, and they immediately told Jesus about her. {1:31} So he went to her, took her hand and helped her up. The fever left her, and she began to wait on them. {1:32} That evening after sunset the people brought to Jesus all the sick and demon-possessed. {1:33} The whole town gathered at the door, {1:34} and Jesus healed many who had various diseases. He also drove out many demons, but he would not let the demons speak because they knew who he was. {1:35} Very early in the morning, while it was still dark, Jesus got up, left the house and went off to a solitary place, where he prayed. {1:36} Simon and his companions went to look for him, {1:37} and when they found him, they exclaimed: "Everyone is looking for you!" {1:38} Jesus replied, "Let us go somewhere else—to the nearby villages—so I can preach there also. That is why I have come." {1:39} So he traveled throughout Galilee, preaching in their synagogues and driving out demons. {1:40} A man with leprosy came to him and begged him on his knees, "If you are willing, you can make me clean." {1:41} Jesus was filled with compassion. He reached out his hand and touched the man. "I am willing," he said. "Be clean!" {1:42} Immediately the leprosy left him and he was cleansed. {1:43} Jesus sent him away at once with a strong warning: {1:44} "See that you don't tell this to anyone. But go, show yourself to the priest and offer the sacrifices that Moses commanded for your cleansing, as a testimony to them." {1:45} Instead he went out and began to talk freely, spreading the news. As a result, Jesus could no longer enter a town openly but stayed outside in lonely places. Yet the people still came to him from everywhere.

{2:1} After some days, Jesus entered Capernaum again, and news spread that he was at home. {2:2} Soon, so many people gathered that there was no room left, not even outside the door. And he preached the word to them. {2:3} Some people came, bringing a paralyzed man, carried by four of them. {2:4} Since they could not get him to Jesus because of the crowd, they made an opening in the roof above Jesus by digging through it and then lowered the mat the man was lying on. {2:5} When Jesus saw their faith, he said to the paralyzed man, "Son, your sins are forgiven." {2:6} Now some teachers of the law were sitting there, thinking to themselves, {2:7} "Why does this fellow talk like that? He's blaspheming! Who can forgive sins but God alone?" {2:8} Immediately Jesus knew in his spirit that this was what they were thinking in their hearts, and he said to them, "Why are you thinking these things? {2:9} Which is easier: to say to this paralyzed man, 'Your sins are forgiven,' or to say, 'Get up, take your mat and walk'? {2:10} But I want you to know that the Son of Man has authority on earth to forgive sins." So he said to the man, {2:11} "I tell you, get up, take your mat and go home." {2:12} He got up, took his mat and walked out in full view of them all. This amazed everyone and they praised God, saying, "We have never seen anything like this!" {2:13} Once again Jesus went out beside the lake. A large crowd came to him, and he began to teach them. {2:14} As he walked along, he saw Levi, son of Alphaeus, sitting at the tax collector's booth. "Follow me," Jesus told him, and Levi got up and followed him. {2:15} While Jesus was having dinner at Levi's house, many tax collectors and sinners were eating with him and his disciples, for there were many who followed him. {2:16} When the teachers of the law who were Pharisees saw him eating with the sinners and tax collectors, they asked his disciples: "Why does he eat with tax collectors and sinners?" {2:17} On hearing this, Jesus said to them, "It is not the healthy who need a doctor, but the sick. I have not come to call the righteous, but sinners." {2:18} Now John's disciples and the Pharisees were fasting. Some people came and asked Jesus, "How is it that John's disciples and the disciples of the Pharisees are fasting, but yours are not?" {2:19} Jesus answered, "How can the guests of the bridegroom fast while he is with them? They cannot, so long as they have him with them. {2:20} But the time will come when the bridegroom will be taken from them, and on that day they will fast. {2:21} "No one sews a patch of unshrunk cloth on an old garment. Otherwise, the new piece will pull away from the old, making the tear worse. {2:22} And no one pours new wine into old wineskins. Otherwise, the wine will burst the skins, and both the wine and the wineskins will be ruined. No, they pour new wine into new wineskins." {2:23} One Sabbath Jesus was going through the grainfields, and as his disciples walked along, they began to pick some heads of grain. {2:24} The Pharisees said to him, "Look, why are they doing what is unlawful on the Sabbath?" {2:25} He answered, "Have you never read what David did when he and his companions were hungry and in need? {2:26} In the days of Abiathar the high priest, he entered the house of God and ate the consecrated bread, which is lawful only for priests to eat. And he also gave some to his companions." {2:27} Then he said to them, "The Sabbath was made for man, not man for the Sabbath. {2:28} So the Son of Man is Lord even of the Sabbath."

{3:1} Jesus entered the synagogue again, and there was a man with a withered hand. {3:2} Some people were watching closely to see if Jesus would heal the man on the Sabbath, so they could accuse him. {3:3} Jesus said to the man with the withered hand, "Come and stand in front of everyone." {3:4} Then Jesus asked the people, "Is it lawful to do good on the Sabbath or to do evil? To save a life or to kill?" But they remained silent. {3:5} Jesus looked around at them with anger, deeply distressed at their stubborn hearts. He said to the man, "Stretch out your hand." The man stretched it out, and his hand was completely restored. {3:6} The Pharisees went out and immediately began to plot with the Herodians against Jesus, how they might kill him. {3:7} Jesus withdrew with his disciples to the lake, and a large crowd from Galilee followed him. {3:8} People also came to him from Judea, Jerusalem, Idumea, and the regions across the Jordan and around Tyre and Sidon. There was a great crowd, hearing about all he was doing, came to him. {3:9} Jesus told his disciples to have a small boat ready for him because of the crowd, to keep them from crowding him. {3:10} He had healed many, and those with diseases were pushing forward to touch him. {3:11} Whenever the impure spirits saw him, they fell down before him and cried out, "You are the Son of God." {3:12} But he gave them strict orders not to tell others about him. {3:13} Jesus went up on a mountainside and called to him those he wanted, and they came to him. {3:14} He appointed twelve that they might be with him and that he might send them out to preach {3:15} And to have authority to drive out demons. These are the twelve he appointed: Simon (to whom he gave the name Peter), {3:16} James son of Zebedee and his brother John (to them he gave the name Boanerges, which means "sons of thunder"), {3:17} Andrew, Philip, Bartholomew, Matthew, Thomas, James son of Alphaeus, Thaddaeus, Simon the Zealot {3:18} And Judas Iscariot, who betrayed him. Jesus went into a house. {3:19} The crowd gathered again so that they could not even eat. {3:20} When his family heard about this, they went to take charge of him, for they said, "He is out of his mind." {3:21} And the teachers of the law who came down from Jerusalem said, "He is possessed by Beelzebul! By the prince of demons, he is driving out demons." {3:22} So Jesus called them over to him and began to speak to them in parables: "How can Satan drive out Satan? {3:23} If a kingdom is divided against itself, that kingdom cannot stand. {3:24} If a house is divided against itself, that house cannot stand. {3:25} And if Satan opposes himself and is divided, he cannot stand; his end has come. {3:26} In fact, no one can enter a strong man's house without first tying him up. Then he can plunder the strong man's house. {3:27} Truly I tell you, people can be forgiven all their sins and every slander they utter, {3:28} But whoever blasphemes against the Holy Spirit will never be forgiven; they are guilty of an eternal sin." {3:29} He said this because they were saying, "He has an impure spirit." {3:30} Then Jesus' mother and brothers arrived. Standing outside, they sent someone in to call him. {3:31} Then Jesus' brothers and mother came to see him. They stood outside and sent word for him to come out and talk with them. {3:32} A crowd was sitting around Jesus, and someone said, "Your mother and your brothers are outside asking for you." {3:33} Jesus replied, "Who is my mother? Who are my brothers?" {3:34} Then he looked at those around him and said, "Look, these are my mother and brothers. {3:35} Anyone who does God's will is my brother and sister and mother."

{4:1} Once again Jesus began teaching by the lakeshore. A large crowd soon gathered around him, so he got into a boat. Then he sat in the boat while all the people remained on the shore. {4:2} He taught them by telling many stories in the form of parables, saying: {4:3} "Listen! A farmer went out to plant some seeds. {4:4} As he scattered them across his field, some seeds fell on a footpath, and the birds came and ate them. {4:5} Other seeds fell on shallow soil with underlying rock. The seeds sprouted quickly because the soil was shallow. {4:6} But the plants soon wilted under the hot sun, and since they didn't have deep roots, they died. {4:7} Other seeds fell among thorns that grew up and choked out the tender plants so they produced no grain. {4:8} Still other seeds fell on fertile soil, and they sprouted, grew, and produced a crop that was thirty, sixty, and even a hundred times as much as had been planted." {4:9} Then he said, "Anyone with ears to hear should listen and understand." {4:10} Later, when Jesus was alone with the twelve disciples and with the others who were gathered around, they asked him what the parables meant. {4:11} He replied, "You are permitted to understand the secret of the Kingdom of God. But I use parables for everything I say to outsiders, {4:12} so that the Scriptures might be fulfilled: 'When they see what I do, they will learn nothing. When they hear what I say, they will not understand. Otherwise, they will turn to me and be forgiven.'" {4:13} Then Jesus said to them, "If you can't understand the meaning of this parable, how will you understand all the other parables? {4:14} "The farmer plants seed by taking God's word to others. {4:15} The seed that fell on the footpath represents those who hear the message, only to have Satan come at once and take it away. {4:16} The seed on the rocky soil represents those who hear the message and immediately receive it with joy. {4:17} But since they don't have deep roots, they don't last long. They fall away as soon as they have problems or are persecuted for believing God's word. {4:18} The seed that fell among the thorns represents others who hear God's word, {4:19} but all too quickly the message is crowded out by the worries of this life, the lure of wealth, and the desire for other things, so no fruit is produced. {4:20} And the seed that fell on good soil represents those who hear and accept God's word and produce a harvest of thirty, sixty, or even a hundred times as much as had been planted." {4:21} Jesus said to them, "Does anyone light a lamp and then put it under a basket or under a bed? Of course not! A lamp is placed on a stand, where its light will shine. {4:22} Everything that is hidden will eventually be brought into the open, and every secret will be brought to light. {4:23} Anyone with ears to hear should listen and understand." {4:24} Then he added, "Pay close attention to what you hear. The closer you listen, the more understanding you will be given—and you will receive even more. {4:25} To those who listen to my teaching, more understanding will be given. But for those who are not listening, even what little understanding they have will be taken away from them." {4:26} Jesus also said, "The Kingdom of God is like a farmer who scatters seed on the ground. {4:27} Night and day, while he's asleep or awake, the seed sprouts and grows, but he does not understand how it happens. {4:28} The earth produces the crops on its own. First a leaf blade pushes through, then the heads of wheat are formed, and finally the grain ripens. {4:29} And as soon as the grain is ready, the farmer comes and harvests it with a sickle, for the harvest time has come." {4:30} Jesus asked, "How can I describe the Kingdom of God? What story should I use to illustrate it? {4:31} It is like a mustard seed planted in the ground. It is the smallest of all seeds, {4:32} but it becomes the largest of all garden plants; it grows long branches, and birds can make nests in its shade." {4:33} Jesus used many similar stories and illustrations to teach the people as much as they could understand. {4:34} In fact, in his public teaching he never taught without using parables; but afterward, when he was alone with his disciples, he explained everything to them. {4:35} As evening came, Jesus said to his disciples, "Let's cross to the other side of the lake." {4:36} So they took Jesus in the boat and started out, leaving the crowds behind (although other boats followed). {4:37} But soon a fierce storm came up. High waves were breaking into the boat, and it began to fill with water. {4:38} Jesus was sleeping at the back of the boat with his head on a cushion. The disciples woke him up, shouting, "Teacher, don't you care that we're going to drown?" {4:39} When Jesus woke up, he rebuked the wind and said to the waves, "Silence! Be still!" Suddenly the wind stopped, and there was a great calm. {4:40} Then he asked them, "Why are you afraid? Do you still have no faith?" {4:41} The disciples were absolutely terrified. "Who is this man?" they asked each other. "Even the wind and waves obey him!"

{5:1} Jesus and his disciples crossed over to the other side of the sea, to the region of the Gadarenes. {5:2} As soon as Jesus stepped out of the boat, he was met by a man with an unclean spirit, who had come from the tombs. {5:3} This man lived among the tombs, and despite attempts to restrain him with chains and fetters, he could not be subdued. {5:4} Night and day, he would cry out in the mountains and among the tombs, cutting himself with stones. {5:5} When he saw Jesus from a distance, he ran and fell on his knees in front of him. {5:6} With a loud cry, he shouted, "What do you want with me, Jesus, Son of the Most High God? In God's name, don't torture me!" {5:7} Jesus commanded the unclean spirit to come out of the man. {5:8} "What is your name?" Jesus asked. The man replied, "Legion, for we are many." {5:9} The demons begged Jesus not to send them out of the country. {5:10} Nearby, a large herd of pigs was feeding on the mountainside. {5:11} The demons begged Jesus to send them into the pigs, and he allowed them. {5:12} The demons came out of the man and went into the pigs, causing the whole herd to plunge down the steep bank into the sea and drown. {5:13} Those tending the pigs ran off and reported this in the town and countryside, and people went out to see what had happened. {5:14} When they came to Jesus, they saw the man who had been possessed by the legion of demons, sitting there, dressed and in his right mind; and they were afraid. {5:15} Those who had seen it told the people what had happened to the demon-possessed man and the pigs. {5:16} Then the people began to plead with Jesus to leave their region. {5:17} As Jesus was getting into the boat, the man who had been demon-possessed begged to go with him. {5:18} Jesus did not let him, but said, "Go home to your own people and tell them how much the Lord has done for you, and how he has had mercy on you." {5:19} So the man went away and began to tell Decapolis how much Jesus had done for him. And all the people were amazed. {5:20} So the man departed and began to tell people in the region of Decapolis about all the great things Jesus had done for him. And everyone was amazed. {5:21} When Jesus had again crossed over by boat to the other side of the lake, a large crowd gathered around him while he was by the lake. {5:22} Then one of the synagogue leaders, named Jairus, came, and when he saw Jesus, he fell at his feet. {5:23} He pleaded earnestly with him, "My little daughter is dying. Please come and put your hands on her so that she will be healed and live." {5:24} So Jesus went with him. A large crowd followed and pressed around him. {5:25} And a woman was there who had been bleeding for twelve years. {5:26} She had suffered a great deal under the care of many doctors and had spent all she had, yet instead of getting better she grew worse. {5:27} When she heard about Jesus, she came up behind him in the crowd and touched his cloak, {5:28} because she thought, "If I just touch his clothes, I will be healed." {5:29} Immediately her bleeding stopped and she felt in her body that she was freed from her suffering. {5:30} At once Jesus realized that power had gone out from him. He turned around in the crowd and asked, "Who touched my clothes?" {5:31} "You see the people crowding against you," his disciples answered, "and yet you can ask, 'Who touched me?'" {5:32} But Jesus kept looking around to see who had done it. {5:33} Then the woman, knowing what had happened to her, came and fell at his feet and, trembling with fear, told him the whole truth. {5:34} He said to her, "Daughter, your faith has healed you. Go in peace and be freed from your suffering." {5:35} While Jesus was still speaking, some people came from the house of Jairus, the synagogue leader. "Your daughter is dead," they said. "Why bother the teacher anymore?" {5:36} Overhearing what they said, Jesus told him, "Don't be afraid; just believe." {5:37} He did not let anyone follow him except Peter, James and John the brother of James. {5:38} When they came to the home of the synagogue leader, Jesus saw a commotion, with people crying and wailing loudly. {5:39} He went in and said to them, "Why all this commotion and wailing? The child is not dead but asleep." {5:40} But they laughed at him. After he put them all out, he took the child's father and mother and the disciples who were with him, and went in where the child was. {5:41} He took her by the hand and said to her, "Talitha koum!" (which means "Little girl, I say to you, get up!"). {5:42} Immediately the girl stood up and began to walk around (she was twelve years old). At this they were completely astonished. {5:43} He gave strict orders not to let anyone know about this, and told them to give her something to eat.

{6:1} After that, Jesus left that place and returned to his hometown, accompanied by his disciples. {6:2} When the Sabbath came, he began to teach in the synagogue, and many who heard him were amazed. They asked, "Where did this man get these things? What is this wisdom that has been given to him? What are these remarkable miracles he is performing? {6:3} Isn't this the carpenter, the son of Mary and the brother of James, Joseph, Judas, and Simon? Aren't his sisters here with us?" And they took offense at him. {6:4} But Jesus said to them, "A prophet is not without honor except in his own town, among his relatives, and in his own home." {6:5} He could not do any miracles there, except lay his hands on a few sick people and heal them. {6:6} And he was amazed at their lack of faith. Then Jesus went around teaching from village to village. {6:7} Jesus called the twelve disciples to him and sent them out two by two. He gave them authority over impure spirits {6:8} and instructed them to take nothing for the journey except a staff—no bread, no bag, no money in their belts. {6:9} They were, however, to wear sandals but not put on extra shirts. {6:10} Then he told them, "Wherever you enter a house, stay there until you leave that town. {6:11} And if any place will not welcome you or listen to you, leave that place and shake the dust off your feet as a testimony against them." {6:12} So they went out and preached that people should repent. {6:13} They drove out many demons and anointed many sick people with oil and healed them. {6:14} King Herod heard about this, for Jesus' name had become well known. Some were saying, "John the Baptist has been raised from the dead, and that is why miraculous powers are at work in him." {6:15} Others said, "He is Elijah." And still others claimed, "He is a prophet, like one of the prophets of long ago." {6:16} But when Herod heard this, he said, "John, whom I beheaded, has been raised from the dead!" {6:17} For Herod himself had given orders to have John arrested, and he had him bound and put in prison. He did this because of Herodias, his brother Philip's wife, whom he had married. {6:18} For John had been saying to Herod, "It is not lawful for you to have your brother's wife." {6:19} So Herodias nursed a grudge against John and wanted to kill him. But she was not able to, {6:20} because Herod feared John and protected him, knowing him to be a righteous and holy man. When Herod heard John, he was greatly puzzled; yet he liked to listen to him. {6:21} Finally the opportune time came. On his birthday Herod gave a banquet for his high officials and military commanders and the leading men of Galilee. {6:22} When the daughter of Herodias came in and danced, she pleased Herod and his dinner guests. {6:23} The king said to the girl, "Ask me for anything you want, and I'll give it to you." And he promised her with an oath, "Whatever you ask I will give you, up to half my kingdom." {6:24} **She went out and said to her mother, "What shall I ask for?" "The head of John the Baptist," she answered.** {6:25} At once the girl hurried in to the king with the request: "I want you to give me right now the head of John the Baptist on a platter." {6:26} The king was greatly distressed, but because of his oaths and his dinner guests, he did not want to refuse her. {6:27} So he immediately sent an executioner with orders to bring John's head. The man went, beheaded John in the prison, {6:28} brought back his head on a platter. He presented it to the girl, and she gave it to her mother. {6:29} On hearing of this, John's disciples came and took his body and laid it in a tomb. {6:30} The apostles gathered around Jesus and reported to him all they had done and taught. {6:31} Then, because so many people were coming and going that they did not even have a chance to eat, he said to them, "Come with me by yourselves to a quiet place and get some rest." {6:32} So they went away by themselves in a boat to a solitary place. {6:33} But many who saw them leaving recognized them and ran on foot from all the towns and got there ahead of them. {6:34} When Jesus landed and saw a large crowd, he had compassion on them, because they were like sheep without a shepherd. So he began teaching them many things. {6:35} By this time it was late in the day, so his disciples came to him. "This is a remote place," they said, "and it's already very late. {6:36} Send the people away so that they can go to the surrounding countryside and villages and buy themselves something to eat." {6:37} But he answered, "You give them something to eat." They said to him, "That would take more than half a year's wages! Are we to go and spend that much on bread and give it to them to eat?" {6:38} "How many loaves do you have?" he asked. "Go and see." When they found out, they said, "Five—and two fish." {6:39} Then Jesus directed them to have all the people sit down in groups on the green grass. {6:40} So they sat down in groups of hundreds and fifties. {6:41} Taking the five loaves and the two fish and looking up to heaven, he gave thanks and broke the loaves. Then he gave them to his disciples to distribute to the people. He also divided the two fish among them all. {6:42} They all ate and were satisfied, {6:43} and the disciples picked up twelve baskets of broken pieces of bread and fish. {6:44} The number of the men who had eaten was five thousand. {6:45} Immediately Jesus made his disciples get into the boat and go on ahead of him to Bethsaida, while he dismissed the crowd. {6:46} After leaving them, he went up on a mountainside to pray. {6:47} Later that night, the boat was in the middle of the lake, and he was alone on land.{6:48} Jesus saw his disciples straining at the oars, because the wind was against them. Shortly before dawn he went out to them, walking on the lake. He was about to pass by them, {6:49} but when they saw him walking on the lake, they thought he was a ghost. They cried out, {6:50} because they all saw him and were terrified. Immediately he spoke to them and said, "Take courage! It is I. Don't be afraid." {6:51} Then he climbed into the boat with them, and the wind died down. They were completely amazed, {6:52} for they had not understood about the loaves; their hearts were hardened. {6:53} When they had crossed over, they landed at Gennesaret and anchored there. {6:54} As soon as they got out of the boat, people recognized Jesus. {6:55} They ran throughout that whole region and carried the sick on mats to wherever they heard he was. {6:56} And wherever he went—into villages, towns, or countryside—they placed the sick in the marketplaces. They begged him to let them touch even the edge of his cloak, and all who touched it were healed.

{7:1} Then the Pharisees and some of the scribes came together to Jesus from Jerusalem. {7:2} And when they saw some of his disciples eating bread with defiled, unwashed, hands, they found fault. {7:3} For the Pharisees and all the Jews do not eat unless they wash their hands in a special way, holding fast to the tradition of the elders. {7:4} When they come from the marketplace, they do not eat unless they wash. And there are many other things which they have received and hold, like the washing of cups, pitchers, copper vessels, and couches. {7:5} Then the Pharisees and scribes asked him, "Why do your disciples not walk according to the tradition of the elders, but eat bread with unwashed hands?" {7:6} He answered and said to them, "Well did Isaiah prophesy you hypocrites, as it is written: 'This people honors Me with their lips, but their heart is far from Me. {7:7} And in vain they worship Me, teaching as doctrines the commandments of men.' {7:8} For laying aside the commandment of God, you hold the tradition of men—the washing of pitchers and cups, and many other such things you do." {7:9} He said to them, "All too well you reject the commandment of God, that you may keep your tradition. {7:10} For Moses said, 'Honor your father and your mother'; and, 'He who curses father or mother, let him be put to death.' {7:11} But you say, 'If a man says to his father or mother, "Whatever profit you might have received from me is Corban"—' (that is, a gift to God), {7:12} then you no longer let him do anything for his father or his mother, {7:13} making the word of God of no effect through your tradition which you have handed down. And many such things you do." {7:14} When He had called all the multitude to Himself, He said to them, "Hear Me, everyone, and understand: {7:15} There is nothing that enters a man from outside which can defile him; but the things which come out of him, those are the things that defile a man. {7:16} If anyone has ears to hear, let him hear!" {7:17} When He had entered a house away from the crowd, His disciples asked Him concerning the parable. {7:18} So He said to them, "Are you thus without understanding also? Do you not perceive that whatever enters a man from outside cannot defile him, {7:19} because it does not enter his heart but his stomach, and is eliminated, thus purifying all foods?" {7:20} And He said, "What comes out of a man, that defiles a man. {7:21} For from within, out of the heart of men, proceed evil thoughts, adulteries, fornications, murders, {7:22} thefts, covetousness, wickedness, deceit, lewdness, an evil eye, blasphemy, pride, foolishness. {7:23} All these evil things come from within and defile a man." {7:24} From there He arose and went to the region of Tyre and Sidon. And He entered a house and wanted no one to know it, but He could not be hidden. {7:25} For a woman whose young daughter had an unclean spirit heard about Him, and she came and fell at His feet. {7:26} The woman was a Greek, a Syro-Phoenician by birth, and she kept asking Him to cast the demon out of her daughter. {7:27} But Jesus said to her, "Let the children be filled first, for it is not good to take the children's bread and throw it to the little dogs." {7:28} And she answered and said to Him, "Yes, Lord, yet even the little dogs under the table eat from the children's crumbs." {7:29} Then He said to her, "For this saying go your way; the demon has gone out of your daughter." {7:30} And when she had come to her house, she found the demon gone out, and her daughter lying on the bed. {7:31} Again, departing from the region of Tyre and Sidon, He came through the midst of the region of Decapolis to the Sea of Galilee. {7:32} Then they brought to Him one who was deaf and had an impediment in his speech, and they begged Him to put His hand on him. {7:33} And He took him aside from the multitude, and put His fingers in his ears, and He spat and touched his tongue. {7:34} Then, looking up to heaven, He sighed, and said to him, "Ephphatha," that is, "Be opened." {7:35} Immediately his ears were opened, and the impediment of his tongue was loosened, and he spoke plainly. {7:36} Then He commanded them that they should tell no one; but the more He commanded them, the more widely they proclaimed it. {7:37} And they were astonished beyond measure, saying, "He has done all things well. He makes both the deaf to hear and the mute to speak."

{8:1} In those days, the multitude was very great and had nothing to eat. Jesus called his disciples to him and said, {8:2} "I have compassion on the multitude because they have now been with me for three days and have nothing to eat. {8:3} And if I send them away fasting to their own houses, they will faint by the way, for some of them have come from far." {8:4} His disciples answered him, "How can anyone satisfy these people with bread here in the wilderness?" {8:5} Jesus asked them, "How many loaves do you have?" And they said, "Seven." {8:6} So he commanded the people to sit down on the ground. Then he took the seven loaves, gave thanks, broke them, and gave them to his disciples to set before them. And they set them before the people. {8:7} They also had a few small fish. He blessed them and commanded them to set them before the people. {8:8} So they ate and were filled, and they took up seven baskets of leftover fragments. {8:9} Now those who had eaten were about four thousand. Then he sent them away. {8:10} Immediately he entered a ship with his disciples and came into the parts of Dalmanutha. {8:11} The Pharisees came forth and began to question him, seeking a sign from heaven, tempting him. {8:12} And he sighed deeply in his spirit and said, "Why does this generation seek after a sign? Truly I say to you, no sign will be given to this generation." {8:13} And he left them, and entered the ship again, and departed to the other side. {8:14} Now the disciples had forgotten to take bread, and they had only one loaf with them on the ship. {8:15} Jesus cautioned them, saying, "Take heed, beware of the leaven of the Pharisees and of Herod." {8:16} And they reasoned among themselves, saying, "It's because we have no bread." {8:17} When Jesus knew it, he said to them, "Why do you reason because you have no bread? Do you not yet perceive or understand? Is your heart still hardened? {8:18} Having eyes, do you not see? And having ears, do you not hear? And do you not remember? {8:19} When I broke the five loaves among five thousand, how many baskets full of fragments did you take up?" They said to him, "Twelve." {8:20} "And of the seven loaves among four thousand, how many baskets full of fragments did you take up?" And they said, "Seven." {8:21} Then he said to them, "How is it that you do not understand?" {8:22} Jesus came to Bethsaida, and they brought a blind man to him, begging him to touch him. {8:23} Taking the blind man by the hand, Jesus led him out of the town. He spat on his eyes, put his hands on him, and asked if he could see anything. {8:24} The blind man looked up and said, "I see men as trees, walking." {8:25} Jesus put his hands on his eyes again, made him look up, and his sight was restored. He could see clearly. {8:26} Jesus sent him home, instructing him not to go into the town or tell anyone in the town what had happened. {8:27} Then Jesus and his disciples went to the towns of Caesarea Philippi. Along the way, he asked his disciples, "Who do people say that I am?" {8:28} They replied, "Some say John the Baptist; others say Elijah, and still others, one of the prophets." {8:29} Jesus asked them, "But who do you say that I am?" Peter answered, "You are Christ." {8:30} Jesus warned them not to tell anyone about him. {8:31} He began to teach them that the Son of Man must suffer many things, be rejected by the elders, the chief priests, and the scribes, be killed, and rise again after three days. {8:32} He spoke openly about this. Peter took him aside and began to rebuke him. {8:33} But when Jesus turned and looked at his disciples, he rebuked Peter, saying, "Get behind me, Satan! You do not have in mind the concerns of God, but merely human concerns." {8:34} Then Jesus called the crowd to him along with his disciples and said, "Whoever wants to be my disciple must deny themselves and take up their cross and follow me. {8:35} For whoever wants to save their life will lose it, but whoever loses their life for my sake and for the gospel will save it. {8:36} What good is it for someone to gain the whole world, yet forfeit their soul? {8:37} Or what can anyone give in exchange for their soul? {8:38} If anyone is ashamed of me and my words in this adulterous and sinful generation, the Son of Man will be ashamed of them when he comes in his Father's glory with the holy angels."

{9:1} Jesus said to them, "Truly I tell you, some of you standing here will not taste death until they see the kingdom of God come with power." {9:2} After six days, Jesus took Peter, James, and John, and led them up a high mountain apart from the others. There, he was transfigured before them. {9:3} His clothing became dazzling white, whiter than anyone on earth could bleach them. {9:4} Then appeared before them Elijah and Moses, who were talking with Jesus. {9:5} Overwhelmed, Peter said to Jesus, "Master, it's good for us to be here. Let's make three shelters—one for you, one for Moses, and one for Elijah." {9:6} He didn't know what to say, they were so frightened. {9:7} Then a cloud appeared and covered them, and a voice came from the cloud: "This is my beloved Son. Listen to him." {9:8} Suddenly, when they looked around, they saw no one with them except Jesus. {9:9} As they were coming down the mountain, Jesus instructed them not to tell anyone what they had seen until the Son of Man had risen from the dead. {9:10} They kept this to themselves, wondering what "rising from the dead" meant. {9:11} They asked Jesus, "Why do the scribes say that Elijah must come first?" {9:12} He replied, "Elijah does come first and restores all things. Why then is it written that the Son of Man must suffer much and be rejected? {9:13} But I tell you, Elijah has indeed come, and they have done to him everything they wished, just as it is written about him." {9:14} When Jesus came to his disciples, he saw a large crowd around them and the teachers of the law arguing with them. {9:15} As soon as all the people saw Jesus, they were overwhelmed with wonder and ran to greet him. {9:16} "What are you arguing about with them?" he asked. {9:17} A man in the crowd answered, "Teacher, I brought you my son, who is possessed by a spirit that has robbed him of speech. {9:18} Whenever it seizes him, it throws him to the ground. He foams at the mouth, gnashes his teeth, and becomes rigid. I asked your disciples to drive out the spirit, but they could not." {9:19} "You unbelieving generation," Jesus replied, "how long shall I stay with you? How long shall I put up with you? Bring the boy to me." {9:20} So they brought him. When the spirit saw Jesus, it immediately threw the boy into a convulsion. He fell to the ground and rolled around, foaming at the mouth. {9:21} Jesus asked the boy's father, "How long has he been like this?" "From childhood," he answered. {9:22} "It has often thrown him into fire or water to kill him. But if you can do anything, take pity on us and help us." {9:23} "'If you can'?" said Jesus. "Everything is possible for one who believes." {9:24} Immediately the boy's father exclaimed, "I do believe; help me overcome my unbelief!" {9:25} When Jesus saw that a crowd was running to the scene, he rebuked the impure spirit. "You deaf and mute spirit," he said, "I command you, come out of him and never enter him again." {9:26} The spirit shrieked, convulsed him violently, and came out. The boy looked so much like a corpse that many said, "He's dead." {9:27} But Jesus took him by the hand and lifted him to his feet, and he stood up. {9:28} After Jesus had gone indoors, his disciples asked him privately, "Why couldn't we drive it out?" {9:29} He replied, "This kind can come out only by prayer and fasting." {9:30} They left that place and passed through Galilee. Jesus did not want anyone to know where they were, {9:31} because he was teaching his disciples. He said to them, "The Son of Man is going to be delivered into the hands of men. They will kill him, and after three days he will rise." {9:32} But they did not understand what he meant and were afraid to ask him about it. {9:33} They came to Capernaum. When he was in the house, he asked, "What were you arguing about on the road?" {9:34} But they kept quiet because on the way they had argued about who was the greatest. {9:35} Sitting down, Jesus called the Twelve and said, "Anyone who wants to be first must be the very last, and the servant of all." {9:36} He took a little child whom he placed among them. Taking the child in his arms, he said to them, {9:37} "Whoever welcomes one of these little children in my name welcomes me; and whoever welcomes me does not welcome me but the one who sent me." {9:38} John said to Jesus, "Master, we saw someone driving out demons in your name and we told him to stop, because he was not one of us." {9:39} "Do not stop him," Jesus said. "For no one who does a miracle in my name can in the next moment say anything bad about me, {9:40} because whoever is not against us is for us. {9:41} Truly I tell you, anyone who gives you a cup of water in my name because you belong to the Messiah will certainly not lose their reward. {9:42} "If anyone causes one of these little ones—those who believe in me—to stumble, it would be better for them if a large millstone were hung around their neck and they were thrown into the sea. {9:43} If your hand causes you to stumble, cut it off. It is better for you to enter life maimed than with two hands to go into hell, where the fire never goes out. {9:44} [And if your foot causes you to stumble, cut it off. It is better for you to enter life crippled than to have two feet and be thrown into hell. {9:45} And if your eye causes you to stumble, pluck it out. It is better for you to enter the kingdom of God with one eye than to have two eyes and be thrown into hell, {9:46} 'where their worm does not die, and the fire is not quenched' {9:47} 'the worms that eat them do not die,and the fire is not quenched.' {9:48} "Everyone will be salted with fire.{9:49} "For everyone will be salted with fire, and every sacrifice will be salted with salt. {9:50} Salt is good, but if the salt has lost its saltiness, how will you season it? Have salt in yourselves, and have peace with one another."

{10:1} "And he arose from there and came into the coasts of Judea by the farther side of the Jordan; and the people gathered to him again, and as he was accustomed, he taught them again. {10:2} And the Pharisees came to him, and asked him, 'Is it lawful for a man to put away his wife?' tempting him. {10:3} And he answered and said unto them, 'What did Moses command you?' {10:4} And they said, 'Moses suffered to write a bill of divorce, and to put her away.' {10:5} And Jesus answered and said unto them, 'For the hardness of your heart he wrote you this precept. {10:6} 'But from the beginning of the creation, God made them male and female. {10:7} 'For this cause shall a man leave his father and mother, and cleave to his wife; {10:8} 'And they twain shall be one flesh: so then they are no more twain, but one flesh. {10:9} **'What therefore God hath joined together, let no man put asunder.'** {10:10} "And in the house his disciples asked him again about the same matter. {10:11} "And he saith unto them, 'Whosoever shall put away his wife, and marry another, committeth adultery against her. {10:12} 'And if a woman shall put away her husband, and be married to another, she committeth adultery.' {10:13} "And they brought young children to him, that he should touch them: and his disciples rebuked those that brought them. {10:14} "But when Jesus saw it, he was much displeased, and said unto them, 'Suffer the little children to come unto me, and forbid them not: for of such is the kingdom of God. {10:15} 'Verily I say unto you, Whosoever shall not receive the kingdom of God as a little child, he shall not enter therein.' {10:16} "And he took them up in his arms, put his hands upon them, and blessed them. {10:17} "And when he was going forth into the way, there came one running, and kneeled to him, and asked him, 'Good Master, what shall I do that I may inherit eternal life?' {10:18} "And Jesus said unto him, 'Why callest thou me good? There is none good but one, that is, God. {10:19} 'Thou knowest the commandments: Do not commit adultery, Do not kill, Do not steal, Do not bear false witness, Defraud not, Honor thy father and mother.' {10:20} "And he answered and said unto him, 'Master, all these have I observed from my youth.' {10:21} "Then Jesus, beholding him, loved him, and said unto him, 'One thing thou lackest: go thy way, sell whatsoever thou hast, and give to the poor, and thou shalt have treasure in heaven: and come, take up the cross, and follow me.' {10:22} "And he was sad at that saying, and went away grieved: for he had great possessions. {10:23} "And Jesus looked round about, and said unto his disciples, 'How hardly shall they that have riches enter into the kingdom of God!' {10:24} "And the disciples were astonished at his words. But Jesus answereth again, and saith unto them, 'Children, how hard is it for them that trust in riches to enter into the kingdom of God! {10:25} 'It is easier for a camel to go through the eye of a needle, than for a rich man to enter into the kingdom of God.' {10:26} "And they were astonished out of measure, saying among themselves, 'Who then can be saved?' {10:27} "And Jesus looking upon them saith, 'With men it is impossible, but not with God: for with God all things are possible.' {10:28} "Then Peter began to say unto him, 'Lo, we have left all, and have followed thee.' {10:29} "And Jesus answered and said, 'Verily I say unto you, There is no man that hath left house, or brethren, or sisters, or father, or mother, or wife, or children, or lands, for my sake, and the gospel's, {10:30} 'But he shall receive a hundredfold now in this time, houses, and brethren, and sisters, and mothers, and children, and lands, with persecutions; and in the world to come eternal life. {10:31} 'But many that are first shall be last; and the last first.' {10:32} "And they were on the way going up to Jerusalem; and Jesus went before them: and they were amazed; and as they followed, they were afraid. And he took again the twelve, and began to tell them what things should happen unto him, {10:33} [Saying,] 'Behold, we go up to Jerusalem; and the Son of man shall be delivered unto the chief priests, and unto the scribes; and they shall condemn him to death, and shall deliver him to the Gentiles: {10:34} 'And they shall mock him, and shall scourge him, and shall spit upon him, and shall kill him: and the third day he shall rise again. {10:35} "And James and John, the sons of Zebedee, come unto him, saying, 'Master, we would that thou shouldest do for us whatsoever we shall desire.' {10:36} "And he said unto them, 'What would ye that I should do for you?' {10:37} "They said unto him, 'Grant unto us that we may sit, one on thy right hand, and the other on thy left hand, in thy glory.' {10:38} "But Jesus said unto them, 'Ye know not what ye ask: can ye drink of the cup that I drink of? and be baptized with the baptism that I am baptized with?' {10:39} "And they said unto him, 'We can.' And Jesus said unto them, 'Ye shall indeed drink of the cup that I drink of; and with the baptism that I am baptized withal shall ye be baptized: {10:40} 'But to sit on my right hand and on my left hand is not mine to give; but [it shall be given to them] for whom it is prepared.' {10:41} "And when the ten heard [it,] they began to be much displeased with James and John. {10:42} "But Jesus called them [to him,] and saith unto them, 'Ye know that they which are accounted to rule over the Gentiles exercise lordship over them; and their great ones exercise authority upon them. {10:43} 'But so shall it not be among you: but whosoever will be great among you, shall be your minister: {10:44} 'And whosoever of you will be the chiefest, shall be servant of all. {10:45} 'For even the Son of man came not to be ministered unto, but to minister, and to give his life a ransom for many. {10:46} "And they came to Jericho: and as he went out of Jericho with his disciples and a great number of people, blind Bartimaeus, the son of Timaeus, sat by the highway begging. {10:47} "And when he heard that it was Jesus of Nazareth, he began to cry out, and say, 'Jesus, [thou] Son of David, have mercy on me.' {10:48} "And many charged him that he should hold his peace: but he cried a great deal, '[Thou] Son of David, have mercy on me.' {10:49} "And Jesus stood still, and commanded him to be called. And they call the blind man, saying unto him, 'Be of good comfort, rise; he calleth thee.' {10:50} "And he, casting away his garment, rose, and came to Jesus. {10:51} "And Jesus answered and said unto him, 'What wilt thou that I should do unto thee?' The blind man said unto him, 'Lord, that I might receive my sight.' {10:52} "And Jesus said unto him, 'Go thy way; thy faith hath made thee whole.' And immediately he received his sight, and followed Jesus in the way."

{11:1} "And when they came nigh to Jerusalem, unto Bethphage and Bethany, at the mount of Olives, he sendeth forth two of his disciples, {11:2} "And saith unto them, 'Go your way into the village over against you: and as soon as ye be entered into it, ye shall find a colt tied, whereon never man sat; loose him, and bring [him.]' {11:3} "And if any man says unto you, 'Why do ye this?' say ye that the Lord hath need of him; and straightway he will send him hither. {11:4} "And they went their way, and found the colt tied by the door without in a place where two ways met; and they lost him. {11:5} "And certain of them that stood there said unto them, 'What do ye, losing the colt?' {11:6} "And they said unto them even as Jesus had commanded: and they let them go. {11:7} "And they brought the colt to Jesus, and cast their garments on him; and he sat upon him. {11:8} "And many spread their garments in the way: and others cut down branches off the trees, and strawed [them] in the way. {11:9} "And they that went before, and they that followed, cried, saying, 'Hosanna; Blessed [is] he that cometh in the name of the Lord: {11:10} 'Blessed [be] the kingdom of our father David, that cometh in the name of the Lord: Hosanna in the highest.' {11:11} "And Jesus entered into Jerusalem, and into the temple: and when he had looked roundabout upon all things, and now the eventide was come, he went out unto Bethany with the twelve. {11:12} "And on the morrow, when they were come from Bethany, he was hungry: {11:13} "And seeing a fig tree afar off having leaves, he came, if haply he might find any thing thereon: and when he came to it, he found nothing but leaves; for the time of figs was not [yet.] {11:14} "And Jesus answered and said unto it, 'No man eat fruit of the hereafter for ever.' And his disciples heard [it.] {11:15} "And they come to Jerusalem: and Jesus went into the temple, and began to cast out them that sold and bought in the temple, and overthrew the tables of the moneychangers, and the seats of them that sold doves; {11:16} "And would not suffer that any man should carry [any] vessel through the temple. {11:17} "And he taught, saying unto them, 'Is it not written, My house shall be called of all nations the house of prayer? but ye have made it a den of thieves.' {11:18} "And the scribes and chief priests heard [it,] and sought how they might destroy him: for they feared him, because all the people were astonished at his doctrine. {11:19} And when even was come, he went out of the city. {11:20} And in the morning, as they passed by, they saw the fig tree dried up from the roots. {11:21} And Peter calling to remembrance saith unto him, 'Master, behold, the fig tree which thou cursed is withered away.' {11:22} "And Jesus answering saith unto them, 'Have faith in God. {11:23} 'For verily I say unto you, That whosoever shall say unto this mountain, Be thou removed, and be thou cast into the sea; and shall not doubt in his heart, but shall believe that those things which he saith shall come to pass; he shall have whatsoever he saith. {11:24} 'Therefore I say unto you, What things soever ye desire, when ye pray, believe that ye receive [them,] and ye shall have [them.] {11:25} 'And when ye stand praying, forgive, if ye have ought against any: that your Father also which is in heaven may forgive you your trespasses. {11:26} 'But if ye do not forgive, neither will your Father which is in heaven forgive your trespasses. {11:27} And they come again to Jerusalem: and as he was walking in the temple, there come to him the chief priests, and the scribes, and the elders, {11:28} And say unto him, 'By what authority doest thou these things? and who gave thee this authority to do these things?' {11:29} And Jesus answered and said unto them, 'I will also ask of you one question, and answer me, and I will tell you by what authority I do these things. {11:30} 'The baptism of John, was [it] from heaven, or of men? answer me.' {11:31} "And they reasoned with themselves, saying, 'If we shall say, From heaven; he will say, Why then did ye not believe him? {11:32} 'But if we shall say, Of men; they feared the people: for all [men] counted John, that he was a prophet indeed.' {11:33} "And they answered and said unto Jesus, 'We cannot tell.' And Jesus answering saith unto them, 'Neither do I tell you by what authority I do these things.'"

{12:1} "And he began to speak unto them by parables. A [certain] man planted a vineyard, and set an hedge about [it,] and digged [a place for] the winefat, and built a tower, and let it out to husbandmen, and went into a far country. {12:2} "And at the season he sent to the husbandmen a servant, that he might receive from the husbandmen of the fruit of the vineyard. {12:3} "And they caught [him,] and beat him, and sent [him] away empty. {12:4} "And again he sent unto them another servant; and at him they cast stones, and wounded [him] in the head, and sent [him] away shamefully handled. {12:5} "And again he sent another; and him they killed, and many others; beating some, and killing some. {12:6} "Having yet therefore one son, his wellbeloved, he sent him also last unto them, saying, They will reverence my son. {12:7} "But those husbandmen said among themselves, This is the heir; come, let us kill him, and the inheritance shall be ours. {12:8} "And they took him, and killed [him,] and cast [him] out of the vineyard. {12:9} "What shall therefore the lord of the vineyard do? he will come and destroy the husbandmen, and will give the vineyard unto others. {12:10} "And have ye not read this scripture; The stone which the builders rejected is become the head of the corner: {12:11} "This was the Lord's doing, and it is marvellous in our eyes?" {12:12} "And they sought to lay hold on him, but feared the people: for they knew that he had spoken the parable against them: and they left him, and went their way. {12:13} "And they sent unto him certain of the Pharisees and of the Herodians, to catch him in [his] words. {12:14} "And when they were come, they say unto him, 'Master, we know that thou art true, and carest for no man: for thou regardest not the person of men, but teachest the way of God in truth: Is it lawful to give tribute to Caesar, or not? {12:15} "Shall we give, or shall we not give? But he, knowing their hypocrisy, said unto them, 'Why tempt ye me? bring me a penny, that I may see [it.]' {12:16} "And they brought [it.] And he said unto them, 'Whose [is] this image and superscription?' And they said unto him, 'Caesar's.' {12:17} "And Jesus answering said unto them, 'Render to Caesar the things that are Caesar's, and to God the things that are God's.' And they marveled at him. {12:18} "Then come unto him the Sadducees, which say there is no resurrection; and they asked him, saying, {12:19} "'Master, Moses wrote unto us, If a man's brother die, and leave [his] wife [behind him,] and leave no children, that his brother should take his wife, and raise up seed unto his brother. {12:20} "'Now there were seven brethren: and the first took a wife, and dying left no seed. {12:21} "'And the second took her, and died, neither left any seed: and the third likewise. {12:22} "And the seven had her, and left no seed: last of all the woman died also. {12:23} "'In the resurrection therefore, when they shall rise, whose wife shall she be of them? for the seven had her to wife.' {12:24} "And Jesus answering said unto them, 'Do ye not therefore err, because ye know not the scriptures, neither the power of God? {12:25} "For when they shall rise from the dead, they neither marry, nor are given in marriage; but are as the angels which are in heaven. {12:26} "'And as touching the dead, that they rise: have ye not read in the book of Moses, how in the bush God spake unto him, saying, I [am] the God of Abraham, and the God of Isaac, and the God of Jacob? {12:27} "'He is not the God of the dead, but the God of the living: ye therefore do greatly err.' {12:28} "And one of the scribes came, and having heard them reasoning together, and perceiving that he had answered them well, asked him, 'Which is the first commandment of all?' {12:29} "And Jesus answered him, 'The first of all the commandments [is,] Hear, O Israel; The Lord our God is one Lord: {12:30} "'And thou shalt love the Lord thy God with all thy heart, and with all thy soul, and with all thy mind, and with all thy strength: this is the first commandment. {12:31} "'And the second [is] like, [namely] this, Thou shalt love thy neighbor as thyself. There is none other commandment greater than these.' {12:32} "And the scribe said unto him, 'Well, Master, thou hast said the truth: for there is one God; and there is none other but he: {12:33} "'And to love him with all the heart, and with all the understanding, and with all the soul, and with all the strength, and to love [his] neighbor as himself, is more than all whole burnt offerings and sacrifices.' {12:34} "And when Jesus saw that he answered discreetly, he said unto him, 'Thou art not far from the kingdom of God.' And no man after that durst asked him [any question.] {12:35} "And Jesus answered and said, while he taught in the temple, 'How do the scribes say that Christ is the Son of David? {12:36} "'For David himself said by the Holy Ghost, The Lord said to my Lord, Sit thou on my right hand, till I make thine enemies thy footstool. {12:37} "'David therefore himself calleth him Lord; and whence is he [then] his son?' And the common people heard him gladly. {12:38} "And he said unto them in his doctrine, 'Beware of the scribes, which love to go in long clothing, and [love] salutations in the marketplaces, {12:39} "'And the chief seats in the synagogues, and the uppermost rooms at feasts: {12:40} "'Which devour widows' houses, and for a pretense make long prayers: these shall receive greater damnation.' {12:41} Jesus sat across from the treasury and watched as people put money into it. Many rich people threw in large amounts. {12:42} Then a poor widow came and threw in two small coins worth only a few cents. {12:43} Jesus called his disciples to him and said, "Truly I tell you, this poor widow has put more into the treasury than all the others. {12:44} They all gave out of their wealth; but she, out of her poverty, put in everything—all she had to live on."

{13:1} As Jesus left the temple, one of his disciples remarked about the impressive stones and buildings there. {13:2} Jesus replied, "Do you see these great buildings? Not one stone here will be left on another; everyone will be thrown down." {13:3} Later, while he was sitting on the Mount of Olives opposite the temple, Peter, James, John, and Andrew asked him privately, {13:4} "Tell us, when will these things happen? And what will be the sign that they are all about to be fulfilled?" {13:5} Jesus answered, "Watch out that no one deceives you. {13:6} Many will come in my name, claiming, 'I am he,' and will deceive many. {13:7} When you hear of wars and rumors of wars, do not be alarmed. Such things must happen, but the end is still to come. {13:8} Nation will rise against nation, and kingdom against kingdom. There will be earthquakes in various places, and famines. These are the beginning of birth pains. {13:9} "You must be on your guard. You will be handed over to the local councils and flogged in the synagogues. On account of me you will stand before governors and kings as witnesses to them. {13:10} And the gospel must first be preached to all nations. {13:11} Whenever you are arrested and brought to trial, do not worry beforehand about what to say. Just say whatever is given you at the time, for it is not you speaking, but the Holy Spirit. {13:12} "Brother will betray brother to death, and a father his child. Children will rebel against their parents and have them put to death. {13:13} Everyone will hate you because of me, but the one who stands firm to the end will be saved. {13:14} **"When you see 'the abomination that causes desolation' standing where it does not belong—let the reader understand—then let those who are in Judea flee to the mountains.** {13:15} Let no one on the housetop go down or enter the house to take anything out. {13:16} Let no one in the field go back to get their cloak. {13:17} How dreadful it will be in those days for pregnant women and nursing mothers! {13:18} Pray that this will not take place in winter, {13:19} because those will be days of distress unequaled from the beginning, when God created the world, until now—and never to be equaled again. {13:20} "If the Lord had not cut short those days, no one would survive. But for the sake of the elect, whom he has chosen, he has shortened them. {13:21} At that time if anyone says to you, 'Look, here is the Messiah!' or, 'Look, there he is!' do not believe it. {13:22} For false messiahs and false prophets will appear and perform signs and wonders to deceive, if possible, even the elect. {13:23} So be on your guard; I have told you everything ahead of time. {13:24} "But in those days, following that distress, "the sun will be darkened, and the moon will not give its light; {13:25} the stars will fall from the sky, and the heavenly bodies will be shaken.' {13:26} "At that time people will see the Son of Man coming in clouds with great power and glory. {13:27} And he will send his angels and gather his elect from the four winds, from the ends of the earth to the ends of the heavens. {13:28} "Now learn this lesson from the fig tree: As soon as its twigs get tender and its leaves come out, you know that summer is near. {13:29} Even so, when you see these things happening, you know that it is near, right at the door. {13:30} Truly I tell you, this generation will certainly not pass away until all these things have happened. {13:31} Heaven and earth will pass away, but my words will never pass away. {13:32} "But about that day or hour no one knows, not even the angels in heaven, nor the Son, but only the Father. {13:33} Be on guard! Be alert! You do not know when that time will come. {13:34} It's like a man going away: He leaves his house and puts his servants in charge, each with their assigned task, and tells the one at the door to keep watch. {13:35} **Therefore keep watch because you do not know when the owner of the house will come back—whether in the evening, or at midnight, or when the rooster crows, or at dawn.** {13:36} If he comes suddenly, do not let him find you sleeping. {13:37} What I say to you, I say to everyone: 'Watch!'"

{14:1} Two days before the Passover and the Festival of Unleavened Bread, the chief priests and the scribes were scheming to arrest Jesus covertly and have him killed. {14:2} But they agreed, "Not during the festival, or there may be a riot among the people." {14:3} Meanwhile, in Bethany, at the house of Simon the leper, Jesus was reclining at the table when a woman came with an alabaster jar of very expensive perfume, made of pure nard. She broke the jar and poured the perfume on Jesus' head. {14:4} Some of those present were indignant and said to one another, "Why this waste of perfume? {14:5} It could have been sold for more than three hundred denarii and the money given to the poor." And they rebuked her harshly. {14:6} But Jesus said, "Leave her alone. Why are you bothering her? She has done a beautiful thing to me. {14:7} The poor you will always have with you, and you can help them whenever you want. But you will not always have me. {14:8} She did what she could. She poured perfume on my body beforehand to prepare for my burial. {14:9} Truly I tell you, wherever the gospel is preached throughout the world, what she has done will also be told, in memory of her." {14:10} Then Judas Iscariot, one of the Twelve, went to the chief priests to betray Jesus to them. {14:11} They were delighted to hear this and promised to give him money. So he watched for an opportunity to hand him over. {14:12} On the first day of the Festival of Unleavened Bread, when it was customary to sacrifice the Passover lamb, Jesus' disciples asked him, "Where do you want us to go and make preparations for you to eat the Passover?" {14:13} So he sent two of his disciples, telling them, "Go into the city, and a man carrying a jar of water will meet you. Follow him. {14:14} Say to the owner of the house he enters, 'The Teacher asks: Where is my guest room, where I may eat the Passover with my disciples?' {14:15} He will show you a large room upstairs, furnished and ready. Make preparations for us there." {14:16} The disciples left, went into the city and found things just as Jesus had told them. So they prepared the Passover. {14:17} When evening came, Jesus arrived with the Twelve. {14:18} While they were reclining at the table eating, he said, "Truly I tell you, one of you will betray me—one who is eating with me." {14:19} They were saddened, and one by one they said to him, "Surely you don't mean me?" {14:20} "It is one of the Twelve," he replied, "one who dips bread into the bowl with me. {14:21} The Son of Man will go just as it is written about him. But woe to that man who betrays the Son of Man! It would be better for him if he had not been born." {14:22} While they were eating, Jesus took bread, and when he had given thanks, he broke it and gave it to his disciples, saying, "Take it; this is my body." {14:23} Then he took a cup, and after he had given thanks, he gave it to them, and they all drank from it. {14:24} "This is my blood of the covenant, which is poured out for many," he said to them. {14:25} "Truly I tell you, I will not drink again from the fruit of the vine until that day when I drink it again in the kingdom of God." {14:26} After singing a hymn, they went out to the Mount of Olives. {14:27} Jesus said to them, "You will all fall away, for it is written: 'I will strike the shepherd, and the sheep will be scattered.' {14:28} But after I have risen, I will go ahead of you into Galilee." {14:29} Peter declared, "Even if all fall away, I will not." {14:30} "Truly I tell you," Jesus answered, "today—yes, tonight—before the rooster crows twice you yourself will disown me three times." {14:31} But Peter insisted emphatically, "Even if I have to die with you, I will never disown you." And all the others said the same. {14:32} They went to a place called Gethsemane, and Jesus said to his disciples, "Sit here while I pray." {14:33} He took Peter, James and John along with him, and he began to be deeply distressed and troubled. {14:34} "My soul is overwhelmed with sorrow to the point of death," he said to them. "Stay here and keep watch." {14:35} Going a little farther, he fell to the ground and prayed that if possible the hour might pass from him. {14:36} "Abba, Father," he said, "everything is possible for you. Take this cup from me. Yet not what I will, but what you will." {14:37} Then he returned to his disciples and found them sleeping. "Simon," he said to Peter, "are you asleep? Couldn't you keep watch for one hour? {14:38} Watch and pray so that you will not fall into temptation. The spirit is willing, but the flesh is weak." {14:39} Once more he went away and prayed the same thing. {14:40} When he came back, he again found them sleeping, because their eyes were heavy. They did not know what to say to him. {14:41} Returning the third time, he said to them, "Are you still sleeping and resting? Enough! The hour has come. Look, the Son of Man is delivered into the hands of sinners. {14:42} Rise! Let us go! Here comes my betrayer!" {14:43} Just as he was speaking, Judas, one of the Twelve, appeared. With him was a crowd armed with swords and clubs, sent from the chief priests, the teachers of the law, and the elders. {14:44} Now the betrayer had arranged a signal with them: "The one I kiss is the man; arrest him and lead him away under guard." {14:45} Going at once to Jesus, Judas said, "Rabbi!" and kissed him. {14:46} The men seized Jesus and arrested him. {14:47} Then one of those standing nearby drew his sword and struck the servant of the high priest, cutting off his ear. {14:48} "Am I leading a rebellion," said Jesus, "that you have come out with swords and clubs to capture me? {14:49} Every day I was with you, teaching in the temple courts, and you did not arrest me. But the Scriptures must be fulfilled." {14:50} Then everyone deserted him and fled. {14:51} A young man, wearing nothing but a linen garment, was following Jesus. When they seized him, {14:52} he fled naked, leaving his garment behind. {14:53} They took Jesus to the high priest, where all the chief priests, the elders, and the scribes were assembled. {14:54} Peter followed him at a distance, right into the courtyard of the high priest. There he sat with the guards and warmed himself at the fire. {14:55} The chief priests and the whole Sanhedrin were looking for evidence against Jesus so that they could put him to death, but they did not find any. {14:56} Many testified falsely against him, but their statements did not agree. {14:57} Then some stood up and gave this false testimony against him: {14:58} "We heard him say, 'I will destroy this temple made with human hands and in three days will build another, not made by human hands.'" {14:59} Yet even then their testimony did not agree. {14:60} The high priest stood up before them and asked Jesus, "Are you not going to answer? What is this testimony that these men are bringing against you?" {14:61} But Jesus remained silent and gave no answer. Again the high priest asked him, "Are you the Messiah, the Son of the Blessed One?" {14:62} "I am," said Jesus. "And you will see the Son of Man sitting at the right hand of the Mighty One and coming on the clouds of heaven." {14:63} The high priest tore his clothes. "Why do we need any more witnesses?" he asked. {14:64} "You have heard the blasphemy. What do you think?" They all condemned him as worthy of death. {14:65} Some began to spit on him; they blindfolded him, struck him with their fists, and said, "Prophesy!" And the guards took him and beat him. {14:66} While Peter was below in the courtyard, one of the servant girls of the high priest came by. {14:67} When she saw Peter warming himself, she looked closely at him. "You also were with Jesus of Nazareth," she said. {14:68} But he denied it. "I don't know or understand what you're talking about," he said, and went out into the entryway. {14:69} When the servant girl saw him there, she said again to those standing around, "This fellow is one of them." {14:70} Again he denied it. After a little while, those standing near said to Peter, "Surely you are one of them, for you are a Galilean." {14:71} He began to call down curses, and he swore to them, "I don't know this man you're talking about." {14:72} Immediately the rooster crowed the second time. Then Peter remembered the word Jesus had spoken to him: "Before the rooster crows twice you will disown me three times." And he broke down and wept.

{15:1} Early in the morning, the chief priests, along with the elders, the scribes, and the whole council, held a meeting. They bound Jesus, led him away, and handed him over to Pilate. {15:2} Pilate asked him, "Are you the King of the Jews?" Jesus replied, "You have said so." {15:3} The chief priests accused him of many things, but Jesus remained silent. {15:4} Pilate asked him again, "Aren't you going to answer? See how many things they are accusing you of." {15:5} But Jesus still made no reply, and Pilate was amazed. {15:6} Now it was Pilate's custom at the feast to release a prisoner whom the people requested. {15:7} A man called Barabbas was in prison with the insurrectionists who had committed murder in the uprising. {15:8} The crowd came up and asked Pilate to do for them what he usually did. {15:9} "Do you want me to release you to the King of the Jews?" asked Pilate, {15:10} knowing it was out of envy that the chief priests had handed Jesus over to him. {15:11} But the chief priests stirred up the crowd to have Pilate release Barabbas instead. {15:12} "What shall I do, then, with the one you call the King of the Jews?" Pilate asked them. {15:13} "Crucify him!" they shouted. {15:14} "Why? What crime has he committed?" asked Pilate. But they shouted all the louder, "Crucify him!" {15:15} Wanting to satisfy the crowd, Pilate released Barabbas to them. He had Jesus flogged, and handed him over to be crucified. {15:16} The soldiers led Jesus away into the palace (that is, the Praetorium) and called together the whole company of soldiers. {15:17} They put a purple robe on him, then twisted together a crown of thorns and set it on him. {15:18} And they began to call out to him, "Hail, king of the Jews!" {15:19} Again and again they struck him on the head with a staff and spit on him. Falling on their knees, they paid homage to him. {15:20} After they had mocked him, they took off the purple robe and put his own clothes on him. Then they led him out to crucify him. {15:21} A certain man from Cyrene, Simon, the father of Alexander and Rufus, was passing by on his way in from the country, and they forced him to carry the cross. {15:22} They brought Jesus to the place called Golgotha (which means "the place of the skull"). {15:23} Then they offered him wine mixed with myrrh, but he did not take it. {15:24} And they crucified him. Dividing up his clothes, they cast lots to see what each would get. {15:25} It was nine in the morning when they crucified him. {15:26} The written notice of the charge against him read: The King of the Jews. {15:27} They crucified two rebels with him, one on his right and one on his left. {15:28} And the scripture was fulfilled that says, "He was counted among the transgressors." {15:29} Those who passed by hurled insults at him, shaking their heads and saying, "So! You who are going to destroy the temple and build it in three days, {15:30} come down from the cross and save yourself!" {15:31} In the same way the chief priests and the teachers of the law mocked him among themselves. "He saved others," they said, "but he can't save himself! {15:32} Let this Messiah, this king of Israel, come down now from the cross, that we may see and believe." Those crucified with him also heaped insults on him. {15:33} At noon, darkness came over the whole land until three in the afternoon. {15:34} And at three in the afternoon Jesus cried out in a loud voice, "Eloi, Eloi, lema sabachthani?" (which means "My God, my God, why have you forsaken me?"). {15:35} When some of those standing nearby heard this, they said, "Listen, he's calling Elijah." {15:36} Someone ran, filled a sponge with wine vinegar, put it on a staff, and offered it to Jesus to drink. "Now leave him alone. Let's see if Elijah comes to take him down," he said. {15:37} With a loud cry, Jesus breathed his last. {15:38} The curtain of the temple was torn in two from top to bottom. {15:39} When the centurion, who stood facing him, saw how Jesus breathed his last, he said, "Truly this man was the Son of God." {15:40} There were also women watching from a distance. Among them were Mary Magdalene, Mary the mother of James the younger and of Joses, and Salome. {15:41} These women had followed Jesus and cared for him while he was in Galilee. Many other women who had come up with him to Jerusalem were there too. {15:42} Now when evening had come, since it was the day of Preparation (that is, the day before the Sabbath), {15:43} Joseph of Arimathea, a respected member of the council who was also himself looking forward to the kingdom of God, went boldly to Pilate and asked for Jesus' body. {15:44} Pilate was surprised to hear that he was already dead. Summoning the centurion, he asked him if Jesus had been dead for some time. {15:45} When he learned from the centurion that it was so, he gave the body to Joseph. {15:46} Joseph bought some linen cloth, took down the body, wrapped it in the linen, and placed it in a tomb cut out of rock. Then he rolled a stone against the entrance of the tomb. {15:47} Mary Magdalene and Mary the mother of Joses saw where he was laid.

{16:1} After the Sabbath had passed, Mary Magdalene, Mary the mother of James, and Salome bought sweet spices to anoint Jesus. {16:2} Very early on the first day of the week, at sunrise, they went to the tomb. {16:3} They wondered who would roll away the stone from the tomb's entrance. {16:4} But when they arrived, they saw that the stone had already been rolled away, even though it was large. {16:5} Entering the tomb, they saw a young man dressed in a long white robe sitting on the right side, and they were frightened. {16:6} But the young man said to them, "Don't be afraid. You're looking for Jesus of Nazareth, who was crucified. He has risen; he is not here. See the place where they laid him. {16:7} But go, tell his disciples and Peter, 'He is going ahead of you into Galilee. There you will see him, just as he told you.'" {16:8} Trembling and amazed, the women fled from the tomb. They said nothing to anyone, because they were afraid. {16:9} Jesus rose early on the first day of the week and appeared first to Mary Magdalene, out of whom he had cast seven demons. {16:10} She went and told those who had been with him and who were mourning and weeping. {16:11} When they heard that Jesus was alive and had been seen by her, they did not believe it. {16:12} Afterward, Jesus appeared in another form to two of them as they were walking in the countryside. {16:13} They went and told the rest, but they did not believe them either. {16:14} Later, Jesus appeared to the eleven as they were eating, and he rebuked them for their lack of faith and their stubborn refusal to believe those who had seen him after he had risen. {16:15} He said to them, "Go into all the world and preach the gospel to all creation. {16:16} Whoever believes and is baptized will be saved, but whoever does not believe will be condemned. {16:17} And these signs will accompany those who believe: In my name they will drive out demons; they will speak in new tongues; {16:18} they will pick up snakes with their hands; and when they drink deadly poison, it will not hurt them at all; they will place their hands on sick people, and they will get well." {16:19} After the Lord had spoken to them, he was taken up into heaven and sat at the right hand of God. {16:20} Then the disciples went out and preached everywhere, and the Lord worked with them and confirmed his word by the signs that accompanied it. Amen.

Luke

{1:1} Many have tried to explain the beliefs we hold dear. {1:2} They passed on what they saw and learned firsthand. {1:3} I've also decided to write to you, Theophilus, so you can understand clearly. {1:4} I want you to be sure about what you've been taught. {1:5} In the time of King Herod of Judea, there was a priest named Zacharias, and his wife was Elisabeth, from the family of Aaron. They lived righteously and followed God's commandments. {1:6} But they didn't have children because Elisabeth couldn't conceive, and they were both old. {1:7} One day, while Zacharias was serving in the temple, an angel appeared to him. {1:8} The angel told Zacharias that his prayers were answered and Elisabeth would have a son named John, who would bring joy and turn many to God. {1:9} Zacharias questioned the angel because of his old age, and as a sign, the angel made him unable to speak until John's birth. {1:10} When Zacharias left the temple, people realized he had seen a vision. {1:11} Elisabeth became pregnant and stayed hidden for five months, grateful for God's kindness. {1:12} In the sixth month, the angel Gabriel was sent to a virgin named Mary, engaged to Joseph, from the family of David. {1:13} The angel greeted Mary, saying she was blessed and would conceive and bear a son named Jesus, who would be called the Son of God. {1:14} Mary wondered how this could happen since she was a virgin. {1:15} The angel explained that the Holy Spirit would come upon her, and the child would be holy. {1:16} Many of the children of Israel will turn to the Lord through him. {1:17} He will go before the Lord with the spirit and power of Elijah, to reconcile fathers with their children and the disobedient to the wisdom of the just, preparing people for the Lord. {1:18} Zacharias doubted, asking for a sign due to his old age and Elisabeth's barrenness. {1:19} The angel Gabriel identified himself and assured Zacharias of the truth of his words. {1:20} Zacharias was struck dumb until the prophecy's fulfillment because of his disbelief. {1:21} People waited for Zacharias outside the temple and were surprised by his delay. {1:22} When he came out, he couldn't speak, indicating he had seen a vision. {1:23} After his time of service, Zacharias returned home. {1:24} Elisabeth conceived and stayed hidden for five months, {1:25} grateful to God for removing her reproach. {1:26} In the sixth month, Gabriel was sent to Mary in Nazareth, engaged to Joseph of David's house. {1:27} Gabriel greeted Mary, calling her favored by God. {1:28} Mary was troubled by Gabriel's words and wondered about his greeting. {1:29} When Mary saw the angel, she was troubled by his words and wondered what kind of greeting this was. {1:30} The angel told her not to fear, for she had found favor with God. {1:31} He said she would conceive and give birth to a son named Jesus. {1:32} Jesus would be great, called the Son of the Most High, and given the throne of his ancestor David. {1:33} He would reign over Jacob's descendants forever, with an everlasting kingdom. {1:34} Mary asked how this could happen since she was a virgin. {1:35} The angel explained that the Holy Spirit would come upon her, and the power of the Most High would overshadow her, making her child the Son of God. {1:36} The angel also told Mary that her cousin Elisabeth, despite her old age and being called barren, was expecting a son. {1:37} The angel reminded Mary that nothing is impossible with God. {1:38} Mary humbly accepted God's plan, and the angel left. {1:39} Mary went quickly to a city in Judea's hill country.{1:40} Mary went to Zacharias' house and greeted Elisabeth. {1:41} When Elisabeth heard Mary's greeting, her baby leaped in her womb, and she was filled with the Holy Spirit. {1:42} Elisabeth exclaimed with a loud voice, blessing Mary and the child in her womb. {1:43} She asked why the mother of her Lord would come to her. {1:44} Elisabeth said that when she heard Mary's greeting, her baby leaped for joy in her womb. {1:45} She praised Mary for believing, knowing that what was told to her by the Lord would be fulfilled. {1:46} Mary praised the Lord, rejoicing in God her Savior. {1:47} She acknowledged God's favor upon her, despite her humble status. {1:48} Mary declared that all generations would call her blessed. {1:49} She recognized the mighty deeds of God and His holiness. {1:50} Mary spoke of God's mercy for those who fear Him throughout generations. {1:51} God has shown His strength, scattering the proud and lifting up the humble. {1:52} He has brought down the powerful and raised up the lowly. {1:53} He has filled the hungry with good things, while sending the rich away empty-handed. {1:54} He has helped His servant Israel, remembering His mercy,{1:55} as He promised to Abraham and his descendants forever. {1:56} Mary stayed with Elisabeth for about three months before returning home. {1:57} When Elisabeth's time came, she gave birth to a son. {1:58} Her neighbors and relatives heard about the Lord's mercy towards her and rejoiced with her. {1:59} On the eighth day, they came to circumcise the child and wanted to name him Zacharias after his father. {1:60} But his mother insisted he be called John. {1:61} They objected, saying no one in their family had that name. {1:62} They asked Zacharias how he wanted to name the child. {1:63} Zacharias wrote, "His name is John," and everyone was amazed.

{1:64} Immediately, Zacharias could speak again, praising God. {1:65} Fear spread among the people in the surrounding area, and news of these events spread throughout the hill country of Judea. {1:66} And all they that heard [them] laid [them] up in their hearts, saying, What manner of child shall this be! And the hand of the Lord was with him. {1:67} And his father Zacharias was filled with the Holy Ghost, and prophesied, saying, {1:68} Blessed [be] the Lord God of Israel; for he hath visited and redeemed his people, {1:69} And hath raised up an horn of salvation for us in the house of his servant David; {1:70} As he spake by the mouth of his holy prophets, which have been since the world began: {1:71} That we should be saved from our enemies, and from the hand of all that hate us; {1:72} To perform the mercy [promised] to our fathers, and to remember his holy covenant; {1:73} The oath which he sware to our father Abraham, {1:74} That he would grant unto us, that we being delivered out of the hand of our enemies might serve him without fear, {1:75} In holiness and righteousness before him, all the days of our life. {1:76} And thou, child, shalt be called the prophet of the Highest: for thou shalt go before the face of the Lord to prepare his ways;{1:77} To give knowledge of salvation unto his people by the remission of their sins, {1:78} Through the tender mercy of our God; whereby the dayspring from on high hath visited us, {1:79} To give light to them that sit in darkness and [in] the shadow of death, to guide our feet into the way of peace. {1:80} And the child grew, and waxed strong in spirit, and was in the deserts till the day of his shewing unto Israel.

{2:1} And it came to pass in those days, that there went out a decree from Caesar Augustus, that all the world should be taxed. {2:2} ([And] this taxing was first made when Cyrenius was governor of Syria.) {2:3} And all went to be taxed, every one into his own city. {2:4} And Joseph also went up from Galilee, out of the city of Nazareth, into Judaea, unto the city of David, which is called Bethlehem; (because he was of the house and lineage of David:) {2:5} To be taxed with Mary his espoused wife, being great with child. {2:6} And so it was, that, while they were there, the days were accomplished that she should be delivered. {2:7} And she brought forth her firstborn son, and wrapped him in swaddling clothes, and laid him in a manger; because there was no room for them in the inn. {2:8} And there were in the same country shepherds abiding in the field, keeping watch over their flock by night. {2:9} And, lo, the angel of the Lord came upon them, and the glory of the Lord shone round about them: and they were sore afraid. {2:10} And the angel said unto them, Fear not: for, behold, I bring you good tidings of great joy, which shall be to all people. {2:11} For unto you is born this day in the city of David a Saviour, which is Christ the Lord. {2:12} And this [shall be] a sign unto you; Ye shall find the babe wrapped in swaddling clothes, lying in a manger. {2:13} And suddenly there was with the angel a multitude of the heavenly host praising God, and saying, {2:14} Glory to God in the highest, and on earth peace, good will toward men. {2:15} And it came to pass, as the angels were gone away from them into heaven, the shepherds said one to another, Let us now go even unto Bethlehem, and see this thing which is come to pass, which the Lord hath made known unto us.{2:16} And they came with haste, and found Mary, and Joseph, and the babe lying in a manger. {2:17} And when they had seen [it,] they made known abroad the saying which was told them concerning this child. {2:18} And all they that heard [it] wondered at those things which were told them by the shepherds. {2:19} But Mary kept all these things, and pondered [them] in her heart. {2:20} And the shepherds returned, glorifying and praising God for all the things that they had heard and seen, as it was told unto them. {2:21} And when eight days were accomplished for the circumcising of the child, his name was called JESUS, which was so named of the angel before he was conceived in the womb. {2:22} And when the days of her purification according to the law of Moses were accomplished, they brought him to Jerusalem, to present [him] to the Lord; {2:23} (As it is written in the law of the Lord, Every male that openeth the womb shall be called holy to the Lord;) {2:24} And to offer a sacrifice according to that which is said in the law of the Lord, A pair of turtledoves, or two young pigeons. {2:25} And, behold, there was a man in Jerusalem, whose name [was] Simeon; and the same man [was] just and devout, waiting for the consolation of Israel: and the Holy Ghost was upon him. {2:26} And it was revealed unto him by the Holy Ghost, that he should not see death, before he had seen the Lord's Christ. {2:27} And he came by the Spirit into the temple: and when the parents brought in the child Jesus, to do for him after the custom of the law, {2:28} Then took he him up in his arms, and blessed God, and said, {2:29} Lord, now lettest thou thy servant depart in peace, according to thy word: {2:30} For mine eyes have seen thy salvation, {2:31} Which thou hast prepared before the face of all people; {2:32} A light to lighten the Gentiles, and the glory of thy people Israel. {2:33} And Joseph and his mother marvelled at those things which were spoken of him. {2:34} And Simeon blessed them, and said unto Mary his mother, Behold, this [child] is set for the fall and rising again of many in Israel; and for a sign which shall be spoken against; {2:35} (Yea, a sword shall pierce through thy own soul also,) that the thoughts of many hearts may be revealed. {2:36} And there was one Anna, a prophetess, the daughter of Phanuel, of the tribe of Aser: she was of a great age, and had lived with an husband seven years from her virginity;{2:37} And she [was] a widow of about fourscore and four years, which departed not from the temple, but served [God] with fastings and prayers night and day. {2:38} And she coming in that instant gave thanks likewise unto the Lord, and spake of him to all them that looked for redemption in Jerusalem. {2:39} And when they had performed all things according to the law of the Lord, they returned into Galilee, to their own city Nazareth. {2:40} And the child grew, and waxed strong in spirit, filled with wisdom: and the grace of God was upon him. {2:41} Now his parents went to Jerusalem every year at the feast of the passover. {2:42} And when he was twelve years old, they went up to Jerusalem after the custom of the feast. {2:43} And when they had fulfilled the days, as they returned, the child Jesus tarried behind in Jerusalem; and Joseph and his mother knew not [of it.]{2:44} But they, supposing him to have been in the company, went a day's journey; and they sought him among [their] kinsfolk and acquaintance. {2:45} And when they found him not, they turned back again to Jerusalem, seeking him. {2:46} And it came to pass, that after three days they found him in the temple, sitting in the midst of the doctors, both hearing them, and asking them questions. {2:47} And all that heard him were astonished at his understanding and answers. {2:48} And when they saw him, they were amazed: and his mother said unto him, Son, why hast thou thus dealt with us? behold, thy father and I have sought thee sorrowing. {2:49} And he said unto them, How is it that ye sought me? wist ye not that I must be about my Father's business? {2:50} And they understood not the saying which he spoke unto them. {2:51} And he went down with them, and came to Nazareth, and was subject unto them: but his mother kept all these sayings in her heart. {2:52} And Jesus increased in wisdom and stature, and in favor with God and man.

{3:1} Now in the fifteenth year of the reign of Tiberius Caesar, Pontius Pilate being governor of Judaea, and Herod being tetrarch of Galilee, and his brother Philip tetrarch of Ituraea and of the region of Trachonitis, and Lysanias the tetrarch of Abilene, {3:2} Annas and Caiaphas being the high priests, the word of God came unto John the son of Zacharias in the wilderness. {3:3} And he came into all the country about Jordan, preaching the baptism of repentance for the remission of sins; {3:4} As it is written in the book of the words of Esaias the prophet, saying, The voice of one crying in the wilderness, Prepare ye the way of the Lord, make his paths straight. {3:5} Every valley shall be filled, and every mountain and hill shall be brought low; and the crooked shall be made straight, and the rough ways [shall be] made smooth; {3:6} And all flesh shall see the salvation of God. {3:7} Then said to the multitude that came forth to be baptized of him, O generation of vipers, who hath warned you to flee from the wrath to come? {3:8} Bring forth fruits worthy of repentance, and begin not to say within yourselves, We have Abraham to [our] father: for I say unto you, That God is able of these stones to raise up children unto Abraham. {3:9} And now also the ax is laid unto the root of the trees: every tree therefore which bringeth not forth good fruit is hewn down, and cast into the fire. {3:10} And the people asked him, saying, What shall we do then? {3:11} He answereth and saith unto them, He that hath two coats, let him impart to him that hath none; and he that hath meat, let him do likewise. {3:12} Then also came the publicans to be baptized, and said unto him, Master, what shall we do? {3:13} And he said unto them, Exact no more than that which is appointed you. {3:14} And the soldiers likewise demanded of him, saying, And what shall we do? And he said unto them, Do violence to no man, neither accuse [any] falsely; and be content with your wages. {3:15} And as the people were in expectation, and all men mused in their hearts of John, whether he were the Christ, or not; {3:16} John answered, saying unto [them] all, I indeed baptize you with water; but one mightier than I cometh, the latchet of whose shoes I am not worthy to unloose: he shall baptize you with the Holy Ghost and with fire: {3:17} Whose fan [is] in his hand, and he will throughly purge his floor, and will gather the wheat into his garner; but the chaff he will burn with fire unquenchable. {3:18} And many other things in his exhortation preached he unto the people. {3:19} But Herod the tetrarch, being reproved by him for Herodias his brother Philip's wife, and for all the evils which Herod had done, {3:20} Added yet this above all, that he shut up John in prison.{3:21} Now when all the people were baptized, it came to pass, that Jesus also being baptized, and praying, the heaven was opened, {3:22} And the Holy Ghost descended in a bodily shape like a dove upon him, and a voice came from heaven, which said, Thou art my beloved Son; in thee I am well pleased. {3:23} And Jesus himself began to be about thirty years of age, being (as was supposed) the son of Joseph, which was [the son] of Heli, {3:24} Which was [the son] of Matthat, which was [the son] of Levi, which was [the son] of Melchi, which was [the son] of Janna, which was [the son] of Joseph, {3:25} Which was [the son] of Mattathias, which was [the son] of Amos, which was [the son] of Naum, which was [the son] of Esli, which was [the son] of Nagge, {3:26} Which was [the son] of Maath, which was [the son] of Mattathias, which was [the son] of Semei, which was [the son] of Joseph, which was [the son] of Juda, {3:27} Which was [the son] of Joanna, which was [the son] of Rhesa, which was [the son] of Zorobabel, which was [the son] of Salathiel, which was [the son] of Neri, {3:28} Which was [the son] of Melchi, which was [the son] of Addi, which was [the son] of Cosam, which was [the son] of Elmodam, which was [the son] of Er, {3:29} Which was [the son] of Jose, which was [the son] of Eliezer, which was [the son] of Jorim, which was [the son] of Matthat, which was [the son] of Levi, {3:30} Which was [the son] of Simeon, which was [the son] of Juda, which was [the son] of Joseph, which was [the son] of Jonan, which was [the son] of Eliakim, {3:31} Which was [the son] of Melea, which was [the son] of Menan, which was [the son] of Mattatha, which was [the son] of Nathan, which was [the son] of David, {3:32} Which was [the son] of Jesse, which was [the son] of Obed, which was [the son] of Booz, which was [the son] of Salmon, which was [the son] of Naasson, {3:33} Which was [the son] of Aminadab, which was [the son] of Aram, which was [the son] of Esrom, which was [the son] of Phares, which was [the son] of Juda, {3:34} Which was [the son] of Jacob, which was [the son] of Isaac, which was [the son] of Abraham, which was [the son] of Thara, which was [the son] of Nachor, {3:35} Which was [the son] of Saruch, which was [the son] of Ragau, which was [the son] of Phalec, which was [the son] of Heber, which was [the son] of Sala, {3:36} Which was [the son] of Cainan, which was [the son] of Arphaxad, which was [the son] of Sem, which was [the son] of Noe, which was [the son] of Lamech, {3:37} Which was [the son] of Mathusala, which was [the son] of Enoch, which was [the son] of Jared, which was [the son] of Maleleel, which was [the son] of Cainan, {3:38} Which was [the son] of Enos, which was [the son] of Seth, which was [the son] of Adam, which was [the son] of God

{4:1} And Jesus being full of the Holy Ghost returned from Jordan, and was led by the Spirit into the wilderness, {4:2} Being forty days tempted by the devil. And in those days he did eat nothing: and when they were ended, he afterward hungered. {4:3} And the devil said unto him, If thou be the Son of God, command this stone that it be made bread. {4:4} And Jesus answered him, saying, It is written, That man shall not live by bread alone, but by every word of God. {4:5} And the devil, taking him up into a high mountain, shewed unto him all the kingdoms of the world in a moment of time. {4:6} And the devil said unto him, All this power will I give thee, and the glory of them: for that is delivered unto me; and to whomsoever I will I give it. {4:7} If thou therefore wilt worship me, all shall be thine. {4:8} And Jesus answered and said unto him, Get thee behind me, Satan: for it is written, Thou shalt worship the Lord thy God, and him only shalt thou serve. {4:9} **And he brought him to Jerusalem, and set him on a pinnacle of the temple, and said unto him, If thou be the Son of God, cast thyself down from hence:** {4:10} For it is written, He shall give his angels charge over thee, to keep thee: {4:11} And in [their] hands they shall bear thee up, lest at any time thou dash thy foot against a stone. {4:12} And Jesus answering said unto him, It is said, Thou shalt not tempt the Lord thy God. {4:13} And when the devil had ended all the temptation, he departed from him for a season. {4:14} And Jesus returned in the power of the Spirit into Galilee: and there went out a fame of him through all the region roundabout. {4:15} And he taught in their synagogues, being glorified of all. {4:16} And he came to Nazareth, where he had been brought up: and, as his custom was, he went into the synagogue on the sabbath day, and stood up to read. {4:17} And there was delivered unto him the book of the prophet Esaias. And when he had opened the book, he found the place where it was written, {4:18} The Spirit of the Lord is upon me, because he hath anointed me to preach the gospel to the poor; he hath sent me to heal the brokenhearted, to preach deliverance to the captives, and recovering of sight to the blind, to set at liberty them that are bruised, {4:19} To preach the acceptable year of the

Lord. {4:20} And he closed the book, and he gave [it] again to the minister, and sat down. And the eyes of all them that were in the synagogue were fastened on him. {4:21} And he began to say unto them, This day is this scripture fulfilled in your ears. {4:22} And all bare him witness, and wondered at the gracious words which proceeded out of his mouth. And they said, Is not this Joseph's son? {4:23} And he said unto them, Ye will surely say unto me this proverb, Physician, heal thyself: whatsoever we have heard done in Capernaum, do also here in thy country. {4:24} And he said, Verily I say unto you, No prophet is accepted in his own country. {4:25} But I tell you of a truth, many widows were in Israel in the days of Elias, when the heaven was shut up three years and six months, when great famine was throughout all the land; {4:26} But unto none of them was Elias sent, save unto Sarepta, [a city] of Sidon, unto a woman [that was] a widow. {4:27} And many lepers were in Israel in the time of Eliseus the prophet; and none of them was cleansed, saving Naaman the Syrian. {4:28} And all they in the synagogue, when they heard these things, were filled with wrath, {4:29} And rose up, and thrust him out of the city, and led him unto the brow of the hill whereon their city was built, that they might cast him down headlong. {4:30} But he passing through the midst of them went his way, {4:31} And came down to Capernaum, a city of Galilee, and taught them on the sabbath days. {4:32} And they were astonished at his doctrine: for his word was with power. {4:33} And in the synagogue there was a man, which had a spirit of an unclean devil, and cried out with a loud voice, {4:34} Saying, Let [us] alone; what have we to do with thee, [thou] Jesus of Nazareth? art thou come to destroy us? I know thee who thou art; the Holy One of God. {4:35} And Jesus rebuked him, saying, Hold thy peace, and come out of him. And when the devil had thrown him in the midst, he came out of him, and hurt him not. {4:36} And they were all amazed, and spoke among themselves, saying, What a word [is] this! For with authority and power he commandeth the unclean spirits, and they come out. {4:37} And the fame of him went out into every place of the country round about. {4:38} And he arose out of the synagogue, and entered into Simon's house. And Simon's wife's mother was taken with a great fever; and they besought him for her. {4:39} And he stood over her, and rebuked the fever; and it left her: and immediately she arose and ministered unto them. {4:40} Now when the sun was setting, all those that had any sickness with diverse diseases brought them unto him; and he laid his hands on every one of them, and healed them. {4:41} And devils also came out of many, crying out, and saying, Thou art Christ the Son of God. And he rebuking [them] suffered them not to speak: for they knew that he was Christ. {4:42} And when it was day, he departed and went into a desert place: and the people sought him, and came unto him, and stayed him, that he should not depart from them. {4:43} And he said unto them, I must preach the kingdom of God to other cities also: for therefore am I sent. {4:44} And he preached in the synagogues of Galilee.

{5:1} And it came to pass, that, as the people pressed upon him to hear the word of God, he stood by the lake of Gennesaret, {5:2} And saw two ships standing by the lake: but the fishermen were gone out of them, and were washing [their] nets. {5:3} And he entered into one of the ships, which was Simon's, and prayed him that he would thrust out a little from the land. And he sat down, and taught the people out of the ship. {5:4} Now when he had left speaking, he said unto Simon, Launch out into the deep, and let down your nets for a draught. {5:5} And Simon answering said unto him, Master, we have toiled all the night, and have taken nothing: nevertheless at thy word I will let down the net. {5:6} And when they had this done, they enclosed a great multitude of fishes: and their net brake. {5:7} And they beckoned unto [their] partners, which were in the other ship, that they should come and help them. And they came, and filled both the ships, so that they began to sink. {5:8} When Simon Peter saw [it,] he fell down at Jesus' knees, saying, Depart from me; for I am a sinful man, O Lord. {5:9} For he was astonished, and all that were with him, at the draught of the fishes which they had taken: {5:10} And so [was] also James, and John, the sons of Zebedee, which were partners with Simon. And Jesus said unto Simon, Fear not; from henceforth thou shalt catch men. {5:11} And when they had brought their ships to land, they forsook all, and followed him. {5:12} And it came to pass, when he was in a certain city, behold a man full of leprosy: who seeing Jesus fell on [his] face, and besought him, saying, Lord, if thou wilt, thou canst make me clean. {5:13} And he put forth [his] hand, and touched him, saying, I will: be thou clean. And immediately the leprosy departed from him. {5:14} And he charged him to tell no man: but go, and shew thyself to the priest, and offer for thy cleansing, according as Moses commanded, for a testimony unto them. {5:15} But so much the more there was a fame abroad of him: and great multitudes came together to hear, and to be healed by him of their infirmities. {5:16} And he withdrew himself into the wilderness, and prayed. {5:17} And it came to pass on a certain day, as he was teaching, that there were Pharisees and doctors of the law sitting by, which were come out of every town of Galilee, and Judaea, and Jerusalem: and the power of the Lord was [present] to heal them. {5:18} And, behold, men brought in a bed a man who was taken with a palsy: and they sought [means] to bring him in, and to lay [him] before him. {5:19} And when they could not find by what [way] they might bring him in because of the multitude, they went upon the housetop, and let him down through the tiling with [his] couch into the midst before Jesus. {5:20} And when he saw their faith, he said unto him, Man, thy sins are forgiven thee. {5:21} And the scribes and the Pharisees began to reason, saying, Who is this which speaketh blasphemies? Who can forgive sins, but God alone? {5:22} But when Jesus perceived their thoughts, he answered and said unto them, What reason ye in your hearts? {5:23} Which is easier, to say, Thy sins be forgiven there; or to say, Rise up and walk? {5:24} But that ye may know that the Son of man hath power upon earth to forgive sins, (he said unto the sick of the palsy,) I say unto thee, Arise, and take up thy couch, and go into thine house. {5:25} And immediately he rose up before them, and took up that whereon he lay, and departed to his own house, glorifying God. {5:26} And they were all amazed, and they glorified God, and were filled with fear, saying, We have seen strange things today. {5:27} And after these things he went forth, and saw a publican, named Levi, sitting at the receipt of custom: and he said unto him, Follow me. {5:28} And he left all, rose up, and followed him. {5:29} And Levi made him a great feast in his own house: and there was a great company of publicans and of others that sat down with them. {5:30} But their scribes and Pharisees murmured against his disciples, saying, Why do ye eat and drink with publicans and sinners? {5:31} And Jesus answering said unto them, They that are whole need not a physician; but they that are sick. {5:32} I came not to call the righteous, but sinners to repentance. {5:33} And they said unto him, Why do the disciples of John fast often, and make prayers, and likewise [the disciples] of the Pharisees; but thine eat and drink? {5:34} And he said unto them, Can ye make the children of the bridechamber fast, while the bridegroom is with them? {5:35} But the days will come, when the bridegroom shall be taken away from them, and then shall they fast in those days. {5:36} And he spake also a parable unto them; No man putteth a piece of a new garment upon an old; if otherwise, then both the new maketh a rent, and the piece that was taken out of the new agreeth not with the old. {5:37} And no man putteth new wine into old bottles; else the new wine will burst the bottles, and be spilled, and the bottles shall perish. {5:38} But new wine must be put into new bottles; and both are preserved. {5:39} No man also having drunk old [wine] straightway desireth new: for he saith, The old is better.

{6:1} And it came to pass on the second sabbath after the first, that he went through the corn fields; and his disciples plucked the ears of corn, and did eat, rubbing [them] in [their] hands. {6:2} And certain of the Pharisees said unto them, Why do ye do that which is not lawful to do on the sabbath days? {6:3} And Jesus answering them said, Have ye not read so much as this, what David did, when himself was an hungred, and they which were with him; {6:4} How he went into the house of God, and did take and eat the shewbread, and gave also to them that were with him; which it is not lawful to eat but for the priests alone? {6:5} And he said unto them, That the Son of man is Lord also of the sabbath. {6:6} And it came to pass also on another sabbath, that he entered into the synagogue and taught: and there was a man whose right hand was withered. {6:7} And the scribes and Pharisees watched him, whether he would heal on the sabbath day; that they might find an accusation against him. {6:8} But he knew their thoughts, and said to the man who had the withered hand, Rise up, and stand forth in the midst. And he arose and stood forth. {6:9} Then said Jesus unto them, I will ask you one thing; Is it lawful on the sabbath days to do good, or to do evil? to save life, or to destroy [it?] {6:10} And looking roundabout upon them all, he said unto the man, Stretch forth thy hand. And he did so: and his hand was restored whole as the other. {6:11} And they were filled with madness; and communed one with another what they might do to Jesus. {6:12} And it came to pass in those days, that he went out into a mountain to pray, and continued all night in prayer to God. {6:13} And when it was day, he called [unto him] his disciples: and of them he chose twelve, whom also he named apostles; {6:14} Simon, (whom he also named Peter,) and Andrew his brother, James and John, Philip and Bartholomew, {6:15} Matthew and Thomas, James the [son] of Alphaeus, and Simon called Zelotes, {6:16} And Judas [the brother] of James, and Judas Iscariot, which also was the traitor. {6:17} And he came down with them, and stood in the plain, and the company of his disciples, and a great multitude of people out of all Judaea and Jerusalem, and from the sea coast of Tyre and Sidon, which came to hear him, and to be healed of their diseases; {6:18} And they that were vexed with unclean spirits: and they were healed. {6:19} And the whole multitude sought to touch him: for there went virtue out of him, and healed [them] all. {6:20} And he lifted up his eyes on his disciples, and said, Blessed [be ye] poor: for yours is the kingdom of God. {6:21} Blessed [are ye] that hunger now: for ye shall be filled.

Blessed [are ye] that weep now: for ye shall laugh. {6:22} Blessed are ye, when men shall hate you, and when they shall separate you [from their company,] and shall reproach [you,] and cast out your name as evil, for the Son of man's sake. {6:23} Rejoice ye in that day, and leap for joy: for, behold, your reward [is] great in heaven: for in the like manner did their fathers unto the prophets. {6:24} But woe unto you that are rich! for ye have received your consolation. {6:25} Woe unto you that are full! for ye shall hunger. Woe unto you that laugh now! for ye shall mourn and weep. {6:26} Woe unto you, when all men shall speak well of you! For so did their fathers to the false prophets. {6:27} But I say unto you which hear, Love your enemies, do good to them which hate you, {6:28} Bless them that curse you, and pray for them which despitefully use you. {6:29} And unto him that smiteth thee on the [one] cheek offer also the other; and him that taketh away thy cloke forbid not [to take thy] coat also. {6:30} Give to every man that asketh of thee; and of him that taketh away thy goods ask [them] not again. {6:31} And as ye would that men should do to you, do ye also to them likewise. {6:32} For if ye love them which love you, what thank have ye? for sinners also love those that love them. {6:33} And if ye do good to them which do good to you, what thank have ye? for sinners also do even the same. {6:34} And if ye lend [to them] of whom ye hope to receive, what thank have ye? for sinners also lend to sinners, to receive as much again. {6:35} But love ye your enemies, and do good, and lend, hoping for nothing again; and your reward shall be great, and ye shall be the children of the Highest: for he is kind unto the unthankful and [to] the evil. {6:36} Be ye therefore merciful, as your Father also is merciful. {6:37} **Judge not, and ye shall not be judged: condemn not, and ye shall not be condemned: forgive, and ye shall be forgiven:** {6:38} Give, and it shall be given unto you; good measure, pressed down, and shaken together, and running over, shall men give into your bosom. For with the same measure that ye mete withal it shall be measured to you again. {6:39} And he spake a parable unto them, Can the blind lead the blind? shall they not both fall into the ditch? {6:40} The disciple is not above his master: but every one that is perfect shall be as his master. {6:41} And why beholdest thou the mote that is in thy brother's eye, but perceivest not the beam that is in thine own eye? {6:42} Either how canst thou say to thy brother, Brother, let me pull out the mote that is in thine eye, when thou thyself beholdest not the beam that is in thine own eye? Thou hypocrite, cast out first the beam out of thine own eye, and then shalt thou see clearly to pull out the mote that is in thy brother's eye. {6:43} For a good tree bringeth not forth corrupt fruit; neither doth a corrupt tree bring forth good fruit. {6:44} For every tree is known by his own fruit. For of thorns men do not gather figs, nor of a bramble bush gather they grapes. {6:45} A good man out of the good treasure of his heart bringeth forth that which is good; and an evil man out of the evil treasure of his heart bringeth forth that which is evil: for of the abundance of the heart his mouth speaketh. {6:46} And why call ye me, Lord, Lord, and do not the things which I say? {6:47} Whosoever cometh to me, and heareth my sayings, and doeth them, I will shew you to whom he is like: {6:48} He is like a man which built an house, and digged deep, and laid the foundation on a rock: and when the flood arose, the stream beat vehemently upon that house, and could not shake it: for it was founded upon a rock. {6:49} But he that heareth, and doeth not, is like a man that without a foundation built a house upon the earth; against which the stream did beat vehemently, and immediately it fell; and the ruin of that house was great.

{7:1} Now when he had ended all his sayings in the audience of the people, he entered into Capernaum. {7:2} And a certain centurion's servant, who was dear unto him, was sick, and ready to die. {7:3} And when he heard of Jesus, he sent unto him the elders of the Jews, beseeching him that he would come and heal his servant. {7:4} And when they came to Jesus, they besought him instantly, saying, That he was worthy for whom he should do this: {7:5} For he loveth our nation, and he hath built us a synagogue. {7:6} Then Jesus went with them. And when he was now not far from the house, the centurion sent friends to him, saying unto him, Lord, trouble not thyself: for I am not worthy that thou shouldest enter under my roof: {7:7} Wherefore neither thought I myself worthy to come unto thee: but say in a word, and my servant shall be healed. {7:8} For I also am a man set under authority, having under me soldiers, and I say unto one, Go, and he goeth; and to another, Come, and he cometh; and to my servant, Do this, and he doeth [it.] {7:9} When Jesus heard these things, he marveled at him, and turned him about, and said unto the people that followed him, I say unto you, I have not found so great faith, no, not in Israel. {7:10} And they that were sent, returning to the house, found the servant whole that had been sick. {7:11} And it came to pass the day after, that he went into a city called Nain; and many of his disciples went with him, and many people. {7:12} Now when he came nigh to the gate of the city, behold, there was a dead man carried out, the only son of his mother, and she was a widow: and many people of the city were with her. {7:13} And when the Lord saw her, he had compassion on her, and said unto her, Weep not. {7:14} And he came and touched the bier: and they that bare [him] stood still. And he said, Young man, I say unto thee, Arise. {7:15} And he that was dead sat up, and began to speak. And he delivered him to his mother. {7:16} And there came a fear on all: and they glorified God, saying, That a great prophet is risen up among us; and, That God hath visited his people. {7:17} And this rumor of him went forth throughout all Judaea, and throughout all the region roundabout. {7:18} And the disciples of John shewed him of all these things. {7:19} And John calling [unto him] two of his disciples sent [them] to Jesus, saying, Art thou he that should come? or look we for another? {7:20} When the men were to come unto him, they said, John Baptist hath sent us unto thee, saying, Art thou he that should come? or look we for another? {7:21} And in that same hour he cured many of [their] infirmities and plagues, and of evil spirits; and unto many [that were] blind he gave sight. {7:22} Then Jesus answering said unto them, Go your way, and tell John what things ye have seen and heard; how that the blind see, the lame walk, the lepers are cleansed, the deaf hear, the dead are raised, to the poor the gospel is preached. {7:23} And blessed is [he,] whosoever shall not be offended in me. {7:24} And when the messengers of John were departed, he began to speak unto the people concerning John, What went ye out into the wilderness to see? A reed shaken with the wind? {7:25} But what did ye see? A man clothed in soft raiment? Behold, they which are gorgeously apparelled, and live delicately, are in kings courts. {7:26} But what went ye out to see? A prophet? Yea, I say unto you, and much more than a prophet. {7:27} This is [he,] of whom it is written, Behold, I send my messenger before thy face, which shall prepare thy way before thee. {7:28} For I say unto you, Among those that are born of women there is not a greater prophet than John the Baptist: but he that is least in the kingdom of God is greater than he. {7:29} And all the people that heard [him,] and the publicans, justified God, being baptized with the baptism of John. {7:30} But the Pharisees and lawyers rejected the counsel of God against themselves, being not baptized by him. {7:31} And the Lord said, Whereunto then shall I liken the men of this generation? and what are they like? {7:32} They are like unto children sitting in the marketplace, and calling one to another, and saying, We have piped unto you, and ye have not danced; we have mourned to you, and ye have not wept. {7:33} For John the Baptist came neither eating bread nor drinking wine; and ye say, He hath a devil. {7:34} The Son of man is coming, eating and drinking; and ye say, Behold a gluttonous man, and a winebibber, a friend of publicans and sinners! {7:35} But wisdom is justified for all her children. {7:36} And one of the Pharisees desired him that he would eat with him. And he went into the Pharisee's house, and sat down to meat. {7:37} And, behold, a woman in the city, which was a sinner, when she knew that [Jesus] sat at meat in the Pharisee's house, brought an alabaster box of ointment, {7:38} And stood at his feet behind [him] weeping, and began to wash his feet with tears, and did wipe [them] with the hairs of her head, and kissed his feet, and anointed [them] with the ointment. {7:39} Now when the Pharisee which had bidden him saw [it,] he spake within himself, saying, This man, if he were a prophet, would have known who and what manner of woman [this is] that toucheth him: for she is a sinner. {7:40} And Jesus answering said unto him, Simon, I have somewhat to say unto thee. And he saith, Master, say on. {7:41} There was a certain creditor which had two debtors: the one owed five hundred pence, and the other fifty. {7:42} And when they had nothing to pay, he frankly forgave them both. Tell me therefore, which of them will love him most? {7:43} Simon answered and said, I suppose that [he,] to whom he forgave most. And he said unto him, Thou hast rightly judged. {7:44} And he turned to the woman, and said unto Simon, Seest thou this woman? I entered into thine house, thou gavest me no water for my feet: but she hath washed my feet with tears, and wiped [them] with the hairs of her head. {7:45} Thou gavest me no kiss: but this woman since the time I came in hath not ceased to kiss my feet. {7:46} My head with oil thou didst not anoint: but this woman hath anointed my feet with ointment. {7:47} Wherefore I say unto thee, Her sins, which are many, are forgiven; for she loved much: but to whom little is forgiven, [the same] loveth little. {7:48} And he said unto her, Thy sins are forgiven. {7:49} And they that sat at meat with him began to say within themselves, Who is this that forgiveth sins also? {7:50} And he said to the woman, Thy faith hath saved thee; go in peace.

{8:1} And it came to pass afterward, that he went throughout every city and village, preaching and showing the glad tidings of the kingdom of God: and the twelve [were] with him, {8:2} And certain women, which had been healed of evil spirits and infirmities, Mary called Magdalene, out of whom went seven devils, {8:3} And Joanna the wife of Chuza Herod's steward, and Susanna, and many others, which ministered unto him of their substance. {8:4} And when much people were gathered together, and were come to him out of every city, he spake by a parable: {8:5} A sower went out to sow his seed: and as he sowed, some fell by the wayside; and it was trodden down, and the fowls of the air devoured it.

{8:6} And some fell upon a rock; and as soon as it sprung up, it withered away, because it lacked moisture. {8:7} And some fell among thorns; and the thorns sprang up with it, and choked it. {8:8} And others fell on good ground, and sprang up, and bare fruit a hundredfold. And when he had said these things, he cried, He that hath ears to hear, let him hear. {8:9} And his disciples asked him, saying, What might this parable be? {8:10} And he said, Unto you it is given to know the mysteries of the kingdom of God: but to others in parables; that seeing they might not see, and hearing they might not understand. {8:11} Now the parable is this: The seed is the word of God. {8:12} Those by the wayside are they that hear; then cometh the devil, and taketh away the word out of their hearts, lest they should believe and be saved. {8:13} They on the rock [are they,] which, when they hear, receive the word with joy; and these have no root, which for a while believe, and in time of temptation fall away. {8:14} And that which fell among thorns are they, which, when they have heard, go forth, and are choked with cares and riches and pleasures of [this] life, and bring no fruit to perfection. {8:15} But on the good ground are they, which in an honest and good heart, having heard the word, keep [it,] and bring forth fruit with patience. {8:16} No man, when he hath lighted a candle, covereth it with a vessel, or putteth [it] under a bed; but setteth [it] on a candlestick, that they which enter in may see the light. {8:17} For nothing is secret, that shall not be made manifest; neither [any thing] hid, that shall not be known and come abroad. {8:18} Take heed therefore how ye hear: for whosoever hath, to him shall be given; and whosoever hath not, from him shall be taken even that which he seemeth to have. {8:19} Then came to him [his] mother and his brethren, and could not come at him for the press. {8:20} And it was told him [by certain] which said, Thy mother and thy brethren stand without, desiring to see thee. {8:21} And he answered and said unto them, My mother and my brethren are these which hear the word of God, and do it. {8:22} Now it came to pass on a certain day, that he went into a ship with his disciples: and he said unto them, Let us go over unto the other side of the lake. And they launched forth. {8:23} But as they sailed he fell asleep: and there came down a storm of wind on the lake; and they were filled [with water,] and were in jeopardy. {8:24} And they came to him, and awoke him, saying, Master, master, we perish. Then he arose, and rebuked the wind and the raging of the water: and they ceased, and there was a calm. {8:25} And he said unto them, Where is your faith? And they, being afraid, wondered, saying one to another, What manner of man is this! For he commandeth even the winds and water, and they obeyed him. {8:26} And they arrived at the country of the Gadarenes, which is over against Galilee. {8:27} And when he went forth to land, there met him out of the city a certain man, which had devils long time, and wear no clothes, neither abode in [any] house, but in the tombs. {8:28} When he saw Jesus, he cried out, and fell down before him, and with a loud voice said, What have I to do with thee, Jesus, [thou] Son of God most high? I beseech thee, torment me not.{8:29} (For he had commanded the unclean spirit to come out of the man. For oftentimes it had caught him: and he was kept bound with chains and in fetters; and he broke the bands, and was driven off the devil into the wilderness.) {8:30} And Jesus asked him, saying, What is thy name? And he said, Legion: because many devils were entered into him. {8:31} And they besought him that he would not command them to go out into the deep. {8:32} And there was a herd of many swine feeding on the mountain: and they besought him that he would suffer them to enter into them. And he suffered them. {8:33} Then went the devils out of the man, and entered into the swine: and the herd ran violently down a steep place into the lake, and were choked. {8:34} When they fed [them] saw what was done, they fled, and went and told [it] in the city and in the country. {8:35} Then they went out to see what was done; and came to Jesus, and found the man, out of whom the devils had departed, sitting at the feet of Jesus, clothed, and in his right mind: and they were afraid. {8:36} They also which saw [it] told them by what means he that was possessed of the devils was healed. {8:37} Then the whole multitude of the country of the Gadarenes round about besought him to depart from them; for they were taken with great fear: and he went up into the ship, and returned back again. {8:38} Now the man out of whom the devils were departed besought him that he might be with him: but Jesus sent him away, saying, {8:39} Return to thine own house, and shew how great things God hath done unto thee. And he went his way, and published throughout the whole city how great things Jesus had done unto him. {8:40} And it came to pass, that, when Jesus was returned, the people [gladly] received him: for they were all waiting for him. {8:41} And, behold, there came a man named Jairus, and he was a ruler of the synagogue: and he fell down at Jesus' feet, and besought him that he would come into his house: {8:42} For he had one only daughter, about twelve years of age, and she lay a dying. But as he went the people thronged him. {8:43} And a woman having an issue of blood twelve years, which had spent all her living upon physicians, neither could be healed of any, {8:44} Came behind [him,] and touched the border of his garment: and immediately her issue of blood stanched. {8:45} And Jesus said, Who touched me? When all denied, Peter and those that were with him said, Master, the multitude throng thee and press [thee,] and sayest thou, Who touched me? {8:46} And Jesus said, Somebody hath touched me: for I perceive that virtue is gone out of me. {8:47} And when the woman saw that she was not hiding, she came trembling, and falling down before him, she declared unto him before all the people for what cause she had touched him and how she was healed immediately. {8:48} And he said unto her, Daughter, be of good comfort: thy faith hath made thee whole; go in peace. {8:49} While he spoke, there cometh one from the ruler of the synagogue's [house,] saying to him, Thy daughter is dead; trouble not the Master. {8:50} But when Jesus heard [it,] he answered him, saying, Fear not: believe only, and she shall be made whole. {8:51} And when he came into the house, he suffered no man to go in, save Peter, and James, and John, and the father and the mother of the maiden. {8:52} And all wept, and bewailed her: but he said, Weep not; she is not dead, but sleepeth. {8:53} And they laughed him to scorn, knowing that she was dead. {8:54} And he put them all out, and took her by the hand, and called, saying, Maid, arise. {8:55} And her spirit came again, and she arose straightway: and he commanded to give her meat. {8:56} And her parents were astonished: but he charged them that they should tell no man what was done.

{9:1} Then he called his twelve disciples together, and gave them power and authority over all devils, and to cure diseases. {9:2} And he sent them to preach the kingdom of God, and to heal the sick. {9:3} And he said unto them, Take nothing for [your] journey, neither staves, nor scrip, neither bread, nor money; neither have two coats apiece. {9:4} And whatsoever house ye enter into, there abide, and then depart. {9:5} And whosoever will not receive you, when ye go out of that city, shake off the very dust from your feet for a testimony against them. {9:6} And they departed, and went through the towns, preaching the gospel, and healing everywhere. {9:7} Now Herod the tetrarch heard of all that was done by him: and he was perplexed, because that it was said of some, that John was risen from the dead; {9:8} And of some, that Elias had appeared; and of others, that one of the old prophets was risen again. {9:9} And Herod said, John have I beheaded: but who is this, of whom I hear such things? And he desired to see him. {9:10} And the apostles, when they were returned, told him all that they had done. And he took them, and went aside privately into a desert place belonging to the city called Bethsaida. {9:11} And the people, when they knew [it,] followed him: and he received them, and spake unto them of the kingdom of God, and healed them that had need of healing. {9:12} And when the day began to wear away, then came the twelve, and said unto him, Send the multitude away, that they may go into the towns and country round about, and lodge, and get victuals: for we are here in a desert place. {9:13} But he said unto them, Give ye them to eat. And they said, We have no more but five loaves and two fishes; except we should go and buy meat for all these people. {9:14} There were about five thousand men. And he said to his disciples, Make them sit down by the fifties in a company. {9:15} And they did so, and made them all sit down. {9:16} Then he took the five loaves and the two fishes, and looking up to heaven, he blessed them, and brake, and gave to the disciples to set before the multitude. {9:17} And they did eat, and were all filled: and there was taken up of fragments that remained to them twelve baskets. {9:18} And it came to pass, as he was alone praying, his disciples were with him: and he asked them, "Who say the people that I am? {9:19} They answered, John the Baptist; but some [say,] Elias; and others [say,] that one of the old prophets is risen again. {9:20} He said unto them, But whom say ye that I am? Peter answered, The Christ of God. {9:21} And he straitly charged them, and commanded [them] to tell no man that thing; {9:22} Saying, The Son of man must suffer many things, and be rejected of the elders and chief priests and scribes, and be slain, and be raised the third day. {9:23} And he said to [them] all, If any [man] will come after me, let him deny himself, and take up his cross daily, and follow me. {9:24} For whosoever will save his life shall lose it: but whosoever will lose his life for my sake, the same shall save it. {9:25} For what is a man advantaged, if he gains the whole world, and loses himself, or is cast away? {9:26} For whosoever shall be ashamed of me and of my words, of him shall the Son of man be ashamed, when he shall come in his own glory, and [in his] Father's, and of the holy angels. {9:27} But I tell you of a truth, there be some standing here, which shall not taste of death, till they see the kingdom of God {9:28} And it came to pass about eight days after these sayings, he took Peter and John and James, and went up into a mountain to pray. {9:29} And as he prayed, the fashion of his countenance was altered, and his raiment [was] white [and] glistering. {9:30} And, behold, there talked with him two men, which were Moses and Elias: {9:31} Who appeared in glory, and spake of his decease which he should accomplish at Jerusalem. {9:32} But Peter and those that were with him were heavy with sleep: and when they were awake, they saw his glory, and the two men that stood with him. {9:33} And it came to pass, as they departed from him, Peter said unto Jesus,

Master, it is good for us to be here: and let us make three tabernacles; one for thee, and one for Moses, and one for Elias: not knowing what he said. {9:34} While he was speaking, there came a cloud, and overshadowed them: and they feared as they entered into the cloud. {9:35} And there came a voice out of the cloud, saying, This is my beloved Son: hear him. {9:36} And when the voice was past, Jesus was found alone. And they kept [it] close, and told no man in those days any of those things which they had seen. {9:37} And it came to pass, that on the next day, when they were coming down from the hill, many people met him. {9:38} And, behold, a man of the company cried out, saying, Master, I beseech thee, look upon my son: for he is mine only child. {9:39} And, lo, a spirit taketh him, and he suddenly crieth out; and it teareth him that he foameth again, and bruising him hardly departeth from him. {9:40} And I begged thy disciples to cast him out; and they could not. {9:41} And Jesus answering said, O faithless and perverse generation, how long shall I be with you, and suffer you? Bring thy son hither. {9:42} And as he was yet a coming, the devil threw him down, and tare [him.] And Jesus rebuked the unclean spirit, and healed the child, and delivered him again to his father. {9:43} And they were all amazed at the mighty power of God. But while they wondered every one at all things which Jesus did, he said unto his disciples, {9:44} Let these sayings sink down into your ears: for the Son of man shall be delivered into the hands of men. {9:45} But they understood not this saying, and it was hidden from them that they perceived it not: and they feared asking him of that saying. {9:46} Then there arose a reasoning among them, which of them should be greatest. {9:47} And Jesus, perceiving the thought of their heart, took a child, and set him by him, {9:48} And said unto them, Whosoever shall receive this child in my name receiveth me: and whosoever shall receive me receiveth him that sent me: for he that is least among you all, the same shall be great. {9:49} And John answered and said, Master, we saw one casting out devils in thy name; and we forbade him, because he followeth not with us. {9:50} And Jesus said unto him, Forbid [him] not: for he that is not against us is for us. {9:51} And it came to pass, when the time was come that he should be received up, he steadfastly set his face to go to Jerusalem, {9:52} And sent messengers before his face: and they went, and entered into a village of the Samaritans, to make ready for him. {9:53} And they did not receive him, because his face was as though he would go to Jerusalem. {9:54} And when his disciples James and John saw [this,] they said, Lord, wilt thou that we command fire to come down from heaven, and consume them, even as Elias did? {9:55} But he turned, and rebuked them, and said, Ye know not what manner of spirit ye are of. {9:56} For the Son of man is not come to destroy men's lives, but to save [them.] And they went to another village. {9:57} And it came to pass, that, as they went in the way, a certain [man] said unto him, Lord, I will follow thee whithersoever thou goest. {9:58} And Jesus said unto him, Foxes have holes, and birds of the air [have] nests; but the Son of man hath not where to lay [his] head. {9:59} And he said unto another, Follow me. But he said, Lord, suffer me first to go and bury my father. {9:60} Jesus said unto him, Let the dead bury their dead: but go thou and preach the kingdom of God. {9:61} And another also said, Lord, I will follow thee; but let me first go bid them farewell, which are at home at my house. {9:62} And Jesus said unto him, No man, having put his hand to the plough, and looking back, is fit for the kingdom of God.

{10:1} After these things the Lord appointed another seventy also, and sent them two and two before his face into every city and place, whether he himself would come. {10:2} Therefore said he unto them, The harvest truly [is] great, but the laborers [are] few: pray ye therefore the Lord of the harvest, that he would send forth laborers into his harvest. {10:3} Go your ways: behold, I send you forth as lambs among wolves. {10:4} Carry neither purse, nor scrip, nor shoes: and salute no man by the way. {10:5} And into whatsoever house ye enter, first say, Peace [be] to this house. {10:6} And if the son of peace be there, your peace shall rest upon it: if not, it shall turn to you again. {10:7} And in the same house remain, eating and drinking such things as they give: for the laborer is worthy of his hire. Go not from house to house. {10:8} And into whatsoever city ye enter, and they receive you, eat such things as are set before you: {10:9} And heal the sick that are therein, and say unto them, The kingdom of God is come nigh unto you. {10:10} But into whatsoever city ye enter, and they receive you not, go your ways out into the streets of the same, and say, {10:11} Even the very dust of your city, which cleaveth on us, we do wipe off against you: notwithstanding be ye sure of this, that the kingdom of God is come nigh unto you. {10:12} But I say unto you, that it shall be more tolerable on that day for Sodom, than for that city. {10:13} Woe unto thee, Chorazin! woe unto thee, Bethsaida! for if the mighty works had been done in Tyre and Sidon, which have been done in you, they had a great while ago repented, sitting in sackcloth and ashes.{10:14} But it shall be more tolerable for Tyre and Sidon at the judgment, than for you. {10:15} And thou, Capernaum, which art exalted to heaven, shalt be thrust down to hell. {10:16} He that heareth you heareth me; and he that despiseth you despiseth me; and he that despiseth me despiseth him that sent me. {10:17} And the seventy returned again with joy, saying, Lord, even the devils are subject unto us through thy name. {10:18} And he said unto them, I beheld Satan as lightning fall from heaven. {10:19} Behold, I give unto you power to tread on serpents and scorpions, and over all the power of the enemy: and nothing shall by any means hurt you. {10:20} Notwithstanding in this rejoice not, that the spirits are subject unto you; but rather rejoice, because your names are written in heaven {10:21} In that hour Jesus rejoiced in spirit, and said, I thank thee, O Father, Lord of heaven and earth, that thou hast hid these things from the wise and prudent, and hast revealed them unto babes: even so, Father; for so it seemed good in thy sight. {10:22} All things are delivered to me of my Father: and no man knoweth who the Son is, but the Father; and who the Father is, but the Son, and [he] to whom the Son will reveal [him]. {10:23} And he turned him unto [his] disciples, and said privately, Blessed [are] the eyes which see the things that ye see: {10:24} For I tell you, that many prophets and kings have desired to see those things which ye see, and have not seen [them;] and to hear those things which ye hear, and have not heard [them]. {10:25} And, behold, a certain lawyer stood up, and tempted him, saying, Master, what shall I do to inherit eternal life? {10:26} He said unto him, What is written in the law? how readest thou? {10:27} And he answering said, Thou shalt love the Lord thy God with all thy heart, and with all thy soul, and with all thy strength, and with all thy mind; and thy neighbour as thyself. {10:28} And he said unto him, Thou hast answered right: this do, and thou shalt live. {10:29} But he, willing to justify himself, said unto Jesus, And who is my neighbour? {10:30} And Jesus answering said, A certain [man] went down from Jerusalem to Jericho, and fell among thieves, which stripped him of his raiment, and wounded [him,] and departed, leaving [him] half dead. {10:31} And by chance there came down a certain priest that way: and when he saw him, he passed by on the other side. {10:32} And likewise a Levite, when he was at the place, came and looked [on him,] and passed by on the other side. {10:33} But a certain Samaritan, as he journeyed, came where he was: and when he saw him, he had compassion [on him], {10:34} And went to [him,] and bound up his wounds, pouring in oil and wine, and set him on his own beast, and brought him to an inn, and took care of him. {10:35} And on the morrow when he departed, he took out two pence, and gave [them] to the host, and said unto him, Take care of him; and whatsoever thou spendest more, when I come again, I will repay thee. {10:36} Which now of these three, thinkest thou, was neighbour unto him that fell among the thieves? {10:37} And he said, He that shewed mercy on him. Then said Jesus unto him, Go, and do thou likewise. {10:38} Now it came to pass, as they went, that he entered into a certain village: and a certain woman named Martha received him into her house. {10:39} And she had a sister called Mary, who also sat at Jesus' feet, and heard his word. {10:40} But Martha was over-serving, and came to him, and said, Lord, dost thou not care that my sister hath left me to serve alone? bid her therefore that she help me. {10:41} And Jesus answered and said unto her, Martha, Martha, thou art careful and troubled about many things: {10:42} But one thing is needful: and Mary hath chosen that good part, which shall not be taken away from her.

{11:1} And it came to pass, that, as he was praying in a certain place, when he ceased, one of his disciples said unto him, Lord, teach us to pray, as John also taught his disciples. {11:2} And he said unto them, When ye pray, say, Our Father which art in heaven, Hallowed be thy name. Thy kingdom come. Thy will be done, as in heaven, so in earth. {11:3} Give us day by day our daily bread. {11:4} And forgive us our sins; for we also forgive every one that is indebted to us. And lead us not into temptation; but deliver us from evil. {11:5} And he said unto them, Which of you shall have a friend, and shall go unto him at midnight, and say unto him, Friend, lend me three loaves; {11:6} For a friend of mine in his journey is come to me, and I have nothing to set before him? {11:7} And he from within shall answer and say, Trouble me not: the door is now shut, and my children are with me

✝ he New Testament ✣ 26

in bed; I cannot rise and give thee. {11:8} I say unto you, Though he will not rise and give him, because he is his friend, yet because of his importunity he will rise and give him as many as he needeth. {11:9} And I say unto you, Ask, and it shall be given you; seek, and ye shall find; knock, and it shall be opened unto you. {11:10} For every one that asketh receiveth; and he that seeketh findeth; and to him that knocketh it shall be opened. {11:11} If a son shall ask bread of any of you that is a father, will he give him a stone? or if he asks a fish, will he for a fish give him a serpent? {11:12} Or if he shall ask for an egg, will he offer him a scorpion? {11:13} If ye then, being evil, know how to give good gifts unto your children: how much more shall your heavenly Father give the Holy Spirit to them that ask him? {11:14} And he was casting out a devil, and it was dumb. And it came to pass, when the devil was gone out, the dumb spake; and the people wondered. {11:15} But some of them said, He casteth out devils through Beelzebub the chief of the devils. {11:16} And others, tempting him, sought of him a sign from heaven. {11:17} But he, knowing their thoughts, said unto them, Every kingdom divided against itself is brought to desolation; and a house divided against a house falleth. {11:18} If Satan also be divided against himself, how shall his kingdom stand? because ye say that I cast out devils through Beelzebub. {11:19} And if I by Beelzebub cast out devils, by whom do your sons cast them out? therefore shall they be your judges. {11:20} But if I with the finger of God cast out devils, no doubt the kingdom of God will come upon you. {11:21} When a strong man armed keepeth his palace, his goods are in peace: {11:22} But when a stronger than he shall come upon him, and overcome him, he taketh from him all his armor wherein he trusted, and divideth his spoils. {11:23} He that is not with me is against me: and he that gathereth not with me scattereth. {11:24} When the unclean spirit is gone out of a man, he walketh through dry places, seeking rest; and finding none, he saith, I will return unto my house whence I came out. {11:25} And when he cometh, he findeth it swept and garnished. {11:26} Then goeth he, and taketh to him seven other spirits more wicked than himself; and they enter in, and dwell there: and the last state of that man is worse than the first. {11:27} And it came to pass, as he spake these things, a certain woman of the company lifted up her voice, and said unto him, Blessed is the womb that bare thee, and the paps which thou hast sucked. {11:28} But he said, Yea rather, blessed are they that hear the word of God, and keep it. {11:29} And when the people were gathered thick together, he began to say, This is an evil generation: they seek a sign; and there shall no sign be given it, but the sign of Jonas the prophet. {11:30} For as Jonas was a sign unto the Ninevites, so shall also the Son of man be to this generation. {11:31} The queen of the south shall rise up in judgment with the men of this generation, and condemn them: for she came from the utmost parts of the earth to hear the wisdom of Solomon; and, behold, a greater than Solomon is here. {11:32} The men of Nineveh shall rise up in the judgment with this generation, and shall condemn it: for they repented at the preaching of Jonah; and indeed, someone greater than Jonah is here. {11:33} No one, when he has lit a candle, puts it in a secret place, or under a basket, but on a candlestick, so that those who come in may see the light. {11:34} The light of the body is the eye: therefore when your eye is single, your whole body also is full of light; but when your eye is evil, your body also is full of darkness. {11:35} Take heed therefore that the light which is in you is not darkness. {11:36} If your whole body therefore is full of light, having no part dark, the whole shall be full of light, as when the bright shining of a candle gives you light. {11:37} And as he spoke, a certain Pharisee invited him to dine with him: and he went in, and sat down to eat. {11:38} And when the Pharisee saw it, he marveled that he had not first washed it before dinner. {11:39} And the Lord said to him, Now you Pharisees make clean the outside of the cup and the dish; but inside you are full of greed and wickedness. {11:40} [You] fools, did not he who made that which is without make that which is within also? {11:41} But rather give alms of such things as you have; and indeed, all things will be clean to you. {11:42} But woe to you, Pharisees! for you tithe the mint and rue and all manner of herbs, and pass over judgment and the love of God: these you ought to have done, and not to leave the other undone. {11:43} Woe to you, Pharisees! for you love the best seats in the synagogues, and greetings in the markets. {11:44} Woe to you, scribes and Pharisees, hypocrites! for you are as graves which appear not, and the men that walk over them are not aware [of them]. {11:45} Then one of the lawyers answered, and said to him, Master, by saying these things you are also reproaching us. {11:46} And he said, Woe to you also, [you] lawyers! for you load men with burdens grievous to be borne, and you yourselves touch not the burdens with one of your fingers. {11:47} Woe to you! for you built the sepulchers of the prophets, and your fathers killed them. {11:48} Truly you bear witness that you allow the deeds of your fathers: for they indeed killed them, and you build their sepulchers. {11:49} Therefore also said the wisdom of God, I will send them prophets and apostles, and [some] of them they shall slay and persecute: {11:50} That the blood of all the prophets, which was shed from the foundation of the world, may be required of this generation; {11:51} From the blood of Abel to the blood of Zacharias, who perished between the altar and the temple: truly I say to you, It shall be required of this generation. {11:52} Woe to you, lawyers! for you have taken away the key of knowledge: you did not enter in yourselves, and those who were entering in you hindered. {11:53} And as he said these things to them, the scribes and the Pharisees began to urge [him] vehemently, and to provoke him to speak of many things: {11:54} Laying wait for him, and seeking to catch something out of his mouth, that they might accuse him.

{12:1} In the meantime, when there were gathered together a large crowd of people, so much so that they trod one upon another, he began to say to his disciples first of all, Beware of the leaven of the Pharisees, which is hypocrisy. {12:2} For there is nothing covered that will not be revealed, nor hidden that will not be known. {12:3} Therefore whatever you have spoken in darkness will be heard in the light, and what you have spoken in the ear in closets will be proclaimed upon the housetops. {12:4} And I say to you my friends, do not be afraid of those who kill the body, and after that have no more that they can do. {12:5} But I will forewarn you whom you shall fear: Fear him, who after he has killed has power to cast into hell; yes, I say to you, Fear him {12:6} Are not five sparrows sold for two farthings, and not one of them is forgotten before God? {12:7} But even the very hairs of your head are all numbered. Fear not therefore: you are of more value than many sparrows. {12:8} Also I say to you, Whoever shall confess me before men, him shall the Son of man also confess before the angels of God: {12:9} But he who denies me before men shall be denied before the angels of God. {12:10} And whoever shall speak a word against the Son of man, it shall be forgiven him: but to him that blasphemes against the Holy Ghost it shall not be forgiven. {12:11} And when they bring you to the synagogues, and to magistrates, and powers, do not take thought how or what thing you shall answer, or what you shall say: {12:12} **For the Holy Ghost shall teach you in the same hour what you ought to say.** {12:13} And one of the crowd said to him, Master, tell my brother to divide the inheritance with me. {12:14} And he said to him, Man, who made me a judge or a divider over you? {12:15} And he said to them, Take heed, and beware of covetousness: for a man's life does not consist in the abundance of the things which he possesses. {12:16} And he spoke a parable to them, saying, The ground of a certain rich man brought forth plentifully: {12:17} And he thought within himself, saying, What shall I do, because I have no room where to bestow my fruits? {12:18} And he said, This will I do: I will pull down my barns, and build greater; and there will I bestow all my fruits and my goods. {12:19} And I will say to my soul, Soul, you have much goods laid up for many years; take your ease, eat, drink, and be merry. {12:20} But God said to him, [You] fool, this night your soul shall be required of you: then whose shall those things be, which you have provided? {12:21} So [is] he that lays up treasure for himself, and is not rich toward God. {12:22} And he said to his disciples, Therefore I say to you, Take no thought for your life, what you shall eat; neither for the body, what you shall put on. {12:23} Life is more than food, and the body [is more] than clothing. {12:24} Consider the ravens: for they neither sow nor reap; which neither have a storehouse nor barn; and God feeds them: how much more are you better than the fowls? {12:25} And which of you with taking thought can add to his stature one cubit? {12:26} If you then are not able to do that at least, why take thought for the rest? {12:27} Consider the lilies how they grow: they toil not, they spin not; and yet I say to you, that Solomon in all his glory was not arrayed like one of these. {12:28} If then God so clothes the grass, which is today in the field, and tomorrow is cast into the oven; how much more [will he clothe] you, O you of little faith? {12:29} And do not seek what you shall eat, or what you shall drink, neither be of doubtful mind. {12:30} For all these things do the nations of the world seek after: and your Father knows that you have need of these things. {12:31} But rather seek the kingdom of God; and all these things shall be added unto you. {12:32} Fear not, little flock; for it is your Father's good pleasure to give you the kingdom. {12:33} Sell what you have, and give alms; provide yourselves bags which do not grow old, a treasure in the heavens that does not fail, where no thief approaches, neither moth corrupts. {12:34} For where your treasure is, there will your heart be also. {12:35} Let your loins be girded about, and your lights burning; {12:36} And you yourselves like men who wait for their lord, when he will return from the wedding; that when he comes and knocks, they may open to him immediately. {12:37} Blessed are those servants, whom the lord when he comes shall find watching: truly I say to you, that he shall gird himself, and make them sit down to eat, and will come forth and serve them. {12:38} And if he shall come in the second watch, or come in the third watch, and find them so, blessed are those servants. {12:39} And know this, that if the master of the house had known what hour the thief would come, he would have watched, and not have allowed his house to be broken into. {12:40} Therefore be ready also: for the Son of man comes at an hour when you think not. {12:41} Then Peter said to him, Lord, do you speak this parable to us, or even to all? {12:42} And the Lord said, Who then is that faithful and wise steward, whom his lord shall make ruler over his household, to give them their portion of food in due season? {12:43} Blessed is that servant, whom his lord when he comes shall find so doing. {12:44} Truly I say to you, that he will make him ruler over all that he has. {12:45} But if that servant says in his heart, My lord delays his coming; and shall begin to beat the menservants and maids, and to eat and drink, and to be drunken; {12:46} The lord of that servant will come in a day when he looks not for him, and at an hour when he is not aware, and will cut him apart, and will appoint him his portion with the unbelievers. {12:47} And that servant, who knew his lord's will, and prepared not himself, neither did according to his will, shall be beaten with many stripes. {12:48} But he who knew not, and did commit things worthy of stripes, shall be beaten with few stripes. For to whomsoever much is given, of him shall be much required: and to whom men have committed much, of him they will ask the more. {12:49} I am come to send fire on the earth; and what will I do if it is already kindled? {12:50} But I have a baptism to be baptized with; and how am I constrained till it is accomplished! {12:51} Do you suppose that I am come to give peace on earth? I tell you, No; but rather division: {12:52} For from now on there shall be five in one house divided, three against two, and two against three. {12:53} The father shall be divided against the son, and the son against the father; the mother against the daughter, and the daughter against the mother; the mother in law against her daughter in law, and the daughter in law against her mother in law. {12:54} And he said also to the people, When you see a cloud rise out of the west, immediately you say, There comes a shower; and so it is. {12:55} And when you see the south wind blow, you say, There will be heat; and it comes to pass. {12:56} Hypocrites, you can discern the face of the sky and of the earth; but how is it that you do not discern this time? {12:57} Yes, and why even of yourselves do you not judge what is right? {12:58} When you go with your adversary to the magistrate, as you are on the way, give diligence that you may be delivered from him; lest he drag you to the judge, and the judge deliver you to the officer, and the officer casts you into prison. {12:59} I tell you, you shall not depart from there, till you have paid the very last mite.

{13:1} At that time, some people told Jesus about the Galileans whose blood Pilate had mixed with their sacrifices. {13:2} Jesus answered them, "Do you think that these Galileans were worse sinners than all the other Galileans because they suffered this way? {13:3} I tell you, no! But unless you repent, you too will all perish. {13:4} Or those eighteen who died when the tower in Siloam fell on them—do you think they were more guilty than all the others living in Jerusalem? {13:5} I tell you, no! But unless you repent, you too will all perish." {13:6} Then Jesus told this parable: "A man had a fig tree growing in his vineyard, and he went to look for fruit on it but did not find any. {13:7} So he said to the man who took care of the vineyard, 'For three years now I've been coming to look for fruit on this fig tree and haven't found any. Cut it down! Why should it use up the soil?' {13:8} 'Sir,' the man replied, 'leave it alone for one more year, and I'll dig around it and fertilize it. {13:9} If it bears fruit next year, fine! If not, then cut it down.'" {13:10} Jesus was teaching in one of the synagogues on the Sabbath. {13:11} A woman was there who had been crippled by a spirit for eighteen years. She was bent over and could not straighten up at all. {13:12} When Jesus saw her, he called her forward and said to her, "Woman, you are set free from your infirmity." {13:13} Then he put his hands on her, and immediately she straightened up and praised God. {13:14} Indignant because Jesus had healed on the Sabbath, the synagogue leader said to the people, "There are six days for work. So come and be healed on those days, not on the Sabbath." {13:15} The Lord answered him, "You hypocrites! Doesn't each of you on the Sabbath untie your ox or donkey from the stall and lead it out to give it water? {13:16} Then should not this woman, a daughter of Abraham, whom Satan has kept bound for eighteen long years, be set free on the Sabbath day from what bound her?" {13:17} When he said this, all his opponents were humiliated, but the people were delighted with all the wonderful things he was doing. {13:18} Then Jesus asked, "What is the kingdom of God like? What shall I compare it to? {13:19} It is like a mustard seed, which a man took and planted in his garden. It grew and became a tree, and the birds perched in its branches." {13:20} Again he asked, "What shall I compare the kingdom of God to? {13:21} It is like yeast that a woman took and mixed into about sixty pounds of flour until it worked all through the dough." {13:22} Then Jesus went through the towns and villages, teaching as he made his way to Jerusalem. {13:23} Someone asked him, "Lord, are only a few people going to be saved?" {13:24} He said to them, "Make every effort to enter through the narrow door, because many, I tell you, will try to enter and will not be able to. {13:25} Once the owner of the house gets up and closes the door, you will stand outside knocking and pleading, 'Sir, open the door for us.' But he will answer, 'I don't know you or where you come from.' {13:26} Then you will say, 'We ate and drank with you, and you taught in our streets.' {13:27} But he will reply, 'I don't know you or where you come from. Away from me, all you evildoers!' {13:28} There will be weeping there, and gnashing of teeth, when you see Abraham, Isaac and Jacob and all the prophets in the kingdom of God, but you yourselves thrown out. {13:29} People will come from east and west and north and south, and will take their places at the feast in the kingdom of God. {13:30} Indeed there are those who are last who will be first, and first who will be last." {13:31} At that time some Pharisees came to Jesus and said to him, "Leave this place and go somewhere else. Herod wants to kill you." {13:32} He replied, "Go tell that fox, 'I will keep on driving out demons and healing people today and tomorrow, and on the third day I will reach my goal.' {13:33} In any case, I must press on today and tomorrow and the next day—for surely no prophet can die outside Jerusalem! {13:34} "O Jerusalem, Jerusalem, you who kill the prophets and stone those sent to you, how often I have longed to gather your children together, as a hen gathers her chicks under her wings, and you were not willing. {13:35} Look, your house is left to you desolate. I tell you, you will not see me again until you say, 'Blessed is he who comes in the name of the Lord.'"

{14:1} One Sabbath day, Jesus went to eat bread at the house of a chief Pharisee. They were watching him closely. {14:2} In front of him was a man with dropsy. {14:3} Jesus addressed the lawyers and Pharisees, asking, "Is it lawful to heal on the Sabbath day?" {14:4} They remained silent. So Jesus healed the man and let him go. {14:5} Then he said to them, "Which of you, if your donkey or ox falls into a pit on the Sabbath day, will not immediately pull it out?" {14:6} They couldn't answer him. {14:7} Jesus also told a parable to those who were invited, noticing how they chose the best seats. {14:8} He said to them, "When you are invited to a wedding, don't sit in the highest place, lest someone more honorable than you is invited, and the host asks you to move down, causing you embarrassment. {14:9} Instead, sit in the lowest place, so that when the host comes, he may say, 'Friend, move up higher,' and you will be honored in front of all the guests. {14:10} For whoever exalts himself will be humbled, and whoever humbles himself will be exalted.{14:11} Jesus taught, "For whoever exalts himself will be humbled, and he who humbles himself will be exalted." {14:12} Then Jesus said to the one who invited him, "When you host a dinner or supper, don't invite your friends, brothers, relatives, or rich neighbors, lest they invite you back and you are repaid. {14:13} Instead, when you host a feast, invite the poor, the maimed, the lame, and the blind. {14:14} You will be blessed because they cannot repay you. You will be repaid at the resurrection of the righteous. {14:15} One of the guests said to Jesus, "Blessed is he who will eat bread in the kingdom of God." {14:16} Jesus replied with a parable: "A man prepared a great supper and invited many guests. {14:17} At supper time, he sent his servant to tell those who were invited, 'Come, for everything is ready now.' {14:18} But they all began to make excuses. The first said he had bought a piece of land and needed to see it, so he asked to be excused. {14:19} Another said he had bought five yoke of oxen and needed to test them, so he asked to be excused. {14:20} Another said he had just gotten married and couldn't come. {14:21} The servant reported these excuses to his master. Angered, the master instructed his servant to go out quickly into the streets and lanes and bring in the poor, maimed, blind, and lame. {14:22} The servant did as commanded, but there was still room. {14:23} So the master told him to go out into the highways and hedges and compel people to come in, so that his house would be full. {14:24} Jesus concluded, "None of those who were originally invited will taste my supper. {14:25} Many people were following Jesus, and he turned to them and said, {14:26} "If anyone comes to me and does not hate his own father, mother, wife, children, brothers, sisters, and even his own life, he cannot be my disciple. {14:27} And whoever does not bear his own cross and follow me cannot be my disciple. {14:28} For which of you, desiring to build a tower, does not first sit down and count the cost, whether he has enough to complete it? {14:29} Otherwise, when he has laid a foundation and is not able to finish, all who see it will mock him, saying, 'This man began to build and was not able to finish.' {14:30} Or what king, going out to encounter another king in war, will not sit down first and deliberate whether he is able with ten thousand to meet him who comes against him with twenty thousand? {14:31} And if not, while the other is yet a great way off, he sends a delegation and asks for terms of peace. {14:32} So, therefore, any one of you who does not renounce all that he has cannot be my disciple.{14:33} Likewise, whoever of you does not forsake all that he has cannot be my disciple. {14:34} Salt is good, but if salt has lost its taste, how shall its saltiness be restored? {14:35} It is of no use either for the soil or for the manure pile. It is thrown away. He who has ears to hear, let him hear."

{15:1} Then all the tax collectors and sinners came near to him to hear him. {15:2} And the Pharisees and scribes complained, saying, "This man receives sinners and eats with them." {15:3} So he spoke this parable to them, saying: {15:4} "What man among you, having a hundred sheep, if he loses one of them, does not leave the ninety-nine in the wilderness, and go after the one which is lost until he finds it? {15:5} And when he has found it, he lays it on his shoulders, rejoicing. {15:6} And when he comes home, he calls together his friends and neighbors, saying to them, 'Rejoice with me, for I have found my sheep which was lost!' {15:7} I tell you that likewise there will be more joy in heaven over one sinner who repents than over ninety-nine just persons who need no repentance. {15:8} "Or what woman, having ten silver coins, if she loses one coin, does not light a lamp, sweep the house, and search carefully until she finds it? {15:9} And when she has found it, she calls her friends and neighbors together, saying, 'Rejoice with me, for I have found the piece which I lost!' {15:10} Likewise, I say to you, there is joy in the presence of the angels of God over one sinner who repents." {15:11} Then he said: "A certain man had two sons. {15:12} And the younger of them said to his father, 'Father, give me the portion of goods that falls to me.' So he divided to them his livelihood. {15:13} And not many days after, the younger son gathered all together, journeyed to a far country, and there wasted his possessions with prodigal living. {15:14} But when he had spent all, there arose a severe famine in that land, and he began to be in want. {15:15} Then he went and joined himself to a citizen of that country, and he sent him into his fields to feed swine. {15:16} And he would gladly have filled his stomach with the pods that the swine ate, and no one gave him anything. {15:17} "But when he came to himself, he said, 'How many of my father's hired servants have bread enough and to spare, and I perish with hunger! {15:18} I will arise and go to my father, and will say to him, "Father, I have sinned against heaven and before you, {15:19} and I am no longer worthy to be called your son. Make me like one of your hired servants."' {15:20} And he arose and came to his father. But when he was still a great way off, his father saw him and had compassion, and ran and fell on his neck and kissed him. {15:21} And the son said to him, 'Father, I have sinned against heaven and in your sight, and am no longer worthy to be called your son.' {15:22} "But the father said to his servants, 'Bring out the best robe and put it on him, and put a ring on his hand and sandals on his feet. {15:23} And bring the fatted calf here and kill it, and let us eat and be merry; {15:24} for this my son was dead and is alive again; he was lost and is found.' And they began to be merry. {15:25} "Now his older son was in the field. And as he came and drew near to the house, he heard music and dancing. {15:26} So he called one of the servants and asked what these things meant. {15:27} And he said to him, 'Your brother has come, and because he has received him safe and sound, your father has killed the fatted calf.' {15:28} But he was angry and would not go in. Therefore his father came out and pleaded with him. {15:29} So he answered and said to his father, 'Lo, these many years I have been serving you; I never transgressed your commandment at any time; and yet you never gave me a young goat, that I might make merry with my friends. {15:30} But as soon as this son of yours came, who has devoured your livelihood with harlots, you killed the fatted calf for him.' {15:31} And he said to him, 'Son, you are always with me, and all that I have is yours. {15:32} It was right that we should make merry and be glad, for your brother was dead and is alive again, and was lost and is found.'"

{16:1} Then Jesus also said to his disciples: "There was a certain rich man who had a steward, and an accusation was brought to him that this man was wasting his goods. {16:2} So he called him and said to him, 'What is this I hear about you? Give an account of your stewardship, for you can no longer be steward.' {16:3} "Then the steward said within himself, 'What shall I do? For my master is taking the stewardship away from me. I cannot dig; I am ashamed to beg. {16:4} I have resolved what to do, that when I am put out of the stewardship, they may receive me into their houses.' {16:5} "So he called every one of his master's debtors to him, and said to the first, 'How much do you owe my master?' {16:6} And he said, 'A hundred measures of oil.' So he said to him, 'Take your bill, and sit down quickly and write fifty.' {16:7} Then he said to another, 'And how much do you owe?' So he said, 'A hundred measures of wheat.' And he said to him, "Take your bill, and write eighty.' {16:8} "So the master commended the unjust steward because he had dealt shrewdly. For the sons of this world are more shrewd in their generation than the sons of light. {16:9} And I say to you, make friends for yourselves by unrighteous mammon, that when you fail, they may receive you into an everlasting home. {16:10} He who is faithful in what is least is faithful also in much; and he who is unjust in what is least is unjust also in much. {16:11} Therefore if you have not been faithful in the unrighteous mammon, who will commit to your trust the true riches? {16:12} And if you have not been faithful in what is another man's, who will give you what is your own? {16:13} "No servant can serve two masters; for either he will hate the one and love the other, or else he will be loyal to the one and despise the other. You cannot serve God and mammon." {16:14} Now the Pharisees, who were lovers of money, also heard all these things, and they derided him. {16:15} And he said to them, "You are those who justify yourselves before men, but God knows your hearts. For what is highly esteemed among men is an abomination in the sight of God. {16:16} "The law and the prophets were until John. Since that time the kingdom of God has been preached, and everyone is pressing into it. {16:17} And it is easier for heaven and earth to pass away than for one tittle of the law to fail. {16:18} "Whoever divorces his wife and marries another commits adultery; and whoever marries her who is divorced from her husband commits adultery. {16:19} "There was a certain rich man who was clothed in purple and fine linen and fared sumptuously every day. {16:20} But there was a certain beggar named Lazarus, full of sores, who was laid at his gate, {16:21} desiring to be fed with the crumbs which fell from the rich man's table. Moreover the dogs came and licked his sores. {16:22} "So it was that the beggar died, and was carried by the angels to Abraham's bosom. The rich man also died and was buried. {16:23} And being in torments in Hades, he lifted up his eyes and saw Abraham afar off, and Lazarus in his bosom. {16:24} "Then he cried and said, 'Father Abraham, have mercy on me, and send Lazarus that he may dip the tip of his finger in water and cool my tongue; for I am tormented in this flame.' {16:25} "But Abraham said to him, 'Son, remember that in your lifetime you received your good things, and likewise Lazarus evil things; but now he is comforted and you are tormented. {16:26} And besides all this, between us and you there is a great gulf fixed, so that those who want to pass from here to you cannot, nor can those from there pass to us.' {16:27} "Then he said, 'I beg you therefore, father, that you would send him to my father's house, {16:28} for I have five brothers, that he may testify to them, lest they also come to this place of torment.' {16:29} Abraham said to him, 'They have Moses and the prophets; let them hear them.' {16:30} And he said, 'No, father Abraham; but if one goes to them from the dead, they will repent.' {16:31} But he said to him, 'If they do not hear Moses and the prophets, neither will they be persuaded though one rise from the dead.'"

{17:1} Then Jesus said to his disciples, "Offenses will come, but woe to the one through whom they come! {17:2} It would be better for him to have a millstone hung around his neck and be thrown into the sea than to cause one of these little ones to stumble. {17:3} So, if your brother sins against you, rebuke him; and if he repents, forgive him. {17:4} Even if he sins against you seven times in a day, and seven times returns to you saying, 'I repent,' you must forgive him." {17:5} The apostles said to the Lord, "Increase our faith." {17:6} And the Lord said, "If you have faith as small as a mustard seed, you can say to this mulberry tree, 'Be uprooted and planted in the sea,' and it will obey you. {17:7} But which of you, having a servant plowing or tending sheep, will say to him when he has come in from the field, 'Come at once and sit down to eat'? {17:8} Instead, won't he say to him, 'Prepare my supper, and dress yourself to serve me until I have finished eating and drinking, and then you may eat and drink'? {17:9} Does he thank that servant because he did what he was told to do? I don't think so. {17:10} So you also, when you have done everything commanded of you, should say, 'We are unworthy servants; we have only done our duty.'" {17:11} As Jesus was traveling to Jerusalem, he passed through the region between Samaria and Galilee. {17:12} As he entered a village, ten men with leprosy met him. They stood at a distance {17:13} and called out in a loud voice, "Jesus, Master, have mercy on us!" {17:14} When he saw them, he said, "Go, show yourselves to the priests." And as they went, they were cleansed. {17:15} One of them, when he saw that he was healed, came back, praising God in a loud voice. {17:16} He threw himself at Jesus' feet and thanked him. This man was a Samaritan. {17:17} Jesus asked, "Were not all ten cleansed? Where are the other nine? {17:18} Has no one returned to give praise to God except this foreigner?" {17:19} Then he said to him, "Rise and go; your faith has made you well." {17:20} Once, on being asked by the Pharisees when the kingdom of God would come, Jesus replied, "The kingdom of God does not come with observation; {17:21} nor will people say, 'Here it is,' or 'There it is,' because the kingdom of God is within you." {17:22} Then he said to his disciples, "The time will come when you will long to see one of the days of the Son of Man, but you will not see it. {17:23} People will tell you, 'Look, there he is!' or 'Look, here he is!' Do not go out or chase after them. {17:24} For just as the lightning flashes and lights up the sky from one end to the other, so will be the Son of Man in his day. {17:25} "But first he must suffer many things and be rejected by this generation. {17:26} Just as it was in the days of Noah, so also will it be in the days of the Son of Man. {17:27} People were eating, drinking, marrying, and being given in marriage up to the day Noah entered the ark. Then the flood came and destroyed them all. {17:28} "It was the same in the days of Lot: People were eating and drinking, buying and selling, planting and building. {17:29} But on the day Lot left Sodom, fire and sulfur rained down from heaven and destroyed them all. {17:30} That is how it will be on the day the Son of Man is revealed. {17:31} "On that day, let no one on the housetop come down to retrieve his possessions, and likewise, let no one in the field return for anything. {17:32} Remember Lot's wife! {17:33} Whoever tries to keep their life will lose it, and whoever loses their life will preserve it. {17:34} I tell you, on that night two people will be in one bed; one will be taken and the other left. {17:35} Two women will be grinding grain together; one will be taken and the other left." {17:36} "Where, Lord?" they asked. He replied, "Wherever there is a carcass, there the vultures will gather."{17:37} When they asked him, "Where, Lord?" He replied, "Wherever there is a carcass, there the vultures will gather."

{18:1} Jesus told his disciples a story to show that they should always pray and never give up. {18:2} "There was a judge in a certain city," he said, "who neither feared God nor cared about people. {18:3} A widow of that city came to him repeatedly, saying, 'Give me justice in this dispute with my enemy.' {18:4} The judge ignored her for a while, but finally he said to himself, 'I don't fear God or care about people, {18:5} but this woman is driving me crazy. I'm going to see that she gets justice, because she is wearing me out with her constant requests!'" {18:6} Then the Lord said, "Learn a lesson from this unjust judge. {18:7} Even he rendered a just decision in the end. So don't you think God will surely give justice to his chosen people who cry out to him day and night? Will he keep putting them off? {18:8} I tell you, he will grant justice to them quickly! But when the Son of Man returns, how many will he find on the earth who have faith?" {18:9} Then Jesus told this story to some who had great confidence in their own righteousness and scorned everyone else: {18:10} "Two men went to the Temple to pray. One was a Pharisee, and the other was a despised tax collector. {18:11} The Pharisee stood by himself and prayed this prayer: 'I thank you, God, that I am not like other people—cheaters, sinners, adulterers. I'm certainly not like that tax collector! {18:12} I fast twice a week, and I give you a tenth of my income.' {18:13} "But the tax collector stood at a distance and dared not even lift his eyes to heaven as he prayed. Instead, he beat his chest in sorrow, saying, 'O God, be merciful to me, for I am a sinner.' {18:14} I tell you, this sinner, not the Pharisee, returned home justified before God. For those who exalt themselves will be humbled, and those who humble themselves will be exalted." {18:15} One day some parents brought their little children to Jesus so he could touch and bless them. But when the disciples saw this, they scolded the parents for bothering him. {18:16} Then Jesus called for the children and said to the disciples, "Let the children come to me. Don't stop them! For the Kingdom of God belongs to those who are like these children. {18:17} I tell you the truth, anyone who doesn't receive the Kingdom of God like a child will never enter it." {18:18} Once a religious leader asked Jesus this question: "Good Teacher, what should I do to inherit eternal life?" {18:19} "Why do you call me good?" Jesus asked him. "Only God is truly good. {18:20} But to answer your question, you know the commandments: 'You must not commit adultery. You must not murder. You must not steal. You must not testify falsely. Honor your father and mother.'" {18:21} The man replied, "I've obeyed all these commandments since I was young." {18:22} When Jesus heard his answer, he said, "There is still one thing you haven't done. Sell all your possessions and give the money to the poor, and you will have treasure in heaven. Then come, follow me." {18:23} But when the man heard this he became very sad, for he was very rich. {18:24} When Jesus saw this, he said, "How hard it is for the rich to enter the Kingdom of God! {18:25} In fact, it is easier for a camel to go through the eye of a needle than for a rich person to enter the Kingdom of God!" {18:26} Those who heard this said, "Then who in the world can be saved?" {18:27} He replied, "What is impossible for people is possible with God." {18:28} Peter said, "We've left our homes to follow you." {18:29} "Yes," Jesus replied, "and I assure you that everyone who has given up house or wife or brothers or parents or children, for the sake of the Kingdom of God, {18:30} will be repaid many times over in this life, and will have eternal life in the world to come." {18:31} Then Jesus took the twelve aside and said to them, "Look, we are going up to Jerusalem, and everything that is written by the prophets about the Son of Man will be fulfilled. {18:32} He will be handed over to the Gentiles, and he will be mocked, treated shamefully, and spit upon. {18:33} They will flog him and kill him, but on the third day he will rise again." {18:34} But they didn't understand any of this. The significance of his words was hidden from them, and they failed to grasp what he was talking about. {18:35} As Jesus approached Jericho, a blind beggar was sitting beside the road. {18:36} When he heard the noise of a crowd going past, he asked what was happening. {18:37} They told him that Jesus of Nazareth was passing by. {18:38} So he began shouting, "Jesus, Son of David, have mercy on me!" {18:39} "Be quiet!" the people in front yelled at him. But he only shouted louder, "Son of David, have mercy on me!" {18:40} When Jesus heard him, he stopped and ordered that the man be brought to him. As the man came near, Jesus asked him, {18:41} "What do you want me to do for you?" {18:42} "Lord," he said, "I want to see!" {18:43} And Jesus said, "Receive your sight; your faith has healed you." Instantly the man could see, and he followed Jesus, praising God. And all who saw it praised God too.

{19:1} Jesus entered Jericho and was passing through. {19:2} A man named Zacchaeus was there. He was a chief tax collector and was very wealthy. {19:3} He wanted to see who Jesus was, but because he was short, he could not see over the crowd. {19:4} So he ran ahead and climbed a sycamore-fig tree to see him, since Jesus was coming that way. {19:5} When Jesus reached the spot, he looked up and said to him, "Zacchaeus, come down immediately. I must stay at your house today." {19:6} So Zacchaeus came down at once and welcomed him gladly. {19:7} All the people saw this and began to mutter, "He has gone to be the guest of a sinner." {19:8} But Zacchaeus stood up and said to the Lord, "Look, Lord! Here and now I give half of my possessions to the poor, and if I have cheated anybody out of anything, I will pay back four times the amount." {19:9} Jesus said to him, "Today salvation has come to this house, because this man, too, is a son of Abraham. {19:10} For the Son of Man came to seek and to save the lost." {19:11} While they were listening to this, he went on to tell them a parable, because he was near Jerusalem and the people thought that the kingdom of God was going to appear at once. {19:12} He said: "A man of noble birth went to a distant country to have himself appointed king and then to return. {19:13} So he called ten of his servants and gave them ten minas. 'Put this money to work,' he said, 'until I come back.' {19:14} "But his subjects hated him and sent a delegation after him to say, 'We don't want this man to be our king.' {19:15} "He was made king, however, and returned home. Then he sent for the servants to whom he had given the money, in order to find out what they had gained with it. {19:16} "The first one came and said, 'Sir, your mina has earned ten more.' {19:17} " 'Well done, my good servant!' his master replied. 'Because you have been trustworthy in a very small matter, take charge of ten cities.' {19:18} "The second came and said, 'Sir, your mina has earned five more.' {19:19} "His master answered, 'You take charge of five cities.' {19:20} "Then another servant came and said, 'Sir, here is your mina; I have kept it laid away in a piece of cloth. {19:21} I was afraid of you, because you are a hard man. You take out what you did not put in and reap what you did not sow.' {19:22} "His master replied, 'I will judge you by your own words, you wicked servant! You knew, did you, that I am a hard man, taking out what I did not put in, and reaping what I did not sow? {19:23} Why then didn't you put my money on deposit, so that when I came back, I could have collected it with interest?' {19:24} "Then he said to those standing by, 'Take his mina away from him and give it to the one who has ten minas.' {19:25} " 'Sir,' they said, 'he already has ten!' {19:26} "He replied, 'I tell you that to everyone who has, more will be given, but as for the one who has nothing, even what they have will be taken away. {19:27} But those enemies of mine who did not want me to be king over them—bring them here and kill them in front of me.'" {19:28} After Jesus had said this, he went on ahead, going up to Jerusalem. {19:29} As he approached Bethphage and Bethany at the hill called the Mount of Olives, he sent two of his disciples, saying to them, {19:30} "Go to the village ahead of you, and as you enter it, you will find a colt tied there, which no one has ever ridden. Untie it and bring it here. {19:31} If anyone asks you, 'Why are you untying it?' say, 'The Lord needs it.'" {19:32} Those who were sent ahead went and found it just as he had told them. {19:33} As they were untying the colt, its owners asked them, "Why are you untying the colt?" {19:34} They replied, "The Lord needs it." {19:35} They brought it to Jesus, threw their cloaks on the colt and put Jesus on it. {19:36} As he went along, people spread their cloaks on the road. {19:37} When he came near the place where the road goes down the Mount of Olives, the whole crowd of disciples began joyfully to praise God in loud voices for all the miracles they had seen; {19:38} "Blessed is the king who comes in the name of the Lord!" "Peace in heaven and glory in the highest!" {19:39} Some of the Pharisees in the crowd said to Jesus, "Teacher, rebuke your disciples!" {19:40} "I tell you," he replied, "if they keep quiet, the stones will cry out." {19:41} As he approached Jerusalem and saw the city, he wept over it {19:42} and said, "If you, even you, had only known on this day what would bring you peace—but now it is hidden from your eyes. {19:43} The days will come upon you when your enemies will build an embankment against you and encircle you and hem you in on every side. {19:44} They will dash you to the ground, you and the children within your walls. They will not leave one stone on another, because you did not recognize the time of God's coming to you." {19:45} Then he entered the temple area and began driving out those who were selling. {19:46} "It is written," he said to them, "'My house will be a house of prayer'; but you have made it 'a den of robbers.'" {19:47} Every day he was teaching at the temple. But the chief priests, the teachers of the law and the leaders among the people were trying to kill him. {19:48} Yet they could not find any way to do it, because all the people hung on his words.

{20:1} On one of those days, as Jesus was teaching the people in the temple and preaching the gospel, the chief priests and the scribes, together with the elders, came up to him. {20:2} They said to him, "Tell us, by what authority are you doing these things? Who gave you this authority?" {20:3} Jesus replied, "I will also ask you a question. Tell me: {20:4} John's baptism—was it from heaven, or of human origin?" {20:5} They discussed it among themselves and said, "If we say, 'From heaven,' he will ask, 'Why didn't you believe him?' {20:6} But if we say, 'Of human origin,' all the people will stone us, because they are persuaded that John was a prophet." {20:7} So they answered that they did not know where it came from. {20:8} Jesus said to them, "Neither will I tell you by what authority I am doing these things." {20:9} Then he began to tell the people this parable: "A man planted a vineyard, rented it to some farmers and went away for a long time. {20:10} At harvest time he sent a servant to the tenants so they would give him some of the fruit of the vineyard. But the tenants beat him and sent him away empty-handed. {20:11} He sent another servant, but that one also they beat and treated shamefully and sent away empty-handed. {20:12} He sent still a third, and they wounded him and threw him out. {20:13} Then the owner of the vineyard said, 'What shall I do? I will send my son, whom I love; perhaps they will respect him.' {20:14} But when the tenants saw him, they talked the matter over. 'This is the heir,' they said. 'Let's kill him, and the inheritance will be ours.' {20:15} So they threw him out of the vineyard and killed him. What then will the owner of the vineyard do to them? {20:16} He will come and kill those tenants and give the vineyard to others." When the people heard this, they said, "God forbid!" {20:17} Jesus looked directly at them and asked, "Then what is the meaning of that which is written: 'The stone the builders rejected has become the cornerstone' ? {20:18} Everyone who falls on that stone will be broken to pieces; anyone on whom it falls will be crushed." {20:19} The teachers of the law and the chief priests looked for a way to arrest him immediately, because they knew he had spoken this parable against them. But they were afraid of the people. {20:20} Keeping a close watch on him, they sent spies, who pretended to be sincere. They hoped to catch Jesus in something he said so that they might hand him over to the power and authority of the governor. {20:21} So the spies questioned him: "Teacher, we know that you speak and teach what is right, and that you do not show partiality but teach the way of God in accordance with the truth. {20:22} Is it right for us to pay taxes to Caesar or not?" {20:23} He saw through their duplicity and said to them, {20:24} "Show me a denarius. Whose image and inscription are on it?" "Caesar's," they replied. {20:25} He said to them, "Then give back to Caesar what is Caesar's, and to God what is God's." {20:26} They were unable to trap him in what he had said there in public. And astonished by his answer, they became silent. {20:27} Some of the Sadducees, who say there is no resurrection, came to Jesus with a question. {20:28} "Teacher," they said, "Moses wrote for us that if a man's brother dies and leaves a wife but no children, the man must marry the widow and raise up offspring for his brother. {20:29} Now there were seven brothers. The first one married a woman and died childless. {20:30} The second {20:31} and then the third married her, and in the same way the seven died, leaving no children. {20:32} Finally, the woman died too. {20:33} Now then, at the resurrection, whose wife will she be, since the seven were married to her?" {20:34} Jesus replied, "The people of this age marry and are given in marriage, {20:35} But those who are considered worthy of taking part in the age to come and in the resurrection from the dead will neither marry nor be given in marriage, {20:36} and they can no longer die; for they are like the angels. They are God's children, since they are children of the resurrection. {20:37} But in the account of the burning bush, even Moses showed that the dead rise, for he calls the Lord 'the God of Abraham, and the God of Isaac, and the God of Jacob.' {20:38} He is not the God of the dead, but of the living, for to him all are alive." {20:39} Then some of the scribes responded, "Teacher, you have spoken well." {20:40} After that, they dared not ask him any more questions. {20:41} Jesus then said to them, "Why do they say that the Messiah is the son of David? {20:42} For David himself says in the Book of Psalms: 'The Lord said to my Lord, "Sit at my right hand {20:43} until I make your enemies a footstool for your feet."' {20:44} David calls him 'Lord.' How can he be his son? {20:45} As all the people listened, Jesus said to his disciples, {20:46} "Beware of the scribes, who like to walk around in long robes, and love to be greeted with respect in the marketplaces, and have the best seats in the synagogues and the places of honor at banquets. {20:47} They devour widows' houses and for a show make lengthy prayers. These men will receive greater punishment."

{21:1} Jesus looked up and saw the rich putting their gifts into the treasury. {21:2} He also saw a poor widow putting in two small copper coins. {21:3} "Truly I tell you," he said, "this poor widow has put in more than all the others. {21:4} All these people gave their gifts out of their wealth; but she out of her poverty put in all she had to live on. {21:5} Some of his disciples were remarking about how the temple was adorned with beautiful stones and with gifts dedicated to God. But Jesus said, {21:6} "As for what you see here, the time will come when not one stone will be left on another; every one of them will be thrown down." {21:7} "Teacher," they asked, "when will these things happen? And what will be the sign that they are about to take place?" {21:8} He replied: "Watch out that you are not deceived. For many will come in my name, claiming, 'I am he,' and, 'The time is near.' Do not follow them. {21:9} When you hear of wars and uprisings, do not be frightened. These things must happen first, but the end will not come right away." {21:10} Then he said to them: "Nation will rise against nation, and kingdom against kingdom. {21:11} There will be great earthquakes, famines and pestilences in various places, and fearful events and great signs from heaven. {21:12} "But before all this, they will seize you and persecute you. They will hand you over to synagogues and put you in prison, and you will be brought before kings and governors, and all on account of my name. {21:13} And so you will bear testimony to me. {21:14} But make up your mind not to worry beforehand how you will defend yourselves. {21:15} For I will give you words and wisdom that none of your adversaries will be able to resist or contradict. {21:16} You will be betrayed even by parents, brothers and sisters, relatives and friends, and they will put some of you to death. {21:17} Everyone will hate you because of me. {21:18} But not a hair of your head will perish. {21:19} Stand firm, and you will win life. {21:20} "When you see Jerusalem being surrounded by armies, you will know that its desolation is near. {21:21} Then let those who are in Judea flee to the mountains, let those in the city get out, and let those in the country not enter the city. {21:22} For this is the time of punishment in fulfillment of all that has been written. {21:23} How dreadful it will be in those days for pregnant women and nursing mothers! There will be great distress in the land and wrath against these people. {21:24} They will fall by the sword and will be taken as prisoners to all the nations. Jerusalem will be trampled on by the Gentiles until the times of the Gentiles are fulfilled. {21:25} "There will be signs in the sun, moon and stars. On the earth, nations will be in anguish and perplexity at the roaring and tossing of the sea. {21:26} People will faint from terror, apprehensive of what is coming on the world, for the heavenly bodies will be shaken. {21:27} At that time they will see the Son of Man coming in a cloud with power and great glory. {21:28} When these things begin to take place, stand up and lift up your heads, because your redemption is drawing near." {21:29} He told them this parable: "Look at the fig tree and all the trees. {21:30} When they sprout leaves, you can see for yourselves and know that summer is near. {21:31} Even so, when you see these things happening, you know that the kingdom of God is near. {21:32} "Truly I tell you, this generation will certainly not pass away until all these things have happened. {21:33} Heaven and earth will pass away, but my words will never pass away. {21:34} "Be careful, or your hearts will be weighed down with carousing, drunkenness and the anxieties of life, and that day will close on you suddenly like a trap. {21:35} For it will come on all those who live on the face of the whole earth. {21:36} Be always on the watch, and pray that you may be able to escape all that is about to happen, and that you may be able to stand before the Son of Man." {21:37} Each day Jesus was teaching at the temple, and each evening he went out to spend the night on the hill called the Mount of Olives, {21:38} and all the people came early in the morning to hear him at the temple.

{22:1} As the Feast of Unleavened Bread, known as the Passover, approached, {22:2} the chief priests and scribes plotted how to kill Jesus, fearing the people. {22:3} Then Satan entered Judas Iscariot, one of the twelve disciples. {22:4} Judas went to the chief priests and captains, discussing how he could betray Jesus to them. {22:5} They were pleased and agreed to pay him. {22:6} Judas agreed and sought an opportunity to betray Jesus away from the crowds. {22:7} On the day of Unleavened Bread, when the Passover lamb had to be sacrificed, {22:8} Jesus sent Peter and John, saying, "Go and prepare the Passover meal for us to eat." {22:9} They asked him where they should prepare it. {22:10} Jesus instructed them to follow a man carrying a pitcher of water into a house, and to ask the homeowner about using his guest chamber. {22:11} They found everything as Jesus had told them and prepared the Passover. 22:12] He will show you a big room upstairs with furniture. Get everything ready there. {22:13} So they went and found exactly what Jesus had told them, and they prepared the Passover meal.{22:14} When the hour came, Jesus sat down with the twelve apostles. {22:15} He expressed his desire to eat this Passover with them before his suffering. {22:16} He stated he wouldn't eat it again until the kingdom of God was fulfilled. {22:17} Jesus took the cup, gave thanks, and told them to share it among themselves. {22:18} He said he wouldn't drink again until the kingdom of God had come. {22:19} Then he took bread, gave thanks, broke it, and gave it to them, saying, "This is my body given for you; do this in remembrance of me." {22:20} Likewise, after supper, he took the cup, saying, "This cup is the new covenant in my blood, which is poured out for you. {22:21} "But look, the hand of the one who will betray me is with me on the table. {22:22} The Son of Man will go as it has been decreed, but woe to that man who betrays him!" {22:23} The disciples began to wonder among themselves who would do such a thing. {22:24} Then a dispute arose among them about who should be considered the greatest. {22:25} Jesus told them that in the Gentile world, kings lord it over their subjects, but among them, it should be different. {22:26} The greatest among them should be like the youngest, and the leader like one who serves. {22:27} Jesus explained that although he was among them as one who serves, they had stood by him in his trials. {22:28} He promised them a kingdom, just as his Father had promised him. {22:29} Jesus said, "I appoint to you a kingdom, just as my Father has appointed one to me. {22:30} You will eat and drink at my table in my kingdom, and you will sit on thrones judging the twelve tribes of Israel." {22:31} Jesus told Simon Peter, "Satan has asked to sift all of you as wheat. {22:32} But I have prayed for you, Simon, that your faith may not fail. And when you have turned back, strengthen your brothers." {22:33} Peter replied, "Lord, I am ready to go with you to prison and to death." {22:34} Jesus answered, "I tell you, Peter, before the rooster crows today, you will deny three times that you know me." {22:35} Jesus then asked the disciples if they lacked anything when he sent them out without money, bags, or sandals. They replied, "Nothing." {22:36} He advised them that now, if they had a purse, they should take it, and likewise a bag; and if they didn't have a sword, they should sell their cloak and buy one. {22:37} Jesus explained that what was written about him needed to be fulfilled: 'He was counted among the transgressors.' He added, "This must be fulfilled in me." {22:38} The disciples said they had two swords, and Jesus told them, "That is enough." {22:39} Jesus went to the Mount of Olives as usual, and his disciples followed him. {22:40} When they reached the place, he said, "Pray that you won't give in to temptation." {22:41} He went on, about a stone's throw away, and knelt down and prayed, {22:42} "Father, if you are willing, please take this cup of suffering away from me. Yet I want your will to be done, not mine." {22:43} Then an angel from heaven appeared and strengthened him. {22:44} He prayed more fervently, and he was in such agony of spirit that his sweat fell to the ground like great drops of blood. {22:45} At last he stood up again and returned to the disciples, only to find them asleep, exhausted from grief. {22:46} "Why are you sleeping?" he asked them. "Get up and pray, so that you will not give in to temptation." {22:47} But even as Jesus said this, a crowd approached, led by Judas, one of the twelve disciples. Judas walked over to Jesus to greet him with a kiss. {22:48} But Jesus said, "Judas, would you betray the Son of Man with a kiss?" {22:49} When the other disciples saw what was about to happen, they exclaimed, "Lord, should we fight? We brought the swords!" {22:50} And one of them struck at the high priest's slave, slashing off his right ear. {22:51} But Jesus said, "No more of this." And he touched the man's ear and healed him. {22:52} Then Jesus spoke to the leading priests, the captains of the Temple guard, and the elders who had come for him. "Am I some dangerous revolutionary," he asked, "that you come with swords and clubs to arrest me? {22:53} Why didn't you arrest me in the Temple? I was there every day. But this is your moment, the time when the power of darkness reigns." {22:54} So they arrested him and led him to the high priest's home. And Peter followed at a distance. {22:55} The guards lit a fire in the courtyard and sat around it, and Peter joined them there. {22:56} A servant girl noticed him in the firelight and began staring at him. Finally she said, "This man was one of Jesus' followers!" {22:57} But Peter denied it. "Woman," he said, "I don't even know him!" {22:58} After a while someone else looked at him and said, "You must be one of them!" "No, man, I'm not!" Peter retorted. {22:59} About an hour later someone else insisted, "This must be one of them, because he is a Galilean, too." {22:60} But Peter said, "Man, I don't know what you are talking about." And immediately, while he was still speaking, the rooster crowed. {22:61} At that moment the Lord turned and looked at Peter. Suddenly, the Lord's words flashed through Peter's mind: "Before the rooster crows tomorrow morning, you will deny three times that you even know me." {22:62} And Peter left the courtyard, weeping bitterly. {22:63} The men who held Jesus mocked him and beat him. {22:64} They blindfolded him and demanded, "Prophesy! Who hit you?" {22:65} They hurled many other insults at him. {22:66} As soon as it was morning, the elders of the people, the chief priests, and the scribes assembled and led Jesus to their high council. They said, {22:67} "Are you the Christ? Tell us." But Jesus replied, "Even if I told you, you wouldn't believe me. {22:68} And if I asked you a question, you wouldn't answer. {22:69} But from now on, the Son of Man will be seated in the place of honor at God's right hand." {22:70} They all asked, "So, are you the Son of God then?" He replied, "You say that I am." {22:71} "Why do we need any more witnesses?" they said. "We ourselves have heard him say it."

{23:1} The entire crowd got up and took Jesus to Pilate. {23:2} They began to accuse him, saying, "We found this man misleading our nation, forbidding us to pay taxes to Caesar, and saying that he himself is Christ, a king." {23:3} Pilate asked him, "Are you the King of the Jews?" He answered, "You have said so." {23:4} Then Pilate said to the chief priests and the crowds, "I find no guilt in this man." {23:5} But they were urgent, saying, "He stirs up the people, teaching throughout all Judea, from Galilee even to this place." {23:6} When Pilate heard this, he asked whether the man was a Galilean. {23:7} And when he learned that he belonged to Herod's jurisdiction, he sent him over to Herod, who was himself in Jerusalem at that time. {23:8} When Herod saw Jesus, he was very glad, for he had long desired to see him, because he had heard about him, and he was hoping to see some sign done by him. {23:9} So he questioned him at some length, but he made no answer. {23:10} The chief priests and the scribes stood by, vehemently accusing him. {23:11} And Herod with his soldiers treated him with contempt and mocked him. Then, arraying him in splendid clothing, he sent him back to Pilate. {23:12} And Herod and Pilate became friends with each other that very day, for before this they had been at enmity with each other. {23:13} Pilate then called together the chief priests and the rulers and the people, {23:14} and said to them, "You brought me this man as one who was misleading the people. And after examining him before you, behold, I did not find this man guilty of any of your charges against him. {23:15} Neither did Herod, for he sent him back to us. Look, nothing deserving death has been done by him. {23:16} I will therefore punish and release him." {23:17} [Now he was obliged to release one man to them at the feast.] {23:18} But they all cried out together, "Away with this man, and release to us Barabbas"— {23:19} a man who had been thrown into prison for an insurrection started in the city and for murder. {23:20} Pilate addressed them once more, desiring to release Jesus, {23:21} but they kept shouting, "Crucify, crucify him!" {23:22} A third time he said to them, "Why? What evil has he done? I have found in him no guilt deserving death. I will therefore punish and release him." {23:23} But they were urgent, demanding with loud cries that he should be crucified. And their voices prevailed. {23:24} So Pilate decided that their demand should be granted. {23:25} He released the man who had been thrown into prison for insurrection and murder, for whom they asked, but he delivered Jesus over to their will. {23:26} And as they led him away, they seized one Simon of Cyrene, who was coming in from the country, and laid on him the cross, to carry it behind Jesus. {23:27} And there followed him a great multitude of the people and of women who were mourning and lamenting for him. {23:28} But turning to them Jesus said, "Daughters of Jerusalem, do not weep for me, but weep for yourselves and for your children. {23:29} For behold, the days are coming when they will say, 'Blessed are the barren and the wombs that never bore and the breasts that never nursed!' {23:30} Then they will begin to say to the mountains, 'Fall on us,' and to the hills, 'Cover us.' {23:31} For if they do these things when the wood is green, what will happen when it is dry?" {23:32} Two others, who were criminals, were led away to be put to death with him. {23:33} And when they came to the place that is called The Skull, there they crucified him, and the criminals, one on his right and one on his left. {23:34} And Jesus said, "Father, forgive them, for they know not what they do." And they cast lots to divide his garments. {23:35} And the people stood by, watching, but the rulers scoffed at him, saying, "He saved others; let him save himself, if he is the Christ of God, his Chosen One!" {23:36} The soldiers also mocked him, coming up and offering him sour wine {23:37} and saying, "If you are the King of the Jews, save yourself!" {23:38} There was also an inscription over him, "This is the King of the Jews." {23:39} One of the criminals who were hanged railed at Jesus, saying, "Are you not the Christ? Save yourself and us!" {23:40} But the other rebuked him, saying, "Do you not fear God, since you are under the same sentence of condemnation? {23:41} And we indeed justly, for we are receiving the due reward of our deeds; but this man has done nothing wrong." {23:42} Then he said, "Jesus, remember me when you come into your kingdom." {23:43} And Jesus said to him, "Truly, I say to you, today you will be with me in paradise." {23:44} It was now about the sixth hour, and there was darkness over the whole land until the ninth hour, {23:45} while the sun's light failed. And the curtain of the temple was torn in two. {23:46} Then Jesus, calling out with a loud voice, said, "Father, into your hands I commit my spirit!" And having said this he breathed his last. {23:47} Now when the centurion saw what had taken place, he praised God, saying, "Certainly this man was innocent!" {23:48} And all the crowds that had assembled for this spectacle, when they saw what had taken place, returned home beating their breasts. {23:49} And all his acquaintances and the women who had followed him from Galilee stood at a distance watching these things. {23:50} Now there was a man named Joseph, from the Jewish town of Arimathea. He was a member of the council, a good and righteous man, {23:51} who had not consented to their decision and action; and he was looking for the kingdom of God. {23:52} This man went to Pilate and asked for the body of Jesus. {23:53} Then he took it down and wrapped it in a linen shroud and laid him in a tomb cut in stone, where no one had ever yet been laid. {23:54} It was the day of Preparation, and the Sabbath was beginning. {23:55} The women who had come with him from Galilee followed and saw the tomb and how his body was laid. {23:56} Then they returned and prepared spices and ointments. On the Sabbath they rested according to the commandment.

{24:1} On the first day of the week, very early in the morning, they came to the tomb, bringing the spices they had prepared. Some others were with them. {24:2} They found the stone rolled away from the tomb. {24:3} When they entered, they did not find the body of Jesus. {24:4} While they were puzzled about this, two men appeared to them in dazzling clothes. {24:5} Frightened, they bowed their faces to the ground. The men said to them, "Why do you seek the living among the dead? {24:6} He is not here; he has risen! Remember how he told you while he was still in Galilee: {24:7} 'The Son of Man must be delivered over to the hands of sinners, be crucified and on the third day be raised again.'" {24:8} Then they remembered his words. {24:9} They returned from the tomb and told all these things to the eleven and to all the others. {24:10} It was Mary Magdalene, Joanna, Mary the mother of James, and the other women with them who told this to the apostles. {24:11} But their story seemed like nonsense to them, and they did not believe them. {24:12} Peter, however, got up and ran to the tomb. Bending over, he saw the strips of linen lying by themselves, and he went away, wondering to himself what had happened. {24:13} That same day two of them were going to a village called Emmaus, about seven miles from Jerusalem. {24:14} They were talking with each other about everything that had happened. {24:15} As they talked and discussed these things with each other, Jesus himself came up and walked along with them; {24:16} but they were kept from recognizing him. {24:17} He asked them, "What are you discussing together as you walk along?" They stood still, their faces downcast. {24:18} One of them, named Cleopas, asked him, "Are you the only one visiting Jerusalem who does not know the things that have happened there in these days?" {24:19} "What things?" he asked. "About Jesus of Nazareth," they replied. "He was a prophet, powerful in word and deed before God and all the people. {24:20} The chief priests and our rulers handed him over to be sentenced to death, and they crucified him; {24:21} but we had hoped that he was the one who was going to redeem Israel. And what is more, it is the third day since all this took place. {24:22} In addition, some of our women amazed us. They went to the tomb early this morning {24:23} but didn't find his body. They came and told us that they had seen a vision of angels, who said he was alive. {24:24} Then some of our companions went to the tomb and found it just as the women had said, but they did not see Jesus." {24:25} He said to them, "How foolish you are, and how slow to believe all that the prophets have spoken! {24:26} Did not the Messiah have to suffer these things and then enter his glory?" {24:27} And beginning with Moses and all the Prophets, he explained to them what was said in all the Scriptures concerning himself. {24:28} As they approached the village to which they were going, Jesus continued on as if he were going farther. {24:29} But they urged him strongly, "Stay with us, for it is nearly evening; the day is almost over." So he went in to stay with them. {24:30} When he was at the table with them, he took bread, gave thanks, broke it and began to give it to them. {24:31} Then their eyes were opened and they recognized him, and he disappeared from their sight. {24:32} They asked each other, "Were not our hearts burning within us while he talked with us on the road and opened the Scriptures to us?" {24:33} They got up and returned at once to Jerusalem. There they found the Eleven and those with them, assembled together {24:34} and saying, "It is true! The Lord has risen and has appeared to Simon." {24:35} Then the two told what had happened on the way, and how Jesus was recognized by them when he broke the bread. {24:36} While they were talking about this, Jesus himself stood among them and said to them, "Peace be with you." {24:37} They were startled and frightened, thinking they saw a ghost. {24:38} He said to them, "Why are you troubled, and why do doubts rise in your minds? {24:39} Look at my hands and my feet. It is I myself! Touch me and see; a ghost does not have flesh and bones, as you see I have." {24:40} When he had said this, he showed them his hands and feet. {24:41} And while they still did not believe it because of joy and amazement, he asked them, "Do you have anything here to eat?" {24:42} They gave him a piece of broiled fish, {24:43} and he took it and ate it in their presence. {24:44} He said to them, "This is what I told you while I was still with you: Everything must be fulfilled that is written about me in the Law of Moses, the Prophets, and the Psalms." {24:45} Then he opened their minds so they could understand the Scriptures. {24:46} He told them, "This is what is written: The Messiah will suffer and rise from the dead on the third day, {24:47} and repentance for the forgiveness of sins will be preached in his name to all nations, beginning at Jerusalem. {24:48} You are witnesses of these things. {24:49} I am going to send you what my Father has promised; but stay in the city until you have been clothed with power from on high." {24:50} When he had led them out to the vicinity of Bethany, he lifted up his hands and blessed them. {24:51} While he was blessing them, he left them and was taken up into heaven. {24:52} Then they worshiped him and returned to Jerusalem with great joy. {24:53} And they stayed continually at the temple, praising God.

John

{1:1} In the beginning was the Word, and the Word was with God, and the Word was God. {1:2} The same was in the beginning with God. {1:3} All things were made by him; and without him was not anything that was made. {1:4} In him was life; and life was the light of men. {1:5} And the light shines in darkness; and the darkness didn't understand it. {1:6} There was a man sent from God, whose name was John. {1:7} The same came for a witness, to bear witness of the Light, that all men through him might believe. {1:8} He was not that Light, but was sent to bear witness of that Light. {1:9} That was the true Light, which lights every man that comes into the world. {1:10} He was in the world, and the world was made by him, and the world knew him not. {1:11} He came to his own, and his own people did not receive him. {1:12} But as many as received him, to them he gave power to become the sons of God, even to them that believe on his name: {1:13} Who were born, not of blood, nor of the will of the flesh, nor of the will of man, but of God. {1:14} And the Word was made flesh, and dwelt among us, (and we beheld his glory, the glory as of the only begotten of the Father,) full of grace and truth. {1:15} John bore witness to him, and cried, saying, "This was he of whom I spoke, He that comes after me is preferred before me: for he was before me." {1:16} And of his fullness have we all received, and grace for grace. {1:17} For the law was given by Moses, but grace and truth came by Jesus Christ. {1:18} No man has seen God at any time; the only begotten Son, which is in the bosom of the Father, he has declared him. {1:19} And this is the record of John, when the Jews sent priests and Levites from Jerusalem to ask him, "Who are you?" {1:20} And he confessed, and denied not; but confessed, "I am not the Christ." {1:21} And they asked him, "What then? Are you Elijah?" And he said, "I am not." "Are you that prophet?" And he answered, "No." {1:22} Then they asked him, "Who are you? so we can give an answer to those who sent us. What do you say about yourself?" {1:23} He said, "I am the voice of one crying in the wilderness, 'Make straight the way of the Lord,' as said the prophet Isaiah." {1:24} And they who were sent were of the Pharisees. {1:25} And they asked him, and said to him, "Why do you baptize then, if you are not the Christ, nor Elijah, neither that prophet?" {1:26} John answered them, saying, "I baptize with water: but there stands one among you, whom you don't know; {1:27} He it is, who coming after me is preferred before me, whose shoe's latchet I am not worthy to unloose." {1:28} These things were done in Bethabara beyond Jordan, where John was baptizing. {1:29} The next day John saw Jesus coming to him and said, "Look, the Lamb of God, who takes away the sin of the world! {1:30} This is he of whom I said, 'After me comes a man who is preferred before me: for he was before me.' {1:31} I didn't know him, but I came baptized with water so that he would be revealed to Israel." {1:32} Then John testified, "I saw the Spirit descending from heaven like a dove, and it remained on him. {1:33} I didn't know him, but the one who sent me to baptize with water told me, 'The one on whom you see the Spirit descending and remaining, this is he who baptizes with the Holy Spirit.' {1:34} And I have seen and testified that this is the Son of God." {1:35} Again the next day John stood, and two of his disciples, {1:36} And seeing Jesus walk by, he said, "Look, the Lamb of God!" {1:37} The two disciples heard him speak, and they followed Jesus. {1:38} Then Jesus turned and saw them following, and asked, "What are you seeking?" They said to him, "Rabbi" (which means Teacher), "where are you staying?" {1:39} He said to them, "Come and see." They went and saw where he was staying, and remained with him that day, for it was about the tenth hour. {1:40} One of the two who heard John speak, and followed him, was Andrew, Simon Peter's brother. {1:41} He first found his own brother Simon and said to him, "We have found the Messiah" (which is translated as Christ). {1:42} And he brought him to Jesus. Jesus looked at him and said, "You are Simon the son of John; you shall be called Cephas" (which means Peter, or Rock). {1:43} The next day Jesus decided to go to Galilee. He found Philip and said to him, "Follow me." {1:44} Now Philip was from Bethsaida, the city of Andrew and Peter. {1:45} Philip found Nathanael and said to him, "We have found him of whom Moses in the Law and also the prophets wrote, Jesus of Nazareth, the son of Joseph." {1:46} Nathanael said to him, "Can anything good come out of Nazareth?" Philip said to him, "Come and see." {1:47} Jesus saw Nathanael coming toward him and said of him, "Behold, an Israelite indeed, in whom there is no deceit!" {1:48} Nathanael said to him, "How do you know me?" Jesus answered him, "Before Philip called you, when you were under the fig tree, I saw you." {1:49} Nathanael answered him, "Rabbi, you are the Son of God! You are the King of Israel!" {1:50} Jesus answered him, "Because I said to you, 'I saw you under the fig tree,' do you believe? You will see greater things than these." {1:51} And he said to him, "Truly, truly, I say to you, you will see heaven opened, and the angels of God ascending and descending upon the Son of Man."

{2:1} On the third day, there was a wedding in Cana of Galilee, and Jesus' mother was there. {2:2} Jesus and his disciples were also invited to the wedding. {2:3} When they ran out of wine, Jesus' mother said to him, "They have no more wine." {2:4} Jesus replied to her, "Woman, what does this have to do with me? My time has not yet come." {2:5} His mother said to the servants, "Whatever he tells you to do, do it." {2:6} Now there were six stone water jars there for Jewish purification rites, each holding twenty to thirty gallons. {2:7} Jesus said to the servants, "Fill the jars with water." So they filled them to the brim. {2:8} Then he told them, "Now draw some out and take it to the master of the banquet." So they did. {2:9} When the master of the banquet tasted the water that had been turned into wine, he did not realize where it had come from, though the servants who had drawn the water knew. Then he called the bridegroom aside {2:10} and said, "Everyone brings out the choice wine first and then the cheaper wine after the guests have had too much to drink; but you have saved the best till now." {2:11} What Jesus did here in Cana of Galilee was the first of the signs through which he revealed his glory; and his disciples believed in him. {2:12} After this, he went down to Capernaum with his mother and brothers and his disciples. There they stayed for a few days. {2:13} When it was almost time for the Jewish Passover, Jesus went up to Jerusalem. {2:14} In the temple courts he found people selling cattle, sheep and doves, and others sitting at tables exchanging money. {2:15} So he made a whip out of cords, and drove all from the temple courts, both sheep and cattle; he scattered the coins of the money changers and overturned their tables. {2:16} To those who sold doves he said, "Get these out of here! Stop turning my Father's house into a market!" {2:17} His disciples remembered that it is written: "Zeal for your house will consume me." {2:18} The Jews then responded to him, "What sign can you show us to prove your authority to do all this?" {2:19} Jesus answered them, "Destroy this temple, and I will raise it again in three days." {2:20} They replied, "It has taken forty-six years to build this temple, and you are going to raise it in three days?" {2:21} But the temple he had spoken of was his body. {2:22} After he was raised from the dead, his disciples recalled what he had said. Then they believed the scripture and the words that Jesus had spoken. {2:23} While he was in Jerusalem at the Passover Festival, many people saw the signs he was performing and believed in his name. {2:24} But Jesus would not entrust himself to them, for he knew all people. {2:25} He did not need any testimony about mankind, for he knew what was in each person's heart.

{3:1} There was a Pharisee named Nicodemus, a Jewish leader, {3:2} who came to Jesus at night and said to him, "Rabbi, we know that you are a teacher who has come from God. For no one could perform the signs you are doing if God were not with him." {3:3} Jesus replied, "Very truly I tell you, no one can see the kingdom of God unless they are born again." {3:4} "How can someone be born when they are old?" Nicodemus asked. "Surely they cannot enter a second time into their mother's womb to be born!" {3:5} Jesus answered, "Very truly I tell you, no one can enter the kingdom of God unless they are born of water and the Spirit. {3:6} Flesh gives birth to flesh, but the Spirit gives birth to spirit. {3:7} You should not be surprised at my saying, 'You must be born again.' {3:8} The wind blows wherever it pleases. You hear its sound, but you cannot tell where it comes from or where it is going. So it is with everyone born of the Spirit." {3:9} "How can this be?" Nicodemus asked. {3:10} "You are Israel's teacher," said Jesus, "and do you not understand these things? {3:11} Very truly I tell you, we speak of what we know, and we testify to what we have seen, but still you people do not accept our testimony. {3:12} I have spoken to you of earthly things and you do not believe; how then will you believe if I speak of heavenly things? {3:13} No one has ever gone into heaven except the one who came from heaven—the Son of Man. {3:14} Just as Moses lifted up the snake in the wilderness, so the Son of Man must be lifted up, {3:15} that everyone who believes may have eternal life in him." {3:16} For God so loved the world that he gave his one and only

Son, that whoever believes in him shall not perish but have eternal life. {3:17} For God did not send his Son into the world to condemn the world, but to save the world through him. {3:18} Whoever believes in him is not condemned, but whoever does not believe stands condemned already because they have not believed in the name of God's one and only Son. {3:19} This is the verdict: Light has come into the world, but people loved darkness instead of light because their deeds were evil. {3:20} Everyone who does evil hates the light, and will not come into the light for fear that their deeds will be exposed. {3:21} But whoever lives by the truth comes into the light, so that it may be seen plainly that what they have done has been done in the sight of God. {3:22} After this, Jesus and his disciples went into the Judean countryside, where he spent some time with them, and was baptized. {3:23} Now John also was baptizing at Aenon near Salim, because there was plenty of water, and people were coming and being baptized. {3:24} (This was before John was put in prison.) {3:25} An argument developed between some of John's disciples and a certain Jew over the matter of ceremonial washing. {3:26} They came to John and said to him, "Rabbi, that man who was with you on the other side of the Jordan—the one you testified about—look, he is baptizing, and everyone is going to him." {3:27} To this John replied, "A person can receive only what is given them from heaven. {3:28} You yourselves can testify that I said, 'I am not the Messiah but am sent ahead of him.' {3:29} The bride belongs to the bridegroom. The friend who attends the bridegroom waits and listens for him, and is full of joy when he hears the bridegroom's voice. That joy is mine, and it is now complete. {3:30} He must become greater; I must become less." {3:31} The one who comes from above is above all; the one who is from the earth belongs to the earth, and speaks as one from the earth. The one who comes from heaven is above all. {3:32} He testifies to what he has seen and heard, but no one accepts his testimony. {3:33} Whoever has accepted it has certified that God is truthful. {3:34} For the one whom God has sent speaks the words of God, for God gives the Spirit without limit. {3:35} The Father loves the Son and has placed everything in his hands. {3:36} Whoever believes in the Son has eternal life, but whoever rejects the Son will not see life, for God's wrath remains on them.

{4:1} When the Lord learned that the Pharisees had heard that Jesus was gaining and baptizing more disciples than John— {4:2} though in fact it was not Jesus who baptized, but his disciples— {4:3} he left Judea and went back once more to Galilee. {4:4} Now he had to go through Samaria. {4:5} So he came to a town in Samaria called Sychar, near the plot of ground Jacob had given to his son Joseph. {4:6} Jacob's well was there, and Jesus, tired as he was from the journey, sat down by the well. It was about noon. {4:7} When a Samaritan woman came to draw water, Jesus said to her, "Will you give me a drink?" {4:8} (His disciples had gone into the town to buy food.) {4:9} The Samaritan woman said to him, "You are a Jew and I am a Samaritan woman. How can you ask me for a drink?" (For Jews do not associate with Samaritans.) {4:10} Jesus answered her, "If you knew the gift of God and who it is that asks you for a drink, you would have asked him and he would have given you living water." {4:11} "Sir," the woman said, "you have nothing to draw with and the well is deep. Where can you get this living water? {4:12} Are you greater than our father Jacob, who gave us the well and drank from it himself, as did also his sons and his livestock?" {4:13} Jesus answered, "Everyone who drinks this water will be thirsty again, {4:14} but whoever drinks the water I give them will never thirst. Indeed, the water I give them will become in them a spring of water welling up to eternal life." {4:15} The woman said to him, "Sir, give me this water so that I won't get thirsty and have to keep coming here to draw water." {4:16} He told her, "Go, call your husband and come back." {4:17} "I have no husband," she replied. Jesus said to her, "You are right when you say you have no husband. {4:18} The fact is, you have had five husbands, and the man you now have is not your husband. What you have just said is quite true." {4:19} "Sir," the woman said, "I can see that you are a prophet. {4:20} Our ancestors worshiped on this mountain, but you Jews claim that the place where we must worship is in Jerusalem." {4:21} "Woman," Jesus replied, "believe me, a time is coming when you will worship the Father neither on this mountain nor in Jerusalem. {4:22} You Samaritans worship what you do not know; we worship what we do know, for salvation is from the Jews. {4:23} Yet a time is coming and has now come when the true worshipers will worship the Father in the Spirit and in truth, for they are the kind of worshipers the Father seeks. {4:24} God is spirit, and his worshipers must worship in the Spirit and in truth." {4:25} The woman said, "I know that Messiah (called Christ) "is coming. When he comes, he will explain everything to us." {4:26} Then Jesus declared, "I, the one speaking to you—I am he." {4:27} Just then his disciples returned and were surprised to find him talking with a woman. But no one asked, "What do you want?" or "Why are you talking with her?" {4:28} Then, leaving her water jar, the woman went back to the town and said to the people, {4:29} "Come, see a man who told me everything I ever did. Could this be the Messiah?" {4:30} They came out of the town and made their way toward him. {4:31} Meanwhile, his disciples urged him, "Rabbi, eat something." {4:32} But he said to them, "I have food to eat that you know nothing about." {4:33} Then his disciples said to each other, "Could someone have brought him food?" {4:34} "My food," said Jesus, "is to do the will of him who sent me and to finish his work. {4:35} Don't you have a saying, 'It's still four months until harvest'? I tell you, open your eyes and look at the fields! They are ripe for harvest. {4:36} Even now the one who reaps draws a wage and harvests a crop for eternal life, so that the sower and the reaper may be glad together. {4:37} Thus the saying 'One sows and another reaps' is true. {4:38} I sent you to reap what you have not worked for. Others have done the hard work, and you have reaped the benefits of their labor." {4:39} Many of the Samaritans from that town believed in him because of the woman's testimony, "He told me everything I ever did." {4:40} So when the Samaritans came to him, they urged him to stay with them, and he stayed two days. {4:41} And because of his words many more became believers. {4:42} They said to the woman, "We no longer believe just because of what you said; now we have heard for ourselves, and we know that this man really is the Savior of the world." {4:43} After the two days he left for Galilee. {4:44} (Now Jesus himself has pointed out that a prophet has no honor in his own country.) {4:45} When he arrived in Galilee, the Galileans welcomed him. They had seen all that he had done in Jerusalem at the Passover Festival, for they also had been there. {4:46} Once more he visited Cana in Galilee, where he had turned the water into wine. And there was a certain royal official whose son lay sick at Capernaum. {4:47} When this man heard that Jesus had arrived in Galilee from Judea, he went to him and begged him to come and heal his son, who was close to death. {4:48} "Unless you people see signs and wonders," Jesus told him, "you will never believe." {4:49} The royal official said, "Sir, come down before my child dies." {4:50} "Go," Jesus replied, "your son will live." The man took Jesus at his word and departed. {4:51} While he was still on the way, his servants met him with the news that his boy was living. {4:52} When he inquired as to the time when his son got better, they said to him, "Yesterday, at one in the afternoon, the fever left him." {4:53} Then the father realized that this was the exact time at which Jesus had said to him, "Your son will live." So he and his whole household believed. {4:54} This was the second sign Jesus performed after coming from Judea to Galilee.

{5:1} After this, there was a Jewish festival, and Jesus went up to Jerusalem. {5:2} Now in Jerusalem near the Sheep Gate, there is a pool, which in Aramaic is called Bethesda and which is surrounded by five covered colonnades. {5:3} Here a great number of disabled people used to lie—the blind, the lame, the paralyzed. {5:4} One who was there had been an invalid for thirty-eight years. {5:5} When Jesus saw him lying there and learned that he had been in this condition for a long time, he asked him, "Do you want to get well?" {5:6} "Sir," the invalid replied, "I have no one to help me into the pool when the water is stirred. While I am trying to get in, someone else goes down ahead of me." {5:7} Then Jesus said to him, "Get up! Pick up your mat and walk." {5:8} At once the man was cured; he picked up his mat and walked. The day on which this took place was a Sabbath. {5:9} The Jewish leaders said to the man who had been healed, "It is the Sabbath; the law forbids you to carry your mat." {5:10} But he replied, "The man who made me well said to me, 'Pick up your mat and walk.'" {5:11} So they asked him, "Who is this fellow who told you to pick it up and walk?" {5:12} The man who was healed had no idea who it was, for Jesus had slipped away into the crowd that was there. {5:13} Later Jesus found him at the temple and said to him, "See, you are well again. Stop sinning or something worse may happen to you." {5:14} The man went away and told the Jewish leaders that it was Jesus who had made him well. {5:15} So, because Jesus was doing these things on the Sabbath, the Jewish leaders began to persecute him. {5:16} In his defense Jesus said to them, "My Father is always at his work to this very day, and I too am working." {5:17} For this reason they tried all the more to kill him; not only was he breaking the Sabbath, but he was even calling God his own Father, making himself equal with God. {5:18} Jesus gave them this answer: "Very truly I tell you, the Son can do nothing by himself; he can do only what he sees his Father doing, because whatever the Father does the Son also does. {5:19} For the Father loves the Son and shows him all he does. Yes, and he will show him even greater works than these, so that you will be amazed. {5:20} For just as the Father raises the dead and gives them life, even so the Son gives life to whom he is pleased to give it. {5:21} Moreover, the Father judges no one, but has entrusted all judgment to the Son, {5:22} that all may honor the Son just as they honor the Father. Whoever does not honor the Son does not honor the Father, who sent him. {5:23} "Very truly I tell you, whoever hears my word and believes him who sent me has eternal life and will not be judged but has crossed over from death to life. {5:24} "Very truly I tell you, a time is coming and has now come when the dead will hear the voice of the Son of God and those who hear will live. {5:25} For as the Father has life in himself, so he has granted the Son also to have life in himself. {5:26} And he has given him authority to judge because he is the Son of Man. {5:27} "Do not be amazed at this, for a time is coming when all who are in their graves will hear his voice {5:28} and come out—those who have done what is good will rise to live, and those who have done what is evil will rise to be condemned. {5:29} Those who have done good will rise to live, and those who have done evil will rise to be condemned. {5:30} I can do nothing on my own. I judge as God tells me. Therefore, my judgment is just, because I carry out the will of the one who sent me, not my own will. {5:31} If I were to testify on my own behalf, my testimony would not be valid. {5:32} There is another who testifies about me, and I know that his testimony about me is true. {5:33} You have sent it to John and he has testified to the truth. {5:34} Not that I accept human testimony; but I mention it that you may be saved. {5:35} John was a lamp that burned and gave light, and you chose for a time to enjoy his light. {5:36} "I have testimony weightier than that of John. For the works that the Father has given me to finish—the very works that I am doing—testify that the Father has sent me. {5:37} And the Father who sent me has himself testified concerning me. You have never heard his voice nor seen his form, {5:38} nor does his word dwell in you, for you do not believe the one he sent. {5:39} You study the Scriptures diligently because you think that in them you have eternal life. These are the very Scriptures that testify about me, {5:40} yet you refuse to come to me to have life. {5:41} "I do not accept glory from human beings, {5:42} but I know you. I know that you do not have the love of God in your hearts. {5:43} I have come in my Father's name, and you do not accept me; but if someone else comes in his own name, you will accept him. {5:44} How can you believe since you accept glory from one another but do not seek the glory that comes from the only God? {5:45} "But do not think I will accuse you before the Father. Your accuser is Moses, on whom your hopes are set. {5:46} If you believed in Moses, you would believe me, for he wrote about me. {5:47} But since you do not believe what he wrote, how are you going to believe what I say?"

{6:1} After these things, Jesus crossed the Sea of Galilee, also known as the Sea of Tiberias. {6:2} A large crowd followed him because they saw the miracles he performed on the sick. {6:3} Jesus went up on a mountainside and sat down with his disciples. {6:4} The Jewish Passover feast was near. {6:5} When Jesus looked up and saw a great crowd coming toward him, he said to Philip, "Where shall we buy bread for these people to eat?" {6:6} He asked this only to test him, for he already had in mind what he was going to do. {6:7} Philip answered him, "It would take more than half a year's wages to buy enough bread for each one to have a bite!" {6:8} Another of his disciples, Andrew, Simon Peter's brother, spoke up, {6:9} "Here is a boy with five small barley loaves and two small fish, but how far will they go among so many?" {6:10} Jesus said, "Have the people sit down." There was plenty of grass in that place, and they sat down (about five thousand men were there). {6:11} Jesus then took the loaves, gave thanks, and distributed to those who were seated as much as they wanted. He did the same with the fish. {6:12} When they had all had enough to eat, he said to his disciples, "Gather the pieces that are left over. Let nothing be wasted." {6:13} So they gathered them and filled twelve baskets with the pieces of the five barley loaves left over by those who had eaten. {6:14} After the people saw the sign Jesus performed, they began to say, "Surely this is the Prophet who is to come into the world." {6:15} Jesus, knowing that they intended to come and make him king by force, withdrew again to a mountain by himself alone. {6:16} When evening came, his disciples went down to the lake, {6:17} where they got into a boat and set off across the lake for Capernaum. By now it was dark, and Jesus had not yet joined them. {6:18} A strong wind was blowing, and the waters grew rough. {6:19} When they had rowed about three or four miles, they saw Jesus approaching the boat, walking on the water; and they were frightened. {6:20} But he said to them, "It is I; don't be afraid." {6:21} Then they were willing to take him into the boat, and immediately the boat reached the shore where they were heading. {6:22} The next day, the crowd that had stayed on the opposite shore of the lake realized that only one boat had been there, and that Jesus had not entered it with his disciples, but that they had gone away alone. {6:23} Then some boats from Tiberias landed near the place where the people had eaten the bread after the Lord had given thanks. {6:24} Once the crowd realized that neither Jesus nor his disciples were there, they got into the boats and went to Capernaum in search of Jesus. {6:25} When they found him on the other side of the lake, they asked him, "Rabbi, when did you get here?" {6:26} Jesus answered, "Very truly I tell you, you are looking for me, not because you saw the signs I performed but because you ate the loaves and had your fill. {6:27} Do not work for food that spoils, but for food that endures to eternal life, which the Son of Man will give you. For on him God the Father has placed his seal of approval." {6:28} Then they asked him, "What must we do to do the works God requires?" {6:29} Jesus answered, "The work of God is this: to believe in the one he has sent." {6:30} So they asked him, "What sign will you give that we may see it and believe you? What will you do? {6:31} Our ancestors ate the manna in the wilderness; as it is written: 'He gave them bread from heaven to eat.'" {6:32} Jesus said to them, "Very truly I tell you, it is not Moses who has given you the bread from heaven, but it is my Father who gives you the true bread from heaven. {6:33} For the bread of God is the bread that comes down from heaven and gives life to the world." {6:34} "Sir," they said, "always give us this bread." {6:35} Then Jesus declared, "I am the bread of life. Whoever comes to me will never go hungry, and whoever believes in me will never be thirsty. {6:36} But as I told you, you have seen me and still you do not believe me. {6:37} All those the Father gives me will come to me, and whoever comes to me I will never drive away. {6:38} For I have come down from heaven not to do my will but to do the will of him who sent me.{6:39} And this is the will of him who sent me, that I shall lose none of all those he has given me, but raise them up at the last day. {6:40} For my Father's will is that everyone who looks to the Son and believes in him shall have eternal life, and I will raise them up at the last day. {6:41} At this the Jews there began to grumble about him because he said, "I am the bread that came down from heaven." {6:42} They said, "Is this not Jesus, the son of Joseph, whose father and mother we know? How can he now say, 'I came down from heaven'?" {6:43} "Stop grumbling among yourselves," Jesus answered. {6:44} "No one can come to me unless the Father who sent me draws them, and I will raise them up at the last day. {6:45} It is written in the Prophets: 'They will all be taught by God.' Everyone who has heard the Father and learned from him comes to me. {6:46} No one has seen the Father except the one who is from God; only he has seen the Father. {6:47} Very truly I tell you, the one who believes has eternal life. {6:48} I am the bread of life. {6:49} Your ancestors ate the manna in the wilderness, yet they died. {6:50} But here is the bread that comes down from heaven, which anyone may eat and not die. {6:51} I am the living bread that came down from heaven. Whoever eats this bread will live forever. This bread is my flesh, which I will give for the life of the world." {6:52} Then the Jews began to argue sharply among themselves, "How can this man give us his flesh to eat?" {6:53} Jesus said to them, "Very truly I tell you, unless you eat the flesh of the Son of Man and drink his blood, you have no life in you. {6:54} Whoever eats my flesh and drinks my blood has eternal life, and I will raise them up at the last day. {6:55} For my flesh is real food and my blood is real drink. {6:56} Whoever eats my flesh and drinks my blood remains in me, and I in them. {6:57} Just as the living Father sent me and I live because of the Father, so the one who feeds on me will live because of me. {6:58} This is the bread that came down from heaven. Your ancestors ate manna and died, but whoever feeds on this bread will live forever." {6:59} He said this while teaching in the synagogue in Capernaum. {6:60} On hearing it, many of his disciples said, "This is a hard teaching. Who can accept it?" {6:61} Aware that his disciples were grumbling about this, Jesus said to them, "Does this offend you? {6:62} Then what if you see the Son of Man ascend to where he was before! {6:63} The Spirit gives life; the flesh counts for nothing. The words I have spoken to you—they are full of the Spirit and life. {6:64} Yet there are some of you who do not believe." For Jesus had known from the beginning which of them did not believe and who would betray him. {6:65} He went on to say, "This is why I told you that no one can come to me unless the Father has enabled them." {6:66} From that time, many of his disciples turned back and no longer followed him. {6:67} "You do not want to leave too, do you?" Jesus asked the Twelve. {6:68} Simon Peter answered him, "Lord, to whom shall we go? You have the words of eternal life. {6:69} We have come to believe and to know that you are the Holy One of God." {6:70} Jesus replied, "Have I not chosen you, the Twelve? Yet one of you is a devil!" {6:71} (He meant Judas, the son of Simon Iscariot, who, though one of the Twelve, was later to betray him.)

{7:1} After these things, Jesus stayed in Galilee because he did not want to go about in Judea, as the Jewish leaders there were plotting to kill him.

{7:2} Now the Jewish Festival of Tabernacles is near. {7:3} Jesus' brothers said to him, "Leave Galilee and go to Judea, so that your disciples there may see the works you do. {7:4} No one who wants to become a public figure acts in secret. Since you are doing these things, show yourself to the world." {7:5} Even his own brothers did not believe in him. {7:6} Therefore Jesus told them, "My time is not yet here; for you anytime will do. {7:7} The world cannot hate you, but it hates me because I testify that its works are evil. {7:8} You go to the festival. I am not going to this festival, because my time has not yet fully come." {7:9} After he had said this, he stayed in Galilee. {7:10} However, after his brothers had left for the festival, he went also, not publicly, but in secret. {7:11} Now at the festival the Jewish leaders were watching for Jesus and asking, "Where is he?" {7:12} Among the crowds there was widespread whispering about him. Some said, "He is a good man." Others replied, "No, he deceives the people." {7:13} But no one would say anything publicly about him for fear of the Jewish leaders. {7:14} During the middle of the festival, Jesus went up into the temple courts and began to teach. {7:15} The Jews there were amazed and asked, "How did this man get such learning without having been taught?" {7:16} Jesus answered, "My teaching is not my own. It comes from the one who sent me. {7:17} Anyone who chooses to do the will of God will find out whether my teaching comes from God or whether I speak on my own. {7:18} Whoever speaks on their own does so to gain personal glory, but he who seeks the glory of the one who sent him is a man of truth; there is nothing false about him. {7:19} Has not Moses given you the law? Yet not one of you keeps the law. Why are you trying to kill me?" {7:20} "You are demon-possessed," the crowd answered. "Who is trying to kill you?" {7:21} Jesus said to them, "I did one miracle, and you are all amazed. {7:22} Yet, because Moses gave you circumcision (though actually it did not come from Moses, but from the patriarchs), you circumcise a boy on the Sabbath. {7:23} Now if a boy can be circumcised on the Sabbath so that the law of Moses may not be broken, why are you angry with me for healing a man's whole body on the Sabbath? {7:24} Stop judging by mere appearances, but instead judge correctly." {7:25} At that point some of the people of Jerusalem began to ask, "Isn't this the man they are trying to kill? {7:26} Here he is, speaking publicly, and they are not saying a word to him. Have the authorities really concluded that he is the Messiah? {7:27} But we know where this man is from; when the Messiah comes, no one will know where he is from." {7:28} Then Jesus, still teaching in the temple courts, cried out, "Yes, you know me, and you know where I am from. I am not here on my own authority, but he who sent me is true. You do not know him, {7:29} but I know him because I am from him and he sent me." {7:30} At this they tried to seize him, but no one laid a hand on him, because his hour had not yet come. {7:31} Still, many in the crowd believed in him. They said, "When the Messiah comes, will he perform more signs than this man?" {7:32} When the Pharisees heard the crowd whispering such things about Jesus, they and the chief priests sent temple guards to arrest him. {7:33} Jesus said, "I am with you for only a short time, and then I am going to the one who sent me. {7:34} You will look for me, but you will not find me; and where I am, you cannot come." {7:35} The Jews said to one another, "Where does this man intend to go that we cannot find him? Will he go where our people live scattered among the Greeks, and teach the Greeks? {7:36} What did he mean when he said, 'You will look for me, but you will not find me,' and 'Where I am, you cannot come'?" {7:37} On the last and greatest day of the festival, Jesus stood and said in a loud voice, "Let anyone who is thirsty come to me and drink. {7:38} Whoever believes in me, as Scripture has said, rivers of living water will flow from within them." {7:39} By this he meant the Spirit, whom those who believed in him were later to receive. Up to that time the Spirit had not been given, since Jesus had not yet been glorified. {7:40} On hearing his words, some of the people said, "Surely this man is the Prophet." {7:41} Others said, "He is the Messiah." Still others asked, "How can the Messiah come from Galilee? {7:42} Does not Scripture say that the Messiah will come from David's descendants and from Bethlehem, the town where David lived?" {7:43} Thus the people were divided because of Jesus. {7:44} Some wanted to seize him, but no one laid a hand on him. {7:45} Finally the temple guards went back to the chief priests and the Pharisees, who asked them, "Why didn't you bring him in?" {7:46} "No one ever spoke the way this man does," the guards replied. {7:47} "You mean he has deceived you also?" the Pharisees retorted. {7:48} "Have any of the rulers or of the Pharisees believed in him? {7:49} No! But this mob that knows nothing of the law—there is a curse on them." {7:50} Nicodemus, who had gone to Jesus earlier and who was one of their own number, asked, {7:51} "Does our law condemn a man without first hearing him to find out what he has been doing?" {7:52} They replied, "Are you from Galilee, too? Look into it, and you will find that a prophet does not come out of Galilee." {7:53} Then they all went home.

{8:1} Jesus went to the Mount of Olives. {8:2} Early in the morning he came again to the temple, and all the people came to him, and he sat down and taught them. {8:3} The scribes and Pharisees brought a woman caught in adultery, and having set her in the midst, {8:4} they said to him, "Teacher, this woman was caught in the act of adultery. {8:5} In the Law, Moses commanded us to stone such women. Now what do you say?" {8:6} They were saying this to test him, so that they could have grounds for accusing him. But Jesus bent down and started to write on the ground with his finger. {8:7} When they continued to question him, he straightened up and said to them, "Let him who is without sin among you be the first to throw a stone at her." {8:8} Then he bent down again and continued writing on the ground. {8:9} When they heard this, they began to go away one by one, starting with the older ones, until only Jesus was left, with the woman still standing there. {8:10} Jesus straightened up and asked her, "Woman, where are they? Has no one condemned you?" {8:11} "No one, sir," she said. "Then neither do I condemn you," Jesus declared. "Go now and leave your life of sin." {8:12} Jesus spoke to them again, saying, "I am the light of the world. Whoever follows me will never walk in darkness, but will have the light of life." {8:13} The Pharisees challenged him, "Here you are, appearing as your own witness; your testimony is not valid." {8:14} Jesus answered, "Even if I testify on my own behalf, my testimony is valid, for I know where I came from and where I am going. But you have no idea where I come from or where I am going. {8:15} You judge by human standards; I pass judgment on no one. {8:16} But if I do judge, my decisions are true, because I am not alone. I stand with the Father, who sent me. {8:17} In your own Law it is written that the testimony of two witnesses is true. {8:18} I am one who testifies for myself; my other witness is the Father, who sent me." {8:19} Then they asked him, "Where is your father?" "You do not know me or my Father," Jesus replied. "If you knew me, you would know my Father also." {8:20} He spoke these words while teaching in the temple courts near the place where the offerings were put. Yet no one seized him, because his hour had not yet come. {8:21} Once more Jesus said to them, "I am going away, and you will look for me, and you will die in your sin. Where I go, you cannot come." {8:22} This made the Jews ask, "Will he kill himself? Is that why he says, 'Where I go, you cannot come'?" {8:23} But he continued, "You are from below; I am from above. You are of this world; I am not of this world. {8:24} I told you that you would die in your sins; if you do not believe that I am he, you will indeed die in your sins." {8:25} "Who are you?" they asked. "Just what I have been telling you from the beginning," Jesus replied. {8:26} "I have much to say in judgment of you. But he who sent me is trustworthy, and what I have heard from him I tell the world." {8:27} They did not understand that he was telling them about his Father. {8:28} So Jesus said, "When you have lifted up the Son of Man, then you will know that I am he and that I do nothing on my own but speak just what the Father has taught me. {8:29} The one who sent me is with me; he has not left me alone, for I always do what pleases him." {8:30} Even as he spoke, many believed in him. {8:31} To the Jews who had believed him, Jesus said, "If you hold to my teaching, you are really my disciples. {8:32} **Then you will know the truth, and the truth will set you free."** {8:33} They replied, "We are Abraham's descendants and have never been slaves to anyone. How can you say that we shall be set free?" {8:34} Jesus answered them, "Truly, truly, I tell you, everyone who sins is a slave to sin. {8:35} Now a slave has no permanent place in the family, but a son belongs to it forever. {8:36} So if the Son sets you free, you will be free indeed. {8:37} I know that you are Abraham's descendants, yet you are trying to kill me because you have no room for my word. {8:38} I am telling you what I have seen in the Father's presence, and you are doing what you have heard from your father." {8:39} "Abraham is our father," they answered. "If you were Abraham's children," said Jesus, "then you would do what Abraham did. {8:40} As it is, you are looking for a way to kill me, a man who has told you the truth that I heard from God. Abraham did not do such things. {8:41} You are doing the works of your own father." "We are not illegitimate children," they protested. "The only Father we have is God himself." {8:42} Jesus said to them, "If God were your Father, you would love me, for I have come here from God. I have not come on my own; God sent me. {8:43} Why is my language not clear to you? Because you are unable to hear what I say. {8:44} You belong to your father, the devil, and you want to carry out your father's desires. He was a murderer from the beginning, not holding to the truth, for there is no truth in him. When he lies, he speaks his native language, for he is a liar and the father of lies. {8:45} Yet because I tell the truth, you do not believe me! {8:46} Can any of you prove me guilty of sin? If I am telling the truth, why don't you believe me? {8:47} Whoever belongs to God hears what God says. The reason you do not hear is that you do not belong to God." {8:48} The Jews answered him, "Aren't we right in saying that you are a Samaritan and demon-possessed?" {8:49} "I am not possessed by a demon," said Jesus, "but I honor my Father and you dishonor me. {8:50} I am not seeking glory for myself; but there is one who seeks it, and he is the judge. {8:51} Very truly I tell you, whoever obeys my word will never see death." {8:52} At this they exclaimed, "Now we know that you are demon-possessed!

Abraham died and so did the prophets, yet you say that whoever obeys your word will never taste death. {8:53} Are you greater than our father Abraham? He died, and so did the prophets. Who do you think you are?" {8:54} Jesus replied, "If I glorify myself, my glory means nothing. My Father, whom you claim as your God, is the one who glorifies me. {8:55} Though you do not know him, I know him. If I said I did not, I would be a liar like you, but I do know him and obey his word. {8:56} Your father Abraham rejoiced at the thought of seeing my day; he saw it and was glad." {8:57} "You are not yet fifty years old," they said to him, "and you have seen Abraham!" {8:58} "Very truly I tell you," Jesus answered, "before Abraham was born, I am!" {8:59} At this, they picked up stones to stone him, but Jesus hid himself, slipping away from the temple grounds.

{9:1} **As Jesus passed by, he saw a man who had been blind from birth.** {9:2} His disciples asked him, "Master, who sinned, this man or his parents, that he was born blind?" {9:3} Jesus answered, "Neither this man nor his parents sinned, but this happened so that the works of God might be displayed in him. {9:4} As long as it is day, we must do the works of him who sent me. Night is coming, when no one can work. {9:5} While I am in the world, I am the light of the world." {9:6} After saying this, he spit on the ground, made some mud with the saliva, and put it on the man's eyes. {9:7} "Go," he told him, "wash in the Pool of Siloam" (this word means "Sent"). So the man went and washed, and came home seeing. {9:8} His neighbors and those who had formerly seen him begging asked, "Isn't this the same man who used to sit and beg?" {9:9} Some claimed that he was. Others said, "No, he only looks like him." But he himself insisted, "I am the man." {9:10} "How then were your eyes opened?" they asked. {9:11} He replied, "The man they call Jesus made some mud and put it on my eyes. He told me to go to Siloam and wash. So I went and washed, and then I could see." {9:12} "Where is this man?" they asked him. "I don't know," he said. {9:13} They brought the man who had been blind to the Pharisees. {9:14} Now the day on which Jesus had made the mud and opened the man's eyes was a Sabbath. {9:15} Therefore the Pharisees also asked him how he had received his sight. "He put mud on my eyes," the man replied, "and I washed, and now I see." {9:16} Some of the Pharisees said, "This man is not from God, for he does not keep the Sabbath." But others asked, "How can a sinner perform such signs?" So they were divided. {9:17} They turned again to the blind man, "What have you to say about him? It was your eyes he opened." The man replied, "He is a prophet." {9:18} They still did not believe that he had been blind and had received his sight until they sent for the man's parents. {9:19} "Is this your son?" they asked. "Is this the one you say was born blind? How is it that now he can see?" {9:20} "We know he is our son," the parents answered, "and we know he was born blind. {9:21} But how he can see now, or who opened his eyes, we don't know. Ask him. He is of age; he will speak for himself." {9:22} His parents said this because they were afraid of the Jewish leaders, who already had decided that anyone who acknowledged that Jesus was the Messiah would be put out of the synagogue. {9:23} That was why his parents said, "He is of age; ask him." {9:24} A second time they summoned the man who had been blind. "Give glory to God by telling the truth," they said. "We know this man is a sinner." {9:25} He replied, "Whether he is a sinner or not, I don't know. One thing I do know. I was blind but now I see!" {9:26} Then they asked him, "What did he do to you? How did he open your eyes?" {9:27} He answered, "I have told you already and you did not listen. Why do you want to hear it again? Do you want to become his disciples too?" {9:28} Then they hurled insults at him and said, "You are this fellow's disciple! We are disciples of Moses! {9:29} We know that God spoke to Moses, but as for this fellow, we don't even know where he comes from." {9:30} The man answered, "Now that is remarkable! You don't know where he comes from, yet he opened my eyes. {9:31} We know that God does not listen to sinners. He listens to the godly person who does his will. {9:32} Nobody has ever heard of opening the eyes of a man born blind. {9:33} If this man were not from God, he could do nothing." {9:34} To this they replied, "You were steeped in sin at birth; how dare you lecture us!" And they threw him out. {9:35} Jesus heard that they had thrown him out, and when he found him, he said, "Do you believe in the Son of Man?" {9:36} "Who is he, sir?" the man asked. "Tell me so that I may believe in him." {9:37} Jesus said, "You have now seen him; in fact, he is the one speaking with you." {9:38} Then the man said, "Lord, I believe," and he worshiped him. {9:39} Jesus said, "For judgment I have come into this world, so that the blind will see and those who see will become blind." {9:40} Some Pharisees who were with him heard him say this and asked, "What? Are we blind too?" {9:41} Jesus said, "If you were blind, you would not be guilty of sin; but now that you claim you can see, your guilt remains."

{10:1} Jesus said, "Truly, truly, I tell you, anyone who does not enter the sheep pen by the gate, but climbs in by some other way, is a thief and a robber. {10:2} The one who enters by the gate is the shepherd of the sheep. {10:3} The gatekeeper opens the gate for him, and the sheep listen to his voice. He calls his own sheep by name and leads them out. {10:4} When he has brought out all his own, he goes on ahead of them, and his sheep follow him because they know his voice. {10:5} But they will never follow a stranger; in fact, they will run away from him because they do not recognize a stranger's voice." {10:6} Jesus used this figure of speech, but the Pharisees did not understand what he was telling them. {10:7} Therefore Jesus said again, "Truly, truly, I tell you, I am the gate for the sheep. {10:8} All who have come before me are thieves and robbers, but the sheep have not listened to them. {10:9} I am the gate; whoever enters through me will be saved. They will come in and go out, and find pasture. {10:10} The thief comes only to steal and kill and destroy; I have come that they may have life, and have it to the full. {10:11} I am the good shepherd. The good shepherd lays down his life for the sheep. {10:12} The hired hand is not the shepherd and does not own the sheep. So when he sees the wolf coming, he abandons the sheep and runs away. Then the wolf attacks the flock and scatters it. {10:13} The man runs away because he is a hired hand and cares nothing for the sheep. {10:14} I am the good shepherd; I know my sheep and my sheep know me— {10:15} just as the Father knows me and I know the Father—and I lay down my life for the sheep. {10:16} I have other sheep that are not of this sheep pen. I must bring them also. They too will listen to my voice, and there shall be one flock and one shepherd. {10:17} The reason my Father loves me is that I lay down my life—only to take it up again. {10:18} No one takes it from me, but I lay it down of my own accord. I have authority to lay it down and authority to take it up again. This command I received from my Father." {10:19} The Jews who heard these words were again divided. {10:20} Many of them said, "He is demon-possessed and raving mad. Why listen to him?" {10:21} But others said, "These are not the sayings of a man possessed by a demon. Can a demon open the eyes of the blind?" {10:22} It was winter, and the Feast of Dedication was being celebrated in Jerusalem. {10:23} Jesus was walking in the temple area, known as Solomon's Colonnade. {10:24} The Jews gathered around him, demanding, "How long will you keep us in suspense? If you are the Messiah, tell us plainly." {10:25} Jesus answered, "I did tell you, but you do not believe. The works I do in my Father's name testify about me, {10:26} but you do not believe because you are not my sheep. {10:27} My sheep listen to my voice; I know them, and they follow me. {10:28} I give them eternal life, and they shall never perish; no one will snatch them out of my hand. {10:29} My Father, who has given them to me, is greater than all; no one can snatch them out of my Father's hand. {10:30} I and the Father are one." {10:31} Again his Jewish opponents picked up stones to stone him, {10:32} but Jesus said to them, "I have shown you many good works from the Father. For which of these do you stone me?" {10:33} "We are not stoning you for any good work," they replied, "but for blasphemy, because you, a mere man, claim to be God." {10:34} Jesus answered them, "Is it not written in your Law, 'I have said you are "gods"'? {10:35} If he called them 'gods,' to whom the word of God came—and Scripture cannot be set aside— {10:36} what about the one whom the Father set apart as his very own and sent into the world? Why then do you accuse me of blasphemy because I said, 'I am God's Son'? {10:37} Do not believe me unless I do the works of my Father. {10:38} But if I do them, even though you do not believe me, believe the works, that you may know and understand that the Father is in me, and I in the Father." {10:39} Again they tried to seize him, but he escaped their grasp. {10:40} Then Jesus went back across the Jordan to the place where John had been baptizing in the early days. There he stayed, {10:41} and many people came to him. They said, "Though John never performed a sign, all that John said about this man was true." {10:42} And in that place many believed in Jesus.

{11:1} There was a man named Lazarus who lived in Bethany with his sisters, Mary and Martha. {11:2} Mary was the one who had anointed the Lord with perfume and wiped his feet with her hair. It was her brother Lazarus who was sick. {11:3} So the sisters sent a message to Jesus telling him, "Lord, your dear friend is very sick." {11:4} But when Jesus heard about it, he said, "Lazarus's sickness will not end in death. No, it happened for the glory of God so that the Son of God will receive glory from this." {11:5} Although Jesus loved Martha, Mary, and Lazarus, {11:6} he stayed where he was for the next two days. {11:7} Finally, he said to his disciples, "Let's go back to Judea." {11:8} But his disciples objected. "Rabbi," they said, "only a few days ago the people in Judea were trying to stone you. Are you going there again?" {11:9} Jesus replied, "There are twelve hours of daylight every day. During the day, people can walk safely. They can see because they have the light of this world. {11:10} But at night, there is danger of stumbling because they have no light." {11:11} Then he said, "Our friend Lazarus has fallen asleep, but now I will go and wake him up." {11:12} The disciples said, "Lord, if he is sleeping, he will soon get better!" {11:13} They thought Jesus meant Lazarus was simply sleeping, but Jesus meant Lazarus had died. {11:14} So he told them plainly, "Lazarus is dead. {11:15} And for your sakes, I'm glad I wasn't there, for now you will really believe. Come, let's go see him." {11:16} Thomas, nicknamed the Twin, said to his fellow disciples, "Let's go, too—and die with Jesus." {11:17} When Jesus arrived at Bethany, he was told that Lazarus had already been in his grave for four days. {11:18} Bethany was only a few miles down the road from Jerusalem, {11:19} and many of the people had come to console Martha and Mary in their loss. {11:20} When Martha got word that Jesus was coming, she went to meet him. But Mary stayed in the house. {11:21} Martha said to Jesus, "Lord, if only you had been here, my brother would not have died. {11:22} But even now I know that God will give you whatever you ask." {11:23} Jesus told her, "Your brother will rise again." {11:24} "Yes," said Martha, "he will rise when everyone else rises, at the last day." {11:25} Jesus told her, "I am the resurrection and the life. Anyone who believes in me will live, even after dying. {11:26} Everyone who lives in me and believes in me will never ever die. Do you believe this, Martha?" {11:27} "Yes, Lord," she told him. "I have always believed you are the Messiah, the Son of God, the one who has come into the world from God." {11:28} Then she returned to Mary. She called Mary aside from the mourners and told her, "The Teacher is here and wants to see you." {11:29} So Mary immediately went to him. {11:30} Jesus had stayed outside the village, at the place where Martha met him. {11:31} When the Jewish people who were comforting Mary in the house saw her leave hastily, they assumed she was going to the tomb to weep there. So they followed her. {11:32} When Mary came to where Jesus was and saw him, she fell at his feet, saying, "Lord, if you had been here, my brother would not have died." {11:33} Seeing her weeping, and the Jews who had come with her also weeping, Jesus was deeply moved and troubled. {11:34} He asked, "Where have you laid him?" They replied, "Come and see, Lord." {11:35} Jesus wept. {11:36} The Jews said, "See how much he loved Lazarus!" {11:37} But some of them questioned, "Could not this man who opened the eyes of the blind have kept this man from dying?" {11:38} Once more deeply moved, Jesus approached the tomb. It was a cave with a stone laid across the entrance. {11:39} Jesus said, "Take away the stone." Martha, Lazarus's sister, objected, "Lord, he has been dead for four days. There will be a bad odor." {11:40} Jesus replied, "Did I not tell you that if you believe, you will see the glory of God?" {11:41} So they removed the stone. Then Jesus looked up and said, "Father, I thank you that you have heard me. {11:42} I knew that you always hear me, but I said this for the benefit of the people standing here, that they may believe that you sent me." {11:43} After he had said this, Jesus called in a loud voice, "Lazarus, come out!" {11:44} The dead man came out, his hands and feet wrapped with strips of linen, and a cloth around his face. Jesus said to them, "Take off the grave clothes and let him go." {11:45} Many of the Jews who had come to visit Mary saw what Jesus did and believed in him. {11:46} But some of them went to the Pharisees and told them what Jesus had done. {11:47} Then the chief priests and the Pharisees called a meeting of the Sanhedrin. "What are we accomplishing?" they asked. "Here is this man performing many signs. {11:48} If we let him go on like this, everyone will believe in him, and then the Romans will come and take away both our temple and our nation." {11:49} Then one of them, named Caiaphas, who was high priest that year, spoke up, "You know nothing at all! {11:50} You do not realize that it is better for you that one man die for the people than that the whole nation perish." {11:51} He did not say this on his own, but as high priest that year he prophesied that Jesus would die for the Jewish nation, {11:52} and not only for that nation but also for the scattered children of God, to bring them together and make them one. {11:53} So from that day on they plotted to take his life. {11:54} Therefore Jesus no longer moved about publicly among the people of Judea. Instead he withdrew to a region near the wilderness, to a village called Ephraim, where he stayed with his disciples. {11:55} When it was almost time for the Jewish Passover, many went up from the country to Jerusalem for their ceremonial cleansing before the Passover. {11:56} They kept looking for Jesus, and as they stood in the temple courts, they asked one another, "What do you think? Isn't he coming to the festival at all?" {11:57} But the chief priests and the Pharisees had given orders that anyone who found out where Jesus was should report it so that they might arrest him.

{12:1} Six days before the Passover, Jesus went to Bethany, where Lazarus, whom he had raised from the dead, was. {12:2} There they prepared supper for him; Martha served, and Lazarus was among those at the table with him. {12:3} Mary took a pound of very costly spikenard ointment, anointed Jesus' feet, and wiped them with her hair, filling the house with the fragrance of the ointment. {12:4} Judas Iscariot, one of his disciples who would betray him, objected, "Why was this ointment not sold for three hundred pence and given to the poor?" {12:5} Judas Iscariot, one of Jesus' disciples, questioned why the expensive ointment was not sold for three hundred pence and given to the poor. {12:6} However, he didn't genuinely care for the poor; rather, he said this because he was a thief and responsible for carrying the money bag, taking what was put into it. {12:7} Jesus responded, "Leave her alone. She has kept this ointment for the day of my burial. {12:8} You will always have the poor with you, but you will not always have me." {12:9} Many Jews came not only to see Jesus but also Lazarus, whom he had raised from the dead. {12:10} The chief priests plotted to kill Lazarus too, {12:11} because many Jews were turning away and believing in Jesus because of him. {12:12} The next day, a large crowd that had come to the feast heard Jesus was coming to Jerusalem. {12:13} They took palm branches, went out to meet him, and cried, "Hosanna! Blessed is the King of Israel who comes in the name of the Lord!" {12:14} Jesus found a young donkey and sat on it, fulfilling the prophecy, {12:15} "Fear not, daughter of Zion; behold, your King is coming, sitting on a donkey's colt." {12:16} At first, his disciples did not understand these things, but after Jesus was glorified, they remembered the prophecies and realized how they applied to him. {12:17} The people who had witnessed Lazarus being raised from the dead testified about it. {12:18} Because of this miracle, many people also came out to meet Jesus. {12:19} The Pharisees, seeing this, said to each other, "You see? You're getting nowhere. Look, the whole world is following him!" {12:20} Some Greeks who had come to Jerusalem to worship during the festival approached Philip, who was from Bethsaida in Galilee. {12:21} They made their request to him: "Sir, we want to see Jesus." {12:22} Philip went to tell Andrew about it, and then Andrew and Philip went to inform Jesus. {12:23} Jesus responded, "The time has come for the Son of Man to be glorified. {12:24} Truly, truly, I tell you, unless a kernel of wheat falls to the ground and dies, it remains only a single seed. But if it dies, it produces many seeds. {12:25} Anyone who loves their life will lose it, while anyone who hates their life in this world will keep it for eternal life. {12:26} Whoever serves me must follow me; and where I am, my servant also will be. My Father will honor the one who serves me. {12:27} Now my soul is troubled, and what shall I say? 'Father, save me from this hour'? No, it was for this very reason I came to this hour. {12:28} Father, glorify your name!" Then a voice came from heaven, "I have glorified it, and will glorify it again." {12:29} The crowd that was there and heard it said it had thundered; others said an angel had spoken to him. {12:30} Jesus said, "This voice was for your benefit, not mine. {12:31} Now is the time for judgment on this world; now the prince of this world will be driven out. {12:32} And I, when I am lifted up from the earth, will draw all people to myself." {12:33} He said this to show the kind of death he was going to die. {12:34} The crowd spoke up, "We have heard from the Law that the Messiah will remain forever, so how can you say, 'The Son of Man must be lifted up'? Who is this 'Son of Man'?" {12:35} Then Jesus told them, "You are going to have the light just a little while longer. Walk while you have the light, before darkness overtakes you. Whoever walks in the dark does not know where they are going. {12:36} Believe in the light while you have the light, so that you may become children of light." When he had finished speaking, Jesus left and hid himself from them. {12:37} Although Jesus had performed so many signs in their presence, they still did not believe in him. {12:38} This was to fulfill the word of Isaiah the prophet: "Lord, who has believed our message and to whom has the arm of the Lord been revealed?" {12:39} For this reason they could not believe, because, as Isaiah says elsewhere: {12:40} "He has blinded their eyes and hardened their hearts, so they can neither see with their eyes, nor understand with their hearts, nor turn—and I would heal them." {12:41} Isaiah said this because he saw Jesus' glory and spoke about him. {12:42} Yet at the same time many even among the leaders believed in him. But because of the Pharisees they would not openly acknowledge their faith for fear they would be put out of the synagogue; {12:43} for they loved human praise more than praise from God. {12:44} Jesus cried out and said, "Whoever believes in me is not only believing in me but also in the one who sent me. {12:45} The one who sees me sees the one who sent me. {12:46} I have come as a light into the world so that whoever believes in me may not remain in darkness. {12:47} If anyone hears my words but does not keep them, I do not judge that person. For I did not come to judge the world, but to save the world. {12:48} There is a judge for the one who rejects me and does not accept my words. The very words I have spoken will condemn them on the last day. {12:49} For I did not speak on my own, but the Father who sent me commanded me to say all that I have spoken. {12:50} I know that his command leads to eternal life. So whatever I say is just what the Father has told me to say."

{13:1} Before the Passover festival, Jesus knew that his hour had come to leave this world and go to the Father. Having loved his own who were in the world, he loved them to the end. {13:2} The evening meal was in progress, and the devil had already prompted Judas, the son of Simon Iscariot, to betray Jesus. {13:3} Jesus knew that the Father had put all things under his power, and that he had come from God and was returning to God; {13:4} so he got up from the meal, took off his outer clothing, and wrapped a towel around his waist. {13:5} After that, he poured water into a basin and began to wash his disciples' feet, drying them with the towel that was wrapped around him. {13:6} He came to Simon Peter, who said to him, "Lord, are you going to wash my feet?" {13:7} Jesus replied, "You do not realize now what I am doing, but later you will understand." {13:8} "No," said Peter, "you shall never wash my feet." Jesus answered, "Unless I wash you, you have no part with me." {13:9} "Then, Lord," Simon Peter replied, "not just my feet but my hands and my head as well!" {13:10} Jesus answered, "Those who have had a bath need only to wash their feet; their whole body is clean. And you are clean, though not every one of you." {13:11} For he knew who was going to betray him, and that was why he said not everyone was clean. {13:12} When he had finished washing their feet, he put on his clothes and returned to his place. "Do you understand what I have done for you?" he asked them. {13:13} "You call me 'Teacher' and 'Lord,' and rightly so, for that is what I am. {13:14} Now that I, your Lord and Teacher, have washed your feet, you also should wash one another's feet. {13:15} I have set you an example that you should do as I have done for you. {13:16} Very truly I tell you, no servant is greater than his master, nor is a messenger greater than the one who sent him. {13:17} Now that you know these things, you will be blessed if you do them." {13:18} "I am not referring to all of you; I know those I have chosen. But this is to fulfill this passage of Scripture: 'He who shared my bread has turned against me.' {13:19} I am telling you now before it happens, so that when it does happen you will believe that I am who I am. {13:20} Very truly I tell you, whoever accepts anyone I send accepts me; and whoever accepts me accepts the one who sent me." {13:21} After he had said this, Jesus was troubled in spirit and testified, "Very truly I tell you, one of you is going to betray me." {13:22} His disciples stared at one another, at a loss to know which of them he meant. {13:23} One of them, the disciple whom Jesus loved, was reclining next to him. {13:24} Simon Peter motioned to this disciple and said, "Ask him which one he means." {13:25} Leaning back against Jesus, he asked him, "Lord, who is it?" {13:26} Jesus answered, "It is the one to whom I will give this piece of bread when I have dipped it in the dish." Then, dipping the piece of bread, he gave it to Judas, the son of Simon Iscariot. {13:27} As soon as Judas took the bread, Satan entered into him. So Jesus told him, "What you are about to do, do quickly." {13:28} But no one at the meal understood why Jesus said this to him. {13:29} Since Judas had charge of the money, some thought Jesus was telling him to buy what was needed for the festival, or to give something to the poor. {13:30} As soon as Judas had taken the bread, he went out. And it was night. {13:31} So, when Judas had left, Jesus said, "Now the Son of Man is glorified, and God is glorified in him. {13:32} If God is glorified in him, God will also glorify him in himself, and will glorify him at once. {13:33} My children, I will be with you only a little longer. You will look for me, and just as I told the Jews, so I tell you now: Where I am going, you cannot come. {13:34} A new command I give you: Love one another. As I have loved you, so you must love one another. {13:35} By this everyone will know that you are my disciples, if you love one another." {13:36} Simon Peter asked him, "Lord, where are you going?" Jesus replied, "Where I am going, you cannot follow now, but you will follow later." {13:37} Peter asked, "Lord, why can't I follow you now? I will lay down my life for you." {13:38} Then Jesus answered, "Will you really lay down your life for me? Very truly I tell you, before the rooster crows, you will disown me three times."

{14:1} "Do not let your hearts be troubled. You believe in God; believe also in me. {14:2} My Father's house has many rooms; if that were not so, would I have told you that I am going there to prepare a place for you? {14:3} And if I go and prepare a place for you, I will come back and take you to be with me that you also may be where I am. {14:4} You know the way to the place where I am going." {14:5} Thomas said to him, "Lord, we don't know where you are going, so how can we know the way?" {14:6} Jesus answered, "I am the way and the truth and the life. No one comes to the Father except through me. {14:7} If you really know me, you will know my Father as well. From now on, you do know him and have seen him." {14:8} Philip said, "Lord, show us the Father and that will be enough for us." {14:9} Jesus answered: "Don't you know me, Philip, even after I have been among you such a long time? Anyone who has seen me has seen the Father. How can you say, 'Show us the Father'? {14:10} Don't you believe that I am in the Father, and that the Father is in me? The words I say to you I do not speak on my own authority. Rather, it is the Father, living in me, who is doing his work. {14:11} Believe me when I say that I am in the Father and the Father is in me; or at least believe in the evidence of the works themselves. {14:12} "Very truly I tell you, whoever believes in me will do the works I have been doing, and they will do even greater things than these, because I am going to the Father. {14:13} And I will do whatever you ask in my name, so that the Father may be glorified in the Son. {14:14} You may ask me for anything in my name, and I will do it. {14:15} "If you love me, keep my commandments. {14:16} And I will pray the Father, and he shall give you another Comforter, that he may abide with you forever; {14:17} the Spirit of truth, whom the world cannot receive, because it neither sees him nor knows him. But you know him, for he dwells with you and will be in you. {14:18} I will not leave you comfortless; I will come to you. {14:19} Yet a little while and the world will see me no more, but you will see me. Because I live, you will live also. {14:20} In that day you will know that I am in my Father, and you in me, and I in you. {14:21} He who has my commandments and keeps them, it is he who loves me. And he who loves me will be loved by my Father, and I will love him and manifest myself to him." {14:22} Judas (not Iscariot) said to him, "Lord, how is it that you will manifest yourself to us, and not to the world?" {14:23} Jesus answered and said to him, "If anyone loves me, he will keep my word; and my Father will love him, and we will come to him and make our home with him. {14:24} He who does not love me does not keep my words; and the word which you hear is not mine but the Father's who sent me. {14:25} These things I have spoken to you while being present with you. {14:26} But the Comforter, the Holy Spirit, whom the Father will send in my name, he will teach you all things, and bring to your remembrance all things that I said to you. {14:27} Peace I leave with you, my peace I give to you; not as the world gives do I give to you. Let not your heart be troubled, neither let it be afraid. {14:28} "You have heard me say to you, 'I am going away and coming back to you.' If you loved me, you would rejoice because I said, 'I am going to the Father,' for my Father is greater than I. {14:29} And now I have told you before it comes, that when it does come to pass, you may believe. {14:30} I will no longer talk much with you, for the ruler of this world is coming, and he has nothing in me. {14:31} But the world may know that I love the Father, and as the Father gave me commandment, so I do. Arise, let us go from here."

{15:1} "I am the true vine, and my Father is the husbandman. {15:2} Every branch in me that does not bear fruit, he takes away; and every branch that bears fruit, he prunes it, so that it may bear more fruit. {15:3} You are already clean because of the word which I have spoken to you. {15:4} Abide in me, and I in you. As the branch cannot bear fruit of itself, unless it abides in the vine, neither can you, unless you abide in me. {15:5} I am the vine, you are the branches. He who abides in me, and I in him, bears much fruit; for without me you can do nothing. {15:6} If anyone does not abide in me, he is cast out as a branch and is withered; and they gather them and throw them into the fire, and they are burned. {15:7} If you abide in me, and my words abide in you, you will ask what you desire, and it shall be done for you. {15:8} By this my Father is glorified, that you bear much fruit; so you will be my disciples. {15:9} As the Father loved me, I also have loved you; abide in my love. {15:10} If you keep my commandments, you will abide in my love, just as I have kept my Father's commandments and abide in his love. {15:11} These things I have spoken to you, that my joy may remain in you, and that your joy may be full. {15:12} "This is my commandment, that you love one another as I have loved you. {15:13} Greater love has no one than this, than to lay down one's life for his friends. {15:14} You are my friends if you do whatever I command you. {15:15} No longer do I call you servants, for a servant does not know what his master is doing; but I have called you friends, for all things that I heard from my Father I have made known to you. {15:16} You did not choose me, but I chose you and appointed you that you should go and bear fruit, and that your fruit should remain, that whatever you ask the Father in my name he may give you. {15:17} These things I command you, that you love one another. {15:18} If the world hates you, you know that it hated me before it hated you. {15:19} If you were of the world, the world would love its own. Yet because you are not of the world, but I chose you out of the world, therefore the world hates you. {15:20} Remember the word that I said to you, 'A servant is not greater than his master.' If they persecuted me, they will also persecute you. If they kept my word, they will keep yours also. {15:21} But all these things they will do to you for my name's sake, because they do not know him who sent me. {15:22} If I had not come and spoken to them, they would have no sin, but now they have no excuse for their sin. {15:23} He who hates me hates my Father also. {15:24} If I had not done among them the works which no one else did, they would have no sin; but now they have seen and also hated both me and my Father. {15:25} But this happened that the word might be fulfilled, which is written in their law, 'They hated me without a cause.'

{15:26} "But when the Helper comes, whom I shall send to you from the Father, the Spirit of truth who proceeds from the Father, he will testify of me. {15:27} And you also will bear witness, because you have been with me from the beginning."

{16:1} "I have told you these things so that you will not be offended. {16:2} They will put you out of the synagogues; yes, the time is coming that whoever kills you will think that he is offering a service to God. {16:3} And they will do these things to you because they have not known the Father nor me. {16:4} But I have told you these things so that when the time comes, you will remember that I warned you about them. I did not tell you these things at the beginning because I was with you. {16:5} But now I am going away to him who sent me, and none of you asks me, 'Where are you going?' {16:6} Yet because I have said these things to you, sorrow has filled your heart. {16:7} Nevertheless, I am telling you the truth: it is to your advantage that I go away, for if I do not go away, the Comforter will not come to you; but if I depart, I will send him to you. {16:8} And when he has come, he will convict the world of sin, and of righteousness, and of judgment: {16:9} of sin, because they do not believe in me; {16:10} of righteousness, because I go to my Father and you will see me no more; {16:11} of judgment, because the ruler of this world is judged. {16:12} "I still have many things to say to you, but you cannot bear them now. {16:13} However, when he, the Spirit of truth, has come, he will guide you into all truth; for he will not speak on his own authority, but whatever he hears he will speak; and he will tell you things to come. {16:14} He will glorify me, for he will take of what is mine and declare it to you. {16:15} All things that the Father has are mine. Therefore I said that he will take of mine and declare it to you. {16:16} A little while, and you will not see me; and again a little while, and you will see me, because I go to the Father." {16:17} Then some of his disciples said among themselves, "What is this that he says to us, 'A little while, and you will not see me; and again a little while, and you will see me'; and, 'because I go to the Father'?" {16:18} They said therefore, "What is this that he says, 'A little while'? We do not know what he is talking about." {16:19} Now Jesus knew that they desired to ask him, and he said to them, "Are you inquiring among yourselves about what I said, 'A little while, and you will not see me; and again a little while, and you will see me'? {16:20} Most assuredly, I say to you that you will weep and lament, but the world will rejoice; and you will be sorrowful, but your sorrow will be turned into joy."{16:21} "When a woman is in labor, she has sorrow because her time has come; but as soon as she gives birth to the child, she no longer remembers the anguish, for joy that a human being has been born into the world. {16:22} So you now indeed have sorrow, but I will see you again and your heart will rejoice, and your joy no one will take from you. {16:23} And in that day you will ask me nothing. Most assuredly, I say to you, whatever you ask the Father in my name, he will give you. {16:24} Until now you have asked nothing in my name. Ask, and you will receive, that your joy may be full. {16:25} These things I have spoken to you in figurative language; but the time is coming when I will no longer speak to you in figurative language, but I will tell you plainly about the Father. {16:26} In that day you will ask in my name, and I do not say to you that I shall pray the Father for you; {16:27} for the Father Himself loves you, because you have loved me, and have believed that I came forth from God. {16:28} I came forth from the Father and have come into the world. Again, I leave the world and go to the Father." {16:29} His disciples said to him, "See, now you are speaking plainly, and using no figure of speech! {16:30} Now we are sure that you know all things, and have no need that anyone should question you. By this we believe that you came forth from God." {16:31} Jesus answered them, "Do you now believe? {16:32} Indeed, the hour is coming, yes, has now come, that you will be scattered, each to his own, and will leave me alone. And yet I am not alone, because the Father is with me. {16:33} These things I have spoken to you, that in me you may have peace. In the world you will have tribulation; but be of good cheer, I have overcome the world."

{17:1} After Jesus said these things, he looked up to heaven and said, "Father, the time has come. Glorify your Son, that your Son may glorify you. {17:2} For you granted him authority over all people that he might give eternal life to all those you have given him. {17:3} Now this is eternal life: that they know you, the only true God, and Jesus Christ, whom you have sent. {17:4} I have brought you glory on earth by finishing the work you gave me to do. {17:5} And now, Father, glorify me in your presence with the glory I had with you before the world began. {17:6} "I have revealed you to those whom you gave me out of the world. They were yours; you gave them to me and they have obeyed your word. {17:7} Now they know that everything you have given me comes from you. {17:8} For I gave them the words you gave me and they accepted them. They knew with certainty that I came from you, and they believed that you sent me. {17:9} I pray for them. I am not praying for the world, but for those you have given me, for they are yours. {17:10} All I have is yours, and all you have is mine. And glory has come to me through them. {17:11} I will remain in the world no longer, but they are still in the world, and I am coming to you. Holy Father, protect them by the power of your name, the name you gave me, so that they may be one as we are one. 17:12} While I was with them, I protected them and kept them safe by that name you gave me. None has been lost except the one doomed to destruction so that Scripture would be fulfilled. {17:13} "I am coming to you now, but I say these things while I am still in the world, so that they may have the full measure of my joy within them. {17:14} I have given them your word and the world has hated them, for they are not of the world any more than I am of the world. {17:15} My prayer is not that you take them out of the world but that you protect them from the evil one. {17:16} They are not of the world, even as I am not of it. {17:17} Sanctify them by the truth; your word is truth. {17:18} As you sent me into the world, I have sent them into the world. {17:19} For them I sanctify myself, that they too may be truly sanctified. {17:20} "My prayer is not for them alone. I pray also for those who will believe in me through their message, {17:21} that all of them may be one, Father, just as you are in me and I am in you. May they also be in us so that the world may believe that you have sent me. {17:22} I have given them the glory that you gave me, that they may be one as we are one: {17:23} I in them and you in me. May they be brought to complete unity to let the world know that you sent me and have loved them even as you have loved me. {17:24} "Father, I want those you have given me to be with me where I am, and to see my glory, the glory you have given me because you loved me before the creation of the world. {17:25} "Righteous Father, though the world does not know you, I know you, and they know that you have sent me. {17:26} I have made you known to them, and will continue to make you known in order that the love you have for me may be in them and that I myself may be in them."

{18:1} After Jesus had spoken these words, he went out with his disciples across the Kidron Valley to a place where there was a garden, which he and his disciples entered. {18:2} Now Judas, who betrayed him, also knew the place, because Jesus often met there with his disciples. {18:3} So Judas brought a detachment of soldiers and some officials from the chief priests and the Pharisees and came there with lanterns, torches, and weapons. {18:4} Then Jesus, knowing all that was going to happen to him, stepped forward and asked them, "Who is it you want?" {18:5} "Jesus of Nazareth," they replied. "I am he," Jesus said. (And Judas the traitor was standing there with them.) {18:6} When Jesus said, "I am he," they drew back and fell to the ground. {18:7} Again he asked them, "Who is it you want?" And they said, "Jesus of Nazareth." {18:8} "I told you that I am he," Jesus answered. "If you are looking for me, then let these men go." {18:9} This happened so that the words he had spoken would be fulfilled: "I have not lost any of those you gave me." {18:10} Then Simon Peter, who had a sword, drew it and struck the high priest's servant, cutting off his right ear. (The servant's name was Malchus.) {18:11} Jesus commanded Peter, "Put your sword away! Shall I not drink the cup the Father has given me?" {18:12} Then the detachment of soldiers with its commander and the Jewish officials arrested Jesus. They bound him {18:13} and brought him first to Annas, who was the father-in-law of Caiaphas, the high priest that year. {18:14} Caiaphas was the one who had advised the Jewish leaders that it would be good if one man died for the people. {18:15} Simon Peter and another disciple were following Jesus. Because this disciple was known to the high priest, he went with Jesus into the high priest's courtyard, {18:16} but Peter had to wait outside at the door. The other disciple, who was known to the high priest, came back, spoke to the servant girl on duty there, and brought Peter in. {18:17} "You aren't one of this man's disciples too, are you?" she asked Peter. He replied, "I am not." {18:18} It was cold, and the servants and officials stood around a fire they had made to keep warm. Peter also was standing with them, warming himself. {18:19} Then the high priest questioned Jesus about his disciples and his teaching. {18:20} "I have spoken openly to the world," Jesus replied. "I always taught in synagogues or at the temple, where all the Jews come together. I said nothing in secret. {18:21} Why question me? Ask those who heard me. Surely they know what I said." {18:22} When Jesus said this, one of the officials nearby slapped him in the face. "Is this the way you answer the high priest?" he demanded. {18:23} "If I said something wrong," Jesus replied, "testify as to what is wrong. But if I spoke the truth, why did you strike me?" {18:24} Then Annas sent him bound to Caiaphas the high priest. {18:25} Meanwhile, Simon Peter was still standing there warming himself. So they asked him, "You aren't one of his disciples too, are you?" He denied it, saying, "I am not." {18:26} One of the high priest's servants, a relative of the man whose ear Peter had cut off, challenged him, "Didn't I see you with him in the garden?" {18:27} Again Peter denied it, and at that moment a rooster began to crow. {18:28} Then the Jewish leaders took Jesus from Caiaphas to the palace of the Roman governor. By now it was early morning, and to avoid ceremonial uncleanness they did not enter the palace, because they wanted to be able to eat the Passover. {18:29} So Pilate came out to them and asked, "What charges are you bringing against this man?" {18:30} "If he were not a criminal," they replied, "we would not have handed him over to you." {18:31} Pilate said, "Take him yourselves and judge him by your own law." "But we have no right to execute anyone," they objected. {18:32} This took place to fulfill what Jesus had said about the kind of death he was going to die. {18:33} Pilate then went back inside the palace, summoned Jesus, and asked him, "Are you the king of the Jews?" {18:34} "Is that your own idea," Jesus asked, "or did others talk to you about me?" {18:35} "Am I a Jew?" Pilate replied. "Your own people and chief priests handed you over to me. What is it you have done?" {18:36} Jesus said, "My kingdom is not of this world. If it were, my servants would fight to prevent my arrest by the Jewish leaders. But now my kingdom is from another place." {18:37} "You are a king, then!" said Pilate. Jesus answered, "You say that I am a king. In fact, the reason I was born and came into the world is to testify to the truth. Everyone on the side of truth listens to me." {18:38} "What is truth?" retorted Pilate. With this he went out again to the Jews gathered there and said, "I find no basis for a charge against him. {18:39} But it is your custom for me to release to you one prisoner at the time of the Passover. Do you want me to release 'the king of the Jews'?" {18:40} They shouted back, "No, not him! Give us Barabbas!" Now Barabbas had taken part in an uprising.

{19:1} So Pilate took Jesus and had him flogged. {19:2} The soldiers twisted together a crown of thorns and put it on his head. They clothed him in a purple robe {19:3} and went up to him again and again, saying, "Hail, king of the Jews!" And they slapped him in the face. {19:4} Once more Pilate came out and said to the Jews gathered there, "Look, I am bringing him out to you to let you know that I find no basis for a charge against him." {19:5} When Jesus came out wearing the crown of thorns and the purple robe, Pilate said to them, "Here is the man!" {19:6} As soon as the chief priests and their officials saw him, they shouted, "Crucify! Crucify!" But Pilate answered, "You take him and crucify him. As for me, I find no basis for a charge against him." {19:7} The Jewish leaders insisted, "We have a law, and according to that law he must die, because he claimed to be the Son of God." {19:8} When Pilate heard this, he was even more afraid, {19:9} and he went back inside the palace. "Where do you come from?" he asked Jesus, but Jesus gave him no answer. {19:10} "Do you refuse to speak to me?" Pilate said. "Don't you realize I have power either to free you or to crucify you?" {19:11} Jesus answered, "You would have no power over me if it were not given to you from above. Therefore the one who handed me over to you is guilty of a greater sin." {19:12} From then on, Pilate tried to set Jesus free, but the Jewish leaders kept shouting, "If you let this man go, you are no friend of Caesar. Anyone who claims to be a king opposes Caesar." {19:13} When Pilate heard this, he brought Jesus out and sat down on the judge's seat at a place known as the Stone Pavement (which in Aramaic is Gabbatha). {19:14} It was the day of Preparation of the Passover; it was about noon. "Here is your king," Pilate said to the Jews. {19:15} But they shouted, "Take him away! Take him away! Crucify him!" "Shall I crucify your king?" Pilate asked. "We have no king but Caesar," the chief priests answered. {19:16} Finally Pilate handed him over to them to be crucified. So the soldiers took charge of Jesus. {19:17} Carrying his own cross, he went out to the place of the Skull (which in Aramaic is called Golgotha). {19:18} There they crucified him, and with him two others—one on each side and Jesus in the middle. {19:19} Pilate had a notice prepared and fastened to the cross. It read: JESUS OF NAZARETH, THE KING OF THE JEWS. {19:20} Many of the Jews read this sign, for the place where Jesus was crucified was near the city, and the sign was written in Aramaic, Latin and Greek. {19:21} The chief priests of the Jews protested to Pilate, "Do not write 'The King of the Jews,' but that this man claimed to be king of the Jews." {19:22} Pilate answered, "What I have written, I have written." {19:23} When the soldiers crucified Jesus, they took his clothes, dividing them into four shares, one for each of them, with the undergarment remaining. This garment was seamless, woven in one piece from top to bottom. {19:24} "Let's not tear it," they said to one another. "Let's decide by lot who will get it." This happened that the scripture might be fulfilled that said, "They divided my clothes among them and cast lots for my garment." So this is what the soldiers did. {19:25} Near the cross of Jesus stood his mother, his mother's sister, Mary the wife of Clopas, and Mary Magdalene. {19:26} When Jesus saw his mother there, and the disciple whom he loved standing nearby, he said to her, "Woman, here is your son," {19:27} and to the disciple, "Here is your mother." From that time on, this disciple took her into his home. {19:28} After this, Jesus, knowing that all things were now accomplished, that the scripture might be fulfilled, said, "I thirst." {19:29} Now a vessel full of sour wine was sitting there; and they filled a sponge with sour wine, put it on hyssop, and put it to His mouth. {19:30} So when Jesus had received the sour wine, He said, "It is finished!" And bowing His head, He gave up His spirit. {19:31} Therefore, because it was the Preparation Day, that the bodies should not remain on the cross on the Sabbath (for that Sabbath was a high day), the Jews asked Pilate that their legs might be broken, and that they might be taken away. {19:32} Then the soldiers came and broke the legs of the first and of the other who was crucified with Him. {19:33} But when they came to Jesus and saw that He was already dead, they did not break His legs. {19:34} But one of the soldiers pierced His side with a spear, and immediately blood and water came out. {19:35} And he who has seen has testified, and his testimony is true; and he knows that he is telling the truth, so that you may believe. {19:36} For these things were done that the Scripture should be fulfilled, "Not one of His bones shall be broken." {19:37} And again another Scripture says, "They shall look on Him whom they pierced." {19:38} After this, Joseph of Arimathea, being a disciple of Jesus, but secretly, for fear of the Jews, asked Pilate that he might take away the body of Jesus; and Pilate gave him permission. So he came and took the body of Jesus. {19:39} And Nicodemus, who at first came to Jesus by night, also came, bringing a mixture of myrrh and aloes, about a hundred pounds. {19:40} Then they took the body of Jesus, and bound it in strips of linen with the spices, as the custom of the Jews is to bury. {19:41} Now in the place where He was crucified there was a garden, and in the garden a new tomb in which no one had yet been laid. {19:42} So there they laid Jesus, because of the Jews' Preparation Day, for the tomb was nearby.

{20:1} **On the first day of the week, Mary Magdalene went to the tomb early, while it was still dark, and saw that the stone had been taken away from the tomb.** {20:2} So she ran and went to Simon Peter and the other disciple, whom Jesus loved, and said to them, "They have taken the Lord out of the tomb, and we do not know where they have laid Him." {20:3} Peter therefore went out, and the other disciple, and they came to the tomb. {20:4} So they both ran together, and the other disciple outran Peter and came to the tomb first. {20:5} And he, stooping down and looking in, saw the linen cloth lying there; yet he did not go in. {20:6} Then Simon Peter came, following him, and went into the tomb; and he saw the linen cloths lying there, {20:7} and the handkerchief that had been around His head, not lying with the linen cloths, but folded together in a place by itself. {20:8} Then the other disciple, who came to the tomb first, went in also; and he saw and believed. {20:9} For as yet they did not know the Scripture, that He must rise again from the dead. {20:10} Then the disciples went away again to their own homes. {20:11} But Mary stood outside by the tomb weeping, and as she wept she stooped down and looked into the tomb. {20:12} And she saw two angels in white sitting, one at the head and the other at the feet, where the body of Jesus had lain. {20:13} Then they said to her, "Woman, why are you weeping?" She said to them, "Because they have taken away my Lord, and I do not know where they have laid Him."{20:14} Now when she had said this, she turned around and saw Jesus standing there, and did not know that it was Jesus. {20:15} Jesus said to her, "Woman, why are you weeping? Whom are you seeking?" She, supposing Him to be the gardener, said to Him, "Sir, if You have carried Him away, tell me where You have laid Him, and I will take Him away."{20:16} Jesus said to her, "Mary!" She turned and said to Him, "Rabboni!" (which is to say, Teacher).{20:17} **Jesus said to her, "Do not cling to Me, for I have not yet ascended to My Father; but go to My brethren and say to them, 'I am ascending to My Father and your Father, and to My God and your God.'"** {20:18} Mary Magdalene came and told the disciples that she had seen the Lord, and that He had spoken these things to her. {20:19} Then, the same day at evening, being the first day of the week, when the doors were shut where the disciples were assembled, for fear of the Jews, Jesus came and stood in the midst, and said to them, "Peace be with you." {20:20} When He had said this, He showed them His hands and His side. Then the disciples were glad when they saw the Lord. {20:21} So Jesus said to them again, "Peace to you! As the Father has sent Me, I also send you." {20:22} And when He had said this, He breathed on them, and said to them, "Receive the Holy Spirit. {20:23} If you forgive the sins of any, they are forgiven them; if you retain the sins of any, they are retained." {20:24} Now Thomas, called the Twin, one of the twelve, was not with them when Jesus came. {20:25} The other disciples therefore said to him, "We have seen the Lord." So he said to them, "Unless I see in His hands the print of the nails, and put my finger into the print of the nails, and put my hand into His side, I will not believe." {20:26} And after eight days His disciples were again inside, and Thomas with them. Jesus came, the doors being shut, and stood in the midst, and said, "Peace to you!" {20:27} Then He said to Thomas, "Reach your finger here, and look at My hands; and reach your hand here, and put it into My side. Do not be unbelieving, but believing." {20:28} And Thomas answered and said to Him, "My Lord and my God!" {20:29} **Jesus said to him, "Thomas, because you have seen Me, you have believed. Blessed are those who have not seen and yet have believed."** {20:30} And truly Jesus did many other signs in the presence of His disciples, which are not written in this book; {20:31} but these are written that you may believe that Jesus is the Christ, the Son of God, and that believing you may have life in His name.

{21:1} After these things, Jesus showed Himself again to the disciples at the Sea of Tiberias; and in this way He showed Himself: {21:2} Simon Peter, Thomas called Didymus, Nathanael of Cana in Galilee, the sons of Zebedee, and two other disciples were together. {21:3} Simon Peter said to them, "I am going fishing." They said to him, "We will also go with you." They went out and immediately got into the boat, and that night they caught nothing. {21:4} But when the morning had now come, Jesus stood on the shore; yet the disciples did not know that it was Jesus. {21:5} The Jesus said to them, "Children, have you any food?" They answered Him, "No." {21:6} And He said to them, "Cast the net on the right side of the boat, and you will find some." So they cast, and now they were not able to draw it in because of the multitude of fish. {21:7} Therefore that disciple whom Jesus loved said to Peter, "It is the Lord!" Now when Simon Peter heard that it was the Lord, he put on his outer garment (for he had removed it), and plunged into the sea. {21:8} But the other disciples came in the little boat (for they were not far from land, but about two hundred cubits), dragging the net with fish. {21:9} Then, as soon as they had come to land, they saw a fire of coals there, and fish laid on it, and bread. {21:10} Jesus said to them, "Bring some of the fish which you have just caught." {21:11} Simon Peter went up and dragged the net to land, full of large fish, one hundred and fifty-three; and although there were so many, the net was not broken. {21:12} Jesus said to them, "Come and eat breakfast." Yet none of the disciples dared ask Him, "Who are You?"—knowing that it was the Lord. {21:13} Jesus then came and took the bread and gave it to them, and likewise the fish. {21:14} This is now the third time Jesus showed Himself to His disciples after He was raised from the dead. {21:15} So when they had eaten breakfast, Jesus said to Simon Peter, "Simon, son of Jonah, do you love Me more than these?" He said to Him, "Yes, Lord; You know that I love You." He said to him, "Feed My lambs." {21:16} He said to him again a second time, "Simon, son of Jonah, do you love Me?" He said to Him, "Yes, Lord; You know that I love You." He said to him, "Tend My sheep." {21:17} He said to him the third time, "Simon, son of Jonah, do you love Me?" Peter was grieved because He said to him the third time, "Do you love Me?" And he said to Him, "Lord, You know all things; You know that I love You." Jesus said to him, "Feed My sheep. {21:18} Most assuredly, I say to you, when you were younger, you girded yourself and walked where you wished; but when you are old, you will stretch out your hands, and another will gird you and carry you where you do not wish." {21:19} This He spoke, signifying by what death he would glorify God. And when He had spoken this, He said to him, "Follow Me." {21:20} Then Peter, turning around, saw the disciple whom Jesus loved following, who also had leaned on His breast at the supper, and said, "Lord, who is the one who betrays You?" {21:21} Peter, seeing him, said to Jesus, "But Lord, what about this man?" {21:22} Jesus said to him, "If I will that he remain till I come, what is that to you? You follow Me." {21:23} Then this saying went out among the brethren that this disciple would not die. Yet Jesus did not say to him that he would not die, but, "If I will that he remain till I come, what is that to you?" {21:24} This is the disciple who testifies of these things, and wrote these things; and we know that his testimony is true. {21:25} And there are also many other things that Jesus did, which if they were written one by one, I suppose that even the world itself could not contain the books that would be written. Amen.

Acts

{1:1} The former account I made, O Theophilus, of all that Jesus began both to do and teach, {1:2} until the day in which He was taken up, after He through the Holy Spirit had given commandments to the apostles whom He had chosen, {1:3} to whom He also presented Himself alive after His suffering by many infallible proofs, being seen by them during forty days and speaking of the things pertaining to the kingdom of God; {1:4} and being assembled together with them, He commanded them not to depart from Jerusalem, but to wait for the Promise of the Father, "which," He said, "you have heard from Me; {1:5} for John truly baptized with water, but you shall be baptized with the Holy Spirit not many days from now." {1:6} Therefore, when they had come together, they asked Him, saying, "Lord, will You at this time restore the kingdom to Israel?" {1:7} And He said to them, "It is not for you to know times or seasons which the Father has put in His own authority. {1:8} But you shall receive power when the Holy Spirit has come upon you; and you shall be witnesses to Me in Jerusalem, and in all Judea and Samaria, and to the end of the earth." {1:9} Now when He had spoken these things, while they watched, He was taken up, and a cloud received Him out of their sight. {1:10} And while they looked steadfastly toward heaven as He went up, behold, two men stood by them in white apparel, {1:11} who also said, "Men of Galilee, why do you stand gazing up into heaven? This same Jesus, who was taken up from you into heaven, will so come in like manner as you saw Him go into heaven." {1:12} Then they returned to Jerusalem from the mount called Olivet, which is near Jerusalem, a Sabbath day's journey. {1:13} And when they had entered, they went up into the upper room where they were staying: Peter, James, John, and Andrew; Philip and Thomas; Bartholomew and Matthew; James the son of Alphaeus and Simon the Zealot; and Judas the son of James. {1:14} These all continued with one accord in prayer and supplication, with the women and Mary the mother of Jesus, and with His brothers. {1:15} And in those days Peter stood up in the midst of the disciples (altogether the number of names was about a hundred and twenty), and said, {1:16} "Men and brethren, this Scripture had to be fulfilled, which the Holy Spirit spoke before by the mouth of David concerning Judas, who became a guide to those who arrested Jesus; {1:17} for he was numbered with us and obtained a part in this ministry." {1:18} (Now this man purchased a field with the wages of iniquity; and falling headlong, he burst open in the middle and all his entrails gushed out. {1:19} And it became known to all those dwelling in Jerusalem; so that field is called in their own language, Akel Dama, that is, Field of Blood.) {1:20} "For it is written in the Book of Psalms: 'Let his dwelling place be desolate, and let no one live in it'; and, 'Let another take his office.' {1:21} "Therefore, of these men who have accompanied us all the time that the Lord Jesus went in and out among us, {1:22} beginning from the baptism of John to that day when He was taken up from us, one of these must become a witness with us of His resurrection." {1:23} And they proposed two: Joseph called Barsabbas, who was surnamed Justus, and Matthias. {1:24} And they prayed and said, "You, O Lord, who know the hearts of all, show which of these two You have chosen {1:25} to take part in this ministry and apostleship from which Judas by transgression fell, that he might go to his own place." {1:26} And they cast their lots, and the lot fell on Matthias. And he was numbered with the eleven apostles.

{2:1} When the Day of Pentecost had fully come, they were all with one accord in one place. {2:2} And suddenly there came a sound from heaven as of a rushing mighty wind, and it filled all the house where they were sitting. {2:3} Then appeared to them divided tongues, as of fire, and one sat upon each of them. {2:4} And they were all filled with the Holy Spirit and began to speak with other tongues, as the Spirit gave them utterance. {2:5} And there were dwelling in Jerusalem Jews, devout men, from every nation under heaven. {2:6} And when this sound occurred, the multitude came together, and were confused, because everyone heard them speak in his own language. {2:7} Then they were all amazed and marveled, saying to one another, "Look, are not all these who speak Galileans? {2:8} And how is it that we hear, each in our own language in which we were born? {2:9} Parthians and Medes and Elamites, those dwelling in Mesopotamia, Judea and Cappadocia, Pontus and Asia, {2:10} Phrygia and Pamphylia, Egypt and the parts of Libya adjoining Cyrene, visitors from Rome, both Jews and proselytes, {2:11} Cretans and Arabs—we hear them speaking in our own tongues the wonderful works of God." {2:12} So they were all amazed and perplexed, saying to one another, "Whatever could this mean?" {2:13} Others mocking said, "They are full of new wine." {2:14} But Peter, standing up with the eleven, lifted up his voice and addressed them: "Men of Judea and all who dwell in Jerusalem, let this be known to you, and heed my words: {2:15} These people are not drunk, as you suppose, since it is only the third hour of the day. {2:16} But this is what was spoken by the prophet Joel: {2:17} *'And it shall come to pass in the last days, says God, that I will pour out of my Spirit on all flesh; your sons and your daughters shall prophesy, your young men shall see visions, your old men shall dream dreams.* {2:18} *And on My menservants and on My maidservants I will pour out My Spirit in those days; and they shall prophesy.* {2:19} *I will show wonders in heaven above and signs in the earth beneath: blood and fire and vapor of smoke.* {2:20} *The sun shall be turned into darkness, and the moon into blood, before the coming of the great and awesome day of the Lord.* {2:21} *And it shall come to pass that whoever calls on the name of the Lord shall be saved.'* {2:22} "Men of Israel, hear these words: Jesus of Nazareth, a Man attested by God to you by miracles, wonders, and signs which God did through Him in your midst, as you yourselves also know— {2:23} Him, being delivered by the determined purpose and foreknowledge of God, you have taken by lawless hands, have crucified, and put to death; {2:24} whom God raised up, having loosed the pains of death, because it was not possible that He should be held by it. {2:25} For David says concerning Him: 'I foresaw the Lord always before my face, For He is at my right hand, that I may not be shaken. {2:26} Therefore my heart rejoiced, and my tongue was glad; Moreover, my flesh also will rest in hope. {2:27} For You will not leave my soul in Hades, nor will You allow Your Holy One to see corruption. {2:28} You have made known to me the ways of life; You will make me full of joy in Your presence.' {2:29} "Men and brethren, let me speak freely to you of the patriarch David, that he is both dead and buried, and his tomb is with us to this day. {2:30} Therefore, being a prophet, and knowing that God had sworn with an oath to him that of the fruit of his body, according to the flesh, He would raise up the Christ to sit on his throne, {2:31} he, foreseeing this, spoke concerning the resurrection of the Christ, that His soul was not left in Hades, nor did His flesh see corruption. {2:32} This Jesus God has raised up, of which we are all witnesses. {2:33} "Therefore being exalted to the right hand of God, and having received from the Father the promise of the Holy Spirit, He poured out this which you now see and hear. {2:34} For David did not ascend into the heavens, but he says himself: 'The Lord said to my Lord, "Sit at My right hand, {2:35} Till I make Your enemies Your footstool."' {2:36} "Therefore let all the house of Israel know assuredly that God has made this Jesus, whom you crucified, both Lord and Christ." {2:37} When they heard this, they were deeply moved and asked Peter and the other apostles, "Men and brethren, what shall we do?" {2:38} Peter replied, "Repent and be baptized, every one of you, in the name of Jesus Christ for the forgiveness of your sins. And you will receive the gift of the Holy Spirit. {2:39} This promise is for you, for your children, and for all who are far off, as many as the Lord our God will call." {2:40} And with many other words, Peter testified and exhorted them, saying, "Save yourselves from this corrupt generation." {2:41} Those who welcomed his message were baptized, and about three thousand souls were added to them that day. {2:42} They devoted themselves to the apostles' teaching and fellowship, to the breaking of bread, and to prayer. {2:43} Fear came upon every soul, and many wonders and signs were done through the apostles. 2:44} All who believed were together and had everything in common. {2:45} They sold their possessions and goods and distributed them to all, as anyone had need. {2:46} Every day they continued to gather together in the temple, breaking bread from house to house, sharing their meals with gladness and sincerity of heart. {2:47} They praised God and enjoyed the favor of all the people. And the Lord added to their number daily those who were being saved.

{3:1} Peter and John went up to the temple together at the time of prayer, around three in the afternoon. {3:2} A man who had been lame from birth was being carried to the temple gate called Beautiful, where he was placed every day to beg from those entering the temple courts. {3:3} When he saw Peter and John about to enter, he asked them for money. {3:4} Peter looked straight at him, as did John. Then Peter said, "Look at us!" {3:5} So the man gave them his attention, expecting to receive something from them. {3:6} But Peter said, "Silver or gold I do not have, but what I do have I give you. In the name of Jesus Christ of Nazareth, walk." {3:7} Taking him by the right hand, he helped him up, and instantly the man's feet and ankles became strong. {3:8} He jumped to his feet and began to walk. Then he went with them into the temple courts, walking and jumping, and praising God. {3:9} When all the people saw him walking and praising God, {3:10} they recognized him as the same man who used to sit begging at the temple gate called Beautiful, and they were filled with wonder and amazement at what had happened to him. {3:11} While the man held on to Peter and John, all the people were astonished and came running to them in the place called Solomon's Colonnade. {3:12} When Peter saw this, he said to them: "Fellow Israelites, why does this surprise you? Why do you stare at us as if by our own power or godliness we had made this man walk? {3:13} The God of Abraham, Isaac and Jacob, the God of our fathers, has glorified his servant Jesus. You handed him over to be killed, and you disowned him before Pilate, though he had decided to let him go. {3:14} You disowned the Holy and Righteous One and asked that a murderer be released to you. {3:15} You killed the author of life, but God raised him from the dead. We are witnesses of this. {3:16} By faith in the name of Jesus, this man whom you see and know was made strong. It is Jesus' name and the faith that comes through him that has completely healed him, as you can all see. {3:17} Now, fellow Israelites, I know that you acted in ignorance, as did your leaders. {3:18} But this is how God fulfilled what he had foretold through all the prophets, saying that his Messiah would suffer. {3:19} Repent, then, and turn to God, so that your sins may be wiped out, that times of refreshing may come from the Lord, {3:20} and that he may send the Messiah, who has been appointed for you—even Jesus. {3:21} Heaven must receive him until the time comes for God to restore everything, as he promised long ago through his holy prophets. {3:22} For Moses said, 'The Lord your God will raise up for you a prophet like me from among your own people; you must listen to everything he tells you. {3:23} Anyone who does not listen to him will be completely cut off from their people.' {3:24} "Indeed, beginning with Samuel, all the prophets who have spoken have foretold these days. {3:25} And you are heirs of the prophets and of the covenant God made with your fathers. He said to Abraham, 'Through your offspring all peoples on earth will be blessed.' {3:26} When God raised up his servant, he sent him first to you to bless you by turning each of you from your wicked ways."

{4:1} While Peter and John were speaking to the people, the priests, the captain of the temple guard, and the Sadducees came up to them. {4:2} They were greatly disturbed because the apostles were teaching the people, proclaiming in Jesus the resurrection of the dead. {4:3} They seized Peter and John and, because it was evening, they put them in jail until the next day. {4:4} But many who heard the message believed; so the number of men who believed grew to about five thousand. {4:5} The next day the rulers, the elders, and the teachers of the law met in Jerusalem. {4:6} Annas the high priest was there, and so were Caiaphas, John, Alexander and others of the high priest's family. {4:7} They had Peter and John brought before them and began to question them: "By what power or what name did you do this?" {4:8} Then Peter, filled with the Holy Spirit, said to them: "Rulers and elders of the people! {4:9} If we are being called to account today for an act of kindness shown to a man who was lame and are being asked how he was healed, {4:10} then know this, you and all the people of Israel: It is by the name of Jesus Christ of Nazareth, whom you crucified but whom God raised from the dead, that this man stands before you healed. {4:11} Jesus is 'the stone you builders rejected, which has become the cornerstone.' {4:12} Salvation is found in no one else, for there is no other name under heaven given to mankind by which we must be saved." {4:13} When they saw the courage of Peter and John and realized that they were unschooled, ordinary men, they were astonished and they took note that these men had been with Jesus. {4:14} But since they could see the man who had been healed standing there with them, there was nothing they could say. {4:15} So they ordered them to withdraw from the Sanhedrin and then conferred together. {4:16} "What are we going to do with these men?" they asked. "Everyone living in Jerusalem knows they have performed a notable sign, and we cannot deny it. {4:17} But to stop this thing from spreading any further among the people, we must warn them to speak no longer to anyone in this name."{4:18} Then they called them in again and commanded them not to speak or teach at all in the name of Jesus. {4:19} But Peter and John replied, "Which is right in God's eyes: to listen to you, or to him? You be the judges! {4:20} As for us, we cannot help speaking about what we have seen and heard." {4:21} After further threats they let them go. They could not decide how to punish them, because all the people were praising God for what had happened. {4:22} For the man who was miraculously healed was over forty years old. {4:23} After they were released, Peter and John went back to their own people and reported all that the chief priests and the elders had said to them. {4:24} When they heard this, they raised their voices together in prayer to God. "Sovereign Lord," they said, "you made the heavens and the earth and the sea, and everything in them. {4:25} You spoke by the Holy Spirit through the mouth of your servant, our father David: 'Why do the nations rage and the peoples plot in vain? {4:26} The kings of the earth rise up and the rulers band together against the Lord and against his anointed one.' {4:27} Indeed Herod and Pontius Pilate met together with the Gentiles and the people of Israel in this city to conspire against your holy servant Jesus, whom you anointed. {4:28} They did what your power and will had decided beforehand should happen. {4:29} Now, Lord, consider their threats and enable your servants to speak your word with great boldness. {4:30} Stretch out your hand to heal and perform signs and wonders through the name of your holy servant Jesus." {4:31} After they prayed, the place where they were meeting was shaken. And they were all filled with the Holy Spirit and spoke the word of God boldly. {4:32} All the believers were one in heart and mind. No one claimed that any of their possessions was their own, but they shared everything they had. {4:33} With great power the apostles continued to testify to the resurrection of the Lord Jesus. And God's grace was so powerfully at work in them all {4:34} that there were no needy persons among them. For from time to time those who owned land or houses sold them, brought the money from the sales {4:35} and put it at the apostles' feet, and it was distributed to anyone who had need. {4:36} Joseph, a Levite from Cyprus, whom the apostles called Barnabas (which means "son of encouragement"), {4:37} sold a field he owned and brought the money and put it at the apostles' feet.

{5:1} There was a man named Ananias who, with his wife Sapphira, sold some property. {5:2} However, they kept back some of the money for themselves, and brought only a part of it and laid it at the apostles' feet. {5:3} Peter said to Ananias, "Why has Satan filled your heart to lie to the Holy Spirit and keep back part of the proceeds of the land? {5:4} While it remained unsold, did it not remain your own? And after it was sold, was it not at your disposal? Why is it that you have contrived this deed in your heart? You have not lied to men but to God." {5:5} Upon hearing these words, Ananias fell down and died. And great fear came upon all who heard of it. {5:6} The young men rose and wrapped him up and carried him out and buried him. {5:7} About three hours later, his wife came in, not knowing what had happened. {5:8} And Peter said to her, "Tell me whether you sold the land for so much." And she said, "Yes, for so much." {5:9} But Peter said to her, "How is it that you have agreed together to test the Spirit of the Lord? Behold, the feet of those who have buried your husband are at the door, and they will carry you out." {5:10} Immediately she fell down at his feet and breathed her last. When the young men came in they found her dead, and they carried her out and buried her beside her husband. {5:11} And great fear came upon the whole church and upon all who heard of these things.{5:12} Now many signs and wonders were regularly done among the people by the hands of the apostles. And they were all together in Solomon's Portico. {5:13} None of the rest dared join them, but the people held them in high esteem. {5:14} And more than ever believers were added to the Lord, multitudes of both men and women, {5:15} so that they even carried out the sick into the streets and laid them on cots and mats, that as Peter came by at least his shadow might fall on some of them. {5:16} The people also gathered from the towns around Jerusalem, bringing the sick and those afflicted with unclean spirits, and they were all healed. {5:17} But the high priest rose up, and all who were with him (that is, the party of the Sadducees), and filled with jealousy {5:18} they arrested the apostles and put them in the public prison. {5:19} But during the night an angel of the Lord opened the prison doors and brought them out, and said, {5:20} "Go and stand in the temple and speak to the people all the words of this Life." {5:21} Now when the high priest came, and those who were with him, they called together the council, all the senate of the people of Israel, and sent them to the prison to have them brought. {5:22} But when the officers came, they did not find them in the prison, so they returned and reported, {5:23} "We found the prison securely locked and the guards standing at the doors, but when we opened them we found no one inside." {5:24} Now when the captain of the temple and the chief priests heard these words, they were greatly perplexed about them, wondering what this would come to. {5:25} And someone came and told them, "Look! The men whom you put in prison are standing in the temple and teaching the people." {5:26} Then the captain with the officers went and brought them, but not by force, for they were afraid of being stoned by the people. {5:27} And when they had brought them, they set them before the council. And the high priest questioned them, {5:28} saying, "We strictly charged you not to teach in this name, yet here you have filled Jerusalem with your teaching, and you intend to bring this man's blood upon us." {5:29} Then Peter and the other apostles replied, "We must obey God rather than human beings. {5:30} The God of our ancestors raised Jesus from the dead—whom you killed by hanging him on a cross. {5:31} God exalted him to his own right hand as Prince and Savior that he might bring Israel to repentance and forgive their sins. {5:32} We are witnesses of these things, and so is the Holy Spirit, whom God has given to those who obey him." {5:33} When they heard this, they were furious and wanted to put them to death. {5:34} But a Pharisee named Gamaliel, a teacher of the law, who was honored by all the people, stood up in the Sanhedrin and ordered that the men be put outside for a little while. {5:35} Then he addressed the Sanhedrin: "Men of Israel, consider carefully what you intend to do to these men. {5:36} Some time ago Theudas appeared, claiming to be somebody, and about four hundred men rallied to him. He was killed, all his followers were dispersed, and it all came to nothing. {5:37} After him, Judas the Galilean appeared in the days of the census and led a band of people in revolt. He too was killed, and all his followers were scattered. {5:38} Therefore, in the present case I advise you: Leave these men alone! Let them go! For if their purpose or activity is of human origin, it will fail. {5:39} But if it is from God, you will not be able to stop these men; you will only find yourselves fighting against God." {5:40} His speech persuaded them. They called the apostles in and had them flogged. Then they ordered them not to speak in the name of Jesus, and let them go. {5:41} The apostles left the Sanhedrin, rejoicing because they had been counted worthy of suffering disgrace for the Name. {5:42} Day after day, in the temple courts and from house to house, they never stopped teaching and proclaiming the good news that Jesus is the Messiah.

{6:1} In those days, as the number of disciples was multiplying, there arose a complaint from the Greek-speaking Jews against the native Hebrews. The issue was that their widows were being overlooked in the daily distribution of food. {6:2} So the twelve apostles called a meeting of all the believers and said, "It is not right for us to neglect the ministry of the word of God in order to handle administrative tasks. {6:3} Therefore, brothers and sisters, select from among you seven men of good reputation, full of the Spirit and wisdom, whom we may appoint to oversee this task. {6:4} Then we can devote ourselves to prayer and to the ministry of the word." {6:5} This proposal pleased the whole group. They chose Stephen, a man full of faith and the Holy Spirit, along with Philip, Prochorus, Nicanor, Timon, Parmenas, and Nicolas from Antioch, who had converted to Judaism. {6:6} These men were presented to the apostles, who prayed for them and laid their hands on them. {6:7} As a result, the word of God spread, and the number of disciples in Jerusalem increased rapidly. Even a large number of priests became obedient to the faith. {6:8} Stephen, full of grace and power, performed great wonders and signs among the people. {6:9} But some members of the Synagogue of the Freedmen (as it was called)—Jews from Cyrene, Alexandria, Cilicia, and Asia—began to argue with Stephen. {6:10} However, they could not stand up against his wisdom or the Spirit by whom he spoke. {6:11} Then they secretly persuaded some men to claim, "We heard Stephen speak blasphemous words against Moses and against God." {6:12} This stirred up the people, the elders, and the teachers of the law. They seized Stephen and brought him before the Sanhedrin. {6:13} They produced false witnesses who testified, "This fellow never stops speaking against this holy place and against the law. {6:14} For we have heard him say that Jesus of Nazareth will destroy this place and change the customs Moses handed down to us." {6:15} All who were sitting in the Sanhedrin looked intently at Stephen, and they saw that his face was like the face of an angel.

{7:1} The high priest then asked Stephen, "Are these accusations against you true?" {7:2} Stephen replied, "Brothers and fathers, listen to me. The God of glory appeared to our ancestor Abraham while he was still in Mesopotamia, before he lived in Harran. {7:3} God told him, 'Leave your native land and your relatives, and come into the land that I will show you.' {7:4} So Abraham left the land of the Chaldeans and lived in Harran until his father died. Then God brought him here to the land where you now live. {7:5} But God gave him no inheritance here, not even one square foot of land. God did promise, however, that eventually the whole land would belong to Abraham and his descendants—though he had no children yet. {7:6} God also told him that his descendants would live in a foreign land, where they would be oppressed as slaves for 400 years. {7:7} 'But I will punish the nation that enslaves them,' God said, 'and in the end they will come out and worship me here in this place.' {7:8} "God also gave Abraham the covenant of circumcision at that time. So when Abraham became the father of Isaac, he circumcised him on the eighth day. Isaac became the father of Jacob, and Jacob became the father of the twelve patriarchs. {7:9} "These patriarchs were jealous of their brother Joseph, and they sold him to be a slave in Egypt. But God was with him {7:10} and rescued him from all his troubles. And God gave him favor before Pharaoh, king of Egypt. God also gave Joseph unusual wisdom, so that Pharaoh appointed him governor over all of Egypt and put him in charge of the palace. {7:11} "But then a famine struck all of Egypt and Canaan, bringing great suffering. Our ancestors couldn't find any food. {7:12} When Jacob heard that there was grain in Egypt, he sent our ancestors to Egypt. {7:13} The second time they went, Joseph revealed his identity to his brothers, and Pharaoh learned about Joseph's family. {7:14} Joseph sent for his father, Jacob, and all his relatives to come to Egypt, seventy-five persons in all. {7:15} So Jacob went to Egypt, where he died, as did our ancestors. {7:16} Their bodies were taken to Shechem and buried in the tomb Abraham had bought for a certain price from Homer's descendants in Shechem. {7:17} "As the time drew near when God would fulfill his promise to Abraham, the number of our people in Egypt greatly increased. {7:18} But then a new king came to the throne of Egypt who knew nothing about Joseph. {7:19} This king exploited our people and oppressed them, forcing parents to abandon their newborn babies so they would die. {7:20} "At that time Moses was born—a beautiful child in God's eyes. His parents cared for him at home for three months. {7:21} When they had to abandon him, Pharaoh's daughter adopted him and raised him as her own son. {7:22} Moses was taught all the wisdom of the Egyptians, and he was powerful in both speech and action. {7:23} "One day, when Moses was forty years old, he decided to visit his relatives, the people of Israel. {7:24} He saw an Egyptian mistreating an Israelite. So Moses came to the man's defense and avenged him, killing the Egyptian. {7:25} Moses assumed his fellow Israelites would realize that God had sent him to rescue them, but they didn't. {7:26} "The next day he visited them again and saw two men of Israel fighting. He tried to be a peacemaker. 'Men,' he said, 'you are brothers. Why are you fighting each other?' {7:27} But the man in the wrong pushed Moses aside. 'Who made you a ruler and judge over us?' he asked. {7:28} 'Are you going to kill me as you killed that Egyptian yesterday?' {7:29} When Moses heard that, he fled the country and lived as a foreigner in the land of Midian. There his two sons were born. {7:30} "Forty years later, in the desert near Mount Sinai, an angel appeared to Moses in the flame of a burning bush. {7:31} Moses saw it and wondered what it was. As he went to take a closer look, the voice of the Lord called out to him, {7:32} 'I am the God of your ancestors—the God of Abraham, Isaac, and Jacob.' Moses shook with terror and dared not look. {7:33} "Then the Lord said to him, 'Take off your sandals, for you are standing on holy ground. {7:34} I have certainly seen the oppression of my people in Egypt. I have heard their groans and have come down to rescue them. Now go, for I am sending you back to Egypt.' {7:35} "So God sent back the same man his people had previously rejected when they demanded, 'Who made you a ruler and judge over us?' Through the angel who appeared to him in the burning bush, God sent him to be their ruler and savior. {7:36} And by means of many wonders and miraculous signs, he led them out of Egypt, through the Red Sea, and through the wilderness for forty years." {7:37} This is the same Moses who told the people of Israel, 'God will raise up for you a Prophet like me from among your own people.' {7:38} Moses was with the assembly of God's people in the wilderness. He was there with the angel who spoke to him on Mount Sinai, and with our ancestors. Moses received living words to pass on to us. {7:39} But our ancestors refused to obey him. Instead, they rejected him and turned back to Egypt in their hearts. {7:40} They told Aaron, 'Make us some gods who can lead us, for we don't know what has become of this Moses, who brought us out of Egypt.' {7:41} So they made an idol shaped like a calf, and they sacrificed it and celebrated over this thing they had made with their own hands. {7:42} Then God turned away from them and abandoned them to serve the stars of heaven as their gods. As the prophets say, 'Was it to me you were bringing sacrifices and offerings during those forty years in the wilderness, Israel? {7:43} No, you carried your pagan gods— the shrine of Molech, the star of your god Rephan, and the images you made to worship them. So I will send you into captivity far away in Babylon.' {7:44} Our ancestors had the Tabernacle of the Covenant with them in the wilderness. It was constructed according to the plan God had shown to Moses. And God had commanded Moses to make it exactly like the pattern he had seen.

{7:45} Later, when Joshua led our ancestors in battle against the nations that God drove out of this land, the Tabernacle was taken with them into their new territory. And it stayed there until the time of King David. {7:46} David found favor with God and asked for the privilege of building a permanent Temple for the God of Jacob. {7:47} But it was Solomon who actually built it. {7:48} However, the Most High doesn't live in temples made by human hands. As the prophet says, {7:49} 'Heaven is my throne, and the earth is my footstool. Could you build me a temple as good as that?' asks the Lord. 'Could you build me such a resting place? {7:50} Didn't my hands make both heaven and earth?' {7:51} "You stubborn people! You are heathen at heart and deaf to the truth. Must you forever resist the Holy Spirit? That's what your ancestors did, and so do you! {7:52} Name one prophet your ancestors didn't persecute! They even killed the ones who predicted the coming of the Righteous One—the Messiah whom you betrayed and murdered. {7:53} You deliberately disobeyed God's law, even though you received it from the hands of angels." {7:54} The Jewish leaders were infuriated by Stephen's accusation, and they shook their fists at him in rage. {7:55} "But Stephen, full of the Holy Spirit, gazed steadily into heaven and saw the glory of God, and he saw Jesus standing in the place of honor at God's right hand. {7:56} And he told them, "Look, I see the heavens opened and the Son of Man standing in the place of honor at God's right hand!" {7:57} Then they put their hands over their ears and began shouting. They rushed at him {7:58} and dragged him out of the city and began to stone him. His accusers took off their coats and laid them at the feet of a young man named Saul. {7:59} As they stoned him, Stephen prayed, "Lord Jesus, receive my spirit." {7:60} He fell to his knees, shouting, "Lord, don't charge them with this sin!" And with that, he died.

{8:1} Saul agreed completely with killing Stephen. A great wave of persecution began that day, sweeping over the church in Jerusalem; and all the believers except the apostles were scattered through the regions of Judea and Samaria. {8:2} (Some devout men came and buried Stephen with great mourning.) {8:3} But Saul was going everywhere to destroy the church. He went from house to house, dragging out both men and women to throw them into prison. {8:4} But the believers who were scattered preached the Good News about Jesus wherever they went. {8:5} Philip, for example, went to the city of Samaria and told the people there about the Messiah. {8:6} Crowds listened intently to Philip because they were eager to hear his message and see the miraculous signs he did. {8:7} Many evil spirits were cast out, screaming as they left their victims. And many who had been paralyzed or lame were healed. {8:8} So there was great joy in that city. {8:9} A man named Simon had been a sorcerer there for many years, amazing the people of Samaria and claiming to be someone great. {8:10} Everyone, from the least to the greatest, often spoke of him as "the Great One—the Power of God." {8:11} They listened closely to him because for a long time he had astounded them with his magic. {8:12} But now the people believed Philip's message of Good News concerning the Kingdom of God and the name of Jesus Christ. As a result, many men and women were baptized. {8:13} Then Simon himself believed and was baptized. He began following Philip wherever he went, and he was amazed by the signs and great miracles Philip performed. {8:14} When the apostles in Jerusalem heard that the people of Samaria had accepted God's message, they sent Peter and John there. {8:15} As soon as they arrived, they prayed for these new believers to receive the Holy Spirit. {8:16} The Holy Spirit had not yet come upon any of them, for they had only been baptized in the name of the Lord Jesus. {8:17} Then Peter and John laid their hands upon these believers, and they received the Holy Spirit. {8:18} When Simon saw that the Spirit was given when the apostles laid their hands on people, he offered them money to buy this power. {8:19} "Let me have this power, too," he exclaimed, "so that when I lay my hands on people, they will receive the Holy Spirit!" {8:20} But Peter replied, "May your money be destroyed with you thinking God's gift can be bought! {8:21} You can have no part in this, for your heart is not right with God. {8:22} Repent of your wickedness and pray to the Lord. Perhaps he will forgive your evil thoughts, {8:23} for I can see that you are full of bitter jealousy and are held captive by sin." {8:24} "Pray to the Lord for me," Simon exclaimed, "that these terrible things you've said won't happen to me!" {8:25} After testifying and preaching the word of the Lord in Samaria, Peter and John returned to Jerusalem. And they stopped in many Samaritan villages along the way to preach the Good News.{8:26} Then an angel of the Lord spoke to Philip, saying, "Arise and go toward the south along the road which goes down from Jerusalem to Gaza." This road is deserted. {8:27} So Philip got up and went. And there he saw a man from Ethiopia, a eunuch of great authority under Candace, the queen of the Ethiopians, who was in charge of all her treasury. This man had come to Jerusalem to worship, {8:28} and he was now returning home. Seated in his chariot, he was reading aloud from the book of the prophet Isaiah. {8:29} The Spirit said to Philip, "Go over and walk along beside the carriage." {8:30} Philip ran over and heard the man reading from the prophet Isaiah. Philip asked, "Do you understand what you are reading?" {8:31} The man replied, "How can I, unless someone instructs me?" And he urged Philip to come up into the carriage and sit with him. {8:32} The passage of Scripture he had been reading was this:"He was led like a sheep to the slaughter. And as a lamb is silent before the shearers, he did not open his mouth {8:33} He was humiliated and received no justice. Who can speak of his descendants? For his life was taken from the earth." {8:34} The eunuch asked Philip, "Tell me, was the prophet talking about himself or someone else?" {8:35} So beginning with this same Scripture, Philip told him the Good News about Jesus. {8:36} As they rode along, they came to some water, and the eunuch said, "Look! There's some water! Why can't I be baptized?" {8:37} Philip said, "If you believe with all your heart, you may." The eunuch answered, "I believe that Jesus Christ is the Son of God." {8:38} So Philip commanded the chariot to stop, and both Philip and the eunuch went down into the water, and Philip baptized him. {8:39} When they came up out of the water, the Spirit of the Lord snatched Philip away. The eunuch never saw him again but went on his way rejoicing. {8:40} Meanwhile, Philip found himself farther north at the town of Azotus. He preached the Good News there and in every town along the way until he came to Caesarea.

{9:1} Saul, still breathing out threats and murder against the disciples of the Lord, went to the high priest {9:2} and asked him for letters to the synagogues in Damascus, so that if he found any followers of Jesus there, whether men or women, he could bring them bound to Jerusalem. {9:3} As he journeyed and came near Damascus, suddenly a light from heaven shone around him. {9:4} He fell to the ground and heard a voice saying to him, "Saul, Saul, why are you persecuting me?" {9:5} Saul asked, "Who are you, Lord?" The Lord replied, "I am Jesus, whom you are persecuting. It is hard for you to kick against the goads." {9:6} Trembling and astonished, Saul said, "Lord, what do you want me to do?" The Lord said to him, "Arise and go into the city, and you will be told what you must do." {9:7} The men traveling with Saul stood speechless, hearing the voice but seeing no one. {9:8} Saul got up from the ground, but when he opened his eyes, he could see nothing. So they led him by the hand and brought him into Damascus. {9:9} For three days he was blind and did not eat or drink anything. {9:10} Now there was a disciple in Damascus named Ananias. The Lord spoke to him in a vision, "Ananias." Ananias answered, "Here I am, Lord." {9:11} The Lord told him, "Go to the street called Straight and inquire at the house of Judas for a man from Tarsus named Saul. He is praying, {9:12} and in a vision he has seen a man named Ananias coming to restore his sight by placing his hands on him." {9:13} Ananias replied, "Lord, I have heard many reports about this man and all the harm he has done to your saints in Jerusalem. {9:14} And now he has come here with authority from the chief priests to arrest all who call on your name." {9:15} But the Lord said to Ananias, "Go! This man is my chosen instrument to proclaim my name to the Gentiles and their kings and to the people of Israel. {9:16} I will show him how much he must suffer for my name." {9:17} So Ananias went to the house and entered it. Placing his hands on Saul, he said, "Brother Saul, the Lord Jesus, who appeared to you on the road as you were coming here, has sent me so that you may see again and be filled with the Holy Spirit." {9:18} Immediately, something like scales fell from Saul's eyes, and he could see again. He got up and was baptized. {9:19} After taking some food, he regained his strength. Saul spent several days with the disciples in Damascus. {9:20} And immediately he began to preach in the synagogues that Jesus is the Son of God. {9:21} All who heard him were amazed and said, "Is this not the same man who caused havoc in Jerusalem among those who called on this name? And hasn't he come here to take them as prisoners to the chief priests?" {9:22} But Saul grew more and more powerful and confounded the Jews living in Damascus by proving that Jesus is the Messiah. {9:23} After many days had passed, the Jews plotted to kill Saul. {9:24} But Saul learned of their plan. They were watching the city gates day and night to kill him. {9:25} So the disciples took him by night and lowered him in a basket through an opening in the wall. {9:26} When Saul arrived in Jerusalem, he tried to join the disciples, but they were all afraid of him, not believing that he was truly a disciple. {9:27} However, Barnabas took him and brought him to the apostles. He told them how Saul had seen the Lord on the road to Damascus, how the Lord had spoken to him, and how boldly Saul had preached in the name of Jesus in Damascus. {9:28} Saul was with them, coming in and going out of Jerusalem, speaking boldly in the name of the Lord Jesus and debating with the Hellenists. Yet, they attempted to kill him. {9:29} When the believers learned of this, they took Saul down to Caesarea and sent him off to Tarsus. {9:30} Then the churches throughout Judea, Galilee, and Samaria had peace and were edified. {9:31} They grew in number, walking in the fear of the Lord and in the comfort of the Holy Spirit. {9:32} Meanwhile, Peter traveled throughout the region and went to visit the believers in Lydda. {9:33} There he found a man named Aeneas, who had been bedridden for eight years, paralyzed. {9:34} Peter said to him, "Aeneas, Jesus Christ heals you. Get up and roll up your mat." Immediately Aeneas got up. {9:35} All the people in Lydda and Sharon saw him and turned to the Lord. {9:36} In Joppa there was a disciple named Tabitha (in Greek her name is Dorcas); she was always doing good and helping the poor. {9:37} About that time she became sick and died, and her body was washed and placed in an upstairs room. {9:38} Lydda was near Joppa, so when the disciples heard that Peter was in Lydda, they sent two men to him and urged him, "Please come at once!" {9:39} Peter went with them, and when he arrived, he was taken upstairs to the room. All the widows stood around him, crying and showing him the robes and other clothing that Dorcas had made while she was still with them. {9:40} Peter sent them all out of the room; then he got down on his knees and prayed. Turning toward the dead woman, he said, "Tabitha, get up." She opened her eyes, and seeing Peter she sat up. {9:41} He took her by the hand and helped her to her feet. Then he called for the believers, especially the widows, and presented her to them alive. {9:42} This became known all over Joppa, and many people believed in the Lord. {9:43} Peter stayed in Joppa for some time with a tanner named Simon.

{10:1} In Caesarea, there was a man named Cornelius, a centurion in the Italian regiment. {10:2} He was a devout man who feared God with all his household, gave generously to those in need, and prayed to God regularly. {10:3} One day at about three in the afternoon, he had a vision. He distinctly saw an angel of God who came to him and said, "Cornelius!" {10:4} Cornelius stared at him in fear. "What is it, Lord?" he asked. The angel answered, "Your prayers and gifts to the poor have come up as a memorial offering before God. {10:5} Now send men to Joppa to bring back a man named Simon who is called Peter. {10:6} He is staying with Simon the tanner, whose house is by the sea." {10:7} When the angel who spoke to him had gone, Cornelius called two of his servants and a devout soldier who was one of his attendants. {10:8} He told them everything that had happened and sent them to Joppa. {10:9} About noon the following day as they were on their journey and approaching the city, Peter went up on the roof to pray. {10:10} He became hungry and wanted something to eat, and while the meal was being prepared, he fell into a trance. {10:11} He saw heaven opened and something like a large sheet being let down to earth by its four corners. {10:12} It contained all kinds of four-footed animals, as well as reptiles and birds. {10:13} Then a voice told him, "Get up, Peter. Kill and eat." {10:14} "Surely not, Lord!" Peter replied. "I have never eaten anything impure or unclean." {10:15} The voice spoke to him a second time, "Do not call anything impure that God has made clean." {10:16} This happened three times, and immediately the sheet was taken back to heaven.{10:17} While Peter was wondering about the meaning of the vision, the men sent by Cornelius found out where Simon's house was and stopped at the gate. {10:18} They called out, asking if Simon, who was known as Peter, was staying there. {10:19} While Peter was still thinking about the vision, the Spirit said to him, "Simon, three men are looking for you. {10:20} So get up and go downstairs. Do not hesitate to go with them, for I have sent them." {10:21} Peter went down and said to the men, "I'm the one you're looking for. Why have you come?" {10:22} The men replied, "We have come from Cornelius the centurion. He is a righteous and God-fearing man, who is respected by all the Jewish people. A holy angel told him to ask you to come to his house so that he could hear what you have to say." {10:23} Then Peter invited the men into the house to be his guests. The next day Peter started out with them, and some of the believers from Joppa went along. {10:24} The following day he arrived in Caesarea. Cornelius was expecting them and had called together his relatives and close friends. {10:25} As Peter entered the house, Cornelius met him and fell at his feet in reverence. {10:26} But Peter made him get up. "Stand up," he said, "I am only a man myself."{10:27} While talking with Cornelius, Peter went inside and found a large gathering of people. {10:28} He said to them: "You are well aware that it is against our law for a Jew to associate with or visit a Gentile. But God has shown me that I should not call anyone impure or unclean. {10:29} So when I was sent for, I came without raising any objection. May I ask why you sent it to me?" {10:30} Cornelius answered: "Four days ago I was praying in my house at three in the afternoon. Suddenly a man in shining clothes stood before me {10:31} and said, 'Cornelius, your prayer has been heard, and your gifts to the poor have come up as a memorial offering before God. {10:32} Now send to Joppa for Simon who is called Peter. He is a guest in the home of Simon the tanner, who lives by the sea.' {10:33} So I sent for you immediately, and it was good of you to come. Now we are all here in the presence of God to listen to everything the Lord has commanded you to tell us." {10:34} Then Peter began to speak: "I now realize how true it is that God does not show favoritism {10:35} but accepts from every nation the one who fears him and does what is right. {10:36} You know the message God sent to the people of Israel, announcing the good news of peace through Jesus Christ, who is the Lord of all. {10:37} You know what has happened throughout the province of Judea, beginning in Galilee after the baptism that John preached— {10:38} how God anointed Jesus of Nazareth with the Holy Spirit and power, and how he went around doing good and healing all who were under the power of the devil because God was with him. {10:39} We are witnesses of everything he did in the country of the Jews and in Jerusalem. They killed him by hanging him on a cross, {10:40} but God raised him from the dead on the third day and caused him to be seen. {10:41} He was not seen by all the people, but by witnesses whom God had already chosen—by us who ate and drank with him after he rose from the dead. {10:42} He commanded us to preach to the people and to testify that he is the one whom God appointed as judge of the living and the dead. {10:43} All the prophets testify about him that everyone who believes in him receives forgiveness of sins through his name." {10:44} While Peter was still speaking these words, the Holy Spirit came on all who heard the message. {10:45} The circumcised believers who had come with Peter were astonished that the gift of the Holy Spirit had been poured out even on Gentiles. {10:46} For they heard them speaking in tongues and praising God. Then Peter said, {10:47} "Surely no one can stand in the way of their being baptized with water. They have received the Holy Spirit just as we have." {10:48} So he ordered that they be baptized in the name of Jesus Christ. Then they asked Peter to stay with them for a few days.

{11:1} When the apostles and believers in Judea heard that the Gentiles had also received the word of God, {11:2} they raised objections with Peter. {11:3} They said, "You went into the house of uncircumcised men and ate with them." {11:4} But Peter began to explain everything to them, step by step. He said, {11:5} "I was in Joppa praying, and in a trance I saw a vision. I saw a large sheet being let down from heaven by its four corners, and it came down to where I was. {11:6} I looked into it and saw four-footed animals of the earth, wild beasts, reptiles, and birds. {11:7} Then I heard a voice saying to me, 'Get up, Peter; kill and eat.' {11:8} But I replied, 'Surely not, Lord! Nothing impure or unclean has ever entered my mouth.' {11:9} The voice spoke from heaven a second time, 'Do not call anything impure that God has made clean.' {11:10} This happened three times, and then it was all pulled up to heaven again. {11:11} Right then three men who had been sent to me from Caesarea stopped at the house where I was staying. {11:12} The Spirit told me to have no hesitation about going with them. These six brothers also went with me, and we entered the man's house. {11:13} He told us how he had seen an angel appear in his house and say, 'Send to Joppa for Simon who is called Peter. {11:14} He will bring you a message through which you and all your household will be saved.' {11:15} As I began to speak, the Holy Spirit came on them as he had come on us at the beginning. {11:16} Then I remembered what the Lord had said: 'John baptized with water, but you will be baptized with the Holy Spirit.' {11:17} So if God gave them the same gift he gave us who believed in the Lord Jesus Christ, who was I to think that I could stand in God's way?" {11:18} When they heard this, they had no further objections and praised God, saying, "So then, even to Gentiles God has granted repentance that leads to life." {11:19} Now those who had been scattered by the persecution that broke out when Stephen was killed traveled as far as Phoenicia, Cyprus, and Antioch, spreading the word only among Jews. {11:20} Some of them, however, men from Cyprus and Cyrene, went to Antioch and began to speak to Greeks also, telling them the good news about the Lord Jesus. {11:21} The Lord's hand was with them, and a great number of people believed and turned to the Lord. {11:22} News of this reached the church in Jerusalem, and they sent Barnabas to Antioch. {11:23} When he arrived and saw what the grace of God had done, he was glad and encouraged them all to remain true to the Lord with all their hearts. {11:24} He was a good man, full of the Holy Spirit and faith, and a great number of people were brought to the Lord. {11:25} Then Barnabas went to Tarsus to look for Saul, {11:26} and when he found him, he brought him to Antioch. So for a whole year Barnabas and Saul met with the church and taught great numbers of people. The disciples were called Christians first at Antioch. {11:27} During this time some prophets came down from Jerusalem to Antioch. {11:28} One of them, named Agabus, stood up and through the Spirit predicted that a severe famine would spread over the entire Roman world. (This happened during the reign of Claudius.) {11:29} The disciples, as each one was able, decided to provide help for the brothers and sisters living in Judea. {11:30} This they did, sending their gift to the elders by Barnabas and Saul.

{12:1} At that time, King Herod began to persecute some of the church members. {12:2} He executed James, the brother of John, with a sword. {12:3} Seeing that this pleased the Jews, he arrested Peter as well. (This happened during the feast of Unleavened Bread.) {12:4} Herod had Peter seized and thrown into prison, placing him under the guard of four squads of four soldiers each. He intended to bring Peter out for public trial after the Passover. {12:5} While Peter was in prison, the church prayed earnestly to God for him. {12:6} The night before Herod was to bring him to trial, Peter was sleeping between two soldiers, bound with two chains, with sentries standing guard at the entrance. {12:7} Suddenly, an angel of the Lord appeared, and a light shone in the cell. The angel struck Peter on the side and woke him up. "Quick, get up!" he said, and the chains fell off Peter's wrists. {12:8} Then the angel told him, "Get dressed and put on your sandals." And Peter did so. "Wrap your cloak around you and follow me," the angel ordered. {12:9} Peter followed him out of the prison, but he had no idea that what the angel was doing was really happening; he thought he was seeing a vision. {12:10} They passed the first and second guards and came to the iron gate leading to the city. It opened for them by itself, and they went through it. When they had walked the length of one street, suddenly the angel left him. {12:11} Then Peter came to himself and said, "Now I know without a doubt that the Lord has sent his angel and rescued me from Herod's clutches and from everything the Jewish people were hoping would happen." {12:12} When this had dawned on him, he went to the house of Mary the mother of John, also called Mark, where many people had gathered and were praying. {12:13} Peter knocked at the outer entrance, and a servant named Rhoda came to answer the door. {12:14} When she recognized Peter's voice, she was so overjoyed that she ran back without opening it and exclaimed, "Peter is at the door!" {12:15} "You're out of your mind," they told her. When she kept insisting that it was so, they said, "It must be his angel." {12:16} But Peter kept on knocking, and when they opened the door and saw him, they were astonished. {12:17} Peter motioned with his hand for them to be quiet and described how the Lord had brought him out of prison. "Tell James and the other brothers and sisters about this," he said, and then he left for another place. {12:18} In the morning, there was no small commotion among the soldiers as to what had become of Peter. {12:19} After Herod had a thorough search made for him and did not find him, he cross-examined the guards and ordered that they be executed. Then Herod went from Judea to Caesarea and stayed there. {12:20} He had been quarreling with the people of Tyre and Sidon; they now joined together and sought an audience with him. After securing the support of Blastus, a trusted personal servant of the king, they asked for peace, because they depended on the king's country for their food supply. {12:21} On the appointed day Herod, wearing his royal robes, sat on his throne and delivered a public address to the people. {12:22} They shouted, "This is the voice of a god, not of a man." {12:23} Immediately, because Herod did not give praise to God, an angel of the Lord struck him down, and he was eaten by worms and died. {12:24} But the word of God continued to spread and flourish. {12:25} When Barnabas and Saul had finished their mission, they returned from Jerusalem, taking with them John, also called Mark.

{13:1} In the church at Antioch, there were prophets and teachers: Barnabas, Simeon (called Niger), Lucius of Cyrene, Manaen (who had been brought up with Herod the tetrarch), and Saul. {13:2} While they were worshiping the Lord and fasting, the Holy Spirit said, "Set apart for me Barnabas and Saul for the work to which I have called them." {13:3} So after they had fasted and prayed, they placed their hands on them and sent them off. {13:4} The two of them, sent on their way by the Holy Spirit, went down to Seleucia and sailed from there to Cyprus. {13:5} When they arrived at Salamis, they proclaimed the word of God in the Jewish synagogues. John was with them as their helper. {13:6} They traveled through the whole island until they came to Paphos. There they met a Jewish sorcerer and false prophet named Bar-Jesus, {13:7} who was an attendant of the proconsul, Sergius Paulus. The proconsul, an intelligent man, sent for Barnabas and Saul because he wanted to hear the word of God. {13:8} But Elymas the sorcerer (for that is what his name means) opposed them and tried to turn the proconsul from the faith. {13:9} Then Saul, who was also called Paul, filled with the Holy Spirit, looked straight at Elymas {13:10} and said, "You are a child of the devil and an enemy of everything that is right! You are full of all kinds of deceit and trickery. Will you never stop perverting the right ways of the Lord? {13:11} Now the hand of the Lord is against you. You are going to be blind for a time, not even able to see the light of the sun." Immediately mist and darkness came over him, and he groped about, seeking someone to lead him by the hand. {13:12} When the proconsul saw what had happened, he believed, for he was amazed at the teaching about the Lord. {13:13} From Paphos, Paul and his companions sailed to Perga in Pamphylia, where John left them to return to Jerusalem.{13:14} After leaving Perga, they went to Pisidian Antioch. On the Sabbath they entered the synagogue and sat down. {13:15} After the reading from the Law and the Prophets, the leaders of the synagogue sent word to them, saying, "Brothers, if you have a word of exhortation for the people, please speak." {13:16} Standing up, Paul motioned with his hand and said: "Fellow Israelites and you Gentiles who worship God, listen to me! {13:17} The God of the people of Israel chose our ancestors; he made the people prosper during their stay in Egypt; with mighty power he led them out of that country. {13:18} For about forty years he endured their conduct in the wilderness; {13:19} and he overthrew seven nations in Canaan, giving their land to his people as their inheritance. {13:20} All this took about 450 years. "After this, God gave them judges until the time of Samuel the prophet. {13:21} Then the people asked for a king, and he gave them Saul, son of Kish, of the tribe of Benjamin, who ruled forty years. {13:22} After removing Saul, he made David their king. God testified concerning him: 'I have found David son of Jesse, a man after my own heart; he will do everything I want him to do.' {13:23} "From this man's descendants God has brought to Israel the Savior Jesus, as he promised. {13:24} Before the coming of Jesus, John preached repentance and baptism to all the people of Israel. {13:25} As John was completing his work, he said: 'Who do you suppose I am? I am not the one you are looking for. But there is one coming after me whose sandals I am not worthy to untie.' {13:26} "Fellow children of Abraham and you God-fearing Gentiles, it is to us that this message of salvation has been sent. {13:27} The people of Jerusalem and their rulers did not recognize Jesus, yet in condemning him they fulfilled the words of the prophets that are read every Sabbath. {13:28} Though they found no proper ground for a death sentence, they asked Pilate to have him executed. {13:29} When they had carried out all that was written about him, they took him down from the cross and laid him in a tomb. {13:30} But God raised him from the dead, {13:31} and for many days he was seen by those who had traveled with him from Galilee to Jerusalem. They are now his witnesses to our people. {13:32} "We tell you the good news: What God promised our ancestors {13:33} he has fulfilled for us, their children, by raising up Jesus. As it is written in the second Psalm: "'You are my son; today I have become your father.' {13:34} God raised him from the dead so that he will never be subject to decay. As God has said, "'I will give you the holy and sure blessings promised to David.' {13:35} So it is also stated elsewhere: "'You will not let your holy one see decay.' {13:36} "Now when David had served God's purpose in his own generation, he fell asleep; he was buried with his ancestors and his body decayed. {13:37} But the one whom God raised from the dead did not see decay. {13:38} So, my friends, I want you to know that through Jesus the forgiveness of sins is proclaimed to you. {13:39} Through him everyone who believes is set free from every sin, a justification you were not able to obtain under the law of Moses. {13:40} Take care that what the prophets have said does not happen to you: {13:41} "'Look, you scoffers, wonder and perish, for I am going to do something in your days that you would never believe, even if someone told you.'" {13:42} As Paul and Barnabas were leaving the synagogue, the people invited them to speak further about these things on the next Sabbath. {13:43} When the congregation was dismissed, many of the Jews and devout converts to Judaism followed Paul and Barnabas, who talked with them and urged them to continue in the grace of God. {13:44} On the next Sabbath almost the whole city gathered to hear the word of the Lord. {13:45} When the Jews saw the crowds, they were filled with jealousy. They began to contradict what Paul was saying and heaped abuse on him. {13:46} Then Paul and Barnabas answered them boldly: "We had to speak the word of God to you first. Since you reject it and do not consider yourselves worthy of eternal life, we now turn to the Gentiles. {13:47} For this is what the Lord has commanded us: "'I have made you a light for the Gentiles, that you may bring salvation to the ends of the earth.'" {13:48} When the Gentiles heard this, they were glad and honored the word of the Lord; and all who were appointed for eternal life believed. {13:49} The word of the Lord spread through the whole region. {13:50} But the Jewish leaders incited the God-fearing women of high standing and the leading men of the city. They stirred up persecution against Paul and Barnabas, and expelled them from their region. {13:51} So they shook the dust off their feet as a warning to them and went to Iconium. {13:52} And the disciples were filled with joy and with the Holy Spirit.

{14:1} In Iconium, Paul and Barnabas went together to the synagogue and preached in such a way that a great number of Jews and Greeks believed. {14:2} But some Jews who refused to believe stirred up the Gentiles and poisoned their minds against the believers. {14:3} Paul and Barnabas spent considerable time there, speaking boldly for the Lord, who confirmed the message of his grace by enabling them to perform signs and wonders. {14:4} The people of the city were divided; some sided with the Jews, others with the apostles. {14:5} There was a plot afoot among both Gentiles and Jews, together with their leaders, to mistreat them and stone them. {14:6} But they found out about it and fled to the Lycaonian cities of Lystra and Derbe and to the surrounding country, {14:7} where they continued to preach the gospel. {14:8} In Lystra there sat a man who was lame. He had been that way from birth and had never walked. {14:9} He listened to Paul as he was speaking. Paul looked directly at him, saw that he had faith to be healed {14:10} and called out, "Stand up on your feet!" At that, the man jumped up and began to walk. {14:11} When the crowd saw what Paul had done, they shouted in the

Lycaonian language, "The gods have come down to us in human form!" {14:12} Barnabas they called Zeus, and Paul they called Hermes because he was the chief speaker. {14:13} The priest of Zeus, whose temple was just outside the city, brought bulls and wreaths to the city gates because he and the crowd wanted to offer sacrifices to them. {14:14} But when the apostles Barnabas and Paul heard of this, they tore their clothes and rushed out into the crowd, shouting: {14:15} "Friends, why are you doing this? We too are only human, like you. We are bringing you good news, telling you to turn from these worthless things to the living God, who made the heavens and the earth and the sea and everything in them. {14:16} In the past, he let all nations go their own way. {14:17} Yet he has not left himself without testimony: He has shown kindness by giving you rain from heaven and crops in their seasons; he provides you with plenty of food and fills your hearts with joy." {14:18} Even with these words, they had difficulty keeping the crowd from sacrificing to them. {14:19} Then some Jews came from Antioch and Iconium and won the crowd over. They stoned Paul and dragged him outside the city, thinking he was dead. {14:20} But after the disciples had gathered around him, he got up and went back into the city. The next day he and Barnabas left for Derbe. {14:21} They preached the gospel in that city and won a large number of disciples. Then they returned to Lystra, Iconium and Antioch, {14:22} strengthening the disciples and encouraging them to remain true to the faith. "We must go through many hardships to enter the kingdom of God," they said. {14:23} Paul and Barnabas appointed elders for them in each church and, with prayer and fasting, committed them to the Lord, in whom they had put their trust. {14:24} After going through Pisidia, they came into Pamphylia, {14:25} and when they had preached the word in Perga, they went down to Attalia. {14:26} From Attalia they sailed back to Antioch, where they had been committed to the grace of God for the work they had now completed. {14:27} On arriving there, they gathered the church together and reported all that God had done through them and how he had opened a door of faith to the Gentiles. {14:28} And they stayed there a long time with the disciples.

{15:1} Some men came down from Judea to Antioch and were teaching the believers: "Unless you are circumcised, according to the custom taught by Moses, you cannot be saved." {15:2} This brought Paul and Barnabas into sharp dispute and debate with them. So Paul and Barnabas were appointed, along with some other believers, to go up to Jerusalem to see the apostles and elders about this question. {15:3} The church sent them on their way, and as they traveled through Phoenicia and Samaria, they told how the Gentiles had been converted. This news brought great joy to all the believers. {15:4} When they came to Jerusalem, they were welcomed by the church and the apostles and elders, to whom they reported everything God had done through them. {15:5} Then some of the believers who belonged to the party of the Pharisees stood up and said, "The Gentiles must be circumcised and required to keep the law of Moses." {15:6} The apostles and elders met to consider this question. {15:7} After much discussion, Peter got up and addressed them: "Brothers, you know that some time ago God made a choice among you that the Gentiles might hear from my lips the message of the gospel and believe. {15:8} God, who knows the heart, showed that he accepted them by giving the Holy Spirit to them, just as he did to us. {15:9} He did not discriminate between us and them, for he purified their hearts by faith. {15:10} Now then, why do you try to test God by putting on the necks of Gentiles a yoke that neither we nor our ancestors have been able to bear? {15:11} No! We believe it is through the grace of our Lord Jesus that we are saved, just as they are." {15:12} The whole assembly became silent as they listened to Barnabas and Paul telling about the signs and wonders God had done among the Gentiles through them. {15:13} When they finished, James spoke up. "Brothers," he said, "listen to me. {15:14} Simon has described to us how God first intervened to choose a people for his name from the Gentiles. {15:15} The words of the prophets are in agreement with this, as it is written: {15:16} "After this I will return and rebuild David's fallen tent. Its ruins I will rebuild, and I will restore it, {15:17} that the rest of mankind may seek the Lord, even all the Gentiles who bear my name, says the Lord, who does these things— {15:18} things known from long ago. {15:19} It is my judgment, therefore, that we should not make it difficult for the Gentiles who are turning to God. {15:20} Instead we should write to them, telling them to abstain from food polluted by idols, from sexual immorality, from the meat of strangled animals and from blood. {15:21} For the law of Moses has been preached in every city from the earliest times and is read in the synagogues on every Sabbath." {15:22} Then the apostles and elders, with the whole church, decided to choose some of their own men and send them to Antioch with Paul and Barnabas. They chose Judas (called Barsabbas) and Silas, men who were leaders among the believers. {15:23} With them they sent the following letter: The apostles and elders, your brothers, To the Gentile believers in Antioch, Syria and Cilicia: Greetings. {15:24} We have heard that some went out from us without our authorization and disturbed you, troubling your minds by what they said. {15:25} So we all agreed to choose some men and send them to you with our dear friends Barnabas and Paul— {15:26} men who have risked their lives for the name of our Lord Jesus Christ. {15:27} Therefore we are sending Judas and Silas to confirm by word of mouth what we are writing. {15:28} It seemed good to the Holy Spirit and to us not to burden you with anything beyond the following requirements: {15:29} You are to abstain from food sacrificed to idols, from blood, from the meat of strangled animals and from sexual immorality. You will do well to avoid these things. Farewell. {15:30} So the men were sent off and went down to Antioch, where they gathered the church together and delivered the letter. {15:31} The people read it and were glad for its encouraging message. {15:32} Judas and Silas, who themselves were prophets, said much to encourage and strengthen the believers. {15:33} After spending some time there, they were sent off by the believers with the blessing of peace to return to those who had sent them. {15:34} But Silas decided to remain there. {15:35} Paul and Barnabas remained in Antioch, where they and many others taught and preached the word of the Lord. {15:36} Some time later Paul said to Barnabas, "Let us go back and visit the believers in all the towns where we preached the word of the Lord and see how they are doing." {15:37} Barnabas wanted to take John, also called Mark, with them, {15:38} but Paul did not think it wise to take him, because he had deserted them in Pamphylia and had not continued with them in the work. {15:39} They had such a sharp disagreement that they parted company. Barnabas took Mark and sailed for Cyprus, {15:40} but Paul chose Silas and left, commended by the believers to the grace of the Lord. {15:41} He went through Syria and Cilicia, strengthening the churches.

{16:1} When Paul came to Derbe and Lystra, he found a disciple named Timothy, the son of a Jewish woman who was a believer, but his father was a Greek. {16:2} The believers at Lystra and Iconium spoke well of him. {16:3} Paul wanted to take him along on the journey, so he circumcised him because of the Jews who lived in that area, for they all knew that his father was Greek. {16:4} As they traveled from city to city, they delivered the decisions reached by the apostles and elders in Jerusalem for the people to obey. {16:5} So the churches were strengthened in the faith and grew daily in numbers. {16:6} Paul and his companions traveled throughout the region of Phrygia and Galatia, having been kept by the Holy Spirit from preaching the word in the province of Asia. {16:7} When they came to the border of Mysia, they tried to enter Bithynia, but the Spirit of Jesus would not allow them to. {16:8} So they passed by Mysia and went down to Troas. {16:9} During the night Paul had a vision of a man from Macedonia standing and begging him, "Come over to Macedonia and help us." {16:10} After Paul had seen the vision, we got ready at once to leave for Macedonia, concluding that God had called us to preach the gospel to them. {16:11} From Troas we put out to sea and sailed straight for Samothrace, and the next day we went on to Neapolis. {16:12} From there we traveled to Philippi, a Roman colony and the leading city of that district of Macedonia. And we stayed there several days. {16:13} On the Sabbath we went outside the city gate to the river, where we expected to find a place of prayer. We sat down and began to speak to the women who had gathered there. {16:14} One of those listening was a woman from the city of Thyatira named Lydia, a dealer in purple cloth. She was a worshiper of God. The Lord opened her heart to respond to Paul's message. {16:15} When she and the members of her household were baptized, she invited us to her home. "If you consider me a believer in the Lord," she said, "come and stay at my house." And she persuaded us. {16:16} Once when we were going to the place of prayer, we were met by a female slave who had a spirit by which she predicted the future. She earned a great deal of money for her owners by fortune-telling. {16:17} She followed Paul and the rest of us, shouting, "These men are servants of the Most High God, who are telling you the way to be saved." {16:18} She kept this up for many days. Finally Paul became so annoyed that he turned around and said to the spirit, "In the name of Jesus Christ I command you to come out of her!" At that moment the spirit left her. {16:19} When her owners realized that their hope of making money was gone, they seized Paul and Silas and dragged them into the marketplace to face the authorities. {16:20} They brought them before the magistrates and said, "These men are Jews, and are throwing our city into an uproar {16:21} by advocating customs unlawful for us Romans to accept or practice." {16:22} The crowd joined in the attack against Paul and Silas, and the magistrates ordered them to be stripped and beaten with rods. {16:23} After they had been severely flogged, they were thrown into prison, and the jailer was commanded to guard them carefully. {16:24} When he received these orders, he put them in the inner cell and fastened their feet in the stocks. {16:25} About midnight Paul and Silas were praying and singing hymns to God, and the other prisoners were listening to them. {16:26} Suddenly there was such a violent earthquake that the foundations of the prison were shaken. At once all the prison doors flew open, and everyone's chains came loose. {16:27} The jailer woke up, and when he saw the prison doors open, he drew his sword and was about to kill himself because he thought the prisoners had escaped. {16:28} But Paul shouted, "Don't harm yourself! We are all here!" {16:29} The jailer called for lights, rushed in and fell trembling before Paul and Silas. {16:30} He then brought them out and asked, "Sirs, what must I do to be saved?" {16:31} They replied, "Believe in the Lord Jesus, and you will be saved—you and your household." {16:32} Then they spoke the word of the Lord to him and to all the others in his house. {16:33} At that hour of the night the jailer took them and washed their wounds; then immediately he and all his household were baptized. {16:34} The jailer brought them into his house and set a meal before them; he was filled with joy because he had come to believe in God—he and his whole household. {16:35} When it was daylight, the magistrates sent their officers to the jailer with the order: "Release those men." {16:36} The jailer told Paul, "The magistrates have ordered that you and Silas be released. Now you can leave. Go in peace." {16:37} But Paul said to the officers: "They beat us publicly without a trial, even though we are Roman citizens, and threw us into prison. And now do they want to get rid of us quietly? No! Let them come themselves and escort us out." {16:38} The officers reported this to the magistrates, and when they heard that Paul and Silas were Roman citizens, they were alarmed. {16:39} They came to appease them and escorted them from the prison, requesting them to leave the city. {16:40} After Paul and Silas came out of the prison, they went to Lydia's house, where they met with the brothers and sisters and encouraged them. Then they left.

{17:1} After passing through Amphipolis and Apollonia, Paul and his companions reached Thessalonica, where there was a Jewish synagogue. {17:2} As was his custom, Paul went into the synagogue, and on three Sabbath days he reasoned with them from the Scriptures, {17:3} explaining and proving that the Messiah had to suffer and rise from the dead. "This Jesus I am proclaiming to you is the Messiah," he said. {17:4} Some of the Jews were persuaded and joined Paul and Silas, along with a large number of God-fearing Greeks and quite a few prominent women. {17:5} But other Jews were jealous; so they rounded up some bad characters from the marketplace, formed a mob and started a riot in the city. They rushed to Jason's house in search of Paul and Silas in order to bring them out to the crowd. {17:6} But when they did not find them, they dragged Jason and some other believers before the city officials, shouting: "These men who have caused trouble all over the world have now come here, {17:7} and Jason has welcomed them into his house. They are all defying Caesar's decrees, saying that there is another king, one called Jesus." {17:8} When they heard this, the crowd and the city officials were thrown into turmoil. {17:9} Then they made Jason and the others post bond and let them go. {17:10} As soon as it was night, the believers sent Paul and Silas away to Berea. On arriving there, they went to the Jewish synagogue. {17:11} Now the Berean Jews were of more noble character than those in Thessalonica, for they received the message with great eagerness and examined the Scriptures every day to see if what Paul said was true. {17:12} As a result, many of them believed, as did also a number of prominent Greek women and many Greek men. {17:13} But when the Jews in Thessalonica learned that Paul was preaching the word of God at Berea, some of them went there too, agitating the crowds and stirring them up. {17:14} The believers immediately sent Paul to the coast, but Silas and Timothy stayed at Berea. {17:15} Those who escorted Paul brought him to Athens and then left with instructions for Silas and Timothy to join him as soon as possible. {17:16} While Paul was waiting for them in Athens, he was greatly distressed to see that the city was full of idols. {17:17} So he reasoned in the synagogue with both Jews and God-fearing Greeks, as well as in the marketplace day by day with those who happened to be there. {17:18} A group of Epicurean and Stoic philosophers began to debate with him. Some of them asked, "What is this babbler trying to say?" Others remarked, "He seems to be advocating foreign gods." They said this because Paul was preaching the good news about Jesus and the resurrection. {17:19} Then they took him and brought him to a meeting of the Areopagus, where they said to him, "May we know what this new teaching is that you are presenting? {17:20} You are bringing some strange ideas to our ears, and we would like to know what they mean." {17:21} (All the Athenians and the foreigners who lived there spent their time doing nothing but talking about and listening to the latest ideas.) {17:22} Paul then stood up in the meeting of the Areopagus and said: "People of Athens! I see that in every way you are very religious. {17:23} For as I walked around and looked carefully at your objects of worship, I even found an altar with this inscription: to an unknown god. So you are ignorant of the very thing you worship—and this is what I am going to proclaim to you. {17:24} The God who made the world and everything in it is the Lord of heaven and earth and does not live in temples built by human hands. {17:25} And he is not served by human hands, as if he needed anything. Rather, he himself gives everyone life and breath and everything else. {17:26} From one man he made all the nations, that they should inhabit the whole earth; and he marked out their appointed times in history and the boundaries of their lands. {17:27} God did this so that they would seek him and perhaps reach out for him and find him, though he is not far from any one of us. {17:28} 'For in him we live and move and have our being.' As some of your own poets have said, 'We are his offspring.' {17:29} "Therefore since we are God's offspring, we should not think that the divine being is like gold or silver or stone—an image made by human design and skill. {17:30} In the past God overlooked such ignorance, but now he commands all people everywhere to repent. {17:31} For he has set a day when he will judge the world with justice by the man he has appointed. He has given proof of this to everyone by raising him from the dead." {17:32} When they heard about the resurrection of the dead, some of them sneered, but others said, "We want to hear you again on this subject." {17:33} At that, Paul left the Council. {17:34} Some of the people became followers of Paul and believed. Among them was Dionysius, a member of the Areopagus, also a woman named Damaris, and a number of others.

{18:1} After leaving Athens, Paul went to Corinth. {18:2} There he met a Jew named Aquila, a native of Pontus, who had recently come from Italy with his wife Priscilla because Claudius had ordered all Jews to leave Rome. Paul went to see them, {18:3} and because he was a tentmaker as they were, he stayed and worked with them. {18:4} Every Sabbath he reasoned in the synagogue, trying to persuade Jews and Greeks. {18:5} When Silas and Timothy came from Macedonia, Paul devoted himself exclusively to preaching, testifying to the Jews that Jesus was the Messiah. {18:6} But when they opposed Paul and became abusive, he shook out his clothes in protest and said to them, "Your blood be on your own heads! I am innocent of it. From now on I will go to the Gentiles." {18:7} Then Paul left the synagogue and went next door to the house of Titius Justus, a worshiper of God. {18:8} Crispus, the synagogue leader, and his entire household believed in the Lord; and many of the Corinthians who heard Paul believed and were baptized. {18:9} One night the Lord spoke to Paul in a vision: "Do not be afraid; keep on speaking, do not be silent. {18:10} For I am with you, and no one is going to attack and harm you, because I have many people in this city." {18:11} So Paul stayed in Corinth for a year and a half, teaching them the word of God. {18:12} While Gallio was proconsul of Achaia, the Jews of Corinth made a united attack on Paul and brought him to the place of judgment. {18:13} "This man," they charged, "is persuading the people to worship God in ways contrary to the law." {18:14} Just as Paul was about to speak, Gallio said to them, "If you Jews were making a complaint about some misdemeanor or serious crime, it would be reasonable for me to listen to you. {18:15} But since it involves questions about words and names and your own law—settle the matter yourselves. I will not be a judge of such things." {18:16} So he drove them off. {18:17} Then the crowd there turned on Sosthenes the synagogue leader and beat him in front of the proconsul; and Gallio showed no concern whatsoever. {18:18} Paul stayed on in Corinth for some time. Then he left the brothers and sisters and sailed for Syria, accompanied by Priscilla and Aquila. Before he sailed, he had his hair cut off at Cenchreae because of a vow he had taken. {18:19} They arrived at Ephesus, where Paul left Priscilla and Aquila. He himself went into the synagogue and reasoned with the Jews. {18:20} When they asked him to spend more time with them, he declined. {18:21} But as he left, he promised, "I will come back if it is God's will." Then he set sail from Ephesus. {18:22} When he landed at Caesarea, he went up to Jerusalem and greeted the church and then went down to Antioch. {18:23} After spending some time in Antioch, Paul set out from there and traveled from place to place throughout the region of Galatia and Phrygia, strengthening all the disciples. {18:24} Meanwhile a Jew named Apollos, a native of Alexandria, came to Ephesus. He was a learned man, with a thorough knowledge of the Scriptures. {18:25} He had been instructed in the way of the Lord, and he spoke with great fervor and taught about Jesus accurately, though he knew only the baptism of John. {18:26} He began to speak boldly in the synagogue. When Priscilla and Aquila heard him, they invited him to their home and explained to him the way of God more adequately. {18:27} When Apollos wanted to go to Achaia, the brothers and sisters encouraged him and wrote to the disciples there to welcome him. When he arrived, he was a great help to those who by grace had believed. {18:28} For he vigorously refuted his Jewish opponents in public debate, proving from the Scriptures that Jesus was the Messiah.

{19:1} While Apollos was in Corinth, Paul traveled through the upper regions and came to Ephesus. There he found some disciples {19:2} and asked them, "Did you receive the Holy Spirit when you believed?" They answered, "No, we have not even heard that there is a Holy Spirit." {19:3} So Paul asked, "Then what baptism did you receive?" "John's baptism," they replied. {19:4} Paul said, "John's baptism was a baptism of repentance. He told the people to believe in the one coming after him, that is, in Jesus." {19:5} On hearing this, they were baptized in the name of the Lord Jesus. {19:6} When Paul placed his hands on them, the Holy Spirit came upon them, and they spoke in tongues and prophesied. {19:7} There were about twelve men in all. {19:8} Paul entered the synagogue and spoke boldly there for three months, arguing persuasively about the kingdom of God. {19:9} But some of them became obstinate; they refused to believe and publicly maligned the Way. So Paul left them. He took the disciples with him and had discussions daily in the lecture hall of Tyrannus. {19:10} This went on for two years, so that all the Jews and Greeks who lived in the province of Asia heard the word of the Lord. {19:11} God did extraordinary miracles through Paul, {19:12} so that even handkerchiefs and aprons that had touched him were taken to the sick, and their illnesses were cured and the evil spirits left them. {19:13} Some Jews who went around driving out evil spirits tried to invoke the name of the Lord Jesus over those who were demon-possessed. They would say, "In the name of the Jesus whom Paul preaches, I command you to come out." {19:14} Seven sons of Sceva, a Jewish chief priest, were doing this. {19:15} One day the evil spirit answered them, "Jesus I know, and Paul I know about, but who are you?" {19:16} Then the man who had the evil spirit jumped on them and overpowered them all. He gave them such a beating that they ran out of the house naked and bleeding. {19:17} When this became known to the Jews and Greeks living in Ephesus, they were all seized with fear, and the name of the Lord Jesus was held in high honor. {19:18} Many of those who believed now came and openly confessed what they had done. {19:19} A number who had practiced sorcery brought their scrolls together and burned them publicly. When they calculated the value of the scrolls, the total came to fifty thousand drachmas. {19:20} In this way the word of the Lord spread widely and grew in power. {19:21} After these events, Paul decided by the Spirit to travel through Macedonia and Achaia and then go to Jerusalem. "After I have been there," he said, "I must also see Rome." {19:22} He sent Timothy and Erastus, two of his helpers, to Macedonia, while he stayed in the province of Asia a little longer. {19:23} During that time, there was a great disturbance about the Way. {19:24} A silversmith named Demetrius, who made silver shrines of Artemis, brought in a lot of business for the craftsmen there. {19:25} He called them together, along with the workers in related trades, and said: "You know, my friends, that we receive a good income from this business. {19:26} And you see and hear how this fellow Paul has convinced and led astray large numbers of people here in Ephesus and in practically the whole province of Asia. He says that gods made by human hands are no gods at all. {19:27} There is danger not only that our trade will lose its good name, but also that the temple of the great goddess Artemis will be discredited; and the goddess herself, who is worshiped throughout the province of Asia and the world, will be robbed of her divine majesty." {19:28} When they heard this, they were furious and began shouting: "Great is Artemis of the Ephesians!" {19:29} Soon the whole city was in an uproar. The people seized Gaius and Aristarchus, Paul's traveling companions from Macedonia, and all of them rushed into the theater together. {19:30} Paul wanted to appear before the crowd, but the disciples would not let him. {19:31} Even some of the officials of the province, friends of Paul, sent him a message begging him not to venture into the theater. {19:32} The assembly was in confusion: Some were shouting one thing, some another. Most of the people did not even know why they were there. {19:33} The Jews in the crowd pushed Alexander to the front, and they shouted instructions to him. He motioned for silence in order to make a defense before the people. {19:34} But when they realized he was a Jew, they all shouted in unison for about two hours: "Great is Artemis of the Ephesians!" {19:35} The city clerk quieted the crowd and said: "Fellow Ephesians, doesn't all the world know that the city of Ephesus is the guardian of the temple of the great Artemis and of her image, which fell from heaven? {19:36} Therefore, since these facts are undeniable, you ought to calm down and not do anything rash. {19:37} You have brought these men here, though they have neither robbed temples nor blasphemed our goddess. {19:38} If, then, Demetrius and his fellow craftsmen have a grievance against anybody, the courts are open and there are proconsuls. They can press charges. {19:39} If there is anything further you want to bring up, it must be settled in a legal assembly. {19:40} As it is, we are in danger of being charged with rioting because of what happened today. In that case, we would not be able to account for this commotion, since there is no reason for it." {19:41} After he had said this, he dismissed the assembly.

{20:1} When the uproar had ended, Paul gathered the disciples, embraced them, and departed to go into Macedonia. {20:2} He traveled through those areas, giving them much encouragement, and eventually arrived in Greece. {20:3} He stayed there for three months. But when the Jews plotted against him as he was about to sail for Syria, he decided to go back through Macedonia. {20:4} Several men accompanied him: Sopater from Berea, Aristarchus and Secundus from Thessalonica, Gaius from Derbe, Timothy, and Tychicus and Trophimus from the province of Asia. {20:5} These men went on ahead and waited for us at Troas. {20:6} We sailed from Philippi after the Feast of Unleavened Bread and five days later joined the others at Troas, where we stayed for seven days. {20:7} On the first day of the week we came together to break bread. Paul spoke to the people and, because he intended to leave the next day, kept on talking until midnight. {20:8} There were many lamps in the upstairs room where we were meeting. {20:9} Seated in a window was a young man named Eutychus, who was sinking into a deep sleep as Paul talked on and on. When he was sound asleep, he fell to the ground from the third story and was picked up dead. {20:10} Paul went down, threw himself on the young man and put his arms around him. "Don't be alarmed," he said. "He's alive!" {20:11} Then he went upstairs again and broke bread and ate. After talking until daylight, he left. {20:12} The people took the young man home alive and were greatly comforted. {20:13} We went on ahead to the ship and sailed for Assos, where we were going to take Paul aboard. He had made this arrangement because he was going there on foot. {20:14} When he met us at Assos, we took him aboard and went on to Mitylene. {20:15} The next day we set sail from there and arrived off Chios. The day after that we crossed over to Samos, and on the following day arrived at Miletus. {20:16} Paul had decided to sail past Ephesus to avoid spending time in the province of Asia, for he was in a hurry to reach Jerusalem, if possible, by the day of Pentecost. {20:17} From Miletus, Paul sent to Ephesus for the elders of the church. {20:18} When they arrived, he said to them: "You know how I lived the whole time I was with you, from the first day I came into the province of Asia. {20:19} I served the Lord with great humility and with tears and in the midst of severe testing by the plots of my Jewish opponents. {20:20} I did not hesitate to proclaim to you anything that was helpful, but taught you publicly and from house to house. {20:21} I have declared to both Jews and Greeks that they must turn to God in repentance and have faith in our Lord Jesus. {20:22} And now, compelled by the Spirit, I am going to Jerusalem, not knowing what will happen to me there. {20:23} I only know that in every city the Holy Spirit warns me that prison and hardships are facing me. {20:24} However, I consider my life worth nothing to me; my only aim is to finish the race and complete the task the Lord Jesus has given me—the task of testifying to the good news of God's grace. {20:25} "Now I know that none of you among whom I have gone about preaching to the kingdom will ever see me again. {20:26} Therefore, I declare to you today that I am innocent of the blood of any of you. {20:27} For I have not hesitated to proclaim to you the whole will of God. {20:28} Keep watch over yourselves and all the flock of which the Holy Spirit has made you overseers. Be shepherds of the church of God, which he bought with his own blood. {20:29} I know that after I leave, savage wolves will come in among you and will not spare the flock. {20:30} Even from your own number men will arise and distort the truth in order to draw away disciples after them. {20:31} So be on your guard! Remember that for three years I never stopped warning each of you night and day with tears. {20:32} "Now I commit you to God and to the word of his grace, which can build you up and give you an inheritance among all those who are sanctified. {20:33} I have not coveted anyone's silver or gold or clothing. {20:34} You yourselves know that these hands of mine have supplied my own needs and the needs of my companions. {20:35} In everything I did, I showed you that by this kind of hard work we must help the weak, remembering the words the Lord Jesus himself said: 'It is more blessed to give than to receive.'" {20:36} When Paul had finished speaking, he knelt down with all of them and prayed. {20:37} They all wept as they embraced him and kissed him. {20:38} What grieved them most was his statement that they would never see his face again. Then they accompanied him to the ship.

{21:1} After we had left them and set sail, we made a straight course to Coos, the next day to Rhodes, and from there to Patara. {21:2} Finding a ship crossing over to Phoenicia, we boarded and set sail. {21:3} When we sighted Cyprus, we passed it on the left and sailed to Syria, landing at Tyre, where the ship unloaded its cargo. {21:4} We sought out the disciples there and stayed with them for seven days. Through the Spirit, they urged Paul not to go up to Jerusalem. {21:5} When our time there was ended, we left and continued on our journey, accompanied by all of them, with their wives and children, until we were out of the city. After kneeling down on the beach to pray together, we said goodbye to one another. {21:6} Then we boarded the ship, and they returned home. {21:7} When we completed our voyage from Tyre, we arrived at Ptolemais, where we greeted the brothers and sisters and stayed with them for a day. {21:8} The next day we left and came to Caesarea, where we went to the house of Philip the evangelist, who was one of the Seven, and stayed with him. {21:9} He had four unmarried daughters who prophesied. {21:10} After staying there for several days, a prophet named Agabus came down from Judea. {21:11} Coming over to us, he took Paul's belt, bound his own hands and feet with it, and said, "The Holy Spirit says, 'In this way the Jewish leaders in Jerusalem will bind the owner of this belt and will hand him over to the Gentiles.'" {21:12} When we heard this, we and the people there pleaded with Paul not to go up to Jerusalem. {21:13} Then Paul answered, "Why are you weeping and breaking my heart? I am ready not only to be bound, but also to die in Jerusalem for the name of the Lord Jesus." {21:14} When he would not be dissuaded, we gave up and said, "The Lord's will be done." {21:15} After this, we started on our way up to Jerusalem. {21:16} Some of the disciples from Caesarea accompanied us and brought us to the home of Mnason, where we were to stay. He was from Cyprus and had been an early disciple. {21:17} When we arrived in Jerusalem, the brothers and sisters welcomed us warmly. {21:18} The next day Paul and the rest of us went to see James, and all the elders were present. {21:19} Paul greeted them and reported in detail what God had done among the Gentiles through his ministry. {21:20} When they heard this, they praised God. Then they said to Paul: "You see, brother, how many thousands of Jews have believed, and all of them are zealous for the law. {21:21} They have been informed that you teach all the Jews who live among the Gentiles to turn away from Moses, telling them not to circumcise their children or live according to our customs. {21:22} What shall we do? They will certainly hear that you have come, {21:23} so do what we tell you. There are four men with us who have made a vow. {21:24} Take these men, join in their purification rites and pay their expenses, so that they can have their heads shaved. Then everyone will know there is no truth in these reports about you, but that you yourself are living in obedience to the law. {21:25} As for the Gentile believers, we have written to them our decision that they should abstain from food sacrificed to idols, from blood, from the meat of strangled animals and from sexual immorality." {21:26} The next day Paul took the men and purified himself along with them. Then he went to the temple to give notice of the date when the days of purification would end and the offering would be made for each of them. {21:27} When the seven days were nearly over, some Jews from the province of Asia saw Paul at the temple. They stirred up the whole crowd and seized him, {21:28} shouting, "Fellow Israelites, help us! This is the man who teaches everyone everywhere against our people and our law and this place. And besides, he has brought Greeks into the temple and defiled this holy place." {21:29} (They had previously seen Trophimus the Ephesian in the city with Paul and assumed that Paul had brought him into the temple.) {21:30} The whole city was aroused, and the people came running from all directions. Seizing Paul, they dragged him from the temple, and immediately the gates were shut. {21:31} While they were trying to kill him, news reached the commander of the Roman troops that the whole city of Jerusalem was in an uproar. {21:32} He at once took some officers and soldiers and ran down to the crowd. When the rioters saw the commander and his soldiers, they stopped beating Paul. {21:33} The commander came up and arrested him and ordered him to be bound with two chains. Then he asked who he was and what he had done. {21:34} Some in the crowd shouted one thing and some another, and since the commander could not get at the truth because of the uproar, he ordered that Paul be taken into the barracks. {21:35} When Paul reached the steps, the violence of the mob was so great he had to be carried by the soldiers. {21:36} The crowd that followed kept shouting, "Get rid of him!" {21:37} As the soldiers were about to take Paul into the barracks, he asked the commander, "May I say something to you?" "Do you speak Greek?" he replied. {21:38} "Aren't you the Egyptian who started a revolt and led four thousand terrorists out into the wilderness some time ago?" {21:39} Paul answered, "I am a Jew, from Tarsus in Cilicia, a citizen of no ordinary city. Please let me speak to the people." {21:40} After receiving the commander's permission, Paul stood on the steps and motioned to the crowd. When they were all silent, he said to them in Aramaic:

{22:1} Listen to my defense, my fellow men, brothers, and fathers." {22:2} (When they heard him speak to them in Hebrew, they became even more silent. Then he said,) {22:3} "I am indeed a Jew, born in Tarsus of Cilicia, but brought up in this city at the feet of Gamaliel, educated strictly in the ancestral law, being zealous for God, just as you all are today. {22:4} I persecuted this Way to the death, binding and putting both men and women into prisons, {22:5} as the high priest and all the Council of the elders can testify. From them I also received letters to the brethren, and started off for Damascus in order to bring even those who were there to Jerusalem as prisoners to be punished. {22:6} "But it happened that as I was on my way, approaching Damascus about noontime, a very bright light suddenly flashed from heaven all around me, {22:7} and I fell to the ground and heard a voice saying to me, 'Saul, Saul, why are you persecuting Me?' {22:8} And I answered, 'Who are You, Lord?' And He said to me, 'I am Jesus the Nazarene, whom you are persecuting.' {22:9} "And those who were with me saw the light, to be sure, but did not understand the voice of the One who was speaking to me. {22:10} "And I said, 'What shall I do, Lord?' And the Lord said to me, 'Get up and go on into Damascus, and there you will be told of all that has been appointed for you to do.' {22:11} "But since I could not see because of the brightness of that light, I was led by the hand by those who were with me and came into Damascus. {22:12} "A certain Ananias, a man who was devout by the standard of the Law and well spoken of by all the Jews who lived there, {22:13} came to me, and standing near said to me, 'Brother Saul, receive your sight!' And at that very time I looked up at him. {22:14} "And he said, 'The God of our fathers has appointed you to know His will, and to see the Righteous One, and to hear an utterance from His mouth. {22:15} 'For you will be a witness for Him to all men of what you have seen and heard. {22:16} 'Now why do you delay? Get up and be baptized, and wash away your sins, calling on His name.' {22:17} "It happened when I returned to Jerusalem and was praying in the temple, that I fell into a trance, {22:18} and I saw Him saying to me, 'Make haste, and get out of Jerusalem quickly, because they will not accept your testimony about Me.' {22:19} "And I said, 'Lord, they themselves understand that in one synagogue after another I used to imprison and beat those who believed in You. {22:20} 'And when the blood of Your witness Stephen was being shed, I also was standing by approving, and watching out for the coats of those who were slaying him.' {22:21} "And He said to me, 'Go! For I will send you far away to the Gentiles.'" {22:22} They listened to him up to this statement, and then they raised their voices and said, "Away with such a fellow from the earth, for he should not be allowed to live!" {22:23} And as they were crying out and throwing off their cloaks and tossing dust into the air, {22:24} the commander ordered him to be brought into the barracks, stating that he should be examined by scourging so that he might find out the reason why they were shouting against him that way. {22:25} But when they stretched him out with thongs, Paul said to the centurion who was standing by, "Is it lawful for you to scourge a man who is a Roman and uncondemned?" {22:26} When the centurion heard this, he went to the commander and told him, saying, "What are you about to do? For this man is a Roman." {22:27} The commander came and said to him, "Tell me, are you a Roman?" And he said, "Yes." {22:28} The commander answered, "I acquired this citizenship with a large sum of money." And Paul said, "But I was actually born a citizen." {22:29} Therefore those who were about to examine him immediately let go of him; and the commander also was afraid when he found out that he was a Roman, and because he had put him in chains. {22:30} But on the next day, wishing to know for certain why he had been accused by the Jews, he released him and ordered the chief priests and all the Council to assemble, and brought Paul down and set him before them.

{23:1} Paul, looking intently at the council, said, "Brothers, I have lived my life with a clear conscience before God up to this day." {23:2} At this, the high priest Ananias ordered those standing near Paul to strike him on the mouth. {23:3} Then Paul said to him, "God will strike you, you whitewashed wall! You sit there to judge me according to the law, yet you yourself violate the law by commanding me to be struck." {23:4} Those who stood nearby said, "Do you dare to insult God's high priest?" {23:5} Paul replied, "Brothers, I did not realize that he was the high priest, for it is written, 'You shall not speak evil of a ruler of your people.'" {23:6} Realizing that some were Sadducees and others Pharisees, Paul called out in the council, "Brothers, I am a Pharisee, the son of a Pharisee. I am on trial because of my hope in the resurrection of the dead." {23:7} When he said this, a dispute broke out between the Pharisees and the Sadducees, and the assembly was divided. {23:8} For the Sadducees say that there is no resurrection, nor an angel, nor a spirit, but the Pharisees acknowledge them all. {23:9} There was a great uproar, and some of the scribes of the Pharisees' party stood up and argued vehemently, saying, "We find nothing wrong with this man. What if a spirit or an angel has spoken to him?" {23:10} As the argument became violent, the commander feared that Paul would be torn to pieces by them. He ordered the soldiers to go down and rescue him from among them and take him into the barracks. {23:11} That night the Lord stood near Paul and said, "Take courage! As you have testified about me in Jerusalem, so you must also testify in Rome." {23:12} When it was daylight, some Jews formed a conspiracy and bound themselves with an oath not to eat or drink until they had killed Paul. {23:13} There were more than forty who had taken this oath. {23:14} They went to the chief priests and elders and said, "We have taken a solemn oath not to eat anything until we have killed Paul. {23:15} Now then, you and the Sanhedrin petition the commander to bring him down to you on the pretext of wanting more accurate information about his case. But we are ready to kill him before he gets here." {23:16} But when Paul's nephew heard about the plot, he went into the barracks and told Paul. {23:17} Then Paul called one of the centurions and said, "Take this young man to the commander; he has something to tell him." {23:18} So the centurion took him to the commander. The centurion said, "Paul the prisoner sent for me and asked me to bring this young man to you because he has something to tell you." {23:19} The commander took the young man by the hand, drew him aside, and asked, "What is it you want to tell me?" {23:20} He said, "The Jews have agreed to ask you to bring Paul before the Sanhedrin tomorrow on the pretext of wanting more accurate information about him. {23:21} Don't give in to them, because more than forty of them are waiting in ambush for him. They have taken an oath not to eat or drink until they have killed him. They are ready now, waiting for your consent to their request." {23:22} The commander dismissed the young man with a warning: "Don't tell anyone that you have reported this to me." {23:23} Then he called two of his centurions and ordered them, "Get ready a detachment of two hundred soldiers, seventy horsemen, and two hundred spearmen to go to Caesarea at nine tonight. {23:24} Provide mounts for Paul so that he may be taken safely to Governor Felix." {23:25} He wrote the following letter: {23:26} "Claudius Lysias, To His Excellency Governor Felix: Greetings. {23:27} This man was seized by the Jews and they were about to kill him, but I came with my troops and rescued him, for I had learned that he is a Roman citizen. {23:28} I wanted to know why they were accusing him, so I brought him to their Sanhedrin. {23:29} I found that the accusation had to do with questions about their law, but there was no charge against him deserving death or imprisonment. {23:30} When I was informed that there was a plot against the man, I sent him to you at once. I also ordered his accusers to present their case against him before you." {23:31} So the soldiers carried out their orders. They took Paul with them during the night and brought him as far as Antipatris. {23:32} The next day they let the cavalry go on with him, while they returned to the barracks. {23:33} When the cavalry arrived in Caesarea, they delivered the letter to the governor and handed Paul over to him. {23:34} The governor read the letter and asked what province Paul was from. Learning that he was from Cilicia, {23:35} he said, "I will hear your case when your accusers arrive." Then he ordered that Paul be kept under guard in Herod's palace.

{24:1} After five days, the high priest Ananias went down to Caesarea with some elders and a lawyer named Tertullus. They presented their case against Paul to the governor. {24:2} When Paul was called in, Tertullus began to accuse him, saying, "Since we enjoy great peace because of you, and reforms are taking place for the benefit of this nation because of your foresight, {24:3} we acknowledge this with all gratitude. {24:4} But I don't want to bore you, so please indulge us briefly and hear our plea with your customary graciousness. {24:5} We have found this man to be a troublemaker, stirring up riots among the Jews all over the world. He is a ringleader of the sect of the Nazarenes. {24:6} He even tried to desecrate the temple, so we arrested him. {24:7} [But] Lysias the commander came and violently took him from our hands {24:8} and ordered his accusers to come before you. By examining him yourself, you will be able to learn the truth about all these charges we are bringing against him." {24:9} The Jews joined in the accusation, asserting that these things were true. {24:10} Then Paul, after the governor motioned for him to speak, replied: "Because you have been a judge of this nation for many years, I am happy to present my defense before you. {24:11} You can verify that it is no more than twelve days since I went up to Jerusalem to worship. {24:12} Neither in the temple nor in the synagogues nor anywhere else in the city did they find me arguing with anyone or stirring up a crowd. {24:13} And they cannot prove to you the charges they are now making against me. {24:14} However, I admit that I worship the God of our ancestors as a follower of the Way, which they call a sect. I believe everything that is in accordance with the Law and that is written in the Prophets, {24:15} and I have the same hope in God as these men themselves have, that there will be a resurrection of both the righteous and the wicked. {24:16} So I strive always to keep my conscience clear before God and man. {24:17} After an absence of several years, I came to Jerusalem to bring my people gifts for the poor and to present offerings. {24:18} I was ceremonially clean when they found me in the temple, neither with a crowd nor with a disturbance. {24:19} But there are some Jews from the province of Asia who ought to be here before you and bring charges if they have anything against me. {24:20} Or these who are here should state what crime they found in me when I stood before the Sanhedrin— {24:21} unless it was this one thing I shouted as I stood in their presence: 'It is concerning the resurrection of the dead that I am on trial before you today.'" {24:22} Then Felix, who was well acquainted with the Way, adjourned the proceedings. "When Lysias the commander comes," he said, "I will decide your case." {24:23} He ordered the centurion to keep Paul under guard but to give him some freedom and permit his friends to take care of his needs. {24:24} Several days later Felix came with his wife Drusilla, who was Jewish. He sent for Paul and listened to him as he spoke about faith in Christ Jesus. {24:25} As Paul talked about righteousness, self-control, and the judgment to come, Felix was afraid and said, "That's enough for now! You may leave. When I find it convenient, I will send for you." {24:26} At the same time, he was hoping that Paul would offer him a bribe, so he sent for him frequently and talked with him. {24:27} When two years had passed, Felix was succeeded by Porcius Festus. And because Felix wanted to grant a favor to the Jews, he left Paul in prison.

{25:1} After Festus arrived in the province, he went up to Jerusalem from Caesarea after three days. {25:2} The chief priests and Jewish leaders presented their case against Paul to him and urged him, {25:3} asking for a favor, that he would send for Paul to come to Jerusalem, planning to ambush him along the way and kill him. {25:4} But Festus replied that Paul would be kept in Caesarea and that he himself would be heading there shortly. {25:5} He said, "Let those among you who are able, go down with me, and if there is anything wrong with this man, let them accuse him." {25:6} After staying among them for more than ten days, Festus went down to Caesarea, and the next day he sat on the judgment seat and ordered Paul to be brought in. {25:7} When Paul came, the Jews who had come down from Jerusalem stood around him, bringing many serious charges that they couldn't prove. {25:8} As Paul defended himself, he said, "I have not done anything against the Jewish law, the temple, or Caesar." {25:9} But Festus, wanting to do the Jews a favor, asked Paul, "Are you willing to go up to Jerusalem and stand trial before me there?" {25:10} Paul replied, "I am standing before Caesar's judgment seat, where I ought to be tried. I have done no wrong to the Jews, as you well know. {25:11} If, however, I am guilty of doing anything deserving death, I do not refuse to die. But if the charges brought against me by these Jews are not true, no one has the right to hand me over to them. I appeal to Caesar." {25:12} Then Festus, after conferring with his council, answered, "You have appealed to Caesar. To Caesar you will go." {25:13} After some days, King Agrippa and Bernice arrived in Caesarea and greeted Festus. {25:14} Since they stayed there for many days, Festus laid Paul's case before the king, saying, "There is a man here whom Felix left as a prisoner. {25:15} When I was in Jerusalem, the chief priests and elders of the Jews brought charges against him, asking for a sentence of condemnation against him. {25:16} I told them that it is not the Roman custom to hand over anyone before they have faced their accusers and have had an opportunity to defend themselves against the charges. {25:17} So when they came here with me, I didn't delay the case, but convened the court the next day and ordered the man to be brought in. {25:18} When his accusers got up to speak, they did not present any of the charges I had expected. {25:19} Instead, they had some points of dispute with him about their own religion and about a dead man named Jesus whom Paul claimed was alive. {25:20} I was at a loss how to investigate such matters, so I asked if he would be willing to go to Jerusalem and stand trial there on these charges. {25:21} But when Paul appealed to be kept in custody for the decision of the Emperor, I ordered him to be held until I could send him to Caesar." {25:22} Then Agrippa said to Festus, "I would like to hear this man myself." "Tomorrow," he said, "you will hear him." {25:23} The next day, Agrippa and Bernice came with great pomp and entered the audience room with the military commanders and the prominent men of the city. At Festus's command, Paul was brought in. {25:24} Festus said, "King Agrippa, and all present with us, you see this man about whom the whole Jewish community has petitioned me, both in Jerusalem and here, shouting that he ought not to live any longer. {25:25} But I found that he had done nothing worthy of death. Yet because he appealed to the Emperor, I decided to send him. {25:26} I have nothing definite to write to my lord about him, so I have brought him before all of you, and especially before you, King Agrippa, so that after he has been examined, I may have something to write. {25:27} For it seems unreasonable to me to send a prisoner without specifying the charges against him."

{26:1} Agrippa then said to Paul, "You may speak for yourself." So Paul stretched out his hand and began his defense: {26:2} "I consider myself fortunate, King Agrippa, because today I am able to defend myself before you regarding all the accusations made against me by the Jews, {26:3} especially since you are knowledgeable about all Jewish customs and controversies. Therefore, I beg you to listen to me patiently. {26:4} All the Jews know about my way of life from my youth, which was spent from the beginning among my own people in Jerusalem. {26:5} They knew me from the outset, if they were willing to testify, that I lived as a Pharisee, adhering strictly to the most rigorous sect of our religion. {26:6} And now I stand on trial because of the hope in the promise made by God to our fathers, {26:7} a promise our twelve tribes hope to attain as they earnestly serve God day and night. It is because of this hope, O King Agrippa, that I am accused by the Jews. {26:8} Why should any of you consider it incredible that God raises the dead? {26:9} I myself was convinced that I ought to do many things in opposition to the name of Jesus of Nazareth. {26:10} And that is what I did in Jerusalem. With authority from the chief priests, I put many of the saints in prison, and when they were condemned to death, I cast my vote against them. {26:11} I frequently punished them in the synagogues and tried to make them blaspheme. I was so furiously enraged against them that I even pursued them to foreign cities. {26:12} On one of these journeys, I was going to Damascus with the authority and commission of the chief priests. {26:13} About noon, O King, as I was on the road, I saw a light from heaven, brighter than the sun, shining around me and those traveling with me. {26:14} We all fell to the ground, and I heard a voice saying to me in Aramaic, 'Saul, Saul, why are you persecuting me? It is hard for you to kick against the goads.' {26:15} 'Who are you, Lord?' I asked. 'I am Jesus, whom you are persecuting,' the Lord replied. {26:16} 'Now get up and stand on your feet. I have appeared to you to appoint you as a servant and as a witness of what you have seen and will see of me. {26:17} I will rescue you from your own people and from the Gentiles. I am sending you to them {26:18} to open their eyes and turn them from darkness to light, and from the power of Satan to God, so that they may receive forgiveness of sins and a place among those who are sanctified by faith in me.' {26:19} "So then, King Agrippa, I was not disobedient to the vision from heaven. {26:20} First to those in Damascus, then to those in Jerusalem and in all Judea, and then to the Gentiles, I preached that they should repent and turn to God and demonstrate their repentance by their deeds. {26:21} That is why some Jews seized me in the temple courts and tried to kill me. {26:22} But God has helped me to this very day; so I stand here and testify to small and great alike. I am saying nothing beyond what the prophets and Moses said would happen— {26:23} that the Messiah would suffer and, as the first to rise from the dead, would bring the message of light to his own people and to the Gentiles." {26:24} As Paul was making his defense, Festus exclaimed loudly, "You are out of your mind, Paul! Your great learning is driving you insane!" {26:25} But Paul replied, "I am not insane, most excellent Festus. What I am saying is true and reasonable. {26:26} The king is familiar with these things, and I can speak freely to him. I am convinced that none of this has escaped his notice, because it was not done in a corner. {26:27} King Agrippa, do you believe the prophets? I know you do." {26:28} Then Agrippa said to Paul, "Do you think that in such a short time you can persuade me to be a Christian?" {26:29} Paul replied, "Short time or long—I pray to God that not only you but all who are listening to me today may become what I am, except for these chains." {26:30} After Paul had spoken, the king and the governor, along with Bernice and those sitting with them, got up {26:31} and left the room. They began saying to one another, "This man is not doing anything worthy of death or imprisonment." {26:32} Agrippa said to Festus, "This man could have been set free if he had not appealed to Caesar."

{27:1} When it was decided that we would sail to Italy, Paul and some other prisoners were handed over to a centurion named Julius, who belonged to the Imperial Regiment. {27:2} We boarded a ship from Adramyttium about to sail for ports along the coast of Asia, and we put out to sea. Aristarchus, a Macedonian from Thessalonica, was with us. {27:3} The next day we landed at Sidon, and Julius, in kindness to Paul, allowed him to go to his friends so they might provide for his needs. {27:4} From there we put out to sea again and passed to the lee of Cyprus because the winds were against us. {27:5} When we had sailed across the open sea off the coast of Cilicia and Pamphylia, we landed at Myra in Lycia. {27:6} There the centurion found an Alexandrian ship sailing for Italy and put us on board. {27:7} We made slow headway for many days and had difficulty arriving off Cnidus. When the wind did not allow us to hold our course, we sailed to the lee of Crete, opposite Salmone. {27:8} We moved along the coast with difficulty and came to a place called Fair Havens, near the town of Lasea. {27:9} Much time had been lost, and sailing had already become dangerous because by now it was after the Day of Atonement. So Paul warned them, {27:10} "Men, I can see that our voyage is going to be disastrous and bring great loss to ship and cargo, and to our own lives also." {27:11} But the centurion, instead of listening to what Paul said, followed the advice of the pilot and of the owner of the ship. {27:12} Since the harbor was unsuitable to winter in, the majority decided that we should sail on, hoping to reach Phoenix and winter there. This was a harbor in Crete, facing both southwest and northwest. {27:13} When a gentle south wind began to blow, they saw their opportunity; so they weighed anchor and sailed along the shore of Crete. {27:14} Before very long, a wind of hurricane force, called the Northeaster, swept down from the island. {27:15} The ship was caught by the storm and could not head into the wind; so we gave way to it and were driven along. {27:16} As we passed to the lee of a small island called Cauda, we were hardly able to make the lifeboat secure, {27:17} so the men hoisted it aboard. Then they passed ropes under the ship itself to hold it together. Because they were afraid they would run aground on the sandbars of Syrtis, they lowered the sea anchor and let the ship be driven along. {27:18} We took such a violent battering from the storm that the next day they began to throw the cargo overboard. {27:19} On the third day, they threw the ship's tackle overboard with their own hands. {27:20} When neither sun nor stars appeared for many days and the storm continued raging, we finally gave up all hope of being saved. {27:21} After they had gone a long time without food, Paul stood up before them and said: "Men, you should have taken my advice not to sail from Crete; then you would have spared yourselves this damage and loss. {27:22} But now I urge you to keep up your courage, because not one of you will be lost; only the ship will be destroyed. {27:23} Last night an angel of the God to whom I belong and whom I serve stood beside me {27:24} and said, 'Do not be afraid, Paul. You must stand trial before Caesar; and God has graciously given you the lives of all who sail with you.' {27:25} So keep up your courage, men, for I have faith in God that it will happen just as he told me. {27:26} Nevertheless, we must run aground on some island." {27:27} On the fourteenth night we were still being driven across the Adriatic Sea, when about midnight the sailors sensed they were approaching land. {27:28} They took soundings and found that the water was a hundred and twenty feet deep. A short time later they took soundings again and found it was ninety feet deep. {27:29} Fearing that we would be dashed against the rocks, they dropped four anchors from the stern and prayed for daylight. {27:30} In an attempt to escape from the ship, the sailors let the lifeboat down into the sea, pretending they were going to lower some anchors from the bow. {27:31} Then Paul said to the centurion and the soldiers, "Unless these men stay with the ship, you cannot be saved." {27:32} So the soldiers cut the ropes that held the lifeboat and let it drift away. {27:33} Just before dawn Paul urged them all to eat. "For the last fourteen days," he said, "you have been in constant suspense and have gone without food—you haven't eaten anything. {27:34} Now I urge you to take some food. You need it to survive. Not one of you will lose a single hair from his head." {27:35} After he said this, he took some bread and gave thanks to God in front of them all. Then he broke it and began to eat. {27:36} They were all encouraged and ate some food themselves. {27:37} Altogether there were 276 of us on board. {27:38} When they had eaten as much as they wanted, they lightened the ship by throwing the grain into the sea. {27:39} When daylight came, they did not recognize the land, but they saw a bay with a sandy beach, where they decided to run the ship aground if they could. {27:40} Cutting loose the anchors, they left them in the sea and at the same time untied the ropes that held the rudders. Then they hoisted the foresail to the wind and made for the beach. {27:41} But the ship struck a sandbar and ran aground. The bow stuck fast and would not move, and the stern was broken to pieces by the pounding of the surf. {27:42} The soldiers planned to kill the prisoners to prevent any of them from swimming away and escaping. {27:43} But the centurion wanted to spare Paul's life and kept them from carrying out their plan. He ordered those who could swim to jump overboard first and get to land. {27:44} The rest were to get there on planks or on other pieces of the ship. In this way everyone reached land safely.

{28:1} After we were safely ashore, we learned that the island was called Malta. {28:2} The islanders showed us unusual kindness. They built a fire and welcomed us all because it was raining and cold. {28:3} Paul gathered a pile of brushwood and, as he put it on the fire, a viper, driven out by the heat, fastened itself on his hand. {28:4} When the islanders saw the snake hanging from his hand, they said to each other, "This man must be a murderer; for though he escaped from the sea, the goddess Justice has not allowed him to live." {28:5} But Paul shook the snake off into the fire and suffered no ill effects. {28:6} The people expected him to swell up or suddenly fall dead; but after waiting a long time and seeing nothing unusual happened to him, they changed their minds and said he was a god. {28:7} There was an estate nearby that belonged to Publius, the chief official of the island. He welcomed us to his home and showed us generous hospitality for three days. {28:8} His father was sick in bed, suffering from fever and dysentery. Paul went in to see him and, after prayer, placed his hands on him and healed him. {28:9} When this had happened, the rest of the sick on the island came and were cured. {28:10} They honored us in many ways; and when we were ready to sail, they furnished us with the supplies we needed {28:11} After three months we put out to sea in a ship that had wintered in the island—it was an Alexandrian ship with the figurehead of the twin gods Castor and Pollux. {28:12} We put in at Syracuse and stayed there three days. {28:13} From there we set sail and arrived at Rhegium. The next day the south wind came up, and on the following day we reached Puteoli. {28:14} There we found some brothers and sisters who invited us to spend a week with them. And so we came to Rome. {28:15} The brothers and sisters there had heard that we were coming, and they traveled as far as the Forum of Appius and the Three Taverns to meet us. At the sight of these people Paul thanked God and was encouraged. {28:16} When we got to Rome, Paul was allowed to live by himself, with a soldier to guard him. {28:17} Three days later he called together the local Jewish leaders. When they had assembled, Paul said to them: "My brothers, although I have done nothing against our people or against the customs of our ancestors, I was arrested in Jerusalem and handed over to the Romans. {28:18} They examined me and wanted to release me, because I was not guilty of any crime deserving death. {28:19} The Jews objected, so I was compelled to make an appeal to Caesar. I certainly did not intend to bring any charge against my own people. {28:20} For this reason I have asked to see you and talk with you. It is because of the hope of Israel that I am bound with this chain." {28:21} They replied, "We have not received any letters from Judea concerning you, and none of our people who have come from there has reported or said anything bad about you. {28:22} But we want to hear what your views are, for we know that people everywhere are talking against this sect." {28:23} They arranged to meet Paul on a certain day, and came in even larger numbers to the place where he was staying. He witnessed them from morning till evening, explaining about the kingdom of God, and from the Law of Moses and from the Prophets he tried to persuade them about Jesus. {28:24} Some were convinced by what he said, but others would not believe. {28:25} They disagreed among themselves and began to leave after Paul had made this final statement: "The Holy Spirit spoke the truth to your ancestors when he said through Isaiah the prophet: {28:26} 'Go to this people and say, "You will be ever hearing but never understanding; you will be ever seeing but never perceiving." {28:27} For this people's heart has become calloused; they hardly hear with their ears, and they have closed their eyes. Otherwise they might see with their eyes, hear with their ears, understand with their hearts and turn, and I would heal them.' {28:28} "Therefore I want you to know that God's salvation has been sent to the Gentiles, and they will listen!" {28:29} After he said this, the Jews left, arguing vigorously among themselves. {28:30} For two whole years Paul stayed there in his own rented house and welcomed all who came to see him. {28:31} He proclaimed the kingdom of God and taught about the Lord Jesus Christ—with all boldness and without hindrance!

Romans

{1:1} From: Paul, a servant of Jesus Christ, called to be an apostle and set apart for the gospel of God— {1:2} the gospel he promised beforehand through his prophets in the Holy Scriptures {1:3} regarding his Son, who as to his earthly life was a descendant of David, {1:4} and who through the Spirit of holiness was appointed the Son of God in power by his resurrection from the dead: Jesus Christ our Lord. {1:5} Through him we received grace and apostleship to call all the Gentiles to the obedience that comes from faith for his name's sake. {1:6} And you also are among those Gentiles who are called to belong to Jesus Christ. {1:7} To all in Rome who are loved by God and called to be his holy people: Grace and peace to you from God our Father and from the Lord Jesus Christ. {1:8} First, I thank my God through Jesus Christ for all of you, because your faith is being reported all over the world. {1:9} God, whom I serve in my spirit in preaching the gospel of his Son, is my witness how constantly I remember you {1:10} in my prayers at all times; and I pray that now at last by God's will the way may be opened for me to come to you. {1:11} I long to see you so that I may impart to you some spiritual gift to make you strong— {1:12} that is, that you and I may be mutually encouraged by each other's faith. {1:13} I do not want you to be unaware, brothers and sisters, that I planned many times to come to you (but have been prevented from doing so until now) in order that I might have a harvest among you, just as I have had among the other Gentiles. {1:14} I am obligated both to Greeks and non-Greeks, both to the wise and the foolish. {1:15} That is why I am so eager to preach the gospel also to you who are in Rome. {1:16} For I am not ashamed of the gospel, because it is the power of God that brings salvation to everyone who believes: first to the Jew, then to the Gentile. {1:17} For in the gospel the righteousness of God is revealed—a righteousness that is by faith from first to last, just as it is written: "The righteous will live by faith." {1:18} The wrath of God is being revealed from heaven against all the godlessness and wickedness of people, who suppress the truth by their wickedness, {1:19} since what may be known about God is plain to them, because God has made it plain to them. {1:20} For since the creation of the world God's invisible qualities—his eternal power and divine nature—have been clearly seen, being understood from what has been made, so that people are without excuse. {1:21} For although they knew God, they neither glorified him as God nor gave thanks to him, but their thinking became futile and their foolish hearts were darkened. {1:22} Although they claimed to be wise, they became fools {1:23} and exchanged the glory of the immortal God for images made to look like a mortal human being and birds and animals and reptiles. {1:24} Therefore God gave them over in the sinful desires of their hearts to sexual impurity for the degrading of their bodies with one another. {1:25} They exchanged the truth about God for a lie, and worshiped and served created things rather than the Creator—who is forever praised. Amen. {1:26} Because of this, God gave them over to shameful lusts. Even their women exchanged natural sexual relations for unnatural ones. {1:27} In the same way the men also abandoned natural relations with women and were inflamed with lust for one another. Men committed shameful acts with other men, and received in themselves the due penalty for their error. {1:28} Furthermore, just as they did not think it worthwhile to retain the knowledge of God, so God gave them over to a depraved mind, so that they do what ought not to be done. {1:29} They have become filled with every kind of wickedness, evil, greed and depravity. They are full of envy, murder, strife, deceit and malice. They are gossips, {1:30} slanderers, God-haters, insolent, arrogant and boastful; they invent ways of doing evil; they disobey their parents; {1:31} they have no understanding, no fidelity, no love, no mercy. {1:32} Although they know God's righteous decree that those who do such things deserve death, they not only continue to do these very things but also approve of those who practice them.

{2:1} So, no matter who you are, if you judge others, you have no excuse. When you judge another person, you condemn yourself, since you, the judge, do the same things. {2:2} We know that God's judgment against those who do such things is based on truth. {2:3} So when you, a mere human being, pass judgment on them and yet do the same things, do you think you will escape God's judgment? {2:4} Or do you show contempt for the riches of his kindness, forbearance, and patience, not realizing that God's kindness is intended to lead you to repentance {2:5} But because of your stubbornness and your unrepentant heart, you are storing up wrath against yourself for the day of God's wrath, when his righteous judgment will be revealed. {2:6} God "will repay each person according to what they have done." {2:7} To those who by persistence in doing good seek glory, honor, and immortality, he will give eternal life. {2:8} But for those who are self-seeking and who reject the truth and follow evil, there will be wrath and anger. {2:9} There will be trouble and distress for every human being who does evil: first for the Jew, then for the Gentile; {2:10} but glory, honor, and peace for everyone who does good: first for the Jew, then for the Gentile. {2:11} For God does not show favoritism {2:12} All who sin apart from the law will also perish apart from the law, and all who sin under the law will be judged by the law. {2:13} For it is not those who hear the law who are righteous in God's sight, but it is those who obey the law who will be declared righteous. {2:14} (Indeed, when Gentiles, who do not have the law, do by nature things required by the law, they are a law for themselves, even though they do not have the law. {2:15} They show that the requirements of the law are written on their hearts, their consciences also bearing witness, and their thoughts sometimes accusing them and at other times even defending them.) {2:16} This will take place on the day when God judges people's secrets through Jesus Christ, as my gospel declares. {2:17} Now you, if you call yourself a Jew; if you rely on the law and boast in God; {2:18} if you know his will and approve of what is superior because you are instructed by the law; {2:19} if you are convinced that you are a guide for the blind, a light for those who are in the dark, {2:20} an instructor of the foolish, a teacher of little children, because you have in the law the embodiment of knowledge and truth— {2:21} you, then, who teach others, do you not teach yourself? You who preach against stealing, do you steal? {2:22} You who say that people should not commit adultery, do you commit adultery? You who abhor idols, do you rob temples? {2:23} You who boast in the law, do you dishonor God by breaking the law? {2:24} As it is written: "God's name is blasphemed among the Gentiles because of you. {2:25} Circumcision has value if you observe the law, but if you break the law, you have become as though you had not been circumcised. {2:26} So then, if those who are not circumcised keep the law's requirements, will they not be regarded as though they were circumcised? {2:27} The one who is not circumcised physically and yet obeys the law will condemn you who, even though you have the written code and circumcision, are a lawbreaker. {2:28} A person is not a Jew who is one only outwardly, nor is circumcision merely outward and physical. {2:29} No, a person is a Jew who is one inwardly; and circumcision is circumcision of the heart, by the Spirit, not by the written code. Such a person's praise is not from other people, but from God.

{3:1} So what's the advantage of being a Jew, or what value is there in circumcision? {3:2} Well, there are many advantages. First of all, the Jews were entrusted with the very words of God. {3:3} But what if some were unfaithful? Does their faithlessness nullify the faithfulness of God? {3:4} Not at all! Let God be true, and every human being a liar. As it is written: "So that you may be proved right when you speak and prevail when you judge." {3:5} But if our unrighteousness brings out God's righteousness more clearly, what shall we say? That God is unjust in bringing his wrath on us? (I am using a human argument.) {3:6} Certainly not! If that were so, how could God judge the world? {3:7} Someone might argue, "If my falsehood enhances God's truthfulness and so increases his glory, why am I still condemned as a sinner?" {3:8} Why not say—as some slanderously claim that we say—"Let us do evil that good may result"? Their condemnation is just! {3:9} What shall we conclude then? Do we have any advantage? Not at all! For we have already made the charge that Jews and Gentiles alike are all under the power of sin. {3:10} As it is written: "There is no one righteous, not even one; {3:11} there is no one who understands; there is no one who seeks God. {3:12} All have turned away, they have together become worthless; there is no one who does good, not even one." {3:13} "Their throats are open graves; their tongues practice deceit." "The poison of vipers is on their lips." {3:14} "Their mouths are full of cursing and bitterness." {3:15} "Their feet are swift to shed blood; {3:16} ruin and misery mark their ways, {3:17} and the way of peace they do not know." {3:18} "There is no fear of God before their eyes."{3:19} Now we know that whatever the law says, it says to those who are under the law, so that every mouth may be silenced and the whole world held accountable to God. {3:20} Therefore no one will be declared righteous in God's sight by the works of the law; rather, through the law we become conscious of our sin. {3:21} But now apart from the law the righteousness of God has been made known, to which the Law and the Prophets testify. {3:22} This righteousness is given through faith in Jesus Christ to all who believe. There is no difference between Jew and Gentile, {3:23} **for all have sinned and fall short of the glory of God**, {3:24} **and all are justified freely by his grace through the redemption that came by Christ Jesus**. {3:25} God presented Christ as a sacrifice of atonement, through the shedding of his blood—to be received by faith. He did this to demonstrate his righteousness, because in his forbearance he had left the sins committed beforehand unpunished— {3:26} he did it to demonstrate his righteousness at the present time, so as to be just and the one who justifies those who have faith in Jesus {3:27} Where, then, is boasting? It is excluded. Because of what law? The law that requires works? No, because of the law that requires faith {3:28} For we maintain that a person is justified by faith apart from the works of the law {3:29} Is God the God of Jews only? Is he not the God of Gentiles too? Yes, of Gentiles too {3:30} since there is only one God, who will justify the circumcised by faith and the uncircumcised through that same faith. {3:31} Do we, then, nullify the law by this faith? Not at all! Rather, we uphold the law.

{4:1} So what can we say about our ancestor Abraham? What did he discover about being made right with God? {4:2} If his good deeds had made him acceptable to God, he would have had something to boast about. But that was not God's way. {4:3} For the Scriptures tell us, "Abraham believed in God, and God counted him as righteous because of his faith." {4:4} When people work, their wages are not a gift, but something they have earned. {4:5} But people are counted as righteous, not because of their work, but because of their faith in God who forgives sinners. {4:6} David also spoke of this when he described the happiness of those who are declared righteous without working for it: {4:7} "Oh, what joy for those whose disobedience is forgiven, whose sins are put out of sight. {4:8} Yes, what joy for those whose record the Lord has cleared of sin." {4:9} Now, is this blessing only for the Jews, or is it also for uncircumcised Gentiles? Well, we have been saying that Abraham was counted as righteous by God because of his faith. {4:10} But how did this happen? Was he counted as righteous only after he was circumcised, or was it before he was circumcised? Clearly, God accepted Abraham before he was circumcised! {4:11} Circumcision was a sign that Abraham already had faith and that God had already accepted him and declared him to be righteous—even before he was circumcised. So Abraham is the spiritual father of those who have faith but have not been circumcised. They are counted as righteous because of their faith. {4:12} And Abraham is also the spiritual father of those who have been circumcised, but only if they have the same kind of faith Abraham had before he was circumcised. {4:13} Clearly, God's promise to give the whole earth to Abraham and his descendants was based not on his obedience to God's law, but on a right relationship with God that comes by faith. {4:14} If God's promise is only for those who obey the law, then faith is not necessary and the promise is pointless. {4:15} For the law always brings punishment on those who try to obey it. (The only way to avoid breaking the law is to have no law to break!) {4:16} So the promise is received by faith. It is given as a free gift. And we are all certain to receive it, whether or not we live according to the law of Moses, if we have faith like Abraham. For Abraham is the father of all who believe. {4:17} That is what the Scriptures mean when God told him, "I have made you the father of many nations." This happened because Abraham believed in the God who brings the dead back to life and who creates new things out of nothing. {4:18} Even when there was no reason for hope, Abraham kept hoping—believing that he would become the father of many nations. For God had said to him, "That's how many descendants you will have!" {4:19} And Abraham's faith did not weaken, even though, at about 100 years of age, he figured his body was as good as dead—and so was Sarah's womb. {4:20} Abraham never wavered in believing God's promise. In fact, his faith grew stronger, and in this he brought glory to God. {4:21} He was fully convinced that God is able to do whatever he promises. {4:22} And because of Abraham's faith, God counted him as righteous. {4:23} And when God counted him as righteous, it wasn't just for Abraham's benefit. It was recorded {4:24} for our benefit, too, assuring us that God will also count us as righteous if we believe in him, the one who raised Jesus our Lord from the dead. {4:25} He was handed over to die because of our sins, and he was raised to life to make us right with God.

{5:1} So now, because we are made right with God by faith, we have peace with him through our Lord Jesus Christ. {5:2} Through Christ, God has given us access by faith into this undeserved kindness in which we now stand. So we are very happy, because we hope we will enjoy God's glory. {5:3} And we also have joy with our troubles, because we know that these troubles produce patience. {5:4} And patience produces character, and character produces hope. {5:5} And this hope will never disappoint us, because God has poured out his love to fill our hearts. He gave us his love through the Holy Spirit, whom God has given to us. {5:6} Christ died for us when we were unable to help ourselves. We were living against God, but at the right time, Christ died for us. {5:7} Very few people will die to save the life of someone else, even if it is for a good person. Someone might be willing to die for an especially good person. {5:8} But Christ died for us while we were still sinners, and by this God showed how much he loves us. {5:9} Now that Christ's blood has made us right with God, we can be even more sure that Christ will save us from God's anger. {5:10} If we were God's enemies, we were brought back to him through the death of his Son. It is even more certain that we will be saved by Christ's life. {5:11} And we are happy with God through our Lord Jesus Christ. Through Jesus we are now God's friends again. {5:12} Sin came into the world because of what one man did. And with sin came death. This is why everyone must die—because everyone sinned. {5:13} Sin was in the world before the law was given. But sin is not judged as sin when there is no law. {5:14} Even though people were sinning from the time of Adam to the time of Moses, death still had power over them, even though they did not break a command as Adam did. In some ways Adam is like Christ who was to come. {5:15} But the gift that God was kind enough to give was very different from Adam's sin. That one sin brought death to many others. Yet the gift of God was great enough to bring grace to many others, who are made right with God by the gift that comes through one man, Jesus Christ. {5:16} And the result of God's gracious gift is very different from the result of that one man's sin. That one sin brought condemnation, but God's gift of forgiveness brings a justification that makes people right with him. {5:17} Because of one man's sin, death ruled over all people. But through that one man, Jesus Christ, those who receive God's full grace and the gift of being made right with him will surely have true life and rule through Christ. {5:18} So as one sin of Adam brought punishment to all people, one good act that Christ did makes all people right with God. And that brings true life for all. {5:19} One man disobeyed God, and many became sinners. In the same way, one man obeyed God, and many will be made right. {5:20} The law came to make people's sins increase. But when sin increased, God's grace increased even more. {5:21} Sin once used death to rule us, but God gave people more of his grace so that grace could rule by making people right with him. And this brings life forever through Jesus Christ our Lord.

{6:1} So what should we say about this? Should we continue to sin so that God's kindness will continue? {6:2} No, of course not! Since we have died to sin, how can we continue to live in it? {6:3} Don't you know that all of us who were baptized into Christ Jesus were baptized into his death? {6:4} When we were baptized into his death, we were buried with him, so that we could be raised up with him in a new life. Just as Christ was raised from the dead by the glorious power of the Father, now we also may live new lives. {6:5} Since we have been united with him in his death, we will also be raised to life as he was. {6:6} We know that our old sinful selves were crucified with Christ so that sin might lose its power in our lives. We are no longer slaves to sin. {6:7} For when we died with Christ we were set free from the power of sin. {6:8} And since we died with Christ, we know we will also live with him. {6:9} We are sure of this because Christ was raised from the dead, and he will never die again. Death no longer has any power over him. {6:10} When he died, he died once to break the power of sin. But now that he lives, he lives for the glory of God. {6:11} So you also should consider yourselves to be dead to the power of sin and alive to God through Christ Jesus. {6:12} Do not let sin control the way you live; do not give in to sinful desires. {6:13} Do not let any part of your body become an instrument of evil to serve sin. Instead, give yourselves completely to God, for you were dead, but now you have new life. So use your whole body as an instrument to do what is right for the glory of God. {6:14} Sin is no longer your master, for you no longer live under the requirements of the law. Instead, you live under the freedom of God's grace. {6:15} So since God's grace has set us free from the law, does that mean we can go on sinning? Of course not! {6:16} Don't you realize that you become the slave of whatever you choose to obey? You can be a slave to sin, which leads to death, or you can choose to obey God, which leads to righteous living. {6:17} Thank God! Once you were slaves of sin, but now you wholeheartedly obey this teaching we have given you. {6:18} Now you are free from your slavery to sin, and you have become slaves to righteous living. {6:19} Because of the weakness of your human nature, I am using the illustration of slavery to help you understand all this. Previously, you let yourselves be slaves to impurity and lawlessness, which led ever deeper into sin. Now you must give yourselves to be slaves to righteous living so that you will become holy. {6:20} When you were slaves to sin, you were free from the obligation to do right. {6:21} And what was the result? You are now ashamed of the things you used to do, things that end in eternal doom. {6:22} But now you are free from the power of sin and have become slaves of God. Now you do those things that lead to holiness and result in eternal life. {6:23} **For the wages of sin is death, but the free gift of God is eternal life through Christ Jesus our Lord.**

{7:1} Brothers and sisters, let me speak to those of you who know the law. Don't you understand that the law applies only while a person is living? {7:2} For example, when a woman marries, the law binds her to her husband as long as he is alive. But if he dies, the laws of marriage no longer apply to her. {7:3} So while her husband is alive, she would be committing adultery if she married another man. But if her husband dies, she is free from that law and does not commit adultery when she remarries. {7:4} In the same way, my dear brothers and sisters, you have died to the law through the body of Christ. And now you belong to another, to him who was raised from the dead, so that we may bear fruit for God. {7:5} When we were controlled by our old nature, sinful desires were at work within us, and the law aroused these evil desires that produced a harvest of sinful deeds, resulting in death. {7:6} But now we have been released from the law, for we died to it and are no longer captive to its power. Now we can serve God, not in the old way of obeying the letter of the law, but in the new way of living in the Spirit. {7:7} Well then, am I suggesting that the law of God is sinful? Of course not! In fact, it was the law that showed me my sin. I would never have known that coveting is wrong if the law had not said, "You must not covet." {7:8} But sin used this command to arouse all kinds of covetous desires within me! If there were no law, sin would not have that power. {7:9} At one time I lived without understanding the law. But when I learned the command not to covet, for instance, the power of sin came to life, {7:10} and I died. So I discovered that the law's commands, which were supposed to bring life, brought spiritual death instead. {7:11} Sin took advantage of those commands and deceived me; it used the commands to kill me. {7:12} But still, the law itself is holy, and its commands are holy and right and good. {7:13} But how can that be? Did the law, which is good, cause my death? Of course not! Sin used what was good to bring about my condemnation to death. So we can see how terrible sin really is. It uses God's good commands for its own evil purposes. {7:14} So the trouble is not with the law, for it is spiritual and good. The trouble is with me, for I am all too human, a slave to sin. {7:15} I don't really understand myself, for I want to do what is right, but I don't do it. Instead, I do what I hate. {7:16} But if I know that what I am doing is wrong, this shows that I agree that the law is good. {7:17} So I am not the one doing wrong; it is sin living in me that does it. {7:18} And I know that nothing good lives in me, that is, in my sinful nature. I want to do what is right, but I can't. {7:19} I want to do what is good, but I don't. I don't want to do what is wrong, but I do it anyway. {7:20} But if I do what I don't want to do, I am not really the one doing wrong; it is sin living in me that does it. {7:21} I have discovered this principle of life—that when I want to do what is right, I inevitably do what is wrong. {7:22} I love God's law with all my heart. {7:23} But there is another power within me that is at war with my mind. This power makes me a slave to the sin that is still within me. {7:24} Oh, what a miserable person I am! Who will free me from this life that is dominated by sin and death? {7:25} Thank God! The answer is in Jesus Christ our Lord. So you see how it is: In my mind I really want to obey God's law, but because of my sinful nature I am a slave to sin.

{8:1} So now there is no condemnation for those who belong to Christ Jesus. {8:2} And because you belong to him, the power of the life-giving Spirit has freed you from the power of sin that leads to death. {8:3} The law of Moses was unable to save us because of the weakness of our sinful nature. So God did what the law could not do. He sent his own Son in a body like the bodies we sinners have. And in that body God declared an end to sin's control over us by giving his Son as a sacrifice for our sins. {8:4} He did this so that the just requirement of the law would be fully satisfied for us, who no longer follow our sinful nature but instead follow the Spirit. {8:5} Those who are dominated by the sinful nature think about sinful things, but those who are controlled by the Holy Spirit think about things that please the Spirit. {8:6} So letting your sinful nature control your mind leads to death. But letting the Spirit control your mind leads to life and peace. {8:7} For the sinful nature is always hostile to God. It never did obey God's laws, and it never will. {8:8} That's why those who are still under the control of their sinful nature can never please God. {8:9} But you are not controlled by your sinful nature. You are controlled by the Spirit if you have the Spirit of God living in you. (And remember that those who do not have the Spirit of Christ living in them do not belong to him at all.) {8:10} And Christ lives within you, so even though your body will die because of sin, the Spirit gives you life because you have been made right with God. {8:11} The Spirit of God, who raised Jesus from the dead, lives in you. And just as God raised Christ Jesus from the dead, he will give life to your mortal bodies by this same Spirit living within you. {8:12} Therefore, dear brothers and sisters, you have no obligation to do what your sinful nature urges you to do. {8:13} For if you live by its dictates, you will die. But if through the power of the Spirit you put to death the deeds of your sinful nature, you will live. {8:14} For all who are led by the Spirit of God are children of God. {8:15} So you have not received a spirit that makes you fearful slaves. Instead, you received God's Spirit when he adopted you as his own children. Now we call him, "Abba, Father." {8:16} For his Spirit joins with our spirit to affirm that we are God's children. {8:17} And since we are his children, we are his heirs. In fact, together with Christ we are heirs of God's glory. But if we are to share his glory, we must also share his suffering. {8:18} Yet what we suffer now is nothing compared to the glory he will reveal to us later. {8:19} For all creation is waiting eagerly for that future day when God will reveal who his children really are. {8:20} Against its will, all creation was subjected to God's curse. But with eager hope, {8:21} the creation looks forward to the day when it will join with God's children in glorious freedom from death and decay. {8:22} For we know that all creation has been groaning as in the pains of childbirth right up to the present time. {8:23} And we believers also groan, even though we have the Holy Spirit within us as a foretaste of future glory, for we long for our bodies to be released from sin and suffering. We, too, wait with eager hope for the day when God will give us our full rights as his adopted children, including the new bodies he has promised us. {8:24} We were given this hope when we were saved. (If we already have something, we don't need to hope for it. {8:25} But if we look forward to something we don't yet have, we must wait patiently and confidently.) {8:26} And the Holy Spirit helps us in our weakness. For example, we don't know what God wants us to pray for. But the Holy Spirit prays for us with groanings that cannot be expressed in words. {8:27} And the Father who knows all hearts knows what the Spirit is saying, for the Spirit pleads for us believers in harmony with God's own will. {8:28} **And we know that God causes everything to work together for the good of those who love God and are called according to his purpose for them.** {8:29} For God knew his people in advance, and he chose them to become like his Son, so that his Son would be the firstborn among many brothers and sisters. {8:30} And having chosen them, he called them to come to him. And having called them, he gave them right standing with himself. And having given them right standing, he gave them his glory. {8:31} What shall we say about such wonderful things as these? If God is for us, who can ever be against us? {8:32} Since he did not spare even his own Son but gave him up for us all, won't he also give us everything else? {8:33} Who dares accuse us whom God has chosen for his own? No one—for God himself has given us the right standing with himself. {8:34} Who then will condemn us? No one—for Christ Jesus died for us and was raised to life for us, and he is sitting in the place of honor at God's right hand, pleading for us. {8:35} Can anything ever separate us from Christ's love? Does it mean he no longer loves us if we have trouble or calamity, or are persecuted, or hungry, or destitute, or in danger, or threatened with death? {8:36} (As the Scriptures say, "For your sake we are killed every day; we are being slaughtered like sheep.") {8:37} No, despite all these things, overwhelming victory is ours through Christ, who loved us. {8:38} And I am convinced that nothing can ever separate us from God's love. Neither death nor life, neither angels nor demons, neither our fears for today nor our worries about tomorrow—not even the powers of hell can separate us from God's love. {8:39} No power in the sky above or in the earth below—indeed, nothing in all creation will ever be able to separate us from the love of God that is revealed in Christ Jesus our Lord.

{9:1} Let me say clearly and truthfully in the name of Christ—I am not lying—my conscience is clear through the Holy Spirit. {9:2} I have great sorrow and unceasing anguish in my heart. {9:3} For I would wish that I myself were cursed and cut off from Christ for the sake of my brothers and sisters, my own flesh and blood. {9:4} They are the people of Israel, chosen to be God's adopted children. God revealed his glory to them. He made covenants with them and gave them his law. He gave them the privilege of worshiping him and receiving his wonderful promises. {9:5} Abraham, Isaac, and Jacob are their ancestors, and Christ himself was an Israelite as far as his human nature is concerned. And he is God, the one who rules over everything and is worthy of eternal praise! Amen. {9:6} Well then, has God failed to fulfill his promise to Israel? No, for not all who are born into the nation of Israel are truly members of God's people! {9:7} Being descendants of Abraham doesn't make them truly Abraham's children. For the Scriptures say, "Isaac is the son through whom your descendants will be counted," though Abraham had other children, too. {9:8} This means that Abraham's physical descendants are not necessarily children of God. Only the children of the promise are considered to be Abraham's children. {9:9} For God had promised, "I will return about this time next year, and Sarah will have a son." {9:10} This son was our ancestor Isaac. When he married Rebekah, she gave birth to twins. {9:11} But before they were born, before they had done anything good or bad, she received a message from God. (This message shows that God chooses people according to his own purposes; {9:12} he calls people, but not according to their good or bad works.) She was told, "Your older son will serve your younger son." {9:13} In the words of the Scriptures, "I loved Jacob, but I rejected Esau." {9:14} Are we saying, then, that God was unfair? Of course not! {9:15} For God said to Moses, "I will show mercy to anyone I choose, and I will show compassion to anyone I choose." {9:16} So it is God who decides to show mercy. We can neither choose it nor work for it. {9:17} For the Scriptures say that God told Pharaoh, "I have appointed you for the very purpose of displaying my power in you and to spread my fame throughout the earth." {9:18} So you see, God chooses to show mercy to some, and he chooses to harden the hearts of others so they refuse to listen. {9:19} Well then, you might say, "Why does God blame people for not responding? Haven't they simply done what he makes them do?" {9:20} No, don't say that. Who are you, a mere human being, to argue with God? Should the thing that was created say to the one who created it, "Why have you made me like this?" {9:21} When a potter makes jars out of clay, doesn't he have a right to use the same lump of clay to make one jar for decoration and another to throw garbage into? {9:22} In the same way, even though God has the right to show his anger and his power, he is very patient with those on whom his anger falls, who are destined for destruction. {9:23} He does this to make the riches of his glory shine even brighter on those to whom he shows mercy, who were prepared in advance for glory. {9:24} And we are among those whom he selected, both from the Jews and from the Gentiles. {9:25} Concerning the Gentiles, God says in the prophecy of Hosea, "Those who were not my people, I will now call my people. And I will love those whom I did not love before." {9:26} And, "Then, at the place where they were told, 'You are not my people,' there they will be called 'children of the living God.'" {9:27} And concerning Israel, Isaiah the prophet cried out, "Though the people of Israel are as numerous as the sand of the seashore, only a remnant will be saved. {9:28} For the Lord will carry out his sentence upon the earth quickly and with finality." {9:29} And Isaiah said the same thing in another place: "If the Lord of Heaven's Armies had not spared a few of our children, we would have been wiped out like Sodom, destroyed like Gomorrah." {9:30} What does all this mean? Even though the Gentiles were not trying to follow God's standards, they were made right with God. And it was by faith that this took place. {9:31} But the people of Israel, who tried so hard to get right with God by keeping the law, never succeeded. {9:32} Why not? Because they were trying to get right with God by keeping the law instead of by trusting in him. They stumbled over the great rock in their path. {9:33} God warned them of this in the Scriptures when he said, "I am placing a stone in Jerusalem that makes people stumble, a rock that makes them fall. But anyone who trusts in him will never be disgraced."

{10:1} Brothers and sisters, my deepest wish and prayer to God for Israel is that they may be saved. {10:2} I can testify about them that they are zealous for God, but their zeal is not based on knowledge. {10:3} Since they did not know the righteousness of God and sought to establish their own righteousness, they did not submit to God's righteousness. {10:4} Christ is the culmination of the law so that there may be righteousness for everyone who believes. {10:5} Moses writes about the righteousness that is by the law: "The person who does these things will live by them." {10:6} But the righteousness that is by faith says: "Do not say in your heart, 'Who will ascend into heaven?'" (that is, to bring Christ down) {10:7} "or 'Who will descend into the deep?'" (that is, to bring Christ up from the dead). {10:8} But what does it say? "The word is near you; it is in your mouth and in your heart," that is, the message concerning faith that we proclaim: {10:9} If you declare with your mouth, "Jesus is Lord," and believe in your heart that God raised him from the dead, you will be saved. {10:10} For it is with your heart that you believe and are justified, and it is with your mouth that you profess your faith and are saved. {10:11} As Scripture says, "Anyone who believes in him will never be put to shame." {10:12} For there is no difference between Jew and Gentile—the same Lord is Lord of all and richly blesses all who call on him, {10:13} for, "Everyone who calls on the name of the Lord will be saved." {10:14} How, then, can they call on the one they have not believed in? And how can they believe in the one of whom they have not heard? And how can they hear without someone preaching to them? {10:15} And how can anyone preach unless they are sent? As it is written: "How beautiful are the feet of those who bring good news!" {10:16} But not all the Israelites accepted the good news. For Isaiah says, "Lord, who has believed our message?" {10:17} Consequently, faith comes from hearing the message, and the message is heard through the word about Christ. {10:18} But I ask: Did they not hear? Of course they did: "Their voice has gone out into all the earth, their words to the ends of the world." {10:19} Again I ask: Did Israel not understand? First, Moses says, "I will make you envious by those who are not a nation; I will make you angry by a nation that has no understanding." {10:20} And Isaiah boldly says, "I was found by those who did not seek me; I revealed myself to those who did not ask for me." {10:21} But concerning Israel he says, "All day long I have held out my hands to a disobedient and obstinate people."

{11:1} So I ask, has God rejected his own people? Absolutely not! For I myself am an Israelite, a descendant of Abraham, from the tribe of Benjamin. {11:2} God has not rejected his people whom he foreknew. Don't you know what Scripture says about Elijah, how he appealed to God against Israel: {11:3} "Lord, they have killed your prophets, they have torn down your altars, and I am the only one left, and they are trying to take my life!" {11:4} But what was God's answer to him? "I have reserved for myself seven thousand who have not bowed the knee to Baal. {11:5} So too, at the present time there is a remnant chosen by grace. {11:6} And if it is by grace, then it cannot be based on works; if it were, grace would no longer be grace. {11:7} What then? What the people of Israel sought so earnestly they did not obtain. The elect among them did, but the others were hardened, {11:8} as it is written: "God gave them a spirit of stupor, eyes that could not see and ears that could not hear, to this very day." {11:9} And David says: "May their table become a snare and a trap, a stumbling block and a retribution for them. {11:10} May their eyes be darkened so they cannot see, and their backs be bent forever." {11:11} Again I ask: Did they stumble so as to fall beyond recovery? Not at all! Rather, because of their transgression, salvation has come to the Gentiles to make Israel envious. {11:12} But if their transgression means riches for the world, and their loss means riches for the Gentiles, how much greater riches will their full inclusion bring! {11:13} I am talking to you Gentiles. Inasmuch as I am the apostle to the Gentiles, I take pride in my ministry {11:14} in the hope that I may somehow arouse my own people to envy and save some of them. {11:15} For if their rejection brought reconciliation to the world, what will their acceptance be but life from the dead? {11:16} If the part of the dough offered as firstfruits is holy, then the whole batch is holy; if the root is holy, so are the branches. {11:17} If some of the branches have been broken off, and you, though a wild olive shoot, have been grafted in among the others and now share in the nourishing sap from the olive root, {11:18} do not consider yourself to be superior to those other branches. If you do, consider this: You do not support the root, but the root supports you. {11:19} You will say then, "Branches were broken off so that I could be grafted in." {11:20} Granted. But they were broken off because of unbelief, and you stand by faith. Do not be arrogant, but tremble. {11:21} For if God did not spare the natural branches, he will not spare you either. {11:22} Consider therefore the kindness and sternness of God: sternness to those who fell, but kindness to you, provided that you continue in his kindness. Otherwise, you also will be cut off. {11:23} And if they do not persist in unbelief, they will be grafted in, for God is able to graft them in again. {11:24} After all, if you were cut out of an olive tree that is wild by nature, and contrary to nature were grafted into a cultivated olive tree, how much more readily will these, the natural branches, be grafted into their own olive tree!

{11:25} I do not want you to be ignorant of this mystery, brothers and sisters, so that you may not be conceited: Israel has experienced a hardening in part until the full number of the Gentiles has come in, {11:26} and in this way all Israel will be saved. As it is written: "The deliverer will come from Zion; he will turn godlessness away from Jacob. {11:27} And this is my covenant with them when I take away their sins." {11:28} As far as the gospel is concerned, they are enemies for your sake; but as far as election is concerned, they are loved on account of the patriarchs, {11:29} for God's gifts and his call are irrevocable. {11:30} Just as you who were at one time disobedient to God have now received mercy as a result of their disobedience, {11:31} so they too have now become disobedient in order that they too may now receive mercy as a result of God's mercy to you. {11:32} For God has bound everyone over to disobedience so that he may have mercy on them all. {11:33} Oh, the depth of the riches of the wisdom and knowledge of God! How unsearchable his judgments, and his paths beyond tracing out! {11:34} "Who has known the mind of the Lord? Or who has been his counselor?" {11:35} "Who has ever given to God, that God should repay them?" {11:36} For from him and through him and for him are all things. To him be the glory forever! Amen.

{12:1} Brothers and sisters, I urge you, in view of God's mercy, to offer your bodies as a living sacrifice, holy and pleasing to God—this is your true and proper worship. {12:2} Do not conform to the pattern of this world, but be transformed by the renewing of your mind. Then you will be able to test and approve what God's will is—his good, pleasing, and perfect will. {12:3} For by the grace given me I say to every one of you: Do not think of yourself more highly than you ought, but rather think of yourself with sober judgment, in accordance with the faith God has distributed to each of you. {12:4} For just as each of us has one body with many members, and these members do not all have the same function, {12:5} so in Christ we, though many, form one body, and each member belongs to all the others. {12:6} We have different gifts, according to the grace given to each of us. If your gift is prophesying, then prophesy in accordance with your faith; {12:7} if it is serving, then serve; if it is teaching, then teach; {12:8} if it is to encourage, then give encouragement; if it is giving, then give generously; if it is to lead, do it diligently; if it is to show mercy, do it cheerfully. {12:9} Love must be sincere. Hate what is evil; cling to what is good. {12:10} Be devoted to one another in love. Honor one another above yourselves. {12:11} Never be lacking in zeal, but keep your spiritual fervor, serving the Lord. {12:12} Be joyful in hope, patient in affliction, faithful in prayer. {12:13} Share with the Lord's people who are in need. Practice hospitality. {12:14} Bless those who persecute you; bless and do not curse. {12:15} Rejoice with those who rejoice; mourn with those who mourn. {12:16} Live in harmony with one another. Do not be proud, but be willing to associate with people of low position. Do not be conceited. {12:17} Do not repay anyone evil for evil. Be careful to do what is right in the eyes of everyone. {12:18} If it is possible, as far as it depends on you, live at peace with everyone. {12:19} Do not take revenge, my dear friends, but leave room for God's wrath, for it is written: "It is mine to avenge; I will repay," says the Lord. {12:20} On the contrary: "If your enemy is hungry, feed him; if he is thirsty, give him something to drink. In doing this, you will heap burning coals on his head." {12:21} Do not be overcome by evil, but overcome evil with good.

{13:1} Let every soul be subject unto the higher powers. For there is no power but of God: the powers that be are ordained of God. {13:2} Whosoever therefore resisteth the power, resisteth the ordinance of God: and those that resist shall receive to themselves damnation. {13:3} For rulers are not a terror to good works, but to evil. Wilt thou then not be afraid of the power? do that which is good, and thou shalt have praise of the same: {13:4} For he is the minister of God to thee for good. But if thou do that which is evil, be afraid; for he beareth not the sword in vain: for he is the minister of God, a revenger to execute wrath upon him that doeth evil. {13:5} Wherefore ye must be subject, not only for wrath, but also for conscience's sake. {13:6} For for this cause pay ye tribute also: for they are God's ministers, attending continually upon this very thing. {13:7} Render therefore to all their dues: tribute to whom tribute is due; custom to whom custom; fear to whom fear; honour to whom honour. {13:8} Owe no man any thing, but to love one another: for he that loveth another hath fulfilled the law. {13:9} For this, Thou shalt not commit adultery, Thou shalt not kill, Thou shalt not steal, Thou shalt not bear false witness, Thou shalt not covet; and if there be any other commandment, it is briefly comprehended in this saying, namely, Thou shalt love thy neighbour as thyself. {13:10} Love worketh no ill to his neighbour: therefore love is the fulfilling of the law. {13:11} And that, knowing the time, that now it is high time to awake out of sleep: for now is our salvation nearer than when we believed. {13:12} The night is far spent, the day is at hand: let us therefore cast off the works of darkness, and let us put on the armor of light. {13:13} Let us walk honestly, as in the day; not in rioting and drunkenness, not in chambering and wantonness, not in strife and envying. {13:14} But put ye on the Lord Jesus Christ, and make not provision for the flesh, to fulfill the lusts thereof.

{14:1} Him that is weak in the faith receive ye, but not to doubtful disputations. {14:2} For one believeth that he may eat all things: another, who is weak, eateth herbs. {14:3} Let not him that eateth despise him that eateth not; and let not him which eateth not judge him that eateth: for God hath received him. {14:4} Who art thou that judgest another man's servant? to his own master he standeth or falleth. Yea, he shall be holden up: for God is able to make him stand. {14:5} One man esteemeth one day above another: another esteemeth every day alike. Let every man be fully persuaded in his own mind. {14:6} He that regardeth the day, regardeth it unto the Lord; and he that regardeth not the day, to the Lord he doth not regard it. He that eateth, eateth to the Lord, for he giveth God thanks; and he that eateth not, to the Lord he eateth not, and giveth God thanks. {14:7} For none of us liveth to himself, and no man dieth to himself. {14:8} For whether we live, we live unto the Lord; and whether we die, we die unto the Lord: whether we live therefore, or die, we are the Lord's. {14:9} For to this end Christ both died, and rose, and revived, that he might be Lord both of the dead and living. {14:10} But why dost thou judge thy brother? or why dost thou set at nought thy brother? for we shall all stand before the judgment seat of Christ. {14:11} For it is written, As I live, saith the Lord, every knee shall bow to me, and every tongue shall confess to God. {14:12} So then every one of us shall give account of himself to God. {14:13} Let us not therefore judge one another any more: but judge this rather, that no man put a stumblingblock or an occasion to fall in his brother's way. {14:14} I know, and am persuaded by the Lord Jesus, that there is nothing unclean of itself: but to him that esteemeth anything to be unclean, to him it is unclean. {14:15} But if thy brother be grieved with thy meat, now walkest thou not charitably. Destroy not him with thy meat, for whom Christ died. {14:16} Let not then your good be evil spoken of: {14:17} For the kingdom of God is not meat and drink; but righteousness, and peace, and joy in the Holy Ghost. {14:18} For he that in these things serveth Christ is acceptable to God, and approved of men. {14:19} Let us therefore follow after the things which make for peace, and things wherewith one may edify another. {14:20} For meat to destroy is not the work of God. All things indeed are pure; but it is evil for that man who eateth with offence. {14:21} It is good neither to eat flesh, nor to drink wine, nor anything whereby thy brother stumbleth, or is offended, or is made weak. {14:22} Hast thou faith? have it to thyself before God. Happy is he that condemneth not himself in that thing which he alloweth. {14:23} And he that doubteth is damned if he eats, because he eateth not of faith: for whatsoever is not of faith is sin.

{15:1} We then that are strong ought to bear the infirmities of the weak, and not to please ourselves. {15:2} Let every one of us please his neighbor for his good to edification. {15:3} For even Christ pleased not himself; but, as it is written, The reproaches of them that reproached thee fell on me. {15:4} For whatsoever things were written before were written for our learning, that we through patience and comfort of the scriptures might have hope. {15:5} Now the God of patience and consolation grants you to be like minded one toward another according to Christ Jesus: {15:6} That ye may with one mind and one mouth glorify God, even the Father of our Lord Jesus Christ. {15:7} Wherefore receive ye one another, as Christ also received us to the glory of God. {15:8} Now I say that Jesus Christ was a minister of the circumcision for the truth of God, to confirm the promises made unto the fathers: {15:9} And that the Gentiles might glorify God for his mercy; as it is written, For this cause I will confess to thee among the Gentiles, and sing unto thy name. {15:10} And again he saith, Rejoice, ye Gentiles, with his people. {15:11} And again, Praise the Lord, all ye Gentiles; and praise him, all ye people. {15:12} And again, Esaias saith, There shall be a root of Jesse, and he that shall rise to reign over the Gentiles; in him shall the Gentiles trust. {15:13} Now the God of hope fill you with all joy and peace in believing, that ye may abound in hope, through the power of the Holy Ghost. {15:14} And I myself also am persuaded of you, my brethren, that ye also are full of goodness, filled with all knowledge, able also to admonish one another. {15:15} Nevertheless, brethren, I have written the more boldly unto you in some sort, as putting you in mind, because of the grace that is given to me of God, {15:16} That I should be the minister of Jesus Christ to the Gentiles, ministering the gospel of God, that the offering up of the Gentiles might be acceptable, being sanctified by the Holy Ghost. {15:17} I have therefore whereof I may glory through Jesus Christ in those things which pertain to God. {15:18} For I will not dare to speak of any of those things which Christ hath not wrought by me, to make the Gentiles obedient, by word and deed, {15:19} Through mighty signs and wonders, by the power of the Spirit of God; so that from Jerusalem, and round about unto Illyricum, I have fully preached the gospel of Christ. {15:20} Yea, so have I strived to preach the gospel, not where Christ was named, lest I should build upon another man's foundation: {15:21} But as it is written, To whom he was not spoken of, they shall see: and they that have not heard shall understand. {15:22} For which cause also I have been much hindered from coming to you. {15:23} But now having no more place in these parts, and having a great desire these many years to come unto you; {15:24} Whensoever I take my journey into Spain, I will come to you: for I trust to see you in my journey, and to be brought on my way thitherward by you, if first I be somewhat filled with your company. {15:25} But now I go unto Jerusalem to minister unto the saints. {15:26} For it hath pleased them of Macedonia and Achaia to make a certain contribution for the poor saints which are at Jerusalem. {15:27} It hath pleased them verily; and their debtors they are. For if the Gentiles have been made partakers of their spiritual things, their duty is also to minister unto them in carnal things. {15:28} When therefore I have performed this, and have sealed to them this fruit, I will come by you into Spain. {15:29} And I am sure that, when I come unto you, I shall come in the fullness of the blessing of the gospel of Christ. {15:30} Now I beseech you, brethren, for the Lord Jesus Christ's sake, and for the love of the Spirit, that ye strive together with me in your prayers to God for me; {15:31} That I may be delivered from them that do not believe in Judaea; and that my service which I have for Jerusalem may be accepted of the saints; {15:32} That I may come unto you with joy by the will of God, and may with you be refreshed. {15:33} Now the God of peace be with you all. Amen.

{16:1} I commend unto you Phebe our sister, who is a servant of the church at Cenchreae: {16:2} That you receive her in the Lord, as befits saints, and assist her in whatever business she may have need of you; for she has been a helper of many, including myself. {16:3} Greet Priscilla and Aquila, my fellow workers in Christ Jesus, {16:4} Who risked their own necks for my life, to whom not only I give thanks, but also all the churches of the Gentiles. {16:5} Likewise, greet the church that is in their house. Greet my beloved Epaenetus, who is the firstfruits of Achaia unto Christ. {16:6} Greet Mary, who has worked hard for us. {16:7} Salute Andronicus and Junia, my kinsmen and fellow prisoners, who are esteemed among the apostles, and who were in Christ before me. {16:8} Greet Ampliatus my beloved in the Lord. {16:9} Salute Urbanus, our fellow worker in Christ, and Stachys my beloved. {16:10} Salute Apelles approved in Christ. Greet those who belong to the household of Aristobulus. {16:11} Salute Herodion my kinsman. Greet those in the household of Narcissus, who are in the Lord. {16:12} Salute Tryphaena and Tryphosa, who labour in the Lord. Salute the beloved Persis, who has worked hard in the Lord. {16:13} Salute Rufus chosen in the Lord, and his mother and mine. {16:14} Salute Asyncritus, Phlegon, Hermes, Patrobas, Hermas, and the brothers who are with them. {16:15} Salute Philologus, Julia, Nereus and his sister, and Olympas, and all the saints who are with them. {16:16} Greet one another with a holy kiss. The churches of Christ greet you. {16:17} Now I urge you, brothers, to watch out for those who cause divisions and obstacles contrary to the doctrine that you have learned; avoid them. {16:18} For such people do not serve our Lord Christ, but their own appetites, and by smooth talk and flattery they deceive the hearts of the naive. {16:19} For your obedience has reached to all; therefore I rejoice over you. But I want you to be wise about what is good, and innocent about what is evil. {16:20} And the God of peace will soon crush Satan under your feet. The grace of our Lord Jesus be with you. {16:21} Timothy, my fellow worker, and Lucius, Jason, and Sosipater, my kinsmen, send you their greetings. {16:22} I, Tertius, who wrote down this letter, greet you in the Lord. {16:23} Gaius, host to me and to the whole church, greets you. Erastus, the city's director of public works, and Quartus, our brother, greet you. {16:24} The grace of our Lord Jesus Christ be with you all. Amen. {16:25} Now to him who is able to strengthen you according to my gospel and the preaching of Jesus Christ, according to the revelation of the mystery that was kept secret for long ages {16:26} But has now been disclosed and through the prophetic writings has been made known to all nations, according to the command of the eternal God, to bring about the obedience of faith— {16:27} To the only wise God be glory forevermore through Jesus Christ! Amen.

1 Corinthians

{1:1} Paul, called to be an apostle of Jesus Christ by the will of God, and Sosthenes our brother, {1:2} To the church of God which is at Corinth, to those who are sanctified in Christ Jesus, called to be saints, with all who in every place call on the name of Jesus Christ our Lord, both theirs and ours: {1:3} Grace to you and peace from God our Father and the Lord Jesus Christ. {1:4} I thank my God always concerning you for the grace of God which was given to you by Christ Jesus, {1:5} that you were enriched in everything by Him in all utterance and all knowledge, {1:6} even as the testimony of Christ was confirmed in you, {1:7} so that you come short in no gift, eagerly waiting for the revelation of our Lord Jesus Christ, {1:8} who will also confirm you to the end, that you may be blameless in the day of our Lord Jesus Christ. {1:9} God is faithful, by whom you were called into the fellowship of His Son, Jesus Christ our Lord. {1:10} Now I plead with you, brethren, by the name of our Lord Jesus Christ, that you all speak the same thing, and that there be no divisions among you, but that you be perfectly joined together in the same mind and in the same judgment. {1:11} For it has been declared to me concerning you, my brethren, by those of Chloe's household, that there are contentions among you. {1:12} Now I say this, that each of you says, "I am of Paul," or "I am of Apollos," or "I am of Cephas," or "I am of Christ." {1:13} Is Christ divided? Was Paul crucified for you? Or were you baptized in the name of Paul? {1:14} I thank God that I baptized none of you except Crispus and Gaius, {1:15} lest anyone should say that I had baptized in my own name. {1:16} Yes, I also baptized the household of Stephanas. Besides, I do not know whether I baptized any other. {1:17} For Christ did not send me to baptize, but to preach the gospel, not with wisdom of words, lest the cross of Christ should be made of no effect. {1:18} For the message of the cross is foolishness to those who are perishing, but to us who are being saved it is the power of God. {1:19} For it is written: "I will destroy the wisdom of the wise, And bring to nothing the understanding of the prudent." {1:20} Where is the wise? Where is the scribe? Where is the dispute of this age? Has not God made foolish the wisdom of this world? {1:21} For since, in the wisdom of God, the world through wisdom did not know God, it pleased God through the foolishness of the message preached to save those who believe. {1:22} For Jews request a sign, and Greeks seek after wisdom; {1:23} but we preach Christ crucified, to the Jews a stumbling block and to the Greeks foolishness, {1:24} but to those who are called, both Jews and Greeks, Christ the power of God and the wisdom of God. {1:25} Because the foolishness of God is wiser than men, and the weakness of God is stronger than men. {1:26} For you see your calling, brethren, that not many wise according to the flesh, not many mighty, not many noble, are called. {1:27} But God has chosen the foolish things of the world to put to shame the wise, and God has chosen the weak things of the world to put to shame the things which are mighty; {1:28} and the base things of the world and the things which are despised God has chosen, and the things which are not, to bring to nothing the things that are, {1:29} that no flesh should glory in His presence. {1:30} But of Him you are in Christ Jesus, who became for us wisdom from God—and righteousness and sanctification and redemption— {1:31} that, as it is written, "He who glories, let him glory in the Lord."

{2:1} And when I came to you, brethren, I did not come with excellence of speech or of wisdom declaring to you the testimony of God. {2:2} For I am determined not to know anything among you except Jesus Christ and Him crucified. {2:3} I was with you in weakness, in fear, and in much trembling. {2:4} And my speech and my preaching were not with persuasive words of human wisdom, but in demonstration of the Spirit and of power, {2:5} so that your faith should not be in the wisdom of men but in the power of God. {2:6} However, we speak wisdom among those who are mature, yet not the wisdom of this age, nor of the rulers of this age, who are coming to nothing. {2:7} But we speak the wisdom of God in a mystery, the hidden wisdom which God ordained before the ages for our glory, {2:8} which none of the rulers of this age knew; for had they known, they would not have crucified the Lord of glory. {2:9} But as it is written: "Eye has not seen, nor ear heard, Nor have entered into the heart of man The things which God has prepared for those who love Him." {2:10} But God has revealed them to us through His Spirit. For the Spirit searches all things, yes, the deep things of God. {2:11} For what man knows the things of a man except the spirit of the man which is in him? Even so no one knows the things of God except the Spirit of God. {2:12} Now we have received, not the spirit of the world, but the Spirit who is from God, that we might know the things that have been freely given to us by God. {2:13} These things we also speak, not in words which man's wisdom teaches but which the Holy Spirit teaches, comparing spiritual things with spiritual. {2:14} But the natural man does not receive the things of the Spirit of God, for they are foolishness to him; nor can he know them, because they are spiritually discerned. {2:15} But he who is spiritual judges all things, yet he himself is rightly judged by no one. {2:16} For "who has known the mind of the Lord that he may instruct Him?" But we have the mind of Christ.

{3:1} And brethren, I could not speak to you as spiritual people but as to carnal, as to babes in Christ. {3:2} I fed you with milk and not with solid food; for until now you were not able to receive it, and even now you are still not able. {3:3} For you are still carnal. For where there are envy, strife, and divisions among you, are you not carnal and behaving like mere men? {3:4} For when one says, "I am of Paul," and another, "I am of Apollos," are you not carnal? {3:5} Who then is Paul, and who is Apollos, but ministers through whom you believed, as the Lord gave to each one? {3:6} I planted, Apollos watered, but God gave the increase. {3:7} So then neither he who plants is anything, nor he who waters, but God who gives the increase. {3:8} Now he who plants and he who waters are one, and each one will receive his own reward according to his own labor. {3:9} For we are God's fellow workers; you are God's field, you are God's building. {3:10} According to the grace of God which was given to me, as a wise master builder I have laid the foundation, and another builds on it. But let each one take heed of how he builds on it. {3:11} For no other foundation can anyone lay than that which is laid, which is Jesus Christ. {3:12} Now if anyone builds on this foundation with gold, silver, precious stones, wood, hay, or straw, {3:13} each one's work will become clear; for the Day will declare it, because it will be revealed by fire; and the fire will test each one's work, of what sort it is. {3:14} If anyone's work which he has built on it endures, he will receive a reward. {3:15} If anyone's work is burned, he will suffer loss; but he himself will be saved, yet so as through fire. {3:16} Do you not know that you are the temple of God and that the Spirit of God dwells in you? {3:17} If anyone defiles the temple of God, God will destroy him. For the temple of God is holy, which temple you are. {3:18} Let no one deceive himself. If anyone among you seems to be wise in this age, let him become a fool so that he may become wise. {3:19} For the wisdom of this world is foolishness with God. For it is written, "He catches the wise in their own craftiness"; {3:20} and again, "The Lord knows the thoughts of the wise, that they are futile." {3:21} Therefore let no one boast about men. For all things are yours: {3:22} whether Paul or Apollos or Cephas, or the world or life or death, or things present or things to come—all are yours. {3:23} And you are Christ's, and Christ is God's.

{4:1} Let people regard us as servants of Christ and stewards of the mysteries of God. {4:2} Moreover, it is required of stewards that they be found faithful. {4:3} But it matters very little to me that I should be judged by you or by human judgment; indeed, I do not even judge myself. {4:4} For I am aware of nothing against myself, yet I am not justified by this; but He who judges me is the Lord. {4:5} Therefore judge nothing before the time, until the Lord comes, who will both bring to light the hidden things of darkness and reveal the counsels of the hearts. Then each one's praise will come from God. {4:6} Now, brethren, I have figuratively applied these things to myself and Apollos for your sake, that you may learn in us not to think beyond what is written, that none of you may be puffed up on behalf of one against the other. {4:7} For who makes you differ from another? And what do you have that you did not receive? Now if you did indeed receive it, why do you boast as if you had not received it? {4:8} You are already full! You are already rich! You have reigned as kings without us—and indeed I could wish you did reign, that we also might reign with you! {4:9} For I think that God has displayed us, the apostles, last, as men condemned to death; for we have been made a spectacle to the world, both to angels and to men. {4:10} We are fools for Christ's sake, but you are wise in Christ! We are weak, but you are strong! You are distinguished, but we are dishonored! {4:11} To the present hour we are both hungry and thirsty, and we are poorly clothed, and beaten, and homeless {4:12} And we labor, working with our own hands. Being reviled, we bless; being persecuted, we endure; {4:13} being defamed, we entreat. We have been made as the filth of the world, the offscouring of all things until now. {4:14} I do not write these things to shame you, but as my beloved children I warn you. {4:15} For though you might have ten thousand instructors in Christ, yet you do not have many fathers; for in Christ Jesus I have begotten you through the gospel. {4:16} Therefore I urge you, imitate me. {4:17} For this reason I have sent Timothy to you, who is my beloved and faithful son in the Lord, who will remind you of my ways in Christ, as I teach everywhere in every church. {4:18} Now some are puffed up, as though I were not coming to you. {4:19} But I will come to you shortly, if the Lord wills, and I will know, not the word of those who are puffed up, but the power. {4:20} For the kingdom of God is not in word but in power. {4:21} What do you want? Shall I come to you with a rod, or in love and a spirit of gentleness?

{5:1} It's commonly reported that there is sexual immorality among you, and such immorality as is not even named among the Gentiles, that one should have his father's wife. {5:2} And you are arrogant, instead of mourning, that he who has done this deed might be taken away from you. {5:3} For I, though absent in body, but present in spirit, have already judged as though I were present concerning him who has so done this deed. {5:4} In the name of our Lord Jesus Christ, when you are gathered together, and my spirit, with the power of our Lord Jesus Christ, {5:5} to deliver such a one to Satan for the destruction of the flesh, that his spirit may be saved in the day of the Lord Jesus. {5:6} Your boasting is not good. Do you not know that a little leaven leavens the whole lump? {5:7} Therefore purge out the old leaven, that you may be a new lump, since you truly are unleavened. For indeed Christ, our Passover, was sacrificed for us. {5:8} Therefore let us keep the feast, not with old leaven, nor with the leaven of malice and wickedness, but with the unleavened bread of sincerity and truth. {5:9} I wrote to you in my epistle not to keep company with sexually immoral people. {5:10} Yet I certainly did not mean with the sexually immoral people of this world, or with the covetous, or extortioners, or idolaters, since then you would need to go out of the world. {5:11} But now I have written to you not to keep company with anyone named a brother, who is sexually immoral, or covetous, or an idolater, or a reviler, or a drunkard, or an extortioner—not even to eat with such a person. {5:12} For what do I have to do with judging those also who are outside? Do you not judge those who are inside? {5:13} But those who are outside God judge. Therefore, "put away from yourselves the evil person."

{6:1} Should any of you, having a dispute with another, dare to go to court before the unjust rather than before the saints? {6:2} Do you not know that the saints will judge the world? And if the world will be judged by you, are you unworthy to judge the smallest matters? {6:3} Do you not know that we shall judge angels? How much more, then, should we judge matters pertaining to this life? {6:4} If you have disputes regarding earthly matters, appoint those who are least esteemed in the church to judge them. {6:5} I say this to your shame: Is it so that there is not a wise person among you, not even one who can arbitrate between his brethren? {6:6} Instead, brother goes to court against brother, and before unbelievers at that. {6:7} Now therefore, there is already a fault among you, because you go to court against one another. Why not rather accept the wrong? Why not rather be defrauded? {6:8} Instead, you yourselves do wrong and defraud, and this to your brethren. {6:9} Do you not know that the unrighteous will not inherit the kingdom of God? Do not be deceived: neither fornicators, nor idolaters, nor adulterers, nor those who practice homosexuality, {6:10} nor thieves, nor covetous, nor drunkards, nor revilers, nor extortioners will inherit the kingdom of God. {6:11} And such were some of you. But you were washed, you were sanctified, you were justified in the name of the Lord Jesus and by the Spirit of our God. {6:12} All things are lawful for me, but not all things are helpful; all things are lawful for me, but I will not be brought under the power of any. {6:13} Foods for the stomach and the stomach for foods, but God will destroy both it and them. Now the body is not for sexual immorality but for the Lord, and the Lord for the body. {6:14} And God both raised up the Lord and will also raise us up by His power. {6:15} Do you not know that your bodies are members of Christ? Shall I then take the members of Christ and make them members of a harlot? Certainly not! {6:16} Or do you not know that he who is joined to a harlot is one body with her? For "the two," He says, "shall become one flesh." {6:17} But he who is joined to the Lord is one spirit with Him. {6:18} Flee sexual immorality. Every sin that a man does is outside the body, but he who commits sexual immorality sins against his own body. {6:19} Or do you not know that your body is the temple of the Holy Spirit who is in you, whom you have from God, and you are not your own? {6:20} For you were bought at a price; therefore glorify God in your body and in your spirit, which are God's.

{7:1} Regarding the matters you wrote to me about: It is good for a man not to have sexual relations with a woman. {7:2} But because of the temptation to sexual immorality, each man should have his own wife and each woman her own husband. {7:3} The husband should fulfill his marital duty to his wife, and likewise the wife to her husband. {7:4} The wife does not have authority over her own body, but the husband does. Likewise, the husband does not have authority over his own body, but the wife does. {7:5} Do not deprive one another, except perhaps by mutual consent for a limited time, that you may devote yourselves to prayer. Then come together again, so that Satan may not tempt you because of your lack of self-control. {7:6} I say this as a concession, not as a command. {7:7} I wish that all were as I am myself. But each has his own gift from God, one of one kind and one of another. {7:8} To the unmarried and the widows I say that it is good for them to remain single, as I am. {7:9} But if they cannot exercise self-control, they should marry. For it is better to marry than to burn with passion. {7:10} To the married I give this charge (not I, but the Lord): the wife should not separate from her husband. {7:11} But if she does, she should remain unmarried or else be reconciled to her husband, and the husband should not divorce his wife. {7:12} To the rest I say (I, not the Lord) that if any brother has a wife who is an unbeliever, and she consents to live with him, he should not divorce her. {7:13} If any woman has a husband who is an unbeliever, and he consents to live with her, she should not divorce him. {7:14} For the unbelieving husband is made holy because of his wife, and the unbelieving wife is made holy because of her husband. Otherwise your children would be unclean, but as it is, they are holy. {7:15} But if the unbelieving partner separates, let it be so. In such cases the brother or sister is not enslaved. God has called you to peace. {7:16} Wife, how do you know whether you will save your husband? Husband, how do you know whether you will save your wife? {7:17} Only let each person lead the life that the Lord has assigned to him, and to which God has called him. This is my rule in all the churches. {7:18} Was anyone at the time of his call already circumcised? Let him not seek to remove the marks of circumcision. Was anyone at the time of his call uncircumcised? Let him not seek circumcision. {7:19} For neither circumcision counts for anything nor uncircumcision, but keeping the commandments of God. {7:20} Each one should remain in the condition in which he was called. {7:21} Were you a bondservant when called? Do not be concerned about it. (But if you can gain your freedom, avail yourself of the opportunity.) {7:22} For he who was called in the Lord as a bondservant is a freedman of the Lord. Likewise he who was free when called is a bondservant of Christ. {7:23} You were bought with a price; do not become bondservants of men. {7:24} So, brothers, in whatever condition each was called, they let him remain with God. {7:25} Now concerning virgins, I have no command from the Lord, but I give my judgment as one who by the Lord's mercy is trustworthy. {7:26} I think that in view of the present distress it is good for a person to remain as he is. {7:27} Are you bound to a wife? Do not seek to be free. Are you free from a wife? Do not seek a wife. {7:28} But if you do marry, you have not sinned, and if a betrothed woman marries, she has not sinned. Yet those who marry will have worldly troubles, and I would spare you that. {7:29} This is what I mean, brothers: the appointed time has grown very short. From now on, let those who have wives live as though they had none, {7:30} and those who mourn as though they were not mourning, and those who rejoice as though they were not rejoicing, and those who buy as though they had no goods, {7:31} and those who deal with the world as though they had no dealings with it. For the present form of this world is passing away. {7:32} I want you to be free from anxieties. The unmarried man is anxious about the things of the Lord, how to please the Lord. {7:33} But the married man is anxious about worldly things, how to please his wife, {7:34} and his interests are divided. And the unmarried or betrothed woman is anxious about the things of the Lord, how to be holy in body and spirit. But the married woman is anxious about worldly things, how to please her husband. {7:35} I say this for your own benefit, not to lay any restraint upon you, but to promote good order and to secure your undivided devotion to the Lord. {7:36} If anyone thinks that he is not behaving properly toward his betrothed, if his passions are strong, and it has to be, let him do as he wishes: let them marry—it is no sin. {7:37} But whoever is firmly established in his heart, being under no necessity but having his desire under control, and has determined this in his heart, to keep her as his betrothed, he will do well. {7:38} So then he who marries his betrothed does well, and he who refrains from marriage will do even better. {7:39} A wife is bound to her husband as long as he lives. But if her husband dies, she is free to be married to whom she wishes, only in the Lord. {7:40} Yet in my judgment she is happier if she remains as she is. And I think that I too have the Spirit of God.

{8:1} Now concerning food offered to idols: we know that we all have knowledge. Knowledge puffs up, but love builds up. {8:2} If anyone imagines that he knows something, he does not yet know as he ought to know. {8:3} But if anyone loves God, he is known by God. {8:4} Therefore, as to the eating of food offered to idols, we know that "an idol has no real existence," and that "there is no God but one." {8:5} For although there may be so-called gods in heaven or on earth—as indeed there are many "gods" and many "lords"— {8:6} yet for us there is one God, the Father, from whom are all things and for whom we exist, and one Lord, Jesus Christ, through whom are all things and through whom we exist. {8:7} However, not all possess this knowledge. But some, through former association with idols, eat food as really offered to an idol, and their conscience, being weak, is defiled. {8:8} Food will not commend us to God. We are no worse off if we do not eat, and no better off if we do. {8:9} But take care that this right of yours does not somehow become a stumbling block to the weak. {8:10} For if anyone sees you who have knowledge eating in an idol's temple, will he not be encouraged, if his conscience is weak, to eat food offered to idols? {8:11} And so by your knowledge this weak person is destroyed, the brother for whom Christ died. {8:12} Thus, sinning against your brothers and wounding their conscience when it is weak, you sin against Christ. {8:13} Therefore, if food makes my brother stumble, I will never eat meat, lest I make my brother stumble.

{9:1} Am I not an apostle? Am I not free? Have I not seen Jesus Christ our Lord? Are you not my work in the Lord? {9:2} If to others I am not an apostle, at least I am to you, for you are the seal of my apostleship in the Lord. {9:3} This is my defense to those who would examine me. {9:4} Do we not have the right to eat and drink? {9:5} Do we not have the right to take along a believing wife, as do the other apostles and the brothers of the Lord and Cephas? {9:6} Or is it only Barnabas and I who have no right to refrain from working for a living? {9:7} Who serves as a soldier at his own expense? Who plants a vineyard without eating any of its fruit? Or who tends a flock without getting some of the milk? {9:8} Do I say these things to human authority? Does not the Law say the same? {9:9} For it is written in the Law of Moses, "You shall not muzzle an ox when it treads out the grain." Is it for oxen that God is concerned? {9:10} Does he not certainly speak for our sake? It was written for our sake, because the plowman should plow in hope and the thresher thresh in hope of sharing in the crop. {9:11} If we have sown spiritual things among you, is it too much if we reap material things from you? {9:12} If others share this rightful claim on you, do we not? Nevertheless, we have not made use of this right, but we endure anything rather than put an obstacle in the way of the gospel of Christ. {9:13} Do you not know that those who are employed in the temple service get their food from the temple, and those who serve at the altar share in the sacrificial offerings? {9:14} In the same way, the Lord commanded that those who proclaim the gospel should get their living by the gospel. {9:15} But I have made no use of any of these rights, nor am I writing these things to secure any such provision. For I would rather die than have anyone deprive me of my ground for boasting. {9:16} For if I preach the gospel, that gives me no ground for boasting. For necessity is laid upon me. Woe to me if I do not preach the gospel! {9:17} For if I do this of my own will, I have a reward, but if not of my own will, I am still entrusted with a stewardship. {9:18} What then is my reward? That in my preaching I may present the gospel free of charge, so as not to make full use of my right in the gospel. {9:19} For though I am free from all, I have made myself a servant to all, that I might win more of them. {9:20} To the Jews I became a Jew, in order to win Jews. To those under the law I became as one under the law (though not being myself under the law) that I might win those under the law. {9:21} To those outside the law I became as one outside the law (not being outside the law of God but under the law of Christ) that I might win those outside the law. {9:22} To the weak I became weak, that I might win against the weak. I have become all things to all people, that by all means I might save some. {9:23} I do it all for the sake of the gospel, that I may share with them in its blessings. {9:24} Do you not know that in a race all the runners run, but only one receives the prize? So run that you may obtain it. {9:25} Every athlete exercises self-control in all things. They do it to receive a perishable wreath, but we are imperishable. {9:26} So I do not run aimlessly; I do not box as one beating the air. {9:27} But I discipline my body and keep it under control, lest after preaching to others I myself should be disqualified.

{10:1} Brothers and sisters, I want to remind you that our ancestors were all under the cloud and they all passed through the sea. {10:2} They were all baptized into Moses in the cloud and in the sea. {10:3} They all ate the same spiritual food {10:4} and drank the same spiritual drink; for they drank from the spiritual rock that accompanied them, and that rock was Christ. {10:5} Nevertheless, God was not pleased with most of them; their bodies were scattered in the wilderness. {10:6} Now these things occurred as examples to keep us from setting our hearts on evil things as they did. {10:7} Do not be idolaters, as some of them were; as it is written: "The people sat down to eat and drink and got up to indulge in revelry." {10:8} We should not commit sexual immorality, as some of them did—and in one day twenty-three thousand of them died. {10:9} We should not test Christ, as some of them did—and were killed by snakes. {10:10} And do not grumble, as some of them did—and were killed by the destroying angel. {10:11} These things happened to them as examples and were written down as warnings for us, on whom the culmination of the ages has come. {10:12} So, if you think you are standing firm, be careful that you don't fall! {10:13} **No temptation has overtaken you except what is common to mankind. And God is faithful; he will not let you be tempted beyond what you can bear. But when you are tempted, he will also provide a way out so that you can endure it.** {10:14} Therefore, my dear friends, flee from idolatry. {10:15} I speak to sensible people; judge for yourselves what I say. {10:16} Is not the cup of thanksgiving for which we give thanks a participation in the blood of Christ? And is not the bread that we break a participation in the body of Christ? {10:17} Because there is one loaf, we, who are many, are one body, for we all share the one loaf. {10:18} Consider the people of Israel: Do not those who eat the sacrifices participate in the altar? {10:19} Do I mean then that food sacrificed to an idol is anything, or that an idol is anything? {10:20} No, but the sacrifices of pagans are offered to demons, not to God, and I do not want you to be participants with demons. {10:21} You cannot drink the cup of the Lord and the cup of demons too; you cannot have a part in both the Lord's table and the table of demons. {10:22} Are we trying to arouse the Lord's jealousy? Are we stronger than him? {10:23} "I have the right to do anything," you say—but not everything is beneficial. "I have the right to do anything"—but not everything is constructive. {10:24} No one should seek their own good, but the good of others. {10:25} Eat anything sold in the meat market without raising questions of conscience, {10:26} for, "The earth is the Lord's, and everything in it." {10:27} If an unbeliever invites you to a meal and you want to go, eat whatever is put before you without raising questions of conscience. {10:28} But if someone says to you, "This has been offered in sacrifice," then do not eat it, both for the sake of the one who told you and for the sake of conscience. {10:29} I am referring to the other person's conscience, not yours. For why is my freedom being judged by another's conscience? {10:30} If I take part in the meal with thankfulness, why am I denounced because of something I thank God for? {10:31} So whether you eat or drink or whatever you do, do it all for the glory of God. {10:32} Do not cause anyone to stumble, whether Jews, Greeks or the church of God— {10:33} even as I try to please everyone in every way. For I am not seeking my own good but the good of many, so that they may be saved.

{11:1} Follow my example, as I follow the example of Christ. {11:2} I commend you for remembering me in everything and for maintaining the traditions just as I passed them on to you. {11:3} But I want you to realize that the head of every man is Christ, and the head of the woman is man, and the head of Christ is God. {11:4} Every man who prays or prophesies with his head covered dishonors his head. {11:5} But every woman who prays or prophesies with her head uncovered dishonors her head—it is the same as having her head shaved. {11:6} For if a woman does not cover her head, she might as well have her hair cut off; but if it is a disgrace for a woman to have her hair cut off or her head shaved, then she should cover her head. {11:7} A man ought not to cover his head, since he is the image and glory of God; but woman is the glory of man. {11:8} For man did not come from woman, but woman from man; {11:9} neither was man created for woman, but woman for man. {11:10} It is for this reason that a woman ought to have authority over her own head, because of the angels. {11:11} Nevertheless, in the Lord woman is not independent of man, nor is man independent of woman. {11:12} For as woman came from man, so also man is born of woman. But everything comes from God. {11:13} Judge for yourselves: Is it proper for a woman to pray to God with her head uncovered? {11:14} Does not the very nature of things teach you that if a man has long hair, it is a disgrace to him, {11:15} but that if a woman has long hair, it is her glory? For long hair is given to her as a covering. {11:16} If anyone wants to be contentious about this, we have no other practice—nor do the churches of God. {11:17} What I am about to say, I cannot commend you for. It seems when you come together, it's not for the better but for the worse. {11:18} I've heard that there are divisions among you when you gather as a church, and I partly believe it. {11:19} It's inevitable that there will be disagreements among you to show who is genuine. {11:20} But when you come together, it's not really to eat the Lord's Supper. {11:21} Instead, each of you eats your own meal without waiting for others. One person goes hungry while another gets drunk. {11:22} Don't you have homes to eat and drink in? Or do you despise the church of God by humiliating those who have nothing? What can I say to you? Can I praise you for this? Certainly not! {11:23} For I received from the Lord what I also passed on to you: On the night when Jesus was betrayed, he took bread, {11:24} and after giving thanks, he broke it and said, "This is my body, which is for you; do this in remembrance of me."

{11:25} In the same way, he took the cup after supper, saying, "This cup is the new covenant in my blood; do this, whenever you drink it, in remembrance of me." {11:26} For whenever you eat this bread and drink this cup, you proclaim the Lord's death until he comes. {11:27} So then, whoever eats the bread or drinks the cup of the Lord in an unworthy manner will be guilty of sinning against the body and blood of the Lord. {11:28} Everyone ought to examine themselves before they eat the bread and drink from the cup. {11:29} For those who eat and drink without discerning the body of Christ eat and drink judgment on themselves. {11:30} That is why many among you are weak and sick, and a number of you have fallen asleep. {11:31} But if we were more discerning with regard to ourselves, we would not come under such judgment. {11:32} Nevertheless, when we are judged in this way by the Lord, we are being disciplined so that we will not be finally condemned with the world. {11:33} So then, my brothers and sisters, when you gather to eat, you should wait for one another. {11:34} If anyone is hungry, they should eat at home, so that when you meet together it may not result in judgment. And when I come, I will give further instructions.

{12:1} Brothers and sisters, I don't want you to be unaware about spiritual gifts. {12:2} You remember how you were once Gentiles, led astray to worship mute idols. {12:3} So, understand this: No one speaking by the Spirit of God would curse Jesus, and no one can confess Jesus as Lord without the Holy Spirit. {12:4} There are various gifts, but it's the same Spirit. {12:5} There are different kinds of service, but the same Lord. {12:6} And there are different activities, but the same God who empowers them all. {12:7} The manifestation of the Spirit is given to each person for the common good. {12:8} To one person is given the message of wisdom, to another the message of knowledge by the same Spirit, {12:9} to another faith by the same Spirit, to another gifts of healing, {12:10} to another miraculous powers, to another prophecy, to another distinguishing between spirits, to another speaking in different kinds of tongues, and to still another the interpretation of tongues. {12:11} All these are the work of one and the same Spirit, who distributes them to each one, just as he determines. {12:12} Just as a body, though one, has many parts, but all its many parts form one body, so it is with Christ. {12:13} For we were all baptized by one Spirit so as to form one body—whether Jews or Gentiles, slave or free—and we were all given the one Spirit to drink. {12:14} Even so the body is not made up of one part but of many. {12:15} If the foot should say, "Because I am not a hand, I do not belong to the body," it would not for that reason stop being part of the body. {12:16} And if the ear should say, "Because I am not an eye, I do not belong to the body," it would not for that reason stop being part of the body. {12:17} If the whole body were an eye, where would the sense of hearing be? If the whole body were an ear, where would the sense of smell be? {12:18} But in fact God has placed the parts in the body, every one of them, just as he wanted them to be. {12:19} If they were all one part, where would the body be? {12:20} As it is, there are many parts, but one body. {12:21} The eye cannot say to the hand, "I don't need you!" And the head cannot say to the feet, "I don't need you!" {12:22} On the contrary, those parts of the body that seem to be weaker are indispensable, {12:23} and the parts that we think are less honorable we treat with special honor. And the parts that are unpresentable are treated with special modesty, {12:24} while our presentable parts need no special treatment. But God has put the body together, giving greater honor to the parts that lacked it, {12:25} so that there should be no division in the body, but that its parts should have equal concern for each other. {12:26} If one part suffers, every part suffers with it; if one part is honored, every part rejoices with it. {12:27} Now you are the body of Christ, and each one of you is a part of it. {12:28} And God has placed in the church first of all apostles, second prophets, third teachers, then miracles, then gifts of healing, of helping, of guidance, and of different kinds of tongues. {12:29} Are all apostles? Are all prophets? Are all teachers? Do all work miracles? {12:30} Do all have gifts of healing? Do all speak in tongues? Do all interpret? {12:31} But eagerly desire the greater gifts. And yet I will show you the most excellent way.

{13:1} If I speak with the tongues of men and of angels but do not have love, I am only a resounding gong or a clanging cymbal. {13:2} Even if I have the gift of prophecy and can fathom all mysteries and all knowledge, and if I have a faith that can move mountains but do not have love, I am nothing. {13:3} Even if I give all I possess to the poor and give over my body to hardship that I may boast, but do not have love, I gain nothing. {13:4} **Love is patient, love is kind. It does not envy, it does not boast, it is not proud.** {13:5} It does not dishonor others, it is not self-seeking, it is not easily angered, it keeps no record of wrongs. {13:6} Love does not delight in evil but rejoices with the truth. {13:7} **It always protects, always trusts, always hopes, always perseveres.** {13:8} Love never fails. But where there are prophecies, they will cease; where there are tongues, they will be stilled; where there is knowledge, it will pass away. {13:9} For we know in part and we prophesy in part, {13:10} but when completeness comes, what is in part disappears. {13:11} When I was a child, I talked like a child, I thought like a child, I reasoned like a child. When I became a man, I put the ways of childhood behind me. {13:12} For now we see only a reflection as in a mirror; then we shall see face to face. Now I know in part; then I shall know fully, even as I am fully known. {13:13} And now these three remain: faith, hope, and love. But the greatest of these is love.

{14:1} Pursue love, and earnestly desire spiritual gifts, especially that you may prophesy. {14:2} For one who speaks in a tongue speaks not to men but to God; for no one understands him, but he utters mysteries in the Spirit. {14:3} On the other hand, the one who prophesies speaks to people for their upbuilding and encouragement and consolation. {14:4} The one who speaks in a tongue builds up himself, but the one who prophesies builds up the church. {14:5} Now I want you all to speak in tongues, but even more to prophesy. The one who prophesies is greater than the one who speaks in tongues, unless someone interprets, so that the church may be built up. {14:6} Now, brothers, if I come to you speaking in tongues, how will I benefit you unless I bring you some revelation or knowledge or prophecy or teaching? {14:7} If even lifeless instruments, such as the flute or the harp, do not give distinct notes, how will anyone know what is played? {14:8} And if the bugle gives an indistinct sound, who will get ready for battle? {14:9} So with yourselves, if with your tongue you utter speech that is not intelligible, how will anyone know what is said? For you will be speaking into the air. {14:10} There are doubtless many different languages in the world, and none is without meaning, {14:11} but if I do not know the meaning of the language, I will be a foreigner to the speaker and the speaker a foreigner to me. {14:12} So with yourselves, since you are eager for manifestations of the Spirit, strive to excel in building up the church. {14:13} Therefore, one who speaks in a tongue should pray that he may interpret. {14:14} For if I pray in a tongue, my spirit prays but my mind is unfruitful. {14:15} What am I to do? I will pray with my spirit, but I will pray with my mind also; I will sing praise with my spirit, but I will sing with my mind also. {14:16} Otherwise, if you give thanks with your spirit, how can anyone in the position of an outsider say "Amen" to your thanksgiving when he does not know what you are saying? {14:17} For you may be giving thanks well enough, but the other person is not being built up. {14:18} I thank God that I speak in tongues more than all of you. {14:19} Nevertheless, in church I would rather speak five words with my mind in order to instruct others, than ten thousand words in a tongue. {14:20} Brothers, do not be children in your thinking. Be infants in evil, but in your thinking be mature.{14:21} In the law it is written, "With people of strange tongues and by the lips of foreigners will I speak to this people, and even then they will not listen to me, says the Lord." {14:22} Thus, tongues are a sign not for believers but for unbelievers, while prophecy is a sign not for unbelievers but for believers. {14:23} If, therefore, the whole church comes together and all speak in tongues, and outsiders or unbelievers enter, will they not say that you are out of your minds? {14:24} But if all prophesy, and an unbeliever or outsider enters, he is convicted by all, he is called to account by all, {14:25} the secrets of his heart are disclosed, and so, falling on his face, he will worship God and declare that God is really among you. {14:26} What then, brothers? When you come together, each one has a hymn, a lesson, a revelation, a tongue, or an interpretation. Let all things be done for building up. {14:27} If any speak in a tongue, let there be only two or at most three, and each in turn, and let someone interpret. {14:28} But if there is no one to interpret, let each of them keep silent in church and speak to himself and to God. {14:29} Let two or three prophets speak, and let the others weigh what is said. {14:30} If a revelation is made to another sitting there, let the first be silent. {14:31} For you can all prophesy one by one, so that all may learn and all be encouraged, {14:32} and the spirits of prophets are subject to prophets. {14:33} For God is not a God of confusion but of peace. As in all the churches of the saints, {14:34} the women should keep silent in the churches. For they are not permitted to speak, but should be in submission, as the Law also says. {14:35} If there is anything they desire to learn, let them ask their husbands at home. For it is shameful for a woman to speak in church. {14:36} Or was it from you that the word of God came? Or are you the only ones it has reached? {14:37} If anyone thinks that he is a prophet, or spiritual, he should acknowledge that the things I am writing to you are a command of the Lord. {14:38} If anyone does not recognize this, he is not recognized. {14:39} So, my brothers, earnestly desire to prophesy, and do not forbid speaking in tongues. {14:40} But all things should be done decently and in order.

{15:1} Brothers and sisters, I want to remind you of the gospel I preached to you, which you received and on which you have taken your stand. {15:2} By this gospel you are saved, if you hold firmly to the word I preached to you. Otherwise, you have believed in vain. {15:3} **For what I received I passed on to you as of first importance: that Christ died for our sins according to the Scriptures,** {15:4} **that he was buried, that he was raised on the third day according to the Scriptures,** {15:5} and that he appeared to Cephas, and then to the Twelve. {15:6} After that, he appeared to more than five hundred of the brothers and sisters at the same time, most of whom are still living, though some have fallen asleep. {15:7} Then he appeared to James, then to all the apostles, {15:8} and last of all he appeared to me also, as to one abnormally born. {15:9} For I am the least of the apostles and do not even deserve to be called an apostle, because I persecuted the church of God. {15:10} But by the grace of God I am what I am, and his grace to me was not without effect. No, I worked harder than all of them—yet not I, but the grace of God that was with me. {15:11} Whether, then, it is I or they, this is what we preach, and this is what you believed. {15:12} But if it is preached that Christ has been raised from the dead, how can some of you say that there is no resurrection of the dead? {15:13} If there is no resurrection of the dead, then not even Christ has been raised. {15:14} And if Christ has not been raised, our preaching is useless and so is your faith. {15:15} More than that, we are then found to be false witnesses about God, for we have testified about God that he raised Christ from the dead. But he did not raise him if in fact the dead are not raised. {15:16} For if the dead are not raised, then Christ has not been raised either. {15:17} And if Christ has not been raised, your faith is futile; you are still in your sins. {15:18} Then those also who have fallen asleep in Christ are lost. {15:19} If only for this life we have hope in Christ, we are of all people most to be pitied. {15:20} But Christ has indeed been raised from the dead, the firstfruits of those who have fallen asleep. {15:21} For since death came through a man, the resurrection of the dead comes also through a man. {15:22} For as in Adam all die, so in Christ all will be made alive. {15:23} But each in turn: Christ, the firstfruits; then, when he comes, those who belong to him. {15:24} Then the end will come, when he hands over the kingdom to God the Father after he has destroyed all dominion, authority and power. {15:25} For he must reign until he has put all his enemies under his feet. {15:26} The last enemy to be destroyed is death. {15:27} For he "has put everything under his feet." Now when it says that "everything" has been put under him, it is clear that this does not include God himself, who put everything under Christ. {15:28} When he has done this, then the Son himself will be made subject to him who put everything under him, so that God may be all in all. {15:29} Now if there is no resurrection, what will those who are baptized for the dead do? If the dead are not raised at all, why are people baptized for them? {15:30} And as for us, why do we endanger ourselves every hour? {15:31} I face death every day—yes, just as surely as I boast about you in Christ Jesus our Lord. {15:32} If I fought wild beasts in Ephesus with no more than human hopes, what have I gained? If the dead are not raised, "Let us eat and drink, for tomorrow we die." {15:33} Do not be misled: "Bad company corrupts good character." {15:34} Come back to your senses as you ought, and stop sinning; for there are some who are ignorant of God—I say this to your shame. {15:35} But someone will ask, "How are the dead raised? With what kind of body will they come?" {15:36} How foolish! What you sow does not come to life unless it dies. {15:37} When you sow, you do not plant the body that will be, but just a seed, perhaps of wheat or of something else. {15:38} But God gives it a body as he has determined, and to each kind of seed he gives its own body. {15:39} Not all flesh is the same: People have one kind of flesh, animals have another, birds another and fish another. {15:40} There are also heavenly bodies and there are earthly bodies; but the splendor of the heavenly bodies is one kind, and the splendor of the earthly bodies is another. {15:41} The sun has one kind of splendor, the moon another and the stars another; and the star differs from star in splendor. {15:42} So will it be with the resurrection of the dead. The body that is sown is perishable, it is raised imperishable; {15:43} it is sown in dishonor, it is raised in glory; it is sown in weakness, it is raised in power; {15:44} it is sown a natural body, it is raised a spiritual body. If there is a natural body, there is also a spiritual body.

{15:45} So it is written: "The first man Adam became a living being"; the last Adam, a life-giving spirit. {15:46} The spiritual did not come first, but the natural, and after that the spiritual. {15:47} The first man was of the dust of the earth; the second man was of heaven. {15:48} As was the earthly man, so are those who are of the earth; and as is the heavenly man, so also are those who are of heaven. {15:49} And just as we have borne the image of the earthly man, so shall we bear the image of the heavenly man. {15:50} I declare to you, brothers and sisters, that flesh and blood cannot inherit the kingdom of God, nor does the perishable inherit the imperishable. {15:51} Listen, I tell you a mystery: We will not all sleep, but we will all be changed— {15:52} in a flash, in the twinkling of an eye, at the last trumpet. For the trumpet will sound, the dead will be raised imperishable, and we will be changed. {15:53} For the perishable must clothe itself with the imperishable, and the mortal with immortality. {15:54} When the perishable has been clothed with the imperishable, and the mortal with immortality, then the saying that is written will come true: "Death has been swallowed up in victory." {15:55} "Where, O death, is your victory? Where, O death, is your sting?" {15:56} The sting of death is sin, and the power of sin is the law. {15:57} But thanks be to God! He gives us victory through our Lord Jesus Christ. {15:58} Therefore, my dear brothers and sisters, stand firm. Let nothing move you. Always give yourselves fully to the work of the Lord, because you know that your labor in the Lord is not in vain.

{16:1} Now about the collection for the Lord's people: Do what I told the Galatian churches to do. {16:2} On the first day of every week, each one of you should set aside a sum of money in keeping with your income, saving it up, so that when I come no collections will have to be made. {16:3} Then, when I arrive, I will give letters of introduction to the men you approve of and send them with your gift to Jerusalem. {16:4} If it seems advisable for me to go also, they will accompany me. {16:5} After I go through Macedonia, I will come to you—for I will be going through Macedonia. {16:6} Perhaps I will stay with you for a while, or even spend the winter, so that you can help me on my journey, wherever I go. {16:7} For I do not want to see you now and make only a passing visit; I hope to spend some time with you, if the Lord permits. {16:8} But I will stay on at Ephesus until Pentecost, {16:9} because a great door for effective work has opened to me, and there are many who oppose me. {16:10} When Timothy comes, see to it that he has nothing to fear while he is with you, for he is carrying on the work of the Lord, just as I am. {16:11} No one, then, should treat him with contempt. Send him on his way in peace so that he may return to me. I am expecting him along with the brothers. {16:12} Now about our brother Apollos: I strongly urged him to go with the brothers. He was quite unwilling to go now, but he will go when he has the opportunity. {16:13} Be on your guard; stand firm in the faith; be courageous; be strong. {16:14} Do everything in love. {16:15} You know that the household of Stephanas were the first converts in Achaia, and they have devoted themselves to the service of the Lord's people. I urge you, brothers and sisters, {16:16} to submit to such people and to everyone who joins in the work and labors at it. {16:17} I was glad when Stephanas, Fortunatus and Achaicus arrived, because they have supplied what was lacking from you. {16:18} For they refreshed my spirit and yours also. Such men deserve recognition. {16:19} The churches in the province of Asia send you greetings. Aquila and Priscilla greet you warmly in the Lord, and so does the church that meets at their house. {16:20} All the brothers and sisters here send you greetings. Greet one another with a holy kiss. {16:21} I, Paul, write this greeting in my own hand. {16:22} If anyone does not love the Lord, let that person be cursed! Come, Lord! {16:23} The grace of the Lord Jesus be with you. {16:24} My love to all of you in Christ Jesus. Amen.

2 Corinthians

{1:1} From Paul, chosen by the will of God to be an apostle of Christ Jesus, and from our brother Timothy. To God's church in Corinth and to all of his holy people throughout Achaia. {1:2} May God our Father and the Lord Jesus Christ give you grace and peace. {1:3} All praise to God, the Father of our Lord Jesus Christ. God is our merciful Father and the source of all comfort. {1:4} He comforts us in all our troubles so that we can comfort others. When they are troubled, we will be able to give them the same comfort God has given us. {1:5} For the more we suffer for Christ, the more God will shower us with his comfort through Christ. {1:6} Even when we are weighed down with troubles, it is for your comfort and salvation! For when we ourselves are comforted, we will certainly comfort you. Then you can patiently endure the same things we suffer. {1:7} We are confident that as you share in our sufferings, you will also share in the comfort God gives us. {1:8} We think you ought to know, dear brothers and sisters, about the trouble we went through in the province of Asia. We were crushed and overwhelmed beyond our ability to endure, and we thought we would never live through it. {1:9} In fact, we expected to die. But as a result, we stopped relying on ourselves and learned to rely only on God, who raises the dead. {1:10} And he did rescue us from mortal danger, and he will rescue us again. We have placed our confidence in him, and he will continue to rescue us. {1:11} And you are helping us by praying for us. Then many people will give thanks because God has graciously answered so many prayers for our safety. {1:12} We can say with confidence and a clear conscience that we have lived with a God-given holiness and sincerity in all our dealings. We have depended on God's grace, not on our own human wisdom. That is how we have conducted ourselves before the world, and especially toward you. {1:13} Our letters have been straightforward, and there is nothing written between the lines and nothing you can't understand. I hope someday you will fully understand us, {1:14} even if you don't fully understand us now. Then on the day when the Lord Jesus returns, you will be proud of us in the same way we are proud of you. {1:15} Since I was so sure of your understanding and trust, I wanted to give you a double blessing by visiting you twice—{1:16} first on my way to Macedonia and again when I returned from Macedonia. Then you could send me on my way to Judea. {1:17} You may be asking why I changed my plan. Do you think I make my plans carelessly? Do you think I am like people of the world who say "Yes" when they really mean "No"? {1:18} As surely as God is faithful, our word to you does not waver between "Yes" and "No." {1:19} For Jesus Christ, the Son of God, does not waver between "Yes" and "No." He is the one whom Silas, Timothy, and I preached to you, and as God's ultimate "Yes," he always does what he says. {1:20} For all of God's promises have been fulfilled in Christ with a resounding "Yes!" And through Christ, our "Amen" (which means "Yes") ascends to God for his glory. {1:21} It is God who enables us, along with you, to stand firm for Christ. He has commissioned us, {1:22} and he has identified us as his own by placing the Holy Spirit in our hearts as the first installment that guarantees everything he has promised us. {1:23} Now I call upon God as my witness that I am telling the truth. The reason I didn't return to Corinth was to spare you from a severe rebuke. {1:24} But that does not mean we want to dominate you by telling you how to put your faith into practice. We want to work together with you so you will be full of joy, for it is by your own faith that you stand firm.

{2:1} I decided that I would not make another painful visit to you. {2:2} For if I cause you grief, who will make me glad? Certainly not someone I have grieved. {2:3} That is why I wrote to you as I did, so that when I do come, I won't be grieved by the very ones who ought to give me the greatest joy. Surely, you all know that my joy comes from your being joyful. {2:4} I wrote that letter in great anguish, with a troubled heart and many tears. I didn't want to grieve you, but I wanted to let you know how much love I have for you. {2:5} I am not overstating it when I say that the man who caused all the trouble hurt all of you more than he hurt me. {2:6} Most of you opposed him, and that was punishment enough. {2:7} Now, however, it is time to forgive and comfort him. Otherwise, he may be overcome by discouragement. {2:8} So I urge you now to reaffirm your love for him. {2:9} I wrote to you as I did to test you and see if you would fully comply with my instructions. {2:10} When you forgive this man, I forgive him, too. And when I forgive whatever needs to be forgiven, I do so with Christ's authority for your benefit, {2:11} so that Satan will not outsmart us. For we are familiar with his evil schemes. {2:12} When I came to the city of Troas to preach the Good News of Christ, the Lord opened a door of opportunity for me. {2:13} But I had no peace of mind because my dear brother Titus hadn't yet arrived with a report from you. So I said good-bye and went on to Macedonia to find him. {2:14} But thank God! He has made us his captives and continues to lead us along in Christ's triumphal procession. Now he uses us to spread the knowledge of Christ everywhere, like a sweet perfume. {2:15} Our lives are a Christ-like fragrance rising up to God. But this fragrance is perceived differently by those who are being saved and by those who are perishing. {2:16} To those who are perishing, we are a dreadful smell of death and doom. But to those who are being saved, we are a life-giving perfume. And who is adequate for such a task as this? {2:17} You see, we are not like the many hucksters who preach for personal profit. We preach the word of God with sincerity and with Christ's authority, knowing that God is watching us.

{3:1} Do we need to start recommending ourselves again? Do we need letters of recommendation to you or from you like some other people do? {3:2} You yourselves are our letter, written on our hearts, known and read by everyone. {3:3} It's clear that you are a letter from Christ, written by us. This letter is not written with ink but with the Spirit of the living God. It's not written on tablets of stone but on human hearts. {3:4} We have this kind of confidence through Christ before God. {3:5} It's not that we are competent in ourselves to claim anything as coming from ourselves, but our competence is from God. {3:6} He has made us competent as ministers of a new covenant—not of the letter but of the Spirit; for the letter kills, but the Spirit gives life. {3:7} Now if the ministry that brought death, which was engraved in letters on stone, came with glory so that the Israelites couldn't gaze steadily at Moses' face because of its glory, even though it was fading, {3:8} will not the ministry of the Spirit be even more glorious? {3:9} If the ministry that brought condemnation was glorious, how much more glorious is the ministry that brings righteousness! {3:10} For what was glorious has no glory now in comparison with the surpassing glory. {3:11} And if what was transitory came with glory, how much greater is the glory of that which lasts! {3:12} Therefore, since we have such a hope, we are very bold. {3:13} We are not like Moses, who would put a veil over his face to prevent the Israelites from seeing the end of what was passing away. {3:14} But their minds were made dull, for to this day the same veil remains when the old covenant is read. It has not been removed, because only in Christ is it taken away. {3:15} Even to this day when Moses is read, a veil covers their hearts. {3:16} But whenever anyone turns to the Lord, the veil is taken away. {3:17} Now the Lord is the Spirit, and where the Spirit of the Lord is, there is freedom. {3:18} And we all, who with unveiled faces contemplate the Lord's glory, are being transformed into his image with ever-increasing glory, which comes from the Lord, who is the Spirit.

{4:1} Since we have this ministry through God's mercy, we do not lose heart. {4:2} Instead, we have renounced secret and shameful ways; we do not use deception, nor do we distort the word of God. On the contrary, by setting forth the truth plainly we commend ourselves to everyone's conscience in the sight of God. {4:3} And even if our gospel is veiled, it is veiled to those who are perishing. {4:4} The god of this age has blinded the minds of unbelievers, so that they cannot see the light of the gospel that displays the glory of Christ, who is the image of God. {4:5} For what we preach is not ourselves, but Jesus Christ as Lord, and ourselves as your servants for Jesus' sake. {4:6} For God, who said, "Let light shine out of darkness," made his light shine in our hearts to give us the light of the knowledge of God's glory displayed in the face of Christ. {4:7} But we have this treasure in jars of clay to show that this all-surpassing power is from God and not from us. {4:8} We are hard pressed on every side, but not crushed; perplexed, but not in despair; {4:9} persecuted, but not abandoned; struck down, but not destroyed. {4:10} We always carry around in our body the death of Jesus, so that the life of Jesus may also be revealed in our body. {4:11} For we who are alive are always being given over to death for Jesus' sake, so that his life may also be revealed in our mortal body. {4:12} So then, death is at work in us, but life is at work in you. {4:13} It is written: "I believed; therefore, I have spoken." Since we have that same spirit of faith, we also believe and therefore speak, {4:14} because we know that the one who raised the Lord Jesus from the dead will also raise us with Jesus and present us with you to himself. {4:15} All this is for your benefit, so that the grace that is reaching more and more people may cause thanksgiving to overflow to the glory of God. {4:16} Therefore we do not lose heart. Though outwardly we are wasting away, yet inwardly we are being renewed day by day. {4:17} For our light and momentary troubles are achieving for us an eternal glory that far outweighs them all. {4:18} ***So we fix our eyes not on what is seen, but on what is unseen, since what is seen is temporary, but what is unseen is eternal.***

{5:1} We know that if our earthly tent, which is our temporary home, is destroyed, we have a building from God, an eternal house in heaven, not built by human hands. {5:2} While we are in this tent, we groan and are burdened, because we do not wish to be unclothed but to be clothed instead with our heavenly dwelling, so that what is mortal may be swallowed up by life. {5:3} Now the one who has fashioned us for this very purpose is God, who has given us the Spirit as a deposit, guaranteeing what is to come. {5:4} Therefore, we are always confident and know that as long as we are at home in the body, we are away from the Lord. {5:5} For we live by faith, not by sight. {5:6} We are confident, I say, and would prefer to be away from the body and at home with the Lord. {5:7} So we make it our goal to please him, whether we are at home in the body or away from it. {5:8} For we must all appear before the judgment seat of Christ, so that each of us may receive what is due us for the things done while in the body, whether good or bad. {5:9} Since, then, we know what it is to fear the Lord, we try to persuade others. What we are is plain to God, and I hope it is also plain to your conscience. {5:10} We are not trying to commend ourselves to you again, but are giving you an opportunity to take pride in us, so that you can answer those who take pride in what is seen rather than in what is in the heart {5:11} If we are "out of our mind," as some say, it is for God; if we are in our right mind, it is for you. {5:12} For Christ's love compels us, because we are convinced that one died for all, and therefore all died. {5:13} And he died for all, that those who live should no longer live for themselves but for him who died for them and was raised again. {5:14} So from now on we regard no one from a worldly point of view. Though we once regarded Christ in this way, we do so no longer. {5:15} Therefore, if anyone is in Christ, the new creation has come: The old has gone, the new is here! {5:16} All this is from God, who reconciled us to himself through Christ and gave us the ministry of reconciliation: {5:17} **that God was reconciling the world to himself in Christ, not counting people's sins against them. And he has committed to us the message of reconciliation.** {5:18} We are therefore Christ's ambassadors, as though God were making his appeal through us. We implore you on Christ's behalf: Be reconciled to God. {5:19} To clarify, God was in Christ, reconciling the world to himself, not counting people's sins against them, and he has entrusted to us the message of reconciliation. {5:20} Therefore, we are ambassadors for Christ, as though God were making his appeal through us. We implore you on Christ's behalf: Be reconciled to God. {5:21} For God made him who had no sin to be sin for us, so that in him we might become the righteousness of God.

{6:1} As fellow workers with God, we urge you not to receive the grace of God in vain. {6:2} For he says, "In the time of my favor I heard you, and in the day of salvation I helped you." I tell you, now, now is the time of God's favor, now is the day of salvation. {6:3} We don't want to cause anyone to stumble, so we strive to live blamelessly in our ministry. {6:4} We demonstrate ourselves as ministers of God through patience, afflictions, hardships, and distresses. {6:5} We endure beatings, imprisonments, riots, hard work, sleepless nights, and hunger. {6:6} We maintain purity, knowledge, patience, kindness, genuine love, {6:7} truthfulness, and the power of God. We wield the weapons of righteousness in the right hand and in the left. {6:8} We are honored and dishonored, slandered and praised. We are viewed as deceivers, yet we are truthful; {6:9} as unknown, yet well-known; as dying, yet we live on; as punished, yet not killed; {6:10} as sorrowful, yet always rejoicing; as poor, yet making many rich; as having nothing, yet possessing everything. {6:11} O Corinthians, we have spoken openly to you, and our hearts are wide open. {6:12} You are not restricted by us, but you are restricted by your own affections. {6:13} In return, I speak to you as my children: Open your hearts to us as well. {6:14} Do not be unequally yoked with unbelievers. For what partnership can righteousness have with wickedness? Or what fellowship can light have with darkness? {6:15} What harmony is there between Christ and Belial? Or what does a believer have in common with an unbeliever? {6:16} What agreement is there between the temple of God and idols? For we are the temple of the living God. As God has said: "I will live with them and walk among them, and I will be their God, and they will be my people." {6:17} Therefore, "Come out from them and be separate, says the Lord. Touch no unclean thing, and I will receive you." {6:18} "I will be a Father to you, and you will be my sons and daughters, says the Lord Almighty."

{7:1} Dear friends, since we have these promises, let us cleanse ourselves from all filthiness of the flesh and spirit, perfecting holiness in the fear of God. {7:2} Please welcome us back. We have wronged no one, corrupted no one, and cheated no one. {7:3} I say this not to condemn you. I have already told you that you hold a special place in our hearts, to live and die with you. {7:4} I am very bold when I speak to you; I take great pride in you. I am greatly encouraged; in all our troubles my joy knows no bounds. {7:5} When we came into Macedonia, we had no rest. We were harassed at every turn—conflicts on the outside, fears within. {7:6} But God, who comforts the downcast, comforts us by the coming of Titus, {7:7} and not only by his coming but also by the comfort you had given him. He told us about your longing for me, your deep sorrow, your ardent concern for me, so that my joy was greater than ever. {7:8} Even if I caused you sorrow by my letter, I do not regret it. Though I did regret it—I see that my letter hurt you, but only for a little while— {7:9} yet now I am happy, not because you were made sorry, but because your sorrow led you to repentance. For you became sorrowful as God intended and so were not harmed in any way by us. {7:10} Godly sorrow brings repentance that leads to salvation and leaves no regret, but worldly sorrow brings death. {7:11} See what this godly sorrow has produced in you: what earnestness, what eagerness to clear yourselves, what indignation, what alarm, what longing, what concern, what readiness to see justice done. At every point you have proved yourselves to be innocent in this matter. {7:12} So even though I wrote to you, it was neither on account of the one who did the wrong nor on account of the injured party, but rather that before God you could see for yourselves how devoted to us you are. {7:13} By all this we are encouraged. {7:14} In addition to our own encouragement, we were especially delighted to see how happy Titus was, because his spirit has been refreshed by all of you. {7:15} I had boasted to him about you, and you have not embarrassed me. But just as everything we said to you was true, so our boasting about you to Titus has proved to be true as well. {7:16} And his affection for you is all the greater when he remembers that you were all obedient, receiving him with fear and trembling. I am glad I can have complete confidence in you.

{8:1} Brothers and sisters, we want you to know about the grace of God that was given to the churches of Macedonia. {8:2} In the midst of a very severe trial, their overflowing joy and their extreme poverty welled up in rich generosity. {8:3} For I testify that they gave as much as they were able, and even beyond their ability. Entirely on their own, {8:4} they urgently pleaded with us for the privilege of sharing in this service to the Lord's people. {8:5} And they exceeded our expectations: They gave themselves first of all to the Lord, and then by the will of God also to us. {8:6} So we urged Titus, just as he had earlier made a beginning, to also bring to completion this act of grace on your part. {8:7} But since you excel in everything—in faith, in speech, in knowledge, in complete earnestness and in the love we have kindled in you—see that you also excel in this grace of giving. {8:8} I am not commanding you, but I want to test the sincerity of your love by comparing it with the earnestness of others. {8:9} For you know the grace of our Lord Jesus Christ, that though he was rich, yet for your sake he became poor, so that you through his poverty might become rich. {8:10} And here is my judgment about what is best for you in this matter. Last year you were the first not only to give but also to have the desire to do so. {8:11} Now finish the work, so that your eager willingness to do it may be matched by your completion of it, according to your means. {8:12} For if the willingness is there, the gift is acceptable according to what one has, not according to what one does not have. {8:13} Our desire is not that others might be relieved while you are hard pressed, but that there might be equality. {8:14} At the present time your plenty will supply what they need, so that in turn their plenty will supply what you need. The goal is equality, {8:15} as it is written: "The one who gathered much did not have too much, and the one who gathered little did not have too little." {8:16} Thanks be to God, who put into the heart of Titus the same concern I have for you. {8:17} For Titus not only welcomed our appeal, but he is coming to you with much enthusiasm and on his own initiative. {8:18} And we are sending along with him the brother who is praised by all the churches for his service to the gospel. {8:19} What is more, he was chosen by the churches to accompany us as we carry the offering, which we administer in order to honor the Lord himself and to show our eagerness to help. {8:20} We want to avoid any criticism of the way we administer this liberal gift. {8:21} For we are taking pains to do what is right, not only in the eyes of the Lord but also in the eyes of man. {8:22} In addition, we are sending with them our brother who has often proved to us in many ways that he is zealous, and now even more so because of his great confidence in you. {8:23} As for Titus, he is my partner and co-worker among you; as for our brothers, they are representatives of the churches and an honor to Christ. {8:24} Therefore show these men the proof of your love and the reason for our pride in you, so that the churches can see it.

{9:1} Concerning the collection for the Lord's people, I don't really need to write to you. {9:2} I know how eager you are to help, and I have been boasting to the Macedonians that since last year you in Achaia were ready to give; and your enthusiasm has stirred most of them to action. {9:3} But I am sending the brothers in order that our boasting about you in this matter should not prove hollow, but that you may be ready, as I said you would be. {9:4} For if any Macedonians come with me and find you unprepared, we—not to say anything about you—would be ashamed of having been so confident. {9:5} So I thought it necessary to urge the brothers to visit you in advance and finish the arrangements for the generous gift you had promised. Then it will be ready as a generous gift, not as one grudgingly given. {9:6} Remember this: Whoever sows sparingly will also reap sparingly, and whoever sows generously will also reap generously. {9:7} Each of you should give what you have decided in your heart to give, not reluctantly or under compulsion, for God loves a cheerful giver. {9:8} And God is able to bless you abundantly, so that in all things at all times, having all that you need, you will abound in every good work. {9:9} As it is written: "They have freely scattered their gifts to the poor; their righteousness endures forever." {9:10} Now he who supplies seed to the sower and bread for food will also supply and increase your store of seed and will enlarge the harvest of your righteousness. {9:11} You will be enriched in every way so that you can be generous on every occasion, and through us your generosity will result in thanksgiving to God. {9:12} This service that you perform is not only supplying the needs of the Lord's people but is also overflowing in many expressions of thanks to God. {9:13} Because of the service by which you have proved yourselves, others will praise God for the obedience that accompanies your confession of the gospel of Christ, and for your generosity in sharing with them and with everyone else. {9:14} And in their prayers for you their hearts will go out to you, because of the surpassing grace God has given you. {9:15} Thanks be to God for his indescribable gift!

{10:1} I, Paul, urge you by the meekness and gentleness of Christ—I who am "timid" when face to face with you, but "bold" toward you when away! {10:2} I beg you that when I come I may not have to be as bold as I expect to be toward some people who think that we live by the standards of this world. {10:3} For though we live in the world, we do not wage war as the world does. {10:4} The weapons we fight with are not the weapons of the world. On the contrary, they have divine power to demolish strongholds. {10:5} We demolish arguments and every pretension that sets itself up against the knowledge of God, and we take captive every thought to make it obedient to Christ. {10:6} And we will be ready to punish every act of disobedience, once your obedience is complete. {10:7} You are judging by appearances. If anyone is confident that they belong to Christ, they should consider again that we belong to Christ just as much as they do. {10:8} So even if I boast somewhat freely about the authority the Lord gave us for building you up rather than tearing you down, I will not be ashamed of it. {10:9} I do not want to seem to be trying to frighten you with my letters. {10:10} For some say, "His letters are weighty and forceful, but in person he is unimpressive and his speaking amounts to nothing." {10:11} Such people should realize that what we are in our letters when we are absent, we will be in our actions when we are present. {10:12} We do not dare to classify or compare ourselves with some who commend themselves. When they measure themselves by themselves and compare themselves with themselves, they are not wise. {10:13} We, however, will not boast beyond proper limits, but will confine our boasting to the sphere of service God himself has assigned to us, a sphere that also includes you. {10:14} We are not going too far in our boasting, as would be the case if we had not come to you, for we did get as far as you with the gospel of Christ. {10:15} Neither do we go beyond our limits by boasting of work done by others. Our hope is that, as your faith continues to grow, our sphere of activity among you will greatly expand, {10:16} so that we can preach the gospel in the regions beyond you. For we do not want to boast about work already done in someone else's territory. {10:17} But, "Let the one who boasts boast in the Lord." {10:18} For it is not the one who commends himself who is approved, but the one whom the Lord commends.

{11:1} I wish you would bear with me in a little foolishness, but indeed you are bearing with me. {11:2} For I am jealous for you with godly jealousy. I promised you to one husband, to Christ, so that I might present you as a pure virgin to him. {11:3} But I am afraid that just as Eve was deceived by the serpent's cunning, your minds may somehow be led astray from your sincere and pure devotion to Christ. {11:4} For if someone comes to you and preaches a Jesus other than the Jesus we preached, or if you receive a different spirit from the Spirit you received, or a different gospel from the one you accepted, you put up with it easily enough. {11:5} I do not think I am in the least inferior to those "super-apostles." {11:6} I may indeed be untrained as a speaker, but I do have knowledge. We have made this perfectly clear to you in every way. {11:7} Was it a sin for me to lower myself in order to elevate you by preaching the gospel of God to you free of charge? {11:8} I robbed other churches by receiving support from them so as to serve you. {11:9} And when I was with you and needed something, I was not a burden to anyone, for the brothers who came from Macedonia supplied what I needed. I have kept myself from being a burden to you in any way, and will continue to do so. {11:10} As surely as the truth of Christ is in me, nobody in the regions of Achaia will stop this boasting of mine. {11:11} Why? Because I do not love you? God knows I do! {11:12} And I will keep on doing what I am doing in order to cut the ground from under those who want an opportunity to be considered equal with us in the things they boast about. {11:13} For such people are false apostles, deceitful workers, masquerading as apostles of Christ. {11:14} And no wonder, for Satan himself masquerades as an angel of light. {11:15} It is not surprising, then, if his servants also masquerade as servants of righteousness. Their end will be what their actions deserve. {11:16} Let no one think I am a fool. But if you do, then at least receive me as a fool, so that I too may do a little boasting. {11:17} What I am saying with this boastful confidence, I am saying not as the Lord would, but as a fool. {11:18} Since many are boasting according to the flesh, I will also boast. {11:19} You gladly put up with fools since you are so wise yourselves! {11:20} Indeed, you tolerate anyone who enslaves you or exploits you or takes advantage of you or puts on airs or slaps you in the face. {11:21} To my shame, I admit that we were too weak for that! But whatever anyone else dares to boast about—I am speaking as a fool—I also dare to boast about. {11:22} Are they Hebrews? So am I. Are they Israelites? So am I. Are they Abraham's descendants? So am I. {11:23} Are they servants of Christ? (I am out of my mind to talk like this.) I am more. I have worked much harder, been in prison more frequently, been flogged more severely, and been exposed to death again and again. {11:24} Five times I received from the Jews the forty lashes minus one. {11:25} Three times I was beaten with rods, once I was pelted with stones, three times I was shipwrecked, I spent a night and a day in the open sea, {11:26} I have been constantly on the move. I have been in danger from rivers, in danger from bandits, in danger from my fellow Jews, in danger from Gentiles; in danger in the city, in danger in the country, in danger at sea; and in danger from false believers. {11:27} I have labored and toiled and have often gone without sleep; I have known hunger and thirst and have often gone without food; I have been cold and naked. {11:28} Besides everything else, I face daily the pressure of my concern for all the churches. {11:29} Who is weak, and I do not feel weak? Who is led into sin, and I do not inwardly burn? {11:30} If I must boast, I will boast of the things that show my weakness. {11:31} The God and Father of the Lord Jesus, who is to be praised forever, knows that I am not lying. {11:32} In Damascus the governor under King Aretas had the city of the Damascenes guarded in order to arrest me. {11:33} But I was lowered in a basket from a window in the wall and slipped through his hands.

{12:1} I shouldn't really be boasting like this, but I need to talk about the visions and revelations I've received from the Lord. {12:2} I know a man in Christ who, fourteen years ago—whether in the body or out of the body, I don't know; God knows—was caught up to the third heaven. {12:3} And I know that this man—whether in the body or apart from the body, I don't know; God knows— {12:4} was caught up into paradise and heard inexpressible things, things that no one is permitted to tell. {12:5} I will boast about such a man, but I won't boast about myself, except about my weaknesses. {12:6} Even if I wanted to boast, I wouldn't be a fool, because I would be telling the truth. But I'll refrain, so that no one will think more of me than is warranted by what I do or say, {12:7} or because of these surpassingly great revelations. Therefore, to keep me from becoming conceited, I was given a thorn in my flesh, a messenger of Satan, to torment me. {12:8} Three times I pleaded with the Lord to take it away from me. {12:9} **But he said to me, "My grace is sufficient for you, for my power is made perfect in weakness." Therefore I will boast all the more gladly about my weaknesses, so that Christ's power may rest on me.** {12:10} That is why, for Christ's sake, I delight in weaknesses, in insults, in hardships, in persecutions, in difficulties. For when I am weak, then I am strong. {12:11} I have made a fool of myself, but you drove me to it. I ought to have been commended by you, for I am not in the least inferior to the "super-apostles," even though I am nothing. {12:12} I persevered in demonstrating among you the marks of a true apostle, including signs, wonders and miracles. {12:13} How were you inferior to the other churches, except that I was never a burden to you? Forgive me this wrong! {12:14} Now I am ready to visit you for the third time, and I will not be a burden to you, because what I want is not your possessions but you. After all, children should not have to save up for their parents, but parents for their children. {12:15} So I will very gladly spend everything I have and expand myself as well. If I love you more, will you love me less? {12:16} Be that as it may, I have not been a burden to you. Yet, crafty fellow that I am, I caught you by trickery! {12:17} Did I exploit you through any of the men I sent to you? {12:18} I urged Titus to go to you and I sent our brother with him. Titus did not exploit you, did he? Did we not walk in the same footsteps by the same Spirit? {12:19} Have you been thinking all along that we have been defending ourselves to you? We have been speaking in the sight of God as those in Christ; and everything we do, dear friends, is for your strengthening. {12:20} I am afraid that when I come again my God will humble me before you, and I will be grieved over many who have sinned earlier and have not repented of the impurity, sexual sin and debauchery in which they have indulged.

{13:1} This is the third time I am coming to visit you. "Every matter must be established by the testimony of two or three witnesses." {13:2} I already warned you when I was with you the second time. Now I am away, and I repeat the warning to those who sinned earlier and to all the others. I said it before, and I say it again now: If I come again, I will not spare those who sinned. {13:3} You are demanding proof that Christ is speaking through me. He is not weak in dealing with you; he is powerful among you. {13:4} For to be sure, he was crucified in weakness, yet he lives by God's power. Likewise, we are weak in him, yet by God's power we will live with him in our dealing with you. {13:5} Examine yourselves to see whether you are in the faith; test yourselves. Do you not realize that Christ Jesus is in you—unless, of course, you fail the test? {13:6} And I hope you will discover that we have not failed the test. {13:7} Now we pray to God that you will not do anything wrong—not so that people will see that we have stood the test but so that you will do what is right even though we may seem to have failed. {13:8} For we cannot do anything against the truth, but only for the truth. {13:9} We are glad whenever we are weak but you are strong; and our prayer is that you may be fully restored. {13:10} This is why I write these things when I am absent, that when I come I may not have to be harsh in my use of authority—the authority the Lord gave me for building you up, not for tearing you down. {13:11} Finally, brothers and sisters, rejoice! Strive for full restoration, encourage one another, be of one mind, live in peace. And the God of love and peace will be with you. {13:12} Greet one another with a holy kiss. {13:13} All God's people here send their greetings. {13:14} May the grace of the Lord Jesus Christ, and the love of God, and the fellowship of the Holy Spirit be with you all.

Galatians

{1:1} This letter is from Paul, an apostle. I was not appointed by any group of people or any human authority, but by Jesus Christ himself and by God the Father, who raised Jesus from the dead. {1:2} I am writing to all the believers in Galatia who are joined together in fellowship with us and to all who are with me. {1:3} May God the Father and our Lord Jesus Christ give you grace and peace. {1:4} Jesus gave his life for our sins, just as God our Father planned, in order to rescue us from this evil world in which we live. {1:5} All glory to God forever and ever! Amen. {1:6} I am shocked that you are turning away so soon from God, who called you to himself through the loving mercy of Christ. You are following a different way that pretends to be the Good News {1:7} but is not the Good News at all. You are being fooled by those who deliberately twist the truth concerning Christ. {1:8} Let God's curse fall on anyone, including us or even an angel from heaven, who preaches a different kind of Good News than the one we preached to you. {1:9} I say again what we have said before: If anyone preaches any other Good News than the one you welcomed, let that person be cursed. {1:10} Obviously, I'm not trying to win the approval of people, but of God. If pleasing people were my goal, I would not be Christ's servant. {1:11} Dear brothers and sisters, I want you to understand that the gospel message I preach is not based on mere human reasoning. {1:12} I received my message from no human source, and no one taught me. Instead, I received it by direct revelation from Jesus Christ. {1:13} You know what I was like when I followed the Jewish religion—how I violently persecuted God's church. I did my best to destroy it. {1:14} I was far ahead of my fellow Jews in my zeal for the traditions of my ancestors. {1:15} But even before I was born, God chose me and called me by his marvelous grace. Then it pleased him {1:16} to reveal his Son to me so that I would proclaim the Good News about Jesus to the Gentiles. When this happened, I did not rush out to consult with any human being. {1:17} Nor did I go up to Jerusalem to consult with those who were apostles before I was. Instead, I went away into Arabia, and later I returned to the city of Damascus. {1:18} Then three years later I went to Jerusalem to get to know Peter, and I stayed with him for fifteen days. {1:19} The only other apostle I met at that time was James, the Lord's brother. {1:20} I declare before God that what I am writing to you is not a lie. {1:21} After that visit I went north into the provinces of Syria and Cilicia. {1:22} And still the Christians in the churches in Judea didn't know me personally. {1:23} All they knew was that people were saying, "The one who used to persecute us is now preaching the very faith he tried to destroy!" {1:24} And they praised God because of me.

{2:1} Fourteen years later I went back to Jerusalem again, this time with Barnabas; and Titus came along, too. {2:2} I went there because God revealed to me that I should go. While I was there I met privately with those considered to be leaders of the church and shared with them the message I had been preaching to the Gentiles. I wanted to make sure that we were in agreement, for fear that all my efforts had been wasted and I was running the race for nothing. {2:3} And they supported me and did not even demand that my companion Titus be circumcised, though he was a Gentil. {2:4} Even that question came up only because of some so-called believers there—false ones, really—who were secretly brought in. They sneaked in to spy on us and take away the freedom we have in Christ Jesus. They wanted to enslave us and force us to follow their Jewish regulations. {2:5} But we refused to give in to them for a single moment. We wanted to preserve the truth of the gospel message for you. {2:6} And the leaders of the church had nothing to add to what I was preaching. (By the way, their reputation as great leaders made no difference to me, for God has no favorites.) {2:7} Instead, they saw that God had given me the responsibility of preaching the gospel to the Gentiles, just as he had given Peter the responsibility of preaching to the Jews. {2:8} For the same God who worked through Peter as the apostle to the Jews also worked through me as the apostle to the Gentiles. {2:9} In fact, James, Peter, and John, who were known as pillars of the church, recognized the gift God had given me, and they accepted Barnabas and me as their co-workers. They encouraged us to keep preaching to the Gentiles, while they continued their work with the Jews. {2:10} Their only suggestion was that we keep on helping the poor, which I have always been eager to do. {2:11} But when Peter came to Antioch, I had to oppose him to his face, for what he did was very wrong. {2:12} When he first arrived, he ate with the Gentile believers, who were not circumcised. But afterward, when some friends of James came, Peter wouldn't eat with the Gentiles anymore. He was afraid of criticism from these people who insisted on the necessity of circumcision. {2:13} As a result, other Jewish believers followed Peter's hypocrisy, and even Barnabas was led astray by their hypocrisy. {2:14} When I saw that they were not following the truth of the gospel message, I said to Peter in front of all the others,

"Since you, a Jew by birth, have discarded the Jewish laws and are living like a Gentile, why are you now trying to make these Gentiles follow the Jewish traditions? {2:15} You and I are Jews by birth, not 'sinners' like the Gentiles. {2:16} Yet we know that a person is made right with God by faith in Jesus Christ, not by obeying the law. And we have believed in Christ Jesus, so that we might be made right with God because of our faith in Christ, not because we have obeyed the law. For no one will ever be made right with God by obeying the law." {2:17} But suppose we seek to be made right with God through faith in Christ and then we are found guilty because we have abandoned the law. Would that mean Christ has led us into sin? Absolutely not! {2:18} Rather, I am a sinner if I rebuild the old system of law I already tore down. {2:19} For when I tried to keep the law, it condemned me. So I died to the law—I stopped trying to meet all its requirements—so that I might live for God. {2:20} **My old self has been crucified with Christ. It is no longer I who live, but Christ lives in me. So I live in this earthly body by trusting in the Son of God, who loved me and gave himself for me.** {2:21} I do not treat the grace of God as meaningless. For if keeping the law could make us right with God, then there was no need for Christ to die.

{3:1} O foolish Galatians! Who has tricked you? Before your very eyes, Jesus Christ was clearly portrayed as crucified. {3:2} Let me ask you this one question: Did you receive the Holy Spirit by obeying the law of Moses? Of course not! You received the Spirit because you believed the message you heard about Christ. {3:3} How foolish can you be? After starting your new lives in the Spirit, why are you now trying to become perfect by your own human effort? {3:4} Have you experienced so much for nothing? Surely it was not in vain, was it? {3:5} I ask you again, does God give you the Holy Spirit and work miracles among you because you obey the law? Of course not! It is because you believe the message you heard about Christ. {3:6} Consider Abraham: He believed in God, and God counted him as righteous because of his faith. {3:7} The real children of Abraham, then, are those who put their faith in God. {3:8} What's more, the Scriptures looked forward to this time when God would make the Gentiles right in his sight because of their faith. God proclaimed this good news to Abraham long ago when he said, "All nations will be blessed through you." {3:9} So all who put their faith in Christ share the same blessing Abraham received because of his faith. {3:10} But those who depend on the law to make them right with God are under his curse, for the Scriptures say, "Cursed is everyone who does not observe and obey all the commands that are written in God's Book of the Law." {3:11} So it is clear that no one can be made right with God by trying to keep the law. For the Scriptures say, "It is through faith that a righteous person has life." {3:12} This way of faith is very different from the way of law, which says, "It is through obeying the law that a person has life." {3:13} But Christ has rescued us from the curse pronounced by the law. When he was hung on the cross, he took upon himself the curse for our wrongdoing. For it is written in the Scriptures, "Cursed is everyone who is hung on a tree." {3:14} Through Christ Jesus, God has blessed the Gentiles with the same blessing he promised to Abraham, so that we who are believers might receive the promised Holy Spirit through faith. {3:15} Dear brothers and sisters, here's an example from everyday life. Just as no one can set aside or amend an irrevocable agreement, so it is in this case. {3:16} God gave the promises to Abraham and his child. And notice that the Scripture doesn't say "to his children," as if it meant many descendants. Rather, it says "to his child"—and that, of course, means Christ. {3:17} This is what I am trying to say: The agreement God made with Abraham could not be canceled 430 years later when God gave the law to Moses. God would be breaking his promise. {3:18} For if the inheritance could be received by keeping the law, then it would not be the result of accepting God's promise. But God graciously gave it to Abraham as a promise. {3:19} Why, then, was the law given? It was given alongside the promise to show people their sins. But the law was designed to last only until the coming of the child who was promised. God gave his law through angels to Moses, who was the mediator between God and the people. {3:20} Now a mediator is helpful if more than one party must reach an agreement. But God, who is one, did not use a mediator when he gave his promise to Abraham. {3:21} Is there a conflict, then, between God's law and God's promises? Absolutely not! If the law could give us new life, we could be made right with God by obeying it. {3:22} But the Scriptures declare that we are all prisoners of sin, so we receive God's promise of freedom only by believing in Jesus Christ. {3:23} Before the way of faith in Christ was available to us, we were placed under guard by the law. We were kept in protective custody, so to speak, until the way of faith was revealed. {3:24} Let me put it another way. The law was our guardian until Christ came; it protected us until we could be made right with God through faith. {3:25} And now that the way of faith has come, we no longer need the law as our guardian. {3:26} For you are all children of God through faith in Christ Jesus. {3:27} And all who have been united with Christ in baptism have put on Christ, like putting on new clothes. {3:28} **There is no longer Jew or Gentile, slave or free, male and female. For you are all one in Christ Jesus.** {3:29} And now that you belong to Christ, you are the true children of Abraham. You are his heirs, and God's promise to Abraham belongs to you.

{4:1} Let me explain further. As long as an heir is underage, he is no different from a slave, even though he owns the entire estate. {4:2} The heir is subject to guardians and trustees until the time set by his father. {4:3} That's the way it was with us before Christ came. We were like children; we were slaves to the basic spiritual principles of this world. {4:4} But when the right time came, God sent his Son, born of a woman, subject to the law. {4:5} God sent him to buy freedom for us who were slaves to the law, so that he could adopt us as his very own children. {4:6} And because we are his children, God has sent the Spirit of his Son into our hearts, prompting us to call out, "Abba, Father." {4:7} Now you are no longer a slave but God's own child. And since you are his child, God has made you his heir. {4:8} Before you Gentiles knew God, you were slaves to so-called gods that do not even exist. {4:9} So now that you know God (or should I say, now that God knows you), why do you want to go back again and become slaves once more to the weak and useless spiritual principles of this world? {4:10} You are trying to earn favor with God by observing certain days or months or seasons or years. {4:11} I fear for you. Perhaps all my hard work with you was for nothing. {4:12} Dear brothers and sisters, I plead with you to live as I do in freedom from these things, for I have become like you Gentiles—free from those laws. You did not mistreat me when I first preached to you. {4:13} Surely you remember that I was sick when I first brought you the Good News. {4:14} But even though my condition tempted you to reject me, you did not despise me or turn me away. No, you took me in and cared for me as though I were an angel from God or even Christ Jesus himself. {4:15} Where is that joyful and grateful spirit you felt then? I am sure you would have taken out your own eyes and given them to me if it had been possible. {4:16} Have I now become your enemy because I am telling you the truth? {4:17} Those false teachers are so eager to win your favor, but their intentions are not good. They are trying to shut you off from me so that you will pay attention only to them. {4:18} If someone is eager to do good things for you, that's all right; but let them do it all the time, not just when I'm with you. {4:19} Oh, my dear children! I feel as if I'm going through labor pains for you again, and they will continue until Christ is fully developed in your lives. {4:20} I wish I were with you right now so I could change my tone. But at this distance I don't know how else to help you. {4:21} Tell me, you who want to live under the law, do you know what the law actually says? {4:22} The Scriptures say that Abraham had two sons, one from his slave wife and one from his freeborn wife. {4:23} The son of the slave wife was born in a human attempt to bring about the fulfillment of God's promise. But the son of the freeborn wife was born as God's own fulfillment of his promise. {4:24} These two women serve as an illustration of God's two covenants. The first woman, Hagar, represents Mount Sinai where people received the law that enslaved them. {4:25} And now Jerusalem is just like Mount Sinai in Arabia, because she and her children live in slavery to the law. {4:26} But the other woman, Sarah, represents the heavenly Jerusalem. She is the free woman, and she is our mother. {4:27} As Isaiah said, "Rejoice, O childless woman, you who have never given birth! Break into a joyful shout, you who have never been in labor! For the desolate woman now has more children than the woman who lives with her husband!" {4:28} And you, dear brothers and sisters, are children of the promise, just like Isaac. {4:29} But you are now being persecuted by those who want you to keep the law, just as Ishmael, the child born by human effort, persecuted Isaac, the child born by the power of the Spirit. {4:30} But what do the Scriptures say about that? "Get rid of the slave and her son, for the son of the slave woman will not share the inheritance with the free woman's son." {4:31} So, dear brothers and sisters, we are not children of the slave woman; we are children of the free woman.

{5:1} So, stand firm in the freedom that Christ has given us. Don't get tied up again in slavery to the law. {5:2} Listen! I, Paul, tell you this: If you are counting on circumcision to make you right with God, then Christ will be of no benefit to you. {5:3} I'll say it again. If you are trying to find favor with God by being circumcised, you must obey every regulation in the whole law of Moses. {5:4} For if you are trying to make yourselves right with God by keeping the law, you have been cut off from Christ! You have fallen away from God's grace. {5:5} But we who live by the Spirit eagerly wait to receive by faith the righteousness God has promised to us. {5:6} For when we place our faith in Christ Jesus, there is no benefit in being circumcised or being uncircumcised. What is important is faith expressing itself in love. {5:7} You were running the race so well. Who has held you back from following the truth? {5:8} It certainly isn't God, for he is the one who called you to freedom. {5:9} This false teaching is like a little yeast that spreads through the whole batch of dough! {5:10} I am trusting the Lord to keep you from believing false teachings. God will judge that person, whoever he is, who has been confusing you. {5:11} Dear brothers and sisters, if I were still preaching that you must be circumcised—as some say I do—why am I still being persecuted? If I were no longer preaching salvation through the cross of Christ, no one would be offended. {5:12} I just wish that those troublemakers who want to mutilate you by circumcision would mutilate themselves. {5:13} For you have been called to live in freedom, my brothers and sisters. But don't use your freedom to satisfy your sinful nature. Instead, use your freedom to serve one another in love. {5:14} For the whole law can be summed up in this one command: "Love your neighbor as yourself." {5:15} But if you are always biting and devouring one another, watch out! Beware of destroying one another. {5:16} So I say, let the Holy Spirit guide your lives. Then you won't be doing what your sinful nature craves. {5:17} The sinful nature wants to do evil, which is just the opposite of what the Spirit wants. And the Spirit gives us desires that are the opposite of what the sinful nature desires. These two forces are constantly fighting each other, so you are not free to carry out your good intentions. {5:18} But when you are directed by the Spirit, you are not under obligation to the law of Moses. {5:19} When you follow the desires of your sinful nature, the results are very clear: sexual immorality, impurity, lustful pleasures, {5:20} idolatry, sorcery, hostility, quarreling, jealousy, outbursts of anger, selfish ambition, dissension, division, {5:21} envy, drunkenness, wild parties, and other sins like these. Let me tell you again, as I have before, that anyone living that sort of life will not inherit the Kingdom of God. {5:22} **But the Holy Spirit produces this kind of fruit in our lives: love, joy, peace, patience, kindness, goodness, faithfulness,** {5:23} **gentleness, and self-control. There is no law against these things!** {5:24} Those who belong to Christ Jesus have nailed the passions and desires of their sinful nature to his cross and crucified them there. {5:25} Since we are living by the Spirit, let us follow the Spirit's leading in every part of our lives. {5:26} Let us not become conceited, or provoke one another, or be jealous of one another.

{6:1} Brothers and sisters, if someone is caught in a sin, you who live by the Spirit should restore that person gently. But watch yourselves, or you also may be tempted. {6:2} Carry each other's burdens, and in this way you will fulfill the law of Christ. {6:3} If anyone thinks they are something when they are not, they deceive themselves. {6:4} Each one should test their own actions. Then they can take pride in themselves alone, without comparing themselves to someone else, {6:5} for each one should carry their own load. {6:6} Nevertheless, the one who receives instruction in the word should share all good things with their instructor. {6:7} Do not be deceived: God cannot be mocked. A man reaps what he sows. {6:8} Whoever sows to please their flesh, from the flesh will reap destruction; whoever sows to please the Spirit, from the Spirit will reap eternal life. {6:9} Let us not become weary in doing good, for at the proper time we will reap a harvest if we do not give up. {6:10} Therefore, as we have the opportunity, let us do good to all people, especially to those who belong to the family of believers. {6:11} See what large letters I use as I write to you with my own hand! {6:12} Those who want to impress people by means of the flesh are trying to compel you to be circumcised. The only reason they do this is to avoid being persecuted for the cross of Christ. {6:13} Not even those who are circumcised keep the law, yet they want you to be circumcised so that they may boast about your circumcision in the flesh. {6:14} May I never boast except in the cross of our Lord Jesus Christ, through which the world has been crucified to me, and I to the world. {6:15} Neither circumcision nor uncircumcision means anything; what counts is the new creation. {6:16} Peace and mercy to all who follow this rule—to the Israel of God. {6:17} From now on, let no one cause me trouble, for I bear on my body the marks of Jesus. {6:18} The grace of our Lord Jesus Christ be with your spirit, brothers and sisters. Amen.

Ephesians

{1:1} This letter is from Paul, chosen by the will of God to be an apostle of Jesus Christ. It is addressed to the saints in Ephesus, who are faithful in Christ Jesus: {1:2} May God our Father and the Lord Jesus Christ give you grace and peace {1:3} Praise be to the God and Father of our Lord Jesus Christ! He has blessed us with every spiritual blessing because we are united with Christ in the heavenly realms. {1:4} Long ago, even before he made the world, God chose us to be his holy and blameless people. He did this out of his love for us. {1:5} He decided in advance to adopt us into his own family through Jesus Christ. This is what he wanted to do, and it gave him great pleasure. {1:6} So we praise God for the glorious grace he has poured out on us who belong to his dear Son. {1:7} He is so rich in kindness and grace that he purchased our freedom with the blood of his Son and forgave our sins. {1:8} He has showered his kindness on us, along with all wisdom and understanding. {1:9} God has now revealed to us his mysterious plan regarding Christ, a plan to fulfill his own good pleasure. {1:10} And this is the plan: At the right time he will bring everything together under the authority of Christ—everything in heaven and on earth. {1:11} Furthermore, because we are united with Christ, we have received an inheritance from God, for he chose us in advance, and he makes everything work out according to his plan. {1:12} God's purpose was that we Jews who were the first to trust in Christ would bring praise and glory to God. {1:13} And now you Gentiles have also heard the truth, the Good News that God saves you. And when you believed in Christ, he identified you as his own by giving you the Holy Spirit, whom he had promised long ago. {1:14} The Spirit is God's guarantee that he will give us the inheritance he promised and that he has purchased us to be his own people. He did this so we would praise and glorify him. {1:15} Ever since I first heard of your strong faith in the Lord Jesus and your love for God's people everywhere, {1:16} I have not stopped thanking God for you. I pray for you constantly, {1:17} asking God, the glorious Father of our Lord Jesus Christ, to give you spiritual wisdom and insight so that you might grow in your knowledge of God. {1:18} I pray that your hearts will be flooded with light so that you can understand the confident hope he has given to those he called—his holy people who are his rich and glorious inheritance. {1:19} I also pray that you will understand the incredible greatness of God's power for us who believe in him. This is the same mighty power {1:20} that raised Christ from the dead and seated him in the place of honor at God's right hand in the heavenly realms. {1:21} Now he is far above any ruler or authority or power or leader or anything else—not only in this world but also in the world to come. {1:22} God has put all things under the authority of Christ and has made him head over all things for the benefit of the church. {1:23} And the church is his body; it is made full and complete by Christ, who fills all things everywhere with himself.

{2:1} God has brought you to life, even though you were dead because of your sins and failures. {2:2} You used to live in sin, just like the rest of the world, obeying the devil—the commander of the powers in the unseen world. He is the spirit at work in the hearts of those who refuse to obey God. {2:3} All of us used to live that way, following the passionate desires and inclinations of our sinful nature. By our very nature, we were subject to God's anger, just like everyone else. {2:4} But God is so rich in mercy, and he loved us so much, {2:5} that even though we were dead because of our sins, he gave us life when he raised Christ from the dead. (It is only by God's grace that you have been saved!) {2:6} For he raised us from the dead along with Christ and seated us with him in the heavenly realms because we are united with Christ Jesus. {2:7} So God can point to us in all future ages as examples of the incredible wealth of his grace and kindness toward us, as shown in all he has done for us who are united with Christ Jesus. {2:8} **God saved you by his grace when you believed. And you can't take credit for this; it is a gift from God.** {2:9} **Salvation is not a reward for the good things we have done, so none of us can boast about it.** {2:10} For we are God's masterpiece. He has created us anew in Christ Jesus, so we can do the good things he planned for us long ago. {2:11} So don't forget that you Gentiles used to be outsiders. You were called "uncircumcised heathens" by the Jews, who were proud of their circumcision, even though it affected only their bodies and not their hearts. {2:12} In those days you were living apart from Christ. You were excluded from citizenship among the people of Israel, and you did not know the covenant promises God had made to them. You lived in this world without God and without hope. {2:13} But now you have been united with Christ Jesus. Once you were far away from God, but now you have been brought near to him through the blood of Christ. {2:14} For Christ himself has brought peace to us. He united Jews and Gentiles into one people when, in his own body on the cross, he broke down the wall of hostility that separated us. {2:15} He did this by ending the system of law with its commandments and regulations. He made peace between Jews and Gentiles by creating in himself one new people from the two groups. {2:16} Together as one body, Christ reconciled both groups to God by means of his death on the cross, and our hostility toward each other was put to death. {2:17} He brought this Good News of peace to you Gentiles who were far away from him, and peace to the Jews who were near. {2:18} Now all of us can come to the Father through the same Holy Spirit because of what Christ has done for us. {2:19} So now you Gentiles are no longer strangers and foreigners. You are citizens along with all of God's holy people. You are members of God's family. {2:20} Together, we are his house, built on the foundation of the apostles and the prophets. And the cornerstone is Christ Jesus himself {2:21} We are carefully joined together in him, becoming a holy temple for the Lord. {2:22} Through him you Gentiles are also being made part of this dwelling where God lives by his Spirit.

{3:1} I, Paul, am a prisoner because of my relationship with Jesus Christ for your benefit, you Gentiles. {3:2} Surely you have heard about the responsibility God gave me to share his grace with you. {3:3} God revealed his mysterious plan to me, as I wrote about briefly earlier. {3:4} As you read what I have written, you will understand my insight into this plan regarding Christ. {3:5} This mystery was not made known to people in earlier generations, but now it has been revealed by the Holy Spirit to God's holy apostles and prophets. {3:6} And this is the secret: that the Gentiles are to be fellow heirs, members of the same body, and partners together in the promise given in Christ Jesus through the Good News. {3:7} I became a servant of this Good News by the gift of God's grace given me through the working of his power. {3:8} Though I am the least deserving of all God's people, he graciously gave me the privilege of telling the Gentiles about the endless treasures available in Christ. {3:9} God's purpose in all this was to use the church to display his wisdom in its rich variety to all the unseen rulers and authorities in the heavenly places. {3:10} This was his eternal plan, which he carried out through Christ Jesus our Lord. {3:11} Because of Christ and our faith in him, we can now come boldly and confidently into God's presence. {3:12} So please don't lose heart because of my trials here. I am suffering for you, so you should feel honored. {3:13} When I think of all this, I fall to my knees and pray to the Father, {3:14} the Creator of everything in heaven and on earth. {3:15} I pray that from his glorious, unlimited resources he will empower you with inner strength through his Spirit. {3:16} Then Christ will make his home in your hearts as you trust in him. Your roots will grow down into God's love and keep you strong. {3:17} And may you have the power to understand, as all God's people should, how wide, how long, how high, and how deep his love is. {3:18} May you experience the love of Christ, though it is too great to understand fully. Then you will be made complete with all the fullness of life and power that comes from God. {3:19} Now all glory to God, who is able, through his mighty power at work within us, to accomplish infinitely more than we might ask or think. {3:20} Now to him who is able to do far more abundantly than all that we ask or think, according to the power at work within us, {3:21} to him will be glory in the church and in Christ Jesus throughout all generations, forever and ever. Amen.

{4:1} Therefore, I, a prisoner for serving the Lord, beg you to lead a life worthy of your calling, for you have been called by God. {4:2} Always be humble and gentle. Be patient with each other, making allowance for each other's faults because of your love. {4:3} Make every effort to keep yourselves united in the Spirit, binding yourselves together with peace. {4:4} For there is one body and one Spirit, just as you have been called to one glorious hope for the future. {4:5} There is one Lord, one faith, one baptism, {4:6} one God and Father of all, who is over all, in all, and living through all. {4:7} However, he has given each one of us a special gift through the generosity of Christ. {4:8} That is why the Scriptures say, "When he ascended to the heights, he led a crowd of captives and gave gifts to his people." {4:9} Notice that it says "he ascended." This clearly means that Christ also descended to our lowly world. {4:10} And the same one who descended is the one who ascended higher than all the heavens, so that he might fill the entire universe with himself. {4:11} Now these are the gifts Christ gave to the church: the apostles, the prophets, the evangelists, and the pastors and teachers. {4:12} Their responsibility is to equip God's people to do his work and build up the church, the body of Christ. {4:13} This will continue until we all come to such unity in our faith and knowledge of God's Son that we will be mature in the Lord, measuring up to the full and complete standard of Christ. {4:14} Then we will no longer be immature like children. We won't be tossed and blown about by every wind of new teaching. We will not be influenced when people try to trick us with lies so clever they sound like the truth. {4:15} Instead, we will speak the truth in love, growing in every way more and more like Christ, who is the head of his body, the church. {4:16} He makes the whole body fit together perfectly. As each part does its own special work, it helps the other parts grow, so that the whole body is healthy and growing and full of love. {4:17} With the Lord's authority I say this: Live no longer as the Gentiles do, for they are hopelessly confused. {4:18} **Their minds are full of darkness; they wander far from the life God gives because they have closed their minds and hardened their hearts against him.** {4:19} They have no sense of shame. They live for lustful pleasure and eagerly practice every kind of impurity. {4:20} But that isn't what you learned about Christ. {4:21} Since you have heard about Jesus and have learned the truth that comes from him, {4:22} throw off your old sinful nature and your former way of life, which is corrupted by lust and deception. {4:23} Instead, let the Spirit renew your thoughts and attitudes. {4:24} Put on your new nature, created to be like God—truly righteous and holy. {4:25} So stop telling lies. Let us tell our neighbors the truth, for we are all parts of the same body. {4:26} And "don't sin by letting anger control you." Don't let the sun go down while you are still angry, {4:27} for anger gives a foothold to the devil. {4:28} **If you are a thief, quit stealing. Instead, use your hands for good hard work, and then give generously to others in need.** {4:29} Don't use foul or abusive language. Let everything you say be good and helpful, so that your words will be an encouragement to those who hear them. {4:30} And do not bring sorrow to God's Holy Spirit by the way you live. Remember, he has identified you as his own, guaranteeing that you will be saved on the day of redemption. {4:31} Get rid of all bitterness, rage, anger, harsh words, and slander, as well as all types of evil behavior. {4:32} **Instead, be kind to each other, tenderhearted, forgiving one another, just as God through Christ has forgiven you.**

{5:1} Therefore, imitate God, since you are his dear children. {5:2} Live a life filled with love, following the example of Christ. He loved us and offered himself as a sacrifice for us, a pleasing aroma to God. {5:3} Let there be no sexual immorality, impurity, or greed among you. Such sins have no place among God's people. {5:4} Obscene stories, foolish talk, and coarse jokes—these are not for you. Instead, let there be thankfulness to God. {5:5} You can be sure that no immoral, impure, or greedy person will inherit the Kingdom of Christ and of God. For a greedy person is an idolater, worshiping the things of this world. {5:6} Don't be fooled by those who try to excuse these sins, for the anger of God will fall on all who disobey him. {5:7} Don't participate in the things these people do. {5:8} For once you were full of darkness, but now you have light from the Lord. So live as people of light! {5:9} For this light within you produces only what is good and right and true. {5:10} Carefully determine what pleases the Lord. {5:11} Take no part in the worthless deeds of evil and darkness; instead, expose them. {5:12} It is shameful even to talk about the things that ungodly people do in secret. {5:13} But their evil intentions will be exposed when the light shines on them, {5:14} for the light makes everything visible. This is why it is said, "Awake, O sleeper, rise up from the dead, and Christ will give you light." {5:15} So be careful how you live. Don't live like fools, but like those who are wise. {5:16} Make the most of every opportunity in these evil days. {5:17} Don't act thoughtlessly, but understand what the Lord wants you to do. {5:18} Don't be drunk with wine, because that will ruin your life. Instead, be filled with the Holy Spirit, {5:19} singing psalms and hymns and spiritual songs among yourselves, and making music to the Lord in your hearts. {5:20} And give thanks for everything to God the Father in the name of our Lord Jesus Christ. {5:21} And further, submit to one another out of reverence for Christ. {5:22} For wives, this means to submit to your husbands as to the Lord. {5:23} For a husband is the head of his wife as Christ is the head of the church. He is the Savior of his body, the church. {5:24} As the church submits to Christ, so you wives should submit to your husbands in everything. {5:25} For husbands, this means love your wives, just as Christ loved the church. He gave up his life for her {5:26} to make her holy and clean, washed by the cleansing of God's word. {5:27} He did this to present her to himself as a glorious church without a spot or wrinkle or any other blemish. Instead, she will be holy and without fault. {5:28} In the same way, husbands ought to love their wives as they love their own bodies. For a man who loves his wife actually shows love for himself. {5:29} No one hates his own body but feeds and cares for it, just as Christ cares for the church. {5:30} And we are members of his body. {5:31} As the Scriptures say, "A man leaves his father and mother and is joined to his wife, and the two are united into one." {5:32} This is a great mystery, but it is an illustration of the way Christ and the church are one. {5:33} So again I say, each man must love his wife as he loves himself, and the wife must respect her husband.

{6:1} Children, obey your parents in the Lord, for this is the right thing to do. {6:2} Honor your father and mother. This is the first commandment with a promise: {6:3} If you honor your father and mother, "things will go well for you, and you will have a long life on the earth." {6:4} Fathers, do not provoke your children to anger by the way you treat them. Rather, bring them up with the discipline and instruction that comes from the Lord. {6:5} Slaves, obey your earthly masters with deep respect and fear. Serve them sincerely as you would serve Christ. {6:6} Try to please them all the time, not just when they are watching you. As slaves of Christ, do the will of God with all your heart. {6:7} Work with enthusiasm, as though you were working for the Lord rather than for people. {6:8} Remember that the Lord will reward each one of us for the good we do, whether we are slaves or free. {6:9} Masters, treat your slaves in the same way. Don't threaten them; remember, you both have the same Master in heaven, and he has no favorites. {6:10} **A final word: Be strong in the Lord and in his mighty power. {6:11} Put on all of God's armor so that you will be able to stand firm against all strategies of the devil.** {6:12} For we are not fighting against flesh-and-blood enemies, but against evil rulers and authorities of the unseen world, against mighty powers in this dark world, and against evil spirits in the heavenly places. {6:13} Therefore, put on every piece of God's armor so you will be able to resist the enemy in the time of evil. Then after the battle you will still be standing firm. {6:14} Stand your ground, putting on the belt of truth and the body armor of God's righteousness. {6:15} For shoes, put on the peace that comes from the Good News so that you will be fully prepared. {6:16} In addition to all of these, hold up the shield of faith to stop the fiery arrows of the devil. {6:17} Put on salvation as your helmet, and take the sword of the Spirit, which is the word of God. {6:18} Pray in the Spirit at all times and on every occasion. Stay alert and be persistent in your prayers for all believers everywhere. {6:19} And pray for me, too. Ask God to give me the right words so I can boldly explain God's mysterious plan that the Good News is for Jews and Gentiles alike. {6:20} I am in chains now, still preaching this message as God's ambassador. So pray that I will keep on speaking boldly for him, as I should. {6:21} To bring you up to date, Tychicus will give you a full report about what I am doing and how I am getting along. He is a beloved brother and faithful helper in the Lord's work. {6:22} I have sent him to you for this very purpose—to let you know how we are doing and to encourage you. {6:23} Peace be with you, dear brothers and sisters, and may God the Father and the Lord Jesus Christ give you love with faithfulness. {6:24} May God's grace be eternally upon all who love our Lord Jesus Christ.

Philippians

{1:1} Paul and Timothy, servants of Jesus Christ, send greetings to all the believers in Philippi, including the elders and deacons. {1:2} May God our Father and the Lord Jesus Christ give you grace and peace. {1:3} I thank my God every time I remember you. {1:4} In all my prayers for all of you, I always pray with joy {1:5} because of your partnership in the gospel from the first day until now, {1:6} being confident of this, that he who began a good work in you will carry it on to completion until the day of Christ Jesus. {1:7} It is right for me to feel this way about all of you, since I have you in my heart and, whether I am in chains or defending and confirming the gospel, all of you share in God's grace with me. {1:8} God can testify how I long for all of you with the affection of Christ Jesus. {1:9} And this is my prayer: that your love may abound more and more in knowledge and depth of insight, {1:10} so that you may be able to discern what is best and may be pure and blameless for the day of Christ, {1:11} filled with the fruit of righteousness that comes through Jesus Christ—to the glory and praise of God. {1:12} Now I want you to know, brothers and sisters, that what has happened to me has actually served to advance the gospel. {1:13} As a result, it has become clear throughout the whole palace guard and to everyone else that I am in chains for Christ. {1:14} And because of my chains, most of the brothers and sisters have become confident in the Lord and dare all the more to proclaim the gospel without fear. {1:15} It is true that some preach Christ out of envy and rivalry, but others out of goodwill. {1:16} The latter do so out of love, knowing that I am put here for the defense of the gospel. {1:17} The former preach Christ out of selfish ambition, not sincerely, supposing that they can stir up trouble for me while I am in chains. {1:18} But what does it matter? The important thing is that in every way, whether from false motives or true, Christ is preached. And because of this I rejoice. {1:19} Yes, and I will continue to rejoice, for I know that through your prayers and God's provision of the Spirit of Jesus Christ what has happened to me will turn out for my deliverance. {1:20} I eagerly expect and hope that I will in no way be ashamed, but will have sufficient courage so that now as always Christ will be exalted in my body, whether by life or by death. {1:21} For to me, to live is Christ and to die is gain. {1:22} If I am to go on living in the body, this will mean fruitful labor for me. Yet what shall I choose? I do not know! {1:23} I am torn between the two: I desire to depart and be with Christ, which is better by far; {1:24} but it is more necessary for you that I remain in the body. {1:25} Convinced of this, I know that I will remain, and I will continue with all of you for your progress and joy in the faith, {1:26} so that through my being with you again your boasting in Christ Jesus will abound on account of me. {1:27} Whatever happens, conduct yourselves in a manner worthy of the gospel of Christ. Then, whether I come and see you or only hear about you in my absence, I will know that you stand firm in the one Spirit, striving together as one for the faith of the gospel {1:28} without being frightened in any way by those who oppose you. This is a sign to them that they will be destroyed, but that you will be saved—and that by God. {1:29} For it has been granted to you on behalf of Christ not only to believe in him, but also to suffer for him, {1:30} since you are going through the same struggle you saw I had, and now hear that I still have.

{2:1} If there is any encouragement in Christ, any comfort from love, any participation in the Spirit, any affection and sympathy, {2:2} then make my joy complete by being like-minded, having the same love, being united in spirit, and intent on one purpose. {2:3} Do nothing out of selfish ambition or conceit, but in humility consider others as more important than yourselves. {2:4} Let each of you look not only to your own interests, but also to the interests of others. {2:5} **Have the same attitude in yourselves which was also in Christ Jesus, {2:6} who, although He existed in the form of God, did not regard equality with God a thing to be grasped, {2:7} but emptied Himself, taking the form of a bond-servant, and being made in the likeness of men. {2:8} And being found in appearance as a man, He humbled Himself by becoming obedient to the point of death, even death on a cross.** {2:9} Therefore God highly exalted Him, and bestowed on Him the name which is above every name, {2:10} so that at the name of Jesus every knee will bow, of those who are in heaven and on earth and under the earth, {2:11} and that every tongue will confess that Jesus Christ is Lord, to the glory of God the Father. {2:12} So then, my beloved, just as you have always obeyed, not as in my presence only, but now much more in my absence, work out your salvation with fear and trembling; {2:13} for it is God who is at work in you, both to will and to work for His good pleasure. {2:14} Do all things without grumbling or disputing; {2:15} so that you will prove yourselves to be blameless and innocent, children of God above reproach in the midst of a crooked and perverse generation, among whom you appear as lights in the world, {2:16} holding firmly the word of life, so that in the day of Christ I will have reason to glory because I did not run in vain nor toil in vain. {2:17} But even if I am being poured out as a drink offering upon the sacrifice and service of your faith, I rejoice and share my joy with you all. {2:18} You too, I urge you, rejoice in the same way and share your joy with me. {2:19} But I hope in the Lord Jesus to send Timothy to you shortly, so that I also may be encouraged when I learn of your condition. {2:20} For I have no one else of kindred spirit who will genuinely be concerned for your welfare. {2:21} For they all seek after their own interests, not those of Christ Jesus. {2:22} But you know of his proven worth, that he served with me in the furtherance of the gospel like a child serving his father. {2:23} Therefore I hope to send him immediately, as soon as I see how things go with me; {2:24} and I trust in the Lord that I myself also will be coming shortly. {2:25} But I thought it necessary to send to you Epaphroditus, my brother and fellow worker and fellow soldier, who is also your messenger and minister to my need; {2:26} because he was longing for you all and was distressed because you had heard that he was sick. {2:27} For indeed he was sick to the point of death, but God had mercy on him, and not on him only but also on me, so that I would not have sorrow upon sorrow. {2:28} Therefore I have sent him all the more eagerly so that when you see him again you may rejoice and I may be less concerned about you. {2:29} Receive him then in the Lord with all joy, and hold men like him in high regard; {2:30} because he came close to death for the work of Christ, risking his life to complete what was deficient in your service to me.

{3:1} Finally, my brothers and sisters, rejoice in the Lord. It's not troublesome for me to repeat these things to you, and it's safe for you. {3:2} Watch out for those who cause trouble, those who do evil, those who mutilate the body. {3:3} We, however, are the true circumcised people, who serve God by his Spirit, who boast in Christ Jesus, and who do not rely on our own efforts. {3:4} Although I could have confidence in my own efforts. If anyone else thinks they have reason to trust in their own efforts, I have more: {3:5} circumcised on the eighth day, from the people of Israel, of the tribe of Benjamin, a Hebrew of Hebrews; in regard to the law, a Pharisee; {3:6} as for zeal, persecuting the church; as for righteousness based on the law, faultless. {3:7} But whatever were gains to me I now consider loss for the sake of Christ. {3:8} What is more, I consider everything a loss because of the surpassing worth of knowing Christ Jesus my Lord, for whose sake I have lost all things. I consider them garbage, that I may gain Christ {3:9} and be found in him, not having a righteousness of my own that comes from the law, but that which is through faith in Christ—the righteousness that comes from God on the basis of faith. {3:10} I want to know Christ—yes, to know the power of his resurrection and participation in his sufferings, becoming like him in his death, {3:11} and so, somehow, attaining to the resurrection from the dead. {3:12} Not that I have already obtained all this, or have already arrived at my goal, but I press on to take hold of that for which Christ Jesus took hold of me. {3:13} **Brothers and sisters, I do not consider myself yet to have taken hold of it. But one thing I do: Forgetting what is behind and straining toward what is ahead,** {3:14} **I press on toward the goal to win the prize for which God has called me heavenward in Christ Jesus.** {3:15} All of us, then, who are mature should take such a view of things. And if on some point you think differently, that too God will make clear to you. {3:16} Only let us live up to what we have already attained. {3:17} Join together in following my example, brothers and sisters, and just as you have us as a model, keep your eyes on those who live as we do. {3:18} For, as I have often told you before and now tell you again even with tears, many live as enemies of the cross of Christ. {3:19} Their destiny is destruction, their god is their stomach, and their glory is in their shame. Their mind is set on earthly things. {3:20} But our citizenship is in heaven. And we eagerly await a Savior from there, the Lord Jesus Christ, {3:21} who, by the power that enables him to bring everything under his control, will transform our lowly bodies so that they will be like his glorious body.

{4:1} So, my beloved brothers and sisters, whom I long for, you are my joy and my crown. Stand firm in the Lord, dear friends. {4:2} I plead with Euodia and I plead with Syntyche to be of the same mind as the Lord. {4:3} Yes, and I ask you, my true companion, help these women since they have contended at my side in the cause of the gospel, along with Clement and the rest of my co-workers, whose names are in the book of life. {4:4} Rejoice in the Lord always. I will say it again: Rejoice! {4:5} Let your gentleness be evident to all. The Lord is near. {4:6} **Do not be anxious about anything, but in every situation, by prayer and petition, with thanksgiving, present your requests to God.** {4:7} **And the peace of God, which transcends all understanding, will guard your hearts and your minds in Christ Jesus.** {4:8} Finally, brothers and sisters, whatever is true, whatever is noble, whatever is right, whatever is pure, whatever is lovely, whatever is admirable—if anything is excellent or praiseworthy—think about such things. {4:9} Whatever you have learned or received or heard from me, or seen in me—put it into practice. And the God of peace will be with you. {4:10} I rejoiced greatly in the Lord that at last you renewed your concern for me. Indeed, you were concerned, but you had no opportunity to show it. {4:11} I am not saying this because I am in need, for I have learned to be content whatever the circumstances. {4:12} I know what it is to be in need, and I know what it is to have plenty. I have learned the secret of being content in any and every situation, whether well fed or hungry, whether living in plenty or in want. {4:13} I can do all this through him who gives me strength. {4:14} Yet it was good of you to share in my troubles. {4:15} Moreover, as you Philippians know, in the early days of your acquaintance with the gospel, when I set out from Macedonia, not one church shared with me in the matter of giving and receiving, except you only; {4:16} for even when I was in Thessalonica, you sent me aid more than once when I was in need. {4:17} Not that I desire your gifts; what I desire is that more be credited to your account. {4:18} I have received full payment and have more than enough. I am amply supplied, now that I have received from Epaphroditus the gifts you sent. They are a fragrant offering, an acceptable sacrifice, pleasing to God. {4:19} And my God will meet all your needs according to the riches of his glory in Christ Jesus. {4:20} To our God and Father be glory forever and ever. Amen. {4:21} Greet all God's people in Christ Jesus. The brothers and sisters who are with me send greetings. {4:22} All God's people here send you greetings, especially those who belong to Caesar's household.

Colossians

{1:1} From Paul, an apostle of Jesus Christ by the will of God, and our brother Timothy, {1:2} To the saints and faithful brothers and sisters in Christ who are in Colossae: Grace and peace to you from God our Father and the Lord Jesus Christ. {1:3} We always thank God, the Father of our Lord Jesus Christ, when we pray for you, {1:4} because we have heard of your faith in Christ Jesus and of the love you have for all God's people— {1:5} the faith and love that spring from the hope stored up for you in heaven and about which you have already heard in the true message of the gospel {1:6} that has come to you. In the same way, the gospel is bearing fruit and growing throughout the whole world—just as it has been doing among you since the day you heard it and truly understood God's grace. {1:7} You learned it from Epaphras, our dear fellow servant, who is a faithful minister of Christ on our behalf, {1:8} and who also told us of your love in the Spirit. {1:9} For this reason, since the day we heard about you, we have not stopped praying for you. We continually ask God to fill you with the knowledge of his will through all the wisdom and understanding that the Spirit gives, {1:10} so that you may live a life worthy of the Lord and please him in every way: bearing fruit in every good work, growing in the knowledge of God, {1:11} being strengthened with all power according to his glorious might so that you may have great endurance and patience, {1:12} and giving joyful thanks to the Father, who has qualified you to share in the inheritance of his holy people in the kingdom of light. {1:13} For he has rescued us from the dominion of darkness and brought us into the kingdom of the Son he loves, {1:14} in whom we have redemption, the forgiveness of sins. {1:15} *He is the image of the invisible God, the firstborn over all creation.* {1:16} *For in him all things were created: things in heaven and on earth, visible and invisible, whether thrones or powers or rulers or authorities; all things have been created through him and for him.* {1:17} He is before all things, and in him all things hold together. {1:18} And he is the head of the body, the church; he is the beginning and the firstborn from among the dead, so that in everything he might have the supremacy. {1:19} For God was pleased to have all his fullness dwell in him, {1:20} and through him to reconcile to himself all things, whether things on earth or things in heaven, by making peace through his blood, shed on the cross. {1:21} Once you were alienated from God and were enemies in your minds because of your evil behavior. {1:22} But now he has reconciled you by Christ's physical body through death to present you holy in his sight, without blemish and free from accusation— {1:23} if you continue in your faith, established and firm, and do not move from the hope held out in the gospel. This is the gospel that you heard and that has been proclaimed to every creature under heaven, and of which I, Paul, have become a servant. {1:24} Now I rejoice in what I am suffering for you, and I fill up in my flesh what is still lacking in regard to Christ's afflictions, for the sake of his body, which is the church. {1:25} I have become its servant by the commission God gave me to present to you the word of God in its fullness— {1:26} the mystery that has been kept hidden for ages and generations, but is now disclosed to the Lord's people. {1:27} To them God has chosen to make known among the Gentiles the glorious riches of this mystery, which is Christ in you, the hope of glory. {1:28} He is the one we proclaim, admonishing and teaching everyone with all wisdom, so that we may present everyone fully mature in Christ. {1:29} To this end I strenuously contend with all the energy Christ so powerfully works in me.

{2:1} I want you to know how hard I am contending for you and for those at Laodicea, and for all who have not met me personally. {2:2} My goal is that they may be encouraged in heart and united in love, so that they may have the full riches of complete understanding, in order that they may know the mystery of God, namely, Christ, {2:3} in whom are hidden all the treasures of wisdom and knowledge. {2:4} I tell you this so that no one may deceive you with fine-sounding arguments. {2:5} For though I am absent from you in body, I am present with you in spirit and delight to see how disciplined you are and how firm your faith in Christ is. {2:6} So then, just as you received Christ Jesus as Lord, continue to live your lives in him, {2:7} rooted and built up in him, strengthened in the faith as you were taught, and overflowing with thankfulness. {2:8} See to it that no one takes you captive through hollow and deceptive philosophy, which depends on human tradition and the elemental spiritual forces of this world rather than on Christ. {2:9} For in Christ all the fullness of the Deity lives in bodily form, {2:10} and in Christ you have been brought to fullness. He is the head over every power and authority. {2:11} In him you were also circumcised with a circumcision not performed by human hands. Your whole self ruled by the flesh was put off when you were circumcised by Christ, {2:12} having been buried with him in baptism, in which you were also raised with him through your faith in the working of God, who raised him from the dead. {2:13} When you were dead in your sins and in the uncircumcision of your flesh, God made you alive with Christ. He forgave us all our sins, {2:14} having canceled the charge of our legal indebtedness, which stood against us and condemned us; he has taken it away, nailing it to the cross. {2:15} And having disarmed the powers and authorities, he made a public spectacle of them, triumphing over them by the cross. {2:16} Therefore do not let anyone judge you by what you eat or drink, or with regard to a religious festival, a New Moon celebration, or a Sabbath day. {2:17} These are a shadow of the things that were to come; the reality, however, is found in Christ. {2:18} Do not let anyone who delights in false humility and the worship of angels disqualify you. Such a person also goes into great detail about what they have seen; they are puffed up with idle notions by their unspiritual mind. {2:19} They have lost connection with the head, from whom the whole body, supported and held together by its ligaments and sinews, grows as God causes it to grow. {2:20} Since you died with Christ to the elemental spiritual forces of this world, why, as though you still belonged to the world, do you submit to its rules: {2:21} "Do not handle! Do not taste! Do not touch!"? {2:22} These rules, which have to do with things that are all destined to perish with use, are based on merely human commands and teachings. {2:23} Such regulations indeed have an appearance of wisdom, with their self-imposed worship, their false humility and their harsh treatment of the body, but they lack any value in restraining sensual indulgence.

{3:1} **Since you have been raised with Christ, set your hearts on things above, where Christ is, seated at the right hand of God.** {3:2} **Set your minds on things above, not on earthly things.** {3:3} For you died, and your life is now hidden with Christ in God. {3:4} When Christ, who is your life, appears, then you also will appear with him in glory. {3:5} Put to death, therefore, whatever belongs to your earthly nature: sexual immorality, impurity, lust, evil desires and greed, which is idolatry. {3:6} Because of these, the wrath of God is coming. {3:7} You used to walk in these ways, in the life you once lived. {3:8} But now you must also rid yourselves of all such things as these: anger, rage, malice, slander, and filthy language from your lips. {3:9} Do not lie to each other, since you have taken off your old self with its practices {3:10} and have put on the new self, which is being renewed in knowledge in the image of its Creator. {3:11} Here there is no Gentile or Jew, circumcised or uncircumcised, barbarian, Scythian, slave or free, but Christ is all, and is in all. {3:12} Therefore, as God's chosen people, holy and dearly loved, clothe yourselves with compassion, kindness, humility, gentleness and patience. {3:13} Bear with each other and forgive one another if any of you has a grievance against someone. Forgive as the Lord forgave you. {3:14} And over all these virtues put on love, which binds them all together in perfect unity. {3:15} Let the peace of Christ rule in your hearts, since as members of one body you were called to peace. And be thankful. {3:16} Let the message of Christ dwell among you richly as you teach and admonish one another with all wisdom through psalms, hymns, and songs from the Spirit, singing to God with gratitude in your hearts. {3:17} And whatever you do, whether in word or deed, do it all in the name of the Lord Jesus, giving thanks to God the Father through him. {3:18} Wives, submit yourselves to your husbands, as is fitting in the Lord. {3:19} Husbands, love your wives and do not be harsh with them. {3:20} Children, obey your parents in everything, for this pleases the Lord. {3:21} Fathers, do not embitter your children, or they will become discouraged. {3:22} Slaves, obey your earthly masters in everything; and do it, not only when their eye is on you and to curry their favor, but with sincerity of heart and reverence for the Lord. {3:23} Whatever you do, work at it with all your heart, as working for the Lord, not for human masters, {3:24} since you know that you will receive an inheritance from the Lord as a reward. It is the Lord Christ you are serving. {3:25} Anyone who does wrong will be repaid for their wrongs, and there is no favoritism.

{4:1} Masters, treat your servants justly and fairly, knowing that you also have a Master in heaven. {4:2} Devote yourselves to prayer, being watchful and thankful. {4:3} And pray for us too, that God may open a door for our message, so that we may proclaim the mystery of Christ, for which I am in chains. {4:4} Pray that I may proclaim it clearly, as I should. {4:5} Be wise in the way you act toward outsiders; make the most of every opportunity. {4:6} Let your conversation be always full of grace, seasoned with salt, so that you may know how to answer everyone. {4:7} Tychicus will tell you all the news about me. He is a dear brother, a faithful minister and fellow servant in the Lord. {4:8} I am sending him to you for the express purpose that you may know about our circumstances and that he may encourage your hearts. {4:9} He is coming with Onesimus, our faithful and dear brother, who is one of you. They will tell you everything that is happening here. {4:10} Aristarchus, my fellow prisoner, sends you his greetings, as does Mark, the cousin of Barnabas. (You have received instructions about him; if he comes to you, welcome him.) {4:11} Jesus, who is called Justus, also sends greetings. These are the only Jews among my co-workers for the kingdom of God, and they have proved a comfort to me. {4:12} Epaphras, who is one of you and a servant of Christ Jesus, sends greetings. He is always wrestling in prayer for you, that you may stand firm in all the will of God, mature and fully assured. {4:13} I vouch for him that he is working hard for you and for those at Laodicea and Hierapolis. {4:14} Our dear friend Luke, the doctor, and Demas send greetings. {4:15} Give my greetings to the brothers and sisters at Laodicea, and to Nympha and the church in her house. {4:16} After this letter has been read to you, see that it is also read in the church of the Laodiceans and that you in turn read the letter from Laodicea. {4:17} Tell Archippus: "See to it that you complete the ministry you have received in the Lord." {4:18} I, Paul, write this greeting in my own hand. Remember my chains. Grace be with you. Amen.

1 Thessalonians

{1:1} From Paul, Silvanus, and Timothy to the church of the Thessalonians, who belong to God the Father and the Lord Jesus Christ. Grace and peace to you from God our Father and the Lord Jesus Christ. {1:2} We always thank God for all of you and continually mention you in our prayers. {1:3} We remember before our God and Father your work produced by faith, your labor prompted by love, and your endurance inspired by hope in our Lord Jesus Christ. {1:4} For we know, brothers and sisters loved by God, that he has chosen you, {1:5} because our gospel came to you not simply with words but also with power, with the Holy Spirit and deep conviction. You know how we lived among you for your sake. {1:6} You became imitators of us and of the Lord, for you welcomed the message in the midst of severe suffering with the joy given by the Holy Spirit. {1:7} And so you became a model to all the believers in Macedonia and Achaia. {1:8} The Lord's message rang out from you not only in Macedonia and Achaia—your faith in God has become known everywhere. Therefore we do not need to say anything about it, {1:9} for they themselves report what kind of reception you gave us. They tell how you turned to God from idols to serve the living and true God, {1:10} and to wait for his Son from heaven, whom he raised from the dead—Jesus, who rescues us from the coming wrath.

{2:1} Brothers and sisters, you yourselves know that our coming to you was not without results. {2:2} Even though we had previously suffered and been treated outrageously in Philippi, as you know, we were bold in our God to declare to you the gospel of God amidst much opposition. {2:3} Our appeal to you is not based on error, impurity, or deceit. {2:4} On the contrary, as servants approved by God to be entrusted with the gospel, we speak not to please men, but God, who examines our hearts. {2:5} You know that we never used flattery, nor did we put on a mask to cover up greed—God is our witness. {2:6} We were not looking for praise from people, not from you or anyone else, even though as apostles of Christ we could have asserted our authority. {2:7} Instead, we were gentle among you, like a nursing mother caring for her children. {2:8} Because we loved you so much, we were delighted to share with you not only the gospel of God but our lives as well, because you had become so dear to us. {2:9} Surely you remember, brothers and sisters, our toil and hardship; we worked night and day in order not to be a burden to anyone while we preached the gospel of God to you. {2:10} You are witnesses, and so is God, of how holy, righteous, and blameless we were among you who believed. {2:11} For you know that we treated each of you as a father treats his own children. {2:12} We encouraged, comforted, and urged you to live lives worthy of God, who calls you into his kingdom and glory. {2:13} And we also thank God continually because, when you received the word of God, which you heard from us, you accepted it not as a human word, but as it actually is, the word of God, which is indeed at work in you who believe. {2:14} For you, brothers and sisters, became imitators of the churches of God in Judea, which are in Christ Jesus: You suffered from your own people the same things those churches suffered from the Jews, {2:15} who killed the Lord Jesus and the prophets and also drove us out. They displease God and are hostile to everyone {2:16} in their effort to keep us from speaking to the Gentiles so that they may be saved. In this way they always heap up their sins to the limit. The wrath of God has come upon them at last. {2:17} But, brothers and sisters, when we were orphaned by being separated from you for a short time (in person, not in thought), out of our intense longing we made every effort to see you. {2:18} For we wanted to come to you—certainly I, Paul, did, again and again—but Satan blocked our way. {2:19} After all, what is our hope, our joy, or the crown in which we will glory in the presence of our Lord Jesus when he comes? Is it not you? {2:20} Indeed, you are our glory and joy.

{3:1} So when we could no longer endure it, we thought it best to be left in Athens alone. {3:2} We sent Timothy, our brother and fellow worker for God in the gospel of Christ, to strengthen and encourage you in your faith, {3:3} so that no one would be unsettled by these trials. For you yourselves know that we are destined for this. {3:4} In fact, when we were with you, we kept telling you that we would be persecuted. And it turned out that way, as you well know. {3:5} That's why, when I could not bear it any longer, I sent to find out about your faith. I was afraid that in some way the tempter had tempted you and that our labors might have been in vain. {3:6} But Timothy has just now come to us from you and has brought good news about your faith and love. He has told us that you always have pleasant memories of us and that you long to see us, just as we also long to see you. {3:7} Therefore, brothers and sisters, in all our distress and persecution we were encouraged about you because of your faith. {3:8} For now we really live, since you are standing firm in the Lord. {3:9} How can we thank God enough for you in return for all the joy we have in the presence of our God because of you? {3:10} Night and day we pray most earnestly that we may see you again and supply what is lacking in your faith. {3:11} Now may our God and Father himself and our Lord Jesus clear the way for us to come to you. {3:12} May the Lord make your love increase and overflow for each other and for everyone else, just as ours does for you. {3:13} May he strengthen your hearts so that you will be blameless and holy in the presence of our God and Father when our Lord Jesus comes with all his holy ones.

{4:1} Furthermore, we urge and encourage you, brothers and sisters, in the name of the Lord Jesus, to live in a way that pleases God, just as you have learned from us. And we encourage you to do this more and more. {4:2} You already know the instructions we gave you on behalf of the Lord Jesus. {4:3} God's will is for you to be holy, so stay away from all sexual sin. {4:4} Each of you should learn to control your own body in a way that is holy and honorable. {4:5} Don't be controlled by your sexual desires like the Gentiles who do not know God. {4:6} Never harm or cheat a fellow believer in this matter by violating his rights, because the Lord avenges all such sins, as we have already told you and warned you. {4:7} For God has called us to live holy lives, not impure lives. {4:8} Therefore, anyone who refuses to live by these rules is not disobeying human teaching but is rejecting God, who gives his Holy Spirit to you. {4:9} Now concerning love for your fellow believers, you have no need for anyone to write to you, for you yourselves have been taught by God to love one another. {4:10} Indeed, you already show your love for all the believers throughout Macedonia. But we urge you, brothers and sisters, to do so more and more. {4:11} Make it your goal to live a quiet life, minding your own business and working with your hands, just as we instructed you before. {4:12} Then people who are not believers will respect the way you live, and you will not need to depend on others for anything. {4:13} And now, dear brothers and sisters, we want you to know what will happen to the believers who have died so you will not grieve like people who have no hope. {4:14} For since we believe that Jesus died and was raised to life again, we also believe that when Jesus returns, God will bring back with him the believers who have died. {4:15} We tell you this directly from the Lord: We who are still living when the Lord returns will not meet him ahead of those who have died. {4:16} **For the Lord himself will come down from heaven with a commanding shout, with the voice of the archangel, and with the trumpet call of God. First, the Christians who have died will rise from their graves.** {4:17} **Then, together with them, we who are still alive and remain on the earth will be caught up in the clouds to meet the Lord in the air. Then we will be with the Lord forever.** {4:18} So encourage each other with these words.

{5:1} Brothers and sisters, there's no need for me to write to you about the times and seasons, {5:2} because you already know perfectly well that the day of the Lord comes like a thief in the night. {5:3} When people are saying, "Everything is peaceful and secure," then disaster will fall on them suddenly, as a pregnant woman's labor pains begin. And there will be no escape. {5:4} But you aren't in the dark about this, brothers and sisters, for that day won't catch you by surprise like a thief. {5:5} You are all children of the light and of the day. We don't belong to darkness or night. {5:6} So let's not be asleep like the others. Let's stay alert and be sober. {5:7} Those who sleep, sleep at night, and those who get drunk, get drunk at night. {5:8} But let us who live in the light be clearheaded, protected by the armor of faith and love, and wearing as our helmet the confidence of our salvation. {5:9} For God chose to save us through our Lord Jesus Christ, not to pour out his anger on us. {5:10} Christ died for us so that, whether we are dead or alive when he returns, we can live with him forever. {5:11} So encourage each other and build each other up, just as you are already doing. {5:12} Brothers and sisters, we urge you to appreciate those who work hard among you, who lead you in the Lord and teach you. {5:13} Respect them highly and love them because of their work. Live in peace with each other. {5:14} Brothers and sisters, we urge you to warn those who are lazy. Encourage those who are timid. Take tender care of those who are weak. Be patient with everyone. {5:15} See that no one pays back evil for evil, but always try to do good to each other and to all people. {5:16} **Always be joyful.** {5:17} **Never stop praying.** {5:18} **Be thankful in all circumstances, for this is God's will for you who belong to Christ Jesus.** {5:19} Do not stifle the Holy Spirit. {5:20} Do not scoff at prophecies, {5:21} but test everything that is said. Hold on to what is good. {5:22} Stay away from every kind of evil. {5:23} Now may the God of peace make you holy in every way, and may your whole spirit and soul and body be kept blameless until our Lord Jesus Christ comes again. {5:24} God will make this happen, for he who calls you is faithful. {5:25} Brothers and sisters, pray for us. {5:26} Greet all the brothers and sisters with a sacred kiss. {5:27} I command you in the name of the Lord to read this letter to all the brothers and sisters.

2 Thessalonians

{1:1} Paul, Silvanus, and Timothy, to the church of the Thessalonians in God our Father and the Lord Jesus Christ: {1:2} Grace and peace to you from God our Father and the Lord Jesus Christ. {1:3} Brothers and sisters, we always thank God for you because your faith is flourishing and your love for one another is increasing. {1:4} We boast about you in the churches of God for your endurance and faith in all the persecutions and trials you are enduring. {1:5} This is evidence of the righteous judgment of God, that you may be considered worthy of the kingdom of God, for which you are also suffering. {1:6} It is a righteous thing for God to repay with affliction those who afflict you, {1:7} and to give relief to you who are troubled and to us as well. This will happen when the Lord Jesus is revealed from heaven with his mighty angels {1:8} in blazing fire, inflicting vengeance on those who do not know God and do not obey the gospel of our Lord Jesus. {1:9} These will pay the penalty of eternal destruction, away from the presence of the Lord and the glory of his power, {1:10} when he comes to be glorified among his saints and admired by all who have believed, because our testimony to you was believed. {1:11} With this in mind, we constantly pray for you, that our God may make you worthy of his calling, and that by his power he may fulfill every good purpose of yours and every act prompted by your faith. {1:12} We pray this so that the name of our Lord Jesus may be glorified in you, and you in him, according to the grace of our God and the Lord Jesus Christ.

{2:1} Now concerning the coming of our Lord Jesus Christ and our being gathered to him, we ask you, brothers and sisters, {2:2} not to become easily unsettled or alarmed by the teaching allegedly from us—whether by a prophecy or by word of mouth or by letter—asserting that the day of the Lord has already come. {2:3} Don't let anyone deceive you in any way, for that day will not come until the rebellion occurs and the man of lawlessness is revealed, the man doomed to destruction. {2:4} He will oppose and exalt himself above every so-called god or object of worship, so that he sits in the temple of God, proclaiming himself to be God. {2:5} Don't you remember that when I was with you, I used to tell you these things? {2:6} And now you know what is holding him back, so that he may be revealed at the proper time. {2:7} For the secret power of lawlessness is already at work; but the one who now holds it back will continue to do so till he is taken out of the way. {2:8} And then the lawless one will be revealed, whom the Lord Jesus will overthrow with the breath of his mouth and destroy by the splendor of his coming. {2:9} The coming of the lawless one will be in accordance with how Satan works. He will use all sorts of displays of power through signs and wonders that serve the lie, {2:10} and all the ways that wickedness deceives those who are perishing. They perish because they refuse to love the truth and so be saved. {2:11} For this reason God sends them a powerful delusion so that they will believe the lie {2:12} and so that all will be condemned who have not believed the truth but have delighted in wickedness. {2:13} But we ought always to thank God for you, brothers and sisters loved by the Lord, because God chose you as firstfruits to be saved through the sanctifying work of the Spirit and through belief in the truth. {2:14} He called you to this through our gospel, that you might share in the glory of our Lord Jesus Christ. {2:15} **So then, brothers and sisters, stand firm and hold fast to the teachings we passed on to you, whether by word of mouth or by letter.** {2:16} May our Lord Jesus Christ himself and God our Father, who loved us and by his grace gave us eternal encouragement and good hope, {2:17} encourage your hearts and strengthen you in every good deed and word.

{3:1} Finally, brothers and sisters, pray for us that the message of the Lord may spread rapidly and be honored, just as it was with you. {3:2} And pray that we may be delivered from wicked and evil people, for not everyone has faith. {3:3} But the Lord is faithful, and he will strengthen you and protect you from the evil one. {3:4} We have confidence in the Lord that you are doing and will continue to do the things we command. {3:5} May the Lord direct your hearts into God's love and Christ's perseverance. {3:6} Now we command you, brothers and sisters, in the name of our Lord Jesus Christ, to keep away from any believer who is idle and disruptive and does not live according to the teaching you received from us. {3:7} For you yourselves know how you ought to follow our example. We were not idle when we were with you, {3:8} nor did we eat anyone's food without paying for it. On the contrary, we worked night and day, laboring and toiling so that we would not be a burden to any of you. {3:9} We did this, not because we do not have the right to such help, but in order to offer ourselves as a model for you to imitate. {3:10} *For even when we were with you, we gave you this rule: "The one who is unwilling to work shall not eat."* {3:11} We hear that some among you are idle and disruptive. They are not busy; they are busybodies. {3:12} Such people we command and urge in the Lord Jesus Christ to settle down and earn the food they eat. {3:13} And as for you, brothers and sisters, never tire of doing what is good. {3:14} Take special note of anyone who does not obey our instructions in this letter. Do not associate with them, in order that they may feel ashamed. {3:15} Yet do not regard them as an enemy, but warn them as you would a fellow believer. {3:16} **Now may the Lord of peace himself give you peace at all times and in every way. The Lord be with all of you.** {3:17} I, Paul, write this greeting in my own hand, which is the distinguishing mark in all my letters. This is how I write. {3:18} The grace of our Lord Jesus Christ be with you all.

1 Timothy

{1:1} This letter is from Paul, an apostle of Jesus Christ, appointed by the command of God our Savior and Jesus Christ, who is our hope. {1:2} I am writing to Timothy, my true son in the faith. May God our Father and Jesus Christ our Lord give you grace, mercy, and peace. {1:3} When I left for Macedonia, I urged you to stay in Ephesus and command certain people not to teach false doctrines. {1:4} They should not waste their time on endless genealogies and myths. These things only lead to meaningless speculation rather than the edification that comes from God-ordained faith. {1:5} The goal of this command is love, which comes from a pure heart and a good conscience and a sincere faith. {1:6} Some have departed from these and turned to meaningless talk. {1:7} They want to be teachers of the law, but they do not know what they are talking about or what they so confidently affirm. {1:8} We know that the law is good if one uses it properly. {1:9} We also know that the law is made not for the righteous but for lawbreakers and rebels, the ungodly and sinful, the unholy and irreligious, for those who kill their fathers or mothers, for murderers, {1:10} for the sexually immoral, for those practicing homosexuality, for slave traders and liars and perjurers—and for whatever else is contrary to the sound doctrine {1:11} that conforms to the gospel concerning the glory of the blessed God, which he entrusted to me. {1:12} I am thankful to Christ Jesus our Lord, who has given me strength, that he considered me trustworthy, appointing me to his service. {1:13} Even though I was once a blasphemer and a persecutor and a violent man, I was shown mercy because I acted in ignorance and unbelief. {1:14} The grace of our Lord was poured out on me abundantly, along with the faith and love that are in Christ Jesus. {1:15} This is a trustworthy saying that deserves full acceptance: Christ Jesus came into the world to save sinners—of whom I am the worst. {1:16} But for that very reason I was shown mercy so that in me, the worst of sinners, Christ Jesus might display his immense patience as an example for those who would believe in him and receive eternal life. {1:17} Now to the King eternal, immortal, invisible, the only God, be honor and glory forever and ever. Amen. {1:18} Timothy, my son, I am giving you this command in keeping with the prophecies once made about you, so that by recalling them you may fight the battle well, {1:19} holding on to faith and a good conscience, which some have rejected and so have suffered shipwreck with regard to the faith. {1:20} Among them are Hymenaeus and Alexander, whom I have handed over to Satan to be taught not to blaspheme.

{2:1} So, I urge you, first of all, to pray for all people. Ask God to help them; intercede on their behalf, and give thanks for them. {2:2} Pray this way for kings and all who are in authority so that we can live peaceful and quiet lives marked by godliness and dignity. {2:3} This is good and pleases God our Savior, {2:4} who wants everyone to be saved and to understand the truth. {2:5} **For there is only one God and one Mediator who can reconcile God and humanity—the man Christ Jesus.** {2:6} **He gave his life to purchase freedom for everyone. This is the message God gave to the world at just the right time.** {2:7} And I have been chosen as a preacher and apostle to teach the Gentiles this message about faith and truth. I'm not exaggerating—just telling the truth. {2:8} In every place of worship, I want men to pray with holy hands lifted up to God, free from anger and controversy. {2:9} And I want women to be modest in their appearance. They should wear decent and appropriate clothing and not draw attention to themselves by the way they fix their hair or by wearing gold or pearls or expensive clothes. {2:10} For women who claim to be devoted to God should make themselves attractive by the good things they do. {2:11} Women should learn quietly and submissively. {2:12} I do not let women teach men or have authority over them. Let them listen quietly. {2:13} For God made Adam first, and afterward he made Eve. {2:14} And it was not Adam who was deceived by Satan. The woman was deceived, and sin was the result. {2:15} But women will be saved through childbearing, assuming they continue to live in faith, love, holiness, and modesty.

{3:1} Here is a trustworthy saying: If someone aspires to be an overseer, he desires a noble task. {3:2} An overseer, then, must be above reproach, the husband of one wife, temperate, self-controlled, respectable, hospitable, able to teach, {3:3} not given to drunkenness, not violent but gentle, not quarrelsome, not a lover of money. {3:4} He must manage his own family well and see that his children obey him, and he must do so in a manner worthy of full respect. {3:5} (If anyone does not know how to manage his own family, how can he take care of God's church?) {3:6} He must not be a recent convert, or he may become conceited and fall under the same judgment as the devil. {3:7} He must also have a good reputation with outsiders, so that he will not fall into disgrace and into the devil's trap. {3:8} In the same way, deacons are to be worthy of respect, sincere, not indulging in much wine, and not pursuing dishonest gain. {3:9} They must keep hold of the deep truths of the faith with a clear conscience. {3:10} They must first be tested; and then if there is nothing against them, let them serve as deacons. {3:11} In the same way, the women are to be worthy of respect, not malicious talkers but temperate and trustworthy in everything. {3:12} A deacon must be faithful to his wife and must manage his children and his household well. {3:13} Those who have served well gain an excellent standing and great assurance in their faith in Christ Jesus. {3:14} Although I hope to come to you soon, I am writing you these instructions so that, {3:15} **if I am delayed, you will know how people ought to conduct themselves in God's household, which is the church of the living God, the pillar and foundation of the truth.** {3:16} Beyond all question, the mystery from which true godliness springs is great: He appeared in the flesh, was vindicated by the Spirit, was seen by angels, was preached among the nations, was believed on in the world, was taken up in glory.

{4:1} The Spirit clearly says that in later times some will abandon the faith and follow deceiving spirits and things taught by demons. {4:2} Such teachings come through hypocritical liars, whose consciences have been seared as with a hot iron. {4:3} They forbid people to marry and order them to abstain from certain foods, which God created to be received with thanksgiving by those who believe and who know the truth. {4:4} For everything God created is good, and nothing is to be rejected if it is received with thanksgiving, {4:5} because it is consecrated by the word of God and prayer. {4:6} If you point these things out to the brothers and sisters, you will be a good minister of Christ Jesus, nourished on the truths of the faith and of the good teaching that you have followed. {4:7} Have nothing to do with godless myths and old wives' tales; rather, train yourself to be godly. {4:8} For physical training is of some value, but godliness has value for all things, holding promise for both the present life and the life to come. {4:9} This is a trustworthy saying that deserves full acceptance. {4:10} That is why we labor and strive, because we have put our hope in the living God, who is the Savior of all people, and especially of those who believe. {4:11} Command and teach these things. {4:12} Don't let anyone look down on you because you are young, but set an example for the believers in speech, in conduct, in love, in faith and in purity. {4:13} Until I come, devote yourself to the public reading of Scripture, to preaching and to teaching. {4:14} Do not neglect your gift, which was given to you through prophecy when the body of elders laid their hands on you. {4:15} Be diligent in these matters; give yourself wholly to them, so that everyone may see your progress. {4:16} Watch your life and doctrine closely. Persevere in them, because if you do, you will save both yourself and your hearers.

{5:1} Don't scold an older person, but talk to them respectfully, as you would to a father. Treat younger men like brothers, {5:2} older women like mothers, and younger women like sisters, always with purity in mind. {5:3} Take care of widows who are truly in need. {5:4} But if a widow has children or grandchildren, they should learn to take care of their own family first. This pleases God. {5:5} A widow who is truly alone puts her trust in God and continues to pray night and day. {5:6} But a widow who lives only for pleasure is spiritually dead even while she is alive. {5:7} These instructions should be taken seriously so that no one can criticize the church. {5:8} But if someone doesn't provide for their own family, they have denied the faith and are worse than unbelievers. {5:9} Don't enroll a widow for support unless she is at least sixty years old, has been faithful to her husband, {5:10} and is well known for her good deeds—such as raising children, welcoming strangers into her home, washing the feet of believers, helping those in trouble, and always doing good. {5:11} Refuse to help younger widows, for when their desires draw them away from Christ, they want to remarry. {5:12} This brings them condemnation because they have broken their first pledge. {5:13} Besides, they learn to be lazy and go around from house to house. And not only are they lazy, but they are also gossips and busybodies, saying things they shouldn't. {5:14} So I advise these younger widows to marry again, have children, and take care of their homes. Then the enemy will not be able to say anything against them. {5:15} For some have already turned away to follow Satan. {5:16} If any woman who is a believer has relatives who are widows, she should help them. The church should not be burdened with them, because then it wouldn't be able to help those who are truly widows. {5:17} Elders who do their work well should be respected and paid well, especially those who work hard at both preaching and teaching. {5:18} For the Scripture says, "Do not muzzle an ox while it is treading out the grain," and "The worker deserves his wages." {5:19} Don't listen to a charge against an elder unless it is confirmed by two or three witnesses. {5:20} Publicly rebuke those who sin, so that the others will be afraid to sin. {5:21} In the presence of God, Christ Jesus, and the holy angels, I solemnly charge you to follow these instructions without showing favoritism to anyone. {5:22} Don't be too quick to appoint anyone as an elder, and don't share in the sins of others. Keep yourself pure. {5:23} Don't drink only water; you ought to drink a little wine for the sake of your stomach because you are sick so often. {5:24} Remember, some people's sins are obvious, leading them to certain judgments. But there are others whose sins will not be revealed until later. {5:25} Similarly, good deeds are obvious, and even those that are not obvious cannot remain hidden forever.

{6:1} Slaves, respect your masters, whether they are good or bad, so that the name of God and his teaching will not be shamed. {6:2} If your master is a believer, don't treat them with disrespect just because they are fellow believers. Instead, serve them even better because they are dear to you as fellow believers. Teach and encourage these things. {6:3} Anyone who teaches differently and doesn't agree with the accurate and healthy teaching of our Lord Jesus Christ and godly living {6:4} is full of pride and doesn't know anything. They are always quibbling over questions and controversies. These lead to jealousy, fighting, slander, and evil suspicions. {6:5} They are always arguing and thinking that godliness is a way to make money. Stay away from such people. {6:6} But true godliness with contentment is itself great wealth. {6:7} After all, we brought nothing with us when we came into the world, and we can't take anything with us when we leave it. {6:8} So if we have enough food and clothing, let us be content. {6:9} But people who long to be rich fall into temptation and are trapped by many foolish and harmful desires that plunge them into ruin and destruction. {6:10} For the love of money is the root of all kinds of evil. And some people, craving money, have wandered from the true faith and pierced themselves with many sorrows. {6:11} But you, Timothy, are a man of God; so run from all these evil things. Pursue righteousness and a godly life, along with faith, love, perseverance, and gentleness. {6:12} Fight the good fight for the true faith. Hold tightly to the eternal life to which God has called you, which you have declared so well before many witnesses. {6:13} I charge you before God, who gives life to all, and before Christ Jesus, who gave a good testimony before Pontius Pilate, {6:14} that you obey this command without wavering. Then no one can find fault with you from now until our Lord Jesus Christ comes again. {6:15} For at just the right time Christ will be revealed from heaven by the blessed and only almighty God, the King of all kings and Lord of all lords. {6:16} He alone can never die, and he lives in light so brilliant that no human can approach him. No human eye has ever seen him, nor ever will. All honor and power to him forever! Amen. {6:17} Teach those who are rich in this world not to be proud and not to trust in their money, which is so unreliable. Their trust should be in God, who richly gives us all we need for our enjoyment. {6:18} Tell them to use their money to do good. They should be rich in good works and generous to those in need, always being ready to share with others. {6:19} By doing this, they will be storing up their treasure as a good foundation for the future so that they may experience true life. {6:20} Timothy, guard what God has entrusted to you. Avoid godless, foolish discussions with those who oppose you with their so-called knowledge. {6:21} Some people have wandered from the faith by following such foolishness. May God's grace be with you all. Amen

2 Timothy

{1:1} This letter is from Paul, chosen by the will of God to be an apostle of Jesus Christ. I am writing to Timothy, my dear son in the faith. May God the Father and Christ Jesus our Lord give you grace, mercy, and peace. {1:2} I am thankful to God, whom I serve with a clear conscience, as my ancestors did. I constantly remember you in my prayers, day and night. {1:3} I long to see you again, for I remember your tears as we parted. And I will be filled with joy when we are together again. {1:4} I remember your genuine faith, for you share the faith that first filled your grandmother Lois and your mother, Eunice. And I know that same faith continues strong in you. {1:5} This is why I remind you to fan into flames the spiritual gift God gave you when I laid my hands on you. {1:6} For God has not given us a spirit of fear and timidity, but of power, love, and self-discipline. {1:7} **So never be ashamed to tell others about our Lord. And don't be ashamed of me, either, even though I'm in prison for him. With the strength God gives you, be ready to suffer with me for the sake of the Good News.** {1:8} For God saved us and called us to live a holy life. He did this, not because we deserved it, but because that was his plan from before the beginning of time—to show us his grace through Christ Jesus. {1:9} And now he has made all of this plain to us by the appearance of Christ Jesus, our Savior. He broke the power of death and illuminated the way to life and immortality through the Good News. {1:10} And God chose me to be a preacher, an apostle, and a teacher of this Good News. {1:11} That is why I am suffering here in prison. But I am not ashamed of it, for I know the one in whom I trust, and I am sure that he is able to guard what I have entrusted to him until the day of his return. {1:12} Hold on to the pattern of wholesome teaching you learned from me—a pattern shaped by the faith and love that you have in Christ Jesus. {1:13} Through the power of the Holy Spirit who lives within us, carefully guard the precious truth that has been entrusted to you. {1:14} As you know, everyone from the province of Asia has deserted me—even Phygelus and Hermogenes. {1:15} May the Lord show special kindness to Onesiphorus and all his family because he often visited and encouraged me. He was never ashamed of me because I was in chains. {1:16} When he came to Rome, he searched everywhere until he found me. {1:17} May the Lord show him special kindness on the day of Christ's return. {1:18} And you know very well how helpful he was in Ephesus.

{2:1} So, my son, be strong in the grace that is in Christ Jesus. {2:2} Take the teachings you heard from me and pass them on to faithful people who will be able to teach others also. {2:3} Endure suffering along with me, as a good soldier of Christ Jesus. {2:4} Soldiers don't get tied up in the affairs of civilian life, for then they cannot please the officer who enlisted them. {2:5} And athletes cannot win the prize unless they follow the rules. {2:6} And hardworking farmers should be the first to enjoy the fruit of their labor. {2:7} Think about what I am saying. The Lord will help you understand all these things. {2:8} Always remember that Jesus Christ, a descendant of King David, was raised from the dead. This is the Good News I preach. {2:9} And because I preach this Good News, I am suffering and have been chained like a criminal. But the word of God cannot be chained. {2:10} So I am willing to endure anything if it will bring salvation and eternal glory in Christ Jesus to those God has chosen. {2:11} This is a trustworthy saying: If we die with him, we will also live with him. {2:12} If we endure hardship, we will reign with him. If we deny him, he will deny us. {2:13} If we are unfaithful, he remains faithful, for he cannot deny who he is. {2:14} Remind everyone about these things, and command them in God's presence to stop fighting over words. Such arguments are useless, and they can ruin those who hear them. {2:15} Work hard so you can present yourself to God and receive his approval. Be a good worker, one who does not need to be ashamed and who correctly explains the word of truth. {2:16} Avoid worthless, foolish talk that only leads to more godless behavior. {2:17} This kind of talk spreads like cancer, as in the case of Hymenaeus and Philetus. {2:18} They have left the path of truth, claiming that the resurrection of the dead has already occurred; in this way, they have turned some people away from the faith. {2:19} But God's truth stands firm like a foundation stone with this inscription: "The Lord knows those who are his," and "All who belong to the Lord must turn away from evil." {2:20} In a wealthy home, some utensils are made of gold and silver, and some are made of wood and clay. The expensive utensils are used for special occasions, and the cheap ones are for everyday use. {2:21} If you keep yourself pure, you will be a special utensil for honorable use. Your life will be clean, and you will be ready for the Master to use you for every good work. {2:22} Run from anything that stimulates youthful lusts. Instead, pursue righteous living, faithfulness, love, and peace. Enjoy the companionship of those who call on the Lord with pure hearts. {2:23} Again I say, don't get involved in foolish, ignorant arguments that only start fights. {2:24} A servant of the Lord must not quarrel but must be kind to everyone, be able to teach, and be patient with difficult people. {2:25} Gently instruct those who oppose the truth. Perhaps God will change those people's hearts, and they will learn the truth. {2:26} Then they will come to their senses and escape from the devil's trap. For they have been held captive by him to do whatever he wants.

{3:1} Understand this: In the last days there will be very difficult times. {3:2} People will love only themselves and their money. They will be boastful and proud, scoffing at God, disobedient to their parents, and ungrateful. They will consider nothing sacred. {3:3} They will be unloving and unforgiving; they will slander others and have no self-control. They will be cruel and hate what is good. {3:4} They will betray their friends, be reckless, be puffed up with pride, and love pleasure rather than God. {3:5} They will act religious, but they will reject the power that could make them godly. Stay away from people like that! {3:6} They are the kind who work their way into people's homes and win the confidence of vulnerable women who are burdened with the guilt of sin and controlled by various desires. {3:7} Such women are always learning but never able to come to a knowledge of the truth. {3:8} These teachers oppose the truth just as Jannes and Jambres opposed Moses. They have depraved minds and a counterfeit faith. {3:9} But they won't get away with this for long. Someday everyone will recognize what fools they are, just as with Jannes and Jambres. {3:10} But you, Timothy, certainly know what I teach, and how I live, and what my purpose in life is. You know my faith, my patience, my love, and my endurance. {3:11} You know how much persecution and suffering I have endured. You know all about how I was persecuted in Antioch, Iconium, and Lystra—but the Lord rescued me from all of it. {3:12} Yes, and everyone who wants to live a godly life in Christ Jesus will suffer persecution. {3:13} But evil people and impostors will flourish. They will deceive others and will themselves be deceived. {3:14} But you must remain faithful to the things you have been taught. You know they are true, for you know you can trust those who taught you. {3:15} You have been taught the holy Scriptures from childhood, and they have given you the wisdom to receive the salvation that comes by trusting in Christ Jesus. {3:16} **All Scripture is inspired by God and is useful to teach us what is true and to make us realize what is wrong in our lives. It corrects us when we are wrong and teaches us to do what is right.** {3:17} **God uses it to prepare and equip his people to do every good work.**

{4:1} I solemnly urge you in the presence of God and Christ Jesus, who will someday judge the living and the dead when he comes to set up his Kingdom: {4:2} Preach the word of God. Be prepared, whether the time is favorable or not. Patiently correct, rebuke, and encourage your people with good teaching. {4:3} For a time is coming when people will no longer listen to sound and wholesome teaching. They will follow their own desires and will look for teachers who will tell them whatever their itching ears want to hear. {4:4} They will reject the truth and chase after myths. {4:5} But you should keep a clear mind in every situation. Don't be afraid of suffering for the Lord. Work at telling others the Good News, and fully carry out the ministry God has given you. {4:6} As for me, my life has already been poured out as an offering to God. The time of my death is near. {4:7} I have fought the good fight, I have finished the race, and I have remained faithful. {4:8} And now the prize awaits me—the crown of righteousness, which the Lord, the righteous Judge, will give me on the day of his return. And the prize is not just for me but for all who eagerly look forward to his appearing. {4:9} Timothy, please come as soon as you can. {4:10} Demas has deserted me because he loves the things of this life and has gone to Thessalonica. Crescens has gone to Galatia, and Titus has gone to Dalmatia. {4:11} Only Luke is with me. Bring Mark with you when you come, for he will be helpful to me in my ministry. {4:12} I sent Tychicus to Ephesus. {4:13} When you come, be sure to bring the coat I left with Carpus at Troas. Also bring my books, and especially my papers. {4:14} Alexander the coppersmith has done me much harm, but the Lord will judge him for what he has done. {4:15} Be careful of him, for he fought against everything we said. {4:16} The first time I was brought before the judge, no one came with me. Everyone abandoned me. May it not be counted against them. {4:17} But the Lord stood with me and gave me strength so that I might preach the Good News in its entirety for all the Gentiles to hear. And he rescued me from certain death. {4:18} Yes, and the Lord will deliver me from every evil attack and will bring me safely into his heavenly Kingdom. All glory to God forever and ever! Amen. {4:19} Give my greetings to Priscilla and Aquila and those living in the household of Onesiphorus. {4:20} Erastus stayed at Corinth, and I left Trophimus sick in Miletus. {4:21} Do your best to get here before winter. Eubulus sends you greetings, and so do Pudens, Linus, Claudia, and all the brothers and sisters {4:22} May the Lord be with your spirit. And may his grace be with all of you.

Titus

{1:1} I, Paul, am a servant of God and an apostle of Jesus Christ. I have been sent to proclaim faith to those God has chosen and to teach them to know the truth that shows them how to live godly lives. {1:2} This truth gives them the confidence of eternal life, which God, who does not lie, promised them before the world began. {1:3} And now at the right time he has revealed this message, and we announce it to everyone. It is by the command of God our Savior that I have been entrusted with this work. {1:4} I am writing to Titus, my true son in the faith. May God the Father and Christ Jesus our Savior give you grace, mercy, and peace. {1:5} **I left you on the island of Crete so you could complete our work there and appoint elders in each town as I instructed you.** {1:6} An elder must live a blameless life. He must be faithful to his wife, and his children must be believers who don't have a reputation for being wild or rebellious. {1:7} A church leader is a manager of God's household, so he must live a blameless life. He must not be arrogant or quick-tempered; he must not be a heavy drinker, violent, or dishonest with money. {1:8} Rather, he must enjoy having guests in his home and must love what is good. He must live wisely and be just. He must live a devout and disciplined life. {1:9} He must have a strong and steadfast belief in the trustworthy message he was taught; then he will be able to encourage others with wholesome teaching and show those who oppose it where they are wrong. {1:10} For there are many rebellious people who engage in useless talk and deceive others. This is especially true of those who insist on circumcision for salvation. {1:11} They must be silenced, because they are turning whole families away from the truth by thei false teaching. And they do it only for money. {1:12} Even one of their own men, a prophet from Crete, has said about them, "The people of Crete are all liars, cruel animals, and lazy gluttons." {1:13} This is true. So reprimand them sternly to make them strong in the faith. {1:14} They must stop listening to Jewish myths and the commands of people who have turned away from the truth. {1:15} Everything is pure to those whose hearts are pure. But nothing is pure to those who are corrupt and unbelieving, because their minds and consciences are corrupted. {1:16} Such people claim they know God, but they deny him by the way they live. They are detestable and disobedient, worthless for doing anything good.

{2:1} But you speak the things that are consistent with sound doctrine. {2:2} Encourage the older men to be sober, sensible, and self-controlled. They should be sound in their faith, love, and endurance. {2:3} Likewise, encourage the older women to live in a way that is appropriate for someone serving the Lord. They should not be slanderers or addicted to much wine. Instead, they should teach what is good. {2:4} These older women should train the younger women to love their husbands and their children, {2:5} to live wisely and be pure, to work in their homes, to do good, and to be submissive to their husbands. Then they will not bring shame on the word of God. {2:6} In the same way, encourage the young men to live wisely. {2:7} And you yourself must be an example to them by doing good works of every kind. Let everything you do reflect the integrity and seriousness of your teaching. {2:8} Teach the truth so that your teaching can't be criticized. Then those who oppose us will be ashamed and have nothing bad to say about us. {2:9} Slaves must always obey their masters and do their best to please them. They must not talk back {2:10} or steal but should show themselves to be entirely trustworthy and good. Then they will make the teaching about God our Savior attractive in every way. {2:11} **For the grace of God has been revealed, bringing salvation to all people.** {2:12} **And we are instructed to turn from godless living and sinful pleasures. We should live in this evil world with wisdom, righteousness, and devotion to God,** {2:13} while we look forward with hope to that wonderful day when the glory of our great God and Savior, Jesus Christ, will be revealed. {2:14} He gave his life to free us from every kind of sin, to cleanse us, and to make us his very own people, totally committed to doing good deeds. {2:15} You must teach these things and encourage the believers to do them. You have the authority to correct them when necessary, so don't let anyone disregard what you say.

{3:1} Remind them to submit to rulers and authorities, to be obedient, and ready to do good. {3:2} Tell them not to speak evil of anyone but to be peaceful and gentle, showing true humility to everyone. {3:3} For we ourselves were once foolish, disobedient, and misled. We were slaves to many kinds of lusts and pleasures. Our lives were full of evil and envy, and we hated each other. {3:4} **But then God our Savior showed us his kindness and love.** {3:5} **He saved us, not because of the good things we did, but because of his mercy. He washed away our sins and gave us a new life through the Holy Spirit.** {3:6} He generously poured out the Spirit upon us through Jesus Christ our Savior. {3:7} Because of his grace, he declared us righteous and gave us confidence that we will inherit eternal life. {3:8} This is a trustworthy saying, and I want you to insist on these teachings so that all who believe in God will devote themselves to doing good. These teachings are good and beneficial for everyone. {3:9} But avoid foolish controversies, genealogies, quarrels, and fights about the law. They are useless and worthless. {3:10} If someone is causing divisions among you, give a first and second warning. After that, have nothing more to do with that person. {3:11} For people like that have turned away from the truth, and their own sins condemn them. {3:12} I am planning to send either Artemas or Tychicus to you. As soon as one of them arrives, do your best to join me at Nicopolis, for I have decided to stay there for the winter. {3:13} Do everything you can to help Zenas the lawyer and Apollos with their trip. See that they are given everything they need. {3:14} Our people must learn to do good by meeting the urgent needs of others; then they will not be unproductive. {3:15} All who are with me send greetings to you. Greet all who love us in the faith. Grace be with you all. Amen.

Philemon

{1:1} This letter is from Paul, who is currently in prison because of his faith in Jesus Christ, and Timothy, our brother. It's addressed to Philemon, whom we dearly love and who works alongside us. {1:2} It's also for our beloved sister Apphia, and Archippus, our fellow soldier in Christ, as well as the church that meets in your home. {1:3} We pray that you will experience God's grace and peace, which come from our Father God and the Lord Jesus Christ. {1:4} Philemon, I always thank God for you and mention you in my prayers. {1:5} I've heard about your love and faith in Jesus and how you treat all of God's people with kindness. {1:6} **I pray that your faith will be active in sharing what you have with others, so that you will understand all the good things we have in Christ.** {1:7} Your love has brought great joy and encouragement to God's people because you refresh their hearts. {1:8} Although I could command you to do what is right, I prefer to appeal to you out of love. {1:9} After all, I am an old man now and a prisoner of Jesus Christ. {1:10} So I appeal to you for my son Onesimus, who became a believer while I was in prison. {1:11} In the past, he was not very helpful to you, but now he is very helpful to both of us. {1:12} I am sending him back to you, and I ask that you welcome him as you would welcome me. {1:13} I would have liked to keep him with me so that he could help me in your place while I am in prison for preaching the Good News. {1:14} But I didn't want to do anything without your consent, so that your act of kindness would be voluntary and not forced. {1:15} *Maybe God allowed him to be separated from you for a little while so that you could have him back forever—* {1:16} *not as a slave anymore, but as much more than a slave, as a dear brother. He is especially dear to me, but how much more to you, both as a fellow man and as a brother in the Lord.* {1:17} So if you consider me your partner, welcome him as you would welcome me. {1:18} If he has done you any wrong or owes you anything, charge it to me. {1:19} I, Paul, am writing this with my own hand: I will repay it. And I won't mention that you owe me your very soul! {1:20} Yes, my brother, please do me this favor for the Lord's sake. Give me this encouragement in Christ. {1:21} I am confident as I write this letter because I know you will do what I ask and even more. {1:22} And please prepare a guest room for me, for I hope that God will answer your prayers and let me return to you soon. {1:23} Epaphras, my fellow prisoner in Christ Jesus, sends you his greetings. {1:24} So do Mark, Aristarchus, Demas, and Luke, my co-workers. {1:25} May the grace of our Lord Jesus Christ be with your spirit. Amen.

Hebrews

{1:1} Long ago, God spoke to our ancestors through various prophets in many different ways. {1:2} But now, in these last days, he has spoken to us through his Son. God appointed his Son to inherit everything, and through him, he created the universe. {1:3} The Son radiates God's own glory and expresses the very character of God. He sustains everything by the mighty power of his command. When he had cleansed us from our sins, he sat down in the place of honor at the right hand of the majestic God in heaven. {1:4} This shows that the Son is far greater than the angels, just as the name God gave him is greater than their names. {1:5} For God never said to any angel what he said to Jesus: "You are my Son. Today I have become your Father." God also said, "I will be his Father, and he will be my Son." {1:6} And when he brought his supreme Son into the world, God said, "Let all of God's angels worship him." {1:7} Regarding the angels, he says, "He sends his angels like the winds, his servants like flames of fire." {1:8} But to the Son he says, "Your throne, O God, endures forever and ever. You rule with a scepter of justice. {1:9} You love justice and hate evil. Therefore, O God, your God has anointed you, pouring out the oil of joy on you more than on anyone else." {1:10} He also says to the Son, "In the beginning, Lord, you laid the foundation of the earth and made the heavens with your hands. {1:11} They will perish, but you remain forever. They will wear out like old clothing. {1:12} You will fold them up like a cloak and discard them like old clothing. But you are always the same; you will live forever." {1:13} And God never said to any of the angels, "Sit in the place of honor at my right hand until I humble your enemies, making them a footstool under your feet." {1:14} Therefore, angels are only servants—spirits sent to care for people who will inherit salvation.

{2:1} So we must pay the most careful attention to what we have heard, so that we do not drift away. {2:2} For since the message spoken through angels was binding, and every violation and disobedience received its just punishment, {2:3} how shall we escape if we ignore so great a salvation? This salvation, which was first announced by the Lord, was confirmed to us by those who heard him. {2:4} God also testified to it by signs, wonders, and various miracles, and by gifts of the Holy Spirit distributed according to his will. {2:5} It is not to angels that he has subjected the world to come, about which we are speaking. {2:6} But there is a place where someone has testified: "What is mankind that you are mindful of them, a son of man that you care for him? {2:7} You made them a little lower than the angels; you crowned them with glory and honor {2:8} and put everything under their feet." In putting everything under them, God left nothing that is not subject to them. Yet at present we do not see everything subject to them. {2:9} But we do see Jesus, who was made lower than the angels for a little while, now crowned with glory and honor because he suffered death, so that by the grace of God he might taste death for everyone. {2:10} In bringing many sons and daughters to glory, it was fitting that God, for whom and through whom everything exists, should make the pioneer of their salvation perfect through what he suffered. {2:11} Both the one who makes people holy and those who are made holy are of the same family. So Jesus is not ashamed to call them brothers and sisters. {2:12} He says, "I will declare your name to my brothers and sisters; in the assembly I will sing your praises." {2:13} And again, "I will put my trust in him." And again he says, "Here am I, and the children God has given me." {2:14} Since the children have flesh and blood, he too shared in their humanity so that by his death he might break the power of him who holds the power of death—that is, the devil— {2:15} and free those who all their lives were held in slavery by their fear of death. {2:16} For surely it is not angels he helps, but Abraham's descendants. {2:17} For this reason he had to be made like them, fully human in every way, in order that he might become a merciful and faithful high priest in service to God, and that he might make atonement for the sins of the people. {2:18} Because he himself suffered when he was tempted, he is able to help those who are being tempted.

{3:1} So, my fellow believers, who share in the heavenly calling, fix your thoughts on Jesus, whom we acknowledge as our Apostle and High Priest. {3:2} He was faithful to the one who appointed him, just as Moses was faithful in all God's house. {3:3} Jesus has been found worthy of greater honor than Moses, just as the builder of a house has greater honor than the house itself. {3:4} For every house is built by someone, but God is the builder of everything. {3:5} Moses was faithful as a servant in all God's house, bearing witness to what would be spoken by God in the future. {3:6} But Christ is faithful as the Son over God's house. And we are his house, if indeed we hold firmly to our confidence and the hope in which we glory. {3:7} So, as the Holy Spirit says: "Today, if you hear his voice, {3:8} do not harden your hearts as you did in the rebellion, during the time of testing in the wilderness, {3:9} where your ancestors tested and tried me, though for forty years they saw what I did. {3:10} That is why I was angry with that generation; I said, 'Their hearts are always going astray, and they have not known my ways.' {3:11} So I declared on oath in my anger, 'They shall never enter my rest.'" {3:12} See to it, brothers and sisters, that none of you has a sinful, unbelieving heart that turns away from the living God. {3:13} But encourage one another daily, as long as it is called "Today," so that none of you may be hardened by sin's deceitfulness. {3:14} We have come to share in Christ, if indeed we hold our original conviction firmly to the very end. {3:15} As has just been said: "Today, if you hear his voice, do not harden your hearts as you did in the rebellion." {3:16} Who were they who heard and rebelled? Were they not all those Moses led out of Egypt? {3:17} And with whom was he angry for forty years? Was it not with those who sinned, whose bodies perished in the wilderness? {3:18} And to whom did God swear that they would never enter his rest if not to those who disobeyed? {3:19} So we see that they were not able to enter, because of their unbelief.

{4:1} So, let us be cautious, lest any of us appear to fall short of the promise of entering his rest. {4:2} For the good news was proclaimed to us just as to them. But the message they heard did not benefit them, because it was not united with faith in those who heard it. {4:3} For we who have believed enter that rest, as he has said, "So I declared on oath in my anger, 'They shall never enter my rest.'" And yet God's works have been finished since the creation of the world. {4:4} For somewhere he has spoken about the seventh day in these words: "On the seventh day God rested from all his works." {4:5} And again in the passage above he says, "They shall never enter my rest." {4:6} Therefore, since it still remains for some to enter that rest, and since those who formerly had the good news proclaimed to them did not go in because of their disobedience, {4:7} God again set a certain day, calling it "Today." This he did when a long time later he spoke through David, as in the passage already quoted: "Today, if you hear his voice, do not harden your hearts." {4:8} For if Joshua had given them rest, God would not have spoken later about another day. {4:9} There remains, then, a Sabbath-rest for the people of God; {4:10} for anyone who enters God's rest also rests from their works, just as God did from his. {4:11} Let us, therefore, make every effort to enter that rest, so that no one will perish by following their example of disobedience. {4:12} **For the word of God is alive and active. Sharper than any double-edged sword, it penetrates even to dividing soul and spirit, joints and marrow; it judges the thoughts and attitudes of the heart.** {4:13} Nothing in all creation is hidden from God's sight. Everything is uncovered and laid bare before the eyes of him to whom we must give account. {4:14} Therefore, since we have a great high priest who has ascended into heaven, Jesus the Son of God, let us hold firmly to the faith we profess. {4:15} For we do not have a high priest who is unable to empathize with our weaknesses, but we have one who has been tempted in every way, just as we are—yet he did not sin. {4:16} Let us then approach God's throne of grace with confidence, so that we may receive mercy and find grace to help us in our time of need.

{5:1} Every high priest is chosen from among the people and is appointed to represent them in matters related to God, to offer gifts and sacrifices for sins. {5:2} He is able to deal gently with those who are ignorant and going astray, since he himself is subject to weakness. {5:3} This is why he has to offer sacrifices for his own sins, as well as for the sins of the people. {5:4} And no one takes this honor on himself, but he receives it when called by God, just as Aaron was. {5:5} In the same way, Christ did not take on himself the glory of becoming a high priest. But God said to him, "You are my Son; today I have become your Father." {5:6} And he says in another place, "You are a priest forever, in the order of Melchizedek." {5:7} During the days of Jesus' life on earth, he offered up prayers and petitions with fervent cries and tears to the one who could save him from death, and he was heard because of his reverent submission. {5:8} Son though he was, he learned obedience from what he suffered {5:9} and, once made perfect, he became the source of eternal salvation for all who obey him {5:10} and was designated by God to be high priest in the order of Melchizedek. {5:11} We have much to say about this, but it is hard to make it clear to you because you no longer try to understand. {5:12} In fact, though by this time you ought to be teachers, you need someone to teach you the elementary truths of God's word all over again. You need milk, not solid food! {5:13} Anyone who lives on milk, being still an infant, is not acquainted with the teaching about righteousness. {5:14} But solid food is for the mature, who by constant use have trained themselves to distinguish good from evil.

{6:1} Therefore, let us move beyond the elementary teachings about Christ and be taken forward to maturity, not laying again the foundation of repentance from acts that lead to death, and of faith in God, {6:2} instruction about cleansing rites, the laying on of hands, the resurrection of the dead, and eternal judgment. {6:3} And God permitting, we will do so. {6:4} It is impossible for those who have once been enlightened, who have tasted the heavenly gift, who have shared in the Holy Spirit, {6:5} who have tasted the goodness of the word of God and the powers of the coming age {6:6} and who have fallen away, to be brought back to repentance. To their loss they are crucifying the Son of God all over again and subjecting him to public disgrace. {6:7} Land that drinks in the rain often falling on it and that produces a crop useful to those for whom it is farmed receives the blessing of God. {6:8} But land that produces thorns and thistles is worthless and is in danger of being cursed. In the end it will be burned. {6:9} Even though we speak like this, dear friends, we are convinced of better things in your case—the things that have to do with salvation. {6:10} God is not unjust; he will not forget your work and the love you have shown him as you have helped his people and continue to help them. {6:11} We want each of you to show this same diligence to the very end, so that what you hope for may be fully realized. {6:12} We do not want you to become lazy, but to imitate those who through faith and patience inherit what has been promised. {6:13} When God made his promise to Abraham, since there was no one greater for him to swear by, he swore by himself, {6:14} saying, "I will surely bless you and give you many descendants." {6:15} And so after waiting patiently, Abraham received what was promised. {6:16} People swear by someone greater than themselves, and the oath confirms what is said and puts an end to all arguments. {6:17} Because God wanted to make the unchanging nature of his purpose very clear to the heirs of what was promised, he confirmed it with an oath. {6:18} God did this so that, by two unchangeable things in which it is impossible for God to lie, we who have fled to take hold of the hope set before us may be greatly encouraged. {6:19} We have this hope as an anchor for the soul, firm and secure. It enters the inner sanctuary behind the curtain, {6:20} where our forerunner, Jesus, has entered on our behalf. He has become a high priest forever, in the order of Melchizedek.

{7:1} This Melchizedek was king of Salem and priest of God Most High. He met Abraham returning from the defeat of the kings and blessed him, {7:2} and Abraham gave him a tenth of everything. First, the name Melchizedek means "king of righteousness"; then also, "king of Salem" means "king of peace." {7:3} Without father or mother, without genealogy, without beginning of days or end of life, resembling the Son of God, he remains a priest forever. {7:4} Just think how great he was: Even the patriarch Abraham gave him a tenth of the plunder! {7:5} Now the law requires the descendants of Levi who become priests to collect a tenth from the people—that is, from their fellow Israelites—even though they also are descended from Abraham. {7:6} This man, however, did not trace his descent from Levi, yet he collected a tenth from Abraham and blessed him who had the promises. {7:7} And without doubt the lesser is blessed by the greater. {7:8} In one case, the tenth is collected by people who die; but in the other case, by him who is declared to be living. {7:9} One might even say that Levi, who collects the tenth, paid the tenth through Abraham, {7:10} because when Melchizedek met Abraham, Levi was still in the body of his ancestor. {7:11} If perfection could have been attained through the Levitical priesthood—and indeed the law given to the people established that priesthood—why was there still need for another priest to come, one in the order of Melchizedek, not in the order of Aaron? {7:12} For when the priesthood is changed, the law must be changed also. {7:13} He of whom these things are said belonged to a different tribe, and no one from that tribe has ever served at the altar. {7:14} For it is clear that our Lord descended from Judah, and in regard to that tribe Moses said nothing about priests. {7:15} And what we have said is even more clear if another priest like Melchizedek appears, {7:16} one who has become a priest not on the basis of a regulation as to his ancestry but on the basis of the power of an indestructible life. {7:17} For it is declared: "You are a priest forever, in the order of Melchizedek."

{7:18} The former regulation is set aside because it was weak and useless {7:19} (for the law made nothing perfect), and a better hope is introduced, by which we draw near to God. {7:20} And it was not without an oath! Others became priests without any oath, {7:21} but he became a priest with an oath when God said to him: "The Lord has sworn and will not change his mind: 'You are a priest forever.'" {7:22} Because of this oath, Jesus has become the guarantor of a better covenant. {7:23} Now there have been many of those priests, since death prevented them from continuing in office; {7:24} but because Jesus lives forever, he has a permanent priesthood. {7:25} Therefore he is able to save completely those who come to God through him, because he always lives to intercede for them. {7:26} Such a high priest truly meets our need—one who is holy, blameless, pure, set apart from sinners, exalted above the heavens. {7:27} Unlike the other high priests, he does not need to offer sacrifices day after day, first for his own sins, and then for the sins of the people. He sacrificed for their sins once for all when he offered himself. {7:28} For the law appoints as high priests men in all their weakness; but the oath, which came after the law, appointed the Son, who has been made perfect forever.

{8:1} So here is the main point: We have a high priest who sits in the place of honor beside the throne of the majestic God in the heavens. {8:2} There he ministers in the heavenly Tabernacle, the true place of worship that was built by the Lord and not by human hands. {8:3} And since every high priest is required to offer gifts and sacrifices, our High Priest must make an offering, too. {8:4} If he were here on earth, he would not even be a priest, since there already are priests who offer the gifts required by the law. {8:5} They serve in a system of worship that is only a copy, a shadow of the real one in heaven. For when Moses was getting ready to build the Tabernacle, God gave him this warning: "Be sure that you make everything according to the pattern I have shown you here on the mountain." {8:6} But now Jesus, our High Priest, has been given a ministry that is far superior to the old priesthood, for he is the one who mediates for us a far better covenant with God, based on better promises. {8:7} If the first covenant had been faultless, there would have been no need for a second covenant to replace it. {8:8} But when God found fault with the people, he said: "The day is coming, says the Lord, when I will make a new covenant with the people of Israel and Judah. {8:9} This covenant will not be like the one I made with their ancestors when I took them by the hand and led them out of the land of Egypt. They did not remain faithful to my covenant, so I turned my back on them, says the Lord. {8:10} But this is the new covenant I will make with the people of Israel on that day, says the Lord: I will put my laws in their minds, and I will write them on their hearts. I will be their God, and they will be my people. {8:11} And they will not need to teach their neighbors,nor will they need to teach their relatives, saying, 'You should know the Lord.' For everyone, from the least to the greatest, will know me already {8:12} And I will forgive their wickedness, and I will never again remember their sins." {8:13} When God speaks of a "new" covenant, it means he has made the first one obsolete. It is now out of date and will soon disappear.

{9:1} The first covenant had regulations for worship and a worldly sanctuary. {9:2} There was a tabernacle constructed, the first one, containing the lampstand, the table, and the consecrated bread. This part was called the sanctuary. {9:3} Behind the second curtain was another section called the Most Holy Place, {9:4} which contained the golden altar of incense and the Ark of the Covenant covered with gold. Inside the Ark were the golden pot of manna, Aaron's staff that had budded, and the stone tablets of the covenant. {9:5} Above the Ark were the cherubim of glory overshadowing the atonement cover. We won't discuss these details now. {9:6} With these arrangements, the priests regularly entered the first section of the tabernacle to perform their duties. {9:7} But only the high priest entered the inner room, and that just once a year, and never without blood, which he offered for himself and for the sins the people had committed in ignorance. {9:8} The Holy Spirit was indicating that the way into the Most Holy Place had not yet been disclosed while the first tabernacle was still functioning. {9:9} This is an illustration for the present time, showing that the gifts and sacrifices being offered were not able to clear the conscience of the worshiper. {9:10} These regulations were only about food and drink and various ceremonial washings—external regulations imposed until the time of the new order. {9:11} But when Christ came as high priest of the good things that are now already here, he went through the greater and more perfect tabernacle that is not made with human hands, that is to say, is not a part of this creation. {9:12} He did not enter by means of the blood of goats and calves; but he entered the Most Holy Place once for all by his own blood, thus obtaining eternal redemption. {9:13} The blood of goats and bulls and the ashes of a heifer sprinkled on those who are ceremonially unclean sanctify them so that they are outwardly clean.

{9:14} How much more, then, will the blood of Christ, who through the eternal Spirit offered himself unblemished to God, cleanse our consciences from acts that lead to death, so that we may serve the living God! {9:15} For this reason Christ is the mediator of a new covenant, that those who are called may receive the promised eternal inheritance—now that he has died as a ransom to set them free from the sins committed under the first covenant. {9:16} In the case of a will, it is necessary to prove the death of the one who made it, {9:17} because a will is in force only when somebody has died; it never takes effect while the one who made it is living. {9:18} This is why even the first covenant was not put into effect without blood. {9:19} When Moses had proclaimed every command of the law to all the people, he took the blood of calves, together with water, scarlet wool and branches of hyssop, and sprinkled the scroll and all the people. {9:20} He said, "This is the blood of the covenant, which God has commanded you to keep." {9:21} In the same way, he sprinkled with the blood both the tabernacle and everything used in its ceremonies. {9:22} In fact, the law requires that nearly everything be cleansed with blood, and without the shedding of blood there is no forgiveness. {9:23} It was necessary, then, for the copies of the heavenly things to be purified with these sacrifices, but the heavenly things themselves with better sacrifices than these. {9:24} For Christ did not enter a sanctuary made with human hands that was only a copy of the true one; he entered heaven itself, now to appear for us in God's presence. {9:25} Nor did he enter heaven to offer himself again and again, the way the high priest enters the Most Holy Place every year with blood that is not his own. {9:26} Otherwise Christ would have had to suffer many times since the creation of the world. But he has appeared once for all at the culmination of the ages to do away with sin by the sacrifice of himself. {9:27} Just as people are destined to die once, and after that to face judgment, {9:28} so Christ was sacrificed once to take away the sins of many; and he will appear a second time, not to bear sin, but to bring salvation to those who are waiting for him.

{10:1} The law was like a shadow of the good things to come, not the reality itself. It could never make those who approached God perfect by the same sacrifices they continually offered year after year. {10:2} If it could, would they not have stopped being offered? For the worshipers would have been cleansed once for all, and their consciences would no longer have felt guilty for their sins. {10:3} But instead, those sacrifices are an annual reminder of sins. {10:4} It's impossible for the blood of bulls and goats to take away sins. {10:5} Therefore, when Christ came into the world, he said: "Sacrifice and offering you did not desire, but a body you prepared for me; {10:6} with burnt offerings and sin offerings you were not pleased. {10:7} Then I said, 'Here I am—it is written about me in the scroll— I have come to do your will, my God.'" {10:8} First he said, "Sacrifices and offerings, burnt offerings and sin offerings you did not desire, nor were you pleased with them"—though they were offered in accordance with the law. {10:9} Then he said, "Here I am, I have come to do your will." He sets aside the first to establish the second. {10:10} And by that will, we have been made holy through the sacrifice of the body of Jesus Christ once for all. {10:11} Day after day every priest stands and performs his religious duties; again and again he offers the same sacrifices, which can never take away sins. {10:12} But when this priest had offered for all time one sacrifice for sins, he sat down at the right hand of God, {10:13} and since that time he waits for his enemies to be made his footstool. {10:14} For by one sacrifice he has made perfect forever those who are being made holy. {10:15} The Holy Spirit also testifies to us about this. First he says: {10:16} "This is the covenant I will make with them after that time, says the Lord. I will put my laws in their hearts, and I will write them on their minds." {10:17} Then he adds: "Their sins and lawless acts I will remember no more." {10:18} And where these have been forgiven, sacrifice for sin is no longer necessary. {10:19} Therefore, brothers and sisters, since we have confidence to enter the Most Holy Place by the blood of Jesus, {10:20} by a new and living way opened for us through the curtain, that is, his body, {10:21} and since we have a great priest over the house of God, {10:22} let us draw near to God with a sincere heart and with the full assurance that faith brings, having our hearts sprinkled to cleanse us from a guilty conscience and having our bodies washed with pure water. {10:23} Let us hold unswervingly to the hope we profess, for he who promised is faithful. {10:24} And let us consider how we may spur one another on toward love and good deeds, {10:25} not giving up meeting together, as some are in the habit of doing, but encouraging one another—and all the more as you see the Day approaching. {10:26} If we deliberately keep on sinning after we have received the knowledge of the truth, no sacrifice for sins is left, {10:27} but only a fearful expectation of judgment and of raging fire that will consume the enemies of God. {10:28} Anyone who rejected the law of Moses died without mercy on the testimony of two or three witnesses. {10:29} How much more severely do you think someone deserves to be punished who has trampled the Son of God underfoot, who has treated as an unholy thing the blood of the covenant that sanctified them, and who has insulted the Spirit of grace? {10:30} For we know him who said, "It is mine to avenge; I will repay," and again, "The Lord will judge his people." {10:31} It is a dreadful thing to fall into the hands of the living God. {10:32} Remember those earlier days after you had received the light, when you endured a great conflict full of suffering. {10:33} Sometimes you were publicly exposed to insult and persecution; at other times you stood side by side with those who were so treated. {10:34} You suffered along with those in prison and joyfully accepted the confiscation of your property, because you knew that you yourselves had better and lasting possessions. {10:35} So do not throw away your confidence; it will be richly rewarded. {10:36} You need to persevere so that when you have done the will of God, you will receive what he has promised. {10:37} For, "In just a little while, he who is coming will come and will not delay." {10:38} And, "But my righteous one will live by faith. And I take no pleasure in the one who shrinks back." {10:39} But we do not belong to those who shrink back and are destroyed, but to those who have faith and are saved.

{11:1} **Faith is being sure of what we hope for and certain of what we do not see.** {11:2} This is what the ancients were commended for. {11:3} By faith we understand that the universe was formed at God's command, so that what is seen was not made out of what was visible. {11:4} By faith Abel brought God a better offering than Cain did. By faith he was commended as righteous, when God spoke well of his offerings. And by faith Abel still speaks, even though he is dead. {11:5} By faith Enoch was taken from this life, so that he did not experience death: "He could not be found, because God had taken him away." For before he was taken, he was commended as one who pleased God. {11:6} And without faith it is impossible to please God, because anyone who comes to him must believe that he exists and that he rewards those who earnestly seek him. {11:7} By faith Noah, when warned about things not yet seen, in holy fear built an ark to save his family. By his faith he condemned the world and became heir of the righteousness that is in keeping with faith. {11:8} By faith Abraham, when called to go to a place he would later receive as his inheritance, obeyed and went, even though he did not know where he was going. {11:9} By faith he made his home in the promised land like a stranger in a foreign country; he lived in tents, as did Isaac and Jacob, who were heirs with him of the same promise. {11:10} For he was looking forward to the city with foundations, whose architect and builder is God. {11:11} By faith Sarah, even though she was barren and past the age, was enabled to bear children because she considered him faithful who had made the promise. {11:12} And so from this one man, and he as good as dead, came descendants as numerous as the stars in the sky and as countless as the sand on the seashore. {11:13} All these people were still living by faith when they died. They did not receive the things promised; they only saw them and welcomed them from a distance, admitting that they were foreigners and strangers on earth. {11:14} People who say such things show that they are looking for a country of their own. {11:15} If they had been thinking of the country they had left, they would have had the opportunity to return. {11:16} Instead, they were longing for a better country—a heavenly one. Therefore God is not ashamed to be called their God, for he has prepared a city for them. {11:17} By faith Abraham, when God tested him, offered Isaac as a sacrifice. He who had embraced the promises was about to sacrifice his one and only son, {11:18} even though God had said to him, "It is through Isaac that your offspring will be reckoned." {11:19} Abraham reasoned that God could even raise the dead, and so in a manner of speaking he did receive Isaac back from death. {11:20} By faith Isaac blessed Jacob and Esau in regard to their future. {11:21} By faith Jacob, when he was dying, blessed each of Joseph's sons, and worshiped as he leaned on the top of his staff. {11:22} By faith Joseph, when his end was near, spoke about the exodus of the Israelites and gave instructions concerning the burial of his bones. {11:23} By faith Moses' parents hid him for three months after he was born, because they saw he was no ordinary child, and they were not afraid of the king's edict. {11:24} By faith Moses, when he had grown up, refused to be known as the son of Pharaoh's daughter. {11:25} He chose to be mistreated along with the people of God rather than to enjoy the fleeting pleasures of sin.{11:26} Moses considered the disgrace for the sake of Christ as greater wealth than the treasures of Egypt, because he was looking ahead to his reward. {11:27} By faith he left Egypt, not fearing the king's anger; he persevered because he saw him who is invisible. {11:28} By faith he kept the Passover and the application of blood, so that the destroyer of the firstborn would not touch the firstborn of Israel. {11:29} By faith the people passed through the Red Sea as on dry land; but when the Egyptians tried to do so, they were drowned. {11:30} By faith the walls of Jericho fell, after the army had marched around them for seven days. {11:31} By faith the prostitute Rahab, because she welcomed the spies, was not killed with those who were disobedient. {11:32} And what more shall I say? I do not have time to tell about Gideon, Barak,

Samson and Jephthah, about David and Samuel and the prophets, {11:33} who through faith conquered kingdoms, administered justice, and gained what was promised; who shut the mouths of lions, {11:34} quenched the fury of the flames, and escaped the edge of the sword; whose weakness was turned to strength; and who became powerful in battle and routed foreign armies. {11:35} Women received back their dead, raised to life again. There were others who were tortured, refusing to be released so that they might gain an even better resurrection. {11:36} Some faced jeers and flogging, and even chains and imprisonment. {11:37} They were put to death by stoning; they were sawed in two; they were killed by the sword. They went about in sheepskins and goatskins, destitute, persecuted and mistreated— {11:38} the world was not worthy of them. They wandered in deserts and mountains, living in caves and in holes in the ground. {11:39} These were all commended for their faith, yet none of them received what had been promised, {11:40} since God had planned something better for us so that only together with us would they be made perfect.

{12:1} Since we are surrounded by such a great cloud of witnesses, let us throw off everything that hinders and the sin that so easily entangles. And let us run with perseverance the race marked out for us, {12:2} fixing our eyes on Jesus, the pioneer and perfecter of faith. For the joy set before him he endured the cross, scorning its shame, and sat down at the right hand of the throne of God. {12:3} Consider him who endured such opposition from sinners, so that you will not grow weary and lose heart. {12:4} In your struggle against sin, you have not yet resisted to the point of shedding your blood. {12:5} And have you completely forgotten this word of encouragement that addresses you as a father addresses his son? It says, "My son, do not make light of the Lord's discipline, and do not lose heart when he rebukes you, {12:6} because the Lord disciplines the one he loves, and he chastens everyone he accepts as his son." {12:7} Endure hardship as discipline; God is treating you as his children. For what children are not disciplined by their father? {12:8} If you are not disciplined—and everyone undergoes discipline—then you are not legitimate, not true sons and daughters at all. {12:9} Moreover, we have all had human fathers who disciplined us and we respected them for it. How much more should we submit to the Father of spirits and live! {12:10} They disciplined us for a little while as they thought best; but God disciplines us for our good, in order that we may share in his holiness. {12:11} No discipline seems pleasant at the time, but painful. Later on, however, it produces a harvest of righteousness and peace for those who have been trained by it. {12:12} Therefore, strengthen your feeble arms and weak knees. {12:13} "Make level paths for your feet," so that the lame may not be disabled, but rather healed. {12:14} Make every effort to live in peace with everyone and to be holy; without holiness no one will see the Lord. {12:15} See to it that no one falls short of the grace of God and that no bitter root grows up to cause trouble and defile many. {12:16} See that no one is sexually immoral, or is godless like Esau, who for a single meal sold his inheritance rights as the oldest son. {12:17} Afterward, as you know, when he wanted to inherit this blessing, he was rejected. Even though he sought the blessing with tears, he could not change what he had done. {12:18} You have not come to a mountain that can be touched and that is burning with fire; to darkness, gloom and storm; {12:19} to a trumpet blast or to such a voice speaking words that those who heard it begged that no further word be spoken to them, {12:20} because they could not bear what was commanded: "If even an animal touches the mountain, it must be stoned to death." {12:21} The sight was so terrifying that Moses said, "I am trembling with fear." {12:22} But you have come to Mount Zion, to the city of the living God, the heavenly Jerusalem. You have come to thousands upon thousands of angels in joyful assembly, {12:23} to the church of the firstborn, whose names are written in heaven. You have come to God, the Judge of all, to the spirits of the righteous made perfect, {12:24} to Jesus the mediator of a new covenant, and to the sprinkled blood that speaks a better word than the blood of Abel. {12:25} See to it that you do not refuse him who speaks. If they did not escape when they refused him who warned them on earth, how much less will we, if we turn away from him who warns us from heaven? {12:26} At that time his voice shook the earth, but now he has promised, "Once more I will shake not only the earth but also the heavens." {12:27} The words "once more" indicate the removal of what can be shaken—that is, created things—so that what cannot be shaken may remain. {12:28} Therefore, since we are receiving a kingdom that cannot be shaken, let us be thankful, and so worship God acceptably with reverence and awe, {12:29} for our "God is a consuming fire."

{13:1} Keep showing love to each other like brothers and sisters. {13:2} Don't forget to welcome strangers, for some who have done this have welcomed angels without realizing it. {13:3} Remember those in prison, as if you were there yourself. Remember also those who are suffering, as if you were going through their pain. {13:4} Marriage should be honored by all, and the marriage bed kept pure, for God will judge the adulterer and all the sexually immoral. {13:5} Keep your lives free from the love of money and be content with what you have, because God has said, "Never will I leave you; never will I forsake you." {13:6} So we say with confidence, "The Lord is my helper; I will not be afraid. What can mere mortals do to me?" {13:7} Remember your leaders, who spoke the word of God to you. Consider the outcome of their way of life and imitate their faith. {13:8} Jesus Christ is the same yesterday and today and forever {13:9} Do not be carried away by all kinds of strange teachings. It is good for our hearts to be strengthened by grace, not by eating ceremonial foods, which is of no benefit to those who do so. {13:10} We have an altar from which those who minister at the tabernacle have no right to eat. {13:11} The high priest carries the blood of animals into the Most Holy Place as a sin offering, but the bodies are burned outside the camp. {13:12} And so Jesus also suffered outside the city gate to make the people holy through his own blood. {13:13} Let us, then, go to him outside the camp, bearing the disgrace he bore. {13:14} For here we do not have an enduring city, but we are looking for the city that is to come. {13:15} Through Jesus, therefore, let us continually offer to God a sacrifice of praise—the fruit of lips that openly profess his name. {13:16} And do not forget to do good and to share with others, for with such sacrifices God is pleased. {13:17} Have confidence in your leaders and submit to their authority, because they keep watch over you as those who must give an account. Do this so that their work will be a joy, not a burden, for that would be of no benefit to you. {13:18} Pray for us. We are sure that we have a clear conscience and desire to live honorably in every way. {13:19} I particularly urge you to pray so that I may be restored to you soon. {13:20} Now may the God of peace, who through the blood of the eternal covenant brought back from the dead our Lord Jesus, that great Shepherd of the sheep, {13:21} equip you with everything good for doing his will, and may he work in us what is pleasing to him, through Jesus Christ, to whom be glory for ever and ever. Amen. {13:22} Brothers and sisters, I urge you to bear with my word of exhortation, for in fact I have written to you quite briefly. {13:23} I want you to know that our brother Timothy has been released. If he arrives soon, I will come with him to see you. {13:24} Greet all your leaders and all the Lord's people. Those from Italy send you their greetings.

James

{1:1} James, a servant of God and of the Lord Jesus Christ, to the twelve tribes scattered among the nations: Greetings. {1:2} My brothers and sisters, consider it pure joy whenever you face trials of many kinds, {1:3} because you know that the testing of your faith produces perseverance. {1:4} Let perseverance finish its work so that you may be mature and complete, not lacking anything. {1:5} *If any of you lacks wisdom, you should ask God, who gives generously to all without finding fault, and it will be given to you.* {1:6} But when you ask, you must believe and not doubt, because the one who doubts is like a wave of the sea, blown and tossed by the wind. {1:7} That person should not expect to receive anything from the Lord. {1:8} Such a person is double-minded and unstable in all they do. {1:9} Believers in humble circumstances ought to take pride in their high position. {1:10} But the rich should take pride in their humiliation—since they will pass away like a wildflower. {1:11} For the sun rises with scorching heat and withers the plant; its blossom falls and its beauty is destroyed. In the same way, the rich will fade away even while they go about their business. {1:12} Blessed is the one who perseveres under trial because, having stood the test, that person will receive the crown of life that the Lord has promised to those who love him. {1:13} When tempted, no one should say, "God is tempting me." For God cannot be tempted by evil, nor does he tempt anyone; {1:14} but each person is tempted when they are dragged away by their own evil desire and enticed. {1:15} Then, after desire has conceived, it gives birth to sin; and sin, when it is full-grown, gives birth to death. {1:16} Don't be deceived, my dear brothers and sisters. {1:17} Every good and perfect gift is from above, coming down from the Father of the heavenly lights, who does not change like shifting shadows. {1:18} He chose to give us birth through the word of truth, that we might be a kind of firstfruits of all he created. {1:19} My dear brothers and sisters, take note of this: Everyone should be quick to listen, slow to speak and slow to become angry, {1:20} because human anger does not produce the righteousness that God desires. {1:21} Therefore, get rid of all moral filth and the evil that is so prevalent, and humbly accept the word planted in you, which can save you. {1:22} Do not merely listen to the word, and so deceive yourselves. Do what it says. {1:23} Anyone who listens to the word but does not do what it says is like someone who looks at his face in a mirror {1:24} and, after looking at himself, goes away and immediately forgets what he looks like. {1:25} But whoever looks intently into the perfect law that gives freedom, and continues in it—not forgetting what they have heard, but doing it—they will be blessed in what they do. {1:26} Those who consider themselves religious and yet do not keep a tight rein on their tongues deceive themselves, and their religion is worthless. {1:27} Religion that God our Father accepts as pure and faultless is this: to look after orphans and widows in their distress and to keep oneself from being polluted by the world.

{2:1} My brothers and sisters, do not show favoritism as you hold on to the faith in our glorious Lord Jesus Christ. {2:2} Suppose a man comes into your meeting wearing a gold ring and fine clothes, and a poor man in filthy old clothes also comes in. {2:3} If you show special attention to the man wearing fine clothes and say, "Here's a good seat for you," but say to the poor man, "You stand there" or "Sit on the floor by my feet," {2:4} have you not discriminated among yourselves and become judges with evil thoughts? {2:5} Listen, my dear brothers and sisters: Has not God chosen those who are poor in the eyes of the world to be rich in faith and to inherit the kingdom he promised those who love him? {2:6} But you have dishonored the poor. Is it not the rich who are exploiting you? Are they not the ones who are dragging you into court? {2:7} Are they not the ones who are blaspheming the noble name of him to whom you belong? {2:8} If you really keep the royal law found in Scripture, "Love your neighbor as yourself," you are doing right. {2:9} But if you show favoritism, you sin and are convicted by the law as lawbreakers. {2:10} For whoever keeps the whole law and yet stumbles at just one point is guilty of breaking all of it. {2:11} For he who said, "You shall not commit adultery," also said, "You shall not murder." If you do not commit adultery but do commit murder, you have become a lawbreaker. {2:12} Speak and act as those who are going to be judged by the law that gives freedom, {2:13} because judgment without mercy will be shown to anyone who has not been merciful. Mercy triumphs over judgment. {2:14} What good is it, my brothers and sisters, if someone claims to have faith but has no deeds? Can such faith save them? {2:15} Suppose a brother or a sister is without clothes and daily food. {2:16} If one of you says to them, "Go in peace; keep warm and well fed," but does nothing about their physical needs, what good is it? {2:17} In the same way, faith by itself, if it is not accompanied by action, is dead. {2:18} But someone will say, "You have faith; I have deeds." Show me your faith without deeds, and I will show you my faith by my deeds. {2:19} You believe that there is one God. Good! Even the demons believe that—and shudder. {2:20} You foolish person, do you want evidence that faith without deeds is useless? {2:21} Was not our father Abraham considered righteous for what he did when he offered his son Isaac on the altar? {2:22} You see that his faith and his actions were working together, and his faith was made complete by what he did. {2:23} And the scripture was fulfilled that says, "Abraham believed God, and it was credited to him as righteousness," and he was called God's friend. {2:24} You see that a person is considered righteous by what they do and not by faith alone. {2:25} In the same way, was not even Rahab the prostitute considered righteous for what she did when she gave lodging to the spies and sent them off in a different direction? {2:26} *As the body without the spirit is dead, so faith without deeds is dead.*

{3:1} My brothers and sisters, not many of you should become teachers, because you know that we who teach will be judged more strictly. {3:2} We all stumble in many ways. Anyone who is never at fault in what they say is perfect, able to keep their whole body in check. {3:3} When we put bits into the mouths of horses to make them obey us, we can turn the whole animal. {3:4} Or take ships as an example. Although they are so large and are driven by strong winds, they are steered by a very small rudder wherever the pilot wants to go. {3:5} Likewise, the tongue is a small part of the body, but it makes great boasts. Consider what a great forest is set on fire by a small spark. {3:6} The tongue also is a fire, a world of evil among the parts of the body. It corrupts the whole body, sets the whole course of one's life on fire, and is itself set on fire by hell. {3:7} All kinds of animals, birds, reptiles and sea creatures are being tamed and have been tamed by mankind, {3:8} but no human being can tame the tongue. It is a restless evil, full of deadly poison. {3:9} With the tongue we praise our Lord and Father, and with it we curse human beings, who have been made in God's likeness. {3:10} Out of the same mouth come praise and cursing. My brothers and sisters, this should not be. {3:11} Can both fresh water and salt water flow from the same spring? {3:12} My brothers and sisters, can a fig tree bear olives, or a grapevine bear figs? Neither can a salt spring produce fresh water. {3:13} Who is wise and understanding among you? Let them show it by their good life, by deeds done in the humility that comes from wisdom. {3:14} But if you harbor bitter envy and selfish ambition in your hearts, do not boast about it or deny the truth. {3:15} Such "wisdom" does not come down from heaven but is earthly, unspiritual, demonic. {3:16} For where you have envy and selfish ambition, there you find disorder and every evil practice. {3:17} But the wisdom that comes from heaven is first of all pure; then peace-loving, considerate, submissive, full of mercy and good fruit, impartial and sincere. {3:18} Peacemakers who sow in peace reap a harvest of righteousness.

{4:1} Where do wars and fights among you come from? Do they not come from your desires for pleasure that war in your members? {4:2} You lust and do not have. You murder and covet and cannot obtain. You fight and war. Yet you do not have because you do not ask. {4:3} You ask and do not receive, because you ask amiss, that you may spend it on your pleasures. {4:4} Adulterers and adulteresses! Do you not know that friendship with the world is enmity with God? Whoever therefore wants to be a friend of the world makes himself an enemy of God. {4:5} Or do you think that the Scripture says in vain, "The Spirit who dwells in us yearns jealously"? {4:6} But He gives more grace. Therefore He says: "God resists the proud, but gives grace to the humble." {4:7} Therefore submit to God. Resist the devil and he will flee from you. {4:8} Draw near to God and He will draw near to you. Cleanse your hands, you sinners; and purify your hearts, you double-minded. {4:9} Lament and mourn and weep! Let your laughter be turned to mourning and your joy to gloom. {4:10} Humble yourselves in the sight of the Lord, and He will lift you up. {4:11} Do not speak evil of one another, brethren. He who speaks evil of a brother and judges his brother, speaks evil of the law and judges the law. But if you judge the law, you are not a doer of the law but a judge. {4:12} There is one Lawgiver, who is able to save and to destroy. Who are you to judge another? {4:13} Come now, you who say, "Today or tomorrow we will go to such and such a city, spend a year there, buy and sell, and make a profit"; {4:14} whereas you do not know what will happen tomorrow. For what is your life? It is even a vapor that appears for a little time and then vanishes away. {4:15} Instead you ought to say, "If the Lord wills, we shall live and do this or that." {4:16} But now you boast in your arrogance. All such boasting is evil. {4:17} Therefore, to him who knows to do good and does not do it, to him it is sin.

{5:1} Come now, you rich, weep and howl for your miseries that are coming upon you! {5:2} Your riches are corrupted, and your garments are moth-eaten. {5:3} Your gold and silver are corroded, and their corrosion will be a witness against you and will eat your flesh like fire. You have heaped up treasure in the last days. {5:4} Indeed the wages of the laborers who mowed your fields, which you kept back by fraud, cry out; and the cries of the reapers have reached the ears of the Lord of Sabaoth. {5:5} You have lived on the earth in pleasure and luxury; you have fattened your hearts as in a day of slaughter. {5:6} You have condemned, you have murdered the just; he does not resist you. {5:7} Therefore be patient, brethren, until the coming of the Lord. See how the farmer waits for the precious fruit of the earth, waiting patiently for it until it receives the early and latter rain. {5:8} You also be patient. Establish your hearts, for the coming of the Lord is at hand. {5:9} Do not grumble against one another, brethren, lest you be condemned. Behold, the Judge is standing at the door! {5:10} My brethren, take the prophets, who spoke in the name of the Lord, as an example of suffering and patience. {5:11} Indeed we count them blessed who endure. You have heard of the perseverance of Job and seen the end intended by the Lord—that the Lord is very compassionate and merciful. {5:12} But above all, my brethren, do not swear, either by heaven or by earth or with any other oath. But let your "Yes" be "Yes," and your "No," "No," lest you fall into judgment. {5:13} Is anyone among you suffering? Let him pray. Is anyone cheerful? Let him sing psalms. {5:14} Is anyone among you sick? Let him call for the elders of the church, and let them pray over him, anointing him with oil in the name of the Lord. {5:15} And the prayer of faith will save the sick, and the Lord will raise him up. And if he has committed sins, he will be forgiven. {5:16} Confess your trespasses to one another, and pray for one another, that you may be healed. The effective, fervent prayer of a righteous man avails much. {5:17} Elijah was a man with a nature like ours, and he prayed earnestly that it would not rain; and it did not rain on the land for three years and six months. {5:18} And he prayed again, and the heaven gave rain, and the earth produced its fruit. {5:19} Brethren, if anyone among you wanders from the truth, and someone turns him back, {5:20} let him know that he who turns a sinner from the error of his way will save a soul from death and cover a multitude of sins.

1 Peter

{1:1} Peter, an apostle of Jesus Christ, to the strangers scattered throughout Pontus, Galatia, Cappadocia, Asia, and Bithynia, {1:2} Chosen according to the foreknowledge of God the Father, through sanctification of the Spirit, for obedience and sprinkling of the blood of Jesus Christ: Grace to you, and peace, be multiplied. {1:3} Blessed be the God and Father of our Lord Jesus Christ, who, according to his abundant mercy, has given us a new birth into a living hope through the resurrection of Jesus Christ from the dead, {1:4} To an inheritance incorruptible, undefiled, and unfading, reserved in heaven for you, {1:5} Who are kept by the power of God through faith for salvation ready to be revealed in the last time. {1:6} In this you greatly rejoice, though now for a little while, if need be, you have been grieved by various trials, {1:7} That the genuineness of your faith, much more precious than gold that perishes, though it is tested by fire, may be found to praise, honor, and glory at the revelation of Jesus Christ, {1:8} Whom having not seen, you love; in whom, though now you do not see him, yet believing, you rejoice with joy unspeakable and full of glory, {1:9} Receiving the end of your faith, the salvation of your souls. {1:10} Of which salvation the prophets have inquired and searched diligently, who prophesied of the grace that should come to you: {1:11} Searching what, or what manner of time the Spirit of Christ which was in them did signify, when it testified beforehand the sufferings of Christ, and the glory that should follow. {1:12} To whom it was revealed, that not to themselves, but to us they ministered the things, which are now reported to you by those who have preached the gospel to you with the Holy Ghost sent down from heaven; which things the angels desire to look into. {1:13} Therefore, gird up the loins of your mind, be sober, and hope to the end for the grace that is to be brought to you at the revelation of Jesus Christ; {1:14} As obedient children, not fashioning yourselves according to the former lusts in your ignorance: {1:15} But as he who has called you is holy, so be holy in all manner of conversation; {1:16} Because it is written, "Be ye holy; for I am holy." {1:17} And if you call on the Father, who without respect of persons judges according to every man's work, pass the time of your sojourning here in fear: {1:18} For as much as you know that you were not redeemed with corruptible things, such as silver and gold, from your vain conversation received by tradition from your fathers; {1:19} But with the precious blood of Christ, as of a lamb without blemish and without spot: {1:20} **Who was verily foreordained before the foundation of the world, but was manifest in these last times for you,** {1:21} **Who by him do believe in God, that raised him up from the dead, and gave him glory; that your faith and hope might be in God** {1:22} Seeing you have purified your souls in obeying the truth through the Spirit to unfeigned love of the brethren, love one another fervently with a pure heart, {1:23} Being born again, not of corruptible seed, but of incorruptible, by the word of God, which lives and abides forever. {1:24} For all flesh is as grass, and all the glory of man as the flower of grass. The grass withers, and its flower falls away: {1:25} But the word of the Lord endures forever. And this is the word which by the gospel is preached to you.

{2:1} Therefore, rid yourselves of all malice, deceit, hypocrisy, envy, and slander of every kind. {2:2} Like newborn babies, crave pure spiritual milk, so that by it you may grow up in your salvation, {2:3} now that you have tasted that the Lord is good. {2:4} As you come to him, the living Stone—rejected by humans but chosen by God and precious to him— {2:5} you also, like living stones, are being built into a spiritual house to be a holy priesthood, offering spiritual sacrifices acceptable to God through Jesus Christ. {2:6} For in Scripture it says: "See, I lay a stone in Zion, a chosen and precious cornerstone, and the one who trusts in him will never be put to shame." {2:7} Now to you who believe, this stone is precious. But to those who do not believe, "The stone the builders rejected has become the cornerstone," {2:8} and, "A stone that causes people to stumble and a rock that makes them fall." They stumble because they disobey the message—which is also what they were destined for. {2:9} But you are a chosen people, a royal priesthood, a holy nation, God's special possession, that you may declare the praises of him who called you out of darkness into his wonderful light. {2:10} Once you were not a people, but now you are the people of God; once you had not received mercy, but now you have received mercy. {2:11} Dear friends, I urge you, as foreigners and exiles, to abstain from sinful desires, which wage war against your soul. {2:12} Live such good lives among the pagans that, though they accuse you of doing wrong, they may see your good deeds and glorify God on the day he visits us. {2:13} Submit yourselves for the Lord's sake to every human authority: whether to the emperor, as the supreme authority, {2:14} or to governors, who are sent by him to punish those who do wrong and to commend those who do right. {2:15} For it is God's will that by doing good you should silence the ignorant talk of foolish people. {2:16} Live as free people, but do not use your freedom as a cover-up for evil; live as God's slaves. {2:17} Show proper respect to everyone, love the family of believers, fear God, honor the emperor. {2:18} Slaves, in reverent fear of God submit yourselves to your masters, not only to those who are good and considerate, but also to those who are harsh. {2:19} For it is commendable if someone bears up under the pain of unjust suffering because they are conscious of God. {2:20} But how is it to your credit if you receive a beating for doing wrong and endure it? But if you suffer for doing good and you endure it, this is commendable before God. {2:21} To this you were called, because Christ suffered for you, leaving you an example, that you should follow in his steps. {2:22} "He committed no sin, and no deceit was found in his mouth." {2:23} When they hurled their insults at him, he did not retaliate; when he suffered, he made no threats. Instead, he entrusted himself to him who judges justly. {2:24} "He himself bore our sins" in his body on the cross, so that we might die to sins and live for righteousness; "by his wounds you have been healed." {2:25} For "you were like sheep going astray," but now you have returned to the Shepherd and Overseer of your souls.

{3:1} In the same way, you wives, be submissive to your own husbands so that, if any of them do not believe the word, they may be won over without words by the behavior of their wives, {3:2} when they see the purity and reverence of your lives. {3:3} Your beauty should not come from outward adornment, such as elaborate hairstyles and the wearing of gold jewelry or fine clothes. {3:4} Rather, it should be that of your inner self, the unfading beauty of a gentle and quiet spirit, which is of great worth in God's sight. {3:5} For this is the way the holy women of the past who put their hope in God used to adorn themselves. They submitted themselves to their own husbands, {3:6} like Sarah, who obeyed Abraham and called him her lord. You are her daughters if you do what is right and do not give way to fear {3:7} Husbands, in the same way be considerate as you live with your wives, and treat them with respect as the weaker partner and as heirs with you of the gracious gift of life, so that nothing will hinder your prayers. {3:8} Finally, all of you, be like-minded, be sympathetic, love one another, be compassionate and humble. {3:9} **Do not repay evil with evil or insult with insult. On the contrary, repay evil with blessing, because to this you were called so that you may inherit a blessing.** {3:10} For, "Whoever would love life and see good days must keep their tongue from evil and their lips from deceitful speech. {3:11} They must turn from evil and do good; they must seek peace and pursue it. {3:12} For the eyes of the Lord are on the righteous and his ears are attentive to their prayer, but the face of the Lord is against those who do evil." {3:13} Who is going to harm you if you are eager to do good? {3:14} But even if you should suffer for what is right, you are blessed. "Do not fear their threats; do not be frightened." {3:15} But in your hearts revere Christ as Lord. Always be prepared to give an answer to everyone who asks you to give the reason for the hope that you have. But do this with gentleness and respect, {3:16} keeping a clear conscience, so that those who speak maliciously against your good behavior in Christ may be ashamed of their slander. {3:17} For it is better, if it is God's will, to suffer for doing good than for doing evil. {3:18} For Christ also suffered once for sins, the righteous for the unrighteous, to bring you to God. He was put to death in the body but made alive in the Spirit. {3:19} After being made alive, he went and made proclamation to the imprisoned spirits— {3:20} to those who were disobedient long ago when God waited patiently in the days of Noah while the ark was being built. In it only a few people, eight in all, were saved through water, {3:21} and this water symbolizes baptism that now saves you also—not the removal of dirt from the body but the pledge of a clear conscience toward God. It saves you by the resurrection of Jesus Christ, {3:22} who has gone into heaven and is at God's right hand—with angels, authorities and powers in submission to him.

{4:1} Since Christ suffered for us in the flesh, arm yourselves with the same attitude, because whoever suffers in the flesh has ceased from sin; {4:2} so that you no longer live the rest of your time in the flesh for human desires, but for the will of God. {4:3} For you have spent enough time in the past doing what the Gentiles like to do—living in debauchery, lust, drunkenness, orgies, carousing, and detestable idolatry. {4:4} They are surprised that you do not join them in their reckless, wild living, and they heap abuse on you. {4:5} But they will have to give an account to him who is ready to judge the living and the dead. {4:6} For this is the reason the gospel was preached even to those who are now dead, so that they might be judged according to human standards in regard to the body, but live according to God in the spirit. {4:7} The end of all things is near. Therefore be alert and of sober mind so that you may pray. {4:8} Above all, love each other deeply, because love covers over a multitude of sins. {4:9} Offer hospitality to one another without grumbling. {4:10} Each of you should use whatever gift you have received to serve others, as faithful stewards of God's grace in its various forms. {4:11} If anyone speaks, they should do so as one who speaks the very words of God. If anyone serves, they should do so with the strength God provides, so that in all things God may be praised through Jesus Christ. To him be the glory and the power for ever and ever. Amen. {4:12} Dear friends, do not be surprised at the fiery ordeal that has come on you to test you, as though something strange were happening to you. {4:13} But rejoice in as much as you participate in the sufferings of Christ, so that you may be overjoyed when his glory is revealed. {4:14} If you are insulted because of the name of Christ, you are blessed, for the Spirit of glory and of God rests on you. {4:15} If you suffer, it should not be as a murderer or thief or any other kind of criminal, or even as a meddler. {4:16} However, if you suffer as a Christian, do not be ashamed, but praise God that you bear that name. {4:17} For it is time for judgment to begin with God's household; and if it begins with us, what will the outcome be for those who do not obey the gospel of God? {4:18} And, "If it is hard for the righteous to be saved, what will become of the ungodly and the sinner?" {4:19} So then, those who suffer according to God's will should commit themselves to their faithful Creator and continue to do good.

{5:1} I urge the elders among you, as a fellow elder and a witness of Christ's sufferings, and also a partaker of the glory that will be revealed: {5:2} Shepherd the flock of God among you, exercising oversight willingly, not under compulsion, but voluntarily; not for shameful gain, but eagerly; {5:3} not lording it over those entrusted to you, but being examples to the flock. {5:4} And when the Chief Shepherd appears, you will receive the unfading crown of glory. {5:5} Likewise, you who are younger, be subject to the elders. And all of you, clothe yourselves with humility toward one another, because "God opposes the proud but shows favor to the humble. {5:6} Humble yourselves, therefore, under the mighty hand of God, so that he may exalt you at the proper time, {5:7} casting all your cares on him, because he cares for you. {5:8} Be sober-minded and alert. Your adversary the devil prowls around like a roaring lion, seeking someone to devour. {5:9} Resist him, standing firm in the faith, because you know that the family of believers throughout the world is undergoing the same kind of sufferings {5:10} And the God of all grace, who called you to his eternal glory in Christ, after you have suffered a little while, will himself restore you and make you strong, firm, and steadfast. {5:11} To him be the power for ever and ever. Amen. {5:12} With the help of Silas, whom I regard as a faithful brother, I have written to you briefly, encouraging you and testifying that this is the true grace of God. Stand firm in it. {5:13} She who is in Babylon, chosen together with you, sends you her greetings, and so does my son Mark. {5:14} Greet one another with a kiss of love. Peace to all of you who are in Christ.

2 Peter

{1:1} Simon Peter, a servant and apostle of Jesus Christ, to those who have received a faith as precious as ours through the righteousness of our God and Savior Jesus Christ: {1:2} Grace and peace be multiplied to you through the knowledge of God and of Jesus our Lord. {1:3} His divine power has given us everything we need for a godly life through our knowledge of him who called us by his own glory and goodness. {1:4} Through these he has given us his very great and precious promises, so that through them you may participate in the divine nature, having escaped the corruption in the world caused by evil desires. {1:5} For this very reason, make every effort to add to your faith goodness; and to goodness, knowledge; {1:6} and to knowledge, self-control; and to self-control, perseverance; and to perseverance, godliness; {1:7} and to godliness, mutual affection; and to mutual affection, love. {1:8} For if you possess these qualities in increasing measure, they will keep you from being ineffective and unproductive in your knowledge of our Lord Jesus Christ. {1:9} But whoever does not have them is nearsighted and blind, forgetting that they have been cleansed from their past sins. {1:10} Therefore, my brothers and sisters, make every effort to confirm your calling and election. For if you do these things, you will never stumble, {1:11} and you will receive a rich welcome into the eternal kingdom of our Lord and Savior Jesus Christ. {1:12} So I will always remind you of these things, even though you know them and are firmly established in the truth you now have. {1:13} I think it is right to refresh your memory as long as I live in the tent of this body, {1:14} because I know that I will soon put it aside, as our Lord Jesus Christ has made clear to me. {1:15} And I will make every effort to see that after my departure you will always be able to remember these things. {1:16} For we did not follow cleverly devised stories when we told you about the coming of our Lord Jesus Christ in power, but we were eyewitnesses of his majesty. {1:17} He received honor and glory from God the Father when the voice came to him from the Majestic Glory, saying, "This is my Son, whom I love; with him I am well pleased." {1:18} We ourselves heard this voice that came from heaven when we were with him on the sacred mountain. {1:19} We also have the prophetic message as something completely reliable, and you will do well to pay attention to it, as to a light shining in a dark place, until the day dawns and the morning star rises in your hearts. {1:20} Above all, you must understand that no prophecy of Scripture came about by the prophet's own interpretation of things. {1:21} For prophecy never had its origin in the human will, but prophets, though human, spoke from God as they were carried along by the Holy Spirit.

{2:1} There were false prophets in the past, and there will be false teachers among you. They will secretly introduce destructive heresies, even denying the Lord who bought them, bringing swift destruction upon themselves. {2:2} Many will follow their depraved conduct and because of them, the way of truth will be blasphemed. {2:3} In their greed, they will exploit you with deceptive words. Their condemnation has been long hanging over them, and their destruction has not been sleeping. {2:4} For if God did not spare angels when they sinned, but cast them into hell, delivering them in chains of darkness to be reserved for judgment; {2:5} and if He did not spare the ancient world, but saved Noah, a preacher of righteousness, along with seven others, when He brought a flood upon the world of the ungodly; {2:6} and if He condemned the cities of Sodom and Gomorrah to destruction by reducing them to ashes, having made them an example of what is coming upon the ungodly; {2:7} and if He rescued righteous Lot, who was oppressed by the unrestrained conduct of the immoral {2:8} (for that righteous man, while living among them day after day, was tormented in his righteous soul by the lawless deeds he saw and heard)— {2:9} **then the Lord knows how to rescue the godly from trials and to hold the unrighteous for punishment on the day of judgment,** {2:10} especially those who follow the corrupt desire of the flesh and despise authority. Bold and arrogant, they are not afraid to slander celestial beings; {2:11} whereas angels, though greater in might and power, do not bring a slanderous judgment against them before the Lord. {2:12} These people, like irrational animals, born as creatures of instinct to be captured and killed, slander what they do not understand, and in their destruction they too will be utterly destroyed, {2:13} suffering wrong as the wages of doing wrong. They consider it a pleasure to carouse in broad daylight. They are blots and blemishes, reveling in their deceitful pleasures while they feast with you. {2:14} With eyes full of adultery, they never stop sinning; they seduce the unstable; they are experts in greed—an accursed brood! {2:15} They have left the straight way and wandered off to follow the way of Balaam son of Beor, who loved the wages of wickedness. {2:16} But he was rebuked for his wrongdoing by a donkey—a beast without speech—who spoke with a human voice and restrained the prophet's madness. {2:17} These people are springs without water and mists driven by a storm. Blackest darkness is reserved for them. {2:18} With lofty but empty words, they appeal to the sensual passions of the flesh and entice those who are just escaping from those who live in error. {2:19} They promise them freedom, while they themselves are slaves of depravity—for "people are slaves to whatever has mastered them." {2:20} If they have escaped the corruption of the world by knowing our Lord and Savior Jesus Christ and are again entangled in it and are overcome, they are worse off at the end than they were at the beginning. {2:21} It would have been better for them not to have known the way of righteousness than to have known it and then to turn their backs on the sacred command that was passed on to them. {2:22} Of them the proverbs are true: "A dog returns to its vomit," and, "A sow that is washed returns to her wallowing in the mud."

{3:1} Beloved, I am writing this second letter to you to stir up your pure minds by way of reminder. {3:2} I want you to remember the words previously spoken by the holy prophets and the commandment of us, the apostles of the Lord and Savior. {3:3} First of all, understand that in the last days scoffers will come, following their own evil desires {3:4} and saying, "Where is the promise of His coming? Ever since our ancestors died, everything goes on as it has since the beginning of creation." {3:5} But they deliberately forget that long ago by God's word the heavens came into being and the earth was formed out of water and by water. {3:6} By these waters also the world of that time was deluged and destroyed. {3:7} By the same word the present heavens and earth are reserved for fire, being kept for the day of judgment and destruction of the ungodly. {3:8} But do not forget this one thing, dear friends: With the Lord a day is like a thousand years, and a thousand years are like a day. {3:9} **The Lord is not slow in keeping His promise, as some understand slowness. Instead, He is patient with you, not wanting anyone to perish, but everyone to come to repentance.** {3:10} But the day of the Lord will come like a thief. The heavens will disappear with a roar; the elements will be destroyed by fire, and the earth and everything done in it will be laid bare. {3:11} Since everything will be destroyed in this way, what kind of people ought you to be? You ought to live holy and godly lives {3:12} as you look forward to the day of God and speed its coming. That day will bring about the destruction of the heavens by fire, and the elements will melt in the heat. {3:13} But in keeping with His promise, we are looking forward to a new heaven and a new earth, where righteousness dwells. {3:14} So then, dear friends, since you are looking forward to this, make every effort to be found spotless, blameless and at peace with Him. {3:15} Bear in mind that our Lord's patience means salvation, just as our dear brother Paul also wrote to you with the wisdom that God gave him. {3:16} He writes the same way in all his letters, speaking in them of these matters. His letters contain some things that are hard to understand, which ignorant and unstable people distort, as they do the other Scriptures, to their own destruction. {3:17} Therefore, dear friends, since you have been forewarned, be on your guard so that you may not be carried away by the error of the lawless and fall from your secure position. {3:18} But grow in the grace and knowledge of our Lord and Savior Jesus Christ. To Him be glory both now and forever! Amen.

1 John

{1:1} This is what we proclaim to you: what was from the beginning, what we have heard, what we have seen with our own eyes, what we have gazed upon, and what our hands have handled, concerning the Word of life— {1:2} the life was revealed, and we have seen it and testify to it, and proclaim to you the eternal life that was with the Father and was revealed to us— {1:3} what we have seen and heard, we also proclaim to you, so that you may have fellowship with us. And truly our fellowship is with the Father and with His Son Jesus Christ. {1:4} We are writing these things so that our joy may be complete. {1:5} This is the message we have heard from Him and declare to you: God is light, and in Him there is no darkness at all. {1:6} If we claim to have fellowship with Him and yet walk in the darkness, we lie and do not live out the truth. {1:7} But if we walk in the light, as He is in the light, we have fellowship with one another, and the blood of Jesus, His Son, purifies us from all sin. {1:8} If we claim to be without sin, we deceive ourselves and the truth is not in us. {1:9} ***If we confess our sins, He is faithful and just to forgive us our sins and to cleanse us from all unrighteousness.*** {1:10} If we claim we have not sinned, we make Him out to be a liar, and His word is not in us.

{2:1} My dear children, I am writing this to you so that you will not sin. But if anyone does sin, we have an advocate with the Father—Jesus Christ, the Righteous One. {2:2} He is the atoning sacrifice for our sins, and not only for ours but also for the sins of the whole world. {2:3} We know that we have come to know him if we keep his commands. {2:4} Whoever says, "I know him," but does not do what he commands is a liar, and the truth is not in that person. {2:5} But if anyone obeys his word, love for God is truly made complete in them. This is how we know we are in him: {2:6} Whoever claims to live in him must live as Jesus did. {2:7} Dear friends, I am not writing you a new command but an old one, which you have had since the beginning. This old command is the message you have heard. {2:8} Yet I am writing you a new command; its truth is seen in him and in you, because the darkness is passing and the true light is already shining. {2:9} Anyone who claims to be in the light but hates a brother or sister is still in the darkness. {2:10} Anyone who loves their brother and sister lives in the light, and there is nothing in them to make them stumble. {2:11} But anyone who hates a brother or sister is in the darkness and walks around in the darkness. They do not know where they are going, because the darkness has blinded them. {2:12} I am writing to you, dear children, because your sins have been forgiven on account of his name. {2:13} I am writing to you, fathers, because you know him who is from the beginning. I am writing to you, young men, because you have overcome the evil one. {2:14} I write to you, dear children, because you know the Father. I write to you, fathers, because you know him who is from the beginning. I write to you, young men, because you are strong, and the word of God lives in you, and you have overcome the evil one. {2:15} Do not love the world or anything in the world. If anyone loves the world, love for the Father is not in them. {2:16} For everything in the world—the lust of the flesh, the lust of the eyes, and the pride of life—comes not from the Father but from the world. {2:17} The world and its desires pass away, but whoever does the will of God lives forever. {2:18} Dear children, this is the last hour; and as you have heard that the antichrist is coming, even now many antichrists have come. This is how we know it is the last hour. {2:19} They went out from us, but they did not really belong to us. For if they had belonged to us, they would have remained with us; but their going showed that none of them belonged to us. {2:20} But you have an anointing from the Holy One, and all of you know the truth. {2:21} I do not write to you because you do not know the truth, but because you do know it and because no lie comes from the truth. {2:22} Who is the liar? It is whoever denies that Jesus is the Christ. Such a person is the antichrist—denying the Father and the Son. {2:23} No one who denies the Son has the Father; whoever acknowledges the Son has the Father also. {2:24} As for you, see that what you have heard from the beginning remains in you. If it does, you also will remain in the Son and in the Father. {2:25} And this is what he promised us—eternal life. {2:26} I am writing these things to you about those who are trying to lead you astray. {2:27} As for you, the anointing you received from him remains in you, and you do not need anyone to teach you. But as his anointing teaches you about all things and as that anointing is real, not counterfeit—just as it has taught you, remain in him. {2:28} And now, dear children, continue in him, so that when he appears we may be confident and unashamed before him at his coming. {2:29} If you know that he is righteous, you know that everyone who does what is right has been born of him.

{3:1} Look at how much love the Father has given us, that we should be called children of God! And that is what we are! The reason the world does not know us is that it did not know him. {3:2} Dear friends, now we are children of God, and what we will be has not yet been made known. But we know that when Christ appears, we shall be like him, for we shall see him as he is. {3:3} All who have this hope in him purify themselves, just as he is pure. {3:4} Everyone who sins breaks the law; in fact, sin is lawlessness. {3:5} But you know that he appeared so that he might take away our sins. And in him is no sin. {3:6} No one who lives in him keeps on sinning. No one who continues to sin has either seen him or known him. {3:7} Dear children, do not let anyone lead you astray. The one who does what is right is righteous, just as he is righteous. {3:8} The one who does what is sinful is of the devil, because the devil has been sinning from the beginning. The reason the Son of God appeared was to destroy the devil's work. {3:9} No one who is born of God will continue to sin, because God's seed remains in them; they cannot go on sinning, because they have been born of God. {3:10} This is how we know who the children of God are and who the children of the devil are: Anyone who does not do what is right is not God's child, nor is anyone who does not love their brother and sister. {3:11} For this is the message you heard from the beginning: We should love one another. {3:12} Do not be like Cain, who belonged to the evil one and murdered his brother. And why did he murder him? Because his own actions were evil and his brother's were righteous. {3:13} Do not be surprised, my brothers and sisters, if the world hates you. {3:14} We know that we have passed from death to life, because we love each other. Anyone who does not love remains in death. {3:15} Anyone who hates a brother or sister is a murderer, and you know that no murderer has eternal life residing in him. {3:16} This is how we know what love is: Jesus Christ laid down his life for us. And we ought to lay down our lives for our brothers and sisters. {3:17} If anyone has material possessions and sees a brother or sister in need but has no pity on them, how can the love of God be in that person? {3:18} Dear children, let us not love with words or speech but with actions and in truth. {3:19} This is how we know that we belong to the truth and how we set our hearts at rest in his presence: {3:20} If our hearts condemn us, we know that God is greater than our hearts, and he knows everything. {3:21} Dear friends, if our hearts do not condemn us, we have confidence before God {3:22} and receive from him anything we ask, because we keep his commands and do what pleases him. {3:23} And this is his command: to believe in the name of his Son, Jesus Christ, and to love one another as he commanded us. {3:24} The one who keeps God's commands lives in him, and he in them. And this is how we know that he lives in us: We know it by the Spirit he gave us.

{4:1} My dear friends, do not believe every spirit, but test the spirits to see whether they are from God, because many false prophets have gone out into the world. {4:2} This is how you can recognize the Spirit of God: Every spirit that acknowledges that Jesus Christ has come in the flesh is from God, {4:3} but every spirit that does not acknowledge Jesus is not from God. This is the spirit of the antichrist, which you have heard is coming and even now is already in the world. {4:4} You, dear children, are from God and have overcome them, because the one who is in you is greater than the one who is in the world. {4:5} They are from the world and therefore speak from the viewpoint of the world, and the world listens to them. {4:6} We are from God, and whoever knows God listens to us; but whoever is not from God does not listen to us. This is how we recognize the Spirit of truth and the spirit of falsehood. {4:7} Dear friends, let us love one another, for love comes from God. Everyone who loves has been born of God and knows God. {4:8} **Whoever does not love does not know God, because God is love.** {4:9} This is how God showed his love among us: He sent his one and only Son into the world that we might live through him. {4:10} This is love: not that we loved God, but that he loved us and sent his Son as an atoning sacrifice for our sins. {4:11} Dear friends, since God so loved us, we also ought to love one another. {4:12} No one has ever seen God; but if we love one another, God lives in us and his love is made complete in us. {4:13} This is how we know that we live in him and he in us: He has given us of his Spirit. {4:14} And we have seen and testify that the Father has sent his Son to be the Savior of the world. {4:15} If anyone acknowledges that Jesus is the Son of God, God lives in them and they in God. {4:16} And so we know and rely on the love God has for us. God is love. Whoever lives in love lives in God, and God in them. {4:17} This is how love is made complete among us so that we will have confidence on the day of judgment: In this world we are like Jesus. {4:18} There is no fear in love. But perfect love drives out fear, because fear has to do with punishment. The one who fears is not made perfect in love. {4:19} We love because he first loved us. {4:20} Whoever claims to love God yet hates a brother or sister is a liar. For whoever does not love their brother and sister, whom they have seen, cannot love God, whom they have not seen. {4:21} And he has given us this command: Anyone who loves God must also love their brother and sister.

{5:1} Whoever believes that Jesus is the Christ is born of God, and everyone who loves the Father loves his child as well. {5:2} This is how we know that we love the children of God: by loving God and carrying out his commands. {5:3} In fact, this is love for God: to keep his commands. And his commands are not burdensome. {5:4} For everyone born of God overcomes the world. This is the victory that has overcome the world, even our faith. {5:5} Who is it that overcomes the world? Only the one who believes that Jesus is the Son of God. {5:6} This is the one who came by water and blood—Jesus Christ. He did not come by water only, but by water and blood. And it is the Spirit who testifies, because the Spirit is the truth. {5:7} For there are three that testify: {5:8} the Spirit, the water and the blood; and the three are in agreement. {5:9} We accept human testimony, but God's testimony is greater because it is the testimony of God, which he has given about his Son. {5:10} Whoever believes in the Son of God accepts this testimony. Whoever does not believe God has made him out to be a liar, because they have not believed the testimony God has given about his Son. {5:11} And this is the testimony: God has given us eternal life, and this life is in his Son. {5:12} Whoever has the Son has life; whoever does not have the Son of God does not have life. {5:13} I write these things to you who believe in the name of the Son of God so that you may know that you have eternal life. {5:14} This is the confidence we have in approaching God: that if we ask anything according to his will, he hears us. {5:15} And if we know that he hears us—whatever we ask—we know that we have what we asked of him. {5:16} If you see any brother or sister commit a sin that does not lead to death, you should pray and God will give them life. I refer to those whose sin does not lead to death. There is a sin that leads to death. I am not saying that you should pray about that. {5:17} All wrongdoing is sin, and there is sin that does not lead to death. {5:18} We know that anyone born of God does not continue to sin; the One who was born of God keeps them safe, and the evil one cannot harm them. {5:19} We know that we are children of God, and that the whole world is under the control of the evil one. {5:20} We also know that the Son of God has come and has given us understanding, so that we may know him, who is true. And we are in him who is true by being in his Son Jesus Christ. He is the true God and eternal life. {5:21} Dear children, keep yourselves from idols.

2 John

{1:1} From the elder, to the chosen lady and her children, whom I love in truth—and not only I, but also all who know the truth— {1:2} because of the truth that abides in us and will be with us forever. {1:3} Grace, mercy, and peace will be with us from God the Father and from Jesus Christ, the Son of the Father, in truth and love. {1:4} I was very glad to find some of your children walking in truth, just as we have received commandment to do from the Father. {1:5} And now I urge you, dear lady—not as if I were writing you a new commandment, but one we have had from the beginning—that we love one another. {1:6} **And this is love: that we walk in obedience to his commands. As you have heard from the beginning, his command is that you walk in love.** {1:7} Many deceivers have gone out into the world, those who do not acknowledge Jesus Christ as coming in the flesh. Such a person is the deceiver and the antichrist. {1:8} Watch out that you do not lose what we have worked for, but that you may be rewarded fully. {1:9} Anyone who runs ahead and does not continue in the teaching of Christ does not have God; whoever continues in the teaching has both the Father and the Son. {1:10} **If anyone comes to you and does not bring this teaching, do not take them into your house or welcome them.** {1:11} **Anyone who welcomes them shares in their wicked work.** {1:12} I have much to write to you, but I do not want to do so with pen and ink. Instead, I hope to visit you and talk with you face to face, so that our joy may be complete. {1:13} The children of your sister, who is chosen by God, send their greetings. Amen.

3 John

{1:1} From the elder, to the beloved Gaius, whom I love in truth. {1:2} Beloved, I pray that you may prosper in all things and be in health, just as your soul prospers. {1:3} For I rejoiced greatly when brethren came and testified of the truth that is in you, as you walk in truth. {1:4} **I have no greater joy than to hear that my children walk in truth.** {1:5} Beloved, you do faithfully whatever you do for the brethren and for strangers, {1:6} who have borne witness of your love before the church. If you send them forward on their journey in a manner worthy of God, you will do well, {1:7} because they went forth for His name's sake, taking nothing from the Gentiles. {1:8} We therefore ought to receive such, that we may become fellow workers for the truth. {1:9} I wrote to the church, but Diotrephes, who loves to have the preeminence among them, does not receive us. {1:10} Therefore, if I come, I will call to mind his deeds which he does, prating against us with malicious words. And not content with that, he himself does not receive the brethren, and forbids those who wish to, putting them out of the church. {1:11} **Beloved, do not imitate what is evil, but what is good. He who does good is of God, but he who does evil has not seen God.** {1:12} Demetrius has a good testimony from all, and from the truth itself. And we also bear witness, and you know that our testimony is true. {1:13} I had many things to write, but I do not wish to write with pen and ink. {1:14} But I hope to see you shortly, and we shall speak face to face. Peace be to you. Our friends greet you. Greet the friends by name.

Jude

{1:1} From Jude, a servant of Jesus Christ and brother of James, to those who are sanctified by God the Father and preserved in Jesus Christ, called: {1:2} May mercy, peace, and love be multiplied to you. {1:3} **Beloved, while I was eager to write to you about our common salvation, I found it necessary to exhort you to earnestly contend for the faith which was once delivered to the saints.** {1:4} For certain men have crept in unnoticed, who were long ago marked out for this condemnation, ungodly men, turning the grace of our God into lewdness and denying the only Lord God and our Lord Jesus Christ. {1:5} But I want to remind you, though you once knew this, that the Lord, having saved the people out of the land of Egypt, afterward destroyed those who did not believe. {1:6} And the angels who did not keep their proper domain, but left their own abode, He has reserved in everlasting chains under darkness for the judgment of the great day; {1:7} as Sodom and Gomorrah, and the cities around them in a similar manner to these, having given themselves over to sexual immorality and gone after strange flesh, are set forth as an example, suffering the vengeance of eternal fire. {1:8} Likewise also these dreamers defile the flesh, reject authority, and speak evil of dignitaries. {1:9} Yet Michael the archangel, in contending with the devil, when he disputed about the body of Moses, dared not bring against him a reviling accusation, but said, "The Lord rebuke you!" {1:10} But these speak evil of whatever they do not know; and whatever they know naturally, like brute beasts, in these things they corrupt themselves. {1:11} Woe to them! For they have gone in the way of Cain, have run greedily in the error of Balaam for profit, and perished in the rebellion of Korah. {1:12} These are spots in your love feasts, while they feast with you without fear, serving only themselves. They are clouds without water, carried about by the winds; late autumn trees without fruit, twice dead, pulled up by the roots; {1:13} raging waves of the sea, foaming up their own shame; wandering stars for whom is reserved the blackness of darkness forever. {1:14} Now Enoch, the seventh from Adam, prophesied about these men also, saying, "Behold, the Lord comes with ten thousands of His saints, {1:15} to execute judgment on all, to convict all who are ungodly among them of all their ungodly deeds which they have committed in an ungodly way, and of all the harsh things which ungodly sinners have spoken against Him." {1:16} These are grumblers, complainers, walking according to their own lusts; and they mouth great swelling words, flattering people to gain advantage. {1:17} But you, beloved, remember the words which were spoken before by the apostles of our Lord Jesus Christ: {1:18} how they told you that there would be mockers in the last time who would walk according to their own ungodly lusts. {1:19} These are sensual persons, who cause divisions, not having the Spirit. {1:20} But you, beloved, building yourselves up on your most holy faith, praying in the Holy Spirit, {1:21} **keep yourselves in the love of God, looking for the mercy of our Lord Jesus Christ unto eternal life.** {1:22} And on some have compassion, making a distinction; {1:23} but others save with fear, pulling them out of the fire, hating even the garment defiled by the flesh. {1:24} Now to Him who is able to keep you from stumbling, and to present you faultless before the presence of His glory with exceeding joy, {1:25} to God our Savior, who alone is wise, be glory and majesty, dominion and power, both now and forever. Amen.

Revelation

{1:1} This is the Revelation of Jesus Christ, which God gave to him to show to his servants the things that must shortly come to pass. He sent and signified it by his angel to his servant John, {1:2} who bore witness to the word of God and to the testimony of Jesus Christ, and to all things that he saw. {1:3} Blessed is the one who reads aloud the words of this prophecy, and blessed are those who hear and keep what is written in it, for the time is near. {1:4} John, to the seven churches which are in Asia: Grace and peace to you from him who is, and who was, and who is to come, and from the seven Spirits who are before his throne; {1:5} and from Jesus Christ, the faithful witness, the firstborn from the dead, and the ruler of the kings of the earth. To him who loved us and washed us from our sins in his own blood, {1:6} and has made us kings and priests to his God and Father, to him be glory and dominion forever and ever. Amen. {1:7} Behold, he is coming with clouds, and every eye will see him, even those who pierced him. And all the tribes of the earth will mourn because of him. Even so, Amen. {1:8} "I am the Alpha and the Omega, the Beginning and the End," says the Lord, "who is, and who was, and who is to come, the Almighty." {1:9} I, John, both your brother and companion in tribulation, and in the kingdom and patience of Jesus Christ, was on the island that is called Patmos for the word of God and for the testimony of Jesus Christ. {1:10} I was in the Spirit on the Lord's Day, and I heard behind me a loud voice, like a trumpet, {1:11} saying, "I am the Alpha and the Omega, the First and the Last," and, "What you see, write in a book and send it to the seven churches which are in Asia: to Ephesus, to Smyrna, to Pergamos, to Thyatira, to Sardis, to Philadelphia, and to Laodicea." {1:12} Then I turned to see the voice that spoke with me. And having turned, I saw seven golden lampstands, {1:13} and in the midst of the seven lampstands one like the Son of Man, clothed with a garment down to the feet and girded about the chest with a golden band. {1:14} His head and hair were white like wool, as white as snow, and his eyes like a flame of fire; {1:15} his feet were like fine brass, as if refined in a furnace, and his voice as the sound of many waters; {1:16} he had in his right hand seven stars, out of his mouth went a sharp two-edged sword, and his countenance was like the sun shining in its strength. {1:17} And when I saw him, I fell at his feet as dead. But he laid his right hand on me, saying to me, "Do not be afraid; I am the First and the Last. {1:18} I am he who lives, and was dead, and behold, I am alive forevermore. Amen. And I have the keys of Hades and of Death. {1:19} Write the things which you have seen, and the things which are, and the things which will take place after this. {1:20} The mystery of the seven stars which you saw in my right hand, and the seven golden lampstands: The seven stars are the angels of the seven churches, and the seven lampstands which you saw are the seven churches.

{2:1} Write to the angel of the church in Ephesus: "These are the words of the one who holds the seven stars in his right hand and walks among the seven golden lampstands: {2:2} I know your deeds, your hard work, and your patience. I know that you cannot tolerate those who are evil, and you have tested those who claim to be apostles but are not, and have found them to be false. {2:3} You have persevered and have endured hardships for my name, and have not grown weary. {2:4} Yet I hold this against you: you have forsaken your first love. {2:5} Remember therefore from where you have fallen; repent and do the things you did at first. If you do not repent, I will come to you and remove your lampstand from its place. {2:6} But you have this in your favor: you hate the practices of the Nicolaitans, which I also hate. {2:7} Whoever has ears, let them hear what the Spirit says to the churches. To the one who is victorious, I will give the right to eat from the tree of life, which is in the paradise of God. {2:8} Write to the angel of the church in Smyrna: "These are the words of the First and the Last, who was dead and came to life: {2:9} I know your afflictions and your poverty—yet you are rich! I know about the slander of those who say they are Jews but are not, but are a synagogue of Satan. {2:10} Do not be afraid of what you are about to suffer. I tell you, the devil will put some of you in prison to test you, and you will suffer persecution for ten days. Be faithful, even to the point of death, and I will give you life as your victor's crown. {2:11} Whoever has ears, let them hear what the Spirit says to the churches. The one who is victorious will not be hurt at all by the second death. {2:12} Write to the angel of the church in Pergamum: "These are the words of the one who has the sharp, double-edged sword: {2:13} I know where you live—where Satan has his throne. Yet you remain true to my name. You did not renounce your faith in me, not even in the days of Antipas, my faithful witness, who was put to death in your city—where Satan lives. {2:14} Nevertheless, I have a few things against you: There are some among you who hold to the teaching of Balaam, who taught Balak to entice the Israelites to sin so that they ate food sacrificed to idols and committed sexual immorality. {2:15} Likewise, you also have those who hold to the teaching of the Nicolaitans. {2:16} Repent therefore! Otherwise, I will soon come to you and will fight against them with the sword of my mouth. {2:17} Whoever has ears, let them hear what the Spirit says to the churches. To the one who is victorious, I will give some of the hidden manna. I will also give that person a white stone with a new name written on it, known only to the one who receives it {2:18} Write to the angel of the church in Thyatira: "These are the words of the Son of God, whose eyes are like blazing fire and whose feet are like burnished bronze: {2:19} I know your deeds, your love and faith, your service and perseverance, and that you are now doing more than you did at first. {2:20} Nevertheless, I have this against you: You tolerate that woman Jezebel, who calls herself a prophet. By her teaching she misleads my servants into sexual immorality and the eating of food sacrificed to idols. {2:21} I have given her time to repent of her immorality, but she is unwilling. {2:22} So I will cast her on a bed of suffering, and I will make those who commit adultery with her suffer intensely, unless they repent of her ways. {2:23} I will strike her children dead. Then all the churches will know that I am he who searches hearts and minds, and I will repay each of you according to your deeds. {2:24} Now I say to the rest of you in Thyatira, to you who do not hold to her teaching and have not learned Satan's so-called deep secrets, 'I will not impose any other burden on you, {2:25} except to hold on to what you have until I come.' {2:26} To the one who is victorious and does my will to the end, I will give authority over the nations— {2:27} that one 'will rule them with an iron scepter and will dash them to pieces like pottery'—just as I have received authority from my Father. {2:28} I will also give that one the morning star. {2:29} Whoever has ears, let them hear what the Spirit says to the churches."

{3:1} Write to the angel of the church in Sardis: "These are the words of the one who holds the seven spirits of God and the seven stars: I know your deeds; you have a reputation of being alive, but you are dead. {3:2} Wake up! Strengthen what remains and is about to die, for I have found your deeds unfinished in the sight of my God. {3:3} Remember, therefore, what you have received and heard; hold it fast, and repent. But if you do not wake up, I will come like a thief, and you will not know at what time I will come to you. {3:4} Yet you have a few people in Sardis who have not soiled their clothes. They will walk with me, dressed in white, for they are worthy. {3:5} The one who is victorious will, like them, be dressed in white. I will never blot out the name of that person from the book of life, but will acknowledge that name before my Father and his angels. {3:6} Whoever has ears, let them hear what the Spirit says to the churches. {3:7} Write to the angel of the church in Philadelphia: "These are the words of the Holy One, the True One, who holds the key of David. What he opens, no one can shut; and what he shuts, no one can open. {3:8} I know your deeds. See, I have placed before you an open door that no one can shut. I know that you have little strength, yet you have kept my word and have not denied my name. {3:9} I will make those who are of the synagogue of Satan, who claim to be Jews though they are not, but are liars—I will make them come and fall down at your feet and acknowledge that I have loved you. {3:10} Since you have kept my command to endure patiently, I will also keep you from the hour of trial that is going to come on the whole world to test the inhabitants of the earth. {3:11} I am coming soon. Hold on to what you have, so that no one will take your crown. {3:12} The one who is victorious I will make a pillar in the temple of my God. Never again will they leave it. I will write on them the name of my God and the name of the city of my God, the new Jerusalem, which is coming down out of heaven from my God; and I will also write on them my new name. {3:13} Whoever has ears, let them hear what the Spirit says to the churches. {3:14} Write to the angel of the church in Laodicea: "These are the words of the Amen, the faithful and true witness, the ruler of God's creation. {3:15} I know your deeds, that you are neither cold nor hot. I wish you were either one or the other! {3:16} So, because you are lukewarm—neither hot nor cold—I am about to spit you out of my mouth. {3:17} You say, 'I am rich; I have acquired wealth and do not need a thing.' But you do not realize that you are wretched, pitiful, poor, blind and naked. {3:18} I counsel you to buy from me gold refined in the fire, so you can become rich; and white clothes to wear, so you can cover your shameful nakedness; and salve to put on your eyes, so you can see. {3:19} Those whom I love I rebuke and discipline. So be earnest and repent. {3:20} **Here I am! I stand at the door and knock. If anyone hears my voice and opens the door, I will come in and eat with that person, and they with me.** {3:21} To the one who is victorious, I will give the right to sit with me on my throne, just as I was victorious and sat down with my Father on his throne. {3:22} Whoever has ears, let them hear what the Spirit says to the churches."

{4:1} After this, I looked, and behold, a door was opened in heaven. The first voice I heard sounded like a trumpet and said, "Come up here, and I will show you what must happen after this." {4:2} Immediately, I was in the spirit, and I saw a throne set in heaven, and someone was sitting on it. {4:3} The one who sat there looked like jasper and carnelian, and a rainbow, resembling an emerald, encircled the throne. {4:4} Surrounding the throne were twenty-four other thrones, and seated on them were twenty-four elders. They were dressed in white and had crowns of gold on their heads. {4:5} From the throne came flashes of lightning, rumblings, and peals of thunder. In front of the throne, seven lamps were blazing. These are the seven spirits of God. {4:6} Also in front of the throne, there was what looked like a sea of glass, clear as crystal. In the center, around the throne, were four living creatures, full of eyes in front and behind. {4:7} The first living creature was like a lion, the second was like an ox, the third had a face like a man, the fourth was like a flying eagle. {4:8} Each of the four living creatures had six wings and was covered with eyes all around, even under its wings. Day and night they never stop saying: "Holy, holy, holy is the Lord God Almighty, who was, and is, and is to come." {4:9} Whenever the living creatures give glory, honor, and thanks to the one who sits on the throne and who lives forever and ever, {4:10} the twenty-four elders fall down before him who sits on the throne and worship him who lives forever and ever. They lay their crowns before the throne and say: {4:11} "You are worthy, our Lord and God, to receive glory and honor and power, for you created all things, and by your will they were created and have their being."

{5:1} Then I saw in the right hand of the one seated on the throne a scroll with writing on both sides and sealed with seven seals. {5:2} And I saw a mighty angel proclaiming in a loud voice, "Who is worthy to break the seals and open the scroll?" {5:3} But no one in heaven or on earth or under the earth could open the scroll or even look inside it. {5:4} I wept and wept because no one was found who was worthy to open the scroll or look inside. {5:5} Then one of the elders said to me, "Do not weep! See, the Lion of the tribe of Judah, the Root of David, has triumphed. He is able to open the scroll and its seven seals." {5:6} Then I saw a Lamb, looking as if it had been slain, standing at the center of the throne, encircled by the four living creatures and the elders. The Lamb had seven horns and seven eyes, which are the seven spirits of God sent out into all the earth. {5:7} He went and took the scroll from the right hand of him who sat on the throne. {5:8} And when he had taken it, the four living creatures and the twenty-four elders fell down before the Lamb. Each one had a harp and they were holding golden bowls full of incense, which are the prayers of God's people. {5:9} And they sang a new song, saying: "You are worthy to take the scroll and to open its seals, because you were slain, and with your blood you purchased for God persons from every tribe and language and people and nation. {5:10} You have made them to be a kingdom and priests to serve our God, and they will reign on the earth." {5:11} Then I looked and heard the voice of many angels, numbering thousands upon thousands, and ten thousand times ten thousand. They encircled the throne and the living creatures and the elders. {5:12} In a loud voice they were saying: "Worthy is the Lamb, who was slain, to receive power and wealth and wisdom and strength and honor and glory and praise!" {5:13} Then I heard every creature in heaven and on earth and under the earth and on the sea, and all that is in them, saying: "To him who sits on the throne and to the Lamb be praised and honor and glory and power, forever and ever!" {5:14} The four living creatures said, "Amen," and the elders fell down and worshiped.

{6:1} Then I watched as the Lamb opened one of the seals, and I heard one of the four living creatures say in a voice like thunder, "Come!" {6:2} I looked, and there before me was a white horse! Its rider held a bow, and he was given a crown, and he rode out as a conqueror bent on conquest. {6:3} When the Lamb opened the second seal, I heard the second living creature say, "Come!" {6:4} Then another horse came out, a fiery red one. Its rider was given power to take peace from the earth and to make people kill each other. To him was given a large sword. {6:5} When the Lamb opened the third seal, I heard the third living creature say, "Come!" I looked, and there before me was a black horse! Its rider was holding a pair of scales in his hand. {6:6} Then I heard what sounded like a voice among the four living creatures, saying, "Two pounds of wheat for a day's wages, and six pounds of barley for a day's wages, and do not damage the oil and the wine!" {6:7} When the Lamb opened the fourth seal, I heard the voice of the fourth living creature say, "Come!" {6:8} I looked, and there before me was a pale horse! Its rider was named Death, and Hades was following close behind him. They were given power over a fourth of the earth to kill by sword, famine and plague, and by the wild beasts of the earth. {6:9} When he opened the fifth seal, I saw under the altar the souls of those who had been slain because of the word of God and the testimony they had maintained. {6:10} They called out in a loud voice, "How long, Sovereign Lord, holy and true, until you judge the inhabitants of the earth and avenge our blood?" {6:11} Then each of them was given a white robe, and they were told to wait a little longer, until the full number of their fellow servants, their brothers and sisters, were killed just as they had been. {6:12} I watched as he opened the sixth seal. There was a great earthquake. The sun turned black like a sackcloth made of goat hair, the whole moon turned blood red, {6:13} and the stars in the sky fell to earth, as figs drop from a fig tree when shaken by a strong wind. {6:14} The heavens receded like a scroll being rolled up, and every mountain and island was removed from its place. {6:15} Then the kings of the earth, the princes, the generals, the rich, the mighty, and everyone else, both slave and free, hid in caves and among the rocks of the mountains. {6:16} They called to the mountains and the rocks, "Fall on us and hide us from the face of him who sits on the throne and from the wrath of the Lamb! {6:17} For the great day of their wrath has come, and who can withstand it?"

{7:1} Then I saw four angels standing at the four corners of the earth, holding back the four winds of the earth to prevent any wind from blowing on the land or on the sea or on any tree. {7:2} And I saw another angel coming up from the east, having the seal of the living God. He called out in a loud voice to the four angels who had been given power to harm the land and the sea: {7:3} "Do not harm the land or the sea or the trees until we put a seal on the foreheads of the servants of our God." {7:4} Then I heard the number of those who were sealed: 144,000 from all the tribes of Israel. {7:5} From the tribe of Judah 12,000 were sealed, from the tribe of Reuben 12,000, from the tribe of Gad 12,000, {7:6} from the tribe of Asher 12,000, from the tribe of Naphtali 12,000, from the tribe of Manasseh 12,000, {7:7} from the tribe of Simeon 12,000, from the tribe of Levi 12,000, from the tribe of Issachar 12,000, {7:8} from the tribe of Zebulun 12,000, from the tribe of Joseph 12,000, from the tribe of Benjamin 12,000. {7:9} After this I looked, and there before me was a great multitude that no one could count, from every nation, tribe, people and language, standing before the throne and before the Lamb. They were wearing white robes and were holding palm branches in their hands. {7:10} And they cried out in a loud voice: "Salvation belongs to our God, who sits on the throne, and to the Lamb." {7:11} All the angels were standing around the throne and around the elders and the four living creatures. They fell down on their faces before the throne and worshiped God, {7:12} saying: "Amen! Praise and glory and wisdom and thanks and honor and power and strength be to our God for ever and ever. Amen!" {7:13} Then one of the elders asked me, "These in white robes—who are they, and where did they come from?" {7:14} I answered, "Sir, you know." And he said, "These are they who have come out of the great tribulation; they have washed their robes and made them white in the blood of the Lamb. {7:15} Therefore, "they are before the throne of God and serve him day and night in his temple; and he who sits on the throne will shelter them with his presence. {7:16} 'Never again will they hunger; never again will they thirst. The sun will not beat down on them,' nor any scorching heat. {7:17} For the Lamb at the center of the throne will be their shepherd; 'he will lead them to springs of living water.' 'And God will wipe away every tear from their eyes.'"

{8:1} When the seventh seal was opened, there was silence in heaven for about half an hour. {8:2} Then I saw the seven angels who stand before God, and seven trumpets were given to them. {8:3} Another angel, who had a golden censer, came and stood at the altar. He was given much incense to offer, with the prayers of all God's people, on the golden altar in front of the throne. {8:4} The smoke of the incense, together with the prayers of God's people, went up before God from the angel's hand. {8:5} Then the angel took the censer, filled it with fire from the altar, and hurled it on the earth; and there came peals of thunder, rumblings, flashes of lightning and an earthquake. {8:6} The seven angels who had the seven trumpets prepared to sound them. {8:7} The first angel sounded his trumpet, and there came hail and fire mixed with blood, and it was hurled down on the earth. A third of the earth was burned up, a third of the trees were burned up, and all the green grass was burned up. {8:8} The second angel sounded his trumpet, and something like a huge mountain, all ablaze, was thrown into the sea. A third of the sea turned into blood, {8:9} a third of the living creatures in the sea died, and a third of the ships were destroyed. {8:10} The third angel sounded his trumpet, and a great star, blazing like a torch, fell from the sky on a third of the rivers and on the springs of water— {8:11} the name of the star is Wormwood. A third of the waters turned bitter, and many people died from the waters that had become bitter. {8:12} The fourth angel sounded his trumpet, and a third of the sun was struck, a third of the moon, and a third of the stars, so that a third of them turned dark. A third of the day was without light, and also a third of the night. {8:13} As I watched, I heard an eagle that was flying in midair call out in a loud voice: "Woe! Woe! Woe to the inhabitants of the earth, because of the trumpet blasts about to be sounded by the other three angels!"

{9:1} When the fifth angel sounded his trumpet, I saw a star that had fallen from the sky to the earth. The star was given the key to the shaft of the Abyss. {9:2} When he opened the Abyss, smoke rose from it like the smoke from a gigantic furnace. The sun and sky were darkened by the smoke from the Abyss. {9:3} And out of the smoke locusts came down on the earth and were given power like that of scorpions of the earth. {9:4} They were told not to harm the grass of the earth or any plant or tree, but only those people who did not have the seal of God on their foreheads. {9:5} They were not allowed to kill them but only to torture them for five months. And the agony they suffered was like that of the sting of a scorpion when it strikes. {9:6} During those days people will seek death but will not find it; they will long to die, but death will elude them. {9:7} The locusts looked like horses prepared for battle. On their heads they wore something like crowns of gold, and their faces resembled human faces. {9:8} Their hair was like women's hair, and their teeth were like lions' teeth. {9:9} They had breastplates like breastplates of iron, and the sound of their wings was like the thundering of many horses and chariots rushing into battle. {9:10} They had tails with stingers, like scorpions, and in their tails they had the power to torment people for five months. {9:11} They had as king over them the angel of the Abyss, whose name in Hebrew is Abaddon and in Greek is Apollyon (that is, Destroyer). {9:12} The first woe is past; two other woes are yet to come. {9:13} The sixth angel sounded his trumpet, and I heard a voice coming from the four horns of the golden altar that is before God. {9:14} It said to the sixth angel who had the trumpet, "Release the four angels who are bound at the great river Euphrates." {9:15} And the four angels who had been kept ready for this very hour and day and month and year were released to kill a third of mankind. {9:16} The number of the mounted troops was twice ten thousand times ten thousand. I heard their number. {9:17} The horses and riders I saw in my vision looked like this: Their breastplates were fiery red, dark blue, and yellow as sulfur. The heads of the horses resembled the heads of lions, and out of their mouths came fire, smoke and sulfur. {9:18} A third of mankind was killed by the three plagues of fire, smoke and sulfur that came out of their mouths. {9:19} The power of the horses was in their mouths and in their tails; for their tails were like snakes, having heads with which they inflicted injury. {9:20} The rest of mankind who were not killed by these plagues still did not repent of the work of their hands; they did not stop worshiping demons, and idols of gold, silver, bronze, stone and wood—idols that cannot see or hear or walk. {9:21} Nor did they repent of their murders, their magic arts, their sexual immorality or their thefts.

{10:1} Then I saw another mighty angel coming down from heaven. He was clothed with a cloud, and a rainbow was over his head. His face was like the sun, and his feet were like pillars of fire. {10:2} In his hand, he held a little open scroll. He planted his right foot on the sea and his left foot on the land. {10:3} He cried out with a loud voice, like the roar of a lion. And when he cried out, the voices of seven thunders spoke. {10:4} When the seven thunders spoke, I was about to write down what they said. But I heard a voice from heaven saying, "Seal up what the seven thunders have said, and do not write it down." {10:5} Then the angel I saw standing on the sea and on the land lifted up his hand to heaven {10:6} and swore by Him who lives forever and ever, who created the heavens and all that is in them, the earth and all that is in it, and the sea and all that is in it, that there will be no more delay. {10:7} But in the days when the seventh angel is about to sound his trumpet, the mystery of God will be accomplished, just as He announced to His servants the prophets. {10:8} Then the voice then I had heard from heaven spoke to me again, saying, "Go, take the open scroll from the hand of the angel standing on the sea and on the land." {10:9} So I went to the angel and asked him to give me the little scroll. He said to me, "Take it and eat it. It will make your stomach bitter, but it will be as sweet as honey in your mouth." {10:10} I took the little scroll from the angel's hand and ate it. It was as sweet as honey in my mouth, but when I ate it, my stomach turned bitter. {10:11} Then the angel said to me, "You must prophesy again about many peoples, nations, languages, and kings."

{11:1} Then a reed like a measuring rod was given to me, and the angel stood, saying, "Rise and measure the temple of God, the altar, and those who worship there. {11:2} But leave out the court which is outside the temple, and do not measure it, for it has been given to the Gentiles. And they will tread the holy city underfoot for forty-two months. {11:3} "And I will give power to my two witnesses, and they will prophesy one thousand two hundred and sixty days, clothed in sackcloth. {11:4} These are the two olive trees and the two lampstands standing before the God of the earth. {11:5} And if anyone wants to harm them, fire proceeds from their mouth and devours their enemies. And if anyone wants to harm them, he must be killed in this manner. {11:6} These have power to shut heaven, so that no rain falls in the days of their prophecy; and they have power over waters to turn them to blood, and to strike the earth with all plagues, as often as they desire. {11:7} "When they finish their testimony, the beast that ascends out of the bottomless pit will make war against them, overcome them, and kill them. {11:8} And their dead bodies will lie in the street of the great city which spiritually is called Sodom and Egypt, where also our Lord was crucified. {11:9} Then those from the peoples, tribes, tongues, and nations will see their dead bodies three-and-a-half days, and not allow their dead bodies to be put into graves. {11:10} And those who dwell on the earth will rejoice over them, make merry, and send gifts to one another, because these two prophets tormented those who dwell on the earth. {11:11} "Now after three-and-a-half days the breath of life from God entered them, and they stood on their feet, and great fear fell on those who saw them. {11:12} And they heard a loud voice from heaven saying to them, 'Come up here.' And they ascended to heaven in a cloud, and their enemies saw them. {11:13} In the same hour there was a great earthquake, and a tenth of the city fell. In the earthquake, seven thousand people were killed, and the rest were afraid and gave glory to the God of heaven. {11:14} "The second woe is past. Behold, the third woe is coming quickly. {11:15} "Then the seventh angel sounded: And there were loud voices in heaven, saying, 'The kingdoms of this world have become the kingdoms of our Lord and of His Christ, and He shall reign forever and ever!' {11:16} And the twenty-four elders who sat before God on their thrones fell on their faces and worshiped God, {11:17} saying: 'We give You thanks, O Lord God Almighty, the One who is and who was and who is to come, because You have taken Your great power and reigned. {11:18} The nations were angry, and Your wrath has come, and the time of the dead, that they should be judged, and that You should reward Your servants the prophets and the saints, and those who fear Your name, small and great, and should destroy those who destroy the earth.' {11:19} "Then the temple of God was opened in heaven, and the ark of His covenant was seen in His temple. And there was lightning, noises, thunderings, an earthquake, and great hail."

{12:1} Then a great wonder appeared in heaven: a woman clothed with the sun, with the moon under her feet, and on her head a crown of twelve stars. {12:2} She was pregnant and cried out in labor and pain to give birth. {12:3} Another wonder appeared in heaven: a great red dragon with seven heads, ten horns, and seven crowns on its heads. {12:4} Its tail swept a third of the stars out of the sky and flung them to the earth. The dragon stood in front of the woman who was about to give birth so that it might devour her child the moment he was born. {12:5} She gave birth to a son, a male child, who will rule all the nations with an iron scepter. And her child was snatched up to God and to his throne. {12:6} The woman fled into the wilderness to a place prepared for her by God, where she might be taken care of for 1,260 days. {12:7} Then war broke out in heaven. Michael and his angels fought against the dragon, and the dragon and his angels fought back. {12:8} But he was not strong enough, and they lost their place in heaven. {12:9} The great dragon was hurled down—that ancient serpent called the devil, or Satan, who leads the whole world astray. He was hurled to the earth, and his angels with him. {12:10} Then I heard a loud voice in heaven say: "Now have come the salvation and the power and the kingdom of our God, and the authority of his Messiah. For the accuser of our brothers and sisters, who accuses them before our God day and night, has been hurled down. {12:11} They triumphed over him by the blood of the Lamb and by the word of their testimony; they did not love their lives so much as to shrink from death. {12:12} Therefore rejoice, you heavens and you who dwell in them! But woe to the earth and the sea, because the devil has gone down to you! He is filled with fury, because he knows that his time is short." {12:13} When the dragon saw that he had been hurled to the earth, he pursued the woman who had given birth to the male child. {12:14} The woman was given the two wings of a great eagle, so that she might fly to the place prepared for her in the wilderness, where she would be taken care of for a time, times and half a time, out of the serpent's reach. {12:15} Then from his mouth the serpent spewed water like a river, to overtake the woman and sweep her away with the torrent. {12:16} But the earth helped the woman by opening its mouth and swallowing the river that the dragon had spewed out of his mouth. {12:17} And the dragon was enraged at the woman and went off to wage war against the rest of her offspring—those who keep God's commands and hold fast their testimony about Jesus.

{13:1} I stood on the sandy shore of the sea, and I saw a beast rising out of the sea. It had seven heads and ten horns, with ten crowns on its horns, and blasphemous names on its heads. {13:2} The beast resembled a leopard, but it had feet like those of a bear and a mouth like that of a lion. The dragon gave the beast his power and throne and great authority. {13:3} One of the beast's heads seemed to have been fatally wounded, but the mortal wound was healed. The whole world was amazed and followed the beast. {13:4} They worshiped the dragon because he had given authority to the beast, and they also worshiped the beast and asked, "Who is like the beast? Who can wage war against it?" {13:5} The beast was given a mouth to utter proud words and blasphemies and to exercise its authority for forty-two months. {13:6} It opened its mouth to blaspheme God, and to slander his name and his dwelling place and those who live in heaven. {13:7} It was given power to wage war against God's holy people and to conquer them. And it was given authority over every tribe, people, language and nation. {13:8} All inhabitants of the earth will worship the beast—all whose names have not been written in the Lamb's book of life, the Lamb who was slain from the creation of the world. {13:9} Whoever has ears, let them hear. {13:10} "If anyone is to go into captivity, they will go. If anyone is to be killed with the sword, with the sword they will be killed." This calls for patient endurance and faithfulness on the part of God's people. {13:11} Then I saw a second beast, coming out of the earth. It had two horns like a lamb, but it spoke like a dragon. {13:12} It exercised all the authority of the first beast on its behalf, and made the earth and its inhabitants worship the first beast, whose fatal wound had been healed. {13:13} And it performed great signs, even causing fire to come down from heaven to the earth in full view of the people. {13:14} Because of the signs it was given power to perform on behalf of the first beast, it deceived the inhabitants of the earth. It ordered them to set up an image in honor of the beast who was wounded by the sword and yet lived. {13:15} The second beast was given power to give breath to the image of the first beast, so that the image could speak and cause all who refused to worship the image to be killed. {13:16} It also forced all people, great and small, rich and poor, free and slave, to receive a mark on their right hands or on their foreheads, {13:17} so that they could not buy or sell unless they had the mark, which is the name of the beast or the number of its name. {13:18} This calls for wisdom. Let the person who has insight calculate the number of the beast, for it is the number of a man. That number is 666.

{14:1} As I looked, I saw a Lamb standing on Mount Zion, and with him were 144,000 who had his Father's name written on their foreheads. {14:2} I heard a voice from heaven, like the roar of rushing waters and loud thunder. The voice was accompanied by the music of harpists playing their harps. {14:3} They sang what seemed to be a new song before the throne, the four living creatures, and the elders. Only the 144,000 who had been redeemed from the earth could learn this song. {14:4} They were those who did not defile themselves with women, for they remained virgins. They followed the Lamb wherever he went. They were purchased from among mankind and offered as firstfruits to God and the Lamb. {14:5} No lie was found in their mouths; they are blameless. {14:6} Then I saw another angel flying in midair, and he had the eternal gospel to proclaim to those who live on the earth—to every nation, tribe, language, and people. {14:7} He said in a loud voice, "Fear God and give him glory, because the hour of his judgment has come. Worship him who made the heavens, the earth, the sea, and the springs of water." {14:8} A second angel followed and said, "Fallen! Fallen is Babylon the Great, which made all the nations drink the maddening wine of her adulteries." {14:9} A third angel followed them and said in a loud voice, "If anyone worships the beast and its image and receives its mark on their forehead or on their hand, {14:10} they, too, will drink the wine of God's fury, which has been poured full strength into the cup of his wrath. They will be tormented with burning sulfur in the presence of the holy angels and of the Lamb. {14:11} And the smoke of their torment will rise for ever and ever. There will be no rest day or night for those who worship the beast and its image, or for anyone who receives the mark of its name." {14:12} This calls for patient endurance on the part of the people of God who keep his commands and remain faithful to Jesus. {14:13} Then I heard a voice from heaven say, "Write this: Blessed are the dead who die in the Lord from now on." "Yes," says the Spirit, "they will rest from their labor, for their deeds will follow them." {14:14} I looked, and there before me was a white cloud, and seated on the cloud was one like a son of man with a crown of gold on his head and a sharp sickle in his hand. {14:15} Then another angel came out of the temple and called in a loud voice to him who was sitting on the cloud, "Take your sickle and reap, because the time to reap has come, for the harvest of the earth is ripe." {14:16} So he who was seated on the cloud swung his sickle over the earth, and the earth was harvested. {14:17} Another angel came out of the temple in heaven, and he too had a sharp sickle. {14:18} Still another angel, who had charge of the fire, came from the altar and called in a loud voice to him who had the sharp sickle, "Take your sharp sickle and gather the clusters of grapes from the earth's vine, because its grapes are ripe." {14:19} The angel swung his sickle on the earth, gathered its grapes and threw them into the great winepress of God's wrath. {14:20} They were trampled in the winepress outside the city, and blood flowed out of the press, rising as high as the horses' bridles for a distance of 1,600 stadia.

{15:1} Then I saw another astounding sign in heaven: seven angels with the seven last plagues, for with them God's wrath is completed. {15:2} And I saw what looked like a sea of glass glowing with fire, and standing beside the sea were those who had been victorious over the beast and its image and over the number of its name. They held harps given them by God {15:3} and sang the song of God's servant Moses and of the Lamb: "Great and marvelous are your deeds, Lord God Almighty. Just and true are your ways, King of the nations. {15:4} Who will not fear you, Lord, and bring glory to your name? For you alone are holy. All nations will come and worship before you, for your righteous acts have been revealed." {15:5} After this, I looked, and the temple—the tabernacle of the covenant law—in heaven was opened. {15:6} Out of the temple came the seven angels with the seven plagues. They were dressed in clean, shining linen and wore golden sashes around their chests. {15:7} Then one of the four living creatures gave to the seven angels seven golden bowls filled with the wrath of God, who lives for ever and ever. {15:8} And the temple was filled with smoke from the glory of God and from his power, and no one could enter the temple until the seven plagues of the seven angels were completed.

{16:1} Then I heard a loud voice from the temple saying to the seven angels, "Go, pour out the seven bowls of God's wrath on the earth." {16:2} The first angel went and poured out his bowl on the land, and ugly, festering sores broke out on the people who had the mark of the beast and worshiped its image. {16:3} The second angel poured out his bowl on the sea, and it turned into blood like that of a dead person, and every living thing in the sea died. {16:4} The third angel poured out his bowl on the rivers and springs of water, and they became blood. {16:5} Then I heard the angel in charge of the waters say: "You are just in these judgments, O Holy One, you who are and who were; {16:6} for they have shed the blood of your holy people and your prophets, and you have given them blood to drink as they deserve." {16:7} And I heard the altar respond: "Yes, Lord God Almighty, true and just are your judgments." {16:8} The fourth angel poured out his bowl on the sun, and the sun was allowed to scorch people with fire. {16:9} They were seared by the intense heat and they cursed the name of God, who had control over these plagues, but they refused to repent and glorify him. {16:10} The fifth angel poured out his bowl on the throne of the beast, and its kingdom was plunged into darkness. People gnawed their tongues in agony {16:11} and cursed the God of heaven because of their pains and their sores, but they refused to repent of what they had done. {16:12} The sixth angel poured out his bowl on the great river Euphrates, and its water was dried up to prepare the way for the kings from the East. {16:13} Then I saw three impure spirits that looked like frogs; they came out of the mouth of the dragon, out of the mouth of the beast and out of the mouth of the false prophet. {16:14} They are demonic spirits that perform signs, and they go out to the kings of the whole world, to gather them for the battle on the great day of God Almighty. {16:15} "Look, I come like a thief! Blessed is the one who stays awake and remains clothed, so as not to go naked and be shamefully exposed." {16:16} Then they gathered the kings together to the place that in Hebrew is called Armageddon. {16:17} The seventh angel poured out his bowl into the air, and out of the temple came a loud voice from the throne, saying, "It is done!" {16:18} Then came flashes of lightning, rumblings, peals of thunder and a severe earthquake. No earthquake like it has ever occurred since mankind has been on earth, so tremendous was the quake. {16:19} The great city split into three parts, and the cities of the nations collapsed. God remembered Babylon the Great and gave her the cup filled with the wine of the fury of his wrath. {16:20} Every island fled away and the mountains could not be found. {16:21} From the sky huge hailstones, each weighing about a hundred pounds, fell on people. And they cursed God on account of the plague of hail, because the plague was so terrible.

{17:1} Then one of the seven angels who had the seven bowls came and talked with me, saying to me, "Come, I will show you the judgment of the great prostitute who sits on many waters. {17:2} With her the kings of the earth committed adultery, and the inhabitants of the earth were intoxicated with the wine of her adulteries." {17:3} So he carried me away in the Spirit into the wilderness. There I saw a woman sitting on a scarlet beast that was covered with blasphemous names and had seven heads and ten horns. {17:4} The woman was dressed in purple and scarlet, and was glittering with gold, precious stones and pearls. She held a golden cup in her hand, filled with abominable things and the filth of her adulteries. {17:5} The name written on her forehead was a mystery: "Babylon the Great, the Mother of Prostitutes and of the Abominations of the Earth." {17:6} I saw that the woman was drunk with the blood of God's holy people, the blood of those who bore testimony to Jesus. When I saw her, I was greatly astonished. {17:7} Then the angel said to me: "Why are you astonished? I will explain to you the mystery of the woman and of the beast she rides, which has the seven heads and ten horns. {17:8} The beast, which you saw, once was, now is not, and yet will come up out of the Abyss and go to its destruction. The inhabitants of the earth whose names have not been written in the book of life from the creation of the world will be astonished when they see the beast, because it once was, now is not, and yet will come. {17:9} "This calls for a mind with wisdom. The seven heads are seven hills on which the woman sits. {17:10} They are also seven kings. Five have fallen, one is, the other has not yet come; but when he does come, he must remain for only a little while. {17:11} The beast who once was, and now is not, is an eighth king. He belongs to the seven and is going to his destruction. {17:12} "The ten horns you saw are ten kings who have not yet received a kingdom, but who for one hour will receive authority as kings along with the beast. {17:13} They have one purpose and will give their power and authority to the beast. {17:14} They will wage war against the Lamb, but the Lamb will triumph over them because he is Lord of lords and King of kings—and with him will be his called, chosen and faithful followers." {17:15} Then the angel said to me, "The waters you saw, where the prostitute sits, are peoples, multitudes, nations and languages. {17:16} The beast and the ten horns you saw will hate the prostitute. They will bring her to ruin and leave her naked; they will eat her flesh and burn her with fire. {17:17} For God has put it into their hearts to accomplish his purpose by agreeing to hand over to the beast their royal authority, until God's words are fulfilled. {17:18} The woman you saw is the great city that rules over the kings of the earth."

{18:1} After these things, I saw another angel coming down from heaven, having great authority, and the earth was illuminated with his glory. {18:2} And he cried mightily with a loud voice, saying, "Babylon the great is fallen, is fallen, and has become a dwelling place of demons, a prison for every foul spirit, and a cage for every unclean and hated bird! {18:3} For all the nations have drunk of the wine of the wrath of her fornication, the kings of the earth have committed fornication with her, and the merchants of the earth have become rich through the abundance of her luxury." {18:4} And I heard another voice from heaven saying, "Come out of her, my people, lest you share in her sins, and lest you receive of her plagues. {18:5} For her sins have reached to heaven, and God has remembered her iniquities. {18:6} Render to her just as she rendered to you, and repay her double according to her works; in the cup which she has mixed, mix double for her. {18:7} In the measure that she glorified herself and lived luxuriously, in the same measure give her torment and sorrow; for she says in her heart, 'I sit as queen, and am no widow, and will not see sorrow.' {18:8} Therefore her plagues will come in one day—death and mourning and famine. And she will be utterly burned with fire, for strong is the Lord God who judges her. {18:9} "The kings of the earth who committed fornication and lived luxuriously with her will weep and lament for her when they see the smoke of her burning, {18:10} standing at a distance for fear of her torment, saying, 'Alas, alas, that great city Babylon, that mighty city! For in one hour your judgment has come.' {18:11} "And the merchants of the earth will weep and mourn over her, for no one buys their merchandise anymore: {18:12} merchandise of gold and silver, precious stones and pearls, fine linen and purple, silk and scarlet, every kind of citron wood, every kind of object of ivory, every kind of object of most precious wood, bronze, iron, and marble; {18:13} and cinnamon and incense, fragrant oil and frankincense, wine and oil, fine flour and wheat, cattle and sheep, horses and chariots, and bodies and souls of men. {18:14} The fruit that your soul longed for has gone from you, and all the things which were rich and splendid have gone from you, and you shall find them no more at all. {18:15} The merchants of these things, who became rich by her, will stand at a distance for fear of her torment, weeping and wailing, {18:16} and saying, 'Alas, alas, that great city that was clothed in fine linen, purple, and scarlet, and adorned with gold and precious stones and pearls! {18:17} For in one hour such great riches came to nothing.' Every shipmaster, all who travel by ship, sailors, and as many as trade on the sea, stood at a distance {18:18} and cried out when they saw the smoke of her burning, saying, 'What is like this great city?' {18:19} "They threw dust on their heads and cried out, weeping and wailing, and saying, 'Alas, alas, that great city, in which all who had ships on the sea became rich by her wealth! For in one hour she is made desolate.' {18:20} "Rejoice over her, O heaven, and you holy apostles and prophets, for God has avenged you on her!" {18:21} Then a mighty angel took up a stone like a great millstone and threw it into the sea, saying, "Thus with violence the great city Babylon shall be thrown down, and shall not be found anymore. {18:22} The sound of harpists, musicians, flutists, and trumpeters shall not be heard in you anymore. No craftsman of any craft shall be found in you anymore, and the sound of a millstone shall not be heard in you anymore. {18:23} The light of a lamp shall not shine in you anymore, and the voice of bridegroom and bride shall not be heard in you anymore. For your merchants were the great men of the earth, for by your sorcery all the nations were deceived. {18:24} And in her was found the blood of prophets and saints, and of all who were slain on the earth."

{19:1} After these things, I heard a great voice of many people in heaven, saying, "Hallelujah! Salvation and glory and honor and power belong to the Lord our God, {19:2} for true and righteous are His judgments, because He has judged the great harlot who corrupted the earth with her fornication; and He has avenged on her the blood of His servants shed by her." {19:3} Again they said, "Hallelujah! Her smoke rises up forever and ever!" {19:4} And the twenty-four elders and the four living creatures fell down and worshiped God who sat on the throne, saying, "Amen! Hallelujah!" {19:5} Then a voice came from the throne, saying, "Praise our God, all you His servants and those who fear Him, both small and great!" {19:6} And I heard, as it were, the voice of a great multitude, as the sound of many waters, and as the sound of mighty thunderings, saying, "Hallelujah! For the Lord God Omnipotent reigns! {19:7} Let us be glad and rejoice and give Him glory, for the marriage of the Lamb has come, and His wife has made herself ready." {19:8} And to her it was granted to be arrayed in fine linen, clean and bright, for the fine linen is the righteous acts of the saints. {19:9} Then he said to me, "Write: 'Blessed are those who are called to the marriage supper of the Lamb!'" And he said to me, "These are the true sayings of God." {19:10} And I fell at his feet to worship him. But he said to me, "See that you do not do that! I am your fellow servant, and of your brethren who have the testimony of Jesus. Worship God! For the testimony of Jesus is the spirit of prophecy." {19:11} Now I saw heaven opened, and behold, a white horse. And He who sat on him was called Faithful and True, and in righteousness He judges and makes war. {19:12} His eyes were like a flame of fire, and on His head were many crowns. He had a name written that no one knew except Himself. {19:13} He was clothed with a robe dipped in blood, and His name is called The Word of God. {19:14} And the armies in heaven, clothed in fine linen, white and clean, followed Him on white horses. {19:15} Now out of His mouth goes a sharp sword, that with it He should strike the nations. And He Himself will rule them with a rod of iron. He Himself treads the winepress of the fierceness and wrath of Almighty God. {19:16} And He has on His robe and on His thigh a name written: KING OF KINGS AND LORD OF LORDS. {19:17} Then I saw an angel standing in the sun; and he cried with a loud voice, saying to all the birds that fly in the midst of heaven, "Come and gather together for the supper of the great God, {19:18} that you may eat the flesh of kings, the flesh of captains, the flesh of mighty men, the flesh of horses and of those who sit on them, and the flesh of all people, free and slave, both small and great." {19:19} And I saw the beast, the kings of the earth, and their armies, gathered together to make war against Him who sat on the horse and against His army. {19:20} Then the beast was captured, and with him the false prophet who worked signs in his presence, by which he deceived those who received the mark of the beast and those who worshiped his image. These two were cast alive into the lake of fire burning with brimstone. {19:21} And the rest were killed with the sword which proceeded from the mouth of Him who sat on the horse. And all the birds were filled with their flesh.

{20:1} Then I saw an angel descending from heaven, holding the key to the bottomless pit and a great chain in his hand. {20:2} He laid hold of the dragon, that ancient serpent, who is the Devil and Satan, and bound him for a thousand years. {20:3} The angel cast him into the bottomless pit, shut it, and sealed it over him so that he could not deceive the nations anymore until the thousand years were fulfilled. After that, he must be released for a short time. {20:4} I also saw thrones, and they sat on them, and judgment was given to them. And I saw the souls of those who had been beheaded for their witness to Jesus and for the word of God, who had not worshiped the beast or his image, and had not received his mark on their foreheads or hands. They lived and reigned with Christ for a thousand years. {20:5} The rest of the dead did not live again until the thousand years were finished. This is the first resurrection. {20:6} Blessed and holy is the one who has a part in the first resurrection. Over such the second death has no power, but they shall be priests of God and of Christ and shall reign with Him for a thousand years. {20:7} When the thousand years are completed, Satan will be released from his prison {20:8} and will go out to deceive the nations in the four corners of the earth, Gog and Magog, to gather them for battle. Their number is like the sand of the sea. {20:9} They marched across the breadth of the earth and surrounded the camp of the saints and the beloved city. But fire came down from heaven and consumed them. {20:10} Then the devil who had deceived them was cast into the lake of fire and brimstone where the beast and the false prophet are, and they will be tormented day and night forever and ever. {20:11} Then I saw a great white throne and Him who sat on it, from whose face the earth and the heaven fled away. And there was no place for them. {20:12} And I saw the dead, small and great, standing before God. And books were opened. Also another book was opened, which is the Book of Life. And the dead were judged according to their works, by the things which were written in the books. {20:13} The sea gave up the dead who were in it, and Death and Hades delivered up the dead who were in them. And they were judged, each one according to his works. {20:14} Then Death and Hades were cast into the lake of fire. This is the second death. {20:15} And anyone not found written in the Book of Life was cast into the lake of fire.

{21:1} **Then I saw a new heaven and a new earth, for the first heaven and the first earth had passed away, and there was no more sea.** {21:2} I, John, saw the holy city, New Jerusalem, descending from God out of heaven, prepared as a bride adorned for her husband. {21:3} And I heard a great voice from heaven saying, "Behold, the tabernacle of God is with men, and He will dwell with them, and they shall be His people, and God Himself shall be with them and be their God. {21:4} And God shall wipe away all tears from their eyes; and there shall be no more death, neither sorrow, nor crying, neither shall there be any more pain: for the former things are passed away." {21:5} And He who sat upon the throne said, "Behold, I make all things new." And He said to me, "Write, for these words are true and faithful." {21:6} And He said to me, "It is done. I am Alpha and Omega, the beginning and the end. I will give unto him who is a thirst of the fountain of the water of life freely. {21:7} He who overcomes shall inherit all things; and I will be his God, and he shall be My son. {21:8} But the fearful, and unbelieving, and the abominable, and murderers, and whoremongers, and sorcerers, and idolaters, and all liars, shall have their part in the lake which burns with fire and brimstone: which is the second death." {21:9} Then one of the seven angels who had the seven vials full of the seven last plagues came to me and talked with me, saying, "Come here, I will show you the bride, the Lamb's wife." {21:10} And he carried me away in the spirit to a great and high mountain, and showed me that great city, the holy Jerusalem, descending out of heaven from God, {21:11} Having the glory of God. Her light was like a most precious stone, like a jasper stone, clear as crystal. {21:12} And it had a great and high wall, with twelve gates, and at the gates twelve angels, and names written on them, which are the names of the twelve tribes of the children of Israel: {21:13} On the east three gates; on the north three gates; on the south three gates; and on the west three gates. {21:14} The wall of the city had twelve foundations, and in them were the names of the twelve apostles of the Lamb. {21:15} And he who talked with me had a golden reed to measure the city, its gates, and its wall. {21:16} The city is laid out as a square; its length is as great as its breadth. And he measured the city with the reed: twelve thousand furlongs. Its length, breadth, and height are equal. {21:17} Then he measured its wall: one hundred and forty-four cubits, according to the measure of a man, that is, of an angel. {21:18} The construction of its wall was of jasper; and the city was pure gold, like clear glass. {21:19} The foundations of the wall of the city were adorned with all kinds of precious stones: the first foundation was jasper, the second sapphire, the third chalcedony, the fourth emerald, {21:20} the fifth sardonyx, the sixth sardius, the seventh chrysolite, the eighth beryl, the ninth topaz, the tenth chrysoprase, the eleventh jacinth, and the twelfth amethyst. {21:21} The twelve gates were twelve pearls: each individual gate was of one pearl. And the streets of the city were pure gold, like transparent glass. {21:22} But I saw no temple in it, for the Lord God Almighty and the Lamb are its temple. {21:23} The city had no need of the sun or of the moon to shine in it, for the glory of God illuminated it. The Lamb is its light. {21:24} And the nations of those who are saved shall walk in its light, and the kings of the earth bring their glory and honor into it. {21:25} Its gates shall not be shut at all by day (there shall be no night there). {21:26} And they shall bring the glory and the honor of the nations into it. {21:27} But there shall by no means enter it anything that defiles, or causes an abomination or a lie, but only those who are written in the Lamb's Book of Life.

{22:1} Then he showed me a pure river of water of life, clear as crystal, proceeding out of the throne of God and of the Lamb. {22:2} In the midst of the street of it, and on either side of the river, there was the tree of life, which bore twelve kinds of fruits, yielding its fruit every month. And the leaves of the tree were for the healing of the nations. {22:3} And there shall be no more curse: but the throne of God and of the Lamb shall be in it; and his servants shall serve him: {22:4} And they shall see his face; and his name shall be in their foreheads. {22:5} And there shall be no night there; and they need no candle, neither light of the sun; for the Lord God gives them light: and they shall reign forever and ever. {22:6} And he said to me, "These sayings are faithful and true: and the Lord God of the holy prophets sent his angel to show to his servants the things which must shortly be done. {22:7} "Behold, I come quickly: blessed is he that keeps the sayings of the prophecy of this book." {22:8} And I, John, saw these things, and heard them. And when I had heard and seen, I fell down to worship before the feet of the angel who showed me these things. {22:9} Then he said to me, "See you do it not: for I am your fellow servant, and of your brethren the prophets, and of them who keep the sayings of this book: worship God." {22:10} And he said to me, "Seal not the sayings of the prophecy of this book: for the time is at hand. {22:11} "He that is unjust, let him be unjust still: and he which is filthy, let him be filthy still: and he that is righteous, let him be righteous still: and he that is holy, let him be holy still." {22:12} "And, behold, I come quickly, and my reward is with me, to give every man according as his work shall be. {22:13} "I am Alpha and Omega, the beginning and the end, the first and the last." {22:14} "Blessed are they that do his commandments, that they may have right to the tree of life, and may enter in through the gates into the city. {22:15} "For without are dogs, and sorcerers, and whoremongers, and murderers, and idolaters, and whoever loves and makes a lie. {22:16} "I, Jesus, have sent my angel to testify to you these things in the churches. I am the root and the offspring of David, and the bright and morning star." {22:17} "And the Spirit and the bride say, Come. And let him that hears say, Come. And let him that is thirsty come. And whoever will, let him take the water of life freely." {22:18} "For I testify to every man that hears the words of the prophecy of this book, If any man shall add to these things, God shall add to him the plagues that are written in this book: {22:19} "And if any man shall take away from the words of the book of this prophecy, God shall take away his part out of the book of life, and out of the holy city, and from the things which are written in this book." {22:20} "He who testifies these things says, 'Surely I come quickly.' Amen. Even so, come, Lord Jesus."

Free Gifts

Thank you so much for diving into what we believe is the most important book on the planet. Your journey through our translation of the New Testament, tailored especially for GenZ, is a big deal to us, and we're thrilled you chose to embark on this adventure. Your engagement with these timeless teachings is not just a personal milestone; it's a ripple in the larger stream of connecting a vibrant, young generation with profound, ancient wisdom.

We're reaching out with a small favor to ask. If you found value in this journey, could you please take a moment to leave a review? Your feedback is more than just words; it's a beacon that guides others in the GenZ community towards this enlightening experience. Sharing your thoughts helps us extend our mission, touching more lives and sparking more minds with the transformative power of faith adapted for the modern world.

Now, let's sweeten your journey even further! Who doesn't love a good bonus, right? Especially when it's tailor-made for GenZ, like you. We're excited to offer you some exclusive gifts that complement your recent journey through the New Testament. Dive into our special questionnaire designed for self-reflection, daily practices that resonate with your lifestyle, and embrace your faith with relevance in today's fast-paced world. That's not all—we've also crafted an engaging, fun-filled version of the Old & New Testament Stories, designed with care and creativity, just for you. And guess what? As we develop more quality resources—like top-notch audiobooks—you'll get access to these at unbeatable prices!

Claiming these gifts is a breeze. Simply scan the QR Code below, send us a screenshot of your order via our email, and voila! We'll whisk your gifts to you in the fastest time possible, getting you all set for the next leg of your spiritual journey.

As we wrap up, we want to express our heartfelt gratitude once more. Your choice to explore this translation is a step toward a life enriched with deeper understanding, wisdom, and faith. We're honored to walk this path with you and excited to continue providing you with resources that inspire, challenge, and uplift. Thank you for being part of this journey, for embracing the spirit of exploration, and for contributing to a world that appreciates the fusion of timeless wisdom with the vibrant energy of Gen Z. Keep shining your light, and remember, this journey is just the beginning.

Made in United States
Troutdale, OR
02/07/2025